ENCYCLOPEDIA
OF
BLACK
AMERICA

W. Augustus Low

Editor
Professor of History
University of Maryland Baltimore County

Virgil A. Clift

Associate Editor
Professor Emeritus
New York University

McGraw-Hill Book Company

New York   St. Louis   San Francisco   Auckland
Bogotá   Hamburg   Johannesburg   London   Madrid
Mexico   Montreal   New Delhi   Panama   Paris
São Paulo   Singapore   Sydney   Tokyo   Toronto

Library of Congress Cataloging in Publication Data

Main entry under title:

Encyclopedia of Black America.

  Includes index.
  1. Afro-Americans—Dictionaries and encyclopedias.
I. Low, W. Augustus. II. Clift, Virgil A.
E185.E55   973'.0496073   80-13247
ISBN 0-07-038834-2

1234567890   HDHD   8987654321

The editors for this book were Daniel Fischel and Patricia Allen-
Browne, the designer was Naomi Auerbach, and the production
supervisor was Teresa F. Leaden. It was set in Melior by University Graphics, Inc.

Printed and bound by Halliday Lithograph.

CONTENTS

Preface

PREFACE

INTRODUCTION

Our purpose has been to produce a reliable and readable reference that represents in large measure the totality of the past and present life and culture of Afro-Americans. We have attempted to fill a long-neglected need for a volume that is comprehensive in scope, accurate and authentic in quality, and factual as well as interpretative in conception and synthesis. We have attempted to survey and to summarize the various major and minor facets of the history and life of Afro-Americans in such a way as has never been done before. In essence, we believe that we have produced within a single volume the first significant and major encyclopedic history of black Americans. We have evaluated facts and ideas carefully and judiciously and have treated them in such a manner as to give meaning and perspective, clarity and reflection, and balance and proportion to the total Afro-American experience. Having accumulated a massive amount of valuable material, easily enough for several volumes, we were influenced greatly in our selections by limitations of space, and we make no claim to all-inclusiveness.

However, we do claim massive research, review, and coverage. Relying upon numerous persons and sources—upon the services of archivists, librarians, researchers, consultants, contributors, and photographers—we believe that our synthesis and its presentation is a notable achievement.

TITLE AND DEFINITIONS

Our initial title for the *Encyclopedia* was tentative, and we indicated this fact in our communications with potential contributors, authors, and researchers. It really was not until we were well into the accumulation of data and manuscripts that agreement was reached on the present title: *Encyclopedia of Black America*. The title was essentially a compromise between the use of two words: *black* and *Afro-American*. These two words perhaps appear with more frequency and regularity than any other words in the volume. Their use is interchangeable.

Throughout the *Encyclopedia*, unless noted otherwise, we have used the words *black* and *Afro-American*—or related words—to refer to people who regard themselves, or identify themselves, as being black or Afro-American, and people who are, or have been, generally regarded as being black or Afro-American. Additionally, we refer to people who are essentially English-speaking in origin and usage and who live, or have lived historically, in what is now the United States.

For us, this definition is a broad working one that may be at variance in degree or kind in law, biology, or the U.S. Census. We believe, however, that in its use we have avoided narrow racial and cultural stereotypes. Our own reflection upon the meaning of *black* or *Afro-American*, or what is race, led us to include the entries ONOMATOLOGY and RACE. Whether real or imagined, racial discrimination has persisted in the United States and elsewhere, and blacks have shouldered—but not exclusively—its great burdens. Indeed, as implied or stated in several places in this volume, overcoming racial and cultural discrimination may be regarded as the central theme in Afro-American life and history.

The fact that Afro-Americans have endured such burdens is a tribute to their moral stamina and courage. The fact, also, that they have made significant achievements despite this adversity— as shown so clearly and abundantly in this volume—is further tribute to their cultural originality, vibrancy, and resiliency.

ENTRIES

Entries in the *Encyclopedia* are divided into three types: articles, biographies, and cross references.

Articles define, describe, or elaborate upon a topic, term, or word, and treat subjects of a non-biographical nature. They are classified as being either major or minor. Generally, we regard a major article as being an entry amounting to about one page or more in length. A minor article is less than one page. By this classification, there are approximately 125 major articles and 200 minor ones. Articles make up about two-thirds of the *Encyclopedia*.

Many major articles are designed and grouped as clusters. A cluster contains two or more distinct but related major articles, usually by different authors. Our clusters connote a sense of unity and cohesion within the *Encyclopedia*. More importantly, they suggest and emphasize a fundamental continuity underlying the reality of the subject. Altogether, the *Encyclopedia* contains eleven clusters which are composed of sixty-one major articles, or about thirty percent of the *Encyclopedia*. The cluster entry AFRO-AMERICAN HISTORY, containing nine major articles, is the largest; the cluster entry RACE is the smallest. The clusters, alphabetically, are as follows: AFRICA; AFRICAN LEGACY / SURVIVALS; AFRO-AMERICAN HISTORY; CIVIL DISORDERS; CIVIL RIGHTS; EDUCATION; LITERATURE: MUSIC; NEWSPAPERS; RACE; SLAVERY.

We must emphasize, however, that almost an equal number of major articles, including four biographies, are not in any cluster at all. Constituting about thirty percent of the *Encyclopedia*, they are too diverse and varied to be clustered. A good example is shown in the numerous entries, both major and minor, that treat the subject of *religion*. Instead of resorting to a cluster, we have treated separately and individually practically all religious bodies of blacks in the United States. No other single volume in print has so captured and presented this great religious variety and diversity, an abiding and fundamental force in Afro-American life and history.

In addition to religious persuasions, other nonclustered major articles treat a variety of subjects as shown in the titles. If minor articles were shown, the variety would be even more pronounced. For example, whereas we have a major article on colleges and universities within the cluster entitled EDUCATION, we have also treated each college and university separately, making a total of more than one hundred entries.

Whether major or minor, our articles not only treat conventionally studied subjects, they also give special attention to topics that have not been explored in the literature on Afro-Americans. Examples can be found in such pioneering entries as AVIATORS, COSMETOLOGY, NURSES, ONOMATOLOGY, and PENTECOSTALS.

Biographies are necessarily more concise than the major articles, or even minor articles. There are in the *Encyclopedia* approximately 1400 biographies. All but four are less than one page in length. The four biographies which are given the extended coverage of a major article are those for Frederick Douglass, W. E. B. Du Bois, Martin Luther King, Jr., and Booker T. Washington.

Cross references follow the conventional *See* and *See also* type. The cross references are useful as a self-indexing guide and, in a limited sense, supplement or substitute additional entries, thus saving valuable space.

Lastly, in regard to all entries, we realize that between the time of the collection of data and their appearance in a finished publication many changes have taken place. Generally, most of the data in the *Encyclopedia* do not extent beyond the year 1976–1977, the year of the completion of the manuscript. Yet, in a work of this scope and comprehensiveness, we recognize the ongoing need to update, especially in regard to biographies and bibliographical references. Although we are aware of the problem, and actually made many changes after the manuscript was in production, the updating process had to be controlled in order to prevent delays in publication.

BIBLIOGRAPHICAL REFERENCES

Special attention has been given to bibliographical references. These references have been listed conventionally at the end of entries, frequently in alphabetical sequence, but sometimes in order of substantive or chronological importance. Occasionally, a reference is briefly annotated. As expected, the overwhelming bulk of the references come at the end of major articles; and without doubt they are the best, or among the best, on the subject. In addition, many references have been listed for minor articles and some biographies. In numerous biographies we have taken care to call attention to the subject's books, writings, or compositions; and we hope this will add greatly to the bibliographical value of the *Encyclopedia*. We venture to suggest that if our references were taken collectively they would constitute a formidable, highly selective, and qualitative library on Afro-Americans.

Additionally, one of our major articles is entitled BIBLIOGRAPHIES/BIOGRAPHIES/GUIDES. This entry may be regarded as a general bibliography, or bibliographic guide, if such is allowable, for the entire *Encyclopedia*. It is essentially a concise bibliography of bibliographies that also shows collective biographies, catalogs, and guides. Many of the items have been annotated. A reader who has consulted references appended to major or minor articles, or in biographies, may turn to this entry for further search. Indeed, many of our entries refer the reader to this section.

Beyond these references and sources, the reader may then turn to our entry entitled ARCHIVES for more intensive research. As pointed out at the beginning of this Preface, our references can help both the casual reader and the serious researcher. But whether for the casual reader or serious researcher, we believe that all our bibliographical listings enhance the authenticity and scholarship of the volume.

BEGINNING OF THE ENCYCLOPEDIA

The suggestion for the publication of this encyclopedia was made by Daniel Fishel, who in the early 1970s was serving as Editor of Professional and Reference Books at the McGraw-Hill Book Company. He indicated his interest to Virgil A. Clift, then a professor at New York University, who in turn suggested that I should be contacted for possible consideration as the editor. Although my initial response was one of interest, I accepted conditionally. The first condition was that the volume be authoritative; the exact word that I used was *scholarly*. The second condition was that Clift should help in the editing.

With these two preliminary conditions agreed upon, we set out to prepare a tentative prospectus that the publisher was later to send out for competitive review. Responses from reviewers were satisfactory and encouraging, and we were given the assignment, the enviable task of implementing the prospectus and producing the *Encyclopedia*.

Virgil Clift and I first met on the eve of World War II when we were young faculty members at the A & T College in Greensboro, North Carolina [which is entered in the *Encyclopedia* as North Carolina Agricultural and Technical (A & T) State University]. Over the years, we developed many mutual, personal, and intellectual interests. Not the least of these interests was a profound regard for the study and appreciation of Afro-American life and history. This interest deepened and matured as the years passed. In a sense, this *Encyclopedia* reflects both this depth and its maturity. Without a formal dedication, we would like to pass this volume along to the youth of a future generation in the hope that their lives will be enriched and their nourishment and strength renewed, as ours have been, by an appreciation of contemporaries and by a remembrance of ancestors.

W. A. Low
Editor

CONTRIBUTORS

To achieve our purpose we were fortunate to enlist a large number of scholars and authorities in many diversified fields and specialties. We believe that in no other single volume relating to Afro-Americans are so many distinguished and able contributors to be found. Their only limitation has been editorial, one of space, while their method of treatment or interpretation developed virtually without prescription. We believe further that they have responded superbly, despite the limitations imposed by space. Though easily prolific or potentially prolific in their respective fields, our contributors have produced excellent works—gems of scholarship—in which value has not been compromised. They have greatly increased our understanding and knowledge of Afro-Americans, and for this we are grateful.

ARNOLD, JOSEPH L. *(Associate Professor of History, University of Maryland Baltimore County)* Ph.D. Ohio State University; author of *The New Deal in the Suburbs: A History of the Greenbelt Town Programs* (1971). POVERTY

BELLAMY, DONNIE D. *(Professor of History, Fort Valley State College, Georgia)* Ph.D. University of Missouri-Columbia; author of *Glory Road: The Visible Black Man, 1930–1954* (1971). SLAVERY IN MISSOURI

BENNETT, ROBERT A., JR. *(Associate Professor, The Episcopal Theological School, Cambridge, Massachusetts)* Ph.D. Harvard University; contributor to *Harvard Theological Review* and *Theological Education.* EPISCOPALIANS

BERRY, MARY FRANCES *(Associate Professor of History, University of Maryland College Park)* Ph.D. University of Michigan (Ann Arbor); author of *Black Resistance/White Law* (1971) and *Military Necessity and Civil Rights Policy* (1977); see biographical entry. CIVIL RIGHTS: ACTS; CIVIL RIGHTS:CASES

BERWANGER, EUGENE H. *(Professor of History, Colorado State University, Fort Collins)* Ph.D. University of Illinois; author of *The Frontier Against Slavery: Western Anti-Negro Prejudice and the Slavery Extension Controversy* (1977). SLAVERY ON THE FRONTIER

BISHOP, DAVID W. *(Professor of History, North Carolina Central University, Durham)* Ph.D. Catholic University; state civil rights leader. CIVIL RIGHTS: SELECTED STATES/NORTH CAROLINA

BLASSINGAME, JOHN W. *(Professor of History, Yale University, New Haven, Connecticut)* Ph.D. Yale University; author of *The Slave Community* (1972) and *Black New Orleans, 1860–1880* (1973); see biographical entry. AFRO-AMERICAN HISTORY:RECONSTRUCTION TO REVOLT, 1877–1977; NATIONALISM; SLAVERY:REFERENCES

BLOCH, HERMAN D. *(Professor of Economics, St. John's University, Jamaica, New York)* Author of *The Circle of Discrimination: An Economic and Social Study of the Black Man in New York City* (1969). COAUTHOR LABOR UNIONS

BRADLEY, DAVID H. *(Editor, The A.M.E. Zion Quarterly Review)* Graduate of Livingstone College, A.M. University of Pittsburgh; author of *History of the A.M.E. Zion Church* (2 vols., 1956, 1970). AFRICAN METHODIST EPISCOPAL ZION CHURCH

BROWN, INA CORINNE *(Professor Emeritus, Scarritt College, Nashville, Tennessee)* Ph.D. University of Chicago; *Understanding Race Relations* (1973). RACE AND CULTURE

BROWN, MARIAN TALLEY *(Professor, Florida Junior College at Jacksonville)* Ph.D. Indiana University, Bloomington. COAUTHOR MUSIC: BLUES

BROWN, WILLIAM A. *(Associate Professor of Voice, University of North Florida)* M.A. Indiana University, Bloomington. COAUTHOR MUSIC:BLUES

CASTEL, ALBERT E. *(Professor of History, Western Michigan University, Kalamazoo)* Ph.D. University of Chicago; author of *Frontier State at War: Kansas, 1861–1865* (1958) and *General Sterling Price and the Civil War in the West* (1968). SLAVERY IN KANSAS

CLIFT, ARLENE *(Associate Professor of English, Fisk University, Nashville, Tennessee)* Ph.D. Harvard University. COAUTHOR LITERATURE: FOLKLORE

CLIFT, VIRGIL A. *(Professor Emeritus, New York University, New York City)* Ph.D. Ohio State University; editor of *Negro Education in America* and associate editor of *Encyclopedia of Black America*; see biographical entry. COAUTHOR BLACK PANTHER PARTY; EDUCATION

COBB, W. MONTAGUE *(Professor Emeritus, College of Medicine, Howard University, Washington, D.C.)* PHYSICIANS

COLES, ANNA B. *(Professor and Dean, School of Nursing, Howard University, Washington, D.C.)* Graduate of the School of Nursing, Freedman's Hospital (Howard University Hospital); M.S. Catholic University. COAUTHOR NURSES

CONTEE, CLARENCE G. *(Professor of History, Howard University, Washington, D.C.)* Ph.D. American University; contributor to *Journal of Politics* and *Journal of Negro History*. PAN-AFRICANISM

CORNELY, PAUL B. *(Professor, Department of Community Health Practice, College of Medicine, Howard University, Washington, D.C.)* M.D. and Dr.P.H. University of Michigan; past president of American Public Health Association; see biographical entry. HEALTH

CRIPPS, THOMAS R. *(Professor of History, Morgan State University, Baltimore, Maryland)* Ph.D. University of Maryland College Park; author of *Slow Fade to Black: The Negro in American Film, 1900–1942* (1976). MOTION PICTURES

DAAKU, KWAME Y. *(Professor of History, University of Ghana, Legon, Ghana)* Author of *Trade and Politics on the Gold Coast* (1970). AFRICA:IMPACT OF THE ATLANTIC SLAVE TRADE UPON AFRICA

DANIEL, W. HARRISON *(Professor of History, University of Richmond, Richmond, Virginia)* Ph.D. Duke University. SLAVERY AND THE CHURCHES

DILLARD, J. L. *(Professor, Ferkauf Graduate School, Yeshiva University, New York City)* Ph.D. University of Texas; author of *Black English: Its History and Usage in the United States* (1972). AFRICAN LEGACY/SURVIVALS: LANGUAGE

DYSON, ERNEST F. *(Former Assistant Professor of Music/Jazz History, Federal City College/University of the District of Columbia.)* MUSIC: JAZZ

FLADELAND, BETTY L. *(Professor of History, Southern Illinois University)* Ph.D. University of Michigan; author of *James Gillespie Birney: Slaveholder to Abolitionist* (1955) and *Men and Brothers: Anglo-American Antislavery Cooperation* (1972). SLAVERY:THE ABOLITIONISTS

FLEMING, G. JAMES *(Professor Emeritus, Morgan State University, Baltimore, Maryland)* Ph.D. University of Pennsylvania; see biographical entry. VIRGIN ISLANDS

FORBES, JACK D. *(Professor of Anthropology, University of California, Davis)* AFRICAN LEGACY/SURVIVALS:SUMMARY; COAUTHOR AFRO-AMERICAN HISTORY:THE WEST

FORNAY, ALFRED R., JR. *(Cosmetologist, Director of Training and Beauty Seminars, Fashion Fair Cosmetics Division, Johnson Publishing Company, Chicago, Illinois)* Graduate of Fashion Institute of Technology, State University of New York; former associate beauty editor for *Essence* magazine. COSMETOLOGY

FORTUNE, HILDA O. *(Professor of Sociology, York College, City University of New York)* Ed.D. New York University; see biographical entry. WOMEN

FREEMAN, EDWARD A. *(Pastor, First Baptist Church, Kansas City, Kansas)* Graduate of Clark College and Central Theological Seminary; see biographical entry. BAPTISTS

GARA, LARRY *(Professor of History, Wilmington College, Wilmington, Ohio)* Ph.D. University of Wisconsin; author of *Liberty Line: The Legend of the Underground Railroad* (1961). SLAVERY:THE UNDERGROUND RAILROAD

GATEWOOD, WILLARD B. *(Alumni Distinguished Professor, University of Arkansas, Fayetteville)* Ph.D. Duke University; author of *Theodore Roosevelt and the Art of Controversy* (1970) and *"Smoked Yankees" and the Struggle for Empire: Letters from Negro Soldiers, 1898–1902* (1971). BOOKER T. WASHINGTON

GAYMON, NICHOLAS E. *(Director of Libraries, Florida Agricultural and Mechanical University, Tallahassee)* Ph.D. Florida University, Tallahassee. CIVIL RIGHTS:SELECTED STATES/ FLORIDA

GIBSON, DONALD B. *(Professor of English, Rutgers University, New Brunswick, New Jersey)* Ph.D. Brown University (Providence, R.I.); author of *Black and White: Stories of American Life* (1971) and *Modern Black Poets: A Collection of Critical Essays* (1973). LITERATURE: POETRY

GILBERT, ABBY L. *(Economist, Office of the Comptroller of the Currency, Washington, D.C.)* Graduate of Goucher College and the Johns Hopkins University School of Advanced International Studies; contributor to *Bankers Magazine* and *Journal of Negro History.* COAUTHOR BANKS

GRAHAM, HUGH DAVIS *(Professor of History, University of Maryland Baltimore County)* Ph.D. Stanford University; coauthor with Ted Robert Gurr of *Violence in America: Historical and Comparative Perspectives* (1969) and with Numan V. Bartley, *Southern Politics and the Second Reconstruction* (1975). CIVIL DISORDERS, 1943–PRESENT

GRAVES, EARL G. *(Publisher, Black Enterprise magazine)* Graduate of Morgan State College; see biographical entry. BUSINESS

GRIFFIN, RICHARD W. *(Professor of History, Northern Virginia Community College, Annandale)* Ph.D. Ohio State University; coauthor of *A History of the Georgia Textile Industry, 1798–1865* (1968). SLAVERY:SLAVES IN INDUSTRY

HALL, CHARLOTTE P. *(National Bankers Association, Washington, D.C.)* Graduate of Morgan State College, attended the Johns Hopkins University School for Advanced International Studies; first editor of the National Bankers Association's newsletter *Quick Ratio.* COAUTHOR BANKS

HICKS, JOHNNYE McMILLIAN *(Assistant Professor of Nursing, University of Maryland at Baltimore)* M.S. Yale University (Connecticut). CUISINE

HUNT, ALFRED N. *(Assistant Professor of History, State University of New York, College of Purchase)* Ph.D. University of Texas. COLONIZATION

JACKSON, JACQUELYNE JOHNSON *(Associate Professor of Medical Sociology, Duke University, Durham, North Carolina)* Ph.D. Ohio State University; see biographical entry. FAMILY

JACKSON, SARA DUNLAP *(Archivist, National Historical Publications Commission, National Archives, Washington, D.C.)* Graduate of Johnson C. Smith University, graduate study at Catholic University and American University; contributor to *Journal of Negro History.* ARCHIVES

JAY, JAMES M. *(Professor of Biology, Wayne State University, Detroit, Michigan)* Ph.D. Ohio State University; author of *Negroes in Science: Natural Science Doctorates, 1876–1969* (1971). SCIENTISTS:BIOLOGICAL, PHYSICAL

JONES, CLIFTON R. *(Professor of Sociology, Howard University, Washington, D.C.)* Ph.D. University of Iowa; see biographical entry. SOCIAL CLASSES

JOYNER, CHARLES W. *(Associate Professor of History and Anthropology, St. Andrews Presbyterian College, Laurinburg, North Carolina)* Ph.D. (history) University of South Carolina, Ph.D. (folklore) University of Pennsylvania. MUSIC:ORIGINS OF SPIRITUALS

KELLOGG, CHARLES FLINT *(Professor of American History, Dickson College, Carlisle, Pennsylvania)* Ph.D. The Johns Hopkins University; The NAACP was the subject of his dissertation, which was published by The Johns Hopkins University Press (1967). NATIONAL ASSOCIATION FOR THE ADVANCEMENT OF COLORED PEOPLE [NAACP]

KING, ANNIE G. *(Librarian, Tuskegee Institute, Tuskegee, Alabama)* Graduate of North Carolina Central University, B.S.L.S. University of Illinois. CIVIL RIGHTS:SELECTED STATES/ALABAMA

LABRIE, HENRY G. III *(Journalist)* Ph.D. University of Iowa. NEWSPAPERS: CONTEMPORARY

LAMON, LESTER C. *(Associate Professor of History, Indiana University at South Bend)* Ph.D. University of North Carolina, Chapel Hill; author of *Black Tennesseans, 1900–1930* (1977). CIVIL DISORDERS, 1861–1917

LANGLEY, HAROLD D. *(Associate Curator, Naval History, Smithsonian Institute, Washington, D.C.)* Ph.D. University of Pennsylvania; author of *Social Reform in the United States Navy, 1798–1962* (1967). WARS

LOW, W. AUGUSTUS *(Professor of History, University of Maryland Baltimore County)* Ph.D.

University of Iowa; past editor of *Journal of Negro History*; editor of *Encyclopedia of Black America.* AFRICA:THE ATLANTIC SLAVE TRADE IN PERSPECTIVE; AFRICAN LEGACY/SURVIVALS: INTRODUCTION; COAUTHOR AFRO-AMERICAN HISTORY:COLONIAL PERIOD, 1600s–1783; COAUTHOR AFRO-AMERICAN HISTORY:THE WEST; AVIATORS; BIBLIOGRAPHIES/BIOGRAPHIES/GUIDES; CHURCHES; CIVIL RIGHTS:ENFORCEMENT; CIVIL RIGHTS:SELECTED STATES/INTRODUCTION; CRIME; DISCRIMINATION; DU BOIS, WILLIAM EDWARD BURGHARDT; EMPLOYMENT; HARLEM; HISTORIANS; HOUSING; HOWARD UNIVERSITY; INCOME; JIM CROW; COAUTHOR LAWYERS; LYNCHING; ONOMATOLOGY; COAUTHOR POPULATION; SCIENTISTS:SOCIAL; SEGREGATION; SLAVERY:SLAVERY IN SELECTED STATES/INTRODUCTION; SLAVERY: SLAVERY IN SOUTH CAROLINA; COAUTHOR SLAVERY:SLAVE NARRATIVES

MACEACHEREN, ELAINE *(Reference Librarian, Central Intelligence Agency, Washington, D.C.)* M.S. Simmons College, Boston; contributor to *Journal of Negro History.* SLAVERY IN MASSACHUSETTS

MARSHALL, ALBERT P. *(Librarian, Eastern Michigan University, Ypsilanti, Michigan)* Graduate of Lincoln University (Mo.), B.S.L.S. University of Illinois; see biographical entry. FRATERNAL SOCIETIES

McCOLLEY, ROBERT M. *(Professor of History, University of Illinois, Urbana-Champaign)* Ph.D. University of California, Berkeley; author of *Slavery and Jeffersonian Virginia* (1973). SLAVERY IN VIRGINIA

MOHR, JAMES C. *(Professor of History, University of Maryland Baltimore County)* Ph.D. Stanford University; author of *The Radical Republicans in New York During Reconstruction* (1973) and *Abortion in America: The Origins and Evolution of National Policy, 1800–1900* (1978). AFRO-AMERICAN HISTORY:THE CIVIL WAR, 1861–1865; AFRO-AMERICAN HISTORY:RECONSTRUCTION, 1865–1877

MOONEY, CHASE C. *(Professor of History, Indiana University, Bloomington)* Ph.D. Vanderbilt University; author of *Slavery in Tennessee* (1957) and *Civil Rights and Liberties* (1965). SLAVERY IN TENNESSEE

MOSELEY, HELEN JEWEL *(Associate Professor of Nursing, University of Maryland at Baltimore)* R.N. Provident Hospital (Baltimore, Md.), M.S. University of Maryland at Baltimore. COAUTHOR NURSES

MURRAY, ANDREW EVANS *(Professor of Religion, Lincoln University, Pennsylvania)* Th.D. (Doctor of Theology) Princeton Theological Seminary; author of *Presbyterians and the Negro:A History* (1967). PRESBYTERIANS

O'ROURKE, JAMES RALPH *(Librarian, Kentucky State College, Frankfort)* Graduate of Talladega College, M.S.L.S. University of Kentucky. CIVIL RIGHTS:SELECTED STATES/KENTUCKY

PARKS, JAMES DALLAS *(Professor of Art, Lincoln University, Jefferson City, Missouri)* M.A. University of Iowa; painter as well as art historian, his works are exhibited in permanent collections at several universities, including Atlanta University, Howard University, and the University of Iowa. ARTISTS

PINKETT, HAROLD T. *(Archivist, National Archives, Washington, D.C.)* Ph.D. American University; past editor of *American Archivist*; author of *Gifford Pinchot, Private and Public Forester* (1970); see biographical entry. AGRICULTURE

PORTER, HERMAN A. *(Pastor, St. Therese Parish, Aurora, Illinois)* M.A. University of Notre Dame; ordained a Roman Catholic priest in 1947. CATHOLICS

QUARLES, BENJAMIN *(Professor of History, Morgan State University, Baltimore, Maryland)* Ph.D. University of Wisconsin; author of *The Negro in the American Revolution* (1961); see biographical entry. AFRO-AMERICAN HISTORY:FREE NEGROES, 1600–1860; FREDERICK DOUGLASS

RICHARDSON, JOE M. *(Professor of History, Florida State University, Tallahassee)* Ph.D. Florida State University; author of *The Negro in the Reconstruction of Florida* (1965). AFRO-AMERICAN HISTORY:THE FREEDMEN'S BUREAU, 1865–72; AMERICAN MISSIONARY ASSOCIATION; FREEDMAN'S SAVINGS BANK

ROBINSON, DONALD L. *(Professor of Government, Smith College, Northampton, Massachusetts)* Ph.D. Cornell University; author of *Slavery in the Structure of American Politics, 1765–1820* (1971). AFRO-AMERICAN HISTORY: SLAVERY AND THE CONSTITUTION

ROGERS, WILLIAM WARREN *(Professor of History, Florida State University, Tallahassee)* Ph.D. University of North Carolina; author of *The One-Gallused Rebellion:Agrarianism in Alabama, 1865–1896* (1970). POPULISTS

ROSENBERG, ELAINE *(Instructor, Language Arts, New York City Public Schools)* M.A. New York University. COAUTHOR RADIO AND TELEVISION

ROSENBLOOM, JANE *(Instructor, Physical Education, New York City Public Schools)* M.S. New York University; former member of Wrightman Cup Team (tennis). ATHLETES

SCHRAUFNAGEL, NOEL *(Associate Professor of English, Alcorn State University, Lormans, Mississippi)* LITERATURE:THE NOVEL

SCOTT, ROLAND E. *(Professor, Department of Pediatrics, Howard University, Washington, D.C.)* COAUTHOR RACE:RACE AND BIOLOGY

SHEELER, JOHN REUBEN *(Distinguished Professor of History, Texas Southern University, Houston)* Ph.D. University of West Virginia; see biographical entry. SLAVERY:RESTRICTIONS ON AFRO-AMERICANS

SHOCKLEY, GRANT S. *(President, Interdenominational Theological Center, Atlanta, Georgia)* Ed.D. Columbia University; see biographical entry. AFRICAN METHODIST EPISCOPAL CHURCH; METHODISTS/UNITED METHODIST CHURCH

SLAVENS, GEORGE EVERETT *(Professor of History, Ouachita Baptist University, Arkadelphia, Arkansas)* Ph.D. University of Missouri. NEWSPAPERS:HISTORY AND DEVELOPMENT

SOUTHERN, EILEEN JACKSON *(Professor of Music, Harvard University, Cambridge, Massachusetts)* Ph.D. New York University; author of *The Music of Black Americans: A History* (1971); see biographical entry. MUSIC:HISTORY AND DEVELOPMENT; MUSIC:SPIRITUALS/PERFORMANCE

SPARKS, DAVID S. *(Professor of History, University of Maryland College Park)* AFRO-AMERICAN HISTORY:SECTIONAL CONFLICT OVER SLAVERY, 1820-1860

SWEAT, EDWARD F. *(Professor of History, Clark College, Atlanta, Georgia)* Ph.D. Indiana University; see biographical entry. SLAVERY IN GEORGIA

TAYLOR, ORVILLE W. *(Professor of History, Georgia College, Milledgeville)* Ph.D. Duke University; author of *Negro Slavery in Arkansas* (1958). SLAVERY IN ARKANSAS

TINNEY, JAMES S. *(Assistant Professor of Journalism, Howard University, Washington, D.C.)* M.A. Howard University; editor of *Spirit:A Journal of Issues Incident to Black Pentecostalism.* PENTECOSTALS

TUTTLE, WILLIAM M. *(Professor of History, University of Kansas, Lawrence)* Ph.D. University of Wisconsin; author of *Race Riot:Chicago in the Red Summer of 1919* (1970). CIVIL DISORDERS, 1917-1943

WALKER, JAMES D. *(Instructor of English, School of Continuing Education, New York University)* M.A. New York University. COAUTHOR LITERATURE:DRAMA/THEATER

WALTON, HANES, JR. *(Professor of Political Science, Savannah State College, Savannah, Georgia)* Ph.D. Howard University; author of *Black Political Parties: An Historical and Political Analysis* (1972) and *The Political Philosophy of Martin Luther King* (1971); see biographical entry. MARTIN LUTHER KING, JR.

WARE, GILBERT *(Associate Professor of Politics, Drexel University, Philadelphia, Pennsylvania)* Ph.D. Princeton University; editor of *From the Black Bar:Voices for Equal Justice* (1976). COAUTHOR LAWYERS

WATT, LOIS B. *(Librarian and Specialist in Children's Literature)* M.A. University of Maryland, M.S.L.S. Catholic University. LITERATURE:CHILDREN'S LITERATURE

WAX, DAROLD D. *(Professor of History, Oregon State University, Corvallis)* Ph.D. University of Washington; coauthor with Max Savelle of *A History of Colonial America* (1973). SLAVERY IN PENNSYLVANIA

WEINBERG, MEYER *(Editor of Integrated Education, Department of History, City Colleges of Chicago, The Loop College)* M.A. University of Chicago; compiler of *The Education of the Minority Child:A Bibliography of 10,000 Selected Entries* (1970); author of *A Chance to Learn:The History of Race and Education in the United States* (1977). EDUCATION:DESEGREGATION IN PERSPECTIVE

WILLINGHAM, ALEX *(Associate Professor of Political Science, Atlanta University, Atlanta, Georgia)* COAUTHOR BLACK PANTHER PARTY; BLACK POWER

WOOD, PETER H. *(Associate Professor of History, Duke University, Durham, North Carolina)* Ph.D. Harvard University; author of *Black Majority:Negroes in Colonial South Carolina from 1670 Through the Stone Rebellion*

(1974). AFRICA:THE ATLANTIC SLAVE TRADE WITH THE CAROLINA RICE COAST

WYNN, DANIEL W. *(Associate Director, The Board of Education, The United Methodist* Church, Nashville, Tennessee) Ph.D. The Johns Hopkins University; author of *NAACP Versus Negro Revolutionary Protest* (1955) and *The Black Protest Movement* (1974). CIVIL RIGHTS:MOVEMENT/INTRODUCTION

ACKNOWLEDGMENTS

We owe our deep thanks to many persons, institutions, and organizations. It is impossible to list all of them here, but we would like to give special acknowledgment to some of the most outstanding.

CONSULTANTS

Anderson, Bernard *Professor of Business Administration, Fort Lewis College, Durango, Colorado*

Anderson, Charles "Chief" *Former Flight Instructor, Tuskegee Institute, Tuskegee, Alabama*

Backman, R. Dwight *Reporter and Producer, WTOP Radio Station, Washington, D.C.*

Bailey, Martin G. *Former Agricultural Supervisor, University of Maryland College Park*

Banks, Earl *Director of Athletics, Morgan State University, Baltimore, Maryland*

Bradley, William H. *Deputy Director, Equal Opportunity Employment Commission (EOEC), Baltimore, Maryland*

Chambers, Frederick *Associate Professor of Secondary Education, Kent State University, Kent, Ohio*

Clarke, Robert *Archivist, National Archives, Washington, D.C.*

Clayton, William L. *Pastor, Macedonia Baptist Church, Baltimore, Maryland*

Couch, William *Former Provost, Federal City College, Washington, D.C.*

Dandridge, William M. *Retired army officer, United States Army*

Darlington, Roy Clifford *Professor of Pharmacy, Howard University, Washington, D.C.*

Fisher, Sethard *Professor of Sociology, University of California, Santa Barbara, California*

Forbes, James Alexander *Professor of Homiletics, Union Theological Seminary, New York City*

Gandy, Samuel L. *Former Professor of Religion, Howard University, Washington, D.C.*

Grace, Patti *Television Producer, WJZ-TV, Channel 13, Baltimore, Maryland*

Greene, Lorenzo J. *Professor Emeritus of History, Lincoln University, Jefferson City, Missouri*

Jackson, Blyden *Professor of English, University of North Carolina, Chapel Hill*

Knighton, Stanley A. *Pastor, Peoples Congregational Church, Washington, D.C.*

Lewis, David T. *Professor of Sociology, University of Maryland Baltimore County*

Low, Patricia *Assistant Professor of Science Education, Morgan State University, Baltimore, Maryland*

Marshall, Pluria *Director, National Black Media Coalition, Washington, D.C.*

Martin, Robert E. *Professor of Political Science, Howard University, Washington, D.C.*

Qualls, Youra *Professor of English, Tuskegee Institute, Tuskegee, Alabama*

Richardson, Earl *Professor of Education, University of Maryland Eastern Shore*

Schwartz, Martin *Professor of Biology, University of Maryland Baltimore County*

Slaiman, Don *AFL-CIO, Washington, D.C.*

Smith, Willie Lamousé *Professor of Sociology, University of Maryland Baltimore County*

Stout, Charles O. *Professor Emeritus, University of Maryland Eastern Shore*

Stout, Juanita Kidd *Judge, Court of Common Pleas, Philadelphia, Pennsylvania*

Taylor, Nathaniel *Assistant Athletic Director, Morgan State University, Baltimore, Maryland*

Toles, Edward B. *U.S. Referee in Bankruptcy, U.S. District Court, Chicago, Illinois*

Wolfgang, Marvin B. *Professor of Sociology and Law, University of Pennsylvania, Philadelphia*

MATERIALS FROM INDIVIDUALS

Many persons were helpful in permitting the use of materials. We would especially like to thank Sherman Briscoe, Constance Britt, John R. Compton, Charles A. Davis, C. Gerald Frazier, Gussie H. Hudson, W. DuBois Johnson, Paul G. Partington, Robert C. Queen, Bennie G. Rodgers, H. D. Singleton, W. Mae Watson, and George R. Woolfolk.

LIBRARIES AND MUSEUMS

University of Maryland Baltimore County
The university's librarian, Antonio Raimo, and the entire staff were most helpful—and delightfully charitable. We give special thanks to members of the reference staff: Mary-Jean Whittaker, Simmona E. Simmons, Howard Curnoles, Binnie Braunstein, Nancy Gonce, Suzanne Thompson, Kathy Hann, Pat Stegal, Helen Williams, and Diane Fishman.

Library of Congress Special thanks are due from us to the photographic services; and we know that, individually and collectively, our consultants and contributors would also acknowledge the library's resources and services in many areas of wide interest. We obtained many illustrations from this source, as is evident in our credit lines.

National Archives Likewise, use was made of photographic collections, but not exclusively so. We give thanks to the archival services of Robert Clarke and James D. Walker; and the services of two contributors, Sara D. Jackson and Harold T. Pinkett.

Howard University Outstanding services were also provided by the university's faculty and staff. The librarians and curators were helpful, especially at the Moorland-Spingarn Research Center to which we assigned a special researcher. Among the librarians and curators were: Ethel Williams of the School of Religion, Michael R. Winston of the Moorland-Spingarn Research Center, and Marilyn Mahanand, Curator of the Theater Collection.

New York Public Library, Schomburg Center for Research in Black Culture Special thanks go to Jean Blackwell Hutson, the chief, and to Ernest Kaiser, curator.

Other libraries included the following: Soper Library, Morgan State University; Milton S. Eisenhower Library, The Johns Hopkins University; Shimkin Library, New York University; and the Welch Medical Library, Johns Hopkins Hospital. Limited use was made of several governmental libraries of the National Institute of Education and the U.S. Office of Education.

Though not a library as such, most significant were the services provided by the Public Information Office, Social and Economic Statistics Administration, U.S. Department of Commerce. We are grateful here to Kenneth C. Field and Beulah Land for their assistance.

Among the museums, we acknowledge the following: Museum of the City of New York, Hart Nautical Museum of the Massachusetts Institute of Technology, Peabody Museum, Baltimore Museum of Art, Mystic Seaport/Marine Historical Association, and the Mariner's Museum. For the latter two, we are especially grateful for materials and data supplied respectively by John F. Leavitt, and John L. Lochhead and Robert H. Burgess. Although most of the materials and data from museums were photographic or illustrative in nature, we also received permission to cite a publication by the Mariner's Museum, for which we give recognition in a later section of these Acknowledgments.

CONSULTANTS ON COLLEGES AND UNIVERSITIES

BENEDICT COLLEGE
Lewis W. Bone
BENNETT COLLEGE
Marvin H. Watkins
CENTRAL STATE UNIVERSITY
Lewis A. Jackson
CHEYNEY STATE COLLEGE
Wade Wilson
CLAFLIN UNIVERSITY
T. K. Blythewood
COPPIN STATE COLLEGE
Calvin W. Burnett
DELAWARE STATE COLLEGE
Luna I. Mishoe
DILLARD UNIVERSITY
Evelyn K. Stampley
EDWARD WATERS COLLEGE
Elma R. Minor
ELIZABETH CITY STATE UNIVERSITY
Thurman J. Andrews, Jr.
FISK UNIVERSITY
Joe M. Richardson
HAMPTON INSTITUTE
Mack M. Greene
HARRIS TEACHERS COLLEGE
Doris L. Mueller
JACKSON STATE COLLEGE
John A. Peoples, Jr.
KENTUCKY STATE UNIVERSITY
Carl M. Hill
LANGSTON UNIVERSITY
James L. Mosley

LeMoyne-Owen College
Robert M. Ratcliffe
Mary Holmes College
Helen E. Pfeifer
Mobile State Junior College
Arthur R. Simpson
Morehouse College
Theda Jackson
Morgan State University
Stewart A. Brooks
Morristown College
James T. Northern
North Carolina Central University
J. E. Jeffries
Paul Quinn College
L. C. Wood
Prairie View Agricultural and Mechanical (A&M) College
Alvin I. Thomas
Prentiss Institute
Harris E. Lee
Rust College
Kathy W. Smith
Saint Augustine's College
Purdie Andus
South Carolina State College
R. L. Hurst
Spelman College
Albert E. Manley
Stillman College
Richard W. Looser
Tennessee State University
A. P. Torrence
Texas College
W. E. Williams
Tougaloo College
Charles W. Porter
Tuskegee Institute
Luther H. Foster
Virginia State College
William E. Terry
Virginia Union University
Allix B. James
Winston-Salem State University
W. Archie Blunt
Xavier University of Louisiana
Paul Keith

COPYRIGHT SOURCES/BY ENTRY

We gratefully acknowledge our indebtedness to authors and publishers for permission to use materials from their publications.

Africa: Land and Peoples of West Africa Robert O. Collins, "The Guinea Coast," in *African History: Text and Readings*, © Random House, Inc., New York, 1971, pp. 129–130.

Africa: The Atlantic Slave Trade with the Chesapeake Tobacco Coast Arthur P. Middleton, *Tobacco Coast: A Maritime History of the Chesapeake Bay in the Colonial Era*, © Mariners Museum, Newport News, Va., 1953, selections from Chapter Five.

Africa: The Atlantic Slave Trade with the Carolina Rice Coast Peter H. Wood, *Black Majority: Negroes in Colonial South Carolina from 1670 Through the Stone Rebellion*, © Peter H. Wood, Alfred A. Knopf, Inc., New York, 1974, with adaptations by the author.

African Legacy/Survivals: African Art Warren M. Robbins, "Introduction," in *The deHavenon Collection*, © Museum of African Art, Washington, D.C., 1971.

African Methodist Episcopal Church Grant S. Shockley, "African Methodist Episcopal Church," in Emory Stevens Bucket (ed.), *The History of American Methodism*, © Abingdon Press, New York, 1964, pp. 547–550.

African Methodist Episcopal Zion Church David H. Bradley, "A History of the A.M.E. Zion Church," *The A.M.E. Zion Quarterly Review*, volume 84, number 3, 1972, pp. 154–156, revised by the author.

Afro-American History: Free Negroes, 1600s–1860 Benjamin Quarles, "The Antebellum Free Negro," *Baltimore Bulletin of Education*, volume 45, numbers 2, 3, 1968–1969, pp. 22–27, revised by the author.

Afro-American History: Colonial Period, 1600–1783 (The Southern Economy) Norman A. Graebner, Gilbert C. Fite, and Philip L. White, *A History of the American People*, © McGraw-Hill Book Company, New York, 1970, pp. 67–72, 101, 120, 159.

Afro-American History: Sectional Conflict over Slavery, 1820–1860 David S. Sparks, "Sectional Conflict in Wesley M. Gewehr et al. (eds.), *The United States: A History of a Democracy*, © McGraw-Hill Book Company, New York, 1960, revised by the author.

Baptists Edward A. Freeman, "National Baptist Convention, U.S.A., Inc.," *Baptist Advance: The Achievements of Baptists in North America for a Century and a Half*, © Boardman Press, Nashville, Tenn., 1964, pp. 190–226, revised and adapted by the author.

ACKNOWLEDGMENTS

CIVIL RIGHTS: AFTERMATH Robert H. Brisbane, *Black Activism*, © Judson Press, Valley Forge, Pa., 1974, from the section entitled "Postscript" and the chapter entitled "Black Politics and the Black Center City."

DANCE Lynne Fauley Emery, *Black Dance in the United States from 1619 to 1970*, © National Press Books, Palo Alto, California, 1972, pp. 325–328.

EDUCATION Virgil A. Clift, "Educating The American Negro," in John Davis (ed.), *The American Negro Reference Book*, © Prentice-Hall, Inc., Englewood Cliffs, N.J., 1966, revised and adapted by the author.

LITERATURE: FOLKLORE (The Centrality of Folklore) Langston Hughes and Arna Bontemps (eds.), *The Book of Negro Folklore*, © Dodd, Mead & Company, Inc., New York, 1965, pp. vii–xi, xiv.

LITERATURE: THE NOVEL Noel Schraufnagel, *The Black American Novel: From Apology to Protest*, © Everett/Edwards, Inc., Deland, Florida, 1973, selections from the Introduction and Chapter One.

LITERATURE: DRAMA/THEATER (History and Development) William Couch (ed.), *New Black Playwrights*, © Louisiana State University Press, Baton Rouge, La., 1968, from the "Introduction."

LITERATURE: DRAMA/THEATER (Lorraine Hansberry) Arthur P. Davis, *From the Dark Tower: Afro-American Writers, 1900-1960*, © Howard University Press, 1974.

MUSIC: SPIRITUALS/PERFORMANCE (except selected spirituals shown) Eileen Southern, *The Music of Afro-Americans*, © W. W. Norton, New York, 1971.

PHYSICIANS W. Montague Cobb, "The Black Physician in America," in *The New Physician*, the official journal of the Student American Medical Association, copyright © 1970, volume 19, pp. 912–916.

POLITICS (Southern Politics) Numan V. Bartley and Hugh D. Graham, *Southern Politics and the Second Reconstruction*, © The Johns Hopkins University Press, Baltimore, Md., 1975, from the section entitled "Conclusion."

POLITICS (Northern Big Cities) Robert H. Brisbane, *Black Activism*, © Judson Press, Valley Forge, Pa., 1974, from the section entitled "Postscript"and the chapter entitled "Black Politics and the Black Center City."

POPULATION (Fertility) Reynolds Farley, *Growth of the Black Population: A Study of Demographic Trends*, © Markham Publishing Company, Chicago, Ill., 1970.

RACE: RACE AND BIOLOGY (Biology) Glenford E. Mitchell and Daniel C. Jordan, *What is Race? Questions and Answers on the Most Challenging Issue*, © National Spiritual Assembly of the Bahá'ís of the U.S.A., Bahá'í Publishing Trust, Wilmette, Illinois, 1967.

RACE: RACE AND BIOLOGY (Sickle-Cell Disease) Roland B. Scott, "A Commentary on Sickle Cell Disease." *Journal of the National Medical Association*, volume 63, number 1, 1971, pp. 1–3.

RACE: RACE AND CULTURE Ina Corinne Brown, "Anthropological and Sociological Factors in Race Relations," in Virgil A. Clift et al. (eds.), *Negro Education in America: Its Adequacy, Problems, and Needs*, © Harper and Row, New York, 1963, revised and adapted by the author.

RACE: RACISM (Persistence) I. A. Newby, *The Development of Segregationist Thought*, © The Dorsey Press, Homewood, Illinois, 1968, pp. 17–20.

SLAVERY: INTRODUCTION Phillis Bate Sparks, "Economic Development—North and South," in Wesley M. Gewehr et al. (eds.), *The United States: A History of a Democracy*, © McGraw-Hill Book Company, New York, 1960.

WOMEN (Individual Women in the 1970s) Virgil A. Clift, "Black America," in *1976 World Topics Yearbook*, © United Educators, Inc., Lake Bluff, Illinois, 1976.

OTHER MATERIALS

Some selected government documents included the following:

U.S. Commission on Civil Rights, *Report 1961: Housing*, U.S. Government Printing Office, Washington, D.C., 1961.

U.S. Department of Commerce, Social and Economic Statistics Administration, *The Social and Economic Status of the Black Population in the United States, 1974*, Ser. P-23, No. 54, U.S. Government Printing Office, Washington, D.C., 1975.

U.S. Commission on Civil Rights, *Twenty Years After Brown: Equal Opportunity in Housing*, U.S. Government Printing Office, Washington, D.C., 1975. U.S. Department of Labor, Bureau of Labor Statistics, *The Negro Employment*

Situation, Report 391, U.S. Government Printing Office, Washington, D.C., 1971.

U.S. Bureau of the Census, *Detailed Occupations of Employed Persons by Race and Sex for the United States: 1970*, PC(S1)-32, March 1973, tables 1 through 7 were adopted from a supplementary report; see table 223 of Final Report PC(1)-D1.

U.S. Department of Labor, Bureau of Labor Statistics, *Black Americans: A Chartbook*, Bulletin 1699, U.S. Government Printing Office, Washington, D.C., 1971. U.S. Bureau of the Census, *A Statistical Portrait of Women in the United States*, Current Population Reports, Special Studies, Ser. P-23, no. 58, U.S. Government Printing Office, Washington, D.C., April 1976.

Other materials included:

Disciples of Christ, *Preliminary Guide to Black Materials in the Disciples of Christ Historical Society* (under the direction of Marvin D. Williams), Nashville, Tennessee, 1971.

Jack D. Forbes, *Afro-Americans in the Far West: A Handbook for Educators*, U.S. Government Printing Office, Washington, D.C., 1967.

Clayton Torrence, *Old Somerset on the Eastern Shore*, reprinted by Regional Publishing Company, Baltimore, 1966.

ILLUSTRATIONS, PHOTOGRAPHS, PHOTOGRAPHERS

Whereas museums supplied a very limited but important number of prints, the great bulk of our illustrations came from other sources: libraries, collections, individuals, and photographers. Since credit lines have been given with our illustrations, we mention briefly here the main sources: Library of Congress, National Archives, Moorland-Spingarn Research Center, Scurlock Studios, special collections at universities or in press or media files, individual photographers, and private collections. We call special attention to services rendered by Tom Beck, Curator of the Edward L. Bafford Photography Collection at the University of Maryland Baltimore County. (Bafford was a Maryland pictorialist and photographer whose work was the first to be exhibited by the Special Collections Library of the university.) Beck introduced and guided us through this collection. The two Civil War photos from this collection on pages 63 and 64 are believed to be printed here for the first time. Although we also included selections from the famous Matthew Brady collection on the Civil War, we were of the opinion that these two photos brought a new freshness that the much-used Brady photos lack.

Beck also supplied us with data on several black contemporary photographers; and his service in this regard enriched the minor article PHOTOGRAPHERS (page 670). The works of several photographers mentioned in this article are represented in the *Encyclopedia*. Two of them, Leroy Henderson and Arnold Hinton, permitted us to select from a wide range of prints, many never before reproduced.

Moreover, we are grateful to Bill and Jeff Morganstern, professional photographers of Woodlawn, Maryland, likewise represented in the *Encyclopedia*, who shot on assignment for us and made many reproductions as well.

Special thanks are also due to the librarians of Talladega College, who sent us printed color copies of the Amistad Murals (see page 120); to James E. Lewis, professor of art at Morgan State University, whose art is represented on pages 319 and 833; to Fritz Achtoh of the Ghanian Embassy, who permitted us to examine a collection in his office; to the Scurlock Studios, who permitted our researcher to examine copies there; to Robert Duncan, who on assignment for us covered Harlem, New York City; to Esme and Lancelot Swann of Bermuda, who sent us unreproduced copies of black American visitors; to Dennis Starks of West Palm Beach, Florida, who permitted us to make reproductions of black musicians and their bands that were photographed in his club, Sunset Lounge, years ago; to Joan Sandler of the Black Theater Alliance, who sent us striking photos of her group; to Elaine and Gilbert Brown, who permitted us as guests in their home to examine their family collection; and last, but not least, to Jacquelyn Low, who shot pictures while sometimes accompanying her father on missions for the *Encyclopedia*, or on jaunts for family pleasure.

BIOGRAPHIES, RESEARCH, CLERICAL

The thankless task of collecting, validating, composing, and typing the numerous biographies was performed primarily by the Editors and the Editorial Staff. Special thanks, however, should go to Patricia Allen-Browne. Moreover, our thanks also go to two nonstaff members who gave very substantial help in the composition and typing: Marilyn Geels of New York City and Louisa Pacetti of New Jersey. Janette Hoston Harris of Washington, D.C., also helped in the composition and typing of some biographies, and we acknowledge her services. We also want to thank the many persons who responded to our queries in regard to biographies—or on other topics.

Lastly, in a project of this sort, the paper work can be, and was, mountainous. We are grateful to many helping hands that served to keep it in reasonable working order through such duties as typing, copy making, collating, cataloging, and filing. Without mentioning professional typists, we do say that family and friends pitched in: Albert Johnson, a former student; the Robinson family: "Robby," Duncan, and Lisa; and Doris, Sharon, William, and Jacquelyn Low.

A

AARON, HENRY LOUIS (HANK) (1934–   ), professional baseball player; born in Mobile, Ala. After playing with teams in black leagues, including the Indianapolis Clowns, Aaron was purchased by the Milwaukee (later Atlanta) Braves of the National League and became a regular outfielder with that club at the start of the 1954 season. His .328 batting average led the National League in 1956; a year later he led the league in home runs (44) and runs batted in (132) and was named its Most Valuable Player while leading the Braves to a world championship and starring in the World Series against the New York Yankees. His production of home runs continued to mount steadily. In his first appearance at bat in 1974, on April 4 in Cincinnati, he hit the 714th home run of his career, thereby tying the major-league record belonging to Babe Ruth for almost 40 years. Four days later, in Atlanta Stadium, he hit his 715th home run (off Al Downing of the Los Angeles Dodgers) to become the most prolific home-run hitter in major-league history—a feat that attracted national attention and won for Aaron congratulatory messages from officials in many areas of American life. By the close of the 1974 season, when he was traded to the Milwaukee Brewers of the American League, Aaron had hit 733 career home runs in 21 seasons in the major leagues. He ended his career with a .310 lifetime batting average, 755 home runs, and 2,202 runs batted in. His autobiography entitled *Aaron,* was published in 1974. In 1975 he was awarded the Spingarn Medal by the National Association for the Advancement of Colored People (NAACP). *See also* ATHLETES: BASEBALL; SPINGARN MEDAL.

ABBOTT, ROBERT SENGSTACKE (1870–1940), editor, publisher; born in St. Simon Island, Ga. Abbott attended Claflin College (Orangeburg, S.C.) and Hampton Institute (Hampton, Va.), and received a LL.B. from Kent College. In 1905 Abbott founded the *Chicago Defender,* later becoming president and treasurer of the Robert S. Abbott Publishing Company. He served on Governor Frank O. Lowden's Race Relations Commission following the Chicago race riot of 1919. Abbott's *Defender* was the most influential black newspaper of its day. It attacked discrimination, segregation, and lynching, and it encouraged blacks to migrate from the South. Abbott increased the *Defender's* circulation from a few hundred in the beginning to more than 200,000 by the end of his career. While engaging in many crusades, he also recruited able writers for the *Defender,* including Gwendolyn Brooks (later a Pulitzer Prize winner) and Willard Motley. *See also* NEWSPAPERS.

ABEL, ELIJAH (? –1884), clergyman. Abel became a member of the Mormon faith (Church of Jesus Christ of Latter-day Saints) in 1832, and much of his career was intimately tied to Mormonism, despite that church's long-standing ban on admitting Afro-Americans to its clergy. Abel was a mortician in Nauvo, Ill., an early Mormon stronghold, and then joined the church's migra-

1

tion to Salt Lake City, Utah, where he was a hotel manager. He was ordained an elder in 1836; as such he is the first black known to have served as a Mormon minister. Abel became a missionary in Canada, and at the time of his death he was engaged in church business in Ohio.

ABERNATHY, RALPH DAVID (1926–   ), civil rights leader, clergyman; born in Linden, Ala. Abernathy, whose grandfather was a slave, received a B.S. degree from Alabama State College in 1950, but his interests changed and he enrolled at Atlanta University to do graduate work in sociology. It was not long before he met Martin Luther King, Jr. He and King each presided over Baptist congregations in Montgomery, Ala., and became fast friends, gaining national prominence in the successful Montgomery bus boycott. From this victory Abernathy and King moved to mobilize the forces of black protest into the formation of the Southern Christian Leadership Conference (SCLC) with King as president and Abernathy as secretary-treasurer. The SCLC soon became the leading proponent of nonviolence, a philosophy that came under attack by the more militant factions in the black movement. But King reasserted his belief in this form of protest by announcing in 1961 that Abernathy would be his successor. Following King's assassination, Abernathy organized the spectacular Poor People's Campaign in Washington, D.C. Dressed in laborer's clothes and carrying tools, he launched the building of Resurrection City, U.S.A.—a site of huts that remained in the center of Washington for more than a month. Abernathy was arrested for refusing to comply with police efforts to dismantle Resurrection City and was jailed for 20 days. Later, in Atlanta, he organized the SCLC's Operation Breadbasket in which economic pressure by means of selective buying was brought against companies that had refused equal opportunities to blacks. In addition to his efforts in the field of civil rights, Abernathy also retained his ministry. After 1961 he served as pastor of the West Hunter Baptist Church in Atlanta, Ga. He also was awarded several honorary degrees. See also MONTGOMERY IMPROVEMENT ASSOCIATION; SOUTHERN CHRISTIAN LEADERSHIP CONFERENCE (SCLC).

ABYSSINIAN BAPTIST CHURCH One of the oldest and largest of Baptist congregations, the church has roots back to 1808/09 when a number of black worshippers (18) split with the parent white membership of the First Baptist Church on Gold Street in lower Manhattan, New York City and began their own services about a mile away on Anthony Street (later named Worth Street). Illustrative of a major migratory pattern of the black population in Manhattan, the church later moved northward to West 40th Street; in 1923 it moved again into a new Gothic building, that cost then about $350,000, at 132 West 138th Street in Harlem. The mortgage was symbolically burned five years later. Throughout its history, the church has played an important, role, locally and nationally, in serving as a public forum for religious, social, and political issues of concern to Afro-Americans. Two of its nationally known ministers, father and son, supplied much of the church's leadership in the 20th century: Adam Clayton Powell, Sr., served as pastor from 1908 to 1937; he was followed shortly thereafter by his son, a U.S. Congressman, whose tenure lasted until the early 1970s when he was succeeded by Samuel D. Proctor. With a letterhead indicating that it was the "church of the masses", Abyssinian at one time claimed to be—and perhaps was—the largest Protestant church in the world, with a membership of 14,-000. See also BAPTISTS; POWELL, ADAM CLAYTON, JR.; POWELL, ADAM CLAYTON, SR.; PROCTOR, SAMUEL D.

ACTORS See LITERATURE: DRAMA/THEATER; MOTION PICTURES.

ADAMS, ALGER L. (1910–   ), editor, publisher, author; born in Omaha, Nebr. Adams received a B.A. degree from Hobart College (later Hobart-William Smith Colleges, Geneva, N.Y.) in 1932 and a M.A. degree from Columbia University Teacher's College in 1967. Adams also attended General Theological Seminary and Columbia University School of Journalism. He served as editor and publisher of the *Westchester County Press* after 1948, and was assistant to the editor and publisher of the New York *Amsterdam News* from 1940 to 1947. Adams was one of the first black instructors at Columbia University Teacher's College and at Manhattan College. He has published two novels: *Taffy* (1949) and *With My Eyes Wide Open* (1952).

ADAMS, ALTON AUGUSTUS (1889– ?), bandmaster, composer; born in St. Thomas, Virgin Islands. Adams organized and conducted an orchestra when he was 14 years old. After study at the University of Pennsylvania and with private teachers, he organized a band in the Virgin Islands in 1917 for the U.S. Navy, becoming the first Afro-American bandmaster in that branch of the service. Other positions held during his career include assistant director of the municipal band of St. Thomas and supervisor of music in the public school system of the Virgin Islands. The composer of several marches, Adams is best known for "Virgin Islands March" and "Spirit of the United States Navy." See also VIRGIN ISLANDS.

ADAMS, CLARA ISABEL (1933–   ), chemist, educator; born in Baltimore, Md. Adams received a B.S. degree from Morgan State College (Baltimore, Md.) in 1954, a M.S. degree from Iowa State University (Ames, Ia.) in 1957, and the Ph.D. from Smith College (Northampton, Mass.) in 1970. In 1975 Adams became dean of the graduate school at Morgan State after serving as chairperson of the department of chemistry. See also MORGAN STATE UNIVERSITY.

ADAMS, JOHN HURST (1929–   ), clergyman, bishop; born in Columbia, S.C. Adams received his B.A. from Johnson C. Smith University (Charlotte, N.C.) in 1948; his S.T.B. and S.T.M. from Boston University (Boston, Mass.); he did further study at Harvard University and Union Theological Seminary. He served as minister for several African Methodist Episcopal (AME) churches, including Bethel in Lynn, Mass., 1950–1952; First AME in Seattle, Wash., 1963–1968; and Grant AME in Los Angeles, Calif., from 1968 until his election as bishop. He also served on faculties to two AME-affiliated institutions of higher education: Payne Theological Seminary, Wilberforce, Ohio, 1952–1956; and, as president, Paul Quinn College, Waco, Texas, 1956–1962. He received several honors and awards, including an honorary doctorate (D.D.) from Wilberforce University, and Man of the Year Award from B'nai B'rith, Seattle, Wash.

ADAMS, NUMA POMPILIUS GARFIELD (1885–1940), physician, educator; born in Delaplane, Va. Adams received a B.A. degree from Howard University (Washington, D.C.) in 1911, a M.A. degree from Columbia University in 1912, and his M.D. degree from Rush Medical School of the University of Chicago in 1923. He taught chemistry at Howard University from 1912 to 1919, and was assistant medical director of the Victory Life Insurance Company from 1927 to 1929. An instructor in neurology at Provident Hospital,

Baltimore, Md., Adams became the first Afro-American dean of medicine at Howard University, Medical College, a post he held from 1929 to 1940. See also HOWARD UNIVERSITY.

ADAMS, SAMUEL CLIFFORD, JR. (1920–   ), government official; born in Waco, Tex. Adams attended Fisk University (Nashville, Tenn.), from which he graduated in 1940. After a tour of duty in the U.S. Air Force, he returned to Fisk and received a M.A. degree in 1947. The same year he was named director of the Marion Cooperative Center of the American Missionary Association. In 1950 Adams became a research assistant in the race relations division of the School of Social Sciences at the University of Chicago. In 1954 he began a government career as acting chief in the education division of the U.S. Operations Mission to Vietnam. In 1955 he was sent to Cambodia, also on an education mission. Three years later, having spent a year at the London School of Economics, he was assigned to educational projects in Niger and Mali. In 1965 Adams was appointed by President Lyndon B. Johnson as overseas director of the Agency for International Development (AID), with administrative control over the U.S. mission to Morocco. In 1972 he became AID's assistant administrator for Africa.

ADDERLEY, HERB See ATHLETES: FOOTBALL.

ADEN, ALONZO JAMES (1906–   ), painter, curator; born in Spartanburg, S.C. Aden was best known for assembling the significant exhibition entitled Art of the American Negro in Chicago, Ill., in 1940. He received a B.A. degree from Howard University (Washington, D.C.) in 1933. From 1940 to 1943 Aden was curator of the Howard University Gallery of Art. He opened the Barnett-Aden Gallery in Washington, D.C., in 1943.

ADOWA A traditional Ghanaian (Gold Coast) dance. See also AFRICA: THE ATLANTIC SLAVE TRADE / AFRICAN IMPACT.

AFAM / AFRAM Abbreviations used for African-American, especially in reference to black studies at colleges and universities.

AFL-CIO (AMERICAN FEDERATION OF LABOR-CONGRESS OF INDUSTRIAL ORGANIZATIONS) See LABOR UNIONS.

AFRICA

Although many ancestors of Afro-Americans descended from ethnic groups in Europe and the Americas, the continent of Africa, particularly West Africa, may be regarded as the principal historic homeland of Afro-Americans. The word "Afro," of course, is derived from the word "Africa," whose linguistic origins are rather obscure. Less obscure, however, is the probable origin of the word "Niger," which derives from the Latin word meaning *black* and which is preserved in the name of the great river in West Africa as well as in corruptions of the word "Negro," a word that has often been misapplied and abused in reference to peoples of African ancestry.

West Africa is a vast land of diverse peoples and cultures. With an area of about 2.4 million square miles, it constitutes about five-sixths the size of the United States; yet, it occupies only about 20 percent of the total land area of Africa, the second largest continent.

Land and Peoples of West Africa* Stretching from Dakar in the west to the Cameroons in the east, the West African coast forms a 2000-mile belt of smooth beaches interspersed by river mouths and inlets forming mangrove swamps and quiet lagoons. Beyond are the rain forests, where the average rainfall ranges from thirty to over one hundred inches a year. In these well-watered

Contemporary view looking north into West Africa from the top of Elmina castle, which is located on the waterfront of the Atlantic Ocean at Elmina, Ghana. The view looks across the Benya River away from the ocean. *(Courtesy of Ghana Information Services Department, Accra.)*

Elmina ("the mine") was the first important castle/port built (1482) by the Portuguese to serve the European-African gold trade; and the region of its location, with its center in Kumasi, thus came to be known as the Gold Coast. Elmina provided many European sailors and traders with their first sight of Africans. It also provided the local Akan-speaking peoples with their first view of seaborne Europeans, who were called *boroni* (in Ashanti) or *borenyi* (in Fanti)—literally *he who came swimming on the surface*—a name later applied to any white person. The emphasis was thus on how whites arrived, not on the difference in black-white skin color. By the mid-1600s slaves had replaced gold as the chief export of the area; and Elmina, as a slave detention depot, had passed to Dutch control. However, when many of the slave ancestors of Afro-Americans passed through Elmina, mainly in the 1700s, the castle was under British rule, remaining so until 1957, when the Gold Coast became the independent nation of Ghana.

forests, shifting cultivation is practiced to support a relatively dense, sedentary population. A minimal amount of group cooperation is required to clear the land and cultivate the corn, manioc, yams, and bananas, the staple crops of the coastal peoples. Beyond the coast the rainfall decreases, and the dense forests turn into parklands and the savanna of the western Sudan. Here the irregular, uneven rainfall supports fewer farmers and encourages pastoralism, which demands vast tracts of land and a sparse population compared with the forest belt further south. In the past, West Africa was more accessible from the north, across the Sahara and Sudan, than from the sea. Except for Dakar and Lagos, the coast of West Africa had few natural harbors and only three estuaries that offered sheltered anchorages—the Gambia, the Senegal, and the Niger. Landings along the rest of the coast had to be made through heavy surf or in mangrove swamps, beyond which lay the dark, brooding forests, penetrated only by narrow, tortuous footpaths that were suitable only for human porterage because the presence of the tsetse fly prohibited the use of animals. Malaria, yellow fever, and other tropical diseases struck down the incomer until the discovery of prophylactics in the nineteenth century.

Despite these formidable and discouraging obstacles to outsiders coming from the sea, the forest region has supported large and prosperous African populations. Many unsuccessful attempts have been made to classify the peoples of West Africa according to political, social, or even physical typologies, but the only rational basis for comparison remains language. With few exceptions, the inhabitants of the forest zone speak related languages of what Professor [Joseph H.] Greenberg has called the Niger-Congo language family. In Senegal reside the Wolof, Serer, Tucolor, and Susu, whereas further down the coast there are a host of small groups, chief among which are the Temne, Vai, Bussa, and Kru. Further in the interior, in the uplands where the Senegal and the Niger rivers take their rise, dwell the Mande-speaking peoples, who have played such a prominent role in the history of the western Sudan and whose trade contacts with the forest regions have spread their influence to the coastal peoples. In the Gold Coast to the east live the Ashanti and Fanti, who are Akan-speaking, and the less numerous Gã and Ewe of the coast, who are not. Dahomey is dominated by the Fon and the Egba, and in the forest zone of Nigeria live the powerful Yoruba in the west and the Ibo in the east, both surrounded by clusters of smaller groups.

The Stateless Societies The history of the coastal regions of the west, like those of East Africa, has polarized around stateless societies on the one

Contemporary map of West Africa showing coast along the Atlantic Ocean from Dakar (upper left) to the Cameroons (lower right). (*Text and map from Robert O. Collins, chap. 2, "The Guinea Coast," *African History: Text and Readings,* copyright © Random House, New York, 1971.)

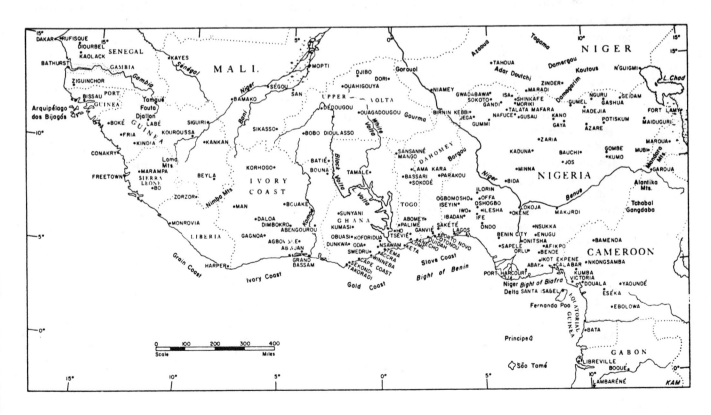

hand and well-organized African state systems on the other. Along the lower Ivory Coast, within the interior of Liberia, and in parts of Guinea and Sierra Leone live small, fragmented groups that never developed the political organization which characterized African state systems further to the east. The dense forests of this region have traditionally hampered movement, particularly between east and west, whereas the rivers of the area provide no access from south to north. The rainy season is long and continually renders communications difficult, if not virtually impossible. Thus, although the density of the rain forest has hindered the evolution of complex political organizations, it has provided a refuge for peoples under pressure from the surrounding states, mixing diverse groups and contributing to the proliferation of tribal names that all but defy classification. Nevertheless, these stateless societies clearly are culturally related to the surrounding peoples, and although it is still hopelessly confused, their history has undoubtedly been deeply influenced by the well-recorded history of the Mande to the north and the Akan to the east. Until more adequate information is supplied by comparative ethnographic studies, the history of these stateless societies remains a mosaic of tribal movements that have split into smaller and smaller political units.

The Forest States Beyond the clusters of stateless societies huddled on the headland of West Africa, a series of forest kingdoms, whose sophisticated political and social organization enabled them to exert widespread cultural and economic influence, existed from the Ivory Coast to the Cameroons. Three factors have conditioned the rise and development of these states. The oldest and probably least-appreciated influence on the forest kingdoms was their contact with the Sudanic states to the north. The trade routes that spanned the Sahara did not always terminate in the great market towns of the western Sudan. Before the arrival of the Europeans in the fifteenth century, a well-established trade route connected the gold-bearing regions of the Gold Coast with the great Sudanic trading entrepôt of Djenné. Commercial centers were founded by Mande and Muslim traders south of the Mali Empire at Bobo Dioulasso, Kong, and even further south at Begho. The wanderings of these merchants almost certainly took them through the heart of Ashanti to the coast, where there may possibly have been a pre-European waterborne trade between the markets of the Gold Coast and the commercial centers of Benin and the Niger Delta. Thus, from the fifteenth to the nineteenth century, gold, kola nuts, and slaves were sent north in exchange for brassware, cloth, and salt—the products of the western Sudan and North Africa. The economic influence of the north was accompanied by political and cultural influences. Islam was carried further south, and groups of Mande warriors who came with the caravans to protect them remained behind to create small, centralized states. A similar northern influence penetrated south from Hausaland in northern Nigeria through Nupe and into the Yoruba state of Oyo. Like the rulers of Ashanti in the Gold Coast, the Yoruba claim a northern origin, though the evidence for this still consists mostly of myth, legend, and selected cultural similarities to the inhabitants of the Sudan and the Nile Valley.

A second influence that shaped the forest kingdoms was the arrival of the Europeans and the development of the slave trade. Many authors have attributed the rise and growth in power of these states to the acquisition of European firearms in return for slaves, and the slave trade has been regarded by past historians of Africa as the sole and sufficient explanation for the rise and fall of the coastal states. Once equipped with guns, the Ashanti, the Fon, the Oyo, and the Benin were able to expand at the expense of their neighbors, founding kingdoms on the spiral of violence—slaves for guns, which led to more slaves for more guns. Certainly the European factor contributed to the growth as well as the ultimate decay of the forest states, but it is an increasingly unsatisfactory basis for the interpretation of their origins.

No history of the forest states can be properly understood without recognizing a third factor, the anatomy or internal dynamics of their political, social, and cultural institutions and the way in which these have precipitated historical change within the states. The manner in which the Ashanti confederacy was organized, the power of the hereditary nobility in Oyo, and the relative weakness of the hereditary class in Benin have, for example, played critical roles in the evolution of these kingdoms. So, too, have the relations of these states to the myriads of their less well-organized neighbors, as well as the development of culture and technology, conditioned the history of the forest states and placed the role of the slave trade in proper historical perspective.

The Atlantic Slave Trade in Perspective "The Atlantic slave trade," says Philip D. Curtin, "lay at the heart of a wide net of commerce and production that touched every shore of the Atlantic basin." Known as the South Atlantic System, this complex had its origins in the Mediterranean areas of Europe in the wake of the Crusades when Europeans were used as slaves to produce the system's first and most important crop: sugar. Revolutionary improvements in the quality of navigation and sailing ships, achieved largely by Portuguese seamen, plus nature's gift of the trade winds, made it possible to draw laborers from West Africa, then to extend the system to the Azores in the Atlantic, and finally to extend the system across the ocean to Brazil and elsewhere during the 1500s and later. A new kind of plantation thus arose in the New World, stretching from Brazil through what is now the southern United States, employing new types of organization and labor unknown before in either Europe or Africa. The laborer became dehumanized, a commodity unit oriented to the export market: this is the essential difference between slavery wherever it developed in the New World and slavery in Africa or the ancient world of Greece and Rome. For every export crop—sugar, tobacco, coffee, cotton, or rice—there was an accompanying large-scale demand for slaves.

The demand for slave labor in the New World led to a highly organized trade in Africa that was supplied by peaceful means or purchase or outright warfare and raids. Sufficient European merchandise (rum, gunpowder, metal, denims) was imported into Africa to support the slaving, and it was brought from ships or supply depots often by caravans or in large canoes. Often soldiers had to accompany the canoes or coffles to ward off piracy, especially on the return trip from the hinterland. Stockades (barracoons) were used for security purposes whenever necessary. Once back on the coast, the purchased or captured slaves, always in coffles and yokes, were placed in forts that served temporarily as prisons until the slave ship, waiting ashore, could receive its quota. Elmina, for example, which had been used in the spice and gold trade, became a slave dungeon. Other well-known slave forts were Cape Coast Castle, Christianborg, Cormantine, Fort Metal Cross, and Goree. Forty-five such forts were built on the Gold Coast (Ghana) alone. As a fort, Elmina was well-suited for the purposes of holding slaves until they were ready for the Atlantic voyage: It was accessible to slave-carrying ships; there were quarters upstairs for merchants and traders; and there were dark,

Eighteenth-century map of the Gold Coast showing location of slave-detention castle/forts. (Flags of European nationals are used as markers.) The map was published by an English writer and economist, Malachy Postlewayt (1707?–1767).

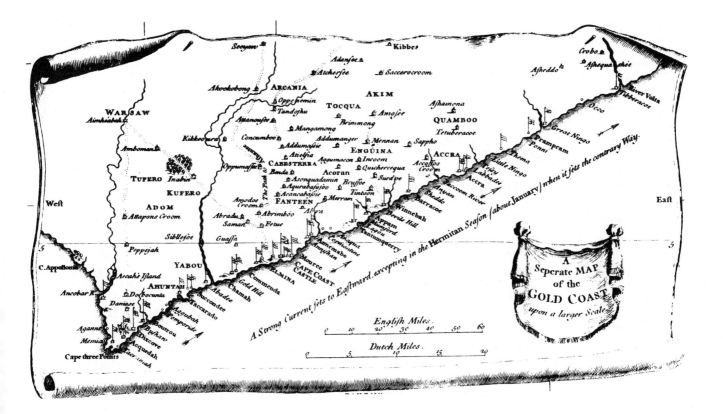

airless dungeons walled with manacles for the slaves below. There was also a courtyard for the branding of slaves.

Slaves were brought to the New World in specially built ships so that large cargoes could be carried. Ships were literally packed with human cargo, for there was not even standing room on slave ships, except on the top deck when, in chains, the slaves were exercised (usually) once per day and doused down with seawater. Below the top deck, there was only crawling room for the slaves. Considering the month-long voyage across the Atlantic and the overcrowding, it is understandable that many slaves died in the crossing (called the "Middle Passage"). About one out of every six or eight slaves forced aboard in Africa never landed in America. It is said that sharks often followed slave ships, feeding upon bodies that were sure to be tossed overboard.

In the early period of the slave trade, the greatest carriers were the Portuguese, Dutch, and Spanish (not excluding other European nationals, however). In the later period, the English were the principal carriers. Headquarters for English operations were Liverpool and Bristol. Much of the trade was triangular, involving rum, slaves, and sugar in shipments between America, Africa, and the West Indies.

The eighteenth century saw the greatest importations of slaves to the West Indies and America. When the British Board of Trade made a survey of the slave trade in 1726, it found that trade to the American colonies, with Virginia the ultimate destination, amounted to 30,000 slaves per year. Bristol alone was operating 63 ships capable of carrying 16,930 slaves.

The next few decades, however, saw the spectacular rise of the Liverpool trade. By 1752 Liverpool merchants had 88 ships that transported upward of 24,730 slaves. In 1786 Liverpool slavers sold 31,690 slaves for £1,282,690, making a profit of £298,462 or nearly a quarter of their investment. The merchants were especially pleased that year and commissioned a local artist, Thomas Stothard, to paint one of their famous slave ships, the *Sable Venus*.

No exact or systematic accounts have been preserved of the slave trade in all of its ramifications. Thus, much data as to number of imports, prices, origins in Africa, and destinations in the New World are speculative. There are, however, some good scholarly estimates. Using documents in the British Museum, Frank Wesley Pitman was one of the early modern English-speaking scholars to investigate aspects of the trade in his book entitled *The Development of the British West Indies, 1700–1763* (1917). Pitman estimated that the total imports of slaves to the British American colonies from 1680 to 1786 was about 2,130,000, or an annual average of 20,095. The high-water mark, he claimed, came in the year 1768 when 104,100 slaves were imported from Africa, of whom the British transported 53,100 during the year; the North Americans, 6,300; the French, 23,500; the Dutch, 11,100; and the Danes, 1,200. A more recent historian, Philip D. Curtin, has lowered these estimates somewhat, indicating that the total imports to British America were about 2,064,000 for the *entire* period of the trade. Curtin's estimates for *all* imports into the Americas are shown below.

TOTAL SLAVE IMPORTS INTO THE AMERICAS, 1451–1870, IN THOUSANDS (ADD 000)

Region and country	Total
British North America	399.0
Spanish America	1,552.1
British Caribbean	1,665.0
Jamaica	747.5
Barbados	387.0
Leeward Islands	346.0
St. Vincent, St. Lucia, Tobago, and Dominica	70.1
Trinidad	22.4
Grenada	67.0
Other BWI	25.0
French Caribbean	1,600.2
Saint Dominigue	864.3
Martinique	365.8
Guadeloupe	290.8
Louisiana	28.3
French Guiana	51.0
Dutch Caribbean	500.0
Danish Caribbean	28.0
Brazil	3,646.8
Old World	175.0
Europe	50.0
São Thomé	100.0
Atlantic Island	25.0
Total	9,566.1
Annual average	22.8

SOURCE: Philip D. Curtin, *The Atlantic Slave Trade: A Census*, University of Wisconsin Press, Madison, 1969.

Depending upon the time and the trader, slave imports came from varying places along the African Atlantic coast. British traders dealt mainly with the Gold Coast (Ghana) during the first half of the eighteenth century. During the second half of the century, however, their operations shifted further to the east along the Guinea Coast, to that portion between the Volta River and the Cameroons, that is, the "slave coast" or the Bight of Benin (from the Volta River to Benin) and the Bight of Biafra (from the Niger Delta

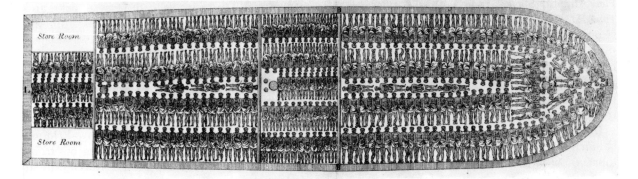

Stowage aboard a slave ship, 1780s. This sketch shows the tightly packed lower deck of the *Brookes* with 292 slaves in the frequently used prone position for shipment from Africa to America. In addition to the 292 on the lower deck, the *Brookes* carried, elsewhere on board, an additional 162 slaves: 130 on platforms or shelves (especially constructed on many slavers) around the wings or sides of its lower deck, and 32 divided between the hold (where provisions were stowed) and shelves beneath the poop deck (at the stern of the ship). Slaves stowed on or beneath these shelves had a height of only about two and a half feet between the beams of the ship and far less space under the beams. With a tonnage of 320, a length of 100 feet, and a width of 25 feet, the three-masted *Brookes,* based in Liverpool, England, was supposed to carry a slave complement of 454, according to a regulatory act passed by Great Britain's Parliament in 1788. Before this regulation was passed, however, and probably afterwards, the *Brookes* carried as many as 609 slaves. Its crew numbered 45. The *Brookes* was considerably larger in tonnage and complement than slavers of an earlier period (the 1740s, for example), but whatever the size or time, slave ships were invariably overcrowded, a fact that contributed to a higher mortality than on other seagoing vessels.

   The *Brookes* was highly publicized during and after an investigation of the slave trade by the British Parliament; for this reason, it was—and still remains in the literature—the best known of all slave ships. A model of the *Brookes,* showing stowage, was used by advocates for the abolition of the trade, including William Wilberforce. Moreover, drawings of the tightly packed *Brookes* were published. The above reproduction was made from one of these prints, preserved in the Library of Congress. Another print, made from another drawing, is preserved in the Hart Nautical Museum, Massachusetts Institute of Technology, Cambridge. There are doubtless similar prints in other libraries and museums.

to the Cameroons). At the end of the eighteenth century, the British had made notable shifts from the Cameroons along the north-south coast extending from Gabon through Angola. Bryan Edwards, a Jamaican slaveholder and historian, showed British participation in the trade for the year 1771, about the time the trade had peaked.

   The destination of the slaves for this particular year (1771) varied. It is likely that of the 47,000 imported, only about 3,000 were carried directly from Africa to the North American colonies; the remainder went to the Caribbean and foreign colonies. However, during the same year, about 2,000 "seasoned" (acculturated) slaves were imported from the West Indies to the mainland American colonies, bringing the total to about 5,000 for this year. Nearly 2,000 of this 5,000 entered at the port of Charleston, S.C. Throughout the period of the Atlantic slave trade, Virginia and South Carolina were the largest importers on the North American mainland, receiving

their human cargoes mainly from British-owned ships, captained and manned by British crews.

British Port of Origin		
Port	Ships	Negroes
Liverpool	107	29,250
Bristol	23	8,810
London	58	8,136
Lancaster	4	950
Total	192	47,146

African Source of Slaves		
Area	Ships	Negroes
Bight of Benin	63	23,301
Windward Coast	56	11,960
Gold Coast	29	7,525
Senegambia	40	3,310
Angola	4	1,050
Total	192	47,146

SOURCE: Bryan Edwards, *The History, Civil and Commercial, of the British Colonies in the West Indies,* Dublin 1793, vol. II, p. 53; reprinted by Arno Press, 1972, for Research Library of Colonial Americana.

The Atlantic Slave Trade with the Chesapeake Tobacco Coast* Virginia and Maryland were regarded by English mercantilists as the two most satisfactory colonies on the North American continent, because their inhabitants consumed enormous quantities of British goods and produced almost nothing that competed with the manufactures of the mother country.

During the 77 years from 1697 to 1775, the balance of trade between Great Britain and the tobacco colonies, as reflected in the British customs records, was normally in favor of the colonies. Even so, the colonists were usually in debt to British merchants. Thomas Jefferson in a well-known remark said that these debts became "hereditary from father to son for many generations, so that the planters were a species of property annexed to certain mercantile houses in London," and estimated that Virginians owed at least £2,000,000 sterling to British creditors on the eve of the Revolution.

The explanation of this paradox lies in the fact that import and export statistics ignored services, taxes, and carrying and handling charges such as freight rates, customs duties, insurance, and commissions. The various carrying and service charges swallowed up the difference between imports and exports, and increased the indebtedness of the Chesapeake colonies to Great Britain despite the apparently favorable balance of trade.

Another invisible export of Great Britain was accounted for by the slave trade, carried on largely by British capital, yet not appearing in the statistics of British exports to the Chesapeake because ships involved in it cleared from Great Britain for Africa.

From its establishment in 1663 until the trade was thrown open to all English subjects in 1698, the Royal African Company had a monopoly on the slave trade to England's American colonies. The depression in the tobacco colonies during the two decades following the Restoration, by limiting the demand for Negroes in the Chesapeake colonies, discouraged the Royal African Company from transporting sufficient slaves to meet even the small demand of these colonies. The apparent indifference of the Royal Company to the needs of the Chesapeake caused much complaint and paved the way for "separate traders," as ships not belonging to the Royal Compa-

ny were called, to trade to the Chesapeake and for colonial vessels to bring Negroes from the West Indies. After 1680, when the rise of tobacco prices brought an increased demand for slaves in Virginia and Maryland, the Royal African Company made several halfhearted attempts to supply them, sending the ship *Speedwell* to Gambia River in January, 1685, for 200 slaves to be carried to Potomac River, and the ship *Two Friends* to the Gambia in March, 1685, for Negroes to be taken to James River. As these efforts proved inadequate, the Chesapeake colonies continued to be supplied by separate traders and by colonial vessels, either under license of the Royal African Company or in violation of its monopoly.

The combined trade of the Royal African Company and the separate traders to the Chesapeake amounted to little during the last three decades of the seventeenth century. Between 1671 and 1700, the number of Negroes in Virginia rose from 2,000 to 6,000. It was not until after the opening of the trade in 1698 that slave imports into the Chesapeake became considerable. After 1698, however, the activity of the separate traders to Africa increased, and by the second decade of the eighteenth century the Chesapeake received slightly over half its Negroes from Africa. By the middle of the century, the volume of imports from Africa reached 90 percent of the total. Generally speaking, the African trade was largely carried on by British capital and British vessels, while the slaves imported into the Chesapeake colonies from the West Indies were brought in colonial vessels. From 1718 to 1727 Virginia imported slightly over 11,000 Negroes from Africa in 76 vessels, of which only six vessels carrying 649 of them were from Virginia. The remaining 70 ships carrying 10,442 Africans were from Bristol, Liverpool, and London.

Of the 66 British vessels that imported Negroes into Virginia during the years 1710–18, some 23 were from Bristol, 20 from London, 11 from Liverpool, and 12 from other British ports. By 1751–63, however, the distribution of British vessels in the Chesapeake slave trade was 25 from Liverpool, 18 from Bristol, 6 from London, and 3 from other ports.

The extent of colonial participation in the traffic was small, especially after the rise of the direct African trade. During the years 1751–63, when the total slave imports into Virginia were 10,548, only 1,293 were brought in by colonial vessels. It is commonly asserted that New England vessels imported large numbers of

*Excerpted from Arthur P. Middleton, Chapter Five, "British and African Trade," *Tobacco Coast: A Maritime History of the Chesapeake Bay in the Colonial Era*, Newport News, copyright © by the Mariners' Museum, 1953.

Negroes from the West Indies to the Chesapeake, but this is not so. New England participation in the Chesapeake slave trade was small and largely confined to importations from Africa. Between 1727 and 1738, some 16 New England vessels brought 540 Negroes into Virginia—an average of only 45 a year. Of these, 447 came from Africa and only 85 from the West Indies. Between 1753 and 1763, some 13 New England vessels brought 869 slaves to Virginia, 755 of them from Africa, and only 2 from the West Indies.

As the slave trade was regarded as being by far the most profitable trade of the Chesapeake colonies, participation in it was eagerly sought after by colonial merchants and planters. Purchasing Negroes on the African coast at a prime cost of between £4 and £6 per head, the slavers sold them in Virginia and Maryland at average prices ranging from £16 to £20 at the end of the seventeenth century, from £28 to £35 during the first half of the eighteenth, and at about £40 after the middle of the century. Considerable variation existed in the sale price depending upon the age, sex, physical condition, and accomplishments of the slave; young adults were preferred to old or to children, males preferred to females, and craftsmen preferred to unskilled laborers. The price was also subject to seasonal variation. In the spring and early summer the planters were "abundantly more fond of them," and would give greater prices for them because they were sure of the advantage of their labor in that year's crop, whereas Negroes bought at the latter end of the year would be of little service until the next spring.

Many colonial merchants and planters desiring to enter the slave trade and partake of its rich profits were deterred by want of capital. If they had enough to build and operate a ship, they were in most cases obliged to use it in the British trade to carry their tobacco overseas and import manufactured goods, or in the West India trade to dispose of their surplus grain and procure rum, sugar, molasses, coin, and bills of exchange without which their other commercial activities would have been hampered. In consequence, few Virginians and Marylanders maintained ships in the African trade. However, Chesapeake merchants and planters occasionally acquired part interest in an African voyage, usually in partnership with British merchants. More commonly, they imported Negroes in small numbers from the West Indies, an undertaking that was an adjunct to their ordinary commerce with that part of the empire rather than a separate trade like the African slave trade.

Colonial merchants might also participate in the trade by receiving consignments of slaves imported in British ships. As Negroes could not be sold at high prices for ready money because of the shortage of currency in the colonies, the extension of credit—often for six months or a year—was an essential feature of the system of disposing of them. This required the services of a merchant resident in the colony who knew the planters in the area and could estimate the extent to which their credit was good. As a form of participation in the trade, the handling of slaves on consignment involved little capital and little risk, yet proved quite lucrative. The usual commission amounted to 5 percent on the sales and 5 percent on the remittances—or about 7½ or 8 percent on the gross sales. Among the Virginians to import slaves or to receive them on consignment were some of the leading men of the colony: William Byrd, Robert Carter, and Benjamin Harrison, several Nelsons, Randolphs, and Braxtons, as well as such merchants as Andrew Sprowle, William Allason, and Neil Jamieson. Among the prominent Marylanders were Daniel Dulany, Samuel Chew, Edward Lloyd, and John Ridout, and such merchants as Galloway, Ringgold, Callister, Robert Morris, and Daniel of St. Thomas Jennifer.

Although enormously profitable, the slave trade was extremely hazardous. Masters and crews of slaving vessels bound to the African

Mutiny aboard a slave ship. Despite stringent security, there were some mutinies aboard slave ships. This sketch, first published in London, England, in 1789, shows a ship's crew directing gunfire from the vicinity of the poop deck (at the stern or rear of the ship) against rebellious slaves, some of whom are shown jumping overboard from the bowsprit. *(Library of Congress.)*

coast were exposed to excessive heat, unaccustomed diseases, and the violence and plundering of pirates and the king's enemies. An even more serious risk was the mortality of the slaves during the passage. A vessel that reached Virginia in 1702 brought 230 Negroes from Africa, having lost 100 at sea. The normal rate was somewhat lower, but occasional instances of high mortality usually received attention in the provincial newspapers. The Boston *News-Letter* in 1760 carried a news item from New York concerning the Bristol slaver *Diamond*, bound from Bonny in Africa to Maryland with 329 Negroes, of which 99 were lost "with the Flux." Other factors in the mortality of slaves were the region from which they came, and the suitability of the vessels for the trade—those not able to "turn well to windward" often lost many slaves before the vessels could clear the African coast.

Another difficulty was the general prejudice against slaving vessels as suitable ships to carry tobacco to Great Britain. They frequently advertised for cargoes in Virginia and Maryland, but usually had to take tobacco at freight rates lower than the prevailing ones in order to obtain full cargoes. It was the general belief that slavers were "never after in a Condition to take in Tobacco." One irate slaver, John Simpson, master of the Guineaman *Black Prince* of London, publicly protested against this idea as "very absurd and ungenerous, and a great Discouragement to bring Negros here." Asserting that his ship was seaworthy, he offered to have a survey made "to clear up all Doubts."

During the late seventeenth and early eighteenth centuries, the assemblies of the Chesapeake colonies levied duties on imported slaves as a means of raising revenue either for general purposes or for specific ones such as building a statehouse, a capitol, or finishing the governor's palace at Williamsburg. As the volume of slave imports became considerable, however, there arose a desire on the part of the colonists to check the rising black tide. The large number of slaves threatened the Chesapeake colonies with the evils of overproduction of tobacco. Owners of large plantations well stocked with Negroes desired to prevent their poorer neighbors from becoming serious competitors. A few wise ones perceived that the increase of slaves had a detrimental effect upon the whites, inflating their pride, ruining their industry, and disposing them to idleness. Others saw in the increasing numbers of "descendents of Ham" a weakening of the colony from a military point of view and a danger of revolt, which might one day "tinge our Rivers as wide as they are with blood."

The Atlantic Slave Trade with the Carolina Rice Coast*

African slaves, if taken together, were the largest single group of non-English-speaking migrants to enter the North American colonies in the pre-Revolutionary era. Indeed, they were the earliest major contingent of ethnic immigrants to reach the continent from across the Atlantic. The proportion of Negroes in the population would never again be so high as it was during the eighteenth century. But for the most part, in the Chesapeake tobacco region and further north, thousands of Afro-Americans were dispersed among an even larger number of European settlers. As a result, most Americans still find it hard to conceive that the population of one of the 13 original colonies was well over half black at the time the nation's independence was declared. This was the case in South Carolina where the black majority played an active, significant, and often determinative part in the evolution of the colony.

Black slaves were present in the South Carolina colony from the year of its founding, and by the second generation they constituted a majority of the population. Here was a thin neck in the hourglass of the Afro-American past, a place where individual grains from all along the West African coast had been funneled together, only to be fanned out across the American landscape with the passage of time. Sullivan's Island, the sandy spit on the northeast edge of Charlestown harbor where incoming slaves were briefly quarantined, might well be viewed as the Ellis Island of Afro-Americans. In fact, the colonial ancestors of present-day Afro-Americans are more likely to have first confronted North America at Charlestown than at any other port of entry. It has been established that well over 40 percent of the slaves reaching the British mainland colonies between 1700 and 1775 arrived in South Carolina, while most of the remainder were scattered through the Chesapeake region, and a comparative few (often from the West Indies rather than Africa) entered through northern ports.

Apart from Africans who had accompanied earlier Spanish explorers of the Southern coast, the first blacks to reach the Sea Islands region

*Reprinted, with some adaptations by the author, from Peter H. Wood, *Black Majority: Negroes in Colonial South Carolina from 1670 through the Stono Rebellion*, Alfred A. Knopf, New York, 1974; copyright © 1974 by Peter H. Wood.

arrived in 1670 alongside the earliest permanent white migrants. The *Carolina*, under Capt. Henry Brayne, reached the coast in late March, bringing settlers from England. When the remainder of the company had joined them on the west bank of the Ashley River in late spring, Brayne was dispatched to Virginia for more men and supplies by Gov. William Sayle. Capt. Brayne was a propertied Barbadian with settlement ambitions of his own, and when he returned from Virginia with livestock and supplies on August 23, he also imported for his own advancement "one lusty negro man 3. christian servants and a oversear."

The fact that this first fully documented Negro arrival reached the colony alongside Europeans is indicative of a pattern of black and white imports that was to predominate for several decades. Three slaves who arrived several weeks later represent two other patterns that would be frequent in the early years. In the first place, they appear to have been united by kinship ties, and secondly, they were imported by leaders of the settlement, in this case the Sayle family. Captain Nathaniel Sayle had ventured to Bermuda in the *Three Brothers* in June, and when he returned in September 1670 he brought back to his father, the governor, three white servants and three Negroes. The latter were listed as John Sr., Elizabeth, and John Jr. This small black family from Bermuda constituted the first group of Negro arrivals to be recorded by name, and they were among the last people considered technically to have arrived with the "first fleet" (a distinction that held benefits for their white master). In the same month, Joseph Dalton could write to Ashley, "The Collony is indeed safely setled and . . . there only remaines the preservation of it."

"Preservation" and survival meant the development of a food supply, and since the time and skills necessary for farming and hunting were initially limited, attention turned to the raising of cattle. The settlement was so sparse and the land so abundant that animals could be allowed to graze freely, requiring almost no time from the limited labor force. Furthermore, the climate proved mild enough and the forage so plentiful that there was no necessity for annual butchering. As a result, livestock multiplied at an unanticipated and unprecedented rate while demanding minimal attention from the owners. This situation was so unfamiliar for Englishmen that it aroused concern among the Proprietors. It has been "our designe," they stated indignantly, "to have Planters there and not Graziers."

While white settlers felt uneasy about open grazing at first, numerous black newcomers understood this practice. In Africa, although domesticated cattle were absent from the area near the Congo due to the presence of the tsetse fly, such animals were common across much of the western region, and many of the slaves entering South Carolina after 1670 may have had experience in tending large herds. People from along the Gambia River, a location for which South Carolina slave dealers came to hold a steady preference, were expert horsemen and herders. English visitors expressed high admiration for their standards of cleanliness with respect to dairy products, and contemporary descriptions of local animal husbandry bear a striking resemblance to what would later appear in Carolina. Gambian herds grazed on the savannas bordering the river and in the low-lying paddy fields when the rice crop was off; at night they were tethered within a cattlefold and guarded by several armed men. African stock was even traded for export occasionally during the seventeenth century.

As early as the 1670s there is evidence of absentee investors relying upon Negro slaves to develop herds of cattle in Carolina. Even when the white owners lived within the province, the care of their livestock often fell to a black slave. The slave would build a small "cowpen" in some remote region, attend the calves, and guard the grazing stock at night. When Denys Omahone sold a 50-acre tract (still inhabited by Indians) to a new white arrival in the 1680s, the property contained four calves, three steers, five sows, one boar, and a "Negro man by name Cato." Upon the death in 1692 of Bernard Schenckingh, a well-to-do Barbadian migrant with four estates, the appraisers of his James Island holdings reported that "In sight and by account apeareth 134 head of Cattle [and] one negro man." Half a century later, the estate of Robert Beath at Ponpon included, "a Stock of Cattle . . . said to be from Five Hundred to One Thousand Head. . . . Also a Man used to a Cow Pen and of a good Character." It is even possible that the very word "cowboy" originated in part through this set of circumstances.

While rice would dominate the colony's later economy even more than livestock shaped the earliest phase, it was the so-called forest industries that particularly characterized Carolina in the early eighteenth century. The same trees that posed an obstacle to planting proved a valued resource, and the necessary process of clearing land became a lucrative enterprise in its own right, demanding more labor than cattle grazing but less capital than rice planting. This natural frontier pursuit took numerous forms, based on the diversity of the coastal forests and the varied demands of consumers; wood was needed by Charlestown carpenters for new houses, by Bermuda shipwrights for their vessels, and by Caribbean planters for the fires that boiled their sugarcane. Many Negroes from this generation, usually working in pairs, spent most of their lives chopping and sawing timber, and many slaves would at some point have used a wedge to split fence rails, a froe to slice shingles, or an adz to square beams.

Afro-Americans shared and even dominated the cooper's art in South Carolina almost from its beginning. Well before the turn of the century, they were shaping staves for export to older colonies that had diminished wood supplies and well-established staples, and as the local economy expanded, this production necessarily increased. Saplings were cut steadily to provide the coopers with sufficient hoops, and in 1714 an act was passed to impose uniform dimensions upon the thousands of barrels being made for beef, pork, rice, and naval stores. It was this last category, including tar, pitch, resin, and turpentine, which formed the heart of South Carolina's forest industry, in fact of its whole economy, during the early eighteenth century. From the outset, black workers were involved in every aspect of producing naval stores.

Clearing forests and providing timber products were by no means the only pioneering tasks in which Afro-Americans participated, as is apparent from an examination of the fur trade. During the first 15 years of the century, England imported annually from Carolina an average of 50,000 deerskins plus other assorted pelts. While most of the hunting and trapping was done by Indians and the procurement and export was managed by whites, Afro-Americans were active in most intermediate stages of the trade and were among those who regularly rowed up the Savannah River, which Col. John Barnwell described as "the ordinary thorowfare to the Westward Indians," and returned downstream with boatloads of skins. Other slaves in Port Royal and Charlestown were engaged in trimming, weighing, and packing these skins for shipment.

Robin, a Negro man owned by Barnwell, earned £4 per month for his master through "doing the Work and Labour of the Storehouse and Trade in Charles Town" in the spring of 1717. Later in the same year, Robert Graham organized a pack train of 22 horses to carry nearly £1,000 in trade goods to the factors at Savannah Town and beyond. Among the six men he hired for the overland trek were two slaves, including a Negro "named Timboe, who was imployed in the said Trade . . . to tend the Pack-Horses [and] . . . to serve as Interpreter." Timboe's presence was so clearly essential to the success of this major venture that his owner managed to collect more than £60 from the Commissioners of the Indian Trade "in Consideration of his said Negro's extraordinary Service, and being Linguist."

No development had greater impact upon the course of South Carolina history than the successful introduction of rice. The plant itself, shallow-rooted and delicate, is now rare on the landscape it once dominated, but its historical place in the expansion of the colony and state is deep-seated and secure, hedged round by a tangle of tradition and lore almost as impenetrable as the wilderness swamps near which it was first grown for profit. Despite its eventual prominence, the mastery of this grain took more than a generation, for rice was a crop about which Englishmen, even those who had lived in the Caribbean, knew nothing at all. White immigrants from elsewhere in northern Europe were equally ignorant at first, and local Indians, who gathered small quantities of wild rice, had little to teach them. But gradually, after discouraging initial efforts, rice emerged as the mainstay of the lowland economy during the first 50 years of settlement, and the cultivation of this grain for export came to dominate Carolina life during the major part of the eighteenth century. "The only Commodity of Consequence produced in South Carolina is Rice," commented James Glen in 1761, "and they reckon it as much their staple Commodity as Sugar is to Barbadoes and Jamaica, or Tobacco to Virginia and Maryland."

Since rice cultivation had a halting beginning that stretched over several decades, numerous bags of imported seed could have contributed to its growth. Documentary evidence is scanty concerning its precise origins. In 1726 a Swiss correspondent stated that "it was by a woman that Rice was transplanted into Carolina," and occasional mention was made of the idea that the first seeds came aboard a slaving ship from Africa. "Opinions differ about the manner in which rice hath been naturalized in Carolina," wrote the Abbé Raynal at the end of the eighteenth century. "But whether the province may have acquired it by a shipwreck, or whether it may have been carried there with slaves, or whether it be sent from England, it is certain that the soil is favourable for it."

The planting and processing of rice involved considerable obstacles for the early European settlers, which may explain why they had discarded the crop initially. "The people being unacquainted with the manner of cultivating rice," recalled an Englishman during the eighteenth century, "many difficulties attended the first planting and preparing it, as a vendable commodity, so that little progress was made for the first nine or ten years, when the quantity produced was not sufficient for home consumption. Similarly, Gov. Glen would later claim that even after experimenters had begun to achieve plausible yields from their renewed efforts around 1690, they still remained "ignorant for some Years how to clean it." Thomas Lamboll recalled how in 1704, as a ten-year-old boy walking to school near Charlestown, "he took notice of some planters, who were essaying to make rice grow."

In contrast to north Europeans, Negroes from the West Coast of Africa were widely familiar with rice planting. Ancient speakers of a proto-Bantu language in the sub-Sahara region are known to have cultivated the crop. An indigenous variety (Oryza glaberrima) was a staple in the western rain-forest regions long before Portuguese and French navigators introduced Asian and American varieties of O. sativa in the 1500s. By the seventeenth and eighteenth centuries, West Africans were selling rice to slave traders to provision their ships. The northernmost English factory on the coast, James Fort on the Gambia River, was in a region where rice was grown in paddies along the riverbanks. In the Congo-Angola region, which was the southernmost area of call for English slavers, a white explorer once noted rice to be so plentiful that it brought almost no price.

The most significant rice region, however, was the "Windward Coast," the area upwind or westward from the major Gold Coast trading station of Elmina in present-day Ghana. Through most of the slaving era, a central part of this broad stretch was designated as the Grain Coast, and a portion of this in turn was sometimes labeled more explicitly as the Rice Coast. An Englishman who spent time on the Windward Coast (Sierra Leone) at the end of the eighteenth century claimed that rice "forms the chief part of the

African's sustenance." He went on to observe, "The rice fields or lugars are prepared during the dry season, and the seed sown in the tornado season, requiring about four or five months growth to bring it to perfection."

Throughout the era of slave importation into South Carolina, references can be found concerning African familiarity with rice. Ads in the local papers occasionally made note of slaves from rice-growing areas, and a notice from the *Evening Gazette*, July 11, 1785, announced the arrival aboard a Danish ship of "a choice cargo of windward and gold coast negroes, who have been accustomed to the planting of rice." Needless to say, by no means every slave entering South Carolina had been drawn from an African rice field, and many, perhaps even a great majority, had never seen a rice plant. But it is important to consider the fact that literally hundreds of black immigrants were more familiar with the

TO BE SOLD on board the Ship *Bance-Island*, on tuesday the 6th of *May* next, at *Ashley-Ferry*; a choice cargo of about 250 fine healthy NEGROES, just arrived from the Windward & Rice Coast. —The utmost care has already been taken, and shall be continued, to keep them free from the least danger of being infected with the SMALL-POX, no boat having been on board, and all other communication with people from *Charles-Town* prevented. *Austin, Laurens, & Appleby.*

N. B. Full one Half of the above Negroes have had the SMALL-POX in their own Country.

Advertisement for a sale of slaves in Charleston, S.C., ca. 1760s. Slaves from the Rice Coast of West Africa were sold at a premium in Charleston, the main port (receiving about 40 percent) for all slave arrivals in British mainland colonies. The reference to smallpox is part of the sales pitch: many African peoples had pioneered many years earlier in the immunization and prevention of the disease. *(Library of Congress.)*

planting, hoeing, processing, and cooking of rice than were the European settlers who purchased them.

During precisely those two decades after 1695 when rice production took permanent hold in South Carolina, the African portion of the population drew equal to, and then surpassed, the European portion. Black inhabitants probably did not actually outnumber whites until roughly 1708. But whatever the exact year in which a black majority was established, the development was unprecedented within England's North American colonies. Were Negro slaves simply the

15

cheapest and most numerous individuals available to a young colony in need of labor? Or were there other variables involved in determining the composition of the Carolina work force?

It now appears that the transition to an African work force in lowland Carolina at the start of the eighteenth century may have depended in part upon variables beyond those familiar to traditional historians of slavery: the cheapness of chattel labor, the availability of Africans in large numbers, and the racism of European masters. Clearly, a number of Africans possessed prior familiarity with rice cultivation, which could have greatly enhanced their value as workers, particularly in the years when this commodity was first being established. Furthermore, West Africans, like Sicilians and others who have lived in malarious climates for centuries, had retained a high incidence of sickle-cell trait, a genetic characteristic the negative effects of which were balanced by its positive contribution: the ability to inhibit malaria among humans constantly exposed to infectious mosquitoes, as was the case among the swamps and marshes of the Carolina rice country.

Whatever the importance of these hypotheses, Africans brought with them distinctive strengths and skills that suited them to life in the Carolina lowlands, and that, ironically but understandably, contributed to the steady growth of their numbers in the frontier province. This early and rapid growth, based more upon importation than upon natural increase, is well illustrated in an eighteenth-century chart of the Charlestown slave trade, reprinted here as a table. By 1739, the year of the Stono Rebellion in South Carolina and the year when this listing ends, the colony contained roughly 39,000 blacks and 20,000 (or scarcely half as many) whites.

Only in 1741, as a result of the Stono Rebellion and other disturbances, was a prohibitive duty imposed upon new slaves in an effort to curtail further growth of the black majority. But by then the racial demography of the colony had been firmly established. "Carolina," commented a Swiss newcomer in 1737, "looks more like a negro country than like a country settled by white people." Another prohibition on slave imports was in effect for several years in the 1760s, but by the end of that decade the colony's black population had again doubled to more than 80,000. Plantation agriculture built on the profits of slave labor had spread to the new, neighboring colony of Georgia. When the white settlers succeeded in achieving political independence from England without granting freedom to black Americans held in bondage, the stage was set for an extended era of agricultural exploitation that would stretch far beyond the

RECORD OF ANNUAL SLAVE IMPORTS, 1706–1739, INTO CHARLESTOWN, S.C., AS IT APPEARS IN GENTLEMAN'S MAGAZINE OF 1755 (XXV, 344)

Years	Negr	Vessels
1706	24	68
[a]1707	22	66
1708	53	81
[b]1709	107	70
1710	131	92
1711	170	81
1712	76	82
1713	159	99
1714	419	121
[c]1715	81	133
[c]1716	67	162
[d]1717	573	127
1718	529	114
1719	541	137
1720	601	129
1721	165	121
1722	323	120
1723	463	116
	4,504	1,919

Years	Negr	Vessels
	4,504	1,919
1724	604	122
1725	439	134
[e]1726	1,728	146
1727	1,794	126
1728	1,201	141
1729	1,499	157
1730	941	165
1731	1,514	184
1732	1,199	182
1733	2,792	222
1734	1,651	209
1735	2,907	248
1736	3,097	229
1737	2,246	239
1738	2,415	195
1739	1,702	225
	32,233	4,843

[a]The trade of this province to 1708 was only in exporting provisions to the sugar islands, from whence they had their supply of *European* goods, *&c.* and there were not above 200 negroes in the province, although now there is above 50,000 [The total of "200 negroes" given by the English author falls short by a factor of 20.]

About this time they began to make tar, pitch, and turpentine.

[b]At this time they began to make and export rice.

[c]Time of the great *Indian* war, when many inhabitants left the prov.

[d]Before this time the trade was chiefly carried on in small coasting vessels, who made three or four voyages *per ann.* but after this in large ships to *Europe*, and smaller vessels to *America*.

[e]About this time two new ports of entry, *&c.* for shipping was allowed, *viz. Port Royal*, to the southward, and *George Town*, to the northward, each about 60 miles from *Charles Town*, and the number of negroes or vessels in those parts are not in this account.

legal termination of the African slave trade to North America in the early nineteenth century.

REFERENCES*: Ajayi, J. F. A. and Michael Crowder, *History of West Africa*, Columbia University Press, New York, 1972, vol. I; Bohannon, Paul and Philip D. Curtin, *Africa and Africans* rev. ed., The Natural History Press, Garden City; published for the American Museum of Natural History, 1971; Collins, Robert O. (ed.), *African History: Text and Readings*, Random House, New York, 1971; Curtin, Philip D. (ed.), *Africa Remembered: Narratives by West Africans from the Era of the Slave Trade*, University of Wisconsin Press, Madison, 1968; Curtin, Philip D., *The Atlantic Slave Trade: A Census*, University of Wisconsin Press, Madison, 1969; Davidson, Basil, *Africa in History: Themes and Outlines*, rev. ed., Collier Books, New York, 1974; Donnan, Elizabeth, *Documents Illustrative of the History of the Slave Trade to America*, Carnegie Foundation, Washington, D.C., 1931; Dunn, Richard S., *Sugar and Slaves: The Rise of the Planter Class in the English West Indies*, University of North Carolina Press, Chapel Hill, published for the Institute of Early American History and Culture at Williamsburg, Va., 1972; Fage, John D., "Slavery and the Slave Trade in the Context of West African History," *Journal of African History*, vol. 10, pp. 393–404, 1969. Greenberg, Joseph H., *The Languages of Africa*, Indiana University Press, Bloomington, 1963; Harvard University, *African History and Literature: Classification Schedule, Classified List of Call Numbers, Chronological Listing and African Documents Listing by Call Number*, Harvard University Press, Cambridge, Widener Shelflist No. 36, 1971: "This volume is without doubt the most inclusive [bibliographical] listing to be found in a single volume of interest to historians and others" (Hans E. Panofsky, *A Bibliography of Africana* Contributions in Librarianship and Information Science, No. 11, Greenwood Press, Westport, 1975, p. 65); Higgins, W. Robert, "Charlestown Merchants and Factors in the External Negro Trade, 1735–1775," *South Carolina Historical Magazine*, vol. 65, pp. 205–17, 1964, lists number of merchants (405) and imported slaves by year; Klein, Herbert S., *Slavery in the Americas: A Comparative Study of Cuba and Virginia*, University of Chicago Press, Chicago, 1967; Mannix, Daniel P., and Cowley, Malcolm, *Black Cargoes*, Viking Press, New York, 1962; Middleton, Arthur P., *Tobacco Coast: A Maritime History of the Chesapeake Bay in the Colonial Era*, Newport News, The Mariners' Museum, (ed. by George Carrington Mason), 1953; Polanyi, Karl, *Dahomey and the Slave Trade*, University of Washington Press, Seattle, 1966; Rodney, Walter, "Gold and Slaves on the Gold Coast," *Transactions of the Historical Society of Ghana*, vol. 10, pp. 13–28, 1969; Sheridan, Richard B., "Africa and the Atlantic Slave Trade," *American Historical Review*, February 1972, pp. 15–35; Sheridan, Richard B., "The Commercial and Financial Organization of the British Slave Trade, 1750–1807," *Economic History Review*, 2d series, vol. 11, pp. 249–63, 1958; Ward, W. E. F., *The Royal Navy and the Slavers: The Suppression of the Atlantic Slave Trade*, (Sourcebooks in Negro History), Shocken Books, New York, 1970; Wax, Darold D., "Negro Import Duties in Colonial Virginia: A Study of British Commercial Policy," *Virginia Magazine of History and Biography*, vol. 79, pp. 29–44, 1971; Williams, Eric, *Capitalism and Slavery*, University of North Carolina Press, Chapel Hill, 1944; Wood, Peter H., *Black Majority: Negroes in Colonial South Carolina from 1670 through the Stono Rebellion*, Alfred A. Knopf, New York, 1974. In addition, two other helpful references are: Anstey, Roger, *The Atlantic Slave Trade and British Aboli-*

*N.B.: These references are for the following entries above on AFRICA: LAND AND PEOPLES OF WEST AFRICA; THE ATLANTIC SLAVE TRADE IN PERSPECTIVE; THE ATLANTIC SLAVE TRADE WITH THE CHESAPEAKE TOBACCO COAST; THE ATLANTIC SLAVE TRADE WITH THE CAROLINA RICE COAST

tion, 1760–1810 (1975); and Craton, Michael, *Sinews of Empire: A Short History of British Slavery* (1974).

Impact of the Atlantic Slave Trade Upon West Africa African-European contacts during ancient and medieval times had almost exclusively embraced the Mediterranean–North African sphere, largely in the interactions of ancient Egypt, Rome, and medieval Islam. With the coming of the Crusades, however, a new dimension began to develop that had a notable impact on European-African contacts, particularly under Islamic influences. Within 150 years, that is by A.D. 1450 or the end of the Middle Ages, a new Europe was emerging, changing from within and expanding abroad. The great upheavals within the new Europe in the acquisition of new religions (Protestantism), new learning and science (Renaissance), new nation-states (nationalism), and new commerce (commercial revolution) had a profound impact upon Africa and the New World. An expansive, aggressive, competitive, and capitalistic western Europe went beyond its old Mediterranean and continental confines to explore other lands and coasts along the Atlantic Ocean. In so doing, sub-Saharan Africa—long separated by the great desert—was made accessible to western Europe by sea. The new nations of Portugal and Spain, nearest to the west coast of Africa, were first to send their ships and seamen to Africa (and eventually all over the earth) in search of trade. Later, with the explorations and activities of Holland, France, and England, the sub-Saharan world took on new importance in the eyes of Europeans, providing maritime stations for provisions, and sources for such commodities as gold, kola nuts, and slaves.

The Gold Trade When the Europeans arrived along the west coast of Africa in the 1440s, they did not have to create any trade in the area, because West Africa had already been involved with the trans-Saharan trade that had led to the rise of such empires as Ghana and Mali. In the forest area of West Africa, especially in modern Ghana, gold and kola nuts—the principal exports to the northern markets—were in abundant supply. This pre-European trade was more than north-south in orientation—there were intricate networks of footpaths crisscrossing West Africa in all directions along which trade was carried. West Africans had also developed regional and local specializations. The coastal regions produced fish and salt that were sent into the inland states in exchange for food and fabrics. Gold from the Gold Coast (Ghana) was also traded in Benin and other places where it was exchanged for cotton cloths, beads, leopard skins, and iron implements. There was much intercommunication along the coast by means of dugout canoes.

The high degree of sophistication of the West African trade and culture explains why initially the crude and coarse manufactures of Portugal could make so little headway in the traditional trading nexus. To achieve any commercial success, it was essential for the Portuguese to become middlemen traders in African goods.

Fabrics were one of many commodities in West African trade. Wearing their traditional *adinkra*, an Ashanti woman and man dance the *adowa* at a modern Ghanaian festival. *(Ghana Information Services Department, Accra.)*

Traders had clear priorities in West Africa: where gold was not easily available, they concentrated on the exportation of human beings as commodities. The markets of Portuguese and Spanish colonies in the New World were supplied with slaves mainly from the Senegambia region, while gold from the Gold Coast was sent to bolster up the economy of Portugal. By the end of the fifteenth century Portugal was annually exporting between 2,000 and 3,000 pounds of gold or £100,000 from West Africa. This was about one-tenth of the total world supply of gold at the time. Soon the Europeans began to divide West Africa into commodity zones denoted by such names as the Grain Coast, Gold Coast, Ivory Coast, and Slave Coast. The Portuguese attempts to safeguard their trade monopoly by the erection of fortified forts and castles proved ineffective. Their first castle, the most impressive European building on the whole of West Africa, was built at Elmina in 1482 to safeguard the gold trade. Had

the Portuguese alone been engaged in West Africa, the slave trade might have gradually died out, since the European markets would not have been able to absorb as many African slaves. But developments outside of Europe and Africa soon came to change the history of West Africa. This was the discovery and settlement of the New World.

Growth of the Slave Trade The growth of the Atlantic slave trade led to the proliferation of firearms in West Africa and particularly in the Gold Coast. By 1658 it was being reported that only muskets would sell well there. Indeed, the Africans became so alarmed at the rate with which firearms were being sold that they unsuccessfully attempted to prevent their European importation. By the end of the 1600s the Dutch alone were annually selling as much as 20,000 tons of gunpowder. At the same time their closest rivals, the English, were earnestly requesting that there be sent to their post in Guinea 500 carbines, 100 blunderbusses, 10,000 flints, 5,000 knives, 50 sword hangers, 800 half barrels of gunpowder, 50 cases of spirits, and 200 tons of Barbados rum. Contemporary European writers marveled at the dexterity with which the Africans were able to handle these weapons. It became fashionable for the European traders on the coast to loan firearms to African rulers, and to pay the ground rents in firearms and spirits in order to facilitate the slave trade.

The correlation between the increased supply of firearms and the high incidence of African wars and the change from the gold to the slave trade is most significant. By the beginning of the eighteenth century the Dutch were exporting as many as 6,000 slaves while the English sent an annual average of 5,000 from the Gold Coast. When the slave exports of the Danes, the Brandenburg Prussians, and the French, as well as a host of other European interlopers, are taken into account, the annual slave export from the Gold Coast alone might have numbered some 15,000 people. It is no wonder then that the Gold Coast, formerly a gold mine, became a slave mart. Indeed, some of the European traders were beginning to wonder why it should not be called the Slave Coast instead of the Gold Coast.

Nevertheless, only a few years before, virtually the whole of the gold coinage of the United Provinces of Holland had been made from Guinean gold. This gold from Guinea had also come to increase the economy of England as well as its monetary vocabulary. Between 1674 and 1714 over half a million fine English coins, known as guineas, were minted from gold from the Guinea

(Gold) Coast. By the seventeenth century the evidence suggests that the Europeans had submerged whatever religious zeal they may have had in venturing into West Africa. Their devotion to gold so surprised the Africans that they began to ask whether gold was the European's god. This devotion, however, soon changed into a zeal for slaves, and by the end of the seventeenth century slaves were the hottest-selling commodity in Afro-European trade.

Effects of the Slave Trade Upon West Africa How did the increased demand for slaves affect West Africa? Had the Europeans desired to trade only natural commodities and not people in West Africa, there is no doubt that all West African societies would have benefited from European presence. On the Gold Coast in particular, the Portuguese were known to have helped with the labor shortage by importing slaves from Benin to Elmina. The increased demand for gold required that output should be increased, and labor problems became frequent in the West African forest where human porterage was the only means of transportation. With the arrival of many Europeans on the coast with various goods for trade, the Africans were faced with a shortage of porters to convey the heavy European commodities, such as pots, brass pans, pewter, and gunpowder from the coast into the interior. Under such a system, the draining effects of the slave trade on the economy of such a state as Ghana, where people were needed to mine gold and carry goods, are easily imagined.

There can be no doubt that the depletion of human resources resulting from the Atlantic slave trade adversely affected the sociopolitical and economic orders of West Africa. The Atlantic slave trade led to the rise and fall of states, perverted the social system, and inhibited economic growth in West Africa.

Admittedly, West Africa, like all places, had known wars in pre-European times. Most of these wars, however, were political wars fought over territories in which the defeated were often assimilated into the group of the conquering peoples. Slavery, too, must have been practiced in West African societies in pre-European times. Undoubtedly, victims of wars could be and were enslaved before they were finally absorbed. What must be emphasized, however, is that slavery in West Africa carried none of the racial connotations that later developed in the New World. Instead, it was a means whereby families and clans replenished and augmented their numbers. A "slave" who was brought into an African family was soon completely absorbed into it and on occasion could rise to become the head of his adopted family. Among the Ashanti, for example, it was a crime to allude to one's ancestry. In pre-European West Africa, therefore, human beings remained human beings—they were not considered commodities. It was the Atlantic-African slave trade that made people marketable.

Politics and War It can be asserted that the Atlantic slave trade had far-reaching political effects on the whole of West Africa. In the first place, it revolutionized the sociopolitical theories of the West African states. Before the arrival of the Europeans, most of the states were organized along kinship lines with each family unit regarding the other in familial terms—such as brother, uncle, or in-law—and each family member being willing and prepared to submit disputes to the arbitration and sanctions of elders and traditional deities. With the increase in the slave trade, the new emphasis on the acquisition of wealth showed that the old order could not prevail. In the Akan states of Ghana, for instance, the struggle for political supremacy was to scatter people from their ancestral homes into all parts of the forest. In Dahomey, the Ebi social theory, which had held together the Aja peoples, completely broke down under the European demand for slaves.

It was this inadequacy of the traditional systems to accommodate the new economic exploitation that led to the rise of powerful states in the West African forest region. Whatever the desires of the founders of the seventeenth-century states, there could be no escape from the pressures and influences of the slave trade. Even Dahomey was squarely caught up in it despite the efforts of Agaja (1708–40) to avoid the slave trade. Without any gold mines, and with the presence of several European slave traders who were prepared to sell firearms to whomever would supply them with slaves, Agaja could not help but take part in the slave trade. Despite the flow of gold from the Gold Coast, the sad spectacle of unsuccessful attempts to insulate the area from the slave trade developed.

Although the gold trade persisted into the succeeding centuries, the shift of emphasis to slaves adversely affected the gold supply. By the end of the seventeenth century some of the European traders were reporting that there could be as much gold as slaves but that their company directors wanted more slaves than gold. To ensure the quick dispatch of the slave ships, Europeans began to lend firearms to the Africans to fight their wars in order to capture more slaves for sale. One of the constant refrains of the coastal traders was that "wars made gold scarce and negroes plenty." When in the 1780s the English provided one warring faction on the coast with firearms, they looked forward with enthusiasm to the victory of their supporters, in which case they noted, "There will be a glorious trade in slaves."

With the wide array of firearms at their disposal, the Africans were not loath to fight wars for real or imaginary wrongs in order to supply the Europeans with victims. It is probably true that without the slave trade, African rulers would still have fought their own wars with the newly acquired firearms in order to gain control over the sources of such commodities, as gold, kola nuts, and ivory. Ashanti and Dahomey, for example, had concentrated their efforts in gaining control over the kola-nut-producing areas and the northern market routes. Like Agaja in the early years of the trade, the rulers were initially unconcerned with slaving activity, yet later succumbed to it in order to preserve their extensive territories. From the beginning of the eighteenth century there was a vast increase in the number of slaves exported from these areas. Initially, the Ashanti did not sell their war captives. In fact, it is known that several towns around the Ashanti capital, Kumasi, were peopled with captives from many of their wars. Some of these towns, such as Fumasua and Ahwaa, were peopled with craftsmen from such conquered states as Denkyira and Sefwi. One of the interesting questions raised by the slave trade is whether wars were fought to procure slaves or whether slaves were incidental to the political wars. There can be no doubt that some of the wars were fought to extend territories or to punish recalcitrant subjects or for various other political motives.

Slave Raids A good deal of the so-called wars were, however, nothing but slave raids intended to satisfy the European demand for slaves. As many of the Europeans, such as John Barbot in the 1680s, realized that during periods of prolonged peace the trade in slaves languished, it became the duty of the European servants along the Guinea Coast to manufacture wars for their African friends. Walter Rodney, a historian, has shown how slavers often teased the Bijago islanders of the Upper Guinea Coast as being unmanly when slaves were in short supply. They plied them with alcohol, which inevitably led to "wars" in which their less powerful neighbors became victims. Many of the tribal wars that the Europeans reported in West Africa were nothing more than slave raids. In wars created by the slave trade, it became necessary for smaller states to submit to more powerful ones or to become the helpless victims of their predatory neighbors. It also became essential to survival for states to try to insulate their nationals from being sold as slaves. Few states, however, were able to do this. With the exception of Ashanti, Dahomey, and a few other states that grew strong enough to be able to protect their nationals, most West African states went the way of Akwamu and the Congo, both of which were forced to supply their own nationals to meet the quotas of the slavers, thus prolonging a national suicide that eventually led to their disintegration. Most West African states remained small and weak, easy prey to the incessant wars that fed the slave markets of the New World. By the middle of the eighteenth century slave raiding was being carried out far into the interior parts of the African continent, eventually leading to the fall of such states as Denkyira, Akwamu, and others.

Effects of the Slave Trade upon Internal Industry Economically, Africa was also the loser in the unequal slave trade system. It has been argued that such items as firearms and iron rods were considered as capital investment in Africa. With the former, some African rulers were able to build powerful states within which they could protect their own citizens. With the latter, the argument continues, more and better iron tools could be manufactured to increase the output of gold, to enable hunters to procure more game and ivory, and to bring much of the forest under cultivation. There can be no doubt that such developments took place, but it must not be forgotten that only a few African states grew stronger as a result of the slave trade. Many more tribes became so involved in wars that it became impossible for them to turn their attention to other serious economic pursuits. In a situation in which "one fortunate marauding makes a native rich in a day," it is understandable that Africans would seek to exert themselves in war, robbery, and plunder rather than in their old business of digging and collecting gold. Nor was this only a phenomenon of the Gold Coast; in the Upper Guinea Coast, the slave trade displaced the trade in camwood and gum.

The slave trade also contributed to the failure of the local crafts industries to develop and improve. Whereas in the early years such locally made goods as beads and cotton cloths had featured prominently in the Afro-European trade, by the end of the seventeenth century cheap European and Indian goods had flooded the market at the expense of African goods. The craftsman, apart from being faced with the uneven competition from Europe, was beset with the many uncertainties that went with the slave trade. He, too, was lucky when he escaped capture in war or forcible seizure by man stealers. One must also take into account the fact that the slavers always wanted the young and virile members of the society—the very people upon whose efforts the well-ordered development of the state depended. These were the peoples through whose energies West Africa could have launched itself into the industrial age. It has been fashionable for some economic historians to assert that the overall demographic map of Africa was unlikely to have undergone much change on the basis that the Europeans introduced new food crops that aided the growth of population, which, in turn, offset the rigors of the slave trade. This argument loses sight of the fact that the slave trade and the high rate of mortality that were the lot of Africa could only have been the main beneficiaries of any such population growth.

Europeans made deliberate attempts to discourage anything that would lead to a plantation agriculture that would have benefited the people. Both the Dutch and the English tried to establish plantations of cotton, indigo, and sugarcane on the Upper Guinea Coast, as well as the Gold Coast, but were discouraged by the powerful West Indian interests. At the beginning of the eighteenth century Sir Dalby Thomas, the English agent-general on the Gold Coast, requested that all kinds of crops be sent to him since they could do equally well in West Africa. Nothing ever came of the suggestion. Though at the beginning of the eighteenth century, the Dutch were exporting cotton, which they claimed was as good as any cotton that came from other parts of the world, they soon gave up its export and concentrated on the slave trade. Those enterprising local officials who wanted to devote more time to agriculture were sharply reprimanded for neglecting the slave trade. A letter (1751) from the British Board of Trade to the governor of the Gold Coast neatly sums up not only the mercantilist-capitalist policy of western Europe but also the unashamed English calculation to make West Africa nothing but the supplier of slaves. The board pointed out that

"the introduction of culture and industry among the Negroes is contrary to the known established policy of this country; there is no saying where this might stop, and that it might extend to tobacco, sugar, and every other commodity which we now take from our colonies, and thereby the Africans, who now support themselves by wars, would become planters and their slaves be employed in the culture of these articles in Africa, which they are employed in America." With such a policy it is no wonder that West African interests were permanently subordinated to those of Europe and the Americas.

Conclusion The Atlantic slave trade brought disaster to the West African peoples. It deprived West Africa of the young and active people on whose efforts the defense and development of the area depended. As to trade, few of the local productive industries, such as gold mining and the collection of gum, camwood, and ivory, could be pursued in peace. The proliferation of firearms, together with the acquisitive norms that were introduced, led to the disintegration of the old traditional order and to the forcible subjugation of people. Admittedly, it also led to the rise of powerful and broad-based political units, and states such as Futa Jallon, Denkyira, Akwamu, Ashanti, Oyo, and Dahomey, came into being. However, all these states were involved in the unrewarding practice of either selling their nationals or conducting disastrous raids on their less-organized neighbors in order to feed the slave market and thereby obtain the necessary European goods with which they could protect themselves and become still more powerful.

Much effort has been expended to show how and why West Africans became slaves. The conclusions so far have been sterile and unhelpful. Understandably, many of these explanations were first adduced by Europeans who as either abolitionists or antiabolitionists sought to justify or disprove popular notions. It was often asserted, among other things, that there was a large number of unprivileged people who could be easily sold by their masters when the Europeans first initiated the trade. Such arguments have also found favor with some historians. Others have asserted that the slave trade was of immense value to the Africans for it enabled some of them to avoid famine and to escape the sacrificial knives of their bloodthirsty rulers. Much of this is myth; for, in fact, if Africans had been so willing to submit themselves to the slavers, it is not likely that they would have made efforts to escape and to revolt before they were aboard the slave ships. Admittedly, the West African diet was much improved with the introduction of exotic New World foodcrops, such as maize (corn) and cassava, but there is no evidence to show that in pre-European times West Africans were living at the point of starvation, as was much of medieval Europe. This is not to deny, however, that in the calamitous times of rain shortages and locust plagues, famine was not a threat to the peoples of West Africa. It appears, however, that such occasions were few and far between.

There is not much evidence to support the claim that most Africans who were exported as slaves were criminals who had been duly convicted by the laws of their countries. Criminals had been sold into slavery; however, there is very little evidence to show that they formed any appreciable proportion of the victims of the transatlantic slave trade. Indeed, throughout the latter part of the seventeenth and in the eighteenth century, both British and Dutch records show that not more than 20 criminals were exported from the Gold Coast.

During nearly four centuries of slave trading, West African societies came face to face with the capitalist demands of western Europeans. The resolve of these societies to insulate themselves from the evil effects of the Afro-European confrontation was eventually weakened by the lure of Europe's well-developed technological system. Africans became victims of a new order that was controlled from Europe and America. Trapped in an alien system, Africans sacrificed much in return for little, having only small gains to carry themselves forward into a well-advanced economy and technology. Ruthless, aggressive, competitive, and capitalist, the slave trade sent enduring shock waves through West African history—and across the Atlantic to the New World.

Far right: However remote, legacies in music and other arts are reminiscent of an African past. This photograph was taken by Roland L. Freeman of a group in a public park in Baltimore in 1975. (Courtesy of Roland L. Freeman.)

REFERENCES: Ajayi, J. F. A. and Michael Crowder, *History of West Africa*, Columbia University Press, New York, 1972; Akinjogbin, I. A., *Dahomey and Its Neighbours, 1708–1818*, Cambridge University Press, Cambridge, 1967; Barbot, John, *North and South Guinea*, London, 1732; Blake, J. W., *European Beginnings in West Africa, 1454–1578*, Greenwood, London, 1937; Bovill, E. W., *The Golden Trade of the Moors*, 4th ed., Oxford University Press, New York, 1958; Cheyney, E. P., *The European Background of American History, 1300–1600*, Macmillan, New York, 1961; Daaku, K. Y., *Trade and Politics on the Gold Coast*, Oxford University Press, New York, 1970; Fage, John D., *An Introduction to the History of West Africa*, Cambridge University Press, Cambridge, 1961; Fage, John D., "Slavery and the Slave Trade in the Context of West African History," *Journal of African History*, vol. 10, pp. 393–404, 1969; and Rodney, Walter, *A History of the Upper Guinea Coast*, Oxford University Press, New York, 1969.

AFRICAN LEGACY / SURVIVALS

Introduction The impact of the Atlantic slave trade produced new peoples and new cultures in the New World; and the southern regions of the continental United States were no exception, although the dimensions of this development were of lesser magnitude. In this process of great cultural diffusion and interaction, there was no clear and abrupt break with the West African past. On the contrary, the cultural effect of the slave trade and the subsequent development of the New World cultures were extremely diverse and dynamic, and their complexity eludes precise description and analysis. However, several main developments may be noted: (1) As "creolization" took place, Africa and its "Africanisms" or "Africanness" or "Negritude" seem to have literally and figuratively receded or changed; just *how much* of the African heritage persisted and in what shape is difficult to establish. (2) Survivals were strongest during the earliest generations of colonization and settlement; they appear to have grown less intense in the course of time. (3) Survivals were less apparent in the continental United States than in areas of Latin America and the Caribbean. (4) Whether within

or outside the continental United States, Africanisms were strongest in music, folklore, and language.

Factors in demography, economics, culture, and chronology contributed to the weakness of survivals in the United States. Demographically, the flow of West Africans into Brazil and the Caribbean, in contrast to the United States, eventually produced population densities in which Europeans were greatly outnumbered. By 1775, black slaves in Jamaica outnumbered whites by a ratio of 8 to 1. Conversely, on the continental mainland that became the United States, whites always exceeded the black minority by ratios of at least 4 to 1. Only one mainland colony—South Carolina—ever had a black majority, and even here Afro-Americans barely outnumbered whites in the mid-eighteenth century. Though the evidence is not always conclusive, it appears that the larger black populations maintained a higher prevalence of Africanisms.

Moreover, the economic impact of the commercial and industrial revolutions effected the retention of Africanisms. From their English origins, these revolutions permeated the entire British-American mercantile system. The slave trade, as part of this complex, reached the British mainland later than non-British areas and Jamaica. This meant that "creolized" or "seasoned" slaves who were transshipped from the Caribbean to the mainland tended to hasten further creolization as opposed to Africanization. There was practically no reverse transshipment of slaves from the mainland to the Caribbean.

Furthermore, there were no great or enduring maroon settlements on the mainland. Though there were many runaway slaves (maroons) on the mainland who formed camps or settlements in isolated areas and swamps, such settlements never enjoyed the longevity or stability of maroon societies elsewhere in the Americas. Only in these larger and more stable camps, such as Palmares in Brazil or Maroon Town in Jamaica, was the retention of Africanisms very strong.

While Africanisms survived in the United States, their visibility or identification had become so modified by the mid-twentieth century that they could best be detected and traced by experts. Certainly, the typical Afro-American in mid-twentieth-century United States who had a West African name or nickname (Buba, Cootie, Cuffe) or who enjoyed certain foods (gumbo, okra) is not likely to be conscious of their African origins. More important, linguistic retentions or modifications, sometimes referred to as black English, may have similarly eluded teachers and educators. Such retentions and modifications in the language are discussed below, followed by an entry on the African legacy in art.

Language The two most striking factors in the development of languages both during and after the impact of the Atlantic slave trade are the amazing uniformity of the underlying grammatical systems and the degree to which the study of this linguistic exchange has long been neglected. Though the New World slaves and their descendants spoke a variety of languages and dialects—English, French, Portuguese, Spanish, and others—an examination of the records of spoken English during the British slave trade in the eighteenth century reveals a great similarity to the languages of West Africa, the West Indies, and the continental United States (of which the Georgia-South Carolina Sea Islands are unusual only in the extent to which they have continued to be a focus of an obvious "daughter" dialect). Still more impressive similarities, though more difficult to comprehend without careful study, are those that exist, and have existed, across language varieties that are considered to be dialects of French, Spanish, or English.

The most obvious relationship between New World varieties of English, French, and Portuguese (or Spanish) spoken in the West Indies and the continental United States, mainly by black populations, is that of "relexification" (rewording). For a preverbal particle indicating past action, there are the following:

ENGLISH	bin	*from*	been
FRENCH	té	*from*	était
PORTUGUESE ("SPANISH")	taba	*from*	estaba

All of these can be combined with another preverbal particle to indicate ongoing action:

ENGLISH	bin	*plus*	(d)a	bina
FRENCH	té	*plus*	ap	tap
PORTUGUESE ("SPANISH")	taba	*plus*	ta	tabata

These forms may be translated, in conjunction with another verb, as follows:

SRANAN TONGO (SURINAM)	bina nyam	
HAITIAN CREOLE	tap mangé	have been eating
PAPIAMENTO	tabata come	

However, the overlap with the English present perfect progressive tense is not complete, any more than, for example, a word in one language always translates to a word in another.

In the continental United States, this relexification relationship is not immediately obvious except in Gullah, the language of the Sea Islands of Georgia and South Carolina and part of northeastern Florida. The forms given for Sranan Tongo (and also for the dialects of Jamaica and other islands in the Caribbean) are approximately those of Gullah. In the other black dialects of the United States—and in those of the West Indies that are not "deep" Creole—one is more likely to find that the ending -ing has replaced the continuative particle (a, ap, ta).

Academic failure to appreciate the degree of these relationships is, in this context, fairly easy to understand. It has been traditional to look not at

You bina eat > you been eating

but at the Standard English:

You have been eating > you been eating

and to consider the black English form (on the right) as a stylistic reduction from Standard English.

There are, however, several objections to this traditional academic approach. First, from a nonlinguistic view, it is improbable that so large a segment of the population (approximately 20 million Americans) is merely associated with the stylistic reductions of the language of the majority group. From the technically linguistic standpoint, forms such as you been eat and you been know that are not traceable to any stylistic reduction from British—derived English dialects. It seems obvious that we are dealing with a language variety that, historically, has been more nearly inherent in the black community and less dependent upon norms received from the white community than has been generally believed.

An investigation into the history of black English (whether continental or West Indian) bears out such a conclusion. Mixed in terms of language and ethnic groups by traders for 300 years, slaves found it necessary to have a lingua franca, primarily for verbal communication among themselves. From the outset, some of the slave population learned the "standard" languages—English, French, Spanish, and Dutch—and then served as spokesmen to white owners. The real problem was internal communication within the slave community, and not one West African language or group of languages could fulfill that function. It is, therefore, reasonable to conclude from what is known of language-contact situations, and verifiable from written records, that the slave population turned to pidginized versions of Portuguese, French, and English.

Historically, these pidgins were loosely based upon Sabir, the lingua franca of the Mediterranean Sea trade. The Portuguese, especially, utilized a version of Sabir containing a very heavy proportion of Portuguese words—the Portuguese Trade Pidgin. As pioneers of European maritime expansion, the Portuguese used the Trade Pidgin as far away as Japan. The English and others, when they later entered the world-trade picture, made use of the same Portuguese variety—although they gradually refitted it with English or French or Dutch words. Transferred to the West African slavers and slaves, this language originally of the European sailors formed the base of those languages used in the vast population movement involved in slaving.

Although historically of European origin, these linguistic varieties (Portuguese in the seventeenth century, then English and French relexifications of the Portuguese Trade Pidgin in the eighteenth century and later) came to be of great utility to Africans of mixed ethnic groups who had to deal with each other in the rapidly expanding slave-trade relationships. Although lingua franca elements remained in the grammar, which was as much European as African, vocabulary was rather freely culled from African languages, and pronunciation reflected the phonological habits of speakers who had not been native speakers of the contact language. Most of the Africans were bilingual or polyglot, and the words that they took into the trade language were those (such as nyam nyam, meaning "eat") that were represented in several or sometimes in many West African languages. If, in speaking Pidgin French, the African could not remember the word for mud, he simply said "poto poto" as he does today in Douala, Cameroon. Among themselves, the slaves referred to the white owner by the not entirely complimentary word bakra/buckra. In a similar fashion, they carried over African phonological features, such as imploded stop consonants, which were foreign to European phonology.

Some of these Pan-West Africanisms are represented in nearly all black English varieties, where acculturation to European norms has been negligible. *Buckra* ("white man") is known in virtually all of the West Indies and in the Gullah-speaking Sea Islands; in an earlier century, it was carried west by English Creole-speaking black cowboys and, in contact with the Spanish *vaquero*, became *buckaroo*. *Nyam* or *nyam nyam* in Gullah ("eat") is known throughout the West Indies and Puerto Rico; in the Harlem jive talk of the 1920s, *yam* ("eat") was still preserved. There is also a secondary feature of replacement, a kind of secondary relexification: *buckra* becomes "white folks" (singular) in many places.

Many other words persisted. The pioneer black linguist, Lorenzo D. Turner, found several thousand words of African origin (the majority were personal names), representing approximately 30 West African languages existing in the Gullah-speaking Sea Islands. Excluding personal names, Turner's list included the following:

bubu, insect
cooter, tortoise
cush-cush, corn meal dough sweetened and fried
fufu, mush
ganja, gingerbread
goober, peanut
gumbo, okra
jigger, a species of flea
juju, magic
nanse, spider
ninny, female breast
oola, louse, bedbug
oona (hoona), you, your
pinda, peanut
pojo, heron
samba, a dance, to dance
sibby, lima bean
swanga, proud
tabby (as in *tabby house*), a house made of cement, oyster shells, pieces of brick, etc.
tote, to carry
tutu, excrement
voodoo, charm, witchcraft
wanga, charm, witchcraft
yam, sweet potato

Though it has been argued that *tote* is British in origin, *cooter*, *goober*, *gumbo*, and *tutu* ("doo-doo") have persisted in southern areas of the United States.

The black slaves who were arriving in Jamestown, Va., in 1619, Manhattan Island in 1635, and Massachusetts in 1638 seem to have used the Afro-European varieties for communication among themselves. The slaves had been so mixed up ethnically and linguistically that no West African language was adequate for the purpose. The early records we have show names such as Paul d'Angola, Simon Congo, Anthony Portuguese, and John Francisco; we know that aside from English other language varieties were involved because in Louisiana French Creole is still used, and because a Dutch patois was spoken in Suffern, N.Y., as late as 1910. Quotations from black English speakers became abundant in the records of Northern states by about 1750, nearly half a century before the earliest records in the Southern colonies were found in Charleston, S.C. In New York City, a significant quotation from a slave suspected as a ringleader in an alleged slave conspiracy of 1741 (Daniel Horsmanden, *The New York Conspiracy*, 1744, p. 127) has been recorded:

His master live in tall house Broadway. Ben ride de fat horse.

From the same source, which labeled this speaker's dialect "so perfectly negro and unintelligible" that it retarded the testimony considerably, we also discover that

... *Backara* ... in Negro language, signifies white people (p. 331)

and that ...

the house ... This in the Negroes' dialect signifies houses, i.e., the town (p. 209).

Virtually ignored by all but a few observers and regarded as a "corrupted" or "deteriorated" version of Standard English, the black English variety was looked down upon even by its own users, who acknowledged the viewpoint imposed on them that Afro-American customs were inferior to those of the white man. Linguistic survivals are as obvious as other cultural survivals such as jazz and the blues, but their history is seldom to be found in the writings of fully sympathetic observers.

There were, however, some observers who were relatively unprejudiced because black English (Plantation Creole in the nineteenth century) was literally their own language, even though they were white. Sons and daughters of southern plantation owners played with large groups of Creole-speaking slave children and learned Plantation Creole as their peer-group language. Sons of southern aristocrats were sent away to school where they either developed a separate "standard" dialect or lost the Creole completely; but daughters were kept at home and never completely lost their "slave speech." Nineteenth-century British observers, such as the novelist Charles Dickens and the geologist

Charles Lyell, report the striking similarity—which Ralph Ellison has recorded again in the twentieth century—between the speech of southern white belles and Afro-American slaves. Many of the whites who had learned black English as children (Ambrose Gonzales, J. W. Page, Julia Peterkin, Charles Colcock Jones, Jr., perhaps even Joel Chandler Harris) wrote occasionally in this dialect. By the time of the Civil War period, they had been joined by such black authors as Martin Delaney (*Blake, or The Huts of America*) and William Wells Brown (*Clotelle*).

Those closest to white norms among the black community were the few favored slaves who constituted the house-servant class and the skilled artisans. The field hands, once the child play relationship with the young master and mistress had been dissolved, would have little contact with white people except for the slave driver or perhaps a "pateroller" now and then. Manumission invariably tended to favor the house servant, who in many cases had been able to learn to read and write and who sometimes even received money and property from his master. Emancipation signaled rapid social mobility for that small group, but not for the field hands and their descendants, over whom the "shadow of the plantation" remained.

Decreolization (the merger of Plantation Creole English with Standard English) had always been a feature of black English, and it became especially noticeable after emancipation. It was always more successful in surface than in underlying forms, so that the black English forms before decreolization

me/I go
you go
him/he go

might afterward become

I goes
you goes
he goes

Since opportunity, especially economic, was generally in terms of the white man's norms, both cultural and linguistic, upwardly mobile blacks tended to forsake the old patterns. The most traditional African-related forms remained in isolated places, especially the Sea Islands. Rural Mississippi was, of course, "blacker" in this sense than urban Harlem. But the "white" linguistic forms were to some degree a veneer, and many older forms were retained by a black

group that had simply not had time to acquire that veneer—the children.

When American educators finally got around to studying the language of black children in the 1960s, they had neither the professional preparation nor the theoretical framework to account for such a sentence as

Me got juice.

Their reactions varied from the naïve—that the phrase could mean "juice has me" or "I have juice"—to the slightly more sophisticated—that the five-year-old culturally isolated or "deprived" black child had a language acquisition pronoun form (*me* for *I*) that a middle-class child drops from his repertoire at the age of from 30 to 36 months. Students of Creole languages recognized, in fact, that many full-fledged adult language varieties use the objective form of the pronoun (*me, him, her, us, you,* and the Africanism *unu,* meaning you plural) in the subject position. Unfortunately, since IQ tests and other evaluation devices are highly biased in terms of language and culture, educationists tended to judge the black child "deficient." Elaborate environmental theories were evolved to show how the lack of a *be* auxiliary in *he goin'* was a result of slum deprivation; however, Creolists pointed out that a contrasting *be* in *he be goin'* fills roughly an old slot of the Creole idiom.

Modern students of black English know much about the many positives of that variety. They know that *rappin', shuckin', jivin', coppin' a plea, riftin',* and *the dozens* (also called *soundin'* and *jonin'*) are elaborate discourse patterns that adult black Americans produce with great variety and skill. They know that the storefront preacher incorporates a basically African call-and-response pattern into a sermon that gives him far more rapport with his congregation than most white preachers achieve. They know that the black child who lacks a *be* auxiliary in *he makin'* is able to convey a grammatical notion in *he be makin'* that the middle-class child, black or white, cannot approximate, and that the nuances of *he done go* and *he been go* are partially or completely missing for most whites. *See also* MUSIC: BLUES; MUSIC: HISTORY AND DEVELOPMENT: MUSIC; SPIRITUALS; ONOMATOLOGY; RACE: CULTURE.

REFERENCES: See especially the references under the entry following, entitled AFRICAN LEGACY / SURVIVALS: AFRICAN ART.

African Art The "discovery" of African sculpture by artists in France and Germany in the first decade of the twentieth century was a milestone in the long era of eclecticism in art that had begun in earnest with the Neoclassicist and Romanticist movements following the French Revolution.

The greatest eclectic of them all, Picasso, had drawn upon such diverse sources as El Greco's

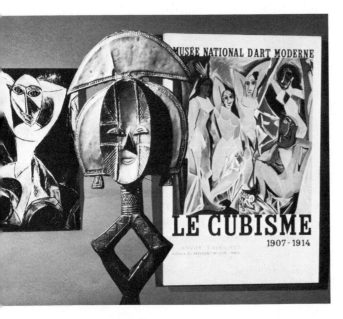

Mannerism and Romanesque Iberian sculpture. Then, in the works of African tribal carvers, he and his colleagues recognized a highly sophisticated use of abstraction and distortion, which corroborated many of their own and Cézanne's ideas about form and sculpture. Their discovery was first reflected in Picasso's 1907 painting *Les Demoiselles d'Avignon*, which set off an aesthetic explosion helping to change the face of modern art.

One should not assume that Picasso and his friends were unmoved by the spirituality expressed in African sculpture, but their overriding preoccupation was with form rather than content. In contrast, the German expressionists, working independently from the same sources of inspiration, were primarily concerned with the spiritual qualities of African sculpture.

The Western art world's new-found enthusiasm for African art was soon manifest in numerous public events. A series of exhibitions and publications followed World War I, as the contents of ethnographic collections and the curio cabinets of colonial officials and missionaries were reexamined in a light that until then had shone only on the bronzes of Benin. Early writings on African art had been, more often than not, filled with romantic nonsense about the unspoiled vision of the "noble savage." Gradually, however, art historians, with the indispensable assistance of anthropologists, began searching for accurate tribal attributions and for a clearer understanding of the original African meanings and cultural roles of particular masks and images.

African art did not, however, receive wider public acceptance until World War II, and even then recognition was far from general. Most devotees of the fine arts were slow to abandon their ethnocentric concepts of what was appropriate to the art museum. Today the art of Africa takes its rightful place beside the other great art traditions of the world, and there is scarcely a museum in this country that is not receptive to the idea of its exposition.

From an historical point of view, this wider appreciation is a function of the world social revolution that has been going on throughout this century. It has taken two world wars and a considerable number of smaller upheavals to break down the structure of international colonialism, but the self-justifying myths that it spawned die hard, leaving behind such misnomers as "primitive art," which, like the once derogatory term "Gothic," appears here to stay. Westerners are now compelled to respect the cultural heritage and aspirations of diverse peoples, as all of us together are caught up in an inexorable trend toward a single world community where understanding is vital to survival.

The same eclecticism that first brought African art to the attention of the Western world has produced an international style of art. Attending an exhibition of contemporary painting, one would find it difficult to distinguish the works of artists in Buenos Aires and Bangkok from those in New York and Paris. The role of art in industrial society is vastly different from what it is in traditional African life. In modern society, art is inextricably tied to urban living and its architectural setting. Paintings are made to hang on walls and sculpture designed to occupy niches or pedestals. Western art is public, and while it may memorialize an individual or event, or express a point of view, its primary role is decorative. Paintings and sculpture are valued to the

Far left: The influence of the abstract shapes of African art on modern Western art is clear in this photograph of a Bakota (Gabon) figure in wood and metal (center) juxtaposed against Picasso's 1907 works *Grand Dancer of Avignon* (left) and *Les Demoiselles d'Avignon* (right). (Museum of African Art, Eliot Elisofon Archives.)

extent that they are the identifiable expressions of a particular individual. While modern artists may attempt to provide visions of order in a chaotic world, titillate the senses, or enrich lives, they play no vital social role as did the artists and craftsmen of our medieval past.

By contrast, African art was functional and, for the most part, mobile. It was created to be viewed on special occasions and in prearranged contexts. It often appeared in motion as an inseparable element of ceremony, dance, costume, and music. Most African art was intensely private, not to be seen by anyone outside the tribal group, and often restricted to members of special societies or initiates of specific rank within them. The success of the African artist was measured by the degree to which he fulfilled the exacting requirements of tribal tradition and ritual function. The carving of an object was itself a ceremonial act, which often took place in secret. Traditional African sculpture, in contrast with our own art, was essential to the orderly functioning and survival of society.

Africa is a continent of natural contrasts in climate and topography as well as great physical and cultural diversity among the peoples who comprise its more than 300 million inhabitants. Although its diversity and complexity defy generalization, many misconceptions persist: for example, the belief that tribal Africans are jungle people when in fact most of Africa's inhabitants live in the savanna, a broad area of gently rolling grassland sparsely scattered with trees. Its population centers range in size from small clusters of dwellings to large, well-organized cities. Black African societies are neither culturally nor physically homogeneous. They are divided into innumerable tribes and subtribes, each with its own distinctive culture and language.

The region of the continent where its most important traditional art originates is that of sub-Saharan West and Central Africa. This area is usually subdivided into three stylistic regions: the Western Sudan area, comprising much of the present-day countries of Mali, Upper Volta, and northeastern Ivory Coast; the coastal countries of Guinea, Sierra Leone, Liberia, Ivory Coast, Ghana, Togo, Dahomey, Nigeria, and northern Cameroon; and the region of the Congo river basin: Gabon, the two Congos (Kinshasa and Brazzaville), and northern Angola. To a lesser extent, traditional art is also found in the neighboring regions to the east of these areas.

Although the concept of "tribe" has come to have pejorative connotations in the modern con-text, it is nevertheless essential to an understanding of African art. Tribal identity was a vital factor in African life, nurtured and preserved by closely held traditions, ancient mythology, religious beliefs and ritual, language, and social customs. Outwardly, it was manifest in distinctive coiffures, scarification, body paint, and costume, while inwardly it was the source of a people's pride and sense of well-being, the object of uncompromising loyalty. Identification with tribal groups in African society was far more intense than the allegiances of Western nationalism, since African societies were more closely knit than European ones and possessed a far greater sense of community.

The religious system served as the repository for the cumulative wisdom of the past and preserved the oral tradition for future generations. It instructed the members of each tribe in their origin and history and explained life and death and man's relation to the spirit world. It gave order and meaning to every aspect of daily living and protected the group from the powerful natural forces that threatened its survival.

Though African religions varied markedly from tribe to tribe, they shared a fundamental concept: all things, animate and inanimate, possess a "life force" that must be properly directed for the welfare of the individual or community. The death or destruction of an entity in which such a life force resided was a critical time for everyone. A new "home," such as a mask or an image, had to be provided and steps taken to pacify and nurture it so that its power could be controlled. Each religion provided ceremonies for the manipulation of the life force to insure such vital factors as human and animal fertility, rain, the fecundity of the soil, control of disease and blight, success in hunting, and the invincibility of warriors. These complex beliefs and practices have often been described in such oversimplified terms as ancestor worship, animism, fetishism—words that focus only on the superficial aspects of what Albert Schweitzer called "reverence for life."

It is just as precarious to generalize about the great diversity of sculptural styles as it is to do so about the religious beliefs to which they give expression. However, a few basic principles may be applied. Traditional African art does not attempt to be narrative or to suggest action. Figures stand rigidly frontal, their faces passive in Buddhalike contemplation. Their expressive power lies in the juxtaposition and subtle interplay of carefully controlled lines and forms that produce a highly selective abstraction and distortion of the human body.

The natural forms and proportional relationships of human and animal bodies and facial features are simplified and altered in order to intensify their expressive unity. The head, home of the intelligence and all the senses and, by analogy, of the individual's life force, is given special importance and often constitutes a third or more of the height of the figure. The legs are usually shortened and flexed to transform the figure into an integral whole.

There is in all African sculpture a studied relationship of forms comparable to the rhythmic variations on a theme in a musical score. The same quality of line and volume is echoed and repeated throughout the figure or mask, giving it coherence and purity of statement. This is equally true whether that quality consists of serene emphasis on verticality, a sensuous inter-

play of curves, or the dynamic and forceful juxtaposition of sharp angular movements. The successful sculpture is one in which forms are harmoniously interrelated to convey a special quality of feeling.

African carvers mastered these principles of plastic abstraction and employed them with purpose and effectiveness long before their works were discovered by Western artists.

When viewing African art in museums or private homes, we must constantly remind ourselves that we are seeing it out of context. Even figures, which are sculpturally self-contained, lose a great deal when removed from their original setting and from the ritual and ceremony in which they were intended to play a part.

To the African, a mask was a living thing, the residence of a very specific spirit—inseparable from the headdress and costume of the wearer and the dance or ceremony in which it functioned. It was seen only on such special occasions as the investitures of chiefs, puberty rites in which young men or women were initiated into adulthood, funerals of important personages, or at times of planting and harvest. With the identity completely hidden by mask and costume, the wearer was believed to be possessed by the mask's spirit and entirely subject to its will.

The occasions on which masked religious functionaries appeared varied greatly as to purpose and audience. They might appear as entertainers for everyone in the village to see, ridiculing human frailties or performing dances of remarkable gymnastic skill; or bull-roarers, drums, and other terrifying sounds in the dark of night might send everyone into hiding, after which masked priests would appear to judge and punish a violator of tribal law. The unseen and unknown wearers of the masks were actually familiar elders, but to the people it was the supernatural power of the masks that carried out the sentence.

When a mask was discarded, it was stripped of its headdress, which often contained magical substances and charms essential to the presence of its power. Sometimes masks were ceremonially deactivated and their spirit force transferred to another suitable residence.

Thus, when a mask or figure is seen in isolation, its full reality can never be perceived. Neither the intellectual concepts that it represents nor its ceremonial context are accessible to the modern viewer. The forms we see tell us little of the generations of religious belief, technical experimentation, and aesthetic refinement that lie behind it. Yet while we may never comprehend its symbolic vocabulary nor grasp its total significance, we can be moved by the dynamism and the spiritual force of African art. *See also* ARTISTS.

REFERENCES: For bibliographic references, see Hans E. Panofsky, *A Bibliography of Africana*, Greenwood, Westport, Conn., 1975, pp. 108–110.

Far left: The legacy of African art is visible in the sculpture of William Ellsworth Artis. (National Archives Gift Collection.)

African Legacy: Summary* Americans of African descent comprise one of the most significant groups of people to be found in the Americas. Perhaps 100 million strong, Afro-Americans dominate the population of most of the Caribbean republics and constitute a sizeable proportion of the citizenry of Brazil, Surinam, Guyana, Venezuela, Colombia, Panama, and the United States. Significant strains of African ancestry are also to be found among the people of Argentina, Peru, Ecuador, Costa Rica, Guatemala, Mexico, and elsewhere, but in these countries the African component is often already absorbed or is rapidly disappearing into the general population.

The Afro-American people, considered in the larger dimension, do not comprise a single ethnic group. People of part-African descent, often with American Indian and European as well as occasional Asiatic ancestors, are ordinarily to be classified with the national population of the country in which they reside. Thus, a part-African Brazilian is in no sense ethnically Afro-American (and still less, "Negro") but rather is simply a Brazilian. The same is usually also true for persons who are of predominantly African ancestry. A darkskinned Cuban with Negroid characteristics is simply a Cuban who happens to be *negro* (the word "negro" means *black* in the Spanish language).

In discussing Afro-Americans, then, we are making reference to a large mass of people who have only one thing in common—the possession of some degree of African ancestry. Most such people are simply to be identified as Venezuelans, Puerto Ricans, Dominicans, or Colombians, and have so thoroughly mixed with Indians and Europeans as to have lost any black identity. Others, while still remaining Negroid in physical appearance, have also become part of a national culture and are now also simply Haitians, Jamaicans, Panamanians, or Cubans.

The cultural legacy from Africa, rich as it is in the region from Haiti to Brazil, does not always provide any kind of Afro-American identity. All of the national cultures in the region have become Africanized to such an extent that all citizens, whether of African descent or not, share an African cultural legacy. For example, there is no Afro-Brazilian culture that belongs exclusively to Brazilians of African descent. All Brazilians live a way of life that is a complex mixture of African, American Indian, and European traits,

*The term "Afro-American" used here includes all peoples of African descent throughout the Americas; it is a qualifying exception to the definition in the PREFACE.

and one that varies primarily from region to region or class to class rather than from racial strain to racial strain.

The United States would seem, at first glance, to present an exception to the above generalizations. It is true that in an official sense the United States is composed of people who are "Negroes" and people who are "whites" and often the dividing line is made to seem rather sharp. In the United States, an "American Negro" identity has developed and, to some degree, at least there also exists a Negro subculture or black culture that is not shared by the balance of the population. On the other hand, the situation in the United States is not altogether distinct, since millions of United States citizens of part-African ancestry are currently classified not as "Negroes" but as Puerto Ricans, Mexican-Americans, American Indians, Cubans, Louisiana Creoles, or simply as "whites."

Likewise, the African cultural heritage of the United States, from yams and coffee to jazz and calypso, is shared by all citizens and not merely by persons of African descent.

The significance of people of varying African ancestry is, then, a much larger subject than would be the significance of the "American Negro," or Afro-Americans in the United States. A new race is being created throughout the Americas, a race that is amalgamating African, European, and American Indian strains, as well as Asiatic elements in certain regions. This new "cosmic" or "universal" race will vary in the relative proportions of African, Indian, and European background but in the region from Brazil through much of the United States and all around the Caribbean the African element will be of great significance.

In a similar manner, the cultures of the Americas are becoming composites of traits derived from Africa and other portions of the world. The African impact upon Europe has always been considerable, from the beginnings of civilization in ancient Egypt to the legacy of the Muslim civilizations and the impact of non-Muslim black Africa, and thus the culture brought by Europeans to the New World (especially by the Portuguese and Spanish) was already part-African. In the course of the last five centuries, this European-Middle Eastern-African legacy has been still further enriched by cultural elements introduced by black Africans and by their Afro-American descendants.

Throughout the Americas then, regional national cultures are developing that are unique composites of worldwide legacies. From Brazil to the United States, the African component in these composites looms very large indeed.

But the significance of the Afro-American people cannot be summarized solely by reference to racial and cultural contributions. For five centuries Americans of African descent have labored alongside their fellow Americans to produce the modern civilizations of this hemisphere. Serving as explorers, sailors, unpaid slaves, soldiers, artisans, architects, statesmen, revolutionaries, diplomats, musicians, poets, novelists, and in a multitude of other capacities, Americans of African descent have made major contributions whether functioning within the framework of an Afro-American cultural legacy or within the context of the larger national cultures.

In the United States, for instance, it can be conservatively asserted that the wealth of the Southern states, and most of the architectural, literary, and artistic accomplishments springing therefrom were built up through the efforts of black labor, free or slave. Without the Afro-American slave and the free Afro-American artisan there never would have been any aristocratic culture in the Old South and no country gentlemen of the type of George Washington and Thomas Jefferson. Similarly, modern Southern economic development and wealthy-class leisure society rests upon a base of low-wage labor, principally Negro. When one considers that the Negro (and Indian) slaves were rarely paid over a period of three centuries and that since the Civil War Afro-American laborers have been largely underpaid, it becomes quite obvious that the financial debt that the white American owes to the Afro-American (and Indian) is large indeed.

Elsewhere, Afro-Americans played crucial roles in the development of Spanish Florida, French–Spanish Louisiana, Spanish-Mexican Texas, and the balance of the West. Without the participation of people of color, whether slave or free, French-Spanish Louisiana and Spanish Florida would doubtless have never existed or, at the very least, would have remained extremely underdeveloped. Especially by the late seventeenth century, and all through the eighteenth century, Spanish soldiers of "mulatto" or other mixed-blood racial character were absolutely essential to the defense of the territory from Florida (where they fought against the English and Scots of South Carolina) to California (where they helped to control the Indian population).

In summary, the Afro-American legacy of the United States and of the balance of the Americas is of profound significance and has become, in great part, the collective legacy of all Americans. Americans may not all be part-African in terms of ancestry, but they are all participants in a part-African historical and cultural heritage. *See also* HISTORY: COLONIAL PERIOD, 1600–1783; MUSIC; NATIONALISM; PAN-AFRICANISM.

REFERENCES: Abraham, Roger D., "Rapping and Capping: Black Talk as Art," in Szwed, John F. (ed.), *Black America,* Basic Books, New York, 1970; Brasch, Ila Wales, *A Comprehensive Annotated Bibliography of American Black English,* Louisiana State University Press, Baton Rouge, 1974; Dillard, J. L., *Black English: Its History and Usage in the United States,* Random House, New York, 1972; Herskovits, Melville J., *The Myth of the Negro Past,* Harper & Brothers, New York, 1941; Kochman, Clarence, *Rappin' and Stylin' Out: Communication in Urban Black America,* University of Illinois Press, Urbana, 1972; McMillan, James B., *Annotated Bibliography of Southern American English,* University of Miami Press, Coral Gables, 1971; Mintz, Sidney W. (ed.), *Slavery, Colonialism, and Racism,* W. W. Norton, Inc., New York, 1974, a volume by 12 contributors that gives particular attention to the historical and contemporary experience of black peoples in the Caribbean and Latin America; Price, Richard (ed.), *Maroon Societies: Rebel Slave Communities in the Americas,* Anchor Press/Doubleday, Garden City, 1973; Smith, Arthur L., *Language, Communication and Rhetoric in Black America,* Harper & Row, New York, 1972; Turner, Lorenzo D., *Africanisms in the Gullah Dialect,* Arno Press, New York, 1969, originally published in 1949; Whitten, Norman E., Jr. and John F. Szwed (eds.), *Afro-American Anthropology,* The Free Press, New York, 1970; and Wood, Peter H., *Black Majority: Negroes in Colonial South Carolina from 1670 through the Stono Rebellion,* Alfred A. Knopf, New York, 1974. See especially Chapter VI, "Gullah Speech: The Roots of Black English".

AFRICAN MEETING HOUSE The oldest extant Afro-American church building in the United States, it was built in Boston, Mass., ca. 1806 with funds raised by Cato Gardner, a freed slave. Although it was originally constructed as a church, the building also served as a community center. William Lloyd Garrison founded the New England Abolitionist Society here. A school was operated in its basement until its relocation in 1834 when the city of Boston, through an endowment, built the Smith School. Located on the North Slope of Beacon Hill in Boston, the meeting house remained active as a Baptist church until the 1900s. It was (1970s) restored by the Museum of Afro-American History under the direction of Byron Rushing.

The meeting house, now the home of the Museum of Afro-American History, has been included in the National Register for Historic Landmarks. For a brief account of the meeting house and museum, see Mark B. Mitchell, "Afro-American Museum Settles on Smith Court," *Beacon Hill News,* Boston, September, 1971.

AFRICAN METHODIST EPISCOPAL CHURCH

AFRICAN METHODIST EPISCOPAL (AME) CHURCH* The development of the African Methodist Episcopal Church, the oldest organization of any kind established by Negroes in the

A 1961 plaque on modern Mother Bethel commemorates Richard Allen, who led the first congregants in 1787 to worship in an abandoned blacksmith's shop on the site. *(Photo by Jacquelyn Low.)*

United States, has passed through several phases. It originated in 1786 at Philadelphia as a small prayer band in St. George's Church under the leadership of Richard Allen (1760–1831). This group subsequently developed into the Free African Society in 1787. With Allen was Absalom Jones, the founder and organizer of St. Thomas's Protestant Episcopal Church in 1794, also an outgrowth of the Free African Society. He was the first Afro-American rector-priest of the Episcopal Church in America. From the Free African Society also emerged the semi-independent Bethel Church, which later became com-

*Excerpted from Grant S. Shockley, "The A.M.E. and the A.M.E. Zion Churches," chap 23, in Emory Stevens Bucke (ed.), *The History of American Methodism*, vol. 2, copyright © Abington Press, Nashville, Tenn., 1964.

pletely autonomous and the organizing nucleus for the new denomination in 1816.

The singular fact that characterizes the several African Methodist societies that met at Philadelphia in 1816 to form a united body was their desire to be free from control and discrimination and to have wider participation and fuller expression in the total life of the church than had been available in the churches from which they had seceded. In the words of Benjamin T. Tanner, in his famous *An Apology for African Methodism,* Afro-American Methodists then as now were anxious "to think for themselves, . . . to talk for themselves, . . . to act for themselves; [and to] support from their own substance, however scanty, the ministration of the Word which they receive." This fact pervades the record of the earliest churches that united with the denomination and those throughout its history. It is true of the blacks who remained in the Methodist churches as well as of those who left. It also accounted for the attempt on the part of the Methodist Episcopal Church to finally ameliorate the situation. The founding of Zoar Church in Philadelphia, the mother church of Afro-American Methodism, is the classic example. "In 1794 . . . the Methodists of St. George's, viewing with . . . chagrin the widespread withdrawal of Afro-Americans, . . . established a mission at Camperdown . . . which eventually became the present Zoar Church."

It was following discrimination, together with gross personal indignities, that the sizable group of blacks withdrew in a body from St. George's Church in Philadelphia in 1787 and formed the Free African Society.

African Methodism in Maryland had a similar background. It began as early as 1787 when the white members of the Log Meeting House, Lovely Lane, and Strawberry Alley Societies in Baltimore refused to let Negroes occupy the same pews or receive the sacrament of Holy Communion with them in the same church buildings. This situation precipitated the withdrawal of the Afro-American membership of these societies and the formation of a Baltimore African Church. This body, while Methodistic in doctrine and polity, was for all practical pruposes an independent organization until 1812, at which time Daniel Coker, the organizer of African Methodism in Maryland, formed the Afro-American membership of this and of other Methodist congregations in Baltimore and vicinity into the society that presented itself at the Organizing Convention.

Publications The literary efforts of the AME Church include the publication of the *Discipline*, official *General Conference Minutes*, church periodicals, hymnals, Sunday school literature, histories, and miscellaneous writings by members of the connection.

The first *Discipline* was published in 1817. The first major revision of the *Discipline* was made in 1836, and since that time periodic revisions and changes have been made as needed. The first printing of the *General Minutes* of the denomination was in 1822. After this they were published intermittently until after the Civil War. In 1840 the first discussion of a connectional periodical occurred. This came to fruition in the founding of the *A.M.E. Church Magazine* in 1841. George Hogarth was the first editor. This paper, originally intended to be a weekly, became a quarterly in its first year and continued in existence for seven years. In 1848 it was made a weekly, renamed the *Christian Herald*, and published by Major Delany's militant race newspaper, *Pittsburgh Mystery*, which was purchased by the denomination for that purpose. Augustus R. Green was its first editor, and in 1852 the *Christian Herald* became the *Christian Recorder* by action of the General Conference. There have been two other regional *Recorders*. The *Southern Recorder*, authorized by the General Conferences of 1880 and 1884, was finally started in 1886 by Henry M. Turner. It was purchased by the denomination in 1888 and became the *Southern Christian Recorder*. The *Western Christian Recorder* was founded by Frank M. McDonald as a private venture in 1891. In 1900 it became one of the official organs of the church, and in 1912 its editor became a general officer of the church.

Between 1858 and 1864, the need for a more sophisticated type of journal began to crystallize, and a new type of publication was instituted "to furnish the race with the thoughts of the leading men and women," and to give "opportunity to [those] who have talent as writers." The earlier of the two forms of this journal was the *Repository of Religion and Literature*, edited by John M. Brown and published at Indianapolis for the first time in April, 1858. This effort expired

in 1864. In 1883 a revival of this type of publication was suggested by Benjamin T. Tanner, which eventuated in the action of the ensuing General Conference of 1884 authorizing the publication of the *A.M.E. Church Review*. Tanner became the first editor.

Two AME missionary periodicals have been developed. The *Voice of Missions*, the official organ of the missionary department of the General Conference, was begun in 1892 and continues until the present. The *Woman's Missionary Recorder*, established in 1912, served as the editorial organ of the womens' auxiliary missionary societies.

The first hymnbook compiled and published by Afro-Americans was the *AME Hymnal*. Its history reaches back to an 1807 copy of the *Pocket Hymn Book, Selected from Different Authors*. This early collection by Richard Allen was apparently published privately by him in 1807 and revised in 1818 with the assistance of Jacob Tapsico. The preface to this edition states:

Having become a distinct and separate body of people, there is no collection of hymns we could with propriety adopt. However, we have for some time been collecting materials for the present work. . . . We have not passed over a selection of hymns because esteemed and used by a particular denomination, but have endeavoured to collect such as were applicable to the various states of Christian experience.

From 1818 to 1835 no reference to a hymnal can be found. Payne, in his *History of the A.M.E. Church*, insisted that up to 1826 there is no proof of the existence of a hymnal and that "probably the Hymn Book of the M. E. Church was used." This statement may indicate the fact that the 1818 edition was not connectional but local; or, if connectional, it was not used widely. There have been several editions of the hymnbook since these early days. Payne related that the subject of the publication of a hymnal was discussed by the Philadelphia Conference in 1835; and that Joseph M. Corr, then general book steward, reported that a thousand copies had been published. In 1854 the Philadelphia Conference learned that a revision of the hymnal was nearly complete, and that "it was the design of the book steward to publish two forms of the hymnbook, one for the pews, . . . the other for the pulpit." The General Conference of 1856 voted "to revise the present hymnbook, [and] to publish it as soon as practicable." A revision with minor changes was ordered by the General Conference of 1864. The 1868 body appointed Henry M. Turner to revise the old hymnbook completely, "which was equivalent to authorizing him to compile a new one." This revision, which appeared in 1873, served as the authorized revision until 1893. It was the first of the omnibus hymnals including "spiritual songs" and chants, liturgies, rituals, and other church ordinances. In 1888 the General Conference appointed another hymnal-revision committee and instructed it to compile what became known as the 1893 hymnbook. Under the editorship of J. C. Embry, a smaller edition, with the hymns grouped according to meter, was presented to the church. Chants were deleted from this edition, and the rituals for the administration of baptism and holy communion, which had been deleted from some former editions, were restored. The first musically scored hymnal was published in 1897, again under the editorship of Embry. This edition was not revised until 1941.

In connection with the movement to organize the council of the bishops of the three major Afro-American Methodist bodies in 1908, an attempt was made to develop a common hymnal and liturgy. These failed to materialize, as did the continuance of the council.

AME Sunday school literature, "the first . . . ever published in this country for the exclusive use of Afro-American Sunday schools," has been successfully published and widely used since the late 1880s through the facilities of their Sunday School Union Press, the publishing unit for religious education materials. By 1881 a *Child's Recorder* was being published and in popular demand by all the Sabbath schools. H. M. Turner's *Catechism* was also in general use as teaching material. The second Annual Report of the publication department in 1882 indicated a continued demand for the *Child's Recorder*, and the interesting fact that "We have also, by authority of the Publishing Board, arranged for, and secured with our imprint on it, a Teacher's Quarterly, Scholar's Quarterly, and Little Learner's Paper."

In addition, the then traditional catechisms, "Milk for Babes" and "Children's Bread," were being printed. In the 1884 report of the Sunday School Department, it was learned that in January 1883, a new publication, *Our Sunday School Review*, had been introduced, and in March of that same year the *Jubilee Gem* had been presented. Curriculum materials such as the *Teacher's Quarterly, Scholar's Quarterly, Juvenile Lesson Paper, Gem Lesson Paper, Primary Lessons for Beginners,* and the *Young Allenite* had been

AME centennial (1876) publication by John H. W. Burley. Richard Allen (center), the first AME bishop, is surrounded (from top clockwise) by: Morris Brown, William Paul Quinn, Daniel Payne, Jabez Campbell, Thomas Ward, John M. Brown, James Shorter, Alexander Wayman, Willis Nazrey, and Edward Waters. Many of the bishops have been commemorated in the names of churches and schools. *(Library of Congress.)*

added. The ten graded publications were "fully adapted to every feature of . . . Sunday School work." In the youth field, by 1912 the Allen Christian Endeavor League was publishing "all kinds of literature;" for example, a *Young Peoples Quarterly* was being published by Augustus Young of Akron, and there was a connectional youth organ, the *Allen Christian Endeavorer.* By 1916 a teacher's guide and quarterlies for each age group in the Sunday school had been developed and improved, and the *Allen C. E. League Star,* a youth periodical, had appeared.

Membership and Churches (1973)* Membership approximates one million in 4,500 churches; the ordained clergy is about 6,000. The bishops of the church in order of rank in seniority (February, 1973) are (number indicates the episcopal district): Decatur Ward Nichols (7th), Joseph Gomez (retired); Isaiah Hamilton Bonner (8th), William Reid Wilks (13th), Howard Thomas Primm (4th), Frederick Douglass Jordan (official), Ernest Lawrence Hickman (1st), William Franklin Ball (unassigned), Odie Lee Sherman (retired), George Wayman Blakeley (unassigned), Harrison J. Bryant (5th), Harold I. Bearden (3rd), Hubert N. Robinson (11th), Henry W. Murph (2nd), John Hurst Adams (10th), Richard Allen Hildebrand (6th), Samuel S. Morris (12th), Vinton R. Anderson (9th), H. Hartford Brookings (17th), Fred H. Tolbert (15th), Fred C. James (15th and 18th), and Frank Madison Reid, Jr. (14th).

The historic and large AME churches include the following: Mother Bethel (Philadelphia), Greater Mount Olive (Philadelphia), Bethel (Baltimore), Payne Memorial (Baltimore), First AME Church (Los Angeles), Allen Temple (Cleveland), Greater Bethel (Cleveland), Bethel (Chicago), Carey AME Temple (Chicago), Allen Temple (Detroit), St. Paul (Detroit), Vernon Chapel (Detroit), Union Bethel (New Orleans), Metropolitan (Washington, D.C.), St. Paul (St. Louis), St. Phillips (Atlanta), Alexander Memorial (Atlanta), and Bethel (New York City). *See also* ALLEN, RICHARD; METHODISTS.

REFERENCES: See the section above entitled "Publications." See also Bucke, Emory Stevens (ed.), *The History of American Methodism,* Abingdon Press, New York, 1964; and Williams, Ethel L. and Clifton T. Brown, *Afro-American Religious Studies: A Comprehensive Bibliography with Locations in American Libraries,* Scarecrow Press, Metuchen, 1972, pp. 167–77 and a more recent general account in Richardson, Harry V., *Dark Salvation: The Story of Methodism Among Blacks in America,* Anchor Press, 1976.

*By the editors.

AFRICAN METHODIST EPISCOPAL ZION (AMEZ) CHURCH The first meetings of the African Methodists in New York City took place January 27, 1771, five years after the founding of the John Street Methodist Society, according to the journal of Joseph Pilmore. For the next 25 years intermittent meetings were evidently held by this group until the African Society was officially sanctioned and the formal organization of the African Chapel took place. In 1799 initial plans were laid to purchase property and build a chapel. The charter was applied for in 1800 and granted in March of the same year. In April 1801, articles of agreement were drawn with Rev. John McClaskey acting for the General Conference of the Methodist Episcopal Church. Twenty-six years later the African Chapel, called Zion, and the companion chapel, Asbury, withdrew from the Methodist Episcopal Church, when it was understood through their pastor, Rev. William Stillwell, that a sizable number of members were withdrawing in the dispute over property rights of the lay members. While Zion and Asbury chapels refused to join the Stillwell Secession as such, they left the mother body because of their concern over these property rights. The first yearly conference of the group took place in New York, June 21, 1821, with 6 societies represented, 22 preachers and a total membership of 1,410. James Varick was elected general superintendent. In 1968 there were 12 bishops, one of them a native African in charge of the work in Liberia, Ghana, and Nigeria, and the 11 assigned to America, South America, Bahamas, Jamaica, Barbados, Trinidad, and England. In 1972 the membership totaled 805,256. There were 4,589 churches. Six educational institutions and inservice centers were supported by the church.

Polity Throughout its history, the church has recognized three classes of members: baptized children, probationers, and full members. The original and present concept of organization provided for the joint responsibility of ministers and lay people for the affairs of the church, lay people aiding in the formation of the first discipline and participating in the early General Conferences. Under the Wesleyan concept, members were organized into classes and these classes formed the society, all with lay leadership. This prevails today. The minister is held responsible for the society, the societies being members of that which is termed the presiding elder district, and these districts compose the annual conferences. Membership, therefore, of the annual conference consists of a delegated body with representation from each society or cluster of societies (all lay people) and three classes of ministers: traveling but not ordained clergy, deacons, and elders, the highest rank.

In the first 50 years of the church, the General Conference designated a person or persons (ministers) who were styled *superintendents*. The superintendent had appointive power in office, but was not consecrated to that office. In an effort to bring about organic union with the AME Church, the denomination agreed to the changing of the title *superintendent* to bishop, but again, as with the case of the superintendent, he was elected for a four-year term only. It was not until 1880 that the bishop was elected for life and consecration took place. The basic concept for the office of bishop is administrative.

Publications The first publication was the *Discipline*, which was used without revision until 1840. By 1860 a newspaper, the *Anglo-African*, was the official organ of the church. By 1873 the *Zion Church Advocate* was being published. In 1884 the *Star of Zion*, a weekly, became the official church organ under the editorship of A. S. Richardson. In addition, Bishop Joseph J. Clinton founded the *A.M.E. Zion Quarterly Review* in 1899; the present editor is the Rev. David H. Bradley. The latter two publications have continued. Other publications include hymnals, disciplines, and minutes. The main publishing headquarters is located in Charlotte, N.C.

REFERENCES: A list of selective references includes: *The A.M.E. Zion Quarterly Review*; Bradley, David H., Sr., *History of the A.M.E. Zion Church*, 1956, vol. I; Bradley, David H., Sr., *History of the A.M.E. Zion Church*, 1970, vol II; Harris, Cicero R., *Historical Catechism*, Charlotte, N.C., 1916; Hood, James Walker, *One Hundred Years of Zion Methodism*, The A.M.E. Zion Church, 1895; Jones, Bishop E. D. W., *Comprehensive Catechism of the A.M.E. Zion Church*, Washington, D.C., 1934; Minutes of the General Conferences; Moore, John Jamison, *History of the A.M.E. Zion Church*, 1884; Rush, Christopher, *A Short Account of the Rise and Progress of the African Methodist Episcopal (Zion) Church*, 1843; *The Discipline of the A.M.E. Zion Church*; Small, Bishop John Bryan, *Code of the Discipline of the African Methodist Episcopal Zion Church*, 1898.

SOME AME ZION CHURCHES AND PASTORS (1972)

Alleyne Memorial AME Zion Church, Philadelphia, Pa.: R. S. Lomax
†Blackwell Memorial AME Zion Church, Chicago, Ill.: Carroll M. Felton, Jr.
†St. Paul AME Zion Church, Detroit, Mich.: William Ardrey
*First AME Zion Church, San Francisco, Calif.: B. Leon Carson

Metropolitan AME Zion Church, St. Louis, Mo.: R. L. Fisher
*Mother AME Zion Church, New York, N.Y.: G. W. McMurray
*Wesley AME Zion Church, Philadelphia, Pa.: W. R. Kennedy
†National Church of Zion Methodism, Washington, D.C.: E. Franklin Jackson
*Wesley Metropolitan AME Zion Church, Washington D.C.: J. D. McArthur
*Wesley Center AME Zion Church, Pittsburgh, Pa.: George Kendall
†St. Mark AME Zion Church, Durham, N.C.: L. A. Miller
*Evans Metropolitan AME Zion Church, Fayetteville, N.C.: H. E. Haggler
*Clinton Chapel AME Zion Church, Charlotte, N.C.: Morgan Tann
*State Street AME Zion Church, Mobile, Ala.: R. E. Stevens
†St. Paul AME Zion Church, Cleveland, Ohio: Novie Chaney
*Clinton Memorial AME Zion Church, Neward, N.J.: C. E. Bourne

  *HISTORICAL CHURCHES
  †SIGNIFICANT FOR SIZE.

BISHOPS OF THE AME ZION CHURCH (1972)

Coleman, Clinton R., 3513 Ellamont Road, Baltimore, Md. 21215
Dunston, Alfred G., Jr., P.O. Box 19788, Philadelphia, Pa. 19143
Foggie, Charles H., 1200 Windermere Drive, Pittsburgh, Pa. 15218
Hilliard, William Alexander, 690 Chicago Boulevard, Detroit, Mich. 48202
Hoggard, J. Clinton, 6401 Sunset Lane, Indianapolis, Ind. 46260
Leake, George J., 508 Grandin Road, Charlotte, N.C. 28208
Marshall, Arthur, Jr., P.O. Box 41138, Ben Hill Station, Atlanta, Ga. 30331
Miller, John H., 6211 Red Bird Court, Dallas, Tex. 75232
Shaw, Herbert Bell, 520 Red Cross Street, Wilmington, N.C. 28401
Smith, William M., 3753 Springhill Avenue, Mobile, Ala. 36608
Speaks, Reuben L., 365 Brookside Avenue, Roosevelt, N.Y. 11575
Wactor, James W., 709 Edgehill Road, Fayetteville, N.C. 28302

AFRICAN ORTHODOX CHURCH A New York-based body that grew out of the Protestant Episcopal Church in 1919 under the leadership of George Alexander McGuire, a native clergyman of Antigua, West Indies, the African Orthodox Church had a membership in the United States of nearly 10,000 in 1971. At that time, its officers were Gladstone St. Clair Nurse (primate archbishop, metropolitan), G. Duncan Hinson (chancellor), and St. Clement Roett (secretary general).

REFERENCES: Rushing, Byron, "A Note on the Origins of the African Orthodox Church," *Journal of Negro History*, January 1972, pp. 37–39; Williams, Ethel L. and Clifton F. Brown, *Afro-American Religious Studies*, 1972, pp. 177–180.

AFRO-AMERICAN See PREFACE; ONOMATOLOGY

AFRO-AMERICAN HISTORY

Beginning of a lease of land on Maryland's Eastern Shore in 1670 to Mary Johnson, widow ("relict") of Anthony Johnson. Settling in 1622, or earlier, the Johnsons were probably the first Afro-American family in what is now the United States. *(Courtesy of the Hall of Records of Maryland, Annapolis, Md.)*

Free Negroes, 1600s–1860

Introduction It is highly probable that the first identifiable English-speaking person of African descent in what is now the United States was a free person. His family name was Johnson. The earliest member, Anthony, is shown by records to have been a free black as early as 15 years after the first settlement by Englishmen at Jamestown, Va., in 1607. His origins and background are quite obscure. He may have come from Angola by way of South America, or by way of Europe, or by way of Bermuda; but this is conjecture. It is also probable that he was a contract laborer ("indentured servant") who had worked off his debtor obligations by 1622. Though the records are scant or nonexistent, the first person to make a thorough investigation of the Johnsons was William Clayton Torrence (1884–1953), a minister and later editor of the reputable *Virginia Magazine of History and Biography,* who wrote *Old Somerset on the Eastern Shore of Maryland* (1935).

The name "John Johnson, Negro" was mentioned in the record of the court held on July 2, 1667, in Somerset County, on Maryland's Eastern Shore. It is the earliest discovered reference to a Negro within the boundaries of the original Somerset County (from Nanticoke River south to the Maryland-Virginia boundary line). Then, too, of yet greater interest, is the fact that these Johnsons (of whom there are records of several generations) were "free negroes" and came to the Eastern Shore of Maryland in late 1661 or early 1662, from Northampton County in Virginia, where they had resided for many years as "free Negroes." This family had its origin in Anthony Johnson and Mary, his wife, "free Negroes," who were residing as early as 1622 in old Accomack, later Northampton County, on the Eastern Shore of the colony of Virginia, and stated to have been the first free blacks in Virginia. In 1652 these Johnsons suffered great property loss from a devastating fire and were thereafter exempted from payment of taxes.

These Johnsons not only were owners of landed property, but also apparently held other Afro-Americans as slaves. Anthony and Mary Johnson were the parents of at least two sons, John Johnson and Richard Johnson, who were grown men by the year 1654, when they appear in land transactions in the records of Northampton County, Va. When settlement was made on the Eastern Shore of the province of Maryland under proclamation of Lord Baltimore, dated November 6, 1661, two of the "headrights" of Randall Revell and Ann Toft to their patent for "Double Purchase," dated November 10, 1662, were Anthony and Mary Johnson who came into the Manokin River section of the Eastern Shore Maryland settlement, transported by Randall Revell and Anne Toft. Anthony Johnson and Mary, his wife, certainly came among the first settlers of the area which later became Somerset County and lived for a while in the Manokin section. On August 10, 1666, "Stephen Horsey, of Annemessex, in the province of Maryland, Gentleman," leased to "Anthony Johnson, of Manonoakin, in the province aforesaid, planter," a tract of 300 acres of land called "Tonies Vineyard," on the south side of Wiccocomoco Creek and lying by the creek side adjoining William Bosman's land. The tract had been granted to Horsey by patent February 24, 1665–66. This lease was for the term of 200 years to Johnson and his wife at the yearly rent of "one pepper corne" and the payment of his lordship's rents and other dues. The lease was entered on the Somerset records September 10, 1666, with William Thorne and William Stevens as witnesses.

The exact date of Anthony Johnson's death is not known, but it took place prior to June, 1670, for on the tenth day of that month Stephen Horsey, of Somerset County, made a 99-year lease of the land called "Tonies Vineyard," on the south side of Wiccocomoco Creek, to Mary Johnson, "relict of Anthony Johnson, late of Somerset County, deceased," and after her death to John Johnson and Richard Johnson and their, or either of their, heirs. The yearly rent again was stated as one ear of Indian corn. On September 3, 1672, Mary Johnson, of Somerset County, ("relict of Anthony Johnson, late of the said county, Negro, deceased"), made deed of gift for cattle, to her grandchildren: Anthony Johnson, son of John Johnson, Negro, and Francis and Richard Johnson, sons of Richard Johnson. On the same date, Mary Johnson, Negro, of Somerset County (widow and relict of Anthony Johnson, late of Somerset, Negro, deceased), gave a power of attorney to her son, "John Johnson, Negro, of Somerset County." This power of attorney was witnessed by Edmund Beauchamp and "John Cazara, Negro."

Besides the Johnsons, other free blacks lived on the Eastern Shore of Maryland and Virginia during the second half of the 1600s. It is likely that one of the first free black communities in British America developed in Northampton County, Va. The names of Drigges (Driggers, Digges) and Vaughan have been preserved. Indeed, at least one family of Vaughans in Hare Valley, Va. (near Nassawaddox), was in existence in the 1970s.

Development The free black class came into existence in a number of ways. Many slaves, having kindly masters who encouraged them to save, obtained their freedom by self-purchase. Many were runaway slaves. Some had been manumitted by the death of their masters. Others obtained their freedom because of meritorious service, particularly in the wars. There was, of course, a natural increase among the free blacks. By 1860 about 11 percent of the Afro-American population was free. Of the 488,000 free blacks, 250,000 were in the South. Maryland had more free blacks in 1860 than any other state (84,000); and Baltimore had more free blacks (26,000) than any other city in the United States. The master-slave ratio, however, was not high in Maryland. At the end of the antebellum period, nearly half of Maryland's black population (49 percent) was free. It is not surprising then that a host of antebellum free blacks in Maryland, such as Benjamin Banneker, Frederick Douglass, and Harriet Tubman earned unusually outstanding reputations.

An Urban Class This free black class tended to be an urban class. For example, in Louisiana, 10,000 of the 18,000 free blacks were located in New Orleans. Except in North Carolina, the free black was predominantly an urban dweller.

The antebellum free black was characterized by a high percentage of mixed ancestry. The census of 1860 reveals that only 8 percent of the slave population was listed as mulatto or mixed, whereas 37 percent of the free black population was listed as mulatto or mixed.

The class of free blacks was as uncomplicated to the outsider as the Afro-American community often appears to outsiders today. But among the free black class, as among any other free class, there were social stratifications. A book entitled *William Johnson's Natchez: The Ante-Bellum Diary of a Free Negro* (edited by W. R. Hogan and E. A. Davis, 1951) divides the Afro-Americans there into four groups: slaveholders, skilled workers, laborers, and domestics. Each group lived between more or less stratified lines, having its own churches, organizations, and clubs.

To be free was a tremendous distinction for all free blacks. Many of them put FMC (Free Man of Color) or FWC (Free Woman of Color) after their names. It was quite a status symbol to be free when the predominant Afro-American mass was not.

It is to be noted that free blacks were restricted to a considerable degree, especially in the South where the Afro-American slave population was so numerous. The historian Ulrich B. Phillips called the free black a third element in a society built for two, meaning obviously the slave and the master.

The free black class in the South was held to be a dangerous class: free blacks might become a public charge; they might make the slave uneasy with his status; they might help the slaves plot insurrection. Free blacks in the antebellum South, therefore, were generally an element unwanted by the white population.

Restrictions in the South The first and most obvious restriction on free blacks was the necessity to carry free papers. There were rewards for catching a free black without his papers. In the South, color presumed status; if you were an Afro-American it was evidence that you were a slave unless you could prove the contrary. Generally, for the Afro-American the ordinary rules of English law, of American law, and of Anglo-Saxon jurisprudence did not obtain. An Afro-American was presumed to be guilty rather than innocent.

Free blacks in some counties had to register every year. They had to go to the courthouse periodically where they registered to indicate that they had behaved themselves since their last appearance.

Free Negroes in Georgia, Florida, and Alabama had to have white guardians to whom they reported periodically to guarantee that they were behaving themselves. Many of these Afro-Americans particularly in South Carolina, had Brown Fellowship clubs and were people of some learning and some ability; nevertheless, on paper at least, they too were required to have legal guardians.

The free black class also suffered legal disabilities in the South. They did not serve on a jury nor were they tried by jury. They could not testify against whites. This was quite a burdensome limitation. A white man murdered William Johnson of Natchez, who was a member of the so-called black aristocracy, an unusual Afro-American. The only witnesses were three Afro-Americans who could not testify. The murderer went free.

The free black in the South was not free to go where he wanted. In some places, if he left his county or his state, he could not return. Moreover, he was not welcome in many places. Some states forbade free Negroes to enter. Some refused to allow any newly emancipated slaves to remain; for this reason, some blacks held other blacks as slaves under a system called benevolent slaveholding. They held relatives and friends as slaves in order to avoid having to send them out of the state.

In Maryland, for example, after 1839 a free black coming in from another state would be fined $20 for the first offense, $500 for the sec-

ond offense. If he could not pay the $500, his labor would be sold until the fine was paid.

In the antebellum South, Afro-Americans had to show that they were gainfully employed; there was always a fear that the free black might become a public charge. He had to have a job that was productive and that society needed or else he could be charged with vagrancy and fined. If he could not pay the fine, his labor could be sold; thus, virtual slavery (peonage) of free blacks could exist.

Restrictions in the North The northern black met a great number of discriminations, not only before the law but also in job opportunity. A book by Leon F. Litwack, *North of Slavery* (1961), gives some idea of the restrictions on the Negro in the North. Some northern states (Ohio, Indiana, Illinois), which bordered the southern states, had laws against the entry of Afro-Americans. In the three states mentioned, plus Iowa and California, Negroes could not testify against whites. Suffrage in the North was also denied the free black except in Massachusetts and Connecticut. In New York, the free black could vote if he had $250 worth of property, whereas other males

Despite many restrictions, free blacks were leaders in Afro-American cultural life and in protest against discrimination and slavery. The sketch shows congregants at worship in their church. *(Library of Congress.)*

could vote simply by having attained the age of 21. In a period in American history when manhood suffrage was extended to all the states that came into the Union, Negro voting was restricted in the North.

There was school segregation in the North. Beginning in 1830, the abolitionists and others tried to end it. A notable breakthrough occurred in Boston in 1855, when the schools were desegregated.

Accomplishments In the antebellum South, Afro-American accomplishments were generally in the area of property owning; free blacks in the antebellum South could make contracts and own property. The shortage of free labor in the South gave free blacks opportunities to get jobs, many of them skilled jobs. It was in this way that they had a chance to become economically self-sufficient and eventually to own property.

One of the surprising things about the Afro-American in the antebellum South was that he was economically well-off by comparison with the Afro-American in the North, where there was a fiercer labor competition.

There was, in the antebellum South, a cluster of Afro-Americans who were quite well-to-do. The Afro-American scholar, Luther P. Jackson, has documented the extent to which free blacks in Virginia held property, some of it in slaves. In Baltimore, there was a group of Afro-Americans who were relatively prosperous. In 1860, 15 Baltimore schools were supported by the Afro-Americans themselves. These schools had teachers of some ability, one of them being Frances E. W. Harper.

Because of his economic advances, the free Negro had many societies of his own, his own church life, and other such organizations that required financing.

Churches In the North, one of the outstanding accomplishments of the Afro-American in the antebellum period was the emergence of the so-called Afro-American church. The Afro-American church, like many organizations in the antebellum period, really came as the result of discrimination on the part of white churches.

On a winter's day in 1787 in Philadelphia, the great church leaders Absalom Jones and Richard Allen were ordered up into the balcony of St. George's Church. Not wishing to create a disturbance, they obeyed; but they never returned to St. George's Church to worship.

It was Richard Allen who became the first bishop of the African Methodist Episcopal (AME) Church. Five years later the African Methodist Episcopal Zion (AMEZ) Church emerged. These were two of the great antebellum Afro-American churches. Doctrine, theology, and tenets were the same in the Afro-American church as in the white church. The black Methodist Church, for example, was like all other Methodist churches except that it was controlled by blacks with their own bishops and

their own leaders. The black church, begun about 1815 but really going back to about 1800, emerged as an outstanding institution. The churchmen, generally, were the best educated Afro-Americans. They furnished leadership, direction, and inspiration. Leadership emerged in the Afro-American churches because Afro-Americans did not want to sit in a balcony and because they wanted to exercise the prerogatives of Christian leadership. They wanted to be preachers, deacons, and deaconesses.

Newspapers In the North, there was another important feature: the emergence of Afro-American newspapers. Seventeen of these newspapers were issued before the Civil War and were basically dedicated to the theme of liberty. One of the first Afro-American journals, *Freedom's Journal*, was published in 1827. Its editor was John Russwurm, who a year earlier had been one of the first two Afro-Americans to graduate from college. The second periodical was called *Rights of All*, which likewise struck a note for freedom, for democracy, and for equality. Great pride came to Afro-Americans who read articles written by men of their own race and letters to the editor, written perhaps by themselves or their friends. The success of such Afro-American editors as Frederick Douglass, who began in 1847 with the *North Star* in Rochester, N.Y., and ended in 1860 in Washington with *Douglass' Monthly*, gave black people a feeling of self-sufficiency and pride, which let the Afro-American know that he too was able to shape public opinion.

The composition in some of these antebellum newspapers is quite surprising in quality. Douglass was a very meticulous editor. He would not allow a typographical error to appear in the *North Star*. He, along with other Afro-Americans, felt that people judged them by their papers and, therefore, he saw to it that there were no gross inaccuracies, misspellings, or bad grammar.

These Afro-American newspapers contributed greatly to the work of the abolitionist movement and to a feeling of accomplishment on the part of blacks.

In addition to newspapers, free blacks also wrote and published other abolitionist materials, including books and journals.

The Abolitionist Movement The northern Negro played a very important and dynamic role in the abolitionist movement, which gradually created a mind-set leading to a clash between the North and the South and, ultimately, achieved the abolition of slavery. When the abolitionist movement began its vigorous attacks on slavery in the 1830s, white Southerners played up such white "malcontents" as William Lloyd Garrison and Wendell Phillips. They conveniently ignored the Afro-American abolitionists because discontent on the part of Afro-Americans was contrary to their fundamental teachings that Afro-Americans did not want to change the slave system. Yet, there were those 17 newspapers put out by Afro-Americans in the North. Moreover, there were Afro-American conventions held annually in the North after 1830 to plan strategy and to make known black wishes regarding freedom and equal rights. The abolitionists, white and black, pressing for freedom, were not only concerned for the slave; they were also concerned with American freedom. They took pains to make it clear that they were not pressing for "Negro rights"; rather, they were pressing for a larger concept of American rights. They stressed that they were helping America to become what it had projected itself as becoming: a land of the free.

Self-Improvement Societies The antebellum Afro-American formed self-improvement societies. Among Afro-Americans in the antebellum South, one of the most common organizations was the mutual aid society, developed for protection in times of distress. These societies grew on an unprecedented scale. Members insured themselves by paying something like 50 cents a month. Thus, they protected themselves against sickness or death.

There were also literary societies, located mainly in the North. Many of them were exclusively women's societies, some were for children, and some were open to all. These self-improvement societies, particularly where Afro-Americans were barred from the public schools, proved to the world that the Afro-American was prepared to handle the responsibilities of citizenship. Such societies were common as a whole in antebellum America, but Afro-Americans very frequently were not permitted into white societies. Even if they were, they often were accepted only on a restricted basis, which hurt their pride.

Political Interest Despite discrimination, blacks worked for freedom through politics. They kept pressing for the vote in order to elect people who had abolitionist sentiments, people who would go to the state capital or to Washington to work against slavery.

One of the outstanding stories of the antebel-

lum black is how he tried to get suffrage despite the law and the constitution of his state. His interest in politics began formally with the Liberty Party, started in 1840. Eight years later, he was present at the formation of the Free Soil Party, which worked against the extension of slavery. He rejoiced when the Republican Party came into existence in 1854, and he supported it in 1856 and 1860. He reasoned that even if these parties did not stamp out slavery, they would contain it and not permit it to extend to the territories. This political interest on the part of black people, who themselves could not vote, was very great.

The Underground Railroad Negroes also worked in the Underground Railroad. The greatest of these underground operators, of course, was Harriet Tubman of Maryland. She worked zealously in the antebellum period and worked all the harder when a price was put on her head. See also AFRICAN METHODIST EPISCOPAL (AME) CHURCH; AFRICAN METHODIST EPISCOPAL ZION (AMEZ) CHURCH; COLONIZATION; FRATERNAL SOCIETIES; NEWSPAPERS: HISTORY AND DEVELOPLMENT; SLAVERY: THE ABOLITIONISTS; SLAVERY: UNDERGROUND RAILROAD.

REFERENCES: Berlin, Ira, *Slaves Without Masters; the Free Negro in the Antebellum South*, Oxford University Press, New York, 1974; Brown, Letitia, *Free Negroes in the District of Columbia, 1790–1846*, Oxford University Press, New York, 1972; Franklin, John Hope, *The Free Negro in North Carolina, 1790–1860*, University of North Carolina Press, Chapel Hill, 1943; Hershberg, Theodore, "Free Blacks in Antebellum Philadelphia," *Journal of Social History*, Winter 1971–72, pp. 183–209; Jackson, Luther P., *Free Negro Labor and Property Holding in Virginia, 1830–1860*, D. Appleton Century Co., New York, 1942; Litwack, Leon F., *North of Slavery: The Negro in the Free States, 1790–1860*, University of Chicago Press, Chicago, 1961; Pease, William and Jane Pease, *Black Utopia: Negro Communal Experiments in America*, State Historical Society of Wisconsin, Madison, 1963; Perlman, Daniel, "Organizations of the Free Negro in New York City, 1800–1860," *Journal of Negro History*, July 1971, pp. 181–97; Quarles, Benjamin, *Black Abolitionists*, Oxford University Press, New York, 1969; Reinders, Robert C., "The Decline of the New Orleans Free Negro in the Decade Before the Civil War," *Journal of Mississippi History*, April 1962, pp. 88–98; Russell, John, *The Free Negro in Virginia, 1830–1860*, Johns Hopkins University Press, Baltimore, 1913; Schoen, Harold, "The Free Negro in the Republic of Texas," *Southwestern Historical Quarterly*, April 1936, pp. 292–308, and October 1936, pp. 85–113; Sydnor, Charles S., "The Free Negro in Mississippi Before the Civil War," *American Historical Review*, July 1927; Turner, Edward R., *The Negro in Pennsylvania, 1639–1861*, American Historical Association, Washington, D.C., 1911; Woodson, Carter G., *The Education of the Negro Prior to 1861*, reprint of 2d ed., 1919, Arno Press, New York, 1968; Woodson, Carter G., "The Negroes of Cincinnati Prior to the Civil War," *Journal of Negro History*, January 1916, pp. 1–22; and Wright, James M., *The Free Negro in Maryland*, Columbia University Press, New York, 1921. See also REFERENCES under SLAVERY IN SELECTED STATES: VIRGINIA and related articles.

Colonial Period, 1600s–1783

Introduction Despite the presence of free Negroes, the great masses of Afro-Americans lived as slaves during the colonial period of American history. However, this essential truth has sometimes been overshadowed by the incessant honor, or eulogy, accorded a few outstanding free blacks—Crispus Attucks, Paul Cuffe, and Prince Hall—who lived under different circumstances in northern regions, far removed from plantation slavery in the South.

The southern colonies were by far the most important colonies from the standpoints of population, economy, and cultural development. Virginia was the oldest and largest colony. The number of its slaves in 1750, nearly 100,000, totaled more than the entire populations of Rhode Island, Delaware, North Carolina, South Carolina, and Georgia. Slave labor in Virginia and neighboring Maryland, the area known as the Tobacco Coast, was vital in the production of tobacco, which was the most important product in the whole system of British-American mercantilism. The British Empire was literally founded upon the tobacco trade, which eventually depended very heavily upon slave labor. Whether on tobacco farms in Virginia and Maryland, or in rice fields farther to the south, slave

Scene at a tobacco wharf on the shoreline of the Chesapeake Bay (Tobacco Coast) about 1750. Somewhat idealized and romanticized, the sketch shows tobacco planters (one being served a drink) and their slave workers at the loading of a shipment of tobacco for the voyage to England. The sketch was made by Elmo Jones after Charles Grignion's engraving of Francis Hayman's cartouche on a map by Joshua Fry and Peter Jefferson entitled *Map of Virginia and Maryland*, published in London in 1751. *(From* Tobacco Coast, *courtesy of the Mariner's Museum.)*

labor was hard and punishments were often severe. Coming mainly from West Africa, blacks were forced to adapt to their new environment, and in the process much of the African heritage was stamped out or drastically modified as demands of a new way of life were met.

During the eighteenth century, four great determinants greatly affected the system of American slavery. The first one was the decision and effort by the British to christianize blacks, although still maintaining them as slaves despite the Christian belief in the brotherhood of man. This decision also led to America's first great moral dilemma in regard to blacks.

Arguments of justification, or rationalization, undergirded the religious sanction of slavery. One of the earliest to appear was that slavery made the fruits of civilization available to the "inferior" African. Other arguments held that the Bible sanctioned slavery; that slavery was a good thing for both the blacks and the country. Some of these arguments could still be heard as late as the eve of the Civil War, and, indeed, traces of them survived as racism. Nevertheless, despite doubts, opposition, and the severe conditions of the colonial experience, the Christianization of the Negro proceeded as the first great step in his larger Americanization.

There is, for example, evidence that the Puritans favored conversion. In a tract published in London in 1673, Richard Baxter favored Christian instruction of slaves. John Eliot and Cotton Mather of New England favored instruction, also. And Samuel Sewall, a judge in Massachusetts, not only favored instruction but was quite outspoken against slavery, believing it to be a curse against God and humanity.

The Church of England, moreover, made efforts at conversion through its Society for the Propagation of the Gospel in Foreign Parts, organized in London in 1701. For example, an early catechizing school was founded in New York City at Trinity Church in 1704. Instruction was given by Elia Neau regularly until 1712, when blame for a local slave uprising was attributed by some masters to Neau's work. High officials disagreed, but enrollment was temporarily curtailed. Neau died in 1722, but instruction continued under others until about midcentury. Reverend Thomas Bray in Maryland was another who encouraged instruction and conversion. His followers, known as Bray's Associates, continued his work, notably in Philadelphia and North Carolina, until the 1760s. These specific attempts by the Church of England are singularly noteworthy, though of greater importance to the movement was the prestige of the Church and of influential clergymen.

The second great determinant was the tremendous rise in the black population through both importations and natural increases. The century began with a population of about 27,000 Afro-Americans, and it ended with nearly 1,000,000. The population increase awoke fears in whites, in some areas, of the increasing black presence.

The third great determinant was the beginning of efforts, some successful, to abolish the Atlantic slave trade with Africa. Notably, the Constitution of the new American republic (1787) abolished the slave trade after 1808. The British had abolished the trade earlier (1807/8) under the persistent leadership of such men as Thomas Clarkson and William Wilberforce.

The fourth great determinant involved successful attempts to free slaves through manumissions and wills. These legal acts formed the beginnings of the abolition movement, which, toward the end of the eighteenth century, resulted in the formation of the Pennsylvania Abolition Society, some of whose members, such as Benjamin Franklin, William Pitt, Noah Webster, and Thomas Paine, were internationally known. These four determinants were very manifest in the colonial South and in its economy.

The Southern Economy*   Below the Mason-Dixon line, which separated Pennsylvania from Maryland, a longer growing season permitted cultivation of crops that could not be grown commercially in the North or in Britain. A wide coastal plain abounding in natural waterways provided Southerners with both favorable conditions for tillage and inexpensive avenues of transportation. Thus, Southern settlers could expect to market their large crops cheaply and without competition from producers in Britain itself or in the northern colonies. Accordingly, those southern settlers who could afford to do so invested heavily both in land and in bound laborers in order to produce a staple agricultural commodity for export. The plantation became a characteristic feature of the southern economy.

*Text reprinted from Norman A. Graebner, Gilbert C. Fite, and Philip L. White, *A History of the American People,* chap. 3, copyright © by McGraw-Hill, New York, 1970.

Tobacco, produced largely in the Chesapeake Bay area, was the most important plantation crop and by far the most important of all American exports throughout the colonial period. The European market for tobacco had grown rapidly, despite much intense opposition to the Indian habit of smoking. In the 1630s Britain was importing as much as 3 million pounds of American tobacco yearly; by the 1670s, roughly 14 million pounds; by the 1770s, about 100 million pounds. Such a production record was possible only because the Caribbean region had largely abandoned tobacco at an early date in order to concentrate on growing sugar, a product in even greater demand.

Securing land was the first step in becoming a tobacco planter. Throughout much of the seventeenth century, men of wealth could claim 50 acres for each immigrant whose passage they had paid. By exploiting this "head-right" law, often corruptly, many men built up extensive holdings. Purchasing from the government or even from speculators was also relatively easy. "Every person," a traveler claimed in 1759, "may with ease procure a small plantation, can ship his tobacco at his own door, and live independently." He exaggerated, of course, but many immigrants were able to save enough as laborers or tenants to purchase land. By 1760 thousands of such small farmers were competing with the great planters in raising tobacco for export.

Whatever the extent of his land holdings, a tobacco planter remained a "one-hogshead man," able to produce only one or two hogsheads of cured tobacco yearly, unless he could secure bound laborers. Most free persons would not long remain agricultural laborers when they could so easily become landowners. Recognizing the labor problem at a very early date, the London Company sent over poor orphan children to be bound to planters as apprentices. From this practice, there evolved the tradition of indentured servitude, or contract labor. Shippers transported poor Englishmen to the Tobacco Coast and sold them to planters. The planters' payment compensated the shipper for affording passage; the indentured servant then worked for the planter, usually for about four years, to repay him. The system financed immigration, alleviated the labor shortage, and afforded immigrants both assurance of a livelihood on their arrival and training for making a living in America. "Freedom dues" fixed by local custom, sometimes including land, helped the immigrant to get started on his own. By 1666, three of every four Virginians had been or was then an indentured servant.

Not all indentured servants came voluntarily. Some were kidnap victims (though not as many as was claimed); some 20,000 were convicts, including major offenders as well as those jailed merely for debt. "Transportation" and 14 years of indentured servitude were long an alternative to execution for those convicted of capital crimes in England. Oddly, some such convicts "did chuse to be hanged ere they would go thither, and were."

Indentured servants were chiefly English until about 1660. Thereafter, prosperity plus government concern over depopulation brought a decline in English emigration. Families from northern Ireland, Scotland, and Germany, however, took up the slack. Upon their arrival, families of "redemptioners" or "free willers" usually sold one or more members of the family into servitude to pay for the passage of all. In the eighteenth century, Pennsylvania replaced the Tobacco Coast as the chief market for indentured servants. Tobacco planters by then had come to prefer another bound labor system involving blacks.

A passing Dutch warship, John Rolfe wrote in 1619, "sold us twenty negars." This arrival, it is worth noting, preceded that of the Pilgrims at Plymouth by one year. Considered as indentured servants rather than slaves, some of these blacks acquired freedom, property, and even the right to vote. Gradually, however, the white population began to impose slave status upon imported Negroes. By the 1660s Virginia laws declared that imported Negro laborers and the offspring of all slavewomen would be slaves for life.

No known evidence explains clearly why Virginia made Negroes slaves rather than indentured servants. Part of the explanation is probably historical. Slavery had long existed among West African Negroes, as it had in some parts of Europe until about the time of Columbus, chiefly in order to provide domestic servants, however, rather than workers for commercial enterprise. After the discovery of America, a great market for slaves developed in the mines and the plantations of the Spanish and Portuguese colonies. Capitalizing upon this new market, coastal tribes in West Africa began to capture and sell greatly increased numbers of their inland neighbors in order to enlarge their own purchases of European goods, chiefly textiles, weapons, and liquor. Thus, by the time the first blacks arrived in Virginia, a century of precedent existed elsewhere in the Americas for fixing slave status upon those Negroes offered for sale as workers.

Prejudice and economic interest also contributed to fixing slave status upon Virginia Negroes. As the name "Negro" suggests (negro is Spanish for "black"), what impressed Europeans most about the West Africans was the darkness of their skin. Whatever the psychological explanation, this difference in color created for many Europeans a prejudice against Negroes and with it a desire for a social system that would hold them permanently apart as an inferior caste. Slave status served that purpose. Slave status was also economically advantageous to the purchaser. Not only did slaves serve for life rather than only a few years but also their progeny were similarly bound, not free as was the case with the offspring of indentured servants.

Despite the economic advantages they offered, Negro slaves did not become a major factor in the development of the Tobacco Coast until the eighteenth century. For most of the seventeenth century, the Dutch had been the principal purveyors of slaves, and British mercantilist principles discouraged purchasing from them. Late in the century, the British replaced the Dutch as the world's leading slave sellers, but until the end of the century the trade was monopolized legally by the somewhat complacent Royal African Company. The opening of the slave trade to free competition at the end of the century greatly increased the supply and reduced the price. By 1750 four of every ten Virginians were black. In Maryland, the proportion was roughly three in ten.

Historians have established relatively few points concerning slavery in the eighteenth century. Contrary to a legend of some popularity in the South, merchants in the northern colonies played a relatively small role in the slave trade. They found it difficult to compete with English merchants in supplying what the West Africans wanted in exchange. Slave mortality was high, not only on the notorious "middle passage" across the Atlantic, but also in the "seasoning" period after arrival. No study of this subject exists for the Tobacco Coast, but in Barbados, where admittedly work was harder, food less plentiful, and the climate less healthy, nearly half of the new slaves died within three years. To the planters there it seemed that slaves would "revenge the slightest mistreatment by dying." Most slave-holders in Virginia held only a few, although many large planters owned more than

100. Accustomed to agricultural work at home, Africans took to tobacco culture more readily than did the few enslaved Indians. Many of them, reflecting a high level of artisan skills in Africa, became skilled craft workers whose services the master rented out.

British regulation was an important factor in the development of the Tobacco Coast. From

son, "so that the planters were a species of property annexed to certain mercantile houses in London." Probably not even the planters themselves understood clearly why this was so, but overproduction was certainly one cause. By oversupplying the world market, Chesapeake planters repeatedly depressed the price of their product. Neither crop-destroying riots nor

Tobacco producers during colonial days used Afro-American slaves in the planting, cultivating, and harvesting, and in the curing (b, d), packing (c), and storing (e), of the South's major crop and America's main export. Sketches are from William Tatham (1752—1819), *An Historical and Practical Essay on the Culture and Commerce of Tobacco* (London, 1800).

1660, one of Britain's famous Navigation Acts required that tobacco, as an "enumerated" commodity, be sent only to British ports. Initially, American production was expected only to supply the British market, but by the eve of the Revolution, Britain was reexporting 60 to 70 percent of its tobacco imports from America, sometimes more than 90 percent. Thus, while Americans produced the world's supply of tobacco, it was the British who sold it to foreign markets.

Debt was a major problem for nearly all tobacco planters. "Debts had become hereditary for many generations," wrote planter Thomas Jeffer-

restrictive legislation, both of which the British condemned, could solve the overproduction problems.

In the Lower South, the first settlers hoped to establish plantations, but they had trouble finding suitable crops. While they were experimenting, an export economy based on deer hides, cattle, naval stores, and lumber developed. Deer hides, secured in trade with the Indians, were used extensively in Europe for clothing and long remained an important export. Frontier "crackers" (so called from the noise of the whips they used) drove cattle from the wild lands of the interior to seaboard slaughterhouses, which prepared meat for export. Lumbering, often a sideline industry for those who were clearing land for agriculture, enjoyed a vast market, although competition from frontier settlers in every colonial region kept prices low. On the eve of the Revolution, lumber products ranked behind only tobacco, wheat, flour, rice and fish in export value.

Naval stores (tar, pitch, turpentine, and resin) became significant exports from the Carolinas after Britain began to subsidize their production during the War of the Spanish Succession (1702–1713). Britain did so in order to be sure of a supply of materials indispensable for ship construction. Production had declined considerably, however, before the Revolution.

Rice became the export staple of the Lower South within a few years after the introduction of superior seed from Madagascar in 1695. Parliament normally taxed rice imports into Britain heavily in order to favor domestic grain growers, but rice was also enumerated; i.e., it could be exported only to British ports so that British rather than American merchants could derive the major profit from selling it to foreign consumers, chiefly in northern Europe. After 1730 Americans could sell rice directly to southern Europe, but roughly 60 percent of the crop still went via Britain to northern Europe. Because rice production required heavy investment in labor and machinery, only very wealthy individuals could become rice planters. Unlike tobacco planters, colonial rice producers did not oversupply the market and thus continued to enjoy ample returns throughout the eighteenth century.

After 1748 indigo joined rice as a major plantation product in the Lower South. When properly processed, the indigo plant produced a blue-violet dye that was widely used in the British textile industry and by farm families that produced their own cloth. The Lower South could usually secure two crops of indigo yearly, as opposed to four or more in the Caribbean area, but preoccupation with sugar in the British West Indies pushed out indigo as it had tobacco. When war with France (War of the Austrian Succession, 1740–1748) interrupted the supply from the French islands, Britain began to subsidize production in her continental colonies. Instructed by Eliza Lucas, who had emigrated from the West Indies, Carolina planters produced indigo profitably from 1748 until the Revolution.

Unlike the Tobacco Coast, which had no port city and was indeed an exclusively rural society, the Lower South developed a true metropolis, the city of Charleston. Large ships could not reach individual plantations as they did along Chesapeake Bay, but came to Charleston as a point of transshipment. Merchants in Charleston, as in other colonial ports, often acted as agents for British merchants, selling imported items, chiefly textiles and slaves, and buying rice, indigo, or other commodities for export. Their compensation for such services was a commission, usually about five percent, on both sales and purchases.

"Negro men," as merchant Henry Laurens frequently reminded his British correspondents, were "the most certain Article" for Charleston's market. Indigo planters, Laurens observed in 1755, had secured "such large Sums" for their crops that they were "all mad for more Negroes." At that time, Charleston imported about 2,000 slaves annually; in 1773 the figure had soared to nearly 8,000, and blacks outnumbered whites in the province by about six to four. In Georgia, where the trustees had barred slavery until 1749, Afro-Americans by 1770 were roughly half of the population. In North Carolina, where problems of navigation impeded the growth of the plantation system in many areas, only about 35 percent of the people were black.

Economic development in the American colonies proceeded rapidly within the mercantilist framework fixed by British policy. Abundant land enabled American families to work larger plots than could most Europeans and thus to enjoy a higher standard of living. A chronic labor shortage not only raised wages above European standards but also led to the importation of impoverished Europeans as indentured servants and later of thousands of African Negroes as slaves. Plantation agriculture—large-scale production for the European market—developed from Maryland southward where the climate permitted production of crops that could not be grown commercially in northern Europe. North of Maryland, farmers produced crops identical to those of northern Europe and consequently had to look elsewhere for a market, turning chiefly to the West Indian sugar plantations and to southern Europe. New Englanders, not well endowed for commercial farming, sold fish from the nearby Grand Banks region to the same markets. Northerners in particular made some progress in manufacturing such products as lumber, flour, iron, and ships, but America as a whole imported most of its manufactured goods and paid for them with exports of less valuable raw or processed materials.

Controversy over enforcement of commercial regulations became more intense after 1767 when "Champagne Charlie" Townshend, then Britain's chief financial officer, instituted drastic reforms. Townshend's program included parliamentary authorization for the hated writs of assistance, juryless vice-admiralty courts with jurisdiction over cases involving alleged evasion of customs duties, and creation of an American Board of Customs Commissioners at Boston.

Britain's dogmatic insistence upon the right of Parliament to bind Americans in any way it chose invited violence. It began at Lexington under circumstances that convinced many Americans of the barbarity of the king's troops. Initially, Americans fought only to compel restitution of what they regarded as "our former just and unalienable Rights and Privileges," but various considerations, and particularly British intransigence, led them in 1776 to declare their independence and to solicit French assistance in attaining it.

Slavery and the American Revolution

Southern slaveholders led in the conflict with England and the colonies. To them, the American Revolution was a "war for political liberty," which, among other rights, included the right to hold slaves. This contradictory stance was obvious to masters, slaves, and the British. Masters became more concerned about slavery and its abolition than at any other previous time, as thousands of slaves fled to the British, who promised them freedom. About 5,000 slaves served with the revolutionary (Continental) armies, while an estimated 30,000 (according to Thomas Jefferson) went over to the British.

The Revolution aided in the creation of a favorable movement to free some slaves. In Massachusetts, for example, the legal inclination against slavery was established. Philadelphia Quakers decided against slavery in the same year that Thomas Jefferson's Declaration of Independence was written (1776). Indeed, there were even some official moves to curtail slavery, notably through the initiative of Jefferson (who allegedly sired children by a black mistress, Sally Hemmings). Jefferson suggested freedom for slaves in his original draft of the Declaration of Independence. He also drew up a plan to abolish slavery in Virginia, his native state. Later, in 1784, he authored an ordinance to abolish slavery in unsettled Western territories. Jefferson's suggestions were never officially enacted. Yet, the last one (1784) failed by only one vote in the Continental Congress, which, three years later (1787), banned slavery in the Old Northwest through the Northwest Ordinance. Moreover, southern states abolished the slave trade with Africa: Virginia was one of the first to act in 1778, and Georgia was the last in 1798. In addition to official inclinations that would place restrictions upon slavery, many individual actions were taken by masters who freed slaves through manumissions and wills.

Many of the southern slaveholders who had provided leadership against Britain during the Revolution were also active as the "founding fathers" during the period of the formation of the Constitution and the establishment of the republic. As during the Revolution, Virginia's role as the largest state and largest slaveholding state was important. With well-established leaders of state and national reputations, Virginians were invariably among the largest owners of slaves: George Washington, 390; Thomas Jefferson, 149; Patrick Henry, 66; Richard Henry Lee, 138; and George Mason, 118. The issue of slavery was thus an important one in the framing of the Constitution. *See also* AFRICA: THE ATLANTIC SLAVE TRADE IN PERSPECTIVE; SLAVERY: SLAVERY IN SELECTED STATES: MASSACHUSETTS, PENNSYLVANIA, SOUTH CAROLINA, VIRGINIA; WARS.

REFERENCES: Andrews, Charles M., *The Colonial Background of the American Revolution,* rev. ed., Yale University Press, New Haven, 1931; Greene, Lorenzo J., *The Negro in Colonial New England, 1620–1776,* Columbia University Press, New

Far left: Influenced by Paul Revere's famous sketch, an artist of the Works Progress Administration in the 1930s showed British soldiers mortally wounding Crispus Attucks, an Afro-American, in the Boston Massacre of 1770. *(National Archives.)*

York, 1942; Jordan, Winthrop D., *White Over Black: American Attitudes Toward the Negro, 1550–1812*, University of North Carolina Press, Chapel Hill, 1968; Middleton, Arthur P., *Tobacco Coast: A Maritime History of the Chesapeake Bay in the Colonial Era*, Newport News, Mariners' Museum, 1953; Nettels, Curtis P., *The Roots of American Civilization*, New York, Quarles, Benjamin, *The Negro in the American Revolution*, University of North Carolina Press, Chapel Hill, 1961; Wax, Darold D., "Slave Preferences in Colonial America," *Journal of Negro History*, October 1973; Wood, Peter H., *Black Majority: Negroes in Colonial South Carolina From 1670 Through the Stono Rebellion*, Alfred A. Knopf, New York, 1974; and Zilversmit, Arthur, *The First Emancipation: The Abolition of Slavery in the North*, University of Chicago Press, Chicago, 1967. See also Smith, Dwight L., *Afro-American History: A Bibliography*, pp. 83–102, under entry BIBLIOGRAPHIES/BIOGRAPHIES/GUIDES.

The Constitution The U.S. Constitution was written during the summer of 1787, 11 years after the colonies had declared their independence from the British Empire. During and after the Revolutionary War, the new nation had been governed by the Continental Congress under a constitution called the Articles of Confederation. But by 1787 it was obvious that a stronger central government would be necessary.

The country was called "the United States," but the feeling of union among the 13 former colonies was not very strong. An important factor that kept the states from trusting one another was the institution of slavery. There were about 500,000 slaves in the United States at that time, all of them black. These slaves constituted about 20 percent of the total population. The slaves were not evenly distributed throughout the country—more than 90 percent of them lived in the five southern states. Already, by 1787, two northern states had abolished slavery, and three others had put it "on the road to extinction" by enacting programs of gradual emancipation. By 1804 all states north of Maryland, except Delaware, would be committed to abolition.

However, the South was moving in the opposite direction. In Virginia, in the aftermath of the Revolutionary War, a program of voluntary emancipation had been tried, but by 1787 a negative reaction to it had already begun to settle in. In the other southern states, the commitment to slavery as the normal status for Afro-Americans never wavered.

The delegates to the federal convention of 1787—all white males—were agreed on many matters. They agreed, for example, that the new government should be "popular," by which they meant that it ought to be based on the consent of the governed, expressed through regular elections. On slavery, however, there was no agreement. In parts of the country where there were few slaves, it was readily seen that slavery was inconsistent with the ideals set forth in the Declaration of Independence. But in sections where Afro-Americans were numerous, most white people thought slavery was necessary—an evil, perhaps, but certainly necessary. Without slavery, they argued, Afro-Americans would abuse their liberty, and the economy of the South, based on plantation agriculture, would collapse.

Thus, there was a profound difference of situation, and an emerging difference of attitude, that separated North and South on slavery. One of the most trying tasks for the framers of the Constitution was to bridge this ever-widening chasm.

The Slavery Issue Most of the delegates would have been happy simply to ignore the slavery issue, but that was not possible. Slavery was related to the two most fundamental questions before the convention: the problem of representation, and the problem of what powers to assign to the federal government.

On the question of representation, the leading delegates were determined to change the one state–one vote system that prevailed in the Continental Congress. As long as Rhode Island had the same vote as New York, and Delaware the same as Virginia, politicians in the larger states were unwilling to give the federal government the power to raise revenue, regulate commerce, or conduct foreign relations. The system of representation had to be changed to reflect the contribution that various regions were capable of making to the nation's strength.

But what should the new basis be? Should representation be tied to population or to wealth? After some discussion, the delegates agreed that it was not necessary to decide this issue. Since population tended to follow wealth, the number of persons in a given area was a reliable index to its wealth. But what about slaves? Were they "persons" in this sense or not? Did their presence indicate wealth, as most Southerners argued, or were they a detriment to the nation's strength, as many Northerners insisted?

The debate on this point was long and heated. In the search for a solution, several delegates recalled an earlier debate in the Continental Congress. In 1783 the problem had been to distribute the tax burden among the various states. Southerners, to reduce their share of the tax burden, sought to eliminate slaves from the formula altogether, while northerners tried to have slaves included equally with free men. A compromise had been struck whereby slaves counted as three-fifths of a free person. Now, in 1787, the shoe was on the other foot: it was the turn for northerners to argue that slaves were not persons, while southerners insisted that slaves should be counted as equal to free persons. It was perhaps inevitable, under these circumstances, that the difference would be compromised as it had been in 1783.

Interestingly, no one at the convention, from North or South, proposed that slaves as such be represented in the Continental Congress or in the Electoral College. What was at stake was whether to give the southerners any additional representation for their slaves. The answer was finally yes: count five slaves as the equivalent of three free persons in calculating representation for the southern states. No one in the convention dreamed that southern representatives would truly "represent" the slaves. It is sometimes said that the Constitution, as originally framed, held a black slave to be only three-fifths of a person. The truth is really worse than that. The Constitution confirmed a system in which slaves were politically not persons at all; yet, at the same time, slaveholders were given more weight in the government than men who owned no slaves.

The second major issue before the convention concerned the powers to be committed to the federal government. On this point, as it affected slavery, southerners were adamant. The hand of the federal government must never touch slavery.

Rather than challenge this determination, most northern delegates were inclined to agree that slavery should be considered a "local" institution, not subject to federal regulation. Northerners whose consciences were troubled by this approach consoled themselves with the belief that slavery was dying away.

In fact, however, this was an illusion. Deep southerners at the convention were quite candid about their reliance on slavery and their intention to keep black people enslaved. The foolish, careless optimism of the New England delegates did have one important effect: it helped the convention to believe that since slavery was a temporary, local phenomenon, its effect on the nation, if any, could safely be ignored.

Thus, it was agreed that the federal government should have no power over the system of slavery. As the convention wore on, however, this solution had to be modified. In two respects,

at least, it was impossible to ignore that slavery affected relations between the states. One issue was the African slave trade. Despite the participation of Yankee merchants in the trade, public opinion in the North was extremely hostile to it. In addition, planters in many parts of the South, including most of Virginia and Maryland, believed that they already had enough slaves and were willing to outlaw the trade immediate-

Ranaway

From my house (No. 14 Commerce-street) on the 6th inst. my Negro Slave HARRIET. She is about the common height, has a very large mouth, thick lips, and flat nose, of rather a copper complexion: she said she intended to go either to Annapolis or Philadelphia. I will give to any person who will apprehend and deliver her to me at the above mentioned place, the sum of *Thirty Dollars*, and pay any reasonable expences: she is a good seamstress. If taken out of the state and delivered as above, I will give *Fifty Dollars*.

Since writing the above, I have reason to believe she may have gone to Alexandria.

JOSEPH NATTALI.

April 7.   d12t

The right of an owner to recover his or her runaway slaves, as illustrated in this advertisement in the Baltimore *Gazetter* for 1808, was acknowledged in the Constitution. *(Courtesy of Joseph Arnold.)*

ly—but the Deep southerners felt differently. As John Rutledge of South Carolina put it, "If the Convention thinks that North Carolina, South Carolina, and Georgia will ever agree to the [Constitution], unless their right to import slaves be untouched, the expectation is in vain."

Here, however, the Deep southerners were unable to raise support for their position. In this case, it was the northerners and Virginians who were adamant. If the Deep southerners continued to import slaves, it was argued, the nation's defenses would be weakened (it was agreed that slavery had made the South more difficult to defend during the Revolutionary War), and those who imported the slaves would be rewarded by gaining increased representation in Congress, due to the three-fifths rule. Again, the argument was resolved by compromise: the Carolinians and Georgians would be permitted, if they wished, to import slaves for 20 more years until 1808, at which time Congress would be authorized to outlaw the trade.

The other issue over which slavery threatened to cause friction between the states was the type of action to be taken against those Afro-Americans who sought to escape from bondage by fleeing to states where slavery was prohibited. To deal with this problem, Pierce Butler, of

South Carolina, demanded the inclusion of a "fugitive slave clause." Northerners objected to this demand arguing that public authorities in the North would be put to the expense of rounding up fugitives. Butler quickly amended his proposal: the right to recover the fugitives would be established by law, but the burden of recovery would fall to the owners. In this form, the clause passed without objection. It represented a substantial and easily gained achievement for southern interests. There could now be no place in the United States that would provide a legal sanctuary for slaves. No northerner expressed concern that the clause might endanger the liberty and safety of free blacks. The only issue debated was the right of the slaveholder to his property.

Slavery and Ratification By September 1787 the convention had finished its work and was ready to submit the Constitution to ratification by the states. In each state, special ratifying conventions were called to consider the new framework. In several of these conventions, the controversy was sharp and the decision close. Occasionally, opponents of ratification criticized the arrangements set forth in the Constitution that affected slavery. Joshua Atherton, of New Hampshire, announced his intention to vote against ratification, insisting that he would not enter into covenant with "manstealers." On the southern side, Rawlins Lowndes, of South Carolina, who strenuously opposed ratification, said that northerners insisted upon ending the slave trade because they had no slaves themselves and "therefore want to exclude us from this great advantage." Lowndes added that, in his opinion, the African slave trade "could be justified on the principles of religion, humanity and justice; for certainly to translate a set of human beings from a bad country to a better, was fulfilling every part of those principles."

Another source of controversy in the South was the suggestion by Patrick Henry, of Virginia, that the "necessary and proper" clause implied a power to emancipate slaves if, for example, a majority of Congress found such an act necessary to the general defense. "Among ten thousand *implied powers* which [Congress] may assume," said Henry, "they may, if we be engaged in war, liberate every one of your slaves, if they please."

However, these dissenting voices were exceptions. Defenders of the Constitution had little difficulty deflecting these assaults. In South Carolina, where suspicions arising from the stated

Northern attitudes toward slavery were striking the nerve of opposition, the Constitution was ratified handily. In other states, where the verdict was closer (New Hampshire, Massachusetts, New York, Pennsylvania, and Virginia), and in Rhode Island and North Carolina, where the Constitution was initially rejected, opposition centered on other grounds. Though information about these ratifying conventions is vague, it seems safe to conclude that the clauses affecting slavery were not, by themselves, a serious threat to ratification. Most of the nation's politicians seemed satisfied with the way that the authors of the Constitution had handled the slavery issue.

Yet despite this lack of serious controversy over slavery, the ratifying conventions, taken as a whole, revealed an ominous cleavage between North and South with respect to slavery. The best illustration comes in comparing the reception given to the clause on the slave trade in Pennsylvania and in South Carolina.

In Pennsylvania, the burden of interpretation was assumed by James Wilson, who rose December 3, 1787, to respond to the criticism that the Constitution left the government impotent to deal with "this reproachful [slave] trade" for 20 years. Wilson pointed out that "Under the present confederation, the states may admit the importation of slaves as long as they please; but by this article, after the year 1808, the Congress will have power to prohibit such importation, notwithstanding the disposition of any state to the contrary." According to Wilson, this clause laid "the foundation for banishing slavery out of this country . . . [by] the same kind, gradual change which was pursued in Pennsylvania." Wilson went on to argue that "the new states which are to be formed will be under the control of Congress in this particular, and slaves will never be introduced among them." He seemed to be referring to the power of Congress, contained in Article IV, Section 3, "to. . . . make all needful rules and regulations respecting the territory or other property belonging to the United States." The exception from Congressional interference with the "migration or importation" of slaves is specifically limited to "states now existing." Wilson apparently concluded that the power of Congress over the new territories included the power to prohibit the "migration" of slaves by land as well as their importation from abroad by sea.

Wilson left the impression that the federal convention had dealt firmly with slavery by starting it on the road to extinction, and that

Congress had power to keep slavery out of the territories. Madison later insisted that no power over the domestic movements of slaves was implied in the Constitution, and that Wilson implying so was the only attempt during the debates over ratification to advance such an interpretation. Had this construction gained currency, Madison argued, "it is easy to imagine the figure it would have made in many of the states, among the objections to the Constitution, and among the numerous amendments to it proposed by the state conventions, not one of which amendments refers to the clause in question. . . ."

Madison's point is a good one. Though the words of the Constitution are susceptible to the construction Wilson put on them, it is almost certain that they would not have been adopted by the federal convention if this interpretation had been hinted at or foreseen. If southerners had learned of Wilson's construction before their ratifying conventions had met, and if they had suspected that it contained a grain of justification, the conventions in Virginia and South Carolina would surely have refused to accept the Constitution. Maryland, too, might have withheld ratification, and Georgia would have tried very hard to retract its (unanimous) approval, granted only one month after Wilson's speech far to the north. Since North Carolina held aloof on other grounds, the result of Wilson's speech, if it had been heard and believed in the South, might well have been to scuttle the Constitution.

Meanwhile, at the other end of the slavery spectrum, words were spoken in South Carolina that would certainly have given offense, had they been heard in Pennsylvania. As a slaveholder Gen. C. C. Pinckney's problem was the reverse of Wilson's. He had to convince his neighbors in Charleston that "considering all circumstances, we have made the best terms for the security of this species of property [slaves] it was in our power to make."

Noting that he and his colleagues "had to contend with the religious and political prejudices" of New England and Pennsylvania and with "the interested and inconsistent opinion of Virginia" (favorable to slavery, but opposed to importations from Africa), Pinckney justified Article I, Section 9, on the grounds of necessity. He asserted his belief that "the nature of our climate, and the flat, swampy situation of our country, oblige us to cultivate our lands with Negroes." Without slaves, he said, "South Carolina would soon be a desert waste." He repeated the basic Northern argument against the trade: that an increase in the number of slaves in the South would weaken the nation's defenses, and increase the South's share of representation in the government. Finally, he said that "after a great deal of difficulty," the northern delegates promised "to restrain the religious and political prejudices" of their constituents, if a date were set when the importation might be stopped altogether. By this arrangement, said Pinckney, South Carolina gained the right to "an unlimited importation of negroes for twenty years" and the opportunity to resist the termination of the trade after 1808 by political means. Robert Barnwell, a leader in the fight for ratification in South Carolina, added his "opinion" that the economic interests of northerners—their desire to transport the products of a vigorous southern agriculture— would counteract their desire to prohibit the foreign slave trade, even after the constitutional moratorium had expired.

A comparison of these expressions in South Carolina with Wilson's remarks at the Pennsylvania Convention suggests the existence of two completely different worlds of experience and discourse on this issue, an unnoticed foreshadowing of the catastrophe that lay ahead.

National Consensus on Slavery As the Constitution of 1787 was being ratified, the authors were satisfied that they had disposed of the issue of slavery to the satisfaction of everyone. Everyone, it seems, judged the Constitution in light of the Articles of Confederation, and nearly everyone found the Constitution superior.

Northerners exulted in their belief that the slave trade was finally under a sentence of death. Slavery had "received a mortal wound, and would die of consumption." Furthermore, power had been given to Congress to keep slavery out of the territories. Surely it was a blessing that an institution that had already "blackened half the plains of America" would now be restrained from spreading its contamination to the rest. Inasmuch as it would be wrong "to abolish slavery, by an act of Congress, in a moment, and so destroy what our southern brethren consider property," the framers were to be commended for doing the right thing: isolating slavery in the South, setting a date when its supply could be cut off, and waiting for historical processes to work their miraculous cleansing effect.

Southerners were equally pleased. As General Pinckney told the South Carolinians, "we have a security that the general government can never emancipate [slaves], for no such authority is granted, and it is admitted, on all hands, that the general government has no powers but what are expressly granted by the Constitution.'' In addition, the Constitution gave ''much better security'' than presently existed for owners whose slaves might escape across state lines. As far as the western territories were concerned, no southerner appears to have dreamed that slavery would be prohibited there. As for the slave trade, Virginians looked upon it as having been put under a sentence of death. To the Deep southerners, who ''were now in want of hands to cultivate their lands,'' there was an opportunity in the next 20 years to be ''fully supplied,'' and even then, there was no guarantee that the power to abolish the trade would be exercised.

Thus, most southerners and northerners alike were convinced that they were better off under the Constitution than they had been under the Articles, with regard to slavery as well as to most other things. The authors had dealt with slavery by seeking, so far as possible, to take it out of the national political arena. They were unable in 1787 to settle the issue one way or the other. They could not establish straightforward constitutional guarantees against emancipation, as the South Carolinians desired, because many northerners, and perhaps even some southerners, would not permit it. Nor could they give Congress power to regulate slavery in any way,

much less abolish it, because southerners refused to yield control over the institution.

Realizing that it was utterly impossible to fashion a national consensus on slavery, or to ''govern'' the issue in the absence of one, the framers sought merely to prevent friction over slavery. Thus, when it was determined to tie representation to population, a date was set when the slave trade could be terminated in order to preserve the relationship the trade now bore to the balance of political forces in the country. When Pierce Butler, of South Carolina, raised the question of escaped slaves, the convention granted his request because most northerners were as reluctant for Afro-Americans to flee North as southern slaveholders were to lose their property. The fugitive slave clause, like the slave trade clause, was intended to remove a potential sore point between the states. Yet, it is possible that by steering clear of the slavery issue in 1787, some framers may have had more in mind than the desire to avoid collison. The word ''slavery'' is never used in the text of the Constitution. Toward the end of the convention, Gouverneur Morris proposed to ''avoid the ambiguity'' in the clause on the slave trade by amending it to read that the ''importation of slaves into North Carolina, South Carolina and Georgia'' could not be prohibited until 1808. However, Madison remarked that it would be ''wrong to

The *Wanderer*, at the right, illegal under the Constitution, is believed to be the last slave ship to arrive in the United States. Although the framers of the Constitution set a date for ending the Atlantic slave trade (1808), some sea captains eluded enforcement, which was undertaken almost alone by the British Navy. (An excellent account of these enforcement efforts is found in W.E.F. Ward, *The Royal Navy and the Slavers: The Suppression of the Atlantic Slave Trade*, Schocken, New York, 1970.) The *Wanderer* was built as a schooner yacht on Long Island, N.Y., during 1856–57. The painting is attributed to Warren Sheppard. *(Courtesy of John F. Leavitt, the Marine Historical Association, Inc., Mystic Seaport, Conn.)*

admit in the Constitution the idea that there could be property in men." To the end, Madison and others remained vigilant against any explicit reference to slavery.

This great concern to avoid the word "slavery" may have represented a desire to save options for an uncertain future. If the Constitution did not sanction slavery, and if fate smiled on the young nation, perhaps in the future a way would be found to abolish slavery.

There is no evidence that any framer thought the Constitution contained power to abolish slavery, as matters stood in 1787. They all knew how the Deep southerners felt about slavery. Many of the framers disapproved of slavery, but they were all sympathetic to the determination of Deep southerners to resist abolition under the present circumstances. This was what Madison meant when he told the ratifying convention in Virginia that slave-owners were safe under the Constitution, that it would be madness for the federal government to abolish slavery, that Northerners knew this, and that, therefore, the Constitution should be accepted as a compact between sane and honorable men who would not commit mayhem on their fellow citizens.

Conclusion No guarantee, however, existed to ensure that powers of emancipation would forever be denied to the federal government. Patrick Henry was right, as Abraham Lincoln later proved, when he argued that the power to abolish slavery might come to inhere in the power to wage war, and General Pinckney was wrong when he stated that the federal government was confined to powers "expressly" listed in the Constitution. If the framers had intended, as Pinckney said (and Madison implied), to deny forever the power to abolish slavery, they could have said so in the Constitution. Export taxes were flatly and "expressly" prohibited; so was the granting of "titles of nobility." States were forbidden to enter into treaties or alliances with foreign powers. The whole ninth and tenth sections of Article I were full of such express prohibitions. However, denial of the power to emancipate slaves or to abolish or regulate slavery was not on that list.

The framers did not intend for the Constitution to include a veiled power to abolish slavery. There is no evidence that any framer foresaw the day when slavery could be abolished, or even regulated in its internal aspects, by an act of government. Yet, the evidence permits the conclusion that the future, with respect to possible public action against slavery, was purposely left open at the insistence of such delegates as James Madison, Gouverneur Morris, and James Wilson.

These speculations are important to an assessment of the political skill and intention of the framers. As history actually developed, however, it was more important to the nation that the framers placed the institution of slavery beyond national regulation. Those Americans who wrote and ratified the Constitution may have believed that they were dealing with slavery as they had dealt with several other issues that were excluded from national politics. There were many institutions, many features of American life, that the federal government was forbidden to touch. Slaveholders were by no means unique in insisting on local control over local institutions.

But the case of slavery *was* different. It was unique in the extent of its impact on national development, in its tendency to polarize the country, and in its relevance to the fundamental principles of future governments. Slavery pulled its proprietors in one direction, in economic, social, political, and moral terms. The main currents of modernity pulled the rest of the country in another. When this tension began to bear on public policy, men who were affected only indirectly by slavery began to wish they could exercise some control over a factor so important to the nation's development as a whole. In reaction, the owners of slaves began to dread the desire of outsiders to interfere with an institution upon which their safety and prosperity seemed to depend, and their resistance to constitutional evolution on this point stiffened.

Americans of the founding generation are often cited for their political genius. In circumstances that were economically and socially rather primitive, they laid the constitutional foundations for a great nation. However, the problem of slavery proved ungovernable, even for these brilliant politicians. The greed and fear of white men prevented them from meeting the demands of justice.

Would it have been better to insist, in 1787, that slavery be made subject to federal regulation, and thus to abolition in due course? If the leading framers had insisted on that, there would have been no union, no new Constitution, and no benefit for those suffering under the curse of slavery. No effort by the framers could have eliminated slavery in 1787. Neither was it possible to build a truly unified nation on the foundation of the Declaration of Independence until slavery had been overthrown. This dilemma had no political solution. It required a bloody civil war to produce, indirectly, the abolition of slavery—a cause that no leading national politician had ever, before 1860, openly espoused. *See also* all entries under SLAVERY.

REFERENCES: Brant, Irving, *James Madison, Father of the Constitution, 1787-1800*, Bobbs-Merrill, Indianapolis, vol. 3, pp. 94-157; Hofstader, Richard, *The American Political Tradition and the Men who Made it*, Alfred A. Knopf, New York, 1948; and Robinson, Donald L., *Slavery in the Structure of American Politics*, Harcourt Brace Jovanovich, New York, 1971.

Sectional Conflict over Slavery, 1820-60 There can be no doubt that the existence of human slavery in one portion of the nation after it had been abandoned in the remainder was a constant threat to the life of the nation. The authors of the Constitution were aware of the threat that slavery presented, but they were unwilling to jeopardize the experiment in political federation by taking any determined action. They retreated from the advanced position taken by Thomas Jefferson in the Northwest Ordinance, when slavery had been prohibited north of the Ohio River. Instead, they left slavery in the hands of the states and provided no clear statement concerning its status in the territories. Sensing that anything so fundamental as property in human beings would inevitably divide the nation, they put a mild check on its future growth by limiting the importation of slaves after 20 years. They then sat back and hoped that something might happen that would lead the South to follow the North in its abandonment of the institution. But slavery did not die. The cotton gin made cotton production immensely profitable. Since cotton cultivation requires tremendous quantities of unskilled labor, the demand for slaves skyrocketed. The hopes of the founding fathers went glimmering as the ownership of human beings became more deeply entrenched in the South.

Far right: State capitol, Jefferson City, Mo. The expansion of slavery led to the Missouri Compromise in 1820, by which Missouri was admitted to the union as a slave state. (Library of Congress.)

Slavery and Expansion In 1820 Americans again found themselves confronted with the issue of slavery. The institution had become a social system as well as a labor system. It allowed a minority of white masters to live among and direct the great masses of black slaves and to retain a reasonable sense of security in the process. Few southerners defended the system on grounds other than economic necessity. Most apologized for the institution and pointed out, quite reasonably, that slavery was as much their heritage as was the language they spoke, the religion they professed, the nation they loved, or the lands

they farmed. But the hard fact remained: slavery existed in only half the nation. When settlement spread beyond the Mississippi River, the question had to be faced again. Was slavery to expand with the nation, or was it to be confined to the area it already dominated? If it were to be confined to existing slave states, a severe strain would be placed upon the nation. Southerners who knew that both their prosperity and their way of life rested on chattel slavery were sure to weigh carefully the value of a nation that threatened both. But if slavery were allowed to expand, the question of a nation "divided against itself" was merely postponed, and a subsequent generation would have to face the problem again. When the Missouri Compromise was passed in 1820, many Americans feared that failure to limit the expansion of slavery threatened the very life of the nation. Jefferson described the decision as "a reprieve only, not a final sentence." He said the news came and "like a fire bell in the night, awakened and filled me with terror. . . . In the gloomiest hour of the Revolutionary War, I never had any apprehensions equal to those which I feel from this source." Other statesmen of the period shared Jefferson's fear for the fate of the nation.

Slavery, fundamental as it was, did not alone destroy the sense of unity that was the American nation. There was a conflict between two economic systems. The North was rapidly becoming industrialized. More and more of its capital and labor were being absorbed in the building of factories and railroads. Even though a majority of northerners still made their living tilling the soil, the spokesmen of the section increasingly represented the interests of industry and transport. The South, on the other hand, remained an agricultural economy. In spite of the zealous efforts of crusaders, the South was wedded to agriculture. While J. D. B. De Bow's *Review* extolled the virtues of a more diversified economy and a few others sought to convert the South to manufacturing by establishing successful factories as examples of what could be done, industry made little headway. The South possessed labor, raw materials, and water power, but it could not develop industrially for want of capital. Its capital was absorbed in a system whereby one portion of the population owned the remainder. Northern capital was not available to the South, since it was already drawing heavy profits from northern factories and railroads and from financing the southern money crops. "And anyway, why turn to industry when such handsome profits are to be made in cotton, cane, hemp, and tobacco?" asked the average planter.

The conflict between farm and factory showed up in a thousand ways. It was revealed in the sectional division over national legislation on tariffs, land, and internal improvements. During the 1850s, it was at the heart of the bitter fight over an eastern terminus of the proposed transcontinental railroad. It filled the pages of southern newspapers as they sought to prove that northern capital, labor, and industry lived off the sweat of southern farmers. Books were published to prove that northern wage earners were more truly enslaved than Afro-Americans. The conflict was presented as a phase of the traditional one between Thomas Jefferson's "chosen people of God" (the Virginia farmers) and Alexander Hamilton's "monocrats" (who lived on "paper and patronage"). The North replied that only southern backwardness prevented the United States from becoming the greatest industrial power in the world. Southern obstinacy deprived the western farmer of free land, a railroad to the Pacific, and a fair wage. Labor could never possess dignity in a land where only the slave worked with his hands.

There is no denying that this clash between two economic sections was one of the deeper causes of the destruction of national loyalties. However, it must be remembered that southern crops sold in northern markets, just as northern crops and manufactured products sold in southern markets. The two economies complemented each other, and at the same time, they competed.

It is a truism of history that men act on the basis of what they *think* has happened rather than what has *actually* happened. Applying this thought to the antebellum period of American history reveals some very interesting attitudes. Starting with slavery, it is apparent to us today

that the institution of Afro-American slavery changed very little between 1850 and 1860. To be sure, the number of slaves in the South increased another 700,000 during the decade, to bring the total to about 4 million in 1860. But compared with the 2.6 million immigrants who entered the country during the same period or the total population increase of 8.3 million during the decade, the increased number of slaves was not remarkable. In fact, the slave population was not increasing as fast as the free population. Slavery moved westward during the 1850s as new lands were opened in Alabama, Mississippi, Louisiana, and Texas. The Black Codes that governed the conduct of slaves were tightened up in areas where the Afro-American population increased radically, and they were relaxed in those areas where the number of slaves dropped. There was no great upsurge in the number or intensity of slave revolts during the decade. Nor was there any apparent increase in the punishment meted out to slaves who resisted their bondage. The number of fugitive slaves escaping into the North increased very little after 1850. June of 1860 ended a year in which some 800 slaves were reported as runaways, while some 3,000 had been voluntarily manumitted by their masters. These annual figures on runaway slaves and manumissions were about the same for the two decades 1840–1860.

But Americans of the 1850s did not have the statistics and records that are available to us today. They thought slavery was changing radically. Southerners read the reports of runaway slaves in their newspapers or heard friends report losses. Rumor exaggerated the numbers until virtually every southerner was convinced that losses from this source alone were costing the South millions of dollars a year. Northerners read of the pathetic plight of poor old Uncle Tom and Eliza, and visualized the inhumanity of Simon Legree. They watched the growth of southern pressure for a reopening of the slave trade and the acquisition of Caribbean territory and became convinced of the existence of a great "aggressive slavocracy." They fought off the demands of the South for access to the territories of Kansas and the Far West, little knowing that slavery would never seriously attempt to move beyond Texas. Both North and South worked themselves into a frenzy of opposition to the doctrine of popular sovereignty, unaware that popular sovereignty actually determined the limits of slavery throughout the entire United States and its territories. Slavery changed very little during the decade of the 1850s, but men's attitudes toward it changed radically. Reality was lost in a conflict over symbols.

Fugitive Slave Act, 1850 Though the South lost few fugitive slaves and retrieved even fewer, the runaway slave became an important symbol of the deeper conflict between the sections. The new law (Fugitive Slave Law) aroused the hostility of men who feared what might be done under it far more than they feared disunion. It had three provisions that were particularly odious to most northerners. In spite of the constitutional provision that in all "suits at common law, where the value in controversy shall exceed twenty dollars, the right of trial by jury shall be preserved," the Fugitive Slave Law allowed no jury trial even though any slave was worth far more than $20 if considered as property. If by chance it was admitted that the slave was a person rather than chattel property, the new law was equally unjust, for it deprived a person of the protection of the Sixth Amendment guaranteeing a jury trial in all criminal prosecutions. Second, the penalties of the law were excessively harsh. Officers charged with the duty of arresting a fugitive were subject to a fine of $1,000 for refusal to execute their assignment, and citizens who refused to assist or who obstructed the officers recapturing runaways were subject to penalties totaling $2,000 and a six-month jail sentence. Finally, the fugitive was to be taken before a special commissioner, rather than a regular court, where the affidavit of the purported owner was sufficient to establish ownership. When the commissioner found the alleged fugitive to be the slave claimed, he received a fee of $10. If he found the charge false, he received only $5. In the light of these provisions, even moderate northerners were ready to agree with the abolitionists who had maintained all along that the South was ready to violate the Constitution in order to protect its "peculiar institution." And to cap it all, the South had now put the price of human liberty at $5. Ralph Waldo Emerson lost all semblance of philosophic calm and wrote of the new Fugitive Slave Law in his journal: "This filthy enactment was made in the nineteenth century, by people who could read and write. I will not obey it, by God!"

Northern resistance to the act began almost immediately and became widespread before the decade was done. The "personal-liberty law" adopted by Massachusetts is typical of the laws adopted in many northern states to nullify the Fugitive Slave Law. It provided that a writ of habeas corpus might be issued in cases involving a fugitive. It also provided for a jury trial and banned the testimony of both the claimant and the alleged fugitive while it put the burden of proof upon the claimant. The law thus made it necessary for the purported owner to prove his title to a particular Afro-American by affidavits from his friends and neighbors back home, and this before a Massachusetts judge and jury! The importance of the personal-liberty laws lies quite outside any question of their effectiveness, for they apparently did not free a single slave. Their significance rests on the fact that a majority of northerners were now ready to nullify a federal law on slavery, whereas prior to 1850 such action would have been countenanced by only the hard core of militant abolitionists. The new Fugitive Slave Law was making abolitionism respectable. The Underground Railroad which spirited slaves across the North to Canada and freedom, now became more active, even fashionable.

Two things brought about this remarkable change in the moral climate of the North. The first was a series of well-publicized cases involving alleged runaway slaves. Eight days after the passage of the Fugitive Slave Act, a man appeared in New York City. He was armed with a power of attorney signed with an "X" by an illiterate Baltimore woman. He filed an affidavit that a certain James Hamlet was the runaway slave of his client. Hamlet was placed under arrest and sent off to Baltimore before his two children were even informed of his whereabouts. In 1851 Euphemia Williams, who claimed she had lived her entire life as a free black in Pennsylvania, was seized and carried off to Maryland by a man who swore she had run away from him 22 years before. He also demanded possession of her six children, including a healthy young lad of seventeen. The most famous case of the period was that of Anthony Burns, a Virginia slave. Burns managed to stow away in a ship at Richmond and reach Boston safely. There he foolishly sent a letter to his brother back in Richmond. His owner traced him to Boston, and since Burns readily recognized his master, there was no question of identification. He was taken before a federal commissioner, who ordered him remanded to his master. The people of Boston organized a protest demonstration, and the authorities, prompted by a fear that some attempt might be made to free Burns, called for extra police forces to escort Burns from the courthouse to the ship that was to carry him back to Virginia. In the end, the hapless fugitive was escorted by more than 1,100 soldiers as well as a host of policemen and extra deputies. The total cost to the United States government of returning Anthony Burns to slavery was about $50,000.

Uncle Tom's Cabin Of even greater significance in solidifying and popularizing abolitionist sentiment in the North was the publication of Harriet Beecher Stowe's *Uncle Tom's Cabin.* Appearing in 1851 in serial form, it was published as a book the following year. Mrs. Stowe had little intimate knowledge of slavery, for she had never lived in a slave state. She had, however, lived in Cincinnati for 17 years, just across the river from slavery. While there, she had been

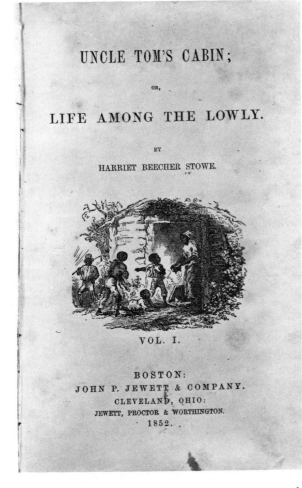

UNCLE TOM'S CABIN;

OR,

LIFE AMONG THE LOWLY.

BY

HARRIET BEECHER STOWE.

VOL. I.

BOSTON:
JOHN P. JEWETT & COMPANY.
CLEVELAND, OHIO:
JEWETT, PROCTOR & WORTHINGTON.
1852.

active in helping runaways make contact with those who operated the Underground Railroad to the North. She had also visited with relatives in Kentucky who were slaveholders. Largely ignorant of the personal side of slavery, she made up in fervor what she lacked in knowledge. Daughter of one of the greatest American

preachers of his day and sister of another, she was married to a classics professor who displayed the quiet courage of his convictions by many years of teaching in the abolitionists' Lane Theological Seminary. Neither Mrs. Stowe nor her publisher was prepared for the reception her story received. Within a year 300,000 copies had been sold and eight power presses were running night and day to meet the demand. Soon translated into half the languages of the world, its influence was nearly as great abroad as it was at home. Russian landowners, moved by her story, even freed some of their serfs. The book was soon transformed into a play that moved audiences in Oslo, Antwerp, and Rome quite as much as it did those of Philadelphia, Cleveland, and Detroit. Hostile reception by the press and leaders of the South did not prevent a great many southerners from reading of the fate of poor old Uncle Tom, one of the prototypes of whom was Josiah Henson of Maryland.

The personal-liberty laws and *Uncle Tom's Cabin* served to make abolitionism respectable in the North. They also allowed northerners to maintain that they favored the "final settlement" while they resisted it in practice. Southerners were at a distinct disadvantage under the Compromise of 1850, for there was no single act of the bargain that they could isolate and resist. They were forced to either accept or reject the entire compromise. Since popular sentiment was obviously strongly supporting the settlement, southern radicals were forced to bide their time while the abolitionists were having a field day. When their opportunity finally arrived, these southern radicals embraced it with a fervor that stemmed from hopes long deferred. Their opportunity was the introduction of a bill to organize the territories of Kansas and Nebraska.

The Kansas-Nebraska Question It was early in 1854 when Stephen A. Douglas, chairman of the Senate Committee on Territories, reported out a bill to organize Kansas and Nebraska. The action was long overdue. The country to the west of Iowa and Missouri had been owned by the United States since the Louisiana Purchase. It had remained unorganized after Texas and California had achieved statehood and the remainder of the Mexican cession had been organized into territories. Much of the delay was caused by failure to clear the land of the Indian titles to it, but this was rectified by a series of treaties in 1853. Some opposition to the organization had come from radical southerners who insisted that the barrier to slave expansion north of 36°30′ in

Far left: Title page of *Uncle Tom's Cabin.* A fictional work, the book is about a good and devoted slave, Uncle Tom, who flees after his kind master dies because of harsh treatment by the cruel Simon Legree. The book is based on accounts by Josiah Henson, an escapee from Maryland whose autobiography was published in 1858 and republished in 1962 with an introduction by Walter Fisher. *(Library of Congress.)*

the Louisiana Territory, established in the Missouri Compromise, discriminated against the South, which had shared in the cost of the Louisiana Purchase. Important opposition appears to have come from promoters of a transcontinental railroad who hoped to win federal support for a southern route. So long as the territory west of the Missouri River remained unorganized, the federal government could not possibly support a northern route, and the southern plans were safe.

Pushed both by northern promoters of a Pacific railroad and by the settlers in Iowa and Missouri who were demanding access to the new lands, Douglas hoped to organize the territories without bringing the slavery question back into national politics. He attempted to do this by providing that the territories be organized under the principle of popular sovereignty. He reasoned that popular sovereignty had been applied to Utah and New Mexico in 1850 without serious protest, so there could be no reasonable objection in 1854. In point of fact, southerners had Douglas over a barrel, and they knew it. Their votes had killed previous attempts to organize the area, and they could kill the new attempt. They also knew that Douglas' future in the Democratic Party (and he was being pushed for the presidency) depended upon them. Making the most of their advantage, they proposed that Douglas make a slight change in his bill. Since the system of popular sovereignty, which allowed the actual settlers to determine the status of slavery, revoked the Missouri Compromise prohibition by implication, they demanded that Douglas revoke the prohibition outright. Caught in the trap of his own logic as well as his political ambitions, Douglas agreed. The Kansas-Nebraska bill was amended to repeal the Missouri Compromise prohibition of slavery north of 36°30'. Douglas firmly believed that popular sovereignty was right and just, and he was convinced that any opposition to it would come only from irresponsible abolitionist agitators, whom he despised.

Douglas had miscalculated the depth and intensity of northern opposition to the extension of slavery. For 33 years the North had believed that the 36°30' line constituted a permanent barrier to the northward expansion of slavery. Few agreed with Douglas that the establishment of popular sovereignty in Utah and New Mexico constituted a precedent for the Louisiana Purchase territory. They saw only that a solemn compromise, made and upheld in perfect good

faith, had been broken by the South. Douglas himself was soon being burned in effigy by the same Chicago crowds that had lionized him a short time before. He was accused of selling out to the "slavocracy" in order to further his presidential ambitions.

The Douglas bill was a godsend to radical abolitionists and Free-Soilers. It made them even more popular than had the Fugitive Slave Law agitation. Typical of northern newspapers' reaction was the Ohio editor who called the Kansas-Nebraska bill "the scheme of a weak and imbecile administration; of a corrupt and ambitious demagogue; of grasping dishonorable slaveholders—[it] has filled the cup of bitterness which has been pressed to Northern lips so long. . . ."

In communities all over the North, anti-Nebraska meetings were called. Men calling themselves Anti-Nebraska or Independent Whigs and Democrats joined Conscience Whigs and Proviso Democrats in adopting resolutions condemning Douglas, the Democratic Party, and southern slaveholders. Many announced their readiness to form a new political party. Soon these dissident elements succeeded in electing governors, representatives to Congress, and many local officials. The Kansas-Nebraska bill thus had a double significance: it hastened the disintegration of the two national political parties, just as Calhoun had feared, and it paved the way for the birth of the Republican Party. As men shifted their loyalty from the national parties to a sectional one, they were abandoning one more of the bonds that held them to their nation.

In the crisis of the Kansas-Nebraska controversy, the nation could no longer rely on the elder statesmen who had created the Compromise of 1850. Henry Clay and Daniel Webster died within six months of each other in 1852. Thomas Hart Benton, defeated for the Senate in 1850, was now in the House, but his influence was gone. Lewis Cass was still in the Senate, but he had lost his fire. In their place was a new set of leaders, younger men with reputations to make. For example, Webster's seat was occupied by Charles Sumner, who would prove one of the most effective and determined enemies of slavery and the South. Of the great compromisers, only Douglas retained a position of leadership, and he had failed to judge the temper of the people.

The Kansas-Nebraska bill provided that the settlers themselves would determine whether slavery would be prohibited or permitted in the new lands. Since the settlers would determine the status of slavery in the course of writing a state constitution, a race developed between North and South to push enough settlers into Kansas to win a majority in the coming constitutional convention. Before long, the air was thick with charges and countercharges. Free states accused Missouri "border ruffians" of crossing into Kansas on election days and, after recording their vote, returning to their homes in Missouri. No one mentioned that Iowans were doing the same thing in Nebraska, for there was no conflict there. Southerners pointed to the Emigrant Aid Societies that were formed in the North to win Kansas for freedom by encouraging northern settlement there. Such societies were formed, but their contribution to the population of Kansas was negligible. The North was also accused of sending Sharps rifles, "not the ordinary weapon used in the chase, or for the protection of the domestic hearth, but a weapon of war," in boxes marked "Bibles." Before long reports of conflict began to filter back to the East: reports of the "Wakarusa War" and the "Sack of Lawrence."

Even today it is difficult to determine exactly what did go on in Kansas in 1855 and 1856. That there was bloodshed there can be no doubt.

The Dred Scott Case "It can now be asserted with finality," said Walter Ehrlich in the *Journal of Negro History*, April 1974, "that the Dred Scott case originated not for mercenary or political reasons, but rather for the humanitarian purpose of obtaining freedom of the slaves involved,"

specifically Dred Scott and his family. One of the most celebrated cases in American history, the decision of the U.S. Supreme Court in 1857 was the culmination of events that began in 1833, when Dr. John Emerson, a physician in St. Louis, Mo., began a tour of duty at Fort Armstrong, Ill., and later at Fort Snelling, Minn. (then in Wisconsin Territory), in company with Scott, his slave. By 1846, Emerson had died, leaving Scott to his wife, Irene; Scott, too, had acquired a wife, Harriet, and a daughter, Eliza. Early litigation for Scott's freedom began in this year by Scott's friends, mainly Henry Taylor Blow.

Scott sued for his freedom on the grounds that his residence in a territory from which slavery was excluded by the terms of the Missouri Compromise (the area north of 36°30′ within the Louisiana Purchase and excluding Missouri itself) made him free even after his return to a slave state. The local Missouri court freed Scott, but the Missouri Supreme Court reversed the decision on the ground that whatever his status while in free territory Scott was a slave when he returned to Missouri.

By arranging a legal sale of Scott to a New Yorker by the name of Sanford (a relative of the former Mrs. Emerson), Scott's friends hoped to get the case into the federal courts on the ground that it became a case of a citizen of Missouri suing a citizen of New York. The hope was to carry the case to the U.S. Supreme Court, where the entire question of slavery in the territories might be decided. Thus, the heart of the case centered on the power of Congress to exclude slavery from the territories belonging to the nation. The Republican contention that Congress had always possessed this power, and had exercised it in the ordinance of 1787 as well as in the Missouri Compromise of 1820, was at issue. Scott's personal freedom was not at stake, for he would be freed by his friends if he lost in the courts.

Far left: Dred Scott. His case, strongly supported by a white friend, Henry Blow, was a symbol of the sectional conflict over slavery. *(The New York Historical Society.)*

Southerners were confident that the court would uphold the Kansas-Nebraska Act repeal of the Missouri Compromise restriction on slavery and would deny the power of Congress to exclude the "peculiar institution" from the territories won with common blood and treasure. Seven of the nine justices were Democrats, five of whom were from the South. Furthermore, there were indications that a majority of the Court were eager to use the power of the Court to get the whole subject of slavery out of the halls of Congress.

Chief Justice Roger B. Taney, the old Jacksonian, gave the majority decision, speaking for the seven Democratic justices. He declared that the lower federal court had lacked jurisdiction because, under the laws of Missouri, Scott was not a citizen. This much was in accord with precedent, and if he had stopped there Taney would have given the Republicans and abolitionists no opening. After all, if the lower federal courts lacked jurisdiction, so did the federal Supreme Court. But Taney went on to declare that Afro-Americans had not been citizens at the time of the adoption of the Constitution and had not become citizens of the nation since. Thus, Scott had been a slave even while at Fort Snelling, for Congress had exceeded its authority in adopting the Missouri Compromise prohibition on slavery. The corollary was that the Missouri Compromise restriction was contrary to the federal Constitution, and Taney so declared it.

Both President James Buchanan and the justices had hoped that a decision of the highest tribunal in the land would carry sufficient prestige and authority to bury permanently the entire question of slavery in the territories. Instead of pronouncing a requiem, the court had exploded a bombshell.

Republicans were nearly speechless with anger (but they quickly recovered their voices), for the court had struck down a solemn compromise. Strong words in the North soon evoked equally harsh replies from the South. The significance of the Dred Scott decision was soon apparent. Existing divisions within the Democratic Party were greatly deepened. Many Democratic leaders, understanding that the only hope for union lay in the continued health and vigor of a truly national party, were helpless. The position of Stephen A. Douglas was typical. As the only national leader left to the party, Douglas' primary job was to reconcile northern and southern wings of the party. After the Dred Scott decision, this meant that he must try to get northern Democrats to acquiesce in the Dred Scott decision while he convinced southern Democrats that they must not insist on the abstract right to take their slaves into all the territories. Personally convinced that the issue of slavery in the territories was dead because the soil and climate would never make slavery profitable in the Far West, Douglas set out to find a formula that would unite the two wings of his party.

A plain-speaking popular attorney, nominated by the Republicans to go after Douglas' Senate seat in 1858, was quick to see the broad canyon Douglas was trying to straddle. Over and over again in a series of debates with Douglas, Abraham Lincoln asked how the people of a territory might prevent slavery from being established among them, since the Supreme Court in the Dred Scott case had decreed that slavery must be protected everywhere in the territories. Douglas' answer, which became known as the Freeport Doctrine, makes more sense to us than it did to his listeners. He pointed out that slavery required positive and friendly local legislation (such as it had received everywhere in the South); failure to pass such laws in territorial legislatures would as effectively prohibit slavery as any act of the federal government. But the damage had been done. Lincoln and the Supreme Court made it impossible for southern Democrats to follow the lead of even so moderate a northern Democrat as Douglas. Dred Scott and the Lincoln-Douglas debates became two more milestones on the long road down to war. However, it would take more heat, more emotion, and more misunderstandings before Americans would be ready to abandon their deeply ingrained loyalty to the union.

John Brown at Harpers Ferry It was in October 1859 that John Brown with a small band of followers, including five blacks, tried to capture the United States Arsenal at Harpers Ferry, Va. Brown had some vague ideas of freeing and arming the slaves in the neighborhood, who would then provide the nucleus for a kind of chain-reaction slave revolt. Harpers Ferry, situated in the mountains at the northern end of the Shenandoah Valley and protected on two sides by the Potomac and Shenandoah rivers, gives the false impression of being easily defensible. Because of its location at the head of the valley, Brown apparently thought it would be accessible to fugitive slaves coming from the South along mountain pathways. Whatever his plans were, none of them were realized. His first victim in the attack was Heyward Shepherd, a free Negro employed at the railroad depot. The arsenal was easily captured, but Brown foolishly allowed a train to go on to Baltimore after the conductor had seen the state of affairs in Harpers Ferry. The conductor spread the alarm, and militia and United States marines soon reinforced the townspeople who had trapped Brown in a firehouse. Seven citizens and soldiers were killed; several of Brown's followers were captured, ten were killed, and a few escaped. One of the escapees was a free black, and printer by trade, Osborn Perry Anderson, who later fought in the Civil

War. The two blacks killed were Lewis Leary and Dangerfield Newby, both North Carolinians. Both were free: Leary's father was white and Newby's wife was a slave. Newby was the first of Brown's group to die. Brown, himself, seriously wounded, was captured, tried for treason by the state of Virginia, and speedily hanged. The two blacks hanged were Shields Green and John Copeland. Green was a student at Oberlin College (Oberlin, Ohio); Copeland was a native of North Carolina. No slaves willingly joined Brown's revolt, but as with previous slave insurrections, the South took no chances. Governor Henry A. Wise of Virginia called out the militia, took command of cadets at the Virginia Military Institute, issued proclamations, and marched his men back and forth across the state.

What John Brown did is unimportant; how Americans reacted to his action is of the first importance. The first reaction, of both North and South, was shock. Once that was past, everyone began to think of the implications of Brown's deed. Most southerners, like most northerners, were primarily interested in what advantage might be gleaned from Harpers Ferry.

The presidential election of the following year (1860) reflected the nation's disunity. Abraham

Lincoln became a minority president. His vote came exclusively from the North; he received not a single vote from the states that later joined the Confederacy, with the exception of a few votes in the area that later became West Virginia. When all analysis of the vote is done, the fact remains that the American people had elected a president who led a sectional party, and to the other section he was a symbol—a "Black" Republican. Because of that symbol, national loyalties were abandoned and sectional loyalties were built. A nation had come to war—against itself. *See also* the following entries under SLAVERY: THE ABOLITIONISTS; THE UNDERGROUND RAILROAD; SLAVERY IN SELECTED STATES; ON THE FRONTIER.

REFERENCES: Abels, Jules, *Man on Fire, John Brown and the Cause of Liberty*, Macmillan, New York, 1971; Berwanger, Eugene H., *The Frontier Against Slavery: Western Anti-Negro Prejudice and the Slavery Extension Controversy*, University of Illinois Press, Urbana, 1967; Craven, Avery O., *The Coming of the Civil War*, 2d ed., University of Chicago Press, Chicago, 1957; Donald, David, *Charles Sumner and the Coming of the Civil War*,; Dumond, Dwight L., *Antislavery Origins of the Civil War in the United States*, University of Michigan Press, Ann Arbor, 1939; Erhlich, Walter, "The Origins of the Dred Scott Case," *Journal of Negro History*, April 1974, pp. 132–42; Milton, George F., *The Eve of Conflict; Stephen A. Douglas and the Needless War*, Houghton Mifflin, Boston, 1934; Nichols, Roy F., *The Disruption of American Democracy*, Macmillan, New York, 1948; Nichols, Roy F., "The Kansas-Nebraska Act: A Century of Historiography," *Mississippi Valley Historical Review*, September 1956; Nevins, Allan, *Ordeal of the Union*, 2 vols., Scribner, New York, 1947; Rawley, James A., *Race and Politics: "Bleeding Kansas" and the Coming of the Civil War*, J. B. Lippincott Company, New York, 1969; Rozwenc, Edwin C. (ed.), *Slavery as a Cause of the Civil War*, Heath, Boston, 1949; and Shapiro, Samuel, "The Rendition of Anthony Burns," *Journal of Negro History*, June 1959, pp. 34–51. See also Quarles, Benjamin, *Allies for Freedom: Blacks and John Brown*, Oxford University Press, 1974.

Far left: Memorial to Heyward Shepherd, the first casualty of John Brown's raid. *(Harpers Ferry Historical Park.)*

The Civil War, 1861–65 The Civil War, which lasted from 1861 to 1865, probably had a greater impact on Afro-Americans than any other single event in the nation's history. Before the war, the vast majority of black Americans were legally slaves; after the war, America's "peculiar institution" had been stamped out. Before the war, according to the Dred Scott decision of 1857, Afro-Americans could not be citizens of the United States; after the war, constitutional amendments, legal statutes, and subsequent U.S. Supreme Court decisions all affirmed the citizenship of Afro-Americans. Freedom and citizenship: these were the great legacies for Afro-Americans of the Civil War. But it is important to realize that these legacies were not just incidental by-products of the conflict. Black men and women worked hard to help win them.

One of the two major ways in which Afro-Americans helped to insure these Civil War legacies was by participating in the military effort itself. This participation was not, however, a simple matter. Though both the North and the South believed the fate of the Afro-American to be a focal point in the crisis of the nation, neither side really welcomed him as a participating military ally during the period immediately after the shelling of Fort Sumter. Ironically, Afro-Americans had to struggle for the right to die in the one war that affected them more dramatically than any other in American history.

Oddly, the Confederacy responded first to black offers to fight. The long-established free black population of New Orleans organized a unit called the Native Guards, and Louisiana's Confederate governor, Thomas O. Moore, officially recognized it as part of the Louisiana militia. In some areas of the South, blacks volunteered for various positions in the Confederate service, including the heavy labor tasks involved in building fortifications. Southern Afro-Americans apparently decided to aid the Confederacy for a number of reasons. Loyalty to their local areas may have proved decisive for some; for others, the hope of winning a better position within a nation they expected to have to deal with permanently may have been the reason for opting for Confederate service; and for many the fear of being impressed into even more intolerable positions no doubt prompted their early activity on behalf of the South. Black Americans never saw battle action in defense of the Confederacy, however, and as the war began to go against the South, greater and greater numbers of southern Negroes went over to the Union lines. Not until its near collapse did the Confederacy change its official policy toward the recruitment, enlistment, and combat service of blacks.

Blacks in the North were also in a difficult quandary, and they debated among themselves concerning the best course of action to pursue. Although some black spokesmen argued that it was folly to force their services upon a government that did not want those services and that might be considered almost as racist as the Confederacy, the majority of northern Afro-Americans probably agreed with the New York *Anglo-African* that the Union war effort could be transformed into a crusade more noble than a narrow exercise in constitutional necessity.

The free colored Americans cannot be indifferent to the progress of this struggle. . . . Out of this strife will come freedom, though the methods are not yet clearly apparent. . . . Public opinion purified by the fiery ordeal through which the nation is about to pass, will rightly appreciate the cause of its political disquiet, and apply the remedy. . . . It must be that the key to the solution of the present difficulties, is the abolition of slavery; not as an act of retaliation on the master, but as a measure of justice to the slave—the sure and permanent basis of "a more perfect Union."

The influential Frederick Douglass, who certainly agreed with this position, took the lead not only in urging blacks to fight for the Union but also in urging the Union to let the blacks fight. "Let the slaves and free colored people be called into service, and formed into a liberating army . . . ," he declared boldly in his influential *Douglass' Monthly* at the outset of the war. For more than a year, he and many others kept the pressure up through newspapers, public speeches, petitions, and private meetings with influential members of the Union government, including finally President Abraham Lincoln himself.

In the meantime, individual blacks had already begun to fight in unofficial ways for the Union. Such men as Nicholas Biddle, the 65-year-old former slave who was wounded in the face while accompanying the first Pennsylvania troops through Baltimore in April 1861 and George Scott, who acted as scout and intelligence agent for the Union Army in its very first engagements at Big Bethel, served heroically from the beginning. In Kansas, in a theater of the war only loosely supervised from Washington, D.C., General James Lane made early and extensive use of Afro-American irregulars in guerrilla skirmishing along the Missouri border. Private black citizens such as William Tillman and Robert Smalls executed daring and successful exploits against Confederate shipping. Tillman, captured aboard a Union ship by Confederate raiders and declared a slave, single-handedly recaptured the Union ship from its new Confederate crew and sailed it back into New York harbor; Smalls, a slave from Charleston, led a band of black shipmen and dockmen who sailed a Confederate steamer past Castle Pinckney, Fort Moultrie, and Fort Sumter out to the blockading Union Navy.

Furthermore, the Union Navy, unlike the Union Army, had never barred blacks from service. Instead, the Navy treated Afro-Americans well, relied upon them, and rewarded their efforts. When the *Kearsarge* ended the famous raiding career of the *Alabama* in the waters off

Cherbourg harbor, there were 15 black sailors aboard the victorious Union ship. One of those men, Joachim Pease, earned the Medal of Honor in that engagement, and three other black sailors subsequently earned the same decoration during the Civil War. Approximately one quarter of the Navy's 3,222 battle casualties were sustained by black seamen. Nevertheless, the Lincoln Administration continued to shy away from enlisting black soldiers in the Union Army.

Not until the summer of 1862 did the government in Washington, D.C., begin to shift its policy. The public pressure of Douglass and his black associates, the exploits of individual Afro-Americans already engaged unofficially in the war effort, and the steadily reliable performance of Afro-Americans in the Union Navy all played a part in the transformation of Lincoln's policy. Both the evolution of the emancipation policy, which was undertaken specifically as a war measure, and the sharp decline in white enlistments played a part in the shift of Lincoln's attitude. Drawing legal authority from the Confiscation Act of July 17, 1862, and the Militia Act of the same date, the Lincoln administration began to enlist black soldiers into the formation of black units during the late summer of 1862. The Louisiana Native Guards, who had previously shifted their allegiance to the Union, the 1st South Carolina Volunteers, consisting largely of former slaves from the Sea Islands, and the 54th Massachusetts Regiment, manned mainly by free blacks from throughout the North, were among the first Afro-American units to be recognized. By March 1863 Adjutant General Lorenzo Thomas had been sent into the vast Mississippi valley to organize black outfits from among the Afro-American populations under Union Army control, and during May of that same year the War Department established a special Bureau of Colored Troops. Altogether a total of 178,895 black

men eventually entered the Union Army, and by the end of the war black troops accounted for somewhere between 10 and 12 percent of the Union forces. Moreover, a number of black women served as military nurses, including the two legendary figures, Harriet Tubman and Sojourner Truth.

What ultimately made this large-scale participation meaningful, indeed, what allowed it to become large scale in the first place, were the courage and the ability of individual black soldiers when tested in battle. Although black units fought in 449 engagements during the Civil War, including 39 major battles, three early clashes proved most crucial. The three—Port Hudson, Milliken's Bend, and Fort Wagner—were important because the black troops involved displayed to both the Confederacy that would enslave them and to the Union that would spurn them that they were a fighting force to be reckoned with. At Port Hudson, on May 27, 1863, the Native Guards made a series of heroic charges over difficult terrain in the face of intense enemy fire. Recently enlisted former slaves passed a dramatic test at Milliken's Bend on June 7, 1863, when they withstood a Confederate attack in savage hand-to-hand combat. And at Fort Wagner in the twilight of July 18, 1863, the 54th Massachusetts made one of the most courageous charges of the war against an impenetrable Confederate stronghold. Though the assault was turned back, the individual foot soldiers provided an unforgettable demonstration of inspired bravery.

The conduct of black troops had a profound impact upon the northern population in general and upon influential Union military and political leaders in particular. In the nineteenth century, the notion of fighting and dying for one's country held almost mystical power, and the performance of individual black soldiers in the Union Army helped to win some of that power

Rare photograph shows troops of the 14th U.S. Colored Infantry at Ship Island, Miss. Despite discrimination and unequal pay, blacks constituted 10 to 12 percent of the Union's forces toward the end of the war. *(Edward L. Bafford Photography Collection, University of Maryland Baltimore County Library.)*

for their twin causes of freedom and citizenship. Moreover, this performance was undertaken despite the hardships of a year and a half of inferior wages, the absence of promotion, the suffering of families back home, and all-too-frequent assignments to fatigue or heavy-labor duties. In May 1864 a government commission summarized the impact of the black soldier this way:

The whites have changed, and are still rapidly changing, their opinion of the negro. And the negro, in his new condition as freedman, is himself, to some extent, a changed being. No one circumstance has tended so much to these results as the display of manhood in negro soldiers. Though there are higher qualities than strength and physical courage, yet, in our present state of civilization, there are no qualities which command from the masses more respect.

The second major way in which Afro-Americans worked to insure the twin legacies of freedom and citizenship during the Civil War was through a continuous program of public information and political activity behind the lines. This effort on the home front was directed toward the eradication of slavery, the breakdown of institutionalized discrimination, and the enactment of a positive legal bulwark for black citizens.

The Afro-American campaign against slavery had, of course, been going on for generations prior to the outbreak of the Civil War. But the war gave black men and women a fresh impetus and a new hope for final success. Though sometimes divided on other issues, and frequently upset with the slow evolution of Lincoln's emancipation policy, the black community was united and outspoken in its belief that the Civil War should be more than a war to preserve the constitutional forms of the American Union. With characteristic force, Frederick Douglass cut to the heart of the issue: "The negro is the key of the situation—the pivot upon which the whole rebellion turns. . . . Teach the rebels and traitors that the price they are to pay for the attempt to abolish this Government must be the abolition of slavery." Anticipating what would later become a white war aim also, Douglass urged, "Henceforth let the war cry be down with treason, and down with slavery, the cause of treason."

After the Lincoln administration finally adopted a policy of emancipation during the summer of 1862 and the northern people began to accept

Refugees from slavery during the Civil War, regarded as war "contraband" by the Union Army, worked and soldiered at military posts, often receiving their first—though unequal—wages, as at Aquia Creek, Va., in winter 1862–63. *(Edward L. Bafford Photography Collection, University of Maryland Baltimore County Library.)*

government of the United States, including the military and naval authorities thereof, will recognize and maintain the freedom of said persons.

And I hereby enjoin upon the people so declared to be free to abstain from all violence, unless in necessary self-defence; and I recommend to them that, in all cases when allowed, they labor faithfully for reasonable wages.

And I further declare and make known, that such persons of suitable condition, will be received into the armed service of the United States to garrison forts, positions, stations, and other places, and to man vessels of all sorts in said service.

And upon this act, sincerely believed to be an act of justice, warranted by the Constitution, upon military necessity, I invoke the considerate judgment of mankind, and the gracious favor of Almighty God.

In witness whereof, I have hereunto set my hand and caused the seal of the United States to be affixed.

Done at the city of Washington, this first day of January, in the year of our Lord one thousand eight hundred and sixty three, and of the Independence of the United States of America the eighty-seventh.

Abraham Lincoln

By the President:

William H. Seward, Secretary of State.

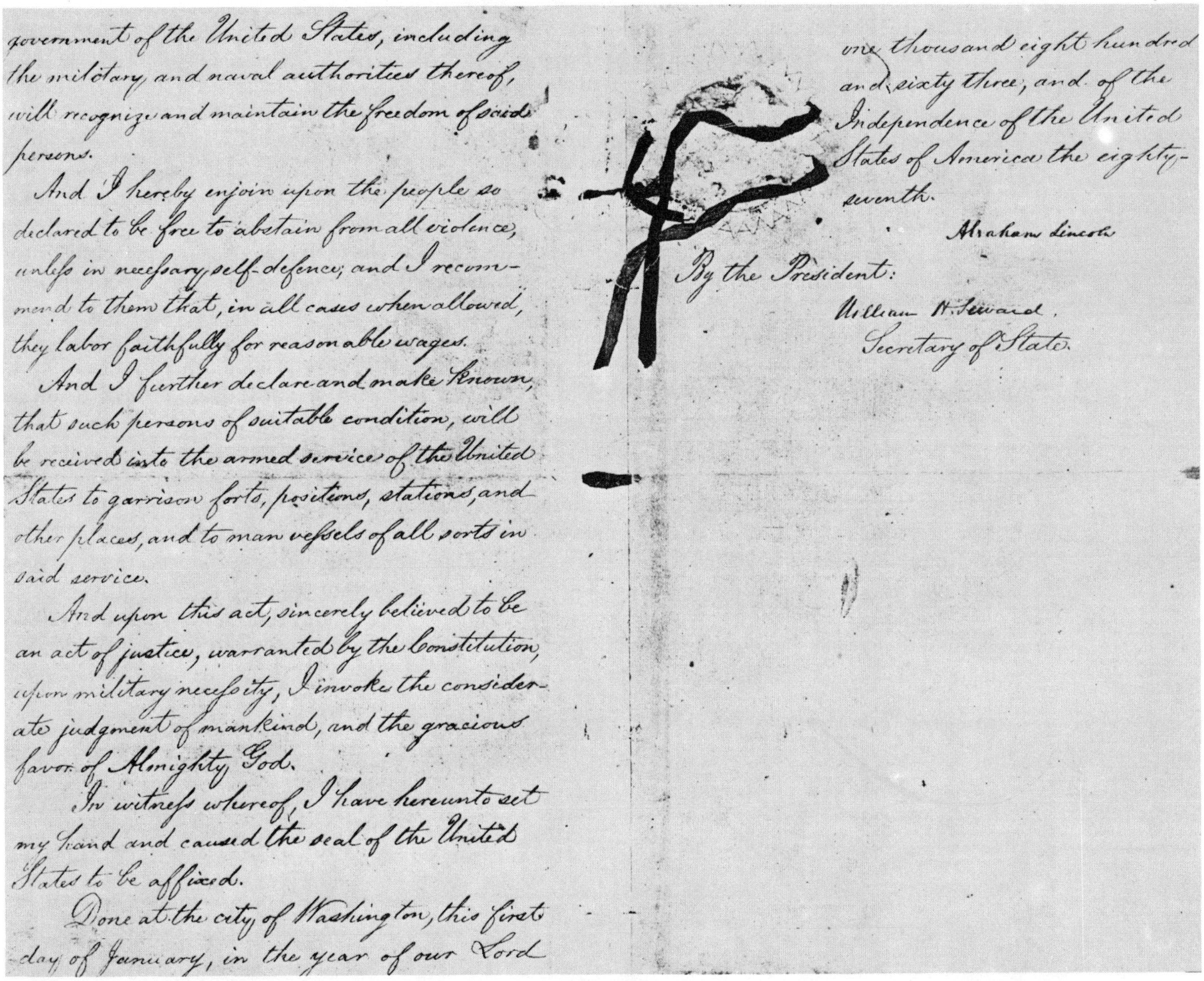

Emancipation Proclamation. Shown above is the last part of the Emancipation Proclamation, one of the great documents of American freedom. The Proclamation was issued by President Abraham Lincoln in September, 1862, and became effective the following January. The seal is shown opposite the signatures. ***(National Archives.)***

the destruction of America's "peculiar institution" as a Union war aim, the blacks of the North felt justifiably proud of their efforts. Meetings were held in most of the major northern cities on New Year's Day, 1863, the date when Lincoln's final Emancipation Proclamation was scheduled to go into effect. A huge gathering at Boston's Tremont Temple, for example, brought together some of the leading black figures in the movement for freedom: William C. Nell, president of the Union Progressive Association (UPA); William Wells Brown, the abolitionist speaker and author; Edwin M. Bannister, then secretary of the UPA and already gaining fame as an artist; J. B. Smith, the wealthy Boston caterer and prominent antislavery benefactor; John Rock, who shortly became the first Afro-American admitted to the bar of the U.S. Supreme Court; and Frederick Douglass, the voice of black idealism, who had joined the ranks of the freedom movement in nearby New Bedford some two decades before. When the telegraph wires from Washington, D.C., carried the news of Lincoln's final Emancipation Proclamation, the celebrants adjourned to the Twelfth Baptist Church of Boston—once known commonly as "the Fugitive Slaves' Church"—for a night of rejoicing. It was, in more ways than one, *their* celebration. The legal capstone of the emancipation movement would come a little more than two years later in the form of the Thirteenth Amendment, adopted by the U.S. Congress on January 31, 1865.

Though less dramatic than the emancipation movement, the black attack upon overt racial discrimination during the Civil War must not be overlooked. It is impossible to dispute and easy to demonstrate with historical evidence that the vast majority of mid-nineteenth-century Americans considered Afro-Americans inferior. Although neither the exact reasons for nor the precise degree of this inferiority were spelled out, the racial prejudice of white Americans was painfully obvious. Socially, blacks were generally shunned, and the segregation of public facilities was common. Educationally, blacks were frequently the victims of wretchedly maintained

separate schools or, sometimes, no schools at all. Politically, black men were able to vote on an equal basis with white men only in the five northeasternmost New England states. In New York state, Afro-Americans had to meet a $250 property qualification, which was not imposed upon whites, in order to exercise the franchise. In every other state in the Union, black citizens were simply barred outright from the polls.

In the face of this second-class citizenship, northern blacks began to chip away at the façade of institutionalized white racism. Such black spokesmen as Frederick Douglass, John Rock, and Robert Purvis spoke out eloquently during the war in opposition to the supposed inferiority of the black race. John Jones, a wealthy tailor from Chicago, led a successful drive against Illinois statutes that barred Afro-American immigration into the state and excluded Afro-American testimony in state courts. William Still organized the black community of Philadelphia in opposition to the segregation of that city's streetcar system, and the movement finally succeeded when Still carried his case into the Pennsylvania state legislature. The prominent caterer and restauranteur George T. Downing spearheaded another successful effort by another local black community: the desegregation of Rhode

Shortly after word of emancipation reached the South, these former slaves joined Union forces at New Bern, N.C., in February 1863. *(Library of Congress.)*

Island's school system. Blacks won a suit to end educational separation in Detroit; John Mercer Langston of Ohio began to organize Equal Rights Leagues across the nation; and Frederick Douglass helped to insure the success of the National Convention of Colored Citizens of the United States in 1864, which outlined black demands for legal equality.

Both in the field and on the home front, then, individual blacks worked to gain the legacies of freedom and full citizenship from the Civil War. Perhaps what most Afro-Americans were struggling for during that crisis was best summarized by a prominent Afro-American clergyman from New York City, the Rev. Henry Highland Garnet. The following excerpt is from a sermon he delivered in the U.S. House of Representatives two months before Lee's surrender effectively ended the American Civil War:

It is often asked when and where will the demands of the reformers of this and coming ages end? It is a fair question, and I will answer.

When all unjust and heavy burdens shall be removed from every man in the land. When all invidious and proscriptive distinctions shall be blotted out from our laws, whether they be constitutional, statute, or municipal laws. When emancipation shall be followed by enfranchisement, and all men holding allegiance to the government shall enjoy every right of American citizenship. When our brave and gallant soldiers shall have justice done unto them. When the men who endure the sufferings and perils of the battlefield in the defense of their country, and in order to keep our rulers in their places, shall enjoy the well-earned privilege of voting for them. When in the army and navy, and in every legitimate and honorable occupation, promotion shall smile upon merit without the slightest regard to the complexion of a man's face. When there shall be no more class-legislation, and no more trouble concerning the black man and his rights, than there is in regard to other American citizens. When, in every respect, he shall be equal before the law, and shall be left to make his own way in the social walks of life. *See also* SLAVERY: THE ABOLITIONISTS; WARS.

REFERENCES: The literature on the Afro-American's role in the Civil War, already voluminous, continues to grow steadily. Three volumes provide an excellent starting place for further study: Cornish, Dudley Taylor, *The Sable Arm: Negro Troops in the Union Army, 1861–1865*, Norton, New York, 1956; McPherson, James M., *The Negro's Civil War: How American Negroes Felt and Acted During the War for the Union*, Vintage Books, New York, 1965; and Quarles, Benjamin, *The Negro and the Civil War*, Little, Brown, New York, 1969. Though it does not focus on the role of blacks specifically, Randall, James G. and David Donald, *The Civil War and Reconstruction*, Heath, Boston, 1969, is the best one-volume study of the period. See also REFERENCES under entry WARS.

Reconstruction, 1865–77 The word *reconstruction* has a fairly literal meaning in American history. The bloody Civil War, from 1861 to 1865, had blown the old American political system completely apart, and the American people had to decide upon the best way to put it back together again—literally, how to reconstruct it. The decision was not an easy one. It took several unsuccessful experiments, alterations of the U.S. Constitution over 12 years, and a great deal of human tragedy before the shape of that decision finally became clear in 1877. During the course of this agonizing process, no question loomed larger than the place of 4 million Afro-Americans in the reconstructed American system.

There is no question that Afro-Americans themselves were clear about the place that they should occupy in the new system. The Civil War

Afro-Americans voted en masse for the first time during Reconstruction, as illustrated in *Harper's Weekly*, Nov. 16, 1867. *(Library of Congress.)*

and the Thirteenth Amendment to the U.S. Constitution had made Afro-Americans citizens of the United States, and they desired a place characterized by functional equality, economic independence, and political power according to their numbers and their contributions to American society. Political power, especially the right to vote, proved to be the focal point of the Reconstruction debate over the status of Afro-Americans. Throughout the war, such black spokesmen as Frederick Douglass and Robert Purvis had called for the enfranchisement of black men, and their call was echoed in the black press, in the public meetings of black communities North and South, and in petitions to all levels of government. When Douglass lectured in 1865 on the subject "What the Black Man Wants," his answer stressed one notion: political power based upon equal suffrage.

The debate over the place of the Afro-American in postwar American life, which had begun during the war itself, continued unresolved through 1865 and 1866. During those years the ex-Confederate states were permitted by President Andrew Johnson to form governments that excluded blacks from the political process altogether. Indeed, the Black Codes passed by many of these regimes appeared to be barely disguised returns to legal peonage, and news reports from the South testified to a large number of racial atrocities committed by whites against free blacks. Blacks were being subjugated; the Democratic Party was threatening to upset the political security of the victorious Republicans; the same men who had led the Confederacy out of the Union in 1861 were back in control under the Johnsonian governments; and the war seemed to have been fought for nothing. In the absence of additional guarantees to free persons, the South appeared to be returning to its antebellum patterns.

In the face of this situation, an increasing number of northerners began to see that they would have to build a more formidable legal foundation under the citizenship that had been granted to Afro-Americans. When President Johnson tried to block the initial safeguards suggested by Congress, safeguards that included an extension of the Freedmen's Bureau and a moderate federal civil rights proposal, a rift was opened between the executive branch and the legislative branch that culminated finally in President Johnson's celebrated impeachment trial in 1868. Well before then, however, in the wake of the congressional elections of 1866, Congress had been able to seize effective control over the Reconstruction process and had begun to erect the kind of legal foundations for which Afro-Americans had been calling.

As finally enacted, these legal foundations seemed substantial indeed. In 1866 Congress had extended the life and the power of the Freedmen's Bureau in order to provide an agency that would help to ease the transition from slavery to full citizenship, and it had also passed

Black New Yorkers honored the adoption of the Fifteenth Amendment in a parade on April 8, 1870. Similar parades were held in Baltimore, Md., and Washington, D.C. *(Library of Congress.)*

a moderate civil rights law in order to provide federal protection for the political rights granted to black citizens. By the terms of the Reconstruction Act of March 2, 1867, and its three subsequent refinements, black citizens in the former Confederate states entered the political arena as full participants. Furthermore, these commitments were backed up by no less powerful a force than the U.S. Army, which continued to occupy the former Confederate states and helped to enforce congressional policy. And eventually capping this entire structure were the Fourteenth and Fifteenth amendments to the U.S. Constitution. The highest law in the land, the very document for which the Civil War had been fought, would henceforth forever guarantee that no citizen could be stripped of any of his rights by the arbitrary action of those more powerful and that no citizen could be deprived of his right to vote "on account of race, color, or previous condition of servitude." In ratifying these constitutional proposals the people of the victorious Union had apparently resolved the dilemma over the place of the black man in postwar America. Frederick Douglass himself could hardly have asked for more.

With the passage of the first Reconstruction Act of 1867, black citizens in the former Confederacy began responsibly to assume the place promised them in the reconstructed United States. They sat in constitutional conventions and helped to draft state constitutions that served as models for a democratized South until the end of the century. Black citizens supported the first comprehensive programs of state education in the South, and with the cooperation of the Freedmen's Bureau they began to make promising inroads into the illiteracy that had been enforced under slavery. Where compromises could be made for the benefit of all, as in the Mississippi constitutional convention, blacks made them; where cooperation with southern whites seemed to be the most effective political approach, as in Louisiana, this was the course pursued by the freedmen; where leadership could best be obtained from black and white men trained in the northern states, as in South Carolina, Afro-Americans supported that leadership. In no state did black citizens attempt to wreak any sort of vengeance against the white population.

Blacks did begin to exercise the functions of officeholders for the first time. Though no Afro-American was elected governor in any of the reconstructed states, Alonzo J. Ransier and

Richard H. Gleaves in South Carolina; A. K. Davis in Mississippi; and Oscar J. Dunn, P. B. S. Pinchback, and C. C. Antoine in Louisiana all served as lieutenant-governors. Pinchback acted as governor of Louisiana for six weeks in 1873, following the removal of the elected white governor. Prominent among a substantial number of

The first black senator and representatives to the United States Congress, 1872 (left to right): Sen. Hiram R. Revels (Miss.) and Reps. Benjamin S. Turner (Ala.), Robert C. DeLarge (S.C.), Josiah T. Wells (Fla.), Jefferson F. Long (Ga.), Joseph H. Rainey (S.C.), and Robert B. Elliott (S.C.). Well publicized as a print, the original was a lithograph (first published by Currier & Ives, New York, 1872) entitled *The First Colored Senator and Representatives in the 41st and 42d Congress of the United States. (Library of Congress.)*

other able black state officials in the South were Francis L. Cardozo, who served as South Carolina's secretary of state and later as its treasurer, and John Roy Lynch, who was speaker of the Mississippi house and then elected to the U.S. House of Representatives. Lynch had taught himself to read before the war by watching the lessons through a window of the white schoolhouse.

In addition to occupying state and local offices, blacks also represented their states in Washington, D.C. Two Afro-Americans, both from Mississippi, served in the U.S. Senate. They were Hiram R. Revels, who was elected in 1870 to complete an unexpired term, and Blanche K. Bruce, whose election to a full term in 1874 was not repeated until Edward Brooke was elected from Massachusetts in 1966. In one of history's supreme bits of exquisite symbolism, Revels, the first black man elected to the U.S. Senate, filled the seat vacated in 1861 by Jefferson Davis. The first Afro-American elected to the U.S. House of Representatives was Joseph H.

Rainey of South Carolina, who served five consecutive terms. He was joined by Robert Smalls, a largely self-educated man, who was also sent to the federal House five consecutive times by the people of South Carolina; John R. Lynch, who served three terms from Mississippi; J. T. Walls, who served three terms from Florida; and 16 other black Congressmen, who served at least one term during the period between 1869 and 1901.

Notwithstanding the legal foundation provided by the national government and notwithstanding the responsible and effective participation of blacks in the political processes of the former Confederate states, some very serious problems remained for the vast majority of free blacks. Perhaps their most significant difficulty lay in their economic status. A few experiments in land redistribution had proved that former

Land tenancy for blacks was a serious economic issue during Reconstruction. This sketch of a black family's cabin in Tennessee appeared in *Scribner's Monthly* in 1874. *(Library of Congress.)*

slaves were perfectly capable of successful farming on their own. Hardworking black farmers on the Sea Islands off South Carolina were able to improve their circumstances substantially during the last years of the war, and an experiment in black yeomanry undertaken on Mississippi plantation land once owned by the Davis brothers likewise proved successful because of the conscientious efforts of the black men and women involved. But these successful projects were never followed up. Despite the urging of Afro-Americans throughout the nation, despite the opinions of several prominent Republican leaders, and despite an attempt by Gen. William T. Sherman to resettle some 40,000 black citizens on former Confederate lands in South Carolina,

Georgia, and Florida, the nation acquiesced in President Johnson's policy of returning all land titles to their prewar owners. Although many Afro-American farmers resisted dispossession as best they could, even the Freedmen's Bureau eventually gave in to the president's policy. As a result, black citizens throughout the agricultural South were kept landless and forced into economically subordinate relationships to white landlords.

At least three alternative arrangements were possible as the basis of agreements between white landowners and black agricultural workers. One of these was rental, but this arrangement was not widely adopted owing to white lack of trust of black lessees and to white pacts against surrendering control over land to Afro-Americans. A second possible arrangement involved wages, but this system also broke down when the whites generally failed to pay reasonable rates and frequently refused to deal with the Freedmen's Bureau, which was eventually charged with supervising labor contracts in the South. This left the third major alternative: sharecropping. Under this arrangement, which became widespread throughout the South, the landowner provided certain minimal capital advantages—tools, sheds, seed, and the like—plus the use of his land in exchange for a predetermined amount, or "share", of the crop produced.

Nothing was inherently unfair about the sharecropping system without the addition of another crucial factor. This factor was the standard southern credit arrangement whereby the landowner extended additional help to the farmer during the lean months of the year and deferred collecting until the farmer was able to cash in his share of the crop. The high initial prices and the exorbitant rates of interest accumulated during the year left the farmer so far in debt by crop time that he was fortunate to break even after cashing in. Without profits, indeed frequently still owing money, the "cropper" had no way to purchase land of his own and no way to meet his obligations except by starting still another season of "shares." And so the system went on.

Thus, the sharecropping and debt cycle came to dominate the economic life of the majority of southern Afro-Americans. In 1883, for example, the South Carolina board of agriculture reported the results of its 1880 survey of conditions in that state's various counties. For Clarendon County, characterized by absentee white landowning and black sharecropping, the survey noted that "the liens for advances on the growing crops . . . numbered 2,716, or one to every farm save nine, and aggregate $283,317.18." In nearby Horry County, by comparison, where most of the farm labor was white, the survey stated that "the liens on the growing crop . . . numbered twenty-seven, and aggregate $1,179.80." Under the sharecropping and debt cycle, many southern blacks were reduced to little more than agricultural serfs, despite their hard work year after year, while the white landowners actually provided little more for their black laborers than they had under slavery and still continued to receive practically the entire profit. Nor did a steadily collapsing cotton market help. After 35 years of struggle under this cycle, black men and women had accumulated only about 600,000 acres of land in the entire South.

The second major difficulty facing the free blacks was that southern whites, with a few exceptions, remained irrevocably opposed to granting blacks a position of functional equality in the reconstituted United States. White racist preconceptions, fanned by the frustrations of military and political defeat, were in no way eliminated by the actual behavior of black men and women. Regardless of their thirst for learning, their acceptance of economic hardship, and their lack of political vengeance against their former masters, Afro-Americans were quickly identified as a bitter enemy to be resisted at all costs and with every means available. At first, the means employed were orderly attempts to block black political activities by court action and by peaceful petition, the same tactics used by the blacks themselves in the period before emancipation. But the whites of the South very quickly grew impatient, and since they wanted to achieve their own ends rather than a modus vivendi in any event, their methods rapidly became violent.

Best known of the white terror organizations that began to spread across the South was the Ku Klux Klan, which originated in Pulaski, Tenn. But the Klan was only one of a large number of similar groups that included, among others, the Knights of the White Camellia, the White Line, the White League, and the White Brotherhood. The stock in trade of these organizations was systematic violence for political ends. Both blacks and their white allies were intimidated, beaten, and assassinated. Racial incidents were intentionally provoked by well-prepared white forces in the manner of the bloody affair at Hamburg, S.C., in 1876. The entire state of Mississippi existed in virtual anarchy for the first half decade of the 1870s, and a single local gang in that state, Higgie's Scouts, claimed to have murdered 116 Afro-Americans. In many other parts of the South the situation was nearly as bad. Attempts by blacks to organize legal militia units for self-protection were frustrated in part by a lack of nerve in some of their white allies and in part by the open lawlessness of white groups who intercepted black weapons shipments and raided state armories. The southern whites, basing their campaign on the two pillars of economic supremacy and political terrorism, were engaged in a counter-Reconstruction of their own. They would not accept the black man's new place as outlined by the Constitution and as practiced by the black man. If blacks were to receive the help they needed in order to protect the position promised them in America's political structure, they would have to receive it from the federal government.

The situation in the North, however, was shifting quickly. Memories of the war grew more vague and the nation's worsening economic position commanded more and more attention during the early 1870s. Also crucial were alterations in the political situation. In 1868 President Ulysses S. Grant had depended for his election upon the votes of the reconstructed southern states and their black constituencies. A Republican Congress had responded to this dependency in 1870 and 1871 by passing the so-called Enforcement and Ku Klux Klan acts designed to protect black citizens. By 1872, however, in the face of continuing agitation, steady violence, and northern misgivings, the reconstructed governments began to appear as possible liabilities rather than as essential allies. When the Democratic Party made a disastrous nomination, and Grant's reelection was secured easily, the administration in Washington, D.C., began to turn its back upon the black citizens to whom it had made such hopeful promises only a few years before. In a famous response to a request for help in Mississippi, President Grant's attorney general observed that the American people were "tired of these annual autumnal outbreaks in the South," and that he would send no more federal assistance. Mississippi's Governor Adelbert Ames, who was painfully aware that these "autumnal outbreaks" were white terror campaigns at election time, recognized that with this "flippant utterance the executive branch of the

National Government announced that it had decided that the reconstruction acts of congress were a failure."

One by one, beginning in the late 1860s, the former Confederate states reverted to exclusively white rule. Though hanging onto the places promised them where they could, blacks were more and more effectively excluded by new regimes that rode to power on waves of political intimidation and economic ascendancy. As if to make obvious that the Northern people were acquiescing in this systematic undoing of their carefully established Reconstruction plans, the U.S. Supreme Court virtually nullified the racially protective aspects of the Fourteenth and Fifteenth amendments. In the case of *United States v. Cruikshank*, in 1874, a distinction was drawn between those rights protected under the Fourteenth Amendment by the federal government and those rights protected under the Fourteenth Amendment by the individual state governments. Since voting was a state right, the individual states involved should protect the constitutional rights of their citizens to vote. In white hands, however, the individual southern states had no intention of protecting the voting rights of their black citizens. In the case of *United States v. Reese*, also in 1874, the court reminded the South that the Fifteenth Amendment was framed in negative terms, that discrimination could not be legally practiced on the grounds of "race, color, or previous condition of servitude." Any other grounds, however, regardless of racial intent, such as criteria based upon whether or not one's grandfather had been an eligible voter, might be acceptable.

By November 1876 blacks clung to power only in South Carolina, Louisiana, and Florida, the last three states still occupied by the Union Army. In the rest of the South the grand plans for vital black participation in a reconstructed America were being quickly dismantled. The presidential election of 1876, contested between Republican Rutherford B. Hayes and Democrat Samuel Tilden, eventually came to hinge on the disputed electoral votes of these three states. Democrats claimed these states on the face of the ballots, but Republicans claimed that the ballots were not indicative because substantial numbers of Afro-American voters had been intimidated from going to the polls. Behind a complicated legal procedure, a political deal was struck. Included in the terms of this arrangement was an agreement by the Democratic forces to grant the disputed votes to Hayes, thereby electing him

president, in return for his prompt withdrawal of all the remaining federal troops in the South, thereby leaving the all-white Democrats a completely free hand in the internal affairs of the former Confederate states. This much of the so-called Compromise of 1877, a bargain struck at the expense of Afro-Americans, was adhered to by both sides, and it had the effect of ending the Reconstruction period of the nation's history. Reconstruction was an era full of promise and bitter with tragic disappointment. In a sense, black men and women worked in the civil rights movement 100 years later to fulfill that promise and to wipe out that disappointment. See *also* AFRO-AMERICAN HISTORY: THE FREEDMEN'S BUREAU, 1865–72; CIVIL RIGHTS: CIVIL RIGHTS CASES, 1865–1975.

REFERENCES: There is a great deal of detailed material that treats various aspects of black history during Reconstruction, including some excellent studies of the situation in various states. Three of the best volumes include: Richardson, Joe, *The Negro in the Reconstruction of Florida*, Florida State University Press, Tallahassee, 1965; Williamson, Joel, *After Slavery: The Negro in South Carolina During Reconstruction, 1861–1877*, University of North Carolina Press, Chapel Hill, 1965; and Wharton, Vernon Lane, *The Negro in Mississippi, 1865–1890*, University of North Carolina Press, Chapel Hill, 1947; Vincent, Charles, *Black Legislators in Louisiana During Reconstruction*, Louisiana State University Press, 1976. Somewhat older, though still valuable, are studies of the Afro-American in Tennessee, North Carolina, and Virginia undertaken by A. A. Taylor, which may be read in back issues of the *Journal of Negro History*. For more general works, the reader may start with either of two volumes by distinguished black historians: Du Bois, W. E. B., *Black Reconstruction in America, 1860–1880*, Atheneum, New York, 1969; or Franklin, John Hope, *Reconstruction After the Civil War*, University of Chicago Press, Chicago, 1961. A very adequate and helpful bibliography of the various aspects of the entire period was compiled by David Donald, *The Nation in Crisis, 1861–1877* (Golden-Tree Bibliographies in American History, 1969).

The Freedmen's Bureau, 1865–72 The Civil War brought freedom to approximately 4 million slaves, a majority of whom were poverty-stricken and uneducated. Hundreds of thousands of displaced Afro-Americans lacked the bare necessities of life. There was a need for a unified and comprehensive service to aid freedmen in their transition from a life of dependency to one of independent responsibility. The rendering of such assistance fell primarily to the Freedmen's Bureau created by the U.S. Congress in March 1865. The act empowered the president to appoint a commissioner who in turn could select as many as ten assistant commissioners to aid him in promoting the general welfare of freedmen and white refugees. Under the leadership of Gen. Oliver Otis Howard, the bureau furnished food, clothing, and medical supplies; established schools; supervised labor contracts between former slaves and employers; intervened to protect blacks from hostile white courts and legislators; managed confiscated and abandoned lands; and helped a few freedmen acquire land.

One of the first problems facing the bureau was the prevention of starvation. In the last months of the war and afterward, both blacks and whites in the South suffered acutely. The lack of food, clothing, and housing and economic displacement, caused by the war and emancipation, was especially distressing for blacks. Numerous freedmen had left their homes, and others, particularly the old and disabled, had been ejected from the plantations. Thousands, both black and white, were without any source of food. The bureau had no power of appropriation with which to meet these needs, but it was authorized to secure food from the commissary general of the army and clothing from the quartermaster. By August the bureau was handing out 148,000 rations daily. Between 1865 and 1869, 21 million rations were distributed, approximately 15 million of them to blacks. Each ration was supposed to contain sufficient food to sustain an adult for one week. Contrary to claims of some southern whites, the bureau did not support freedmen in idleness. Generally, rations were issued only to the obviously needy.

Closely connected with the bureau's distribution of food was the establishment of hospitals and medical centers. The freedmen were in dire need of medical care. Since they were undernourished and inadequately sheltered, diseases often assumed epidemic proportions. In Florida, smallpox was controlled only by a systematic campaign of vaccination by bureau physicians. By 1867 the bureau had established more than 40 hospitals and eventually treated nearly one-half million cases of illness. The medical department spent more than 2 million dollars in improving the health of freedmen. The bureau also established colonies for the aged and infirm, and undertook to reunite families that had been scattered by slavery and war. One of the great anxieties of many former slaves was how to reunite their scattered families—to bring back the mother, child, or wife who had been sold away years before, or who had been separated in the confusion of war and emancipation. A type of missing persons agency was established by the bureau and free transportation was provided for those returning to their families.

Another bureau duty was to try to protect black civil rights in the hostile South. One of the fundamental failures of Reconstruction was the inability or unwillingness to secure justice for black citizens. Court records reveal thousands of cases of discriminatory punishments. Freedmen were arrested for petty offenses and given large sentences while whites went unpunished for major crimes against Afro-Americans. Black men were sometimes given greater sentences for petty theft than the sentences some white men received for murder. Black Codes passed by most southern states in 1865 and 1866 discriminated against blacks. Though without specific authorization, the Freedmen's Bureau frequently intervened in cases of flagrant misjustice. It was a common bureau practice to appeal to the governor for executive clemency in cases of unreasonably severe penalties. The bureau sometimes overruled civil courts in cases where special

Upper: Tickets for rations being issued by the Freedmen's Bureau. *(Library of Congress.)*

Lower: A sewing class under the sponsorship of the Freedmen's Bureau. *(Library of Congress.)*

punishments such as whipping and pillorying were used. In a few instances, martial law was declared in more unruly counties. In May 1865 Commissioner Howard directed the assistant commissioners of each state, either by themselves or through appointed officers, to adjudicate difficulties between black and white in areas where freedmen's rights were being disregarded. Howard suggested the use of a court composed of three persons: a bureau agent, a native white, and a representative of the freedman involved. Such courts could hear and determine civil cases between blacks and whites which involved less than $300. These courts could also try offenses committed by or against blacks, provided the punishment imposed did not exceed a $100 fine or imprisonment at hard labor for 30 days.

In 1866 the bureau received specific congressional authority to protect Afro-Americans. The civil rights bill authorized bureau officials to take into district court any person they found guilty of depriving freedmen of the legal rights enjoyed by whites. When the bureau was extended in July 1866, it was given new power. Under this legislation, it could use military tribunals as well as courts. In some areas the bureau established its own courts, and when civil officials refused to act against those abusing free blacks, bureau agents often made arrests and acted as judges. These courts were used only in instances where agents were convinced that impartial justice could not be rendered in any other way. Most frequently, agents observed trials in the local courts and when they believed the decision to be unjust to black defendants, the case was appealed to appellate courts. If the appellate court verdict was considered unfair, the case could be appealed to the U.S. District Court, which was considered final. Actually, the bureau courts were seldom used after 1866. The bureau only cautiously interfered with Johnsonian governments.

Whites charged that bureau agents, in an attempt to secure justice, were partial to blacks. Such charges were rarely true. A close examination of bureau records indicates that a majority of agents made every attempt to be fair to native whites. Indeed, some agents were openly prejudiced against the ex-slaves and permitted discriminatory treatment. The bureau had only limited success in its attempt to secure justice for blacks. It was of value in seeking to obtain equal rights for freedmen in an area where two standards of justice were commonly practiced, but it

was only able to extend protection for the short period it was in existence and left little permanent benefit. Most agents were aware, even before the bureau ended, that they had not gained enough courtroom protection for black citizens from the violence of white people.

One of the most pressing problems of the postwar period was that of labor. The slave had been the chief source of southern labor, and the destruction of slavery made the creation of a new labor system necessary. Many whites still "hugged the ghost of slavery" and apparently hoped that the southern states could be restored to the Union with such loose guarantees that slavery could be reinstituted in some form. Even those who realized that slavery was dead seemed to think, nonetheless, that blacks existed to serve whites. In some areas the labor system changed little after the war. Physical punishment was still used. Many whites claimed that free blacks would not work without physical compulsion. In 1866 a South Carolina planter inserted a provision into his hiring contracts that required his laborers to call him "master," and as late as 1868 another planter drew up a contract that bound his employees "to be strictly as my slaves" in obeying orders.

The bureau immediately began to urge both employers and employees to sign labor contracts. In some areas where contracts had already been made, and the bureau considered them unfair, it pressured planters to draw up new ones. The bureau also induced free blacks to work by warning them that idleness would not be tolerated, promising fair wages, and providing transportation to areas where work was available. Some blacks were reluctant to contract for paltry wages and difficult labor under conditions not too dissimilar from slavery. Moreover, there was continually a vague rumor of land distribution among freedmen. Some were hesitant to contract for a year as a laborer when land of their own might become available. In such cases the bureau used force. "A little wholesome constraint" could not be avoided, said Commissioner Howard. Patrols were sent to towns and throughout the countryside to apprehend idlers and convey them to plantations. Even the bureau, reputedly the free black's friend, apparently believed that Afro-American men and women had no right to decide that they would not work.

After having persuaded employers and employees to contract freedmen, the bureau assumed responsibility for enforcing these agreements. Planters who failed to keep faith were sometimes taken to court, and on rare occasions soldiers were used to compel fair settlements. Many officials seemed even more eager to force blacks to keep their part of the bargain. In Florida, a free black who had reservations about working on a particular plantation was placed in a bureau jail on bread and water until he agreed to return; in South Carolina, two men accused of malingering were tied up by the thumbs. The bureau was absolutely insistent that free blacks should work.

Though the bureau undoubtedly protected black workers from dishonest employers, its activities were not unfavorable to landowners. Agents often approved contracts that stipulated low wages and permitted agreements worded in such a manner that workers could get nothing in a poor crop year. Ordinarily, laborers were paid in shares of the crop—anywhere from one-fourth to one-third. Since a majority of blacks were destitute, the planter furnished food and other necessary provisions, which were eventually deducted from the final payment. At settlement time, freedmen not only received no money, but, frequently, found themselves in debt to the planter. Many blacks preferred to work for money wages rather than for crop shares, but the wage system usually failed wherever it was tried. In many cases, employers simply lacked the necessary cash to meet regular payrolls. Other employers opposed the system on principle—wages would render the worker too independent and he would be bound to the employer for too short a period. Thus, the system of slavery soon turned into sharecropping; black men had little choice. They had to accommodate themselves to the harsh realities of a labor market over which they had little power. As economic conditions gradually grew worse, blacks were the first to suffer. When planters were in debt to merchants, and cotton prices were falling, one solution was to reduce laborers' wages and cut allowances to bare subsistence and housing to a wretched minimum. Despite bureau assistance, Afro-American farm workers sank into a position of semi-peonage. Those in nonfarm occupations usually suffered somewhat less than farm workers.

For the black man to have achieved a semblance of economic independence after the war, it would have been necessary for him to own some of the instruments of production, and in the south this meant land. The law that created the bureau had also provided that confiscated and abandoned land controlled by the bureau be rented to blacks with the option to buy. Though a few freedmen secured land in this manner, President Andrew Johnson's Amnesty Act of May 29, 1865, and his later liberal pardoning policy, which restored to owners all property except slaves, took most of the land from under bureau supervision. Some freedmen who had already settled upon and improved land (assured that it was their property) were forced to return it to original owners. In June 1866 Congress made a halfhearted attempt to provide freedmen with land by passing a new homestead act that opened government-owned lands in Arkansas, Mississippi, Alabama, Louisiana, and Florida for entry. The bureau vigorously cooperated with blacks in this enterprise. It provided locating agents, free transportation to the homestead, and sometimes free rations while land was being cleared. Within a year almost 2,500 homesteads were settled in Florida alone. Altogether, more than 4,000 families took up land under the law. Unfortunately, the homesteaders all too frequently failed. The land was often poor; white neighbors were hostile. In addition, there were certain basic necessities for successfully operating a farm and most Afro-Americans were in no position to get them. Farm implements, houses, a mule or horse, and provisions while crops were being cultivated were essential to beginning homesteads and unavailable to most freedmen. Although a few men with hard work, unusual initiative, and good luck managed to succeed on homesteads, most either failed completely or managed to eke out only a bare subsistence. The bureau has been criticized for its failure to provide freedmen with land, but there may have been little more the bureau could have done: it did not control much land. To assist black citizens in gaining economic independence, massive federal aid or land confiscation and redistribution was necessary—and Congress was unwilling to take these steps. Black folk remained a peasant class, subservient to white owners of land and wealth. And without economic independence, political independence was all but impossible.

Perhaps the bureau's most important contribution to freedmen was in education. Although the original act made no provision for educational activities, Commissioner Howard rendered what assistance he could by furnishing school buildings, free transportation, and cheap provisions for teachers. Numerous benevolent associations were sending teachers South, and the bureau was valuable in superintending and coordinating their activities. Moreover, many whites who disapproved of Afro-American education displayed their hostility through acts of violence. Attempts were made to protect teachers and pupils. In areas where whites refused to rent or sell buildings for schools and teacher housing, bureau agents gave assistance; and though they were not authorized to do so, a few assistant commissioners, notably Wager Swayne in Alabama, paid teachers' salaries. Swayne expended more than $34,000 for salaries in 1865 and 1866.

When the bureau was extended in July 1866, formal appropriations were made for Afro-American education, but the bureau still was not permitted to pay teachers. The bureau circumvented this obstacle by giving buildings for school purposes, and then paying rentals on those same buildings, which were used for salaries. Rental payments varied, but the bureau commonly paid associations operating the school $10 per month for each 30 pupils. In addition, the bureau constructed scores of schoolhouses. Almost every black college and university established during Reconstruction owes a considerable debt to the bureau. Talladega College (Talladega, Ala.) was created through aid given by the bureau. Assistant Commissioner Swayne urged the establishment of Talladega and it was only upon his promise to assist that the American Missionary Association agreed to do so. Buildings at Talladega were purchased by the bureau at a cost of $20,000. Additional funds went to the school for rent, repairs, and teacher transportation.

Commissioner Howard preferred to work through the various benevolent societies, but in areas where societies sent no teachers, local agents were responsible for founding schools. The bureau also cooperated closely with states in organizing public school systems. The state superintendent of education was often also appointed bureau superintendent of education so the bureau could pay his salary and more closely coordinate activities. After state systems were organized, the bureau frequently deeded its buildings to the local school system. In 1869, even after Florida had established a fledgling public school system, the bureau spent three times more money for education than the state did for both black and white children. During the 1866−67 school year in South Carolina, a total of $107,000 was spent for Afro-American education. The bureau contributed $25,000, benevolent associations about $65,000, and freedmen themselves gave nearly $17,000. In 1867−68 the bureau furnished $57,000 of the

$127,000 spent on black education in South Carolina. Between October 1865 and February 1870 the bureau spent more than $156,000 for black education in Alabama. During its five years of operation in the South, Commissioner Howard claimed the bureau was instrumental in initiating 4,239 separate schools that employed 9,307 teachers and instructed 247,333 pupils.

Bureau agents have been vigorously condemned for their role in southern politics. They were charged with using their offices to recruit Afro-American votes and propagandizing to gain votes for the Republican Party. It is true that many agents correctly believed that President Andrew Johnson's Reconstruction policy was unfavorable to blacks and that they supported congressional Reconstruction. But propaganda was unnecessary to make Republicans of black voters. Bureau activity was not needed to convince former slaves to support the party of emancipation rather than the party of slavery. Agents played a significant role in registering black voters, but only a small minority of agents were ever personally involved in politics.

In conclusion, it might be said that the Freedmen's Bureau was a qualified failure; it provided much needed relief and medical care; it helped establish a semi-free labor system; it provided temporary protection for large numbers of freedmen; and its assistance in establishing an educational system for Afro-Americans was one of the truly significant accomplishments of Reconstruction. However, it did not provide first-class citizenship for black folk. What freedmen really needed after emancipation was a change in white racist attitudes, massive doses of federal aid to assist in the achievement of economic independence, and a commitment by Americans to guarantee racial equality and justice. The bureau was unable to do these things under the circumstances. It did not have the necessary funds, personnel, or federal commitment. The failure of the bureau was a failure of American democracy.

REFERENCES: Abbott, Martin L., *The Freedmen's Bureau in South Carolina, 1865−1872,* University of North Carolina Press, Chapel Hill, 1967; Bentley, George R., *A History of the Freedmen's Bureau,* University of Pennsylvania, Philadelphia, 1955; Cox, John and LaWanda, "General O. O. Howard and the 'Misrepresented' Bureau," *Journal of Southern History,* vol. 19, pp. 427−56, 1953; Elliott, Claude, "The Freedmen's Bureau in Texas," *Southwestern Historical Quarterly,* vol. 56, pp. 1−24, 1962; Low, W. A., "The Freedmen's Bureau and Civil Rights in Maryland," *Journal of Negro History,* vol. 37, pp. 221−76, 1952; Low, W. A., "The Freedmen's Bureau and Education in Maryland," *Maryland Historical Magazine,* vol. 47, pp. 29−39, 1952; Richardson, Joe M., "An Evaluation of the Freedmen's Bureau in Florida,"

Florida Historical Quarterly, vol. 41, pp. 223–38, 1963; and White, Howard A., *The Freedmen's Bureau in Louisiana*, Louisiana State University Press, Baton Rouge, 1970.

The West

The Spanish Heritage* In the early years of the sixteenth century, long before any Englishmen had established colonies in the Americas, Africans and part-Africans began coming to the West Indies. Some were black Africans purchased by the Spaniards from Portuguese slave traders. Others were Christian blacks born in Spain itself. Still others were Moorish (Muslim) captives of various colors. Some of these Africans were free, but the majority were captives (slaves). These slaves could become free under a number of circumstances and were, in any case, provided with many rights by virtue of their status as human beings and subjects of the Spanish Crown.

Between 1520 and the 1560s, the number of black Africans in the West Indies increased very rapidly. By the latter date, Puerto Rico had 15,-000 Africans and fewer than 500 Spaniards; Haiti (Santo Domingo) had over 30,000 Negroes and about 2,000 Spaniards; and Cuba and the coasts of the mainland from Vera Cruz, Mexico, to Cartagena, Colombia, possessed a similar ratio of blacks to Europeans. In all of these areas race mixture occurred rapidly, with the surviving Indians being absorbed into the African and Spanish communities and with a new mulatto class developing as well.

Virtually every Spanish expedition that reached the mainland of North America included numbers of Africans of Muslim or non-Muslim background; and in the 1520s blacks became permanent residents in Mexico and the Carolinas. The latter event occurred when, in 1525–27, the Lucas Vásques de Ayllón expeditions attempted to found a colony along the Carolina coast. Indian hostility and fever plagued the Spaniards while the Negro slaves rebelled and apparently some were left behind by the fleeing European survivors. It is, therefore, very likely that these blacks intermarried with the Carolina Indians and became the first permanent non-Indian residents of what is now the United States, 80 years before Jamestown.

Africans also became early "settlers" elsewhere in North America. Several other Spanish

*The use of the term "Afro-American" in this section, unless indicated otherwise, refers to non-English-speaking blacks, an exception to common usage throughout the ENCYCLOPEDIA.

expeditions left Negroes behind who had run away or hidden with the Indians. Hundreds of Negroes accompanied the Vásques de Coronado expedition to New Mexico and Kansas in 1539–42 and several blacks remained in New Mexico. A mulatto woman was left with Indians in Kansas in the 1590s by the Leyva de Bonilla-Umaña expedition. A number of blacks may well have settled in the South during the period from the 1520s to the 1560s as a result of escaping from expeditions led by de Soto, Narváez, and others. A black Muslim survivor of the Narváez party, Estebán, or "Little Stephen," traveled with Cabeza de Vaca from Texas to Sonora and then became the first non-Indian known to have entered New Mexico. By 1565, when the Spaniards successfully founded St. Augustine, Fla., their first permanent settlement in the United States, blacks or descendants of blacks were already living with Indians in the Carolinas, Kansas, New Mexico, and probably in scatterings from Arizona to the Atlantic seaboard. From its very beginning, St. Augustine included among its population a significant number of persons of African background.

The Settlement of California In 1769 the Spanish Empire was expanded to include coastal California. Because Sonora, Sinaloa, and Baja California included so many part-Africans among their Spanish-speaking residents, it is not at all surprising that from the outset Afro-Americans played an important role in the occupation of California. The Portolá expedition, which founded San Diego and Monterey, and which explored the coast numbered among its members at least one mulatto soldier, Juan Antonio Coronel (a soldado de cuera, or leather-jacket soldier, so called because these troops wore thick cowhide jackets and carried leather shields and lances). They were crack frontier troops, used to control and fight Indians. Several mulatto mule drivers were also with the expedtion, including one who traveled alone through the strange land in February, 1770.

The Juan Bautista de Anza expedition of 1775, very important in the annals of California settlement, included seven mulatto soldiers out of a total of 29, or virtually one out of four. These and other early Afro-Americans in California blazed trails, fought Indians, suffered from near-starvation, and finally settled down to help found towns and develop ranches. All of the early African pioneers in California were free men and women, serving either as soldiers or civilian settlers. Later, in the 1790s and early 1800s, some convicts were sent to California to serve out their sentences, and of one such group in 1798, four (18 percent) were mulattos. Generally, convicts of this type had been convicted of petty crimes and soon became free men in California.

Overall, at least 20 percent of the Spanish-speaking settlers and soldiers in California in the 1790s were of African or part-African background. Since the Spaniards' position was at best precarious, with perhaps 200,000 Indians to pacify and control, the Afro-American's contribution in terms of manpower can be seen as absolutely essential.

Several Spanish settlements in California could not have been founded without Afro-Americans, since the latter constituted a large enough percentage of the settlers so that the settlement would not have been feasible without their presence. This was certainly the case in the founding of the now-great city of Los Angeles in 1781.

The Coming of English-Speaking Afro-Americans The first English-speaking Afro-American to settle permanently in California was "Bob," who arrived on the *Albatross* in January, 1816, probably coming from Boston. Baptized in 1819 as Juan Cristobal, he apparently settled at Santa Barbara and became absorbed into the California population. At the same time, the first Anglo-American white (Thomas Doak) also settled in the province.

In 1818 several Afro-Americans arrived in California as members of the Bouchard expedition, an Argentine effort to liberate the Americas from Spain. Norris or Fisher, a Negro, served at San Juan Capistrano as a cook but later left California. Mateo José Pascual, probably an Argentine Negro or mulatto, was captured by the Spanish near Santa Barbara but was later exchanged for Californians taken prisoner by the Argentinians. Still later, Pascual deserted the Argentine expedition and stayed in California. Francisco, an Afro-American, was captured by the Spanish and apparently also remained permanently in California, being absorbed into the general population.

Other Afro-Americans undoubtedly arrived in California between 1821 and 1848, many of them escaping from U.S. vessels. For example, one Afro-American ran away from the U.S. warship *Cyane* (1842). He took refuge with the Pomo Indians at Clear Lake, Calif., only to be later murdered by Mexicans in 1842, when the latter massacred a large number of Clear Lake Indians.

A black runaway who became prominent was Allen B. Light, who probably deserted from the *Pilgrim* in 1835 and thereafter became a successful otter-hunter along the California coast. Light participated in several California rebellions in the period from 1836 to 1838 and became a Mexican citizen. In 1839 he was appointed by Governor Alvarado to the post of "comisario general" in charge of the suppression of illegal otter hunting. Subsequently he settled in the San Diego region, still a hunter in 1846–48.

Advancing toward the Far West during the period from 1800 to the 1840s were numbers of English- and French-speaking fur trappers, hunters, and adventurers, sometimes called "mountain men." These rugged frontiersmen were often of racially mixed ancestry and a number were Afro-Americans. One such individual was York, the Negro who helped to keep the Lewis and Clark expedition's members alive by obtaining food from Indians in return for his performing feats of strength. Two of the most famous black mountain men, Moses "Black" Harris and Edward Rose, got as far west as the Great Salt Lake and the Oregon Country but apparently never entered California. Other Afro-Americans did, however, reach Mexican territory.

In 1826 the first overland party of Anglo-Americans to reach California (led by Jedidiah Smith) included Peter Ranne (or Ranee), a "man of color." The party traveled from the Great Salt Lake to Los Angeles. Leaving the rest of the party near Los Angeles, Smith and Ranne traveled to San Diego for an interview with Governor Echeandia and then the entire party journeyed north to the Great Central Valley of California. Some of the men, including Ranne, spent the winter of 1826–27 in California while Smith returned to the Great Salt Lake. In the latter year, Smith returned to California with a new group of men, half of whom were killed by Mohave Indians on the Colorado River. Among the dead was Polette Labross, a mulatto.

The balance of Smith's men rejoined the party left in California the previous winter, and then the combined group trekked north to Oregon. There the Umpqua River Indians killed all but three of the trappers and among those killed was Peter Ranne.

James Beckwourth, the famous mulatto mountain man and scout, never became a permanent settler in California, but he was a frequent visitor. After spending many years as a fur trapper and as a leading man among the Crow Indians, Beckwourth, from 1838 to 1840, joined with Pegleg Smith and Ute and Shawnee Indians in stealing large herds of horses in southern California (an acceptable job for a mountain man). In 1840 he married a Mexican girl in New Mexico. From 1844 to 1846, Beckwourth was back in California, taking part in a rebellion in 1845. In 1846 he stole 1,800 horses in the Los Angeles area and drove them to Colorado.

During 1847 and 1848, Beckwourth served as a scout for the U.S. Army, operating between California and Missouri. In 1847 he served as the mail carrier from Monterey to southern California, in true "pony express" style. Beckwourth was described an "an old trapper . . . , a counterpart of Jim Bridger. . . ." He participated in the California Gold Rush and became one of the first settlers in Plumas County, Calif. But in 1857 he returned to the New Mexico-Colorado region and finally died while living with the Crow Indians in 1866.

One of the most successful Afro-Americans arriving late in the Mexican period was William Alexander Leidesdorff, whose mother was a St. Croix (Virgin Islands) mulatto. From 1841 to 1845, Leidesdorff operated as a ship captain and trader between San Francisco and Hawaii. The wealth that he accumulated allowed him to purchase extensive property in still-undeveloped San Francisco. In 1844 he became a Mexican citizen and acquired a rancho grant in the Sacramento Valley. The following year he became the U.S. vice-consul, serving under Consul Thomas Larkin. Leidesdorff's business enterprises were both successful and important pioneering efforts. In 1846 he built the City Hotel at Clay and Kearny Streets in San Francisco, and in 1847 he launched the first steamship ever to sail on San Francisco Bay.

H. H. Bancroft, the historian of California, notes that Leidesdorff "was not only one of [San Francisco's] most prominent businessmen, but a member of the council, treasurer, and member of the school committee, taking an active part in local politics. . . . He was an intelligent man of fair education, speaking several languages; active, enterprising, and public-spirited." He died as a young man in 1848, one year before "descendants of Africans" were legally stigmatized in California.

Other Afro-Americans entered California with various overland parties coming from the United States. For example, one black came with the Joseph B. Chiles party in 1843, settling at Sonoma. Jacob Dodson, a free black from the United States, was a volunteer member of the exploring expeditions of John C. Frémont and entered California in 1843–44 and again in 1845. During 1846–47, Dodson participated in many campaigns against the Californians and appears to have been much relied upon by Frémont.

In the meantime, many other persons of African ancestry were moving westward, especially in connection with the expansion of slavery. As early as 1803, the population of upper Louisiana (mostly Missouri) included 1,500 English-speaking Afro-Americans or 15 percent of the population. Negro slaves were taken into Texas in large numbers from the 1820s on and kept in slavery by Anglo-Texans, in spite of Mexican laws requiring that they be set free. Other slaves were taken to Kansas during the 1850s by white southerners seeking to establish slavery in that state, to Indian Territory from the 1820s on by southern Indians, and, in smaller numbers, to New Mexico, Arizona, and elsewhere by southern slaveholders.

Free persons of color were also active in the Trans-Mississippi West, especially those with French or Spanish surnames and who had originated in Florida or Louisiana. In the area of east Texas, for example, free mulattos established themselves and were strong enough to carry on an armed struggle with some of their Anglo-Texan neighbors during the mid-1850s. Other Afro-Americans escaped from slavery by joining Indian tribes, and many of the southern Indians who came to Oklahoma were already part-African, including especially the Seminoles and Creeks. George Catlin, a visitor to the West during the 1830s, remarked that "the finest built and most powerful men I have ever yet seen, have been some of the . . . Negro and the North American Indian mixed, of equal blood. These

Far left: The West had its share of black cowboys, like this group shown at a fair in Bonham, Tex., in the early 1900s. (Courtesy of Mary Alice Pettis, from the Erwin E. Smith collection, Library of Congress.)

79

instances are rare, to be sure, yet are occasionally to be found amongst the Seminoles and Cherokees, and also amongst the Comanchees [sic] even, and the Chaddoes [Caddos]."

California Statehood and Slavery As indicated earlier, a few English-speaking blacks entered California during the early 1840s, and their number was augmented during the 1848 Gold Rush. It would appear that they did not at first suffer from any serious discrimination since California was still largely Hispano-Mexican and the gold miners were tolerant of diversity during the first few months of the "rush." The mining districts were not overly crowded, gold was abundant, and even Indians were allowed to dig for mineral (either on their own or in the employ of others). During 1849, on the other hand, the Anglo-American became dominant in the gold region and the intense rivalry for riches led to antipathy towards all non-Anglos. Indians, Mexicans, and other groups became targets for assaults, and a discriminatory society began to appear.

The California constitutional convention of 1849 marks the formal close of the era of Mexican racial tolerance. In spite of the partial objections of a few Mexican-American and Californianized Anglo-American delegates, the convention voted to disfranchise "Indians, Africans, and the descendants of Africans."

Ironically, at least one of the delegates, Antonio Mariá Pico, was approximately one-eighth African and one-eighth Indian, but he apparently kept his silence, anticipating perhaps that wealthy mixed-bloods would be able to exercise their political rights. In this he was correct, since Spanish-speaking mixed-bloods were able to hold political office for several decades, especially in southern California.

Many blacks were brought to California as slaves and were held in slavery by their owners in spite of the state constitution. The legislature did not choose to adopt any rules governing the freeing of slaves, and, thus, each case was left up to the individual court. Additionally, a number of ex-slaves were forced back into a status of slavery due, in part, to the Fugitive Slave Law, described earlier.

Many free blacks and friendly whites were able to liberate individual slaves, but it was not until 1857 that general interest was aroused. In that year, the state supreme court (under pro-southern control) ruled that an ex-slave, Archy Lee, was really free but because it was the first case of its kind to reach the Supreme Court, the white claimant could return Lee to slavery. This decision, "giving the law to the North and the Negro to the South," was denounced by many, and Lee was liberated in San Francisco—partly through the efforts of Mary Pleasants, a prominent black woman in that city. The executive committee of the Colored Citizens' Convention also raised funds for the Lee case.

It is alleged that some Negroes were maintained in a status of slavery during the 1860s, and peonage laws served to enslave Indians until well after the dates of the Emancipation Proclamation and Thirteenth Amendment.

The Negro in the California Gold Rush Several thousands of English-speaking Negroes (along with other Afro-Americans) participated in the West's greatest gold rush. At least 1,000 new blacks were in California by 1850 and more than 4,000 by 1860, but many hundreds of others undoubtedly spent brief periods of time in the state or were unrecorded by the census. During the general Gold Rush period, English-speaking Negroes constituted from one-half to one percent of the total non-Indian population, but the percentage was significantly higher in the San Francisco, Sacramento, and "Mother Lode" regions, where most Negroes were concentrated.

Afro-Americans came to California during this era by all of the overland routes as well as by sea (via Panama and Nicaragua or around Cape Horn). Many (probably a majority) were free persons of color who came west to make their fortune in mining or business. Many were slaves brought by southern whites who hoped to use slave labor in the mines, while a few were slaves who were allowed to come to California on their own (with a chance to work for their freedom or merely to earn money for the owner back home). Some were runaways, seeking their freedom in the Far West.

The initial target of most Negroes was undoubtedly the gold mining region of the Sierra Nevada foothills, but during the 1850s a trend toward residence in cities or towns is evident. By 1860 one-third of the state's Negroes resided in San Francisco or Sacramento counties while those who continued to live in the mining regions were more and more becoming artisans, cooks, and barbers rather than miners.

We do not know the precise status of the black miner after 1848 because much of the first hand testimony is contradictory. In most mining camps the miners refused to allow a man to hire (or control) another man's labor, and, thus, the use of Indian or Negro workers was ruled out (the use of hired workers or slaves would have given one miner an advantage over his competitors who could not afford hired help or who had no slaves). Southern slaveholders were, however, occasionally able to use slave labor by either congregating together in certain camps or by making it appear that their slaves were individual miners working on their own claims.

Local and state law enforcement agencies, as such, rarely interfered with the practice of slavery in California, except in a few instances where a forced return of the slave to the South was involved.

It is evident from early photographs and diaries that individual black miners were tolerated in some areas throughout the mining period. On the other hand, the general tendency was for Anglo-American miners to drive non-Anglos away from desirable locations, and cases are recorded where black claims were seized by whites. Perhaps for this reason, more and more Afro-Americans appear to have given up mining in favor of occupations that they tended to dominate in this period, such as cooks, waiters, and barbers, or serving as general laborers. On the other hand, there were a number of individual Afro-Americans and some Negro-organized mining companies that did manage to remain in the gold region and make profitable discoveries.

In the mining camps and newly-constructed towns of northern California, segregation was not always strictly enforced, and there is some indication that color lines were often obscured in the saloons and hotels, and that interracial marriages occasionally took place (the 1850 Negro population was predominantly male, which probably encouraged liasons with women of other races). Nevertheless, enough discrimination was regularly encountered to encourage the people of color to begin organizing their own separate institutions, including churches, social organizations, and newspapers. Likewise, active anti-Negro legislation led to the establishment of separate "colored schools" and protective organizations. The establishment of a distinct "Negro" or "colored" community, with separate institutions, was, however, not a unique California phenomenon but was rather an extension of northern attitudes and practices to the West Coast.

San Francisco and Sacramento were the earliest centers for organized activity by English-speaking blacks, with the years from 1852 to 1856 witnessing the establishment of Baptist, African Methodist Episcopal (A.M.E.), and African Methodist Episcopal Zion (A.M.E.Z.)

churches; an educational-cultural organization (the San Francisco Athenaeum with its own library); a newspaper (The Mirror of the Times); and private schools. Private black schools were organized in both cities in 1854 because non-white children were barred from the public schools. Gradually these, and other black schools, were supported by the local white school boards and became segregated "colored" public schools.

Education Black Californians established their own schools in San Francisco and Sacramento in 1854 and shortly thereafter these schools became segregated public schools; after 1854, most schooling for Negroes, Orientals, and Indians, when available, was segregated, but not universally. Segregation was sometimes carried to extremes, as when the Watsonville school board hired a white teacher to teach the children of its two colored families rather than integrate.

In 1859 the state superintendent of public instruction denounced what little integration existed and said that "If this attempt to force Africans, Chinese, and Diggers [Indians] into our white schools is persisted in, it must result in the ruin of our schools." The 1860 legislature responded by cutting off all state funds from integrated schools, and the 1870 legislature formally established a statewide segregated school system.

Between 1871 and 1875, Afro-Americans waged a successful campaign to eliminate the state segregation policy, winning an initial success when the legislature (in 1874) decided that nonwhite children could go to the white school if no colored school existed. Afro-American parents boycotted segregated schools, won court tests, and petitioned for integration, and after 1875, the dual school system disappeared as a *formal* element in California education.

Afro-Americans Elsewhere in the West Americans of African ancestry tended to concentrate largely in California, doubtless because the more urbanized environment of that state afforded economic opportunities not available elsewhere. Negroes were largely denied the possibility of becoming agricultural "pioneers" by adverse legislation and prejudice, and relatively plentiful Indian and Mexican labor inhibited their settlement in much of the Southwest. Nevertheless, opportunities were available in the mining industry and in transportation, and these two fields of enterprise helped to establish small black colonies in virtually every western region.

Blacks were among the first prospectors in the

Colorado mines, and they continued to be active
in mining there for several decades—a few being
able to make significant discoveries. Others were
active in mining in Nevada, Utah, British Columbia, South Dakota, and elsewhere, although
always working under more or less severe handicaps. As in California, these Afro-Americans
gradually abandoned mining in favor of urban-
style occupations or employment in the transportation industry.

Generally speaking, wherever blacks were
forced to associate with a predominantly Anglo-
American community, they were subjected to
the general pattern of Jim Crow relationships
current in the North. In a few regions, where
Hispano-Mexican or Indian attitudes persisted,
the style of life was radically altered by greater
interethnic tolerance. Two examples may serve
to illustrate this variation. In 1857 Frederick Law
Olmsted found that the Mexican-Americans of
south Texas "consort freely with the Negroes,
making no distinction from pride of race. A few,
of old Spanish blood, have purchased Negro servants, but most of them regard slavery with
abhorrence. . . . [The Mexicans] are regarded by
[Anglo] slaveholders with great contempt and
suspicion for their intimacy with slaves and
competition with plantation labor."

The Buffalo Soldiers Although largely denied
access to the riches of the West, Afro-Americans
were given an opportunity to help the white man
conquer the native Indians of the region. Afro-
American troops had performed exceedingly
well during the Civil War (some fighting in
regions west of the Mississippi), and it was,
therefore, logical to recruit Afro-Americans to do
some of the white man's fighting in the Plains
and Southwest.

In 1866 legislation was adopted that allowed
Afro-Americans to serve in the regular peace-
time army in up to six regiments of segregated
troops. By 1867 several units were operational
and were assigned to garrison duty of Oklahoma
and Kansas. Thereafter, and until 1891, they
fought with great courage and ultimate success
against Indians in New Mexico, Arizona, west
Texas, Oklahoma, Colorado, and in the Dakotas,
earning the nickname "Buffalo Soldiers,"
bestowed upon them by their native enemies.

More than 12,000 Afro-Americans served in
the Indian wars of the West, constituting one-
fifth of the cavalry assigned to that struggle.
Their heroism and fortitude never received just
recognition at the time, nor, of course, has Hollywood chosen to portray correctly the racial char-

acter of the "Indian-fighting" Army in the multitude of Western motion pictures produced in
recent decades. Most of the troops actively fighting against the Apaches over many years were
black.

Separatists Although the majority of black separatists held the view that colonies of black citizens should be formed in lands outside the United States, there were those who held that
autonomous colonies or communities should be
set up within the territorial boundaries of this
country. The West beckoned as a "safety valve"
for black frustrations; it would provide the
promise of economic opportunity as it did for
other Americans. One of the best-known promoters of the idea of separate colonies within the
United States was Benjamin "Pap" Singleton, a
native of Tennessee, who organized a successful
movement of settlers to the state of Kansas in
1879. Other settlers moved into the Oklahoma
Territory, and there began two well-known all-
black towns—Boley and Langston— as well as
several others. According to historian Arthur L.
Tolson in *The Black Oklahomans, A History:
1541–1972* (1972), the black towns that sprang
up as a result of this westward movement
included Arkansas Colored, Bailey, Bookertee,
Canadian Colored, Chase, Ferguson, Foremen,
Gibson Station, Lewisville, Liberty, Lima, Lincoln City, Lincoln (later named Clearview), Marshalltown (sometimes called Marshall Town),
North Fork Colored, Overton, Red Bird, Rentiesville, Summit, Taft, Tatums, Tullahassee, Wer-
non, Wellston Colony, Wild Cat (later named
Grayson), and Wybark.

Far left: "Westward Ho!" was the caption that appeared with this sketch in *Scribner's Monthly* in 1874. This migrant from Mississippi was one of many to settle in the West after the Civil War. *(Library of Congress.)*

not enough to initiate a period of racial justice and tolerance. On the contrary, California Afro-Americans were forced to make their way as a separate people, largely segregated in fact, if not in law.

California "custom" until after World War II required that black children, wherever numerous, be assigned to separate schools; that black teachers teach in black schools; that black swimmers not swim with whites; that black customers eat in their own restaurants; and that many kinds of occupations, such as that of streetcar operator, be reserved solely for whites. In short, California possessed a society every bit as Jim Crow as any state outside of the Deep South, but a Jim Crow society difficult to change because its forms of discrimination stemmed largely from attitude rather than law.

Within the limitations imposed by such a discriminatory social order, black Californians erected their own society (as Afro-Americans did everywhere) with their own churches, clubs, fraternal organizations, newspapers, cultural societies, and black-oriented businesses. They developed their own leadership (within the Colored Convention organization and then later in the National Association for the Advancement of Colored People (NAACP) and other more transitory groups), acquired their own attorneys, formed their own veterans' groups, and developed a full-blown black bourgeosie culture with debutante balls and all of the other trimmings of middle-class white society.

Segregation, on the other hand, was never complete in the Far West. A handful of Afro-American teachers, beginning in the late 1850s, had non-Negro pupils in their classrooms, and in 1919 Frederick Madison Roberts became the first English-speaking black to serve in the California legislature. In 1914 Bessie B. Burke became Los Angeles' first Afro-American teacher and four years later she was named principal of Holmes Avenue School.

The greatest migration of Afro-Americans to the West came after 1940, or after World War II. The first official census ever taken of blacks in the West (1850) gave their number as 1,241, compared to 178,818 whites. By 1930 the Afro-American population had increased to about 120,000, or about one percent of the total population, while that of whites was about 12,000,-000. By 1960, however, the black population had grown to slightly more than 1,000,000, largely through in-migration, or to nearly four percent of the total population. Ten years later, in 1970,

Several such towns were to develop in Mississippi. Some black leaders sought to make Oklahoma an all-black state. Edwin P. McCabe, a former state auditor of Kansas who came to Oklahoma in 1879, and who was one of the founders of the town of Langston, had ambitions to be governor of Oklahoma; he was active in the First Black Independent Brotherhood (FBIB) which like a kindred group, the Oklahoma Immigration Association, favored making Oklahoma an all-black state. Another black adherent of separatism was W. L. Eagleson of Topeka, Kans. In fact, there was an influx of blacks into Oklahoma, but it is doubtful that most immigrants had as their purpose the creation of a black state. The idea of separatism within the nation was later revived by W. E. B. Du Bois in 1940, when the phrase "the 49th State" was given currency.

Civil Rights The period after 1875 was in many respects strikingly like that which has ensued after 1965. In both cases, periods of active progress in furthering minority rights at the legislative level were followed by the grim and frustrating task of reforming white society at the behavioral and attitudinal level. The Colored Citizen's Convention, California's major Afro-American organization until the World War I era, and individual Afro-Americans found that the legal gains made in the 1863–75 period were about one-half million more Afro-Americans had been added to the West's total population; and Afro-Americans made up about five percent (4.9) of the total population.

Fleeing from poverty and second-class citizenship elsewhere, the newcomers sought jobs, decent housing, and a better life in the West (mainly in California), as did other migrants before them. However, as in other regions of the nation, migrants were victims of discrimination in jobs and housing opportunities, and they were forced to congregate in overcrowded central-city residential areas. As blacks were funneled into ever-crowding ghettoes, whites fled to often hastily-built suburbs while neighborhood after neighborhood in the central city became increasingly black. This, in turn, affected the schools, city services, police, industry (which was moving to the suburbs also), downtown business areas, and, of course, the countryside itself, which was often transformed from fertile garden or scenic hills into a series of vast, virtually all-white communities.

The effect, then, of being unprepared for the heavy in-migration of Afro-Americans has been manifold and extends far beyond the problems of the black community itself. The cost of segregation and discrimination, in other words, was borne by the total population not only in terms of expenses directly connected with serving the Afro-American community but also in terms of expenses created by that proportion of urban "sprawl" traceable to the flight of whites from racially-changing neighborhoods.

The more than one million Afro-Americans who have sought homes and opportunity in the Far West since 1940 have been forced to wage battles on many fronts, with the old fight against Jim Crow practices occupying the center of the stage for much of the period. Civil rights organizations, supported by mass black action in many cases, have been able to eliminate segregated swimming pools, theaters, restaurants, hotels, motels, and the like. Afro-Americans are now free, generally speaking, to utilize any public or privately-owned facility open to the public without restriction if they can afford it. This struggle to knock down the more visible elements in the West's Jim Crow system was, of course, immeasurably aided by national reforms along the same lines, but many local battles were won in the West by the National Association for the Advancement of Colored People and allied groups before national changes were effected.

The elimination of the more obvious forms of discrimination has, however, brought to the surface other, more fundamental problems. Basic to the latter is the fact that although black southerners have worked for more than three centuries to create wealth for the South (and the nation), the vast majority were not legally able to accumulate any capital from the first two centuries of labor and have been practically prevented from retaining any significant share of the wealth produced during the past century. In short, southern Afro-Americans migrate to the North and West with a collective work experience record in the United States of 300 years but with little or no capital accumulation.

This is to say not only that black Americans are, by and large, "poor," but also, and perhaps more significantly in psychological terms, that they are poor because they have been the victims of long-term exploitation. Frustrations and disappointments that lead to violence in the urban ghetto are, in part at least, the end product of three centuries of thwarted potentialities.

See also AFRICA: THE ATLANTIC SLAVE TRADE IN PERSPECTIVE; AFRICA: AFRICAN LEGACY / SURVIVALS; BECKWOURTH, JAMES P.; DISCRIMINATION; LEIDESDORFF, WILLIAM; POPULATION; SLAVERY: SLAVERY ON THE FRONTIER; WARS.

REFERENCES: Beasley, Delilah L., *Negro Trail Blazers of California*, Mirror Printing, Los Angeles, 1919; Bonner, T. D., *The Life and Adventures of James P. Beckwourth*, Harper & Brothers, New York, 1856; Caughey, John W., *Segregation Blights Our Schools*, Quail Books, Los Angeles, 1967, deals with problems of segregation in the Los Angeles area; Conot, Robert, *Rivers of Blood, Years of Darkness*, Bantam Books, New York, 1967, treats the Los Angeles riot (Watts) of 1965 and race relations in southern California; Durham, Philip and Everett L. Jones, *The Negro Cowboy*, Dodd, Mead, New York, 1965; Forbes, Jack D., *Afro-Americans in the Far West: A Handbook for Educators*, U.S. Government Printing Office, Washington, D.C., 1967; Forbes, Jack D., "Black Spaniards: The Spanish-Speaking Afro-Americans of the Southwest," *Phylon*, Fall 1966, pp. 233–46; Harris, Theodore H. (ed.), *Henry O. Flipper, Negro Frontiersman*, Texas Western College Press, El Paso, 1963; Katz, William Loren, *The Black West*, Doubleday, Garden City, 1971; Lapp, Rudolph M., "The Negro in Gold Rush California," *Journal of Negro History*, January 1965, pp. 81–98; Leckie, William H., *The Buffalo Soldiers: A Narrative of the Negro Calvary in the West*, University of Oklahoma Press, Norman, 1967; Littlefield, Daniel F. and Lonnie E. Underhill, "Negro Marshals in the Indian Territory," *Journal of Negro History*, April 1971, pp. 77–87; Porter, Kenneth W., "Relations Between Negroes and Indians Within the Present Limits of the United States," *Journal of Negro History*, October 1932, pp. 287–367; Savage, W. Sherman, "The Negro in the History of the Pacific Northwest," *Journal of Negro History*, July 1928, pp. 255–64; Savage, W. Sherman, "The Negro on the Mining Frontier," *Journal of Negro History*, January 1945, pp. 30–46; Savage, W. Sherman, *Blacks in the West*, Greenwood Press, 1976; and Tannenbaum, Frank, *Slave and Citizen, the Negro in the Americas*, Alfred A. Knopf, New York, 1947. See also Abajian, James De T., *Blacks and Their Contributions to the American West, A*

Bibliography and Union List of Library Holdings Through 1970 under BIBLIOGRAPHIES/BIOGRAPHIES/GUIDES.

Reconstruction to Revolt, 1877–1977 The years of Reconstruction (1865–77) were marked by a dramatic improvement in the status of blacks, who now held in their posession the right to vote and to hold office, and the promise of equality. Undoubtedly, the high point of the drive for equality came in 1875 with the passage of the Civil Rights Act, which banned discrimination in public accommodations and in jury selection. The promise given, however, did not materialize. From 1875 to 1920, race relations reached a low ebb, "the nadir," according to Rayford W. Logan in his book, *The Betrayal of the Negro: From Rutherford B. Hayes to Woodrow Wilson (1965).* Many whites in both North and South, seeking assurances against black political and economic predominance after the Reconstruction, and after the establishment of the separate-but-equal doctrine, turned gratefully to the accommodative philosophy of Booker T. Washington, who advised blacks to "cast down your bucket where you are," to educate their hands, to work diligently and with patience for the economic advancement that would in turn bring equality. To the more militant, such as W. E. B. Du Bois, this philosophy was anathema, a surrender of the hopes for political equality nurtured in the Reconstruction.

Ironically, the first spoiler of the dream of equality for blacks was the Republican Party, the party of "the Great Emancipator," Abraham Lincoln. After the election of Rutherford B. Hayes in 1877, the Republican Party abandoned southern Afro-Americans to the local white populations who, once assured that they would be free from northern interference, began a systematic curtailment of black political power. Mississippi led the way in this movement in 1890. Between 1890 and 1910, a majority of southern states disfranchised blacks. Toward this end, one of the most ingenious devices was the "grandfather clause" in Louisiana, a ruling that excused any man from meeting the stringent voting requirements if his grandfather had voted before 1867. (Of course, no blacks in the South had voted before 1867.) Disfranchisement was accomplished in many other ways: violence, gerrymandering, stuffing ballot boxes, secret shifting of polling places, muddling potential voters with extremely complicated ballots, and enforcing cumulative poll taxes.

Deprived of political power and confronted with the vindictiveness of the post-Reconstruction South, Afro-Americans faced a reign of terror after 1877. For example, between 1882 and 1900, most of the approximately 3,000 lynchings in the United States occurred in the South and most of the victims were blacks. Race riots devastated Wilmington, Del. (1898), and Atlanta, Ga. (1905). Southern politicians pilloried Afro-Americans from 1890 to 1920. One of the most infamous of the white supremacists, James K. Vardaman of Mississippi, asserted that the very idea that the Afro-American was human and thus capable of improvement was "the most damnable and dangerous doctrine . . . in America." Others,—Hoke Smith of Alabama, and Cole Blease and Ben Tillman of South Carolina—had similar philosophies.

The U.S. Supreme Court was the second spoiler of the black dream of equality. In almost every case concerning blacks after 1877, the court ruled against blacks and in favor of white supremacy. It delivered its heaviest blow in 1883, when it ruled that the public accommodations section of the Civil Rights Act of 1875, the bill that enhanced the rights granted by Congress during Reconstruction, was unconstitutional. The court concluded its anti-black record in 1896 when it ruled in the case of *Plessy v. Ferguson* that a Louisiana statute segregating railroad passengers was constitutional as long as the separate accommodations were equal. It also held that the Constitution had not intended, in the Fourteenth Amendment, "to abolish distinction based on color, or to enforce social . . . equality. . . ." In his dissent, Justice John Marshall Harlan said, "The thin disguise of equal accommodations . . . will not mislead anyone nor atone for the wrong this day done."

The third spoiler of the black dream was the communications media. Northern newspapers, magazines, and dramas attempted to justify southern oppression of blacks, seemed to approve of lynching, and, in general, took the position that blacks were stupid and morally degraded and deserved an inferior position in society. Producers and playwrights stood out in this regard. The stage Negro was irrepressibly happy; instinctively servile and loyal to whites; cowardly; stupid; and given to drinking hard liquor, playing the "numbers," eating watermelons and chicken, and flashing razors.

Scientists were worse than the playwrights. Darwinian insistence that in evolution only the fittest survive was also applied to social and international relations. Since scientists argued that Negroes were inferior, as shown in studies such as I. A. Newby's *Jim Crow's Defense: Anti-Negro Thought in America, 1900–1930* (1965), rather than trying to uplift them, many whites helped to push blacks down. One of the most detrimental of these pushes was America's late-nineteenth- and early-twentieth-century imperialistic ventures in Santo Domingo, Haiti, Cuba, Puerto Rico, and the Philippines. The relationship between America's "manifest destiny" to occupy the lands of allegedly backward colored people, and the oppression of the Afro-American was clear. If black or colored people in Haiti, Cuba, and the Philippines were too degraded to govern themselves, then Afro-Americans who were so similar to them, should not be given the opportunity to rule whites or to bring all their corrupt practices into politics.

From this background, a caste system that came to be known as "Jim Crow" permeated American life. Historian C. Vann Woodward, in his book *The Strange Career of Jim Crow* (revised 1966), stated that segregation in the South was a creation of the late nineteenth and twentieth centuries. Strikingly, southern whites were willing to live for many years with the nonsegregated patterns established during Reconstruction. For example, in South Carolina the Public Accommodations Act of 1870 was not repealed until 1889. In many states, segregation bills were defeated several times between 1877 and 1890. However, national policies encouraged segregation. As a direct result of the Interstate Commerce Commission rulings and the case of *Plessy v. Ferguson* (1896), segregated travel arrangements received national sanction. Southern-born President Woodrow Wilson reinforced that sanction. As president of Princeton University, Wilson had barred Afro-American students from the school; now he had taken these ideas with him into the White House in

1913. Almost immediately some of his cabinet officers, sometimes at the insistence of Mrs. Wilson, began segregating public facilities in federal office buildings.

Blacks reacted in several ways to white proscriptions. Barred from politics, they stressed self-help, both economic and moral, and protested in any way they could against discrimination. They attacked the Supreme Court for its 1883 civil rights decision: one Afro-American newspaper asserted that the decision proved the American government to be "a farce, and a snare, and the sooner it is overthrown and an empire established upon its ruins the better." Afro-Americans petitioned Congress for a new civil rights bill. Failing this, they began agitating for state civil rights laws in the North. In the next few years, California, Colorado, Connecticut, Illinois, Indiana, Iowa, Kansas, Massachusetts, Michigan, Minnesota, Nebraska, New Jersey, New York, Ohio, Pennsylvania, Rhode Island, Washington, and Wisconsin passed or strengthened civil rights acts. In general, the new laws barred discrimination in public amusement, travel, inns, and theaters. Nine states prohibited discrimination in advertisements.

One of the most persistent of the blacks' campaigns was the protest against Jim Crow travel arrangements. State laws were challenged in the U.S. Supreme Court, and, between 1887 and 1910, six cases were brought before the Interstate Commerce Commission. Many black leaders spoke out against segregated travel; they called it immoral, unchristian, inconvenient, tyrannical, and an attempt to fasten a badge of inferiority on blacks. Most effective was the protest against segregation on streetcars (trolleys). When most southern states or municipalities passed Jim Crow laws pertaining to local transportation between 1891 and 1909, blacks immediately stopped riding. From 1892 to 1899, Afro-Americans in Atlanta, Augusta, and Savannah, Ga., were so successful in their boycotts that the public transportation companies dropped the segregated seating arrangements. From 1901 to 1905, black boycotts were partially successful in Jacksonville and Pensacola, Fla., and Montgomery and Mobile, Ala. However, victory was temporary as white-supremacy crusades relentlessly and stringently enforced the lines of caste.

Protest by blacks continued intermittently into the twentieth century. Beginning with CORE's (Congress of Racial Equality) first freedom ride in 1947, blacks became increasingly militant in their demands for integration after World War II.

The promises and dreams of Reconstruction were actually followed by widespread repression of blacks, as shown in this photo of a chain gang in South Carolina in the early 1900s. *(National Archives.)*

Joined by sympathetic young whites, drawing pride from the liberation of African peoples, winning worldwide moral support due to press coverage and the presence of the United Nations, Afro-Americans gained a number of victories. In 1956 Martin Luther King, Jr., led a successful boycott against segregated buses in Montgomery, Ala.; Tallahassee Afro-Americans quickly followed suit. Four years later, a group of black students in North Carolina began the "sit-in movement," which led to the desegregation of facilities in 100 cities by 1962.

Two forces have influenced the black response to America: urbanization and black nationalism. In 1910, 73 percent of all blacks lived in rural areas; no American city had as many as 100,000 black residents. In 1960, 73 percent of the black population lived in urban areas and more than one-third lived in the 25 largest cities. Afro-Americans left the boll weevil and the lynch mob in the South only to face economic deprivation and increasing segregation in the North.

In spite of the deprivations and discomforts of the city, urbanization was important in the political regeneration of black America. The concentration of blacks in northern cities led to greater political sophistication. Perusing the records of the legislators from their new northern districts,they began to vote with greater discernment. In 1923 they voted against those who had

Martin Luther King, Jr., (center) leaving the courthouse in Montgomery, Ala., with Ralph D. Abernathy (left) and Bayard Rustin (right) after their arraignment in February 1956 as leaders in the Montgomery bus boycott. *(Schomburg Collection, New York Public Library.)*

defeated the Dyer antilynching bill. In 1930 they defeated two senators who had voted for the confirmation of the North Carolina racist John J. Parker as Supreme Court justice. In addition, they began to shift their political allegiance to the Democratic party; by 1936 the swing was virtually complete. Blacks first demonstrated their political muscle when they elected a black Republican, dapper Oscar DePriest of Chicago, to Congress in 1928. In 1934 Chicago's Arthur W. Mitchell became the first Afro-American Democrat elected to Congress. The urban concentration of Afro-Americans was reflected in the election of 30 blacks to state legislatures in 1946, and the election to Congress of Harlem's Adam Clayton Powell in 1944, and Chicago's William L. Dawson and Detroit's Charles Diggs in 1954. By 1967 there were six black representatives and one black senator in Congress; in 1972 there were 13. In many states black voters held the balance of power in state and municipal elections, and, as a result, they began to win more important political posts.

The political regeneration of black America was aided by successful suits launched by the NAACP against disfranchisement in the South. In 1915 the Supreme Court struck down Oklahoma's "grandfather clause." Most southern states reacted as Texas did in 1923, by barring Afro-Americans from participating in primaries, a move tantamount to disfranchisement. In the 1927 *Nixon v. Herndon* case, (not to be confused with the case of Angelo Herndon), the court struck down these voting laws, holding that to bar blacks from primaries in the solidly Democratic South was indeed disfranchisement. Still, only a small increase in registration of southern blacks was accomplished until 1947, when the court declared the South Carolina white primary law to be unconstitutional. The next year, 35,000 blacks registered in the state. In retaliation, most southern states increased the discretionary power of registrars in an effort to minimize the surge of newly eligible black voters in the 1960s.

At this time, Mississippi devised a way in which to blackmail economically prospective black voters: according to local law, the names of new voters were printed in the newspapers for several days, after which time black registrants found it difficult to find jobs. It was only after the passage of the Civil Rights Act of 1964 and the Voting Rights Act of 1965 that blacks received federal protection of their voting rights. Armed with this protective legislation, blacks elected 280 black candidates to public office, including

90 state legislators in 1964. The number of elected officeholders rose to 1,185 in 1969; to 3,979 before the November elections of 1976.

The flight of whites to the suburbs led to an increasingly larger percentage of blacks in the cities. By 1967 this new electorate had elected mayors in Cleveland, Ohio; Gary, Ind.; and Flint, Mich. In 1967, 12 Afro-Americans were on the federal bench, 7 were ambassadors, and 57 were foreign-service officers. In New York City, in 1960, many Afro-Americans held administrative and judicial positions: there were 17 black judges, 2 supreme court justices, 1 general sessions judge, 4 city magistrates, 3 domestic relations court judges, 6 municipal court judges, and 1 city court judge. In such southern cities as Atlanta, Houston, and Memphis, blacks, having voted throughout the twentieth century, were elected and appointed to important offices during the 1950s.

Despite political advances, the duality of being black in a white America lingered in the consciousness of twentieth-century Afro-Americans. The American system of caste, of Jim Crow laws, and segregation still affected their lives—in war and peace, in migrating and emigrating, finding jobs, and securing civil rights. In war, for example, blacks had fought in segregated divisions during World War I and World War II, and had shared in the glory and agony. In in-migrating (a striking phenomenon of the twentieth century) from farm to city or from South to North, there were always pressures to remain in the South. Discrimination in housing and employment and a host of other problems usually awaited the migrant at the northern terminus. Discrimination plagued him even as it had "down home" in the South, and blacks protested by every means available to them.

Angry voices were raised in a movement known as the Harlem Renaissance—a release during the 1920s of the cultural and intellectual forces that had concentrated in the great urban centers. Law and the courts were turned to for relief and adjustment. Black lawyers—the two giants were William H. Hastie and Charles H. Houston—working mainly through the NAACP, achieved brilliant successes. Outside the courts, appeals were directed to the public, in the streets and highways, in marches and demonstrations, in Montgomery, Selma, Washington, D.C., and scores of other cities. Martin Luther King, Jr., a new hero from Montgomery's bus boycott, won massive support for his dream of black-white unity, equality, and nonviolence.

But the protests, the appeals, and the dream

Demonstrators against lynching and legalized racism march by the White House in 1933. The words "Angelo Herndon" and "Scottsboro Boys" on the placards refer to two of the most celebrated criminal cases in Afro-American history. Angelo Herndon, born in Ohio and openly affiliated with the Communist Party, led a march in Georgia to protest discrimination against blacks. He was convicted in 1933 and sentenced to a 20-year prison term, under a hundred-year-old Georgia slave law, for inciting insurrection. His conviction was reversed in 1937 on appeal to the U.S. Supreme Court. The nine Scottsboro youths, two of whom were ages 13 and 14, were convicted of raping two white women. All except one of the youths were sentenced to death. However, litigation lasted for many years and included appeals to the U.S. Supreme Court, which acted favorably on behalf of the youths in two cases: *Powell v. Alabama* (1932) and *Norris v. Alabama* (1935). Careful historians of the Scottsboro affair would agree that the youths were innocent victims of racism. Two excellent studies have been made of the Scottsboro and Herndon cases, one by Dan T. Carter (*Scottsboro: A Tragedy of the American South,* 1969) and one by Charles H. Martin (*The Angelo Herndon Case and Southern Justice,* 1976). *(Library of Congress.)*

had turned into frustrated rage and riot. Afro-Americans themselves became the victims of the very cities to which they had turned for freedom and opportunity. The ghetto became a new reality on the American scene—several exploding into riots that necessitated military or police control. Throughout the period from Reconstruction to revolts, blacks maintained their churches, their organizations, their schools, and a virile press. They remained devoted to their music and dance, and to the American Dream. New creativity developed despite discrimination. In this way, the bitter historic forces of the past lived within Afro-Americans despite their new "consciousness" and "identity" in the 1960s and 1970s. *See also* CIVIL DISORDERS; CIVIL RIGHTS: CIVIL RIGHTS ACTS; CIVIL RIGHTS: CIVIL RIGHTS CASES, 1865–1975; CIVIL RIGHTS MOVEMENT; DISCRIMINATION; EDUCATION; HOUSING; LABOR UNIONS; LITERATURE; LYNCHING; NATIONAL ASSOCIATION FOR THE ADVANCEMENT OF COLORED PEOPLE (NAACP); NATIONALISM; POLITICS; POPULATION; WARS.

REFERENCES: Davis, Arthur P., *From the Dark Tower: Afro-American Writers, 1900–1960*, Howard University Press, Washington, D.C., 1974; Franklin, John Hope and Isadore Starr (eds.), *The Negro in Twentieth Century America*, Vintage Books, New York, 1967; Logan, Rayford W., *The Betrayal of the Negro*, Collier Books, New York, 1965 (a reissue with some revision of *The Negro in American Life and Thought: The Nadir, 1877–1901*, 1954); Low, W. A., "Historical Developments," Virgil A. Clift, *et al* (eds.), *Negro Education In America: Its Adequacy, Problems, and Needs*, Harper and Row, New York, 1962, pp. 27–59; Meier, August and Elliott M. Rudwick, *From Plantation to Ghetto: An Interpretative History of American Negroes*, Hill and Wang, New York, 1966, pp. 156–252; Fishel, Leslie H. and Benjamin Quarles, *The Black American: A Documentary History*, Scott, Foresman and Company, Glenview, 1976, chs. 8–12; Woodward, C. Vann, *The Burden of Southern History*, rev. ed., Louisiana State University Press, Baton Rouge, 1968; and Woodward, C. Vann, *The Strange Career of Jim Crow*, 2d rev. ed., Oxford University Press, New York, 1966.

AFRO-AMERICAN LEAGUE In 1887 journalist T. Thomas Fortune called for the formation of the Afro-American League. It was one of the great early efforts to establish a continuing, national group to work for equality for Afro-Americans. *See also* FORTUNE, TIMOTHY THOMAS.

AGRICULTURE

AGRICULTURE Prior to the Civil War, most black Americans lived as slaves on farmlands in the Southern states where they performed much of the field work in the production of the leading agricultural commodities of those states: cotton, tobacco, sugar, and rice. At the same time, they took an important part in other agricultural activities such as livestock production, logging operations, cutting of firewood, and cultivation and harvesting of fruits and vegetables. A small number of free Negroes in the South were owners of large estates on which there was considerable agricultural production. In spite of the physically and mentally depressive effects of slave labor, Negroes were often observed to be skillful farm workers, and some were credited with inventing devices for improving the processing of cotton, corn, and sugar.

After the collapse of the slave economy, black Americans in the agricultural areas of the southern United States, lacking land and capital, became primarily hired laborers and farm tenants (especially sharecroppers). Under a "stand-ing-wage system," the hired laborers worked for white landowners for a period of six months or a year prior to complete settlement of wages. Rations were issued periodically, and clothing and shelter were sometimes furnished. The wages paid the laborers (between $50 and $100 a year) were dependent upon the nature of the work performed and the amount of other necessities furnished by the landowners. This arrangement was designed to keep laborers working throughout the crop year. Under a modified form of this arrangement, the laborers were given monthly wages ($5–$7) and three or four acres of land to cultivate for their own use. There was also a plan of cropping under which black farmhands worked four days for landlords who in turn provided them with land, stock, stock feed, and farming implements with which to cultivate land for themselves in the remaining weekdays.

Sharecropping By the close of the nineteenth century, these wage-earning systems tended to be less important in Negro agricultural life than new types of farm tenancy. Foremost among these was the *sharecropping* system in which white landowners furnished black farmers land, shelter, fuel, workstock, stock feed, seed, farm implements, and one-half the necessary fertilizers. The farmers, in turn, provided labor and the remaining fertilizers, and received from one-third to one-half of the harvest. Somewhat similar to this arrangement was a form of tenancy known as *share renting*; under this system, black farmers received from landlords shelter, land, fuel, and one-fourth or one-third of the necessary fertilizers, and were required to provide labor, workstock, feed for stock, implements, seed, and three-fourths or two-thirds of the necessary fertilizers. In return, they received three-fourths or two-thirds of the total crop yield. A third type of tenancy, known as *cash renting* or *fixed renting*, called for the landlord to supply land, shelter, and fuel while farmers were required to furnish labor, workstock, feed for stock, implements, seed, and fertilizers. In return, farmers were entitled to crops less fixed amounts of produce or cash that were due the landlords. A fourth relationship between landlord and farmer was a system known as *share-cash tenancy* in which the farmers might pay for use of single tracts of land with fixed amounts of cash, produce, or labor, or proportionate shares of the crops, or by the rental of tracts of land on other bases.

Contracts stipulating the terms by which black farm tenants were to cultivate and divide crops usually made no provision for tenant credit allowances toward purchases of food, clothing, and items needed in farm work. Terms for such allowances were made separately with landlords and local merchants who secured themselves against losses by taking liens on growing crops and often upon unplanted crops. The black tenants, often only semiliterate and always socially subordinate, were compelled to pay high rates of interest for credit and to accept the rendition of farm accounts made by the landlords and merchants. After the settlement of the crop year, the tenants were likely to be indebted to their creditors. Out of this situation there grew a system of *debt peonage* under which many insolvent black farmers, unable to pay their debts from year to year, were legally bound to work for landlords until their debts were paid. This condition, equivalent to involuntary servitude, still persisted many years after it was declared unconstitutional by the U.S. Supreme Court in 1911.

In spite of adversities, black Americans continued to make advances and had become important participants in the nation's agricultural economy by the beginning of the twentieth century. Some had overcome handicaps of inadequate capital, burdensome credit, poor lands, and uncertain prices to become self-reliant tenants or farm owners. In 1910 more than 50 percent of the nation's gainfully employed Negroes were engaged in agriculture. Some 893,370 of them (14 percent of all American farmers) were farm operators. This group included 218,972 farm owners and 1,434 managers. These farm owners operated 211,087 farms in the South, 7,498 in the North, and 387 in the West. The farms held a total of 15,691,536 acres valued at $272,992,238. In the South, they tended to average 70 acres per farm with more than 50 percent of the acreage free of mortgage.

The importance of the agricultural activities of the black population of the South at the begin-

Sharecropping 1918: A cotton field near Sumter, S.C., at picking season. The woman at right has been posed on her opened sack. *(National Archives.)*

ning of the century was further illustrated by the extent to which the principal crops of this region were grown on farms operated by black farmers. Of the total acreage of staple crops in 1909, Negro farmers held the following percentages: 52.7 of cotton, 28.5 of sweet potatoes, 28.2 of dry peas, 27.2 of peanuts, 19.2 of corn, 16.2 of tobacco, and 10.6 of potatoes. The value of their yield was estimated at some $373 million. At the time, however, three-quarters of all black farmers in the South were share or cash tenants. Black-tenanted farms averaged only 40 acres in size, while those of white tenants averaged 94 acres. Similarly, the average value of their farms differed from those of their white counterparts—$1,138 and $2,732, respectively. There was also a large occupational group of black agricultural laborers in excess of 2 million persons. Of these, 57 percent were employed on home farms and nearly 40 percent worked away from homes. Of the home-farm workers nearly three out of four were female laborers.

Southern black tenant farmers and farm workers suffered from a crushing poverty and discrimination unequaled by any other group in the United States. The tenants were increasingly dependent upon excessive credit arrangements, and the laborers lived from hand to mouth, earning a few dollars whenever work was available. Both groups were compelled to live in overcrowded, flimsy dwellings, to wear shabby clothes, and to subsist on a diet of fatback, corn bread, molasses, and potatoes. During this era, Southern Negroes were frequent victims of disfranchisment and violence that continually increased their social subordination.

Decline of Sharecropping Since 1910 the proportion of gainfully employed black Americans in agriculture has steadily declined. By 1920 employment had decreased to 44.2 percent. Several factors had begun to cause a major movement of Negroes away from farm operations. For example, by 1915, cotton-field workers were being displaced because of the ravages of the boll weevil. At the same time, much agricultural activity in the lower Mississippi valley was being disrupted by unusual floods. A beginning of considerable crop diversification by white landlords resulted in the use of fewer black agricultural laborers than had been employed in cotton culture. Then, too, the increased demand for industrial labor in urban areas after the outbreak of World War I, and the lure of higher urban wages induced large numbers of Negroes to

leave the farms. Furthermore, impressions created of the northern city as a "land of promise" and a place of greater social privileges attracted many black Americans away from their agricultural life in the South.

In the decade after 1910, there was a sharp decrease in the number of black farm operators. Since 1920 the number has continued to decrease. Nevertheless, on the eve of the Great Depression in 1930, there were 882,850 black farmers, constituting 14 percent of all farm operators, while the black population represented only 9.7 percent of the total population of the United States. As in the past, 98 percent of the black farmers were in the South, although there were a few in every non-Southern state. More than 79 percent were tenants, and in the South more than two-fifths were sharecroppers. Black farm owners (15 percent of all black farmers) tended to have farms larger in size than those of tenants. The average size of all farms operated by Negroes, however, was only 14.6 acres, as compared with 176 acres for white farms. This limited acreage, however, yielded 10 to 30 percent of the South's total production of staple crops such as cotton, sweet potatoes, tobacco, corn, and Irish potatoes.

Since the 1930s, the number of black farm operators has declined markedly. By 1940 the number had decreased to 681,790 and by 1964 had fallen to approximately 200,000 or about 6 percent of the total number of all farm operators in the United States. This figure contrasts sharply with the 14 percent that black farm operators comprised in 1930. Similarly, since 1930 the number of Negro farm owners has decreased from 218,972 to approximately 100,000, and the number of farm tenants from some 600,000 to about 75,000. Of the tenanted farmers in the South, 65 percent still operate under a crop-share lease. Statistics from the latest agricultural census in 1969 continue to show a similar decline.

The decline of Negro farmers has been most noticeable in the South; whereas in 1930 nearly half the gainfully employed Negroes were in agriculture, by the 1960s only one-fifth were so employed. These trends have been caused by increasing mechanization of southern agriculture, especially in the use of the cotton picker; erosion and exhaustion of many older farmlands; the spread of cotton culture to mechanized farms in the West; more diversified land use practices in the South, including cattle and poultry production; and the persistent feeling that greater social and economic opportunities for blacks exist in nonrural areas of the nation.

Hired Farmers and Migrant Workers It is important to note, however, that the decline of black farm operators has not been matched by a similar decline in black hired farm workers. During the decade after 1954, when the number of nonwhite farmers and managers decreased by 63 percent, the number of nonwhite farm laborers fell only 14 percent, from 589,000 to 506,000. Related occupationally to this class of workers, there has existed since the 1930s a sizable number of black *migratory workers*. These migrants, often without permanent homes and always drawn from low-income groups, follow crop cycles in search of seasonal day labor. They include unsuccessful farm operators, displaced tenants, and unskilled, unemployed city dwellers recruited mainly in the southeastern United States and the West Indies. The families of these two groups of agricultural laborers are among the nation's most economically and socially underprivileged people.

Recent Changes In recent years, some individual black farmers have made progress in obtaining ownership of farms and in improving their operations. Most Negroes, however, have been struggling with farms that are too small and infertile for profitable, productive farming. Moreover, the difficulties of small-scale farming have been increased by the requirements of expensive mechanization brought on by competition from varied agricultural enterprises, At the same time, a great number of black farmers have remained shackled with the vestiges of the sharecropper system, and more than half a million black agricultural laborers continue to be among an extremely insecure labor force. Accordingly, Negroes engaged in agricultural activities today (1972) include a large number of persons considered to be living in poverty (i.e., those in families with annual incomes of less than $3,000 or unrelated individuals with incomes of less than $1,500). In 1960, for example, 88.4 percent of the nation's nonwhite farm families, compared with 47.1 percent of white farm families, were living in poverty. In the South, these nonwhite families included some 1.3 million black farm residents.

Agricultural Extension Since the 1910s, black Americans in agricultural pursuits have received varying amounts of assistance from agencies of the federal government. The oldest of these agencies, the Extension Service—conducted jointly by the Department of Agriculture and the land-grant colleges—has disseminated information concerning better methods of farming and rural home improvement to both black and white farmers. In the South, this agency employed a number of black agricultural and home-demonstration agents to give advice and guidance to black farmers and their families. These agricultural agents placed major emphasis on activities designed to produce sufficient food and foodstuffs for home use, such as the cultivation of year-round gardens and possession of poultry, hogs, and milk cows. Agents also conducted demonstrations in the growing of cotton, corn, peanuts, and other crops to improve production. In recent years, they have performed some educational work involving the explanation of various federal agricultural programs to black farmers. The home-demonstration agents organized clothing, cooking, and canning projects for farm women, and other agents have organized clubs for training farm youths in agricultural tasks.

Black agricultural-extension agents also provided important assistance to black farmers, but were severely handicapped in several ways. To begin with, they were paid lower salaries and provided with less adequate administrative facilities than white agricultural agents. Moreover, they were less numerous in proportion to the farmers to be assisted than their white counterparts. Then, too, for many years they had no significant role in planning or administering subsidy and protective programs for farm tenants and laborers, who included among them the great majority of black Americans in agriculture.

Officials of the U.S. Department of Agriculture under the Civil Rights Act of 1964 made some effort to equalize employment opportunities for black agricultural-extension workers, but the effort met stubborn resistance by southern officials of the Extension Service and failed to eliminate widespread racial discrimination in work loads, occupational classification, and promotions. Moreover, the situation deprived many thousands of black farmers of services that would help them to increase and diversify farm production and to provide their families with adequate diets and improved home management.

In a related area of agricultural education involving 17 Negro land-grant colleges, federal assistance to Negroes has been inadequate and unequal. These colleges have long needed substantial funds for an effective agricultural research program. As late as 1967, the federal allocation to these colleges for all research work amounted to only $441,000.

Federal Programs other than Extension Federal assistance to agriculture, prompted by the economic depression of the 1930s, brought some new programs by which black farmers benefited and others by which they suffered losses. The most beneficial programs were those conducted by the Farm Security Administration (FSA), which provided three forms of assistance: (1) rehabilitation loans, (2) tenant purchase loans, and (3) the establishment of resettlement communities. FSA rehabilitation loans were made to obtain credit from banks or other lending institutions. These loans, begun in 1933 and continued by other agencies, enabled many Negro borrowers to acquire livestock, seed, farm equipment, fertilizer, and other supplies that they needed to become better farm producers. Associated with these loans were relief grants that enabled many poor black tenant farmers to purchase necessary food and clothing. During the period 1935–1940, this rehabilitation program gave aid to nearly 200,000 black families. Tenant purchase loans under the FSA were given to tenant farmers lacking other sources of credit to enable them to purchase their own family-size farms. Southern blacks, who comprised 23.8 percent of the South's population during the 1930s, received 21 percent of all the tenant purchase loans made during this decade. At the same time, the FSA community resettlement program included 32 projects on which some 1,400 black families were relocated from submarginal lands to areas more suitable for farming. In general, the FSA programs, which were altered after 1940, represented well-directed steps toward aiding black farmers. They were far too limited in financial resources, however, to offer the vast and long-term assistance needed by most blacks in southern agriculture. These programs gave favorable consideration to the applications of only a small fraction of the thousands of poor black farmers who sought loans and other assistance.

The Farmers Home Administration, which replaced the Farm Security Administration in 1946, also provided considerable credit assistance to black farmers. Nevertheless, this assistance, in the form of loans and technical guidance, tended to differ from that furnished to white farmers in the same economic class. Negro borrowers were given smaller loans in relation to their net worth and received fewer loans for major farm improvements and less technical guidance in farm operations. The Farmers Home Administration also insured loans made by private lenders to black farmers for farm purchase and other expenses. Among the lenders in this program were several leading Negro insurance companies.

Federal agricultural programs, greatest in scope and financial resources during the 1930s, aggravated rather than improved the lot of the nation's black sharecroppers. These programs, carried on by the Agricultural Adjustment Administration (AAA), were designed principally to raise and stabilize farm prices through payments to farmers for restricting their acreage of basic crops. It was presumed that sharecroppers and other tenant farmers would receive payments in proportion to reduced acreage of their farms. In practice, however, this usually did not happen, since the AAA made all payments to landowners who were free to manipulate credit accounts with their tenants to the latter's finan-

The Farm Security Administration (FSA), a New Deal agency (1937–1946), offered low-interest 40-year loans to rural Southern farmers. The percentage of black recipients was just under the percentage of black farmers in the population. *(Library of Congress.)*

FARM SECURITY ADMINISTRATION AIDS THE NEGRO FARMER

THE NEGRO FARMER'S PROBLEM IS THE SOUTHERN FARMER'S PROBLEM
95 PERCENT OF NEGRO FARMERS ARE IN THE SOUTH. 47 PERCENT OF THESE ARE SHARECROPPERS. 32 PERCENT ARE TENANTS. — ONLY 21 PERCENT ARE OWNERS.

Toward

From

FARM SECURITY HELPS THROUGH ...
1. REHABILITATION LOANS FOR EQUIPMENT, LIVESTOCK, SEED, FERTILIZER.
2. TENANT PURCHASE LOANS TO MAKE OWNERS OUT OF CROPPERS AND TENANTS.
3. DEBT ADJUSTMENT TO REDUCE INTEREST, RE-SCALE PAYMENTS TO THE FARMER'S CAPACITY.
4. CO-OPERATIVE COMMUNITIES TO ENABLE SMALL FARMERS TO COMPETE WITH LARGE, MECHANIZED FARMS.

cial loss. Moreover, landowners (usually white) found it advantageous to reduce the number of their tenants and to hire wage laborers in their place in order to keep a larger share of the AAA payments for reduced acreage. Consequently, some 192,000 Negro tenants were forced off farms during the 1930s and were drawn increasingly to urban ghettos. In a sense, these programs of the AAA, central to the New Deal, were disastrous to black farmers.

In later years, the Agricultural Stabilization and Conservation Service and other bureaus charged with administering agricultural production stabilization programs likewise failed to bring about the equal participation of black farmers. Typically, Negroes have been given smaller acre projections of crop yields than whites and, thus, have received smaller yields subsidy payments. Negro farmers have received inadequate information concerning stabilization program rules and alternatives to the use of land for cotton. Only since the 1960s have steps been taken to eliminate discriminatory practices in nominations and elections for the county committees that administer the stabilization programs; only recently have blacks been employed in county and state program offices. The Farm Credit Administration, established in 1933, provided relief for a few black farm owners but gave little aid to most farm tenants and laborers. It made available long-term, low-interest loans to farmers who could offer first mortgages on farm property as security. Tenants could not offer such mortgages and were normally only eligible for possible short-term production credit if they could promise security from unencumbered mortgages on chattel property or crops. Most black tenants did not own chattel property and were usually unable to persuade landlords to waive first liens on their crops. These requirements for loan security made impossible most credit assistance to black farmers.

In the 1970s the picture of the black farmer continued to be dismal. The farm population continued to decline among owners, operators, tenants, and sharecroppers due primarily to: (1) the high cost of farm operation; (2) greater mechanization; (3) lack of available capital; (4) the continued absence of government assistance; and (5) and the growth of the agro-industrial complex, which affects all agricultural life in America.

Decline of Land Ownership The decline of Afro-Americans in agriculture is vividly revealed in the decline of black-owned land, reflected by the drastic desertion of farms for urban living. Since 1950, blacks have lost half of their land. In 1950 black Americans held about 12 million acres of farmland; in 1969 they held 5.5 million acres. These 5.5 million acres represented 79,000 farms owned and operated by blacks, and 17,000 farms run by black tenant farmers. The decline in ownership was dramatic in the 11 states of the former Confederacy, which, until 1930, contained the preponderant bulk of the black population. Many blacks sold their land—some were swindled or persuaded to sell—and then moved to urban areas. The decline reflects a fundamental social and economic phenomenon in Afro-American life, namely, the exchange of economic instability and the deterioration of an older rural order in the South for a questionable living in the urban ghetto. Though farming has ceased to be a profitable investment for most blacks, investment in ghetto living has proved to be often as precarious. *See also* AFRO-AMERICAN HISTORY; DISCRIMINATION; POPULATION; POVERTY.

REFERENCES: There is no single, definitive reference on Afro-Americans in agriculture. There are, however, many important sources. Among them are the various censuses of agriculture. The bibliographic resources of the cooperative project of the Agricultural History Branch of the U.S. Department of Agriculture and the Agricultural History Center, University of California at Davis, are the best available. Some older published lists of references still available are "A List of References for the History of Agriculture in the United States, 1790–1840," by Douglas E. Bowers; "A List of References for the History of Agriculture in the Southern United States, 1865–1900," by Helen H. Edwards; "A List of References for the History of Agriculture in the Mountain States," by Earl M. Rogers; and "A List of References for the History of the Farmer and the Revolution, 1763–1790," by Douglas E. Bowers. More recent (1973) are "A List of References for the History of Agriculture in the Midwest, 1840–1900," compiled by Douglas E. Bowers and James B. Hoehn, and "A List of References for the History of the Farmers' Alliance and the Populist Party," compiled by Henry C. Dethloff. Multilithed, a fourteenth section (116 pp.) of this comprehensive bibliography, entitled *A List of References for the History of Black Americans in Agriculture, 1619–1974*, was compiled by Joel Schor and Cecil Harvey, 1975. Four books that provide general treatments of southern agriculture and life are Gray, Lewis C., *History of Agriculture in the Southern United States*, Washington, D.C., 1933; Raper, Arthur F., *Preface to Peasantry*, University of North Carolina Press, Chapel Hill, 1936; Tindall, George B., *The Emergence of the New South, 1913–1945*, Louisiana State University Press, Baton Rouge, 1967; and Woodward, C. Vann, *The Origins of the New South, 1877–1913*, Louisiana State University Press, Baton Rouge, 1951. A good specialized study of peonage is Pete Daniel, *The Shadow of Slavery: Peonage in the South, 1901–69*, University of Illinois Press, 1972.

AILEY, ALVIN (1931–   ), choreographer; born in Rogers, Tex. Ailey gained international recognition after the founding of the Alvin Ailey City Center Dance Theater in 1958. Between 1971 and 1973 he choreographed nine new works for his company. In 1966 Ailey created the dances for Samuel Barber's opera *Antony and Cleopatra,* which opened the new Metropolitan Opera House in Lincoln Center in New York City. He choreographed and collaborated on the musical staging of Leonard Bernstein's *Mass,* which officially opened the John F. Kennedy Center for the Performing Arts in Washington, D.C. (1972). Ailey's international tours have taken his company to six continents, to nearly every European country, and to the Soviet Union. He has received honorary degrees of doctor of fine arts from Cedar Crest College and Princeton University. *See also* DANCE.

ALABAMA AGRICULTURAL AND MECHANICAL (A & M) UNIVERSITY Alabama Agricultural and Mechanical (A & M) University, at Normal, Ala,, was founded in 1875 as a teaching–training (normal) school. A state-supported, land-grant institution, its eight coeducational schools are situated on a campus of 650 acres. The university offers bachelor's and master's degrees and provides liberal arts, teacher education, and vocational curricula. Its enrollment in 1975 was about 3,500. It granted 480 degrees, of which 120 were master's, in 1974.

Beginning in 1876, and for many years thereafter, the school was influenced by its executive head, William Hooper Councill (born of slave parents), a prominent educator, editor, and associate of Booker T. Washington.

ALABAMA CHRISTIAN MOVEMENT FOR HUMAN RIGHTS (ACMHR) The ACMHR was founded in 1956 under the leadership of the Rev. Fred L. Shuttlesworth and Rev. Vernon Johns, both Baptist ministers (Shuttlesworth at the First Baptist and Bethel Baptist Church in Birmingham, Ala., and Johns at the Dexter Avenue Baptist Church in Montgomery, Ala.). Shuttlesworth, a veteran civil rights leader in Baltimore, was the organizer and first president of the ACMHR. As president, he organized demonstrations at such public facilities as lunch counters—demonstrations that led to rioting and bloodshed, and, in turn, new protest for government action and legislation. ACMHR was operative between 1956 and 1962. It was the forerunner of the Montgomery Improvement Association (MIA), which was later succeeded by the Southern Christian Leadership Conference (SCLC). Coming to the Dexter

Avenue Baptist Church, Martin Luther King, Jr., an organizer of both the MIA and the SCLC, found a responsive and supportive atmosphere that had been created, in part, by his predecessors, Shuttlesworth and Johns. *See also* CIVIL RIGHTS MOVEMENT; MONTGOMERY IMPROVEMENT ASSOCIATION (MIA); SHUTTLESWORTH, FRED LEE; SOUTHERN CHRISTIAN LEADERSHIP CONFERENCE (SCLC).

ALABAMA STATE COLLEGE *See* ALABAMA STATE UNIVERSITY.

ALABAMA STATE COLLEGE FOR NEGROES *See* ALABAMA STATE UNIVERSITY.

ALABAMA STATE COLLEGE MOBILE CENTER *See* MOBILE STATE JUNIOR COLLEGE.

ALABAMA STATE UNIVERSITY Alabama State University, at Montgomery, Ala., was founded at Salem in 1874 as the State Normal School and University for Colored Students and Teachers, largely through the efforts of William Burns Patterson. It was the first state-supported institution for the training of black teachers in the United States. The coeducational university continues to serve as a teacher education and liberal arts institution. By the mid-1970s about two-thirds of all Afro-American teachers in Alabama were graduates of the university. In 1975 its enrollment was about 3,900; in the previous year, it granted 449 bachelor's and 115 master's degrees.

In 1887 the school was moved from Salem to Montgomery, and its name was changed to the State Normal School for Colored Students. Before 1969, when the school acquired university status, it was also known by three other names: State Teachers College, Alabama State College for Negroes, and Alabama State College. The changes in name reflect, in part, the upgrading of the curriculum. Alabama State has evolved from a teacher education institute, with a staff numbering fewer than 20, to a multipurpose university of 400 faculty and support persons.

ALBANY BIBLICAL AND MANUAL TRAINING INSTITUTE *See* ALBANY STATE COLLEGE.

ALBANY STATE COLLEGE Albany State College, at Albany, Ga., was founded in 1903 as the Albany Biblical and Manual Training Institute.

The institution is urban and state-supported, offers the bachelor's degree, and provides liberal arts and teacher education curricula. Its 1973 enrollment was 1,926.

The coeducational school traces its origins to Dr. Joseph Winthrop Holley, a Lincoln University (Lincoln University, Pa.) educator who came to Albany seeking aid in the establishment of a school for Afro-American youth. With the financial help of the Hazard family of Rhode Island, and several of the leading white citizens of Albany, Holley founded and maintained the institute. He remained its president until 1943. In 1917, however, the state of Georgia assumed responsibility for the college's operation, and its name was changed to Georgia Normal and Agricultural College. In 1943, the school was upgraded to a four-year curriculum, becoming a degree-granting institution in the fields of elementary education and home economics. At that time its name was changed to Albany State College, In 1970 the college's academic structure was again completely reorganized into three main divisions: arts and sciences, business, and education.

ALBERT, ROBERT L. (1928–   ), educational consultant, business executive; Born in New York, N.Y. Albert is the president of Robert L. Albert & Associates in Sudbury, Mass., a consultant firm on matters in higher education, that is particularly active in eliminating discrimination on the basis of sex and race in higher institutions. Albert received his college training at the University of Washington. He is a special assistant to the president of Tufts University and also the director of Equal Opportunity Intergroup Relations at Tufts.

ALCORN STATE UNIVERSITY Alcorn State University, at Lorman, Miss., was founded in 1871 as a land-grant institution and named in honor of a Reconstruction governor of the state. Known until the 1970s as Alcorn Agricultural and Mechanical (A & M) College, Alcorn is the oldest land-grant college for Afro-Americans in the United States. A state-supported institution, Alcorn has consistently provided programs in land-grant education, though not to the exclusion of offerings in liberal arts and teacher education. With about 100 buildings situated on a campus of 239 acres, the college has nearly 1,500 additional acres devoted to agricultural purposes. In 1975 its enrollment was approximately

2,500; 542 bachelor's degrees were awarded the previous year.

ALDRICH, JAMES THOMAS (1894–1968), physician. Aldrich received his M.D. degree from Meharry Medical College (Nashville, Tenn.) in 1920. He became president of the National Medical Association, chairman of its board of trustees, and speaker of its house of delegates, one of two men in the history of the association to have held all three posts. *See also* NATIONAL MEDICAL ASSOCIATION (NMA).

ALDRIDGE, IRA F. (ca.1805–67), actor. A leading Shakespearean actor of the nineteenth century, Aldridge was born in obscurity. His birthplace has been variously reported as Africa, New York City, and Maryland, and his date of birth anywhere from 1804 to 1807. It is somewhat more certain that he attended the African Free School in New York City, married an English woman and later a Swedish opera singer, and

Far right: Ira Aldridge as Aaron in Titus Andronicus: *Act 4, scene 2: "He dies upon my scimetar's sharp point / That touches this my first-born son and heir!" (Museum of the City of New York, Theatre and Music Collection.)*

had three children. In 1821 he joined an African theater company in New York City, after which he moved to Europe. He studied in Glasgow, and then in 1826 began a stage career, at first in the provinces and then in London and on the Continent that lasted until 1865. He gave command performances before, and was honored by, the monarchs of Sweden, Prussia, Austria, and Russia. His best-known portrayal, Othello, was never seen on stage in America. He died in Poland while arrangements were being made for an American tour. *See also* LITERATURE: DRAMA/ THEATER.

ALEXANDER, ARCHIE (1888–1958) engineer, governor; born in Des Moines, Iowa. Alexander received a B.S. degree in civil engineering from the University of Iowa in 1912. He studied at the University of London, and in 1914 became a designer for Marsh Engineering, Co. Soon thereafter he opened his own construction business for large-scale construction jobs such as highways, municipal power and sewer plants, and bridges. Among the bridges his firm built is the Tidal Basin Bridge in the District of Columbia. In 1954 President Dwight D. Eisenhower appointed Alexander governor of the Virgin Islands of the United States. He was the second Afro-American to hold this post.

ALEXANDER, BENJAMIN H. *See* SCIENTISTS: BIOLOGICAL, PHYSICAL.

ALEXANDER, CLIFFORD L., JR. (1933–), lawyer, government official; born in New York, N.Y. Alexander received a B.A. degree from Harvard University in 1955 and his LL.B. degree from Yale Law School in 1958. Following two years as assistant district attorney for New York County, he became program and executive director of Harlem Youth Opportunities Unlimited, Inc., in 1962. In 1965 he was appointed associate special counsel to President Lyndon B. Johnson, and a year later deputy special counsel. He became chairman of the Equal Employment Opportunity Commission in 1967, but was fired two years later by the new Nixon administration. Later in 1969 Alexander accepted a partnership with the law firm of Arnold and Porter in Washington, D.C. In 1974 he ran for mayor of that city but lost to Walter Washington. In 1977 Alexander was appointed Secretary of the Army by President Carter.

ALEXANDER, LESLIE L. (1917–), physician; born in Jamaica, British West Indies. Alexander received B.A. and M.A. degrees from New York University, and his M.D. degree from Howard University Medical College (Washington, D.C.) in 1952. He served as acting chairman of the department of radiology, and director of the division of radiation therapy and nuclear medicine, Kings County Hospital Center, and professor of radiology, College of Medicine, State University of New York Downstate Medical Center.

ALEXANDER, MARGARET WALKER (1915–), poet; born in Birmingham, Ala. Alexander received a B.A. degree from Northwestern University (Evanston, Ill.) in 1935, and her M.A. degree from the University of Iowa in 1940. In the 1940s she served on the faculties of Jackson State College (Jackson, Miss.) and Livingstone College (Salisbury, N.C.). Her first book of poems, *For My People* (1942), won the Yale Younger Poets competition. Her first novel, *Jubilee* (1966), won a Houghton–Mifflin Literary Fellowship. She received a Rosenwald Fellowship in 1944. Her other books include *Prophets for a New Day* (1970) and *October Journey* (1973). In 1968 Alexander became director of the Institute for the Study of the History, Life, and Culture of Black People at Jackson State College.

ALEXANDER, RAYMOND PACE (1898–1975), lawyer, judge; born in Philadelphia, Pa. Alexander graduated from the University of Pennsylvania with a B.S. degree in economics in 1920, and received his LL.B. degree from Harvard Law School in 1923. He was admitted to the Pennsylvania bar in 1923, and he quickly established a fine reputation for his civil and criminal trial practice. He served as counsel to many important church, civic, and government groups and, from 1952 to 1958, was active in civic and public affairs as a member of the city council of Philadelphia. Alexander served as co-founder and editor of the *National Bar Journal*; as national director of the March of Dimes and the Free Europe Committee; and as board member of such organizations as the Young Men's Christian Association (YMCA) and the Young Women's Christian Association (YWCA), the Philadelphia Grand Opera Company, the Philadelphia Council of Churches, and the Crime Prevention Association. In 1959 he became judge of the court of common pleas in Philadelphia, and 11 years later, in 1970, he was appointed senior judge of that court. Many of his decisions on the bench became landmarks; one of them, the Community Legal Services, Inc., case, opened the way for government subsidized legal services for persons unable to pay for them. He received honorary degrees from several universities. His papers are housed at the Amistad Research Center, Dillard University (New Orleans, La.).

Clifford L. Alexander, Jr. *(U.S. Army Photograph.)*

ALEXANDER, SADIE TANNER MOSSELL (1898–   ), lawyer; born in Philadelphia, Pa. Alexander received a B.S. degree (1918), an M.A. degree (1919), a Ph.D. degree (1921), and her LL.B. degree (1927) from the University of Pennsylvania; she was the first black woman to be awarded a law degree by the University of Pennsylvania. She married Raymond Pace Alexander in 1923. Admitted to the Pennsylvania bar in 1927, she was also the first woman to practice law in Pennsylvania. As a young lawyer in 1921, she authored a study entitled "Standards of Living Among 100 Negro Migrant Families in Philadelphia." From 1928 to 1930 she was assistant city solicitor in Philadelphia; she resumed that post from 1934 to 1938. In 1946 Alexander was appointed a member of the President's Committee on Civil Rights, and later she was named by President John F. Kennedy as a member of the Lawyers Committee on Civil Rights. Her affiliation with the American Civil Liberties Union was long-lived, ranging from membership on the National Advisory Council to membership on the board of directors of the Greater Philadelphia branch.

ALEXANDER, SANFORD *See* NEWSPAPERS: CONTEMPORARY.

ALEXANDER, WALTER GILBERT (1880–1953), physician; born in Lynchburg, Va. Alexander received a B.A. degree from Lincoln University (Lincoln University, Pa.) in 1899, and his M.D. degree from the College of Physicians and Surgeons (Boston, Mass.) in 1903. He practiced medicine in West Virginia (1903–04) and in Orange, N.J., after 1904, where he later became assistant city physician in 1935. Alexander was appointed to the New Jersey state board of health, and he served as state vice-president and president (in 1926) of the National Medical Association.

ALI, MUHAMMAD (CASSIUS CLAY) (1942–   ), pugilist; born in Louisville, Ky. As an amateur fighter, Ali was the winner of the Golden Gloves and Amateur Athletic Union (AAU) titles and the Olympic Games light heavyweight championship in 1960, the year he became a professional. In 1964 Ali won the professional heavyweight championship from a heavily favored Charles "Sonny" Liston, whom he knocked out in seven rounds, and whom Ali defeated even more decisively the next year. Ali adopted the Black Muslim faith in 1957 and took the name

Muhammad Ali in 1964. He was barred from the ring for four years and stripped of his heavyweight title because of conscientious objection, on religious grounds, to serving in the armed forces. A court order in 1970 overturned his suspension from boxing, and in that year he launched a remarkable comeback. Though he lost

to Joe Frazier in a title match in 1971, Ali regained the championship in 1974, at the age of 32, by knocking out George Foreman in eight rounds. In 1978, he lost his title to Leon Spinks but regained it before his retirement in 1979. One of the most idolized fighters of all time, especially in black communities, Ali was known for his witty poetry and rhymes and his outspoken opposition to racism. *See also* ATHLETES; MUSLIMS.

ALI, NOBLE DREW (TIMOTHY DREW) (1886–?), religious leader, cultist; born in North Carolina. With little formal religious training, Ali established his first temple in Newark, N.J., in 1913 and later founded other temples in Pittsburgh, Pa.; Detroit, Mich.; and Chicago, Ill. The Chicago temple, known as the Moorish Science Temple of America, was the most famous. Ali taught initiates the necessity of nationality. Upon becoming a full member, the initiate was given an identification card showing symbols for

Far right: Muhammad Ali regained the world heavyweight boxing championship in his bout in Zaire with George Foreman on October 30, 1974. (Sonia Katchian.)

Allah, Islam, and Unity, with the following inscription:

This is your Nationality and Identification Card for the Moorish Science Temple of America, and Birthrights for the Moorish Americans, etc. We honor all divine prophets, Jesus, Mohammed, Buddha and Confucius. May the blessings of the God of our Father Allah, be upon you that carry this card. I do hereby declare that you are a Moslem under the Divine Laws of the Holy Koran of Mecca, Love, Truth, Peace, Freedom, and Justice.

"I AM A CITIZEN OF THE U.S.A."
NOBLE DREW ALI, THE PROPHET, 3603 INDIANA AVE., CHICAGO, ILL.

Circumstances surrounding his death remain obscure, but speculation holds that he was a victim of a power struggle. His movement split into various factions after his death. See also MUSLIMS.

ALLEN, ARIS T. (1910–   ), physician, state legislator; born in San Antonio, Tex. Allen received his M.D. degree from Howard University Medical College (Washington, D.C.) in 1944, and then completed further studies at the University of Buffalo and at Harvard University. He served in the U.S. Air Force (1953–55), and was a member of the Maryland state legislature after 1966. He served on the board of directors of the Bank and Trust Co. of Annapolis, Md., and on numerous civic and professional boards. In 1977 he was elected to chair the Maryland Republican Committee. He ran for Lieutenant Governor the following year but was defeated.

ALLEN, HENRY JAMES, JR. (RED) (1900–69), jazz trumpeter; born in Algiers, La. Allen first studied the violin with Peter Bocage, later abandoning it in favor of the trumpet. In 1917 he joined King Oliver in St. Louis, Mo., at the start of a long career that included stints with many jazz greats (Walter "Fats" Pichon, pianist; Louis Russell; Fletcher Henderson; Lucky Millinder; and Louis Armstrong). Allen formed his own orchestra in 1941. His tours included one of Europe in 1959 with Kid Ory and another in 1964. See also MUSIC: JAZZ.

ALLEN, MILTON B. (1917–   ), lawyer, public official; born in Baltimore, Md. Allen received a B.A. degree from Coppin State College (Baltimore, Md.) in 1938, and a LL.B. degree (1941) and his J.D. degree (1971) from the University of Maryland Law School. He practiced law in Baltimore for 25 years. In 1970 Allen was elected state's attorney for Baltimore, where he supervised a staff of 90 assistant state's attorneys. He has served on the governor's commission on law enforcement. Allen was appointed to the Baltimore Superior Court in 1976.

ALLEN, RICHARD (1760–1831), clergyman, bishop; born in Philadelphia, Pa., Allen was the founding bishop of the African Methodist Episcopal (AME) Church. The AME Church was the first major black institution in America, and Allen was the first major leader of Afro-Americans in the United States. Born of slave parentage, he grew up in slavery in Delaware and became a zealous Methodist minister whose many converts included his master, who let him buy his freedom. Allen settled in Philadelphia about 1786, where he brought so many Afro-Americans into St. George's Methodist Church that friction soon developed in the church between whites and blacks. He proposed a separate church for blacks and by 1787 had formed the Free African Society, one of the first official organizations of Afro-Americans. It was dedicated to self-improvement and advancement. In the same year, whites segregated blacks by assigning them to the gallery at St. George's Church. Allen and Absalom Jones led an exodus of black parishioners from that church, and Jones and members of the Free African Society established St. Thomas's Free African Church within the Protestant Episcopal Church. Allen, in turn, formed the Bethel African Methodist Episcopal Church (Mother Bethel). He was ordained a bishop in 1799. After winning a court case in 1816, he gained complete independence for his congregation and legally established the AME Church. See also AFRICAN METHODIST EPISCOPAL (AME) CHURCH; ALLEN UNIVERSITY; METHODISTS; RICHARD ALLEN CENTER FOR CULTURE AND ART.

ALLEN, SAMUEL W. (pseud. PAUL VESEY) (1917–   ), lawyer, folklorist, poet; born in Columbus, Ohio. After having studied at Fisk University (Nashville, Tenn.) and the Sorbonne, Allen received his LL.D. degree from Harvard Law School. His first book, a collection of poetry entitled Elfenbeinzaehne (Ivory Tusks), was published under the name of Paul Vesey in Germany in 1956. In his role as a lawyer, he was assistant general counsel in the legal department of the United States Information Agency and worked with the Community Relations Service of the Department of Justice. His literary career continued as English editor of the magazine

Presence Africaine and as lecturer in colleges throughout the country. He soon became a poet in residence at Tuskegee Institute (Tuskegee Institute, Ala.) and later Avalon Professor of Humanities (an endowed chair for creative work) at Tuskegee. He then went to Boston University as professor of English in African literature. His works include *Pan-Africanism Reconsidered* 1962, coeditor; *Ivory Tusks and Other Poems,* 1968; and *Poems From Africa* (1973), editor.

ALLEN UNIVERSITY Allen University, at Columbia, S.C., was founded in 1870 as Payne Institute, in Cokesbury, S.C., by the African Episcopal (AME) Church. A private coeducational school, it grants the bachelor's degree and provides liberal arts and teacher education curricula. Its 1975 enrollment was about 460.

The school was originally named after Daniel Alexander Payne (1811–93), an apostle of Afro-American education. In 1880 the church voted to transfer the institute to a more central location at Columbia. A charter was procured and the institute was renamed Allen University in honor of Bishop Richard Allen (1760–1831), founder of the AME Church—the first church in the United States entirely controlled and supported by Afro-Americans. Allen University was the first institution of higher learning for Afro-Americans in South Carolina. During its early years, however, it had to serve its students at all educational levels from law, theology, and the arts to elementary school subjects. At one time, a student might enter Allen at first-grade level and leave as a college graduate. The grammar school was discontinued in the mid-1920s, and the high school ended with the graduating class of 1929. *See also* ALLEN, RICHARD; PAYNE, DANIEL ALEXANDER.

ALLEN, WILLIAM DUNCAN (1908–), pianist, educator; born in Portland, Oreg. Allen received his musical education at the Oberlin Conservatory of Music (Oberlin, Ohio), the Juilliard School of Music (New York, N.Y.), and Columbia University. He was instructor of piano at Howard University (Washington, D.C.) from 1929 to 1935, and at Fisk University (Nashville, Tenn.) from 1936 to 1943. Allen then became accompanist for Todd Duncan, baritone, and he also gave many recitals in the United States and abroad.

ALLEN, WILLIAM EDWARD (1903–), physician; born in Pensacola, Fla. Allen received a B.S. degree from Howard University (Washington, D.C.) in 1927 and his M.D. degree from Howard University Medical College in 1930. He was resident in radiology at City Hospital, St. Louis, Mo., and a member of the American College of Radiology in 1940. After military service, he became a fellow of the college in 1945. Allen was a consultant in roentgenology and radiology at the University of Missouri from 1950 to 1959; instructor in radiology at St. Louis University School of Medicine; a member of the department of radiology, St. Louis University Hospitals; and a member of the board of directors, St. Louis Institute of Medical Education and Research. Allen received the Distinguished Service Medal of National Medical Association (NMA) in 1967.

ALSTON, CHARLES *See* ARTISTS.

AMERICAN CIVIL LIBERTIES UNION (ACLU) The ACLU was founded in 1920 by whites whose stated aim was to "champion the rights of man set forth in the Declaration of Independence and the Constitution." Its activities have been mainly legal and have encompassed many varieties of court cases and public protests. Among its landmark test cases were the Scopes trial in the 1920s, and the case involving the right of school children of the Jehovah's Witnesses to refuse to salute the flag. In the field of black civil rights, it fought civil rights cases all over the country involving such issues as jury service, freedom to demonstrate, voting rights, and jury representation. In the five-year period 1964–69, its newly formed Southern Regional Office litigated more than 160 cases in the South, and won 69. In the 1970s, the ACLU's activities encompassed an even broader spectrum of legal and moral fights: government intrusion of privacy by surveillance; rights of prisoners, women, and homosexuals; freedom of the press; and amnesty for draft evaders. Signaling the wide interests of the organization is its large variety of committees: academic freedom, church-state, communications media, due process, equality, free speech association, labor/business, and privacy. Claiming to be the oldest of the civil rights organizations the ACLU has expanded through the years to 46 states and has grown to have an annual budget of $5.5 million. In 1973 its executive director was Areyh Neier, and its chairman, Edward J. Ennis.

AMERICAN COLONIZATION SOCIETY Founded in 1816, the purpose of the society was to send free blacks to Africa. With headquarters in Washington, D.C., the society was the first positive attempt to carry out an old idea common to many whites but to only a few blacks—to return blacks to their "ancestral home." The founders and first members, often motivated by humane as well as utilitarian impulses, were men of wealth and education, and included Henry Clay, senator; Francis Scott Key, attorney and author of the "Star Spangled Banner"; and Bushrod Washington, a judge and relative of George Washington.

The society's efforts resulted in the founding in 1821 of a colony known as Liberia (after "liberty") in West Africa. Its first principal settlement was on Cape Mesurado. Monrovia, the capital city, was named after President James Monroe. After many difficulties under the leadership of the society's energetic and colorful agent, Jehudi Ashmun, for whom Lincoln University (Lincoln University, Pa.) was originally named, the colony survived both internal and external pressures and eventually became, in 1847, the Republic of Liberia. The name of one of its counties, Maryland County, reflects both the connection with the border state that sent over its emancipated slaves as settlers, and also the efforts of white sponsors of the Maryland State Colonization Society, whose story is told by Penelope Campbell in her book, *Maryland in Africa: The Maryland State Colonization Society, 1831–1857* (1971).

Besides actually financing the first Liberian settlement, the society encouraged emigration through correspondence and through its official publication, *African Repository*. The society also worked toward the manumission of slaves and the suppression of the slave trade. Records of its activities can be studied in the Library of Congress where about 190,000 letters, reports, accounts, and financial records are housed.

Though free blacks generally opposed the society in its main program of colonization (slaves, in contrast, favored *any* movement against bondage), the society successfully sent over several thousand settlers and encouraged more to migrate. It published the number of actual settlers in its thirty-fifth *Annual Report* (Washington, D.C., 1860). Nearly half (2,409) came from the state of Virginia. The best account of the society and its colonization activity is found in P. J. Staudenraus, *The African Coloni-*

zation Movement, 1816–1865, Columbia University Press, New York, 1961, *See also* COLONIZATION; NATIONALISM; PAN-AFRICANISM.

AMERICAN FEDERATION OF LABOR *See* LABOR UNIONS.

AMERICAN FREE PRODUCE ASSOCIATION This association was founded in 1836 by abolitionists under the leadership of Lewis Tappan. Short-lived, its purpose was to boycott the purchase or use of slave-produced goods. *See also* SLAVERY: THE ABOLITIONISTS.

AMERICAN MISSIONARY ASSOCIATION (AMA) The American Missionary Association (AMA) grew out of a committee organized in 1839 to defend those blacks who had mutinied and seized the Spanish slave ship, *Amistad*. Abolitionist from the beginning, the association drew its major support from Congregationalists as well as from other denominations. In 1865 the AMA became the official agency of Congregational churches for conducting educational work among freedmen. It founded outright, supported, or aided in the establishment of scores of schools for blacks in the South. It supported or supplied teachers for many schools.

Organized September 3, 1846, as a protest against the relative silence on the issue of slavery of other missionary societies, the association for years carried on nondenominational work in an attempt to convince Southerners of the evils of slavery. Agents were sent into the western and the border states to organize churches with antislavery principles. Missions were established among black fugitives in Canada, West Africa, Hawaii, Jamaica, Siam, Egypt, and on a few Indian reservations. The association's early leadership was evangelical-abolitionist. Lewis Tappan was the first treasurer and, until his death, the dominant figure. Gerrit Smith served on the committee that called for the organizational meeting in 1846. A rebel from Lane College (Jackson, Tenn.) and confident of Theodore Weld, George Whipple was the first corresponding secretary. The association was supported by the same faction that sponsored the American and Foreign Antislavery Society.

Before the Civil War, the American Missionary Association was both an abolitionist and a missionary society. After the war had begun, it concentrated its work primarily in providing relief and education to freedmen. Its first school was established in September, 1861, at Hampton, Va., with a black woman, Mary Peake, as teacher. As new areas were opened by the Union Army, more teachers were sent. By 1863 the AMA had 83 teachers in the South. The number increased to 250 in 1864, and to 320 in 1865. Finally, by 1868 the association had 532 teachers and missionaries in the southern and border states.

American Missionary Association officials were motivated in their work by "Christian abolitionism." Emancipation meant more to them than striking off slaves' fetters. It meant divesting freedmen of the shackles of "ignorance, superstition and sin." The association advocated not only equality before the law but full citizenship as well. Lewis Tappan claimed the black man would never have his rights until he had a musket in one hand and a ballot in the other. At its 1865 annual meeting, the AMA advocated black suffrage and denounced distinctions made because of color.

American Missionary Association teachers in the South frequently lived and worked with black families. Southern whites often accused the AMA instructors (and others) of teaching social equality. In 1874 the Georgia state superintendent of education condemned Atlanta University in the following way: Instructors and students were both well qualified, he candidly admitted, but the school taught social equality. Social equality should not be formally taught in the classroom, he said, because it was taught in a more effective way by example. None of the AMA's schools practiced racial distinction in admissions. Black teachers were sent south when possible. The first principal of Avery Institute, Charleston, S.C., was F. L. Cardozo, later a well-known black politician. Ten of Avery's twenty teachers were black.

Though the AMA proclaimed lofty ideals, its representatives sometimes failed to live up to those ideals. Teachers often failed to recognize the richness of black culture, and racial prejudice was not uncommon. Though on occasion the glories of ancient Africa and black pride were taught, the general educational aim seems to have been to make black folk as much like whites as possible. Black teachers were often sent south not because of respect for black teachers, but simply because they were more readily accepted by the black community and, therefore, were more effective. In the 1870s the association began to compromise some features of its program. The egalitarian position of Lewis Tappan

was gradually changed to accommodate, at least partially, Southern attitudes and the Northern desire for reconciliation. Still the AMA came closer to full recognition of black needs than most American institutions.

The first AMA schools were elementary, but from the beginning the association had been concerned with normal schools and colleges. The association had early decided that black people would eventually furnish their own teachers. No race, AMA officials thought, could or should be dependent permanently upon another race for its development. Though whites should assist, black people would have to work out their own future with their own educators and teachers. As soon as southern states began to establish more extensive public school systems, the AMA began to de-emphasize common schools and concentrate on graded schools, normal schools, and colleges. In some states the AMA provided almost the only normal training available for black youth. Of the 20 teachers in Kentucky black normal schools in 1870, 17 were from the AMA. In 1887 Alabama had only two secondary schools for blacks, both AMA-sponsored.

While the AMA played an important role in founding common schools and in providing thousands of dollars of relief to poverty-stricken freedmen, its most permanent contribution was the establishment of several black colleges. Among the colleges founded by the AMA were Fisk University, Berea College, Atlanta University, Talladega College, Straight University (now Dillard), Hampton Normal and Agricultural Institute, Tougaloo College, Tillotson College, and Lemoyne Institute. Though some of its initial idealism had disappeared over the years, the association continued to pursue its "ministry of reconciliation." Its official stance was always against caste, though it recognized class lines. It was usually found to be involved in antilynching battles and in forming interracial commissions. In 1942 the association decided to concentrate its attention on the field of race relations. In doing so, the association was merely reaffirming its original policy, though it now sought to utilize the methods and resources developed in broader areas of social action rather than just the simple appeal to Christian brotherhood. In 1944 the AMA organized its first annual conference on race relations at Fisk University under the guidance of the famed sociologist, Charles S. Johnson. The AMAs major focus remains black folk in America. *See also* EDUCATION: DEVELOP-

MENTS IN ELEMENTARY AND SECONDARY EDUCATION; EDUCATION: COLLEGES AND UNIVERSITIES.

REFERENCES: Beard, Augustus Field, *A Crusade of Brotherhood: A History of the American Missionary Association,* AMS Press, Boston, 1909; Brownlee, Frederick L., *New Day Ascending,* Pilgrim Press, Boston, 1946; Drake, Richard B., "The American Missionary Association and the Southern Negro, 1861–1888," unpublished Ph.D. thesis, Emory University, Atlanta, 1957; and Johnson, Clifton H., "The American Missionary Association, 1846–1861: A Study in Christian Abolitionism," unpublished Ph.D. thesis, University of North Carolina, Durham, 1959.

AMERICAN NEGRO ACADEMY An organization that began in 1897 under the leadership of Alexander Crummell, its aims were to promote black interest in literature, science, and art; to publish scholarly works by and about blacks; and to promote more advanced and more highly refined tastes among educated Afro-Americans. It published a score of *Occasional Papers* from 1897 to 1916. The academy was a forerunner of the Association for the Study of Negro Life and History. *See also* CRUMMELL, ALEXANDER; SCHOMBURG, ARTHUR; SCIENTISTS: SOCIAL/SOCIOLOGISTS.

AMERICAN REVOLUTION *See* AFRO-AMERICAN HISTORY: COLONIAL PERIOD, 1600s–1783; WARS.

AMERICAN SOCIETY OF AFRICAN CULTURE Founded in New York City in 1957, the society was an outgrowth of the Society of African Culture in Paris. Its purpose was to create an understanding and an appreciation of Africa's cultural heritage by means of its periodic publications and cultural exchanges. Now defunct, the society published a newsletter, the *African Forum,* and several special volumes by Afro-Americans about black Africa. Its executive director was John A. Davis.

AMERICAN TEACHERS ASSOCIATION (ATA) The ATA was founded at the beginning of the twentieth century largely through the leadership of black educators: J. R. E. Lee, R. R. Wright, and W. T. B. Williams. It served as the principal national organization representing Afro-American teachers until its incorporation in the 1960s with the National Education Association (NEA). The following were the presidents (1904–66): J. R. E. Lee, Alabama (1904–1908); R. R. Wright, Sr., Georgia (1909–10); W. T. B. Williams, Virginia (1911–12); M. W. Dogan, Texas (1913–14); Nathan B. Young, Florida (1915); John Hope, Georgia (1916); W. H. Singleton, Tennessee (1917); J. S. Clark, Louisiana (1918); S. G. Atkins, North Carolina (1919); John M. Gandy, Virginia (1920); Levi J. Rowan, Mississippi (1921); H. L. McCrorey, North Carolina (1922); J. A. Gregg, Ohio (1923); Mary McLeod Bethune, Florida (1924); William W. Saunders, West Virginia (1925); R. S. Grosley, Delaware (1926); William A. Robinson, North Carolina (1927); William J. Hale, Tennessee (1928); John W. Davis, West Virginia (1929); Mordecai W. Johnson, Washington, D.C. (1930); Fannie C. Williams, Louisiana (1931); H. Council Trenholm, Alabama (1932); Francis W. Wood, Maryland (1933); J. M. Scott, Ohio (1934); Garnet C. Wilkinson, Washington, D.C. (1935); Rufus E. Clement, Georgia (1936); Willa Carter Burch, Washington, D.C. (1937); Alphonse Heningburg, North Carolina (1938); Carrington Davis, Maryland (1939–40); Mary L. Williams, West Virginia (1941–44); Walter N. Ridley, Virginia (1945–47); John Brodhead, Pennsylvania (1948–49); George W. Gore, Jr., Tennessee (1950–51); Robert C. Hatch, Alabama (1952–53); Gerard Anderson, South Carolina (1954); Lillian Rogers Johnson, Mississippi (1955); Elmer T. Hawkins, Maryland (1956); Theodore R. Speigner, North Carolina (1957); Charles W. Orr, Alabama (1958); Lucius T. Bacote, Georgia (1959); George W. Brooks, Tennessee (1960); Lelia A. Bradby, South Carolina (1961); Lucius H. Pitts, Georgia (1962); Richard V. Moore, Florida (1963); J. Rupert Picott, Virginia (1964); C. J. Duckworth, Mississippi (1965); and R. J. Martin, Georgia (1966).

AMISTAD *See* ARCHIVES (DILLARD UNIVERSITY); ARTISTS; SLAVERY: THE ABOLITIONISTS.

AMOS AND ANDY One of the longest-lived radio comedy serials in history, *Amos 'n' Andy* was created by two white men, Freeman F. Gosden (Amos) from Virginia and Charles J. Correll (Andy) from Illinois. The first program was heard in 1928 over a Chicago radio station. Its airing introduced to the radio audience two young black men from Georgia who had come North to seek their fortune. Amos, the gentle soul, drove their "Fresh-Air Taxicab," and did most of the work. Andy, more calculating and domineering, "supervised." Gosden and Correll played all the male voices until 1943; after that date they played a large percentage of them. In 1947 the program was rated the fourth most popular program on radio. With the transition to television, black actors took over all the roles. The part of Kingfish, who became the protagonist, was played by Jim Moore. Early in the 1950s, the National Association for the Advancement of Colored People (NAACP) became active in trying to have the show taken off the air. The reasons were set forth in an article entitled "Why the *Amos 'n' Andy* Show Should be Taken Off the Air":

1. The show tends to strengthen the conclusion among uninformed and prejudiced people that Negroes are inferior, lazy, dumb, and dishonest.
2. Every character is a clown or a crook.
3. Negro doctors are shown as quacks and thieves.
4. Negro lawyers are shown as slippery cowards, ignorant of their profession, and without ethics.
5. Negro women are seen as cackling screaming shrews in big-mouth close-ups, using street slang just short of vulgarity.
6. All Negroes are shown as dodging work of any kind.
7. An entire race of 15,000,000 Americans are being slandered each week by this one-sided caricature.

Along with other pressure groups, the NAACP finally succeeded in having the program removed from the air. *See also* RADIO AND TELEVISION.

AMSTERDAM NEWS James Henry Anderson started this New York weekly newspaper in 1909 with six sheets of paper and two pencils. One of the few black papers to have been fully unionized, it was forced into receivership by a six-week strike by the Newspaper Guild in 1935. It was sold to two black physicians, Clilan B. Powell and P. M. H. Savory, who operated the paper as a speculative venture on the basis of its earning power rather than because of their own interest in journalism. It was sold again in 1971 to a group of black politicians and businessmen, including Percy E. Sutton, Clarence B. Jones, and H. Carl McCall. From four-page issues selling at two cents a copy, the *Amsterdam News* became a standard black weekly. Its staff has included such well-known journalists as Dan Burley and T. Thomas Fortune.

ANDERSON, CHARLES (CHIEF) *See* AVIATORS.

ANDERSON, CHARLES H. (1924–   ), lawyer, judge. After attending Roosevelt University (Chicago, Ill.), Anderson received his LL.B. degree from Lincoln University (Jefferson City, Mo.). He served as a referee on the Kentucky workmen's compensation board and on the Kentucky state board of claims from 1960 to 1968, after which he became a judge in the Third Magisterial District Court of Louisville, Ky.

ANDERSON, EDDIE (ROCHESTER) (1906–1977), actor; born in Oakland, Calif. Best known for his role as Jack Benny's factotum, Rochester, on radio, television, and the screen, Anderson began his acting career in the 1920s and 1930s as a song and dance man in small clubs in the West. His single-shot appearance with Benny in 1937 grew into a long-lived and successful association. Despite his preoccupation and association with the character of "Rochester", he appeared in several movies, including *Star-Spangled Rhythm* and *Cabin in the Sky. See also* RADIO AND TELEVISION.

ANDERSON, JAMES HENRY (1868– ?), editor, publisher; born in Columbia, S.C. From 1905 to 1908 Anderson was a billposter; in 1909 he founded the New York *Amsterdam News,* of which he became managing editor. In 1913 he was a Republican candidate for alderman. *See also* AMSTERDAM NEWS; NEWSPAPERS.

ANDERSON, JOHN WESLEY (1861–1947), physician, philanthropist; born in Lexington, Mo. Anderson attended Kansas University, and received his M.D. degree from Meharry Medical College (Nashville, Tenn.) in 1885. He also studied at the University of Michigan and at Chicago University. Anderson practiced medicine in Dallas, Tex., for more than 50 years and made generous gifts to Meharry Medical College, the Young Men's Christian Association (Dallas), Wiley College (Marshall, Tex.), Freedmen's Hospital (Washington, D.C.), and several orphanages. Anderson was perhaps the leading Afro-American philanthropist of his day.

ANDERSON, MARCELLUS J., SR. (1900–   ), business executive; born in Anderson, S.C. Anderson received his B.A. degree at Ohio State University and later taught at Livingstone College (Salisbury, N.C.) and at Huston-Tillotson College (Austin, Tex.). He was president of the Federation of Masons of the World and of the Pan Texas Mortgage Investment Co., Austin, Tex. He also served on the board of directors of the Citizens National Bank of Austin, Tex., and was on the board of the Texas Association of Real Estate Brokers.

ANDERSON, MARIAN (1902–   ), singer; born in Philadelphia, Pa. One of the most beloved and admired celebrities of her time, she received her early training and inspiration in church choirs. Anderson was the first black singer to be admitted to the Metropolitan Opera Company in New York City. Having studied voice with Giuseppe Boghetti, she entered and won a major competition that resulted in an appearance with the New York Philharmonic in August 1925. She won a Rosenwald Fellowship

soon after, and made her European debut in Berlin in 1930. The next five years were spent concertizing throughout Europe where her reputation as one of the world's most remarkable contraltos was firmly established. On her return to America in 1935, she triumphed in a tour that included recitals at New York City's Town Hall and Carnegie Hall. For the next several years she toured both Europe and America, sometimes performing in as many as 100 concerts a season. In 1939 national attention was focused on her when she was barred from singing in Constitution Hall in Washington, D.C., by the Daughters of the American Revolution (DAR) because of her race. This blatant act of discrimination led to the intervention of Eleanor Roosevelt, who responded by sponsoring an Easter concert at the Lincoln Memorial in Washington; the performance was attended by 75,000 people. In 1942 she established the Marion Anderson Award for young singers. It was not until 1955 that Anderson appeared at the Metropolitan Opera as Ulrica in Verdi's *Un ballo in maschera*. Later, in 1957, she toured India and the Far East as an

emissary of the U.S. Department of State. She was signally honored in India at the shrine of Mahatma Gandhi. In 1958 she was appointed by President Dwight D. Eisenhower as a delegate to the 13th General Assembly of the United Nations. Her autobiography, *My Lord, What a Morning*, was published in 1956.

ANDERSON, VINTON RANDOLPH (1927–), clergyman, bishop; born in Somerset, Bermuda. Anderson received a B.A. degree from Wilberforce University (Wilberforce, Ohio) in 1952, a B.D. degree from Payne Theological Seminary in 1952, a M.A. degree from Kansas University in 1962, and a honorary D.D. degree from Paul Quinn College (Waco, Tex.) in 1964. Anderson was pastor of African Methodist Episcopal (AME) churches in Topeka, Parsons, Lawrence, and Wichita (all in Kansas), from 1952 to 1964. He was the pastor of St. Paul's Church in St. Louis, Mo., after 1964. Anderson was a member of the general board of education of the African Methodist Episcopal (AME) Church; first vice-president of the Wichita branch of the National Association for the Advancement of Colored People (NAACP); and a member of Zeta Sigma Pi, the national honorary social science fraternity. He was appointed to the President's Commission on Equal Employment Opportunities in 1963, and was elected bishop of the AME Church in 1972.

ANDERSON, VIOLETTE N. (1882–?), lawyer; born in London, England. Anderson attended the Chicago Athenaeum, the Chicago Seminar of Sciences, and received her LL.B. degree from the University of Chicago Law School in 1920. She was the first black woman admitted to practice law in the state of Illinois; the first admitted to practice in the United States District Court, Eastern Division; and the first woman assistant city prosecutor in Chicago.

ANDERSON, WALTER F. (1915–); organist, educator; born in Zanesville, Ohio. Anderson received his musical education at the Oberlin Conservatory of Music (Oberlin, Ohio) where he concentrated on the organ, of which instrument he became a distinguished exponent. He began his teaching career at Kentucky State College (1939–43), later becoming chairman of the music department of Antioch College (Yellow Springs, Ohio). He was one of the first Afro-

Far left: Marian Anderson. Her repertoire often included renditions of Afro-American spirituals. *(U.S. Information Agency, National Archives.)*

Americans to receive an appointment to the National Endowment for the Arts.

ANGELOU, MAYA (1928–   ), author, dancer, producer, born in St. Louis, Mo. Angelou was a student of the modern dance under professionals Martha Graham, Pearl Primus, and Ann Halprin, then spent 16 years as a professional dancer and entertainer. She toured 22 countries as part of a U.S. State Department tour in 1954–55, during which time she taught dancing in several countries. She wrote for the *African Review* in Accra, Ghana; the *Arab Observer* in Cairo, Egypt; and several other publications in the period from 1962 to 1965. She wrote songs for B. B. King, and has written, produced, and appeared in many shows for National Educational Television. The story of her difficulties and unhappy childhood was told in her best-selling autobiography, *I Know Why the Caged Bird Sings* (1970). Her other books include *Just Give Me a Cool Drink of Water 'Fore I Die* (1971); *Gather Together in My Name*

Maya Angelou.
(Photo by Bill Price/ Vision.)

(1974); and *Singin' and Swingin' and Gettin' Merry Like Christmas* (1976).

ANTHOLOGIES *See* Bibliographies/Biographies/Guides

A. PHILIP RANDOLPH INSTITUTE Founded by A. Philip Randolph in 1964, the institute serves the Afro-American community in the field of civil rights actions and in the promotion of cooperation with organized labor. It favors full employment and the unionization of Afro-Americans, and it works toward these ends by organizing affiliate groups and coalitions to achieve political change. Among its many functions, the institute maintains close ties with several unions, distributes literature, watchdogs social and welfare legislation by the federal government, and works for voter registration. In 1973 the institute had 3 affiliates in 45 cities in 20 states. *See also* Randolph, Asa Philip; Rustin, Bayard.

ARCHIVES

ARCHIVES Through the years, numerous libraries, historical societies, and archival institutions have collected and preserved materials, manuscripts, and records as well as printed matter pertinent to American history. The following summary is a sampling from that rich array of irreplaceable source materials so necessary for the study and understanding of the Afro-American and his history. The partial list of holdings of the few institutions described below indicate sources of information on the social, educational, economical, religious, and political life of the Afro-American as it relates to the total American picture.

Many institutions have published guides to and lists and inventories of their collections, which can be made available upon request or for use at the institution or which may be available in larger universities or research libraries. The prospective researcher who has exhausted the secondary sources would do well to contact the curator of the collection in which he is interested before attempting to visit the institution.

The size of the holdings is not indicated here,

and only a minimum of biographical information is included. Detailed descriptions of these and many other collections are contained in the following publications:

Hamer, Philip M. (ed.), *A Guide to Archives and Manuscripts in the United States* (New Haven, Yale University Press, 1961).

Harvard Guide to American History (The Belknap Press, Cambridge, Harvard University Press, 1954).

Library of Congress: *National Union Catalog of Manuscript Collections, 1968* (Washington, D.C., 1969).

Schatz, Walter (ed.), *Directory of Afro-American Resources* (New York, R. R. Bowker Company, 1971).

Dillard University, Amistad Research Center, New Orleans, La. 70122. Clifton H. Johnson, director.

American Missionary Society Archives, 1817–1920 Multidenominational society that established missions and schools throughout the United States and Canada; later sponsored by the Congregational church. Reports, financial statements, contracts, clippings, and correspondence of field ministers relating to conditions and church matters are part of the center's collection; the correspondence reflects the dichotomy between ministers serving churches with slave-holding members and those with abolitionist congregations. Also included in the collection are documents relating to the successful efforts of the society to aid and educate Southern blacks from 1855 to 1875.

American Missionary Association Archives (1839–1879) Correspondence, constitutions, circulars, proclamations, pamphlets, photographs, and papers relating to slavery, abolitionists and their movement, the underground railroad, colonization in Africa, education, Reconstruction, Fisk University, Berea College, and the Ku Klux Klan. The archive collection includes the constitution of the American Freedman's Aid Commission, the journal of H. M. Ladd's exploration in Africa for a location for a mission, and the correspondence of Lewis and Arthur Tappan with and for the AMA. Other correspondents include Samuel A. Armstrong, Henry Lyman and Thomas Beecher, Gail Borden, Salmon P. Chase, Clinton B. Fisk, James Garfield, O. O. Howard, John Jay, Owen Lovejoy, and Charles Sumner.

Bethune, Mary McCleod, 1875–1955, educator. Papers (1919–50).

Cartwright, Margaret Dorsey, social worker, educator, and diplomat. Papers: Correspondence and other materials relating to her career as a newspaper correspondent, lecturer, and teacher cover such subjects as the Negro theater and press, the United Nations, Africa, and the Peace Corps.

Race Relations Department, American Missionary Association Archives (1942–   ): Correspondence, studies, notes, pamphlets, and some papers that pertain to the 25 annual institutes on race relations and race-relation activities.

Voorhees, Lillian Welch, 1898–   , playwright; professor of English, speech, and drama. Papers (1917–68): Correspondence and teaching contracts (1917–67), manuscripts of plays and undated poems, abstract of doctoral dissertation (1925), programs and clippings, personal letters (1945–64) from Voorhees' mother and Rev. F. L. Brownlee and his wife. These letters contain information concerning Campbell Folk School and Berea College. Persons mentioned include W. E. B. Du Bois, Charles S. Johnson, and Mary E. Spence.

Duke University, William R. Perkins Library, Durham, N.C. 27706. Mattie Russell, director, manuscript division.

Agricultural Papers (1777–1923:) Plantation diaries, year and day books, and other records and papers of farmers that relate to Southern agricultural activities mainly in the nineteenth century. These papers include detailed information on the use of slave and free Negro labor and agricultural conditions in the South before, during, and after the Civil War.

Bennett, Bryant, merchant and planter. Papers (1767–1802): Correspondence and business papers include plantation account books containing household and farm records, and lists of slaves and supplies issued to them.

Boyd, Archibald H., businessman. Papers (1841–97): Personal and business correspondence of Boyd and his son, James E., attorney and political leader, include Civil War letters commenting on living conditions, military activities, and relating to the areas around Richmond and Petersburg, Va. The correspondence contains letters of Samuel R. Browning, slave trader of Louisiana, relating to conditions of the slave market, health of slaves, effects of cholera epidemics on the slave trade, and accounts of his various transactions.

British Political Papers (1628–1915) Various papers that relate to emancipation in the West Indies, the slave trade, and other subjects.

Cable, George Washington, 1844–1925, author. Papers (1879–1917): Letters (mainly from 1885 to 1891) concerned with Cable's literary activities reflect his gradual break with the South and his work as a reformer. Contents include references to the Negro problem, criticism of himself by Southern newspapers, and other issues.

Cain, Patrick H, merchant, tobacco salesman, and representative in the North Carolina assembly. Papers (1783–1940): Legal documents, correspondence, and other papers, mainly of a business nature, include documents indicating the value of slaves, purchase and sales prices, and, after the Civil War, the wages and tenancy of freedmen.

Fox, John, politician and South Carolina legislator. Papers (1784–1892): Correspondence and other papers (chiefly from 1825 to 1892) relate to slave purchasing and management, crime and law enforcement in the Confederacy, Reconstruction in South Carolina, and the political activities of Negroes in 1872.

Fuller, Stephen, 1716–1808, British iron manufacturer and colonial agent, Jamaica. Papers: (1702–96): Correspondence and other papers (chiefly from 1786 to 1796) include discussions of slavery, the slave trade, and the Wilberforce movement for abolition.

Hunter, Charles N., ca. 1851–1931, Negro educator, North Carolina. Papers (1818–1931): Correspondence, scrapbooks of clippings, and other papers. The material concerns the Negro problem shortly after the Civil War, the attitude of whites toward Negroes, Negro education, temperance, and other matters. Correspondents include Charles B. Aycock, Josephus Daniels, William Borah, Charles Dawes, Charles Sumner, Theodore Roosevelt, Franklin Roosevelt, and Booker T. Washington.

Negroes (slave and free), 1770–1944 Papers and correspondence, relating to slaves and free Negroes, especially in the South in the nineteenth century. Includes information on the manumission, price, trading, and marketing of slaves; Quaker interest in education of slaves; conditions among slaves; treatment of free Negroes in the North and South prior to the Civil War; the underground railroad; slaves during the war; Negroes during Reconstruction; the Wilmington, N.C., race riot; and the campaign for white supremacy in North Carolina.

Wilberforce, William, 1759–1833, philanthropist and member of Parliament. Papers (1788–1872): Mainly letters (1814 to 1815) relating to Wilberforce's activities in the antislave trade and abolition movements with references to English politics and missionary activities in East Africa and various British colonies.

Fisk University Library, Nashville, Tenn. 37203. Jessie Carney Smith, librarian.

Chestnut, Charles Waddell, 1858–1932, author and lawyer. Papers (1857–1950): Correspondence, journal (1874–1885), scrapbooks, certificates, contracts, Spingarn Medal, photographs, and drafts of manuscripts. Correspondents include *Atlantic Monthly, Boston Evening Transcript, Century Magazine,* Newton D. Baker, Benjamin G. Brawley, George Washington Cable, W. E. B. Du Bois, Doubleday Page & Co., Harper Brothers, James Weldon Johnson, Kelly Miller, Emmett J. Scott, Albion W. Tourgee, and Booker T. Washington.

Cullen, Countee, 1903–46, author. Papers (1921–47): Correspondence, literary manuscripts, a plan book from high school classes, certificates, photographs, and diaries. Correspondents include Arna Bontemps, Sterling Brown, Langston Hughes, Charles S. Johnson, Helen Keller, Alain Locke, and Carl Van Vechten.

Du Bois, W. E. B., 1868–1963, author, historian, and founding editor of the *Crisis* (1911–33).

Miscellaneous (1900–60): Books, clippings, journals, correspondence, diaries, literary manuscripts, notebooks, minutes, and memorabilia

concerning his writings, the NAACP, and aspects of the civil rights movement.

Hughes, Langston, 1902–67, writer and lecturer. Papers (1921–): Clippings, notices of appearances, reviews of books and plays, interviews, articles, correspondence, ads, playbills, announcements, awards, and other materials relating to his career.

Johnson, Charles Spurgeon, 1893– , sociologist, author, and college president. Papers (1870–1956): Correspondence, addresses, interviews, memoranda, studies, abstracts, printed matter, and other papers. Most of the materials are from 1928 to 1956, when Johnson was head of the social science department and president of Fisk. Subjects included are race relations, Ku Klux Klan, Chicago Riot of 1919, Negro education, housing and health, TVA, NAACP, and American slavery. Correspondents include Franz Boas, Horace Mann Bond, Katherine Dunham, Richard T. Greener, A. S. Schomburg, National Urban League, and the Civil Liberties Union.

Julius Rosenwald Fund Archives (1917–48): Correspondence, evaluations, manuscripts of unpublished writings, memoranda, minutes, reports, and financial papers. Relates to various aspects of Negro life, rural education, school construction, teacher training, race relations, health, hospitals, and such institutions as Atlanta and Fisk universities and Meharry Medical College. Some of the persons whose work is involved include Marian Anderson, William S. Braithwaite, Owen Dodson, Charles Drew, W. E. B. Du Bois, John Hope Franklin, Robert Hutchins, John Work, and Monroe Work.

Toomer, Jean, poet. Papers (ca. 1920–50): Clippings, magazine articles, literary manuscripts, correspondence, photographs, memorabilia, notes, paper discourses, plays, and periodicals in which his work appeared. Correspondents include Sterling Brown, Sherwood Anderson, Hart Crane, Jessie R. Fauset, and Aldous Huxley.

Historical Society of Pennsylvania Library, 1300 Locust Street, Philadelphia, Pa. 19107. Nicholas Wainwright, director.

American Colonization Society, 1832–1972 Papers: Includes biographical sketches of the society's members and information concerning American activities in Africa.

American Negro Historical Society Records (1790–1901): Minutes, constitutions, and business and legal papers, including stock certificates, bonds and deeds, and correspondence. Some of the names included in these records are Jacob

White, Benjamin Banneker, Isaiah Wears, and Frederick Douglass. Among the institutions and organizations mentioned are the Daughters of Africa Society, Agricultural and Mechanic Association of Pennsylvania, New Jersey Banneker Institute, Equal Rights League, Frederick Douglass Memorial Hospital, and the First and Second Presbyterian churches.

Papers Relating to Negroes 16th–19th centuries. A miscellaneous collection relating to slavery, admission of the free states to the Union, colonization, Reconstruction, and the mutual aid movements.

Howard University 2401 Sixth Street, NW, Washington, D.C. 20001. Michael R. Winston, director, Moorland-Spingarn Research Center.

Negro Collections Created as The Moorland Foundation, the Library of Negro Life and History by the board of trustees in 1914, it is now a

voluminous collection covering the arts, humanities, social and physical sciences, medicine, journalism, and sports. Included are books, periodicals, newspapers, pamphlets, theses, dissertations, manuscripts, correspondence, clippings, photographs, sheet music, and other materials. Among the manuscript collections are the following:

Anderson, Marian, 1902–   , singer. Papers (1939): Mainly clippings relating to Anderson and the DAR controversy, together with letters, telegrams, minutes, memoranda, and pictures.

Brawley, Benjamin G., 1882–1939, educator, author, and professor of English at Howard University. Papers: Consist of letters, notes, programs, pamphlets, photographs, clippings, essays, poems, and documents relating to Brawley's father, Edward K. Brawley.

Bruce, Blanche Kelso, 1841–98, politician, lecturer, and United States senator from Mississippi. Papers: Correspondence, documents, clippings, family papers, and other materials. The correspondence relates to Bruce's career as a senator (1874–80) and reflects the political, economic, and social conditions in the South, specifically Mississippi during the Reconstruction. Correspondents include James Hill, John R. Lynch, and P. B. S. Pinchback. This collection is related to the library's Josephine Bruce and Roscoe C. Bruce Collection.

Clarkson, Thomas, 1760–1846, English philanthropist and abolitionist. Papers (1791–1887): Correspondence relates primarily to the abolitionist movement; a diary (1791–92) of the abolitionist mission in America contains the memorial and petition of Thomas Peters, free Negro and sergeant in the Regiment of Guides and Pioneers in North America under the command of General Henry Clinton; it also contains material on the efforts of the Sierra Leone Company to establish a settlement of free Negroes on the coast of Africa.

Douglass, Frederick, 1817–1895. Papers, correspondence, addresses, documents, picture albums, clippings, poetry, and other papers. Correspondents include Gerrit Smith, Mordecai Johnson, George F. Hoar, and J. E. Rankins.

Grimké, Angelina Weld, 1880–1958, author and teacher.

Grimké, Archibald Henry, 1849–1930, lecturer, lawyer, author, and diplomat.

Grimké, Francis James, 1850–1937, Presbyterian minister, lecturer, and trustee of Howard University. Papers (1834–1958): Correspondence; diaries; manuscripts of short stories and poems; financial papers; school reports and records; business, official, and personal papers of the diplomat; and sermons and addresses of the minister and papers of his wife, Charlotte Forten Grimké. The correspondents include Langston Hughes, Alain Locke, Emmett Scott, W. E. B. Du Bois, Paul Lawrence Dunbar, John Greenleaf Whittier, the Committee of Twelve, the Association for the Study of Negro Life and History, and government agencies.

Howard University Papers: Minutes of the trustees (1867–75); executive committee minutes

Far left: Dorothy B. Porter, for many years the curator of the Moorland-Spingarn Research Center, is shown examining a volume in the collection. *(Moorland-Spingarn Research Center, Howard University.)*

(1867, 1872, 1877); correspondence; the plan of organization of Howard Normal and Theological Institute; legal papers including deeds, leases, and bonds; reports, contracts, and notes of incorporation. Includes correspondence by or related to Henry H. Garnett, Oliver O. Howard, E. Whittlesley, George Vashon, John M. Langston, and S. C. Pomeroy.

National Association for the Advancement of Colored People Washington, D.C., branch. Papers (1920–46): Correspondence, membership papers, clippings, legal and financial papers, and periodicals relating to such subjects as lynching, the National Negro Congress, education, poll tax, citizens' committees on race relations, Fair Employment Practices Commission, police brutality, housing discrimination, and the Armed Forces.

Works Progress Administration Papers (1934–51): Manuscripts and reports of and correspondence to officials of the WPA concerning welfare, relief, labor, the Negro in the federal government, defense employment, Negro workers, rural Negroes, rehabilitation, and the Negro WPA.

Henry E. Huntington Library and Art Gallery 1151 Oxford Road, San Marino, Calif. 91108. Daniel H. Woodward, librarian.

Alexander Collection, 1848–1939 Papers of a freedman, James M. Alexander, who was active in Arkansas politics and his son, John H., the second Negro to graduate from the U.S. Military Academy at West Point. Included is a journal kept during the march of the son's army unit in Wyoming, 1888.

American Tract Society Collection Papers (1864–75): Correspondence of the society's agency in Richmond, Va. Letters concern the distribution of religious books and tracts, and work with freedmen and refugees, prisoners of war, Sunday schools, juvenile instruction, and funds for rehabilitation.

Clarkson, Thomas 1760–1846, British philanthropist. Correspondence, drafts of speeches, and other papers, including letters about the abolition of slavery and the slave trade.

Hill, Lewis and Robert Papers (1778–1857): Correspondence of the Hills, who worked as commission merchants, bill collectors, and agents for the hiring of Negroes.

Pleasant Family Papers (1745–1838): Letters and documents of a prominent Quaker family of Virginia containing references to the family's land holdings and mercantile business interests, manumission of slaves, and the education of Negroes. These papers include epistles, reports, and other papers relating to various local Quaker meetings and correspondence with Quakers elsewhere.

Virginia General Assembly Papers (1861–65): Contains, among other topics, a discussion of legislation pertaining to Negro volunteers.

The New York Public Library The Schomburg Center for Research in Black Culture 103 West 135th Street, New York, N.Y. 10030. Jean Blackwell Hutson, chief; Ernest Kaiser, curator.

This is a reference and research library. The nucleus of this voluminous collection is the private library and collection assembled by Arthur A. Schomburg, a Puerto Rican of African descent.

Aldridge, Ira 1807–67, Shakespearean actor. Papers: Scrapbook, playbills, photographs, and letters, chiefly of Amanda Ira Aldridge (1866–1956), his daughter.

Art Collection: Oil paintings Includes work by such artists as Richmond Barthé, E. Simms Campbell, Aaron Douglas, Lois M. Jones, Augusta Savage and Henry O. Tanner. Also included are watercolors, etchings, lithographs, and engravings.

Civil Rights Congress (CRC) Papers (1946–ca. 1956): The congress was formed from a merger of the International Labor Defense and the Federation for Constitutional Liberties. Correspondence, press releases, photographs, clippings, phono-discs, films, tapes, and trial transcripts. The collection includes cases, correspondence, and publications of the CRC's Prisoners' Relief Committee, law and literature departments, and material of the U.S. Communist Party relating to the "Trial of the 12" (1949).

Crummell, Alexander 1819–1898, Episcopal minister, scholar, and founder of the America Negro Academy. Papers (ca. 1837–90s): Correspondence, addresses, and manuscripts. Includes material relating to Crummell's ministry, his study in England, work in Liberia, and founding of St. Luke's Church in Washington, D.C. (1873), and the American Negro Academy (1897). Persons and correspondents mentioned include Paul Lawrence Dunbar, James McCune Smith, Lemuel Haynes, Henry Highland Garnet, John Jay, Archibald and Francis Grimké, Kelly Miller, and others.

National Negro Congress Files (1933–47): Correspondence, statements, documents, statistics, speeches, reports, financial papers, photographs, and related materials. This collection also includes files of the Negro Industrial League, Joint Committee on National Recovery, and files relating to other committees. Among the many subjects and correspondents represented are the American Peace Mobilization, Ku Klux Klan, Adam Clayton Powell, Jr., NAACP, CIO, Fair Employment Practices Committee, March on Washington (1943), Africa, Urban League, Armed Forces, voter registration, Henry Wallace, and Harry S. Truman.

Tape Recording Collection Interviews, speeches, readings, and recordings by a large number of persons. Among the subjects covered are the Democratic party, Brotherhood of Sleeping Car Porters, racism, White Citizens Council, housing, and the Black Muslim movement.

Slavery and Abolition Collection Papers (1700–1890s): Letters, slave sales, passes, certificates of registry, manumission papers, wills, speeches, and other papers. Includes letters from Frederick Douglass, William Wilberforce, Granville Sharp, Theodore Weld, and materials relating to the Amistad and other slave cases, the Haitian Revolution, miscegenation, Sherman's march to the sea, labor unions, education, and the Ku Klux Klan.

Tuskegee Institute, Hollis Burke Frissell Library Tuskegee, Ala. Annie G. King, librarian; Daniel T. Williams, archivist.

Calloway, C. J., 1916–1930. Correspondence and reports including material concerning Tuskegee's Extension Service and the school's role in administering the rural schools programs and Rosenwald Schools, 1916–43.

Carver, George Washington Papers (1887–1943): Reports, documents, correspondence, affidavits, scrapbooks, citations, and other papers containing George Washington Carver's personal thoughts and aims, material on experiments and patents, a study of his early life, copies of documents relating to the U.S. Extension Service and the Department of Agriculture, and articles on Carver's life and work.

Derbigny, Irving Anthony Papers: Letters received and sent as vice president of Tuskegee, relating to his work at the institute, education in Alabama and the South, the Carnegie Fund, and the organization of Alpha Mu National Honorary Society.

Holsey, Albon L. Papers (1904–47): Documents relating to his work as a member of Tuskegee's faculty, executive secretary of the National Negro Business League, assistant to the president, and director of public relations. Correspondence relating to his activities at the institute and the NNBL.

Lynch Reports, 1882– Papers: A detailed record of all known lynchings, giving dates, state, race of victim, cause, and place.

Moton, Robert R. President, Tuskegee Institute. Papers (1916–35): Correspondence relating to activities of the institute and the role of the Negro in American education, political and business activities, and race relations. Included is material concerning the Negro in World War I, correspondence about Moton's activities and interest in Hampton Institute, the National Negro Business League, the General Education Board, and the National Urban League. The correspondents include Mary McCleod Bethune, T. H. Cardoza, Calvin Coolidge, Herbert Hoover, Theodore Roosevelt, Oscar DePriest, Marcus Garvey, W. E. B. Du Bois, Thomas Edison, and Thomas Fortune.

Photographs Collection Thirty-five hundred photographs depicting early and contemporary life of Tuskegee and the history of the Negro.

Southern Conference for Human Welfare, Southern Conference Educational Fund, Inc. (SCEF) Papers: Minutes, correspondence, financial papers, clippings, booklets, photographs, and documents relating to civil rights and liberties in the South and to the lives and activities of Carl and Anne Braden and James A. Drombowski; information on the Southern Regional Council, Southern Tenant Farmers' Union, American Peace Mobilization, the CIO, and the National Citizens Political Action Committee

Tuskegee Collection Papers (ca. 1881–   ): Miscellaneous materials pertaining to programs and presentations at Tuskegee, departmental materials on the city of Tuskegee and Macon County and phases of academic life and development at the institute; papers relating to the Negro in the South, farmers conferences, and interracial programs.

Washington, Booker T. (1856–1915), educator, statesman, founder and president of Tuskegee Institute. (1881–1915): Correspondence; printed material by, to, and about Washington; manuscripts; and other papers. The collection contains manuscripts of Washington's Atlanta Exposition speech, extensive student correspondence, material concerning the "Committee of the 12"; the personal and business correspondence of Margaret Murray Washington, including references to her role in establishing the National Association of Colored Women (1896), and materials concerning publications of the institute and the National Negro Business League.

U.S. General Services Administration, National Archives and Records Service, Washington, D.C. 20408 James B. Rhoads, archivist of the United States. The National Archives and Records Service (NARS) is responsible for selecting, preserving, and making available to the federal government and the public the permanently valuable noncurrent records of the federal government and for promoting improved current-records management and paper practices in federal agencies. It is also responsible for publishing the laws, constitutional amendments, presidential documents, and administrative regulations having general applicability and legal effect, and for administration of the presidential libraries and records centers. The holdings of the National Archives are classified according to record groups (RG), of which there are more than 400.

RG–11, General Records of the U.S. Government Records (1778–1945): File of constitutional and statutory enactments and of treaties, including source material on slavery and the trade, colonization, emancipation, civil and political rights. Antislave treaties include two with Great Britian—the Webster-Ashburton Treaty (1842) and one in 1870—and the Statute of Brussels (1890) with European powers multilaterally. Records relating to the ratification of the Thirteenth, Fourteenth, and Fifteenth amendments include correspondence between the secretary of state and the governors of the states and some messages of governors to the legislatures. The file of unperfected treaties contains the treaty of December 15, 1863, with the Netherlands concerning emigration of freedmen to Surinam.

RG–21, U.S. District Courts Records (1685–1929): Among the many court records are materials concerning the following districts:

District of Columbia. Minutes of the circuit court (1801–63) contain entries on the commitments of fugitive slaves. There are separately filed manumission papers (deeds, wills, affidavits, bills of sale—1821–62); manumission and emancipation papers (1857–62) relating to voluntary manumissions, emancipation under the act of April 16, 1862, and claims for emancipation filed by slaves whose masters had failed to file schedules under that act; fugitive slave materials (1862–63); and case materials dealing with civil rights during Reconstruction, and with discrimination, civil and political rights, from Reconstruction to 1929.

Eastern District of North Carolina. Records include case materials from 1791 dealing with slavery; material during Reconstruction pertaining to civil rights, Ku Klux Klan and other intimidation cases, and case records to 1911 relating to civil and political rights, discrimination, and similar matters.

Southern District of New York and Eastern District of Pennsylvania. The earliest of these records are dated 1685 and relate to the landing of eight Negroes near Rye, N.Y. Included from 1789 are case files in admiralty and criminal matters arising out of the slave trade; and materials during Reconstruction and to 1912 pertaining to civil and political rights, discrimination, and similar matters.

RG–29, Bureau of the Census Records (1790–1930): Population schedules or their equivalents for the censuses of 1790–1880 inclusive, the censuses of 1910 and 1930, and the separate slave censuses of 1850 and 1860. The slave schedules for the 1860 census give for each slaveholder the number of his slaves and their age, sex, and color; those who were fugitives; the number manumitted; those who were "deaf and dumb," blind, insane, or "idiotic"; and the number of slave houses. Also included for the 1860 census are photographic copies of printed maps of the Southern states with symbols showing for each county the number of whites, free Negroes, and slaves as well as agricultural information and information on slaves and freedmen on an Indian reservation west of Arkansas.

RG–45, Naval Records Collection, Office of Naval Records and Library Records: Correspondence, logbooks, and letterbooks of the African Squadron and a roll of slaves employed by the engineer office at Charleston, S.C. (1862–64). Included in the material of the African Squadron is considerable correspondence, from 1819 to 1861, between the Secretary of the Navy and commanding officers of the squadron; U.S. agents on the Guinea coast; federal, executive, and judicial officials; the American Colonization Society; private individuals and firms relating to the seizure of American slaving vessels and their condemnation in U.S. District Courts; arrangement for shipment of liberated Africans to reception centers at Sherbro Island and along the Liberian coast; the establishment, maintenance, and supply of these centers; U.S. naval vessels in combating the traffic in slaves and in facilitating African and Afro-American colonization in Liberia; and the activities of the American Colonization Society and state societies. Separately filed is the letterbook (1843–45) of the first commander of the African Squadron, Matthew C. Perry, and that of his successor, William C. Bolton (1847–49).

RG–46, U.S. Senate Records: 37th–82d Congresses. Materials, particularly memorials and petitions of such senate standing committees as:

Committee on the The District of Columbia. Petitions and memorials concerning such matters as the employment of freedmen or contrabands in the district, opposition to the abolition of slavery, extension of voting irrespective of color, and legislation to put all white men who are citizens and residents of the district "upon an equal footing with Negros."

Committee on Education and Labor. Petition for appropriations to Wilberforce University, Wilberforce, Ohio, for education of freedmen, and the testimony (1883) of Mrs. George R. Ward dealing with Southern life before the Civil War, Negro superstitions, matrimony, religion and service servants.

Joint Select Committee to Inquire into the Condition of the Late Insurrectionary States. The committee gave attention to the Ku Klux Klan activities.

Select Committee on Slavery and the Treatment of Freedmen. Memorials, including letters and scrolls with signatures and often addresses and occupations on the following subjects: liberation of slaves in the seceded states, abolition of slavery, suppression or reopening of the African Slave Act, extension of the right of suffrage to freed slaves, suppression of rebellions, and other subjects.

There are similar records in RG–233, Records of the U.S. House of Representatives.

RG–59, General Records of the State Department Correspondence (1774–1942): The diplomatic correspondence, especially from Great Britian and Brazil, contains information on the slave trade as well as the correspondence of many Negroes who serve in diplomatic capacities, particularly in Haiti, Liberia, Santo Domingo, and Madagascar, and the applications and recommendations filed in connection with their appointments. The miscellaneous correspondence includes letters from various colonization societies, and material as late as the early 1900s that reveals a continued interest in Negro colonization and that also concerns the restriction of immigration of American Negroes to other countries. This record group is supplemented and complemented by the records contained in RG–84, Foreign Service Posts.

RG–94, Records of the Office of the Adjutant General General correspondence and related records.

Included are papers concerning the Memphis riots, 1866, and the Baltimore riot, 1861; records of the American Freedmen's Inquiry Commission; and opinions of the solicitor of the War Department concerning a slave if drafted.

Military Service Records. Muster rolls and returns of Regular Army and volunteer units, regimental papers, description and letterbooks of volunteer regiments, registers of enlistments (1798–1914), reports of examination of recruits (1884–1912), registers of physical examinations (1864–1912), compiled service records of soldiers serving with the U.S. Colored Troops (USCT), register of appointments in USCT (1863–66), carded medical records of the Regular Army (1861–86), and records of commissioned Regular Army officers, such as Major Charles Young, Chaplain Theopolis Steward, and Lieutenant Henry O. Flipper.

Records of the U.S. Military Academy. Appointment papers and correspondence concerning cadets at West Point.

Generals' Papers and Books.

Thomas, Lorenzo, Adjutant General, U.S. Army Papers (April 1, 1863 to July, 1864): Orders, letters, and telegrams sent. Includes records of Thomas' recruitment and organization of colored troops in the Mississippi Valley, list of officers selected for commission in the USCT, and information concerning the problems connected with his activities.

Colored Troops Division. Records (1863–89): Correspondence, applications for appointment, registers and rosters, and other papers concerning recruitment, organization, and service of Negro units and their officers. Included in this series is an eight-volume compilation (1885) containing copies of official records, state papers, and historical extracts of various kinds relating to the Negro in the military service dating from the colonial period to 1885.

Freedmen's Branch. Records (1872–79): Formed after the discontinuance of the Bureau of Refugees, Freedmen, and Abandoned Lands. Correspondence, employee records, reports, financial and legal papers, and bounty records.

Material relates to the functions of the bureau, which were essentially receiving, passing upon, and paying claims of Negro soldiers and sailors or their heirs for bounty, pensions, arrears of pay, commutation of rations, and prize money.

RG–105, Bureau of Refugees, Freedmen, and Abandoned Lands The bureau was established in the War Department by an act of Congress approved March 3, 1865. Its functions were to supervise and manage lands in the Southern states that had been abandoned by their owners and to "control all subjects relating to refugees and Freedmen." Military officers, special agents of the Treasury Department, and benevolent societies had dealt in various ways with all the problems. On June 2, 1865, President Andrew Johnson ordered the agents and officers to transfer to authorized representatives of the bureau all abandoned lands, funds, and property set apart for the use of freedmen.

Major-General Oliver O. Howard was appointed commissioner of the bureau on May 12, 1865. His headquarters staff in Washington, D. C. included an assistant adjutant general; an assistant inspector general; medical, quartermaster, and disbursing officers; land, claims, and education divisions. Field officers, under assistant commissioners, were organized to carry on the work of the bureau in the Southern and border states.

Assistant Commissioners' Headquarters. Records of the assistant commissioners headquarters in the following states: Alabama, Arkansas, Florida, Georgia, Kentucky, Tennessee, Louisiana, Maryland (sometimes Delaware and West Virginia), Mississippi, Missouri, North Carolina, South Carolina, Texas, and Virginia. The District of Columbia is also included.

The records consist of registered letters received, letters received and sent, orders, circulars, claims, employment registers, contracts, records of freedmen's courts, complaints, hospital records, marriages, rations issued, and bounty registers. Included for the District of Columbia is material relating to Freedmen's Village, Arlington, Va; sick and wounded freedmen and refugees at Freedmen's Hospital, the industrial and home schools for freed children, and the Commission for the Relief of Destitute Colored Persons. There are also similar records for the states.

Education Division. Correspondence: Letters received by the superintendent of education (1866–70), including letters from benevolent societies, individuals interested in the education of freedmen, and state superintendents of education; and reports and schedules of schools, rental accounts, lists of teachers, and histories of societies and organizations supporting the schools. This series contains information pertinent to the history of such schools as Johnson C. Smith, Shaw, and Atlanta universities.

Records Division. Records: Correspondence, relating to all aspects of the bureau's functions addressed to or received from the secretary of war and other bureaus of the government, the assistant commissioner in the states, state governors, societies, and individuals interested in the freedmen. Also included are lists of appointments, circulars, and orders; reports of assistant commissioners; offenses against freedmen; letters received from the Executive Mansion; letters received by T. D. Eliot, chairman of the House Committee on Freedmen's Affairs, and by O. O. Howard; inspection reports of buildings at Howard University; and papers relating to the operation of the bureau.

RG–153, Judge Advocate General's Office Records (1812–1942): Investigations, trials, and opinions in such cases as the court-martial of Henry O. Flipper, first Negro graduate of West Point; J. S. Whitaker, cadet; the Brownsville (Tex.) affray; the Houston riots; and the activities of the Order of American Knights of the Golden Circle.

RG–183, U.S. Employment Service (USES) Records (1930–39): The file of J. A. Otley, advisor on Negro affairs and field representative of the USES, includes correspondence, memoranda, conference minutes, and reports on the availability of USES services to Negro applicants. The reports cover many aspects of the status of Negro labor, such as population trends, chief occupations, amount of unemployment, available relief, and evaluation of the local activities of the USES. Correspondence is particularly concerned with discrimination in employment and placement of Negroes.

RG–391, U.S. Regular Army Mobile Units Regimental records of the 9th and 10th U.S. Cavalry and the 24th and 25th U.S. Infantry, including descriptive and letterbooks, orders, returns rolls, and miscellaneous materials.

RG-393, U.S. Army Continental Commands Records (1821–1920): Divisions, departments, and districts. Twenty-fifth Army Corps, 1864–1866. Records contain information relating to the status of Negroes' protection by law in courts, interracial relations, Ku Klux Klan activities, and registration and elections.

Divisions and departments. Records contain

information relating to the Bureau of Negro Affairs and Free Labor, 1862–65; activities of, and attitudes toward, Negro units stationed in various areas. Similar information is contained in the records of the Army posts.

Embracing the NARS holdings is an extensive audiovisual collection of motion pictures, film, still pictures, and sound recordings. Included are 81 photographs taken by Matthew Brady and his associates, which document the experience of the Negro in the Civil War, photographs depicting Negro troops in the Spanish-American War and later wars, and the Harmon Foundation Archives, 1922–67, which includes 1,400 black-and-white photographs of paintings and sculpture by Negro artists. Among the films is the Federal Extension Service's "Helping Negroes to Become Better Farmers and Home Makers" (1921), and the U.S. Air Force's "Wings for This Man" (1945).

Yale University Memorial Library Box 1603A Yale Station, New Haven, Connecticut 06520. Lawrence E. Dowler, Head, Manuscripts and Archives.

Baldwin Family Papers (1584–1947): Correspondence and other papers of Roger Sherman Baldwin (1793–1863) relating to the Amistad case (1839–41). Baldwin was later governor of the state of Connecticut.

Beecher Family Papers (1706–1953): Correspondence, sermons, travel accounts, diaries, newspaper clippings, and other papers of Henry Ward Beecher (1813–87), clergyman and orator, and of other members of his family, including Lyman Beecher (1775–1863), clergyman. The collection includes professional correspondence from H. W. Beecher to leading nineteenth-century clergymen and the letters of Harriet Beecher Stowe (1811–96) to her brothers as well as other Stowe material.

James Weldon Johnson Memorial Collection of Negro Art and Letters Founded by Carl Van Vechten, the collection consists of books, periodicals, pamphlets, photographs, objects of art, newspapers, clippings, manuscripts, letters, phonograph records, scrapbooks, sheet music, posters, bulletins, concert and theatrical programs, calling cards, handbills, signatures, and other materials. The emphasis is on the accomplishments of Negroes in the field of the fine arts, belle lettres, and sports in the twentieth century. Included in the collection are the papers, pictures, paintings, manuscripts, and phonograph records of Harry T. Burleigh, Countee Cullen, Langston Hughes,

Paul Robeson, William Grant Still, Joel Spingarn, Carl Van Vechten, Walter White, and Hale Woodruff.

Phillips, Ulrich B. 1877–1934. Papers (1712–1933): Materials, mainly from 1790 to 1865, collected and prepared in connection with Phillips's historical studies of the Old South. Included are family papers and records and individual documents of plantation owners.

Stimson, Henry Lewis 1867–1950. Papers (1870–1950): Consists of information in diaries and papers concerning Negro troops in World War II when Stimson served as Secretary of War.

Todd Family Papers (1834–70): Includes the papers of John A. Wilder (1834–70) and Charles B. Wilder (1852–70), which relate to their work with Negro troops during and immediately following the Civil War. John Wilder commanded the 2d Regiment U.S. Colored Troops; Charles was superintendent of contrabands at Fortress Monroe. *See also* BIBLIOGRAPHIES/BIOGRAPHIES/GUIDES; HARSH, VIVIAN G.

REFERENCES: *See* the beginning of this entry.

ARKANSAS AGRICULTURAL MECHANICAL AND NORMAL (AM&N) COLLEGE *See* UNIVERSITY OF ARKANSAS AT PINE BLUFF.

ARKANSAS BAPTIST COLLEGE Arkansas Baptist College, at Little Rock, Ark. was founded in 1884 by the Baptist church. A small four-year coeducational college, it grants the bachelor's degree and provides liberal arts and teacher education curricula. The enrollment increased from 170 in 1970 to about 500 in 1975.

ARMISTEAD, JAMES also **JAMES LAFAYETTE** (1760–1832), soldier; born in New Kent County, Va. In March 1781, Armistead, with his master's permission, joined the Revolutionary Army at Williamsburg, Va., and was attached to General Lafayette's camp where he acted as courier and double agent. He worked as a spy behind British lines, and for a time, the British General Cornwallis thought he was in Britain's employ. Armistead was warmly respected by Lafayette, whose name he later adopted. On November 21, 1784, Lafayette wrote of Armistead:

. . . he [Armistead] properly acquitted himself with some important communications I gave him . . . his intelligence from the enemy camp were industriously collected and most faithfully delivered.

His Army service and Lafayette's testimonial

prompted the Virginia state legislature to grant Armistead his freedom in 1786. He remained in New Kent County, becoming a property owner and head of a large family. Lafayette visited him on his return to the United States in 1824–25.

ARMSTRONG, HENRY (HANK) (1912–   ), pugilist, clergyman; born Henry Jackson in Columbus, Miss. Armstrong was raised in St. Louis, where he attended Vashon High School. He boxed professionally from 1932 to 1945, winning 144 of 175 bouts, 97 by knockouts. He won the featherweight title in 1937 and voluntarily relinquished it the next year. He won the lightweight championship in 1938 and held it for a year in an era of outstanding fighters. Armstrong won the welterweight crown in 1938 and defended it successfully 20 times until 1940. Armstrong was the only professional fighter to hold three world titles simultaneously. Elected to boxing's Hall of Fame in 1954, Armstrong returned to St. Louis, where he became an ordained minister and associate pastor of a Baptist church and assistant director of the Herbert Hoover Boys' Club. See *also* ATHLETES.

ARMSTRONG, LILIAN HARDIN (LIL) (1898–1971), jazz pianist; born in Memphis, Tenn. Hardin gained an early reputation as a barrelhouse player. One of her most notable professional associations was with King Oliver's band. Married to Louis "Satchmo" Armstrong from 1924 to 1938, she collapsed and died in Chicago, Ill., while performing at a memorial service in honor of her former husband. *See also* ARMSTRONG, (DANIEL) LOUIS.

Louis Armstrong with King Oliver's Creole Jazz Band (left to right): Baby Dodds, drums; Honoré Dutrey, trombone; King Oliver, cornet; Louis Armstrong, trumpet; Bill Johnson, bass; Johnny Dodds, clarinet; Lil Hardin, piano. *(Courtesy of David Stuart.)*

ARMSTRONG, (DANIEL) LOUIS (SATCHMO) (1900–71), jazz musician; born in New Orleans, La. One of the most influential and famous of all jazz artists, Armstrong was born in the black ghetto of New Orleans. A boyish prank, played when he was 13, caused him to be sent to the Negro Waifs Home for a year. There he learned to play the cornet and to read music. Although he was skilled enough to begin to perform after his release in 1915, he was too young to get work in a band. King Oliver, one of the outstanding exponents of the new Dixieland jazz, befriended him, gave him trumpet lessons, and, in 1917, when he moved on to an engagement in Chicago, left his place in the Kid Ory Band to Armstrong.

In 1922 Oliver asked Armstrong to join him in Chicago as second cornet with his Original Creole Jazz Band. Two years later, Armstrong joined Fletcher Henderson's band at New York City's Roseland Ballroom. By this time, he was playing the trumpet and doing some vocalizing. It was in 1925 that Armstrong began the "four golden years" of his "Hot Five" and "Hot Seven" recordings in which his technique for free improvisation and rhythmic inventiveness reached its greatest heights. Only five years later, he turned to leading large bands and using popular songs rather than Dixieland as his material, to the dismay of jazz purists. His rasping voice and vaudeville-like performances, however, along with virtuoso handling of his instrument, led the way to the era of the swing band. About 1947 he again returned to leading small groups, which, in the end, served merely as backdrops for his personal performances.

Although he had appeared on European stages in 1932 and had acquired international popularity, he became a habitual traveler after the close of World War II, often as a goodwill ambassador of the United States. Through the years, he appeared in a variety of films: *Pennies from Heaven*, 1936; *Cabin in the Sky*, 1943; *The Glenn Miller Story*, 1953; *Hello Dolly*, 1969; and on countless television programs. He also appeared on Broadway in the *Hot Chocolates* (1929) revue and in *Swingin' the Dream* (1939) in which he played Shakespeare's character Bottom. His music, however, especially his early jazz, remains his most important legacy. *See also* ARMSTRONG, LILIAN HARDIN (LIL); MUSIC: JAZZ.

ARMSTRONG, WILEY THURBER (1905–   ), physician; born in Rocky Mount, N.C. Armstrong received a B.S. degree from Shaw University (Raleigh, N.C.) in 1929 and his M.D. degree from Meharry Medical College (Nashville, Tenn.) in 1944. He did postgraduate work at New York, Columbia, and Howard universities. As a member of the National Medical Association, he served as speaker of the house of delegates (1961–62), as chairman of the board of trustees (1964–68), and as president in 1970.

ARMY *See* WARS.

ARNEZ, NANCY LEVI (1928–   ), educator, poet, author; born in Baltimore, Arnez received a B.A. degree from Morgan State University (Baltimore, Md.) in 1949 and her Ed.D. degree from Columbia University in 1958. She taught in the Baltimore public schools (1949–62). Arnez was director of student teaching at Morgan State University (1962–66), professor for the Inner City Studies Project at Northeastern Illinois University (1966–73), and a professor of education and acting dean of the school of education at Howard University (Washington, D.C.) in 1973. Her articles have appeared in the *Journal of Teacher Education, Journal of Negro Education, NASSP Bulletin, Improving College and University Teaching, Phylon, School and Society,* and other professional publications. Arnez was also author of *Partners in Urban Education: Teaching the Inner City Child.* Listed in more than a dozen *Who's Who* publications of educators, authors, and community leaders, she also published poetry in a number of magazines, as well as a book of poems, *The Rocks Cry Out.*

ARROYO, MARTINA (1936–   ), soprano; born in New York, N.Y. Arroyo graduated from Hunter College of the City University of New York, and pursued vocal studies until winning the Metropolitan Opera Auditions in 1958. As her career expanded, she sang in all the great opera houses of the world (Vienna, Berlin, Buenos Aires, London, Hamburg), making her Metropolitan Opera debut in February 1965 in the title role in *Aida.* One of the foremost operatic sopranos of the 1970s, Arroyo has sung many roles at the Metropolitan Opera, including Donna Anna in *Don Giovanni,* Liu in *Turandot,* Leonora in *Il Trovatore,* Elsa in *Lohengrin,* and the title role in *Madam Butterfly.*

Martina Arroyo as Aida. *(Courtesy of Metropolitan Opera House.)*

ARTIS, WILLIAM ELLSWORTH (1914–   ), ceramist, sculptor, educator; born in Washington, D.C. Artis received a B.S. degree from Chadron State College (Chadron, Nebr.), and B.F.A. and M.F.A. degrees from Syracuse University (Syracuse, N.Y.). His awards include a Rosenwald Fellowship in 1947, Outstanding Educator of America and Outstanding Afro-American Artist in 1970, and nine purchase awards in sculpture from Atlanta University between 1944 and 1965. His work, which shows a gift for communicating ideas through shape and intensities, has been exhibited at the Harmon Foundation, New York N.Y. 1933; Whitney Museum of American Art, New York, N.Y. 1940; Art of the American Negro, Chicago, Ill., 1940; and elsewhere. Artis has works in several important collections, including the Smithsonian Institution, Washington, D.C. He taught at Nebraska State Teacher's College and at the Harlem Young Men's Christian Association (YMCA) in New York City. *See also* ARTISTS.

ARTISTS

Art has been the least-known contribution of the Afro-American to American culture. Since the latter part of the eighteenth century, there have been black painters, sculptors, printmakers, and craftsmen of excellence, but until very recently they have been largely ignored or forgotten by critics, historians, and the great museums, almost as if they did not exist at all.

Many Afro-Americans have ancestors from West Africa, where the visual arts such as wood carving, bone carving, fetish making, and bronze casting were well-developed throughout many centuries. The arts of Nok, Ife, Benin, Nigeria, and the Ashanti reveal the artistry of the black man, which suffered near-extinction under American slavery. Beyond doubt, some skilled sculptors and craftsmen came over to America on the slave ships, but the conditions of slavery and caste removed any opportunity for them to practice their traditional tribal arts.

By the latter part of the eighteenth century, black artists had learned the prevailing American art genres. Most of these artists were freemen from Boston, Philadelphia, and New York. They were self-taught, since formal art training was not yet available to them. Few of their works have been preserved, and some are known only by written descriptions.

Slaveholders soon recognized the manual dexterity of the slaves, who became artisans of wrought iron for southern mansions, bricklayers, stonemasons, pewterers, wheelwrights, cabinetmakers, seamstresses, and carvers of designs on furniture, coffins, and houses. Examples of their skills may still be seen in the architecture and artifacts of Charleston, New Orleans, Savannah, Natchez, and other southern cities.

One of the first Afro-American artists was G. W. Hobbs, whose pastel of Richard Allen, founder of the African Methodist Episcopal (AME) Church, was made in 1785. Another early portrait painter was Scipio Moorhead. Patrick Reason, an engraver from New York City who was associated with the antislavery movement, worked about the same time. There were some Afro-American artists in New Orleans, notably Julien Hudson and Eugene Warburg, who showed considerable talent as portrait painter and sculptor, respectively. Black artists of the period followed the American trend in portrait painting, for which there was a lively market.

Joshua Johnston (1765?–1830) was probably the best-known and most successful black painter of his time. He was reputed to have once been a slave, but at least 30 years of his life were spent as a freeman. He earned his living as a portrait painter and enjoyed the patronage of upper-class whites of Baltimore. Today, several of his paintings still hang in well-to-do homes of the area; Johnston's painting entitled The James

McCormick Family (ca. 1804) is in the collection of the Maryland Historical Society. Johnston's works have the stylized stiffness and two-dimensional quality of the limners of New England. Later works, perhaps influenced by Charles and Rembrandt Peale, who also worked in Baltimore at that time, show considerably more sophistication and realism.

In the early 1800s, Afro-American artists of greater competence than their colonial predecessors appeared. William Simpson (1830–72) of Boston was a highly skilled portrait painter; unfortunately, few of his works remain. Other skilled artists, such as Robert Douglas (1809–55) and J. W. Chaplin, worked in Philadelphia.

The first Afro-American artist to gain international, as well as national recognition, was Robert Scott Duncanson (1817–72). Duncanson was the son of a white Scottish-Canadian father and a fair-skinned mother. A prolific painter of portraits, still lifes, murals, and landscapes, who lived and worked chiefly in Cincinnati and Detroit, Duncanson maintained a studio and made a comfortable living from his art. His place in the history of American art rests mainly on his handsome landscapes that were painted in the Hudson River School tradition. One of his patrons was Nicholas Longworth the elder, who was at that time one of the richest men in Cincinnati. Longworth, along with members of the Antislavery League, financed one of Duncanson's trips to Europe.

Duncanson was the first Afro-American muralist, and three of his most noted paintings, Blue Hole, Flood Waters, and Little Miami River, can be seen today in the Cincinnati Art Museum. During one of his trips to Europe, he exhibited successfully in London and Glasgow and sold a number of paintings. Queen Victoria bought one of his paintings for Balmoral Castle. However, in spite of his success, Duncanson lived a frustrated life. In 1872, at the height of his career, he became mentally ill and died in an insane asylum in Detroit. In addition to Cincinnati, Duncanson is also represented in major museums in St. Louis (City), Boston (Museum of Fine Arts), and Detroit (Institute of Arts).

Edward Bannister (1828–1901) was another competent landscape painter and a contemporary of Duncanson. He first gained recognition in Boston, where he had received his formal training. Bannister later went to Providence, R.I., where he spent most of his career. Among his achievements was the award of the Gold Medal at the Centennial Exposition in Philadelphia in 1876.

Joshua Johnston, *The James McCormick Family.* The faces in this otherwise highly stylized portrait are particularly realistic. *(Courtesy of the Maryland Historical Society.)*

Edmonia Lewis (1845–90) was the first black woman to achieve widespread recognition in art. A sculptor of unusual talent, she attended Oberlin College (Oberlin, Ohio) and received formal training in Boston. She created portrait sculpture and medallions, and many works in marble. With the help of white patrons, Lewis went to Rome where she increased her knowledge of antique sculpture. She received a number of commissions for historical portraits including ones for Charles Sumner and Wendell Phillips.

Another promising nineteenth-century sculptor was Eugene Warburg (1825–61) of New Orleans who specialized in portraits. He died in Rome following a stay in Paris.

These early black artists often faced insurmountable barriers of prejudice, and a number of them expatriated themselves to Europe for training and an opportunity to sell their works.

The period from the close of the Civil War to the turn of the century was a time during which the struggle of the talented black artist for recognition was as bitter and as difficult as in the earlier years. One step forward in this struggle was that Afro-American artists, especially in the North and East, could now secure formal art training. The market for their works, however, remained extremely limited.

Out of this period came the painter regarded as one of the finest artists produced in America. Henry Ossawa Tanner (1859–1937), the son of an AME bishop, graduated from the Pennsylvania Academy of Fine Arts in 1888, where he was the pupil of Thomas Eakins. In his early career, Tanner painted genre pictures of Afro-American life. As a teacher of art at Morris Brown College (Atlanta, Ga.), he found the existence of a black artist in America too difficult and unrewarding. In 1891 he expatriated himself to France, where he spent the remainder of his life. Tanner became the dean of American painters in Paris. He won a Gold Medal at the Salon in Paris, and his painting, *Raising of Lazarus*, was purchased for the Luxemburg Palace. Tanner concentrated on the painting of religious subjects, winning numerous high awards during his lifetime.

Although Tanner was widely acclaimed in Europe, he received meager recognition in America. Recently, however, he has been rediscovered, and a retrospective exhibit of his paintings toured American museums in the early 1970s.

Meta Warrick Fuller (1877–1967) was an outstanding sculptor. Like Tanner, she studied at the Pennsylvania Academy of Fine Arts. She later went to Paris and studied with the renowned sculptor Auguste Rodin, who had much praise for her work. Fuller exhibited at the Paris Salon in 1898 and 1899. She has works in the Cleveland Museum and the Schomburg Collection in New York City.

Other noteworthy black artists appeared at the beginning of the twentieth century. May Howard Jackson (1877–1931), a sculptor, was another talented black graduate of the Pennsylvania Academy of Fine Arts. She was noted for her portraits of Afro-Americans. Isaac Hathaway, a native of Pine Bluff, Ark., was a portrait sculptor of considerable merit who lived and worked in comparative obscurity. His portraits of such distinguished Afro-Americans as Frederick Douglass, Booker T. Washington, and Paul Lawrence Dunbar occupy places of prominence in many black institutions. Malvin Gray Johnson (1896–1934) died at an early age but was a brilliant painter of Afro-American life in the Deep South. He is represented in the Whitney Museum of American Art in New York City. Horace Pippin (1888–1946) was one of the few black painters to attract the attention of the critics of the white art world. He was entirely self-taught and ranks as one of the truly great American primitive painters. He is represented in the famous Barnes Collection (Marion, Pa.) and the Pennsylvania Academy of Fine Arts. William Harper (1873–1910) was one of the most promising black artists of his day, but his career, like Johnson's, was cut short by death. He studied in Paris and for a time was the student of Henry O. Tanner. William Edward Scott (1884 – ?) was a highly trained artist who had also studied with Tanner and at the Academie Julien in Paris. After Duncanson, he was one of the first black American artists to turn to mural painting. His murals may be seen in public buildings in Illinois, Indiana, and New York. Scott traveled and painted in Haiti and has exhibited in many cities throughout the world. Nancy Elizabeth Prophet (1890 – ?) was another expatriate black sculptor. After she graduated from the Rhode Island School of Design, she went to Paris to study at the École des Beaux-Arts, residing in Paris for 13 years. Her honors include an award from the Whitney Biennial in 1935.

During the Harlem Renaissance of the 1920s and the Great Depression in the 1930s, a number of promising black artists began to emerge against great odds. Except for the primitive painters, most black artists of that period were still creating art in the current dominant American styles. Although decades before, in the early 1900s in Paris, such painters as Picasso, Matisse,

AMISTAD MURALS

Hale Woodruff painted his masterful murals of a mutiny that took place in 1839 aboard the slave ship *Amistad*. The artist's three panels, commissioned by Talladega College on the 100th anniversary of the mutiny, celebrate the artist's own personal belief as well as the central theme of Afro-American history: freedom. The successful mutineers ordered the ship sailed east to Africa, but the two slave traders steered north at night, and the ship landed at Montauk Point, Long Island Sound, in 1839. After a famous trial in Hartford, Conn., the case was reviewed before the Supreme Court, which decided for the Africans.

PANEL 1 (lower left) The first panel shows the forty-odd kidnapped Africans in revolt on the *Amistad* while en route from Havana, where they had been sold. Their leader, Cinque, is seen full-face on the left, struggling with the ship's cook (back turned). Kenna, back turned, behind the cook, brandishes a weapon. Montez, one of the slave traders, just behind Cinque, is about to be hit by Pona. Ruiz, the other slave trader, lies on the ship's deck; Yuang is about to strike. Ship's captain Ferrer (with hat) is at the mercy of Gaby, one of the slaves. Two crew members escape in a boat; Antonio, the mulatto cabin boy, escapes up the rigging of the ship. One of the slaves has been slain (lower right).

PANEL 2 (top) The second panel shows the trial of the captive slaves on charges of murder and piracy brought by the two slave traders. Cinque is standing defiantly near the center of the panel. Behind him are, right, Banna, and left, Cinque's aide, Gaby. The three white men in the left foreground are, left to right, Rev. Simeon Jocelyn, Arthur Tappan, and Roger Baldwin. Kale wearing a cap, sits just behind Jocelyn. The little girl in extreme lower left is Margue, one of three young girl captives, who later had a son who returned to America and graduated from the Yale School of Religion. Woodruff has included a self-portrait (seated in third row to right of Joceylyn, chin on right hand). Judge Smith Thompson is presiding. The prosecution lawyer sits with back turned; behind him is James Covey, the translator, a cabin boy who could speak both English and the captives' language, Mendi.

PANEL 3 (lower right) The third panel shows the repatriation of the 32 remaining mutineers to Sierra Leone as a Mendi mission. Cinque stands in the center; behind him, missionary James Steele, Banna unpacks the books destined for the mission school; Margue is at his right. Missionary William Raymond stands with hat in hand; behind him is George Wilson, a black missonary. *(Courtesy of Savery Library, Talladega College.)*

and Modigliani had seen in primitive African sculpture those aesthetic qualities that were to form the basis of both modern painting and modern sculpture, the black painter, as a rule, had still not thought of looking into his own heritage.

However, one painter, Aaron Douglas (1899–), did rediscover the qualities of African sculpture during the Harlem Renaissance, and his murals attracted more attention than had the work of any other black painter in many years. Particularly in his singular, individualistic style with its elongation of figures and rhythmic movement, there is to be found a quality reminiscent of primitive African sculpture. These murals stand in striking contrast to his later more academic and detailed portraits.

Douglas was born in Topeka, Kan., and he studied at the University of Kansas. His murals were painted at Fisk University (Nashville, Tenn.), where he was a professor of art for many years; Bennett College (Greensboro, N.C.); and the New York Public Library at 135th Street (the Schomburg Center for Research in Black Culture). More than any other black painter, Douglas pointed the way for other black artists to look back into their cultural heritage for inspiration.

E. Simms Campbell (1906–71) achieved a degree of recognition in the field of commercial art that was never accorded any of his predecessors. Campbell, whose early art training was gained in St. Louis, was a facile illustrator and cartoonist, who won great fame for his work in such magazines as *Esquire* and *The New Yorker*. His syndicated cartoon, "Cuties," was carried in more than 100 daily papers in the United States and Latin America. Many Americans were unaware that this popular artist was black.

The number of Afro-American sculptors, painters, and printmakers increased enormously from 1927 to 1965, an increase that may be attributed to a number of reasons. In the South, for example, the new proliferation of art departments in many black colleges made art training more available. These art departments were strengthened by a staff of highly trained black artists. There were, among others, several outstanding art professors, such as James A. Porter, Lois Jones Pierre-Noel, and James Herring at Howard University; James D. Parks at Lincoln University (Jefferson City, Mo.); Jack Jordan at Langston University (Langston, Okla.) and Southern University (New Orleans, La.); James E. Lewis and Charles Stallings at Morgan State College; Jimmie Mosely at Maryland State College; H. L. Oubre at Alabama State; and David C. Driskell who served at Fisk University from 1966 to 1976. By building strong art departments, black colleges have influenced ever-increasing numbers of Afro-American youths.

Moreover, art and community centers in large Northern cities, such as the Karamu House in Cleveland and the People's Art Center in St. Louis, provided further instruction and incentive for black youth. In Chicago, a large group of black artists developed, including Charles White, Bernard Goss, Margaret Burroughs, Eldzier Cortor, and William Carter.

The Federal Art Project furnished much assistance to black artists during the Great Depression. In the 1920s and 1930s, the awards and the

exhibits of the Harmon Foundation were the chief source of national visibility for Afro-American art. It was joined in 1942 by the now famous Atlanta University Art Show, which, with the Harmon awards, became the outstanding showplace of black art. In addition, the National Archives, Washington, D.C., has a photographic collection showing representative works of many black artists.

Since the Afro-American artist found himself almost entirely excluded from the great museums of the country, black colleges began to assemble collections of works by black artists. The largest and most comprehensive collections are at Howard University and Atlanta University. Smaller but growing collections are at Hampton, Tuskegee, Lincoln, Bennett, Morgan, Fisk, and Talladega. Without the foresight shown by these institutions, there would be no large collections of Afro-American art.

A generation of black artists survived the Great Depression and World War II. Lois Jones Pierre-Noel has been called the finest Afro-American woman painter. She studied at the Beaux-Arts and the Academie Julien in Paris, spending considerable time in France, Haiti, and Africa. She

Lois Mailou Jones (Lois Jones Pierre-Noel) in her studio. A designer and watercolorist, she served as a professor of art at Howard University from the 1930s to the 1970s. *(Courtesy of the artist, Lois Mailou Jones.)*

has exhibited in one-man shows in cities in Europe and America and has won numerous awards. Several of her paintings were purchased recently for the presidential palace in Haiti.

Hale Woodruff (1900–   ), a native of Cairo, Ill., became one of America's outstanding painters. He received his early formal training at the John Herrin Institute in Indianapolis. Later, he went to Paris where he studied at the Academie Scandinave and with Henry O. Tanner. Woodruff has been not only a fine easel painter but also a distinguished muralist with such major works as the Amistad murals at Talladega College. Woodruff has made other murals for Atlanta University and the Golden Gate Insurance Company in Los Angeles, Calif. While teaching at Atlanta University, Woodruff helped develop a number of young painters—among them, William Hayden, Albert Wells, John Howard, and Lawrence Jones. Until 1968, he was professor of art education at New York University. He is represented in numerous museums and private collections.

Charles Alston (1907–1977), has had an impressive career as a painter, muralist, sculptor, and teacher. He studied at Columbia University and was awarded a Rosenwald Fellowship. His murals are powerful in force and design. He is represented in the collections of the Metropolitan Museum of Art (New York City), the Whitney Museum of American Art (New York City), and several universities (Nebraska, Atlanta, and Howard). In 1972 he was a teacher at New York University and at the Art Students League.

James D. Parks is a painter, lithographer, and historian of Afro-American art. Born in St. Louis, Mo., and educated at Bradley University and the University of Iowa, his paintings and lithographs deal with the many diverse aspects of Negro life. Parks is represented in the permanent collections of Atlanta University, Texas Southern University, Lincoln University, Springfield (Missouri) City Art Museum, and the Dunbar School in Kansas City.

James A. Porter (1905–71) was not only a fine painter but also the leading historian of Afro-American art. He received his B.A. degree at Howard University and his M.A. degree in art history from New York University; later, he studied at the Sorbonne, in Paris. He is the author of *Modern Negro Art* (1969) and numerous monographs and articles. His paintings are chiefly about Afro-American life. Porter was dedicated and diligent in his efforts to preserve for posterity the deeds of the black artist.

Elizabeth Catlett (born 1915) was one of the most brilliant of present-day black sculptors. Born in Washington, D.C., she is a graduate of Howard University and the University of Iowa. Her carvings of Afro-American mothers are strong and forceful.

Archibald Motley (1891–?) distinguished himself as a fine painter during his long lifetime. A strongly individualistic painter, he won numerous awards (a Guggenheim fellowship) and exhibited widely. From 1935 to 1939, he worked for the mural division of the Illinois Federal Arts Project. His paintings hang in numerous Midwestern museums. Motley's genre studies of Afro-American life rank among his best work, although he has also been an outstanding portrait painter.

Richmond Barthé (1901–   ) was one of the most outstanding sculptors in America in the twentieth century. Barthé studied at the Art Institute of Chicago and the Art Students League, New York, N.Y. Much of his sculpture is devoted to the portrayal of black personalities and groups. His works are monumental and forceful.

Charles White (1918–   ) began his brilliant career as a painter during the 1930s when he attended the Art Institute of Chicago. He joined the mural division of the Federal Arts Project from 1938 to 1940. White was a master of drawing, easel painting, printmaking, and mural painting. His style was basically realist.

This middle portion of the century would not be complete without the mention of Romare Bearden (1912–   ), one of the most inventive of Afro-American painters, whose artistic career, like that of Charles White, extended into the period after 1955. His work in lively colors is appealing.

Another artist, William Artis (1914–   ), is an outstanding sculptor, potter, and printmaker.

Beyond doubt, however, the Afro-American painter who achieved the most fame in the post-World War II period was Jacob Lawrence (1917–   ). More than any other Afro-American painter, Lawrence was accepted by critics and art historians. Born in Atlantic City, N.J., Lawrence studied with Charles Alston and Henry Bannarn; later, he attended the Harlem Art Center. He works primarily in tempera. His paintings are owned by several large American museums, and his work has been exhibited in many American cities.

As it did for practically all aspects of black life in America after 1950, the civil rights movement focused attention on the black artist. Like the black cowboy, the black artist, who had also been around for a long time, was "discovered." For the first time since the Great Depression, some promising young artists found more encouragement for study and work. Like his fellow black intellectuals in literature, music, and drama, the Afro-American artist revived his interest in the black past, black protest, civil rights, and négritude.

Present-day Afro-American artists, most of whom were born after or during the Great Depression, but who are not necessarily endorsers of the artistic concept of négritude, include the following: Roland Ayers (1932–   ), Betty Blayton (1937–   ), Frank Bowling (1936–   ), James Brantley (1945–   ), Marvin Brown (1943–   ), John E. Chandler (1943–   ), Barbara Chase-Riboud (1936–   ), Walter Davis (1937–   ), Avel DeKnight (1933–   ), Frederick John Eversley (1941–   ), Ernest Frazier (1942–   ), Sam Gilliam (1933–   ), William Howard Henderson (1943–   ), Barkley L. Hendricks (1945–   ), Manuel Hughes (1938–   ), Richard Hunt (1936–   ), Lester Johnson (1937–   ), B. Nathaniel Knight (1942–   ), Alvin Loving (1935–   ), Phillip Lindsay Mason (1939–   ), Lloyd G. McNeill, Jr. (1935–   ), Algernon Miller (1945–   ), Howardardena Pindell (1943–   ), Stephanie Pogue (1944–   ), Faith Ringgold (1934–   ), Henry Rollins (1937–   ), Walter Allen Rogers (1942–   ), Joseph

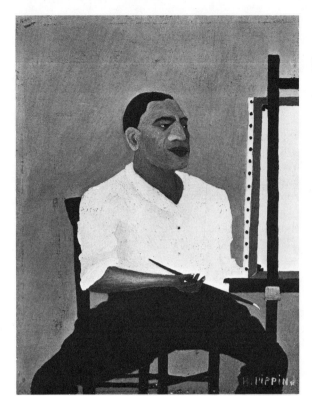

Horace Pippin's *Self-Portrait* (1941) reveals some of the intensity with which he rendered his vision. *(Courtesy of Terry Dintenfass, Inc.)*

B. Ross, Jr. (1943–   ), Raymond Saunders (1934–   ), Evelyn P. Terry (1946–   ), Robert Thompson (1937–   ), Franklin A. White, Jr. (1943–   ), Reginald Wickham (1931–   ), and Todd Williams (1939–   ).

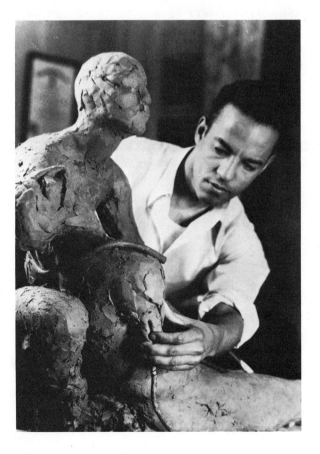

REFERENCES: Writings about Afro-American artists and their art increased notably after the 1960s. A list of selective references includes the following: Atkinson, Edward J. (ed.), *Black Dimensions in Contemporary Art*, New American Library, New York, 1971; Bearden, Romare, *Six Black Masters of American Art*, Doubleday, New York, 1972 (the six artists are Johnston, Duncanson, Tanner, Pippin, Savage, and Lawrence); Cederholm, Theresa Dickison, *Afro-American Artists: A Bio-Bibliographical Directory*, Boston Public Library, Boston, 1973; Chase, Judith Wragg, *Afro-American Art and Craft*, Van Nostrand, New York, 1972; Doty, Robert, *Contemporary Black Artists in America*, Whitney Museum of American Art, New York, 1971; Dover, Cedric, *American Negro Art*, New York Graphic Society, Greenwich, 1960; Fax, Elton, C., *17 Black Artists*, Dodd, Mead, New York, 1971; Lawrence, Jacob, *Harriet and the Promised Land*, Windmill Books, Simon & Schuster, New York, 1968; Lewis, Samella, and Ruth G. Waddy (eds.), *Black Artists on Art*, Contemporary Crafts Publishers, Los Angeles, 1970; Matthews, Marcia M., *Henry Ossawa Tanner: American Artist*, University of Chicago Press, Chicago, 1969; Pleasants, J. Hall, "Joshua Johnston, the First American Negro Portrait Painter," *Maryland Historical Magazine*, June, 1972, pp. 5–39. Porter, James A., *Modern Negro Art*, Dryden Press, New York, 1943 (reprinted with a new preface in 1969) is an excellent older account. A more recent account is Driskell, David C., *Two Centuries of Black American Art*, Random House, New York, 1976.

Far left: Richmond Barthé at work on his *Negro Number 140*. *(National Archives.)*

Far right: Arthur
Ashe making a
forehand return.
(AP Wirephoto,
Tennis Hall of
Fame.)

ASANTE / ASHANTI *See* Africa: Land and Peoples of West Africa; Africa: The Atlantic Slave Trade in Perspective.

ASBURY, JOHN CORNELIUS (1862–1941), lawyer, state legislator, business executive; born in Washington County, Pa. Asbury attended Washington and Jefferson College (Washington, Pa.) and received his LL.B. and LL.M. degrees from Howard University (Washington, D.C.). He served as commonwealth attorney of Norfolk County, Va.; as assistant city solicitor of Philadelphia; and as representative in the state legis-

ASHE, ARTHUR (1943–   ), tennis player; born in Richmond, Va. Ashe began playing tennis at the age of seven under his coach Dr. Robert "Whirlwind" Johnson, of Lynchburg, Va. He won the national junior indoor singles title in 1960 and defended it successfully the next year, and in 1963, was the first black player named to the American Davis Cup team. At the University of California at Los Angeles, from which he graduated in 1966, Ashe led the school's team to the National Collegiate Athletic Association (NCAA) championship in 1965, and he won NCAA singles and doubles titles in 1966. He was the American clay-court champion in 1967; a year later, he became the first Afro-American to win a major title when he achieved the national amateur

men's singles championship. In 1970 he won the Australian Open tournament. In 1975 he became the first black male to win the men's singles title at Wimbledon. *See also* Athletes: Tennis.

ASHFORD, EMMETT *See* Athletes: Baseball.

ASSOCIATION FOR THE STUDY OF NEGRO LIFE AND HISTORY *See* Historians.

ATHLETES

The history of the Afro-American athlete in the United States is one of great courage, ability, and achievement. Until 1947, when Jackie Robinson joined the Brooklyn Dodgers and became the first black major-league baseball player, most college and professional sports were segregated or were discriminatory against blacks.

Once the color barrier was dropped, however, black athletes became an even more outstanding and integral part of the sports scene in the United States. Though only one American in ten is a Negro, by the 1970s black athletes represented one-quarter of the regulars in major-league baseball, one-third of the regulars in professional

football, and one-half of the regulars in professional basketball. Moreover, there were untold numbers of blacks on high school and college teams throughout the nation. Currently, the highly skilled black athlete is in tremendous demand, despite a discriminatory past that still lingers, for example, in the placement of blacks in managerial and administrative positions, or in the admission to exclusive golf and racing clubs.

Baseball Baseball is considered America's national pastime and is its oldest major team sport. Though baseball's origin has long been in dispute, the sport probably derived from the

English games cricket and rounders and gradually developed into its present form in the first half of the nineteenth century, with New York, New England, and Philadelphia as major centers. It is not known to what extent Negroes played baseball before the Civil War. However, during the war, black soldiers copied the game from soldiers who played it in the Army camps.

In 1885, Frank Thompson organized the first Negro team composed of paid members. Thompson was the headwaiter at the Argyle Hotel in Babylon, New York, and the other waiters at the hotel made up the team. Hoping to avoid the strong prejudice against blacks, they were billed as the Cuban Giants. The illusion was enhanced by players feigning to speak Spanish.

As early as 1893, Negroes were playing baseball at universities and colleges in the North and West. During the years from 1893 to 1898, J. Francis Gregory played at Amherst and Eugene Gregory at Harvard. William Clarence Matthews was a shortstop and second baseman at Harvard in 1902. Syracuse University's 1908 team included Oscar Brown, and in the same year Howard Robinson was the catcher at Oberlin College in Ohio. William Kindle was the most valuable player at Springfield College (Springfield, Mass.) in the 1914–15 season. The great black athlete, Paul Robeson, was at Rutgers in 1918, Earl Brown pitched at Harvard in 1923, and George Grossen was Boston University's short-

stop and most valuable player in 1924. John W. Copeland was the shortstop and captain of the Oberlin Team in 1937.

Andrew "Rube" Foster was the founding father of black baseball in the United States. Foster was a brilliant pitcher, promoter, and manager. After he retired as a player, he managed a team called the Giants and was the first black manager to arrange exhibition games between Negro teams and major-league clubs (those in organized professional baseball, at that time exclusively white). In 1920 he successfully formed the first Negro professional league called the National Negro Baseball League. Other leagues soon followed. In 1921 the Eastern League was organized; then in the 1930s the American Association League was established, together with the Mid-Western Baseball League and the Negro International League. Some of the most famous Negro-league teams were the Homestead Grays, American Giants, Chicago Giants, Kansas City Monarchs, and the St. Louis Stars. The first world series between Negro-league teams was played in 1924. One of the most notable power hitters of the leagues was Josh Gibson.

Color Barrier and Integration The tradition of segregation before World War II prevented professional major-league clubs from signing outstanding black baseball players. James "Cool Papa" Bell, Walter "Buck" Leonard, John Henry Lund, and Satchel Paige were only a few of the qualified black players to be denied major-league contracts prior to the admission of black players into the major leagues after World War II. (Paige eventually became a major-league pitcher, crossing the racial barrier in 1948; "Buck" Leonard was voted into the Baseball Hall of Fame in 1972; and "Cool Papa" Bell was voted into the Baseball Hall of Fame in 1976). In the 1920s, John McGraw of the New York Giants had a black first baseman named Charlie Grant, who was passed off as an Indian until some of his Negro friends gave him a party and the secret became known. At that point, McGraw let Grant go.

World War II and the civil rights movement helped bring about integration in professional baseball. The first test came with the admission, in 1947, of Jack Roosevelt Robinson. Robinson's major-league performance was brilliant. It didn't take long for Jackie Robinson to become something of a national hero to both black and white Americans through his skill, courage, and restraint.

Far left: Satchel Paige was a star in Negro leagues, where he played for about 22 years before becoming the first black pitcher in the American League. *(Burt Goldblatt.)*

Jackie Robinson was an all-around athlete before he broke the color bar in the major leagues. *(Schomburg Collection, New York Public Library.)*

Far right: Hank Aaron hit his 715th home run in 1974, breaking Babe Ruth's career record. *(Baseball Hall of Fame.)*

Other blacks soon began to appear on major-league teams. In many ways, the era initiated by Jackie Robinson's admission to the Brooklyn Dodgers was historic. Brooklyn and several other National League teams were quite active in recruiting black and Latin-American players soon after Robinson's arrival; the American League, in contrast, continued to depend more heavily on the traditional (white) supply of players. Soon thereafter the balance of power between the leagues in professional baseball changed drastically. The American League, which had been superior to the National League in most respects before World War II, was largely surpassed by the National after World War II, both in standard of play and in attendance. The factor that was most responsible for this increase in the strength and popularity of the National League was the rich flow of black and Latin-American players into that league.

Such black players as Jackie Robinson, Willie Mays, Henry "Hank" Aaron, and Frank Robinson ranked with the great white stars—and box-office attractions—of the postwar years. During the period from 1954 to 1964, blacks led the National League in batting average seven of eleven times, and in home runs eight of eleven.

Other measures of this progress are equally impressive. Jackie Robinson, appropriately, became the first black player to win election (in 1962) to the Baseball Hall of Fame in Cooperstown, N.Y. Henceforth, all players, regardless of race, were eligible for such an honor. Further, baseball recognized its debt to the many black players of the pre-Robinson era by establishing a special Baseball Hall of Fame division for those players who had been deprived of recognition because their careers were spent wholly or largely in the Negro leagues, not by their own choice.

In 1971 Satchel Paige became the first black player admitted on this special basis at Cooperstown, though his selection also recognized his work in the major leagues beginning in 1948.

Major-league baseball was slower in initiating change on other levels, but even on those there has been significant progress. In 1962 Buck O'Neil became the first black coach when he was named to such a position by the Chicago Cubs of the National League. In 1966 Emmett Ashford became the first black major-league umpire; this time it was the American League that broke the racial barrier. Black coaches are no longer the rarity they once were, but Ashford remains unique among umpires.

The year 1974 was crucial to black baseball history in two respects. First, Hank Aaron of the Atlanta Braves became the all-time major-league home-run leader; his 715th career home run surpassed the long-standing home-run record of Babe Ruth, the most famous record in the sport's history. Then on October 3, 1974, Frank Robinson was named manager of the Cleveland Indians of the American League and, thus, became the first black elevated to one of the game's foremost positions.

A few simple facts illustrate the story of black players' economic rise during the 18 years following Jackie Robinson's admission into the major leagues. Willie Mays, who received a bonus of just $5,000 when he joined the New

York Giants early in the 1950s, was earning 21 times that amount by 1964. In the inflationary decade following 1964, salaries became even more impressive. Bob Gibson, for example, was one of several black stars whose earnings rose well over $100,000 by the 1970s. Salaries over the $200,000 mark were reportedly earned by Hank Aaron and Richie Allen.

Outstanding Professional Baseball Players Since 1940

Henry "Hank" Aaron began in baseball with a black team called the Mobile Bears, and then played with one of the most famous of all black teams, the Indianapolis Clowns. The Milwaukee (now Atlanta) Braves later signed him as a shortstop. Aaron became a regular infielder by 1954, and then switching to the outfield, he led the Milwaukee Braves to two pennants, and won the National League's Most Valuable Player award in 1957 when he hit 44 home runs. Home runs became his specialty. In 1974 he made baseball history by breaking Babe Ruth's record for career home runs (714), and by the close of the 1974 season, Aaron had hit 733. He was then traded to the Milwaukee Brewers of the American League. See AARON, HENRY.

Richie Allen joined the Philadelphia Phillies in 1964 and was voted Rookie of the Year in the National League with a .318 batting average. His baseball prowess continued, and in 1966 his batting average was .317. He hit 41 home runs, and batted in 110 runs that season. Allen achieved superstar status in spite of fielding trouble (he made 41 errors in his first year), problems in getting along with teammates and bosses, and two damaged tendons in his right hand. He was later outstanding in the American League with the Chicago White Sox, and then again with the Philadelphia Phillies.

Ernie Banks and Gene Baker were the first Negro players with the Chicago Cubs, having been signed in 1953. Banks distinguished himself as the leading home-run hitter among shortstops in the history of the major leagues. He was the first slugger to use a light bat, and he is credited with having introduced the "era of the light-but-lively bat" to the major leagues. The baseball career of Ernie Banks is studded with records. Between 1955 and 1960, he hit more home runs (248) than any other player. Banks was the first National League player to win the Most Valuable Player award two years in succession (1958, 1959). His 47 home runs and 129

runs batted in in 1958, and the 45 home runs and 143 runs batted in in 1959, earned him the awards. By 1971 Ernie Banks was a lifetime home-run leader with 509.

Roy Campanella was the regular catcher for the Brooklyn Dodgers from 1948 to 1958. During that time, he contributed substantially to the Dodger pennants in 1949, 1952, 1953, 1955, and 1956. He was named the National League's Most Valuable Player three times during his career (1951, 1953, 1955). Campanella's days as an active player were ended quickly and tragically when he became paralyzed after an automobile accident in 1958. See also CAMPANELLA, ROY.

Larry Doby, an outfielder, was the first Negro to play in the American League, signed in 1947 by the Cleveland Indians. In 1948 Doby's heavy hitting enabled the Indians to go to the World Series; Doby batted .318 in the series and the Indians won. In 1950, he hit 25 home runs and batted in 102 runs; his hitting average for the year was .326. Doby led Cleveland to another pennant in 1954 with league-leading totals of 32 home runs and 126 runs batted in. The Indians traded Doby to the Chicago White Sox, and he eventually finished his playing career at Baltimore. He was a coach for the Indians in 1974 and managed the Chicago White Sox in 1978.

Curt Flood was a brilliant center fielder for the St. Louis Cardinals throughout the 1960s. When the Cardinals decided to trade him to the Philadelphia Phillies after the 1969 season, Flood refused to report to Philadelphia and brought suit against the National League, challenging the "reserve clause" under which a player remains the property of the club owning his contract unless the club trades him to another club or releases him outright. Flood's suit reached the U.S. Supreme Court in 1972 where it was rejected. Though he lost, Flood focused national attention on a baseball practice that is at variance with the normal employee right to bargain with all employers in an open market. The court recognized this contradiction, but said that it was up to the U.S. Congress to review baseball's special status, originally granted by Congress in 1922. The special status enables baseball to operate outside federal antitrust laws.

Josh Gibson was prevented by racial discrimination from receiving the national fame he deserved. He played professional ball for the Homestead Grays as a catcher from the 1920s to the 1940s. As a batter, he earned the nickname of "the Babe Ruth of Negro Baseball." It is reported that he once hit 80 home runs in one season. When he died in 1947, Gibson had lived long enough to see a black athlete play in the major leagues. In 1972 he was voted posthumously into the Baseball Hall of Fame.

Elston Howard was signed by the Yankees in 1950, though he was not brought up from the minor leagues until 1955. In his rookie season, he played outfield, caught, played first base, and hit .290. Finally, in the twilight of Yogi Berra's playing career, Howard became the number one catcher for the Yankees and batted .348 in 1961. In 1962 he caught 135 games, batted .287, and, in general, played brilliantly during a year when Roger Maris and Mickey Mantle were injured. He was the first black American League player to win the Most Valuable Player award (1963).

Reginald (Reggie) Martinez Jackson began his professional baseball career in 1967 and played his first World Series game in the early 1970s. He became one of the highest paid players in 1976 and in the following year he broke Babe Ruth's record of home runs in World Series competition.

Willie Mays was brought up to the major leagues in 1951. At that time, Mays was an undeniable asset (he hit .274) to the New York Giants in their successful quest for the pennant. The U.S. Army then drafted Mays, and when he returned to the Giants in 1954, he was even more impressive a hitter than before. He batted .345, hit 41 home runs, led the Giants to pennant and World Series victories, and won the National League's Most Valuable Player award. In 1956 his 40 stolen bases led both leagues, and he hit three triples in one game in 1961. The "Amazing Mays" won the Most Valuable Player award again in 1965 as a member of the San Francisco Giants. In 1971 Mays was elected to the Living All-Time Baseball Team, and in the same year was one of the lifetime home-run leaders with 628. He retired in 1973 after playing briefly for the New York Mets.

Don Newcombe's career as a pitcher for the Brooklyn Dodgers was a distinguished one. In 1949, his rookie year, he won 20 games. He served in the Armed Forces in 1952 and 1953, returning to the Dodgers in 1954, a year Newcombe won only 8 games. His talents quickly revived though, and in 1955 and 1956 he had the the best won-lost percentage in the National League. He was awarded the National League's Most Valuable Player award in 1956 and retired two years later.

Leroy Robert "Satchel" Paige had an enormous assortment of pitches and fantastic control. Some say he was the greatest pitcher in the history of baseball. Paige began his baseball career in the 1920s. Fans of the Pittsburgh Crawfords saw him win 31 games, 21 in succession, in 1933. He pitched five winning games in one week in 1933, allowing a total of only three runs for all five games. When he went to South America in 1939, he won 54 games and lost just 5. As a pitcher with the Kansas City Monarchs in 1946, Paige threw 64 consecutive scoreless innings.

In 1948, although Paige was over 40 years old, he became a rookie with the Cleveland Indians, finally being admitted to baseball's major leagues. Paige pitched a winning shutout in his first game with the Indians. He pitched for the St. Louis Browns from 1951 to 1953, after which he retired. Before retiring, however, Paige was chosen by Casey Stengel as a pitcher for the 1952 All-Star Game. In 1968, while in his sixties, Paige was signed by the Atlanta Braves in order to make him eligible for the major-league pension plan. His final honor was his election to the Baseball Hall of Fame on August 9, 1971.

Frank Robinson began his major-league career with the Cincinnati Reds in 1956. When the Reds won the pennant in 1961, Robinson won the National League's Most Valuable Player award with 37 home runs, 124 runs batted in, and a batting average of .342. Before leaving the Reds, he played in six All-Star games.

While leading the Baltimore Orioles to pennant and World Series victories in 1966, Frank Robinson became the first player to win the triple crown since 1956. He led the American League in batting with a .316 average, led the league in runs batted in with 122, and led in home runs with 49. When he won the American League's Most Valuable Player award in 1966, he became the first player ever to earn that coveted distinction in both leagues. When he was named manager of the Cleveland Indians after the 1974 season, he achieved an even more historic distinction—that of being the first black to manage a major-league team.

Jackie Roosevelt Robinson's athletic career began at the University of California at Los Angeles (UCLA) where he played on the football, baseball, basketball, and track teams. In 1946 he chose baseball as his professional career and was signed as second baseman for the Montreal club in the Brooklyn Dodgers' organization. When he entered the professional sports world, he carried the dreams, good wishes, and aspirations of most black people on his shoulders. Signing in 1947 with the Dodgers, he was selected by Branch Rickey to break the color barrier of major-league baseball. Robinson responded magnificently. *See* ROBINSON, JACK ROOSEVELT.

Maury Wills was called in as shortstop by the Los Angeles Dodgers in 1959 after a discouraging eight-and-a-half years in the minor leagues. In that year, he hit .260 to help win the pennant, and he hit .250 and fielded brilliantly to help Los Angeles win the World Series. Wills earned the 1962 National League's Most Valuable Player award for stealing 104 bases, batting .299, and scoring 130 runs. During his eight years with the Dodgers, Wills led the league in stolen bases for six straight years, and Los Angeles won four pennants while he was on the team. In 1967 he was traded to Pittsburgh where he continued his fine play as a shortstop; he batted .302 and stole 29 bases that year. Wills' major-league record for stolen bases in a single season, 104, lasted until 1974 when Lou Brock of the St. Louis Cardinals, another outstanding black player, stole 118. Brock also broke Ty Cobb's 1928 record (892) for bases stolen on August 29, 1977.

Basketball It is not known exactly when black athletes first began playing basketball, but the game was included in physical education classes at Howard University in 1904. By 1906 there were some league teams in Washington, D.C., and by 1911 nearly every high school had a basketball team.

Basketball truly began in Negro colleges around 1909 or 1910. At that time, Hampton Institute (Hampton, Va.) had the only gymnasium large enough to house a regulation court. Along with Hampton Institute, Lincoln University (Oxford, Pa.), Wilberforce University (Wilberforce, Ohio), and Virginia Union University (Richmord, Va.) were the first schools to have basketball teams before 1911. Xavier University (New Orleans, La.) had one of the greatest Negro college teams from 1934 to 1938; four other fine teams of this period were from Wiley College (Marshall, Tex.), Alabama State (Montgomery, Ala.), Virginia Union, and Lincoln University (Jefferson City, Mo.). In four seasons, Xavier won 67 games and lost only 2. The five regulars were Bray, Rhodes, Colege, Gant, and McQuitter.

Because of discrimination in the larger colleges, only a few blacks were notable as basketball players prior to 1945. From 1908 to 1937,

there were such stars as Wilbur Woods (Nebraska), Paul Robeson (Rutgers), John Johnson and George Gregory (Columbia), Charles Drew (Amherst), James and Samuel Barnes (Oberlin), Cleveland Abbot and Owen Ross (South Dakota), Bob Yancy and Ben Franklin (Boston).

Early Professional Basketball Club basketball teams, such as the Smart Set Athletic Club of Brooklyn and the St. Christopher Club of New York City, appeared in New York City and New Jersey in 1906. These clubs really became popular with the commencement of intercity games among the Brooklyn, New York City, and Washington, D.C., clubs. In 1908 the first important game was played: the Smart Set versus the winning team of the Washington, D.C., Interscholastic Athletic Association.

One early basketball club of note was the Chicago Romas, a girls' team that existed for a long period after World War I. The team—Corinne Robinson, Mignon Burns, Lillian Ross, Virginia Willis, Lula Porter, and Isadore Channels—was never defeated.

The Renaissance (Rens) was the most outstanding team of New York City. The team played over a period of 16 years, from 1923 to 1939, winning 1,588 games and losing 239. Winner of the first professional basketball tournament on record, the Rens team consisted of William "Wee Willie" Smith, Charles "Tarzan" Cooper, John Isaacs, William "Pop" Gates, Clarence "Puggy" Bell, Eyrie Saitch, Zack Clayton, and Clarence "Fats" Jenkins.

The Philadelphia Tribune girls' team was organized in 1931 by Ora Washington. In nine years the team lost only six games to black teams that played "boys" rules. Ora Washington was captain. Gladys Walker, Virginia Woods, Lavinia Morre, Myrtle Wilson, Rose Wilson, Marie Leach, and Florence Campbell were other members of the team.

In 1927 Abe Saperstein took over a team from Chicago called the Savoy Big Five. The team was rechristened the Harlem Globetrotters so that people would think they had "been around," although not one member of the original team was from Harlem or had ever been outside of the United States. Since 1927, however, the Globetrotter teams have traveled more than 5 million miles, have been to more than 100 countries, and have played for more than 60 million fans. Under Saperstein's promotion, the Globetrotters became an outstanding box-office attraction—a team that combined phenomenal basketball talent with slapstick comedy routines. The Globetrotters' overall record by the 1950s was 9,200 wins in 9,600 games.

Some of the early Globetrotter players were Willie "Sweet Willie" Oliver, Al "Runt" Pullins, Reece "Goose" Tatum, and Marques Haynes. Tatum played with the Trotters from 1942 to 1955 and was their center attraction as the "Clown Prince of Basketball." Haynes was with the team from 1946 to 1952 as the "World's Greatest Dribbler." When Tatum left the Globetrotters, "Meadowlark" Lemon took over the clowning and "Curley" Neal took over the dribbling from Haynes. In recent years, some of the young players with the Globetrotters have gone on to the major professional basketball leagues, as did Nat "Sweetwater" Clifton, Wilt Chamberlain, and Connie Hawkins.

Professional basketball was slower than baseball and football in eliminating racial segregation. In 1951, when Chuck Cooper was signed by the Boston Celtics, he became the first Negro to play in the National Basketball Association (NBA), the leading professional league of the present era. Although professional basketball was the last of the major professional sports to integrate its teams, it was the first to hire a black coach. Bill Russell, who became coach for the Boston Celtics in 1966, was the first Negro to coach a major-league sports team. Since their entry into professional basketball, black athletes have dominated the game in numbers and ability—more than half are black.

Outstanding Professional Basketball Players

Kareem Abdul-Jabbar (Lew Alcindor) played for the University of California, Los Angeles,

Kareem Abdul-Jabbar. *(National Basketball Association.)*

team in 1966, and led the team to an undefeated season and the national championship. UCLA did not lose another game until 1968 when Alcindor (7 feet 1⅞ inch) was injured. They did, however, in that year go on to win a third consecutive National Collegiate Athletic Association (NCAA) championship. After college, he signed an NBA contract with the Milwaukee Bucks. In the 1969–70 and 1971–72 seasons, Jabbar was the top NBA scorer. In 1971 he was the scoring leader with 2,822 points, a game-average of 34.8, and, in both 1971 and 1972, Jabbar was the league's Most Valuable Player. (He adopted the name Kareem Abdul-Jabbar during his professional career.)

Elgin Baylor played for Seattle University during its 23–4 season in 1958. The Los Angeles Lakers signed Baylor in 1959, and in 1968 he led the Lakers into the finals of the NBA championship playoffs. Baylor became the Lakers' top scorer—in one game against the New York Knickerbockers, he scored 71 points, a total second only to Wilt Chamberlain's record total (100) for a single game.

Walt Bellamy (6 feet 11 inches) was so distinguished as a center at Indiana University that he was chosen to play on the 1960 U.S. Olympic basketball team. In his first professional season (1961–62), Bellamy played with the Chicago Packers (now the Baltimore Bullets). At that time, he set what was then an NBA record with a field-goal percentage of .513. His 2,495 points were five short of making him the second man in NBA history to score 2,500 points in one season.

Dave Bing played for the Syracuse University basketball team, and led the Orangemen in scoring, rebounding, and assists. The 1966–67 season was his first with the Detroit Pistons. During that season, he became the sixth rookie in NBA history to score more than 1,600 points. He was named NBA Rookie of the Year while leading Detroit to its first NBA championship playoff in six years. In 1967–68 Bing led the NBA in scoring and was named to the league All-Star team. By the 1970–71 season, he was the NBA's individual-scoring-average leader.

Wilt Chamberlain, standing 7 feet tall, became the greatest offensive player in the history of basketball and the holder of numerous NBA records. Chamberlain was, for example, the top NBA scorer in seven straight seasons, 1959 to 1966. By 1971 he was the all-time NBA scorer, averaging 50.4 points per game. He led the NBA in rebounds for four straight seasons, 1959 to 1963, and then for five straight from 1966 to

1971. When he retired in 1974, he held the NBA career marks for total points scored (31,419) and rebounds (23,924). He also held the record for points scored in a single game (100). In the NBA, he played for Philadelphia (twice), San Francisco, and Los Angeles. His last season was spent as coach of the San Diego Conquistadors of the now defunct American Basketball Association (ABA).

Elvin Hayes, nicknamed the "Big E" (6 feet 9 inches), was the first black to play for the University of Houston. Hayes was named Player of the Year in college basketball over the brilliant Lew Alcindor in 1968. As a senior, he led Houston to a 31–0 regular-season college record. In 1968 Hayes signed with the San Diego Rockets of the NBA even though the ABA's Houston Mavericks offered him much more money; he later played with the Washington Capitals. The 1968–69 season saw Hayes become the top NBA scorer; in the 1969–70 season, he was an NBA rebound leader; and by the 1970–71 season, he was the individual-scoring-average leader of the NBA.

Julius Irving was an outstanding college player at the University of Virginia. Playing professionally for the New York Nets, he earned the ABA Most Valuable Player award in 1974, 1975, and 1976. Displaying dazzling offensive skills, "Dr. J" led the Nets to the ABA championships in 1974 and 1975. After being traded to the Philadelphia 76ers, he led the team to the NBA finals in 1977.

Tex Harrison, *Sam Jones*, and *Earl Lloyd* all attended black colleges, where they were outstanding basketball players toward the end of the segregation era (1950s). Thus, in entering organized professional basketball, they may be regarded as being among the pioneers, among the early pros. Harrison and Jones played at North Carolina State College (Durham). Harrison later joined the Globetrotters, while Jones played for the Boston Celtics. Lloyd attended West Virginia State College and later became the first black scout for the NBA. While in college, Harrison and Jones were coached by John McLendon, himself outstanding as a black coach.

Earl "the Pearl" Monroe was drafted by the Baltimore Bullets in 1967. He was named the NBA Rookie of the Year for the 1967–68 season. In 1968–69 and 1970–71, he was the NBA individual scoring leader. Monroe was traded to the New York Knickerbockers in November, 1971.

Willis Reed, in his first year as center for the New York Knicks, was named the NBA Rookie of the Year. Though hampered by a muscle injury, his determination and presence in the seventh game of the 1970 NBA finals inspired the Knicks to victory in the decisive game. He received the 1970 Most Valuable Player award. In 1977, Reed became coach of the New York Knicks.

Oscar Robertson, "the Big O," began his outstanding basketball career at the University of Cincinnati. During his three years there, the team won 79 games and lost only 9; Robertson scored a record 2,973 points. In 1960 Robertson starred for the U.S. Olympic basketball team, and it won a gold medal. The Cincinnati Royals of the NBA drafted Robertson, and he went on to lead the team to six straight playoffs. From 1960 to 1966, Robertson was the NBA assist leader, and in the 1967–68 season he led the league in scoring average. Robertson was on the NBA All-Star team each year throughout his career.

William "Bill" Russell (6 feet 10 inches) led the University of San Francisco's basketball team to two consecutive NCAA championships in 1954–55 and 1955–56. He was voted the 1956 college Player of the Year for this achievement. As a member of the U.S. Olympic basketball team in 1956, he was largely responsible for the team's gold-medal victory. In 1957 Russell signed with the Boston Celtics. He was the NBA rebound leader in 1957–58, 1958–59, 1963–64, and 1964–65. In 1969 he was an all-time NBA leading scorer. Arnold "Red" Auerbach of the Celtics offered Russell the opportunity of becoming the first Negro in a managerial position in professional sports; Russell accepted the job as coach for the Celtics in 1966. In 1973 Russell was made coach and general manager of the NBA Seattle SuperSonics.

Cazzie Russell was a triple-threat man at the University of Michigan, playing defense as a forward, offense as a center, and both as an all-around guard. The New York Knickerbockers first signed him to play guard, though Russell did not play well at this position in his first NBA year. In 1967, however, he fared better as a forward, the position he generally played. In 1971 he was traded to the San Francisco Warriors (later the Golden State Warriors).

Nate Thurmond (6 feet 11 inches) was an outstanding center with the San Francisco Warriors, perhaps one of the best all-around players in the NBA. In 1967 he helped the Warriors into the NBA championship final against Chamberlain and the Philadelphia 76ers. In that same year, he had shut out Wilt Chamberlain from the floor—no one had ever done that before.

Boxing Boxing is the only major professional sport that never excluded black athletes. This does not mean that black boxers received equal treatment; on the contrary, as one famous sportswriter observed (Paul Gallico, *Farewell to Sport*), black boxers were in competition from "behind the eight ball." During the days of the large plantations in the South, in the era of slavery, the sons of wealthy planters were often sent to England for their education where they came into contact with the sporting places of that country. Returning home, they brought with them the fashionable custom of pitting the strongest slave of one plantation against the strongest of another.

Early Boxers, 1800–1904

Andy Bowen established a record for ring fights. In 1893 he fought a 101–round draw with Jack Burke.

George Dixon was a bantamweight and featherweight fighter, and he was a champion in one class or the other for 11 years, 1889 to 1900. Dixon has been rated the greatest bantamweight of all time.

Joe Gans (1874–1910), native of Philadelphia, was the first black to hold the lightweight championship. He won it by defeating Frank Erne by a first-round knockout in 1901. He lost the title to "Battling" Nelson on a knockout in the seventeenth round in 1908. Gans also competed successfully against opponents outside his division, even against heavyweights.

George Godfrey was billed as the first black heavyweight champion of America. He wanted to fight John L. Sullivan, recognized as the official champion of the division, but Sullivan refused the challenge, invoking the color line.

Peter Jackson, a West Indian who became champion of Australia in 1886, defeated George Godfrey in a California bout in 1888. Jackson fought James J. Corbett in 1891, but that contest was declared a draw after 60 rounds. Again, Sullivan would not fight a black champion (though he fought Corbett and lost his title to him in 1892).

Tom Molyneux, whose father and grandfather were famous boxers among plantation slaves, began fighting in 1809 in the Catherine Markets of New York City. He fought and defeated all comers. He was the first black American champion to fight an international bout.

Bill Richmond, who fought between 1800 and 1818, was the first Negro to win honors in the ring. Taken to London as a boy, he was revered as a fighter there.

Joe Walcott, the welterweight champion from 1901 to 1904, was chosen as the greatest welterweight of all time by the highly respected Nat Fleischer.

Jim Wharton fought nine championship-caliber bouts and was never beaten. He had his most notable fight with Tom Britton in 1836—it was a 200-round contest and was declared a draw after four hours and seven minutes.

Heavyweights

Jack Johnson won the heavyweight crown from Tommy Burns in Sydney, Australia, in 1908. Johnson was the first Negro to win the world heavyweight championship. As recently as 1959, Nat Fleischer ranked him as the greatest ever in this division, boxing's foremost. The white establishment of that day, however, was so distressed by the fact that no white could beat Johnson that, in search of a "white hope," they brought Jim Jeffries (champion from 1899 to 1905) out of retirement. The resulting knockout by Johnson established his position as champion

Far right: Jack Johnson. (Library of Congress.)

beyond doubt and elated blacks. (*Question:* "What do you want to eat?" *Answer:* "A cup of coffee as strong as Jack Johnson and a steak beat up like Jim Jeffries.") Even though on April 5, 1915, Johnson lost his title to Jess Willard in Havana (with the usual claims of foul play), he held the title longer than any other heavyweight in modern boxing up to that time. Johnson died in 1946 and was elected to the Boxing Hall of Fame. *See also* JOHNSON, JACK.

Joe Louis (Joseph Louis Barrow), the "Brown Bomber," began his professional career in 1934 and lost only once during his entire career (excluding comeback failures), to Max Schmeling in 1936. On the return match, however, Louis avenged his earlier loss by a devastating knockout (kidney punch) in New York City in 1938. There was national rejoicing by blacks, as boxing had recently become a "white" sport. On June 22, 1937, however, the 23-year-old Joe Louis knocked out James J. Braddock, winning the world heavyweight title. Louis had also scored first-round victories in matches with John Henry Lewis, Jack Roper, Buddy Baer, and Tami Mauriello. In his long ring career, Louis successfully defended his title 25 times, a record in the

history of boxing. Louis formally retired in 1949 but failed in comeback attempts in 1950 and 1951 against Ezzard Charles and Rocky Marciano, respectively. *See* LOUIS, JOE.

Ezzard Charles. When Joe Louis retired from the ring in 1949, as undefeated world heavyweight champion, a title match was arranged between Ezzard Charles and Jersey Joe Walcott. Charles emerged victorious from that fight, and became the new holder of the heavyweight crown. New York State, however, still listed Joe

Louis as the champion. So, in 1950, to ensure his championship in all states, Charles fought Louis and won. Charles held the heavyweight crown from 1949 to 1951.

Jersey Joe Walcott (Arnold Cream) began fighting in 1936 but left the ring in 1941. He was poorly managed and exploited to such an extent that, although he was winning fights, he was barely earning enough to eat. Walcott returned to boxing, under new management, in 1945 and after bouts with Joe Baksi, Jimmy Bivens, Joey Maxim, and Joe Louis, he won the title from Ezzard Charles in 1951, becoming, at 37, the oldest fighter ever to become heavyweight champion. In that year, also, he won the Edward J. Neil Memorial Award, given annually by the Boxing Writers' Association of New York to the person who has contributed the most to boxing in that year. Walcott was dethroned by Rocky Marciano in 1952.

Floyd Patterson first distinguished himself as a boxer in 1952 when he won a gold medal in the Olympics at Helsinki. He then turned professional and was undefeated in his first 12 bouts. When Rocky Marciano retired from the ring in 1956, a fight was arranged between Patterson and Archie Moore for the vacant title. Patterson defeated Moore and became the youngest boxer ever to hold the heavyweight championship crown. In that year, he won the Edward J. Neil Memorial Award. Ingemar Johansson took the title from Patterson in 1959, but in a rematch with Johansson in 1960, Floyd became the first fighter in boxing history to regain the world heavyweight championship. Patterson lost his title for good to Charles "Sonny" Liston in 1962.

Muhammad Ali (Cassius Clay), like Floyd Patterson, first exhibited his talents when he won a gold medal in the 1960 Olympics. Later, as a professional, Ali was managed by a syndicate of ten businessmen from Louisville, the place of his birth. Ali was unbeaten in his first 19 professional bouts, and he won the heavyweight title from Sonny Liston in 1964. In 1965 he received the Edward J. Neil Memorial Award.

Ali, always a colorful and very talented boxer, experienced publicity problems when he adopted Islam as his religion. Some sportswriters refused to refer to him by his new Muslim name, although they never seemed to mind calling Arnold Cream "Jersey Joe Walcott," or Walker Smith "Sugar Ray Robinson." When Ali refused to be drafted into the U.S. Army in 1967, on the grounds that he was a minister of the Islamic

Far left: Joe Louis (left) with Sugar Ray Robinson. Kenny Seaman (right). Louis's trainer, is binding Louis's hands. *(Moorland-Spingarn Research Center, Howard University.)*

faith, his championship title and his boxing license were officially rescinded. Granted a new license to fight in 1970, Ali began a comeback, but he was unsuccessful in his attempt to dethrone Joe Frazier in 1971. However, in 1974, in Zaire (Africa), Ali became only the second man to regain the heavyweight title, by knocking out George Foreman, who had taken the title from Frazier in 1973. Ali was then 32. In 1978, he lost his title to Leon Spinks. See ALI, MUHAMMAD.

Jimmy Ellis was never really considered by many people as the champ, although he held the title of heavyweight champion after it was taken away from Ali. After all, they contended, Ali was never beaten in the ring. To add to the confusion, some states regarded Ellis as the champion and other states officially recognized Joe Frazier. While Ali's appeal against induction into the Armed Forces was pending in the courts, the World Boxing Association (WBA) and the New York State Athletic Commission ruled the championship vacant. Ellis won the WBA crown in 1968 by defeating Jerry Quarry. Frazier won the New York version of the title in 1968 by knocking out Buster Mathis (and also gained recognition as champion in Massachusetts and Illinois). Frazier was accepted as champion by all states, and by Europe and the Orient as well, when he defeated Ellis in 1970.

Joe Frazier, born in Beaufort, S.C. (1944), won the Olympic heavyweight championship in 1964. His victories over Buster Mathis (1968) and Jimmy Ellis (1970) gave the heavyweight division an undisputed champion after three years of confusion. He successfully defended his title against Muhammad Ali in 1971, but in 1973 Frazier lost the title to George Foreman in a match staged in Kingston, Jamaica. A year later, Foreman lost to Muhammad Ali in an eighth-round knockout in Zaire. See also FRAZIER, JOE.

Light Heavyweights

Archie Moore won the light-heavyweight championship from Joey Maxim in 1952, and he kept the title until 1961. In 1958 he was honored with the Edward J. Neil Memorial Award. However, he was unsuccessful in all his attempts to become the heavyweight champion, although he knocked out more opponents than any other man in boxing.

Middleweights

Sugar Ray Robinson (Walker Smith), the most spectacular fighter since "Tiger" Flowers in the 1920s, fought 202 bouts in his professional boxing career, which lasted 25 years, from 1940 to 1965. After holding the welterweight title from 1946 to 1951, he later ruled the middleweights; in the latter division, he won the title five times between 1951 and 1958. As "Kid Chocolate" (a champion in his own right) once stated, in comparing him with other middleweights, Robinson was "the master."

Lightweights

Henry ("Hammering Hank") Armstrong was the only man to hold the championship in three different classes at the same time. In a ten-month period, during 1937 and 1938, he held the featherweight, lightweight, and welterweight championships. He gave up the featherweight title without a fight when he could no longer make the 126-pound weight limit. He lost the lightweight title in 1939 to Lou Ambers, and the welterweight title in 1940 to Fritzie Zivic. Altogether, Armstrong fought 175 professional fights, winning 144 and scoring 97 knockouts. He made $4 million during his career, and Armstrong was elected to the Boxing Hall of Fame in 1954.

Joe Brown, at the age of 32, won the lightweight crown from Wallace "Bud" Smith in 1956. He defended his title until 1962, when at the age of 38, he lost to Carlos Ortiz.

Featherweights

Sandy Saddler, was the featherweight champion during most of the 1950s. He originally won the title from Willie Pep in 1948, lost it to Pep in 1949, and regained it in 1950. Saddler then kept the title until 1957 when he retired following an automobile accident.

Football

Dominance at Black Colleges Save for a few black players who became stars at white colleges and universities in the North, the great bulk of black participation in the early history of college football centered on programs at black colleges. So completely segregated was athletics in the South, for example, that tickets were not sold to blacks for the Rose Bowl game held at Duke University in 1942. Thus, for the black spectator and participant, the black college was almost the exclusive source for football competition and training. Athletic programs in black institutions were developed mainly around football and basketball, especially the former, at the expense, critics claimed, of academic programs. Nonetheless, well-attended and organized schedules were maintained by several athletic conferences, including the Central Intercollegiate Athletic Association (CIAA) and the Southern Intercollegiate Athletic Conference (SIAC). Except for a few white spectators or the news media, everything was entirely black—spectators, bands, players, coaches, referees, and officials. Most of the larger colleges participated, and, considering the meager resources of the black college, the performances were not lacking in terms of prevailing American football standards.

The high-water mark of the programs was reached during the 1950s, in the prosperity following World War II and the years prior to desegregation—before white institutions made offers to potential black athletes. Some black colleges developed consistently winning football programs. Before 1930, Tuskegee, Hampton, Wilberforce, Lincoln University (Oxford, Pa.), and Howard dominated. Between the mid-1930s and the mid-1950s, Langston, Kentucky State, Morgan State, and Tennessee A & I dominated. In the 1950s and 1960s, Florida A & M, Grambling, Morgan State, and Maryland State became the top black football powers.

In the 1960s and 1970s, black college teams appeared in postseason classics at several bowls. The Orange Blossom classic (originally played in Jacksonville, Fla.; later changed to Miami), under the sponsorship as well as dominance of Florida A & M University (FAMU), has been among the best-known postseason bowl games. Other black-sponsored bowl games have been played in Washington, D.C., Philadelphia, and New York City. Grambling College and Morgan State College have been featured in these games (the 1970s). Some black colleges, generally very small and always beset with financial problems, are revamping (or have revamped) their athletic programs in the face of competition for their athletes over whom they once had a virtual monopoly. Some schools have actually stopped playing against traditional black conference opponents. Integration has tended to hamper athletics at black colleges even if it has been a boon to individual athletes.

Some notable college football coaches throughout the years were Gideon Smith (Hampton), Harry R. Jefferson (Hampton), Henry A. Kean (Tennessee A & I), Edward P. Hurt (Morgan), Talmadge I. Hill (Morgan), Earl Banks (Morgan), Nathaniel "Nat" Taylor (Morgan), Vernon E. "Skip" McCain (Maryland State), B. T. Harvey (Morehouse), Alonzo S. "Jake" Gaither (Florida A & M), Cleve Abbott (Tuskegee), Johnny McLendon (Tennessee A & I), Ernest Marshall (Howard), George Johnson (Lincoln University at Oxford, Pa.), R. W. E. Jones (Grambling), Fred T. "Pop" Long (Wiley), W. J. Nicks (Prairie View A & M), J. W. Barco (Virginia Union), Tom Harris (Virginia Union), John T. Williams (Kentucky State), Robert "Bob" White (Kentucky State), and William Bell (North Carolina A & T).

Early Black Football Stars at White Colleges Eastern and New England colleges with their long traditions of admitting a few blacks (though not without discrimination) have been the schools for some of the earliest black football players, many of whom later became professionals. Some of these players are mentioned below.

William H. Lewis was a center at Amherst College in the early 1890s. He was named an All-American by Walter Camp for the 1892–93 season, and he went on to become a line coach at Harvard, an exceptional accomplishment even by 1970 standards. Lewis climaxed his career in 1911 by becoming the first black assistant attorney general of the United States.

William H. Craighead became the first black captain of a white college football team at Massachusetts State in 1905.

Frederick "Fritz" Pollard was a halfback at Brown University and was named an All-American in 1916. When the forerunner of the modern National Football League was founded in 1920, he soon became one of its stars. He played for the Akron Indians, the Milwaukee Badgers, the Hammond Pros, and the Providence Steamrollers until he retired in 1926.

Paul Robeson, who won four varsity letters at Rutgers, was a football All-American in 1917 and 1918. Robeson played professionally with the Hammond Pros, the Akron Indians, and the Milwaukee Badgers. After his football career, Robeson, an outstanding actor and singer, emigrated to the U.S.S.R. but later returned to the United States. *See* ROBESON, PAUL.

Wilmeth Sadat-Singh was a great quarterback and passer for Syracuse University. Although he had been accepted to play on a white team, he suffered scorn and prejudice from other white teams. In 1937, for example, the University of Maryland, then completely segregationist and "lily-white," had an at-home game with Syracuse in which Sadat-Singh was barred from playing. In a rescheduled game in Syracuse, in which Sadat-Singh played, Maryland was thoroughly routed, 53–0.

Jerome Hartwell "Brud" Holland, an end who made the "end-around" play famous, was the first Negro to play football for Cornell University. He began playing in 1939, and at the end of his college career, he was named a member of the university's all-time football team. Holland was later appointed to the presidencies of Delaware State College and Hampton Institute and was American ambassador to Sweden.

· *Kenny Washington* was a halfback for the University of California, Los Angeles (UCLA), and was named to the All-American team in 1939. Segregation and World War II prevented Washington from continuing his football career as a professional. However, professional football had changed by the end of the war, and Washington signed with the Los Angeles Rams in 1946 and played with them until he retired in 1949. Other notable black players, at white institutions, include: Duke Slater (All-America, Iowa, 1919, 1921), Homer Harris (first black football captain, Iowa, 1938), Levi Jackson (captain, Yale, 1949), Horace Bell (Minnesota), Willis Ward (Michigan), Matthew Bullock (Dartmouth), Robert Marshall (Minnesota), Bernard Jefferson (Northwestern), Chester Pierce (Harvard), Gene Derricote (Michigan), George Talliaferro (Indiana), Ozzie Simmons (Iowa), and Lenny Lyle (Indiana). (For information about more recent players, see the professional players discussed below.)

National Football League: Offensive Stars

Marion Motley, at the end of World War II, became one of the first Negroes to play a major-league professional sport. He was signed as a fullback in 1946 by the Cleveland Browns and played until 1953. Throughout his career, Motley always averaged over 4.27 yards per carry. Because of his outstanding ability on the field, he was voted into the Professional Football Hall of Fame. Although he wanted to remain in professional football as a coach, he was never offered such a position, probably because of the color barrier.

Fletcher Joe Perry was signed by the San Francisco 49ers in 1948, becoming their first black player. Perry, a fullback, led the NFL in ground gaining in 1953 and 1954, with more than 1,000 yards per season. He was elected to the Professional Football Hall of Fame, and as of 1971 he was one of the NFL's all-time leaders in rushing yardage with 8,378 yards.

Lenny Moore had two football careers. One was as a pass-catching halfback and the other,

after injuries, as a running halfback. In 1956 he was signed by the Baltimore Colts and was named Rookie of the Year, and he went on to become an all-star NFL flanker for four years in a row—1957–60. Liddell Mitchell, playing twenty years later for the Colts, surpassed Moore's rushing record.

Claude "Buddy" Young left the University of Illinois to play professional football with the New York Yankees of the All-America Conference, a professional league founded in 1946. When that league merged with the National Football League in 1949, he continued his career with the Baltimore Colts. In six seasons with the NFL, Young rushed for 1,275 yards, and caught passes for a total of 1,978 yards. When Young retired, the Colts gave him the rare honor of retiring his number (22) along with him. In 1968 he was elected to the professional Football Hall of Fame. Young served as a public-relations representative for the Colts, and, later, the NFL appointed him as a special assistant to the commissioner.

Jim Brown's professional football career began in 1957 with the Cleveland Browns. Brown was the greatest runner in the history of professional football. He led the NFL in rushing in eight of his nine seasons; by the early 1970s, he was the NFL's all-time leader in rushing yardage with 12,312, and had scored 126 touchdowns, an NFL career record. Brown is in the Professional Football Hall of Fame.

Charley Taylor graduated from Maryland State College and joined the Washington Redskins in 1964, when he was named Rookie of the Year in the National Football League. In 1966 he caught 72 passes, the top total in the NFL, and he also earned the NFL's star receiver award in 1967. By 1971 he was the NFL's active statistical leader in pass receptions with 396, and in points with 366.

Leroy Kelly, as a Cleveland Brown in 1965, was the National Football League punt-return champion with a 15.6-yard average. In 1966 he was made a regular halfback and in 1967 led the NFL in rushing with 1,205 yards, an average of 5.1 yards a carry. By 1971 Kelly was one of the NFL's all-time leaders in rushing yardage with 5,209 yards, and in points scored with 420.

Gale Sayers joined the Chicago Bears in 1965 from the University of Kansas. In that year, he scored 22 touchdowns, a league record, and led the league in scoring with 132 points. He rushed for 867 yards, averaging 5.2 yards per carry and was named Rookie of the Year in the National

Football League. In 1966 and again in 1969 he was the top rusher in the NFL, and by 1971 Sayers was a National Football Conference active statistical leader in rushing with 4,917 yards. He retired in 1972 at the age of 29 after numerous leg injuries.

Roosevelt Brown was named to the black college All-American team after four years of active playing at Morgan State College. In 1953 he started his professional football career with the New York Giants. Until he retired in 1965, Brown was football's most awesome and respected offensive tackle.

Jim Parker, a two-time All-American while a student at Ohio State University, signed with the Baltimore Colts in 1957. He is said to have been the best offensive interior lineman in professional football. He was an All-Professional Tackle for five years as well as an All-Professional Guard. He was a mainstay of the Colts in 1958 and 1959 when they won NFL championships, and again in 1964 when they won the division title but lost to Cleveland in the postseason championship game.

National Football League: Defensive Stars

Gene "Big Daddy" Lipscomb was one of the few professionals who never attended college. He signed with the Los Angeles Rams in 1953 and was traded to the Baltimore Colts in 1956. In 1959 he led the Colts in number of tackles and was thought by many to be the best defensive lineman in the game. He ended his professional career with the Pittsburgh Steelers and later turned to a career as a professional wrestler.

Willie Wood was the University of Southern California's quarterback for three years, but he was not drafted by professional football teams (blacks are usually not placed in the quarterback position by professional teams). However, in 1960 he tried out for the safety position on the Green Bay Packers, and quickly became an outstanding defensive back. In 1962 he intercepted nine passes and was second in the league in punt returns with an average of 11.9 yards. By 1971 he was a National Football Conference active statistical leader in interceptions with 71.

Herb Adderley was an All-American at Michigan State, and was signed by the Green Bay Packers in 1961. In 1962 he intercepted seven passes and was the league's third best kickoff-return man with a 27.9 average, returning one kickoff 103 yards. He held the NFL record (six) for most touchdowns from interceptions. The National Football Conference records him as an active statistical leader in interceptions with 42, and in kickoff returns with an average yardage of 25.7.

David "Deacon" Jones became an outstanding defensive end with the Los Angeles Rams in the mid-1960s, when that team was noted for its defensive line.

Other great black NFL players of the modern (postwar) era were Emlen Tunnell (New York Giants) and Dick "Night Train" Lane (Detroit Lions), defensive backs; and Ollie Matson (Chicago Cardinals) and Larry Brown (Washington Redskins), running backs.

American Football League Stars The American Football League began operation in 1960 as a rival of the National Football League. In 1970 the leagues completed a merger, whereby the NFL included a National Conference (composed of earlier NFL teams) and an American Conference (comprised mainly of former AFL teams). Some of the players noted in the following paragraphs played in the AFL when it was an independent league, and some have played when it was independent (AFL) and then as a division (AFC) of the NFL.

Abner Haynes played for the Dallas Texans in 1960, the first year of the American Football League. That year he led the league in rushing and punt returns; he was fifth in pass catching, seventh in scoring, and eighth in kickoff returns. This impressive play was responsible for his becoming the AFL's first Player of the Year. By 1969, Haynes was an outstanding AFL rusher and pass receiver.

Paul Lowe was a virtually unnoticed halfback until he began to play for the San Diego Chargers. In 1963 he gained 1,010 yards for an average of 5.7 yards per carry, and in 1965 he gained 1,121 yards and was the AFL's Player of the Year. In 1971 he was a statistical leader in the American Football Conference in rushing yardage (4,860 yards).

Mike Garrett was a halfback All-American at the University of Southern California, and in 1965 he won the Heisman Trophy. Garrett was drafted by Kansas City Chiefs of the AFL. That year as a rookie, he tied for second in rushing with 801 yards, averaging 5.5 yards per carry. His 77-yard run from scrimmage was the longest of the season. In 1967 he carried for 192 yards against the New York Jets, the best single-game performance in the AFL for that year. By 1971, he was an active statistical leader in rushing with 3,392 yards.

Otis Taylor became a regular flanker for the

Kansas City Chiefs in 1965. His performance in 1966 included catching 58 passes for 1,297 yards, having the league-leading average of 22.4 yards per catch, and scoring 8 touchdowns. In 1967 he caught 59 passes and scored 11 touchdowns, and by 1971 he was the American Football Conference's leading pass receiver.

Orenthal James ("O. J.") Simpson was recognized as a great football player while still at the

O. J. Simpson—
"Juice." *(Photo by
Robert L. Smith,
Courtesy of Buffalo
Bills.)*

University of Southern California (U.S.C.) in the mid 1960s. While at U.S.C., Simpson led the nation in rushing with 1,415 yards, and he was voted an All-American Halfback. In 1967 he was voted the college Player of the Year by the National Sportscasters and Sportswriters Association and by United Press International. The Heisman Trophy was awarded him in 1968. After college, he was signed by the Buffalo Bills (AFC) and in 1971 he was an active statistical leader (AFC) in kickoff returns with an average of 30.8 yards per return. In 1973 Simpson set a new single-season professional record for rushing when he gained 2,003 yards, bettering the previous mark held by Jim Brown.

Ernie Ladd was a defensive tackle with the San Diego Chargers when they were a championship team (AFL). Ladd won a reputation for hard-driving, aggressive play. After playing for the Chargers, he was traded to the Houston Oilers and then to the Kansas City Chiefs.

Buck Buchanan signed with the Kansas City Chiefs in 1962, and by 1966 he was an all-star AFL performer at defensive tackle. At 275

pounds, he was one of the biggest players in professional football.

Bobby Bell was an All-American Tackle in his junior and senior years while playing football at the University of Minnesota. He won the Outland Trophy as the nation's best college lineman in 1962, and he later became an outstanding linebacker for the Kansas City Chiefs.

Heisman Trophy Winners In addition to Ernie Davis (1961), Mike Garrett (1965), and O. J. Simpson (1968), mentioned above, recent black winners of the Heisman Trophy were Archie Griffin (1975, 1976), Ohio State University, Tony Dorsett (1977), University of Pittsburgh, Billy Simms (1978), University of Oklahoma, and Charles White (1980) of the University of Southern California. Griffin was the first athlete to win the trophy twice.

Horse Racing Until the end of the nineteenth century, racing jockeys were mostly black. From the early colonial days of the sport in America, black jockeys, handlers, trainers, and grooms were everywhere evident. It was, of course, the expected duty of slaves and servants to care for the livery. Thus, knowledge and skills related to the sport were entrusted to blacks. The names of some of the earliest jockeys, like much of Afro-American history, have been lost to history. Now and then, a name like Cato or Pompey appears. (It was a common practice to name some slaves after Romans during the colonial period.) The tradition of black participation, nevertheless, continued after emancipation from slavery and well through the next generation. For example, in the first Kentucky Derby (1875), 14 of the 15 jockeys were black; and, expectedly, a black jockey (Oliver Lewis) was astride the winner (Aristides). The last black jockey (from the United States) in the Kentucky Derby was Jess Conley (1911).

Though black handlers or an occasional jockey and owner are still to be seen at racetracks, the black presence, save for the spectators, is not nearly as much in evidence as in football, basketball, track, or baseball. The twentieth-century black jockey has been largely excluded from participation. On June 15, 1971, Cheryl White, a seventeen-year-old Ohioan, rode her first mount and, thus, became the first black female jockey. There have been three truly great black jockeys: Isaac Murphy, Willie Simms, and Jimmy Winkfield.

Isaac Murphy won his first horse race astride Glentina when he was only 14 years of age in

1875. He went on winning races, including three Kentucky Derbies, most famous of all American horse races. In 1884 he rode Buchanan, in 1890 he rode Riley, and in 1891 he rode to the winner's circle on Kingman. Murphy is in the Hall of Fame established by two famous race courses (Pimlico, Md., and Saratoga Springs, N.Y.). He is one of a handful of jockeys whose fame is almost legendary.

Willie Simms won the Kentucky Derby in 1896 and 1898 riding Ben Brush and Plaudit, respectively. Simms was the first Negro jockey to gain international fame. When he raced in England, he was the first American jockey ever to win on an English racetrack with an American horse.

Jimmy Winkfield, together with Isaac Murphy, was one of only two jockeys to have ever won the Kentucky Derby twice in succession. Winkfield won in 1901 on His Eminence and in 1902 on Alan-a-Dale. Winkfield left the United States to race in France, Russia, and other European countries where he became a rider of great renown and a very successful trainer. He did not leave France until 1940 when Hitler invaded that country. After World War II, he returned to Europe and continued his career as an outstanding trainer.

Auto Racing As black jockeys were shunted out of horse racing, the new sport of auto racing, ever on the increase after 1910, was essentially closed to black drivers from the outset, and remained so. One of the first blacks to participate on a restricted basis, and with little or no recognition or acclaim, was Rojo Jack. His career extended from 1923 to 1954. Since that time up to the present, there have been two notable black drivers: George Wiltshire and Wendell Scott, a native of Danville, Va.

Track and Field From the standpoint of integration, track-and-field sports were somewhat akin to boxing. Blacks did not always receive the same considerations as whites, but they were never barred from participating in track-and-field events.

In 1946 the National Amateur Athletic Union outdoor championships were to be held in San Antonio, Tex., and many athletes wondered if they should compete in a part of the nation that enforced segregation. Although many athletes went to the meet, the members of the Pioneer Club of New York did not. Blacks who attended were received cordially, but hotel accommodations were not available to them. In 1947 Washington, D.C., was host to the first indoor track meet open to all races; it was held in the National Guard building.

Runners

George Poage, a hurdler and quarter miler, became the first Negro track-and-field participant in the Olympic Games when he competed in St. Louis in 1904.

Howard P. Drew was probably the world's best sprinter before World War I, although he was never able to enter the Olympics. He was injured before the 1912 Olympics, and the 1916 games were cancelled because of World War I. By 1920 he was past his prime. The track records he set before the war, however, stood for many years. In 1912 and 1913 he won the National Amateur Athletic Union championship in the 100-yard dash, and in 1913 he won the 220-yard dash. In 1914 he was coholder, with Arthur Duffy, of the world record for the 100-yard dash, having run it in 9.6 seconds. He later became the sole official holder of that record when Duffy admitted accepting money for competing in track meets.

Eddie Tolan, along with Ralph Metcalfe, dominated the 1932 Olympic Games. In the 100-meter dash, Tolan ran with Metcalfe to a photo finish in a world-record time of 10.3 seconds, and it was the first time a Negro had won an Olympic gold medal. Tolan also won the 200-meter dash in 21.2 seconds, another world record.

Ralph Metcalfe was captain of Marquette University's track team, and although he never won an Olympic gold medal, he had a notable track career. In 1932 he broke previous records for the 220-yard dash, and the 100- and 200-meter sprints, and tied Eddie Tolan's record of 9.5 seconds in the 100-yard dash.

Jesse Owens, literally and figuratively, ran away with the 1936 Olympics in Berlin, where he won four gold medals. He tied the world record for the 100-meter dash in 10.3 seconds; he set an Olympic broad-jump record by leaping 26 feet 5⁵/₁₆ inches; he set a new Olympic record with a time of 20.7 seconds in the 200-meter dash; and he ran the first leg of the 400-meter relay, helping his team set an Olympic and world record of 39.8 seconds. Sportswriters have voted Owens the greatest track-and-field star ever. *See also* OWENS, JESSE.

Eulace Peacock, a contemporary of Owens, was upstaged by Owens at the 1932 Olympics

Isaac Murphy.
(Library of Congress.)

because of an injured tendon. However, along with Owens, Peacock was one of the nation's great sprinters.

Harrison Dillard was another black track-and-field athlete who starred at the Olympic Games. In the 1948 Olympics, he was the first American track-and-field entrant to win a gold medal, win-

Jesse Owens after receiving one of his four gold medals in the 1936 Olympics, with silver medalist Lutz Long (right) and bronze medalist Tajiman (left). *(Wide World Photos.)*

ning the 100-meter sprint with a time of 10.3 seconds that tied Eddie Tolan's 1932 record. In the 1952 Olympics, he won a gold medal in the 100-meter high hurdles.

Mal Whitfield turned in a remarkable performance in the 1948 Olympics, setting a new Olympic record of 1 minute and 49.2 seconds in the 800-meter run. He ran the anchor-leg and was instrumental in winning the 1,600-meter relay, and he took third place in the 400-meter dash, achieving the highest individual total score of the 1948 games. Later, in the 1952 Olympics, he won a gold medal in the 800-meter race with the same record time as in 1948.

Otis Davis was the only American to win a gold medal in a track event in the 1960 Olympic Games. He won his medal in the 400-meter dash while setting a new Olympic and world record of 44.9 seconds.

Wilma Rudolph, with great courage and fortitude, overcame scarlet fever and double pneumonia that had left her crippled at the age of

four. She went on to earn a reputation as the fastest woman runner in the world. While competing in the 1960 Olympic Games, held in Rome, she won the 100-meter dash, defeated her opponents in the 200-meter dash with an Olympic record time of 23.3 seconds, and anchored the winning 400-meter relay team. With those three victories, she became the first American woman to win three Olympic medals in track. A graduate of Tennessee A & I University, she was also voted the female athlete of the year (1960) by the Associated Press, and named the most outstanding athlete of the year by the European Sportswriters Association. Wilma Rudolph did not compete in the 1964 Olympics—she retired on top.

Henry Carr, who ran in the 1964 Olympics at Tokyo, was another record breaker. He set an Olympic and world record in the 200 meters (20.2 seconds) and in the 220 meters (20.3 seconds). He also played a significant part in winning the gold medals in the 400-meter and 1,600-meter relays for the United States. Following the Tokyo games, Carr began a career in professional football with the New York Giants and was later traded to the Baltimore Colts.

Hayes Jones, with weak vision and a right leg three-quarters of an inch shorter than the left, won the Amateur Athletic Union's title in 1961 and the 110-meter high hurdles in the 1964 Olympics. Together with Henry Carr, Jones was a member of the victorious 400- and 1,600-meter relay teams. He retired from track competition after realizing his dream of winning an Olympic gold medal.

Bob Hayes won the 100-meter race in 10 seconds flat and made up four yards to win the 400-meter relay during the 1964 Olympics. In 1965 he joined professional football with the Dallas Cowboys and became one of the NFL's top receivers.

Wyomia Tyus won many Amateur Athletic Union events while she was attending Tennessee A & I State University on a track scholarship. She became an Olympic champion in 1964 by winning the 100-meter dash in 11.4 seconds. In 1965, while competing in Russia, she equaled the women's world record for the 100 meters with a time of 11.1 seconds.

Decathlon Champions

Milt Campbell, when only 18 years of age, entered the decathlon in the 1952 Olympics in Helsinki and finished second to Bob Mathias. Later, in the 1956 Melbourne Olympics, he won the 110-meter high hurdles, the 100-meter dash, and the shot-put event; his point total of 7,937 set a new Olympic decathlon record. Rather than continue with decathlon, Campbell went to college on a football scholarship and later played professional football with the Cleveland Browns.

Rafer Johnson finished second to Milt Campbell in the 1956 Olympics decathlon, but later in a triangular meet, he became America's fastest high hurdler with a time of 22.7 seconds. In 1958, at the "Little Olympics" in Moscow, he set a world decathlon record of 8,302 points by establishing a new decathlon discus distance of 161 feet, throwing a javelin 238 feet, pole-vaulting almost 13 feet, and running the 400-meter race in 48.2 seconds. Johnson was determined to be number one in the 1960 Olympics decathlon event and he was. He won easily with a phenomenal point total of 8,392, far above all previous records. Aside from being the finest all-around athlete in the history of track-and-field competition, Johnson had an A average at UCLA, was UCLA's student-body president, and headed three campus honorary societies. He went on to work for California's State Recreation Commission and became a sportscaster. His interest in politics brought him close to Senator Robert Kennedy, by whose side he stood when the senator was fatally shot by Sirhan Sirhan.

High Jumpers

Cornelius Johnson, David Albritton, and Melvin Walker, by clearing the bar at 6 feet 9¾ inches, had jumped higher than any other athletes. Their record stood from 1932 to 1939.

John Thomas was 17 and a freshman at Boston University in 1959, when at the Melrose Games, he became the first man to jump seven feet indoors. Unfortunately, the judges did not measure the bar after his jump, and the record did not become official. Two weeks later, at the New York Athletic Club, Thomas duplicated his 7-foot feat. This time it was recorded, and he had set a new world record. In 1960 he twice cleared the bar at 7 feet 2 inches, and though he only won a bronze medal in the 1960 Olympics, he set a new world record for the high jump (7 feet 3¾ inches) at the trials for the games.

Broad Jumpers *See* HUBBARD, DEHART; OWENS, JESSE.

Weight Champions

Theodore Cable was the first black athlete to win an intercollegiate weight championship. In 1912 he threw the hammer 162 feet 4½ inches.

Charley Fonville captured the American shot-put record with a throw of 58 feet ¼ inches in 1948.

Notable Black Athletes in Other Sports

Tennis Tennis was introduced into the United States not long after Maj. Walter C. Wingfield, a British army officer, devised the modern game in 1873. Although it was a completely segregated sport, it had become popular in the black community by the early 1880s.

One of the first black sponsors of tennis was the Rev. W. W. Walker. He was responsible for the first interstate tennis tournament, which was held in Philadelphia in 1898. The singles' champion of that tournament was Thomas Jefferson, and his first prize was a tennis racket. Walker won the interstate tournaments in 1899 and 1900. The American Tennis Association (ATA) was founded in 1916 by H. S. McCard, William H. Wright, B. M. Rhetta, Ralph V. Cook, Henry Freeman, John F. N. Wilkinson, and Talley Holmes. The ATA's first national championships were held in Baltimore in 1917 and were won by Talley Holmes and Sylvester Smith. The ATA first held two national championships—men's singles and doubles. Then, in 1917, women's singles were established; in 1928 women's doubles and mixed doubles were introduced; and in 1933 veterans' singles were played. In 1935 the ATA added girls' singles and in 1937 junior doubles and boys' singles.

Althea Gibson was the daughter of a poor sharecropper who earned the right to play tennis against whites in the big tournaments. Her first tournaments were won as a member of the American Tennis Association (ATA). She won the association's championships in 1942, 1944, and 1945. In 1952 she was ranked ninth nationally, and in 1953 she was seventh.; in 1954 she dropped to thirteenth. In 1956 she took her first big tournament by winning the French women's singles championship. In 1957 and 1958, she won the United States and Wimbledon singles titles; in 1958 and 1959, she was the top-ranked woman tennis player in the United States, the first black to attain that status. She retired from amateur tennis in 1958. In 1972 she was named to the National Lawn Tennis Hall of Fame. During her long and successful tennis career, she had become an outstanding competitive golfer as well.

Arthur Ashe, like Althea Gibson, also made some tennis "firsts" as a black athlete. Under the tutelage of R. Walter "Whirlwind" Johnson, a black physician, he was the first black to com-

Althea Gibson warming up for a match at Forest Hills in 1950, when she was the first black athlete to play in a national U.S. Lawn Tennis Association tourney. *Photoworld.)*

pete on the U.S. Davis Cup Team (1963). When Ashe won the U.S. National men's singles championship, in 1968, he became the first black to win a major men's tennis title. Again in 1968, when he won the first U.S. National Open title at Forest Hills, he triumphed over the strongest field ever assembled for a single American tennis tournament. In 1975, Ashe became the first black male to win the Wimbledon singles. *See* ASHE, ARTHUR.

Golf Like tennis, golf had been a segregated and elitist sport during its early years. Negroes did play it shortly after it was introduced in this country, however, and the use of Negro caddies was a factor that encouraged an interest in the sport among blacks. Some golf clubs even sponsored caddy tournaments.

Since most golf courses were (and are) owned by private country clubs that discriminated against blacks, the black golfer found his best opportunity to play on public golf courses. Even here, however, there was exclusion and discrimination. The first Negro golf courses were at Mapledalex in Stowe, Mass., the Asbury Park course in New Jersey, and the Sunset Hills course in Kankakee, Ill. The earliest country clubs, with nine-hole courses, that were owned or operated by Negroes included the Shady Rest Country Club in Westfield, N.J., and the Lincoln

Country Club in Atlanta, Ga.

The United Golf Association (UGA) was formed for men in the mid-1920s and joined by women in 1930. Its national tournaments were held annually beginning in 1926. Each year, about 150 or more black golfers entered the National Open and Amateur and the Southern Open and Amateur championship tournaments. Unfortunately, early black golfers had few opportunities to test their skills nationally because they were often barred from white courses and tournaments; but conditions were to change after the civil rights movement (1960s).

Professional Golfers

Charlie Sifford may be the best-known black golfer. In 1957 he won the Long Beach, Calif., Open tournament, and earned $8,000 on the Professional Golfers' Association (PGA) tour in that year. By 1967 he had won enough tournament money ($47,025) to rank number 25 among leading PGA money winners.

Lee Elder was not able to achieve his full potential as a golfer because, as a black man, he was barred from most of the best courses that would have enabled him to train properly for a national tournament. Nevertheless, he began his professional golfing career by winning 18 out of 21 tournaments as a member of the UGA. Unchallenged by the UGA play, he attended the Professional Golfers' Association school to obtain credentials to play on the PGA tour. Elder earned $25,000 in his first year's tour with the PGA. In 1968 he was barely defeated by Jack Nicklaus in the American Golf Classic in Akron, Ohio. In 1974 Elder made golf history by becoming the first black player ever to qualify for the Masters tournament, one of the sport's four greatest events. He won the Houston Open in 1976.

Bicycle Racing

Major Taylor was the world's fastest bicycle rider. At first, Taylor was not allowed to participate in the American Spring championships because of his color. He was determined to do so, however, and marshaled the support of his white friends and the press to force the management of the big racing syndicates to admit him. Once allowed to compete, Taylor won the 1898, 1899, and 1900 American Sprint championships and continued on to Europe and Australia, where he defeated all the competing cyclists on those continents.

Versatile Women Pioneers

Anita Grant was a pioneer in developing the interest of women in athletics and a versatile athlete who won honors in several sports. When she was captain of the YWCA basketball team, the team lost only three intercity games over a period of nine years. As a tennis player, she won the women's Washington city matches in 1925 and 1926. She was the female partner on the team that won the national mixed-doubles title of the American Tennis Association in 1929 and 1930, and she was a member of the national women's doubles championship team in 1933.

Inez Patterson fought for the right to compete in sports regardless of racial background, and she was persistent, ladylike, and successful in this fight. At Temple University she played on six varsity teams: hockey, tennis, basketball, track, volleyball, and dancing. She broke the color barrier that restricted black women from participating in the May Day festival, the American Red Cross examiners' course, and the Women's Athletic Association swimming meet. When her active career in sports was over, Patterson devoted her energies toward training other black women in athletics.

Lula Hymes was a member of the Tuskegee girls' track team, which from 1936 to the present, has had almost unbroken success. In 1937 and 1938, the team won the National Amateur Athletic Union's women's track-and-field championship. Hymes was high-point winner of the 1938 AAAU meet, winning the 100-meter dash and the broad jump.

Alice Coachman was a very notable female member of the U.S. Olympic team in 1948. She won a gold medal in the running high jump with a jump of 5 feet 6⅛ inches, breaking the previous record for that event set in 1932, and she was the only woman member of that Olympic team to win a track event. In addition, she earned an Olympiad Champion crown.

Notes on the Black Athlete Sports have provided some athletes a way to the very top, but this conclusion is misleading. For every Kareem Abdul-Jabbar, or Muhammed Ali, athletes who command the highest salaries, there are hundreds of aspiring black athletes who do not make successful careers. More important, though the black athlete has been a morale builder and a symbol of racial achievement, and though his income often places him in the category of the elite and the celebrity, his employment (undoubtedly beneficial to himself and family) does very little to uplift financially the black community as a whole. Like most other blacks, however, the athlete has also faced the problems of discrimination.

REFERENCES: There is an extensive popular literature on individual athletes and sports. Helpful guides to this periodical literature may be found in *Guide to Negro Periodical Literature,* compiled in the 1940s by Albert P. Marshall. It was one of the first such guides to be published. Continuations of this guide follow in the *Index to Periodical Articles By and About Negroes* (formerly *Index to Selected Periodicals*) by the Hallie Q. Brown Memorial Library and the New York Public Library's Schomburg Collection. Several good but aging comprehensive references include: Fleischer, Nathaniel S., *Black Dynamite: The Story of the Negro in the Prize Ring from 1782 to 1938,* C. J. O'Brien, New York, 1938–47; Henderson, Edwin B., *The Negro in Sports,* rev. ed., Associated Publishers, Washington, D.C., 1949; and Young, Andrew S. N., *Negro Firsts in Sports,* Johnson Publishing Co., Chicago, 1963. An increasing number of autobiographies and biographies of Afro-American athletes has appeared since the 1960s. *See also* BIBLIOGRAPHIES/BIOGRAPHIES/GUIDES.

ATKINS, HANNAH D. (1923–   ) librarian, state legislator; born in Winston-Salem, N.C. Atkins received a B.S. degree from Saint Augustine's College (Raleigh, N.C.) and a B.L.S. degree from the University of Chicago. She studied law for a time at Oklahoma City University and the University of Oklahoma. Starting in 1963, she was chief of the general reference division and acting law librarian of the Oklahoma State Library. In 1969 Atkins was elected to the Oklahoma house of representatives, and became the first Afro-American woman to chair a legislative committee.

ATKINS, SIMON G. (1863–1934), educator; born in Haywood, N.C. Atkins graduated from Saint Augustine's Normal and Collegiate Institute (Raleigh, N.C.; now Saint Augustine's College) in 1884. He served on the faculty of Livingstone College (Salisbury, N.C.) for six years and was superintendent of the Afro-American schools of Winston-Salem for five years. In 1892 Atkins founded the Slater Industrial and State Normal School, which, in 1969, became Winston-Salem State University. For 40 years, Atkins was a delegate to the quadrennial conferences of the African Methodist Episcopal Zion (AMEZ) Church. *See also* WINSTON-SALEM STATE UNIVERSITY.

ATLANTA BAPTIST FEMALE SEMINARY *See* SPELMAN COLLEGE.

ATLANTA BAPTIST SEMINARY *See* MOREHOUSE COLLEGE.

ATLANTA UNIVERSITY Atlanta University, at Atlanta, Ga., was founded at the end of the Civil War to teach the children of slaves. Atlanta University now consists of four undergraduate colleges—Morehouse, Spelman, Clark, and Morris Brown (see entries under separate college names)—all of which adjoin the campus of the university. The coeducational university offers degrees through the doctorate. It is an independent school with a 1975 enrollment of nearly 1,150. The first classes, however, were held in a church and a railroad boxcar. Its formal work under its present name did not begin until 1869, though it was chartered two years before; the school was active as early as November 1865. Its first normal class was graduated in 1873 and its first college class in 1876.

Of necessity, the school began with students of low academic standing. During the first year, only one student ranked higher than first year in high school; yet, by 1894, all work below the high school level was discontinued. In 1925 the high school classes were also discontinued, and by the fall of 1928 no students below freshman and junior normal classification were admitted.

In 1929 an arrangement was reached among Atlanta University and Morehouse and Spelman colleges for the affiliation of the three institutions in a university system: graduate and professional educations to be offered by Atlanta University; undergraduate courses to be available through Morehouse and Spelman colleges.

More recently, Clark College, Interdenominational Theological Center, and Morris Brown College have joined the university affiliation. Each institution is independently organized, but all facilities are available to all students in the university. Atlanta University offers a limited number of undergraduate-graduate courses. It has been, and remains, one of the most prestigious black institutions of higher learning in the United States. See also CLARK COLLEGE; INTERDENOMINATIONAL THEOLOGICAL CENTER; MOREHOUSE COLLEGE; MORRIS BROWN COLLEGE; SPELMAN COLLEGE.

Alexander Augusta. *(Moorland-Spingarn Research Center, Howard University.)*

ATLANTA WORLD The first Afro-American daily newspaper in the United States, beginning in 1932. It was founded as a weekly in 1928, in Atlanta Ga., by the Scott family. The editor and general manager was Cornelius Adolphus Scott, born in Edwards, Miss., in 1908. See also NEWSPAPERS.

ATTUCKS, CRISPUS (1723–70), patriot, martyr, hero; born in Framingham, Mass. The first martyr in an event prior to the Revolutionary War, Attucks was the son of Prince Attucks, a native African, and Nancy Attucks, a native Natick American Indian. When the British were in central Boston at Dock Square near Custom House, March 5, 1770, he was with a band of leaders that was the first to defy the red coats. The black patriot was the first to die in the melee and be buried with honor. By age eleven, Attucks had become unhappy with the difference he had observed between slavery and freedom. As a child, he had been sold from one slave owner to another but eventually ran away to become a sailor and whaler. Attucks learned to read and write and to understand the fundamental principles that underlay different forms of government. Prior to the Boston Massacre, he attended several meetings with other patriots to discuss burdensome taxes levied by England. Attucks later wrote a letter of protest to Governor Thomas Hutchinson, the Tory governor of the province, which showed wisdom, insight, and his devotion to the cause of freedom. The Boston Massacre Monument on Boston Common preserves Attucks' memory. See also AFRO-AMERICAN HISTORY: COLONIAL PERIOD; HISTORIANS.

AUGUSTA, ALEXANDER (1825– ?), physician, soldier; born in Va. Augusta received his M.D. degree from Trinity Medical College (Toronto, Canada) in 1836. Augusta was quite young when he arrived in Canada. He practiced as a doctor for some time in Toronto and had mostly white patients. In 1863 he joined the Union Army and was appointed "surgeon to the U.S. Colored Troops" with the rank of lieutenant colonel. In the following year, two of his white assistants complained to President Abraham Lincoln about the "unnatural situation" involved in serving under a black officer. In February 1864 Augusta was transferred to another unit. Augusta was the first black doctor to head a hospital in the United States—the Freedmen's Hospital in Washington, D.C. See also PHYSICIANS; WARS.

AUGUSTA INSTITUTE See MOREHOUSE COLLEGE.

AUNT JEMIMA The name of a particular brand of pancake flour, "Aunt Jemima" was also the name of the character that advertised the product on radio and television. She was a round and jolly black woman, her head covered with a colorful kerchief. She became a stereotypical figure of the black "mammy."

AVIATORS

AVIATORS Eugene Jacques Bullard, born in Columbus, Ga., in 1894, was one of the first Afro-Americans who sought to break the racial barrier and enter the field of aviation. Failing in the United States, he went to France and joined the Foreign Legion in 1914. Eventually, he became a pilot in the Lafayette Escadrille, gaining fame as one of the Lafayette Flying Four. He returned to the United States in 1940 and died in 1961. Between the end of World War I and 1939, 23 blacks were licensed to fly private craft and 4 to fly commercial craft. One of the private-craft

flyers was Hubert Julian, a flamboyant pilot known as the "Black Eagle." During the Italo-Ethiopian War (1935), he went to Ethiopia and offered his services to the emperor Haile Selassie. On his return to the United States, he made many lecture tours, but he was not accepted for flight duty in the United States Army Air Force during World War II.

Other black private-craft flyers in the 1930s formed a group known as the Negro Airmen International, Inc., in Chicago, Ill., in 1933 under the leadership of Ed Gibbs. About the same time in Chicago, some of the earliest black pilots, or student pilots, were accommodated at a black-operated flying school and local airport (Harlem).

One of the four commercially licensed pilots in the country before World War II was Robert Terry

of East Orange, N.J. Terry had been a stunt flyer before the war and taught flying at A & T college, in Greensboro, N.C., under the Civilian Pilot Training (CPT) program in 1940–41. One of his first graduates was the college's youthful dean of men, William H. Gamble. Another CPT flight program was conducted at West Virginia State College where there were several graduates, including a young Ph.D. on the faculty of mathematics, William S. Claytor. There were also CPT programs at three other black colleges, then segregated. There were programs at Howard University, Washington, D.C.; Hampton Institute, Hampton, Va.; and Tuskegee Institute, Tuskegee, Ala. Charles "Chief" Anderson, another of the four commercially licensed black pilots before World War II was in charge of the CPT program at Tuskegee Institute. (One of his students was Daniel "Chappie" James, a fighter pilot in World War II who later became a four-star general in the United States Air Force.)

Born in 1907, "Chief" Anderson was a native of Pennsylvania. However, he remained a permanent resident at Tuskegee long after the Army Air Force closed the base. He also remained an excellent pilot of his own personal plane after he had passed his seventieth birthday. With an extensive knowledge of Afro-Americans in aviation, Anderson preserved memories of his former students and pilot friends, including "Chappie" James. One of his fondest recollections was of a goodwill flight to Trinidad in the early 1930s with a former student and friend, Albert E. Forsythe. Another one of Anderson's recollections was of the time that he obliged Eleanor Roosevelt by taking her on a flight over the Tuskegee area in a Piper Cub. Mrs. Roosevelt and President Franklin D. Roosevelt were visiting Tuskegee at the time, preparatory to the decision of the army to put an air base nearby in order to train black pilots for World War II.

After the war began, Robert Terry went to the air base at Tuskegee, serving as a civilian instructor in the pilot training program, and was later commissioned. Two of his students, Sam Bruce and Graham Smith, preceded him there as the first pilot-training students, receiving their "wings" in the 99th Pursuit Squadron, which became the famous 332nd, commanded by Ben-

Far left: This group of Harlem aviators assembled in 1935 in the interest of aiding Emperor Haile Selassie in the Italo-Ethiopian War. (U.S. Information Agency. National Archives.)

jamin O. Davis, Jr. Bruce was later killed in his fighter plane (a P-40) over Sicily, and Smith was reported missing in the Korean War.

James O. Plinton, Jr., another pilot with a commercial license, also went to the Tuskegee air base as a flight instructor. He became the first black to serve as a top executive (vice president) of a major airlines (Eastern) in 1971.

Certainly, World War II provided the first important entry of blacks into aviation. After the war, however, commercial flying remained almost exclusively closed to black pilots, and flight activity among black pilots decreased. By the time of the civil rights movement of the late 1960s, however, a few black pilots were serving as flight officers on commercial lines. One of

This picture was taken by the parents of Jill Brown immediately after her solo flight in 1967. *(Courtesy of Elaine and Gilbert Brown.)*

these was Warren Wheeler of Durham, N.C., who became a pilot for Piedmont Airlines at the age of 22. In 1969, Wheeler began his own airline (Wheeler) at the Raleigh-Durham Airport.

Although he did not fly for a commercial airline, one Afro-American commercially licensed pilot, William M. Dandridge, maintained a life-long interest in flying that went back (though not service-connected) to his days as a commissioned officer in World War II. Of the 49,694 airplane pilots in the nation in 1970, however, only 162 were black (5 of these were women), according to census reports. One of the women flyers, Jill Brown of Millersville, Md., later gained distinction when she became the first Afro-American woman to serve as a captain on a major commercial airline (Texas International). *See also* JAMES, DANIEL "CHAPPIE"; PLINTON, JAMES O., JR.; WARS.

REFERENCES: Very little attention has been given to the subject of black aviators. In the 1970s, however, two biographies, one on Jacques Bullard (Carisella, P. J., *Black Swallow of Death*, 1972) and the other on Hubert Julian (John Peer, Nugent, *Black Eagle*, 1971), appeared, showing increasing interest in the subject. (An early reference by Charles E. Francis, *The Tuskegee Airmen: The Story of the Negro in the U.S. Air Force*, 1955, is concerned almost entirely with combat activity.) Also, an article in the *Charlotte Observer*, Feb. 5, 1978, featured Warren Wheeler; and *Ebony* magazine, in the same year, carried a feature on Jill Brown.

B

BABER, GEORGE W. (1898–1971), African Methodist Episcopal bishop; born in Cleveland, Ohio. Baber received a B.A. degree from Payne Theological Seminary, a B.D. degree from Chicago Theological Seminary, and honorary D.D. degrees from Wilberforce University, Morris Brown College, Shorter College, Daniel Payne College, and Campbell College. He was elected bishop in the African Methodist Episcopal (AME) Church in 1944. Baber served as trustee and chairman of the finance board of Payne Seminary, as a member of the Detroit Interracial Committee, as president of the Bishops' Council, and with the National Association for the Advancement of Colored People (NAACP). A housing project was named for him in Baltimore, Md.

BACK-TO-AFRICA-MOVEMENT *See* COLONIZATION; NATIONALISM; PAN-AFRICANISM.

BACOTE, CLARENCE ALBERT (1906–), historian; born in Kansas City, Mo. Bacote graduated from the University of Kansas in 1926. He then attended the graduate school and received a M.A. degree in 1929. In 1955 he received his Ph.D. degree in history from the University of Chicago. During the period from 1926 to 1955, Bacote was first a professor of history at Florida Agricultural and Mechanical (A&M) University (1928–30), and then assistant professor and professor at Atlanta University (1930–55). Bacote

was also a member of the Georgia advisory committee to the U.S. Civil Rights Commission. His published works include: *History of Atlanta University, 1865–1965* (1968); "Negro Proscription, Protests, and Proposed Solutions in Georgia, 1880–1908," *Journal of Southern History,* 1959; and "Negro Officeholders in Georgia under President McKinley," *Journal of Negro History,* 1959.

BAHÁ'Í FAITH One of the world's newest religious faiths, the Bahá'í faith emphasizes peace and the brotherhood of man—"the oneness and wholeness of the human race." It was founded in Persia shortly after the middle of the nineteenth century by Bahá'u'lláh, who wrote more than 100 books and tablets, which have been translated into more than 428 languages (as of 1970). Bahá'ís are established in 42,000 localities throughout the world, including 3,300 in the United States. The National Bahá'í Center in America is located in Wilmette, Ill. Believing in the essential unity of all mankind, the Bahá'ís have been active in fighting prejudice, discrimination, and racism. This faith has appealed to some blacks, but it seems to have gained its greatest number of converts among those groups from the middle class. The highest Bahá'í award for human rights is named in honor of an Afro-American, Louis G. Gregory. The director of the North American Bahá'í Office for Human Rights in the early 1970s was a black woman, Juliette B. Buford.

BAILEY, JOHN SETH (1896–   ), clergyman; born in Mobile, Ala. Bailey attended Trinity Hall College and Seminary. He was the founder (1926) and first pastor of the Bailey Temple Church of God in Christ, Inc., and of the Seth Temple Church of God in Christ, Inc. (1953), in Detroit, Mich. In 1951 he was ordained bishop of the Michigan diocese.

BAILEY, MARGARET E. (active 1930s–1960s), nurse, army officer; born in Selma, Ala. Bailey received her R.N. degree from the Fraternal Hospital School of Nursing (Montgomery, Ala.), and a B.A. degree from San Francisco State College in 1959. After joining the Army Nurse Corps in 1944, she became assistant chief nurse at the U.S. Army Medical Center, Camp Zama, Japan, and later chief nurse at the U.S. Army 130th General Hospital, Chinon, France. In 1964 Bailey became the first black nurse to achieve the rank of lieutenant colonel.

BAILEY, MINNIE T. (ca. 1922–   ), historian, educator; born in Pulaski, Tenn. Bailey received a B.S. degree from Tennessee State University in 1945, a M.S. degree from State University of Iowa in 1950, and her Ed.D. degree from Oklahoma State University in 1967. She taught at elementary and secondary schools in Tennessee before joining the faculty of history at Grambling College (Grambling, La.) (1959). She became a professor (1967), and chairperson of the department of American history also. Her publications include: *Reconstruction in Indian Territory: A Story of Avarice, Discrimination and Opportunism* (1972), and "The Attitude of Thomas Jefferson Toward Negro Slavery During the Revolutionary and Early National Period."

BAILEY, PEARL (MAE) (1918–   ), singer, actress; born in Newport News, Va. Bailey's career began at 15 years of age when she entered an amateur-night contest at the Pearl Theater in Philadelphia and won a two-week engagement in a local theater. From there she went to New York to win another amateur night at the Apollo Theater. These two events catapulted her into show business. She appeared as a specialty dancer with Noble Sissle's band; as a chorus girl in Philadelphia nightclubs; and as a vocalist with the Edgar Hayes orchestra, with Cootie Williams, and with the Sunset Royal Band. About 1944 she made her debut as a soloist at the Village Vanguard, a popular New York City nightclub. Later, she made a stunning eight-

Pearl Bailey. *(Photo by Carl Van Vechten, Moorland-Spingarn Research Center, Howard University.)*

month appearance at another nightclub in New York City, the Blue Angel. After an appearance with Cab Calloway at the Strand Theater and the Zanzibar nightclub on Broadway, she made her Broadway debut in *St. Louis Woman* (1946). Her motion picture debut came a year later in *Variety Girl* (1947), for which she was given a special "Tony" award in 1968. Other motion pictures in which she played were: *Carmen Jones* (1954), *That Certain Feeling* (1956), *St. Louis Blues* (1958), *Porgy and Bess* (1959), and *All the Fine Young Cannibals* (1960). She made her first concert appearance at Philharmonic Hall in New York City's Lincoln Center, in 1966. Her autobiography, *The Raw Pearl*, was published in 1968.

BAILEY, ROBERT L. (1885–?), lawyer; born in Florence, Ala. Bailey attended Talladega College (Talladega, Ala.) in 1906. Graduating from Indiana University Law School in 1912, he became one of the outstanding black lawyers in the state of Indiana, and the only black lawyer in the Indianapolis Bar Association.

BAKER, AUGUSTA (ALEXANDER) librarian; born in Baltimore, Md. Baker received a B.A. degree (1934) and her B.S. degree in library science (1937) from New York State University at Albany. She served in the New York Public Library from 1937 to 1943. Baker was a consultant to the library services in Trinidad, British West Indies (1953), and an instructor of library science at Columbia University (1956), and at Rutgers University (1967). She received the Dutton-McRea Award (1953), the Parents Magazine Medal (1966), and the American Library Association (ALA) Crolier Award (1968). Baker wrote many articles on children's literature, and served on several commissions and boards related to children's literature and to library science. *See also* LITERATURE: CHILDREN'S.

BAKER, GEORGE (FATHER DIVINE) (ca. 1880–1965), religious leader, cultist; born in Hutchinson's Island, Ga. The son of sharecropping parents on a rice plantation, Baker spent much of his early life in Georgia and in the area of Baltimore, where he came under the influence of Samuel Morris ("Father Jehovia"), a cultist and junk peddler. About 1900, Baker opened his own mission for the distribution of aid and alms to the needy and assumed the name of Major J. Divine. He moved to the New York City area about 1915. His original base (the first of what he termed "heavens") was located in Sayville, Long Island, where his followers lived in communal fashion. Thereafter, he became one of the best-known religious leaders in all America, and his movement, the Father Divine Peace Mission, established communal branches nationwide (though chiefly in large northern cities). Father

Divine's following was composed of a hard core of several thousand lower-income blacks, a much smaller number of whites, and countless more well-wishers. By the 1960s the movement controlled property estimated to have a value of $10 million. Father Divine proclaimed that he was God and his official weekly periodical, *New Day*, reiterated his views: peace is wonderful, heaven is on earth, and the love of God (Father Divine) "has caused you to do things the government tried to get you to do: stop committing vice and crime and sin and debauchery of every kind." His peace missions provided low-priced or free food and other aid for thousands of impoverished blacks during the Depression, and also offered physical and spiritual havens. Besides providing employment, the missions attempted to reclaim many criminals. Father Divine, small in size and elusive in speech, provided for no successor, and when he died on September 10, 1965, so did the soul of his movement.

BAKER, HOUSTON A., JR. (1943–   ), educator, critic; born in Louisville, Ky. Baker received a B.A. degree from Howard University (Washington, D.C.) in 1965 and a B.A. degree from the University of California at Los Angeles in 1967.

He did most of his postgraduate work at the University of Edinburgh (1967–68), and received his Ph.D. from the University of California at Los Angeles in 1968. Baker was a John Hay Whitney and NDEA Fellow. He served as an instructor at Howard University and at Yale University (1968–69), and became a professor of English at the University of Virginia (1970). He wrote *Long Black Song: Essays in Black Literature and Culture* (1972) and *Twentieth Century Interpretations of Native Son* (1972). Baker frequently contributed to professional journals and anthologies.

BAKER, JOSEPHINE (1906–1975), singer and dancer; born St. Louis, Mo. Baker began working part-time when she was eight to help support her family; she first worked as a chorus girl while still in grade school. At 17 she was dancing in Noble Sissle's *Shuffle Along* (1923). Her dancing in *La Revue Negre* (1925), an American jazz revue which played in Paris, led her to international fame as an expatriate. Her vivacity and flamboyance as the "Dark Star" of the Folies Bergere, at the Casino de Paris, in musical comedy, and on film (*Black Shadows*, 1923; *Moulin Rouge*, 1944; *The French Way*, 1959) were enhanced by her grand public gestures offstage. She was awarded the French Legion of Honor for her work during World War II. In the 1920s she adopted and raised a number of orphan children of many races. To support them she returned from retirement to star in *Paris, Mes Amours*, a musical modeled on her life. She died in Paris. A biography by Stephen Papich, *Remembering Josephine*, was published in 1976.

BALDWIN, JAMES (1924–   ), writer; born in Harlem, New York City. In his early teens Baldwin became a Pentecostal preacher. He edited the literary magazine at his high school, and after graduation he worked at a defense plant and then moved to Greenwich Village, where he worked at odd jobs and continued to write. His articles began to be published in the *Nation, New Leader*, and *Commentary*. A Rosenwald fellowship in 1948 enabled him to go to Paris, where he stayed for ten years partially supported by a Guggenheim fellowship (1954) and a *Partisan Review* fellowship (1956). His best novels include *Go Tell It on the Mountain* (1953), which in part uses his experience of Pentecostal religion; *Giovanni's Room* (1956); *Another Country* (1962); and *Tell Me How Long the Train's Been Gone* (1968). His plays are *Blues for Mister Charlie*, based on

Far left: George Baker (Father Divine) and his wife (Mother Divine) who is holding a copy of Divine's official weekly, *New Day.* (Scurlock Studio.)

the Emmett Till murder case, and *The Amen Corner* (1964), about a Pentecostal preacher. His essays, which helped establish his national reputation, have been collected as *Notes of a Native Son* (1955), *Nobody Knows My Name* (1960), and *The Fire Next Time* (1963). He served as a member of the national advisory board of the Congress of Racial Equality (CORE). Among his awards are a National Institute of Arts and Letters Award, 1956, and Ford Foundation grant-in-aid, 1959. *See also* LITERATURE: THE, NOVEL.

BAMBARA, TONI CADE (1939–   ), author; born in New York, N.Y. Bambara received a B.A. degree from Queens College of the City University of New York in 1959 and a M.A. degree from City College (New York, N.Y.) in 1964. She did community organizing and social work, and she also taught at Livingston College of Rutgers University (New Brunswick, N.J.) from 1969 to 1974. Later Bambara was an associate at the Institute of the Black World in Atlanta, Ga. Her essays and stories have appeared in many magazines and anthologies. Bambara was the editor of *The Black Woman: An Anthology* (1970), as well as the author of 2 books of short stories: *Gorilla, My Love,* published in 1972, and *The Seabirds Are Still Alive: Collected Stories*, 1977.

BANDS See MUSIC: JAZZ.

BANKS

BANKS Banking among blacks began in 1833. During the 30 years prior to the Civil War, financial endeavors were supplementary to other business efforts. Individual wealthy, free Negroes in New Orleans, Richmond, Natchez, New York, Philadelphia, and smaller cities made loans from their own resources and the savings of others, which had been entrusted to their care.

Three attempts were made in the 1850s to establish Negro banks. A convention of Negroes in March, 1851, discussed the possibility of a mutual savings bank in New York City. It was hoped that the $40,000 to $50,000 belonging to black depositors held in Wall Street banks would be placed in the new institution. Another convention in 1855 proposed the creation of a fund to encourage new Negro enterprises. Plans to establish Negro banks were considered, but without success, and no black-owned bank was formed prior to the Civil War, in part because of the difficulties faced by free blacks in investing their funds.

Three banks were established during the Civil War for free Negroes and black soldiers: the Free Labor Bank of New Orleans, established by Gen. Nathaniel P. Banks; a military savings bank at Norfolk, Va., established by Gen. Benjamin F. Butler; and a second military savings bank at Beaufort, S.C. which had deposits of $200,000 by the end of the war, established by Gen. Rufus Saxon. As a Reconstruction measure, the Freedman's Savings and Trust Company was established in 1865 by the federal government as a depository for the savings of blacks. Controlled and operated largely by whites, this bank established 34 branches between 1865 and 1871.

Until 1870 it was managed conservatively and remained sound, but when its operators overinvested in the commercial paper of the First National Bank of Washington, D.C., a run on the Freedman's Savings and Trust Company was precipitated by that bank's failure. In June, 1874, the Freedman's closed its doors—owing almost

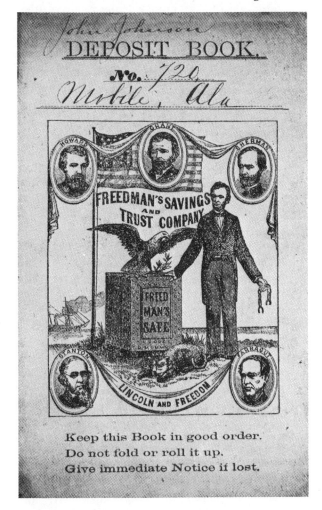

Keep this Book in good order.
Do not fold or roll it up.
Give immediate Notice if lost.

$3 million to 61,000 depositors. Although it had been owned and operated by whites for blacks, its failure led to a loss of confidence in banking for blacks—a feeling that remained until the end of the century.

After Reconstruction, 1877–1900 Several powerful forces led to the establishment of black banks during this period. There was the incentive provided by Negro churches, fraternal organizations, and secret societies which were unable to obtain credit from white banks. Second, despite its disastrous end, the Freedman's Savings Bank had instilled in many blacks the ideal of business enterprise. Another impetus was the lack of depositories for Negro savings; while prejudice

lay at the root of this situation, the lack of such depositories was largely caused by the simple economic fact that deposits by blacks were extremely small and the cost of carrying them relatively great. Finally, with the development of Afro-American business in a segregated economy, a persistent demand for the organization of black banks developed.

As a result of these forces, more than a dozen banks were established during the nineteenth century. The first was the True Reformers Bank, a subsidiary corporation of the Grand Fountain United Order of True Reformers, chartered by the Commonwealth of Virginia on March 2, 1888. Located in Richmond, the bank, capitalized at $100,000, was authorized to serve as a depository for the order and to do a general banking business. It began operating in April 1889, and by the end of the decade its deposits totaled $235,875—45 percent of which were demand deposits. The True Reformers Bank was the only bank in Richmond to pay specie during the crisis of 1893, and it loaned the city $150,000 to pay its schoolteachers.

The second Negro bank founded was an unincorporated joint-stock company opened in Washington, D.C., on October 1, 1888. The Capital Savings Bank began with a capital of $6,000, later increased to $50,000, and it, too, successfully withstood the Panic of 1893.

The Alabama Penny Savings Bank was opened in Birmingham, Ala., on October 15, 1890, by W. R. Pettiford, with a capital of $25,000. Pettiford, a preacher, personally solicited deposits among rural blacks, demonstrating to them the social prestige that a bank account brought and the bank's aid in buying homes. Cooperation with white banks helped to solve early management problems. Three branches were established in Selma, Anniston, and Montgomery; further expansion was stopped by Alabama's laws limiting branch banking. The bank attracted more than 10,000 customers and deposits of $200,000.

Other banks opened during the decade included the Mutual Savings and Trust Company of Chattanooga, Tenn., in 1889; the Capital Trust Company of Jacksonville, Fla., in 1894, with a capital of $25,000; the Nickel Savings Bank in Richmond, Va., in 1896; the Mutual Aid Banking Company in New Bern, N.C., in 1897; the Dime Bank in Kingston, N.C., in 1898; and the People's Savings Bank in Birmingham, Ala., with a capital by 1898 of $50,000.

Given the few resources, lack of knowledge, inexperience, and racial climate, it is surprising

Far left: Bankbook of the Freedman's Savings and Trust Company. *(Library of Congress.)*

that these small institutions were able to begin operations at all. Most learned by trial and error. The banks had difficulty in relating to a Negro clientele. In order to win the confidence of blacks, it was necessary to show that the Freedman's Savings Bank, a well-known failure, had been managed by whites for blacks. A great deal of social work and education was necessary, along with the bank work. These banks were not reservoirs of accumulated savings for investment capital or commercial credit. Their contribution was social—teaching thrift and cooperation, and pointing to the future possibilities of economic power for blacks.

Turn of the Century, 1900–14 Between 1900 and 1914, approximately seventy-five Negro banks were established. In 1906 there were 30 banks; in 1912, 56; and in 1914, 75. These banks were concentrated in the South, despite the fact that efforts to create black banks had formerly been conducted primarily in the North. In the early years of the twentieth century, most of the banks were related to fraternal orders, such as the St. Luke's Penny Savings Bank of Richmond, Va., which was founded in 1903 by Maggie L. Walker, who remained its president for many years. At the same time, banks were formed that had as their nucleus funds of societies, but they were not subsidiaries of the societies. By 1908, banks were being established without any special fraternal connections, one of which was in Philadelphia, one in Chicago, and another in Durham, N.C.

Although the organization of these banks was predicated on the need for developing business enterprise, none ever rendered much assistance to agriculture—the main enterprise in which southern blacks were engaged for profit. It was not until after World War I that black bankers belatedly acknowledged this problem. Actually, the majority of black banks were begun either as depositories for Negro fraternal societies or as responses to exhortations by Negro leaders that blacks should become thrifty and accumulate funds. Blacks were further urged to buy property. In order to satisfy this demand, the banks were forced to engage in mortgage financing; short-term funds were used for long-term purposes, and bank investments became frozen in fixed assets. The banks had a pronounced tendency to expand loans out of proportion to deposits. Usually when a black bank made a loan, the money left the bank permanently until repayment: the white bank received the loan as a

deposit. Thus, one direct result of the establishment of a Negro bank was the increase of black deposits in white banks. Cash on deposit lay idle, and little was invested in government bonds, which would have maintained liquidity. The tying up of capital in bank buildings led to further impairment of assets.

Ignorance of elementary banking principles, dishonest and inefficient management, and the difficulties inherent in financing racial businesses often led to failure. Instability was intimately tied up with the segregated economy and the laxity of bank supervision in the states of the Deep South where many states did not organize banking departments until 1910.

Black bankers created a trade organization in 1906, the National Negro Bankers Association (NNBA), an affiliate of the National Negro Business League, which Booker T. Washington had formed six years earlier. Because black banks provided a source of otherwise unobtainable loans for a large number of worthy Negro citizens, the NNBA called for more banks. Negro banks faced a major difficulty in relying primarily upon customers who were wage earners rather than businessmen, and regaining the confidence of blacks remained a continuing problem. In the years before the formation of the Federal Reserve System, the NNBA discussed the creation of some form of a central black bank. As early as 1906, it was suggested that black banks start their own central clearinghouse. By 1911 black bankers were working on plans for a central depository to aid Negro banks during times of emergency and during panics.

World War I and after, 1914–30 During World War I, Negro banks participated in the Liberty Loan drives. The government made its first deposit of public funds in black banks in 1918 when black bankers became especially concerned with the lack of Negro patronage. The limited support of Negro businessmen for black banking resulted in the inadequate development of black banks. These banks were thus unable to provide capital for Negro businesses and were confronted with the absence of industrial and commercial firms of any importance requiring the productive use of capital. The nature of existing black businesses made it difficult, if not impossible, for commercial loans to be extended, since in lending to very small businessmen, the management skill of the borrower is of utmost importance. In addition, the financial position of small firms was often hard to determine because of inadequate or nonexistent records. Because Negroes were engaged in amusement and recreational businesses, real estate, retail trade, and personal services, with an average of four persons employed in each enterprise, they made poor commercial loan risks and Negro banks seemed locked into their limited function as savings institutions promoting thrift, home ownership, and the purchase of safe securities.

Difficulties stemming from the lack of business customers were compounded by the exclusion of black banks from clearinghouse participation and the inaccessibility to certain bond issues. Thus, they were forced to confine themselves to mortgage real-estate loans, which resulted in inelastic funds and an inability to meet financial stress.

The characteristics of the segregated marketplace were reflected in the earning capacity, financial structure, and stability of black banks. In the late 1920s a bench-mark ratio of fixed assets to capital investments was 21 percent; the ratio of loans and discounts to total deposits was 66 percent. The ratio of fixed assets to capital investments of black banks fluctuated from a high of 109.7 percent in 1920 to a low of 56.9 percent in 1924, and to 80 percent in 1930. This fluctuation had an important bearing on the ability of black banks to liquidate their investments and to build up a surplus. The loan-to-deposit ratio went from 79.7 percent in 1915 to 99.7 percent in 1930, and for most of this 15-year period was 15 points higher than the norm. Black banks were overcapitalized, nonliquid, and undiversified. They had too large a capital structure for the amount of deposit business they did. Most of the deposits were ill-structured, with many small savings accounts that averaged about $30, and some as low as $2 or less. As in prewar years, black banks tended to expand loans disproportionately to total deposits, partially because they were unable to secure sufficient deposits and partially because they desired to maximize returns. Security behind most of the loans was either real estate or chattel property. Negro banks continued to include few stocks, bonds, and government securities in their investments. They also faced the problem of inadequate management stemming, in part, from an inability to gain experience in white banks.

Black banks did not increase at the same rate in the 1920s as in the past. Thirty-seven banks were chartered in that decade. Failures were often related to unemployment of black laborers and to the migration of others who withdrew their savings, draining the bank of most of its resources. In 1916 there were 48 banks; in 1918, 52; in 1927, 33; in 1928, 28; in 1929, 27, and in 1930, 23. These banks were located in 14 states, including the North, Midwest, and Southwest.

The early 1920s saw the chartering of the first two Negro national banks: the First National Bank in the all-black town of Boley, Okla., with a capital of $25,000, in 1921; and the Douglass National Bank of Chicago with a capital of $200,000, in 1922. Under the leadership of John D. Rockefeller, Jr., the Dunbar National Bank of New York City (1928–38) was, like the Freedman's Savings Bank, organized by whites for Negroes, with minority membership on the board of directors and an almost all-black staff of tellers, bookkeepers, clerks, and typists.

Despite the decline in the number of banks, however, capital, loans, and demand deposits increased during the 1920s. Black banks even developed a small trust business. Moreover, the National Bankers Association (NBA), the bankers' trade organization, was founded in 1927 by Maj. R. R. Wright, Sr. The NBA became independent of the National Negro Business League and excluded all but commercial banks.

The Great Depression The handful of black banks left in 1930 were further reduced by the Great Depression. Of the 8,812 banks to fail between 1930 and 1933, twelve were black: eight in 1930, one in 1931, one in 1932, and two in 1933. Eleven banks remained, with $3 million in deposits, at the end of the four-day Bank Holiday (closing of U.S. banks by executive order) called by President Franklin D. Roosevelt on March 6, 1933. These were the Citizens and Southern Bank and Trust Company, Philadelphia, Pa.; Citizens Savings Bank and Trust Company, Nashville, Tenn.; Citizens Trust Company, Atlanta, Ga.; Consolidated Bank and Trust Company, Richmond, Va.; Crown Savings Bank, Newport News, Va.; Danville Bank and Trust Company, Danville, Va.; Fraternal Bank and Trust Company, Fort Worth, Tex.; Industrial Savings Bank, Washington, D.C.; Mechanics and Farmers Bank, Durham, N.C.; Tuskegee Institute Savings Bank, Tuskegee, Ala.; and Victory Savings Bank, Columbia, S.C. No Negro bank operating immediately prior to the holiday was refused permission to reopen. Following their relicensing, Negro banks sold preferred stock or capital notes to the Reconstruction Finance Corporation, which had been created in 1932 to prevent further deflation and disintegration of the banking system. Only two black banks were chartered during the 1930s, one in Washington, D.C., in 1934, and one in Boley, Okla., in 1935.

As with American banking in general, a major reform for black banks which was a result of the Depression, was the insurance of deposits by the Federal Deposit Insurance Corporation. The creation of deposit insurance immediately increased confidence in Negro banks and deposits grew from 100 to 300 percent between 1933 and 1936. Deposit insurance even attracted white customers. However, the problem of increasing the number of black depositors remained. In a survey conducted in 1937, slightly fewer than 5 percent of Negroes carried checking accounts in black banks, and only 10 percent had savings accounts.

Portfolios were invariably filled with loans secured by generally unmarketable real estate in black neighborhoods. Small deposits and frequent withdrawals continued to plague the development of black banks, reflecting the limited resources of blacks as a group. Nevertheless, Negro banks had an impact during this period. Loan sharks, who chronically preyed on blacks, lost some of their power in cities where black banks were in operation.

Another change brought about by the Depression was a new willingness to purchase government bonds. Although black banks still purchased few federal government bonds because of their extremely low yield, they did provide funds to local governments by successfully bidding for and purchasing municipal securities. In 1936 such securities made up about 33 percent of earning assets.

World War II and After, 1940–60 Of the 136 Negro banks that were established after 1888, only 12 remained by 1940. As in World War I, black banks participated fully in war-bond drives during World War II. In 1942 more than $1,180,000 of war bonds were sold by black banks.

The investments of black banks showed a decided change from past policy. One change was the large increase in the holding of government securities, a direct result of the war-financing campaign. In 1941 government obligations rose to $1,405,125, an increase in one year of more than $1 million, or 53.5 percent. By 1943, cash and government obligations constituted 75.8 percent of total resources, just slightly above the ratio of 74.4 percent for all banks and 73.8 percent for all nonblack banks. More significant was the shift in the historical pattern of investment from bank buildings and other real estate to bonds and securities. Real estate was less than one percent of total resources by the end of 1943. During the war years, loans were reduced because of restrictions on housing construction, consumer credit, and installment loans.

Three banks were established during the postwar years in Memphis, Tenn., Savannah, Ga., and Kansas City, Mo. No banks were chartered during the next 12 years. The stability and strength of the 15 black banks far exceeded that of their early predecessors. They engaged more actively in commercial banking, and the role of savings decreased. United States government obligations had fallen from 58 percent of total assets in 1945 to 46.4 percent in 1947. The percentage of loans increased from 14.6 to 28.2, a reflection of increased business lending following the war. Capital growth was attributable to the three new banks rather than expansion of existing banks.

The early 1950s were influenced by an inflationary trend caused by the Korean War. Credit demands by industry for loans to finance defense production stimulated the rise of total loans of Negro-owned banks to more than $12 million, amounting to 39.3 percent of total assets. By 1951 the rate of increase of total assets, 9.5 percent, surpassed all annual increases since World War II. Each of the black banks had total assets in excess of all the Negro banks combined in 1933. Compared with all commercial banks, black banks held a slightly smaller proportion of loans as part of total assets, and a slightly larger proportion of securities and real estate. This reflected the risks inherent in a small bank lending to small borrowers in a segregated market with little opportunity to diversify.

Black banks also felt the impact of increased costs in the 1950s. Net earnings and profits were reduced by rising costs for maintenance, operations, salaries and taxes. So despite the increased growth, Negro-owned banks remained insignificant, reflecting the economics of poverty and discrimination. Aggregate total assets were equal to only one of the nation's average small community white banks. Negro bankers were neither part of the national banking nor Federal Reserve systems because of their high capital and reserve requirements.

Black Banks since 1960 The most dramatic development for black-owned banks since their beginnings in 1888 came in the 1960s. Stimulated by the social and political successes of the civil rights movement, Afro-Americans became increasingly aware of economics as a pivotal force in their development. Economic growth became an objective for all blacks. A new philosophy of black economic growth emerged, emphasizing black entrepreneurship and community development and control. A new interest arose in existing black-owned banks, long ignored, and opportunities for organizing additional banks became a matter of national and local concern.

In 1960, 12 black-owned banks, with aggregate assets of almost $58 million, operated primarily in the Deep South. The majority of stock was held by small groups of investors, usually the boards of directors. However, a new era for black banking opened in 1963 with the chartering of Riverside National Bank in Houston, Tex., the third black-owned bank to receive a national charter. Riverside National Bank was the catalyst for a resurgence of black-owned banks. Between 1963 and 1969, 12 banks were organized, and the rate of growth of black banks greatly exceeded that achieved by all insured commercial banks. The faster expansion was due primarily to the newly chartered banks. All of these new banks were organized in major industrial cities with significant black populations: five in the Midwest, one in the Southwest, three in the West, and three in the East. Eight of these new banks operated under national charters issued by the Office of the Comptroller of the Currency, one of the federal bank-regulatory agencies, while only four were chartered by state authorities. In contrast to earlier years, the majority of the stock was held by a large number of small investors in the communities in which these banks operated.

Black banking continued to expand through new bank entry in the early 1970s. Six black-owned banks were chartered in 1970 and 1971: three received national charters, and three were organized under state auspices. In 1970 the average black-owned bank held assets of $12.5 million, and had a capital of $860,000. At the end of 1971, there were 30 black banks. At this rate, at least 75 black-owned banks will be operating in the United States by 1980.

The National Bankers Association (NBA), the national trade association of black bankers, emerged as a vital force in the national financial community during this period. Until 1968, the NBA's major function had been the convening of an annual convention to discuss problems confronting black banking. However, in 1968, the NBA received a grant from the Economic Development Authority, a division of the Department of Commerce, to establish a national office in Washington, D.C., and to conduct programs of technical services for its membership. In 1969 the NBA sponsored a bank-management training program jointly with the American Bankers Association to recruit young black men and women for a one-year intensive mid-career training program in banking. By 1971 some 60 blacks had been trained and were employed either by NBA or ABA member banks. In 1971 the NBA established a national award in memory of its founder, R. R. Wright, for minority economic development. The first recipient was Rev. Jesse Jackson for his work with Operation Breadbasket. In the 1960s, the NBA ceased being solely a black banking organization and membership was opened up to other minority-owned banks. In 1971 six Mexican-American and Spanish-American banks joined the NBA, bringing total membership to 36 banks. The National Bankers Association had emerged as a relevant force to assist the entry of minorities into the financial sector of the American economy.

During the 1960s and early 1970s, black banks expanded their loans to the black community and the results have been varied. Black banks continued to hold government securities, 27.8 percent of total assets; however, the expansion of state and municipal securities was much smaller. Some of the banks continued to rely on sales of federal funds, engaging in short-term lending to other banks of excess reserves of Federal Reserve member banks.

Industrial Bank of Washington, D.C., chartered in 1934, is one of the oldest of black banks. *(Jacquelyn Low.)*

PRESIDENTS OF THE NATIONAL BANKERS ASSOCIATION

Richard Robert Wright	President, Citizens and Southern Bank and Trust Company, Philadelphia, Pa.	1927–42
Jesse H. Mitchell	President, Industrial Bank of Washington, Washington, D.C.	1942–45
Lorimer D. Milton	President, Citizens Trust Company, Atlanta, Ga.	1945–48
LeRoy F. Riley	President, Crown Savings Bank, Newport News, Va.	1948–50
John H. Wheeler	President, Mechanics and Farmers Bank, Durham, N.C.	1950–52
Macco C. Martin, Sr.	President, First State Bank, Danville, Va.	1952–59
B. Doyle Mitchell	President, Industrial Bank, Washington, D.C.	1959–66
Jesse H. Turner	Executive Vice-President, Tri-State Bank of Memphis, Memphis, Tenn.	1966–68
Edward E. Tillmon	President, Bank of Finance, Los Angeles, Calif.	1968–70
William R. Hudgins	President, Freedom National Bank, New York, N.Y.	1970–71
I. Owen Funderburg	Executive Vice-President, Gateway National Bank, St. Louis, Mo.	1971–

Deposits flowed into black banks at a faster rate than that experienced by the banking system as a whole. Since 1970 this growth has been fairly evenly divided between demand deposits and time and savings deposits. On September 30, 1970, the federal government, with strong endorsement by President Richard M. Nixon, launched a combined government-private campaign to increase deposits in minority banks by $1 billion at the end of one year. Of this total amount, $35 million was to come from approximately 24 government agencies, departments, and federal courts; and $65 million from state and local governments and the private sector. The private phase of the program operated under the general direction of the President's Advisory Council on Minority Business Enterprise, and the Office of Minority Business Enterprise (OMBE) in the Department of Commerce. The program was carried out through Capital Formation, Inc., and the National Bankers Association. The program was successful and operated on a continuing basis. At the end of 15 months, on December 31, 1971, total deposits had grown by $242 million, an increase of 61 percent.

General Summary: An Overview The success and failure of the black bank has been everywhere influenced by the segregated economy that provided incentives to Negro entrepreneurs. Racial reasons more than economic reasons have been responsible for the establishment of Negro banks. The growth and failure of Negro banks and their relative prosperity were not highly dependent on general economic conditions, and until recently their development seems to have been countercyclical. Part of the explanation lies in the segregation and nonindustrialization of the black economy. Failures (131 out of 157 banks have failed since 1888) were no more numerous than for other banks of similar size, but they constituted a terribly heavy drain on the meager resources of an impoverished group. Failures common to all banks (overcapitalization, speculation, misappropriation, and mismanagement) were erroneously attributed to dis-

ASSETS AND LIABILITIES OF BLACK BANKS

Year	Loans and discounts	Total assets	Total deposits	Total capital
1900*	$ 19,902	$ 447,320	$ 247,200	$ 195,237
1910*	1,070,738	1,865,973	1,317,999	405,704
1920*	4,677,677	8,180,389	6,112,044	404,000
1930*	2,642,846	6,006,700	4,093,834	1,266,821
1940	2,942,803	7,404,475	6,276,177	1,092,410
1950	12,600,957	32,103,568	29,133,105	2,278,435
1960	29,953,893	57,952,160	51,980,208	5,101,373
1970	135,943,915	322,722,605	278,895,266	23,180,238

*Reporting banks only
SOURCE: Compiled by authors

honest management by blacks who sought safety for their deposits in white banks.

The relative success of the protected black banks, which provided worthwhile but marginal financial services, helped to make the Negro bank the symbol of the concept of business enterprise, which would provide the solution to the race's economic and social problems. Yet by the 1920s, objective observers were beginning to question the soundness of banks based on racial interest and pride alone. Progress toward desegregation in the wake of the civil rights movement had eroded the black banks' protected markets. One result has been increasing competition for the black bankers' traditional labor supply. Since the late 1960s, blacks have been eagerly recruited by large white banks. The heritage of racial discrimination that prevented a large number of blacks from receiving economic, financial, and business-management training has continued the critical problem of a dearth of skilled employees and officers. Small black banks are unable to retain qualified employees. The black bank in 1969 provided jobs for only 0.092 percent of all workers employed in insured commercial banks, while blacks totaled 4.1 percent of all employees in white banks. Finally, the black banker has found increased competition for black customers, thus aggravating the historic difficulty of attracting black depositors.

The legacy of a segregated economy has also shaped the environment in which the Negro banker works. Median income for blacks is generally about two-thirds of the median income for whites and Negro families are in a poorer net financial position than comparable white families. Businesses are not the types of borrowers to either expand black banks rapidly or to utilize the black bank's funds to provide mainsprings for long-run economic development. An inadequate market for capital in the past led Negro

DIRECTORY OF BLACK BANKS

Name of bank	Location of bank	Opening date
American State Bank	Tulsa, Okla.	November 1970
Atlantic National Bank	Norfolk, Va.	September 1971
Bank of Finance	Los Angeles, Calif.	November 1964
Carver State Bank	Savannah, Ga.	April 1947
Citizens Savings Bank & Trust Company	Nashville, Tenn.	January 1904
Citizens Trust Company	Atlanta, Ga.	June 1921
Consolidated Bank & Trust Company	Richmond, Va.	July 1903
Douglass State Bank	Kansas City, Kans.	August 1947
First Enterprise Bank	Oakland, Calif.	June 1972
First Independence National Bank of Detroit	Detroit, Mich.	May 1970
First Independence State Bank	Oakland, Calif.	June 1972
First Plymouth National Bank	Minneapolis, Minn.	February 1969
First State Bank	Danville, Va.	September 1919
Freedom Bank of Finance	Portland, Oreg.	August 1969
Freedom National Bank	New York, N.Y.	December 1964
Gateway National Bank	St. Louis, Mo.	June 1965
Greensboro National Bank	Greensboro, N.C.	November 1971
Highland Community Bank	Chicago, Ill.	November 1970
Independence Bank of Chicago	Chicago, Ill.	December 1964
Industrial Bank of Washington	Washington, D.C.	August 1934
Liberty Bank of Seattle	Seattle, Wash.	May 1968
Liberty Bank and Trust Company	New Orleans, La.	November 1972
Mechanics and Farmers Bank	Durham, N.C.	March 1908
Medical Center State Bank	Oklahoma City, Okla.	January 1973
Midwest National Bank	Indianapolis, Ind.	November 1972
National Industrial Bank	Miami, Fla.	April 1964
North Milwaukee State Bank	Milwaukee, Wis.	February 1971
Peoples National Bank of Springfield	Springfield, Ill.	September 1970
Riverside National Bank	Houston, Tex.	August 1963
Seaway National Bank	Chicago, Ill.	January 1965
Skyline National Bank	Denver, Colo.	December 1971
Swope Parkway National Bank	Kansas City, Mo.	July 1968
Tri-State Bank of Memphis	Memphis, Tenn.	December 1946
United Community National Bank	Washington, D.C.	August 1964
Unity Bank and Trust Company	Roxbury, Mass.	June 1968
Unity State Bank	Dayton, Ohio	August 1970
Vanguard National Bank	Hempstead, N.Y.	May 1972
Victory Savings Bank	Columbia, S.C.	October 1921

banks to make investments of dubious economic worth: loans to churches, fraternal lodges, theaters, not-easily-negotiable real estate, and small salaried wage earners for consumption.

The ghetto of the 1970s was a very risky place for small banks to lend money. The lack of diversification in the earning assets of black banks stems from the fact that they are small banks influenced by the qualitative and quantitative character of Negro businesses. These factors are interconnected: the black bank is small because Negro business is small; Negro banks, like all small banks, have high operating costs and are unable to distribute their loanable funds among sound borrowers to acquire a large capital. Thus, the deficiency of small Negro banks is an economic as well as racial dilemma.

Expansion in the 1960s and 1970s demonstrated that the black bank cannot survive in isolation. It appears that the majority of its customers will remain on the bottom of the economic scale for some time to come, while reliance on a segregated economy for growth is doubtful. Compelling economics seem to dictate that black banks can become instruments of economic development only as large stable institutions operating in an integrated economy. See also BUSINESS; DISCRIMINATION; FREEDMAN'S SAVINGS BANK; HOUSING; INCOME; INSURANCE; NATIONAL ASSOCIATION FOR THE ADVANCEMENT OF COLORED PEOPLE (NAACP).

REFERENCES: Writings on black banks are far from numerous. A good reference to begin with is an annotated bibliographic study by Abby L. Gilbert entitled *Black Banks: A Bibliographic Survey* (1971), a reprint publication (with addendum) of the U.S. Treasury Department, Office of the Comptroller of the Currency, from *The Bulletin of Bibliography*, vol. 28, April–June 1971. The following references are especially noteworthy: Becker, Gary S., *The Economics of Discrimination*, University of Chicago Press, Chicago, 1957; Brimmer, Andrew F., "The Negro in the National Economy" in Davis, John P. (ed.), *The American Negro Reference Book*, Educational Heritage, New York, 1966; Harris, Abraham L., *The Negro as a Capitalist: A Study of Banking and Business Among American Negroes*, American Academy of Political and Social Science, Philadelphia, 1936 (reprint, Peter Smith, 1968); Gilbert, Abby L., "The Comptroller of the Currency and the Freedman's Savings Bank," *Journal of Negro History*, April 1972, pp. 125–43; Irons, Edward D., "A Positive View of Black Capitalism," *The Bankers Magazine*, Spring 1970, pp. 43–47; Osthaus, Carl R., "The Rise and Fall of Jesse Binga, Black Financier," *Journal of Negro History*, January 1973, pp. 39–60; and Osthaus, Carl R., *Freedmen, Philanthropy, and Fraud: A History of the Freedman's Saving Bank*, University of Illinois Press, Urbana, 1976.

BANKS, ELOISE HARDISON (1926–   ), publisher, editor; born in Indianapolis, Ind. Banks received a B.A. degree from Indiana Central College in 1947 and her M.A. degree from Arizona State University in 1953. She married Edward Banks in 1957 while teaching English in Phoenix, Ariz., and from 1958 to 1969 was copublisher and coeditor (with her husband) of the Arizona *Tribune*. She assumed full duties as publisher and editor after his death in 1969.

BANKS, JAMES ALBERT (1941–   ), educator; born in Marianna, Ark. Banks received a B.Ed. degree from Chicago Teachers College in 1964 and a M.A. degree (1967) and his Ph.D. degree (1969) from Michigan State University. He was an assistant professor of education at the University of Washington in 1969 and became a full professor in 1973. He authored several publications including: *March Toward Freedom: A History of Black Americans* (1970); *Teaching the Black Experience* (1970); and *Teaching Strategies for Social Studies* (1973). He was coeditor of *Black Self-Concept* (1972).

BANKS, WILLIAM SAMUEL MARON (1915–   ), sociologist, educator; born in Amite County, Miss. Banks received an A.B. degree from Dillard University in 1937, an A.M. degree from Fisk University in 1940, and his Ph.D. degree from Ohio State University in 1949. He served as a commissioned officer (captain) in the 92d Infantry during World War II. After the war, he returned to Fort Valley State College, where he served as a professor, departmental chairman, and administrative dean (since 1967). His studies in sociology tested some of the conclusions in Gunnar Myrdal's *An American Dilemma*.

BANNEKER, BENJAMIN (1731–1806), mathematician, scientist; born in Ellicott Mills, Md. Banneker received his early schooling with the friendly assistance of a Quaker family. About 1773, he began making astronomical calculations for almanacs, accurately predicting an eclipse in 1789. He assisted in a survey of the District of Columbia in 1790; published an annual almanac for farmers from 1792 to 1802, the first scientific book written by an Afro-American; published a treatise on bees; and computed the cycle of the 17-year locust. Banneker became a national hero for blacks, and a number of schools have been named in his honor. For a biography, see Silvio A. Bedini's book, *The Life of Benjamin Banneker*, 1972. See also SCIENTISTS: PHYSICAL.

BAPTISTS

BAPTISTS With a long tradition of religious freedom and diversity in both pulpit and pew, Baptists constitute the largest family of black denominations in North America. Most black Baptists belong to one of the largest single organized religious groups in the United States—the National Baptist Convention, U.S.A., Inc., whose membership was estimated in 1972 at 6,300,000, more than one-fourth of the entire black population of the United States. Black Baptist groups are among the oldest and the newest, the richest and the poorest, and the largest and the smallest of religious bodies. Their churches may be storefronts or elaborate edifices; their preachers may

be "jacklegs" with little formal schooling, or they may be powerful national leaders or erudite college professors. Despite their diversity, however, Baptist preachers all seem to have an abundance of at least three characteristics in common: individuality, devotion to their congregation, and eloquence.

Both black and white Baptist churches are commonly formed into various associations at local, state, and national levels for purposes of fellowship. Most meet annually in state conventions, representing the various individual congregations in a given area. The largest black national organization (after the National Baptist Conven-

Funeral service at the Abyssinian Baptist Church, New York City, for Bill "Bojangles" Robinson, 1949. The minister, Adam Clayton Powell, Jr., is seated on the dais at the far left. *See also* ABYSSINIAN BAPTIST CHURCH. *(National Archives.)*

tion, U.S.A., Inc.) is the National Baptist Convention of America. It is frequently referred to as the "unincorporated convention" and the larger group as the "incorporated convention"; the distinction reflects a schism that took place during the early part of the twentieth century.*

Early Churches During the latter half of the eighteenth century, the black Baptists began to establish independent churches in various parts of the country. Although there is some controversy as to the name of the very first Negro Baptist church in America, there is complete agreement that it was in the South. Whether the first church was at Savannah, Ga., as is held by some historians, or at Silver Bluff, S.C., as other historians point out, is uncertain; but according to the dates quoted by black historians, the church at Silver Bluff seems to be the oldest black Baptist Church on record in the United States. Evidence indicates it was organized before 1775, perhaps as early as 1750, as recorded on the cornerstone of the present church building.

Other historic churches were the First African Baptist Church of Savannah (ca. 1778); the Harrison Street Baptist Church, organized at Petersburg, Va. (1786); the Negro Baptist Church at Williamsburg, Va. (1785); and the African Baptist Church of Lexington, Ky. (1790). Thirteen black members were dismissed from the white Baptist church in Philadelphia to form the first African Baptist Church in 1809. They worshiped for a while in the edifice of the First Baptist Church. In 1805 the Joy Baptist Church at Boston was organized by Thomas Paul, who served as pastor for nearly 25 years. While he was still serving in Boston, in 1809, Paul was requested to go to New York City and organize what is now the Abyssinian Baptist Church. This church today is probably the largest black Baptist church in the world.

By 1814 a number of Baptist churches were composed entirely of Negro members—both freedmen and slaves; however, the majority of Negro Baptists were members of the same churches as their owners. Black churches were included in district associations along with white churches.

Luther Rice found Negroes receptive to the

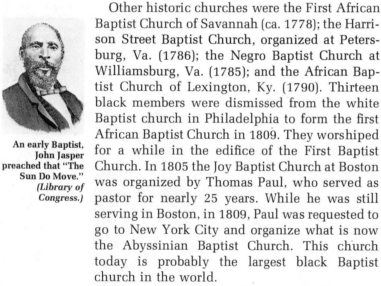

An early Baptist, John Jasper preached that "The Sun Do Move." *(Library of Congress.)*

*This article was adapted by the author, Freeman, Edward A., from a chapter in Wooley, Davis C. (ed.), *Baptist Advance: The Achievements of the Baptists in North America for a Century and a Half,* copyright © Boardman Press, Nashville, Tenn., 1964.

idea of missions and often recorded in his journals the receipts of gifts from "black" men. Lott Cary, a member of the First Baptist Church, Richmond, Va., and inspired by Rice, organized The Richmond African Baptist Missionary Society (April 1815). Carey and Collin Teague were appointed missionaries to Africa by the board of the Baptist General Convention in 1819 and sailed for Liberia in January 1821.

After this, many Negro churches sprang up throughout the eastern, southern, and midwestern sections of the country. In 1839 the first black Baptist church in the District of Columbia was founded, the Nineteenth Street Baptist Church. The first black Baptist church in Tennessee was organized at Columbia, in 1843, with seven members. Ten years later at Nashville, the Spruce Street Baptist Church was organized, with Nelson G. Merry as pastor. In 1859 the First Baptist Church at Kansas City, Kan., was organized, along with the First AME Church in that city.

Early Pioneers / George Lisle George Lisle (or Liele) was a Baptist preacher in antebellum days—one of quite a long and brilliant list of preachers. The date of his birth was not known by him, but he would frequently make guesses about his age in important letters written to his friends. However, Carter G. Woodson states "that Lisle was born in Virginia, about 1750, and moved with his master, Henry Sharp, to Burke County, Georgia, a few years before the Revolutionary War." He was converted and baptized by Rev. Matthew Moore. In the archives of black American Baptists, the career of Lisle is an immortal legend that ranks along with those of such missionary pioneers as William Carey, Adoniram Judson, Robert Morrison, Robert Moffatt, David Livingstone, and others. It was Lisle who was the first Christian missionary to launch out on the missionary endeavor at least 15 years before any of the others named here.

Another Baptist pioneer was John Jasper, noted for the antiscientific views of his most famous sermon, "The Sun Do Move," which, according to his biographer William E. Hatcher, the author of *John Jasper* (1908), was effectively preached 250 times.

Slavery, Civil War, and Reconstruction Organized church work above the local level from post-Revolutionary times to the Civil War period was totally outside the Negroes' sphere of operation. Blacks participated only in the larger organizations by virtue of their having been accepted as congregations by the larger white bodies. The first attempt at an organization beyond the local church level among black Baptists was the Providence Baptist Association, organized in Ohio in 1836. This group was composed of Negro churches of the West. Among the early leaders of the new movement were Richard DeBaptiste of Detroit and Chicago and James Poindexter of Columbus. The second oldest body of this kind was the Wood River Baptist Association of Illinois, comprising the churches of St. Clair and Madison counties and of the city of Chicago. John Livingston was chosen its first moderator.

The progress of the larger organizations among Negroes in the West continued uninterrupted until the passage of the Fugitive Slave Law in 1850, when many Negroes who had escaped from the South and had settled in these western cities were forced to flee to Canada for safety. One of the direct results of this flight was the formation of several Negro Baptist churches in Canada, among which is the historic First Baptist Church of Toronto, which was flourishing as early as 1846.

The abolition movement accelerated the desire for larger organizations: the feeling was evidenced that for the salvation and continued progress of church work, larger Negro organizations were necessary. Therefore, the churches of the western area of "territory" were organized into the Colored Baptist Convention in 1853. State conventions were organized as follows: Louisiana, 1865; North Carolina, 1866; Alabama and Virginia, 1867; Arkansas, 1868; Kentucky and Mississippi, 1869; and Georgia, 1870. These Baptist organizations were avenues toward the unification of blacks along religious and social lines and were used by the leaders in the abolition movement as a medium to give momentum to their cause. The Methodist and Baptist churches acquired dominant positions in the institutional life of blacks, and eventually, the church became a repository of the Negroes' older traditions. The biggest boon to the abolition movement was given by Methodist, Baptist, Presbyterian, Quaker, and Episcopal ministers of both races when they declared themselves favorable to its principles and exerted tremendous pressure in it.

Despite the many methods used to circumvent the moral responsibility involved in the slave controversy, the split among the church organizations inevitably came: the Methodists in 1844;

the Baptists in 1845; and the Presbyterians in 1861, when the churches in the South shut their doors to blacks. This caused trouble for the free Negro in the communities of the South, and many were forced to leave these areas. More severe regulations throughout the South to hold the Negro in check and continual agitation in response to these checks made the condition for blacks much more unbearable. In some places laws were passed forbidding the Negro to preach except in compliance with rigid regulations and in the presence of certain slaveholders.

The free Negroes, having to migrate north and west in large numbers, along with runaway slaves, contributed to their own betterment through these larger black denominational bodies. In 1840 the American Baptist Missionary Convention was organized by the Negro Baptists who lived in the New England and the Middle Atlantic states.

The American Baptist Missionary Convention seems to have had plans for assisting the wives of ministers as well as some definite rules for the missionaries. For the missionaries, it required that a report be made to the corresponding secretary quarterly. This report was to contain the number of sermons preached, the probable number of persons attending, the number of persons ministered to, the number of persons attending Sabbath School, the number of members, the methods of reception, the number excluded, and the number decreased. It was stipulated that the appropriations be made quarterly only when the above requisitions were complied with.

Edmond Kelley, one of the prominent leaders in the Convention, relates that the Convention made a draft on the ordained preachers throughout the North and the East, hundreds of whom in various ways had escaped slavery. Several of these ministers had availed themselves of the opportunity to attend schools in the North and had fitted themselves for leadership. Many of these men were appointed as missionaries and teachers to work among the freedmen of the South, under the protection of the Union Army.

When the Convention met in its twenty-third annual meeting in Washington, D.C., in 1863, a committee went to see President Abraham Lincoln to discuss the protection their missionaries would get on Southern soil.

These missionaries were warmly received and their presence welcomed in the South by their brethren, and because of this, they made rapid progress for some time.

The Consolidated American Baptist Missionary Convention was organized in 1866, as the result of a merger between the Northwestern Convention and the American Baptist Missionary Convention. This act united the efforts of most blacks in all sections of the country. There are records of this new group until 1879, the year before the Foreign Mission Convention was founded. The Consolidated Convention met triennially, but the executive board met annually and kept the people informed through the official organ, *The National Monitor*.

The report of the annual meeting of the Consolidated Convention in New York in November 1876 shows that 46 schools were aided and 18 new schools were organized with more than 500 baptisms. Delegates arrived from Pennsylvania, New Jersey, Connecticut, New York, North Carolina, South Carolina, Georgia, Florida, Alabama, Mississippi, Louisiana, Texas, Arkansas, and Kansas, and reports were heard from Haiti. The officers for 1876 were: president, William Gray, Mississippi; secretary, W. C. Phillips, Illinois; corresponding secretary, R. L. Perry, New York. In the report of 1877, 26 states reported a total enrollment of 600,000 black Baptists. They proposed to build a new church at Port aú Prince. Also, they voted to meet annually instead of triennially. In 1878 the Committee on Foreign Missions recommended the formation of a Foreign Board, and the recommendation was accepted. Richard DeBaptiste of Chicago was elected the corresponding secretary. The total receipts that year were $3,614. It was also recommended that in addition to the work in Haiti, work would be started in Africa at once, with C. H. Richardson, who was then in England or en route to Africa, as their missionary. The Committee ordered an investigation of the status of the Von Brun Missions among the Bassa people in Liberia and, if possible, the adoption of that work. The headquarters was to be in Chicago with three field agents—R. H. Duling and Mrs. Duling for the states west of the Alleghenies, and Walter H. Brooks for all states east of these mountains. The Committee on Education urged the need of an educated ministry and commended those institutions of learning, in the North and the South, that were open to such Negroes, as were qualified by training and ability to enter.

The Foreign Mission Convention A desperate appeal, coupled with a disagreement between black and white missionaries with reference to the treatment of natives on the African mission fields, produced the atmosphere that called into being the Foreign Mission Convention of the United States of America. The moving spirit of the new endeavor was W. W. Colley, returned missionary of the Southern Baptist Convention. According to E. M. Brawley, in his book *The Negro Baptist Pulpit* (1890), Colley was sent to Africa by the Foreign Mission Board of the Southern Baptist Convention in 1875, and served until 1879. Upon his return, he was employed by the Negro Baptists of Virginia to canvass the United States in order to organize a general denominational convention among black Baptists. His genial character was not endowed with any special gifts of eloquence but Colley was deeply consecrated to the purpose of serving God by bringing the Word of God to "darkest Africa." He urged upon his brethren the moral responsibility that, since God had blessed them with the light of his Word, it was their sacred responsibility to send it to their brethren in Africa. He pointed out in his many speeches that, although the white missionaries were doing good work, they were greatly limited and restricted in dealing with the natives. He traveled near and far, pouring out his soul for Africa. It is said that his appeals were so earnest that whenever he would call a conference of pastors together to discuss the matter, he would get a most favorable response. Thus, it seems that Colley was the proper person to initiate this call for a national effort in foreign missions.

On November 24, 1880, at Montgomery, Ala., 150 persons, principally ministers and church workers from 11 states, answered Colley's call. Colley served as temporary chairman of the meeting, and as he raised the gavel to open the meeting officially, after a 30-minute devotion, he was restrained by tears that flowed down his cheeks and long beard. After a moment of silence and with a radiant face, he lifted the gavel and pounded it on the desk with the announcement of the purpose of the meeting. The Foreign Mission Convention was brought into being. W. H. McAlpine of Alabama was elected president; eleven vice-presidents, two secretaries, and a treasurer were also chosen.

The organization of this Convention gave black Baptists of the United States a new sense of national power and responsibility, as witnessed by various types of denominational advancement. Only foreign missions, however, claimed the attention of the delegates. This new national consciousness gained more definite expression in the further efforts of the leaders to organize a board of directors with headquarters in Richmond, Va. The special function of this board was to wage a continuous campaign of enlistment of churches, associations, state conventions, and other larger Baptist bodies to raise the necessary funds for the support of foreign mission work in Africa and other places.

The Convention then set up the Foreign Mission Board and elected A. Binga, Jr., of South Richmond as first chairman, with Colley as first corresponding secretary or executive secretary and field agent at a salary of $1,000 per year. He was acclaimed its father and progenitor, for it was through his efforts that this foreign mission idea had been made workable among Negro Baptists. The achievements and influence of this board are inestimable.

Formed in 1880, the Foreign Mission Convention was not without problems. As with any new movement, there was an initial struggle for survival until enough confidence and achievements rendered it secure. However, it was the intention of Colley to unite the whole of Negro America in the cause of foreign missions, and the facts will show that various groups across the country fell into line with his movement. However, such organizations as the New England Convention, the Baptist African Mission Convention, and various smaller groups did not join the movement in 1880. Still, the feeling that there should be a concentration of the efforts of all Baptists directed through one national body to a particular point of service persisted, and this situation led to the birth of another national group.

At the suggestion of William J. Simmons of Louisville, Ky., who was a national figure himself, and upon a call issued by him, nearly 600 delegates met at St. Louis, Mo., and organized the American National Baptist Convention. Simmons was elected its first president; J. R. Young and T. L. Johnson, vice-presidents; L. R. DeBaptiste, corresponding secretary; T. S. Clanton and W. H. Steward, recording secretaries; D. A. Gaddie, treasurer; and L. W. Smith, historian. An interesting constitution was formed and adopted. One of the main objectives of this convention was to work for the unification of all Negro Baptists of America in support of mission work. T. J. Johnson said at this meeting, "Knox lifted Scotland, Luther lifted Germany, and it remains for us to lift up the heathen in the land of our fathers—Africa." A radiant passion for the evangelization of Africa actuated the founders of the National Baptist work.

It appears that the National Baptist Convention attempted to exist apart from the Foreign Mission Convention, which was less than six years older and whose missionaries had been in Africa only two years. A resolution was adopted at the second meeting of the American National Baptist Convention to send a committee to the Foreign Baptist Convention, asking permission to meet with it; it seems that this committee's proposal was favorably accepted. The forming of this body did not as yet solve the problem of unifying the multiplicity of national and missionary agents among the Negro Baptists. In 1893, another organization, proposing to be national in scope, was founded in Washington, D.C.; it was known as the Baptist National Educational Convention. The chief emphasis of this group was an educated ministry in the leadership of the churches.

An account exists that helps to point the way through the state of confusion that existed among the Baptist leaders. "In the same year, 1893, it was suggested that what was called the Tripartite Union" be formed, consisting of the New England Convention (organized in 1875), the African Foreign Mission Convention, and the Foreign Mission Convention of America (organized in 1880). An attempt was made to unite the financial resources of the three conventions in order to secure and expand the work in foreign fields; however, this effort failed.

Formation of the National Baptist Convention, 1895–97   The floundering national Baptist bodies met at Montgomery, Ala., in 1894. After the reports of the main committees were given, an earnest appeal was made for the national union of Negro Baptists. It was then that A. W. Pegues, graduate of Bucknell University, scholar, and orator, offered a resolution that reflected his deep insight into the fundamental causes of the problem that threatened the Negro Baptists with national failure. Yet, the meeting adjourned without any real advance toward unification, though with a committee formed to investigate and draft solutions for the next year's session.

This session was held in Atlanta, Ga., in 1895, with the committee that was appointed at Montgomery ready to report. Their report was adopted with the understanding that whatever action that had been undertaken by the bodies previously would be rendered null and void, unless

William J. Simmons, first president of the American National Baptist Convention, a forerunner of national Baptist organizations. (Library of Congress.)

163

such purpose or action was definitely set forth in the new constitution. It should be noted here that under the new constitution the Foreign Mission Convention no longer existed. Instead, it became the Foreign Mission Board—only an agency for foreign missions of the National Baptist Convention. The committee sent out in 1894, at Montgomery, was composed of the following members: W. H. McAlpine, Pegues, Joseph E. Jones, A. S. Jackson, J. H. Frank, A. Hobbs, Jacob Bennette, Wesley G. Parks, and A. J. Stokes.

E. C. Morris of Arkansas was elected president of the Foreign Mission Board; also named were 16 vice-presidents—two from Texas and one from each of the other states represented; three secretaries; and a treasurer. The three new boards selected by the Convention were the Foreign Mission Board, the Home Mission Board, and the Educational Board.

The Foreign Mission Board was elected and its headquarters was retained at Richmond for a few months. L. M. Luke of Georgia was elected the first corresponding secretary under the new organization. His services were limited to three months, from September 1895 to December 31 of the same year. While he was preaching in the Old Fifth Street Baptist Church at Louisville, Ky., he was fatally stricken and died a few hours later.

In October, 1896, L. G. Jordan, who was then pastor of the Union Baptist Church of Philadelphia, was selected the capable successor of Luke. Little was it known that this able man was beginning an illustrous career during which the missionary movement among Negro Baptists would soar to unprecedented heights and take its place beside the many other distinguished boards of the denomination. This giant was the first of his race to produce most of the records, statistics, and data that are found in his report and that are so freely used as a basic source for history.

Shortly after Jordan was elected corresponding secretary of the Baptist Foreign Mission Board, he moved its headquarters from Richmond to Louisville, where it remained for some time. Some very unfavorable repercussions accompanied this transfer: a breach was created that has not until this day been filled. The support of the brethren in Richmond and the surrounding area was lost to the Board and Convention. It may be noted that the Lott Cary Missionary Society thrives in this area today.

The First Schism of the National Baptist Convention, 1897–1915 One of the early divisive problems of the Convention was control over publications. When the Publishing Board made its first report, the Lott Cary supporters were very dissatisfied with it and immediately inaugurated a plan of organization of their own (they later seceded from the Convention). This new Publishing Board was first placed under the Home Mission Boards of which R. H. Boyd was corresponding secretary, and administered by a committee of nine men (Boyd was to become the corresponding secretary for the Publishing Board also). This later proved quite disastrous to the Convention.

The board was organized under the title The National Baptist Publishing Board and not designated "of the National Baptist Convention," as were other boards. It was chartered as such and was under the exclusive management of the Board's own members. This and other facts led to the division in 1915. The plan of publishing national Baptist material made it a great economic success because the writing was done by some of the best Baptist minds—writers who could interpret the Negroes' feelings and needs, their yearnings and aspirations. This material was very popular and was well received by practically all the churches across the country. Its growth was rapid and phenomenal to the extent that it soon became very influential upon the whole Convention.

The amazing success of the Publishing Board soon put this group in the best financial position of any agent of the Convention. The leaders of this group soon became rather recalcitrant and indifferent to the overall program of the Convention. Unfortunately, there were signs of disloyalty and corruption, which focused the eyes of the parent body upon the Publishing Board. It was hoped that this Board would render for the Convention the same service that the Publishing Board of the Southern Baptist Convention was rendering for that group. In 1915 it was reported that the income of the Publishing Board had reached an aggregate total of $2,400,000 for the nine years of its existence.

These yearly reports were happily accepted with the understanding and acknowledgment that this board was the property of the Convention. When E. C. Morris recommended that the Publishing Board be separated from the Home Mission Board, this suggestion was vigorously opposed by Boyd, who was serving as secretary and treasurer of both boards and using state missionaries as book agents for the Publishing Board. At this time there ensued a state of confusion and turmoil that was to last for nearly ten years. The most debated question was: "Who owns the publishing house?"

After the secession of what was called the Boyd faction from the National Baptist Convention, the name chosen by this faction was the National Baptist Convention, Unincorporated, with the Publishing House as the center of the group, while the Foreign Mission Board became the center of the National Baptist Convention, Incorporated. Upon separation, *The National Baptist Union-Review*, the former national organ of the Publishing Board, continued with the Unincorporated Convention.

The full account of the happenings surrounding this most regrettable event among the National Baptists is given by Jordan. It is sufficient here to say that the leaders of the Convention lost respect for R. H. Boyd (secretary of the Publishing Board). Though their suspicions were unexplained, the rapid growth and success of the Publishing Board was offset by a growing lack of confidence in the business relations of its secretary. The two factions continued to gain in strength and to oppose each other until the breaking point. Boyd refused to give certain requested information about the operation and expense of the Publishing Board, and after he was called in question regarding the ownership of properties and the final ownership and control of the Publishing Board, the Convention sued for control.

However, Boyd and his followers won the subsequent decision of the Tennessee court and the Convention bowed to defeat. The Convention lost its publishing board and a number of churches, but it was incorporated and made a new start by organizing the Sunday School Publishing Board of the National Baptist Convention. After S. P. Harris and William Haynes had served short terms as secretary, this new board elected A. M. Townsend in 1920, and he served with distinction.

Inasmuch as the Unincorporated Convention began with only one board (all other boards remained with the incorporated group), its first task was to organize other boards. Through a joint commission with the Lott Cary Convention in 1924, it was agreed that each convention was to remain autonomous; yet all foreign mission work would be channeled through the Lott Cary Convention. The advantage was clear. It gave the National Unincorporated group a wide field in which to distribute its literature and the Lott Cary Convention would gain in national prominence.

The Second Schism: The Progressive National Baptist Convention, Inc. Some old unresolved stresses within the National Baptist Convention, U.S.A., Inc., and the new thrusts of the civil rights movement were two factors that precipitated the second great schism in the early 1960s. The president of the Convention, Joseph H. Jackson, had encouraged the blacks of America to rise up and break the chains of economic slavery, just as his predecessors had done for blacks in the days prior to and during Reconstruction. A leader of the direct action thrust of the civil rights movement, Martin Luther King, Jr., a Baptist minister and member of the Convention, was elected vice-president of one of its large auxiliary bodies—the National Sunday School and Baptist Training Union Congress—in 1958. Two groups of supporters formed behind the different approaches of the two national black leaders to the civil rights struggle. After an attempt to unseat Jackson as president of the Convention failed in Philadelphia in 1960, King was replaced as vice-president of the National Congress in Kansas City in 1961. In Kansas City, too, in a showdown struggle that precipitated a brief period of physical violence, the King-backed candidate, Gardner C. Taylor, pastor of the Concord Baptist Church of Brooklyn, N.Y., was decisively defeated by a vote of 2,732 to 1,321. Thus, the Jackson supporters prevailed as did Jackson, as head of the six-million-member body.

In 1962, in a meeting called by Rev. L. Venchael Booth, pastor of the Zion Baptist Church in Cincinnati, Ohio, many of Taylor's supporters gathered to form the Progressive National Baptist Convention; in its first annual meeting in Los Angeles, Calif., T. M. Chambers, pastor of the Zion Hill Baptist Church of Los Angeles, was elected president. Thus, a third national Baptist group was formed.

Unlike episcopal or apostolic groups, the real power of Baptist bodies lies more decisively within each individual congregation rather than in any collective association, convention, or conference. This is not to say, however, that individual congregations in non-Baptist groups do not provide a strong power base for some influential clergymen. With Baptists, however, the position of the pastor is more closely related to the sover-

Joseph H. Jackson. *(Courtesy of Boardman Press.)*

eignty of the church as expressed in the unity, or apparent unity, of pastor, deacons, and laity.

REFERENCES: For general bibliography (annotated) on black Baptists, see Crismon, Leo T., "Baptists and Religious Literature," *Baptist Advance: The Achievements of the Baptists of North America for a Century and a Half*, Boardman Press, Nashville, 1964, pp. 404–18. For additional references, see Williams, Ethel L., and Clifton R. Brown, *Afro-American Religious Studies: A Comprehensive Bibliography with Locations in American Libraries*, The Scarecrow Press, Inc., Metuchen, 1972. Two additional references are Freeman, Edward A., "National Baptist Convention, U.S.A., Inc.," *Baptist Advance*, pp. 190–226, and Woodson, Carter G., *The History of the Negro Church*, Associated Publishers, Washington, D.C., 1921.

Some Historic Baptist Churches and Their Pastors, 1970s

Abyssinian Baptist Church	Samuel D. Proctor	New York, N.Y.
Abyssinian Baptist Church	Austin Jefferson, Jr.	Philadelphia, Pa.
Central Baptist Church	T. E. Huntley	St. Louis, Mo.
City Temple of Baltimore	William W. Payne	Baltimore, Md.
Concord Baptist Church	Gardner Taylor	Brooklyn, N.Y.
Cornerstone Baptist Church	Sandy Ray	Brooklyn, N.Y.
Ebenezer Baptist Church	William J. Cook	Richmond, Va.
Ebenezer Baptist Church	Martin Luther King, Sr.	Atlanta, Ga.
First African Baptist Church	Charles Sumner Lee	Philadelphia, Pa.
First Baptist Church	Edward A. Freeman	Kansas City, Kans.
Greater Harvest Baptist Church	Henry Bracken	Chicago, Ill.
King Solomon Baptist Church	T. S. Boone	Detroit, Mich.
Nineteenth Street Baptist Church	Jerry Moore	Washington, D.C.
Olivet Baptist Church	Joseph H. Jackson	Chicago, Ill.
Starlight Baptist Church	Cornell E. Talley	Detroit, Mich.
Union Baptist Church	Baxter L. Matthews	Baltimore, Md.
Union Second Baptist Church	E. C. Copeland	Detroit, Mich.
Wheat Street Baptist Church	William Holmes Borders	Atlanta, Ga.
Zion Hill Baptist Church	T. M. Chambers	Los Angeles, Calif.

BARAKA, IMAMU AMIRI (LEROI JONES) (1934–), poet, playwright, political activist; born in Newark, N.J. After attending the Newark extension of Rutgers University, Baraka received a B.A. degree from Howard University (Washington, D.C.) in 1953 and then did graduate work at Columbia University and the New School for Social Research, both in New York City. As LeRoi Jones, the name under which much of his writing was published, he first gained national recognition during the 1950s as a leading poet of the "Beat Generation" literary movement in Greenwich Village, New York, when he and his wife published the poetry magazine *Yugen*. In 1960–61 he won a Whitney Fellowship. In 1961 he was one of the founders of the American Theater for Poets, an avant-garde organization. Among his writings of this period are the plays *Dutchman*, winner of an Obie Award as the best American play of 1964 presented Off Broadway; *The Toilet*; and *The Slave*, which played Off Broadway in 1964 and deals with a recurrent theme in his work: the interracial confrontation in America during the time of the civil rights movement. Later, Baraka settled in Harlem, where he wrote his powerful autobiographical novel, *The System of Dante's Hell* (1965), and founded the Black Arts Repertory Theater. In 1966 he again took up residence in Newark, becoming a leading spokesman for black nationalism and an exponent of Afro-Islamic culture. Thereafter, he took the name Imamu Amiri Baraka, and adopted the Kawaida branch of Islam as his faith. Meanwhile, Baraka had continued his literary career, winning a Guggenheim Fellowship (1965–66). His major works of poetry include: *Preface to a Twenty-Volume Suicide Note* (1961), *The Dead Lecturer* (1964), and *Black Magic: Collected Poetry 1961–67* (1969). Among his later writings for the stage were such works as *Four Black Revolutionary Plays* (1969) and *Jello* (1970). His prose works include: *Blues People: Negro Music in White America* (1963), *Home: Social Essays* (1966), and *Raise Race Rays Raze: Essays Since 1965* (1971). He edited *The Moderns: An Anthology of New Writings in America* (1963) and, with Larry Neal, *Black Fire* (1968). A number of his plays have been produced in Paris, Berlin, and Dakar, Senegal. *See also* LITERATURE: DRAMA/THEATER; LITERATURE: POETRY.

BARBER-SCOTIA COLLEGE Barber-Scotia College, at Concord, N.C., was founded as Scotia

Seminary in 1867 by the Freedmen's Committee of the Presbyterian Church. (It is still affiliated with the Presbyterian Church.) This private and coeducational college offers the bachelor's degree and provides liberal arts and teacher education curricula. The enrollment in 1975 was about 470.

The school was established to educate newly freed slaves; it opened in a one-room building with one teacher and ten students and offered elementary, secondary, and normal work to prepare black women to be teachers and social workers. In 1916 junior-college-level courses were first offered, and the institution's name was changed to Scotia Women's College. In 1930 it merged with Barber Memorial College of Anniston, Ala., which raised its endowment, and the institution changed its name again, becoming Barber-Scotia College. In 1954 it admitted students without regard to race or sex.

BARKSDALE, RICHARD K. *See* ANTHOLOGIES.

BARNES, ROBERT P. *See* SCIENTISTS: BIOLOGICAL, PHYSICAL.

BARNETT, CHARLIE *See* MUSIC: JAZZ.

BARNETT, CLAUDE A. (1889–1967), journalist; born in Sanford, Fla. After receiving an engineering degree from Tuskegee Institute (Tuskegee Institute, Ala.) in 1906, Barnett spent three years working for the U.S. Post Office in Chicago, Ill., and later became an ad salesman for the Chicago *Defender*. In 1919 he founded the Associated Negro Press, which supplied news to black newspapers. Like the Associated Press, it worked on a cooperative basis, receiving news from subscribers about their own areas. From 1942 until after World War II, Barnett was a special assistant to the U.S. Secretary of Agriculture, advising on the problems of black farmers. By the time the ANP was sold in 1964, Barnett had made some 15 trips to Africa in order to expand his coverage, and added more than 200 new subscribers. His work helped to build and to stabilize the Afro-American press. *See also* NEWSPAPERS.

BARNETT, CONSTANTINE CLINTON (1869–1935), physician; born in New Canton, Va. Barnett attended the University of Michigan and received his M.D. degree from Howard University Medical College (Washington D.C.) in 1899.

He worked at first as a civil servant for the federal government and later at the West Virginia Hospital for the Insane. Barnett started a private practice in Huntington, W. Va., and founded the Barnett Hospital there. He helped to establish a mental hospital for Afro-Americans in West Virginia in 1926.

BARNETT, IDA WELLS *See* WELLS, IDA BARNETT.

BARNWELL, SIDNEY FITZ C. (1926–   ), surgeon; born in Guyana. Barnwell received his M.D. degree from Howard University Medical College (Washington, D.C.) in 1955. He was a resident at Provident Hospital, Baltimore, Md. (1957–59), and later a diplomate of the American Board of Surgery (1964). Barnwell became assistant chief of general surgery at the Veterans Hospital, Tuskegee, Ala., and an attending surgeon at the Craven County Hospital, New Bern, N.C. Barnwell had a private practice in general surgery after 1965.

BARRACOONS Stockades or places of security that temporarily held slaves enroute from the African interior to coastal forts on the Atlantic coast.

BARRELHOUSE The term refers to (1) any good-time place, and (2) a popular song entitled "Barrel House Blues." The term's origin is obscure, perhaps deriving from the barrels found on the premises of saloons and clubs.

BARROW, JOSEPH LOUIS *See* LOUIS, JOE.

BARTHÉ, RICHMOND (1901–   ), sculptor; born in Bay St. Louis, Miss. After he was refused admission to a New Orleans art school because he was black, Barthé attended the Art Institute of Chicago in 1924 and the Art Students League, New York, N.Y., in 1931. Among his awards were a Rosenwald Fellowship (1928–29) and a Guggenheim Fellowship (1940–41). His forceful, monumental works, often looking to African art for their inspiration, include oil paintings of black individuals and groups, and theater themes in sculpture. Some of his exhibits in New York City have been at the Harmon Foundation, 1929, 1931, 1933; at the Whitney Museum of American Art 1933; at the 1939 World's Fair; and at the Grand Central Gallery, 1947. Barthé's work is included in the collections of the Whitney Museum of American Art, and the Metropolitan

Museum of Art, and the New York Public Library (Schomburg Collection), all in New York City. Among his finest pieces are *Shoe Shine Boy*, *The Boxer*, and *Booker T. Washington*. A bas-relief by Barthé is displayed at Harlem River Houses, New York, N. Y. *See also* ARTISTS.

BASEBALL See ATHLETES.

BASHFUL, EMMETT WILFORT (1917–   ), political scientist, educator; born in New Roads, La. Bashful received a B.S. degree from Southern University (Baton Rouge, La.) in 1940 and an M.A. degree from the University of Illinois in 1947. He was awarded his Ph.D. degree in political science in 1955. After an instructorship in political science at Florida Agricultural and Mechanical (A&M) University from 1948 to 1950, Bashful became an assistant professor there, and later he served as professor and chairman of the department. In 1958 he returned to his alma mater to become professor for one year. Immediately thereafter, he was appointed dean of Southern University, and ten years later he became the vice-president at the university's New Orleans (La.) campus.

BASIE, WILLIAM (COUNT) (1904–   ), jazz pianist, bandleader; born in Red Bank, N.J. Basie began playing the piano in his early teens, later studying with "Fats" Waller. During the early 1920s, he toured the eastern vaudeville circuit, joining Benny Moten in Kansas City, Mo., in 1926. He formed his own band in 1936, and its special brand of jazz made Count Basie and his band famous into the 1970s. Basie's long career was marked by many "firsts." For example, his was the first American band to play a royal command performance for the Queen of England (in 1957). As a composer, Basie wrote many of his band's most popular numbers. Perhaps his best-known work is "One O'Clock Jump," written in 1937 with Otho Lee Gaines. *See also* MUSIC: JAZZ.

BASKETBALL See ATHLETES.

BASSETT, EBENEZER DON CARLOS (1833–1908), government official; born in Litchfield, Conn. Bassett was educated at Connecticut State Normal School, Yale College, and the University of Pennsylvania. He was a high school principal in New Haven, Conn., and Philadelphia, Pa., until President Ulysses S. Grant appointed him minister resident of the U.S. to Haiti in 1869.

Ebenezer D. Bassett. (Photo by J. W. Hurn, Moorland-Spingarn Research Center, Howard University.)

This was the first diplomatic appointment outside the United States ever given an Afro-American by the U.S. government. In 1879 he became consul-general of Haiti in New York, and in 1888 he returned to Haiti where he remained until 1892. Back in the United States, Bassett engaged in the literary studies that resulted in the publication of the *Handbook of Haiti*.

BATEMAN, MILDRED MITCHELL psychiatrist. Mitchell was graduated with a B.S. degree from Johnson C. Smith University (Charlotte, N. C.) and her M.D. degree from the Woman's Medical College of Pennsylvania in 1946. She served a psychiatric residency and fellowship at the Menninger School of Psychiatry (Topeka, Kans.). Bateman was clinical director of Lakin State Hospital, West Virginia; supervisor of professional services and later director of the West Virginia department of mental health; and diplomate of the American Board of Psychiatry and Neurology. Her Honors included: Woman of the Year Award from the *Gazette-Mail* (1962); honorary doctorate of science degree from Johnson C. Smith University; and a special award from the West Virginia Medical Society.

BATES, DAISY (1922–   ), civil rights leader; born in Huttig, Ark. Bates acquired prominence in Little Rock, Ark., when in 1941 she and her husband organized what was to become one of the most widely read weekly newspapers in the South, the *Arkansas State Press*. In 1957 she gained national recognition when, as president of the Arkansas chapter of the National Association for the Advancement of Colored People (NAACP), she played an active role in the Little Rock, Ark., school crisis—an incendiary incident brought about by the action of Arkansas Governor Orville Faubus to prevent black children from entering the Little Rock Central High School. State guardsmen, blocking the entrance of the school to black children, were preempted by federal troops, ordered there by President Dwight D. Eisenhower. Bates stood firm with the children, submitted herself to arrest, and declared that the students would return to the school only with assurances of protection from the president of the United States. She and the nine arrested students received the NAACP's Spingarn Medal in 1958 for their courage in accomplishing the integration of the high school. Her book, *The Long Shadow of Little Rock: A Memoir*, was published in 1962. *See also* SPINGARN MEDAL.

BATES, NATHANIEL (1921–), public official, mayor; born in Cason, Tex. Before graduating from San Francisco State University in 1963, Bates did military service in Korea. Later, he was employed as deputy probation officer of the Alameda County Probation Department in Oakland, Calif. In 1967 Bates was elected to the Richmond, Calif., city council, the first of many prominent positions he held in that city. In 1971 he became mayor of Richmond.

BATTLES See WARS.

BAXTER, CHARLES F. (1927–), scientist; born in Washington, D.C. Baxter received a bachelor's degree in chemical engineering from the Polytechnic Institute of Brooklyn (Brooklyn, N.Y.), a M.S. degree in management from the Massachusetts Institute of Technology, and has done further graduate work at the International Institute of Nuclear Science and Engineering at the Argonne National Laboratory. He served as a project engineer, program manager, and the U.S. Atomic Energy Commission's (AEC) interagency representative for space missions in the U.S. Navy's Transit Navigational Satellite Program, the U.S. Coast Guard's Navigational Aids Program, and the National Aeronautics and Space Administration's (NASA), Nimbus, Pioneer, and Viking projects. Baxter was a member of the United States Energy Research and Development Administration, and also served the New York State Energy Research and Development Authority as its manager of research under the Intergovernmental Personnel Assistance Act of 1970. He served on the staff of the U.S. ERDA (formerly the U.S. Atomic Energy Commission) after 1955.

BAYLOR, ELGIN See ATHLETES: BASKETBALL.

BAYLOR, SOLOMON (1922–), lawyer, judge; born in King William, Va. Baylor attended Coppin State Teachers College (Baltimore, Md.), and graduated from the University of Maryland Law School in 1951. He established a private law practice in Baltimore, which he subsequently abandoned in 1970 when he was appointed to the bench of the housing and rent court of the District Court of Maryland.

BEARDEN, BESSYE J. (1891–1943), educator, born in Goldsboro, N. C. After graduating from Virginia Normal and Industrial Institute (now Virginia State College), Bearden became the New York representative of the Chicago *Defend-* er. After becoming the first woman member of a New York City school board, Bearden became a nationally known black leader. She was appointed to local board 15 in 1922, and was elected chairman after it was changed to 12. Among many other accomplishments, she was a deputy collector for the Internal Revenue Service (1935), the national treasurer of the Council of Negro Women, and the founder and president of the Colored Women's Democratic League. Her son, Romare, became a prominent painter. *See also* BEARDEN, ROMARE.

BEARDEN, ROMARE (1912–), artist, author; born in Charlotte, N.C. Bearden received a B.S. degree from New York University and attended Pittsburgh and Columbia universities. He also attended the Art Students League in New York City, where he studied under George Grosz. At the Sorbonne in 1950–51, Bearden began to discover the works of Brancusi, Léger, and Braque, and he developed enthusiasm for Picasso and the Cubists. Intending to paint the life of his people, Bearden experimented with photomontage and other media, including collage. His collages have been used on the covers of such magazines as *Time, Fortune,* and *The New Yorker.* Bearden's oils and other works have been exhibited at the Carnegie Museum, Pittsburgh, Pa., 1937; the Institute of Modern Art, Boston, Mass., 1943; the Corcoran Gallery, Washington, D.C., 1965; the Boston Museum of Fine Arts, 1970; and elsewhere. His work is in the permanent collections of the Museum of Modern Art, the Whtney Museum of American Art, and the New York Public Library (Schomburg Collection), all in New York City; and the Museum of Fine Arts, Boston. Bearden was a member of the National Institute of Letters, and he directed the Cinque Gallery for young black artists in New York City. He wrote *The Painter's Mind* with Carl Holty (1969) and *Six Black Masters of American Art* (1972).

BEASLEY, DELILAH LEONTIUM (1871–1934), historian, journalist; born in Cincinnati, Ohio. Beasley wrote for the Cleveland *Gazette* before she was 13 years old, and by the age of 15, she was writing a column for the Cincinnati *Enquirer.* Her first published book was *The Negro Trail Blazers of California* (1919; 1968); she also contributed articles to the Oakland *Tribune.* Beasley was a member of several groups favoring the entry of the United States into the World Court, and she belonged to such other disarmament and international peace organizations as the League of Nations Association for Northern California and the World's Forum.

BEBOP *See* MUSIC: JAZZ.

BECHET, SIDNEY (1891–1959), jazz clarinetist, soprano saxophonist, composer; born in New Orleans, La. Bechet was the first jazzman to achieve recognition on the soprano saxophone and one of the first to win acceptance in classical circles as a serious musician. After World War I, Bechet played in England and on the Continent with Will Marion Cook's Southern Syncopated Orchestra. During the 1920s, he made a series of records with Clarence Williams' Blue Five; in the 1930s, he played throughout the United States and Europe before forming his own trio. His best-known songs, written with Noble Sissle after 1929, include: "Petite Four"; "The Fishseller"; "As-tu la Cafard"; "Viper Mad"; "Southern Sunset"; "Delta Mood"; and "The Broken Windmill." *See also* MUSIC: JAZZ.

BECKWOURTH, JAMES P. (1798–ca. 1867), frontiersman; born in Fredericksburg, Va. Beckwourth's father was white and his mother of black and Indian ancestry. In 1823 he became a fur trapper, and in 1824 joined the expeditions of W. H. Ashley and Andrew Henry as a scout and trapper. He is known to have "married" into several Indian tribes. He lived with the Crow Indians ca. 1826–34. During his lifetime he was a miner, guide, fur trapper, company agent, army scout, soldier, and hunter. As a scout in the early 1850s, he discovered a pass through the Sierra Nevada Mountains to the Sacramento Valley. In 1864 he took part in the Apache Wars on the American side, later dying in Denver, Colo. Beckwourth's life as a frontiersman is recorded in T. B. Bonner (ed.), *The Life and Adventures of James P. Beckwourth, Mountaineer, Scout, and Pioneer and Chief of the Crow Nation* (1856), written at Beckwourth's request and supposedly in his own words. *See also* AFRO-AMERICAN HISTORY: THE WEST.

James P. Beckwourth. *(Library of Congress.)*

BECTON, GEORGE WILSON (? –1933), cultist. Becton was the leader of a Harlem-based sect known as the World's Gospel Feast, rival and competitor of similar groups. With 12 selected disciples, an orchestra, gospel singers, and his own oratory, he delighted followers in New York and other large cities with programs for "consecrated dimes" during the Great Depression (1930s). Becton advocated thrift and abstention from such worldly vices as drink and gambling. Becton was riddled by bullets from unknown assailants in his automobile and died in Philadelphia, Pa.

BECTON, JULIUS W., JR. (1927–   ), army officer. Becton received a B.S. degree from Prairie View Agricultural and Mechanical (A&M) College (Prairie View, Tex.) and M.A. degree from the University of Maryland. He served as chief of the armored branch in the office of personnel of the U.S. Army, and was awarded the Distinguished Flying Cross and the Legion of Merit. Becton was promoted to the rank of major general in 1974.

BELAFONTE, HAROLD GEORGE, JR. (HARRY) (1927–   ), singer, actor; born in New York, N. Y. Belafonte lived in Jamaica from 1935 to 1940, but during World War II, he served in the U.S. Navy. He began his successful career as a popular singer and actor by appearing in nightclubs in New York City in 1949–50. His first motion pictures, *Bright Road* and *Carmen Jones*, were made in the early 1950s, the time also of his debut on Broadway in *Three for Tonight* (1953). During the 1950s and 1960s, Belafonte toured all the American states and many other areas of the world, ranking as one of the most popular performers of that era. His career was also distinguished by association with the civil rights movement and with many other black causes.

BELCHER, FANNIN S. *See* LITERATURE: DRAMA/THEATER.

BELL, AL (1940–   ), businessman; born in Little Rock, Ark. Bell received a B.S. degree from Philander Smith College (Little Rock, Ark.). Before he joined the Memphis, Tenn., staff of Stax Records, Inc., in 1966, he earned his living as a disc jockey. In 1967 Bell was named executive vice-president and chairman of the board of the company, becoming one of the most influential Afro-Americans in the recording industry.

BELL, DENNIS (ca. 1870–1953), soldier; born in Washington, D.C. Bell was one of four privates of the 10th U.S. Cavalry who rowed through heavy Spanish gunfire to rescue 15 members of an all-white landing party off the coast of Tayabocoa, during the Spanish-American War in 1898. All four soldiers, Bell, Private Fitz Lee, Private William H. Thompkins, and Private George Wauton, were cited for gallantry and were awarded the Congressional Medal of Honor in 1899. *See also* WARS.

BELL, DERRICK A., JR. (1930–   ), lawyer, educator; born in Pittsburgh, Pa. Bell received a B.A. degree from Duquesne University (Pittsburgh, Pa.) in 1952, after which he served in the U.S. Air Force and then went on to study law at the University of Pittsburgh, receiving his LL.B. degree in 1957. He worked for two years on the issues of conscientious objection and civil rights in the U.S. Department of Justice, served for a year as executive director of the Pittsburgh branch of the National Association for the Advancement of Colored People (NAACP), and was a staff attorney on the NAACP's legal defense and education fund until 1966. He spent the next two years with the U.S. Department of Health, Education, and Welfare, in the civil rights division, later becoming executive director of the Western Center on Law and Poverty, a division of the Office of Equal Opportunity. In 1971 Bell was appointed professor of law at Harvard University after two years there as lecturer. He published articles in various law journals on conscientious objection, school litigation, black studies, and minority admissions, and wrote a book entitled *Race, Racism, and American Law* (1973).

BELL, EDWARD F. (1929–   ), lawyer, judge; born in Grand Rapids, Mich. Bell received a B.A. degree from the University of Michigan in 1951 and his J.D. degree from the Detroit College of Law in 1954. After spending three years with the Children's Aid Society in Detroit as a social worker, he began practicing law in 1959. Ten years later, he became a judge on the Wayne County Circuit Court. However, in 1972, he resigned in order to run for the office of mayor of Detroit, but lost the race to Coleman Young. *See also* YOUNG, COLEMAN.

BELL, HOWARD E. (1920–   ), lawyer judge; born in Norfolk County, Va. Bell received a B.A. degree from Virginia Union University in 1944 and his LL.B. degree from Brooklyn Law School (Brooklyn, N.Y.) in 1947. He practiced law until 1958, when he became an attorney in the Controller's Office of the city of New York, remaining there for two years. Bell was later appointed assistant counsel to the Housing and Redevelopment Board of the City of New York. In May 1969 he was appointed by Mayor John V. Lindsay for

an interim term on the Civil Court of the City of New York—a term that expired in December 1969. Bell subsequently ran for election to a full term on that bench in November 1969, and won.

BELL, JAMES M. (1921–   ), psychiatrist; born in Portsmouth, Va. Bell received a B.S. degree from North Carolina College in 1943 and his M.D. degree from Meharry Medical College (Nashville, Tenn.) in 1947. He served his internship at Harlem Hospital. Bell was assistant physician and clinical director of Lakin State Hospital (1948–51); a captain in the U.S. Army Medical Corps (1951–53); and a resident in psychiatry at Winter Veterans Hospital, Topeka, Kans. He was a civilian consultant in psychiatry at Irwin Army Hospital, Fort Riley, Kans.; instructor at the Menninger School of Psychiatry Topeka, Kans.; and psychiatrist and director of the Berkshire Farm for Boys, Canaan, N.Y.

BELL, JAMES MADISON (1826–1902), political activist, poet; born in Gallipolis, Ohio. Bell befriended abolitionist John Brown in Canada in 1854 and helped him recruit support for the movement. A prominent antislavery orator, Bell moved to California in 1860, returning to Ohio after the Civil War. He was a delegate to the 1868 Republican National Convention, which nominated Ulysses S. Grant for his first presidential term. Bell's poetry came second to his activism, and was primarily meant to be recited. A volume of his verse, *Poetical Works,* was published in 1901.

BELL, PHILIP A. (1807–89), journalist. Bell managed the *Colored American* in New York City, and he appointed Samuel Cornish as its editor. In 1857 he became associate editor of *The Pacific Appeal* in San Francisco, Calif., and although it was perhaps the leading black newspaper on the West Coast at that time, Bell began his own newspaper in 1865. This journal, *The Elevator,* was devoted to reporting developments in the arts and sciences, and its orientation to technological issues and their effect on American life was considerably greater than most of the paper's competitors. Although *The Elevator* was a success at first, Bell died in poverty. *See also* CORNISH, SAMUEL JAMES.

BELLAMY, WALT *See* ATHLETES: BASKETBALL.

BENEDICT COLLEGE Benedict College, at Columbia, S.C., was founded in 1870 by the Baptist

Church and remained a strongly church-related institution. The coeducational college is private, offers the bachelor's degree (including B.D. and B.Th. degrees) and provides a liberal arts curriculum.

Begun with the aid of Bathsheba A. Benedict, of Rhode Island, the school was founded to meet the needs of newly freed slaves and at one time offered precollege education. The enrollment increased from 39 students in 1870 to approximately 1,500 in 1975. The faculty grew from 2 to 83 during that period. More than half the black teachers in South Carolina have been Benedict graduates, and seven college presidents were Benedict alumni. A survey of the period from 1955 to 1969 showed that 35 percent of Benedict's graduates went on to advanced studies, and 80 percent went into education. Its black presidents include: J. J. Starks, 1929–44; J. A. Bacotes, 1944–65; T. J. Hansberry (Acting), 1965; and Benjamin F. Payton, 1965–

BENNETT COLLEGE Bennett College, at Greensboro, N.C., was founded in 1873 by the Freedman's Aid Society and the Southern Education Society of the Methodist Episcopal Church. Still church-related, but with private support, this women's college offers the bachelor's degree, and provides liberal arts and teacher education curricula. Its 1975 enrollment was about 550.

Originally coeducational, Bennett became a women's junior college in 1926 under the auspices of the Woman's Home Missionary Society of the Methodist Church. By 1930, it had become a four-year college and graduated its first class of four students. By 1976, Bennett conducted a special study program for extraordinary students, exchange programs with other women's colleges, and extensive field work in various disciplines.

Lerone Bennett, Jr.

BENNETT, LERONE, JR. (1928–   ), journalist, historian, educator; born in Clarksdale, Miss. As a teenager, Bennett worked as a reporter on the Jackson *Advocate* and the Mississippi *Enterprise*. Before receiving his B.A. degree from Morehouse College (Atlanta, Ga.) in 1949, he served as a reporter and as city editor for the Atlanta *Daily World*. In 1953 Bennett joined the Johnson Publishing Company in Chicago, Ill., as associate editor of *Jet*. In 1958 he became senior editor of *Ebony*. Bennett received the Capital Press Club's Book of the Year Award for *Before the Mayflower: A History of the Negro in America 1619–1962*. He has also written *What Manner*

of Man: A Biography of Martin Luther King, Jr. (1964); *Black Power U.S.A.: The Human Side of Reconstruction, 1867–1877* (1968); *Pioneers in Protest* (1968); and *The Challenge of Blackness* (1972). Bennett was a visiting professor of history at Northwestern University (Evanston, Ill.) in 1969, and he became the chairman of the black studies program there in 1973.

BENNETT, ROBERT See PREFACE: LIST OF CONTRIBUTORS.

BERKLEY, TOM See NEWSPAPERS: CONTEMPORARY.

BERNARD, CANUTE CLIVE (1924–   ), surgeon; born in Costa Rica. Bernard received a B.S. degree from Howard University (Washington, D.C.) in 1949 and his M.D. degree from the University of Geneva, Switzerland. He was an attending surgeon at Harlem and Jamaica hospitals, New York, N.Y., and he later became surgeon and founding partner of the Carter Community Health Center.

BERRY, BENJAMIN DONALDSON (1939–   ), clergyman; born in Washington, D.C. Berry received a B.A. degree from Morehouse College (Atlanta, Ga.) in 1962 and his S.T.B. degree from Harvard Divinity School in 1966. He was associate dean of the Chapel of Fisk University (Nashville, Tenn.) from 1964–1965. Berry became a social worker in Cambridge, Mass., and later served as pastor of the Plymouth United Church of Christ, Louisville, Ky.

BERRY, EDWIN CARLOS (BILL) (1910–   ), civil rights organizer, sociologist, civic leader; born in Oberlin, Ohio. Berry received a B.A. degree from Oberlin College (Oberlin, Ohio) in 1934 and then attended the University of Pittsburgh, where he received his M.S.W. degree in 1943. From 1945 to 1955, Berry was executive director of the Portland, Oreg., branch of the Urban League, and from 1956 until his retirement in 1969, he served as executive director of the Chicago Urban League. As executive director, Berry bridged the gap between the Chicago Urban League and the somewhat more militant black civil rights movement, and he developed more traditional league ties to the business and civic community. Berry taught in the sociology departments of several leading universities, including: Duquesne University, University of Chicago, Northern Illinois University, Northwestern University, and Loyola College. He received the American Civil Liberties Union fourth annual Civil Liberties Award in 1964, and in 1965 he was named Chicagoan of the Year in welfare work.

BERRY, JESSE F. (1932–   ), engineer; born in Asheville, N.C. Berry received a B.S. degree from the University of Southern California in 1962 and a M.S. degree from California State University in 1969. Prior to his graduation from Southern California, he worked on research projects at North American Aviation in Los Angeles. Berry then became an electronic engineer for Interstate Electronics Company in Anaheim, Calif., for four years, and from 1966 to 1971, he was systems engineer at Hughes Aircraft Company in Fullerton, Calif. Berry was principal engineer at Honeywell-Marine Systems Division in Seattle, Wash., after 1971.

BERRY, MARY FRANCES (1938–   ), historian, educator; born in Nashville, Tenn. Berry received the B.A. and M.A. degrees from Howard University, 1961 and 1962, and a Ph.D. in 1966 from the University of Michigan, Ann Arbor. She received her law degree (J.D.) in 1970. During the 1970s she served in several high-ranking executive positions, among them head of black studies at the University of Maryland, College Park; chancellor of the University of Colorado at Boulder; and assistant secretary for education in the U.S. Department of Health, Education, and Welfare (HEW). In addition to articles, she has authored two books: *Black Resistance / White Law*, 1971, and *Military Necessity and Civil Rights Policy*, 1977. *See also* Preface: List of Contributors.

BERRY, THEODORE MOODY (1905–   ), lawyer, public official, mayor; born in Maysville, Ky. Berry received a B.A. degree (1928) and his LL.B. degree (1931) from the University of Cincinnati (Cincinnati, Ohio). Although he opened his own law office, he eventually became a member of two other law firms, one in Cincinnati and one in Washington, D.C. In 1949 he was elected city councilman in Cincinnati, and in 1956 he was chosen vice-mayor of the city. In 1965 President Lyndon B. Johnson appointed him director of the community action programs within the

U.S. Office of Economic Opportunity (OEO). In 1972 Berry was elected mayor of Cincinnati by his fellow councilmen.

BETHUNE-COOKMAN COLLEGE Bethune-Cookman College, at Daytona Beach, Fla., was founded by a merger in 1923 of two Florida institutions: Cookman Institute of Jacksonville, founded in 1872 by Rev. D. S. B. Darnell; and the Daytona Normal and Industrial Institute for Negro Girls of Daytona Beach, founded in 1904 by Mary McLeod Bethune. The school is private, coeducational, and strongly church-related (United Methodist); it offers the bachelor's degree and provides liberal arts, teacher education, and vocational curricula. Its 1975 enrollment was about 1200.

After the 1923 merger, the institution was renamed the Daytona-Cookman Collegiate Institute and was administered by the board of education of the Methodist Episcopal Church. High school work was discontinued, and emphasis was placed on a two-year college program. In 1941 the four-year college program in liberal arts and teacher training was instituted. In 1960 Bethune-Cookman was voted into full membership in the Southern Association of Colleges and Schools.

Bethune-Cookman's presidents include: Mary McLeod Bethune, 1904–42 and 1946–47; James E. Colston, 1942–46; Richard V. Moore, beginning in 1947, and Oswald P. Bronson. *See also* Bethune, Mary McLeod.

BETHUNE, MARY McLEOD (1875–1955), educator, civic leader; born near Mayesville, S.C. Bethune left the cotton fields of her childhood to attend Scotia College in North Carolina (1888–95), and the Moody Bible Institute in Chicago (1895–97), where she was the only Negro student. In 1904, she founded the normal and industrial school for young Negro women at Daytona Beach, Fla.—starting with $1.50 in cash, five pupils, and a rented cottage—that became Bethune-Cookman College in 1923, and which she served as president until 1947. Bethune also was president of the National Association of Colored Women's Clubs (1924–28), and she was the founder of the National Headquarters for the National Association of Colored Women (1926) and founder-president of the National Council of Negro Women (1935–49). Bethune was also a member of the Hoover Committee for Child Welfare and director of the National Business League, the National Urban

League, and the Commission on Interracial Cooperation. Bethune directed the Division of Negro Affairs of the National Youth Administration. She was the first Negro woman to head a federal office, and as such she created the informal Black Cabinet of the New Deal. A national memorial in Washington, D.C., was erected in her honor in July 1974. *See also* BETHUNE-COOKMAN COLLEGE; WOMEN.

BETHUNE, THOMAS GREENE (BLIND TOM) (1849–1908), pianist, composer; born in Columbus, Ga. Bethune, born blind and a slave, was sold to Colonel Bethune, who realized his remarkable musical talents and encouraged his career as a pianist. A child prodigy, Bethune made his debut at a recital in Savannah, Ga., in 1858, and afterward for more than 40 years amazed his audiences with his artistry and his gift for total recall. Bethune could play more than 700 pieces from memory. *See also* MUSIC: HISTORY AND DEVELOPMENT.

BIBLE WAY CHURCH OF OUR LORD JESUS CHRIST WORLD WIDE, INC. This pentecostal religious body of about seventy churches withdrew in 1957 from the Church of Our Lord of the Apostolic Faith. Under the leadership of Smallwood Edmund Williams, presiding bishop, the church has its headquarters in Washington, D.C., and a membership of about 40,000 (1976).

◆◆

BIBLIOGRAPHIES/BIOGRAPHIES/GUIDES

BIBLIOGRAPHIES / BIOGRAPHIES / GUIDES Books about Afro-Americans were relatively few during the nineteenth century, and, thus, there were few bibliographies. One of the earliest noteworthy attempts at bibliographic formation was made by W. E. B. Du Bois in the Atlanta University studies in his short *A Select Bibliography of the American Negro*, 1905, 71 pp. Another milestone came in 1928 when Tuskegee Institute published Monroe N. Work's monumental compilation (see listing below).

However, it was not until after the turn of the mid-century, under the impetus of the civil rights movement, that books and bibliographies proliferated. Never before had so many books appeared about Afro-Americans as during the decade of the 1960s. Many old books about Afro-Americans were reprinted, notably by such publishers as the Johnson Reprint Corporation (*The Basic Afro-American Reprint Library*), Negro Universities Press, Johnson Publishing Company (*Ebony Classics*), and Arno Press. Some established publishers issued many new titles about blacks; outstanding among these houses were: Oxford University Press, University of Illinois Press, R. R. Bowker Company, and McGraw-Hill Book Company.

By the end of the 1960s publications had become so numerous that R. R. Bowker Company gave special attention to this fact in several issues of *Paperbound Books in Print*, and Appleton-Century-Crofts issued its *Afro-American Writers* in its Goldentree Bibliographies series. (See listings below under R. R. Bowker Company and Turner, Darwin T.).

The following references, including bibliographies, biographies, guides, directories, and indexes are representative of the vast sources available for studying Afro-Americans.

Abajian, James De T., *Blacks and Their Contributions to the American West: A Bibliography and Union List of Library Holdings Through 1970*, G.K. Hall, Boston, 1974. Compiled for the Friends of the San Francisco Public Library and published in cooperation with the American Library Association, it contains 4,300 entries.

Arata, Esther Spring, and Nicholas John Rotoli, *Black American Playwrights, 1800 to the Present: A Bibliography*, Scarecrow Press, Inc., Metuchen, N.J., 1976, 295 pp.; not annotated. It contains information on 530 black playwrights.

Baker, Augusta, *The Black Experience in Children's Books*, New York Public Library, New York, 1971, 109 pp.; gives a comprehensive and highly selective bibliography of children's books.

Bardolph, Richard, *The Negro Vanguard*, Vintage Books, New York, 1959. A collective biography that spans Afro-American history from 1770 to 1959; a basic bibliography is included in the author's section on "Essay on Authorities," pp. 463–95.

Barksdale, Richard K., and Kenneth Kinnamon, *Black Writers in America: A Comprehensive Anthology,* Macmillan, New York, 1972.

Brasch, Ila Wales, and Walter Milton Brasch, *A Comprehensive Bibliography of American Black English,* Louisiana State University Press, Baton Rouge, 1974; contains descriptions of 1,800 sources.

Broderick, Dorothy, *Image of the Black in Children's Literature,* R. R. Bowker Company, New York, 1973; more than 100 titles are examined.

Burr, Nelson R., *A Critical Bibliography of Religion in America,* Princeton University Press, Princeton, N.J., 1961. Most of the citations deal with the period before the 1930s.

Chambers, Fredrick, *Black Higher Education in the United States: A Selected Bibliography on Negro Higher Education and Historically Black Colleges and Universities,* Greenwood Press, Westport, Conn., 1978. Institutional histories and doctoral dissertations are included among the contents.

Chapman, Dorothy, *Index to Black Poetry,* G. K. Hall, Boston, 1974. This is an index of poets included in 94 books and pamphlets and in 33 anthologies.

Chicago Public Library, *The Chicago Afro-American Union Analytic Catalog: An Index to Materials of the Afro-American in the Principal Libraries of Chicago,* G. K. Hall, Boston, 1972, 5 vols. A major publication comprising more than 75,000 entries that are housed at the George C. Hall Branch of the Chicago Public Library.

Davis, Arthur P., *From the Dark Tower: Afro-American Writers from 1900 to 1960,* Howard University Press, Washington, D.C., 1974. This volume contains a highly selective bibliography, pp. 230–89, for each writer considered.

Davis, John P., *The American Negro Reference Book,* Prentice-Hall, Englewood Cliffs, 1966, 969 pp. This volume includes scholarly references on a variety of topics.

Davis, Lenwood G., *The Black Woman in American Society: An Annotated Bibliography,* G. K. Hall, Boston, 1975, contains 700 listings (of which 300 are books) alphabetized by author.

Dickinson, Donald C., *A Bio-Bibliography of Langston Hughes, 1902–1967,* Archon Books, 2d ed., 1972.

Disciples of Christ Historical Society, *Preliminary Guide to Black Materials in the Disciples of Christ Historical Society,* 1971, 31 pp. It lists more than 625 books, pamphlets, periodicals, theses, personal papers, and manuscripts. The preface and introduction include further details

on the guide, the history of black Disciples of Christ, and the historical society's Black Materials Project.

Dumond, Dwight L., *A Bibliography of Anti-Slavery in America,* University of Michigan Press, Ann Arbor, 1961. This volume is perhaps the most important bibliography on the subject and was compiled by an outstanding author and scholar.

Dunmore, Charlotte J., *Black Children and Their Families: A Bibliography,* Rand E Research Associates, San Francisco, Calif., 1976, 103 pp.

Editors of *Ebony, The Ebony Success Library: 1,000 Successful Blacks,* Johnson Publishing Company, Chicago, 1973; gives contemporary profiles with reliable biographical data and without listings of sources or bibliographies.

Edmonds, Helen G., *Black Faces in High Places: Negroes in Government,* Harcourt, Brace, Jovanovich, New York, 1971, 271 pp.; gives short biographical sketches for figures at all levels of government.

Fisk University, *Dictionary Catalog of the Negro Collection of the Fisk University Library,* G. K. Hall, Boston, 1974.

Foner, Philip S., *History of Black Americans: From Africa to the Emergence of the Cotton Kingdom,* Greenwood Press, Westport, 1975; a topical bibliography, pp. 595–662, is included.

Gilbert, Abby L., *Black Banks: A Bibliographic Survey,* Office of the Comptroller of the Currency, Washington, D.C., reprinted from *The Bulletin of Bibliography,* vol. 28, April–June 1971, with addendum.

Glenn, Robert W., *Black Rhetoric: A Guide to Afro-American Communication,* Scarecrow Press, Inc., Metuchen, N.J., 1976, 386 pp.; not annotated. It lists 40 bibliographies, 182 anthologies, 1,270 books, and more than 2,400 speeches and essays. This volume provides an identification of and guide to the accessible texts of many speakers and writers, and directs students and teachers of Afro-American communication to secondary materials that will assist in the study of those texts.

Hampton Institute, *Dictionary Catalog of the George Peabody Collection of Negro Literature and History,* Greenwood Press, Westport, 1972, 2 vols.; it lists about 15,000 items.

Hatch, James V., *Black Image on the American Stage: A Bibliography of Plays and Musicals, 1770–1970,* DBS Publications, Inc., New York, 1970, 162 pp.; without annotation; title and author index, pp. 123–60. Contains about 2,000 entries, pp. 1–121. Entries are arranged chronologically from the 1800s to 1970. The compiler states the following criteria for his selections in the "Introduction" (p. ix):

"In most cases, a play included in this bibliography must meet two of four criteria: 1.) it contains at least one black character; 2.) it was written by a black playwright; 3.) it is on a black theme; 4.) the play was written or produced in America between the years 1767 and 1970."

This bibliography includes full-length plays, one acts, musicals, revues, operas, and in some cases, dance dramas. The names of composers are listed only when there was an indication that they had written either part of the book and/or the lyrics. This compiler, with Omanii Abdullah, has a more comprehensive and annotated bibliography published later. *Black Playwrights, 1823–1977: An Annotated Bibliography of Plays*, R. R. Bowker, 1977, 280 pp.

Haywood, Charles, *A Bibliography of North American Folklore and Folksong*, 2d rev. ed., Dover, New York, 1961; see Vol. 1 for its section on the Negro, pp. 430–560.

Heller, Murray, (ed), *Black Names in America: Origins and Usage*, G. K. Hall, Boston, 1975. This volume is an edition of a collection made by Newbell Niles Puckett, who gathered about 340,000 names dating from the 1600s to the mid-1940s. It also indicates names of African origin.

Ho, James K. K., *Black Engineers in the United States—A Directory*, Howard University Press, Washington, D.C., 1974; provides biographical data on 1,500 persons.

Holway, John, *Voices From the Great Black Baseball Leagues*, Dodd, Mead, New York, 1975.

Howard University, *Dictionary Catalog of the Jesse E. Moorland Collection of Negro Life and History*, Howard University, Washington, D.C., G. K. Hall, Boston, 1970; a catalogue of about 100,000 items in the well-known Moorland Collection.

Howe, Mentor A., and Roscoe E. Lewis (comps.), *A Classified Catalogue of the Negro Collection in the Collis P. Huntington Library*, Hampton Institute, Hampton, 1940; republished in 1971 by Scholarly Press, Inc., 341 pp. This volume covers the collection up to 1940, and it lists more than 14,000 books and 1,300 documents.

Jenkins, Betty Lanier, and Susan Phillis, *Black Separatism: A Bibliography*, Greenwood Press, Westport, 1976, 163 pp.; annotated. The subject is divided into two parts: the separatism vs. integration controversy and its institutional and psychological dimensions.

Josey, E. J., and Ann A. Shockley, (eds.), *Handbook of Black Librarianship*, Libraries Unlimited, Littleton, Colo., 1977.

Katz, Bill, *Magazines for Librarians*, 2d ed., R. R. Bowker, New York, 1972; Xerox; pages 105–15 give descriptions of black magazines.

Kidd, Foster, *Profile of the Negro in American Dentistry*, Howard University Press, Washington, D.C., 1976.

Library Company of Philadelphia and the Historical Society of Pennsylvania, *Afro-Americana, 1553–1906: Author Catalogue of The Library Company of Philadelphia and The Historical Society of Pennsylvania*, G. K. Hall, Boston, 1973.

McPheeters, Annie L., *Negro Progress in Atlanta, Georgia, 1961–1970*, originally published by the author, Atlanta, 1972; reprinted by University Microfilms, Ann Arbor, 225 pp.; no index; no annotation. References are made to many articles that appeared in Atlanta newspapers during the 1960s.

McPherson, James M., et al., *Blacks in America: Bibliographical Essays*, Doubleday, New York, 1972, 432 pp. Gilbert Osofsky, *Journal of American History*, June 1972, wrote: "[It has] the best listing of writings on race in America from slavery to the present to appear in the literature.... One finds not only citations for books and essays, but page and chapter notations helping the reader to special themes within these writings and notations about abbreviated editions and changed titles. The book is organized both thematically and chronologically, it has ... asterisks to denote paperback and hardbound editions, dates of original as well as reprint publication. It is a work of exactitude that will surely find its way quickly to the desks of serious researchers and college students hunting for term papers in black history and literature: the central subjects of this volume."

Marshall, Albert P. (comp.), *Guide to Negro Periodical Literature*. This volume is a pioneer work and reference. Marshall began it when he was librarian at Winston-Salem-Teachers College (now Winston-Salem State University), but work on it was interrupted during World War II when Marshall was on duty in the armed forces and again when he attended graduate school. During the years from 1950 to 1954, the Hallie Q. Brown Memorial Library, Wilberforce, Ohio, issued the title as *Index to Selected Negro Periodicals*; in the spring of 1954, the title became

Index to Selected Periodicals, and it appeared quarterly. Now decennial, the publication is issued by G. K. Hall, Boston. *See also* MARSHALL, ALBERT PRINCE.

Matney, William C. See listing below as *Who's Who Among Black Americans.*

Matthews, Daniel G. (ed.), *A Current Bibliography on African Affairs,* African Bibliographic Center, Washington, D.C.; a periodical publication.

Matthews, Geraldine O. et al., *Black American Writers, 1773–1949: A Bibliography and Union List,* G. K. Hall, Boston, 1975. This study was made in cooperation with the African-American Materials Staff of the School of Library Science, North Carolina Central University. The works of more than 1,600 black authors are covered from the 1700s to 1949, and this volume provides information about many authors and their works for the first time. The compilation covers materials found in more than 60 institutions in several southern states: Alabama, Georgia, North Carolina, South Carolina, Tennessee, and Virginia. Entries are arranged by author, and there is an author index.

Miller, Elizabeth W., and Mary L. Fisher, *The Negro in America: A Bibliography,* 2d rev. ed., with foreword by Thomas F. Pettigrew, Harvard University Press, Cambridge, 1970, 351 pp.

Miller, Wayne Charles, et al., *A Comprehensive Bibliography for the Study of American Minorities,* New York University Press, New York, 1976, 2 vols. Pages 3–262 treat Afro-Americans.

New York Public Library, *Dictionary Catalogue of the Schomburg Collection of Negro Literature and History,* G. K. Hall, Boston, 1962, 9 vols.; additional vols. issued in 1967. These volumes constitute a catalogue of one of the great collections relating to Afro-Americans.

New York Public Library, *No Crystal Stair: A Bibliography of Black Literature,* New York Public Library, New York, 1971, 63 pp.; index by author and title, pp. 55–63; general listings with limited annotation. This bibliography is arranged topically as follows: reference, history, politics and government, the contemporary scene in literature and the arts, sociology and psychology, religion, economics, education, and sports.

New York Times Company, *The New York Times Biographical Edition: A Compilation of Current Biographical Information of General Interest,* published monthly, New York, N.Y. Increasingly, more Afro-Americans have appeared in this monumental series during the 1970s.

Oaks, Priscilla, *Minority Studies: A Selected Annotated Bibliography,* G. K. Hall, Boston, 1975.

Obudho, Constance E., *Black-White Racial Attitudes: An Annotated Bibliography,* Greenwood Press, Westport, 1976, 180 pp. Contains 475 entries.

Partington, Paul G., *W. E. B. Du Bois: A Bibliography of His Published Writings,* published by the author, Whittier, Calif., 1977, 202 pp.

Perry, Margaret, *A Bio-Bibliography of Countee P. Cullen 1903–1946,* Greenwood Press, Westport, 1971, 134 pp. This volume consists of two parts: the man and his poetry, and a bibliography.

Perry, Margaret, *Silence to the Drums: A Survey of the Literature of the Harlem Renaissance,* Greenwood Press, Westport, 1976.

Porter, Dorothy B., *The Negro in the United States: A Selected Bibliography,* Library of Congress, U.S. Government Printing Office, Washington, D.C., 1970, 313 pp.; index, pp. 279–313. Contains 1,781 listings, mostly selected books in history and literature. Porter based her selections, especially in history and literature, "on the frequency of requests for particular works in large library collections on the Negro and on their inclusion in the numerous bibliographies and reading lists now being compiled for use in junior colleges, colleges, and universities."

Reardon, William R., and Thomas D. Pawley, *The Black Teacher and the Dramatic Arts,* Negro Universities Press, Westport, 1970, 489 pp.; not annotated. Norman Parks Ragland, *Journal of Negro History,* October 1971, wrote: "William Reardon and Thomas D. Pawley have presented a thorough bibliography (pp. 70–121) of available works related to the theater and an anthology of excellent plays for study and performance."

Robinson, Wilhelmina S., *Historical Negro Biographies,* Publishers Co., New York, 1968,

291 pp.; a volume in the International Library of Negro Life and History. This volume contains biographical sketches of more than 500 blacks important throughout world history.

Rogers, Joel A., *World's Great Men of Color*, rev. ed., originally published in 1946; edited with an introduction by John Henrik Clarke, Macmillan, New York, 1972, 2 vols. This volume contains biographies of important blacks from ancient through modern times.

R. R. Bowker Company, *Paperbound Books in Print*, "Black Literature," vol. 14, no. 11, pp. 4–24, November 1969; annotated.

R. R. Bowker Company, *Paperbound Books in Print*, "Black History—An Afro-Amercian Resource Guide," vol. 15, no. 4, pp. 4–32, April 1970; annotated.

R. R. Bowker Company, *Paperbound Books in Print*, "Blacks Today—A Modern Afro-American Library," vol. 15, no. 5, pp. 4–56, May 1970; annotated.

Rush, Theresa Gunnels, *Black American Writers Past and Present: A Biographical and Bibliographical Dictionary*, Scarecrow Press, Inc., Metuchen, N.J., 1975.

Schatz, Walter (ed.), *Directory of Afro-American Resources*, R. R. Bowker Company, New York, 1970, 485 pp. This work, a general guide, resulted from the cooperative efforts of many librarians, archivists, and directors.

Shockley, Ann, and Sue Chandler, *Living Black American Authors: A Biographical Directory*, Bowker, New York, 1973.

Schor, Joel, and Cecil Harvey, *A List of References for the History of Black Americans in Agriculture, 1619–1974.* See REFERENCES under AGRICULTURE for further description.

Smith, Dwight L. (ed.), *Afro-American History: A Bibliography*, American Bibliographical Center—Clio Press, Inc., Santa Barbara, 1974, introduction by Benjamin Quarles; 856 pp.; index, pp. 779–840. This volume contains about 3,000 abstracts, averaging about 100 words each, of articles appearing in about 400 periodicals, including professional magazines. Professor Saunders Redding wrote that "the area of American Studies dealing with the Negro experience has at last won academic respectability among humanistic scholars of the first rank."

Smith, Jessie Carney, *Black Academic Libraries and Research Collections: An Historical Survey*, Greenwood Press, Westport, 1977.

Smythe, Mabel (ed.), *The Black American Reference Book*, Prentice-Hall, Englewood Cliffs, N.J., 1976.

Texas Southern University, *Catalogue: Heartman Negro Collection*, Texas Southern University, Houston, 1956, 325 pp.

Thompson, Edgar Tristram, and Alma Macy Thompson, *Race and Religion, A Descriptive Bibliography Compiled with Special Reference to the Relations Between Whites and Negroes in the United States*, University of North Carolina Press, Chapel Hill, 1949, 194 pp.

Toppin, Edgar A., *A Biographical History of Blacks in America Since 1528*; David McKay Co., New York, 1971. The first half of the volume is historical; the second half gives short biographies of 145 representative men and women who "demonstrate the range of achievement of black Americans."

Turner, Darwin T., *Afro-American Writers*, Appleton-Century-Crofts, New York, 1970, 117 pp.; without annotation; author index. The first 36 pages of this Goldentree Bibliographies series contain listings for "Aids to Research," "Backgrounds," and "Literary History and Criticism." The bulk of this paperback (pp. 37–87) gives references for a wide variety (about 135) of Afro-American authors, beginning with Alston Anderson and ending with Frank Yerby. Periodical listings predominate.

Tuskegee Institute, *Negro Year Book*. A landmark publication first issued in 1912 under the editorship of Monroe N. Work, who was editor from 1912 to 1938. He was followed in this position by Jessie P. Guzman and Vera Chandler. *Negro Year Book* ceased publication in 1952 (no editions were published in 1920, 1923, 1927, and 1929). These volumes treat a variety of subjects, including bibliographical and biographical notations. *See also* WORK, MONROE NATHAN.

U.S. Department of Agriculture, *The Poor: A Selected Bibliography*, Economic Research Service, Miscellaneous Publications, U.S. Government Printing Office, Washington, D.C., May 1969, 56 pp. This bibliography is a selected compilation of literature dealing with aspects of poverty in the United States. Most references are reports of field investigations. Although this work mainly emphasizes the dynamics of poverty and the characteristics of the poor, sources dealing with proposals for alleviating poverty are also listed.

Walters, Mary Dawson, *Afro-Americana: A Comprehensive Bibliography of Resource Materials in the Ohio State University Libraries By Or About Black Americans*, The Ohio State University Libraries, Columbus, 1969, 220 pp. This volume contains more than 3,000 comprehensive titles.

Walton, Hanes, Jr., *A Study and Analysis of Black Politics: A Bibliography*, Scarecrow Press, Inc., Metuchen, N.J., 1973, 161 pp. This volume contains bibliographies relating to blacks in regard to major political parties, national elections, state and local pressure groups, political candidacies, political behavior, political science methodology, urban politics, public policy, and the U.S. Supreme Court.

Wasserman, Paul, and Esther Herman (eds.), *Library Bibliographies and Indexes: A Subject Guide to Resource Material Available from Libraries, Information Centers, Library Schools and Library Associations in the United States and Canada*, Gale Research Company, Detroit, 1975; see pp. 60–63 for topical listings relating to blacks.

Weinberg, Meyer, *The Education of the Minority Child: A Comprehensive Bibliography of 10,000 Selected Entries*, Integrateducation Associates, Evanston, 1970, 530 pp. This volume is the most complete bibliography on the subject, covering especially the education of black, Mexican-American, Indian, and Puerto Rican children. It contains numerous citations from the literatures of education, history, law, and the social sciences.

West, Earle H., *A Bibliography of Doctoral Research on the Negro, 1933–1966*, Xerox Company, New York, 1969.

Westmoreland, Guy T., *An Annotated Guide to Basic Reference Books on the Black Experience*, Scholarly Resources, Inc., Wilmington, 1974, 134 pp.; comprehensive and annotated. This guide is divided into two major parts. Part One treats such general reference works as library catalogues, biographical sources, and multisubject bibliographies; Part Two deals with such subjects as history and literature.

Who's Who Among Black Americans, ed. by William C. Matney, Who's Who Among Black Americans, Inc, Northbrook, Ill., 1976. The editor acknowledges that 10,000 individual, abbreviated biographical sketches are included in alphabetical order; no accompanying photographs.

Who's Who in Colored America: A Biographical Dictionary of Notable Living Persons of African Descent in America, Christian E. Burckel & Associates, Yonkers, 1950. This work was published in seven editions between 1927 and 1950. The editions from the period 1924–41 were published by Who's Who In America Corporation, New York City. Most of the sketches treat profes-

sional men and women. *See also* FLEMING, G. JAMES. One of the last editors of the series was G. James Fleming.

Williams, Ethel L., and Clifton F. Brown, *Afro-American Religious Studies*, Scarecrow Press, Inc., Metuchen, N.J., 1972, 454 pp.; appendixes, pp. 393–409; index, pp. 411–54. This volume contains about 6,000 listings, many annotated.

Williams, Daniel T., *Eight Negro Bibliographies*, Kraus Reprint Co., New York, 1970. A reprint of bibliographies, compiled mostly in the 1960s, with the exceptions of bibliography nos. 1, 2, and 7, previously available only for reference at Tuskegee Institute. Contents are:

1. The Freedom Rides: A Bibliography. 1961.
2. The Southern Students' Protest Movement: A Bibliography. 1961.
3. The University of Mississippi and James H. Meredith: A Bibliography. 1963.
4. The Black Muslims in the United States: A Selected Bibliography. 1964.
5. Martin Luther King, Jr. 1929–1968: A Bibliography. 1968.
6. The Awesome Thunder of Booker T. Washington: A Bio-Bibliographical Listing. 1969.
7. The Lynching Records at Tuskegee Institute; with Lynching in America: A Bibliography. 1969.
8. The Perilous Road of Marcus M. Garvey: A Bibliography, and some correspondence with Booker T.Washington, Emmett J. Scott, and Robert Russa Moton. 1969.

Williams, Ora, *American Black Women in the Arts and Social Sciences: A Bibliographic Survey*, Scarecrow Press, Metuchen, N.J., 1978.

Work, Monroe N. (comp.), *Bibliography of the Negro in Africa and America*, Argosy-Antiquarian, New York, 1965. This classic was originally published by H. W. Wilson, New York, 1928. This volume contains about 17,000 entries, but some have been supplemented by more recent bibliographies. *See also* ARCHIVES; WORK, MONROE NATHAN.

Wright, Richard R., ed., *The Encyclopaedia of the African Methodist Episcopal Church*, Philadelphia, 1916. "It is indeed a notable work," said Jean Blackwell [Hutson], curator, Schomburg Collection, New York Public Library, in the introduction to the 7th edition (1950) of *Who's Who in Colored America*.

Young, Henry J., *Major Black Religious Leaders, 1755–1940*, Abingdon, Nashville, Tenn., 1977.

BIDDLE UNIVERSITY *See* JOHNSON C. SMITH UNIVERSITY.

BIGGERS, CHARLES A. (1887– ?), educator, journalist; born in Oswego, Kans. Biggers attended George R. Smith College, received a M.A. degree from Baker University (Baldwin City, Kans.), and studied at Eastman Business College. Biggers served as a court reporter for three years in the deposition department of the Dawes Commission. Later, he established the Biggers Business College and the 20th Century Correspondence School, in Oklahoma City and Los Angeles, respectively. Biggers Business College won the First Award of Merit at the Second Annual Conclave of the All-American League (1917), and, as a result, it also won funding for a number of scholarships.

BILLINGSLEY, ORZELL, JR. (1924–), lawyer, judge; born in Birmingham, Ala. Billingsley received a B.A. degree from Talladega College (Talladega, Ala.) in 1946 and his J.D. degree from the Howard University School of Law (Washington, D.C.) in 1950. As a young lawyer in 1967 Billingsley was one of the first participants in the move to incorporate black municipalities in the South. Roosevelt City, Ala. was created from this effort, with Billingsley its founder and municipal judge. Noted as a civil rights attorney, Billingsley's clients included corporations, credit unions, and cooperatives for whom he served as consultant.

BILLINGSLY, ANDREW (1926–), educator, administrator; born in Marion, Ala. Billingsly received a B.A. degree from Grinnell College (Grinnell, Iowa) in 1951, a M.S. degree from Boston University School of Social Work in 1956, a M.A. degree from the University of Michigan in 1960, and his Ph.D. degree from the Florence Heller Graduate School for Advanced Studies in Social Welfare, Brandeis University (Waltham, Mass.) in 1964. He was assistant chancellor for academic affairs at the University of California at Berkeley from 1968 to 1970, vice-president for academic affairs at Howard University (Washington, D.C.) from 1970 to 1975, and president of Morgan State University (Baltimore, Md.) after 1975. Billingsly also published *Black Families in White America* (1968), and *Children of the Storm*, with Jeanne Giovannoni (1972).

BING, DAVE See ATHLETES: BASKETBALL.

BINGA, JESSE (1865–1950), banker; born in Detroit, Mich. A Chicago real-estate broker, Bin-

ga founded in 1908 the first black-owned-and-operated bank in Chicago, Ill., the Binga State Bank, and served as its president. Deposits grew to $1.5 million by 1932, at which time depression conditions forced the bank to close—largely because of Binga's refusal to foreclose on real estate mortgages. Binga was criminally charged for his part in the bank failure and was sentenced to prison; though he was pardoned by President Franklin D. Roosevelt in 1933, he was never able to rebuild his personal fortune. *See also:* BANKS.

BIOGRAPHIES See BIBLIOGRAPHIES / BIOGRAPHIES / GUIDES.

BIRCH, ADOLPHO A. (1898–), clergyman; born in British Honduras. Birch attended Hampton Institute (Hampton, Va.), received a B.Th. from Howard University (Washington, D.C.), and also studied at Virginia Theological Seminary. He was pastor of Protestant Episcopal churches in Virginia, Texas, and Washington, D.C., and chaplain at Howard University, from which he received the alumni award of the School of Religion.

BIRCH, ADOLPHO A., JR. (1932–), lawyer, judge; born in Washington, D.C. Birch graduated from Howard University (Washington, D.C.) in 1953 and later studied at the Howard University School of Law, receiving his J.D. degree in 1956. After serving in the U.S. Navy, Birch became assistant district attorney general in the 10th Judicial Circuit Court in Nashville, Tenn., and later he was appointed judge of the Court of General Sessions in the 10th Circuit.

BISHOP COLLEGE Bishop College, at Dallas, Tex., was founded in 1881 by Baptists, and it has continued to be strongly church-related. A private, coeducational school, it confers the bachelor's degree and provides liberal arts and teacher education curricula. Its 1975 enrollment was about 1600.

The school's curricula have always emphasized general studies and the humanities. Bishop College is accredited by the Texas Association of Colleges and Universities and the Southern Association of Colleges and Secondary Schools.

BISHOP, DAVID W. See PREFACE: LIST OF CONTRIBUTORS; HISTORIANS.

BLACHE, JULIAN OWEN (1900–1964), physician; born in Trinidad, British West Indies. Blache attended New York University and received his M.D. from Howard University Medical College (Washington, D.C.) in 1932, after interning at City Hospital No. 2, St. Louis. Blache was head of the department of pathology at the Homer G. Phillips Hospital and later served as the hospital's acting medical director.

BLACK ACADEMY OF ARTS AND LETTERS, INC. Formed in 1970 with Julia Prettyman as executive director, the academy's objectives are to recognize black artists and scholars of excellence, to give encouragement to young Afro-Americans, and to foster the arts and letters among black people. The roster of its members, though neither inclusive nor exhaustive, is virtually a representative checklist of black talent (mostly in the arts and letters) in contemporary America.

BLACK AMERICAN See PREFACE; ONOMATOLOGY.

BLACKAMOOR See ONOMATOLOGY.

BLACKBURN, CLEO W. (1909–   ), educator; born in Port Gibson, Miss. Blackburn received a B.A. from Butler University (Indianapolis, Ind.) in 1932, a M.A. from Fisk University (Nashville, Tenn.) in 1936, a D.D. from Northwest Christian College (Eugene, Oreg.) in 1955, a doctorate in humanities from Indiana Central College (Indianapolis) in 1966, and D.H.L. degrees from Wabash College (Crawfordsville, Ind.) in 1968 and Butler University in 1970. Blackburn taught sociology at Fisk University in 1932, at Knoxville College (Knoxville, Tenn.) in 1934, and at Tuskegee Institute (Tuskegee Institute, Ala.) in 1935. He served as president of Jarvis Christian College (Hawkins, Tex.) from 1953 to 1964. Blackburn was also executive director of the Board for Fundamental Education in Indianapolis, beginning in 1954; vice-president and director of the National Federation Settlements from 1947 to 1950; a member of the Federal Council of Churches; director of the National Council of Family Relations; and active in many other groups. In 1940 Blackburn received a distinguished service award from the Indianapolis Junior Chamber of Commerce, and he was appointed director of the U.S. Chamber of Commerce in 1971.

BLACK ENGLISH See AFRICAN LEGACY / SURVIVALS: LANGUAGE.

BLACK JEWS The Black Jews are a small religious group numbering nearly 40,000 and located mainly in New York City and Chicago. The claims of the Black Jews that they are true Jews have at times been questioned by nonblack Jews. It has been estimated that several hundred Afro-Americans have emigrated to Israel (mainly to Dimona), where their reception has been mixed. Rabbi Abel Respes became one of the principal leaders in the black Jewish community of New York City, the largest congregation.

REFERENCES: Brotz, Howard, *The Black Jews of Harlem: Negro Nationalism and the Dilemmas of Negro Leadership*, Free Press, New York, 1964; Erhman, Albert, "Exploration and Responses," *Journal of Ecumenical Studies*, Winter 1971; and Wartgker, H., "Black Judaism in New York," *Harvard Journal of Negro Affairs*, 1967, pp. 12–44. For a related study, see Diner, Hasia R., *In the Almost Promised Land: American Jews and Blacks, 1915–1935*, Greenwood Press, Westport, 1977.

BLACK MUSLIMS See MUSLIMS; NATIONALISM.

BLACK NATIONALISM See NATIONALISM.

BLACK P. STONE NATION A Chicago-based youth group, the Black P. (for peace) Stone Nation took its name from an avenue on Chicago's South Side. Its members, known as the Blackstone Rangers, were well-organized and disciplined in the 1960s. The Rangers received national publicity when a congressional committee charged them with extortion and illegal drug practices.

BLACK PANTHER PARTY The Black Panther Party was organized in October 1966 in Oakland, Calif., by Huey Newton and Bobby Seale, two disillusioned and impatient young workers in the state poverty program of California. The Black Panther Party spearheaded a revolutionary movement that departed from the nonviolent philosophies of other national black groups. Starting from the theory that the police—the arm of the suppressive white establishment in the area of the ghetto—must be monitored by blacks, they took to the streets with loaded cameras and guns, thus claiming for themselves and the black youths of the ghetto the respect and due process they felt was lacking.

Self-defense and self-determination for the oppressed black community became their watchwords. Their motto, "We are advocates of the abolition of war; but war can only be abolished through war; and in order to get rid of the gun it is necessary to pick up the gun," was inspired by Mao Tse-tung. Between 1966 and 1971, the Panthers were called "the vanguard of the North American revolution movement." The party's theories, characterized as violently militant, were explained by Eldridge Cleaver, who joined Newton, Seale, and Bobby Hutton in the movement in 1967. He said violence took two forms: "violence directed at you to keep you in your place and violence to defend yourself against that suppression and to win your freedom."

Armed with these theories of revolution, the Panthers quickly became anathema to the police, the prime target of their vigilance. Gun battles and other violent confrontations between party members and police were numerous, and the killing took its toll on the leadership of the group: Hutton, only 17 years old, was shot and killed; Cleaver went into exile; Fred Hampton, chairman of the Panthers in Illinois, was shot and killed; Mark Clark, also a member of the Illinois group, was shot and killed. Many major cities reported armed clashes between the Panthers and the police. Panthers were arrested for bomb plots and public harrassment in New York and around the country. With Newton and Seale in jail and with Cleaver in exile, the Panthers claimed they were the target of systematic police vengeance. In 1968 and 1969 they reported 28 deaths in their ranks as a result of police actions.

The Panthers often referred to themselves as "the children of Malcolm," having evolved many of their ideas from those held by Malcolm X during his later years. Eventually, the Panthers welcomed the cooperation and support of whites and emphasized that their quarrel was not with whites in general, but rather with the actions of white racists. They stressed self-defense against the ongoing murder of blacks in the black community—defining murder as inadequate hospital care, lead poisoning from peeling paint in neglected slum tenements, malnutrition, diseases due to poverty, provoked shoot-outs, and police brutality.

Having ideologically separated blacks from the rest of society, which they contended was at war with the black community, the Panthers stressed education as a means of creating the pride and self-reliance they believed was absent in black youth. They held classes to train young

blacks to wage the war already in progress and, in a broader sense, to prepare themselves as soldiers and educators of the future. In 1971 the party instituted a breakfast program for black ghetto youths in 44 major cities, and a shoestring operation of free health clinics was successfully maintained in many cities.

With party chapters throughout the nation, the Panthers represented the first nationwide black political movement. Although its views tended toward extremism, the party functioned in revealing the hidden implications of ghetto life. Probing and raising questions about the capacity of the American system to provide justice and equality for Afro-Americans, the Panthers contended that it would be blacks alone, better educated and better armed, who would lift from themselves the yoke of white colonialism:

"We start with the basic [assumption] that black people in America are a colonized people . . . and that white America as an organized imperialist force holding black people in colonial bondage. . . . [Violence] against the police and other agents . . . of authority is not crime, but heroism, not merely an unlawful act but a revolutionary gesture against an illegitimate goat."

Panthers and the Law   By 1969 some of the leaders of the Black Panther Party were having serious difficulties with the law. Huey Newton was in jail despite protests by blacks and whites that he had been unjustly charged with killing a policeman; Bobby Seale was on probation for a gun-law violation; Eldridge Cleaver was in Algeria evading a parole-violation charge. Twenty-one Panthers were being held in New York charged with a conspiracy to bomb department stores, railroad tracks, and police stations. Bails of $100,000 each kept 12 Panthers in jail

Far right: Eldridge Cleaver, information minister of the Black Panther Party, standing beside a bullet-riddled campaign poster for his presidential candidacy on the Peace and Freedom Party ticket in the 1968 campaign. *(Wide World Photos)*

for several months, but they were finally acquitted and set free. A police raid in Chicago in 1970 claimed the life of two Panther leaders, Fred Hampton and Mark Clark. Federal and state investigations following the raid led to the conclusion that "performance of law enforcement agencies, at least in this case, serves as a reasonable basis for public doubt of their efficiency or even of their credibility." Scholarly books and articles on the Panthers and the law were appearing by the end of 1971. According to these works, trials of Panther Party members revealed the callous, racist nature of law enforcement and judicial action in the United States. These accounts demonstrated clearly that black militants were unfairly treated by law-enforcing groups. *See also* CLEAVER, LEROY ELDRIDGE; NEWTON, HUEY; SEALE, ROBERT G. (BOBBY).

REFERENCES: A great deal of literature, mostly periodical, was published about the Black Panthers and black power during the 1960s and 1970s. A selective list of these references includes: Anthony, Earl, *Picking Up the Guns: The Story of the Black Panthers*, Dial, New York, 1970; Chandler, Christopher, "Black Panther Killings in Chicago," *New Republic*, vol. 162, pp. 21–24, January 10, 1970; Cleaver, Eldridge, "Revolution in the White Mother Country and National Liberation in the Black Colony," *North American Review* (new series), vol. 5, pp. 13–15, July-August 1968; Cleaver, Eldridge, "Tears for the Pigs," *Humanist*, vol. 29, p. 5 and pp. 8–10, March-April 1969; Keating, Edward M., *Free Huey: The True Story of the Trial of Huey P. Newton for Murder*, Ramparts Press, 1971; Moore, Gilbert, *A Special Rage*, Harper and Row, New York, 1971; Rogers, R., "Black Guns on Campus: Black Panthers and U.S.," *Nation*, vol. 208, pp. 558–60, May 5, 1969; Sayre, Nora, "Black Panthers," *Progressive*, vol. 31, pp. 20–23, July 1969; and Sheehy, Gail, *Panthermania: The Clash of Black Against Black in One American City*, Harper and Row, New York, 1971. See also G. Louis Heath (ed.), *Off the Pigs: The History and Literature of the Black Panther Party*, Scarecrow Press, Metuchen, N.J., 1976.

BLACK POWER The slogan "Black Power" was not an unknown term when Stokely Carmichael popularized it during the march of James Meredith through northern Mississippi in 1966. In fact, 12 years earlier Richard Wright had written a book with that very title. However, the use of the term, within the framework of what purported to be an interracial society, tended to provoke some of the most extreme reactions. Terms such as these, which were used frequently among activists of the civil rights movement, came to create general confusion about the intentions of black people during the critical period of escalating black political protest.

The era of Black Power may be effectively dated from the Meredith March to the breakup in 1968 of the coalition (that has also been called a merg-

er) formed between such leaders of the Student Nonviolent Coordinating Committee (SNCC) as Rap Brown and James Foreman—as well as Carmichael and Willie Ricks of the Student Organization for Black Unity (SOBU)—and the Black Panther Party of Oakland Black Power thus reigned for two years as a makeshift consensus for the most militant sectors of the black movement.

BLACK REPUBLICANS *See* AFRO-AMERICAN HISTORY: SECTIONAL CONFLICT OVER SLAVERY, 1820–60.

BLACKSHEAR, WILLIAM *See* NEWSPAPERS: CONTEMPORARY.

BLACK STUDIES *See* EDUCATION: BLACK STUDIES.

BLACK THEATER ALLIANCE *See* LITERATURE: DRAMA.

BLACKWELL, DAVID H. (1919–), educator, mathematician; born in Centralia, Ill. Blackwell received a B.A. degree (1938), a M.A. degree (1939), and his Ph.D. degree (1941) in mathematics from the University of Illinois. Blackwell became a Rosenwald Fellow at the Institute for Advanced Study at Princeton University. He taught at Southern University (Baton Rouge, La.) from 1942 to 1943, at Clark College (Atlanta, Ga.) from 1943 to 1944, at Howard University (Washington, D.C.) from 1944 to 1954, and at the University of California at Berkeley, after 1954. Blackwell was a Fellow of the Institute of Mathematical Statistics prior to becoming its president in 1955, and he was elected to the National Academy of Sciences in 1965. Blackwell was coauthor of *Theory of Powers and Statistical Decisions* (1954). *See also* SCIENTISTS: BIOLOGICAL, PHYSICAL.

David H. Blackwell. *(Courtesy of David H. Blackwell.)*

BLACKWELL, JAMES E. *See* SCIENTISTS: SOCIAL.

BLAIR, EZELL *See* CIVIL RIGHTS MOVEMENT IN SELECTED STATES: NORTH CAROLINA.

BLAKELY, GEORGE WAYMAN (1905–), African Methodist Episcopal bishop; born in Ashley County, Ark. Blakely received a B.A. degree from Western University in 1924, a B.D. degree from Iliff School of Theology in 1928, and honorary D.D. degrees from Payne Theological Seminary, Daniel Payne College (Birmingham, Ala.), Monrovia College, and Kittrell College (Kittrell, N.C.). Blakely was pastor of African Methodist Episcopal (A.M.E.) churches in Missouri, Wyoming, Colorado, Kansas, and Arkansas, and he was elected and consecrated a bishop in 1964. He was a delegate to the World Council of Churches in Amsterdam in 1948.

BLAKEY, DUROCHER LON (1909–   ), clergyman, publisher; born in Macon City, Ala. Blakey received a B.A. degree from Livingstone College (Salisbury, N.C.) in 1947, attended Johnson C. Smith University (Charlotte, N.C.), Miles College (Birmingham, Ala.), and Hood Theological Seminary, and then received a B.D. degree from Southern Baptist Theological Seminary in 1963. He was pastor of churches in Alabama, North Carolina, Georgia, and Arkansas. In 1963 Blakey became general manager of the African Methodist Episcopal Zion Churches Publishing House.

BLANCHET, WALDO WILLIE EMERSON (1910-   ), educator; born in New Orleans, La. Blanchet received a B.A. degree from Talladega College (Talladega, Ala.) in 1931, and a M.S. degree (1936) and his Ph.D. degree (1946) from the University of Michigan. He taught science at Fort Valley Normal and Industrial School (1932–35) and served as appointed dean there (1936–38). He was later professor of physical science (1939–66), dean (1939–66), president (1966–73), and president emeritus of Fort Valley State College. Blanchet has been a member of or consultant to many associations, such as the National Science Foundation (NSF), Science Institutes in Albany and Atlanta (1960–61), and the National Association for Research Science Teaching, of which he was president from 1956 to 1957.

James A. Bland.
(Moorland-Spingarn Research Center, Howard University.)

BLAND, JAMES A. (1854–1911), actor, composer; born in Flushing, N.Y. The young Bland moved to Washington, D.C., with his father, Allan M. Bland, who was appointed an examiner in the U.S. Patent Office. Bland attended Howard University (Washington, D.C.) for a short time, but left college to perform in Haverly's Colored Minstrels. When the troupe played in London in the early 1880s, he received popular acclaim and stayed abroad for the next 20 years. Bland composed more than 600 popular songs, including: "Oh Dem Golden Slippers," "In the Evening by the Moonlight," and "Carry Me Back to Old Virginny." The latter became Virginia's official state song almost 30 years after Bland's death.

BLANTON, JIMMY (1921–42), jazz bassist; born in St. Louis, Mo. Blanton was recognized as the first true bass master and as the musician who established the bass as a solo instrument. Before joining Duke Ellington's band in 1939, Blanton had played in the 1930s with Fate Marable's band on Mississippi River excursion boats. *See also* Music: Jazz.

BLASSINGAME, JOHN W. (1940—   ), historian; born in Covington, Ga. He received a B.A. degree from Fort Valley State College, Fort Valley, Ga., in 1960 and an M.A. degree from Howard University, Washington, D.C., in 1961. Additional graduate degrees came from Yale University, New Haven, Conn.: M. Phil. in 1968 and Ph.D. in 1971. He taught at Howard (1961–65) and at the University of Maryland, College Park (1968–70). In the 1970s he joined the Yale faculty, serving as chairman of Afro-American studies and later as both an associate and professor of history. As a scholar and historian, Blassingame has specialized in Afro-American history, particularly in subjects related to slavery. His writings have appeared in many reputable journals and magazines, including the *Journal of Negro History* and the *Journal of Southern History*. He is the author of several books, including *The Slave Community: Plantation Life in the Antebellum South* (1972) and *Black New Orleans, 1860–1880* (1973). Moreover, he has served in several editorial capacities, including the editorship of the Frederick Douglass papers. *See also* Preface: List of Contributors.

BLEDSOE, JULIUS C. (1898–1943), singer, composer; born in Texas. Bledsoe received a B.A. degree from Bishop College (Dallas, Tex.) in 1918. He began to study medicine but turned to singing. After studying music in New York, Paris, and Rome, Bledsoe made his singing debut at Aeolian Hall in New York City in 1924. Unable to pursue an opera career in the United States because of his color, Bledsoe performed on European stages in such roles as Amonasro in *Aida* and Boris Godunov. Finally, he appeared on the vaudeville stage and in musical comedy in the United States. A member of the cast of *Show Boat* in 1927, he created the role of Joe and sang "Ole Man River." Bledsoe also sang with the Boston Symphony and with the Municipal Opera Company of Cleveland, Ohio. A composer as well, he wrote several songs and an *African Suite* for violin and orchestra.

BLOUNT, CLARENCE W. (1921–   ), educator, state legislator; born in Beaufort, N.C. Blount received a B.A. degree from Morgan State University (Baltimore, Md.) and a M.A. degree from Johns Hopkins University (Baltimore, Md.). He also studied international law and international relations at Georgetown University (Washington, D.C.). Blount was a high school principal in Baltimore, Md., before entering politics, and after several years in the Maryland legislature, he was elected to the state senate from Baltimore; he later served as chairperson of the Baltimore city senatorial delegation.

BLUEFIELD STATE COLLEGE Bluefield State College, at Bluefield, W.Va., was founded in 1895. Bluefield is a coeducational state-supported school that offers both four-year and two-year programs and that provides liberal arts, teacher education, and vocational curricula. Its student body and faculty were predominantly black until about 1950, after which time Afro-Americans became a minority. The college's 1975 enrollment was about 1,200.

BLUES *See* MUSIC: BLUES.

BLUFORD, LUCILLE *See* NEWSPAPERS: CONTEMPORARY.

BOLDEN, CHARLES (BUDDY THE KING) (1868–1931), jazz cornetist and trumpeter, bandleader; born in New Orleans, La. Bolden formed one of the first jazz bands before 1895. His cornet style was the starting point for many other musicians, extending from King Oliver to Louis Armstrong. In 1907, having been diagnosed as a paranoid, Bolden was committed to the East Louisiana State Hospital, where he spent the rest of his life. His active career as a musician predated the recording of jazz. *See also* MUSIC: JAZZ.

BOLDEN, THEODORE F. *See* SCIENTISTS: BIOLOGICAL, PHYSICAL.

BOLIN, JANE M. (MRS. WALTER P. OFFUTT, JR.) (1908–   ), lawyer, judge; born in Poughkeepsie, N.Y. Bolin graduated from Wellesley College (Wellesley, Mass.) in 1928 and from Yale Law School in 1931. In 1937 she became assistant corporation counsel of the city of New York, a post she held for two years. When, in 1939, Bolin was appointed judge of the Domestic Relations Court of the city of New York by Mayor Fiorello LaGuardia, she became the first black woman judge in the United States.

BOND, HORACE MANN (1904–1972), educator, author; born in Nashville, Tenn. Bond received a B.A. degree (1923) and a LL.D. degree (1941) from Lincoln University (Lincoln University, Pa.), a M.A. degree (1926) and a Ph.D. degree (1936) from the University of Chicago, and a LL.D. degree from Temple University (Philadelphia, Pa.) in 1952. He taught education courses at Lincoln University (1923–1924), at Langston University (1924–1926), and then at Alabama State Teachers College (1927–1928), Fisk University (1928–1934), Dillard University (1934–1938), and again at Fisk University (1939). Bond was president of Fort Valley State College (Fort Valley, Ga.) (1939–1945), president of Lincoln University (1945–1957), and the dean of the School of Education, Atlanta University (1957–1966). In 1936, he received the Susan Colver Rosenberger prize for an outstanding thesis in social science at the University of Chicago that was also published as a book, *Education in Alabama: A Study in Cotton and Steel* (1940), for which he received the Educational Research Association of America Award. Bond's other books include: *The Education of the Negro in the American Social Order* (1934). His brother, J. Max Bond, was an educator and a foreign service specialist. His son, Julian Bond, was a member of the Georgia state legislature. *See also* BOND, J. MAX; BOND, JULIAN.

BOND, J. MAX (1902– ?), educator, government official. Bond received a B.P.E. degree from George Williams College (Downers Grove, Ill.), a M.A. degree from the University of Pittsburgh, and his Ph.D. degree from the University of Southern California in 1936. Bond was dean of the School of Education at Tuskegee Institute (Tuskegee Institute, Ala.) and he was made both a Rosenwald Fellow and a General Education Board Fellow. A contributor to many journals. Bond was also a service officer in the U.S. State Department's Agency for International Development (AID). His brother was Horace Mann Bond.

BOND, J. MAX, JR. (1935–   ), architect, urbanist; born in Louisville, Ky. Bond received a B.A. degree magna cum laude (1955) from Harvard College and an M.Arch. degree from Harvard University Graduate School of Design (1958). He held a Harvard College National

Scholarship as an undergraduate (1951–1955). After service abroad, he was an associate professor in the Graduate School of Architecture and Planning at Columbia University (New York, N.Y.). Since 1968 he has been a partner in Bond-Ryder Associates, a Harlem-based firm of architects who focus on urban structures. His father was J. Max Bond.

Julian Bond.
(Courtesy of National Educational Television.)

BOND, JULIAN (1940–   ), state legislator, civil rights leader; born in Nashville, Tenn. While studying at Morehouse College (Atlanta, Ga.), Bond became one of the founders of the Committee on Appeal for Human Rights. Soon thereafter he helped organize and became communications director of the Student Nonviolent Coordinating Committee (1960–66). After working as reporter, feature writer, and managing editor on the Atlanta *Inquirer*, Bond won election to the Georgia House of Representatives in 1965. For a year, because of his outspoken opposition to U.S. military involvement in Vietnam, fellow legislators prevented him from taking his seat, until the U.S. Supreme Court ruled their action unconstitutional. In 1968 he was a vice-presidential candidate at the Democratic National Convention. His father was Horace Mann Bond.

BONGA, STEPHEN (ca. 1789– ?), trader, trapper. Bonga lived in the region of Lake Superior and was called the "first white man at head of lake," which indicated that the Indians considered anyone who was not Indian to be either white or associated with Anglo-Saxons.

BONTEMPS, ARNA WENDELL (1902–73), author, critic; born in Alexandria, La. Bontemps became a teacher at the Harlem Academy after receiving a B.A. degree from Union Pacific College in 1923. He quickly became a leading figure in the Harlem Renaissance, after he left the West Coast for Harlem. Bontemps received a M.A. degree from the University of Chicago in 1943 with the aid of two Rosenwald Fellowships, then became librarian at Fisk University until 1965. He taught at the University of Illinois in 1966, and at Yale University in 1972. Bontemps was the author of *God Sends Sunday* (1931), which he and Countee Cullen adapted for Broadway in 1946 as *St. Louis Woman*. Another novel, *Black Thunder* (1936), was based on Gabriel Prosser's slave rebellion in 1800. Bontemps worked on W. C. Handy's autobiography, *Father of the Blues* (1941), and joined Langston Hughes in editing

The Poetry of the Negro 1746–1949 (1949) and *The Book of Negro Folklore* (1958). Bontemps' awards include: *Opportunity* magazine's Pushkin Awards for Poetry in 1926 and 1927, and a Guggenheim Fellowship in 1949. Bontemps was a central figure in the discovery and dissemination of Afro-American literature, and he showed that black music, art, and poetry have their own mainstreams with a rich heritage. *See also* CULLEN, COUNTEE; HANDY, W. C.; HUGHES, LANGSTON.

BOOGIE-WOOGIE *See* MUSIC: JAZZ.

BOOKS *See* BIBLIOGRAPHIES/BIOGRAPHIES/GUIDES.

BOONE, RAYMOND HAROLD (1938–   ), journalist; born in Suffolk, Va. Boone received a B.S. degree from Boston University in 1960, and then worked as a reporter for the Suffolk *News Herald* and the Norfolk *Journal and Guide* (Virginia), and the Quincy *Patriot-Ledger* (Massachusetts). Boone was the White House reporter for the Washington *Afro-American* (1964–65), and he became editor of the Richmond *Afro-American* (Virginia) in 1965. *See also* NEWSPAPERS: CONTEMPORARY.

BOONE, THEODORE SYLVESTER (1896– ?), clergyman, educator, author; born in Winchester, Tex. Boone received a B.A. degree from Des Moines College (Des Moines, Iowa) in 1918, a B.A. degree from Sioux Falls College in 1918; an LL.B. degree from Chicago Law School in 1922, and an M.A. degree from Arkansas Baptist College in 1924. He became pastor of Baptist churches in Texas and Michigan. Boone was also a lecturer at Bishop College (Dallas, Tex.). He received the Most Famous Negro Citizen Award of Fort Worth, Tex., in 1933.

BOOTH, L. VENCHAEL *See* BAPTISTS.

BOOTH, WILLIAM H. (1922–   ), lawyer, judge. A graduate of Queens College of the City University of New York, and of New York University Law School where he earned both LL.B. and LL.M. degrees, Booth was admitted to the New York state bar in 1950. He became eligible to practice before the U.S. Supreme Court in 1956, and later became a judge of the Criminal Court in New York City. By 1974 he had become one of the most controversial judges in New York because of his sensitivity to social and economic problems as they related to criminal behavior. His liberal attitude earned him the nickname of "William 'turn 'em aloose' Booth."

BORDERS, WILLIAM HOLMES (1905–   ), clergyman; born in Bibb County, Ga. Borders received a B.A. degree from Morehouse College (Atlanta, Ga.) in 1929, a B.D. degree from Garrett Theological Seminary in 1932, a M.A. degree from the University of Chicago in 1936, and his L.H.D. degree from Wilberforce University (Wilberforce, Ohio) in 1962. He was pastor of Baptist churches in Illinois and Georgia, and a professor of psychology at Morehouse College. Borders received the Omega Psi Phi Social Action Achievement Award in 1949. He was the author of several books and religious poems in which he formulated the motto "I'm Somebody."

BOTTOMS, LAWRENCE WENDELL (1908–   ), clergyman; born in Selma, Ala. Bottoms received a B.A. degree from Beaver College (Glenside, Pa.) and a B.D. degree from the Presbyterian Seminary in Pittsburgh. He studied further at Atlanta University and was ordained by the Presbyterian Church in 1936. Bottoms was pastor of the Grace Presbyterian Church in Louisville, Ky. (1938–49), and he served on many boards and commissions in the Presbyterian Church. In June 1975, Bottoms was elected moderator of the Presbyterian Church (southern region), and he was the first Afro-American to hold such a position.

BOUCHET, EDWARD ALEXANDER (1852–1918), physicist, educator; born in New Haven, Conn. Bouchet received a B.A. degree from Yale University and his Ph.D. degree from Yale University in 1876—the first Afro-American to receive the degree in the United States and also the first elected to Phi Beta Kappa. Despite his high achievements, he continued to teach in high schools throughout his life. Bottoms was an instructor in physics and chemistry at the Institute for Colored Youth for 26 years from 1876 to 1902, an instructor in physics and mathematics at Summer High School, St. Louis, Mo., in 1903, and an instructor in physics and mathematics at St. Paul Normal and Industrial School, Lawrenceville, Va., from 1906 to 1908. Bouchet was also principal of Lincoln High School, Gallipolis, Ohio, in 1908.

BOURNE, JOHN STANHOPE RAY (1873– ?), editor, lawyer; born in Barbados, British West Indies. Bourne received a LL.B. degree from Northeastern University (Boston, Mass.) in 1916 and a LL.M. degree from Boston University in 1926. Before coming to the United States, Bourne had become, in 1891, the founder and first editor of *The Barbados Bulletin*, the first daily newspaper there. Journalism occupied him until 1896, at which time he went to South America to engage in gold-placer mining. Bourne soon returned to the British West Indies, and by 1899 he had started proofreading for the British Government Printing Office while at the same time contributing to various newspapers. In 1904 he traveled to Boston where, after several years as a compositor and then chief of the typographical department at the *Atlantic Monthly,* he received his law education, and eventually began to practice law.

BOUSEFIELD, MIDIAN O. (1885–1948), physician, civic leader; born in Tipton, Mo. Bousefield received a B.A. degree from Kansas State University in 1907 and his M.D. degree from Northwestern University School of Medicine (Evanston, Ill.) in 1909. After serving his internship at the Freedmen's Hospital, Washington, D.C., Bousefield practiced medicine in Chicago from 1914 to 1948. He was medical director and president of Liberty Life Insurance Company, medical director and vice-president of Supreme Liberty Life Insurance Company, and the director of Afro-American health of the Julius Rosenwald Fund. Bousefield helped establish the infantile paralysis units at Tuskegee Institute (Tuskegee Institute, Ala.) and at Provident Hospital, Chicago, Ill., and he organized, staffed, and directed the Station Hospital, Fort Huachuca, Ariz. Bousefield was made president of the National Medical Association from 1933 to 1934, and was a member of the Chicago Board of Education in 1939.

BOWEN, JOHN WESLEY EDWARD (1855–1933), educator, theologian; born in New Orleans, La. Bowen was awarded a B.A. degree from the University of New Orleans in 1878, a B.D. degree from Boston University in 1885, and Ph.D. (1887) and D.D. degrees from Gammon Theological Seminary. He also served as a pastor of churches in New Jersey, Maryland, and Washington, D.C. Bowen taught at Central Tennessee College (1878–82), Morgan State College (Baltimore, Md.; now Morgan State University), Howard University (Washington, D.C.), and Gammon Theological Seminary, where he was the first

Afro-American to be appointed a regular professor. He was the editor of *The Voice of the Negro*, and was coeditor with I. Garland Penn of *The United Negro*.

BOWEN, RUTH J. (1930–   ), business executive; born in Danville, Va. Bowen attended New York University and the University of California. She established her own booking and talent agency with headquarters in New York City—the first such firm to be headed by a black woman—after having done public relations work for Dinah Washington and other entertainers. Her firm, the Queen Booking Corporation, annually topped the million dollar mark in earnings and represented such black artists as Sammy Davis, Jr., Aretha Franklin, and Ray Charles.

BOWIE STATE COLLEGE Bowie State College, at Bowie, Md., was founded in 1867 under the auspices of the Quakers as the Colored Normal School in Baltimore. It is currently state supported and coeducational; it grants the bachelor's and the master's degree, and provides liberal arts and teacher education curricula. It's 1975 enrollment was about 1,160.

The school was moved to Bowie, Md., in 1911, and it was renamed Bowie State Teacher's College. In the 1960s it developed a newer system of higher education that emphasized liberal arts as well as teacher education and general education. During the 1960s changes occurred in the composition of the student body, and the proportion of white students increased.

BOWIE STATE TEACHER'S COLLEGE See BOWIE STATE COLLEGE.

BOXERS, BOXING See ATHLETES.

BOYCOTTS See CIVIL RIGHTS: CIVIL RIGHTS MOVEMENT; CIVIL RIGHTS MOVEMENT IN SELECTED STATES: ALABAMA.

BOYD, JOHN DEWEY (1899–   ), educator, agronomist; born in Doloroso, Miss. Boyd received a B.S. degree from Alcorn Agricultural and Mechanical (A & M) College (Lorman, Miss.) in 1931 and his M.S. degree from the University of Illinois in 1949. Boyd served as president of Alcorn A & M College (1957–1969). He was also vice-president of the State Mutual Savings and Loan Association and a delegate to the White House Conference on Education.

BOYD, MILLER W., JR. (1934–   ), psychologist. Boyd received a B.A. degree from Fisk University (Nashville, Tenn.) in 1955, and a M.S. degree (1968) and his Ph.D. degree (1970) from St. Louis University. Boyd was first an instructor and then director of special projects at Southern Illinois University (1969–71), an instructor at Parks Aeronautical College (1968), and became co-director and research psychologist at the Academy of Urban Service, Inc., in St. Louis, Mo. (1971).

BOYD, ROBERT FULTON (1858–1912), physician, dentist; born in Pulaski, Tenn. Boyd attended Central Tennessee College and Fisk University (Nashville, Tenn.), and he received his M.D. degree (1882) and D.D.S. degree (1887) from Meharry Medical College (Nashville, Tenn.). He did postgraduate work in diseases of women and children at the Postgraduate Medical School and Hospital in Chicago, and he practiced dentistry in Nashville, Tenn., after 1887. Boyd held chairs in the departments of anatomy, physiology, hygiene, gynecology, and surgery at Meharry Medical College, was superintendent and chief surgeon at Mercy Hospital, and was one of the founders and the first president of the National Medical Assocation. Boyd was also president of the Peoples' Savings Bank and Trust Company, Nashville, Tenn., one of the first banks owned and managed by blacks. *See also* BANKS; NATIONAL MEDICAL ASSOCIATION (NMA).

BOYER, JAMES ALEXANDER (1909–   ), educator; born in Raleigh, N.C. Boyer received a B.A. degree from Morehouse College (Atlanta, Ga.) in 1931, a M.A. degree from Atlanta University in 1934, and his Ed.D. degree from the University of Michigan in 1949. He taught at Saint Augustine's College (Raleigh, N.C.) and later became its president.

BOYKINS, E. A. (1931–   ), educator, administrator; born in Vicksburg, Miss. Boykins received a B.S. degree from Xavier University in 1953, a M.S. degree from Texas Southern University in 1958, and his Ph.D. degree from Michigan State University in 1964. He served as director of the division of arts and sciences at Alcorn Agricultural and Mechanical (A & M) College (Lorman, Miss.), before being appointed college president in 1971. His publications include: "DDT in the Food Chains of Wild

Birds" and "The Effects of DDT-Contaminated Earthworms in the Diet of Birds."

BRADFORD, ARVINE M. (1915–   ), surgeon, educator; born in Alcoa, Tenn. Bradford received a M.A. degree from Fisk University (Nashville, Tenn.) and his M.D. degree from Howard University Medical College (Washington, D.C.) in 1949. He interned at Harlem Hospital, New York, N.Y. (1949–50), and was resident there from 1955–1959. Bradford was a physician on the faculty of Maryland State College, and he opened his first office in Pocomoke City, Md., becoming the first Afro-American to practice medicine there. Bradford was on the courtesy staffs of the Washington Hospital Center, Columbia Hospital for Women, and Morris Cafritz Hospital, all in Washington, D.C. He also was on the faculty of the department of obstetrics and gynecology at Howard University Medical College and the staff of Freedmen's Hospital, Washington, D.C. Bradford was made a fellow of the American College of Surgeons.

BRADLEY, ANDREW M. (1906–   ), accountant, public official; born in Neville Island, Pa. Bradley studied at the Wharton Extension School of the University of Pennsylvania, Cades CPA School, and Thompson Business College (Harrisburg, Pa.). In 1955 Bradley was appointed state budget secretary, becoming the first Afro-American to serve in the cabinet of a governor of Pennsylvania. From 1940 to 1964 Bradley headed the Afro-American division of the Democratic State Committee for all statewide elections, and he served as a delegate-at-large at the Democratic National Conventions from 1948 to 1968.

BRADLEY, DAVID H.   See PREFACE: LIST OF CONTRIBUTORS.

BRADLEY, THOMAS (1917–   ), civil servant, lawyer, mayor; born near Calvert, Tex. Bradley moved to Los Angeles, Calif., at the age of seven, and at ten he began working to help support his family. He attended Polytechnic High School, where he was a star on the track team, and later went on to the University of California at Los Angeles on an athletic scholarship. In 1940 he joined the Los Angeles police department where he remained for 21 years, rising through the ranks to lieutenant—the highest police rank ever held by an Afro-American. Having studied law at night, Bradley was admitted to the California bar in 1956, and in 1961 he retired from the Los

Angeles police department to practice law. In 1963 Bradley won a seat on the city council in Los Angeles, thus becoming the first elected black official in that city and only the second California black to be elected to public office. Bradley was later elected first vice-president of the National League of Cities, the only nonmayor to have led the prestigious organization of 15,000 municipalities. In the 1973 Los Angeles mayoral election, he defeated Sam Yorty, who had served for three terms; and Bradley became the first Afro-American mayor of America's third largest city, where only 15 percent of the voters were black.

BRADSHAW, BOOKER TALMADGE, SR. (1904–   ), business executive; born in St. Louis, Mo. Bradshaw received a B.S. degree from the University of Illinois and his LL.D. degree from Virginia State College. He was the founder of the Virginia Mutual Benefit Life Insurance Company in Richmond and was later its president and treasurer. Bradshaw was a member of the board of directors of the Consolidated Bank and Trust Company and the Jefferson Virginia Townhouse Corporation.

BRAGG, GEORGE F., JR. (1863–1940), clergyman, editor; born in Warrenton, N.C. After serving as a page in the Virginia legislature in 1882, Bragg founded a weekly newspaper, the *Lancet,* in Petersburg, Va. Ordained an Episcopal minister in 1887, he served churches in Virginia and Maryland. Bragg organized and founded the Maryland Home for Friendless Colored Children. For 34 years, he edited the *Church Advocate,* a religious paper. *See also* EPISCOPALIANS.

BRAILEY, TROY *See* NATIONAL AFRO-AMERICAN LABOR COUNCIL.

BRAITHWAITE, WILLIAM STANLEY (1878–1962), poet, editor; born in Boston, Mass. Braithwaite was educated at home, became interested in poetry while working in a bookstore, and published his first volume of poetry, *Lyrics of Love,* in 1904. He was the literary editor of the Boston *Transcript* from 1908 to 1929, and edited the annual *Anthology of Magazine Verse* (1913–29), which helped launch the careers of such poets as Vachel Lindsay and Carl Sandburg. His own delicate verse was published in *Selected Poems* (1948). Braithwaite also wrote an autobiography, *The House Under Arcturus* (1941). In 1918 he received the National Association for the

William Stanley Braithwaite. *(Library of Congress.)*

Advancement of Colored People's (NAACP) Spingarn Medal. See also LITERATURE: POETRY.

BRAMWELL, HENRY (1919–   ), lawyer, judge; born in Brooklyn, N.Y. Bramwell attended Brooklyn College of the City University of New York from 1937 to 1941. Several years in the Armed Forces delayed his law education until 1945, when he entered Brooklyn Law School. Bramwell received his LL.B. degree in 1948, and he was admitted to the New York state bar that same year. From 1953 to 1961 he was an assistant district attorney for the Eastern District Court of New York. Bramwell served as associate chief enforcement attorney for the New York State Rent Commission from 1961 to 1963, and as special hearing officer for the U.S. Department of Justice from 1962 to 1966. Appointed judge to fill a vacant seat on the Civil Court of the City of New York in 1966, Bramwell stood for election to a full term in 1969 and won.

BRANCH, DOROTHY SUTTON (1922–   ), clergywoman; born in Chicago, Ill. Branch received a B.S. degree from Judson Baptist College in 1938, a M.A. degree from Garrett Theological Seminary in 1941, and her Ph.D. degree from the University of Colorado in 1960. She established the Youth Fellowship at the Commonwealth Funeral Home in 1942, and served on the board of the City Colleges of Chicago. She was pastor of the Junior Church of Cosmopolitan Community Church in Chicago (1939) and of the Commonwealth Community Church in Chicago.

BRANCH, EMANUEL SYLVESTRE (1921–   ), clergyman; born in Philadelphia, Pa. Branch received a B.A. degree from Yale University in 1950 and his B.D. degree from Yale Divinity School in 1955. He was pastor of Baptist churches in Connecticut and Ohio. Branch was appointed lecturer at Western Reserve University (Cleveland, Ohio; now Case Western Reserve University) and became a member of the delegate assembly of the National Urban League. He was president of the board of directors of the Urban League of Cleveland.

BRANCH, GEORGE MURRAY (1914–   ), clergyman; born in Prince Edward County, Va. Branch received a B.S. degree from Virginia Union University in 1938, a B.D. degree from Andover Newton Theological School in 1944, and a M.A. degree from Drew University (Madi-

son, N.J.) in 1946. He served as pastor of Baptist churches in New Hampshire and New Jersey. Branch was an assistant professor at Morehouse College (Atlanta, Ga.) from 1947 to 1956, an associate professor at the Interdenominational Theological Center (Atlanta, Ga.), and a member of the board of directors of the Atlanta branch of the American Civil Liberties Union.

BRANCH, JOHN H., JR. (1931–   ), army officer. Branch received a B.S. degree (1955) and his M.S. degree (1972) from Morgan State University (Baltimore, Md.). He served in the U.S. Army from 1956 to 1976, retiring as a lieutenant-colonel. Branch was appointed director of transportation of city schools in Baltimore in 1976.

BRANCH, MARY E. (1882–1945), educator; born in Farmville, Va. Branch graduated from Virginia State College and received her Ph.B. degree (1922) and M.A. degree (1925) from the University of Chicago. She taught English at Virginia State College (1924), at Sumner High School (1925–26), and was a supervisor at Vashon High School, St. Louis, Mo. (1926–30). In 1930 Branch became president of Tillotson College (Austin, Tex.; now Huston-Tillotson College).

BRANCH NORMAL See UNIVERSITY OF ARKANSAS AT PINE BLUFF.

BRANCH, WILLIAM B. (1929–   ), author, producer, playwright; born in New Haven, Conn. Branch received a B.S. degree from Northwestern University (Evanston, Ill.) in 1949, his M.F.A. degree from Columbia University in 1958, and did further study as a resident fellow at Yale University from 1965 to 1966. He received a Guggenheim Fellowship (1959–60), the Yale University ABC Fellowship (1965–66), and the Film Festival Blue Ribbon Award for *Still a Brother: Inside the Negro Middle Class* (1969). Branch was a free-lance writer, producer, and director after 1959, and, in addition to newspaper articles and anthologies, he produced *A Medal for Willie; In Splendid Error* (1954–55); and *A Wreath for Udomo* (1961). See also LITERATURE: DRAMA/THEATER.

BRANSON, HERMAN RUSSELL (1914–   ), educator, scientist; born in Pocahontas, Va. Branson received a B.S. degree from Virginia State College in 1936 and his Ph.D. degree from the University of Cincinnati (Cincinnati, Ohio) in 1939. He taught mathematics and physics at Dillard University (New Orleans, La.) from 1939 to 1941, physics and chemistry at Howard University (Washington, D.C.) from 1941 to 1968, and he served as president of Central State University (Wilberforce, O.) from 1968 to 1970 and of Lincoln University (Lincoln University, Pa.) in 1970. Branson was a National Science Foundation Faculty Fellow at the University of Hamburg and at the French Atomic Energy Commission at Saclay (1962–63), a member of evaluation teams for the Middle States Association of Colleges and Secondary Schools (1965), and a consultant for the National Science Foundation and Science Education in India (1966–67). He became one of the first educators to design and successfully direct federally funded compensatory education programs for disadvantaged black youth seeking college admission. Branson was a consultant and adviser for many federal programs that aimed at upgrading science curricula at Afro-American colleges. *See also* SCIENTISTS: BIOLOGICAL, PHYSICAL.

BRANTON, WILEY A. (1923–   ), lawyer; born in Pine Bluff, Ark. Branton studied at Arkansas Agricultural, Mechanical, and Normal (A M & N) College receiving a B.S. degree in 1950, and at the University of Arkansas, where he received his LL.B. degree in 1953. He practiced law in Pine Bluff from 1952 to 1962, and he distinguished himself in 1957 as chief counsel for the "Little Rock Nine"—the nine students who were plaintiffs in the cases arising from the stormy attempts to desegregate Little Rock's schools. Branton was director of the Voter Education Project of the Southern Regional Council, Inc. (1962–65), a special assistant to U.S. attorney generals Nicholas Katzenbach and Ramsey Clark (1965–67), and the executive director of several community and social action groups including the Council for United Civil Rights Leadership, Inc., in New York City. In 1971 he became a partner in a Washington, D.C. law firm, although he maintained professional affiliations with a firm in Little Rock.

BRATHWAITE, YVONNE WATSON *See* BURKE, YVONNE WATSON BRATHWAITE.

BRAWLEY, BENJAMIN G. (1882–1939), educator, author; born in Columbia, S.C. Brawley received B.A. degrees from Morehouse College (Atlanta, Ga.) in 1901 and from the University of Chicago in 1906, and a M.A. degree from Harvard University in 1908. He taught at Morehouse College from 1902 to 1910 and at Howard University (Washington, D.C.) from 1910 to 1912, and then became dean of Morehouse in 1912. Brawley was a pastor for a year in Brockton, Mass. from 1921 to 1922, and then returned to teaching at Shaw University (Raleigh, N.C.) from 1923 to 1931. He was author of many books, including: *A Short History of the American Negro* (1913); *A Social History of the American Negro* (1921); *The Negro in Literature and Art* (1918); and *A Short History of English Drama* (1921).

BRAYBOY, THOMAS L. (1919–   ), psychiatrist, educator; Brayboy attended West Virginia State College, and received his M.D. degree from Meharry Medical College (Nashville, Tenn.). He later attended William Alanson White Institute, interned at Harlem Hospital, New York, N.Y. (1949–50), and was a resident in psychiatry at Virginia Hospital, Northport, L.I. (1950–51). Brayboy was a psychiatric supervisor at the Rockland State Hospital, Orangeburg, N.Y. (1953–55), an associate director at the Rockland County Mental Health Center, Monsey, N.Y. (1955–57), an assistant clinical professor of psychiatry at New York Medical College, and a professor of psychiatry at the Northern New Jersey College of Medicine. He was also the director of the Youth Development Center in Newark, N.J.

BREATHETT, GEORGE (1926–   ), historian, educator. Breathett received a B.S. degree from Tennessee State University in 1948, a M.A. degree from the University of Michigan in 1950, and his Ph.D. degree from the University of Iowa in 1954. He taught history at Bennett College (Greensboro, N.C.) from 1953 to 1960, where he became chairman of the division of social sciences (1964). His publications include: "Haiti in the French Revolution" (1967), "Religious Protectionism and the Slave in Haiti" (1969).

BREEDEN, JAMES PLEASANT (1934–   ), clergyman; born in Minneapolis, Minn. Breeden received a B.A. degree from Dartmouth College (Hanover, N.H.) and a B.D. degree from Union Theological Seminary in 1960. He was curate of the St. James Episcopal Church, Roxbury, Mass.; canon and advisor to the bishop of St. Paul's Cathedral, Boston, Mass.; and a member of the U.S. Civil Rights Commission.

BREWER, THOMAS HENRY, SR. (1894–1956), physician; born in Saco, Ala. Brewer attended Selma University (Selma, Ala.) and received his M.D. degree from Meharry Medical College (Nashville, Tenn.) in 1920. He started a medical practice in Columbus, Ga., in 1920. Brewer was a member of the Georgia Committee on Interracial Cooperation and a member of the house of delegates of the National Medical Association. He later became the president of the Georgia State Medical, Dental, and Pharmaceutical Association.

BREWER, WILLIAM MILES (1889–1970), educator, historian, editor; born in Elberton, Ga. Brewer received a B.A. degree (1919) and a M.A. degree (1929) from Harvard University, and his LL.D. degree from Johnson C. Smith University (Charlotte, N.C.) in 1951. He taught at Johnson C. Smith University (1919–20), Nashville State College (1921–22), and in high schools in Baltimore and Washington, D.C. (1923–31). Brewer became supervisor of history for the public schools of Washington, D.C., and he edited the *Journal of Negro History* from 1951 until his health failed in 1969.

BRICE, CAROL (1920–), singer; born in Indianapolis, Ind. After graduating from Talladega College (Talladega, Ala.) with a bachelor of music degree in 1939, Brice received further training at the Juilliard School of Music in New York City. Winner of the Naumburg Award in 1944, she made her singing debut in a Town Hall recital in New York City a year later. Her appearances on stage began in 1959 in the role of Kakou in the musical *Saratoga*. Her debut was followed by performances as Maude in *Finian's Rainbow* (1960); Queenie in *Show Boat* (1961); Marie in *Porgy and Bess* (1961); and Harriet Tubman in *Gentlemen Be Seated* (1963).

BRIGHT, JOHN DOUGLAS (1917–72), African Methodist Episcopal bishop; born in Americus, Ga. Bright received a B.A. degree from Wilberforce University (Wilberforce, Ohio) and his Th.B. degree from Payne Seminary in 1942. After serving as pastor of African Methodist Episcopal (AME) churches in Ohio and Pennsylvania, he was elected bishop in 1960. His first assignment was in Central Africa (1960–62), but, during the next two years, he was based in Arkansas and Oklahoma. From May 1964 until his death, Bright was the presiding bishop of the

Edward W. Brooke in 1966 became the first Afro-American U.S. senator in the twentieth century when he was elected as a Republican to represent Massachusetts. *(Courtesy of Edward W. Brooke.)*

First Episcopal District of the AME Church. He was a member of the World Council of Churches, the National Council of Churches, and the National Association for the Advancement of Colored People (NAACP).

BRIMMER, ANDREW FELTON (1926–), economist, government official, educator; born in Newellton, La. The son of a sharecropping warehouseman, Brimmer received a B.A. degree from the University of Washington in 1950 and a M.A. degree in economics a year later while on a John Hay Whitney Foundation Fellowship there. He studied at the Delhi School of Economics and the University of Bombay on a Fulbright Fellowship, then became a teaching fellow at Harvard University, where he received his Ph.D. degree in 1957. Brimmer worked as an economist for the Federal Reserve Bank in New York (1955–58). He was an assistant professor of economics at Michigan State University (1958–61) and taught at the Wharton School of Finance and Commerce, University of Pennsylvania (1961–66). In 1965 Brimmer was made U.S. assistant secretary of commerce for economic affairs, and in 1966 he became the first Afro-American appointed to the Federal Reserve Board. Later, he served for two years as a visiting professor at Harvard University.

BRISBANE, ROBERT H. political scientist, educator; born in Florida. Brisbane graduated from Saint John's University (Jamaica, N.Y.) and received his Ph.D. degree from Harvard University. He was later chairman of the department of political science at Morehouse College (Atlanta, Ga.). Brisbane was a Fulbright senior lecturer in India (1958–59), and he received many other travel grants, including a study trip to Russia (1973). He was the author of *The Black Vanguard* (1970) and *Black Activism* (1974). *See also* Pref-ace: Acknowledgements.

BRONZEVILLE This term has at least three meanings: (1) a reference frequently used by journalists from 1930 to 1960 to designate *any* black community; (2) a specific section of Chicago, Ill., referred to in the poetry of Gwendolyn Brooks; and (3) a general reference to a specific area or section inhabited by blacks before integration.

BROOKE, EDWARD W. (1919–), lawyer, U.S. Senator; born in Washington, D.C. Brooke attended Howard University (Washington, D.C.) and received a B.S. degree there in 1941. After serving as an infantry officer in World War II, he received his LL.B. degree from Boston University in 1948, and two years later he received his LL.M. degree there. In 1962 he was elected attorney general of Massachusetts, the only Republican within the state to win a statewide election that year. In 1964 he was reelected by a majority of nearly a million votes at the same time many Republicans were following Barry Goldwater to defeat. In 1966 Brooke was elected to the U.S. Senate, and with his election, he not only became the first Afro-American to be elected to the Senate by popular vote, but also the first to sit in the Senate since Reconstruction. A Republican and a Protestant, Brooke showed his tremendous political strength by handily winning districts where blacks comprised only two percent of the population. He was the recipient of many awards, including the Charles Evans Hughes Award of the National Conference of Christians and Jews and, in 1967, the Spingarn Medal. He lost his senatorial seat in the elections of 1978.

BROOKS, GLENWOOD C., JR. See EDUCATION: REFERENCES; SCIENTISTS: SOCIAL.

BROOKS, GWENDOLYN (1917–), poet, educator; born in Topeka, Kans. Brooks graduated from Chicago's Wilson Junior College in 1936 and joined the faculty of the Chicago Teacher's College a year later. Since then, she has taught at many Chicago schools, sometimes at as many as three at once. Brooks was chosen by *Mademoiselle* magazine as one of the Ten Women of the Year in 1945—the same year her first collection of poetry was published, *A Street in Bronzeville.* She received a Guggenheim Fellowship in 1946. Her second volume of verse, *Annie Allen* (1949), was awarded the first Pulitzer Prize ever received by an Afro-American. Brooks became poet laureate of Illinois in 1969, and she was named a consultant on literature to the Library of Congress in 1973. Brooks has been credited with starting a trend in poetry of going back to the issues and problems of urban life and away from academic detachment. Her other books include a short novel, *Maud Martha* (1963); *Selected Poems* (1963); and an autobiography, *Report from Part One* (1972). See also LITERATURE: POETRY.

BROOKS, HARRY W., JR. (1929–), army officer; born in Indianapolis, Ind. Brooks received a B.A. degree from the University of Omaha in 1962. Before his promotion to brigadier general in 1972, he was chief of the Equal Employment Opportunity Programs in Washington, D.C. Brooks received many medals and awards during his 25 years in the U.S. Army, including, the Legion of Merit and the Bronze Star. He also conducted an important study on race relations among Army troops stationed overseas.

BROOKS, LYMAN BEECHER (1910–), educator; born in Mathews, Va. Brooks received a B.S. degree from Virginia Union University in 1929, and a M.A. degree (1937) and his Ph.D. degree (1942) from the University of Michigan. He taught in Virginia schools from 1929 to 1936, and he became provost of the Norfolk division of Virginia State College in 1938. Brooks was president of the Virginia Teachers Association, and he served on the board of trustees of Virginia Union University.

BROOKS, WALTER HENDERSON (1851–1945), clergyman; born in Richmond, Va., Brooks studied at Wilberforce Institute (Wilberforce, Ohio; now Wilberforce University), received a B.A. degree from Lincoln University (Lincoln University, Pa.), and was awarded honorary degrees from Howard University (Washington, D.C.) and Lincoln University. Ordained a Baptist minister in 1876, he served as Sunday School Missionary for the American Baptist Publication Society for two years and then as pastor of the Second African Baptist Church of Richmond for four years. In 1882, Brooks became pastor of the Nineteenth Street Baptist Church of Washington, D.C., and served there until his death. He was an ardent temperance worker and was chaplain of the Anti-Saloon League of the District of Columbia throughout the league's existence. See also BAPTISTS.

BROTHERHOOD OF SLEEPING CAR PORTERS (BSCP) See LABOR UNIONS; RANDOLPH, ASA PHILIP.

BROWN, AARON (1906–), educator; born in Pensacola, Fla. Brown received a B.A. degree from Talladega College (Talladega, Ala.) in 1928, a M.A. degree from Atlanta University in 1933, and his Ph.D. degree from the University of Chicago in 1943. He was head of the science department at LeMoyne College (Memphis, Tenn.) from 1928 to 1932, principal of Moultrie High School from 1933 to 1935, dean of State Teachers College (Forsythe, Ga.) in 1935, dean of Ft. Valley State College (Ft. Valley, Ga.) from 1939 to 1941, and president of Albany State College (Albany, Ga.) from 1943 to 1954. He taught education at Long Island University and was assistant to the provost from 1965 to 1969, and assistant to the president after 1969. Brown wrote *An Evaluation of the Secondary Schools for Negroes in the South* (1943), *The Albany Negro* (1948), and *Ladders to Improvement* (1960).

BROWN, CALVIN SCOTT (1859– ?), clergyman, educator; born in Salisbury, N.C. Brown received a B.A. degree (1886), a D.D. degree (1898), and a M.A. degree (1900) from Shaw University (Raleigh, N.C.). He founded Waters Training School (Winston, N.C.) and became its principal in 1886. Brown was a delegate to the World Sunday School Convention in Rome (1896) and to the World Baptist Convention in Stockholm (1924).

BROWN, CHARLOTTE HAWKINS (1882–1961), educator; born in Henderson, N.C. Brown studied at State Normal School (Salem, Mass.) in 1901, at Harvard University, and at Simmons College (Boston, Mass.). She was the founder and principal of Palmer Memorial Institute (Sedalia, N.C.) from 1901 to 1952, which she founded from the remnants of a church congregation and which she named in honor of Alice Freeman Palmer, who was her early benefactor. Brown was highly active in many civic affairs and was the first black woman to be elected (1928) to the 20th Century Club of Boston, whose membership includes persons of distinction in education, art, science, and religion.

BROWN, CLAUDE (1937–), author; born in New York, N.Y. Brown received a B.A. degree from Howard University (Washington, D.C.) in 1965, and his plays were performed by the Afro-Negro Theater Guild in 1960–61. Brown wrote *Manchild in the Promised Land* (1968), which was the best-selling autobiography of his Harlem youth.

BROWN, DOROTHY L. (1919–), surgeon, state legislator. Brown spent the first 12 years of her life in an orphanage. She graduated from Bennett College (Greensboro, N.C.) in 1941, and received her M.D. degree from Meharry Medical College in 1948. Brown interned at Harlem Hospital, New York, N.Y., and was resident in surgery at George W. Hubbard Hospital, Nashville, Tenn. She became clinical professor of surgery at Meharry Medical Center, Nashville, Tenn., chief of surgery at Riverside Hospital; and she was elected to be a member of the Tennessee state legislature. Brown was also a member of the National Medical Association and was made a fellow of the American College of Surgeons.

BROWN, FRANK REGINALD (1902–), clergyman, educator; born in New York, N.Y. Brown received a B.A. degree from Lincoln University (Lincoln University, Pa.) in 1932, a M.A. degree from Columbia University in 1936, and his Ed.D. degree from Union Theological Seminary in 1952. He was ordained a Baptist chaplain in 1937 and a minister in the African Methodist Episcopal Zion (AMEZ) Church in 1943; he served as pastor of churches in New England and New York, as well as pastor of the Allegheny, West Central, and Western North Carolina Conference of the AMEZ Church. Brown was professor and dean at Hood Seminary and head of the science department of Virginia Seminary and College (1936–39).

BROWN, GEORGE L. (1925–), state legislator, lieutenant governor; born in Lawrence, Kans. Brown received a B.S. degree in journalism from the University of Kansas in 1950, and later did graduate work at the University of Colorado. In 1955 he was appointed to the Colorado House of Representatives, and in 1956 he was elected to the State Senate, the first Afro-American to achieve that distinction. Brown was reelected to four successive terms in 1960, 1964, 1968, and 1972. Meanwhile, in 1960, he joined the writing staff of the Denver *Post*. In 1962 Brown was asked by the U.S. Department of State to give lectures on communications in Europe and Africa, and in 1965 he was appointed assistant executive director of the Denver Housing Authority. In 1969 he was selected as the first executive director of the Metro-Denver Urban Coalition. Brown was elected lieutenant governor of Colorado in 1974, the first Afro-American to hold that office.

BROWN, GRAFTON TYLER (1841–1918), painter, lithographer; born in Harrisburg, Pa. Brown was perhaps the first noteworthy black artist to work in California, where he established his own lithography business in San Francisco. He was known for his drawings of towns and landscapes in California and the Pacific Northwest, some of which later appeared as engravings on stock certificates, and several of which were recreated by the artist in oil. In 1872 he sold his business and traveled throughout the West, painting landscapes. His work was exhibited at and collected by the Oakland Museum, Oakland, Calif. See also ARTISTS.

BROWN, H. RAP (1943–   ), civil rights militant; born in Baton Rouge, La. He was active in the 1960s, and was popular with young blacks, who admired his militant rhetoric. In 1967 he succeeded Stokely Carmichael as chairman of the Student Nonviolent Coordinating Committee (SNCC). Throughout his career, Brown was frequently in trouble with the law in several states: in Maryland, he was accused of inciting a race riot; in Louisiana, he appealed a federal conviction for transporting firearms across state lines; in Virginia and New York, he was charged with a violation of his bail. In 1970 after years of charges and trials, Brown disappeared. Two of his friends had been killed in a suspicious automobile explosion, and his defense attorney claimed Brown would be in danger if he reappeared. In 1971, however, Brown was wounded in a gun battle with police after a bar holdup in New York City. He was arrested, brought to trial in 1972, found guilty in 1973, and began serving a prison sentence. His book, *Die Nigger Die!*, was published in 1969.

BROWN, J. HAROLD (1909–   ), composer, choral conductor; born in Shellman, Ga. Brown received a B.A. degree from Fisk University (Nashville, Tenn.) in 1923 and a M.A. degree from Indiana University in 1931. His teaching career included positions at Florida Agricultural and Mechanical (A & M) College and at Southern University (Baton Rouge, La.). During the 1950s Brown was music director at Karamu House and at the Huntington Playhouse, Cleveland, Ohio. Best known as a composer, Brown wrote the oratorio *Job, The Saga of Rip Van Winkle* (for chorus), and the cantata *The African Chief*.

BROWN, JAMES (1933–   ), singer, business executive; born in Augusta, Ga. Brown began to perform for small change at the age of 12. A little more than two years later, his first hit record

began his rise to fame as "Mr. Dynamite" and later as "Soul Brother Number 1." Brown became owner of a publishing firm, a production company, and three radio stations. His interests also included two record companies and various real estate holdings.

BROWN, JAMES NATHANIEL (JIM) (1936–   ), professional football player, actor; born in St. Simons Island, Ga. Brown won ten varsity letters in athletics at Syracuse University (Syracuse, N.Y.), and in 1956 he was chosen to the NCAA All-American football team. During his nine seasons with the Cleveland Browns (1957–65), Brown was the most publicized player in the National Football League (NFL) and was considered by many to be the greatest running back to play modern professional football. Brown led the NFL in rushing in eight of nine seasons, rushed for 12,312 career yards, compiled a career rushing average of 5.2 yards per carry, and scored 126 career touchdowns. Brown's career records continued to stand in the mid-1970s. Following his retirement in 1965, he became a well-known actor in such films as *Rio Conchos, The Dirty Dozen, Slaughter,* and *Black Gunn. See also* ATHLETES: FOOTBALL.

BROWN, LETITIA WOODS (1915–76), historian, educator; born in Tuskegee, Ala. Brown received a B.S. degree from Tuskegee Institute (Tuskegee Institute, Ala.) in 1935, a M.A. degree from Ohio State University in 1937, and her Ph.D. degree in history from Harvard University in 1966. She taught history at Tuskegee Institute from 1937 to 1940, and was an instructor at LeMoyne-Owen College (Memphis, Tenn.) from 1940 to 1945. She was an associate professor at Howard University (Washington, D.C.) from 1961 to 1970 and at George Washington University (Washington, D.C.) after 1971. She wrote *Washington from Banneker to Douglass, 1791–1870,* and coauthored *Free Negroes in the District of Columbia, 1790–1864* (1971).

BROWN, MILDRED *See* NEWSPAPERS: CONTEMPORARY.

BROWN, RICHARD ALGER (1905–   ), physician; born in Steelton, Pa. Brown received a B.A. degree from Lincoln University (Lincoln University, Pa.) in 1927 and his M.D. degree from Howard University Medical College (Washington, D.C.) in 1932. He interned at St. Louis City Hospital No. 2 and did postgraduate work at New

England Medical Center and at Tufts College Medical School (Medford, Mass.). Brown practiced medicine in York, Pa. (1932–42) and in Harrisburg, Pa., after 1942. He was a staff member of Harrisburg Hospital and president of the Crispus Attucks Community Center, York, Pa. (1935–42).

BROWN, ROBERT TURNER (1868– ?), clergyman, educator; born in Courtland, Ala. After receiving his M.D. degree from Meharry Medical College (Nashville, Tenn.) in 1888, Brown received a B.A. degree (1889) and a M.A. degree (1892) from Walden University (Nashville, Tenn.) and a D.D. degree from Philander Smith College (Little Rock, Ark.) in 1898. He was editor of the *Christian Index* for eight years, and in 1922 was made a bishop of the Christian Methodist Episcopal (CME) Church. In addition, Brown was dean of Lane College (Jackson, Tenn.) and president of Miles Memorial College.

BROWN, ROOSEVELT See ATHLETES: FOOTBALL.

BROWN, ROSCOE C., JR. (1922–), educator, author; born in Washington, D.C. Brown received a B.S. degree from Springfield College (Springfield, Mass.) in 1943 and a M.A. degree (1949) and his Ph.D. degree (1951) from New York University. He taught physical education at West Virginia State College and then joined the School of Education at New York University (1951), where he became director of the Institute of Afro-American Affairs (1960–). Brown coauthored *The Negro Almanac* (1967) and became president of Bronx Community College (N.Y.) in 1977.

BROWN, ROSCOE C., SR. (1884–1962), dentist, public official. Brown attended Howard University (Washington, D.C.) and received his D.D.S. degree from Howard University College of Dentistry in 1906. He practiced dentistry in Richmond, Va. (1907–15), and he became active in public health as a lecturer on the health problems of Afro-Americans after 1919. Brown was chief of the special programs branch of the U.S. Public Health Service in 1954 and was editor of *National Negro News,* a quarterly bulletin of the U.S. Public Health Service. He was a member of President Franklin D. Roosevelt's "Kitchen Cabinet," and he was made a fellow of the American Public Health Association.

BROWN, RUSSELL W. See SCIENTISTS: BIOLOGICAL, PHYSICAL.

BROWN, STERLING ALLAN (1901–), poet, critic; born in Washington, D.C. Brown received a B.A. degree from Williams College (Williamstown, Mass.) in 1925, where he was a member of Phi Beta Kappa, and a M.A. degree from Harvard University in 1930. He later taught English at Howard University (Washington, D.C.) and was a visiting lecturer at Vassar College (Poughkeepsie, N.Y.) and at the University of Minnesota, among other schools. Brown was a staff member of the 1944 Gunnar-Myrdal study of the Negro in American life and editor of Negro affairs for the Federal Writers Project (1936–39). He received a Guggenheim Fellowship in 1937. Brown emphasized in his writings the importance of folk tradition, and he helped achieve recognition for folk artists, such as Ma Rainey, Bessie Smith, and Blind Lemon Jefferson. He is the author of *The Negro in American Fiction* (1937). In 1941 he became senior editor of *The Negro Caravan,* a standard reference source on black literature. Brown, who belonged to the Harlem Renaissance and whose first poems appeared in *Southern Road* (1932), has been called "the dean of American Negro poets." *See also* LITERATURE: POETRY.

BROWN THEOLOGICAL INSTITUTE See EDWARD WATERS COLLEGE.

BROWN, TOMMIE FLORENCE (1934–), social worker; born in Rome, Ga. Brown received a B.A. degree from Dillard University (New Orleans, La.) in 1957 and her M.S.W. degree from George Washington University (Washington, D.C.) in 1964, and did further postgraduate work at Atlanta University. She worked with the Tennessee department of public welfare after 1957, becoming a field supervisor in 1961. Brown was president of the Southeastern Tennessee Chapter of the National Association of Social Workers (NASW) from 1967 to 1969, and served as its national secretary from 1972 to 1973. In 1969 she became a member of the Chattanooga Model Cities Board, and in 1971 she taught at the University of Tennessee at Chattanooga. Her awards include: the NASW Member of the Year Award (1970), the Howard Gustafson Memorial Award (1970), and the Alpha Kappa Alpha Woman of the Year Award (1968–69).

BROWN, TONY See RADIO AND TELEVISION.

BROWN UNIVERSITY *See* EDWARD WATERS COLLEGE.

BROWN, WILLIE L., JR. (1934–   ), lawyer, state legislator; born in Mineola, Tex. Brown received a B.A. degree from San Francisco State College in 1955 and his J.D. degree from Hastings College of Law at the University of California in 1958. After being admitted to the California bar in 1959, he was elected to the California state assembly for the first time in 1964, and maintained his seat in every election thereafter; he became minority whip in 1969. In the Democratic National Conventions of both 1968 and 1972, Brown played prominent roles: in 1968 in the movement to remove Georgia Governor Lester Maddox, and in 1972 as cochairman of the California delegation.

BRUCE, BLANCHE KELSO (1841–1898), U.S. Senator, government official; born in Farmville, Va. Bruce was taken to Missouri, where he learned the printer's trade, before the outbreak of the Civil War. In 1861 he escaped to Hannibal, Mo., and started a school for blacks. After the war, Bruce spent two years studying at Oberlin College (Oberlin, Ohio) and then moved to Mississippi, where he eventually became a wealthy planter. Bruce was a member of the Mississippi levee board, sheriff, tax collector, and county superintendent of schools. In 1874, having become a prominent Republican, he was elected by the Mississippi state legislature to the U.S. Senate, the first Afro-American to serve a full term (1875–81). After taking up residence in Washington, D.C., he was appointed by President James A. Garfield as registrar of the U.S. Treasury in 1881. Under President Benjamin Harrison, Bruce was recorder of deeds for the District of Columbia (1889–93), and in 1895 he was reappointed registrar of the Treasury, a position he retained until his death.

BRUCE, JOHN EDWARD (BRUCE GRIT, DUKE OF UGANDA) (1856–1924), journalist, publisher; born in Piscataway, Md. Bruce was born of slave parents and moved to Washington, D.C., with his mother at an early age. He attended several private schools and studied three months at Howard University (Washington, D.C.) in 1872. Bruce received his first lessons in journalism on the New York *Times* in 1874 and soon became a correspondent for a large number of weekly newspapers, including the *Progressive Ameri-*

can, and the *Cherokee Advocate,* published by the Cherokee Nation. In 1879 he started his own newspaper, *The Argus,* in Washington, D.C., and the following year published the *Sunday Item,* the first Sunday newspaper founded by an Afro-American. In 1884 Bruce began to use the pen name "Bruce Grit" and was widely known by it during the remainder of his 40 years in journalism. Deliberately refusing to address a white audience or join any nonblack organization, Bruce was an early militant who opposed interracial marriages, urged racial pride and solidarity, and advocated the use of defensive force. He joined Marcus Garvey's black nationalist movement in 1918, in which he was known as the "Duke of Uganda." In 1911 Bruce organized The Negro Society for Historical Research with Arthur Schomburg. He was one of the most widely read and influential black journalists and more than 5,000 people attended his funeral, at which Garvey delivered the oration. *See also* GARVEY, MARCUS; NEWSPAPERS; SCHOMBURG, ARTHUR ALFONSO.

BRYANT, HAZEL J. (1939–   ), singer, actress, producer; born in Zanesville, Ohio. Bryant appeared in European opera houses and on the Off Broadway stage. She was a member of the theater panel of the New York State Council on the Arts, president of the Black Theater Alliance, and a co-producer of the Lincoln Center Street Theater Festival in New York City. Bryant was the founder and director of the Richard Allen Center for Culture and Art and also the director of the Afro-American Total Theater Arts Foundation, Inc., in New York City, which sponsored the Richard Allen Center. *See also* RICHARD ALLEN CENTER FOR CULTURE AND ART.

BRYANT, WILLIAM B. (1911–   ), lawyer, educator, judge; born in Wetumpka, Ala. Bryant graduated from Howard University (Washington, D.C.) in 1932 and received his LL.B. degree from the Howard University School of Law in 1936. He was a member of the Howard University Law School faculty (1935–43), and after four years as a lieutenant colonel in the U.S. Army (1943–47), he started practicing law in Washington, D.C. From 1951 to 1954, he served as an assistant U.S. attorney, leaving that post to open a private law practice. In 1965 Bryant was appointed judge in the U.S. District Court for the District of Columbia, and in 1965 he became professor of law at the Howard University School of Law.

BRYSON, WINFRED OCTAVIUS, JR. (1915–), economist, business executive, educator; born in Tennessee. Bryson received a B.A. degree from Morehouse College (Atlanta, Ga.) in 1936, and a M.A. degree from Atlanta University in 1937, and his Ph.D. degree from the University of Pennsylvania in 1947. He organized, developed, and served as chairman of the department of economics at Morgan State University (Baltimore, Md.) from 1937 to 1972. In 1972 Bryson became director of student activities and professor at the graduate school of Morgan State University. In 1963 he founded and served as president of the Advance Federal Savings and Loan in Baltimore.

BUCKNER, GEORGE WASHINGTON (1855– ?), physician, government official; born in Green County, Ky. Buckner taught school in Kentucky and Indiana (1873–90) and received his M.D. degree from Indiana Eclectic Medical College (ca. 1890). He practiced medicine in Evansville, Ind., for 23 years and was appointed by President Woodrow Wilson as minister to Liberia in 1913. Buckner resigned this post and returned to general practice in Evansville after 1915.

BUCKRA / BAKRA A term of West African origin and use; in early America, reference to a white slave master, or to any white person; *buckaroo* is thought to be derivative. *See also* AFRICAN LEGACY/SURVIVALS.

BUFORD, JULIETTE B. *See* BAHÁ'Í FAITH.

BULLARD, EUGENE JACQUES *See* AVIATORS.

BULLINS, ED (1935–), playwright; born in Philadelphia, Pa. A cofounder of Black Arts West in San Francisco and a member of the Black Arts Alliance, Bullins became associate director and resident playwright of the New Lafayette Theater in New York City's Harlem. He was the editor of *Black Theatre* magazine, of an anthology of contemporary black plays entitled *New Plays From the Black Theatre* (1969), and of *The New Lafayette Theatre Presents: Plays with Aesthetic Comments by 6 Black Playwrights* (1974). Bullins' other works include: *Five Plays* (1968), *How Do You Do: A Nonsense Drama* (1968), *The Hungered One: Early Writ-*

ings (1970), *The Duplex: A Black Love Fable in Four Movements* (1971), *Four Dynamite Plays* (1972), *The Theme Is Blackness: The Corner and Other Plays* (1972), and the novel *The Reluctant Rapist* (1973). *See also* LITERATURE: DRAMA/THEATER.

BULLOCK, WILLIAM HORACE *See* RACE: RACE AND BIOLOGY.

BUNCHE, RALPH JOHNSON (1904–1971), political scientist, educator, government official; born in Detroit, Mich. One of the most prominent Afro-Americans of his generation, Bunche, born in the slums of Detroit, was the son of a barber and his wife—both of whom died when he was a child of eleven—and the grandson of a former slave, who raised him. He went to the University of California on an athletic scholarship, graduating with honors in 1927. The next year, Bunche received a M.A. degree from Harvard University, and afterward he began teaching at Howard University (Washington, D.C.), where he eventually became chairman of the political science department. He returned to Harvard in 1932, and in 1934 completed work on his Ph.D. In the following years, Bunche pursued further graduate

Far right: Ralph Bunche was the first Afro-American to receive the Nobel Peace Prize, which was awarded to him in 1950 for his negotiations in the Arab-Israeli armistice agreements in 1948–49. *(United Nations.)*

studies at Northwestern University, the London School of Economics, and the University of Cape Town, South Africa. He continued his teaching at Howard University for a great part of his career, while at the same time traveling widely in order to expand his research on colonial administration and race relations. Bunche began government service in 1941 in a position with the Office of Strategic Services. He contributed to Gunnar Myrdal's *An American Dilemma* (1944), and later he joined the U.S. Department of State. In two years of service with the state department, he attended numerous conferences, from San Francisco to Paris, distinguishing himself as a statesman and diplomat. In 1946, having helped draw up the portions of the United Nations (UN) charter for all trusteeships and territories, Bunche was selected to head the Trusteeship Division of the UN, and later (1948–1954) served as director of the Department of Trusteeship and Non-Self-Governing Territories. From 1957 to 1967 he served as undersecretary of Special Political Affairs. In 1968 he became undersecretary general, the highest rank held by an American at the UN. During these UN years, Bunche carried out several special diplomatic missions that made his name and reputation familiar throughout the world. In 1948 he headed the peace-seeking Palestine commission that brought temporary peace to the Arab-Israel conflict in 1949. As a result of these efforts, he was awarded the Nobel Prize for Peace in 1950. In 1960 he was the special UN representative to the Congo and in 1963 to Yemen. As a special emissary, he also visited the Suez, Kashmir, and Cyprus. In 1963 he received the Presidential Medal of Freedom.

BUNTON, HENRY CLAY (1903–   ), Christian Methodist Episcopal bishop; born in Tuscaloosa County, Ala. Bunton received a B.D. degree from Florida Agricultural and Mechanical (A & M) College in 1941, and his Th.M. degree from Iliff School of Theology in 1952. He was pastor of Christian Methodist Episcopal (CME) churches in Alabama, Florida, Arkansas, Texas, Colorado, and Tennessee. In 1962 Bunton was elected bishop of the Seventh Episcopal District of the CME Church.

BURDICK, BENJAMIN D. (1903–   ), lawyer, judge; born in Lawrence, Mass. After receiving his J.D. degree from Wayne State University Law School (Detroit, Mich.) in 1928, Burdick served as chief public administrator of Wayne County

for six years. He was appointed judge of the Circuit Court of Wayne County in 1963 and was later reelected for a full term. In 1972 Burdick became a judge of the U.S. Third Judicial Circuit.

BUREAU OF REFUGEES FREEDMEN AND ABANDONED LANDS *See* AFRO-AMERICAN HISTORY: THE FREEDMEN'S BUREAU, 1865–1872.

BURGESS, JOHN MELVILLE (1909–   ), Episcopal bishop; born in Grand Rapids, Mich. Burgess received B.A. and M.A. degrees from the University of Michigan, and his B.D. degree from the Episcopal Theological Seminary. He served mission churches in Michigan and Ohio for 12 years, was the Episcopal chaplain at Howard University (Washington, D.C.) from 1946 to 1951 and canon at Washington Cathedral from 1951 to 1956. In 1956 Burgess became archdeacon of Boston and supervisor of the Episcopal City Mission. He was elected bishop in 1969, heading the diocese of Massachusetts, and thus becoming the first Afro-American to preside over a diocese of the Protestant Episcopal Church in America. *See also* EPISCOPALIANS.

BURKE, LILLIAN W. (1917–   ), lawyer, judge; born in Thomaston, Ga. Burke graduated from Ohio State University in 1947 and from the Cleveland-Marshall College of Law at Cleveland State University in 1951. She was admitted to the Ohio bar in 1951. Burke was an assistant attorney general for the State of Ohio, vice-chairman of the Ohio Industrial Commission, and president of the National Council of Negro Women. In 1969 she was appointed to complete an unexpired term on the municipal court in Cleveland. That same year, Burke won election for a full term as municipal court judge and became the first Afro-American woman judge elected to an Ohio bench.

BURKE, YVONNE WATSON BRATHWAITE lawyer, U.S. Representative; born in Los Angeles, Calif. Burke received a B.A. degree from the University of California at Los Angeles and her LL.B. degree from the University of Southern California in 1956, the same year she was admitted to the California bar. Burke served as deputy corporation commissioner for the state of California and hearing officer for the police commission. She was an attorney for the McCone Commission, which investigated the Watts rebellion of 1965, and was elected to the California assembly in 1966 and again in 1968. Burke presided over several sessions of the 1972 Democratic National Convention, and she was elected representative to the U.S. Congress from the 37th Congressional District in Los Angeles in 1972.

BURLEIGH, HARRY T. (THACKER) (1866–1949), singer, composer; born in Erie, Pa. Burleigh received a scholarship to study at the National Conservatory of Music in New York, and he remained there for four years. In 1894, having applied for a position as soloist in the choir of St. George's Episcopal Church in New York, he began more than 50 years of singing and soloing in this church. At the turn of the century, Burleigh joined the choir of Temple Emanu-El in New York, singing there for 25 years, the only black singer in one of the largest synagogue choirs in the country. On the concert stages of the United States and Europe, he was one of the first performers to introduce Negro spirituals; in fact, he began to set down and arrange spirituals that had never been written down. Burleigh made concert arrangements for more than 100 spirituals, thus preserving a body of music that otherwise would have been lost. He also composed more than 250 songs, ballads, anthems, and violin pieces. Toward the end of his career, he was musical editor for G. Ricordi and Sons, music publisher, in New York. In 1941 Burleigh became the first Negro to serve on the board of directors of the American Society of Composers, Authors, and Publishers. *See also* MUSIC: SPIRITUALS/ORIGINS.

BURLEY, DAN (1907–62), journalist; born in Lexington, Ky. After having lived briefly in Texas, Burley and his family moved North, where he graduated from high school and later joined the staff of the Chicago *Defender* as a copy boy. He worked on the staffs of the *Bee* and the *Telegram* in Chicago, before becoming managing editor of the *New Crusader*. Subsequently, Burley moved to New York City, where he was sports writer, columnist, and editor of the *Amsterdam News* (1937–48). He became an associate editor for Johnson Publications upon his return to Chicago, and there he began a small news magazine of his own, a weekly called *The Owl*. Burley's column in the Chicago *Defender* and the *Amsterdam News*, "Back Door Stuff," sounded like a "hep" Walter Winchell, and displayed his sharp wit. As an amateur pianist performing at rent parties, he was credited with inventing the tech-

nique known as "riffling" the keys. Burley's jive columns have been anthologized several times, and he was the author of *The Original Dictionary of Harlem Jive* (1944).

BURNS, HAYWOOD (1941–   ), lawyer, educator. Burns was an honor student in history at Harvard University, where he received a B.A. degree in 1962. He attended Cambridge University in England as a Lionel de Jersey Harvard Student and received his LL.D. degree from Yale University. Burns was a staff member in the Civil Rights Division of the U.S. Department of Justice, a legal intern with the New Haven Legal Assistance Association, and a law clerk for the Hon. Constance B. Motley, the first black woman to serve as a district court judge in the United States. He was also a faculty member of the New York University Law School. Burns defended the Black Panthers, black students at Cornell University, and Angela Davis. He was the author of "Can a Black Man Get a Fair Trial," published in the New York *Times* in 1970.

BURRELL, BERKELEY GRAHAM (1919–79), business executive, civic and social leader; born in Washington, D.C. After attending Howard University (Washington, D.C.) Burrell became an executive of a dry-cleaning firm, and in 1962 he was named president of the National Business League. He served as vice-chairman of the President's Advisory Council on Minority Business Enterprises and was a member of the National Business Council for Consumer Affairs.

BURROWS, VINIE *See* LITERATURE: DRAMA/THEATER.

BURTON, JOHN H. (1910–   ), labor union leader, mayor; born in St. Louis, Mo. Burton served on the city council of Ypsilanti, Mich., for 18 years, after which he was elected mayor. He served on many civic boards and received the Man of the Year citation from the Ford Motor Company. Burton was a representative of the International United Auto Workers Union in Detroit.

BUSH, MYRON B. (? –1971), lawyer; born in Cincinnati, Ohio. Bush received his LL.D. degree from the University of Iowa, and practiced law in Cincinnati until his death. He was the first Afro-American to be elected to the city council in Cincinnati.

BUSINESS

BUSINESS Some blacks managed and owned small businesses throughout the slave period. However, they were free persons. For example, Samuel Fraunces was a successful tavern owner in New York City (1770s); Paul Cuffe was a shipper and merchant of New England (ca. 1790–1810); James Wormley (1820–85) was a well-known hotel proprietor in Washington, D.C.; William Johnson was a well-to-do barber-businessman in antebellum Natchez, Miss.; and Isaac Myers was an owner and organizer of a marine drydock company in Baltimore, Md., after the Civil War. However, like so much of a free black's life in slaveholding America, black businesses were precarious.

After slavery, Afro-Americans began to acquire more property and relatively more capital. An increasing number began to set up establishments that rendered personal services, especially for the needs of blacks who were victims of discrimination and segregation imposed by white businesses. For example, barbering had historically been a source of both black employment and business; it was a type of activity expected of blacks, in the North and the South, as was bootblacking, food catering, and table-waiting. Later, hairstyling and beauty culture (especially for women) provided sources of employment. Two of the earliest and greatest fortunes among Afro-Americans were made by Annie M. Turnbo Malone and Madame C. J. Walker in the manufacture and marketing of hair preparations for blacks (products such as "Poro," "Heroline," and "Black and White") during the first half of the twentieth century. (*See* COSMETOLOGY.) Funeral services were another personal-service business almost exclusively under black ownership and control.

Supplying personal services has remained an outstanding feature of black businesses. Though such black pursuits as barbering and funeral services still remain almost exclusively for blacks,

The Chesapeake Marine Railway and Dry Dock Company in a lithograph (1870s) by E. A. Sachse. The business was owned and operated by black Americans, 1866–1884; a principal organizer was Isaac Myers, a free-born black caulker of Baltimore. *(Reproduced by permission of the Enoch Pratt Free Library, Baltimore, Md.)*

the position, priority, and magnitude of these services have been superseded by filling stations, restaurants, and food stores.

Characteristics Whether in services or other areas, black business has certain common characteristics that may be summarized as follows: (1) Black business is only a small fraction of the total American business system. While blacks constitute about 11 percent of the total population (1975), they own less than one percent of all businesses. If all of American business was represented by one dollar, the size of the black amount would be about half a penny. The supreme fact of economic life is that blacks have been—and remain—essentially laborers in the American economy, not owners and managers; and even as laborers, they were and are discriminated against in wage earnings. Discrimination has also prevented access to finance markets, so essential in business enterprise. (2) Nearly half of all black business is concentrated in three retail businesses in this order of rank: filling stations, food stores, and restaurants. (3) The average black business employs only about 3 or 4 persons. (4) There were nearly 195,000 black-owned firms in 1972; of these, 182,000 (93.6 percent) were sole proprietorships that accounted for 57.8 percent of gross receipts; 8,500 (4.3 percent) were partnerships that accounted for 11.3 percent of gross receipts; and 4,000 (2.1 percent) were corporations that accounted for 30.9 percent of gross receipts. (5) Most black firms are located in the Southern Atlantic states. (6) The greatest need in black business is finance capital. This recognized need led to two developments in the 1960s and 1970s: one was *black capitalism*, a political-economy philosophy asserting that black businessmen must ultimately own and control black economic destiny (more orthodox economists have questioned this concept). The other was the recognized need for government aid, which was provided through the federal Office of Minority Business Enterprise (OMBE).

Leading Firms Excluding banks, insurance companies, and savings-and-loan establishments, the 100 individual firms listed below were owned or managed by Afro-Americans in 1975:

100 LARGEST AFRO-AMERICAN FIRMS: 1975

Rank, Company, location	Chief executive	Business	Year started	Employees	1975 Sales: (million dollars)
1 MOTOWN INDUSTRIES Los Angeles, Calif.	Berry Gordy, Jr.	Entertainment	1959	300	$43.50
2 JOHNSON PUBLISHING CO., INC. Chicago, Ill.	John H. Johnson	Publishing and cosmetics	1942	300	41.00
3 JOHNSON PRODUCTS CO., INC. Chicago, Ill.	George E. Johnson	Hair products and cosmetics mfg.	1954	459	39.00
4 FEDCO FOODS CORP. Bronx, N.Y.	J. Bruce Llewellyn	Supermarkets	1969	500	36.00
5 THE GREAT PHILADELPHIA TRADING CO., LTD. Philadelphia, Pa.	Kenny Gamble	Music, record production	1967	40	16.10
6 GARLAND FOODS, INC. Dallas, Tex.	Mildred M. Montgomery	Ham processing	1969	165	15.87
7 H. G. PARKS, INC. Baltimore, Md.	Henry G. Parks, Jr.	Sausage and meat specialties mfg.	1951	240	13.06
8 SUPER PRIDE MARKETS Baltimore, Md.	Charles Burns	Supermarkets	1970	219	12.00
9 DICK GIDRON CADILLAC Bronx, N.Y.	Richard D. Gidron	Automobile dealership	1972	72	11.80
10 CAPITOL CITY LIQUOR CO., INC. Washington, D.C.	Chester C. Carter	Wine and liquor import and distribution	1970	57	10.50
11 SECURITY MEAT INDUSTRIES, INC. Philadelphia, Pa.	Roderick G. Thomas	Beef boning	1971	68	9.61

100 Largest Afro-American Firms: 1975 (Continued)

12 DRUMMOND DISTRIBUTING CO., INC. Compton, Calif.	Lance E. Drummond	Wholesale liquor distribution	1969	40	9.00
13 WALLACE & WALLACE FUEL OIL CO., INC. St. Albans, N.Y.	Charles Wallace	Retail petroleum products	1969	40	8.79
14 WALLACE & WALLACE CHEMICAL & OIL CORP. St. Albans, N.Y.	Charles Wallace	Refining; wholesale and import of crude oil	1972	31	8.62
15 H. J. RUSSELL CONSTRUCTION CO., INC. Atlanta, Ga.	Herman J. Russell	Construction and development	1958	300	8.50
16 AL JOHNSON CADILLAC Chicago, Ill.	Al W. Johnson, Sr.	Automobile dealership	1967	90	8.00
17 CENTURY CHEVROLET, INC. Upper Darby, Pa.	Robert L. Myers, Jr.	Automobile dealership	1971	50	7.50
18 CONYERS FORD, INC. Detroit, Mich.	Nathan G. Conyers	Automobile dealership	1970	68	7.25
19 UNIQUE PLASTICS DIV., INC., OF ECEER, INC. Cincinnati, Ohio	Samuel Reece	Design, development, and manufacture of plastic products	1968	69	6.80
20 SENGSTACKE ENTERPRISES, INC. Chicago, Ill.	John H. Sengstacke	Newspaper publishing	1936	190	6.49
21 ALL-PRO ENTERPRISES, INC. Pittsburgh, Pa.	Brady Keys, Jr.	Fast-food restaurants	1968	525	6.10
22 WATTS MFG. CORP. Lynwood, Calif.	Mark E. Rivers, Jr.	Metal & fabric products mfg.	1970	260	6.00
23 THE KENWOOD CO., INC. New York, N.Y.	Kenneth N. Sherwood	Furniture, retailing, and property management	1965	55	5.70
24 THACKER CONSTRUCTION CO. Alton, Ill.	Floyd O. Thacker	Road and airport heavy construction	1970	200	5.67
25 MICON CONSTRUCTION & DEVELOPMENT CORP. Lynbrook, N.Y.	Charles Peay	General construction	1972	5	5.62
26 SYPHAX ENTERPRISES Arlington, Va.	William T. Syphax	Construction and management	1969	40	5.51
27 BILL NELSON CHEVROLET, INC. Richmond, Calif.	William W. Nelson	Automobile dealership	1969	50	5.50
27 WILLIE DAVIS DISTRIBUTING CO. Los Angeles, Calif.	Willie Davis	Beer distributor	1970	43	5.50
29 FIESTA LINCOLN/MERCURY, INC. Queens Village, N.Y.	William J. Phillips	Automobile dealership	1969	35	5.40
30 BLANCHARD MANAGEMENT CORP. New York, N.Y.	Blanchard W. Robinson	Food service management	1973	187	5.33
31 D.P.S. PROTECTION SYSTEMS, INC. New York, N.Y.	Dale R. Michael	Security services and products	1974	830	5.27
32 ESSENCE COMMUNICATIONS, INC. New York, N.Y.	Edward Lewis	Magazine publishing	1969	39	5.20
33 PARKER HOUSE SAUSAGE CO. Chicago, Ill.	Daryl F. Grisham	Sausage mfg.	1921	104	5.20
34 TUESDAY PUBLICATIONS, INC. Chicago, Ill.	W. Leonard Evans, Jr.	Publishing	1965	40	5.19
35 R. L. DUKES OLDSMOBILE, INC. Chicago, Ill.	Rufus L. Dukes	Automobile dealership	1971	40	5.11

100 Largest Afro-American Firms: 1975 (Continued)

36 GOLDEN BIRD, INC. Los Angeles, Calif.	Willie J. Stennis	Fast-food chain	1958	235	5.10
37 B & T METALS CO. Columbus, Ohio	Lawrence J. Tolbert	Aluminum extrusion and decorative trims	1930	200	5.00
37 CHIOKE INTERNATIONAL CORP. New York, N.Y.	Christopher E. Chioke	Equipment marketing and leasing, automotive exports	1970	8	5.00
37 COCOLINE CHOCOLATE CO., INC. Brooklyn, N.Y.	Leonard Halpert	Chocolate products mfg.	1973	100	5.00
37 TOMBS & SONS, INC. Bonner Springs, Kans.	Leroy C. Tombs	Food-catering service	1971	1,500	5.00
41 TRANS-BAY ENGINEERS & BUILDERS, INC. Oakland, Calif.	Ray Dones	General contracting	1969	26	4.99
42 T.W.O./HILLMAN'S, INC, Chicago, Ill.	Lawrence W. Carroll	Supermarkets	1968	63	4.93
43 VASSALL MOTORS, INC. Philadelphia, Pa.	Ivan Vassall	Automobile dealership	1969	37	4.65
44 GORDON BUICK, INC. Philadelphia, Pa.	Darrell R. Gordon	Automobile dealership	1972	29	4.63
45 BOB SMITH CHEVROLET, INC. Louisville, Ky.	Robert W. Smith	Automobile dealership	1972	64	4.60
46 MERCER CADILLAC, INC. Alton, Ill.	Calvin Mercer	Automobile dealership	1973	29	4.52
47 CALIFORNIA GOLDEN OAK PRODUCTS, INC. Los Angeles, Calif.	William M. Alexander	Wood office furniture mfg.	1968	107	4.51
48 KC DODGE, INC. San Francisco, Calif.	Todd S. Cochran	Automobile and truck dealership	1968	35	4.50
49 PROGRESS AEROSPACE ENTERPRISES, INC. Philadelphia, Pa.	Frederick E. Miller	Electronics products mfg.	1968	115	4.49
50 CEDAR LEE CHRYSLER PLYMOUTH, INC. Cleveland Hts., Ohio	Burton D. Clemons	Automobile dealership	1974	37	4.46
51 EDMUNDS BUICK, INC. Kansas City, Mo.	McKinley H. Edmunds	Automobile dealership	1974	35	4.43
52 BUSH CONSTRUCTION CO., INC. Chicago, Ill.	Ernest Bush	General contracting	1963	41	4.34
53 MAIN FOOD SERVICE OF BUFFALO, INC. Buffalo, N.Y.	Carl A. Mackin	Supermarket	1972	75	4.25
54 PORTERFIELD WILSON PONTIAC, INC. Detroit, Mich.	Porterfield Wilson	Automobile dealership	1970	43	4.00
55 SAM JOHNSON METRO LINCOLN/ MERCURY, INC. East St. Louis, Ill.	Sam Johnson	Automobile dealership	1973	29	3.99
56 WHITE BUICK, INC. Mandhester, N.H.	Luther J. White	Automobile dealership	1974	24	3.98
57 C. H. JAMES & CO. Charleston, W. Va.	Charles H. James III	Wholesale foods	1883	30	3.98
58 JONES & ARTIS CONSTRUCTION CO., INC. Washington, D.C.	Carl D. Jones	Concrete and underground construction; paving	1972	125	3.83

100 Largest Afro-American Firms: 1975 (Continued)

59	HORACE NOBLE LINCOLN/MERCURY, INC. Chicago, Ill.	Horace Noble	Automobile dealership	1970	29	3.76
60	GREEN GARDENS, INC. Jersey City, N.J.	Rudolph V. Green	Supermarket	1972	60	3.71
61	THE AFRO-AMERICAN CO. OF BALTIMORE CITY Baltimore, Md.	John H. Murphy III	Newspaper publishing	1892	205	3.63
62	CHUCK WHITE BUICK, INC. Chicago, Ill.	Charles H. White	Automobile dealership	1971	30	3.60
63	DELTA ENTERPRISES, INC. Greenville, N.C.	Charles D. Bannerman	Diversified mfg.	1969	250	3.56
64	E. G. GRAVES PUBLSHING CO., INC. New York, N.Y.	Earl G. Graves	Publishing	1970	39	3.55
65	URBAN MECHANICAL CO., INC. Bronx, N.Y.	Fred Clarke	Mechanical contractor	1969	100	3.54
66	E. SIMMONS MOVING & WRECKING CONTRACTOR, INC. Syracuse, N.Y.	Eric Simmons, Sr.	Demolition, paving, and excavating	1945	34	3.50
67	ASKEW DISTRIBUTING CO. Chicago, Ill.	James R. Askew	Wholesale beer distributor	1973	18	3.50
67	EBONY OIL CORP. Jamaïca, N.Y.	Lawrence J. Cormier	Retail fuel oil and heating equipment	1956	40	3.50
69	OASIS FORD Newhall, Calif.	David J. Babb	Automobile dealership	1972	27	3.49
70	BOB ROSS BUICK, INC. Richmond, Ind.	Robert P. Ross	Automobile and truck dealership	1974	46	3.46
71	JIM BRADLEY PONTIAC-GMC, INC. Ann Arbor, Mich.	James H. Bradley	Automobile and truck dealership	1973	35	3.44
72	LOWERY DISTRIBUTING CO., INC. Chicago, Ill.	Winifred E. Lowery	Beer distributor	1969	20	3.40
73	PRO-LINE CORP. Gardena, Calif.	Comer J. Cottrell	Cosmetics mfg.	1970	53	3.26
74	ROBERTS MOTELS, INC. Chicago, Ill.	Herman Roberts, Sr.	Motel	1961	297	3.20
75	EWING ENTERPRISES, INC. Indianapolis, Ind.	Robert L. Ewing	Grocery retailing	1972	52	3.12
76	INNER CITY BROADCASTING CORP. New York, N.Y.	Pierre Sutton	Broadcasting	1972	48	3.10
76	RICHFIELD PACKING CO. Palmetto, Fla.	James Woodson	Produce shipping and cultivation	1964	400	3.10
76	STATUM CHEVROLET, INC. Salem, Va.	H. S. Statum	Automobile dealership	1974	35	3.10
79	OZANNE CONSTRUCTION CO., INC. Cleveland, Ohio	Leroy Ozanne	Commercial and industrial construction	1956	11	3.05
80	ALL-STAINLESS, INC. Hingham, Mass.	Eugene V. Roundtree	Stainless steel industrial supplies	1952	40	3.00
81	LAWNDALE PACKAGING CORP. Chicago, Ill.	Dennis Manthe	Box and container mfg.	1968	72	2.90
82	YONKERS PLATE GLASS, INC. Yonkers, N.Y.	Delton Walker	Architectural metalwork; glass and glazing	1960	45	2.80

100 Largest Afro-American Firms: 1975 (Continued)

83 JAMES PONTIAC, INC. Oakland, Calif.	Claude I. James	Automobile dealership	1971	34	2.76
84 BOB NEAL PONTIAC-TOYOTA, INC. Chicago, Ill.	Robert P. Neal	Automobile dealership	1966	20	2.75
85 H. F. HENDERSON INDUSTRIES West Caldwell, N.J.	Henry F. Henderson, Jr.	Mfg. weighing systems and control panels	1954	35	2.75
86 AMNEWS CORP. New York, N.Y.	John L. Procope	Newspaper publishing	1909	105	2.70
87 G. E. WASH CONSTRUCTION CO. Detroit, Mich.	Glen E. Wash	General contracting	1968	36	2.64
88 GEORGE WHITE OLDSMOBILE, INC. Cincinnati, Ohio	George W. White	Automobile dealership	1974	29	2.62
89 TERRY MFG. CO., INC. Roanoke, Ala.	Roy Terry	Apparel mfg.	1963	95	2.57
90 CENTRAL NEWS-WAVE PUBLICATIONS, INC. Los Angeles, Calif.	Chester L. Washington	Newspaper publishing	1971	84	2.53
91 D & H TIRE SERVICE CO. Kansas City, Kans.	Luther Davis White	Tire sales and service	1965	50	2.50
91 TOP VALUE FOOD MART, INC. Cleveland, Ohio	Davis Collier	Retail groceries	1972	30	2.50
91 MITCHOM GENERAL CONTRACTING CO. East St. Louis, Ill.	Robert Mitchom	General contracting	1969	20	2.50
94 LANCE INVESTIGATION SERVICE, INC. Bronx, N.Y.	Ralph V. Johnson	Security guard service	1962	380	2.42
95 FOSTER CHEMICALS, INC. Detroit, Mich.	George H. Hill	Cleaning compound and water treatment product mfg.	1971	30	2.40
95 NATIONAL BLACK NETWORK New York, N.Y.	Eugene D. Jackson	Radio broadcasting	1972	50	2.40
97 L. H. SMITH OIL CORP. Indianapolis, Ind.	Lannie H. Smith, Jr.	Fuel oil	1964	32	2.34
98 WM. CARGILE CONTRACTOR, INC. Cincinati, Ohio	William Cargile III	General contracting	1957	20	2.32
99 BLATCHE'S FOODS, INC. Hartford, Conn.	Emerson Blatche	Supermarket	1973	18	2.30
100 AULT INC. Minneapolis, Minn.	Luther T. Prince, Jr.	Magnetic components and power supplies mfg.	1967	100	2.27

Insurance Insurance grew out of the need for mutual aid among free blacks. Like so much else in the history of Afro-Americans, mutual aid developed within religious bodies or groups closely associated with churches. The Free African Society, founded by Absalom Jones and Richard Allen, was a pioneer organization for mutual aid in the last quarter of the eighteenth century. Mutual aid was also one of the benefits offered by membership in scores of fraternal societies founded before the Civil War. The pool-ing of mutual aid interests and savings from various churches, fraternal societies, and mutual benefit and burial societies eventually led to the formation of the first black insurance company after the Civil War. This development received impetus in 1884 when more than 2,000 delegates, representing 40 Afro-American organizations, met in Baltimore, Md., to discuss the problems of mutual aid among Afro-Americans. Nine years later the Southern Aid Society was chartered in Richmond, Va., a company whose existence may be regarded as the formal beginning of Afro-American life insurance.

The increase of black insurance companies after the turn of the century led to the establishment of the National Insurance Association (NIA). The NIA was formed in 1921 at a meeting held at the home office of the North Carolina Mutual Life Insurance Company in Durham by 60 men representing 13 black insurance companies (the group was then known as the National Negro Insurance Association). Among the principal founders of the association were: C. C. Spaulding (who became the first president), W. Ellis Stewart, W. S. Hornsby, C. B. Gilpin, G. W. Cox, W. A. Attaway, E. M. Martin, W. H. Lee, M. S. Stuart, L. T. Burbridge, Anthony Overton, Wayne W. Cox, Harry H. Pace, J. E. Walker, A. L. Lewis, Fred L. Gillespie, T. K. Gibson, C. A. Shaw, and J. L. Wheeler.

Data on black insurance companies are given in the table below:

Main office of North Carolina Mutual Insurance Company, Durham, N.C. *(Courtesy of the company.)*

AFRO-AMERICAN INSURANCE COMPANIES: 1975

Company	Location	Chief executive 1976	Year started	Total assets*	Insurance in force* (million dollars)
1 NORTH CAROLINA MUTUAL LIFE INSURANCE CO.	Durham, N.C.	W. J. Kennedy III	1898	145.696	2,256.419
2 SUPREME LIFE INSURANCE CO. OF AMERICA	Chicago, Ill.	John H. Johnson	1919	46.144	2,002.427
3 GOLDEN STATE MUTUAL LIFE INSURANCE CO.	Los Angeles, Calif.	Ivan J. Houston	1925	59.223	1,729.951
4 CHICAGO METROPOLITAN MUTUAL ASSURANCE CO.	Chicago, Ill.	Anderson M. Schweich	1927	32.656	524.303
5 ATLANTA LIFE INSURANCE CO.	Atlanta, Ga.	Jesse Hill, Jr.	1905	87.814	502.280
6 UNIVERSAL LIFE INSURANCE CO.	Memphis, Tenn.	A. M. Walker, Sr.	1923	46.633	299.625
7 BOOKER T. WASHINGTON INSURANCE CO., INC.	Birmingham, Ala.	A. G. Gaston, Sr.	1923	13.525	182.540
8 MAMMOTH LIFE & ACCIDENT INSURANCE CO.	Louisville, Ky.	Julius E. Price, Sr.	1915	23.700	167.200
9 PILGRIM HEALTH AND LIFE INSURANCE CO.	Augusta, Ga.	W. S. Hornsby	1898	14.499	130.298
10 PURPLE SHIELD LIFE INSURANCE CO.	Baton Rouge, La.	Homer J. Sheeler, Sr.	1949	1.112	125.523
11 AFRO-AMERICAN LIFE INSURANCE CO.	Jacksonville, Fla.	James L. Lewis, Jr,	1901	10.929	123.828

Afro-American Insurance Companies: 1975 (*Continued*)

12	WINSTON MUTUAL LIFE INSURANCE CO.	Winston-Salem, N.C.	Selena Hayes Hall	1906	4.609	58.398
13	AMERICAN WOODMEN'S LIFE INSURANCE CO.	Denver, Colo.	James H. Browne	1966	9.701	52.294
14	UNITED MUTUAL LIFE INSURANCE CO.	New York, N.Y.	Nathaniel Gibbon, Jr.	1933	9.464	45.227
15	WINNFIELD LIFE INSURANCE CO.	Natchitoches, La.	Ben D. Johnson	1936	2.649	44.468
16	SOUTHERN AID LIFE INSURANCE CO.	Richmond, Va.	E. S. Thomas III	1893	4.449	37.310
17	CENTRAL LIFE INSURANCE CO.	Tampa, Fla.	Edward D. Davis	1922	6.702	36.849
18	PEOPLES LIFE INSURANCE CO. OF ALABAMA	New Orleans, La.	Benjamin J. Johnson	1922	4.128	33.899
19	PROTECTIVE INDUSTRIAL INSURANCE CO. OF ALABAMA	Birmingham, Ala.	Virgil L. Harris	1923	4.562	30.542
20	VIRGINIA MUTUAL BENEFIT LIFE INSURANCE CO.	Richmond, Va.	Richard W. Foster	1933	4.201	20.729
21	UNITY LIFE INSURANCE CO.	Mobile, Ala.	Roger E. Allen	1928	1.584	20.336
22	UNION PROTECTIVE LIFE INSURANCE CO.	Memphis, Tenn.	C. A. Rawls	1933	3.569	19.409
23	GERTRUDE GEDDĒS WILLIS LIFE INSURANCE CO.	New Orleans, La.	Joseph O. Misshore, Jr.	1941	1.777	17.035
24	GOLDEN CIRCLE LIFE INSURANCE CO.	Brownsville, Tenn.	C. A. Rawls	1958	3.213	16.719
25	WRIGHT MUTUAL INSURANCE CO.	Detroit, Mich.	Wardell C. Croft	1942	2.742	15.518
26	RELIABLE LIFE INSURANCE CO.	Monroe, La.	Joseph H. Miller, Jr.	1940	0.765	14.420
27	CHRISTIAN BENEVOLENT INSURANCE CO., INC.	Mobile, Ala.	W. Madison Cooper	1926	1.004	13.041
28	KEYSTONE LIFE INSURANCE CO.	New Orleans, La.	Jesse Hill, Jr.	1941	1.175	11.970
29	BENEVOLENT LIFE INSURANCE CO.	Shreveport, La.	Granville L. Smith	1934	0.878	10.879
30	NATIONAL SERVICE INDUSTRIAL LIFE INSURANCE CO.	New Orleans, La.	Duplain W. Rhodes	1948	1.368	9.543
31	SECURITY LIFE INSURANCE CO. OF THE SOUTH	Jackson, Miss.	W. H. Williams	1940	1.039	7.582
32	MAJESTIC LIFE INSURANCE CO.	New Orleans, La.	Adam R. Haydel	1947	0.624	6.632
33	BRADFORD'S INDUSTRIAL INSURANCE CO.	Birmingham, Ala.	Daniel Kennon, Jr.	1932	1.137	6.321
34	LIGHTHOUSE LIFE INSURANCE CO.	Shreveport, La.	Bunyan Jacobs, Sr.	1945	0.456	5.713

ARO-AMERICAN INSURANCE COMPANIES : 1975 (*Continued*)

35	SUPERIOR LIFE INSURANCE CO.	Baton Rouge, La.	J. K. Haynes	1954	0.346	5.089
36	LOVETT'S LIFE AND BURIAL INSURANCE CO.	Mobile, Ala.	L. M. Lovett	1950	0.409	5.073
37	SOUTHERN LIFE INSURANCE CO.	Baltimore, Md.	Milton E. Branch, Jr.	1906	1.215	3.706
38	UNITED FIDELITY VICTORY LIFE INSURANCE CO.	New Orleans, La.	Duplain W. Rhodes	1971	0.658	2.926

*As of December 31, 1975. Companies are ranked by insurance in force.
Source: *Black Enterprise*, June 1976.

See *also* BANKS; EMPLOYMENT; FRATERNAL SOCIETIES; PORO.

REFERENCES: In addition to the references listed at the end of BANKS, the following are also suggested: Brimmer, Andrew F., "The Black Revolution and the Economic Future of Negroes in the United States," *American Scholar*, vol. 38, pp. 629–43, 1969; Bell, Carolyn Shaw, *The Economics of the Ghetto*, Pegasus, New York, 1972; Thomas, Bettye C., "A Nineteenth Century Black Operated Shipyard, 1866–1884: Reflections Upon Its Inception and Ownership," *Journal of Negro History*, January 1974, pp. 1–12; and Weare, Walter B., *Black Business in the New South: A Social History of the North Carolina Mutual Life Insurance Company*, University of Illinois Press, Urbana, 1973. Two serials are also helpful. The first is *Survey of Minority-Owned Businesses*, special reports by the U.S. Bureau of the Census, first published in 1969 and again in 1974 (data for 1972); the two studies are parallel for the most part and cover such statistical data as number of firms, gross receipts, and number of employees distributed geographically. The other serial is *Black Enterprise* (circulation 175,000 in 1975), a monthly magazine that was begun in New York City in 1970 by Earl G. Graves; it supplies information on black economic development and marketing.

BUSINESS SCHOOLS The history of business education in the United States as a whole falls roughly into three periods: the beginning or experimental period, when business training first began to move beyond the apprenticeship system into evening training classes (1834–50); the private school evolution, when public education systems took little or no notice of business education, which was available only for a fee in institutions that offered the most rudimentary instruction (1850–90); and the emergence of business education in secondary schools, colleges, and universities, when private schools were forced by competition to upgrade their courses (1890 to present).

For Afro-Americans, however, little access to business training was available prior to the end of World War II. As long as occupational opportunities were restricted in the general business mainstream, Afro-Americans were not encouraged to enroll in available business courses in public schools, and they were sometimes prevented from attending such courses by prohibitive prerequisites. Chiefly for those reasons, as well as the lack of trained leadership, no black private business schools existed before that time.

On the college level, as far back as 1899, a conference sponsored by Atlanta University recommended that Negroes participate more in business and that colleges offer courses that would prepare them for business activity. However, until Fisk University offered "applied economics" studies in 1917, black colleges and universities concentrated on classical and theological curricula to prepare graduates for the occupations most open to them, teaching and preaching. By 1924 six Afro-American colleges offered business courses leading to a degree; by 1940 there were more than 20; and by the 1970s a business curriculum existed in most black colleges.

Following the war years, as business opportunities opened up for blacks, private business schools began to appear. Among the first were Durham Business College (Durham, N.C.) founded in 1947, and the Cortez Peters Business School (Washington, D.C., with a branch in Baltimore, Md.). In answer to increasing demand, black private business schools were rapidly founded in almost every major city across the country.

An important development in business training available to blacks was the formation of the Institute for Minority Business Education (MBE) at Howard University (Washington, D.C.) under the auspices of the federal government in 1970–71. See *also* BUSINESS; EDUCATION.

BUSING See EDUCATION: DEVELOPMENTS IN ELEMENTARY AND SECONDARY EDUCATION.

BUTCHER, GEORGE H. (1879–1950), dentist; born in Washington, D.C. Butcher received his D.D.S. degree from Howard University College of Dentistry (Washington, D.C.) in 1903 and joined the Robert T. Freeman Dental Society, Inc., of Washington, D.C., in 1904. He was the first visiting dentist to Freedmen's Hospital, Washington, D.C.; dentist for the children in the Industrial Home, Blue Plains (1920–50); and one of the organizers of the Tri-State Dental Society, comprised of black dentists from Maryland, Virginia, and the District of Columbia (1913). Butcher served as secretary, vice-president, chairman of the executive board, and president of the Robert T. Freeman Dental Society, Inc., and he was an honorary member of the National Dental Association. *See also* NATIONAL DENTAL ASSOCIATION.

BUTCHER, MARGARET JUST *See* LOCKE, ALAIN LEROY.

BUTCHER, PHILIP (1918–   ), educator, administrator; born in Washington, D.C. Butcher received a B.A. degree from Howard University (Washington, D.C.) in 1942 and a M.A. degree (1947) and his Ph.D. degree (1956) from Columbia University. He served on the faculty at Morgan State University (Baltimore, Md.) after 1947 and later became dean of the graduate school there. Butcher contributed many articles to scholarly journals, and wrote several books, including: *George W. Cable: The Northampton Years* (1959), *George W. Cable* (1962), and *The William Stanley Braithwaite Reader* (1972).

BUTLER, BROADUS NATHANIEL (1920–   ), educator; born in Mobile, Ala. Butler received a B.A. degree from Talladega College (Talladega, Ala.) in 1941, and a M.A. degree (1947) and his Ph.D. degree (1952) from the University of Michigan. He taught philosophy at Saint Augustine's College (Raleigh, N.C.) in 1953 and at Talladega College from 1953 to 1956, and he served as assistant to the dean and in the graduate office at Wayne State University (Detroit, Mich.) from 1959 to 1969. Butler was assistant to the commissioner, U.S. Office of Education, Washington, D.C., from 1964 to 1967, and associate director of Project PRESCAD (Preschool and Adolescent Children), Wayne State University after 1966. He served as dean of Texas Southern University in 1969 and as president of Dillard University (New Orleans, La.) from 1969 to 1973. Butler was appointed director of the Office of Leadership Development, Higher Education, American Council of Education in 1974.

BUTLER, FRANK S. (1883– ?), educator, composer; born in Philadelphia, Pa. Butler attended the Institute of Musical Art (New York, N.Y.). He became a piano teacher of note, and founded the Butler Piano School in 1914. All of his knowledge of technique, theory, and composition were expounded in his instruction book, *Master School of Professional Piano Playing,* for which he is best known. Additionally, he composed many pieces for the piano.

BUTTS, HUGH F. (1926–   ), psychiatrist; born in New York, N.Y. Butts received a B.S. degree from City College (New York, N.Y.) in 1949 and his M.D. degree from Meharry Medical College (Nashville, Tenn.) in 1953. He interned at Morrisania City Hospital, Bronx, N.Y., did a two-year residency in psychiatry at the Bronx Veterans Administration Hospital, and became an instructor in psychiatry at Columbia University Psychoanalytic Clinic for Training and Research. Butts was on the faculty of the College of Physicians and Surgeons of Columbia University, was clinical director of Floyd Patterson House of the Wiltwyck School for Boys, psychiatric consultant at Hillcrest Center for Children and for the Jewish Board of Guardians, and chief of the in-patient service of the department of psychiatry at Harlem Hospital, New York, N.Y.

BYNUM, GEORGE S. (1910–   ), labor union leader; born in Chicago, Ill. Bynum studied at Chicago State Teachers College, University of Notre Dame (1956–58), the University of Chicago (1957–60), and Cornell University (1958–59). He led a thousand members out of the International Journeyman Barbers Union of America (AFL-CIO) in 1946 and formed a local independent union. Bynum later became the secretary-treasurer of Local 939, Chicago Barbers Union. He was the founder and editor of the *Illinois Union Barber,* and was appointed board member of the Service Federal Savings & Loan Association of Chicago.

BYRD, HANNAH ELIZABETH (1907–1968), judge. Byrd graduated from Duncan's Business College and was appointed to complete her husband's term as magistrate in Pennsylvania from 1950 to 1952. In doing so, she became the first Afro-American woman magistrate in that state.

CAIN, HERBERT R., JR. (1916–   ), lawyer, judge; born in New York, N.Y. Cain graduated from Lincoln University (Lincoln University, Pa.) and Howard University School of Law (Washington, D.C.). Later, he became a judge of the Court of Common Pleas in Philadelphia, Pa.

CAIN, RICHARD H. (1825–1887), African Methodist Episcopal bishop, state legislator, U.S. Representative; born in Greenbrier County, Va. After studying at Wilberforce University (Wilberforce, Ohio), Cain served as pastor of several different churches in New York. In 1865 he was sent to Charleston, S.C., by the African Methodist Episcopal (AME) Church council to assist newly freed slaves. Cain served in both houses of the South Carolina legislature and then for two terms in the U.S. House of Representatives, beginning in 1873. He later became a bishop of the AME Church, and in 1885 he founded *The Missionary Record.* Cain was also president of Paul Quinn College (Waco, Tex.).

CALDWELL, CHARLES (? –1875), state legislator; born in Mississippi. Caldwell was one of 16 black delegates who attended the state constitutional convention of 1868. When an attempt was made on his life by the son of a white judge, Caldwell killed his attacker while defending himself. He was tried by an all-white jury and acquitted; thus, he is believed to be the first black man alleged to have killed a white person in Mississippi to be acquitted on that charge. Caldwell was elected to the state senate of the first Reconstruction legislature in 1870. Five years later, he was assassinated after he had quelled a riot at a Republican parade.

CALDWELL, JOSIAH S. (1862– ?), African Methodist Episcopal bishop; born in Charlotte, N.C. After receiving a B.A. degree from Livingstone College (Salisbury, N.C.), Caldwell entered the ministry of the African Methodist Episcopal (AME) Church in 1890 and served churches in North Carolina, Virginia, New York, and Philadelphia. Elected bishop in 1904, he later became chairman of the board of bishops and served as a delegate to the ecumenical conferences in London (1901 and 1921) and Toronto (1911).

CALEB, JOSEPH (1937–72), labor union leader; born in Savannah, Ga. Caleb moved to Miami in the 1950s, and by 1963 he had become president of Local 478 of the International Union of North American Laborers. Under his leadership, the local grew into one of the largest union locals in the country, with a predominantly black membership of more than 6,000. Caleb was shot on February 6, 1972, by unknown gunmen for what police said were nonunion-related motives. Active in civic affairs, he was named outstanding citizen of 1970 by the Dade County Better Government League. Caleb was chairman of the Model Cities Administering Board in Miami at the time of his death, and in 1974 the Joseph

Caleb Comprehensive Community Center was named in his honor.

CALHOUN, EUGENE CLAYTON (1912–   ), clergyman, educator. Calhoun received his B.A. degree from Florida Southern College in 1939. He was pastor of churches in Florida and North Carolina (1934–37; 1941–45; and 1948–56), and a missionary in China (1946–47). Calhoun became president of Paine College (Augusta, Ga.) in 1956. He was the author of *Men Who Ventured Much and Far* (1961) and *The Forgiving Forgiven*.

CALIVER, AMBROSE (1894–1962), educator. Caliver received a B.A. degree from Knoxville College (Knoxville, Tenn.) in 1915 and attended Tuskegee Institute (Tuskegee Institute, Ala.) the next year. He received his diploma in personnel management from Harvard University in 1919, a M.A. degree from the University of Wisconsin in 1920, and his Ph.D. degree from Columbia University Teachers College in 1932. Caliver served in high schools in Tennessee and Texas, and was head of the manual arts department (1918–25), assistant dean (1925–27), and then dean (1927–30) of Fisk University (Nashville, Tenn.). He was appointed specialist in black education in the U.S. Office of Education in 1940. His writings include: *A Personnel Study of Negro College Students; Secondary Education for Negroes; and Education of Negro Teachers in the United States*.

CALLENDER, EUGENE ST. CLAIR (1926–   ), civic leader, clergyman; born in Cambridge, Mass. Callender received a B.A. degree from Boston University in 1947 and his B.D. degree from Westminster Theological Seminary (Philadelphia, Pa.) in 1950. He then did graduate studies at Union Theological Seminary, became associate pastor of a church in New Jersey, and later became pastor of the Church of the Master in New York City. Callender founded the Mid-Harlem Community Parish in New York City, and as a concerned and influential New York citizen, he was active in many community and civil rights groups. He was chairman of the committee that spearheaded the formation of Harlem Youth-Action, the first federal program for ghetto youths; he was executive director of the New York Urban League; he organized the Harlem street academies and Harlem Prep; and he was a member of the President's Task Force on Manpower and Urban Unemployment. In 1969 Cal-

Cab Calloway.
(National Educational Television.)

lender was elected head of the New York Urban Coalition. In addition to lecturing at schools and colleges, he was the host of a weekly television show in New York City entitled "Positively Black."

CALLOWAY, BLANCHE (1902–   ), entertainer, business executive; born in Baltimore, Md. Calloway attended Morgan State University (Baltimore, Md.), but because of her interest in show business, she left college to perform in local revues and stage shows. In 1928 she went to Chicago and appeared in nightclubs before she and her brother, Cab Calloway, joined forces—he led a dance band and she was the featured vocalist. By 1930 she had formed her own band and became the first black woman to lead an all-male band, which toured the country and enjoyed enormous success. Calloway retired from the entertainment world in 1941 and settled in Philadelphia, Pa., where she took an active interest in politics, eventually becoming a Democratic committeewoman. About 1953 she moved to Florida and founded Afram House, a cosmetic firm catering to the needs of the black community, and also continued her political activities there—becoming the first black woman to vote in Miami in 1958. In 1956 she reentered the entertainment world when she became the first black woman disc jockey at Miami's radio station WFEC. In 1957 Calloway moved to radio station WMBM in Miami, where she served as executive director and conducted her own radio show until 1971.

CALLOWAY, CAB (1907–   ), bandleader, singer; born in Rochester, N.Y. Calloway studied at Crane College after moving to Chicago with his family. He worked at odd musical jobs for several years until 1928, when he began to work with the Missourians in New York City and the Alabamians in Chicago. Within a year, he was featured in the "Hot Chocolates" revue in New York City and was leader of the Alabamians in their New York City appearance at the Savoy. By 1930 the Missourians had become Cab Calloway and his Orchestra, and in 1931 they began a resoundingly successful engagement at the Cotton Club in New York City. With its newly acquired national reputation, the band toured Europe in 1934, and during that decade and the next, it became one of the ten most successful bands in the United States. Toward the end of the 1940s, the band was dissolved and Calloway formed a sextet, reforming large bands only for special engagements. From 1952 to 1954 he toured the United States and Europe as Sportin' Life in *Porgy and Bess*. After a solo tour of England in 1955, occasional tours with *Porgy*, and a few big band appearances, Calloway appeared in *Hello Dolly* with Pearl Bailey in the late 1960s. As a songwriter, perhaps Calloway's best-known tune is "Minnie the Moocher." Through the years he appeared in several films, including *The Big Broadcast* (1932), *The Singing Kid* (1936), *Stormy Weather* (1943), and *St. Louis Blues* (1939). *See also* MUSIC: JAZZ.

CALLOWAY, DEVERNE LEE (1916–), state legislator; born in Memphis, Tenn. Calloway attended LeMoyne-Owen College (Memphis, Tenn.), and did graduate work at Atlanta University and Northwestern University (Evanston, Ill.). She was elected to the Missouri house of representatives from St. Louis for the first time in 1962 and was reelected six times subsequently. The first black woman to be elected to the state government in Missouri, Calloway served on the Elections Committee and the Accounts Committee, as chairman of the Federal-State Relations Committee, and as secretary of the legislature's Democratic caucus. During her tenure, she worked for fair employment, women's rights, nonsegregated housing, and more community control of school boards.

CALLOWAY, NATHANIEL O. (1907–), surgeon, scientist; born in Tuskegee, Ala. Calloway received a B.S. degree (1930) and his Ph.D. degree (1933) from the University of Iowa, and his M.D. degree from the University of Illinois College of Medicine in 1944. He was head of the department of chemistry at Tuskegee Institute (Tuskegee Institute, Ala.) from 1933 to 1935, a faculty member of Fisk University (Memphis, Tenn.) from 1936 to 1940, and a research fellow (1940), and assistant instructor (1942) in the department of pharmacology at the University of Chicago. Calloway was a staff member of the University of Illinois Hospital in Chicago (1944) where, as head of the research ward, he conducted studies in endocrinology.

CALVIN, FLOYD JOSEPH (1902–39), journalist; born in Washington, Ark. Calvin attended Shover State Teacher Training College in Arkansas and City College (New York, N.Y.) from 1916 to 1921. He became associate editor of the now-defunct magazine, *Messenger*, in 1922. After serving as writer and editor for the Pittsburgh

Courier from 1924 to 1935, Calvin started Calvin's News Service, which was used by nearly 150 weeklies at the time of his death. Providing a fuller schedule than other services, Calvin's service offered recipes, features, and opinions, as well as news. His column, "Calvin's Digest," appeared in scores of papers. In 1927 his radio talk show for the *Courier* on Negro journalism was the first radio program ever sponsored by a black newspaper.

CAMBRIDGE, GODFREY (1933–1978), comedian, actor, civil rights advocate; born in New York, N.Y. The son of devoutly religious parents, Cambridge was sent to Nova Scotia, Canada, the home of his grandparents, and there he attended elementary school. He returned to New York City, where his parents had bought a house in a white neighborhood in Queens, for high school. After graduating in three years, Cambridge attended Hofstra University on Long Island and later the College of the City of New York. He began his acting career in 1956 in an Off Broadway revival of *Take a Giant Step*. The show led to appearances on television and other parts in *Nature's Way*, *Detective Story*, and *Lost in the Stars*. His first major role, however, came in 1961 in Jean Genet's *The Blacks*, for which he received much critical acclaim. The same year he opened in a Broadway production of *Purlie Victorious*, with his friend Ossie Davis, in which he played the archetypal Uncle Tom. Following the great success of *Purlie*, Cambridge appeared in many motion pictures and television programs. His satirical brand of humor was particularly popular on college campuses and, although he preferred student audiences, he also appeared in many nightclubs. In addition to his active stage career, Cambridge found time to write several articles, and a book entitled *Put Downs and Put Outs* (1967). *See also* RADIO AND TELEVISION.

CAMPANELLA, ROY (1921–), professional baseball player; born in Homestead, Pa. Campanella began his professional baseball career as a catcher with the Baltimore Elite Giants of the Negro National League and also played winter baseball in Central America. Purchased by the Brooklyn Dodgers of the National League, he made his major-league debut in 1948. Campanella was voted the Most Valuable Player in the National League in 1951, 1953, and 1955. In 1953 he set major-league records for home runs (41), runs batted in (142), and putouts (807) by a catcher in a single season. An automobile accident in January 1958, which left him paralyzed, cut short his brilliant career. In 1969 Campanella was elected to the Baseball Hall of Fame. His autobiography is *It's Good to Be Alive. See also* ATHLETES.

CAMPBELL, CLOVES C. (1931–), state legislator; born in Elizabeth, La. Campbell graduated from Arizona State University in 1958 with a B.A. degree in education. He was elected to the Arizona house of representatives in 1962 and was reelected in 1964. In 1967 Campbell became the first Afro-American elected to the Arizona senate.

CAMPBELL, EGBERT ALEXANDER (1927–), clergyman; born in Montego Bay, Jamaica. Campbell received a B.A. degree from Virginia Union University in 1952, a B.D. degree from Virginia Union Theological Seminary in 1955, and his M.A. degree from Hartford Seminary in 1957. Ordained to the ministry of the United Church of Christ in 1959, he served as director of religious education for the Middlefield Federated Church of Connecticut, and was also active in churches in Rhode Island and New Jersey.

CAMPBELL, ELMER SIMMS (1906–71), painter, cartoonist; born in St. Louis, Mo. After having made a name for himself as a cartoonist during his high school days, Campbell attended the University of Chicago and the Chicago Art Institute. Later, he became the first Afro-American artist to work for national publications, his work appearing in such magazines as *The New Yorker, Esquire, Cosmopolitan, Playboy,* and *Ebony.* His syndicated cartoon, "Cuties," was carried in more than 100 newspapers, with most readers unaware that the artist was black. Campbell had great skill in working with pen, pencil, and colors, and his watercolor sketches of Haitian scenes are especially notable. His work has been exhibited at the Harmon Foundation, New York, N.Y., 1929 and 1935; at the National Gallery of Art, Washington, D.C., 1929; and at the Art of the American Negro, Chicago, Ill., 1940. *See also* ARTISTS.

CAMPBELL, HAYWARD *See* SCIENTISTS: BIOLOGICAL, PHYSICAL.

CAMPBELL, LEE L. (1919–), educator; born in Austin, Tex. Campbell received a B.S. degree

from Prairie View Agricultural and Mechanical (A & M) College (Prairie View, Tex.) in 1940, a M.A. degree from Columbia University Teachers College in 1947, and his Ed.D. degree from New York University in 1952. He taught at Tuskegee Institute (Tuskegee Institute, Ala.) and was dean of the college at Knoxville College (Knoxville, Tenn.).

CAMPBELL, LEWIS *See* NEWSPAPERS: CONTEMPORARY.

CAMPBELL, ROBERT LEE *See* WARS.

CAMPBELL, THOMAS (1883–1956), agriculturalist; born in Bowman, Ga. Campbell was admitted to Tuskegee Institute (Tuskegee Institute, Ala.) as a work student, and he spent eight years there. He then became a field agent training black farmers in agricultural techniques, the first black agent in the South. Later, Campbell became an agricultural aide for the U.S. Department of Agriculture.

CANSLER, CHARLES W. (1871– ?), educator, lawyer, mathematician; Cansler attended Freedman's Normal Institute and Maryville College, both in Tennessee. He was a lawyer in Knoxville, Tenn. (1894–96), principal of Burnside School (1896–98), a teacher in Austin High School (1898–1910), and principal of Colored High School (1910–28) and of Green School after 1928. He wrote *Cansler's Short Methods in Arithmetic* (1895) and lectured and gave exhibitions of "lightning calculations" in many northern states (1891–92). Cansler had a remarkable—almost unique—mathematical talent, and he could instantly give the day of the week for any date. He worked in many civic groups to improve the life of blacks, including the committee in charge of supervising the building of a Carnegie library. The city of Knoxville, Tenn., named one of its major streets for his family.

CAREY, ARCHIBALD JAMES (1868– ?), African Methodist Episcopal bishop; born in Atlanta, Ga. Carey received a B.A. degree from Atlanta University in 1889, M.A. and Ph.D. degrees from Brown University (Providence, R.I.), and his D.D. degree from Wilberforce University (Wilberforce, Ohio). Ordained to the African Methodist Episcopal (AME) ministry in 1891, he served as pastor of churches in Georgia, Florida, and Illinois, and was elected a bishop in 1920. See also CAREY, ARCHIBALD JAMES, JR.

CAREY, ARCHIBALD JAMES, JR. (1908–), lawyer, judge, clergyman; born in Chicago, Ill. After attending the University of Chicago for two years Carey received a B.S. degree from Lewis Institute in 1928, a B.D. degree from Northwestern University (Evanston, Ill.) in 1932, and his LL.B. degree from Chicago Kent College of Law in 1935. He was ordained a minister in the African Methodist Episcopal (AME) Church in 1930 and, after serving as pastor of the Woodlawn Church in Chicago (1930–49) and the Quinn Chapel in Chicago (1949–67), he was named pastor emeritus of Quinn Chapel. Meanwhile, in 1936, Carey was admitted to the Illinois bar and began practicing law. He was a member of the Chicago City Council (1947–55), a U.S. delegate to the 8th General Assembly of the United Nations in 1953, and a member of the President's Committee on Government Employment Policy (1955–61). In 1966 Carey became a judge of the Circuit Court of Cook County, Ill. See also CAREY, ARCHIBALD JAMES.

CARMICHAEL, STOKELY, (1941–), civil rights leader; born in Port-of-Spain, Trinidad. Carmichael attended Howard University (Washington, D.C.) in 1960, in preference to the white universities that had offered him scholarships, and he joined the young people from the Congress of Racial Equality (CORE) —who ranged throughout the South—with their "direct action" protest activities at lunch counters and other public facilities. After his graduation in 1964, Carmichael began work on voter registration in Lowndes County, Miss., with the Student Nonviolent Coordinating Committee (SNCC). From these activities in 1964 in Mississippi sprang the Lowndes County Freedom Organization, a political group separate from and independent of both Republican and Democratic parties, and a forerunner of the Black Panther Party. In 1966 the charismatic Carmichael was elected head of SNCC, and soon thereafter he used the rallying phrase "Black Power" during James Meredith's Freedom March in Mississippi. In 1973 he and his wife (Miriam Makeba) became citizens of Uganda. Carmichael published two books: *Black Power; the Politics of Liberation in America* (1967) with Charles V. Hamilton, and *Stokely Speaks; Black Power Back to Pan-Africanism.* See also BLACK PANTHER PARTY; BLACK POWER; STUDENT NATIONAL COORDINATING COMMITTEE (SNCC).

CARNEY, WILLIAM (1840–1904?), soldier; Born in either New Bedford, Mass., or Norfolk, Va. Carney worked at many odd jobs, though he was primarily interested in the ministry. In February 1863 he enlisted in Company C of the 54th Massachusetts Infantry, the first Union regiment of Northern free blacks; in July 1863 the 54th led the Union assault on Fort Wagner at Charleston, S.C. When the color bearer fell, Carney seized the flag and led a renewed charge. He was severely wounded twice during the battle. Carney was awarded the Congressional Medal of Honor in 1900.

CARRINGTON, ELSIE (active 1930s–1970s), nurse; born in Darlington Heights, Va. Carrington received her R.N. degree from Provident Hospital School of Nursing and her certificate for psychiatric nursing from Columbia University. She was charge nurse at Brooklyn Jewish Hospital, Memorial Hospital, New York-Cornell Medical Center, Kingsbridge Veterans Hospital, and Presbyterian Hospital (all in New York City). Carrington was also psychiatric nurse–counselor at the Henry Ittelson Center for emotionally disturbed children. She became the executive director of the Community Participation Education Program (New York City) in 1972. See also NURSES.

CARROLL, DIAHANN (1935–), singer, actress; born in Bronx, N.Y. Carroll began acting in school plays and singing with the children's church choir as a very young child, and at 10 she won a Metropolitan Opera scholarship for singing lessons. After graduating from the High School of Music and Art, she entered New York University, but was soon launched on a show-business career by virtue of winning top place on a television talent show. In 1954 Carroll appeared in the movie *Carmen Jones*, was a guest on several television shows, and played in the Broadway musical *House of Flowers*. Other movies in which she played were *Porgy and Bess* and *Paris Blues*. In 1962 Carroll starred in *No Strings*, the Broadway musical written for her by Richard Rodgers. In the following years, she continued to appear in nightclubs and on television shows, and in 1968 Carroll began her own television series entitled "Julia." See also RADIO AND TELEVISION.

Stokely Carmichael. *(National Educational Television.)*

CARROLL, EDWARD GONZALEZ (1910–   ), United Methodist bishop; born in Wheeling, W. Va. Carroll received a B.A. degree from Morgan State University (Baltimore, Md.) in 1930, a B.D. degree from Yale University in 1933, a M.A. degree from Union Theological Seminary in 1941, and an honorary LL.D. degree from Morgan State in 1967. Ordained to the ministry of the United Methodist Church in 1935, he served as pastor of churches in Maryland, Virginia, West Virginia, and New York. Carroll was an instructor at Morgan State University (1937–41) and a U.S. Army chaplain (1941–45). In 1972 he was elected a bishop of the United Methodist Church.

CARROLL, GEORGE D. (1923–   ), lawyer, judge, mayor; born in Brooklyn, N.Y. Carroll received a B.A. degree from Brooklyn College of the City University of New York in 1943 and his LL.B. degree from Brooklyn Law School in 1950; he was admitted to the New York bar in 1950. Subsequently, Carroll became a judge in the Municipal Court of Richmond, Calif., and later mayor of Richmond in 1964.

CARSON, SIMEON LEWIS (1881–1954), surgeon; born in Marion, N.C. Carson received his M.D. degree from the University of Michigan Medical School in 1903. He accepted a medical civil service appointment to the Indian reservations in South Dakota, working there for five years. Carson was appointed assistant surgeon-in-chief at the Freedmen's Hospital, Washington, D.C., in 1908, and he was professor of surgery at Howard University Medical College (Washington, D.C.) until 1919. He was the founder and first director of Carson Private Hospital (1919–39) and a consultant at Johns Hopkins Hospital.

CARTER, CHESTER (1921–   ), lawyer, business executive, government official, born in Emporia, Kans. Carter received a B.A. degree (1950) and a M.A. degree (1952) from the University of Southern California. He went on to the law school at Loyola Marymount University in Los Angeles and received his J.D. degree there in 1958. Carter was a first lieutenant in the U.S. Army during World War II (1942–46) and a major during the Korean War (1950–52). As a young veteran, he became a court officer in the probation department of the Superior Court of Los Angeles and later a traffic hearing officer.

Carter was a deputy Peace Corps representative in Ethiopia and director of Peace Corps activities in Tunisia and the Cameroons (1962–63). He served as deputy assistant superintendent for congressional relations in the U.S. State Department, and President Lyndon B. Johnson accorded him the rank of ambassador in 1967 while he was deputy chief of protocol of the State Department. In 1968 he became an executive of the Seagrams Overseas Sales Company.

CARTER, CHURCHILL (1922–   ), clergyman; born in Louisville, Ky. Carter received a B.S. degree from Wilberforce University (Wilberforce, Ohio) in 1945, a B.D. degree from Payne Theological Seminary in 1945, and his M. Litt. degree from the University of Pittsburgh in 1947. He was pastor of African Methodist Episcopal (AME) churches in Pennsylvania, parole advisor for the Pennsylvania state parole board, and probation officer for the Juvenile Court of Pittsburgh.

CARTER, GWENDOLEN MARGARET (1906–   ), political scientist, educator; born in Hamilton, Ontario, Canada. Carter received a B.A. degree from the University of Toronto in 1929, and B.A. and M.A. degrees from Oxford University (Oxford, England) in 1931 and 1935, respectively. She came to the United States to work toward her Ph.D. at Radcliffe College (Cambridge, Mass.) and received another M.A. degree there in 1936 and her Ph.D. degree in 1938. Carter began her teaching career as an instructor at McMaster University (Hamilton, Ontario, Canada) from 1932 to 1935, and then taught at Wellesley College (Wellesley, Mass.) from 1938 to 1941. She was a research associate at the Harvard Bureau of International Affairs for a year and an instructor at Tufts College (Medford, Mass.) the next year. Carter joined the faculty of Smith College (Northampton, Mass.) in 1943 and remained there until 1964, by which time she had become Sophia Smith Professor. An expert in African affairs, she was placed on the advisory council for the African Bureau in the U.S. Department of State in 1962, a post she held until 1967. In 1964 she went to Northwestern University (Evanston, Ill.), where she directed the African studies program as professor of political science and Melville J. Herskovits Professor of African Affairs. A member of many groups and associations, Carter was active in the African Studies Association and was a member of the board of the African-American Institute. She was the author and coauthor of many books on government.

CARTER, LISLE C., JR. (1925–), lawyer, government official, educator; born in New York, N.Y. A graduate of Dartmouth College (Hanover, N.H.) in 1944 and Saint John's University School of Law (Jamaica, N.Y.) in 1950, Carter began practicing law in New York City. As a young lawyer he was on the legal staff of the National Association for the Advancement of Colored People (NAACP), and by 1961 he had become deputy assistant secretary in the Department of Health, Education, and Welfare (HEW). Carter remained in that position for three years until he was appointed assistant director of intergroup relations in the Office of Economic Opportunity. In 1966 he returned to HEW as assistant secretary. Subsequent to that position, he became vice-president of Cornell University (Ithaca, N.Y.), resigning in 1971 to return to teaching and writing.

CARTER, MATTHEW GAMALIEL (1913–), clergyman, civic leader; born in Danville, Va. Carter received a B.A. degree (1939) and his B.D. degree (1942) from Virginia Union University. He was pastor of Baptist churches in Virginia and held a number of official positions with the Young Men's Christian Association (YMCA), including assistant director of the publication department, National Council, YMCA. Carter was deputy mayor and director of public works of Montclair, N.J., and the recipient of the Man of the Year Award of the Philadelphia YMCA in 1962.

CARTER, RANDALL ALBERT (1867–1954), Christian Methodist Episcopal bishop; born in Fort Valley, Ga. After being ordained a minister in the Christian Methodist Episcopal (CME) conference of South Carolina in 1887, Carter enrolled at Paine College (Augusta, Ga.), from which he graduated in 1891. Prior to 1914, when he was elected a bishop, he served as pastor in Georgia churches. Carter then served as bishop in dioceses in Texas, Mississippi, the District of Columbia, Georgia, and several midwestern states. In 1919 Carter moved to Chicago, where he resided for 34 years and where he was instrumental in the building and purchase of more than 250 churches. He was a delegate from the CME Church to ecumenical conferences in London (1901) and in

Toronto (1921). Carter also served on the federal council of the Churches of Christ in America.

CARTER, REGINALD (1916–), editor, publisher; born near Kimball, W. Va. After studying at a New York dental college, Carter went to West Virginia and became the assistant to the publisher of the *Independent Observer*, and later became an artist and photographer for the *Mountain Mirror*. He formed the Carter Printing Company in Bluefield, Va., in 1940, moved the company to Los Angeles in 1959, and started the Los Angeles *News* the same year. Carter founded a quarterly magazine, *Negro Reporter*, in 1969. He was the vice-presidential candidate of the Afro-American Negro Party in 1960. *See also* NEWSPAPERS: CONTEMPORARY.

CARTER, REGINALD C. clergyman; born in Miami, Fla. Carter received a B.A. degree from Morehouse College (Atlanta, Ga.) in 1960 and his M.Rel.Ed. degree from the Interdenominational Theological Center (Atlanta, Ga.) He studied further at Hunter College of the City University of New York and Fordham University (New York, N.Y.). As chaplain of the 560th Engineering Battalion, Carter became Georgia's first Afro-American National Guard officer.

CARTER, WALTER (1923–71), educator, civil rights leader. After having been an assistant professor of sociology at Loyola College (Baltimore, Md.), Carter became chairman of the Baltimore chapter of the Congress of Racial Equality (CORE) in 1960. He was Maryland coordinator for the historic civil rights march on Washington, D.C., in 1963, and in 1965 he coordinated the largest local project of the Federation of Civil Rights Organizations—The March Against Segregated Housing and Slums. Carter organized freedom rides in the early 1960s to protest the segregation of public accommodations in Maryland.

CARTER, WILLIAM JUSTIN (1866–1947), lawyer; born in Richmond, Va. After attending Virginia Normal and Collegiate Institute (now Virginia State College), Carter studied law at Howard University (Washington, D.C.). From 1892 to 1894 he was assistant principal of the Afro-American public school in Annapolis, Md., after which he went to Harrisburg, Pa., to begin practicing law. Since the black clientele in Harrisburg was small and poor, his practice lagged, and he thus accepted an offer to become assistant district attorney for Dauphin County, Pa. In 1910 he was chosen as a delegate to the Universal Race Congress in London. Carter was one of the promoters of the Niagara Movement, which was first active in 1905, and which is considered a forerunner of the National Association for the Advancement of Colored People (NAACP). *See also* CIVIL RIGHTS MOVEMENT: INTRODUCTION.

CARTWRIGHT, MARGUERITE DORSEY (1914–), educator; born in Boston, Mass. Cartwright received a B.A. degree (1932) and a M.A. degree (1933) from Boston University, and her Ph.D. degree from New York University in 1948. She subsequently taught at Hunter College, Brooklyn College, and the New School for Social Research (all in New York City). Cartwright was an accredited correspondent in the United Nations Press Corps, and a member of the provisional council and board of trustees of the University of Nigeria (1972). She conducted independent fieldwork among the Mayan Indians in Yucatan and in Dutch Guiana.

CARTWRIGHT, ROSCOE C. (1919–), Army officer; born in Kansas City, Mo. Cartwright was educated at San Francisco State College and at the University of Missouri. He joined the Armed Forces in 1941, and in 1972 he was named assistant division commander of U.S. Military Headquarters (USAREUR) and the 7th Army, 3d Infantry Division. His job, to assist in the administering, housing, and training of several thousand troops and officers, had been held by a black man only once before in American military history.

CARVER, GEORGE WASHINGTON (1864–1943), botanist; born near Diamond Grove, Mo. His mother and he were kidnapped and sold as slaves in Arkansas. However, his owner, Moses Carver, secured the return of the young Carver, who then worked his way through high school, received a B.S. degree (1894) and a M.S. degree (1896) in agriculture from Iowa Agricultural College, and was then placed in charge of the college's greenhouse. Carver was persuaded by Booker T. Washington to come to Tuskegee Institute, where Carver became a teacher in 1896 and later the director of agricultural research. He was a collaborator in the division of mycology

and disease survey for the Bureau of Plant Industry, U.S. Department of Agriculture, in 1935. Carver concentrated his research on industrial uses of the peanut, sweet potato, pecan, and cotton. His discoveries helped improve the agrarian industry of the South. Although he never attempted to patent any of the hundreds of uses that he found for these products, he did set up, with his life's savings, the George Washington Carver Foundation in 1938 to continue his work for the benefit of mankind. Frequently honored during his lifetime by professional organizations and by political groups, he received recognition for his works and deeds in a postage stamp issued in his honor and in the Carver National Monument, located near Diamond, Mo., the first national monument erected in honor of an Afro-American. Carver was named a Fellow of the Royal Academy of England in 1916, given the National Association for the Advancement of Colored People's (NAACP) Spingarn Medal in 1923, and awarded the Roosevelt Medal for distinguished service to science in 1939. In April of 1977, he was enshrined in the Hall of Fame for Great Americans (located at Bronx Community College, formerly the Bronx campus of New York University, New York City, N.Y.).

George Washington Carver. *(Photo by Prentice H. Polk, Tuskegee Institute.)*

CARY, LOTT (1780–1828), missionary; born in Charles City County, Va. About 1813, after his wife had died, Lott purchased his freedom and that of his two children for $850. He received a license to preach from the First Baptist Church of Richmond, Va., and in 1815 he helped to organize the Richmond African Baptist Missionary Society. Determined to go to Africa himself, Lott was received for service by the Baptist Board of Foreign Missions in 1819, and in 1826 he became vice-agent of the colony of Liberia. In 1828, while he was assisting in the defense of the colony, a powder explosion killed Lott and several other persons. *See also* BAPTISTS.

CARY, W. STERLING (1927–   ), clergyman; born in Plainfield, N.J. Cary studied at Morehouse College (Atlanta, Ga.) and Union Theological Seminary, and was ordained to the ministry of the Baptist Church in 1948. From 1958 to 1968 he was pastor of Grace Congregational Church in New York City. In December, 1972, Cary was elected president of the National Council of Churches, becoming the first Afro-American to hold that office.

CASEY, EDMUND C. (1923–   ), physician, educator; born in Marion, Ind. Casey received a B.A. degree from Earlham College (Richmond, Ind.) and his M.D. degree from Meharry Medical College (Nashville, Tenn.) in 1948. He served in the U.S. Army during World War II and later was a captain in the Medical Corps of the U.S. Air Force. With a practice in Cincinnati, he was an active member of many regional and local health-related organizations and associations, and became chairman of the board of the National Medical Association in 1970.

CASEY JONES (BALLAD OF) *See* SAUNDERS, WALLACE.

CASHIN, JOHN L., JR. (1928–   ), dentist; born in Huntsville, Ala. Cashin was a graduate of Tennessee State University and Meharry Medical College (Nashville, Tenn.), and practiced dentistry in Alabama. He was a successful political leader in the early 1970s and was the principal founder and chairman of the national Democratic Party of Alabama. Cashin was frequently requested to speak before youth and college groups.

CASTE *See* RACE; RACISM; SEGREGATION.

CATCHINGS, LINCOLN MAYNARD (1914–   ), clergyman, educator; born in Houston, Tex. Catchings received a B.S. degree from Prairie View Agricultural and Mechanical (A&M) College (Prairie View, Tex.) in 1935 and a B.D. degree (1941) and a M.A. degree (1942) from Howard University (Washington, D.C.). He was pastor of Plymouth Congregational Church, Washington, D.C. from 1947 to 1953, assistant professor in the department of social sciences at Fisk University (Nashville, Tenn.) from 1954 to 1957, and later chaplain of Congregational students at Howard University. *See also* CONGREGATIONALISTS.

CATHOLICS

CATHOLICS Maryland was established by a group of Roman Catholic colonists under the leadership of Sir George Calvert, who became the first Lord Baltimore. Though Maryland came under Protestant leadership at a later time, Roman Catholics always enjoyed greater freedom of religion in this colony than anywhere else, except in Louisiana. The first native-born Catholic bishop in the United States, John Carroll of Baltimore, wrote to the pope in 1785: "There are in Maryland about 15,800 Catholics; of these, there are about 3,000 of African origin, called Negroes." For many years, Maryland remained the center of Roman Catholic life in the United States. It was there (in Baltimore) that the first catechistic school for black Catholics was established in 1796 by Father William Valentine Dubourg. Father Dubourg later became bishop of New Orleans.

Southern Louisiana, particularly New Orleans, has been predominantly Catholic from the outset of the European presence, as a result of Spanish and, later, French influence. The French and Spanish never attempted to justify slavery on the ground that blacks were subhuman or in any way inferior. They advocated the exploitation of blacks purely on the premise of expediency. The French and Spanish, for example, did not hesitate to take a black woman as a lawful spouse.

At the time of the Civil War, more than 60,000 free blacks lived in Louisiana; they were referred to as *libres l'hommes de couleur* ("free men of color"). These Catholic freedmen maintained schools for their children in New Orleans and often sent their children to Canada, and even to France, for higher education. A persistent legend states that one of the early bishops of New Orleans came from one of the old quadroon families, popularly known now as Creoles.

Smaller pockets of black Catholics lived in other parts of the South—in and around Louisville and Bardstown, Ky.; Natchez, Miss.; Mobile, Ala.; and Port Arthur, Tex. As the white Catholic population grew and spread elsewhere in the country, so, too, black Catholics were to be found, albeit in small numbers, in virtually every state of the Union. The ranks of black Catholics were notably augmented in the United States as a result of the 1793 uprisings in Santo Domingo and Haiti. Many of the well-to-do blacks and mulattoes fled from their islands and settled in New York, Baltimore, and New Orleans. Several black Catholic families in those cities today are descendants of West Indian refugees.

After the Civil War, the Roman Catholic Church established a bureau to help the freedmen in their transition from slaves to citizens. The Sisters of the Holy Family, a congregation of black nuns founded in 1842, worked zealously with adults and children in establishing schools, orphanages, and homes for the elderly in New Orleans and in other parts of Louisiana.

In 1871, Father Herbert Vaughn, an English priest who had organized a small band of other English priests for missionary activity in Africa, sent the first of his missionaries to America instead. They were the first group of missionary priests to devote themselves exclusively to the spiritual welfare of Afro-Americans. Coming from Mill Hill, England, they came to be known as the Mill Hill Fathers; later, they changed their name to Priests of the Society of St. Joseph. They established their first parish for black Catholics in Baltimore, at St. Francis Xavier Church, in 1871. Soon they formed other parishes in Baltimore and Washington, D.C., and in a short time they had established a parish for blacks in Covington, Ky. Today the Fathers of St. Joseph, or Josephite fathers (as they are best known), have more than 30 parishes in the South, and operate equally as many grade schools and several high schools.

Several other orders joined the Josephite fathers in this missionary effort among American blacks. Noteworthy contributions were made by the Benedictine fathers and by the Jesuits, who had begun work with blacks in Balitmore even before the Revolutionary War. The Holy Ghost fathers, now best known for their presence at Duquesne University (Pittsburgh, Pa.), began late in the nineteenth century to lend their efforts to the evangelization of American blacks. They established the famous St. Emma's Industrial and Military Academy for black students in Rock Castle, Va., in 1895. More recently, the Divine Word priests, who came to America from Germany just before the start of World War I, established a seminary in Northbrook, Ill., for the training of priests to work among blacks in the South. Later, they extended their activities to several parishes in the black ghettos of the urban North. Their method of operation was quite the same as that established by the Josephite fathers, who had become the experts and authorities in the mission fields of the South: they established schools first and later built small mission churches.

Catholic Women The first order of black nuns in the United States was established in Baltimore in 1827 by a young black woman who had migrated to the United States from Santo Domingo in 1795. Marie Joubert was her name, and members of that order still work in schools throughout the South and Southeast. Presently they number nearly 300, and this figure is still growing. Before Fidel Castro's rise to power in Cuba, nuns of the order founded by Joubert staffed several schools in that country. Another order of black nuns, the Sisters of the Most Pure Heart of Mary, was established about 1920 and is now based in New York City, where its members operate day-care, catechistic, and recreation centers for Afro-American youth in Harlem and Brooklyn.

Credit must also be paid to the hundreds of white nuns of more than a dozen orders who have dedicated themselves to the education of Afro-American boys and girls throughout the country. An especially noteworthy contribution was made by Katharine Drexel (1858–1955), daughter of the millionaire Philadelphia banker Francis Drexel. When her father died in 1885, she inherited a fortune. Having toured the South and

and West with her father shortly before his death, she was said to have been shocked by the deplorable living conditions of the Indians and blacks. Her socialite friends were even more shocked when, four years after his death, this immensely wealthy, talented, and beautiful young woman entered a convent and then established an order of nuns, the Sisters of the Blessed Sacrament for Indians and Colored People, which dedicated itself to work exclusively among blacks and Indians. She herself devoted more than $20 million to her missionary efforts, which included the establishment of more than 50 grade schools and high schools for blacks throughout the South. Xavier University (New Orleans, La.), the first black Catholic college in the United States, stands as a monument to her charity and zeal. Scores of nationally known black professional men and women have graduated from that school, founded by Sister Katharine Drexel in 1915. More than 1,000 of her religious sisters continue her work in the South among Afro-Americans and in the West among the Indians.

Black Catholics Today Of about 47 million Roman Catholics in the United States in the 1970s, nearly 850,000 are black. New Orleans has the largest number of black Catholics, with about 200,000. The Diocese of Lafayette, La., ranks second with more than 100,000. Other cities having 50,000 or more black Catholics include: Chicago, New York, Washington, D.C., Baltimore, Detroit, Louisville, and Los Angeles.

Three orders of black nuns currently have about 800 members in aggregate; nearly 300 black nuns belong to about 50 orders that are predominately white. Even though the black man has had no difficulty in finding a bishop

willing to welcome him as a candidate for the priesthood within the last 25 years, there are comparatively few black priests in the Roman Catholic Church in America. Still, about 25 years ago, there were only 33 black priests in the United States and now the number is 175. The problem faced by the Roman Catholic Church, with respect to ordaining men to the priesthood, is one without a pattern of racial discrimination. Not enough young men, black or white, are seeking entrance to seminaries at the present time.

REFERENCES: There is no definitive reference. However, the listings under Williams, Ethel L. and Clifton L. Brown, *Afro-American Religious Studies* (1972), should be consulted: pp. 114–116, 271–276, 331–335. Limited attention is called to Gillard, John Thomas, *The Catholic Church and the American Negro* (1929, 1968) and LaFarge, John, "American Catholics and the Negro," *Social Order* (April, 1962, pp. 153–61).

CATLETT, ELIZABETH (1915–   ), sculptor, painter; born in Washington, D.C. Catlett received a B.A. degree from Howard University (Washington, D.C.) and her M.F.A. degree from the State University of Iowa, where she studied under Grant Wood. Later, she attended the Art Institute of Chicago and the Art Students League, New York, N.Y. Catlett is best known as a sculptor in marble, wood, and terracotta of monumental works charged with social realism and emotion. She exhibited at Atlanta University in 1942, 1943, and 1951; in "Black Experience," the Museum of Modern Art, Mexico City, Mexico; at the National Center of Afro-American Artists, Boston, 1970; and at the Studio Museum, Harlem, 1971–72. Catlett is represented in the collections of the Museum of Modern Art, Mexico City; the Library of Congress and Howard University, Washington, D.C.; as well as others. She lived in Mexico and taught at the University of Mexico at Mexico City. Her sculpture, *Mother and Child*, won first prize at the Art of the American Negro Exhibition, Chicago, 1940. *See also* ARTISTS.

CAYTON, HORACE ROSCOE (1903–70), sociologist, educator; born in Seattle, Wash. Cayton received a B.A. degree from the University of Washington in 1931, after supporting himself for two years as a deputy sheriff. He was a special assistant to the U.S. secretary of the interior (1934–35), and then an instructor at Fisk University (Nashville, Tenn.) from 1935 to 1936. There he began a long career on the staffs of many academic institutions. In 1937 Cayton received a Rosenwald Fellowship. His works include *Black*

Far left: Bishop Harold R. Perry of the archdiocese of New Orleans celebrated the tenth anniversary of his consecration with a mass at Our Lady of Lourdes in New Orleans, where he was pastor. *(Photo by George Gurtner, Catholic News Service.)*

Metropolis (with St. Clair Drake), which won the Anisfield-Wolf Award in 1945 as one of the year's two best books on race relations, and *Black Workers and the New Unions* (with George S. Mitchell), an exploration of the role of Afro-Americans in industralized life, published in 1935. Cayton died in Paris while working on a biography of his friend, the novelist Richard Wright.

CENTENARY BIBLICAL INSTITUTE See MORGAN STATE UNIVERSITY.

CENTRAL INTERCOLLEGIATE ATHLETIC ASSOCIATION See ATHLETES.

CENTRAL STATE COLLEGE See CENTRAL STATE UNIVERSITY.

CENTRAL STATE UNIVERSITY Central State University, at Wilberforce, Ohio, came into being in 1887 when the Ohio general assembly, in order to improve teacher education and to introduce industrial training, passed an act establishing the Combined Normal and Industrial Department. A coeducational state-supported school, it offers the bachelor's degree (including the B.S.Ed.), and provides liberal arts, teacher education, and vocational curricula. The 1975 enrollment was about 2,300.

The Combined Normal and Industrial Department was housed at Wilberforce University but it had its own separate board of trustees, separate legal status, and separate identity. By a 1941 state statute this institution became the College of Education and Industrial Arts at Wilberforce University in Greene County, and in 1951 it became Central State College. Central State had been academically affiliated with Wilberforce University, but in 1947 the African Methodist Episcopal (AME) Church—which supported Wilberforce—and the state of Ohio—which supported Central State—changed their academic arrangements, and the college established independent academic programs. In 1965 it became Central State University as graduate studies in education and in English had been authorized by the Board of Regents in 1964.

CENTRAL TENNESSEE COLLEGE See MEHARRY MEDICAL COLLEGE.

CHAD SCHOOL See FEDERATION OF PAN-AFRICAN EDUCATIONAL INSTITUTIONS.

CHAMBERLAIN, WILT (1936–   ), professional basketball player; born in Philadelphia, Pa. Towering more than 7 feet in height, Chamberlain was named Wilton Norman Chamberlain at birth, but at the beginning of his basketball career, fans dubbed him "Wilt the Stilt." After an outstanding sports career at Overbrook High School in Philadelphia, Pa., during which he scored 2,252 points, Chamberlain had an equally brilliant record at the University of Kansas before leaving to join the Harlem Globetrotters for a year. He began a 14-season career in the National Basketball Association (NBA) in 1959 with the Philadelphia (later San Francisco) Warriors; subsequently, he played for the Philadelphia 76ers (1965–68) and the Los Angeles Lakers (1968–73) of the NBA. His autobiography is *Wilt*. See also ATHLETES.

CHAMBERS, FREDRICK See EDUCATION: COLLEGES AND UNIVERSITIES.

CHAMBERS, JORDAN (? –1962), politician; born in Nashville, Tenn. His family moved to St. Louis, Mo., when he was one year old. He attended but did not finish Sumner High School. Remembering his father, who was a Pullman porter, Chambers formed and was a leader in Railway Coach Cleaners Union 16088 during the period 1918 to 1923. He entered politics at the local level in St. Louis; and, although he held no official political office, by 1931 the St. Louis *Post-Dispatch* regarded him as the "Negro Mayor of St. Louis," so effective was his political power, which only a few black leaders could wield then in large metropolitan areas. He received the Distinguished Public Service Award from the St. Louis *Argus* six months before his death.

CHAMBERS, YOLANDE HARGRAVE lawyer, business executive; born in Danville, Va. Chambers graduated from Hampton Institute (Hampton, Va.) in 1950 and from Yale University School of Law in 1953. After admission to the Virginia bar in 1954, she began six years of private practice in Norfolk and Portsmouth (Virginia), combined with a two-year instructorship at Virginia State College (1955–57). Chambers then moved to Michigan, was admitted to the bar there, and in 1962 became senior urban renewal assistant with the Detroit Housing Commission. In 1963 her career shifted to the business world, and she became vice-president and personnel director of Davidson Bros., Inc., a firm that operates department stores throughout the country. In addition to her business affiliations, Chambers' interest in public affairs and community life led to memberships on the boards of many important organizations.

CHANDLER, SUE PINKSTON librarian; born in Nashville, Tenn. Chandler received a B.A. degree from Xavier University in 1953 and her M.A.L.S. from George Peabody College (Nashville, Tenn.) in 1960. She joined the library staff at Fisk University (Nashville, Tenn.) in 1960. After becoming head librarian, she co-edited *Living Black American Authors: A Biographical Directory*, in association with Ann Allen Shockley (1973). *See also* SHOCKLEY, ANN ALLEN.

CHAPIN, ARTHUR A. (1915–   ), government official; born in Philadelphia, Pa. Chapin began his career as assistant to the head of New Jersey's state Congress of Industrial Organizations (CIO) council, in which position, from 1947 to 1958 he researched and drafted civil rights, housing, and unemployment compensation legislation. He also served as a member of the New Jersey Committee on Housing, and as a member of the state's wage panel for restaurant employees. Eventually, Chapin became civil rights counsel to the mayor of Newark. He began his association with the U.S. Department of Labor in 1961 when he received the post of minority groups consultant in the Bureau of Employment Security; soon he became the department's specialist in minority group problems. As such, Chapin was later named director of the Office of Equal Employment Opportunity.

CHAPPELLE, THOMAS OSCAR (1915–   ), clergyman; born in Sapulpa, Okla. Chappelle received a B.A. degree from Bishop College (Dallas, Tex.) in 1934 and a B.Th. degree from American Baptist Theological Seminary the following year. He served as dean of the Oklahoma School of Religion (1940–42) and subsequently became pastor of Morning Star Baptist Church in Tulsa, Okla. Chappelle was the owner of Rest Haven Nursing Home in Tulsa and he served as president of the board of Moton Memorial Hospital. He was the author of *How Do We Do It* (1960).

CHAPPELLE, WILLIAM D. (1857– ?), clergyman; born in Fairfield County, S.C. Chappelle

studied at Fairfield Normal Institute and Allen University (Columbia, S.C.). In 1883 he was ordained a deacon in the African Methodist Episcopal (AME) Church, and in 1885 an elder. In 1887 Chappelle was elected a delegate to the church's General Conference, and three years later he became corresponding secretary and editor of the Sunday school periodicals of the AME Church. Chappelle became president of Allen University (Columbia, S.C.) in 1897.

CHARLES, EZZARD *See* ATHLETES: BOXING.

CHARLES, RAY (1930–   ), singer, pianist, composer; born in Albany, Ga. Charles moved to Florida with his family when he was very young. He became blind from glaucoma at about the age of six and both parents died when he was in his mid-teens. In a school for the blind in Florida, Charles learned to read and write Braille, and to play the piano and clarinet. At a still young age, he left the school for band engagements around the state of Florida. His travels with singer Lowell Fulsome led to an important engagement at the Apollo Theater in New York City. In Seattle, Wash., about 1950, Charles formed a fairly successful trio, but in 1954 he organized a larger rhythm and blues group. He first recorded in 1951, and five years later he cut his first hit, "I Got a Woman." New record sales were broken with his "Georgia on My Mind" in 1959. For many years, jazz critics rated him America's top male vocalist, and Charles won several awards from the National Academy of Recording Arts and Sciences. In 1964 he completed an international tour that included 90 concerts in nine weeks.

CHARLTON, MELVILLE (1883– ?), organist, composer; born in New York, N.Y. Charlton studied at the National Conservatory of Music and City College (New York, N.Y.), and received his Mus.D. degree from Howard University (Washington, D.C.) in 1924. His career as an organist included several distinguished positions in New York City—musical director of the Temple of the Covenant (1914–24); of Temple Emanu-El; of Union Theological Seminary; and of St. Philip's Episcopal Church. Charlton also composed many pieces for both organ and piano.

CHASE, WILLIAM CALVIN (1854–1921), lawyer, journalist; born in Washington, D.C. Chase studied at Howard University (Washington, D.C.), was admitted to the Virginia bar in 1889, and later was heard before the U.S. Supreme Court. From 1879 to 1891 he was a reporter for the Washington *Plaindealer*. Chase became editor of the *Free Lance*, another weekly newspaper, in 1880, and he started the Washington *Bee* in 1882 and quickly made it known for its social and political sting. The *Bee* served as a powerful and effective lobbying base for civil rights and for increased government hiring of blacks.

CHAVIS, JOHN (1763–1838), educator; born near Oxford, N.C. Chavis attended Princeton University, and in the late 1790s he enrolled at Washington Academy (Lexington, Va.). He fought in the Revolutionary War then became a licensed minister and a missionary among blacks in Maryland and Virginia. In about 1805 he moved to North Carolina, and by 1808 was operating schools—teaching whites during the day and blacks at night. His students included the children of North Carolina's chief justice, two pupils who later became state governors, and two who became congressmen. Chavis reputedly administered the best college preparatory schools in North Carolina; however, restrictions imposed after Nat Turner's Revolt (1831) ended his teaching and ministerial carreers.

CHEATHAM, HENRY PLUMMER (1857–1935), U.S. Representative, public official; born near Henderson, N.C. Cheatham graduated from Shaw University (Raleigh, N.C.) in 1883, and the same year he became principal of the State Normal School in Plymouth, N.C. His first political position was that of register of deeds of Vance County from 1884 to 1888. In 1888 Cheatham won election to the U.S. Congress from North Carolina. Reelected in 1890, he served in both the fifty-first and fifty-second congresses from 1889 to 1893. In 1897 he became recorder of deeds in the District of Columbia and served throughout the administrations of William McKinley. In 1901 Cheatham moved to Oxford, N.C., and he became the superintendent of the North Carolina Colored Orphanage (having been one of its founders in 1887), a post he held until his death.

CHEEK, JAMES EDWARD (1932–), educator; born in Roanoke Rapids, N.C. Cheek received a B.A. degree from Shaw University (Raleigh, N.C.) in 1955, a B.D. degree from Colgate-Rochester Divinity School in 1958, and his

James E. Cheek. *(Moorlland-Spingarn Research Center, Howard University.)*

Ph.D. degree from Drew University (Madison, N.J.) in 1962. He received an honorary LL.D. degree from North Carolina Agricultural and Technical (A & T) State University in 1971, an honorary D.HC. degree from the University of Haiti in 1972, an honorary Ed.D. degree from Providence College in 1972, and an honorary LL.D. degree from Delaware State College in 1972. Cheek taught at Drew Theological School (1959–60), Union Junior College (1959–60), Virginia Union University (1960–63), and then became president of Shaw University (1963–69) and president of Howard University (Washington, D.C.) after 1969. He also served as special consultant to the president on black colleges and universities (1970) and was a member of the President's Commission on Campus Unrest (1970). Cheek also worked as a member of the task force on adult education of the Department of Health, Education, and Welfare, and on the steering committee of the National Urban Coalition.

CHEEK, KING VIRGIL, JR. (1937–), educator; born in Weldon, N.C. Cheek received B.A. and M.A. degrees from Bates College (Lewiston, Maine), and his J.D. degree from the University of Chicago. He joined the faculty of Shaw University (Raleigh, N.C.) in 1964 and became its president in 1969. Cheek was also president of Morgan State University (Baltimore, Md.) from 1972 to 1975.

CHESNUTT, CHARLES WADDELL (1854–1932), author; born in Cleveland, Ohio. Chesnutt was educated in both Ohio and North Carolina, and became principal of the State Normal School in Fayetteville, N.C., in 1880. He then taught himself to take shorthand dictation and obtained a job as legal stenographer for Dow Jones, Inc., on Wall Street, moonlighting as a gossip columnist for the New York *Mail and Express*. In 1887 Chestnutt was admitted to the Ohio bar, but found legal stenography too lucrative a profession to give up in order to practice law. That same year his first short story, "The Gophered Grapevine," was published by the *Atlantic Monthly*, and a volume of short stories, *The Conjure Woman*, was issued in 1889. His first novel, *The House Behind the Cedars* (1900), dealt with a young black girl's attempt to pass for white. Chesnutt worked in the area of the "problem" novel, dealing with racial themes from a black viewpoint. Considered the first serious craftsman among Afro-American writers, his work broke the color line in publishing, and was praised by the great critic William Dean Howells. Later, however, the members of the Harlem Renaissance rejected the basically ingratiating approach he typified. *See also* LITERATURE: THE NOVEL.

CHESS, SAMMIE, JR. (1934–   ), lawyer, judge; born in Allendale, S.C. Chess graduated with both a B.A. degree and a LL.B. degree from North Carolina Central University, and began to practice law in North Carolina. In 1970 he was named judge of the Superior Court of North Carolina, becoming the first Afro-American jurist in the state's history. Previously, Chess had served on the Warren Commission appointed to study the state's educational system.

CHEYNEY STATE COLLEGE Cheyney State College, at Cheyney, Pa., was founded in 1837 in Philadelphia through a bequest made by Richard Humphreys, a Quaker philanthropist. It is coeducational, state-supported, offers the bachelor's and master's degrees, and provides chiefly a teacher education curriculum. Its 1975 enrollment was about 2,300.

Cheyney State College has had a long history as an institution for the training of teachers, although that aim was not immediately realized. It began as a farm school before the Civil War, and then successively became an evening school for apprentices, a high school for training teachers, a normal school, a teachers college, and a state college with extended curricular emphases. A graduate program leading to the master of education degree in elementary education and in industrial arts was initiated in 1968–69. In the early 1970s, 85 percent of its students were black.

CHICAGO DEFENDER Founded in 1905 by Robert S. Abbott, the newspaper grew from a circulation of a few hundred copies a week to more than 250,000 in 1929. Abbott's policy of sensationalism and outrage made the *Defender* a national forum on racial injustice. The paper urged black southerners to migrate North, and attacked oppression in the South. Its strong support of black soldiers and its opposition to military segregation and the inferior treatment of black soldiers during World War I also swelled circulation, although it displeased government officials and brought the paper under federal scrutiny. One of the most influential Afro-American newspapers, the *Defender* produced many distin-

guished writers and reporters. It became a daily in 1956. *See also* ABBOTT, ROBERT SENGSTACKE; NEWSPAPERS.

CHILDRESS, ALICE (1920–   ), playwright, editor; born in Charleston, S.C. Childress studied at the American Negro Theater School and was on the faculty of Radcliffe Institute (1966–68). Her works include: *Trouble in Mind* (1956), which won a "Best Play" Obie Award; *Wine in the Wilderness* (1969), produced on Boston television; and *Wedding Band*, which was performed at Joseph Papp's Public Theater in New York in 1972 and for ABC-TV in 1973. Childress became editor of *Black Scenes* magazine in 1971. *See also* LITERATURE: DRAMA/THEATER.

CHISHOLM, SHIRLEY ANITA (1924–   ), state legislator, educator, U.S. Representative; born in Brooklyn, N.Y. Born and bred in the deprived Bedford-Stuyvesant section of Brooklyn (the constituency that eventually elected her to the U.S. Congress), Chisholm became the first black women ever elected to Congress. She received a B.A. degree from Brooklyn College of the City University of New York in 1946, and she received her M.A. degree from Columbia University in 1952. From 1946 to 1953 she worked as a nursery school teacher, after which she became the director of a child-care center in New York City. For five years following 1959, she was educational consultant in the division of day care of the New York City Bureau of Child Welfare. In 1964 Chisholm began her political career as a member of the assembly in the New York state legislature. She had served for four years when, in 1968, she was elected on the Democratic ticket to serve in the Ninety-first Congress; in 1971 Chisholm was reelected to the Ninety-second Congress. A year later, in 1972, she ran in the New York Democratic primary for president of the United States, and although she lost, she had established another first for a black woman. Chisholm continued to hold her seat as a representative after the elections of 1976.

CHOW, KENNETH (1937–   ), publisher, business executive; born in Greenville, Miss. Chow received his high school diploma in 1965 while in Terre Haute Federal Penitentiary. He founded the *Black Progress Shopper-News* (Kansas City, Kans.) in 1968, the first paper of its kind in Kansas and Missouri. Chow also founded the United Struggle for Black Employment (1968), an organization designed to create self-help pro-

Shirley Chisholm. *(Courtesy of Shirley Chisholm.)*

grams without the assistance of federal, state, or city funds. He also owned several black enterprises, including a clothing store and a catering service.

CHRISTIAN, CHARLIE (1917–42), jazz guitarist; born in Dallas, Tex. Christian was an early and important contributor to the jazz revolution later named Bop and was the first electric guitarist to use single-string solos. Christian played in Benny Goodman's band from 1939 to 1941; during the 1940s he performed at Minton's Playhouse in Harlem with Thelonius Monk (pianist), Kenny Clark (drummer), and Dizzy Gillespie (trumpeter), during the historic developmental period of Bop. *See also* MUSIC: JAZZ.

CHRISTIAN CHURCH, DISCIPLES OF CHRIST, CHURCHES OF CHRIST Almost from its beginnings in the early nineteenth century, blacks have been deeply involved in the movement whose churches today are variously known as Christian Churches, Churches of Christ, and Disciples of Christ. Most of the early black Disciples were slaves attending the churches of their masters. There were, however, some significant departures from the usual practice. In 1853, for example, the Christian Church sent to Africa its first missionary, Alexander Cross, a former slave whose freedom had been purchased by the people of Christian County, Ky.

Because of the congregational polity of the Christian Church, the activities of the churches in regard to race varied in the years immediately following the Civil War. By the turn of the century, however, as a result of their desire for independence and self-identity, most, if not all, Afro-American Disciples had organized their own congregations along racial lines. This was not entirely true of the educational institutions of the Church. Several of the colleges and universities related to the Christian Church did not have racial bars in their admission policies. Also, by the turn of the century, several missions were carried on by the white churches to evangelize blacks, the most notable being the Board of Negro Education and Evangelization.

In recent years, the black membership of the Christian Churches has received some recognition, and several blacks have been elected to prominent positions within the Church. This has not been an easy task, however, as in the 1950s and early 1960s, several churches fired their ministers because of racial issues. Actually, it could be said that the history of blacks within

the Disciples movement is a microcosm of the religious history of blacks in America, a story little known but worthy of note.

CHURCHES AND MINISTERS

Alabama	10	Missouri	10
Arkansas	6	New Jersey	2
California	7	New York	10
Colorado	1	North Carolina	49
Florida	4	Ohio	15
Georgia	4	Oklahoma	5
Illinois	5	Pennsylvania	1
Indiana	3	South Carolina	13
Kansas	5	Tennessee	6
Kentucky	13	Texas	38
Maryland	3	Virginia	14
Michigan	2	Washington, D.C.	1
Mississippi	9	West Virginia	1

Some notable ministers from various states include: *Alabama:* Earl Murphy (Birmingham), C. J. Hinson (Montgomery), Nathaniel Chambliss (Mobile); *Kentucky:* Walter Bingham (Louisville), Isaac Hunt (Lexington), H. Earl Jackson (Paducah); *Missouri:* Henry Berry (St. Louis), James L. Blair (Kansas City); *New York:* Theodore N. Friedy (Bronx), Richard L. Saunders (Brooklyn); *North Carolina:* Amos Artis (Goldsboro), L. L. Graves (Reidsville), C. C. Crawford (Greensboro), C. W. McLaurin (Fayetteville), James Pugh (Concord), C. W. Sutton (Kinston); *Ohio:* F. T. Barnett (Cleveland), Frank T. Garner, Jr. (Cincinnati), Ozark Grange (Columbus); *South Carolina:* Hezikiah Dore (Burton), Jacob Jamerson (Moncks Corner); and *Texas:* Joseph E. Blair, Jr. (Houston), Augustus Burke (Beaumont), Melvin C. Dickson (Dallas), King David Cole (Dallas), E. B. Washington (Waco), Paul A. Sims (Fort Worth).

CHRISTIAN METHODIST EPISCOPAL (CME) CHURCH The roots of the Christian Methodist Episcopal (CME) Church have their origins in American Methodism. Whereas black Methodists of the African Methodist Episcopal (AME) and African Methodist Episcopal Zion (AMEZ) churches formed their own congregations at the end of the eighteenth century (or the early years of the nineteenth), black Methodists of the CME Church did not form a separate body until after the Civil War. At the outbreak of the Civil War, there were about 250,000 slave communicants in the Methodist Episcopal (ME) Church, South (established after a schism over slavery in 1844). With emancipation, a mass exodus of blacks from the ME Church, South, took up membership, for the most part, in the older, well-established black Methodist bodies—the AME Church and the

AMEZ Church (largely the former). Those who remained in the ME Church, South, requested (1866) that their own conferences be formed into a separate body, and in 1870 the Colored Methodist Episcopal Church was established. Later, at its General Conference in Memphis, Tenn. (May 1954), the same month of the famous *Brown v. Board of Education of Topeka* decision of the U.S. Supreme Court, the body voted overwhelmingly to change its name to Christian Methodist Episcopal Church. The name became official in January 1956.

Current Status The Church is the third largest black Methodist body in the United States; its membership is nearly 500,000 (mid-70s), and it has more than 2,000 clergymen and 2,000 churches. The greatest geographical concentration of the Church remains in the South, and a number of its national offices (boards) are in Memphis, Tenn. The official church organ is the *Christian Index*, which has been published continuously since 1867. Its bishops, as of 1973, were: B. W. Doyle (retired), J. Claude Allen, B. Julian Smith, P. R. Shy, Henry C. Bunton, N. S. Curry, W. H. Amos, E. P. Murchison, N. S. Curry, Joseph A. Johnson, Jr., and C. A. Kirkendoll. Some of its general officers were: M. C. Pettigrew, C. D. Coleman, Pauline Grant, Alexander Chambers, O. T. Peeples, and D. S. Cunningham.

A slected list of some large and/or historic churches includes: Brown Memorial CME Church, Louisville, Ky.; Calvary Tabernacle CME Church, New Orleans, La.; Carter Institutional CME Church, St. Louis, Mo.; Hays Tabernacle CME Church, Los Angeles, Calif.; Lane Memorial CME Church, Washington, D.C.; Lane Metropolitan CME Church, Cleveland, Ohio; Lane Tabernacle CME Church, Houston, Tex.; Miles Memorial CME Church, Washington, D.C.; Miles Chapel CME Church, Houston, Tex.; Phillips Temple CME Church, Los Angeles, Calif.; Russell Tabernacle CME Church, Philadelphia, Pa.; Scruggs Memorial CME Church, St. Louis, Mo.; Williams Institutional CME Church, New York, N.Y.; and Williams Temple CME Church, Philadelphia, Pa. *See also* METHODISTS.

REFERENCES: For additional information, see Cade, John B., *Holsey, The Incomparable*, Pageant Press, 1964; Carter, Randall A., *A Century of Progress in Christian Journalism: The Christian Index* (1967); Holsey, Lucius Henry, *Autobiography, Sermons, Addresses, and Essays of Bishop L. H. Holsey* (1898); Pettigrew, M. C., *From Miles to Johnson* (1970); Phillips, Charles Henry, *The History of the Colored Methodist Episcopal Church in America* (1898).

CHRISTIAN RECORDER *See* AFRICAN METHODIST EPISCOPAL (AME) CHURCH; NEWSPAPERS.

CHURCHES Blacks are members of, affiliated with, or related in polity and belief to practically every religious body in the United States. A wide variety and spectrum of Afro-Americans embrace many shades of religious faith and activity. The highest concentrations of Afro-Americans are in Protestant and Roman Catholic churches; smallest numbers are in bodies of the Islamic and Jewish faiths. Protestant bodies predominate, overwhelmingly in Baptist and Methodist congregations. The distribution of membership is shown in the accompanying diagram.

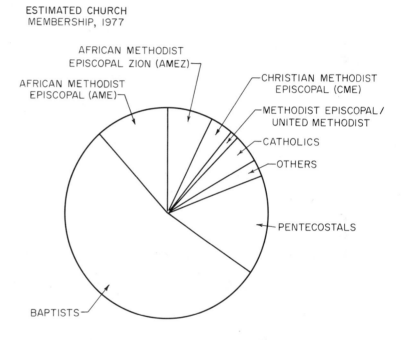

ESTIMATED CHURCH MEMBERSHIP, 1977

AFRICAN METHODIST EPISCOPAL ZION (AMEZ)

AFRICAN METHODIST EPISCOPAL (AME)

CHRISTIAN METHODIST EPISCOPAL (CME)

METHODIST EPISCOPAL / UNITED METHODIST

CATHOLICS

OTHERS

PENTECOSTALS

BAPTISTS

Principal Beliefs Religious beliefs vary widely. Some of the main beliefs to which Afro-American members of religious bodies adhere are outlined below. Congregations are listed in order of Afro-American membership, more or less.

Baptists. Freedom of interpretation allowed members; informal unity of belief; practice of total immersion; Communion taken as a remembrance of Christ's death.

Methodists. Doctrine is subordinate to the love of God and personal religious experience; baptism usually by sprinkling; Communion symbolizes salvation through the death of Christ, who is present in spirit.

Pentecostals. Stress free will; brotherhood.

Catholics. Sacraments confer grace (life in Christ) on the believer; Communion is Christ's body and blood in the Mass.

Presbyterians. Sovereignty of God is revealed in Jesus Christ the Son; much freedom of religious thought.

Episcopalians. Generally accept the Trinity and doctrine of incarnation; use Book of Common Prayer; Christ is present in spirit in Communion.

Christian Church, Disciples of Christ. Close to Baptists with "no creed but Christ"; Communion in remembrance of Christ (not a sacrament).

Congregationalists. Considerable freedom to interpret God's word as revealed in Jesus Christ, his Son.

Muslims. Acclaim Allah and the Koran (Qúran); favor separation and Nation of Islam.

Lutherans. Christ was both God and man; stress Luther's doctrine of justification by faith; Christ is present in spirit, not body, of Communion.

Seventh Day Adventists. Have some similarities with Baptists; stress Second Coming and Last Judgment.

Quakers (Friends). Stress direct experience of God's Inner Light (guiding spirit) and peace.

Unitarians. God is one; no belief in the Trinity; Christ was human.

See also AFRICAN METHODIST EPISCOPAL (AME) CHURCH; AFRICAN METHODIST EPISCOPAL ZION (AMEZ) CHURCH; AFRICAN ORTHODOX CHURCH; BAHÁ'Í FAITH; BAPTISTS; BIBLE WAY CHURCH OF OUR LORD JESUS CHRIST WORLD WIDE, INC.; BLACK JEWS; CATHOLICS; CHRISTIAN CHURCH, DISCIPLES OF CHRIST, CHURCHES OF CHRIST; CHRISTIAN METHODIST EPISCOPAL (CME) CHURCH; CHURCH OF OUR LORD JESUS CHRIST OF THE APOSTOLIC FAITH, INC.; CONGREGATIONALISTS; EPISCOPALIANS; LUTHERANS; METHODISTS; MUSLIMS; PENTECOSTALS; PRESBYTERIANS; QUAKERS; SEVENTH DAY ADVENTISTS.

CHURCHES OF CHRIST See CHRISTIAN CHURCH.

CHURCH OF OUR LORD JESUS CHRIST OF THE APOSTOLIC FAITH, INC. A religious body of approximately 50,000 members in 1973, it is based in Philadelphia, Pa. (22d Street and Bainbridge), under the leadership of S. McDonald Shelton, its bishop.

CINQUE, JOSEPH See ARTISTS: AMISTED MURALS; SLAVERY: THE ABOLITIONISTS.

◆◆◆

CIVIL DISORDERS

CIVIL DISORDERS

1861–1917 Violent racial disorders have been a part of American history since the late seventeenth and early eighteenth centuries. The early violence generally erupted in the form of slave revolts or out of fear of such slave uprisings. In the turbulent decades from 1830 to 1860, however, rapid city growth, interlaced with mass immigration and attendant nativism, gave birth to the urban race riot visualized in the twentieth century. During this period between 1830 and 1860, New York, Boston, Cincinnati, and Philadelphia experienced anti-abolitionist rioting, and Philadelphia earned a reputation for being "the northernmost southern city" with outbreaks in 1834, 1835, 1838, 1842, and 1849 that

were clearly anti-Negro. Violent precedents were plainly established by the time of the Civil War.

The Civil War and Reconstruction Years A central theme throughout early American history was the relationship of the black minority to the majority white population. The Civil War brought this issue into sharp focus. The events that preceded the war made it clear that not all northerners accepted the viewpoint of the abolitionists, and the diversity of opinion in the North was made more manifest by racially activated civil disorders during the Civil War years.

Violence flared in Cincinnati, Chicago, Newark, Buffalo, and New York City. These riots originated in a complex combination of wartime grievances, all of which involved the presence of black men. Rioting in Cincinnati began in July 1862 among the Irish and Afro-American roustabouts who competed for jobs on Ohio riverboats. The immediate cause concerned the use of blacks as waterfront strikebreakers, but the Irish and other white laborers also viewed an end to slavery as a beginning of massive low-wage competition. The burning of the Negro section of town led to retaliation against the Irish neighborhood. Six days of violence left scores injured and hundreds of people homeless.

Similar motives sparked the so-called New York Draft Riots in July 1863. Again, real and feared competition among blacks and newly immigrated Irish laborers heightened tensions, and economic conflict —all was intensified by dire predictions of a glutted postwar labor market by the northern Democratic press. The spark that ignited the bloodiest rioting in American history was the drawing of names for the National Conscription Act on July 11, 1863. Now finding themselves called upon to fight a war to "free the niggers," Irish laborers, unable to hire substitutes on their meager $15 weekly earnings, denounced conscription as a form of economic suicide. Why risk life and limb when the end result would be increased unemployment? After four days of virtually uninterrupted violence, more than 1,000 whites and perhaps twice as many blacks lost their lives. The impersonal force of the "draft" had easily been translated into a race question, and the "draft riot" became a "race riot." The mobs had not only attacked blacks, but also men and women who employed blacks. Even the Colored Orphan Asylum was burned.

The conclusion of the Civil War hardly eased racial tensions. The appearance of Afro-Americans in blue military uniforms created special problems in the minds of southern whites, who had long been conditioned to a fear of armed slave revolts. The presence in the postwar South of black "occupation" troops and discharged black soldiers who kept their arms inevitably led to numerous racial disorders. Norfolk, New Orleans, Franklin, and Memphis were among those southern towns and cities that were racked by antiblack rioting.

The violence that erupted in Memphis followed weeks of tension that had been created by the concurrent and reciprocal practice of black soldiers arresting white policemen and white policemen arresting black soldiers. Arrest procedures in both cases had often been unduly harsh.

A regiment of black troops was discharged on April 30, 1866, and in the celebration that followed, several of the former soldiers were arrested. Serious rioting began when a crowd of blacks tried to prevent the arrests and, in turn, were fired upon by the police. During the three-day melee that followed the arrests, it was necessary to call in federal troops from other parts of the state to quell the fighting. Official government sources put the death toll at 46 blacks and two whites. In addition to fatalities in the Memphis violence, a large part of the black section of the city was burned to the ground.

Perhaps surprisingly, the withdrawal of federal troops from the South following the Compromise of 1877 did not signal a beginning of racial war. In the North, the feared influx of freedmen did not materialize on the massive scale often predicted. A steady trickle of Afro-Americans made its way to northern urban centers, but not

In the Draft Riots of 1863, mobs attacked at random, and rioters pursued and killed fleeing blacks in New York City. (*Museum of the City of New York.*)

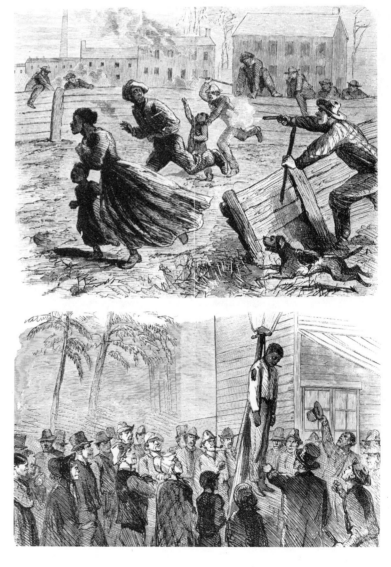

in any greater proportion than southern whites. Most of these migrants in the 1870s and 1880s were absorbed by the expanding opportunities for unskilled labor that industrialization was creating. In the South, white southerners used a variety of measures to reassert their control. Most of these measures were related to the return

of local political autonomy. Local political leaders and local law enforcement officials no longer had to compete with the presence of federal troops. Social mores and prejudices quickly found their ways, undisguised, back into "official" practice. The black euphoria of freedom seemed to vanish with the presence of federal troops. The struggle for economic survival and the desire to avoid the deadly and omnipresent power of the Ku Klux Klan, the White Cappers, or unjust law enforcement officers encouraged the black man to "know his place." Violence came to be used as a measure of personal racial control rather than as an expression of mass hysteria. Lynchings, floggings, and mysterious disappearances punctuated life in virtually all black communities.

Jim Crow Laws and Disfranchisement Individual and symbolic repression proved unsatisfactory. For the South, mentally accustomed to Negro slavery and white supremacy, the slightest hint of racial equality served as a constant reminder of past defeat and attendant economic and political impotency. By the late 1880s an unmistakable campaign was building in the southern states to sweep away all vestiges of Reconstruction's

attempts at political and social equality between the races. A caste system, meticulously defined, came into being. Blacks were effectively deprived of the franchise and reduced to second-class citizens before the law. The disfranchisement and Jim Crow campaigns occurred in an atmosphere of emotional and abusive rhetoric. Predictions as to the impact of black equality upon southern tradition, and especially upon southern womanhood, resembled, in effect, the fearful economic prognosis of the Democratic press during the Civil War. Tensions and fears mounted, and so did the potential for violent rioting.

Tension and fear were ever-present from 1890 to 1917, and, on occasion, these feelings infected areas outside the South. While estimates of "forty major race riots" have been made for the period 1898–1910, the massive civil disorders of these years exploded around the old issues of black military personnel, economic competition, and the increasingly controversial political role of blacks.

Few blacks had held office since 1877, but the specter of the black voter and "black rule" continued to haunt the South. The Populist movement of the 1890s raised clearly, but hesitantly, the possibility of the black vote as a means to attain the balance of power between the agrarian insurgents and the aristocracy. North Carolina continued to send one black congressman to Washington, D.C., throughout most of the 1880s and the 1890s. In 1894 Populists and Negro Republicans entered into a "fusionist" agreement, which succeeded in electing representatives of both races to state offices in that year and also in 1896. Georgia, meanwhile, experienced the most spectacular attempt to enlist black voter support for the Populist ticket. Tom Watson, the agrarian leader, openly endorsed the cause of black opportunity and, on occasion, defended his Negro backers against violence. Georgia also maintained a black state legislator until 1908, longer than any other state in the nation.

It is not surprising, then, that North Carolina and Georgia responded most violently to the caste-directed racial campaigns around the turn of the century; here the political challenges to black suppression were strongest and, therefore, most aggravating. The elections of 1898 in North Carolina carried a call for a constitutional convention to deal with Negro disfranchisement. Not only was such a convention approved, but also the "fusionist" ticket was rejected in a campaign that involved intimidation, violence, inflammatory newspaper rhetoric, and stump oratory. Emphasis was placed on the sexual and the emotional rather than on the "rational" appeal of disfranchisement. Much attention was given to an editorial written by the black editor of the Wilmington *Record*, an editorial in which the writer was interpreted as having cast interracial slurs on the honor of southern womanhood. Wilmington became a focal point, representing to whites the dangers of black equality. The election success of the white supremacists subsequently turned into a bloodbath for that city's blacks. On November 10, 1898, more than 400 whites invaded the black section of town, burned the *Record* office and proceeded to chase as many Negroes out of the area as possible. Evidence exists to indicate that some actual battle plans had been drawn up far in advance of the attack, which took the lives of at least 30 blacks.

Georgia, meanwhile, did not get involved in a full-fledged disfranchisement campaign until 1906. By this time, Tom Watson had made an about-face on the race issue and had joined other white politicians in the state in calling for the removal of Afro-Americans from politics. The election of 1906 coincided with a statewide crusade for prohibition, and the race issue became entwined with prohibition in the political campaign. It was charged that a direct correlation existed between alcohol and Negro crime and that prohibition could only be achieved by the exclusion of black voters from the polls. The speeches of the day included support for the "Wilmington revolution" and a willingness to "imitate" the actions of that North Carolina city. An Atlanta "imitation" was also made. The copyists of that city had learned their lesson well: on September 24, the rioting began. Hundreds of blacks were beaten, many as they were seeking sanctuary in the Negro colleges of the city. The rioting was not all one-sided, as blacks gathered arms and occasionally fought back, but the casualty toll showed far more deaths among Negroes than whites. For several days the city was paralyzed: factories were closed and all transportation stopped. In the constitutional convention that followed, black disfranchisement was duly ratified.

Brownsville Riot While the Wilmington and Atlanta riots were greatly indicative of the emerging fate of black southerners, the greatest national attention turned to an event in the small town of Brownsville, Tex. On August 13, 1906, a group of men "shot up" the town, killing one

white man and wounding two others, including a police officer. Black soldiers of the 25th Infantry, who were stationed on the edge of town, were charged with the violence. Arresting authorities overlooked the lack of positive identification, concentrating instead on what they felt was a clear-cut motive: the soldiers had been complaining for some time about their discriminatory treatment in restaurants, in stores, and at the hands of law enforcement officers.

Despite the successful service of black cavalry units in the West and the valor shown by black regiments in the Spanish-American War and in the occupation of the Philippine Islands, white Americans never fully accepted the sight of the black man in a military uniform. Brownsville was not the first instance of racial prejudice openly flaunted against black soldiers, and it would not be the last. During the Spanish-American War, there had been incidents in such cities as Tampa, Fla., and Macon, Ga., and the Brownsville companies of the 25th Infantry had experienced similar treatment in 1903 at Fort Riley, Kans.

The Brownsville affair particularly caught the attention of the nation, however, because of the harsh treatment (dishonorable discharge) that President Theodore Roosevelt meted out to the entire black garrison. The black press was indignant, and Senator Joseph B. Foraker of Ohio demanded an investigation of the harsh penalties. No concrete evidence was unearthed against any of the soldiers, but only 14 of the men were ever allowed to return to the service.

Northern Riots Not all blacks accepted the imposition of caste restrictions peacefully; many fought back. However, most southern blacks who attempted to avoid increased oppression, instead of resisting, moved North. Other factors also influenced this migration, including the boll weevil's fording of the Mississippi River in 1907 and the resulting economic depression in the cotton fields of the Deep South. Yet, northern cities were hardly the "promised land" that many black migrants envisioned.

Altercations between the races occurred in most large cities, but the first northern city to "explode" in racial disorders during this period was New York. In August 1900, a heat wave exacerbated racial tensions in the expanding Harlem ghetto and created potential riot conditions. A fight between a white policeman and a black man, ending in the policeman's death, provided the spark that ignited the entire neighborhood. "Men and women poured by the hundreds from the neighboring tenements," said the New York *Daily Tribune.* "Negroes were set upon wherever they could be found and brutally beaten." Two days of rioting, with little interference from the police, were finally halted by a severe summer thunderstorm. Only blacks had been arrested during the affray, and known casualties among blacks far exceeded those of whites.

As with the Civil War riots, many of the tensions created by the migration to northern cities were economic in origin. Job competition had also led to violence in the South, particularly in the coal fields of Tennessee and Kentucky during the summer of 1908. Economic riots, however, were most common in the North because the southern caste structure limited the areas of job competition, i.e., in the South there were "Negro jobs" and "white jobs."

The most violent economic riots before 1917 occurred in Abraham Lincoln's hometown, Springfield, Ill., in 1908. Springfield, an area largely settled by people of southern extraction and sentiment, had recently received a sizable influx of black migrants. Tensions arising from the use of black miners as strikebreakers combined with general resentment against black competition for wages, and together these forces created a widespread feeling that the town's Negroes needed a lesson in the racial facts of life. "Why, the niggers came to think they were as good as we are," said one rioter after the crisis passed. Incensed by false accusations of rape of a white woman by a black handyman, white mobs destroyed the black neighborhood in the city on August 14 and 15. By the time the state militia had quelled the violence, eight blacks were dead and an estimated 2,000 had fled the city. The alleged leaders of the riot escaped punishment, and the community engaged in a political and economic boycott to drive out the remaining Negro residents. Whites who refused to fire their black employees received anonymous threats of violence.

The epidemic of racially motivated civil disorder was far from over in 1917. Some steps, however, had been taken to deal with the growing problems of caste restrictions and migration pressures. After the Atlanta rioting in 1906, a small group of whites and blacks organized the Atlanta Civic League as a "sounding board" to diffuse potential trouble in the future. This organization served as the seminal body for the Commission on Interracial Cooperation of the 1920s, which was operative throughout the entire South. After the Springfield riot, greater concern

developed among certain northern white liberals and race-conscious blacks. These parties met in Springfield in 1909, and the concept of the National Association for the Advancement of Colored People (NAACP) emerged.

However, the worst was yet to come, and the impact of the Interracial Commission and the NAACP lay mostly in the future. There was still a war to be fought, both at home and abroad.

See also SLAVERY: SLAVERY IN SELECTED STATES.

REFERENCES: Relevant books and articles include: Crouthamel, James L., "The Springfield Race Riot of 1908," *Journal of Negro History,* vol. 45, pp. 164–81, July 1960; Crowe, Charles, "Racial Violence and Social Reform—Origins of the Atlanta Riot of 1906," *Journal of Negro History,* vol. 58, pp. 234–56, July 1968; Edmonds, Helen Gray, *The Negro and Fusion Politics in North Carolina, 1894–1901,* University of North Carolina Press, Chapel Hill, 1951; Graham, Hugh Davis and Ted Robert Gurr (eds.), *Violence in America: Historical and Comparative Perspectives,* U.S. Government Printing Office, Washington, D.C., 1969; Grimshaw, Allen D., "Lawlessness and Violence in America and Their Special Manifestations in Changing Negro-White Relationships," *Journal of Negro History,* vol. 44, pp. 52–72, January 1959; Lane, Ann J., *The Brownsville Affair: National Crisis and Black Reaction,* Kennikat Press, Port Washington, 1971; Lofton, Williston H., "Northern Labor and the Negro During the Civil War," *Journal of Negro History,* vol. 34, pp. 251–73, July 1949; Meier, August and Elliott M. Rudwick, *From Plantation to Ghetto,* Hill and Wang, New York, 1966; Osofsky, Gilbert, *Harlem: The Making of a Ghetto,* Harper and Row, New York, 1963; Werstein, Irving, *July, 1863,* Julian Messner, New York, 1957; Wilson, Frederick T., *Federal Aid in Domestic Disturbances, 1787–1903,* Arno Press, New York, 1969; and Woodward, C. Vann, *Origins of the New South, 1877–1913,* Louisiana State University Press, Baton Rouge, 1951.

Civil Disorders: 1917–1943

The World War I Years, 1917 and 1918 The United States went to war in Europe in 1917, and that same year warfare erupted several times within the country's own borders—between the white and black races. The bloodiest of these race riots occurred in July in East St. Louis, Ill., where nine whites and nearly 40 blacks were murdered by mobs. Many of these victims suffered horrible deaths. White mobs put torches to the homes of Afro-Americans, leaving them with the choice of burning alive or fleeing to their deaths by gunfire. Black men were hanged; black women and children were clubbed, shot, and stabbed. Law enforcement officials were completely absent; in fact, police and militiamen, instead of trying to quell the violence and bloodshed, worked in collusion with the mobs. State troops fraternized with lawbreaking whites, and many were seen helping with murder and arson.

Although the riot in East St. Louis was the

bloodiest of 1917, it was not the only outbreak of racial civil disorder that year. In August three blacks and three whites died as a result of rioting in Chester, Pa. In the same month, there was racial bloodshed in Houston, Tex., where the black 24th Infantry had been stationed by the U.S. Army. After weeks of racial slurs and discrimination, black troops in Houston were angry and ready to strike back. Why, they asked, should they have to endure segregated streetcars and brutal treatment and taunts from police? To add to their frustration, they were deprived of their weapons by Army officials who feared that the soldiers might retaliate against Houston's whites. The precipitating incident inevitably came on August 26. After arresting a black woman on a charge of using abusive language, two white policeman were asked for an explanation by a black military policeman. Replying, "I don't report to any Negro," one of the officers then struck the soldier over the head with his pistol and fired at him as he fled. Rumors spread that the soldier had been mortally wounded, and the policeman's overreaction was soon matched by that of the black troops. They stormed into the arms and ammunition tent, seized weapons, marched to town, and murdered 17 whites. The next year, though quieter than 1917, was also a time of many outbreaks of racial civil disorder. In Philadelphia, for example, three white men were killed in late July during rioting involving blacks.

Why were the years 1917 and 1918 witness to such racial turmoil? Throughout American history, times of war have provided settings conducive to racial violence: during the Civil War, there were draft and labor riots; during World War II, riots in Detroit and Harlem shattered the domestic calm; and during the Vietnam era of the 1960s, many ghettos rioted. World War I was no exception. Generative of rapid social and economic change, wars also seem to stimulate a climate of violence and to foster an atmosphere that accepts violence as normal in everyday life. Perhaps a more important reason for the 1917–18 racial turmoil was the wartime migration. Whites had long been hostile to the strivings of blacks but during World War I this hostility became even more intense when more than 500,-000 southern blacks migrated to the North. There, in crowded cities, the new arrivals continuously confronted whites over jobs, housing, political power, and facilities for education, transportation, and relaxation. In Chicago, for example, when blacks threatened to move into all-white neighborhoods, white residents responded angrily. "If we can't get them out any other way," one white Chicagoan warned, "we are going to . . . bomb them out." Indeed, bombs did explode: in Chicago in the two-year period from the summer of 1917 to the eruption of the Chicago riot in July 1919, two dozen bombs damaged the homes of blacks and the offices of those realtors who dealt with them.

Black migrants were convenient scapegoats for whites who feared that their economic and social status would suffer because of the influx from the South. The employment of a new black worker in a shop or the arrival of a black family on the block often prompted the ancient fear of "social equality." White hostility to individual blacks who threatened white's livelihoods eventually became generalized into categorical hatred of the entire race.

The "Red Summer" of 1919 If 1917 and 1918 were bloody years, 1919 was even bloodier. Lynch mobs murdered 78 blacks in 1919, an increase of more than 15 over the number killed in 1918 and more than 30 over the 1917 total. Ten of the victims were war veterans, several of them still in uniform. Throughout the South, hangings, burnings, and shootings increased in brutality and frequency as summer approached. The National Association for the Advancement of Colored People (NAACP) had expressed shock in 1918 when lynch mobs had murdered two black men by fire; now, in 1919, 11 men were burned alive at the stake.

Even more destructive of life than the lynchings were the race riots. The factors that earlier caused East St. Louis, Houston, and Philadelphia to explode were now evident in varying degrees in several other American cities in 1919. In fact, the atmosphere during the first year of peace after World War I seemed even more conducive to racial violence than it had been during the war itself. When James Weldon Johnson of the NAACP spoke of the "Red Summer," he was referring to that miserable season when the race riots bloodied the streets of 25 towns and cities in the six-month period from April to early October 1919. The death toll was staggering: 38 dead in Chicago, including 23 blacks and 15 whites, and considerably more than 500 of both races injured; 7 reported killed in Knoxville, Tenn.; 6 dead in Washington, D.C.; 7 dead in Millen, Ga.; and 4 killed in Longview, Tex. On a main street in Omaha, a white mob hanged, shot, and burned to death a black prisoner accused of having raped a white girl. In rural Phillips County,

Ark., between 20 and 120 blacks were slaughtered after black tenant farmers and sharecroppers attempted to organize a labor union.

This unparalleled eruption of racial violence in 1919 was caused, first of all, by the continued migration of blacks from the South to the North, exacerbating the already disquieting competition between urban blacks and whites for jobs, housing, and other necessities. Thousands of black and white war veterans who preferred not to return to the rural and sometimes isolated existence of their prewar homes joined the large postwar influx to the cities. Moreover, there prevailed in 1919, beyond the racial disquiet, a climate of unrest, evident in the wave of antiforeign and antiradical sentiment that swept the country. This outburst of angry mistrust, which historians have called the "Red Scare," manifested itself in the beatings by vigilantes of foreign-born Americans, in raids on the offices of left-wing organizations and newspapers, and in mass arrests and deportations by the federal government of alleged radicals and enemies of the country. The Red Scare was an extension of the emotionalism of the war, of superpatriotism, and of scapegoatism. Although, in 1919 the common enemy—the external threat posed by Germany— had been vanquished, American citizens, emotionally unsatisfied with the fruits of military victory, began searching for domestic "enemies." By midyear the void left by the removal of the external threat had been filled with indiscriminate hatred for the enemy from within— aliens, dissenters and noncomformists, alleged radicals, and, in many cases, Afro-Americans.

For their part, black men and women in both the North and the South began the new year (1919) with aspirations for a larger share of both the nation's political power and its wealth. With the armistice, black men and women eagerly awaited reward for their contributions as soldiers and war workers to the Allied victory. But that satisfaction was not forthcoming. Tension mounted as black aspirations met with a general determination to reinforce the prewar status of blacks on the bottom rung of the nation's political and economic ladders. In addition, blacks in 1919 were strongly cynical about the ability and willingness of government at all levels to protect them. Legally constituted authority was viewed as the armed representative of white racism and hostility—the white arm of the law. As a result, many blacks who had previously condemned nonviolence in the face of white aggression now armed themselves. Black retaliatory violence

was not unique in 1919, but it had never been so widespread nor, on occasion, so fierce.

In 1919 the "New Negro" emerged resolved to stand fast and retaliate if attacked. "If we must die," wrote the black poet Claude McKay in 1919, "let it not be like hogs. . . . If we must die—oh, let us nobly die. . . . Like men we'll face murderous, cowardly pack, pressed to the wall, dying but fighting back!" McKay's was not a solitary voice calling for self-assertion, manliness, and resolute self-defense; there were many "New Negroes" in the Red Summer of 1919.

Racial Massacres: Florida Election Day Riots, 1920, and Tulsa, 1921 "We Americans," Warren G. Harding said early in his presidency, "are united in the sweetest concord that ever united men." Events of that same period, however, belied Harding's cheerful observation. For on election day in 1920, racial warfare was waged by whites against blacks in towns throughout the state of Florida; and in early June of 1921 much of Tulsa's black housing lay in smoking ruins after assaults by white arsonists.

In the autumn of 1920 two events occurred simultaneously in such Florida towns as Ocoee and Orlando in the central part of the state, in Palmetto on the west-central coast, and in Jacksonville, Quincy, Greenville, and Live Oak to the north. One was the resurgence of the Ku Klux Klan and the other was the concerted efforts by black citizens to register and vote. The Ku Klux Klan held huge parades prior to the elections on November 2. In Jacksonville, for example, 1,000 men wearing full Klan regalia marched on the evening of October 30. The Klan also sent threatening letters to those advocating black enfranchisement. "We have been informed," the Grand Master, Florida Ku Klucks wrote a white lawyer, "that you have been telling Negroes to register. . . ." Reminding the lawyer of the Klan's role in subverting Reconstruction, the Grand Master noted that, with the reappearance of the Klan in 1920, "now you know that history repeats itself. . . . We shall always enjoy WHITE SUPREMACY in this country and he who interferes must face the consequences." The word also went out to blacks; in Ocoee, the local Klan notified the black citizenry that no blacks would be allowed to vote and that violence would result if any even tried to do so. Despite these efforts at intimidation, blacks continued to try to register, and on election day thousands appeared at the polling places.

In Jacksonville on November 2, a black minister reported that "more than 3,000 [black] men and women stood in line from 8 A.M. to 5:40 P.M. . . . and were not allowed to vote." Elsewhere there was bloodshed and burning. In Ocoee, a mob surrounded the black residential area, doused buildings with kerosene, and burned eighteen houses, two churches, a schoolhouse, and a lodge hall. Several blacks, including a mother and her baby, were cremated in their houses. Although the total of fatalities was never determined, it was believed that as many as 32 blacks were murdered in Ocoee. In Palmetto, a prospective black voter was gunned down and died the next day. The Klan threatened to kill several black leaders in Live Oak unless they left town. And from Gadsden County in northern Florida there came pathetic news from an anonymous author describing election day: " . . . I want to say that did not a Negro vote in my Co[unty]. They [the whites] wint around by the 2 and three hundred in auto with white Caps over they faces and Rifles furbide Negroes to vote. . . . one of our (NAACP) Members . . . was taking out by Mob at night and linch . . . and was thrown in to the Ocklockonee River (after being shot, his hands tied behind his back, and weighted with a sack of sand fastened to his neck). . . ."

Like so many other outbreaks of racial violence, an alleged rape of a white girl by a black youth was the spark that ignited the Tulsa race riot of May 31–June 1, 1921. The real reasons, however, were more substantive. Tulsa was a city that had almost quintupled its population in ten years. Throughout that time, corrupt politics were controlled by a vice ring, blacks were demanding equal rights, and persistent and undeterred violence raged against both blacks and whites. Fearing that the accused rapist would be lynched, 75 blacks had marched to the jail to set up vigil, but having been assured by the sheriff that the prisoner would be safe, they had begun to disperse. At this point, a white man tried to disarm one of the blacks, a shot was fired, and then, according to the sheriff, "all hell broke loose." There were further shots, and twelve men were fatally wounded, ten of them white and two black. Upon hearing of the shootings, several thousand white men armed with clubs, cans of oil, torches, rifles, and even machine guns massed for an attack on "Little Africa," the city's black section. Block after block of homes were burned to the ground. The official death toll of the slaughter was twenty-six blacks and ten whites. The unofficial estimate of the NAACP was that 50 whites and between 150 and 200 blacks were killed. "What," Walter

White asked, "is America going to do after such a horrible carnage . . . ? How much longer will America allow these pogroms to continue unchecked?"

The Decline in Major Race Riots Although spectacular incidents of racial violence occurred in the late 1920s, there was a marked decline in the number of large-scale riots. At least for the time being, racial wars on the scale of those in East St. Louis, in Chicago, and in Tulsa had come to an end. Tension continued to exist in racially contested neighborhoods in the urban North and, on occasion, there was violence. One such instance occurred in 1925 in Detroit, after a black physician, Dr. Ossian H. Sweet, purchased a house in an all-white neighborhood. During the Sweets' second day of occupancy, a mob numbering about 1,000 surrounded the house and bombarded it with rocks. A shot was fired from the house, mortally wounding a white man, and initiating one of the most famous criminal trials in Afro-American history. The NAACP hired Clarence Darrow to defend Sweet and a friend who had been visiting in the house. The final verdict, after one hung jury, was acquittal.

Racial Violence During the Great Depression For many people in the United States, the Great Depression arrived with shattering suddenness in October 1929. However, for hundreds of thousands of farmers, coal miners, and railroad and textile workers, the 1920s had been a time of almost unrelieved economic hardship. For them, the Great Depression was only an additional disaster, and in certain parts of the country, this disaster precipitated racial violence. In the South, lynchings increased from 12 (including four whites) in 1929 to 25 (all but one black) in 1930. "For the Negro in the South is in deep trouble now . . . ," *Outlook* magazine declared in late 1930. "Intense anti-Negro feeling has the states of the cotton belt in its grip, and every few days it strikes down a victim."

To combat economic deprivation and lack of political power some black tenant farmers and sharecroppers formed labor unions. But this action, too, brought on violence. In July 1931, in an incident reminiscent of the Phillips County, Ark., riot of 1919, an armed white mob stormed a black church in Camp Hill, Ala., where a sharecroppers' union was meeting. Gunfire was exchanged, a number of blacks were wounded, and in the next few days a posse of 500 whites roved the countryside hunting blacks. Officially, one black was killed and five wounded, but the toll was probably far higher. "It wasn't much," a local marshall later recalled. "The sheriff heard the niggers were having a Communist meeting and we went with him to break the meeting up— and shooting started." The efforts by numerous tenants and sharecroppers to overcome their lot continued despite the violence. Some of these efforts were biracial: blacks and whites joined together in 1934 to form the Southern Tenant Farmers' Union. But violence persisted as well: in 1935, 25 blacks were lynched, five of them leaders of an Alabama sharecroppers' union engaged in a cotton pickers' strike.

The South also suffered other kinds of labor-related racial violence in the 1930s. In the early 1930s, for example, the Mississippi division of the Illinois Central Railroad hired black firemen. By mid-1933, seven of these firemen had been ambushed and murdered, seven wounded, and one brutally flogged.

The "New-Style" Riot in Harlem, 1935 In addition to the physical violence, an enormous amount of psychological and symbolic violence damaged the pride and self-esteem of individual blacks, who were often unable to defend themselves and their families against the abuses and the insults of second-class citizenship. Hunger and dispossession from the land aggravated the problems of

In mid-Depression 1935, bleak economic prospects and urban pressures spurred a riot in Harlem. (*National Archives.*)

these blacks in the 1930s. Thus uprooted, tens of thousands migrated to the cities of the North.

Unlike the mood of the migration during World War I, the atmosphere of the 1930s migration was not hopeful. In the cities, unemployment, poverty, dilapidated housing, filth, neglect, and disease already existed, despite several attempts by blacks to organize in protest against these conditions. Blacks formed unions of apartment tenants to demand reasonable rents and adequate upkeep, and organizations were established to boycott businesses that practiced discriminatory hiring. "Don't Buy Where You Can't Work," was the advice of Harlem's Negro Industrial and Clerical League. But these actions did not alleviate the frustrations of the urban North's black slumdwellers. At best, the boycotts and rent strikes brought only transitory relief. More gratifying for many blacks, at least in the short run, was violence, especially violence against white landlords and merchants.

In March 1935, after rumors had spread of the killing of a black youth caught stealing a knife by a white shopkeeper, Harlem exploded into furious smashing and looting. "The looting was brazen and daring . . . ," the black writer Claude McKay reported. "But," he added, "the mass riot in Harlem was not a race riot. . . . there was no manifest hostility between colored and white as such. . . . white persons, singly and in groups, walked the streets of Harlem without being molested." Unlike the riots of the Red Summer (1919)—and like the civil disorders of the 1960s—the Harlem riot was black-initiated, and the objects of assault were not people but property; (especially stores), the symbols of the white man's economic domination over the black man. Two hundred stores were wrecked by black mobs, accounting for millions of dollars in damage. A riot commission reported that the basic causes of the Harlem disorders were "resentments against racial discrimination and poverty in the midst of plenty." A new style of race rioting, one that would be repeated scores of times in the 1960s, appeared on the streets of Harlem in 1935.

World War II The United States finally emerged from the Great Depression during World War II. Priming the economic pump were billions of federal dollars for war production, creating jobs for both blacks and whites. For a while, as war industries practiced discrimination in hiring, it seemed that blacks would not benefit equally from the sudden availability of jobs. But the threat of a March on Washington, D.C., by tens of thousands of blacks in 1941 produced a presidential order encouraging the hiring of blacks for war work.

Many blacks, however, argued that war service should produce guarantees of democracy as well as of jobs. "A community is democratic," A. Philip Randolph, the leader of the all-black march on Washington, D.C., stated in 1942, "only when the humblest and weakest person can enjoy the highest civil, economic, and social rights that the biggest and most powerful possess. . . . By fighting for their rights now, American Negroes are helping to make America a moral and spiritual arsenal of democracy." However, many whites felt threatened by such uncompromising demands for equality. To them, Randolph and other civil rights activists in 1941 and 1942 were "agitators" and "rabble-rousers." "Extremist Negro leaders and Negro newspapers in this country," Virginius Dabney, a white southerner, wrote early in 1943, "are demanding an overnight revolution in race relations." "Unless saner counsels prevail," Dabney warned, "we may have the worst internal clashes since Reconstruction, with hundreds, if not thousands, killed. . . ."

As is 1917–19, widespread violence occurred in 1942 as once again black aspirations were in collision with white determination to reaffirm the status quo. In several cities and towns, shootouts and pitched battles between black soldiers and white soldiers and policemen resulted from this collision: 29 black soldiers were injured in a battle with white military policemen in Alexandria, La.; three soldiers—two black, one white—were killed in a riot at Fort Dix, N.J.; race riots involving troops occurred at Tuskegee, Ala.; Flagstaff, Ariz.; New Orleans, La.; Florence, S.C.; and Vallejo, Calif. However, the old type of black-white rioting was passing away during the years of World War II, and new patterns of civil disorders would emerge. See also NATIONAL ASSOCIATION FOR THE ADVANCEMENT OF COLORED PEOPLE (NAACP); POPULATION.

REFERENCES: Relevant books for consultation include: Chalmers, David M., Hooded Americanism: The History of the Ku Klux Klan, Doubleday, Garden City, 1965; Garfinkel, Herbert, When Negroes March: The March on Washington Movement . . . , Atheneum, New York, 1969; Graham, Hugh Davis and Ted Robert Gurr (eds.), Violence in America: Historical and Comparative Perspectives, U.S. Government Printing Office, Washington, D.C., 1969; Grubbs, Donald H., Cry from the Cotton: The Southern Tenant Farmers' Union and the New Deal, University of North Carolina Press, Chapel Hill, 1971; Rudwick, Elliott, Race Riot at East St. Louis, July 2, 1917, Meridian, Cleveland, 1966; Seligmann, Herbert J., The Negro Faces America, Harper & Brothers, New York, 1920; Tindall, George B., The Emergence of the New South, 1913–1945, Louisiana State University Press, Baton Rouge, 1967; Tuttle, William M., Jr., Race Riot: Chicago in the Red Summer of 1919, Atheneum, New York, 1970; Waskow, Arthur I., From Race Riot to Sit-In, 1919 and the 1960s, Doubleday, Garden City, 1966; White, Walter F., A Man Called White: The Autobiography of Walter White, Viking, New York, 1948; and Wolters, Raymond, Negroes and the Great Depression: The Problem of Economic Recovery, Greenwood Press, Westport, 1970.

Civil Disorders: 1943–Present

In recent years, students of America's long history of urban racial violence have come to distinguish between the "old style" race riots that generally characterized the years prior to World War II, and the "new style" civil disorders that have dominated ever since. According to this distinction, the older or traditional racial conflicts were basically ecological or communal in character in that they involved pitched battles between large numbers of white and black citizens. These outbursts were customarily sparked by incidents that occurred in peripheral areas dividing white and black neighborhoods; and the ensuing battles more often than not involved aggressive white mobs, defensive blacks, and police control that was generally ineffective and frequently sympathetic to whites. This older type of racial violence, although linked through the years by the continuity of white aggression against blacks, can nonetheless, be divided into three periods: (1) the pre-Civil War period when violence was inherent in the master-slave relationship; (2) the period of Reconstruction and adjustment when lynchings increased following emancipation and peaked in 1892; (3) the post-Populist and World War I periods when racial incidents occurred in such cities as Wilmington, N.C. (1896); Springfield, Ill. (1908); East St. Louis, Ill. (1917); Washington, D.C. (1919); Tulsa, Okla. (1921); and most notably in Chicago, Ill. (1919).

The new style riot since World War II has been characterized more as a "commodity" than as a communal disorder: the violence generally has been confined to the black ghettos and has not involved white mobs. Black aggression has been less directed against the lives of white civilians and more symbolically directed against white-owned property and, increasingly, against the police—the guardsmen and soldiers who represent the authority of the white establishment. This fundamental transition in the pattern of collective racial violence was conditioned by the great migration of blacks into the nation's inner cities; by confining racial discrimination that created the ghetto and strangled its economic life and civic health; and also to some extent by the growth and modernization of urban police forces, which, with radios and patrol cars, quickly seal off exploding ghettos from surrounding white communities.

A Definite New Style: 1943 The year 1943 provides a useful demarcation between old style and new style racial disturbances, not because it neatly separates them—in fact, the Harlem riot of 1935 more closely resembles the new pattern, and conversely, persistent communal flare-ups (1970s) in such smaller cities and towns as Cairo, Ill., and York, Pa., continue to reflect the older patterns—but because two major riots in that year most clearly reflect this change.

In Detroit in 1943, 9 whites and 25 blacks were killed in an eruption that in many ways reflected the older pattern: confrontations between recently arrived black migrants and aggressive white mobs, precipitated by an incident that occurred in a peripheral, congested area (the Belle Isle). In fact, the fuel for the riot was provided at the Belle Isle Amusement Park when black teenagers, who a few days earlier had been ejected from the white-controlled Eastwood Park, had a fistfight with a white man. Rumors of atrocities (none had occurred) quickly spread to the heart of the ghetto, and vengeful blacks began stoning passing cars driven by whites and then smashing and looting the ghetto's white-owned businesses.

The Harlem riot of the same year was even more characteristic of the new type of rioting. In this case, the ghetto population was composed of many blacks who were long-time residents of the community; the riot was started within the Negro community, not at the periphery; it did not involve a confrontation between black and white civilians; its looting and destruction were directed against property and retail establishments owned mainly by outside white proprietors; and the casualties and deaths resulted mainly from the use of force against the black population by police and by units of the National Guard.

Although the basic ingredients of the commodity-type civil disorder had been established during World War II, these new style riots did not occur in any significant degree until the middle 1960s. The sudden outbreak of urban violence in these years coincided with two paradoxical events: the successful enactment of civil rights laws for which the civil rights movement had fought for so many years, and the disintegration of the civil rights movement and the upsurge of the separatist, anti-integrationist rhetoric of Black Power.

Clearly, the burgeoning, nonviolent civil rights movement of the 1950s and the early 1960s had instilled new hope and great expectations in the hearts of millions of Afro-Americans. These sentiments were encouraged by the erosion of white racial antagonism and of the de jure structure of segregation, and by such biracial demonstrations as the March on Washington, D.C., of 1963 and the optimistic rhetoric of liberal reformers. In the 1950s and the early 1960s, racial violence continued and even quickened in the South; but, ironically, black courage and determination combined with the new age of televised exposure to transform such celebrated symbols of southern racial brutality as Sheriff "Jim" Clark of Selma, Ala., and Police Commissioner "Bull" Connor of Birmingham, Ala., into unwitting allies of the civil rights movement. The U.S. Congress passed a comprehensive civil rights act in 1964, and in 1965 issued a voting rights act with genuine teeth. A joint session of Congress listened and cheered as President Lyndon B. Johnson, himself a southerner, affirmed that "We *shall* overcome."

The summer violence of 1963 in Birmingham, Ala., for all its outrage and despair, also carried a promise of hope. Nonetheless, this outburst was followed in 1964 by additional explosions of racial anger in Rochester, N.Y., and in Harlem and in the Bedford-Stuyvesant section of Brooklyn (New York City)—and the accelerating series of "long hot summers" in the urban ghettos of the North and the West had begun. Racial violence also flared that summer in Chicago, Ill., Cleveland, Ohio, and Philadelphia, Pa.; in Jersey City, Elizabeth, and Patterson, N.J.; and in St. Augustine and Jacksonville, Fla.

Riots of the 1960s The most destructive race riot (since those in 1943) exploded in the Watts section of Los Angeles, Calif., in the summer of 1965: more than 4,000 citizens were arrested, 34 were killed, hundreds were wounded, and an estimated $35 million in property damage occurred. The following summer (1966), Chicago erupted: 4,200 National Guardsmen joined the police in making 533 arrests, and 3 blacks were killed. Violence also flared in Dayton, Ohio, and in the Hough section of Cleveland, Ohio. During the spring of 1967, bellwether disruptions occurred on predominantly black college campuses in Nashville, Tenn., Houston,

Tex., and Jackson, Miss., and during that summer another riot, larger than the Watts riot, took place in Detroit: 7,200 arrests, 43 dead (33 blacks and 10 whites), and more than $40 million property damage. Another major riot shook Newark, N.J., and lesser riots flared in Cincinnati, Ohio, Tampa, Fla., Atlanta, Ga., and several cities in northern New Jersey (Elizabeth, Englewood, Jersey City, Plainfield, and New Brunswick). In response to the growing turmoil, President Lyndon B. Johnson created the National Advisory Commission on Civil Disorders, headed by Governor Otto Kerner of Illinois. The Kerner Commission reported that during the first nine months of 1967 there were 164 disorders in 128 cities: 8 (5 percent) of these riots were classified as major, 33 (20 percent) as serious, and 123 (75 percent) as minor. In its final report, the Kerner Commission forcefully isolated "white racism" as the fundamental cause of the racial violence: "What white Americans can never fully understand—but what the Negro can never forget—is that white society is deeply implicated in the ghetto. White institutions maintain it, and white society condones it." In conclusion, the Kerner Commission bluntly warned that "our Nation is moving toward two societies, one black, one white—separate and unequal."

The *Report of the National Advisory Commission on Civil Disorders* was issued in March 1968. On April 4, 1968, Rev. Martin Luther King, Jr., was murdered by a white man in Memphis,

Tenn., and in the following week, urban America's brief respite from violence was shattered by protesting blacks. Memphis, closest to the tragedy, blew up first; but as news of the assassination quickly spread through the news media, riots erupted once again in Harlem, Bedford-Stuyvesant (Brooklyn), Nashville, and Jackson. Disorders then broke out in such previously riotless cities as Boston, Mass., and Hartford, Conn.; in Greensboro, Raleigh, Winston-Salem, Durham, Charlotte, and New Bern, N.C.; and most explosively of all in Washington, D.C., where heavily armed units of the 82d Airborne Division were flown in from Fort Bragg, N.C., to help restore order. This marked the first time that the Army had been summoned to quell civil insurrection in Washington, D.C., since Gen. Douglas MacArthur had routed the "bonus army" from Anacostia Flats in 1932. In Washington, D.C., 8 people were killed and 705 were injured.

On the day following King's death, massive rioting once again erupted in Chicago, where 6,000 guardsmen and 5,000 army troops joined the overwhelmed police: 11 demonstrators were killed (7 blacks and 4 whites) and 350 were arrested. Violence also flared that day in Detroit, Mich., Toledo, Ohio, Pittsburgh, Pa., Philadelphia, Pa., Savannah, Ga., Tallahassee, Fla., and San Francisco, Calif. On April 6 further rioting occurred in Cincinnati, Ohio, Newark and Trenton, N.J., and particularly in Baltimore, Md., where 6,000 guardsmen and 2,000 federal troops

A pall of smoke hangs over Detroit, Mich. after the first day of racial violence in Detroit, Mich. When the disorder had abated after the second day (July 23–24, 1967), more than 24 people had been killed and property damage had reached $150 million. *(Wide World Photos.)*

were brought in (5 people were killed and 258 were injured). In April alone more National Guard troops were called out than in all of 1967 (34,900 to 27,700) and far more federal troops were used (23,700 to 4,800).

Riots and Radicalism During the summer of 1968, two additional events occurred that signified yet another fundamental transformation in the evolving patterns of American racial violence. In August the violence that broke out at the Democratic National Convention in Chicago—which the Walker Report to the National Commission on the Causes and Prevention of Violence labeled a "police riot"—involved blacks only minimally and peripherally. Though most black leaders denounced the war in Indochina, the large part of the political protesters were white students, young radicals, and white middle-class liberals.

More significant—and certainly more ominous—were the implications of the shooting that occurred in Cleveland, Ohio, that same summer. On the evening of July 5, a full-scale gun battle broke out in Glenville, on Cleveland's racially troubled East Side, between city police and black snipers. The gunfire and arson continued for five days, and in its smoldering aftermath 63 business establishments were damaged or destroyed and property losses were in excess of $2 million (this was considerably less than the destruction of April). Four salient characteristics distinguished the pattern of the Cleveland outbreak from previous disorders. First, it began not as property-oriented but as people-oriented violence, with heavily armed blacks (snipers) and whites (police) shooting at each other. Second, there were more white casualties than black, an unprecedented situation in the history of major American racial violence. After the first hour of shooting, the official casualty list reported: 3 police killed, 12 injured; 3 suspects killed, 1 wounded; 1 civilian killed, 2 injured—out of a total of 22 casualties, 15 were police. Third, the shooting occurred in the first major American city to have elected a black mayor, Carl B. Stokes. Fourth, Mayor Stokes, who had been successful in preventing violence in Cleveland after the assassination of Martin Luther King, Jr., introduced a new and highly controversial technique for quelling the violence. At the urging of local black leaders, he placed control of the troubled neighborhood in the residents' hands and barred white policeman, National Guardsmen, and white nonresidents from the area. This technique was only partially successful in calming the Cleveland disorder, and after one trial night the incensed white police and guardsmen were reintroduced into the neighborhood, chiefly to protect property.

In view of the relative absence of large-scale civil disorders after 1968, and in light of the subsequent development of open warfare between city police and such radical black groups as the Black Panthers, it appeared that yet another type of civil disorder had evolved, one characterized by small but tightly organized and heavily armed groups of radicals waging guerrilla warfare against the police and the system of authority they represent. Yet, such revolutionaries represented only a tiny minority of Afro-Americans.

Conclusion Behavioral scientists have probed the large-scale riots of the 1960s in an attempt to determine their origins and dynamics, and especially to ascertain who participated in them and why. One early attempt, now largely discredited, was that made by the McCone Commission on the Watts riot of 1965. That commission's explanation rested chiefly on what has been called the "riffraff" theory, which holds that urban unrest is a product of a deprived class of recent unassimilated migrants to the cities. Yet survey data reveal that no significant difference in income between rioters and nonrioters existed, that rioters were neither the poorest of the poor nor the hard-core unemployed, and that those most likely to riot were not migrants but long-term residents. Indeed, the data revealed that the blacks most likely to riot and to respond favorably to the slogan "Black Power" were employed, long-term residents whose social outlook and political attitudes were rooted not in the paternalistic culture of the rural South but in the cosmopolitan, secularized environment typical of northern cities. For these blacks, the influence of the church had waned, as had faith in the benevolence of paternalistic friends and allies, especially in government. Probably only the church-dominated, essentially peasant culture of the rural and small-town South had endowed the nonviolent and long suffering followers of Martin Luther King, Jr., with the strength to endure. When Reverend King attempted to bring his nonviolent tactics to the brittle, angry culture of the northern ghettos, the discipline of the protesters cracked under the first strain. Too, southern cities were rapidly coming to resemble, both physically and culturally, their counterparts to the North and West.

In all the urban riots since 1943, black leaders

sought with varied success to stem the tide of violence, which was in part inevitably self-destructive. An uneasy calm followed the massive summer disorders of 1968, despite the occasional outbursts of guerrilla-type warfare that shattered that implicit armistice. Only time will determine whether Martin Luther King, Jr.'s celebrated dream will free American cities from their legacy of racial carnage. *See also* CIVIL RIGHTS MOVEMENT; DISCRIMINATION; HOUSING; NATIONAL ASSOCIATION FOR THE ADVANCEMENT OF COLORED PEOPLE (NAACP); POPULATION.

REFERENCES Suggested references include: Baskin, Joseph (ed.), *Urban Racial Violence in the Twentieth Century*, Glencoe Press, Beverly Hills, 1969; Caplan, Nathan S. and Jeffrey M. Paige, "A Study of Ghetto Rioters," *Scientific American*, August 1968, pp. 15–21; Graham, Hugh Davis and Ted Robert Gurr, *The History of Violence in America*, Praeger, New York, 1969, especially chaps. 2, 9, 10, and 11; *Report of the National Advisory Commission on Civil Disorders*, E. P. Dutton, New York, 1968; *Rebels in Eden*, Little, Brown, Boston, 1970, especially chap. 6; Skolnick, Jerome H., *The Politics of Protest*, Ballantine, New York, 1969, especially chaps. 4, 5, and 6; and *To Establish Justice, To Insure Domestic Tranquility: Final Report of the National Commission on the Causes and Prevention of Violence*, U.S. Government Printing Office, Washington, D.C., 1969.

CIVIL RIGHTS

Civil Rights: Movement

Introduction Protest is deeply rooted in the Afro-American experience. Even as they were being involuntarily and forcibly taken from their homelands and shipped to the New World, ancestors of today's American blacks expressed protest against enslavement through individual acts that ranged from passive reluctance to starvation, self-mutilation, and suicide by drowning. Mutinies at sea were strongly guarded against, but nevertheless some have been recorded—the most publicized uprising having taken place aboard the ship *Amistad*. Once settled in the New World, slaves continued to protest in many ways, including deception, malingering, pilferage, flight, and rebellion. Likewise, northern free blacks in the United States, taking advantage of the freedom of assembly and of speech, met in national pre-Civil War conventions to protest slavery. However, with the collapse of Reconstruction after the Civil War, and its subsequent replacement with massive discrimination and Jim Crow laws, Afro-Americans made special, organized efforts in behalf of civil rights.

In a very real sense, the first meaningful civil rights movement came into being at the end of the nineteenth century when racism by whites was conducted in the form of disfranchisement, lynching, terror, and the numerous degrading indignities imposed by segregation and discrimination. This first movement was essentially passive, being strongly tempered by black fears of southern white repression and reprisal.

The second, more important movement came after World War II. It was essentially activist in nature; it had massive appeal to and support of blacks, and it affected a greater and more sympathetic national response. With two distinct but interrelated phases, one of direct nonviolent action and the other of direct militant action, the second movement was variously referred to by such names as the "Negro Revolt," the "Black Revolution," the "Civil Rights Revolution," and the "Second Reconstruction." The movement climaxed in the late 1960s, most probably in 1968, in the reaction of both black and white Americans to the assassination of the well-known civil rights leader, Martin Luther King, Jr.

Protest Collaboration (Accommodation) A protest collaboration movement originated and developed mainly under the leadership of two Afro-American school principals: Booker T. Washington of Tuskegee, Ala. and W. H. Councill of Normal, Ala. This movement was centered on the theory that it was in the best interest of Afro-Americans to get along with white people. Judging the temper of their times skillfully and pragmatically, Washington and Councill sought compromise and accomodation within the framework of the establishment. While Washington mainly endorsed the idea of Afro-Americans lifting themselves up within the segregated system, Councill tended to define their role in terms of the fallen planter class. Emerging as the most distinguished and enduring collaboration leader, Washington used his school at Tuskegee as a base

CIVIL RIGHTS:Movement

for the training of blacks as common, industrial, and technical workers, and as leaders within the black community. He founded the National Negro Business League in 1900, the purpose of which, as stated in its constitution, was the "promotion of commercial achievement" for blacks.

Protest collaboration was not accepted by all blacks despite Washington's immense popularity. W. E. B. Du Bois, one of the most vocal opponents of Washington's leadership, once referred to Washington as the "Tuskegee Machine." In 1905 Du Bois organized an ill-fated movement that became known as the Niagara

Movement (named after the locale of its first meeting, Niagara Falls, N.Y.). Four years later, the Niagara Movement was superseded by the organization of the National Association for the Advancement of Colored People (NAACP), in which Du Bois played an important role. The NAACP occupies a supreme and special place in the civil rights movement of the twentieth century; its goals were the integration of Afro-Americans into the American mainstream; its methods sought redress largely through the courts, the ballot, and the press.

Nonviolent Direct Action One of the first notable

In protest for civil rights, an estimated quarter million demonstrators, from places throughout the nation, assembled peaceably near the Washington Monument in Washington, D.C., in August of 1963. *(National Archives.)*

attempts at direct nonviolent action was made by A. Philip Randolph, president of the Brotherhood of Sleeping Car Porters, when he threatened to organize a mass march on Washington, D.C., at the beginning of World War II. The idea of the mass march was revived in the early 1960s and culminated in 1963, when an estimated 250,000 Afro-Americans from all over the nation converged on the nation's capital to protest discrimination. Many placards displayed the words "FREEDOM NOW"; others indicated the need for fair treatment in such matters as housing and employment.

The movement of nonviolent direct action found its greatest success in the organized efforts of the Southern Christian Leadership Conference (SCLC), whose roots extended to civil rights actions in Montgomery, Ala. Under the principal leadership of Martin Luther King Jr., the SCLC organized a successful boycott of the segregated public buses of Montgomery in 1955. King's leadership in the boycott emphasized the Christian doctrine of love: it is better to receive violence than to inflict it upon others. His nonviolent principles and approach were reminiscent of Mohandas K. Gandhi (1869–1948), the internationally known Indian reformer and nationalist.

Included in the strategy of the nonviolent movement in general and of the SCLC in particular were the following: (1) to coordinate local protest centers and agencies throughout the nation that would adhere to a philosophy of nonviolence; (2) to implement national civil rights laws by peacefully disobeying local laws that promoted segregation and discrimination; (3) to dramatize the evils of local segregation laws and of the system of segregation; and (4) to desegregate large cities in the South and in other parts of the nation.

Included among the effects of the movement were the following: (1) arousing sympathy for the black cause throughout the United States and abroad; (2) implementing some of the civil rights laws and court decisions that the NAACP had succeeded in getting on the books; (3) building up adequate moral pressure to secure the passage of new and more effective civil rights legislation at the national level; and (4) inspiring and motivating many whites and blacks, particularly youths, to participate in the civil rights movement.

Militant Direct Action The phase of militant direct action of the civil rights movement grew out of the failure of civil rights enforcement and

the violent treatment suffered by blacks at the hands of white racists, particularly in the South. This treatment included: (1) white police brutality against Afro-Americans; (2) terrorist activities against Afro-Americans and the lack of police protection; (3) lack of redress for Afro-Americans, especially in lower and state courts; (4) racist pressures from white southern politicians; and (5) economic deprivation (in general) and reprisals (in particular) against Afro-Americans who either passively or actively sought change.

A close-up of some of the protesting demonstrators in Washington shows (from left, with white badges): Roy Wilkins of the NAACP; A. Philip Randolph, pioneer labor leader; and Walter Reuther of the United Automobile Workers (UAW). (National Archives.)

The Student Nonviolent Coordinating Committee (SNCC) is properly associated with this phase of the movement. This organization, mainly formed of students from black colleges in the South, was founded in 1960 in order to take more dynamic and more militant action against segregation than that espoused by the SCLC. One of SNCC's aims was to desegregate public facilities; another was to register to vote masses of Afro-Americans in the South. It also attempted to organize a third political party in Mississippi and Alabama. Stunned by reprisals, SNCC eventually denounced nonviolence as a technique, particularly after Stokely Carmichael succeeded John Lewis as the national chairman in 1966. About the same time, members of the Congress of Racial Equality (CORE), who had also suffered bitter experiences and reprisals in the Deep South, adopted Carmichael's "Black Power" slogan in 1965. The most violent-prone of the militant direct action organizations was the Black Panther Party.

Expressing a mood rather than a program, the so-called Black Power movement of the late

1960s was articulated in varying degrees by several militant civil rights groups. Especially for youths, the movement symbolized black awareness, black pride, black self-respect, and black consciousness, all of which were ingredients of the rationale, rhetoric, fashion, hairstyle, and life-styles of an ever-increasing number of Afro-Americans by the late 1960s. Black Power was adopted as a symbol of CORE, SNCC, and the Mississippi Freedom Democratic Party (MFDP); the NAACP and the National Urban League objected to the use of the slogan. The SCLC had initially disagreed with the slogan, but later endorsed its underlying ideology. Basic to that ideology was an old principle of race consciousness—positive beliefs in racial identity and in racial pride that would serve as adhesive and guiding forces in the movement toward equal rights. Fundamental to the belief, therefore, was the attainment of greater political power by blacks. Indeed, blacks did gain some political power as a result of the civil rights movements; but those who held power were not the militants of Black Power rhetoric.

The civil rights movement was universal and diverse, representing the aspirations of Afro-Americans of all classes in all regions of the nation. The movement's impact, however, was particularly manifest in the South, where eight or nine out of every ten blacks lived, where segregation and discrimination were most apparent, and where the problems of poverty, health, and race relations seemed most acute. The nature, extent, and diversity of the civil rights movement can, therefore, be best illustrated by tracing its history in various selected states in the South. The national dimensions of the movement, however, can be traced through civil rights acts, civil rights cases, and civil rights enforcement.

Civil Rights: Acts

Introduction The history of federal civil rights legislation began during the period of Reconstruction with the adoption of the Thirteenth Amendment, which abolished slavery in 1865; the Fourteenth Amendment, which affirmed black citizenship under the Constitution in 1868; and the Fifteenth Amendment, which forbade interference with the right to vote on the basis of race, color, or previous condition of servitude in 1870. These three constitutional amendments have provided the U.S. Congress with the authority for enacting the civil rights legislation that has become law since 1865.

Reconstruction Acts Of the seven acts passed during Reconstruction under the authority of the new amendments to the Constitution and concerned directly with black people, five were general civil rights acts. While several of these were limited in their scope, others were quite comprehensive.

The Civil Rights Act of April 9, 1866, was passed over President Andrew Johnson's veto and was fashioned to prevent him and southern conservatives from continuing black servitude with the sanction of the Black Codes. Based on the Thirteenth Amendment, the act consisted of ten wide-ranging sections. The most important provisions were as follows: blacks were declared citizens and as such were granted equal rights to contracts, suits, access to trials, purchases, and properties. All citizens were made subject to "like punishment, pains, and penalties." Any person found guilty of depriving citizens of the stated rights because of race, color, or previous condition of servitude could be fined up to $1000, imprisoned, or both. United States district and circuit courts were given jurisdiction over cases arising under the statute, and officials prosecuted by the states for complying with the federal law were granted removal by habeas corpus to federal court. The President was authorized to direct other officials to enforce the Act and to use the army or navy as a last resort in its execution.

The Enforcement Act of May 31, 1870, while designed principally to guarantee black suffrage, was even broader than its predecessor. Basically, this act directed that all citizens otherwise qualified to vote in any election should not be denied that privilege because of race. States were allowed to set up prerequisites for voting, but all persons were to have equal access to the right to vote. Two or more persons acting to obstruct voting in violation of the act were guilty of felonious conspiracy and subject to a fine of not more than $5,000 and imprisonment for up to ten years.

The Act of February 28, 1871, amending the Enforcement Act of 1870, was designed to eliminate fraudulent registration practices. This Act established a complex system of federal machinery to supervise elections in the states. Upon petition, the circuit courts of the United States could commission election supervisors who were granted the authority to oversee both registration and voting. Again the federal courts were given jurisdiction over all cases arising under the act.

The Act of April 20, 1871, the third enforcement act, commonly called the Ku Klux Act, was designed primarily to prevent intimidation of blacks by illegal action where states were unwilling or unable to provide protection. The act contained a provision granting the President the right to employ the militia in cases where insurrection obstructed the execution of the laws. The President was further authorized to suspend the right of habeas corpus where "unlawful combinations" acted to endanger public safety.

Another Reconstruction measure, the Civil Rights Act of 1875, guaranteed to all persons, regardless of race or color, the "full and equal enjoyment" of inns, public conveyances, and public places of amusement; granted the right to sue for personal damages; gave the federal courts exclusive jurisdiction over all cases arising under the act; and made it a misdemeanor to bar any qualified person from serving as a grand or petit juror. This was the last piece of civil rights legislation passed by the U.S. Congress until 1957.

Two other acts may be included within this general category of legislation. The Act of May 1866 provided for the punishment of kidnapping with intent to carry into involuntary servitude. One year later, Congress passed an act forbidding "the holding of any person to service or labor under the system known as peonage" or in any way returning any person to such a condition.

Reaction to Reconstruction During Reconstruction, a number of southern states passed laws designed to protect the civil rights of blacks, but as soon as Reconstruction was overthrown, many states enacted discriminatory statutes. Some laws prohibited intermarriage; other laws provided unequal punishment for blacks for the same crime if committed by whites, excluded blacks from jury service, provided separate schools, and provided for separate public accommodations.

Although discriminatory statutes were the rule in the South, a number of northern state legislatures enacted laws to protect civil rights in the early part of the twentieth century. For example, in Illinois in 1919 and in California in 1925, acts were passed that forbade the open defamation and disparagement of blacks or the publication of inflammatory materials calculated to engender hatred among minorities. Additionally, some southern as well as northern states passed new laws to prevent lynching and to strengthen older laws prohibiting terrorism or vigilante activity. A few northern states, including Pennsylvania in 1911, passed laws forbidding the establishment of racially segregated schools, and several modest bans against discrimination in employment were enacted. However, the rarity of civil and criminal cases arising under these laws and the impediments placed in the way of their enforcement give credence to the theory that they were largely ineffective efforts.

Despite the few measures to the contrary, the period from 1875 to 1957, during which no federal civil rights legislation was passed, was dominated by extreme racism and restrictive Jim Crow legislation. Racism was reinforced by pseudoscientific sanction and by religious primitivism, and aggravated by the flow of immigrants from Europe that led to increased nativism. Together, these factors stiffened the determination of white Americans to maintain (by statute or otherwise) the status quo of blacks. The passage of civil rights legislation became impossible in such a setting, even after the successful organization of the National Association for the Advancement of Colored People (NAACP), which, in desperate attempts to reverse the tide of oppression, argued a number of cases before the U.S. Supreme Court involving the right to vote, residential segregation, separate public education, and segregated interstate and local transportation.

Little changed in the legal framework that supported the structure of racism and discrimination in the first few decades of the twentieth century. An increasingly urbanized black population suffered the effects of legal racism throughout World War I, the postwar "Red Scare," and the Ku Klux Klan and antiforeign activity that pervaded the 1920s. The major effort toward legislative reform during these years was the lobbying of the NAACP in favor of antilynching and antipoll tax legislation.

Impact of World War II In 1941, responding to A. Phillip Randolph's threat to organize a march on Washington, D.C., for July 1, 1941, that would publicize the black demand for employment in the booming American defense industry, President Franklin D. Roosevelt issued his celebrated Executive Order No. 8802. The order, carrying the force of law, provided that there would be no discrimination in the national defense program on the basis of race, creed, color, or national origin. Departments and agencies of the government, as well as federal contracting agencies, were instructed to comply with the order. A Fair

Employment Practices Commission was established, and it was empowered to receive and investigate complaints and to take appropriate steps to redress grievances. Although largely ignored by other government agencies, and without power of enforcement, the commission successfully dealt with some 10,000 complaints during its five-year existence. In 1951 President Harry S. Truman created, by Executive Order No. 10308, a Committee on Contract Compliance to handle complaints of violation of nondiscrimination provisions in government contracts. Three years later President Dwight D. Eisenhower maintained the committee as a part of his first administration.

President Harry S. Truman frequently exercised his presidential authority in behalf of civil rights. In 1946 he established a commission on higher education that included in its report a warning that discriminatory legislation must be repealed. More important, in the same year, President Truman established a Committee on Civil Rights that prepared the historic document entitled *To Secure These Rights*, which appraised the nation's shortcomings in the area of racial discrimination. The committee suggested the enactment of no fewer than 27 civil rights acts. President Truman did not ignore the report; in fact, in 1948 he presented to Congress a comprehensive program of federal civil rights legislation. These measures were met with strong opposition in the Senate, and they failed to pass. In July 1948, President Truman issued two more executive orders on the same day. The most far-reaching one, Executive Order No. 99881, stated that discrimination in the Armed Forces was to be eradicated. The second order declared that fair employment practices should be universally instituted and very carefully followed throughout all federal agancies to insure that blacks would find equal employment and treatment.

President Truman's executive orders not only reflected the practical politics of the Democratic Party, but also represented the burden of America's assumed role after World War II as the leader of democracy in the battle for the allegiance of underdeveloped nations. These political changes, as well as pressure from blacks and from white liberals, prompted Congress in 1957 to enact the first federal civil rights law since 1875. However, the legislation that emerged was a weak compromise, which reflected the nation's continued ambivalence toward the racial issue.

In the 1950s, American liberals continued to believe that securing the right to vote for blacks would be a solution to the problems resulting from racism. It was common knowledge, reinforced by surveys conducted by the Southern Regional Council, that the right of blacks in the South to vote was constantly denied to them. In several predominantly black counties in the South, not a single black in the twentieth century had ever cast a ballot. Although the white primary and the poll tax were falling into disuse, southern whites increasingly relied upon literacy and comprehension tests as well as upon intimidation to prevent blacks from voting. The Civil Rights Act of 1957 was passed in an effort to remedy these difficulties. The act created a Commission on Civil Rights with the purpose of making a broad study of racial conditions in the United States. It gave additional aid to the civil rights division in the U.S. Department of Justice and empowered the Attorney General to institute suits in behalf of blacks who were denied the franchise in federal elections. However, the act, with its many loopholes, proved to be largely ineffective in guaranteeing the right to vote. Nonetheless, the Civil Rights Commission (still in existence in 1977) conducted useful studies, surveys, and investigations, issuing its findings to legislative and administrative agencies as well as to the public.

The 1960s Continued interference with the right to vote and terrorist activity against Afro-Americans led to the enactment of the Civil Rights Act of 1960. This Act was designed to end the duplicity of registrars in southern states who would resign on the eve of a federal suit so there would be no party to sue, or who refused to make registration and voting records available for inspection. The Act provided that state election officials must preserve records for at least 22 months for inspection by the U.S. Attorney General. The Act made it a federal crime to obstruct any federal court order by threat or force and provided penalties for crossing state boundaries to avoid prosecution. It also authorized the U.S. Department of Justice to sue in federal courts on behalf of persons denied their right to vote in federal elections. If the plaintiff was upheld by the court, the Attorney General could ask the court to determine whether a pattern or practice of discrimination against blacks existed in that community. If the court decided that such a pattern did exist, federal referees would supervise the registration of voters in that area.

However, the Civil Rights Act of 1960 was largely ineffective because its terms did not provide for stringent measures of enforcement.

Incessant delays and court action devitalized the act. Before a broad, all-encompassing, and enforceable civil rights bill could be passed, it was necessary that white indignation against the extremism of racism in the South be increased sufficiently to make Congress believe that the passage of such legislation was politically expedient. The ground was laid for such advocacy by the continued brutality and violence reported in the news media, even after the passage of the act of 1960. Such events as the violence at the University of Mississippi when James Meredith was admitted; the shooting of Medgar Evers and the release of his murderer after two mistrials; the bombing of the homes of black civil rights workers; the murder by bombing in 1963 of four black children in a Sunday school in Birmingham, Ala.—all these fanned the embers of public indignation. Yet, despite the violence and the indignant reaction, the new civil rights bill that was before Congress in 1963 might not have passed if President John F. Kennedy had not been assassinated in November 1963. However, after the assassination, Kennedy's successor, President Lyndon B. Johnson, made this bill "must" legislation; and, reflecting the nation's shock and sorrow over Kennedy's death, Congress passed it in 1964.

The Civil Rights Act of 1964 contained 11 sections (titles), each strengthening the provisos in former civil rights acts, or, on occasion, creating new guidelines for the administration and preservation of civil liberties. It was the most far-reaching legislation of its kind since Reconstruction. Title I addressed the issue of voting: it guaranteed protection against the arbitrary application of a different standard to black voters by biased registrars. Title II outlawed the exclusion of blacks from restaurants, hotels, theaters, and other public accommodations, and empowered the Attorney General to bring suits against defiers. Title III guaranteed Afro-Americans access to all public facilities such as parks, stadiums, and swimming pools. The Attorney General was again empowered to bring suits. Title IV provided that the federal government give financial aid to all schools in the process of desegregation. Again the Attorney General was enabled to bring suits. Title V extended the life of the Civil Rights Commission for four more years. Title VI provided that federal funds should not be given to maintain and operate educational institutions or programs that practiced discrimination. Title VII prohibited discrimination by employers and unions. Title VIII

directed that the U.S. Census Bureau's voting statistics be gathered by race, but only in areas designated by the Civil Rights Commission. Title IX prevented a federal court from sending a civil rights case back to state or local courts. Title X established the Community Relations Service (CRS) to arbitrate local race problems. The final section, Title XI, provided the right of jury trial in any case that arose from any section of the act.

Under this new act, federal agencies were given the task of preparing guidelines for compliance with Title VI; and the Department of Health, Education, and Welfare (HEW) was empowered to set school desegregation guidelines and standards under Title IV. Several cabinet-level departments as well as such agencies as the General Services Administration, the Housing and Home Finance Agency, the National Science Foundation, the Atomic Energy Commission, and the Agency for International Development have issued guidelines under Title VII. An assurance-of-compliance form was required as a condition of participation in federally assisted programs under the act.

A new amendment to the Constitution, designed to abolish the poll tax as a prerequisite for voting in federal elections, was also enacted in 1964. Until that time, the poll tax was in use in many southern states as it had been since the end of Reconstruction; it was one of the most common methods of keeping Afro-American voters away from the polls. A number of attempts had been made previously to pass an act of Congress that would outlaw the poll tax, but doubts about the constitutionality of such legislation had existed. Now in the wake of enthusiasm for civil rights legislation that followed the passage of the Civil Rights Act of 1964, the Twenty-fourth Amendment was passed.

The Voting Rights Act of 1965 originated in the same atmosphere of enthusiasm. Before the passage of the Civil Rights Act of 1957, persons who were deprived of the right to vote had to sue at their own expense. In 1957, for the first time, the U.S. Attorney General was given the authority to institute suits in behalf of these persons. However, the weaknesses of this act, as well as those of the act of 1960, became immediately obvious, and Title I in the Civil Rights Act of 1964 was designed to strengthen the voting rights measures in both. Notwithstanding, no significant increase in black voting or registration occurred. Violence and intimidation continued in those areas where blacks attempted to register or to exercise their right to vote. Yet, with restricted primaries barred by law, southern whites instituted other restraining tactics such as literary tests. Protracted litigation was the norm when private suits were brought to court. The continued exclusion of Afro-Americans from politics, the harassment of voter-registration workers and demonstrators, and the murder of Mrs. Viola Liuzzo and other civil rights workers prompted Congress to pass the Voting Rights Act of 1965, which was a departure from the patterns of the acts of 1957, 1960, and 1964.

The Voting Rights Act provided for direct federal examination of voter registration. It outlawed knowledge, character, and literacy tests—those devices that had been used by local registrars to prevent blacks from voting. The effects of the act were soon evident: in less than two years the percentage of black registered voters promptly rose from 27 to 53 percent in Georgia, from 19 to 52 percent in Alabama, and from less than 7 to 60 percent in Mississippi. By 1968 more than 50 percent of the black voting-age population in every southern state was registered. In addition to influencing the electoral outcome where white candidates were involved, and having some effect on the policy position of the political parties, the greatly increased black vote also resulted in the election of black officeholders. By the end of 1969, at least 1200 black public officeholders were elected in the country, more than 400 of them in the South. In Georgia, no fewer than 14 black legislators were sent to the state assembly. Though much of this increase was accomplished under the supervision of federal examiners provided by the act, far more resulted from the supervision of local voting registrars who were now convinced the federal government intended to enforce the law.

Even as the Civil Rights Act of 1964 and the Voting Rights Act of 1965 were being passed, Afro-Americans were turning increasingly to economic problems. These problems, more militant black spokesmen believed, could not be resolved by participation in the political process alone or by merely having equal access to public accommodations. Increased militancy by a vocal and active sector of the black community created a white "backlash" that mobilized both popular and congressional opinion against further civil rights legislation. A civil rights act was proposed in 1966 and transmitted to the Congress by the Attorney General; it passed in the House but it was killed in the Senate. A mild measure to protect civil rights workers from harassment, the vetoed act was revived in 1967 and again passed in the House. An open-housing provision was added in the Senate, and the act was sent back to the House in a greatly expanded form. The House, still in a conservative mood, might not have passed the law but for an event that shook the country and in its wake generated a great surge of indignation against racial discrimination. The event was the assassination of Dr. Martin Luther King, Jr., on April 4, 1968. The bill was subsequently passed, but again at great cost. The shock of Dr. King's assassination impelled Congress to pass the 1968 Civil Rights Act, just as the assassination of President Kennedy provoked Congress to pass the 1964 Civil Rights Act.

The most important section of the Act of 1968 was Title VII, which concerned open housing. This section provided that there should be no discrimination in the renting, selling, or offering (to sell) of houses because of race, color, or national origin. The antiriot clauses in the act were directed against black militancy and rebellions in the cities; a lengthy section aimed at black reprisals against whites outlined penalties for interfering by violence or intimidation with any person's enjoyment of his federally protected rights.

The Civil Rights Act of 1968 marked the end of an era of civil rights legislation. Indeed, black leaders virtually stopped agitating for such legislation. The possibilities, they believed, of what could be written into law had been exhausted; the newer problems centered about the manner and intent of enforcement rather than whether statutes existed on the books. Afro-Americans, they concluded, would have to look to the U.S. Supreme Court and the executive branch for enforcement. In fact, many black leaders believed that much of the civil rights legislation of the 1960s was simply a reenactment of Reconstruction statutes, and that if the old Reconstruction measures had ever been enforced, there would have been no necessity for the later legislation—during the so-called Second Reconstruction. Disillusionment with the acts of Congress and the law pervaded the black community, and increased attention was given to enforcement. Recent laws could only prove effective through interpretation by the U.S. Supreme Court and the willingness of the president and the executive branch to enforce them. *See also* CIVIL RIGHTS: CIVIL RIGHTS CASES, 1865–1975; CIVIL RIGHTS: CIVIL RIGHTS ENFORCEMENT; NATIONAL

ASSOCIATION FOR THE ADVANCEMENT OF COL-
ORED PEOPLE (NAACP); POLITICS.

REFERENCES: For additional information, see: Berger, Morroe, *Equality by Statute: The Revolution in Civil Rights*, Double-day, New York, 1967; Blaustein, Albert P. and Robert L. Zangrando (eds.), *Civil Rights and the American Negro*, Trident Press, New York, 1968; McCord, John H. (ed.), *With All Deliberate Speed: Civil Rights Theory and Reality*, University of Illinois Press, Urbana, 1969; Schwartz, Bernard, *Statutory History of the United States: Civil Rights*, Chelsea House Publishers in association with McGraw-Hill Book Co., New York, 1970; Strong, Donald S., *Negroes, Ballots, and Judges: National Voting Rights Legislation in the Federal Courts*, University of Alabama Press, Birmingham, 1968; and U.S. Laws, Statutes, *Civil Rights Acts of 1957, 1960, 1964, 1968, and Voting Rights Act of 1965*, Washington, D.C., U.S. Congress, House of Representatives, 91st Congress, 1st Session. (These are texts of the laws printed for a House committee.)

Civil Rights: Cases

Introduction The Thirteenth, Fourteenth, and Fifteenth Amendments to the U.S. Constitution and the subsequent enforcement legislation that was enacted to establish and to protect the post-Civil War citizenship of Afro-Americans became almost ineffective as soon as they were written into law. For more than half a century after the end of the first Reconstruction, the U.S. Supreme Court repeatedly interpreted the Constitution in a manner that resulted more in weakening than in strengthening the civil rights of Afro-Americans. Essentially, the U.S. Supreme Court decreed that the Reconstruction amendments, especially the Fourteenth and the Fifteenth, applied only to action taken by the states themselves or by agents of the states, and not to individual actions against blacks. The U.S. Supreme Court presumed that the law was, in effect, *not* discriminatory unless it was clearly so. When the Supreme Court balanced the police power of the states against an Afro-American who claimed denial of equal treatment, it generally ruled in favor of the priority of police power. Moreover, the Supreme Court held rather steadily to the position that, although discrimination was forbidden by the Constitution, racial distinctions were permissible.

The Impact of the Slaughterhouse Cases The Supreme Court first laid out these new doctrines in a series of decisions beginning with the Slaughterhouse Cases in 1873 and culminating in the *Civil Rights Cases* ten years later. These principles remained the law on the subject until the mid-twentieth century.

The *Slaughterhouse Cases* involved the claim of some white butchers in New Orleans, La., that they had a right to practice their trade, despite a Louisiana statute that granted a private corporation a 25-year monopoly on slaughtering operations in and around New Orleans. In this case, the court narrowly interpreted the privileges and immunities clause of the Fourteenth Amendment. It decided that state and national citizenship are separate and distinct, and that the Fourteenth Amendment forbade only state impairment of those privileges and immunities intrinsic to citizens of the United States. Thus, in its implication for and application to the rights of Afro-Americans, the Fourteenth Amendment was virtually nullified by the *Slaughterhouse Cases* since the civil rights infringements suffered by Afro-Americans commonly resulted from interference with the privileges and immunities under state citizenship.

In subsequent cases, the Supreme Court weakened other sections of the Reconstruction amendments and legislation. For example, in *United States v. Reese* in 1876, the Supreme Court declared portions of the Enforcement Act of 1870 to be unconstitutional. This act had imposed heavy penalties upon individuals who undertook to prevent citizens from voting. The Court struck down the legislation with the argu-

Decades of litigation climaxed in 1954 with the historic *Brown v. Board of Education of Topeka* decision, which ordered school desegregation. Standing on the Supreme Court steps are the lawyers who successfully argued the case (from left to right): Howard Jenkins, James N. Nabrit, Spotswood W. Robinson III, Frank Reeves, Jack Greenberg, Thurgood Marshall, Louis Redding, U. Simpson Tate, and George E. C. Hayes. *(Courtesy of NAACP.)*

ment that the Fifteenth Amendment did not guarantee the right to vote, but merely prohibited both federal and state governments from excluding persons from voting on account of race, color, or previous conditions of servitude. The Court found that the act did not limit itself to unlawful discrimination on account of race, and that it was, therefore, unconstitutional. Moreover, in *United States v. Cruikshank*, also decided in 1876, the white defendant had been charged with breaking up a meeting of Afro-Americans and conspiring to prevent them from voting by force and intimidation. The court decided that interference with civil rights by a private individual could be a federal crime only if the meeting had some object connected with national citizenship. The court held that since the blacks had assembled to discuss a state matter, namely the Louisiana elections, they were, therefore, not under the protection of the federal Constitution or federal statutes. A result of the *Reese* and *Cruikshank* cases was to render the Fourteenth and Fifteenth amendments and the enforcement acts practically useless in protecting the voting rights of blacks.

Another area of importance to Afro-Americans was the right of Afro-Americans to sit on juries and the right of black defendants to be judged by juries that included members of their race. The equal protection clause of the Fourteenth Amendment seemed to make this a requirement. In March 1880, the Supreme Court handed down several decisions relating to jury service and equal protection under the law. In one decision, a West Virginia statute that confined jury service to white male citizens only was held to be unconstitutional. In this case, *Strauder v. West Virginia* in 1880, the court found it particularly obnoxious that the intention to discriminate was clearly asserted by unambiguous language in the legislation.

On the same day that *Strauder v. West Virginia* was decided, another favorable decision was made in *Ex parte Virginia* wherein the court denied relief to a judge in Virginia who declared that he had been falsely arrested for deliberately keeping blacks off juries. He petitioned for release under a writ of habeas corpus on the ground that his conduct had been a judicial act and, therefore, not within the reach of an act of Congress. The court disagreed. A few weeks later, however, all hope of protecting the right of blacks to serve on juries was discarded when, in *Virginia v. Rivers,* the court ruled that, where state statutes did not specifically exclude blacks from juries, the mere absence of Afro-Americans on a jury was not a valid obstacle to conviction. In order to prove discrimination, a complainant had also to show that there was discrimination on the part of state officials who prevented blacks from serving on a jury. This was, of course, difficult to show.

When the court decided *Ex parte Siebold,* also in 1880, a glimmer of hope remained that the equal protection clause of the Fourteenth Amendment might still serve some protective purpose for blacks. Election officials in Maryland had been indicted for stuffing the ballot box in a congressional election, an act defined as a criminal offense by federal civil rights legislation. The argument was made by the attorneys for the election officials that the authority of a state in such matters is equal to that of the nation. The Supreme Court rejected that argument and upheld federal authority.

However, it soon became evident that the *Siebold* ruling did not constitute a new interpretation in support of the equal protection clause. In 1883, for example, the case of *Pace v. Alabama* involved an Alabama statute that provided for more severe punishment for adultery and fornication between whites and blacks than between perpetrators of the same race. A racially mixed couple claimed that this provision violated the equal protection clause. The court rejected their argument on the grounds that the punishment of both parties to the offense was the same. Furthermore, in *United States v. Harris* in 1883, the Supreme Court found the Ku Klux Act of April 20, 1871, to be unconstitutional in part when applied to the case of 20 members of a lynch mob in Tennessee who snatched four black prisoners from jail and beat them so severely that one of them died. In effect, the court again announced that the Fourteenth Amendment applied only to state action and not the action of individuals so that any remedy for that action must be sought in the state courts.

In the *Civil Rights Cases* of 1883 yet another blow was struck against the enforcement of the rights of black people under Reconstruction amendments and acts. At issue was the Civil Rights Act of March 1875, which granted equal accommodations without discrimination to blacks in public places. The Supreme Court decided that this act was unconstitutional on grounds that, although it was based on the Fourteenth Amendment, which prohibits only state action, it purported to punish the private actions of an individual who refused admission of an Afro-American to a public place. Furthermore, the court said that the Civil Rights Act of 1875 could not have been held unconstitutional under the authority of the Thirteenth Amendment, which was only designed to end slavery and not every act of discrimination. The court further said that it would be stretching the slavery argument too far to make the act apply to such instances of discrimination as the choice of guests a person may entertain or the choice of people he may take into his coach, cab, or car.

The unwillingness of the Supreme Court to advance minority rights, conforming with public opinion of the day, persisted throughout the next few years. The court had effectively whittled down any interpretation of the Reconstruction amendments and statutes that might guarantee rights to blacks. The privileges and immunities clause of the Fourteenth Amendment had been effectively neutralized; the due process clause had been used to protect property rights rather than minority rights; and the equal protection clause had been rendered practically meaningless.

The Impact of *Plessy v. Ferguson* The court extended this pattern of decision-making to the subject of public transportation. For example, in the case of *Hall v. DeCuir* in 1878, it decided that a Reconstruction law of Louisiana (the guarantee of equal rights and privileges to blacks on public conveyances) was unconstitutional because it interfered with the power of Congress to regulate commerce. The court held, therefore, that the plaintiff (a black woman) had no right to obtain cabin space on a steamboat plying the Mississippi River between New Orleans, La., and Vicksburg, Miss. Like other southern states, Louisiana revoked old Reconstruction acts in the 1890s with Jim Crow laws: such was the statute of 1890 that required separate accommodations in public facilities for blacks and whites. In the famous case of *Plessy v. Ferguson* in 1896, the Supreme Court was called upon by the Afro-American plaintiff, Homer Adolph Plessy, to decide the constitutionality of Louisiana's Jim Crow law.

Plessy was arrested for refusing to ride in the Jim Crow ("colored") railway coach on a 60-mile intrastate trip from New Orleans to Covington, La. Legally, his refusal was a violation of the state law that required "equal but separate accommodations for the white and colored races" in public facilities. The defendant in the case, Ferguson, was the Louisiana judge who conducted the trial on criminal charges. Albion W. Tourgée was retained as counsel for Plessy. Tourgée, a white lawyer from upstate New York, had served briefly as a state judge in North Carolina during Reconstruction. His brief to the court stated that "Justice is pictured blind and her daughter, the Law, ought at least to be color-blind." The only dissenting justice, John Marshall Harlan, who had also dissented 13 years

earlier in *Civil Rights Cases,* caught this expression in his written dissent and reduced it to the more famous phrase: "Our Constitution is color-blind."

Unlike in *Hall* in 1876, the court did not take the position in *Plessy* that the Louisiana law was an interference with the power of Congress to regulate commerce (an argument later used in civil rights cases of the 1960s). Instead, the court declared that Louisiana's action brought *Plessy* within the province of the equal protection clause of the Fourteenth Amendment, and that the Fourteenth Amendment required only that separate accommodations be equal. The *Plessy* decision thus confirmed the court's later decision in *Cumming v. Richmond County Board of Education* in 1899. Later in 1908, the precedent of *Plessy* prevented Berea College, Berea, Ky. (which had pioneered in admitting black students before the Civil War), from reopening its doors to Afro-Americans in the case of *Berea College v. Kentucky.* Sanction for segregation as the supreme law of the land was thus established in *Plessy,* and it was to remain in force, de jure, for the next 58 years.

On the matter of jury service and equal protection, the court decided in *Carter v. Texas* in 1900 that when it could be demonstrated that Afro-Americans had been systematically excluded from a jury because of their race, such action would constitute a violation of the Fourteenth Amendment's equal protection clause. Although the attorneys in *Carter* had been able to show positive exclusionary action by state officials, the decision did not, however, substantially improve the position of Afro-Americans as prospective jurors or as defendants. Whereas it was easy to demonstrate that blacks were not on the jury or were not in the pool from which jurors were chosen, it was not so easy to prove positive systematic exclusion in every case—so old abuses continued.

It was also difficult to outlaw peonage, which was imposed on blacks after the Civil War in the rural South by the sharecropper system and crop lien laws. Peonage was encouraged by the practice of permitting employers to pay the fines for blacks who had been convicted for petty crimes for which they themselves could not afford to pay; these blacks would be required to work to pay off such debts. The Peonage Abolition Act was passed by Congress on March 2, 1867, under the authority of the Thirteenth Amendment, and was finally upheld as being constitutional by the

Supreme Court in *Clyatt v. United States* in 1905. However, peonage continued and did not really lose its legal sanction until 1911. In that year, in *Bailey v. Alabama,* the Supreme Court found that state laws that provided for peonage were in violation of the statute. In reality, however, peonage continued after 1910.

Between 1910 and 1938, the Supreme Court not only reaffirmed the separate but equal doctrine in a number of cases, but it also elaborated on the requirements of "equality." In *McCabe v. Atchison, Topeka and Santa Fe Railway Company* in 1914, the court upheld Oklahoma's Jim Crow railway law, but declared that in order to make the facilities equal the railway must in fact make such facilities as coaches and observation, sleeping, and dining cars accessible to Afro-Americans.

Residential housing had long been a sensitive matter in black-white relations, both in the North and the South. As an ever-increasing number of black migrants moved into northern and southern cities during the twentieth century, pressures from the migration generated social and economic responses that were reflected in the courts. In *Buchanan v. Warley* in 1917, the Supreme Court declared an ordinance of Louisville, Ky., to be unconstitutional. The ordinance had provided for segregation in housing, forbidding a person of one race the right to move into a neighborhood occupied predominantly by people of another race. The court ruled that this principle "destroyed the right of the individual to acquire, enjoy, and dispose of his property."

After the decision in *Buchanan v. Warley,* restrictive covenants (that is, private agreements or contracts by which members of minorities

were prevented from buying real estate in certain communities) became the chief means of discrimination. Several complaints brought action in state courts. The Supreme Court, in considering the case of *Corrigan and Curtis v. Buckley* in 1926, upheld the lower court ruling, which held that a restrictive covenant was permissible because the restraint it imposed on the use of property was not protected under the Fourteenth Amendment. Despite this action, the court in *Harmon v. Tyler,* also decided in 1926, extended the rule laid down in *Buchanan v. Warley* and invalidated a city ordinance barring Afro-Americans from establishing residences in white communities except with the written consent of a majority of the white residents. Although the decisions in *Buchanan* and *Harmon* were steps against discrimination in housing, it should be noted that the opinions in both cases were based on the premise that white sellers were being deprived of the right to alienate their property without due process of law, and not on the intention of giving Afro-Americans access to neighborhoods outside of their ghettos.

The Dismantling of Slaughterhouse The Supreme Court did, however, extend the influence of the equal protection clause in the areas of the administration of justice and of the rights of accused criminals. In the case of *Moore v. Dempsey* in 1923, the court overturned the convictions of black defendants who were tried in an atmosphere wherein a mob was prevented from lynching the defendants only by the promise of a committee of seven governor-appointed members that the blacks would be speedily and fully punished. In *Aldridge v. United States* in 1931, the court declared that it was a reversible error for a district judge in the District of Columbia to refuse the request of a black defendant, accused of murder, to have every prospective juror questioned concerning racial prejudice.

The most famous of the criminal cases were those associated with Scottsboro, Ala., in the 1930s. These cases arose out of the arrest of nine black youths, ages 13 to 19, who were charged with the rape of two white girls. These cases, *Powell v. Alabama* in 1932 and *Norris v. Alabama* in 1935, were known respectively as the first and second Scottsboro cases. In the first, the court ruled that the due process clause of the Fourteenth Amendment was violated when the state failed to provide a defendant in a criminal case with adequate legal counsel. In the second Scottsboro case, the court found that there was

Below, left: Clarence Norris, one of the 9 Scottsboro boys, as he appeared in the 1970s. *(Photo by Bill Price/Vision.)*

Below, right: Appealing for White House intervention in 1934 were the mothers of some of the Scottsboro boys, Richard B. Moore of the International Labor Defense (ILD), and Ruby Bates, one of the alleged victims (from left to right): Ida Norris, Janine Patterson, Bates, Mamie Williams, Viola Montgomery, and Moore. *(Photoworld.)*

systematic exclusion of blacks from the trial jury. The court restated the principle of *Carter v. Texas* in 1900, that wherever there is systematic exclusion of blacks from a jury, equal protection provided for in the Fourteenth Amendment is denied. The court found that there was a sufficient number of qualified Afro-Americans in the population of the county to have accounted for the presence of some Afro-Americans in the jury pool, despite the fact that the clerk of the jury commission and the circuit court had never known a black to serve on a jury. With powerful assistance from NAACP lawyers, Afro-Americans won significant concessions in voting rights cases. The so-called grandfather clause, which permitted persons to vote without regard to other qualifications if their ancestors had been eligible to vote before the end of slavery, was declared unconstitutional by the Supreme Court in 1915 in *Guinn v. United States*—although by that time, the practice had already outlived its usefulness. In a subsequent case, *Nixon v. Herndon,* a Texas case of 1927, the exclusion of black voters from primary elections, called "the white primary," was found unconstitutional under the Fourteenth and Fifteenth Amendments. In response, Texas legislators passed a law under which the Democratic Party could prescribe the qualifications of its own members: the Democratic Party then adopted a white primary rule. The Supreme Court, in *Nixon v. Condon* in 1932, disposed of this device also. Democratic Party officials in Texas then adopted their own party rules in 1932, which still excluded black voters, though ostensibly, not in response to any legislative or executive committee action. The Supreme Court ignored the effect and the motivation of this action and upheld it as a private and not a state action in *Grovey v. Townsend* in 1935. By 1945, however, the court had finally reversed the tactic of private action and had overturned *Grovey* when, in *Smith v. Allwright,* it ruled that a state's delegation of its rights to a political party to determine the qualifications of its own members was indeed a state action. Texans retaliated against the decision in *Smith* by setting up private and totally unofficial primaries in order to continue the exclusion of blacks. The Democratic Party in Texas relinquished its duties to the Jaybird Association, a private organization that limited its membership to whites only. Finally, in the fifth and last of the Texas primary cases litigated since 1927, the Supreme Court, in *Terry v. Adams* in 1953, ruled that Afro-Americans could not be barred from Jaybird's elections.

Higher Education and the End of *Plessy v. Ferguson* Black plaintiffs likewise successfully challenged the discriminatory doctrine of separate but equal laid down in *Plessy*. A series of cases related to public education between 1938 and 1954 eventually reached the Supreme Court. At first, the cases were limited mainly to the field of higher education and sought the admission of black students to white state colleges and universities. The first of such state cases was that of Donald Gaines Murray, a graduate of Amherst College (Amherst, Mass.), who unsuccessfully applied to the law school of the all-white University of Maryland. Supported by the NAACP through his counsel, Charles Hamilton Houston, Murray claimed the right to admission under the equal protection clause of the Fourteenth Amendment. Local courts in Baltimore, Md., the seat of the law school, denied admission to Murray, but the state Court of Appeals reversed the decision. Murray, the first and only black in his class, entered the law school in 1935, from which he graduated a few years later, seemingly without overt racist incidents.

Murray's case, brilliantly handled by Houston, prompted other state action in Missouri where Sidney Redmond and other Afro-American attorneys in touch with Houston prevailed upon Lloyd Lionel Gaines to seek admission to the law school of the all-white University of Missouri. Gaines was a well-liked honor student at Vashon High School in St. Louis, Mo., and at Lincoln University in Jefferson City, Mo. After working his way through Lincoln University, he graduated in August 1935. His case against the University of Missouri became a celebrated precedent. Known officially as *Missouri ex rel Gaines v. Canada,* it finally reached the Supreme Court, which ruled in Gaines' favor in 1938. The court ordered the state (legally through Canada, the registrar) either to admit Gaines to the law school or to provide *equal* facilities *within* the state for him. Of course, Missouri chose not to admit Gaines. Instead, within a few years after the decision, the state hastily set up a short-lived school as part of Lincoln University for black law students. The school was located in St. Louis in the old Poro Building, a structure once owned and operated by a hairdressing company belonging to Annie Malone.

Lloyd Gaines, as he appeared in a special graduating issue of the student newspaper, the *Lincoln Clarion,* May, 1935, at Lincoln University, Jefferson City, Mo. Gaines permitted the suit to be filed in his name, as *Missouri ex rel Gaines v. Canada,* for admission to the law school of the all-white University of Missouri at Columbia, Mo. The U.S. Supreme Court ordered Missouri in 1938 either to admit Gaines or to set up a law school for him. The state chose to set up a makeshift law school while Gaines chose to attend the University of Michigan from which he strangely disappeared.

Gaines never attended the makeshift law school erected as a result of his case, nor did he ever enroll at the University of Missouri. Instead, during the long litigation, Gaines attended the University of Michigan, at Ann Arbor, from which he reportedly disappeared, his whereabouts forever unknown to his contemporaries. There was speculation that he had become a victim of foul play as a result of his being the principal in the case. But some old fraternity brothers from high school and college—including Frank T. Lyerson, Jesse Askew, Horatio McNeil, Shelby T. Freeman, and "Gus" Low—reflecting on his dislike of publicity and social ritual, have suggested that Gaines possibly went into exile incognito. In any event, Gaines became one of the many casualties of the civil rights movement, thousands of whom never achieved his celebrity.

Legal cases that followed in the wake of the *Gaines* decision involving segregated white universities ultimately raised the following question: Is any segregated school expressly established for blacks really equal to similar schools for whites already in existence? This question was broached in *Sipuel v. Board of Regents of the University of Oklahoma* in 1948 and in *Sweatt v. Painter* in 1950. The latter case centered around Heman Sweatt, who had applied for admission to the University of Texas Law School for the February term of 1946. He was not admitted, and the Texas courts did not uphold his legal plea; instead, the courts allowed the state six months in which to set up a separate law school. It was obvious to Sweatt and his counsel that such a hastily established law school would hardly qualify as being legally or educationally equal to the all-white University of Texas Law School. Through his persuasive counsel, Thurgood Marshall of the NAACP, Sweatt convinced the Supreme Court of the existing inequality, and the court reversed the Texas courts, ordering the admission of Sweatt. Within the next few years following *Sweatt*, another legal victory involving admission was achieved in the case of *McLaurin v. Oklahoma State Regents* in 1950.

Increasingly, it became clear to the court that segregated educational facilities were not, in fact, equal, and, therefore, doubts were raised about the constitutional validity of the doctrine of separate but equal as set forth in *Plessy*. The social implications were immense, for the whole structure and function of segregation in the

nation were involved. Doubts were expressly raised in a cluster of cases during the early 1950s. There were five different legal cases from five separate places, known collectively as the *School Desegregation Cases:* from Delaware, *Gebhart v. Belton;* from the District of Columbia, *Bolling v. Sharpe;* from Kansas, *Brown v. Board of Education of Topeka;* from South Carolina, *Briggs v. Elliott;* and from Virginia, *Davis v. County School Board of Prince Edward County.* It is one of the ironies of history that the least important of these five cases from a legal viewpoint became the best known. That case was the suit of Oliver Brown against the Board of Education of Topeka, Kans., a case that simply happened to be the first name alphabetically in the first case (set of cases) on the Supreme Court's docket for the October term of 1953. The cluster of cases, therefore, were issued under *Brown,* first as the unanimous opinion of the court on May 17, 1954, and then as the enforcement decree the next year. The opinion was one of the most far-reaching in the history of American jurisprudence: *Plessy* was overturned. "We conclude," said the court, "that in the field of public education the doctrine of 'separate but equal' has no place." Segregated facilities were found to be "inherently unequal." In its enforcement decree the following year, the court ordered "a prompt and reasonable start . . . with all deliberate speed" toward compliance.

The Impact of *Brown v. Board of Education of Topeka*
With the decisions in *Brown,* a new era of civil rights litigation began. Southern states embarked upon programs to avoid compliance. Opposition ranged from the militant response in Little Rock, Ark.—where federal troops were called in at Central High School—to the abandonment of the public school system in Prince Edward County, Va., and to pupil relocation and other devices elsewhere.

The Supreme Court was asked to declare as unconstitutional each one of these devices. For example, in *Cooper v. Aaron* in 1958, a case that grew out of the confrontation over the integration of schools in Little Rock, Ark., the court decided that state officials must obey the interpretation given the Constitution in *Brown.* In *Griffin v. County School Board of Prince Edward County* in 1964, the court ruled that the creation and use of private schools for whites only, with the use of public funds, denied to blacks the protection provided by the Fourteenth Amendment. Speaking for the court in this case, Justice

Hugo L. Black stated that the situation in Prince Edward County, Va.—where no black child had attended any public-supported school from 1959 to 1963—showed "entirely too much deliberation and not enough speed." Prince Edward County was ordered to open and desegregate its schools.

Two other important cases followed *Griffin*. In *Green v. County School Board of New Kent County* in 1968 (and companion cases) the court decided that the so-called freedom-of-choice plans (basically, evasive devices resorted to by segregationists) did not meet the requirements handed down by *Brown*. Indeed, said the court, any such plan that did not in fact result in a reduction of segregation was not in conformity with *Brown*. And yet in another case, *Alexander v. Holmes County Board of Education* in 1969, a court wary of evasion announced that the "all deliberate speed" formula was no longer in effect—that all dual school systems must be terminated at once.

As evasive tactics by segregationists were ruled unconstitutional by the court, busing of school pupils became the new focus of legal and constitutional arguments in the late 1960s and early 1970s. Preserving the "neighborhood" became the new rallying tactic of segregationists. A number of school systems attempted to avoid federal court orders to desegregate by arguing that busing was unconstitutional inasmuch as it violated the neighborhood school concept. The Supreme Court decided in 1971 in *Swann v. Charlotte-Mecklenburg Board of Education* (and companion cases) that busing is a remedy that may be required to establish racial balance in schools where de jure segregation had existed in the past. By 1975, busing had become a national and unresolved political issue. Another impact of *Brown* was the split decision in the "reverse discrimination" case of *Regents of the University of California v. Bakke* (1978). The U.S. Supreme Court ruled that a white student who had been denied admission to the university's medical school because of existing quotas there for blacks should be admitted; but it did not rule out race as a factor for admission. Thurgood Marshall, now a sitting judge on the court, dissented.

Issues of Housing and Public Transportation On the issue of residential housing, the Supreme Court reversed its earlier decision in *Corrigan and Curtis v. Buckley*, which upheld the enforcement of restrictive covenants in state courts in 1926, in *Shelley v. Kraemer*. In this case, decided in 1948, the court declared that it was unconstitutional for any state to enforce such covenants in the state courts. The next important case on the subject of housing was *Jones v. Alfred H. Mayer Company*, decided in 1968, in which the court upheld the constitutionality of the old Civil Rights Act of 1866, and declared that since 1866 Afro-Americans had always had the right to buy, lease, rent, and sell property without discrimination.

By the time the court decided *Jones*, the important issues in the area of housing related to efforts by whites to avoid residential desegregation by claiming that such residential segregation was in fact economic and not racial. Even as whites had opposed desegregation in public schools with the sophisticated argument that the quality of the neighborhood school was what really interested them and not whether their children went to school with children of a different race, so now opposition centered on the effects of the existence of public housing or low-income housing in white neighborhoods—opposition, segregationists claimed, that had nothing to do with racial discrimination. Thus, in the case of *James v. Valtierra* in 1971, the Supreme Court upheld a California statute that required that low-income housing projects could not be built unless they were first approved by local referendum in the communities where such projects would be placed. The effect of *James* practically excluded Afro-Americans and other minorities from white neighborhoods. On the other side of the coin, in another case decided in 1971, the court confirmed the lower-court ruling that the city of Lackawanna, N.Y., by refusing to permit low-income housing to be constructed in a white neighborhood, had been guilty of supporting racial segregation.

On the subject of transportation, the court held in *Mitchell v. United States* in 1941 that Congress could forbid discrimination in interstate commerce. In *Morgan v. Virginia* in 1946, the court declared that a state statute that required separate seating of passengers by race placed an undue burden on interstate commerce. However, in *Henderson v. United States* in 1950 the court clearly stated that racial segregation of dining-room car facilities on trains involved in interstate commerce was unconstitutional, since the law forbade any kind of racial classification in interstate commerce. Furthermore, the 1964 Civil Rights Act prohibited racial segregation in public accommodations. Tested almost immediately, the constitutionality of the public accommodations section of the act was upheld in *Heart of Atlanta Motel v. United States* in 1964 as a proper exercise of congressional power to regulate interstate commerce.

Triumph in Voting Rights After *Terry v. Adams* in 1953, the Supreme Court ruled in *United States v. Raines* in 1960 that such devices as literacy tests and comprehension clauses violated the Fourteenth and Fifteenth Amendments. In *Gomillion v. Lightfoot,* also in 1960, it was decided that the gerrymandering of Tuskegee, Ala., had the effect of disfranchising black voters. Redistricting was found to be a denial of equal protection because of its discriminatory results. The Voting Rights Act of 1965, which provided for federal regulation of the right to vote in those states where there had been discrimination in the past, seemed to be the ultimate in the legal use of legislation to enforce the right to vote. The act was upheld when challenged in *South Carolina v. Katzenbach* in 1966.

On the subject of jury service, the Supreme Court in 1970 still seemed to be unsure of just how far the constitutional right of fair trials for Afro-Americans applied. Although the court did strike down some of the more brazen procedures that were used to keep Afro-Americans off jury lists, as in *Avery v. Georgia* in 1953, the court was still upholding schemes in 1970 that were insurmountable barriers to the selection of more than an occasional black juror. Time after time, black appellants submitted evidence to show that state laws made it extremely easy for officials to keep blacks off jury lists or to disqualify prospective black jurors on the grounds that they did not meet such subjective requirements as honesty, intelligence, good character, and sound judgment. The court, however, in *Carter v. Jury Commission of Green County* in 1971, ruled that it would be improper to conclude that such statutes were so clearly discriminatory in intent that judicial interference with a state's rights to regulate its own jury selection was justified.

The specter of states' rights continued to inhibit the court in this area. A Georgia case, *Turner v. Fouche* in 1970, arose in Taliaferro County, where no Afro-American had ever served on the school board, a body that was appointed by the county grand jury. Grand jury lists for January 1968 numbered 130 county citizens, but only 11 of these were black, whereas 62 percent of the county's population was black. Appellants centered their pleas upon this gross underrepresentation of blacks. Again, the

Supreme Court ruled that while there was potential for discrimination in the Georgia statute—because jurors could be eliminated by reasons of poor health, old age, or lack of intelligence—the court would defer to states' rights since it was not clear that the statute was inherently unfair. Not primarily a southern practice, the same subtle form of exclusion continued in nonsouthern states and municipalities having high percentages of blacks. As long as the court permits such criteria as discretion, intelligence, uprightness, and moral character in the choosing of a pool of jurors, challenges to the absence of Afro-Americans from juries are indeed fraught with legal difficulty.

Conclusion The impact of civil rights cases on Afro-American history in the United States has been limited. Supreme Court decisions, while important, were few in number compared to the thousands of cases that filled lower-court calendars every day of the year. Thus, a true examination of the history of Afro-Americans in the court system must focus also on these lower courts throughout the country. Moreover, with social and legal barriers precluding some cases from ever coming into any courtroom, an examination of civil rights as seen through the court system can at best be only limited.

The road of civil rights enforcement since Reconstruction has been rough and uneven, filled with many pitfalls. One of the major difficulties has been the paucity of federal attorneys, marshalls, and interested and dedicated officials; another has been an unwillingness on the part of state officials to enact legislation; and still another has been an inordinately long lead time on litigation and appeals (for reasons inherent in judicial procedure) so that the rights of the plaintiff have become moot by the time the cases were decided. These difficulties reflect the attitudes of the majority at large toward the right of the black minority.

The history of civil rights cases illustrates the axiom that laws are effective only to the extent that they are enforced, and that the will of society directs that laws be interpreted in a fair and enlightened manner. Thus, it has been incumbent upon Afro-Americans to try to influence public policy and politics, and to obtain power, so that in the end the courts can interpret equitable laws in a society better adjusted to the needs of its minorities. *See also* Civil Rights: Civil Rights Acts; Civil Rights: Civil Rights Enforcement; Civil Rights Movement; Civil Rights Movement: Civil Rights Movement in

Selected States; Discrimination; Education: Desegregation in Perspective; National Association for the Advancement of Colored People (NAACP); Politics; Segregation.

REFERENCES: For additional information, see: Berger, Morroe, *Equality by Statute: The Revolution in Civil Rights*, Doubleday, New York, 1967; Blaustein, Albert P. and Robert L. Zangrando (eds.), *Civil Rights and the American Negro: A Documentary History*, Trident Press, New York, 1968; Carter Emerson, Thomas I. and David Haber, *Political and Civil Rights in the United States: A Collection of Legal and Related Materials*, 2 vols., Little, Brown, Boston, 1967; Fraenkel, Osmond K., *The Rights We Have*, rev. ed., Thomas Y. Crowell, New York, 1974; revised to include important decisions of the Supreme Court through 1973; Marshall, Thurgood, "The Rise and Collapse of the 'White Democratic Primary,'" *Journal of Negro Education*, Summer 1958, pp. 249–254; McWilliams, Carey, "Race Discrimination and the Law," *Science and Society*, vol. 9, no. 1, pp. 1–22, Winter 1945; Miller, Loren, *The Petitioners: The Story of the Supreme Court of the United States and the Negro*, Pantheon Books, New York, 1966; *Race Relations Law Reporter*, February 1956–May 1970. Vol. 1, no. 2, April 1956, contains a select bibliography, pp. 501–508; and Schwartz, Bernard, *Statutory History of the United States: Civil Rights*, 2 vols., Chelsea House Publishers, New York, 1970.

Specific cases cited in this article are:
Aldridge v. United States, 283 U.S. 308 (1931)
Alexander v. Holmes County Board of Education, 396 U.S. 19 (1969)
Avery v. Georgia, 345 U.S. 559 (1958)
Bailey v. Alabama, 219 U.S. 219 (1911)
Berea College v. Kentucky, 211 U.S. 458 (1908)
Brown v. Board of Education of Topeka, 347 U.S. 483 (1954)
Brown v. Board of Education of Topeka, 349 U.S. 294 (1955)
Buchanan v. Warley, 245 U.S. 60 (1917)
Carter v. Jury Commission of Green County, 396 U.S. 320 (1971)
Carter v. Texas, 177 U.S. 442 (1900)
Civil Rights Cases, 109 U.S. 3 (1883)
Clyatt v. United States (1905)
Cooper v. Aaron, 358 U.S. 1 (1958)
Corrigan and Curtis v. Buckley, 271 U.S. 323 (1926)
Cumming v. Richmond County Board of Education, 175 U.S. 528 (1899)
Ex parte Siebold, 100 U.S. 371 (1880)
Ex parte Virginia, 100 U.S. 339 (1880)
Gomillion v. Lightfoot, 364 U.S. 339 (1960)
Green v. County School Board of New Kent County, 391 U.S. 430 (1968)
Griffin v. County School Board of Prince Edward County, 375 U.S. 391 (1964)
Grovey v. Townsend, 295 U.S. 347 (1935)
Guinn v. United States, 238 U.S. 347 (1915)
Hall v. DeCuir, 95 U.S. 485 (1878)
Harmon v. Tyler, 273 U.S. 668 (1926)
Heart of Atlanta Motel v. United States, 379 U.S. 241 (1964)
Henderson v. United States, 339 U.S. 816 (1950)
James v. Valtierra, 402 U.S. 137 (1971)
Jones v. Alfred H. Mayer Company, 392 U.S. 409 (1968)
McCabe v. Atchinson, Topeka and Santa Fe Railway Company, 235 U.S. 151 (1914)
McLaurin v. Oklahoma State Regents (1950)
Missouri ex rel Gaines v. Canada, 305 U.S. 337 (1938)
Mitchell v. United States, 313 U.S. 80 (1941)
Moore v. Dempsey, 261 U.S. 86 (1923)
Morgan v. Virginia, 328 U.S. 373 (1946)
Nixon v. Condon, 286 U.S. 73 (1932)
Nixon v. Herndon, 273 U.S. 536 (1927)
Norris v. Alabama, 294 U.S. 587 (1935)

Pace v. Alabama, 106 U.S. 583 (1883)
Plessy v. Ferguson, 163 U.S. 537 (1896)
Powell v. Alabama, 287 U.S. 45 (1932)
Regents of the University of California v. Bakke, (1978)
Shelley v. Kraemer, 334 U.S. 1 (1948)
Sipuel v. Board of Regents of the University of Oklahoma, 332 U.S. 631 (1948)
Slaughterhouse Cases, 83 U.S. (16 Wall.) 36 (1873)
Smith v. Allwright, 321 U.S. 649 (1944)
South Carolina v. Katzenbach, 383 U.S. 301 (1966)
Strauder v. West Virginia, 100 U.S. 303 (1880)
Swann v. Charlotte-Mecklenburg Board of Education, 402 U.S. 1 (1971)
Sweatt v. Painter, 339 U.S. 629 (1950)
Terry v. Adams, 345 U.S. 461 (1953)
Turner v. Fouche, 369 U.S. 396 (1970)
United States v. Cruikshank, 92 U.S. 542 (1876)
United States v. Harris, 106 U.S. 629 (1883)
United States v. Raines, 172 F. Supp. 552 (M.D. Ga. 1959), rev'd., 362 U.S. 17 (1960)
United States v. Reese (1876)
Virginia v. Rivers, 100 U.S. 313 (1880)

Civil Rights: Enforcement

The enforcement of civil rights on behalf of Afro-Americans was a dismal failure throughout the period from the close of the first Reconstruction (1877) to the time of World War II. After nearly three-quarters of a century of governmental indifference and impotence, it was not until the 1940s that the federal government demonstrated a growing concern toward the fulfillment of constitutional and legislative promises made during the decade after the Civil War. The U.S. Supreme Court led the way by providing substantive meaning to civil rights in its interpretations of the broad constitutional mandates decreed in the equal protection and due process clauses of the Constitution. The executive branch followed, though hesitatingly, with a series of orders directing that, first, the federal establishment must end its own discrimination and insisting, second, that all federal contractors must do likewise. Congress was the most reluctant to act; it was not until the late 1950s that it passed its first civil rights act since Reconstruction.

Although all three branches of the federal government recognized the failure of enforcement, their actions were cautious; it was not until the so-called civil rights revolt of the 1960s, with both its violence and nonviolence, that the federal government began to consider stronger enforcements. Yet, even with stronger legal and administrative machinery, enforcement was far from complete as shown in a significant and far-reaching report by the U.S. Commission on Civil Rights in 1971 entitled *The Federal Civil Rights Enforcement Effort*.

Presidential Enforcement Enforcement has been a constitutional responsibility of the president.

The actions of the president's office, however, have been frequently influenced by those of the other two branches of government and, significantly, by public opinion. Thus, even when the great prestige and power of the office itself pointed in the direction of more meaningful enforcement, the president's approach was often cautious; and complicance was open to indeterminate delays. Enforcement actions themselves sometimes required additional enforcements; and these in turn required other reinforcements.

The first meaningful and widespread civil rights enforcement applied to the federal establishment itself, which, like American society in general, had a persistent history of discrimination against Afro-Americans. Presidents Franklin D. Roosevelt and Harry S. Truman issued important executive orders. For example, in the wake of the Ramspeck Act of 1940, President Roosevelt issued Executive Order No. 8587, which barred discrimination in employment and promotion within the federal service.

Roosevelt also issued Executive Order No. 8802 in 1941, which set up the Fair Employment Practices Commission (FEPC), whose aim was to prevent discrimination by federal contractors who, at the time, were becoming increasingly vital in the war effort. The FEPC had no enforcement powers, however. It relied upon negotiations, moral suasion, and public opinion. As a remedial measure, President Truman issued Executive Order No. 10308 in 1951, which established the Committee on Contract Compliance. The committee was empowered merely to study the effectiveness of compliance; it did not provide for the use of sanctions. President John F. Kennedy issued Executive Order No. 10925 in 1961 in behalf of compliance.

President Lyndon B. Johnson followed four years later with Executive Order No. 11246. Unlike prior orders, this one empowered the secretary of labor through the Office of Federal Contract Compliance (OFCC) to issue regulations implementing the order and imposing sanctions. This order not only required all federal contractors to assure the federal government that they would not discriminate in employment practices but also that they would undertake "affirmative action" toward equal opportunity and protection. Johnson's order was important in that it provided for sanctions against all federal contractors (about 100,000 firms), who employed about one-third of the nation's labor force. Affirmative-action regulations required

each contractor to complete a thorough plan and evaluation of the use of minority personnel, including promotions, transfers, and upgradings. In later regulations, issued notably in 1968 and in 1970, the OFCC established three basic requirements and eight additional guidelines for affirmative-action programs. The three basic requirements obliged contractors to: (1) perform an analysis of the use of minorities in all job categories; (2) establish goals and timetables to correct deficiencies; and (3) collect data systematically and report plans documenting progress toward achieving the goals of affirmative action. Regulations also called for the OFCC to assist, evaluate, monitor, and guide the federal contracting agencies toward achievement of OFCC goals.

Truman's Executive Orders President Harry S. Truman's actions were outstanding in the effort toward a more effective enforcement of civil rights. Following a plea by the NAACP in 1946, for example, Truman issued Executive Order No. 9808, which established the President's Committee on Civil Rights. The committee had only investigative powers; but its report entitled *To Secure These Rights*, submitted in 1947, was a landmark in recommending redress on a variety of grounds: civil, economic, international, and moral. Truman boldly followed up the report with a special address to Congress on February 2, 1948, in which he recommended that Congress enact legislation in regard to the following ten objectives: (1) establishing a permanent Commission on Civil Rights, a joint congressional Committee on Civil Rights, and a civil rights division in the Department of Justice; (2) strengthening existing civil rights statutes; (3) providing federal protection against lynching; (4) protecting more adequately the right to vote; (5) establishing a Fair Employment Practices Commission to prevent unfair discrimination in employment; (6) prohibiting discrimination in interstate transportation facilities; (7) providing home rule and suffrage in presidential elections for residents in the District of Columbia; (8) providing statehood for Hawaii and Alaska and a greater measure of self-government for island possessions; (9) equalizing opportunities for residents of the United States to become naturalized citizens; and (10) settling the evacuation claims of Japanese-Americans. Truman also followed with an address to the NAACP, an unprecedented presidential action.

Claiming Congress to be a "do nothing" one

for its inaction, Truman used further executive powers. He issued Executive Order No. 9981 on July 26, 1948. Calling for equality of opportunity, this order abolished segregation in the military establishment and set up a special committee to assure its enforcement. Moreover, Truman insisted upon ending segregation within the federal establishment, achieving notably desegregation of dual food services (restaurants) in Washington, D.C.

Congressional Action Congress did not respond with enforcement legislation until the 1960s. It had set up the U.S. Commission on Civil Rights in 1957; but it had given the commission only investigative and reportorial powers: to investigate complaints; to study and collect information concerning legal developments; to appraise federal laws and practices; to act as a clearinghouse for information; and to submit reports, findings, and recommendations to the president and to Congress.

However, the Civil Rights Act of 1964 (with amendments in 1972) provided for more relative enforcement. Under Title VII, the Act created the Equal Employment Opportunity Commission (EEOC) with the purpose of eliminating discrimination in employment based upon race, color, sex, religion, or national origin. Designed to influence the private sector of the economy, the EEOC became a national counterpart to state and local fair employment commissions, some of which had already been in existence for 20 years. EEOC's coverage embraced approximately 75 percent of the nation's private employment, excluding the self-employed. Many employers were not covered, however, in certain types of urban wholesale and retail trade where black minorities would be most affected.

The EEOC could recommend legal suits to the attorney general for prosecution and file as amicus curiae in federal courts. Through its Office of Federal Contract Compliance, the EEOC was empowered to process complaints and to apply sanctions. However, though the EEOC investigated and processed thousands of complaints, the U.S. Civil Rights Commission in a special report of 1971, entitled *Federal Civil Rights Enforcement Effort,* found that EEOC's effectiveness was hampered because of its failure to apply sanctions. Indeed, this monumental report revealed failures in the enforcement of civil rights in some 40 governmental agencies with varying duties and obligations related to civil rights. Another study by the Commission in 1979

(*The Federal Fair Housing Enforcement Effort*) found similar failures.

Summary and Conclusion Although the role of government is important, the enforcement of civil rights transcends federal actions. Enforcement is rather a larger responsibility of American society; its failure lies within the confines of the nation's morals and mores. Enforcement thus raises two basic questions. One is moral (Is it right to deny civil rights to Afro-Americans?). The other is practical (What can be done about this denial?). Basic American ideals, with strong conceptions of fair play (as shown, for example, in the Bill of Rights to the Constitution), have long and consistently in principle answered the first question in the negative, though the application of such ideals was not easily and readily extended to blacks. The answer to the second question is less obvious and more complex because of the many factors involved, not the least being the nature of power and psychological relationships. Particularly after the 1950s, moral and legal suasion have been in long supply in attempts to bring racist realities into line with prevailing American ideals. However, there can be little doubt that practical social changes have come about, reflecting the changes in American attitudes toward Afro-Americans and civil rights. Entirely too slowly for American blacks and yet entirely too rapidly for American racists, the old order of segregation with its massive discrimination has been constitutionally dismantled. Though discrimination and de facto segregation persist, American society became more open to Afro-Americans than ever before; and, importantly but slowly, anticivil rights action seemed more in permanent retreat than in ascendancy by the time of the nation's bicentennial or the *Bakke* decision two years later.

Gains toward the enforcement of civil rights after the 1950s came largely through nonviolent means of moral and legal suasion, though the potential and real effects of the violent civil disorders of the 1960s cannot be overlooked. Not without many allies, Afro-Americans themselves were central in protest movements, reminding the nation repeatedly of the American dream while demonstrating relentlessly the harsh realities of segregation and discrimination. Protest was symbolized and personified by many black leaders, notably Martin Luther King, Jr., whose eloquence and reiterative theme ("I have a dream") did much to set a moral climate of opinion for civil rights enforcement. *See also*

CIVIL DISORDERS; CIVIL RIGHTS: CIVIL RIGHTS
ACTS; CIVIL RIGHTS: CIVIL RIGHTS CASES, 1865–
1975; CIVIL RIGHTS: CIVIL RIGHTS MOVEMENT;
DISCRIMINATION; EMPLOYMENT; NATIONAL ASSO-
CIATION FOR THE ADVANCEMENT OF COLORED PEO-
PLE (NAACP); SEGREGATION.

REFERENCES: For additional information, see: Berger, Morroe, *Equality by Statute: The Revolution in Civil Rights*, Double-day, New York, 1967; Blaustein, Albert P. and Robert L. Zangrando (eds.), *Civil Rights and the American Negro*, Trident Press, New York, 1968; Brink, William and Louis Harris, *Black and White: A Study of U.S. Racial Attitudes Today*, Simon and Schuster, New York, 1967; Dulles, Foster Rhea, *The Civil Rights Commission 1957–1965*, Michigan State University Press, East Lansing, 1968; Fleming, Harold C., "The Federal Executive and Civil Rights," *Daedalus*, Fall 1965, pp. 921–48; Hamiton, Charles V., "Race, Morality and Political Solutions," *Phylon*, September 1959, pp. 242–47; Lichtman, Allan, "The Federal Assault Against Voting Discrimination in the Deep South, 1957–1967," *Journal of Negro History*, October 1969, pp. 346–67; Marshall, Burke, *Federalism and Civil Rights*, Columbia University Press, New York, 1964; Marshall, Thurgood, "Law and the Quest for Equality," *Washington University Law Quarterly*, Winter 1967, pp. 1–9; President's Committee on Civil Rights, *To Secure These Rights*, U.S. Government Printing Office, Washington, D.C., 1947; and U.S. Commission on Civil Rights, *Federal Civil Rights Enforcement Effort*, U.S. Government Printing Office, Washington, D.C., for the years 1971, 1973, 1975.

Civil Rights: Selected States

Introduction In many ways, the national civil rights movement originated in, developed from, and merged with activities within individual states and local communities. Indeed, the national movement was frequently reinforced through local actions, a historic fact especially apparent during the activist phase of the movement that followed World War II. Though the national goals of the movement remained basically unchanged within each state, there were many local variations in implementation due to variables in such local factors as history, geography, demography, politics, and economics. In contrast to the topic of slavery, however, the story of the civil rights movement at state and local levels remains almost completely untold, despite the voluminous amount of materials and data that exists; no doubt this fact can be attributed to the relatively recent historical moment of the movement, which provides only a short span of time for study and reflection.

Nevertheless, the movement at state and local levels is illustrated in the separate accounts that follow of the history of the movement in four states: Alabama, Florida, Kentucky, and North Carolina. All four states showed many common similarities, nationally and regionally, in regard to the civil rights movement: (1) All were part of the South, the region that experienced the greatest political and social impact of the movement; (2) All largely shared a common regional history and demography, including a system of slaveholding and of rigid segregation; (3) All largely shared a common heritage from the movement, namely, a change in the political and social roles of Afro-Americans.

Yet, there were variations among the four states. For example, though each state had a past history of slaveholding and of rigid segregation, one state did not join the Confederacy: the border or "rim" state of Kentucky remained in the Union despite strong sympathies with the southern cause. In addition, although Florida did join the Confederacy, its modern politics would have likewise placed it in the "rim" South. On the other hand, Alabama belonged to the Deep South: to many observers, the state lay geographically, historically, and politically deep "in the heart of Dixie."

Demographically, there were also variations. During the civil rights movement, Alabama had some of the highest densities of rural blacks in the nation, and its total black population (in 1940, for example) was surpassed only by that of Mississippi and by that of Georgia. On the other hand, with the exclusion of Oklahoma, Kentucky had the smallest black population of any state in the South; furthermore, its blacks were overwhelmingly urban and lived in only a few cities—chiefly in Louisville.

Florida was quite different demographically from either Alabama, Kentucky, or North Carolina in the nonsouthern composition of much of its white population. As a coastal and "sunshine" state, it attracted northern whites after the 1920s who, less attached to southern mores, sought tourism, retirement, or employment. On the other hand, many of Florida's rural blacks, seeking to escape harsh and persistent peonage on turpentine farms, looked for freedom and employment in such coastal cities as Jacksonville, Miami, and Tampa. (In 1970 these three cities ranked the state below only Ohio and California in having the most cities with the largest black populations among the nation's 50 largest cities.)

North Carolina's agriculture and educational facilities made it unique among southern states. An overwhelming number of blacks and whites lived on small farms (among the smallest in the nation) or worked in factories devoted to the state's chief economic activity: tobacco. While cotton was declining in the South, the tobacco economy was comparatively healthy in North Carolina. Educationally, the state was rated the best in the South; and with the exception of Texas, it had far more black colleges (13) than any other state in the nation.

In each of these four selected states—Alabama, Florida, Kentucky, and North Carolina—as elsewhere in the nation, the activist phases of the civil rights movement brought great changes (de jure and de facto) within the American social order. This accomplishment, however, did not come without resistance or violence.

Civil Rights: Selected States/Alabama

The Tuskegee Story. Particularly in regard to voting rights, the small town of Tuskegee (the seat of Macon County) best illustrates the course of the civil rights movement in the state of Alabama. Throughout most of the twentieth century, black life in the town had revolved around two institutions: Tuskegee Institute, made famous by Booker T. Washington, and the Veterans Administration Hospital.

The story of the struggle of Afro-Americans for the right to vote in Tuskegee may be divided into six phases. (1) The period before 1943 may be designated as the "permissive phase." Available records show, for example, that in 1928 there were only 32 registered black voters; by 1940 the number had increased to 77 as a result of a highly selective process of registration. (2) The years between 1943 and 1948 may be called the "legal action phase." During this period, many Afro-Americans sought to become registered voters without success. As a result, a number of suits were filed against the Macon County board of registrars. (3) During 1949 and 1950, the "harmony phase," 85 percent of those Afro-Americans filing applications were given certificates of registration.(4) The period from 1951 to 1956 may be characterized as the "obstructive delaying phase," a time when many evasive tactics were used by registrars: for example, blacks were required to write long passages of the state constitution, to wait in line for long periods of time, and to take tests not required of whites. (5) The "community crisis phase" followed in the years 1956–57. During this period a boycott of white merchants took place in which the black students of Tuskegee Institute were very active. In retaliation, the state legislature gerrymandered the town in such a way as to exclude all except 10 of the 420 registered black voters. The gerrymander in turn was countered in a legal suit by Charles G. Gomillion, a faculty member at the Institute. His case eventually reached the U.S Supreme Court, which decided in his favor in *Gomillion v. Lightfoot* in 1960. In November of the following year, Gomillion was elected to the Macon County board of education, one of the

Alabama state troopers clubbed down demonstrators demanding voting rights for black citizens in Selma, Ala. early in March 1965. The nonviolent freedom marchers responded by organizing bigger demonstrations. *(Wide World Photos.)*

261

first blacks ever to hold elective office in the county. (6) The phase that followed the decision in *Gomillion* was closely related to civil rights actions at the national level, as shown in the implementation of the Voting Rights Act of 1965 that provided for strong federal enforcement of the voting rights of blacks. Tuskegee's implementation, however, had actually preceded the passage of this important national legislation.

Freedom Riders Although the origin of freedom rides is perhaps traceable to similar but ill-fated attempts in North Carolina at the close of World War II, this aspect of the civil rights movement began on May 4, 1961, when six whites and seven blacks boarded a Greyhound bus in Washington, D.C., en route through the South to New Orleans, La., in order to test accommodation facilities for blacks at bus terminals. Based on a strategy of nonviolent resistance, the tour was planned by the Congress of Racial Equality (CORE).

Several repercussions followed when the freedom riders passed through North Carolina and South Carolina; but in Alabama dramatic and violent scenes developed. After arriving in Anniston, the riders were beaten while local police looked on with apparent approval. At the stop in Birmingham, the riders were attacked by an estimated 40 to 50 whites brandishing pipes and key rings, according to an account by news commentator Howard K. Smith. At this point, the ride took on greater national proportions because several out-of-state groups joined the protest. For example, the Student Nonviolent Coordinating Committee (SNCC) in Nashville, Tenn., sent in reinforcements.

When the riders arrived in Montgomery on

May 20, they were immediately attacked by a waiting mob of whites that increased (according to estimates) from 200 to 1,000. In the mounting disorder, President John F. Kennedy ordered the Attorney General (who was his brother, Robert) to take any necessary steps to keep the peace. Accordingly, several hundred federal marshalls were dispatched. On the next day, tensions and violence continued, despite the presence of marshalls, as an angry mob of about 1,000 whites formed outside a mass meeting of nearly 1,500 blacks at the First Baptist Church under the direction of its pastor, Rev. Ralph D. Abernathy. Rev. Martin Luther King, Jr., joined the nonviolent protest inside the church; later, he expressed his opinion to the Attorney General that more protection of blacks was necessary. Subsequently, the Governor of Alabama, John Patterson, called in the National Guard.

In the wake of this tension in Montgomery, 11 participants or sympathizers with the freedom riders were arrested for attempting to desegregate a lunch counter. Three were white ministers or college professors: John McGuire, Gaylord B. Noyce, and David Swift; and several were black ministers: Ralph D. Abernathy, Fred L. Shuttlesworth, and Wyatt Tee Walker. However, U.S. District Court Judge Frank M. Johnson, Jr., in response to action initiated by the U.S. Attorney General, issued a restraining order against civil rights groups as well as against the Montgomery police, the Ku Klux Klan, and the National States Rights Party.

Birmingham Nevertheless, the civil rights campaign was renewed in Birmingham. In the spring of 1963, several blacks resorted to the use of sit-ins and boycotts. An intensive drive was led by Rev. Martin Luther King, Jr., in an effort to desegregate lunch counters and public facilities and to end discrimination in employment. King and many of his followers were arrested several times by Birmingham's public safety commissioner, Eugene "Bull" Connor, who on one occasion ordered the use of water hoses and police dogs to disperse the black demonstrators. Hundreds of blacks were jailed, including children and students; both King and Abernathy were also imprisoned. It was during this confinement that King wrote his famous, long "Letter from a Birmingham Jail," dated April 23, 1963, in which he expressed disagreement with some white clergymen about the civil rights movement, including their commendation of the Birmingham police.

Violence in Birmingham continued, and fed-

Members of SNCC and Freedom Riders integrated the lunch counter at the Montgomery, Ala. bus station on May 24, 1961, when they breakfasted there before leaving for Jackson, Miss. and New Orleans. *(Wide World Photos.)*

eral troops were eventually alerted. Through efforts of the offices of the U.S. attorney general (in the person of Burke Marshall, who was on the scene) and the president, blacks and prominent white citizens reached an agreement in order to end the demonstrations. The agreement called for: (1) desegregation of lunch counters, rest rooms, sitting rooms, and drinking fountains in downtown department stores; (2) promotion and employment of blacks in selected cases; (3) release of demonstrators from jail; and (4) establishment of a fair employment committee and a biracial committee.

This agreement appeared to be doomed, however, when violence erupted again after two bombings on May 11: at the home of Rev. A. D. King, who was at that time being visited by his brother, Rev. Martin Luther King, Jr., and at the A. G. Gaston Motel, a well-known, black-owned business establishment being used as headquarters by civil rights groups. More than 2,000 blacks rioted in the wake of the bombings. Supporting the agreement, President Kennedy now authorized the use of federal troops to restore calm.

Opposition to civil rights continued, however, on two notable occasions: the first occurred on May 20 when the school board in Birmingham, over the objection of the superintendent, suspended or expelled approximately 1,000 black students for their participation in the demonstrations; the second, on September 15, involved the bombing of the Sixteenth Street Baptist Church during the Sunday School hour. The explosion, injuring 14 persons and damaging five cars in a nearby street, killed four black girls, ages 11 to 14; Addie Mae Collins, Denise McNair, Carol Robertson, and Cynthia Wesley. Mayor Boutwell of Birmingham, moved to tears, called the bombing "just sickening," and President Kennedy called it "cruel and tragic."

College Desegregation The use of federal military force was invoked again in the desegregation of the University of Alabama at Tuscaloosa. Back in 1953, the NAACP had obtained the admission to the university of Autherine Lucy after strong local opposition, including vicious harassment and threats that eventually contributed to her hasty withdrawal after entry. Now, ten years later, Vivian Malone and James Hood had been ordered to be admitted. When they arrived to register on June 11, they were confronted by Governor George C. Wallace, who, in view of national press and television, ritualistically barred their entrance. However, after a

short speech, Wallace stepped aside, as expected, when U.S. Deputy Attorney General Nicholas de B. Katzenbach, with the support of a presidential proclamation and of federal troops, remarked that "from the outset, governor, all of us have known that the final chapter of this history will be the admission of these students." That evening, President Kennedy, in a nationwide telecast in support of the two students, stated that "a great change is at hand and our task, our obligation, is to make the revolution [civil rights], that change, peaceful and constructive for all." Though Hood never finished, Vivian Malone graduated in 1965.

The Selma to Montgomery March Efforts of Afro-Americans to register and to vote in Dallas County, one of the "black belt" counties of the state, had been long blocked through intimidation and coercion by officials in Selma, the county seat. In protest, a group of more than 500 black

citizens attempted to march from Selma to the state capital of Montgomery. Setting out on Sunday, March 7, 1965, they were met by a charging force of Alabama state troopers, who later said they were carrying out Governor George C. Wallace's orders to ban the march. The beatings and tear gas to which the black demonstrators were subjected led to an influx of civil rights advocates from all across the country, who demanded the right to demonstrate.

A second attempt, led by Martin Luther King, Jr., was made two days later. It was foiled again by a restraining order against the march issued by a federal judge. On March 17, however, the

A church service led by Dr. Martin Luther King, Jr., at Selma, Ala., on March 21, 1965 initiated a five-day 54-mile march to the state capitol at Montgomery, Ala., to protest against restrictions on black voting rights. *(Wide World Photos.)*

march was sanctioned by the court, which ordered Governor Wallace to supply the necessary protection. The march finally began on March 21; and in the five days it took to reach the state capitol in Montgomery, the ranks of marchers, both black and white, had swelled to nearly 25,000. King advocated a withdrawal of federal

support from Alabama and a boycott of Alabama products. After several rebuffs, he presented an equal rights petition to the Governor.

See also the cross-references and references at the end of CIVIL RIGHTS: AFTERMATH; STUDENT NATIONAL COORDINATING COMMITTEE (SNCC).

Civil Rights: Selected States / Florida

Introduction The U.S. Supreme Court decision in *Brown* v. *Board of Education of Topeka* (1954) had little or no effect on Florida school desegregation for several years. It was not until the early 1960s that suits were filed in federal courts against the two most geographically separated counties in Florida, Dade and Escambia. The number of suits continued to increase during the mid-1960s when the U.S. Department of Justice took 14 additional school districts to court. Counties not under the jurisdiction of the federal courts prior to 1964 were required by the Civil Rights Act of 1964 to begin desegregation.

School Desegregation The pace of desegregation was slow. Counties under federal court orders were desegregating at the rate of one grade per year. Counties operating under directions from the Department of Health, Education, and Welfare (HEW) began their desegregation on a percentage quota basis. The initial step was ten percent student desegregation the first year with

an increase in student desegregation and one faculty member per school for the second year forward until an acceptable racial mix was attained. A variety of subsequent rulings relative to dual school systems was common during the late 1960s. Consequently, as of September 1970, 33 counties in Florida were conducting their desegregation plans under federal court order and the remaining 34 were operating under volunteer plans under the jurisdiction of HEW. By September 1970 physical desegregation in Florida was near completion. As for the desegregation of faculties, the ratio of black to white teachers in each school approximated the ratio of blacks to whites within the entire school system.

Public Accommodations In protest of the arrest of the two co-eds who had refused to move to the rear of a segregated bus, students at Florida Agricultural and Mechanical (A & M) University in Tallahassee stopped using local buses in mid-1956. Later in the same year, the bus service was suspended. After a seven-month boycott, Afro-Americans resumed riding the buses under slightly improved conditions. However, in January 1957 three white students and three black students from Florida State University and Florida A & M, respectively, were arrested for violating a bus ordinance that gave Tallahassee bus drivers the authority to assign seats. Three students, two of them blacks, were convicted of this offense; they were freed early in 1958.

In 1959 swimming pools, parks, and other facilities in Miami were opened to blacks. Simultaneously, a group of Afro-Americans in Jacksonville was suing the city in order to prevent the sale to private interest of two public golf courses; the sale, they believed, was a method of circumventing integration. The decade of the 1960s saw both the beginning and the climax of sit-ins, swim-ins, and similar protest activities. Many of the cities in Florida experienced swim-ins early in the 1960s. St. Petersburg, for example, integrated its public beach and swimming pool in early 1961. Five students sued the Tallahassee city commissioners, city manager, and local police for their arrest in September 1961 at the bus station's restaurant, where they were refused service. In succeeding years, Afro-Americans picketed in many cities, including Tallahassee and St. Augustine, against businesses that practiced discrimination.

Riots A race riot erupted in Jacksonville in the spring of 1964; one black woman was killed and several other Afro-Americans were hurt. This was reportedly the worst racial flare-up in Jacksonville since the one that occurred in August 1960. More than 200 persons were arrested. Two other key incidents took place in 1964 in St. Augustine: a biracial group of 18 was arrested for demonstrating against segregated dining facilities at a motor lodge; and a group of other demonstrators was attacked by a white mob. A series of suits were filed throughout the state by individuals and by groups asking for compliance with the Civil Rights Act of 1964 as it related to restaurants and similar public facilities. In fact, recourse to the courts became the trend in the years after the passage of the Civil Rights Act of 1964. The highest number of suits was filed between 1964 and 1968.

As was the case throughout the country, the assassination of Rev. Martin Luther King, Jr., in 1968 ignited a series of racial upheavals throughout Florida. Violence erupted in Tampa, where 50 national guardsmen were mobilized; 200 guardsmen were alerted during the nights of violence near Florida A & M University in Tallahassee. Disorders of varying degree occurred in Gainesville, Jacksonville, and Miami. Violence continued during the summer of 1968 in the Miami area, including eruptions in Liberty City, a section of Miami.

Racial violence subsided very little in 1969 and 1970. Alleged fire bombings of buildings by blacks in Pompano Beach and Fort Lauderdale occurred in August 1970, and mass marching and window breaking erupted in Quincy following the wounding of a black man by a black patrolman in October 1970.

See also the cross-references and references at the end of CIVIL RIGHTS: AFTERMATH.

Civil Rights: Selected States / Kentucky

Desegregation of Colleges and Universities In 1904 the state legislature of Kentucky passed the "Day Law," which made it illegal to educate white and black students on the same campus. The Day Law was enforced until 1950. However, the walls of Kentucky's segregated educational system began to crumble in 1948 when a bill was introduced by Kentucky's only black legislator, attorney Charles W. Anderson, that provided that nursing schools could accept members of both races; it was amended to permit black physicians to take residencies at white hospitals. After continued pressure by Afro-American students to whom postgraduate courses were not available in the state, the University of Kentucky

began to admit Afro-Americans to its law, engineering, pharmacy, and graduate schools in 1949. Eventually, as the result of efforts of black leaders, in a federal suit filed by Lyman T. Johnson, a public school teacher, the entire University of Kentucky was desegregated. In 1950 Paducah Junior College was also ordered to admit black students. The Louisville Municipal College, which had been maintained exclusively for blacks, was closed in June 1951. Of its 14 staff members, including two librarians and an administrative assistant, only one was selected to join the University of Louisville faculty: Dr. C. H. Parrish, Jr., a black professor, was named chairman of the sociology department of the newly integrated university in 1959.

The repeal of the Day Law also opened the doors of three Louisville Catholic Colleges: Nazareth, Bellarmine, and Ursuline. Berea College, the last and most reluctant college to close its doors to Afro-Americans (1904), had been among the first to open them (1955).

Desegregation of Public Schools When the U.S. Supreme Court announced its decision in the case of *Brown v. Board of Education of Topeka* in 1954, the governor of Kentucky, Lawrence W. Weatherly, stated that "Kentucky will do whatever is necessary to comply with the law." Attorney General J. D. Buckman, Jr., announced that the *Brown* decision removed all legal barriers to integration in Kentucky.

The first desegregated Kentucky schools opened in the fall of 1955. Five black teachers were assigned to former all-white schools. The greatest number of Kentucky pupils entered desegregated schools in the fall of 1956. There was comparatively little trouble with the exception of incidents at two high schools. Governor A. B. Chandler acted swiftly to quell these outbursts. On opening day, a crowd of local citizens blocked the entrance to Sturgis High School as black students attempted to enter. Deciding not to force their way through the crowd, the students returned to their homes. When Governor Chandler ordered out 200 National Guardsmen and 200 state troopers to protect the students, many white students stayed at home. A similar incident occurred at Clay. On September 13 the state attorney general ruled that since Webster County had made no provisions for an "orderly process" of school desegregation, black students could not yet be admitted. By January 1956, following a suit filed by the National Association for the Advancement of Colored People

(NAACP), both Clay and Sturgis high schools were opened to Afro-Americans. During the next ten years, NAACP lawyers filed suits in federal courts to desegregate schools in 13 Kentucky counties. In each case, the court ordered desegregation. By the mid-1970s the flight of whites from these counties had left resegregated school conditions. Efforts to achieve racial balance by busing pupils became controversial, especially in Louisville, where near-riot tensions prevailed at the opening of the school year in 1975.

The National Guard served as a buffer to protect orderly desegregation at the high school in Sturgis, Ky., in autumn 1956. *(Photoworld)*

Desegregation of Public Facilities As early as 1945, Afro-Americans in Henderson learned that no state law prohibited them from using the state parks there. Thus, large groups of families simply paid their admission and entered Audubon Park. In 1947 Dr. P. C. Sweeney, a Louisville physician, filed a suit against the city of Louisville when he was not allowed to play golf on a city-owned golf course. It was five years before a federal judge ruled that Louisville must allow Dr. Sweeney and other blacks to play golf on city-owned courses until separate courses could be provided for blacks. On December 16, 1955, the Kentucky Court of Appeals banned segregation in all public recreational facilities.

As late as 1969, some swimming pool owners and managers were operating their facilities as private clubs in order to remain exempt from civil rights legislation. Complaints filed against so-called private pools in Franklin and Clinton resulted in public hearings. The Human Rights Commission ruled in both cases that the pools were public accommodations and, thus, must serve the public without regard to race. The commission noted that it had recorded no problems in Kentucky with desegregated swimming pools.

Housing Following World War II, Afro-Americans throughout Kentucky were faced with housing problems. New subdivisions were built around towns and cities, but blacks, living mostly in the crowded central cities, could not buy homes in the new areas. In the spring of 1954, a white couple, Carl and Ann Braden, bought a newly constructed house in an all-white subdivision and sold it to a black family. After many threatening phone calls, cross burnings, and broken windows from rifle shots, the house was partially destroyed by a bomb. After a grand jury investigation, Carl and Ann Braden were tried and convicted on a charge of sedition. Carl Braden served seven months in prison before the Kentucky Court of Appeals reversed his conviction.

In 1960 Louisville was granted funds for urban renewal. For Louisville's blacks, who comprised 25 percent of the population in this the largest of Kentucky's cities, urban renewal meant "urban removal," since the majority of families affected were black. The need for adequate housing increased, and blacks became more determined than ever to end the unwritten discrimination that barred them from such housing. Bardstown and Nelson counties became the first Kentucky areas to pass open-housing laws. The Committee on Open Housing in Louisville presented a plan based on the Bardstown "model" to the board of aldermen in September 1966 and to the county judge in October. Failing to obtain results, black leaders resorted to more drastic and dramatic action. For several months, blacks marched, demonstrated, and boycotted businesses. The city issued an injunction against the marchers who continued despite the injunction, submitting nonviolently to police arrest while whites jeered, threw sticks and rocks, and shouted obscenities. In the meantime, several other cities, including Covington and Lexington, passed open-housing ordinances. Louisville's black leaders warned the mayor and the board of aldermen that other cities were becoming far more progressive than Louisville in the field of civil rights. Then in March 1968, the General Assembly passed a fair-housing act. It was approved by the senate by a vote of 27 to 3 and by the house by a vote of 54 to 12.

Kentucky became the first state in the South to enact a statewide housing law. On March 15, 1968, the Kentucky House of Representatives passed the Kentucky Civil Rights Act, which cleared the senate by a majority of 27 to 3. The act banned discrimination in all housing sold or rented through real estate agencies and most housing sold or rented directly by an owner.

Racial Violence Racial tensions within the state erupted into violence in 1968. Black churches and businesses were bombed; blacks were beaten and fired upon; and stores belonging to white owners were looted and vandalized. In Louisville, the National Guard was mobilized. In Lexington, ten persons were injured when a drugstore owned by a member of the Commission on Human Rights was bombed. The owner believed that the bombing was a plot by white terrorists. During this period, four persons were killed; 25 persons were injured; and 525 persons were arrested. The loss of property was estimated at approximately $500,000.

In the 1970s, Kentuckians faced some of the same problems as in the past. Resegregation due to changing housing patterns occurred. The Commission on Human Rights had much work to do in such areas as public accommodation, employment, and housing. Yet, enforcement provided greater hope for further progress in race relations.

See also the cross-references and references at the end of CIVIL RIGHTS: AFTERMATH.

Civil Rights: Selected States / North Carolina

The senatorial election of 1950 in North Carolina exposed latent racial issues and antagonisms in the most industrialized and racially harmonious southern state. In contrast to most southern states, white supremacy in North Carolina had not been an issue in post-World War II election campaigns. The States Rights Democratic Party of 1948 (viewed as being antiblack) had no state officers on its ballots, for example, and it did not carry a single county in the state. In fact, the state board of elections had ruled against the party, but the state's supreme court had allowed its candidates to be placed on the official ballot.

In the last three days before the 1950 senatorial election, a Kinston afternoon newspaper contained printed handbills for distribution entitled "White People Wake Up." The message spread across the state by means of paid political advertisements and broadcasts: "Political End of Segregation Proposed," "Do You Know That 28% of N.C.'s Population Is Colored?" and "The Southern Working Man Must Not Be Sacrificed By FEPC." The senatorial opponents were incumbent Frank Graham and Willis Smith, an attorney from Raleigh. The latter allegedly accused Graham of being a "nigger lover" and a proponent of compulsory FEPC (Fair Employment Practices Commission) legislation (although Graham had denounced this legislation publicly), stated that Graham favored political appointments of blacks over whites, and argued that a vote for Graham meant a vote for integration at the University of North Carolina. (In fact, a recent U.S. Supreme Court decision had ruled that the universities of Texas and Oklahoma must admit blacks.) Previously, labor had opposed Smith, but racial issues now split the vote and Smith won by a majority of about 3 percent.

Education Blacks continued to combat racial problems by following local black leadership and the leadership of the National Association for the Advancement of Colored People (NAACP), the Congress of Racial Equality (CORE), and the National Urban League. Before 1957 there were no integrated public schools in North Carolina, despite the *Brown* decision. On the university level, three Hillside High (Durham) graduates, Leroy B. Frasier, John L. Brandon, and Ralph Kennedy, sued for admission to the University of North Carolina, and the federal district court upheld their suit in 1956.

White public officials were the most vigorous opponents of the implementation of the *Brown* decision. Governor Umstead considered the decision "a terrible dissappointment," and official methods were sought to maintain segregated schools. The two Pearsall committees, appointed in 1954 and in 1955, which included two Afro-American college presidents, made several unanimous recommendations (known collectively as the Pearsall Plan) that warned the public that Carolinians "would not support mixed schools." North Carolina's General Assembly authorized local boards of education to assign pupils to public schools, and it submitted proposed amendments to Article IX of the Constitution. These amendments, ratified by the voters, authorized local boards to suspend operation of public schools, to grant public funds for students attending nonpublic schools when public schools were closed, and to exempt parents from compulsory school-attendance laws.

Blacks seeking redress through the courts were confronted not with one opponent—the state's department of public instruction—but with 100 separate local boards. In two important cases, Carson v. McDowell County and Jeffreys v. Whitley, both in 1955, the federal district courts ruled that blacks had not exhausted all administrative remedies. By September 1957, out of a total black student enrollment of 23,787 in three major city systems, only 11 blacks were assigned to white schools: 4 to Charlotte; 6 to Greensboro; and 1 to Winston-Salem. (No whites were assigned to black schools.) To many black teachers and students, it became clear that the exercise of a constitutional right meant one thing for whites and quite another thing for blacks.

Voting The federal Civil Rights Act of 1957 extended the vote in federal elections to all qualified citizens regardless of race or color; it became a federal crime to interfere with this right. No longer armed with the poll tax as a weapon, some public officials used violence, intimidation, and harassment to impede enforcement of the law. It was reported that one county registrar demanded that black applicants answer a list of 20 questions, among which were: Name all the candidates running for office. Define the word *primary*. State if you are a member or supporter of the NAACP. In another county, officials required a no-error reading and writing test for blacks but not for whites. In this county, the black majority was 2 to 1, but only four blacks were registered from 1954 to 1956.

Belatedly, the Civil Rights Act of 1960 permitted federal voting referees in areas where a pattern of racial discrimination existed. North Carolina's congressional representation unanimously opposed passage of the bill.

College students were becoming disillusioned and restless. Although Martin Luther King, Jr., and other civil rights leaders were still popular, white political leaders were not responding effectively to the voices of the people. Racism was the dominant attitude and Jim Crow laws were still prevalent, even though they were unconstitutional. Not until 1960 did it become an established legal principle that state and local Jim Crow laws violated the equal protection clause of the Fourteenth Amendment. Immediate relief was needed in the view of many students.

The First Sit-In On Monday, February 1, 1960, four black freshmen from the Agricultural and Technical College in Greensboro—Ezell Blair (the leader), Franklin McCain, Joseph McNeill, and David Richmond—sat down at the lunch counter of a dime store on Greene Street and ordered coffee. Thus began the historic student sit-ins of the 1960s, supported by CORE and adopted by Martin Luther King, Jr.

Responses to sit-ins were swift. Reactions by several black and most white school officials in North Carolina were negative; and at least 141 students and 58 professors were later dismissed in reprisal. Police officials in the major cities responded with violence against blacks even though no laws had been violated. With the exception of the Park Central Hotel in Raleigh, the Adcock Restaurant in Durham, and houses of ill repute, the movement succeeded in making local businessmen integrate restaurants, motels, and hotels before the passage of the Civil Rights Act of 1964. Local public officials and elitist groups repeatedly used their influence to persuade these businessmen to integrate their businesses. Governor Sanford responded immediately by calling a conference with blacks in the spring of 1963 to discuss differences. Subsequently, plans were made with college students and teachers to involve them in voter registration drives, adult political education programs, and other projects.

Black Political Action By 1964 blacks were convinced that there would have to be more meaningful participation within the Democratic Party, lest segregationists continue to dominate party power. Reginald A. Hawkins (a Charlotte dentist), Jacquelyne J. Jackson (a professor of sociology), and D. W. Bishop (a professor of history) spearheaded the organization of the North Carolina Committee for More Representative Political Participation (NCCFMRPP). Hawkins announced his candidacy for governor. The organization had solid statewide support from all segments of the black population, and its representatives met with the State Democratic Party Platform Committee at the state convention in June 1968. Hawkins presented a resolution from NCCFMRPP demanding 25 percent black representation within the party at all levels, including delegates to the national Democratic Party Convention to be held in Chicago in August 1968. Party leaders rejected these demands. Subsequently, Hawkins announced that the organization would send its own delegates to Chicago and make local demands into national issues. The national Democratic Party eventually accepted the basic proposals of NCCFMRPP and recommended a uniform plan for all state and local parties. The North Carolina Democratic Party accepted the plan in January 1970.

At the State Democratic Party Convention of 1970, blacks were represented in meaningful decision-making positions at all levels. The party presented for adoption a weak civil rights platform, and D. W. Bishop, state treasurer of NCCFMRPP, presented a strong civil rights platform. Bishop's platform was the one finally adopted by the party:

> Whereas institutionalized racism is disrupting American democracy and damaging the personalities of all Americans. . . . Therefore be it Resolved, That the Democratic Party in North Carolina commits itself to work in concert with Afro-Americans in bringing about the total and immediate integration of every area of American life. . . . That the Party . . . commits itself to the development and implementation of humanitarian, social, and economic programs in concert with Afro-Americans.

This was the strongest civil rights platform ever adopted by any political party in a southern state.

The years between 1950 and 1970 were probably the most meaningful in North Carolina history in terms of strategies and sacrifices made by Afro-Americans in behalf of civil rights. Protests were forthright, and the results became apparent despite some resistance by white elected public officials. One of the most important achievements of Afro-Americans was convincing public officials, elitist groups, and party officials to change old attitudes and to respond positively to the solution of racial problems.

See also the cross-references and references at the end of CIVIL RIGHTS: AFTERMATH.

Civil Rights: Aftermath

Civil Rights Movement During the early years of the 1970s, there was a growing tendency among blacks generally to shrug off the black revolution and the question of whether it brought about any positive, measurable improvement in the condition of blacks in the United States. Among other things, Afro-Americans pointed to the disproportionately high percentage of blacks on public welfare, the high unemployment rate of black males, the apparent impregnability of de facto segregation in the cities, and the widespread white hysteria against busing to achieve public school desegregation. While these contentions are essentially sound, whether they constitute a fair and proper judgment of the black revolution is open to question. One could, of course, quibble about the use of the term "revolution" as a designation of black activism during the decade, but the problem here is not really one of semantics.

Essentially, the so-called black revolution was a social movement that began spontaneously in the Deep South during the mid-1950s. Over the next 15 years the movement divided into two distinct phases, each with its own goals, its own leadership, and its own ideology. Each also made its individual impact upon American society. The first phase of the movement, which is sometimes characterized as the "Era of Nonviolence," or the Age of Martin Luther King, Jr., spanned the ten-year period between 1955 and 1965. Originating out of the bus boycott in Montgomery, Ala., it later encompassed the sit-in crusade of 1960 and the freedom rides of 1961. In 1962 the movement took on the dangerous and difficult task of reenfranchising the millions of voteless blacks in the southern states. In all of these campaigns, the movement was successful. In less than 18 months, black college students changed the face of the South. Challenging age-old traditions, customs, and entrenched racism, they managed to bring about the desegregation of public accommodations at a time and in a place where it was thought impossible. They had brought about a major social change. When the federal government enacted the Civil Rights Act of 1964, it was belatedly endorsing an institutional change brought about by the movement some three years earlier.

Of equal importance was the movement's success in restoring political rights to southern blacks. Although the funding and some of the supervision came from sources outside of the movement, the hard, dangerous work of voter education and voter registration was undertaken by virtually the same young blacks who had served on the sit-ins and the freedom rides. In the two-year period between 1962 and 1964, these youths were instrumental in adding more than 700,000 new black voters to the registration rolls in the states of the Old Confederacy. They thus laid the foundation for the federal Voting Rights Act of 1965. During the next five years, the black vote in the region became a patent political force. It placed hundreds of blacks into political office for the first time since Reconstruction and brought an end to much of the "red neck" demagoguery for which the region was so well known. In short, after the lapse of more than one hundred years, the promises of the Fifteenth Amendment were finally being fulfilled.

Several specific reasons lay behind the success of the first phase of the black revolution. For one thing, all of its goals were unmistakenly system-oriented. Invoking the American creed itself, blacks demanded that the age-old disparity between the expressed ideals and the actual performance of American democracy be ended. Beyond this, there was an effective appeal to the conscience of white America. Perhaps the most vital accomplishment of Martin Luther King, Jr., was his success in getting the so-called Negro question recognized and accepted as the basic moral issue before the country. King was thus able to isolate the white South while providing the rest of the nation's whites with an opportunity to expiate their collective guilt. This was the prime reason for the white northern support of the Civil Rights Act of 1964 and the Voting Rights Act of 1965.

Of equal importance with the goals of the first phase of the movement were the means employed to achieve them. As modes of social protest, nonviolence and "love" were new and confusing on the American scene. Nevertheless, they were inherent in the Judeo-Christian tradition that undergirded the American ethos. Morally, the American people could not openly invoke retaliation and repression. Skeptical at first, white America was moved ultimately to give unprecedented support to nonviolence and the goals to which it was directed. Nonviolence won for Dr. King, at least, the qualified support of two national administrations, that of President John F. Kennedy and that of President Lyndon B. Johnson. And beyond this it won almost universal approval abroad. Indeed, it was because of his philosophy and his ability to implement it that Dr. King won the Nobel Peace Prize.

Because of the excitement, the agitation, and the tumult associated with it, the black nationalist phase of the movement has managed to obscure the period from 1955 to 1965. Indeed, in the minds of a growing number of Americans, the black revolution is associated only with militant black nationalism and the images of Stokely Carmichael, Huey P. Newton, and LeRoi Jones. However, in terms of its material impact upon American institutions, black nationalism was far less revolutionary than nonviolence. Over a five-year period, the goals of black nationalism were broadcast first as "Black Power" and then as "Black Liberation." At no time was there ever any consensus on what either of the terms really envisioned.

Equally as nebulous and visionary were the black militant projections of black armed uprisings and mass slaughter of white. None of this activity ever moved beyond the talking stage. On the other hand, evidence existed of some serious study of the possibilities of adopting the guerrilla warfare theories of Ché Guevara, Vo-Nguyen-Giap, and Mao Tse-tung for black ghetto use. The Revolutionary Action Movement (RAM) and the Republic of New Africa (RNA) probably went further with this work than any other group. In this, as in other things, however, the activities of the militants received far more notoriety than they merited. The nation's press invariably magnified and spread any rumor it received of black urban guerrilla activity. There is almost a certainty that no sizable group of black militants ever received all of the training and know-how necessary to mount successful guerrilla activity in urban America. Even if one group had, the community support necessary to sustain such a campaign would not have been forthcoming. Urban blacks are not given to that kind of violence. Black militant confrontations with the local police, however, were another matter. They fascinated the black community, especially the "block boys," and they were acceptable substitutes for the mass slaughter of whites that was forever being promised. Essentially, the confrontation was a public display of machismo, that is, virility, courage, and bravado. These were the qualities historically denied the black male by American society.

If there was one common tie among all black militants, college youths and block boy, it was their special brand of speech or "rhetoric." Almost a new language, it consisted of words, phrases, and even metaphors culled from "black English" and from the writings of Fanon, Malcolm X, and socialist revolutionary literature. The rhetoric also employed a good deal of profanity and obscenity, the purpose of which was to shock and distress listeners. All things considered, their rhetoric was perhaps the most effective thing the militants had going for them. While it did not produce the revolution, it did have a discernible effect upon the minds of the ghetto youth. Such admonitions as "Kill the pig upon the hill" and "get the honkey" were bound to be taken literally by some ghetto juveniles. In effect, they were indoctrination for crime disguised as revolutionary catechisms.

By mid-1970, revolutionary black nationalism was definitely beginning to lose its aura for an increasing number of black youth. They had been led to expect what in effect was a Second Coming, a final apocalypse. They had given of their hopes, their enthusiasm, and their labor, and still there was no deliverance, or any sign of deliverance. There were only promises and interminable rhetoric. The result for many of these youths was moodiness and despair, even despondency. Some of the college militants accepted the proffered embrace of the Black Muslims; others, reluctantly, made peace with the establishment. For the block boys, the result was far more critical. The aggression and hostility that only recently had been directed toward whites were once again turned on the black community and produced a crime rate unprecedented in the history of the nation. Moreover, the need to escape from utter hopelessness was perhaps not unrelated to the alarming rise of narcotic addiction in the black communities.

For all this, however, militant black nationalism did have a positive discernible impact upon blacks and especially upon Afro-American culture. The black studies crusade, which it launched during the mid-1960s, was initially a political movement, but others came to recognize its intrinsic worth and developed it into a legitimate academic pursuit. The more than 600 colleges and universities that were offering black studies courses in 1972 all owed a debt to the movement. Less concrete but far more pervasive was the movement's influence on the growth of black consciousness within the race. The obsequious, docile, and apologetic "Uncle Tom" had vanished from the scene, and the young blacks who were reaching maturity in the 1970s were evidencing a greater pride in their blackness than had any generation before them.

In the arts and letters, the dominant theme for Afro-American craftsmen was also the black awakening. The struggle to produce a new black poetry was meeting with success, and black playwrights were winning their battle for recognition of the black theater. In the motion picture area, however, the movement had its most dramatic impact. Gone from the scene were such slack-jawed versions of Uncle Tom as Stepin Fetchit, Manton Moreland, and Eddie "Rochester" Anderson. The so-called black film made its debut, and it presented black audiences with such new characters as "Shaft," "Nigger Charlie," and "Superfly." The new films were popular enough, but they did not meet universal approval. They tended to make heroes of black narcotic pushers, pimps, and miscellaneous hustlers. In the view of many observers, they were producing new black stereotypes. From others, mostly of the motion picture industry, the rebuttal was that the films were producing unprecedented opportunities for black directors, black producers, black technicians, and black actors. As the controversy continued, the demand grew for the establishment of a black review board.

As with any new cause, the singular pursuit of black consciousness began to produce excesses. The growing tendency to apply the "black perspective" to all social problems regardless of their nature reflected this excess. Thus, by 1970, upwards of 25 black professional groups, almost all of which had achieved "liberation" by separating themselves from the predominantly white national organizations, had come into being. Calling this a "new tribalism," Bayard Rustin observed (*Newsweek*, November 13, 1972): "Their various manifestos and agendas reflect a narrow vision of society in which racial awareness replaces political organization and lifestyle is a substitute for economic and social progress."

See also AFRO-AMERICAN HISTORY: RECONSTRUCTION TO REVOLT, 1887–1977; BLACK PANTHER PARTY; BLACK POWER; CIVIL RIGHTS ACTS; CIVIL RIGHTS CASES, 1865–1975; CIVIL RIGHTS ENFORCEMENT; CONGRESS OF RACIAL EQUALITY (CORE); MISSISSIPPI FREEDOM DEMOCRATIC PARTY (MFDP); NATIONAL ASSOCIATION FOR THE ADVANCEMENT OF COLORED PEOPLE (NAACP); NATIONALISM; PAN-AFRICANISM; POLITICS; SEGREGATION; SOUTHERN CHRISTIAN LEADERSHIP CONFERENCE (SCLC); STUDENT NATIONAL COORDINATING COMMITTEE (SNCC).

REFERENCES: For additional information, see: Bennett, Lerone, Jr., *Confrontation: Black and White,* Johnson Publishing Co., Chicago, 1965; Bennett, Lerone, Jr., *The Negro Mood,* Johnson Publishing Co., Chicago, 1964; Brink, William and Louis Harris, *The Negro Revolution in America,* Simon & Schuster, New York, 1964; Brisbane, Robert H., *Black Activism: Racial Revolution in the United States, 1954–1970,* Judson Press, Valley Forge, 1974; Broderick, Francis L. and August Meier (eds.), *Negro Protest Thought in the Twentieth Century,* Bobbs-Merrill, Indianapolis, 1965; Carmichael, Stokely and Charles V. Hamilton, *Black Power: The Politics of Liberation in America,* Random House, New York, 1967; Clark, Kenneth B., "The Civil Rights Movement: Momentum and Organization," *Daedalus,* Winter 1966, pp. 237–67; Kaiser, Ernest, "Recent Literature on Black Liberation Struggles and the Ghetto Crisis," *Science and Society,* Spring 1969, pp. 168–96; Katzenbach, Nicholas de B., "The Protection of 'Political Rights,'" *Federal Bar Journal,* Winter 1964, pp. 18–30; King, Coretta, *My Life with Martin Luther King, Jr.,* Holt, Rinehart, and Winston, New York, 1969; King, Martin Luther, Jr., *Stride Toward Freedom: The Montgomery Story,* Harper and Row, New York, 1958; Lomax, Louis E., *The*

Negro Revolt, Signet Books, New York, 1962; Malcolm X, *The Autobiography of Malcolm X,* Grove Press, New York, 1964; McCord, William, *Mississippi, The Long Hot Summer,* W. W. Norton, New York, 1965; Meier, August and Elliott Rudwick, *CORE: A Study in the Civil Rights Movement, 1942–1968,* Oxford University Press, New York, 1973; Minnis, Jack, "The Mississippi Freedom Democratic Party: A New Declaration of Inedependence," *Freedomways,* Spring 1965; Muse, Benjamin, *The American Negro Revolution: From Nonviolence to Black Power, 1963–1967,* Indiana University Press, Bloomington, 1968; Sellers, Cleveland and Robert Terrell, *The River of No Return: The Autobiography of a Black Militant and the Life and Death of SNCC,* William Morrow, New York, 1973; Silver, James W., *Mississippi: The Closed Society,* Harcourt, Brace & World, New York, 1964; Slaiman, Donald, *Civil Rights in the Urban Crisis,* U.S. Department of Labor, Manpower Administration, Washington, D.C., 1968; Strong, Augusta, "Negro Women in Freedom's Battles," *Freedomways,* Fall 1967, pp. 302–15; U.S. Commission on Civil Rights, *Law Enforcement: A Report on Equal Protection in the South,* U.S. Government Printing Office, Washington, D.C., 1965; U.S. Commission on Civil Rights, *Political Participation: A Study of the Participation by Negroes in the Electoral and Political Processes in 10 Southern States,* U.S. Government Printing Office, Washington, D.C., 1968; Wynn, Daniel Webster, *The NAACP Versus Negro Revolutionary Protest,* New York, Exposition Press, 1955; Wynn, Daniel Webster, *The Black Protest Movement,* Philosophical Library, New York, N.Y., 1974; and Zinn, Howard, *SNCC: The New Abolitionists,* Beacon Press, Boston, 1964.

CLAFLIN UNIVERSITY Claflin University, at Orangeburg, S.C., was founded in 1869 and named in honor of Leo Claflin—a prominent Methodist of Boston—and his son William Claflin—governor of Massachusetts—who were both instrumental in buying the property for the original site. The coeducational school, private and still church-related, offers the bachelor's degree and provides liberal arts and teacher education curricula. In 1975 it had an enrollment of about 700.

The original site was selected by Rev. T. Willard Lewis, the first missionary sent by the Methodist Church to the emancipated people of South Carolina, and by Alonzo Webster, a minister from Vermont who served as a chaplain in the U.S. Army during the Civil War. Admission requirements for the first prospective students were good moral character and a conscientious desire to learn. In 1896 the General Assembly of South Carolina separated the State A & M College from Claflin. The college was later admitted to full membership in the Southern Association of Colleges and Schools.

CLAIR, MATTHEW WESLEY (1865–1943), Methodist Episcopal bishop; born in Union, W.Va. Clair graduated from Morgan State University (Baltimore, Md.) in 1889, received his Ph.B. degree from Bennett College (Greensboro, N.C.) in 1897, and was ordained to the ministry of the Methodist Episcopal (ME) Church in 1889. He was pastor of churches in Harpers Ferry, W.Va.; Staunton, Va.; and Washington, D.C., where he served as presiding elder of the Washington, D.C., district of the ME Church. Elevated to bishop in 1920, Clair was assigned to the diocese of Monrovia, Liberia.

CLARK COLLEGE Clark College, at Atlanta, Ga., was founded by Methodists in 1869 and is still affiliated with the Methodist Episcopal (ME) Church. A private coeducational school, it offers the bachelor's degree, and provides liberal arts and teacher education curricula. In 1975 its enrollment was about 1,300.

Clark was named for a Methodist bishop who was active during Reconstruction, when the Freedmen's Aid Society was establishing Methodist schools for Afro-Americans in the South. Although Clark College is part of the Atlanta University system, it retains its independence. *See also* ATLANTA UNIVERSITY; METHODISTS.

CLARK, FELTON GRANDISON (1903– ?), educator; born in Baton Rouge, La. Clark received a B.A. degree from Beloit College (Beloit, Wisc.) in 1924, and a M.A. degree (1925) and his Ph.D. degree (1933) from Columbia University. He taught at Wiley College (1925–27), at Howard University (1931–33), and at Southern University, where he served as dean (1934–38) and then president, beginning in 1938. Clark was a member of Phi Beta Kappa and served on several national educational and civic commissions and committees.

CLARK, ISAAC RUFUS (1925–), clergyman, educator; born in New Castle, Pa. Clark received a B.A. degree from Wilberforce University (Wilberforce, Ohio) in 1951, a B.D. degree from Payne Theological Seminary in 1952, and his Th.D. degree from Boston University School of Theology in 1958. He was pastor of African Methodist Episcopal (AME) churches in Massachusetts and served in an educational post at Paul Quinn College (Waco, Tex.).

CLARK, JAMES I. (1906–), Bible Way bishop; born in Trinidad. Clark received a Th.B. degree from Paterson State College (Paterson, N.J.), and Th.D. and D.D. degrees from American Bible College (Chicago, Ill.). In 1932 he was ordained in the Bible Way Church of Our Lord Jesus Christ World Wide, Inc., and he served as pastor of churches in New Jersey and New York. Clark became dean of the Bible Institute, and in 1962 he was consecrated bishop of the diocese of New York and the West Indies. *See also* BIBLE WAY CHURCH OF OUR LORD JESUS CHRIST WORLD WIDE, INC.

CLARK, JOSEPH SAMUEL (1871–1944), educator; born in Sparta, La. Clark received a B.A. degree from Leland University in 1901, a M.A. degree from Selma University (Selma, Ala.) in 1913, and two hon. degrees, one from Leland University in 1914 and one from Arkansas Baptist College in 1921. He was president of Baton Rouge College (1901–12) and president of Southern University (1913–40)—the first black president of that university. Clark also reorganized the Louisiana State Colored Teachers Association and served as its president for eight years. In 1928 he was appointed a member of the National Survey Committee, which was made up of 72 leading educators—mostly white. In 1930 Clark became a member of President Herbert Hoover's White House Conference on Child Welfare and Protection. Hoover appointed him to other positions in 1931 and, of special interest, to the Interracial Commission in 1932.

CLARK, KENNETH BANCROFT (1914–), educator, psychologist; born in the Panama Canal Zone. Clark received a B.A. degree (1935) and a M.S. degree (1936) from Howard University (Washington, D.C.), and his Ph.D. degree from Columbia University in 1940. He taught at Hampton Institute (1940–41) and at City College of New York (1942–), and was co-founder and research director of the Northside Center for Child Development (1946–66). Clark was a member of a commission on integration of the board of education of New York City (1954–58), president of the Metropolitan Applied Research Center, Inc., a member of the board of trustees, Howard University (1959), and also a member of the New York board of regents (1966). He received the Spingarn Medal in 1961. His writings include: *Desegregation: An Appraisal of the Evidence* (1953), *Prejudice and Your Child* (1955), and *Dark Ghetto* (1965).

CLARK, KENNETH SPEARMAN (KENNY) (1914–), jazz drummer; born in Pittsburgh, Pa. Clark was one of the originators of the Bop revolution in jazz and a pioneer figure in the use of drums as a solo instrument. His early professional experience was gained with Roy Eldridge and Edgar Hayes. In the 1940s Clark played with Teddy Hill before moving to Minton's Playhouse in Harlem. At one time or another Clark worked with many jazz greats: Dizzy Gillespie, Charlie Christian, Coleman Hawkins, Sidney Bechet (1940–41), and Red Allen (1942–46). In the 1950s Clark toured with Billy Eckstine, and in 1952 he helped found the Modern Jazz Quartet. *See also* MUSIC: JAZZ.

CLARK, PETER HUMPHRIES (1829–ca. 1895), educator, journalist; born in Cincinnati, Ohio. Clark served as teacher and principal of black schools in Cincinnati for more than 30 years. He worked with Frederick Douglass on a newspaper in Rochester, N.Y., and earlier, in 1854, published a newspaper, *Herald of Freedom*.

CLARKE, JOHN HENRIK (1915–), historian, educator; born in Union Springs, Ala. After studying at New York University, Clarke became the first licensed teacher of African and Afro-American history in New York state and later an associate professor of black and Puerto Rican studies at Hunter College (New York City). He won several awards for his work in television, notably as a consultant on the CBS-TV "Black Heritage" series, which he created. His books include: *Rebellion in Rhyme* (1948), *Harlem, a Community in Transition* (1964), *Malcolm X: The Man and his Times* (1969), and *Marcus Garvey and the Vision of Africa* (1974). Clarke also served on the staffs of five publications, including *Freedomways*, *Ghana Evening News*, and *Negro History Bulletin*. He was a founding member of the Black Academy of Arts and Letters.

CLARKE, RICHARD V. (1927–), business executive; born in New York, N.Y. Clarke graduated from City College of the City University of New York in 1955. He was founder and president of Richard Clarke Associates, Inc. (1964), located in New York City and Chicago, the largest minority group counseling and recruiting organization in the United States. Clarke was also publisher of *Contact* magazine and *Opportunities for the College Grad*. He became a consultant to the Federal Equal Employment Opportunity Commission, to the Community Relations Service, and to the Agency for International Development, and he was a member of the New York Urban Coalition Manpower Task Force (1970). Clarke also served on the Manhattan Advisory Subcommittee to the Urban League and on the Interracial Council for Business Opportunity. He lectured at Harvard College, the College of the City of New York, Northwestern University, Boston University, New York University, and Brookings Institute.

CLAXTON, RICHARD See GREGORY, DICK.

CLAY, CASSIUS See ALI, MUHAMMAD.

CLAY, WILLIAM LACY (1931–   ), U.S. Representative; born in St. Louis, Mo. Clay received a B.S. degree from St. Louis University (St. Louis, Mo.) in 1953. As manager of a life insurance company in St. Louis from 1959 to 1961, and as a long-time activist member of black civil rights groups in St. Louis, he was elected to the city's board of aldermen from the 26th Ward in 1959 and again in 1963. From 1961 to 1964, Clay was business representative of the city employees union, and in 1966 he became education coordinator of Steamfitters Local No. 562. In January 1969 he took his seat in the Ninety-first U.S. Congress as a Democratic representative from Missouri. Clay was reelected to several congresses thereafter.

CLAYTON, XERNONA (1933–   ), television personality; born in Muskogee, Okla. A graduate of Tennessee State University in 1952, Clayton was a teacher in Chicago and Los Angeles before she became involved with the Southern Christian Leadership Conference (SCLC). Active in civic affairs, she became a consultant for the Atlanta Model Cities Program. Clayton later became the first Afro-American to host a television show in the South—"The Xernona Clayton Show"—televised in Atlanta, Ga.

CLAYTOR, WILLIAM SCHIEFFELIN (1908–60), mathematician, educator; born in Virginia. Claytor received a B.S. degree from Howard University (Washington, D.C.) in 1929 and his Ph.D. degree from the University of Pennsylvania in 1933. He was a Rosenwald Fellow and did postdoctoral study at the University of Michigan in mathematics (1935–36). Claytor taught mathematics at West Virginia State College and at Howard University from the mid-1940s until 1960. A veteran of World War II, several of his writings have appeared in scholarly journals. See also AVIATORS.

CLEAGE, ALBERT BUFORD (1911–   ), clergyman, civil rights leader; born in Indianapolis, Ind. Cleage received a B.A. degree from Wayne State University (Detroit, Mich.) in 1937 and his B.D. degree from Oberlin School of Theology. He was a caseworker for the Detroit department of public welfare in 1937 and 1938. For ten years, beginning in 1942, Cleage was pastor of churches in Kentucky, California, Massachusetts, and Michigan; in 1952 he became pastor of the Shrine of the Black Madonna in Detroit. He was a member of the executive board of the National Association for the Advancement of Colored People (NAACP) and Michigan state chairman of the Freedom Now political party. Cleage wrote *The Black Messiah* (1968) and *Black Christian Nationalism: New Directions for the Black Church* (1972). Hiley H. Ward's *Prophet of the Black Nation* (1969) is a biography of Cleage.

CLEAVER, JIM See NEWSPAPERS: CONTEMPORARY.

CLEAVER, LEROY ELDRIDGE (1935–   ), author, civil rights activist; born in Wabaseka, Ark. Cleaver entered reform school in 1954 and later was sent to Soledad Prison in California for selling marijuana. Paroled after two-and-a-half years, he was returned to prison for assault and received a 14-year sentence, but was paroled again in December 1966. By that time Cleaver had become a senior editor of *Ramparts* magazine, which helped wage a campaign on his behalf. In 1968 he and Bobby Hutton (his Black Panther bodyguard) were attacked by police in Oakland, Calif., and Hutton was slain while he tried to surrender. Cleaver was arrested as a parole violator, freed two months later, and then ordered back to prison as the result of an appellate court ruling. Instead of returning to prison, on Nov. 25, 1968, he fled first to Cuba and later to Algeria and to France. Cleaver was minister of information for the Black Panther Party in 1967, the Peace and Freedom Party presidential candidate in 1968, and a guest lecturer at the University of California in 1968. His books include an autobiography, *Soul on Ice* (1968), and a collection of essays, *Post Prison Writings and Speeches* (1969). He returned voluntarily from exile in 1976. See also BLACK PANTHER PARTY.

CLEM, CHARLES DOUGLAS (1875–1934), poet; born in Greensville, Tenn. Clem's first book, *Oklahoma, Her People and Professions* (1892), appeared six years before he graduated from Greensville College. He was also the author of *Rhymes of a Rhymster* (1896), and he edited a weekly newspaper, *The Western World*, in Oklahoma City in 1901 and 1902. Clem traveled widely, giving poetry recitals and lecturing on metaphysics, telepathy, and hypnotism. His autobiography is entitled *Fourteen Years in Metaphysics* (1913).

CLEM, WILLIAM WEBSTER (1918–   ), educator; born in Convent, La. Clem received a B.A. degree from Southern University (Baton Rouge, La.) in 1938, a M.A. degree from Fisk University (Nashville, Tenn.) in 1939, and his Ph.D. degree from the University of Wisconsin in 1949. He taught education at Edward Waters College (1939–40) and at Southern University, where he became critic, teacher, and principal of the laboratory school (1942–51); professor of education and director of extension services (1951–58); and dean of the college of education in 1958. Clem was a contributor to the *Journal of Negro Education*.

CLEMENT, GEORGE CLINTON (1871–1934), African Methodist Episcopal Zion bishop; born in Davie County, N.C. Clement received a B.A. degree (1898), a M.A. degree (1904), and his D.D. degree (1906) from Livingstone College (Salisbury, N.C.). Ordained to the ministry of the African Methodist Episcopal Zion (AMEZ) Church in 1893, he served as pastor of churches in North Carolina and Kentucky. Clement was editor of the *Star of Zion*, the official church paper, from 1904 to 1916, and also became manager of the AMEZ Publishing House in Charlotte, N.C. He was elected bishop in 1916, and under his supervision churches were erected or purchased in many towns. Clement also served as chairman of the Commission on Race Relations of the Federal Council of Churches of Christ in America.

CLEMENT, RUFUS EARL (1900–67), educator; born in Salisbury, N.C. Clement received a B.A. degree from Livingstone College (Salisbury, N.C.) in 1919, a B.S. degree from Garrett Biblical Institute in 1922, and his Ph.D. degree from Northwestern University (Evanston, Ill.) in 1930. He was awarded many honorary degrees, including a LL.D. degree from the University of Liberia, a L.F.D. degree from Virginia Union University, a LL.D. degree from Manhattanville College of the Sacred Heart (Purchase, N.Y.) in 1962, and a LL.D. degree from Virginia State College in 1963. Clement taught at Louisville Municipal College (1931–37) and served as president of Atlanta University for 30 years (1937–67). In 1954 he became a member of the board of education in Atlanta, Ga. Clement was the first Afro-American to serve as a school board member in a major city in the Deep South since Reconstruction. He was also a member of the board of trustees of Livingstone College, and Morehouse and Spelman colleges (both in Atlanta, Ga.), and was vice-chairman of Georgia's Commission on Interracial Cooperation (1937–44). Clement was a member of the executive committee of the United Negro College Fund.

CLIFFORD, MAURICE C. (1920–   ), gynecologist. Clifford received his M.D. degree from Meharry Medical College (Nashville, Tenn.) in 1947 and was resident in obstetrics and gynecology at Philadelphia General Hospital from 1948 to 1951. He was associate professor of clinical obstetrics and gynecology at the Medical College of Pennsylvania and had a private medical practice in Philadelphia. Clifford was elected president of the Philadelphia Council for Community Advancement in 1968.

CLIFFORD, PAUL INGRAHAM (1914–   ), educator; born in Martinsburg, W.Va. Clifford received a B.S. degree from Shippensburg State College (Shippensburg, Pa.) in 1938, a M.A. degree from Atlanta University in 1948, and his PH.D. degree from the University of Chicago in 1933. He taught at Paine College (Augusta, Ga.) and at Atlanta University (1948–54), where he also served as registrar after 1954.

CLIFT, VIRGIL A. (1912–   ), educator; born in Princeton, Ind. Clift received a B.A. degree from Indiana University in 1934, a M.A. degree from Indiana State University in 1939, and his Ph.D. degree from Ohio State University in 1944. He taught at North Carolina Agricultural and Technical (A & T) State University from 1940 to 1948 and at Morgan State University (Baltimore, Md.) from 1948 to 1963, and served as a professor of social sciences at New York University from 1963 to 1975. Clift was a Fulbright lecturer in Pakistan from 1954 to 1955 and educational advisor to the ministry of education of Libya for the Agency for International Development (AID) from 1956 to 1968. He was coauthor and coeditor of *Negro Education in America* (1963) and a frequent contributor to journals of education. *See also* PREFACE: LIST OF CONTRIBUTORS.

CLYMER, LEWIS W. (1910–   ), lawyer, judge; born in Neosho, Mo. Clymer graduated from Lincoln University (Jefferson City, Mo.) and from Howard University School of Law (Washington, D.C.) in 1939. He was admitted to the Missouri bar in 1939. In 1941 Clymer began serving on the War Manpower Commission as a minority group specialist, returning to his law practice in Kansas City, Mo., in 1945. He became assistant prosecuting attorney there in 1947 and assistant attorney general in 1953. In 1960 Clymer was appointed judge of the Municipal Court of Kansas City. Ten years later, the governor of Missouri named him judge of the 16th Judicial Circuit Court of that state.

CME [CHRISTIAN METHODIST EPISCOPAL] HIGH SCHOOL See LANE COLLEGE.

COAHOMA JUNIOR COLLEGE Coahoma Junior College, at Clarksdale, Miss., was founded as the Coahoma County Agricultural High School in 1924. It is state and locally controlled, and offers terminal occupational programs and studies toward the bachelor's degree. Its 1975 coeducational enrollment was about 1,000.

In 1949 a junior college curriculum was added, and during the next year the institution became eligible to share in state funds. Increased support made possible the expansion of physical and instructional facilities.

COAN, JOSEPHUS ROOSEVELT (1902–), clergyman, educator; born in Spartanburg, S.C. Coan received a B.A. degree from Howard University (Washington, D.C.) in 1930, a B.D. degree (1933) and a M.A. degree (1934) from Yale University, and his Ph.D. degree from Hartford Seminary in 1961. He then served as pastor of churches in Rhode Island and Georgia. Coan was a missionary to South Africa and Central Africa (1938–47) and later became associate editor of the African Methodist Episcopal (AME) Church's *Journal of Religious Education.* He taught at Morris Brown College (Atlanta, Ga.) and later became a professor of Christian education and missions at the Interdenominational Theological Center (Atlanta, Ga.).

COBB, HENRY EARL (1917–), historian, educator, born in Anderson, S.C. Cobb received a B.A. degree from Benedict College (Columbia, S.C.) in 1941, and a M.A. degree (1948) in education and his Ph.D. degree in education (1952) from Temple University (Philadelphia, Pa.). He was an instructor and then an assistant professor

at Tuskegee Institute (Tuskegee Institute, Ala.) from 1948 to 1952. After five years as professor at Florida Agricultural and Mechanical (A & M) University from 1952 to 1957, Cobb transferred to Southern University (Baton Rouge, La.), where he became chairman of the history department and later, in 1972, dean of the graduate school. In addition to his academic work, he was director of the Peace Corps Training Program in 1965, consultant for the U.S. Office of Education in 1966, and director of the National Defense Education Act Historical Institute in 1966 and in 1967. A member of many scholarly associations, Cobb contributed articles to several journals.

COBB, JAMES A. (1876–1958), judge; born in Arcadia, La. Cobb attended Straight University (New Orleans, La; now Dillard University) and Fisk University (Memphis, Tenn.) before he received a LL.M. degree (1900) and his Pd.B. degree (1902) from Howard University (Washington, D.C.). He began practicing law in Washington, D.C., after his admission to the District of Columbia bar in 1901. By 1907 Cobb was special assistant to the U.S. attorney, a post he held until 1915. He was a delegate to the Republican National Convention in 1920. After serving as a professor of constitutional law and as vice-dean of Howard University School of Law, Cobb was appointed municipal judge of the District of Columbia in 1926. He left the bench in 1935 to resume private practice in a law firm in Washington, D.C.

COBB, ROBERT S. (1888– ?), educator, lawyer; born in Cape Girardeau, Mo. Cobb attended Knoxville College (Knoxville, Tenn.) and received his LL.B. degree from the Chicago School of Law in 1925. He taught in Missouri public schools from 1908 to 1918, was the secretary of the YMCA in 1918, and served as executive secretary of the Missouri Negro Industrial Commission from 1919 to 1927.

COBB, W. MONTAGUE (1904–), physician, editor; born in Washington, D.C. Cobb received a B.A. degree from Amherst College (Amherst, Mass.) in 1925, a M.D. degree from Howard University Medical College (Washington, D.C.) in 1929, and his Ph.D. degree from Case Western Reserve University (Cleveland, Ohio) in 1932. He was an instructor at Howard University in 1928 and later became the chairman of the department of anatomy of the College of Medi-

W. Montague Cobb in 1946. *(National Medical Association.)*

cine. Cobb was president of the National Medical Association (1964–65), of the American Association of Physical Anthropologists, and of the Anthropological Society of Washington, D.C. He was editor of the *Journal of the National Medical Association* after 1949, and he was cited by *Modern Medicine* in 1970 as the "principal historian of the Negro in medicine." *See also* acknowledgements in the PREFACE; NATIONAL MEDICAL ASSOCIATION (NMA).

COLE, NAT (KING) (1919–65), singer, pianist; born Nathaniel Adams Coles in Montgomery, Ala. Cole's family moved to Chicago when he was five; by the time he reached 12, he was a pianist and a church organist. In 1936 Cole played piano for a touring black revue, *Shuffle Along*. When the show closed in Los Angeles, Calif., a year later, he performed solo in various small nightclubs until one manager wanted a quartet. Cole hired a quartet, the drummer failed to appear, and the King Cole Trio was born, with Cole as singer-pianist. In 1941 it toured the country, and in 1943 the trio began recording for Capitol Records. His first record, "Straighten Up and Fly Right," sold more than 500,000 records. After that, one success followed another. In the 1940s Cole was the only black performer with his own commercial network radio program. He served as a summer replacement for Bing Crosby's "Kraft Music Hall" in 1946. Later, the trio

appeared in several motion pictures, toured the country, performed in jazz concerts, and in 1950 toured Europe as a quartet. In 1956 Cole became the first black entertainer with his own national television show. Some of hit songs were: "It's Only a Paper Moon," "Too Young," "Walking My Baby Back Home," "The Christmas Song," and "Nature Boy." *See also* RADIO AND TELEVISION.

COLE, ROBERT A. (BOB) (1863–1911), composer, singer, vaudeville actor; born in Athens, Ga. Cole attended Atlanta University and after graduation moved to New York City, where he began his career as a singer and vaudeville actor. Teaming up with Billy Johnson, he wrote, produced, and directed a string of successful Broadway shows, in several of which he performed. Some of the team's most successful shows were *The Wedding of the Chinese and the Coon* (1897), *Chicken* (1899), and *Louisiana Lize* (1899). Cole's most popular songs include: "Under the Bamboo Tree," "The Maiden with the Dreamy Eyes," "Oh, Didn't He Ramble," and "Lazy Moon." *See also* MUSIC: HISTORY AND DEVELOPMENT.

COLE, THOMAS WINSTON, SR. (1913–   ), educator; born in Navasota, Tex. Cole received a B.S. degree from Wiley College (Marshall, Tex.) in 1934, a M.S. degree from the University of Wisconsin in 1947, and his Ed.D. degree from the University of Texas in 1955. He taught at Wiley College (1950–54), and became its president in 1958. Cole was a member of the executive committee of the United Negro College Fund.

COLEMAN, FREDERICK M. (1917–   ), lawyer; born in Lilly, Ga. Coleman attended Case Western Reserve University (Cleveland, Ohio) and received his LL.B. degree from the Cleveland-Marshall College of Law (now part of Cleveland State University) in 1953. He engaged in a private law practice from 1953 to 1967, and he served as first assistant public defender from 1963 to 1967. For three years Coleman was a municipal judge in Cleveland, and, in 1970, he became U.S. attorney for the Northern District of Ohio.

COLEMAN, JAMES H., JR. lawyer, judge; born Lawrenceville, Va. After his graduation from Virginia State College in 1956, Coleman attended Howard University School of Law (Washington, D.C.), from which he received a degree in 1959. Admitted to the New Jersey bar in 1960, he forthwith became director of the New Jersey Second Injury Fund and a consultant to the New Jersey Rehabilitation Committee. Four years later, Coleman was appointed judge of the New Jersey Workmen's Compensation Court.

COLEMAN, ORNETTE (1930–   ), jazz alto saxophonist; born in Fort Worth, Tex. Coleman was largely self-taught as a musician, although he attended the school of jazz at Lenox, Mass., and also studied on a Guggenheim Fellowship. After playing with a rhythm and blues band in New Orleans, La., Coleman formed his own band in Fort Worth, later moving to Los Angeles, Calif., and recording on the alto saxophone in Hollywood, Calif. In 1959 he formed his own quartet. In the 1960s and 1970s Coleman made his home in New York, N.Y., where he played regularly in several nightclubs. He often performed with John Coltrane, tenor saxophonist, and Eric Allan Dolphy, clarinetist. Coleman's most famous instrumentals include "Lonely Woman," "Sadness," "Ramblin'," and "Turnaround." See also MUSIC: JAZZ.

COLEMAN, WILLIAM T., JR. (1920–   ), lawyer, government official; born in Philadelphia, Pa. Coleman received a B.A. degree from the University of Pennsylvania in 1941, his LL.B. degree from Harvard University Law School in 1946, and did further study at Harvard Business School. He was secretary to Judge Herbert F. Goodrich of the U.S. Court of Appeals and also to U.S. Supreme Court Justice Felix Frankfurter. Coleman was a senior partner in the firm of Dilworth, Paxson, Kalish, and Coleman of Philadelphia, Pa. He served on the board of directors of such major corporations as Pan American World Airways, Penn Mutual Insurance Co., First Penn Corp., First Penn Banking and Trust Co., and Brookings Institute. Coleman held more than 25 federal, state, and community appointive positions. He also served as president of the National Association for the Advancement of Colored People (NAACP) Legal Defense and Education Fund. Coleman was appointed by President Gerald Ford as secretary of transportation.

COLES, ANNA B. See PREFACE: LIST OF CONTRIBUTORS.

COLLEGE OF EDUCATION AND INDUSTRIAL ARTS See CENTRAL STATE UNIVERSITY.

COLLEGE OF THE VIRGIN ISLANDS College of the Virgin Islands, at St. Thomas, Virgin Islands, was founded in 1963. It is coeducational, state-controlled, and offers the bachelor's degree as well as terminal occupational work. It provides liberal arts, teacher education, and vocational curricula. Its 1975 enrollment was approximately 1,700, including students attending the branch at St. Croix, Virgin Islands.

COLLEGES See EDUCATION: COLLEGES AND UNIVERSITIES.

COLLIER, ARTHUR JAMES, JR. (1930–   ), clergyman; born in Macon, Ga. Collier received a B.S. degree from Florida Normal and Industrial Memorial College in 1957 and his B.D. degree from Howard University School of Religion (Washington, D.C.) in 1960. He then became, successively, minister to migrant workers in New York and Florida, pastor of a Baptist church in Florida, and project director of Adult Migrant Education for the Florida State Department of Education.

COLLINS, CARDISS ROBINSON (1932–   ), U.S. Representative; born in St. Louis, Mo. Collins received a B.A. degree from Northwestern University (Evanston, Ill.) in 1967 and later was an auditor for the Illinois department of labor. She ran for and won (receiving 87 percent of the vote) a seat in the U.S. House of Representatives from the 7th Congressional District in Chicago, Ill., in 1974. This seat had been held by her husband, George Collins, who had been killed in a plane crash. In 1975 Collins was appointed whip-at-large in the House of Representatives, the first Afro-American to hold this office. See also COLLINS, GEORGE.

COLLINS, GEORGE (1925–   ) U.S. Representative; born in Chicago, Ill. Collins studied business law at Northwestern University (Evanston, Ill.), and during World War II he served with the Army in the South Pacific. After his discharge, he worked in the Cook County sheriff's office, in the Chicago court system, and on the Chicago board of health. In 1963 Collins became administrative assistant to the health commissioner. The next year he served as alderman on the Chicago City Council, a position he maintained until

1970 when he was elected as a Democrat to the U.S. House of Representatives to fill an unexpired term. Collins was reelected to a full term in the Ninety-second Congress, which convened in 1971. He was killed in a plane crash in 1972. *See also* COLLINS, CARDISS ROBINSON.

COLLINS, JANET (1923–), dancer; born in New Orleans, La. When a child, Collins moved to Los Angeles, Calif., with her family, where she later attended Los Angeles City College and Los Angeles Art Center School. After participating in the initial tour of the Katherine Dunham dance troupe and performing a solo concert at Las Palmas Theater in Los Angeles, Calif., in 1947, she made her New York City debut in 1949 in a solo concert. From 1950 to 1951, Collins was lead dancer in Cole Porter's Broadway musical, *Out of This World,* following which she joined the corps de ballet of the Metropolitan Opera (New York City) in 1951 as prima ballerina.

◆◆◆

COLONIZATION

COLONIZATION The attempt by white Americans in the nineteenth century to remove Afro-Americans to Africa indicates that they regarded the United States as a white man's country: no blacks were wanted except as servants or slaves. While not all whites supported such institutions as the American Colonization Society, the oldest and best known of the colonizing organizations, most undoubtedly hoped that the "Negro problem" would somehow disappear. Since slavery acted as a stabilizing force that defined, however inequitably, racial relationships, only free blacks at best were considered "problems" while slaves at worst were considered "troublesome property." Thus, colonizing free blacks was one specific remedy that caught the imagination of many white Americans. Colonization also greatly appealed to erstwhile humanitarians. However, it later became the solution advocated by slavery's apologists in the Deep South. To those men the free black was a dangerous anomaly who contradicted and undermined their defense of slavery and, therefore, should be removed. Regardless of the motives, colonization offered selfish benefits to its white originators. And to those who saw blacks as semibarbaric Africans, colonization had great emotional appeal.

Since mass migrations of peoples have not been unknown in history, it is odd that most critics of colonization dismiss the movement as either chimerical or absurd. This is especially bewildering since American history illustrates that the strategy of removing the object of oppression, instead of the oppression itself, was a common solution to social ills throughout the nineteenth century. Indian resettlement was

Several Liberians watch Afro-American troops of World War II on a road in Liberia, first colonized by the American Colonization Society in the early 1800s. *(U.S. Department of the Army.)*

national policy during this same period, while the concept of the frontier as a safety valve exerted a continuing impact on American thought. The reasoning here seems to have been that because colonization failed, *ipso facto,* it could never have succeeded. Admittedly, the American Colonization Society, for example, was frustrated in its attempt to interest free blacks in wholesale emigration. Lack of funds and increasing internal conflicts along sectional lines contributed to its ineffectiveness. But a factor in its failure, invariably underestimated, was the strong black opposition that it aroused. This opposition, like the general debate over the removal of Afro-Americans, establishes that, contrary to popular opinion, black men in antebellum America had a substantial voice in determining their destinies.

The idea of colonization—that is, sponsoring the settlement of blacks in an area removed from contact with whites—was current long before the organization of the American Colonization Society. Strangely, it was the man most responsible for articulating the desires of Afro-Americans who first publicly advocated removal. Thomas Jefferson, whose Declaration of Independence gave expression to the concept of equality, five years earlier had suggested in his *Notes on the State of Virginia* that freedmen be "removed beyond the reach of mixture." Jefferson said what many whites felt: get rid of the embarrassing black problem by sending what caused it away. At this early date, many Afro-Americans also favored colonization, though for different reasons. In 1789 The Free African Society, a group of Afro-Americans in Newport, R.I., espoused emigration to Africa as the best means of escaping discrimination in the United States. Nevertheless, it was not until 1811 when the shrewd Afro-American mariner, Paul Cuffe, negotiated with the British African Institute for permission to trade with Sierra Leone that actual attempts at colonization began. Cuffe had the backing of such influential black leaders as Philadelphia merchant James Forten, who was, however, more interested in commercial advantage— trading rights in exchange for skilled black emigrants—than in the redemption of Africa.

This wood engraving of Paul Cuffe, a pioneer colonizer, after a drawing by John Pole, 1812, is the only known reliable likeness of him. *(Library of Congress.)*

With these precedents in mind, concerned whites formed the American Colonization Society in 1816. The society appealed mostly to border-state whites who felt that the black man would remain permanently inferior in America. African colonization would rectify this situation and also free the country of its racial problem. The general reform milieu in which this organization was born reflected the mild antislavery position of most of the tidewater South at the turn of the century. Secondary issues raised by the society included a desire to Christianize and "civilize" Africa and put an end to the slave trade.

Since the American Colonization Society was the most prominent institutional symbol of black removal during the years from 1817 to 1850, the free black opposition to removal focused upon the white-oriented society's activities. This controversy centered in the free black communities of the North, which led one participant to comment on the irony of agitating an issue that deeply concerned the South but that could not be publicly debated there because the slave South was a closed society.

A group of free blacks, among them Rev. Richard Allen, Absalom Jones, and James Forten, met in Philadelphia in January 1817 to denounce the society's aims. This first rebuttal to African colonization set the tone for anticolonization agitation in the years to come. For one thing, these men expressed shock at the notion that they were considered Africans:

Whereas our ancestors (not of choice) were the first successful cultivators of the wilds of America, we their descendants feel ourselves entitled to participate in the blessings of her soil, which their blood and sweat manured.

These blacks considered themselves American citizens and went to great lengths to show that they had won their rights in the Revolutionary War and the War of 1812. They also complained about the degrading manner in which colonizationists alluded to free blacks, describing them as a "dangerous and useless part of the community" and a "living pestilence." These men also had a positive reason for rejecting colonization. Many of them were satisfied with their present situation; this fact is understandable since the meeting took place in Philadelphia, where a relatively substantial free black bourgeoisie lived. Also, their optimism came at a period when Afro-Americans still thought of America as a land of opportunity and believed hopefully that emancipation was inevitable. Not only were they personally content, but also they questioned the practicality of sending American blacks into the "savage wilds of Africa" and doubted that yesterday's unlettered slaves could be tomorrow's missionaries.

In spite of these remonstrances, during the 1820s Afro-Americans were urged to undertake the task of converting the African "heathens"— thus benefiting God, country, and self, and establishing a link with their "homeland." Following several abortive attempts by others, a black missionary, Lott Cary, became the first American Baptist to proselytize in Africa. Cary was motivated, he admitted, as much by the desire to escape discrimination in America as to Christianize blacks in Africa. His response perhaps indicates why a sense of missionary spirit did not permeate the black community despite the efforts of the American Colonization Society to foster such a spirit. Black missionary work reflected individual need rather than a general spirit of philanthropy. In fact, both Cary and his colleague, Colin Teague, were agents of the American Colonization Society, as were other black missionaries in West Africa, notably Elijah Johnson and Daniel Coker. They preceded the rise of militant abolitionism.

In the 1830s the rise of militant abolitionism affected the black response to removal. With Thomas Dew and John C. Calhoun now arguing that slavery was a positive good, abolitionists began to demand immediate emancipation, instead of gradual freedom with eventual colonization. Dew, the standard bearer of the new southern philosophy, discussed colonization at length—that is, colonization as a method of strengthening the bonds of slavery.

In their fight against colonization, blacks helped to convert two important allies. William L. Garrison once favored colonization, but he was persuaded to adopt a militant anticolonizationist stand by his fellow black Bostonian, David Walker. Garrison's abolitionist newspaper, *The Liberator,* later became an important instrument in the fight against colonization. *The Liberator* regularly published news items, letters to the editor, and editorials opposing the scheme. Garrison published a collection of letters from blacks in a most influential polemic, *Thoughts on Colonization* (1832). The tract received wide circulation, and it was still being recommended by a black convention as late as 1853.

The other significant white convert to the anticolonization camp was James G. Birney, once an important official in the American Colonization Society. Birney renounced that organization in 1833. Although the white abolitionist Theodore Weld was directly responsible for Birney's change of heart, increasing black opposition to removal was also an influential factor. Both conversions, Garrison's and Birney's, were significant accomplishments that aided the anticolonizationist cause immeasurably.

The black activists who attended the annual conventions after 1830 gave notice to the white man that they were seeking to cure a sick body politic: the "moral disease, slavery, is in America," they said, "and not in Africa." After waiting a decade for some signs of improvement, they decided to prescribe a stronger medicine, an even more active crusade against slavery and its "twin sister," colonization. The first sign of impatience came in 1840 when many black abolitionists broke away from the nonpolitical, doctrinaire aloofness of the Garrisonian abolitionists in favor of direct political action. Aside from a more militant stand on abolition and the demand that all available resources be used to combat slavery, black abolitionists found new approaches to the problem. Slave narratives became very popular and influential in the North, as did the fugitives themselves, many of whom went on long speaking tours haranguing slavery and colonization. Indeed, many blacks in the North were so caught up in the different movements that the very idea of withdrawing from the battle was unthinkable.

One of the restraining forces that kept blacks from approving of African colonization was their preoccupation with their own uplift in America. Frederick Douglass, an ardent foe of colonization, insisted that he was an American, and that this was his native land. If he often criticized his country, it was not because he opposed her institutions, he said, but because he cherished them, and thus could not tolerate slavery and slaveholders. Despite oppressive conditions in many areas, Douglass, like most anticolonizationists, saw cause for amazing optimism.

This type of black response to removal eventually forced the American Colonization Society to alter its direction. The failure of Liberia as a company-controlled colony—partly as a result of anticolonizationist blacks at home—led to its reorganization as the independent black Republic of Liberia in 1847. Reluctantly, the American Colonization Society was forced to "retreat to emigration." Although the society found its failure hard to swallow, there were some blacks who welcomed the change.

Since not all Afro-Americans agreed with Douglass' assessment of the future of the black man in America, some of them advocated bolder action against recalcitrant whites. A young black pastor, Henry Highland Garnet, epitomized the nascent stage of a new development in black thought. Admittedly influenced by David Walker's *Appeal* of 1829, Garnet concluded his "Address to the Slaves of the United States" with this ominous call to action:

. . . Awake, awake; millions of voices are calling you! Your dead fathers speak to you from the grave. Heaven, as with a voice of thunder, calls on you to arise from the dust. Let your motto be resistance! resistance! RESISTANCE!. . . . remember that you are FOUR MILLIONS.

This militant call to arms, and a renewed awareness of black colonies elsewhere, helped create an atmosphere conducive to Pan-Africanism among young Afro-Americans. Sons of the older black anticolonizationists, William Cornish, Robert Douglass, and George Vashon, among others, visited such black areas as Jamaica, Haiti, and the newly independent Liberia. They began to see the struggle for equality in a new and larger light. These young men found in the assertion of "négritude" a reply in kind to white discrimination. Instead of seeing colonization as removal by whites, they viewed leaving as black emigration. The distinction was crucial, for it transformed what was originally a negative solution to the racial problem into a positive one from their point of view.

This new development intensified a schism that had developed within the black community. Blacks considered a unilateral withdrawal from white America. As early as 1818, a black named Prince Saunders had urged the American Convention of Abolitionist Societies to keep Haiti open as an asylum for American blacks. Even such ardent anticolonizationists as Rev. Richard Allen served as president of the Haitian Emigration Society. Haiti had a definite emotional appeal to blacks. Just as freedmen in the North became a symbol of the capabilities of the Negro race, Haiti stood for what a black nation could accomplish. Through the most successful slave revolt in history, and the subsequent victory over European forces, it had *won* its independence. Thus, Haiti was a legitimate source of black pride. Black newspaper editors and lecturers constantly apotheosized the black Jacobin, Toussaint L'Ouverture, and portrayed Haiti as a vision of tropical splendor. Blacks exploited this image during the 1850s when black nationalism became a viable movement.

The principal advocate of emigration to Haiti was James Theodore Holly, a frequent visitor who became involved in the country's affairs. He argued for a limited black migration to the island, one that would introduce skilled Afro-Americans into an already thriving colony. Haiti was preferable to Liberia, he felt, because it was not dependent upon white philanthropy. Like most black emigrationists, Holly explained away the effect that voluntary removal would have upon those Afro-Americans left behind. A successful Haitian emigration would benefit black slaves by "reflex influence," he wrote, for white America would be confronted with a powerful black nation that would not tolerate mistreatment of blacks in America. Holly's international scheme to "nationalize" blacks marks him as a precursor of Pan-Africanism.

Although not as attractive as Haiti, Jamaica and certain areas in Central America and Mexico also interested blacks. In fact, one Afro-American remarked that he believed that the whole colored population of the United States was in search of a place to live in freedom, and Henry Garnet, for one, suggested Jamaica as a good emigration spot. Runaway slaves established a thriving colony in Vera Cruz, Mexico, and entrepreneurs tried unsuccessfully to develop another one through the Central American Land Company. The appeal of such places was obvious. They allowed blacks to raise their children "virtuously and not face discrimination," while still remaining in the New World. That this was a consideration at all suggests that they, too, accepted the distinction between the Old and New Worlds and shared in the dream of America as the promised land.

If many blacks were still hesitant to give emigration their wholehearted consideration, the Fugitive Slave Law of 1850 caused them at least to accept emigration as a possible safety valve. The law gave slaveholders the right to claim alleged runaways without adjudication, and this further humiliation convinced many Afro-Americans that they would never enjoy equality or freedom in the United States.

Blacks were not only concerned about their personal liberty, but also they were disappointed that the national government would abandon them for the sake of sectional harmony. Indeed, there was little to give blacks hope after 1850, for the slavocracy seemed to be in control of the country. Under these conditions, the emigration movement blossomed into a full-fledged nationalism: black, militant, and urgent in tone. While some blacks dreamed of a nation of their own in the Caribbean, others scattered across the unsettled West hoping to find relief from oppression. By 1855 some 4,000 blacks had migrated to California, but even there the Fugitive Slave Law was in force.

Canada, once a wartime outlet, remained an easily accessible haven for blacks. In the antebellum period perhaps as many as 40,000 blacks fled to Canada, half of them as a direct result of the Fugitive Slave Law and the later *Dred Scott* decision, which denied Afro-Americans citizenship. Many others settled in areas close to the Canadian border from which they could quickly cross to safety.

Canada's first significant migration came in 1829 when a large number of blacks flocked there in the aftermath of a race riot in Cincinnati. These blacks organized a commune, Wilberforce, which was self-supporting and self-governing in the best tradition of "Middle Period equalitarianism." Soon four such communities developed, but they were only successful as temporary homes for fugitive slaves and transients. The emigration of a prosperous Rochester merchant and former slave, Austin Steward, illustrates this point. Steward left for Canada in 1829 because of white discrimination, but he never escaped the attraction of home, and after seven years as a leader of Wilberforce he returned to the United States. This northern asylum had the approval of all of the Negro conventions and major black spokesmen as a temporary haven, especially after 1850. Blacks in Canada, like proponents of Haiti, did not forget that they were committed to the fight against slavery in the United States. Canada was the terminus of the Underground Railroad, and blacks there published several newspapers, such as Henry Bibb's *Voice of the Fugitive* and Samuel Ward's *Provincial Freeman*. Abolitionist newspapers frequently carried articles and laudatory editorials by Canadian blacks, urging their American brethren to emigrate if conditions became unbearable. Afro-American expatriates in Canada also served an important role as exemplars of the black man's capabilities. They pointed with pride to their achievement in developing a viable colony out of a wilderness area. This desire to demonstrate worthiness was a significant aspect of black thought, indicating that Afro-Americans were concerned about influencing white opinion in the States. Their hope was not only to ameliorate the condition of those who remained behind, but also to return home themselves when the situation improved.

Most blacks, however, argued that they were in America to stay. Frederick Douglass, for example, delivered a lecture, "The Claims of the Negro Ethnologically Considered," in which he supported the theory of a single creation (monogenesis) as opposed to that of the separate creation of each race (pologenesis). He used the American Indian as a contrast to the Negro, citing the widely held theory that the red man was vanishing because of his contact with civilization, whereas the black man flourished within it and continued to increase in number. Early nineteenth-century black thought on race reveals the same flaws that marred white theories. Eternally utilitarian, black theoreticians devised explanations to suit their purpose, without a thought for the consistency of their argument. They almost universally expounded the theory of monogenesis, but saw no contradiction in claiming special characteristics, such as "adaptability," that allowed them to survive while the Indian per-

ished. It was environment alone that caused their misery, while the Indian was doomed because of his nature.

Thus, in spite of the fact that blacks in America had reached their nadir during the 1850s, Frederick Douglass continued his attacks on emigration in his newspaper. He saw emigration—white- or black-sponsored—as a form of segregation, and as an assimilationist, he was violently opposed to it. James McCune Smith joined him in denouncing emigration. Smith thought that it was ridiculous to say, as colonizationists and emigrationists did, that the intermingling of the races was revolting to whites. Why each day, Smith chided, Negro slaves in the South gave birth to mulatto offspring. Thus, "admixture is progress, isolation is retrogression. . . . What God has joined together let no man put asunder." Meetings called to discuss colonization and emigration, however, ended in disruption, and name-calling became endemic. Emigrationists were labeled as "Judas" to the cause of the black in America, while they in turn accused assimilationists of lacking pride and dignity.

A crucial juncture in the debate came in 1852 when New York Governor Washington Hunt endorsed colonization in a message to the state legislature. Blacks reacted immediately to his remarks, condemning both the governor and the American Colonization Society. One suggested that Garrison's *Thoughts on Colonization* be reprinted so that whites would know, once and for all, that black Americans did not desire to return to Africa. Removal was both "unchristian" and "unconstitutional." Meetings held in other cities, such as Cincinnati, also passed resolutions against colonization. Despite everything, the assimilationists maintained an almost incredible faith in their future. Even adverse legislation could not long repress their optimism. To many, such sanguine faith was folly. Years of disappointment, combined with the nascent self-help philosophy with its overtones of racial pride, had created a desire for black nationalism. This desire was recognized in a hastily written tract by a militant, activist black, Martin R. Delany, whose *The Condition, Elevation, Emigration, and Destiny of the Colored People of the United States* marked the coming of age of black nationalism in America. Frederick Douglass summed up his protagonist's character in one pithy sentence: "I thank God for making me a man simply; but Delany always thanks Him for

Martin R. Delany. *(Library of Congress.)*

making him a *black* man." Delany, his sense of alienation complete, chose to reject the white society that had rejected him. He wrote:

We are a *superior race,* being endowed with properties fitting us for all parts of the earth, while they [whites] are only adopted to certain parts. Of course, this proves our right and duty to live wherever we may *choose:* while the white race may live only where it *can* [sic].

Like every racial chauvinist, Delany had arrived at the ultimate conclusion: his race was superior to all others. As the location for black regeneration, Delany originally favored Central America; however, he added an appendix to his pamphlet proposing East Africa instead. There the black race could establish a vital transcontinental railroad between the Far East and America. Ironically, even the most radical black nationalist reflected certain American values.

Delany was instrumental in organizing the first black National Emigration Convention. Taking their cue from the long-standing tradition of black political conventions, emigrationists assembled at Cleveland, Ohio, in 1854. Only those who favored emigration were invited, a fact that offended Douglass and other assimilationists. They worried about the adverse effect that the meeting would have upon black unity and wondered if it might not open the gates for wholesale deportation. Characterizing themselves as full citizens, the assimilationists expressed their faith in America.

Nevertheless, the National Emigration Convention did meet once every two years, and in 1858 assigned several black leaders to explore the possibilities of certain proposed sites. With this mandate, J. Theodore Holly left for Haiti, and Delany, along with Robert Campbell, journeyed to West Africa. Both expeditions returned with optimistic reports, but nothing was to come of them.

By 1860 national events had overshadowed emigration. The black man's attention was riveted on the Civil War. Symbolically, one of the first black officers commissioned in the war was Martin R. Delany, erstwhile separatist. The promise of a new future in America was enough to make the black forget his African dreams. There were no black emigrationists about on September 22, 1862, when President Abraham Lincoln, himself a colonizationist, promulgated the Emancipation Proclamation.

Thus, the black response to removal—colonization and emigration—was a response based upon the circumstances as Afro-Americans saw them. Removal could only mean defeat or escape from oppression; in all of its manifestations, it was fundamentally a negative response to repressive conditions at home. Although some blacks did actually leave America, few of them ever completely gave up hope that they might one day return. Because of their involvement in both national affairs and national myths, most blacks never desired to leave their New World home. *See also* AMERICAN COLONIZATION SOCIETY; NATIONALISM; PAN-AFRICANISM.

REFERENCES: For additional information, see: Bell, Howard, "Negro Nationalism: A Factor in Emigration Projects, 1858–1861," *Journal of Negro History,* January 1962, pp. 42–53; Bell, Howard, "The Negro Emigration Movement, 1849–54: A Phase of Negro Nationalism," *Phylon,* vol. 20, 1959; Campbell, Penelope, *Maryland in Africa: The Maryland State Colonization Society, 1831–1857,* University of Illinois Press, Urbana, 1971; Fisher, Miles Mark, "Lott Cary, the Colonizing Missionary," *Journal of Negro History,* October 1922, pp. 380–418; Foster, Charles, "The Colonization of Free Negroes in Liberia, 1816–1835," *Journal of Negro History,* January 1953, pp. 41–56; Miller, Floyd J., *The Search for a Black Nationality: Black Colonization and Emigration, 1787–1863,* University of Illinois Press, Urbana, 1975; and Staudenraus, P. J., *The African Colonization Movement, 1816–1865,* Columbia University Press, New York, 1961; see also Walker, James W. St. G., *The Black Loyalists: The Search for a Promise Land in Nova Scotia and Sierra Leone 1783–1870,* Dalhousie University Press, Halifax, Nova Scotia, 1976.

COLOR BAR, COLOR LINE *See* DISCRIMINATION; ONOMATOLOGY; RACE: BIOLOGY; RACE: RACISM; SEGREGATION.

COLORED *See* ONOMATOLOGY.

COLORED DOUGLASS HIGH AND TRAINING SCHOOL *See* COPPIN STATE COLLEGE.

COLORED FARMERS ALLIANCE *See* POPULISTS.

COLORED METHODIST EPISCOPAL CHURCH *See* CHRISTIAN METHODIST EPISCOPAL (CME) CHURCH.

COLORED, NORMAL, INDUSTRIAL, AGRICULTURAL AND MECHANICAL COLLEGE OF SOUTH CAROLINA *See* SOUTH CAROLINA STATE COLLEGE.

COLORED NORMAL SCHOOL *See* BOWIE STATE COLLEGE; FLORIDA AGRICULTURE AND MECHANICAL (A & M) UNIVERSITY.

COLSTON, JAMES ALLEN (1909–   ), educator; born in Quincy, Fla. Colston received a B.S.

degree from Atlanta University, his Ph.D. degree from New York University in 1950, and an honorary L.H.D. degree from Westminister College in 1966. He served as president of Bethune-Cookman, Georgia State, and Knoxville colleges before becoming president of the Bronx Community College of the City University of New York in 1966.

COLTRANE, JOHN (1926–1967), jazz tenor saxophonist; born in Hamlet, N.C. Coltrane was one of the greatest of all saxophonists. In the 1940s he played with a small combo in Philadelphia, Pa., and then in a U.S. Navy band in Hawaii. During the 1950s Coltrane played with Dizzy Gillespie, Miles Davis, and Thelonius Monk. He frequently performed with Eric Allan Dolphy, clarinetist, and Ornette Coleman, alto saxophonist. *See also* MUSIC: JAZZ.

COMBINED NORMAL AND INDUSTRIAL DEPARTMENT *See* CENTRAL STATE UNIVERSITY.

COMBS, WALTER A. (1924–   ), physician; born in Washington, D.C. Combs received his M.D. degree from Howard University Medical College (Washington, D.C.) in 1948. He was an attending staff member of Children's Hospital, Providence Hospital, and Washington Hospital Center, and he was appointed chief of pediatric service at Wheelus Air Force Base Hospital, Tripoli, Libya in 1954. Combs became clinical assistant professor of pediatrics at Howard University Medical College in 1955.

COMER, JAMES P. (1934–   ), physician, psychiatrist, educator; born in East Chicago, Ind. Comer received a B.A. degree from Indiana University in 1956, a M.D. degree from Howard University Medical College (Washington, D.C.) in 1960, and his M.P.H. degree from the University of Michigan School of Public Health in 1964. He received his training in psychiatry at Yale University, where he now serves as associate professor of psychiatry in the School of Medicine. Comer wrote *Beyond Black and White,* and he has contributed many articles to scholarly journals in the field of psychiatry.

COMMUNITY DEVELOPMENT CORPORATIONS (CDCs) These corporations are a group of organizations designed to promote business, economic, and social development in large black urban areas. Under the terms of the Housing and Urban Development Act (84 Stat. 1770) enacted in 1970, the National Community Corporation Certification Board (NCCCB) was created to grant federal charters and send money in the form of an initial allocation of federal funds (through MESBIC, Minority Enterprise Small Business Investment Company) to community development corporations. Further funding came from private sources. Some examples of CDCs are the Zion Investment Associates (ZIA), Operation Breadbasket, and Hough Area Development Corporation. *See also* BUSINESS.

COMPTON, JAMES W. (1939–   ), administrator; born in Aurora, Ill. Compton received a B.A. degree from Morehouse College (Atlanta, Ga.) in 1960 and did graduate study under a Merrill Scholar award from 1959 to 1961. He was in charge of the Urban League in Binghamton, N.Y., and he later served as director of a community service program in Chicago, Ill. Compton became a staff member of the Chicago Urban League in 1965 and was appointed the executive director of the Chicago Urban League in 1972. He was selected by the Chicago Junior Association of Commerce and Industry as one of its Ten Outstanding Young Men in 1972.

John Coltrane. *(New York Public Library.)*

CONE, JAMES HAL (1938–   ), clergyman, educator; born in Fordyce, Ark. Cone received a B.A. degree from Philander Smith College (Little Rock, Ark.) in 1958, a B.D. degree from Garrett Theological Seminary in 1961, and a M.A. degree (1961) and his Ph.D. degree (1965) from Northwestern University (Evanston, Ill.). He then began a career in teaching, becoming a professor at Philander Smith College, Adrian College, and Union Theological Seminary. Cone wrote *Black Theology and Black Power* (1969).

CONGO SQUARE A section of New Orleans, La., that was frequented by blacks, mainly during the nineteenth century, for various activities, including festivals and dancing.

CONGREGATIONALISTS / UNITED CHURCH OF CHRIST With an estimated membership of about 35,000 in the mid-1970s, Congregationalists have demonstrated an importance far in excess of their size. They grew historically out of Calvinist-oriented white churches that predominated in New England. Like their parent bodies, black Congregationalists placed strong emphasis upon education. In fact, in the Congregational tradition there was no separation of religion and education. This tradition was strongly shown in the work and influence of the missionary agency of Congregationalism, the American Missionary Association (AMA). Altogether, Congregationalists set up or aided in the development of about five hundred schools for Afro-Americans, mainly in the South where most blacks lived.

Culturally related to New England rather than to the South, Congregationalists were among the main teachers of emancipated slaves and their children. Many of the northern teachers who went into the South during and after Reconstruction were Congregationalist in background. Acting largely through the AMA, they established or aided in the development of schools for blacks. Although many of the schools passed out of existence, some remained as landmarks in the history of higher education for Afro-Americans: Hampton Institute, Fisk University, Atlanta University, Tougaloo College, Dillard University, Lemoyne-Owen College, Huston-Tillotson College, and Talladega College.

John Conyers, Jr., at a political convention in Gary, Ind., 1972. *(Photo by Leroy Henderson.)*

Although Congregationalists supported rural schools during and after Reconstruction, their principal churches remained essentially urban-oriented, first in New England and then later in other regions. Dixwell Congregational Church (renamed Dixwell Avenue Congregational Church), established in 1820 in New Haven, Conn., is regarded as the oldest church. Later, churches were founded elsewhere, including Lincoln Congregational Temple, Washington, D.C.; St. Marks Congregational, Boston, Mass.; Plymouth Congregational, Washington, D.C.; Peoples Congregational, Washington, D.C.; Central Congregational, New Orleans, La.; Beecher Congregational, New Orleans, La.; Lemuel Haynes Congregational, Brooklyn, N.Y.; Church of Christian Fellowship, Los Angeles, Cal.; and First Congregational, Atlanta, Ga. *See also* AMERICAN MISSIONARY ASSOCIATION; CHURCHES; EDUCATION.

CONGRESS OF INDUSTRIAL ORGANIZATIONS (CIO) *See* LABOR UNIONS.

CONGRESS OF RACIAL EQUALITY (CORE) A
pioneer civil rights organization that rose to prominence during the civil rights movement of the 1960s. CORE was founded in 1942 by James Farmer at the University of Chicago. Its techniques and tactics included the use of sit-ins (first employed against Jack Spratt's restaurant in Chicago, Ill., in 1943) and freedom rides. *See also* CIVIL RIGHTS: CIVIL RIGHTS MOVEMENT; CIVIL RIGHTS MOVEMENT IN SELECTED STATES: ALABAMA; CIVIL RIGHTS MOVEMENT IN SELECTED STATES: NORTH CAROLINA; FARMER, JAMES L.; MCKISSICK, FLOYD BIXLER.

CONTEE, CLARENCE G. *See* PREFACE: LIST OF CONTRIBUTORS; HISTORIANS.

CONYERS, JAMES E. *See* SCIENTISTS: SOCIAL.

CONYERS, JOHN, JR. (1929–   ), lawyer, U.S. Representative; born in Detroit, Mich. Conyers received a B.S. degree (1957) and his LL.B. degree (1958) from Wayne State University (Detroit, Mich.). He began the practice of law in Detroit, Mich. at the same time that he became legislative assistant to Congressman John D. Dingell. In addition, Conyers assumed the responsibilities of general counsel for three union locals. From 1961 to 1963, he refereed for the Michigan Workman's Compensation Department, and in 1964 he was elected to the U.S. House of Representatives from Michigan. Conyers subsequently became the first black member of the House Judiciary Committee.

COOK, CELESTINE STRODE (1924–   ), business executive, civic leader; born in Teague, Tex. After receiving a B.S. degree from Tuskegee (Tuskegee Institute, Ala.) in 1944, Cook taught in Houston, Tex., public schools and at Houston Negro College (1944–45). In 1948, as a young widow, she directed her late husband's investment and real estate interests in Galveston, Tex., until 1958, when she remarried and moved to New Orleans, La. There, from 1959 to 1973, Cook served as corporate secretary for Good Citizens Life Insurance Company, Good Citizens Funeral System, Inc., and Good Citizens Realty Corporation, Inc. In 1972 she became the first black woman ever to be elected to the multiracial board of directors of Liberty Bank and Trust Company in New Orleans, La., and was the first black woman to serve on the National Business Committee for the Arts in 1973. In 1974 Cook became the first Afro-American selected by the city of New Orleans as one of its ten most outstanding women; that same year she was elected National Financial Secretary of Links, Inc. Furthermore, in 1975 she became the first black woman named to the selection board of the U.S. Navy ROTC.

COOK, GEORGE WILLIAM (1855–1931), educator; born in Winchester, Va. Cook, born a slave, moved to Pennsylvania when he was very young. Entering Howard University (Washington, D.C.) as a work student, he received a B.A. degree in 1881, and later he earned both bachelor of law and master of law degrees. He was subsequently professor, secretary, acting president, alumni secretary, and a member of the board of trustees of Howard University. Cook was appointed by three consecutive U.S. presidents to serve on the board of charities of the District of Columbia, a post he held for 12 years. He was a member of the board of directors of the National Association for the Advancement of Colored People (NAACP) from the time of its inception until his death, and he served for many years as president of the Colored Social Settlement, an organization that did much to improve housing conditions among Afro-Americans in Washington, D.C.

COOK, MERCER (1903–   ), educator, government official; born in Washington, D.C. Cook received a B.A. degree from Amherst College (Amherst, Mass.) in 1925, a teacher's diploma from the University of Paris in 1926, and a M.A. degree (1931) and his Ph.D. degree (1936) from Brown University (Providence, R.I.). After a short term as an instructor at North Carolina Agricultural & Technical State University in 1926, he joined the staff of Howard University (Washington, D.C.) and remained there until 1936 as an assistant professor of French. Cook then moved to Atlanta University where he taught until 1943, when he became supervisor of English at the University of Haiti. In 1945 he returned to Howard as full professor. After almost 35 years of teaching, in 1961 Cook was appointed U.S. ambassador to Niger; in 1964 he became ambassador to Senegal and Gambia. His published books include: *Le Noir* (1934), *Five French Negro Authors* (1944), a translation of Senghor's *On African Socialism* (1964), and *Militant Black Writers in Africa and the United States* (1969), which he coauthored. *See also* LITERATURE: DRAMA/THEATER.

COOK, SAMUEL LECOUNT, JR. (1887–1952), physician, educator; born in Washington, D.C. Cook attended Phillips Exeter Academy (preparatory school) and received his M.D. degree from the University of Illinois College of Medicine in 1913. He interned at Provident Hospital, Chicago, Ill., and at Freedmen's Hospital in Washington, D.C., and he became a faculty member and later a clinical professor of obstetrics and gynecology at Howard University Medical College (Washington, D.C.). Cook served as president of the John A. Andrew Clinical Society of Tuskegee, Ala. (1930–31) and was a member of the National Medical Association.

COOK, WILL MARION (1869–1944), composer; born in Washington, D.C. Cook began studying violin at the Oberlin Conservatory of Music (Oberlin, Ohio) when he was 13 years old. When he was 15, he won a scholarship to study with Joseph Joachim at the Berlin Conservatory, Berlin, Germany. In 1898 Cook composed the ragtime operetta, *Clorinda*, which introduced syncopated ragtime music to New York City's theater-going audiences. *Jes Lak White Folks*, written in 1899, was also a success on the New York stage. Some of Cook's best-known songs are: "That's How the Cake Walk Is Done," "Emancipation Day," "I May Be Crazy But I Ain't No Fool," "I'm Comin' Virginia," and "Rain Song." Cook formed a jazz band during the early 1900s, and in 1914 Cook's Southern Syncopated Orchestra began its notable career, which included tours throughout the United States and engagements in London, Paris, and Berlin. *See also* MUSIC: HISTORY AND DEVELOPMENT.

COOKE, PAUL PHILIPS (1917–   ), educator; born in New York, N.Y. Cooke received a B.S. degree from Miner Teachers College (Washington, D.C.) in 1937, M.A. degrees from New York University in 1941 and Catholic University of America (Washington, D.C.) in 1943, and his Ed.D. degree from Columbia University in 1947. He taught at public schools in Washington, D.C. (1941–44), and he was a teacher of illiterate adults for the War Department in Baltimore, Md. (1944). Cooke then taught at Miner Teachers College (1944–55) and became dean of the District of Columbia Teachers College (1955–64). He served as director of the model school division of the public Schools of Washington, D.C. (1964–65), as president of the District of Columbia Teachers College (1966), and as consultant to the U.S. Office of Education (1964–69).

COOKERY / COOKING *See* CUISINE.

COOKMAN INSTITUTE *See* BETHUNE-COOKMAN COLLEGE.

COOKS, STONEY (1943–), civil rights leader; born in Uniontown, Ala. Cooks joined the Southern Christian Leadership Conference (SCLC) as a field organizer, and in 1967 he was appointed SCLC's director of student affairs. He became administrative assistant to the SCLC president in 1968, and in 1970 he served as director of public relations. In 1971 Cooks was named executive director of SCLC.

COOL *See* MUSIC: JAZZ.

COON A term of contempt applied to Afro-Americans, mainly during the nineteenth and early twentieth centuries. Perhaps it derived from *raccoon. See also* ONOMATOLOGY.

COON SHOWS A stereotypical name applied to musical comedies in contrast to minstrel shows and town shows of the second half of the nineteenth century. Bert Williams and George Walker, a very popular black song-and-dance duo in the late 1800s, billed themselves as "Two Real Coons" in order to distinguish themselves from similar white performers who used blackface (burnt cork), the customary disguise of minstrels. *See also* MUSIC: HISTORY AND DEVELOPMENT.

COONTOWN A stereotypical and general term used in the nineteenth century and early twentieth century to denote a black community. For example, a very popular show written in 1898 by Bob Cole, an Afro-American, that starred another Afro-American, Sam Lucas, as Uncle Tom, was entitled *A Trip to Coontown. See also* LITERATURE: DRAMA/THEATER; ONOMATOLOGY.

COOPER, JEANNE *See* NEWSPAPERS: CONTEMPORARY.

COPPIN, FANNY M. JACKSON (1836–1913), educator; born in Washington, D.C. An aunt bought Coppin's freedom for $125, after which Coppin attended Rhode Island State Normal School and later Oberlin College (Oberlin, Ohio). She taught special night classes for newly freed slaves, and in 1865 Coppin began teaching at the Institute for Colored Youth in Philadelphia, Pa., where she later served as principal (1869–1900). Her autobiography is *Reminiscences of School Life, and Hints on Teaching* (1913).

COPPIN NORMAL SCHOOL *See* COPPIN STATE COLLEGE.

COPPIN STATE COLLEGE Coppin State College, at Baltimore, Md., was founded in 1900 by the Baltimore school board. Coppin is state-supported, coeducational, offers the bachelor's and master's degrees, and provides a teacher education curriculum. The 1975 enrollment was about 2,600.

The school began as a "normal department," with a one-year training class for the preparation of black elementary school teachers, that shared facilities with the Colored Douglass High and Training School. By 1926 Coppin's one-year training class had expanded into a three-year program and had become a separate institution with its own principal. The institution was named Coppin Normal School in honor of Fanny M. Jackson Coppin, a former slave, who had become one of the first black women in the United States to receive a college degree, and who had introduced teacher training programs into the educational system of Philadelphia, Pa. The college moved to its present site in 1952, occupying its own buildings for the first time in its history. The school features such unusual majors as teacher education for exceptional children and training for work with disadvantaged youth.

CORE *See* CONGRESS OF RACIAL EQUALITY.

CORNELY, PAUL BERTAU 1906–), physician; born in Guadeloupe, French West Indies. Cornely received his M.D. degree (1931) and his D.P.H. degree (1934) from the University of Michigan Medical School. He was assistant professor (1934–36) and professor (after 1947) of preventive medicine and public health at Howard University (Washington, D.C.), and medical director at Freedmen's Hospital, Washington, D.C. 1947–58. Cornely sponsored demonstrations organized by the Medical Committee for Human Rights (1965–66) and later served as president of the American Public Health Association. *See also* PREFACE: LIST OF CONTRIBUTORS.

CORNISH, SAMUEL E. (ca. 1795–1859), clergyman, editor; born in Delaware. After graduating from the Free African School in New York City, Cornish went to Philadelphia, Pa., where he became an ordained minister. In 1821 he organized the first black Presbyterian church in New York City. With John B. Russwurm, Cornish founded the first black newspaper in the United States in 1827; originally named *Freedom's Journal*, it was renamed *The Rights of All* in

1828 and continued publication until 1829. Cornish's service as senior editor of the newspaper was interrupted for a year when he became an agent for the Free African School. He was one of the leaders of the first National Negro Convention, which met in Philadelphia in 1830, and until 1840 Cornish was active in the American Antislavery Society. In 1837 and 1838 he served as editor of another newspaper, *The Colored American,* in New York City. *See also* NEWSPAPERS: HISTORY AND DEVELOPMENT.

CORTEZ PETTERS BUSINESS SCHOOL   *See* BUSINESS SCHOOLS.

COSBY, BILL (1937–   ), comedian, television personality; born in Germantown, Pa. While a student at Temple University (Philadelphia, Pa.), Cosby began performing on stage, and it was not long before he left Temple and went to New York City to try out his comedy routines in the nightclubs there. He soon went further afield to such cities as Los Angeles, Calif., and Las Vegas, Nev. In 1965 Cosby began a three-year run in the television series "I Spy," becoming the first Afro-American to star in a network television series. Cosby's recordings, which have also won awards, include "Bill Cosby is a Very Funny Fellow-Right?" *See also* RADIO AND TELEVISION.

COSMETOLOGY

COSMETOLOGY   Choices in hairstyles and facial cosmetics for Afro-Americans were always conditioned by the fact that black people were an identifiable presence in a white-oriented, largely closed society wherein physical differences in hair and skin color were linked pervasively to slavery, caste, or class. The Afro-American response has varied. For example, illustrations and photographs of blacks during the first three-quarters of the 1800s reveal generally "natural" hair styling devoid of excessive grooming. By the end of the 1800s, however, hair "straightening" by use of hot combs (straightening combs) and oils or pomades had come into vogue for women. About the same time, but definitely later, Afro-American males "slicked" or "laid down" their hair by using pomades and a tight fitting skull cap, sometimes called a "stocking cap," that could be made at home by simply cutting off and knotting the upper end of a woman's stocking. Many young males reached elaborate extremes in "slicking down" styles, or fancy marcelling, at the time of World War II and shortly thereafter when with the use of pomades and hot combs or curlers, they "conked" or "processed" their hair themselves or had it done by amateur or professional hairstylists.

The straightening and slicked down styles of the first half of the 1900s provided ventures for amateur and professional hairdressers and man-ufacturers. Beauty shops or parlors proliferated; and much "hair dressing" or "dressing hair" took place in private homes. Among the notable manufacturers of cosmetics during the period, mainly of pomades, were Madame C. J. Walker of Indianapolis, Ind. and Annie M. Malone of St. Louis, Mo., who amassed fortunes out of the cosmetic business and who were reputed to be the wealthiest black women in America. Trade products by manufacturers of this period (about 1900–1950) carried such brand names as Poro, Black and White, and Murray's. The trademarked non-black-produced product Vaseline was for all practical purposes universally in use for hair and skin. The use of lard was not uncommon by low-income families, especially in poverty stricken areas of the South.

Facial cosmetology in the same period (about 1900–1950) was strongly influenced by several attitudes. Two of the main attitudes appeared to be contradictory. One attitude held that black or "colored" skin was natural and should be treated, or made up, with cosmetics in order to bring out or to enhance the natural beauty of the skin. This view often found expression in the old Afro-American folk phrase, "the blacker the berry, the sweeter the juice." This view of the use of cosmetics was related to a consciousness of "race" or "blackness" in a predominantly white oriented society. It received widespread publicity and acknowledgment during and following the civil rights movement of the 1960s and 1970s in the slogan "black is beautiful." The other attitude toward facial cosmetology, while not necessarily denying the truth of the natural view, supported the use of cosmetics in order to "lighten up" or to "whiten" the skin. Commercial or household cosmetics were used to support these two attitudes in keeping with individual preferences. For example, Afro-American manufacturers of cosmetics unabashedly advertised products that claimed to "lighten up" or to "whiten" dark skins.

A new era in cosmetology was ushered in with the civil rights movement of the 1960s. The natural look, or some expression of individual tastes, prevailed. Special grooming was required for "Afro" or "Bush" styles; special combs and picks had to be used in their upkeep. The old straightening comb gave way—but did not vanish—to a proliferation of rollers, hair pins, clips, curling irons (with temperature controls), hair bleaching machines, hair blowers, and professional salon dryers. The old pomades likewise gave way to newer natural products aimed at conditioning and adding lustrous sheens and color. The old dyeing of hair also gave way to new techniques: hair coloring for black women ceased to be a fad. In fact, 2 out of every 5 Afro-American women were using some form of hair coloring by the mid-1970s. In short, cosmeticians and their black clientele had learned and accepted the fact that the hair of Afro-Americans could be styled in any way desired without damaging the skin or hair (as some of the older processes may have).

Wigs and hairpieces, varying in color and style, became fashionable, especially for women of financial means.

The new era also saw the decline—but not the end—of skin "whitening." Realistically, professional and amateur cosmetologists applied their skills to satisfy a clientele with varying shades of blackness, realizing (as one noted cosmetologist said) that "the best looks effect a sense of cleanliness, clarity, and naturalness." Cosmeticians became ever more aware of appropriate color foundation and the use of color for eye, cheek, and lips to compliment black skin tones. They classified and knew how to apply their skills to six colors: blue, brown, olive, olive-brown, yellow, and beige, realizing that these categories can be further enlarged to a cosmetology involving some 33 shades of blackness.

With the new era came new growth in the cosmetics industry. For example, blacks began to publish beauty magazines, both trade and retail: *Beauty Trade,* a trade publication edited and published by Bernice Calvin; and *Essence,* a highly successful magazine whose beauty editor was Susan Taylor, a licensed cosmetologist. Another example of growth came in new boutiques or salons, such as one owned and operated by Jim Williams in New York City and those directed by Thomas Hayden, Creative Style Director for the new Ultra Sheen Boutiques, sponsored by Johnson Products Co., Inc., of Chicago, Ill.

In addition to Johnson Products, there were 14 Afro-American manufacturers of cosmetics in the mid-1970s. Moreover, according to the U.S. census for 1970, some 35,000 blacks (of whom 1,800 were males) were employed as professional hairdressers and cosmetologists. Many of these professionals were, and had been, organized into a group known as the National Beauty Culturists League under the leadership of Katie Wickham since 1958.

Growth in the new cosmetics opened new career opportunites for such positions as directors, laboratory technicians, fashion photographers, and cosmetics chemists. On the retail level, black cosmetics establishments trained and placed licensed black makeup artists as demonstrators *in front* of the counter and black sales people—who had knowledge, skills, and understanding of black women—*behind* the counter. Following this lucrative cue, white cosmetics businesses (and publications) began to create makeup for and appeal expressly to black females and, in so doing, provided some new employment opportunities for Afro-Americans.

See also BUSINESS; EMPLOYMENT; RACE: RACE AND CULTURE; SOCIAL CLASSES.

REFERENCES: There is no adequate reference. This article can serve as a beginning point with a follow-up search of periodical literature.

COTTON, COTTON GIN *See* AGRICULTURE; SLAVERY: SLAVERY IN SELECTED STATES.

COTTRELL, CLAYTON J. (1923–   ), educator, labor administrator; born in Huntington, W. Va. After receiving a B.S. degree from Central State University (Wilberforce, Ohio) in 1949, Cottrell did graduate work at the University of California and at Ohio State University. He was associate professor of physics and mathematics at Alabama A & M University (1949–53), before leaving the field of education to enter industry. He was an engineer and manager for General Electric in Utica, N.Y. (1955–60), manager for General Dynamics Corporation, Rochester, N.Y. (1960–70), and was named deputy regional manpower administrator in Atlanta, Ga., in early 1970. In September 1970 Cottrell became special assistant to the deputy manpower administrator for employment of the U.S. Department of Labor in New York City. In 1972 he was appointed regional director of the U.S. Department of Labor for Region II, which includes New York, New Jersey, Puerto Rico, and the Virgin Islands.

COTTRELL, ELIAS (1853– ?), Christian Methodist Episcopal bishop; born in Holly Springs, Miss. Cottrell attended Walden University (Nashville, Tenn.) and received his D.D. degree from Rust College (Holly Springs, Miss.) in 1895. In 1875, he became a minister in the Colored (now Christian) Methodist Episcopal (CME) Church, and in 1894 he was elected a bishop.

COUNCILL, WILLIAM HOOPER (1849– ?), clergyman, educator; born in Fayetteville, N.C. After his family was separated in a slave sale in Richmond, Va., Councill attended the school of the Freedmen's Bureau. He entered politics during Reconstruction and served as clerk of the Alabama legislature (1872–74). Councill was elected president of the State Normal School in Alabama (now Alabama A & M University) in 1876 and served in that position for many years. *See also* CIVIL RIGHTS: CIVIL RIGHTS MOVEMENT.

COUSINS, WILLIAM, JR. (1927–), lawyer; born in Swiftown, Miss. Cousins received a B.A. degree from the University of Illinois in 1948 and his LL.B. degree from Harvard University Law School in 1951. He served in the U.S. Army in Korea and later became a staff judge advocate in the U.S. Army Reserve. Cousins became an alderman in Chicago, Ill., where he served on many important committees and where he maintained a private law practice after 1953.

COVINGTON, BENJAMIN JESSE (1869–1961), physician; born in Marlin, Tex, Covington attended Hearne Baptist Academy and received his M.D. degree from Meharry Medical College (Nashville, Tenn.) in 1900. He practiced medicine in Houston, Tex., for 58 years and during that time helped to reorganize the Lone Star Medical Association.

COWAN, JAMES RANKIN (1916–), physician, public official; born in Washington, D.C. Cowan received a B.S. degree from Howard University (Washington, D.C.) in 1937, a M.A. degree from Fisk University (Nashville, Tenn.) in 1940, and his M.D. degree from Meharry Medical College (Nashville, Tenn.) in 1944. He served as a captain in the Armed Forces and as chief of surgery at the 26th Station Hospital in Germany. Cowan later became attending physician at East Orange General Hospital in East Orange, N.J. Then he was appointed to the governor's cabinet as state commissioner of health in New Jersey, and was in charge of a department with more than 1,000 persons and a budget in excess of $40 million.

COX, BENJAMIN ELTON (1931–), clergyman, civil rights leader; born in Whileville, Tenn. Cox received a B.A. degree from Livingstone College (Salisbury, N.C.) in 1954 and his B.D. degree from Howard University School of Religion (Washington, D.C.) in 1957. He served as pastor of African Methodist Episcopal Zion (AMEZ) churches in Illinois, North Carolina, and Washington, D.C., and later as pastor of the United Church of Christ in North Carolina. Cox served as assistant chaplain of Boys' Village of Maryland, as a high school teacher in North Carolina, and as national youth secretary for the National Association for the Advancement of Colored People (NAACP) and field secretary for the Congress of Racial Equality (CORE). Active in civil rights, he was one of the first of the freedom riders.

COX, OLIVER CROMWELL (1901–), sociologist; born in Trinidad, West Indies. Cox received a B.A. degree from Northwestern University (Evanston, Ill.), and a M.A. degree and his Ph.D. degree (1938) from the University of Chicago. He taught at Wiley College, at Tuskegee Institute, and at Lincoln University (Jefferson City, Mo.). His most important work is *Caste, Class and Race* (1948), a critical view of the caste-class structure of American society. Cox attacked the school of sociologists who view the black man as belonging to a caste. This theme was reiterated in many articles and book reviews between 1945 and 1949.

CRAIG, WALTER F. (1854– ?), violinist; born in Princeton, N.J. Craig made his musical debut in New York City in 1870. By 1886 he had been labeled by the New York *Freeman* as the "Prince of Negro Violinists." Craig organized a band in New York in 1872, and with it he toured throughout the United States. Craig's Celebrated Orchestra was one of post-Civil War America's most popular musical institutions.

CRAWFORD, DAVID EUGENE (1869– ?), banker, lawyer; born in Lynchburg, Va. Crawford attended Hampton Institute (Hampton, Va.) and Northeastern College (Boston, Mass., now Northeastern University). In 1910 he founded the Eureka Cooperative Bank, the first black cooperative bank in America. After being admitted to the Virginia bar in 1908, Crawford was appointed to the chancery of Suffolk County, Virginia, in 1915 and appointed as public administrator of Suffolk County in 1924.

CRAWFORD, EVANS EDGAR (1923–), clergyman, educator; born in Temple, Tex. Crawford received a B.A. degree from Sam Houston State College (Huntsville, Tex.) in 1943, and a S.T.B. degree (1946) and his Ph.D. degree (1957) from Boston University. He was pastor of churches in Massachusetts and Rhode Island. Crawford later became a teacher of theology and dean of chapel at Howard University (Washington, D.C.).

CRAWFORD, HENRY ROBERT (1890– ?), administrator; born in Belden, Tex. Crawford attended Central Young Men's Christian Association (YMCA) Community college in Chicago, Ill., and became executive secretary and later physical director of the YMCA in that city. He was also a member of the board of directors of the Cook County Athletic Federation. Crawford's affiliations included memberships in the Illinois State Physical Directors Society and the National Physical Directors Society.

CRICHLOW, ERNEST (1914–), painter, illustrator; born in New York, N.Y. Crichlow studied at New York University. His notable illustrations for *Two is a Team,* a children's book written by Jerrold Beim (1945), helped establish Afro-American youngsters as characters in general children's stories. Such early oil paintings as *Lend Me a Hand* showed great sympathy with the joys and fears of childhood, adolescence, and motherhood. His later works are equally as sensitive and realistic. Crichlow exhibited at the Harlem Community Center, New York, N.Y., 1938; Art of the American Negro Exhibition, Chicago, 1940; Library of Congress, Washington, D.C., 1940; and elsewhere. *See also* ARTISTS; LITERATURE: CHILDREN'S.

CRIME

Statistical Conditions Blacks, whether they are male or female, are far more likely than whites to be the victims of such serious crimes of violence as murder, rape, robbery, and aggravated assault. However, black females are the most vulnerable group of all. Burglary and larceny (more than $50) are also greater threats to black than white women, but there is no significant difference between black and white men. On the other hand, black men and women are somewhat more likely to be the victims of auto theft than are whites.

Afro-Americans are more likely to be the victims of serious crimes than whites, no matter what their income group. Crimes of violence against the person—including murder and other homicide, forcible rape, robbery, and aggravated assault—are most likely to affect the poorest blacks. However, even blacks in the higher income groups are much more likely than whites to suffer such crimes. Crimes against property are also more likely to victimize a black than a white at every income level. However, the incidence of such crimes is much greater against higher-income blacks, and the black-white differences are larger in the high-income than in the lower-income groups.

More blacks than whites are arrested for serious crimes of violence, but arrests for crimes against property take place mainly among whites. Even in cities, where more blacks live, Afro-Americans are not the major group responsible for such serious property crimes as burglary, larceny (more than $50), and auto theft. In the suburbs, a greater proportion of arrests for serious crimes involves whites, whether violent crimes (homicide, rape, robbery, and aggravated assault) or property crimes. However, arrest data alone are not necessarily good measures of criminality, since an arrest may not result in conviction in court and since some groups are more subject to arrest than others.

The two accompanying tables show (1) types of crime and (2) their relative occurrence against blacks in major American cities.

Underlying Social Conditions There are several underlying social factors that relate to crime. First, violence traditionally underlies the history of the nation. Since the 1950s, moreover, violence has taken on new meanings. Conditions have existed that reinforced a general erosion of an older way of life in American society, as shown in the civil rights movement and the campus unrest of the 1960s. These civil disorders resulted largely from rapid urbanization, especially of the black population, and a notable reduction in the average age of the total population. Second, a feeling of *powerlessness* exists among blacks, as pointed out in the *Report of the National Advisory Commission on Civil Disorders* (1968). "The frustrations of powerlessness," the commision observed, "have led some to the conviction that there is no effective alternative to violence as a means of expression and redress. . . . More generally, the result is alienation and hostility toward the institutions of law and government and the white society which controls them." Third, the ghettos are regarded by many as a breeding ground for crime. With

poor housing and very high unemployment rates, Afro-Americans tend to turn to crime. Fourth, and finally, there is the factor of police. As the cornerstone of criminal law enforcement, the job of policemen has become very complex and demanding due to such recent social developments as drug traffic and addiction. In addition, complications of law enforcement arise in the matter of intergroup relations: a great many policemen in ghettos are white. Blacks have long been distrustful and suspicious of white policemen and have been known to interfere with or deter the proper enforcement of the law against blacks. On the other hand, some white policemen have exhibited prejudice against blacks. The President's Commission on Law Enforcement and the Administration of Justice (1967) gave special attention to this problem. It recommended that every large police department, especially in communities with substantial minority problems, should "make special efforts

NUMBER AND RATE OF PERSONAL VICTIMIZATIONS, BY TYPE OF CRIME: 1973

Race of victim and type of crime	Victimizations		Victimization rate[1]
	Number (thousands)	Percent	
BLACK			
Total	2,255	100	132
Crimes of violence (total)	801	36	47
Rape and attempted rape	29	1	2
Robbery and attempted robbery	245	11	14
Assault and attempted assault	527	23	31
Crimes of theft (total)	1,454	64	85
Personal larceny with contact	118	5	7
Personal larceny without contact	1,336	59	78
WHITE			
Total	18,211	100	127
Crimes of violence (total)	4,642	25	32
Rape and attempted rape	129	1	1
Robbery and attempted robbery	856	5	6
Assault and attempted assault	3,657	20	26
Crimes of theft (total)	13,569	75	95
Personal larceny with contact	381	2	3
Personal larceny without contact	13,188	72	92

Note: Data in this table on criminal victimization in 1973 were gathered from surveys of a National Crime Panel, conducted by the U.S. Bureau of the Census. The surveys were sponsored by the U.S. Department of Justice, Law Enforcement Assistance Administration.

[1]The victimization rate, a measure of occurrence among population groups at risk, was computed on the basis of the number of victimizations per 1,000 population age 12 and over.

SOURCE: U.S. Department of Justice, Law Enforcement Assistance Administration.

to recruit minority group officers and to deploy and promote them fairly. . . . They should have rigorous internal investigation units to examine complaints of misconduct." Some cities have begun to implement these recommendations.

Inmates of Local Jails Nearly 142,000 persons were confined in local jails in this country as of mid-1972. Black inmates numbered 59,000 and comprised 42 percent of the jail population. (In some cities the percentage of black prisoners amounts to between 60 and 80 percent.) A jail is a locally administered institution that has authority to retain adults for 48 hours or longer. The jail population includes those sentenced, and those awaiting arraignment, transfer to other authorities, trial, or final sentencing.

Black inmates were generally young (under 30), poorly educated, and unmarried (single, divorced, separated, or widowed). Also, sizable

proportions of inmates were low-paid wage earners or unemployed prior to their arrest. The same pattern prevailed among white inmates even though some differences between blacks and whites were evident. For example, 69 percent of the black inmates were not high school graduates as compared to 62 percent for the white inmates.

Black and white inmates differed in relation to the type of offense with which they were charged. Crimes of violence were more prevalent among blacks, regardless of their confinement status: 37 percent of black inmates compared with 17 percent of whites. In regard to crimes of violence, the proportion of blacks charged was larger than that of whites only for the crimes of murder, kidnapping, and robbery. No difference existed between blacks and whites in the proportion charged with rape or assault. Blacks were less likely than whites to have been charged

PERSONAL VICTIMIZATION RATES FOR BLACK RESIDENTS OF SELECTED CITIES, BY TYPE OF CRIME: 1972 AND 1973 (Rate per 1,000 population age 12 and over)

Year of survey	Selected cities	All crimes against persons	Crimes of violence				Crimes of theft	
			Total	Rape	Robbery	Assault	Personal larceny with contact	Personal larceny without contact
a	Atlanta	115	38	2	15	21	13	64
a	Baltimore	120	58	2	30	26	15	47
b	Boston	171	70	[1]2	32	36	26	75
b	Buffalo	128	57	2	22	34	7	64
a	Chicago	163	72	4	39	29	18	72
b	Cincinnati	170	65	1	17	46	8	96
a	Cleveland	146	66	2	34	30	12	67
a	Dallas	96	34	3	11	20	4	58
a	Denver	182	65	2	14	49	8	110
a	Detroit	173	78	2	40	36	11	83
b	Houston	178	58	3	25	31	8	112
a	Los Angeles	166	79	5	29	45	6	81
b	Miami	88	39	[1]2	16	22	7	42
b	Milwaukee	203	74	3	25	46	11	118
b	Minneapolis	206	66	[1]4	19	44	[1]7	133
a	Newark	105	52	2	37	13	18	34
b	New Orleans	116	40	3	16	21	11	65
a	New York	81	42	1	30	11	11	27
b	Oakland	129	44	2	15	27	7	77
a	Philadelphia	179	88	2	44	42	18	73
b	Pittsburgh	139	61	3	20	39	11	67
a	Portland	219	67	2	16	49	8	143
b	San Diego	173	47	[1]1	10	36	[1]2	124
b	San Francisco	174	64	[1]4	23	36	16	94
a	St. Louis	87	36	2	18	16	8	44
b	Washington, D.C.	73	26	1	16	9	10	37

Note: Statistics on criminal victimization for the 26 cities were gathered as part of the National Crime Panel by the U.S. Bureau of the Census for the U.S. Department of Justice, Law Enforcement Assistance Administration. The victimization rate for crimes against persons is a measure of occurrence among population groups at risk and is computed on the basis of the number of victimizations per 1,000 population, age 12 and over.
[a]Survey covers year 1972.
[b]Survey covers year 1973.
[1]Estimate based on about 10 or fewer sample cases is statistically unreliable.
SOURCE: U.S. Department of Justice, Law Enforcement Assistance Administration.

with crimes relating to forgery, fraud, or drugs, as well as such minor crimes as drunkeness and traffic offenses.

Among inmates not on appeal, the average sentences were generally longer for blacks than for whites for all of the crimes of violence. The most marked spread between the racial groups was for murder or kidnapping: the median number of months sentenced was 66.1 for blacks and 5.8 for whites. Among the less serious crimes, the average sentences for blacks were more severe only for petty larceny, auto theft, and drug-related crimes. *See also* DISCRIMINATION; EMPLOYMENT; HOUSING; POVERTY.

REFERENCES: Some selective references include: *Black Americans: A Chartbook* (1971); Brown, Ina Corinne, *Understanding Race Relations*, U.S. Department of Labor, Bureau of the Census, Washington, D.C., 1973; U.S. President's Commission of Law Enforcement and Administration of Justice, *Task Force Report: Crime and Its Impact—An Assessment*, U.S. Government Printing Office, Washington, D.C., 1967; U.S. President's Commission on Law Enforcement and Administration of Justice, *Task Force Report: Juvenile Delinquency and Crime*, U.S. Government Printing Office, Washington, D.C., 1967; U.S. President's Commission on Law Enforcement and Administration of Justice, *Task Force Report: The Police*, U.S. Government Printing Office, Washington, D.C., 1967; and Wolfgang, Marvin E. and Bernard Cohen, *Crime and Race: Conceptions and Misconceptions* (1970).

CROCKETT, GEORGE W., JR. (1909–   ), lawyer, judge; born in Jacksonville, Fla. Crockett received a B.A. degree from Morehouse College (Atlanta, Ga.) in 1931 and his J.D. degree from the University of Michigan Law School in 1934. From 1939 to 1943 he served as senior attorney in the U.S. Department of Labor. Crockett was hearing commissioner for the U.S. Fair Employment Practices Committee in Washington, D.C. (1943), executive director of the UAW-CIO Fair Practice Committee in Detroit, Mich. (1944–46), and associate general counsel for the International UAW-CIO (1946–47). He was elected judge of the Recorder's court in Detroit, Mich., and he was reelected in 1972. Regarded as one of the most outspoken members of the bench, Crockett fought racism wherever he encountered it—even among his colleagues on the bench. He was known to be very reluctant to sentence defendants in cases in which there was evidence of police brutality.

CROCKETT, GWENDOLYN (1932–   ), lawyer, educator; born in Monroe, La. Crockett received her J.D. degree from Southern University (Baton Rouge, La.) in 1958, after which she practiced law in her native city. In 1961 Crockett returned to Baton Rouge, La., to teach at Southern University Law School, and later she served as director of the Legal Aid Society there. In 1972 she became a lawyer in the office of the solicitor of labor in the U.S. Department of Labor.

CROGMAN, WILLIAM HENRY (1841–1931), educator; born in St. Martin, Dutch West Indies. Orphaned at the age of twelve, Crogman became a seaman for 11 years. He then graduated from Pierce Academy (Marlborough, Mass.) in 1870, received a B.A. degree (1876), a M.A. degree (1879), and his Litt.D. degree (1901) from Atlanta University, and his LL.D. from Clark University (Atlanta, Ga.) in 1901. Crogman served as professor of classics at Clark from 1876 to 1903, and he was president of the college from 1903 to 1910. In 1895 he was chosen as chief exposition commissioner for the blacks of Georgia for the Cotton States and International Exposition in Atlanta, Ga. Crogman was a trustee of Gammon Theological Seminary and of Clark University. *See also* HISTORIANS.

CROMWELL, JOHN WESLEY (1864–1927), journalist; educator; born in Portsmouth, Va. Cromwell moved to Philadelphia, Pa., as a youth and studied in the public schools there. He received a law degree from Howard University (Washington, D.C.) in 1874 and was admitted to the bar the same year. Cromwell became the first Afro-American to practice before the Interstate Commerce Commission when he successfully argued a case involving the Georgia Railroad. In 1876 he helped found a weekly newspaper, *The People's Advocate*, and within three months was left in sole charge. He moved the newspaper from Alexandria, Va., to Washington D.C., and, with T. T. Fortune doing the mechanical work, Cromwell produced issues at home. Although the paper became a success, in 1889 Cromwell began a 30-year career as a teacher in the Washington, D.C., public schools. He was the author of *The Negro in American History* (1914); and the American Negro Academy, of which he was corresponding secretary, published several of his papers.

CROMWELL, OTELIA (1873–1972), educator. Cromwell received two B.A. degrees, one from Smith College (Northampton, Mass.) another from Columbia University, and received her Ph.D. degree from Yale University. She was the first black graduate of Smith, where, in 1950, she received an honorary LL.D degree. Cromwell served as chairman of the division of languages and literature at Miner Teachers College. She was the author of *Negro Reading for Schools and Colleges* and of biographies of Lucretia Mott and Thomas Haywood.

CROSS, EDWARD B. (1922–   ), physician, government official; born in Forrest City, Ark. Cross received a B.S. degree from Philander Smith College (Little Rock, Ark.) in 1943 and his M.D. degree from Howard University Medical College (Washington, D.C.) in 1952. He interned at Public Health Hospital, Chicago, Ill. From 1958 to 1959 Cross worked for the Public Health Service as an administrator of public hospitals in Detroit, Seattle, San Francisco, Boston, and New York City. He served as medical director of the Peace Corps in Ethiopia for two years, and he was the first black physician to become U.S. assistant surgeon general. Cross became director of the U.S. Office of Health and Medical Care of the Department of Health, Education, and Welfare, and he was named vice-provost for health sciences at the University of Missouri in 1970.

CROSSON, JAMES D. (1909–   ), lawyer, judge; born in Newberry, S.C. Crosson was educated at the Jewish People's Institute and at the Lewis Institute of Technology in Illinois. He received a J.D. degree (1940) and his LL.M. degree (1947) from the Cleveland-Marshall Law School of Cleveland State University. Crosson was one of the first graduates of the National College of State Trial Judges at the University of Colorado. During World War II, he became well known in southern France as an able trial lawyer through his defense of American soldiers charged with major crimes. After the war, Crosson began practicing law as a partner in a Chicago, Ill. law firm. From 1954 to 1961, he served first as a referee in the Municipal Court of Chicago and then as administrative assistant to the chief justice of that court. Crosson soon became known as the "lawman" in the chief justice's Office. In 1962 he was appointed a judge of the Circuit Court of Cook County, Ill.

CRUMMELL, ALEXANDER (1819–98), clergyman, author; born in New York, N.Y. The son of free parents, Crummell was a descendant of West African royalty since his paternal grandfather was a tribal king. He attended Mulberry Street School in New York City, and in 1831 he was enrolled briefly in a new high school in

Alexander Crummell. *(Moorland-Spingarn Research Center, Howard University.)*

Canaan, N.H., before the school was destroyed by neighborhood residents. In 1836 Crummell attended Oneida Institute (Whitesboro, N.Y.), a manual labor school. He was received as a candidate for Holy Orders in 1839 and applied for admission to the General Theological Seminary of the Episcopal Church, but was not admitted because of his color. Crummell was eventually received in the diocese of Massachusetts and ordained to the diaconate there. After study at Queen's College, Cambridge, England, he went to Africa as a missionary, becoming rector of a parish and professor of mental and moral science in Liberia. While there, Crummell became widely known as a public figure; in 1862 he published a volume of his addresses, most of which had been delivered in Africa. After spending 20 years on that continent, Crummell returned to the United States and became rector of St. Luke's Church, Washington, D.C. In 1897 he capped his career by founding the American Negro Academy in Washington, D.C. *See also* AMERICAN NEGRO ACADEMY; EPISCOPALIANS.

CUFFE, PAUL (1759–1817), merchant, seaman; born in Cuttyhunk Island, near New Bedford, Mass. Cuffe, whose mother was a Wampanoag Indian and whose father was a West African, went to sea as a teenager. At the age of 25, he became master of his own ship, and he became involved in the coastwise trade in such vessels as the *Ranger,* the *Traveller,* and the *Alpha.* After 1800 Cuffe arranged with friends in Philadelphia, Pa., to cooperate in establishing missionary activity in Sierra Leone. Subsequently, he established a lucrative trade with Sierra Leone. Cuffe believed that colonies in Africa would help to bring about the abolition of slavery in America. To this end, he favored emigration of blacks and actually transported black colonists in his ships. Two good accounts of Cuffe's life and activities are Harris, Sheldon H., *Paul Cuffe: Black American and the African Return* (1972) and Miller, Floyd J., "Paul Cuffe: From Missionary-Entrepreneur to Black Emigrationist," in *The Search for a Black Nationality: Black Colonization and Emigration, 1787–1863* (1975). *See also* AMERICAN COLONIZATION SOCIETY; COLONIZATION.

CUISINE Many aspects of traditional Afro-American cuisine have their roots in the slave period, especially in the eating practices of the Old South. Modern "soul food" largely originated in traditional slave and southern foods and in their preparation. The principal foods and dishes related to and still largely relate to pork products: chitterlings (chitlin's, without the r sound), fatback, pig feet, pig ears, and pork chops; to greens: collard, turnip, and mustard; to black-eyed peas; to sweet potatoes (called "yams," after the African word *nyam*, meaning "to eat"); to okra (also an African word); to cornbread (fried in a skillet, baked on a hearth, or used for stuffing); to chicken (fried or "smothered"); and to fish (catfish and perch—frequently fried as for "fish frys"). Many of these foods were not regularly eaten by slaves. On the contrary, the most regular slave menu consisted of the "3 M's": meat (sow belly), meal, and molasses. Nevertheless, the above list contains the principal foods that were traditional among Southerners, making allowance, of course, for regional varieties and preferences.

Black cooks were important in the preparation of foods, and black hands were essential to its service throughout the nation, but nowhere as principally as in the South, where most blacks lived. In general, black chefs tended to favor strong seasonings, especially hot pepper. Fats ("grease") were very liberally used. Some dishes carried such distinctive regional flavors as shell fish (crabs and oysters) in the Chesapeake Bay areas and rice in the Carolinas and Georgia. When prepared and savored with okra, vegetables, and sauces, shrimp gumbo was a favorite in the Gulf regions. When prepared with blackeyed peas, rice dishes could be universal and yet as distinctive as "hopping john." Served with hog jowl or other pork parts, hopping john was a favorite New Year's meal, regarded as an omen of good luck and good health, as it is often today.

Either as domestics or as commercial professionals, Afro-Americans have had a long tradition in cookery and catering. In countless cases, however, the art of the black chef, whether with "soul" or other foods, has disappeared. The skills and artistry of many cooks have been forgotten along with their names and their recipes. Yet, a great deal of cooking knowledge remains among Afro-Americans, as any good gourmet can testify. From time to time, a few prized Afro-American recipes have appeared in black newspapers and magazines, and some recipes have been preserved in various cookbooks.

REFERENCES: For additional information, see: Bivins, S. Thomas, *The Southern Cookbook*, 1912; De Knight, Freda, *The Ebony Cookbook*, 1962; Gaskins, Ruth L., *A Good Heart and a Light Head: Ruth L. Gaskins' Collection of Negro Recipes*, 1968; National Council of Negro Women, *The Historical Cookbook of the American Negro*, 1958; and Ott, Eleanore, *Plantation Cookery in Old Louisiana*, 1938. For a good economic account, see Hilliard, S. B., *Hogmeat and Hoecake: Food Supply in the Old South*, 1972.

CULLEN, COUNTEE (1903–46), poet; born Countee Porter in Baltimore, Md. Adopted by Rev. and Mrs. Frederick Cullen, the young poet received a B.A. degree from New York University in 1925 and a M.A. degree from Harvard University in 1926. Cullen was probably the best-known member of the Harlem Renaissance of the 1920s, his work combining racial consciousness with a poet's sensitivity. He was assistant editor of *Opportunity* magazine from 1926 to 1928 and taught French at Frederick Douglass High School after 1934. Cullen wrote several volumes of poetry, including *Color* (1925), *Copper Sun* (1927), and *The Ballad of The Brown Girl* (1927); his selected poems were published posthumously in a volume entitled *On These I Stand* (1947). He received the Witter Bynner Poetry Award in 1925, a Guggenheim Fellowship in 1928, and the National Association for the Advancement of Colored People's (NAACP) Spingarn Medal. At the time of Cullen's death, the Broadway play he coauthored, *St. Louis Woman*, was beginning rehersals. *See also* LITERATURE: POETRY.

CUNEY, WILLIAM W. (1906–), singer, poet; born in Washington, D.C. Cuney was educated at Howard University (Washington, D.C.), Lincoln University (Lincoln University Pa.), and the New England Conservatory of Music (Boston, Mass.). He also studied voice in Rome. In 1926 Cuney won first prize in *Opportunity* magazine's poetry competition. He also wrote song lyrics, some of which were sung by Josh White in the 1930s on his *Southern Exposure* album. Cuney's books include *Puzzles* (1961) and *Storefront Church* (1973). *See also* LITERATURE: POETRY.

CUNNINGHAM, FRANK (1912–), educator; born in Okolona, Miss. Cunningham received a B.A. degree from Mount Union College (Alliance, Ohio) in 1937, and M.A., S.T.B. (1940), and Ph.D. (1951) degrees from Boston University. He taught at Wilberforce University (Wilberforce, Ohio) from 1942 to 1945, and then at Morris Brown College (Atlanta, Ga.) in 1945. Cunningham also served as dean of the school of religion at Morris Brown College and became its president in 1958.

CURRY, NORRIS SAMUEL (1910–), Christian Methodist Episcopal bishop; born in Naples,

Tex. Curry received a B.A. degree (1942) and a B.D. degree from Texas College, and his LL.D. degree (1957) from Drew University (Madison, N.J.) in 1947. He became pastor of churches in Texas and New Jersey and later in California. In 1958 Curry was made editor of the *Christian Index,* and four years later he was elected a bishop of the Christian Methodist Episcopal (CME) Church. He became the presiding bishop of the CME Fourth Episcopal District (Louisiana and Mississippi).

CURTIS, AUSTIN MAURICE (1868–1939), surgeon; born in Raleigh, N.C. Curtis graduated from Lincoln University (Lincoln University, Pa.) in 1888 and received his M.D. degree from Northwestern University Medical School (Evanston, Ill.) in 1891. He was the first intern and house physician at Provident Hospital, Chicago, Ill. (1891–92) and served as the first black on the medical staff of Cook County Hospital (1896–98). Curtis became chief surgeon of Freedmen's Hospital, Washington, D.C. He also served as head of the department of surgery at Howard University Medical College for 40 years.

CURTIS, JAMES L. (1922–   ), psychiatrist; born in Jeffersonville, Ga. Curtis received his M.D. degree from the University of Michigan Medical School in 1946. He became director of psychiatry of the Community Mental Health Board of the New York City Department of Social Services and was clinical assistant professor of psychiatry at the State University of New York Downstate Medical Center. Curtis served as associate dean and associate professor of psychiatry at Cornell University Medical College (Ithaca, N.Y.) after 1969.

DANCE

Africans danced at home in Africa and on the ships carrying them to the New World. In the United States, as Afro-Americans, they continued to dance, sometimes forced by the whip, and sometimes in religious ecstasy, in competition, or as entertainers.

The dances most frequently observed in the Caribbean were of the African hip-shaking variety: the Calenda, the Chica, and the Juba. Some African dance traditions were maintained in the islands, such as the John Canoe and Gombay dancers. Funeral dance customs remained close to their African origins, while wedding dances among the blacks were frequently imitative of white customs. Dance played a large role in religious observance, since the religious ceremonies developed in the New World derived in part from African beliefs. In Africa, dance was meant to induce the ultimate state of religious ecstasy, "possession," an objective prominent in the New World practice of Voodoo, Shango, and Nañigo.

West Indian dance remained an influence on the dance performed by blacks in the United States. Funeral dances, for example, were the same. Traces of the Calenda and Chica were found on the plantations, and while the Juba changed from a sacred to a secular dance, it was widely known throughout the South. Other dances of African origin included those performed with containers of water carried on the head and such animal dances as the Buzzard Lope, Pigeon Wing, and Buck. A state of reli-

gious ecstasy could be achieved through the Ring-Shout, which was the Protestant counterpart of Voodoo or Shango.

While the Breakdowns and Cake-Walks were being danced on the plantation, the blacks in the North were dancing on such occasions as Pinkster Day, when a dance much like the Calenda was performed. On the levees of the Ohio and Mississippi rivers a dance called the Coonjine developed, while in New Orleans a wide variety of dances were performed, covering the spectrum from the European social dances performed at the Quadroon Balls to the Bamboula, Calenda, and Chica of Congo Square, to the Voodoo dances held in the Bayou St. John.

Wherever black people gathered to dance, white people came to be entertained. Soon white

The breakdown, in an 1861 wood engraving. Its derivatives were related to the hoedown. *(Library of Congress.)*

performers were imitating the black dancers. The most famous of these early white performers was Thomas "Jim Crow" Rice. Imitating the dance and song of an old lame Negro, Rice developed the stereotype of the comic Negro that was maintained in the later minstrel shows. Though the minstrels purported to imitate the

The cakewalk, about 1890, a popular dance of the period that is thought to contain elements of mockery and mimicry of well-to-do whites. *(Library of Congress.)*

plantation Negro, the distortion was so great that by 1890 any resemblance between the Negro and his blackface stereotype was incidental. Yet in the minds of many of the minstrel audience, the real Negro was exactly that caricature, that stereotype that minstrelsy so carefully created and cultivated.

The stereotype developed by minstrelsy has been one of the greatest influences on the life of the black American. This distorted image has had both a positive and negative effect on the dance of the Afro-American. It has exerted a positive effect in that people believed the black had a natural talent for dance, rhythm, and music; because of this belief the door to the entertainment world opened more readily for the black dancer. The great black dancers of the entertainment world—Master Juba, the Behee Brothers, Williams and Walker, Bill Robinson, and Earl Tucker—were readily accepted because the stereotype allowed the Negro to entertain by dancing.

Yet even though there were strong positive

effects from the minstrel caricature, the negative far outweighed any advantages gained. The stereotype restricted the black dancer to the role of an entertainer, as opposed to a serious artist. It proscribed the thematic material available for black dance and later limited the dancer to either ethnic African or West Indian material as used by Dafora, Dunham, and Primus, or to strictly Negro thematic material such as spirituals, jazz, plantation dances, and themes traditionally recognized as belonging to Negro life. Pearl Primus and Talley Beatty, in particular, have utilized this type of thematic material. The minstrel image has fostered rejection of the serious black artist when he has attempted to step outside the proscribed thematic limits.

Because the stereotype has been so all-pervasive in American life, few Americans have avoided believing in at least some part of it. Dance critics have often allowed the stereotype to influence their reviews.

While Talley Beatty, Alvin Ailey, and Donald McKayle have broken out of the proscribed material to a certain degree, their most successful compositions still remain within the realm of "Negro" material. In the work of these three men, however, the experience of being black in America has been dramatized for white audiences and a bridge of understanding has been created.

Some dancers believe that critics have limited their aspirations by lavishly overpraising the *efforts* rather than the actual *accomplishments* of black dancers. By claiming that the Afro-American was a natural dancer and complimenting his "inherent" abilities, critics have upheld

Far right: The jitterbug, here performed at a dance in Harlem, New York City, 1939, calls for a straight upper torso swiveled on the hips, rapid two-step footwork, intermittent hand contact, and spectacular acrobatics. The Erskine Hawkins Band is in the background. *(Museum of the City of New York.)*

the concept that black dancers did not need the extensive training and strict discipline so necessary to white dancers. The value of discipline, however, has been shown in the work of Carmen de Lavallade, Mary Hinkson, Matt Turney, William Louther, Clive Thompson, and Dudley Williams. These artists, all well trained and highly disciplined, have demonstrated the supreme position a black dancer may attain in the international world of dance.

The ballet world has demonstrated the strongest bias against the black dancer. The entire basis of ballet was alien to the *white's conception of the black*. The white who enslaved the black could not think of him as either noble or majestic. Neither did the white consider the black to be graceful. Black dance was considered instinctive and improvised, sometimes savage and licentious, sometimes comic, but never controlled or precise. The concept of beauty also entered into the discrimination against black dancers in the ballet and it was only when such dancers as Janet Collins and Arthur Mitchell approached the white ideal of beauty that they were accepted.

Such West Indian dancers as Jean-Léon Destiné, Geoffrey Holder, and Percival Borde contributed to the overall success of black concert dance. The young dancer-choreographers Louis Johnson, Eleo Pomare, and Rod Rodgers, and on the West Coast Ruth Beckford and Carleton Johnson achieved a reputation through their choreography and teaching efforts. Indeed, Afro-Americans contributed more and have been more influential in the American dance than nearly any other factor throughout the years.

REFERENCES: For additional references, see: Emery, Lynne Fauley, *Black Dance in the United States From 1619 to 1972*, copyright © National Press Books, Palo Alto, 1972, from which this entry was adapted with special permission of author and publisher.

DANDRIDGE, PAUL A. (1926–), lawyer, judge. Dandridge received a B.A. degree from Lincoln University (Lincoln University, Pa.) and a LL.B. degree from Temple University (Philadelphia, Pa.). He was admitted to the Pennsylvania bar in 1966 and became a judge of the Municipal Court in Philadelphia, Pa.

DANIEL PAYNE COLLEGE Daniel Payne College, at Birmingham, Ala., was founded in 1889 at Selma, Ala., by Brown Chapel of the African Methodist Episcopal (AME) Church of Selma.

The school is coeducational, private, continues to be church-related, offers the bachelor's degree, and provides liberal arts and general teacher preparatory curricula. In 1975 its enrollment was approximately 350.

The school began with two regular teachers, M. E. Bryant and W. H. Mixon, as well as W. B. Johnson, who acted as leader of the college and structured a classical curriculum. In 1922, under the direction of Bishop William Alfred Fountain, Sr., the institution was discontinued at Selma and moved to Birmingham, where the college has since been located.

DANIEL, WALTER CLARENCE (1922–), educator; born in Macon, Ga. Daniel received a B.A. degree from Johnson C. Smith University (Charlotte, N.C.) in 1944, a M.S. degree from South Dakota State University in 1962, his Ph.D. degree from Bowling Green State University (Bowling Green, Ohio) in 1962, and an honorary L.H.D. degree from Lincoln University (Jefferson City, Mo.) in 1972. He taught in Los Angeles, Calif., public schools (1946–60). Daniel was an instructor of English at Saint Augustine's College (Raleigh, N.C.) from 1962 to 1963 and at North Carolina Agricultural and Technical (A & T) State University from (1963–70). He served as president of Lincoln University (Jefferson City, Mo.) from 1970 to 1973 and as vice-chancellor of the University of Missouri beginning in 1973.

DANIELS, HAYZEL BURTON (1907–), lawyer, judge; born in Fort Clark, Tex. Daniels received a B.A. degree (1939), a M.A. degree (1941), and his J.D. degree (1948) from the University of Arizona. He was admitted to the Arizona bar in 1948 after serving in the U.S. Air Force during World War II. From 1950 to 1952, Daniels was a representative in the Arizona legislature, and from 1954 to 1960 he served as an assistant attorney general. He was appointed one of the ten city magistrates in Phoenix, Ariz., in 1965, and was, in 1973, the only black judge in Arizona.

DARLINGTON, ROY CLIFFORD (1908–), educator, pharmacist. Darlington received a B.S. degree (1941), a M.S. Degree (1943), and his Ph.D. degree (1947) from Ohio State University. Orphaned and homeless as a child and youth, he became the first Afro-American to receive a Ph.D. degree in pharmacy in the United States. Darlington taught at Howard University (Wash-

Street dancing, accompanied by a jazz band, in New Orleans, La. 1974. Many Afro-American dances are combined to create a traditional festive parade which often followed a funeral cortege. *(Photo by Arnold Hinton.)*

ington, D.C.), where he became professor of pharmacy in 1949 and later served as chairman of the department of pharmacy, as assistant dean (1971–73), and as associate dean (1973–76). He was appointed historian of the Washington, D.C., section of the American Pharmaceutical Association and was elected chairman of the editorial board of the *Journal of the National Pharmaceutical Association.* Darlington's articles on over-the-counter medications in the *Handbook of Non-Prescription Drugs,* one of the most widely used references in pharmacy, have been read and discussed in seminars throughout the United States. Darlington received the Distinguished Alumni Award from Ohio State University. *See also* NATIONAL PHARMACEUTICAL ASSOCIATION.

DAVENPORT, ERNEST H. (1917–   ), accounting executive, government official; born in Lima, Ohio. Davenport received a B.A. degree from Morris Brown College (Atlanta, Ga.) in 1940 and did graduate work at Wayne State University (Detroit, Mich.). From 1941 to 1946, he was on active duty with the Army Reserve, from which he retired. In 1971 Davenport was called to Washington, D.C., to head the audit division of the U.S. Office of Economic Opportunity (OEO), the first black to hold the position as supervisory auditor for OEO. After leaving his post in OEO in 1973, Davenport became assistant director of the U.S. General Accounting Office. He was a director of the Bank of the Commonwealth (Detroit, Mich.) from 1967 to 1973, received the Michigan Minuteman Award in 1968, and served as national president of Kappa Alpha Psi fraternity from 1967 to 1970.

DAVENPORT, RONALD ROSS (1937–   ), lawyer, educator; born in Philadelphia, Pa. Davenport received a B.S. degree in economics from Pennsylvania State University in 1958, a LL.B. degree from Temple University School of Law (Philadelphia, Pa.) in 1962, and his LL.M. degree from Yale University Law School in 1968. He became dean of the Duquesne Law School (Pittsburgh, Pa.) in 1970. Davenport won the Pennsylvania State University Presidential Scholarship in 1958 and was associate editor of the *Temple Law Quarterly.* He became associate justice of the Moot Court Board and a faculty research associate (1961–62), and received the Temple University Law School Scholarship (1961–62). Davenport served on the staff for the Legal

Defense Fund of the National Association for the Advancement of Colored People (NAACP) in 1964, as general counsel of the Mayor's Committee on Human Resources, Inc. (1964–68), and on the Equal Educational Opportunity Program of the Department of Health, Education, and Welfare (HEW) in 1968. Davenport wrote many scholarly articles, including: "The Unions, the Implicit Ememy," and "The Second Justice Marshall and the Supreme Court and the Negro."

DAVIS, ALLISON (1902–   ), psychologist, educator; born in Washington, D.C. Davis received a B.A. degree from Williams College (Williamstown, Mass.), in 1924, a M.A. degree from Howard University (Washington, D.C.) in 1925, and his Ph.D. degree from the University of Chicago in 1942. He taught at the University of Chicago after 1939, where he eventually became the John Dewey Distinguished Service Professor of Education. Davis served as a visiting professor at Columbia University, the University of Michigan, the University of California at Berkeley, and as a George A. Miller Distinguished Service Professor at the University of Illinois in 1965. He was a member of the Conference to Insure Civil Rights (1965) and of the White House Task Force on the Gifted (1968). Davis was the first man, black or white, from the field of education to become a fellow in the American Academy of Arts and Sciences. He was one of the first to point out the inadequacies of intelligence (IQ) tests for measuring accurately the educational potential of children from low-income families. Davis wrote several books, including: *Children of Bondage,* coauthored with John Dollard (1940); *Deep South: A Social Anthropological Study of Caste and Class,* coauthored with Burleigh and Mary Gardner (1941); *Psychology of the Child in the Middle Class* (1960); and *Relationship Between Achievement in High School, College and Occupation: A Follow-up Study* (1963). He also contributed many articles to professional journals.

DAVIS, ANGELA (1944–   ), civil rights activist, educator; born in Birmingham, Ala. Davis graduated magna cum laude from Brandeis University in 1965 and received her M.A. degree from the University of California at San Diego. She served as an instructor at the University of California at Los Angeles. The California board of regents declined to renew her contract and she was dropped from the staff. Subsequently, Davis became involved in an alleged kidnapping attempt of three San Quentin prisoners from the Marin County Civic Center; she was accused of planning the incident and supplying the gun that killed four people during the incident. Charged with murder, kidnapping, and conspiracy, Davis was finally incarcerated. However, in 1972, after 16 months in jail, she was tried and acquitted of the charges. A celebrity, Davis travelled to the Soviet Union and several other communist countries, and lectured in the United States. Her publications include: *If They Come in the Morning: Voices of Resistance* (1971); the pamphlet *Lectures on Liberation* (1972); *Angela Davis: With My Mind on Freedom, An Autobiography* (1974).

DAVIS, AUTHUR P. (1904–   ), educator, author; born in Hampton, Va. Davis received a B.A. degree (1927), a M.A. degree (1929), and his Ph.D. degree (1942) from Columbia University. His teaching career began in 1927 at North Carolina College at Durham (now North Carolina Central University). Davis later taught at Virginia Union University and at Hampton Institute (Hampton, Va.), and he became professor of English at Howard University (Washington, D.C.) in 1969. He coedited, with Sterling Brown and Ulysses Lee, *The Negro Caravan* (1941). Davis contributed many book reviews and articles to professional journals, and he wrote several books, including *From the Dark Tower: Afro-American Writers, 1900 to 1960* (1975).

DAVIS, BENJAMIN OLIVER, JR. (1912–   ), Air Force officer; born in Washington, D.C. The son of Gen. Benjamin O. Davis, Sr., Davis graduated from the U.S. Military Academy at West Point in 1936, the fourth black student ever to do so. He transferred to the Air Corps when he received his wings in 1942. Davis became commander of the 99th Fighter Squadron, which fought in North Africa, Sicily, and Northern Italy during World War II, and after that, he commanded the 332d Fighter Group. By the end of the war, he had won the Silver Star and the Distinguished Flying Cross. Subsequently, Davis was appointed commander of the 51st Fighter-Interceptor Wing during the Korean War in 1952, and later he became director of operations and training of the Far East Air Forces. In 1954 he was made a brigadier general, becoming the first black

general in the Air Force. In 1965 Davis was promoted to lieutenant general, the rank he held on his retirement from the Air Force in 1970. After serving as director of public safety in Cleveland, Ohio, during that year, Davis was appointed assistant secretary in charge of civil aviation security of the U.S. Department of Transportation. *See also* DAVIS, BENJAMIN OLIVER, SR.

Brigadier Gen. Benjamin O. Davis, Sr., (right) pins the Distinguished Flying Cross on his son, Col. Benjamin O. Davis, Jr., in Italy during World War II. Awaiting their turn to be decorated are other officers of the 332d Fighter Group: Capt. Joseph D. Elsberry of Langston, Okla., 1st Lt. Jack D. Holsclaw of Spokane, Wash., and 1st Lt. Clarence D. Lester of Chicago, Ill. *(U.S. Air Force photo.)*

DAVIS, BENJAMIN OLIVER, SR. (1877–1970), Army officer, educator, government official; born in Washington, D.C. Father of Gen. Benjamin O. Davis, Jr., of the U.S. Air Force, Davis attended Howard University (Washington, D.C.), after which he enlisted as a private in the Regular Army in 1899 (after a year in the infantry during the war with Spain). He served for two years in the Philippines, and in 1901 he was commissioned a second lieutenant in the cavalry. In the following years, Davis served in various posts in the United States, until he was sent to Monrovia, Liberia, as military attaché, a post he held until 1912. He joined and rejoined the faculty of Wilberforce University (Wilberforce, Ohio) several times throughout his career, teaching military science both there and at Tuskegee Institute (Tuskegee Institute, Ala.). Rising in rank through the years, Davis was promoted to major during World War I and to full colonel in 1930. He was further promoted to brigadier general under President Franklin D. Roosevelt in 1940, the first Afro-American to attain that rank in the Army. After his retirement in 1941, Davis was recalled to active duty to serve as special adviser to the commander of the European Theater (ETO) during World War II and as assistant to the inspector general in Washington, D.C. Davis finally retired from the Armed Forces in 1948. *See also* DAVIS, BENJAMIN OLIVER, JR.

DAVIS, ERNIE See ATHLETES: FOOTBALL.

DAVIS, FRANK MARSHALL (1905–   ), journalist; born in Arkansas City, Kas. After attending Kansas State College, Davis helped start the Atlanta *Daily World* in 1931. He served as executive editor of the Associated Negro Press (1935–40) and as executive editor of the Chicago *Star* (1946–48). Davis was a Rosenwald Fellow in 1937. Before retiring to Hawaii, he published three volumes of poetry: *Black Man's Verse* (1935), *I Am the American Negro* (1937), and *47th Street* (1949).

DAVIS, GEORGE E. See EDUCATION.

DAVIS, GEORGIA M. (1923–   ), business executive, state legislator; born in Springfield, Ky. Davis attended Louisville Municipal College (Louisville, Ky.) and received certificates in business from the Central Business School and the I.B.M. Supervisory School. Davis was a successful business executive in Louisville, Ky., before her election to the Kentucky state senate in 1967. Active in civil rights, she served on several important commissions and boards.

DAVIS, LAWRENCE ARNETT (1914–   ), educator; born in McCrory, Ark. Davis received a B.A. degree from the Agricultural, Mechanical, and Normal (A M & N) College (Pine Bluff, Ark; now University of Arkansas at Pine Bluff) in 1937, a M.A. degree from the University of Kansas in 1941, and his Ed.D. degree from the University of Arkansas in 1960. He taught (1937–39) and later became dean at the A M & N College at Pine Bluff and its president in 1943.

DAVIS, MILES See MUSIC: JAZZ.

DAVIS, NATHAN T. (1937–   ), musician, composer, educator; born in Kansas City, Kans. Davis received a B.A. degree from the University of Kansas and studied at the Kansas City Conservatory of Music and at the Sorbonne. He received his Ph.D. degree in ethnomusicology from Wesleyan University (Middletown, Conn.) in 1965. Davis has made several recordings, including "Happy Girl," "Hip Walk," and

"Peace Treaty." He was vice-president of Seque Recording Company and became an assistant professor of music at the University of Pittsburgh.

DAVIS, OSSIE (1917–   ), actor, playwright, director; born in Cogdell, Ga. From 1938 to 1941 Davis attended Howard University (Washington, D.C.), from which he received an honorary doctorate in 1973. In 1941 he joined the Rose McClendon Players, a small theater group in New York City's Harlem. After serving in the U.S. Army, Davis made his Broadway debut as the title character in *Jeb.* Subsequently, he played many roles both on tour and on Broadway. During the 1950s, he appeared in larger roles in such plays as *Green Pastures* and *A Raisin in the Sun.* In 1961 Davis triumphed with the Broadway production of his own satirical comedy, *Purlie Victorious,* in which he also played the lead, and which later became a successful Broadway musical called *Purlie.* He and his wife, actress Ruby Dee, made their nightclub debut in 1964 at the Village Vanguard in New York City. A performer in almost all the media, Davis first appeared on television in 1955 in *The Emperor Jones,* and he subsequently starred in numerous television plays. He also recorded the poetry and stories of Langston Hughes and others and appeared in several films. Davis was director and producer of such films as *Black Girl, Cotton Comes to Harlem,* and *Kongi's Harvest.* Always aware of the problems of Afro-Americans, he testified at a Congressional inquiry in 1962 into racial discrimination in show business. In 1975 Davis represented Afro-Americans at meetings of the World Festival of Black and African Arts and Culture in preparation for its second festival in Nigeria. *See also* DEE, RUBY; LITERATATURE: DRAMA/THEATER.

DAVIS, SAMMY, JR. (1925–   ), entertainer; born in New York, N.Y. Davis was on stage before he was two as a walk-on in his parents' vaudeville act, and he was there ever afterward. By 1930 he was a regular member of the Will Mastin Trio, which consisted of his father, his uncle (Mastin), and Davis. In 1946 Davis became the star of the act, and two years later, with the others' retirement, he launched his show business career as a solo performer. He made his stage debut on Broadway in 1956 as Charley Welch in *Mr. Wonderful.* In the following years, Davis appeared in such films as *Anna Lucasta*

(1959); as "Sportin' Life" in *Porgy and Bess* (1959); and in *Oceans 11* (1960). In 1964 he returned to Broadway in the role of Joe Wellington in the musical version of *Golden Boy.* Davis' popularity seemed to increase as he went from stage to films to records. His recordings, beginning in 1954, sold well; his nightclub appearances were spectacular successes; and his forays into television, as both guest and host, were equally well received. His autobiography, *Yes, I Can,* was published in 1966.

DAVIS, TONY *See* Newspapers: Contemporary.

DAVISON, FREDERIC E. (1917–   ), Army officer; born in Washington, D.C. Davison received a B.A. degree (1938) and his M.S. degree (1940) from Howard University (Washington, D.C.). A member of the Army ROTC, he was commissioned a lieutenant in the U.S. Army Reserve in 1939 and was ordered to active duty in 1941, serving later (World War II) as a captain in the 92d Infantry Division. By 1959 Davison had reached the rank of lieutenant colonel and went to Korea as chief of personnel services for the Eighth Army. Returning home, he studied at the Army War College and at George Washington University (Washington, D.C.), where he received a M.A. degree in international affairs. Serving in various military positions in the United States until 1967, Davison requested an assignment in Vietnam, and he was sent to Saigon as deputy commander of an infantry brigade. The next year he was promoted from colonel to brigade commander and soon after to brigadier general. In 1969, after returning from Vietnam, he was inspector general of the U.S. Army for a year and then deputy chief of staff for Army personnel in Europe for a year. By this time, Davison had been promoted to major general, and in 1972 he served as commanding general of the 8th Infantry Division in Germany. In 1973, now the U.S. Army's ranking black officer, he took command of the military district of Washington, D.C. *See also* Wars.

DAWSON, WILLIAM L. (1886–1970), U.S. Representative; born in Albany, Ga. Dawson graduated from Fisk University (Nashville, Tenn.) in 1909. He studied law at Kent College and received a law degree from Northwestern University (Evanston, Ill.) after moving to Chicago, Ill. Dawson was admitted to the Illinois bar in 1920, after serving overseas in Europe during World War I. He began his political career in Chicago as a precinct worker, and then became a state central committeeman, and alderman of the second ward of Chicago, and a Democratic national committeeman. These positions enabled Dawson to win election to the U.S. Congress as a representative. The first black man to head a standing committee in the Congress, Dawson served as chairman of the House Committee on Government Operations. He remained in Congress for 14 terms, longer than any other black representative.

DAWSON, WILLIAM LEVI (1898–1971), musician, composer; born in Anniston, Ala. Dawson received his education at Tuskegee Institute (Tuskegee, Ala.); Horner Institute for Fine Arts (Kansas City, Mo.); Chicago Musical College (Chicago, Ill.); and the American Conservatory of Music, from which he received his Mus.M. degree in 1927. Dawson directed the Tuskegee Institute Choir for many years, relinquishing that post in 1955. Dawson's best-known composition is *Negro Folk Symphony.*

DAYTONA-COOKMAN COLLEGIATE INSTITUTE *See* Bethune-Cookman College.

DAYTONA NORMAL AND INDUSTRIAL INSTITUTE FOR GIRLS *See* Bethune-Cookman College.

DEADWOOD DICK *See* Love, Nat.

DEAN, WILLIAM HENRY (1910–52), economist; born in Lynchburg, Va. Dean graduated from Bowdoin College (Brunswick, Maine) in 1930, a summa cum laude and Phi Beta Kappa student. He continued his studies at Harvard University, where he was a Rosenwald Fellow, and from which he received a M.A. degree (1932) and his Ph.D. degree (1938). In 1933 Dean joined the faculty of Atlanta University and remained there until 1942. He later served with the National Resources and Planning Board in Washington, D.C., and the Office of Price Administration in the U.S. Virgin Islands. In 1944 Dean became director of a community relations project for the National Urban League. Two years later he was appointed chief of the Africa unit in the Division of Economic Stability and Development of the United Nations.

DE BERRY, WILLIAM NELSON (1870– ?), clergyman, civic official; born in Nashville, Tenn.

Ruby Dee and Ossie Davis on a National Educational Television program 1970s. *(Public Broadcasting Service.)*

De Berry graduated from Fisk University (Nashville, Tenn.) in 1896 and from Oberlin Theological Seminary in 1899. He was minister of St. John's Congregational Church in Springfield, Mass., from 1899 to 1931 and then resigned from the ministry to devote his time to welfare and interracial work in Springfield. De Berry served as a member of the Springfield board of public welfare and the Massachusetts state committee on religious and interracial understanding. In addition, he held elective offices in the National Council of the Congregational Churches in the United States and in the American Missionary Association. De Berry was also a trustee of Fisk University. He received medals from the Harmon Foundation of New York and from the city of Springfield for distinguished public service.

DEBOW, RUSSELL ROBINSON (1913–   ), lawyer, judge; born in Lovejoy, Ill. Debow graduated from Illinois State Normal University in 1935, and received his J.D. degree from De Paul University (Chicago, Ill.) in 1954. Soon after, he began work as assistant to a U.S. Congressman at the same time that he practiced law in Chicago, Ill. From 1965 to 1967, Debow served as administrative assistant to Mayor Richard T. Daley of Chicago. In 1971 he became an associate judge of Cook County, Ill.

DECARAVA, ROY See PHOTOGRAPHERS.

DEE, RUBY (1923–   ), actress; born in Cleveland, Ohio. A graduate of Hunter College of the City University of New York in 1945, Dee prepared for her stage career at the American Negro Theater in New York City from 1941 to 1944. In 1946, after several small roles on Broadway, she appeared with Ossie Davis in *Jeb;* two years later she married Davis and appeared with him in several different shows. Her other Broadway performances include appearances in *A Raisin in the Sun* in 1959 and in *Purlie Victorious,* written by Ossie Davis, in 1961. Her movie career began with *The Jackie Robinson Story* and included roles in *Take A Giant Step, A Raisin in the Sun,* and *The Balcony.* In 1965 she joined the American Shakespeare Festival in Stratford, Conn., becoming the first black actress to play major parts there. Her roles ranged from classical to existential parts and took her to many areas of the country. The Ruby Dee Scholarship in Dramatic Art was established to help talented young black women realize a career in the theater. In

1970 she and her husband were presented with the Frederick Douglass Award by the New York League. *See also* DAVIS, OSSIE.

DEJOIE, CONSTANT CHARLES, JR. (1914–   ), editor; born in New Orleans, La. A graduate of Talladega College (Talladega, Ala.), DeJoie received his M.A. degree from the University of Michigan in 1938. That same year he joined the staff of the Louisiana *Weekly,* a newspaper of which he became editor and then president. DeJoie served as president of the National Newspaper Publishers Association from 1954 to 1956, and was treasurer of this organization for several years. He was also one of the corporate owners of the New Orleans Saints. *See also* NEWSPAPERS: CONTEMPORARY.

DELANEY, CLARISSA SCOTT (1901–1927), poet, educator; born in Tuskegee Institute, Ala. The daughter of Emmett J. Scott, secretary to Booker T. Washington, she married Hubert Delaney in 1926. Delaney was educated at Tuskegee Institute (Tuskegee Institute, Ala.), Bradford Academy, and Wellesley College (Wellesley, Mass.), before she began teaching at Dunbar High School in Washington, D.C. Delaney studied delinquency and neglect among black children in Washington, D.C. Her poem, "Solace," was included in many anthologies.

DELANEY, HAROLD (1919–   ), educator; born in Philadelphia, Pa. Delaney received B.S. (1941), M.S. (1943), and Ph.D. (1958) degrees from Howard University (Washington, D.C.). He taught chemistry at North Carolina Agricultural and Technical State University from 1945 to 1948, and was professor and dean at Morgan State University (Baltimore, Md.) from 1948 to 1969. Delaney served as dean and acting chancellor of the State University of New York (1969–72), and then as associate provost (1972). He later became vice president of the University of North Carolina (1972–74) and then served as president of Manhattanville College (Purchase, N.Y.), beginning in 1974.

DELANY, MARTIN ROBISON (1812–1885), physician, abolitionist; born in Charlestown, Va. Delany's family moved to Chambersburg, Pa., soon after his birth. Later, as an active abolitionist, he lived in Pittsburgh, Pa., serving as an agent of the Underground Railroad. Delany became cofounder and coeditor of the newspaper *The North Star.* He was also an apprentice-trained physician, studying under the Pittsburgh doctors A. N. McDowell, J. P. Gazzan, and F. J. Lemoyne. Denied admission to several medical schools because of his color, Delany applied to and was accepted by Harvard Medical School for the 1850–51 term; however, he left Harvard before attaining his degree. He returned to Pittsburgh, where he distinguished himself as a physician during the cholera epidemic of 1854. As an active emancipationist, Delany attempted to set up a Negro state in Nicaragua, and he explored the Niger River Valley of Africa for the same purpose in 1859. During the Civil War, Delany was commissioned a regular major in the infantry, the first black to achieve that rank. He published *Principles of Ethnology* in 1879. *See also* COLONIZATION; PAN-AFRICANISM; SLAVERY: ABOLITIONISTS.

DELARGE, ROBERT CARLOS (1842–1874), state legislator, U.S. Representative; born in Aiken, S.C. After graduating from high school, DeLarge became a farmer. In 1868 he was a delegate to the South Carolina Constitutional Convention and in that same year was elected to the South Carolina house of representatives. In 1870 DeLarge was elected to the South Carolina State Land Commission, and in 1871 to the U.S. House of Representatives from South Carolina. Two years later, however, the Republicans contested his election, and his seat was declared vacant. DeLarge retired from the national political scene and lived his last year as a local magistrate in Charleston, S.C.

DELAWARE STATE COLLEGE Delaware State College, at Dover, Del., was founded in 1891 when the Delaware General Assembly passed "an Act to establish and maintain a College for the education of colored students in Agriculture and Mechanic Arts." The college is coeducational, and state-supported; it offers the bachelor's degree and provides liberal arts and teacher education curricula. Its 1975 enrollment was approximately 2,000.

The college was founded to instruct students in such vocational and industrial arts as agriculture and mechanics, as well as in the liberal arts and sciences. It was also intended that a normal school to prepare teachers would be connected with the college. It opened with 2 faculty members, 12 students, and 3 buildings. Although its early growth was slow, by 1960 the college had 386 students and 42 faculty members. More than

half of its graduates have become teachers. The school was fully integrated after 1971.

Ronald V. Dellums. *(Photo by Leroy Henderson.)*

DELLUMS, RONALD V. (1935–), U.S. Representative; born in Oakland, Calif. Dellums attended Oakland City College and received a B.A. degree from San Francisco State College in 1960. In 1962 he received a M.S.W. degree from the University of California at Berkeley. Dellums began his professional career in 1962 as a psychiatric social worker, and he continued in that field in various community and youth centers until 1970. That year he was elected to the U.S. House of Representatives from the 7th Congressional District of California.

DELTA A section (Yazoo Basin) of the state of Mississippi that extends more than 150 miles north from Vicksburg and eastward from the Mississippi River. The Delta has a large black population (50 percent or more). Greenville, a river port and cotton-growing center, was known as the "Queen City of the Delta" during the 1920s and 1930s. Black migrants leaving the Delta after World War I settled in large numbers in Chicago, Ill.

DENT, ALBERT WALTER (1904–), educator; born in Atlanta, Ga. Dent received a B.A. degree from Morehouse College (Atlanta, Ga.) in 1926. He taught at Dillard University (New Orleans, La.) in 1928, where he later became president. Dent also served as president of the National Health Council, vice-president of the United Negro College Fund, and director of the National Tuberculosis and Respiratory Disease Association. He was also a member of the board of directors of the National Merit Scholarships.

DENTISTS *See* NATIONAL DENTAL ASSOCIATION.

DEPRIEST, JAMES (1936–), musician, conductor; born in Philadelphia, Pa. DePriest received a B.S. degree (1958) and his M.A. degree (1961) from the University of Pennsylvania. He did further graduate study at the Philadelphia Conservatory of Music (1959–61). DePriest served as the director of music for WCAU-TV in Philadelphia (1965–66), as director of summer music programs in Westchester County, N.Y. (1965–66), and as a guest conductor in several foreign countries before becoming assistant conductor to Leonard Bernstein of the

Oscar DePriest
*(Library of
Congress.)*

New York Philharmonic. In 1972 he became the associate conductor of the National Symphony Orchestra, Washington, D.C.

DEPRIEST, OSCAR (1871–1951) U.S. Representative, business executive; born in Florence, Ala. The young DePriest moved to Kansas with his family in 1878 and then to Chicago, Ill., in 1889, where he became a real estate broker. After years of participating in the political life of Chicago as a member of the board of commissioners of Cook County and as a member of the city council, he was elected as a Republican to the U.S. House of Representatives in 1928. He held his congressional seat for three terms. In 1935 DePriest returned to his real estate business and further political involvements in Chicago, including the vice chairmanship of the Cook County Republican Central Committee and renewed membership on the city council.

DERBIGNY, IRVIN ANTHONY (1900– ?), educator. Derbigny received a B.A. degree from Talladega College (Talladega, Ala.); two M.A. degrees (one from Cornell University, Ithaca, N.Y., and one from the University of Minnesota); and his Ph.D. degree from Columbia University in 1932. He served as administrative dean at Tuskegee Institute (Tuskegee Institute, Ala.) beginning in 1936. Derbigny wrote *General Education in the Negro College* (1947).

DERHAM, JAMES C. (ca. 1762– ?), physician; born in Philadelphia, Pa. Derham's masters, all doctors, taught him how to handle patients and a knowledge of pharmacy and therapeutics. About 1783 his owner, Dr. Robert Dove, allowed him to buy his freedom, and Derham went to New Orleans, La., where he established a very successful practice, treating both black and white patients. Derham met Dr. Benjamin Rush in Philadelphia in 1788, and the two physicians discussed diseases and medicines. Afterward, Derham and Rush corresponded for many years on diseases, their treatments and new medicines. *See also* PHYSICIANS.

DESEGREGATION *See* CIVIL RIGHTS: MOVEMENT; EDUCATION: DESEGREGATION IN PERSPECTIVE; SEGREGATION.

DETT, ROBERT NATHANIEL (1882–1943), composer, arranger; born in Drummondville, Quebec, Canada. Dett was educated at the Oberlin Conservatory of Music (Oberlin, Ohio), Columbia University (New York, N.Y.), and the University of Pennsylvania (Philadelphia, Pa.). Dett combined a career in teaching with another as a composer. In these capacities he developed choral groups at Bennett College (Greensboro, N.C.), Hampton Institute (Hampton, Va.), Lane College (Jackson, Tenn.), and Lincoln Institute (Jefferson City, Mo.). His best-known compositions include "Oh Holy Land" and "Listen to the Lambs" for chorus; "The Magnolia Suite," "The Enchantment Suite," and "In the Bottoms" for piano; and the motet "Chariot Jubilee." Dett's oratorio, *The Ordering of Moses,* was widely performed in the 1940s. The first American composer to use Negro folk tunes for classical compositions, Dett also wrote and edited *The Dett Collection of Negro Spirituals* (1937). *See also* MUSIC: SPIRITUALS/PERFORMANCE, COLLECTIONS.

DIASPORA A Greek word used historically to refer to the dispersal of Jews throughout the Old World in successive periods after the Babylonian captivity, *diaspora* has been used by scholars and Pan-Africanists of the mid-twentieth century and afterward to refer principally to the dispersal of Africans in the New World during the Atlantic slave trade. *See also* AFRICA: THE ATLANTIC SLAVE TRADE IN PERSPECTIVE.

DIBBLE, EUGENE HERIOT (1893–1968), surgeon; Dibble attended Atlanta University and received his M.S. degree from Howard University Medical College (Washington, D.C.) in 1919. He served as medical director of J. A. Andrew Memorial Hospital and as chief of the surgical section of the U.S. Veterans Hospital, Tuskegee, Ala. Dibble was the 17th Distinguished Medalist of the National Medical Association.

DICKENS, HELEN OCTAVIA (1909–), physician, educator; born in Dayton, Ohio. Dickens received a B.M. degree (1932) and her M.D. degree (1934) from the University of Illinois College of Medicine, and she received a second B.M. degree from the University of Pennsylvania Graduate School of Medicine in 1945. Dickens served as director of the department of obstetrics and gynecology at Mercy-Douglass Hospital (1950–67), as chief of obstetrics and gynecology at Woman's Hospital, Philadelphia, Pa. (1956), and as associate dean and associate professor of obstetrics and gynecology at the University of Pennsylvania School of Medicine after 1970.

DICKERSON, EARL BURRUS (1891–), lawyer, business executive; born in Canton, Miss. Dickerson graduated from the University of Illinois in 1914, and received a J.D. degree from the University of Chicago in 1920 and his H.H.D. degree from Wilberforce University (Wilberforce, Ohio) in 1961. In 1921 he began an association with the Supreme Life Insurance Company of America that lasted more than 50 years. In addition to his duties at Supreme Life, he served as assistant corporation counsel of Chicago (1923–27), as assistant state attorney general (1933–39), as a member of the city council of Chicago (1939–43), and as a member of the President's Committee on Fair Employment Practices (1941–43). *See also* BUSINESS: INSURANCE.

DIGGS, CHARLES COLES, JR. (1922–), state legislator, U.S. Representative; born in Detroit, Mich. Diggs attended the University of Michigan (1940–42) and then went to Fisk University (Nashville, Tenn.) for a short while before he entered the U.S. Army. He eventually graduated from Wayne State University (Detroit, Mich.) in 1946 and later received his law degree from the Detroit College of Law. A licensed mortician, he was elected as a Democrat to the U.S. House of Representatives in 1954, maintaining his congressional seat through 12 succeeding terms.

DIGGS, ESTELLA B. (1916–), public official; born in St. Louis, Mo. Educated at the New York Institute of Dietetics, Pace College (New York, N.Y.), City College of the City University of New York, and New York University, Diggs became a teacher in the New York State Career Development program, a free-lance writer for the *Amsterdam News*, and a home economist in product promotion for food and baking companies. She then entered politics, and was elected to the state legislature as an assemblywoman from Bronx County in 1972.

DILLARD, OLIVER W. (1926–), Army officer; born in Margaret, Ala. Dillard graduated in 1959 from the University of Omaha (later the University of Nebraska at Omaha) and received a M.S. degree from George Washington University (Washington, D.C.) in 1965. However, his army career started before he earned his college degrees. In 1945 Dillard was inducted into the U.S. Army, and in 1947 he was commissioned a second lieutenant. After service in Europe, Africa, and the Far East, Dillard attained the rank of brigadier general in 1972.

DILLARD UNIVERSITY Dillard University, at New Orleans, La., originated indirectly in 1869. The school is private and independent, although it maintains strong ties with Congregational, Methodist, and other Protestant churches. It offers the bachelor's degree and provides liberal arts and teacher education curricula. The 1975 coeducational enrollment was about 1,000.

In 1869, both Straight University, later renamed Straight College, and the Union Normal School, later renamed New Orleans University, were founded. In 1930, these two institutions merged to form Dillard. Straight College had been founded by the American Missionary Association of the Congregational Church, and New Orleans University had been established by the Freedmen's Aid Society of the Methodist Episcopal (ME) Church. Dillard continued these relationships with the Congregational and Christian Churches and the United Methodist Church (as they are now known) and also continued its practice of making no distinction regarding religion, race, color, or sex so far as its students, faculty, and staff were concerned.

In 1935, Dillard University (named in honor of James Hardy Dillard, a white man who distinguished himself in the education of blacks in the South) began instruction. The educational quality of the institution is attested to by the fact that 65 percent of its alumni attend graduate schools and also by the many areas of education it pioneered. Dillard was the first college in Louisiana to offer a nationally accredited program in nursing, and among the first colleges in the nation to establish an intensive prefreshman program to help incoming freshmen improve their language skills. Dillard also originated the first undergraduate general education curriculum in the South.

Some of Dillard's outstanding alumni are Mack J. Spears, the first black president of the Orleans Parish (Louisiana) school board; Revius O. Ortique, Jr., former president of the National Bar Association; and Peter Marshall Murray, the first Afro-American to be elected to the American Medical Association's House of Delegates.

DISCIPLES OF CHRIST See CHRISTIAN CHURCH, DISCIPLES OF CHRIST, CHURCHES OF CHRIST.

DISCRIMINATION

Introduction The word *discrimination* has a very special albeit dark meaning in Afro-American life and history. The term itself probably derived from the Latin noun *discriminatus* and the Latin verb *discriminare,* which mean a cry out against an offense or wrongdoing that may not be clearly defined in law. Whatever the etymology of the word, for Afro-Americans the term has basically one meaning: the wrongdoing of white people against black people. Discrimination has come to denote unfair actions or practices of racial prejudice and of racism. Even when blacks admit that discrimination may indicate only private or individual preferences or choices, they have been conditioned to believe, and have usually found confirmation of that belief, that such preferences or choices may carry anti-black overtones in the complex spectrum of black-white relations.

Indeed, discrimination against blacks is an established truism in American history and life. Whether overt or covert, subtle or blatant, mild or rabid, discrimination against blacks has been an ever-present reality within the American social order. For blacks, this reality is invariably associated with oppression, racism, white supremacy, segregation, inequality, brutality, and racial hatred. In this sense, the struggle to overcome discrimination has persisted as the central theme of Afro-American history and life.

In 1944 Gunnar Myrdal gave clarity and scope to the nature of discrimination in his book entitled *An American Dilemma.* He held that whites discriminated against blacks in the following order: (1) intermarriage and sexual intercourse involving white women; (2) etiquette and personal relations; (3) use of public facilities; (4) political action (voting); (5) law courts and the police; and (6) earning a living. Of course, revolutionary changes have occurred since Myrdal's book first appeared. The civil rights movement, for example, brought an end to many discriminatory practices within the American social order. However, although the order of the discriminatory practices listed by Myrdal was hardly valid by the 1970s, discrimination remained.

Progress to End Discrimination under Civil Rights Laws and Policies Since World War II, the federal government and many interested citizens and groups have showed a growing concern for the rights of Afro-Americans and other minorities. The courts led the way, providing substantive civil rights meanings to the broad constitutional mandates of the equal protection clause of the Fourteenth Amendment and the due process clause of the Fifth Amendment. The executive branch followed the judicial lead through a series of executive orders that directed federal departments and agencies to ensure against discrimination in their own activities and in the practices of those with whom they associated. Congress was the last of the three branches of the federal government to act. Beginning in 1957, Congress enacted several civil rights laws, including such landmark acts as the Civil Rights Act of 1964, the Voting Rights Act of 1965, and the Civil Rights Act of 1968 (the federal fair housing law).

These laws, together with judicial decisions and executive orders, constitute a formidable array of civil rights guarantees. They provide broad protections against discrimination in virtually every aspect of Afro-American life: access to public accommodations, administration of justice, education, employment, housing, voting, and participation in federally assisted programs. Further, while some of the remedies require the aggrieved individual to take the initiative in securing his own rights, in most cases responsibility is also placed on federal departments and agencies to act affirmatively in support of the rights guaranteed against discrimination. However, many federal agencies, charged with enforcement of civil rights, did not, or could not, fulfill their responsibilities.

Public Accommodations One of the most dramatic examples of the weight a civil rights law can carry is seen in the field of public accommodations. Until the early 1960s, segregation of restaurants, motels, hotels, and theaters was the rule throughout the South and parts of the North. So rigid and inflexible was adherence to this rule that in cases where African diplomats, who traveled frequently between New York City and Washington, D.C., were denied service in restaurants along the route, even the urgent pleas of the U.S. Department of State could not induce a change in racially discriminatory policies. In 1964 Title II of the Civil Rights Act of 1964 was passed outlawing racial discrimination in most places of public accommodation. While the law has not brought a complete end to this kind of discrimination, thousands of hotels, motels, restaurants, and theaters have abandoned their discriminatory policies. A number of factors are responsible for this success. For example, the sit-ins of the early 1960s had brought about some change before Title II was enacted. Other private and public efforts to achieve voluntary desegregation of public accommodations before passage of the Civil Rights Act of 1964 helped to create a climate of opinion ready to accept desegregation. One other factor that undoubtedly contributed to the impact of this law was the quick action taken by the U.S. Department of Justice immediately after the law was passed. Within a few months after enactment, the Department of Justice brought several enforcement actions that tested the constitutionality of the public accommodations law. The law was upheld by the U.S. Supreme Court; it was made clear that equal access to places of public accommodation was, and would remain, the law of the land.

Voting The Voting Rights Act of 1965 has also resulted in historic, statistically measurable progress. Before its passage, registration of black citizens of voting age in the six southern states affected by the law was less than 31 percent. By the spring of 1969, approximately 57 percent of eligible blacks in those states were registered; black registration in the deep southern states increased by more than 740,000 persons. To be sure, the Voting Rights Act did not result in full use of the franchise. Means other than disqualification, such as the exploitation of continued economic dependence of rural Afro-Americans, still constitute deterrents to the exercise of the right to vote in the South. Nonetheless, impressive progress was made as a result of the Voting Rights Act of 1965.

Health Hospital and health facility practices reflect an outstanding example of salutary change resulting directly from civil rights laws. The combination of the existence of the Civil Rights Act of 1964, the introduction of a new federal program—Medicare—and a large-scale compliance effort by the Department of Health, Education, and Welfare (HEW) brought a swift and almost total end to discrimination and segregation as an official policy of hospitals.

The Medicare program was enacted in 1965. In 1966, HEW's Office of Equal Health Opportunity undertook a massive compliance effort, using a large staff of reviewers—sometimes as many as 500—to conduct thousands of visits to hospitals and other health facilities to determine whether the requirements of Title VI were being met. Anxious to obtain federal certification for participation in Medicare, many of these institutions abolished long-standing discriminatory practices in order to qualify for the substantial aid offered by the new program. No longer were black patients refused admission; no longer,

Far left: Protest to end discriminaton continued after passage of civil rights laws, as shown in this photo of Angela Davis addressing a rally in New York City. (*Photo by Leroy Henderson.*)

311

when admitted, were they segregated in wards, wings, and services. By January 1, 1968, HEW was able to report that 97 percent of the nation's hospitals were committed to nondiscrimination in the provision of services. More than 3,000 hospitals and other health facilities changed previous policies and practices to comply with Title VI.

Education In school desegregation as well, progress, however slow, resulted directly from the enactment of civil rights laws. Ten years after the famous decision in *Brown v. Board of Education of Topeka* (1954) that held that legally compelled school segregation was unconstitutional, only three percent of the black school children in the South were attending public schools with white children. By the 1968–69 school year, however, five years after enactment of the Civil Rights Act of 1964, more than 20 percent of the black school children attended desegregated schools in the region. Energetic use of the administrative mechanism of Title VI by HEW was the principal factor responsible for this significant acceleration of southern school desegregation.

Employment Equal opportunity in employment is mandated by a host of federal enactments—statutes, judicial decisions interpreting the Constitution, and executive orders and regulations. Taken together, they constitute a comprehensive ban on job discrimination, covering all federal, state, and local jobs and nearly all private employment. Almost any act of discrimination by a government or private employer violates some aspect of federal law. The remedies available to eradicate such discrimination, however, vary widely in their scope and efficacy.

The most complete federal policy of equal job opportunity is that dealing with federal employment. Every federal department and agency is required to take necessary steps to assure that the goals of executive orders are achieved. For example, each agency is required to provide sufficient resources to carry out its equal employment opportunity program, to ensure that recruitment methods reach all sources of job candidates, to utilize fully the skills of employees, and to provide maximum opportunity for employees to develop their abilities and to advance accordingly.

The Civil Service Commission is the agency chiefly responsible for implementing the order. The commission is directed to provide leadership and guidance to other executive depart-

Far right: Once barred from even applying for certain employment, Afro-American workers were later protected from job discrimination by a complex, often baffling maze of regulations and laws. (National Archives.)

ments and agencies in the conduct of equal employment opportunity programs. It is also directed to review and evaluate agency performance and report to the president, and to assure fair consideration of complaints of discrimination including impartial review within the various agencies.

In a very general sense, it may be said that federal law is as comprehensive in prohibiting discrimination in state and local government employment as it is in barring discrimination in federal jobs, for the courts have held that discrimination by state and local governments—including job discrimination—violates the fourteenth amendment. But in actuality, protection against discrimination by state and local governments is not nearly as complete, because—with certain exceptions—there is no federal administrative machinery to assist the victim of discrimination. In most cases, a private lawsuit is the only means such a victim has to secure his constitutional right.

The exceptions pertain to certain areas where Congress and the executive branch have acted to provide an administrative remedy because the federal and state governments participate jointly in furnishing the government service. For example, an administrative remedy is provided by the Federal Merit Standards System, which applies to a variety of federally funded programs and covers approximately 250,000 state employees.

Originally promulgated under a 1939 amendment to the Social Security Act of 1935, the merit standards require that state employees administering these programs be selected, promoted, and compensated according to a federally approved, state-administered merit system. Among the specific criteria established in the 1939 standards was a prohibition against discrimination on the basis of religious and political affiliation. In 1963 the prohibition was extended to include race and national origin, and state regulations were required to provide an appeal procedure in cases of alleged discrimination.

The major programs covered by the merit standards provision are: aid to families with dependent children, old age assistance, other federally aided public assistance programs, and certain state health programs financed by HEW; state employment services and unemployment insurance systems, which are funded by the U.S. Department of Labor; and civil defense activities supported by the U.S. Department of Defense (DOD).

Each federal agency authorized to grant financial assistance has the final responsibility for assuring the implementation of approved state plans for program operation. For administrative convenience, however, supervision of the implementation of all aspects of merit standards, including the nondiscrimination clause, rests with the Office of State Merit Systems in HEW.

In addition to protection against state employment discrimination provided by the Federal Merit Standards System, such discrimination is also prohibited by contractual requirements of the U.S. Department of Housing and Urban Development (HUD) in two important programs it administers—urban renewal and public housing. Under these requirements, nearly 900 local urban renewal agencies and 2,000 local public housing authorities, which are state agencies, are required to be equal opportunity employers.

Title VI of the Civil Rights Act of 1964, which prohibits discrimination in programs and activities receiving federal financial assistance, also forbids employment discrimination by states or localities in programs and activities where a primary purpose of the assistance is to provide employment. These include apprenticeship training, work-study, or economic development programs. Under Title VI, discriminatory employment practices also are prohibited if they tend to result in discriminatory or unequal treatment for such intended beneficiaries of the program or activity as teachers in a federally aided school system, doctors or nurses in a federally aided hospital, or agricultural extension workers.

Since World War II, presidents have used the federal contracting power to require nondiscrimination in employment by government contractors. Executive Order No. 11246, issued in 1965, prohibits employment discrimination by government contractors or federally assisted construction contractors, and requires them to take affirmative action to remedy the effects of past discrimination. In addition, banks that are depositories of federal funds or that handle federal savings bonds are subject to the same mandate.

The Office of Federal Contract Compliance (OFCC) in the Department of Labor is responsible for establishing overall policy and for overseeing the entire program of equal employment opportunity by federal contractors. Primary responsibility for securing compliance in specific industries, however, rests with several federal agencies called "predominant interest agencies." Sanctions available to these agencies and to the OFCC under the executive order include cancellation of contracts, debarment of contractors from future federal contracts, and public identification of noncomplying contractors.

Title VII of the Civil Rights Act of 1964 prohibits employment discrimination by all employers with 25 or more employees, labor unions that have 25 or more members or that operate a hiring hall, and employment agencies that regularly obtain employees for an employer covered by the title.

It also created the Equal Employment Opportunity Commission (EEOC) with responsibility to administer the title and conciliate and negotiate differences between aggrieved individuals and the accused parties. The EEOC also may make studies, provide technical assistance, and carry on other activities designed to stimulate employers, unions, and employment agencies to develop effective equal employment opportunity policies. The EEOC is granted no power to require a discriminatory party to cease engaging in prohibited activities. Lawsuits, however, may be brought by private parties or by the Department of Justice.

Section 1 of the Civil Rights Act of 1866 provides that all persons shall have the same right to make and enforce contracts as white citizens of the United States. A 1968 Supreme Court decision indicated that a similar provision of the 1866 law prohibits racial discrimination in housing. Similarly, lower court decisions have ruled that this law prohibits employment discrimination. Thus, despite limitations in coverage of other equal employment opportunity provisions, any individual who believes he has been discriminated against in employment because of his race may bring federal suit for relief under the Civil Rights Act of 1866.

The National Labor Relations Act (NLRA) and related laws regulate the conduct of employers and unions. Although not specifically designed to provide relief for employment discrimination, the NLRA has a significant impact on the federal effort to end such discrimination. The act creates an obligation on the part of all unions representing employees under the act to do so fairly, impartially, and without discrimination. A union failing to comply with this obligation would be in violation of its duty of fair representation. In addition, a union's discriminatory membership policy constitutes an unfair labor practice under the act. With respect to employers, a U.S. Court of Appeals opinion in 1969 indicated that discrimination by an employer in his employment practices can constitute an unfair labor practice.

Persons who have been subjected to discrimination covered by the act may file a complaint with the National Labor Relations Board. The board is empowered, after a finding of discrimination, to issue a cease and desist order against an employer or union, to revoke or deny certification or exclusive representation status of a union, or to refuse to require an employer to bargain with an offending union.

Housing Like employment, equal opportunity in housing is a broadly protected federal right. Almost all housing, federally assisted or not, must be made available without discrimination.

Executive Order No. 11063, issued in November 1962, constituted the first significant federal requirement on nondiscrimination in housing. Discrimination is prohibited in the sale or leasing of all federally assisted housing provided after the order's issuance, including housing owned by the government, housing purchased in whole or in part with government loans (such as low-rent public housing), housing provided through loans insured or guaranteed by the government (such as Federal Housing Administration and Veterans Administration housing), and housing provided through slum clearance or urban renewal programs. The prohibition also extends to lending practices insofar as those practices relate to loans insured or guaranteed by the federal government. Finally, the order directs all executive departments and agencies with functions relating to housing to "take all action necessary and appropriate to prevent discrimination because of race, color, creed, or national origin. . . ."

The order provides for the following remedies to be applied in cases where discrimination is found and conciliation and persuasion fail to bring about compliance: cancellation or termination of agreements or contracts with offenders; refusal to extend further aid under any program to offenders; refusal to approve a lending institution as a beneficiary under any program that is affected by the order; and revocation of such approval if previously granted.

Title VI of the Civil Rights Act of 1964 covers all federally assisted housing except those instances in which the assistance provided is solely in the form of contracts of insurance or guaranty. (Although this exclusion exempts FHA home mortgage insurance and VA home loan guaranty programs, they are covered by Executive Order No. 11063.) Title VI does apply to such varied housing programs as urban renewal, housing rehabilitation, relocation grants, low-rent public housing, and code enforcement programs. Remedies under Title VI include suspension or termination of federal financial assistance, or refusal to grant or to continue such assistance. In addition, HUD may refer noncompliance matters to the Department of Justice for litigation.

The Civil Rights Act of 1968 The federal fair housing law covers not only federal assisted housing, but most private housing as well. The only significant exceptions from coverage are rental housing with fewer than five units, one of which is owner-occupied, and single family houses owned by a private individual and sold without the use of a real estate broker. It is estimated that 80 percent of all housing is covered by Title VIII. In addition to prohibiting discrimination in the sale or rental of housing, Title VIII requires all federal departments and agencies with functions relating to housing to administer their programs and activities affirmatively to further the purposes of fair housing.

Although the coverage of Title VIII is much broader than that of the executive order or Title

VI, the remedies are not nearly so strong. Compliance with Title VIII can be brought about through administrative conciliation by HUD, through action by a state or local enforcement agency, through private litigation, or, in the case of patterns or practices of discrimination, through lawsuits brought by the U.S. attorney general. Administrative enforcement is not available under Title VIII.

A provision of the Civil Rights Act of 1866, which grants to black citizens the same rights as white citizens to rent or to purchase property, was construed by the Supreme Court in 1968 in *Jones v. Mayer and Co.* to prohibit racial discrimination in all housing, private as well as public. The means of enforcement, however, appear to be limited to privately instituted litigation.

In addition to HUD, there are a number of other federal departments and agencies with direct responsibility to ensure that minority group citizens are not deprived of their right to equal housing opportunity. These include: the Department of Justice, which has authority under Title VIII to institute lawsuits to eliminate patterns or practices of discrimination; agencies that supervise mortgage lending institutions; the General Services Administration (GSA), the federal government's real estate agent that is responsible for ensuring that housing problems of low-income and minority group employees are taken into consideration when sites for federal installations are selected; the Department of Defense, which has the obligation of ensuring that its minority group servicemen are able to secure adequate, nonsegregated off-base housing; and the Veterans Administration, which administers a major program of housing loans.

Persistence of Discrimination Despite the progress made possible by civil rights laws and policies, substantial evidence exists that discrimination still persists in many areas. Generally, civil rights laws have been most successful in dealing with practices that do not require complex institutional change. Thus, desegregation of public facilities, places of public accommodation, and hospitals and other health facilities required basic but simple changes in conduct that were accomplished without either violent opposition or massive federal enforcement efforts.

In the area of voting, progress may be attributed primarily to the fact that the federal government—by suspending literacy tests and authorizing the appointment of federal examiners to register citizens—intervened more directly to protect the rights of individuals in this context than it has in other civil rights areas.

In fields where complicated institutional change is required and the federal government has not intervened so directly, progress has come slowly and, in some cases, at a pace that can barely be discerned. As the following seven examples suggest, equal opportunity still is far from a way of American life.

(1) In the area of federal employment, where the degree of federal control is absolute, minority group representation has increased substantially but black and Spanish surnamed Americans are still grossly underrepresented in the higher salary brackets. According to a survey of minority group employment in the federal government as of 1969, by the U.S. Civil Service Commission, less than 2 percent of General Schedule (GS) grade-13 and above of classified workers were black. The employment record of some individual agencies is even worse. For example, the Federal Aviation Administration, an agency of the Department of Transportation, employed more than 20,000 air traffic controllers as of June 30, 1969. Of these, only 547 were minority employees. Moreover, only 13 minority group employees existed among the 1,600 supervisory and administrative personnel at GS grade-14 or above.

(2) Despite nondiscrimination requirements in the merit system applicable to federally aided state programs, minority group employment often remains low. For example, the Mississippi Welfare Department had only 38 blacks on its staff of more than 1,500 in 1967. Data for 1968 indicated that only 5.3 percent of the employees of the Louisiana State Employment Security Agencies were black. In both these states, most minority group employees were in nonprofessional positions.

When the state of Alabama refused to amend its standards for the Merit System of Personnel Administration to include a nondiscrimination clause, the Department of Justice filed suit against the state. Evidence introduced at the trial indicated that in 1968 the six state agencies involved in the merit system had one black among 988 clerical employees and 26 blacks on their staffs of 2,019 professional, technical, and supervisory employees. Of the 70 custodial, labor, and laboratory helper positions, however, 67 were occupied by blacks.

(3) Despite the fact that equal employment

opportunity requirements have been imposed on government contractors since the 1940s and that since 1964 Title VII has extended that requirement to most other employers, evidence gathered by the U.S. Commission on Civil Rights indicates that employment discrimination in the private sector is still prevalent throughout the United States.

At an April 1966 hearing of the U.S. Commission on Civil Rights in Cleveland, Ohio, for example, testimony showed that there were 139 federal contractors with facilities in Cleveland with 50 or more employees. These firms had a total work force of more than 93,000 employees. Although blacks constituted 34 percent of Cleveland's population, 21 of the firms employed none at all and 86 employed less than 10 percent in their work forces.

(4) In a 1968 hearing in Montgomery, Ala., the U.S. Commission on Civil Rights examined employment opportunities in a 16-county area in that state and found that, while 62 percent of the area's population was black, companies filing employment data with EEOC in 1967 reported that only 22 percent of their employees were black. More significantly, Afro-Americans were hired almost exclusively for the more menial jobs. They held 63 percent of unskilled positions compared with 8 percent of the white-collar and skilled jobs. The hearing revealed that the Dan River Mills textile plant, a federal contractor in Greenville, Ala., had only three black employees out of a total of 200 and that the American Can Company, also a federal contractor, owned a segregated company town, complete with segregated schools and homes.

(5) In June 1969, statements received at an open meeting of the Commission's Massachusetts State Advisory Committee in Boston showed that of approximately 1,000 building trades apprentices in the Boston area only 58 were black, and that the skilled building trades in the Boston area had a total journeyman nonwhite membership of 1.4 percent out of a total of 11,120 members. But 6 percent of the population of the Boston metropolitan area is black.

(6) The denial of equal opportunity in housing also remained a severe and persistent problem. In 1959, before adoption of any federal fair housing laws or policies, it was estimated that less than 2 percent of the new houses provided through FHA mortgage insurance since 1946 had been available to minorities. In 1967, nearly 5 years after issuance of Executive Order No.

11063, the situation had not improved appreciably. A 1967 national FHA survey of minority group occupancy in subdivisions built after the date of the executive order, and subject to its provisions, found that of the more than 400,000 units surveyed, only 3.3 percent were reported as having been sold to black families.

In a detailed, 3-year study completed in 1977, the American Bar Association (ABA) reported that post-World War II urban growth in the United States has been accompanied by "serious racial and economic polarizaton." The study concluded that exclusionary zoning and other local governmental action "have prevented access to decent housing and have reinforced and aggravated patterns of racial and economic segregation." Furthermore, "courts and legislatures have done far too little to prevent this governmental abuse of power."

The ABA study predicted that without basic changes in the future direction of urban development, planning, and housing programs, "greater numbers of Americans will be denied housing choice, our cities will continue to decline, and racial and economic segregation will be perpetuated." The study challenged local governmental bodies to assume the "affirmative legal duty to. . . (1) plan for present and prospective housing in a regional context; (2) eliminate those local regulatory barriers that make it difficult to provide housing for persons of low and moderate incomes; and (3) offer regulatory concessions and incentives to the private sector in this regard."

(7) Discrimination has also persisted in the operation of Department of Agriculture programs. For example, the Agricultural Stabilization and Conservation Service, which administers programs to stabilize farm income through price support payments and crop allotments, runs its program through a system of locally elected farmer committees. In addition to administering the programs, committees serve as an informational link to farmers who participate in and receive the benefits of the programs. Prior to 1968, no black farmer had ever been elected to any committee at the county level in the South. Even in 1970, although the 1964 Census of Agriculture indicated that blacks comprised a majority of the farm operator population in 58 counties in the South, only two blacks were among the more than 4,100 such committeemen in the region.

These seven types of persistent discrimination

do not purport to be exhaustive. Rather, they represent some of the instances of continuing discrimination and inequity that have come to the attention of the U.S. Commission on Civil Rights in the normal course of its work. They indicate, however, a national pattern of continuing abridgement of the rights of Afro-Americans.

They also demonstrate that while progress has been made in eliminating discriminatory practices, many of the problems that existed before civil rights laws were passed, before various executive orders were issued, and before key court decisions were rendered, continue to exist. The adoption of these civil rights laws and policies has given hope to black citizens that they would be freed from the second-class status to which they had been relegated for generations and could assume the role of equal members of American society. Their expectations of equal status have been reasonable, but in many cases they have been frustrated.

It is clear that the full potential of civil rights laws and policies has not been realized. The promise of equal protection of the law for all citizens has not yet been redeemed.

See also CIVIL RIGHTS: CIVIL RIGHTS ACTS; CIVIL RIGHTS: CIVIL RIGHTS CASES, 1865–1975; CIVIL RIGHTS: CIVIL RIGHTS ENFORCEMENT; EDUCATION; EMPLOYMENT; HOUSING; LABOR UNIONS; NATIONAL ASSOCIATION FOR THE ADVANCEMENT OF COLORED PEOPLE (NAACP); POLITICS; RACE: RACISM; SEGREGATION.

REFERENCES: Banks, W. S. M., II, "The Rank Order of Sensitivity to Discrimination of Negroes in Columbus, Ohio," American Sociological Review, August 1950, pp. 529–34; Becker, Gary S., The Economics of Discrimination, University of Chicago Press, Chicago, 1957; Bell, Carolyn Shaw, The Economics of the Ghetto, Pegasus, New York, 1972; Bloch, Herman D., The Circle of Discrimination: An Economic and Social Study of the Black Man in New York, New York University Press, New York, 1969; Clark, Kenneth B., "Desegregation: An Appraisal of the Evidence," Journal of Social Issues, October 1953, pp. 2–76; Countryman, Vern (ed.), Discrimination and the Law, University of Chicago Press, Chicago, 1965; Duncan, Otis Dudley, "Discrimination Against Negroes," Annals of the American Academy of Political and Social Science, May 1967, pp. 85–103; Hill, Herbert, "Racial Inequality in Employment," Annals of the American Academy of Political and Social Science, January 1965, pp. 30–47; Myrdal, Gunnar, An American Dilemma, Harper Brothers, New York, 1944; Pettigrew, Thomas F., "Complexity and Change in American Racial Patterns: A Social Psychological View," Daedalus, Fall 1965, pp. 974–1008; Rose, Arnold M. and Caroline Rose (eds.), The Minority Problem: A Book of Readings, Harper and Row, New York, 1965; Ross, Arthur M. and Herbert Hill (eds.), Employment, Race and Poverty, Harcourt, Brace & World, New York, 1967; Taeuber, Karl E., "Residential Segregation," Scientific American, August 1965, pp. 12–19; U.S. Commission on Civil Rights, Federal Civil Rights Enforcement Effort, U.S. Government Printing Office, Washington, D.C., 1971; U.S. Commission on Civil Rights, Racial Isolation in the Public Schools, U.S. Government Printing Office, Washington, D.C., 1967; Weaver, Robert C., Dilemmas of Urban America, Harvard University Press, Cambridge, 1965; and Woodward, C. Vann, The Strange Career of Jim Crow, Oxford University Press, New York, 1966. For other references, see Constance E. Obudho, Black-White Attitudes: An Annotated Bibliography, Greenwood Press, Westport, 1976.

DISFRANCHISEMENT See CIVIL RIGHTS: ACTS; CIVIL RIGHTS: CASES.

DISTRICT OF COLUMBIA TEACHERS COLLEGE District of Columbia Teachers College, at Washington, D.C., originated indirectly in 1851. The coeducational college is city-supported and controlled, offers the bachelor's degree, and provides a teacher education curriculum. The 1975 enrollment was about 3,175.

The college was formed by a merger of Miner Teachers College and Wilson Teachers College in 1955. Miner Teachers College was founded in 1851 as the Normal School for Colored Girls in the City of Washington by Myrtilla Miner, a native of New York City and one-time teacher of planters' daughters in Mississippi. In 1879 the school became part of the public school system of the District of Columbia and was renamed Washington Normal School No. 2. Wilson Teachers College was established in 1873 as the Washington Normal School. Its name was changed to James Ormond Wilson Normal School in 1913 in honor of the superintendent of schools when it was founded. Both normal schools became four-year teachers colleges in 1929.

The District of Columbia Teachers College came under the authority of the board of higher education in 1969, after nearly one hundred years as part of the public school system of the District of Columbia. It is fully accredited by the Middle States Association of Colleges and Secondary Schools.

DITON, CARL ROSSINI (1886–1969), composer, pianist, educator; born in Philadelphia, Pa. Diton graduated from the University of Pennsylvania (Philadelphia, Pa.) in 1909, and then studied in Germany. He combined a successful career as a concert pianist with one in teaching, at first in colleges (Paine College, Augusta, Ga.; Talladega College, Talladega, Ala.) and then in his own studio in New York, N.Y. Diton was the first black pianist to make a transcontinental tour. He wrote compositions for mixed choruses, vocal solos, and organ, mostly based on spirituals. The best known are *Four Spirituals* (1914) and *The Hymn of Nebraska* (an oratorio, 1921).

DIUGUID, WILLIAM SHERWOOD (1910–   ), lawyer, judge; born in Lynchburg, Va. Diuguid received a B.A. degree from West Virginia State College in 1934 and graduated from Howard University School of Law (Washington, D.C.) in 1937. Admitted to the Virginia bar in 1937, he practiced law in Lynchburg (1939–46). Then, in 1946, after admission to the Missouri bar, Diuguid became a member of a firm along with Myron Bush in St. Louis, Mo. He served as assistant attorney general of the state of Missouri (1953), as a provisional judge in St. Louis (1952–54), and as a magistrate (1954–62).

DIXON, DEAN (1915–1976), conductor; born in New York, N.Y. Dixon was the first black to achieve fame as a symphonic conductor. He was educated at the Juilliard School of Music, receiving his Mus.B. degree in 1936, and at Columbia University (New York, N.Y.), from which he gained his M.A. degree three years later. In 1941 Dixon was invited to conduct the NBC Symphony Orchestra in two concerts, and the same year he became the first black to conduct the New York Philharmonic. In order to make a career as a conductor, Dixon moved to Europe, where he

Mattiwilda Dobbs
(Moorland-Springarn Research Center.)

Dean Dixon rehearses the American Youth Orchestra. *(Photoworld.)*

became the conductor of the Göteborg Symphony in Göteborg, Sweden, serving in that post from 1949 to 1960. In the latter year, he was appointed conductor of the Hessian Radio Symphony in Frankfort, Germany, and thereafter he frequently conducted at the Frankfort Opera and with major orchestras throughout Europe.

DIXON, RUSSELL A. (1898–   ), dentist; born in Kansas City, Mo. Dixon received a D.D.S. degree (1929) and his M.D.S. degree (1933) from the College of Dentistry, Northwestern University (Evanston, Ill.). He served as dean of the College of Dentistry, Howard University (Washington, D.C.) and was the first black named to the Veterans Administration Special Medical Advisory Group. Dixon served as president of the National Dental Association and was the recipient of the Dentist of the Year Award from the Washington, D.C., Dental Society.

DOBBS, MATTIWILDA (1925–   ), coloratura soprano; born in Atlanta, Ga. Dobbs graduated from Spelman College (Atlanta, Ga.) in 1946, and then studied at Columbia University (New York, N.Y.) and for two years in Paris, France. Although a career in opera was almost an impossibility in the United States, Dobbs sang in all the major European opera houses. She was the first Afro-American to sing a principal role at La Scala, Milan, Italy. Dobbs, who made her New York City debut at Town Hall in 1954, sang for many years in Sweden.

DOBY, LARRY   See ATHLETES: BASEBALL.

DODSON, OWEN (1914–   ), poet, playwright; born in Brooklyn, N.Y. Dodson received a B.A. degree from Bates College (Lewiston, Maine) in 1936 and his M.F.A. degree from Yale University in 1939. He taught at Atlanta University, Hampton Institute (Hampton, Va.) and Howard University (Washington, D.C.), at which latter institution he was professor of drama from 1936 to 1939. Dodson received a Rosenwald Fellowship, and a Guggenheim Fellowship in 1953. One of the first serious black dramatists, Dodson wrote many poems and plays, including *Divine Comedy* (1938) and *Garden of Time*, both of which were produced at Yale University and by many smaller theater groups. His short story, "The Summer Five," won an award from the Paris Review and is anthologized in *Best Short Stories of the Paris Review* (1961). His books include a novel, *Boy at the Window* (1951), and a collection of poems, *Powerful Long Ladder* (1970).

DOGAN, MATTHEW WINIFRED (1863–1947), educator; born in Pontotoc, Miss. Dogan received a B.A. degree (1884) and a M.A. degree from Rust College (Holly Springs, Miss.). He was an instructor of mathematics at Central Tennessee College (1889–96), and he served as president of Wiley College (Marshall, Tex.) for forty-six years (1896–1942). Dogan founded and organized the Intercollegiate Athletic and Oratorical Association among the black colleges in Texas. He also founded the Southern Athletic Conference.

DOMINO, ANTOINE, JR. (FATS) (1928–   ), pianist, bandleader, composer; born in New Orleans, La. Domino began working with bands at the age of 19, some time after hurting his hand while working in a bedspring factory. Later, he appeared in nightclubs and films. His best-known songs include "Poor Me," "I'm Walkin'," and "Ain't That a Shame." *See also* MUSIC: HISTORY AND DEVELOPMENT.

DOUGLAS, AARON (1899–   ), painter, illustrator; born in Topeka, Kans. Douglas received a B.A. degree from the University of Kansas in 1923 and a M.F.A. degree from Columbia University Teachers College (New York, N.Y.). In 1928 and in 1929, he studied in Paris on a Barnes Foundation grant, and also received Rosenwald grants in 1931 and 1938. Douglas illustrated books by Countee Cullen, Langston Hughes, and James Weldon Johnson; and his work also appeared in contemporary magazines: *Vanity Fair, Theatre Arts,* and *American Mercury.* Douglas was among the first to apply the qualities of African sculpture to painting, and those qualities—flat angularities and abrupt changes of line and mass—appear most dramatically in his murals on Afro-American themes. His murals were in the Club Ebony (Harlem), the Hotel Sherman (Chicago, Ill.), and Fisk University (Nashville, Tenn.). *See also* ARTISTS.

DOUGLASS, FREDERICK

*FREDERICK   DOUGLASS: CHALLENGE   AND   RESPONSE

by Benjamin Quarles

(Courtesy of James A. Holley, Public Relations, Morgan State University.)

I have always found it stimulating to turn my attention to Frederick Douglass and it is especially gratifying to do so in this particular city and under such happy auspices. Born in Maryland, Frederick Douglass spent eight years of his young manhood in Baltimore and was a frequent visitor to the city after the Civil War. On the

Morgan campus stands a striking eight-foot bronze sculpture of Frederick Douglass, a proud addition to the public statuary of a historic metropolis which likes to call itself "the monumental city," a statue which is the work of James E. Lewis, chairman of the art department at this college. . . .

This very day marks the sesquicentennial of his [Douglass'] birth and three hours from now a new twenty-five cent Frederick Douglass stamp of general issue will be unveiled by the Post Office in Washington, D.C., where within the past five years a bridge has been named after Douglass and where his Anacostia Heights home has been taken over as a national shrine by the United States Department of the Interior. . . .

For in the career of this son of the Eastern

*Title of an address delivered in 1967 by the distinguished historian and scholar, Benjamin Quarles, at Morgan State College (now Morgan State University), Baltimore, Md., on the occasion of the 150th anniversary of the birth of Frederick Douglass, abolitionist and editor, (ca. 1817–1895), who was born in Tuckahoe, Maryland. Except for a few minor omissions permitted by the author, the address is reproduced here in its entirety. The statue of Douglass by James Lewis, erected in 1956 and mentioned at the beginning of the address, can be seen in the illustration on the right.

Shore the usable past comes into its own. His words have a contemporary ring and his outlook is scarcely less instructive for our day than for his . . .

A figure of heroic proportions, one who contributed notably to making American democracy a viable force, Douglass was destined to cast a

The escape of Douglass from slavery in 1837 was romanticized in this song and lithograph of 1845. *(Library of Congress.)*

long shadow. "Were ever so many miracles crowded into a single life?" asked a contemporary. The day and year of his birth are uncertain, for he was born a slave. But when he died five state legislatures adopted resolutions of regret, and at his last rites, held in Washington on a winter afternoon in 1895, two United States Senators and a Supreme Court Justice were numbered among the honorary pall bearers. A *Washington Post* editorial stated that he "died in an epoch which he did more than any other to create."

Douglass indeed did symbolize many characteristic American traits, perhaps most obviously the driving force to pull oneself up by his bootstraps. After twenty years in slavery he fled to New Bedford, Massachusetts, where for three years he lived a hand-to-mouth existence. Things took a turn for the better in 1841 when he became an abolitionist lecturer, following the accidental discovery of a fluent tongue and a talent for the public platform.

His subsequent career reflected the central issues of his times. In 1847 at Rochester, New York, he became editor of an anti-slavery weekly which he published for sixteen years. In 1848 he

took a prominent part in the Seneca Falls Convention in New York which formally inaugurated the woman's rights movement in the United States. During the Civil War he recruited troops for the Union Army, and he urged the Lincoln administration to strike forcefully against slavery. After the war he worked for a Reconstruction policy that would guarantee the right to vote without respect to race. Beginning in 1877 he received high federal appointments from three successive presidents, becoming in turn Marshal of the District of Columbia, Recorder of Deeds for the District, and United States Minister to the Republic of Haiti.

What is it that makes Douglass a figure worthy of our attention? Let four of his well-known contemporaries suggest an answer. Frederick Law Olmsted, who traveled extensively in the slave states, wrote of Douglass in 1854: "All the statesmanship and kind mastership of the South has done less, in fifty years, to elevate and dignify the African race, than he in ten." Another contemporary opinion of Douglass was expressed by Mark Twain in a letter to President-elect James A. Garfield on January 12, 1881, urging him to reappoint Douglass as Marshal of the District: "I offer this position with peculiar pleasure and strong desire," wrote Twain, "because I honor this man's high and blemishless character and so admire his brave, long crusade for the liberties and elevation of his race."

Writing ten years earlier Senator (and later Vice President) Henry Wilson struck an even broader note: "The main interest and importance of Mr. Douglass' career are public, rather than personal. Full of thrilling adventure, striking contrasts, brilliant passages, and undoubted usefulness, as his history was, his providential relations to some of the most marked facts and features of American history constitute the chief elements of that interest and importance which by common consent belong to it." This more rounded view of Douglass was expressed by Governor Theodore Roosevelt when he went to Rochester on June 10, 1899, to speak at the unveiling of a monument to Douglass: "I am proud to be able to do my part in paying respect to a man who was a worthy representative of his race because he was a worthy representative of the American nation. . . ."

To say that Douglass' career was strewn with obstacles is to put him in the general class of achievers. The odds against Douglass, however, were especially great and they stand in stark contrast to the unusual kind of man he became—

well-rounded, high principled, and of a spacious outlook. Hence, the distinctive, indeed peculiar, nature of his up-stream career would seem to warrant our appraisal. What circumstances enabled Frederick Douglass to emerge from the shadows?

If anyone were entitled to be called a self-made man, surely it was Douglass. But even in his case there were outward circumstances that cannot be ignored. To begin with, Douglass came to manhood in a day when reformist movements were in forment. The quarter of a century preceding the Civil War was characterized by crusades, among them woman's rights, temperance, world peace, universal education, and prison improvement. Foremost of these reforms in shaping this country's destiny was the abolitionist crusade—the movement to wipe out slavery. Hence when Frederick Douglass joined the abolitionists in 1841, the times were favorable for a man of his antecedents and his talents. The anti-slavery platform was a school for the training of orators, and Douglass did not take long to become "a cataract that roared."

If the times operated to the advantage of Douglass, so did the locale—the particular places he lived. True he was born a slave, but at the age of eight he was sent to Baltimore. City slavery was less oppressive than plantation slavery, the former offering far more "elbow room." "A city slave," wrote Douglass, "is almost a freeman, compared with a slave on the plantation." "Going to live in Baltimore laid the foundation, and opened the gateway, to all my subsequent prosperity."

His first ten years in freedom Douglass spent in Massachusetts. At New Bedford, his first place of residence, he soon learned of an abolition society made up of Negroes. He joined their ranks, leaving only to become a full-time agent of the Massachusetts Anti-Slavery Society. Here he met William Lloyd Garrison, Wendell Phillips and their fellow reformers. These dedicated men and women gave Douglass a helping hand. "To these friends, earnest, courageous, inflexible, ready to own me as a man and brother, against all the scorn, contempt, and derision of a slavery-polluted atmosphere, I owe my success in life," he wrote in later years. And, as Douglass himself noted, his early befrienders numbered many Negroes. The first two of these were David Ruggles, secretary of the New York Vigilance Committee, with whom he spent his first two weeks in freedom, and Nathan Johnson of New Bedford, who provided a roof for the young run-

away and his bride, and bestowed upon him the surname Douglass.

After nearly ten years in Massachusetts, Douglass in 1847 moved to Rochester where he was to spend the next twenty five years. Again during the shaping years of his life, he was fortunate in his place of residence. Douglass never regretted coming to Rochester. "I know of no place in the Union," he wrote in 1882, "where I could have located at the time with less resistance, or received a larger measure of sympathy and cooperation, and I now look back to my life and labors there with unalloyed satisfaction."

A final outward circumstance contributing to the rise of Douglass was his personal appearance. His looks helped him. He was well-proportioned, being tall and broad-shouldered. A newspaper editor, N. P. Rogers, described Douglass as he looked in 1841—the year in which he became an abolitionist lecturer. "A commanding person—over six feet, we should say, in height, and of most manly proportions. His head would strike a phrenologist amid a sea of them, and his voice would ring like a trumpet in the field. Let the South congratulate itself that he is a fugitive. It would not have been safe for her if he had remained about the plantations a year or two longer."

Like Rogers, James Russell Lowell, who saw the youthful Douglass frequently, was impressed by what he saw: "The very look and bearing of Douglass are eloquent," wrote Lowell in 1844, "and are full of an irresistible logic against the oppression of his race." Even after the first flush of youth, Douglass retained his power to make a lasting impression on people seeing him for the first time. . . .

His arresting appearance and the times in which he lived by no means account for the full measure of Douglass' accomplishments. Paul Lawrence Dunbar did not have Douglass in mind when he said that some men are born great, some men achieve greatness, and some men lived during Reconstruction times. Fame did not come to Douglass unearned. "Greatness was inherent in his being, and circumstances simply evoked it," wrote William H. Crogman, a late nineteenth-century Negro college president.

His own qualities of mind enabled Douglass to move inexorably toward his goals. At the base of these mental qualities was a thirst for knowledge. The first great ambition of the young Douglass was to master the printed page. As a slave boy of 12 years old in Baltimore, he took the first pennies he ever owned and bought a popular book of orations. He then bribed white boys on the docks to teach him to read. Often he had no money left to buy writing materials. "During this time," as he tells it himself, "my copy-book was the board fence, brick wall and pavement, my pen and ink was a lump of chalk."

To Douglass freedom from chattel slavery was but half a victory unless followed by a liberation of the mind. He expressed the opinion that there was no useful thing a man might do that could not be better done by an educated man than an uneducated one. Referring to his slavery background, he wryly observed that some know the value of education by having it. "I know its value by not having it." Speaking at Storer College in 1880, Douglass shared his credo with students. "If," said he, "a man is without education, he is but a pitiable object; a giant in body, but a pigmy in intellect, and, at best, but half a man. . . . Education, on the other hand, means emancipation; it means light and liberty."

Throughout his life he exhibited this desire to learn, to lead a rich life in the brain. He acquired a personal library of over ten thousand volumes; he started to learn French when he was over seventy. Always to make a new man of himself—this was his goal.

Douglass was a learner because of his desire to increase his effectiveness as a reformer and to improve the quality of life itself. This twin purpose made Douglass a hard worker, one to whom conscientious preparation became a way

This rare photograph of Douglass in old age displays his commanding presence. *(Sophia Smith Collection, Smith College.)*

of life. He never wrote an article or gave a speech without first doing his homework carefully. Richard T. Greener, first Negro graduate of Harvard College, in speaking of Douglass at memorial exercises held by the city of Boston on December 20, 1895, took note of his thoroughness. "He seemed to have the grand miltonic scorn of coming into a contest of thought unprepared; with his blade not well sharpened, the hilt untried, and the point not tested."

As careful as he was with facts, Douglass was equally as meticulous in putting his thoughts in writing. The most cursory examination of his papers will show that he wrote over and over again, striving for clarity and precision. It may be that Douglass was so careful in composing his sentences because he knew that almost everything he wrote would find its way into print and perhaps into posterity. At any rate, Douglass would have agreed fully with a present-day literary critic, Herbert Hill, that "the urgencies of social protest cannot be invoked as an excuse for shoddy undisciplined writing. For writing without artistic quality can only lead to dull and ineffective protest literature. Indeed, for the writer, a serious and purposeful commitment to racial justice and social action requires the most intense devotion to literary technique and artistic discipline."

The sense of personal responsibility that went into his literary efforts was characteristic of Douglass. He did not believe in waiting for things to take a turn for the better. As a slave he made two attempts to escape, not losing heart because the first was thwarted. Desirous of freedom he began, as he put it, to pray with his legs. In 1894 Douglass was paid a visit by Daniel Hale Williams, first physician in the world to operate successfully on the human heart, and a charter member of the American College of Surgeons. Having his troubles as head of Freedman's Hospital in Washington, D.C., Williams drove out to the Douglass residence seeking advice. The words of the aged reformer, then 77, might have been a capsule of his own career: "The only way you can succeed, Dan, is to override the obstacles in your way. By the power that is within you, do what you hope to do."

These words to Dr. Williams were typical of Douglass. He was always urging Negroes to be up and doing whatever betide. He knew what it was to be black in his native land but he did not believe that prejudice absolved its victims from the exercise of personal responsibility. In the very first issue of his newspaper, the *North Star*, he stated his credo: "While advocating your rights, the *North Star* will strive to throw light on your duties: while it will not fail to make known your virtues, it will not shun to discover your faults."

To say that Douglass believed in racial self-reliance does not mean that he was against cooperating with whites. "It is gallant to go forth single-handedly, but is it wise?" he said in a speech on John Brown. Douglass was opposed to separate, all-Negro organizations, believing that a solid colored minority would tend to polarize racial resentments. Hence, he took a stand, for example, against the formation in 1888 of a woman's suffrage association of colored women. "I have associated with white people in various societies," wrote he, "in anti-slavery societies, temperance societies, literary societies, woman's suffrage societies, and I see no reason why educated and well-informed colored women should not do the same."

Douglass reasoned that the Negro was an American and that inasmuch as there could be but one America, a nation within a nation would be an anomaly. In delivering the commencement address to the Colored High School of Baltimore in the closing year of his life, Douglass pointed out that "the evils now crushing us to earth have their root and sap in this narrow spirit of race and color, and we have no more right to foster it than men of any other race."

Douglass did not advocate a policy of "go-it-alone." But he did hold that the Negro's white friends could not do for him what he could do for himself. Douglass held it as an article of faith that the Negro's destiny was largely in his own hands. "If we succeed in the race of life, it must be by our own energies, and our own exertions," he said over and over. The Negro should be his own man, speaking up for himself. This was necessary, affirmed Douglass, not merely to inspire the colored people themselves but to furnish doubting whites with an object lesson in the Negro's readiness for equality.

Douglass knew what it was to become one's own spokesman, having taken this step in 1847 while on the threshold of his career. In that year he had broken with the Massachusetts abolitionists. As much as he admired them he left their ranks when he became convinced that their attitude toward him was to some degree patronizing, smacking of "father knows best." They wanted Douglass to stick to a script they had written for him, confining his speeches to his experiences as a slave rather than his reflections

as a man. Douglass refused, having opened his eyes, as he phrased it, and looked out of them through another telescope. No people, observed Douglass, ever "stood forth in the attitude of freedom" unless some one from among themselves had arisen to lead them on to victory.

A final consideration of Douglass as a nineteenth century mover and shaker must take note of his qualities of the spirit. Foremost among these was a sense of humanity that crossed the barrier of race and color. Douglass was broad and encompassing in his outlook and sympathies. This ecumenical spirit was perhaps the more unusual inasmuch as Douglass was pro-Negro to the core. "Whatever character or capacity you ascribe to us," he told a New York audience in May 1853, "I am not ashamed to be numbered with this race. I utterly abhor and spurn with all contempt possible that cowardly meanness which leads any colored man to repudiate his connection with the race." One of Douglass' Negro critics in the 1880s T. Thomas Fortune, editor of the New York *Freeman,* paid tribute to his battle for the Negro. On April 2, 1886, Fortune wrote as follows: "Of course I do not agree to all your views, but the fight for the race is there and that satisfies me."

But Douglass was not ethnocentric; instead, his interests embraced the family of man. As he said on one occasion, the black people were his people, the yellow people were his people and the white people were his people. "Now, as always," he wrote in a private letter in April 1884, "I am for any movement whenever there is a good cause to promote, a right to assert, a chain to be broken, a burden to be removed, or a wrong to be redressed."

In part Douglass's broad outlook stemmed from his early association with such figures as William Lloyd Garrison and Wendell Phillips, whose reform interest were far-ranging. In part, too, Douglass's broad sympathies may have resulted from being a Negro. Paradoxically, it would seem, his belonging to a despised group had given him a deeper, more inclusive sense of human brotherhood. Douglass' deep interest in the plight of his fellow men may be viewed as a mark of maturity if we are to believe the new school of "ego psychology."

But whatever the reasons Douglass belonged to "the fellowship of the concerned." His own success never lulled his conscience, leading him to murmur, "Soul, take thine ease." He could be numbered among those who mourned man's inhumanity to man. Oppressed peoples in other lands evoked his words of support—the Irish under England, the Hungarians under Austria and the Cubans under Spain.

Of the non-racial domestic reforms that engaged Douglass' attention, woman's rights took highest rank. "Right is of no sex," said Douglass in 1847, and throughout his life no man was a more zealous woman's righter. Ignoring volleys of criticism and abuse, he took part in many of the state and national conventions held by the embattled women's groups. Age did not diminish his interest. On his last afternoon he attended a meeting of the National Council of Women in Washington, D.C., at which he was warmly received. He returned home and as he and his wife were talking after dinner, his heart gave away.

Nearly two hours later, as the National Council of Women opened their evening session, Mary Wright Sewall, the presiding officer, took solemn note of his passing. It was a historic coincidence, she said, that the man who embodied the struggle between liberty and oppression should have spent his last day in company with the seekers of "a new expression of freedom." It was a sentiment Douglass would not have quarreled with, being not wide of the mark.

In leaving Douglass it hardly need be added that most of what he said and stood for has a relevance for our times. His social insights were, on the whole, remarkable. Two brief final illustrations may be noted. A careful reader of the American character, Douglass knew that his countrymen, as heirs of the Declaration of Independence, were committed to the call of freedom and equality. In the dark days of the Dred Scott decision he had proclaimed that "the best defense of free American institutions is the hearts of the American people."

But Douglass also knew that America's dedication to freedom and equality could not be taken for granted—that his countrymen were prone to infringe upon the rights of the Negro. In a speech in Washington in 1889, under the auspices of the Bethel Literary and Historical Association, Douglass summed up the attitude of the mass of Americans, his statement as cogent now as it was then. "Justice and magnanimity are elements of the American character. They may do much for us. But we are in no position to depend upon these qualities exclusively. Depend upon it, whenever the American people shall become convinced that they have gone too far in recognizing the rights of the Negro, they will find some way to abridge these rights. The Negro is great but the welfare of the nation will be considered greater. They will forget the Negro's service in the late war. They will forget his loyalty to the republic."

Finally, Douglass saw the Negro as the touchstone of American democracy, its inescapable test. In the main an optimist, he did not believe that human problems were so vast as to defy solution. But neither did he believe that they would go away of themselves. Hence one of Douglass' major contributions was in holding up a mirror to America, in making her face up to the unfinished business of democracy. The land of the free must needs come to grips with itself. America's inevitable self-confrontation was a theme of one of Douglass' greatest speeches, delivered in the nation's capital on the occasion of the twenty-first anniversary of emancipation in the District of Columbia, and subsequently reprinted upon the request of twenty prominent Negroes, headed by former United States Senator B. K. Bruce. The words of Douglass on that occasion could almost have been written today:

"What Abraham Lincoln said in respect of the United States is as true of the colored people as of the relations of those states. They cannot remain half slave and half free. You must give them all or take from them all. Until this half-and-half condition is ended, you will have an aggrieved class, and this discussion will go on. Until the public schools shall cease to be caste schools in every part of our country, this discussion will go on. Until color shall cease to be a bar to equal participation in the offices and honors of the country, this discussion will go on. Until the trades-unions and the workshops of the country shall cease to proscribe the colored man, this discussion will go on. In a word, until truth and humanity shall become living ideas, this discussion will go on."

See also AFRO-AMERICAN HISTORY; MORGAN STATE UNIVERSITY; NEWSPAPERS; SLAVERY: THE ABOLITIONISTS; QUARLES, BENJAMIN.

REFERENCES: There are several adequate references to be noted. Benjamin Quarles wrote a full-length biography of Douglass (1948) for the Associated Publishers. He also authored, in 1968, a biography for Prentice-Hall. Philip S. Foner, another scholar, showed an early interest in Douglass by editing selections from his writings (1945); a later study (1976) revealed Douglass' interest in women's rights. There are, of course, many articles on Douglass; several have appeared in the *Journal of Negro History*. Moreover, Douglass spoke ably of himself in his own accounts: *Life and Times of Frederick Douglass* (Collier Books, 1962; reprinted from rev. ed. of *My Bondage and My Freedom*, 1892); and *Narrative of the Life of Frederick Douglass, An American Slave, Written by Himself* (Belknap Press, 1960; reprinted from an original edition of 1845).

DOUGLASS, HALEY GEORGE (1881–1954), educator; born in Canandaigua, N.Y. Douglass, the last surviving grandson of Frederick Douglass, attended Phillips Exeter Academy and received a B.A. degree from Harvard University in 1905. Douglass taught in high schools for 46 years in Washington, D.C., and served as mayor of Highland Beach, Md. *See also* DOUGLASS, FREDERICK.

DOWDY, LEWIS CARNEGIE (1917–   ), educator; born in Eastover, S.C. Dowdy received a B.A. degree from Allen University (Columbia, S.C.) in 1939, a M.A. degree from Indiana State College in 1949, and his Ed.D. degree from Indiana University in 1965. He was a high school principal (1939–51) in South Carolina before he became an instructor of education at North Carolina Agricultural and Technical (A & T) State University (1951–56), where he eventually was appointed president (1964). Dowdy was active in many education groups, including the National Association of State Universities and Land-Grant Colleges, of which he served as president from 1974 to 1975.

DOYLE, BERTRAM WILBUR (1897– ?), Christian Methodist Episcopal bishop; born in Lowndesboro, Ala. Doyle received a B.A. degree from Ohio Wesleyan University in 1921, a M.A. degree (1924) and his Ph.D. degree (1934) from the University of Chicago, and his D.D. degree from Lane College (Jackson, Tenn.) in 1934. Ordained in the Christian Methodist Episcopal (C.M.E.) Church in 1925, he served as pastor of churches in South Carolina and Tennessee before being elected a bishop in 1950. Doyle taught at Sam Houston State College, Claflin College, Clark College, and Fisk University, and served as dean at Fisk and at Paine College. He was a member of Phi Beta Kappa and wrote *Etiquette of Race Relations in the South* (1937).

DOZENS A colloquial or conversational term used in connection with the expressions "playing the dozens" or being "put in the dozens." The usage has deep roots in the psychology, humor, personality, and social relationships of Afro-Americans. "Playing the dozens" carries references to one's relatives, especially one's mother; the expression means to talk about such a person by implying, taunting, kidding, "jiv-

ing," teasing, or insulting. The frequency and importance of this usage, never much of a middle-class preference (and not a white colloquial expression), seems to have declined after the mid-twentieth century. *See also* ONOMATOLOGY.

DRAKE, ST. CLAIR (1911–   ), anthropologist, educator; born in Suffolk, Va. Drake taught anthropology at Roosevelt University (Chicago, Ill.) for 23 years. He coauthored *Black Metropolis: A Study of Negro Life in a Northern City* (1945) and wrote *Black Diaspora* (1972). Drake also contributed articles to *Negro Americans*, edited by Talcott Parsons and Kenneth Clark.

DRAMA See LITERATURE: DRAMA/THEATER.

DREER, HERMAN See HISTORIANS.

DREW, CHARLES RICHARD (1904–50), physician, scientist; born in Washington, D.C. Drew graduated from Amherst College (Amherst, Mass.) in 1926 and received his M.D. degree from McGill Medical College (Montreal, Quebec, Canada) in 1933. He interned at Montreal General Hospital, where he pioneered in blood research, and was on the faculty of Howard Medical College in 1935. Drew was awarded a General Education Board Fellowship to Columbia University Medical School in 1935 in order to research a specific project on the preservation of blood and its use for transfusions. In 1940 he published *Banked Blood: A Study in Blood Preservation*, and at the request of Dr. John Beattie (Royal College of Surgeons), Drew started the "Blood for Britain" project in 1940, which consisted of collecting and drying blood plasma to be used for transfusions on the battlefield. In recognition of his achievements abroad, Drew was awarded an honorary D.Sc. degree from Columbia University in 1940. He served as the director of the American Red Cross Blood Bank in 1941, as assistant director of blood procurement for the National Research Council, and later as chief surgeon of Freedmen's Hospital, Washington, D.C. Drew continually disputed any scientific basis indicating blood differences according to race. In April 1950 he was killed in an auto accident in North Carolina, a tragedy sharpened by the irony of its circumstances. Drew was traveling to a professional meeting by automobile in order to avoid segregated public accommodations in the South when he crashed, and the segregated hospital to which he was

Charles R. Drew
(Scurlock Studio.)

admitted did not have any blood plasma that might have saved his life. *See also* RACE: BIOLOGY.

DREW, KENNETH (1915–   ), publisher; born in Burlington, Ohio. Drew studied at Lewis Institute of Technology from 1941 to 1942 and at Columbia University (New York, N.Y.) from 1963 to 1964. In 1957 he became a licensed real estate broker and founded Cardonta Realty. Drew also served as a civil engineer for the city of New York, and as a special investigator for the state attorney general's office from 1958 to 1959. In 1959 he founded the Corona-East Elmhurst *News*, later known as the *Voice* and then as the *New York Voice*. Drew was a member of the board of directors of the National Newspapers Publisher's Association for many years.

DREW, TIMOTHY   *See* ALI, NOBLE DREW.

DRISKELL, DAVID C.   *See* ARTISTS.

DRIVER, RICHARD (SONNY)   *See* NEWSPAPERS: CONTEMPORARY.

DU BOIS, SHIRLEY LOLA GRAHAM (1906–1977), author, composer; born in Indianapolis, Ind. Graham received advanced musical training in Paris from 1926 to 1928, and in 1929 earned a French Certificate from the Sorbonne. She received a B.A. degree (1934) and her M.A. degree (1935) from Oberlin College (Oberlin, Ohio). Graham served as chairman of the fine arts department of Tennessee State College (1935–36), as director of the Negro unit of the Chicago Federal Theater (1936–38), and as a director of the USO and of the YMCA (1940–42). In 1951 she married W. E. B. Du Bois. Graham was the founding editor of *Freedomways*, and in 1964, the year after her husband's death, she became the founding director of Ghana Television. In 1968 Graham served as the English editor of the Afro-Asian Writers Bureau in Peking. Her awards include a Rosenwald Fellowship in 1938, a Guggenheim Fellowship in 1945, and the Anisfield-Wolf Award in 1950 for *Your Most Humble Servant*, (Benjamin Banneker). Her other books include: *Paul Robeson: City of the World* (1946, 1971), *Booker T. Washington* (1955), and *His Day is Marching On: A Memoir of W. E. B. Du Bois* (1973). *See also* LITERATURE: CHILDREN'S.

DU BOIS, W. E. B.

WILLIAM EDWARD BURGHARDT DU BOIS (1868–1963), author, editor, educator; born in Great Barrington, Mass. Du Bois received a B.A. degree in 1888 from Fisk University (Nashville, Tenn.) and a second B.A. degree in 1890 from Harvard University. His M.A. degree (1891) and his Ph.D. degree (1895) came from Harvard University. He later studied at the University of Berlin and was awarded honorary degrees from Howard University, Atlanta University, Fisk University, and Wilberforce University. Du Bois taught Greek and Latin at Wilberforce University (1894–1896) and sociology at the University of Pennsylvania (1896–1897). He taught at Atlanta University (1897–1910), returning in 1933 as head of the Department of Sociology until 1944. He served as director of publications for the National Association for the Advancement of Colored People (NAACP), as editor of Crisis magazine (1910–1932), as editor of Atlanta University Studies (1897–1911), and as editor of *Phylon* quarterly review (1940–1944).

Whether as editor, college professor, or public lecturer, Du Bois advocated the elimination of discrimination and inequality against Afro-Americans. Although his emphases and directions changed at different times, throughout his life he remained essentially a critic of the American social order and its suppression of blacks. His solutions embraced a variety of suggestions such as: equalitarian democracy, pan-Africanism, economic and cultural self-determinism, and Marxian socialism. His views or personality often brought him into conflict with contemporaries of differing ideologies, including such able Afro-Americans as Booker T. Washington, William Monroe Trotter, Marcus Garvey, and Walter White. Controversy with White, secretary of the

NAACP, eventually led to Du Bois' second and final break with the NAACP in 1948. (See NATIONAL ASSOCIATION FOR THE ADVANCEMENT OF COLORED PEOPLE.)

Du Bois' personal and ideological response to the Afro-American presence and destiny in the United States can be categorized under two main but paradoxical views. One view encompassed integrationism; the other, nationalism. Du Bois was aware of this duality and dilemma, this "twoness" as he once referred to it; and his response varied with times and circumstances. Early in his career (toward the end of the 1890s), he placed much importance upon the value of scholarship and liberal education as a means of solving the Afro-American dilemma. He advocated leadership and uplift of the masses through an educated (preferably "college-bred") black elite, which he defined as the "talented tenth." Still believing in the talented tenth, he was disturbed by the rising racist blacklash in disfranchisement and segregation that was so pervasive at the turn of the century. Raising his voice in protest, he opposed accommodationist views and actions that were symbolized in the philosophy and programs of the popular national black leader, Booker T. Washington. To this end, Du Bois founded and led the Niagara Movement, a protest organization whose membership consisted of many northern black intellectuals. Short of funds and under attack by Washington's followers, the movement survived only a few annual conferences: at Niagara, Canada, 1905, where it first convened after denial of hotel accommodations at nearby Niagara, N.Y.; at Harpers Ferry, W. Va., 1906, a site reminiscent and symbolic to delegates of the radical abolitionist, John Brown; at Boston, Mass., 1907, where controversy between Du Bois and Trotter was a factor in the breakup of the organization. Du Bois then turned to the emerging NAACP, 1909–1912.

He also turned about this time to the Progressives of former president Theodore Roosevelt (TR) for support. However, when they failed to include a platform plank on the rights of Afro-Americans, he urged the support of Woodrow Wilson, the Democratic party's presidential nominee in 1912. Disappointed with the newly elected president's anti-black policies, he urged blacks to support the Socialist party's candidate in the election of 1916. Although Du Bois protested against segregation, discrimination, and Wilson, he urged Afro-Americans to support the nation's war effort in World War I.

After World War I, his attention seemed to have focused increasingly on pan-Africanism and Marxian socialism. Through his efforts, the first significant pan-African congress was held in 1919; and his interest in the communist revolution and experiment in Russia led to an invitation to Russia in 1926. By 1935 he had come to accept Marxist views in the study and writing of Afro-American history as shown in his book, *Black Reconstruction*. In the late 1940s and in the decade of the 1950s he was linked increasingly with communist groups or their fellow travelers. Such linkage led to an indictment by the U.S. Justice Department; but Du Bois was acquitted. At an all African conference held in Accra, Ghana, in 1958, he urged the acceptance of socialism over capitalism. Three years later, at the age of 93, he joined the Communist party, returning to Ghana as a voluntary exile upon invitation of that

W. E. B. Du Bois in his study during his editorship of the *Crisis. (National Association for the Advancement of Colored People.)*

nation's first prime minister, Kwame Nkrumah. He died in Ghana at the age of 95, having devoted his last two years to directing the writing of an encyclopedia of Africa, a project that he had proposed in his early life.

Du Bois was a prolific writer, contributing many articles to outstanding magazines and journals. His books include: *The Suppression of the African Slave Trade* (1896); *The Philadelphia Negro* (1899); *The Souls of Black Folk* (1903); *John Brown* (1909); *Quest of the Silver Fleece* (1911); *The Negro* (1915); *Darkwater* (1920); *The Gift of Black Folk* (1924); *Dark Princess* (1928); *Black Reconstruction* (1935); *Black Folk: Then and Now* (1939); *Dusk of Dawn* (1940); *Color and Democracy* (1945); and *The World and Africa* (1946). See also AFRO-AMERICAN HISTORY: RECONSTRUCTION TO REVOLT, 1877–1977; HISTORIANS; LITERATURE: THE NOVEL; NATIONAL ASSOCIATION FOR THE ADVANCEMENT OF COLORED PEOPLE (NAACP); PAN-AFRICANISM; SCIENTISTS: SOCIAL.

REFERENCES: For a good reference that treats the major profiles of Du Bois, see Rayford, Logan (ed.), *W. E. B. Du Bois: Profile*, 1972. For other references, see Ernest F. Kaiser's biobibliography that was published in *Freedomways* shortly after Du Bois' death. For a more comprehensive bibliography, see Partington, Paul G., *W. E. B. Du Bois: A Bibliography of His Published Writings*, published by the author, Whittier, Calif., 1977.

DUDLEY, EDWARD RICHARD (1911–   ), lawyer, judge, government official; born in South Boston, Va. Dudley graduated from Johnson C. Smith University (Charlotte, N.C.) in 1932 and Saint John's University Law School (Jamaica, N.Y.) in 1941. Admitted to the New York bar in 1941, he soon became assistant attorney general for the state of New York. From 1948 to 1953, Dudley served as U.S. ambassador to Liberia, following which he served in 1953, as director of the National Association for the Advancement of Colored People (NAACP) Freedom Fund. In 1955 he became judge of the Domestic Relations Court of New York City. After five years on the bench, Dudley resigned to become president of the Borough of Manhattan in 1961; he also became chairman of the New York County Democratic Committee in 1963. In 1964 Dudley was elected justice of the Supreme Court of the State of New York. Dudley was designated administrative judge of the Criminal Court of New York City in 1967 and, subsequently, administrative judge of the Supreme Court of New York (First Department) in 1971.

Paul Laurence Dunbar. *(Library of Congress.)*

DUKE, CHARLES SUMNER (1879–1952), engineer, educator; born in Selma, Ala. Duke attended Howard University (Washington, D.C.) and received a B.A. degree from Harvard University in 1904 and his C.E. degree from the University of Wisconsin in 1913. From 1905 to 1908, he was a teacher and principal in Indianapolis, Ind., public schools, after which he became a draftsman for the city of Chicago, Ill., until 1922, when he founded his own firm in architectural engineering. In 1940 Duke was named associate estimating and cost engineer for the U.S. Housing Authority, and in 1945 he joined the Federal Works Agency. During his long career, Duke served as construction engineer with the General Services Agency in the Virgin Islands, aided in the formation of the National Technical Association and was its president, and served on numerous Illinois housing commissions. He was a member of the subcommittee on housing and chairman of the Congress on Industrial Organization in Washington, D.C., chairman of the Housing Committee of the Industrial Housing Council in Washington, D.C., and housing director of the Improved Benevolent Protective Order of Elks of the World.

DUMPSON, JAMES R. (1919–   ), educator, administrator; born in Philadelphia, Pa. Dumpson received a B.S. degree from Pennsylvania State Teachers College in 1932, and a B.A. degree (1947) and his M.A. degree (1950) from the New School for Social Research (New York, N.Y.). He served as consultant on corrections and delinquency for the Welfare Council of New York City (1948–51), as a consultant for the Protestant Welfare Agencies of New York (1951–54), and as director of the Bureau of Child Welfare (1955–58). Dumpson became commissioner of welfare of New York City in 1959, and in 1965 he became professor and associate dean of the School of Social Work at Hunter College of the City University of New York. He was later appointed dean of the School of Social Work at Fordham University (1967). In 1974 Dumpson left Fordham to serve as the administrator of the Human Resources Administration and as the commissioner of social services in New York City.

DUNBAR, PAUL LAURENCE (1872–1906), poet; born in Dayton, Ohio. The son of former slaves, Dunbar started writing poems at the age of six and gave a public recital of his poetry when he was 13. His father had died when he was 12, and he and his mother struggled to maintain themselves; he delivered laundry bundles and worked part time in hotels. Dunbar attended Dayton's only high school and was the only black in his graduating class. He was elected president of the school literary society and editor of the school newspaper, and he wrote the class song for his graduating class. His teachers encouraged his literary talent, but, since he lacked money to go to college, he sought employment in journalism and clerical work. Dunbar was rejected by newspapers and offices because of his color, but he finally found work, holding a job as an elevator operator when his first volume of poems, *Oak and Ivy*, was published in 1893. This volume was followed by *Majors and Minors* (1895) and *Lyrics of a Lonely Life* (1896), the latter book winning for him national recognition. His *Complete Poems* was published in 1913. *See also* LITERATURE: POETRY; NELSON, ALICE RUTH MOORE DUNBAR.

DUNBAR, RUDOLPH (1917–   ), composer, conductor, clarinetist; born in British Guiana. Dunbar received his musical education at the Institute of Musical Art (New York, N.Y.) and in Paris and Leipzig. He conducted widely in Great Britain and in the United States. Dunbar made his New York City debut with the NBC Symphony Orchestra and his London debut with the London Philharmonic Orchestra (1942). Perhaps his best-known composition is *Dance of the 20th Century*. Dunbar was also the author of a popular text, *A Treatise on Clarinet Playing*.

DUNCAN, ROBERT MORTON (1927–   ), lawyer, judge; born in Urbana, Ohio. Duncan received a B.S. degree from Ohio State University in 1948 and his LL.B. degree from the Ohio State College of Law in 1952. Several legal positions with the city of Columbus, Ohio, and with the state of Ohio preceded his appointment to the Franklin County (Ohio) Municipal Court in 1966. He remained on that bench for three years until, in 1969, he became an associate justice of the Supreme Court of the state of Ohio. In 1971 Duncan was appointed by President Richard M. Nixon to the U.S. Court of Military Appeals in Washington, D.C. He was the first Afro-American judge to serve on that court.

DUNCAN, ROBERT TODD (1903–   ), baritone; born in Danville, Ky. Duncan graduated from Butler University (Indianapolis, Ind.) in 1925 and received his M.A. degree from Columbia University in 1930. He was selected to play the role of Porgy in George Gershwin's *Porgy and Bess* in 1935, and during his career he performed the role more than 1,800 times. Duncan gave recitals throughout the United States and Europe, and also appeared in such other shows as *The Sun Never Sets* (London, 1938) and *Cabin in the Sky* (London, 1940).

DUNCANSON, ROBERT SCOTT (1817–72), painter; born in Cincinnati, Ohio. Duncanson's reputation rests mainly on his landscapes in the tradition of the Hudson River School, of which *Blue Hole, Little Miami River,* and *Flood Waters* are among the best-known examples. He was also a prolific painter of portraits, receiving many commissions from Cincinnati society. (He later opened a studio in Detroit, Mich., to cater to a similar clientele.) Duncanson's *Portrait of Richard Sutton Rust, I* is typical of his portrait style, but he also painted romantic allegories (*Uncle Tom and Little Eva*) and comedies (*The Drunkard's Plight*). Four of Duncanson's murals are in the Taft Museum (Cincinnati, Ohio). During a trip to Europe, Duncanson did a painting of Balmoral Castle that was bought by Queen Victoria. His style was highly detailed and meticulous. His works have been shown at the Art of the American Negro Exhibition, Chicago, Ill., (1940); at the Boston Museum of Fine Arts and at the National Center of Afro-American Artists, Boston; at Howard University, Washington, D.C.; and elsewhere. Duncanson's work is included in the collections of the Boston Museum of Fine Arts; the National Archives, Washington, D.C.; and the Glasgow Art Gallery, Scotland. Duncanson was perhaps the first Afro-American artist to win international recognition. *See also* ARTISTS.

DUNGEE, JOHN *See* NEWSPAPERS: CONTEMPORARY.

DUNGEE, ROSCOE (1883–1965), journalist; born in Harpers Ferry, W. Va. Dungee attended Langston University (Langston, Okla.). In 1915, after ten years with various Oklahoma newspapers, he became editor of the *Black Dispatch* of Oklahoma City. His editorials consistently and strongly advocated full civil rights for Afro-Americans. *See also* NEWSPAPERS: CONTEMPORARY.

DUNHAM, KATHERINE (1910–   ), dancer, choreographer; born in Chicago, Ill. Dunham attended the University of Chicago, where she majored in anthropology, and spent a year of field study in the West Indies on a Rosenwald Fellowship. This training in anthropology was the foundation for the new dance forms that she later introduced. Through her work, African and Caribbean rhythms and movements were seen for the first time on American stages. *Cabin in the Sky,* a Broadway musical choreographed by Dunham, in which she also acted and danced, was the first of several stage productions and films with which she was connected. Others included such films as *Stormy Weather* (1943) and *Pardon My Sarong* (1942), which she choreographed, and the musical *Windy City* (1946), also choreographed by her. During the 1940s, Dunham formed the Katherine Dunham School of Cultural Arts, and the Katherine Dunham Dance Company, which toured the United States and (after the war) Europe, performing dances staged and choreographed by Dunham as producer-director. In 1943 the company presented her *Tropical Revue* on tour; three years later it provided dancers for her work, *Bal Nègre,* in which she also performed. Since 1947 the company has performed in nearly 60 countries. Dunham appeared as a guest artist with several symphony orchestras, and in 1963 she became the first black choreographer to work at the Metropolitan Opera House in New York City, when she choreographed the dances for a new production of *Aida.* In the 1970s, in addition to directing the Performing Arts Training Center and Dynamic Museum at Southern Illinois University and serving as technical adviser for the John F. Kennedy Center for the Performing Arts in Washington, D.C., Dunham directed *Treemonisha,* a ragtime opera by Scott Joplin, at the Wolf Trap Farm for the Performing Arts in Virginia. Her autobiography, *Touch of Innocence,* was published in 1959, and a biography by Terry Harnan, *African Rhythm–American Dance; A Biography of Katherine Dunham,* was published in 1974. *See also* DANCE.

DUNSTON, ALFRED G., JR. (1915–   ), African Methodist Episcopal Zion bishop; born in Coinjock, N.C. Dunston attended Livingstone College (Salisbury, N.C.) and Hood Seminary, and received a M.A. degree from Drew University (Madison, N.J.) and his D.C.L. degree from Monrovia College (Liberia). He served churches in North Carolina, New Jersey, Tennessee, Pennsylvania, and New York, and was elected a bishop of the African Methodist Episcopal Zion (AMEZ) Church in 1964. Dunston helped found the Opportunities Industrialization Center in Philadelphia, Pa., in 1963. He was a member of the Commission on Human Relations in Philadelphia, Pa., and a trustee of Berea College.

DURHAM, CHARLES J. (1927–   ), lawyer, judge. Durham attended the University of Illinois and received his LL.B. from De Paul University (Chicago, Ill.). Admitted to the Illinois bar in 1955, he became magistrate of the Circuit Court of Chicago.

DU SABLE, JEAN-BAPTISTE POINT (? –1818), pioneer, entrepreneur. The origins of Du Sable, the first settler in the area of Chicago, Ill., are unknown. He was of French and African descent, and his place of birth has been listed as Santo Domingo, Haiti, and French Canada. Sometime before 1773, Du Sable settled in what is today Chicago. In 1773 he purchased 30 acres of land, built a house with several rooms, and lived in relative prosperity with his Indian wife and growing family. Du Sable participated briefly in the Revolutionary War, spying for the British. However, he was jailed by the English authorities for a few months because they thought his sympathies were "too French." In 1780 Du Sable served as a liaison officer between Indians of the Port Huron region and white officials, having been appointed to this post by the territorial governor, Patrick Sinclair, at the request of the Indians. Du Sable returned to Chicago in about 1782 where he became a fur trapper and trading post owner. As he prospered, he added 400 acres to his original tract, and his post grew to include a house (renowned for its elaborate furnishings and modern conveniences), two barns, a mill, a bakehouse, a poultry house, and large livestock holdings. In 1800, for reasons still obscure, Du Sable sold the Chicago post for a total sum of $1,200 and moved to St. Charles, Mo., to live with one of his sons. He died a pauper in 1818.

EAGLESON, HALSON VASHON (1903–   ), physicist, educator; born in Bloomington, Ind. Eagleson received a B.A. degree (1926), a M.A. degree (1931), and his Ph.D. degree (1939) from Indiana University. He was a professor of mathematics and physics at Morehouse College (Atlanta, Ga.) from 1927 to 1935, chairman of the department of physics at Howard University (Washington, D.C.) from 1935 to 1947, and chairman of the department of physics at Clark College (Atlanta, Ga.) from 1940 to 1947. Eagleson received a General Education Board Fellowship in 1935.

EBONY A popular magazine published in Chicago, Ill., by Afro-Americans. *See also* NEWSPAPERS: CONTEMPORARY.

EBONY SPOTS A popular singing quartet based in Chicago, Ill., in the 1930s and 1940s.

EDELMAN, MARIAN WRIGHT (1939–   ), lawyer; born in Bennettsville, S.C. Edelman received a B.A. degree from Spelman College (Atlanta, Ga.) in 1960 and her LL.B. degree from Yale Law School in 1963. She began to work for the National Association for the Advancement of Colored People (NAACP) Legal Defense and Education Fund, Inc., first in New York City and then, from 1964 to 1968, in Jackson, Miss. Returning North in 1968, Edelman became a partner in the Washington Research Project, and two years later she was appointed director of the

Harvard Center of Law and Education. In 1972 Edelman became the first black female elected to the Yale University board of trustees.

EDMONDS, HELEN GREY (1911–   ), historian, educator; born in Lawrenceville, Va. Edmonds received a B.A. degree from Morgan State University in 1933, and a M.A. degree (1938) and Ph.D. degree (1946) from Ohio State University. She served as dean of women and teacher at St. Paul Normal School in Virginia (1935–40). Edmonds later became professor and dean of the graduate school (arts and sciences) at North Carolina Central University. She wrote for professional journals on topics relating to Afro-Americans in politics and authored *The Negro in North Carolina's Fusion Politics 1894–1901* (1951) and *Black Faces in High Places* (1971).

EDMONDS, SHEPPARD RANDOLPH (1900–   ), educator, playwright; born in Lawrenceville, Va. Edmonds received a B.A. degree from Oberlin College (Oberlin, Ohio) in 1926 and a M.A. degree from Columbia University in 1932. He then studied at the University of Dublin on a General Education Board Fellowship, and at the London School of Speech and Drama on a Rosenwald Fellowship (1938). Edmonds became a professor of English and drama at Morgan State University (Baltimore, Md.) from 1925–26, and he also taught at Florida Agricultural and Mechanical (A & M) College and at Hampton

Institute (Hampton, Va.). Edmonds wrote *Shades and Shadows* (1930), *Six Plays for the Negro Theatre* (1934), and *The Land of Cotton* (1942). He received special invitational perfor-mances for his plays at the University of North Carolina, Grinnell College, the University of Miami, Fisk University, and many other institu-tions. See *also* LITERATURE: DRAMA / THEATER.

EDUCATION

Developments in Elementary and Secondary Educa-tion Since the importation of the first blacks in the 1600s into the Jamestown colony, the ques-tion of Negro education in the United States has invited controversy. During the Colonial period, slavery was recognized as being incompatible with education: Education could be a factor in destroying slavery. There are reports, however, of organizations that sought to provide some education for slaves. For example, Christianiza-tion of blacks was usually the first great step in their larger American education. Considerable evidence exists that shows that the Puritans favored conversion. Richard Baxter published a tract in London favoring Christian instruction (1673); in 1674 John Eliot, who had worked among the Indians, turned his attention to instructing blacks. In 1717 Cotton Mather began his evening school for Indians and blacks. Samu-el Sewall (1652–1730), a judge in Massachu-setts, not only favored instruction but was out-spoken against slavery. In 1728 Nathaniel Pigott announced that he was opening a school for the "instruction of Negroes in reading, catechizing, and writing."

A few other notable efforts to educate Afro-Americans were attempted. In 1700 William Penn was instrumental in establishing a Month-ly Meeting (Quaker) for blacks. Many colonists taught their slaves, and a few free blacks, such as the prosperous Paul Cuffe (1759–1817), estab-lished their own schools. In Maryland, the Rev. Thomas Bray, a founder of the Society for the Propagation of the Gospel (1701), encouraged instruction and, at times, white and black chil-dren were taught together. An early catechizing school was founded by Trinity Church (New York City) in 1704.

Because of their concern with Christianiza-tion, French and Spanish settlers were more active in educating slaves than were the English. In 1727 the Roman Catholics in New Orleans, led by the Ursuline Nuns, taught Afro-Ameri-cans and Indians, and in 1734 established a school for blacks. The English followed a similar policy only after provincial statutes and the bishop of London had established the principle that conversion did not lead to liberty. In 1740 the Society for the Propagation of the Gospel in Foreign Parts sought to raise the level of living of all people in the South and urged that slaves be given the opportunity to be converted, to study the Scriptures, and, toward that end, to learn to read and write. Occasionally, members of the society taught the slaves themselves, and in one notable instance they established a school in Charleston, N.C., in which the teachers were slaves.

The most conscientious efforts to improve conditions among the slaves were made by such Quakers as George Fox. They labored both to abolish slavery and, in the meantime, to urge slaveholders to give instruction to their charges. In 1774 the Quakers of Philadelphia, Pa., estab-lished a school. Anthony Benezet, another Quak-er, began an evening school in his home in Phil-adelphia in 1750, and it continued until 1770. Benezet continued his activities after the Revo-lutionary War, and throughout that time spoke out against the idea of Negro inferiority. In 1776 the Quakers of Philadelphia decided to put an end to slaveholding. The Philadelphia Abolition Society, whose members included Benjamin Franklin, William Pitt, Noah Webster, and Thomas Paine, aimed also to establish schools for blacks whenever possible.

From the Revolution to the Civil War The doctrine of the "natural rights" of man, part of the philoso-phy of the American Revolution, reinforced the idea of the rights of Afro-Americans to educa-tion. Benjamin Franklin encouraged full educa-tion. Thomas Jefferson favored industrial and agricultural education only; he did not believe in the intellectual equality of blacks.

Despite legal restrictions and the contentions of such Southerners as John C. Calhoun that blacks were not educable, slaves did receive limited education in parts of the South after the American Revolution—sometimes from their masters and mistresses. The case of Frederick Douglass having been taught by his mistress is perhaps the best-known instance of an owner teaching a slave. One Mississippi planter boasted that all 20 of his slaves could read. In some cases the children of masters taught slaves to read and to write.

Instruction of one or of two slaves, although against the law, was not regarded as a serious offense and was rarely prosecuted. However, the insurrection of 1800, led by the slave Gabriel Prosser, so frightened southern planters that education of blacks was discouraged. This insurrection was followed by two other revolts, in 1822 and 1831, led by Denmark Vesey and Nat Turner, respectively—both of whom were also slaves. Thus, in the nineteenth century, southern blacks had to content themselves for the most part with clandestine schools and private teachers. In some isolated instances blacks did attend mixed schools. In 1840 they were permitted to attend schools with white children in Wilmington, Del. Julius Melbourn was sent by his mistress to a white academy near Raleigh, N.C., and remained there until it was discovered he was black. There is no way, however, of knowing how many blacks attended white schools, or even, with any accuracy, of knowing how many were literate before the Civil War. Estimates of literacy run from one in fifty to one in eighty. Yet, most blacks who learned to read were self-taught.

During the post-Revolutionary period, northern blacks benefited from the trend to establish and improve schools in the new nation. Whites in Boston taught black children both privately and in public institutions. New Jersey began educating black children in separate schools in 1777. In addition, Quakers and other humanitarian groups taught black children privately, and Quaker philanthropist Anthony Benezet provided funds to enlarge the Quaker program begun with the school session of 1774. In 1787 a school for Afro-Americans was built in Philadelphia, and by 1797 at least seven schools had been established. Also in 1787, the Manumission Society established one of the best-known schools of the period, the New York African Free School. It began with 40 students, and the number never exceeded 60 during its first decade of existence. At first great opposition to the school reigned, but in 1800 interest in it increased and

new impetus came for its growth in 1810 when New York required masters to teach all slave children to read the Scriptures. By 1830 the institution had enrolled more than 500 children. By 1824 the New York Common Council had begun to support African Free Schools, and in 1834 it took them over altogether.

In 1798, in Boston, a white teacher established a separate school for black children in the home of Primus Hall, a prominent Afro-American. Two years later, blacks asked the city for a separate school but were refused. They established one anyway and hired two Harvard alumni as instructors. Finally, in 1820, Boston opened an elementary school for blacks. Rhode Island and Connecticut also maintained separate schools. Pennsylvania continued to give both public and private support to its black schools, and they increased in number, particularly in the western part of the state. New York permitted black children to attend white schools, but in 1841 the state made it clear that any district could establish separate schools.

It was not until 1849 that the theory of separate schools was challenged. Charles Sumner, in the case of *Roberts v. The City of Boston*, appeared before the Massachusetts Supreme Court on behalf of a black girl who had been barred from a white school. The court held against the girl, but by 1855 public opinion had persuaded the legislature to repudiate the court and, in that year, segregation in Massachusetts public schools ended.

From the Civil War to the Twentieth Century The main changes that took place in education during this period were in the South during Reconstruction (1866–77). Before the Civil War, only 1.7 percent of blacks of school age were enrolled

Butler School House, the first permanent schoolbuilding for freedmen in Hampton, Va., was one of many freedmen's schools set up by the American Missionary Association. *(Courtesy of American Missionary Association Archives.)*

in scattered schools throughout the North. After the Civil War and during Reconstruction (until 1877), education for blacks took on a new course. In the border states, support for black public schools came from the taxes paid by blacks. This was true even in the District of Columbia, where, in 1862, Congress passed a bill setting aside 10 percent of these taxes to support black schools. West Virginia, which became a separate state in 1863, was the first southern state to provide in its constitution for the "separate but equal" education of the Afro-American. In some sections of Florida and Louisiana that were under the jurisdiction of the Union military forces and in the border states, efforts to set up public school systems for blacks were numerous. In 1865 Missouri included blacks in its school system. The major issue during the period was not support for schools, but whether the two races should be obliged to attend them together.

During Reconstruction, the attitude of the South toward the education of freedmen was determined not only by the traditional attitudes toward the status of the Afro-American, but also by the outlook and interests of the various groups that emerged with the collapse of the traditional class and economic structure. Three elements in southern society arose: (1) The conservatives, who attempted (through the Black Codes) to reinstate as much as possible the servile status of the black. This class was opposed to any form of education for blacks. (2) The moderates, who realized that slavery was dead and that the new status of the black should be recognized in creating a new society in the

An Early one-room schoolhouse. (Library of Congress.)

South. This moderate group consisted of many large plantation owners who were willing to provide some education for blacks in order to secure a stable and reliable labor supply. (3) The radicals, comprised of unpropertied whites and small farmers, who had no real interest in the slave system. Because of the cooperation of this group with blacks during the early years of Reconstruction, they have been called renegades and scalawags. Education for blacks was neglected by all three groups because the power struggle among them created a negative climate for education.

Historically, the South had always been opposed to education of children at public expense. Slavery and its concomitant historical cultural, social, and economic value systems were contrary to a doctrine that supported education at public expense. In general, this feeling also carried over to the education of blacks.

Therefore, the chief educational achievement of the Reconstruction government was the establishment in the South of a precedent for public tax-supported education for the masses as a democratic right to which citizens were entitled. However, the education of whites and blacks in the same school was not attempted on a large scale. In Louisiana and South Carolina, where attempts were made to educate the children of both races together, either violence or boycotts by whites attended the efforts. On the whole, black leaders accepted separate schools as an inevitable consequence of traditional attitudes. But they lost a strategic position when they accepted the well-intentioned assurance of philanthropic whites that if they surrendered the right to attend mixed schools, they would receive their fair share of public funds.

The famous case of *Plessy v. Ferguson* (1896) had an important influence on the education of blacks until 1954. This case involved an attack upon a Louisiana statute requiring segregation on intrastate railroads. Plessy asked the court to invalidate the Louisiana law as a violation of his personal rights under the Thirteenth and Fourteenth Amendments. The court refused his demand. Consequently, the "separate but equal" doctrine of education was given the sanction of federal law by virtue of a dictum, or remark, of the court. The Supreme Court actually went out of its way to recognize "that segregation in education was a general American practice, not an uniquely southern one." Thus, the court firmly embedded the durable doctrine of "separate but equal," the determinant in litigation involving the dual school system.

From 1896 to 1954, the dual system of education was developed and expanded in the South. Permissive segregation was maintained in the border states. Schools remained, in fact, separate and unequal.

Developments during the Twentieth Century In the early years of the twentieth century, public education for blacks in the South received significant impetus from the outside through the contributions of such philanthropists as John D. Rockefeller and George Peabody. In 1908 the Anna T. Jeanes Fund inaugurated the Jeanes Teacher program to improve the quality of instruction in rural black schools. Beginning in 1913, the Julius Rosenwald Fund provided grants for black school construction, and by 1932 more than 5,000 school buildings in 883 counties of 15 southern and border states had been built with Rosenwald aid. George E. Davis (1862–1959), of North Carolina and a teacher at Biddle University, was the first Afro-American appointed by Rosenwald for the building program. Rosenwald grants provided an invaluable incentive and accounted for about 15 percent of the money spent on school construction for blacks. In addition, 17 percent came from direct contributions made by blacks themselves. Nevertheless, at the end of the Rosenwald building program, the per-pupil value of black school property was less than one-fifth that of white schools. Even more telling is a comparison of teachers' salaries. Between 1900 and 1930, the average white salary rose from slightly less than $200 to $900, while the average black salary rose from $100 to $400. (These figures reflect the peak of a national boom, both in national income and in school population.)

The effects of this disparate policy were evident in the concentration of black children in the lower grades during the first half of the twentieth century. Poor and inadequate, or often no facilities, were available for higher grades. As late as 1920, 85 percent of all black pupils in the South were enrolled in the first four grades. In 1916 only 67 black public high schools existed, with fewer than 20,000 students.

Challenges to the *Plessy* Decision Between 1896, when the *Plessy* decision was handed down, and 1930, only three cases involving black education came before the Supreme Court. However, in none of these was school segregation directly challenged, nor did the court order relief of any

kind for black plaintiffs. In 1899 the Supreme Court heard an appeal by a group of blacks from Augusta, Ga., who demanded an end to public support for two white high schools after the sole black high school had been discontinued. The majority opinion in this case, *Cumming v. Richmond County,* held that the relief requested was improper. In 1908 the Supreme Court heard the case of *Berea College v. Kentucky,* which involved the right of a privately chartered college to teach both races in defiance of a Kentucky law making segregation mandatory. The Supreme Court ruled against Berea on technical grounds. In 1927 the court heard the case of *Gong Lum v. Rice.* The issue was whether the state of Mississippi could properly classify a Chinese child as "colored" and therefore require her to attend a black school. The court upheld the local state law and Chief Justice William Howard Taft offered a reminder that the "separate but equal" doctrine was still in effect: "Had the petition alleged specifically that there was no colored school in Martha Lum's neighborhood to which she could conveniently go, a different question would have been presented." None of these cases directly challenged the constitutionality of segregation in education.

In 1935 the doctrine of separate but equal received a fourth challenge, that of Donald Murray, a black who had applied for admission to the law school of the University of Maryland and had been refused in accordance with Maryland's segregation statutes.

An exhibit of the Farm Security Administration (FSA). This federal agency sought to improve rural black life while it existed (1937–1946), operating through low-interest, repayable loans to farmers and rehabilitation loans for education. *(Library of Congress.)*

During the decade and a half that followed, the South spent unprecedented sums on the education of blacks out of fear that further litigation might be successful in overcoming the "separate but equal" doctrine. However, the amount spent was still too little and came too late to repair the many inequalities. Thus, in 1952, the long course of litigation over separate education in America brought before the U.S. Supreme Court five separate cases that challenged the Plessy doctrine head on.

Each of these cases raised the basic issues of segregation in education in a somewhat different way. The implications pervaded the entire nation's segregated pattern, as laid down by the *Plessy* decision, as well as the basic division of authority between the federal government and the sovereign states. In addition, the moral overtones had practical repercussions on America's effort in international politics to keep black, brown, and yellow peoples of the world from swinging into the Communist orbit.

The most celebrated of the cases brought before the Supreme Court was *Brown v. Board of Education of Topeka,* under the leadership of Thurgood Marshall, chief counsel for the National Association for the Advancement of Colored People (NAACP). Precedent-setting social science testimony provided by Kenneth B. Clark supported the view that segregated education damaged the personality of black children, lowered their motivation, and contributed to their development of negative self-images. These factors, it was held, damaged the aspirational levels of black children and therefore had a negative effect on academic achievement. On the basis of this evidence, on May 17, 1954, the U.S. Supreme Court ruled unanimously and unequivocally that segregation of the races in public education was unconstitutional.

Desegregation Desegregation had been progressing slowly, even in the South, before this historic and far-reaching decision. In the fall of 1954, in compliance with the *Brown* decision, it began in earnest in a few large cities, notably Wilmington, Del., Baltimore, Md., and Washington, D.C., and in some scattered counties in Missouri, Arkansas, and West Virginia. By the fourth anniversary of the Supreme Court's original decision, desegregation was underway in ten out of seventeen states that previously had compulsory school segregation. In keeping with the court-ordained "deliberate speed" clause, desegregation moved faster in Kentucky, Oklahoma, and Texas than in Tennessee and North Carolina. But it did spread. Out of 2,889 southern school districts with both white and black pupils, desegregation had begun in 764 by the end of four years. Of these, fewer than 40 districts were compelled to act by specific court order.

Then, in the fall of 1958, southern hostility abruptly brought desegregation almost to a standstill. New efforts at integration were limited to 13 school districts in the entire South, and in Little Rock, Ark., and in sections of Virginia, schools were closed to avoid integration. Desegregation had been stopped short by seven states willing to dispense with public schools rather than to yield to racial mixing.

In the middle of the 1958–59 school year, the situation took yet another turn. Black pupils entered white schools in Alexandria, Va., without incident, bringing a third new community into the sphere of desegregation—and not in a border state but in a former center of massive resistance. Desegregation thus met the ultimate test of school closing and proved, at least in Virginia, that parents placed sufficiently high value on public education for their children to endure a limited amount of integration. Georgia, Alabama, and Mississippi still seemed ready to provide strong resistance. Yet, the solid front had been broken, and, in its sixth year, desegregation made marked advances.

The decade of the 1960s brought a shift in the racial conflict in schools from the South to the urban cities of the North. By 1970 more black children attended segregated schools than ever before in the history of America because mass migration to the black ghettos of the northern

Three of the nine black students aiming to attend legally integrated Central High School, Little Rock, Ark., arrive at the school on October 2, 1957. They were protected by Army paratroopers, called out by President Eisenhower to enforce the court order of desegregation after several weeks of mob action prevented the students from entering the school. The nine students and their leader, Daisy Bates, were later awarded the Spingarn Medal. *(Photoworld, Inc.)*

cities created de facto segregated schools, as evidenced by the table below.

PERCENT OF BLACK STUDENTS ATTENDING SCHOOLS 80 PERCENT OR MORE BLACK IN 34 BIG CITY SCHOOL DISTRICTS WITH ONE-THIRD OR MORE BLACK ENROLLMENT IN 1968 AND 1971[a]

District	1968	1971
Washington, D.C.	96.5	97.6
Compton, Calif.		97.8
Atlanta, Ga.	91.8	85.9
Newark, N.J.	88.4	91.3
Orleans Parish, La.	83.3	80.8
Richmond, Va.	88.6	36.5
Baltimore, Md.	83.8	84.1
St. Louis, Mo.	89.0	89.8
Gary, Ind.	90.7	95.7
Detroit, Mich.	79.1	78.6
Philadelphia, Pa.	76.9	80.2[b]
Oakland, Calif.	77.1	73.1
Cleveland, Ohio	90.8	91.3
Birmingham, Ala.	92.7	74.7
Chicago, Ill.	90.3	91.6
Memphis, Tenn.	95.4	89.2
Kansas City, Mo.	78.1	86.4
Caddo Parish, La.	97.4	66.6
Louisville, Ky.	64.9	82.3
Chatham County, Ga.	86.5	7.6
Charleston County, S.C.	84.2	62.4
Norfolk, Va.	82.3	1.2
Cincinnati, Ohio	50.9	54.9
Mobile County, Ala.	87.5	44.2
Dayton, Ohio	82.7	78.1
Pittsburgh, Pa.	60.0	61.6
Flint, Mich.	42.4	46.6
Buffalo, N.Y.	65.1	59.0
Baton Rouge Parish, La.	94.2	72.0
Houston, Tex.	90.9	86.0
Indianapolis, Ind.	62.5	60.1
Dallas, Tex.	93.0	83.4
Rochester, N.Y.	34.4	33.7
New York, N.Y.	60.5	69.2

SOURCE: U.S. Senate Select Committee on Equal Educational Opportunity, 1972, pp. 116–17.
[a]Ranked according to 1971 black percentage in enrollment.
[b]1970 figure.

Busing During the two decades following the U.S. Supreme Court decision outlawing de jure segregated education (*Brown v. Board of Education of Topeka,* 1954), various methods were employed to eliminate racial segregation in schools. Busing became one of the methods used to correct racial imbalance: sending black children (in school buses) to predominantly white schools away from their own neighborhoods and white children to predominantly black schools, also in other neighborhoods.

Few issues in the movement toward desegregation in education generated so much emotionalism and controversy. In some communities, both northern and southern, feelings erupted into rage and violence. The busing issue became a problem of national significance after the 1968 Supreme Court decision that "free choice" plans were acceptable only if they actually abolished racially segregated schools. It held also that school districts must submit a desegregation plan "which promises realistically to work now."

In August 1970 the U.S. Congress passed a $75 million Emergency School Assistance Program Act to assist in school desegregation. The federal courts had been requiring busing in urban areas to remedy racial imbalances. By 1971, after a long series of court cases and controversies in communities, the Supreme Court in *Swann v. Charlotte-Mecklenburg Board of Education* decided on a desegregation plan that would require a substantial increase in busing: "An objection to the transportation of students may have validity when the time or distance traveled is so great as to risk either the health of the children or significantly impinge on education progress."

Congressional reaction came quickly. Antibusing amendments were added to pending educational legislation. Comprehensive legislation was proposed that would limit the power of the courts as well as the use of busing. A constitutional amendment prohibiting busing was proposed and received great support.

The Nixon administration changed positions on the busing controversy several times between 1970 and 1974, resulting in more confusion and conflict. The Department of Health, Education, and Welfare (HEW) appeared to the public to shift its positions on policy from time to time; it often changed policy on the provision of funds to enable districts to desegregate schools by busing. Antibusing amendments to educational legislation frequently delayed the passage of much needed educational reforms.

Then, in July 1974, the Supreme Court ruled in a five-to-four decision in *Milliken v. Bradley* that interdistrict busing between Detroit, Mich., and its suburbs was not an appropriate remedy for segregated schools in the city. The court maintained that the plaintiffs had not demonstrated that actions of suburban school districts had resulted in segregation, but it did not close the door on all cross-district busing plans. However, the *Milliken* decision did place the burden of proof on those who seek to desegregate schools by busing.

History and experience have taught Afro-Americans that it is impossible to have equal

By 1970, educational attainment of young black adults was within one-half year of young white people this age. Lack of education is often a barrier to employment in better-paid jobs for both black and white workers, whether education is required for performance of the job or not.

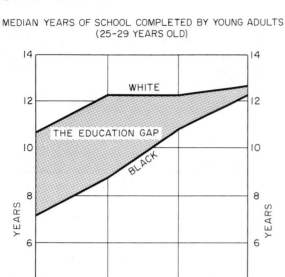

MEDIAN YEARS OF SCHOOL COMPLETED BY YOUNG ADULTS (25-29 YEARS OLD)

Source: U.S. Department of Labor, Bureau of Labor Statistics (1960–1974).

opportunities when facilities and institutions are segregated. Historically, the "separate but equal" doctrine has not worked. Since education is of such great significance in the improvement of the quality of life for any individual, many blacks view the desegregation issue as the most compelling one confronting them today. *See also* AFRICAN MEETINGHOUSE; AMERICAN MISSIONARY ASSOCIATION (AMA); AFRO-AMERICAN HISTORY; CIVIL RIGHTS: CIVIL RIGHTS CASES, 1865–1975; NATIONAL ASSOCIATION FOR THE ADVANCEMENT OF COLORED PEOPLE (NAACP).

REFERENCES: For additional information, see: Ashmore, Harry S., *The Negro and the Schools*, University of North Carolina Press, Chapel Hill, 1954; Bond, Horace Mann, *The Education of the Negro in the American Social Order*, 2d ed., Octagon, New York, 1966; Bullock, Henry Allen, *A History of Negro Education in the South: From 1619 to the Present*, Harvard University Press, Cambridge, 1967; Clift, Virgil A., Archibald W. Anderson, and H. Gordon Hullfish, *Negro Education in America: Its Adequacy, Problems and Needs*, Harper, New York, 1962; Clift, Virgil A., "Educating the American Negro," in J. P. Davis (ed.), *American Negro Reference Book*, Prentice-Hall, Englewood Cliffs, 1965, pp. 360–95; and Coleman, James S., *Equality of Educational Opportunity*, U.S. Government Printing Office, Washington, D.C., 1966. *See also* listings of the *Journal of Negro Education* under REFERENCES for the entry on colleges and universities. In addition, more recent references, especially in regard to desegregation, are found in the introductory chapter ("Introduction: The Desegregation Controversy in Context," pp. 44–55) in the edition by Daniel U. Levine and Robert J. Havighurst, *The Future of Big-City Schools: Desegregation Policies and Magnet Alternatives*, McCutchan Publishing Corporation, Berkeley, 1977. Of further value is Benjamin S. Bloom, *Human Characteristics and School Learning*, McGraw-Hill Book Co., New York, 1976; and Reynolds Farley "Residential Segregation and its Implications for School Integration," Duke University, School of Law, *Law and Contemporary Problems*, vol. 39, Winter, 1975.

Colleges and Universities Organized higher education for blacks started immediately following the Civil War, and for the most part it began in one of two ways: either with the help of religious groups and sometimes assistance from individual philanthropists or philanthropic groups; or, after 1890, through legislative acts. State help came mainly after the Land Grant Act (Second Morrill Act) of 1890 when no federal aid was to be given to any white agricultural and mechanical school unless the state had also provided for a similar school for blacks.

Although the first schools were called anything from seminaries to universities, they almost all began with the basic reading and writing and other elementary subjects necessary to train the mostly illiterate, newly freed slaves. In addition, many schools emphasized religion, education, and vocational activities. Religion, of course, was inherent in the many church-related schools. Teacher training was automatically recognized as necessary; learning had to be spread, and quickly. Vocational and agricultural studies were likewise a necessity.

These historic black schools changed rapidly. As one need was filled, it was replaced by another. Secondary schools and college-level courses were added, and gradually the lower levels of teaching were dropped and left for the regular lower schools that arose. Between 1930 and 1950, graduate work was added in many black colleges and universities. Most of these historic black schools still exist, and many are among the most prominent higher institutions in the nation, although their names may have been changed several times, as well as their curricula and even their sites. Of course, they have all moved from the first makeshift "school houses"—that may have been anything from space in a church basement, a one-room wooden cabin, or perhaps an actual house or small building—to modern school complexes of various types and sizes. The schools have also evolved from original student bodies of fewer than 12 to hundreds or thousands of students, and from a faculty of one to whatever size of faculty the current student body requires.

Some of the most important of the church-founded schools include Atlanta University (1865), in Atlanta, Ga.; Fisk University (1866), in Nashville, Tenn.; Talladega College (1867), in Talladega, Ala.; and Tougaloo University (1869), in Tougaloo, Miss. All four schools were established by the American Missionary Association (AMA). The Arkansas Agricultural, Mechanical, and Normal (AM&N) College began as Branch Normal in 1873 at Pine Bluff, Ark. Morehouse College, of Atlanta, Ga., was originally established in 1867 as the Augusta Institute in Augusta, Ga. Morehouse was initially supported by the American Baptist Home Mission Society, which was also instrumental in the founding and support of Virginia Union University (1865), in Richmond, Va., Shaw University (1865), in Raleigh, N.C., and Benedict College (1870), in Columbia, S.C. The Methodist Episcopal (ME) Church established an institution at Holly Springs, Miss., in 1867, a school later known as Shaw University and as Rust College. The Presbyterians in North Carolina established Scotia Seminary, which today is known as Barber-Scotia College. Biddle University was founded the same year at Charlotte, N.C., and is known today as Johnson C. Smith University. The Methodist Episcopal (ME) Church founded the Centenary Biblical Institute in Baltimore, Md., in 1866, which became Morgan College, then Morgan State College, and is today Morgan State University. Howard University in Washington, D.C., was established in 1867. These are a few of the institutions of higher education, significant in America today, that can trace their roots to the post-Civil War period.

Large-scale philanthropy for whites and blacks, as opposed to the individual philanthropy that often went hand in hand with church efforts, provided buildings, endowments, scholarships, and support for teacher training and industrial education. These funds included the Samuel F. Slater Fund, the Rosenwald Fund,

A rare photograph of Howard University in 1870, three years after its founding. (*Moorland-Spingarn Research Center.*)

and funds established by George Peabody, Andrew Carnegie, and John D. Rockefeller. The Daniel Hand Fund and the Anna T. Jeanes Fund were established exclusively for blacks.

Land-grant colleges for blacks were established under the provisions of the Second Morrill Act (1890), which was one of the first legislative actions to assure land-grant funds for Negro

Founded as Ashmun Institute in 1854, The Lincoln University, situated in Chester County, Pa., was renamed in 1866. (*Courtesy of The Lincoln University.*)

339

education in areas where the dual system of education existed. On the other hand, the act also gave strength to the doctrine of "separate but equal," with the result that the 17 southern states maintained colleges that came to be known as Negro land-grant colleges, upon which much of the public system of higher education for blacks in the South was based.

Tuskegee Institute, early 1900s. Vocational education and home economics were taught, in keeping with the land-grant idea in general and the insistence of founder Booker T. Washington in particular. (Tuskegee Institute.)

After Reconstruction (1877), the South deprived blacks not only of citizenship rights but also of educational privileges. From 1876 to 1895, in the southern states as a whole, the enrollment of whites increased markedly (106 percent) and that of blacks only moderately (59 percent). During the 1890s, blacks were disfranchised by state constitutional provisions and their subordinate status was given legal basis in the South. As a result, their education became more segregated in those areas where mixed schools had existed, and subsequently inequalities developed in teachers' salaries and in other provisions for education.

Students in home economics at Tougaloo College, early 1900s. (Tougaloo College.)

In 1890 the influence of Booker T. Washington began to spread. His campaign to establish an educational program for blacks that would be acceptable to the South was widely discussed and approved. During this period, philanthropy also became an important factor in the support of black education in the South. Ironically, seizing upon these two factors, southern states soon introduced inequality into their support of black and white education. Gains that had been made toward the racial mixing of schools were quickly stamped out.

A dictum from the famous case of Plessy v. Ferguson (1896) became the basis for the "separate but equal" doctrine of education in the South. The U.S. Supreme Court actually went out of its way to recognize "that segregation in education was a general American practice, not an uniquely Southern one." From 1896 to 1954, the dual system of education was developed and expanded.

Supreme Court and Higher Education In 1935, almost 40 years after the Supreme Court handed down the Plessy decision permitting "separate but equal" public educational facilities, Donald Murray, a black, applied for admission to the law school of the University of Maryland and was refused. His complaint was that the state of Maryland provided no law school for blacks within its boundaries but had attempted to meet the implications of the Plessy doctrine by offering a limited number of scholarships for blacks in institutions outside the state. The Maryland Court of Appeals upheld Murray's contention and accepted the argument that out-of-state scholarships, which covered only the cost of tuition, placed black students at an economic disadvantage.

The Gaines case in 1938 was the real forerunner of the court decisions of the 1940s that opened graduate schools in the South to blacks. Lloyd Gaines sued for admission to the law school of the University of Missouri on the grounds that no separate law school was provided in the state and that the out-of-state scholarships available to him did not satisfy the requirement of equal treatment. The Supreme Court reversed the courts of Missouri in a majority opinion that announced a new point of law.

The Gaines decision set into motion a feverish expansion of state-supported black graduate and professional schools, an expansion designed especially to deny blacks admission to white state-supported colleges and universities. The decade following the Murray and Gaines cases witnessed the most revolutionary change in the history of education in the South: the entire region began to spend an unprecedented proportion of its income for the education of black children in public schools (in order to avoid possible court orders to admit them to white schools).

It came as a surprise to southern state officials and legislators that blacks were not impressed with the makeshift graduate schools, the increased expenditure on capital improvements, the attempts to equalize salaries, and the general increase in expenditures for black education. Educational opportunities were greatly improved, to be sure, but Afro-American citizens were unimpressed when they compared their condition with that of their white fellow citizens and with the promises long tendered to them by the American system.

Therefore, blacks prepared to make direct attacks on the validity of segregation in higher education. In cases against the University of Oklahoma and against the University of Texas, black plaintiffs, between 1946 and 1949, carried to the U.S. Supreme Court issues that sharply tested the right of states to alter in any substantial particular the opportunities for graduate and professional study offered to blacks in terms of that offered to whites. Indeed, in the Texas case, *Sweatt v. Painter*, the plaintiff's attorneys argued that no segregated black school actually could provide an equal education. They not only declared that the new black law school established by Texas was materially inferior, but also they offered the testimony of anthropologists, psychologists, and educators to show that blacks were as capable of learning as were whites, that classification of students by race was arbitrary and unjust, and that segregation was harmful to personality adjustment. The court obviously gave weight to these contentions in that it ruled out segregation in specific instances in college-level education, and to a large extent in the field of graduate and professional training.

Meanwhile, the southern states had pooled their resources to set up regional programs for higher education that would serve both the black and white students of all participating states. This plan was denounced by black leaders as another device for preserving segregation. The Southern Regional Educational Board and the regional compact were immediately challenged in 1949 when Esther McCready was denied admission to the University of Maryland School of Nursing on the grounds that she was entitled under the regional plan to out-of-state training at

Meharry Medical College, a black institution at Nashville, Tenn. The Maryland Court of Appeals ordered McCready admitted to the state university. Following this decision, more public institutions admitted blacks, although enrollment was restricted primarily to graduate and professional schools.

The relentless legal assault upon segregated education was planned and executed with great care. Black leaders reasoned that the anachronistic system of segregation in public elementary and secondary schools perpetuated segregation and discrimination in all other phases of public life of the nation. They maintained that such segregation was a divisive and antidemocratic device perpetuating an obsolete caste system that was in clear conflict with the basic ethical concepts of the American Judeo-Christian tradition.

By this time, some Afro-Americans were demanding that the National Association for the Advancement of Colored People (NAACP) press harder for equal rights in all fields. Large segments of Afro-Americans, in the North and in the South, were making such great demands that in many instances their leaders were actually being pressured into actions that otherwise they may have been reluctant to take.

Blacks in Nonblack Colleges From emancipation to the 1930s, blacks were excluded by law from white colleges in southern states. Even though many blacks attended white colleges elsewhere in the nation, it was not until 1972 that the number attending white colleges equaled the number attending colleges regarded historically as black.

The dramatic increase in black enrollments in white colleges came after the death of Martin Luther King, Jr., in 1968. The civil rights movement throughout the 1960s had produced a dramatic rise in black enrollment in white institutions as a result of new open admissions policies at many white institutions. In addition, the number of community colleges in urban areas increased, and these new schools were attended by large numbers of blacks. These two factors (new open admissions policies and an increase in the number of community colleges) were largely responsible for the rapid rise of general black enrollment in schools of higher education between 1968 and 1974 and also accounted for the fact that during that period more blacks enrolled in white institutions than in historically black colleges.

In 1974 about 750,000 blacks were enrolled in

colleges and post-secondary educational institutions. This figure included graduate and undergraduate students and students in professional schools, evening schools, community colleges, evening classes, terminal courses, and vocational courses. Of this number, more than 250,000 full-time undergraduates (larger than a similar enrollment at the historic black colleges) attended white institutions. In 1976 the total post-secondary black enrollment had reached 817,-000; in 1977, it was more than 1 million.

In 1971, among predominantly white, four-year institutions, Wayne State University (Detroit, Mich.) and the City College of the City University of New York had the most black full-time students—Wayne with 3,649 and City College with 2,046. About a dozen other mostly white universities—among them Rutgers, Southern Illinois, Michigan State, Illinois, Memphis State, California at Los Angeles, California at Berkeley, Michigan, Maryland, and New York—each enrolled more than 1,000 blacks.

The largest of the predominantly black colleges (1975) were Howard University, Southern University, Jackson State College, and Morgan State University.

Problems of the Historic Black Colleges Although the faculties and student bodies of many historic black colleges were becoming increasingly integrated, these institutions seem destined to remain, for some decades to come, the major college alternative for black youth. It is important, therefore, to consider those obstacles that prevent these schools from providing the highest quality of education. The four most pressing problems are discussed below.

Adequate Financial Support Financial support remains woefully inadequate. Historically, segregation in education has always been used as a weapon for discrimination. The doctrine of separate but unequal is deeply embedded in the culture of the South. Indeed, any land-grant university with an enrollment of 20,000 or more has an annual budget that far exceeds the combined budgets of all the black state colleges and the additional 32 private liberal arts colleges that are supported by the United Negro College Fund.

Adequately Trained Faculty It is difficult to recruit and hold a competent faculty. Many other employment opportunities are now open to trained blacks and these professionals are increasingly lured away from teaching. (Formerly teaching was almost the only employment in which Afro-Americans could use their advanced training.) These new professional employment opportunities are especially attractive because they frequently pay more than the inadequately supported college. Other teachers leave these historic black colleges because they want to move to the North where, generally, there is less discrimination. Still others find positions at white universities where it is much easier to gain recognition as a scholar.

Adequately Prepared Student Body The problem of an inadequately prepared student body can be attributed to two factors. First, the lower schools most blacks attend are inferior due to lack of financial support, teachers with little training and experience, and deprived school neighborhoods. Thus, many youths who enter college are not properly prepared. Second, the most capable students, whose parents are more economically sufficient and are of a higher social class, are sent to prestigious white colleges and

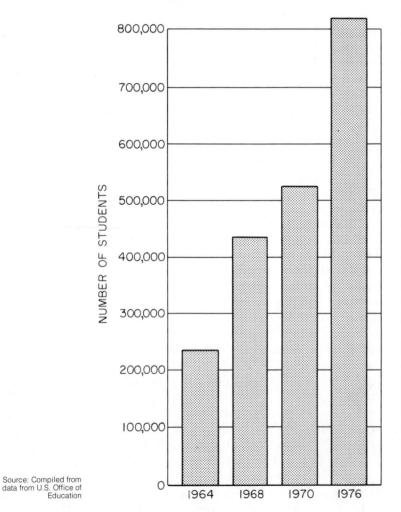

AFRO-AMERICANS ENROLLED IN COLLEGES

NUMBER OF STUDENTS

800,000
700,000
600,000
500,000
400,000
300,000
200,000
100,000
0

1964 1968 1970 1976

Source: Compiled from data from U.S. Office of Education

state universities. This practice skims the cream from the academic crop that once attended only all-black colleges.

Consequences of Inferior Status Assigned Black Colleges by the White Culture This last problem, relating to the inferior status assigned to black colleges, is difficult to assess in all its ramifications. The white majority never seems to hold black colleges in as high esteem as it does white institutions. In the South, black students are stigmatized because of their race, and they therefore have a double stigma to overcome when the institutions they attend, which are for the most part still segregated, are also regarded as inferior.

In the face of these problems, some black leaders feared that many black colleges might be dismantled or merged into white institutions unless their financial problems could be solved, and there seemed little hope of receiving adequate financial support from state and federal sources. In addition, enrollments were declining (thus compounding the financial crisis) as larger numbers of black high school graduates were attracted to white institutions.

"Save the Black Colleges" campaigns have not solved the problem. The United Negro College Fund, for example, was providing helpful financial assistance to more than 30 private colleges, but even this considerable effort was far from adequate. Several institutions also feared the loss of their identity as a result of being incorporated into the white university system or of having white state universities establish a branch nearby.

Black educators were caught up in the problem of trying to preserve the identity of the black college, on the one hand, while attempting to achieve integrated education on the other. Yet, by 1974, educators and the black community alike were firm in their conviction that their colleges should survive, should be made stronger and more competitive, and should not merge with white institutions. Afro-Americans wished to maintain control over their own institutions, regardless of the racial composition of the student body. They knew that black colleges provided great strengths, including: sources of ethnic pride; opportunities to develop leadership; opportunities for wholesome social relationships that were not possible in some white institutions; programs designed to meet the special and unique needs of the black community; and repositories for black heritage.

Profiles of the following colleges and universities are entered individually in this encyclopedia:

Alabama Agricultural and Mechanical (A & M) University
Alabama State University
Albany State College
Alcorn State University
Allen University
Arkansas Baptist College
Atlanta University
Barber-Scotia College
Benedict College
Bennett College
Bethune-Cookman College
Bishop College
Bluefield State College
Bowie State College
Central State University
Cheyney State College
Claflin University
Clark College
Coahoma Junior College
College of the Virgin Islands
Coppin State College
Daniel Payne College
Delaware State College
Dillard University
District of Columbia Teachers College
Edward Waters College
Elizabeth City State University
Fayetteville State University
Federal City College
Fisk University
Florida Agricultural and Mechanical (A & M) University
Florida Memorial College
Fort Valley State College
Friendship Junior College
Grambling College
Hampton Institute
Harris Teachers College
Howard University
Huston-Tillotson College
Interdenominational Theological Center
Jackson State College
Jarvis Christian College
Johnson C. Smith University
Kentucky State College
Kittrell College
Knoxville College
Lane College
Langston University
Lemoyne-Owen College
Lincoln University (Missouri)
Lincoln University (Pennsylvania)
Livingstone College
Lomax–Hannon Junior College
Mary Holmes College
Meharry Medical College
Miles College
Mississippi Industrial College
Mississippi Valley State College
Mobile State Junior College
Morehouse College
Morgan State University
Morris Brown College
Morris College
Morristown College
Natchez Junior College
Norfolk State College
North Carolina Central University
Oakwood College
Paine College

Paul Quinn College
Philander Smith College
Prairie View Agricultural and Mechanical (A & M)
    University
Prentiss Normal and Industrial Institute
Rust College
Saint Augustine's College
Saint Paul's College
Savannah State College
Selma University
Shaw University
Shorter College
Simmons University Bible College
South Carolina State College
Southern University Agriculture and Mechanical (A&
    M) College
Southwestern Christian College
Spelman College
Stillman College
Talladega College
Tennessee State University
Texas College
Texas Southern University
Theodore Alfred Lawson State Junior College
Tougaloo College
Tuskegee Institute
University of Arkansas at Pine Bluff
University of the District of Columbia
University of Maryland Eastern Shore
Utica Junior College
Virginia State College
Virginia Union University
Voorhees College
West Virginia State College
Wilberforce University
Wiley College
Winston-Salem State University
Xavier University of Louisiana

Libraries and Archives The problems of black libraries and archives are much the same as those of the colleges: lack of funds. Yet these libraries are exceptional. Although they may be lacking in some areas, many black schools have developed libraries with rich collections of black studies materials. *See* ARCHIVES.

The importance of the history of black people and their heritage was only beginning to be fully recognized by many blacks as well as whites in the 1970s. It is a heritage with tremendous ramifications and one that, as with the historically black colleges, black educators and the black community alike seem determined to preserve.

Attitude of Black Students on Campus During the 1950s and early 1960s, black students sought integration and equality through the civil rights movement. By 1969, these students had begun to develop the concepts of black identity, black independence, black pride, and black power. By the spring of 1969, several white institutions had become targets of black student strikes, lockouts, and sit-ins. Demands for black studies, open admissions, black curricula, and in some cases separate accommodations on campus left a number of educators—both black and white—confused, bewildered, and even traumatized.

Black students were concerned with the problems of the institutionalized racism that had done little to combat poor housing, poor schools, poor physical and mental health, and poor job opportunities for Afro-Americans. The challenge to the black students and to higher eduction was one of trying to bring culturally separate worlds closer together, enabling black students to help their own people and to find identity and self-esteem while developing essential competencies and skills. *See also* AMERICAN MISSIONARY ASSOCIATION (AMA); ARCHIVES; CIVIL RIGHTS CASES, 1865–1975; FEDERATION OF PAN-AFRICAN EDUCATIONAL INSTITUTIONS; RACE: RACISM; SEGREGATION; UNITED NEGRO COLLEGE FUND.

REFERENCES: Some general references that are noteworthy include the following: Ashmore, Harry S., *The Negro and the Schools*, University of North Carolina Press, Chapel Hill, 1954; Bond, Horace Mann, *The Education of the Negro in the American Social Order, 1934*, Octagon, New York, 1966; Clift, Virgil A., Archibald W. Anderson, and H. Gordon Hullfish, *Negro Education in America: Its Adequacy, Problems and Needs*, Harper and Row, New York, 1962; *Journal of Negro Education* (all issues on the subject): "A Survey of Negro Higher Education," vol. 2, July 1933; "The Relationship of the Federal Government to Negro Education," vol. 7, July 1938; "Negro Higher and Professional Education in the U.S.," vol. 17, Summer, 1948; Desegregation and the Negro College," vol. 27, Summer 1958; "The Negro Private and Church-Related College," vol. 29, Summer 1960; "The Negro Public College," vol. 31, Summer 1962; "Studies in the Higher Education of Negro Americans," vol. 35, Fall 1966; "The Higher Education of Negro Americans: Prospects and Programs," vol. 36, Summer 1967; all of these issues appeared under the guidance of Charles A. Thompson who, while serving as a faculty member at Howard University, devoted 30 years (1934–1964) as editor. In addition, see also the best bibliographic treatment of black colleges as historic institutions in Chambers, Frederick, *Black Higher Education in the United States: A Selected Bibliography on Negro Higher Education and Historically Black Colleges and Universities*, Greenwood, Westport, Conn., 1978. Chambers, a professor of education at Kent State University (Kent, Ohio) pioneered in the long-neglected area of histories of black colleges. Contents of the volume include doctoral dissertations, institutional histories, masters theses, and selected books and general references.

Black Studies Black studies may be broadly defined as intensive and scholarly studies of the black experience in the United States, including some related experiences in Africa. However, no universally accepted definition exists. Roscoe C. Brown, director of the Institute of Afro-American Affairs, New York University, defined black studies as a scholarly examination of the culture and the history of black people, and of the social, economic, and political influences on black people in Africa, the Caribbean, and the United States.

Emergence of Black Studies Unprecedented in its dramatic and rapid implementation, the idea of teaching black history was ushered into higher education in the United States during the period of turmoil on college campuses in the late 1960s, although some historic black colleges had taught such topics a generation earlier. The annual meeting of the American Association of University Professors (1969) acknowledged that this turmoil, with its confrontations and demonstrations, grew out of "deep and sometimes profound moral discontent arising out of social injustices, public policy, and in some cases, out of inefficiency, irresponsibility, and unresponsiveness within the institutions themselves."

Among the discontented were black students who felt that college personnel were insensitive to their particular needs, especially the teaching of their own history. Seemingly overnight, prestigious and less well-known colleges alike accepted black studies programs and faculty integration as being long overdue, and hastily introduced courses of varying types and quality. Efforts to define black studies continued simultaneously with steps to design curricula; to prepare teachers; and to establish departments, institutes, centers, and/or coordinated interdisciplinary programs.

Some promoters maintained that the programs should be purely educational with educational goals and should not be used as forums for propaganda or reverse racism. Others held that a thorough and well-organized black studies curriculum was indispensable to the cultural liberation of black people.

Curriculum Most advocates of black studies attempted to avoid "black-white" courses, and instead worked for courses relevant to the black experience, which consisted in most instances of a marriage between theory and action. Most educators and administrators agreed on the theory side, for example, that an undergraduate major in black studies should be coupled with a traditional academic discipline in order to increase opportunities for employment or admission to graduate school. On the action side, black studies advocates attempted to relate learning to the black community. For example, students in the Africana Studies and Research Center at Cornell University (Ithaca, N.Y.) dug ditches in Tanzania and worked on voter registration in Mississippi. Courses too hastily instituted and taught by unprepared instructors were soon discontinued, if not avoided by black students themselves who sometimes derisively referred to them as "Chitterling 101" or "Advanced Cornbread."

Most black studies advocates recommended the inclusion of bibliographies of works of such black scholars as W. E. B. DuBois, Benjamin Brawley, Rayford W. Logan, E. Franklin Frazier, John Hope Franklin, and Benjamin Quarles. In a critique on black studies entitled "Realism in Afro-American Studies," Martin Kilson criticized the emotionalism of black militants who had little regard for the objectivity of scholars. Other writers whose works were popular with black students included Eldridge Cleaver, James Baldwin, Malcolm X, Claude Brown, Frantz Fanon, and Frederick Douglass.

Course offerings seemed unlimited in possibility, and a small sampling of typical courses included: African and Afro-American art; Contemporary Education of Afro-Americans; Afro-American Writers; Afro-American History; Africa: A Study in the Problems of Emerging Nations; Sociology of Afro-Americans; Black Capitalism; Jazz Styles and Techniques; Pan-Africanism: The Politics of Integration; The Caribbean and the West Indies; Community Studies: Problems in Community Living; Black Religion; Arabic; Swahili; Hausa; and The Afro-American Cultural Revolution and New Ethic.

The proliferation of black studies programs in the closing years of the 1960s depleted the supply of trained teachers, black or white. The black colleges in the South, which had long included courses on black history, literature, and music, became a major source for the recruitment of trained faculty members. Northern recruiters offered such enticements as salary increases and assistance in research projects and publication. Another source of teachers was the hastily trained self-proclaimed "expert" on blacks. Knowledgeable blacks—and some whites—were in high demand. Some black professors, as "adjunct," shuttled back and forth between two or more positions or appointments, recipients of a financial windfall that was in sharp contrast to the long, lean past that had previously confined them almost exclusively to black colleges.

John Hope Franklin, who first taught at a black college, held in an article entitled "On Negro American History and Black Studies," that universities themselves were responsible for this dearth of trained professors, pointing out that not until recently had institutions "encouraged whites to study and write about the history of Negro Americans." He concluded that when the history of the United States became integrated with the history of the black man, American history could then be written by any person, white or black, for nothing is so "irrelevant in telling the truth as the color of a man's skin." In any case, owing to the shortage of faculty prepared to conduct black studies courses, a number of colleges formed consortia. In addition, the Ford Foundation in 1969 provided $1 million to several institutions—Morgan State, Howard, and Yale—to help prepare faculty members to teach Afro-American courses. The black studies program at Morgan State University, regarded by some as exemplary, is thorough and interdisciplinary. It consists of (1) the undergraduate program; (2) the graduate program in black history; (3) the postdoctoral program in black culture; (4) special minority-related courses; and (5) the center for urban studies.

Whatever the approach, black studies programs survived the 1960s and early 1970s, but by the mid-1970s the elimination or curtailment of these programs at some institutions because of low enrollments and lack of financial support caused some concern about the permanent survival of such programs in colleges and universities.

REFERENCES: For additional information, see: Altman, Robert A. and Patricia O. Snyder, *The Minority Student on the Campus*, Western Interstate Commission for Higher Education, Boulder, 1970; Bernard, Cleveland, "Black Studies and Higher Education," *Phi Delta Kappan*, 1969; Brown, Roscoe C., "Black Studies in Perspective," *New York University Education Quarterly*, New York University School of Education, New York, 1971; *College Board Review*, "The Black Agenda for Higher Education," College Entrance Examination Board, no. 71, 1969; Edwards, Harry, *Black Students*, Free Press, New York, 1970; *IRCD Bulletin*, Eric Information Retrieval Center on the Disadvantaged, Horace Mann-Lincoln Institute, Teachers College, New York, 1969; Kilson, Martin, "Realism in Afro-American Studies," *Educational Annual, Teacher News*, New York State Federation of Teachers, vol. 2, no. 3, 1970; Morton, Carol, "Black Studies for Black Survival," *Essence*, May 1971; Reid, Inez Smith (ed.), *The Black Prism, Perspectives on the Black Experience*, City University of New York, New York, 1970; and Trent, Richard (ed.), *Afro-American Studies*, vol. 1, no. 1, Bordon and Breach, New York, 1970. In addition, see also the last four references under EDUCATION: DEVELOPMENTS IN ELEMENTARY AND SECONDARY EDUCATION.

Desegregation in Perspective Segregation is a socially patterned separation of people, usually accompanied by an unequal allocation of resources and accomplished by compulsion of politically and socially powerful community groups. The subordinate group, subjugated by legal and/or extralegal influences—including at times violence—is often seen as consisting of persons of an inferior mentality or morality. The powerful majority views the educational system as a principal means of ensuring its dominance. Thus, segregation is best understood as an adjunct to the doctrines of racial superiority. Doctrines that assert the equal dignity of all men are incompatible with the fact of segregation. While racial doctrines attain their own virulent momentum, they tend also to merge into the general ideological framework of society. The racial order is thus incorporated within the social order at large: the one comes to define the normality of the other.

The legal distinction between de facto and de jure segregation has been found to have no effect on the impact of a segregation upon children.

The essential mark of a segregated school is not the presence of a certain ethnic mixture, but rather the view of the community that the school is inferior and unsuitable for privileged children. A school is segregated when it becomes known as a "Negro school"; in a society that applies the doctrines of racial superiority, this term stigmatizes the school. The stigma imposed upon the school by the community makes it segregated. Such a school almost invariably will be deprived of an equal share of community resources inasmuch as the control of resources, as well as the thought-orientation, is socially patterned. If a school is considered by the community to be adequate for minority children but not for majority children, then that school is deemed segregated.

Desegregation is a process of dismantling the racial order by abolishing structural barriers in institutional life. The goal of school desegregation is to create a setting for productive learning by removal of policies and practices that inhibit the treatment of children as individual learners. A desegregated school is thus one in which children are not marked for failure or success because of their social identities.

Historical Aspects Until the Civil War, schools were segregated by law in both the North and South, with occasional exceptions in such New England cities as Portland, Maine, and New Bedford, Mass. Black children traditionally were placed in separate classrooms or sometimes even in a separate part of one room. Conditions differed within states; in southern Ohio, separate schools were the rule, while in Cleveland, black and white children learned together. During Reconstruction, when blacks gained considerable political power in the South, black legislators favored interracial schooling. It was, however, only rarely achieved, as in New Orleans, La., one of the few liberal cities. The end of Reconstruction led to extreme segregation in the public schools of the South. Many black children had no access to schools, segregated or desegregated. In the North, segregation persisted without benefit of law in some cases, and in violation of the law in many other instances. After World War I, northern cities swelled with the northward migration of blacks, and schools were forced to enroll large numbers of black children. By that time, residential segregation in these cities was a fait accompli, planned by white-controlled real estate organizations. White school boards chose to base public school boundaries on these manipulated residential

areas. Thus, school segregation in the North was an amalgam of deliberate policy and fortuitous population movement.

American higher education, private and public, was also severely segregated. Princeton University long excluded blacks; not until 1947 did an Afro-American student graduate from that institution. As late as the 1930s, black students were not permitted to share rooming or recreational facilities or extracurricular activities with white students at Ohio State University. This practice was approved by the Ohio Supreme Court. In the 1920s, black women were accepted at the University of Chicago but were not allowed to sleep in the women's dormitory. A scattering of black students were permitted to study at these and other white colleges, but they were also expected to "stay in their place." In the South, separate schools constituted a multiple burden upon the black community. They were meagerly furnished, and supplies and books were scarcely adequate. This very fact caused Afro-Americans to depend upon their own private schools which, because of black poverty, were even more meagerly supported.

Meanwhile, many black public schools were deprived of a fair measure of tax support; politically impotent, black communities rarely received their full share of tax money allocated through state aid. White school authorities—representing the county, especially—would send part of the allocation to black schools, but would shift the remainder to white schools. Thus, it became advantageous for a white community to have a large reservoir of Afro-American children to report to the state for purposes of state aid; it was implicit that black parents would not raise an effective protest against the shortchanging of their children. The more Negroes in a county, the greater the disparity between per capita school expenditures and types of education for black and white students. With Negro state-aid resources to draw on, white authorities, representing primarily the landowners of the area, could keep local school taxes low and relieve the largest property holders of a financial burden. What W. A. Davis wrote about Texas a generation ago can probably be applied to the entire South of the period: "The Texas educational system has been a dual system in name only; the Texas system is essentially a white system with Negro education incidental to it."

Similar tendencies operate in contemporary urban education in both the North and South.

Total expenditures on city schools rise with an increase of complaints about the inferior quality of inner-city education. Because of this inflated expenditure, academic achievement levels rise in more privileged suburbs and in schools located at the outer fringes of the central city. Inner-city education improves only slightly. The factor of residence has replaced the county school board as the mechanism for unequal distribution of public funds, and superior political power operates as the enforcing agent.

In neither elementary nor higher education was the practice of separate-but-unequal schooling challenged successfully. During the 1930s, segregation in public education was more prevalent than ever. The principle of "separate but equal" as applied to colleges and universities was reaffirmed by the U.S. Supreme Court (*Sweatt*, 1938), which insisted that practice must accord with the principle; "separate," the court said, must be "equal." In fact, however, equality in education was not the case either before or after 1938.

Problems of Enforcement The *Brown v. Board of Education of Topeka* decision in 1954 made school desegregation a constitutional requirement where deliberate state action toward segregation could be proved. W. E. B. Du Bois, the black educator, commented on the decision in 1955: "At best, it will be a generation before the segregated Negro public school entirely disappears. . . . It is going to be difficult for the South and the northern copperheads to treat the . . . decision as they have treated disfranchisement since 1876."

However, evasion proved easier than Du Bois imagined.

Southern states continued separate schools, and the federal government accepted the practice. Recourse to the courts brought, at best, admission of single black children to hitherto white schools. By 1959, Kenneth B. Clark, educator and social psychologist, warned: "If northern communities are able to preserve segregated schools, with their inequities and inherent damage, by adminstrative action, neglect, and indifference, merely because they have no laws which stipulate that this should be done, then southern communities may follow this example as an effective way of evading the letter and spirit of the May 17th decision of the United States Supreme Court. If this loophole is not removed, then that historic decision would be made hollow."

Segregation in northern schools continued to expand along carefully orchestrated residential lines. Southern cities adopted the same strategy, clearing black occupants from white residential areas and creating a geographical base for school segregation. Legal barriers were overcome in a variety of other ways, as the following account of an incident in Georgia shows.

In January 1958, ten Negro parents and the National Association for the Advancement of Colored People (NAACP) filed suit to desegregate Atlanta's public school system. Under existing state law, if such a suit were successful, it would become necessary to close all the public schools in Atlanta. From Atlanta, especially, there came a call for the state legislature to pass a local-option law, permitting the voters in any federally desegregated school district to decide whether the schools should be' closed. The state's oligarchs refused to concede the right of voters to decide the fate of their schools. In February 1959 the state legislature passed several laws: one permitted a single desegregated school to be closed rather than all the schools in the district; another prohibited any desegregated school district from levying school taxes; and a third offered a refund credit on the state income tax to those parents who sent their children to a private school so as to avoid attending a desegregated school. In June 1959 an Atlanta federal court ordered the city's school board to prepare a plan for desegregation. Five months later, the board presented a plan to desegregate one grade a year, starting with the last year of high school. Afro-American children were to be tested before being transferred to white schools. The court studied the plan.

Meanwhile, it was clear that Atlanta could not desegregate under federal court order and still obey the state law that required the closing of a school in the event of desegregation. Cries arose to keep the public schools open. In a way, this was a neutral position. No white group called for desegregation. But very wide circles of whites openly refused to permit schools to be closed to protest segregation. In the midst of this widespread debate—the state's first on any such issue since 1954—the political oligarchy temporized. After 40 days in session, the state legislature was still unable to resolve the question of whether to desegregate or close the schools. Instead, a 19-man study commission was appointed by the governor to make recommendations. In May 1960 the commission, by a vote of 11 to 8, came out in favor of a local-option law. The next month, a federal judge gave the Atlanta board one year to effectuate its desegregation plan.

Clearly, segregation in the schools was starting to give way. Legislators could see that they needed to grant some concessions. On the other hand, they were wedded to the ideal of segregation. Their problem was resolved by a suggestion from Newell Edenfield, president of the Georgia Bar Association. In June 1960 he publicly advocated that the legislature repeal all laws requiring school segregation. "Where a state by its solemn statutes admits and even brags that enforced segregation is being practiced," observed Edenfield, "there is nothing left for the [federal] court to decide and a blanket injunction follows automatically." He noted that in states that had no formal structure of school segregation laws—North Carolina and Alabama—black plaintiffs had been uniformly unsuccessful in loosening the grip of school segregation. The most the courts had done in such cases was to see to it that the individual plaintiffs—but no one else—were permitted to enter a white school, if they were qualified. Edenfield thus suggested the legal basis of "tokenism": concede on individual cases while maintaining the general pattern of segregation.

Hard-line segregationists seized upon this suggestion, although not without some initial suspicion. In January 1961 the governor asked the state legislature to repeal all the state's school segregation laws and to open all schools to any black applicant who could prove he was qualified; he also requested a local-option law. He was granted both. In September 1961, nine Afro-American children were transferred into four Atlanta high schools attended by a total of 4,600 white students. In July 1962 the desegregated Atlanta school system had 57,000 white students and 48,500 black students. Only 48 black students were in schools with white students.

When the so-called pupil placement laws were finally held unconstitutional, they were succeeded by new evasions, the chief of which was "free choice" or "open enrollment." According to this system, a white school was declared eligible for desegregation if individual black children applied. While some did, many were dissuaded from doing so by physical and economic coercion. In 1968, in the Green decision, the Supreme Court declared that any desegregation plan was constitutionally accepta-

ble so long as it resulted in effective desegregation. Hereafter, emphasis was laid on the practical effects of a plan. The following year, in Alexander, the court ordered Mississippi schools to desegregate immediately. In 1971 the court decided that wide-scale mandatory busing could be used if necessary to achieve a unitary (nonsegregated) school system.

Community Support Black communities, especially throughout the North, had opposed exclusion of their children from publicly supported schools. In the late 1840s blacks in Boston successfully fought school segregation. The pages of William Lloyd Garrison's Liberator (1831–66) are filled with instances of black opposition to separate schooling at public expense. During the years between 1890 and 1930, a number of school boycotts occurred in Alton, Ill., East Orange, N.J., and Springfield and Dayton, Ohio, among other places. Numerous court actions were undertaken by black parents throughout the North. In the South, political oppression prevented similar public protests.

After the Brown decision in 1954, school segregation became a prime target of the civil rights movement, especially in the North. In 1963 and 1964, mass black boycotts were undertaken in Boston, Mass., Chicago, Ill., New York City, and elsewhere. By the mid-1960s, school segregation had become a central issue among black people in the South. Black protests were mainly aimed against desegregation that was accomplished by closing black schools. The first such sustained black mass protest occurred in Swan Quarter, N.C., in 1967. In the following years, demands spread for more equitable desegregation: the exchange of white as well as black students. A large number of mass actions on behalf of this demand occurred in the South; only rarely was this demand pursued in the North. Black student and parent-organized actions also called for equal treatment after black and white students attended the same schools.

Present Situation In 1954 about 2.2 million black students attended all-black schools. By 1960 barely 235,000 black students attended formerly all-white schools. Over the next decade, significant changes occurred. In the fall of 1970 some 1.1 million black students were attending all-minority schools, half the number in 1954. At the same time, 3.4 million attended schools with some number of whites. This figure represented an enormous increase since 1954. In 1970, also, it could be said for the first time in American history that a higher percentage of southern schools was desegregated than of northern schools: in that year, 27.7 percent of all black students in the North attended predominantly nonminority schools; the figure for the South was 38.1 percent. This was a reversal of the situation that had existed only two years earlier.

Effects of Desegregation Numerous studies clearly demonstrate that desegregation helps close the academic achievement gap between black and white. A typical study was done at Duke University by Katzenmeyer in 1962. Katzenmeyer studied the effect of social interaction on the achievement of black and white pupils in the public schools of Jackson, Mich. He hypothesized that "the measured intelligence of the group of Negro children will be significantly changed as the consequence of school experience which enhances their opportunities for social interaction with the dominant white culture." The positive effects of integration on the achievement of black students had been cited in studies by James E. Coleman (Johns Hopkins University) and Christopher Jencks (Harvard University).

All children entering kindergarten in October and November, 1957 and 1958, were given a standard intelligence test. Included were 193 blacks and 1,061 whites. All were retested in the second grade in October 1959 and October 1960. Treating the blacks as an experimental group and the whites as a control, the mean IQ scores were as follows:

	1957/1958	1959/1960
Experimental group	83.06	89.74
Control group	102.04	103.91

The change in the experimental group was found to be statistically significant beyond the .001 level. Katzenmeyer concluded that the change was to be explained principally by the social interaction between black and white children.

Other research at the University of South Carolina reported the results of a specific study done after one year of desegregation in a southern city. Instead of tracing the progress of individual children, it was concerned with the effect of the racial composition of classes on achievement. It reported that "no significant relations were found between percent of Negroes in the class and amount of achievement." The results of the study, it was observed, "suggest that fears of necessary detrimental effects of desegregation on classroom achievement may not be firmly based."

Another study of certain factors in school achievement compared Afro-American achievement in two racially balanced and five imbalanced schools in an upstate New York city over a two-year period. On a global comparison, no significant achievement differences were found between children in either type of school. However, when students were divided into groups who had attended balanced or imbalanced schools for two years or longer, a significant difference emerged in favor of the children in the racially balanced schools. Research in the area of aspirations and self-concept permits the following generalizations to be made:

(1) Black students' aspirations are as high and often higher than those of white students.

(2) If realism is defined by its correspondence with the status quo, then Afro-American youth in colleges are highly realistic aspirants.

(3) The social climate of the school constitutes an autonomous influence upon aspirations.

(4) If the community as a whole were to raise its aspirations for the low-status student, including the Afro-American, an enormous educational stride forward would probably result.

(5) To disentangle the separate effects of race and class upon self-concept is extremely difficult.

(6) Desegregation has most often benefited the black child's self-esteem and has virtually never harmed it.

(7) Such historical factors as the civil rights movement are critical in raising the self-esteem of black children.

(8) Desegregation has facilitated black acceptance of color as a constructive factor, while heightening black willingness to live and learn with whites.

Much was heard in the 1970s about raising the self-conception of black children. Implied were the contentions that the self-conception of black children was poor and that self-conception and oppression are inversely related. Both contentions are misleadingly stated. If black self-conception and aspirations were only discovered by social scientists in the 1970s, it is not because they only then arose. Oliver C. Cox has pointed out: "Even as far back as the days of slavery Negro aspiration was everywhere evident. We could not conceive of any institution of hope, such as the Negro spirituals, developing among the lower castes of India. . . ." Horace Mann

Bond sardonically explained years ago: "For it is self-respect that gives to the American Negro that inner security in the face of real or fancied injuries which was accorded him as a member of a group definitely in its place." A contemporary researcher, Stanley Coopersmith, accounts for the coexistence of oppression and high self-esteem: " . . . It is not discrimination per se but the person's acceptance of his oppressor's judgment and standards, and rejection of his own standards that is likely to produce self-devaluation."

Student relations under desegregation were marked by toleration, for the most part, and less prominently by either violence or positive respect. Many interracial friendships developed. The old saw about students being more "liberal" than their parents was proven true by various studies. Whether in Syracuse, N.Y., or Detroit, Mich., students from the most varied social circumstances learned to cooperate to their mutual benefit. However, very few studies have afforded insights into the behavior of white students under desegregation.

Most administrative planning for desegregation concerned political and (white) community problems; very little dwelt on changes in classroom and curriculum. By and large, however, teachers seem to have attended to the single most important change in the classroom: they made Afro American children feel welcome. This is not to say that interracial classrooms were typically operating at the maximum benefit to black and to white children. Press reports of desegregation in some areas of the Deep South strongly suggested that numerous teachers and principals lent themselves to the humiliation of black children. Stated summarily, the major effects of school desegregation were as follows:

(1) Academic achievement rose as the minority child learned more and the advantaged majority child continued to learn at his accustomed rate. Thus, the achievement gap narrowed. This finding was, for all practical purposes, established in relation to black children. It is less firm with regard to American Indians and Mexican-American children.

(2) Black aspirations, already high, were positively affected; self-esteem rose; and self-acceptance as an Afro-American grew. With some exceptions, this was firmly established for black children, indicated for Mexican-American children, and true in an indeterminate degree for children of American Indians.

(3) Toleration, respect, and occasional friendships were the chief characteristics of student and teacher relations in desegregated schools. Little informal socializing occurred outside school. Exceptions were numerous, with physical violence playing a diminishing role.

(4) While culturally different from Afro-Americans, American Indians and Mexican-Americans did not seem to respond to desegregation in any culturally unique ways.

(5) The U.S. Office of Education's Equal Educational Opportunity Study and the U.S. Commission on Civil Rights' Racial Isolation Study lent strong support to both the learning and attitudinal effects of desegregation. The latter study afforded the stronger support but in no sense could the former be properly interpreted in the contrary direction.

(6) The effects of desegregation on Afro-Americans were evident; the support the Afro-American community lent to desegregation was widespread. The movement toward black nationalism has thus far, at least, not created disillusionment with the value of desegregation.

(7) Virtually none of the negative predictions by segregationists—lower achievement, aggravated self-concepts of black children, and growing disorder in desegregated schools—found support in the studies of actual desegregation. See also CIVIL RIGHTS: CIVIL RIGHTS CASES, 1865–1975; DISCRIMINATION; RACE: RACISM; SEGREGATION.

REFERENCES: For additional information see: Ashmore, Harry, *The Negro and the Schools*, University of North Carolina Press, Chapel Hill, 1954; Bullock, Henry Allan, *A History of Negro Education in the South from 1619 to the Present*, Harvard University Press, Cambridge, 1967, chs. 9–11; Mack, Raymond W. (ed.), *Our Children's Burden: Studies of Desegregation in Eight American Communities*, Random House, New York, 1968; Orfield, Gary, *The Reconstruction of Southern Education: The Schools and the 1964 Civil Rights Act*, Wiley-Interscience, New York, 1969; Panetta, Leon E. and Peter Gall, *Bring Us Together: The Nixon Team and the Civil Rights Retreat*, J. B. Lippincott Company, Philadelphia, 1971; Sarratt, Reed, *The Ordeal of Desegregation*, Harper and Row, New York, 1966; U.S. Commission on Civil Rights, *Racial Isolation in the Public Schools*, 2 vols., U.S. Government Printing Office, Washington, D.C., 1967; Weinberg, Meyer, *Desegregation Research: An Appraisal*, 2d ed., Phi Delta Kappa, Bloomington, 1970; Weinberg, Meyer (comp.), *The Education of the Minority Child: A Comprehensive Bibliography of 10,000 Selected Entries*, Integrated Education Associates, Chicago, 1970; and Weinberg, Meyer, *A Chance to Learn: The History of Race and Education in the United States*, Cambridge University Press, New York, 1977. See also the last four references under EDUCATION: DEVELOPMENT IN ELEMENTARY AND SECONDARY EDUCATION.

EDWARDS, ALFRED LEROY (1920–), public official; born in Key West, Fla. Edwards received a B.A. degree from Livingstone College (Salisbury, N.C.) in 1948, a M.A. degree from the University of Michigan in 1949, and his Ph.D. degree from the University of Iowa in 1958. All of his degrees were earned in economics. After a career in teaching at several universities, Edwards became an adviser in economics to the University of Nigeria at Nsukka. Appointed in 1963 as deputy assistant secretary for rural development and conservation in the U.S. Department of Agriculture, Edwards became one of the key coordinators in that department's Rural Renaissance Movement.

EDWARDS, DENNIS, JR. (1922–), lawyer, judge; born in New York, N.Y. Edwards graduated from New York University in 1941 and from Harvard Law School in 1944. He served as a law secretary to a justice of the New York State Supreme Court from 1948 to 1965, after which he became a judge of the Criminal Court of the City of New York.

EDWARDS, ESTER GORDY business executive; born in Oconee, Ga. Edwards attended Howard University (Washington, D.C.) from 1940 to 1941 and Wayne State University (Detroit, Mich.) from 1941 to 1942. In 1959 she joined Motown Record Corporation of Detroit, Mich., and became its senior vice-president and director of international operations. She also served as corporate secretary and director of Jobete Publishing Company of Detroit after 1959. Edwards was named chairman of the Wayne County Democratic Women's Committee in 1956, and in 1960 she was the only black woman delegate-at-large from Michigan to the Democratic National Convention. Edwards was appointed to the board of directors of the Central Business District Association of Detroit in 1970. *See also* GORDY, BERRY, JR.

EDWARDS, GILBERT FRANKLIN (1915–) sociologist, educator; born in Charleston, S.C. Edwards received a B.A. degree from Fisk University (Nashville, Tenn.) and his Ph.D. degree from the University of Chicago, where he was a Rosenwald Fellow. He taught at Fisk and at Howard University (Washington, D.C.) from the 1950s to the 1970s. Edwards also wrote *The Negro Professional Class* (1959) and edited *E. Franklin Frazier on Race Relations: Selected Papers* (1968).

EDWARDS, HERBERT OLIVER (1929–), clergyman, educator. Edwards received a B.A. degree from Morgan State University (Baltimore, Md.) in 1956, a B.D. degree from Harvard Divinity School, and his Ph.D. degree from Brown University (Providence, R.I.) in 1973. He was pastor of churches in Massachusetts, Maryland, and North Carolina. Edwards taught at Morgan State University, the University of Rhode Island, Roger Williams Junior College, and Harvard University. He was appointed associate professor of black studies at the Divinity School of Duke University in 1974. Edwards published some articles on theology and ethics, and he wrote *Non-Violence, Shame and the Future: The Social Ethics of Martin Luther King, Jr.* (1976).

EDWARDS, NELSON JACK (1917–), labor union leader; born in Lowndes County, Ala. Edwards left high school because of economic hardship, working first as a farm laborer and, in 1935, for the Southern Oil Company. In 1937 he moved to Detroit, Mich., and found work in a foundry making parts for Dodge autos. There Edwards was introduced to union activities, and in the late 1930s he was elected chairman of United Auto Workers (UAW) Local 900, whose membership was predominantly white. In 1962 Edwards became the first black member of the UAW executive board. In 1970 he was elected a union vice-president, the first black to hold that position. A champion of civil rights, Edwards worked with Martin Luther King, Jr., in Birmingham, Ala., in 1963 as an official representative of the UAW. He was a frequent contributor to *Free Labor World*, the official publication of the International Confederation of Trade Unions.

EDWARD WATERS COLLEGE Edward Waters College, at Jacksonville, Fla., was founded in 1866 at Live Oak, Fla., under the auspices of the African Methodist Episcopal (AME) Church. (It is still affiliated with that church.) A private coeducational school, it offers the bachelor's degree and provides liberal arts and teacher education curricula. In 1975 its enrollment was about 500.

Edward Waters College was the first institution of higher learning for blacks in Florida and was originally intended to provide an educated ministry, beginning with the first primary grade and continuing through the higher grades. In 1872 the school was chartered as Brown Theological Institute, and two years later it was renamed Brown University. In 1883 Brown University moved to Jacksonville, and in 1892 it was incorporated as Edward Waters College. In 1901 the college was destroyed by a fire, but it was rebuilt (1905) on its present site. It continued with programs from elementary school through the bachelor's degree until 1934. In 1934 the elementary school was discontinued, and in 1952 the high school programs were terminated. In 1955 the school became a junior college, and in 1958 it became a four-year college.

ELAM, LLOYD CHARLES (1928–), psychiatrist, educator; born in Little Rock, Ark. Elam received a B.S. degree from Roosevelt University (Chicago, Ill.) in 1950, his M.D. degree from the University of Washington in 1957, an honorary L.H.D. degree from Roosevelt University in 1974, and an honorary U.D. degree from Harvard University in 1973. He taught at Meharry Medical College (Nashville, Tenn.), beginning in 1961, and became its president in 1968.

ELDER, LEE (1934–), professional golfer; born in Dallas, Tex. Beginning as a caddie in Dallas, Elder became one of the leading players on the United Golf Association (UGA) tour after turning professional in 1962. He was the first Afro-American to play in the South African Professional Golfers' Association competition, and won the Nigerian Open in 1971. In the United States Elder qualified for Professional Golfers' Association (PGA) competition in 1967 and joined the integrated PGA tour a year later. His victory in the 1974 Monsanto Open made him the first black player ever to qualify for the Masters tournament (in 1975). Elder won the Houston Open in 1976. *See also* ATHLETES.

ELDER, LONNE, III (1931–), playwright; born in Americus, Ga. Elder studied at New Jersey State University, and after his discharge from the U.S. Army, he joined the Harlem Writer's Guild. He wrote the play *Ceremonies in Dark Old Men*, produced by the Negro Ensemble Company in New York in 1965, a play that won numerous awards and that was second in the voting for the 1969 Pulitzer Prize. Elder studied drama at Yale University and received a Whitney Fellowship. He worked on scripts for the television series "McCloud" and "NYPD" and wrote the script for the film *Sounder* (1974). *See also* LITERATURE: DRAMA/THEATER.

ELDRIDGE, ROY (LITTLE JAZZ) (1911–), jazz trumpeter, singer; born David Roy Eldridge in Pittsburgh, Pa. Eldridge began his career in the late 1920s with Speed Webb and Zach Whyte. During the next decade he performed with McKinney's Cotton Pickers, Teddy Hall, and Fletcher Henderson. During the 1940s, he played with Sammy Kaye, Gene Krupa, and Artie Shaw. One of the most influential trumpeters in jazz history, Eldridge formed his own quintet in the 1950s and also played with several small bands. *See also* MUSIC: JAZZ.

ELIZABETH CITY STATE TEACHERS COLLEGE *See next entry below.*

ELIZABETH CITY STATE UNIVERSITY Elizabeth City State University, at Elizabeth City, N.C., was founded in 1891 as the State Colored Normal School. The coeducational, four-year college is state-supported, offers a bachelor's degree, and provides liberal arts and teacher education curricula. The 1975 enrollment was about 1,140.

Hugh Cale, a black delegate from Pasquotank County, introduced a bill in the North Carolina general assembly to found the school. In 1912 the school moved to its present site. It has had six presidents since 1891: Peter W. Moore, John H. Bias, Harold L. Trigg, Sidney D. Williams, Walter N. Ridley, and Marion D. Thorpe.

The university offers remedial assistance in reading, speech, and general grammar. Special laboratory experiences are provided through observation and student teaching in the public schools, and through business intern programs. A university-established nursery school and kindergarten also serve as laboratory centers for students in early childhood education. In 1968 a Basic Education and Enrichment Program was begun to help all freshmen to achieve a higher level of performance.

ELLINGTON, EDWARD KENNEDY (DUKE) (1899–1974), jazz bandleader, pianist, composer; born in Washington, D.C. Ellington achieved one of the most legendary careers in American jazz. Educated in Washington, D.C., and with private teachers, Ellington formed his first jazz band in 1918 in Washington, D.C., and another in New York City in 1922. Many of jazz's greats performed with Ellington's band throughout its long period of popularity. Ellington's best-known popular tunes include "Mood Indigo," "Down Beat," "I Got It Bad and That Ain't Good," "Don't Get Around Much Anymore," and "Indigo Echoes." He also wrote many piano suites, the most important being "Black, Brown, and Beige," "Liberation Suite" (1947), "Harlem"

(1951), and "Blue Bells of Harlem" (1953). Ellington pioneered in the use of the wordless voice as a musical instrument in orchestration. The recipient of many awards and honors, including the Spingarn Medal and the Grammy Award, Ellington also established a scholarship

Duke Ellington. *(Columbia Broadcasting System.)*

fund and Ellington Collection at Yale University. *See also* MUSIC: JAZZ.

ELLIOTT, DAISY (1919–   ), public official, state legislator; born in Filbert, W.Va. After having become a resident of Michigan, Elliott graduated from the Detroit Institute of Commerce, and thereafter studied at Wayne State University (Detroit, Mich.) and the University of Detroit. A delegate to the Michigan constitutional convention, she authored the civil rights portion of the new constitution and was instrumental in creating a civil rights commission in Michigan. In 1962 Elliott was elected to the Michigan state legislature as a representative from Detroit, and subsequently she aided in the passage of more than 80 bills that bear her name, many of which are in the fields of education, and senior citizen and child welfare.

ELLIOTT, ROBERT B. (1842–84), state legislator, U.S. Representative; born in Boston, Mass. Elliott attended schools in Boston, Jamaica, and London, and graduated from Eton College in England in 1859. He first practiced law in England, and then in South Carolina where he became editor of the Charleston *Leader* newspaper. After attending the State constitutional con-

vention in 1868, Elliott served in the lower house of the state legislature until 1870. From 1869 to 1871 he was assistant adjutant general of South Carolina, after which he was elected as a Republican representative to the Forty-second Congress, which convened in 1871. Elliott resigned his House seat in 1874 and returned to the state legislature as speaker of the house for two years. He moved to New Orleans, La., at the age of 39, where he practiced law until his death three years later.

ELLIS, EFFIE O'NEAL (1913–   ), physician; born in Pulaski County, Ga. Ellis received her M.A. degree in biology from Atlanta University and later studied at the University of Illinois College of Medicine and at Johns Hopkins University (Baltimore, Md.), specializing in pediatrics. She served as special assistant for health services for the American Medical Association (1970) and was widely acclaimed for her work in the area of food and nutritional problems of the poor.

ELLIS, E. FRANK (1918–   ), physician, educator; born in Pittsburgh, Pa. Ellis received a B.S. degree from Boston University in 1940, his M.D. degree from Meharry Medical College (Nashville, Tenn.) in 1944, and his M.P.H. degree from the University of Michigan in 1968. He interned at Kansas City Hospital No. 2 and was medical superintendent there from 1946 to 1956. Ellis served as assistant administrator and director of outpatient services at Kansas City General Hospital and Medical Center, as a faculty member in community medicine at the University of Missouri, and as director of the Department of Public Health and Welfare, Cleveland, Ohio (1968). He then became assistant professor of community medicine at Case Western Reserve University (Cleveland, Ohio).

ELLIS, GEORGE C. (1890– ?), physician. Ellis attended the University of Illinois and received his M.D. degree from Rush Medical College in 1918. He interned at Illinois Central Hospital and was later neurologist for Cook County Hospital and Psychopathic Hospital. Ellis received a Rosenwald Fellowship for study at Queens Hospital, London. He served as head of the division of neurology at Provident Hospital, Chicago, Ill.

ELLISON, JOHN MARIUS (1893– ?), educator; born in Richmond, Va. Ellison received a B.A. degree from Virginia Union University in 1925, a M.A. degree from Oberlin College (Oberlin, Ohio) in 1927, studied at Union Theological Seminary, and received his Ph.D. degree from Drew University (Madison, N.J.) in 1933. He founded and was principal of Northumberland County High School (Reedville, Va.) from 1918 to 1926, chaplain and professor of sociology at Virginia State College from 1927 to 1934, instructor in religious education at Howard University (Washington, D.C.), and professor of sociology at Virginia Union University after 1936. In 1936 Ellison was appointed by the federal government to study social and economic conditions in Michigan.

ELLISON, NOLEN M. (1941–   ), educator; born in Kansas City, Kans. Ellison received a B.A. degree from the University of Kansas in 1963 and his Ph.D. degree from Michigan State University in 1971. He served as assistant to the president of Michigan State University (1970–71), and as assistant to the chancellor of the Metropolitan Junior College District in St. Louis, Mo. (1971–72). In 1972 Ellison was appointed president of Central Community College (Seattle, Wash.).

ELLISON, RALPH WALDO (1914–   ), author; born in Oklahoma City, Okla. Ellison studied music for three years at Tuskegee Institute (Tuskegee Institute, Ala.), but moved to New York City in 1936 without finishing his studies. In 1942 and 1943 he edited the *Negro Quarterly*. A Rosenwald Fellowship enabled him to write a novel, *Invisible Man* (1952), which won a National Book Award and which was termed in a 1965 poll "the most distinguished single work" published in the United States since 1945. In the mid-1950s Ellison lectured in Germany, Austria, and Italy, and he studied in Rome on a fellowship before returning to the United States in 1958. After his return to the United States, he taught at Bard College, Rutgers University, and the University of Chicago. He was named Albert Schweitzer Professor of Humanities at New York University in 1970. *See also* LITERATURE: THE NOVEL.

EMANCIPATION CELEBRATION Held on January 6, 1863, at the Second Baptist Church, Detroit, Mich., the Emancipation Celebration (as it was known) is reputed to be the first such celebration to follow Lincoln's famous proclamation.

EMANCIPATION OAK A tree on the campus of Hampton Institute (Hampton, Va.), the Emancipation Oak was named in remembrance of the coming of freedom.

EMANCIPATION PROCLAMATION *See* AFRO-AMERICAN HISTORY: CIVIL WAR, 1861–1865.

EMPLOYMENT

Background Blacks were first brought forcibly to America to fulfill labor needs. The earliest employment was slave labor used basically in the production of tobacco in colonial America, mainly in the colony of Virginia. To a lesser extent (yet still very important), slave labor was used in the production of naval stores in North Carolina and of rice in South Carolina. Later, in the nineteenth century, slave labor became a principal factor in the cotton-dominated economy of the South, where 9 out of every 10 blacks lived. With the collapse of the slave economy at the close of the Civil War, much of black labor was diverted and redirected into the cotton-tenancy (sharecropping) system of the new South; with the decline of cotton tenancy in the twentieth century, black labor flowed into industrial centers in the North and South. The flow corresponded with the great migrations that came during World War I and World War II, or during periods of economic prosperity.

Throughout Afro-American history, black labor has been both skilled and unskilled, though largely the latter. Moreover, job discrimination has always existed. Yet, despite discrimination, the position of the black worker relative to the entire economy has shown gradual increases and gains. The most spectacular gains began to occur about the time of the New Deal and World War II, with the advocacy of fair employment practices. The civil rights movement of the 1960s strengthened both this advo-

A self-employed craftsman, early 1900s, who repaired streets, roads, and walks. *(George L. Bafford Collection, University of Maryland Baltimore County Library.)*

Women who worked as domestics, ca. 1900. *(U.S. Bureau of Agricultural Economics, National Archives.)*

A colonial cobbler may well have worked in a shop like this one, his tools ready on the wall. Black slaves as well as black freemen did become skilled laborers. *(Colonial Williamsburg Photograph, The Williamsburg Collection of Antique Furnishings.)*

cacy and the programs of fair employment. Despite gains, however, some of the old discriminatory practices still prevail. Though unionism has been generally advantageous to black workers (though not without its own discrimination), unemployment rates for blacks have persistently remained twice as high as for whites. (Within certain cities—Chicago, Ill., for example—and certain age groups (18–25) unemployment rates reached estimates of 30–45 percent during the 1970s.) The table opposite, showing persons 16 years old and over, gives data on employment and unemployment after 1950.

Contemporary Perspectives: The 1960s and 1970s

Labor Force Status The black civilian labor force continued to expand in 1970 at a fast pace despite the reduced availability of jobs (see Table 1). At 9.2 million, the black labor force was up 250,000 from the 1969 level, the largest annual advance since 1960. Three-fifths of the 1969–70 expansion occurred among adult men, primarily in the 20-to-34-year-old category. A large part of the adult male increase reflected the return to civilian life of young men separated from the armed forces during the year. The adult female labor force rose somewhat less, and the teenage labor force showed no growth over the year.

Continuing the trend that has been in evidence for the past decade, the black labor force participation rate registered a small decline in 1970. However, the reduction in participation was comparatively smaller than in the past several years. This decline continued to be particularly evident among males, primarily teenagers and young men 20 to 24 years of age. However, the 1969–70 decline in participation rates for 20-to-24-year-old black males occurred at a time when the participation rate for young adult white males was rising. For the latter group, the rise in participation rates represented a reversal of a trend, because rates for both black and white men in this age group had been declining since the mid-1960s (although the decline for whites had been at a somewhat slower pace than that for blacks). Labor-force participation among black female teenagers and young women 20 to 24 years of age also declined in 1970; in contrast, among white women, participation rates for both age categories increased significantly in 1970. This declining participation among young blacks became pronounced in the third quarter of 1970 and corresponded with an upsurge in their jobless rate; this rise suggests increased

TABLE 1. CIVILIAN LABOR FORCE, 1950–70
(IN MILLIONS)

Year	Noninstitutional population[1]	Labor force	Total	Percent employed in— Agriculture	Nonagriculture	Percent unemployed	Not in labor force
Total							
1950	107	64	62	11.5	83.2	5.3	43
1955	113	68	65	9.9	85.7	4.4	45
1960	120	72	70	7.8	86.6	5.5	48
1965	129	77	74	5.9	89.6	4.5	52
1967	133	81	77	5.0	91.2	3.8	53
1968	136	82	79	4.8	91.6	3.7	53
1969	138	84	81	4.5	92.0	3.5	54
1970	140	86	83	4.2	90.9	4.9	54
Male: White							
1950	52	45	44	13.7	81.2	5.1	7
1955	55	47	44	11.8	84.0	4.2	8
1960	58	49	46	9.6	85.0	5.4	9
1965	62	51	48	7.4	88.7	4.0	12
1967	64	52	49	6.5	90.5	3.1	12
1968	65	53	50	6.7	93.3	3.0	12
1969	66	54	50	5.9	91.3	2.8	13
1970	67	54	51	5.6	90.0	4.4	13
Male: Afro-American and other[2]							
1955	5	(NA)	4	16.3	75.5	8.2	1
1960	6	(NA)	5	13.9	75.4	10.7	1
1965	7	(NA)	5	10.0	82.4	7.6	2
1967	7	5	5	7.3	86.7	6.0	1
1968	7	5	5	8.0	92.0	5.7	1
1969	7	5	5	6.1	88.6	5.3	2
1970	7	5	5	5.8	86.8	7.3	2
Female: White							
1950	54	18	18	6.3	88.0	5.7	36
1955	58	21	21	5.8	89.4	4.9	37
1960	62	23	23	4.2	89.9	5.9	38
1965	67	26	26	3.1	91.4	5.5	41
1967	69	28	28	2.4	92.4	5.2	41
1968	70	29	29	2.4	97.6	5.0	41
1969	71	31	31	2.1	93.2	4.7	41
1970	73	32	32	1.9	92.2	5.9	41
Female: Afro-American and other[2]							
1955	6	(NA)	3	11.5	81.0	7.5	3
1960	7	(NA)	3	8.9	81.6	9.5	4
1965	8	(NA)	4	5.2	85.6	9.3	4
1967	7	4	4	2.8	88.1	9.1	4
1968	6	3	3	2.8	97.2	11.2	4
1969	8	4	4	2.0	90.3	7.8	4
1970	8	4	4	1.6	89.1	9.3	4

NA Not available.
[1] For Negro and other, civilian only, through 1965.
[2] Excludes white.
SOURCE: U.S. Bureau of the Census, *Pocket Data Book, U.S.A. 1976*, U.S. Government Printing Office, Washington, D.C., 1976, table 193, p. 157.

discouragement over job prospects in the last half of the year.

Occupational Changes During the decade of the 1960s, employment for blacks in the better-paying occupations rose rapidly, while employment in the lower-paying, less secure occupations declined.

In 1967, for the first time, substantially more than half of all black workers held white-collar, craftsmen, or operative jobs. The proportion increased to 58 percent in 1969 and to 60 percent in 1970. Employment of blacks in these occupations was 70 percent larger in 1970 than in 1960, compared with a 25 percent gain for whites.

However, the proportion of white workers in these jobs was still higher than for blacks: 8 in every 10 whites compared with 6 in every 10 blacks. In 1970, despite the economic slowdown, Afro-Americans continued to make further progress up the occupational ladder.

Although the rise (60,000) in total employment was small, the number of blacks employed in white-collar occupations rose 7 percent, or 160,000. This increase primarily reflected a significant advance in the number of blacks securing jobs in the professional, technical, and managerial fields. As a result, the proportion of all black workers who were employed in white-collar jobs reached 28 percent in 1970 compared with 26 percent in 1969. Nevertheless, the proportion of blacks in white-collar jobs still remained well below that of white workers, of whom 50 percent were in white-collar jobs in 1970. However, younger black workers (the newer jobholders) were concentrated more heavily in these jobs than older black workers; the same was true among whites but to a much lesser degree.

Breaking down the major occupational groupings into detailed classifications makes it clear that the largest gains for black men between 1963 and 1970 were as factory operatives, especially in durable goods manufacturing. About 185,000 new jobs were opened to black men in durable goods factories in the seven-year period and another 94,000 in nondurable goods. Next largest were increases in clerical jobs, some of which paid fairly high wages. In terms of future

trends, increases in professional and technical occupations, salaried management positions, craft occupations, and police and other protective service occupations may prove to be more important. Consistent with recent trends, employment of farm and private household workers continued to decline in 1970. Only 13 percent of all employed Afro-Americans held professional, technical, and managerial positions in 1970, compared with 26 percent for whites. Similarly, among skilled craftsmen and foremen, the proportions were 8 percent for blacks and 14 percent for whites. Twenty-two percent of all employed blacks were engaged in private household work, farm, and laboring jobs, more than twice the proportion for whites (9 percent). However, in 1960, the proportion of Afro-Americans employed in these jobs had been much higher (40 percent). Overall, although black employment gains for the year were achieved in the high-skill, higher-level occupations, they still constituted a disproportionate share of the workers in most low-paying occupations.

Tables 2–7 show the distribution of blacks among employed occupational groups. All data come from the U.S. Bureau of the Census and follow official definitions and symbols: (1) Employed persons comprise all civilians 16 years old and over who were either (a) "at work"—those who did any work at all as paid employees or in their own business or profession, or on their own farm, or who worked 15 hours or more as unpaid workers on a family

Blast-furnace workers changing shifts at Bethlehem Steel Corporation's Sparrows Point plant in the mid-1970s. *(Baltimore Sunpapers, Ellis Malashuk.)*

TABLE 2. EMPLOYMENT OF AFRO-AMERICANS AND OTHER RACES BY OCCUPATION ANNUAL AVERAGES, 1960–70
(Number in thousands)

Occupation	1970	1969	1965	1960	Change					
					1960–69		1965–69		1969–70	
					Number	Percent	Number	Percent	Number	Percent
Total	**8,445**	**8,384**	**7,643**	**6,927**	**1,457**	**21.0**	**741**	**9.7**	**61**	**0.7**
White-collar workers	**2,356**	**2,197**	**1,493**	**1,113**	**1,084**	**97.4**	**704**	**47.2**	**159**	**7.2**
Professional and technical	766	695	524	331	364	110.0	171	32.6	71	10.2
Managers, officials, and proprietors	297	254	204	178	76	42.7	50	24.5	43	16.9
Clerical workers	1,113	1,083	630	503	580	115.3	453	71.9	30	2.8
Salesworkers	180	166	135	101	65	64.4	31	23.0	14	8.4
Blue-collar workers	**3,561**	**3,591**	**3,133**	**2,780**	**811**	**29.2**	**458**	**14.6**	**−30**	**−.8**
Craftsmen and foremen	692	709	521	415	294	70.8	188	36.1	−17	−2.4
Operatives	2,004	2,004	1,646	1,414	590	41.7	358	21.7	0	0
Nonfarm laborers	866	877	966	951	−74	−7.8	−89	−9.2	−11	−1.3
Service workers	**2,199**	**2,239**	**2,419**	**2,196**	**43**	**2.0**	**−180**	**−7.4**	**−40**	**−1.8**
Private household	652	714	963	982	−268	−27.3	−249	−25.9	−62	−8.7
Other	1,546	1,525	1,456	1,214	311	25.6	69	4.7	21	1.4
Farm workers	**328**	**356**	**599**	**841**	**−485**	**−57.7**	**−243**	**−40.6**	**−28**	**−7.9**
Farmers and farm managers	87	84	138	219	−135	−61.6	−54	−39.1	3	3.6
Laborers and foremen	241	272	461	622	−350	−56.3	−189	−41.0	−31	−11.4

SOURCE: U.S. Department of Labor, Bureau of Labor Statistics, *The Negro Employment Situation*, U.S. Government Printing Office, Washington, D.C., Report 391, 1971, p. 8.

TABLE 3. OCCUPATIONAL DISTRIBUTION OF EMPLOYMENT BY RACE, ANNUAL AVERAGES, 1960–70

Occupation	Afro-Americans and other races				White			
	1970	1969	1965	1960	1970	1969	1965	1960
Thousands of employed persons	**8,445**	**8,384**	**7,643**	**6,927**	**70,182**	**69,518**	**63,445**	**58,850**
Percent distribution	**100.0**	**100.0**	**100.0**	**100.0**	**100.0**	**100.0**	**100.0**	**100.0**
White-collar workers	**27.9**	**26.2**	**19.5**	**16.1**	**50.8**	**49.8**	**47.9**	**46.6**
Professional and technical	9.1	8.3	6.9	4.8	14.8	14.5	13.2	12.1
Managers, officials, and proprietors	3.5	3.0	2.7	2.6	11.4	11.1	11.2	11.7
Clerical workers	13.2	12.9	8.2	7.3	18.0	17.7	16.6	15.7
Salesworkers	2.1	2.0	1.8	1.5	6.7	6.5	6.9	7.0
Blue-collar workers	**42.2**	**42.8**	**41.0**	**40.1**	**34.5**	**35.5**	**36.4**	**36.2**
Craftsmen and foremen	8.2	8.5	6.8	6.0	13.5	13.6	13.7	13.8
Operatives	23.7	23.9	21.5	20.4	17.0	17.8	18.4	17.9
Nonfarm laborers	10.3	10.5	12.6	13.7	4.1	4.0	4.3	4.4
Service workers	**26.0**	**26.7**	**31.6**	**31.7**	**10.7**	**10.5**	**10.3**	**9.9**
Private household	7.7	8.5	12.6	14.2	1.3	1.3	1.6	1.7
Other	18.3	18.2	19.1	17.5	9.4	9.2	8.7	8.2
Farm workers	**3.9**	**4.2**	**7.8**	**12.1**	**4.0**	**4.2**	**5.4**	**7.4**
Farmers and farm managers	1.0	1.0	1.8	3.2	2.4	2.5	3.3	4.3
Laborers and foremen	2.9	3.2	6.0	9.0	1.6	1.7	2.1	3.0

[1]Statistics for Afro-Americans and other minority races are used to indicate the situation for black workers. Afro-Americans constitute about 92 percent of this larger group.

SOURCE: U.S. Department of Labor, Bureau of Labor Statistics, *The Negro Employment Situation*, U.S. Government Printing Office, Washington, D.C., Report 391, 1971, p. 9.

TABLE 4. EMPLOYMENT: PROFESSIONAL, TECHNICAL, AND KINDRED WORKERS, 1970

	Number			
	Total		Afro-American	
	Male	Female	Male	Female
Total employed, 16 years old and over	**47,623,754**	**28,929,845**	**4,052,063**	**3,309,080**
Total	**6,800,554**	**4,550,584**	**237,293**	**374,041**
Accountants	520,601	182,945	9,026	7,495
Architects	54,233	1,981	1,151	107
Computer specialists	204,614	49,923	5,803	2,655
Computer programers	124,956	36,381	4,008	1,829
Computer systems analysts	68,213	11,736	1,548	707
Computer specialists, n.e.c.	11,445	1,806	247	119
Engineers	1,187,932	19,577	12,995	684
Aeronautical and astronautical	64,508	1,075	696	19
Chemical	51,404	668	364	40
Civil	170,684	2,293	2,359	99
Electrical and electronic	276,556	4,684	3,637	147
Industrial	178,716	5,509	1,602	204
Mechanical	175,586	1,626	1,743	72
Metallurgical and materials	15,115	199	110	5
Mining	4,464	51	35	—
Petroleum	10,876	153	62	5
Sales	53,872	398	71	6
Engineers, n.e.c.	186,151	2,921	2,316	87
Farm management advisors	6,345	1,247	337	131
Foresters and conservationists	38,217	1,591	638	89
Home management advisors	216	5,177	16	618
Lawyers and judges	259,221	13,180	3,231	497
Judges	11,380	869	298	51
Lawyers	247,841	12,311	2,933	446
Librarians, archivists, and curators	26,818	101,916	1,412	6,808
Librarians	22,001	99,851	1,201	6,735
Archivists and curators	4,817	2,065	211	73
Mathematical specialists	23,041	12,048	643	737
Actuaries	3,810	1,150	34	63
Mathematicians	5,927	1,716	235	113
Statisticians	13,304	9,182	374	561
Life and physical scientists	175,892	26,597	4,845	1,486
Agricultural	11,694	1,011	310	23
Atmospheric and space	5,255	520	34	34
Biological	19,126	10,254	784	714
Chemists	95,599	12,887	3,322	635
Geologists	19,085	715	46	21
Marine	2,992	161	59	9
Physicists and astronomers	21,075	866	260	45
Life and physical, n.e.c.	1,066	183	30	5
Operations and systems researchers and analysts	71,841	7,637	1,112	443
Personnel and labor relations workers	201,446	89,310	8,334	6,276
Physicians, dentists, and related practitioners	493,081	45,665	9,581	1,855
Chiropractors	12,602	1,127	103	11
Dentists	87,691	3,110	1,983	115
Optometrists	16,527	692	87	12
Pharmacists	96,610	13,032	1,913	588
Physicians, medical and osteopathic	255,105	25,824	5,055	1,051
Podiatrists	5,566	460	195	55
Veterinarians	18,450	985	234	18
Health practitioners, n.e.c.	530	435	11	5
Registered nurses, dietitians, and therapists	53,152	891,831	6,808	69,620
Dietitians	3,222	36,909	919	7,514
Registered nurses	22,332	807,359	3,318	59,007
Therapists	27,598	47,563	2,571	3,099

TABLE 4. EMPLOYMENT: PROFESSIONAL, TECHNICAL, AND KINDRED WORKERS, 1970 *(Continued)*

	Number			
	Total		Afro-American	
	Male	Female	Male	Female
Health technologists and technicians	78,946	180,893	8,007	16,151
Clinical laboratory technologists and technicians	32,965	84,641	3,812	7,288
Dental hygienists	942	14,863	46	234
Health record technologists and technicians	881	10,283	69	490
Radiologic technologists and technicians	16,767	35,463	1,501	2,489
Therapy assistants	1,093	2,118	172	310
Health technologists and technicians, n.e.c.	26,298	33,525	2,407	5,340
Religious workers	227,614	26,062	12,840	1,031
Clergymen	211,830	6,237	12,350	500
Religious workers, n.e.c.	15,784	19,825	490	531
Social scientists	87,712	20,801	2,013	1,075
Economists	58,558	7,390	1,081	362
Political scientists	689	215	26	3
Psychologists	17,200	10,630	461	501
Sociologists	851	467	43	65
Urban and regional planners	7,954	1,099	362	97
Social scientists, n.e.c.	2,460	1,000	40	47
Social and recreation workers	109,901	156,053	15,013	25,778
Social	80,810	135,813	11,098	22,771
Recreation	29,091	20,240	3,915	3,007
Teachers (college and university)	348,158	138,063	9,211	7,599
Biology	16,332	4,260	382	166
Chemistry	13,875	1,839	234	47
Engineering	15,592	931	186	36
Physics	13,297	664	108	28
Other life and physical sciences	8,341	526	78	11
Mathematics	21,014	4,935	528	291
Economics	9,123	731	88	15
English	22,402	16,067	477	671
History	13,457	2,823	376	127
Miscellaneous social sciences	23,809	7,731	567	446
Other specified teachers	94,741	55,979	2,478	2,421
Not specified teachers	96,175	41,577	3,709	3,340
Teachers (except college and university)	815,783	1,926,165	50,891	172,372
Adult education	27,129	23,037	1,643	1,905
Elementary school	231,028	1,182,887	19,492	113,544
Prekindergarten and kindergarten	2,637	122,359	370	13,941
Secondary school	510,020	491,489	27,491	39,689
Teachers (except college and university)n.e.c.	44,969	106,393	1,895	3,293
Engineering and science technicians	715,316	87,837	21,836	4,820
Agriculture and biological (except health)	21,655	10,060	922	509
Chemical	51,333	9,034	2,421	688
Draftsmen	262,858	22,257	7,033	731
Electrical and electronic engineering	145,565	8,612	4,827	574
Industrial engineering	17,934	2,400	376	100
Mechanical engineering	12,746	503	325	31
Mathematical	678	92	36	—
Surveyors	57,678	1,690	867	126
Engineering and science, n.e.c.	144,869	33,189	5,029	2,061
Technicians (except health, engineering, and science) ..	137,856	17,636	2,993	1,075
Airplane pilots	49,694	710	157	5
Air traffic controllers	23,923	1,370	643	76
Embalmers	4,528	221	313	64
Flight engineers	6,181	164	48	—
Radio operators	21,069	7,307	459	268
Tool programers, numerical control	2,585	498	81	61
Technicians, n.e.c.	29,876	7,366	1,292	601
Vocational and educational counselors	60,123	46,556	4,414	5,469

TABLE 4. EMPLOYMENT: PROFESSIONAL, TECHNICAL, AND KINDRED WORKERS, 1970 (Continued)

	Number			
	Total		Afro-American	
	Male	Female	Male	Female
Writers, artists, and entertainers	526,718	227,239	18,236	6,643
Actors	5,846	3,882	327	224
Athletes and kindred workers	34,971	13,522	1,957	270
Authors	17,933	7,443	321	142
Dancers	1,072	4,878	73	383
Designers	83,117	25,671	1,352	874
Editors and reporters	87,565	59,360	1,624	1,445
Musicians and composers	56,341	31,493	4,726	1,096
Painters and sculptors	64,614	36,279	1,782	535
Photographers	55,785	8,906	1,891	368
Public relations men and publicity writers	54,368	19,376	1,512	720
Radio and television announcers	19,766	1,460	606	60
Writers, artists, and entertainers, n.e.c.	45,340	14,969	2,065	526
Research workers (not specified)	86,045	29,912	1,999	1,284
Professional, technical, and kindred workers (allocated) .	289,732	242,742	23,908	31,243

TABLE 5. EMPLOYMENT: CRAFTSMEN AND KINDRED WORKERS

	Number			
	Total		Afro-American	
	Male	Female	Male	Female
Total	**10,088,483**	**521,147**	**618,029**	**47,372**
Automotible accessories installers	6,430	294	682	75
Bakers	76,634	32,558	9,023	4,207
Blacksmiths	9,978	249	430	11
Boilermakers	29,174	371	1,435	35
Bookbinders	14,593	19,441	1,298	1,998
Brickmasons and stonemasons	160,208	2,034	26,323	398
Bulldozer operators	87,313	1,135	9,750	224
Cabinetmakers	64,100	3,413	2,936	270
Carpenters	831,363	10,978	43,530	999
Carpet installers	43,219	748	2,685	47
Cement and concrete finishers	64,675	904	20,247	397
Compositors and typesetters	135,496	23,907	6,855	1,351
Cranemen, derrickmen, and hoistmen	150,332	1,939	19,473	346
Decorators and window dressers	29,709	40,251	1,391	1,775
Dental laboratory technicians	20,586	6,022	1,001	440
Electricians	459,843	8,616	13,408	737
Electric power linemen and cablemen	100,448	1,444	3,764	123
Electrotypers and stereotypers	6,730	283	168	8
Engravers (except photoengravers)	6,368	2,326	250	103
Excavating, grading, and road machine operators (except bulldozer)	219,040	2,495	12,766	250
Floor layers (except tile setters)	20,974	359	1,377	18
Foremen, n.e.c.	1,462,820	127,607	51,711	8,202
Construction	150,420	1,613	5,586	133
Manufacturing	847,050	77,886	26,340	4,100
Durable goods	536,915	25,634	15,651	1,537
Nondurable goods (including not specified manufacturing) ..	310,135	52,252	10,689	2,563
Transportation, communications, and other public utilities	150,283	5,704	4,739	294
All other industries	315,067	42,404	15,046	3,675
Forgemen and hammermen	14,649	724	1,510	75
Furniture and wood finishers	17,655	3,589	1,974	614
Farriers	2,206	461	77	55
Glaziers	24,241	779	1,002	82
Heat treaters, annealers, and temperers	19,711	598	1,846	58
Inspectors, scalers, and graders (log and lumber)	15,188	1,864	2,013	530

TABLE 5. EMPLOYMENT: CRAFTSMEN AND KINDRED WORKERS (Continued)

	Number			
	Total		Afro-American	
	Male	Female	Male	Female
Inspectors, n.e.c.	108,953	8,855	4,658	1,604
Construction	22,331	334	383	19
Railroads and railway express service	24,376	247	897	25
Jewelers and watchmakers	32,839	4,280	681	362
Job and die setters (metal)	84,489	2,221	4,982	98
Locomotive engineers	49,948	392	790	20
Locomotive firemen	12,869	151	462	16
Machinists	366,899	11,754	16,693	1,396
Mechanics and repairmen	2,394,798	49,114	137,776	4,592
Air conditioning, heating, and refrigeration	116,531	1,061	4,269	70
Aircraft	136,214	4,001	6,364	422
Automobile body repairmen	106,306	1,332	6,676	100
Automobile mechanics	793,727	11,045	62,518	1,300
Data processing machine repairmen	30,844	864	1,021	77
Farm implement	33,141	416	983	30
Heavy equipment mechanics (including diesel)	571,762	10,713	26,602	1,009
Household appliance and accessory installers and mechanics	120,284	2,539	5,148	229
Loomfixers	20,566	437	481	21
Office machine	38,812	688	1,331	43
Radio and television	132,438	5,011	6,543	414
Railroad and car shop	55,105	510	4,094	45
Miscellaneous mechanics and repairmen	168,804	7,790	7,389	641
Not specified mechanics and repairmen	70,264	2,707	4,357	191
Millers (grain, flour, and feed)	6,973	157	548	11
Millwrights	77,519	903	2,073	81
Molders (metal)	48,314	5,749	10,242	707
Motion picture projectionists	14,831	631	504	37
Opticians, and lens grinders and polishers	21,279	6,101	647	507
Painters (construction and maintenance)	314,026	13,303	28,733	1,055
Paperhangers	9,149	1,111	332	24
Pattern and model makers (except paper)	37,066	1,858	587	79
Photoengravers and lithographers	28,828	3,842	569	244
Piano and organ tuners and repairmen	6,539	330	191	19
Plasterers	28,275	435	5,210	108
Plumbers and pipe fitters	377,769	4,110	17,371	365
Power station operators	17,752	557	479	38
Pressmen and plate printers (printing)	143,326	13,346	7,751	1,476
Rollers and finishers (metal)	18,378	1,264	2,158	135
Roofers and slaters	57,539	735	6,570	101
Sheetmetal workers and tinsmiths	151,309	2,898	4,594	303
Shipfitters	10,478	123	1,113	36
Shoe repairmen	24,820	6,343	3,282	420
Sign painters and letterers	17,334	1,609	772	92
Stationary engineers	168,259	2,467	7,807	221
Stonecutters and stonecarvers	5,864	445	388	29
Structural metal craftsmen	73,098	868	1,733	49
Tailors	46,338	21,244	4,208	2,228
Telephone installers and repairmen	230,444	8,285	9,566	741
Telephone linemen and splicers	51,274	756	1,859	64
Tile setters	31,224	378	2,760	66
Toolmakers and diemakers	197,754	4,191	2,964	249
Upholsterers	52,144	9,955	4,219	1,157
Craftsmen and kindred workers, n.e.c.	77,878	7,249	5,449	451
Former members of the Armed Forces	369	69	27	11
Craftsmen and kindred workers (allocated)	598,855	27,679	78,356	4,752

TABLE 6. EMPLOYMENT: OPERATIVES (EXCEPT TRANSPORT), 1970

	Number			
	Total		Afro-American	
	Male	Female	Male	Female
Total	**6,483,532**	**4,014,993**	**793,990**	**533,496**
Asbestos and insulation workers	23,842	498	995	58
Assemblers	489,296	454,611	64,042	51,082
Blasters and powdermen	6,776	311	498	26
Bottling and canning operatives	30,568	15,909	3,505	1,877
Chainmen, rodmen, and axmen (surveying)	10,398	163	441	36
Checkers, examiners, and inspectors (manufacturing)	362,643	327,530	25,942	28,533
Clothing ironers and pressers	44,806	136,394	13,527	55,384
Cutting operatives, n.e.c.	128,706	45,530	15,890	5,170
Dressmakers and seamstresses (except factory)	4,706	92,114	759	8,223
Drillers (earth)	53,803	3,405	3,059	327
Dry wall installers and lathers	43,134	566	1,927	25
Dyers	21,806	2,031	3,541	342
Filers, polishers, sanders, and buffers	90,508	23,665	10,831	3,732
Furnacemen, smeltermen, and pourers	62,455	2,761	14,493	448
Garage workers and gas station attendants	412,221	12,084	31,924	879
Graders and sorters (manufacturing)	13,656	24,352	2,065	2,977
Produce graders and packers (except factory and farm)	7,174	19,356	819	1,343
Heaters (metal)	6,551	224	998	28
Laundry and drycleaning operatives, n.e.c.	62,353	108,022	13,877	29,997
Meatcutters and butchers (except manufacturing)	190,435	10,446	11,414	1,891
Meatcutters and butchers (manufacturing)	49,883	17,608	8,904	4,375
Meatwrappers (retail trade)	2,983	41,112	323	1,716
Metalplaters	28,286	2,828	2,754	255
Milliners	183	1,855	15	182
Mine operatives, n.e.c.	151,697	3,359	6,945	263
Mixing operatives	65,443	2,806	11,325	574
Oilers and greasers (except auto)	44,007	1,496	4,386	160
Packers and wrappers (except meat and produce)	201,449	314,067	33,837	38,513
Painters (manufactured articles)	97,506	16,457	14,372	2,213
Photographic process workers	33,734	28,780	2,363	2,256
Precision machine operatives	373,619	37,474	23,729	2,834
Drill press operatives	53,788	14,831	4,264	1,124
Grinding machine operatives	125,432	7,882	10,652	662
Lathe and milling machine operatives	133,209	7,566	5,565	517
Precision machine operatives, n.e.c.	61,190	7,195	3,248	531
Punch and stamping press operatives	111,003	48,377	12,760	4,250
Riveters and fasteners	14,253	10,941	1,947	967
Sailors and deckhands	24,241	466	2,653	74
Sawyers	91,036	8,717	15,828	1,114
Sewers and stitchers	54,686	812,716	7,658	78,346
Shoemaking machine operatives	24,064	36,419	1,037	1,495
Solderers	7,400	32,851	770	3,328
Stationary firemen	89,474	4,813	9,977	493
Textile operatives	196,730	232,578	31,221	29,330
Carding, lapping, and combing operatives	14,859	4,565	2,667	721
Knitters, loopers, and toppers	10,317	18,089	1,008	1,802
Spinners, twisters, and winders	56,867	99,222	9,585	11,799
Weavers	23,461	26,680	2,564	2,324
Textile operatives, n.e.c.	91,226	84,022	15,397	12,684
Welders and flamecutters	506,429	31,273	43,289	3,576
Winding operatives, n.e.c.	29,800	30,939	1,947	2,617
Miscellaneous and not specified operatives	1,806,132	714,372	241,200	98,855
Occupation:				
Machine operatives (miscellaneous specified)	733,381	285,810	91,706	34,953
Machine operatives (not specefied)	414,753	151,943	66,270	23,456
Miscellaneous operatives	442,680	187,750	57,855	30,331
Not specified operatives	215,318	88,869	25,369	10,115

TABLE 6. EMPLOYMENT: OPERATIVES (EXCEPT TRANSPORT), 1970 (Continued)

	Number			
	Total		Afro-American	
	Male	Female	Male	Female
Industry:				
Manufacturing	1,512,349	629,011	199,235	82,907
Durable goods	879,534	305,308	120,588	38,485
Lumber and wood products (except furniture)	61,930	10,357	12,628	2,452
Furniture and fixtures	36,199	13,324	5,015	2,455
Stone, clay, and glass products	81,736	18,062	10,861	1,568
Primary metal industries	161,762	11,477	27,430	1,457
Blast furnaces, steelworks, and rolling and finishing mills	58,155	1,241	11,364	404
Fabricated metal industries (including not specified metal)	105,699	29,962	13,249	3,453
Machinery (except electrical)	129,350	23,599	10,371	2,215
Electrical machinery (equipment and supplies)	88,993	105,031	9,283	13,085
Transportation equipment	130,989	23,041	22,138	2,942
Motor vehicles and motor vehicle equipment	72,939	13,382	14,956	1,904
Professional and photographic equipment and watches	19,865	18,049	1,468	1,670
Ordnance	15,619	7,246	2,337	1,242
Miscellaneous manufacturing industries	43,383	44,113	5,159	5,812
Durable goods (allocated)	4,009	1,047	649	134
Nondurable goods	621,270	317,041	76,254	42,949
Food and kindred products	135,783	63,259	21,043	13,803
Tobacco manufacturers	9,256	8,665	2,885	1,672
Apparel and other fabricated textile products	22,463	67,853	2,978	9,292
Paper and allied products	134,521	40,063	13,922	4,162
Printing, publishing, and allied industries	41,866	33,771	3,348	3,086
Chemicals and allied industries	121,837	23,527	14,533	3,121
Petroleum and coal products	28,141	585	2,485	78
Rubber and miscellaneous plastic products	107,223	53,992	12,915	5,718
Leater and leather products	18,126	23,766	1,839	1,855
Nondurable goods (allocated)	2,054	1,560	306	162
Not specified manufacturing industries	11,545	6,662	2,393	1,473
Nonmanufacturing industries	293,783	85,361	41,965	15,948
Construction	31,854	966	4,143	172
Transportation, communications, and other public utilities	62,617	3,918	7,968	526
Wholesale and retail trade	102,603	43,231	16,136	7,858
Business and repair services	44,790	7,438	4,799	1,011
Public administration	18,780	3,529	3,606	1,112
All other industries	33,139	26,279	5,313	5,269
Operatives, except transport (allocated)	414,657	302,717	94,203	63,332

farm or in a family business; or (b) "with a job, but not at work"—those who did not work during the reference week, but had jobs or businesses from which they were temporarily absent due to illness, bad weather, industrial dispute, vacation, or other personal reasons. Excluded from the employed are members of the U.S. Armed Forces. (2) For employed persons, the data on occupation refer to the job held during the reference week. For persons employed at two or more jobs, the data refer to the job at which the person worked the greatest number of hours. The occupation statistics presented here are based on the detailed system developed for the 1970 census. (3) The abbreviation "n.e.c." refers to managers, officials, and proprietors. The reader should bear in mind, however, that statistics based on such major occupational groupings as "craftsmen" and "operatives" mask important differences within the groups. Within any of the broad occupation groups for which data are available, there are occupations with a wide range of earnings levels and status, and blacks may have entered the lower levels in greater proportions than they have entered the higher levels. Moreover, differences in pay exist even within a specific occupation, and these too could result in a greater degree of occupational inequality than is apparent from the broad occupational group data.

Tables 4–8 are adapted from a supplementary report of the U.S. Bureau of the Census, taken from Table 223 of Final Report PC(1)–D1,

Detailed Occupation of Employed Persons by Race and Sex for the United States: 1970, PC(S1)–32, March 1973.

Unemployment Developments Despite the fact that blacks represent only 11 percent of the civilian labor force, they (or members of other minority races) were 18 percent (750,000) of the nation's

About one out of every 17 black workers were federal employees in the 1970s. Afro-Americans numbered about 400,000 of the 2.5 million government workers in 1972, or about 15 percent of the total. One out of every three black federal workers was employed in the Post Office, totalling 127,000 in 1972. Black federal workers were also employed in large numbers in Defense, 111,000; Veterans Administration (VA), 42,000; and Health, Education, and Welfare (HEW), 26,000.

Source: U.S. Department of Labor, Bureau of Labor Statistics, Bulletin 1960, Revised 1972.

ly (about 20 percent each). The jobless rate for adult women rose from 5.8 to 6.9 percent, while the teenage rate increased from 24 to 29.1 percent.

Of the 750,000 jobless Afro-Americans in 1970, about 265,000 were adult men, 250,000 were adult women, and 235,000 were teenagers. About three-fifths each of the jobless adult men and women were in the central age group—25 to 54 years of age. Joblessness among teenagers in 1970 was distributed about equally between boys and girls. Most of the unemployed adult men had lost their previous jobs, the majority of the jobless adult women were returning to the labor force after a period of absence, and most of the teenagers were seeking their first jobs.

Full Time/Part Time The increase in black joblessness over the year was concentrated among adult male full-time jobseekers. The rate for all Afro-American full-time jobseekers increased from 5.8 to 7.7 percent, while the rate for Afro-American part-time workers rose at a somewhat slower pace (from 10.0 to 11.5 percent).

Despite the reduced availability of jobs, more than four-fifths of the jobless black workers in 1970 were seeking a full-time job. These included 250,000 unemployed adult men (nine-tenths of all unemployed adult men), 215,000 adult women (four-fifths of all unemployed adult women), and 155,000 teenagers (two-thirds of all unemployed teenagers). Teenagers comprised about three-fifths of the 140,000 black part-time jobseekers in 1970.

Duration of Unemployment The incidence of joblessness among blacks in 1970 was primarily of a short-term nature. Among those blacks unemployed at any point of time in 1970, the average length of time they had been unemployed (through the reference week of the survey) was 9.0 weeks in 1970; this number was up only moderately over the 1969 level of 8.5 weeks. These figures compare with an average duration of unemployment for whites of 8.7 and 7.8 weeks in 1970 and 1969, respectively.

In the average week in 1970, about 380,000, or one-half of the jobless black workers, had been unemployed for 1 month or less, while 250,000, or one-third, had been jobless 5 to 14 weeks. At the other extreme, however, 125,000, or 16 percent, were among the long-term unemployed, that is, had looked for work for 15 weeks or longer. About 50,000 of these long-term unemployed were household heads.

Comparative Unemployment Trends One way of looking at comparative unemployment trends

4.1 million jobless workers in 1970 and 20 percent of the total (570,000) in 1969.

As a whole, unemployment was most prevalent among lesser-skilled black workers in 1970. Unskilled laborers, service workers (private household and other), and semiskilled operatives together represented more than three-fifths of the experienced unemployed blacks, about equal to their proportion of total employment.

Age/sex Distribution Between 1969 and 1970, unemployment among adult Afro-American men rose much more sharply than among adult Afro-American women or Afro-American teenagers. Their unemployment increased about 60 percent and their unemployment rate rose from 3.7 to 5.6 percent, reaching its highest point since 1965. Joblessness among black adult women and teenagers increased somewhat less rapid-

TABLE 7. EMPLOYMENT: TRANSPORT EQUIPMENT OPERATIVES AND LABORERS, 1970

	Number			
	Total		Afro-American	
	Male	Female	Male	Female
Transport equipment operatives (Total)	**2,825,883**	**132,052**	**403,605**	**13,195**
Boatmen and canalmen	4,631	324	247	27
Bus drivers	169,942	66,000	29,645	4,084
Conductors and motormen (urban rail transit)	9,322	235	4,251	79
Deliverymen and routemen	600,609	19,691	57,416	1,755
Forklift and tow motor operatives	213,017	3,842	42,407	707
Motormen (mine, factory, logging camp, etc.)	9,642	153	1,286	12
Parking attendants	29,395	1,096	6,504	157
Railroad brakemen	46,844	537	2,220	82
Railroad switchmen	51,396	867	3,758	112
Taxicab drivers and chauffeurs	143,132	8,512	30,328	1,606
Truck drivers	1,359,505	20,120	181,658	3,247
Transport equipment operatives (allocated)	188,448	10,675	43,885	1,327
Laborers, except farm (Total)	**3,146,982**	**284,300**	**639,681**	**49,435**
Animal caretakers (except farm)	31,503	14,763	3,841	538
Carpenters' helpers	42,525	953	9,526	200
Construction laborers (except carpenters' helpers)	547,381	9,571	121,377	2,371
Fishermen and oystermen	25,959	1,147	1,881	139
Freight and material handlers	500,803	38,760	103,183	8,598
Garbage collectors	70,260	1,157	26,401	455
Gardeners and groundskeepers (except farm)	286,396	8,424	50,183	1,746
Longshoremen and stevedores	42,349	705	15,326	234
Lumbermen, raftsmen, and woodchoppers	77,741	1,766	19,132	430
Stock handlers	481,815	104,292	37,811	12,859
Teamsters	7,138	301	1,413	53
Vehicle washers and equipment cleaners	104,384	12,155	26,518	3,272
Warehousemen, n.e.c.	102,812	3,861	13,754	621
Miscellaneous and not specified laborers	554,687	66,252	121,035	12,730
Occupation:				
Miscellaneous laborers	184,029	18,199	42,549	3,065
Not specified laborers	370,658	48,053	78,486	9,665
Industry:				
Manufacturing	281,889	38,239	61,934	6,247
Durable goods	192,539	20,806	43,057	3,236
Lumber and wood products (except furniture)	21,712	1,561	5,883	469
Furniture and fixtures	4,761	1,430	811	243
Stone, clay, and glass products	20,356	1,473	3,733	184
Primary metal industries	69,147	1,673	17,477	403
Blast furnaces, steelworks, and rolling and finishing mills	39,394	692	9,695	251
Fabricated metal industries (including not specified metal)	20,270	3,912	3,811	392
Machinery (except electrical)	16,603	1,337	2,393	209
Electrical machinery (equipment, and supplies)	8,251	3,794	1,153	446
Transportation equipment	21,688	1,647	5,952	312
Motor vehicles and motor vehicle equipment	11,246	735	3,226	164
Professional and photographic equipment, and watches	1,186	740	168	54
Ordnance	2,763	1,135	630	258
Miscellaneous manufacturing industries	3,917	2,008	552	231
Durable goods (allocated)	1,885	96	494	35
Nondurable goods	87,379	17,063	18,370	2,929
Food and kindred products	33,589	4,354	6,265	1,222
Tobacco manufactures	1,128	343	505	176
Textile mill products	8,583	2,401	2,577	375
Apparel and other fabricated textile products	1,705	1,654	320	299
Paper and allied products	12,141	1,267	2,399	158
Printing, publishing, and allied industries	3,135	1,065	472	137
Chemicals and allied products	12,727	1,328	3,313	243
Petroleum and coal products	3,593	95	931	13
Rubber and miscellaneous plastic products	7,396	2,073	1,097	178
Leather and leather products	2,446	1,302	229	90
Nondurable goods (allocated)	936	181	262	38

TABLE 7. EMPLOYMENT: TRANSPORT EQUIPMENT OPERATIVES AND LABORERS, 1970 (*Continued*)

| | Number | | | |
| | Total | | Afro-American | |
	Male	Female	Male	Female
Not specified manufacturing industries	1,971	370	507	82
Nonmanufacturing industries	272,798	28,013	59,101	6,483
Transportation, communications, and other public utilities.....	96,379	2,952	25,446	790
Wholesale and retail trade.................................	78,068	10,364	13,787	1,948
Business and repair services	17,846	2,015	2,347	539
Public administration	17,374	1,352	4,572	466
All other industries	63,131	11,330	12,949	2,740
Laborers, except farm (allocated).............................	271,229	20,193	88,300	5,189
Farmers and farm managers (Total)	**1,347,974**	**70,772**	**36,651**	**5,518**
Farmers (owners and tenants)	1,220,432	58,988	28,138	2,101
Farm managers	57,986	2,570	1,450	97
Farmers and farm managers (allocated)	69,556	9,214	7,063	3,320
Farm laborers and farm foreman (Total)	**795,008**	**153,301**	**140,394**	**34,648**
Farm foremen	30,740	1,882	1,999	277
Farm laborers (wage workers)	648,316	94,903	119,864	25,856
Farm laborers (unpaid family workers)	55,510	37,232	2,150	1,053
Farm service laborers (self-employed)	3,477	506	133	125
Farm laborers and farm foremen (allocated)...................	56,965	18,778	16,248	7,337

between black and white workers is to examine the relative unemployment rates of the two groups. In doing this, it must be recognized that the comparison of overall rates is affected by the age/sex composition of the two groups, since women and youth tend to have higher unemployment rates than adult men, and the age/sex composition of the black and of the white labor force is both different and changing over time. It also must be acknowledged that changes in labor-force participation rates are sometimes associated with changes in unemployment: when unemployment rises, some people tend to drop out of the labor force.

As indicated earlier, the number of both black and white jobless workers rose sharply during 1970. Between 1969 and 1970, black unemployment increased by 180,000 (31.9 percent) and joblessness among whites rose by 1.1 million (47.6 percent). As a result, the ratio of black-to-white jobless rates, which had averaged 2 to 1 or higher every year since 1953, dropped from 2.1 to 1 in 1969 and to 1.8 to 1 in 1970.

The narrowing of the differential between the two rates began to take place around mid-1969, when the first employment effects of the nation's economic slowdown became noticeable, and the differential continued to edge downward throughout 1970 and early 1971.

A lowering of the black jobless rate relative to the white rate first became apparent for adults in the mid-1960s: for example, in 1964 the black-white ratios were 2.3 to 1 for adult men and 2 to 1 for adult women, at a time when the overall ratio was 2.1 to 1. By 1969 these ratios had dropped to 2 to 1 for men and 1.7 to 1 for women, whereas the overall ratio remained unchanged at 2.1 to 1. The reason for this shift is that the unemployment rate for Afro-American teenagers deteriorated considerably relative to that for whites over this period at the same time

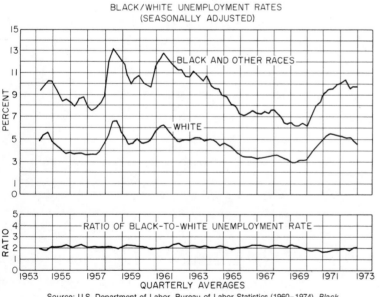

BLACK/WHITE UNEMPLOYMENT RATES
(SEASONALLY ADJUSTED)

Source: U.S. Department of Labor, Bureau of Labor Statistics (1960–1974). *Black Americans: A Chartbook* (1971).

TABLE 8. EMPLOYMENT: SERVICE AND PRIVATE HOUSEHOLD WORKERS, 1970

	Number			
	Total		Afro-American	
	Male	Female	Male	Female
Service workers, except private household (Total)	**3,837,317**	**4,790,043**	**632,437**	**843,345**
Cleaning service workers	1,265,664	595,838	301,841	205,045
Chambermaids and maids (except private household) ..	10,107	186,660	3,557	72,581
Cleaners and charwomen	186,640	252,423	63,855	92,745
Janitors and sextons	1,068,917	156,755	234,429	39,719
Food service workers	863,694	1,909,879	110,878	230,411
Bartenders	149,388	39,381	7,770	1,344
Busboys	80,884	13,528	7,094	3,223
Cooks (except private household)	305,492	523,485	48,890	112,404
Dishwashers	102,119	63,991	14,157	12,301
Food counter and fountain workers	35,818	115,563	2,247	11,556
Waiters	111,934	907,466	17,724	45,320
Food service workers, n.e.c. (except private household)	78,059	246,465	12,996	44,263
Health service workers	138,846	1,041,667	35,912	223,556
Dental assistants	1,866	86,309	141	2,834
Health aides (except nursing)	18,305	100,602	3,731	18,689
Health trainees	1,106	16,549	100	1,186
Lay midwives	138	537	47	226
Nursing aides, orderlies, and attendants	108,946	609,022	29,962	150,666
Practical nurses	8,485	228,648	1,931	49,955
Personal service workers	385,223	768,985	45,816	79,675
Airline stewardesses	1,364	31,290	81	682
Attendants (recreation and amusement)	51,757	16,335	3,383	1,063
Attendants (personal service, n.e.c.)	22,530	37,262	4,203	5,903
Baggage porters and bellhops	18,158	482	6,508	184
Barbers..	159,442	7,814	14,499	2,026
Boarding and lodging house keepers	2,087	5,284	114	418
Bootblacks	3,270	389	2,179	71
Child care workers (except private household)	9,196	122,062	1,409	17,234
Elevator operators	25,643	9,561	5,814	4,249
Hairdressers and cosmetologists	46,663	424,873	1,809	31,782
Housekeepers (except private household)	29,076	74,256	3,955	9,379
School monitors	2,539	23,468	348	1,594
Ushers (recreation and amusement)	9,906	4,197	430	220
Welfare service aides	3,592	11,712	1,084	4,870
Protective service workers	894,705	57,532	60,804	7,860
Crossing guards and bridge tenders	17,726	23,919	1,098	3,118
Firemen (fire protection)	174,922	1,976	4,279	99
Guards and watchmen	302,002	16,262	31,714	2,636
Marshals and constables	4,913	203	232	27
Policemen and detectives	362,396	13,098	22,023	1,773
Sheriffs and bailiffs	32,746	2,074	1,458	207
Service workers, except private household (allocated)	289,185	416,142	77,186	96,798
Private household workers (Total)	**36,037**	**1,109,854**	**17,717**	**590,549**
Occupation:				
Child care workers	4,010	208,177	596	26,020
Cooks...	1,803	29,494	912	18,571
Housekeepers	3,773	96,922	1,582	39,894
Laundresses	545	11,206	141	4,322
Maids and servants	22,686	644,178	12,154	417,600
Private household workers (allocated)	3,220	119,877	2,332	84,142
Living arrangement:				
Living in	3,022	72,281	48	16,636
Living out	33,015	1,037,573	16,969	573,913

that teenagers were becoming a larger proportion of the total unemployment figure.

For black teenagers, the jobless rate in 1970 (29.1 percent) continued to be more than double the rate for white teenagers (13.5 percent), and the ratio of their unemployment rates was not significantly changed during the economic

Black employment rate 1970, was about 8%—much higher than the white rate.

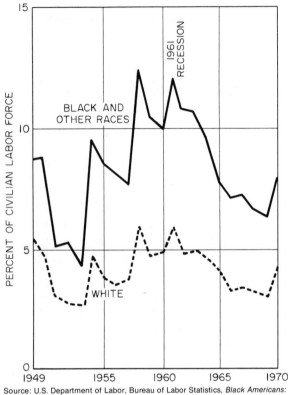

Source: U.S. Department of Labor, Bureau of Labor Statistics, *Black Americans: A Chartbook* (1971).

slowdown. The ratio of black-to-white teenage joblessness was last below 2 to 1 in 1964 (1.8 to 1). In 1965 the black teenage rate rose to double the white rate, and by 1967 it was 2.4 times as high. In both 1969 and 1970 the rate for black teenagers was about 2.2 times as high as that for white teenagers.

The problem of joblessness among black teenagers continued to be most serious among girls. In 1970 the unemployment rate for black teenage girls increased from 27.6 to 34.4 percent, while the rate for black teenage boys rose from 21.2 to 24.9 percent. Thus, although the 1970 ratio of black-to-white joblessness among male teenagers dropped below the 2-to-1 pattern that had held since 1965 (1.8 to 1), the ratio of black-to-white jobless rates of female teenagers increased from 2.4 to 1 in 1969 to 2.6 to 1 in 1970.

Some Factors in the Declining Ratio of Black-White Joblessness To understand better the 1969–70 change in the ratio of black-white unemployment rates, it is necessary to bear in mind that blacks and members of other minority races have historically constituted a disproportionate share of the unemployed. Prior to the fall of 1969 blacks made up 2 out of every 10 of the total unemployed, twice their proportion of the civilian labor force. During the period of rising unemployment, the number of Afro-Americans added to the swelling jobless total continued to exceed their 1 to 10 labor-force ratio. They accounted for approximately 1½ of every 10 persons added to the unemployed rolls, although this figure is less than the historical 2 out of 10 proportion. Therefore, the "narrowing" in black-white joblessness differentials in 1969 was not quite as dramatic as might appear at first glance. Proportionate to the size of their labor force, more blacks than whites were still unemployed in 1970.

A number of factors may have played a part in the narrowing of the black-white unemployment rate differential. First, the industrial distribution of black employment appears to have played a major role. The narrowing of the ratio between the two rates first began to take place about mid-1969, when the slowdown in employment growth was generally confined to a few "sophisticated" industries where the work force was disproportionately white. In particular, substantial job cutbacks in defense and aerospace indus-

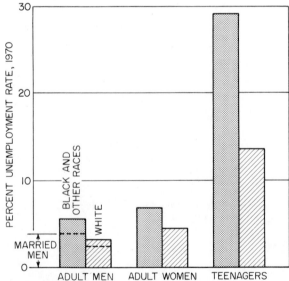

Source: U.S. Department of Labor, Bureau of Labor Statistics, *Black Americans: A Chartbook* (1971).

tries—mainly in ordnance and aircraft—tended to exert upward pressure on the white unemployment rate but had little or no effect on the rate for Afro-Americans, who were not employed in these industries in large numbers. Conversely, relatively few cutbacks occurred in the service industries and government, where

many blacks are employed. This explanation is supported by the fact that most of the narrowing of the black-white jobless ratio took place prior to 1970.

Second, as mentioned earlier, labor force participation rates for black youth between the ages of 16 and 24, particularly among males, fell at the same time that rates for white young persons were rising. This decline was an indication that a disproportionate number of young black workers were becoming discouraged over job prospects and leaving or refraining from entering the labor force. These differential movements in labor-force participation appear to have had some effect upon the narrowing in the black-white jobless rate ratio, particularly during the latter half of 1970 when the discouragement became more pronounced, since it is generally assumed that higher participation for this age group would partially be reflected in higher unemployment.

Third, it is possible that employers became more conscious of both public and private efforts to alleviate the social and economic ills of Afro-Americans during the mid-1960s through the mid-1970s. To the extent that they were aware of these moves, they made special efforts to improve hiring standards for blacks and to retain them or at least to refrain from laying them off discriminately during periods of employment reductions. However, no clear statistical evidence to support this contention exists.

Finally, the long-term rise in the levels of education and skill among blacks enabled many to enter occupations where joblessness tended to be lower than in those where blacks were employed earlier. Moreover, the effect of the government manpower programs permitted large numbers of blacks to move into, and gain some seniority in, better-paying jobs. Nonetheless, as indicated earlier, Afro-Americans remain heavily concentrated in comparatively low-paying jobs within the service-producing industries, which, in any case, have been less affected by the slowdown in economic activity.

Some Additional Considerations Although the above factors appear to have contributed to the recent narrowing of the black-white unemployment rate ratio, during previous cyclical economic swings short-lived narrowings of the ratio also have taken place in the initial stages of economic slowdowns. During the recovery phases, the ratio typically reverted to its previous pattern. In none of the previous slowdowns, however, did the ratio remain below 2 to 1 for an extended period.

Far Left: Organized protests against unemployment, like this picket line, in the 1970s, were influenced by high unemployment rates. *(Photo by Arnold Hinton.)*

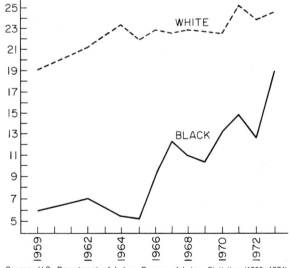

Source: U.S. Department of Labor, Bureau of Labor Statistics (1960–1974). *Black Americans: A Chartbook.*

The black-to-white jobless rate differential narrowed markedly during the 1970 slowdown in economic activity, as the ratio fell below 2 to 1 for the first time since 1953. However, earlier experience suggests that a permanent reduction of the ratio of black and of white jobless rates cannot be verified until the recovery phase of the slowdown of the 1970s is passed. See also BUSINESS; CIVIL RIGHTS: CIVIL RIGHTS ENFORCEMENT; CIVIL RIGHTS MOVEMENT; HOUSING; INCOME; LABOR UNIONS; NATIONAL ASSOCIATION FOR THE ADVANCEMENT OF COLORED PEOPLE (NAACP); POPULATION.

REFERENCES: Early works that provide background information on employment include: Greene, Lorenzo J. and Carter G. Woodson, *The Negro Wage Earner*, Association for the Study of Negro Life and History, Washington, D.C., 1931; Spero, Sterling D. and Abram L. Harris, *The Black Worker: The Negro and the Labor Movement*, Kennikat Press, Port Washington, 1966, first published in 1931; and Wesley, Charles H., *Negro Labor in the United States, 1850–1925: A Study in American Economic History*, Russell & Russell, New York, 1967; first printed in 1927.

For a recent background study, see Ross, Arthur M. and Herbert Hill (eds.), *Employment, Race and Poverty*, Harcourt, Brace & World, New York, 1967. Recent developments in employment have been investigated and published by the Industrial Research Unit, Wharton School of Finance and Commerce, University of Pennsylvania, Philadelphia, Pa., under the direction of Herbert R. Northrup. Thirty titles in the series had been published by 1972. Each volume deals with a separate, major American industry. A companion volume by the director is entitled *Negro Employment in Southern Industry* (1970). Another recent study (focusing basically upon segments of the electrical equipment and appliance industries) is Purcell, Theodore G. and Gerald F. Cavanagh, *Blacks in the Industrial World: Issues for the Manager*, Free Press, New York, 1972. For additional references, the reader should also consult the references at the end of the article LABOR UNIONS. More important, the section entitled "Employment" (pp. 151–75) in Miller, Elizabeth W. and Mary L. Fisher (comps.), *The Negro in America: A Bibliography*, Cambridge, 1970, should also be consulted. A specific account is given in Rittenoure, R. Lynn, *Black Employment in the South: the Case of the Federal Government*, U. of Texas Business Research, Austin, 1976.

ENCYCLOPEDIAS   See PREFACE.

ENGINEERS   See HO, JAMES K. K., under BIBLIOGRAPHIES/BIOGRAPHIES/GUIDES; EMPLOYMENT.

EPISCOPALIANS

Introduction   In writing one of the first comprehensive histories of the black church in 1903, W. E. B. Du Bois noted that the Episcopal Church had "probably done less for black people than any other aggregation of Christians." Subsequent historians have not been quite so candid, but they have all agreed that the impact and attraction of the Episcopal Church in the black community have not always been great. Several reasons have been suggested for this, including the identification of the Episcopal Church with urban society and the upper class, quite distinct from the black agrarian proletariat; and the intellectual sophistication of its ritual, of its Prayer Book, unattractive to blacks and allowing no opportunity for the emotional and unrestrained religious expression somehow associated with the religion of Afro-Americans. It has almost become a cliché that if a black Christian is neither a Baptist nor a Methodist "someone has been fooling around with his religion." In other words, because of their contrary histories and temperaments, the Afro-American and the Episcopal Church do not belong together. Still another and perhaps more serious view is that blacks who do belong to the Episcopal Church are social climbers and, worse, seek to deny their peculiarly black religious heritage. The black Episcopalian has been marked as the "black bourgeois" par excellence; he has been seen as attempting to escape the black community or, if he must remain in it, as attempting to avoid being thought of as an integral part of it.

The truth of the matter is that black Episcopalians have always accepted and shared the well-established view that the black church (collectively) is the most vital force within the black community. They have demonstrated the authenticity of their religious commitment by struggling persistently to maintain an ethnic identity within the larger Episcopal Church, which historically has not readily acknowledged the black presence. The reality of the response of Afro-Americans to both the church's doctrine and its mode of worship is based upon the conviction that Christian faith is vital in life. Black Episcopalians have decided, in common with other Christians, not to abandon their participation in a predominantly white church body. Indeed, they have continued their allegiance and faith not as a means to escape black involvement but rather as a recognition of the reality that their church, no less than society as a whole, struggles with the dilemma of racism.

The Antebellum Church In the Colonial period and in the early days of the republic, the vast majority of black Christians in America were Anglicans. The strength of the Church of England, or the Anglican Church, lay primarily in the middle and southern colonies where the landowners were mostly Anglican, and where often, as in Maryland and Virginia, the Church of England was the established church or "state" church. Here, in the Anglican South, lived the masses of America's black ancestors, and though the white settlers and planters themselves were not interested in the conversion of the African slaves, the Mother Church was. The story of the black Episcopalian begins with the concerted effort of English missionaries sent to America by the Society for the Propagation of the Gospel (SPG) to christianize blacks and Indians. Established by royal charter in 1701, the SPG introduced blacks to the Christian gospel through the Anglican Chruch, later called the Episcopal Church. The response of the slaves to the Gospel and the zeal of their English missionizers laid the basis for the continuing strength of the black church in a time when the spiritual health of Anglican landowners and planters seemed to be at a particularly low ebb.

The Episcopal Church, as its very name implies, is structurally and theologically dependent upon the bishop as its chief pastor. Yet, from the founding of the Jamestown colony in 1607 until the consecration of Samuel Seabury in 1784 as the first American bishop (177 years), there was neither a chief pastor in America nor very many priests, except for the ordained missionaries of the SPG. This fact, coupled with the depressed state of the Church of England in America after the Revolutionary War, meant that the Anglican-Episcopal church of the eighteenth century was physically as well as spiritually weak. Furthermore, the deistic philosophy of the revolutionary period, denying God's intervention in human history and replacing belief in the supernatural with human reason and morality, became coupled with the weakness of the church, and this combination left the planters' exploitive designs unbridled. It was this situation that contributed to the evolution of the kind of chattel slavery that was peculiar to Protestant America. Winthrop Jordan, in *White Over Black: American Attitudes Toward the Negro 1550–1812* (1968), chronicled the black-white relationship in America for that period and concluded that the weakness of the white church and the thus unrestrained designs of the Anglican settlers and planters led eventually to the development of the "peculiar institution" of racial slavery in America, so different from ancient slavery and contemporary slavery forms in Latin America.

The early eighteenth-century Christianization of African slaves by Anglican missionaries was barely tolerated by the colonists whose initial lack of concern gave way to fears that conversion implied freedom. It is interesting that the slaveholder's first view of conversion and baptism into the faith did not separate the spiritual from the mundane, but instead saw a relationship between "freedom in Jesus" and "political freedom," a fact that eased the slaveholder's conscience over the denial of baptism to blacks. The Church of England and the SPG arrived at a compromise by maintaining that conversion did not indeed imply manumission or freedom for the slave. This dilution of the Gospel, the lack of concern on the part of most of the colonials, the question of just how many slaves were reached, and, when reached, how many were truly converted, all combined to lend some ambiguity to the fact that the first Afro-American Christians were Anglican. From the beginning and into the early nineteenth century, those slaves closest to the master's household were more readily touched by missionary efforts than those perhaps more physically distant from it. Yet, even this qualification of Anglicanism among the slaves must be placed against the phenomenon of the "invisible" black church, that bond of oral communication between ranks within the slave community.

Early examples of the conversion effort occurred in 1695 under the Rev. Samuel Thomas at Goose Creek Parish, S.C., and the training of

Afro-Americans themselves for missionary work began in 1743 by the SPG. It is clear that a major aim of the SPG was to educate the slave, as shown, for example, in the establishment of schools in Charleston, S.C., Frederick, Md., and Talbot County on the Eastern Shore of Maryland, the latter school dating from 1755. Perhaps the most important person in this effort was Rev. Thomas Bray of the SPG, who held the important post of commissary for Maryland. Thorough surveys and evaluations of the English missionary work among the slaves have been made. George F. Bragg aptly summarized this initial stage of the black Episcopalian Church: "In brief, all of the Church's efforts among the Negroes, previous to emancipation, was of a patronizing and charitable sort. However, much practical good was realized, but there was no serious endeavor at Church extension among Negroes, nor could such have obtained in the presence of human bondage. The great body of the Church was wholly indifferent to the work of Negro evangelization."

The black Episcopalian was indeed part of the "invisible" church of which E. Franklin Frazier speaks. Soon after the Revolutionary War, slaves and free blacks sought to establish themselves as an identity within the newly reorganized Anglican (Episcopal) Church. George Bragg's comment is significant: "It was reserved for poor, and almost helpless, Negro priests, to become 'founders' and initiate the real constructive, self-respecting work of the Church in the great centers of Negro population." The story of Richard Allen (1760–1831) and Absalom Jones (1746–1818) represents the beginning of the black church in America as an institutional, "visible" form, providing the northern black after the Revolution with a separate means for his own religious development. The story is told by Bragg in his book, *History of the Afro-American Group* (1922), and in his pamphlets, "Heroes of the Eastern Shore: Absalom Jones, The First of the Blacks" (1939) and "Richard Allen and Absalom Jones" (1916). The latter writing tells of the two Methodists who, expelled from St. George's Methodist Church in Philadelphia, Pa., in 1787 formed the "Free African Society," which later became an "undenominational" African Church with the dedication of its building in 1794. The membership voted (with Richard Allen dissenting) to join the Episcopal Church on three conditions: (1) that they be recognized as an organized body; (2) that they be guaranteed local control of their affairs; and (3) that one of their number be placed over them and, subsequently, ordained. Richard Allen would not leave the Methodist fold, though he later founded and became the first bishop of the African Methodist Episcopal (AME) Church in 1816. The Episcopal diocese of Pennsylvania, under Bishop William White, accepted the terms, and St. Thomas African Episcopal Church became the first black Episcopal parish in the United States (1794). Absalom Jones was ordained deacon by Bishop White in 1795 and priest in 1804. This first black Episcopal priest had been born a slave in Delaware, later moving with his master to Philadelphia, Pa. He married, purchased his wife's freedom and his own later, became involved in real estate, and with Allen helped to establish the African Society. Before his death at the age of 71, Jones participated in the consecration of his comrade Richard Allen as bishop of the AME Church.

Two important movements affected the development of the black church during the close of the eighteenth and the beginning of the nineteenth centuries: first, the increased concern for personal freedom following the Revolutionary War; second, the dramatic effect of the Great Revival on American religious life. The antislavery crusade, in the North at least, led to greater freedom for blacks and undoubtedly affected their own sense of participation in American religious institutions. However, as indicated by the expulsion of blacks from St. George's and the slowness of the Episcopal diocese to give St. Thomas' vote in its convention (1863), all was not well "north of slavery." Nevertheless, at least a foothold had been established in these nascent black religious institutions prior to the Civil War. It was the spiritual revival of the Great Awakening that led to the rapid growth of the Baptist and Methodist churches in this era. Yet even here, the Afro-American was touched only toward the end of the period when Baptists and Methodists finally began to evangelize the black man. In other words, the movement of black communicants from a nominal Anglicanism, or, perhaps better, an undenominational Christianity, was a relatively late and slow process in the antebellum period.

At the same time, much of the emotionalism and unrestrained religious expression so often equated with black communicants was a phenomenon originally associated with the Great Awakening. The question may well be raised whether it was the emotionalism alone or the effect of active evangelization by the larger movement that brought the black fathers into the

Methodist and Baptist churches. The spirit of the Revolution aided from within and from without the concept of self-determination and the initiation of the fledgling black institutions. This was the first appearance of the visable black church. But it was the influence of the Great Awakening that moved that emerging black church into evangelical, revivalistic Protestantism. These ingredients, combined with the turmoil of the Civil War and the floundering of the white churches on the issue of race, constitute the foundations of the historical religion of the black churches.

The first distinctly black Episcopalians did not prosper, but neither did they die out. Their number spread in the coastal cities, first in the North and then in the South. After the establishment of St. Thomas' Church in Philadelphia, Pa. (1794), St. Philip's, in New York, N.Y., was founded (1819), whose rector, Peter Williams, Jr. (ordained priest in 1826 by Bishop Hobart of New York) was the son of Peter Williams, Sr., a founder of the African Methodist Episcopal Zion (AMEZ) Church. St. Thomas' had been formed by dissident black Methodists, and St. Philip's members had been parishioners of New York's Trinity Church.

However, the founding of St. James' Church in Baltimore, Md. in 1827, represented the first true missionary effort by a black priest below the Mason-Dixon Line. William Levington of New York City, ordained in St. Thomas', Philadelphia, Pa. (1824), established a church in Baltimore, Md., and his sons went forth to aid in the founding of other churches. William Douglass, the first black ordained in Maryland (deacon, 1834; priest, in Philadelphia, Pa., 1836) became rector of St. Thomas'. Eli Stokes, ordained deacon at St. James' (1843), founded St. Luke's, New Haven, Conn. (1844); he was made priest in 1846 and died a missionary in Africa. St. James', Baltimore, Md., nurtured the mother of AME Bishop Levi J. Coppin, an alumnus of the Episcopal Philadelphia Divinity School. St. Luke's, New Haven, where W. E. B. Du Bois was baptized, had as its rector (1856–61) James T. Holly, who was to become founder and first bishop of the Church of Haiti (1874–1911). It was a former Baptist minister, William C. Munroe (deacon, 1846; priest, 1849), who helped to establish St. Matthew's, Detroit, Mich. (1851), which served as a terminus for the Underground Railroad. Munroe went to Liberia as a missionary in 1859 and died there. It was at St. Matthew's that James T. Holly was ordained (deacon, 1855; priest, at

St. Luke's, New Haven, 1856). Several other congregations were formed in the mid-nineteenth century: Christ Church, Providence, R.I. (1843); Crucifixion Church, Philadelphia, Pa. (1852); St. Philip's, Newark, N.J. (1856); and St. Philip's, Buffalo, N.Y. (1865). Such black parishes as St. Stephen's, Savannah, Ga., and St. Mark's, Charleston, S.C., were formed in southern coastal cities. The southern parishes had white clergy in this early period.

Prior to emancipation, southern black Episcopalians were under the paternalistic control of southern bishops, while their more independent brethren in the North suffered under the benign neglect of northern bishops. Black Episcopalians in the South received religious instruction and the sacramental ministration of the church. It was in the church that many Afro-Americans first learned to read and write through instruction in the catechism. They were baptized, confirmed, received Communion, were buried by the priest, and increasingly married in the church. Yet, they were not incorporated into the fellowship of the church, being forced into slave galleries or accepting services held for them at special hours or in separate buildings. Their priests were white; often the bishop of the diocese took the black parishioners as his special responsibility.

St. Philip's Protestant Episcopal Church, established in 1819, New York, NY. *(Photo by Ronald Duncan.)*

Though the rise of independent black parishes has been noted above, all did not go well with blacks in northern congregations just prior to the Civil War. For example, St. James' in Baltimore, Md., struggled to stay alive, as did the Bethel AME Church, the only two congregations with black pastors in Baltimore. The struggle of

St. James Episcopal Church, established in 1824, Baltimore, Md. *(Photo by Jacquelyn Low.)*

northern parishes to gain full admission into their dioceses with the right to vote in church conventions was symptomatic of attitudes of the period. St. Philip's, New York, N.Y., though founded in 1819, was not given one right to vote until 1853; and St. Thomas', Philadelphia, Pa., could not vote in Pennsylvania conventions until 1863. Black applicants for the church's General Theological Seminary, New York, N.Y., were discouraged or refused outright. Isaiah DeGrasse was told in 1836, for example, that he could not become a regular student at the General Theological Seminary; the following year Alexander Crummell was refused admission to the seminary outright. Crummell, who was to become the black church's leading spokesman, went then to the Congregational Andover Seminary in Boston, Mass., and was ordained deacon at St. Paul's Cathedral, Boston, by Bishop Griswold (1842) and priest in Pennsylvania (1844). St. Matthew's, Detroit, had its congregation scattered several times as a result of the Fugitive Slave Law of 1850. It was in this period of repression prior to and during the Civil War that black Episcopalians became active in missionary activity in the black republics of Haiti and Liberia. James T. Holly, rector of St. Luke's, New Haven, established Holy Trinity Church in Port-au-Prince, Haiti (1861), and Crummell, after study at Queens College, Cambridge, England (1852–53), taught at the College of Liberia, returning to the United States only after the Civil War in 1873. Numerous other clergy followed the lead of these men.

Civil War through Post-Reconstruction The most significant aspect of the Episcopal Church during the Civil War and Reconstruction was its failure to take any definitive policy actions. Unlike some denominations prior to the outbreak of hostilities, the Episcopal Church did not split into North-South branches over the issue of slavery. During the war, the southern bishops formed a grouping that was welcomed back into the national church at the end of hostilities. The southern black Episcopalians had no recourse but to acquiesce to the southern bishops or to leave the church, which the vast majority did. Although it has been argued that the failure of the church to split over slavery was a sign of its "catholic" aspect, which could not be disrupted by social and political issues, the fact of the matter is that the church's silence signaled disaster for its already unenthusiastic mission among Afro-Americans. This was especially true in the South where the vast majority of black Episcopalians lived. The official silence of the church over slavery, combined with its continued "hands-off" policy with regard to the freed black Episcopalian during Reconstruction, led to mass defections by black communicants.

It has been estimated that in some southern states 90 percent of the black Episcopalians left the Episcopal Church to join either the AME or CME African churches. The exit of significant numbers of black churchmen was hastened by the missionary zeal of the emerging visible black church. In the postwar period, black Protestant churches grew so rapidly that by 1890 the AME, AMEZ, CME, and Baptist churches claimed 9 out of every 10 of all Afro-American Protestants. Yet during this period the Episcopal Church resisted granting autonomy or the right of leadership to its Afro-American membership.

Though greatly diminished, those black Episcopalians who remained in the church pressed the fight not for independence, but for the development of their own leadership within the church and an arena in which to exercise a voice and vote within the church's general convention. Though initially rebuffed, St. Mark's, in Charleston, S.C., persisted in efforts to be seated in the South Carolina convention.

Samuel D. Ferguson of Charleston, S.C., served as bishop in Liberia (1885–1916) and was the first black bishop to sit in the American

House of Bishops. In 1918, Edward T. Demby and Henry B. Delany became suffragan bishops, that is, bishops without right of franchise or succession.

Twentieth Century At least three vital phenomena have brought the black Episcopalian to the present position of hope. First, the massive increase of their numerical strength due to the large immigration of Anglicans from the West Indies in the first half of this century has reinforced their representative position. Second, the pervasive impact of the civil rights movement of the 1950s and 1960s has led the nation and its churches to become more receptive to the aspirations of black America. This was particularly evident in the Episcopal Church in the formation of the interracial action group known as the Episcopal Society for Cultural and Racial Unity (ESCRU) and in the establishment of the General Convention Special Program (GCSP) in 1967. Third, the formation in 1968 of a black caucus, known as the Union of Black Episcopalians (UBE), provided a forum and lobby for black interests in the church, as the Conference of Church Workers had done previously. These three factors—increase in number, a more responsive national church, and a vocal black leadership—have reversed that depressing situation that led Du Bois to condemn the Episcopal Church in 1903.

Though small in comparison with the largest black church bodies, the black Episcopalian church is showing strength in the 1970s never contemplated in previous generations. Approximately 100,000 baptized black Episcopalians (or 3.5 percent of the nearly 3.5 million total membership of the Episcopal Church) are found (mostly) in nearly 220 black parishes and missions, while a not insignificant number are members of predominantly white congregations. There are about 290 black priests and an average of 25 men in the seminary (1972). Six black bishops recently ordained in the Episcopal Church were: John M. Burgess, bishop of Massachusetts (suffragan, 1962; diocesan, 1970); Cedric E. Mills, bishop of the Virgin Islands (1963); Richard B. Martin, suffragan bishop of Long Island (1967); George D. Browne, bishop of Liberia (1970); John T. Walker, suffragan bishop of Washington, D.C. (1971); and Luc Garnier, bishop of Haiti (1971). Gains in the status as well as in the strength of black Episcopalians are evidenced by the greater representation and voice in diocesan conventions and by the laity in executive positions as well as in the church's missionary outreach, particularly in urban centers. As a sign of the church's new readiness to serve and evangelize in the black community, the traditionally urban-oriented Episcopal Church is placing black priests at the head of its outreach programs to the black city dweller. A dozen or more priests have been attached to cathedral staffs as Urban Missioners. Dillard Robinson, for example, became dean of the Episcopal Cathedral in Newark, N.J., and Walter Dennis became canon on the staff of New York City's Cathedral Church of St. John the Divine. In theological education, Quinland Gordon was named dean of the Absalom Jones Theological Institute in the Interdenominational Theological Center, Atlanta, Ga., and Joseph Pelham became dean of students at the Colgate-Rochester Bexley Hall Seminary in Rochester, N.Y., and Robert Bennett became professor at the Episcopal Theological School in Cambridge, Mass. The overall national church leadership of black Episcopalians, the position once held by Tollie L. Caution (executive secretary for racial minorities, 1946–67) passed after 1967 into the hands of the Union of Black Episcopalians. *See also* AFRICAN METHODIST EPISCOPAL (AME) CHURCH; AFRICAN METHODIST EPISCOPAL ZION (AMEZ) CHURCH; ALLEN, RICHARD; BAPTISTS; CHRISTIAN METHODIST EPISCOPAL (CME) CHURCH; CHURCHES; CRUMMELL, ALEXANDER; METHODISTS/UNITED METHODIST CHURCH; SOCIETY FOR THE PROPAGATION OF THE GOSPEL IN FOREIGN PARTS (SPG).

REFERENCES: For additional information, see: Clifton, Denzil T., "Anglicanism and Negro Slavery in Colonial America," *Historical Magazine of the Protestant Episcopal Church*, vol. 39, no. 1, pp. 24–70, March 1970; "The Domestic and Foreign Missionary Society Papers—The Liberia Papers: 1822–1939; The Haiti Papers: 1855–1939," *Historical Magazine of the Protestant Episcopal Church*, vol. 39, no. 1, pp. 90–95, March 1970; "The Episcopal Church and the Negro Race," *Historical Magazine of the Protestant Episcopal Church*, vol. 4, no. 1, p. 49, March 1935; Ferris, William H., *Alexander Crummell, An Apostle of Negro Culture*, American Negro Academy, Washington, D.C., 1920; Franklin, John Hope, "Negro Episcopalians in Ante-Bellum North Carolina," *Historical Magazine of the Protestant Episcopal Church*, vol. 13, no. 3., pp. 216–34, September 1944; Frazier, E. Franklin, *The Negro Church in America*, Schocken, New York, 1963; "Negro Bishops and Diocesan Segregation in the Protestant Episcopal Church: 1870–1957," *Historical Magazine of the Protestant Episcopal Church*, vol. 31, pp. 231–42, 1962; Reimers, David, *White Protestantism and the Negro*, Oxford University Press, New York, 1965; and Woodson, Carter, *The Negro Church*, Associated Publishers, Washington, D.C., 1921.

ERVING, JULIUS WINFIELD See ATHLETES: BASKETBALL.

ESTEBAN /ESTEVANICO (LITTLE STEPHEN) *See* AFRO-AMERICAN HISTORY: THE WEST.

EVANS, HERBERT B. (1919–), lawyer, judge; born in Kansas City, Mo. Evans graduated from Howard University (Washington, D.C.) in 1947 and received his LL.B. degree from Saint John's University (Jamaica, N.Y.) in 1950. He was admitted to the New York bar in 1951, and subsequently became a member of a law firm in New York City. In 1955 Evans served as counsel to the governor of New York, a post he held until 1958, when he became a member of the State Parole Commission. Beginning in 1960, he served on the Housing and Redevelopment Board, and part of the time he acted as commissioner of that board. In 1961 Evans was appointed to the city council of New York, serving with the council for two years. He was elected judge of the Civil Court of New York City in 1967, and subsequently became a judge on the New York State Supreme Court.

EVANS, MARI *See* LITERATURE: POETRY

EVANS, W. LEONARD, JR. (1914–), publisher, editor; born in Louisville, Ky. Evans was president of Tuesday Publications, Inc., and editor and publisher of *Tuesday,* a magazine supplement appearing in nearly 20 Sunday newspapers. In 1972 Evans was the recipient of the Business Achievement Award of the Interracial Council for Business Opportunity.

EVERS, JAMES CHARLES (1922–), civil rights leader, mayor; born in Decatur, Miss. Evers received his early and college education in Mississippi schools, graduating from Alcorn Agricultural and Mechanical (A & M) College (Lorman, Miss.; now Alcorn State University) in 1950. After serving in the U.S. Army during the Korean conflict, he took over his family's considerable business interests in Philadelphia, Miss., but in 1957 decided to move to Chicago, Ill. Evers remained in Chicago and pursued various careers (successful nightclub owner, real estate agent, and disc jockey) until the assassination of his brother Medgar in 1963 brought him back to Mississippi. He assumed his brother's post as field director of the National Association for the Advancement of Colored People (NAACP) in Mississippi, and as such, several years later, ran

Far right: James Charles Evers with the other members of the Mississippi delegation to a convention held in Gary, Ind., in 1972. (Photo by LeRoy Henderson.)

for election as mayor of the town of Fayette, Miss. Fayette, the county seat of Jefferson County with a population of about 2,000, elected Evers mayor in 1969, thus installing the first black mayor in a racially mixed southern town since Reconstruction. He was reelected in 1973, after an unsuc-

cessful attempt for the governorship on an independent ticket in 1972. His autobiography, *Evers,* was published in 1971. *See also* EVERS, MEDGAR WILEY.

EVERS, MEDGAR WILEY (1925–63), civil rights leader, lawyer; born in Decatur, Miss. Evers, the brother of James Charles Evers, graduated from Alcorn Agricultural and Mechanical (A & M) College (Lorman, Miss.; now Alcorn State University) and then studied law at the University of Mississippi Law School. He was active in civil rights movements in Mississippi from 1954 until he was assassinated at the entrance of his home in Jackson, Miss., in 1963. After his death, his role as state leader of the National Association for the Advancement of Colored People (NAACP) was assumed by his brother James Charles. *See also* EVERS, JAMES CHARLES.

EXODUSTERS A term used in reference to Afro-American separatist settlements in the West, particularly in the state of Kansas under Pap Singleton. With this term as a main title, a book dealing with the subject was written by Nell Irvin Painter, *Exodusters: Black Migration to Kansas after Reconstruction* (Alfred A. Knopf, 1977). *See also* AFRO-AMERICAN HISTORY: THE WEST.

FAMILY

FAMILY Much existing literature on black families remains pathologically oriented. The traditional use of white middle-class families as the standard for measuring black families frequently results in an unnecessary utilization of a deficit model disadvantageous to the latter. Often ignoring their heterogeneity, generalizations arising from specific samples of black families, bound by time and space, are overextended to include the population of *all* black families without sufficient assurance of their aptness, or of the specific environmental situations in which they resided.

Significant gaps continue to persist in our knowledge about black familial institutions, especially when one seeks valid data beyond their structural characteristics. No substantial agreement about or action on respective black-white complementary roles has yet emerged from any of the historical and contemporary controversies about optimal interaction between black families and the American society, though an upsurge of literature, especially by black writers, in the 1960s and the 1970s promises to bear more fruit (e.g., Staples, 1971). Such gaps in research and literature currently prohibit any definitive theory of *the black family*. Much of the existing divergence in the literature about and policies and programming for black families may be at least partially attributed to conceptual usages. In reality, there is no *the black family*; there are, however, *black families*. This limited focus upon black families is principally con-

cerned with their demography, and, to a lesser extent, with a brief specification of certain central issues surrounding them.

(Courtesy of Roland L. Freeman.)

Demography In general, recent demographic comparisons of the categories of *the black fami-*

ly and *the white family* suggest that certain gaps between them continue to exist in several important ways directly related to their different histories, socioeconomic positions, and family structures; but they do not suggest that black families should become more like white families. During the 1960s and early 1970s, it appears that blacks failed to make any widespread, relative progress in reducing gaps in education, occupation, income, and employment between themselves and whites, or in increasing the likelihood that their children would be reared in husband-wife families during childhood and adolescence.

While approximately 97 percent of all blacks and whites resided within households in 1970 (and the remaining within group quarters), proportionately fewer household heads were found among blacks (27.4 percent) than among whites (32.6 percent), a function, no doubt, of their larger average household size (3.68 persons for blacks, 3.11 for whites) and greater inaccessibility to adequate neolocal housing. More primary individuals were found among blacks (22.1 percent) than among whites (19.4 percent).

Also, in 1970, far more husband-wife groupings (73 percent) were found among white families than among blacks (55 percent), while the latter were slightly larger (4.31 persons) than the former (3.54 persons). Black families, reflecting their younger average ages, were less likely to have members 65 years of age and over, but more likely to have younger ones, especially under 18 years. About 57 percent of all black families were in central cities, as compared with only 26 percent of all white families. Black families were thus more likely to be impacted by urban blight.

While males most often headed families, about three times as many black (27.8 percent) as white (9 percent) families were headed by females. This racial variation should be seen in the light of racial differences in marital statuses, life expectancies, and sex ratios. In 1970 the vast majority of blacks and whites, 14 years of age and over, were married, but those most likely to be without spouses were black famales, due principally to higher rates of widowhood, separation, and divorce (rates affected certainly by longevity and sex ratios). Females among both racial groups tended to marry earlier than did the males, but black females were slightly older at age of first marriage than were white females. As of 1970, however, 64.8 percent of black females, 69.8 percent of white females, 45.3 percent of black males, and 51.1 percent of white males married or ever married were all first married prior to becoming 25 years old.

Blacks—and especially males—continued to experience significantly shorter life expectancies than whites, contributing thereby to greater family disruption through death. One outcome is greater widowhood—and at earlier ages—for black females, thus contributing further to the proportion of female-headed families among blacks.

The sex ratio may be even more significant. In 1970 it was 90.8 among blacks (about 91 males for every 100 females) and 95.3 among whites. Excessive white females only appeared in the 1950 census (99.1), while every census after 1850 has shown excessive black females. The 1970 data also showed a significant, inverse relationship among blacks in their state-by-state sex ratio and their percentage of female family heads. In other words, the more the males, the fewer the female heads.

One critical difference between black and white families, which rarely receives sufficient attention, is simply that of the diminished availability of black males. Although intermarriage rates between both groups are yet quite small, the fact that the typical black mate is male further diminishes the male supply available to black females, with adverse consequences for black family life. Barring a dramatic reversal, continued female excesses are likely to persist among both groups in the decades ahead, thereby inviting less conformity to conventional familial norms. It is quite probably that a continuing white female excess could well produce greater similarity to familial variations found already among the black population, since, in this respect, the latter has a headstart upon nonconventional patterns. For example, although the reported illegitimacy rates continue to be higher among blacks than whites, the actual percentage change in the white illegitimate rate from 1955–59 to 1968 was almost eight times as great as that of the black: plus 53 percent for the whites, as compared with minus 8 percent for the blacks.

Black fertility rates were higher at every age-specific level during the childbearing years than were those of whites, and especially so at the extreme ends, 15–19 and 40–44 years of age, as shown in the accompanying table.

Yet, fertility rates, inversely related to education and income, showed clearly lower rates for black than for white females completing four or more years of college. Black females were also more likely either to have no children, one child, or five or more children than were whites, while the latter were much more likely to have borne two to four children. Thus, *blacks were those both more likely to have the lowest and the highest fertility rates.*

In 1969, both blacks and whites continued to contribute toward the possibility of overpopulation, for their respective replacement indices were 175 and 142. The highest black replacement indices occurred among those blacks in the South not in metropolitan areas, not in the labor force, and with less than a ninth-grade educa-

CHILDREN EVER BORN PER WOMAN BY MARITAL STATUS AND AGE: 1965, 1970, AND 1974

Marital status and age	Black		
	1974	1970	1965
Total Women[1]			
Total, 15 to 44 years	**1.6**	**2.0**	**2.1**
15 to 19 years	0.1	0.1	0.2
20 to 24 years	0.7	0.9	1.2
25 to 29 years	1.6	2.0	2.6
30 to 34 years	2.5	3.0	3.4
35 to 39 years	3.5	3.5	3.5
40 to 44 years	3.5	3.5	3.1
Women Ever Married			
Total, 15 to 44 years	**2.7**	**3.0**	**3.1**
15 to 19 years	0.9	1.0	(B)
20 to 24 years	1.3	1.6	1.8
25 to 29 years	2.1	2.5	3.0
30 to 34 years	3.0	3.4	3.9
35 to 39 years	3.8	3.8	3.8
40 to 44 years	3.8	3.8	3.4

Marital status and age	White		
	1974	1970	1965
Total Women[1]			
Total, 15 to 44 years	**1.4**	**1.6**	**1.7**
15 to 19 years	0.1	—	—
20 to 24 years	0.6	0.7	0.9
25 to 29 years	1.4	1.7	2.1
30 to 34 years	2.3	2.6	2.7
35 to 39 years	2.8	2.9	2.8
40 to 44 years	3.0	2.9	2.7
Women Ever Married			
Total, 15 to 44 years	**2.1**	**2.3**	**2.4**
15 to 19 years	0.5	0.6	0.6
20 to 24 years	0.9	1.0	1.3
25 to 29 years	1.6	1.9	2.3
30 to 34 years	2.4	2.7	2.8
35 to 39 years	2.9	3.1	2.9
40 to 44 years	3.2	3.0	2.8

—Rounds to zero.
[B]Base too small for rate to be shown.
[1]Includes single (never married) women, not shown separately.
SOURCE: U.S. Department of Commerce, Bureau of the Census, *Current Population Reports,* ser. P-23, no. 54.

tion. Conversely, the lowest black replacement indices occurred among those in the Northeast, in central cities, in the labor force, and with more than eight years of formal education. These replacement variations among blacks imply that family planning resources have been far less accessible to those with the higher rates. What may be of at least equal importance is the implication that families with potentially greater resources for successful childrearing, culminating in substantially improved upward vertical mobility for their offspring, are those least likely to overreproduce themselves, whereas those with the least resources are most likely to contribute toward black replacement. Further, many more less sufficient blacks are more likely to produce larger numbers of offspring, reducing thereby available child resources for each offspring, which has the net effect of diminishing their educational, occupational, employment, and income achievement levels. These diminutions threaten the child's potentialities for sufficient support and the maintenance of his or her family.

More than one-third of all black families (about three times as many as whites) live below the poverty level, as do more than one-half of all black children. But less than half of these black families are welfare recipients. Most black families have a working head, employed full time. More than three-fourths of all black males and about one-half of all black females participate actively within the labor force. In 1969 about 45 percent of black females with children under six years of age were working mothers, although many were without adequate child care resources. Even when the heads of black families are employed, however, racism continued to plague them. In 1970 the median black family income was only 71.2 percent that of whites, but the number of employed members within a black family was often greater than that of a white family. Black wives contributed substantially more to the family income when employed than did typical white wives. Again, in 1970, the median income of *both* the employed husband and wife in a black family was only $23 more ($9,134) that that of a white family *without* a working wife ($9,111). Also important is the fact that the median 1970 income of a black female-headed family was only 36.7 percent as much as that of a white family without a working wife, although that black family typically contained more persons (4.22) than did that white family

(3.54), merely another indication of the greater accessibility of whites to societally supportive family resources.

It should be stressed that what is indisputable in any composite description of *the black family* is that it is statistically dominated by the nuclear family (i.e., husband, wife and offspring in neolocal residence) with a working head employed full time, and whose wife is equally likely to be a labor-force participant or a housewife. The structure of most black families dissolves through death. Variations do exist, for one minority pattern is that of female-headed households, whose resources are usually far more restricted than those of male heads, due partially to greater constrictions imposed upon the females by their more severely limited occupational and income levels. Black families differ only in degrees, not in kind, from white families, for the same minority patterns exist among the latter as well.

Issues Briefly, it may be suggested that almost no one assumes that there is nothing wrong with *the black family*. With such rare exceptions as those of Jackson (1972) and Staples (1971), almost all sociologists assume that the *ideal black family* is the *ideal patriarchal, white middle-class family*. Most existing controversy about black families now may be broadly subsumed under the issues of: (a) blame objects for "the black condition;" (b) needed changes and change agents for condition modification; (c) actual change methods; and (d) existence of black familial advantages.

Three of the major writers on the black family easily illustrate most of those issues. Moynihan (1965) clearly attempted to exculpate white guilt by citing the black family as the cause of the deterioration of the fabric of black society, as if a black society and culture existed apart from the American society or culture. While explicitly acknowledging Frazier's insistence (1939) upon slavery, urbanization, and economic deprivation (especially housing and employment) as the root causes of black family disorganization, Moynihan actually turned Frazier upside down, for the latter squarely placed primary blame upon white society. Rainwater (1967) took a middle-of-the-road position by blaming both. Frazier emphasized societal responsibility (especially governmental) for rectifying disorganizing elements found largely within social conditions, while Moynihan suggested, it appears, federal intervention within the family interior (through increased male employment, reduced illegitimacy, and reduced welfare dependency in particular), and Rainwater contended that it would probably "make more sense to change [the black] ... socioeconomic situation and then depend upon the people involved to make new adaptations as time goes on." All authors operated under the assumption that black families should be changed, in essence, to become more like ideal white families. Frazier clearly regarded the black matriarchy as a nondominant family pattern among blacks and recognized its historical evolution and functionality. He did not regard it harshly, as did Moynihan, Rainwater, Bernard (1966), Scanzoni (1971), and Billingsley (1968), among others. Clearly too much over generalization of the black matriarchy is now apparent, but that theory has been most useful in simply blaming black mothers for situations over which they were and remain essentially powerless [see, e.g., Jackson (1972), Hyman and Reed (1969), Ladner (1971), and Mack (1971)].

Actual change methods, as incorporated in such programs of the 1960s as the Job Corps, Project Headstart, and Upward Bound, appear highly ineffective in bringing about any significant changes in black familial patterns. If significant educational gains could be produced in higher education and occupational employment, at significantly higher-income levels, it is quite likely that familial variations among blacks may ensue. Essentially, what is required is a significant reduction of racism and significant upward mobility of the black population so that the majority of black families will be middle-class families, if that is the goal. In the meantime, it appears very likely that black families will continue in the future, as they surely have in the past, to adapt to existing situations where they are powerless to change them, to continue to muster strength and courage to effect desired changes, and to maintain much love for and concern about their family members, regardless of the proclamations of social scientists and social planners.

Social researchers and social planners should pay greater heed to the significant gaps characterizing knowledge about and conditions of black families. They should also, following Rainwater, be far more concerned about reducing racism and inequities in education, housing, and income. One of the great advantages of most black families has been their tremendous adaptive flexibility, that stoical ability to survive. In many ways, with such changes as those noted of the increasingly excessive number of females now found among whites, whites may well benefit by learning more about a black familial advantage—how do you make it, indeed, with less than one male for every female. See also DISCRIMINATION; EMPLOYMENT; HEALTH; HOUSING; INCOME; POPULATION; POVERTY; WOMEN.

REFERENCES Bernard, Jessie, Marriage and Family Among Negroes, Prentice-Hall, Englewood Cliffs, 1966; Billingsley, Andrew, Black Families in White America, Prentice-Hall, Englewood Cliffs, 1968; Dollard, John, Caste and Class in a Southern Town, 3d ed., Doubleday, Garden City, 1957; Frazier, E. Franklin, The Negro Family in the United States, University of Chicago Press, Chicago, 1939; Hyman, Herbert H. and John S. Reed, "'Black Matriarchy' Reconsidered: Evidence from Secondary Analysis of Sample Surveys," Public Opinion Quarterly, vol. 33, pp. 346–54, 1969; Gutman, Herbert George, The Black Family in Slavery and Freedom, 1750–1925, Pantheon Books, New York, 1976; Jackson, Jacquelyne J., "Negro Aged: Toward Needed Research in Social Gerontology," The Gerontologist, vol. 11, pp. 52–57, 1971a; Jackson, Jacquelyne J., "Sex and Social Class Variations in Black Older Parent-Adult Child Relationships," Aging and Human Development, 1971b; Ladner, Joyce. Tomorrow's Tomorrow, The Black Woman, Doubleday, Garden City, 1971; Mack, Delores, "Where the Black Matriarchy Theorists Went Wrong," Psychology Today, vol. 4, pp. 24ff., 1971; Moynihan, Daniel P., The Negro Family, The Case For National Action, U.S. Government Printing Office, Washington, D.C., 1965; Rainwater, Lee, "Crucible of Identity: The Negro Lower-Class Family," in Talcott Parsons and Kenneth Clark (eds.), The Negro American, Beacon Press, Boston, 1967, pp. 160–204; Scanzoni, John H., The Black Family in Modern Society, Allyn and Bacon, Boston, 1971; and Staples, Robert, "Towards a Sociology of the Black Family: A Theoretical and Methodological Assessment," Journal of Marriage and the Family, vol. 33, pp. 119–38, 1971.

FARMER, JAMES L. (1920–   ), civil rights leader; born in Marshall, Tex. The son of a professor, Farmer was educated at Wiley College (Marshall, Tex.) and at Howard University (Washington, D.C.), receiving a divinity degree in 1941 from the latter institution. Refusing to be ordained as a religious leader in a segregated society, he concerned himself instead with civil rights activities. In 1942, in Chicago, Ill., Farmer formed the Congress of Racial Equality (CORE) and became its director. As such, he led protests against discrimination, especially in public facilities. His protests were nonviolent and employed the techniques of passive resistance that had not previously been utilized in the civil rights movement: sit-ins, standing lines, freedom rides, pilgrimages, and marches, all of which became trademarks of the movement and especially of CORE. Opposing the new trend toward separatism that was taking hold in the cadres of CORE, Farmer left the organization, after its great successes in the 1950s and early

1960s, in 1966. For the next two years, he served as professor of social welfare at Lincoln University (Lincoln, Pa.) and as adjunct professor at New York University. After having served as vice-chairman of the Liberal Party in New York from 1954 to 1961, he ran for the U.S. Congress in 1968, but was defeated by Shirley Chisholm. In 1969 President Richard M. Nixon appointed him assistant secretary of Health, Education, and Welfare, a position he held until his resignation in 1970. Farmer wrote Freedom When? (1965) and was the author of numerous articles and essays. See also CONGRESS OF RACIAL EQUALITY (CORE).

FARMERS, FARMING   See AGRICULTURE.

FARRIS, JEROME (1930–   ), lawyer, judge; born in Birmingham, Ala. Farris was admitted to the Washington bar in 1958, after having received a B.S. degree from Morehouse College (Atlanta, Ga.), a M.S.W. degree from Atlanta University, and his J.D. degree from the University of Washington. He soon became a judge on the State Court of Appeals in Seattle, Wash.

FARRISON, WILLIAM EDWARD (1902–   ), educator; born in Orangeburg County, S.C. Farrison received a B.A. degree from Lincoln University (Lincoln University, Pa.), a M.A. degree from the University of Pennsylvania, and his Ph.D. degree from Ohio State University in 1936. He taught at North Carolina Central University and wrote William Wells Brown: Author and Reformer (1969).

FATHER DIVINE   See BAKER, GEORGE.

FAUNTLEROY, JOHN DOUGLAS (1920–   ), lawyer, judge; born in Washington, D.C. Fauntleroy attended Rutgers University (New Brunswick, N.J.), after which he studied law at the Robert H. Terrell Law School (Washington, D.C.), receiving his LL.B. degree in 1941. He earned a B.S. degree in government at American University (Washington, D.C.) in 1953, and he did further graduate study at Georgetown University (Washington, D.C.) in 1954. Fauntleroy began to practice law in the District of Columbia in 1947. After two and a half years in military service, he returned to law, and beginning in 1960 he served as a member of the Judicial Conference of the District of Columbia Circuit until 1967. In 1962 Fauntleroy was appointed presi-

James Farmer (Photoworld.)

dent of the Washington Bar Association, a post he held for two years. In 1967 he became associate judge of the Juvenile Court (now Superior Court) in the District of Columbia.

FAUNTROY, WALTER E. (1933–   ), civil rights leader, U.S. Representative; born in Washington, D.C. A graduate of Virginia Union University in 1955, Fauntroy received a B.D. degree from Yale Divinity School in 1958. The next year he became pastor of the New Bethel Baptist Church in Washington, D.C. During the 1960s, in addition to his civic and religious activities, Fauntroy was an active participant in the civil rights movement: helping to coordinate the 1963 March on Washington, D.C., and the 1965 Selma to Montgomery March; serving as national coordinator of the Poor People's Campaign in 1969; and heading the Southern Christian Leadership Conference (SCLC) in the District of Columbia. In 1971 he was elected to Congress as a representative from the District of Columbia, the only elected black official in the district with a seat in Congress.

FAUSET, ARTHUR HUFF (1899–   ), author, educator; born in Flemington, N.J. A graduate of the University of Pennsylvania where he received his B.A., M.A., and Ph.D. degrees, Fauset was a teacher and principal in Philadelphia, Pa., public schools (1918–46). He wrote several articles that appeared in such magazines as *Crisis* and *Opportunity*. His books include *Sojourner Truth: God's Faithful Pilgrim* (1938), a biography, and *Black Gods of the Metropolis: Negro Religious Cults of the Urban North* (1944, 1970). *See also* FAUSET, JESSIE REDMON.

FAUSET, JESSIE REDMON (1886–1961), author, educator; born in Philadelphia, Pa. Fauset received a B.A. degree from Cornell University (Ithaca, N.Y.) in 1905 and her M.A. degree from the University of Pennsylvania the following year, where she met her future husband (Arthur Huff Fauset). From 1920 to 1921 she worked on the short-lived children's magazine *The Brownie's Book*. In 1921 Fauset attended sessions of the Pan-African Congress abroad, and later returned to Europe to study French at the Sorbonne. In 1944, after having been a member of the staff of *Crisis* magazine of the National Association for the Advancement of Colored People (NAACP), she resumed her interrupted career as a teacher. In 1949 Fauset was appointed visiting

Jessie Fauset
(Library of
Congress.)

professor of English at Hampton Institute (Hampton, Va.). Her novel, *There Is Confusion,* was published in 1924. *See also* FAUSET, ARTHUR HUFF; LITERATURE: THE NOVEL.

FAYETTEVILLE STATE COLLEGE See FAYETTEVILLE STATE UNIVERSITY.

FAYETTEVILLE STATE TEACHERS COLLEGE See FAYETTEVILLE STATE UNIVERSITY.

FAYETTEVILLE STATE UNIVERSITY Fayetteville State University, at Fayetteville, N.C., was founded in 1877 by the general assembly of North Carolina under the bill known as the Act to Establish Normal Schools. The coeducational school is state-supported, offers the bachelor's degree, and provides a teacher education curriculum. In 1975 its enrollment was about 1,800. The faculty and staff number more than 200.

The university has been variously named the State Colored Normal School (1877), State Colored Normal and Industrial School (1916), State Normal School for the Negro Race (1921), State Normal School (1926), Fayetteville State Teachers College (1939), Fayetteville State College (1963), and Fayetteville State University (1969).

Prior to 1960 the only major offered was in elementary education. In 1959, however, the general assembly revised the university's charter and authorized expansion of the curriculum to include a major in secondary education. The university now offers 16 majors and a cooperative program with North Carolina State University, which adds ten additional majors.

Fayetteville State graduated its first four-year class in 1939 and its first white student in 1964.

FEDERAL CITY COLLEGE Federal City College, at Washington, D.C., was founded in 1968. The college is federally supported and coeducational, offers the bachelor's and the master's degrees, and provides liberal arts, teacher education, and professional curricula. In 1974 its enrollment was about 7,800.

Having been established by the federal government as the only urban land-grant college, Federal City set out to combine traditional and contemporary elements in a program that would be relevant to the new urban student body. From the beginning, it was decided that within the framework of providing high-quality academic and intellectual programs, attention would be focused on the problems within Washington,

D.C., a city of great political power and wealth, yet one with many black people impoverished and constantly subject to the ills of a decaying metropolis.

The college determined that it would not stop with traditional higher education; it would also serve the city by taking an active part in reversing the process of urban decay. The programs at Federal City place strong emphasis upon African, Afro-American, and urban studies.

FEDERATION OF PAN-AFRICAN EDUCATIONAL INSTITUTIONS An organization founded in 1971, the federation was composed of six institutions: the Chad School, Newark, N.J.; the Pan-African Work Center, Atlanta, Ga.; Malcolm X Liberation University, Greensboro, N.C.; the Marcus Garvey School, Youngstown, Ohio; the Clifford McKissick Community School, Milwaukee, Wisc.; and the Marcus Garvey Memorial Institute, Monrovia, Liberia.

FEREBEE, DOROTHY See HEALTH.

FERGUSON, CLARENCE CLYDE, JR. (1924–), lawyer, government official; born in Wilmington, N.C. Upon graduation from Ohio State University in 1948, Ferguson went to Harvard Law School and received his LL.B. degree in 1951. After a year as a teaching fellow at Harvard, he became an assistant U.S. attorney in New York. In 1955 Ferguson joined the faculty of Rutgers University (New Brunswick, N.J.) for six years as professor of law, after which he served as general counsel to the U.S. Civil Rights Commission. In 1963 he became dean of Howard University School of Law (Washington, D.C.), and in 1970 he became U.S. ambassador to Uganda.

FERGUSON, LLOYD NOEL (1918–), chemist, educator; born in Oakland, Calif. Ferguson received a B.S. degree (1940) and his Ph.D. degree (1943) from the University of California at Berkeley. He was a research assistant of the National Defense Project, University of California at Berkeley (1941–44), an assistant professor at North Carolina Agricultural and Technical (A & T) State University (1944–45), and a faculty member at Howard University (1945–65) and head of its chemistry department (1958–65). Ferguson did extensive research on the biochemical aspects of the sense of taste. He also wrote extensively, contributing more than 40 articles to scholarly journals. See also SCIENTISTS: BIOLOGICAL, PHYSICAL.

FERGUSON, ROSETTA (1920–), state legislator; born in Florence, Miss. Ferguson received her higher education at the Detroit Institute of Technology. After serving as general manager of a real-estate firm, she was elected a member of the Michigan state house of representatives in 1964. In this position, she was responsible for the passage of Michigan's Fair Textbook Law.

FERGUSON, SAMUEL DAVID See EPISCOPALIANS.

FERRIS, WILLIAM H. (1874–1941), editor, author; born in New Haven, Conn. After receiving his early education in local schools, Ferris earned a M.A. degree from Yale University in 1899 and a second M.A. degree from Harvard Divinity School in 1900. He then became a teacher, lecturer, preacher, and writer on behalf of Marcus Garvey's Universal Negro Improvement Association. Ferris worked for various newspapers, including *The Champion* (associate editor, 1916–17), *Negro World* (literary editor, 1919–23), and *The Spokesman* (literary editor, 1925–27). Ferris was the author of a two-volume study, *The African Abroad* (1913).

FETCHIT, STEPIN (1902–), actor, comedian; born as Lincoln Theodore Monroe Andrew Perry. Fetchit was the first black actor to receive feature billing. He appeared in many movies during the 1920s and the 1930s, including *Stand Up and Cheer* (1934), always portraying a shuffling, laconic character who rolled his eyes in fright at the complexities of the world. Despite the stereotype he portrayed of an unsophisticated, subservient black man, he broke down many segregation barriers in show business. See also MOTION PICTURES.

FICKLING, AUSTIN L. (1914–), lawyer, judge; born in Washington, D.C. Fickling received his LL.B. degree from the Robert H. Terrell Law School (Washington, D.C.) in 1942, and was admitted to the District of Columbia bar in 1943. He practiced law from 1942 to 1954. Fickling served as assistant U.S. attorney, as associate judge of the U.S. Municipal District Court for the District of Columbia, and as counsel for the National Association for the Advancement of Colored People (NAACP). He was a member of the Republican State Central Committee and a judge of the Court of General Sessions, Washington, D.C.

FICTION *See* LITERATURE: THE NOVEL.

FIELDS, BARTON A. (1903–   ), public official; born in Philadelphia, Pa. Fields graduated from Pennsylvania State University. In 1957 he began a career in government that included service with the Pennsylvania state government in the department of education, the department of property and supplies, the Public Utility Commission, and the department of state. Meanwhile, he became state conference education chairman for the Pennsylvania National Association for the Advancement of Colored People (NAACP).

FIERCE, HUGHLYN F. banker, civic leader; born in New York, N.Y. Fierce received a B.A. degree from Morgan State University (Baltimore, Md.) and a M.A. degree from New York University Graduate School of Business Administration in 1967. In 1972 he became a vice president of Chase Manhattan Bank of New York, resigning in 1975 to become president of the Freedom National Bank in New York City.

FILMS *See* MOTION PICTURES.

FINLEY, HAROLD E. *See* SCIENTISTS: BIOLOGICAL, PHYSICAL.

FISHER, MILES MARK (1889–1971), clergyman, historian, educator; Fisher received a B.A. degree from Morehouse College (Atlanta, Ga.), a B.D. degree from the Northern Baptist Theological Seminary, and his Ph.D. degree from the University of Chicago. He was professor of history at Shaw University and at Virginia Union University, and author of *Negro Slave Songs in the United States* (1954). *See also* MUSIC: SPIRITUALS.

FISHER, RUDOLPH (1897–1934), physician, author; born in Washington, D.C. Fisher received a B.A. degree and a M.A. degree from Brown University (Providence, R.I.) and his M.D. degree with honors from Howard University Medical College (Washington, D.C.), before moving to New York City in 1927 to further his medical studies at Columbia University, and later to practice medicine. His first story, "The City of Refuge," was published in *Atlantic Monthly*

in 1923. Fisher was associated with the Harlem Renaissance, but was less ideological than most of the other writers involved with this movement. He wrote two novels, *The Walls of Jericho* (1928) and *The Conjure-Man Dies* (1932), the latter the first full-length detective novel by a black writer.

FISHER, SETHARD (1929–   ), sociologist, educator. A native of Arkansas, Fisher received a B.A. degree (1952), a M.A. degree (1958), and his Ph.D. degree (1964) from the University of California at Berkeley. After a number of community and social service positions, he served as an assistant professor of sociology at Los Angeles State College (Los Angeles, Calif.) from 1961 to 1964 and as an associate professor of sociology at the University of Alberta (Edmonton, Alberta, Canada) from 1967 to 1969. In 1971 Fisher became professor of sociology at the University of California at Santa Barbara. In addition to many articles and scholarly research papers, Fisher wrote a book entitled *Power and the Black Community* (1970). *See also* PREFACE: ACKNOWLEDGMENTS.

FISHER, WALTER *See* HISTORIANS.

FISK FREE SCHOOL *See* FISK UNIVERSITY.

FISK JUBILEE SINGERS Five years after its founding in 1860, Fisk University (Nashville, Tenn.) seemed on the verge of collapse. Not even local debts for food and fuel could be paid. The decaying buildings used for classes were virtually beyond repair, and new buildings were badly needed. It was at this point that a dramatic story in the history of education began.

From the time the school had opened, Fisk students and teachers had demonstrated considerable interest in music; during leisure hours students sang together the songs they had learned as slaves. George L. White, treasurer of the school, whose love for music was exceeded only by his desire to raise money for the foundering institution, organized a group of talented student singers. The group gave local concerts with considerable success, and White was convinced that they could earn money for the school. Thus, in October 1871, a small band of recently emancipated slaves, who called themselves the Fisk Jubilee Singers, and their untrained musical director set out for the Midwest on a trial fund-raising tour.

At first the concerts, composed of "white man's music," attracted little attention, but when slave songs were added audiences became enthusiastic. The rise in popularity of spirituals can be traced largely to the pioneer efforts of the Fisk Jubilee Singers. People began to understand the quality of the contributions blacks had already made and could eventually make to American culture.

After a few weeks in the Midwest, the Jubilee Singers went East where they sang to wildly excited crowds. By May 1872, when they returned to the Fisk campus, they had earned $20,000 and had made Fisk the best-known black college in the United States.

Only a week elapsed before the Jubilee Singers went on another tour. In June 1872 they interrupted their travels long enough to participate in the Second World's Peace Jubilee in Boston, Mass., where they electrified a crowd of 40,000. Their fame having spread across the ocean, the Jubilee Singers went to Europe in May 1873, the first of two European tours in the next five years. They were praised by royalty, music critics, and the public; non-English speaking audiences applauded, wept, or smiled, enjoying the concerts without understanding the words.

When the Jubilee Singers finally disbanded in 1878, they had raised $150,000 for their struggling university. They had paid for a new campus and the construction of aptly named Jubilee Hall. They had made Fisk University famous, familiar to hundreds of thousands of Europeans and millions of Americans. The first to popularize and capitalize on slave songs, the Jubilee Singers began a tradition of fund-raising that black colleges were to use for decades to come.

Most important, however, was the by-product of their original fund-raising purpose: the preservation of the spirituals, a purely American body of music. The Fisk Jubilee Singers sang these songs of aspiration, longing, and sorrow into the hearts and consciousnesses of the people of two continents. See also FISK UNIVERSITY; MUSIC: HISTORY AND DEVELOPMENT; MUSIC: SPIRITUALS/PERFORMANCE, COLLECTIONS.

REFERENCES: Marsh, J. B. T., *The Story of the Jubilee Singers with Their Songs*, 3d ed., London, 1876; Pike, Gustavus D., *The Singing Campaign for Ten Thousand Pounds*, rev. ed., New York, 1875; Pike, Gustavus D., *The Jubilee Singers, and their Campaign for Twenty Thousand Dollars*, New York, 1873; Richardson, Joe M., *A History of Fisk University*, Tuscaloosa, 1871; and Spence, Mary E., "The Jubilee of Jubilees at Fisk University," *Southern Workman*, vol. 51, p. 73, February 1922.

FISK UNIVERSITY Fisk University, at Nashville, Tenn., was founded in 1866. A private, coeducational, independent school, Fisk offers the bachelor's and the master's degrees, and provides a liberal arts curriculum. Its 1975 enrollment was about 1,500.

Known at the time it opened its doors as Fisk Free School, Fisk began with commendable and lofty—some thought impractical—aims. Its founders, E. M. Cravath and E. P. Smith of the American Missionary Association (AMA) and John Ogden of the Freedmen's Bureau, proposed to offer a free school (from primary to normal) based upon a "broad Christian foundation." The founders intended to satisfy the desperate need for qualified black teachers, and hoped that Fisk would ultimately become a first-class college that would give black youth the same educational opportunities enjoyed by whites. When Fisk opened, students, old and young alike, enrolled by the hundreds. The first students entered at a primary level, but John Ogden, who had resigned from the bureau to become Fisk's first principal, continued to advocate higher rather than elementary education.

In keeping with Ogden's desire for a black college in Nashville, Fisk School was incorporated in 1867 as Fisk University, with the stated purpose of training youth of all races. College work could not be immediately offered, but the first normal class was accepted in November 1867. Two years later Dr. Barnas Sears, general agent for the Peabody Fund, declared that Fisk was the best normal school he had seen in the South. In 1871 four students were accepted in the college department. The previous year Adam K. Spence had given up a University of Michigan professorship to come to Fisk to take charge of the college. Nevertheless, the college and college preparatory classes remained the smallest in the school for several years. Since public schools for black children in Tennessee were quite poor, Fisk offered primary, secondary, and normal as well as college training.

The period 1870–1915 was critical for Fisk. A constant struggle was waged against financial collapse even though the Fisk Jubilee Singers were earning large sums. White hostility, black poverty, and the craze for vocational education threatened Fisk's aim of becoming a major liberal arts college. Nevertheless, the university built a new campus, increased its faculty, and enlarged the college department.

By 1915 the university had long since passed the experimental stage. Its students and graduates had taught thousands of black children and were engaged in every imaginable profession. The school had received praise from many quarters, but the compliments of Booker T. Washington, sometimes thought to be an opponent of liberal education, may have been the most gratifying of all. Fisk, he said, had been, to an extent, a model for all other schools in the South.

In 1915 Fisk embarked upon a new era. The curriculum was expanded, standards raised, faculty salaries increased, and the physical plant improved. Unfortunately, in the process of making numerous contributions to Fisk, Fayette Avery McKenzie, the new president and a white, alienated those whom he was supposed to be serving—students and alumni. The "new" black students at Fisk resented antiquated regulations, the school's "Jim Crow" practices, McKenzie's seemingly too-close alliance with the white community, and the white faculty, who appeared to have little faith in black students. In 1925 students, with the active support of some alumni, including W. E. B. Du Bois, forced out their president through strikes and agitation.

McKenzie was replaced by Thomas Elsa Jones, who led Fisk into a period of unprecedented growth. By the time Jones retired in 1946, Fisk was recognized as a center of scholarship and culture. Jones had added distinguished black scholars to his faculty, including Charles S. Johnson and James Weldon Johnson. By 1940 the school was doing research on a scale larger than any other black college. Yet despite its impressive growth, Fisk still had problems: a limited physical plant and an unending need for money. Maintenance of the school's status in the educational world was to challenge its next leader and Fisk's first black president, Charles S. Johnson. Under Johnson's leadership, Fisk became and has remained a truly great institution of higher learning. See also ARCHIVES; FISK JUBLIEE SINGERS; JOHNSON, CHARLES SPURGEON; JOHNSON, JAMES WELDON.

FITZBUTLER, HENRY (1842–1901), physician; born in Ontario, Canada. Fitzbutler worked his way through medical school as a farm hand, surveyor, and teacher. He became the first black student accepted at Detroit Medical College in 1869 and received his M.D. degree from the University of Michigan Medical School in 1872. Fitzbutler then set up a medical practice in Louisville, Ky., becoming the first black physician to practice in that state. He was founder

Ella Fitzgerald
(National Educational Television.)

(1888) and dean of the Louisville National Medical College.

FITZGERALD, ELLA (1918–   ), singer; born in Newport News, Va. Fitzgerald began her career at an amateur contest at the Apollo Theater in New York City at the age of 15. She was hired by bandleader Chick Webb to sing with his band, and in 1938 with her recording of "A-Tisket, A-Tasket," her reputation began to grow. A leading jazz interpreter of the popular song, her clear voice and rhythmic control, especially in her famous scat singing, led to fame in the United States and abroad. "The First Lady of Song" recorded many songs, among them: "Love You Madly," "Hard-Hearted Hannah," "Into Each Life Some Rain Must Fall," and "How High the Moon."

FLANIGAN, JAMES C. (1915–   ) lawyer, judge. Flanigan received a B.A. degree from the University of Denver (Denver, Colo.) and his LL.B. degree from the Westminister College of Law (Denver, Colo.). He was admitted to the Colorado bar in 1947, and in 1972 he became a District Court judge in Denver.

FLEMING, G. JAMES (1904–   ), political scientist, educator; born in the Virgin Islands. Fleming graduated from the academy at Hampton Institute (Hampton, Va.), and received a B.A. degree from the University of Wisconsin in journalism (1931), and a M.A. degree (1944) and his Ph.D. degree (1948) in political science from the University of Pennsylvania. He was elected to several scholastic and honor societies, including Phi Beta Kappa, Sigma Delta Chi (journalism), Delta Sigma Rho (speech), Pi Gamma Mu (social science), Gamma Theta Epsilon (geography), and Phi Kappa Phi (scholarship). Fleming was a professor of political science at Morgan State University (Baltimore, Md.) and founder-director of Morgan's Institute for Political Education from 1959 to 1966. He served as a visiting professor at the University of Pennsylvania from 1966 to 1968 and at Lincoln University (Lincoln University, Pa.) from 1968 to 1970. He was the editor of *Who's Who in Colored America* and the supervising editor of *Who's Who in the United Nations*. His writings include *An All-Negro Ticket in Baltimore* (1960), "The Negro Church and Politics" (1968), and *Why Baltimore Failed to Elect a Black Mayor in 1971* (1972). He appeared frequently on television and radio, including the "Voice of America" programs.

Fleming also served on the board of trustees of both the College of the Virgin Islands and Morgan State University. *See also* BIBLIOGRAPHIES/BIO-GRAPHIES/GUIDES; PREFACE: LIST OF CONTRIBU-TORS.

FLETCHER, ARTHUR ALLEN (1924–   ), government official, administrator; born in Phoenix, Ariz. Fletcher received a B.A. degree from Washburn University of Topeka (Topeka, Kans.) in 1950. He was assistant public relations director of the highway commission in Kansas (1954–57), and became involved in politics as a paid staff member of the Nixon-Lodge campaign. Fletcher served as assistant secretary of labor during the Nixon administration, the highest ranking black man in that administration. He was the author of *The Silent Sellout* (1974).

FLIPPER, HENRY OSSIAN (1856–1940), Army officer, engineer; born in Thomasville, Ga. The first black to graduate from the U.S. Military Academy at West Point (cavalry, 1877), Flipper was also educated at Atlanta University. As a second lieutenant, he was court-martialed on a charge of mishandling company funds, acquitted, but later dismissed from the service for "conduct unbecoming an officer and a gentleman," a decision he was never able to have reversed. As a civilian, Flipper practiced civil and mining engineering for 37 years in Mexico. His cashiering was redeemed in 1976 when the Army gave him an honorable discharge.

FLIPPER, JOSEPH SIMEON (1859–1944), African Methodist Episcopal bishop, educator; born in Atlanta, Ga. Flipper was one of the first students to enroll at Atlanta University. He served as bishop of the Florida and South Carolina diocese of the African Methodist Episcopal (AME) Church, and was on the theology faculty of Morris Brown College (Atlanta, Ga.), later becoming its president.

FLOOD, CURT *See* ATHLETES: BASEBALL.

FLORIDA AGRICULTURAL AND MECHANICAL (A & M) COLLEGE *See* FLORIDA AGRICULTURAL AND MECHANICAL (A & M) UNIVERSITY.

FLORIDA AGRICULTURAL AND MECHANICAL (A & M) UNIVERSITY Florida Agricultural and Mechanical (A & M) University, at Tallahassee, Fla., was founded in 1887 as the Colored Normal School. A coeducational, state-supported, land-grant college, Florida A & M offers the bachelor's

and the master's degrees and provides liberal arts, teacher education, professional, and terminal occupational curricula. Its 1975 enrollment was about 5,200.

During the early years of the school's existence, the state provided only the minimum amount of appropriations required by the federal government in order for it to qualify for matching appropriations. In 1891 the original Copeland Street location within the Tallahassee city limits was abandoned for a new site—then outside the city limits—at which the university has remained.

In 1905 the management of the school was transferred from the state board of education (public schools) to the state board of control (higher education), and in 1909 its name was changed to Florida Agricultural and Mechanical College. In 1953 the college became, through legislative enactment, a university.

FLORIDA BAPTIST ACADEMY *See* FLORIDA MEMORIAL COLLEGE.

FLORIDA BAPTIST INSTITUTE *See* FLORIDA MEMORIAL COLLEGE.

FLORIDA MEMORIAL COLLEGE Florida Memorial College, at Miami, Fla., was founded in 1892 by the Baptists and is still a church-related organization. A private, coeducational school, it offers the bachelor's degree and provides liberal arts and teacher education curricula. Its 1973 enrollment was 821. Major current support comes from various Baptist conventions.

Florida Memorial College originated in Live Oak where, in 1879, the American Baptist Home Mission Society established the Florida Baptist Institute for Negroes. In 1892 the Florida Normal and Industrial Institute was founded in Jacksonville and became known as Florida Baptist Academy. In 1917 the institute incorporated the Baptist Academy, and in 1918 the college moved to St. Augustine, where it secured important amendments to its charter, including full college powers and a change of its name from Florida Baptist Academy to Florida Normal and Industrial Institute.

The college graduated its first four-year class in 1945. In 1950 its name was changed to Florida Normal and Industrial Memorial College, and in 1963 its charter was again amended to change its name to Florida Memorial College and to open the institution to students of all races. The college moved to Miami in 1968.

Henry Ossian Flipper *(Gift Collection, National Archives.)*

FLORIDA NORMAL AND INDUSTRIAL INSTITUTE See FLORIDA MEMORIAL COLLEGE.

FLORIDA NORMAL AND INDUSTRIAL MEMORIAL COLLEGE See FLORIDA MEMORIAL COLLEGE.

FOOTBALL See ATHLETES.

FORBES, JAMES ALEXANDER, JR. See PREFACE: ACKNOWLEDGMENTS.

FORD, GERALDINE BLEDSOE lawyer, judge; born in Detroit, Mich. Ford attended Howard University (Washington, D.C.) and received a B.A. degree from the University of Michigan in 1948. After receiving a law degree from Wayne State University Law School (Detroit, Mich.) in 1951, she engaged in private practice for the next ten years. Subsequently, Ford served as assistant U.S. attorney for the Eastern District of Michigan. In 1972 she became judge of the Recorders Court in Detroit.

FORD, HAROLD E. (1945–   ), elected official, Congressman; born in Memphis, Tenn. He received B.S. and M.S. degrees from Tennessee State University, Nashville, Tenn. A professional mortician, he served in the Tennessee Legislature as a representative from 1971 to 1974. He then entered national politics, being elected as a Democrat to the House in 1974.

FORD, JERRY W. (1921–   ), clergyman; born in Pine Bluff, Ark. Ford received B.A. and B.D. degrees from Westminister College (Salt Lake City, Utah), and did graduate work at the University of Utah. Ford was pastor of the Bethel African Methodist Episcopal (AME) Church in Los Angeles, Calif., and was a member of the general board of the AME Church, serving on several commissions of that board. He was a candidate for bishop in 1976.

FORD, NICK AARON (1904–   ), author, educator; born in Ridgeway, S.C. He received the B.A. degree (1926) from Benedict College (Columbia, S.C.) and the M.A. (1934) and Ph.D. (1945) degrees from the University of Iowa, Iowa City, Ia. After service at Langston University, Ford became chairman of the department of English at Morgan State College in 1945, a position he held until retirement. He is the author of several books, including *The Contemporary Negro Novel: A Study in Race Relations* (1936), and *Black Studies: Threat-or-Challenge* (1973).

FOREMAN, GEORGE See ATHLETES: BOXING.

FORMAN, JAMES (1929–   ), civil rights leader; born in Chicago, Ill. Forman graduated from Roosevelt University (Chicago, Ill.) with a degree in public administration and then became a teacher in Chicago. He was executive secretary of the Student Nonviolent Coordinating Committee (SNCC) for several years in the early 1960s. In 1969, as a representative of the National Black Economic Development Conference, he authored "The Black Manifesto," a document that demanded $500 million from white churches and synagogues as reparations for the injustices suffered by blacks under slavery and capitalism. The manifesto, read by Forman in a surprise appearance at New York City's Riverside Church during Communion services, represented the outcome of a meeting of black leaders held a year before to discuss the economics of Black Power. Other works by Forman include: *Sammy Younge, Jr.: The First Black College Student to Die in the Black Liberation Movement* (1968) and *The Making of Black Revolutionaries: A Personal Account* (1972).

FORTEN, JAMES (1766–1842), abolitionist, business executive; born in Philadelphia, Pa. Forten attended a Quaker school until the age of nine when lack of funds forced him to seek employment. He spent several years at sea, enlisting in 1781 on the *Royal Louis*. Returning to Philadelphia in 1786, Forten became apprenticed to Robert Bridges, a white sailmaker, who soon made him foreman of his shop. Forten opened his own sailmaking shop in 1798, employing more than 40 workers, both black and white; his personal fortune soon grew to an estimated $100,000. Dedicated to the cause of racial equality, Forten joined Rev. Richard Allen in 1800 in circulating a petition calling on the U.S. Congress to emancipate the slaves. During the War of 1812, he organized (1814), with the assistance of Revs. Richard Allen and Absolom Jones, a black volunteer force of 2,500 men for the defense of Philadelphia. His efforts throughout the 1820s helped to gain important black support for the radical abolitionist movement, and he was closely associated with such men as William Lloyd Garrison and Theodore Weld. Extremely influential with Garrison, Forten is credited with convincing the future publisher of the *Liberator* to call for emancipation and equality rather than colonization. In 1833 Forten helped to organize the American Antislavery

Society and was active in the society until 1841, when he became seriously ill. A supporter of the women's suffrage and temperance movements, he founded, in 1839, the American Moral Reform Society, which was established for the "promotion of Education, Temperance, Economy, and Universal Liberty." The society also published monthly the *National Reformer*. Several of Forten's children were active in the reform movement, especially his daughter Margaretta, who served as secretary to the Philadelphia Female Antislavery Society, and another daughter Harriet, who married the abolitionist Robert Puvis and was active in the antislavery movement. Best known is Forten's granddaughter, Charlotte Forten Grimké, whose autobiography entitled *A Free Negro in the Slave Era* will always have a permanent place in the history of American literature. *See also* SLAVERY: THE ABOLITIONISTS.

FORTUNE, HILDA O. (ca. 1912–   ), educator; born in Youngstown, Ohio. Fortune received a B.A. degree from Morgan State University (Baltimore, Md.), and a M.A. degree (1958) and her Ed.D. degree (1963) from New York University. She was an associate professor (1970–72) and professor (1972) of social sciences at York College (New York, N.Y.), and prior to that she served on the staff of Brooklyn College of the City University of New York from 1963 to 1968, in the employment department of the Young Men's Christian Association (YMCA) from 1947 to 1952, and with the community services department of New York Urban League from 1952 to 1963. Fortune was also a member of the faculty of New York University on a part-time basis (1963–69). She wrote *Shared Leadership, New Concepts* (1965) and several articles for professional journals. *See also* PREFACE: LIST OF CONTRIBUTORS.

FORTUNE, TIMOTHY THOMAS (1856–1928), journalist; born in Marianna, Fla. Born a slave and freed by proclamation in 1865, Fortune trained as a printer in his youth. He left the profession to work for the post office, but returned to printing, sometimes composing newspaper articles while he created and simultaneously dictated articles to someone else to typeset. He attended Howard University (Washington, D.C.) and was a printer in New York in 1879, where he founded the newspaper New York *Age,* which he sold in 1907. Fortune (and others) took over the failing *Rumor* in 1880, and

brought financial success to that newspaper before he left to publish the New York *Freeman* in 1884. (It later became the New York *Age.*) His varied career involved work on many newspapers, including stints as reporter and editor for the Boston *Transcript* and the New York Sun, two general-circulation newspapers. Fortune was also a close friend and advisor of Booker T. Washington and helped Washington write his autobiography. In 1890 Fortune founded the National Afro-American League, a forerunner of the National Association for the Advancement of Colored People (NAACP); he also helped organize the National Afro-American Press Association. Fortune was the author of pamphlets and several books, including *Black and White: Land, Labor, and Politics in the United States* (1884), *The Negro in Politics* (1886), and *Dreams of Life, Miscellaneous Poems* (1905). Although frequently called "the dean of Negro newspapermen" and treated as the spokesman of the black press, he eventually died in obscurity after a long retirement marked by mental illness. For a biography of Fortune, see Thornbrough, Emma Lou, *T. Thomas Fortune: Militant Journalist* (1972). *See also* NEWSPAPERS: HISTORY AND DEVELOPMENT.

FORT VALLEY HIGH AND INDUSTRIAL SCHOOL See FORT VALLEY STATE COLLEGE.

FORT VALLEY NORMAL AND INDUSTRIAL SCHOOL See FORT VALLEY STATE COLLEGE.

FORT VALLEY STATE COLLEGE Fort Valley State College, at Fort Valley, Ga., was founded in 1895 by leading citizens of an interracial group in Fort Valley. State-supported, the coeducational, land-grant college offers the bachelor's and the master's degrees, and provides liberal arts and teacher education curricula. Its 1975 enrollment was about 1,800.

The college began as Fort Valley High and Industrial School, with 240 students. After 37 years as Fort Valley High and Industrial School (1895–1932), its name was changed to Fort Valley Normal and Industrial School (1932–39), and, in 1939, Fort Valley State College, when it became a unit of the university system of Georgia. In 1947 the Georgia board of regents recognized and designated it as a land-grant college. Six presidents have served the college: John W. Davison, Henry A. Hunt, Horace Mann Bond, Cornelius V. Troupe, Waldo W. E. Blanchet, and Cleveland W. Pettigrew.

T. Thomas Fortune (Moorland-Spingarn Research Center.)

FOSTER, ANDREW *See* ATHLETES: BASEBALL.

FOSTER, LAURENCE (1903– ?) anthropologist, educator. Foster received B.A. (1926) and S.T.B. (1929) degrees from Lincoln University (Lincoln University, Pa.) and his Ph.D. degree (1936) from the University of Pennsylvania. He taught at Stowe Teachers College (St. Louis, Mo.) and Cheyney State College before coming to Lincoln University (Pa.) where he spent most of his professional career as a professsor and chairman of the department of social sciences. Foster served as chairman of the governor's Temporary Commission for the Study of Pennsylvania's Negroes. He wrote *The Functions of a Graduate School in a Democratic Society,* and edited a college textbook on government entitled *An Introduction to American Government* (1954).

FOSTER, LUTHER HILTON, JR. (1913–   ), educator, administrator; born in Lawrenceville, Va. Foster received a B.A. degree from Virginia State College in 1932, a B.S. degree from Hampton Institute (Hampton, Va.) in 1934, a M.B.A. from Harvard University in 1936, and his Ph.D. degree from the University of Chicago in 1951. He was also awarded an honorary LL.D. degree from the University of Michigan in 1967. Foster was on the staff of Howard University (1936–40), then served as business manager (1941–53) and president (after 1953) of Tuskegee Institute (Tuskegee Institute, Ala.). He worked for many education and education-related groups, including the Race Relations Information Center, of which he was chairman of the board (1969–70).

FOWLER, STEPHEN HAMILTON (1881– ?), educator, administrator, editor; born in Fort Worth, Tex. Educated at Prairie View Agricultural and Technical (A & T) State University (Prairie View, Tex.) and at the University of Chicago, Fowler served as executive secretary of the Young Men's Christian Association (YMCA) in the 1920s. Leaving Prairie View in 1901, he immediately began a teaching career that took him to several Texas schools as teacher and as principal. In 1916 Fowler attended the University of Chicago, and three years later he began his position as executive secretary of the YMCA. At about that time, Fowler was made a member of the Texas Commission on Interracial Cooperation, and in 1922 he became editor of the *Western Star.*

FOXX, REDD (1922–   ), entertainer; born John Elroy Sanford in St. Louis, Mo. Foxx began a show business career with his washtub band on the street corners of Chicago, Ill. After World War II, and several lean years of odd jobs, he began performing in nightclubs in New York City and Baltimore, Md., and then in black vaudeville with a partner. Moving to California, he broke with his partner and made the first of a long series of party albums that were very successful. It was not until the 1960s that he began his television career. Guest appearances on many network shows led to top nightclub billing, and finally, to his own television series, "Sanford and Son." *See also* RADIO AND TELEVISION.

FRANCES, NORMAN C. educator; born in Lafayette, La. Frances received a B.A. degree from Xavier University of Louisiana in 1952, and his LL.B. degree from Loyola University (New Orleans, La.) in 1955. He served in many capacities at Xavier University of Louisiana and became its president in 1968. Frances was a member of the President's Commission on School Finance, and a member of the board of directors of the Association of American Colleges and of the board of trustees of the College Entrance Examination Board.

FRANCIS, G. HAMILTON (1885–1963), physician; born in St. Christopher, British West Indies. Francis received his M.D. degree from Meharry Medical College (Nashville, Tenn.) and practiced medicine in Norfolk, Va., for 52 years. He was a member of the National Medical Association and received the association's Distinguished Service Medal in 1953.

FRANCIS, SAMUEL *See* TURNER, NAT.

FRANCIS, YVETTE FAE physician; born in Jamaica, British West Indies. Francis attended Hunter College of the City University of New York, received a M.A. degree from Columbia University, and earned her M.D. degree from Yale University Medical School in 1950. She was a pioneer both in the study of sickle-cell anemia and in the field of etiology. Francis served as the director of the Sickle-Cell Anemia Clinic, Jamaica Hospital, New York, N.Y. *See* RACE: RACE AND BIOLOGY.

FRANKIE AND JOHNNIE A folk legend and ballad about two lovers whose relationship ended in the man being shot to death by the woman because "he done her wrong." Thomas Hart Benton painted a mural in Missouri's State Capitol depicting the shooting scene. At that time (the 1930s), the painting was considered highly con-

troversial. It is likely that the characters in the legend were actually Frankie Baker and Johnny Allen Britt of St. Louis, Mo., where the shooting took place on the night of Oct. 13, 1899, according to Jonathan Benbow in "A Resounding Legacy," St. Louis *American*, bicentennial edition, Sept. 22, 1964, page 5.

> Frankie went to the coffin—
> She looked down in Johnnie's face;
> She said "Oh, Lawd, have mercy on me,
> I wish I could take his place.
> I killed my man 'cause he done me wrong.

Frankie Baker was acquitted of homicide and left for Oregon.

FRANKLIN, ARETHA (1942–   ), singer; born in Memphis, Tenn. Known as the "Queen of Soul," Franklin made her first recording in 1954. Her singing career began with singing the gospels she had learned during her early years from her father, an evangelist minister. Franklin turned to blues in the 1960s, while still retaining some of the qualities of gospel, and in 1967 she recorded two albums that sold more than one million copies each. Many of her later recordings achieved similar spectacular sales figures. Franklin's concert performances and records won her world renown and adulation.

FRANKLIN, CARL MATTHEW (1921–   ), educator, economist, born in New Orleans, La. He received the B.A. degree at Howard University, the M.B.A. at New York University and the Ph.D. degree (1964) at Indiana University. He has served as a professor of economics at Morgan State University in Baltimore since 1967. He has also served on the faculty at Atlanta University, at Elizabeth City State University (North Carolina), and at Johns Hopkins University.

FRANKLIN, ELEANOR I. endocrinologist, educator; born in Dublin, Ga. Franklin was valedictorian of her class at Carver High School (Monroe, Ga.) and received a B.S. degree from Spelman College (Atlanta, Ga.) in 1944, and a M.S. degree (1951) and her Ph.D. degree (1957) from the University of Wisconsin. She taught at Tuskegee Institute (Tuskegee Institute, Ala.) and joined the faculty of Howard University (Washington, D.C.) in 1963. Franklin became the first woman medical administrator at Howard University Medical College in 1970.

FRANKLIN, JIMMIE L. (1939–   ), historian, educator; born in Moscow, Miss. Franklin received a B.A. degree from Jackson State College (Jackson, Miss.) in 1961, and a M.A. degree (1964) and his Ph.D. degree (1970) from the University of Oklahoma. He taught at the University of Wisconsin (1966–69) and at the University of Washington (1969–70). Franklin was a visiting professor at Hyderabad, India (1970) and an associate professor of history at Eastern Illinois University (1970–   ). He was the author of *Born Sober: A History of Prohibition in Oklahoma, 1907–1959* (1971).

FRANKLIN, JOHN HOPE (1915–   ), historian, educator, author; born in Rentiesville, Okla. Franklin received a B.A. degree from Fisk University (Nashville, Tenn.) in 1935, and a M.A. degree (1936) and his Ph.D. degree (1941) from Harvard University. In addition, he was awarded more than 30 honorary degrees. From 1936 to 1964, Franklin taught at several universities, including Fisk, Saint Augustine's, North Carolina State, Howard, Cambridge (England), and Brooklyn College of the City University of New York, where he was chairman of the history department from 1956 to 1964. Franklin became the chairman of the department of history at the University of Chicago in 1964. He received a Rosenwald Fellowship in 1937 and a Guggenheim Fellowship in 1950. His many books include *The Free Negro in North Carolina*

Far left: "Frankie and Johnnie" mural by Thomas Hart Benton. *(Missouri State Council on the Arts.)*

John Hope Franklin *(University of Chicago.)*

(1943), *The Militant South 1800–1860* (1956), and *Color and Race* (1968). He also coauthored the junior high school textbook, *Land of the Free* (1966). Also outstanding is his standard college textbook and reference, *From Slavery to Freedom*, which has achieved several editions since its publication in 1948. Franklin received extraordinary recognition and honor in the 1970s when he was elected as the first Afro-American president of two very prestigious historical organizations: the Southern Historical Association and the American Historical Association. *See also* HISTORIANS.

FRANKLIN, ROBERT VERNON, JR. (1926–   ), lawyer, judge; born in Toledo, Ohio. Franklin received a B.A. degree from Morehouse College (Atlanta, Ga.) in 1947 and his J.D. degree from the University of Toledo College of Law in 1950. Franklin was appointed judge of the Toledo Municipal Court and named Toledo's outstanding young man in 1960. In 1968 he was elected judge of the Common Pleas Court of Toledo. Franklin received Toledo's outstanding citizen's award in 1970.

FRASER, THOMAS PETIGRU (1902–   ), educator; born in Georgetown, S.C. Fraser received a B.S. degree from Claflin College (Orangeburg, S.C.) in 1926, and a M.A. degree (1930) and his Ed.D. degree (1948) from Columbia University. After nearly a quarter century of teaching at Morgan State College, he became the interim president for two years in the 1970s.

FRATERNAL SOCIETIES

FRATERNAL SOCIETIES Fraternal and mutual benefit societies have existed among Afro-Americans from the earliest establishment of free but segregated communities in the mid-seventeenth century. These local organizations provided a forum of ideas that helped in the formulation of programs designed to alleviate undesirable conditions. Through regular meetings of these local societies, members pooled their funds to aid those who suffered financial or physical reverses. A retrospective look at these small groups reveals that they contributed significantly to the development of leadership, and served as an impetus to social and intellectual development among members.

The first formal fraternal organization among

Grand Lodge of Mason No. 1. Masons are the oldest continuous fraternal group, having been founded in 1775 by Prince Hall. This rare photograph was taken in 1897 in Greenville, Mississippi, in the heart of the old slave/cotton belt. It is very likely that some members of this group were former slaves. It is also likely that the only man wearing a hat was E. W. Lampton, later a financial secretary and bishop of the African Methodist Episcopal Church (AME). *(Library of Congress).*

Afro-Americans began on March 6, 1775, when Prince Hall and 14 others were inducted into a British Army Masonic Lodge near Boston, Mass. Hall, who had migrated from Barbados ten years earlier, soon became a minister of the gospel and was deeply concerned with the plight of black people in the colonies. The new Masons enjoyed the fellowship of already established white groups, but Hall believed that a separate lodge would provide the specific kind of camaraderie needed by Afro-American members. He sought permission from the Massachusetts Grand Lodge to establish an African lodge, but his request was denied. He then applied directly to the British Grand Lodge, from which a warrant was issued for African Lodge No. 459 on September 29, 1784, naming Hall as the Worshipful Master. Through a series of circumstances the papers were not received, however, until 1787. On June 24, 1791, the African Grand Lodge was established with Prince Hall as Grand Master. Some five years later, a license was issued for a lodge in Philadelphia, Pa., which was composed initially of 13 Afro-Americans who had been initiated in England and Ireland. In 1808 delegates from Boston, Mass., Providence, R.I., and Philadelphia, Pa., decided to call their organization Prince Hall Masons. By 1815 three grand lodges were in existence. These were often visited by white Masons who cooperated in a number of ways. A "protocol" was issued by the Prince Hall Masons in 1827 declaring that henceforth they were to be "free and independent of any lodge but that of our own."

The recognition of the need for such organizations as effective forces in teaching Afro-Americans the basic principles of economic and social survival in the new country encouraged the establishment of several mutual benefit organizations throughout the postrevolutionary period. Richard Allen and Absalom Jones organized the Philadelphia Free African Society on April 12, 1787, "without regard to religious tenets," and encouraged its members to live "an orderly and sober life . . . to support one another in sickness, and for the benefit of widows and fatherless children." Similar groups soon appeared in Newport, R.I., Boston, Mass., and New York, N.Y., and a steady exchange of correspondence and visits tended to link the members of these cities. The Boston group asserted that it would take "no one into this Society who shall commit any injustice or outrage against the laws of their country." An important provision common to all of these groups was an insurance feature that provided help after membership of one year. Each member was assessed one shilling per week, from which the "needy of this society . . . would receive the sum of three shillings and nine pence per week of said money; provided the necessity is not brought on by their own imprudence."

Other Fraternal Groups Many such benevolent societies were in existence by 1835, though some were not as secretive as others. Among them were the Friendship Benevolence Society for Social Relief, the Star in the East Association, and the Daughters of Jerusalem. These groups were often organized around such occupational groups as mechanics, coachmen, and caulkers. A major objective was integration of Afro-Americans into the political, social, and economic life of the nation.

The Grand United Order of Tents of the J. R. Gidding's and Jolliffe Union was organized in Boston, Mass., in 1819. The Grand Order of Odd Fellows was organized by Peter Ogden, a ship steward, in 1843. Ogden held a membership card from Liverpool, England, and established the Philomethian Lodge No. 646 in New York City.

The United Brothers of Friendship and Sisters of the Mysterious Ten was organized in 1854 and chartered by the legislature of Kentucky in 1861, becoming the first chartered and regularly constituted Afro-American society south of the Ohio River. The Knights of Pythias of North America, South America, Europe, Asia, Africa, and Australia was organized at Washington, D.C., on February 19, 1864.

Other major lodges in order of their formation were: Grand Order of Galilean Fishermen, organized at Baltimore, Md., in 1865; Grand United Order of J. R. Gidding's and Jolliffe Union, organized at Norfolk, Va., in 1866; Independent Order of St. Luke, organized in 1867; Grand United Order of Brothers and Sisters, Sons and Daughters of Moses, organized in 1868; Knights and Daughters of Tabor, organized at Independence, Mo., in 1871; United Order of True Reformers, organized at Richmond, Va., in 1881; National Order of Mosaic Templars of America, organized in Little Rock, Ark., in 1882 by J. A. Bush and C. W. Keatts; Royal Knights of King David, organized at Durham, N.C., in 1884; Colored Brotherhood and Sisterhood of Honor, organized at Franklin, Ky., in 1886; Ancient Order of Gleaners, organized at Caro, Mich., in 1894, by Grant Slocum; Improved Benevolent and Protective Order of Elks of the World, organized by B. F. Howard at Cincinnati, Ohio, in 1899; Grand United Order Sons and Daughters of Peace, organized at Newport News, Va., in 1900; Supreme Camp of American Woodmen, organized in 1901; Royal Circle of Friends of the World, organized at Helena, Ark., in 1909; Woodmen of Union, organized in 1915; African Blood Brotherhood, organized at Louisville, Ky., in 1923; and Knights of the Invisible Colored Kingdom (an anti-Ku Klux Klan group) organized in Tennessee in 1923.

The All-Race Assembly, held in November 1923, ended in the organization of the African Blood Brotherhood designed as a "fraternity of Negro peoples," headquartered in New York City; it asserted as its major objective the "rights and legitimate aspirations of the Negro workers against exploitation." Specific aims of the organization were: (1) a liberated race in the United States; (2) absolute racial equality; (3) fostering of racial self-respect; (4) organized and uncompromising opposition to the Ku Klux Klan; (5) a united Negro front; (6) industrial development; (7) higher wages for Negro labor; (8) education; and (9) cooperation with other dark races and with "openconscious" white workers.

There were other lodges, but little is known of their dates or places of founding. Some of these were: Progressive Order of Men and Women; Colored Consolidated Brotherhood, organized at Atlanta, Tex.; Independent Benevolent Order, organized at Atlanta, Ga.; Pullman Porter Benevolent Association of America; Ancient United Knights and Daughters of Africa; Mutual Link Protective Association of America; Improved Order of Samaritans; and the Supreme Circle of Benevolence.

Fraternal groups played an important role in the development of pride and self-esteem in Afro-Americans. At their meetings, members not only enjoyed the camaraderie of their brothers, but also received encouragement to study in order to progress within the lodge. Meanwhile, leadership qualities were being developed that would eventually be used in later periods. Because these organizations appealed to and attracted many qualified persons, Frederick Douglass complained in a speech entitled "What Are the Colored People Doing for Themselves?" that:

... in popular demonstrations of odd fellowship, free-masonry and the like, we expend annually from ten to twelve thousand dollars. If we put forth a call for a national convention, for the purpose of considering our wrongs, and asserting our rights, and adopting measures for our mutual elevation and the emancipation of our enslaved fellow countrymen, we shall bring together about fifty, but if we call a grand celebration of odd fellowship, or free-masonry, we shall assemble ... from four to five thousand—the expense of which alone would be from seventeen to twenty thousand dollars, a sum sufficient to maintain four or five efficient presses, devoted to our elevation and improvement.

Fraternal organizations did encourage thrift and cooperative enterprise. Their selective nature provided a higher-than-average intelligence among members and a leadership of high quality. The hierarchy of authority did away, for awhile at least, with unscrupulous officers. The extravagance of regalia and tinsel tended to divert the funds of many members into less effective channels, which later contributed to decreases in membership.

The *Negro Yearbook* of 1921–22 reported approximately 60 fraternal organizations "of a more or less national scope," with an estimated membership of 2.2 million. The Knights of Pythias had about $1 million in endowment funds, and more than $50,000 in the Grand Lodge treasury. The Masons owned about $1 million worth of property; the Odd Fellows, $2 million; and the Pythians, $2.5 million. A $20 million estimate was made for all such organizations. By 1965 an estimated 312,000 Prince Hall Masons were located throughout 38 states, Canada, Liberia, and Nassau.

Among the counterparts to Masonic orders that exist in the United States are: the Royal Arch; Councils of Royal and Select Masters; Commanderies of Knights Templar; and Consistories and Supreme Councils of the Scottish Rite. Any 32d degree Mason may join the Ancient Egyptian Arabic Order of Nobles of the Mystic Shrine. There are about 15,000 Afro-American Shriners in 150 temples throughout the United States. These organizations regularly contribute to medical research. The auxiliary, Daughters of Isis, enrolls about 6,500 women in 117 courts. Female relatives of Masons may join the Eastern Star.

Though members of the Roman Catholic Church are systematically excluded from membership in Masonic orders, those Catholics who desired to belong to a lodge organized their own groups. In 1909 the Knights of Peter Claver, a Catholic fraternal organization, was founded by four Josephite priests (Conrad Rebeshler, John Dorsey, Samuel Kelley, and Joseph Van Baast) along with three Catholic laymen. This organiza-

BLACK GREEK-LETTER ORGANIZATIONS: 1975–76

Name of fraternity or sorority	Date founded	National headquarters	Number of chapters	Publication	Membership
Alpha Kappa Alpha	1908	5211 S. Greenwood Avenue, Chicago, Ill. 60615	active 179 alumni 243	Ivy Leaf	75,000
Alpha Phi Alpha	1906	4432 Martin Luther King Drive, Chicago, Ill. 60653	active 467 alumni 243	The Sphinx	50,000
Delta Sigma Theta	1913	1707 New Hampshire Avenue, N.W., Washington, D.C. 20009	active 515	The Delta Journal	80,000
Kappa Alpha Psi	1911	2320 North Broad Street, Philadelphia, Pa. 19132	active 167 alumni 186	Kappa Alpha Psi Journal	74,000
Omega Psi Phi	1911	2714 Georgia Avenue, N.W., Washington, D.C. 20001	active 433 alumni 232	Oracle	42,000
Phi Beta Sigma	1914	1006 Carroll Street, Brooklyn, N.Y. 11225	active 256	Crescent	41,000
Zeta Phi Beta	1920	1734 New Hampshire Avenue, N.W., Washington, D.C. 20009	active 90 alumni 200	Archon	20,000

tion was incorporated at Mobile, Ala., in 1911. In 1965 it had approximately 17,000 members.

Two Catholic orders, Knights of Columbus and Catholic Order of Foresters, have always admitted people of African descent, though until 1964 many were excluded by blackballs, of which only five were required to exclude a person. The blackball rule was then changed so that one-third of the membership must cast a negative vote in order to withhold membership. Thousands of Afro-Americans now belong to both of these organizations, some having served as grand knights of their councils.

Except for the Catholic orders, white fraternal organizations remain as segregated as ever. Though several Masonic historians have admitted the legitimacy of Prince Hall Masonry, no official recognition has ever been given. A statement issued by the Grand Lodge of New York in 1851 that American Indians and Afro-Americans were "unfit" for initiation into the "Craft" seems to have been adopted by most fraternal groups. The Grand Lodge of Washington, D.C., issued a declaration in 1897 that freemasonry knew no color line, and offered to recognize any African lodges within its jurisdiction. Several grand lodges immediately severed connections with the Grand Lodge of Washington, D.C., forcing it to bow to the pressure. The Grand Lodge of Massachusetts decided to offer partial recognition to Prince Hall Masonry in 1947, but when the grand lodges of Texas and Florida severed relations, and California threatened to do so, the offer was withdrawn. Though four white lodges (by the mid-1970s) accepted blacks into membership (two in Brooklyn, N.Y., Adelphia Lodge No. 348 in New York City, and St. Andrew's Lodge in Boston, Mass.), only Prince Hall Masons have opened their ranks without qualification to persons of all nationalities.

Black College Fraternities and Sororities Black Greek-letter fraternities and sororities came into being primarily during the first quarter of the twentieth century. They were founded largely as social organizations; however, since the 1950s some of them have engaged in important civic and service functions. Many of the outstanding black professional and civic leaders in the nation belong to these Greek-letter organizations. Some of the oldest and largest of these organizations are listed in the table above.

See also HALL, PRINCE; LABOR UNIONS.

REFERENCES: Grimshaw, William H., *Official History of Freemasonry Among the Colored People in North America*, Negro Universities Press, Westport, 1969; Preuss, Arthur (comp.), *A Dictionary of Secret and Other Societies*, Herder, 1924; and Whalen, William J., *Handbook of Secret Organizations*, Bruce Publishing Co., 1966. Other references dealing with the official histories of various organizations are: Gill, Robert L., *The History of Omega Psi Phi Fraternity*; Wesley, Charles H., *The History of Alpha Phi Alpha*, 1939; and Wesley, Charles H., *The History of the Prince Hall Grand Lodge of Free and Accepted Masons of the State of Ohio*, 1961. However, there is no single, comprehensive reference that treats either civic or collegiate organizations adequately.

FRAUNCES TAVERN A well-known dining place and tavern popular in New York City during the latter half of the eighteenth century, the Fraunces Tavern was owned and operated in those days by a migrant from the British West Indies, Samuel Fraunces, who was nicknamed "Black Sam." Both British and American soldiers patronized the tavern, and George Washington came there to draw up terms with the British regarding their evacuation of New York in the 1770s. The building was restored in 1905.

Fraunces Tavern
(Moorland-
Spingarn Research
Center).

FRAZIER, E. FRANKLIN (1894–1962); sociologist, educator; born in Baltimore Md. In 1916 Frazier graduated cum laude from Howard University (Washington, D.C.) with a B.A. degree and accepted a position as mathematics instructor at Tuskegee Institute (Tuskegee Institute, Ala.). He received his M.A. degree from Clark University (Worcester, Mass.) in 1920 and his Ph.D. degree from the University of Chicago in 1931. He was awarded a grant from the New York School of Social Work and another from the American Scandinavian Foundation between 1920 and 1922, the latter enabling him to go to Denmark to study "folk" schools. From 1922 to 1924, Frazier taught sociology and African studies at Morehouse College (Atlanta, Ga.), and then served as director of the Atlanta School of Social Work from 1922 to 1927. He was on the faculty at Fisk University (Nashville, Tenn.) from 1931 until 1934, after which he became head of Howard University's department of sociology, a post he held until named professor emeritus in 1959. Frazier lectured extensively in Europe, and in 1940 he was awarded a Guggenheim Fellowship. He was a prolific writer; he was the author of *The Negro Family in Chicago* (1932); *Traditions and Patterns of Negro Family Life* (1934); *The Negro Family in the United States* (1939, rev. ed., 1949), winner of the John Anisfield Award; *Negro Youth at the Crossways* (1940); *The Negro in the United States* (1949); *Race and Culture in the Modern World*; and *The Negro Church in America* (1962). His most widely read and most controversial book was *Black Bourgeoise* (1957). *See also* SCIENTISTS: SOCIAL.

FRAZIER, HORACE MARION (1927–70), physician; born in Greensboro, N.C. Frazier received a B.S. degree from Howard University (Washington, D.C.) and his M.D. degree from Meharry Medical College (Nashville, Tenn.) in 1953. He interned at George W. Hubbard Hospital, Nashville, Tenn., and was an American Cancer Society clinical trainee postdoctoral fellow at the University of Chicago in 1954. Frazier served as professor of the department of pathology at Meharry Medical College in 1957, became its acting chairman in 1958, and its chairman in 1962.

FRAZIER, JOE *See* ATHLETES: BOXING.

FREE AFRICAN SOCIETY *See* AFRICAN METHODIST EPISCOPAL CHURCH; EPISCOPALIANS.

FREEDMAN'S SAVINGS BANK The Freedman's Savings Bank was created through the efforts of Afro-Americans and abolitionists to find a means of assisting recently emancipated slaves in securing a stronger economic position. During the Civil War, several experiments were made with savings banks for Afro-Americans. Military savings banks had been founded in Norfolk, Va.; Beaufort, S.C.; and New Orleans, La. These banks were eventually absorbed by the Freedman's Savings Bank, incorporated by the U.S. Congress in 1865 (officially named the Freedman's Savings and Trust Company of Washington, D.C.).

Though the bank was controlled by individuals, blacks came to think of the institution as a U.S. government bank, in part because of its close relationship to the Freedmen's Bureau. The bureau advertised the bank and encouraged Afro-Americans to make deposits in it. Believing that the bank was guaranteed by the government, thousands of blacks placed their meager, hard-earned savings in the bank. Soon branch banks were located in every southern state. An observer once said that one could go into the bank at any time and find Afro-Americans "depositing little sums of money, drawing little sums, or remitting to distant parts of the country where they had relatives to support or debts to discharge." Within a few years, the number of depositors had reached 72,000. By 1874 a total of $7 million had been deposited in the bank. The bank appeared to have a promising future with the potential of assisting former slaves to economic freedom.

Unfortunately, poor management, hostility to the bank as a black institution, dishonesty and incompetence in various branches, and careless lending of funds resulted in the bank's failure in

1874. In an effort to revive it, Frederick Douglass was elected president, but even his energy and reputation proved insufficient. Eventually, years later, 62 percent of the deposits at the time of its failure were refunded, though small depositors were seldom located. The Freedman's Savings Bank offered a promising plan for assisting freedmen economically, and its failure caused serious economic injury for many years. *See also* BANKS.

REFERENCES: Three helpful references are: Fleming, Walter L., *The Freedman's Savings Bank: A Chapter in the Economic History of the Negro Race*, University of North Carolina Press, Chapel Hill, 1927; Gilbert, Abby L., "The Comptroller of the Currency and the Freedman's Savings Bank," *Journal of Negro History*, April 1972, pp. 125–43; and Osthaus, Carl R., *Freedmen, Philanthropy, and Fraud: A History of the Freedman's Savings Bank*, University of Illinois Press, Urbana, 1976.

FREEDMEN'S BUREAU *See* AFRO-AMERICAN HISTORY: THE FREEDMEN'S BUREAU, 1865–72.

FREEDOM RIDERS *See* CIVIL RIGHTS MOVEMENT.

FREEMAN, CAROL *See* LITERATURE: POETRY.

FREEMAN, EDWARD ANDERSON (1914–   ), clergyman; born in Atlanta, Ga. Freeman received a B.A. degree from Clark College (Atlanta, Ga.) in 1939, and a B.D. degree (1949), a Th.M. degree (1950), and his Th.D. degree (1953) from the Central Baptist Seminary. He was pastor of the First Baptist Church in Kansas City, Kan., after 1946. Freeman served on the Kansas City, Kans., Planning Commission, and was a member of the board of the American Baptist Theological Seminary, the Greater Kansas City Baptist and Community Hospital, and the Kansas City Minister's Alliance. He was author of *The Epoch of Negro Baptists and the Foreign Mission Board* (1953). *See also* PREFACE: LIST OF CONTRIBUTORS.

FREEMAN, FRANKIE MUSE lawyer, civil rights leader; born in Danville, Va. Freeman was educated at Hampton Institute (Hampton, Va.) from 1933 to 1936 and she received a LL.B. degree from Howard University (Washington, D.C.) in 1947. For a year after her admission to the District of Columbia bar in 1947, she taught business law at Sampson College (New York, N.Y.), and then moved to St. Louis, Mo., where she began the practice of law. In 1956 Freeman became associate general counsel of the St. Louis Housing and Land Clearance Authorities, and in 1964 she was appointed a member of the U.S. Commission on Civil Rights by President Lyndon B. Johnson. Freeman was married to Shelby T. Freeman. *See also* FREEMAN, SHELBY T.

FREEMAN, ROLAND L. *See* PHOTOGRAPHERS.

FREEMAN, SHELBY T. (1915–   ), business executive, educator; born in Dorsey, Miss. After receiving a B.S. degree in mathematics and physics at Lincoln University (Jefferson City, Mo.) in 1938, Freeman taught at Sampson College (New York, N.Y.) from 1947 to 1948. After entering the civil service, he served as chief of the financial management branch of the St. Louis Mobility Equipment Command from 1950 to 1970, when he retired and returned to teaching at State Community College in East St. Louis, Ill. He then became active in East St. Louis civic and fraternal affairs. Freeman was married to the former Frankie Muse.

FREEMAN, WILLIAM ADRIAN (1901–   ), physician, philanthropist. Freeman received his M.D. degree from Case Western Reserve Medical School (Cleveland, Ohio) in 1929 and later became chief of traumatic surgery at Harlem Hospital (New York, N.Y.). During his 40 years in practice, he established nursing scholarships at Hampton Institute and the William A. Freeman Scholarship at Case Western Reserve Medical School in 1957. Among his awards were the Centennial Medallion (from Hampton Institute, Hampton, Va.), the 20th Century Award for an outstanding citizen, and the Bronze Medal for an outstanding alumnus. The William A. Freeman Hall at Hampton Institute was named in his honor in 1969.

FREE NEGROES *See* AFRO-AMERICAN HISTORY: FREE NEGROES, 1600s–1860.

FRIENDSHIP JUNIOR COLLEGE Friendship Junior College, at Rock Hill, S.C., was founded in 1891 by Baptists. The church-related, coeducational college has a two-year program that is principally creditable toward the bachelor's degree. Its 1973 enrollment was about 200.

The college was founded as the Friendship Institute with the purpose of training teachers and preachers. Since no public schools existed for blacks in Rock Hill until 1920, the school served as both an elementary school (until 1938) and as a high school (until 1951). After 1951 the institution operated as a two-year college.

FRONTIERS INTERNATIONAL Founded in 1936, Frontiers International is a civic, social, and fraternal organization of several thousand persons, many of whom are professionals.

FULLER, HOYT (1927–   ), editor, author; born in Atlanta, Ga. Fuller received a B.A. degree from Wayne State University (Detroit, Mich.) in 1950. He worked for the Detroit *Tribune* and other newspapers from 1949 to 1954, and then became an associate editor of *Ebony* magazine from 1954 to 1957. From 1957 to 1960 Fuller served as an African correspondent, and then became an assistant editor of *Collier's Encyclopedia*. In 1961 he became executive editor of *Black World* (formerly *Negro Digest*). In 1965 Fuller received a Whitney Fellowship that enabled him to travel to Africa, and a book about his experiences, *Journey to Africa,* was published in 1971. He was the founder of the Organization of Black American Culture in Chicago, Ill., a nonprofit writer's workshop.

FULLER, META VAUX WARRICK (1877–1967), sculptor, illustrator; born in Philadelphia, Pa. After attending the Pennsylvania Academy of Fine Arts in 1907, Fuller went to Paris where she attended the École des Beaux-Arts in 1899, and where she also studied under Auguste Rodin. Fuller was one of the first Afro-American sculptors to turn to antislavery themes, and her sculptures so expressed suffering and toil that she became known as "a delicate sculptor of horrors." She did many portrait sculptures, among them heads or busts of Frederick Douglass, Sojourner Truth, and Harriet Tubman. After exhibiting her works at the Paris salons of 1898, 1899, and 1903, Fuller's sculptures were shown at the Jamestown Tricentennial Exposition, 1907; at the Harmon Foundation, New York, N.Y., 1931–33; at Howard University, Washing-

"Water Boy" by Meta Vaux Warrick Fuller *(Harmon Foundation Collection, National Archives).*

ton, D.C., 1961; at City College of the University of New York, 1967; and elsewhere. Fuller's sculptures are in the collections of the San Francisco Museum of Fine Arts; of Howard University; and the New York Public Library (Schomburg Collection). She was a member of the Boston Art Club, the Players, Zonta (the only black chapter president), and other societies. Among her awards were the George K. Crozier First Prize for Modeling, the Battles First Prize for Pottery (1904), and a 1961 fellowship from the Pennsylvania Academy of Fine Arts. She was the wife of Solomon C. Fuller, the distinguished neurologist. *See also* ARTISTS; FULLER, SOLOMON C.

FULLER, OSCAR ANDERSON (1904–   ), composer, educator; born in Marshall, Tex. Fuller was educated at Bishop College (Marshall, Tex.), the New England Conservatory of Music (Boston, Mass.), and the University of Iowa, from which he received his Ph.D. degree in 1942. Fuller was the first Afro-American to earn a Ph.D. degree in music. His teaching career was mainly concentrated in three institutions of higher learning: North Carolina Agricultural and Technical (A & T) State University, Prairie View Agricultural and Mechanical (A & M) College (Prairie View, Tex.), and Lincoln University (Jefferson City, Mo.).

FULLER, SOLOMON C. (1872–1953), neurologist, psychiatrist; born in Liberia. Fuller came to the United States in 1889, and received a B.A. degree from Livingstone College (Salisbury, N.C.) in 1893 and his M.D. degree from Boston University Medical School in 1897. He interned at Westborough State Hospital, Massachusetts, and did further study at the psychiatric clinic of the University of Munich. Fuller was appointed instructor in neurology and psychiatry at Boston University Medical School in 1899, and served there in various capacities for more than 30 years. He contributed many articles on psychiatry to scholarly journals. He was married to the prominent sculptress, Meta Vaux Warrick Fuller. *See also* FULLER, META VAUX WARRICK.

GAINES, ABRAHAM LINCOLN (1866– ?), African Methodist Episcopal bishop, educator; born in Washington, Ga. Gaines received a B.A. degree and a M.A. degree from Atlanta University, his B.D. degree from Gammon Theological Seminary, and honorary degrees from Wilberforce University (Wilberforce, Ohio) and Paul Quinn College (Waco, Tex.). He was elected a bishop of the African Methodist Episcopal (AME) Church in 1924 after serving as pastor of leading AME churches in the Southeast. Gaines also served as principal of Gray Street School in Atlanta, Ga.

GAINES CASE See CIVIL RIGHTS: CIVIL RIGHTS CASES, 1865–1975.

GAINES, EDYTHE J. (1922–), educator. Gaines received a B.A. degree from Hunter College of the City University of New York, a M.A. degree from New York University, and her Ed.D. degree from Harvard University. She became a district superintendent of schools in the Bronx, N.Y., in 1969, after having held various other posts in the New York City public school system. Gaines was a member of the Montclair State College board of trustees, the educational development board of New York City, and the board of overseers visiting committee for the Harvard Graduate School of Education. She also was the recipient of the Mary McLeod Bethune Award.

GAINES, LLOYD LIONEL See CIVIL RIGHTS: CIVIL RIGHTS CASES, 1865–1975.

GALAMISON, MILTON A. (1923–), clergyman, civil rights leader; born in Philadelphia, Pa. Galamison received a B.D. degree from Lincoln University (Lincoln University, Pa.) before his postgraduate study at Princeton Theological Seminary. He was pastor of Siloam Presbyterian Church of Brooklyn, N.Y. As a member of the New York City board of education, Galamison was regarded as an activist in education; he served as president of the Parents' Workshop for Equality in the New York City school system and as director of the School and Community Organized for Partnership in Education (SCOPE). He was also director of the Center of Urban Affairs at Harvard University.

GALE, DORIS See NEWSPAPERS: CONTEMPORARY.

GAMBLE, WILLIAM H. See AVIATORS.

GANDY, SAMUEL LUCIUS (1916–), educator, clergyman; born in Anderson, S.C. Gandy received a B.S. degree from South Carolina State College in 1935, a B.D. degree from the Howard University School of Religion (Washington, D.C.) in 1938, and his Ph.D. degree from the University of Chicago in 1952. He was assistant dean of students at Fisk University (Nashville, Tenn.) from 1938 to 1941, dean of the chapel at Dillard University (New Orleans, La.) from 1955 to 1961, and dean of Howard University School of Religion after 1964. Gandy did research on the activities of urban churches.

GANS, JOE *See* ATHLETES: BOXING.

GARDNER, J. HORACE (1900–72), state legislator; born in Cairo, Ill. Gardner was elected to the Illinois house of representatives in 1948, one of three black Republican legislators in that body, and he was reelected six times. In 1968 he became a member of the Illinois State Republican Central Committee.

GARNER, ERROLL LOUIS (1921–1977), jazz pianist, composer; born in Pittsburgh, Pa. Garner became one of the most important jazz pianists despite his lack of formal music training. While still in elementary school, he played on Allegheny riverboats, and he gradually developed his unique style of stride-piano playing. Garner was

Erroll Garner. (*From the collection of Martha Glaser.*)

the first jazz instrumentalist to give a solo recital in the United States (in Cleveland, Ohio, in 1950), and later in his career he appeared on television shows and made many recordings. As a composer of popular tunes, Garner achieved his greatest success with "Laura" and "Misty." *See also* MUSIC: JAZZ.

GARRETT, LARRY *See* NEWSPAPERS: CONTEMPORARY.

Marcus Garvey. (*Moorland-Spingarn Research Center.*)

GARRETT, LEONARD PAUL (1925–   ), publisher; born in Wichita, Kans. Garrett was the founder and editor (1966) of the Wichita *News Hawk,* a weekly newspaper, and the founder (1968) of the annual Black Arts and Labor Festival. He was president of Black American to African Starvation (BAATAS) in 1968, and the organizer and founder of Local 701 (AFL-CIO) in 1951.

GARRETT, MIKE *See* ATHLETES: FOOTBALL.

GARROTT, HOMER L., JR. (1914–   ), lawyer, judge. Garrott received his law degree from Southwestern University (Los Angeles, Calif.). Admitted to the California bar in 1960, he became a juvenile court referee in Los Angeles and, subsequently, a Municipal Court commissioner.

GARVEY, MARCUS (1887–1940), Pan-Africanist; born in Jamaica, British West Indies. Garvey served as an apprentice printer in his youth, beginning his self-education with the experiences of hardships suffered by the poor. Later reinforced by his travels to Central and South America, these early lessons formed the foundations of his mature philosophy, which reasoned that Negro independence—economic, military, and political—was the only method by which black people could "uplift" themselves and gain equality with whites. To this end, he founded the Universal Negro Improvement Association (UNIA) in Jamaica in 1911. In 1916 Garvey came to the United States where, in New York City's Harlem, he formed another branch of his organization and began to talk about a "Back to Africa" program. Attracting much interest, he recruited thousands into the UNIA and was able to start the newspaper *Negro World.* Branches of the UNIA were established throughout the country and, with substantial economic support (purchasing of shares) from his constituency, Garvey was able to form an Afro-American steamship company called the Black Star Line. Soon after its founding, his "Back to Africa" advocates began negotiations with Liberia, which, fearful that Garvey would take over the government, subsequently withdrew its support from his plans. Disillusioned by this rejection and embroiled in financial and legal difficulties, Garvey went abroad to raise funds for his foundering steamship company. Meanwhile, the federal government was compiling charges against him for misuse of the U.S. mails to defraud investors in the Black Star Line, and in 1925 Garvey was sentenced to a five-year jail term. After having served two years of the sentence, he was deported to Jamaica in 1927. Once again he attempted to establish a political base for his schemes but failed. In 1935 Garvey went to London, where he died five years later. *See also* COLONIZATION; NATIONALISM; PAN-AFRICANISM; UNIVERSAL NEGRO IMPROVEMENT ASSOCIATION (UNIA).

GARVIN, CHARLES H. (1889–1968), physician; born in Jacksonville, Fla. Garvin received a B.A. degree from Howard University (Washington, D.C.) in 1911 and his M.D. degree from the Howard University Medical College in 1915. He was commissioned a captain in the U.S. Army in 1917. Garvin successfully resisted terror tactics and bomb throwing launched to force his removal from an exclusive residential area in Cleveland, Ohio, in 1927. He served on the board of trustees of Howard University.

GATHINGS, JOSEPH GOUVERNEUR (1898–1965), dermatologist; born in Richmond, Tex. Gathings received his M.D. degree from Howard University Medical College (Washington, D.C.) in 1928, and later served as a faculty member of Howard University.

GAVINS, RAYMOND (1942–), historian, educator; born in Atlanta, Ga. Gavins received a B.A. degree from Virginia Union University (Richmond) in 1964, and a M.A. degree (1967) and his Ph.D. degree (1970) from the University of Virginia (Charlottesville). He was a minister at the Brown Grove Baptist Church in Ashland, Va. (1963–67), and taught history at Duke University (Durham, N.C.) after 1970. Gavins wrote a biography of Gordon B. Hancock. (1977).

GAYLE, ADDISON, JR. (1932–), critic, educator; born in Newport News, Va. After studying at the City College of City University of New York and at the University of California at Los Angeles, Gayle became an English instructor at Baruch College in New York City. Books that he wrote or edited include: *Black Expression* (1969); *The Black Situation* (1970); *Bondage, Freedom and Beyond: The Prose of Black Americans* (1971); *The Black Aesthetic* (1971); *Oak and Ivy: A Biography of Paul Laurence Dunbar* (1972); and *The Way of the New World: The Black Novel in America* (1975).

GAYMON, NICHOLAS E. See PREFACE: LIST OF CONTRIBUTORS.

GAYNOR, FLORENCE S. administrator; born in Jersey City, N.J. After receiving a M.A. degree in public health, Gaynor was appointed administrative director of Lincoln Hospital in the Bronx, N.Y., in 1967. She served as executive director of Sydenham Hospital in Harlem (New York, N.Y.), and then she was named chief administrator of Martland Hospital in Newark, N.J. in 1972.

GEORGIA NORMAL AND AGRICULTURAL COLLEGE See ALBANY STATE COLLEGE.

GEORGIA STATE INDUSTRIAL COLLEGE FOR COLORED YOUTH See SAVANNAH STATE COLLEGE.

GIBBS, MIFFLIN WISTER (1823–1915), publisher, lawyer, government official; born in Philadelphia, Pa. Gibbs traveled to San Francisco in 1849 to find his fortune, beginning there as a bootblack and later forming a partnership in the shoe business. In 1855 he founded *Mirror of the Times,* California's first black newspaper, and published it until its merger with the *Pacific Appeal.* Moving to Victoria, British Columbia, Canada, Gibbs undertook several enterprises as merchant, district councilman, railroad builder, and law student. In 1869 he left Canada to continue his unfinished law education at Oberlin College (Oberlin, Ohio). Within a year Gibbs was admitted to the Arkansas bar, and within three years he was elected municipal judge in Little Rock, Ark. Thereafter, with his reputation well known, he served under several presidents—in the administration of President Rutherford B. Hayes as registrar of U.S. lands in eastern Arkansas and under President Benjamin Harrison as registrar of public moneys received. During the McKinley administration, Gibbs became U.S. consul in Madagascar, and he retained this post through Theodore Roosevelt's presidency. Vigorous and active throughout his long life, Gibbs published an autobiography entitled *Shadow and Light* in 1902.

GIBBS, WARMOTH THOMAS (1892–), historian, educator; born in Baldwin, La. Gibbs received a B.A. degree from Wiley College (Marshall, Tex.) in 1912, and a second B.A. degree (1917) and his Ed.M. degree (1926) from Harvard University. Except for a period of military service during World War I and during his retirement, he devoted his life to North Carolina Agricultural and Technical (A & T) State University mainly as dean and as president (1955–61). After his retirement, Gibbs wrote a history of the college.

GIBSON, ALTHEA (1927–), tennis player, professional golfer; born in Silver, S.C. Reared in Harlem (New York, N.Y.) and educated at Florida Agricultural and Mechanical (A & M) University, Gibson was the first black to compete successfully in major international tennis play.

Nine years after beginning a brilliant career as an amateur, she became the first Afro-American to compete in American national singles play at Forest Hills, N.Y., where she won the women's singles titles in 1957 and in 1958. In the same two years, Gibson won the "All-England" women's singles championships at Wimbledon and became the first black titleholder; she was also a member of the women's championship Wimbledon doubles teams of 1957 and 1958. As a tennis professional, Gibson became the world champion in 1960, three years prior to her becoming a professional golfer. She published her autobiography, *I Aways Wanted to Be Somebody*, in 1958. *See also* ATHLETES.

GIBSON, DONALD *See* PREFACE: LIST OF CONTRIBUTORS.

GIBSON, HARRY H. C. (1913–), lawyer, business executive; born in Atlanta, Ga. Gibson was a practicing attorney who later served as associate general counsel of the United Mortgage Bankers of America. He was director of the Fireside Mutual Life Insurance Co., Columbus, Ohio; vice-chairman of the Chicago Land Clearance Commission; and later senior vice-president and general counsel of the Supreme Life Insurance Company of America, Chicago, Ill.

GIBSON, JOSH *See* ATHLETES: BASEBALL.

GIBSON, KENNETH ALLEN (1932–), engineer, mayor; born in Enterprise, Ala. Gibson moved to Newark, N.J., with his parents (a butcher and a seamstress) when he was 8 years old. After completing his military service requirement, he received a B.S. degree from the Newark College of Engineering in 1963. Gibson subsequently served as chief engineer of urban renewal projects sponsored by the Newark Housing Authority. In 1970 he became the first black mayor of Newark after defeating the white incumbent. He was reelected in 1974 and in 1978.

GIBSON, PAUL (1927–), public official; born in New York, N.Y. Gibson received a B.S. degree from the City University of New York and his J.D. degree from New York University. From 1966 to 1969 he served as legislative counsel to the president of the New York city council. In 1969 Gibson was appointed law secretary to the New York Supreme Court, and from 1971 to 1974 he was vice-president for urban and environmental affairs of American Airlines. In 1974

Gibson became the first Afro-American to serve as deputy mayor of New York City. He was a member of the board of directors of the Jamaica branch of the National Association for the Advancement of Colored People (NAACP) and of the Queens Urban League, and was vice-president of the Jamaica Chamber of Commerce. He also served as a director of the National Aerospace Education Association and was instrumental in the establishment of August Martin High School (for aviation training) in New York City.

GIBSON, TRUMAN KELLA (1882–1972), business executive; born in Macon, Ga. Gibson received a B.A. degree from Atlanta University in 1905 and a second B.A. degree from Harvard University in 1908. He was instrumental in the formation of the Supreme Life Insurance Company of America, one of the foremost black business enterprises, which was created through the merger of the Supreme Life and Casualty Company of Illinois and the Northeastern Life Insurance Company of New Jersey. Gibson served as chairman and then as chairman emeritus of the Supreme Life Insurance Company of America. *See also* BUSINESS.

GILES, JULIAN W. (1923–69), physician; born in Washington, D.C. Giles received a B.S. degree from Howard University (Washington, D.C.) in 1942 and his M.D. degree from Howard University Medical College in 1946. He was a staff member of Freedmen's Hospital, Washington, D.C. (1959–60) and director of the Veterans Administration Hospital, Tuskegee, Ala. (1962–69).

GILES, ROSCOE CONKLING (1890–1970), physician, civil rights leader; born in Albany, N.Y. Giles received a B.A. degree from Cornell University (Ithaca, N.Y.) in 1911 and his M.D. degree from Cornell University Medical College in 1915, the first black graduate of the medical college. He became supervisor of the city health department in Chicago, Ill., in 1917, assistant professor of surgery at the Chicago Medical School in 1946, and attending surgeon at Cook County Hospital in 1953. Giles worked ardently to secure admission of black personnel to all services in the U.S. Navy, to open military hospitals to black officers, and to include black physicians on local boards of the Selective Service System. He received numerous awards and citations throughout his career.

GILLESPIE, JOHN BIRKS (DIZZY) (1917–   ), jazz trumpeter, bandleader; born in Cheraw, S.C. Gillespie studied harmony and theory at Laurinburg Institute (Laurinburg, N.C.) before joining Cab Calloway's band as a trumpeter (1939–41). In the 1940s Gillespie, along with other jazz greats, including Oscar Pettiford and Charlie "Bird" Parker, was a leader in the formation of the revolutionary jazz style known as Bop. Gillespie organized his own band in the 1940s, and in 1956 he became the first jazz musician to take his band on an overseas tour sponsored by the U.S. Department of State. *See also* MUSIC: JAZZ.

GILLIAM, EARL B. (1931–   ), lawyer, judge. Gilliam received a B.A. degree from San Diego State College and his J.D. degree from Hastings College of Law of the University of California at San Francisco. He was admitted to the California bar in 1957, and later Gilliam became judge of the Municipal Court of San Diego.

GILMORE, AL-TONY (1946–   ), historian, educator; born in Spartanburg, S.C. Gilmore received a B.A. degree from North Carolina Central University in 1968, and a M.A. degree (1969) and his Ph.D. degree (1972) from the University of Toledo. He became an assistant professor of history at Howard University (Washington, D.C.) in 1972; later he went to the University of Maryland at College Park as head of black studies. Gilmore is the author of "America's Reaction to Jack Johnson, 1908–15" (1973) and other studies of Johnson, the black heavyweight.

GILPIN, CHARLES SIDNEY (1878–1930), actor; born in Richmond, Va. The son of a white mother and a black father, Gilpin began his working life on a newspaper in Richmond. Until 1916, when he moved to New York City and became manager of the Lafayette Theater Company in Harlem, he held an assortment of jobs with singing groups and stock companies, and he had organized the Gilpin Players, a stock company, in Cleveland, Ohio, in 1915. His debut as a Broadway actor was in the role of William Custis in John Drinkwater's *Abraham Lincoln* in 1919. A year later, Gilpin appeared at the Provincetown Theater (Provincetown, Mass.) in the title role of Eugene O'Neill's *The Emperor Jones*, a role that won Gilpin great acclaim. In 1921 he received the NAACPs Spingarn Medal for that performance. In 1927 he left the cast of the new film version of *Uncle Tom's Cabin*, believing the characterization of Uncle Tom to be insulting to his race. The role was modified after his departure. *See also* LITERATURE: DRAMA/THEATER; MOTION PICTURES.

GIOVANNI, NIKKI (1934–   ), poet; born in Knoxville, Tenn. After receiving a B.A. degree from Fisk University (Nashville, Tenn.), Giovanni did graduate work first at the University of Pennsylvania and then at Columbia University. She was the author of several books of poetry and prose, including *Black Feelings, Black Talk* (1968); *My House* (1972); *Gemini: An Extended Autobiographical Statement*; and with James Baldwin, she wrote *A Dialogue* (1973). Giovanni was on the faculty of Livingston College, Rutgers University (New Brunswick, N.J.) in 1973. *See also* LITERATURE: POETRY.

GLADWIN, WALTER H. (1902–   ), lawyer, judge; born in British Guiana. Gladwin immigrated to the United States in 1924, attended evening sessions at City College of the City University of New York, and received his LL.B. degree from New York University School of Law. He was admitted to the New York bar in 1943, after which he began his law career as assistant deputy collector for the Internal Revenue Service. Gladwin then served as assistant corporation counsel from 1946 to 1948 and as assistant district attorney from 1948 to 1953. He was elected to the New York state legislature from Bronx County, and from 1957 to 1962 he was a magistrate from the Bronx. In 1962 Gladwin became judge of the Criminal Court of the City of New York and served on that bench until his retirement.

GLANTON, LUTHER T., JR. (1913–   ), lawyer, judge. Glanton received a B.S. degree from Tennessee State University and his LL.B. degree from Drake University (Des Moines, Iowa). He was admitted to the Iowa bar in 1942, and after a period of about four years in the U.S. Army, he returned to civilian life and the practice of law. Glanton first became judge of the Municipal Court in Des Moines and later district associate judge.

GLASGOW, DOUGLASS G. (1929–   ), educator; born in New York, N.Y. Glasgow received a B.A. degree from Brooklyn College of the City University of New York, a M.S.W. degree from Columbia University in 1961, and his D.S.W. degree from the University of Southern California in 1968. He became dean of the School of

Charles Gilpin in the title role of Eugene O'Neill's *The Emperor Jones.* (Library of Congress.)

Social Work at Howard University (Washington, D.C.) in 1971, after serving with the School of Social Work at the University of California at Los Angeles.

GLASS, ROBERT D. (1922–   ), lawyer, judge; born in Wetumpka, Ala. Glass received a B.A. degree (1949) and a LL.B. degree (1951) from North Carolina Central University. He practiced law in Charlotte, N.C., from 1951 to 1953, and in New Bern, N.C., from 1953 to 1960. Glass served as claims examiner for the Unemployment Compensation Division of the Connecticut Labor Department in 1961. In 1962 he opened a law practice in Waterbury, Conn., where he practiced for four years. As an assistant U.S. attorney in 1966, he became the first black to serve in this capacity in Connecticut. A year later he was appointed judge of the Connecticut Juvenile Court, again the first Afro-American to hold such a position in Connecticut.

GLENN, EVANS TYREE (1912–   ), jazz trombonist; born in Corsicana, Tex. Glenn became one of the most accomplished of jazz trombonists. During the course of his career he played with many famous bands, including those of Benny Carter, Cab Calloway, Don Redman, and Duke Ellington. Glenn also led his own groups and played many engagements in New York City nightclubs. See also MUSIC: JAZZ.

GLOSTER, HUGH MORRIS (1911–   ), critic, educator; born in Brownsville, Tenn. Gloster received a B.A. degree from Morehouse College (Atlanta, Ga.) in 1931, a M.A. degree from Atlanta University in 1933, and his Ph.D. degree from New York University in 1943. From 1933 to 1967 he taught English at LeMoyne College (Memphis, Tenn., now LeMoyne-Aven College), at Hampton Institute (Hampton, Va.), and at Morehouse College, of which he became president in 1967. Gloster was the founder of the College Language Association (CLA) in 1937 and served as its president from 1937 to 1938 and from 1948 to 1950. From 1948 to 1953 he was a contributing editor of *Phylon*. His best-known book is *Negro Voices in American Fiction* (1948).

GOLAR, SIMEON (1928–   ), lawyer, judge; born in Chester, S.C. Golar received a B.A. degree from City College of the City University of New York and his LL.B. degree from New York University. He served as the chairman of the New York City Housing Authority in the early 1970s, before his appointment to the New York City judiciary.

GOLDEN, CHARLES FRANKLIN (1912–   ), United Methodist bishop; born in Holly Springs, Miss. Golden attended Clark College (Atlanta, Ga.), received a B.D. degree and a honorary D.D. degree from Gammon Theological Seminary, and did further study at Boston University. After holding several pastorates and administrative positions, he became a bishop of the United Methodist Church of California in 1968.

GOLDSBY, RICHARD A. See SCIENTISTS: BIOLOGICAL, PHYSICAL.

GOODLETT, CARLTON B. (1914–   ), physician, publisher; born in Chipley, Fla. He received a B.S. from Howard University (Washington, D.C.) in 1935, a Ph.D. from the University of California (Berkeley) in 1938, and his M.D. from Meharry Medical College (Nashville) in 1944. He established his medical practice in San Francisco, Calif., in 1945; and three years later he became the editor and publisher of the *Sun-Reporter* there. He has served as president of the National Newspaper Publishers Association. See also NEWSPAPERS: CONTEMPORARY.

GORDONE, CHARLES (1926–   ), playwright; born in Cleveland, Ohio. After graduating from California State College in 1952, Gordone became an actor, appearing in several shows Off Broadway. In 1970 his play, *No Place to be Somebody*, received the Pulitzer Prize. See also LITERATURE: DRAMA/THEATER.

GORDY, BERRY, JR. (1929–   ), business executive; born in Detroit, Mich. Gordy attended Northeastern High School in Detroit, from which he dropped out during his junior year. After trying songwriting and boxing, he was inducted into the U.S. Army in 1951. Gordy opened a record shop in Detroit in 1953 that went broke. After working briefly as a plasterer and with the Ford Motor Company, he was encouraged by William (Smokey) Robinson, Jr., to form a recording company. Motown Record Corporation was founded by Gordy in 1959. Motown's first issue was in 1959, and by 1960 the company had published its first gold record, both recorded by Smokey Robinson, who became vice-president of Motown. By 1970 Motown, under Gordy's leadership, grossed more than $50 million annually. Among Motown's most popular recording artists were the Supremes, the Jackson Five, Stevie Wonder, and Marvin Gaye. As president and chairman of the Motown board, Gordy supervised most aspects of the company's operations, and saw Motown grow to become the largest black-owned firm in annual gross income in 1975. *See also* BUSINESS; EDWARDS, ESTER GORDY.

GORE, GEORGE W., JR. (1901–), educator; born in Greencastle, Ind. Gore received a B.A. degree from DePauw University (Greencastle, Ind.) in 1923, an Ed.M. degree from Harvard University in 1928, and his Ph.D. degree from Columbia University in 1940. He taught at Tennessee State University (1923–27) and was dean (1927–50) and then president (1950) of Florida Agricultural and Mechanical (A & M) University (Tallahassee).

GOSPELS *See* MUSIC: HISTORY AND DEVELOPMENT.

GRACE, "DADDY" *See* UNITED HOUSE OF PRAYER FOR ALL PEOPLE.

GRAHAM, HARRY PIERSON (1929–), educator; born in Gaffney, S.C. Graham received a B.S. degree from South Carolina State College in 1950, a M.A. degree from Northwestern University (Evanston Ill.) in 1958, and his Ed.D. degree from the University of Oklahoma in 1969. He was affiliated with the South Carolina Area Trade School (1950–67), leaving his post there as dean of instruction to become vice-president (1969) and later president of Voorhees College (Denmark, S.C.).

GRAHAM, SHIRLEY *See* DU BOIS, SHIRLEY GRAHAM.

GRAMBLING COLLEGE Grambling College, at Grambling, La., was founded in 1901. A state-supported, coeducational college, the school offers the bachelor's degree, provides liberal arts and teacher education curricula, and offers professional and terminal occupational work. Its 1974 enrollment was about 3,600.

Grambling originated as an industrial education school. In 1901 a farmer's relief association of Ruston, La., requested Booker T. Washington to send a man from Tuskegee Institute, Ala., to help start an industrial school. In August Charles P. Adams arrived as the endorsed representative to start the school. The site chosen was two miles west of the present site.

The original purpose of the institution was to teach Afro-Americans how to make a living by improving methods of farming, by preparing and preserving foods, by improving health conditions, and by learning how to buy land and build homes. The education offered was patterned after that of Tuskegee Institute. All students were accepted, the only qualification being that all who entered must work. From 1901 to 1905 Charles P. Adams and his two-man faculty tried to maintain and promote the idea of an industrial school that they hoped could develop enough to gain parish and state support.

In 1905 the school was moved to its present location. A philanthropist, Fidelia Jewett, became interested in the institution and donated a large sum of money to it. Therefore, between 1901 and 1912, the institution was operated under private auspices. In 1912 it became a semi-public institution.

In 1918 the school became known as the Lincoln Parish Training School and was operated under the direction of the Lincoln Parish school board. In 1928 it was made a state junior college to train elementary teachers for small rural schools. In 1940 a four-year program was inaugurated. In 1948 the state board of education granted the college permission to prepare high school teachers, and in 1954 it authorized the institution to provide preliminary training for the study of medicine, law and dentistry. During the 1958–59 school year, the liberal arts program was put into effect, and in 1963 the division of general studies was organized. Probably no other black college has produced as many famous, professional football players as Grambling.

GRANGER, LESTER B. (1896–1976), civil rights leader. Granger received a B.A. degree from Dartmouth College (Hanover, N.H.) in 1918. He taught at Slater Normal School from 1919 to 1920, at Saint Augustine's College (Raleigh, N.C.) from 1920 to 1921, and at Tulane University, Dillard University, Rutgers University, Morehouse College, Hampton Institute, Atlanta University, Park College, Loyola University, and Texas Southern University. In addition, he served as executive director of the National Urban League (1941–61), as chairman of the Federal Advisory Council on Employment Security, as special adviser to Secretary of the Navy James Forrestal during World War II, and as the architect of the policy established by the U.S. Navy for ending racial segregation. Granger received the Navy's

Distinguished Civilian Service Medal in 1946 and the President's Medal for Merit in 1947. *See also* NATIONAL URBAN LEAGUE.

GRANT, EARL (1933–1969) singer, pianist; born in Oklahoma City, Okla. Grant was raised in Kansas City, Mo., and after his graduation from the University of Southern California, he studied at conservatories in Kansas City; in New Rochelle, N.Y.; and at DePaul Conservatory (Chicago, Ill.). The singing competitions he won in the 1950s led to further successes, and eventually to a worldwide reputation. His instrumental recording of "Ebb Tide" was very popular. Grant died in an automobile accident in New Mexico.

Samuel Gravely. *(U.S. Navy Photographic Center.)*

GRAVELY, SAMUEL LEE (1922–   ), Navy officer; born in Richmond, Va. Interrupting his college studies to enlist in the U.S. Navy, Gravely became, in 1944, the first black ensign commissioned in World War II. Released from active duty in 1946, he returned to college and received a B.A. degree from Virginia Union University in 1948, but was recalled by the Navy in 1949. Gravely was the first Afro-American to command a U.S. Navy ship, the *USS Falgout*, in 1962, and eventually became the U.S. Navy's first black rear admiral in 1971. In 1973 he was named commander of a flotilla of 30 ships.

GRAVES, EARL G. (1935–   ), publisher; born in Brooklyn, N.Y. He received his B.A. degree from Morgan State College, Baltimore, Md. After serving on the staff of Senator Robert F. Kennedy, 1966–68, he began to publish *Black Enterprise*, a successful magazine devoted to black business and economic development. *See also* PREFACE: LIST OF CONTRIBUTORS.

GRAY, FRED D. (1930–   ), lawyer, state legislator; born in Montgomery, Ala. Gray received a B.A. degree from Alabama State University at Montgomery and his LL.B. degree from Case Western Reserve University (Cleveland, Ohio). After admission to the Ohio bar in 1954, Gray became immediately involved in the famous *City of Montgomery v. Rosa Parks* case, a lawsuit to determine whether a black woman had the right to refuse a bus seat to a white man. A leader for civil rights and a minister of the Church of Christ, Gray worked as an attorney for the National Association for the Advancement of Colored People (NAACP) and for the city of Tuskegee, Ala., as well as for educational institutions in Ala-

bama. In 1970 he was elected to the Alabama state legislature. *See also* LAWYERS.

GRAY, JESSE (1923–   ), public official, civic leader; born in Tunica, La. Gray attended Xavier University of Louisiana and Southern University (Baton Rouge, La.). In the 1950s, as leader of the Harlem Tenants Council (HTC), he fought for and won rent-control regulations, the right to due process for evicted residents, and a ten-year hiatus of all demolition in the Harlem area of New York City. By 1963, having participated in rent-strike activities for some time, Gray led about 30,000 residents in a strike to protest substandard housing in New York City; this strike resulted in a state rent-strike law that made it permissible for a resident to withhold rent. Gray became a Democratic member of the New York state assembly in 1972.

GRAY, WILLIAM H., III   See POLITICS; NIX, ROBERT N.C., SR.

GREEN, CLIFFORD SCOTT (1923–   ), lawyer, judge. Green received B.S. and LL.B. degrees from Temple University (Philadelphia, Pa.), and was admitted to the Pennsylvania bar in 1952. He later served as a judge of the Court of Common Pleas, Philadelphia, Pa., and as a U.S. District Court judge.

GREEN, HARRY JAMES, SR. (1911–   ), scientist; born in St. Louis, Mo. Green received a B.Ch.E. degree (1932) and his Ph.D. degree (1943) from Ohio State University, and a M.S. degree from Massachusetts Institute of Technology in 1938. He served as instructor in chemistry at North Carolina Agricultural and Technical (A & T) State University (1934–37), and then as assistant professor and later as professor there (1938–44). Green worked at the Stromberg-Carlson Company, Rochester, N.Y., as senior engineer (1944–59) and then as supervising manager of the products engineering department (1959–67). He was on the staff of the research department of Xerox Corporation after 1970.

GREENE, LORENZO JOHNSTON (1899–   ), historian, educator; born in Ansonia, Conn. Greene received a B.A. degree from Howard University (Washington, D.C.) in 1924, and a M.A. degree (1926) and his Ph.D. degree (1942) from Columbia University. In 1928 he began a lifetime affiliation with the Association for the Study of

Afro-American Life and History as assistant to its director. Greene began his teaching career as professor of history at Lincoln University (Jefferson City, Mo.) in the early 1930s, and retired there as acting head of the department in 1971. While at Lincoln, he married the concert pianist, Thomasina Talley. During this period, he also edited the *Midwest Journal*. His book, *The Negro in Colonial New England, 1620–1776* (1942, 1966), has become a classic on the subject. *See also* HISTORIANS.

GREENE, PERCY *See* NEWSPAPERS: CONTEMPORARY.

GREENER, RICHARD T. (1844–1922), lawyer, educator; born in Philadelphia, Pa. Raised in Boston, Mass., Greener was the first Afro-American to graduate from Harvard University (1870). Thereafter, he had an outstanding career as an educator, lawyer, and finally as consul in the U.S. Department of State. Greener taught philosophy at the University of South Carolina until 1877, when Reconstruction (and integration) ended. He then went to Washington, D.C., to become dean of the Howard University School of Law. Resigning that post, Greener served as the U.S. comptroller of the treasury and as U.S. consul in Russia. *See also* LAWYERS.

GREENFIELD, ELIZABETH TAYLOR (1809–1876), singer; born in Natchez, Miss. Greenfield became known as the "Black Swan" of the concert stage. She was trained by a Mrs. Greenfield, a Quaker woman who took her to Philadelphia, Pa. In 1851 Greenfield performed at the Buffalo Musical Association in Buffalo, N.Y. Critics compared her to Jenny Lind, and praised the great range of her voice. From 1851 to 1853 Greenfield toured the United States and Canada, and the next year she went abroad to tour England, where she sang at Buckingham Palace at a command performance before Queen Victoria.

GREER, EDWARD (1924–), Army officer; born in Gary, W. Va. Greer received a B.S. degree from West Virginia State College in 1948 and his M.S. degree from George Washington University (Washington, D.C.) in 1967. Entering the U.S. Army in 1947, he rose to the rank of brigadier general in 1972. Named deputy commanding general of the U.S. Army Training Center, Fort Leonard Wood, Mo., in 1972, Greer became one of the first two Afro-Americans to assume such a command. His awards included the Silver Star, the Legion of Merit with Oak Leaf Cluster, and the Bronze Star Medal with Oak Leaf Cluster.

GREGG, ARTHUR J. (1928–), Army officer; born in Florence, S.C. Gregg received a B.S. degree from Saint Benedict's College (Atchison, Kans.). During a long career in the U.S. Army, he won the Legion of Merit and the Joint Service Commendation Medal, and was promoted to brigadier general in 1972, becoming deputy director of supply and maintenance.

GREGORY, DICK (1932–), comedian, civil rights leader; born Richard Clayton in St. Louis, Mo. Gregory attended Southern Illinois University, where he was an outstanding athlete, until he left college to join the U.S. Army. Entertaining in special service shows kindled his interest in the theater, an interest that developed into a profession in the latter part of the 1950s. By the 1960s Gregory was appearing in large nightclubs across the country, with acts that combined wit, humor, and incisive social comment. In fact, much of his comedic material derived from his interest and participation in the civil rights and antiwar movements. In 1966 Gregory officially entered politics by declaring himself a write-in candidate for mayor of Chicago, Ill., opposing Mayor Richard J. Daley. He was a candidate again in 1968, this time for president of the United States on the Peace and Freedom Party ticket. In addition to making comedy records, Gregory wrote several books, among them *No More Lies; The Myth and Reality of American History* (1971) and *Nigger; An Autobiography* (1964). *See also* RADIO AND TELEVISION.

Dick Gregory. *(National Educational Television.)*

GREGORY, LOUIS (1874–1951), educator, religious leader; born in Charleston, S.C. Gregory was a graduate of Fisk University (Nashville, Tenn.) and Howard University School of Law (Washington, D.C.) in 1902. In 1912 he was visited by international leaders of the Bahá'í faith, and subsequently he became active in the work of that religious system, serving on its first national administrative body in the United States. An award for service to humanity was established in his memory in 1968 by the National Spiritual Assembly of the Bahá'ís of the United States. *See also* BAHÁ Í FAITH.

GRESHAM, JEROME LYNWOOD (1938–), educator; born in Atlanta, Ga. Gresham received a B.A. degree from Allen University (Columbia, S.C.) in 1959 and his M.A. degree from Columbia University in 1963. He taught at Demery's Business College in 1960 and at Sheldon Jackson Junior College (Sitka, Alaska) from 1961 to 1963. He was principal of Sitka Junior High School (Sitka, Alaska) from 1963 to 1965. Gresham served as consultant for the Alaska state department of education, and in 1966 he became president of Barber-Scotia College (Concord, N.C.).

GRIER, ROOSEVELT (ROSEY) (1932–), professional football player, entertainer; born in Cuthbert, Ga. Grier attended Pennsylvania State University where he received a B.A. degree in 1955. He was an outstanding athlete in several sports in college and signed a contract with the New York Giants football team (National Football League) in 1955. During his career with the Giants, Grier became one of the most feared and famous defensive players. He served in the U.S. Army in 1957, after which he returned to professional football and was voted All-Pro twice. Grier was a bodyguard for Robert F. Kennedy at the time of his assassination in 1968. His singing career began at Carnegie Hall in New York City in 1963, and he subsequently appeared in movies and on television. *See also* ATHLETES.

GRIFFITH, THOMAS L., JR. (1902–), lawyer, judge; born in Albia, Iowa. Son of a Baptist minister, Griffith received his LL.B. degree from Southwestern University (Los Angeles, Calif.). He was admitted to the California bar in 1931, after which he practiced law in a private practice for nearly 21 years. In 1953 Griffith was appointed judge of the Municipal Court of Los Angeles; he was reelected unopposed in 1958 and again in 1964. In 1968 Griffith was elected judge of the Superior Court of Los Angeles County by a majority of more than one million votes, and he remained on that bench until his retirement.

GRIMKÉ, ARCHIBALD HENRY (1849–1930), author, editor, civil rights leader; born in Charleston, S.C. Grimké studied under the literary training program at Lincoln University, and later graduated form Harvard University Law School in 1874. He edited *The Hub*, a weekly newspaper in Boston, Mass. (1883–85), and also wrote for the Boston *Herald* and Boston *Traveler*. Grimké served as president of the American Negro Academy and as U.S. consul to Santo Domingo (1894–98). He was a member of the Authors' Club of London (England), the American Social Science

Association, and the Frederick Douglass Memorial and Historical Association. Grimké was an outstanding leader and officer of the National Association for the Advancement of Colored People (NAACP) and a noted champion of the rights of Afro-Americans. He was awarded the Springarn Medal in 1919. *See also* GRIMKÉ, FRANCIS JAMES who was his brother.

GRIMKÉ, FRANCIS JAMES (1850–1937), clergyman, civic leader, author; born in Charleston, S.C. Grimké graduated from Lincoln University (Lincoln University, Pa.) in 1870, studied law at Howard University (Washington, D.C.), and graduated from Princeton Theological Seminary in 1878. He was very active in the work of the American Negro Academy and in the civic affairs of Washington, D.C., where he was pastor of the Fifteenth Street Presbyterian Church and a trustee of Howard University. In 1878 he married Charlotte Forten, daughter of James Forten of Philadelphia, Pa. Charlotte Forten Grimké (1838–1914) became widely known as a teacher and poet. Some excellent references on Grimké include *The Works of Francis J. Grimké* (4 vols., 1942), edited by Carter G. Woodson, and *Life and Writings of the Grimké Family* (1951), largely devoted to the writings of Francis Grimké, edited by Anna Julia Cooper. *See also* GRIMKÉ, ARCHIBALD HENRY; PRESBYTERIANS.

GROSS, LOIN *See* NEWSPAPERS: CONTEMPORARY.

GUNTER, LAURIE MARTIN (1922–), nurse, educator; born in Navarro County, Tex. Gunter received a B.S. degree from Tennessee State University in 1948, a certificate in nursing from the University of Toronto (Toronto, Canada) in 1949, a M.A. degree from Fisk University (Nashville, Tenn.) in 1952, and her Ph.D. degree from the University of Chicago in 1959. She was a nurse and supervisor at George W. Hubbard Hospital, Nashville, Tenn. (1943–48), and then taught at Meharry Medical College of Nursing, the University of California at Los Angeles, Indiana University Medical Center, the University of Washington, and Pennsylvania State University.

GUY, HERMAN C. *See* NEWSPAPERS: CONTEMPORARY.

GUZMAN, JESSIE P. *See* BIBLIOGRAPHIES/BIOGRAPHIES/GUIDES (Tuskegee Institute, *Negro Year Book*); LYNCHING.

H

HAGAN, HELEN EUGENIA (1893–1964), pianist, educator; born in Portsmouth, N.H. Hagan graduated from the Yale University School of Music in 1911, and subsequently was awarded a Samuel Simmons Sanford Fellowship for two years of study abroad. She made her New York City debut in Aeolian Hall. Later she served on the faculty of Bishop College (Dallas, Tex.).

HAIRSTON, LOYLE (1926–   ), author; born in Macon, Miss. After serving in the U.S. Navy during World War II, Hairston moved to New York City and joined the Harlem Writer's Guild. The author of many short stories, he was also a contributing editor to *Freedomways* magazine.

HALE, FRANK WILBUR, JR. (1927–   ), educator, author; born in Kansas City, Mo. Hale received a B.A. degree from the University of Nebraska in 1950, and a M.A. degree (1951) and his Ph.D. degree (1955) from Ohio State University. He was affiliated with Oakwood College (Huntsville, Ala.) from 1952 to 1959 and Central State University (Wilberforce, Ohio) from 1959 to 1966, and then returned to Oakwood College to become its president in 1966. Hale wrote *Sunlight and Shadows* (1967) and *A Manual of Public Speaking* (1969).

HALE, WILLIAM HENRY (1914–   ), educator; born in Krebs, Okla. Hale received a B.S. degree from Langston University (Langston, Okla.) in 1940, a M.A. degree from the University of Wis-

consin in 1941, and his Ph.D. degree from the University of Chicago in 1949. He was affiliated with Fisk University (Nashville, Tenn.) from 1941 to 1942, Langston University from 1942 to 1943, Bethune-Cookman College (Daytona Beach, Fla.) from 1943 to 1946, and Clark College (Atlanta, Ga.) from 1948 to 1960 before becoming president of Langston University in 1960.

HALE, WILLIAM JASPER (1876–1944), educator; born in Retro, Tenn. Hale attended Maryville College (Maryville, Tenn.). He became president of Tennessee Agricultural and Industrial (A&I) University (now Tennessee State University) in 1911, and remained in that position for more than 30 years until he retired in the 1940s. He built what was then known as the Agricultural and Industrial Normal School from a college consisting of only a few frame buildings to a state college with 15 buildings and more than 200 acres of land. Hale was the founder and president of the Interracial League in Tennessee and chairman of the executive committee of the National Association of Teachers of Colored Schools. He was also appointed a member of President Herbert Hoover's Negro Housing Committee.

HALEY, ALEXANDER PALMER (ALEX) (1921–   ), journalist, author; born in Ithaca, N. Y. Haley attended Elizabeth City State Teachers College (Elizabeth City, N. C.) from 1937 to 1939.

He entered the U. S. Coast Guard in 1939, serving later as editor of *Out Post*, the official Coast Guard publication. From 1945 to 1949 he served as a public relations official in Coast Guard District Headquarters. Haley gained further recognition when he assisted in writing *The Autobiography of Malcolm X* (1965), one of the most influential books of the decade. His book, *Roots*, was published in 1976 and serialized on national television. *Roots* won Haley the Pulitzer Prize in 1977 and in 1977 he received the Spingarn Medal for "his unsurpassed effectiveness in portraying the legendary story of every American of African Descent."

HALL, BERTRAND A. (1908–), agriculturalist, civic leader; born in Hartford, Conn. Hall attended the University of Massachusetts and received a B.A. degree from Tuskegee Institute (Tuskegee Institute, Ala.) in 1932. He served as county agricultural extension agent in Guilford County, N.C., for more than a quarter of a century until his retirement in 1973. Hall served on many local, state, and national boards in the fields of agriculture and agricultural extension service. He was active in community and service activities for Afro-Americans in North Carolina and was elected to the Guilford County board of commissioners in 1974; reelected overwhelmingly in 1976.

HALL, FRED P. See NEWSPAPERS: CONTEMPORARY.

HALL, FREDERICK DOUGLASS (1898–1964), organist, educator; born in Atlanta, Ga. Hall received his education at Morehouse College (Atlanta, Ga.), Chicago Musical College, and Columbia University. From the latter institution he earned his Ph.D. degree in music in 1952. Hall's distinguished teaching career spanned positions at Jackson State College (Jackson, Miss.), Clark College (Atlanta, Ga.), Alabama Agricultural and Mechanical (A & M) College, and Dillard University (New Orleans, La.). At Jackson State, Hall organized the conservatory of music.

HALL, GEORGE CLEVELAND (1864–1930), physician, civic leader; born in Ypsilanti, Mich. After receiving a B.A. degree from Lincoln University (Lincoln University, Pa.), Hall earned his M.D. degree from Bennett College of Medicine in 1888. He helped to organize the Provident Hospital, Chicago, Ill., in 1890, and then devised and coordinated a teaching program for black medical students at the hospital. In 1914 he ran for the Chicago board of commissioners on the Progressive slate. Hall was appointed to the Governor's Commission on Race Relations, which investigated the Chicago Riots of 1919. He was the first Afro-American appointed to the Chicago library board, and was an active member of the National Urban League and was briefly its vice-president. Hall participated in the 1913 meeting between Urban League members and trade union leaders.

HALL, JAMES LOWELL, SR. (1892–1965), physician; born in Waxahachie, Tex. Hall received a B.S. degree from the University of Chicago in 1923 and his M.D. degree from the University of Chicago College of Medicine in 1925. He interned at the Homer G. Phillips Hospital, St. Louis, Mo., and trained as a research physician at Billings Hospital, Chicago, Ill. Hall established allergy clinics at Provident and at Freedmen's hospitals, both in Washington, D.C. He served as director of clinics at Provident Hospital in 1936, as head of the department of medicine at Howard University (Washington, D.C.) in 1941, and as director of Freedmen's Hospital.

HALL, LLOYD A. (1894–1971), scientist; born in Elgin, Ill. Hall received a Ph.C. degree (1914) and a B.S. degree (1916) from Northwestern University (Evanston, Ill.). He was sanitary chemist at the department of health laboratories, Chicago, Ill. (1916–18), president and chemical director of Chemical Products Corporation, Chicago (1924–25), consultant to Griffith's Laboratories, Chicago (1925–29), chief chemist and research director of Griffith's Laboratories (1925–46), and technical director there after 1946. Hall held more than 75 patents in the United States, Great Britain, and Canada and made substantial contributions to the meat-packing industry with his various discoveries of and recipes for curing salts, condiments, spices, and flavors.

HALL, PRINCE (1748–1797), fraternal society leader; born in Bridgetown, Barbados. Hall's father was a leatherworker and his mother was a free black of French extraction. In 1765 Hall sailed for Boston, Mass., working en route for his passage. In Boston he worked in the leather trade, acquired real estate, and took lessons at night to overcome his lack of schooling. Hall eventually became a minister of the Methodist Church in Cambridge, Mass., and as leader of the Afro-Americans in Boston, he urged the Com-

HAMILTON, HENRY COOKE

mittee of Safety to let slaves enlist in the colonial armies in 1775. Hall served in the Revolutionary War himself, enlisting for a nine-month term in 1778: After the war, he worked for the education of black children: petitioning the legislature to open schools in 1787; urging his fellow Afro-Americans to open a school of their own in 1792; and requesting the selectmen of Boston to provide a schoolhouse for Afro-Americans in 1796. A month before the fighting broke out at Lexington, Mass., Hall and 14 other free blacks were initiated into masonry in Boston by British Army Lodge No. 441 of the 38th Regiment of Irish infantry and these 15 blacks became the first Afro-American Masons. In 1776 Hall was granted a license, and African Lodge No. 1, the first organized body of Afro-American Masons in the United States, was established (July 3). He subsequently applied for a charter from the white provincial Masonic authorities in America without success, and then wrote to the British Grand Lodge in 1784. Though a charter was granted that year, because of a mix-up, the charter was not delivered until three years later. Under this charter, African lodge No. 459 was formally organized in 1787 with Prince Hall as master. In 1797 Hall was granted warrants to establish lodges in Philadelphia, Pa., and Providence, R.I. *See also* FRATERNAL SOCIETIES.

HALL, WILLIAM MARTIN (1926–), physician, gerontologist; born in Detroit, Mich. Hall received a B.A. degree from Lincoln University (Lincoln University, Pa.) in 1947 and his M.D. degree from Meharry Medical College (Nashville, Tenn.) in 1953. He was an intern at the Medical Center, Jersey City, N.J. in 1953 and later at Harlem Hospital, New York, N.Y. Hall served in the U.S. Navy from 1954 to 1956, becoming a lieutenant commander. He was instrumental in the establishment of the Garwin Medical Center in Baltimore, Md., and became president of the center in 1968. Hall was president of the staff of the Lutheran Hospital, Baltimore, Md., the first black physician to become a staff president in a white hospital in Maryland. He was also on the staff of Provident Hospital, Chicago, Ill.; Sinai Hospital, New York, N.Y.; and the Greater Baltimore Medical Center, Baltimore, Md. Hall served on many civic boards including the board of directors of Planned Parenthood.

HAMER, FANNIE LOU (1917–1977), civil rights leader, farmer; born in Montgomery County, Miss. She was the youngest of 20 children of poor sharecropping parents. Without very much formal education, and leaving her life as a cotton sharecropper, she joined the civil rights activists in 1962. She was a founder of the Mississippi Freedom Democratic Party (MFDP), which challenged the white-ruled regular party for representation, especially at the National Democratic Convention in 1964. *See also* MISSISSIPPI FREEDOM DEMOCRATIC PARTY (MFDP); POLITICS.

HAMILTON, CHARLES V. (1929–), political scientist, educator; born in Muskogee, Okla. Hamilton reveived a B.A. degree from Roosevelt University (Chicago, Ill.) in 1951, his J.D. degree from Loyola University (Chicago, Ill.) in 1954, and a M.A. degree (1957) and his Ph.D. degree (1964) from the University of Chicago. He taught at Albany State College (Albany, Ga.), at Tuskegee Institute (Tuskegee Institute, Ala.), and at Rutgers University (New Brunswick, N.J.) before joining the faculty of Lincoln University as professor of political science in 1964. In 1967 Hamilton returned to Roosevelt University for two years, after which he was appointed professor of political science at Columbia University. He authored many articles and books, including *Black Power: The Politics of Liberation in America* (1967), which he wrote with Stokely Carmichael; *The Black Experience in American Politics* (1973); and *The Bench and the Ballot* (1973).

HAMILTON, GRACE TOWNS 1907–), educator, state legislator; born in Atlanta, Ga. Hamilton received a B.A. degree from Atlanta University in 1927 and her M.A. degree from Ohio State University in 1929. She taught at LeMoyne College (Memphis, Tenn.; now LeMoyne-Owen College) from 1927 to 1928, and the following year at Clark College (Atlanta, Ga.). She directed a survey of white-collar and skilled Afro-American workers in Memphis from 1930 to 1934, and was associate director of the Southern Regional Council in Atlanta from 1935 to 1936. Hamilton was a Rosenwald Fellow from 1947 to 1948, and was executive director of the Atlanta Urban League from 1943 to 1960. In 1966 she was elected to the Georgia house of representatives from the 112th District in Atlanta, the first black woman to be seated in the Georgia legislature.

HAMILTON, HENRY COOKE (1899–), educator; born in Memphis, Tenn. Hamilton received a B.A. degree from Atlanta University in 1921, a M.A. degree from the University of Pittsburgh in 1928, and his Ed.D. degree from the University of Cincinnati (Cincinnati, Ohio) in 1937. He was affiliated with Morehouse College (Atlanta, Ga.) and Atlanta University; was an instructor of mathematics at Alabama Agricultural and Mechanical (A & M) University (Normal, Ala.), and at Durham State Normal School (Durham, N.C.); and was dean of LeMoyne College (Memphis, Tenn.; now LeMoyne-Owen College) from 1928 to 1930. Hamilton wrote *The Vocabulary of Plane Geometry* (1928).

HAMILTON, PAUL L. (1941–   ), state legislator; born in Pueblo, Colo. Hamilton received a B.A. degree from the University of Denver (Denver, Colo.), and then taught in the Denver public school system. In 1969 he was elected a representative to the Colorado legislature, and in 1971 he became a member of the advisory board of the Colorado Commission on Higher Education.

HAMLET, JAMES FRANK (1921–   ), Army officer; born in Alliance, Ohio. After receiving a B.S. degree in business administration from Saint Benedict's College (Atchison, Kans.), Hamlet entered the U.S. Army. His military service included three years in South Vietnam, where he became commanding general of the Third Brigade, First Calvary Division. Subsequently, Hamlet became commanding general of the Fourth Infantry Division (mechanized), Fort Carson, Colo., with the rank of major general.

A class in physics at Hampton Institute, early 1900s. (Hampton Institute.)

HAMMOND, BENJAMIN E. See SCIENTISTS: BIOLOGICAL, PHYSICAL.

HAMPTON INSTITUTE Hampton Institute, at Hampton, Va., was founded in 1868 by Samuel Chapman Armstrong, a 27-year-old brevet brigadier general who commanded the U.S. 8th and 9th black troops during the Civil War. A private, coeducational, independent school, Hampton offers the bachelor's and the master's degrees, and provides liberal arts, teacher education, and vocational curricula. Its 1975 enrollment was about 2,800.

Hampton Normal and Agricultural Institute, as it was first known, opened its doors in 1868 to train selected young Afro-Americans, beginning at the elementary level, to teach and lead their people. Enlisting the support of northern philanthropists and religious groups, General Armstrong was able to secure funds to purchase a waterfront estate within a mile or two of where the Monitor battled the Merrimac. General James A. Garfield served as a member of Hampton's board of trustees from 1870 to 1876, and as president of the United States he traveled to Hampton, where he gave his last public speech. President William H. Taft also served as a member of Hampton's board of trustees from 1909 to 1913 and as chairman of the board from 1914 to 1930.

One of Hampton's most eminent graduates was Booker T. Washington, founder of Tuskegee Institute (Tuskegee Institute, Ala.). In his autobiography, *Up From Slavery,* Washington describes his life as a Hampton student and his work there after his graduation in 1875. In 1878 a group of American Indians came to Hampton to be educated with the help of federal funds. An unusual aspect of Hampton was its famed choirs. Under R. Nathaniel Dett in the 1920s (and Roland Carter in the 1970s), the choirs traveled widely in the United States and abroad and brought to the world's attention Hampton's rich musical heritage. Dorothy Maynor, who trained under Dett, achieved an important career as a concert artist.

In 1922 courses leading to the bachelor of science degree were offered. Courses at the elementary and secondary levels were gradually dropped, and the entire resources of the institution were concentrated upon education at the college level. Unrestricted accreditation as a full-fledged four-year college came in the period 1932–33. In 1961, under the auspices of the Agency of International Development (AID),

Hampton Institute undertook the establishment of its first Rural Training Institute at Kenema, Sierra Leone, West Africa.

The college today is interracial and intercultural in both its student body and its faculty.

HAMPTON, LIONEL (1913–   ), jazz vibraphonist, bandleader; born in Louisville, Ky. Hampton was raised in Birmingham, Ala., and Chicago, Ill. He was a drummer with Les Hite's band in California before he formed his own Los Angeles group, playing both drum and vibraphone solos. Hampton played the vibraphone with Benny Goodman's band (1936–40), after which he formed his own permanent orchestra. During the 1940s and 1950s he toured throughout the United States, Europe, North Africa, the Near East, and Australia. Some of his best-known tunes include "Lady Be Good," "Jumpin' at the Woodside," and "Flyin' Home" (1939). *See also* MUSIC: JAZZ.

HANCOCK, GORDON BLAINE (1884–1970), educator, clergyman, journalist. Based mainly in Richmond, Va. Hancock used the pulpit, classroom, and press to preach black uplift and pride. His first biography was written by Raymond Gavins, *The Perils and Prospects of Southern Black Leadership: Gordon Blaine Hancock, 1884–1970*, Duke, Durham, N.C., 1977.

HANDY, WILLIAM CHRISTOPHER (W. C.) (1873–1958), composer, musician; born in Florence,

Ala. Handy is known as the "Father of the Blues" because he was the first composer to recognize the musical importance of the blues and to write them down. He also composed many spirituals. As a youngster, discouraged by his parents from pursuing a musical career, Handy secretly bought a cornet and later began playing in a band and singing in a minstrel quartet. During the early part of his career, he played with the Hampton Cornet Band and performed with Mahara's Minstrels. After a teaching stint, Handy became director of a black fraternal band in Clarksdale, Miss., and it was here that he decided to arrange and compose music rooted in black folk experience. Moving to Memphis, Tenn., he formed a band that played in Beale Street saloons, at picnics and funerals, and for political campaigns. In 1912 Handy published the first blues composition ever to be published: "The Memphis Blues." Other important blues written by Handy include "St. Louis Blues" (1914), "Joe Turner Blues" (1915), "Beale Street Blues" (1917), and "John Henry Blues." Handy also wrote several marches, "Careless Love," and "Afro-American Hymn." *See also* MUSIC: HISTORY AND DEVELOPMENT. MUSIC: BLUES.

HANSBERRY, LORRAINE (1930–65), playwright; born in Chicago, Ill. After graduating from high school in 1948, Hansberry studied stage design and drama at the University of Wisconsin for two years and painting at the Art Institute of Chicago. Her first play, *A Raisin in the Sun*, opened on Broadway in 1959 with Claudia McNeil, Ruby Dee, and Sidney Poitier in the cast. It had the longest run of any play by a black author up to that time, and won the New York Drama Critics Circle Award. In 1973 it was revived as a musical, *Raisin*, which won the Tony Award for best musical. Her second play, *The Sign in Sidney Brustein's Window*, about white intellectual political involvement, had a brief run, closing on the day of her death. She was also the author of poems, articles, and a book, *To Be Young, Gifted and Black* (1969). Presented as a play in 1968–69, it became the longest running play of the off-Broadway season. Other works include *The Movement: Documentary of a Struggle for Equality* (1964) and *Les Blancs: The Collected Last Plays of Lorraine Hansberry* (1972). *See also* LITERATURE: DRAMA THEATER; LITERATURE: THE NOVEL.

Far left:
W. C. Handy. (Moorland-Spingarn Research Center, Howard University.)

HANSBERRY, WILLIAM LEO (1894–1965), educator; born in Gloster, Miss. Hansberry received a B.A. (1921) and his M.A. (1932) degrees from Harvard University. As professor of African history at Howard University for almost forty years, he helped and inspired many American and African students and scholars in their study of African history, and some of his students have become well-known in their own right as scholars in the field. He himself received the first Haile Selassie Prize Trust Award (1964) for his original work in African history, archaeology, and anthropology. He was co-founder of the African American Institute in Washington, D. C. (1952) and later became trustee and vice president of the Institute. The University of Nigeria's Hansberry College of African Studies, where he was advisor and Distinguished Scholar, was named for him. His book, *The William Leo Hansberry Notebook*, was published posthumously: *Pillars of Ethiopian History*, Vol. I (1974) and *Africa and Africans as Seen by Classical Writers*, Vol. II (1977).

HARALSON, JEREMIAH (1846–1916), congressman; born in Muscogee County, Ga. His parents were slaves and he was self-educated. Haralson entered politics in Alabama after the Civil War and was elected to the House of Representatives in 1874, serving for two years. Having been accused of fraud, he was forced to submit to a run-off election, which he won. He later moved to Colorado.

HARDEN, K. ALBERT (1905–75), physician, educator; born in Bessemer, Ala. Harden received a B.A. degree from the University of Michigan in 1927 and his M.D. degree from the University of Michigan Medical School in 1931. He served in various capacities at Howard University Medical College (Washington, D.C.) from 1941 to 1962, becoming vice-dean in 1962 and dean in 1966.

HARDING, VINCENT (1931–   ), historian, educator; born in New York, N.Y. Harding graduated from the City College of New York in 1952, received a M.S. degree from Columbia University in 1953, and received a M.A. degree (1956) and his Ph.D. degree (1965) from the University of Chicago. A lay pastor for the Seventh Day Adventist Mission Church and the Woodlawn Mennonite Church, both in Chicago, Ill., Harding also served as a representative for the Mennonite Service Committee as a negotiator and troubleshooter in southern civil rights disputes. From 1965 to 1969 Harding was chairman of the department of history and sociology at Spelman College (Atlanta, Ga.). Formerly a director of the Martin Luther King, Jr., Library in Georgia, Harding became

director of the Institute of the Black World, one of the four components of the Martin Luther King, Jr., Memorial Center, which was formed in 1969 for research and analysis of black education.

HARE, MAUD CUNEY (1874–1936), pianist, author; born in Galveston, Tex. Hare received her musical education at the New England Conservatory (Boston, Mass.) and later under private instructors. She became director of music at the Deaf, Dumb, and Blind Institute of Texas and at Prairie View State College (Prairie View, Tex., now Prairie View Agricultural and Mechanical (A & M) College). During her travels, she lectured, performed, and collected songs from Mexico, the Virgin Islands, Puerto Rico, and Cuba. In addition to her contributions to many periodicals, she published several books, including *Creole Songs*, *Negro Musicians and Their Music*, and *The Message of the Trees*.

HAREWOOD, RICHARD ALEXANDER (1900–   ), lawyer, judge, state legislator; born in Barbados, British West Indies. After service in World War I and after becoming a naturalized citizen of the United States in 1918, Harewood received a B.A. degree from the University of Illinois in 1922 and his J.D. degree from the University of Chicago in 1926. After admission to the Illinois bar in 1926, he began practicing law in Chicago, Ill. Harewood became assistant state attorney for Cook County from 1944 to 1947, and served in the Illinois general assembly from 1937 to 1938 and again from 1957 to 1958. He became a judge of Cook County Superior Court in 1962, remaining on that bench until 1970. Harewood then became judge of the Circuit Court of Cook County.

HARGRAVES, JAMES ARCHIE See SHAW UNIVERSITY.

HARGROVE, JOHN R. (1923–   ), lawyer, judge; born in Atlantic City, N.J. Hargrove received a B.A. degree from Howard University (Washington, D.C.) and his LL.B. degree from the University of Maryland. He was admitted to the Maryland bar in 1950. Hargrove began his career on the bench in 1962 as judge of the People's Court of Baltimore, Md., and later became judge of the Municipal Court of Baltimore. Hargrove was then appointed administrative judge of the District Court in Baltimore.

HARLEM

HARLEM Located on Manhattan Island north of Central Park between 8th Avenue and the East and Harlem rivers in New York City, N.Y., Harlem constitutes an area of about six square miles. It is perhaps the best known of all black communities and has been one of the main residential areas for black Americans in the city throughout the 1900s. Although blacks first arrived and lived in Manhattan when it was under Dutch control, they did not settle in Harlem until the late 1800s. Brought in by the Dutch in 1626 as indentured or bonded servants (workers), eleven blacks first lived in lower Manhattan in the vicinity of Fort Amsterdam and Wall Street; later they were freed of their bonds. However, 20 years later, in 1646, the first slave ship arrived at Manhattan Island with most of its human cargo from Curacao, a Dutch colony in the West Indies. Though a free black community was to develop in Manhattan and nearby Brooklyn over the years, slavery remained legal and in force in New York for 200 years, that is, until the period of the 1830s. Meanwhile, the main centers of the black population in the state had grown to about 16,000 by 1830. The 14,000 blacks who lived in Manhattan were confined to areas on the lower part of the island south of 14th Street, including settlements in the vicinity of City Hall, Catherine Street Market, Greenwich Village, and Avenue C. Except for a major settlement near Second Avenue and 29th Street, where draft rioters terrorized blacks during the Civil War, much of the black population remained largely south of 14th Street until 1900. By this date, however, there were a few noticeable pockets of blacks in mid-Manhattan: a neighborhood known as San Juan Hill, west of Central Park in the vicinity of 61st–63rd Streets; and a more famous settlement known as Black Bohemia Behind the El (elevated trains) in the vicinity of West 53rd Street. This area, and especially the Marshal Club on 53rd Street, was frequented by black celebrities of the period like Joe Gans and Sam Langford (pugilists), Bert Williams and George Walker (entertainers), Will Marion Cook and James Europe (musicians), and Paul Laurence Dunbar and James Weldon Johnson (poets and writers).

More significantly, at the turn of the century blacks penetrated well-to-do areas at the northern end of Central Park and beyond into Harlem: first at 99th Street by 1903 and at 125th Street by 1910. Penetration in these areas was abetted by realty speculators who extracted high mortgages or rents from the black newcomers. It was also abetted by population pressures upon black New Yorkers who had a long history of restrictions and discrimination against them in regard to housing, jobs, and education. Most of the realty speculators were white; but two outstanding black ones were Phillip A. Payton, who founded the Afro-American Realty Company in 1904, and John G. Taylor who founded the Harlem Property Owners' Improvement Association in 1913. To pay the landlords—some later called "slumlords"—many black tenants in Harlem took in boarders, or roomers, or gave Saturday night "rent parties." Houses that were once elegant and roomy were partitioned into rooming houses; and it was not unheard of for some lodgers to sleep in bath tubs. Needless to say, overcrowding brought a chain of problems in its wake: crime, squalor, diseases, decay, vermin, and emotional and psychological strain. Inevitably, like many areas in similar circumstances, Harlem deteriorated.

Whether white or black, real estate brokers

A scene on 125th Street near the Apollo Theater in the early 1930s. (*National Archives.*)

reaped large profits from the masses of black immigrants who poured into Harlem during the first three or four decades of the 1900s. Census figures do not show the number of blacks in Harlem in 1900; but they do show Manhattan as having 36,000, a number that was twice the size of all other blacks in New York City, and slightly more than a third the size of all blacks in the state. By 1930, the city's black population had reached 152,000, of which 109,000 were in Manhattan. Either through immigration or natural increase, New York City's black population had reached the million mark in the late 1950s, the first American city to obtain this level. In 1970 the city had a black population of 1,885,000; of this number (in rounded figures), Manhattan had 380,000; the Bronx, 358,000; Queens, 258,000; Richmond, 16,000. Brooklyn was the largest with 656,000. Of Manhattan's 380,000 in 1970, Harlem contained about 300,000, or a population density of about 50,000 blacks per square mile.

With high densities, high unemployment, and low incomes, together with high cultural propensities to "jive" or "rap," it is understandable that Harlemites frequently inhabited their streets, or appreciated the role that streets played in their lives, as revealed in novels by Ann L. Petry (*The Street*, 1946), and Claude Brown (*Manchild in the Promised Land*, 1965).

A scene on 125th Street in the mid-1970s. (*Ronald I. Duncan.*)

Wide and planted with an island of greenery, Seventh Avenue invited some of Harlem's most spectacular parades. Its intersection with 125th Street formed one of the liveliest corners in the area. Here an assortment of speakers—religious, political, or cultural, some eloquent and rational—could mount their stump in hope of finding an audience in the passers-by.

The following description of Lenox Avenue was written by C. Gerald Fraizer, "Harlem, A Myth and Reality," *Black Enterprise* December, 1971, p. 55, 1971:

Lenox Avenue is one of Harlem's most fascinating streets. Its 39 blocks contain almost all the elements of black urban communities. It begins at Central Park North, actually West 110th Street but renamed by Harlemites to give their end of the park equal status with downtown, predominantly white Central Park South. Most prominent at this end of Lenox is the tall, austere Martin Luther King Houses (formerly the Stephen Foster Houses), a low-income housing "project." The avenue ends about two miles north with the equally tall, balconied apartments of Esplanade Gardens, a middle income cooperative housing "development." In between are the storefront churches, the bars, the restaurants, funeral chapels, schools, two-story frame houses and tenements that contribute to the avenue's vast diversity. Lenox is also an avenue of contrasts, but it is large enough to contain them. On the avenue are the massive Mt. Olivet Baptist Church and the magnificent half-million-dollar Muhammad's Mosque No. 7 with its golden dome and rotating star and crescent; the Club Baron, Harlem's only nightspot where contemporary jazz giants can still be heard; Bond-Ryder Associates, Harlem's only black architectural firm, and sitting like a big blue box on the avenue is Harlem Hospital's new Martin Luther King pavilion, which probably employs more people than any other single institution or business in Harlem.

And, crowding the broad sidewalks almost 24 hours every day are the people, the early morning wave of exiting wage earners making it to work, the shopkeepers raising their corrugated and hopefully riot-proof steel gates, school children and then later, the shoppers, the number runners and their customers, the pushers and assorted other hustlers.

Lenox Avenue is more than a street. It is also a symbol of itself as well as of Harlem. It conjures up images or memories of Harlem's past, or of an aging Harlem, faded, jaded, but alive in its history, literature, or lore. Many migrants from many distant places, such as Claude McKay, did indeed find a home in Harlem (*Home to Harlem*, 1928). Like him, many walked its streets or wrote of Lenox Avenue. Some, like Malcolm X of the Black Muslims, found a passionate, fatal misson in Harlem. Others found in Harlem the underlying warmth in the souls of black folk, as did Langston Hughes in his character, Jesse B. Semple. James Baldwin, like others who were born in and grew up in Harlem, escaped its suppressive ghetto and protested against this suppression brilliantly and eloquently in *Tell Me How Long the Train's Been Gone*, 1968.

Harlem was a home or stopover for many celebrities of stage, screen, night club, radio, or television; for artists, musicians, singers, intellectuals, writers, Bohemians and revolutionaries. Whatever the magnitude of its social and economic problems, Harlem's place in Afro-American life and history is secure. *See also* ABYSSINIAN BAPTIST CHURCH; CIVIL DISORDERS: DISCRIMINATION: HOUSING; LITERATURE: POETRY; POPULATION.

REFERENCES: There are many references about Harlem, especially in periodical literature. Four of the best books, however, are James Weldon Johnson, *Black Manhattan*, first published in 1930 and reprinted in 1940 and 1968; Roy Ottley and William J. Weatherby (eds.), *The Negro in New York* (1967); Gilbert Osofsky, *Harlem: The Making of a Ghetto; Negro New York, 1890–1930* (1966); and Seth M. Scheiner, *Negro Mecca: A History of the Negro in New York City* (1965).

HARLEM RENAISSANCE *See* LITERATURE: POETRY; NATIONAL ASSOCIATION FOR THE ADVANCEMENT OF COLORED PEOPLE (NAACP).

HARMON, JOHN H. (1906–   ), economist; born in Houston, Tex. Harmon received a B.S. degree from Howard University (Washington, D.C.) in 1926 and his M.S. degree from Columbia University in 1927. He served as director of the National Business League; was owner of the Harmon Information and Business Service, Inc.; and was founder and executive director of the Afro-American Cultural Foundation in White Plains, N.Y. Harmon wrote *The Negro as Business Man* with Carter G. Woodson.

HARPER, FRANCES ELLEN (1825–1911), poet; born in Baltimore, Md. Born of free parents, Harper was educated in Baltimore at a school run by her uncle. Born Frances Watkins, she married Fenton Harper in 1860. A volume of her verse, *Poems on Miscellaneous Subjects* (1857), sold 10,000 copies in the first five years following publication. Her other works include *Sketches of Southern Life* (1872) and *Moses: A Story of the Nile* (1869). The most popular black poet of her time, she raised the question of whether Afro-American authors should dwell on their own racial problems or address such wider issues as temperance. *See also* LITERATURE: POETRY.

HARRELD, KEMPER (1885–1971), violinist, educator; born in Muncie, Ind. Harreld received his musical education at Chicago Musical College (Chicago, Ill.) and at Stern Conservatory of Music (Berlin, Germany). He joined the faculty of Morehouse College Atlanta, Ga.) in 1911, and taught at Spelman College (Atlanta, Ga.) after 1927. Harreld was one of the founders of the National Association of Negro Musicians in 1919.

HARRINGTON, OLIVER WENDELL (1913–   ), painter, cartoonist; born in Valhalla, N.Y. Harrington received a B.F.A. degree from Yale University in 1938 and later studied at the National Academy of Design. Harrington was art editor of *The Peoples Voice*. Known for his crisply drawn cartoons—including the "Bootsie" series that appeared in the Pittsburgh *Courier*—he has been called America's "socio-artist."

HARRIS, ABRAM L. (1899–1963), economist; born in Richmond, Va. Harris graduated from Virginia Union University in 1922, and received a M.A. degree from the University of Pittsburgh in 1924 and his Ph.D. degree from Columbia University in 1931. After a brief instructorship in economics in 1924 at West Virginia State College, he joined the faculty of Howard University (Washington, D.C.) as assistant professor of economics in 1927. Harris remained at Howard until 1945, having become head of the economics department in 1936. In 1946 he moved to the University of Chicago where, in various capacities, he taught and lectured until 1950. Harris wrote *Economics and Social Reform* (1958), and contributed articles to scientific journals and encyclopedias.

HARRIS, CHARLES F. (1934–   ), editor, publisher; born in Portsmouth, Va. Harris graduated from Virginia State College in 1955 and then did graduate work at New York University. In 1956 he became a research analyst for Doubleday & Co., and in 1960 helped to found its Zenith Books division. Harris later was appointed vice-president and general manager of Portal Press, a division of John Wiley and Sons, and then served as a senior editor at Random House. In 1971 Harris became executive director of the Howard University Press, Washington, D.C.

HARRIS, FRANCO (1950–   ), A native of New Jersey, Harris was recruited from Pennsylvania State University by the Pittsburgh Steelers in

1972. Within a few years, he was established as a leading rusher in the league (averaging about 4.7 yards per attempt) and scoring 20 touchdowns in 38 games. He set a Super Bowl record in 1975 for most yards gained (158). *See also* ATHLETES.

HARRIS, JAMES ALEXANDER (1926–   ), educator; born in Des Moines, Ia. Harris earned a B.A. in fine arts in 1948 and a M.A. in 1955 from Drake University (Des Moines). He also studied at Drake's Divinity College; served in the military; taught at a junior high school. In 1974 he was elected president of the National Education Association (NEA), the first black man to head this organization.

HARRIS, JAMES T. *See* NEWSPAPERS: CONTEMPORARY.

HARRIS, MARQUIS LAFAYETTE (1907–   ), educator, clergyman; born in Armstrong, Ala. Harris received a B.S. degree from Clark College (Atlanta, Ga.) in 1928, a B.D. degree from Gammon Theological Seminary in 1929, a M.A. degree (1930) and a S.T.M. degree (1930) from Boston University, and his Ph.D. degree from Ohio State University in 1933. He taught physics, chemistry, and mathematics at Clark College from 1927 to 1929, physics and religion at Claflin College (Orangeburg, N.C.) from 1930 to 1931, and was a clergyman at the Methodist Episcopal Church in Columbus, Ohio from 1932 to 1933. Harris served as dean and professor of sociology at Samuel Houston College (Dallas, Tex.) in 1933 and at Philander Smith College (Little Rock, Ark.) from 1936 to 1960, where he also became president.

Patricia Roberts Harris. *(Department of Housing and Urban Development.)*

HARRIS, PATRICIA ROBERTS (1924–   ), lawyer, educator; born in Mattoon, Ill. Harris finished her undergraduate studies at Howard University (Washington, D.C.) with a *summa cum laude* B.A. degree in 1945. Before going on to receive her J.D. degree with honors from George Washington University Law School (Washington, D.C.) in 1960, she did postgraduate work at the University of Chicago and at American University (Washington, D.C.). Harris was admitted to practice before the U.S. Supreme Court and to the District of Columbia bar in 1960. After working for the U.S. Department of Justice for a year, she served as associate dean of students and lecturer in law at Howard University from 1961 to

1963. In 1963 Harris became professor of law at Howard, and in 1969 she was made dean of the School of Law. During this period, from 1965 to 1967, she also served as ambassador to Luxembourg. Following her deanship, Harris joined a Washington, D.C., law firm as a partner. By this time her educational recognition had expanded to include several degrees from institutions throughout the country. During her career, Harris was active on numerous committees and commissions dedicated to the fight for civil rights. A political person as well, she was a delegate to the Democratic National Convention in 1964, a presidential elector from the District of Columbia in 1964, chairman of the credentials committee in 1972, and a member-at-large of the Democratic National Committee in 1973. President Jimmy Carter appointed her to his cabinet as Secretary of Housing and Urban Development (HUD) in 1977.

HARRIS TEACHERS COLLEGE Harris Teachers College, at St. Louis, Mo., was founded in 1857 (for whites) as the first public teacher education institution west of the Mississippi River. Now a city-supported interracial school, Harris offers the bachelor's degree and provides a teacher education curriculum. Its 1975 enrollment was about 900.

The school was named after William Torrey Harris, a former U.S. commissioner of education and superintendent of instruction for the St. Louis public school system. In 1954 Harris merged with Stowe Teachers College (for blacks), which had been the companion institution to Harris before the famous case of *Brown v. Board of Education of Topeka.* The college is housed in a building that was once an all-black high school, Vashon, constructed in 1927.

HARRISON, GENERAL LA MAR (1899–   ), educator; born in Terrell, Tex. Harrison received a B.A. degree from Howard University (Washington, D.C.), in 1926, and his Ph.D. degree from Ohio State University in 1935. He was professor and director of elementary teacher training at West Virginia State College (1928–32), and later became president of Langston University (Langston, Okla.).

HARRISON, HAZEL (1881– ?), pianist, educator; born in La Porte, Ind. Harrison studied piano in Chicago, Ill., and later in Berlin, Germany, and from 1903 to 1906 she played with the Berlin Philharmonic Orchestra. She toured the United States in the 1920s, appearing with the Los Angeles, Minneapolis, and Chicago symphony orchestras. Later she taught at Tuskegee Institute (Tuskegee Institute, Ala.), and in the 1940s Harrison became a member of the faculty of Howard University (Washington, D.C.).

HARRISON, HUBERT (1883–1927), socialist, editor; born in St. Croix, Virgin Islands. Harrison arrived in New York City about 1900, where he worked at such odd jobs as waiter, porter, and elevator operator while embarking on an intensive process of self-education. In 1917 he organized the Liberty League, based in New York City's Harlem, which was devoted to the furthering of the black cause; he also founded and edited the league's newspaper, *The Voice*. An outstanding orator, Harrison was able to attract crowds wherever he spoke. He lectured in churches and local halls, and at such schools as the City College of the City University of New York, New York University, and the Modern School. Harrison offered Marcus Garvey his first public platform in New York City on June 12, 1917, at the Bethel African Methodist Episcopal Church. For four years Harrison helped edit the Garveyite paper, the *Negro World*. He lost much of his influence as internal problems began to splinter the Liberty League and many of its members dropped out or joined the Garveyite movement. In 1917 Harrison published *The Negro and the Nation*. He died in New York City, poor and almost entirely forgotten. *See also* GARVEY, MARCUS.

HARRISON, RICHARD BERRY (DE LAWD) (1864–1935), actor, educator; born in Canada. The young Harrison, whose parents had escaped from slavery in the United States, traveled to Detroit, Mich., where his interest in the theater was nourished. He trained in elocution, and began reciting professionally on both the Behymer (L.E. Behymer had been his friend) and Chautauqua circuits. His repertoire included recitations from Shakespeare, Poe, Kipling, and Dunbar. Sometime later, he went to North Carolina Agricultural and Technical (A & T) State University where he taught drama and elocution. It was while Harrison was teaching, in 1929, that he was selected to play "De Lawd" in Marc Connelly's *Green Pastures*. Before the end of his life, he played this role nearly 2,000 times.

Although his fame derived from this popular part, Harrison spent most of his career teaching, lecturing, and arranging festivals for black schools and churches. An auditorium was named in his honor at the North Carolina A & T State University. *See also* LITERATURE: DRAMA/ THEATER; MOTION PICTURES.

HARSH, VIVIAN G. (1894–1960), librarian; born in Chicago, Ill. After attending high school, Harsh went to the Library School of the University of Chicago. In 1932 she began the Harsh Collection on Afro-American History and Literature at the George Cleveland Hall branch of the Chicago Public Library. The collection includes a file on black history in Illinois prepared by the Works Progress Administration (WPA) and such writers as Arna Bontemps and Richard Wright. Original manuscripts and the *Chicago Afro-American Union Analytic Catalogue*, a guide to writings by or about blacks, are also included in the collection. Containing more than 75,000 entries, the catalogue was published in book form in 1972. *See also* BIBLIOGRAPHIES/BIOGRAPHIES/GUIDES (Chicago Public Library).

HART, WILLIAM H. H. (1857–1934), lawyer, educator; born in Eufaula, Ala. Hart graduated from the preparatory department of Howard University (Washington, D.C.) in 1880, from the college department in 1885, and from the law department in 1887. For 25 years he served as professor of criminal law in the Howard University School of Law, meanwhile working in the U.S. Department of the Treasury, the U.S. Department of Agriculture, and the Library of Congress (Washington, D.C.). Hart was also an assistant to the district attorney for the District of Columbia, and was well known for his fight in 1904 against the Jim Crow laws of the state of Maryland.

HARTSHORN, HERBERT HADLEY (1909–   ), educator; born in St. Joseph, Mo. Hartshorn received a B.S. degree from Lincoln University (Jefferson City, Mo.) in 1930, and a M.A. degree (1940) and his Ph.D. degree (1948) from the University of Minnesota. He was dean of Saint Phillips Junior College, director of extension schools at Samuel Houston College (Dallas, Tex.) from 1932 to 1936, and a social worker in St. Louis, Mo., from 1935 to 1936. Hartshorn also taught at the Laboratory High School of Lincoln University from 1936 to 1940, served as its principal from

Richard B. Harrison. *(Moorland-Spingarn Research Center, Howard University.)*

1940 to 1948, and after that became the dean of students at Lincoln University from 1948 to 1950. In 1950 he moved to Texas Southern University, where he became vice-president of the university in 1970.

HARVEY, JOHN W. (1913–), lawyer, judge; born in St. Louis, Mo. Harvey received both his B.S. and LL.B. degrees from Lincoln University (Jefferson City, Mo.). He was admitted to the Missouri bar in 1942. A president of the Mount City Bar Association, Harvey was appointed judge of the Magistrate Court in St. Louis.

HARVEY, MCCLENNON PHILLIP (1917–), editor, publisher; born in Waco, Tex. Harvey received a B.A. degree from Paul Quinn College (Waco, Tex.) in 1939 and studied at Texas Southern University in 1954: He was teacher, business manager, and director of public relations at Paul Quinn College. Harvey then became editor and owner of the Waco *Messenger*, and president of Smith Printing Company after 1961. He was a member of the local Urban Renewal Commission, and of the advisory board of Paul Quinn College.

HASKELL, ROSCOE CHESTER (1881– ?), physician; born in St. Louis, Mo. Haskell attended Genner Medical College (Chicago, Ill.) and Howard University (Washington, D.C.), and received his M.D. degree from Meharry Medical College (Nashville, Tenn.) in 1911. He interned at Mercy Hospital, Nashville, Tenn., and at Kansas City General Hospital, and served as superintendent of City Hospital No. 2, St. Louis, Mo., (1918–26).

HASTIE, WILLIAM HENRY (1904–1976), educator, lawyer, government official, judge; born in Knoxville, Tenn. Hastie received a B.A. degree from Amherst College (Amherst, Mass.) in 1925, and a LL.B. degree (1930) and his S.J.D. degree (1933) from Harvard University. In 1930 he joined the faculty of the School of Law at Howard University (Washington, D.C.), where he remained for seven years. While teaching, Hastie was admitted to the District of Columbia bar and joined the firm of Houston and Houston. During that period, he was also brought into President Franklin D. Roosevelt's New Deal administration and served as assistant solicitor in the U.S. Department of Interior from 1933 to 1937, despite southern objections to his "leftist" leanings and his connections with the National Association for the Advancement of Colored People (NAACP). In 1937 Hastie was appointed by President Roosevelt as judge of the U.S. District Court for the Virgin Islands, the first Afro-American to be appointed to a federal bench. He returned to Howard University in 1939 as professor of law and dean of the School of Law, taking a leave of absence from 1940 to 1943 in order to serve as civilian aide to Secretary of War Henry L. Stimson. In protest over the continued segregation practiced by the U.S. Army and the Army Air Corps, he left this position and returned to Howard University, where he remained for three years until 1946, when President Harry S. Truman appointed him governor of the Virgin Islands. In 1949 President Truman appointed him judge of the U.S. Court of Appeals, Third Circuit. Hastie retired from this position in 1971, after serving for 21 years. *See also* HOUSTON, CHARLES HAMILTON; LAWYERS.

HASTINGS, ALICIA E. physician, educator; Hastings received a B.S. degree from Lincoln University (Jefferson City, Mo.) and her M.D. degree from Howard University Medical College (Washington, D.C.) in 1959. She interned at General Rose Memorial Hospital, Denver, Colo., and was awarded a fellowship in physical medicine and rehabilitation at the University of Colorado Medical Center. Hastings then served as assistant professor and as chief of the department of physical medicine and rehabilitation at Howard University Medical College, becoming chairman of the department in 1967.

HATCHER, ANDREW J. (1925–), journalist, press secretary; born in Princeton, N.J. Hatcher received a B.A. degree from Springfield College (Springfield, Mass.). He then served on the staff of the San Francisco *Sun-Reporter*, and in 1960 President John F. Kennedy appointed him as associate press secretary, a position he resigned after President Kennedy's assassination in 1963.

HATCHER, RICHARD G. (1933–), lawyer, mayor; born in Michigan City, Ind. Hatcher received a B.S. degree from Indiana University in 1956 and a LL.B. degree from Valparaiso University (Valparaiso, Ind.) in 1959. Admitted to the Indiana bar the year of his graduation, he opened a law office in East Chicago, Ind. Hatcher was an active member of the National Association for the Advancement of Colored People (NAACP), and joined with that organization in demonstrations protesting segregation and other curtailments of civil rights. He was one of the founding members of a political/social club called Muigwithania, which became his political base. In 1961 Hatcher was appointed deputy prosecutor of the Criminal Court of Lake County, Ind. But in 1963 he resigned to take a seat on the Gary, Ind., city council as councilman-at-large. Following three years on the city council, Hatcher was elected mayor of Gary in 1967, becoming the first black mayor of a large northern city. He was reelected in 1971. In 1972 Hatcher served as one of the three leaders of the National Black Political Convention along with Imamu A. Baraka and Congressman Charles C. Diggs of Michigan.

HAUGHTON, JAMES G. (1925–), physician, administrator; born in Panama City, Panama. Haughton received a B.A. degree from Pacific Union College (Angwin, Calif.) in 1947 and his M.D. degree from Loma Linda University (Loma Linda, Calif.) in 1950. He did postgraduate medical work at New York University Medical School (1959–60). In the early 1970s Haughton became executive director of the Health and Hospitals Governing Commission of Cook County (Chicago, Ill.), a position that made him responsible for the management of one of the world's largest medical facilities.

HAWKINS, AUGUSTUS FREEMAN (1907–), state legislator, U.S. Representative; born in Shreveport, La. Hawkins moved to California at the age of eleven, attended Los Angeles schools, and graduated from the University of California at Los Angeles in 1931. He spent the next year at the University of Southern California's Institute of Government. Engaged in a real estate and retail business in Los Angeles, Hawkins became active in politics and was sent to the California state assembly from Los Angeles in 1934. He remained a member of that body until 1962. At that time, he was elected to the Eighty-eighth Congress as representative from the 21st Congressional District of California.

HAWKINS, COLEMAN (BEAN) (1904–1969), jazz tenor saxophonist; born in St. Joseph, Mo. Hawkins studied at Washburn College (Topeka, Kans.) before joining Mamie Smith's Jazz Hounds in 1922. Later, he played in Fletcher Henderson's band (1923–34). After organizing his own band, Hawkins toured England and the Continent. His solo record, "Body and Soul," made in 1939, is a jazz classic. In 1944 Hawkins organized an all-star band for the first Bop recording sessions, and he gave encouragement to "Dizzy" Gillespie, Charlie "Bird" Parker, and other performers he admired. During the 1960s, Hawkins played in small combos. *See also* MUSIC: JAZZ.

HAWKINS, JOHN RUSSELL (1862–1939), educator; born in Warrenton, N.C. Hawkins attended Hampton Institute (Hampton, Va.) and graduated from Howard University School of Law (Washington, D.C.) in 1915. He was involved in railway-mail service from 1882 to 1884, before he joined Kittrell College (Kittrell, N.C.) in 1887, becoming its president in 1890.

HAWKINS, MASON ALBERT (1874–1947), educator; born in Charlottesville, Va. Hawkins received a B.A. degree from Harvard University in 1901, a M.A. degree from Columbia University in 1910, and his Ph.D. degree from the University of Pennsylvania in 1930. He served as principal of Douglass High School in Baltimore, Md., from 1909 until his retirement, after which time he became a professor at Morgan State University (Baltimore, Md.).

HAWKINS, REGINALD *See* CIVIL RIGHTS MOVEMENT; CIVIL RIGHTS MOVEMENT IN SELECTED STATES: NORTH CAROLINA.

HAWKINS, REGINALD ARMISTICE (1923–), dentist; born in Beaufort, N.C. Hawkins received a B.S. degree (1944) and a B.D. degree (1962) from Johnson C. Smith University (Charlotte, N.C.), and his D.D.S. degree from Howard University School of Dentistry (Washington, D.C.) in 1948. He practiced dentistry in Charlottesville, N.C., and served as a captain in the U.S. Army Dental Corps.

HAWKINS, W. ASHBY *See* CIVIL RIGHTS: CIVIL RIGHTS CASES, 1865–1975; LAWYERS.

HAWTHORNE, EDWARD W. (1921–), physician, educator; born in Alcorn, Miss. Hawthorne received a B.S. degree from Howard University (Washington, D.C.) in 1941, his M.D. degree from Howard University Medical College in 1946, and a M.S. degree (1949) and his Ph.D. degree in physiology (1951) from the University of Illinois. He was laboratory assistant in physiology at Howard University (1942–44), and an intern and assistant resident in internal medicine at Freedmen's Hospital, Washington, D.C. (1946–48). Hawthorne served as professor and as head of the department of physiology at How-

Coleman Hawkins.
(Burt Goldblatt.)

ard University Medical College (1951–69), becoming assistant dean in 1962 and associate dean in 1967. He also was a special consultant to the National Institutes of Health (1954–57), and he became vice-president-at-large of the American Heart Association in 1971.

HAYDEN, ROBERT (1913–   ), poet; born in Detroit, Mich. After receiving a B.A. degree and a M.A. degree from Wayne State University (Detroit, Mich.), Hayden worked for the Federal Writers' Project, supervising research in local Afro-American history and folklore. He won the Hopwood Award for his poetry in 1938 and again in 1942. Hayden joined the faculty of Fisk University (Nashville, Tenn.) in 1944, and in 1967 he began teaching at the University of Michigan. He received a Rosenwald Fellowship in 1946, a Ford Fellowship in 1954, and the Grand Award for Poetry at the First World Festival of Negro Arts in Senegal, Africa, in 1965. His books include: *The Lion and the Archer* (1948), with Myron O'Higgins; *A Ballad for Remembrance* (1962); *Selected Poems* (1966); *Words in the Mourning Time* (1970); and *The Night-Blooming Cereus* (1972). *See also* LITERATURE: POETRY.

HAYES, ELVIN *See* ATHLETES: BASKETBALL.

HAYES, ISAAC (1942–   ), singer, composer; born in Covington, Tenn. Known as "Little Moses" to his millions of "soul" fans, Hayes began life in a tin shack in a town outside Memphis, Tenn. In 1968 his first album, *Presenting Isaac Hayes,* was released, but it gained momentum only after the appearance of his second album, *Hot Buttered Soul.* Hayes' new "cool" delivery and his introductory "raps" made him a sensation in the soul music industry. By 1969 sales of *Hot Buttered Soul* had exceeded $1 million, and by 1971 more than 3.5 million albums had been sold. His next two releases, *The Isaac Hayes Movement* and *Isaac Hayes . . . To Be Continued,* both reached the $2 million mark in sales. He began giving concerts in 1969, and they were no less spectacular than his other endeavors. With a flair for spectacle, Hayes appeared all across the country with his shaved head and his velvet costumes trimmed with fur; his popularity was immense. In 1971 the film *Shaft,* for which Hayes wrote the score, was released; it received critical and popular approval. Also, the album of Hayes' score became one of the fastest selling discs in history. Hayes later became vice-president of the record company in Memphis that had started him in his career.

HAYES, ROLAND (1887–1977), singer; born in Curryville, Ga. The son of former slaves, Hayes set out from Chattanooga, Tenn., where he had been sent to go to school, to look for further education. He eventually attended Fisk University (Nashville, Tenn.) for four years and there joined the Fisk Jubilee Singers. One of the singers' tours took him to Boston, Mass., in 1911, where he remained to study voice. In 1916 Hayes began concertizing in the United States, winning critical praise for his interpretation of classical lieder and Negro spirituals. He became the first Afro-American to sing in Symphony Hall in Boston, and five years later he traveled to Europe to study and he gave triumphant concerts in many European capitals. A farewell concert in New York City's Carnegie Hall in 1962 celebrated his retirement.

HAYNES, GEORGE EDMUND (1880–1960), sociologist, administrator; born in Pine Bluff, Ark. Haynes received a B.A. degree from Fisk University (Nashville, Tenn.) in 1903 and his M.A. degree from Yale University in 1904. In 1912 Haynes received his Ph.D. degree from Columbia University, the first Afro-American to earn a doctorate there. His thesis, *The Negro at Work in New York,* was published by Columbia University Press in 1912. In 1910 Haynes co-founded the National League on Urban Conditions Among Negroes (now the National Urban League), and served as its executive secretary until 1918. From 1910 to 1921 Haynes was chairman of the department of social sciences at Fisk University, where he organized a training center for social workers. In 1910 he founded the Association of Negro Colleges and Secondary Schools and served as its secretary until 1916. From 1918 to 1920 he was special assistant to the secretary of the U.S. Department of Labor on the problems of Afro-Americans and on child labor conditions, and in 1921 Haynes became a member of the President's Unemployment Conference. In 1930 he conducted an in-depth survey for the Young Men's Christian Association (YMCA) on South Africa, and subsequently he made field studies in the Belgian Congo and Angola. Haynes resumed his teaching career in 1950, lecturing at the City College of New York for the next nine years. His published writings include *The Negro Newcomer in Detroit, Michigan* (1917) and *The Trend of the Races* (1922).

HEALTH

HEALTH The health of blacks in the United States has not been studied extensively. One of the earliest documents in this area was prepared in 1906 under the supervision of W. E. B. Du Bois. Some 30 years later another study was published (in 1935) that dealt with a variety of statistical tables about Afro-Americans in the United States for the period 1920–32. This was a publication of the U.S. Bureau of the Census, entitled *Negroes in the United States, 1920–1932.* Chapter XV dealt specifically with vital statistics concerning Afro-Americans. It is of interest to note that in this volume data were given for blacks and other colored populations, with the statement that for the latter category "the data for states are included in which the Negro population constituted 55% or more of the total colored population." In 1942 Julian Lewis published *The Biology of the Negro,* and for the first time an effort was made to review the literature in reference to racial differences in the prevalence and incidence of disease. The first nationwide conference on the health of the Afro-American was held at Howard University (Washington, D.C.) on March 13–14, 1967, bringing together about 200 persons from 20 states. The conference published a report entitled "The Health Status of the Negro Today and in the Future." It is to be emphasized that the National Center for Health Statistics annually publishes the Vital Statistics summaries, which provide information concerning the statistical difference between white and nonwhite population groups. Furthermore, after 1958, the center (through the National Health Survey) published a number of reports dealing with a variety of health topics, including dental caries, utilization of health services, and morbidity studies, in which racial comparisons are made. In spite of these efforts, it can be said that valid information about the health of Afro-Americans in the United States is scanty and rather inadequate.

Discussions concerning the health of Afro-Americans are generally based on mortality statistics published by the National Center for Health Statistics, which separates data according to white and nonwhite population. Presently, the white segment includes Puerto Rican and Mexican, while the nonwhite portion is made up of Afro-Americans, Indians, Chinese, Japanese, and other so-called colored races. The mortality differences that are found between these two groups (white and nonwhite) are generally publicized, and all too often emphasis is placed on the unfavorable status of the nonwhite population and indirectly on the black population, which makes up 90 percent of the nonwhite group. Even more futile are comparisons using morbidity or illness data on a nationwide basis, possibly because these data are usually incomplete and inadequate. Finally, no comparison is made between the health levels of these two groups, because at present no sound measures of health standards are available. Thus, mortality

Left: Harlem Hospital, built in 1887, one of the oldest and largest health centers for black Americans. *(Harlem Hospital.)* Left, below: The main building of Harlem Hospital at 135th Street and Lenox Avenue in New York City, built in 1907, as it appeared in the 1960s. *(Photo by Edward Entin.)* Below: The Martin Luther King Pavilion, erected in 1969. *(Photo by Edward Entin.)*

and morbidity rates, which are indeed negative measures of health, continue to be used.

The inadequacies of mortality and morbidity data are compounded by racial comparisons. It is an accepted dictum that the forces that really affect the levels of death and disease are social and economic in nature. Education, employment, housing, poverty, neighborhood sanitation, recreational facilities, availability and accessibility of health facilities, and the attitude and mores of a community are the important determinants of death and disease. It is therefore mandatory that at all times in this kind of discussion the effects of these factors be fully considered. Furthermore, it has long been hoped that the National Center for Health Statistics would begin to develop techniques whereby mortality and morbidity rates would be adjusted or related to a selected number of these social and economic factors, and thus the center would eventually remove entirely the constraints of comparing mortality and morbidity data solely on the basis of race.

It is ironic that after making this plea that this article will have to resort to some comparison on the basis of race, but this is the nature of the present techniques of social pathology. When one looks at the available data concerning the mortality and morbidity experience of Afro-Americans in this country, one finds both favorable and unfavorable aspects. It is not the purpose of this article to present these aspects exhaustively; only a few selected examples will be discussed. This discussion will constitute the first part of this article, and the second part will be concerned with possible solutions to some of these problems.

Some Favorable and Unfavorable Aspects of the Health of Afro-Americans It has been customary to dwell at length on the extremely unfavorable position of blacks as noted by some racial comparisons in the field of health. These comparisons have mainly dealt with illegitimacy, venereal diseases, tuberculosis, maternal and infant mortality, prematurity, and homicide rates among young males. However, the force of social and economic factors (as has already been stated) are the real determinants of these racial differences rather than genetics or inherent factors. Nevertheless, the literature is replete with the litany of the unfavorable aspects of the health of Afro-Americans. Not only is this to be found in scientific articles but also in popular magazines and even in the Congressional Record, where congressmen have used data to further the sup-

port for discriminatory and segregated patterns. No effort will be made to repeat such data at length; however, three unfavorable relationships will be mentioned in order to point up the present situation.

The Widening Gap Any objective examination of the available data comparing black and white mortality and morbidity rates shows that the gap between the two is increasing. This is true for most of the important public health indexes used in this country.

Mental Retardation The prevalence of inferior intellectual functioning in the black community is illustrated by recent studies of black school-age children. Eighth-grade pupils in central Harlem were found to have a mean IQ of 87.7, while the average IQ for New York City eighth-graders was 100.1. A normative study of 1,800 Afro-American elementary school children in five southern states yielded a mean IQ of 80.7. According to the most recent classification system accepted by the American Association of Mental Deficiency, which is also used by the U.S. Public Health Service, the average child in the latter study is classified as "borderline retarded." These data do not present any particularly new information; such findings have been reported for more than 50 years. The precursors of and factors associated with mental retardation abound in the Afro-American community. Mental retardation has been found to be associated with prematurity, complications of pregnancy, low socioeconomic status, as well as lower occupational levels, lower educational attainment, and broken homes. Yet, little has been done to alleviate these conditions.

Health Concerns of Unskilled and Semiskilled Workers Unskilled and semiskilled workers have the most serious health problems and receive the least adequate health care. Because of past and present segregation and discriminatory patterns,

Far right: Black workers, along with other Americans, have often been liable to accident risks or health hazards, as were these shipbuilders in World War I. (*National Archives.*)

the great majority of Afro-Americans fall into these occupational groups, and their health problems stem mainly from this fact. The health services received by them tend to be obtained from two sources: (1) charity wards and clinics, and (2) private care by usually overworked and harried general practitioners.

Another factor concerns injury and workmen's compensation. Afro-Americans, who are largely concentrated in unskilled and heavy labor occupations, are often subjected to greater risk of injury and consequent potential loss of health. Because these workers are largely unskilled and poorly educated, even union activity, significant in the past in protecting the workmen's interest in these areas, has largely waned and in some areas has tragically disappeared.

A tendency in many industries to contest all claims made by injured workmen, particularly where disability results, has been growing. This kind of activity on the part of industry forces the claimant in many instances to require legal services in order to establish the merit of his claim, or forfeit, through ignorance and inadequate education, the very benefit that the law was originally established to provide. Afro-Americans tend to be the greatest victims of this treatment.

However, the favorable aspects of the health of Afro-Americans are indeed significant and worthy of attention.

Longevity and the Average Expectation of Life No one can dispute the fact that marked improvements have taken place in the health status of the nonwhite population during the last half century, even though that population has had to live under crowded and insanitary conditions and medical services and hospital facilities have often been sparse or absent. The black population in 1790 was 757,280; 90 years later, in 1880, it had increased eightfold to 6,580,793; and by 1970, it had tripled, to approximately 22 million.

The average life expectation of the Afro-American, as would be expected, has shown a phenomenal increase—much more favorable than that for white individuals—as depicted in the table below and the accompanying graph.

LIFE TABLE VALUE, BY COLOR AND SEX REGISTRATION STATES

Color and Sex	1900–02	1967	Percent Increase
White male	48.23	67.8	40.7
Nonwhite male	32.54	61.1	88.0
White female	51.08	75.1	46.9
Nonwhite female	35.04	67.4	63.5

For nonwhite males and females, the expectation of life increased between 1900 and 1967 by 88 and 63.5 percent, respectively, as contrasted with 40.7 and 46.9 percent for whites. A word of caution must of course be given in these comparisons, because the data are for registration states and the values for 1900–02 reflected the urban northeastern portion of the United States and excluded the majority of the nonwhites, hence the percentage gain during this period was lower. Nevertheless, these figures are suggestive.

The figures for life expectation at single years for ages over 60 and including 85 years show an interesting phenomenon. Up to the age of 68 years, the expectation of life at each single year is lower for nonwhite males and females than for whites, but this tendency is then reversed so that by the age of 85 years the expectations for nonwhite individuals are about one and a half times that of white males and females. It is to be remembered, however, that these expectation-of-life values merely forecast average remaining lifetime for the hypothetical cohorts.

LIFE EXPECTANCY, 1900–1975.

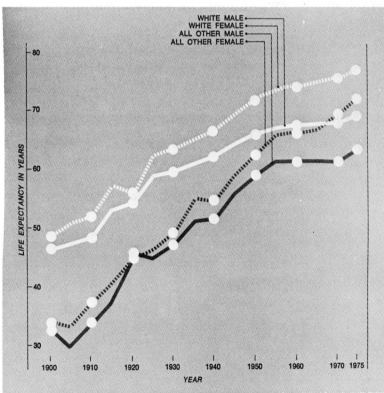

NOTE: The term "All Other" as used in this graph refers to all nonwhites, 90 percent of whom would be Afro-Americans.

SOURCE: *Health, United States, 1976–1977: Chartbook*, National Center for Health Statistics, 1977.

Physical Assets of Blacks The physical prowess of blacks has been amply and repeatedly demonstrated. This attribute is most evident in the amateur sports world in the performance of young Afro-Americans from disadvantaged areas who have excelled in track and field events, including the Olympics. In professional athletics, the consistent performance of Afro-Americans in boxing and their prevalence in baseball, basketball, and football is striking. Nevertheless, investigations of the physical fitness and performance of black children are not plentiful.

A readily available source of data that has not been adequately tapped may be of value for future exploration: the selective service examinations are of particular interest here. As early as 1906, W. E. B. Du Bois called attention to the fact that the Report of the United States Surgeon General for 1902 showed that colored recruits had approximately the same rate of rejection by the Armed Forces as white ones, and that those rejected for vision were approximately twice as high in white as in black recruits. The report published in 1948, which contains results from the examination of millions of young men for induction into the Armed Forces during World War II, illustrates the prevalence of defects among the registrants for the period November 1940 to December 1943. The report shows that the rates of rejection for both black and white individuals were approximately the same, and that the former had lower prevalence rates in 19 of 28 defects. Venereal diseases, educational deficiency, and defects of feet and heart were the only conditions in which Afro-Americans showed higher proportions. A selected list of physical defects in which blacks fared better is found in the following table.

PREVALENCE OF A SELECTED DEFECT PER 1,000 SELECTIVE SERVICE REGISTRANTS EXAMINED BY RACE, NOVEMBER 1940 DECEMBER 1943

Defects	White	Afro-American
Total	1,105.2	1,108.6
Eyes	128.2	67.4
Ears	43.0	14.6
Teeth	125.3	59.5
Nose	45.9	13.4
Neurological	26.6	19.3
Musculoskeletal	91.2	65.9

Blacks had about half of the rejection for vision; one-third for hearing; and half for defects of teeth. Even though not of the same magnitude, Afro-Americans also had lower rejection rates for neurological and musculoskeletal defects. As

far as can be ascertained, these data, over a quarter of a century old, are the only ones available that provide information about rejections according to specific defects.

The low level of disqualifications for medical reasons of blacks appears to be a pattern of long duration; nevertheless, the potential of these data for study and further investigation still remains untapped. Only the data dealing with the low rejection rates for visual acuity have been subject to analysis according to race, and then only statistically. Karpinos reviewed a sample of 273,000 medical reports of selective service registrants—221,310 whites and 51,282 Afro-Americans—and substantiated the findings already mentioned. No significant physiologic, genetic, endocrinologic, or medical studies have been carried out to determine whether genetic or environmental factors, or both, were important. This type of scholarly neglect is amazing when it is realized that these facts, at least in the case of visual acuity, have been known for almost 70 years.

The most recent data that provide information about the favorable position of black individuals in relation to certain physical and laboratory findings are to be found in the reports of the National Health Survey, conducted on a nationwide basis by the National Center for Health Statistics. Some 16 separate reports of findings from the Health Examination Survey for the period 1960–62 consider the question of a differential between rates for Afro-Americans and whites for certain specific conditions. Arthur J. McDowell, director of the Division of Health Examination Statistics, in summarizing these data, states that six of the reports show levels for the Afro-American population that were more favorable than those for the white population. Here again the dental findings confirm the low rate of rejection of recruits by the military. Two of the dental findings show that both DMF (Decayed, Missing, and Filled) and edentulousness rates were more favorable for Afro-Americans. Another report also brings forth the better performance in terms of visual and hearing acuity of black as contrasted with white examinees. In addition to these already known advantages, the serum cholesterol values for Afro-Americans were lower than for white individuals, as were the rates for moderate and severe degrees of osteoarthritis. However, it should be noted again, very little has been done to pursue these leads and determine possible causal associations.

Favorable Morbidity and Mortality Differentials
Morbidity and mortality data that present racial differences are all too often of questionable validity. They are presented here because they have too often been used to show the inadequacies of Afro-Americans. A quick perusal of a number of morbidity studies and mortality reports shows that the incidence and prevalence of many diseases are less in black than in white individuals. This has even been true for such diseases as hookworm and pinworm infestations that are associated with the poor.

The prevalence of cancer in these two segments of the population may be selected for a bit more detailed study. (A survey by the U.S. Public Health Service is the major source for the data quoted.) The incidence of cancer for nonwhite individuals was less than two-thirds that for whites, and even when this was adjusted for age distribution, this differential, although not as great, remained. The incidence of cancer for a number of sites showed lower rates for blacks as contrasted with white individuals, and startling differences were found in certain age groups. The two most interesting contrasts in racial difference were found in cancer of the skin and of the genitals. In the former, the incidence is extremely low for blacks; in the latter, the reverse is true for both male and female. The low incidence of cancer of the skin among blacks has been noted on other occasions, and is generally considered to reflect a true racial difference in susceptibility to skin diseases. In support of this assertion, the low incidence of dermatitis and dermatoses caused by irritating dusts, liquids, and vapors found in industry is generally quoted. Nevertheless, surprisingly little or no research has been done in this area to determine why this apparent low susceptibility exists among black individuals.

Possible Solutions for Selected Health Problems Among Black People

General The unfavorable morbidity and mortality experiences of the black population, as has been reiterated, are not due to any genetic differences, but rather to such socioeconomic and environmental deficiencies as poverty, housing, unemployment, nonavailability and inaccessibility of health services facilities, discrimination and segregation, and inadequate family structure. Therefore, the major thrust to improve the health of blacks must be directed at these factors along the following lines:

(a) A massive, coordinated, and comprehensive attack on the nation's social, economic, and health problems sponsored by the federal government is critically and urgently needed. A press release in the early 1970s in Washington, D.C., reported that Argentina recently sent six Peace Corps volunteers to help in poverty areas in our affluent society. It is possible that after a brief exposure here, these volunteers will ask their country to send surplus beef to feed the starving black children in Mississippi.

(b) Much of the mental retardation in Afro-American communities can be alleviated by positive, significant, and lasting improvement in the overall standard of living. The high incidence of borderline mental retardation among the deprived is acutely susceptible to available remedies. A comprehensive plan of effective action for the black community as a whole, and for the functionally retarded individual in particular, is necessary if a notable decline in the incidence of mental retardation in the black community is to occur.

(c) Research is urgently needed in order to determine the many factors that affect the full utilization of health services by the poor, and in order to find ways and means to develop a health-care system that will reach and be accepted by the poor.

(d) Black health professionals should become actively interested in the correction of factors that promote homicide, drug addiction, illegitimacy, and other behavior problems with high incidence among black youth. Currently, there appears to be considerable apathy among this group of professionals.

(e) Small regional conferences financed by the federal government or foundations should be developed to consider some of the health problems of Afro-Americans. These conferences could bring together specialists in the field for a more careful consideration of such problems. Hopefully, these conferences would stimulate an increase in research in many neglected areas.

Government-Financed Health Care and Blacks The role of the federal government in the organization, financing, and delivery of health services had been a relatively passive one until the action of President Lyndon B. Johnson and the Eighty-ninth Congress. This country has no delivery system that provides high quality medical care for every citizen. The deficiencies in some areas are serious and, in others, shocking. Presently, two important obstacles must be faced and must be resolved: poverty and discrimination.

Aside from the goals of the alleviation of poverty and of discrimination, most admit that if government-financed health programs are to reach the black poor, innovations must be previously made to meet the needs of the ghetto. A renewed approach is certainly necessary for new programs, but it is even more applicable to old programs that have missed the mark. School health services, which have held a prominent place in public health practice in this country during the past 50 years, are a case in point. These services represent an annual expenditure in excess of $250 million. Thousands of nurses are employed in this service system on a full-time basis, and thousands of physicians spend a good part of their professional time working in these programs. School health services have steadfastly steered a course away from the inclusion of medical care, except for an occasional program that provided ophthalmic examinations and eyeglasses. Should such limited programs be continued in the face of huge gaps in facilities and manpower in the medical-care aspects of comprehensive services? The artificial dichotomy of preventive and curative services that is so widely evident in school health service programs should be abolished. School health services should be integrated into the mainstream of medical and health programs. Is there any reason for not offering medical care in the school and utilizing available school health staffs in these activities? Schools located in inner cities and in other areas of poverty should become identified as sites for delivering curative medical care.

Health Manpower and the Black Community The problem of health manpower is two-faced in its dimensions as far as Afro-Americans are concerned. Tremendous shortages in all health professions, which damage the health of all, do exist, especially among the black poor. Conversely, shortages in trained and skilled personnel badly affect the economic base of the black community and maintain it in a welfare posture. Since much has been written about shortages of doctors, dentists, and other professional personnel and about what needs to be done, this section will be devoted to nonprofessional health aides. However, it is mandatory first to call attention to the plight of the black dentist, who is becoming a vanishing American. Dr. Joseph Henry, dean of the Dental School at Howard University (Washington, D.C.), states that in 1940 the proportion of black dentists in this country was 4 percent; in 1950, 3 percent; and in 1965, this figure had been reduced to 2 percent, and has remained at this level. This is, indeed, a critical situation.

The training and use of nonprofessional health aides or health services aides are of great import to the black community. Development and expansion of needed neighborhood community health services have been handicapped by an increasing shortage of trained personnel, and by the major difficulties of reaching, motivating, and involving those people in the neighborhoods who need such services. At the same time, disadvantaged residents of these communities lack realistic employment, training, and career opportunities in all but the most menial or dead-end entry levels of the job market.

A significant answer to this shortage of health services in disadvantaged communities has been the development of experimental programs for the training and employment of local residents in nonprofessional jobs with career possibilities in community health services programs. Several training centers in the country, including those at Howard University (Washington, D.C.), at Lincoln Hospital (New York, N.Y.), and in the California State Department of Health, have developed such nonprofessional positions on a variety of entry levels in health services, and have successfully trained and employed disadvantaged persons for these positions.

As with the professional programs, counseling and recruitment must become more extensive and more aggressive. High schools and junior community colleges need to develop more effective programs to guide students' attention to the possibilities and gratifications inherent in health careers. Such various health agencies as hospitals and health departments in black communities should be used as educational media for health careers. Part-time or summer jobs in these agencies should be made available to both black and white youths. Extensive promotional activities should be carried out through radio, television, and newspapers, which cater to and are used by certain segments of the population.

Health agencies can also help solve this problem by making provisions to take blacks with minimal educational backgrounds, give them on-the-job training, and, subsequently, as they improve, provide them with the opportunity for formal education while at work, and so allow them to move up the occupational ladder. Of course, it is obvious that parallel efforts must be made to raise the salaries and improve the working conditions of health aides, thus allowing health agencies to compete with industry in attracting black youths. In the same sense, boards of education need to approve such training and certify such training centers. Licensing boards must also come to grips with some of the questions raised and be willing to revise their regulations so as to give more recognition to on-the-job training.

Health Attitudes and Behavior of Black and White Individuals that Affect Health Care and Utilization of Services The attitudes and behavior of people—the donors and recipients of health care—adversely or favorably affect the utilization of health services. The professionals—the donors of health care—can be helpful in many ways, some of which can be mentioned. A major difficulty in the reception of health care is the social distance between the provider and the recipient of health care. Inasmuch as the former is in possession of the information that the recipient requires for the care of his health, it is essential that this information be transmitted adequately. Professionals should be more aware of this and be alert to the need to modify their presentation to assure and ensure acceptability and understanding. This involves the attitude that middle-class professionals have toward the poor: the professional tendency is to treat disease and not the patient, and to ignore his way of life, his environment, his problems, and his emotions. All too often it is the professional who is "hard-to-reach" and not the patient. Therefore, a need exists for training programs to include study units that will aid professionals in understanding their own prejudices and altering them. Professionals must also be taught how to communicate effectively with low-income persons; how to develop satisfactory interpersonal relationships; and how to work with others in the community.

Attention must also be called to the fact that most health education material continues to be geared to middle-class vocabulary and attitudes. An experiment worthy of wider application has been made whereby a group of lower socioeconomic individuals prepared their own health education materials. The drawings were a bit crude and the words different from the usual professional language, but the information was effectively transmitted. Another is the approach that the health education division of the District of Columbia Department of Public Health has used. Selected materials, before publication, were submitted to a group of neighborhood

health aides for criticism and suggested changes in the format and wording and then pretested among a group of the families with which these personnel were working.

Just as professionals create certain impediments in the transmission of health education, so, too, do low-income black consumers of

Dorothy Ferebee, physician and community service leader, photographed in the 1950s with children at the Southeast Settlement House, Washington, D.C., which she founded and directed. *(U.S. Information Agency, National Archives.)*

health services. A study by Cornely and Bigman has emphasized some of these, and they need not be repeated here. However, it must be reiterated that these differences in the health attitudes and behavior of low-income black families must be taken into consideration in any program for improvement.

Health of the Worker What can be done about the health problems of unskilled and semiskilled Afro-American workers and their families? First, there seems to be a growing feeling that neither Medicare nor Medicaid will accomplish the objective of providing a single system of medical care for all citizens and that, therefore, the time has come to adopt a new abolition movement— "Abolish Charity Medicine." All minority groups, be they Afro-American, Puerto Rican, or American Indian, are the unwilling victims of the present charity system of medical care. The abolition of charity medicine can only be implemented with the passage of legislation establishing a national health insurance scheme dedicated to the principle that every individual in the United States has a right to medical care. This has become a central political issue of the 1970s. The many national health bills that have been introduced in the Ninety-second Congress attest to this fact. It is hoped that in the years to come, the United States will join other enlightened nations who have had a national health plan for many years.

Second, many inadequacies in workmen's compensation legislation in every state presently exist, and continuing efforts must be made to improve these laws. However, the inequities of each state program, as well as those existing between states, make it imperative to consider the feasibility of a national workmen's compensation law that would assure a minimum level of benefits throughout the nation. The rehabilitation of injured workers should be closely coordinated with workmen's compensation programs. In many states, little cooperation and no coordination exist between these two programs.

Third, the deplorable condition of occupational health programs at the local, state, and federal level is a reflection of the almost total lack of national leadership. It is hoped that the Occupational Safety and Health Act of 1970 will motivate a genuine federal commitment for the improvement and expansion of these services, and perhaps these efforts will bring about a true coordination between in-plant programs and community health services. Parenthetically, it must also be noted that occupational health programs make no effort to overcome the illiteracy of many unskilled and semiskilled workers. It is difficult to implement health and safety programs if the worker is unable to read or understand educational materials.

Racism and Health   The black poor, as well as the black health professional, are convinced that racism in the area of health is a reality and not a myth. The insensitivity, the indifference, the apathy, and the omnipresent barriers convince Afro-Americans that in order to extricate themselves from these locked-in situations, they must increase their participation in and control of health care systems.

The important objective remains to incorporate ethnic minorities into the political structure, thereby increasing the responsiveness of governments to the diversity of all citizens and preventing the "battered adult" syndrome. This has been said many times in recent years, and it would appear that in the health field the time has come to make effective community participation and community control a reality. This is one of the major ways by which this singular domestic problem can be met.

Community participation in the past has come principally from the middle class and the rich. In most instances, this pattern continued even though population composition in urban and rural communities had changed and even though the revolution in democratic participation had gathered momentum. All who have been kept out of the mainstream of influence— the black, the poor, and the young—have been insistent in their demands that they be given the opportunity to share in the determination of the policies and activities that are central in their everyday lives. Representation from all segments of a community is of paramount importance if the organization and delivery of health care is to be meaningful. It is imperative, therefore, that all sectors of our health industry come to grips with this problem and provide opportunities for the unrepresented to become an integral part of the community.

Community control, as contrasted with community participation, must be considered from a different perspective. The power or authority for the health of citizens in this country resides in the state as part of its police power. This authority may be delegated by the state to such political subdivisions as a city, a county, or a district, or to duly constituted groups or bodies that have met such legal requirements as have universities, commissions, hospitals, or prepaid health plans. The legal vehicle for the reception of this authority may be a corporation, a foundation, or a cooperative, but never a neighborhood, or a club, or a church, or an indigenous group of people. The citizens of suburbia can no more control their health institutions than can those in the inner city, unless they have met the legal requirements for the allocation of such authority.

Community control of health institutions is feasible and desirable if the legal requirements prescribed by the state or its political subdivisions are met. If these legal requirements are found to be unreasonable or discriminatory, then the community must move toward the abolition, modification, or complete change of the existing regulations. This is a right that the many ethnic minorities in our country must have if a pluralistic society is to be the true strength of a democracy.

Community participation and control, if fully and equitably granted to the black and the poor and the other nonwhite minorities, and if these minorities are allowed to err even though at times costly (just as the Department of Defense so commonly does in many of its experimental projects), may make a most significant contribution to the health of our society. Modern technologic society in general and American society in particular is ugly, repressive, destructive, and subversive of much that is truly human. Our society's requirement of maximal efficiency and output leads to minimal individuality and eventually to the absence of creativity. Technological man becomes an appendage of the machine and his major aim is to have more and use more. As Eric Fromm has stated, modern man "spends his time doing things in which he is not interested, with people in whom he is not interested, producing things in which he is not interested, and when he is not producing, he is consuming." Modern man tends to be bored, although affluent. The passiveness of man in this industrial society is one of his most characteristic and pathologic features, and this passiveness is one of a host of symptoms in the "syndrome of alienation." This is our societal pathology.

Can the spread of this nationwide pathology be halted? Fromm believes that "if the constructive forces within industrial society, which are choked by a deadening bureaucracy, by artificial consumption and manipulated boredom, are released by a new mood of hope . . . if the individual regains his confidence in himself, and if people make contact with each other in spontaneous and genuine group life, new forms of psychospiritual practices will emerge and grow which might be unified eventually in a total socially acceptable system." *See also* DISCRIMINATION; EMPLOYMENT; HOUSING; INCOME; NURSES; PHYSICIANS; POPULATION; POVERTY; RACE: BIOLOGY; RACE: RACISM.

REFERENCES: Atlanta University, *The Health and Physique of the Negro American*, Atlanta University Press, Atlanta, Publication no. 11, 1906; Cornely, P. B. and S. K. Bigman, "Some Considerations in Changing Health Attitudes," *Children*, January–February, 1963, pp. 23–28; Dorn, H. F. and S. J. Cutler, "Morbidity from Cancer," *U.S. Public Health Monograph No. 56*, Government Printing Office, Washington, D.C., 1959; Howard University College of Medicine, Department of Preventive Medicine and Public Health, *The Health Status of the Negro Today and in the Future*, Washington, D.C., 1967; Kennedy, W. A., et al., *A Normative Sample of Intelligence and Achievement of Negro Elementary School Children in the Southeastern United States*, Monogr. Soc. Res. Child Development 28, ser. 90, no. 6, 1963; Lewis, Julian H., *The Biology of the Negro*, University of Chicago Press, Chicago, 1942; Moynihan, Daniel P., *The Negro Family (The Case for National Action)*, U.S. Department of Labor, Office of Policy Planning and Research, Washington, D.C., 1965; National Center for Vital Statistics, *Vital Statistics of the United States, 1966*, vol. 2, pp. 1–9, Government Printing Office, Washington, D.C., 1968; National Center for Vital Statistics, *Vital Statistics of the United States, 1967*, vol. 2, sect. 5, U.S. Government Printing Office, Washington, D.C., 1969; President's Commission on the Health Needs of the Nation, *Building America's Health, Vol. III*, 1951. Attention is also called to the annual reports of the Secretary of Health, Education, and Welfare (*Health, United States*) required by an act of Congress in 1974; and Richard Allen Williams, ed. *Textbook of Black-Related Diseases*, McGraw-Hill, New York, 1975.

HEALY, JAMES A. (1830–1900), Roman Catholic bishop; born in Macon, Ga. Healy attended Quaker elementary schools in Flushing, N.Y., and in New Jersey. Upon graduating from the College of the Holy Cross (Worcester, Mass.) in 1849, he entered the Sulpician Seminary in Montreal, Canada, and three years later enrolled at a corresponding seminary in Paris, France. Healy was ordained a priest at Notre Dame Cathedral in Paris in 1854, and in the same year went to Boston, Mass., to be an assistant priest of a parish there. After 11 years as a bishop's secretary and diocesan chancellor, he became pastor of St. James Church in South Boston in 1866. In 1875 Pope Pius IX named Healy bishop of Portland, Maine, and he thus became the first Afro-American Roman Catholic bishop in the United States. Healy was made an assistant to the papal throne in 1900 by Pope Leo XIII, but he died two months after his appointment. His brother, Patrick F. Healy, who was president of Georgetown University (Washington, D.C.) from 1873 to 1882, was the first Afro-American to be awarded a doctorate (1865). Edward S. Bouchet's doctorate in physics, awarded by Yale University in 1876, was formerly believed to be the first for an Afro-American.

James A. Healy in 1889; he was the first Afro-American Roman Catholic bishop. *(Library of Congress.)*

HEARD, WILLIAM H. (1850–1937), African Methodist Episcopal bishop; born in Elbert County, Ga. Heard attended Atlanta University and the Divinity School of West Philadelphia and received his D.D. degree from Allen University (Columbia, S.C.) in 1891. Ordained in the African Methodist Episcopal (AME) ministry in 1879, he was made a bishop in 1904. Heard was elected to the South Carolina House of Representatives in 1876, and from 1898 to 1899 he served as minister resident and consul-general to Liberia. He was a trustee of Wilberforce University and Payne Theological Seminary both in Wilberforce, Ohio. His writings include *The Bright Side of African Life* (1900) and *From Slavery to the Bishopric in the A.M.E. Church: An Autobiography* (1924).

Anna Arnold
Hedgeman

HEDGEMAN, ANNA ARNOLD (1899–   ), civic leader; born in Marshalltown, Iowa; reared in Anoke, Minn. Hedgeman received a B. A. degree in English from Hamline University (St. Paul, Minn.) in 1922. In the late 20s, she did postgraduate work at the University of Minnesota and in the 30s she did postgraduate work at the New York School of Social Work. From 1922 to 1924 she was professor of English at Rust College (Holly Springs, Miss.). From 1924 to 1934 she served as Executive Director of the Young Women's Christian Association (YMCA) at several urban branches. In 1933 she married concert artist Merritt A. Hedgeman. In 1934 she became supervisor at the Emergency Relief Bureau in New York City. Later she was named the first New York City Consultant on Racial Problems for the Commissioner. In 1943 Hedgeman was appointed Executive Director of the National Council for a Permanent Fair Employment Practices Committee (FECP), developing a national legislative and educational program. In 1946 she served as assistant to the dean of women at Howard University (Washington, D. C.). From 1949 to 1953 Hedgeman was the assistant to the adminstrator of the Federal Security Agency, now Health, Education, and Welfare (HEW). In 1954 she became the first woman member of the Cabinet of the Mayor of the City of New York. Her numerous awards include the first Human Relations Award (1955); citations from the Farmer's Union of Montana, the National Urban League, the National Association of College Women, the Association for the Study of African American Life and History, and the AFL-CIO. In 1978, the National Conference of Christians and Jews honored Hedgeman as one of the 50 Extraordinary Women of Achievement in New York City. Among her publications are *The Trumpet Sounds* (1964) and *The Gift of Chaos* (1977).

HEIGHT, DOROTHY L. (1913–   ), social worker; born in Richmond, Va. Immediately after receiving a B.S. degree from New York University in 1934, Height joined the New York City department of welfare as a caseworker, and later received her M.S. degree from New York University. In 1937 Height went to work for the Young Women's Christian Association (YWCA), where she eventually became director of the Center for Racial Justice. From 1952 to 1955 she served as consultant to the U.S. Department of Defense Advisory Committee on Women and was visiting professor at the Delhi School of Social Work, Delhi, India, in 1952. From 1958 to 1968 Height was consultant to the New York State Social Welfare Board. Appointed to the President's Committee on the Status of Women, the President's Committee for Equal Employment Opportunity, and the President's Committee for the Employment of the Handicapped, she also served on the Ad Hoc Committee on Public Welfare of the U.S. Department of Health, Education, and Welfare (HEW). In 1957 Height became president of the National Council of Negro Women (NCNW) and was active in the Council for United Civil Rights Leadership. From 1947 to 1958 she was president of Delta Sigma Theta sorority, and she sat on the board of governors of the American Red Cross from 1964 to 1970. Height received honorary L.H.D. degrees from Tuskegee Institute (Tuskegee Institute, Ala.) and from Coppin State College (Baltimore, Md.), as well as honorary LL.D. degrees from Pace College (New York, N.Y.) and from Harvard University. In 1971 she was awarded the Distinguished Service Award of the National Conference on Social Welfare. *See also* WOMEN.

HENDERSON, ELMER A. (1887–1951), educator; born in Gilboa, Md. Henderson received a B.A. degree from Morgan State University (Baltimore, Md.). He began teaching at the age of 15 in Harford County, Md., and went to Baltimore, Md., in 1906. For 45 years he served in the Baltimore school system as a teacher, vice-principal, principal, and director of colored schools. In 1945 Henderson was appointed assistant superintendent of schools, becoming one of the first Afro-Americans in the South to hold such a position.

HENDERSON, FLETCHER (1898–1952), musician, band leader; born in Cuthbert, Ga. A chemistry major at Atlanta University, Henderson went to New York for graduate studies. To pay expenses, he worked with a music publisher (Black Swan) and shortly therafter became a full-time pianist with the company. By 1924 he was performing with his own band at the Roseland, where one of his players was Coleman Hawkins. Later Henderson and his band were in demand at the Savoy and Apollo in New York City. He and his band were also favorites at dance affairs on college campuses, where his swing arrangements added to the popularity of the big jazz bands. Among his arrangements was the *King Porter Stomp*. Some of his arrangements were used by other musicians, including Benny Goodman. *See also* MUSIC: JAZZ.

HENDERSON, FRANCES MURPHY journalist, educator, administrator; born in Baltimore, Md. Henderson received a B.A. degree from the University of Wisconsin, a B.S. degree from Coppin State College (Baltimore, Md.), and his M.Ed. degree from Johns Hopkins University (Baltimore, Md.). He was the director of the news bureau and assistant professor of English at Morgan State College (Baltimore, Md.) from 1964 to 1971, and a teacher in the Baltimore public schools from 1958 to 1964. Henderson also served as a reporter for the Baltimore *Afro-American,* the Richmond *Afro-American,* and the Washington *Afro-American.* He was chairman of the board of directors of the Afro-American Newspaper Company after 1971, and a member of the boards of the National Council of College Publications Advisers, the Urban League, and the National Association for the Advancement of Colored People (NAACP).

HENDERSON, JAMES (1917–   ), scientist; born in Falls Church, Va. Henderson received a B.S. degree from Howard University (Washington, D.C.) in 1939 and a M.Ph. degree (1940) and his Ph.D. degree in plant physiology (1943) from the University of Wisconsin. He was assistant pharmacologist for the National Defense Research Committee in Chicago, Ill., from 1943 to 1945, and worked as research associate professor in plant physiology and in biology at the Carver Research Foundation of Tuskegee Institute (Tuskegee Institute, Ala.) from 1945 to 1968, becoming director of the research foundation and chairman of its natural science division in 1968.

HENDERSON, RAY (1896–1971), popular composer; born in Buffalo, N.Y. Henderson became one of the most popular of American songwriters in the period following World War I. As a member of a successful songwriting team with Lew Brown and Buddy de Sylva, he composed "Button Up Your Overcoat," "The Birth of the Blues," "It All Depends on You," "You're the Cream in My Coffee," and "The Best Things in Life Are Free." Teaming with Billy Rose and Mort Dixon, Henderson wrote "That Old Gang of Mine"; with Bud Green and Buddy de Sylva, "Alabamy Bound"; with Mort Dixon, "Bye, Bye Blackbird"; and with Sam Lewis and Joe Young, "Five Foot Two, Eyes of Blue."

HENDERSON, THOMAS HOWARD (1910–   ), educator; born in Newport News, Va. Henderson

received a B.S. degree from Virginia Union University in 1929, and a M.A. degree and his Ph.D. degree (1941) from the University of Chicago. He served as dean at Virginia Union University (1941–60), becoming its president in 1960.

HENDERSON, VIVIAN WILSON (1923–76), economist, educator; born in Bristol, Tenn. Henderson graduated from North Carolina Central University in 1947, and received a M.A. degree (1949) and his Ph.D. degree (1952) from the University of Iowa. Before becoming president of Clark College (Atlanta, Ga.) in 1965, he taught at Prairie View Agricultural and Mechanical (A&M) College (Prairie View, Tex.) and at Fisk University (Nashville, Tenn.). Henderson wrote a number of books and articles, and he served on several governmental commissions, including the Advisory Committee for the Study of Race and Education, established by President Lyndon B. Johnson, and on the Commission on Rural Poverty.

HENRY, JOSIAH   *See* LAWYERS.

HENRY, REGINA M. GOFF (1917–   ), psychologist, educator; born in St. Louis, Mo. Henry received a B.S. degree from Northwestern University (Evanston, Ill.) in 1936, and a M.A. degree (1940) and her Ph.D. degree (1948) from Columbia University. She taught at Lincoln University (Jefferson City, Mo.) from 1940 to 1947, at Stowe Teachers College from 1947 to 1948, at Florida Agricultural and Mechanical (A&M) State College (Tallahasse, Fla., now Florida A&M University) from 1948 to 1949, at Morgan State University (Baltimore, Md.) from 1950 to 1960, and at the University of Maryland. Henry served as assistant commissioner of education in the U.S. Office of Education from 1964 to 1970, and was an adviser to the minister of education in Iran for the International Cooperation Administration of the U.S. Department of State from 1955 to 1957. Her writings include: "Culture and Personality Development of Minority People," in *Negro Education in America,* edited by V. A. Clift, and a chapter in *Racial Crisis in American Education* (1969). She married Josiah Henry. *See also* HENRY, JOSIAH.

HENRY, WILLIAM EDWARD (1900–   ), educator; born in Snow Hill, Md. Henry received a B.A. degree from Virginia Union University in 1923, and a M.A. degree (1929) and his Ed.D. degree (1945) from the University of Pennsylvania. He taught at Roger Williams College (Providence, R.I.) from 1924 to 1925, at Maryland Normal School from 1925 to 1927, and at North Carolina Agricultural and Technical (A&T) State University from 1928 to 1932. Henry became supervisor of schools for Worcester County, Md. in 1932. He served as dean of instruction at Maryland State College from 1938 to 1942 and as president of Bowie State Teachers College (Bowie, Md.) in the 1940s and the 1950s.

Matthew Henson.
(Library of Congress.)

HENSON, MATTHEW A. (1866–1955), explorer; born in Charles County, Md. Henson went to sea at the age of 12, and then worked as a stevedore, bellhop, coachman, and stock clerk. As a stock clerk, he met Lt. Robert Peary in 1887, who hired Henson to accompany him on a trip to survey a canal route through Nicaragua. After this venture, Henson accompanied Peary on other explorations, including the historic first expedition to the North Pole in 1909. After the expedition, however, Henson was ignored and forgotten, and was forced to find work as a parking attendant. A black politician eventually secured him a job in the custom house as a messenger boy, where he worked his way up to clerk, retiring at the age of 70. Bills to grant him a federal pension as a reward for his Arctic explorations were stalled in Congress four times. Yet in 1937, the Explorers Club made him a member, and in 1944 Congress issued a medal jointly honoring all six of Peary's companions. President Harry S. Truman paid tribute to Henson in ceremonies at the Pentagon in 1950, and President Dwight D. Eisenhower honored him at the White House in 1954. In 1961 the state of Maryland passed a bill providing for a bronze plaque to be erected in its state house in Henson's memory. He published an autobiography in 1912 entitled *A Negro Explorer at the North Pole.*

HERNDON, ANGELO *See* AFRO-AMERICAN HISTORY: RECONSTRUCTION TO REVOLT.

HERNTON, CALVIN S. (1932–   ), author, educator; born in Chattanooga, Tenn. Hernton received a B.A. degree from Talladega College (Talladega, Ala.) in 1954 and his M.A. degree from Fisk University (Nashville, Tenn.) in 1956, before doing post-graduate work at Columbia University. From 1957 to 1961 he taught at several southern colleges, and from 1956 to 1961 he was a social worker in New York City. His books include *The Coming of Chronos to the House of Night Song* (1963), *Sex and Racism in America*

(1965), and *White Papers for White America* (1966). Hernton was associate professor of Afro-American studies at Oberlin College (Oberlin, Ohio).

HERSHAW, LAFAYETTE MCKEENE (1863–1945), lawyer, government official; born in Clay County, N.C. Hershaw received a B.A. degree from Atlanta University in 1886 and his law degree from Howard University School of Law in 1892. He was a teacher and principal in the Atlanta public school system from 1886 to 1890, after which time he went to Washington, D.C., to serve as an executive in the U.S. Civil Service. Attaining the position of land examiner in the U.S. Department of the Interior, Hershaw held this post for 42 years until his retirement. He also taught law at the Robert H. Terrell Law School in Washington, D.C.

HEWELL, GRACE L. (1918–   ), educator, social worker, government official; born in Atlanta, Ga. Hewell received a B.A. degree from Spelman College (Atlanta, Ga.) in 1940, a M.S.W. degree from the Atlanta University School of Social Work in 1943, and a M.A. degree (1952) and her Ed.D. degree (1958) from Columbia University. She taught at Columbia University (1945–56), was a community health educator with the New York City department of health (1954–60), a community organization consultant with the New York City Youth Board (1960–61), and served with the Department of Health, Education, and Welfare (HEW) in Washington, D.C. Hewell became the education chief of the Committee on Education and Labor of the U.S. House of Representatives after 1965.

HICKMAN, ERNEST LAWRENCE (1903–   ), African Methodist Episcopal bishop; born in Fayetteville, Tenn. Hickman received a B.D. degree from Turner College in 1928 and his LL.D. degree from Wilberforce University (Wilberforce, Ohio) in 1956. He was pastor of African Methodist Episcopal (AME) churches in Cleveland, Ohio; and in Chattanooga, Memphis, Knoxville, and Fayetteville, Tenn. Hickman was elected an AME bishop in 1956.

HIGGINBOTHAM, A. LEON, JR. (1928–   ), lawyer, judge; born in Trenton, N.J. Higginbotham attended Purdue University (Lafayette, Ind.) for a year, received a B.A. degree from Antioch College (Yellow Springs, Ohio) in 1949, and received his LL.B. degree from Yale Law School in 1952. After working as an assistant district attorney in Philadelphia, Pa., for two years, he became a partner in a law firm there. In 1956 Higginbotham became special deputy attorney general for Pennsylvania, and in 1962 he was appointed a commissioner of the Federal Trade Commission, the first Afro-American to become head of a federal regulatory commission. Two years later, Higginbotham was sworn in as judge of the U.S. District Court for the Eastern District of Pennsylvania. After his appointment in 1968 to the National Commission on the Causes and Prevention of Violence, he returned in 1969 to the bench as judge of the U.S. District Court in the Virgin Islands. During his career, Higginbotham received many awards and honorary degrees, including the National Human Relations Award of the National Conference of Christians and Jews in 1969. He wrote a masterful book: *In the Matter of Color; Race and the American Legal Process: The Colonial Period*, Oxford U. Pr., New York, 1978.

HIGGINS, RODNEY GONZALES (ca. 1910–65), educator; born in Missouri. Higgins received his Ph.D. degree in economics from the University of Iowa in 1940. He served with the Red Cross in Burma during World War II and then taught at North Carolina Agricultural and Technical (A&T) State University (1940–41). Higgins served as professor of economics and later as chairman of the department of social sciences at Southern University (Baton Rouge, La.) after 1950.

HILDEBRAND, RICHARD ALLEN (1916–), African Methodist Episcopal bishop; born in Winsboro, S.C. Hildebrand received a B.A. degree from Allen University (Columbia, S.C.) in 1938, a B.D. degree from Wilberforce University (Wilberforce, Ohio) in 1941, his S.T.M. degree from Boston University in 1948, and a honorary D.D. degree from Wilberforce in 1951. He served churches in South Carolina, Ohio, Rhode Island, New York, and Delaware, before becoming pastor of the Bethel African Methodist Episcopal Church of New York City in 1954. Hildebrand was the first black president of the Manhattan division of the Protestant Council of New York, and he was also president of the New York City chapter of the National Association for the Advancement of Colored People (NAACP). He was elected an AME bishop in 1972.

HILL, BEN H. *See* NEWSPAPERS: CONTEMPORARY.

HILL, CARL MC CLELLAN (1907–), educator; born in Norfolk, Va. Hill received a B.S. degree from Hampton Institute (Hampton, Va.) in 1931, and a M.S. degree (1935) and his Ph.D. degree (1941) from Cornell University (Ithaca, N.Y.). He taught at Hampton Institute (1931–41), at North Carolina Agricultural and Technical (A&T) State University (1941–44), and at Tennessee State University (1944–62). Hill became president of Kentucky State College in 1962 and served in that post until his retirement in 1975. He worked on chemistry research projects for the Tennessee Valley Authority (1948–52) and was a trustee of Stillman College (Tuscaloosa, Ala.). Hill was a member of the American Chemical Society and the Sigma Xi honor society.

HILL, HENRY AARON (1915–), scientist; born in St. Joseph, Mo. Hill received a B.A. degree from Johnson C. Smith University (Charlotte, N.C.) in 1936 and his Ph.D. degree from Massachusetts Institute of Technology in 1942. He was a Rosenwald Fellow, and then became a research chemist for Atlantic Research Associates, Inc. (1942–43) and then vice-president in charge of research (1944–46). Hill served as president of Riverside Research Laboratories, and after 1952 as assistant manager of National Polychemicals, Inc.

HILL, H. SOLOMON (1909–), clergyman, educator; born in North Little Rock, Ark. Hill received a B.A. degree from Arkansas Agricultural, Mechanical and Normal (AM&N) College in 1931, a B.D. degree from Payne Seminary in 1935, and his M.A. degree from Drew University (Madison, N.J.) in 1942. He was in the ministry until he became president of Shorter College (North Little Rock, Ark.) in 1960.

HILL, JOHN H. (1852–1936), author, educator; born in Charles Town, W. Va. Hill studied at Bowdoin College (Brunswick, Maine), qualified at the bar of Sagadahoc County, Maine, at the age of 27, and served in the 10th Cavalry of the U.S. Army—participating in the campaign against Geronimo. He left military service and became principal of an elementary school in West Virginia and later instructor and principal at the West Virginia Colored Institute. During the Spanish-American War, Hill joined the U.S. 8th Infantry, but returned to the institute as an instructor after the war. In World War I he served as a welfare worker in the coal fields and then as an assistant in the state compensation department of West Virginia until 1929. In 1935 Hill was made president emeritus of West Virginia State College.

HILL, JULIUS WANSER (1917–   ), physician; born in Atlanta, Ga. Hill received a B.A. degree from Johnson C. Smith University (Charlotte, N.C.) in 1933, a B.S. degree (1934) and a M.S. degree (1937) from the University of Illinois, and his M.D. degree from Meharry Medical College (Nashville, Tenn.) in 1951. He interned at Los Angeles County General Hospital, and also did a four-year residency there in orthopedic surgery. Hill became president of the National Medical Association (NMA) in 1969.

HILL, LESLIE PINCKNEY (1880–1960), educator, poet; born in Lynchburg, Va. Hill received a B.A. degree (1903) and his M.A. degree (1904) from Harvard University. He subsequently taught at Tuskegee Institute (Tuskegee Institute, Ala.) from 1904 to 1907, and then served with Manassas Industrial School from 1907 to 1913 and with Cheyney Training School after 1913. Hill was chairman of the Interracial Committee of Philadelphia, Pa. He wrote *The Wings of Oppression* (Poems) and *Toussaint L'Overture* (a dramatic history, 1928). Hill served with distinction as the president of Cheyney State College (Cheyney, Pa.) for two decades. *See also* LITERATURE: POETRY.

HILL, MOZELL C. (1911–1969), sociologist, educator; born in Anniston, Ala. Hill received a B.A. degree (1933) and a M.A. degree (1937) from the University of Kansas, and earned his Ph.D. degree in sociology from the University of Chicago in 1946; he did postgraduate work at the London School of Economics from 1952 to 1953. From 1937 to 1946 he taught sociology at Langston University (Langston, Okla.), and served as chairman of the department of sociology at Atlanta University from 1948 to 1958. From 1958 to 1960, Hill taught at Columbia University, and in the following two years taught abroad, lecturing at Cambridge University (Cambridge, England) and at the University of Nigeria. In 1963 Hill became a professor of educational sociology at New York University. He served on several government commissions, including the Government Committee on Unemployment Relief of Indiana from 1934 to 1935; the U.S. Resettlement Administration from 1935 to 1937; the federal project on juvenile delinquency in St. Louis, Mo., from 1962 to 1963; and the U.S.

Public Health Commission. Hill was also a consultant to several local boards of education, and served on the executive committee of the Southern Sociological Society. He edited the *Southwestern Journal* from 1945 to 1947 and Atlanta University's *Phylon* from 1948 to 1958.

HILL, OLIVER W. (1907–   ), lawyer; born in Richmond, Va. Hill received a B.A. degree and his LL.B. degree from Howard University (Washington, D.C.). In 1934 he was admitted to the Virginia bar, and in 1948 he was elected to the city council of Richmond, Va. Hill was the first Afro-American to be elected to a public office in Richmond since Reconstruction. He was also active in the civil rights movement in Virginia.

HILL, T. ARNOLD (1888–1947), civil rights leader; born in Richmond, Va. Hill received a B.A. degree from Virginia Union University in 1911, and did postgraduate work in sociology at New York University. In 1914 he joined the staff of the National Urban League, an organization in which he was active most of his professional life. In 1917 Hill assisted George Cleveland Hall and others in organizing a Chicago, Ill., branch of the league, and in the same year Hill assumed the post of its executive director. He was also western field secretary for the league, and although Hill helped to organize western branches, he concentrated his attention on the city of Chicago. During the 1919 Chicago race riots, the Chicago Urban League staff took an active part in restoring order. In 1923 Hill ran unsuccessfully for alderman in Chicago, and in March 1925 assumed the directorship of the industrial relations department of the National Urban League in New York City. Working closely with America Federation of Labor (AFL) leaders, Hill stood as a firm supporter of attempts by blacks to organize unions, at one time throwing league support behind A. Philip Randolph and the Brotherhood of Sleeping Car Porters. Under his direction, the league emphasized greater opportunity for Afro-Americans in employment, the right of collective bargaining, and better education of workers in industry. Within the hierarchy of the Urban League, Hill was a militant, stressing direct action and bread-and-butter issues. He served as acting executive director of the National Urban League from 1934 to 1936, while Eugene Kinckle Jones was on leave in Washington, D.C. Hill resigned from the league in 1940 due to an ideological split with Jones. He assisted Gunnar Myrdal in his research on Afro-Americans from 1945 to 1946 by contributing studies on the National Urban League and its branches. *See also* NATIONAL URBAN LEAGUE.

HILL, WENDELL T., JR. *See* SCIENTISTS: BIOLOGICAL, PHYSICAL.

HILYER, AMANDA GRAY (1870–1957), pharmacist; born in Atchison, Kans. Hilyer graduated from Howard University (Washington, D.C.) and operated a drugstore in Washington, D.C., for many years. During World War I, she was director of hostesses in U.S. Army camps at Upton, Dix, and Taylor. Hilyer later served as executive secretary of the Phyllis Wheatley Young Women's Christian Association (YWCA).

HIMES, CHESTER BOMAR (1909–   ), author; born in Jefferson City, Mo. Himes was educated at Ohio State University from 1926 to 1927 and received a Rosenwald Fellowship in 1944. He lived mostly in France and Spain after World War II. His short stories and novels, primarily humorous in nature, include *If He Hollers Let Him Go* (1945); *Lonely Crusade* (1947); *Pinktoes* (1961); *Cotton Comes to Harlem* (1966); *Black on Black: Baby Sister; A Black Greek Tragedy and Selected Writings*. His autobiography is *The Quality of Hurt* (1973). *See also* LITERATURE: THE NOVEL.

HINDERAS, NATALIE (1927–   ), concert pianist; educator; born in Oberlin, Ohio. Hinderas studied at Oberlin College (Oberlin, Ohio), the Juilliard School of Music (New York, N.Y.), and the Philadelphia Conservatory (Philadelphia, Pa.). A performer at the age of three, she made her New York City debut in 1954. Following that, she appeared as soloist with the Los Angeles Philharmonic, the Philadelphia Orchestra, and the New York Philharmonic, and she made several tours of Europe. In the 1970s Hinderas was associate professor at Temple University (Philadelphia, Pa.). Her recordings include *Natalie Hinderas Plays Music by Black Composers.*

HINES, EARL (FATHA) (1905–   ), jazz pianist, bandleader; born in Duquesne, Pa. Hines formed his own trio while still in high school. After moving to Chicago, Ill, he played with Louis Armstrong's band. Hines formed his own band in the 1920s, and he became known for his trumpet-style piano solos that featured hard-hit octaves played by the right hand. Hines has worked with many of jazz's greats, and was active with his own small groups; he toured throughout the United States and the Continent. Hines greatly influenced many other jazz pianists, notably Joe Sullivan and Jess Stacy. Many consider him the greatest of jazz pianists. *See also* MUSIC: JAZZ.

HINSON, EUGENE THEODORE (1873– ?), physician; born in Philadelphia, Pa. Hinson received his M.D. degree from the University of Pennsylvania in 1898, but because of his color was denied an internship at the university hospital. Later, he received an appointment to the staff of Douglass Hospital, a black institution. Hinson was one of a group of physicians who founded Mercy Hospital, Philadelphia, Pa., in 1907. He served on the hospital's board of directors and became chief of its gynecological department.

HINTON, JAMES SIDNEY (1834– ?), state legislator; born in Raleigh, N.C. Hinton moved to Indiana at the age of six in order to attend a subscription school. He was elected to Indiana's house of representatives in 1881, becoming that state's first black legislator.

HINTON, MILTON J. (MILT) (1910–   ), jazz bass player; born in Vicksburg, Miss. Hinton ranks in the annals of jazz as one of the greatest bass performers. He played with many great bands, including those of Cab Calloway (1936–51), Count Basie, Louis Armstrong, Benny Goodman, and Teddy Wilson (in the 1950s). Throughout the 1960s Hinton appeared in concerts and on television shows. *See also* MUSIC: JAZZ.

HINTON, WILLIAM AUGUSTUS (1883–1959), physician, educator; born in Chicago, Ill. Hinton received a B.S. degree from Harvard University in 1905 and his M.D. degree with honors from Harvard Medical School in 1912. He worked at the pathology laboratory, Massachusetts General Hospital (1912–15), and became director of Wassermann Laboratory, Massachusetts Department of Public Health in 1915. Hinton served as chief (1915) and director (1916–52) of the Boston Dispensary Laboratory, and in 1949 was appointed professor of preventive medicine and hygiene at Harvard Medical School, the first black to become a professor at the school. He became world famous for his work in venereal diseases, developing the Hinton test for detecting syphilis, and, with Dr. Davies, developing the Davies-Hinton tests of blood and spinal fluid for the detection of syphilis.

Chester Himes. *(National Educational Television.)*

HISTORIANS

Nineteenth-Century Historians The earliest black American historians were the slave narrators or autobiographers. One of the first and best accounts of slavery was written by Olaudah Equiano. His *The Interesting Narrative of the Life of Olaudah Equiano, or Gustavus Vassa the African, Written by Himself,* was published in 1787. Writing quite vividly, Equiano left a rare account of the Atlantic slave trade, as viewed by one of its victims. Numerous other slave narratives written after this date added much to the literature and history of Afro-Americans. Several nonslave accounts also appeared in the nineteenth century in the works of William C. Nell; Joseph T. Wilson; George Washington Williams; and several clergymen, including William J. Simmons, Daniel A. Payne, and J. W. Hood.

William C. Nell was the first Afro-American significantly to collect and publish the biographies of blacks, especially those of partriots in the Revolutionary War. A native free person of Boston, Mass., Nell wrote in the nationalist idiom and style of nineteenth-century historians, extolling the patriotism of Revolutionary War heroes in his illustrated book of 1855 (reprinted in 1968), *The Colored Patriots of the American Revolution.* Crispus Attucks, Nell's favorite martyr and subject, received his first written biography as Nell's opening subject, along with the more famous sketch (already embellished) of Attucks' death from a volley fired by British soldiers in the Boston Massacre, on March 5, 1770.

Nell pleased the abolitionists: Harriet Beecher Stowe and Wendell Phillips, for example, wrote introductions to his book. Interviewing survivors and scanning tombstones in graveyards, Nell placed later historians in his debt by rescuing Attucks and others from oblivion. More than a hundred years later, Benjamin Quarles, an eminent modern Afro-American historian, wrote ably of the role of blacks in the American Revolution in his volume entitled *The Negro in the American Revolution* (1961); but unlike Nell, he wrote as a professional historian, not as a biographer, and he also wrote without the nationalist bias of Nell.

Military heroes of the Civil War received attention from Joseph T. Wilson and George Washington Williams, both veterans.

George Washington Williams was regarded as "the most eminent Negro historian in the world" in his day. His book, *A History of the Negro Troops in the War of Rebellion, 1861–1865* (1888), for example, long remained distinctively in a class by itself. Regarded with equal respect is Williams' comprehensive history entitled *History of the Negro Race in America from 1619 to 1880: Negroes as Slaves, as Soldiers, and as Citizens* (1883). This work was the first serious historical study to depart from the simple narrative and biographical idiom of earlier histories. Williams was not a popular writer, but he had great influence upon the black historians of his generation, and by the turn of the century more and more writers, though nonprofessional, were turning their hands to histories.

However, before the close of the nineteenth century, William J. Simmons had compiled the best biography of his generation in a massive volume entitled *Men of Mark* (1887). Without this collection, much of nineteenth-century Afro-American biography would be obscure. Altogether, Simmons divided his work into 177 biographies, including a range of selections from lesser-known contemporaries to such famous persons as Frederick Douglass and Toussaint L'Ouverture. Moreover, he illustrated his text with the inclusion of many valuable portrait etchings, among them one of himself. The introduction to the volume was written by Simmons' friend and fellow clergyman, Henry McNeal Turner, an outspoken bishop of the African Methodist Episcopal (AME) Church and an advocate of black nationalism and Pan-Africanism. Although Turner made history in his day and times, he left most of its writing to other churchmen.

Indeed, churchmen frequently also wrote institutional histories, an understandable fact in the light of the central, commanding position that the minister, clergy, and church have held throughout Afro-American history. One of the earliest church histories was written by Christopher Rush and George Collins on the first organized Afro-American denomination and entitled *Short Account of the Rise and Progress of the African Methodist Episcopal Church in America* (1843). Daniel A. Payne, B. T. Tanner, L. M. Haygood, C. H. Phillips, W. J. Gaines, and R. R.

Wright also wrote on various aspects of the AME Church. About the Baptists, several histories were likewise written—by Patrick H. Thompson, N. H. Pius, Lewis G. Jordan, and Charles H. Brooks, mainly in the twentieth century. Also, C. H. Phillips wrote on the history of the Colored Methodist Episcopal (CME) Church in 1898, and J. W. Hood served as historian of the African Methodist Episcopal Zion (AMEZ) Church.

Carter G. Woodson The work of Carter G. Woodson provides a meaningful and convenient dividing line between early and later historians. Woodson was a central, commanding figure in the study, writing, and teaching of Afro-American history, reflecting both the past and the present of Afro-Americans. He was the first historian to use successfully sound scholarship in the refutation of myths and racist views about the Afro-American. Woodson rendered his distinctive service chiefly in his capacity as the principal founder and director of the Association for the Study of Negro Life and History. For 34 years he served as the editor of its official organ, the *Journal of Negro History,* published continuously after January 1916. However, Woodson did not stand alone. An outstanding contemporary was the historian-sociologist W. E. B. Du Bois, one of the first Afro-Americans to be published in the *American Historical Review,* who applied Marxist interpretations to the Reconstruction period of American history in his book entitled *Black Reconstruction* (1935).

The Association for the Study of Negro Life and History (which in the 1970s substituted the word "Afro-American" for "Negro" in its name) was organized in Chicago, Ill., on September 9, 1915, under the leadership of Woodson, George Cleveland Hall, W. B. Hargrove, J. E. Stamps, and Alexander L. Jackson. It was incorporated the same year in the District of Columbia. The purposes of the association are as follows: (1) to promote historical research and writing; (2) to publish books on Afro-American life and history; (3) to promote the study of Afro-American history through schools, colleges, churches, homes, fraternal groups, and clubs; (4) to collect and encourage the collection of historical manuscripts and materials relating to black people. Among the association's presidents (1960s–1970s) were John Reuben Sheeler, J. Rupert Picott, Andrew F. Brimmer, Edgar A. Toppin, and Charles Walker Thomas.

The association is composed of both lay and professional members. Its annual meetings are attended by several thousand scholars from various disciplines and by interested lay persons. Since 1937 it has published the *Negro History Bulletin,* which appeals largely to a lay and public high school audience. In conjunction with Associated Publishers, the association has also published over the years several volumes and éditions on Afro-American history, and it has sponsored and encouraged interest in blacks through the observance of Negro History Week after 1926 (the word "Negro" has in this context been replaced by "black").

But the *Journal of Negro History* remains the greatest achievement of the association, the most reputable landmark and publication in Afro-American history. With the publication of the *Journal,* a new revised history of blacks began to appear, refuting the many old myths that had been largely written and perpetuated by whites, when written at all. Accepting the work of both black and white scholars, the *Journal* revised the prevailing views of American history in regard to slavery and Reconstruction.

Carter G. Woodson (1875–1950) in the late 1940s. *(Scurlock Studio.)*

Although Ulrich B. Phillips' view of slavery as a benign and beneficial institution had prevailed as the dominant view of slavery, Afro-American historians knew otherwise and arrived at conclusions that were later taken up by many revisionists of Phillips. Studies at Fisk University (Nashville, Tenn.) in the early 1930s, for example, revealed the unhappy memories—whippings and other cruelties—of ex-slaves. Moreover, Afro-American scholars began early to revise the prevailing views of William A. Dunning on Reconstruction. For example, Alrutheus A. Taylor, a professor at Fisk University, published studies of Reconstruction in Tennessee and Virginia that were serialized during the early 1930s in the *Journal of Negro History.*

Both the association and Woodson attracted early support from a group of young black professional historians, especially in the 1930s. Among them were Charles H. Wesley, who later served as director of the association; Albert N. D. Brooks, who later became editor of the *Negro History Bulletin;* Luther P. Jackson, a professor at Virginia State College (Petersburg, Va.); W. Sherman Savage and Lorenzo J. Greene, both professors at Lincoln University (Jefferson City, Mo.); Alrutheus A. Taylor; Rayford W. Logan and William M. Brewer, who later served as editors of the *Journal of Negro History;* Merle Eppse, a professor at Tennessee Agricultural and Industrial (A&I) College; Herman Dreer and Irving Dilliard of St. Louis, Mo.; James and E. Horace Fitchett of South Carolina; and Hugo Johnston of Virginia State College.

Contemporary Professionals Still younger professional historians joined these ranks, mainly after the 1950s: Clarence Albert Bacote, Letitia Brown, Robert Clarke, Henry Earl Cobb, Helen G. Edmonds, Walter Fisher, John Hope Franklin, Elsie Lewis, Frenise Logan, W. A. (Gus) Low, Roland McConnell, Harold T. Pinkett, Benjamin Quarles, Lawrence D. Reddick, Wilhelmina S. Robinson, John Reuben Sheeler, Edgar A. Toppin, Lorraine A. Williams, and George Ruble Woolfolk, to mention only a few. These and other contemporary historians have embraced a variety of subjects, but one theme that constantly appears in their work is concern about the effects of discrimination. Like other Afro-Americans, black historians in their writings have reflected the pressures upon the black presence in white America. Especially in the early days, a great many turned to biography. While this approach was less evident among professional historians of the second half of the twentieth century, it was much in vogue among the popularizers. Moreover, whereas Woodson's school placed emphasis upon black achievement or uniqueness (what blacks did for themselves), later black historians turned increasingly toward larger forces operating upon blacks both from inside and outside the black community. Their view is more comprehensive, and their approach tends to be more analytical and theoretical. Black nationalism, for example, became a growing concern after the 1950s. "Our emphasis," said Vincent Harding "is on exposure, disclosure, or reinterpretation of the entire American past." Other black historians, realizing the impact of Afro-Americans upon cities, have turned, like many of their white colleagues, to urban history.

Wherever they turned—to urban history, nationalism, Africa, Latin America, or to biography—a younger generation of Afro-American historians, swelling the ranks of their older contemporaries, emerged during and after the civil rights movement of the late 1960s and early 1970s. Among the group were: Mary F. Berry, Allison Blakely, John W. Blassingame, Al-Tony Gilmore, Jimmie L. Franklin, Bettye Gardner, James E. Haney, Janette H. Harris, Alton Hornsby, Jr., Franklin W. Knight, Tony Martin, Genna Rae McNeil, and Bettye C. Thomas.

Afro-American historians entered in the *Encyclopedia*, as contributors or as biographies (who were active in the 1970s), include the following:

Clarence Albert Bacote; Minnie T. Bailey; Donnie D. Bellamy, a contributor; Mary F. Berry, a contributor; David W. Bishop, a contributor; John W. Blassingame, a contributor; George Breathett; Letitia Woods Brown; Henry Earl Cobb; Clarence Contee, a contributor; Helen G. Edmonds; Jimmie L. Franklin; John Hope Franklin; Raymond Gavins; Al-Tony Gilmore; Lorenzo Johnston Greene; Vincent Harding; Alton Hornsby, Jr.; Nathan I. Huggins; Sarah D. Jackson, a contributor; Franklin W. Knight; Frenise A. Logan; Rayford W. Logan; W. A. Low, a contributor; Hollis R. Lynch; Roland C. McConnell; Paul McStallworth; Robert E. Perdue; Harold T. Pinkett, a contributor; Martha S. Putney; Benjamin Quarles, a contributor; Richard D. Ralston; Lawrence D. Reddick; Wilhelmina S. Robinson; W. Sherman Savage; Otey M. Scruggs; John Reuben Sheeler, a contributor; George Sinkler; Alonzo T. Stephens, Sr.; Arvarh E. Strickland; Edward F. Sweat, a contributor; Merze Tate; Joseph H. Taylor; Earlie E. Thorpe; Edgar A. Toppin; Ernestein Walker; Charles H. Wesley; Rubin F. Weston; and Prince Wilson.

REFERENCES: The most comprehensive reference is the *Journal of Negro History*, which contains several good articles. Two of the more recent ones are in the issue for January 1973: Gray, Daniel Savage, "Bibliographical Essay: Black Views on Reconstruction" and Logan, Rayford W., "Carter G. Woodson: Mirror and Molder of His Times, 1875–1950." For a good critical essay on writings on slavery (by both blacks and whites), see Blassingame, John W., *The Slave Community: Plantation Life in the Antebellum South*, Oxford University Press, New York, 1972. Writings on black historians are few. Earlie E. Thorpe pioneered and practically preempted the field in his several works: *Negro Historians in the United States* (1958), *The Mind of the Negro; An Intellectual History of Afro-Americans* (1961), *Black Historians: A Critique* (1971). For a short, perceptive view of Afro-American historians and their writings, see Benjamin Quarles, "Black History Unbound," in Sidney W. Mintz, ed., *Slavery, Colonialism, and Racism*, W. W. Norton & Company, New York, 1974.

HOGANS, CLARENCE WALKER (1901–69), physician; born in Paterson, N.J. Hogans interned at Harlem Hospital, New York, N.Y. (1929–31) and received clinical training in obstetrics and gynecology at New York Postgraduate and Beth Israel hospitals. He served as chief of a division of the department of obstetrics and gynecology at Harlem Hospital, as attending gynecologist at Mount Morris Hospital, and as a staff member of Sydenham, Misericordia, and Wickersham hospitals.

HOLIDAY, BILLIE (LADY DAY) (1915–59), singer; born Eleanor Fagan Gough in Baltimore, Md.

Holiday moved to New York City as a young girl, and her singing career began in 1929 in the nightclubs of Harlem. During the 1930s, she appeared in downtown clubs in New York City as a vocalist with such bandleaders as Artie Shaw, Benny Carter, Count Basie, and Paul Whiteman. The records she made during this period, in her plaintive blues style, increased her reputation and popularity. It was not long before Holiday was affectionately known as "Lady Day," a name given to her by Lester Young, tenor saxophonist with Count Basie's band. Several of her records became classics in the field of blues singing, among them "Strange Fruit," "God Bless the Child," "My Man," "Mean to Me," and "I Cried For You and You Let Me Down." Her autobiography was published in 1956, and the film *The Lady Sings the Blues*, released in 1973, gave an account of her life, which, in the end, was marked by addiction to drugs and alcohol. *See also* MUSIC: BLUES.

HOLLAND, JEROME HEARTWELL (1916–   ), educator, business executive, government official; born in Auburn, N.Y. Holland received a B.S. degree (1939) and his M.S. degree (1941) from Cornell University (Ithaca, N.Y.), where he played end on the football team. He was an All-American for two seasons and eventually a member of college football's hall of fame. He received his Ph.D. (1950) from the University of Pennsylvania. He was president of Delaware State College from 1953 to 1960, and president of Hampton Institute (Hampton, Va.) from 1960 to 1970. From 1970 to 1972 he was United States ambassador to Sweden, resigning to become the first Afro-American director of the New York Stock Exchange. *See also* ATHLETES.

HOLLOMAN, JOHN LAWRENCE SULLIVAN, JR. (MIKE) (1919–   ), physician, administrator, civic leader; born in Washington, D.C. Holloman graduated from Virginia Union University with honors in chemistry, received his M.D. degree from the University of Michigan, and interned at Harlem Hospital, New York, N.Y., before joining the U.S. Army Air Corps in World War II. After returning from the Armed Forces, he did postgraduate training at Cornell University (Ithaca, N.Y.) and at Bellevue Hospital, New York, N.Y. He also maintained a private practice in Harlem. He served as a vice-president of the Health Insurance Plan, as president of the National Medical Association, and as a trustee or adviser for a dozen health agencies. In 1973 he became the

first black president of the New York City Health and Hospital Corporation.

HOLMAN, M. CARL (1919–   ), journalist, urbanist; born in Minter City, Miss., but grew up in St. Louis, Mo. He received a B.A. degree from Lincoln University (Mo.), an M.A. degree from the University of Chicago and his M.F.A. from Yale University. Holman taught at several black colleges, including Clark, Atlanta University, and Hampton Institute. He also edited the *Atlanta Inquirer*. He joined the National Urban Coalition in 1968, filling the position once held by Whitney M. Young.

HOLMES, DEFIELD T. scientist, educator. Holmes received a B.S. degree from Hampton Institute (Hampton, Va.) in 1948, and a M.S. degree and his Ph.D. degree from Ohio State University. He served as assistant professor of biology and chemistry at Shaw University (Raleigh, N.C.) from 1953 to 1955, and as professor of biology (1958–60) and as chairman of the department of biology (1960–68) at Central State University (Wilberforce, Ohio). In 1967 Holmes became dean of the School of Graduate Studies of Central State University, and in 1968 dean of its College of Arts and Sciences. He became director of the United Board for College Development in Atlanta, Ga. in 1971.

HOLMES, DWIGHT OLIVER WENDELL (1883–1966), educator; born in Lewisburg, W. Va. Holmes received a B.A. degree (1901) and a M.A. degree (1912) from Howard University (Washington, D.C.); a second M.A. degree from Columbia University in 1915; two LL.D. degrees, one from Howard University and one from Wilberforce University (Wilberforce, Ohio); and his Ph.D. degree from Columbia University in 1934. He taught at Howard University, served as dean of the College of Education there (1920–34), and then as dean of the graduate school (1934–37). Holmes was the first black president of Morgan State University (Baltimore, Md.). He was a contributing editor to the *Journal of Negro Education* and the *Negro College Quarterly*, and he wrote *The Evolution of the Negro College* (1934).

HOLT, LEONARD W. *See* LAWYERS.

HOOKS, BENJAMIN LAWSON (1924–   ), lawyer, civic leader; born in Memphis, Tenn. He attended LeMoyne College, Howard University, and received his law degree (J.D.) from De Paul

Billie Holiday. (Photo by Robin Carson.)

University in 1948. Active in church and civic affairs, he served as pastor of the Middle Baptist Church and as a local judge in Memphis. A persuasive speaker, he became the executive director of the National Association for the Advancement of Colored People (NAACP) in 1977.

HOPE, JOHN (1868–1936), educator; born in Augusta, Ga. The son of a former Virginia planter and a free black woman, Hope was robbed of his family's inheritance by executors after his father's death in 1876. Aided by scholarships, Hope worked his way through Worcester Academy (Worcester, Mass.); received a B.A. degree (1894) and a M.A. degree (1907) from Brown University (Providence, R.I.); he became president of Atlanta Baptist College in 1906, one of the first Afro-Americans to head a black college established after the Civil War. In 1929 Hope put together the Atlanta University System, designed to coordinate the six denominational colleges that were competing for black students in Atlanta, Ga., and served as the first president of the new Atlanta University (1929–36). Hope's life is recounted in a biography by Ridgely Torrence entitled *The Story of John Hope* (1948). *See also* ATLANTA UNIVERSITY.

HORNE, FRANK S. (1899–   ), physician, public official, poet; born in New York, N.Y. A graduate of the City College of the City University of New York in 1921. Horne received a degree in ophthalmology from Northern Illinois College of Ophthalmology and Otology in 1923. He practiced optometry in Illinois for three years until he joined the staff of Fort Valley State College (Fort Valley, Ga.) as employment dean and ultimately as acting president. In 1936 his career took another direction, and Horne became involved with federal housing agencies. Until 1946 he served on the Federal Public Housing Authority, and thereafter on the Housing and Home Finance Agency. In addition, his ability as a writer led to the publication of articles and poems in many magazines, and he published a book of poems entitled *Haverstraw* (1963).

HORNE, LENA (1917–   ), singer, actress; born in Brooklyn, N.Y. At the age of 16, not yet finished with high school, Horne secured a job as a chorus girl at the Cotton Club in New York City's Harlem, where she danced and sang for two years. During that time, she appeared in an unsuccessful Broadway play *Dance With Your Gods* in 1934. For the next three years Horne toured and recorded with Noble Sissle's band, a rigorous training period that led to a starring role in the revue *Blackbirds of 1939*, which closed after only nine performances. The next year she joined Charlie Barnet's Band, and in 1941 was hired by Barney Josephson to sing at his Cafe Society Downtown, where within a short time she succeeded in reinvigorating a lagging business. From there Horne went to Hollywood to appear in nightclubs, and later to sign a movie contract that led to roles in such films as *Cabin in the Sky* (1943), *Stormy Weather* (1943), and *Broadway Rhythm* (1944). *See also* MOTION PICTURES.

HORNSBY, ALTON, JR. (1940–   ), historian, educator; born in Atlanta, Ga. Hornsby received a B.A. degree from Morehouse College (Atlanta, Ga.) in 1961, and a M.A. degree (1962) and his Ph.D. degree (1969) from the University of Texas. He was associate professor of history at Morehouse College, and became chairman of the department in 1968. He edited *In the Cage: Eyewitness Accounts of the Freed Negro in Southern Society, 1877–1929* (1971). Hornsby became acting editor of the *Journal of Negro History* in 1976 and, later, its editor.

HORSE RACING   *See* ATHLETES.

HORTON, GEORGE MOSES *See* LITERATURE: POETRY.

HOSPITALS   *See* HEALTH; PHYSICIANS.

HOUSING

HOUSING

Background Restrictions based upon income and racial discrimination have been two underlying historic factors that have long influenced the housing of Afro-Americans. The vast majority of blacks (about 8 or 9 out of 10) lived in poor (substandard) dwellings until the mid-twentieth century. Since then, however, housing conditions have improved substantially, but they still lagged considerably behind those for whites. Thus, a disproportionately greater number of blacks than whites continued to live in substandard and overcrowded housing situated in segregated, low-income areas during the 1970s.

The term "substandard," used here as a measure of housing quality, was first defined as such by the national housing agencies in the 1950s. It is descriptive of the structural quality as well as the basic facilities of a housing unit. In 1950 units in a dilapidated condition were defined as substandard; in 1960 deteriorating housing was added as a classification in the substandard category; in the 1970 census structural quality was not measured. However, units lacking some or all basic plumbing facilities, previously included in the substandard category, were counted in 1970. In metropolitan areas, the U.S. Bureau of the Census defines a low-income area in terms of a census tract in which 20 percent or more of the population was below the poverty-income level in 1969. In nonmetropolitan areas, a low-income area is defined in terms of a township, district, or political subdivision in which 20 percent of the population was below this level. By these definitions, considerably more than half of all Afro-Americans lived in poverty areas in the 1970s, and about 1 out of 4 lived in substandard dwellings.

Whether below or above the poverty-income level, a much greater proportion of blacks than whites lived in poverty areas in 1970, both inside and outside metropolitan areas. In nonmetropolitan areas, 80.2 percent of low-income blacks and 71.3 percent of blacks above the poverty level lived in low-income areas; for whites

the figures are 50.6 percent and 30.9 percent, respectively. In metropolitan areas, 66 percent of low-income blacks and 46.5 percent of blacks above the poverty level lived in low-income areas; for whites the figures were 22.8 percent and 6.1 percent, respectively. Moreover, low-income whites living in metropolitan areas were distributed equally between central cities and suburban areas. For blacks the ratio was 5 to 1.

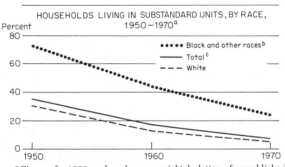

HOUSEHOLDS LIVING IN SUBSTANDARD UNITS, BY RACE, 1950-1970[a]

●●●●● Black and other races[b]
—— Total[c]
– – – White

[a] Figures for 1970 are based on a special tabulation of unpublished data provided by a 1970 Bureau of the Census survey, Components of Inventory Change.

[b] In 1970 "Afro-American and other races" is limited to Afro-Americans only and "White" included white and other races.

[c] For 1960 census data yielded a figure of 16 percent. However, 1960 data had a serious undercounting of dilapidated units. The 1959 Survey of Components of Change and Residential Finance (SCARF) is believed to have yielded more accurate figures regarding dilapidation. Hence, the 17 percent figure is based on SCARF findings.

SOURCE: Executive Office of the President, U.S. Office of Management and Budget, *Social Indicators*, 1973, Table 6/3.

The percentage of all American families living in substandard housing declined drastically from 35 percent in 1950 to approximately 7 percent in 1970. Considerably more black families than white families lived in substandard housing in 1950: 73.2 percent of black families compared to 31.8 percent of white families. Between 1950 and 1970 the proportion of whites living in substandard housing dropped faster than the proportion of blacks. Thus in 1970, 23 percent of black families but only 5.7 percent of white families lived in substandard housing. One factor that created this imbalance was that between

445

1950 and 1960, 9 out of every 10 standard homes that were added to the housing supply went to white occupants, despite the relatively greater need of blacks. Because the incidence of substandard housing rises with declining income and because a larger proportion of the black population than of the white population is poor, it can be expected that a larger proportion of blacks would live in substandard housing conditions. However, this factor holds true for blacks in every income category.

The incidence of overcrowded housing is considerably more frequent among black families of all income levels than among white families. In 1960 one-tenth of all white homes had more than one person per room compared with more than one-fourth (28 percent) for nonwhites. By 1970 the proportion for whites and minorities other than blacks had fallen to 7 percent and for blacks to 19 percent. For families of Spanish origin living in urban areas, crowded conditions were more prevalent than for any other racial or ethnic group in 1970. This was especially true for families of Mexican origin. In rural areas, American Indian families had the highest incidence of overcrowding, followed closely by families of Mexican origin.

Not only is the incidence of overcrowding and inadequate plumbing facilities higher among minority families, but also a greater proportion of minorities at all income levels live in such housing than do whites. For example, 14 percent of the housing occupied by families of whites and other races with income below $2,000

lacked some or all plumbing facilities in 1970, and 3.5 percent were overcrowded. For black families at this income level, the respective figures were 29.9 percent and 12.3 percent. At the other end of the income scale, only 0.7 percent of the white households earning $15,000 or more lived in homes lacking adequate plumbing facilities, and 5.4 percent were overcrowded. For black families with similar incomes, the figures were 2.3 percent and 17.4 percent, respectively.

Even in homes with adequate plumbing facilities, the number of such facilities in black homes lagged well behind the number found in white homes. For example, 26 percent of all white-occupied housing in 1970 had more than one bath as opposed to only 12 percent of black-occupied homes. In terms of such other amenities as clothes washers and dryers, dishwashers, and garbage disposals, minority homes lagged well behind white homes.

Discrimination Discrimination in housing against Afro-Americans has its roots in slavery and racism. Defined legally as property themselves, blacks under slavery could not buy their own households. They could and did frequently live in close proximity to whites, but their conduct was regulated by codes in conformity with white racist supremacy. Free blacks during the slave period could and did own households, but these homes were often severely restricted and segregated as to quality and location.

After slavery, a great number of privately generated and publicly legislated practices were used to create and perpetuate discrimination in housing. Early in the twentieth century, for example, many American communities enacted zoning ordinances requiring block-by-block segregation based upon race. State governments, which delegated zoning powers to local governments, supported the establishment of these ordinances, many of which were upheld in state courts. A number of these ordinances were maintained long after 1917, when they were declared unconstitutional by the U.S. Supreme Court in *Buchanan v. Warley*. Legal attempts to enforce them in the courts were still being made in the 1950s.

A second device that came into widespread use after 1917 was the restrictive covenant. This was a written agreement between the buyer and the seller of a house whereby the buyer promised not to sell, rent, or transfer his property to families of a specific race, ethnic group, or religion. Although the covenants were private agree-

The shacks in this 1874 drawing housed the slaves on a rice plantation in South Carolina. Discrimination against black Americans in housing has its roots in slavery and racism. *(Scribner's Monthly.)*

ments, they achieved the status of law through enforcement by the judicial machinery of the state. Where residents of entire neighborhoods or communities joined together to use restrictive covenants, and to seek their enforcement by the courts, if necessary, blacks were denied access to all or a large portion of the housing inventory.

Perpetrators of the racially restrictive covenants operated freely for three decades before the U.S. Supreme Court ruled in 1948 in *Shelley v. Kraemer* that enforcement of restrictive covenants by state courts was a violation of the 14th Amendment. This ruling made restrictive covenants judicially unenforceable; but, because of entrenched racism and the business interests of white real-estate brokers, their use continued in many communities.

White real estate brokers operated on the assumption that residential segregation was not only a business necessity but also morally correct. Real estate agents promoted the use of restrictive covenants and refused to show houses located in white residential areas to prospective black purchasers. In the 1920s, the National Association of Real Estate Brokers (NAREB) counseled its members not to sell property to individuals of racial groups whose ownership allegedly would diminish the value of other property in the area. As late as 1950, NAREB's Code of Ethics stated, in part: "A Realtor should never be instrumental in introducing into a neighborhood, by character of property or occupancy, members of any race or nationality, or any individual whose presence will clearly be detrimental to property values in the neighborhood."

Private builders and mortgage lending institutions acted in accordance with the separate market principle. Thus, in the period of the late 1940s, during which the building boom supplied a substantial number of new houses in large subdivisions throughout urban areas of the nation, the only new housing available to blacks consisted of a comparatively small number of homes located in enclaves and designated for minority occupancy. Financial institutions refused to finance builders who desired to provide housing on a nondiscriminatory basis and denied loans to home buyers—black or white—who desired to purchase housing in neighborhoods in which most or all of the residents were not the race of the homeseeker. In addition, many mortgage lenders refused outright to provide loans to Afro-Americans, thus greatly diminishing the Afro-American's opportunity to

purchase housing, even in black neighborhoods. Typically, Afro-Americans could only secure mortgages under terms that were unfavorable compared to whites: they were required to pay higher interest rates and to make larger downpayments.

Restrictions upon homeownership imposed by discrimination and racism depressed the level of wealth of black families. Homeownership has been the principal means of capital accumulation for all low- and middle-income families, white or black. The importance of homeownership, for example, has been illustrated by John F. Kain in a paper prepared for the Department of Housing and Urban Development (HUD), entitled "Housing Market Discrimination and Its Implications for Government Housing Policy" (June 1973). He estimates that the average house purchased with a Federal Housing Administration (FHA) mortgage in 1949 had a value of $8,286 and a mortgage of $7,101. If this house

An apartment in a New York City tenement, about 1900. *(Photo by Jacob A. Riis, Jacob A. Riis Collection, Museum of the City of New York.)*

were purchased with a 20-year mortgage by a 30-year-old household head, and the home neither appreciated nor depreciated, the purchaser of this home would have saved more than $7,000 and would own the home free and clear by his or her 50th birthday. However, Kain stated that the average appreciation of single-family houses during the past 20 years must have exceeded 100 percent, which is a conservative estimate. Therefore, the homeowner in Kain's example would have accumulated assets by the age of 50 worth at least $16,000, a considerable sum that he or she could use to reduce housing costs, to borrow against for family needs, or simply to hold for retirement. Writing with John M. Quigley in *The American Economic Review* (June 1972), Kain stated that limitation on black homeownership can increase housing costs for blacks by 30 percent.

For Afro-Americans who had obtained homeownership, the median housing value was considerably less than for whites, and the houses owned before and after 1970 were generally older. For example, in 1970, 60.7 percent of whites owned homes worth $15,000 or more and 35 percent of these homes were constructed after 1960. (Only 29.8 percent of the black-owned homes were constructed after 1960.) On the other hand, 46.3 percent of black homeowners owned homes of less than $10,000 value and 93 percent of these homes were built prior to 1960. Although the age of similar white-owned homes approximated those owned by blacks in this category, only 19.4 percent of whites owned homes under $10,000 in value. Among homes valued the highest ($20,000 or more), those owned by blacks were less likely than those owned by whites to be of recent construction. Similarly, in 1970, 70 percent of black renters—as compared to 59 percent of white renters—lived in housing built in 1949 or earlier.

In general, Afro-Americans pay lower median

Before World War II, 8 out of 10 black Americans lived in housing classed as substandard by then current definitions. This rural Louisiana home was photographed in the early 1940s. *(Library of Congress.)*

This comfortable new home in Sabine Farms, Tex., was built by the Farm Security Administration. *(Library of Congress.)*

rents than whites. Nevertheless, according to some studies, blacks still spend more of their income for housing than whites. These studies tend to show, for example, that 30 percent of black homeowners paid one-quarter of their incomes or more for housing as compared to 18 percent of white homeowners. Approximately 43 percent of black renters, compared to 35 percent of white renters, paid one-quarter of their incomes or more for rent.

Other recent studies, however, have found that blacks actually spend a smaller fraction of their incomes on housing than whites of similar income and family structure because of the higher relative prices of good quality housing to which whites have easy access but that is in short supply in areas of minority concentration. These studies have concluded that blacks would spend as much or more than similarly situated whites if access were the same for both groups to a similar range of housing.

Moreover, other studies confirm that blacks pay more than whites for housing of similar size, quality, and neighborhood amenity. For example, a federal study by the President's Committee on Urban Housing entitled *A Decent Home* (1968) found that blacks in urban areas paid up to 30 percent more than whites to obtain minimally adequate housing in 1960. A study of the housing market in St. Louis, Mo., in 1967 showed a 9 percent markup in rental units and a 15 percent markup in sale units. More recent analyses using later data indicated comparable differences in the 1970s.

Thus, whites not only enjoy better housing conditions than blacks but better neighborhood environments as well, regardless of income. The quality of the immediate neighborhood is at least as important as the physical condition of the housing itself when the concern is for the total home environment of the family or individual. Figures relating the incidence of overcrowded and substandard housing conditions are clearly insufficient to convey the pervasive picture of bad living conditions found in low-income areas, especially in central cities. Such conditions are related to a complex of factors: social, economic, political, and cultural. In central-city poverty areas, for example, housing density is many times greater than anywhere else. Here, too, educational and health-care opportunities tend to be the poorest in quality; the percentage of residents who are victims of crime, the highest; and such public services as trash collection, the least effective.

Federal Involvement and Discrimination The federal government has played a significant though not always effective role in regard to the housing of Afro-Americans. Its concern began during the Great Depression, with such measures as the creation of the federal Home Loan Bank System in 1932 and the Home Owner's Loan Corporation in 1933. More significant federal involvement in housing came through the 1934 National Housing Act, which created the Federal Housing Administration (FHA) and its mortgage insurance programs. The act also established the system of insuring accounts in savings and loan associations whose principal business was home finance.

The principal purposes underlying the federal government's early housing policy were the facilitation of credit and the relief of depressed economic conditions. Thus the 1934 National Housing Act was aimed primarily at revitalizing the nation's credit machinery by stimulating greater activity in the home-finance community. In establishing the low-rent public housing program in 1937, federal housing policy took a somewhat different turn by aiming primarily at the provision of housing for lower-income families. Even here, however, a major purpose also was economic—to relieve unemployment in the construction trades.

In the years that followed, the focus of federal housing activity changed to the emphasis of meeting the housing needs of American families. In 1949 the goal of "a decent home and a suitable living environment for every American family" was set forth as the national housing objective toward which federal housing policy was to be directed. By 1968; when the landmark Housing and Urban Development Act was passed, the goal of producing housing in volume, particularly for families that could not afford housing provided through the ordinary channels of the marketplace, had become a matter of national concern and major priority.

When the federal government first became significantly involved in the housing field, an opportunity was presented to effect salutary changes in the existing discriminatory practices of the private housing and home-finance industry. It was an opportunity that was lost. Early federal policy in the housing field accepted and even magnified the discriminatory practices and attitudes of private industry. FHA, for example, not only acquiesced in discriminatory private industry practices, but it even encouraged them, to the point of recommending a model racially

restrictive covenant to insure against what the agency called "inharmonious racial groups." The Federal Home Loan Bank Board and the Home Owners' Loan Corporation openly espoused policies favoring racial residential exclusion. It is to be noted that such federal and private policies of exclusion coincided in time with black protest efforts to end residential segregation as symbolized in the case of *Shelley v. Kraemer.*

Children playing in DeFrees Alley, Washington, D. C., in 1941. *(Library of Congress.)*

In public housing the federal government adopted a different policy—one based on the equitable participation of minorities, not only as tenants, but also in construction and management. But equitable participation was not construed to preclude segregation, and the majority of public housing projects produced during the first 25 years of the program's operation were either all-black or all-white. Until 1962 this was regarded as a matter strictly within the discretion of local public housing authorities. This was so despite the fact that numerous federal court decisions had made it clear that such segregation was in violation of the U.S. Constitution. Even in such newer programs as urban renewal, established in 1949 with the purpose of revitalizing the nation's cities, discriminatory housing practices by private redevelopers benefiting from government subsidies were not deemed a matter in which government should interfere.

It was not until the early 1960s that federal policy progressed to the point where open occupancy integration was considered desirable but not obligatory. No federal agency concerned with housing and urban development had adopted any measure to assure that this policy was carried out in fact. In 1959 it was estimated that less than 2 percent of the new houses provided in the postwar years through FHA mortgage insurance had been available to minorities. On November 20, 1962, President John F. Kennedy issued Executive Order No. 11063 on equal opportunity in housing, directing: "all departments and agencies in the executive branch of the Federal Government, insofar as their functions relate to the provision, rehabilitation, or operation of housing and related facilities, to take all action necessary and appropriate to prevent discrimination because of race, color, creed, or national origin."

Although the order was couched in broad terms, it was, in fact, legally limited. This was true in at least two senses. First, its command of nondiscrimination by no means affected all housing in which the federal government was involved. For example, in the area of home financing, the order was limited to housing "provided in whole or in part by loans ... insured, guaranteed, or otherwise secured by the credit of the Federal Government. . . ." Thus housing provided through mortgage insurance by FHA or loan guarantees by the Veterans Administration (VA)—representing some 25 percent of the new housing market and less than

1 percent of the nation's entire housing inventory—was made subject to a nondiscrimination requirement. But the great bulk of housing units—those conventionally (non-FHA or non-VA) financed by mortgage lending institutions whose deposits or accounts are insured by the federal government—were excluded from coverage.

Second, the principal content of the order as set up in section 101, referred almost entirely to housing provided through federal aid agreements executed after the order's effective date of November 20, 1962. Thus, existing housing that previously had received federal assistance and housing that was still receiving such assistance were unaffected by section 101 if the assistance agreement has been entered into before the order was issued. Moreover, housing not yet even built was, in many cases, unaffected by section 101 for the same reason. This was of particular significance in connection with the urban renewal and public housing programs because of the long time lag between execution of the agreement for federal financial assistance and the ultimate construction and occupancy of the housing so aided. The critical cutoff date for purposes of section 101 of Executive Order No. 11063, it must be emphasized, was the date on which the financial assistance was agreed to be given, not the date on which the housing was constructed or occupied, or even the date on which money changed hands.

Housing provided under federal aid agreements prior to the order was covered by section 102 of the order, known popularly as the "good offices" section. Although it expressly authorized litigation and other appropriate action, as well as good offices, to bring an end to discrimination in pre-order housing, no enforcement action was ever taken. And experience under Executive Order No. 11063 made it clear that the use of "good offices" alone was inadequate to obtain compliance.

The landmark Civil Rights Act of 1964, containing Title VI, was enacted by Congress and signed into law on July 2, 1964. Title VI provides a broad guaranty of nondiscrimination with respect to federally assisted programs. It states: "No person in the United States shall, on the ground of race, color, or national origin, be excluded from participation in, be denied the benefits of, or be subjected to discrimination under any program or activity receiving Federal financial assistance."

Title VI extended nondiscrimination requirements to many of the urban renewal and public

"Striver's Row" in the 1970s. This block of brownstone dwellings on 139th Street in Harlem, New York City, was designed in 1891 by Stanford White for middle-class occupants. (*Roy DeCarava.*)

housing units left uncovered by section 101 of Executive Order No. 11063. Pursuant to regulations implementing Title VI, all urban renewal projects that had not reached the land disposition stage by January 4, 1965 (the date when the regulations became effective) were subject to the nondiscrimination requirements of Title VI, regardless of the date on which the financial assistance agreement was executed. Since the time lag between execution of the assistance agreement and disposition of the urban renewal land frequently is five years or more, and since the urban renewal program had only begun to have a significant impact in terms of project completion by 1964, Title VI had the effect of subjecting the great bulk of urban renewal activity to the requirement of nondiscrimination.

In public housing, all low-rent projects still receiving federal assistance in the form of annual contributions on January 4, 1965, were made subject to the requirements of Title VI, regardless of the date on which the annual contributions contract was executed. This meant that virtually every public housing project authorized since 1937, when the program was initiated, was subject to the mandatory requirements of Title VI.

The principal programs for which section 102 of Executive Order No. 11063 was still a live issue after Title VI was enacted were those involving assistance solely in the form of insurance or guarantees. Section 602 of Title VI, which is the implementing provision of that law, expressly excludes from coverage, "a contract of insurance or guaranty." This meant, for example, that apartment houses built with the aid of pre-order FHA insurance agreements, but still receiving the benefits of that insurance, were excluded from Title VI coverage. It also meant that housing conventionally financed by federally insured mortgage lending institutions continued to be outside the scope of federal nondiscrimination requirement.

In 1968 Congress acted again, closing both coverage gaps that had existed under Executive Order No. 11063 and under Title VI. On April 11, 1968, Congress passed Title VIII of the Civil Rights Act of 1968, which stated: "It is the policy of the United States to provide, within constitutional limitations, for fair housing throughout the United States."

The act provided coverage in phases. The first phase, extending to the end of 1968, provided for coverage identical to that in section 101 of Executive Order No. 11063 on equal opportunity in housing—that is, housing provided under federal aid agreements entered into after November 20, 1962. The second phase, covering the period January 1, 1969, through December 31, 1969, extended coverage generally to private, nonfederally assisted housing except single-family housing and buildings containing no more than four housing units, one of which is occupied by the owner. A further exception permits religious organizations to sell or rent housing to persons of the same religion and permits private clubs to limit occupancy to their members. The third phase, which went into effect on January 1, 1970, further broadens coverage by limiting the exception of single-family housing to such housing sold or rented without the use of a real-estate broker. In view of the fact that the great majority of single-family housing is sold or rented through a broker, this provision has the effect of bringing most single-family housing within the coverage of Title VII. Title VIII also expressly prohibits discrimination in financing of housing, in the advertising of housing for sale or rent, and in the provision of brokerage services. Further, the practice of "blockbusting" was prohibited. ("Blockbusting" is defined under the statute as: "For profit, to induce or attempt to induce any person to sell or rent any dwelling by representations regarding the entry or prospective entry into the neighborhood of a person or persons of a particular race, color, religion, or national origin.")

While under the order on equal opportunity in housing and Title VI of the Civil Rights Act of 1964 only a small fraction of the nation's housing inventory of some 70 million units was covered, under Title VIII nearly 80 percent became subject to a federal nondiscrimination requirement.

If Executive Order No. 11063 and Title VI were weak in coverage, however, their strength was in the sanctions available for enforcement. Both provided for enforcement through the leverage of the substantial assistance contained in federal housing and urban development programs. Thus, if discrimination persisted, the "recipients"—such as FHA-aided builders, local urban renewal agencies, and local public housing authorities—could be debarred from receiving the benefits of these programs. This was a potentially powerful enforcement weapon.

Under Title VIII, by contrast, while coverage was a strong point, enforcement was weak. In fact, enforcement was limited largely to resort to litigation, either by the person discriminated against or by the U.S. Department of Justice in the case of "pattern or practice" lawsuits. In housing, where the need for relief is frequently urgent, the time involved in litigation, as well as the cost, made it a relatively ineffective enforcement mechanism. However, HUD, charged with the principal responsibility for enforcement and administration of the fair housing law, has only the enforcement weapons expressly at its command of "informal methods of conference, conciliation, and persuasion."

Thus, the fair housing act of 1968 has not been enforced. In a special report in 1979, the U.S. Commission on Civil Rights concluded that the federal government's fair-housing efforts suffered from three main interrelated deficiencies: (1) the act itself (Title VIII of the Civil Rights Act of 1968) did not provide effective enforcement mechanisms, (2) federal agencies and departments charged with ensuring fair housing had not carried out their duties adequately, and (3) federal appropriations in support of fair housing had been inadequate. Beyond the failure of federal enforcement, there also existed the probability of failure when the law was tested under existing local conditions. The two cases below show success and failure under the law.

On June 17, 1968, two months after the federal fair housing law had been enacted, the U.S. Supreme Court, in *Jones v. Alfred H. Mayer Company,* held that a provision of an 1866 civil rights law "bars *all* racial discrimination private as well as public, in the sale or rental of property." The statute, which was enacted under the authority of the 13th Amendment, says: "All citizens of the United States shall have the same right, in every State and Territory, as is enjoyed by white citizens thereof to inherit, purchase, lease, sell, hold, and convey real and personal property."

The *Jones* decision rendered all housing, with no exception, open without regard to race, at least as a matter of legal right. Again, however, the means available to secure this right are limited at present to litigation by persons discriminated against.

Almost ten years later, in 1977, a complaint was made against discriminatory zoning in the case of *Village Arlington Heights v. Metropolitan Housing Development Corporation.* The U.S. Supreme Court refused to invalidate, on constitutional grounds, a zoning ordinance of a community in Illinois that operated to exclude low-income, racially integrated housing even though the effect of the ordinance fell disproportionately on blacks. The Court found no intent to discriminate.

There is, then, a full and complex array of laws that, taken together, provide broad protection against racial discrimination in housing. While the main enforcement mechanism is litigation, in many cases opportunities are afforded for assuring compliance by means other than this time-consuming and burdensome process. The laws also afford authority for a coordinated federal effort by all departments and agencies that have programs and activities relating to housing. These include not only HUD, but also such agencies as the Veterans Administration, which administers a home loan guaranty program; financial regulatory agencies, which supervise and benefit the great majority of the nation's mortgage lending institutions; the General Services Administration, which is responsible for determining where and under what conditions most federal installations shall be located; and the U.S. Department of Defense, which, through the economic benefits generated by the presence of military installations, can be a strong influence on housing patterns in many communities throughout the nation. Further, the Department of Justice, through its authority to bring pattern or practice suits, can play a key role in ending discrimination. Of course, many complex factors underly enforcement, one of which is pervasively political in regard to the role of government.

Despite discrimination, however, housing conditions and patterns showed noticeable changes in the 1970s. Undoubtedly, some of the changes were inspired by the latter phases of the civil rights movement of the 1960s and its accompanying changes in social attitudes and practices. Although many of the old conditions and problems of the past prevailed, an array of criteria showed that blacks were far better off in housing than in any preceding period of Ameri-

Homes of middle-class professional Afro-Americans in Baltimore, Md., 1970s. *(Photo by Bill Morgenstern.)*

can history. The changes were revealed when the U.S. Bureau of the Census, under the sponsorship of HUD, conducted its annual housing survey in 1973. Though there were certainly differences in the quality and cost of housing as pointed out above, many similarities existed, which, in a sense, revealed the extent to which homes in the nation had tended to become standardized. Some selected consumer findings are indicated below.

(1) In the 12-month period between the fall of 1972 and the fall of 1973, a slightly smaller proportion of black households (47 purchases per 100 households) than white households (52 purchases per 100 households) purchased at least one of the major appliances covered in the 1973 survey. Black-and-white television sets and refrigerators were the only commodities for which the "household purchases per 100 households" were greater for blacks than for whites. (2) New automobiles were the most costly item in the survey, and the average price paid per black household was about $4,450, approximately the same as that paid per white household. Also, a smaller proportion of black households (7 percent) than white households (13 percent) reported making a new car purchase. (3) For appliances, no significant differences between the average price paid by blacks and whites appeared. (4) Black households were less likely than white households to have most major appliances. The only exception was black-and-white television sets. (5) Among black households, the three most common appliances were refrigerators and kitchen ranges (which are generally considered items of necessity) and television sets. Dishwashers, central air conditioning, and clothes dryers were the least frequently reported—the proportion of black households owning these durables in 1973 was 4, 6, and 16 percent, respectively. (6) Black households were less likely than white households to have owned an automobile in 1973: 57 and 84 percent, respectively. Moreover, black households tended to have older automobiles than white households. About 38 percent of black households with cars compared with 27 percent of white households had a 1967 or earlier model. (7) Since black households receive less income on the average than white households, the proportion of black households owning many major appliances is lower. Comparing the ownership rates for black and white households in the highest income quartile (households with income of $15,000 or more) reduces, in part, the effect of the income differentials. However, at this high income quar-

tile, some differences still existed between blacks and whites in ownership rates of appliances in 1973. *See also* CIVIL RIGHTS: CIVIL RIGHTS CASES, 1865–1975; CIVIL RIGHTS: CIVIL RIGHTS ENFORCEMENT; CIVIL RIGHTS: DISCRIMINATION; EMPLOYMENT; FAMILY; INCOME; NATIONAL ASSOCIATION FOR THE ADVANCEMENT OF COLORED PEOPLE (NAACP); NATIONAL COMMITTEE AGAINST DISCRIMINATION IN HOUSING.

REFERENCES: Duncan, Otis D., *The Negro Population of Chicago: A Study of Residential Succession*, University of Chicago Press, Chicago, 1957; Kain, John F. and John M. Quigley, "Housing Market Discrimination, Homeownership, and Savings Behavior," *American Economic Review*, vol. 52, pp. 263–277, June 1972; Kain, John F. and John M. Quigley, *Housing Markets and Racial Discrimination*, Columbia University Press, New York, 1975; McGraw, B. T., "Potentials for Equal Opportunity in Housing and Community Development," *Journal of Intergroup Relations*, vol. 3, pp. 126–37, Spring 1962; National Advisory Commission on Civil Disorders, *Report of the National Advisory Commission on Civil Disorders*, U.S. Government Printing Office, Washington, D.C., 1970; Taeuber, Karl E. and Alma F. Taeuber, *Negroes in Cities; Residential Segregation and Neighborhood Change*, Aldine Publishing Co., Chicago, 1965; Taeuber, Karl E., "Residential Segregation," *Scientific American*, vol. 213, pp. 12–19, August 1965; U.S. Commission on Civil Rights, *Federal Civil Rights Enforcement Effort*, U.S. Government Printing Office, Washington, D.C., 1971; U.S. Commission on Civil Rights, *Twenty Years After Brown: Equal Opportunity in Housing*, U.S. Government Printing Office, Washington, D.C., 1975; U.S. Department of Commerce, Social and Economic Statistics Administration, *The Social and Economic Status of the Black Population in the United States, 1974*, ser. p-23, no. 54, U.S. Government Printing Office, Washington, D.C., 1975; and U.S. Department of Labor, *Black Americans: A Chartbook*, Bureau of Labor Statistics Bulletin 1699, U.S. Government Printing Office, Washington, D.C., 1971.

HOUSTON, CHARLES HAMILTON (1895–1950), lawyer, educator; born in Washington, D.C. The son of a prominent Howard University (Washington, D.C.) professor, Houston received a B.A. degree and a Phi Beta Kappa Key at the age of 19 from Amherst College (Amherst, Mass.) in 1915. After two years of teaching at Howard University and another two years in military service, Houston entered Harvard Law School, from which he received a LL.B. degree in 1922 and a D.J.S. degree in 1923. Then, having won a traveling fellowship, he went to Madrid, Spain, where he studied at the university for a year, and earned a D.C.L. degree. A lifelong law partnership with his father began in 1924 under the firm name of Houston and Houston. Although his career took him at many points away from the firm, Houston remained closely associated with his father. From the beginning, he had outside commitments: from 1924 to 1929 he was a law instructor

Charles Houston. *(Moorland-Spingarn Research Center.)*

453

at Howard University; by 1929 he had been elevated to associate professor and to vice-dean of the School of Law, concurrent positions he held until 1935. In addition, from 1933 to 1935 Houston served as a member of the board of education of the District of Columbia. In 1944 he was appointed by President Harry S. Truman to the President's Committee on Fair Employment Practices. From 1935 to 1940 he served as special counsel of the National Association for the Advancement of Colored People (NAACP) at its national headquarters in New York City, returning to private practice in Washington, D.C., in 1940, though remaining a member of the NAACP's national legal committee. Houston served on innumerable national organizations, but much of his greatest distinction came as counsel for the NAACP. He was one of the greatest, unsung heroes of Afro-American history, moving with great skill and ability in his legal attack upon discrimination—upon the old legal theory of "separate but equal"—to tear down the walls of segregation. He spearheaded the strategy that led to favorable U.S. Supreme Court decisions against restrictive real estate covenants and against discrimination in colleges. Houston was posthumously awarded the Spingarn Medal by the NAACP. *See also* CIVIL RIGHTS: CIVIL RIGHTS ACTS; CIVIL RIGHTS: CIVIL RIGHTS CASES, 1865–1975; CIVIL RIGHTS MOVEMENT; LAWYERS; NATIONAL ASSOCIATION FOR THE ADVANCEMENT OF COLORED PEOPLE (NAACP).

HOUSTON, IVAN JAMES (1925–   ), business executive; born in Los Angeles, Calif. Houston received a B.S. degree from the University of California at Berkeley in 1948 and also studied at the University of Manitoba (Winnipeg, Canada). He became an accountant with the Golden State Mutual Life Insurance Company in 1948 and then advanced to the positions of supervisor, administrative assistant, assistant secretary, and actuary (beginning in 1956). Houston served as vice-president of that company from 1962 to 1971, at which time he became president of the company.

HOUSTON, NORMAN O. (1893–   ), business executive; born in San Jose, Calif. Houston was educated at the University of California at Berkeley and at the University of Southern California. In 1920 he became a salesman for the National Life Insurance Company, and in 1924 he was co-organizer of and field secretary of the Liberty Savings and Loan Association of Los Angeles,

Calif. Still later, Houston helped found the Golden State Mutual Life Insurance Company of Los Angeles, which he served as secretary, treasurer, president, and controller.

HOUSTON, ULYSSES L. (1881–1965), physician; born in Evansville, Ind. Houston graduated from the preparatory department of Howard University (Washington, D.C.) in 1898 and received his M.D. degree from Bennett Medical College in 1912. He opened a private practice in Washington, D.C., and served as a faculty member of Howard University Medical College for 40 years. Houston was also chief of the division of otolaryngology at Freedmen's Hospital, Washington, D.C.

HOUSTON, WILLIAM EUGENE, JR. (1920–   ), clergyman, administrator; born in Hot Springs, Ark. Houston received his B.A., B.D., and D.D. degrees from Johnson C. Smith University (Charlotte, N.C.). He served as chaplain of New York Hospital on Welfare Island and of Elmhurst General Hospital, Elmhurst, Long Island, and as chairman of the Central Harlem Council for Community Planning from 1957 to 1959.

HOWARD, ELSTON *See* ATHLETES: BASEBALL ·

HOWARD, JOSEPH C. (1922–   ), lawyer, judge; born in Des Moines, Iowa. Howard attended the University of Iowa, from which he graduated in 1949. He received a LL.B. degree (1954), a M.S. degree (1955), and his J.D. degree (1968) from Drake University (Des Moines, Iowa), having done additional study at Washington and Lee University (Lexington, Va.), Northwestern University Law School (Evanston, Ill.), and the National College of State Trial Judges. A veteran of World War II, he was assistant state's attorney in Maryland from 1964 to 1968 and assistant city solicitor in Baltimore, Md., in 1968. Howard was the first Afro-American candidate in Maryland's history to be elected to the position of associate judge of the Supreme Court of Baltimore.

HOWARD, PERRY WILSON (1877–1961), lawyer, educator; born in Ebeneezer, Miss. Howard received a B.A. degree from Rust College (Holly Springs, Miss.) in 1899, after which he attended Fisk University (Nashville, Tenn.) and the University of Chicago. He received a LL.B. degree from the University of Illinois in 1905, and a LL.D. degree from Campbell College (Jackson,

Miss.) in 1914. Before he began to practice law in Mississippi in 1905, he taught mathematics at Alcorn Agricultural and Mechanical (A & M) College (Lorman, Miss.: now Alcorn State University). Howard was a special assistant U.S. attorney from 1921 to 1929, when he joined a law firm in Washington, D.C. He served as chairman of the Republican State Committee in Mississippi from 1924 to 1932 and as a member of the Republican National Committee for most of his life after 1924. Howard was buried in Arlington National Cemetery in Washington, D.C.

HOWARD UNIVERSITY Howard University, at Washington, D.C., was founded in 1867 largely, but not solely, through the encouragement of Oliver Otis Howard, a veteran Union general and commissioner of the Freedmen's Bureau, for whom the university was named. Howard offers bachelor's, master's, and doctor's degrees. It provides liberal arts, teacher education, professional, and terminal occupation curricula. National and independent, the coeducational university was chartered by the U.S. Congress and receives annual support from the federal government. It is interracial and has an international student body and faculty. Its 1975 enrollment was about 10,000, making it one of the largest predominantly black colleges.

Founded on its present site, then a farm, the university was originally intended to meet the needs of newly freed slaves. It began with two academic departments, four students, and a faculty of one. Howard's complete role, however, has not been restricted solely to the education of Afro-Americans. Throughout its history, it has accepted students who were not Afro-American. Indeed, among its white graduates was the first woman physician in the District of Columbia. Its black graduates, however, in both number and distinction, reflect the significant place that the university has occupied in Afro-American academic and public life. For example, about half of the nation's black physicians, surgeons, and dentists are Howard graduates. About 25 percent of all black lawyers and more than 50 percent of Afro-American engineers and architects are graduates of Howard.

One of the university's foremost distinctions is its long history of excellence in its faculty. In almost any conceivable area—scholarship, writing, university service, public service—the faculty has consisted of some of the most distinguished Afro-Americans. Examples are numerous, but the following teachers, all of whom have separate listings in the *Encyclopedia,* show the range and distinction of the men and women who have served on the university's faculty throughout the years: Numa Pompilius Garfield Adams (medicine), David H. Blackwell (mathematics), Herman Russell Branson (physics), Sterling Allan Brown (literature), Ralph Johnson Bunche (political science), W. Montague Cobb (medicine), Anna B. Coles (nurs-

Howard University's chapel in the mid-1970s. *(Courtesy of Jacquelyn Low.)*

ing), Will Marion Cook (music), Roy Clifford Darlington (pharmacy), Arthur P. Davis (literature), Charles Richard Drew (medicine), Lloyd Ferguson (chemistry), John Hope Franklin (history), E. Franklin Frazier (sociology), Abram L. Harris (economics), William Henry Hastie (law), Charles Hamilton Houston (law), Robert Stewart Jason (medicine), Martin David Jenkins (education), Ernest Everett Just (biology), John Mercer Langston (law), Warner Lawson (music), Alain Leroy Locke (literature-philosophy), Rayford W. Logan (history), Benjamin Elijah Mays (religion), Kelly Miller (sociology), Dorothy B. Porter (library), Charles Henry Thompson (education), Charles Harris Wesley (history), and Carter Godwin Woodson (history).

This list does not mean, however, that Howard University had a monopoly of academic talent among black institutions. Rather, it indicates that Howard's faculty, collectively, seems to have had more distinguished members over a longer period of time or at any given time.

HUBBARD, CHARLOTTE MOTON educator, government official; born in Hampton, Va. Hubbard attended Tuskegee Institute (Tuskegee Institute, Ala.) of which her father was president, graduating in 1931. She then received a B.S. degree in education and physical education from Boston University in 1934. Hubbard began her career as an instructor of physical education at Hampton Institute (Hampton, Va.), where she stayed until 1941. In the following three decades she held a variety of positions in the field of public relations and communications in both government and private industry, culminating in her appointment to the U.S. Department of State as deputy assistant secretary for public affairs, a post she held from 1964 to 1970.

HUBBARD, DEHART (1904–1976), track-and-field athlete; born in Cincinnati, Ohio. Hubbard graduated from the University of Michigan in 1925, and subsequently he began to work in the field of public relations, first for the city of Cincinnati, Ohio, then for the Federal Public Housing Authority in Cleveland, Ohio, and later for the Federal Housing Administration. He was well known, however, for his exploits on the athletic field. He held the national championship in broad jumping from 1922 to 1927, and earned a gold medal in broad jumping at the 1924 Olympics in Paris, the first black American to win an Olympic championship (with a jump of 24 feet, 5⅛ inches). In 1925 Hubbard set the world broad-jump record at 25 feet, 10⅞ inches. He was also the national Amateur Athletic Union (AAU) hop, skip, and jump (later known as the triple jump) champion in 1922 and 1923. *See also* ATHLETES.

HUDSON, LINCOLN THEODORE (1916–   ), business executive; born in Okmulgee, Okla. He received his B.S. degree in 1951 from Loyola University (Chicago) and studied at the University of Chicago Business School. He served with the famous 332d Fighter Group in Italy in World War II, eventually becoming a prisoner-of-war at Nuremburg, Germany, after parachuting from his disabled plane while on escort duty for a bombing mission. After the war, he became an executive in the advertising/sales department of Johnson Publishing Company in Chicago. See also BUSINESS.

HUDSON, ROY DAVAGE (1930–   ), educator; born in Chattanooga, Tenn. Hudson received a B.S. degree from Livingstone College (Salisbury, N.C.) in 1955, and a M.S. degree (1957) and his Ph.D. degree (1962) from the University of Michigan. He taught at the University of Michigan Medical School from 1961 to 1965 and at Brown University (Providence, R.I.) from 1966 to 1970). Hudson became president of Hampton Institute

(Hampton, Va.) in 1970. Hudson was a member of Sigma Xi and Phi Kappa Phi honor societies.

HUGGINS, NATHAN IRWIN (1927–   ), historian; born in Chicago, Ill. Huggins received his B.A. from the University of California, Berkeley, Cal., in 1954, his M.A., 1959, and his Ph.D., 1962, from Harvard University. He taught at several colleges and universities, including the University of Massachusetts, Boston, Mass., and the University of California, Berkeley, Cal., before being appointed a professor at Columbia University, New York, in 1970. He has served as a fellow for the John Hay Whitney Foundation and the Guggenheim Foundation. His writings include *The Harlem Renaissance*, Oxford University Press, 1971.

HUGGINS, WILLIS N. (1886–1940), historian, educator. Huggins received his Ph.D. degree from Fordham University (New York, N.Y.) in 1932, and he taught in the New York City public school system for many years. He wrote *A Guide to Studies in African History* (1934) with John A. Jackson, and he also published *Introduction to American Civilization* (1937). Huggins founded the Blyden Society for the Study of African History. He also reported from Geneva, Switzerland, on the League of Nations meetings on the Italo-Ethopian War for the Chicago *Defender* in the 1930s.

HUGHES, LANGSTON (1902–1967), poet, author; born in Joplin Mo. Hughes attended Central High School in Cleveland, Ohio, but learned a great deal as a young man from extensive travel largely as a waiter or mens servant, in Mexico, Europe, Africa, and the United States. It was as a busboy at a hotel in Washington, D.C. that he met Vachel Lindsay, writer and critic, who encouraged him. Hughes was a prolific writer. His first book of poems was *The Weary Blues* (1926), followed by *Fine Clothes to the Jew* (1927). After completing college (Lincoln University, Pa.) in 1930, Hughes wrote a number of plays, including: *Mulatto* (1935), which had a triumphant Broadway run in 1935–1937, and *Scottsboro Limited* (1932). His first published collection of short stories was *Ways of White Folks* (1934). In the 1950s, he created and told humorous accounts of Jesse B. Semple, a black character, in *Simple Speaks His Mind* (1950) and *Simple Stakes a Claim* (1957). Simple/Semple, was the focus of a Broadway musical he produced, *Simply Heavenly* (1957). Altogether,

Hughes published ten volumes of poetry and sixty-odd short stories and produced dramas, operas, and anthologies in addition to his Semple books. He wrote two autobiographies: *The Big Sea* (1940) and *I Wonder as I Wander* (1956). In 1960, Hughes received the Spingarn Medal as "Poet laureate of the Negro race." *See* LITERATURE: POETRY, DRAMA/THEATER.

HUGHES, S. BERNARD (1879–1952), physician; born in Point of Rocks, Md. Hughes graduated from New York University and received his M.D. degree from Howard University Medical College (Washington, D.C.). He practiced medicine in Baltimore, Md., for 45 years and was a member of the American Medical Association.

HUNT, HENRY ALEXANDER (1867–1938), educator; born in Georgia. Hunt was one of the most influential persons in public education in Georgia during the first third of the twentieth century. Much of his professional life was spent in the development of the Fort Valley Industrial School, which he served as president for 34 years. For his services to education, Hunt was awarded the Spingarn Medal in 1930. *See also* FORT VALLEY STATE COLLEGE.

HUNTON, BENJAMIN L. (1919–), educator, government official; born in Hyattsville, Md. Hunton received a B.A. degree (1940) and a M.A. degree (1942) from Howard University (Washington, D.C.), and his Ph.D. degree from American University (Washington, D.C.) in 1954. From 1942 to 1966 he was a teacher and administrator in Washington, D.C., schools, and from 1966 to 1970 he served in both the U.S. Department of Interior, as assistant director of the Bureau of Mines, and in the U.S. Department of Health, Education, and Welfare. In 1971 Hunton became the first black brigadier general in the Armed Forces reserves. He was a member of the White House Committee on Civil Rights and Minority Affairs and served on the District of Columbia Commission on Academic Facilities.

HURST, CHARLES G., JR. (1928–), educator; born in Atlanta, Ga. Hurst received a B.S. degree (1950) and his Ph.D. degree (1961) from Wayne State University (Detroit, Mich.). He taught at Wayne State from 1955 to 1961 and at Howard University (Washington, D.C.) from 1961 to 1970, where he was the founder and director of the communications science research program. In 1969 Hurst became president of

Crane College (Chicago, Ill.; now Malcolm X College).

HURST, JOHN (1863–1930), African Methodist Episcopal bishop, administrator; born in Port-au-Prince, Haiti. Hurst received a B.D. degree from Wilberforce University (Wilberforce, Ohio) in 1886 and his LL.D. degree from Morris Brown University (Atlanta, Ga.), in 1917. Ordained in the ministry of the African Methodist Episcopal (AME) Church in 1886, he served as pastor of St. Paul's Church, Port-au-Prince, from 1886 to 1887 and as superintendent of AME missions in Haiti from 1888 to 1889. From 1889 to 1893 he was first secretary of the Haitian Legation in Washington, D.C. Hurst was pastor of Waters Church in Baltimore, Md., from 1894 to 1898 and from 1903 to 1908, and of Bethel Church in that city from 1898 to 1903. He was financial secretary of the AME Church from 1908 to 1912, and in May 1912 he was elected an AME bishop. Among his educational posts was that of chancellor of Edward Waters College (Jacksonville, Fla.).

HURSTON, ZORA NEALE (1907–1960), author; born in Eatonville, Fla. Hurston studied at Morgan State University (Baltimore, Md.) and at Howard University, (Washington, D.C.) then moved to New York City. In 1927 she received a Negro Historical Society Fellowship to make a study of the last boatload of slaves to arrive in the United States. In 1928 Hurston received a B.A. degree from Barnard College (New York, N.Y.) and began studying Negro folklore under Franz Boas, Columbia University. She continued her folklore studies on a private grant, traveling to Florida, Louisiana, and Haiti. In 1935 she received a Rosenwald Fellowhip, and from 1936 to 1938 she traveled in the British West Indies and in Haiti studying folklore on a Guggenheim grant. Hurston wrote radio scripts for a Cincinnati, Ohio, station, and later in her career was a drama instructor at North Carolina College. Her books include three novels: *Jonah's Gourd Vine* (1934), *Their Eyes Were Watching God* (1937), and *Seraph on the Suwanee* (1948); an autobiography, *Dust Tracks on the Road* (1943); three articles in the *Encyclopedia Americana*; and several volumes of folklore, including *Mules and Men* (1935). *See also* LITERATURE: THE NOVEL.

HUSTON-TILLOTSON COLLEGE Huston-Tillotson College, at Austin, Tex. was founded in

1876. A coeducational independent school with multiple Protestant affiliations, Huston-Tillotson offers a bachelor's degree and provides liberal arts and teacher education curricula. Its 1975 enrollment was about 660.

The school was formed by the merging of two institutions: Samuel Huston College, founded at Dallas, Tex., in 1876 under the auspices of the West Texas Conference of the Methodist Episcopal Church, and Tillotson College, founded in Austin in the same year under the auspices of the American Missionary Association affliated with the National Council of Congregational Churches. One of its buildings, Allen Hall, constructed on the original Tillotson College campus in 1881, is thought to be the first building erected in the state of Texas and west of the Mississippi River for the higher education of Afro-Americans. The present institution, chartered in 1952, is supported jointly by education and missions boards of both the United Methodist Church and the United Church of Christ. Its campus is a close neighbor of the University of Texas.

HUTCHERSON, WALTER LEONARD (1891–1931), civic leader; born in Amherst, Va. Hutcherson graduated from Tuskegee Institute (Tuskegee Institute, Ala.) in 1914, and later attended the Estes Park Young Men's Christian Association (YMCA) training school in Estes Park, Colo. He became active in the YMCA while still at Tuskegee, and from 1915 to 1917 he was field secretary there. After serving in the U.S. Army as a first lieutenant, Hutcherson went to Buxton, Iowa, in 1919 to serve as general secretary of the black YMCA there. In 1921 he moved to the Wichita, Kans, black branch to serve in the same capacity until 1930. In that year Hutcherson was promoted to executive secretary, and he moved to the Tulsa, Okla., branch. A well-known figure in the midwest, he promoted interracial harmony as a member of the National Interracial Commission of the YMCA and as vice-president of the National Association of Colored YMCA secretaries.

HUTSON, JEAN BLACKWELL (1914–), librarian, curator; born in Summerfield, Fla. Hutson received a B.A. degree from Barnard College (New York, N.Y.) in 1935, her M.A. degree from the Columbia University School of Library Science in 1936, and did further study at the New School for Social Research (New York, N.Y.) and at the Seifert Historical Library. She served as curator of the Schomburg Center for Research and Black Culture (New York, N.Y.) after 1949. *See also* New York Public Library under ARCHIVES.

HYTCHE WILLIAM PERCY (1927–), educator; born in Porter, Okla. He received a B.S. degree in 1950 from Langston University (Langston, Okla.) and an M.S. (1958) and his Ed.D. (1967) degrees from Oklahoma State University. He taught mathematics in Ponca City, Okla., in the 1950s and came to Maryland State College in 1960 as dean of student affairs. He served in several positions at the college, including chairman of liberal studies, before becoming chancellor in 1976. *See also* UNIVERSITY OF MARYLAND EASTERN SHORE.

INCOME

Introduction Incomes have increased since World War II for black and white Americans. For example, the percent of black families with less than $3,000 in annual purchasing power (income adjusted for changes in prices) has been reduced substantially: from about 60 percent in 1947 to about 20 percent in 1970. Incomes of blacks, however, were less than one-third of

MEDIAN INCOME OF FAMILIES: 1950 TO 1974

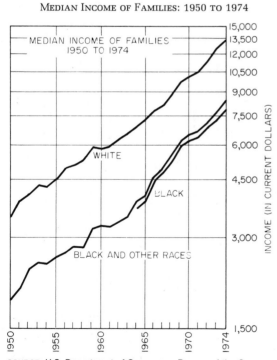

SOURCE: U.S. Department of Commerce, Bureau of the Census, Social and Economic Statistics Administration.

those of whites at the close of the war. Trends since the war show that this gap has been considerably reduced. In fact, incomes of blacks in the mid-1970s ranged from over half of the median income of whites in the South to about three-fourths in the West. Whether they were black or white, men earned more than women. White men earned most, but black men earned more than either black or white women. Families with a man and wife at the head were more likely to have high incomes, whether they were black or white, especially if the wife worked. On the other hand, families headed by a woman alone had the smallest incomes (regardless of age). Black families headed by younger black men had the highest incomes of all black families, most closely approaching the level of incomes of whites. The accompanying illustration shows actual income in current dollars from 1950 to 1974.

Income in the 1970s* The median income in 1971 was about $6,400 for black families and about $10,670 for white families, yielding a black to white median income ratio of 60 percent. In 1971 the relative position of black to white family income was the same as in 1970. However, this 1971 ratio represented a significant improvement over the ratio of 54 percent in

*Adapted from U.S. Department of Commerce, Bureau of the Census, Social and Economic Statistics Administration, *The Social and Economic Status of the Black Population in the United States*, ser. P-23, no. 42, July 1972; and ser. P-23, no. 54, 1975.

459

1964, the first date for which corresponding survey data on Afro-Americans were available.

The proportion of nonwhite families in the $10,000 and over income category increased during the 1960s. By 1970 approximately 28 percent were at this income level, compared to 11 percent in 1960, taking into account changes in prices. The proportion of nonwhite families with relatively high incomes was still far below that of white families, as about half of the white families had incomes of $10,000 or more in 1970.

Significant gains in achieving income parity with whites have been made by only a very small segment of black families. These were young husband-wife families residing in the North and West in which both the husband and wife worked. Among these families, the ratio of black to white income was about 104 percent in 1970 compared to 85 percent in 1959. In the South, for the comparable group of black families, the median income was 75 percent that of whites, an increase over the 56 percent in 1959. The working wife was an important factor in explaining the narrowing of the income differential between young black and white families. Where only the husband worked, the income differential in the North and West remained at about 75 percent in 1970, whereas in the South, the ratio of 63 percent was up from the 52 percent in 1959.

Among the young husband-wife families, black wives were more likely than white wives to have participated in the employed labor force and as year-round workers in 1970. Nationally, about 68 percent of the young black wives contributed to the family income by working, compared to 56 percent for young white wives. In the North and West, a larger percentage of young black wives worked year-round. These black wives earned approximately 30 percent more and also made a larger contribution to the family income than did their white counterparts. For the North and West, the ratio of young wives' earnings to the family income was 35 percent for blacks and 27 percent for whites.

Inflation continued to erode the income levels of both black and white families during the 1970s. For example, in 1974, the median income of black families was estimated at $7,800, an increase of 7.4 percent over the 1973 level. However, after adjusting for the rise in prices, the 1974 median declined by approximately 3.2 percent over the 1973 median. This was not statistically different from the 4.4 percent decline noted for white families. The median income of white families was $13,400 in 1974.

The income status of blacks as reflected by the income distribution of blacks had hardly changed during the 1970s. Of the 5.5 million black families in March 1975, about 19 percent had high incomes in 1974 ($15,000 and above) and 38 percent had incomes of $10,000 and over. At the other end of the income scale, 23 percent of the black families had incomes under $4,000. In constant dollars, these proportions, as well as the median income level, remained essentially unchanged from the corresponding 1970 figures. The overall income differential, as measured by the median income ratio, between black and white families widened after 1970. In 1974 the average median income of black families was 58 percent of the median of white families; it was thus below the 1970 ratio of 0.61. However, the ratio has not changed since 1970, when such factors as family composition and labor force status of wife are taken into account.

As was observed for the entire nation, the income disparity between black and white families, as measured by the median income ratio, has widened in the North and West since 1970—it was 67 percent in 1974 and 73 percent in 1970. On the other hand, southern black families had maintained their income position relative to their white counterparts—the ratio was about 57 percent in both 1974 and 1970. Income levels in 1974 were still lower in the South than in the North and West.

In contrast to the decline in the overall median income ratio for families, the median income ratio of black to white persons has remained essentially unchanged since 1970. In 1974 the median income of black men ($5,400) was about 61 percent of the median income of white men—not statistically different from the 59 percent in 1970. For women, the ratio was about 90 percent in both 1974 and 1970.

Among men who worked year-round, full time, the average income was 70 percent of the median income of the comparable group of white men, about the same as in 1970 (68 percent). However, black women who worked year-round, full time, made gains relative to their white counterparts—the income ratio in 1974 was 91 percent, up from the 82 percent in 1970.

Income Ratio of Black to White Families As noted previously, the median income ratio of black to white families declined in the 1970s, after a rise in the mid- and late 1960s. The decline in the black-white median income ratio reflects many interrelated factors. The analysis that follows does not propose to explain all the reasons for these changes or all the underlying causes for the decline in the median income ratio. Undoubtedly, such social and economic forces as changing attitudes and practices related to the civil rights movement, inflationary pressures, economic slowdown in 1969–70, and the economic recession in 1974, have had diverse impacts upon the black and white communities, as enumerated below.

Families with Wives in the Paid Labor Force Between 1970 and 1974 the proportion of black families with wives in the paid labor force declined from 36 to 33 percent; whereas, the proportion for their white counterparts increased from 34 to 37 percent. Changes in the proportion of all families with working wives are a result of changes in first, the proportion of all families that are husband-wife families and, second, the proportion of husband-wife families who have working wives. Black husband-wife families as a percent of all black families have declined; virtually no changes have been observed for their white counterparts during the period 1970 to 1974 (income year). The husband-wife families generally have median incomes that are higher than those of other types of families, primarily because they are more likely to have at least two earners. In 1974 black husband-wife families had a median income of $12,982 compared to $7,942 for black families headed by a male with no wife present and $4,465 for black families headed by a female. Thus, the decline in the proportion of black husband-wife families would have a downward influence upon the median income of all black families.

In the past, not only have proportionally more black than white wives worked to supplement the income resources of their families, but their contributions have been greater. Since 1970 the proportion of black husband-wife families with wives in the paid labor force has fluctuated; however, the percentage in 1974 (54 percent) was the same as that in 1970. During the same time period, the proportion for their white counterparts had increased from 38 to 42 percent. (From 1967 to 1970 both racial groups had experienced increases in this proportion.) The income levels of black husband-wife families with a wife in the paid labor force had risen from 1970 to 1974; but these families have not improved their income status relative to comparable white families. (Black to white income

ratio was about 78 percent for these families in both 1970 and 1974.) Between 1970 and 1974 the decline in the proportion of black husband-wife families has reduced the proportion of all black families with wives in the paid labor force. This pattern combined with changes that have occurred among white families has produced a downward effect upon the overall income ratio of black to white families in the 1970s.

Families Headed by Women and Men Among families headed by women, the income ratio of black to white did not show a statistically significant change from 1970 to 1974 (62 percent in 1970 and 61 percent in 1974). The same pattern occurred among families headed by men; yet the overall income ratio of black to white families declined. This contradiction can be explained by differential changes in the proportion of black and of white families headed by women and men and incomes received by these families.

Work Experience of the Family Head Shifts have been observed in the work experience patterns between black and white families. The proportion of black families with a head who worked the previous year declined from 78 percent in 1970 to 73 percent in 1974, whereas that for white families dropped slightly from 84 to 82 percent. The reduction for blacks was the result of declines in the proportion who worked among both male and female heads of families. For whites the proportion of female heads who worked in the preceding year did not change from 1970 to 1974; in contrast, a decline was noted for male heads.

As generally assumed, families with heads who held a job the previous year had higher incomes than families whose head did not have a job. Consequently, the relatively larger decline from 1970 to 1974 in the proportion of black heads who had gainful employment the previous year, than the decline for their white counterparts, had a negative effect upon the black-white income ratio.

Number of Earners Per Family Historically, black families have had a greater proportion of multiple earners than white families. However, from 1970 to 1974, the proportion of black families with two or more earners decreased from 55 percent in 1970 to 48 percent in 1974, falling below the 54 percent observed for white families in 1974. The decline in multiple-earner families reflects both the changes in the composition of black families and the work patterns of black wives. Traditionally, most two-earner families were husband-wife families in which both husband and wife were earners. In the past, multiple-earner families have been primarily responsible for the upgrading of income levels among black families. The decline (1970–74) in this proportion had a strong negative effect on the overall income level of black families.

Poverty Levels Poverty or low-income levels are determined annually. The low-income threshold (level) for a nonfarm family of four was $5,038 in 1974, $4,540 in 1973, and $2,973 in 1959. Families and unrelated individuals are classified as being above or below the low-income threshold, using the poverty index adopted by a federal interagency committee in 1969. This index centers around the U.S. Department of Agriculture's Economy Food Plan and reflects the differing consumption requirements of families based on their size and composition, sex and age of the family head, and farm-nonfarm residence. The low-income cutoffs for farm families have been set at 85 percent of the nonfarm levels. These cutoffs are updated every year to reflect the changes in the Consumer Price Index. The low-income data exclude inmates of institutions, members of Armed Forces living in barracks, and unrelated individuals under 14 years of age.

There were 7.5 million blacks below the poverty or low-income level in 1974, comprising about 31 percent of the black population and more than three times the comparable proportion of 9 percent of the white population. In 1959 the percentage of blacks (55 percent) below the poverty level was much higher. About one-third of all people with incomes below the poverty level were blacks in 1974.

The number of poor black families in 1974 was about the same as the 1973 figure; the number of low-income white families increased, returning to the 1972 level. After a rise at the very beginning of the decade (1969–70), the number of poor black families began to level off in the 1970s. The trend represents a mixed composite of declines among low-income black families headed by men and increases among those headed by women.

Female heads have comprised an increasing proportion of both black and white low-income families; however, female heads have become an overwhelming majority only among low-income black families. At the beginning of the decade, about 56 percent of all poor black families were headed by women; by 1974 the proportion had grown to 67 percent. This proportion rose as a result of both the decline in the number of low-income black families headed by men and the concomitant increase in the numbers headed by women. Female heads of low-income families were less likely than the male heads to have worked. In 1973 about 38 percent of poor black female heads of families held a job sometime during the year and about 10 percent worked year-round, full time. For black male heads of low-income families, the corresponding figures were 65 percent and 27 percent, respectively. Of the female heads not working, 7 out of 10 reported keeping house as their main reason for not working. The presence of children and often the lack of adequate low-cost day-care facilities are factors that affect the ability of low-income female heads to seek gainful employment. As most of the poor male heads have wives present, these factors are not delimiting to them.

Among blacks, the low-income families were more likely than those above the poverty level to have one or no earners in the family. For example, about 42 percent of poor black families had one earner in 1973; the comparable proportion for black families above the low-income level was 33 percent. Also, the proportion of low-income black families with no earners (38 percent) was more than five times that for those above the poverty line. Moreover, among poor black families with multi-earners, there is some evidence that the second earner is usually not the wife, but another relative of the head; whereas among those above the low-income level, the wife is usually the secondary earner.

Since a sizable proportion of both black and white poor families had no earners, a substantial number had received unearned income in 1973.

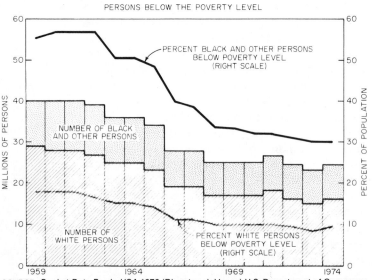

PERSONS BELOW THE POVERTY LEVEL

SOURCE: *Pocket Data Book: USA 1976* (Bicentennial Issue) U.S. Department of Commerce, Bureau of the Census, 1976.

For black families below the low-income level without earnings, public assistance was the major source of unearned income; whereas, among white families, public assistance and Social Security were the two major sources of unearned income. Approximately 3.6 million households purchased food stamps in July 1974; of these, 1.4 million, or about 40 percent, were black households. Households that received food stamps, in contrast to the total number, regardless of the race of the head, were more likely to have a female head, to have lower incomes, to have a greater proportion of large households (5 or more members), and to receive public assistance. *See also* DISCRIMINATION; EMPLOYMENT; FAMILY; LABOR UNIONS; POPULATION; POVERTY.

REFERENCES: U.S. Department of Commerce, Bureau of the Census, Social and Economic Statistics Administration, *The Social and Economic Status of the Black Population in the United States,* ser. P-23, no. 42, July 1972; ser. P-23, no. 54, July 1975; U.S. Department of Commerce, Bureau of the Census, *Current Population Reports,* "Money Income in 1973 of Families and Persons in the United States," ser. P-60, no. 97, 1974; U.S. Department of Labor, *Black Americans: A Chartbook,* Bureau of Labor Statistics, Bulletin 1699, 1971; and U.S. Department of Labor, Bureau of Labor Statistics, *Employment and Earnings,* vol. 18, no. 8, February 1972.

INDEXES *See* BIBLIOGRAPHIES / BIOGRAPHIES / GUIDES.

INDUSTRY *See* BUSINESS; EMPLOYMENT.

INGRAM, EDITH J. (1942–), educator, judge; born in Hancock County, Ga. Ingram received a B.S. degree from Fort Valley State College (Fort Valley, Ga.) in 1963, and was an elementary school teacher in Georgia from 1963 to 1968. In 1972 she was appointed a judge of Hancock County Court of Ordinary in Sparta, Ga., becoming the first black judge in the state of Georgia. Ingram received many civic awards, including the Woman of the Year Award by the Augusta, Ga., *Mirror.*

INK SPOTS *See* RADIO AND TELEVISION.

INNIS, ROY EMILE ALFREDO (1934–), civil rights leader; born in St. Croix, Virgin Islands. Innis attended City College of the City University of New York after his return from military service in Korea. After several years of involvement in the Harlem branch of the Congress of Racial Equality (CORE), he was appointed its national director in 1968. A separatist philosophically, Innis was instrumental in presenting CORE's Community Self-Determination Bill to the U.S. Congress in 1968, advocating black control of education, business, and social services within black communites. Also in 1968, he founded, with William F. Haddad, the *Manhattan Tribune,* an upper west side weekly newspaper.

INSTITUTE OF THE BLACK WORLD Formerly part of the King Center in Atlanta, Ga., the Institute of the Black World became an independent research center in 1969. It was dedicated to examining the education of Afro-Americans with an eye to its efficacy as an instrument of social change and equality.

INSURANCE *See* BUSINESS.

INTEGRATION *See* CIVIL RIGHTS: CIVIL RIGHTS ENFORCEMENT; DISCRIMINATION; EDUCATION: DESEGREGATION IN PERSPECTIVE; SEGREGATION.

INTERDENOMINATIONAL THEOLOGICAL CENTER Interdenominational Theological Center, at Atlanta, Ga., was chartered in 1958 by four schools of theology: Gammon Theological Seminary, Morehouse School of Religion, Phillips School of Theology, and Turner Theological Seminary. The coeducational center offers the master of divinity, master of religious education, and doctor of sacred theology degrees. Its 1975 enrollment was about 200. The center is accredited by the American Association of Theological Schools, and it is a member of the Atlanta University System.

IRBY, RAY (1918–), business executive; born in Meridian, Miss. Irby began a career in insurance in Tuscaloosa, Ala., in the early 1940s, and became president of the Supreme Life Insurance Company of America in Chicago, Ill., in 1973. He was a member of many civic organizations.

IRVIS, K. LEROY (1919–), lawyer, state legislator; born in Saugerties, N.Y. Irvis received a B.A. degree from New York State Teachers College in 1938, a M.A. degree from New York University in 1939, and his LL.B. and J.D. degrees in 1954 from the University of Pittsburgh Law School. He was elected to the Pennsylvania state legislature in the 1950s and became minority whip of the Pennsylvania house of representatives in 1973.

JABBAR, KAREEM ABDUL- *See* Athletes: Basketball.

JACK, HULAN (1907–   ), state legislator; born in St. Lucia in the Windward Islands, British West Indies. Jack graduated from New York University in 1932, having majored in business administration. He was an assemblyman in the New York state legislature from 1941 to 1953 when he was elected borough president of Manhattan. The first black politician to win that post, he held it until 1959, when a grand jury indicted him for conspiracy to obstruct justice and for violation of the city charter. The charge stemmed from a district attorney's investigation of a so-called loan accepted by Jack to remodel his apartment from a realty operator who had business pending before the city board of estimate. Although he refused to resign, Jack agreed to suspend himself from office until the courts had reached a determination of his case. The first trial ended in a hung jury; a second trial, in 1961, resulted in his conviction, a suspended sentence, and removal from office. Jack then joined the Coordinated Community Services, Inc., becoming its president in 1963. In 1967 he was reelected to the New York state assembly, maintaining his seat until 1972.

JACK, ROJO *See* Athletes: Auto Racing.

JACKMAN, HAROLD (1901–   ), educator, philanthropist; born in London, England. Reared and educated in the United States, Jackman became a patron of the arts, with emphasis on black art and literature. He founded the Countee Cullen Memorial Collection of Atlanta University, and contributed to the James Weldon Johnson Collection of Yale University, to the literary collection of Fisk University, and to the Schomburg Collection of the New York City Public Library. Jackman was also co-founder of the Harlem Experimental Theatre.

JACKSON, BLYDEN (1910–   ), critic, educator; born in Paducah, Ky. Jackson earned a B.A. degree from Wilberforce University (Wilberforce, Ohio) in 1930, and a M.A. degree (1938) and his Ph.D. degree (1952) from the University of Michigan. He taught at Florida Agricultural and Mechanical (A & M) University and at Fisk University (Nashville, Tenn.) from 1945 to 1954, and was dean of graduate studies at Southern University (Baton Rouge, La.) from 1962 to 1969. He became a professor of English at the University of North Carolina in 1969. Jackson wrote for several scholarly and professional journals, including the *College Language Association Journal*, *The Journal of Negro History*, and *Phylon*. He was coauthor with Louis D. Rubin, Jr., of *Black Poetry in America: Two Essays in Historical Interpretation* (1974). Later, he published *The Waiting Years: Essays on American Negro Literature* (Louisiana State University Press, 1976).

JACKSON, CLYDE   See NEWSPAPERS: CONTEMPORARY.

JACKSON, EMORY O.   See NEWSPAPERS: CONTEMPORARY.

JACKSON, GEORGE (1941–1971), revolutionary, author; born in Chicago, Ill. Jackson entered prison at the age of 15 to serve a sentence of one year to life for stealing $70 from a gas station. He spent the rest of his life in prison, including seven and a half years in solitary confinement. One of the Soledad Brothers, he killed a white guard at Soledad Prison in January 1970. His younger brother, Jonathan, was killed in August 1970 during the invasion of a courthouse in an unsuccessful rescue attempt. Jackson was killed in a second escape attempt a year later. He was the author of *Soledad Brother: The Prison Letters of George Jackson* (1970) and *Blood in my Eye* (1972). *See also* DAVIS, ANGELA.

JACKSON, JACQUELYNE JOHNSON (1932–), sociologist, educator; born in Winston-Salem, N.C. Jackson received B.S. and M.S. degrees from the University of Wisconsin and her Ph.D. degree from Ohio State University. She taught at Howard University (Washington, D.C.), Southern University (Baton Rouge, La.), and Jackson State College (Jackson, Miss.) before being appointed an associate professor in medical sociology at Duke University (Durham, N.C.) in 1968. Jackson wrote *These Rights They Seek* (1962). *See also* PREFACE: LIST OF CONTRIBUTORS.

JACKSON, JESSE LOUIS (1941–), clergyman, civil rights leader; born in Greenville, S.C. Jackson received a B.A. degree from North Carolina Agricultural and Technical (A & T) State University and studied at Chicago Theological Seminary, which later awarded him a honorary D.D. degree. Ordained to the ministry of the Baptist Church in 1968, he became associate pastor of Fellowship Baptist Church in Chicago, Ill. Jackson was a protégé of Martin Luther King, Jr., with whom he served during civil rights demonstrations in the 1960s. He was chosen by King to organize an alliance of black businessmen and clergy in Chicago for the purpose of promoting job opportunities for blacks with firms doing business in the black community. Known as Operation Breadbasket, this project was a joint effort of the Southern Christian Leadership Conference (SCLC) and the Coordinating Council of Community Organizations, and it had the fur-

Jesse Jackson.
(Photo by Leroy Henderson.)

ther aim of providing sales outlets for black-produced merchandise. The project was a distinct success in Chicago and eventually spread to other large American cities, with Jackson as its national director from 1967 to 1971. Jackson was also a leader of the Poor People's Campaign sponsored by SCLC in 1968, and in 1971 he founded a second economic program, People United to Save Humanity (PUSH), of which he became executive director.

JACKSON, JOSEPH H. (1900–), clergyman; born in Rudyard, Miss. Jackson received a B.A. degree and an honorary D.D. degree from Jackson College (Jackson, Miss.), a B.D. degree from Colgate-Rochester Divinity School, and a M.A. degree from Creighton University (Omaha, Nebr.). He did postgraduate work at the universities of Nebraska, Pennsylvania, and Chicago. Jackson served churches in Mississippi, Nebraska, and Pennsylvania before becoming pastor of Olivet Baptist Church in Chicago, Ill. He was a member of the executive committee of the Baptist World Alliance, and in 1953 became president of the National Baptist Convention, U.S.A., Inc. Jackson was made a Royal Knight of the Republic of Liberia. He wrote *Stars in the Night* (1950), *The Eternal Flame* (1956), and *Many But One: The Ecumenic of Charity* (1964). *See also* BAPTISTS.

JACKSON, JUANITA E.   lawyer, civil rights worker; born in Baltimore, Md. Jackson attended Morgan State University (Baltimore, Md.) and received a M.S. degree in sociology from the University of Pennsylvania in 1934. She was the first Afro-American woman to graduate from the law school of the University of Maryland. Through her work in 1931 in organizing a citywide (Baltimore) Young People's Forum that concentrated on various political, social, and economic problems confronting young blacks, she was recognized by the National Association for the Advancement of Colored People (NAACP) and in 1935 joined its staff as special assistant to the secretary. Meanwhile, Jackson had organized an interracial commission of the Young Women's Christian Association (YWCA) at the University of Pennsylvania. While she was vice-president of the National Council of Methodist Youth in 1934, the group passed a resolution committing itself to frequent only establishments that did not discriminate because of race. Jackson was active in the civil rights movement in Maryland during the 1960s. Her husband

Clarence M. Mitchell, Jr., headed the Washington, D.C., branch of the NAACP, and her son Clarence M. Mitchell, III, served in the Maryland state legislature for more than a decade. Her mother, Lillie Jackson, headed the Baltimore branch of the NAACP for more than two decades, during which time it had the largest membership of any branch of the NAACP in the nation. *See also* MITCHELL, CLARENCE M., JR.

JACKSON, LUTHER PORTER (1892–1950), educator, historian; born in Lexington, Ky. Jackson received a B.A. degree from Fisk University (Nashville, Tenn.) in 1914, a M.A. degree from Columbia University in 1922, and his Ph.D. degree from the University of Chicago in 1937. He taught history at Virginia State College (1922–50), and was founder and president of the Virginia Voters League. Jackson also served with the Association for the Study of Negro Life and History, and became prominent as a historian in the 1920s and the 1930s, working especially to strengthen the field of Afro-American research and study. He wrote *Free Negro Labor and Property Holding in Virginia, 1830–1860; A History of the Virginia State Teachers Association; The Virginia Negro Soldier and Sailor in the American Revolution; Negro Officeholders in Virginia 1865–1895;* and *The Voting Status of the Negro in Virginia* (annual handbook after 1942, published by the Virginia Voters League). *See also* HISTORIANS.

JACKSON, LUTHER PORTER, JR. (1925–), journalist, educator; born in Virginia; Jackson served as a reporter for the Washington *Post* and the Baltimore *Afro-American*, and later as director of Communicating Research on the Urban Poor (CROSS-TELL), Washington, D.C. He was an associate director of public relations for the National Association for the Advancement of Colored People (NAACP), and a board member of the executive council of the Association for the Study of Negro Life and History. Jackson became an associate professor at the Columbia University Graduate School of Journalism in 1972.

JACKSON, MAHALIA (1911–72), gospel singer; born in New Orleans, La. The daughter of a barber-stevedore-preacher and his wife who permitted only sacred music in their home, Jackson sang in her father's choir until, at the age of 16, she went to Chicago, Ill. There she joined the Greater Salem Baptist Church choir and soon

became its soloist. She made her first recording, which enjoyed great popularity in the South among lovers of gospel music, in 1934. It was not until 1945, however, that "Move On Up a Little Higher," her next record, brought her nationwide attention; it was the first gospel record to sell more than a million copies and the first to bring gospel singing to the general public. European critics praised her records, and their reactions led to concerts both in Europe and the United States. Her first concert in New York City's Carnegie Hall in 1950 was a sellout; she toured the United States and Europe with equal success, and refused to sing in nightclubs and theaters. Her richly textured contralto voice, with its great range and expressiveness, combined with her forceful delivery and uninhibited faith earned her the title "Queen of the Gospel Song." Books about Jackson include *Movin' On Up* (1966) and *Mahalia Jackson Cooks Soul* (1970).

JACKSON, MAYNARD (1938–), lawyer, mayor; born in Dallas, Tex. Jackson entered Morehouse College (Atlanta, Ga.) at the age of 14 and received a B.A. degree in 1956; he earned his LL.D. degree with honors from the North Carolina Central University School of Law in 1964. Admitted to the Georgia bar in 1965, he practiced law for only four years before he was elected vice-mayor of Atlanta. In 1968 he ran for the office of U.S. Senator, losing by a surprisingly small margin to the incumbent, Senator Herman Talmadge. Having thus gained statewide recognition, it was no surprise when, the next year, he was elected vice-mayor of Atlanta by a large majority. In 1973, he was elected mayor, thus becoming not only the first black mayor of Atlanta but also the first of a major southeastern city.

Maynard Jackson. *(Photo by Rogers Murphy.)*

JACKSON, MILES MERRILL, JR. (1929–), librarian, educator; born in Richmond, Va. Jackson received a B.A. degree from Virginia Union University in 1955 and his M.S.L.A. degree from Drexel University (Philadelphia, Pa.) in 1956. Beginning in 1956, he served on the staff of the Free Public Library in Philadelphia, Pa., and later was on the library staff at Hampton Institute (Hampton, Va.). Jackson was territorial librarian for the government of Samoa (1962–64), a Fulbright professor at the University of Teheran, Iran (1968–69), and professor at the State University of New York at Geneseo after 1969. He contributed several articles to journals and magazines and was one of the coauthors of *Bibliography of Negro History and Culture for Young Readers* (1969).

JACKSON, PERRY B. (1896–   ), editor, state legislator, lawyer, judge; born in Zanesville, Ohio. Jackson graduated from Adelbert College of Case Western Reserve University (Cleveland, Ohio) in 1919, and received his LL.B. degree there in 1922. Before his appointment as judge of the Municipal Court of Cleveland in 1942, the first black judge to ascend the bench in Ohio, he had a varied career. He was editor of the Cleveland *Call* (1922–29); a representative in the Ohio state legislature; a Cleveland city councilman (1932–34); an assistant police prosecutor (1934–41); and a secretary to the Ohio director of public utilities (1941–42). In 1945 Jackson was elected to a full term on the Municipal Court. Fifteen years later he became judge of the Court of Common Pleas, from which he retired in 1972 to become judge emeritus of the Cuyahoga County Common Pleas Court in Cleveland.

JACKSON, REGINALD (REGGIE)   See ATHELETES: BASEBALL.

JACKSON, ROBERT W. (1949–   ), conductor; born in Portsmouth, Va. Jackson studied theater arts and music at Adelphi University (Garden City, N.Y.) and later did graduate work at New York University. In 1970 he became musical director and conductor of a traveling production of George Gershwin's *Porgy and Bess* that toured throughout 22 European countries. His talent and sense of style made him the most promising Afro-American conductor of the 1970s.

JACKSON, SAMUEL C. (1929–   ), lawyer, government official; born in Kansas City, Kans. Jackson received a B.A. degree (1951) and his J.D. degree (1954) from Washburn University (Topeka, Kans.). He was admitted to the Kansas bar in 1954, and in 1957, after three years of military service began the practice of law in Topeka. In 1965 Jackson was appointed by the president to the U.S. Equal Employment Opportunities Commission—one of the five original appointments. He served as a commissioner until 1968, and a year later he was made assistant secretary for metropolitan planning and development of the U.S. Department of Housing and Urban Development (HUD). Responsible for dispensing more than $700 million in grants and loans to rehabilitate cities and rural areas, Jack-

son was at this time one of the highest ranking black officials in the country. HUD guidelines and requirements were revised during his tenure to reflect his belief that low- and moderate-income families, if given the opportunity, can purchase and meet payments on homes. In 1973 Jackson became general manager of the National Community Development Corporation in Washington, D.C.

JACKSON, SARA DUNLAP   See PREFACE: LIST OF CONTRIBUTORS.

JACKSON STATE COLLEGE Jackson State College, at Jackson, Miss., was founded in 1877. State-supported and coeducational, the college offers the bachelor's and the master's degrees, and provides liberal arts and teacher education curricula. Its 1973 enrollment was more than 5,000.

The institution was founded in 1877 as Natchez Seminary at Natchez, Miss., by the American Baptist Home Mission Society. It opened with 20 students and operated as a private church school for 63 years. Its purpose was to educate teachers, preachers, and agriculture leaders. In 1882 the society moved the college to Jackson, Miss., a more centralized location, and in 1902 the college was moved to its present site. It became a teacher education institution under the control of the Board of Trustees of Institutions of Higher Learning, State of Mississippi, by an act of the 1940 state legislature. In 1967 John A. Peoples, Jr., was elected the sixth president of the college, having been preceded by Charles Ayer, Jr., Luther Barrett, Zackary T. Hubert, B. Baldwin Dansby, and Jacob L. Reddix.

JAMES, ALLIX BLEDSOE (1922–   ), clergyman, educator; born in Marshall, Tex. James received B.A. and B.D. degrees from Virginia Union University, and Th.M. and Th.D. degrees from Union Theological Seminary of Virginia. He began his career as a teacher at Virginia Union as an instructor in religion in 1947, then served as dean of students, and from 1957 to 1970 was dean of the school of theology. James was vice-president of Virginia Union University from 1960 to 1970 and president after 1970.

JAMES, DANIEL, JR. (CHAPPIE) (1920–78), Air Force officer, government official; born in Pensacola, Fla. After receiving a B.P.E. degree from Tuskegee Institute (Tuskegee Institute, Ala.), James was commissioned a second lieutenant in the U.S. Air Force in 1943. He flew 101 combat missions during the Korean War, and in 1957 was named air staff officer, Office of the Deputy Chief of Staff for Operations, Air Defense Division, Washington, D.C. In 1966 James became deputy commander for operations, Eighth Tactical Fighter Wing, Thailand, and led 78 missions over North Vietnam. In 1970 he was made assistant secretary of defense for public affairs with the rank of brigadier general. During his military career, James was awarded the Distinguished Flying Cross with Oak-Leaf Cluster and the Air Medal with seven Oak-Leaf Clusters.

JAMES VAN DER ZEE INSTITUTE An institute that was founded, organized, and based in New York, N.Y., after 1967. Its main purpose was to preserve the work of James Van Der Zee (born in 1884), a photographer of the Harlem community and scene of the 1920s and 1930s. Reginald McGhee, a photographer, was one of its principal organizers. Some of the Van Der Zee photographs have been published in book form.

JAMES, WILLIS LAURENCE (1909–), educator, musicologist; born in Montgomery, Ala. James graduated from Morehouse College (Atlanta, Ga.) and also studied at Chicago Musical College. In addition to composing for voice and chorus, James became a specialist in Negro folk music and jazz. In that capacity he served as a consultant to the Institute of Jazz Studies (New York, N.Y.) and to the Library of Congress survey committee on American music.

JAMISON, JUDITH (1943–), dancer; born in Philadelphia, Pa. An incipient dancer at the age of six, Jamison's private dance lessons ended in 1961 when she matriculated at Fisk University (Nashville, Tenn.). She later studied dance at the Judimar School in Philadelphia, Pa., the Philadelphia Dance Academy, Joan Kerr's School, the Harkness School, and with Paul Sanasardo. Jamison joined American Ballet Theater in 1965. In 1967 Jamison rejoined the Alvin Ailey Dance Company, soon becoming a principal.

JARBORO, CATERINA (1903–), soprano; born in Wilmington, N.C. Jarboro studied voice in Paris, France, and later in Milan, Italy, under Nino Campino. She made her operatic debut in *Aida* at the Puccini Opera House in Milan in 1930. Later, Jarboro appeared in *L'Africaine*, and in 1933 in *Aida* with the Chicago Opera Company.

JARRETT, THOMAS DUNBAR (1912–), educator; born in Union City, Tenn. Jarrett received a B.A. degree from Knoxville College (Knoxville, Tenn.) in 1933, a M.A. degree from Fisk University (Nashville, Tenn.) in 1937, and his Ph.D. degree from the University of Chicago in 1947. He taught high school in Tennessee (1933–37) before serving as professor of English at Knoxville College (1937–40), at Louisville Municipal College (1941–43), and at Atlanta University (1947), of which he became president in 1968. Jarrett received Ford Foundation and Carnegie grants, and spent considerable time (1953–54) in England as a lecturer at various colleges and universities.

JARVIS CHRISTIAN COLLEGE Jarvis Christian College, at Hawkins, Tex., was founded in 1912 by the Disciples of Christ and is still affiliated with that church. Private, coeducational, and church-related, the college offers the bachelor's degree and provides liberal arts and teacher education curricula. Its 1975 enrollment was 624.

Named for two related benefactors (Jarvis) who donated the land on which the college was built (456 acres), Jarvis began its academic life as Jarvis Christian Institute, on an elementary school level. Its high school department, started in 1914 and accredited by the state department of education in 1924, was discontinued in 1938. The college was first accredited by the state department of education in 1941. From 1939 to 1961 the college was approved by the Southern Association of Colleges and Secondary Schools. The next few years marked a transition from the separate accreditation criteria for Afro-American and white institutions to the single standard for all member institutions. In 1967 the college was admitted to full membership and accreditation by the Southern Association of Colleges and Schools, and in 1968 to full membership in the Association of Texas Colleges and Universities.

In a circumstance that may be unique among schools, oil was discovered on Jarvis' property in 1941, and by the 1970s 19 wells were operating. One-fourth of the net income from oil is allocated to the endowment fund, one-fourth to capital reserves, and one-half to operating costs. In 1964 Jarvis Christian College and Texas Christian University of Fort Worth executed a "Memorandum of Understanding" that resulted in a Jarvis Christian College-Texas Christian University affiliation. *See also* CHRISTIAN CHURCH, DISCIPLES OF CHRIST, CHURCHES OF CHRIST.

JARVIS CHRISTIAN INSTITUTE *See* JARVIS CHRISTIAN COLLEGE.

JASON, ROBERT STEWART (1901–   ), physician, educator; born in Santurce, Puerto Rico. Jason graduated from Polytechnic Institute (Puerto Rico) in 1920, received a B.A. degree from Lincoln University (Lincoln University, Pa.) in 1924, a M.D. degree from Howard University Medical College (Washington, D.C.) in 1928, and his Ph.D. degree in pathology from the University of Chicago in 1932. He served as professor of pathology at Howard University (1931–37), and as vice-dean (1946–53) and dean (1955–65) of the College. Jason received numerous awards and citations, including the 24th Distinguished Service Medal of the National Medical Association in 1969.

JAY, JAMES M. *See* PREFACE:CONTRIBUTORS.

JAZZ *See* MUSIC: JAZZ.

JEFFERS, LANCE *See* LITERATURE: POETRY.

Martin D. Jenkins. *(Morgan State University.)*

JEFFERSON, BERNARD S. (1910–   ), lawyer, judge, educator. Jefferson received a B.A. degree from the University of California at Los Angeles in 1931, and received a LL.B. degree (1934) and his S.J.D. degree (1943) from Harvard University. He was admitted to the California bar in 1934, and later served on the faculty of Howard University (Washington, D.C.). Jefferson then became a judge of the California Superior Court in Los Angeles.

JEFFERSON, BLIND LEMON (1897–1929?), blues singer; born near Couchman, Tex. Jefferson is remembered as the best of the early blues shouters. His style influenced many later artists, including Sonny Terry, Muddy Waters, Joe Turner, T-Bone Walker, and Josh White. His 80-or-so recordings form a unique history of the early blues period of American music. Jefferson, who was born blind, was found frozen to death in a snow bank in Chicago, Ill. *See also* MUSIC: BLUES.

JENKINS, HOWARD, JR. (1915–   ), lawyer, educator, government official; born in Denver, Colo. Jenkins received a B.A. degree (1936) and his LL.B. degree (1941) from the University of Denver, the first black to earn a law degree at that university. Indeed, in 1941, Jenkins became the first Afro-American to be admitted to the Colo-

rado bar. During World War II he worked for the Office of Price Administration, the Denver War Labor Board, and the National Wage Stabilization Board in Denver. After the war, he taught labor and administrative law at Howard University School of Law (Washington, D.C.). After ten years at the university, he became, in 1956, an attorney for the U.S. Department of Labor, rising by stages to the post of assistant commissioner in the Bureau of Labor Management Reports in 1962. The next year he was appointed by President John F. Kennedy to a five-year term as a member of the National Labor Relations Board, and in 1968 he was reappointed by President Lyndon B. Johnson.

JENKINS, JOHN L. government official; born in Chattanooga, Tenn. After serving as assistant director of community services in the Office of Minority Business Enterprise (OMBE) of the U.S. Department of Commerce, Jenkins became director of that agency in 1971, filling the vacancy left by Abraham S. Venable, who was also an Afro-American.

JENKINS, MARTIN DAVID (1904–78), educator; born in Terre Haute, Ind. Jenkins received a B.S. degree from Howard University (Washington, D.C.) in 1925, a B.A. degree from Indiana State College in 1930, and a M.S. degree (1933) and his Ph.D. degree (1935) in educational psychology from Northwestern University (Evanston, Ill.). He taught education at Virginia State College (1930–32), North Carolina Agricultural and Technical (A & T) State University (1935–37), Cheyney State College (1937–38), and Howard University (1938–48). Jenkins was a senior specialist in higher education with the U.S. Office of Education (1940–41), president of Baltimore's Morgan State University (1948–70), and director of the Office of Urban Affairs of the American Council on Education (1970–75).

JERVAY, THOMAS, SR. *See* NEWSPAPERS: CONTEMPORARY.

JESSYE, EVA ALBERTA (1897–   ), music director, educator, author; born in Coffeyville, Kans. Jessye graduated from Western University in 1914, and later studied at Langston University (Langston, Okla.). She taught piano in Muskogee, Okla., served as director of music at Morgan State University (Baltimore, Md.) from 1919 to 1920, and worked on the editorial staff of the Baltimore *Afro-American*. Jessye served as director of music for the first all-Negro motion picture, "Hallelujah," directed by King Vidor in 1929. She directed the Dixie Jubilee Singers of Los Angeles, Calif., and managed a training school for radio artists in New York City. Jessye donated her impressive collection of photographs and memorabilia to the University of Michigan in 1973. *See also* MOTION PICTURES.

JIM CROW The origin of the term is obscure. Several probable origins exist, and they all relate to a proper name. One possible origin may relate to a slave trader who bore the name; another might refer to the name of a black slave who escaped from or eluded a slave trader or slave catcher. Another possible source might be local folklore, in which a lame person and dancer bore the name. All of these origins may very well be interrelated or have evolved from a common source. In this connection, the story of Thomas "Daddy" Rice (1808–60), is important. Before he became famous as a minstrel performer, Rice heard a black American singing and dancing "Jump Jim Crow." One version of the story tells how Rice heard and saw a lame black named Jim Crow (or Crowe) entertain other workers between duties at Thomas Crowe's Livery Stable located on Third Street in Louisville, Ky., about 1830. Laurence Hutton, author of a well-read volume in its day entitled *Curiosities of the American Stage* (1890, 1891), quotes a person who claimed to have seen one of Jim Crow's performances:

He was very much deformed, the right shoulder was drawn up high, and the left leg was stiff and crooked at the knee, which gave him a painful, but at the same time ludicrous, limp. He was in the habit of crooning a queer old tune, to which he had applied words of his own. At the end of each verse he gave a peculiar step, "rockin de heel" . . . and these were the words of his refrain: "Wheel about, turn about, do jis so, an' ebery time I wheel about I jump Jim Crow."

Adding his own interpretations, Rice adopted the performance for his own shows, which became very popular.

Another version of the story describes how Rice first observed a black youth on the streets of Cincinnati, Ohio, "jumping Jim Crow." Taking up the idea, Rice would come on stage with a sack slung over his back, and coming downstage he would announce rhythmically to the audience (according to the *Atlantic Monthly*, November 1867): "Ladies and Gentlemen, I'd

have you to know that I have a little darky here that jumps Jim Crow." Then Rice would empty the sack from which emerged his diminutive partner in blackface and rags. In any case "Jump Jim Crow" became a popular hit tune and dance; and minstrel shows performed many different verses and varieties of it.

Still another version of the origin of the term is noted by Monroe N. Work in the *Negro Yearbook* for 1916. According to this description, a hotelkeeper in Charleston, S.C. had two slaves in the early part of the nineteenth century, both named James. To differentiate between them, he instructed one to respond only to "Jim." Because Jim was very black, boarders at the hotel added the further designation of *"Crow."* This story says that Jim Crow was born in Richmond, Va., about 1800 and was later sold to owners in Charleston and then in New Orleans, La.

As the century progressed, a new meaning of the term emerged. Referring less to minstrelsy, the term came to be applied to the legally sanctioned system of segregation of blacks and whites that included Jim Crow laws, Jim Crow schools, and Jim Crow trains. *See also* DISCRIMINATION; ONOMATOLOGY; SEGREGATION.

JOBS *See* EMPLOYMENT; LABOR UNIONS.

JOHN HENRY A legendary Afro-American folk hero of the 1800s, John Henry was endowed with superhuman strength and endurance. The hero challenged a mechanical, steel driving hammer; he won but died after his superhuman victory. His name, however, lived on as an authentic American legend.

The man who invented the steam drill thought he was mighty fine; John Henry drove his fifteen feet and the steam drill only made nine.

See also LITERATURE: FOLKLORE.

JOHNS, VERNON *See* ALABAMA CHRISTIAN MOVEMENT FOR HUMAN RIGHTS (ACMHR).

JOHNSON, CHARLES SPURGEON (1893–1956), sociologist, educator; born in Bristol, Va. Johnson received an early introduction to classical, modern, and theological literature from his father, Rev. Charles Henry Johnson, who was an emancipated slave. In 1916 Johnson received a B.A. degree from Virginia Union University, and the following year he received his Ph.B. degree from the University of Chicago. During World

Charles Spurgeon Johnson. *(Fisk University.)*

471

War I, he saw action in France, receiving upon his return a Carnegie Institute Foundation grant to study the migration of the black population. From 1918 to 1919 Johnson worked as a researcher for the Chicago Urban League, and in 1919 he was appointed to the Governor's Committee to Investigate the Chicago Riots, to which he had been an eyewitness. He coauthored the committee report that was published as a book, in 1922 under the title *The Negro in Chicago*. In 1921 Johnson became director of research and investigation for the National Urban League and founded the league's journal, *Opportunity*. As chairman of the Fisk University (Nashville, Tenn.) department of social sciences (1928–46), he developed the Fisk Institute of Race Relations, which reflected his belief that " . . . the pathological problem of race relations . . . will have to be worked out as part of the general political and economic framework." In 1933 Johnson became director of the Swarthmore College Institute of Race Relations, and in 1943 he directed a program on race-related problems for the American Missionary Association of the Congregational Christian Church, also serving as director of the Julius Rosenwald Fund's interracial relations program that year. Johnson continued thereafter to serve as a trustee of the fund. In 1946 Johnson was appointed the first black president of the integrated Fisk University, retaining the post until his death.

In addition, Johnson was active in several government projects. In 1930 he was part of a three-member League of Nations team that investigated charges of slavery in Liberia. In 1931 Johnson became a consultant to President Herbert Hoover's Conference on Home Building and Home Ownership (Negro Housing Committee). In 1934 he served on the Tennessee Valley Authority (TVA), and from 1936 to 1937 he was a consultant to the U.S. Department of Agriculture, Farm Tenancy Committee. In 1946 Johnson was one of the U.S. delegates to UNESCO and a member of the group sent to Japan by the U.S. Department of State to reorganize the country's educational system in 1946. From 1945 to 1946 he served as president of the Southern Sociological Society as well as co-head of the Southern Council on Regional Development. In addition to his 1922 study of the Chicago riots, Johnson's major books include: *The Negro in American Civilization* (1930) and *The Economic Status of the Negro* (1933), written under the auspices of the Julius Rosenwald Fund; *Shadows on the Plantation* (1934); *The Collapse of Cotton Tenancy:*

1933–1935 (1935); *The Negro College Graduate* (1936), winner of the Wolf-Anisfield Award; *Growing Up in the Black Belt; Negro Youth in the Rural South* (1941); *Patterns of Negro Segregation* (1943), prepared for the University of Stockholm project on the Negro in America, directed by Gunnar Myrdal; *To Stem The Tide: A Study of Racial Tensions in the United States* (1944); *Education and the Cultural Crisis* (1951); and *A Preface to Racial Understanding* (1953). Johnson received honorary doctoral degrees from Harvard University; Columbia University; Howard University; Virginia Union University, and the University of Glasgow, Scotland. *See also* FISK UNIVERSITY; NATIONAL URBAN LEAGUE; SCIENTISTS: SOCIAL.

JOHNSON, CHARLES V. (1928–   ), lawyer, judge; born in Malvern, Ark. Johnson received a B.A. degree from Arkansas Agricultural, Mechanical, and Normal (AM&N) College (now the University of Arkansas at Pine Bluff) and his J.D. degree from the University of Washington. He was admitted to the Washington bar in 1958, and later became a judge of the Municipal Court in Seattle, Wash.

JOHNSON C. SMITH UNIVERSITY Johnson C. Smith University, at Charlotte, N.C., was founded in 1867 by the Presbyterian Church and is still affiliated with it. Private, coeducational, and church-related, the school offers the bachelor's degree, (including the bachelor of divinity) and provides liberal arts and teacher education curricula. Its enrollment in 1975 was about 1,000.

In 1867 Rev. S. C. Alexander and W. L. Miller recognized the need for a school for Afro-Americans in North Carolina; at a meeting of the Catawba Presbytery in the Old Charlotte Presbyterian Church in Charlotte, the movement for a school for boys and young men was formally inaugurated. Alexander and Miller were elected teachers. The main purpose of the school was to train men for the ministry, for catechists, and for teaching.

Information concerning the school was brought to the attention of Mary D. Biddle, a churchwoman of Philadelphia, Pa., who, through appeals in one of the church papers, managed to pledge $1,400. In appreciation of this gift—the first—friends of the project asked to name the school after her late husband, Maj. Henry Biddle. As a result, the school was named The Biddle Memorial Institute and was later so chartered by the state legislature. The school's first site was donated. In 1876 its charter was changed by the state legislature, and the name of the school was also changed to Biddle University, the name it retained until 1923.

In 1921 Jane Berry Smith of Pittsburgh, Pa., gave considerable funds to Biddle, and in addition provided for a handsome endowment in memory of her late husband, Johnson C. Smith. In recognition of her generous donations, the board of trustees voted to change the name of the institution to Johnson C. Smith University. The charter was so amended, and from 1923 until her death in 1929, Mrs. Smith funded the construction of five more buildings, including a church.

In 1932 the institution became coeducational. Until 1941 women were admitted to the senior college division only, but beginning with the school year 1941–42 they were also admitted to the freshman class.

JOHNSON, EDWARD AUSTIN (1860–1944), lawyer, educator, author; born in Raleigh, N.C. Johnson studied at Atlanta University, and received a LL.B. degree (1891) and his LL.D. degree from Shaw University (Raleigh, N.C.). For some ten years at the start of his career and before he became a lawyer, he was the principal of a school in Atlanta, Ga., and one in Raleigh. In 1893 Johnson became an instructor in the law school at Shaw University, later becoming its dean. He entered politics as an alderman in Raleigh, and then served as an assistant U.S. attorney in the Eastern District of North Carolina for several years. An active Republican, Johnson served on various party committees and as a delegate to both local and national conventions. In 1907 he moved to New York City to practice law. In 1928 Johnson made an unsuccessful bid for a seat in Congress, and subsequently spent his remaining years in private law practice. He was the author of several works, including *A School History of the Negro Race in America; History of Negro Soldiers in the Spanish-American War; Light Ahead for the Negro; Negro Almanac and Statistics;* and *Adam vs. Ape-Man and Ethiopian.*

JOHNSON, FENTON (1888–1958), poet, author; born in Chicago, Ill. Johnson attended the University of Chicago, and produced original plays at the Pekin Theater on Chicago's South State Street. The editor and publisher of several literary magazines, he was also the author of several volumes of poetry, including *A Little Dreaming* (1914), *Visions of Dusk* (1915), and *Songs of the*

Soil (1916). His short stories appeared in *Tales of Darkest America* (1920). *See also* LITERATURE: DRAMA/THEATER; LITERATURE: POETRY.

JOHNSON, GEORGIA DOUGLAS (1886–1966), poet; born Georgia Douglas Camp in Atlanta, Ga. Educated at Atlanta University and at the Oberlin Conservatory of Music (Oberlin, Ohio), Johnson was a pioneer in many civic and women's movements and the first black woman after Frances Harper to gain general recognition as a poet. Her tragic 1928 play *Plumes* was performed in New York City. Her four volumes of poetry are *The Heart of a Woman* (1919), *Bronze* (1920), *An Autumn Love Cycle* (1929), and *Share My World* (1962). *See also* HARPER, FRANCES ELLEN; LITERATURE: DRAMA/THEATER; LITERATURE: POETRY.

JOHNSON, GEORGE E. (1927–   ), business executive, civic leader; born in Richton, Miss. Johnson was a laboratory assistant with Fuller Products Company of Chicago, Ill., from 1945 to 1948, when he was made production chemist. In 1954 he founded the Johnson Products Company of Chicago and served that firm as president after that date. Johnson was also president of the Chicago Urban League, vice-president of Junior Achievement of Chicago, and a director of the Lincoln National Bank of Miami, Fla.

JOHNSON, GLENN T. (1917–   ), lawyer, judge; born in Washington, Ark. Johnson received a B.S. degree from Wilberforce University (Wilberforce, Ohio) in 1941, and a LL.B. degree (1949) and his J.D. degree (1950) from the Cleveland-Marshall Law School (Chicago, Ill.). He was admitted to the Illinois bar in 1950 and engaged in private practice until 1957, when he became assistant state attorney general. In 1963 Johnson was appointed assistant attorney for the Metropolitan Sanitary District of Greater Chicago, and by 1966 he had become judge of the Circuit Court in Chicago. He was appointed to the Appellate Court in Chicago in 1972.

JOHNSON, HALL (1888–1970), composer, arranger, choral director; born in Athens, Ga. Johnson was educated at Allen University (Columbia, S.C.), at Hahn School of Music (Philadelphia, Pa.), at the University of Pennsylvania, and at the Institute of Musical Art (New York, N.Y.). In 1925 he organized the Hall Johnson Choir in Harlem in New York City. This group brought black folk music to a wide audience and made him America's best-known choral director. Johnson transcribed many spirituals, and he arranged music for both Broadway shows and motion pictures. Some of his most important compositions include *Song of Man* (an Easter cantata); the operetta *Fi-Yer*; and *The Green Pastures Spirituals*. *See also* LITERATURE: DRAMA/THEATER.

JOHNSON, JACK (JOHN ARTHUR) (1878–1946), pugilist; born in Galveston, Tex. Johnson left school after the fifth grade to enter a world of odd jobs, begging, gambling, wandering, and dock fights. His feat of knocking out a professional boxer traveling with a circus was the major impetus for Johnson's brilliant ring career, which spanned the first quarter of this century. The first black world heavyweight champion, he won the title by defeating Tommy Burns in Sydney, Australia, in 1908. Racist concepts of white superiority popular at that time led to a search for a "great white hope" to reclaim the title and resulted in James J. Jeffries' coming out of retirement to challenge Johnson, unsuccessfully, in 1910. Johnson held the heavyweight title until 1915 when he was knocked out by Jess Willard in the 26th round of their match. He continued to box until 1927. References to Johnson include Gilmore, Al-Tony, *Bad Nigger! The National Impact of Jack Johnson* (1975) and Johnson, Jack, *Jack Johnson Was a Dandy* (1969). *See also* ATHLETES.

JOHNSON, JAMES E. (1926–   ), Marine Corps officer, government official; born in Madison, Ill. Johnson served in the Marine Corps for 21 years, becoming during that time the first Afro-American to be appointed a warrant officer in the Marines. After military retirement, he was named vice-chairman of the Civil Service Commission in 1969 and was assistant secretary of the navy for manpower and reserve affairs from 1971 to 1973. In 1973 Johnson left government service to enter private industry in California.

JOHNSON, JAMES LOUIS (J. J.) (1924–   ), jazz trombonist, composer; born in Indianapolis, Ind., Johnson was the first musician to adapt the trombone to the difficult techniques demanded by the advent of Bop. His skill in performing high-speed and intricate solos, usually of his own composition, became legendary. During the 1940s Johnson played with Benny Carter, Count Basie, and Illinois Jacquet, and later he joined Kai Winding's Jay and Kai Quintet. During the 1960s Johnson led a quartet, and later a sextet

(with Clark Terry and Sonny Stitt), which toured Europe and the United States with great success. As a composer, Johnson's six-part work for orchestra, *Perceptions*, recorded in 1961, is his best-known work. *See also* MUSIC: JAZZ.

JOHNSON, JAMES PRICE (JIMMY) (1891–1955), composer, pianist. Johnson began his professional career at Coney Island, N.Y., in 1912. From then until 1921, when he began recording, he played his special brand of Harlem rhythm in New York and New Jersey clubs and on the southern vaudeville circuit. In the 1920s, in addition to recording with bands and such singers as Bessie Smith and Ethel Waters, Johnson served as musical director for Dudley's *Black Sensations/Smart Set* revues. He also established himself as a composer of note with such songs as "Charleston," "If I Could Be With You" and "Carolina Shout." Devoting much of his time to composing, he wrote the music for the *Runnin' Wild* revue in 1923; in 1928 he wrote *Yamecraw*, a long work that premiered at Carnegie Hall in New York City. Johnson continued composing during the 1930s; his *Symphony Harlem*, written in 1932, was followed by several works for the stage, one (*De Organizer*) in collaboration with Langston Hughes. He also led his own orchestra, and toward the end of the decade returned to solo playing at such clubs as Cafe Society in New York City. In the 1940s Johnson again served in such various musical roles as musical director, band leader and soloist, participant in Eddie Condon's Town Hall concerts, and soloist-composer in his own concert at Carnegie Hall. In 1949 his revue *Sugar Hill* was produced.

JOHNSON, JAMES WELDON (1871–1938), poet, lyricist, government official; born in Jacksonville, Fla. After receiving a B.A. degree (1894) from Atlanta University (Atlanta, Ga.), he enrolled in graduate study at Columbia University. He was admitted to the Florida bar in 1897. From 1901 to 1906 he collaborated with his brother, the composer J. Rosamond Johnson, in writing musical comedies and light operas, including such songs as "Congo Love Song," "Since You Went Away," and "Lift Every Voice and Sing," the latter often referred to as the "black national anthem." Their writing team was broken up when Johnson entered politics and was appointed U.S. consul to Venezuela in 1906. He was transferred to Nicaragua in 1909 before his return to New York City in 1913, where he became editor of the weekly New York *Age*. From 1916 to 1930 Johnson was a prominent member of the National Association for the Advancement of Colored People (NAACP). He was visiting professor at New York University in 1930, and joined Fisk University (Nashville, Tenn.) as a literature instructor the following year. Johnson died in an auto crash in Maine. Primarily known for his poetry, he was the author of *God's Trombones: Seven Negro Sermons in Verse* (1927), based on Negro folk preaching; a novel, *The Autobiography of an Ex-Colored Man* (1912), which many people believed was his own life story; and *Black Manhattan* (1930), the history of black theater in New York. He was also the editor of several books, including *The Book of American Negro Poetry* (1922) and *Negro Spirituals* (1925). *See also* JOHNSON, JOHN ROSAMOND; LITERATURE; DRAMA/THEATER; LITERATURE: THE NOVEL.

JOHNSON, JOHN HAROLD (1918–   ), editor, publisher; born in Arkansas City, Ark. Johnson was an honor student at Du Sable High School in Chicago, Ill., and studied at the University of Chicago from 1936 to 1938 and at Northwestern University's School of Commerce (Evanston, Ill.) from 1938 to 1940. He worked on the house publication of the Supreme Liberty Life Insurance Company from 1936 to 1942, a company of which he later became chief stockholder and board chairman. In 1942 Johnson founded *Negro Digest*, later renamed *Black World*; *Ebony*, a slick picture magazine, was founded in 1945; and *Tan Confessions*, which eventually became *Black Stars*, began publication in 1950. A newsweekly, *Jet*, was introduced in 1951, and the Johnson Publishing Company began publishing books in 1962, in addition to its weeklies and magazines. Johnson was the first Afro-American to be named one of the ten outstanding young men of the year by the Chicago, Ill., Junior Chamber of Commerce. *See also* NEWSPAPERS: CONTEMPORARY.

JOHNSON, JOHN ROSAMOND (1873–1954), composer; born in Jacksonville, Fla. The brother of James Weldon Johnson, an important lyricist, Johnson was educated at Atlanta University and the New England Conservatory of Music (Boston, Mass.). In addition, he studied piano, organ, harmony, and voice in Europe. Throughout his long career, Johnson was at times a teacher, at times the musical director of an opera house, at times a vaudeville performer. He composed the music for the operetta *The Shoo-Fly Regiment* (1906) and for *The Red Moon* (1908). With his lyricist brother, he composed many popular songs and made arrangements of many spirituals. Two of their most enduring hits are "Since You Went Away" and "Lift Every Voice and Sing." *See also* JOHNSON, JAMES WELDON; MUSIC: HISTORY AND DEVELOPMENT.

JOHNSON, LEROY R. (1928–   ), lawyer, state legislator; born in Atlanta, Ga. Johnson received a B.A. degree from Morehouse College (Atlanta, Ga.) in 1948, a M.A. degree from Atlanta University in 1951, and his LL.B. degree from North Carolina Central University in 1957. From 1957 to 1962 he served as a criminal investigator on the staff of the U.S. solicitor-general. In 1962 Johnson was elected state senator from Fulton County. Ga., becoming the first Afro-American elected to that position since 1870.

JOHNSON, MORDECAI WYATT (1890–1976), clergyman, educator, administrator; born in Paris, Tenn. The son of a clergyman, Johnson received a B.A. degree from Morehouse College (Atlanta, Ga.) in 1911, a second B.A. degree (social sciences) from the University of Chicago in 1913, a B.D. degree from the Rochester Theological Seminary in 1916, a M.Th. degree from Harvard University in 1922, and D.D. degrees from Howard University (Washington, D.C.) in 1923 and Gammon Theological Seminary in 1928. Early in his career he was a teacher of English at Morehouse College, later serving as pastor of a Baptist church in Mumford, N.Y., and then of a church in Charleston, W.Va. Johnson was very active in the civic affairs of Charleston, and founded a local branch of the National Association for the Advancement of Colored People (NAACP) there. He traveled throughout the Southwest for the Young Men's Christian Association (YMCA), making studies of black schools and colleges, eventually recommending the formation of the Southwestern Annual Student Conference. In 1926 he became the first Afro-American president of Howard University, and in recognition of his outstanding administration there, which not only revolutionized the physical plant but brought marked advances in scholastic standing, Johnson was awarded the NAACP's Spingarn Medal in 1929. Widely known as a public speaker, Johnson retired from Howard University early in the 1960s. An administration building of the university was named for him in 1973.

Mordecai Johnson, university president, speaking at a Howard University program. *(Moorland-Spingarn Research Center.)*

JOHNSON, RAFER LEWIS (1935–   ), athlete, actor; born in Hillsboro, Tex. Johnson moved with his family to Kingsburg, Calif., at the age of ten. While attending the University of California at Los Angeles (UCLA), where he was elected president of the student body in his senior year, he first competed in the decathlon, a contest in which each entrant participates in 10 different track-and-field events. Johnson finished second in the decathlon in the 1956 Olympic Games in Melbourne, Australia (the winner was Milt Campbell, the first Afro-American athlete to finish first in this demanding competition). In the 1960 Olympics in Rome, Italy, Johnson won the decathlon with a total of 8,392 points, which set new world records. Subsequently, he appeared in motion pictures and on television, and was a sportscaster. *See* ATHLETES.

JOHNSON, ROBERT B. (1904–   ), lawyer, judge. Johnson was graduated from Lincoln University (Lincoln University, Pa.) and received his law degree from the University of Pennsylvania. He was admitted to the New Jersey bar in 1933, and later became judge of the County District Court in Camden, N.J.

JOHNSTON, JOSHUA *See* ARTISTS.

JOINT CENTER FOR POLITICAL STUDIES (JCPS) A nonprofit, nonpartisan organization based in Washington, D.C., the center serves as a research, collection, and dissemination agency in regard to black politics. Founded in 1970 with a grant from the Ford Foundation, JCPS is under the joint sponsorship of Howard University (Washington, D.C.) and the Metropolitan Applied Research Center. It publishes annually a *National Roster of Black Elected Officials.* For a brief but good survey of the center, see Poinsett, Alex, "'The Joint': D.C. Center for Political Studies," *Ebony,* April 1973.

JONES, ABSALOM *See* African Methodist Episcopal (AME) Church; Episcopalians.

JONES, BILLY (1916–   ), judge. Jones graduated from Tennessee State University, and received his LL.B. degree from Howard University (Washington, D.C.) in 1945. He was admitted to the bar in 1947, served as president of the National Bar Association from 1967 to 1968, and later became a judge of the Circuit Court in the state of Illinois.

JONES, CLARA STANTON (1913–   ), librarian; born in St. Louis, Mo. Jones received the B. A. degree from Spelman College (Atlanta, Ga.) in 1934. Later she served on the library staffs at Dillard University and Southern University. In 1944, Jones joined the staff of the Detroit Public Library (Detroit, Mich.), becoming chief of division in 1950. In 1970 she was elected director of the Detroit Public Library System. In 1976 she was elected president of the prestigious American Library Association (ALA).

JONES, CLARENCE BENJAMIN (1931–   ), lawyer, business executive, publisher; born in Philadelphia, Pa. Jones received a B.A. degree from Columbia University in 1953 and his LL.B. degree from Boston University Law School in 1959. As a member of the New York bar, his practice encompassed the worlds of entertainment, corporate finance, and civil rights. He was general counsel, director, and vice-president of the Lawyers Constitutional Defense Committee of the American Civil Liberties Union; general counsel of the Harlem Cultural Council; counsel to Martin Luther King, Jr.; and special counsel to the Southern Christian Leadership Conference (SCLC). An allied member of the New York Stock Exchange, Jones was a director and vice-president of CBWL-Hayden, Stone Inc., a New York City banking and brokerage firm. Later he became the principal founder of the nation's first publicly owned multiracial life insurance enterprise, Intramerican Life Corporation, for which venture he was cited as Businessman of the Month by *Fortune* magazine in June 1965. While Jones was editor and publisher of the New York City newspaper *Amsterdam News,* he was also board chairman and chief executive officer of its parent company, AmNews Corporation. At the same time he chaired the board of Inner City Broadcasting Corp., a company that owned and operated a radio station in New York City.

JONES, CLIFTON RALPH *See* PREFACE: LIST OF CONTRIBUTORS.

JONES, CYRIL J. (1915–   ), surgeon, born in New York, N.Y. Jones received his M.D. degree from Harvard Medical School in 1944. He served as assistant professor of surgery at the College of Medicine of State University of New York Downstate Medical Center, as director of oncology training at Brooklyn-Cumberland Medical Center, and as attending surgeon at Kings County,

State University, St. Johns Episcopal, and Brooklyn hospitals. Jones was selected in 1967 as a U.S.–U.S.S.R. health exchange medical research scientist by the Office of International Health of the Public Health Service of the U.S. Department of Health, Education, and Welfare, to engage in collaborative research in the field of organ transplantation and immunity.

JONES, DAVID DALLAS (1887–1956), educator, administrator; born in Greensboro, N.C. Jones received a B.A. degree from Wesleyan College (Middletown, Conn.) in 1911 and his M.A. degree from Columbia University in 1930. He was traveling secretary for the Young Men's Christian Association (YMCA), and later worked with the YMCA in St. Louis, Mo., where he raised the largest sum of money ever contributed there for an Afro-American cause (the construction of the Pine Street YMCA). Jones served at Bennett College (Greensboro, N.C.) from 1926 to 1956, where as president he successfully initiated the expansion of the college's physical plant and furthered the development of various college programs.

JONES, EDITH IRBY (1927–   ), physician, educator; born in Conway, Ark. Jones received a B.S. degree from Knoxville College (Knoxville, Tenn.), did graduate work at Northwestern University (Evanston, Ill.), and received a B.S. degree and her M.D. degree (1952) from the University of Arkansas (she was the first black student admitted to that university). She interned at University Hospital, Hot Springs, Ark., and was a resident at Baylor Affiliated Hospitals, Houston, Tex. Jones served as clinical instructor in medicine at Baylor College of Medicine after 1962.

JONES, EUGENE KINCKLE (1885–1954), civil rights leader; born in Richmond, Va. Son of a slave father and a freeborn mother, both teachers in Richmond, Va., Jones received a B.A. degree from Virginia Union University in 1906 and his M.A. from Cornell University (Ithaca, N.Y.) in 1908. Reserved and rather quiet while still in college, he later proved to be an excellent public speaker and successful organizer. Jones was active in many university-related activities and helped to organize the Alpha Phi Alpha fraternity, which developed quickly into a nationwide association. He taught at Louisville University (Louisville, Ky.) from 1908 to 1909, and from

1909 to 1911 he was on the faculty of Louisville's Central High School. For most of his active life, Jones worked for the National Urban League, and under his direction it expanded to include more than 40 branches across the nation with a large membership and staff and an ever-increasing financial base. Jones came to New York City to help organize the league at the request of George Haynes in 1911. From 1911 to 1940 he was its executive secretary. In 1941, in severe ill health, he curtailed his activities (becoming general secretary), and in 1950 retired from the league altogether.

Eugene Kinckle Jones. *(National Urban League.)*

An active supporter of attempts by Afro-Americans to get more and better employment, Jones gave league support to the struggle to organize unions and to gain the right of collective bargaining. As early as 1913, he arranged for a meeting between Samuel Gompers and other American Federation of Labor (AFL) executives and the Urban League staff. During the New Deal era, Jones acted as a consultant to several government commissions, and from 1934 to 1937 he took a leave of absence from the league to act as adviser on Afro-American affairs to the U.S. Department of Commerce. As an adviser on New Deal policies, Jones was successful in lobbying for appointments for Afro-Americans to such federal agencies and commissions as the U.S. Department of Commerce, the National Recovery Administration, and the U.S. Employment Service. He was active in the National Conference of Social Work, serving on its board of directors from 1923 to 1930 and as a vice-president from 1932 to 1933. Virginia Union University awarded Jones an honorary LL.B. degree in 1924, and he served on the university's board of trustees from 1932 to 1934. In 1945 Jones was awarded (jointly with L. Hollingworth Wood) the first of the National Urban League's "Two Friends" award.

JONES, JAMES EARL (1931–   ), actor; born in Tate County, Miss. Jones's father is the stage, screen, and television actor Robert Earl Jones. Jones grew up on a farm in Michigan and received a B.A. from the University of Michigan (1953) and, after U.S. Army service, a diploma from the American Theatre Wing (1957). His stage debut came in 1955, his Broadway debut in 1957, and he played in many Shakespearean roles as well as in plays by Genet, Athol Fugard, and others before his Broadway performance as Jack Johnson, the heavyweight champion, in *The Great White Hope* (1969) brought him the Tony award

James Earl Jones. *(National Educational Television.)*

as best actor, the Drama Desk award for best performance for 1968–69, and star status. He had already received the 1962 Village Voice Off-Broadway Obie and the 1962 Theater World award. He has appeared in movies (*The Man*, 1972; *Claudine*, 1973) and television (narrator, *Malcolm X*, 1972) as well as on stage, where his range stretched from Sophocles to the one-character play by Phillip Hayes Dean about the life of Paul Robeson (1977).

JONES, JAMES FRANCIS MARION (PROPHET JONES) (1907–1971), clergyman, cult leader; born in Birmingham, Ala. According to friends, Jones made his first prophecy when not quite two years of age; at six he joined a sect similar to the one he later founded, and he preached his first sermon to its congregation. In 1938 the sect sent him to Detroit, Mich., as a missionary; Detroit was the city that was to become the base for his own cult. His success in attracting converts often resulted in expensive gifts being presented to him, and when a dispute arose over the rightful ownership of the gifts, Jones broke with sect leaders and formed his own group. The new organization became national in scope during the 1940s and 1950s, when it was reported to have 6 million members and when Jones increased his following through a radio show and later a television program. At the peak of his popularity, Prophet Jones, as he became known, was famous for the lavishness of his lifestyle: he lived in a 54-room Detroit mansion and his wardrobe included a full-length white mink coat given to him by the children of a Chicago, Ill., family who credited him with restoring their mother's health. A lengthy series of personal reverses preceded his death in Detroit.

JONES, J. RAYMOND (1900–   ), political leader; born in the Virgin Islands. A participant in precinct politics in New York City from 1921 to the late 1950s, Jones was eventually elected chairman of the New York County Democratic Organization, the city's Tammany Hall political machine. Known as "the Fox" because of his elegant manner and dress and his uncanny instinct for political survival, he resigned his Tammany post in 1967 and retired to the Virgin Islands.

JONES, LAURENCE CLIFTON (1884–1950), educator; born in St. Joseph, Mo. Jones received his Ph.B. degree from the University of Iowa in 1907. He was founder and president of the Piney Woods School in Mississippi, and during World War I was in charge of the thrift-stamp campaign among Afro-Americans in Mississippi. Jones wrote *Up Thru Difficulties* (1910); *Piney Woods and Its Story* (1923); *The Spirit of Piney Woods* (1931); and *The Bottom Rail* (1933). He was also the publisher and editor of *The Piney Woods Torch*.

JONES, LEROI *See* BARAKA, IMAMU AMIRI.

JONES, MARK ELMER, JR. (1920–   ), lawyer, judge; born in Indianapolis, Ind. Although his talent ranged beyond his profession into the arts, Jones became a lawyer in 1950 after receiving his J.B. degree from Loyola University (Chicago, Ill.). Before that time he had been a student at Roosevelt University (Chicago, Ill.) from which, although his student years were interrupted by military service, he graduated in 1948. After five years as assistant state's attorney of Cook County, Jones joined a law firm in Chicago, where he remained until he was appointed associate judge of the Municipal Court of Chicago (Circuit Court, Municipal Department) in 1963. In 1964 he ran for and won a seat on the Cook County Circuit Court. His abstract paintings appeared in bar association exhibits—he won three first prizes—and at the South Side Art Center in Chicago.

JONES, RICHARD L. (1893–   ), business executive, government official; born in Albany, Ga. Jones was educated at the University of Cincinnati and at the University of Illinois. After serving as a second lieutenant in the U.S. Army during World War I, he worked as a journalist and department store executive. Reentering military service in the 1930s, Jones rose to the rank of major during World War II. After the war, he was again a department store executive and insurance company official before he was appointed director of the U.S. Operations Mission in Liberia in 1954. Two years later he was named U.S. ambassador to Liberia and appointed alternate delegate on the U.S. Mission to the Eleventh General Assembly of the United Nations.

JONES, SCIPIO AFRICANUS *See* LAWYERS, NATIONAL ASSOCIATION FOR THE ADVANCEMENT OF COLORED PEOPLE (NAACP): LYNCHING, MOB VIOLENCE, AND REPRESSION.

JONES, SIDNEY A., JR. (1909–   ), lawyer, judge, fraternal and civil leader; born in Sandersville, Ga. Jones graduated from Atlanta University in 1928 and received his J.D. degree with honors from Northwestern University (Evanston, Ill.) in 1931. Admitted to the Illinois bar in 1931, he engaged in a varied and successful law practice. From 1939 to 1946 Jones was an attorney in the U.S. Department of Labor, and from 1955 to 1959 he was alderman on the Chicago City Council for the Sixth Ward. The next year he was appointed judge of the Municipal Court of Chicago (Circuit Court, Municipal Department). In 1964 Jones became an associate judge on the Circuit Court of Cook County, and some time later he became judge of that court.

JONES, SISSIERETTA (BLACK PATTI) (1868–1933), concert singer; born Matilda S. Joyner in Portsmouth, Va. Jones was raised in Providence, R.I., and studied music at the New England Conservatory (Boston, Mass.). She made her professional debut as the first black singer to appear on the stage of Wallack's Theater in Boston. After touring South America and the West Indies,

Jones returned in 1892 to New York City, gave a performance at Madison Square Garden, and resumed concertizing in the United States. That same year she sang at a White House reception given by President Benjamin Harrison. Her next concert tour took her to Europe, where she acquired the nickname "Black Patti" (after Italian soprano Adelina Patti). In 1893 Jones returned to New York City to star in an all-black group known as Black Patti's Troubadours. *See also* MUSIC: HISTORY AND DEVELOPMENT.

JONES, VIRGINIA L. (1912–   ), librarian; born in Cincinnati, Ohio. Jones received a B.S. degree from Hampton Institute (Hampton, Va.) in 1936, a M.S. degree from the University of Illinois in 1938, and her Ph.D. degree from the University of Chicago in 1945. She served as librarian at Louisville Municipal College (Louisville, Ky.), at Hampton Institute, and at Prairie View Agricultural and Mechanical (A & M) College (Prairie View, Tex.) before becoming a member of the Atlanta University staff in 1941. Jones was then dean at Atlanta University (1943–45) and later became the director of the School of Library Science there. She was a former president of the Association of American Library Schools.

JOOK (JUKE), JOOK HOUSE The word was derived from the Gullah *dzuqu*, which had African connotations akin to *wicked* or *evil*. In the American South, however, the term referred to a good-time house, a dance hall, or a barrelhouse. The words *juke* and *jukebox* are derivatives. *See also* AFRICA: AFRICAN LEGACY/SURVIVALS: LANGUAGE.

JOPLIN, SCOTT (1868–1919), composer, pianist; born in Texarkana, Tex. Joplin left home when he was 14 years old to earn his living by playing the piano in the saloons, vaudeville houses, and gambling parlors of St. Louis, and Sedalia, Mo., (and other Mississippi River towns). During the next 15 years, he evolved his unique style, ragtime, based on the displacement of accent. In 1899 Joplin wrote *Maple Leaf Rag*, and many other ragtime compositions followed. *Original Rag* (1899), *Peacherine Rag* (1901), *The Easy Winners* (1901), *Palm Leaf Rag* (1907), *Fig Leaf Rag* (1908), *Stoptime Rag* (1910), *Binks' Waltz*, and *Cleopha March* rank today as his most popular creations. Throughout his life, Joplin fought for recognition that his rags were a

Far left: An advertisement showing Sissieretta Jones. *(Museum of the City of New York.)*

significant development in modern music, but he did not achieve much success. However, he was one of the greatest innovators in the history of American music, and appropriately enough he is known as "King of Ragtime." In 1976 Joplin was awarded the Pulitzer Prize posthumously for his ragtime opera *Treemonisha*, composed 60 years earlier. *See also* MUSIC: HISTORY AND DEVELOPMENT.

JORDAN, BARBARA (1936–   ), state legislator, U.S. Representative; born in Houston, Tex. Jordan received a B.A. degree from Texas Southern University in 1956 and her LL.B. degree from Boston University in 1959. She began the practice of law in Houston, and became administrative assistant to a county judge there. In 1966 she was elected to the Texas State senate, and the following January she became the first Afro-American citizen to sit in the Texas senate since 1883. Having served on most major senate committees, Jordan was named president *pro tempore* of that body in 1972. Later that year she was elected U.S. Representative from the 18th Congressional District of Texas, and she was reelected in 1974.

JORDAN, HOWARD, JR. (1916–   ), educator; born in Beaufort, S.C. Jordan received a B.A. degree from South Carolina State College in 1938 and his Ed.D. degree from New York University. He taught at South Carolina State College (1941), served as dean of the faculty there (1959–63), and became president of Savannah State College (Savannah, Ga.) in 1963.

JORDAN, JOHN Q. *See* NEWSPAPERS: CONTEMPORARY

JORDAN, VERNON FULION, JR. (1935–   ), lawyer, civil rights leader; born in Atlanta, Ga. Jordan attended DePauw University (Greencastle, Ind.), from which he graduated in 1957, and received a J.D. degree from Howard University, 1960. Although not yet a member of the bar, Jordan served as a law clerk in the office of a civil rights attorney from 1960 to 1961. From 1961 to 1963 he was field secretary for the Georgia branch of the National Association for the Advancement of Colored People (NAACP), and led a boycott of Augusta stores that refused to hire blacks. Admitted to the Arkansas bar in 1964, Jordan began practicing law in Pine Bluff, and then became interested in the problem of black voting in the South. Beginning in 1964 he headed the

Voter Education Project of the Southern Regional Council. He spent the year 1970 heading the United Negro College Fund, and in 1972 he was named to succeed the late Whitney M. Young as executive director of the National Urban League. *See also* NATIONAL URBAN LEAGUE.

JOSEY, CHARLES J. (1930–   ), lawyer; born in Pennsylvania. Josey received a B.A. degree from Howard University (Washington, D.C.) and received his LL.B. degree from the University of Pennsylvania. He practiced law in Baltimore, Md., after 1957, the year he was admitted to the bar.

JOSEY, E. J. (1924–   ), librarian; born in Norfolk, Va. He received an A.B. degree from Howard University (Washington, D.C.), an M.A. degree from Columbia University (New York), and his M.S.L.S. degree from the State University of New York in 1953. Since 1966, he has served as an executive librarian with the New York State Education Department. Among his writings are a book, *What Black Librarians Are Saying*, 1972; and an edition with Ann A. Shockley, *Handbook of Black Librarianship*, 1977.

JOURNALISTS *See* NEWSPAPERS. *See also* ABBOTT, ROBERT SENGSTACKE; BEARDEN, BESSYE J.; BENNETT, LERONE, JR.; CORNISH, DAVIS; DOUGLASS, FREDERICK; FRANK, MARSHALL; DEJOIE, CHARLES CONSTANT, JR.; DUNGEE, ROSCOE; FORTUNE, TIMOTHY THOMAS; FULLER, HOYT; GIBBS, WISTAR MIFFLIN; HATCHER, ANDREW J.; JACKSON, PERRY B.; JOHNSON, JOHN H.; MARTIN, LOUIS EMANUEL; MURPHY, CARL J.; MURPHY, JOHN H., III; ROWAN, CARL THOMAS; RUSSWURM, JOHN BROWN; THOMPSON, ERA BELL; VANN, ROBERT LEE; WELLS IDA B.

JUDGES *See* LAWYERS; NATIONAL BAR ASSOCIATION.

JULIAN, EMERSON RICHELIEU (?–1978), physician; born in Montgomery, Ala. Julian received a B.A. degree from DePauw University (Greencastle, Ind.) in 1938 and his M.D. degree from Howard University Medical College (Washington, D.C.) in 1942. He served as a physician and city councilman in Baltimore, Md. Julian and his two brothers and three sisters, all graduates of DePauw University and distinguished members of their respective communities, established a memorial fund at DePauw in honor of their deceased parents, who had moved to Greencastle from Montgomery in 1918 so that their children could attend the university. *See also* JULIAN, PERCY LAVON.

JULIAN, HUBERT FAUNTLEROY *See* AVIATORS.

JULIAN, PERCY LAVON (1899–1975), scientist; born in Montgomery, Ala. Julian received a B.A. degree from DePauw University (Greencastle, Ind.) in 1920, a M.A. degree from Harvard University in 1923, and his Ph.D. degree from the University of Vienna, Austria, in 1931. He was an instructor of chemistry at Fisk University (Nashville, Tenn.) from 1920 to 1925, won a fellowship to Harvard University in 1922, and was an instructor of chemistry at West Virginia State College. Julian became an associate professor of chemistry at Howard University (Washington, D.C.) in 1927 (where he also established the chemistry building), and was a research fellow in organic chemistry at DePauw from 1932 to 1936. Although he had already made notable contributions to the field of chemistry, the board of trustees of DePauw was reluctant to appoint an Afro-American to the university faculty. Julian, therefore, accepted a research position with the Institute of Paper Chemistry in Wisconsin. He was director of research on soya products for the Glidden Company of Chicago, Ill., from 1936 to 1953, in which position he successfully developed new processes for paints and perfected a method of extracting sterols from soybean oil for the manufacture of sex hormones. In 1954 he founded Julian Laboratories, Inc., in Chicago, in Mexico City, and in Guatemala, in which he successfully developed synthetic cortisone. In 1961 Julian sold the Chicago plant to Smith, Kline & French, remaining as president, and the Guatemala plant to Upjohn Company. In 1964 he founded Julian Research Institute. Julian contributed many scholarly papers to journals and registered 105 patents. He was awarded the Spingarn Medal in 1947.

JUST, ERNEST EVERETT (1883–1941), zoologist, educator; born in Charleston, S.C. Just attended Kimball Academy in New Hampshire, and received a B.A. degree from Dartmouth College (Hanover, N.H.) in 1907 and his Ph.D. degree in zoology and physiology from the University of Chicago in 1916. He was on the faculty of Howard University (Washington, D.C.) after 1907, except for short leaves of absence. Just spent 20 summers at the Marine Biological Labo-

Ernest Just was a young man when he posed for this photograph by Addison N. Scurlock. (*Scurlock Studio.*)

ratory, Woods Hole, Mass., in research work, later becoming a member of the ruling board of the laboratory. His primary interest was the fertilization and experimental parthenogenesis of marine eggs. Just published more than 50 papers in this field between 1912 and 1937, and he also published *Basic Methods for Experiments in Eggs of Marine Animals* and *The Biology of the Cell Surface,* both in 1939. During the 1930s he did research in institutes and marine laboratories in Berlin, Germany; Paris, France; and Naples, Italy. Just served as vice-president of the American Zoological Society. Among his many awards was the Spingarn Medal (1915).

K

KAISER, ERNEST (1915–), editor, author, librarian; born in Petersburg, Fla. A student at City College in New York from 1935 to 1938, Kaiser spent five years as a redcap in Jersey City, N.J., and as a shipping clerk, before becoming editor of *Negro Quarterly* and cofounder and associate editor of *Freedomways* magazine. He was an adviser and editor of manuscripts on Afro-American subjects for several publishing companies, and was a longtime staff member and subsequently curator of the Schomburg Collection for Research in Black Culture in New York City. Kaiser wrote and edited *In Defense of the People's Black and White History and Culture* (1971), *Harlem: A Community in Transition* (1964); and *Black Seventies* (1970).

KAY, ULYSSES (1917–), composer; born in Tucson, Ariz. Kay graduated from the Eastman School of Music (Rochester, N.Y.) and served in the U.S. Navy during World War II. He rapidly became the most important Afro-American composer of classical music in the United States, and sustained that reputation throughout his career, which included teaching positions. He taught at Lehman College of the City University of New York after 1968. A list of Kay's important compositions includes *Sinfonietta* and *Five Mosaics,* both for orchestra; *Oboe Concerto* (1940); *Piano Sonata* (1940); *Danse Calinda* (ballet); *Of New Horizons* (1944); *A Short Overture* (1947); the opera, *The Juggler of Our Lady* (1962); *Fantasy Variations* (1963); *Umbrian Scene* (1964); and *Theatre Set* (1968).

KEENE, JESSIE ALSTORK (1901–70), physician, educator; born in Washington, D.C. Keene received a B.S. degree from Howard University (Washington, D.C.) in 1921, a M.D. degree from Howard University Medical College in 1924, and his M.P.H. degree from Harvard University in 1939. He was a faculty member of Howard University (1929–54) and served as an epidemiologist with the District of Columbia Department of Public Health (1943–70).

KEENE, PAUL F., JR. (1920–), painter, sculptor, educator; born in Philadelphia, Pa. After attending the Philadelphia Museum of Art School of Art and the Tyler School of Fine Arts (Philadelphia, Pa.), Keene went to the Academie Julien, (Paris, France) where he received B.F.A., B.S.C.Ed., and M.F.A. degrees. He was past assistant professor of painting at the Philadelphia Museum School of Art and chairman of the fine arts department of Bucks County Community College. Expressing himself both in stone and in oil, Keene is sometimes folksy in his work (as in the painting *Let's Go See Snake Mary*), though other works, such as the Rootman series of pictures, show a sardonic style and fantasized subjects. Keene was a professional member of the Pennsylvania Academy of Fine Arts and received two Whitney fellowships (1970 and 1972). He exhibited at the Pennsylvania Academy of Art Annual, 1953; at the 1st Biennale Internationale of Marine Art, Genoa, Italy, 1951; at the Institute of Modern Art, Boston, 1942; at the Smith College Museum of Art, Northampton,

Mass.; and elsewhere. Keene's work is in the collections of John Hay Whitney; The Hirshhorn Museum, Washington, D.C.; the Tyler School of Fine Arts, Philadelphia, Pa.; and Howard University, Washington, D.C.

KEITH, DAMON JEROME (1922–   ), lawyer, judge; born in Detroit, Mich. Keith received a B.A. degree from West Virginia State College in 1943, a LL.B. degree from Howard University School of Law (Washington, D.C.) in 1949, and his LL.M. degree from Wayne State University (Detroit, Mich.) in 1956. Admitted to the Michigan bar in 1949, he began his career as a lawyer in Detroit, soon becoming partner in a law firm there. During this period, Keith was a member of the Wayne County board of supervisors (1958–63); was appointed by Governor George Romney as cochairman of the Michigan Civil Rights Commission (1964–67) and elected chairman in 1967; was president of the Detroit Housing Commission (1958–67); and was commissioner of the Michigan state bar (1960–67). In 1967 Keith was elected judge of the U.S. District Court for the Eastern District in Michigan. He was awarded the Springarn Medal in 1974.

KEITH, LEROY (1939–   ), educator; born in Chattanooga, Tenn. He received the B.A. degree at Morehouse College (1961), the M.A. (1968) and Ph.D. (1970) at Indiana University. He served as an assistant professor and associate dean at Dartmouth College (1973–75) and later as Chancellor of the Board of Higher Education in Massachusetts. In 1977 he received the Outstanding Alumni Award at Indiana University, Bloomington, Ind.

KELLEY, WILLIAM MELVIN (1894–   ), editor; born in Chattanooga, Tenn. After studying at Wilberforce University (Wilberforce, Ohio) in 1912, Kelley became circulation manager of the New York *Daily News* in 1913. In 1916 he was appointed Brooklyn manager for the *Amsterdam News,* and he worked for *Champion* magazine in Chicago, Ill., the following year. Kelley became editor of the *Amsterdam News* in 1922, and retired in 1973.

KENNEDY, WADARAN L. (1905–   ), agriculturalist, educator. Kennedy received a B.S. degree and a M.S. degree from the University of Illinois, and his Ph.D. degree from Pennsylvania State University in 1936. He taught at and served as first dean of the graduate school of North Carolina Agricultural and Technical (A & T) State University until he retired in 1970. Kennedy was recognized as one of the outstanding agriculturalists of the Negro land-grant colleges for more than three decades, from the 1940s through the 1960s.

KENNEY, HOWARD WASHINGTON (1917–   ), physician; born in Tuskegee, Ala. Kenney received a B.S. degree from Bates College (Lewiston, Maine) in 1940 and his M.D. degree from Meharry Medical College (Nashville, Tenn.) in 1944. He interned at Sydenham Hospital, New York, N.Y., and was resident at Howard University College of Medicine. Kenney served in Veterans Administration hospitals in Alabama and in New Jersey for 17 years, and was appointed regional director of the Veterans Administration in 1969, the highest post then held by an Afro-American physician in the administration. He was medical director of the John A. Andrew Memorial Hospital, Tuskegee, Ala., from 1965 to 1969.

KENNEY, JOHN ANDREW (1874–1950), physician, editor; born in Albemarle County, Va. Kenney received his M.D. degree from Leonard Medical School of Shaw University (Raleigh, N.C.) in 1901; interned at Freedmen's Hospital, Washington, D.C.; and was resident physician at Tuskegee Normal and Industrial Institute (Tuskegee Institute, Ala., now Tuskegee Institute). Kenney was personal physician to Booker T. Washington, and served as director of the John A. Andrew Memorial Hospital, Tuskegee, Ala. He founded *The Journal of the National Medical Association* and edited it for 32 years. After threats from the local Ku Klux Klan, Kenney moved to Newark, N.J., where he established the Kenney Memorial Hospital.

KENTUCKY STATE NORMAL SCHOOL FOR COLORED PERSONS See KENTUCKY STATE UNIVERSITY.

KENTUCKY STATE UNIVERSITY Kentucky State University, at Frankfort, Ky., was founded in 1886 by an act of the Kentucky general assembly. State-supported and coeducational, the university offers the bachelor's and master's degrees and provides liberal arts, teacher education, and vocational curricula. Its 1975 enrollment was about 2,000.

The university was first established as the Kentucky State Normal School for Colored Persons, and its the name was changed in 1902 to

Kentucky Normal and Industrial Institute for Colored Persons, reflecting the institution's identification as a land-grant school. The name was again changed in 1926 to Kentucky Industrial College for Colored Persons, and again in 1938 to Kentucky State College for Negroes. The term "for Negroes" was eventually dropped in 1952. Finally, in 1972, university status was given to the institution. Seven presidents have served the school: John H. Jackson, James E. Givens, James S. Hathaway, G. P. Russell, F. M. Wood, R. B. Atwood, and Carl M. Hill.

KENYATTA, CHARLES 37X (1920–1969), civil rights militant. Formerly known as Charles Morris or Charles Roberts, Kenyatta organized and led a small militant group known as the Harlem Mau Mau Society in the late 1960s. He had been a bodyguard of Malcolm X. Despite his reputation for militancy, he worked with mayor John Lindsay of New York City on slum problems and he campaigned against the open sale of narcotics. In the summer of 1969 Kenyatta was shot at and critically wounded; because of the many and widely differing splinter groups in the Black Power movement, the police were unable to identify his assailants.

KIDD, MAE STREET state legislator; born in Millersburg, Ky. Kidd served overseas with the American Red Cross during World War II and with the United Seaman's Service in Maine and New York. She was associated with Mammoth Life Insurance Company in Louisville, Ky., from 1935 to 1964 as supervisor of policy issue, public-relations counselor, and salesperson. In 1964 Kidd joined Supreme Life Insurance Company of America in Chicago, Ill., as a consultant. Four years later she was elected to the Kentucky house of representatives. Her efforts in the house secured passage in 1972 of a Kentucky housing law that established an agency to finance low-income housing.

KILGORE, THOMAS, JR. (1913–), clergyman; born in Woodruff, S.C. Kilgore received an A.B. degree from Morehouse College (Atlanta) in 1935 and his B.D. degree from Union Theological Seminary (New York) in 1957. He also studied at the Howard University School of Religion (Washington, D.C.). He served long tenures as pastor of Baptist congregations in North Carolina (Friendship Baptist Church, Winston-Salem, 1938-47), New York (Friendship Baptist Church, New York, 1947-63), and California (Second Baptist Church, Los Angeles), after 1963. Kilgore was awarded honorary degrees by Shaw University (Raleigh, N.C.) in 1956 and Morehouse College in 1963.

KILLENS, JOHN OLIVER (1916–), author, educator; born in Macon, Ga. Killens attended Edward Waters College (Jacksonville, Fla.), Morris Brown College (Atlanta, Ga.), Howard University School of Law (Washington, D.C.), and other schools before becoming a teacher at Fisk, Howard, and Columbia universities. In 1936 he became a member of the National Labor Relations Board (NLRB). A founder and longtime chairman of the Harlem Writers Guild, his books include *Youngblood* (1954), *And Then We Heard the Thunder* (1963), *'Sippi* (1967), and *The Cotillion* (1970). Killens contributed articles to many magazines, and wrote the film script *Odds Against Tomorrow* (1960).

KING, B. B. See KING, RILEY B.

KING, CORETTA SCOTT (1927–), singer, civil rights leader; born in Marion, Ala. King received a B.S. degree from Antioch College (Antioch, Ohio) in 1951 and her Mus.B. degree from the New England Conservatory of Music (Boston, Mass.) in 1954. In 1948 she made her concert debut in Springfield, Ohio, and gave numerous performances in this country and in India after that. In 1962 she became a voice instructor at Morris Brown College (Atlanta, Ga.). She married Dr. Martin Luther King, Jr., in 1953. After his death she continued to be active in the civil rights movement, becoming president of the Martin Luther King, Jr., Memorial Center and joining the board of directors of the Southern Christian Leadership Conference (SCLC), which he had founded. She wrote *My Life with Martin Luther King* in 1969. See also KING, MARTIN LUTHER, JR.

KING, JOHN Q. TAYLOR (1921–), educator; born in Memphis, Tenn. King received a B.A. degree from Fisk University (Nashville, Tenn.) in 1941, a B.S. degree from Huston-Tillotson College (Austin, Tex.) in 1947, a M.S. degree from De Paul University (Chicago, Ill.) in 1950, and his Ph.D. degree from the University of Texas in 1957. He taught math, first at Samuel Huston College (1947–50) and then at Tillotson College (1950–52). When the two schools merged, he remained with the new school, of which he became president (1965). King was active in both church (Methodist) and education associations.

KING, MARTIN LUTHER, JR.

KING, MARTIN LUTHER, JR. (1929–1968), civil rights leader; born in Atlanta, Ga.

Despite hard times, King's father, who was a Baptist minister, and his schoolteacher mother, Alberta, were financially secure. King's grandfather on his mother's side, Rev. Alfred Daniel Williams, had founded the Ebenezer Baptist Church in Atlanta, Ga., in 1895. His father, who had become pastor in 1932, built the church into one of the most important and influential black churches in that city. Both King's father and grandfather had used the pulpit and the church to gain rights for Afro-Americans in Atlanta. His grandfather, who was a charter member of the city's chapter of the National Association for the Advancement of Colored People (NAACP), was a leader in the 1920s of a drive to defeat local bond issues until a black public high school was built. During the same period he helped organize a successful boycott against a local newspaper that ridiculed Afro-Americans for seeking equal education. His son, Martin Luther King, Sr., continuing in his father's tradition, protested against the humiliating effects of segregation in the South, while at the same time seeking improvement within the segregated system that cast Afro-Americans into inferior positions. Through all these protests, Martin Luther King, Jr., was present, a witness to the existing racial tensions and the possibilities for change. The young King, whose original name (Michael) had by now been changed by his father, attended Booker T. Washington High School, the first public high school for blacks in Atlanta. Skipping the ninth and twelfth grades, he was admitted to Morehouse College (Atlanta, Ga.), his father's alma mater, at the age of 15. At that time President Benjamin E. Mays of Morehouse had been in office only four years, but he had already launched an educational program that emphasized academic excellence and a sense of community among all races. Mays' influence and that of George D. Kelsey, professor of religion, were instrumental in King's decision to become a minister. King was ordained at his father's church in 1947, and received a B.A. degree in sociology from Morehouse in 1948. Immediately thereafter, he entered Crozer Theological Seminary in Pennsylvania, where he was an excellent student. In 1951 he became president of the senior class; won the Plafker Award as the most outstanding student; and received a fellowship to do graduate work at any university of his choice. He chose Boston University's School of Theology to study for a Ph.D., where he met, courted, and eventually married Coretta Scott of Heiberger, Ala., who was studying voice at the New England Conservatory of Music (Boston, Mass.).

In 1954, after completing his course work, King rejected several job offers to teach and accepted the pastorship of the Dexter Avenue Baptist Church in Montgomery, Ala., succeeding Vernon Johns who had a brilliant record of protest against segregation while minister. During his first year as pastor, King completed his doctoral dissertation, entitled "A Comparison of the Conceptions of God in the Thinking of Paul Tillich and Henry Nelson Wieman," and received his Ph.D. degree in 1955 from Boston University.

At this point in his life, King had been influenced by several ideas and scholars. At Morehouse he had been fascinated by Thoreau's *Essay on Civil Disobedience.* "I was so deeply moved," he wrote, "that I read the work several times. This was my first intellectual contact with the theory of nonviolence and resistance." At Crozer, his perusal of Walter Rauschenbush's *Christianity and the Social Crisis* provided the theological basis for his own social concern. From Rauschenbush, King realized that "in order for Christianity to be relevant to man—be he black or white—it had to deal with not only the spiritual realm but with man's everyday socioeconomic environment." Also at Crozer, he heard Dr. Mordecai Johnson's sermon on the life and teachings of Mohandas Gandhi. The message by Howard University's president electrified King and inspired him to study all of Gandhi's works on nonviolence. As a result, he lost his skepticism of the power of love and began to appreciate its potential usefulness in the area of social reform. The works of Reinhold Niebuhr provided King with an insight into the morality and behavior of groups and individuals; of Hegel, the concept of the dialectic; of Martin Buber, the doctrine of personalism.

The Montgomery bus boycott, which began on December 1, 1955, with the arrest of Rosa Parks, a black seamstress who refused to give up her bus seat to a white person, forced King to merge the divergent intellectual influences that he had acquired into a positive social philosophy. Although Gandhianism was not yet an expressed philosophy, a letter to the editor of the Montgomery *Advertiser* from Juliette Morgan, a white librarian, compared the tactics of Afro-Americans to those used by Gandhi, and what had been implicit to King was now revealed. When Bayard Rustin joined the protest, nonviolent techniques were more widely employed. King also joined, and he subsequently became the voice of the growing nonviolent civil rights movement. In May 1956 NAACP's counsel Robert Carter argued the Montgomery case before the federal District Court. A month later, six months after Parks' arrest, the court ruled against segregated seating on municipal buses. Five months after the District Court ruling, the U.S. Supreme Court upheld the decision and bus segregation came to an end in Montgomery. As the Afro-American author Louis Lomax stated, "Montgomery was the launching pad for Martin Luther King." At the end of the Montgomery bus boycott, King had "gained international fame, the applause of the world was ringing in his ears, eighteen million Negroes were calling him 'Saviour' and the world ethicists were comparing him to Gandhi and Thoreau." Lawrence D. Reddick, an Afro-American historian, professor, and participant, wrote with more restraint but with similar praise in his biography of King.

Before leaving Montgomery in 1959 to become co-pastor with his father of Ebenezer Baptist Church, King organized the Southern Christian Leadership Conference (SCLC) "to carry on nonviolent crusades against the evils of second-class citizenship throughout the South." In 1957 he addressed the Prayer Pilgrimage to Washington, D.C., with his famous "Give Us the Ballot" speech to 35,000 pilgrims who had come from 30 states to stand before the Lincoln Monument on May 17, 1957, three years after the U.S. Supreme Court decision in the case of *Brown v. Board of Education of Topeka.*

King journeyed to Ghana and traveled extensively within the United States delivering speeches and addresses. On September 19, 1958, he was stabbed by a mentally deranged black woman in a New York City (Harlem) department store while autographing copies of his first book,

Stride Toward Freedom (1958), a history of the Montgomery bus boycott. In 1959 he visited India, the home of Gandhi.

By the time he left Montgomery King's philosophy of nonviolence had taken root and in 1960 had formed the underlying principles of what was to become the Student Nonviolent Coordinating Committee (SNCC). In February 1960 four

Martin Luther King, Jr. *(Photoworld)*

students of the North Carolina Agricultural and Technical (A & T) College launched a sit-in campaign to desegregate public eating facilities—a campaign that was to spread rapidly across the South and that was to include such other public facilities as pools, libraries, beaches, and parks.

In December 1961 King began a campaign against segregation in Albany, Ga., at the invitation of several local leaders. It was a failure, and he withdrew in the fall with no victories but a clear insight into his tactical weakness. Thus, in 1963, after reassessment, King launched a series of successful nonviolent demonstrations in Birmingham that led to his arrest and confinement in a Birmingham jail during which time he wrote "Letter from a Birmingham Jail." These demonstrations also led to federal intervention and aided greatly in the passage of the 1964 Civil Rights Act. After his 1963 successes, King was one of the principals in the spectacular "March on Washington" that drew some 250,000 people to demonstrate in behalf of the pending civil rights bill. It was here, at the Lincoln Memorial, that he delivered his famous "I Have a Dream" speech. About this time, *Time* magazine selected King as Man of the Year, and in 1964 he was awarded the Nobel Peace Prize for his adherence to the principles of nonviolence and for setting an example for others who sought to change things peacefully in other areas of the world.

King receiving the Nobel Peace Prize in 1964 from Gunnar Jahn, chairman of the Norwegian Parliament's Nobel Committee. At 35, King was the youngest man ever to receive a Nobel Prize. *(Schomberg Collection, New York Public Library.)*

When riots erupted in northern ghettoes in 1964, King moved North. The reception of his numerous visits to the Watts section of Los Angeles, Calif., was not always highly enthusiastic. However, back in the South in 1965, he helped conduct a march that aided in bringing about the passage of the Voting Rights Act of 1965. After the march, King again moved his campaign North, yet he returned to the South in 1966 after the ambush of black leader James Meredith in order to lead the "Memphis to Jackson March" that culminated in the birth of "Black Power," a phrase that King did not embrace fully until 1968.

In 1967, aware of the anger and restlessness of those young black leaders who championed militance and black power, King denounced the American war in Vietnam. In his view, the war was draining away the country's resources that, he felt, could have been used to eliminate some of the misery, poverty, and disease at home. His move to unite in one coalition the antiwar and civil rights causes gained him harsh criticism, but he nevertheless continued to speak out against the war. In March 1968 he called for the "Poor People's March on Washington" to demonstrate the need for the federal government to review its priorities; to withdraw from the war in Vietnam; and to launch another war, a war on

poverty. However, on April 4, about six o'clock, while on a balcony of the Lorraine Motel in Memphis, Tenn., where he had come to help the local sanitation workers in their strike for higher wages, he was shot by an assassin, allegedly James Earl Ray. King was pronounced dead at 7 P.M. in the emergency room of St. Joseph's Hospital.

King, who had touched the world with his philosophy of nonviolence, met a violent end. His death caused riots, looting, killing, and waves of disorder in more than 120 U.S. cities, with the worst destruction taking place in Washington, D.C., only ten blocks from the White House. In a week or so, the riots subsided, but the anger and frustration that had caused them remained.

In Senate Testimony in 1975, officials of the Federal Bureau of Investigation (FBI) belatedly acknowledged that for six years the FBI had harassed and tried to discredit Dr. King, in spite of the fact that it had no legal authority to do so. Further, J. Edgar Hoover, director of the FBI, had received field reports indicating that King posed no threat to national security. In one instance, the FBI sent to him an anonymous threatening letter in an effort to induce King to commit suicide. The bureau admitted that it tried to prevent King from receiving honorary degrees from colleges, and that it had tried to prevent him from accepting the Nobel Peace Prize and from meeting the pope. Efforts were also made to shut off financial support for his organization. By 1976 Attorney General Edward Levi had ordered his top deputies to find out whether the King murder file should be reopened as a result of FBI misdeeds. *See also* CIVIL RIGHTS: CIVIL RIGHTS

Far right: Model of memorial to Martin Luther King, Jr. Known as the Martin Luther King, Jr. Center for Social Change, the memorial, located in Atlanta, Ga., was designed by Bond-Ryder Associates, architects. *(Courtesy of Bond-Ryder Associates.)*

ACTS; KING, CORETTA SCOTT; MONTGOMERY BUS BOYCOTT; SOUTHERN CHRISTIAN LEADERSHIP CONFERENCE (SCLC).

REFERENCES: Although the literature on King and the civil rights movement is expansive (especially periodical literature), there is no definitive biography. However, it is suggested that further readings should begin with C. Eric Lincoln, ed., *Martin Luther King, Jr.: A Profile*, Hill and Wang, New York, 1970. Contributors to this volume were: Ralph Abernethy, James Baldwin, Lerone Bennett, Jr., Haig Bosmajian, Reese Cleghorn, David Halberstam, Vincent Harding, Louis Lomax, August Meier, William Robert Miller, Lawrence D. Reddick, Carl T. Rowan and Jerry Tallmer. King's own vigorous accounts should be consulted: *Stride Toward Freedom: The Montgomery Story (1958)* and *Why We Can't Wait (1964)*. See also references for various entries under CIVIL RIGHTS.

KING, RILEY B. (B. B.) (1925–   ), singer; born in Indianola, Miss. After a childhood of quartet and street-corner singing, King traveled to Memphis, Tenn., in 1947, his first stop on the way to becoming one of the most popular and commercially successful blues performers in the 1960s and 1970s. In Memphis he began to work for the black radio station there, eventually becoming a disc jockey known as the "Boy from Beale Street" (B. B.). King began recording in 1949, and his first hit, "Three O'Clock Blues," enabled him to leave the radio station and go on the road. However, it was not until the 1960s that his style of blues singing became popular with white audiences; his appearance in New York City's Cafe Au Go Go in 1968 was a sensational success. Also in 1968 he toured Europe and appeared for an extended engagement at the Village Gate in New York City. King's career in the 1970s included television appearances, a concert at Carnegie Hall, and extensive concert tours.

KITCHEN, ROBERT WILSON, JR. (1921–   ), educator, government official; born in Brunswick, Ga. Kitchen received a B.A. degree in economics from Morehouse College (Atlanta, Ga.) in 1943 and his M.S. degree in business administration from Columbia University in 1946. Having worked and taught during his student years, in 1948 he secured a post teaching business administration and public relations at West Virginia State College, where he remained until 1952. Subsequently, Kitchen entered government service, working for foreign missions in Liberia and the Sudan and serving in Washington, D.C., in the fields of international coopera-

tion and economics. A member of the Secretary of State's Advisory Committee on Africa, he became director of the Office for International Training, Agency for International Development (AID) in 1963. In 1970 Kitchen was named AID's international economist to the U.S. Mission to the United Nations.

KITT, EARTHA (1928–   ), singer, actress; born in Columbia, S.C. Kitt was orphaned at the age of six and came to New York City to live with her aunt. She left school at 14 to work in a uniform factory in Brooklyn; two years later she auditioned for Katherine Dunham and won a dance training scholarship. It was not long before Kitt was chosen to join the troupe that toured the United States, and she soon became Dunham's vocalist. After a European tour with the troupe, she decided to stay in Paris, France, and made her nightclub debut there. Subsequently, Orson Welles chose her for the role of Helen of Troy in his European production of *Faust*. Later Kitt starred in two French films, after which she returned to the United States and sang in nightclubs in New York City. She appeared in the Broadway productions *New Faces of 1952* and *Mrs. Patterson* (1954), both of which were extremely popular.

KITTRELL COLLEGE Kittrell College, at Kittrell, N.C. was founded by the African Methodist Episcopal (AME) Church in 1886, and the school still retains this affiliation. From the beginning, Kittrell has offered work-study programs to enable students of limited financial means to gain a higher education. The college offers a two-year course in either terminal vocation or in work that can be credited toward the bachelor's degree. Its 1975 enrollment was 396.

KNIGHT, ETHERIDGE See LITERATURE: POETRY.

KNIGHT, FRANKLIN WILLIS (1942–   ), historian, educator; born in Manchester, Jamaica. Knight received a B.A. degree from the University College of the West Indies in 1964, a M.A. degree from the University of Wisconsin in 1965, and his Ph.D. degree from the State University of New York at Stony Brook in 1969. He became an associate professor of history at Johns Hopkins University (Baltimore, Md.) in 1973. His publications include *Slave Society in Cuba During the Nineteenth Century* (1970) and "Cuba," in *Neither Slave Nor Free* (1972).

KNIGHTS OF PYTHIAS *See* FRATERNAL SOCI-ETIES.

KNOX, CLINTON EVERETT (1908–   ), government official; born in New Bedford, Mass. Knox received a B.A. degree from Williams College (Williamstown, Mass.) in 1930, a M.A. degree from Brown University (Providence, R.I.) in 1931, attended the University of Paris in 1938, and received his Ph.D. degree from Harvard University in 1940. After an instructorship at Morgan State University (Baltimore, Md.), Knox joined the U.S. Department of State as a research analyst in 1945. The next year he was appointed deputy chief of the Western European Section division of research, and in 1947 he became chief of the Northern and Western European Bureau. Through the years Knox rose in the ranks of the state department, was assigned to the North Atlantic Treaty Organization (NATO), and was appointed U.S. ambassador (1964) and then consul general (1965) to Dahomey, West Africa. He became ambassador to the Republic of Haiti in 1969.

KNOXVILLE COLLEGE Knoxville College, at Knoxville, Tenn., was founded in 1875 by the United Presbyterian Church. A private, church-affiliated, coeducational college, Knoxville offers the bachelor's degree and provides liberal arts and teacher education curricula. Its enrollment in 1975 was about 750.

The college originated in the efforts of Presbyterian missionaries to provide education for freedmen and their children after the Civil War. Programs ranged from primary through high school levels until the 1890s when collegiate programs became available. The college was chartered by the state of Tennessee in 1901, receiving state and federal support as a land-grant institution. The land-grant function, however, was removed in 1912, at which time it was transferred to the Agricultural and Industrial Normal School for Negroes, now Tennessee State University. After 1912 the college evolved into a liberal arts institution with strong emphasis upon teacher education, especially in granting the bachelor of science degree in music education.

KOONTZ, ELIZABETH DUNCAN (1919–   ), government official, educator; born in Salisbury, N.C. Koontz received a B.A. degree from Livingstone College (Salisbury, N.C.) in 1938 and her M.A. degree from Atlanta University in 1941. She began early to teach in the public schools of North Carolina and continued until 1965 when she became president of the department of classroom teachers of the National Education Association. Koontz served as vice-president of the association in 1966 and as national president in 1968. In 1969 President Richard M. Nixon appointed her director of the Women's Bureau of the U.S. Department of Labor, the first major black appointee in the Nixon administration. Koontz remained in this post until 1972.

KU KLUX KLAN An antiblack organization for whites only, the KKK grew out of the Civil War and Reconstruction and sought to maintain white supremacy in the South by various means, including terrorism. It was founded in Pulaski, Tenn., in 1866, and organized on a more formal basis in Nashville, Tenn., a year later. Its periods of peak activity came shortly after the Civil War and in the 1920s. Although some remnants of the Klan exist, it is no longer the powerful "invisible empire" of bygone years. For additional information, see Horn, S. F., *The Invisible Empire* (1939). *See also* AFRO-AMERICAN HISTORY: RECONSTRUCTION, 1865–77; RACE: RACISM.

KUYKENDALL, RUFUS CALVIN (1903–   ), lawyer, judge; born in Indianapolis, Ind. Kuykendall received a B.A. degree from Indiana University in 1927 and his LL.B. degree from Indiana Law School (now Indianapolis Law School of Indiana University and Purdue University) in 1942. Admitted to the Indiana bar the year of his graduation, he began to practice law in Indianapolis. Kuykendall was deputy prosecuting attorney for the 19th Judicial Circuit of Indiana from 1943 to 1949; public defender in the Criminal Court from 1950 to 1952 and again from 1963 to 1964; assistant city attorney in Indianapolis from 1962 to 1966; and judge of the Superior Court of Marion County after 1967. He also directed the legal staff of the U.S. Commission on Civil Rights from 1959 to 1960, and served as councilman for the city of Indianapolis from 1964 to 1966.

KYLE, MARY J. *See* NEWSPAPERS: CONTEMPO-RARY.

The elder statesman of Afro-American labor leaders, A. Philip Randolph (left), and his longtime associate Bayard Rustin, first collaborated in 1941 on a demand for equal opportunities in the defense industry. *(Photo by Irene Fertik.)*

LABOR/LABOR FORCE See EMPLOYMENT.

LABOR UNIONS

Exclusion and Restriction Various craft organizations that sought to ensure job security existed long before organized unions became part of the American way of life. The pervading racism against Afro-Americans that prevailed in these organizations, as it did in society in general both before and after the Revolutionary War, became institutionalized in later labor unions. During the early period of American history, it was common practice for authorities and officials to devise and enforce noncompetitive situations between Afro-American and white workers. For example, as early as the 1730s the Caulkers Trade Society of Boston, Mass., opened its membership to whites only. Unions of shipwrights, carpenters, and typographers continued this policy of exclusion throughout the early 1800s.

A half century later, the first outstanding union, the National Labor Union (NLU), took a similar racist stand. The founding of the NLU filled the void left by the disintegration of the International Industrial Association (1864–66). Affiliates of the NLU, which held its first national convention in Baltimore, Md., in 1866, were closed to blacks. For example, the Iron Moulders' Union, headed by William H. Sylvis who was prominent in the formation of the NLU, consisted primarily of highly skilled white, native-born, male craftsmen. Although the NLU later admitted Afro-American delegates to its conventions (after controversy), one of its goals was to secure job monopoly against invasion by foreign-born and Afro-American workers.

The NLU conceded, however, that Afro-Americans should be organized but not integrated into existing white unions. Accordingly, blacks formed the Colored National Labor Union in 1869 largely through the influential leadership of Isaac Myers, a freeborn Afro-American carpenter and caulker of Baltimore, Md., who was also instrumental in organizing a black-operated shipyard—the Chesapeake Marine Railway and Dry Dock Company—in his native city. Actually, Afro-Americans had formed one of their first labor unions, the Caulkers' Association, in Baltimore as early as 1838.

The NLU was superseded by the Noble Order

491

of the Knights of Labor, which in principle but not always in practice sought to eliminate discrimination in union membership based upon race, sex, or skill. The first grand master of the order, Uriah Stephens, stated that he could "see ahead of me an organization that will include men and women of every creed and color." The second grand master, Terence V. Powderly, sought on at least one notable occasion to implement the Knights' goal of nondiscrimination. Whatever his reasons, Powderly proposed that he should be introduced at the national convention in Richmond, Va., in 1886 by a black delegate from New York, Frank J. Ferrell, whose

At a Richmond, Va., convention in 1886, the Knights of Labor revealed their failure to root out racial discrimination when some delegates objected to black delegate Frank J. Ferrell's appearance on the platform. Ferrell was furiously denounced by segregationist delegates after he appeared on the platform to introduce Terence V. Powderly. *(Library of Congress.)*

entry to the building had been contested on racial grounds. Ferrell did indeed enter and make the introduction, emphasizing the Knights' belief in nondiscrimination: "One of the objects of our order," he said, "is the abolition of those distinctions which are maintained by creed or color." Ferrell's appearance infuriated segregationist delegates, especially when they saw him on the same speaker's platform as the governor of the state of Virginia, who bore the revered name of Lee.

While the Knights did, in fact, organize tens of thousands of black workers, much rank and file pressure was mounted to exclude blacks. Powderly seemed forced to moderate his views: "The color line," he said, "cannot be rubbed out, nor can the prejudice against the colored man be overcome in a day." Therefore, he concluded, "it

would be better to organize colored men by themselves."

With the decline of the short-lived Knights of Labor, the American Federation of Labor (AFL) became the official spokesman for organized labor. Unlike the Knights, the AFL emphasized the separation of crafts, exclusive jurisdiction, and autonomy for each of its affiliates. This policy attracted many newly organized craft unions as well as affiliates of the moribund Knights.

Although no specific allusion was made to the Afro-American worker in the AFL's constitution, the organization early required from all unions seeking affiliation a pledge "never to discriminate against a fellow worker on account of color, creed, or nationality." The pledge was rather meaningless: "ritual," an oath taken by incoming members never to propose an Afro-American for membership, permitted the AFL to charter affiliates with policies of exclusion. Yet, the AFL reiterated its nondiscrimination policy at its convention in 1897; but the practical result was that the AFL no longer went through the pretense of requiring nondiscrimination against black membership. Many affiliates simply excluded blacks regardless of pretenses. Sterling D. Spero and Abram L. Harris in their book entitled *The Black Worker* (1931) listed 24 major unions that barred blacks; ten were AFL affiliates, and the others were independents.

To ensure that Afro-American and white workers did not compete, and to provide local craft unions with "job monopoly," various practices were developed by organized labor during the period between the end of the Civil War and the close of World War II in order to control the number of laborers. These practices were: (1) full restriction or complete exclusion; (2) partial restriction that permitted unions to retain control on the one hand while ensuring against strikebreaking by use of black laborers on the other; and (3) full acceptance of Afro-American members, which would, therefore, prohibit competition with fellow unionists. Throughout the period, it may be said that blacks were either excluded from or segregated within the labor movement; in either case, the result was blatant discrimination.

The persistence of discrimination can be readily documented. For example, as late as 1944, the Seafarers' International Union of North America had separate listings for white and for black hiring halls in telephone directories. When the two hiring halls were combined in 1947, blacks were restricted to two occupations, fireman and steward, the former to coal-burning vessels and the latter to all-black sculleries. When this fact was called to the union's attention, an official responded in this way: "You government [officials] are interfering with our hiring hall . . . neither the President [of the United States] nor anyone else is going to tell men with whom they are going to live; and to a seaman a ship is his home."

Other examples of discrimination include the following examples. The United Auto Workers (UAW) had separate seniority lists, one for blacks and one for whites; and some occupations were closed to blacks in plants in Detroit, Mich. Elsewhere, garage car washers and cleaners unions, as well as the Motion Picture Projectionists Union, though maintaining mixed membership, showed preferences that favored whites. Black motion picture projectionists in New York City were limited to employment in Harlem. These are only a few of the thousands of examples of discrimination that black workers faced in the American labor movement.

Samuel Gompers, the first AFL president, defended the exclusionist AFL policy. His successor, William Green, though occasionally outspoken against racism, did not (or could not) stop the exclusionist policy. Excluded from the unions, Afro-Americans sometimes served willingly as strikebreakers, believing that this was the best way to open up the unions. Both the Brotherhood of Sleeping Car Porters (BSCP) and the National Association for the Advancement of Colored People (NAACP) fought the AFL's policy of exclusion and discrimination with little success during the 1930s and 1940s. For example, Charles H. Houston, representing the NAACP, protested at the AFL's convention of 1934. Yet, seven years later, the AFL rejected resolutions introduced by A. Philip Randolph and Milton P. Webster protesting policies of exclusion, Jim Crow practices, and other forms of discrimination. The AFL continued its practices during and after World War II, and though official policy changed in the 1950s some affiliates continued many old practices.

The Brotherhood of Sleeping Car Porters (BSCP) and the Civil Rights Movement The first great changes toward the unionization of black workers occurred in the 1930s with the rise of the Brotherhood of Sleeping Car Porters (BSCP) union under the leadership of A. Philip Randolph, with the New Deal under President Franklin D. Roosevelt, with the Congress of Industrial Organizations (CIO) under Philip Murray, and with the United Automobile Workers (UAW) under Walter Reuther. All initiated sympathetic policies and programs that were later supplemented and made more meaningful by the civil rights movement, changing tremendously the image and reality of Afro-Americans in the American labor movement.

Founded in 1925 and nurtured for more than a generation by its indefatigable and articulate founder, A. Philip Randolph, the BSCP organized railway porters (traditionally an occupation for Afro-Americans) to bargain with the Pullman Company, which held a virtual monopoly on the nation's sleeping-car facilities. Seeking a national charter from the AFL, the BSCP was refused first in 1928 and again in 1934. However, in 1935, the New Deal's National Mediation Board recognized the BSCP, and the next year the AFL followed suit. From within, the BSCP opposed the AFL's practice of exclusion and discrimination. From without, the fight was joined by the National Urban League and the NAACP.

The New Deal, with its political coalition of labor, liberals, and Afro-Americans, passed far-reaching legislation and introduced innovative programs that were to affect white and black workers alike. Such legislation included the National Industrial Recovery Act (wages and hours); the National Labor Relations Act (collective bargaining); and the Fair Labor Standards Act (wages and hours). Although some policies and programs were not applicable to agriculture and domestic services, areas in which Afro-Americans were heavily employed at the time, the New Deal succeeded in establishing a favorable image of itself with the black industrial worker, an image enhanced through the visibility of several black advisers, including Mary McLeod Bethune, a presidential appointee to the National Youth Administration (NYA); Lester Granger of the National Urban League; and A. Philip Randolph. Perhaps as effective as any legislation was the issuance of Executive Order No. 8802 on June 25, 1941, which established the Committee on Fair Employment Practices (FEPC) within the Office of Production Management. The order forbade discrimination by employers or labor unions against blacks in World War II defense industries, and its issuance was prompted by Randolph's threat to protest discrimination by a march on Washington, D.C.

Indeed, Afro-Americans surged into the ranks of organized labor during the years of the New

Deal and World War II when large industries were being massively unionized on the principle of industrial unionism. The secession of the Committee for Industrialization (CIO) from the AFL in 1935 provided opportunities for the unionization of black industrial workers. Irrespective of labor supply, source of labor, or ethnic background, the CIO sought to organize workers on a massive, industry-wide basis. The 1930s witnessed a new dimension in labor history when blacks and whites joined in the common cause of industrial unionism.

Black membership in unions rose rapidly, especially during the war years, and after the war membership continued to increase. By 1970 it had reached approximately 2,131,000, according to the U.S. Department of Labor. If this figure is valid, between 1933 and 1970 black union membership increased about 30 times.

During the latter phase of the civil rights movement (1960s and 1970s), the thrust of unionization took place mainly in service-connected employment: government workers, farm workers, hospital employees, and sanitation workers. Though a few large independent aggregations claimed some black membership (Postal

AFRO-AMERICANS AS A PERCENT OF TOTAL WAGE AND SALARY WORKERS, BY INDUSTRY, AND LABOR UNION MEMBERSHIP, 1970

Industry of longest job held in 1970	Total wage and salary workers		In labor unions		Not in labor unions	
	Number (thousands)	Percent Afro-American[1]	Number (thousands)	Percent Afro-American[1]	Number (thousands)	Percent Afro-American[1]
All industries[2]	84,256	11.6	17,192	12.4	67,063	11.4
Mining	574	4.4	205	4.9	368	4.3
Construction	4,975	10.2	1,948	8.7	3,027	11.2
Manufacturing, total	22,503	10.7	7,600	12.4	14,903	9.8
Durable goods, total	13,094	10.0	4,900	12.4	8,194	8.5
Metal industries	2,874	11.3	1,391	13.9	1,482	8.9
Machinery, including electrical	4,650	6.7	1,489	8.9	3,160	5.7
Transportation equipment	2,403	10.5	1,148	13.2	1,256	8.0
Motor vehicles	1,105	13.4	732	15.4	374	9.4
Other transportation equipment	1,298	8.1	416	9.1	882	7.5
Other durable goods .	3,168	13.1	871	14.9	2,296	12.5
Nondurable goods, total	9,409	11.7	2,700	12.5	6,709	11.3
Food	1,908	14.7	690	15.1	1,218	14.4
Textiles and apparel .	2,712	14.5	622	14.5	2,090	14.5
Printing	1,368	5.6	306	7.5	1,062	5.1
Chemicals	1,249	8.6	295	10.5	954	8.0
Other nondurable goods	2,172	11.0	787	11.6	1,387	10.7
Transportation, communication, and public utilities	5,642	10.7	2,527	10.3	3,115	11.1
Transportation	3,070	10.4	1,589	8.7	1,481	12.2
Communication and other public utilities ..	2,573	11.1	938	13.0	1,634	10.1
Wholesale trade	3,047	8.1	345	11.9	2,701	7.6
Retail trade	13,732	8.0	1,363	9.7	12,368	7.9
Services and finance	27,115	13.9	2,103	18.6	25,012	13.5
Educational	7,426	10.9	803	11.7	6,623	10.9
Hospitals	3,162	20.0	267	37.8	2,895	18.4
Private households	2,481	36.3	16	([3])	2,465	36.3
Insurance and real estate	2,320	7.0	112	17.0	2,208	6.5
Personal	2,205	17.1	272	30.9	1,933	15.2
Other services	9,520	9.3	635	13.5	8,886	9.0
Public administration	4,761	12.8	1,055	16.5	3,706	11.8
Postal	820	21.7	428	20.6	392	23.0
Other Federal	1,596	14.7	213	22.5	1,384	13.4
State	709	6.2	94	6.4	616	6.2
Local	1,636	9.5	321	9.7	1,314	9.4

[1]Columns nonadditive.
[2]Includes agriculture not shown separately.
[3]Base less than 75,000.
NOTE: Due to rounding, sums of individual items may not equal totals.
SOURCE: *Selected Earnings and Demographic Characteristics of Union Members, 1970*, Report 417, U.S. Department of Labor, 1972.

Employees, Letter Carriers, and United Mine Workers), the vast majority of Afro-Americans continued their membership in the AFL-CIO, which, merging at the time (1955) of the civil rights movement, gave valuable support to the cause.

Indeed, although some elements in the rank and file were not in sympathy, the top leadership of the newly created AFL-CIO generally endorsed some of the major national reforms. This was especially true of the AFL-CIO's lobby in support of the landmark Civil Rights Act of 1964, notably Title VII, which concerned fair employment practices. Moreover, the AFL-CIO took a public-relations posture favorable to the movement, holding its first National Trade Union Conference on Civil Rights in 1957; giving some financial support to the Leadership Conference on Civil Rights; and establishing and supporting the civil rights department at its headquarters in Washington, D.C. It cooperated with such groups as the National Urban League and the A. Philip Randolph Institute in providing job opportunities for black youths. For example, writing in *Harper's Magazine* in 1971, Bayard Rustin of the A. Philip Randolph Institute stated that 79 "outreach" programs in as many cities had placed more than 8,000 Afro-American youths in high-paying jobs in the trades.

Good intentions and leadership at national levels, however, have not always been equally implemented at lower levels. In fact, although unions may not have been the worst violators of equal opportunities for Afro-American workers, ample evidence exists to show that discriminatory practices have persisted. For example, the U.S. Department of Labor found evidence of discrimination in 1967 when the heralded "Philadelphia Plan" (which established goals and target dates for hiring Afro-Americans) was under consideration. The agency concluded that a pattern of discrimination existed within eight construction trade unions in the Philadelphia, Pa., area, where, ironically, the plan originated. The pattern was clear: over a period of years, less than one percent of the union membership of electrical workers, ironworkers, pipefitters, steamfitters, sheet-metal workers, and roofers had been black. In effect, Afro-Americans were practically excluded from these unions.

Another example is shown from evidence revealed through the U.S. Department of Justice in 1970 when litigation was underway against a number of labor unions representing such

diverse groups as electrical workers, mineworkers, longshoremen, teamsters, ironworkers, plumbers, and steelworkers. Moreover, a news release by the agency on March 31, 1970, indicated that nine craft locals affiliated with motion picture and television industries practiced discrimination; it appeared that the unions involved had a combined membership of approximately 12,000, including 800 members of other minority groups, but only 45 Afro-Americans.

It cannot be denied, on the one hand, that unions have been important in shaping the economic destiny of great masses of Afro-American workers and that the struggle of blacks and their union allies to overcome exclusion and discrimination was significant in this achievement. It must be acknowledged, on the other hand, that the achievement of unionization, however defined or evaluated, has pointed to the incompleteness and inconsistency of the reality behind the American dream of equal opportunity. For in whatever context the achievement is placed and

Martin Luther King, Jr. joined the picket line at a 1964 International Chemical Workers Union strike against a Scripto plant in Atlanta, Ga., for discrimination against black employees. *(Schomburg Collection, New York Public Library.)*

measured, it is apparent that unionism flows vitally within the economic mainstream of American society; and the denial of its rewards and benefits carries its own built-in punishment. Although the civil rights movement had many facets, that of job opportunity, increasingly measured by union membership, has certainly remained paramount in the minds of Afro-Americans even when more current social or political issues appear on the surface. In a sense, this fact is illustrated in the final public act of the civil rights leader, Martin Luther King, Jr., who, at the time of his assassination in Memphis, Tenn., was supporting a local union of black sanitation workers in their struggle to overcome job discrimination. See also CIVIL RIGHTS: CIVIL RIGHTS ENFORCEMENT; DISCRIMINATION; EMPLOYMENT; FRATERNAL SOCIETIES; NATIONAL ASSOCIATION FOR THE ADVANCEMENT OF COLORED PEOPLE (NAACP); RANDOLPH, ASA PHILIP.

REFERENCES: AFL-CIO, Equal Rights for All, rev. ed., Publication No. 113, May 1970; Bloch, Herman D., "Craft Unions and the Negro in Historical Perspective," Journal of Negro History, January 1958, pp. 10–33; Bloch, Herman D., "Negroes and Organized Labor," Journal of Human Relations, Summer 1962, pp. 357–374; Cahn, William, A Pictorial History of American Labor, Crown Publishers, New York, 1972; Cantor, Milton (ed.), Black Labor in America, Negro Universities Press, Westport, 1969; Greene, Lorenzo J. and Carter G. Woodson, The Negro Wage Earner, Associated Publishers, Washington, D.C., 1931; Hill, Herbert, "Racism within Organized Labor: A Report of Five Years of the AFL-CIO, 1955–1960," Journal of Negro Education, vol. 30, pp. 109–18, Spring 1961; Hill, Herbert, "Employment, Manpower Training and the Black Worker," Journal of Negro Education, vol. 38, pp. 204–17, Spring 1969; Marshall, Ray, The Negro and Organized Labor, John Wiley & Sons, New York, 1965; Northrup, Herbert R., Organized Labor and the Negro, Harper, New York, 1944; Rustin, Bayard, "Blacks and the Unions," Harper's Magazine, April 1971; and Spero, Sterling D. and Abram L. Harris, The Black Worker: The Negro and the Labor Movement, 2d ed., Kennikat Press, Port Washington, 1966; "The Negro in the American Labor Movement: Some Selected Chapters," Labor History (entire issue), vol. 10, Summer 1969 is a good, general treatment. A specific treatment of the important BSCP is found in William H. Harris, Keeping The Faith: A. Philip Randolph, Milton P. Webster, and The Brotherhood of Sleeping Car Porters, 1925–37, University of Illinois Press, Urbana, 1976; and a later period is treated in Gould, William B., Black Workers in White Unions: Job Discrimination in the United States, Cornell University Press, Ithaca, N.Y., 1977.

LAFONTANT, JEWEL STRADFORD (1922–   ), lawyer, government official; born in Chicago, Ill. Lafontant graduated from Oberlin College (Oberlin, Ohio) in 1943 and from the University of Chicago Law School in 1946. As a new member of the Illinois bar, she became a trial lawyer for the Legal Aid Bureau in Chicago until 1954. A year later Lafontant was appointed by President Dwight D. Eisenhower as an assistant U.S. attorney for the Northern District of Illinois, the first black woman named for this position. In 1960 she distinguished herself as an alternate delegate to the Republic National Convention by seconding the nomination of Richard M. Nixon for president. Active on many executive boards, she also served as director of several, including Trans World Airlines; Jewel Companies, Inc.; and the United Nations Association. Lafontant was also respected in private practice and was soon made a partner in a law firm in Chicago. In 1969 she became vice-chairman of the U.S. Advisory Commission on International Educational and Cultural Affairs, a post she held for three years. From 1970 to 1972 Lafontant was a member of the President's Council on Minority Business Enterprise. The year following she was named to the U.S. delegation to the United Nations, and in 1973 she took the position of deputy solicitor-general of the United States. Appointed by the president, she was the first woman deputy solicitor-general and one of the highest-ranking Afro-Americans in Washington, D.C.

LAMB, ARTHUR C. See LITERATURE: DRAMA/THEATER.

LAND-GRANT COLLEGES See EDUCATION: COLLEGES AND UNIVERSITIES.

LANE COLLEGE Lane College, at Jackson, Tenn., was founded by Isaac Lane in 1882 as the Christian Methodist Episcopal (CME) High School. Church-related and coeducational, the college offers the bachelor's degree and provides liberal arts and teacher education curricula. Its 1975 enrollment was 715.

The school began with Jennie E. Lane as its sole teacher. In her honor, the school was renamed Lane Institute. In 1887 Rev. T. F. Saunders, a member of the Memphis Conference of the Methodist Episcopal (ME) Church, South, was appointed the first president and as such made numerous contributions to the institute. It was during this period that the need for a college department was felt. This department was organized in 1896 and the name of the school was changed from Lane Institute to Lane College.

In 1961 the college was admitted to full membership in the Southern Association of Colleges and Secondary Schools. See also LANE, ISAAC.

LANE INSTITUTE See LANE COLLEGE.

LANE, ISAAC (1834–1937), Christian Methodist Episcopal bishop, educator; born in Madison County, Tenn. By the outbreak of the Civil War Lane was recognized as an influential minister. In 1866 he was ordained a deacon and in 1873 elected a bishop of the Colored Methodist Episcopal Church (now Christian Methodist Episcopal Church), which he helped to develop. Active until 1914, he was instrumental in the expansion of that church in such major cities as Cleveland, Ohio; Chicago, Ill.; St. Louis, Mo.; Kansas City, Kans.; Topeka, Kans.; Oklahoma City, Okla.; and

Tulsa, Okla. Meanwhile, in 1882, Lane founded Lane College (Jackson, Tenn.), of which his son, James Franklin Lane, became president (1907–28). *See also* LANE COLLEGE.

LANE, JAMES FRANKLIN (1874–1944), educator; born in Jackson, Tenn. Lane received a normal (teaching) certificate in 1891, B.A. degrees from Walden University (Nashville, Tenn.) (1895) and Harvard College (1897), and his Ph.D. degree from Walden College in 1903. He taught mathematics at Lane College (Jackson, Tenn.), became head of the department of education there, and finally served as president of the college (1907–28). Lane wrote *My Second Trip Abroad* and *Much in Little*.

LANG, XENOPHONE F., SR. (1917–   ), lawyer, judge. Lang graduated from Dillard University (New Orleans, La.). He received a law degree from Southwestern University (Los Angeles, Calif.) and was admitted to the California bar in 1951. Choosing to remain in Los Angeles, Lang became a Municipal Court judge there. In 1974 he resumed the private practice of law.

LANGSTON, JOHN MERCER (1829–97), lawyer, educator, state legislator, government official; born in Louisa, Va. Langston, a former slave, graduated from Oberlin College (Oberlin, Ohio) in 1849 and from the theology school there in 1852. He was Ohio's first black lawyer, the first president of Virginia State College, and Virginia's first black congressman. After studying law in Elyria, Ohio, Langston was admitted to the Ohio bar in 1854 and began a practice in Oberlin. He was active in civic affairs until he moved to Washington, D.C., to practice law. In 1869 Langston became dean of the law department of Howard University (Washington, D.C.), a post he maintained until 1876. Meanwhile, he was appointed a member of the District of Columbia Board of Health by President Ulysses S. Grant in 1871, and some time later he was appointed minister resident and consul general to Haiti and charge d'affaires to Santo Domingo by President Rutherford B. Hayes. Langston's papers are housed at the Amistad Research Center. *See also* LAWYERS.

LANGSTON UNIVERSITY Langston University, at Langston, Okla., was established in 1897 by the Territorial legislature. A state-supported, land-grant, coeducational school, Langston offers the bachelor's degree and provides liberal arts, teacher education, and vocational curricula. Its 1975 enrollment was 1,250.

The school was first chartered as the Colored Agricultural and Normal University, but it was popularly known as Langston, after the name of the village where it is located. The site was named after John Mercer Langston, a congressman from Virginia during Reconstruction. In 1941 the state officially recognized the popular name. The college's first president was Inman E. Page, a graduate of Brown University (Providence, R.I.). He was followed successively by Isaac B. McCutcheon, R. E. Bullit, J. M. Marquess, Isaac W. Young, Z. T. Hubert, J. W. Sanford, G. L. Harrison, William H. Hale (an alumnus of Langston), and William E. Sims.

LARSEN, NELLA (1893–1963), author, nurse; born in Chicago, Ill. Larsen attended Fisk University (Nashville, Tenn.) and graduated from the Lincoln Hospital Training School for Nurses (New York, N.Y.) in 1915. She became superintendent of nurses at Tuskegee Institute (Tuskegee Institute, Ala.), and later served as supervisor of nurses at Lincoln Hospital Training School for Nurses. In 1918 Larsen accepted a position as district nurse in the New York City Department of Health. Three years later she began working in the children's department of the New York Public Library, and in 1929 she was made general assistant librarian. In 1930 Larsen became the first black woman to receive a Guggenheim Award. She wrote two novels: *Quicksand* (1928) and *Passing* (1929, 1971).

LATIMER, LEWIS H. (1848–1928), inventor, scientist; born in Chelsea, Mass. Latimer served in the Union Navy in 1863, studied drafting, and later invented and patented an incandescent light bulb with a carbon filament in 1881. He served as an engineer for the Edison Company for many years, and while with Edison supervised the installation of the electric light system in New York, N.Y.; Philadelphia, Pa.; Montreal, Canada; and London, England. Latimer wrote the first textbook on the lighting system used by the Edison Company, and he was employed by Alexander Graham Bell to make patent drawings for the first telephone. He also served as chief draftsman for General Electric and Westinghouse companies.

LAUREY, JAMES RICHARD (1907–1964), surgeon; born in East St. Louis, Ill. Laurey received a B.A. degree (1929), a M.B. degree (1932), and his M.D. degree (1933) from Wayne State University (Detroit, Mich.). He was professor of thoracic surgery (1936–39), senior and later chief thoracic surgeon (1941–50), and chief surgeon and chairman of the department of surgery (1950–55) at Freedmen's Hospital, Washington, D.C.

LAWLESS, THEODORE KENNETH (1892–1971), dermatologist; born in Thibodaux, La. Lawless received a B.A. degree (1914) and a D.Sc. degree (1915) from Talladega College (Talladega, Ala.), and his M.D. degree (1919) and M.S. degree (1920) from Northwestern University School of Medicine (Evanston, Ill.). He studied dermatology at Harvard Pathological Institute, Freiburg, Germany (1922–23), and was a fellow of dermatology and syphilology at Massachusetts General Hospital, Boston, Mass. (1920–21), at Saint Louis Hospital, Paris, France (1921–22), and at Kaiser Joseph Hospital, Vienna, Austria. Lawless served as an instructor at Northwestern University School of Medicine (1924–41) and as a consulting dermatologist at Geneva Community Hospital (1924–41). He was associate examiner in dermatology for the National Board of Medical Examiners, consultant to the U.S. Chemical Warfare Board, and director of his own dermatological clinic in the heart of Chicago, Ill.'s black belt. Lawless received numerous honors and high awards for his achievements, including the National Association for the Advancement of Colored People's (NAACP) Spingarn Medal in 1954.

LAWRENCE, ANNIE L. (1926–   ), nurse, educator; born in Madisonville, Va. Lawrence received her B.S.N. and M.S.N. degrees from De Paul University (Chicago, Ill.). She was involved in the evaluation and regulation of nursing programs in Illinois, and was the coordinator for the Illinois Department of Registration and Education for nursing education. Her office surveyed, approved, and licensed schools of nursing in the state of Illinois. Lawrence was also adviser to the Illinois State Nurse's Association.

LAWRENCE, JACOB (1917–   ), painter, educator; born in Atlantic City, N.J. Probably one of the best-known Afro-American painters, Lawrence studied at the Art Workshop, the Harlem Art Center, the Harlem Workshop in 1932, and taught at Pratt Institute (Brooklyn, N.Y.). His paintings, mostly in tempera, are noted for simple outlines combined with complex figure groupings in bright color, keen patterning, and a narrative quality with little perspective. Some works are sad in mood, as *Tombstones*; others express frantic joy, as his famous *Dancing at the Savoy*. Lawrence did a series of 60 gouache panels entitled *Migrations of the Negro*; a series of 40 panels in tempera depicting the life of Frederick Douglass; and a similar series, in 40 panels, showing the life of Harriet Tubman. Other works such as *Square Dance* and *John Brown's Body* also have won critical acclaim. Lawrence was the first artist to receive the National Association for the Advancement of Colored People's (NAACP) Spingarn Medal, in 1970, and he had previously won a Rosenwald Fellowship in 1946; a Guggenheim Fellowship in 1946; second prize at the Art of the American Negro, Chicago, Ill., 1940; and other awards. Lawrence's exhibits included ones held at the Harlem Art Center, New York, N.Y., 1936–39; at the Museum of Modern Art, New York, N.Y., at the Ford Foundation Retrospective Exhibit; and at the Whitney Museum of American Art, New York, N.Y., 1971. His work is represented in the Museum of Modern Art, New York, N.Y.; the Harmon Foundation, New York, N.Y.; IBM; Virginia Museum of Fine Arts; and others. Lawrence was a member of the Artists Equity Association and the National Institute of Arts and Letters. He was appointed head of the art department at the University of Washington in 1972. He is the author of *Harriet and the Promised Land* (1968) an illustrated book for children. *See also* ARTISTS; LITERATURE: CHILDREN'S LITERATURE.

LAWRENCE, MARGARET MORGAN (1914–   ), pediatrician; born in New York, N.Y. Lawrence received a B.A. degree from Cornell University (Ithaca, N.Y.) in 1936, and a M.D. degree (1941), a M.P.H. degree (1943), and her certificate in psychoanalytic medicine (1951) from the College of Physicians and Surgeons of Columbia University. She was associate professor of pediatrics at Meharry Medical College (Nashville, Tenn.) and a resident in psychiatry at New York State Psychiatric Institute and Hospital in 1948. Lawrence also served as a member of the College of Physicians and Surgeons, Columbia University, of Rockland County Community Mental Health Center, and of Nyack Hospital. She was a member of the American Psychoanalytic Association.

LAWSON, JAMES RAYMOND (1915–   ), physicist, administrator; born in Louisville, Ky.

Lawson received a B.A. degree from Fisk University (Nashville, Tenn.) in 1935, and a M.S. degree (1936) and his Ph.D. degree (1939) from the University of Michigan. He served as acting vice-president (1966–67), acting president (1967), and president (after 1967) of Fisk University.

LAWSON, MARJORIE (1912–   ), lawyer, judge; born in Pittsburgh, Pa. Lawson was graduated from the University of Michigan in 1933, and received her J.D. degree from Columbia University Law School in 1939. She practiced law until 1962 when she was appointed to the Juvenile Court of the District of Columbia, a post she held for three years. Lawson was the first black woman ever appointed to a judgeship by a U.S. president and approved by the U.S. Senate for a statutory appointment. In 1962 President John F. Kennedy named her to his Committee on Equal Employment Opportunities. Before that, from 1943 to 1946, she had been assistant director, and later director, of the division of review and analysis of the President's Committee on Fair Employment Practices. Lawson wrote a weekly public-affairs column for the Pittsburgh *Courier* for 15 years

LAWSON, WARNER (1903–71), pianist, educator. Lawson was educated at Fisk University (Nashville, Tenn.) and received a B.Mus. degree from Yale University in 1929. He taught at Fisk University and at North Carolina Agricultural and Technical (A&T) State University before joining the faculty of Howard University (Washington, D.C.). At the latter institution he became dean of music and for a quarter of a century directed the Howard University Choir. Under his direction this choir served as the unofficial chorus of the National Symphony Orchestra, singing with it several times each year in the 1950s and 1960s.

- - -

LAWYERS

Background Despite severe discrimination, several Afro-Americans won recognition as lawyers in the nineteenth century. Outstanding among them were George B. Vashon, primarily a teacher in pre-Civil War New York and John M. Langston, a native of Virginia and a graduate of Oberlin College (Oberlin, Ohio). Admitted to practice before the U.S. Supreme Court in 1867, Langston served as one of the first deans of the law department at Howard University (Washington, D.C.). Another pioneer was the versatile John Swett Rock, born in New Jersey in 1825, a physician and civil rights advocate who was admitted to the Massachusetts bar in 1861. With the aid of a white U.S. senator, Charles Sumner, Rock was admitted to plead before the U.S. Supreme Court in 1864. Other midcentury and Reconstruction leaders who were lawyers included: James C. Napier, a native of Tennessee who graduated from the law department of Howard University, Richard T. Greener, a graduate of Harvard (1870), and Judson W. Lyons, a native of Georgia, and a

John M. Langston (left) and Richard T. Greener. (*Library of Congress.*)

graduate of Howard (1884), who practiced for 14 years in Augusta, Ga.

Not all early Afro-American lawyers practiced extensively. Though several were admitted to the U.S. Supreme Court, the first actually to appear there was Samuel Lowery of Huntsville, Ala., on February 2, 1880. Lowery's appearance was reported in Frank Leslie's *Illustrated Newspaper*, March 13, 1880.

The last decades of the nineteenth century saw

Samuel Lowery in the Supreme Court in 1880, as pictured in *Frank Leslie's Illustrated Newspaper.* *(Library of Congress.)*

the appearance of an increasing number of Afro-Americans who established successful practices in local areas. J. T. V. Hill began practice in Indianapolis, Ind. in 1882; James H. Lott began in Indianapolis in the 1890s, as did Robert L. Bailey sometime later; Frederick L. McGhee, born in Aberdeen, Miss., was admitted to the Illinois bar, and in 1885 became a partner with the more celebrated Afro-American lawyer, Edward A. Morris, who was admitted to the bar in 1879 at the age of 21. Later, McGhee established a successful practice in St. Paul, Minn.

By the turn of the century, an increasing number of Afro-Americans were practicing law. They included Simuel McGill, born in Florida in 1877, who served as counsel for the Knights of Pythias; Perry Howard, born in Mississippi in 1877; George E. Hall, born in Kentucky in 1889, who practiced in New York City; William H. H. Hart, born in 1857, who taught criminal law at Howard University for 25 years; Walter Moran Farmer, the first black law graduate of Washington University (St. Louis, Mo.); and Homer G. Phillips, also of St. Louis, whose memory is preserved in a hospital dedicated there in the late 1930s.

Civil Rights Whatever their specialty in law, almost without exception all Afro-American lawyers have supported civil rights causes, professionally, morally, and financially. Invariably, lawyers of older and younger generations have been members of the National Association for the Advancement of Colored People (NAACP) or have aided its program. Numerous

lawyers have served the cause of civil rights, but some of the outstanding ones are as follows: W. Ashby Hawkins, Baltimore NAACP, counsel in *Buchanan v. Warley* (1917); Scipio Africanus Jones of the NAACP in the Arkansas sharecroppers cases of 1919; later more significant work was done by Charles Hamilton Houston, William H. Hastie, James M. Nabrit, Leon Ransom, Raymond Pace Alexander, Sidney Redmond, Loren Miller, and Thurgood Marshall. Much of their work spanned the 1930s, 1940s, and 1950s, often as counsel in such classic civil rights cases as those of Lloyd Lionel Gaines, Ada Sipuel, and Heman Sweatt. Moreover, on numerous local levels, lawyers fought for civil rights. Such lawyers, for example, were Louis Redding of Wilmington, Del., whose activities spanned more than 30 years in the state; and Leonard W. Holt, a graduate of Howard University, who served as counsel in more than 40 school integration cases in Virginia after the 1940s. Mention should also be made of Howard Moore, Jr., born in Georgia in 1932, who defended such civil rights leaders as Martin Luther King, Jr. (1960s) and Angela Davis (1972); and Fred Gray, who defended Rosa Parks.

Women lawyers were also active as civil rights advocates. Charlotte Ray graduated from Howard in 1872 as the first black woman lawyer in the U.S. She was followed by an ever-increasing list that included Jane Bolin (New York, N.Y), Juanita Jackson Mitchell (Baltimore, Md.), Frankie Muse Freeman (St. Louis, Mo.), Constance Baker Motley (New York, N.Y.), Patricia Roberts Harris (Washington, D.C.), Juanita Kidd Stout (Phila-

Far right: Attorney Fred Gray defended Rosa Parks (left), who, after refusing to move to the rear of the bus in Montgomery, Ala., in 1955, was found guilty of breaking a city ordinance. This is a photograph of the reenactment of the Parks case which inspired the Montgomery bus boycott. *(National Educational Television.)*

delphia, Pa.), Ruby Martin (Washington, D.C.), Eleanor Holmes Norton, (Washington, D.C.), and Edith Miller (New York, N.Y.).

Later Trends Indications show that a new generation of lawyers had emerged by the 1970s, born during or after the Great Depression and growing to adulthood during the flowering of the civil rights movement of the 1960s. Some of the later trends observable among Afro-American lawyers include:

(1) Though relative increases in the number of Afro-American lawyers occurred, the increase did not keep abreast of needs and population changes.

(2) Discrimination against Afro-American lawyers still existed in the areas of training and employment opportunities, but there were ever-increasing opportunities for these lawyers in public and private sectors of the economy.

(3) Some black lawyers, contrary to those of the earlier generation, were financially better off as a group in regard to professional fees. This fact may reflect the increase in the prestige of Afro-American lawyers both within and beyond ethnic limitations.

(4) The contemporary generation of black lawyers, like their elders, continued to oppose racial discrimination against Afro-Americans, while looking forward to better opportunities.

Prospects in the 1980s Since the 1960s American society has become more sensitive about the problem of black underrepresentation in the legal profession, and has grudgingly moved to reduce the numerical shortage. But little has been said about, and even less has been done to solve, the more serious problems indigenous to this numerical shortage. The problem has been defined as that of alleviating the shortage in attorneys who can advise, counsel, and defend those Afro-Americans who become subjects of, and are often adversely affected by, the system of criminal laws. The problem embraces, for example, the difficulty of establishing large black law firms. This difficulty, in turn, is inextricably linked to the circumscribed nature of the black practice. Criminal cases, family disputes, divorces, minor real property transactions, welfare rights, and the demands of community leadership have not, and do not now, generate the resources necessary for significant expansion of a law practice, enhancement of skills of the lawyers, or acquisition of the attendant office tools needed by a lawyer in a growing civil practice.

With the rights and remedies of the individual Afro-American directly at stake, and indirectly over the long run those of the black community, it has become clear that these shortcomings in the civil areas are of broader importance than previously recognized.

Black attorneys are effectively foreclosed from certain areas of the law, primarily in the civil areas where specialization would be most profitable. These "profitable" areas are measured not only by the potential pecuniary advantage to the black practitioner, but also by "profitable" advantage to the black community in having a black perspective skillfully and forcefully represented in all substantive areas of the law. Such major areas of legal practice as tax law, patent law, corporate law, labor law, antitrust law, and securities law have been the exclusive and private preserve of the white practitioner and his law firms. The black legal profession and others think that young black lawyers should move into the councils of the large impact-wielding white law firms, and more importantly that they should develop black law firms of equal dignity, competence, and effectiveness. Concurrently, multiple black "power pockets," they think, must develop along with the absorption of blacks into existing "power pockets." Relevant curricula for Afro-American law students may necessarily include, but must also look beyond, a simple definition of "returning to the community."

As law schools recruit and train, and as more black lawyers move into large firms and gather necessary experience, the legal plight of the black community in other than criminal matters is beginning to be alleviated. Further, the prospect of highly qualified black lawyers gives rise to the vision of black law firms in areas of civil specialization. This, in turn, will give Afro-American lawyers the potential to command the respect and wield the power that are necessary adjuncts to the total black struggle for self-determination.

In the late 1960s it seemed that improved opportunities for Afro-Americans in the legal profession would be among the fruits born of the civil rights movement. To some extent, this has been the case. An increase in the number of black law students, lawyers, judges, and law school faculty members has occurred. Even major law firms have taken on greater numbers of Afro-Americans.

But the bright possibilities of the late 1960s

have been far from realized. For example, black representation is minimal among lawyers, especially among those in society's most powerful posts: big law firms, corporations, banks, high government office, and the faculties of leading law schools. Afro-Americans hold only about one percent of the judgeships at the state and local levels, and only about seven percent of those at the federal level (but less than one percent in the South where 53 percent of the Afro-American population resides). Of the prosecutors in 12 major cities containing nearly a quarter of the nation's Afro-Americans, less than one half of one percent are black. The number of black law students increased in the late 1960s but began to decrease several years later under the burden of high tuitions, the discouragement of continuing racism in law school and at bar examinations, an ambivalence in the belief in law as an effective means of advancing the welfare of Afro-Americans, the greater attractiveness of other professions, and the curtailment of efforts to recruit Afro-Americans for legal education.

Insofar as opportunities to study and practice law are concerned, the outlook in the 1980s for Afro-Americans was somewhat, but not very much better than before. What has substantially increased is the challenge they confront, individually and collectively, in the perennial struggle for equal justice under law for themselves as jurists as well as for their people.

See also CIVIL RIGHTS: CIVIL RIGHTS CASES, 1865–1975, CIVIL RIGHTS MOVEMENT; EMPLOYMENT; HOWARD UNIVERSITY; NATIONAL ASSOCIATION FOR THE ADVANCEMENT OF COLORED PEOPLE (NAACP);

REFERENCES: Written references are practically nonexistent and there is no single adequate reference. Among the few, suggested ones include *Harvard Law School Bulletin*, February 1971, an issue devoted entirely to the Afro-American lawyer. See also various issues of the *Howard Law School Journal*. The Winter 1971 issue contains "A Black Lawyers Study" by Jerome Shuman. See also issues of the *Journal of Negro History*, including vol. 15, which contains an article on Afro-American lawyers in Mississippi; and vol. 52, which has a short treatment of John S. Rock. It should also be noted that the first issue of the *Black Law Journal* (Spring 1971) contains several articles of interest, as do the following issues: Winter 1971; Winter 1972; Spring 1972; Spring 1973; vol. 3, nos. 2 and 3 (n.d.); vol. 4, no. 3. (n.d.). In addition, see Ware, Gilbert, "Auction Block Justice," *Focus*, vol. 2, no. 9, pp. 4–5, July 1974; Ware, Gilbert, "The Fallacy of Reverse Discrimination," *Encore American and Worldwide News*, April 7, 1975, pp. 8, 10, 14; Ware, Gilbert (ed.), *From the Black Bar: Voices for Equal Justice*, Putnam, New York, 1976; and Ware, Gilbert (ed.), "Proceedings: Founding Convention of the Judicial Council of the National Bar Association," *Journal of Public Law*, vol. 20, no. 2, pp. 371–441, 1974.

LEADERSHIP CONFERENCE ON CIVIL RIGHTS (LC-CR) A coordinating organization for some 130 national civil rights, labor, business, religious, civic, and fraternal bodies, the LC-CR works toward the passage and enforcement of civil rights legislation. It has been based in Washington, D.C., since its formation in 1949 when it began to lobby and negotiate to achieve its stated purpose.

LEAGUE, JAMES L. (1873–1970), physician; born in De Kalb County, Tenn. League graduated from Walden University (Nashville, Tenn.), and received his M.D. degree from Meharry Medical College (Nashville, Tenn.) in 1917. He was a faculty member of Meharry Medical College for 16 years, and later practiced in Nashville, Tenn., until his retirement in 1968. League received the President's Plaque from Meharry Medical College "for 50 years of service to mankind."

LEDBETTER, HUDDIE (LEADBELLY) (1888–1949), composer, singer; born in Mooringsport, La. Leadbelly made a major contribution to the revival of folk music in the United States and abroad, thereby achieving legendary status. Raised in Texas, he played the accordion and the guitar and sang in Louisiana and Texas before being jailed for murder in 1918. Pardoned seven years later, Leadbelly was jailed again in 1930 for attempted homicide, this time serving four years. Discovered by folklorist Alan Lomax, Leadbelly recorded many songs for the Library of Congress in the 1940s and played many nightclub engagements. Two of his most popular songs are "On Top of Old Smokey" and "Good Night Irene." See also MUSIC: BLUES.

LEE, CANADA (1907–51), actor; born Leonard Lionel Cornelius Canegata. Lee studied violin in New York City until, at the age of fourteen, he ran away to Saratoga Springs, N.Y., to become a jockey. His failure in the horse racing world led him to return to New York City to try his hand at boxing; he won the national amateur lightweight title, and in 1926 he turned professional. As Canada Lee, he fought with great success for several years until an injury forced him to retire from the ring. He then turned to music for a short while, and it was only by a fortunate coincidence that he came to his real profession: he began his acting career in the Works Project Administration (WPA) production of *Brother Mose* in 1934. From that time on he played many and varied roles: Blakesnake in *Stevedore*; Banquo in *Macbeth*; and Jean-Christophe in *Haiti*. Finally, in 1941, Orson Welles chose Lee for the part of Bigger Thomas in Welles' production of Richard Wright's *Native Son*. Unanimously praised by critics, *Native Son* enjoyed a long

run, but Lee's subsequent parts were less impressive until Alfred Hitchcock's film *Lifeboat* was premiered in 1944. Once again, Lee was heralded as a remarkable actor, this time in a role of "dubious significance." The year 1944 also saw Lee appear on Broadway in *Anna Lucasta* and on a Sunday afternoon radio series called *New World A-Coming*, which was devoted to the Afro-American in the United States. His work in radio, in fact, reflected his interest in the myriad problems of blacks. Late in 1944 he appeared in *The Tempest*, and still later in *Set My People Free*. Another great film success came in *Cry, The Beloved Country* in 1952.

LEE, DAVIS See NEWSPAPERS: CONTEMPORARY.

LEE, DON L. See LITERATURE: POETRY.

LEE, HOWARD N. (1934–   ), social worker, business executive, mayor; born in Lithonia, Ga. Lee received a B.A. degree from Fort Valley State College (Fort Valley, Ga.) in 1959 and his M.A. degree in social work from the University of North Carolina in 1966. He was the director of youth services at Duke University (Durham, N.C.) from 1966 to 1968, and was elected mayor of Chapel Hill, N.C., in 1968 and reelected in 1971.

LEE, JOHN ROBERT EDWARD (1870–1944), educator; born in Seguin, Tex. Lee received a B.A. degree (1889) and a M.A. degree (1904) from Bishop College (Dallas, Tex.), and his LL.D. degree from Wilberforce University (Wilberforce, Ohio) in 1918. He taught Latin and history at Bishop College (1889–99) and at Tuskegee Institute (1899–1915), and served as president of Florida Agricultural and Mechanical (A&M) College (1924–28). Lee was founder (1904) and president (1904–09) of the National Association of Teachers in Colored Schools.

LEE, ULYSSES (1913–68), historian; born in Washington, D. C. Lee received his bachelor's degree (summa cum laude) from Howard University and his Ph.D. from the University of Chicago (1942). He served as a staff member in the office of Chief of Military History from 1946 to 1952. A professor of history at Morgan State College, he also served on the staff of the *Journal of Negro History*. He was coeditor, with Sterling Brown, of *The Negro Caravan: Writings by American Negroes* (1941) and author of *The Employment of Negro Troops* (1966), a highly respected study of Afro-Americans in the army during World War II. *See also* WARS

LEE, WILLIAM H. (1936–   ), publisher; born in Austin, Tex. Lee attended Sacramento State College (Sacramento, Calif.) from 1953 to 1955, and received his B.A. degree from the University of California in 1957. He served on the Sacramento County Welfare Commission, and published the Sacramento *Observer*. Lee won the National Newspaper Publisher's Association award along with other outstanding newspaper awards. *See also* NEWSPAPERS: CONTEMPORARY

LEEVY, CARROLL MORTON (1920–   ), physician; born in Columbia, S.C. Leevy received his M.D. degree from the University of Michigan Medical School in 1944. He became professor of medicine at the College of Medicine and Dentistry of New Jersey and professor of medicine and director of the division of hepatic metabolism

Far left:
In his last film, *Cry, the Beloved Country,* Canada Lee (center) worked with newcomer Sidney Poitier (left). *(Museum of Modern Art, Still Archive, New York City.)*

and nutrition, New York College of Medicine, New York, N.Y. Leevy organized the first multidisciplinary clinic for the diagnosis and treatment of alcoholics with liver disease. He also served as president of the International Association for the Study of the Liver.

LEIDESDORFF, WILLIAM (1810–48), merchant, civic leader; born in Saint Croix, Virgin Islands. Of black and Danish ancestry, Leidesdorff migrated from the West Indies to the United States, settling in New Orleans, La., in 1834. Becoming a ship captain, he piloted the schooner *Julia Ann* on a 1841 voyage from New York to California via the southern tip of South America. Leidesdorff then became a California pioneer, built the City Hotel in San Francisco, Calif., set up a public school there, promoted steamboating, and served as a civic and educational leader in the San Francisco area. From 1845 to 1846 he was U.S. vice-consul for the port of San Francisco. A street in that city now bears his name. *See also* AFRO-AMERICAN HISTORY: THE WEST.

LEIGHTON, GEORGE NEVES (1912–   ), lawyer, judge; born in New Bedford, Mass. A graduate of Howard University (Washington, D.C.) in 1940, Leighton went to Harvard Law School and received his LL.B. degree in 1946. Having served in the U.S. Army from 1942 to 1945, he moved to Chicago, Ill., was admitted to the Illinois bar in 1947, and in 1951 opened a law firm with two other partners. Leighton remained in private practice until 1964. During the years before 1969, when he became judge of the Appellate Court for the First District (Cook County) in Illinois, he was active in the American Bar Association, an instructor at Marshall Law School, (Chicago, Ill.), a member of the joint commission to revise the criminal code in Illinois, and chairman of the Illinois advisory committee to the U.S. Commission on Civil Rights.

LEMOYNE COLLEGE   *See* LEMOYNE-OWEN COLLEGE.

LEMOYNE-OWEN COLLEGE LeMoyne-Owen College at Memphis, Tenn., was founded in 1870 by the American Missionary Association of the Congregational Church, now the United Church of Christ. Private, church-related, and coeducational, the college offers the bachelor's degree and provides liberal arts and teacher education curricula. The 1975 enrollment was 852.

The name LeMoyne-Owen resulted from a merger in 1968 of LeMoyne College (named after Julius LeMoyne, a physician) and Owen Junior College. Owen was founded in Memphis, Tenn., in 1954 by the Tennessee Baptist Missionary and Educational Convention. LeMoyne-Owen College had 56 faculty members, 23 administrative officers, and 20 staff members in 1972. More than half of its graduates go into education, and about 12 percent continue their education in graduate and professional schools.

LENEAR, JOHN   *See* NEWSPAPERS: CONTEMPORARY.

LEONARD, WALTER (BUCK) *See* ATHLETES: BASEBALL.

LETTS, JOHN T. (1912–   ), lawyer, judge. Letts received a B.A. degree from Wilberforce University (Wilberforce, Ohio) and his LL.B. degree from Suffolk University (Boston, Mass.). He was admitted to the Michigan bar in 1953, and subsequently became a Circuit Court judge in Grand Rapids, Mich.

LEVISTER, ROBERT L. (1918–   ), lawyer, judge; born in Rocky Mount, N.C. Levister received a B.A. degree from Johnson C. Smith University (Charlotte, N.C.) and his LL.B. degree from Boston University. He was admitted to the Connecticut bar in 1949, and later became a Circuit Court judge in Stamford, Conn.

LEWIS, EDMONIA (ca. 1845–90), sculptor; born in Albany, N.Y. One of the earliest Afro-American women to win fame as a sculptor, Lewis attended Oberlin College (Oberlin Ohio), trained at Edmund Brackett's studio in Boston, Mass., and later went to Rome, Italy, to continue her studies, specializing in portrait busts. In Rome, influenced by Hiram Powers, she abandoned an earlier crude realism and adopted the neoclassical style. Among her best-known works are a medallion head of John Brown; a bust of the Civil War hero Col. Robert Gould Shaw; a fine plaster portrait of Charles Sumner; and the remarkably modern-looking mother-and-children group entitled *Forever Free*. At the Philadelphia Centennial Exhibition in 1876, Lewis and Richard Bannister, also black, received top honors. Her work was exhibited at the Art of the American Negro Exhibition, Chicago, Ill., 1940; at Howard University, Washington, D.C., 1967; at Vassar College, Poughkeepsie, N.Y., 1972; and elsewhere. Lewis is represented in the collections of the Frederick Douglass Institute of Negro Arts & History, Washington, D.C.; Harvard College Library, Cambridge, Mass.; and the Fogg Art Museum, Cambridge, Mass. *See also* ARTISTS.

LEWIS, HENRY (1933–   ), conductor; born in California. Lewis gained national recognition for his conductorial abilities during the 1970s. He became the first Afro-American conductor of a leading American symphony orchestra when he was appointed to head the New Jersey Symphony Orchestra in 1968. Before that, Lewis had served as assistant conductor of the Los Angeles Philharmonic and had formed and conducted his own orchestra, the Los Angeles Chamber Orchestra. Another important milestone in American musical life with which Lewis was associated occurred in 1972 when the Metropolitan Opera, New York, N.Y., engaged him to conduct *La Bohème*. Lewis thereby became the first Afro-American to conduct in that house. *See also* MUSIC : HISTORY AND DEVELOPMENT

LEWIS, IRA FOSTER (1883–   ), publisher; born in Lexington, N.C. Lewis was manager of the Pittsburgh *Courier,* and in 1940 became president of that newspaper upon the death of Robert L. Vann.

LEWIS, JAMES (1832–1914), soldier, government official; born in Woodville, Miss. At the beginning of the Civil War, the talk of emancipation ringing in his ears, Lewis, a riverboat steward, rushed to New Orleans, La., to join in the fray. He raised two companies of black volunteers and served in both. The First Louisiana Volunteers Native Guards and Company K both achieved recognition in the Civil War. After resigning his commission as captain in 1864, Lewis became the traveling agent of the educational department of the Freedmen's Bureau. He was then appointed U.S. inspector of customs at the port of New Orleans, the first Afro-American to receive an appointment from the federal government. In 1870, after rising through the ranks of the metropolitan police, Lewis was made a colonel of the Second Regiment, State Militia, and soon after, in the same year, was elected administrator of police. A Republican, he chaired the Louisiana delegation to the Republican National Convention in 1872. Following that, Lewis became administrator of public improvement in New Orleans.

LEWIS, JAMES E.   *See* ARTISTS; DOUGLASS, FREDERICK; WARS. *See also* ACKNOWLEDGMENTS.

LEWIS, JAMES E.   *See* NEWSPAPERS: CONTEMPORARY.

LEWIS, JOHN GIDEON, JR. (1903–   ), fraternal leader; born in Natchitoches, La. Lewis received a B.A. degree from Fisk University (Nashville, Tenn.) and was awarded an honorary degree from Central State College. He was Grand Master and then Sovereign Master of the Southern Jurisdiction of the Prince Hall Masons (Afro-American lodges), which involved him in many fraternal and civic programs. In 1961 he received the National Urban League Equal Opportunity Award. Lewis was also a member of the Louisiana Educational Association. *See also* FRATERNAL SOCIETIES.

LEWIS, JOHN ROBERT (1940–   ), civil rights leader; born in Troy, Ala. Lewis graduated from the American Baptist Theological Seminary in 1961 and from Fisk University (Nashville, Tenn.) in 1963. Having organized and participated in the sit-ins and freedom rides of 1961, and having submitted to innumerable arrests, he became chairman of the Student Nonviolent (now National) Coordinating Committee (SNCC) in 1963. His resignation from the organization in 1966 because of its growing tendency toward militancy left a void that was filled by Stokely Carmichael. Meanwhile, in 1966, Lewis was appointed to the White House Conference called "To Fulfill These Rights." He subsequently went to the Field Foundation in New York City for a year and then to Atlanta, Ga., to become director of Community Organization Projects for the Southern Regional Council from 1967 to 1970. In 1970 Lewis was named director of the Voter Education Project, Inc. (VEP), another program of the council, and by 1973 the VEP had registered nearly 3.5 million voters in 11 southern states.

LEWIS, JULIAN HERMAN (1891–?), educator, pathologist. Lewis received a B.A. degree from the University of Illinois, a M.A. degree and his Ph.D. degree (1915) from the University of Chicago, and his M.D. degree from Rush Medical College. He served as associate professor of pathology at the University of Chicago, and wrote *The Biology of the Negro* (1942).

Henry Lewis conducting the New Jersey Symphony Orchestra. *(New Jersey Symphony Orchestra.)*

LEWIS, RAMSEY E., JR. (1935–   ), musician, composer; born in Chicago, Ill. Lewis gained nationwide recognition as a pianist when he and his trio recorded *The In Crowd* in 1965. His trio was formed in 1956, but it was nearly a decade later before his albums began to gain popularity, eventually selling more than a million copies. In spite of criticism from some jazz writers, Lewis achieved great success, setting records in audience attendance and in the sale of his recordings. *The In Crowd* won a Grammy in 1965 as the best jazz record by a small group.

LEWIS, WILLIAM H. *See* ATHLETES: FOOTBALL.

LIBRARIANS / LIBRARIES *See* ARCHIVES; BIBLIOGRAPHIES/BIOGRAPHIES/GUIDES. *See also* BAKER, AUGUSTA; BONTEMPS, ARNA; HARSH, VIVIAN G.; JACKSON, MILES MERRILL, JR.; JONES, CLARA STANTON; JOSEY, E.J.; KAISER, ERNEST; MARSHALL, ALBERT P.; PORTER, DOROTHY; SCHOMBURG, ARTHUR; SHOCKLEY, ANN; SMITH, JESSIE CARNEY; WILLIAMS, ETHEL; WORK, MONROE N.

LIELE/LISLE, GEORGE *See* BAPTISTS.

LINCOLN, CHARLES ERIC (1924–   ), clergyman; educator; born in Athens, Ala. Lincoln received a B.A. degree from LeMoyne College (Memphis, Tenn.; now LeMoyne-Owen College) in 1947, a M.A. degree from Fisk University (Nashville, Tenn.) in 1954, a B.D. degree from the University of Chicago in 1956, and his M.E. and Ph.D. degrees from Boston University in 1960. He was pastor of John Calvin Presbyterian Church in Nashville, Tenn. (1953–54). Lincoln taught at Fisk University (1954–57) and was resident chaplain of Boston University School of Theology (1958–59). He then became a faculty member of Union Theological Seminary (New York, N.Y.), before returning to the faculty of Fisk University in 1973. He authored the two books entitled *The Black Muslims in America* (1961) and *My Face is Black* (1964); and edited *Martin Luther King, Jr.: A Profile* (1970).

LINCOLN INSTITUTE *See* LINCOLN UNIVERSITY.

LINCOLN PARISH TRAINING SCHOOL *See* GRAMBLING COLLEGE.

LINCOLN UNIVERSITY Lincoln University, at Jefferson City, Mo., was founded in 1866 as the Lincoln Institute. State-supported and coeducational, the college offers the bachelor's degree and provides liberal arts and teacher education curricula. Its 1975 enrollment was about 2,570.

The school was founded by the officers and enlisted men of the 62d and 65th Infantries (Colored) of the Union Army while stationed in Louisiana. During its early years the school had a difficult time, but later it received federal funds under the Morrill Act and eventually became fully state-supported. Its name was changed from Lincoln Institute to its present one in 1921. It was the only state-supported college for Afro-Americans under segregation. With the impetus of the *Gaines* case, a law school was hastily built in St. Louis, Mo., as an extension of the university. The extension never developed fully, however, and was phased out as integration progressed.

Enrollment was small (under 600) until the late 1950s when an upsurge in enrollment brought in whites, who came to comprise more than 50 percent of the student body within a decade.

LINCOLN UNIVERSITY Lincoln University, at Lincoln University, Pa., was founded in 1854. Independent, state-related, and coeducational, the college offers the bachelor's and master's degrees, and provides liberal arts and teacher education curricula. Its 1975 enrollment was about 1,060.

The university has a history that goes back to the nineteenth century and to the ancestors of its founder, Rev. John Miller Dickey, and his wife, Sarah Emlen Cresson. The maternal grandfather of John Miller Dickey was a Philadelphia, Pa., marble merchant who made contributions to the education of Afro-Americans in that city as early as 1794; his father was minister of the Oxford Presbyterian Church before John Miller Dickey, who, after serving as a missionary and preaching to the slaves in Georgia, became pastor of that same church in 1832. Sarah Emlen Cresson also inherited a long tradition of service and philanthropy through the Society of Friends in Philadelphia.

Reverend Dickey was involved in the American Colonization Society and took an active part in 1851 in the court actions leading to the freeing of a young black girl who had been abducted from southern Chester County by slave raiders from Maryland. At the same time, James Amos, a young freeman who had been unsuccessful in his efforts to gain admission to even the most liberal of schools, was taught by Dickey, who undertook to prepare the young man for the ministry and to open a school for blacks. Eventually, Lincoln University was chartered as Ashmun Institute (named after the white emigrationist, Jehudi Ashmun) "for the scientific, classical, and theological education of colored youth of the male sex." Dickey was also white.

Since the turn of the century the number of Lincoln alumni to have undertaken graduate study in the various professions—most notably medicine, dentistry, law, and education—has increased to include more than 50 percent of Lincoln's graduates. By the end of the 1950s Lincoln had become an integrated, interracial, and coeducational institution with a proud heritage. *See also* PRESBYTERIANS.

LINDE, SHIRLEY MOTTER (1929–   ), editor, publisher; born in Cincinnati, Ohio. Linde received a B.S. degree from the University of Cincinnati and her M.S. degree from the University of Michigan Medical School. She was associate editor of *Together Magazine*, assistant editor of the *Journal of International College of Surgeons*, and edited many newsletters and other publications. Linde was also associated with Pavilion Publishing Company in New York City.

LISTON, HARDY (1889–1956), educator; born in Fairfield County, S.C. Liston graduated from Biddle University (Charlotte, N.C.; now Johnson C. Smith University) in 1911, and received two additional degrees from the University of Chicago in 1925 and in 1928. He taught in the public schools of Spartanburg S.C. from 1912 to 1913, taught mathematics at Kittrell College (Kittrell, N.C.) from 1913 to 1915, served as dean of Kittrell from 1915 to 1931, was dean at Knoxville College (Knoxville, Tenn.) from 1931 to 1943, and was executive vice-president of Johnson C. Smith University from 1947 to 1956.

LITERATURE

Folklore

Background Folklore is initially and primarily oral, a form based on the setting of a speaker and an audience, or more comprehensively, of a group involved in such common activities as work or worship. A storyteller, for example, usually enhances his delivery through pacing, gestures, intonation, and variations in detail and language to suit the occasion. It is generally held that folklore is of anonymous origin and that works by individual, identifiable authors do not fit the category. Still some creations by known authors frequently become part of the folk tradition, so important in the history and culture of Afro-Americans. In addition, most black writers are especially aware of the resources of folklore; thus, one finds in novels, short stories, and poems by Afro-American writers the use of materials and themes that are already a part of the general tradition and creativity of black folk.

The treatment of subject matter ranges from deep reverence to ribald irreverence. Though certain general patterns and motifs recur frequently, folklore is an ever-creative genre.

When looking for precise sources of Afro-American folklore, one has to give attention to individual selections. It is clear, however, that the Old South, Europe, and Africa are the principal geographical areas. After recording and analyzing more than a thousand oral narratives of Afro-Americans born in the South, Richard M. Dorson concluded (*American Negro Folktales,* 1967) that only about ten percent were known in West African folktales. But he also concluded that variations on the same story could have multiple geographical sources.

Even before Dorson began collecting and printing his tales in the 1950s, a sizable body of printed tales was already in existence. Though some interest had been shown previously, after the Civil War especially, whites, many of them northern, began collecting the songs of Afro-Americans with more attention to the accurate recording of material. Even so, only certain material, for example, the religious songs, received emphasis, as collectors made selections and interpretations based on their own interests and predilections. Particular attention was given to the Sea Islands of the Georgia and South Carolina coast; the Gullah dialect of that region showed close relationships to some African languages and thus seemed particularly distinctive and attractive. After the Civil War and Reconstruction, Joel Chandler Harris, a native white of Georgia, popularized for the reading public the Uncle Remus stories (*Nights with Uncle Remus: Myths and Legends of the Old Plantation,* 1883). The Uncle Remus publications featured dialect, animal tales, perhaps the most famous of which were the stories about the trickster, Brer (Brother) Rabbit. Two writers after Harris who published tales were Charles C. Jones (*Negro Myths from the Georgia Coast Told in the Vernacular,* 1888) and A. M. H. Christensen (*Afro-American Folk Lore, Told Round Cabin Fires on the Sea Islands of South Carolina,* 1892).

The trickster tales of Brer Rabbit (the word "Brother" is shortened in various ways, depending on the particular version) deserve comment. In African folktales, the hare was not a major character in the lore as a whole but did frequently appear as a wily trickster, the role in which he is cast by blacks in the United States. In dealing with stronger but essentially stupid animals, Brer Rabbit is a master of psychology and compensates for his physical weakness through his cunning. Though he is sometimes the victim of the joke as well, the implication is usually that he will learn from his experience. Though the Uncle Remus stories were merely charming animal fables depicting a cozy world, other versions of the rabbit tales include more specific references to the general theme of survival on the plantation. In such stories, for example, Brer Bear is frequently cast as the overseer; Brer Fox as the plantation owner.

Trickster tales about plantation life also frequently tell of a slave called John who generally outsmarts his master; like Brer Rabbit, however, he is frequently the butt of the joke himself. Richard Dorson in *American Negro Folktales* notes analogues in tales that deal with the master-servant relationship in Europe. The motif of the stolen animal substituted for a baby in the crib is recognizable as part of the plot of the medieval *Second Shepherd's Play,* for example. Still the "John" tales give a realistic portrayal of existence on the plantation and emphasize the wit and ingenuity of the character.

In addition to animal stories, or fables, other tales relating to the Afro-American experience include those about "hoodoo" (voodoo), conjuring, ghosts, and witches. Witchcraft seems expressly associated with the devil, a feature that links it to the folk beliefs found in other cultures as well. Themes found in ghost stories, another popular story form, include encounters with those who have come back to recover missing parts of their bodies, to help recover buried treasure, or to help others find their way. Again, such themes are found in ghost stories of other countries and cultures as well.

Moreover, tales relating to churches and religious life make up a significant category. Foremost are the preacher tales, those told by or about the preacher. Such tales grew primarily out of the experiences of Afro-Americans in the United States, though the tradition of tales to exemplify or illustrate the teachings of the church and tales that treat the clergy less than reverently had been well established already, as can be seen, for example, in the attitudes toward priests and clergymen in medieval Europe. Afro-Americans, denied in America their traditional religion that was an all-encompassing orientation for their lives, turned to the spiritual sources that were allowed them and shaped those sources to their own situations.

The use of tales in the pulpit by the preacher himself, once Afro-Americans were able to have preachers of their own, may have been aided initially by exposure to white ministers of the more evangelical sects who preached from plantation to plantation and frequently used tales or stories as part of their address to the listeners. Stories about and frequently at the expense of the preacher stemmed first of all from the preacher's stature in society; that is, though fun may be poked at him, it was usually in a good-humored way and the humor increased through the underlying assumption that the preacher was very often seen out of his role as a spiritual leader of dignity and power and as a man with the frailties of his parishioners. Motifs of preacher tales included the results of taking biblical language literally; they also gave attention to such sectarian differences as diverse baptismal rites.

Important as they are, the tales comprise only a part of the great mass of folklore. Sermons, spirituals, work songs, ballads, blues, rhymes, word games (such as the "dozens"), and proverbs have also enriched Afro-American literature. Many examples exist. After hearing a sermon on "The Creation," James Weldon Johnson was inspired to write the first of the sermons that appeared as *God's Trombones.* Before Johnson, Paul Lawrence Dunbar gave attention to folk situations and presented them in dialect. In the 1920s, at the time of what is known as the Harlem Renaissance, Afro-American writers became especially interested in folklore and took advantage of that resource. Langston Hughes was a foremost example. He wrote some of his earliest poems in the three-line blues stanza and gave particular attention to the language used by blacks. His subsequent creation, Jesse B. Semple, or "Simple," embodies the style and wisdom of a speaker of the "Simple" truth. Sterling Brown created a ballad hero in Slim Greer and wrote many other poems that incorporate the religious and secular background of black folk culture. Other writers who used folk themes from the 1920s to the present include Jean Toomer, Zora Neale Hurston, Margaret Walker, Melvin Tolson, Ralph Ellison, Richard Wright, and James Baldwin. The list could be expanded considerably, for there is at least one pertinent folklore example, if not more, in any black writer's work. The centrality of folklore in black culture indicates the reason.

The Centrality of Folklore* The lore of the Afro-American turned out to be a deeper vein than was at first suspected. Once represented principally by Uncle Remus and the Brer Rabbit tales, it has since found its way into such entertainments as the minstrel shows of the late nineteenth and early twentieth centuries and the monologues of Bert Williams (on phonograph records as well as in vaudeville and the *Ziegfeld Follies*), not to mention recent characterizations such as those projected by Stepin Fetchit, Rochester, and the Amos n' Andy ensemble. A carry-over from Afro-American folktales into American writing by and about Afro-Americans, from Mark Twain to William Faulkner and Ralph Ellison, is also conspicuous.

But the tales, as varied and intriguing as they are, give only a partial indication of the range and capacity of the folk who created them. For many Americans these are still apt to evoke memories of favored house servants, trusting and trusted Aunties, Uncles, and Grannies. But a less cozy, less contented side of folk life is recaptured by such ballads as "John Henry," by work and prison songs, by the blues, and even by the spirituals. Still another mood of the folk may be detected in sermons, prayers, and testimonials. These expressions of life's hardship, its stress and strain, did not lend themselves so quickly to exploitation, but ways were eventually found. The blues provided a taproot of tremendous vitality for season after season, vogue after vogue of popular music, and became an American idiom in a broad sense. A time came when "Dry Bones," "When the Saints Go Marching In," and

*See acknowledgements in the PREFACE.

"He's Got the Whole World in His Hand" even seemed to express a national mood. Nor was the art of the old-time Negro preacher overlooked in the scramble.

Interestingly, too, folk expression of this kind continues. The "Black and Unknown Bards," eulogized by James Weldon Johnson as creators of the spirituals, have now emerged as the composers of such gospel songs as those sung by Mahalia Jackson, but their intimate links with the folk, personal as well as musical, remain intact. Louis Armstrong was himself a bridge between the sporting houses in which Jelly Roll Morton introduced his special piano style and "invented" jazz for seduction, and the era of television, goodwill tours, and jazz as a secret weapon of diplomacy. Uncle Remus finds a very "hep" Harlem counterpart in Langston Hughes' "Simple Minded Friend."

Close reading, so called, can become a bad habit, possibly a vice, where simple appreciation is concerned, but never does it start more quarrels than when the folk are involved. So let it be said quickly that Afro-American folklore, like almost any other kind, can be traced in its origins to a dim past when it drew on a common cultural heritage that most of the folk of the world appear to have shared. In any case, the telling of tales is a time-honored custom in Africa. By what steps the *Fables of Aesop* (Ethiop) became the animal stories of West Africa, of the West Indies, and of the slave states of the United States is a lively question but not to the point

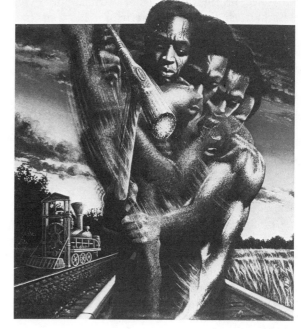

John Henry, Steel Drivin' Man, by Charles Lilly. The lore of John Henry treats the idea of a superman in competition with a machine; John Henry wins, but at the cost of his life. *(Charles Lilly, PepsiCo, Inc.)*

here. What does concern us is that the slaves brought with them to the New World their ancient habit of storytelling as pastime, together with a rich bestiary.

While the masters of slaves went to some length to get rid of tribal languages and such tribal customs as certain practices of sorcery, they accepted the animal stories as a harmless way to ease the time or entertain the master's children. That the folk tales of these Afro-American slaves were actually projections of personal experiences, hopes, and defeats in terms of symbols appears to have gone unnoticed.

In the African prototypes of the Afro-American tales the heroes were generally the jackal, the hare, the tortoise, and the spider. The African jackal survived as the American fox, the African hare as the American rabbit, and the African tortoise as the American dry-land turtle or terrapin. The spider came only as near as the West Indies, where it reappeared in the Anansi tales of Jamaica. As a villain, the African hyena was replaced by the American wolf, but that role is sometimes assigned to the fox or the bear in the American tale. The rest of the cast of characters—the lions, leopards, tigers, and monkeys—were safely transported.

Much has sometimes been made of the fact that a study of some 300 versions of "The Tar Baby" story tends to leave the impression that its origin was in India, or that the well-liked "Playing Godfather," for example, is in the Reynard cycle and reappears in Grimm's *Fairy Tales*. This, however, is not true of the great majority of the tales brought over from Africa, and even where it is, the Afro-American fables, as has been pointed out by anthropologists, "have been so modified with new beasts and local color added, different themes, and different experiences, that an almost new, certainly a quite different thing results." Written literature, of course, does the same thing.

The Afro-American slave, adopting Brer Rabbit as hero, represented him as the most frightened and helpless of creatures. No hero-animals in Africa or elsewhere were so completely lacking in strength. But the slaves took pains to give Brer Rabbit other significant qualities. He became in their stories by turn a practical joker, a braggart, a wit, a glutton, a lady's man, and a trickster. But his essential characteristic was his ability to get the better of bigger and stronger animals. To the slave in his condition the theme of weakness overcoming strength through cunning proved endlessly fascinating.

Also satisfying, for related reasons, were accounts of the defeat, if not destruction, of the powerful Brer Wolf, the stupid Brer Bear, and the sly Brer Fox. Variations on these themes permitted the storytellers to invest Brer Squirrel, Sis Goose, Brer Rooster, Brer Alligator, and the rest with traits equally recognizable, equally amusing, and equally instructive.

The Brer Rabbit lore owes its wide vogue among Americans in general to the Uncle Remus stories of Joel Chandler Harris, but his were not the first or the last collections of these tales. Much of the special appeal of his versions may be attributed to the setting in which the old uncle entertains the young master. To this extent they do not conform as fully to the definition of a folktale as one *by the folk for the folk* as do such versions as "Brer Rabbit Fools Buzzard," collected by Arthur Huff Fauset, or "Brer Fox and the Goobers," collected by Carl Carmer. Such a story as "Ole Sis Goose," collected by A. W. Eddins, appears to belong to a time more recent than the Joel Chandler Harris tales and to suggest, by its reference to the problem of justice in the courts, that the possibilities of this genre have not even yet been exhausted by Afro-Americans.

Another body of Afro-American folktales, equally dear to the slaves themselves, stemmed from the familiar trickster theme. In slavery the trickster, most frequently called John or Jack, had a made-to-order setting. Surprised in his folly or his wrongdoing by Ole Master, Old Miss, the "patterollers," or even the devil, he would attempt to clear himself by his wit. He did not always succeed, but the happy ending was when he avoided a whipping or, better still, obtained his freedom. In the course of the tales the storytellers poked as much fun at themselves as they did at their masters, but pretentiousness was unfailingly exposed.

Stories of enormous exaggeration, sometimes called "lies" by the folk themselves; a large body of "why" stories, accounting humorously for the beginnings of almost everything, from the creation of man and beast to explanations of the peculiar ways of women; and humanized accounts of heaven continue to amuse the folk nearly a century after Emancipation. Equally durable is the preacher story, likewise of slavery-time origin.

The Afro-American "preacher tale" is in the tradition of the religious tales of antiquity and the "exempla" of medieval Europe, as well as of the anecdotes used so effectively by Lorenzo Dow and other Methodist and Baptist preachers

510

in proclaiming Protestantism to the plantation folk in the latter part of the eighteenth century. While frequently failing to moralize and generally taking off into directions not suggested by their respected predecessors, the Afro-American religious tales retained at least one important characteristic of the genre: they aimed to entertain.

Writing about the Afro-American church in the United States in 1903, W. E. B. Du Bois observed that "there is a church organization for every sixty Negro families. This institution, therefore, naturally assumed many functions which the harshly suppressed social organ had to surrender; the church became the center of amusements, of what little spontaneous economic activity remained, of education and of all social intercourse." The picture is still recognizable.

The tempo of the singing, as represented by the Negro spirituals, has been stepped up and a jazz note added to make the gospel songs, and the "moaning" of the preacher has given way (more or less) to a more ordered discourse, but the "gravy" is still there, as the folk themselves would testify.

James Weldon Johnson recognized in the sermons of the old-time black preacher an important form of folk expression. He reproduced a number of these as poetry. Other folklorists have gone to the same sources and made literal transcriptions or prose adaptations. All have confirmed one point: a wonderful creativity existed behind this preaching that fully warrants the esteem in which it was held by its rapt, hand-clapping, foot-patting, and vocally responsive hearers.

Many of the more successful sermons of the old-time Afro-American preacher were repeated time and again and gradually took on the set pattern of a work of folk art. John Jasper of Richmond, Va., became famous for his "De Sun Do Move," and thousands of people, white and black, flocked to his church to hear it. Other old-time preachers imitated it, adapted it, and added it to their own repertoires. The same happened with such numbers as "Dry Bones in the Valley," "The Heavenly March," and the "Train Sermon," sometimes called "The Black Diamond Express, running between here and hell, making thirteen stops and arriving in hell ahead of time."

The old-time Afro-American preacher himself belonged to a unique breed. Entertaining, comic when comedy was needed, he was in every sense the shepherd of the flock. It was he who gave the slave hope and inspiration. It was he who eased the hard journey with the comforting sentiment, "You may have all dis world, but give me Jesus." It was he who created the setting in which the spirituals were born.

Before the American Revolution, the Afro-Americans George Liele and Andrew Bryan were preaching to whites and blacks alike in Augusta and Savannah, Ga., respectively. John Ledman in his *History of the Rise of Methodism in America* tells about Black Harry who preached from the same platform with the other founders of that church in the United States and concludes, "The truth was that Harry was a more popular speaker than Mr. Asbury (Bishop Francis Asbury) or almost anyone else in his day." The old-time preacher was among the first slaves to learn to read and write. He became a teacher. When the time came for courageous action, he took a hand in the Underground Railroad, while his counterpart in the North became an effective abolitionist speaker. So the tradition to which Martin Luther King, Jr., belonged is a long one. The Afro-American preacher has had a vital role, not the least important aspect of which has been the awakening and encouragement of folk expression. He is forever memorialized in the spirituals, the preacher stories, and to a lesser extent, since the whole setting cannot be recaptured (the moaning and the hand-clapping and the responses of the audience, for example), in the sermons themselves.

As an indication of the kind of backing the old-time preacher could count on, we have the testimonials and remembrances of his members. The church folk answered him back, and the answer was strong and affirmative. What he gave, and what they picked up, was hope, confidence, and a will to survive. The lore that stemmed from the religious experiences of the Afro-American in slavery, like that which found expression in the animal tales and the pastime rhymes, was always fundamentally optimistic. But this is not the whole story.

Just as sure as God had his heaven, the devil had his hell. And the box (guitar), as all the older folk know, has always been a special device of the devil's. One writer has recorded what happened to a careless minstrel who made the mistake of wandering onto the church grounds during an intermission between services back in his childhood. The sisters of the church lit into him like a flock of mother hens attacking a garter snake. He protested. He was just fixing to play a couple of hymns, he explained. But this did not save him. He was obliged to leave in a hurry. The deaconesses knew from bitter experience, no doubt, that the churchyard was no place for a box. They also knew that the songs with which the guitar was associated were not for the ears of children.

The blues, like the work and prison songs and most of the folk ballads, seemed at first shockingly incompatible with the new condition and aspirations of freedmen. But this was not actually the case. Behind these earthy lyrics was the beginning of a new racial consciousness and self-conception. It recognized difference but without the usual connotations of disparity. It made no apology, asked no pity, offered no defense. It insisted only on being itself, as the young poets of the Harlem Renaissance loved to say.

Because of this a distinguished sociologist could observe some 30 years ago that "Who would know something of the core and limitations of this life (Negro folk) should go to the blues. In them is the curious story of disillusionment without a saving philosophy and yet without defeat. They mark these narrow limits of life's satisfactions, its vast treacheries and ironies. Stark, full human passions crowd themselves into an uncomplex expression, so simple in their power that they startle. If they did not reveal a fundamental and universal emotion of the human heart, they would not be noticed now as the boisterous and persistent intruders in the polite society of lyrics that they are. . . . Herein lies one of the richest gifts of the Negro to American life. . . . These are the blues, not of the Negro intellectuals any more than of the white ones, but, of those who live beneath the range of polite respect."

Ellison has called the blues "an autobiographical chronicle of personal catastrophe expressed lyrically," and added, "Their attraction lies on this, that they at once express both the agony of life and the possibility of conquering it through sheer toughness of spirit. They fall short of tragedy only in that they provide no solution, offer no scapegoat but the self."

It is not surprising, under the circumstances, that Afro-American writers, and the many others who have used the Afro-American as a subject, should continue to dip into the richness of Afro-American folk life. See also AFRICA; AFRICAN LEGACY/SURVIVALS; MUSIC: HISTORY AND DEVELOPMENT; MUSIC: SPIRITUALS/ORIGINS; MUSIC: BLUES.

REFERENCES: Abrahams, Roger D., *Deep Down in the Jungle . . . : Negro Narrative Folklore from the Streets of Philadelphia*, Folklore Associates, Hatboro, 1964; Brewer, John Mason (comp), *American Negro Folklore*, Quadrangle Books, Chicago, 1968; Brewer, John Mason, *The Word on the Brazos; Negro Preacher Tales from the Brazos Bottoms of Texas*, University of Texas Press, Austin, 1953; Dorson, Richard M. (comp.), *American Negro Folk Tales*, Fawcett, Greenwich, 1967; Dorson, Richard M., *Negro Folktales in Michigan*, Harvard University Press, Cambridge, 1956; Haywood, Charles A., *A Bibliography of North American Folklore and Folksong*, 1961, vol. 1, pp. 430–560; Hughes, Langston and Arna Bontemps (eds.), *The Book of Negro Folklore*, Dodd, Mead, New York, 1965; Jackson, Bruce (comp.), *The Negro and His Folklore in Nineteenth Century Periodicals*, University of Texas Press, Austin, 1967; and Puckett, Newbell N., *Folk Beliefs of the Southern Negro*, 2d ed., Patterson Smith, Montclair, 1968. One of the best compilations is by the noted folklorist, Harold Courlander, *A Treasury of Afro-American Folklore*, Arno Press, New York, 1976.

Children's Literature

From Then To Now One could say that the literature of Afro-American children began with Topsy, and stayed with her, unmoving, for more than half a century. Or one could consider that for black children, as for all children, literature began the first time a gifted human told a great tale to a listener who remembered and who in another time and turn told the same tale.

In either case one must recognize that today, as in the past, Afro-American children, like children of all races and unlike adults, do not write their own literature. They are dependent for the most part upon what adults write for them, publish for them, and choose, buy, and place in libraries for them. Even those few children who buy their own books unchaperoned can choose only what has been produced almost totally by adults.

To go back to that first teller of tales, it is very likely that he or she was an adult. It may have been a brave man eager to share the drama of a wild forest hunt with those kept at home; or it may have been a loving woman who somehow shaped her memories of a day's sunny happenings into a rhythmic chant to soothe a child not yet ready for sleep. Where that first surge of the creative power of words happened, or whether that first storyteller was black or white, is—of course—unknown.

What is known is that children have in hand fruits of a long process in such a book as John Steptoe's *Stevie*. It was written by a black man, young enough to remember childhood, about black children and a universal experience. It is a book wherein children of all races can see themselves, a book whose glowing pictures were painted by the author himself in a magnificent dual sharing of rich gifts.

What about that road from the first story told to *Stevie?* Several landmarks exist, and they are landmarks for all children, not just for black ones. To discover them one must look at the kinds of books that are written for children, consider early examples of those books that represent the black experience, and see which ones of recent years merit attention. This large task is simplified if one limits examination to a single and clearly defined segment of the field. If we focus our attention only on "children's books about black people," we will have a manageable unit and one productive of some significant facts.

What we call "literature" takes several forms, whether it is written for children or adults. There is poetry as well as fiction, and there are informational and eloquent biographies and histories whose power of concept and beauty of language mark them with literary distinction. Unfortunately one finds few books that give children a picture of Afro-Americans as individual human beings of interest and achievement or as a group of power and importance functioning in American life.

Informational Books The first biography of an Afro-American is a very recent one indeed: the earliest children's book about an Afro-American is *Railroad to Freedom* (1932), according to Ruth Hill Viguers writing in *A Critical History of Children's Literature* (1969). Viguers found worthy of comment only eight biographies of Afro-Americans published between 1932 and 1965.

One that she did not include, perhaps because most librarians think of it as a young-adult title, is *Your Most Humble Servant* by Shirley Graham Du Bois, the earliest biography of Benjamin Banneker, published in 1949. Teachers have found that able seventh graders read Du Bois' book with enjoyment. Simpler stories about the man who saved the city of Washington, D.C., were written later to introduce him to younger readers.

Another landmark was the award of the Newbery Medal to Elizabeth Yates for *Amos Fortune: Free Man* as the most distinguished contribution to American literature for children in the year 1950. Its significance is two-fold: Amos Fortune was a person overdue for attention and, moreover, the award recognized the importance of this book for children of all races.

General historical writing about the black experience was even slower to appear than individual biography. Only after 1948 have children had access to a substantial history of Afro-Americans in the United States, *The Story of the Negro* by Arna Bontemps. Other books were published from time to time, and the 1960s brought forth many books to help fill the gap. Of particular interest in that period was the publication of the documentary works of Milton Meltzer (*In Their Own Words*) and Julius Lester (*To Be A Slave*), both of whom collected and reproduced in book form parts of actual diaries, journals, and some spoken words of historical black men and women.

Closely related to the development of historical literature about Afro-Americans and their life in the United States was the need for information about Africa itself. During the 1960s newly independent nations established themselves in Africa, and with this development came an increase in American books about the peoples of these countries. The political facts of life make such books quickly obsolete, but new ones continue to appear. The first edition of *Subject Guide to Children's Books in Print* includes about 150 nonfiction titles about Africa's history, geography, and peoples in 1970.

Among so much information, three books especially represent the increased attention given to African resources of history and culture. *Piankhy the Great,* written and illustrated by E. Harper Johnson, dramatically but accurately shares the facts about the great Kushite king whose empire flourished in the Nubian valley about 725 B.C. In *Playtime in Africa,* African woman educator Efua Sutherland describes children and their games, while the accompanying photographs add to the book's universal appeal. In *The Musical Instruments of Africa,* American educator Betty Warner Dietz and Nigerian musicologist Michael Babatunde Olatunji explain music as a complex communication medium.

Folklore In addition to the facts about Africa and its peoples, the field of traditional literature is relevant as a matter of heritage and the oral transmission of cultures.

Black folk tales were told in the United States long before there was any concern about literature. The earliest collection of folk material, the "Uncle Remus" stories, was begun in the 1880s. The stories are rejected today by many Afro-Americans and are seldom read by any child because of the difficulties posed by the dialect. The work is significant, however, because it dates the first printed flow of African folk elements into the American literary stream, and it substantiates as well the fascination such tales hold for a child who can handle the communication medium.

Every society produces folk heroes. One shadowy figure is Big Road Walker, portrayed in Eula Duncan's 1940 book of that name. He is not very well known, perhaps because of the barrier of the dialect. John Henry is the black hero who seems most familiar to American children. Irving Shapiro's *John Henry and the Double-Jointed Steam Drill* appeared in 1945, and Harold Felton's *John Henry and His Hammer* was published in 1950. Today's children revel in the stunning picture book version, *John Henry: An American Legend,* by Ezra Jack Keats.

In 1969 Julius Lester's *Black Folk Tales* gave open expression to the hatred and contempt some Afro-Americans have for the white race. Whatever the strengths or the provocative elements of the book, it must be looked at as a product of social oppression recorded and presented in the format of literature.

Poetry It is a natural step from folklore to poetry, for some literature such as the 1967 collection *A Crocodile Has Me by the Leg* is both. Sharing with children some of the traditional verse of Africa, the collection is freshly edited by Leonard Doob, a specialist in African studies, and illustrated by a Nigerian educator-artist.

Depending on such various criteria for inclusion as the age level of the intended reader and the race of the poet, along with consideration of literary distinction, a survey of American poetry for young people that has risen out of the black experience is a very long story that began with Phillis Wheatley. Over the intervening years, Paul Laurence Dunbar, Countee Cullen, James Weldon Johnson, and Langston Hughes have all

Jacob Lawrence demonstrating drawing to schoolchildren at Lincoln School about 1950. He wrote *Harriet and the Promised Land* (1968), an illustrated book for young children. *(National Archives Gift Collection)*

been recognized for what they have given to young people.

A different kind of book, *North Star Shining: A Pictorial History of the Negro* by Hildegarde Swift, appeared in 1947, unique for its presentation of notable facts in strong, rhythmic verse. In 1956 *Bronzeville Boys and Girls* showed with what power the Pulitzer Prize-winning author Gwendolyn Brooks was able to speak to children.

A young American poet, June Jordan, produced two unusual volumes in 1969–70: in 1969 *Who Look at Me,* a long poem of pride, bitterness, and dignity, complemented by reproductions of 27 paintings of Afro-Americans by distinguished black and white artists, was published; and in 1970 in her publication, *The Voice of the Children,* she collected the demanding, exciting verses of the city's youngsters, black children among them.

Also in 1970 a series of books began whose content looks like verse and reads like poetry, but each book of which is actually a newly illustrated selection from Lorenz Graham's earlier publication, *How God Fix Jonah.* These Bible stories, collected in Liberia, are told in the idiom of those "newly come to English speech." Three of them have recently been published in picture book format: *Every Man Heart Lay Down,* which is the Christmas story; *A Road Down in the Sea,* the story of Moses and the Promised Land; and *God Wash the World and Start Again,* which tells of Noah and the Flood. They are powerful books, dramatic and moving.

Fiction It is comparatively easy to trace the occurrence of factual and traditional literature for children. Biographies are immediately identifiable, and we see that folklore came to America from Europe, Asia, and Africa through an identifiable transfer medium in each case. However, children's fiction is more difficult to categorize. Present-day writers, critics, and social philosophers frequently disagree about who should write of the black experience for children, whether a white author can adequately develop the character of a black child in fiction, and even whether black children should read at all the stories obviously reflecting only the structure of an all-white society.

One can hope that the disagreement about the relative validity of books about the black experience by nonblack writers will enforce the vital concern that children be given the essence of truth in all things. It should also be recognized that a reflective relationship is observed by literary critics and historians between children's literature and social history. In this context, one can attribute the slow appearance of distinguished fiction about black children in the United States to the slowness of white adults to consider this as an art form to be encouraged.

To return to that beginning that Topsy represents: if we again admit to oversimplification, we can look upon her as a symbol of sorts. She was not the first black child to appear in an American novel, and she can hardly be considered a representative child. Neither is *Uncle Tom's Cabin* a representative book, and very likely it was not meant to be. Nevertheless, it is possible to recognize in Topsy an attempt to create a personality, and to treat her with honesty and sympathy in the hope that she would speak in some measure for the children of her race to the readers of the 1850s. Unfortunately, the demands of classical fiction can seldom be adjusted to the demands of the tract writer. *Uncle Tom's Cabin* developed as a social document and Topsy degenerated into a caricature. Actually, anyone who does not know her would do well, as a matter of historical and human interest, to read the 1966 version of *Uncle Tom's Cabin*, edited by Anne Terry White in an effort to make it understandable for young readers.

After Topsy, it was nearly a hundred years before other Afro-Americans appeared in any numbers in fiction, but they have finally arrived: sturdy and spirited little girls and boys bringing the essence of blackness to the gallery of valid and appealing portraits in American literature for children.

To reach such characters the student must endure the dragging starts of the 1930s, the few products of the 1940s and the 1950s, and finally the rapid and sometimes injudicious proliferations of the 1960s. Because of its history, children's fiction about the American black experience is difficult to define precisely, and it remains open to subjective judgment. In fact, because it has not been defined precisely, one can hardly find out how much of it there is.

Subject Guide to Children's Books in Print 1970 lists no books under the entry "black," but refers the searcher to "Negroes," where about 60 books of fiction are identified in several subsections. Because the *Subject Guide* is not a selective list, this total obviously represented a reporting and computing problem, and undoubtedly subsequent editions will define and list books with greater accuracy.

More information on figures can be gained from a recent survey by Barbara Glancy in which she annotated 328 examples of children's interracial fiction published between 1951 and 1967. She listed about 65 others published from 1968 to 1969, thus identifying about 420 such titles published since mid-century. It should be recognized, of course, that some such books were published before the period covered by the survey, that only a few of these 420 books have literary merit, that some are no longer in print, and that many others have been published since the survey.

The Early Ones. If we agree that children's literature is a part of the whole of creative literature and should be judged by the same standards, we find that selective and critical studies document very little early children's fiction about the black experience that can be called *literature.*

In *The Critical History of Children's Literature*, R. H. Viguers discusses five stories about Afro-American children published between 1937 and 1959. She included five other books from the same period in a discussion of social problems and interest in minority groups. It is interesting to note that the first edition of the book contained no section for children's books about Afro-Americans but that Viguers included seven of these same books in a section about social problems, the Depression, and minority groups.

The seven books common to both editions are (in chronological order of publication): *Sad-Faced Boy* by Arna Bontemps; *Shuttered Windows* by Florence Crannell Means; *Steppin and Family* by Hope Newell; *All-American* by John Tunis; *My Dog Rinty* by Ellen Tarry; *Great Day in the Morning*, also by Means; and *Willow Hill* by Phyllis Whitney. *Lonesome Boy* by Arna Bontemps and *Mary Jane* by Dorothy Sterling were included in the second edition due to their later publication dates.

Because there is no other such work as the *Critical History*, it is not possible to compare the opinions expressed there with other judgments arrived at in the same manner. However, valuable guidance in the study of fiction about Afro-American children can also be found in the substantial selective bibliographies that have developed recently as aids for teachers and librarians. Two of general significance are *The Black Experience in Children's Books*, compiled by Augusta Baker of the New York Public Library, and *We Build Together*, edited by Charlemae Rollins for the National Council of Teachers of English.

Study of these bibliographies, discussions with users of their early editions as well as their current ones, and familiarity with the literature itself lead the writer of the present article to add five books to those identified in the *Critical History*, for these also represent aspects of the black experience first appearing in juvenile literature of the period.

One of the most important of these is Stella Gentry Sharpe's *Tobe*, which tells the everyday life of a black boy living on his family's farm in simple, lucid, natural language, and documents the story with clear and appealing photographs. It looks like, and is, a picture book for easy reading. It has the appearance of a factual book, but the child is not specifically identified and therefore the book is considered fiction. (Incidentally, it is worth comparing *Tobe*, which was published in 1939, with *Sweet Pea* by Jill Krementz, published in 1969, to note how little rural life in the South has changed in 30 years.)

Another "easy reading" book, *Two is a Team* by Jerrold Beim, published in 1945, is a tale of friendship between two little boys presented in such low-key fashion that only the pictures indicate one is black and one white. A few years later, the same author helped poke fun at prejudice in *Swimming Hole*.

If *All-American* is the earliest sports story about a black teenager, *Little Vic* is surely the earliest sports story for younger children, assuming one classes horse racing as a sport. A reader is well along with this story before he realizes that Pony, who wants desperately to ride the horse he grooms so faithfully, is black.

A fifth addition to other noteworthy books of this period is *Chariot in the Sky*, a story by Arna Bontemps, who weaves the moving tale of Cyrus Williams, born a slave, into the authentic tapestry of the founding of the Jubilee Singers and the difficult beginnings of Fisk University.

Recent Fiction. The period from 1960 to the present has produced many examples of fiction about Afro-American children, varying widely in the involvement and essential quality of blackness, and also in literary quality. Curiously, only one of these is an important piece of serious fantasy centering on a black child: *The Time-Ago Tales of Jahdu*, by Virginia Hamilton, a young and talented writer. Another category notably unrepresentative of black interest is science fiction, again with only one book of significance: *The Day of the Drones*, which tells of a small community (the only humans left) in Africa, who educate only the blackest among them in order to keep power from any light-skinned human, because the whites had destroyed the world's population in a holocaust.

The other books of this period, several hundred in number, seem to fall into four groups: historical fiction about Afro-Americans, family stories, books in which black children face contemporary troubles, and books in which black children and white children are seen together in realistic groups and happenings.

Historical Fiction. Of this group, six books merit attention, for different reasons. Ann Petry's book *Tituba of Salem Village* (1964) tells of a strong black woman who kept her own faith and supported others in a time of mounting mass hysteria. *I, Juan de Pareja* by Elizabeth Borton de Treviño is the first treatment for American children of a black artist who was forbidden to paint because he was a slave (of the Spanish artist Velázquez). In *Walk the World's Rim* Betty Baker interprets the heroic figure of black Estaban and his role with Cabeza de Vaca in the exploration of North America. Thomas Fall treats an aspect of the Underground Railroad and its hazards in *Canalboat for Freedom*, with a compelling positive portrait of black Lundius, a freed slave. *Bimby*, Peter Burchard's book published in 1968, is memorable: it seems a fragment, at once haunting and demanding, of a larger story one hopes will be told. In 1970 *The Drinking Gourd* by F. N. Monjo put some of the excitement of the Underground Railroad into an easy reader for younger children.

Family Life and Adventures. Of the books about Afro-American children who meet specific challenges in their own lives, *Stevie* has been universally praised. Many others are outstanding, though not all have such excellence as John Steptoe's first book. Seven of them show black children involved in adventures and solving aggravating problems with family support much in evidence. These are *The Snowy Day*, Ezra Jack Keats' 1963 picture book; *Who's in Charge of Lincoln* by Dale Fife; *Evan's Corner* by Elizabeth Starr Hill; *A Wonderful Terrible Time* by Mary Stolz; two dramatic tales by Virginia Hamilton, *Zeely* and *The House of Dies Drear*; and *Behind the Magic Line* by Betty Erwin.

Children and Courage. Quite different is another group of six. In these books, black children involved in situations not of their own making face desperation and tragedy with courage and forceful spirits, sometimes with no help at all. Frank Bonham tells in *Durango Street* how it was with Rufus and the Moors in the gang life of Los Angeles, Calif., written just before the summer of civil disorders in Watts. *The Jazz Man* by Mary Hayes Weik and *How Many Miles to Babylon* by Paula Fox mirror the heartbreak of two little boys who lived with problems too big for them. Bella Rodman's *Lions in the Way* tells how one group of black youngsters faced the torment of desegregation. Two books in this group won prizes for their authors. Kristin Hunter, author of *The Soul Brothers and Sister Lou*, was a winner in the first contest to locate unpublished manuscripts by minority group writers sponsored by the Council on Interracial Books for Children. *Sounder*, by William Armstrong, was awarded the Newbery Medal in 1969. It was praised by some critics, black and white, and vigorously condemned by others before being made into a popular film starring Cicely Tyson.

Black Children and White Children. In a final group of books, youngsters are seen together—some black, some white—playing together in sports and music; protesting together; sometimes working out problems better than their elders; and sometimes seeming unconscious of their problems. Representative of this kind of book are: *North Town* by Lorenz Graham; *Jazz Country* by Nat Hentoff; *Easy Does It*, a baseball story by Ester Wier; *A Question of Harmony*, Gretchen Sprague's story of a sit-in by high school musicians; and *Queenie Peavy* by Robert Burch, which tells of a troublesome little girl (white) whose black friends are better off than her family. *The Egypt Game* by Zilpha Snyder and *Jennifer, Hecate, Macbeth, William McKinley, and Me, Elizabeth* by E. L. Konigsburg show lively children full of inventive games, with racially mixed groups in both books.

Graphic Art in Juvenile Literature It is not possible to consider at any length the portrayal of Afro-American children by picture book artists and the illustrators of books for older children. There is room in the present article only to identify some recent trends and significant works. Readers concerned with early stereotyped views of Afro-American children will want to note the research of Dorothy Broderick, who documents the persistence into the 1930s of psychologically disastrous and unrepresentative pictures of black children. In contrast more realistic views appeared in the next decade.

In 1943 *Small Rain*, a book of Bible verses compiled by Jessie Orton Jones and illustrated by Elizabeth Orton Jones, showed black children and white children playing matter-of-factly with those of other races in natural situations. The following year the same artist included black children with others in her pictures for Rachel Field's *Prayer for a Child*; in 1945 Elizabeth Jones was awarded the Caldecott Medal for her illustrations in this picture book.

If an awakening conscience seems discernible here, it must be described as confused, because the next step was a backward one. In 1946 Maud and Miska Petersham were awarded the Caldecott Medal for their pictures in *The Rooster Crows*, a collection of rhymes and jingles described as particularly American. Not only Afro-Americans, but also others as well, felt that two pages picturing black children offended Afro-American pride and dignity. In the eleventh printing of the book in 1964 those two pages were deleted.

Some efforts were made in the late 1940s and in the 1950s to illustrate the culture of Afro-Americans more truthfully, but some of these were unacceptable because the pictures seemed little more than "color me brown" exercises. Marguerite De Angeli's *Bright April*, well intentioned though it was, does not picture Afro-Americans with total realism. That book, like *Uncle Tom's Cabin*, must be viewed as a product of its time, a message of goodwill expressed through a faulty medium.

Other illustrations of these years—Harper Johnson's pictures for *Frederick Douglass* (by Arna Bontemps), Ernest Crichlow's for *Two Is a Team* (by Jerrold Beim), and *Mary Jane* (by Dorothy Sterling)—have treated Afro-American children realistically.

In 1963 the Caldecott Medal was awarded to Ezra Jack Keats for *The Snowy Day*, whose major character was a black child. Keats has followed with five other books, with the young hero growing a bit older while he copes with small everyday problems and experiences common to all city children. Still later, in 1968, Jacob Lawrence portrayed black children with dignity and reality in his book, *Harriet and the Promised Land*.

The works of Tom Feelings have become increasingly popular and successful. His illustrations for his wife's 1970 book, *Zamani Goes to Market*, help children feel the blaze of the African sun, and they demonstrate this artist's versatility. Feelings—along with Leo Carty, Don Robertson, George Wilson, George Ford, and others—participated in an innovative project begun by the Council on Interracial Books in the summer of 1970. The project brought children into immediate and simultaneous contact with literature and artists in a unique fashion. Storyteller-illustrator combination teams went to New York City streets and parks. The storyteller read

White Fence Number Two, by Ernest Crichlow, painter and illustrator, whose illustrations for a children's book in 1945 helped establish black youngsters in children's literature as positive, nonstereotyped characters. (*Courtesy of Ernest Crichlow.*)

aloud from a book while the illustrator drew appropriate pictures under watchful young eyes, and later the illustrators gave these same pictures to the children.

Such an exciting development reminds one of literature's beginnings with the storyteller, renews a strengthening of literature's ties with the graphic arts, and reaffirms our recognition that art and literature for children are maintained by adults and children in the mainstream of human creativity.

REFERENCES: Baker, Augusta, *The Black Experience in Children's Books*, New York Public Library, New York, 1971; Glancy, Barbara Jean, *Children's Interracial Fiction: An Unselective Bibliography*, American Federation of Teachers AFL-CIO, Washington, D.C., 1969; Jackson, Miles M., *A Bibliography of Negro History and Culture for Young People*, University of Pittsburgh Press, Pittsburgh, 1969; Meigs, Cornelia, A.T. Eaton, *et al*, *A Critical History of Children's Literature*, rev. ed., Macmillan, New York, 1969; Rollins, Charlemae (ed.), *We Build Together: A Reader's Guide to Negro Life and Literature for Elementary and High School Use*, 3d. ed., National Council of Teachers of English, Champaign, 1967; Soderbergh, Peter A., "Bibliographical Essay: The Negro in Juvenile Series Books, 1899–1930," *Journal of Negro History*, April 1973, pp. 179–186; Watt, Lois B. and Patricia M. Markun, *Bibliography Books for Children*, Association for Childhood Education International (ACEI), Washington, D.C., 1974; and Wisconsin Department of Public Instruction, *Starting Out Right: Choosing Books About Black People for Young Children: Preschool Through Third Grade*, Wisconsin Department of Public Instruction, Division of Administrative Services, Madison, 1972.

(NOTE: Biographical sketches of Baker, Jackson, and Rollins appear in the *Encyclopedia*.)

Poetry   The poetry of Afro-Americans has been as varied in its form and content as the multiplicity of personalities who have contributed to its development. Traditionally, it has had no particular core: that is, it has not been a unified poetry in the sense that the poetry of the English Renaissance or that of the Romantic period were unified. This has been the case except during times of great social stress, such as in the 1920s or the 1960s and 1970s. During such times large numbers of black poets wrote with a commonly shared perspective (general as it might be) on the nature and function of poetry. At other times, in general, the poetry of black poets has closely followed the direction of poetry in the large culture. Indeed, it has never differed from the forms employed by poets of the majority culture; in content, as suggested above, its nature often depends upon the prevailing social and political climate.

Poetry by Afro-American writers is either racial in its orientation, employing subjects, language, attitudes, and scenes from racial experience, or it is nonracial, oriented toward and about experience common to the majority of people, or it is in varying degrees both these at once. Generally considered, poetry by Afro-Americans has no more specific character than poetry as a whole has. Some black poets have written racial protest poems against discrimination or other forms of racism; some have written about Afro-American life and character, describing or commenting on it in unprotesting fashion. Still others have written poems from a completely nonracial perspective, poems indistinguishable from those written by nonblack poets. Ultimately, no terms or categories specifically distinguish the writing of Afro-American poets from that of others. Black poets have tended to be conservative; prior to the 1970s they rarely departed from traditional poetic form and style.

The earliest known Afro-American poets—

Lucy Terry, Jupiter Hammon, and Phyllis Wheatley—were of the eighteenth century, and their poems were constructed on models current at that time. The first of these, Lucy Terry (1730–1821), wrote a brief narrative poem describing an Indian raid, a poem important not for its aesthetic so much as its place in history. Another Terry poem, "Bars Fight," written about 1746, is the first poem known to have been written by an Afro-American poet. Simple doggerel verse, the poem would likely seem humorous today because of its awkward rhymes, its archaic language, and its unsophisticated juxtaposition of ideas:

Eunice Allen see the Indians comeing [sic]
And hoped to save herself by running,
And had not her petticoats stopt her,
The awful creatures had not cotched her,
And tommyhawked her on the head . . .

Whether Lucy Terry (later Mrs. Abijah Prince) wrote other poems is not known.

Jupiter Hammon (ca. 1720–1800), a Long Island slave, wrote poems primarily of a religious or moral character. Conservative in his thinking and devoted to early Methodist piety, he wrote poems intended to serve as moral guides. As might be expected, Hammon was by no means original, either in the form or content of his poems. His first poem, "An Evening Thought: Salvation by Christ with Penitential Cries" (1760), is based on a Methodist hymn, and in its thought and language it echoes hundreds of other such pieces. He knew of the third earliest Afro-American poet, Phyllis Wheatley, and, in fact, wrote an address to her as traditional in language and thought as any of his other works.

Phyllis Wheatley (1753–84) is the best-known early Afro-American poet, Born in Africa and stolen from there at about the age of eight, Wheatley turned out to be something of a prodigy if we consider that after 16 months in her new homeland she was able to read the most difficult parts of the Bible, and after only six years in America she wrote "To the University of Cambridge in New England," an eloquent testimony to her thorough mastery of the language (a mastery far greater than that of most of her contemporaries). Her first published poem appeared in 1770, and her first volume of verse, the first volume published by an Afro-American writer, appeared in 1773 with the title *Poems on Various Subjects, Religious and Moral*. Her poetry is neither original nor highly imaginative, yet it reveals a thorough grasp of the diction and form of conventional neoclassic verse. As were so many of her contemporaries, she was content to follow the practice of the master of the heroic couplet, Alexander Pope.

There is little reference to race in Wheatley's poems. A few such references do occur, but except for these, one would undoubtedly not know her racial identity. This is in part because she followed the tradition of impersonality so characteristic of much of neoclassic verse. Her tendency was to cast her feelings in traditional molds so that her personal feelings remain unspoken. Also her religious inclinations may have been responsible for her silence about personal matters. She was so devoutly religious that she probably felt that the poetic expression of faith was far more significant than writing about personal concerns. If she led a reasonably easy life as the slave of a northern owner and as a house servant, and there is reason to believe she did, she might not have felt a strong enough tension between herself and society to elicit expressions of protest. Her marvelously good ear and her capacity to create clear and logical poems were used in the service of promoting what must have seemed to her the highest good, Christian faith, despite the fact that her later life was extremely miserable and culminated in her death at the age of 31.

During the nineteenth century several more

Phyllis Wheatley is the best known early black American poet. This engraving after a work by the black painter Scipio Moorhead is the only known likeness of her; it appeared in her *Poems on Various Subjects*. (Library of Congress.)

Afro-American poets appeared, including George Moses Horton (ca. 1797–ca. 1883), Frances Ellen Harper (1825–1911), James Madison Bell (1826–1902), and James M. Whitfield (1823–78). Each of these poets was to some degree political, writing against slavery or other wrongs perpetrated by society. Horton's first volume, *Hope of Liberty* (1829), was written with the actual hope that it would earn enough money to allow him to purchase his freedom. In it he describes the ills of slavery, thus becoming the first Afro-American poet to complain openly about slavery's evil.

Frances Ellen Harper was the most widely known of this group because of her general involvement in reform, especially the abolitionist and temperance movements. A large number of her poems are devoted to revealing the horrors of slavery, "The Slave Mother" and "The Slave Auction" being among the best of these. Like her Afro-American contemporaries and forebears in poetry (and like American poets generally during this time), she wrote in conventional ways about the same subjects that interested many others. She wrote, published, and republished her poetry throughout the nineteenth century, and her *Poems on Miscellaneous Subjects* (1854) exceeded 20 editions.

But Harper, as widely known as she was, did not begin to match the accomplishments of a black poet born in Ohio toward the beginning of the final quarter of the nineteenth century, Paul Laurence Dunbar (1872–1906). Dunbar was the first Afro-American poet to achieve national recognition, recognition sustained throughout his brief creative life. Dunbar wrote two kinds of poetry, both dialect poetry and poems in, as he liked to think of them, Standard English. He considered his non-dialect poems his best work, and eventually wrote in dialect only because it was demanded of him by editors and the public to whom he frequently gave readings. His dialect poems are nearly all about Afro-American life and character, and though they are too frequently based on stereotyped characters or situations, they from time to time strike a note of truth when the poet comes upon a phrase, a situation, or a sentiment whose intention is not simply to amuse or support the prejudices of his white audience. Such elements are in "A Negro Love Song," "When Malindy Sings," and "An Antebellum Sermon." Generally romantic, conventional in style and subject matter, and often derivative, Dunbar's poems in Standard English have not been as well remembered as his dialect

works. Dunbar would probably have been a better poet had he been able to be more personal in these poems, to speak freely and openly of his actual thoughts and feelings instead of saying, as he did, conventional things in conventional ways. Dunbar was best when least conventional, when he took off the mask of the poet and spoke as a breathing organism as in (ironically) "We Wear the Mask" and "Ere Sleep Comes Down to Soothe the Weary Eyes."

Dunbar wrote poems that were racial, nonracial, or both. He wrote dialect poems intended to evoke general human response ("Little Brown Baby" and "A Death Song," for example), though he did not, with the possible exception of "We Wear the Mask," write nondialect poems about the black experience. This resulted from his rather rigid idea of what constitutes poetry, what subjects are suitable for poetry, and what poetic form is. Had he been less rigid, his poetry might have been more forward looking than it now appears to be, though no poet other than Stephen Crane was writing in very unconventional ways at the time.

The poetry of Leslie Pinckney Hill (1800–1960), George Marion McClellan (1860–1934), and William Stanley Braithwaite (1878–1962) was written by black writers, who intended to reflect general human (and not specifically black) experience. Their primary end was beauty, though Hill tended to be philosophically inclined. By far the most accomplished of these poets was Braithwaite, who was widely known as an anthologist and particularly for his annual collections of magazine verse. Braithwaite is perhaps the best example of a black writer who consciously set out to be a poet and not a *black* poet. A sophisticated practitioner of the art of poetry for its own sake, he wrote the most successful poetry of this kind before Robert Hayden later in the twentieth century.

Another early twentieth-century poet worthy of brief mention is Fenton Johnson (1888–1958), who, following the modes set forth by the New Poetry movement, wrote untraditional poems largely pessimistic in mood. His "Tired" is an example: "throw the children into the river; civilization has given us too many."

The Harlem Renaissance of the 1920s saw one of the greatest periods of creative activity among Afro-American artists. For the first time large numbers of black writers lived in the same place (Harlem) or were otherwise in contact with one another. It was a time of great social agitation following the large-scale black oppression after

World War I and the first great migration of black peasants from the South. Marcus Garvey, advocating the establishment of a new black nation on African soil to which Afro-Americans would immigrate, commanded the allegiance of large numbers of followers. While none of the major poets writing at the time were specifically followers of Garvey, his black nationalistic teachings were perhaps responsible for a greater sense of unity among black people than had existed before, and they exemplified a new radicalism reflected in the poetry of the times.

In economic terms the 1920s was a period of general prosperity when a little of the fat of the land trickled down to better the lot of black men. This accounts in part for the agitation for equality, the newly expressed pride in blackness, the fact that a large number of black writers had the leisure to write and the inclination to write. It is of significance that nearly all the major black writers were college-educated. These factors point to the economic climate that allowed the Harlem Renaissance to occur. The energy that went into it would not have been available had not times been relatively good.

In general cultural terms the 1920s was a time when Americans tested the moral and social restraints sanctioned by traditional standards of conduct. Freud had begun to capture the popular imagination, and traditional, puritanical American attitudes about sex were called into question. It is in this context that the Harlem Renaissance existed. For many white Americans the Afro-American became a fitting symbol of unrestrained, natural, noninstitutional behavior. In order to be whole and fully human, the reasoning of great numbers of whites ran, one must throw off the restraints of culture and civilization and regain the primitive simplicity of black people. This resulted in a new attitude toward an old stereotype, an attitude no less reprehensible, however, for being new. Many whites imitated Afro-Americans, but always with the implication that black people were by nature uncivilized, amoral, and unhampered by social restraints. The result of such thinking was to reduce the Afro-American to a set of terms fitting the psychological needs of many nonblacks.

In practical and specific terms this line of thinking meant that things related to black life and culture became of great importance. Whites began coming to Harlem nightclubs in great numbers. Such musical shows about black people as "Chocolate Dandies," "Shuffle Along," and "Brown Rhythm" became popular. Eugene

O'Neill wrote *The Emperor Jones;* Sherwood Anderson wrote *Dark Laughter;* Carl Van Vechten wrote *Nigger Heaven;* and Dubose Heyward wrote *Porgy and Bess.* All of these white writers saw the black man as they wanted and needed to see him.

Afro-American writers used this situation in order to attain their own ends though they sometimes, unfortunately, exploited the situation by writing in terms of the white stereotype. However, they frequently did not do this, and the result was the development of thoughts, attitudes, and ideas from the inside, from the black perspective. Thus, during the 1920s, the first large-scale manifestations of black pride, concern for the beauty of blackness, interest in black history and culture, and political awareness of and concern with the use of poetry as a means of exploring and celebrating blackness arose.

Foremost among such writers was Langston Hughes (1902–67), who differed from most of his predecessors and from many of his contemporaries by addressing his poetry specifically to black people. At a time when many poets were turning inward and writing obscure and esoteric poetry, Hughes was turning outward, using language and themes, attitudes and ideas familiar and recognizable to anyone who had the ability to read. He was, unlike most nonblack poets other than Vachel Lindsay and Carl Sandburg, a

Langston Hughes (right) with Arna Bontemps. Foremost in the Renaissance of the 1920s, Hughes was the first black poet whose language, themes, and ideas expressed the aspirations of black Americans. *(Moorland-Spingarn Research Center, Howard University.)*

poet of the people. He often employed a dialect recognizable as belonging to the black urban dweller or the rural black peasant. Throughout his career he was aware of injustice and oppression, and he used his poetry as a means of opposing or mitigating that oppression. Such early poems as "The Negro Speaks of Rivers" and "I, Too" testify to his abiding hope in the fulfillment of the American dream—not only for Afro-Americans, but also for all the dispossessed of the land. Until the time of his death Hughes

Gwendolyn Brooks was awarded the Pulitzer Prize for poetry in 1950. *(Mooreland-Spingarn Research Center, Howard University.)*

spread his message humorously though always seriously to audiences throughout the country, having read his poetry to more people probably than any other American poet.

Claude McKay (1891–1948), Countee Cullen (1903–46), and Jean Toomer (1894–1967) all had an orientation toward the proper uses of poetry somewhat different from that of Langston Hughes. All tended, though in different degrees, to view poetry as having more to do with the rhythmical creation of beauty rather than with the affairs of the world (though Hughes did write some lyrical poems with no social bias). McKay was very much involved in politics, but that interest found only limited expression in his poetry. He wrote about love, nature, religion, and places he had visited; he wrote nostalgically about his early home, Jamaica, and about America. Among this group of poets he was the most like Hughes in that he wrote a number of poems whose orientation is social, including "If We Must Die," "America," "The Lynching," and "The White House."

Countee Cullen and Jean Toomer, though both wrote on social matters, are by no means social poets. Cullen had an especially good ear for metrics and found himself more at home with Keats, Shelley, and Tennyson than with those who were writing experimental verse. Most of his poetry is indistinguishable from that of non-black poets, though he wrote some poems with racial subjects or themes.

Countee Cullen in 1941. *(Moorland-Spingarn Research Center, Howard University.)*

Jean Toomer's case is a much more interesting one because he created in his poetry and prose a mythical black past to which he explored his own relationship. Toomer seems to have sought the roots of race in mysticism and aestheticism, so his relationship to blackness seems more of the imagination than of the real ethnic world (from which he was something of a recluse). He translated imagined black experience into forms so idealized as to be little related to reality.

Far right: Sterling Brown (right) with Roy Wilkins, then (ca. 1940) the editor of the NAACP's *The Crisis. (Moorland-Spingarn Research Center, Howard University.)*

The 1930s was a relatively barren time for poetry—Sterling A. Brown (1901–   ) published his *Southern Road* in 1932 using dialect for its realistic rather than humorous effects—and it was not until the 1940s and early 1950s that a significant number of well-considered Afro-American poets began publishing volumes of verse. These poets, Melvin Tolson (1900–66), Robert Hayden (1913–   ), Margaret Danner (19?–   ), Gwendolyn Brooks (1917–   ), and Margaret Walker (1915–   ), were all, like their predecessors in the 1920s, college-educated (though perhaps even more highly educated

formally). All were strongly influenced by academic tastes and practices, though Gwendolyn Brooks and Margaret Walker perhaps less so than Tolson, Hayden, and Danner. The latter three wrote poetry that by academic standards is very good poetry, but that might not be so easily understood by the average person. Brooks and Walker wrote considerably less esoterically and are closer in this sense to the poetic practice of Langston Hughes. These poets all competed successfully with their contemporaries among non-black poets, as the prizes and awards they won for their poems (with the exception of Tolson, who for strange and complicated reasons has yet to be fully recognized) indicated. Each of these writers was a professional poet (primarily a poet), as opposed to several Afro-American poets of the past who wrote poetry on occasion, or who were novelists, or who did other things as the primary activity of their lives. When LeRoi Jones began to be heard from as a poet in the early 1960s, he was writing poetry not unlike that of this group of poets, complicated and sophisticated.

The most significant Afro-American poet writing after the early 1960s was LeRoi Jones/Imamu Amiri Baraka (1934–   ), looked to as a leader by younger black poets both for the example of his poetry and for the example provided by his life. During the late 1950s and early 1960s Jones was a very successful contemporary poet whose verse, though unique in its way, was not unlike that of other academic poets: complex, obscure, written primarily for academicians and other poets. After a period of transition, traceable in his poems and essays, he turned his back on the established powers responsible for making him a success, and set about working toward the organization of the black community in Newark, N.J., his hometown. His poetry underwent several significant changes (as did his name from Jones to Baraka), becoming less complex, aggressively

militant in its tone and message, and directed, in the manner of Langston Hughes, to the people. Most of the younger black poets have followed his lead insofar as he has defined the nature and proper uses of poetry for black poets.

The result of the great social stress (referred to at the beginning of this article) of the past decade has been responsible for the creation of a significantly definable Afro-American poetry, one having qualities making it more distinguishable than black poetry had ever been in the past. This is because most of the younger black poets share a generally common perspective on the nature and function of poetry. Perhaps the most basic element of similarity among most poetry by younger black writers is its oral nature: most of this poetry, unlike that of most other poets of our time, is written to be read aloud. Its language is simple, such as that which ordinary people use or may easily understand. It is frequently rhetorical in the manner of the sermon of the black church, and as frequently as the black sermon requires or evokes response from the audience. It is either political—setting forth proper political goals, actions, or attitudes—or it is cultural—descriptive of black life or character and at the same time seeking to establish or to validate black cultural norms. Its language and tone frequently derive from black urban dialect. It is positive in its perspective on blackness and strives toward the unconventional, often attempting to shock with its open and frank use of language traditionally considered vulgar or obscene. These generalities are apparent in an anthology of the work of younger black writers, *Black Fire* (1968), prepared by LeRoi Jones and another leader of the movement, Larry Neal.

A great number of young black poets were writing in the 1970s, far too many to mention here. Most of them found an outlet for their writing through Broadside Press, a Detroit based publishing house run by Dudley Randall, himself a black poet. Prominent among this group were Mari Evans, Don L. Lee, Sonia Sanchez, Clarence Major, Lance Jeffers and Conrad Rivers (of an earlier generation), Naomi Long Madgett, Carol Freeman, Nikki Giovanni, and Etheridge Knight.

REFERENCES: Baker, Houston A. Jr., *Black Literature in America*, McGraw-Hill Book Co., New York, 1971; Benston, Kimberly W., *Baraka: The Renegade and the Mask*, Yale University Press, New Haven and London, 1976; Bontemps, Arna (ed.), *American Negro Poetry*, Hill and Wang, New York, 1963; Brawley, Benjamin G., *Early Negro American Writers; Selections with Biographical and Critical Introductions*, University of North Carolina Press, Chapel Hill, 1935; Brooks, Gwendolyn (ed.), *A Broadside Treasury, 1965–1970*, Broadside Press, Detroit, 1971; Brown, Sterling A., *Negro Poetry and Drama*, Arno Press, New York, 1969; Calverton, V. F., *Anthology of American Negro Literature*, Modern Library, New York, 1929; Chapman, Dorothy, *Index to Black Poetry* (See BIBLIOGRAPHIES/BIOGRAPHIES/GUIDES for description); Davis, Arthur P., *From the Dark Tower: Afro-American Writers, 1900 to 1960*, Howard University Press, Washington, D.C., 1974; Dickinson, Donald C., *A Bio-Bibliography of Langston Hughes, 1902–1967*, Archon Books, The Shoe String Press, Hamden, 1967; Gross, Seymour and John E. Hardy (eds.), *Images of the Negro in American Literature: Essays in Criticism*, University of Chicago Press, Chicago, 1966; Hayden, Robert (ed.), *Kaleidoscope, Poems by American Negro Poets*, Harcourt, Brace & World, New York, 1967; Henderson, Stephen E., *Understanding the New Black Poetry, Black Speech and Black Music as Poetic References*, Morrow, New York, 1973; Hughes, Langston and Arna Bontemps (eds.), *The Poetry of the Negro, 1746–1970*, rev. ed., Doubleday, Garden City, 1970; Jackson, Blyden, *Black Poetry in America*, Louisiana State University Press, Baton Rouge, 1974; Locke, Alain, *The New Negro: An Interpretation*, 2d. ed., Atheneum, New York, 1968; Loggins, Vernon, *The Negro Author: His Development in America to 1900*, Columbia University Press, New York, 1964; Perry, Margaret, *A Bio-Bibliography of Countee P. Cullen*, Westport, 1971; Porter, Dorothy B., *North American Negro Poets, A Bibliographical Checklist of Their Writings, 1760–1944*, Brook Farm, Hattiesburg, 1945. For some thoughtful essays, see Gibson, Donald B., *Modern Black Poets: A Collection of Critical Essays*, Prentice-Hall, New York, 1973.

Nikki Giovanni in 1972. *(National Educational Television.)*

The Novel*

Before *Native Son*, 1853–1940 Since the publication of William Wells Brown's *Clotel, or the President's Daughter* (1853), the dominant theme in the Afro-American novel has been the problem black people face living in a racist society. Black novelists in the United States have responded to white oppression by exposing it in their fiction either in an overtly propagandistic manner or by subjugating the protest elements to aesthetic principles in a method that nevertheless covertly condemns discriminatory practices. But the question of what it means to be an Afro-American in a country that has institutionalized racial discrimination has persisted regardless of the style or talent of the author.

The conditions under which blacks were forced to live in the nineteenth century were conducive to the writing of protest fiction, but there were few Afro-Americans who had the freedom, the education, or the time to write. Beginning in the late eighteenth century, though, several white writers produced antislavery novels. Hugh Henry Brackenridge's *Modern Chivalry* (1792–1815), *The Oriental Philanthropist* (1800) by Henry Sherburne, *The Algerine Captive* (1797) by Royall Tyler, *The Slave, or Memoirs of Archy Moore* (1836) by Richard Hildreth, and *Recollections of a Southern Matron* (1836) by Caroline Howard Gilman

*See acknowledgements in the PREFACE.

fit into this category. But it remained for Harriet Beecher Stowe's *Uncle Tom's Cabin* (1852) to catch the imagination of much of the nation. The novel was designed to emphasize the inhumanity of the people who profit from the slave trade as contrasted with the Christian humility of Uncle Tom. In her depiction of Tom and the Harris family, Stowe attempted to destroy the myth of the domestic tranquility of the plantation.

Uncle Tom's Cabin attacked not only the conditions of slavery but also the type of fiction known as the plantation tradition. Produced primarily by white southerners to defend slavery, the plantation tradition created stereotypes of Afro-Americans in an effort to prove that they were naturally inferior, and content only under the protection of the white master on the plantation.

Given impetus by such early nineteenth-century novelists as George Tucker, John Pendleton Kennedy, William Gilmore Simms, and Nathaniel Beverly Tucker, the plantation tradition became a fixture in American literature. It grew to its greatest strength after the publication of *Uncle Tom's Cabin*. Against this literary background, William Wells Brown, an ex-slave who fled to England with the help of a Quaker family, produced *Clotel* (1853). Published in London, the novel is a propagandistic condemnation of slavery designed to advance the abolitionist cause. The plot is interspersed with tales of the inhumanity practiced by whites against slaves. In addition the author inserted his own comments on the evils of slavery in an effort to contradict the plantation tradition as thoroughly as possible.

The plot of *Clotel, or the President's Daughter* revolves around a mulatto woman and her two daughters who are sold as slaves after the mother has been discarded by her white lover. The separate careers of the three women are traced, but the emphasis is on one of the daughters, Clotel, who finally ends her tragic life by drowning in the Potomac River as she is being pursued by a gang of whites. The fact that she dies within sight of the White House, occupied by Thomas Jefferson, is more than a conincidence, as the title of the novel suggests. Brown comments on the suicide of Clotel by stating that it

should be an evidence wherever it should be known, of the inconquerable love of liberty the heart may inherit; as well as a fresh admonition to the slave dealer, of the cruelty and enormity of his crime.

Brown reiterates this thesis throughout the book. Although it adds nothing to the literary value of *Clotel,* the patent propagandistic approach indicates the author's basic concern. He is interested only in exposing the evils of slavery and in refuting the claims of the plantation tradition. Primarily because of the inclusion of Jefferson in the reprobation of the American system of slavery, though, *Clotel* was not published in the United States until 1867. The American edition is in a revised form in which an anonymous senator is substituted for the president. Reference to the president was also deleted from the title.

The first novel by an Afro-American published in this country was Frank Webb's *The Garies and Their Friends* (1857). It deals with a woman of Afro-American ancestry who passes for white. She marries a white man and lives peacefully in Philadelphia, Pa., until the secret of her lineage is discovered. The result is mob violence in which Mr. Garie, her husband, is killed. As in the case of *Clotel,* Webb's novel exposes the effects of racism without showing much concern for literature as art.

Before the Civil War the only other long piece of fiction published by a black was Martin Delany's "Blake, or the Huts of America." A fragment of a novel, "Blake" (1859) appeared in the *Anglo-African Magazine*. The 26 extant chapters extol the virtues of the black characters, including their intelligence and beauty. The protagonist is a runaway slave who travels throughout the South in an effort to organize slave uprisings. The fragment is filled with the horrors of slavery and is modeled to a large degree on *Uncle Tom's Cabin*, the major differences being that the Christian symbol of Uncle Tom is replaced by a militant figure resembling Stowe's George Harris.

Afro-American fiction, then, was born in the protest tradition established by the white abolitionists. Both William Wells Brown and Martin Delany borrowed freely from the model provided by *Uncle Tom's Cabin*.

By the last decade of the nineteenth century, black writers had begun to enter the novelistic arena themselves as an Afro-American middle class started to emerge. The emphasis in most of the novels produced at this time is on the creation of counterstereotypes to combat the degrading images projected by southerners. Frances Harper's *Iola Leroy* (1886), "helped to establish the precedent of developing well-mannered, educated colored characters to offset the stock-characters of the plantation tradition." *Appointed* (1894), a novel by Walter Stowers and William H. Anderson, dealt with a systematic program of oppression as applied by whites. *Hearts of Gold* (1896), by J. McHenry Jones, revealed the injustices practiced against Afro-Americans, while it praised the black upper classes as models of decorum. Pauline E. Hopkins, in *Contending Forces* (1900), followed the example of Jones in "placing the case of worthy but oppressed Negroes before the bar of American justice."

It remained for Sutton Griggs, though, to sound the note of militancy that was not to be matched for over half a century. His first novel, *Imperium in Imperio* (1889), a forerunner of such militant protest novels as *Sons of Darkness, Sons of Light* (1969), and *The Spook Who Sat by the Door* (1969), reveals a plan to take the state of Texas by force under the direction of a secret black organization. The novel begins as a farce when two black youths, Belton Piedmont and Bernard Belgrave, vie for academic honors in a prep school in the South. Both boys are extremely intelligent, but as they go their separate ways after graduation they discover that being black is a handicap that cannot be easily overcome. Belton is actually lynched for helping a white girl find the right page in her hymn book in church and escapes only by feigning death when the whites cut down the rope too soon.

Not much of a market for militant protest existed at the turn of the century, however, and Griggs turned to writing apologetic fiction in his later work, which included *Overshadowed* (1901), *Unfettered* (1902), *The Hindered Hand* (1905), and *Pointing the Way* (1908). Unlike the racial protest novels of the 1940s that explore the psychological effects of racial prejudice, the earlier protests against racism concentrated primarily on physical results in the manner of such antislavery novels as *Uncle Tom's Cabin* or *Clotel*.

The concept of apologizing for a race was not especially conducive to exploring the depths of the black experience. J. Saunders Redding suggests that if a black writer, at the beginning of the twentieth century, wanted an audience he had to conform to the accepted standards of Afro-American behavior or dissemble completely by writing of white characters. This meant, in the absence of a novelist skilled or independent enough to depict the essence of Afro-American life, that a black novelist wrote either in opposition to the plantation tradition, by portraying counterstereotypes, or that he ignored Afro-Americans entirely. Grigg's *Imperium in Imperio* conforms partially to the former pattern, but its militancy violated the code of decorum and the novel achieved little popularity. More to the liking of the white audience was the work of Paul Laurence Dunbar. A popular poet who catered to the tastes of white America, Dunbar wrote four novels that were published around the turn of the century. The first of these, *The Uncalled* (1898), is a relatively competent novel of a white youth who becomes a minister, under the stern guidance of his guardian, only to discover that love is of more consequence than a God of vengeance. Reminiscent of Harold Frederic's famous study of the psychological destruction of a strict Calvinist in *The Damnation of Theron Ware* (1896), *The Uncalled* revealed a potential that was never fulfilled, as Dunbar turned to melodramatic romance in his later works. *The Love of Landry* (1900) and *The Fanatics* (1901) dealt with white lovers who are separated because of class barriers and political differences. Dunbar wrote of black characters in *The Sport of the Gods* (1902), but his thesis corresponds to that of the plantation tradition. In this novel he echoed the philosophy of Booker T. Washington by urging the black masses to remain in the South to provide a labor force for white industry. However, his argument was weakened by the use of the plantation concepts of the wretched freedman and the faithful retainer. Dunbar even resorted to didactic passages about the wicked influence of the urban North on poor and uneducated blacks in an effort to convince his audience that the South was the proper home of Afro-Americans.

Dunbar, though, was not typical of the black author of his time. Patronized by William Dean Howells, he sought to become popular rather than to retain the racial and literary integrity he possessed as a young man. Charles W. Chesnutt sounded the note of racial protest, still basically apologetic, that dominated black fiction early in the twentieth century. His first novel, *House Behind the Cedars* (1900), dealt with the theme of "passing." Rena Walden, reared in a house provided by her mother's white lover, in the colored section of the town, decides to pass for white and to marry her white suitor. Her deception is discovered, and Rena spends the rest of her short life in obscurity. A change of heart by

Charles W. Chesnutt. *(Moorland-Spingarn Research Center, Howard University.)*

the southern lawyer who had dismissed her after he learned of her Afro-American blood comes too late, as the young woman dies before he can confess his love for her.

While *The House Behind the Cedars,* despite its melodrama, is perhaps Chesnutt's best novel, in his two later efforts he dealt more directly with the problem of conflict between the white and black races. in *The Marrow of Tradition* (1901) he based the plot on the riots that occurred in Wilmington, N.C., in 1898 when Afro-Americans tried to vote. Dr. Miller, the black protagonist, is a moderate on the issue of retaliation until his son is killed in the rioting. He is tempted to change his position and commit himself in favor of violent retaliation until his professional ethics enter the picture. He performs an operation that saves the life of a white boy and in the process decides that violence is not the answer to white oppression.

In his third novel, *The Colonel's Dream* (1905), Chesnutt exposed the southern system of exploiting black labor. The tone of the novel is conciliatory, however, as Colonel French, the white protagonist, designs a plan that will provide blacks with adequate opportunities in the labor market. The novel dealt with race relations in a practical manner, but Chesnutt was more concerned with stating his argument than in writing good fiction.

Chesnutt's fiction suffers as a result of his propagandistic purposes. His novels indicate a desire to combat the discrimination typical of his own life, as well as to offset the image of the Afro-American as projected by white writers. At the time that Chesnutt was writing, a relatively new concept of black depravity was presented to the public. The stereotypes of the plantation tradition were joined by the image of the brute Negro that emerged from the work of Hinton Helper, Thomas Nelson Page, and Charles Carroll. The supreme white racist, however, was Rev. Thomas Dixon who, in his *Trilogy of Reconstruction,* attempted to retain the old tradition of the South by appealing to the baser emotions of humanity. *The Leopard's Spots* (1902), *The Clansman* (1905), and *The Traitor* (1907) are defenses of the terrorist tactics of the Ku Klux Klan. The Negro, in the propaganda of Dixon, is displayed as a primitive savage who will commit any crime in his lust for white flesh. In *The Clansman,* from which the infamous 1916 movie *The Birth of a Nation* was created, a brute Negro rapes a white woman only to be identified when it is discovered that his image has been imprint-

James Weldon Johnson. *(Library of Congress)*

ed on the cornea of the dead victim. Negroes, according to Dixon, corrupt everything "white" that they come in contact with, and therefore the Klan is eulogized as the preserver of Aryan culture and the protector of white womanhood.

The literary advent of the brute Negro did not dramatically change the fiction produced by the apologetic black writers. W. E. B. Du Bois and James Weldon Johnson did publish novels that tended to approach the racial protest novels of the 1940s in their systematic and intrinsic condemnation of white oppression, but they were still of the old school of apologetic protest that aggrandizes black characters without getting to the core of the consequences of racism. Du Bois, the famous sociologist, tried his hand at fiction in *The Quest of the Silver Fleece* (1911). The book is an attempt to expose the economic roots of racial discrimination. The black protagonists, Bles and Zora, are robbed of their cotton crop by a southern landowner. As a result they move from the South to Washington, D.C., where they attempt to put political pressure on the plantation system. Failing to accomplish much, they return to the South to organize black sharecroppers into a cooperative system. Their ultimate goal is to join the poor blacks with the poor whites to combat the cotton trust.

The failings of Du Bois were only partially remedied in James Weldon Johnson's *The Autobiography of an Ex-Colored Man* (1912). Published anonymously, the novel, despite its concern with the overworked theme of passing, its pedantic discussions of race relations, and its digressions, presented a panoramic view of Afro-American life and the color problem. Johnson presented most of his insights into black-white relationships in the reflections of the narrator rather than through the action itself; nevertheless, he analyzed many of the major race problems to a greater extent than any other novelist of his era.

Johnson, through his fictional representative, called for a new tradition in literature that would depict the various aspects of Afro-American life, especially the attempts of black people to break away from the limitations set by white society. The novel itself takes a step in this direction, but it is basically a catalogue of grievances against the racial policies of American society. It resembles an essay more than a work of fiction. Yet, in its depiction of Afro-American folk culture, in its analysis of the color problem in American life, and in its suggestions for improved racial relationships, *The Autobiography of an Ex-Col-*

ored Man is one of the important novels of the early twentieth century.

The black population of the United States, the vast majority still subsisting at poverty levels in urban ghettos or depressed rural areas in the South, did not yet, however, produce the literary figures to answer Johnson's plea, and it was again the white novelists who created the popular literary image of the black man after World War I. With the continued migration of Afro-Americans to the North, such places as New York City's Harlem seethed with people looking for a release from the restrictions of life in the ghetto. Marcus Garvey and his "Back to Africa" movement became popular for a while, but his dream died when he was arrested for mail fraud in 1925. With most Afro-Americans resigned to existing in a ghetto, one of the major attractions for them was the night life. The bistros of Harlem enticed white people, as well as black, and one of the results of the white influx was the belief that Afro-Americans were naturally less inhibited.

In fiction this concept became the cult of the primitive in which blacks were depicted as people who obeyed their instincts, regardless of the cost, presumably as a result of their savage African background. At the same time, their intellectual capabilities were virtually ignored. New stereotypes were created as Eugene O'Neill, Sherwood Anderson, Dubose Heyward, and Carl Van Vechten popularized the primitive Negro who lived for the moment. In Anderson's *Dark Laughter* (1925), the uninhibited sexual activity of blacks is glorified. In the same year, Heyward's *Porgy* stressed the gambling, sexual, and drinking habits of a black community. The merits of the novel, and some of the characters, became matters of secondary importance as Sportin' Life emerged as the stereotype of the "typical nigger," especially in the dramatization of the popular story.

Most of the novels produced by Afro-Americans put a greater stress on racial themes, and the Harlem Renaissance had its share of these too. Walter White, Jessie Fauset, and Nella Larsen all wrote novels of passing in which they try to indicate that life on the darker side of the color line is preferable, despite the discrimination that accompanies it. White's *Flight* (1926) dealt with a heroine of mixed blood who marries a white man only to return to the black community when she grows tired of her husband's empty life. Fauset's *Plum Bun* (1929) and *Comedy American Style* (1933) both present Afro-American women who unsuccessfully try to find happiness in the white world. In *Quicksand* (1928) and *Passing* (1929), Nella Larsen also depicted heroines who strive for success in white society, but who are thwarted by a discovery of their black ancestry.

Black writers in the 1930s, as indicated by the historical fiction of Bontemps, Paynter, and Hill, continued to stress racial themes illustrating white oppression. There are, however, a few exceptions. *Ollie Miss* (1935) by George Wylie Henderson is about black sharecroppers in Alabama who exist in an isolated world. The novel emphasized the folk customs of rural Afro-Americans. In a pastoral setting, Ollie, a young woman who works the land as well as most men, renounces an unsatisfactory love affair. Despite her pregnancy, she looks forward to nurturing the green things of her own farm without her former lover. The absence of white people in the novel allowed Henderson to concentrate on Ollie Miss, who learns through suffering and moral awareness the value of being honest with herself.

Zora Neale Hurston's two novels in the 1930s also made use of Afro-American folklore in settings conspicuous for the absence of whites. *Jonah's Gourd Vine* (1934) is the story of a mulatto preacher whose illicit love affairs lead to self-destruction. Although the characterization is not impressive, the author vividly depicts certain phases of Afro-American life in Alabama and Florida. Social problems are not stressed as the blacks are resigned to their inferior status. *Their Eyes Were Watching God* (1937) presented the tempestuous life of Janie Starks in the black community of Eatonville, Fla. Janie stands up to the scorn of her neighbors in an effort to find happiness with Tea Cake, a penniless gambler and drifter. She comes to understand the meaning of love in her wanderings through the villages of the Everglades. When Tea Cake dies, she returns to Eatonville, convinced that she has experienced life at its best. She is thus oblivious to the gossip of the townspeople.

Racial discrimination is simply taken for granted in *Their Eyes Were Watching God*. After a severe hurricane, for instance, the bodies of white people are buried in coffins while black bodies are merely rolled into shallow depressions. Problems develop, though, when a number of badly damaged bodies cannot be identified as to race. This ironical situation is the extent of Hurston's racial protest. William Attaway, in *Let Me Breathe Thunder* (1939), also avoided direct racial confrontations to a large extent, but by presenting white characters instead of black. In its treatment of migrant workers, it is typical of the proletarian novels of the time, although hardly comparable on a literary level to Steinbeck's *The Grapes of Wrath* (1939).

Native Son **and After, 1940–70** The birth of the modern Afro-American novel is marked by the publication of Richard Wright's *Native Son* in 1940, in the same way that the modern English novel is dated by the 1740 edition of Samuel Richardson's *Pamela*. Both authors changed the course of fiction in their respective eras. Before the appearance of *Native Son*, most of the novels of Afro-Americans either avoided racial issues, or were in the apologetic tradition, which portrayed heroic black characters who were physically victimized by white racists. Wright began a new trend in protest literature by presenting a character who is psychologically thwarted by racism.

The psychological impact of racism presented in *Native Son* and the Wrightian protest novels of the 1940s depicted the Afro-American as a depraved victim of American society. Protest fiction eventually changed, however, and the apologetic novel came into vogue following World War II. This trend depicted an exemplary black protagonist who is physically challenged by bigoted whites. At about the same time that apologetic protest emerged, a reaction against protest was launched. The result was the rise of the accommodationist novel. This type of fiction does not avoid racial issues but deals more specifically with the development of an individual black character as he struggles to adjust to white society. This tendency of the characters to accommodate themselves to white America, rather than to fight it, was carried over into another fictional movement. The assimilationist novel, dealing primarily with white characters, became popular in the 1950s as black novelists attempted to escape the shadow of *Native Son*. The protagonist of Wright's novel, though, could not be ignored, and he eventually evolved into the revolutionist of the militant protest novel. The latter trend depicted blacks in an organized retaliation against whites.

The covert form of white oppression portrayed in *Native Son* dehumanized the black protagonist Bigger Thomas. The ghetto inhabitant therefore retaliated with acts of violence that satisfied his sense of helplessness, and thus he emerged as a symbol of rebellion against a racist Ameri-

Richard Wright in 1943. He changed the course of Afro-American fiction with his novel, *Native Son*. (Gordon Parks, Library of Congress.)

can society. Bigger Thomas served as a prototype for the characters that appeared in other novels in the years following the publication of *Native Son*. Wright himself, after achieving international fame, acted the role of a rebel by becoming an expatriate. From his self-imposed exile in Europe, he enjoyed a brief but influential reign in the realm of the Afro-American novel. The Wrightian style of psychological protest was prevalent in the 1940s. With Bigger Thomas as a pattern, such black authors as Ann Petry and Chester Himes presented oppressed figures who were denied the opportunity to develop as individuals. The characters had no ambitions or dreams comparable to those of whites, as a racist atmosphere tended to produce people with inferiority complexes, or some other form of emotional instability. These social misfits, judged from the white point of view, were shown to be the inevitable result of American society.

After World War II, however, the Wrightian protest novel was replaced by several distinct literary trends. The fiction patterned after *Native Son* began to disappear as black authors revealed a preference to depict the diversity of Afro-American life. Racial protest remained popular, but it was treated in different ways. One approach was the revival of the apologetic protest novel by Willard Savoy and William Gardner Smith. In this type of fiction, a talented black protagonist attempts to advance socially, or to oppose the white power structure, and is subsequently victimized by prejudiced whites. This direct confrontation with white authority is in contrast to the method used by Wright and his followers. Rather than portraying the psychological effects of racism, the apologetic writers attempted to show that the blacks who are fortunate enough to escape the ghetto are nevertheless doomed if they try to assert themselves as human beings. Physical retaliation is the primary method of depriving Afro-Americans of their rights.

As the apologetic protest movement was struggling to fill the gap left by the decline of the Wrightian novel in the late 1940s, a different fictional trend made an appearance. Protest elements were relegated to a position of secondary importance by novelists who were more concerned with revealing the individual problems of black characters striving to enter the mainstream of American life. In these accommodationist novels the protagonists do not directly challenge the authority of the whites. They merely attempt to adjust to the special problems created by a hostile world. One of the primary goals is to find a relatively comfortable place in life without altering the society that is controlled by whites. Social aspects are not ignored, but they are not the primary emphasis as in the protest novels. Such writers as William Demby, J. Saunders Redding, Ralph Ellison, and James Baldwin reacted to the overtly propagandistic novels of the era by concentrating on the diversity of the black experience in America. By stressing the unique problems of individuals rather than the evils of racism, the accommodationist authors were generally able to be more objective in their work. Consequently, such prominent novels as Ellison's *Invisible Man* and Baldwin's *Go Tell It on the Mountain* dominated the early 1950s.

While this type of fiction was the major challenge to protest literature, some black authors abandoned racial material completely in an effort to obtain objectivity. The assimilationist novelists, then, by concentrating on white characters, attempted to avoid the label of propagandists. They preferred to become a part of the American literary tradition rather than to become spokesmen for the Afro-American. From an artistic point of view, assimilationism theoretically allowed the author freedom to explore his subject matter without producing a tract. He could portray American life from the viewpoint of a detached observer instead of an embittered victim. The assimilationist novel came into vogue in the 1950s as such former protest and accommodationist writers as Ann Petry, William Gardner Smith, Chester Himes, and James Baldwin experimented in the area; however, these same writers entered the protest realm with later novels. The movement toward a renewed interest in racial pride evolved from the civil rights activities that gained impetus with the growing fame of Martin Luther King, Jr. On almost a reverse ratio the assimilationist trend declined and was virtually abandoned in the 1960s.

The death of assimilationism was accompanied by the rebirth of militant protest. In 1954, the year the U.S. Supreme Court began a new era in civil rights by ruling against segregated schools, John Oliver Killens and William Gardner Smith started a new trend in fiction. The militant protest novel depicts blacks in an organized effort to resist white oppression. Unlike Wrightian protest, in which the protagonist strikes out blindly in an individual act of violence, a planned retaliatory measure is perpetrated. This type of protest novel was first produced by Sutton Griggs. His *Imperium In Imperio* (1899) related how a secret organization of blacks attempted to take over the state of Texas. The novel met with disfavor, however, and militancy was abandoned, with a few exceptions, until its revival by Killens and Smith. The former's *Youngblood* (1954) depicted the rebellion begun by a black laborer in the South who refused, finally, to be cheated by his white employer. Smith's *South Street* (1954) revealed the need for an armed Afro-American organization to combat white violence in the streets of Philadelphia, Pa.

It was not until the 1960s, though, when the American scene was shaken by many violent racial confrontations, that the militant protest novel became popular. The passive tactics of Martin Luther King, Jr., not only challenged the discriminatory practices of much of the country, but also evoked the emergence of such radical leaders as Malcolm X. The latter figure emerged as the archetype of the miltant protagonist in the fiction of John A. Williams, Ronald Fair, James Baldwin, and Sam Greenlee. The militant novels of the period portray violence as a necessary means of shocking whites into realizing that blacks are demanding immediate enactment of their rights, and an end of institutionalized racism. Force is regarded as the only answer to racial oppression in a country that has continually failed to fulfill its obligations to minority groups. The armed revolution depicted in Greenless's *The Spook Who Sat by the Door* (1969) is the ultimate threat to white racism in the militant novel, as well as a gruesome prophecy for the United States.

Along with the emergence of the militant protest novel as a major factor in Afro-American fiction of the 1960s, apologetic protest developed into a more respectable art form. Such young writers as John A. Williams and Ernest J. Gaines gave new life to the trend by presenting protagonists who were less idealized than the typical characters of an earlier era. Rather than dealing with romantic individuals who are destroyed by a white mob, apologetic novelists of the 1960s depicted Afro-Americans who merely tried to escape from poverty and injustice. In rebelling against the denial of their human dignity, they were not the victims of violence, but of the more subtle types of racism. These characters struggled against oppression on an individual basis with a definite goal in mind. Thus, they represent a middle ground between the Wrightian rebels, who commit blind acts of violence, and the organized groups of the militants.

Despite the prevalence of protest fiction in the 1960s, the accommodationist trend also continued to thrive. The number of Afro-American novels increased greatly during this period, and not all of the authors embraced militancy or individual rebellion. As in the previous decade when Ellison and Baldwin led the revolt against protest, accommodationist writers continued to depict the efforts of Afro-Americans to adjust to the middle-class way of life. The typical protagonist, epitomized in Kristin Hunter's *God Bless the Child* (1964), is concerned with moving up the social ladder—in escaping the deprivations of the ghetto. One of the major themes is the quest for an identity within the culture dominated by whites. The movement toward racial pride, so prevalent in protest fiction, is subordinated to the attainment of a relatively comfortable and secure place in American life. Discrimination makes this goal difficult but all the more coveted. The movement toward equality, then, is made within the established rules of conduct rather than through violence or another form of overt challenge to white authority.

The three decades of the Afro-American novel under consideration here consist essentially of three types of protest fiction, as well as accommodationism and assimilationism. James Baldwin's career is perhaps best representative of the novelistic tendencies of the period. He violently objected to the propagandistic intent of *Native Son* and produced *Go Tell It on the Mountain* (1953) as an example of the direction black writers should take. He later changed his attitude by forsaking accommodationism and writing *Giovanni's Room* (1956), a novel with white characters that propagandized for the cause of homosexuality. In the 1960s Baldwin entered the realm of racial protest with *Another Country* (1962), an apologetic novel that revealed how an Afro-American was destroyed by systematic racism. This was followed by a militant book, *Tell Me How Long the Train's Been Gone* (1968). The increasing social commitment of Baldwin, the country's most famous black writer, is indicative of the general mood of black novelists. Once the aesthetic reaction to the pattern protest novel receded, the tendency to concentrate on an exposition of American racist practices ensued. However, the writers have shown, over the years, an ability to combine artistic elements with a social message. The result is that *Native Son*, despite its influence, is no longer the single novel by an

Afro-American to be widely read in this country. Some of the significant American novels since 1950 have been produced by black authors.

REFERENCES: Baker, Houston A., Jr., *Black Literature in America*, McGraw-Hill Book Co., New York, 1971; Bone, Robert A., *The Negro Novel in America*, rev. ed., Yale University Press, New Haven, 1965; Brawley, Benjamin, *The Negro in Literature and Art*, Dodd, Mead, New York, 1929; Brown, Sterling A., "A Century of Negro Portraiture in American Literature," *Massachusetts Review*, Winter 1966; Brown, Sterling A., Arthur P. Davis, and Ulysses Lee (eds.), *The Negro Caravan*, Dryden, New York, 1941; Chapman, Abraham (ed.), *Black Voices*, New American Library, New York, 1968; Corrigan, Robert A., *Afro-American Fiction: A Checklist, 1853–1970*, Midcontinent American Studies Journal, Fall 1970, pp. 114–35; Davis, Arthur P., *From the Dark Tower: Afro-American Writers, 1900 to 1960*, Howard University Press, Washington, D.C., 1974; Ford, Nick Aaron, *The Contemporary Negro Novel, A Study in Race Relations*, Meador Publishing Co., Boston, 1936; Fuller, Hoyt W., "Contemporary Negro Fiction," *Contemporary Southwest Review*, vol. 50, pp. 321–35, 1965; Gloster, Hugh M., *Negro Voices in American Fiction*, University of North Carolina Press, Chapel Hill, 1948; Jackson, Blyden, "The Negro's Image in the Universe as Reflected in His Fiction," *CLA Journal*, September 1960; Loggins, Vernon, *The Negro Author; His Development in America to 1900*, 2d ed., Kennikat Press, Port Washington, 1964; Matthews, Geraldine O., *Black American Writers, 1773–1949: A Bibliography and Union List* (see BIBLIOGRAPHIES/BIOGRAPHIES/GUIDES for a description); O'Daniel, Therman B., (ed.), *James Baldwin: A Critical Evaluation*, Howard University Press, Washington, D.C., 1976; Redding, J. Saunders, "The Problems of the Negro Writer," *Massachusetts Review*, Autumn-Winter 1964–65; Rush, Theressa Gunnels, *Black American Writers Past and Present: A Biographical and Bibliographical Dictionary*, Scarecrow Press, Metuchen, 1975; Schraufnagel, Noel, *The Black American Novel: From Apology to Protest*, Everett/Edwards, Inc., Deland, 1973; Turner, Darwin T., *Afro-American Writers*, Appleton-Century-Crofts, New York, 1970; and Webb, Constance, *Richard Wright, A Biography*, Putman, New York, 1968.

Drama/Theater

History and Development* As early as the mid-eighteenth century, such Negro minstrel companies as the Congo Melodists, the Ethiopian Serenaders, and the Georgia Minstrels were delighting American audiences. Bob Cole's *A Trip to Coontown* (1898) was probably the first show to be organized, produced, and managed by Afro-Americans. By the turn of the century Paul Laurence Dunbar, in collaboration with Will Marion Cook, was producing such successful Broadway theatricals as *Clorindy—the Origin of the Cakewalk* and *Jes Lak White Folks*, titles which clearly bespeak the era. The 1920s saw a spurt in the Afro-American's success in the field of musical comedy, with Broadway productions of Noble Sissle's *Chocolate Dandies* and Miller and Lyle's *Shuffle Along, Runnin' Wild*, and *The Black Birds*. That same period saw the rise to fame of such authentic stars of vaudeville as Bert

*See acknowledgements in the PREFACE.

Williams, Florence Mills, Miller and Lyle, Sissle and Blake, and Bill "Bojangles" Robinson. Though discriminated against, black theatrical entertainers nevertheless found it possible to participate in a sector of the American theater, where they gained considerable prominence and acclaim. This of course does not mean that Afro-Americans did not desire to bring to the more serious side of the theater the same talents that they have demonstrated in the novel, in poetry, and in the lighter side of the theater. In fact a considerable amount of history attests to the black man's determination to establish himself in the great world of the theater. As early as 1821 an actor named James Hewlett formed the African Company in New York City, where he became famous for his performances in Shakespearean roles. In 1833 Ira Aldridge, who entered the theater in this country as a handyman, was appearing on the London, England, stage as Othello opposite Ellen Terry.

Charles Gilpin, who made drama history in 1920 playing the title role of Eugene O'Neill's *The Emperor Jones*, was selected by the New York Drama League, along with David Belasco and Eugene O'Neill, as one of the ten persons who contributed most to the American theater during the year. Paul Robeson, Rutgers University's four-letter man, a member of Phi Beta Kappa, and a graduate of the Columbia University Law School, later won fame in the Gilpin-created role and in O'Neill's *All God's Chillun*. "The Negro is a born actor," wrote George Jean Nathan, and "Robeson, with relatively little experience, and with no training to speak of, is one of the most thoroughly eloquent, impressive, and convincing actors that I have looked at and listened to in the past twenty years of theater going."

Similar accolades went to Leigh Whipper for his Broadway success in John Steinbeck's *Of Mice and Men* and in George Sklar and Paul Peters' *Stevedore*, to Frank Wilson for his role in Paul Green's Pulitzer Prize-winning drama *In Abraham's Bosom*, and to Richard B. Harrison for his masterful portrayal of De Lawd in Marc Connelly's *Green Pastures*. Today the stage artistry of Robert Hooks, Sidney Poitier, and James Earl Jones forms a link with the accomplishments of the great Afro-American performers of the past.

Alain Locke, who in 1927 published an anthology entitled *Plays of Negro Life*, was optimistic about the rise of a national Afro-American theater "where the black playwright and the black actor will interpret the soul of their people

in a way to win the attention and admiration of the world." Through the 1920s and 1930s Afro-Americans, in the spirit of Langston Hughes, did seem to redouble their efforts to "build temples." In 1921 the Howard Players at Howard University (Washington, D.C.) were organized with the hope of establishing a basis for a Little Theater movement among Afro-Americans. The Morgan College Players (Baltimore, Md.), formed by playwright-teacher Randolph Edmonds in 1930, became a distinguished theatrical group. Edmonds also founded the Negro

Opening night at the Lafayette Theater in Harlem, 1936, for a production of *Macbeth* set in Haiti and performed by black actors under the direction of Orson Welles. *(National Archives.)*

Intercollegiate Dramatic Association, which included such predominantly black schools as Morgan State College, Howard University, Virginia State College, Shaw University, North Carolina College at Durham, Lincoln University in Pennsylvania, and North Carolina Agricultural and Technical (A & T) State University. At the same time Fannin Belcher, drama coach at West Virginia State College, was organizing play tournaments among Afro-American high schools in the state "to cultivate in our students a more genuine enthusiasm for drama." [Other drama directors and coaches at black colleges in the 1930s and 1940s included: Frederick W. Bond (West Virginia State College); Arthur C. Lamb (Morgan State University); Thomas D. Pawley (Lincoln University, Missouri); Charles G. Green (North Carolina Agricultural and Technical (A & T) State University); and Mercer Cook and Owen Dodson (Howard University).]

The contagion to perform, to write for, and to become an integral part of the theater spread from black college campuses to black communities across the nation. Drama groups began to spring up—the Gilpin Players in Cleveland, Ohio; the Krigwa Players with ensembles in Washington, D.C., in New York City and on the West Coast; Langston Hughes' Suitcase Theater in New York City; the Rose McClendon Players; the Little Theater of Columbus, Ohio; The Neighborhood Players in Atlantic City, N.J., under the direction of Montgomery Gregory, who with Alain Locke founded the Howard University Players.

Denied access to the full ambience of the theater, yet driven by an understandable urgency to make public their protests, Afro-American playwrights too often have suffered from the twin disasters of racial discrimination and hastily done work. Moreover, the relative preeminence of the black actor over the black playwright is in some degree the result of the public's tendency to regard actors as entertainers, a role traditionally "acceptable" for Afro-Americans. Certainly it can be speculated that the kinds of social involvement attending the function of the playwright, the various contacts in the steps to opening night—the whole sociology of the theater world—restrict the opportunities of a black person. Poets and novelists work in solitude, their task being accomplished when they have had their say; but in the world of the theater, which demands relationships and interaction, the national ritual of race predominates.

From the start Afro-American writers have resisted the restrictions forced on them. William Wells Brown's *The Escape, or a Leap to Freedom* (1858), the first play written in America by an Afro-American, satirized slavery. This play is not known to have been produced, although Brown did give numerous lyceum readings from it. Significantly, while Brown's plays (it is difficult to say how many he wrote, but he read from at least three in his lectures) languished unproduced in America. Victor Séjour, an Afro-American who was born in New Orleans in 1817, achieved a notable success in Europe as playwright and actor. Le Théâtre Français presented Séjour's first play, *Diegarias*, in 1844, and it is believed that the theaters of Paris, France, presented in all some 21 of this black expatriate's works.

Apparently the first successful drama written by a black and interpreted on the stage by black actors was Angeline Grimké's *Rachel*, a play in three acts dealing with the lynching of a girl's father, which was produced in 1916 by the Drama Committee of the National Association for the Advancement of Colored People (NAACP) in Washington, D.C. The tendentious character of the play was evident from the program announcement: "This is the first attempt to use the stage for race propaganda in order to enlighten the American people relative to the lamentable condition of ten millions of colored citizens in this free republic." In April 1917, on the day of America's entrance into World War I, Broadway for the first time witnessed Afro-American actors performing in serious drama, when at the Garden City Theater the all-black Hapgood Players presented Ridgley Torrence's three one-act plays "written for the Negro theatre" (*Granny Maumee*, *The Rider of Dreams*, and *Simon the Cyrenian*). The event marked the beginning of public interest in the legitimate drama of Afro-American life as interpreted by blacks. Six years later, in May 1923, the Colored Folk Theatre, later known as the Ethiopian Art Theater, was organized by Raymond O'Neil in cooperation with Mrs. Sherwood Anderson. It offered such varied theater fare as Oscar Wilde's *Salome*, a jazz interpretation of Shakespeare's *A Comedy of Errors*, and *The Chip Woman's Fortune* by Willis Richardson, a black government clerk who between 1921 and 1927 wrote six plays that were produced.

One of the most talented writers associated with the Harlem Renaissance was Jean Toomer, best known as a writer of fiction (*Cane*), whose almost tragic attempts to turn playwright were frustrated because the techniques he used were regarded as too advanced for the times. *Kabnis* (1923), a play that demonstrates his modernist methods, found no producer. *Balo, A Sketch of Negro Life* (1922), a less mature work dealing with Afro-American peasants in Georgia, was performed by the Howard Players during the 1923–1924 season.

Drama contests sponsored in the 1920s by *Opportunity, A Journal of Negro Life* brought to light several new black playwrights: Frank Wilson, already well known as an actor, who won first prize in 1925 with *Sugar Cane*; John Matheus, a promising literary talent who later turned to college teaching, who won first prize in 1926 with *'Cruiter*, a play that dealt with migrant Afro-American labor from the South after World War I; and Georgia Douglas Johnson, the poet, whose *Plumes* won first prize in 1927.

Almost half the plays contributed to Alain Locke's *Plays of Negro Life* in 1927 were written by Afro-Americans. That most of the white authors in the anthology (Eugene O'Neill, Paul Green, and Ridgley Torrence) were better known than their Afro-American counterparts (Willis Richardson, Frank Wilson, or even Jean Toomer) neither obscured the Afro-Americans' determination to succeed as playwrights nor concealed the progress these black writers had been making in spite of discouraging obstacles. Their achievement could be measured in light years from the days of minstrelsy and coon shows not too many decades before.

The following year, 1928, audiences at the Princess Theater on Broadway were captivated by Frank Wilson's *Meek Mose,* a serious study of Afro-American life. It had been a long journey for Wilson, from postal clerk to the *Opportunity* contests to Broadway as both playwright and actor. In 1929 Wallace Thurman's *Harlem* (written with assistance from William Rapp), which attempted to give an actual reproduction of the average Afro-American's existence in New York City, enjoyed a short run on Broadway before moving to Canada. In 1933 Hall Johnson's *Run Little Chillun* opened on Broadway. A folk play, it was a mixture of fantasy and realism, music and drama, and it revealed Johnson, whose reputation was already high as a composer and choir director, as a dramatist of genuine promise. In spite of weaknesses of plot and the overuse of melodramatic effects, *Run Little Chillun* is still probably one of the best theater works by an Afro-American.

Creation of a Federal Theater Project in 1935 gave Afro-Americans a laboratory for experiment in all areas of the theater. Plays of varying degrees of success devoted to the plight of Afro-Americans were numerous and enjoyed a popularity that was reinforced by the general preoccupation with proletarian art in the 1930s. Project productions of *The Hot Mikado, Haiti,* and *Macbeth* with black casts are still exciting memories. Of the contributions by black playwrights, perhaps the most notable in retrospect were Frank Wilson's *Walk Together Children* (1936), which focused on the race riots and friction that develop when southern black laborers come North, and Augustus Smith and Peter Morrell's powerful depiction in *Turpentine* (1936) of the struggles of workmen, black and white, in the Florida pines. When the Federal Theater Project ended in 1939, it had already served the purposes of revitalizing the interest of Afro-American communities in plays, especially in the larger cities, and had increased the knowledge and interest of black writers and actors in the technique of the theater.

But it is not until we come to Langston Hughes that we find what, without any doubt, has been the most successful and enduring career of any Afro-American playwright. Hughes' *Mulatto,* a study of illicit relationships in the South that centers on the conflict between a mulatto son and his white father, was the first long-run Broadway hit by a black dramatist. Opening at the Vanderbilt Theatre on October 24, 1935, *Mulatto* played continuously until December 9, 1937. Encouraged by this success and loyal to a creative bent that embraced drama, poetry, and the novel, Hughes, unlike many of his contemporaries who after a few militant forays in the theater succumbed to what can only be described as the almost insurmountable difficulties of being a black playwright, continued to write plays for the rest of his life. Thirty years after his first Broadway success, and two years before his death in 1967, Hughes' play *Tambourines to Glory* was running on Broadway. During the intervening years he had courageously accepted the writer's risk of never letting his pen remain idle, and he had steadfastly lived up to his credo that Afro-American artists should express themselves "without fear or shame." The results, in terms of artistry, were not always even. But the passionate confirmation of black life in America in such plays as *Trouble Island, Scottsboro Limited, Angela Herndon Jones,* and *Don't You Want to Be Free?,* not to mention dozens of lesser plays, comprises an honorable legacy to the proletarian drama of this country. Few American playwrights have surpassed the total achievement of Langston Hughes.

Ossie Davis, author of *Purlie Victorious* and

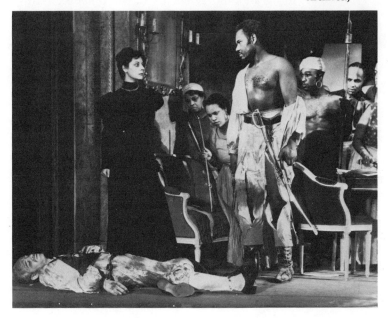

A scene in *Haiti,* a play created by the Federal Theater Project of the Works Progress Administration (1930s), starring Elena Karem (left) and Rex Ingram (right) and performed at the Copley Theatre. *(WPA, National Archives.)*

an astute commentator on the theater, remarked in the early 1970s that "No one can deny that integration has come to Broadway ... that the Negro is now included, meaningfully, in more aspects of Broadway life." *Anna Lucasta* still remains one of the all-time record holders for Broadway runs of straight plays and Paul Robeson's *Othello* holds the record for the Broadway run of a Shakespearean play. Yet Davis is quick to confess "that while there are no impediments to plays about the truth of Negro experiences being produced on Broadway, such productions so far have not succeeded—have not been 'hits' in the sense that *Anna Lucasta* was." The hope that Afro-Americans would be included in the mainstream of American theater, Davis confesses, "has been realized in form, but defeated in substance." Davis disclosed that his own play, *Purlie Victorious,* a stunning comedy-satire on race nonrelations, was kept on Broadway for seven and one-half months with money out of his own pocket and that of his sympathetic producer.

Integration Drama of the 1950s In addition to *Purlie Victorious,* several other important Afro-American plays were produced in the 1950s. Louis Peterson's *Take a Giant Step,* which opened on Broadway in September 1953, tells the poignant story of Spencer Scott, a black youth growing up in the North, and the problems he faces with his white friends. He is thrown out of school after challenging his history teacher about a statement she has made about blacks. His parents strongly condemn him, but his grandmother comes to his defense, telling his parents they were to blame about "that bull" of "staying in place." Spencer represents a kind of "giant step forward" in black characterization, for as he comes of age at the end of the play, he determines to live his own life, free from the white boys of the neighborhood, concentrating on his studies and his music.

In Splendid Error by William Branch ran for three months Off Broadway at the Greenwich Mews Theater in late 1954 and early 1955. It is the story of a little-known incident in the life of Frederick Douglass in which he split with John Brown over the question of tactics just before the raid on Harper's Ferry. The play takes place in the parlor of Douglass' home in Rochester, N.Y., before and after the raid. While some saw the work as a plea for moderation in the civil rights struggle, it is actually about two different ways

of fighting for a cause, and expresses admiration for Brown's efforts.

Trouble in Mind by Alice Childress ran Off-Broadway in 1955, and was revived afterward. It was optioned for Broadway but withdrawn by the author when the producer insisted on trying to turn it into a "heartwarming little story," which it clearly is not. It is a story about the racial conflicts among members of a predominantly black cast during the rehearsals of a topical play on civil rights during part of a week in 1957. It ends on a note of, perhaps, optimism when director Al Manners (white) says, "I, a prejudiced man, ask you, a prejudiced cast, to wait until our prejudiced author arrives tomorrow. I propose that we sit down in mutual blindness and try to find a way to bring some splinter of truth to a prejudiced audience."

A Land Beyond the River by Loften Mitchell opened in 1957 at the Greenwich Mews Theater for a ten-week run, played for most of a year, and then went on tour. It is based on the experiences of Rev. Joseph A. DeLaine, who brought a case to court in South Carolina in 1949 asking for bus transportation for children. The appeal was one of the cases decided by the U.S. Supreme Court in its May 17, 1954, decision outlawing segregation. While the case was before the courts, DeLaine was attacked and his church was burned down. After being shot at, he fled to New York City for asylum; an attempt was made to have him extradited for supposedly having shot at a group of white persons. He was cleared of the charges in a New York City court on January 16, 1956. Mitchell learned of the case from Ossie Davis, who urged him to write a full-length play based on the story. With the assistance of DeLaine, then a Brooklyn pastor, Mitchell did so.

The major conflict of the play is between DeLaine, representing a large portion of the black population, and Reverend Cloud, the school superintendent who supports the white establishment. A secondary conflict is between DeLaine and a school principal, Philip Turnham, who represents "Uncle Tomism" at its most sophisticated level. While DeLaine cannot be easily categorized or labeled, his position is in line with the prevailing civil rights attitudes of the 1950s: that is, to use the system in a nonviolent manner in order to bring about changes.

The most outstanding integrationist drama of the period—and perhaps of all Afro-American drama—is Lorraine Hansberry's *A Raisin in the Sun.*

Lorraine Hansberry's *A Raisin in the Sun** The author of two Broadway plays, *A Raisin in the Sun* and *A Sign in Sidney Brustein's Window*, Lorraine Hansberry had become something of a legend before her death at the early age of 34. In her intensity, in her compassion, and in her ardent defense of and concern with the lowly and oppressed, she embodied and articulated in her works the best spirit of the young of her time. Martin Luther King, Jr., said of her: "Her commitment of spirit . . . her creative literary ability and her profound grasp of the deep social issues confronting the world today will remain an inspiration to generations yet unborn."

Born in Chicago, Ill., in 1930, Lorraine Hansberry was the daughter of successful and highly respected middle-class parents. After graduating from Englewood High School, where she became interested in drama, she studied for two years at the University of Wisconsin. Hansberry subsequently studied painting at the Art Institute of Chicago, Roosevelt College (Chicago, Ill.), and in Guadalajara, Mexico. Finding that her interests and talent were not in art, she went to New York City in 1950 and began what was to be her life work, her career as a writer.

Before her writing began to pay off, Hansberry worked at various jobs. Among other things, she was a clerk in a department store, aide to a young theatrical producer, waitress, hostess, and cashier in a restaurant run by the family of Robert Nemiroff, songwriter and music publisher. She married Nemiroff in 1953. Lorraine Hansberry died of cancer in 1965.

A Raisin in the Sun, after successful tryouts in Philadelphia, New Haven, and Chicago, opened on Broadway on March 11, 1959 and proceeded to win the 1958–1959 New York Drama Critics Award. Significantly it won over entries by Tennessee Williams, Eugene O'Neil, and Archibald MacLeish. Claudia MacNeill, Diana Sands, and Sidney Poitier (in his first Broadway starring role) played the principal parts in this popular play.

A Raisin in the Sun (the title taken from a Langston Hughes poem), like Ossie Davis' successful play, *Purlie Victorious*, has, among its other virtues, that of humor. In recent years this quality has not been found too often in Afro-American drama. Since 1960, most Afro-American writing about the ghetto have forgotten how

*See acknowledgements in the PREFACE.

to laugh. In her doubled-edged attack on blacks and whites alike in *A Raisin in the Sun*, Hansberry joined Dunbar, Schuyler, Hughes, Fisher, Sterling Brown, and other black writers who dipped into that unique and richly supplied reservoir of race humor that the black author has at his disposal.

A Raisin in the Sun, however, is not just a humorous play. It is far more than that. In this heartwarming drama of urban Afro-American life in the North, Hansberry made use—and often brilliant use—of several basic themes, which if handled with any degree of skill, are guaranteed "good theater." The first of these was black motherhood. Mama in this play is not only a strong and appealing character; she also symbolizes the courage, the unselfishness, the resourcefulness, and the endurance that black mothers had to possess if their families were to survive. Black literature after about 1960 has glorified the black woman in poetry and fiction as well as in drama, but few of the more recent portraits have been as effective as Hansberry's Mama.

Another appealing and foolproof theme used by the dramatist was that of the generation gap. Mama—with her old-fashioned common sense and her tried ways of tolerantly listening to the young folk, correcting them when they were wrong, praising and encouraging them when right—dramatizes this relationship between the generations. One of the high points in the play— actually, one of the most effective scenes in

Lorraine Hansberry. *(Schomburg Collection, New York Public Library.)*

Raisin in the Sun starred Claudia MacNeill (left), Sidney Poitier (center), and Diana Sands (right). *(Schomburg Collection, New York Public Library.)*

Afro-American drama—is found in Act I, Scene i, when Mama slaps Beneatha for denying the existence of God. This is a powerful scene. The appeal of the generation gap is enhanced by the religious conflict involved.

Another basic theme in *A Raisin in the Sun* is typically American: the mobility pattern, the upward move of family, manifested spiritually in the better education of the children and physically in the change to a better neighborhood. In this case the basic appeal is strengthened by the race issue. The questions involved go beyond mere housing. It is still the fight of the ambitious poor—whether black or white—to make a better world for the next generation, a conflict that is always with us.

In addition to the "basic" appeals, *A Raisin in the Sun* intrigues the reader and theatergoer because though written in 1958, just before the so-called New Black Renaissance, it looks forward to that movement. The identity theme is there, represented in Beneatha's searching for meaning as a young black girl. The African theme, one that is now so popular, is presented there through the portrait of Asagai, the Nigerian student. The dignity theme, the kind of dignity that old, proud black families have, is there. There is a kind of old-fashioned race pride that is without excessive militancy, without high-sounding rhetoric. When Walter, after learning his lesson the hard way, finds himself, he falls back on the family tradition. He tells Mr. Lindner, who had come to buy him off: "What I am telling you is that we called you over here to tell you that we are very proud and that this is—this is my son, who makes the sixth generation of our family in this country, and that we have all thought about your offer and we have decided to move into our house because my father—my father—he earned it."

This fusing of the old, solid elements in Afro-American life with the promise of the new is beautifully and effectively done by Hansberry. The spirit of *A Raisin in the Sun* is integrationist and quite unlike that of black nationalist drama of the 1960s (that is, most of it); but the work is still appealing, it is still "good theater."

Speaking of black nationalism, Hansberry had, as all who knew her attest, a deep and militant interest in her people, but she never wanted to think of Afro-Americans as being apart from the mainstream. A well-meaning critic once told her that *A Raisin in the Sun* was not "really a Negro play; why this could be about anybody! It's a play about people!" Hansberry's answer was:

Imamu Amiri Baraka, poet, playwright, and novelist. *(Photo by Leroy Henderson.)*

"Well, I hadn't noticed the contradiction because I'd always been under the impression that Negroes *are* people."

Hansberry felt that the artist should write specifically about his subject, as specifically as he can. If he does it well, he will create universal literature. As for *Raisin in the Sun*, Hansberry says, in effect, yes, "it is definitely a Negro play before it is anything else." but it is also more than just that.

The Black Arts Movement Although the Black Arts Movement flowered during the 1960s, its roots extend backward to Alain Locke and W. E. B. Du Bois. It was a movement characterized by expression of a positive black image, conceived and controlled by blacks. Its slogans could be summarized as follows: "Black is beautiful" and "I'm black and I'm proud." During this time new artists and critics came into prominence.

The central figure and spiritual leader was, without doubt, Imamu Amiri Baraka, who began his career as LeRoi Jones. His play *Dutchman* (1963) represented a first step in the development of a black consciousness. The plot is direct: a white woman, Lula, meets a typically middle-class Negro, Clay, on a subway car. She entices and provokes him, and he is tempted. When she then insults him to an intolerable point, he lashes out at her in highly emotional language, drops the facade of a well-mannerd Negro, and tells her what he thinks of white people in general and of her in particular. Lula, outraged, then stabs and kills Clay, and his body is thrown from the subway car. Baraka implies that America will destroy any truly threatening black; thus, blacks must take action on their threats, or collectively they will end up as victims of white oppression, like Clay.

The character who comes full force and full turn from intergrationist to black revolutionary is Walker Vessels in Baraka's *The Slave* (1964). In this play, Walker returns to his former white wife, Grace, now married to a white college professor, Easley, who is the perfect symbol of the white liberal—a symbol that constantly reappears in black revolutionary literature. The confrontation between these three principal characters encapsulates the major arguments for and against black power and black nationalism. Walker, now firmly committed to a total black revolution in America, argues against the neatly packaged, seemingly correct arguments of Grace and Easley. He calls for "No social protest . . . right is in the act!"

The novelist James Baldwin wrote two significant and controversial plays in the 1960s, *Blues* and *Amen Corner*. *Blues* was based on the celebrated Emmett Till murder case of the 1950s. Baldwin's *Amen Corner* deals with an evangelist, Sister Margaret; her son, David; her husband; and a series of characters associated with her church. The action of the play reveals Margaret's own coming to the full awareness that one cannot merely give lip service to the principles of Christianity; one must truly live them. The fact that Margaret is put out of her church is less important than her arrival at a satisfactory and comfortable spiritual position at the end. Her triumph is as a person, not as a religious leader.

A prolific writer (more than three dozen plays), Ed Bullins is also known as a critic, editor, and a director of the New Lafayette Theatre in New York City. One of his most arresting plays is *In the Wine Time* (1966), a lyrical play whose central character, Ray, is a young man who dreams of and sees, passing his corner each and every day during his last wine time, a girl "wearing a light summer dress with big pockets, in small ballerina slippers, swinging her head back and to the side all special like, hearing a private melody in her head." Ray wishes to leave the confines of his aunt's home to find himself as a man. At the end of the play, he finds himself a wiser but sadder young man whose dreams of love are already unfulfilled. In this and other plays, Bullins established himself as a playright who is concerned with the lifestyles of the black people, the search for love, and the need for black unity and collective survival.

Ceremonies in Dark Old Men (1965) by Lonnie Elder III and *No Place To Be Somebody* (1969) by Charles Gordone were two outstanding plays of the late 1960s. A memorable and lyrical play, *Ceremonies* was first produced by the Negro Ensemble Company. It won a series of awards, including the Stanley Drama Award, the Yale Award, the Joseph E. Levine Award, and the Bishop K. Hamilton Award. Richard Watts of the New York *Post* called it "the best American play of the season."

Lindsay Patterson regarded *No Place To Be Somebody* as "the most vital play (black or white) to come out of the sixties." First produced in May 1969 at the New York Shakespeare Festival Public Theater in New York City, the play won a Drama Desk Award in 1969. The next year it was awarded the Pulitzer Prize in drama, the first Pulitzer Prize ever won by a black playwright.

The 1970s The opening years of the 1970s saw a dramatic increase in the number of successful black plays and playwrights. The Afro-American Studio successfully produced a play written in 1968, *El Haji Malik*. The New Heritage Theater produced two one-act plays by Alice Childress, *Mojo* and *Wine in the Wilderness* (November 1970). The Negro Ensemble Company went a step further than many of its fellow theaters and organized a series of plays under the heading of "Themes of the Black Struggle." Perhaps the

A scene from *The River Niger* by Joseph Walker in the production by the Black Theater Alliance/Negro Ensemble Company that was well received by audiences and critics. *(Photo by Bert Andrews.)*

most significant play of this series was Joseph Walker's *Ododo*. Joseph Walker was a co-founder and co-director of the Demi-Gods, one of the three theaters housed in a former brewery complex on 127th Street in New York City's Harlem, later named the Afro-American Studio Center. In some aspects, *Ododo* (the word means "truth" in Yoruba) traces the history of black people through the use of poetry, music, and dance. Walker also wrote *The River Niger*, the great artistic success of the 1973 Broadway season that found warm responses on tour in American cities.

Melvin Van Peebles was a successful artist of the 1970s whose film *Sweet Sweetback's Bad-asssss Song* (1971) ignited a popular explosion in motion pictures. Like his film, his three plays are controversial but all have been produced on Broadway: *Ain't Supposed to Die a Natural Death, Don't Bother Me I Can't Cope*, and *Don't Play Us Cheap*. His dramas follow the general tradition of the musically oriented play, though with important differences. *Ain't Supposed* is a tableau of the aspects of the modern black ghetto, and its characters are typical of the many kinds of people who inhabit such communities as Harlem and Watts.

Other plays of the 1970s included: *The Life and Times of J. Walter Smitheus* by Edgar White; *Jazznite* and *The Boston Party at Annie Mae's House* by Walter Jones; *Sty of the Blind Pig* by Martie Charles; *Black Terror* by Richard Wesley; and *Black Girl* by J. E. Franklin.

Vinnie Burrows (left), affiliate member of the Black Theater Alliance, with Ernie McClintock (center), president of the Alliance and director of the Afro-American Studio Theater, and Joan Sandler (right), director of the Alliance. *(Photo by Ronnie Braithwaite, Black Theater Alliance.)*

Conclusion Like other institutions in American life, the theater remained essentially segregated until the 1950s and 1960s. Both participants and spectators were exposed to discrimination and racism. The American stage in general and most theaters in particular were not receptive to blacks, except on a discriminatory basis, during the segregation era. However, many well-known commercial black theaters, patronized by Afro-American performers and the theatergoers, existed, especially in the large cities: the Lafayette and Apollo in New York City; the Howard and Lincoln in Washington, D.C.; the Pekin and Savoy in Chicago, Ill.; the Royal in Baltimore, Md; the Comet in St. Louis, Mo.; and the Karamu in Cleveland, Ohio. Despite popular and lively entertainment (mostly musical), theaters entered a period of decline with the coming of integration. Although the commercial houses were sig-

nificant, widespread performance continued in local churches, high schools, colleges, community halls, and clubs.

Regardless of the staging, Afro-American theater remained a source of pride and enjoyment, segregation and discrimination notwithstanding. Playwrights, performers, and directors—and the theater collectively, especially vocal in its black playwrights—put forth efforts to overcome discrimination and racism. The Black Arts Movement, for example, flourished in the 1960s and 1970s. Many playwrights and interested groups developed community theaters throughout the nation, especially in New York City (such as the National Black Theater, under Barbara Ann Teer; the New Heritage Repertory Theater, under Roger Furman; the East River Players, under Mical Whittaker; and the New Lafayette Theater). Thirteen of New York City's community-based theaters in the early 1970s were formed into the Black Theater Alliance under Joan Sandler and Marc Primus. Such groups turned out several noteworthy productions (including *The River Niger*) that were warmly received by both black critics and black audiences. *See also* CIVIL RIGHTS; DISCRIMINATION; MUSIC; NATIONALISM.

REFERENCES: Many references exist, but there is no single definitive volume treating either drama or the theater. The best bibliographic reference is Reardon, William R. and Thomas D. Pawley (eds.), *The Black Theatre and the Dramatic Arts: A Dialogue, Bibliography and Anthology*, Negro Universities Press, Westport, 1970. A bibliographic checklist of plays dealing with blacks is Hatch, James V., *Black Image on the American Stage: A Bibliography of Plays and Musicals, 1770–1970*, DBS Publications, Inc., New York, 1970. For brief descriptions of these two bibliographic references, see BIBLIOGRAPHIES/BIOGRAPHIES/GUIDES.

Older treatments, mainly narrative, are helpful: Bond, Frederick W., *The Negro and the Drama*, Associated Publishers, Washington, D.C., 1940; Isaacs, Edith J. R., *The Negro in the American Theatre*, (rev. ed.), McGrath, New York, 1968; Richardson, Willis, (ed.), *Plays and Pageants from the Life of the Negro*, Associated Publishers, Washington, D.C., 1940.

Newer references (narratives and anthologies) include: Bullins, Ed (ed.), *Four Dyamite Plays*, William Morrow, New York, 1971; Couch, William, Jr. (ed.), *New Black Playwrights*, Louisiana State University Press, Baton Rouge, 1968; Davis, Arthur P., *From the Dark Tower: Afro-American Writers, 1900–1960*, Howard University Press, Washington, D.C., 1974; Jones, LeRoi and Larry Neal (eds.), *Black Fire: An Anthology of Afro-American Writing*, William Morrow, New York, 1968; Jones, LeRoi, *Four Black Revolutionary Plays*, Bobbs-Merrill, New York, 1969; Mitchell, Loften, *Black Drama: The Story of the American Negro in the Theatre*, Hawthorne Books, New York, 1967; Patterson, Lindsay (eds.), *Black Theatre: A Twentieth Century Collection of the Works of Its Best Playwrights*, Dodd, Mead, New York, 1971; Ross, Ronald, "The Role of the Blacks in the Federal Theatre, 1935–1939." *Journal of Negro History*, January 1974, pp. 38–50; Thomas, Bettye and Bettye Gardner, "The Cultural

Impact of the Howard Theatre on the Black Community," *Journal of Negro History*, October 1970, pp. 253–265; and Turner, Darwin T., *Black Drama in America: An Anthology*, Fawcett, New York, 1971.

LITTLE, MALCOLM See MALCOLM X.

LIVINGSTONE COLLEGE Livingstone College, at Salisbury, N.C., was founded in 1879 by the African Methodist Episcopal Zion (AMEZ) Church. It was named in honor of David Livingstone, the explorer. A small, church-related school, Livingstone offers the bachelor's degree and provides liberal arts curriculum, although its program also includes teacher education and professional preparation. Its 1975 enrollment was 750.

The college is fully accredited by the Southern Association of Colleges and Secondary Schools. It generally offers a summer program in communications skills for junior and senior high school students who need strengthening in this area before attempting college work.

LOCKE, ALAIN LEROY (1886–1954), educator; born in Philadelphia, Pa. Locke received a B.A. degree (1907) and his Ph.D. degree (1918) from Harvard University. He was also a Rhodes Scholar (1907–10). He taught at and was chairman of the department of philosophy at Howard University (Washington, D.C.) for more than 40 years. Locke wrote many articles and several books, including *The New Negro* (1925); *The Negro in America* (1933); *The Negro and His Music* (1936, 1969); *Negro Art: Past and Present* (1936, 1969); and *The Negro in Art* (1941, 1970). He edited *Plays of Negro Life* (1927, 1970) with Montgomery Gregory and *When Peoples Meet: A Study in Race and Culture Contact* (1941) with Bernhard J. Stern. His work on black culture, left unfinished at his death, was completed by Margaret Just Butcher and published as *The Negro in American Culture* (1956, 1972). Locke's great contribution was that of an interpreter and promoter of black culture. Locke was a member of Phi Beta Kappa and the American Negro Academy. See also LITERATURE: DRAMA/ THEATER.

LOCKER, JESSE DWIGHT (1891–1955) lawyer, government official; born in Cincinnati, Ohio. Locker graduated from Howard University Law School (Washington, D.C.) in 1915. He began practicing law in 1916 and eventually special-

ized as a trial lawyer. In 1941 he was elected to the city council of Cincinnati, Ohio, and he retained his seat for more than ten years. In 1953 Locker was appointed U.S. ambassador to Liberia.

LODGES See FRATERNAL SOCIETIES.

LOGAN, FRENISE A. (1920–   ), historian; born in Albany, Ga. He received an A.B. degree (1943) from Fisk University and his M.A. (1948) and Ph.D. (1953) degrees from Western Reserve University. He taught history at North Carolina College, Bennett, and A & T, predominantly black colleges in North Carolina. His writings have appeared in several professional journals, and he authored a volume entitled *The Negro in North Carolina, 1876-1894* (1964).

LOGAN, RAYFORD W. (1897–   ), historian; born in Washington, D.C. Logan received a B.A. degree (1917) and his M.A. degree (1929) from Williams College (Williamstown, Mass), received his Ph.D. degree from Harvard University in 1936, and was awarded an honorary LL.D. degree from Williams College in 1965. He taught history at both Virginia Union University and Atlanta University before joining the faculty of Howard University (Washington, D.C.) in 1938. In 1942 Logan became head of the department of history at Howard University. He was an editor of the *Journal of Negro History* and *Negro History Bulletin*. Logan is best known for his studies of Africa and Afro-Americans: *Diplomatic Relations of the United States with Haiti* (1941); *The Negro and the Post-War World, A Primer* (1945); *The African Mandates in World Politics* (1948); *The Negro in American Life and Thought; The Nadir 1877–1901* (1954), expanded and revised as *The Betrayal of the Negro; From Rutherford B. Hayes to Woodrow Wilson* (1965).

LOMAX-HANNON COLLEGE Lomax-Hannon college, at Greenville, Ala., was founded in 1893 by the African Methodist Episcopal Zion Church (AMEZ). One of its early presidents was Smart B. Boyd. Beginning as an industrial school, the college has developed a two-year associate's program applicable toward the bachelor's degree. In the mid-1970s the student enrollment was approximately 142.

LOMAX, LOUIS EMANUEL (1922–70), author, journalist, educator; born in Valdosta, Ga.

Lomax received a B.A. degree from Paine College (Augusta, Ga.) in 1942 and then joined the staff of the Baltimore *Afro-American*. He did graduate work at American University (Washington, D.C.) before teaching philosophy at Georgia State College in Savannah, and then went to Yale University for further graduate work. He became a staff writer for the Chicago *American* (later *Chicago Today*), and in 1958 Lomax became a newscaster for WNTA-TV in New York City, the first black journalist to hold such a position. Lomax was professor of humanities and social science at Hofstra University (Hempstead, N.Y.) in 1970 when he was killed in an auto crash. His books include: *When the Word is Given: A Report on Elijah Muhammad, Malcolm X, and the Black Muslim World* (1963); *Thailand: The War That Is, The War That Will Be* (1967); and *To Kill a Black Man* (1968).

LONG, HERMAN HODGE (1912–1976), educator; born in Birmingham, Ala. Long received a B.A. degree from Talladega College (Talladega, Ala.) in 1935, a M.A. degree from Hartford School of Religious Education in 1936, and his Ph.D. degree from the University of Michigan in 1949. He taught at Miles College (Birmingham, Ala.) from 1937 to 1939, was field representative for the race relations department of the American Missionary Association (AMA), and became president of Talladega College in 1964. He wrote *People Verus Property* with Charles S. Johnson and *An American City in Transition: The Baltimore Self-Study on Human Relations.*

LONG, JEFFERSON (1836–1900), U.S. Representative; born near Knoxville, Ga. Long was self-educated. After working in the shop of a merchant tailor, he opened his own tailoring business in Macon, Ga. In 1869 he won the Republican Party congressional nomination to fill a vacancy in the U.S. House of Representatives, and he was elected a representative to the Forty-first Congress, having campaigned for enforcement of the 15th Amendment. Long served only one term and in 1871 returned to his business in Macon. He was the only Afro-American from the state of Georgia to serve in the U.S. Congress in the nineteenth century.

LOOBY, Z. ALEXANDER (1899–1971), educator, public official, civil rights leader; born in Antigua, British West Indies. The young Looby came to the United States in 1914. His education prepared him for a legal career that he began in

1928. In addition to his practice, Looby taught law, medical jurisprudence, and business administration in various colleges through the years, and was a city councilman in Nashville, Tenn., for 20 years. Noted for his work in pioneer civil rights cases throughout the 1950s, he was director of the Legal Defense Division of the National Association for the Advancement of Colored People (NAACP). As such, he defended students arrested in sit-in demonstrations in the early 1960s.

LOUIS, JOE (1911–   ), pugilist, born Joseph Louis Barrow in Chambers County, Ala. Louis' family moved to Detroit, Mich., when he was ten, and it was there that he began a distinguished career as an amateur boxer, eventually winning 54 of 58 matches. In his professional

career, beginning in 1934, Louis won 68 of 71 bouts, 54 by knockouts, and two of his defeats occurred at the very end of his career following his retirement. Louis won the heavyweight title in 1937 when he knocked out Jim Braddock in the eighth round. When he retired in 1949 Louis was undefeated as champion, and one of his successful title defenses was against Max Schmeling, the German boxer who had beaten him in 1936. His autobiography, *My Life Story*, was published in 1947. Louis entered the Boxing Hall of Fame in 1954. *See also* ATHLETES: BOXING.

LOVE, EDGAR AMOS (1891–?), Methodist bishop; born in Harrisonburg, Va. Love was educated at Morgan College (Baltimore, Md.) and received a B.A. degree (1913) and a B.D. degree (1916), from Howard University (Washington, D.C.) and his S.T.B. degree from Boston University in 1918. Ordained to the Methodist ministry in 1915, he served churches in Pennsylvania, Maryland, and West Virginia from 1921 to 1933, and was district superintendent of the Washington

Far right: This medallion celebrates Joe Louis' successful rematch with Max Schmeling. The event was regarded by many as a contest between democracy and Nazism, between the "black" Louis and the "aryan" Schmeling. The medallion was produced in 1973 by the International Numismatic Agency and minted by the Medallic Art Company, both in New York City. It was designed by Paul Calle and executed by Joseph DiLorenzo (Courtesy of Milton Fenster Associates, Inc.)

Conference of Methodist Churches from 1933 to 1940. From 1952 to 1964 Love was the Methodist bishop of Baltimore, Md.

LOVE, NAT (DEADWOOD DICK) (1854–1921), cowboy; born near Nashville, Tenn. Love worked on his father's small farm and on surrounding plantations until 1869, when he headed west to join his fortunes with the cowboys of Dodge City, Kans. Soon he was working on the Duval Ranch in Texas, then after three years at the Gillinger Ranch in Arizona. Love became a matchless range rider, involved in gun battles with Indians and bandits; his expert marksmanship made him well known in the West as "Deadwood Dick," a title he won in open competition in Deadwood, S.D., on July 4, 1876. In 1889 he married, left the range, and became a Pullman porter on the Denver and Rio Grande Railroad. His autobiography, *The Life and Adventures of Nat Love, Better Known in Cattle Country as Deadwood Dick,* was published in 1907.

LOW, W. A. (GUS) *See* PREFACE: LIST OF CONTRIBUTORS.

LUNCEFORD, JIMMIE (1902–47), bandleader; born in Fulton, Mo. Lunceford studied at Fisk University (Nashville, Tenn.) and at the College of the City of New York. Lunceford became proficient on all reed instruments, and in the late 1920s organized a band. He opened at the Cotton Club in New York City in 1933 and rapidly established his own image and style in the field of jazz. His band, known for its discipline, became one of the greatest of all jazz bands, and Lunceford's style influenced many arrangers and bandleaders throughout the 1950s and 1960s. *See also* MUSIC: JAZZ.

LUTHERANS The Lutherans are a religious group with a small Afro-American membership. According to George F. Harkins, secretary of the Lutheran Church in America (with a reported clergy of 7,295 in 1970), there were 17 Afro-American pastors in June 1971: Winston S. Bone (Jamaica, N.Y.); Lynell Hampton Carter (Winnipeg, Canada); Vernon E. Carter (Boston, Mass.); Edward Dixon (Philadelphia, Pa.); Rudolph R. Featherstone (Norwood, Mass.); James E. Gunther (New York, N.Y.); Massie L. Kennard (Chicago, Ill.); Samuel A. Lewis (Jamaica, N.Y.); Cyril A. Lucas (Sacramento, Calif.); John A. Parkinson (Philadelphia, Pa.); Claude T. Peterson (Philadelphia, Pa.); Jesse W. Routte (retired, Staten Island, N.Y.); Robin W. Skyles, III (Chicago, Ill.); James H. Somersille (Washington, D.C.); Harold W. Varner (Palo Alto, Calif.); Lee H. Wesley (New York, N.Y.); and Allen G. Youngblood (Cleveland, Ohio). *See also* CHURCHES.

LYNCH, HOLLIS RALPH See PAN-AFRICANISM.

LYNCH, JOHN ROY (1847-1939), state legislator, U.S. Representative, author; born in Concordia Parish, La. Lynch grew up a slave in Natchez, Miss. After his emancipation, he managed a successful photographic studio in Natchez. In 1867 Lynch was named a justice of the peace by the Republican governor of the state, and in 1869 he became a member of the Mississippi house of representatives. At 24 he was elected speaker of the house, and in 1872 he was elected to the U.S. House of Representatives, where he served for two terms. He is remembered for his support of the 1875 Civil Rights Act that banned discrimination in public accommodations. Lynch wrote *The Facts of Reconstruction* (1913).

Nat Love. *(Library of Congress.)*

LYNCHING The atmosphere of racism and violence in the United States in general, and in particular in the South, provided the breeding ground for the lynching of Afro-Americans. The South had a tradition of active militancy, as the historian John Hope Franklin noted in his *The Militant South, 1800–1860* (1956). It was also a region in which the old master-slave psychology lingered long after the constitutional death of slavery. Gunnar Myrdal suggested in his great study (*An American Dilemma,* 1944) that whites lynched blacks because of fear of losing status and racial supremacy.

Whatever the cause, Afro-Americans were the chief victims of southern vigilance. The table that follows, taken from statistics compiled by Tuskegee Institute (Tuskegee Institute, Ala.) shows the number of blacks lynched between 1882 and 1968. By the latter date, lynching had virtually ceased and records were no longer kept by Tuskegee.

Though Tuskegee took care to record these statistics, no doubt the numbers should be upgraded for blacks. Victimized by lynchings, many blacks simply disappeared, and relatives or friends, fearing reprisal, kept silent. Occasionally, somewhere in the rural South, a body may have turned up, black but otherwise unidentified, suggesting that the victim had been lynched or murdered. Such was the revelation in Jasper County, Ga., in 1921. It so happened that a white boy discovered a body near Allen's Bridge in Newton County. The crowd that gathered speculated about the identity of the slain man and thought that neighboring Jasper County would be the place to look for further information. "County pride and a conscionable group of local officers," explains Pete Daniel in his *The Shadow of Slavery: Peonage in the South, 1901–1969* (1972), "combined to launch one of the South's most unusual murder cases." One of the most unusual aspects of the subsequent cases was that they were brought to light and even into court.

Moreover, statistics on lynchings do not reveal the pervasive atmosphere of terror and sadism, the near-victims who escaped, or the threats of lynching or violence that were always held over the heads of Afro-Americans in many areas of the South. *See also* CIVIL DISORDERS, 1861–1917; NATIONAL ASSOCIATION FOR THE ADVANCEMENT OF COLORED PEOPLE (NAACP); RACE: RACISM; WELLS, IDA B.

REFERENCES: Guzman, Jessie P., Vera Chandler Foster, and W. Hardin Hughes (eds.), *Negro Year Book; A Review of Events Affecting Negro Life, 1941–1946*, Tuskegee Institute, Tuskegee, 1947, pp. 302–11. Records of lynchings have appeared in various issues of this publication since its beginning in 1912; Myrdal, Gunnar, *An American Dilemma*, Harper, New York, 1944; Raper, Arthur, *The Tragedy of Lynching in the United States*, University of North Carolina Press, Chapel Hill, 1933; White, Walter F., *Rope and Faggot: A Biography of Judge Lynch*, Alfred A. Knopf, New York, 1929;

and Williams, Daniel T., "The Lynching Records at Tuskegee Institute," in *Eight Negro Bibliographies*, Kraus Reprint, New York, 1969. This is the best bibliography on the subject.

LYNK, MILES V. (1871– ?), physician; born near Brownsville, Tenn. Lynk received his M.D. degree from Meharry Medical College (Nashville, Tenn.) in 1891. Intently interested in a forum for the expression of medical findings and the opinions of black physicians, he founded and published *The Medical and Surgical Observer* in 1892, the first black medical journal in the United States. In 1900 Lynk founded the Medical College of the University of West Tennessee, and he operated it until it closed in 1923. He was one of the founders and an ardent supporter of the National Medical Association.

Indiana was the scene of these lynchings, which took place in the 1920s. *(Library of Congress.)*

LYNCHING BY STATES, 1882–1968

State	Whites	Blacks	Total
Alabama	48	299	347
Arizona	31	0	31
Arkansas	58	226	284
California	41	2	43
Colorado	65	3	68
Delaware	0	1	1
Florida	25	257	282
Georgia	39	492	531
Idaho	20	0	20
Illinois	15	19	34
Indiana	33	14	47
Iowa	17	2	19
Kansas	35	19	54
Kentucky	63	142	205
Louisiana	56	335	391
Maine	1	0	1
Maryland	2	27	29
Michigan	7	1	8
Minnesota	5	4	9
Mississippi	42	539	581
Missouri	53	69	122
Montana	82	2	84
Nebraska	52	5	57
Nevada	6	0	6
New Jersey	1	1	2
New Mexico	33	3	36
New York	1	1	2
North Carolina	15	86	101
North Dakota	13	3	16
Ohio	10	16	26
Oklahoma	82	40	122
Oregon	20	1	21
Pennsylvania	2	6	8
South Carolina	4	156	160
South Dakota	27	0	27
Tennessee	47	204	251
Texas	141	352	493
Utah	6	2	8
Vermont	1	0	1
Virginia	17	83	100
Washington	25	1	26
West Virginia	20	28	48
Wisconsin	6	0	6
Wyoming	30	5	35
Total	1,297	3,446	4,743

MADGETT, NAOMI LONG *See* LITERATURE: POETRY.

MADISON, ROBERT P. (1923–   ), architect; born in Cleveland, Ohio. Madison received a bachelor of architecture degree from Case Western Reserve University (Cleveland, Ohio) in 1948 and his master of architecture degree from Harvard University in 1952. He was later a Fulbright Scholar and research fellow in Paris, France. Among his more important works are the designs for the Engineering and Nuclear Complex at Tuskegee Institute (Tuskegee Institute, Ala.) and the U.S. Embassy Building in Dakar, Senegal.

MAGAZINES *See* NEWSPAPERS.

MAHONEY, CHARLES H. (1886–1966), lawyer, government official; born in Decatur, Mich. Mahoney received a B.A. degree from Fisk University (Nashville, Tenn.) in 1908 and his LL.B. degree from the University of Michigan in 1911. While an attorney in Michigan he was active in both civic affairs and private enterprise; he was a member of the Detroit Planning Commission and the county board of supervisors, commissioner of the Department of Labor and Industry, and chairman of the board of directors and president of the Great Lakes Mutual Insurance Company of Detroit. In 1954 Mahoney was appointed by President Dwight D. Eisenhower as a permanent member of the U.S. delegation to the United Nations. He served at the UN in this capacity until 1959, and was the first Afro-American permanent member of the delegation.

MAHONEY, MARY ELIZABETH (1845–1926), nurse. Mahoney received her R.N. degree from the New England Hospital for Women and Children (Boston, Mass.) in 1879, the first black graduate nurse in the United States. Because of her unstinting work, both in the field of nursing and in the organization of nurses, the National Association of Colored Graduate Nurses established the Mary Mahoney Award in 1936 for distinguished service in nursing. The American Nurses' Association now awards this honor for outstanding contributions to intergroup relations. *See also* NURSES.

MAJOR, CLARENCE (1936–   ), poet, novelist; born in Atlanta, Ga. Major grew up in Chicago, Ill., and later moved to New York City. He taught creative writing at Sarah Lawrence College (Bronxville, N.Y.). Major's published works include: *No* and *All Night Visitors*, novels; and *Swallow the Lake, Private Line, Symptoms and Madness*, and *The Cotton Club*, volumes of poetry.

MAJORS, MONROE ALPHEUS (1864– ?), physician, editor; born in Waco, Tex. Majors attended Tillotson College, (Austin, Tex; now Huston-Tillotson College), and received a B.A. degree from Central Tennessee College and his M.D. degree from Meharry Medical College (Nashville, Tenn.) in 1886. He organized the Lone Star Medical Association in 1886, but, threatened by segregationist elements, he fled to the West Coast, where in 1888 he became the first Afro-American doctor to pass the medical examinations given by the state board of California. Majors edited the *Texas Searchlight* from 1893 to 1895, and he was associate editor of the Indianapolis *Freeman* and the Chicago *Broad Ax*.

MALCOLM, BENJAMIN J. (1920 –   ), public official. Malcolm worked as a parole and correction official in New York City before he was appointed by Mayor John Lindsay as commissioner of corrections in 1972. He was the first Afro-American to be appointed to this office.

MALCOLM X (AL HAJJ MALIK AL-SHABAZZ) (1925–65), clergyman, civil rights leader; born Malcolm Little in Omaha, Nebr. Malcolm X was the son of a Garveyite Baptist preacher whose early death in Lansing, Mich.,

Malcolm X speaking at 115th Street and Lenox Avenue, New York City, in the summer of 1963. (*Photo by Arnold Hinton*.)

where he had moved his family, left the six-year-old boy and his seven siblings alone with their mother. Soon after, his mother was committed to a mental institution, and Malcolm X was sent to a foster home. Transferred to state institutions and boarding houses, Malcolm X left the Mason City, Iowa, school he attended and headed east

in 1940, just after finishing the eighth grade. In Boston, Mass., living with his sister, he held a variety of jobs—shoeshine boy, waiter, soda jerk; three years later, in New York City, he became involved in the underworld, living a life of crime and drug addiction that resulted in a ten-year jail sentence in 1946. While in jail, Malcolm X was introduced to the Lost-Found Nation of Islam, the Black Muslim religion led by Elijah Muhammad, with whom he began a correspondence. In 1952, on his parole from jail, he began speaking out in the idiom of his newly found philosophy—that the white Christian world was inherently evil and that the black people, to survive, must separate themselves in every way from white culture. Soon a minister of the faith with the given name Malcolm X, he established a mosque in Philadelphia, Pa., founded the newspaper *Muhammad Speaks*, and secured official orthodox (Azhar) recognition for the sect. In 1954 Malcolm X went to Harlem in New York City to head the mosque there. His speeches in behalf of the movement helped spread the messages of racial separation, of black self-defense, of nonparticipation in white society or religion, and of western decadence and immorality. His popularity became a threat to the power of many Muslim leaders, and finally in 1963, after Malcolm X proposed that President John F. Kennedy's assassination was a case of the "chickens coming home to roost," he was suspended from the Black Muslim movement. It was not long before he formed two of his own nationalist groups—the Muslim Mosque, Inc., and the Organization of Afro-American Unity—to work for black unity and freedom in cooperation with other civil rights groups. By this time he had made a pilgrimage to Mecca, changed his name to Al Hajj Malik al-Shabazz, and modified his views to encompass the possibility that all white people were not evil and that progress in the black struggle could be made with the help of world organizations, other black groups, and even progressive white groups. Malcolm X was killed by members of a dissenting black group in New York City. His life, the gradual evolution of his world philosophy, and his violent end had significant impact on the thinking of Afro-Americans for some years. His *Autobiography of Malcolm X* was published posthumously in 1965. Other works published after his death include: *Malcolm X Speaks* (1965); *The Speeches of Malcolm X at Harvard* (1968); *By Any Means Necessary: Speeches, Interviews, and a Letter by Malcolm X* (1970); and *The End of White*

Supremacy: Four Speeches by Malcolm X (1971). *See also* MUSLIMS.

MALCOLM X LIBERATION UNIVERSITY *See* FEDERATION OF PAN-AFRICAN EDUCATION INSTITUTIONS.

MALLORY, ARENIA CONELIA (1908–   ), educator; born in Jacksonville, Ill. Mallory received a B.S. degree from Simmons College (Boston) in 1927 and her M.A. degree from the University of Illinois (Urbana) in 1950. She was founder and president of Saints Junior College (Lexington, Miss.). In 1926 she visited Lexington, saw the deplorable conditions of the blacks (mostly sharecroppers) in that section of the state, and decided to stay there and do something for her people. Mallory founded a small school, on brick stilts, with a few homemade benches. With less than $10 in her purse, she took over the direction of the school, and from it she developed a college. Mallory also served as vice president of the National Council of Negro Women (1954–58), of the National Council of Women of United States (1956–59), and of the Educational Committee of the International Council of Women (1961–63).

MALONE, ANNIE M. TURNBO (1870–1957), business executive, philanthropist; born in Metropolis, Ill. Malone was educated in the public schools of Metropolis and Peoria, Ill., and received honorary M.A. degrees from Kittrell College (Kittrell, N.C.) and Western College. She founded Poro College (St. Louis Mo.) for beauty culture, and invented and manufactured several hair and toilet preparations (one named "Poro") after 1900. She was a generous donor to the Young Men's Christian Association (YMCA) of St. Louis, to the endowment fund of Howard University (Washington, D.C.), and to the St. Louis Colored Orphans Building Fund. At the peak of her career (ca. 1925), she is reputed to have been the richest Afro-American woman in the United States. *See also* BUSINESS; PORO.

MALONE, CAROL *See* NEWSPAPERS: CONTEMPORARY.

MALONE, HUEY PERRY (1935–   ), engineer; born in Bude, Miss. Malone received a B.S. degree from Roosevelt University (Chicago, Ill.) his Ph.D. degree from the University of Illinois in 1970. As a research engineer for the Gulf Oil Corporation, one of his areas of specialization was the development of nonpolluting products from oil, coal, and shale. Malone was a member of the board of the Urban League in Pittsburgh, Pa., and a member of numerous professional organizations.

MANGUM, ROBERT J. (1921–   ), lawyer, government official; born in Petersburg, Va. Mangum graduated from City College of the City University of New York in 1942, and received a M.A. degree in public administration from New York University in 1957, a M.S. degree in administrative medicine from Columbia University in 1964, and his LL.B. degree from New York Law School. He was admitted to the New York bar in 1949. Mangum became deputy police commissioner of New York City but resigned in 1957 to enter politics. A year later he was appointed deputy commissioner of hospitals in New York City, and after that director, Northeastern Region, Office of Economic Opportunity.

MANLEY, ALBERT EDWARD (1908–   ), educator; born in San Pedro Sula, Honduras. Manley received a B.S. degree from Johnson C. Smith University (Charlotte, N.C.) in 1930, a M.A. degree from Columbia University Teachers College in 1938, and his Ed.D. degree from Stanford University (Stanford, Calif.) in 1946. He was professor and dean at North Carolina Central University from 1946 to 1953, and became president of Spelman College (Atlanta, Ga.) in 1953. Manley also served on the board of the United Negro College Fund.

MANLY, JOHN BENSON (1910–   ), surgeon; born in Elmore County, Ala. Manly received his M.D. degree from Howard University Medical College (Washington, D.C.) in 1935, where he also became an instructor in orthopedic surgery. He served as chief of orthopedic surgery at Brooklyn Veterans Hospital, Brooklyn, N.Y., and as director of orthopedic surgery at Queens General Hospital and at Mary Immaculate Hospital, Jamacia, NY., beginning in 1964.

MANN, MARION (1920–   ), physician, educator; born in Atlanta, Ga. Mann received a B.S. degree from Tuskegee Institute (Tuskegee Institute, Ala.) in 1940, and his M.D. degree from Howard University Medical College (Washington, D.C.) in 1954, and his Ph.D. degree in pathology from Georgetown University (Washington, D.C.) in 1961. He was resident in pathology at Georgetown University Medical Center, and was an instructor and professor at George-town University and at Howard University. Mann served as deputy coroner for the District of Columbia (1962–67), and was appointed dean of Howard University in 1970.

MANNING, HUBERT VERNON (1918–), clergyman, educator; born in Cheraw, S.C. Manning received a B.A. degree from Claflin College (Orangeburg, S.C.) in 1940, a B.D. degree from Gammon Theological Seminary in 1945, and his M.A. degree from Boston University in 1947. He served churches in South Carolina before becoming president of Claflin College in 1956.

MARCUS GARVEY MEMORIAL INSTITUTE See FEDERATION OF PAN-AFRICAN EDUCATIONAL INSTITUTIONS.

MARCUS GARVEY SCHOOL See FEDERATION OF PAN-AFRICAN EDUCATIONAL INSTITUTIONS.

MARR, CARMEL CARRINGTON (1921–), lawyer, public official; born in Brooklyn, N.Y. Marr attended Hunter College of the City University of New York, from which she graduated with honors in 1945. She studied law at Columbia University Law School and was admitted to the New York state bar in 1948. After working in New York law firms for five years, Marr became legal adviser to the U.S. Mission to the United Nations, and five years later became senior legal officer in the Secratariat's Office of Legal Affairs. In 1968 Marr began serving as a member of the New York State Human Rights Appeal Board, and in 1971 she became commissioner of the New York State Public Service Commission, the first woman to serve on this body.

MARR, WARREN, II (1916–), administrator, editor; born in Pittsburgh, Pa. As an official of the American Missionary Association (AMA), Marr was in charge of research and planning for the centennial celebration of AMA colleges. He joined the public-relations department of the National Association for the Advancement of Colored People (NAACP) in New York City in 1967, and later became department director. Marr also served as executive director of the Friends of Amistad Research Center of New York City, as an official of Dillard University (New Orleans, La.), and as a trustee of Waltann School of Creative Arts. In 1975 he became the editor of *Crisis* magazine, published by the NAACP.

Thurgood Marshall. *(Administrative Office of the U.S. Supreme Court.)*

MARSHALL, ALBERT PRINCE (1914–), librarian; born in Texarkana, Tex. Marshall received a B.A. degree from Lincoln University (Jefferson City, Mo.) in 1938, a B.S.L.S. degree from the University of Illinois (Urbana) in 1939 and his M.A. degree from the University of Missouri (Columbia) in 1953. Except for two years in the Navy during World War II, he served as librarian at Winston-Salem State Teachers College (now Winston-Salem State University) in North Carolina from 1941 to 1950. He served as librarian at his alma mater from 1950 to 1969 when he joined the faculty of Eastern Michigan University (Ypsilanti). Marshall was very active in library service at state and national levels, serving as a vice president of the Missouri Library Association and the American Library Association (ALA). He received a citation from the Missouri Library Association in 1969 and the Distinguished Alumni Award from Lincoln University in 1964. *See also* BIBLIOGRAPHIES / BIOGRAPHIES / GUIDES; PREFACE: LIST OF CONTRIBUTORS.

MARSHALL, C. HERBERT See NATIONAL MEDICAL ASSOCIATION.

MARSHALL, HARRIET GIBBS (1869–1941), pianist, educator. Marshall attended the Oberlin Conservatory of Music (Oberlin, Ohio), becoming the first Afro-American to graduate from that institution. After additional piano studies in France, she gave piano recitals throughout the United States. Her teaching career included positions in the District of Columbia public school system, in Haiti, and in Kentucky. Marshall founded the Washington Conservatory of Music.

MARSHALL, PAULE (1929–), author; born in Brooklyn, N.Y. Marshall received a B.A. degree from Brooklyn College (Brooklyn, N.Y.) in 1953, and was a staff writer for *Our World* until 1956. After that, she lectured at Oxford, Columbia, and Paris universities, and received a Guggenheim Fellowship in 1960 and a Rosenthal Fellowship in 1961. Marshall wrote many short stories and several novels, incuding *Brown Girl, Brownstones* (1959), *Soul Clap Hands and Sing* (1961), and *The Chosen Place, the Timeless People.*

MARSHALL, THURGOOD (1908–), lawyer, judge, civil rights leader; born in Baltimore, Md. Marshall's grandfather was born in Africa and brought to the United States as a slave; his mother was a teacher in a segregated school; and his father worked as a steward in a country club. Marshall was educated at Lincoln University (Lincoln University, Pa.), receiving a B.A. degree in 1930. He then entered Howard University Law School (Washington, D.C.) and graduated with high honors. Entering private practice, he built up a large clientele with problems relating to civil rights. At the same time, he worked for the National Association for the Advancement of Colored People (NAACP) in Baltimore, Md., and became an assistant to its special counsel, Charles Hamilton Houston. In 1938 Marshall succeeded Houston as special counsel to the NAACP. During the years until 1961, when he was appointed judge of the U.S. District Court for the Second Judicial Circuit, Marshall expended all his efforts on attaining civil rights for Afro-Americans. Many of his cases constituted landmarks of progress. As early as 1938, he prepared the brief that led to the admission of a black student, Lloyd Gaines, to the University of Missouri Law School; in *Smith v. Allwright* (1944), Marshall fought for and won the right for blacks to vote in primary elections in Texas; *Morgan v. Virginia* (1946) signaled the end of segregation on interstate passenger carriers in Virginia; *Shelley v. Kraemer* (1948) held state enforcement of restrictive housing covenants to be unconstitutional; *Sweatt v. Painter* (1950) resulted in the admission of black students to the law school at the University of Texas; and in 1954 *Brown v. Board of Education of Topeka* began the slow process of school desegregation. In 1946 Marshall was awarded the NAACP's Spingarn Medal. Distinguished as an advocate, he became equally distinguished on the bench. After four years on the District Court, to which he was appointed by President John F. Kennedy, Marshall was named U.S. solicitor-general, and two years later, in 1967, he was appointed by President Lyndon B. Johnson as an associate justice of the U.S. Supreme Court. *See also* Civil Rights: Civil Rights Cases, 1865–1975.

MARTIN, JULIA M. (1924–   ), chemist, educator; born in Snow Hill, Md. Martin received both the bachelors and masters degrees from Tuskegee Institute (Tuskegee, Ala.) in 1946 and 1948 respectively. In 1963 she received her Ph.D. degree in biochemistry from Pennsylvania State University (University Park). She taught chemistry at Tuskegee Institute and Florida A & M University (Tallahassee) before joining the faculty at Southern University (Baton Rouge, La.), where she served as acting dean of the graduate

school, 1974–1976. She was cited in 1975 as an outstanding American educator.

MARTIN, LOUIS EMANUEL (1912–   ), editor, publisher; born in Shelbyville, Tenn. After receiving a B.A. degree from the University of Michigan in 1934, Martin became editor and publisher of the Michigan *Chronicle* in 1936. He also served as editor of the Chicago *Defender*, and published a magazine, *Headlines and Pictures*, in New York City during the 1940s.

MARTIN LUTHER KING, JR., MEMORIAL CENTER The center, located in a four-block area near downtown Atlanta, Ga., was begun in 1968. It comprises the frame house in which King was born, the Ebenezer Baptist Church where he once preached, his tomb, and Freedom Hall (library). *See also* King, Martin Luther, Jr.

MARTIN, ROBERT EARLE *See* Politics; and acknowledgments in the Preface.

MARTIN, TONY *See* Universal Negro Improvement Association (UNIA).

MARY HOLMES COLLEGE Mary Holmes College, at West Point, Miss, was founded in 1892 by the Board of Missions for Freedmen of the Presbyterian Church in the U.S.A. An independent and coeducational school, Mary Holmes offers a two-year terminal occupation program as well as work that can be credited toward the bachelor's degree. Its 1975 enrollment was 582.

The school was established through the efforts of Rev. Mead Holmes and Mary Holmes in honor of Mrs. Mead Holmes, who had long served the Board of Missions for Freedmen. It opened with an enrollment of 168 at Jackson, Miss., as a seminary for training Afro-American girls in domestic arts and Christian service. Destroyed by fire two years after its founding, the school was moved to West Point and reopened in 1897 on a tract of land donated by citizens of the community. The school has remained on this site, despite two more disastrous fires. As late as 1965 much of its land was under cultivation as a farm, which at one time was operated by the students, most of whom come from rural Mississippi. Sale of the produce helped to support the institution.

In 1932 the school became coeducational. Boys of high school age were given vocational training in carpentry and mechanics, and some buildings still in use on the campus were built by them. In the same year a college department was added for training elementary teachers. In

1959 the high school department was dropped, and the institution continued solely as a junior college with an expanded curriculum that led to associate degrees in the arts and the sciences, with emphasis on teacher training and preparation for business careers.

MARYLAND STATE COLLEGE *See* UNIVERSITY OF MARYLAND EASTERN SHORE.

MASON, VAUGHAN CARRINGTON (1919–70), surgeon. Mason received his M.D. and C.M. degrees from McGill University (Montreal, Quebec, Canada) in 1941. He served as director of the department of obstetrics and gynecology at Sydenham Hospital; as attending obstetrician at St. Claire's Hospital, New York, N.Y. and as president of the National Medical Association (1961–62).

MASONRY / MASONS *See* FRATERNAL SOCIETIES; HALL, PRINCE.

MASSIE, SAMUEL PROCTOR, JR. (1919–   ), scientist, educator; born in Little Rock, Ark. Massie received a B.S. degree from Arkansas Agricultural, Mechanical, and Normal (A M & N) College (now the University of Arkansas at Pine Bluff) in 1938, a M.A. degree from Fisk University (Nashville, Tenn.) in 1940, and his Ph.D. degree from Iowa State University in 1946. He taught chemistry at Arkansas A M & N College from 1940 to 1941, at Fisk University, from 1946 to 1947, and at Langston University (Langston, Okla.) from 1947 to 1953. Massie was chairman of the department of chemistry at Fisk University from 1953 to 1960, and became program director of the National Science Foundation in Washington, D.C. in 1960, before he returned to teaching at Howard University in 1962. He served as president of North Carolina Central University from 1963 to 1972, and joined the faculty of the U.S. Naval Academy (Annapolis, Md.) in 1972.

MATHIS, JOHNNY (1935–   ), singer; born in San Francisco, Calif. Mathis attended San Francisco State College, where he set new school records as a high jumper. He began his show business career as a singer in San Francisco nightclubs in 1955, soon signing a recording contract that resulted in a number of best-selling albums. His performances in many of the major nightclubs in the United States and his guest appearances on many television shows, always

sticking to what became his specialty and trademark—ballads—made him one of the wealthiest singers in the United States. In 1964 Mathis established and became president of Rojan Productions, a company designed to manage his business affairs as well as those of young, aspiring performers.

MAYNOR, DOROTHY (1910–   ), soprano; born in Norfolk, Va. Maynor's earliest training was received in church choirs. She earned a B.S. degree from Hampton Institute (Hampton, Va.) in 1933, where she studied under the famous musician R. Nathaniel Dett, and later she toured Europe with the college choir. Maynor then studied voice under Wilfred Klamroth and John Alan Haughton, making her debut at the Berkshire Festival in 1939. She appeared in concerts throughout the United States, often with symphonic orchestras. In 1940 Maynor won the Town Hall Endowment Award for her high-caliber performances and the outstanding alumni award from Hampton Institute. Bennett College (Greensboro, N.C.) awarded her an honorary Mus.D. degree in 1945.

MAYS, BENJAMIN ELIJAH (1895–   ), educator; born in Epworth, S.C. Mays received a B.A. degree from Bates College (Lewiston, Maine) in 1920, and a M.A. degree (1925) and his Ph.D. degree (1935) from the University of Chicago. He was awarded honorary degrees from a great number of universities. Mays taught at Morehouse College (Atlanta, Ga.) from 1921 to 1924, and at South Carolina State College from 1925 to 1926. He held several civic positions before he returned to teach at South Carolina State College. Mays then served as dean of the School of Religion at Howard University (Washington, D.C.) from 1934 to 1940 and as president of Morehouse College from 1940 to 1968. He was the author of many works, including *Negro's Church* (1933), *Negro's God,* and the autobiographical *Born to Rebel.* Mays was the first Afro-American president of the school board of Atlanta, Ga. Among his many honors was his inclusion (1944) on the Schomburg Honor Roll of Race Relations as one of 12 Afro-Americans who had done outstanding work in this area.

MAYS, WILLIE (1931–   ), professional baseball player; born in Fairfield, Ala. Mays was an all-around athlete at Fairfield Industrial High School before signing a professional contract with the Birmingham Black Barons when he was

17. He began his major-league career in 1951 with the New York (later San Francisco) Giants and also played with the New York Mets in 1972 and 1973. In 22 major-league seasons, through 1973, Mays compiled a career batting average of .302, and his total of 654 home runs ranks as third highest in the game's history. He led the National League in home runs four times and in stolen bases four times; in addition he was an excellent defensive player and one of the most popular performers in the sport. Mays was the league's Most Valuable Player in 1954 and 1965. His autobiography, *My Life In and Out of Baseball*, was published in 1966. *See also* ATHLETES: BASEBALL.

MAZIQUE, DOUGLAS WILKERSON (1909–64), physician; born in Natchez, Miss. Mazique received a B.S. degree from Morehouse College (Atlanta, Ga.) in 1933 and his M.D. degree from Meharry Medical College (Nashville, Tenn) in 1941. He introduced the first Afro-American newspaper, the *Mississippi World,* into Natchez in 1933, and taught in Natchez public schools (1933–37). Mazique was assistant ophthalmologist at the University of Illinois Infirmary for 19 years; was the first black physician on the staff of Alexin Brothers Hospital, Chicago, Ill.; and was chairman of the department of otolaryngology, Provident Hospital, Chicago, Ill.

McADOO, MARTHA ALLEN (1868–1936), singer, social worker; born in Columbus, Ohio. McAdoo graduated from high school in Washington, D.C., and taught in that city for two years. She was introduced to Orpheus M. McAdoo, manager of a musical company, joined his troupe, and later married him. The troupe toured through the British Isles, South Africa, Australia, Tasmania, and New Zealand, and after the death of her husband abroad, McAdoo returned to the United States. She lived in Boston, Mass., and Cleveland, Ohio, until World War II when she returned to Washington, D.C., to take charge of the Phillis Wheatley Young Women's Christian Association (YWCA). She became one of the first members of the Association for the Study of Negro Life and History.

McBROOM, F. PEARL (1926–   ), physician, cardiologist; born in Louisville, Miss. McBroom received a B.A. degree from the University of Chicago, a B.S. degree from Columbia University, and her M.D. degree from the College of Physicians and Surgeons, Columbia University,

in 1953. She interned at Bellevue Medical Center, New York, N.Y., and was sponsored by the U.S. Public Health Department for four years' research in cardiovascular disease. Her work in coronary artery transplants earned her a listing in the Royal Book of England. McBroom was in practice at Ross Medical Center in Los Angeles, Calif., and received numerous awards for her work in research.

McCLENDON, ROSE (?   –1936), actress. McClendon was active in the little theater movement as well as in radio in the "John Henry Sketches." She performed on stage in *Abraham's Bosom, Porgy, Deep River, Panic,* and other plays, and she promoted the interests of black actors through Actors Equity League.

McCLENNEY, EARL HAMPTON (1907–   ), educator; born in Marion Ala. McClenny received a B.S. degree from North Carolina Agricultural and Technical (A & T) State University in 1930, his M.S. degree from Cornell University (Ithaca, N.Y.) in 1937, and an honorary LL.D. degree from North Carolina Agricultural and Technical (A & T) State University in 1954. He was president of Voorhees School and Junior College (Denmark, S.C.; now Voorhees College) from 1947 to 1950, and president of Saint Paul's College (Lawrenceville, Va.).

McCLINTOCK, ERNIE *See* LITERATURE: DRAMA/THEATER

McCLONEY, LEON H. (1924–   ), clergyman, educator; born in Beaumont, Tex. McCloney received a B.A. degree from the College of Emporia (Emporia, Kans.) and his B.D. degree from Western University Seminary. He was pastor of African Methodist Episcopal (AME) churches in Kansas, Missouri, and Texas from 1943 to 1962, and also served as president of Paul Quinn College (Waco, Tex.).

McCONNELL, ROLAND C. (1910–   ), historian, educator; born in Amherst, Nova Scota, Canada. McConnell received a B.A. degree (1931) and a M.A. degree (1933) from Howard University (Washington, D.C.), and his Ph.D. degree from New York University in 1945. He taught at Elizabeth City State University (Elizabeth City, N.C.) from 1938 to 1939, served as archivist for the National Archives from 1943 to 1947, and returned to teaching (history) at Morgan State University (Baltimore, Md.) in the 1940s, where he later became the chairman of the department of history. McConnell was the author of various works on history, including *Negro Troops of Antebellum Louisiana: A History of the Battalion of Free Men of Color* (1968).

McCREE, WADE HAMPTON, JR. (1920–   ), lawyer, judge; born in Des Moines, Iowa. After having graduated from Fisk University (Nashville, Tenn.) in 1941, McCree received his LL.B. degree from Harvard Law School in 1944, and subsequently received many honorary degrees. Graduate work delayed his admission to the Michigan bar until 1948, at which time he began practicing law in Detroit, Mich. During the following years McCree was workmen's compensation commissioner in Detroit. In 1954 he became judge of the Michigan Circuit Court in Wayne County, and in 1961 judge of the U.S. District Court for the Eastern District, Michigan. McCree remained on the District Court bench until he was appointed to the U.S. Court of Appeals for the Sixth Circuit in 1966. In 1977 he was appointed Solicitor General in the administration of President Jimmy Carter.

McCROREY, HENRY LAWRENCE (1863–1951), clergyman, educator; born in Fairfield County, S.C. In 1888 McCrorey was ordained to the ministry by the Fairfield Presbyterian Synod of Atlantic. He received a B.A. degree (1892), a S.T.B. degree (1895), and a D.D. degree (1902) from Biddle College (Charlotte, N.C.; now Johnson C. Smith University), and his LL.D. degree from Lincoln University in 1924. McCrorey taught at and served as president of Johnson C. Smith University (1907–47). An authority in the Hebrew language, he taught in that field for 22 years.

McCURDY, MERLE M. (1912–   ), lawyer; born in Conneaut, Ohio. McCurdy attended Case Western Reserve University (Cleveland, Ohio) and received his LL.B. degree from the law school in 1947. In 1952 he became assistant county prosecutor for Cuyahoga County, Ohio, serving until 1960 when he was made first county public defender. A year later McCurdy became the U.S. attorney for the Northern District of Ohio.

McDONALD, CHARLES J. (1931–   ), dermatologist; born in Tampa, Fla. McDonald received his M.D. degree from Howard University Medical College (Washington, D.C.) in 1960. He served as assistant professor of medicine and pharmacology at Yale University School of Medicine and as attending physician and head of the division of dermatology at Roger Williams General Hospital, Providence, R.I., beginning in 1968. McDonald became a professor at Brown University (Providence) in 1974.

McGEE, HENRY W., JR. (1932–   ), lawyer; born in Chicago, Ill. McGee received a B.A. degree in journalism from Northwestern University (Evanston, Ill.) in 1954 and a J.D. degree from De Paul University (Chicago, Ill.) in 1957. At De Paul he was editor-in-chief of the De Paul Law Review, the first black to hold that position. McGee received his LL.B. degree from Columbia University in 1968, where he was a Benjamin Cardozo Fellow. He served in the State Attorney General's Office in Chicago, Ill., from 1958 through 1961, after which he entered private practice in Chicago. McGee was active in civil rights cases in the 1960s, and served as regional director of the Office of Equal Opportunity's Legal Service Program. Later he directed the Center for Studies in Criminal Justice at the University of Chicago Law School. McGee taught law at Ohio State University, Columbia University (1968), and at the University of California at Los Angeles. His scholarly articles include "Urban Renewal in the Crucible of Judicial Review" (1970); "Law Advocacy and Legal Services of Youth" (1969); and "Arrests in Civil Distrubances: Reflections on the Use of Deadly Force in Riots" (1968). His teaching materials include *Law, Poverty and the Oppressed,* and *Materials on the American Legal Process and the Poor* (1969).

McGEE, JAMES H. (1918–   ), lawyer, mayor; born in Berryburg, W. Va. McGee finished his undergraduate studies at Wilberforce University (Wilberforce, Ohio) and received his J.D. degree from Ohio State University. He was admitted to the Ohio bar in 1949, and 20 years later he was elected mayor of Dayton, Ohio, the fourth largest city in the United States with a black mayor.

McGHEE, FREDERICK L. See LAWYERS.

McGHEE, NORMAN LEROY (1897–   ), lawyer, editor; born in Austell, Ga. McGhee, having graduated from Montgomery State College (Montgomery, Ala.; now Alabama State University), was admitted to the Ohio bar in 1925. After a year as editor of the Cleveland *Call,* he began to practice law.

McGILL, NATHAN KELLOG (1888– ?), lawyer, editor; born in Quincy, Fla. McGill received his LL.B. degree from Boston University in 1912, and several years later began a private practice in Illinois, although he spent the year 1919–20 as editor and owner of the *Florida Sentinel* in Jacksonville, Fla. From 1925 to 1932 McGill was special counsel in the office of the attorney for Cook County, Ill., and from 1929 to 1933 he served as assistant state attorney general.

McGILL, SIMUEL DECATUR *See* LAWYERS.

McHENRY, DONALD F. (1936–), U. S. career diplomat; born in St. Louis, Mo. He received degrees (B.S., M.S.) from Southern Illinois University, Carbondale, Ill. On duty as a foreign service officer since 1963, he was appointed ambassador to the United Nations in 1979 by President Carter after the resignation of Andrew Young.

McKANE, ALICE WOODBY (1865– ?), physician; born in Bridgewater, Pa. McKane received her M.D. degree from Woman's Medical College of Pennsylvania in 1892. An instructor of nurses at Haines Institute in Georgia, she also established the first training school for nurses in southeast Georgia in 1893. McKane also established the McKane Hospital for Women and Children and the Training School for Nurses at Savannah, Ga. in 1896.

McKAY, CLAUDE (1890–1948), poet, novelist; born in Jamaica, British West Indies. McKay served in the Kingston, Jamaica, constabulary before coming to the United States in 1912. After study at Kansas State College for two years, he went abroad, living and traveling in England, Holland, Germany, France, and Russia. McKay was associate editor of *The Liberator* and *The Masses,* two radical magazines. A prominent member of the Harlem Renaissance, his works include *Harlem Shadows* (1922), *Banjo* (1929), and *A Long Way to Come Home* (1937). He became an American citizen in 1940 and a convert to Roman Catholicism in 1944. After his conversion he worked with a Catholic bishop in Chicago, Ill., until a long final illness curtailed his activities. His *Selected Poems* was published posthumously in 1953. *See also* LITERATURE: POETRY.

McKINLAY, WHITEFIELD (1852–1941), business executive, government official; born in Charleston, S.C. McKinlay studied at Avery Institute and he was one of the black students who were forced to leave the University of South Carolina by the more conservative administration that came to office in 1876. Disqualified from the U.S. Military Academy at West Point on physical grounds, he worked in the U.S. Printing Office as a clerk before entering the real estate business. McKinlay was a personal friend of President Theodore Rossevelt and frequently conferred with him about matters of civil rights for Afro-Americans. In 1907 McKinlay was appointed by President Roosevelt to the Housing Commission in order to investigate housing facilities among the poor of Washington, D.C., and he was later appointed collector of the port of Georgetown.

McKINNEY, RICHARD ISHMAEL (1906–), clergyman, educator; born in Live Oak, Fla. McKinney received a B.A. degree from Morehouse College (Atlanta, Ga.) in 1931, a B.D. degree from Andover Newton Theological School in 1934, and his Ph. D. degree from Yale University in 1942. He also attended Chicago, Paris, and Columbia Universities. McKinney was an assistant professor and director of religious activities at Virginia Union University from 1935 to 1942, and dean of the school of religion there from 1942 to 1944. From 1944 to 1950 McKinney served as president of Storer College, and beginning in 1948 he headed the department of philosophy at Morgan State University (Baltimore, Md.). While on leave from that school, McKinney was appointed an associate of the A. Philip Randolph Institute (New York, N.Y.) in 1971. He wrote *Religion in Higher Education Among Negroes* (1945).

McKINNEY, THEOPHILUS E. (1899– ?), educator; born in Live Oak, Fla. McKinney received a B.A. degree from Morehouse College (Atlanta, Ga.) in 1921 and his M.A. degree from Boston University in 1924. He was dean of North Carolina Agricultrual and Technical (A & T) State University for many years, and taught at Johnson C. Smith University (Charlotte, N.C.) during the 1940s and 1950s. McKinney was founder and first president of the National Association of Collegiate Deans and Registrars in Negro Schools, and he became managing editor of *Quarterly Review of Higher Education Among Negroes* in 1933.

Claude McKay. *(Moorland-Spingarn Research Center.)*

McKINNEY, THOMAS THEODORE (1869–1926), surgeon; born in Alstyne, Tex. McKinney attended Central Tennessee College, and received his M.D. degree from Meharry Medical College (Nashville, Tenn.) in 1895. He did postgraduate work at the Medical School and Hospital of Chicago and at the University of Michigan Medical School before he began practicing medicine and surgery for 31 years.

McKISSICK, FLOYD BIXLER (1922–), civil rights leader, lawyer, business executive; born in Asheville, N.C. McKissick studied at Morehouse College (Atlanta, Ga.) and received a B.A. degree from North Carolina Central University. With the legal help of Thurgood Marshall, he entered the University of North Carolina Law School at Chapel Hill, and became the first black recipient of a LL.B. degree from that institution in 1951. The next year, McKissick set up a law practice in Durham, which occupied him until 1966. He specialized in the hundreds of civil rights cases that were brought before the courts in the 1960s in the burgeoning civil rights movement. Having served as legal counsel for the Congress of Racial Equality (CORE) in those years, in 1966, when James Farmer, then national director of CORE, resigned, McKissick was elected national chairman of that organization. In 1966 McKissick joined Stokely Carmichael in his cry for Black Power during the James Meredith March Against Fear in Mississippi. In 1968 McKissick left CORE to launch Floyd B. McKissick Enterprises, Inc., a corporation involved in organizing and financing businesses. An arm of that company, Warren Regional Planning Corporation, Inc., was formed for the purpose of developing Soul City, a new town in North Carolina. McKissick was the author of *Three-Fifths of a Man*, published in 1968. *See also* CONGRESS OF RACIAL EQUALITY (CORE).

McMILLAN, WILLIAM ASBURY (1920–), educator; born in Winnabow, N.C. McMillan received a B.A. degree from Johnson C. Smith University (Charlotte, N.C.) in 1942, and a M.A. degree (1946) and his Ph.D. degree (1954) from the University of Michigan. He was affiliated with Johnson C. Smith University and Wiley College (Marshall, Tex.), and served as president of Bethune-Cookman College (Daytona Beach, Fla.), and then as president of Rust College (Holly Springs, Miss.) beginning in 1967.

McMILLIAN, THEODORE (1919–), lawyer, judge, educator; born in St. Louis, Mo. McMillian received a B.S. degree from Lincoln University (Jefferson City, Mo.) and his LL.B. degree from St. Louis University Law School. After serving in the armed forces during World War II, he was admitted to the Missouri bar in 1949 and engaged in a private law practice until 1953. McMillian then served as assistant circuit attorney for the city of St. Louis until 1956, when he was appointed judge of the Circuit Court of Missouri. Meanwhile, he taught law for several years at St. Louis University Law School. In 1970 McMillian received the Man of the Year Award from Frontier International. Throughout his career he was associated closely with many legal, civic, and church organizations.

McQUAY, JAMES (ca. 1930–), furrier, designer; born in White Plains, N.Y. McQuay specialized in the design, tailoring, and production of fur coats and other garments for men and women, and operated his own fur company in New York City. He was named Designer of the Year for the fur industry in 1969 and 1971, and in 1972 he was selected as the outstanding Afro-American business executive in New York City.

McSTALLWORTH, PAUL (1910–), historian, educator; born in Flatwood, Ala. McStallworth received a B.A. degree from Geneva College (Beaver Falls, Pa.) in 1936, a M.A. degree from Howard University (Washington, D.C.) in 1940, and his Ph.D. in European history from Ohio State University in 1954. He taught at Saint Augustine's College (Raleigh, N.C.) from 1940 to 1943, at Central State University (Wilberforce, Ohio) from 1947 to 1954, and served as professor of history at Wright State University (Fairborn, Ohio) after 1969. His publications include "The Congolese and Self-Determination" (1958) and "Nigerianization at Dawn."

MECCA FLATS The name given to an area, predominantly black, on the south side of Chicago, Ill. The term was used especially during the 1920s and 1930s.

MEDICINE See HEALTH; PHYSICIANS.

MEHARRY MEDICAL COLLEGE Meharry Medical College, at Nashville, Tenn., was founded in 1876 as the medical department of Central Tennessee College by the Freedmen's Aid Society of the Methodist Episcopal (ME) Church. A private, independent, and coeducational school, Meharry offers a full range of medical and dental programs, including undergraduate studies. Its 1975 enrollment was 683.

The college was named for its principal benefactor, Samuel Meharry, who, together with his four brothers, contributed about one-half of their combined fortune to set up the medical department of Central Tennessee College. In 1886 a department of dentistry was added. In 1900 the parent institution was reorganized as Walden University, and the medical department became Meharry Medical College of Walden University. In 1910 the first unit of George W. Hubbard Hospital was opened as a teaching adjunct for Meharry and a school of nursing was established. In 1915, when Walden University failed under a series of hardships, Meharry was granted a separate charter by the state of Tennessee, and in 1931 the college moved to its present location in Nashville.

Meharry is the only fully accredited, privately endowed, predominantly black medical college in the United States. The college includes the School of Medicine, the School of Dentistry, the Graduate School, and the George W. Hubbard Hospital. It offers courses leading to certification in medical technology, dental hygiene, and X-ray technology. Degrees in health-care administration and planning are given in cooperation with Fisk University and Tennessee State University. Nearly half of the practicing Afro-American physicians and dentists in the United States are graduates of Meharry.

MEREDITH, JAMES HOWARD (1933–   ), civil rights worker; born in Kosciusko, Miss. Meredith's application and subsequent admission to the University of Mississippi in 1961 was the cause célèbre that initiated the desegregation of the university. Having applied in 1961, he was at first refused. A U.S. Supreme Court decision in his favor forced the call-up of U.S. marshalls to escort him to class after the governor of Mississippi refused to comply with the court's decision, personally preventing Meredith's entry. Federal troops arrived on the campus when rioting broke out, and remained there until 1963 when Meredith graduated. The next year Meredith studied in Nigeria, West Africa; then, returning to the United States, he took up the study of law at Columbia University. In 1966, interrupting his studies at Columbia, he led a

march in Mississippi to publicize a drive for voter registration. It was during this drive that an attempt was made on Meredith's life and that Stokely Carmichael was to call for Black Power. Also in 1966 Meredith published *Three Years in Mississippi*. Subsequently, he lectured at colleges and universities on civil rights and racial problems and worked in a stock brokerage house.

MERRITT, EMMA FRANCES GRAYSON (1860–1933), educator; born in Dumfries, Va. Merritt attended George Washington University (Washington, D.C.) from 1887 to 1890. She served as teacher and as principal of Banneker School from 1876 to 1887, and then as principal of Garnet School from 1896 to 1898, as its director of primary instruction from 1898 to 1927, and as its supervising principal from 1927 to 1930. During her long tenure in public education in Washington, D.C., Merritt made many contributions to the improvement of instruction in schools attended by Afro-American children.

MERRITT, ROBERT (1937–   ), health executive; born in Leesburg, Fla. Merritt received a B.S. degree from the University of New Haven (West Haven, Conn.) in 1967 and his M.H.A. degree from Yale University in 1969. He served in several administrative positions connected with health services, including Project Director for the Marcus Garvey Nursing Home.

MERRIWEATHER, FRANK E., JR. See NEWSPAPERS: CONTEMPORARY.

METCALFE, RALPH H. (1910–1978), track-and-field athlete, educator, U.S. Representative; born in Atlanta, Ga. Metcalfe received a B.Ph. degree from Marquette University (Milwaukee, Wis.) in 1936, where he became a world-famous track-and-field star. He was a member of the U.S. Olympic teams in 1932 and 1936, and after Olympic competition returned to school and received his M.A. degree from the University of Southern California in 1939. Metcalfe was political science instructor and coach at Xavier University (New Orleans, La.) from 1936 to 1942. He served on the city council in Chicago, Ill., from 1955 to 1971 and was elected to the U.S. House of Representatives from the state of Illinois in 1972, serving until his death. Metcalfe was founder of the Ralph H. Metcalfe Foundation in Chicago. *See also* ATHLETES.

METHODISTS

METHODISTS / UNITED METHODIST CHURCH

Introduction The development, leadership, and contributions of black Methodists who remained in the organizational structure of the Methodist Episcopal (ME) Church (1784–1939) and its successors, the Methodist Church (1939–1968), and the United Methodist Church (1968–   ), comprise an important chapter in the religious experience of Afro-Americans in the United States.

Black Methodists withdrew early from the former Methodist Episcopal (ME) Church and formed independent bodies, namely, the African Methodist Episcopal (AME) Church (1816), the African Methodist Episcopal Zion (AMEZ) Church (1821), and the Christian Methodist Episcopal (CME) Church (1870). Each of these three churches is treated in separate articles in this *Encyclopedia*.

John Wesley (1703–91), the founder of Methodism, had contact with Afro-Americans in North America prior to his evangelical conversion in the religious society of Aldersgate Street, London, England, in 1738. In 1735 Wesley came to Georgia as an Anglican missionary. His appointment was to convert the Indians and "negro (sic) slaves." Wesley's contact with Afro-Americans began during missionary visits in South Carolina. While in the Charleston vicinity in 1736, he preached to blacks on several occasions.

George Whitefield (1714–70), associated with the Wesleys in the "Holy Club" at Oxford University (Oxford, England), indirectly influenced two of America's first Afro-American writers, Jupiter Hammon (ca. 1720–ca. 1800) and Phillis Wheatley (ca. 1753–84). Hammon, a slave in Queens Village, Long Island, N.Y., wrote and published "An Evening Thought: Salvation by Christ," the first poem by an Afro-American. This "shout-hymn" showed the influence of the Methodist evangelicals of the time. Phillis Wheatley, born in Senegal, Africa, was likewise influenced by the religious fervor of Whitefield's Calvinistic Methodist influence in New England at the time, as shown in her work "Prepare for Eternal Judgment."

Early American Methodism and Afro-Americans In 1760 Philip Embury (ca. 1730–73), an Irish local preacher, migrated to America. In 1776 he con-

The first Methodist Episcopal Church in America (center building), known as Wesley's Chapel, was erected ca. 1768 on Golden Hill (later John Street) between William and Nassau Streets, New York City. Early black and white Methodists worshipped together, more visibly in the larger congregations in Baltimore and Philadelphia. *(From a painting by Joseph C. Smith, ca. 1817, Museum of the City of New York.)*

554

ducted what was probably the first Methodist service in America. Present at that service was an Afro-American servant woman, Betty, employed by Barbara Heck, the cousin of Philip Embury. When the society that grew out of Embury's "meeting" outgrew both his home and later a "rigging loft," the group sought a permanent home (1761). Two black servants, Rachel and Margaret, contributed to the cost of constructing that first Methodist chapel in New York City. Also in New York City, Capt. Thomas Webb (1724–96), a retired British soldier-preacher, reported that after preaching six months there, more than two dozen persons were converted, "half of them white, the rest negroes." Webb also converted Peter Williams and his wife, Mollie. Peter Williams later became the prime mover in the organization of the African Methodist Episcopal Zion (AMEZ) denomination in 1821.

Another Irish lay preacher, Robert Strawbridge (? –1781), settled on Sam's Creek in Frederick County, Md., between 1762 and 1765, and used his living quarters for preaching services. A member of the group that first heard him was a black woman, "Aunt" Annie Sweitzer.

In 1769 Wesley sent Richard Boardman (1738–82) and Joseph Pilmoor (? –1821) to America as missionaries. Boardman was moved by the zeal of the Afro-Americans in his congregation and Pilmoor had formed Afro-American classes by 1770. George Shadford (? –1816) and Thomas Rankin (? –1810), also British missionaries, both reported black converts and members in their societies.

The one man who did more to establish Methodism in America than any other single person, Francis Asbury (1771–1816), had many contacts with Afro-Americans. He preached to blacks in St. John Church in 1771, converted blacks in Maryland in 1773, and catechized them in 1776. In 1772, in Philadelphia, Pa., he commended a Mr. Roberdeau, who refused to keep slaves; back in Maryland in 1783, he condemned a slaveholder, John Worthington.

Two Afro-Americans were present at the historic Christmas Conference held in Lovely Lane Meeting House in Baltimore, Md., in 1784 at which the Methodist Episcopal (ME) Church in America was organized: Richard Allen (1760–1831) and "Black Harry" Hosier (ca. 1750–1806). Thirty-six of the fifty-one societies represented at this conference reported Afro-American members.

Development, 1750–1865 Despite discrimination against them in the early Methodist societies, North and South, Afro-Americans responded to Methodism's outreach and contributed to its development. "Black Harry" Hosier accompanied Freeborn Garrettson (1752–1827) on an evangelistic tour in 1790, going with him as far as Boston, Mass. He preached many times, "to the pleasure and profit of his hearers." Blacks initiated and supported Free African Societies along the eastern seaboard in the late eighteenth century. The first of these mutual self-help organizations was founded by Richard Allen in Philadelphia, Pa., at Bethel Church (1787), the first separate black Methodist Episcopal meetinghouse in America.

African Zoar Church in Philadelphia, Pa., organized in 1794 and dedicated by Asbury in 1796, represented the earliest instance of Afro-American initiative and protest against segregation by Afro-Americans who still remained within the Methodist Episcopal (ME) Church.

In 1799 Richard Allen became the first black Methodist to receive ordination (deacon) in the Methodist Episcopal (ME) Church. Daniel Coker (ca. 1780–1816), one of the organizers of the African Methodist Episcopal (AME) Church and almost its first bishop, was ordained by Asbury about the same time. Other black Methodist local preachers were not ordained until the early 1800s, following General Conference authorization.

Notable Methodist Episcopal (ME) churches organized and firmly established by Afro-Americans before the black exodus to northern and southern cities about 1916 are shown in the table on the next page.

Black ME Annual Conferences, 1886–1939 Agitation for separate black annual conferences began shortly after the North-South division of the Methodist Episcopal (ME) Church in 1844. Several reasons explain this. In the urban North, Afro-American members of the ME Church were taunted by black members of the AME Church and the AMEZ Church for belonging to the "white man's" church. They were reminded of their few black preachers and their lack of "presiding elders," bishops, annual conferences and the like. Also, large numbers of MEs had already begun to defect to these other black denominations. Protesting and seeking to remedy this situation, black MEs in the Philadelphia-Baltimore-Washington, D.C., vicinity formed and held

One of the oldest Methodist congregations, Sharp Street Memorial United Methodist Church was founded in 1802 in Baltimore, Md. Members of the church pioneered in colonizing Liberia and escaped to Canada to avoid slavery. The first classes of the parent body of Morgan State University were housed by the church in the 1860s. (Courtesy of John W. Coleman, Sharp Street Memorial United Methodist Church.)

1802

1976

annual conferences of local preachers and lay-men (1852–63), the predecessors of the first offi-cial black annual conferences. The official con-ferences date from 1864. By 1929, 24 black annual conferences had been formed covering 27 states and every region excepting northern New England and the Far West. This arrangement divided the Methodist Episcopal (ME) Church along racial lines while still including black MEs within the organic structure of the denomination.

At the time of unification in 1939, the 24 black annual conferences, in response to population shifts and membership increases and decreases, had been consolidated into 19.

Black United Methodist Colleges The Methodist Episcopal (ME) Church organized the Freed-men's Aid Society in 1866 to assist ex-slaves in securing a basic education. Between 1866 and 1896 a number of schools were begun as elemen-tary and secondary schools. Several have sur-vived to become strong and accredited Method-ist-related institutions: nine are four-year coeducational colleges; one (Bennett) is a four-year women's college; one (Morristown) is a junior college; and two (Meharry Medical and Gammon Theological) are graduate professional schools. The accompanying table lists all col-leges and universities affiliated with the United Methodist Church.

Preachers and Missionaries The earliest leaders to emerge among black Methodists were preach-ers: "Black Harry" Hosier; Richard Allen; Daniel Coker; John Charleston; Henry Evans; and Fran-cis Brown. First among the black missionaries was John Stewart (ca. 1786–1823), the founder of Methodism's first successful mission to the

HISTORICAL METHODIST EPISCOPAL (ME) CHURCHES

Church	Organized	Location
African Zoar	1794	Philadelphia, Pa.
Sharp Street	1802	Baltimore, Md.
Ezion	1805	Wilmington, Del.
Calvary	1815	Cincinnati, Ohio
Mt. Zion	1816	Washington, D.C.
Asbury	1818	Frederick, Md.
Union Memorial	1818	Boston, Mass.
Wesley Chapel	1820	New Orleans, La.
Jones Temple	1832	Louisville, Ky.
Asbury	1836	Washington, D.C.
Tindley Temple	1837	Philadelphia, Pa.
Union Memorial	1846	St. Louis, Mo.
Mt. Zion	1865	Leesburg, Va.
Trinity	1866	Orangeburg, S.C.
Centenary	1866	Charleston, S.C.
St. Matthew	1866	Greensboro, N.C.
Central	1868	Atlanta, Ga.
St. Mark	1871	New York, N.Y.
Asbury	1871	Savannah, Ga.
Cory Memorial	1875	Cleveland, Ohio
Wesley	1881	Los Angeles, Calif.
Central	1890	Jackson, Miss.
St. Mark	1895	Chicago, Ill.
Salem	1902	New York, N.Y.
Scott Memorial	1904	Denver, Colo.
Scott Memorial	1912	Detroit, Mich.

Wyandot Indian tribe in Ohio in 1819 and insti-gator of the movement that led to the formation of the Missionary and Bible Society of the former Methodist Episcopal (ME) Church, the predeces-sor of the Board of Missions. Three of the four black missionary bishops were missionaries before their consecration: Francis Burns (1809–63), the first black Methodist missionary bishop, elected in 1858; John W. Roberts (1812–75); and Alexander P. Camphor (1865–1919), the first regularly appointed black missionary in the for-mer ME Church. Slave-born Amanda Smith (1837–1915), a Marylander, was a nationally

UNITED METHODIST COLLEGES AND UNIVERSITIES

Institution	Location	Founded	First Afro-American President	President (1972)
Rust College	Holly Springs, Miss.	1866	L. M. McCoy (1924)	W. A. McMillan
Morgan State University[1]	Baltimore, Md.	1867	D. O. W. Holmes (1938)	(see footnote)
Philander Smith College	Little Rock, Ark.	1868	J. M. Cox (1899)	W. R. Hazzard, Sr.
Claflin College	Orangeburg, S.C.	1869	J. B. Randolph (1922)	H. V. Manning
Clark College	Atlanta, Ga.	1869	W. H. Crogman (1907)	V. R. Henderson
Dillard University	New Orleans, La.	1869	A. W. Dent (1930)	B. N. Butler
Bethune-Cookman College	Daytona Beach, Fla.	1872	M. B. Bethune (1923)	R. V. Moore
Bennett College	Greensboro, N.C.	1873	D. D. Jones (1926)	L. H. Miller
Wiley College	Marshall, Tex.	1873	L. B. Scott (1893)	R. E. Hays, Sr.
Huston-Tillotson College	Austin, Tex.	1876	R. S. Lovingood (1900)	J. T. King
Meharry Medical College	Nashville, Tenn.	1876	G. W. Hubbard (1876)	L. C. Elam
Morristown Junior College	Morristown, Tenn.	1881	J. W. Haywood (1936)	J. O. Erwin
Gammon Theological Seminary	Atlanta, Ga.	1883	J. W. E. Bowen, Sr. (1906)	M. J. Jones

[1]Continues the United Methodist presence at Morgan State University founded in 1867 as Centenary Biblical Institute. It became Morgan College in 1890 and Morgan State University in 1975.

known evangelist-missionary in the 1870s. W. H. Riley and his wife of the former Lexington Conference established the first Deaconess Training School for young Afro-American women in the country (1900).

District Superintendents Black presiding elders, known since 1908 as district superintendents, emerged as leaders with the organization of the black annual conferences. The first Afro-Americans appointed were: Isaiah Henson, James Davis, and Wilmore Elzey (Delaware, 1864); Benjamin Brown, and James Harper (Washington, D.C., 1864); T. W. Willard, D. D. Leavitt (South Carolina, 1866); James D. Lynch (Mississippi, 1867); Henry H. Lytle and Hanson Talbot (Lexington, Ky., 1868); Emperor Williams (Mississippi, 1868); and Adam Palmer (Georgia, 1869).

General Conference Delegates, 1868–1968 Elected delegates to the general conference constituted another category of black Methodist leadership. The first Afro-Americans to sit in this body (1868) were: James Davis (Delaware) and Benjamin Brown (Washington, D.C.). The 1868 general conference also authorized lay representation to be equal to that of the clergy in the general conferences beginning with 1872. The first Afro-American lay delegates were: James A. Jones (Delaware); James Harris and Aaron Shoreler (Washington, D.C.); S. H. Toles and James Wells (Mississippi); and C. H. Holloway and Henry Cardoza (South Carolina). Predominantly white

annual conferences have also elected black ministerial delegates to the general conferences: William H. Brooks (New York, 1920) and Alexander P. Shaw (Southern California, 1928).

Afro-American Bishops, 1858–1968 Black Methodists contended for almost a half century for their rightful opportunity to hold the highest office that United Methodism can bestow, the episcopacy. Francis Burns and John W. Roberts had been elected missionary bishops in 1858 and 1866, respectively, on the recommendation of the Liberian Church. The first formal request for a black bishop to be elected by the general conference and assigned for service in the United States came in 1872. At that time Afro-Americans were declared eligible but none were considered qualified. The renewal of this demand in 1876 was futile since the general conference decided not to elect bishops. The general conference of 1880 recommended electing an Afro-American bishop for Afro-Americans. Quadrennially, until 1900, the most highly qualified Afro-American candidates failed to be elected. In 1904 Isaiah B. Scott was finally elected by the general conference as a missionary bishop to Liberia, and in 1916 Alexander P. Camphor was elected to the same post. It was not until 1920 that an Afro-American bishop, Robert E. Jones, was elected to the episcopacy for service in the United States. The accompanying table lists all Afro-American bishops consecrated by the United Methodist Church until 1968.

AFRO-AMERICAN BISHOPS OF THE UNITED METHODIST CHURCH

Name	Born	Consecrated	Annual Conference	Retired	Died
Francis Burns*	1809	1858	Liberia		1863
John W. Roberts*	1812	1866	Liberia		1875
Isaiah B. Scott*	1854	1904	Texas	1916	1931
Alexander P. Camphor	1865	1916	Central Alabama		1919
Robert E. Jones	1872	1920	North Carolina	1936	1960
Matthew W. Clair, Sr.	1865	1920	Washington, D.C.	1936	1943
Alexander P. Shaw	1879	1936	Mississippi	1952	1966
W. A. C. Hughes	1877	1940	Washington, D.C.		1940
Lorenzo H. King	1878	1940	New York		1946
Willis J. King	1886	1944	Texas	1960	
Robert N. Brooks	1888	1944	North Carolina		1953
Edward W. Kelly	1880	1944	Central West	1952	1964
J. W. E. Bowen, Jr.	1889	1948	Louisiana	1960	1962
Edgar A. Love	1891	1952	Washington, D.C.	1964	
Matthew W. Clair, Jr.	1890	1952	Lexington, Ky.	1964	1968
Prince A. Taylor, Jr.	1907	1956	North Carolina		
Charles F. Golden	1912	1960	Lexington, Ky.		
Noah W. Moore, Jr.	1902	1960	Delaware		
M. Lafayette Harris	1909	1960	Lexington, Ky.		1962
James S. Thomas, Jr.	1919	1964	South Carolina		
L. Scott Allen	1918	1967	Georgia		
Roy C. Nichols	1918	1968	New York		

*Missionary bishop

Afro-American Church Executives Significant contributions have been made to the black community and to Methodism through the work of Afro-American Methodists who have served in executive posts. Some of the most important executives include: (1) Marshall W. Taylor (1847–87), first Afro-American editor of the *Central Christian Advocate,* 1884–87; (2) M. C. B. Mason (1859–1918), first Afro-American board of education executive, field secretary 1891–93, assistant corresponding secretary 1893–96, and corresponding secretary 1896–1912; (3) I. Garland Penn (1897–1930), pioneer Afro-American Epworth League executive; (4) G. G. Logan (1871–1931), field agent, board of missions, 1903–10; (5) W. W. Lucas (1872–   ), field agent, board of missions, 1910–12; (6) I. L. Thomas, field agent, board of missions, 1912–17; (7) J. N. C. Coggins (1870–1927), first black staff member, board of temperance, 1914–24; (8) W. A. C. Hughes (1877–1940), director, bureau of Negro work, ca. 1920–40; (9) Frederick H. Butler, first Afro-American executive, board of Sunday schools, 1921–23; (10) Samuel H. Sweeney (1888–1965), first Afro-American field representative, board of pensions, 1930–33; (11) N. J. Crolley, Sweeney's successor, who served from 1930–48; and (12) Daisy M. Bulkey, a staff member of the Woman's Home Missionary Society, a predecessor unit of the Women's Division of Christian Service.

Prior to the creation of the central jurisdiction, approximately 12 Afro-Americans held or had held executive posts in the Church. From 1940 to the present, approximately 48 have held such posts, including: John T. Fletcher (1872–1956), staff, church extension department, board of missions, 1940–45; Edgar A. Love, superintendent, department of Negro work, board of missions, 1940–52; J. W. Golden (1883–1961), staff, board of evangelism, 1940–56; A. R. Howard (1885–1965), staff, board of temperance, 1940–56; C. H. Dubra, staff, board of temperance, 1956–61; J. H. Touchstone, layman, staff, board of lay activities, 1942–64; Charles P. Kellogg, staff, board of lay activities, 1964–68, and assistant general secretary, 1968–   ; John A. Greene, staff, board of education, 1943–52; Timothy B. Echols, staff, board of pensions, 1948–63; Allen M. Mayes, associate secretary, board of pensions, 1963–   ; John W. Haywood, staff, board of world peace, 1948–55; M. S. Davage, secretary, department of higher education for Negroes, 1940–52; James S. Thomas, associate secretary, division of educational institutions, board of education, 1952–64; Daniel W. Wynn, associate director, department of educational institutions, board of education; Frank L. Horton, associate director, department of campus ministry, board of education; H. Walter Willis, staff, division of curriculum resources, 1966–71; James S. Gadsen, staff, division of curriculum resources, 1967–   ; Earnest A. Smith, associate general secretary, board of Christian social concerns, 1966–   ; Grant S. Shockley, executive secretary, Christian education, world division, board of missions, 1966–70; Rose M. Catchings, executive secretary, status of women, world division, board of missions, 1966–   ; Isaac Bivins, associate secretary, joint committee, missionary personnel, 1967–70; John F. Norwood, director, local church, board of health and welfare ministries, 1968–   ; William T. Handy, Jr., publishing representative, board of publications, 1968–71, and vice president, 1971–   ; Woodie W. White, executive secretary, commission on religion and race, 1969–   ; Clayton E. Hammond, associate executive secretary, commission on religion and race, 1969–   ; DePriest W. Whye, associate executive secretary, quadrennial emphasis committee, 1969–   ; Ernest T. Dixon, Jr., assistant general secretary, division of research and planning, program council, 1969–   ; Warren M. Jenkins, assistant general secretary, division of interpretation, program council, 1969–   ; Ernestine A. Calhoun, staff, division of curriculum resources; John W. Heyword, Jr., associate secretary, commission on chaplains and related ministries, 1970–   ; Isaac H. Bivins, assistant general secretary for African affairs, world division, board of missions, 1970–   ; Harry B. Gibson, Jr., assistant general secretary, board of missions, 1971–   ; and Enid M. Belle, comptroller, national division, board of missions. Several Afro-American executives have held positions with the Women's Division of Christian Service and one of its predecessors in the former Methodist Episcopal (ME) Church, the Woman Home Missionary Society (WHMS). Serving as a staff member of WHMS was Daisy Burley of South Carolina. The following Afro-Americans have served since unification (1940): Lillian W. Pope; Vivienne N. Gray; Ethel L. Watkins; Cornelia L. Smith; and Minnie Stein. Theresa Hoover, associate general secretary of the division, holds the highest executive post of any Afro-American in the denomination. Other Afro-American executives include Negoil R. Riley, executive secretary, urban ministries, board of missions, 1967–

; George M. Daniels, director, interpretive services, joint commission, educational cultivation, board of missions; and David W. Briddele, director, audio-visual resources, joint commission on education and cultivation, board of missions.

Central Jurisdiction and Integration The racial issue has been crucial for Methodism throughout its history in the United States. Its first major crisis resulted in the division of the Church in 1844. Ostensibly, the cause of the separation was a North-South dispute over the authority of the General Conference versus the episcopacy. The South generally adhered to the principles of episcopal supremacy, and the North (and West) favored the relative subordination of the episcopacy to the general conference.

The more definitive issue was the position of the Methodist Episcopal (ME) Church on slavery. Those sympathetic to the direction of adjusting church policy to slavery withdrew and formed the Methodist Episcopal (ME) Church, South (1845–1939). Those committed to the eradication of slavery remained in what continued as the Methodist Episcopal (ME) Church, composed largely of northern and western members.

Bishop Willis J. King indicated two main effects of this North-South division on Afro-American Methodist developments in the North: "Despite their espousal of the freedom of the slaves, local attitudes against the admission of Negroes into the churches changed slowly; and in a number of cases Negroes were encouraged to set up their own local congregations or to join the independent Negro denominations." In the South the policy was clear and consistent, namely, that the cause of Afro-Americans could be served best through a program of service outside the organizational structure of the church. This policy eventuated in the creation of the Christian Methodist Episcopal (CME) Church.

The northern-western policy resulted in a highly anomalous situation. With the organization of a system of black annual conferences extending across 27 states, the Methodist Episcopal (ME) Church had erected in effect a de facto segregated church, the largest racially segregated religious body in the nation.

The problem of the place of the Afro-American Methodist was the problem that faced every effort toward unification between the former Methodist Episcopal (ME) Church, the Methodist Episcopal Church, South and the Methodist

Protestant Church from the beginning of union talks in the early 1900s. The issue was resolved, to the dissatisfaction of the vast majority of Afro-Americans and a minority of northern whites, by the creation of the central jurisdiction.

The onus of second-class church membership and the stigma of being related to a religious body whose official structure was racially discriminatory have been heavy burdens for black United Methodists to bear in the period between 1940 and the 1970s. Despite this, Afro-Americans have made considerable achievements. Fourteen Afro-Americans have been elected to the episcopacy; Bishop Prince A. Taylor, Jr., became the first black to head the council of bishops for a term, 1965–66; Bishops James S. Thomas, Jr., Charles F. Golden, Noah W. Moore, Jr., and L. Scott Allen were the first Afro-Americans to be assigned to predominantly white Episcopal areas; and Bishop Roy C. Nichols was the first Afro-American elected to the episcopacy by a predominantly white jurisdiction.

With the phasing out of black annual conferences beginning in 1964, in accordance with General Conference procedure, black district superintendents were appointed to white districts. The first such appointment was that of Charles L. Warren (1911–71) of the New York annual conference in 1964.

Notable Afro-American Methodists and Their Contributions Afro-American Methodists who have made notable contributions to the black community and to the nation include: Prince Hall (1753–1807), Methodist minister and founder of Masonry among Afro-Americans (Prince Hall Grand Masonic Lodge, 1791); Hiram R. Revels (1822–1901), Methodist minister and the first of two Afro-Americans elected to the U.S. Senate (1879–81) prior to 1966; Charles A. Tindley (1855–1933), "Prince of Preachers," builder and pastor of one of American Methodism's largest churches, Tindley Temple, Philadelphia, Pa.; William C. Jason, Sr. (1859–1943), first Afro-American president of Delaware State College; Countee Cullen (1903–46), brilliant poet and important literary figure in the 1920s, the son of Frederick A. Cullen, pastor of Salem Church, New York, N.Y.; Mary McLeod Bethune (1876–1955), Methodist laywoman and Spingarn Medal winner; Emmett J. Scott (1873–1957), special assistant to Secretary of War Newton D. Baker, 1917–18; Melvin B. Tolson (1895–1966), poet laureate of Liberia; and J. Ernest Wilkins (1894–1959), Methodist layman, appointed assistant secretary of labor for international labor affairs, 1954, and a member of the U.S. Civil Rights Commission, 1957–59.

United Methodist notables (1940) included: Thelma Barnes, first national secretary, Delta Ministry Project (Mississippi), National Council of Churches; Oswald P. Bronson, president of the Interdenominational Theological Center, Atlanta, Ga., and first Afro-American religious educator to be elected to the presidency of the 63-year-old Religious Education Association of the United States; Grace Bumbry, internationally known operatic soprano; Ezzard Charles, world heavyweight boxing champion (1949–51), elected to the Boxing Hall of Fame, 1954; Shirley Chisholm, the first Afro-American woman U.S. Representative (Brooklyn, N.Y.); James H. Cone, creative theologian and teacher at Union Theological Seminary, New York, N.Y.; James L. Farmer, first national director of Congress of Racial Equality (CORE); Cain H. Felder, executive director, black Methodists for church renewal; Claire Collins Harvey, first Afro-American to head Church Women United, 1971; Augustus F. Hawkins, first Afro-American elected to the U.S. Congress from California; Walter R. Hazzard, Jr., star professional basketball player; Anna Arnold Hedgeman, former Department of Health, Education, and Welfare executive and former executive director, National Council for Fair Employment Practices Commission; Dorothy L. Height, president, National Council of Negro Women and a member of the Defense Advisory Committee on Women in the (Armed) Services; Aaron E. Henry, courageous leader of the Mississippi Freedom Democratic Party (MFDP); M. Carl Holman, president, National Urban Coalition and brilliant writer; James M. Lawson, Jr., a founding organizer of the Student Nonviolent Coordinating Committee (SNCC) and leading civil rights figure; C. Eric Lincoln, professor of the sociology of religion at Union Theological Seminary, New York, N.Y. and noted author and founder of the Black Academy of Arts and Letters; J. Echols Lowery, chairman, board of directors, Southern Christian Leadership Conference (SCLC); Frederick D. Patterson, former president, Tuskegee Institute, Tuskegee Institute, Ala., and former president of the Phelps-Stokes Fund and founder of the United Negro College Fund; Leontyne Price, world-famous lyric soprano and Spingarn medalist (1965); Harry V. Richardson, first president, Interdenominational Theological Center; Cornish Rogers, associate editor of Protestantism's prestigious and influential *Christian Cen-*

tury; Carl B. Stokes, first Afro-American mayor of Cleveland, Ohio; Louis Stokes, first Afro-American elected to the U.S. Congress from Ohio; William O. Walker, publisher-editor of the nationally famous Afro-American newspaper, Cleveland *Call and Post*; and Joseph R. Washington, noted author and researcher in black religion. *See also* AFRICAN METHODIST EPISCOPAL (AME) CHURCH; AFRICAN METHODIST EPISCOPAL ZION (AMEZ) CHURCH; CHRISTIAN METHODIST EPISCOPAL (CME) CHURCH; CHURCHES.

REFERENCES: For further reading, see the following volumes: Barclay, William C., *History of Methodist Missions*, 3 vols., The Board of Missions and Church Extension of the Methodist Church, New York, 1949; Bucke, Emory S. (ed.), *The History of American Methodism*, 3 vols., Abingdon Press, New York, 1964; Clark, Elmer T., *The Journals and Letters of Francis Asbury* 3 vols., Abingdon Press, New York, 1958; Godbold, Albea, *Forever Beginning: 1766–1966: Historical Papers Presented at American Methodism's Bicentennial Celebration, Baltimore, Maryland (April 21–29, 1966)*, Association of Methodist Historical Societies, Lake Junaluska, 1967; Leete, Frederick D., *Methodist Bishops: Personal Notes and Bibliography*, Parthenon Press, Nashville, 1948; Morrow, Ralph E., *Northern Methodism and Reconstruction*, Michigan State University Press, East Lansing, 1956; Shaw, J. Beverely F., *The Negro in The History of Methodism*, Parthenon Press, Nashville, 1954; Sweet, William W., *Religion on the American Frontier: 1783–1840*, vol. IV, *The Methodists*, University of Chicago Press, Chicago, 1946; and Thomas, I. L., *Methodism and the Negro*, Eaton and Mains, New York, 1910; for a later volume, see Richardson, Harry V., *Dark Salvation: The Story of Methodism among Blacks in America* (1976).

MICHAEL, CYRIL (1898–   ), musician, lawyer, judge; born in Charlotte Amalie, Virgin Islands. After attending Catholic Parochial School in St. Thomas, Virgin Islands, Michael studied music and law through extension at the University of Chicago. Michael worked in various capacities—clerk, court commissioner, interpreter— in the U.S. District Court from 1937 to 1951, and during that same period intermittently sat on the bench of the Police Court as acting judge. From 1951 to 1957 Michael was U.S. attorney and attorney general of the Virgin Islands. In 1957 he became judge of the Municipal Court of St. Thomas and St. John, and in 1965 presiding judge of the Municipal Court of the Virgin Islands.

MICHAUX, HENRY M., JR. (1930–   ), lawyer, government official; born in Durham, N.C. Michaux received both the B.S. (1952) and J.D. (1964) degrees from North Carolina Central University (Durham). He served as assistant district attorney for North Carolina's Middle District, a milestone in bringing an end to the nation's historic practice of having only white federal prosecutors in the South.

MICHEAUX, OSCAR (1884– ?), motion picture producer; born in Metropolis, Ill. Early in his life Micheaux worked as a Pullman porter, farmer, and rancher in South Dakota. He was a novelist and publisher before beginning the production of motion pictures in the early 1920s, making many films thereafter. *See also* MOTION PICTURES.

MIDDLETON, JOHN ALBERT (1914–), educator, clergyman; born in Foreston, S.C. Middleton received a B.A. degree from Allen University (Columbia, S.C.) in 1939, a B.D. degree from Howard University (Washington, D.C.) in 1943, and his Th.M. degree from Iliff School of Theology (Denver, Colo.) in 1956. He then became pastor of several African Methodist Episcopal (AME) churches. Middleton taught at Morris Brown College (Atlanta, Ga.) for 14 years and became president of the college in 1965.

MIGRATORY / MIGRANT WORKERS See AGRICULTURE.

MILES COLLEGE Miles College, at Birmingham, Ala., was founded in 1907 by the Colored Methodist Episcopal Church (now the Christian Methodist Episcopal Church). Church-related and coeducational, Miles offers the bachelor's degree and provides liberal arts and teacher education curricula. Its 1975 enrollment was about 1,200.

The institution was originally chartered as Miles Memorial College in honor of William H. Miles, a bishop. In 1941 the trustees adopted the present name. Since its founding, the college has had ten presidents: James A. Bray, William A. Bell, George Wesley Gilbert, George A. Payne, Robert T. Brown, George L. Word, Mack P. Burley, Brooks Dickens, William Bell (second term), Lucius H. Pitts, and W. Clyde Williams.

The college is concerned with the welfare of people, especially the black community of Birmingham. Miles tries to assist the capable student, regardless of his financial circumstances. To this end, it devised a strong financial-aid program. In 1970–71, for example, Miles dispensed more than one million dollars in scholarships, grants, loans, and wages to about 80 percent of its student body.

MILITARY SERVICE See WARS.

MILLER, EDITH (1930–), lawyer, judge. Miller graduated from Hunter College of the City University of New York and Saint John's University Law School (Brooklyn, N.Y.). She was admitted to the New York bar in 1955, and seven years later she volunteered her services as attorney to the Legal Aid Society of New York. In 1967 Miller was employed as assistant attorney in charge of the Harlem branch office of the Legal Aid Society. She later became judge of the Family Court in New York City.

MILLER, FLOURNOY E. (1887–1971), comedian. Miller attended Fisk University (Nashville, Tenn.) before he formed a comedy team with Aubrey Lyles. Together they appeared in nightclubs in New York City and Chicago, Ill. In 1921, after their return from an engagement in London, England, they starred in their own Broadway show, *Shuffle Along*, with book and score by Noble Sissle and Eubie Blake. Some critics called it "the greatest Negro show ever." They wrote the book for another musical comedy, entitled *Runnin' Wild*, which opened on Broadway in 1923, and four years later they appeared in *Rang Tang*, another musical revue that they also helped to stage. *See also* MUSIC: HISTORY AND DEVELOPMENT.

MILLER, GEORGE W. (1922–), lawyer; born in Rutherfordton, N.C. Miller, a 1943 graduate of North Carolina Agricultural and Technical (A&T) State University, earned a law degree from Brooklyn Law School (Brooklyn, N.Y.) in 1955. He became a member of the New York state assembly in 1971, and later served as counsel to a large New York law firm.

MILLER, JAMES M. (1907–), composer, pianist; born in Pittsburgh, Pa. Miller received his education at the Carnegie Institute of Technology (Pittsburgh, Pa.) and Duquesne University (Pittsburgh, Pa.). He was a concert pianist from 1930 to 1945, and taught music in Pittsburgh schools after 1939. He was also a noted organist and composer and arranger of spirituals. His best-known compositions include "Please Don't Drive Me Away," "I Wanna Be Ready," "I Am Seeking for a City," "Daniel," "You Gonna Reap," and "Didn't My Lord Deliver Daniel?" *See also* MUSIC: SPIRITUALS/PERFORMANCE, COLLECTIONS.

MILLER, J. ERROLL See SCIENTISTS: SOCIAL.

MILLER, KELLY (1863–1939), sociologist, educator; born in Winnsboro, S.C. Miller received a B.A. degree (1886), a M.A. degree (1901), and his LL.B. degree (1903) from Howard University (Washington, D.C.). His mother was a slave and his father a soldier in the Confederate Army. Miller attended Fairfield Institute (1878–80) and won a scholarship to Howard University, from which he graduated in 1886. In 1887–88 he did postgraduate work in mathematics at Johns Hopkins University (Baltimore, Md.). Miller taught high school in Washington, D.C., in 1889, and began his career as a college professor teaching mathematics at Howard University in 1890. He served as dean of the College of Arts and Science at Howard University from 1907 to 1918, and retired as an administrator at Howard in 1935. His most significant writings include: "Howard University," in R. C. Ogden (ed.), *From Servitude to Service* (1905); *Race Adjustment* (1910); *Out of the House of Bondage* (1914); *An Appeal to Conscience* (1918); and *The Everlasting Stain* (1924). Two major contributions to sociology are his "Education of the Negro," in *U.S. Bureau of Education Report* (1901) and "Enumerations of Errors in Negro Population," *Scientific Monthly,* February 1922. See also SCIENTISTS: SOCIAL.

MILLER, LEON PARKER (1899–   ), lawyer, judge; born in Knoxville, Tenn. Having received his LL.B. degree from the University of Pennsylvania Law School in 1922, Miller opened a law firm with Harry J. Capehart in Welch, W. Va. From 1928 to 1932 Miller served as assistant prosecuting attorney of McDowell County, W. Va. Beginning in 1942 he was a member of the State Republican Executive Committee for 12 years, and following that became U.S. attorney to the Virgin Islands until 1962. In 1968 Miller was elected judge of the Criminal Court of McDowell County by a write-in vote, and a few years later he became judge of the Intermediate Court in McDowell County, a post from which he later retired.

MILLER, LOREN (1903–67), lawyer, judge, editor; born in Pender, Nebr. Miller studied at the University of Kansas and Howard University (Washington, D.C.), and received his LL.B. degree from Washburn College of Law (Topeka, Kans.) in 1929. From 1930 to 1934, however, he eschewed the practice of law, and worked as editor of the *California Eagle, California News,* and Los Angeles *Sentinel,* and as European correspondent for the Associated Negro Press. Miller began to practice law in Los Angeles, Calif. in 1934. After 30 years he was appointed judge of the Municipal Court of Los Angeles. His excellent book, *The Petitioners: The Story of the Supreme Court of the United States and the Negro,* was published in 1966. A good reference on Miller is Smith, Warner, "Loren Miller: Advocate for Blacks," *The Black Law Journal,* Spring 1971, pp. 7–15.

MILLER, MELVIN B. See NEWSPAPERS: CONTEMPORARY.

MILLER, THOMAS E. (1849– ?), lawyer, state legislator, U.S. Representative; born in Beaufort County, S.C. Miller graduated from Lincoln University (Lincoln University, Pa.) in 1872. He served in the lower house of the state legislature of South Carolina in 1874, 1876, and 1878, before he was admitted to the South Carolina bar in 1879. In 1880 Miller became a state senator, and almost ten years later he won election to the U.S. House of Representatives as a member of the Fifty-first Congress. Subsequently, he was again elected to the lower house of the state legislature, and in 1895 he was a delegate to the South Carolina Constitutional Convention. Miller was instrumental in persuading the state to establish the South Carolina State Colored College (now South Carolina State College) at Orangeburg, and he helped to organize the institution; after serving the school for 20 years, he returned to private practice. See also SOUTH CAROLINA STATE COLLEGE.

MILLIGAN, DOLFUS See SCIENTISTS: BIOLOGICAL, PHYSICAL.

MILLS, FLORENCE (1895–1927), singer, dancer, comedienne; born in Washington, D.C. Mills started singing and dancing in the salons of Washington D.C., society at the age of 5, and she regularly performed at the residence of the British ambassador for several years. At the age of 6 she made her professional debut in Washington, D.C., with the Bert Williams and George Walker show, *Sons of Ham,* and then she traveled with the show. After moving to New York City's Harlem in 1903, Miller performed in road companies and vaudeville acts, and in 1919 she joined her sisters in a singing act. Later she became part of a cabaret act known as the Panama Four, with Ada "Bricktop" Smith, Cora Greene, and Mattie Hight; still later she joined another group called the Tennessee Ten. Her first notable success, however, came in 1921 as a result of her performance in *Shuffle Along*, the all-black musical revue written by Noble Sissle and Eubie Blake. Subsequently, Miller appeared in *Plantation Revue* (1922), *Dixie to Broadway* (1924), and her own *Blackbirds* revue in London, England, and Paris, France. By the time of her death in 1927, she had achieved enormous popularity in Europe as well as in the United States.

MINER TEACHERS COLLEGE *See* DISTRICT OF COLUMBIA TEACHERS COLLEGE.

MING, WILLIAM ROBERT, JR. (1911–1973), lawyer, educator; born in Chicago, Ill. Ming received a Ph.B. degree (1931) and his J.D. degree (1933) from the University of Chicago. He was admitted to the Illinois bar in 1933, and practiced law in various capacities, public and private, from 1933 to 1961. He taught at Howard University (Washington, D.C.) from 1937 to 1946 and at the University of Chicago from 1947 to 1953. Ming was imprisoned for income tax evasion in Chicago and died there at the age of 62.

MINGUS, CHARLES (CHARLIE) (1922–1979), jazz bass player, bandleader, composer; born in Nogales, Ariz. Mingus played in Los Angeles and San Francisco, Calif., during the 1940s, and became known as a "hard Bop" performer. During his career Mingus played with many jazz greats, including Louis Armstrong, Kid Ory, Lionel Hampton, Charlie Parker, Stan Getz, Duke Ellington, Bud Powell, and Art Tatum. Known as one of jazz's most original bassists, Mingus also achieved success as a composer. *Meditations on Integration* and *The Mingus Dances*, a ballet score, became well-known. Mingus also formed his own combo in New York City. *See also* MUSIC: JAZZ.

MINSTRELS *See* LITERATURE: DRAMA/THEATER; MUSIC: HISTORY AND DEVELOPMENT.

MISCEGENATION *See* RACE: CULTURE.

MISHOE, LUNA ISAAC (1917–), educator; born in South Carolina. Mishoe received a B.S. degree from Allen University (Columbia, S.C.) in 1938, a M.S. degree from the University of Michigan in 1942, and his Ph.D. degree in mathematics from New York University in 1953. He taught mathematics and physics at Kittrell College (Kittrell, N.C.) from 1939 to 1942; joined the U.S. Air Force for four years from 1942 to 1946; and then served as professor at Delaware State College

from 1946 to 1948, as professor at Morgan State University (Baltimore, Md.) from 1948 to 1960, and as president of Delaware State College after 1960. Mishoe was also president of the Delaware Academy of Science and of the Higher Education Advisory Committee of the state of Delaware after 1973.

MISSISSIPPI FREEDOM DEMOCRATIC PARTY (MFDP) An organization composed largely of Afro-Americans, it came into existence in the 1960s. The MFDP worked to obtain more adequate representation of blacks in Mississippi politics. It drew national attention in 1964 by challenging the regular Mississippi delegation to the Democratic National Convention and by winning two seats as special delegates. At the 1968 convention, in coalition with white liberal groups under the name Loyal Democrats of Mississippi, the MFDP again challenged the regular delegation and succeeded in barring it from being seated on the grounds that discrimination, starting at the precinct level, prevented Afro-Americans from participating in politics. In 1972 the party supported Charles Evers for governor. Some of its leaders were Aaron E. Henry, Fannie Lou Hamer, Charles Evers, and the well-known (white) Mississippi publisher, Hodding Carter, III. *See also* POLITICS.

MISSISSIPPI INDUSTRIAL COLLEGE Mississippi Industrial College, at Holly Springs, Miss., was founded in 1905 by the Colored Methodist Episcopal Church, (now the Christian Methodist Episcopal Church). Still church-related, the coeducational college offers the bachelor's degree and provides liberal arts and teacher education curricula. Its 1975 enrollment was 371. Important persons associated with the historical development of the college, most of whom were affiliated with the CME or Methodist churches, include: Elias Cottrell, a bishop; J. D. Hammond, a secretary of the board of education of the Christian Methodist Episcopal Church, South; and Randall A. Carter, a bishop.

MISSISSIPPI VALLEY STATE UNIVERSITY Mississippi Valley State University, at Itta Bena, Miss., was authorized by the state legislature in 1946 but not actually opened until 1950. A state-supported, coeducational institution, the university offers the bachelor's degree and provides liberal arts, teacher education, professional, and terminal curricula. The institution opened in 1950 with 14 regular students, and its 1975

Charlie Mingus. *(National Educational Television.)*

enrollment was about 2,500. Its first president was James H. White; its president in 1975 was Ernest A. Boykins.

Arthur Mitchell. (Courtesy of Martha Swope.)

MITCHELL, ARTHUR (1934–   ), ballet dancer, artistic director; born in New York City. Mitchell won a scholarship to New York City's High School of Performing Arts and was the first male graduate to receive the school's annual Dance Award. In 1952 he studied dance on a scholarship at the School of American Ballet, at the same time continuing to perform in the modern dance idiom in which he trained at the high school and making his Broadway debut in the Harold Arlen-Truman Capote musical, *House of Flowers*. He made his debut with the New York City Ballet in 1955 in George Balanchine's *Western Symphony* as the first black dancer in the nation to become a member of a major classical ballet company. A casting novelty at first, he quickly rose to principal dancer with the company. He electrified audiences in Balanchine's abstract *Agon*, in the comic role of Puck in *A Midsummer's Night Dream*, and in many other ballets. In 1969 on the Johnny Carson *Tonight* show he shattered the television taboo of black-white dance partnership when he danced with Suzanne Farrell in *Agon*. He formed an interracial dance company which performed at the Spoleto Festival of Two Worlds in Italy, and in 1966 formed and was artistic director of the American Dance Company, scheduled to perform at the first World Festival of Negro Art in Dakar, Senegal. Shortly after, at U. S. government request he created the National Ballet Company of Brazil, acting as its choreographer and artistic director. He founded the Dance Theatre of Harlem to teach not only black children, but all children, the art of dance and especially the art of classical ballet. *See also* DANCE.

MITCHELL, CLARENCE M., JR. (1911–   ), lawyer, administrator; born in Baltimore, Md. Mitchell received a B.A. degree from Lincoln University (Lincoln University, Pa.) in 1932, and both LL.B. and J.D. degrees from the University of Maryland Law School. He did graduate studies in the field of social work at the University of Minnesota and at Atlanta University. Although admitted to the Maryland bar, Mitchell became a newspaper reporter, after which he held various government positions until appointed director of the Urban League in St. Paul, Minn. As labor secretary for the National Association for the Advancement of Colored People (NAACP) from 1945 to 1950, he planned and directed the drive to bring about fair employment practices for government employees. In addition his testimony before a civil service commission in 1948 about racial discrimination in post offices led to sweeping reforms. Mitchell's lobbying activities in 1949 prevented the UN Food and Agricultural Organization from locating at the University of Maryland because of the university's discriminatory policies. After 1950 he became director of the Washington, D.C., Bureau of the NAACP, and in addition he took on the job of legislative chairman of the Leadership Council on Civil Rights. Mitchell received the NAACP's Spingarn Medal in 1969 for his pivotal role as civil rights lobbyist in promoting the Civil Rights Act of 1968. *See also* NATIONAL ASSOCIATION FOR THE ADVANCEMENT OF COLORED PEOPLE (NAACP).

MITCHELL, JUANITA E. JACKSON   *See* JACKSON, JUANITA E.

MITCHELL, LOFTEN (1920–   ), playwright, critic; born in New York, N.Y. Mitchell studied playwrighting at night at City College of the City University of New York, graduated with honors from Talladega College (Talladega, Ala.) in 1943, and studied at Columbia University for a year. He performed with the Rose McClendon Players, and in 1958 received a Guggenheim Fellowship. His plays include *A Land Beyond the River, Ballad of the Winter Soldiers,* and *Star of the Morning* (about Bert Williams). Mitchell also authored a novel, *The Stubborn Old Lady Who Resisted Change* (1973), and *Voices of Black Theater: Told in the Words of Its Pioneers* (1974). His personal memoir, *Black Drama* (1967), is the most complete history of Afro-American theater. *See also* LITERATURE: DRAMA / THEATER.

MITCHELL, PARRAN J. (1922–   ), educator, U.S. Representative; born in Baltimore, Md. Mitchell received a B.A. degree from Morgan State University (Baltimore, Md.), and served as an infantry officer in the 92d Infantry Division during World War II. He later became the first Afro-American to be admitted to the graduate school of the University of Maryland, from which he received his M.A. degree in sociology. Mitchell engaged in civil rights activities in the 1960s, serving with various civil rights agencies, and taught at Morgan State University. He was elected to the U.S. House of Representatives in 1968 and reelected in 1970, 1972, 1974, 1976 and

1978. He chaired the caucus of black congressmen. *See also* POLITICS.

MOBILE STATE JUNIOR COLLEGE Mobile State Junior College, at Mobile, Ala., was authorized by the state board of education in 1963. A state-supported, coeducational school, Mobile is a two-year institution that offers terminal occupational programs that can be credited toward the bachelor's degree. Its 1975 enrollment was 656.

Formerly the Mobile Branch of Alabama State College, the school opened in 1936 and offered a two-year college curriculum and extension courses for teachers in service. In 1963 the structural pattern of the college was changed, and the school was renamed the Alabama State College Mobile Center. The college had operated as part of Alabama State College for 28 years.

In 1965 the state legislature ratified the board's 1963 action, thus giving the institution legal independent status and its first actual recognized existence.

MONK, THELONIUS (1920–   ), jazz pianist, composer; born in Rocky Mount, N.C. Monk grew up in New York City, where he began piano lessons when he was 11 years old and began playing in local bands a few years later. During the 1940s he played at Minton's Playhouse in Harlem, and there along with Charlie

Christian (guitarist), Dizzy Gillespie (trumpeter), and Kenny Clark (drummer) was instrumental in the development of the revolutionary jazz style called Bop. In 1959 Monk made his first appearance in New York City's Town Hall. As a composer, he wrote many compositions, including "Round About Midnight," "Blue Monk," "Ruby, My Dear," and "In Walked Bud." Because of his contribution to the development of Bop, he is known as the "High Priest of Bop." *See also* MUSIC: JAZZ.

MONROE, EARL *See* ATHLETES: BASKETBALL.

MONTANTE, JAMES (1907–   ), lawyer, judge; born in Pittston, Pa. Montante completed undergraduate school and law school at the University of Michigan. After having received his LL.B. degree, he was admitted to the Michigan bar in 1930. From then until 1961 he engaged in a private law practice, and in 1961 he became judge of the Circuit Court for Wayne County, Mich.

MONTGOMERY IMPROVEMENT ASSOCIATION (MIA) On December 1, 1955, an Afro-American seamstress, Rosa Parks, refused to give up her seat on a public bus in Montgomery, Ala., to a white man. The subsequent arrest of Parks for this act of defiance prompted two young black ministers of Montgomery, Dr. Martin Luther King, Jr., and Rev. Ralph D. Abernathy, to organize a boycott against the bus system. To coordinate this massive protest action, King formed the Montgomery Improvement Association. After 381 days of walking or using car pools arranged by the MIA, citizens of Montgomery were able to return to a nonsegregated bus system. With the successful ending of the boycott, the MIA also came to an end, yet not before having established Martin Luther King, Jr., as an important black leader and having made Afro-Americans more aware of the effectiveness of unified action. Out of this organization came the leaders of the Southern Christian Leadership Conference (SCLC). *See also* CIVIL RIGHTS: CIVIL RIGHTS MOVEMENT IN SELECTED STATES: ALABAMA; KING, MARTIN LUTHER, JR.; SOUTHERN CHRISTIAN LEADERSHIP CONFERENCE (SCLC).

MOORE, ARCHIE *See* ATHLETES: BOXING.

MOORE, HARRY T. *See* NATIONAL ASSOCIATION FOR THE ADVANCEMENT OF COLORED PEOPLE (NAACP).

Far left: Parran J. Mitchell (left) at the Black Economic Development Conference, held in January, 1972, at Morgan State University (Baltimore). At Mitchell's left is Earl G. Graves, publisher of *Black Enterprise,* a business magazine. *(Photo by Leroy Henderson.)*

MOORE, HOWARD, JR. (1932–   ), lawyer; born in Atlanta, Ga. Moore graduated from Morehouse College (Atlanta, Ga.) in 1954 and Boston University School of Law in 1960. He founded the Southern Legal Assistance Project to help young men in their efforts to resist the draft during the war in Vietnam. As head of a large law firm in Atlanta, Moore defended, among others, such leading figures of the civil rights movement as Dr. Martin Luther King, Jr., Rev. Ralph Abernathy, Stokeley Carmichael, and H. Rap Brown. In 1966 Moore represented Julian Bond in his effort to take the seat in the Georgia legislature to which he had been elected but from which he was banned for his antiwar statements. After his participation as chief defense counsel in the lengthy trial of Angela Davis from 1971 to 1972, Moore opened additional law offices in Berkeley, Calif. *See also* LAWYERS.

Jesse E. Moorland. *(Moorland-Spingarn Research Center.)*

MOORE, NOAH WATSON, JR. (1902–   ), Methodist bishop; born in Newark, N.J. Moore received a B.A. degree (1926) and his LL.D. degree (1961) from Morgan State College (Baltimore, Md.), a B.D. degree from Drew University (Madison, N.J.) in 1931, and his D.D. degree from Gammon Theological Seminary in 1951. He was pastor of Methodist churches in New York, Maryland, and Pennsylvania before being elected a Methodist bishop in 1960.

MOORE, PARLETT LONGWORTH (1907–   ), educator; born in Wetipquin, Md. Moore received a B.A. degree from Howard University (Washington, D.C.) in 1930, a M.A. degree from Columbia University Teachers College in 1935, and his Ed.D. degree from Temple University (Philadelphia, Pa.). He was principal of high schools in Maryland, taught at Morgan State University Summer School from 1938 to 1943, was dean of Carver Junior College in Maryland from 1950 to 1956, and served as president of Coppin State College (Baltimore, Md.) until he retired in the late 1960s.

MOORE, RICHARD B. *See* ONOMATOLOGY.

MOORE, RICHARD V. (1906–   ), educator; born in Quincy, Fla. Moore received a B.E. degree from Knoxville College (Knoxville, Tenn.) in 1932, his M.Ed. degree from Atlanta University in 1944, and honorary LL.D. degrees from Knoxville College in 1950 and from Edward Waters College (Jacksonville, Fla.) in 1948. He became president of Bethune-Cookman College (Daytona Beach, Fla.) in 1947.

MOORE, WINSTON E. (1929–   ), psychologist, public official; born in New Orleans, La. Moore graduated from West Virginia State College in 1952, and received a M.A. degree in psychology from the University of Louisville (Louisville, Ky.) in 1954. Starting his career in Louisville as a psychologist for the Juvenile Court, he moved to Chicago, Ill., where he soon became clinic director for the Illinois Youth Commission, then staff psychologist with the Illinois State Employment Service. From 1968 to 1970 Moore was superintendent of the Cook County Jail. In 1970 he became executive director of the Cook County Department of Corrections.

MOORLAND, JESSE EDWARD (1863–1940), clergyman, educator; born in Coldwater, Ohio. Moorland, whose ancestors had been free for about 200 years, studied at Northwestern Normal University and at Howard University (Washington, D.C.). He pastored Congregational churches in Virginia, Tennessee, and Ohio. Moorland also served with the Young Men's Christian Association (YMCA) in Washington, D.C., from 1898 until his retirement in 1924. Interested in the study of Afro-American history, he began and encouraged contributions to a valuable collection of books and materials at Howard University (the Moorland-Spingarn Research Center). Howard honored him with a D.D. degree in 1906.

MOORLAND-SPINGARN RESEARCH CENTER *See* ARCHIVES. *See also* HOWARD UNIVERSITY; MOORLAND, JESSE EDWARD; PORTER, DOROTHY L.

MOREHOUSE COLLEGE Morehouse College, at Atlanta, Ga., was founded in 1867 as Augusta Institute in Augusta, Ga., under the sponsorship of the American Baptist Home Mission Society. An independent college for men, Morehouse offers the bachelor's degree and provides a liberal arts curriculum. However, it is also strongly oriented toward teacher education, and its religious origins still exert influence. Its 1975 enrollment was about 1,200.

The school was founded by Edmund Turney, Richard Coulter, and William Jefferson, under the sponsorship of the American Baptist Home Mission Society. When it moved to Atlanta in 1879, its name was changed to Atlanta Baptist Seminary. In 1913 this name was changed to Morehouse College, in honor of Rev. Henry L.

Morehouse, corresponding secretary of the society.

From a school that began with a student body of 37 former slaves and 3 faculty members, who met in the basement of Springfield Baptist Church in Augusta, Morehouse has grown to a fully accredited liberal arts college with 75 faculty members. It also features a special program that allows for study abroad. Morehouse leads all predominantly black four-year colleges in the percentage of alumni who have received doctorates: one out of every ten Morehouse men has an academic or professional doctorate. It was estimated in the 1960s that one out of every 18 Afro-Americans who held the earned doctorate (Ph.D.) had received his bachelor's degree from Morehouse. Among the college's alumni who are treated biographically in this *Encyclopedia* are: Lerone Bennett, Jr., editor-historian; Julian Bond, politician; James Allen Colston, educator; Hugh Morris Gloster, critic-educator; Maynard Jackson, politician; and Martin Luther King, Jr., clergyman and civil rights leader. *See also* ATLANTA UNIVERSITY.

MORGAN COLLEGE *See* MORGAN STATE UNIVERSITY.

MORGANFIELD, McKINLEY *See* MUSIC: BLUES; WATERS, MUDDY.

MORGAN, GARRETT A. (1875–1963), inventor; born in Paris, Tenn. Morgan developed his first invention, a belt fastener for sewing machines, in 1901, and he sold it for $150. In 1914 he won the First Grand Prize gold medal at the Second International Exposition of Sanitation and Safety for his breathing helmet and smoke protector; in 1916 he demonstrated the use of this device in the rescue operation following an explosion in a tunnel at the Cleveland Waterworks that trapped many men below Lake Erie. In 1923, Morgan developed an automatic stop sign to aid the movement of traffic, selling the rights to this invention to General Electric for $40,000.

MORGAN, NORMA GLORIA (1928–), painter, printmaker; born in New Haven, Conn. Morgan studied at the Hans Hofmann School of Fine Arts and the Art Students League in New York City. She used an intricate line, especially in her copper engravings, to bring out the features of fantasy landscapes and natural rock patterns. She also painted the prophets of the Bible, as in *David in the Wilderness*, and portrayed the

remoteness of the Scottish moors, as in *Glen in Badenoch*.

MORGAN STATE UNIVERSITY Morgan State University, at Baltimore, Md., was chartered in 1867 as the Centenary Biblical Institute. State-supported and coeducational, Morgan State offers undergraduate and graduate degrees and provides liberal arts and teacher education curricula. Its 1976 enrollment was 6,361.

The history of the university can be divided into three major phases. Chartered in 1867, the institution's first phase was as the Centenary Biblical Institute (1867–90); its second was as Morgan College (1890–1938); and its third phase was as Morgan State College (1938–75).

View of the administration building at Morgan State University (Baltimore) in 1975. (*Photo by Jacquelyn Low*.)

The Centenary Biblical Institute began operation with no classroom of its own, using the lecture rooms of the Sharp Street Methodist Episcopal Church. It was not until 1872 that the school was formally opened, in its own building, with its purpose being to prepare young men for the Christian ministry. When the first building became too small to accommodate the classes, a stone building was erected on a lot donated by Dr. and Mrs. John F. Goucher. The cornerstone was laid in 1880.

The growth of the school was marked by an increase in curriculum offerings (normal and academic subjects especially were added), the admission of young women as students, and the establishment of two branch schools. The first, Princess Anne Academy, was established at Princess Anne, Md., in 1886. This school later became Maryland State College and later the

University of Maryland Eastern Shore. The second branch school, Virginia Collegiate and Industrial Institute, established at Lynchburg, Va., in 1891, was destroyed by fire in 1917. Both of these schools emphasized secondary and industrial training.

Morgan State was launched on its second phase of development in 1890 when Dr. Lyttleton F. Morgan, former chairman of the board of trustees, gave a large sum of money to the institution. Morgan's endowment enabled the school to offer courses on the collegiate level for the first time. In gratitude the school was renamed Morgan College. Following an intensive and frustrating search, a new site was found for the growing school. Title was taken in 1917, and adjoining property was bought in 1919 at the present site.

The school entered its third phase in 1939. By act of the Maryland general assembly, Morgan College officially became a state institution. Its name, accordingly, was changed from Morgan College to Morgan State College. On July 1 of its centennial year (1967), the board of trustees was dissolved. The college then came under the purview of the board of trustees of the state colleges of Maryland, an organizational arrangement that ended, however, in 1975 when the state legislature granted university status to the college.

Morgan's graduates have predominated in public and community services. For example, 4 of the 5 Afro-American Maryland state senators in 1975 were Morgan graduates: Verda Welcome, Clarence Blount, Paul E. Weisengoff, and Clarence M. Mitchell; and 5 of the 14 Afro-Americans in the Maryland House of Delegates were either graduates or had attended the university. In addition to holding prominent positions in government, law, and social services, Morgan graduates make up an imposing array of the chief leaders in education in the state: principals, supervisors, and teachers.

Before the 1930s, all of the institution's presidents were white. After this period, all were Afro-Americans: Dwight O. W. Holmes; Martin D. Jenkins; King V. Cheek, Jr.; and Andrew Billingsley. Many faculty members attained recognition in a variety of areas. See also EDUCATION: COLLEGES AND UNIVERSITIES.

MORIAL, ERNEST NATHAN (1928–), lawyer, judge, state legislator; born in New Orleans, La. Morial received a B.S. degree from Xavier University (Cincinnati, Ohio) in 1951, and his LL.B. degree from Louisiana State Law School in 1954, the first Afro-American student to receive such a degree from that university. In 1967 he was elected to the Louisiana state legislature, becoming the first black to earn this distinction since Reconstruction. Later, Morial attained another "first," when he became a judge of the Juvenile Court of New Orleans in 1970, the first Afro-American judge on this bench. In 1974 Morial was elected to the Court of Appeal for the Fourth Circuit (city of New Orleans), Louisiana; and he became the first Afro-American mayor in 1977.

MORMAN, WILLIAM DANIEL (1901–51), physician; born in Augusta, Ga. Morman received a B.S. degree from Morehouse College (Atlanta, Ga.) in 1925 and his M.D. degree from Howard University Medical College (Washington, D.C.) in 1929. He interned at City Hospital No. 2, St. Louis, Mo.; was hygiene inspector in the public schools of St. Louis (1931–45); was associate director of the department of otolaryngology (1934–51); and was chief of staff at Homer G. Phillips Hospital, St. Louis (1941–51). Morman served as head of the department of otolaryngology at St. Mary's Infirmary and at the Peoples' Hospital, St. Louis, and as instructor in otolaryngology at St. Louis University School of Medicine.

MORRIS BROWN COLLEGE Morris Brown College, at Atlanta, Ga., was founded in 1881 under the patronage of the African Methodist Episcopal (AME) Church. A church-related and coeducational school, Morris Brown offers the bachelor's degree and provides liberal arts and teacher education curricula. Its 1975 enrollment was 1,383.

Morris Brown was a product of the self-help concept generated among Afro-Americans after slavery in an effort to educate their children. It was chartered in 1885 and named in honor of Morris Brown (1770–1849), the second consecrated bishop of the African Methodist Episcopal (AME) Church. The students are predominantly Afro-American, although the faculty is integrated. The college is affiliated with the Atlanta University Center. See also ATLANTA UNIVERSITY.

MORRIS, CARL See NEWSPAPERS: CONTEMPORARY.

MORRIS COLLEGE Morris College, at Sumter, S.C., was founded in 1908 by the Baptist Educational and Missionary Convention of South Carolina, a consortium of Baptist churches. A church-related and coeducational school, Morris offers the bachelor's degree and provides liberal arts and teacher education curricula. Its 1975 enrollment was 350.

At the time of its founding, the purpose of the college was to provide South Carolina youths with greater opportunity for education at the elementary, high school, and college levels. This broad-spectrum service was thought necessary because of the small number of both public and private schools available to Afro-Americans in the state. In later years the elementary and high school programs were discontinued.

The college currently pursues a policy of keeping its enrollment small, and the faculty makes a particular effort to spend as much time as possible with the students in informal surroundings.

MORRIS, EDWARD H. (1858–1944), lawyer, state legislator; born in Flemingsburg, Ky. Morris, whose father was a slave and whose mother was free, studied law in the offices of a Chicago, Ill., lawyer and was admitted to the Illinois bar at the age of 21 in 1879. Because of his color, his law practice started very slowly, but eventually he counted among his clients George Pullman, Marshall Field, Loeb and Company, and International Harvester Company. Before then Morris had served for a year as attorney for Cook County in charge of taxes. In 1881 he was elected to the Illinois legislature in which he sat for eight years.

MORRIS, JAMES B., SR. *See* Newspapers: Contemporary.

MORRIS, SAMUEL SOLOMON (1916–), African Methodist Episcopal bishop; born in Norfolk, Va. Morris received a B.S. degree from Wilberforce University (Wilberforce, Ohio) in 1937 and his B.D. degree from Yale University in 1940; he also attended Ohio State University and the University of Chicago. He was pastor of African Methodist Episcopal (AME) churches in Tennessee, Michigan, Indiana, and Illinois before being elected an AME bishop in 1972. Morris served as president of Shorter College (North Little Rock, Ark.) from 1946 to 1948.

MORRISON, CHLOE ANTHONY (TONI) WOFFORD (1931–), author, editor; born in Lorraine, Ohio. Morrison received a B.A. degree from Howard University (Washington, D.C.) in 1953 and her M.A. degree from Cornell University (Ithaca, N.Y.) in 1955. She taught at Texas Southern University and Howard University before becoming a senior editor with the New York publishing firm, Random House, in 1965. Her works include two novels, *The Bluest Eye* (1970) and *Sula* (1974). Her third novel, *Song of Solomon* (1977), received the National Critics Circle award for fiction (1977).

MORRISON, RICHARD DAVID (1910–), educator; born in Utica, Miss. Morrison received a B.S. degree from Tuskegee Institute (Tuskegee Institute, Ala.) in 1931, a M.Ed. degree from Cornell University (Ithaca, N.Y.) in 1941, and his Ph.D. degree from Michigan State University in 1954. He taught vocational agriculture in Talladega County, Ala. (1932–37) and then joined the staff of Alabama Agricultural and Mechanical (A & M) College in 1937, becoming its president in 1962.

MORRISON, TONI *See* Morrison, Chloe Anthony (Toni) Wofford.

MORRISTOWN COLLEGE Morristown College, at Morristown, Tenn., was founded in 1881 by Rev. Judson S. Hill, a Methodist Episcopal (ME) minister from New Jersey. A church-related and coeducational school, Morristown offers a two-year program, usually credited toward the bachelor's degree. Its 1975 enrollment was 149.

Morristown College was for many years the cultural and educational center of the Afro-American community of East Tennessee, serving as a boarding, elementary, and high school. When it became a two-year college, it achieved a success not realized until then by any black institution of its type—that is, full accreditation by the regional accrediting agency. Morristown College continued in the 1970s as a two-year, liberal arts-oriented institution, affiliated with the United Methodist Church, and awarding the associate in arts degree.

MORROW, E. FREDERIC (1909–), administrator, government official; born in Hackensack, N.J. Morrow graduated from Bowdoin College (Brunswick, Maine) in 1930, and later received his LL.B. degree from the Law School of Rutgers University (New Brunswick, N.J.). In 1952, after holding positions at the National Urban League, the National Association for the Advancement of Colored People (NAACP), and for three years in the public affairs division of the Columbia Broadcasting System (CBS), he joined the

Dwight D. Eisenhower presidential campaign staff. Three years later, President Eisenhower named him an administrative assistant, and Morrow became the first Afro-American to hold an executive position on a presidential staff. He left government service in 1961.

MORROW, JOHN HOWARD (1910–   ), educator, government official; born in Hackensack, N.J. Morrow received a B.A. degree from Rutgers University (New Brunswick, N.J.), and a M.A. degree and his Ph.D. degree from the University of Pennsylvania. He taught in high schools and colleges for 23 years before being appointed ambassador to Guinea by President Dwight D. Eisenhower in 1959. His brother, E. Frederic Morrow, was an administrative assistant to President Eisenhower. Morrow later served as a member of the U.S. delegation to the UN General Assembly. *See also* MORROW, E. FREDERIC.

MORTON, CHARLES EVANS (1926–   ), clergyman, educator; born in Bessemer, Ala. Morton received a B.A. degree from Morehouse College (Atlanta, Ga.) in 1946, a B.D. degree from Union Theological Seminary in 1949, and his Ph.D. degree from Columbia University in 1958. He taught at Knoxville College (Tennessee) 1953-1957 and chaired humanities and philosophy at Dillard University (New Orleans, La.) 1957-1962. He served as pastor of several churches, including Ebenezer Baptist Church (Poughkeepsie, N.Y.) 1951-1953 and Metropolitan Baptist Church (Detroit) since 1964.

Jelly Roll Morton from a sketch in a special edition of the *St. Louis American*, 1964, for the bicentennial of St. Louis, Mo. *(Courtesy of Bennie G. Rodgers. St. Louis American.)*

MORTON, FERDINAND JOSEPH (JELLY ROLL) (1885–1941), composer, pianist; born in New Orleans, La. Morton studied the guitar as a youth, then switched to the piano. He played in bars and cabarets up and down Basin Street in New Orleans along the Gulf Coast, and up the river to cities such as St. Louis. He worked with many of his era's great artists, including Porter King, Skinny Head Pete, Florida Sam, and Baby Gryce. He made the transition from ragtime to jazz, although he is remembered as one of ragtime's greatest exponents. Morton wrote more than 120 songs and he made hundreds of recordings. In 1938 he recorded 116 sides for Alan Lomax, curator of the archives of American folk song at the Library of Congress, Washington, D.C. These recordings represent a monumental contribution to the documentation and preservation of early jazz. *See also* MUSIC: JAZZ.

MORTON, FRANKLIN WHEELER, JR. (1920–   ), lawyer, judge. Morton attended Lincoln University (Lincoln University, Pa.), and received an undergraduate degree from Long Island University in 1941. He studied law at Temple University (Philadelphia, Pa.), and at New York University, from which he received his LL.B. dgree in 1948. From 1951 to 1958 Morton served as assistant district attorney for Kings County, and in 1958 he became judge of the Criminal Court of the City of New York. He later became a judge of the Supreme Court in Brooklyn, N.Y.

MOSELEY, HELEN JEWEL *See* PREFACE: LIST OF CONTRIBUTORS.

MOSS, ELIZABETH MURPHY (1917–   ) business executive, journalist; born in Washington, D.C. Moss received a B.A. degree from Howard University (Washington, D.C.) and the M.A. from the University of Minnesota (1958). She earned a certificate of journalism from Columbia University in 1951. Moss became vice-president and treasurer of the Afro-American Company, publisher of the largest black chain of weekly newspapers in the United States, and served as a member of the board of directors of the company for more than 23 years. In addition, she wrote a weekly column under the pseudonym Bettye M. Moss. During World War II Moss was in England as the first Afro-American woman war correspondent. Morgan State University honored her with the D. Litt. in 1976.

MOSS, OTIS (1935–   ), clergyman; born in La Grange, Ga. Moss received a B.A. degree from Morehouse College (Atlanta) in 1956 and his B.D. also from Morehouse three years later. He has pastored several churches, including Old Mt. Olive Baptist Church (La Grange, Ga.) and Provident Baptist Church (Atlanta) from 1956–1961. Since 1961 he served as minister of Mt. Zion Baptist Church (Lockland, Ohio). He wrote a weekly column for the Atlanta *Inquirer*; and his sermon, "Going from Disgrace to Dignity" appeared in a book entitled *Best Black Sermons* (1972).

MOTEN, BENNY / ETTA *See* MUSIC: JAZZ.

MOTHER BETHEL *See* AFRICAN METHODIST EPISCOPAL (AME) CHURCH.

MOTION PICTURES Motion pictures are slightly older than the twentieth century, and roles in them for Afro-Americans were available from the very beginning. It is a truism that American movies have reflected the beliefs and behavior of the audiences to whom they were directed, but black roles provided a special case altered by conditions within the film industry and by social forces on the cutting edge of American social change. For example, black roles ranged more widely in style and dimensions during times of laissez-faire competition among more-or-less independent studios. On the one hand, black roles grew standardized during times of corporate oligopoly; on the other hand, wartime stresses shifted racial antipathies toward other groups, thus relieving social repressions upon Afro-Americans and encouraging the growth of new and better depictions of black life on the screen. Times of relative prosperity, such as the late 1920s or the late 1930s, stimulated Afro-American protest efforts that in turn opened the way for marginal developments on the screen. On at least one occasion, the introduction of sound film, a technological change provided fresh opportunity for black cinema performers. Because so much of black artistic expression was based on musical foundations, only early sound film seemed to do justice to it. Indeed, in certain Afro-American circles the myth prevailed that only black voices could be recorded accurately by existing sound-recording equipment.

Finally, black contributions to the motion picture industry were often the results of black protest beginning with the editorial complaints of the New York *Age* and other black newspapers in the 1910s; the legal and direct action protests of the National Association for the Advancement of Colored People (NAACP) against the motion picture *The Birth of a Nation* in 1915; the complaints of such individual actors as Charles Gilpin on the set of Universal's *Uncle Tom's Cabin* in 1926; the complaints of other actors on many sets thereafter; the growing protests of ad hoc citizens' committees in the early World War II years; and the NAACP demands in the 1960s and 1970s for broadened job opportunities in cinema and television production guilds.

The First Films During the first ten years of commercial cinema, between 1895 and 1905, Afro-Americans, for many different reasons, appeared in a remarkable range of images—some in a light more favorable than could be expected in late Victorian melodrama and fiction, and certainly in a manner more varied than Americans accepted in their daily lives. However, these early appearances did not leave any permanent mark. They lacked black roots, having come from the traditions of ethnic vaudeville and of topical film-as-record. Eventually, in the end, they were drowned in the publicity surrounding the Civil War semi-centennial, which brought with it a rage for sentimental movies and melodramas that reached a climax in D. W. Griffith's *The Birth of a Nation* in 1915. Such movies created a monopoly for southern literary metaphor in which Afro-Americans had no place except as servile props to the antebellum way of life.

Among the topical films-as-record of the primitive era was *A West Indian Woman Bathing a Baby* (Edison, 1895), followed by other anthropolgically neutral films. The Spanish-American War stimulated many "newsreel" cameramen, who recorded *Colored Troops Disembarking; The Ninth Negro Cavalry Watering Horses;* such reenactments of reality as *The Battle of Mt. Ariat,* which featured, according to a catalogue, the "famous 25th Infantry, colored;" and *The Colored Invincibles,* in which blacks fought with "as much zeal as their white brothers." More rarely, cameramen attempted to record Afro-Americans performing, as in *Ballyhoo Cakewalk* (Edison, 1903). After 1905 the nonfiction films included the broad variety of African life recorded incidentally to the African journey of President Theodore Roosevelt (including a fraud shot in Chicago, Ill.); such anthropological films for commercial screens as *The Military Drill of the Kikuyu Tribes and Other Native Ceremonies;* and several of Jack Johnson's boxing matches.

Black images reflected the broad stream of American racial custom at its most traditional in the form of minstrelsy and southern lore. Thomas Edison's company released several brief reels of blackface minstrelsy. But by 1905 the catalogue pages of most of the eastern studios were thick with the chicken thieves, crapshooters, and proverbial "darkey" stories of southern tradition that reached farther into the racist past than the relatively benign minstrels. *Interrupted Crap Game, Chicken Thieves, A Night in Blackville,* and *Prize Fight in Coon Town* were typical titles from studio catalogues.

Pictures About the Civil War The broadest and most humane roles were offered in films rooted in ethnic vaudeville and in such melodramas as

Harriet Beecher Stowe's *Uncle Tom's Cabin*, the first cinema version of which, by William S. Porter, appeared in 1903. A year later Biograph released *A Bucket of Cream Ale*, a well-worn bit of ethnic conflict that ends with a blackface Negro maid hurling a bucket of ale in the face of a boorish Dutchman.

But then the golden anniversary of the Civil War brought North and South together, embracing the abstract principle of "union" rather than the emotional one of abolition. The mood of intersectional harmony was reflected in scores of Civil War movies that took a nostalgic southern point of view in which Afro-American roles could do no more than retrace old ruts. Biograph's *The Fights of Nations* (1907) foreshadowed the shift. Beginning as a celebration of the many American ethnic groups that lived in harmony together, it omitted Afro-Americans from its final tableau (although they had contributed a fine piece of vernacular jazz dance to the middle, probably the first ever recorded on film). Beginning in 1909 and 1910 many old-fashioned stereotypes increased in films, but the most startling new trend was the rash of movies of the Civil War in which antebellum Negro roles became stock ingredients. These films included *The Empty Sleeve, Or Memories of By Gone Days*; *A Reconstructed Rebel*; *Days of War*; *A Flag of Two Wars*; *The Suwanee River*; *A Fair Rebel*; *A Girl Spy*; *For the Cause of the South*;

The Soldier Brothers of Susannah; *The Only Veteran in Town*; *The Littlest Rebel*; *Old Mammy's Secret Code*; *In the Fall of '64*; *A Gentle Volunteer*; *A Slave's Devotion*; and *Old Mammy's Charge*. Their common feature was faithful Negro servants who sacrificed their own self-interest for the honor of preserving their masters' fortunes and families.

Among the best were *The Battle*, *His Trust*, and *His Trust Fulfilled*, all three by D. W. Griffith, who in these years gradually gave shape to a grand design for a magnificent advance in film making, eventually entitled *The Birth of a Nation* (1915), a celebration of southern virtue under the burden of Reconstruction. Afro-Americans were stratified into loyal servants on the one hand, and insolent and cruel "town Negroes" who abused freedom on the other. The NAACP used the film's release as the occasion for the first national black social protest that combined legislative lobbying in the Massachusetts statehouse, picketing in Boston streets, protests to several mayors, nationwide mail campaigns, and joining forces with white organizations. Indeed, so zealous were they that some branches overreacted to a movie of William Sheldon's *The Nigger* (retitled *The Governor*, with a politesse that would not become common until years later), a melodrama with a clearly neutral and at times pro-black point of view.

At first Griffith's ambitious film, which had received praise from the president of the United States and other public figures, forced the NAACP into an illiberal demand for censorship. However, by 1916 the splash made by *The Birth of a Nation* had spurred the NAACP, Emmett J. Scott of Tuskegee Institute (Tuskegee Institute, Ala.), and a group of black West Coast businessmen to seek means to make all-black movies that would serve as counterpropaganda to Griffith and his imitators. Between 1916 and 1922 a California group known as the Lincoln Company, led by George and Noble Johnson, produced on an average one film per year with such titles as *The Realization of a Negro's Ambition* and *The Trooper of Troop K*. Only the lack of a distribution system and subsequently a nationwide influenza epidemic blocked their plans for an indigenous black cinema. The NAACP and Scott's joint project met worse luck. Their film, *Lincoln's Dream*, was the subject of constant haggling with Universal, and by the end of three years of patchwork it had deteriorated into an

Griffith's *Birth of a Nation* (1915) was flawed by its simplistic depiction of Afro-Americans as either loyal servants or as villainous "town Negroes." *(Museum of Modern Art/Film Stills Archive.)*

expensive overblown failure that barely survived its Chicago, Ill., opening in 1919 as *The Birth of a Race*. Nevertheless, the film represented an early Afro-American attempt to create a black cinema aesthetic beyond mere contributionism. Its rivals for the all-black market, such as Ebony Company of Chicago, by way of contrast produced black mirror images of white pictures, such as *A Black Sherlock Holmes*.

Stereotypes In the ten years after *The Birth of a Nation*, movies became a relatively regressive medium because older metaphorical black roles persisted in the absence of newer images, despite an increase of urbanization and sophistication. However, little of Afro-American urban life found its way to the screen. The studios themselves had grown larger, more conservative, and increasingly satisfied with old ways. Blackface remained a common mode of depicting Afro-American life on the screen, along with the antebellum pictures and the newly minted Tarzan movies with their hapless jungle men. Such movies were the studios' means of standardizing product and minimizing risk.

Nevertheless, a small cadre of Afro-American regulars began to develop as featured players, among them Madame Sul-te-Wan, Onest Conley, Carolynne Snowden, Nathan Curry, Zach Williams, Spencer Williams, Raymond Turner, the boxers Sam Baker and George Godfrey, and others. Noble M. Johnson exemplified both the plight and the achievement of the Afro-American actor. He began with the Lubin studio in Philadelphia, Pa., in the 1910s, and survived into the 1940s in John Ford's *She Wore a Yellow Ribbon*. Later, he joined the Lincoln Company, although Universal, which held another of his contracts, forced him to resign. He had regular roles in Universal's "B" series films: *Bull's Eye, Red Ace,* and *Red Feather Specials.* Johnson played exotic primitives, Orientals, Latins, and Indians in *Adorable Woman, Leopard Woman, Kismet, The Four Horsemen of the Apocalypse, Robinson Crusoe, The Courtship of Miles Standish, The Ten Commandments,* and many more. In one year he appeared in nine movies, including *Flaming Frontier, Aloma of the South Seas, Manon Lescaut, Lady of the Harem,* and *Ben Hur.*

If Afro-Americans appeared in many old conventional roles, their postwar urban lives, especially as they impinged on white lives, began to break down the social conditions that had rein-

forced the stereotypes. Thus small changes, in part exemplified by Johnson's career, began to appear on the screen. In 1916 Bert Williams made two touching, witty comedies for Biograph, *Fish* and *A Natural Born Gambler,* each of which contained Williams' old blackface routines and yet managed to reach beyond them as well. In the same period Vitagraph made two blackface parodies of white boxers whose comedy emerged from their fear of Jack Johnson—*Some White Hope* and the *The Night I Fought Jack Johnson.* Other urbanized bits were featured in Griffith's *Hoodoo Ann* (1916), with its black confidante, and C. B. DeMille's *Manslaughter* (1922), with its derisive black women convicts. As early as the 1910s, several egalitarian children's series were released that eventually matured by the later 1920s into Hal Roach's *Our Gang,* with its regular black performers, Allan Hoskins, Stymie Beard, and their successors—all of whom drew appreciative black crowds on their personal-appearance tours. Afro-American soldiers appeared in footage released to commercial theaters by the U.S. War Department: Goldwyn's *Too Fat to Fight* (1919) and Griffith's *The Greatest Thing in Life* (1918). Black partners, trainers, and wise old hands appeared in most boxing, horse racing, and other sports films, and as flippant rather than obsequious servants in such pictures as *California Straight Ahead.* If such films failed to reach large audiences, they at least attracted critics to racial issues, with the result that subsequent movies would occasionally be found wanting (critically) because of the shabby ways in which they depicted Afro-Americans.

Three of Griffith's pictures are illustrative of change in the 1920s. *One Exciting Night* (1922) included stock black servants, but the crime (the criminals are bootleggers) is solved by a "Kaffir, the dark terror of the bootleg gang." The next year critics turned on Griffith's *The White Rose,* objecting to his "mawkish sickening sentimentality" and "jumbled and pointless" plot. Again he had used the old blackface servants, but this time critics excused him as a "genius out of touch with the world." Next he made, or at least started, *His Darker Self,* an intended vehicle for the blackface singer Al Jolson, who deserted the film in its early stages. In the end the film's urban setting necessarily included tough black hustlers as well as such bourgeois roles as a preacher (and his mass baptism) and the only servant who was also his employer's fishing partner. Symbolically, the picture had begun with Griffith and blackface, had ended with his dismissal, and had generated a number of perhaps unconsciously strong Afro-American roles.

The freewheeling 1920s simply had no room for undiluted racism. There were too many alert black critics such as Lester Walton of the *Age*, Romeo Daugherty of the *Amsterdam News*, J. A. Rogers, D. Ireland Thomas, and others; and too many increasingly sensitive whites, especially those writing for such motion picture trade papers as *Variety*. The Ku Klux Klan tried and failed to produce its own film to counteract the trend. In 1924 Al Woods attempted to release *Free and Equal,* a ten-year-old racist essay, only to find the trade papers warning exhibitors that "it is not only old-fashioned but so crudely done that the Sunday night audience laughed it practically out of the theater."

By the late 1920s studio heads occasionally issued trial-balloon press releases testing public reaction to stronger Afro-American themes. The best opportunity emerged in the form of *Uncle Tom's Cabin.* Abolitionist in tone, it appealed to black and to white audiences alike because, along with its message, it had become glossed with nostalgia. A black love affair already had appeared on the screen in John M. Stahl's film of Charles Dazey's play, *In Old Kentucky.*

The Afro-American press responded to the impending production with encouragement and avid discussion. The mainstream of black thought had moved away from the zionism and nationalism of Marcus Garvey's United Negro Improvement Association (UNIA). The news of

This broadside heralded Micheaux's The Millionaire (1928). (Library of Congress.)

Uncle Tom's Cabin was one of many small evidences of optimism. For the title role Universal signed Charles Gilpin, who was subsequently released, it was said, because of his strong reading of the part. But his successor, James Lowe, gave a fine performance in a movie that cut through much of the sentimental veneer built up by years of treacly roadshow *Toms.* "Never before has the Southern Negro had the good fortune to be selected to take part in a clean-up motion picture," claimed the *Amsterdam News.* Every black actor, it insisted, "should be proud of the opportunity which is his to help portray conditions as they were in the days of oppression." Although the finished picture failed to measure up to the hopes held for it, a series of elaborate openings and several southern protests ensued. Still, in a decade of weak black roles in Hollywood movies, it was unique in bringing a strong, artfully portrayed black figure to the screen. The decade closed with Edgar "Blue" Washington's good hobo role in William Wellman's *Beggars of Life* (1928); with honest Afro-American sailors in DeMille's *Old Ironsides* (1926); with Alan Crosland's *The Sea Beast* (1926); with an accurately crafted urban ambience in Monta Bell's *Man, Woman, and Sin* (1927); and with a few other heartening roles in a time of despair.

Response and Protest: Oscar Micheaux In response to unfulfilled black needs, a kind of "underground" film-making movement grew outside of Hollywood. Largely white-owned, it nonetheless set out to make films for a predominately urban Afro-American audience. Beset by continuing problems of distribution, low budgets, unevenly trained actors, and technical inadequacies, these producers turned out films throughout the silent era. Their most important feature was that they went beyond mere contributionism toward treating Afro-Americans as a genuine presence in American life.

As early as the 1910s Luther Pollard's Ebony Corporation produced Afro-American versions of popular stories, and the Douglass Company of New Jersey attempted "to show the better side of Negro life" and "to inspire in the Negro a desire to climb higher" with war movies, with an adaptation of Paul Laurence Dunbar's *The Scapegoat,* and with *The Colored American Winning His Suit* (1916). Several companies joined Douglass in releasing U.S. War Department footage under such titles as *From Harlem to the Rhine* and *Our Hell Fighters Return.*

By the early 1920s many companies had been established all over the country. "Colored Motion Picutres Are in Great Demand," claimed a New York *Age* headline. Among the producers and their pictures were: Reol's version of Dunbar's *Sport of the Gods;* Sidney P. Jones' *Injustice,* a wartime tale of Afro-Americans and the Red Cross; Democracy Photoplay Corporation's *Democracy, Or a Fight for Right and Loyal Hearts,* "A Smashing Virile Story of Our Race Heroes"; the Renaissance Film Company's newsreels of 1922; Ben Strasser's *His Great Chance;* Norman's *The Green-Eyed Monster;* Dr. A. Porter Davis' *The Lure of a Woman,* the first film made in Kansas City, Mo.; Cotton Blossom's *Undisputed Evidence* and Lone Star's *Wife Hunters,* both made in San Antonio, Tex.; and Norman's *Crimson Skull,* shot in the all-black town of Boley, Okla. In addition scores of companies had announced optimistic prospectuses but failed to survive to release their first production.

The strongest producer throughout the 1920s was Oscar Micheaux, a black midwesterner who produced in Chicago, Ill., and then in New York City. Beginning with *The Homesteader* in 1919, he broke off a negotiation with the Lincoln Company and struck out on his own. In succession through the 1920s he produced *Within Our Gates,* a treatment of the Leo Frank lynching in Atlanta, Ga.; *The Brute,* featuring the black boxer Sam Langford; *The Symbol of the Unconquered,* an indictment of the Ku Klux Klan; *Birthright,* a claim that racism burdened even a Harvard University graduate; *The Conjure Woman* and *The House Behind the Cedars,* two novels by Charles Waddell Chesnutt; *Body and Soul,* starring Paul Robeson in his first movie; and other films. Micheaux's style was an archly cynical mask that indicted racism, but his cinematic flair was hampered by a paucity of funds, a condition above which he could never rise.

Toward the end of the decade the Colored Players of Philadelphia, Pa., a white group fronted by Sherman (Uncle Dud) Dudley (a black impresario from Washington, D.C.) and served by a white technical crew, contributed a black version of *Ten Nights in a Barroom* starring Charles Gilpin. A year later, in 1928, it released *Scar of Shame,* a treatment of color caste within an Afro-American community and its tragic implications. But it was still Micheaux who most consistently dealt with black issues. His *Spider's Web* was a melodrama that expressed the love-hate relationship between the black ghetto and "numbers game." However, Micheaux could never make the melodramatic genre speak consistently to and for Afro-Americans, and he lapsed into bankruptcy at the end of the silent era, leaving the field to Dunbar, the Colored Players, and a few other companies.

Musical Comedies and Dramas One of the high points of black achievement in film came with the widespread distribution of sound films. After the success of *The Jazz Singer* and other sound films in the late 1920s, studios searched for new materials with which to exploit the new medium. Metro Goldwyn Mayer (MGM) and 20th Century-Fox produced two of the most ambitious pictures, *Hallelujah!* and *Hearts in Dixie.* Through the viewpoint of southern white admirers of black life, both films introduced the religion, ambitions, loves, hates, regionalisms, and music of Afro-Americans to a mass white audience. If they were distorted, they nevertheless created a demand for such pictures and gave employment to such actors and actresses as Nina Mae McKinney, Daniel Haynes, Clarence Muse, Stepin Fetchit, and a host of their imitators. Moreover, King Vidor, the MGM director, employed a black assistant director, Harold Garrison, and a black consultant, James Weldon Johnson of the NAACP. Vidor's policy was also followed at Christie Comedies, which employed Spencer Williams as writer and performer.

Despite the success of the black musicals, the studios eschewed making large investments in them though they retained interest in such films. The result was a long run of black musical and variety performances in a generation of one- and two-reel films. At their worst studios resorted to old southern literary metaphors in such vehicles as Paramount-Christie's comedies made from Octavus Roy Cohen's *Saturday Evening Post* "darkey" stories. The Afro-American team of Buck and Bubbles made a similar early sound series for Pathe from Hugh Wiley's *Post* stories. The black performers who appeared in them were like interchangeable parts. Some of the Lafayette Players, a black theater troupe that had moved from New York City to Los Angeles, Calif., regularly supplied casts to Micheaux's "race movies," to Hollywood feature films, and to the all-black two-reelers. For the resulting outpouring of black two-reelers the studios signed Aubrey Lyles and Flournoy Miller of the Afro-American revue, *Shuffle Along;* Duke Ellington; the dancing Covans; Jules Bledsoe; the Hall Johnson Choir; Louis Armstrong in *I'll Be Glad*

When You're Dead You Rascal You; Cab Calloway in *Minnie the Moocher*; Jimmie Mordecai in *Yamecraw*; Noble Sissle in *That's the Spirit*; the Nicholas brothers in *Barbershop Blues* and *The Black Network*; Armstrong and Sidney Easton in *A Rhapsody in Black and Blue*; Ellington in *Black and Tan Fantasy*; Eubie Blake and Sissle in *Pie, Pie Blackbird*; and dozens more. Yet hidden under the busy surface remained the nagging fact that the short films rarely served as trials for larger productions. Instead, because the studios would not risk large sums on black movies, the black performers remained consigned to small films.

Throughout the history of Afro-Americans in the cinema, the fortunes of the race were best served in times of laissez-faire independent production. Conversely, monopolistic conditions tended to encourage stereotypes. The age of the Great Depression was no exception, and after the first splash of *Hallelujah!* and *Hearts in Dixie*, the best work was the product of independent studios. Unlike the 1920s, however, depressed conditions, small distribution facilities, and the need for heavy investments in sound equipment drove most all-black producers from the field. Gradually, such white entrepreneurs as Alfred Sack of Texas, Ted Toddy of Atlanta, Ga., and Bert and Jack Goldberg of New York City took over the race movies.

Serious independents afterward came from theatrical and European backgrounds. The most sanguine product was *St. Louis Blues* by Dudley Murphy. Shot in New York City using new RCA equipment by a director with both Hollywood experience and a minor reputation based on the experimental film *Ballet Mecanique* (done with the avante-garde painter Ferdinand Léger), *St. Louis Blues* featured the singing of Bessie Smith, the dancing of Jimmie Mordecai, the playing of Jimmy Johnson, and the music and arrangements of W. C. Handy and J. Rosamond Johnson. The result was the finest film of Afro-American life up to that time (1930). Like most movies about Afro-Americans, it appeared at the bottom of double bills and caused little excitement even among middle-class blacks.

In 1933 Murphy again made a fine black movie, *The Emperor Jones*, with a script approved by the original author, Eugene O'Neill; musical score by J. Rosamond Johnson; a title role by Paul Robeson; and a production team free of strictures imposed by the Hollywood studios' fears of southern box office reactions. Again, a fine film received a mixed response due to hesitant distributors, a divided black press, and conservative critics.

The mixed results caused Afro-American intellectuals, Robeson among them, to despair and to look to Europe for respite from American racial mores. As early as 1930 Robeson had joined a small group of cineasts (led by Kenneth Macpherson) in Territet, Switzerland, and made *Borderline*, a powerful indictment of racism that subsequently became entangled in customs and in distribution problems. Later in the 1930s Robeson made a number of British films each one an attempt to rise above the ruck of racism and intended to give him a modicum of personal control. But even when they were good, these films (among them were *King Solomon's Mines*, *Sanders of the River*, *Big Fella*, *Proud Valley*, *and Jericho*) failed to appeal to American audiences, black or white.

European films seemed devoid of the worst outrages of American racial arrangements. Among the movies of high reputation and low appeal for Afro-Americans were those of Josephine Baker, the St. Louis, Mo., expatriate of the Folies Bérgère. Her movies, such as *Siren of the Tropics*, were often replicas of exotic primitives. Despite praise by blacks in France, the press attacked the film when it arrived because it "renders the Negro ignoble." Theophilus Lewis concluded that "Miss Baker will never crash the films in a big way." Of all the European projects in the early 1930s, Mezrabpom's Russian production, *Black and White*, attracted the most Afro-American attention. Although it was never completed, it lured Langston Hughes, Ted Poston, Henry Lee Moon, and two dozen other Afro-Americans to Russia to help in its production. It was said that Stalin finally suppressed it as the price of diplomatic recognition. Thus, Afro-Americans were frustrated at every turn in the early 1930s; and, for all its failures, Hollywood provided the only cinematic outlet of nationwide range and acceptable technical proficiency.

The Great Depression Years Throughout the 1930s the Afro-American press praised each small gain, and implicitly chose Hollywood productions as the main means through which black cinema could be expressed. Scores of movies were praised for some small bit of decency, and at the end of the decade one well-known actor concluded "Hollywood is a swell place." Each gain in quality or status promised much.

To take a slice of the period from mid-decade would provide illustration of the range of, though not necessarily typical, black roles. Fox released *The Little Colonel* and *The Littlest Rebel*, which teamed Shirley Temple and the black dancer, Bill Robinson, in an antebellum setting that seemed about the only possible milieu available to present a black dancer's talent. Paramount's *Mississippi* was one of many pictures that featured black performers who had no investment in the plot, in this case the "Cabin Kids." *Escape from Devil's Island* featured Noble Johnson and Daniel Haynes in one of the well-worn prison pictures that provided the few opportunities for black actors actually to emote. John Ford's *Steamboat Round the Bend* was the best example of the slow-moving style of Stepin Fetchit, the black star whom fans admired for his style of life while often resenting the roles that earned him his keep. Warner Brothers' *Bullets of Ballots* lifted Louise Beavers out of the ranks of maids and mammies as Nellie Silvers, the "numbers queen." In another urbane bit Bill Robinson, in a playlet within *Hooray for Love*, appeared as a kind of "mayor" of Harlem who saves Jeni Legon from eviction, a segment supported by the witty piano of Fats Waller. King Vidor, the director of *Hallelujah!*, brought Stark Young's Civil War novel, *So Red the Rose*, to the screen, and depicted both poles of black response to slavery—accommodation *and* rebellion. Ford infused *The Prisoner of Shark Island*, the story of Dr. Samuel Mudd—the man who set John Wilkes Booth's leg—with the strong presence of black soldiers. Warner Brothers' adaptation of Robert E. Sherwood's Broadway success, *The Petrified Forest*, benefited from a central sequence in which two blacks, a gunman and a liveried chauffeur, debate their respective plights with the outlaw as the clear victor. Marc Connelly's black religious fable lifted from the tales of Roark Bradford, *The Green Pastures*, brought another all-black cast to the screen, garnering both the praise and damnation of the black press. Universal's remake of *Showboat* replaced Stepin Fetchit's "Joe" with that of Paul Robeson, who, along with Hattie McDaniel, gave the picture a certain Afro-American strength missing from the older version. In addition to the Afro-American roles, Fritz Lang and Mervyn LeRoy made *Fury* and *They Won't Forget*, two misfired indictments of lynching.

But in spite of the growing range of black roles, Hollywood society and hiring practices continued to conform to the broad outlines of American norms. Therefore the thrust of the depression era films was toward preserving Afro-Americans in the roles of servants and lackeys, at least until the eve of World War II. The black press felt obligated to praise the longevity of black performers, no matter what their roles, while at the same time it singled out for special notice those roles that seemed to advance the cause of the race. Among the breaches with tradition were Lewis Milestone's *Hallelujah, I'm a Bum* (1933), with its egalitarian hoboes, among them Edgar Conner; Etta Moten's silhouetted song, "Remember My Forgotten Man" in LeRoy's *Gold Diggers of 1933* and her "Carioca" in *Flying Down to Rio*; Ivie Anderson and the black chorus of the Marx Brothers' *A Day at the Races*; Louis Armstrong's raucous "Public Melody Number One" with Martha Raye in *Artists and Models*; Clarence Muse and Langston Hughes' writing credits on *Rainbow on the River* and *Way Down South*; Fetchit's role as a servant who joins the French army with his master in *The World Moves On*; and Fox's indictment of an Atlantic "blackbirder" in *Slave Ship*.

In genres that could not adapt to such subtle changes, such as jungle movies, black roles disappeared. The decade of the 1930s opened on MGM's jungle melodramas—*Trader Horn* with its black actor, Mutia Omooloo, and the first *Tarzan*—and ended with Tarzan in New York, Guatemala, and anywhere other than Africa. Late in the decade Africans appeared in authentic (if in a one-sided and simplistic manner) big movies such as *Four Feathers*, *Rhodes of Africa*, and *Stanley and Livingstone*, but remained locked into stereotypical, witless tribal roles in "B" movies.

Not until the late 1930s did the black press offer a countervailing pressure to that of southern exhibitors. Southern circuits had regularly refused to book such films as *Artists and Models* and *One Mile from Heaven*, the latter a story of a black woman (Fredi Washington) who must surrender the white child she has raised. Moreover, southern censors, especially in Memphis, Tenn., and Atlanta, Ga., often elided presumably offensive racial sequences. But in the late 1930s the Afro-American press began to object to scripts for such documentaries as *The March of Time* and to Hollywood's failure to move beyond mere contributionism. It had always praised such occasional parts as Clarence Brooks' West Indian doctor in John Ford's *Arrowsmith* or the attempt at interracial relationships in Universal's adaptation of Fannie Hurst's *Imitation of Life*. For whatever reason, on the eve of World War II maids seemed to grow more flippant (as in *The*

Mad Miss Manton); the South grew more decadent (as in *Jezebel, Another Part of the Forest,* and *The Little Foxes*); and interracial conflict seemed possible, at least in bits (as in *Golden Boy*).

Probably because of Hollywood's apathy toward Afro-American social ambitions, the 1930s marked the zenith for the race movie movement, even though by then the Great Depression would have forced most of the production companies into the hands of a few white entrepreneurs.

In part also the viability of the movement, at least in the short run, may have stemmed from the failure of European imports. Europeans always failed to deal with American racism because they tended to equate it with class consciousness. Such Russian films as G. V. Alexandrov's *The Circus* (1936), which featured a story centering on racism, were so filled with dull propaganda that their messages fell short of Afro-American audiences due to their own ponderous weight. Josephine Baker's movies, including *Princess Tam Tam* and *Siren of the Tropics,* failed to rise above the conventional exotic native girl romance. Victor Trivas' *War is Hell* depicted the impact of war on the "little people," but its "classless" internationalism was undermined by its black soldier, a grinning song-and-dance man. Such French films as Pierre Chenal's *L'Alibi,* Jean Renoir's *Toni,* Jean Benoit-Levy's *La Mort du Cygne,* and Jacques Feyder's *Le Grand Jeu* never deviated from American norms. Afro-Americans were used for a jazz atmosphere, for inclusion in scenes of lower-class life, or were light-skinned enough to be acceptable or included in such exotic locales as the Foreign Legion (the cases in the above

The late Thirties saw several black westerns such as *Bronze Buckaroo* (1939), which starred Herb Jeffries (center). *(Museum of Modern Art/Film Stills Archive.)*

films). British films were more honest, with a longer tradition ranging back to the 1910s. But neither their colonialist films, such as Robeson's *Sanders of the River,* nor such parodies, funny as they were, as *Old Bones of the River,* had much appeal for American audiences.

In the 1920s the Afro-American press and several intellectuals had high hopes for race movies. Ten years later they despaired and opted for Hollywood. The reasons were clear: such age-old disabilities as inadequate distribution, poor facilities, and low budgets combined with the increased financial burdens of sound-recording. Only Micheaux managed to produce consistently throughout the decade; yet he too suffered from the disabilities. Micheaux's *Ten Minutes to Live* (1932) and *The Exile* (1931), Rosebud's *Absent,* and Harry Gant's *Georgia Rose* (1930) all suffered criticism for their faulty technique especially as it related to sound and cutting. Notwithstanding, Donald Heywood attempted a parody of the Garvey movement, *The Black King* (1932), and Robert Mintz and Louis Weiss tried to adapt a genuine black drama to the screen as *Drums o' Voodoo* (1933). But except for an occasional newsreel compilation, by the mid-1930s the movement languished.

Later in the decade a number of white investors entered the field and replaced all the Afro-Americans save Micheaux. On the West Coast the race movies came largely from a single source, Million Dollar Pictures, an amalgam of Harry and Leo Popkin of Hollywood, Ben Rinaldo, and two blacks, Ralph Cooper and George Randol, both of whom had Hollywood experience. Their goal was good quality acceptable to white theater chains, good Afro-American casts, and, where it did not intrude too obviously, an entertaining black theme of uplift or self-help. The logical choice was the popular gangster genre, and all the producers, the Popkins, Micheaux, and the New York group centering on the Goldberg brothers, turned them out—*Dark Manhattan, Gang War, Bargain with Bullets, Underworld, Mystery in Swing, Double Deal,* all the way into the postwar era with *Dirty Gertie from Harlem.* The best were like Gary Cooper's *Am I Guilty?* (1940) in which he plays a doctor who must struggle with the decision to minister to the needs of gangsters or to open a free clinic for poor Harlemites. Some of them, such as *Moon over Harlem* (1939), were directed by whites, such as the German émigré, Edgar G. Ulmer, or Arthur Dreifuss, who made *Murder on Lenox Avenue* (1941).

Outside the gangster genre there were few successes. Clarence Muse made a sentimental and interesting musical drama, *Broken Strings* (1940), a tale in which blacks come to accept the merits of both European music and jazz. Jed Buell's Hollywood Productions in 1938–39 released four derivative westerns, *Harlem Rides the Range, Bronze Buckaroo, Two Gun Man from Harlem,* and *Harlem on the Prairie,* which made good use of the singer, Herb Jeffries, and the comedians, Mantan Moreland and Flournoy Miller. Perhaps the two best pictures of the cycle were Joe Louis' and Henry Armstong's boxing biographies, *The Spirit of Youth* (1937) and *Keep Punching* (1939), both of which made good visual use of the boxing milieu and its ambience.

The World War II Years As World War II approached, Afro-American observers and critics grew more impatient. The Young Communist League picketed Micheaux's *God's Step Children* because "it slandered Negroes, holding them up to ridicule." The black press attacked such pictures as the Popkins' *Reform School* as "overdramatic"; Dixie National's *Mr. Washington Goes to Town* as "undignified"; and so on. Micheaux attempted one last grand scheme in concert with Colonel Hubert Julian, the "Black Eagle" of the Ethiopian Air Force. Together they released *The Notorious Elinor Lee* and *Lying Lips,* but the results were disappointing. By the end of the war the race movies had begun to pall, and except for a few remaining Micheaux films, Goldberg releases, All-America productions, and a clutch of Louis Jordan musicals, the movement waned.

The trade paper, *Variety,* in the spring of 1942 displayed a banner headline—"Better Breaks for Negroes in H'wood." The story referred to an agreement struck by major studio heads, Walter White of the NAACP, and Wendell Willkie, the defeated Republican presidential candidate in 1940, through which Afro-Americans could expect better roles of higher quality, roles in which blacks might normally appear in society, and roles that would depart from the old stereotypes. Ad hoc committees of black actors and citizens, liberal white groups, and the black press became micrometers for measuring the studios' cleaving to the new standards. Organized Afro-Americans gave awards to movies that took liberal stances.

By then blacks were at the mercy of Hollywood because of the slow attrition of race movies. The one exception to white production was the "Soundies," short musical films starring many blacks produced for use in jukeboxes. Fritz Pollard, an old black football star, fronted for the organization but gradually it too fell under white control.

The best indicator of black plight on the eve of the war was *Gone With the Wind,* David O. Selznick's expensive film of Margaret Mitchell's best selling novel of Civil War and Reconstruction. Many films, *His Trust, The Birth of a Nation, The Texans, Dark Command, Belle Starr, The Prisoner of Shark Island, So Red the Rose,* and several biographies of Lincoln had tried to comprehend the period. Selznick took his race angle seriously and tried to see "that the Negroes come out decidedly on the right side of the ledger." Indeed, he tested the blacks as carefully as he did the white principals. Butterfly McQueen appeared as an urbane easterner on the set, and in her shrill role *Time* reported that she went beyond mere servitude toward "sly humor." The black press plugged Hattie McDaniel's Mammy as possessed of "dignity and earnestness" that would raise her to "more than a servant." The film's gaudy premiere, its reception, and the eventual Academy Award given to McDaniel polarized Afro-American opinion for and against the picture. Even the Communist Party organ divided on the subject.

Thenceforward, Afro-American roles slowly improved in *Sullivan's Travels, Birth of the Blues, The Little Foxes, In This Our Life,* and *Casablanca,* and an agreement between NAACP representatives and the studios in the spring of 1942 codified and gave direction to the liberal

The all-black musical *Stormy Weather* (1943) included, in addition to the star-spangled cast list on the poster, Ada Brown, F. E. Miller, Zuttie Singleton, Nicodemus Stewart, Babe Wallace, Ernest Whitman, and Dooley Wilson. *(New York Public Library.)*

changes. War movies gradually included more black roles, sometimes even before the armed services being depicted got around to it. *Mission to Moscow, The Ox-Bow Incident, Cabin in the Sky, Stormy Weather, Sahara, Crash Dive, Lifeboat,* and *Shoe Shine Boy* were all efforts to broaden the contribution of Afro-Americans to musicals, war films, and westerns. The federal government contributed *The Negro Soldier, The Negro College in Wartime, Henry Brown, Farmer,* and others in a propaganda effort against racism forced upon it by a rising awareness of the implication of fighting a war against ideological racists.

As a gauge of wartime social change in racial arrangements, audiences and organized Afro-Americans turned against two innocuous pictures that probably would have been well received in 1936. Walt Disney's *Song of the South* and Julien Duvivier's *Tales of Manhattan* both appeared toward the end of the war. They featured a number of whimsically conceived, well-acted, old black figures, the two best of which were played by the veteran James Baskette and by Paul Robeson. However, when Robeson perceived the hostile black reaction to his film he repudiated it; and Baskette died and received a posthumous Oscar even as pickets walked under marquees of *Song of the South.*

After the war Afro-American roles shifted from contributionism toward surrogates for

American social problems. Stanley Kramer had worked with Carl Foreman and Carlton Moss on *The Negro Soldier,* and after the war he bought Arthur Laurents' polemic against anti-Semitism, *The Brick Foxhole,* turning it into *Home of the Brave,* a secretly produced "message movie" that preached against racism. It was quickly fol-

lowed by Louis DeRochemont's *Lost Boundaries,* Elia Kazan's *Pinky,* Clarence Brown's *Intruder in the Dust,* Sidney Portier's first movie, *No Way Out,* and such lower budget films as the Popkins' *The Well* and Roger Corman's *The Intruder.* Each one revealed Afro-American problems as being at the bottom of white problems of attitude and discriminatory behavior. However, a true black film, Richard Wright's *Native Son,* with the author playing the lead met distribution problems.

Contemporary Films: The 1960s and 1970s As though casting the Afro-American experience in problem form would exacerbate it, the next generation of films resumed the contributionist tradition and the exceptional-Negro storyline. Robert Gordon's *Joe Louis Story,* two versions of the Harlem Globetrotters, Poitier's near-raceless delinquent in *Blackboard Jungle,* Darryl Zanuck's picture postcard of Alec Waugh's *Island in the Sun* with its muted race-politics, and well-scrubbed productions of *Carmen Jones* and *Porgy and Bess* asked little of their audiences save a reserved tolerance of dark skin colors. Gradually this period of respite from the pressure of new ideas on old social attitudes metamorphosed into a new genre of racial films in the 1960s that treated Afro-Americans and their lives as they impinged upon whites who see their value system first threatened then enriched by an Afro-American presence.

Young Man with a Horn followed the career of a white jazzman who learned his art at the feet of an old black sideman. Exploitation films, such as Hugo Haas' *Night of the Quarter Moon* (1959), Stephen Borden's *My Baby is Black,* Larry Buchanan's *Free, White, and 21,* and others, sensationalized and then defused black-white

Far right: Pinky (1949), a story about crossing the color line and "passing," featured (left to right) Ethel Waters, Frederick O'Neal, and Jeanne Crain. (Museum of Modern Arts/Film Stills Archive.)

Home of the Brave (1949), which featured (left to right) Lloyd Bridges, James Edwards, and Frank Lovejoy, focused on racism among U.S. servicemen in World War II. (Museum of Modern Art/Film Still Archive.)

relationships. Except for Shirley Clarke's documentary-style *The Cool World*, most of the well-known pictures came from sources in other media, such as Ossie Davis' *Purlie Victorious*, a barbed satire on the manners of slavery; Lorraine Hansberry's *A Raisin in the Sun*; Leroi Jones' *Dutchman*; and *To Kill a Mockingbird*, adapted from Harper Lee's novel; or, like *One Potato, Two Potato*, they purported to deal in documentary fashion with social problems.

By the late 1960s Afro-Americans had begun to move into all phases of the industry, both because of conscious programs and because of pressure from the NAACP and federal agencies. The Motion Picture Association of America began to keep precise records of studio hiring patterns on racial and ethnic lines. Blacks entered upon aspects of production: Wendell Franklin and Gordon Parks in direction, Vincent Tubbs and Walter Burrell in publicity, Quincy Jones in music, and Harry Belafonte and others in producing. Marcel Camus' Brazilian import, *Orfeo Negro*, scored a hit and demonstrated that perhaps at least one other racial system bore relevance to the American model. Less noticeable, but at least as important, were the ordinary roles in which blacks appeared: Poitier as a psychiatrist in Hubert Cornfield's *Pressure Point*; Sammy Davis' flippant convict in Millard Kaufman's *Convicts Four*; Maidie Norman's sane maid in *What Ever Happened to Baby Jane?*; the middle-class extras and bits in *The Manchurian Candidate* and *Kisses for My President*; the growth of Jim Brown as a sexy star in *Rio Conchos* and other pictures; the reaching of Poitier for more range in *Lillies of the Field*, *The Long Ships*, *The Organization*, *The Lost Man*, and the ill-timed and therefore misjudged *Guess Who's Coming to Dinner*; the old-fashioned burlesque "Toms" played for laughs by Sammy Davis in *Sergeants Three* and Woody Strode in *Two Rode Together*; conservative John Ford's movie about the buffalo soldiers, *Sergeant Rutledge*; Michael Roehmer's *Nothing But a Man* whose black southern ambience was so well rendered that a major urban library bought a print for its documentary collection; and *The Defiant Ones*, Stanley Kramer's obvious allegory of the plight of Americans.

For whatever it was worth, the period provided an evenhanded scenario for solving America's racial problems in a rational way. Unfortunately, events did not fit the model or the rate of social change lagged in the economic sector, and Afro-Americans became nationalized to a degree

unseen since the 1920s. The major studios in 1970 caught the mood and began to produce for an urban Afro-American audience. Gordon Parks, in the midst of a rash of black exploitation movies, preserved his integrity with *The Learning Tree*, *Shaft*, and *Sounder*, moving easily from memoir to melodrama to pastoral lyric.

For his performance in *Lilies of the Field* (1964), with costar Lilia Skala, Sidney Poitier became the first Afro-American to win an Oscar for a starring role. *(Museum of Modern Art/Film Stills Archive.)*

Melvin Van Peebles moved from hand-held cameras to overseas production to studio tutelage (*Watermelon Man* at Columbia) to quasi-independent production of his cause célèbre, *Sweet Sweetback's Baadasss Song*, which grossed $10 million despite its limited distribution. Among the more than fifty titles in the cycle by 1973, there were blatant exploitations by studios hungry for revenues to see them through a slow season, artful black remakes of older white movies, gestures by older black stars to keep up, overcorrections of hoary white myths, and shab-

In *Sounder* (1972), Gordon Parks deals with the struggles of a rural family in the South's recent past; (from left to right) Paul Winfield, Yvonne Jarrell, Eric Hooks, Cicely Tyson, Kevin Hooks, and Taj Mahal. *(Museum of Modern Art/Film Stills Archive.)*

by unions of race and sex and violence. *The Asphalt Jungle* reappeared as *Melinda; Dracula* as *Blacula;* and the U. S. Cavalry as *Soul Soldier. Soul to Soul* and *Wattstax* were compilations of festival films with corresponding low costs and high profits. *The Landlord, The Bus Is Coming, Black Jesus* (a mythic Patrice Lumum-

A scene from *Greased Lightning* (1977) shows Richard Pryor (center), Cleavon Little (left), and Pam Grier (right). (*Museum of Modern Art/Film Stills Archive.*)

ba), *Honky,* Poitier's detective stories, *Buck and the Preacher, Cotton Comes to Harlem, Georgia, Georgia,* Jim Brown's vehicles, *The Angel Levine,* and *The Book of Numbers* were some of the works of the Afro-American market stoked by theaters left empty by migrating whites and filled by urban blacks searching for new mythic lore. Pam Grier, Raymond St. Jacques, William Marshall, Richard Roundtree, Rosalind Cash, and Tamara Dobson were some of the performers whose careers began or were revived in the black boom. *See* also AFRO-AMERICAN HISTORY: RECONSTRUCTION TO REVOLT, 1877–1977; LITERATURE: DRAMA/THEATER; NATIONAL ASSOCIATION FOR THE ADVANCEMENT OF COLORED PEOPLE (NAACP); RACE: RACISM; SEGREGATION.

REFERENCES: Bogle, Donald, *Toms, Coon, Mulattoes, Mammies, and Bucks: An Interpretive History of Blacks in American Films,* Viking, New York, 1973; Cripps, Thomas, "The Reaction of the Negro to the Motion Picture 'Birth of a Nation,'" *Historian,* vol. 25, pp. 244–62, May 1963; Cripps, Thomas, "The Death of Rastus: The Negro in American Films Since 1945," *Phylon,* vol. 28, pp. 267–75, Fall, 1967; Cripps, Thomas, "Movies in the Ghetto Before Poitier," *Negro Digest,* vol. 18, pp. 21–27; 45–48, February 1969; Cripps, Thomas, "The Myth of the Southern Box Office: Factors in the Perpetuation of White Supremacy in Films, 1920–1940," in Lewis Gould and James Curtis, *The Black Experience in America,* University of Texas Press, Austin, 1970; Cripps, Thomas, "Paul Robeson and Black Identity in American Movies," *Massachusetts Review,* vol. 11, pp. 468–85, Summer 1970; Cripps, Thomas, "The Unformed Image: The Negro in the Movies Before *Birth of a Nation,*" *Maryland Historian,* vol. 2, pp. 13–26, Spring, 1970; Cripps, Thomas, "*Native Son* in the Movies," *New Letters,* vol. 38, pp. 49–63,

Winter 1972; Cripps, Thomas, "*The Birth of a Race* Company: An Early Stride Toward a Black Cinema," *Journal of Negro History,* January 1974, pp. 28–37; Jerome, V. J., *The Negro in Hollywood Films,* Masses and Mainstream, New York, 1950; Mapp, Edward, *Blacks in American Films: Today and Yesterday,* Scarecrow Press, Metuchen, 1972; Noble, Peter, *The Negro in Films,* Skelton Robinson, London, 1948; Pines, Jim, *Blacks in the Cinema: The Changing Image,* The British Film Institute, London, 1971; Zito, Stephen F., "The Black Film Experience," in Tom Shales et al. *The American Film Heritage: Impressions from the American Film Institute Archives,* Acropolis Books, Washington, D.C., 1972; and Cripps, Thomas: *Slow Fade to Black: The Negro in American Film, 1900–1942,* Oxford, New York, 1976.

MOTLEY, ARCHIBALD See ARTISTS.

MOTLEY, CONSTANCE BAKER (1921–   ), lawyer, judge; born in New Haven, Conn. Motley attended Fisk University (Nashville, Tenn.) for a time, and received a B.A. degree from New York University in 1943 and her LL.B. from Columbia University in 1946. Even before her graduation from law school, she joined the National Association for the Advancement of Colored People (NAACP) Legal Defense and Educational Fund, Inc., and remained with it until 1965. It was during that period, between 1961 and 1964, that she argued ten and won nine major civil rights cases before the U.S. Supreme Court, and represented James Meredith in his efforts to gain admission to the University of Mississippi. In 1964 Motley was elected to the New York State Senate, the first Afro-American woman in the state's history to sit in the senate. In 1965 the New York City Council elected her Manhattan borough president. A year later President Lyndon B. Johnson named her judge of the U.S. Circuit Court for the Southern District of New York.

MOTLEY, MARION See ATHLETES: FOOTBALL

MOTON, ROBERT RUSSA (1867–1940), educator; born in Rice, Va. Moton was educated primarily at Hampton Institute (Hampton, Va.), but received a Litt.D. degree from Lincoln University (Lincoln University, Pa.) in 1920 and his M.A. degree from Harvard University in 1929. He also attended Wilberforce University, Oberlin College, Williams College and Howard University. Moton was affiliated with Hampton Institute (1890–1915) until he succeeded Booker T. Washington as principal of Tuskegee Institute (Tuskegee Institute, Ala.) in 1915. He was instrumental in organizing the National Negro

Finance Corporation and was its president. Moton wrote an autobiography, *Finding a Way Out* (1920), and *What the Negro Thinks* (1929).

MOULTRIE, H. CARL (1915–   ), civic leader, judge; born in Charleston, S.C. Moultrie received the B.A. from Lincoln University (Penn.), 1936, the M.A. from New York University, 1952, and the J.D. from Georgetown University, Washington, D.C., 1956. He served in a variety of civic capacities, including director of the Wilmington Boys' Club and Hillcrest Housing Project (1941-1949). He was an attorney with Howard, Hayes & Windsor (1957-1972) until his appointment as a judge on the Superior Court, Washington, D.C.

MUHAMMAD, ELIJAH (1896–1975), religious leader; born Elijah Poole in Sandersville, Ga. One of 13 children of tenant farmers who were former slaves, Muhammad worked in the fields at an early age out of necessity, thus severely limiting his formal education. At 16 he left home and began a nomadic life. In 1923 Muhammad settled in Detroit Mich., and worked for a time in an automobile factory. Early in the 1930s during a time of extreme economic distress, he became acquainted with W. D. Fard (Wali Farad, Master Farad Muhammad), and this meeting proved to be the turning point of his life. Fard, then working as a peddler, had already established the first Temple of Islam in Detroit. He is generally credited with having founded the Nation of Islam, or Muslim faith, among blacks in the United States. Upon Fard's disappearance in 1934, Elijah Muhammad (the name conferred on him by Fard) claimed the role of Fard's successor and the custodian of the latter's revelation, and eventually became known as Messenger of Allah or Supreme Minister of the Nation of Islam. Though his policies of strict racial separation were modified somewhat in his later years, and still more in the hands of others after his death, Muhammad's goal of separate self-sufficiency for Afro-Americans set the course of the Muslims outside the mainstream (integration) of the civil rights movement. *See also* MUSLIMS; NATIONALISM.

MULZAC, HUGH (1886–1971), master seaman, born in Union Island, West Indies. Mulzac was the first Afro-American to become the captain of an American merchant marine ship. He went to sea in 1907 and later studied at the Swansea Nautical College (Swansea, Wales). Mulzac became an American citizen in 1918 and worked on American ships between 1922 and 1936. Although Mulzac earned a perfect score on the master seaman's examination, he was unable to rise above the rank of steward for a long time because of racial discrimination. In 1942, however, he was given a captain's berth on the S.S. *Booker T. Washington*. The crew was integrated, 27 percent being Afro-American, and under Mulzac's leadership the *Booker T. Washington* made 22 voyages around the world. Mulzac was also active in the National Maritime Union, and after his retirement from the merchant marine, Mulzac became involved in radical politics. He ran unsuccessfully in 1957 on the American Labor Party ticket for a seat on the New York City Council, and in 1958 he made an unsuccessful bid for New York state controller as a member of the Independent Socialist Party. Mulzac wrote an account of his life in the merchant marine entitled *A Star to Steer By*.

MURCHISON, ELISHA P. (1907–   ), editor, clergyman; born in Fort Worth, Tex. Murchison received a B.A. degree from Clark College (Atlanta, Ga.) in 1929, a B.D. degree from Gammon Theological Seminary in 1930, and his M.A. degree from Boston University in 1932. He was the pastor of Christian Methodist Episcopal (CME) churches in Texas, Georgia, Massachusetts, and Illinois. Murchison served as editor of the *Christian Index* from 1946 to 1954, and was elected bishop of the Christian Methodist Episcopal (CME) Church, Fifth Episcopal District, in 1958. Murchinson was also a missionary to Africa.

MURPHY, CARL J. (1889–1967), editor, publisher; born in Baltimore, Md. Murphy received a B.A. degree from Howard University (Washington, D.C.) and his M.A. degree from Harvard University in 1913. After graduation, he taught German at Howard University until 1918, and then became editor of the Afro-American newspaper chain until 1944. From 1922 to 1961 Murphy was president of the company, and from 1953 to 1967 he served as chairman of the board. In 1955 Murphy received the National Association for the Advancement of Colored People's (NAACP) Spingarn Medal. For 36 years Murphy was on the national board of directors of the NAACP.

MURPHY, ISSAC (1861–96), jockey; born in Pleasant Green Hill, Ky. During his peak years (1884–92), Murphy compiled one of the most impressive records in racing history. Victories in the Kentucky Derby in 1884, 1890, and 1891 made him the first jockey to ride winning mounts in that famous race three times and the first to finish first twice in succession. He also rode the winners in four of the first five runnings of the American Derby in Chicago, Ill., in 1884, 1885, 1886, and 1888. *See also* ATHLETES.

MURPHY, JOHN H., III (1916–   ), publisher; born in Baltimore, Md. Murphy received his B.S. degree from Temple University (Philadelphia, Pa.) in 1937, and attended the American Press Institute Seminars at Columbia University. He joined the Afro-American newspaper publishers of Baltimore, Md., in 1937, worked in many positions in the firm, and rose to the office of president in 1967. Murphy also served on the U.S. Civil Rights Commission and on the Maryland Advisory Committee of the U. S. Civil Rights Commission, as well as being a member of many civic organizations in Baltimore.

MURRAY, GEORGE WASHINGTON (1853–1926), educator, U.S. Representative; born in Rembert, S.C. Murray studied at the University of South Carolina for two years and taught school for some 15 years thereafter. In 1888 he was chosen Republican Party chairman for Sumter County, S.C., after which he served as inspector of customs at the port of Charleston. In 1893 Murray was elected as a Republican to the Fifty-third Congress, a seat he held until 1897. In 1905 he moved to Chicago, Ill., where he became a lecturer and writer.

MURRAY, JOAN (1941–   ), newscaster, business executive; born in Ithaca, N.Y. Murray attended Ithaca College (Ithaca, N.Y.), Hunter College of the City University of New York, and the New School for Social Research (New York, N.Y.). Joining WCBS-TV in 1960, she soon became the first major Afro-American television news correspondent. In 1969 she and a partner formed Zebra Associates, the first integrated advertising agency with black principals. Murray served as executive vice-president of the New York City firm.

MURRAY, PAULI (1910–   ), educator, lawyer, civil rights activist; born in Baltimore, Md. Murray studied at Hunter College of the City University of New York, Howard University

(Washington, D.C.) and the University of California. Murray received her D.J.S. degree from Yale Law School. In 1940 she was arrested and convicted in Petersburg, Va., for refusing to move to a segregated seat on an interstate bus, and later she was one of the Howard University student leaders of the sit-ins in Washington, D.C., restaurants. Murray was named the Outstanding Educator of America in 1971, and became Louis Stulberg professor of law and politics at Brandeis University (Waltham, Mass.) in 1973. She was the author of several works, including *Proud Shoes* (1956), *The Constitution and Government of Ghana*, and a collection of poetry, *Dark Testament and Other Poems*.

MURRAY, PETER MARSHALL (1888– ?), surgeon; born in Houma, La. Murray received a B.A. degree from New Orleans University in 1910 and his M.D. degree from Howard University Medical College (Washington, D.C.) in 1914. He interned at Freedmen's Hospital, Washington, D.C., remaining on its staff as assistant clinical professor of surgery and assistant surgeon-in-chief until 1920. Murray then served as medical inspector in the public schools of the District of Columbia, and he later practiced medicine in New York City from 1921 to 1953, during which time he was on the staff of Harlem Hospital for 25 years. He was president of the medical board of Sydenham Hospital; consulting gynecologist for Harlem and St. Clare's hospitals, New York, N.Y.; and president of the New York County Medical Society from 1954 to 1957, the first Afro-American to serve as its president.

MURRAY, ROBERT R., JR. *See* RACE: RACE AND BIOLOGY.

MUSCOVADO This word was often used generally and synonymously in reference to sugar during the 1600s and 1700s. Specifically, muscovado was a raw, dark sugar that was processed, along with molasses, from the juice of the sugar cane. Produced mainly in the New World with black slave labor from Africa, muscovado was the basis for the revolution in the use of sugar. Its production and importance were thus linked to European-American commercial enterprise and the rise and development of the Atlantic slave trade. *See also* AFRICA: THE ATLANTIC SLAVE TRADE IN PERSPECTIVE.

MUSE, CLARENCE E. (1889– ?), actor, director; born in Baltimore, Md. Muse received his LL.B. degree from Dickinson College (Carlisle, Pa.), and as founder and manager of the Chicago School of Dramatic Art took leading parts in a number of plays. Between 1916 and 1923 he was one of the Lafayette Players. For two years Muse worked on the filming of several of the *Saturday Evening Post* stories by Harris Dixon, and in

1943 he directed a revival of Hall Johnson's folk drama, *Run, Little Chillun'*, on Broadway. *See also* MOTION PICTURES.

MUSEUM OF AFRICAN ART *See* AFRICAN LEGACY / SURVIVALS.

MUSIC

History and Development The contributions of Afro-Americans to the history of music in the United States began with the arrival of the first blacks on the mainland in 1619. Although Africans who were sold into slavery were stripped of their possessions, clamped into irons, and wedged into foul vessels to make the dreaded "middle passage" from Africa to America, they nevertheless brought with them to the new land their memories of the rich music and dance traditions of the lands of their ancestors. They remembered the importance of music in the West African way of life—how almost every activity was accompanied by music appropriate to the occasion and how special kinds of music were provided for festivals (called "customs" in Africa)—and they continued these practices in the New World.

Colonial sources of information include numerous references to the huge slave festivals that took place in the northern colonies. Perhaps worthy of special mention are the Pinkster festivals, held in various cities of New York state, in which Afro-Americans danced traditional dances to the music of drums and singing, while large crowds of white spectators watched the "exotic" scenes. In New England, "'lection Day" celebrations drew similar crowds of whites to watch slaves and free blacks parade, dance, and sing to the accompaniment of drums, woodwinds, and string instruments. Annual fairs provided similar opportunities in Philadelphia, Pa., and in New Orleans, La., the transplanted Africans staged traditional dances on Sunday afternoons in the Place Congo.

Before long, Afro-Americans had adapted to the European traditions of the white colonists. According to newspapers and other printed sources of the colonial period, blacks soon became proficient performers on the violin, flute,

French horn, and trumpet, as well as on the drum. Players of these instruments were pressed into service for country dances and for the many dancing schools that had sprung up throughout the land. Drummers and fifers accompanied military units, and fiddlers and other performers played in the society-dance orchestras that performed for the assemblies of the aristocracy. Blacks attended the meetinghouses (churches) of the white colonists, and there they learned to sing the psalms sung by all Protestant Americans. When a new kind of religious song, called the hymn, began to supplant the psalms during the middle of the eighteenth century, blacks learned to sing hymns. Their favorites were the hymns written by the English minister Dr. Isaac Watts.

Of the more than 5,000 Afro-Americans who fought in colonial wars, the names of several army and navy musicians have come down to us: trumpeter Nero Benson; fifers Primus Lew, Barzillai Lew, and Richard Cozzens; and drummers Nimrod Perkins, Jazeb Jolly, and William Nickens. Army muster rolls frequently referred to black servicemen as "Negro Tom, drummer," or "Negro Bob, drummer," without any further identification. The names of at least three black musicians of the War of 1812 have come down to us: bugler George Brown, fifer Cyrus Tiffany, and fifer Jessie Wall.

After the American Revolution, the cultural life of the young nation, now called the United States of America, developed with amazing vigor, helped along by the immigration of large numbers of European musicians, who soon founded orchestras and other musical organizations, inaugurated concert series, established music publishing houses, and produced musical plays and operas. It was during this period that the first black professional musicians began to appear on the scene. Slavery had been abolished in the North by the end of the 1820s, and blacks were then able not only to cultivate their natural talents but also to study with excellent music teachers.

Newport Gardner seems to have been the nation's first black music teacher of stature. He earned a fine reputation in New England as the master of a "very numerously attended singing school," which attracted both black and white students. Pioneer concert artists were Elizabeth Taylor Greenfield, who was called the "Black Swan," and her younger contemporary, Thomas Bowers, called the "Colored Mario." In New Orleans, during the 1830s, Afro-Americans organized a symphony orchestra of more than a hundred members. Brass bands were founded throughout the North and Midwest during this period, as well as in those large cities of the South where there were communities of free blacks. These cities included New Orleans, La., Charleston, S.C., Richmond, Va., Baltimore, Md., and others. According to the records, at least one of the several choral groups that came into existence during this period was ambitious enough to produce an oratorio (Philadelphia, 1841) with accompaniment provided by a fifty-piece symphony orchestra.

Established music houses printed the music of black composers; chief among these musicians were Francis Johnson, William Brady, A. J. R. Connor, Edmund Dédé, Henry F. Williams, and Justin Holland. Above all, Afro-American musicians achieved recognition for their skills as instrumentalists. Francis (Frank) Johnson was regarded as the nation's leading performer on the Kent bugle and, at the same time, as a superior fiddler, bandmaster, and society-dance orchestra leader. During one of his tours in England, he was called to Buckingham Palace, London, to present a command performance for the reigning English monarch, Queen Victoria, who presented him with a silver bugle in token of her appreciation. Other well-known performers and orchestra leaders of the period included William and Henry Appo, Peter O'Fake, Sy Gilliat, George Walker, Horace Weston, and Henry F. Williams. New Orleans was noted for its Afro-American musicians, particularly the Lambert family, Constantin Deberque, and Thomas Martin.

After the Revolutionary War, the establishment of separate Afro-American congregations gained momentum, resulting in the organization of the nation's first independent black denomination, the African Methodist Episcopal (AME) Church. It was founded in 1794 under the leadership of Richard Allen. One of Allen's most important acts was to publish in 1801 the first hymnal designed exclusively for the use of Afro-Americans, entitled *A Collection of Spiritual Songs and Hymns Selected from Various Sources by Richard Allen, African Minister.* Allen's church expanded rapidly; by midcentury there were congregations throughout the land, and their musical activities included trained choirs, organ accompaniment for congregational singing, and "concerts of sacred music." Similar practices obtained in other black churches, such as the African Methodist Episcopal Zion (AMEZ) Church and the independent black congregations of established white Protestant churches.

In New York a group of enterprising Afro-Americans founded the African Grove Theater, which flourished from about 1821 until 1828. Here ballad operas were staged and musical numbers performed between the acts of plays, as well as before and after their presentation. One of the city's slum districts, the so-called Five Points area, won an international reputation for the "hot music" of its Afro-American performers, which was provided chiefly by fiddlers occasionally joined by drummers and trumpeters, especially on Saturday nights. The English novelist Charles Dickens visited the area in 1841 and witnessed the dancing of a black man known as the "greatest of all dancers," Master Juba (William Henry Lane).

As the century progressed, more and more Afro-Americans became involved in musical activities. Richard Milburn wrote a melody, "Listen to the Mocking Bird," which was the hit song of the 1850s. The antislavery movement was responsible for the development of a body of antislavery songs, and at least one group, the Luca Family Singing Troupe, began its career under the aegis of an antislavery society. Afro-Americans now organized more bands, orchestras, and choral groups; published music manuals as well as compositions; gave music lessons; and in a few instances embarked upon stage careers alongside white "Ethiopian" minstrels (who blackened their faces with burnt cork). The marvel of the times was the blind piano prodigy, Thomas Bethune who was called Blind Tom. A slave, Bethune was started on a concert career by his owner at the age of nine (in 1858); his brilliant playing and prodigious memory amazed the critics, "eminent composers," and audiences of two continents.

The Civil War brought a cessation of conventional musical activities in the United States. In the Union Army black musicians were organized into regimental bands, and according to the records a few slave musicians were pressed into service as drummers and fifers by the Confederates. Above all, however, contemporary sources emphasize the singing of Afro-American soldiers, particularly their singing of their own folksongs. These songs had been in the process of development for more than a hundred years, especially in the South among the slaves on plantations.

It was not until after the Civil War, however, that the first collection of Afro-American folksongs was published; *Slave Songs in the United States,* edited by William Francis Allen, Charles Picard Ware, and Lucy McKim Garrison, appeared in 1867. During the next three decades, several important collections were published, including *Jubilee Songs as Sung by the Fisk Jubilee Singers* (1872) and *Hampton and Its Students . . . with Fifty Cabin and Plantation Songs* (1874). In 1878 the significant first historical survey of the black man's music in the United States, *Music and Some Highly Musical People,* by James Monroe Trotter, was published. This volume includes discussions of concert artists, composers, music organizations, and minstrel troupes, and has an appendix made up of representative musical compositions.

During the 1860s Afro-Americans—many of them ex-slaves—began to form their own minstrel troupes, which toured at home and abroad. The minstrel show came to represent for the time America's contribution to the musical world; during the last decades of the nineteenth century, genuine Afro-American troupes, as distinguished from white minstrels in blackface, enjoyed an international vogue. Minstrelsy offered to black artists the opportunity to acquire experience in the theatrical arts, which could not be obtained in any other way during that period, and the most creative talents of the race entered the field. The celebrated songwriters of minstrelsy were James Bland, the "World's Greatest Minstrel Man"; Sam Lucas, who specialized in humorous songs; and ballad-writer Gussie Davis, who "did more than his share to open up the tear ducts of America." Eventually, minstrelsy lost its popularity and was replaced by vaudeville and musical comedy.

The turn of the century and the early part of the twentieth century witnessed vigorous activity on the part of Afro-American musicians, per-formers, and composers. Blind Tom continued to concertize until 1904. California contributed the Hyer sisters, Anna Madah and Emma Louise, to the concert world. They made their joint debut in 1867 and afterward went on tour. In 1877 the Hyer sisters organized a traveling company that produced musical shows. Soprano

The Fisk Jubilee Singers of Oberlin, Ohio, popularized the beauty of Afro-American spirituals, singing at the White House and touring Europe. *(Library of Congress.)*

Marie Selika began to concertize in the 1880s, winning praise at home and abroad for the "surprising sweetness and extraordinary compass" of her voice. Most renowned of the singers of the time was soprano Sissieretta Jones, called the "Black Patti." Her white managers were deterred by racism in their attempts to build a lasting concert career for their songbird—the fate of all Afro-American concert artists in this period—although Jones' concert tours earned her impressive credentials. As a compromise, "Black Patti's Troubadours" was organized; its shows featured the soprano in the singing of operatic airs. Another popular vocal group of the period, originating at Fisk University, Nashville, Tenn., was the Fisk Jubilee Singers, who toured both the United States and abroad.

During this period Joseph Douglass (grandson of Frederick Douglass) became the first Afro-American violinist to make concert tours, and Carl Diton became the first black pianist to tour. Among other concert artists were pianist Hazel Harrison, and singers Flora Batson and Sidney Woodward. New Afro-American musical organizations established during the period included symphony orchestras, opera companies, and choral societies. The Samuel Coleridge-Taylor Choral Society of Washington, D.C. (named after the Afro-English composer), produced a festival of Coleridge-Taylor's works in 1904 with the composer as conductor.

Among the composers who began to win recognition during the early twentieth century were singer Harry Burleigh, violinist Will Marion Cook, singer J. Rosamond Johnson, folksong collector John Wesley Work, Sr., violinist Clarence Cameron White, and pianist Robert Nathaniel Dett. All these artists, as well as their less well-known contemporaries, were excellently trained, having studied at the nation's leading conservatories and/or with eminent composers abroad. Generally, Afro-American composers wrote in traditional European musical forms, but their music was infused with characteristic Negro idioms and dance rhythms. Burleigh was the first to make solo arrangements of spirituals; his "Deep River" (1916) remains a landmark. White attracted attention for his opera *Ouanga* as well as for his symphonic works; Dett became noted for his piano works and choral compositions, especially his oratorios. Other opera composers of the time included Lawrence Freeman and Scott Joplin. The latter's opera, *Treemonisha*, was frequently revived in the 1970s.

The early twentieth century was also a time of great activity for writers of musical shows. In New York and at the Pekin Theater in Chicago,

Ill., such composers as Cook, Robert Cole, Leubrie Hill, Johnson, and Joe Jordan—to name but a few—produced the music for a steady stream of shows, some of which featured the celebrated comedy team of Bert Williams and George Walker. In the summer of 1898 the first all-black musical, *Clorindy: the Origin of the Cakewalk,* written and directed by a Negro, Will Marion Cook, opened on Broadway and created a sensation. In the fall of the same year Robert Cole presented the first full-length musical written, directed, and produced by Afro-Americans, *A Trip to Coontown.* Cook later wrote: "Negroes were at last on Broadway, and there to stay. . . . Nothing could stop us, and nothing did for a decade." Some of the more successful black shows toured in Europe.

During this period ragtime came into its own, beginning with the immense popularity of "The Maple Leaf Rag" (1899). Its composer, Scott Joplin, regarded as "King of Ragtime," and others active in the St. Louis area, such as Thomas Turpin and James Scott, were mainly responsible for the rise of the ragtime vogue. On the eastern seaboard rag pianist Eubie Blake followed in the tradition of these legendary pianists and was himself followed by Luckey Roberts, Willie-the-Lion Smith, James P. Johnson, and Fats Waller. The acknowledged leader of the New Orleans school was Jelly Roll Morton, who was as famous for his blues as for his rag pianism.

Syncopated dance orchestras flourished everywhere, particularly in the large cities, along with brass bands that played not only military and concert music but also music in syncopated style. Traditionally, Afro-Americans had provided music for white America to dance to since colonial times, and in many places the role of dance musician was reserved by custom for black men. In 1905 a group called the Nashville Students presented for the first time in public a concert of syncopated music at a theater in New York. Its success led to more such concerts and to European tours. One of the musicians associated with the group, James Reese Europe, organized a black musicians' union called the Clef Club in 1910, which eventually developed almost a monopoly in supplying the music for New York's society dances. Jim Europe later organized the Tempo Club, which functioned in a similar way, with such bandleaders as Tim Brymn, Will Tyers, Will Vodery, and Ford Dabney.

An event of major importance was the perfor-

By the turn of the century, black musical theater had established itself on Broadway. The comedy team of George Walker (right) and Bert Williams (left) starred in *Sons of Ham.* Williams later was a headliner in the Ziegfeld *Follies.* (Museum of the City of New York.)

mance of Europe's Clef Club Symphony Orchestra of 145 players at Carnegie Hall in New York City in 1912. The program emphasized light concert music and arrangements of folksongs rather than symphonic works, and the instrumentation was novel, including mandolins, bandores, harp-guitars, saxophones, and pianos, along with traditional orchestral instruments. The effect of syncopated music with its "biting attacks" and "infectious rhythms" upon the Carnegie Hall audience was electrifying. New Yorkers received their first inkling of the power of the new music produced by Afro-Americans—soon to be developed into jazz.

The same kind of music was being played by Afro-Americans in other cities, particularly Baltimore, Md., Philadelphia, Pa., Chicago, Ill., Memphis, Tenn., and New Orleans, La. In New Orleans, there were dozens of marching brass bands, dance orchestras, and strolling groups of players. Bands competed with each other on the streets in "cutting contests," egged on by excited bystanders and children, called the "second line," who danced along in time to the music. At public dances, such players as trumpeter Buddy Bolden and cornetist Bunk Johnson delighted the crowds with their "ragged" versions of street songs and blues. In 1897 New Orleans set off a section of the city, called Storyville, for legalized prostitution. Eventually, the best dance musicians found their way to Storyville, where wages were good, work was regular, and the patrons appreciated sizzling hot music and blues.

Little is known about the origin of the blues. Old-timers who sang the blues asserted that "the blues always been!" William Christopher Handy established himself as the "Father of the Blues" when he popularized the type with his publication in 1912 of "The Memphis Blues" and in 1914 of the immortal "The St. Louis Blues." Although the blues had always been popular among Afro-Americans, it was not until 1920 when the first commercial recording of a blues was made that this popularity became national.

The years preceding World War I marked the end of a musical era for Afro-Americans. Many of the best instrumentalists joined army bands, which played abroad and gave Europe its first sound of syncopated music. Some of the important figures of the previous era died: Scott Joplin, Bob Cole, comedian George Walker, and minstrel stars James Bland, Billy Kersands, and Sam Lucas. New Orleans' Storyville was closed in 1917 by order of the U.S. Navy, and the musicians who had worked there went "up the river"

(the Mississippi) in search of work, many traveling as far as Chicago, Ill. Indeed, a wholesale migration of Afro-Americans to the North and the Midwest to work in war industries took place. They took with them their music, their blues and spirituals, their syncopated band and orchestra music.

The postwar period was a time of new beginnings, with most of the action taking place in the Afro-American communities of large northern cities. Among the labels given to this period are The Black Renaissance, The Harlem Renaissance, and The Jazz Age. The fusion of blues and ragtime, of brass-band music and syncopated music, resulted in the new music called jazz, a music that developed its own characteristics. Jazz evolved its own vocabulary, its own traditions, its own literature, and its own discography. The materials of jazz history are phonograph records, which first began to appear in the early 1920s. But before that time, there had been the legendary pioneers—the men who played in New Orleans' Excelsior, Olympia, Onward, and Tuxedo brass bands; the Clef Club and Tempo Club bandsmen of New York City; the "hot music" dispensers of Chicago's South Side and of other cities; and the nation's first Afro-American touring jazz group, Freddie Keppard and his Original Creole Band.

The origin of the word *jazz* is lost in legend. Ironically, the first groups to use the word in public were white bands from New Orleans: Brown's "Dixieland Jass *(sic)* Band" and Nick LaRocca's "Original Dixieland Jazz Band." But black men were the originators of jazz music, and they had used the word (often with sexual connotations) among themselves many years before whites popularized it as a gimmick for attracting attention. Traditionally, the history of jazz begins with four pioneers, natives of New Orleans, and their Chicago-based groups: trumpeter King Oliver and his Creole Jazz Band; pia-

W. C. Handy was the first musician to print sheet music of the blues in 1912. Two years later he wrote his most famous composition "The St. Louis Blues." *(Moorland-Spingarn Research Center.)*

nist Jelly Roll Morton and his Red Hot Peppers; trumpeter Louis Armstrong and his Hot Five and Hot Seven; and clarinetist Johnny Dodds, whose bands in the 1920s had various names.

The nation's first "big band" was organized by Fletcher Henderson in New York in 1923. The next few years saw the emergence of a number of big bands; for example, Chick Webb's, Jimmie Luncefords's, Andy Kirk's, Erskine Hawkins', Count Basie's (who got his start in the Kansas City school), Duke Ellington's, Erskine Tate's, and Earl "Fatha" Hines'. When white jazzmen began organizing big bands, they used Afro-American arrangers in order to ensure that their music would have an authentic sound; these arrangers included Fletcher and Horace Henderson, Sy Oliver, James Mundy, and Fred Norman.

Jazz was only one of the exciting developments of the postwar years. The period was notable for a number of "firsts": the *Afro-American Symphony* of black composer William Grant Still was performed by a major symphony orchestra (1931); an Afro-American singer, Lillian Evanti, starred in European opera houses in the late 1920s; a Negro singer, Caterina Jarboro, sang the title role of an opera with a major American opera company (1933); musical comedies written and staged by Afro-Americans dominat-

ed the Broadway scene, beginning with Eubie Blake's and Noble Sissle's *Shuffle Along* (1921). It was also during these years that for the first time a black-owned recording company was organized, the Pace Black Swan Recording Company, and Afro-American composer-arrangers began to obtain jobs in the white entertainment industry, for example, in movies and radio. Professional choruses came into being; those directed by Hall Johnson and Eva Jessye received most acclaim.

The midcentury years were marked by the steady expansion of Afro-American musical activities—that is, after the interruption of World War II, which put a damper on most activities for several years. Established composers continued to produce music in all styles; William Grant Still, William Dawson, Howard Swanson, Ulysses Kay, Julia Perry, and Hale Smith were the most notable. New composers appeared on the scene in great numbers. Without exception, Afro-American composers continued to be well trained. Some—for example, Olly Wilson, T. J. Anderson, and George Walker—earned doctorates in music. All of the composers were eclectic, drawing freely upon divergent styles and sources in their compositions. The influence of jazz, blues, gospel music, and the older spirituals was often reflected in the music of both established composers and the younger men—David Baker, Coleridge-Taylor Perkinson, Noel DaCosta, Arthur Cunningham, William Fischer, Stephen Chambers, John Price, and others. Some performer-composers wrote almost exclusively in jazz or jazz-derived styles; this group included Duke Ellington, John Lewis, and Ornette Coleman.

Notable strides were made by Afro-American performers. Jazzmen experimented with new sounds, moving from bebop to "cool jazz" to "hardbop" to "soul" to "third-stream" style. Like the composers, performing groups used electronic techniques, whether in jazz styles or folk music (such as blues and gospel). In the field of opera gifted black singers found it increasingly easy to obtain principal parts after the pioneering efforts of Todd Duncan and Camilla Williams with the New York City Opera in the 1940s and Marian Anderson with the Metropolitan Opera in 1955. Leontyne Price, Martina Arroyo, Grace Bumbry, Shirley Verrett, and George Shirley were leading figures at the Metropolitan Opera in the 1960s and 1970s, and many other black opera stars were associated with the leading opera companies in the United States and Europe. These included

Musical comedies created by Afro-Americans dominated the Broadway scene, commencing with Eubie Blake (seated) and Noble Sissle shown in *Shuffle Along* in 1921. (Courtesy of Burt Goldblatt.)

Mattiwilda Dobbs, Gloria Davy, Adele Addison, Margaret Tynes, Betty Allen, Ellabelle Davis, Dorothy Maynor, and Jessye Norman. Singers moved freely back and forth between the world of opera and the concert stage.

Afro-American instrumentalists and conductors met with markedly less success. Few performers reached the top, as did black pianist Andre Watts, and there was only token placement of instrumentalists in the major symphony orchestras of the country. The Symphony of the New World in New York augured well for the future, however, with more than forty percent of its personnel black, and Leopold Stokowski's American Symphony included a number of Afro-American musicians. Among conductors who earned enviable reputations were Dean Dixon, Everett Lee, James DePriest, Paul Freeman, and Henry Lewis (in 1968 Lewis became the first Afro-American to be appointed permanent conductor of a major American symphony orchestra).

REFERENCES: This article is one of the best short references on the subject. The author, Eileen Southern, gives a full account in her *The Music of Black Americans: A History*, W. W. Norton, New York, 1971. Other references to be noted include: Buerkle, Jack Vincent, *Bourbon Street Black: The New Orleans Black Jazzmen*, Oxford University Press, New York, 1973; Hare, Maud Cuney, *Negro Musicians and Their Music*, Association for the Study of Negro Life and History, Washington, D.C., 1936; Katz, Bernard, *The Social Implications of Early Negro Music in the United States*, Arno Press, New York, 1969; Kofsky, Frank, *Black Nationalism and the Revolution in Music*, Pathfinder Press, New York, 1970; Lovell, John, Jr., *Black Song: The Forge and the Flame*, Macmillan, New York, 1972; Southern, Eileen (ed.), *Readings in Black American Music*, W. W. Norton, New York, 1971; Stearns, Marshall, *The Story of Jazz*, Oxford University Press, New York, 1956; and Walton, Ortiz M., *Music: Black, White & Blue*, William Morrow, New York, 1972.

Spirituals—Origins For more than a century a controversy has raged concerning the origin of the spirituals originally sung by Afro-Americans in the South and about their relationship to the religious songs of whites. Where did the spirituals of Afro-Americans come from? What is their relationship, if any, to the music of West Africa and to that of Europe? Do the spirituals of Afro-Americans exhibit to a high degree or to a low degree cultural traits derived from West Africa? Or are these spirituals primarily borrowings from the culture of the white man?

It was at first assumed that black spirituals represented, in essence, the spontaneous outburst and expression of the anguish experienced by human beings in bondage, that is, of Afro-American slaves. An early writer on the topic, James Weldon Johnson, wrote: "Aframerican folk art, an art by Africa out of America, Negro creative genius working under the spur and backlash of American conditions, is unlike anything else in America or elsewhere, nor could it have been possible in any other place or in any other times" (James Weldon Johnson papers, Yale University, New Haven, Conn.).

The earliest collectors of slave songs were inclined to be tentative rather than dogmatic about the origins of spirituals. Basically, these collectors felt that the main part of Afro-American music was civilized in its character, and that the spirituals had been composed partly under the influence of association with whites and partly actually imitated from their music. The texts of the spirituals, they pointed out, had been largely taken from Scripture and from hymns sung in Protestant churches. Although these collectors found many expressions used in spirituals "abundantly in Methodist hymnbooks," they were, however, unable to trace the tunes employed in the spirituals. Nevertheless, they felt obliged to note that "there are very few which are of an intrinsically barbaric character, and where this character does appear, it . . . may very well be purely African in origin." They felt that if they had been able to collect more secular songs they might have had to revise their opinion regarding "the proportion of the barbaric element." However, it was difficult to persuade the freedmen to sing secular songs because emancipation had produced a sense of dignity. "I never fairly heard a secular song among the

Far left: Leontyne Price as Cleopatra in Samuel Barber's *Antony and Cleopatra*. The opera marked the grand opening of the new Metropolitan Opera house in 1966. (Courtesy of the Metropolitan Opera.)

Port Royal freedmen," William Francis Allen, one of the editors of the first collection of slave songs, declared, "and never saw a musical instrument among them."

After the turn of the century, students began to look to Africa for explanations of the essential characteristics of spirituals. The distinguished musicologist Henry E. Krehbiel published the first extensive analysis of black spirituals in 1914 in his *Afro-American Folksongs*. With his usual zeal and fervor, Krehbiel argued that five characteristics of spirituals indicated the survival of African elements in them: (1) their widespread use of the pentatonic scale; (2) tonal deviations in the major and minor scales, such as flatted sevenths and neutral thirds; (3) prominent rhythmns; (4) the heavy use of syncopation; and (5) the structural pattern of a melodic line statement by a soloist with a choral refrain. Krehbiel, however, made no detailed study of the music of West Africa, but depended upon what he had read in travel accounts for his data on African music.

A decade or so later, N. G. J. Ballanta, a Sierra Leone native who had studied music in the United States, published a collection of Afro-American music from the South Carolina Sea Islands entitled *St. Helena Island Spirituals* (1925). In his forword Ballanta argued the case for the African origins of spirituals.

The publication of Melville J. Herskovits' *The Myth of the Negro Past* in 1941 revealed much more of the complexity of the problem of African origins for spirituals than the earlier volumes had done. Herskovits suggested that not one but two acculturation processes were taking place in the American South during the time when the spirituals were created. He pointed out that there had been not only African accommodation to European culture but also the interaction of various African cultures. This interaction had produced a new set of customs and practices—an American culture, but one with its roots entirely in Africa. Herskovits noted that Ashanti music, for example, is differentiated from Dahomey music by a number of characteristics and that these, in turn, differ from the musical styles of Nigeria and of Togoland. The slaves who came from all these areas combined and recombined their local African styles in the crucible of the American South. The question of the origins of the spirituals thus included not only the influence of British music upon African music but also the effects of the combination of a number of varied West African musics.

The Krehbiel-Ballanta interpretation of the origins of spirituals was widely accepted until the late 1920s when a new line of thought was proposed by the German musicologist Erich M. von Hornbostel. He suggested that almost all the outstanding characteristics of Negro spirituals were derived from European music. He cited the use of the pentatonic scale, the prevalence of the "Scotch snap," and the tendency to harmonize in thirds as well-known traits of European music. One practice only—that of "leading lines sung by a single voice, alternating with a refrain sung by the chorus"—was held by Von Hornbostel to be derived from African musics.

A few years later, Newman Ivey White, in his *American Negro Folk-Songs* (1928), attacked the theory of African origins and pointed to the old revival and camp-meeting songs of the whites of the early nineteenth century as the sources of Negro spirituals. Consulting a number of back-country song books of the period, White emphasized the similarity of form and pattern of the spirituals of black and white southerners; he also found textual antecedents for some of the black spirituals in songs of the whites. Nevertheless, White did not completely deemphasize the African contribution to black spirituals. He regarded it as "reasonable to conclude that the Negro brought African music with him to America, and that it is a considerable element in the songs he sings today."

Several years later, Guy B. Johnson consulted some of the same back-country hymnbooks previously used by White in his own investigation of the sources of Negro spirituals. The results of his study were published in 1930 in *Folk Culture on St. Helena Island, South Carolina*. Through his careful investigation of musical analogies between white and black spirituals, an aspect not considered by White, and through his analysis of scales and modes, pitch intervals, melodic structure, and rhythmic patterns, Johnson gave considerable support to White's thesis that Negro spirituals, instead of falling outside the tradition of the music of the whites, represented in fact a selective adoption of that tradition, influenced by the African musical heritage.

In his *White Spirituals in the Southern Uplands*, published in 1933, George Pullen Jackson provided additional support for the thesis of White and Johnson by tracing the tunes and texts of 20 Negro spirituals back to an equal number of white spirituals. In *Spiritual Folk Songs of Early America*, issued in 1937, he compared some 60 Negro spirituals to as many white spirituals, and then pronounced the white songs to be their "legitimate tune-and-words forebears." Although Jackson emphasized the Negro spirituals as part of the Anglo-American folk music tradition, he recognized the influence of the African heritage upon their development.

In the hands of many scholars in this field the comparative approach has proved to be misleading. Many absurd assertions have been advanced by specialists who undertook to compare two things, about one or both of which they were ignorant. Although they generally expressed their conclusions undogmatically, and occasionally made a tentative nod toward an African musical tradition, Newman Ivey White, Guy B. Johnson, and George Pullen Jackson held the position, in essence, that whatever characteristics of African musics might or might not be present in Negro spirituals the similarities between black and white spirituals are so marked that one need look no further before declaring that black spirituals mainly reflect earlier white ones. Thus, these scholars rested their case on the scrutiny of only one of the two sources they supposedly were comparing. None of the three took seriously into account the possibility of a viable West African folk music tradition engaged in a vigorous interaction with the British folk music tradition in the American South.

Doubt no longer exists that Afro-Americans did, indeed, take over some of the traditional melodies of white spirituals. Examples of such borrowings have been found by the score, and it would be strange, in fact, if this were not the case. Stanley M. Elkins, in his *Slavery* (1959), argued forcefully that the compulsive transfer of black people from freedom in Africa to slavery in America involved a series of culture shocks, including the disruption of family and kinship arrangements, language, tribal religion, taboos, name, and so on. Old values, standards, and sanctions were destroyed.

Nevertheless, it would be difficult to deny that the spirituals of the black southerners are distinguishable from those of the whites. The Afro-Americans gathered their materials from a variety of sources, many of them white, but they shaped them into their own distinctive artistic property.

The important question now becomes: How and why did British and West African folk musics blend so easily? One reason is that the culture of West Africa and the culture that West African immigrants encountered in the New World were more alike in certain respects than has been commonly recognized. Almost all of the regions of West Africa enjoyed stable political, economic, and social institutions. Agriculture formed the basis of a healthy economy that included industry and commerce and that was marked by a tendency toward specialization in production. Well-defined concepts of law and order prevailed within a political system that included a division of powers between a central political organization and local authorities. The definable social structure was firmly undergirded by the cohesive influence of the family. Social stratification ranged from the aristocracy at the top of the scale to slaves at the bottom. Slavery formed an important feature of African social and economic life. West African immigrants thus had come out of a complex political, social, and economic situation. It was this fact that must have made their transition to a New World dominated by the white man's culture—in many ways so similar—less traumatic than it might have been to a more primitive people.

Perhaps an even more important element in the easy blending of folk cultures was the similarity between British folk music and West African tribal music. In the American South, where British and West African cultures confronted each other, the similarities in the underlying patterns of the two traditions tended to coalesce and to reinforce each other. Many characteristics of British folk music paralleled those of West African music, thus furnishing West Africans newly arrived in the South familiar materials on which to build.

For example, the black southerners' practice of singing spirituals in a solo-and-chorus pattern, or a call-and-response pattern, had been considered by Krehbiel and by Ballanta, and reluctantly admitted by Von Hornbostel, to be a survival of African singing styles. Certainly, the call-and-response pattern is an important characteristic of West African musics, and it was echoed in the music of black southerners. At the same time, however, it must be pointed out that the British musical tradition confirmed Afro-Americans in their retention of this West African pattern, and this same tradition assisted in and facilitated the blending of styles. The practice of lining-out hymns—in which the preacher chanted a line of the hymn and the congregation repeated the line—lent itself easily to the West African call-and-response system. Lining-out has been traced back to the Scottish kirk of the seventeenth century. This practice, introduced because of illiteracy and lack of hymnbooks, lasted long after literacy had become widespread and hymnbooks common. It had, in fact, become an important and organic part of the style of the hymns. Thus the lining-out, or "deaconing," of hymns by camp-meeting song leaders provided black southerners with a style that they could both identify with and appreciate.

Thomas Wentworth Higginson, a white who commanded a regiment of black troops in the Civil War, witnessed the creation of a spiritual and documented the importance of the call-and-response pattern. He wrote about this experience in his book, *Army Life in a Black Regiment* (1870):

... one day when I was being rowed across from Beaufort to Ladies' Island, I found myself, with delight, on the actual trail of a song. One of the oarsmen, a brisk young fellow, not a soldier, on being asked for his theory of the matter, dropped out a coy confession. "Some good spirituals," he said, "are start juess out o' curiosity. I been a-raise a sing, myself, once."

My dream was fulfilled, and I had traced out, not the poem alone, but the poet. I implored him to proceed. "Once we boys," he said, "went for tote some rice and de nigger-driver he keep a-callin' on us; and I say, 'Oh, de ole nigger-driver!' Den anudder said, 'Fust ting my mammy tole me was, notin' so bad as nigger-driver.' Den I made a sing, just puttin' a word, and den anudder word." Then he began a singing, and the men, after listening a moment, joined in the chorus, as if it were an old acquaintance, though they evidently had never heard it before. I saw how easily a new "sing" took root among them.

O de ole nigger-driver
O gwine away

Fust ting my mamma tell me
O gwine away

Tell me about de nigger-driver
O gwine away

Nigger-driver second devil
O gwine away

Best ting for do he driver
O gwine away

Knock he down and spoil he labor
O gwine away

Here one can readily see the creation of a new song in a tradition that was able to assume ready familiarity with the call-and-response pattern, with new words spontaneously improvised to fit an old format.

Krehbiel and Ballanta also contended that extensive use of the pentatonic scale in the spirituals was strong evidence of African survivals in them. Interestingly enough, Von Hornbostel

argued that the large number of pentatonic spirituals was evidence of European borrowings. Although pentatonic scales are widely used in West African musics, they are also extensively employed in British folk music, occurring especially frequently in the music of Scotland, and they survived in the folk music brought to the American South by British immigrants. George Pullen Jackson noted that of 19 camp-meeting songs he considered precursors of Negro spirituals, 15 were pentatonic. Black southerners, given the strong pentatonic characteristics of their West African musical heritage, must have found the scales of Anglo-American folk music pleasing to their ears.

Another deviation from the major and minor diatonic scales that ostensibly evidenced African origins for spirituals was the tendency of black spirituals to employ the intervals of the neutral third and minor seventh (the so-called blue notes). These intervals do not constitute a special feature common to African music, although their African use is fairly widespread. On the other hand, both the neutral third and the flatted seventh are found in British music as well as in African. Cecil Sharp has written thus of the English folksinger's varying intonation of the third tone of the scale: "It is often so flat that it is hardly to be distinguished from the minor third. Frequently, too, it is a 'neutral' third, i.e., neither major nor minor . . ." Sharp also noted that "this use of the flatted seventh, as though it were a leading-tone, is often to be found in folk airs, especially in those of England." Like the pentatonic scale, then, the flatted seventh and the neutral third provided black southerners with a bridge between their traditional African music and the Anglo-American musical tradition.

The task of looking for the harmonic sources of the Negro spirituals *as written down* in collections convinced Jackson and others that the harmonics were taken entirely from Anglo-American folk hymns. Certainly, the harmonies employed in Afro-American spirituals rarely depart from the simple harmonic patterns of white spirituals. However, the tendency of black spirituals to harmonize in thirds—evidence to Von Hornbostel of European borrowings—is a usage also quite widespread in West Africa. The Ashanti, for example, harmonize in any other fashion only rarely. The collectors of *Slave Songs of the United States*, moreover, were careful to point out that the spirituals of the Sea Islands were generally sung in unison. Each participant sang his own version of the melody, thus creating a complicated heterophony, or combination of different versions of the same melody being sung together.

This heterophony corresponds to the Anglo-American folk style of singing hymns, which dispensed with all except accidental harmony. In addition, shape-note hymnals, such as *The Southern Harmony* and *The Sacred Harp*, stressed part-singing for these modal tunes rather than harmonizing, with interesting horizontal lines for each part replacing vertical harmonies. This practice provided an interesting polyphonic interplay, which blacks found similar to the highly developed polyphony of West African choral singing. This development in Anglo-American music excited the West African ear and accelerated the blending of African and British musical traditions in the South.

Scholars have generally agreed upon one characteristic of the spirituals: the beat, that regular pulsating rhythm that runs through Afro-American music, cannot be felt to the same degree in Anglo-American music. Perhaps James Weldon Johnson put his finger on the essential difference between the two traditions when he wrote:

The Negro loves nothing better in his music than to play with the fundamental time beat. He will, as it were, take this fundamental throb and pound it out with his left hand almost monotonously; while with his right hand he will take as many liberties with it as he dares to take without losing the beat. (James Weldon Johnson papers, Yale University, New Haven, Conn.)

Nevertheless, even on the subject of rhythm, parallels between West African and British folk music exist. The element of syncopation, for example, so widely prevalent in African music is quite similar to the characteristic of British folk music called the "Scotch snap." It must be noted, however, that syncopation is considerably more pronounced in the Afro-American tradition than is the "Scotch snap" in the Anglo-American tradition.

Thus it appears that with the exception of rhythmic elements, which are more pronounced in black Southern music than in white, virtually all of the musical characteristics of the spirituals are common to both the African and to the British traditions. To point out parallels in British folk music, parallels generally claimed as African survivals in black spirituals, is not the same as saying, however, that these elements in black spirituals came from a British rather than an African source or that these elements were borrowed by blacks from British or Anglo-American

traditions. The major determinant of whether any given African musical element survived or not in the New World, it would seem, would have been its similarity to a parallel element in the folk music tradition of the whites.

Perhaps important questions to ask in this connection are: How many elements of the spirituals could be accounted for if one assumes no survival of African cultural traits? How many could be accounted for if one assumes no contact with white culture? The most important characteristic of the spirituals that cannot be accounted for except with reference to white culture is that they are in the English language. The number of spirituals containing African words is very small. Not one instance is known of parallel texts of an Afro-American song and an African one.

Furthermore, it is obvious that the subject matter of the spirituals is deeply rooted in the Christian religion. As James Weldon Johnson has described it, "The Negro took as his basic materials his native African rhythms and the King James Version of the Bible and out of them created the spirituals." Although Christianity, of course, is not—theologically speaking—a "white man's religion," nevertheless, black southerners adopted it through their contact with white men. Guy B. Johnson noted that the subject matter of the spirituals he collected on St. Helena Island—"Heaven, hell, the judgment, appeals to the sinner, Biblical characters, Satan, the jubilee, the gospel trumpet, the gospel ship, the chariot, the river Jordan, the union band, etc."—were identical to those of white religious songs.

The similarity of symbols in the spiritual songs of black and white southerners, however, is not as close as it may superficially appear. Black spirituals are less concerned with sin than their white counterparts; they dwell more upon the real troubles of the world, and heaven symbolizes an escape, not from the grip of Satan and the weakness of the flesh, but from actual worldly tribulations. Black spirituals are filled with psychological symbols of alienation, oppression, and an intense yearning for escape from slavery into a transcendent freedom. This does not mean that white religious songs do not make references to the burdens of the workaday world nor that black spirituals exhibit no preoccupation with the concept of sin; the remarkable difference between the two is in their emphasis.

Thus, from the musical tradition of West Africa and that of the British Isles, two important spiritual singing traditions developed in the American South, each of which was, to some extent, influenced by the other. The blending of cultures in camp meetings was not a one-sided affair. In no sense are black spirituals mere borrowings from white spirituals, nor are they purely or even chiefly African. Few of the South Carolina spirituals fail to reveal at least some slight influence from Anglo-American folk music, but even fewer lack the essential characteristics of the African tradition. Like so many other things in southern life, the black and white spirituals are the offspring of the mating of African and British folk cultures. This cultural integration was made possible by a unique coincidence of circumstances that did not occur elsewhere. Only in the South was a genuinely biracial folk culture created, and for this distinctive contribution to American culture to emerge both the inheritance from West Africa and the inheritance from the British Isles were essential.

REFERENCES: Some of the best references include the following: Allen, William Francis, Charles P. Ware, and Lucy McKim Garrison (eds.), *Slave Songs of the United States*, New York, 1867; Ballanta, N. G. J., *St. Helena Island Spirituals*, New York, 1925; Fisher, Miles M., *Negro Slave Songs in the United States*, Chicago, 1953; Herskovits, Melville J., *The Myth of the Negro Past*, Boston, 1958; Hornbostel, Erich M. von, "American Negro Songs," *International Review of Missions*, vol. 15, pp. 748–53, 1926; Jackson, George Pullen, *White Spirituals in the Southern Uplands*, Chapel Hill, 1933; Jackson, George Pullen, *Spiritual Folk Songs of Early America*, New York, 1937; Johnson, Guy B., *Folk Culture on St. Helena Island, South Carolina*, Chapel Hill, 1930; Johnson, Guy B., "The Negro Spiritual: A Problem in Anthropology," *American Anthropologist*, vol. 33, pp. 162–63, 1931; Krehbiel, Henry E., *Afro-American Folksongs*, New York, 1914; Lomax, Alan (ed.), *Folk Song U.S.A.*, New York, 1947; Lovell, John, Jr., *Black Song: The Forge and the Flame*, New York, 1972; McLaughlin, Wayman B., "Symbolism and Mysticism in the Spirituals," *Phylon*, 1963; Merriam, Alan P., "Characteristics of African Music," *Journal of the International Folk Music Council*, vol. 11, pp. 13–19, 1959; Merriam, Alan P., "The African Idiom in Music," *Journal of American Folklore*, vol. 75, pp. 120–30, 1962; Nettl, Bruno, *Folk and Traditional Music of the Western Continents*, Englewood Cliffs, 1965; and White, Newman Ivey, *American Negro Folk-Songs*, Cambridge, 1928.

Spirituals—Performance, Collections

Performance* Spirituals form a vital part of the great musical heritage of Afro-Americans. As an art form, they incorporate elements from history, literature, religion, drama, and music. A great variety of ethnic and cultural elements also went into their making.

Perhaps the element of performance should be regarded as the single most important factor in spirituals. It is the performance that shapes the song, that determines its rhythm, melody, tex-

*See acknowledgments in PREFACE; references under MUSIC: HISTORY AND DEVELOPMENT.

ture, tempo, text, and, finally, its effect upon listeners. This is largely due to the importance of improvisation in the African tradition. The song as written down represented only one performance in which the main stable elements were the meter, the refrain texts, and the basic outlines of the melody. All else could change from

Far right: Mahalia Jackson's warm, powerful voice was evident as she sang gospel songs or spirituals. *(U.S. Information Agency National Archives.)*

performance to performance: syncopations and dotted rhythms could be introduced at different places; embellishments and pitch alterations could be added to or eliminated from the melody; the "basers" could join the singing or drop out of it at varying time intervals, and they could provide different harmonizing tones for the melody. Even the general form of the piece might be changed by the repetition of refrain lines or choruses.

In regard to all these matters, William Francis Allen wrote a word of encouragement to the users of his pioneer collection of Negro spirituals, *Slave Songs in the United States*, first published in 1867:

We have aimed to give all the characteristic variations [for the songs] which have come into our hands, whether as single notes or whole lines, or even longer passages; and of words as well as tunes. . . . It may sometimes be a little difficult . . . to determine precisely [the relationship between all these things]. . . . However much latitude the reader may take in all such matters, he will hardly take more than the negroes themselves do. . . . The rests [in the notated songs], by the way, do not indicate a cessation in the music, but only in part of the singers. They overlap in singing, as already described, in such a degree that at no time is there any complete pause.

Adding to all this complexity in the performance of spirituals was the practice of audience participation—indeed, in the strict sense of the term there was no audience. There were only singers and nonsingers. The whites who came to listen might sit quietly, showing their appreciation of a performance by facial expression and by applause at appropriate times, but the Afro-Americans actively participated in the performance, not only by clapping and tapping, but also by constantly interjecting spoken or chanted words in order to reinforce the meaning of the text. Some short phrases commonly interjected include "Yes, Lord," "O Lord," and "I say now." The nature of these interpolations depended upon the occasion. One reporter has recorded that on one occasion the men watching a shout gave encouragement by yelling, "Wake 'em, brother!" and "Stand up to 'em, brother!"

The voice quality cultivated by the early singers of spirituals was high-pitched and of great intensity. Without exception, contemporary accounts refer to the "far-sounding harmony," "vigorous chorus," and the "great billows of sound" produced by the blacks' singing. For example, when Afro-Americans gathered for corn-shucking jubilees, as many as 300 or more would participate in some places; they would sing as they marched along the roads, their "rich, deep voices swelling out" on the refrains. Even the singing of two Afro-Americans as they walked through a forest "would make the dense old woods, for miles around, reverberate with their wild songs." When the blacks sang psalms and hymns during their religious services, they sang "loud and slow." With regard to the individual voice, there are few contemporary references except those noting some slave's unusually wide range. One observer does remark, however, that the voices of the slaves on ·her plantation seemed "oftener tenor than any other quality." A number of other reporters have commented upon the free use of falsetto among the slaves, particularly in the field hollers.

Collections The first important collection of Afro-American spirituals, which included 136 examples, was compiled in 1867 by William Francis Allen, Charles Picard Ware, and Lucy McKim Garrison. *Slave Songs in the United States,* as their volume is entitled, was reprinted by Oak Publications in 1965. Another very famous collection and arrangement of spirituals was made by James Weldon Johnson and J. Rosamond Johnson. Their volume, *The Book of American Negro Spirituals,* was issued by the Viking Press in 1925 and 1926. It was reissued in a Viking Compass edition in 1969.

Other important collections with notes or arrangements include: *Seventy Negro Spirituals* (William Arms Fisher); *American Negro Songs and Spirituals* (Monroe N. Work); *Dett Collec-* *tion of Negro Spirituals* (R. Nathaniel Dett); *The Story of the Jubilee Singers* (J. B. T. Marsh); *Cabin and Plantation Songs* (Hampton Institute collection); and *Old Songs Hymnal* (Harry T. Burleigh).

Unfortunately, many spirituals were never written down, and thus have passed from memory in the course of time. Others, however, survive in many versions with variants in tunes and texts. The Library of Congress, in Washington, D.C., has assembled a collection of more than 6,000 spirituals and variants in its music division.

The Most Popular Spirituals Perhaps the 100 most popular spirituals are listed below in alphabetical order. The ten most popular have been selected by the author and by the staff of the *Encyclopedia,* and they are indicated with an asterisk (*). The titles are written in standard English rather than in Negro dialect.

A Little Talk With Jesus Makes It Right
*All God's Children Got Wings
All I Do, the Church Keep A Grumbling
By and By (When the Morning Comes)
Calvary
Can't You Live Humble?
Chilly Water
Come Here, Lord!
Crucifixion
*Deep River
Didn't My Lord Deliver Daniel?
Didn't Old Pharaoh Get Lost?
Done Found My Lost Sheep
Don't Be Weary Traveler
Every Time I Feel the Spirit
*Ezekiel Saw the Wheel
Give Me That Old Time Religion
*Get on Board, Little Children
Give Me Jesus
Give Me Your Hand
*Go Down Moses
God's Going to Trouble the Waters
Great Camp Meeting in the Promised Land
Great Day
Going to Sing All Along the Way
Hail, Mary, Don't You Weep
Hallelujah!
Heaven Bound Soldier
Humble Yourself, the Bell Done Rung
I Couldn't Hear Nobody Pray
I Feel Like My Time Ain't Long
I Got a Home in the Rock
I Know the Lord's Laid His Hands on Me
I Long to See That Day
I'm Going to Heaven Anyhow
I'm Going to Glory
I'm Troubled in Mind
In That Great Getting Up Morning
It's Me, O Lord
I Want to Be Ready
I Want to Die Easy When I Die

Joshua Fit the Battle of Jericho
Jubilee
Keep Inching Along
Keep Me From Sinking Down
Listen to the Lambs
*Little David Play on Your Harp
Look How They Done My Lord
Lord, I Want to Be a Christian in a My Heart
Mary and Martha Just Gone Home
Mary Had a Baby, Yes, Lord
My Lord Delivered Daniel
My Lord's a Writing All the Time
My Lord Says He's Going to Rain Down Fire
My Lord, What a Morning
My Soul's Been Anchored in the Lord
My Way Is Cloudy
Nobody Knows the Trouble I've Seen
O, Brother, Don't Get Weary
O, Gambler, Git Up Off of Your Knees
O, Rocks, Don't Fall on Me
O, Wasn't That a Wide River?
O, My Good Lord, Show Me the Way
Old Ship of Zion
O, Yes, O, Yes, Wait Until I Git on My Robe
Over the Crossing
Over My Head
Peter, Go Ring Them Bells
Poor Mourner's Got a Home at Last
Ride On, Moses
Rise, Mourner, Rise
Rise Up Shepherd and Follow
Roll the Old Chariot Along
*Roll, Jordan, Roll
Run, Mary, Run
Singing with a Sword in My Hand
Sinner, Please Don't Let This Harvest Pass
Somebody's Knocking at Your Door
*Sometimes I Feel Like a Motherless Child
Stand Still Jordan
Steal Away Jesus
*Swing Low Sweet Chariot
There's A Meeting Here Tonight
To See God's Bleeding Lamb
Until I Reach a My Home
Up on the Mountain
Walk in Jerusalem Just Like John
Walk, Mary, Down the Land
Walk Together Children
We Are Climbing Jacob's Ladder
Weary Traveler
*Were You There When They Crucified My Lord?
What You Going to Do When the Lamp Burns
   Down?
When I Fall on My Knees
Where Shall I Be When the First Trumpet Sounds?
Who That a Coming Over Yonder?
Who Will Be a Witness for My Lord?
You Go, I Go With You
You Got a Right
You May Bury Me in the East

Blues The blues is a musical expression that is an individual form of creative statement. It is a personal statement, a reaction to the life experience in its entirety. The blues can voice complaint, dissatisfaction, or hopelessness; despair at injustices, social conditions, or interpersonal relationships; the need for love, lack of love, or loss of love; or it can simply comment on a situation. Because the blues focuses on elements so common in the human experience, it is easy for people to identify with its texts. This ability of the blues to win people's sympathy easily has helped to make the appeal of this musical form universal.

No single person originated the blues. Its musical characteristics emerged from a storehouse of resources that had been created and maintained by Afro-Americans since the arrival of the first slaves in the new land; and its messages reflect the experiences of generations of blacks in both their collective and individual capacities. Thus, many contributed to the development of the blues and to its influence on other musical genres.

Blues fall into two basic categories: rural or country blues and urban or classic blues.

The early rural blues, or field blues, retained many elements of antebellum shouts, hollers, yells, work songs, cries, and spirituals. Their themes were melancholic, and the singers hummed and moaned them, using an occasional falsetto as well as the rhythmic chanting technique historically associated with Afro-American preachers. The country blues was highly improvisatory. The singer sang for as long as he could conceive ideas about the theme he was presenting. Unlike the style of later country blues, the rural blues did not feature the strong-beat phrasing associated with instrumental accompaniment.

The country blues was usually a folk tale of lament or a song of unrequited love, and it was sung predominantly by men in the rural South. Most of the country blues singers were born in Mississippi, Louisiana, or Texas. They sang their lyrics in a very primitive fashion, usually with accompanying bottleneck guitar and occasionally with a Jew's harp, or harmonica. Their melodies seem to have had no set structure; the singers seemed mainly interested in the expression of their feelings. Later on, these singers began to add a meter and structure that resemble the 12-bar technique. Big Bill Broonzy, one of the major country blues singers, has said: "This is what Mississippi people call dressed-up blues, when you count your time, and each chord is given so many beats." In addition to Broonzy, there were three other major exponents of the country blues technique: Blind Lemon Jefferson, Huddie ("Leadbelly") Ledbetter, and Robert Johnson.

The urban or classic blues is called *classic* because it is music that seems to contain all the diverse and conflicting elements of Afro-American music, plus the emotional appeal of smoother performance. The classic blues is usually presented in the 12-bar form, that is, the first and second lines are the same, with the third line complementing the first. These three lines are augmented by musical phrases called breaks. The musical fill plus the lyric line make up the 12 bars of the blues. However, although the thematic categories of blues have remained rather static, its internal formal structure has become highly variable. The ultimate refinement in true blues performance is the way the singer manipulates the vocal line, that is, his articulation of blue notes, his slides, turns, improvisations, moans, and groans. The form imposes few limitations. Stanzas may fall into any number of bars. Actually, structure is influenced by the talents of the individual performer, who develops his or her ideas according to the capacity of the subject chosen for expansion.

The most prominent classic blues singers have been women, and it was they who brought this form of Afro-American music into the commercial market. The 1920 recording of Mamie Smith singing "Crazy Blues" made history as the first *recording* ever made of Afro-American music. It sold 790,000 copies during its first year of issue and led to a series of records that were advertised as "race records."

The first *performances* of classic blues, however, had taken place in the minstrel shows that toured the South in the late 1800s. One of these shows, the Rabbit Foot Minstrels, featured a woman singer, Gertrude "Ma" Rainey. She was later called the "Mother of the Blues" because she fostered the classic blues style. "Ma" Rainey also gained recognition because of her tutelage of a young singer from Chattanooga, Tenn., named Bessie Smith. The combination of Smith's talent and Rainey's coaching established Bessie Smith as the most commercially successful of the "race record" artists. Bessie Smith's broad vocal intonation and sensitive interpretation of the lyric refrain manifested themselves as vital instruments of ethnic ("soul") expression, earning her the title "Empress of the Blues." Most of Smith's recordings were made with outstanding jazz musicians, including Clarence Williams, Fletcher Henderson, James P. Johnson,

and Louis Armstrong. Four other women who were prominent as blues singers during Bessie Smith's reign were Bertha "Chippie" Hill, Victoria Spivey, Ida Cox, and Alberta Hunter.

The blues were first printed in 1912 when sheet music of W. C. Handy's "The Memphis Blues" was issued. Handy, a southern musician, had joined a black minstrel show at the age of 23. In his travels he had heard and learned about the blues. Although he was never a blues singer, Handy wrote down the music of this genre (he was the first to do so). In 1914 Handy wrote and published what became one of the best-known songs and blues pieces ever written, "The St. Louis Blues." In this composition Handy remembered the St. Louis of the 1890s, recalling the beauty and gaiety of its women and the fascinating life on Market Street, Chestnut Street, and Walnut Street, all within a few blocks of the train station. He also immortalized the "St. Louis woman with her diamond ring." By the time Handy wrote this song, however, the playing of the blues had settled into a standard musical form.

The blues is the most dominant artistic force to emerge from the Afro-American experience in America. Its lyric is the most candid form of rhetoric for depicting the inward feelings of Afro-Americans. Its techniques of musical expression are the barometer by which a great jazz musician is distinguished from a good one. The influence of the blues in black culture has hardly been equaled by that of any other musical element.

Jazz The musical expression called jazz was created by Afro-Americans who lived in the southern United States during the last part of the nineteenth century, although the popular use of this name was delayed until the time of World War I and later. In every sense, jazz is a hybrid—the elements that went into its makeup derived from the folklore of Negro work songs, spirituals, and the blues. However, these were not the only components of jazz; many scholars have cited West African rhythms and European harmony as other major ingredients. Moreover, in spite of the cultural deprivation of southern blacks, both Latin American and West Indian musical elements, prominent in the music of the New World, entered into the formation and makeup of jazz, merging with Old World principles of harmony, melody, and rhythm.

Bessie Smith, classic blues singer, combined with jazzmen like Louis Armstrong and Fletcher Henderson to produce a bonanza in record sales in the 1920s. *(Schomburg Collection, New York Public Library.)*

Huddie (Leadbelly) Ledbetter. *(Photo by Robin Carson.)*

599

From the beginning, the melody of jazz was delivered in a call-and-response technique that traces its origins back to West Africa and the "talking drum." About 90 percent of all jazz melodic themes, either written or improvised, use the call-and-response technique. However, this technique was employed earlier in the United States by the black preacher and his congregation and in field hollers and shouts before its contemporary transmutation into such sophisticated themes and compositions as epitomized, for example, by Miles Davis' "So What."

Jazz melody contains the embellishment of falsetto tones around the pitch, timbre, intervals, and the different rhythmic articulations. The falsetto tones provide tonal colors that emulate the human voice and depict, in musical sounds, the human spirit and emotions. The moans, cries, and hollers of the past, which evidenced the spirit of an oppressed people, after their development into the melodic structure through jazz techniques display these same characteristics in the growl of the trumpet and the heavy vibrato of the saxophone. An outstanding example of jazz melody is, for example, found in the instrumental variations in Johnny Green's "Body and Soul," played by tenor-saxophonist Coleman Hawkins. Hawkins' deep vibrato tones flow through the melody with the passion of a man possessed, and the ability of expressing one's feelings vibrantly, fluidly, and with feeling is the distinguishing mark of technique for jazz musicians.

Perhaps the most important element of Western music used in jazz is that of rhythm, the beat, meter or heart throb of jazz. The beat, or meter, is not restricted to the literal meaning of x number of beats per measure. Instead, it is a combination of rhythmic meter and rhythmic articulation within the melodic phrase. This articulation lengthens and accents notes in order to identify the essence of the jazz melodic theme or phrase.

The rhythmic concept in jazz is a combination of West African and South American rhythmic techniques applied to Western patterns, resulting in a polyrhythmic style not found in any other Western music. This polyrhythmic concept provides rhythmic variations, the most important of which is syncopation. In simple terms, the principle of syncopation is the absence of an accent where one expects it to be and the placing of an accent where one does not expect it. This interruption of rhythmic regularity produces a feeling of unrest in the music, with

consequent arousal of feelings of stimulation and excitement in the listener.

Although the rhythm of jazz originated in West Africa and in Latin America, its harmony derived from European musical models. Harmony is the structural function and relationship of chords, and the chords form the basis of melody. Harmony, as employed in jazz, spirituals, the blues, and most types of improvisations, consists of orderly arrangements of chords based upon long-established European laws of sequence. Harmony is employed in jazz principally in breaks, the intervals between musical phrases, to compensate for the lack of melodic development. The breaks are an improvised variation based on the melodic theme with harmonic interpretations stemming from the black tradition, that is, following instead of establishing the melody. Spirituals without harmony are rare, and jazz without harmony is absolutely unthinkable.

Three main components that went into the formation of jazz are work songs and folklore, spirituals, and the blues.

Work songs were the chants delivered in the African tradition of call-and-response by blacks on the roads, farms, levees, and in the prisons of the southern United States. They served as a means to make laborious tasks easier, and they form a chronicle of the conditions of oppression that black men endured during slavery. The moans, cries, and hollers of the southern plantation field hands (workers) formed the basis for the black esthetics movements of the 1960s and 1970s. Slaves improvised work songs concerning, for example, work in the fields, labor on roads, breaking of rocks, or laying of railroad tracks; one of the best known of these songs is about the folk hero, John Henry, "de steel-drivin' man," who died challenging the machine. All of these songs have a melodic theme and a rhythmic articulation that emphasize the nature of the subject with little or no harmony.

Spirituals, the first original songs created by black slaves on American soil, can very easily be dated from the changes and fluctuations in theological attitudes toward slavery. Most spirituals can be placed in a definite period of American history if such varieties as hymns, ring shouts, revival shouts, camp-meeting songs, and funeral marches are divided into three basic patterns of origin.

The first of the three basic patterns of origins of spirituals includes the adaptations of African ritual music to Christian liturgical requirements. In this group the form and attitude of African worship survived in the guise of Christianity. For example, the Dahomey River God ceremony was incorporated into the rite of Protestant baptism. Another ritual, but one wholly African in origin, was the ring shout, which was performed in churches and meeting houses as a shuffling dance accompanied by the singing of spirituals.

The second pattern consists of songs spontaneously created by Afro-American preachers and their congregations. In these the natural rise and fall of Afro-American speech is intensified by the highly rhythmic and dynamic strain of Afro-American preaching and is accented by the exclamations of the congregation.

Afro-American variations on European ecclesiastical tunes, in which the words, rather than the music, held the greatest interest to the black listener form the third basic pattern of spirituals' origins. The blacks saw their own fate reflected in these chronicles of faith and patience in exile; as the slaves of Rome before them had turned to Judaism, so now they sought comfort in Christianity.

The characteristics of all spirituals can be described in a few words. The spiritual is sung with freedom, independence, and individuality of the vocal line. The leader-and-chorus (call-and-response) pattern predominates. Some melodies resemble familiar European tunes, although others are extremely wild and unconventional. Spirituals were used as working songs as well as at religious meetings. The spirituals include many hymns, mostly Baptist and Methodist in derivation, and the black slaves also adopted many of the revival songs sung by whites at camp meetings. Frequently, psalms and long-metered hymns were adapted to the call-and-response pattern for church singing. The singing of the spirituals was characterized by peculiar vocal effects, difficult—if not impossible—to indicate by regular musical notation.

The influence of spirituals can easily be traced in the development of jazz. A good example of the call-and-response technique is the blues song, "That Too, Do," on "Count Basie in Kansas City: Bennie Moten's Great Band of 1930–32" (RCA Victor Vintage Series LPV–514), which features "that provocative call-and-response between 'preacher' Ed Lewis' trumpet and the band's 'congregation.'" Another example is the contemporary treatment of the spiritual "Swing Low, Sweet Chariot," by the Modern Jazz Quartet, in which John Lewis develops a series of variations on a theme he entitles "The Spiritual."

The second component of jazz, the blues, was the musical sign and symbol of black emancipation. In its singular vigor and incisiveness, the blues bore the characteristic marks of a vast social achievement. At the same time, however, the blues carried the signs of the social and spiritual agonies of an emancipation that brought relief from slavery but did not lead to social, economic, or cultural equality.

The real folk blues told about the empty bed and the easy rider with the casual and unsmirking assurance of a people to whom the impermanence of all loving relationships had been unforgettably demonstrated in the days of slavery, when any two people who loved one another might on any day be callously separated and sold to different owners. Thus, the blues singer sang about lost love; he also sang of the other cares endemic to the lives of black southerners.

At the beginning of the twentieth century, the music of the socially alienated Afro-American became a dominant force in the expression of several white American composers. The three most important composers to use Afro-American musical motifs were Stephen Foster, John Philip Sousa, and Louis M. Gottschalk. Sousa, called "the March King," and Gottschalk employed a particular form of music introduced by blacks in southern cities, where pianists usually played it in bars and dance halls. "Barrelhouse" pianism—it is not known if its name derived from the fact that it became popular in bars where beer was sold from barrels—became popular, and from it developed a highly sophisticated style of musical expression that became know as ragtime.

Ragtime is a strongly accented syncopated rhythm with a series of melodic strains structured in the classic rondo form. Very little of classic ragtime was improvised. Ragtime's rondo form characteristically has a thematic structure that appears as AABACD. The first two themes, A and B, constitute contrasting melodic subjects. Theme C acts as a trio, forming a sort of dance movement within the sonata form, and theme D serves as the finale of the entire work. This format may be seen in many of Sousa's marches, such as "Stars and Stripes." The two contrasting themes (A and B) were generally written in a meter to which one could dance the two-step, polka, or waltz.

Scott Joplin, Thomas Milton Turpin, and James Scott were the three masters of classic ragtime. Of the three, Joplin achieved the most renown. It was his piece, "The Maple Leaf Rag," published in 1897, that set the stage for the recognition of this musical form. James Scott's "Ragtime Oriole" derived in part from the cake-

Scott Joplin was recognized as a master of ragtime, as shown on this cover of one of his compositions. (*Moorland-Spingarn Research Center*.)

walk, which had originally been a prancing dance in which slaves competed for a cake as a prize from their white masters. The reemergence of interest in the cakewalk, along with the popularity of "The Maple Leaf Rag" and other rag pieces, brought ragtime into the big time and established it as a commercially successful music form, mostly through the sale of sheet music.

During the 1970s ragtime experienced a renaissance. Many piano students added the scores of rag masters to their repertoires, and one of Scott Joplin's two ragtime operas, *Treemonisha*, written in 1911, was revived throughout the United States. Joplin's tunes also were featured in the prize-winning movie, *The Sting*. The score of his first opera, *Guest of Honor*, written in 1903, has unfortunately been lost.

Although the classic ragtime fever had outlasted its heyday by 1920, this musical idiom grew into a piano style in the eastern United States that was called stride piano. Ragtime, combined with the motifs of the spiritual and the blues, provided the repertoires of the early jazz band instrumentalists.

The piano form favored on the eastern seaboard had as its hallmark a strongly accented figure in the left hand called striding. Pianists employed this rhythmic technique to provide a walking-bass accompaniment to the melodic theme. The sound generally appeared as a monotonous *oom-pa, oom-pa* meter. This unique use of syncopation brought greater attention to the music of Afro-Americans. Early exponents, such as Eubie Blake and Charles "Lucky" Roberts, performed their pieces in both musical shows and in private entertainments in homes. Blake achieved great success by adopting his style of ragtime piano to the musical scores of such Broadway successes as *Shuffle Along*. Roberts, who performed in the parlors of Harlem houses in New York City, increased the general awareness of the value of the stride style and was the major influence on the three most prominent exponents of the stride school of playing. These masters were James P. Johnson, Willie "The Lion" Smith, and Thomas "Fats" Waller.

Although all three made outstanding contributions in both technique and composition, Johnson was acknowledged by all as the "dean." Johnson's composition, "Carolina Shout," was considered the test of a pianist's ability to play the stride technique, which furnishes evidence of the esteem in which Johnson was held by stride pianists. Other important compositions by Johnson include "The Charleston," "Mule Walk," "Old-Fashioned Love," "A Porter's Love Song," and "If I Could Be With You One Hour Tonight."

One of Johnson's major protégés was "Fats" Waller, who was the youngest of the three and is ranked now as the best composer. Waller is particularly remembered for "Ain't Misbehavin'," composed for the revue *Hot Chocolates*. Willie "The Lion" Smith wrote in his book, *Music on My Mind*: "Beetle [Johnson], 'Fats' and I played all of the rent parties in Harlem and the East Side." Rent parties were characteristic social functions of the 1920s and 1930s, given in order to raise the rent money for the party-giver. Musicians, principally pianists, were invited, and were paid with food and drink. The guests paid a fee for the food and drink, which went toward the rent. It was at rent parties on New York's East Side that George Gershwin, for example, was first exposed to the black musical idiom, and its effect on him is well illustrated in his "Rhapsody in Blue" and in his opera *Porgy and Bess.*

Meanwhile, in the Midwest another style of piano playing had been developing. It was called boogie-woogie, or fast blues, and it emphasized a figure in the left hand. This figure was a repetitive bass line that commonly contained 8 beats to the bar, although it sometimes had 16, to a melodic figure that followed the 12-bar blues concept. The citadel of boogie-woogie was Chicago, Ill., and Jimmy Yancey was its "dean." Yancey's most famous composition is "Yancey's Stomp." Other important contributors to the boogie-woogie style were Pinetop Smith ("Pinetop's Boogie-Woogie") and Meade Lux Lewis ("Honky Tonk Train Blues"). Just as stride piano was played in Harlem and on the East Side of New York City at rent parties, so in Chicago in the South Side's Mecca Flats, boogie-woogie was played at the same kind of parties. This style of playing the blues became one of the primary bases in the development of jazz in the big-band era in Kansas City, and it was a major contributor to the American music known as rock and roll.

All the forms and styles of Afro-American music so far discussed in this article contributed to the art form known as jazz. Although some of these styles developed independently, such as boogie-woogie, they all derived from the emotions, spirit, and imagination of Afro-Americans. They all served as a catalyst in the development of the historical style known as jazz, which began in New Orleans, La.

New Orleans was the birthplace of jazz because of the social, economic, and moral characteristics that typified that city about the turn of the twentieth century. In 1897 a New Orleans alderman named Stanley Story had presented an unusual report to the city council in which, after pointing out the profits to be gained by allowing legalized prostitution in New Orleans, he had recommended that legalized prostitution be confined to a specific 22-block Negro area of the city, which later became known as Storyville. The city accepted Story's idea, and prostitution became legal in this one area of New Orleans in July 1897. Brothels and bordellos soon flourished within the limits of Storyville, and the background music for these houses was provided by black pianists who played ragtime. Some of these pianists who later became famous include Aaron Harris, Tony Jackson, and Ferdinand "Jelly Roll" Morton. However, long before Storyville came into being, the idiom of ragtime had served as the basis of the music of brass

marching bands, which performed for such various city functions as parades, picnics, and funerals. The marching band had become a central part of the city's daily routine, its most notable function being the funeral parade.

The marching bands of New Orleans performed rags, stomps, and church hymns in the ensemble style, with the cornet carrying the lead theme. These bands were composed mainly of musicians attached to a lodge or fraternal organization, such as the Knights of Pythias, and although not all of these musicians played the music later to be known as jazz, each group had outstanding jazz players within its ensemble. At funerals, the bands would accompany the body to the cemetery playing such hymns as "Nearer My God to Thee," and then afterward return to the heart of town playing such joyful mood pieces as "When the Saints Go Marching In." One of these bands, for example, had as its lead cornetist a barber named Charles "Buddy" Bolden.

When Bolden was not playing in parades, he gathered together a number of players and they performed for parties, dances, and picnics. The music that this small ensemble played became known as jazz; the etymology of this word, with its strong sexual connotations, extends back to Africa.

The repertoire of Buddy Bolden's Band consisted of rags, stomps, and blues, the latter played in a slow, low-down manner to imitate the singing voice of a country blues singer. Their music, which would today be called semibaroque, was characterized by the cornet playing the lead, the clarinet the second, and the trombone third. Its approach was augmented by the rhythmic accompaniment of the banjo and drums. Most of the players, including Bolden, were untrained, but Bolden's talent and range on the cornet earned him the title of "King" and set the standard for future cornetists to aim at. Of Bolden's range, legend says that his high notes could be heard throughout New Orleans and that his low notes achieved a deep sad quality when he played the blues.

Buddy Bolden's Band was made up of members of the Eagles Marching Band. After Bolden was committed to the East Louisiana State Hospital on June 5, 1907, where he died in 1931, Frank Dusen, the band's valve trombonist, assumed leadership. Bunk Johnson wrote of Buddy Bolden and his band in his book *Hear Me Talkin' to Ya* (1966): "Now here is the thing that made King Bolden's Band the first band to play jazz. It was because they could not read at all."

White and creole musicians soon organized bands in the tradition of the Negro dance bands, such as Buddy Bolden's. There were creole bands, white bands, Negro bands, Negro bands with creole players, and bands with creoles, whites, and blacks. Many musicians attained fame by perpetuating the tradition begun by Buddy Bolden. This number includes Bunk Johnson, Freddie Keppard, Manuel Perez, "Big Eye" Louis Nelson, Jimmy Noone, Sidney Bechet, Johnny Dodds, Joe "King" Oliver, and others.

In addition to its public performances in parades, picnics, and funerals, and at private parties and dances, the new musical style was soon being played up and down the Mississippi River on riverboats, and its popularity spread beyond the city of New Orleans. One of the main reasons for this popularity derived from the set of dances most often performed to it: the quadrille. The quadrille is a dance consisting of five figures: two 2-step polkas, a mazurka, a waltz, and a schottische.

After Storyville was closed by the U.S. Navy in November 1917, the jazzmen went up the river to Chicago, where jazz found a new home. One white ensemble, Tommy Brown's Band, played jazz in Chicago in 1914–15, but it was not successful. Later when creole and Negro bands from New Orleans migrated to Chicago they were accepted by that city's black population. Many jazz pianists, out of work in New Orleans, were lured north by the favorable conditions in Chicago.

An important historical event in the world of jazz occurred on February 27–28, 1917. A white group of New Orleans musicians, who called themselves the Original Dixieland Jazz Band, recorded two selections on phonograph records. These were "Livery Stable Blues" and "The Dixieland Band One-Step," and were recorded under the auspices of the Victor Phonograph Company, who had earlier asked Freddie Keppard to record with his Creole Jazz Band. However, Keppard had replied: "Nothin' doin', boys. We won't put our stuff on records for everybody to steal." The first nonwhite jazz recording was made in Los Angeles, Calif., in June 1922 by Kid Ory's Sunshine Syncopaters. The two selections recorded were "Ory's Creole Trombone" and "Society Blues." With recordings, jazz entered a new era of commercialization—and, possibly, of corruption and exploitation.

The most successful venture in early Chicago jazz was a creole jazz band led by Joseph "King"

Oliver and featuring a young cornetist named Louis Armstrong. The band played nightly at Lincoln's Garden on the South Side of Chicago, and among the audience were white musicians from the North Side, who learned their craft from this historic group. Some of these "students" included members of the later-formed New Orleans Rhythm Kings and Austin High Gang. They heard a repertoire of blues and stomps, such as the famous "Dippermouth Blues," with the second cornet solo by Armstrong, and "Jazzin' Baby Blues," later called "Royal Garden Blues."

From the Oliver band emerged the famous Louis Armstrong Hot Five, which took over residence in the Sunset Club in 1925. The Hot Five was composed of stellar musicians: Armstrong on cornet, Kid Ory on trombone, Johnny Dodds on clarinet, Johnny St. Cyr on banjo, and Lil Hardin (who later became Mrs. Armstrong) on piano. This group of outstanding jazz performers made some of the most memorable recordings in the entire history of jazz. Their inventive techniques and innovations are still used today as a vital resource in the development of jazz soloists. Some of their famous recordings include such classics as "Gut Bucket Blues," "Heebie Jeebies," "Cornet Chop Suey," "Willie the Weeper," "Lonesome Blues," and "Jazz Lips." The most important characteristics of these recordings are the techniques of ensemble play, solo versatility—particularly Armstrong's handling of the break—, and the total essence of 12-bar blues format. Because of the primitive nature of recording facilities at that time, drummer Warren "Baby" Dodds, brother of the clarinetist, could not appear in these recordings, but he did play with the Hot Five at all live performances.

Other outstanding jazzmen who recorded during that period were "Jelly Roll" Morton and his Hot Peppers. In 1926 they recorded a series that included "The Original Jelly Roll Blues" and "Black Bottom Stomp." These two recordings were the first arranged by a leader (in this case, Morton) for a band without losing the idea of spontaneity necessary—at that time—for pure jazz. The significance of Morton's arrangements is that they showed the way for such other jazzmen as Fletcher Henderson, Duke Ellington, and Quincy Jones to write and arrange jazz pieces without destroying spontaneity.

Morton's conception of arranging jazz pieces was utilized and refined by Fletcher Henderson and Bill McKinney and adapted to larger ensembles. Henderson and McKinney formed the vanguard of the "Big Band Era." The big band consisted of three sections: reeds (tenor, baritone, and alto saxophones; clarinets), brass (trumpets, trombones), and rhythm (drum, piano, bass, and guitar). The hallmark of the big-band ensemble was the predominance of the saxophone as the lead voice carrying the theme with the brass supplying intervals of call-and-response figures in a choral manner. Both Henderson and McKinney had a special talent in writing for ensembles of this type. They were both skilled in orchestration, and were able to arrange compositions that retained the jazz tradition.

Thus, while Louis Armstrong and "Jelly Roll" Morton were entertaining Chicagoans, Fletcher Henderson's Orchestra and Bill McKinney's Cotton Pickers were delighting East Coast listeners with their big-band approach to jazz. The popularity of these two groups soon led to the organization of such others as Sam Wooding's Band, Jesse Europe's Band, Noble Sissle's Band, and Luis Russell's Band. Henderson's style of arranging achieved even greater popularity through his arrangements for Benny Goodman's Band, whose leader became known as the "King of Swing."

Perhaps the most important occurrence in the 1920s for the history of jazz was the appearance in New York City in 1923 of Washington, D.C.'s Edward Kennedy Ellington—for he quickly established himself, and his big-band ensembles reigned from that time into the 1970s.

"Duke," as Ellington was internationally known, was a pianist out of the James P. Johnson/Willie "The Lion" Smith mold. His approach to writing for his big band has often been described as one based on writing for his own instrument because his improvisations for his band were as personal as if he were, indeed, writing for the piano, his own instrument.

Ellington's first success was his appearance at the Cotton Club in New York City in December 1927. From that engagement to appearances at Carnegie Hall, throughout Europe, the Soviet Union, and Asia, Ellington carried the sound of jazz in his own impeccable style to the status of a respected art form. As a composer, Ellington wrote such classics as "East St. Louis Toodle-oo," "Cotton Tail," "Black and Tan Fantasy," "Mood Indigo," "Concerto for Cootie," "Ko-Ko," and "Satin Doll." His extended suites, some for piano, include "Black, Brown and Beige," "Liberian Suite," "A Drum Is a Woman," "My People," and "New Orleans Suite."

Like McKinney's Cotton Pickers, who had sax-

ophonist Don Redman as co-arranger and composer of songs, Ellington employed Billy Strayhorn, a young composer and pianist from Pittsburgh, Pa., to assist him. Strayhorn contributed to Ellington's band such famous compositions as "Take the A Train," adopted by Ellington as his theme, "Chelsea Bridge," "Warm Valley," and "Jack the Bear."

Fletcher Henderson orchestrated much of the transition from spontaneous music to carefully scored ensemble playing, which led to the big bands of the swing era. (University Archives, Universtiy of Kansas.)

One of Ellington's talents, as well as one of the means of his long-sustained success, was his ability to seek out and to attract fine musicians. His band profited from the talents of many outstanding jazzmen, including reedsmen Otto Hardwick, Ben Webster, Johnny Hodges, Harry Carney, Barney Bigard, and Paul Gonzalez; trom-

Harlem's Cotton Club, 1932, was noted for its well-known entertainers, including popular band leaders such as Duke Ellington, Cab Calloway, and Lionel Hampton. (National Archives.)

bonists Joe "Tricky Sam" Nanton, Juan Tizol, and Lawrence Brown; trumpeters Bubber Miley, Rex Stewart, Cootie Williams, Cat Anderson, and Clark Terry; drummers Sonny Greer and Sam Willyard; bassists Wellman Braud, Billy Taylor, Sr., Oscar Pettiford, and Jimmy Blanton, the innovator of the solo bass; and trumpeter Ray Nance, also a violinist. In addition to these instrumentalists, Ellington also employed a corps of talented female singers, including Ivie Anderson, Joya Sherrill, Kay Davis, and Marie Ellington.

During Ellington's reign in New York and abroad, Kansas City had become a mecca for the blues—but within the big-band concept. The history of Kansas City jazz has been told in *Jazz Style in Kansas City and the Southwest,* published by Ross Russell, the personal manager of Charlie Parker, in 1971. Kansas City, close to rural southern areas, attracted musicians who had been exposed to the Mississippi Delta country blues. When instrumentalists began to insert their innovations into big-band renditions, Kansas City music was flavored with the raw, pure sound of the blues. The rhythem context of the big bands employed the boogie-woogie figure, which had been associated with the blues and often called a fast form of the blues. The main bandleader of the Kansas City movement was a trombonist named Bennie Moten. In addition to being a pioneer in big bands in Kansas City in the 1920s, Moten was also a key figure in the political schemes of that city's mayor and boss, Tom Pendergast. For example, all incoming groups of black musicians had to clear with Moten before accepting contracts for work in Kansas City. As a matter of course, Moten's band had the best jobs. Moten also had his pick of the best musicians, and such performers as bassist Walter Paige, who had originally come to Kansas City with his own group from Oklahoma called the Blue Devils, trumpeter "Hot Lips" Page, blues singer Jimmy Rushing, and a pianist from Red Bank, N.J., named William "Count" Basie all performed with his band.

After Moten's death in the mid-1930s, Basie became leader of his band, and soon gave birth to another of jazz history's important styles, known as swing. "Count" Basie's hallmark, during all of his years as a bandleader from the 1930s to the 1970s, was his rhythm section: four performers who kept a steady, smooth, foot-tapping rhythm for ensemble, soloist, and listener. Basie's musical approach was simple: an 8-bar

theme followed by spontaneous improvisation for everyone, including liberal employment of the call-and-response technique. The rhythm section, which was called by Paul Whiteman, acknowledged by many as the king of jazz, the "All-American Rhythm Section," was made up of Basie on piano, Walter Paige on bass, Freddie Green on guitar, and Joe Jones on drums. This section supported such outstanding jazz soloists as Herschel Evans on tenor sax, Lester Young on tenor sax, Dickie Wells on trombone, Buck Clayton on trumpet, and blues shouter Jimmy Rushing.

Basie's early recordings are now collectors' items, locked up in jazz archives. They include "One O'Clock Jump," the Basie theme; "Swingin' the Blues"; "Every Tub"; "Send for You Yesterday, and Here You Come Today"; and "Boogie-Woogie," the last two featuring Rushing on vocal.

Kansas City was a fertile ground for many big bands from the mid-1920s to 1940. Some were known only in that city, such as those of Alonzo Tate, Tommy Douglass, and Harlan Leonard; others, however, achieved national recognition, such as those of Andy Kirk (his Clouds of Joy featured as pianist and arranger-composer Mary Lou Williams and trumpeter Howard McGhee) and Jay McShann (who featured alto-saxophonist Charlie Parker).

During the mid-1930s and early 1940s, several big bands were booked into theaters and halls along the East Coast. Theater marquees headlined "King of the Drums" Chick Webb, featuring Ella Fitzgerald of "A Tisket, A Tasket" fame; "The Twentieth Century Gabriel," Erskine Hawkins, composer of "Tuxedo Junction"; "King of the Hi-De-Ho" Cab Calloway, with such outstanding performers as bassist Milt Hinton, tenor-saxophonist Chu Berry, drummer Cozy Cole, and trumpeter Dizzy Gillespie; Lucky Millinder, featuring alto-saxophonist Tab Smith and vocalist Sister Rosetta Tharpe; and Earl "Fatha" Hines and his orchestra, with vocals by Billie Eckstine and Sarah Vaughan.

One of the first collegiate-formed bands of the 1930s to make an impact on the big-band scene was a group composed mainly of Fisk University alumni, under the direction of Jimmie Lunceford. His instrumental voicing had great influence on such emerging white bands as those of Tommy Dorsey and Glenn Miller. The Lunceford crew had Sy Oliver as arranger, Willie "The Lion" Smith, and Trummy Young as trombonist,

Count Basie created the big band sound in Kansas City that was grounded in a flawless rhythm section, superb sidemen, and a freewheeling spirit. *(Museum of the City of New York.)*

who also wrote "It Ain't What You Do, It's the Way That You Do It." The Alabama State Collegians, a university band, also achieved a measure of national fame during this period.

Jazz instrumentalists who worked in big bands often assembled after hours in small nightclubs for "jam sessions." One of the most popular havens for "jamming" was The Three Deuces in New York City. The musician in residence at this club was Art Tatum, a blind pianist from Toledo, Ohio. Tatum was truly a phenomenon in the annals of jazz; his touch on the piano has been compared to the feel of velvet, and he sent mellow tones running with graceful arpeggios through both jazz and classics. Tatum's genius attracted Lester Young, Coleman Hawkins, Roy Eldridge, and Ben Webster to frequent jam sessions, in which the spontaneity of jazz was truly reincarnated.

At the same time, in New York City's Harlem, at a small club known as Minton's Playhouse, another type of jam session was taking place. Musicians here were working out new innovations in the presentation of the jazz melody, innovations later called bebop. These innovations constituted variations on melodic themes, many of which popular American dance bands had been playing for the past two decades. The new concept involved instantaneous improvisation on the theme stated in unison usually by two or three horn players. The role of the rhythm section was also changed. The drummer relinquished his custodial duty as keeper of the beat, and a new form of placing accents was established for him. The bass player became the pillar of rhythm, and the pianist carried the foundation of the melodic theme in the harmonic chords used to accompany the horn players. The principal architects of this new approach to jazz were Dizzy Gillespie, Charlie Parker, who was nicknamed "Bird," Thelonius Monk, Kenny Clarke, and Charlie Christian.

Of this group, the least known is guitarist Christian. In 1939 Christian was brought to New York City to join the Benny Goodman band, with whom he played for three years, delighting fans and fellow jazzmen with his unique approach to the electric-amplified guitar. Christian brought his instrument to the forefront as a major solo vehicle, and later became one of the major residents of Minton's, contributing a vital influence in his use of the riff phrase. Evidence of Christian's stay at Minton's can be heard on the album *Harlem Jazz Scene - 1941* (Counterpoint/Esoteric

Records, #548). Black and white performers of the 1960s and 1970s, whose forte and style are based upon the electric guitar, all owe a debt, knowingly or not, to Christian.

Some of the tunes that received the bebop approach include "How High the Moon," which, when transmuted into the bop idiom, became "Ornithology"; and "What Is This Thing Called Love," which became a Tad Dameron composition called "Hot House." These variations and others were first recorded on Dial Recordings, and featured Parker, Gillespie, Monk, and Clarke.

Charlie ("Bird") Parker. *(Schomburg Collection, New York Public Library.)*

One of the most significant series of jazz recordings of this era featured the Charlie Parker Quintet. This group, composed of Parker on alto sax, Miles Davis on trumpet, Duke Jordan on piano, Tommy Potter on Bass, and Max Roach on drums, displayed its distinctive style of unison ensemble in these recordings. The theme is stated over unique rhythmic patterns with individual solos that rival those of the Armstrong Hot Five of an earlier era. "Dewey Square," "The Hymn," "Scrapple from the Apple," and "Bird of Paradise" rank among the most important of these recordings. In the Parker composition "The Hymn," Parker assumes the role of a black preacher with three choruses, which resembles a sermon, followed by a close harmony statement with Parker joining Davis in a melodic theme that resembles a church choir. "Bird of Paradise" displays Parker and Davis performing a variation on the Jerome Kern song, "All the Things You Are," complete with counterpoint technique employed to close the composition.

Many other recordings illustrate Parker's genius and illuminate his contributions to this new style of music, but only two more can be discussed. "Parker's Mood" displays his obsession with the blues and documents his Kansas City background. "Repetition," a composition by Neal Hefti, recorded for Norman Granz in *The Jazz Scene* (Clef Records, MGC-674), in which Parker plays an obbligato solo over the theme completely impromptu, illustrates both his compositional authority and his instrumental technique.

Three pianists played an important role in the compositional development of the bop era: Thelonius Monk, Tad Dameron, and John Lewis. Monk was to the new jazz what "Jelly Roll" Morton had been to early jazz. One of Monk's most important contributions was his harmonic scheme, which became the hallmark of such

Thelonious Monk. *(Burt Goldblatt.)*

Monk compositions as "Criss Cross," "Straight, No Chaser," "Well, You Needn't," "Misterioso," and "'Round Midnight." "Misterioso" features a unique use of the simple blues progression I-IV-V-I. "'Round Midnight," a mood ballad, will probably go down in the annals of jazz as one of the ten greatest jazz compositions.

As Monk's hallmark was harmony, Tad Dameron was a composer deeply concerned with melody. Dameron's melodic themes seem to flow endlessly, like water in a brook. Many of his works were written for trumpeters Freddie Webster, Fats Navarro, Kenny Dorham, and Clifford Brown. His best-known compositions include "Good Bait," "Our Delight," "If You Could See Me Now," "Dial B for Beauty," and "The Scene is Clean."

John Lewis entered the jazz world as the result of his friendship with drummer Kenny Clarke, who introduced him to Dizzy Gillespie. Lewis became the pianist in Gillespie's big band, where he worked with Clarke, bassist Ray Brown, and vibraharpist Milt Jackson. The first recordings made by these four soloists led to the formation of the Modern Jazz Quartet. Lewis also wrote "Toccata for Trumpet" for Gillespie's band, and contributed to several pieces for the Miles Davis Nine.

Dizzy Gillespie paralleled Parker's impact with his musical innovations as both trumpeter and composer. He wrote such classics as "Grooving High," a variation of the theme "Whispering"; "A Night in Tunisia"; and the satirical "Salt Peanuts." Gillespie was also instrumental in introducing the new musical concepts into big bands. Gillespie's first experience was as musical director and trumpeter in a band led by Billie Eckstine, former vocalist for Earl Hines. This band was composed of such stars as baritone-saxophonist Leo Parker, tenor-saxophonists Wardell Gray and Dexter Gordon, trombonists J. J. Johnson and Bennie Green, trumpeters Gillespie, Miles Davis, and Fats Navarro, drummer Art Blakey, bassist Nelson Boyd, and pianist John Malachi. In 1947 Gillespie formed his own band and added a new dimension to the modern jazz concepts developed during the bop era. This dimension involved the integration of Cuban rhythms into those of the Afro-American motif. The Afro-Cuban rhythm brought a dynamic new force to the melodic theme and solos of the big band. Three compositions that illustrate this integration of intercontinental rhythmic variations are Gillespie's "Manteca," George Russell's extended opus "Cubana Be, Cubana Bop," and

Walter Fuller's "Swedish Suite." On the recordings of these three pieces Chano Pozo, the brilliant Cuban bongo and conga drummer, is featured.

During this transitional period in jazz, many brilliant musicians came to the fore. One of the most prominent was pianist Earl "Bud" Powell. Powell's pianistic artistry rivaled that of his predecessor, Art Tatum, and was a manifestation of the influence of Charlie Parker. Bud Powell was called by one critic "the first and foremost of bop pianists." Powell was a composer, too, and his compositions include "Parisienne Thorofare," "Hallucinations," and "The Fruit."

By 1948 the new jazz had grown to maturity, and its innovators then began to experiment with new instrumental voicing ideas. These experiments resulted in a close one-voice ensemble presentation augmented by previously foreign instrumental voices. The leading figure in this movement was Miles Davis, the Charlie Parker protégé. Davis assembled an ensemble composed of alto and baritone sax, trombone, French horn, and tuba, and the rhythm section was the Miles Davis Nine. The recordings made by this group in 1949–50 became known as the "Birth of the Cool." Compositions for this group were written by Canadian-born Gil Evans, Gerry Mulligan, and John Lewis. The Capitol record album (T-1974) entitled *Miles Davis: Birth of the Cool* contains the complete repertoire of this distinguished group. The term *cool*, incidentally, was used to describe the attitude of the performer, not the sound of his music.

Another group that demonstrated the ensemble approach to jazz was composed of the Gillespie big-band alumni John Lewis, Milt Jackson, Kenny Clarke, and Ray Brown's replacement, Percy Heath. This group became one of the first cooperative groups in jazz, there being no single leader. The group adopted the name the Modern Jazz Quartet (MJQ), and presented musical offerings in the ensemble style of New Orleans with a hint of the Basie rhythm concept. Lewis, the group's pianist and its musical director, supplied most of the quartet's repertoire. In existence more than two decades by 1975, the quartet has had only one replacement, Connie Kay for Clarke on drums. Perhaps only Louis Armstrong and Duke Ellington have been more widely known on the international scene than the MJQ. Its compositions "Django," "Bag's Groove," "Bluesology," and "Baden-Baden" are deservedly famous.

John Lewis wrote composition for both the

John ("Dizzy") Gillespie, along with "Bird" Parker, Thelonious Monk, Kenny Clarke, and Charlie Christian, created the new sound called bebop. (U.S. Information Agency, National Archives.)

Quartet and other instrumental ensembles that have been described as jazz in a neoclassical setting. Several of these works have employed the baroque technique of counterpoint in a fugal setting. The best known of these are "Vendôme," "Concord," "Versailles," and "Little David's Fugue."

Up until this time jazz had been played with improvisations on a melodic theme or with the use of the blues. The new approach using extended compositions, and symphony orchestras and string quartets to augment jazz players, added a third element to jazz, and it is called the Third Stream Movement.

The Modern Jazz Quartet was the principal participant in the Third Stream Movement; however, other musical concepts emerged and were developed at the same time. In the two decades after 1950 the black musician became deeply concerned with his heritage. In other words, jazz seemed to be returning to its roots—namely, to the pure expression of the blues and of gospel music motifs. Trumpeter Miles Davis formed a star-studded group in the 1950s composed of alto-saxophonist Julian "Cannonball" Adderley, tenor-saxophonist John Coltrane, and a rhythm section featuring bassist Paul Chambers, pianists Red Garland and Wyton Kelly, and drummers "Philly" Joe Jones and Jimmy Cobb. This ensemble placed emphasis on the blues and reflected much of the purity of the old folk art.

Drummer Art Blakey and pianist Horace Silver formed a cooperative group known as the Jazz Messengers. This group featured many compositions written by Silver, including "The Preacher," "Doodling," and "Creeping In." The Messengers' musical repertoire, its chief architect, Silver, and his replacement, Bobby Timmons (author of "Moanin'") displayed the strong influence of gospel music in modern jazz.

A powerful and dynamic quintet, known as the Max Roach/Clifford Brown Quintet, next gave notice of a return to excitement and gusto in the presentation of their musical repertoire. Clifford Brown, trumpeter and co-leader of the group, was one of the finest trumpeters in jazz history, much in the tradition of Bolden, Armstrong, Eldridge, Gillespie, and Navarro. His ability to play tunes at a fast tempo in a clear staccato style was impeccable. The Max Roach/ Clifford Brown Quintet was known for such compositions as "Parisienne Thorofare," "Theme from Samson and Delilah," Clifford Brown's own composition "Joy Spring," and Duke Jordan's "Jordu." Another piece that illus-

The Modern Jazz Quartet, seen here as they performed with Arthur Fiedler and the Boston Pops Orchestra, included John Lewis on piano, Kenny Clarke on drums, Milt Jackson on vibes, and Ray Brown on bass. (National Educational Television.)

trates the quintet's versatility is the use of waltz tempo in the Sonny Rollins opus "Valse Hot." Unfortunately, Clifford Brown and the group's pianist Richie Powell (Bud's brother) were killed in an automobile accident in June 1956.

Bassist Charles Mingus headed an ensemble that gave a hint of the music that was to come; their repertoire utilized blues, gospel, and the freedom of solo limitations. Examples of the Mingus formula may be heard on *Pithecanthropus erectus* (Atlantic 1237) and on *Mingus Ah Um* (Columbia CL 1370).

Other groups proliferated on the jazz scene. One cooperative group, known as the Jazztet, featured composer and tenor-saxophonist Benny Golson and trumpeter Art Farmer, and it followed in the tradition of the Jazz Messengers and the Roach/Brown Quintet. Another quintet, under the leadership of the Adderley brothers, Julian and Nat (trumpeter), was formed in the 1960s, and it followed in the tradition of perpetuating the roots of black esthetics in its reliance on the blues and on the gospel format.

The deep concern for black awareness, both spiritual and physical, that charaterized the 1960s and 1970s found musical expression in the movement that was labeled "Avant-Garde." Some critics have called the new music "black militant" and "black nationalist" music, but in reality this music is a reflection of the creative artist's awareness of his heritage. This movement began with the blossoming of tenor-saxophonist John Coltrane, who assembled a quartet to play the new music, which featured extended solos (lasting, in some instances, for the duration

609

of one side of an LP recording). Although Coltrane's music is complex, as David N. Baker, Jr., the director of jazz studies at Indiana University (Bloomington, Ind.) has pointed out, it is a combination of melody and scale patterns, and Coltrane offers to jazz the most outstanding solo approach since Parker's. Examples of Coltrane's artistry may be heard in such tunes as "Giant Steps" and "My Favorite Things" and in his extended pieces "A Love Supreme" and "Ascension."

Many contemporary jazzmen are in the vanguard of today's musical movements. They include alto-saxophonists Ornette Coleman and Eric Dolphy; tenor-saxophonists Archie Shepp, Pharoah Sanders, John Handy, Wayne Shorter, and Brooker Ervin; trumpeters Albert Ayler, Don Cherry, and Freddie Hubbard; pianists Cecil Taylor and Herbie Hancock; drummers Tony Williams and Elvin Jones; and bassists Ron Carter and Richard Davis. They form, however, part of a long tradition. They have taken the essence of jazz, the innovations of bop that extend backward to the purity of the blues, the spirituals, the cries, the hollers, and the moans of an oppressed people, and they have fused them into a living musical expression of great artistry, an expression that eloquently voices the very essence of jazz and much of Afro-American music—the belief that man must be free. Jazz, seen in this context, becomes one and the same in theme and beauty with Afro-American history. Its universality is everywhere acknowledged, and its creativity as displayed in its magnificent varieties, splendors, dimensions, and ever-changing improvisations and versatility is a lasting tribute to the genius of its makers—Afro-Americans.

REFERENCES: Although many books and articles have been written on jazz, there is no adequate, comprehensive, and definitive written account of jazz and its history. Perhaps, the best manner in which to read about jazz is to begin with the references under MUSIC: HISTORY AND DEVELOPMENT. Then consult several bibliographies on the subject and therein select those titles of books and articles that most nearly seem to reflect individual interest and needs. The best bibliographies to consult are the following: Choice, November 1969; Gillis, Frank and Alan F. Merriam (comps.), Ethnomusicology and Folk Music: An International Bibliography of Dissertations and Theses, 1966; Merriam, Alan F., A Bibliography of Jazz, 1954; Miller, Elizabeth, The Negro in America: A Bibliography, pp. 92–96, 1970; and Porter, Dorothy B., The Negro in the United States: A Selected Bibliography, pp. 206–12, 1970. Several referral centers and agencies specialize in the history of jazz and of folk music. These include the Institute of Jazz Studies (New York, N.Y.); North Texas State University (Denton, Tex.), which has files on Duke Ellington; and the music division of the Library of Congress (Washington, D.C.). There are also several good encyclopedias on the subject: Rose, Al and Edmond Sanchon, New Orleans Jazz: A Family Album (1967), Leonard Feather, An Encyclopedia of Jazz (1960), and Robert S. Gold, A Jazz Lexicon (1964).

MUSLIMS Commonly referred to as Black Muslims, the Muslims are a small religious group that has gained publicity and membership through (1) their official organ, *Muhammed Speaks,* which has the largest circulation of any Afro-American newspaper; (2) publicity in the national media; (3) the leadership and organization of such outstanding personalities as Noble Drew Ali, M. Fard Muhammed, Elijah Muhammad, and Malcolm X; and (4) their economic enterprises. The origins of the Black Muslims go back to the 1930s or earlier. They believe in Allah and sanction the Koran; they further believe in the separation of "so-called Negroes and the so-called white Americans." Well-disciplined, they advocate economic self-sufficiency, and to this end have established business enterprises in several locations, including Chicago, Ill., Detroit, Mich., and New York, N.Y. Estimates of membership vary, though an often quoted number is 100,000. See also BIBLIOGRAPHIES/BIOGRAPHIES/GUIDES; ALI, NOBLE DREW; CHURCHES; MALCOLM X; MUHAMMAD, ELIJAH; NATIONALISM.

REFERENCES: For a standard reference, see Lincoln, C. Eric, The Black Muslims in America, Beacon Press, Boston, 1961. For additional references, see Williams, Ethel L., and Clifton F. Brown, Afro-American Religious Studies, Scarecrow Press, Metuchen, 1972, pp. 201–205, and Williams, Daniel T., "The Black Muslims in the United States: A Selected Bibliography," in Eight Negro Bibliographies, 1970.

MYERS, ISAAC *See* BUSINESS; LABOR UNIONS.

MYERS, SAMUEL LLOYD (1919–), educator, government official; born in Baltimore, Md. Myers received his B.A. degree from Morgan State University (Baltimore, Md.) in 1940, a M.A. degree from Boston University in 1942, and a M.A. degree (1948) and his Ph.D. degree in economics (1949) from Harvard University. He was affiliated with Harvard (1948–49), then became an economist with the Bureau of Labor Statistics (1950) before returning to teach at Morgan State University (1950–63). Myers served with the Bureau of Inter-American Affairs, U.S. Department of State (1963–67), returning to the academic world to become president of Bowie State College (Bowie, Md.) in 1967.

NAACP LEGAL DEFENSE AND EDUCATIONAL FUND, INC. (LDF) A New York City-based organization founded in 1939, LDF is separate from and independent of the National Association for the Advancement of Colored People (NAACP). It represents such civil rights groups as the Congress of Racial Equality (CORE), the Southern Christian Leadership Conference (SCLC), the Student Nonviolent Coordinating Committee (SNCC), and the NAACP, and private citizens as well. Funds are contributed to provide counsel and to train attorneys. Its Herbert Lehman Education Fund and its Earl Warren Training Program both supply scholarships to black students. Community assistance is provided through the Division of Legal Information and Community Services. The Committee of 100, a volunteer group, sponsors the appeal for funds. The LDF supports several publications, and it releases legal materials and press and other reports. Jack Greenberg was its long-time director-counsel. The LDF aided in hundreds of court cases, a list of which embraces the major civil rights cases since 1940. *See also* CIVIL RIGHTS: CIVIL RIGHTS CASES, 1865–1975.

NABRIT, JAMES MADISON, JR. (1910–   ), lawyer, educator, civil rights advocate; born in Atlanta, Ga. Nabrit graduated from Morehouse College (Atlanta, Ga.) in 1923, and received his J.D. degree from Northwestern University (Evanston, Ill.) in 1927. Nabrit later received several honorary degrees. He taught at Leland Col-

lege in Louisiana and served as dean of the Agricultural, Mechanical, and Normal (A M & N) College in Pine Bluff, Ark. (now University of Arkansas at Pine Bluff), before taking up the practice of law in Houston, Tex., for six years. In 1936 Nabrit joined the teaching staff of Howard University Law School (Washington, D.C.). While continuing to teach, he held many other posts in the university, and finally in 1960 became president. He was legal adviser to the governor of the Virgin Islands, and adviser to the U.S. delegation to the ILO Conference in Geneva, Switzerland, in 1959. In 1966 Nabrit was appointed U.S. deputy representative to the UN and the Security Council. He returned to Howard University after a year and a half, and retired from the presidency in 1969. Through the years Nabrit was involved in many civic and civil rights causes as a member of the legal staff of the National Association for the Advancement of Colored People (NAACP). *See also* CIVIL RIGHTS: CIVIL RIGHTS CASES, 1865–1975; HOWARD UNIVERSITY; NABRIT, SAMUEL MILTON.

NABRIT, SAMUEL MILTON (1905–   ), educator; born in Macon, Ga. Nabrit received a B.S. degree from Morehouse College (Atlanta, Ga.) in 1925, and a M.S. degree (1928) and his Ph.D. degree (1932) from Brown University (Providence, R.I.). He taught at Morehouse College and Atlanta University, and became president of Texas Southern University in 1955. During the period he was president of Texas Southern, his brother, James Nabrit, was president of Howard University (Washington, D.C.). Thus, the two brothers simultaneously held the office of president at two of the largest Afro-American colleges in the nation. *See also* NABRIT, JAMES MADISON, JR.

NAMES *See* ONOMATOLOGY.

NANCE, M. MACEO, JR. (1925–   ), educator; born in Columbia, S.C. Nance received a B.A. degree from South Carolina State College in 1949, his M.S. degree from New York University in 1953, and an honorary LL.D. degree from Morris Brown College (Atlanta, Ga.) in 1968. He held many positions at South Carolina State College beginning in 1949, eventually becoming president of the institution in 1968.

NASH, GWENDOLYN V. BROWNLEE (1929–1970), physician; born in Camden, S.C. Nash graduated from North Carolina College at Durham (now North Carolina Central State University) and received her M.S. and M.D. degrees from Howard University (Washington, D.C.). She interned at Freedmen's Hospital, Washington, D.C., and was resident at Provident Hospital, Baltimore, Md. Nash served as assistant professor of physiology and associate professor of cardiorenal research at Howard University Medical College from 1958 to 1965, and she continued there as a fellow in cardiovascular research until 1967.

NATCHEZ JUNIOR COLLEGE   Natchez Junior College, at Natchez, Miss., was founded in 1885 by Baptists. The church-related and coeducational school offers a two-year program, usually credited toward the bachelor's degree. Its 1975 enrollment was 121.

NATCHEZ SEMINARY   *See* JACKSON STATE COLLEGE.

NATIONAL AFRO-AMERICAN LABOR COUNCIL (NALC)   Founded in 1960, NALC was a national association of black trade-union members. It proposed to eliminate discrimination in employment by exposing it, by working to secure union membership for black workers and to establish job training programs, and by confronting and negotiating with unions on discrimination issues. In 1970 the NALC had 20 chapters. One of its leaders was Troy Brailey, long affiliated with the Brotherhood of Sleeping Car Porters (BSCP).

NATIONAL ASSOCIATION FOR THE ADVANCEMENT OF COLORED PEOPLE

The National Association for the Advancement of Colored People (NAACP), more than any other single organization or group, reflects the history and aspirations of Afro-Americans in twentieth-century American society. Politically oriented and national in scope, the NAACP has cut across religious, political, social, and class lines in achieving a high degree of unity among Afro-Americans in its continuous fight against racial discrimination and segregation. Its aims have been to help create a truly democratic society in the United States by integrating Afro-Americans into the mainstream, by eliminating racial injustice and intolerance, and by making equality of opportunity for black people a living reality. In a peaceful way, it has relied upon methods provided by society itself: the press, the petition, the ballot, and the courts. It has persisted in the use of legal and moral suasion even in the face of overt and violent racial hostility.

Founding   The NAACP, a biracial organization, was founded in 1909. In response to the apparent declining status of Afro-Americans in the United States, and in particular as the result of a race riot in August 1908 in Springfield, Ill., William English Walling wrote an article in a Springfield periodical, *The Independent*, asking for citizens to rally to the support of Afro-Americans. Mary White Ovington, the first professional social worker to live and work in New York City's black ghetto, reacted to the article by calling together a small biracial group that began meeting early in 1909.

Charles Edward Russell, a free-lance writer, and Dr. Henry Moskowitz, a social worker, were immediately interested. From the black community, Ovington recruited Bishop Alexander Walters of the African Methodist Episcopal Zion (AMEZ) Church and Rev. William Henry Brooks, pastor of St. Mark's Methodist Episcopal (ME) Church of New York City. Social workers Florence Kelley and Lillian Wald also joined; and Oswald Garrison Villard, influential publisher of the New York *Evening Post* and grandson of the abolitionist William Lloyd Garrison, took an active part from the beginning.

To secure support for a renewal of the old abolitionist struggle for complete emancipation and full citizenship of Afro-Americans a call for a conference, drafted by Villard and signed by 60 prominent blacks and whites, was issued on Abraham Lincoln's birthday in 1909. Meeting at the end of May of that year in New York City as the National Negro Conference, renowned scientists, economists, and educators refuted the popular arguments that Afro-Americans were physically and mentally inferior to whites and therefore incapable of becoming first-class citizens or social equals. The Afro-American problem was also discussed in relation to labor and women's rights. W. E. B. Du Bois, a professor at Atlanta University, presented the political as well as the economic implications of the problem. He believed that there could be no solution to the overall difficulties until the franchise was restored to Afro-Americans.

A national Committee for the Advancement of the Negro Race and a select Committee of Forty on Permanent Organization emerged from the conference of 1909. Villard, a dynamic man of great executive ability, secured funds, formed an effective subcommittee on permanent organization, and engaged (in February 1910) Frances Blascoer, a social worker, as a salaried office worker. Upon her resignation in March 1911, Mary Ovington took charge of the office as a volunteer worker.

The next annual conferences, held in 1910 and 1911, gave attention to problems of internal organization and to themes relating to the disfranchisement of blacks. With incorporation in June 1911, Villard became chairman of the newly created board of directors. He served in this capacity until he withdrew from active participation in 1914 following a series of clashes with Du Bois. Moorfield Storey, a nationally known lawyer, was elected president; John E. Milholland and Bishop Walters, vice-presidents; Mary

Ovington, secretary; and Walter Sachs, treasurer. Du Bois remained in his salaried post as director of publicity and research, giving significant attention to the earliest issues of *The Crisis*, the official organ of the association. Significant also during the early years was the appointment to the board of directors of Joel E. Spingarn, chair-

Cover of the first issue of *The Crisis*, which appeared one year after the founding of the NAACP. *(Library of Congress)*

man of the department of comparative literature at Columbia University.

The earliest conferences worked to end disfranchisement based upon race and sex. Disfranchisement based upon color, for example, was the theme of the second annual conference in 1910. The early boards of directors held that before any real reform could be accomplished, women and blacks would have to become voters. Villard, Milholland, Spingarn, and Du Bois were particularly active in advocating women's rights. A more tangible example of the association's stand for voting rights came in 1915 in the celebrated case of *Guinn v. United States*. In this case, one of the first in which the NAACP participated, the U.S. Supreme Court held that the "grandfather clause," an old Reconstruction device for disfranchising blacks, was unconstitutional. The NAACP's brief was filed with the court, amicus curiae, and joined by Moorfield Storey. From the victory in *Guinn* until the passage of the Voting Rights Act of 1965, the courts were the principal arena of the NAACP in the field of disfranchisement. The issues were defined with each case or set of cases that arose: exclusion of Afro-Americans from primary elections of political parties, or disfranchisement because of literacy tests or poll taxes. Sponsored or aided by the NAACP, many cases were brought before the courts in a slow process that eventually proved essential in establishing the vote for Afro-Americans.

Rift with Booker T. Washington Du Bois brought to the NAACP the remnants of the Niagara Movement, which he and William Monroe Trotter had founded in 1905 to protest Booker T. Washington's dominance of Afro-American affairs and to agitate for full political and civil rights. By 1909 the Niagara Movement had disintegrated, and Du Bois was ready to join with the founders of the new movement. Reasons for the failure of the Niagara Movement included its inability to seek and secure a wide-based support from the black community and white liberals, the continued opposition of Washington, internal disorganization, financial difficulties, and the loss of the Boston *Guardian* as a medium of publicity when Trotter, the editor, broke with Du Bois in 1907.

Washington was greatly disturbed when Du Bois, his chief antagonist, became a salaried official of the new "advancement" association, founded and sponsored by prominent and wealthy white liberals and backed by the New York *Evening Post*. Du Bois seemed to be in a position to menace Washington's immense prestige and leadership. Washington's hostility took the form of skillful undercover maneuvers to counter Du Bois and the influence of the NAACP. Through his influence with the Afro-American press and with his own secretly owned newspaper, the New York *Age*, Washington sought to discredit the NAACP and those blacks who joined the new movement. Until his death in 1915, he and his supporters were in open conflict with the NAACP.

After Washington's death in 1915, Du Bois proposed a conference of black leaders to reconcile the differences and to form a united front. In August 1916 about 50 men and women met at Joel E. Spingarn's estate in Amenia, N.Y. The conferees were equally divided between the followers of Washington and of Du Bois. They adopted resolutions calling for an end to the old suspicions, controversies, and factional alignments. They emphasized the need for a practical working agreement among leaders to secure all types of education and complete political freedom for Afro-Americans. An important by-product of the Amenia Conference was the appointment in November 1916 of James Weldon Johnson, a former protégé of Washington, as national organizer of the NAACP with the title of field secretary.

Publicity and Research In his role as director of publicity and research, Du Bois, in November 1910, published the first issue of *The Crisis* magazine, the official organ of the NAACP. Its success was phenomenal. In six months its circulation reached 10,000; at the end of two years, 24,000; in 1916, 37,000; and by June 1919, 104,000. This surge in circulation was due to the restlessness, tension, and violence of the postwar period, which came to a bloody climax in a score of race riots during the "Red Summer" of 1919. Afterward, *The Crisis* declined both in circulation and influence as it met increasing competition from an emerging Afro-American press.

For the first few years, newspaper publicity for the NAACP was handled by volunteer workers. Among them were professional writers and newsmen: Villard; Paul Kennaday; Mary Dunlop Maclean; James F. Morton, Jr.; and Charles Edward Russell.

With the rapid growth of the association and its broadening range of activities, May (Mary) Childs Nerney, who succeeded Mary Ovington in the national office in 1912, took over the preparation and distribution of news articles. When John R. Shillady succeeded Royal Freeman Nash as secretary in 1918, press coverage was placed on a professional basis with Herbert Seligmann of the *Evening Post* as full-time director of publicity.

Before the advent of radio and television, mass meetings and the lecture platform were the most effective means of reaching the public. To link the new abolition movement with the old, the NAACP celebrated with mass meetings such important anniversaries as the signing of the Emancipation Proclamation and the birthdays of Abraham Lincoln and of such noted abolitionists as William Lloyd Garrison, Charles Sumner, and Wendell Phillips.

Du Bois research activity was another method of bringing the work of the NAACP to the attention of the public. Like other reformers of the progressive era, Du Bois and his colleagues in the NAACP firmly believed that once evils were exposed and understood, reform would follow. Therefore, his research and publications were important not only in bringing the NAACP to public attention but also in combating racism in America.

To foster pride in Afro-American accomplishments and to publicize them in the white world, Joel E. Spingarn endowed a gold medal to be awarded annually by the NAACP for "the highest and noblest achievement of an American Negro." The first Spingarn Medal was presented in 1915 to Ernest Everett Just of Howard University for his research in biology.

Moreover, the NAACP sought to counter untrue and derogatory publicity. Its chief battle in its early years was waged with varying success in seeking to suppress the motion picture, *The Birth of A Nation*, released in 1915, which portrayed the Afro-American in a vicious light and Reconstruction as a failure. The film inflamed public opinion in the North and contributed to mob violence against blacks who were migrating to the North in large numbers.

NAACP Branches From the beginning the NAACP was highly centralized, and the national body maintained strict control over branches and membership. As the association grew, however, fundamental policy stipulated that each branch be biracial; that branches and officers could not engage in partisan politics; and that the NAACP should never use or advocate force or violence, but only peaceful and constitutional means to gain its ends.

Board members as well as staff traveled extensively seeking to enlarge the association from its first branches on the Atlantic Seaboard. In 1914 and 1915, for example, Board Chairman Joel E. Spingarn (at his own expense) made two organizational trips throughout the Midwest, starting branches in St. Louis, Mo.; Columbus, Ohio; Detroit, Mich.; Indianapolis, Ind.; and in other major cities. From 1912 until the arrival of James Weldon Johnson in 1916, the NAACP was forced to depend on part-time promotional agents to supplement the volunteer work of its board members.

To facilitate communication between local branches and the national office, large regions were organized into district conferences, the first in 1916 known as the Great Lakes District Conference. The Dixie District and the Pacific District were added in 1917, and by the end of 1919 eight district conferences—each with its own secretary and annual meeting—had been established. In 1918, in honor of Moorfield Storey's 70th birthday, and in recognition of his great legal and financial contributions to the NAACP, Shillady instituted the Moorfield Storey Drive. Membership rolls jumped in eight months from 9,869 to 43,994, with branches having been established in all Southern states.

The annual conference at Cleveland, Ohio, in the fall of 1919 marked the end of white leadership in conference affairs. The NAACP, founded by white liberals ten years earlier, was now being expanded and controlled by Afro-Americans. In 1920 James Weldon Johnson became the first black secretary; his assistant, Walter White, and most members of the executive committee were Afro-Americans. With a few exceptions, the branches and their boards were controlled by Afro-Americans. Only on the national board did white membership predominate, but its influence waned as more of the actual direction of NAACP affairs passed into the hands of the secretary and the executive committee.

At the end of its first decade, the NAACP had 91,203 members. In response to the geographical shift in balance, with southern membership for the first time exceeding that in the North, the annual conference of 1920 was held in the South—in Atlanta, Ga.

The NAACP, Wilson, and World War I To the leaders of the NAACP and those Afro-Americans disillusioned with the Republican Party, the administrations of President Woodrow Wilson were also disappointing. Wilson had raised hopes when he had assured Bishop Alexander Walters that he would treat Afro-Americans with "absolute fairness" and would not exclude them from governmental office. He later repudiated this statement in both word and deed.

Villard, at first convinced that Wilson was truly liberal, gave him the support of the New York *Evening Post* in his campaign for the governorship of New Jersey and later in his campaign for the presidency. But Villard's NAACP-sponsored plan for a National Race Commission was met with evasion and procrastination and was finally rejected by President Wilson. The commission was to have been a biracial, privately supported body organized to study the economic, health, and educational status of Afro-Americans.

During the Wilson administrations, the NAACP fought against the introduction of segregation into government bureaus in Washington, D.C., which Wilson approved, justifying a segregated policy on the grounds that it would give black officeholders security in their jobs. Instead, the increase of southern influence in Washington, D.C., during Wilson's presidency led to the dismissal of a large number of blacks from the federal service. In addition, segregation spread from government bureaus to the lunchrooms of the District of Columbia Court Building, the Library of Congress, the Senate dining room in the U.S. Capitol, and the galleries of the Senate.

The combined efforts of the Washington, D.C., NAACP branch and the national office brought defeat to hostile legislation that was introduced in the U.S. Congress during 1915 and 1916. Rev. Archibald Grimké, a Harvard Law School graduate, led the lobbying against Jim Crow streetcar bills and anti-intermarriage bills for the District of Columbia. Other proposals that were defeated during these years called for the exclusion of black aliens from the United States and the prevention of Afro-Americans from becoming commissioned or noncommissioned officers in the U.S. Armed Forces, even preventing their enlistment in certain branches of the service. A proposal to disfranchise Puerto Ricans and a request for a U.S. Supreme Court ruling on the validity of the Fourteenth and Fifteenth amendments were also opposed by the association at this time. This treatment of Afro-Americans as second-class citizens by the federal government set a precedent that the nation was quick to follow.

While the National Defense Act of 1916 was pending before the U.S. Congress, the NAACP urged the House and Senate committees on military affairs to allow Afro-Americans to enlist in the new artillery and infantry regiments being created by Congress. Since 1870 opportunities for Afro-Americans to serve in the U.S. Armed Forces had been limite ! primarily in the Navy to mess corpsmen and in the Army to two cavalry and two infantry regiments.

World War I split the NAACP board into a strongly pacifist group—Mary Ovington, John Haynes Holmes, Oswald Garrison Villard, Lillian Wald, and Jane Addams—and a group consisting of Joel and Arthur Spingarn and the secretary, Roy Nash, all of whom quickly volunteered and secured commissions in the U.S. Army. The active opposition to the war effort by most of the pacifists caused the government to look upon the NAACP with suspicion and alarm.

In May 1917 the NAACP called a general Afro-American conference in Washington, D.C., to consider questions of particular importance to blacks growing out of the wartime emergency. This conference, attended by 700 persons, urged Afro-Americans to enlist and to support the war effort. It demanded training for black officers to serve on the field of battle and to lead Afro-American troops in combat.

The independent efforts of Joel E. Spingarn led to the establishment of a separate camp for training black officers at Des Moines, Iowa. This move set off a heated debate in the Afro-American press. The NAACP's position was that since blacks were going to be conscripted anyway, and since admission to white officer training camps was closed, the stigma of being placed in a separate camp could not equal the harm that would ensue if Afro-Americans were denied admission to officer rank. Leadership positions would be denied because of lack of training facilities, separate or integrated.

The NAACP secured the temporary reinstatement to active duty of Col. Charles Young, a West Point graduate and the highest ranking Afro-American officer in the U.S. Army. He had been retired on grounds of physical disability, but investigation revealed that the Army was reluctant to promote a black man to the rank of general.

The NAACP vigorously fought discrimination and the ill treatment of Afro-American soldiers, both on the home front and overseas. Du Bois' reports of conditions in France were publicized in *The Crisis*. Du Bois, Villard, and Storey protested the degrading conditions in camps and on railroads to Emmett J. Scott, black assistant to the secretary of war, and to other high government officials.

Black labor batallion at Brest, France, during World War I. The NAACP fought discrimination against black soldiers during the war, contending that black soldiers were used excessively as labor units. *(U.S. Signal Corps, National Archives.)*

But there was much hostility in the government toward NAACP proposals. Surgeon-General William C. Gorgas, for example, prevented black nurses, physicians, and dentists from serving with nonblack units. In addition to refusing to assign Afro-American professional men and skilled workers to duties for which they were trained, the Army segregated all black officers and troops traveling on the railroads. A disproportionate number were assigned to service and stevedore batallions. After the armistice, the NAACP fought in vain against an order requiring black units to be demobilized at their point of origin—an order that forced many veterans to return to the South against their will.

A riot that took place in Houston, Tex., on August 23, 1917, involving a battalion of the black 24th Infantry was investigated by a representative of the NAACP. The reporter indicated that the soldiers had been provoked into violence by rabid race prejudice. Before order had been restored, 17 whites and 2 blacks had been killed. The NAACP fought the verdict of the court martial that condemned 20 to death (4 were summarily executed without right of appeal), 41 to life imprisonment, and 4 to long prison terms. Through four presidential administrations, the NAACP worked ceaselessly for the reduction of the sentences and the release of the prisoners. Ten lives were eventually saved, and the last prisoner was released in 1938.

To secure black cooperation with the war effort, the U.S. War Department called a conference of Afro-American editors in July 1918. Du Bois represented *The Crisis* and took the lead in drafting a statement of grievances that included lynching, mob violence, the cashiering of Col. Charles Young, the refusal to employ black nurses, and the failure to assign Afro-Americans as war correspondents. Despite the discontent revealed by these demands, the conference united the Afro-American press behind the war effort. Du Bois, whose harsh criticism of the federal government had caused *The Crisis* to come under the scrutiny of the U.S. Department of Justice, now urged blacks to forget their special grievances and to "close ranks" with white Americans in support of the war.

At the close of the war, the NAACP sent Du Bois to Paris, France on a three-pronged mission: to report the Paris Peace Conference for *The Crisis*, to collect material for a history of the Afro-American in World War I, and to call a NAACP–sponsored-and-financed Pan-African Congress. In January 1919, a month prior to the opening of the Pan-African Congress in Paris, the NAACP alerted America to the fate of the African people by holding a mass meeting on "Africa in the World Democracy." The meeting emphasized the theme of the congress: that the League of Nations should have as one of its chief duties the care and protection of the peoples of Middle Africa so that black people could develop unhampered by other races.

The NAACP was well represented at the congress. In addition to Du Bois, NAACP board members Joel E. Spingarn, William English Walling, and Charles Edward Russell were present and addressed the meeting. According to Du Bois, the idea for a Mandates Commission of the League of Nations grew out of the demand of the Pan-African Congress for international supervision of the former German colonies.

NAACP and Haiti   Four years before the Pan-African Congress, the NAACP had shown its concern for black folk outside America by supporting moves for Haitian independence. Villard, on behalf of the NAACP, urged Joseph P. Tumulty, Wilson's secretary, and Robert Lansing, secretary of state, to appoint a commission to make a social and economic survey of the Republic of Haiti as a preliminary step to the withdrawal of United States forces, who had taken control of the country. The proposal, however, was brushed aside.

In spite of rigorous American censorship, news of the brutal treatment and suppression of Haitian liberties continued to reach the outside world. In February 1920 the NAACP sent James Weldon Johnson to Haiti to make an investigation. He toured the island and conferred with former Haitian authorities. At Johnson's suggestion, they established the Union Patriotique, an organization modeled on the NAACP, to advance the cause of Haitian independence. When Union Patriotique officials visited the United States to lobby for the freedom of their country, they used the NAACP offices in New York City as their headquarters.

Upon his return, Johnson wrote four articles for *The Nation,* exposing, among other evils of the U.S. military occupation, the liquidation of 3,000 Haitians as "bandits." He persuaded Warren G. Harding to make Haiti a campaign issue. This move led the Wilson administration to institute an investigation of the Navy, which exonerated the Marines, but which nevertheless brought about a number of reforms.

Continued pressure by the NAACP during

President Harding's administration brought an inquiry by a Senate investigating committee. Although the report also was a "whitewash" of the occupation, it did recommend a change from military to civilian administration. The NAACP continued to agitate the Haitian question with assistance from Ernest Gruening in the editorial pages of *The Nation*. When Walter White became secretary of the NAACP in 1931, he visited Haiti; and the NAACP's persistence was influential in bringing an end to American occupation of Haiti in August 1934.

Lynching, Mob Violence, and Repression The NAACP came into being in response to an act of lynching and mob violence, and for many years considered the suppression of this evil to be its primary task. *The Crisis* annually published the lynching toll. Eight hundred and forty persons were lynched during the 1910s, and 304 between 1920 and 1927.

The NAACP showered protests, memorials, and demands for remedial legislation upon the president of the United States, the vice-president, the speaker of the House of Representatives, and the chairmen of the judiciary committees of both houses of Congress. They put pressure upon state officials, and gave wide publicity to the responses. Southern liberals were also urged to speak out and to organize a movement against lynching within the South.

In 1911 at Coatesville, Pa., a seriously wounded Afro-American, charged with killing a policeman, was taken from the hospital and burned alive. Like the 1908 Springfield, Ill., race riot, this outbreak profoundly disturbed members of the NAACP as it indicated that lynching was

spreading to the North. They immediately entered upon a prolonged and costly investigation that made use of private detectives. However, a conspiracy of silence protected the leaders of the mob from conviction.

May of 1916 brought the "Waco Horror," the burning alive of a mentally retarded teenager convicted of murdering a white woman. He was seized in the courtroom, taken by the mob to the public square, and there tortured and burned before a crowd of 15,000 persons.

This atrocity was followed in August 1916 by a mass lynching at Gainsville, Fla., of five blacks (two of them women) who had become involved in a quarrel with a white man over a pig. In November a wealthy Afro-American was lynched in South Carolina as the result of an altercation with a white man who had attempted to defraud him.

These and many other lynchings in the South, together with abuse and degradation imposed upon blacks by Southern white racists, were among the factors that produced a mass migration of Afro-Americans to northern cities. This flow of thousands of Afro-Americans to the industrial centers of the North and the subsequent competition for housing and jobs aroused animosity among white workers. As a result, race riots, formerly limited to the South, broke out in a number of cities in the North.

Encouraged by philanthropist Philip G. Peabody's offer of $10,000 to the NAACP if it could create an effective program to end lynching, an Antilynching Committee was formed. It proposed a three-fold program: the compilation of data, the investigation of specific cases, and the organization of southern business and political leaders in opposition to lynching. Not impressed, Peabody maintained that $10,000 was too small a sum to make this program effective. He proposed instead to give $1,000 with the promise that if the NAACP raised $9,000 he would give an additional $1,000. The efforts to raise the $9,000 stimulated public interest in the crimes of lynching across the country.

The NAACP also raised funds to provide defense for those indicted for participation in the riots that took place in East St. Louis, Ill., in 1917 and for those who were left homeless and destitute. A "Silent Protest Parade" was held on New York City's Fifth Avenue in July 1917, a protest that drew more prominent Afro-Americans into the NAACP. Increased pressure to act was brought upon state officials and law officers,

The NAACP's Silent Protest Parade on Fifth Avenue in New York City, July 28, 1917. Most of the women in the parade wore white; the men wore dark suits. *(Library of Congress.)*

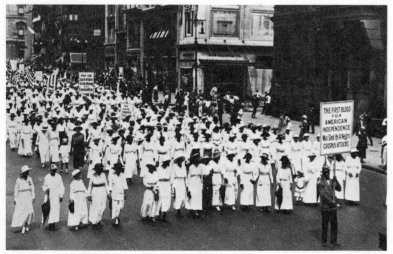

and President Wilson, after repeated urging, finally made a public statement asking all citizens to cooperate in bringing an end to lynching.

Nevertheless, by 1919, lynchings had grown more fierce and more sadistic. Martha Gruening and Helen Boardman undertook an investigation of crimes of violence against Afro-Americans, and the NAACP published their findings as "Thirty Years of Lynching in the United States, 1889–1918." Under the leadership of Mary Talbert, a NAACP board member, black women were aroused in protest, and raised nearly $50,-000 for the NAACP antilynching program.

In May 1919 the NAACP held a national Antilynching Conference in New York City. Its sponsors included such notables as Charles Evans Hughes, Attorney General A. Mitchell Palmer, Elihu Root, William Howard Taft, and Anna Howard Shaw of the woman's suffrage movement.

Despite the organization of such a conference, the summer of 1919 was so filled with tension, violence, lynchings, and riots that it became known as the "Red Summer." A score of serious racial clashes flared up in various parts of the country. John Shillady, NAACP secretary, was beaten unconscious in daylight on the streets of Austin, Tex., by a group of whites, including a county judge and an officer of the law. The governor of Texas later expressed satisfaction with the conduct of the citizens of his state.

The climax of this violent summer came in Phillips County, Ark., when armed whites sought to prevent blacks from organizing against economic exploitation and peonage. It is estimated that more than 200 persons, mostly Afro-Americans, lost their lives during the disturbance. Seventy-nine Afro-Americans were indicted and brought to trial on charges of murder and insurrection. Six were convicted of murder, and the rest were sentenced to long prison terms. The case was handled for the NAACP on the state level by a black attorney, Scipio Africanus Jones, the first Afro-American lawyer to be placed in charge of an important NAACP case in the South. Previously, in deference to local feeling and due to the lack of sufficient black legal talent at that time, Afro-American attorneys had only assisted local white lawyers who had prestige in the community.

Moorfield Storey argued the case *Moore v Dempsey* (1923) before the U.S. Supreme Court. The decision, reversing the conviction, was a triumph for the NAACP in declaring that a trial dominated by a mob constituted a failure to provide for due process of law. In the case of *Moore v. Dempsey,* the court reversed the stand it had taken in *Frank v. Mangum* (1914), which had held that the court could not interfere so long as the form of a trial had been complied with. The new decision guaranteed legal protection to all Americans who might be tried and convicted in courts influenced by mobs.

Throughout the 1920s and 1930s, the major thrust of the NAACP's program was directed toward securing a federal antilynching law. In April 1921, through Representative L. C. Dyer of Missouri, the association introduced a bill into Congress that had Moorfield Storey's approval. Dyer had previously sponsored antilynching legislation in 1918, but Storey, ruling it to be unconstitutional, had not given it NAACP support. The Dyer bill passed in the House, but it lost in the Senate because of the Republican Party's indifference in the face of a southern filibuster.

However, the antilynching fight did not stop. In 1931 Walter White, who succeeded Johnson as secretary of the NAACP, enlisted the sponsorship of Representative Edward Costigan of Colorado and Senator Robert Wagner of New York in behalf of a new antilynching measure. The Costigan-Wagner bill passed the House, but Senator Wagner and Senator Van Nuys (the latter became co-sponsor when Costigan left the Senate) twice failed to break a southern filibuster. In February 1938 the bill was abandoned. The NAACP persisted in agitating for a federal antilynching law. In 1940 a new measure, the Wagner-Gavagan bill, passed the House but was again blocked in the Senate. Although the NAACP failed to persuade Congress to legislate against lynching, the debate and publicity attending the legislation efforts brought a decrease in lynching and a lessening of mob violence. The campaign also stimulated the growth and activity of NAACP branches and increased the financial support of the national office. In addition, the NAACP was unanimously recognized as the leader and spokesman for the Afro-American in the field of civil rights.

The NAACP's attack upon discrimination in the war effort and upon lynching produced a counterattempt to silence *The Crisis.* In 1918, for example, the U.S. Department of Justice had warned the NAACP concerning the radical tone of the magazine. Moreover, Representative James F. Byrnes of South Carolina, holding the

Afro-American press responsible for the race riots of the "Red Summer" of 1919, called upon the Department of Justice to determine if *The Crisis* had violated the Espionage Act and had incited to riot and mob violence. Efforts were made to link black unrest to Russian propaganda and to the radical labor movement, especially to the Industrial Workers of the World (IWW). Attorney General A. Mitchell Palmer, in his report on radical propaganda of November 1919, asserted that such black intellectual leaders as Du Bois and his assistant on the staff of *The Crisis*, Augustus G. Dill, were a source of radical opposition to the government and to law and order. State governments also caught up in the "Red Scare" (such as the Lusk Committee of the New York state legislature) expressed fear of a black revolution and listed some editorials of *The Crisis* as dangerous confirmation.

Though under attack, *The Crisis* survived. Indeed, attempts to silence or to intimidate the magazine greatly increased its circulation and enhanced the prestige of the NAACP among Afro-Americans. Moreover, *The Crisis* enhanced the cultural awakening, known as the Harlem Renaissance, of the black America of the 1920s and 1930s. In the pages of *The Crisis*, Du Bois sought out and encouraged young black poets, writers, and playwrights by evaluating and publishing their work. Among these young race-conscious artists who took their themes from Afro-American life, folklore, and history were Countee Cullen, Georgia Douglass Johnson, Anita Scott Coleman, and Langston Hughes. (Du Bois was also instrumental in founding Krigwa, a black theater with black actors, black writers, and predominantly black audiences.) Joel and Amy Spingarn helped to discover and encourage new talent by providing prizes for literary contests in *The Crisis*. Other NAACP officials who made contributions to the Harlem Renaissance through their writings and through encouraging others were James Weldon Johnson, Jessie Fauset, and Walter White.

The NAACP and Residential Segregation   Since its inception the NAACP has fought patterns of segregation. The U.S. Supreme Court in *Plessy v. Ferguson* in 1896 had established the principal of "separate but equal," giving legal sanction to segregation. On December 10, 1910, the city of Baltimore, Md., enacted the first of a series of ordinances providing for the segregation of Afro-Americans in residential areas. Following Baltimore, other cities in the southern states passed similar ordinances that the NAACP subsequently challenged in the courts. Finally, in 1917, in the Louisville, Ky., segregation case of *Buchanan v. Warley,* the U.S. Supreme Court ruled in favor of Moorfield Storey's contention that segregation ordinances were in violation of the due process clause of the Fourteenth Amendment in that they "destroyed the right of the individual to acquire, enjoy, and dispose of his property." White property owners in Baltimore, Md., New Orleans, La., Washington, D.C., and other cities sought to circumvent the ruling in *Buchanan v. Warley* through the use of racially restrictive covenants that forbade the sale of property to nonwhites.

In *Corrigan v. Buckley* (1926) the U.S. Supreme Court upheld the right of private persons to make contracts concerning the control and disposition of their property despite NAACP legal arguments that the action of a lower court in enforcing a restrictive covenant had the force of a statute. *Corrigan v. Buckley* was a blow to black equality. It came at a time when a new wave of black migration to the cities was beginning and shortly before the federal government became involved in housing. During the 1930s and 1940s, both state courts and the federal housing agencies accepted and acted upon the decision that judicial enforcement of restrictive covenants was constitutional, since the U.S. Supreme Court seemed to say that judicial action was not state action and therefore not in conflict with the Fourteenth Amendment.

For 20 years the U.S. Supreme Court refused to review an increasing number of cases challenging the decision rendered in *Corrigan v. Buckley,* but in 1947 it agreed to review two cases, which were combined in *Shelley v. Kraemer.* Here the court ruled that the Fourteenth Amendment protected the right of Afro-Americans to equality in the enjoyment of property rights, and that this right was basic to the realization of other civil rights.

An attempt was next made to circumvent this decision by bringing damage suits against persons who sold their property to blacks in violation of restrictive covenants. In *Barrows v. Jackson* (1953) this procedure was declared illegal as an attempt to enforce covenants by indirection.

Thus the NAACP, in winning these two decisions, was successful not only in ending the racially restrictive covenants as instruments of segregation, but also in broadening the concept of what constituted state action.

The effect became evident in the area of public

housing. Since the 1930s the federal government had administered the housing acts on the basis of the doctrine of "separate but equal." In 1953 the U.S. Supreme Court refused to review the decision of the California courts in *Bank v. Housing Authority,* which held that segregation in public housing was in violation of the equal protection clause of the Fourteenth Amendment. Finally in 1962 President John F. Kennedy issued an executive order forbidding segregation in future low-rent public housing.

The NAACP and the New Deal Blacks benefited to a limited degree by New Deal measures designed to promote relief, recovery, and reform. Of special concern was the program of the Agricultural Adjustment Act and its administration (AAA), since half of the black labor force was employed in agriculture. Under the sharecropping system, tenant farmers were at the mercy of landlords who frequently defrauded black workers. Under the AAA, the tenant was often cheated by the withholding of payments or the denial of access to credit provided under the terms of the act. The crop reduction program also worked to the Afro-American's disadvantage. Landlords frequently curtailed their acreage, evicted tenants, and shifted to day labor to avoid sharing payments for crop reduction. Under the AAA, the small percentage of very well-to-do farmers received most of the benefits. But more than half the farm population, of which Afro-Americans were the most impoverished group, received very little because of their lack of political power.

The NAACP had traditionally concerned itself with securing civil rights and liberties through legal procedures, leaving unemployment and other economic problems to the National Urban League. Accordingly, it was without experience when it came to the problems of the serious deterioration of the Afro-American's already unsatisfactory economic conditions. Moreover, the NAACP was experiencing severe financial difficulties due to the Great Depression. It is therefore not surprising that measures taken by the NAACP to meet the emergency were the traditional ones it had found to be effective in the field of civil rights—investigation, publicity, agitation, and petition for redress of grievances.

The association, however, went beyond mere publicity and agitation and gave modest financial support to the aggressive biracial Southern Tenant Farmers Union, organized in 1934. But by 1936 the union was declining under the implacable opposition of landlords.

Furthermore, the NAACP expended efforts toward ending discrimination in organized labor. For example, in 1934 the association attempted to get the national American Federation of Labor (AFL) convention to insist that its constituent members cease practicing discrimination. The resolution failed; another also failed the following year, being overshadowed by the struggle within the ranks of organized labor that eventually resulted in the formation of the Congress of Industrial Organizations (CIO).

The Public Works Administration (PWA) of the New Deal was also vitally concerned with the welfare of Afro-Americans. Under its administrator, Harold L. Ickes (a former president of the Chicago branch of the NAACP), the agency decreed that contracts must carry a nondiscrimination clause. Contractors, however, merely resorted to tokenism in order to comply with the regulation, forcing the NAACP to establish a criterion to determine when discrimination existed. The recommendation of the NAACP was that black workers must receive that part of the payroll that was equal to one-half of their percentage of the entire labor force as given in the occupational census of 1930. This provided a basis for determining the existence of discrimination and for proceeding against violators.

In contrast to the Public Works Administration, the Works Progress Administration (WPA) under Harry Hopkins never adopted specific contract provisions to assure equal job opportunities for Afro-Americans. Hopkins did, however, issue a directive forbidding discrimination and put pressure on local authorities to obtain compliance.

The NAACP concentrated its efforts on two aspects of the WPA programs that were especially harmful to Afro-American workers: the tendency of work relief wages to gradually drop to the level of regional wages and the practice in the South of firing large numbers of Afro-Americans at harvest time, thus forcing them to work in the fields at substandard wages.

The Second Amenia Conference and Internal Strife Criticism of the NAACP developed in the early 1930s. Young Afro-American activists and intellectuals—such as economist Abram L. Harris, political scientist Ralph Bunche, attorney Louis Redding, and sociologists Ira DeA. Reid and E. Franklin Frazier—felt that the NAACP was not meeting the demands of the times and had no program to alleviate the economic distress of the black masses. These emerging young leaders, disillusioned with the New Deal, looked inward to the black community for a solution to the problems confronting Afro-Americans during the Depression; they looked to cultural nationalism and to the achievement of integrating the black and white masses into the labor movement.

Acutely conscious of the growing criticism that reached a climax with the NAACP's inept handling of the Scottsboro case, NAACP leadership decided to consult with representative young black activists as to programs and policies. Accordingly, in August 1933, a three-day conference was held at Amenia, N.Y., on the Spingarn estate, the site of the conference in 1916. Thirty-three men and women participated in the discussions, and a wide variety of issues were discussed, including cultural nationalism, a new integrated labor movement of the masses of black and white workers, and the development of bloc voting in order to increase political power. All conferees agreed to the need for the NAACP to evolve a new program to meet the new problems facing the Afro-American population.

Implementation of these ideas was difficult. The NAACP was not yet ready to abandon its traditional interracial approach for black nationalism. Repeated attempts to integrate labor unions had failed, and the New Deal recovery program was just emerging. As for marshaling Afro-American voters to obtain political power, the NAACP had advocated this approach for more than a decade.

The Second Amenia Conference forshadowed a later drafting, adoption, and partial implementation of the Harris Plan or the Future Plan and Program. Before this came to pass, however, the NAACP was shaken and severely weakened by the eruption of a long-standing feud between Du Bois and the association's secretary, Walter White.

Unlike White, Du Bois believed that the NAACP at that time should concentrate its energies on the economic problems of black America. He believed further that in order for Afro-Americans to survive the Great Depression, and ultimately to achieve equality, they must organize and develop a black economy based on self-help. He used the pages of The Crisis to argue his case; but many readers, and nonreaders as well, misunderstanding his emphasis on "voluntary segregation," viewed his position as a retreat and Du Bois himself as a counselor of

Walter White emerged as the principal leader of the NAACP in the 1930's, and the NAACP became more highly centralized under his executive direcction. (Library of Congress.)

despair with an unworkable plan that would lock blacks more firmly into an already detestable system of segregation. Du Bois' campaign for his views, coupled with the existing critical financial situation of both the NAACP and The Crisis, inflamed the deep personal antagonism of the two leaders. In addition to suggesting that an Afro-American far less fairer in complexion than White (who could easily have passed for a white person) should serve as secretary of the association, Du Bois resented White's membership on a special board of control for management and policy making of The Crisis. White, on the other hand, was angry at having to find funds from scarce resources in order to meet the deficits of The Crisis.

Antagonism between Du Bois and White reached the breaking point when White, as part of his financial retrenchment policy, chose to end the employment of two long-tenured and popular NAACP fieldworkers, Robert Bagnall and William Pickens. At the end of several power maneuvers, in which Du Bois resigned and White offered to withdraw from the association, the NAACP choose to accept Du Bois' resignation upon his own insistence.

The Future Plan and Program: The 1930s The resignation of Du Bois and White's tightened control over the national office did nothing to stop the slow decline in membership, finances, and influence of the NAACP. White was reluctant to implement the findings of the Second Amenia Conference, but pressure within the association forced his hand. In July 1934 the board appointed a committee on the Future Plan and Program with the young revisionist economist Abram L. Harris of Howard University (Washington, D.C.) as its chairman.

The Harris Committee was aided by advisory committees composed of other young black revisionists who brought in a proposed program suggesting a thorough revision of the NAACP's objectives. Their chief emphasis was directed toward building an integrated labor movement. As an aid in achieving this objective, an educational program would be developed throughout the branches, to be supported by a program of research into the economic problems of industry and agriculture.

To insure against sabotage of the program by the staff in the national office and to aid in effecting the decentralization of the association, the Harris Committee proposed that a semiautonomous committee on economic activities (composed of professional economists) would direct the economic activities. The board would direct the NAACP's civil rights program, while the national office would function only as a coordinating agency. John P. Davis of the Joint Committee on National Recovery, a group composed of 22 national, racial, and interracial organizations, would be added to the NAACP staff as director of economic affairs. Branches would be revamped to make a greater appeal to the masses of Afro-American workers and would become centers of economic and political education and agitation under the direction of salaried regional secretaries.

The young revisionists felt strongly that the interracial aspect of the NAACP was a source of weakness. The absolute control by Afro-Americans of their leading organization was held to be a necessary component of the new program to develop pride in race and in the institution of a program of self-help.

The program presented by the Harris Committee posed a threat to the executive officers of the NAACP, whose roles would be greatly diminished. White and Assistant Secretary Roy Wilkins attacked the plan, indirectly claiming that it would identify the Afro-American with radicalism, an identity that would increase and justify the racism of white America. They also accused the committee's plan of lacking the emotional appeal necessary for the raising of large amounts of money.

Board members feared that weakening the centralized structure of the NAACP would lead to Communist infiltration or to the use of the association as a tool of self-seeking individuals and politicians. In addition, the feeling that economic problems were properly the sphere of the National Urban League and that the NAACP should limit its program to its traditional role of working for civil rights still persisted.

Nearly a year of consideration and debate brought changes in the Harris Plan. Important revisions left the board in control of the proposed committee on economic activities, appointed by and responsible to the board. Instead of adding Davis (of the joint committee) to the staff, it was now proposed that as soon as funds became available the board should appoint a director of economic activities who would supervise NAACP cooperation with existing agencies in the economic field.

For a time a close relationship was maintained between the joint committee and the NAACP with the association paying half of Davis' small salary. But by the fall of 1935, concern that Davis might turn to the extreme left and the growing stringency of the NAACP led the association to curtail its support of the joint committee. Another probable factor behind this cutback was the threat that the joint committee might become a rival of the NAACP and that the brilliant and capable Davis would supplant Walter White as the preeminent black leader in the United States. By August 1936, the NAACP had severed its connection with the joint committee, a move that led to the demise of the federated group.

However, aside from the brief union with the joint committee and the institution of an educational program for the branches, the rest of the Harris program was never implemented because of several factors. Believing that its economic program lacked sufficient emotional appeal to produce financial support from the NAACP's black middle-class and white liberal constituents, the board was less disposed to that program than toward its traditional civil rights program. The board believed that the antilynching campaign, the drive for equalization of black teachers' salaries, and the fight to end the white primary election provided the emotional appeal essential to raise money during the Depression.

Meanwhile, White moved swiftly to eliminate his opposition and to consolidate his position of leadership. The retirement and death of a number of founders and board members helped that goal. Many functions of the board were taken over by a small committee on administration composed of members of the executive staff; and Mary Ovington was maneuvered out of the board chairmanship into the obscure position of treasurer. In 1935 Dr. Louis T. Wright, an eminent surgeon and ardent supporter of Walter White, became the first black chairman of the board. Following Joel E. Spingarn's death, Arthur B. Spingarn, his brother, was elected to the honorary position of president, vacating the position of chairman of the national legal committee, a post filled by William H. Hastie, dean of the Howard University School of Law. Dr. Channing H. Tobias, former senior secretary of the Young Men's Christian Association (YMCA) for Colored Work, became board chairman in 1953. Thus, the key positions on the board, now filled by White's supporters, assured White control of the NAACP. Instead of becoming decentralized as envisaged by the Harris report, the organization had become highly centralized and more firmly under the direction of its chief executive officer.

The NAACP in World War II Although conditions for Afro-Americans in the U.S. Armed Forces were considerably better during World War II than they had been during World War I, many of the old injustices remained to harass black soldiers and workers. Following the passage of the Selective Service Act in 1940, the chief executives of the NAACP, the National Urban League, and the Brotherhood of Sleeping Car Porters (BSCP) met with President Franklin D. Roosevelt to discuss a joint memorandum concerning the role of black personnel in the U.S. Armed Forces.

The group made a series of demands: the integration of black officers and recruits into all Army units; the integration of black doctors, nurses, and dentists; the end of discrimination in the Navy; the assignment of black reserve officers in the training of troops; the same training for black recruits as for white; the appointment of blacks to draft boards; and finally the appointment of Afro-American civilian aides to the secretaries of war and navy.

When the War Department policy regarding Afro-American recruits was announced a few weeks later, Afro-Americans were shocked to learn how few of their demands had been met. The Navy would admit Afro-Americans only to the mess corps. Blacks, including professional people, were to be placed in segregated Army units on the basis of their proportion to the total population. However, William H. Hastie was appointed as civilian aide to the secretary of war and Col. Campbell Johnson as assistant to the director of the Selective Service. Units of the Reserve Officer Training Corps (ROTC) were extended to more black colleges and a flight training school under the Army Air Corps was set up at Tuskegee, Ala.

Afro-Americans were not to be appeased, however, and a storm of criticism broke out in the black press, protesting the discriminatory treatment of black military personnel as well as the lack of civilian job opportunities in defense industries. In retaliation, a number of Army commanders ordered the prohibition of such "inflammatory" black newspapers. Constant pressure from the NAACP and the black community finally opened the Navy and Marine Corps to black enlistments, and later to black commissions in the officer corps. Black women were also eventually accepted into the WAVES and the WACS.

Representing the NAACP, Walter White visited black service units in the various theaters of war. In *A Rising Wind* (1945), he laid bare the injustices inflicted on black service personnel. The impact of this revelation was second only to that of Du Bois' editorials in *The Crisis* at the close of World War I.

Another target for NAACP action was the discriminatory hiring practices of most defense industries. Together, the Brotherhood of Sleeping Car Porters and the NAACP planned a march on Washington, D.C., to protest these practices. When President Roosevelt learned of these plans (for a march on Washington, D.C., to take place on July 1, 1941), he sought to dissuade the leaders of the two organizations. It was not until he promised to issue an executive order prohibiting discrimination in defense industries and in the government that the march was canceled.

Thus on June 25, 1941, Executive Order No. 8802 was issued, outlawing discrimination in the government just 28 years after it had been instituted under President Woodrow Wilson. An antidiscrimination clause was now placed in all war contracts, and a Fair Employment Practices Commission (FEPC) was set up to investigate complaints of violations.

The NAACP and other organizations moved to

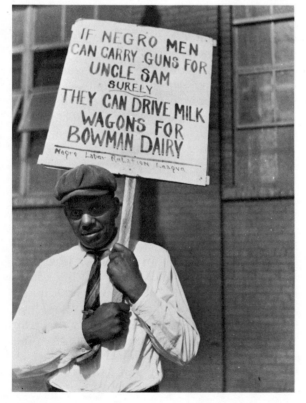

The NAACP supported laborers against discrimination in defense industries in World War II. In the face of threats by the Brotherhood of Sleeping Car Porters and the NAACP, President Roosevelt issued Executive Order No. 8802 outlawing discrimination in government contracts. *(Library of Congress.)*

secure permanent FEPC legislation and a National Committee for a Permanent FEPC was established. Although in 1944 both major political parties endorsed the proposal, the U.S. Congress failed to act. The following year, fulfilling a promise made in his address to the Thirty-eighth Annual Conference of the NAACP on June 29, 1947, President Harry S. Truman issued an executive order requiring fair employment in government service. Furthermore, both he and President Dwight D. Eisenhower instituted committees to prevent discrimination by companies holding government contracts.

The great migration of Afro-Americans to industrial centers, causing friction with whites over jobs, housing, and recreation, led to a series of riots in Detroit, Mich.; New York, N.Y.; and Columbia, Tenn. During this time the NAACP set up relief stations, aided the destitute, and attempted to bring police and white civilians guilty of assault and other outrages to justice.

At the close of the war, returning black veterans met with violence and lynching in the South. Under the leadership of the NAACP, a committee that represented labor, the Federal Council of Churches, the Phelps-Stokes Fund, and the NAACP met with President Truman on September 19, 1946, to discuss violations of civil rights. As a result, the president appointed a commission to investigate these violations and to recommend a program of corrective action. The President's Committee on Civil Rights, as it was called, was a distinguished biracial body that issued its report, *To Secure These Rights,* in the fall of 1947. This document called for a comprehensive program to end segregation and the denial of civil rights to Afro-Americans.

Before this, at the organizational conference of the United Nations in San Francisco, Calif., in 1945, official observers representing the NAACP were W. E. B. Du Bois (who had been recalled to the NAACP in 1944) and Walter White, with Roy Wilkins as alternate. Du Bois supervised the drafting by a group of distinguished Afro-American scholars of an appeal to the UN Commission on Human Rights, presented in October 1947, concerning the inequities suffered by Afro-Americans, that is discrimination and the denial of the ballot. The object of the appeal was to call attention to the plight of the black minority in America and to influence public opinion through discussion and debate in the international forum.

Du Bois had returned to the NAACP (after his retirement from Atlanta University) with the understanding that he was to be assured of a semi-independent position as consultant, with freedom to write and to revive the link between the NAACP and the Pan-African Congress. Walter White, however, expected Du Bois to play a more subservient role. Their continued conflict and clashes finally led to the dismissal of Du Bois by the board in 1948.

Discrimination in Education   As early as 1909 the NAACP had published a pamphlet attacking segregation and discrimination in secondary education. Believing that the solution to this

President Harry S. Truman (foreground, in light suit) attended the NAACP Convention June 29, 1947, when he endorsed a permanent FEPC and supported the NAACP's views. No other president had been as outspoken or had ever appeared on an NAACP program. Flanking the president were (left) Walter White and (right) Mrs. Eleanor Roosevelt. Contralto Carol Brice is at the rostrum leading the audience in a closing hymn. *(James Weldon Johnson Collection, Yale University.)*

problem lay in federal aid to education, the association attempted in 1911 to organize an independent national committee to study methods used by governments in other countries and to work for an improved program in the United States. However, lack of interest among liberals and educators alike delayed the establishment of the independent committee until 1916. NAACP founders were especially interested in agricultural extension legislation, and in generating federal aid to vocational education in public secondary schools with programs that would be of benefit to black farmers and to black school children.

Beginning in 1911, when the Smith-Lever bill for federal aid to agricultural colleges was first introduced, until its passage in 1914, the NAACP opposed the bill because of its discriminatory features. The association sought without success to secure an amendment providing for an equal distribution of federal funds between black and white colleges and to rally public opinion behind their efforts.

By 1918 heavy Afro-American migration from the South led to the introduction of segregation in some northern public schools. This trend was energetically fought by the NAACP. Likewise, some northern colleges and graduate schools introduced the practice, though the NAACP successfully opposed it at Cornell University (Ithaca, N.Y.) and at Smith College (Northampton, Mass.). Johns Hopkins University (Baltimore, Md.), however, refused to admit Afro-Americans for fear of losing grants from the state of Maryland, which required separate schools for the races.

The 1930s witnessed the opening of the NAACP's sustained campaign to end segregation and discrimination in education. A grant from the American Fund for Public Service made possible the employment of an exceptionally able attorney, Nathan R. Margold, to make a study of the legal status of the Afro-American. Charles H. Houston, a Phi Beta Kappa graduate of Amherst College (Amherst, Mass.) and the Harvard Law School, was also engaged under the direction of Arthur B. Spingarn, who had served as volunteer chairman of the National Legal Committee for nearly 25 years.

The plan of attack as evolved by Spingarn and Houston and as carried on by the latter's successor, Thurgood Marshall, was to insist that southern states must comply with the ruling in *Plessy v. Ferguson* that held that separate facilities for Afro-Americans must be equal to those provided for whites. NAACP attorneys believed that by insisting on equal facilities and salaries for both races, the states would find it financially impossible to maintain segregated school systems.

Throughout the 1930s and 1940s, the NAACP and its lawyers worked through the courts to achieve adherence to the law as stated in *Plessy v. Ferguson* and the Fourteenth Amendment. In 1939 a federal district court ruled that the law providing for lower minimum salaries for black teachers in Anne Arundel County, Md., was a violation of the due process and equal protection clauses of the Fourteenth Amendment. The following year a federal circuit court of appeals in Norfolk, Va., ruled that the setting of salary scales was a form of state action and so was subject to the Fourteenth Amendment. The U.S. Supreme Court gave sanction to this decision by its refusal to review the case. In 1941 denial of equal protection of the laws was also the basis of a federal court's decision in a case against the

state of Florida in which it was held that local school officials were agents of the state and that differentials in salary schedules for Afro-Americans with the same qualifications were violations of the Fourteenth Amendment.

Meanwhile, with increasing numbers of college-trained Afro-Americans, the growing demand for graduate and professional training could not be met by the small number of black institutions offering graduate work. In 1935 the NAACP secured the admission of Donald Gaines Murray, an Amherst College graduate, to the University of Maryland Law School. In this case the Maryland Court of Appeals held that the system of out-of-state tuitions for Afro-Americans in lieu of admission to state universities, was a violation of equal protection under the law. Even more important for the success of the NAACP strategy was the U.S. Supreme Court decision in 1938 in the case of *Missouri ex rel Gaines v. Canada*, which declared that equal educational facilities within the state must be provided for Lloyd Lionel Gaines.

When the South failed to respond, and in fact hardened its resistance, the NAACP continued its legal attack. By the early 1950s it had instituted suits that eventually resulted in the famous decision in *Brown v. Board of Education of Topeka* (1954). In this case, an important aspect of the NAACP's brief was its appendix, which cited the testimony of more than a score of prominent social scientists that segregation caused irreparable damage to the personality development of both black and white children. In overturning segregation, the court cited sociological and psychological evidence that segregation of black children produced a sense of inferiority that adversely affected their motivation to learn. This "feeling of inferiority," said the court, "may affect their hearts and minds in a way unlikely ever to be undone." The court declared that "separate educational facilities are inherently unequal." The enforcement of the *Brown* decision, however, ushered in a new era of litigation in which the NAACP continued to fight.

The End of Jim Crow Transportation   Another area of concern in the NAACP's general program was that of Jim Crow transportation. Several factors contributed to a delay in action on this issue until the 1940s. In 1915 Moorfield Storey had refused to argue what was to have been the first test of an Oklahoma law allowing railroads to provide dining and sleeping accommodations for whites only because he believed the suit was improperly drawn. Simultaneously, the NAACP had prepared two more cases to test the Oklahoma law and to arrange to petition the Interstate Commerce Commission (ICC) for relief. At this point, however, the struggle over the role of the Afro-American in the U.S. Army intervened and consumed all the time, energy, and resources of the association. Moreover, Louis Brandeis, who was prepared to represent the NAACP before the ICC, was appointed to the U.S. Supreme Court, making his appearance for the NAACP impossible. Finally, wartime unification of the railroads under a southerner, William G. McAdoo, precluded the cases from coming to trial.

It was not until 1946 that the NAACP turned again to the problem of Jim Crow transportation and won a decision in *Morgan v. Virginia,* reversing the Virginia state courts that had held that the law segregating the races on buses applied to both interstate and intrastate passengers. Four years later, as a result of legal action by the NAACP, the U.S. Supreme Court ordered the end of segregation on railroad dining cars.

Southern Attacks on the NAACP Following the NAACP's legal victory in the famous case of *Brown v. Board of Education of Topeka,* southern states launched an offensive against the NAACP by enacting a series of laws designed to circumscribe its activities and to consume its resources and energies in self-defense.

In 1956 the state of Alabama brought suit to prevent the NAACP from functioning in the state, claiming that the association was an out-of-state corporation that had failed to register to do business in the state as required by law. Legal maneuvers in the Alabama courts, including an order to produce membership lists, forced the NAACP to return to the U.S. Supreme Court four times over a period of eight years before receiving a favorable decision in 1964 holding that there was no reason for banning the NAACP in Alabama.

Meanwhile, both Arkansas and Louisiana tried various devices to secure NAACP membership rolls. In Arkansas, Little Rock and North Little Rock city ordinances were revised to require that out-of-state corporations must file membership lists. The U.S. Supreme Court overruled this action. Arkansas then passed a law requiring schoolteachers to list all the organizations to which they belonged. The U.S. Supreme Court in 1960 also overruled this law as having no bearing on the competence or fitness of a

teacher. Louisiana's law of 1958 attempted to prevent any organization from functioning in the state if any officers or directors of its out-of-state affiliate were a member of a Communist, Communist-front, or subversive organization cited by the House Un-American Activities Committee or the U.S. attorney general. The Supreme Court in 1961 held that the law was not applicable to the NAACP.

Virginia, in its attack on the NAACP, attempted to apply to the association the laws against barratry and the solicitation of litigants. To achieve this, the state laws were extended to require that any organization advocating either integration or segregation, working for legislation in behalf of any race, or raising or spending money for litigation in behalf of any race must list the amount expended and its source, and file a list of its members, officers, and directors. Six other southern states enacted similar legislation. The association, however, brought suit, and in *NAACP v. Button* (1963) the U.S. Supreme Court ruled in favor of the NAACP. Another favorable ruling came in *Gibson v. Florida* in the same year, when the court decided that there was no basis for Florida's investigation of the NAACP as a Communist-infiltrated organization.

In addition to legal attacks by southern states, acts of individual violence were perpetrated against officials and members of the NAACP. From the standpoint of public reaction, some of the most notable terrorist acts included the following killings and/or bombings: (1) Harry T. Moore, an official in Florida, who was killed in his home in Mims, Fla., on December 25, 1951, as the result of a bombing; Moore had spoken out against Florida's treatment of Afro-Americans in a criminal case that was known as the Groveland Case or as The Little Scottsboro Case (see *Ebony,* April 1952); (2) Z. Alexander Looby, a lawyer for the NAACP in Nashville, Tenn., and counsel for more than 100 student sit-in demonstrations, whose home was bombed on April 19, 1960; (3) Medgar W. Evers, NAACP field secretary for nine years, who was ambushed and killed at his home in Jackson, Miss., on the night of June 11, 1963; (4) Aaron Henry, president of the NAACP in Mississippi, whose home in Clarksdale was bombed on April 12, 1963; and (5) Fred D. Alexander, head of the NAACP in North Carolina, whose home in Charlotte was bombed on November 22, 1965.

The NAACP and Civil Rights Activism In 1931, when Walter White became secretary, the

NAACP was suffering badly from the effects of the Great Depression. Membership had decreased to 70,000; income amounted to only $59,081; and the NAACP was running a deficit of $4,359. Although staff and salaries were curtailed, difficulties still existed in meeting the payroll. *The Crisis* was also in serious trouble and had ceased to be self-supporting. Circulation had fallen to 10,000 subscribers and debts were uncollectable. Deficits from 1921 to 1931 amounted to about $9,000, which, in addition to the editor's salary, had to be assumed by the NAACP. At the time of Walter White's death in 1955, the NAACP consisted of more than 1,300 branches, youth councils, and college chapters and a membership of approximately 250,000. Annual income was nearly $500,000.

Roy Wilkins, who joined the staff in 1931, was White's successor. During the Wilkins era of the 1950s and 1960s, a changed climate prevailed in the area of race relations. The first Civil Rights Act in 1957 greatly increased federal activity. Nevertheless, efforts to evade or delay desegregation in education and to nullify the civil rights and voting acts produced an angry and militant response from blacks and from many white supporters of the NAACP.

New protest groups under new leaders came to the fore. The Congress of Racial Equality (CORE), the Southern Christian Leadership Conference (SCLC), and the Student Nonviolent Coordinating Committee (SNCC) received national attention. For a time these organizations wrested the initiative for change away from the NAACP. Their tactics were those of direct action and street demonstrations. Amid mounting tension and resistance, serious riots and disturbances erupted.

The NAACP slogan, "Free by '63," was taken up by other civil rights groups and became the rallying cry of the huge but peaceful "March on Washington for Jobs and Freedom" at the end of August 1963. This was the climax of a series of demonstrations that had occurred during the spring and summer of that year and that had been set off by the unusual police brutality in Birmingham, Ala., against demonstrators led by Dr. Martin Luther King, Jr. Demonstrations continued during the "long hot summer" of 1964, and riots swept northern cities during the following summers of 1965 and 1966.

Under the leadership of Roy Wilkins, the NAACP boldly reaffirmed its commitment to the democratic process and to the goal of integration. It responded by condemning intimidation

Roy Wilkins as he appeared in the 1970s. He boldly reaffirmed the NAACP's commitment to equal opportunity for blacks during his leadership, 1940s-1970s. *(NAACP.)*

and violence as well as racial and economic separatism. But young revisionists within the NAACP were not easily silenced. They insisted that the traditional program was no longer relevant; but again, at the 1968 Annual Conference, they were defeated by the more conservative elements in the association. The same year dissension in the national office erupted in a dramatic manner with the publication of an attack on the U.S. Supreme Court as "racist" by a white member of the legal staff. His subsequent dismissal led to the resignation of the entire legal staff of the NAACP.

Although the association took a firm stand against revisionism and reiterated its faith in its traditional program and values, it was slowly moving toward a more militant position. By the time of the 1971 Annual Conference, harmony was at least outwardly restored in what Bishop Stephen Gill Spottswood, the board chairman, hailed as "the oldest, largest, most experienced, most successful, most consulted, most feared of all civil rights organizations." By 1977, new national officers had been appointed or elected. Margaret Bush Wilson, a lawyer from St. Louis, Mo., became president of the board; Warren Marr, II, became editor of *The Crisis*; and Benjamin Lawson Hooks became executive secretary, replacing Roy Wilkins. *See also* AFRO-AMERICAN HISTORY: RECONSTRUCTION TO REVOLT, 1877–1977; AGRICULTURE; CIVIL DISORDERS; CIVIL RIGHTS; DISCRIMINATION; DU BOIS, WILLIAM EDWARD BURGHARDT; EDUCATION; EMPLOYMENT; HOUSING; LABOR UNIONS; LAWYERS; LYNCHING; MOTION PICTURES; POLITICS; SEGREGATION; SPINGARN MEDAL; WHITE, WALTER FRANCIS.

REFERENCES: Abraham, Henry J., *Freedom and the Court: Civil Rights and Liberties in the United States*, Oxford University Press, New York, 1967; Bardolph, Richard (ed.), *The Civil Rights Record: Black Americans and the Law, 1849–1970*, Thomas Y. Crowell, New York, 1970; Blaustein, Albert and Charles Clyde Ferguson, *Desegregation and the Law*, Rutgers University Press, New Brunswick, 1957; Broderick, Francis, L., *W. E. B. Du Bois: Negro Leader in Time of Crisis*, Stanford University Press, Stanford, 1959; Cooney, Charles F., "Walter White and the Harlem Renaissance," *Journal of Negro History*, vol. 57, no. 3, pp. 231–40, July 1972; Dalfiume, Richard M., *Desegregation of the U.S. Armed Forces Fighting on Two Fronts 1939–1953*, University of Missouri Press, Columbia, 1969; Du Bois, W. E. B., *The Autobiography of W. E. B. Du Bois*, International Publishers, New York, 1968; Franklin, John Hope, *From Slavery to Freedom: A History of Negro Americans*, Alfred A. Knopf, New York, 1967; Garfinkel, Herbert, *When Negroes March*, Atheneum, New York, 1969; Garraty, John A. (ed.), *Quarrels That Have Shaped the Constitution*, Harper and Row, New York, 1964; Hixson, William B., *Moorfield Storey and the Abolitionist Tradition*, Oxford University Press, New York, 1972; Hughes, Langston, *Fight for Freedom: The Story of the*

NAACP, W. W. Norton, New York, 1962; Johnson, James Weldon, *Along This Way: The Autobiography of James Weldon Johnson*, Viking, New York, 1933; Johnson, James Weldon, *Black Manhattan*, Alfred A. Knopf, New York, 1930; Kellog, Charles Flint, *NAACP: A History of the National Association for the Advancement of Colored People, 1909–20*, vol. I, Johns Hopkins University Press, Baltimore, 1967; Key, Vladimir O., Jr., *Southern Politics in State and Nation*, Alfred A. Knopf, New York, 1950; Konvitz, Milton R., *Expanding Liberties: Freedom's Gains in Postwar America*, Viking, New York, 1966; Lee, Ulysses, *The Employment of Negro Troops in the U.S. in World War II*, Special Studies, no. 8, U.S. Government Printing Office, Washington, D.C., 1966; Miller, Loren, *The Petitioners: The Story of the Supreme Court of the United States and the Negro*, World Publishing Co., Cleveland, 1966; Muse, Benjamin, *The American Negro Revolution: From Non-Violence to Black Power 1963–1967*, Indiana University Press, Bloomington, 1970; Muse, Benjamin, *Ten Years of Prelude: The Story of Integration Since the Supreme Court's 1954 Decision*, Macmillan, New York, 1964; Myrdal, Gunnar, *An American Dilemma: The Negro Problem and Modern Democracy*, 2 vols., Macmillan, New York, 1944; Ovington, Mary White, *The Walls Came Tumbling Down*, Schocken, New York, 1970; Raper, Arthur F., *The Tragedy of Lynching*, University of North Carolina Press, Chapel Hill, 1933; Rauchames, Louis, *Race, Jobs, and Politics: The Story of the FEPC*, Harper Brothers, New York, 1953; Record, Wilson, *Race and Radicalism: The NAACP and the Communist Party*, Cornell University Press, Ithaca, 1964; Sterner, Richard, *The Negro's Share*, Harper Brothers, New York, 1943; Sternsher, Bernard, *The Negro in Depression and War: Prelude to Revolution 1930–1945*, Quadrangle Books, Chicago, 1969; Vose, Clement E., *Caucasians Only*, University of California Press, Berkeley, 1959; Waskow, Arthur I., *From Race Riot to Sit-In, 1919 and the 1960's: A Study in the Connections Between Conflict and Violence*, Doubleday, Garden City, 1966; White, Walter, *How Far the Promised Land?*, Viking, New York, 1955; White, Walter, *A Man Called White: The Autobiography of Walter White*, Viking, New York, 1948; White, Walter, *A Rising Wind*, Doubleday, Garden City, 1945; and Wolters, Raymond, *Negroes and the Great Depression: The Problem of Economic Recovery*, Greenwood Press, Westport, 1970.

NATIONAL ASSOCIATION OF COLORED GRADUATE NURSES See NURSES.

NATIONAL BANKERS ASSOCIATION See BANKS.

NATIONAL BAR ASSOCIATION This national association of Afro-American attorneys was founded in 1925. By 1975 the membership had reached approximately 4,000. The purposes of the organization are as follows: "to advance the science of jurisprudence; to improve the administration of justice; to help preserve the independence of the judiciary; to work for a more equitable representation of all racial groups in the judiciary of our cities, States, and Nation; to promote legislation that will improve the economic condition of all the citizens of the United States; to aid all citizens, regardless of race or creed, in their effort to secure a free and untrammeled use of the franchise guaranteed by the Constitution of the United States; to uphold the honor of the legal profession; to protect the civil and political rights of the citizens and residents of the several States of the United States." In 1971 the judicial council of the association was set up with the aim of reconstructing the American system of justice so as to conform to the current needs of society, particularly in matters relating to race and class, and poverty and power. Past presidents of the association (1925–70) include: George H. Woodson of Des Moines, Iowa, elected in Des Moines, Iowa, 1925; Charles Calloway of Kansas City, Mo., elected in Chicago, Ill., 1926; Homer G. Phillips of St. Louis, Mo., elected in St. Louis, Mo., 1927; C. Francis Stradford of Chicago, Ill., elected in Chicago, Ill., 1928; Raymond Pace Alexander of Philadelphia, Pa., elected in Detroit, Mich., 1929 and reelected in Washington, D.C., 1930; Jesse S. Heslip of Toledo, Ohio, elected in Cleveland, Ohio, 1931 and reelected in Indianapolis, Ind., 1932; Eugene Washington Rhodes of Philadelphia, Pa., elected in St. Louis, Mo., 1933, and reelected in Baltimore, Md., 1934; George W. Lawrence of Chicago, Ill., elected in Nashville, Tenn., 1935, and reelected in Pittsburgh, Pa., 1936; William L. Houston of Washington, D.C., elected in Philadelphia, Pa., 1937, and reelected in Durham, N.C., 1938; Sidney R. Redmond of St. Louis, Mo., elected in New York, N.Y., 1939, and reelected in Columbus, Ohio, 1940; Euclid Louis Taylor of Chicago, Ill., elected in Little Rock, Ark., 1941. Due to the World War II restrictions on travel, no meeting was held in 1942, and Taylor served until 1943; Charles W. Anderson of Louisville, Ky., elected in Baltimore, Md., 1943, and reelected in Chicago, Ill., 1944; Earl B. Dickerson of Chicago, Ill., elected in Cleveland, Ohio, 1945, and reelected in Detroit, Mich., 1946; Thurman L. Dodson of Washington, D.C., elected in Washington, D.C., 1947, and reelected in Atlanta, Ga., 1948; James R. Booker of Little Rock, Ark., elected in Indianapolis, Ind., 1949, and reelected in Nashville, Tenn., 1950; Scovel Richardson, elected in St. Louis, Mo., 1951, and reelected in Detroit, Mich., 1952; Harold Flowers of Pine Bluff, Ark., elected in New Orleans, La., 1953; Harold Bledsoe of Detroit, Mich., elected in Kansas City, Mo., 1954; Richard Atkinson, elected in Washington, D.C., 1955, and reelected in New York, N.Y., 1956; William S. Thompson of Washington, D.C., elected in Cleveland, Ohio, 1957, and reelected in Chicago, Ill., 1958; Elmer C. Jackson, Jr., of Kansas City, Kans., elected in

Milwaukee, Wis., 1959, and reelected in Philadelphia, Pa., 1960; Robert E. Lillard of Nashville, Tenn., elected in Los Angeles, Calif., 1961, and reelected 1962; Theodore Coggs of Milwaukee, Wis., elected in Indianapolis, Ind., 1963, and reelected in Baltimore, Md., 1964; Revius O. Ortique of New Orleans, La., elected in New Orleans, La., 1965, and reelected in Detroit, Mich., 1966; Billy Jones of East St. Louis, Ill., elected in Houston, Tex., 1967; Charles M. Waugh of Muskegon Heights, Mich., elected in Washington, D.C., 1968; William E. Peterson of Chicago, Ill., elected in Durham, N.C., 1969; and Edward F. Bell, elected in New York, N.Y., 1970. *See also* LAWYERS.

NATIONAL BEAUTY CULTURALISTS' LEAGUE, INC. (NBCL) One of the largest Afro-American business organizations, the NBCL was founded in 1919 in Philadelphia, Pa. In 1975 it was based in Washington, D.C. It is involved in various activities, including the sponsorship of annual conventions, institutes of cosmetology, and trade shows, and aiding civic organizations. NBCL opposed discrimination on boards of beauty control, inspection, and examiners.

NATIONAL BIBLIOGRAPHIC AND RESEARCH CENTER An organization based in Washington, D.C., the National Bibliographic and Research Center was founded in 1965 with the purpose of furthering knowledge about Afro-Americans. *See also* BIBLIOGRAPHIES/BIOGRAPHIES/GUIDES.

NATIONAL BLACK POLITICAL CONVENTION Held as a unity meeting in Gary, Ind., in March 1972, the National Black Political Convention was organized largely through the efforts of Michigan Congressman Charles C. Diggs, Mayor Richard Hatcher of Gary, Ind., and Imamu Baraka (Leroi Jones). Attended by some 3,500 delegates from 44 states, the Virgin Islands, and the District of Columbia, the convention mapped national political strategies. A National Black Assembly was set up to meet in Chicago, Ill., in October of the same year; it met again in March 1973 in Detroit, Mich. The second National Black Political Convention met in 1974 in Little Rock, Ark., followed by meetings in 1975 of the assembly and another smaller group, the National Political Council. *See also* POLITICS.

NATIONAL BUSINESS LEAGUE The league was founded in 1900 by Booker T. Washington as the National Negro Business League to encourage the development of Afro-American business. It was the first effective national organization of its kind. Based upon Washington's philosophy of self-help, honesty, and thrift, the league had the support of one of the nation's wealthiest industrialists, Andrew Carnegie, a white philanthropist who admired Washington. Since the 1950s the league has been revitalized, claiming more than 13,000 members in 72 local chapters. The goals of the league are to provide ownership interest for minority citizens (local development corporations); to provide advice on mergers and consolidations (business planning); to generate adequate capital for profitable operations (loan packaging); and to provide technical assistance (such as market analysis and management training). *See also* BURRELL, BERKELEY GRAHAM; BUSINESS.

NATIONAL COMMITTEE AGAINST DISCRIMINATION IN HOUSING Founded in 1950, the National Committee develops research and programs aimed to end discrimination in housing. Its programs are in favor of open housing and open communities, against suburban segregation against blacks. Its offices are in Washington, D.C. *See also* HOUSING.

NATIONAL CONFERENCE OF ARTISTS (NCA) The NCA dates its annual conferences from 1958. Its early organizers were James D. Parks and Margaret Burroughs. Each annual conference in the late 1970s attracted several hundred participants. *See also* ARTISTS.

NATIONAL COUNCIL OF NEGRO WOMEN *See* WOMEN.

NATIONAL DEMOCRATIC PARTY OF ALABAMA (NDPA) A black-inspired political organization that was formed in 1967, the NDPA held its first annual convention in Birmingham, Ala. It has among its aims to end discrimination in Alabama, to guarantee the right of protest and equal protection of the law to all citizens, and to elect select candidates to public office. *See also* POLITICS.

NATIONAL DENTAL ASSOCIATION A professional organization embracing Afro-American dentists in 28 affiliates in the United States, the National Dental Association began as a section of the National Medical Association but became a national body following World War II. Strong state groups were already in existence, however, before the national body was formed. The body is representative of Afro-American dentists, who numbered about 2,100 in 1970. *See also* HEALTH.

REFERENCES: Studies of dentists and their profession are few or nonexistent. However, early activities are described in the pages of the *Journal of the National Medical Association*. One source designed to aid in the study of the Afro-American dentist is Kidd, Foster, *Profile of the Negro in American Dentistry*, Howard University Press, Washington, D.C., 1976.

NATIONAL ECONOMIC GROWTH AND RECONSTRUCTION ORGANIZATION (NEGRO) NEGRO is a self-help organization, founded in 1964 by Thomas W. Matthew, an Afro-American surgeon. Opposing welfare payments, NEGRO owns and operates several enterprises designed to employ those who would otherwise, according to its estimates, be welfare recipients.

NATIONAL EDUCATION ASSOCIATION *See* AMERICAN TEACHERS ASSOCIATION (ATA); EDUCATION.

NATIONALISM The origins and dimensions of Afro-American nationalism cannot be easily determined. Some historians point to colonizationist and separatist movements or schemes in the early nineteenth century as identifiable manifestations. The central black personalities in these early schemes were Paul Cuffe and later Martin R. Delany. Both took colonists to Africa, and the latter, a Harvard-educated physician, reputedly coined the phrase "Africa for the Africans." Colonizationist and separatist activities continued after the Civil War. For example, a group of blacks in South Carolina formed the Liberian Exodus and Joint Stock Steamship Company in 1877. Acquiring a ship, the *Azor*, they made the voyage to Liberia in 1878 with 206 passengers. Afterward, the company went bankrupt.

Henry McNeal Turner was the chief supporter of the back-to-Africa idea from 1876 until World War I. As a former Union soldier chaplain and Georgia state legislator, Turner was deeply affected by the increase of Jim Crow legislation, lynching, and what he regarded as the betrayal of Reconstruction. Constantly reiterating his determination never to take up arms again in defense of the United States, he wished misfortune and ruin on his native land. With scorn, he described the U.S. Constitution as a "dirty rag, a cheat, a libel and ought to be spit upon by every Negro in

the land." It was only in Africa, he argued, that a Negro could regenerate the continent culturally, religiously, and economically.

Turner inspired William Ellis, an Afro-American stock broker, who led an expedition to Ethiopia in 1903. A black ship captain, Harry Dean, was also a follower of Turner. A descendant of Paul Cuffe, Dean was proud of his African heritage and dreamed of establishing an African empire. He obtained a concession of land in Basutoland (now Lesotho) but eventually was swindled out of it.

About the time of Turner's death in 1915, a Ghanaian, Alfred C. Sam, started a colonization movement in Oklahoma. Growing racial oppression and the cotton depression of 1913 created an atmosphere in which Sam, allegedly an African chief, sold stock in his Akim Trading Company and formed several emigration clubs. In spite of opposition from *The Crisis*, the magazine of the National Association for the Advancement of Colored People (NAACP), most Afro-American newspapers, and the United States and British governments, Sam created so much enthusiasm for his schemes that thousands of Oklahoma blacks went to Houston, Tex., in the summer of 1914 to await the arrival of Sam's ship, the S.S. *Liberia*. In August, 60 of them sailed to Africa. Arriving in Ghana in 1915, Sam eventually lost his ship through the machinations of British officials and the movement collapsed. By this time, however, the rise of Marcus Garvey had eclipsed all other comparable ventures.

The Garvey Movement The Garvey Movement was fueled by many factors, including rising black discontent; black reaction to the revival of the Ku Klux Klan activities; depression in southern agriculture; and the disillusionment of the black veterans of World War I, who returned from "making the world safe for democracy" in Europe to face northern mobs at home. Garvey, a native Jamaican, exalted blackness and racial purity, showing an undisguised hatred of whites and mulattoes. Blackness, he contended, represented beauty and power. Like Turner, he argued that it was the height of stupidity and self-hatred for blacks to worship white deities. Consequently, he contended that God, Christ, and the Madonna were black; he favored the establishment of an African Church. Believing that there could be no justice for the Afro-American in America, Garvey dreamed of an independent nation in Africa.

Henry McNeal Turner. *(Library of Congress.)*

Garvey was a Pan-Africanist, and to achieve his aims he established the United Negro Improvement Association (UNIA) in Jamaica in 1914. A commanding, charismatic figure, Garvey insisted on "Africa for the Africans," and tried to build a sense of pride and racial solidarity through elaborate ceremonials, uniforms, parades, and titles—all of which were regarded as grandiloquence by his critics. To foster self-sufficiency, the UNIA published a newspaper, *Negro World,* and planned a chain of Afro-American grocery stores; restaurants; nurses corps; and, the largest venture, the Black Star Steamship Line. Designating himself as the provisional president of Africa, Garvey petitioned the League of Nations in 1922 to turn over the former German colonies in Africa to the UNIA. After his conviction for mail fraud in 1925 and his subsequent deportation in 1927, only a few weak organizations supported his ideas in the United States. Garvey's demise did not, however, end interest in Africa. It was during the 1920s, for instance, that Howard University's William Leo Hansberry began his pioneering research into African history and négritude, and Pan-Africanism appeared as a proper theme for art and literature in the Harlem Renaissance. Symbolic of this was Countee Cullen's celebrated 1925 poem, "Heritage."

Other manifestations surfaced in the early 1930s when blacks rallied to the cause of Liberia, whose independence was threatened for nonpayment of European debts and the existence of slave labor. Moreover, extremely proud of the oldest black self-governing nation in the world, Ethiopia, Afro-Americans in the 1930s began raising funds, organizing clubs, and holding mass meetings in sympathy for Ethiopia at the time when Italian armies overran the country in 1935 and 1936. Since World War II a dramatic increase in the Afro-American's sense of indentification with Africa has taken place as old European colonies have gained their independence, beginning with Ghana in 1957. This indentification was also part of a new movement of black consciousness.

Nation of Islam The urban misery of Afro-Americans combined with the Great Depression to produce one of the most significant manifestations of nationalism and separatism in 1930. In that year W. D. Farad Muhammad began organizing the Black Muslims. Farad defined his mission as the preparation of blacks for Armaged-

don, when the white forces of evil and the black forces of good would join in final battle. He contended that the word "Negro" was invented by whites to separate blacks from their African and Asian brothers. Since Christianity was the religion the white man used to enslave blacks, only in Islam could Negroes obtain justice. Civilization had begun with blacks, the chosen people of Allah. According to Farad, "black civilizations flourished [on the continent of Afro-Asia] long before the white man stood up on his hind legs and crept out of the caves of Europe." Further, the "Prophet" said, the white man is a devil by nature; he is the physical embodiment of the principle of evil, and he is incapable of doing good. Farad contended that blacks had been enslaved and robbed of their names and language and given Christian ones and forced to learn the English language, both of which were badges of slavery. Brainwashed by white teachers and lulled into submissiveness by Christianity, blacks were taught to hate themselves and worship a blue-eyed, blond Jesus as their God. The Muslims were taught that as the Lost Found Nation of Islam in the wilderness of North America, blacks were destined to throw off the manacles of slavery. In order to do this, the group stressed the study of African and Afro-American history in an effort to instill self-respect in black men. They insisted that black children be taught by black teachers and learn Arabic in their schools. An important part of their program emphasized protection and respect for black women. Frugality, hard work, and training for self-defense were preached. Since blacks were never protected by the American government, the Muslims rejected U.S. military service. At the same time, they believed in obedience to the laws of the land.

When Farad disappeared in 1934, 8,000 Black Muslims existed in the United States. The new leader, Elijah Poole (later Elijah Muhammad), had come to Detroit, Mich., with his family in the 1920s. Disillusioned by northern discrimination and especially by the fact that blacks were barred from jobs even if they had fought in the U.S. Army, Muhammad eagerly followed the tenets of Farad. Under Elijah Muhammad, the movement spread quickly to Chicago, Ill., and by 1960 there were 80 Islamic temples. Racism, widespread in law enforcement, brought many converts to the Muslims, who proselytized actively on the streets or even in prisons. Their official publication, *Muhammad Speaks,* enjoyed a circulation larger than that of any black newspaper.

The Muslim tenets attracted those Afro-Americans who had been exposed to discrimination in northern cities where, escaping the South, they had dreamed of finding the promised land. Stressing racial pride, the Muslims provided a release for the black man's hatred for and disillusionment in white America. For the Muslims, the enemy was no longer concealed in such abstractions as the "system" or the "establishment": he was the white man, a "blue-eyed devil."

It is indicative of the failure of America to integrate Afro-Americans into the nation that blacks have often faced a conflict of loyalties to America, to each other, and to Africa. W. E. Du Bois summed up the essential conflict in loyalty when he wrote that blacks always felt their twoness: "an American, a Negro, two souls, two thoughts, two unreconciled strivings; two warring ideals in one dark body, whose dogged strength alone keeps it from being torn asunder." It was almost inevitable, given the pervasiveness of racism and discrimination, that many Afro-Americans would favor some form of separatism and racial isolation. NAACP Executive Secretary James Weldon Johnson, for example, once wrote that there were times when "the most persistent integrationist becomes an isolationist, when he curses the white world and consigns it to hell." Separatism, for many, has represented the only apparent alternative. After viewing the growth of Jim Crow and the economic oppression of Afro-Americans, Du Bois reached the conclusion that they "must be a thing apart." See also BLACK POWER; COLONIZATION; GARVEY, MARCUS; MUHAMMAD, ELIJAH; MUSLIMS; PAN-AFRICANISM; UNITED NEGRO IMPROVEMENT ASSOCIATION (UNIA).

REFERENCES: Bittle, W. E., G. Geis, and D. F. Parker, The Longest Way Home: Chief Alfred C. Sam's Back-to-Africa Movement, Wayne State University Press, Detroit, 1964; Clarke, John Henrik, "The New Afro-American Nationalism," Freedomways, vol. 1, no. 3, pp. 285–95, Fall 1961; Cronon, Edmund D., Black Moses: The Story of Marcus Garvey and the Universal Negro Improvement Association, University of Wisconsin Press, Madison, 1962; Fax, Elton C., Garvey: The Story of a Pioneer Black Nationalist, Dodd, Mead, New York, 1972; Miller, Floyd J., The Search for a Black Nationality: Black Colonization and Emigration, 1787–1863, University of Illinois Press, Urbana, 1975; Redkey, Edwin S., Black Exodus: Black Nationalist and Back-to-Africa Movements, 1890–1910, Yale University Press, New Haven, 1970; and Vincent, Theodore G., Black Power and the Garvey Movement, Simon and Schuster, New York, 1971.

NATIONAL LINK, INC. A social and fraternal organization, National Link, Inc., has substantially increased in popularity during the 1960s and 1970s.

NATIONAL MEDICAL ASSOCIATION (NMA) A professional body composed predominantly of Afro-American physicians, the NMA was founded in 1895 at the Cotton States and International Exposition held in Atlanta, Ga. Ironically, the address of Booker T. Washington at this affair has been so publicized as to obscure the founding meeting, which was held in the First Congregational Church and presided over by I. Garland Penn, an Afro-American journalist and national civic leader in charge of the Negro division of the exposition. About 12 physicians were present, including Miles Vardahurst Lynk, who had urged the establishment of "an Association of medical men of color, national in character," in his Medical and Surgical Observer of December 1892, the first national medical journal for blacks. In 1909 the NMA brought out its own official Journal of the National Medical Association, which appeared quarterly until 1939 and bimonthly after then. After 1949 the Journal was edited by W. Montague Cobb, whose wide-ranging editorials treated such topics as medical history (mainly biography), the recruitment of youths for medicine, civil rights, and public health programs. These editorials often reflected the opinions of the NMA as a body.

The NMA was incorporated in St. Louis, Mo., in 1923; the Woman's Auxiliary was organized in Philadelphia, Pa., in 1936. The organization included dentists and pharmacists in its membership during a great part of its history. Membership in the NMA in the early 1970s was about 6,000, distributed throughout 48 states and several foreign countries, in about 70 local and state chapters.

Presidents of the NMA since 1895 are listed below:

PRESIDENTS OF THE NATIONAL MEDICAL ASSOCIATION

Robert F. Boyd, Nashville, Tenn. 1895–97
H. T. Noel, Nashville, Tenn. 1898–1900
O. D. Porter, Bowling Green, Ky. 1901–02
F. A. Stewart, Nashville, Tenn. 1903
Charles V. Roman, Dallas, Tex. 1904
John E. Hunter, Lexington, Ky. 1905
R. E. Jones, Richmond, Va. 1906
Nathan F. Mossell, Philadelphia, Pa. 1907
W. H. Wright, Baltimore, Md. 1908
P. A. Johnson, New York, N.Y. 1909
Marcus F. Wheatland, Newport, R.I. 1910
Austin M. Curtis, Washington, D.C. 1911

PRESIDENTS OF THE NATIONAL MEDICAL ASSOCIATION

H. F. Gamble, Charleston, W.Va. 1912
John A. Kenny, Sr., Tuskegee Institute, Ala. 1913
A. M. Brown, Birmingham, Ala. 1914
F. S. Hargraves, Wilson, N.C. 1915
Ulysses G. Dailey, Chicago, Ill. 1916
D. W. Byrd, Norfolk, Va. 1917
George W. Cabaniss, Washington, D.C. 1918
D. A. Ferguson, Richmond, Va. 1919
J. W. Jones, Winston-Salem, N.C. 1920
John P. Turner, Philadelphia, Pa. 1921
H. M. Green, Knoxville, Tenn. 1922
J. Edward Perry, Kansas City, Mo. 1923
John O. Plummer, Raleigh, N.C. 1924
Michael O. Dumas, Washington, D.C. 1925
Walter G. Alexander, Orange, N.J. 1926
Carl G. Roberts, Chicago, Ill. 1927
C. V. Freeman, Jacksonville, Fla. 1928
T. Spotuas Burwell, Philadelphia, Pa. 1929
L. A. West, Memphis, Tenn. 1930
W. H. Higgins, Providence, R.I. 1931
Peter M. Murray, New York, N.Y. 1932
G. Hamilton Francis, Norfolk, Va. 1933
Midian O. Bousfield, Chicago, Ill. 1934
John H. Hale, Nashville, Tenn. 1935
W. Harry Barnes, Philadelphia, Pa. 1936
Roscoe C. Giles, Chicago, Ill. 1937
Lyndon M. Hill, Atlanta, Ga. 1938
George W. Bowles, York, Pa. 1939
Albert W. Dumas, Sr., Natchez, Miss. 1940
Arthur N. Vaughn, St. Louis, Mo. 1941
Henry Eugene Lee, Houston, Tex. 1942
T. Manuel Smith, Chicago, Ill. 1943
Emory I. Robinson, Los Angeles, Calif. 1944–45
Walter A. Younge, St. Louis, Mo. 1946
J. A. C. Lattimore, Louisville, Ky. 1947
C. Austin Whittier, San Antonio, Tex. 1948
C. Herbert Marshall, Washington, D.C. 1949
Henry H. Walker, Nashville, Tenn. 1950
Joseph C. Gathings, Washington, D.C. 1951
Whittier C. Atkinson, Coatesville, Pa. 1952
A. Porter Davis, Kansas City, Kans. 1953
Matthew Walker, Nashville, Tenn. 1954
A. C. Terrence, Opelousas, La. 1955
T. R. M. Howard, Chicago, Ill. 1956
Arthur M. Townsend, St. Louis, Mo. 1957
R. Stillmon Smith, Macon, Ga. 1958
Edward C. Mazique, Washington, D.C. 1959
James T. Aldrich, St. Louis, Mo. 1960
Vaughan C. Mason, New York, N.Y. 1961
John A. Kenney, Jr., Washington, D.C. 1962
Kenneth W. Clement, Cleveland, Ohio 1963
W. Montague Cobb, Washington, D.C. 1964
Leonidas H. Berry, Chicago, Ill. 1965
John L. S. Holloman, Jr., New York, N.Y. 1966
Lionel F. Swan, Detroit, Mich. 1967
James M. Wittico, Jr., St. Louis, Mo. 1968
Julius W. Hill, Los Angeles, Calif. 1969
W. T. Armstrong, Rocky Mount, N.C. 1970
Emerson C. Walden, Baltimore, Md. 1971
Edmund Casey, Cincinnati, Ohio 1972
Emery Rand, Charlotte, N.C. 1973
Vernal Cave, New York, N.Y. 1974
Jasper Williams, Chicago, Ill. 1975
Arthur Coleman, Oakland, Calif. 1976

See also HEALTH; PHYSICIANS.

REFERENCES: See also REFERENCES under PHYSICIANS. For a study of the characteristics of members of the NMA, see an article by George E. Schwarz and Montague S. Lawrence in the *Journal of the National Medical Association*, vol. 62, no. 1, January 1970.

NATIONAL NEGRO CONGRESS The National Negro Congress was founded in 1935 at Howard University (Washington, D.C.) with the purpose of forming a union of organizations that were interested in the economic betterment of Afro-Americans. The coalition included religious, labor, civic, and fraternal groups. At its first meeting in Chicago, Ill., A. Philip Randolph was elected president and John P. Davis, executive secretary. The aims of the organization were to oppose discrimination and deportation proceedings against foreign-born blacks; to encourage good will between foreign-born and native blacks; to support the foreign-born in their struggles at home; and to foster improved relations among blacks around the world. Although members of the Communist Party were among the founders of the congress, it was not until 1940 that Communist influence was predominant. Membership at that point began to dwindle, and many of the national leaders, including Randolph and Ralph Bunche, left the organization.

NATIONAL NEGRO CONVENTION The first National Negro Convention was held in 1830 in Philadelphia, Pa., "to devise ways and means for the bettering of our condition"; to resist all forms of oppression; to promote universal education; and to encourage Afro-Americans to aspire to mechanical, agricultural, and professional pursuits. Many conventions were held from 1830 to 1865, and several were convened in 1865. After the Civil War, the conventions demanded citizenship rights, the right to vote, fair wages, equal education, and the repeal of discriminatory laws. See also AFRO-AMERICAN HISTORY: FREE NEGROES, 1600s–1860; COLONIZATION.

NATIONAL NEWSPAPER PUBLISHERS ASSOCIATION See NEWSPAPERS.

NATIONAL PHARMACEUTICAL ASSOCIATION This organization grew out of the pharmaceutical section of the National Medical Association (NMA) in the late 1940s. Many local groups of Afro-American pharmacists, however, had originally formed at the turn of the century, such as a group in New York City. The official publication of the association is the *Journal of the National Pharmaceutical Association*, first published in 1954. The seat of the journal is at Howard University (Washington, D.C.); its editor in 1977 was Chauncey I. Cooper, a professor of pharmacy at the university and executive secretary of the association. *See also* HEALTH; PHYSICIANS.

NATIONAL RELIGIOUS TRAINING SCHOOL AND CHAUTAUQUA *See* NORTH CAROLINA CENTRAL UNIVERSITY.

NATIONAL SCHOLARSHIP SERVICE AND FUND FOR NEGRO STUDENTS Founded in New York City in 1948 to help black high school students obtain scholarships to institutions of higher learning, the service is still based in New York City but also maintains a regional office in Atlanta, Ga.

NATIONAL URBAN LEAGUE The National Urban League is an interracial, nonprofit, and nonpartisan community service organization that uses the tools and methods of social work, economics, law, and other disciplines to secure equal opportunities in all sectors of American society for Afro-Americans and other minorities. Its mission is to eliminate segregation in the United States and to help blacks and other minorities share equally in the responsibilities and rewards of full citizenship.

The Urban League has been in existence since 1910 when the Committee on Urban Conditions Among Negroes was established to help black migrants from the rural South find jobs and housing, acquire more education, and adjust to the rigors of an urban environment. A year later this committee merged with three others: the Association for the Protection of Colored Women; the Committee for Improving the Industrial Conditions of Negroes; and the National League for the Protection of Colored Women. These together formed the National League on Urban Conditions Among Negroes, a co-founder of which was George Edmund Haynes. The name was shortened several years later to the National Urban League.

The scope of the agency's services has widened since its inception. From a relatively narrow base of assisting migrants to adjust to life in the North, the league has now become involved in basic problems endemic to the urban and rural poor.

The Urban League is governed nationally by an interracial board of trustees composed of outstanding men and women from the professional, business, industrial, civic, religious, and labor communities. As required by the bylaws, 25 percent of the board's membership is under 30 years of age.

Under the Terms of Affiliation, local Urban Leagues have their own boards that are responsible for local budgets and for adapting national policy to local needs and conditions. The local boards resemble the national board in makeup.

The national headquarters is in New York, New York. There are five regional offices: Eastern—New York, N.Y.; Mideastern—Akron, Ohio; Midwestern—St. Louis, Mo.; Western—Los Angeles, Calif.; and Southern—Atlanta, Ga. Located in Washington, D.C., are a Washington, D.C., bureau and a research department. On the local level, the National Urban League had 101 affiliates located in 34 states and the District of Columbia in the mid-1970's. *See also* BERRY, EDWIN CARLOS; GRANGER, LESTER B.; HAYNES, GEORGE EDMUND; HILL, T. ARNOLD; JOHNSON, CHARLES SPURGEON; JORDAN, VERNON; JONES, EUGENE KINCKLE; YOUNG, WHITNEY MOORE, JR.

REFERENCES: For a brief popular and illustrated historical account, see Simms, William R. (ed.), *The Urban League Story, 1910–1960*, New York, National Urban League, 1961. For a serious, scholarly account with an excellent bibliography, see Strickland, Arvarh E., *History of the Chicago Urban League*, University of Illinois Press, Urbana, 1966. *See also* Parrish, Guichard and Lester Brooks, *Blacks in the City: A History of the National Urban League* (1971) and Weiss, Nancy Joan, *The National Urban League, 1910-1940* (1974).

NATION OF ISLAM *See* CHURCHES; MUSLIMS; NATIONALISM.

NAVY *See* WARS.

NEAL, EARL L. (1928–   ), lawyer; born in Chicago, Ill. Neal received a B.A. degree from the University of Illinois in 1949 and his J.D. degree from the University of Michigan in 1952. He was admitted to the Michigan bar in 1953. Soon after his admission to the Illinois bar in 1955, he joined the staff of the Chicago Land Clearance Commission as associate counsel, a post he held for three years. In 1970 Neal was named special counsel for the city of Chicago; in 1972, special attorney for the Metropolitan Sanitary District; and later, special attorney for the corporation council of the city of Chicago. A private practitioner in Chicago, Neal was a member of several boards of trustees and civic organizations, and served as general counsel for the Service Federal Savings and Loan Corporation.

NEGRO *See* ONOMATOLOGY.

NEGRO ENSEMBLE COMPANY A theater group in New York City, the Negro Ensemble Company was formed in 1967 to establish a black-oriented repertory company and a training ground for Afro-American actors, while simultaneously increasing employment opportunities for black actors. Douglas Turner Ward, artistic director, and Robert Hooks, executive director, planned a pilot season to include Peter Weiss' *Song of the Lusitania Bogey*; a revival of Ray Lawler's *Summer of the 17th Doll*; Wole Soginka's *Kongi's Harvest*; and Louis Sapin's *Daddy Goodness*, adapted by Richard Wright. The second season was highlighted by the well-received *Ceremonies in Dark Old Men* by Lonne Elder, III; subsequent seasons brought such plays as *The Sty of the Blind Pig* by Phillip Hayes Dean (1971) and *The River Niger* by Joseph A. Walker (1973). *See also* LITERATURE: DRAMA/THEATER.

NEGRO FOOT, VA. An officially designated community in the state of Virginia until the 1940s, where, reputedly, a black lynching victim lost one of his feet to a souvenir hunter.

NELL, WILLIAM COOPER (1816–74), historian; born in Boston, Mass. Nell studied law in the office of William I. Bowditch, but when it came time to apply for admission to the bar he refused on grounds that he did not want to take an oath supporting the Constitution of the United States, which he felt compromised the powers of slaves. Thus he became affiliated with the antislavery movement, organizing meetings and lecturing for it. At the same time Nell was active in the movement in Massachusetts to do away with separate public schools for Afro-American children. Concurrently developing some literary skills, he began in 1851 to serve as assistant to Frederick Douglass, who published the *North Star* in Rochester, N.Y. That same year, Nell's own pamphlet, *Services of Colored Americans in the Wars of 1776 and 1812*, was published. Four years later he wrote *The Colored Patriots of the American Revolution*. In 1861 Nell was appointed postal clerk in Boston, Mass., the first Afro-American to hold a federal position. *See also* HISTORIANS.

NELSON, ALICE RUTH MOORE DUNBAR (1875–1935), author, social worker; born Alice Ruth Moore in New Orleans, La. Nelson studied at Straight College (New Orleans, La.; now Dillard University), the University of Pennsylvania, Cornel University (Ithaca, N.Y.), and the School of Industrial Arts (Philadelphia, Pa.), before marrying Paul Laurence Dunbar in 1898. Twelve years after Dunbar's death in 1904, she married Robert J. Nelson. Alice Nelson was a probation and parole officer, and served as associate editor of the *AME Review* of the African Methodist Episcopal Church and as editor of the Wilmington, Del., *Advocate* for three years. A weekly contributor to the Associated Negro Press, she was also executive secretary of the American Interracial Peace Committee in 1928. Her books include a volume of short stories, *Goodness of St. Rocque* (1899), and two books that she edited, *Masterpieces of Negro Eloquence* (1914) and *The Dunbar Speaker* (1920). *See also* DUNBAR, PAUL LAURENCE.

NELSON, WILLIAM STUART (1895–), clergyman, educator; born in Paris, Ky. Nelson received a B.A. degree from Howard University (Washington, D.C.) in 1920, his B.D. degree from Yale University in 1924, and did further study at the Sorbonne and at the Protestant Theological Seminary (Paris, France) from 1921 to 1922. Nelson was dean of the School of Religion at Howard University from 1940 to 1969, and later became a vice-president of the university. He was editor and author of many publications, and his books include *Bases of World Understanding* (1949) and *La Race Noir dans la Democratic Americaine* (1921).

NEWCOMBE, DON *See* ATHLETES: BASEBALL.

NEWSOME, LIONEL H. (1919–), educator; born in Wichita Falls, Tex. Newsome received a B.A. degree from Lincoln University (Jefferson, Mo.), an M.A. degree from the University of Michigan (Ann Arbor), and his Ph.D. degree from Washington University (St. Louis). He taught at Lincoln, at Morehouse College (Atlanta, Ga.), and at Southern University (Baton Rouge, La.). Newsome was president of Barber-Scotia College (Concord, N.C.) from 1964 to 1966, of Johnson C. Smith University (Charlotte, N.C.) from 1969 to 1972, and of Central State University (Wilberforce, Ohio) after 1972. He served on the National Defense Executive Reserve and as chairman of the Georgia Council of Human Relations, and was an executive council member of the Atlanta Negro Voters League. A former president of Alpha Phi Alpha fraternity, Newsome received an honorary doctorate from Davidson College (Davidson, N.C.).

NEWSON, MOSES J. *See* NEWSPAPERS: CONTEMPORARY.

NEWSPAPERS

History and Development During the three decades prior to the Civil War, a number of Afro-Americans published newspapers, all of which devoted their primary attention to the abolitionist movement. They were published by free Afro-Americans living in the North and were read as much by white supporters of the movement as by blacks. Some 30 newspapers are known to have been published for at least a short time during the antebellum period. John B. Russwurm and Samuel Cornish are credited with beginning the first Afro-American newspaper, *Freedom's Journal,* which lasted for three years (1827–30) in the state of New York. Perhaps the best-known paper during the antebellum period was Frederick Douglass' *North Star.* Having escaped from slavery in Maryland, Douglass became known as the editor of the New York *Star* and as a leading spokesman against human bondage. Virtually all Afro-American newspapers that began before 1860 lasted only a few years, primarily because of financial difficulties, and in that respect they set a pattern that characterized their successors until as late as the beginning of World War I (1914).

Although Afro-American newspapers failed to flourish during the Civil War years, the Afro-American gained his freedom and a renewed hope of becoming a full participant in American society with the advent of Reconstruction. However, the promises and hopes of Reconstruction were not fulfilled sufficiently. Thus, between Reconstruction and World War I, when integration into the total community seemed, at best, a distant dream, Afro-Americans displayed much concern for group uplift and cohesion. Many black leaders placed special emphasis on such institutions as the church, the lodge, and the press, that would create racial solidarity. All three of these groups did eventually help to provide a structure within the black community and to provide an outlet for individual newspapers.

By the turn of the twentieth century, the Afro-American newspaper had become primarily a business venture, and a hazardous one at that. Editors found it difficult to obtain advertise-

Cover of special handbook authored by Sherman Briscoe and issued by the National Newspaper Publishers Association (NNPA). Insets show Samuel E. Cornish (left) and John B. Russwurm (right) surrounded by mastheads of historic and contemporary newspapers/magazines. (*Courtesy of Sherman Briscoe and Constance L. Britt, National Newspaper Publishers Association.*)

ments, and they could not afford to reject those of doubtful propriety. This often meant the acceptance of advertisements for useless patent medicines and other panaceas. Political parties provided an additional source of income. The loyalty of the Afro-American to the Republican Party (until the 1930s) made this source more lucrative in the two-party North than in the one-party South. Such dubious sources of income became all the more important to the Afro-American press, which did not have access to the Associated Press and to "boiler plate," both of which had proven invaluable to white weeklies as a source of both news and advertising.

Although hundreds of black newspapers began publication during the late nineteenth and early twentieth centuries, few became successful business ventures. Afro-American weeklies in operation in 1914 included: none founded before 1880, 9 founded in the 1880s, and 19 founded in the 1890s. The tendency of black newspapers to grow in numbers and for each to disappear soon after creation was shared with the white weeklies of the period, but Afro-American papers showed more rapid rates.

Booker T. Washington, the dominant black leader at the turn of the century, frequently gave financial aid to Afro-American newspapers that supported him and his viewpoint. On the other hand, he sought to manipulate those who opposed his views. When he did assist, this assistance came largely from white groups and individuals with whom he had influence. It may seem amazing how anxiously black editors sought financial aid from Washington since his subsidies seldom were substantial. However, this reflected both the desperate financial circumstances of many editors and the great prestige and power of Washington. Even the Republican National Committee contributed financial aid in support of his program of subsidies.

The involvement between Washington and the editors of the Afro-American press constituted a two-way street. While his influence with the white power structure proved helpful to black editors financially, they, in turn, were invaluable to him. Through them he could mold Afro-American public opinion on issues and also create an atmosphere favorable to his leadership. He was fully conscious of the contributions the press made to his program. Moreover, most of the editors genuinely agreed with Washington's doctrines. As self-made businessmen themselves, they believed in his concept of self-help. Further, as products of the middle class, they

Robert S. Abbott. *(Chicago Daily Defender.)*

were committed to order and stability, and they were anxious to do anything they could to perpetuate his kind of leadership.

The second decade of the twentieth century produced major changes in the black community. The census report of 1910 indicated that 90 percent of all Afro-Americans still lived in 11 southern states. During the next decade, a large-scale migration, primarily to border and northern cities, reduced that figure to 80 percent. This migration had a great impact on the character of the Afro-American community in the northern cities. Afro-Americans now sought new freedoms and opportunities previously unknown to them.

Afro-American migration and militancy intensified with the coming of World War I. Even in the segregated U.S. Armed Forces, Afro-American troops traveled and associated with whites as never before. At the same time, the needs of war production made jobs available to Afro-American workers at home who would have been excluded in a more crowded job market.

These changes naturally affected the Afro-American press. Seventy percent of the black newspapers founded before 1910 had been located in the South. By 1945, 52 percent of all black papers were being published in northern cities. Two Chicago, Ill., journalists led the way in making the Afro-American press more comparable to that of the white community. Robert S. Abbott made his Chicago *Defender,* a weekly established in 1905, into one of the most successful black newspapers. The key to his success lay in his use of sensationalism in both content and format. William Randolph Hearst and Joseph Pulitzer had already found this technique lucrative in the white metropolitan press.

In 1919 another Chicago journalist, Claude A. Barnett, organized the Associated Negro Press (ANP). Although his news service was more amateurish than the Associated Press, which had served white papers for several decades, it did facilitate news reporting. Every newspaper that belonged to the ANP served as a local bureau in its community to provide news to the national organization. The agency had no reporters of its own until World War II. However, it did offer increased national coverage to Afro-American papers to which it had previously been unavailable. However, for many years black newspapers continued to obtain most of their stories through volunteer reporters.

Even more significant after 1914 were the changes in the militancy of black papers. Gunnar

Myrdal contends that "it was the Negro press which made the northward migration into a protest movement." Most northern black editors around the turn of the century were descendants of families that had lived in the North more than a generation. The new breed of editors consisted of men who had migrated from the South themselves and who were prepared to offer militant leadership to others who followed them. These new editors expressed themselves boldly on a wide variety of subjects of special significance to Afro-Americans. They insisted upon complete social equality in the areas of education, jobs, housing, and the law. Many of them indicated a frank admiration for the new Bolshevik regime in Russia and for Marcus Garvey's black nationalism, often criticizing members of their own race who were more cautious than they. These editors also expressed concern for the oppressed of all races and all nations.

Thus on the surface it may seem strange that the Afro-American press remained generally critical of labor unions as late as the 1930s. However, it should be noted that this opposition did not extend to the Pullman porters' union. Efforts in the late 1920s to organize locals of this union had led to charges in the white papers of Communism and racketeering, but many black editors spoke out strongly in defense of the union and its leaders. It may well be that discrimination shown against black workers, who were excluded from membership in many unions, was more responsible for opposition to unionism by the black press than was any underlying economic bias.

In the highly sensational black news media, lynchings easily received the most intensive treatment. The second decade of the twentieth century opened with a revival of the Ku Klux Klan and closed with race riots triggered by the tensions of World War I. For the next two decades the Afro-American press gave major attention to atrocities committed against blacks in every part of the country. Every such case gave rise to strong editorials against lynching, in support of law and order, and often to demands for a federal antilynching bill. When, by the 1940s, a decline in lynching was noted, the Afro-American press took most of the credit for itself.

In the decades following World War I, black papers acquired an increased interest in international affairs. While this reflected the broadened horizons of some editors, it also suggested that they conceived of the race issue in a broader context. They felt that the problems of colored peoples in all parts of the world were also their own. (This was particularly so during the Ethiopian crisis of 1935.) Many editors also spoke often of the impact of American race relations on the nation's image abroad.

The same period witnessed a gradual decline in the commitment of the Afro-American and his press to the Republican Party. The old debt of gratitude they had long felt for emancipation had been more than paid. Afro-American voters were now encouraged to support parties and candidates only when they were "right" on the race issue. At first only Republicans seemed to be "right," but by the 1930s more and more Afro-American editors began endorsing Democrats.

The increasing political independence of the black press stemmed both from problems of race and of poverty. Even though relatively little was done during the administrations of President Franklin D. Roosevelt for integration, President Roosevelt did champion responsible federal action on behalf of those who were not sharing fully in the rewards of the economy. Since the Afro-American had been the first to lose his job when the Depression came, programs to stimulate employment were especially meaningful to him.

Black editors became increasingly conscious of what politics could do for them, and also of what they could offer in return. During the time that most Afro-Americans lived in the South and were denied the franchise, they were a constituency that could exert little influence. Now, having moved northward to the great urban areas that were rapidly becoming the center of population and of power, the Afro-American found himself in a new political relationship.

The decade from 1937 to 1947 produced still another important change in the black press. While the Great Depression of the early 1930s had temporarily slowed the growth of such papers, the decade after 1937 brought them to a peak of circulation and sophistication. During that ten-year period the combined circulation of Afro-American newspapers doubled to two million readers. A marked trend for a few large papers in major cities to replace small local publications also occurred. Like its white counterpart, the black press became big business. Although the appearance of the surviving small papers still remained distinctly inferior, the larger publications began to look much like the major white weeklies.

Most major black papers in the decade from 1937 to 1947 began to publish national editions.

Sixty percent of the circulation of black papers now extended across state lines. In 1947 the Chicago *Defender* had a local circulation of 62,300 and a nonlocal circulation of 131,600. More than 66 percent of this nonlocal total went to subscribers in the South.

Perhaps no development highlighted the growth of the Afro-American press in the decade after 1937 more than did the formation of the National Negro Press Association in 1939. This organization reflected a desire on the part of publishers and editors to band together in support of causes that were meaningful to their race. They also hoped to improve the content of their papers and to seek solutions to common professional problems.

Traditionally, black newspapers had been distributed through the mail and at newsstands in large cities. White distributors had been unwilling to handle them, a serious impediment to circulation expansion. However, in 1938 LeRoy Brannic founded the Great Eastern News Corporation in New York City with outlets in cities throughout the country. It was controlled and operated entirely by Afro-Americans.

Increased circulation was followed by improvements in production. By 1938 the Scott Syndicate in Atlanta, Ga., was printing 32 different papers. Contact was maintained with the local community by retaining a small staff there, but the advantages of mass operation were gained in shared news, features, and printing operations.

Quality and uniformity were further enhanced through the growth of news agencies and syndicated columns. The National Feature Service, Calvin's Newspaper Service, Crusader News Service, Tuskegee Institute Service, and the Press Service of the National Association for the Advancement of Colored People (NAACP) all provided feature stories and syndicated columns to member papers. Some of the more successful papers had their own New York reporters, and a few even maintained foreign correspondents. Along with the Associated Negro Press, these innovations did much to broaden the horizons and to improve the quality of local papers.

Improvements also came through the hiring of better qualified staffs. Although many of the older, self-made men still retained ownership of newspapers, they were now able to hire college-trained professional journalists as editors and reporters. The greater number of blacks receiving higher educations and the improved salaries being paid by the papers made this possible. The expanded use of photography and the acquisition of expensive printing equipment were other advancements.

As Afro-American newspapers grew in size and quality, they became increasingly concerned about income. The typical white newspaper obtains about two-thirds of its income from advertising and one-third from subscriptions. With the black press, these proportions have traditionally been reversed.

The most lucrative sources of advertising in white newspapers have been "want ads" and advertisements for products having an appeal to the whole society. However, the economic status of most Afro-Americans limited their purchasing power, and thus advertising occupied only a minor part of the makeup of most Afro-American papers, while 75 percent of them had none at all. Most national advertisers seem to have felt that white periodicals reached the Afro-American market satisfactorily—and they clearly doubted that market's overall value as well.

As in early decades, some advertising in the Afro-American press continued to publicize worthless products and was clearly directed to unsophisticated readers. Indeed, evidence exists that much of the Afro-American reading public strongly objected to the caliber of advertising accepted by their papers. As one of its earliest stated goals, the National Negro Press Association announced its intention to improve both the quality and quantity of advertising appearing in the pages of its membership publications. During the 1940s progress was made toward realizing this goal.

As early as the mid-1930s, the possibilities of the Afro-American market became apparent to a few observers. Burns Roper of the Elmo Roper research organization discussed this potential in 1934, contending that the Afro-American market had an ultimate annual value of $30 billion, of which only about $2 billion was currently being realized. Roper felt that the continued expansion of Afro-American economic activity would make the realization of this market value achievable in the near future.

In the early 1940s two black agencies emphasizing cooperative efforts to increase advertising in the black press made their appearance. Both of these—United Newspapers, Inc., and Associated Publishers, Inc.—had their headquarters in New York City, and both sought to increase the use of the Afro-American press by nationally known corporations. In fact, both agencies grew rapidly and became highly effective in obtaining advertising.

In the late 1930s and 1940s, the black press continued to speak out for the rights of its own people. The most concerted effort by editors in this direction was their crusade for increased job opportunities. They fought for the elimination of discrimination in defense industries during World War II, arguing that a moral victory must come at home as well as on the overseas battle-fronts if American military triumph was to be really meaningful. This campaign evoked a charge of "traitorism" from Westbrook Pegler, whose syndicated column was carried widely by the metropolitan press.

By the 1940s, however, the black publisher had become more a merchant than a protest lead-er. As Afro-American newspapers grew in size, publishers became increasingly aware that cru-sades for social justice might frighten away both the investor and the advertiser. While most Afro-American newspapers continued to support pro-grams for the advancement of their race, they nonetheless became less active in initiating such crusades.

No longer did editorial columns explore the merits of extremist movements as their predeces-sors had in the 1920s. Writing in 1948, V. V. Oak suggested that the Afro-American newspaper was radical only on the race issue and otherwise reflected the viewpoint of any other big busi-ness.

This conservatism can be seen in the attitude of black newspapers during the 1940s toward labor unions. As late as the 1930s the black papers objected to unions only when they dis-criminated against black workers. Their position had hardened considerably by the mid-1940s. The new viewpoint found expression at the June 1947 meeting of the National Negro Press Asso-ciation. Meeting in Detroit, Mich., one of the strongest union cities in the country, that body passed a resolution supporting the Taft-Hartley bill. By a sizable vote, it urged Senator Robert A. Taft to bend every effort to see to it that President Harry S. Truman's veto of the measure was over-riden. This was done despite the strong support of civil rights causes currently being given by large segments of organized labor.

By the mid-1950s some observers were begin-ning to suggest that the Afro-American press might face an uncertain future. Circulation, still the chief source of income, was dropping rapid-ly. The Chicago *Defender* lost 3,000 subscribers from 1952 to 1955, and its circulation by then was down to 49,000 (Chicago's total black popu-lation was 700,000). The *Defender's* national edition had dropped from 62,000 to 37,000 since 1947. The national circulation of the *Afro-Amer-ican* of Baltimore, Md., had lost 50,000 of its 230,000 subscribers by the end of World War II.

Professional journalists and scholars alike were beginning to ask the question, "Can the Negro press survive?" Had this institution, which had contributed so much to the leader-ship of the Afro-American community in its struggle for full equality, begun a steady decline that would lead ultimately to its extinction? Writing in 1944 when the Afro-American press still had a large circulation, Gunnar Myrdal spoke of it in highly complimentary terms, call-ing it an agency of education and power that "influences a large proportion of the Negro pop-ulation."

As early as 1948 V. V. Oak warned that the Afro-American press had lost much of its influ-ence. Unless Afro-American newspapers began to express a real "social consciousness," he felt that they would decline in status. John H. John-son, the editor of the famous Afro-American magazine *Ebony*, expressed much the same viewpoint in an article in *Time* magazine in 1955. He contended that "the Negro press had depended too much on emotion and racial pride." He asserted that the press was originally a product of a segregated community, but now that this segregated community was being inte-grated into the total society, the press must either adjust or face extinction.

On the other hand, one of the leading scholars in the field of Afro-American journalism expressed a more optimistic attitude in 1966. Professor Armistead Scott Pride of Lincoln Uni-versity (Jefferson City, Mo.) felt that the Afro-American newspaper would continue to flour-ish. He held that the Afro-American would con-tinue to identify himself generally with a black community and that such a community would indeed support its own press. Although white dailies were increasing their coverage of Afro-American news under integration, Pride main-tained that they could not hope to offer the in-depth coverage the black press gave to its com-munity. The years subsequent to Pride's remarks have tended to confirm his optimism: the con-temporary black press in the United States is very much a virile institution. *See also* ABBOTT,

John H. Sengstacke.
(Chicago Daily Defender.)

Robert Sengstacke; Afro-American History: Reconstruction to Revolt, 1877–1977; Business; Douglass, Frederick; National Association for the Advancement of Colored People (NAACP).

REFERENCES: No single volume definitively covers the history and development of the Afro-American press. There are, however, four major works on the subject: Detweiler, Frederick, *The Negro Press in the United States,* University of Chicago Press, Chicago, 1922; Oak, V. V., *The Negro Newspaper,* Antioch University Press., Yellow Springs, 1948; Penn, I. Garland, *The Afro-American Press,* Willey and Co., Springfield, 1891; and Wolseley, Richard, *The Black Press, U.S.A.,* Iowa State University Press, Ames, 1971, with a helpful and representative bibliography, pp. 343–52. Several excellent articles are noteworthy: Fleming, G. James, "108 Years of the Negro Press," *Opportunity,* March 1935; Gordon, Eugene, "The Negro Press," *The Annals of the American Academy of Social and Political Sciences,* November 1928; Henderson, Lewis H., "The Negro Press As A Social Instrument," *Journal of Negro Education,* Spring 1951; Meier, August, "Booker T. Washington and the Negro Press," *Journal of Negro History,* January 1953; Pride, Armistead Scott, "Negro Newspapers: Yesterday, Today, and Tomorrow," *Journalism Quarterly,* Spring 1951; Thornbrough, Emma Lou, "American Negro Newspapers, 1880–1914," *Business History Review,* October 1965; and Thornbrough, Emma Lou, "More Light on Booker T. Washington and the 'New York Age,'" *Journal of Negro History,* January 1958.

Contemporary About 1,240 Afro-American newspapers began publication in the nineteenth century. Of this number, only eight were still being published in the mid-1970s. The oldest were three religious publications: *Christian Recorder,* a publication of the African Methodist Episcopal (AME) Church, begun in 1846; *Star of Zion,* a publication of the African Methodist Episcopal Zion (AMEZ) Church, begun in 1867; and *American Baptist,* begun in 1880. The other five newspapers, commercial publications, were the following, in chronological order: Philadelphia *Tribune* (1885), Philadelphia, Pa.; Houston *Informer* (1892), Houston, Tex.; *Afro-American* (1892), Baltimore, Md.; Iowa *Bystander* (1894), Des Moines, Iowa; and *Indianapolis Recorder* (1895), Indianapolis, Ind.

In the twentieth century, about 1,500 Afro-American newspapers began publication; of this number about 200 survived. The total circulation of all black newspapers was approximately 4 million in 1973.

Few of the pre-1900 newspapers had circulations exceeding 10,000. This changed radically in the twentieth century as the literacy rates and economic conditions of Afro-Americans improved. Increased circulation also owed much

to the foresight of such journalists as Robert Sengstacke Abbott of the Chicago *Defender,* Robert Lee Vann of the Pittsburgh *Courier,* and John H. Murphy, Sr., of the Baltimore *Afro-American.* Vann, Abbott, Murphy, and later, W. A. Scott and C. A. Scott of the Atlanta *Daily World,* recognized the market for a nationwide circulation. Abbott relied on his *Defender,* and by 1917 his paper reached into the far corners of the South and circulated more than 250,000 weekly. Vann, Murphy, and the Scotts expanded their operations from their home offices by means of the edition method. For example, cities other than Pittsburgh soon began to issue a *Courier,* including Philadelphia and New York. The climax for the *Courier* chain came in 1947 when a weekly circulation of more than 350,000 copies was reached.

However, shifting priorities redirected the aims of black newspaper publishers toward a new audience level. The old national newspapers passed away. *Muhammad Speaks* (circulation: 625,000), the voice of the Nation of Islam, and *Black Panther* (circulation: 100,000), the voice of the Black Panther Party, were the only two black newspapers that sought a national audience and resembled national newspapers in the 1970s, and this was due largely to the missionary zeal of their leaders.

By 1973 the Chicago *Daily Defender* was selling about 35,000 copies each day. The *Courier* chain had been dissolved, but the Pittsburgh edition averaged about 20,000 per week. The Atlanta *Daily World* averaged 25,000 daily; the *Afro-American* averaged about 32,000 on a twice-a-week basis. Other large circulations in 1973 were: New York's *Amsterdam News* (circulation: 83,000); Jamaica's *Voice* (New York) (circulation: 90,000); Detroit's *Michigan Chronicle* (circulation: 60,000); Houston's *Forward Times* (circulation: 33,000); Norfolk's *Journal and Guide* (circulation: 23,000); and Philadelphia's *Tribune* (circulation: 32,500). All except the New York *Voice* provided audited circulations.

A very recent trend in the Afro-American press was the simultaneous rise of both the black shopper newspaper and the black-controlled circulation advertiser, each offered free to the public. The most successful examples of the latter include the seven newspapers published by the Central *News-Wave* group in Los Angeles, Calif. (circulation: 250,000); the five newspapers of the *Post* chain in Berkeley, Calif. (circulation: 60,500); and the Chicago *Citizen* group of four weeklies (circulation: 75,000). Unlike the controlled circulation papers that guarantee a specified audience and home delivery to the advertiser, the shoppers are either mailed or distributed through neighborhood stores. The St. Louis, Mo., *Metro-Sentinel* (circulation: 58,000); the Dallas, Tex., *In Sepia* (circulation 35,000); the Kansas City, Kans., *Black Progress Shopper* (circulation: 22,000); and the Seattle, Wash., *Medium* (circulation: 10,000) are important examples of the black shopper newspaper.

The total number of employees in the labor force of all Afro-American newspapers was almost 2,500 in 1973. Of this number, about 11 percent were white. Only 39 black newspapers actually had their own printing equipment and did their own printing. Eighty percent of the newspapers were printed "cold type" and used the offset process. Most black newspapers were weeklies, and Thursday was the publication day for two-thirds of all Afro-American weeklies published in 1973.

Only four black dailies were published. The oldest began in 1932 when Scott Brothers Publishing changed their four-year-old weekly, the Atlanta *World,* into a daily. The second active black daily, the Chicago *Daily Defender,* switched from a weekly format in 1956. The paper was founded in 1905 by Robert S. Abbott and is now under the able guidance of Abbott's nephew, John H. Sengstacke, Sr. The third daily began a five-day-a-week publication schedule in 1970. Formerly the Columbus, Ga., *News,* its name was changed to the Columbus *Times.* The fourth, the New York *Daily Challenge,* began in 1972 and with a 1973 circulation of 65,000 was the largest of the group.

Both the *World* and the *Defender* offer examples of chain ownership in the black press. The *World* also publishes the Birmingham, Ala., *World* and the Memphis, Tenn., *World,* and Sengstacke also serves as publisher of Detroit's *Michigan Chronicle,* Memphis' *Tri-State Defender,* and Pittsburgh's *New Pittsburgh Courier.*

Newspapers owned and managed by Afro-Americans are important tributes to black business management. In 1978, 99 of them were grouped into the National Newspaper Publishers Association (NNPA). Originally known as the National Negro Publishers Association, the NNPA worked hard after 1941 to unite the active members of the press. More recently, it gathered support for NNPA journalism scholarships. Eight such scholarships were awarded at its 1972 convention, and they represented a growing awareness in America of the increasing and improved educational opportunities for Afro-Americans in

Some of the members of the National Newspapers Publishers Association (NNPA), late 1970s.

Top row, left to right: John H. Murphy, III, Afro-American Newspapers; Nathaniel A. Sweets, Sr., St. Louis American; Mildred D. Brown, Omaha Star; John L. Procope, New York Amsterdam News.

Bottom row, left to right: C. A. Scott, Atlanta Daily World; Longworth M. Quinn, Michigan Chronicle; Sherman Briscoe, director of NNPA; Robert J. Thomas, Milwaukee Star-Times. *(Courtesy of Sherman Briscoe and Constance L. Britt, National Newspapers Publishers Association.)*

journalism. The University of Iowa School of Journalism established the John H. Sengstacke, Sr., Scholarship (given annually to an incoming freshman student) in January 1972 in an effort to encourage the preparation of minority members for careers in the mass media.

A list (by state) of contemporary (1972) Afro-American newspapers appears below.

NEWSPAPERS (1972)

Newspaper	Year founded	Publisher	Editor	No. on staff	Circulation
ALABAMA					
Birmingham *Baptist Leader*	1912	Alabama Baptist Publishing Board	W. H. Radney	4	3,400
Birmingham *Mirror*	1948	J. H. Williamson	J. H. Williamson	6	14,000
Birmingham *Times*	1964	Jesse J. Lewis	James E. Lewis	32	36,500
Birmingham *World*	1932	Scott Newspaper Syndicate	Emory O. Jackson	4	17,000
Jasper *Walker County Mirror*	1965	J. H. Williamson	M. L. Slaughter	2	2,000
Mobile *Beacon*	1954	Frank P. Thomas	Frank P. Thomas	10	6,000
Montgomery *Mirror*	1955	J. H. Williamson	Mildred Harris	3	5,800
Selma *Mirror*	1965	J. H. Williamson	Ernest L. Doyle	2	3,800
ARIZONA					
Phoenix *Arizona Tribune*	1958	Eloise H. Banks	Eloise H. Banks	4	4,000
ARKANSAS					
Little Rock *Southern Mediator Journal*	1938	Mrs. C. H. Jones	Herman C. Guy	5	36,000
CALIFORNIA					
Bakersfield *Observer*	1955	William Lee	Nettie James	4	4,000
Berkeley *Post Group*	1963	Tom Berkley	Tom Berkley	25	61,652
East Palo Alto *Peninsula Bulletin*	1966	Charles Thrower	Charles Thrower	5	10,000
Fresno *California Advocate*	1967	Les Kimber	Les Kimber	6	8,000
Los Angeles *Central News*	1953	Chester L. Washington	Chester L. Washington	8	40,000
Los Angeles *Herald-Dispatch*	1952	Sanford Alexander	Mrs. E. P. Alexander	8	35,000
Los Angeles *News*	1959	Reginal Carter	Reginal Carter	12	25,000
Los Angeles *The Record Newspapers*	1943	Tim Goodson	Sadie Kelly	6	35,000
Los Angeles *Sentinel*	1934	Leon Washington	Jim Cleaver	50	39,277
Los Angeles *Southwest News*	1953	Chester L. Washington	Chester L. Washington	8	14,000
Los Angeles *Watts Star Review*	1904	Robert Holeman	Robert Holeman	4	2,500
Menlo Park *Ravenwood Post*	1953	Don Wilson	Don Wilson	5	8,000
Oakland *California Voice*	1919	E. A. Daly	Lewis Campbell	6	12,500
Pomona *Clarion*	1970	Strickland Publishing Co.	Otis Bennings	10	8,000
Sacramento *Observer*	1962	William H. Lee	William H. Lee	16	20,000
San Diego *Voice and Viewpoint News*	1959	Earl Davis, Jr.	Earl Davis, Jr.	3	11,000
San Francisco *Sun Reporter*	1944	Carlton Goodlett	Thomas Flemming	23	9,000
San Francisco *The Black Panther*	—	—	—	—	—
San Joaquin *Progressor*	1969	D. L. Harvin	Claudia Hudson	7	25,000
COLORADO					
Denver *Chronicle*	1968	Rick Darnell	Rick Darnell	14	22,000
CONNECTICUT					
Bridgeport *Harambee*	—	Bill Jackson	Edward Miller	—	—
Hartford *Star*	1969	Henry Morris	Henry Morris	6	10,000
New Haven *Crow*	1968	The Crow Publishing Co.	Barbara Winters	10	7,000
DELAWARE					
Wilmington *Delaware Defender*	1962	Defender Publishing Co.	A. G. Hibbert	11	12,000
DISTRICT OF COLUMBIA					
Washington, D.C., *Afro-American*	1892	John H. Murphy, III	Art Carter	25	9,000

NEWSPAPERS (1972)   (Continued)

Newspaper	Year founded	Publisher	Editor	No. on staff	Circulation
Washington, D.C., *Capitol Spotlight*	1953	Dance Hines	R. E. Kendrick	2	40,000
Washington, D.C., *Informer*	1964	Calvin Rolark	Calvin Rolark	7	24,000
Washington, D.C., *National Crusader*	1970	Clay J. Claiborne	Clay J. Claiborne	21	—
Washington, D.C., *Observer*	1960	J. Hugo Warren	J. Hugo Warren	10	25,000
FLORIDA					
Ft. Lauderdale *Tri-City News*	1969	Tri City News	Alma Clayton	7	10,000
Ft. Pierce *Chronicle*	1957	C. E. Bolen	C. E. Bolen	7	10,000
Jacksonville *Florida Star-News*	1950	Eric O. Simpson	Eric O. Simpson	10	18,000
Lakeland *Weekly Bulletin*	1970	William F. Jackson	William F. Jackson	3	10,000
Miami *Times*	1922	Garth Reeves	Garth Reeves	15	17,000
Orlando *Sun Mirror*	1932	L. Lawrence Bowden	L. Lawrence Bowden	8	5,000
Pensacola *Times*	1968	Jesse J. Lewis	Admiral LeRoy	10	18,000
Sarasota *Weekly Bulletin*	1959	William F. Jackson	William F. Jackson	6	10,000
St. Petersburg *Weekly Challenger*	1965	Cleveland Johnson, Jr.	William Blackshear	20	20,000
Tampa *News Reporter*	1958	James A. Jackson	James A. Jackson	5	7,000
Tampa *Sentinel-Bulletin*	1945	C. Blythe Andrews, Sr.	C. Blythe Andrews, Jr.	22	75,000
West Palm Beach *Photo News*	1955	Mrs. M. A. Hall Williams	Mrs. M. A. Hall Williams	6	3,500
GEORGIA					
Albany *Times*	1964	W. L. Russell	W. L. Russell	5	3,000
Albany *Southwest Georgian*	1940	A. C. Searles	A. C. Searles	6	10,000
Atlanta *Inquirer*	1960	Jesse Hill, Jr.	Ernest Pharr and D. L. Stanley	10	30,000
Atlanta *Voice*	1966	J. Lowell Ware	J. Lowell Ware	10	30,000
Atlanta *World*	1928	Scott Family	C. A. Scott	35	25,000
Augusta *Free Press*	1970	Frank Madison	Frank Madison	5	7,500
Savannah *Herald*	1945	Floyd Adams	Floyd Adams	4	4,000
Thomasville *News*	1967	D. L. Inman	D. L. Inman	5	5,400
ILLINOIS					
Chicago *Bulletin*	1958	Bruce Sagan	Hurley Green	—	10,364
Chicago *Citizen*	1965	Gus Savage	Gus Savage	—	50,000
Chicago *Courier*	1959	Fred P. Wall	Fred P. Wall	22	25,000
Chicago *Daily Defender*	1905	John H. Sengstacke, Sr.	John H. Sengstacke, Sr.	100	33,000
Chicago *New Crusader*	1940	Balm L. Leavell	Joseph H. Jefferson	12	30,000
Chicago *Muhammad Speaks*	1961	Nation of Islam	John Niles Woodford	75–100	700,000
East St. Louis *Crusader*	1941	John M. Kirkpatrick	John M. Kirkpatrick	6	7,500
East St. Louis *Monitor*	1962	Clyde C. Jordan	Clyde C. Jordan	10	14,500
Harvey *Chicago South Surburban News*	1964	Charles B. Armstrong	Charles B. Armstrong	10	33,000
Maywood *Suburban Echo-Reporter*	—	John C. Cruzat	Myrtle Jefferson	6	—
INDIANA					
Gary *Crusader*	1959	Joe Jefferson	Dorothy L. Leavell	4	9,000
Gary *Info*	1961	James T. Harris, Jr.	James T. Harris, Jr.	8	14,500
Indianapolis *Indiana Herald*	1959	O. L. Tandy	O. L. Tandy	9	24,000
Indianapolis *Recorder*	1895	Marcus C. Stewart, Sr.	Marcus C. Stewart, Sr.	26	12,000
South Bend *Reformer*	1967	Richard Giloth	Richard Giloth	12	2,000
IOWA					
Des Moines *Iowa Bystander*	1894	James B. Morris, Sr.	James B. Morris, Sr.	4	3,300
KANSAS					
Kansas City *Black Progress Shopper News*	1968	Kenneth Chow	Kenneth Chow	20	35,000
Wichita *News Hawk*	1965	Leonard Garrett	Leonard Garrett	4	7,000
Wichita *Times*	1970	Jack Hudson	Jack Hudson	6	11,000

NEWSPAPERS (1972) (Continued)

Newspaper	Year founded	Publisher	Editor	No. on staff	Circulation
KENTUCKY					
Louisville *Defender*	1933	Frank L. Stanley	Frank L. Stanley	20	7,000
LOUISIANA					
Alexandria *News Leader*	1962	J. K. Land	C. J. Bell	6	12,100
Baton Rouge *News Leader*	1952	J. K. Land	Doris Gale	8	16,000
Bossier City *Hurricane*	1960	Roy Smith	Roy Smith	6	5,000
Lafayette *News Leader*	1970	J. K. Land	Sandra Bonnie	4	10,000
Lake Charles *News Leader*	1965	J. K. Land	Barbara Page	5	10,500
Monroe *News Leader*	1962	J. K. Land	Geraldine Williams	5	11,000
New Orleans *Louisiana Weekly*	1926	C. C. Dejoie	C. C. Dejoie	25	22,000
Shreveport *Sun*	1920	Shreveport Southern, Inc.	Melvin L. Collins, Jr.	7	18,500
MARYLAND					
Baltimore *Afro-American*	1892	John H. Murphy, III	Moses J. Newson	160	34,000
MASSACHUSETTS					
Boston *Bay State Banner*	1965	Melvin B. Miller	Melvin B. Miller	15	16,500
Springfield *Star*	1970	Henry Morris	Henry Morris	3	3,000
MICHIGAN					
Detroit *Ecorse Telegram*	1945	J. C. Wall	J. C. Wall	6	5,000
Detroit *Michigan Chronicle*	1936	John Sengstacke, Sr.	Longworth Quinn	40	63,200
Jackson *Blazer*	1962	Ben Wade	James Murphy	6	4,500
Kalamazoo *Ledger*	1967	Jean Phillips	Jean Phillips	10	7,500
MINNESOTA					
Minneapolis *Spokesman*	1934	Cecil E. Newman	Cecil E. Newman	17	11,000
Minneapolis *Twin Cities Courier*	1966	Mary J. Kyle	Mary J. Kyle	5	12,000
Minneapolis *Twin Cities Observer*	1941	Jeanne Cooper	Jeanne Cooper	11	8,500
St. Paul *Recorder*	1934	Cecil E. Newman	Cecil E. Newman	17	8,500
St. Paul *Sun*	1942	Jeanne Cooper	Jeanne Cooper	2	6,700
MISSISSIPPI					
Jackson *Advocate*	1940	Percy Greene	Percy Greene	3	10,000
Jackson *Mississippi Enterprise*	1939	Willie J. Miller	Sarah Stevens	3	10,000
Greenville *Negro Leader*	—	Albert Jenkins	Albert Jenkins	—	6,000
MISSOURI					
Kansas City *Call*	1919	Ada C. Franklin	Lucille Bluford		16,500
St. Louis *American*	1928	Nathaniel, A. Sweets, Sr.	Bennie G. Rodgers		9,000
St. Louis *Argus*	1912	Eugene Mitchell	Al Wallace	24	23,000
St. Louis *Crusader*	—	Henry Cockrell	Henry Cockrell	8	—
St. Louis *Mirror*	1955	Irving A. Williamson	Irving A. Williamson	6	42,000
St. Louis *Sentinel*	1968	Howard B. Woods	Howard B. Woods	20	21,000
NEBRASKA					
Omaha *Star*	1938	Mildred Brown	Mildred Brown	15	30,000
NEVADA					
Las Vegas *Voice*	1963	C. I. West	Paul Smith	6	6,500
NEW JERSEY					
Atlantic City *Crusader*	1966	Clay J. Claiborne	Clay J. Claiborne	6	23,800
Camden *Jersey Beat*	1955	Charles Nichols	Charles Nichols	4	25,000
Newark *Afro-American*	1892	Afro-American Publishing Co.	Robert C. Queen	5	25,000
Newark *Nite Lite*	1958	L. M. Strothers	L. M. Strothers	8	15,000
Plainfield *Voice*	1968	Voice Associates	Warren Blackshear	5	5,000
NEW YORK					
Brooklyn *New York Recorder*	1958	Thomas Watkins	Thomas Watkins	6	20,000
Buffalo *Challenger*	1962	Ambrose I. Lane	Arthur O. Eve	4	15,000

NEWSPAPERS (1972)   (Continued)

Newspaper	Year founded	Publisher	Editor	No. on staff	Circulation
Buffalo *Criterion*	1925	Frank E. Merriweather, Jr.	Frank E. Merriweather, Jr.	6	12,000
Hastings-on-Hudson *Westchester County Press*	1910	Alger Adams	Alger Adams	10	5,100
Jamaica *Voice*	1958	Elmhurst Times, Inc.	Claire Paisner	12	90,000
Mount Vernon *Westchester Observer*	1947	Ben Anderson	Ben Anderson	15	17,000
New York *Amsterdam News*	1909	C. B. Powell	Jesse Walker	200	83,000
New York *Courier*	1910	P. R. Sutton	P. R. Sutton	15	45,000
New York *Manhattan Tribune*	1968	Bill Haddad and Roy Innis	Harold Holzer	10	40,000

NORTH CAROLINA

Newspaper	Year founded	Publisher	Editor	No. on staff	Circulation
Charlotte *Post*	1940	J. S. N. Tross	J. S. N. Tross	14	12,000
Durham *Carolina Times*	1921	L. E. Austin	L. E. Austin	14	18,000
Greensboro *Carolina Peacemaker*	1965	John M. Stevenson	John M. Stevenson	7	12,000
Greensboro *Future Outlook*	1934	J. F. Johnson	J. F. Johnson	4	8,000
Raleigh *Carolinian*	1940	P. R. Jervay	P. R. Jervay	18	9,000
Wilmington *Journal*	1945	Thomas Jervay, Sr.	Thomas Jervay, Sr.	10	7,000

OHIO

Newspaper	Year founded	Publisher	Editor	No. on staff	Circulation
Bedford Heights *Cleveland Metro*	1955	William Rini	John Lenear	4	27,000
Cincinnati *Call and Post*	1950	William O. Walker	Ben Fair	3	10,000
Cincinnati *Black Dispatch*	1969	Black Communications Commission	Oliva Vaughn	—	20,000
Cincinnati *Herald*	1956	Marjorie Parham	Ray Paul	9	17,500
Cleveland *Call and Post*	1920	William O. Walker	William O. Walker	100	25,000
Columbus *Call and Post*	1960	William O. Walker	Amos Lynch	5	10,000
Dayton *Express*	—	Western Star	Sydney Davis	10	5,000
Toledo *Bronze Raven*	1945	Richard Belcher	Brenda Belcher	3	6,000
Youngstown *Buckeye Review*	1937	Buckeye Review	B. B. Burrowes	4	30,000

OKLAHOMA

Newspaper	Year founded	Publisher	Editor	No. on staff	Circulation
Oklahoma City *Black Dispatch*	1909	John Dungee	John Dungee	10	21,000
Tulsa *Oklahoma Eagle*	1921	E. L. Goodwin, Sr.	Ben H. Hill	19	12,000

OREGON

Newspaper	Year founded	Publisher	Editor	No. on staff	Circulation
Portland *Northwest Clarion Defender*	1944	Gail Black	James B. Walker	8	12,500

PENNSYLVANIA

Newspaper	Year founded	Publisher	Editor	No. on staff	Circulation
Philadelphia *Afro-American Newspaper*	1893	John Murphy, III	Mildred O'Neill	8	20,000
Philadelphia *Nite Lite*	1953	Charles Searles	Charles Searles	4	25,000
Philadelphia *Nite Owl*	1958	Mary Troup	Mary Troup	5	3,000
Philadelphia *Nite Scene*	1967	Fletcher Lone	Sunny Perry	7	—
Philadelphia *Scoop*	1959	Richard "Sonny" Driver	Richard "Sonny" Driver	10	25,000
Philadelphia *Tribune*	1885	Eustace Gay	Jack Saunders	100	30,000
Pittsburgh *New Courier*	1910	John Sengstacke, Sr.	Carl Morris	26	17,100

SOUTH CAROLINA

Newspaper	Year founded	Publisher	Editor	No. on staff	Circulation
Orangeburg *Herald*	1957	Davis Lee	Davis Lee	6	5,000

TENNESSEE

Newspaper	Year founded	Publisher	Editor	No. on staff	Circulation
Memphis *Citizen*	1969	Southern View Corporation	Larry Garrett	13	25,000
Memphis *Tri-State Defender*	1951	John Sengstacke, Sr.	John Sengstacke, Jr.	16	22,000
Memphis *World*	1931	Scott Newspaper Syndicate	J. A. Beauchamp	8	8,500
Nashville *Commentator*	—	L. B. Tomlinson	L. B. Tomlinson	—	—

TEXAS

Newspaper	Year founded	Publisher	Editor	No. on staff	Circulation
Austin *Capital City Argus*	1962	Mason Smith	Mason Smith	3	1,500
Dallas *Express*	1910	Mrs. Carter Wesley	Mrs. Carter Wesley	4	18,000
Dallas *In Sepia*	1953	Tony Davis	Tony Davis	12	35,000
Dallas *Key News*	1960	Al Smith	Al Smith	5	15,000

Newspapers (1972)   (Continued)

Newspaper	Year founded	Publisher	Editor	No. on staff	Circulation
Dallas *Post Tribune*	1949	H. L. Fagan	R. Fagan	15	25,000
Fort Worth *Bronze Texan News*	1964	Freddy Wilson	Freddy Wilson	5	15,000
Fort Worth *Como Monitor*	1940	William H. Wilburn, Sr.	William H. Wilburn, Sr.	3	1,250
Fort Worth *La Vida*	1958	Audrey Pruit	Audrey Pruit	8	13,800
Fort Worth *Mind*	1932	C. R. Wise and R. L. Milton	C. R. Wise and R. L. Milton	2	15,000
Houston *Call*	1969	Samuel Ammons	Mrs. Finis Stewart	7	3,000
Houston *Defender*	1934	C. F. Richardson, Jr.	C. F. Richardson, Jr.	2	8,500
Houston *Forward Times*	1960	Julius Carter	Varee Shields	40	33,000
Houston *Globe Advocate*	—	S. T. McKibben	S. T. McKibben	—	—
Houston *Informer*	1892	Mrs. Carter Wesley	Clyde Jackson	12	8,000
Houston *Voice of Hope*	1967	Earl Allen	Earl Allen	14	16,000
Lubbock *West Texas Times*	1962	Norman Williams	P. J. Patterson	7	3,000
San Antonio *Register*	1933	Blamo C. Bellinger	U. K. Andrews	11	11,000
San Antonio *Snap News*	1958	E. E. Coleman	Clarence Jackson	5	8,000
Tyler *Leader*	1969	S. F. Wilkinson	S. F. Wilkinson	3	1,000
Waco *Messenger*	1929	M. P. Harvey	M. P. Harvey	6	3,600
VIRGINIA					
Charlottesville *Albermarle Tribune*	1954	Randolph L. White	Randolph L. White	6	3,000
Norfolk *Journal and Guide*	1909	John Q. Jordan	John Q. Jordan	50	30,000
Richmond *Afro-American*	1939	John H. Murphy, III	Raymond H. Boone	14	16,000
Roanoke *Tribune*	1940	F. E. Alexander	F. E. Alexander	6	4,000
WASHINGTON					
Seattle *Afro-American Journal*	1967	Loin Gross	Loin Gross	5	5,000
Seattle *Medium*	1970	Chris Bennett	Chris Bennett	6	5,000
Seattle *Facts News*	1961	Fitzgerald Beaver	Fitzgerald Beaver	6	7,500
Tacoma *Northwest Courier*	1969	Northwest Courier, Inc.	Clay Armstrong, Jr.	15	5,000
WISCONSIN					
Milwaukee *Courier*	1963	Jerrell W. Jones	Carol Malone	35	8,000
Milwaukee *Greater Milwaukee Star*	1961	Walter Jones	Walter Jones	11	8,560
Milwaukee *Soul City Times*	1967	Robert Thomas	Gregory Stanford	7	5,000

Source: Compiled by Henry G. LaBrie.

John H. Johnson, president and publisher of the Johnson Publishing Co., Inc., and editor of *Ebony*. (Johnson Publishing Co., Inc.)

Magazines Although there were black magazines as early as the mid-1830s, the growth of this medium never parallelled that of black newspapers. The successful entry of the Afro-American magazine into the consumer field did not occur until 1942 when John H. Johnson launched *Negro Digest* (now titled *Black World*). While Johnson was successful with *Negro Digest*, his good fortune was yet to come. In 1945 Johnson Publications began *Ebony* in Chicago, Ill., and it was not long before that magazine was established as a popular monthly. *Ebony* reportedly had a circulation exceeding 1,250,000 in 1972.

Several other magazines followed the success of *Ebony*. Johnson issued *Tan* in 1950; *Jet*, a small pocket-size newsmagazine, in 1952; and *Copper Romance* in 1953. A competitor of Johnson Publications was Good, Inc., which published *Sepia*. However, although founded in 1955, *Sepia* never successfully challenged the leadership of *Ebony* in its field; in 1972 it had a circulation of about 75,000. Good, Inc., also published *Jive*, *Bronze Thrills*, and *Hep*. Like *Tan*, the latter three were based on the confession-style story format.

The late 1960s and early 1970s saw the birth of several new and specialized magazines intended for the Afro-American community. For women, *Essence* and *New Lady* appeared; by the mid-1970s, the former was perhaps the most rapidly developing black magazine in America. Other journals also appeared: *Black Scholar* appealed to the intellectual; *Black Enterprise*, to the businessman; *Black Sports*, to the sports fan; and *Freedomways*, to a varied audience. These publications sharply contrasted with the much older, established, and scholarly magazines, such as *The Crisis*, *Journal of Negro History*, *Journal of Negro Education*, *Phylon*, and the *CLA Journal*.

The table below gives data about selective basic periodicals that were in circulation in the early 1970s. (For a description of these and other Afro-American magazines, see Katz, Bill, *Magazines for Libraries*, 1972.)

PERIODICALS

Title	Year founded	Circulation	Editor/Publisher
Black Academy Review	1970	5,000	Okechukwu Mezu
Black Careers	1967	93,000	Project Magazines, Inc.
Black Enterprise	1970	110,000	Earl G. Graves
Black Scholar	1969	18,000	Robert Chrisman
Black Theatre	1968	3,000	Ed Bullins
Black World	1942	60,000	Johnson Publishing Co.
CLA Journal	1957	900	Therman B. O'Daniel (College Language Association)
Crisis	1910	115,000	Henry Lee Moon
Ebony	1945	1,250,000	Johnson Publishing Co.
Essence	1970	150,000	The Hollingsworth Group, Inc.
Freedomways	1961	10,000	Esther Jackson
Journal of Negro Education	1932	3,000	Howard University
Journal of Negro History	1916	5,600	Association for the Study of Afro-American Life and History
Negro Braille Magazine	1952	300	Printing House for the Blind
Negro History Bulletin	1937	22,000	Association for the Study of Afro-American Life and History
Negro Traveler & Conventioneer	1942	72,000	Travelers' Research Publishing Co., Inc.
Phylon	1940	2,200	Atlanta University
Sepia	1954	52,000	Good, Inc.

NEWTON, HUEY (1942–   ), political organizer; born in Monroe, La. Newton was raised and schooled in Oakland, Calif., and attended Merritt College (Oakland, Calif.), where he earned an associate in arts degree and was active in the Afro-American Association. With Bobby Seale, whom he met as a college student, he founded the Black Panther Party in Oakland in 1966; they were joined the next year by Eldridge Cleaver. In 1967 Newton was charged with the murder of an Oakland policeman. After a spectacular trial with many thousands of demonstrators, he was convicted of voluntary manslaughter and sentenced from two to fifteen years in prison. His conviction was reversed by the California Court of Appeals in 1970, and this reversal was affirmed by the state Supreme Court. Newton was subsequently released from prison, and two new trials ended in hung juries. Newton later fled the country but returned voluntarily, surrendering to law enforcement officials in July, 1977 to face charges of murder and assault. By this time his political philosophy had softened somewhat: he had moved from a disciplined and militant Marxist revolutionary position to a rejection of the "rhetoric of the gun" and the acceptance of peaceful revolution through participation in and organization of the community. *See also* BLACK PANTHER PARTY.

NIAGARA MOVEMENT see DUBOIS, WILLIAM EDWARD BURGHARDT.

NICHOLS, CHARLES see NEWSPAPERS: CONTEMPORARY.

NICHOLS, ROY C. (1918–   ), United Methodist bishop; born in Hurlock, Md. Nichols received a B.A. degree from Lincoln University (Lincoln University, Pa.) and his B.D. degree from the Pacific School of Religion in California. He was pastor of churches in California and New York before being elected bishop of the Pittsburgh area of the United Methodist Chruch in 1968. Nichols wrote *Motivation for a New Age* (1964).

NICHOLSON, LAWRENCE E. (1915–   ), psychologist, educator; born in St. Louis, Mo. He received the B. A. degree (1938) at Lincoln University (Lincoln, Mo.), the M. A. (1942) at the University of Chicago, and the Ph. D. at Columbia University (New York City). He served as a social case worker as chief of the Veterans Administration Counseling Center (St. Louis). Beginning in 1950 as a professor at Harris Teachers College (St. Louis), he has continued this affiliation. In 1972, he received an award for distinguished service from Omega Psi Phi Fraternity and the Man of the Year award from the Americans for Democratic Action (ADA).

NIGGER See ONOMATOLOGY.

NIGGERDOM A term used by the racist politician, Benjamin (Pitchfork Ben) Ryan Tillman, in reference to the Seventh Congressional District of South Carolina in the 1880s.

NIGGER HEAVEN The title of a 1926 novel by Carl Van Vechten; it is also a slang term that refers to the top balcony or top rows of a balcony in a theater (after about 1850).

NIGGER ROCK This name was given to the burial grounds for Afro-Americans in St. Armand, Canada, in the eighteenth century.

NIGRA See ONOMATOLOGY.

NIPSON, HUBERT (1916–   ), journalist, business executive; born in Asheville, N.C. Nipson received a B.A. degree from Pennsylvania State University in 1940 and his M.F.A. degree in creative writing from the University of Iowa. He was elected to Phi Eta Sigma, the freshman honorary fraternity, and to Sigma Delta Chi, the national honor society in journalism. Nipson won the statewide Iowa Press Photographers Association Award and also worked on the Cedar Rapids Gazette. He became an associate editor of *Ebony* in 1949, a co-managing editor in 1951, and the managing editor in 1964. Nipson was named a distinguished alumnus of Pennsylvania State University in 1973.

NIX, ROBERT NELSON CORNELIUS, SR. (1905–   ), U.S. Representative; born in Orangeburg, S.C. Nix received a B.A. degree from Lincoln University (Lincoln University, Pa.) in 1921 and his LL.B. degree in 1924. He began to practice law in Philadelphia, Pa., in 1925, and from 1934 to 1938 he was special deputy attorney general of Pennsylvania. In 1958 Nix took a seat as a member of the Fifty-fifth Congress, elected as a Democrat to fill a vacancy from the Second district of Pennsylvania. He lost his seat in 1978 to William H. Gray, 3d, the 37-year-old pastor of the Bright Hope Baptist Church (Philadelphia). *See also* NIX, ROBERT NELSON CORNELIUS, JR.

NIX, ROBERT NELSON CORNELIUS, JR. (1928–   ), lawyer, judge; born in Philadelphia, Pa. Nix, the son of Robert N. C. Nix (congressman from Pennsylvania), received a B.A. degree from Villanova University (Villanova, Pa.) in 1950 and his J.D. dgree from the University of Pennsylvania in 1953. After postgraduate studies in business administration and economics at Temple University (Philadelphia, Pa.), Nix was admitted to the Pennsylvania bar in 1956. He became a partner in a Philadelphia law firm. In 1968 Nix left this firm to become a judge of the Common Pleas Court in Philadelphia County, remaining on that bench for three years. In 1972 he was elevated to justice of the Supreme Court of Pennsylvania. *See also* NIX, ROBERT NELSON CORNELIUS, SR.

NORFOLK DIVISION OF VIRGINIA STATE COLLEGE See NORFOLK STATE COLLEGE.

NORFOLK JOURNAL AND GUIDE A newspaper founded in 1909 by Plummer B. Young (1884–1962), a native of Littleton, N.C., who was both the editor and publisher. Avoiding sensationalism, it earned a national reputation for high quality journalism, although it circulated mainly in Virginia and North Carolina. *See also* NEWSPAPERS.

NORFOLK POLYTECHNIC COLLEGE See NORFOLK STATE COLLEGE.

NORFOLK STATE COLLEGE Norfolk State College, at Norfolk, Va., was founded as Norfolk Polytechnic College. A state-supported and coeducational school, Norfolk State offers the bachelor's degree and provides liberal arts, teacher education, and terminal occupational curricula. Its 1973 enrollment was about 5,900.

By an act of the 1944 general assembly of Virginia, Norfolk Polytechnic College became the Norfolk Division of Virginia State College. The school was relocated in buildings that formerly housed a hospital. Since that time, the division has undergone a vast expansion. In recognition of the growth of the college and the demands of the area, the 1956 general assembly of Virginia passed a bill authorizing the Norfolk Division of Virginia State College to offer four-year programs in certain fields. The college became independent in 1969, and its name then became Norfolk State College. *See also* VIRGINIA STATE COLLEGE.

NORFORD, GEORGE (1918–), business executive; born in New York, N.Y. Norford attended Columbia University and the New School for Social Research (New York, N.Y.). He served as the only black staff correspondent on *Yank* magazine during World War II, and later became vice-president-general secretary of Westinghouse Broadcasting Company. In 1972 Norford was elected to that firm's board of directors. He was the first black producer of network television programs and the national coordinator of Broadcast Skills Bank, an industry recruitment-training program for minorities that he helped to create in 1966. Earlier, Norford was a consultant on broadcasting for the New York State Commission on Human Rights and a columnist for the *Amsterdam News*.

NORMAN, JESSYE *See* MUSIC: HISTORY AND DEVELOPMENT.

NORTH CAROLINA AGRICULTURAL AND TECHNICAL (A&T) STATE UNIVERSITY North Carolina Agricultural and Technical (A&T) State University, at Greensboro, N.C., was founded in 1892. State-supported and coeducational, the school offers the bachelor's and master's degrees, and provides liberal arts, teacher education, and professional curricula. Its 1975 enrollment was nearly 4,750.

The school is the largest of the historic black colleges in North Carolina. Founded in Greensboro, the school's training program was geared for many years especially to the needs of rural life and farming. Nearly 90 percent of the state's black professionals and paraprofessionals are graduates of its agricultural programs. Moreover, more than half of the state's black teachers and principals are among its alumni. The university underwent probably its greatest growth during and after World War II. It has had six presidents: J. O. Crosby, 1892–96; James B. Dudley, 1896–1925; F. D. Bluford, 1925–55; War-

moth T. Gibbs, 1955–60; Samuel D. Proctor, 1960–65; and Lewis C. Dowdy, 1965–

NORTH CAROLINA COLLEGE *See* NORTH CAROLINA CENTRAL UNIVERSITY.

NORTH CAROLINA CENTRAL UNIVERSITY North Carolina Central University, at Durham, N.C., was chartered in 1909 and opened in 1910. State-supported and coeducational, the school offers the bachelor's and master's degrees (including the M.Ed., the M.S. in library science, and the J.D), and provides liberal arts, teacher education, and professional curricula. Its 1975 enrollment was 4,062.

The school was first chartered as the National Religious Training School and Chautauqua, and its purpose was to develop the character and the sound academic training necessary for "real service." The founder was James E. Shepard, an Afro-American, who was also president when the institution opened in 1910 with an enrollment of 201 students and 15 faculty members. Originally nondenominational with its primary emphasis on training for church leadership, the school offered an education from the secondary level through the bachelor's degree. Under Shepard's leadership, the school became successively a private academy, a state-supported normal school, and finally in 1925 the nation's first state-supported liberal arts college for Afro-Amercians. Shepard was succeeded by two Afro-American presidents, Aphonso Elder and Albert N. Whiting.

Graduate-level programs were authorized in 1939, as were professional programs in law and library science. By the 1970s the college had acquired its present name.

NORTON, ELEANOR HOLMES (1937–), lawyer; born in Washington, D.C. She received a B.A. degree from Antioch College in 1960; the M.A. (1963); and J.D. (1964) from Yale University. She served with the American Civil Liberties Union (ACLU) for 5 years. In 1970 she was appointed chairperson of the New York City Commission on Human Rights by Mayor John V. Lindsay, an appointment that was renewed in 1974 by Abraham D. Beam. Through this position, supported by her background and inclination, Norton opposed many discriminatory conditions and practices. She was appointed chairperson of the Equal Employment Opportunity Commission (EEOC) in 1977.

NURSES

NURSES Many nurses, both Afro-American and white, were untrained, in the modern sense of the word, in the eighteenth and nineteenth centuries. They acted as midwives, administered folk remedies, and were called upon to minister to the ill in the early days of the United States. Particularly in the South, many of these nurses were blacks. When illness struck, it was sometimes the mistress of the slaveholding household who acted as nurse, but often it was a slave—most likely a house slave—who was called. In most southern cities free black women frequently served as midwives and nurses for both blacks and whites. In this way a tradition of nursing developed among Afro-Americans, as well as among whites, during the slave period. However, when formal training began after the Civil War, nursing was subjected to segregation and discrimination.

Early Pioneers and Schools The first Afro-American nurse on record to be graduated from a white school of professional nursing was Mary E. Mahoney. While other schools remained closed to Afro-Americans, the New England Hospital for Women and Children accepted Mary Mahoney, who graduated in 1879. Mahoney had become interested in nursing when, as the oldest daughter in a family of 25, she acted as midwife at the birth of her younger brothers and sisters.

The oldest Afro-American nursing school, the Provident Hospital Training School, was founded in Chicago, Ill. in 1891 by a surgeon, Daniel

Daniel Hale Williams (seated in chair) with the nurses and physicians of the class of 1899 at Freedmen's Hospital, Washington, D.C. (*Moorland-Spingarn Research Center, Howard University.*)

Hale Williams. One renowned graduate of the fourth graduating class, in 1895, was Jessie Sleet Scales, who had a strong desire to become a district or public health nurse. After numerous unsuccessful attempts, she entered the Charity Organization Society in New York City and worked as a district nurse and visitor for nine years, a position that marked the beginning of paid district nursing and social work in New York City by a black nurse.

The Tuskegee Institute Training School (Tuskegee Institute, Ala.), although not primarily a nursing school, gave service to U.S. Army camps during the Spanish-American War. One male graduate (1894), Oscar R. Gale, was a nurse in the U.S. Army hospital in the Philippines.

The Freedmen's Hospital Training School (Washington, D.C.) began accepting students on November 15, 1894, and graduated its first class of 17 nurses in 1896. An outstanding graduate and pathfinder from this school was Elizabeth Tyler, who became the first Afro-American nurse to be accepted on the visiting nurse staff of the Henry Street Nursing Settlement in New York City. Tyler also received an appointment with the State Health and Welfare Commission of Delaware, where she managed the child hygiene aspects of the clinic and helped to coordinate the health work under one commission. She was the first black to hold such a position. Later, in New Jersey, Tyler became the first Afro-American to be employed by the New Jersey Tuberculosis League, and she was active in health education programs against tuberculosis, the main disease killer of Afro-Americans at that time.

Clara May Harris, a graduate (1904) of Lincoln Hospital School of Nursing (New York, N.Y.), was another pioneer in this field. She passed the federal civil service examination in 1912, and was appointed to the division of child hygiene in the U.S. Department of Health. Harris was the first Afro-American nurse in charge of a baby health station, where she served for five years. Jane Turner, also a graduate (1909) of Lincoln Hospital School of Nursing, was employed by the Philadelphia Visiting Nurse Society. She became the first Afro-American nurse of that staff in 1916. When it became compulsory for nurses to take a board examination before receiving the registered nurse (R.N.) degree in the state of New York, Jane Turner passed the board with a rating of 90 percent.

Another graduate (1912) of Freedmen's Hospital Training School, was Frances Elliott, who became the first Afro-American nurse to take a course in the Town and Country Nursing Service program at Columbia University, which included conferences each week with Adelaide Nutting, practice work at the Henry Street Nursing Settlement, and service on the New York Board of Charities. She remained at Henry Street until July 1917, when the Red Cross called her to Jackson, Tenn., the first city to ask for the services of a black Red Cross nurse. When the United States entered World War I in 1917, all Town and Country Red Cross nurses were automatically enrolled as American Red Cross nurses, and received official pins—except Frances Elliott, who was advised by the Red Cross that black nurses were not to be enrolled.

Later, the director of the Bureau of Public Health Nursing informed her that she was to be the first Afro-American to be enrolled in the Red Cross. She received an official pin, marked Number One—a recognition, to be sure, but also the start of segregation in the labeling of Afro-American nurses. After World War I, Frances Elliott organized the first training school for Afro-American nurses in Michigan.

Mable Keaton Staupers was also a graduate (1917) of Freedmen's Hospital Training School. Her many "firsts" included being the first nurse executive of the National Association of Colored Graduate Nurses (NACGN). Serving as its president for many years, she met the challenge of change in her time by merging the National Association of Colored Graduate Nurses with the American Nurses Association (ANA), into one body in 1951. Staupers was keenly aware of the need to establish a special black nursing organization, and with the NACGN she also helped to bring nurses from all racial and ethnic origins together through the ANA and the National League for Nursing—an early move toward integration.

General Conditions The early pioneers in Afro-American nursing were limited mainly to employment in black institutions or institutions in which the services of black nurses were especially designated for the care of black patients.

The inhibiting influence of color often led to frustrations for both nurse and patient. Services in most hospitals in both the North and the South were definitely segregated and unequal, and few facilities existed for work. The expectation that the Afro-American nurse would become a fully accepted member of the nation's health establishment was very doubtful. Some black nurses were allowed to join the ANA early in the 1900s, but neither anything was done to encourage their participation on any meaningful scale nor any particular concern shown for their special problems.

Afro-Americans set up their own schools for training nurses, usually in black hospitals. By 1928, 36 black nursing schools had been established. Yet even before 1928, the existing white schools had graduated some 2,800 Afro-American nurses. Ten of the largest of these schools and the number of their graduates up to 1928 were: Lincoln School for Nursing (New York, N.Y.), 493; Freedmen's Hospital Training School (Washington, D.C.), 439; Dixie Hampton Training School (Hampton, Va.), 281; Provident Hospital Training School (Chicago, Ill.), 226; Hubbard Hospital Training School (Nashville, Tenn.), 138; Hospital and Training School (Charleston, S.C.), 127; Mercy Hospital (Philadelphia, Pa.), 136; St. Agnes Hospital (Raleigh, N.C.), 172; Flint-Goodridge Hospital (New Orleans, La.), 137; and Tuskegee Institute Training School (Tuskegee Institute, Ala.), 128.

National Association of Colored Graduate Nurses (NACGN) In 1908, under the leadership of Martha Franklin, the National Association of Colored Graduate Nurses (NACGN) was organized with 26 charter members. The three main goals of the NACGN were: (1) to advance the standards and the best interests of trained nurses; (2) to eliminate discrimination in the profession; and (3) to develop leadership within the ranks of Afro-American nurses. Support for the organization came from several black physicians, especially the eminent Daniel Hale Williams, founder of Provident Hospital Training School; Lillian D. Wald, a white friend of Afro-American nursing, also gave much needed support.

In 1936 the NACGN established the Mary Mahoney Award, a medal awarded for distinguished service in nursing. The first recipient of this award was Adah B. Thoms. Since that time 17 other outstanding Afro-American nurses have received this award. They are: Nancy Kemp, Carrie Bullock, Petro Pinn, Lula Warlick, Ellen

Woods Carter, Ruth Logan Roberts, Ludie Andrews, Julia Northcross, Susan Freeman, Estelle Massey Riddle Osbrne, Mable Keaton Staupers, Mary Merritt, Eliza Pillars, Marguerette Creth Jackson, Fay Wilson, Marie Mink, and Helen Miller.

After 40 years of struggle to win full-and-equal status, the NACGN reached the goal that its charter members had established, namely, to dissolve the association and to integrate its program with the American Nurses Association (ANA). This meant that all qualified nurses, regardless of race, could participate on an equal level with all other nurses as members of one association. Also, throughout the years, representatives of the NACGN had fought to gain acceptance and admission into nonblack nursing organizations, and eventually did attend the International Council of Nurses. Such members as Alma John and Alida C. Dailey were also responsible for other nurses attending national and international meetings. In 1949 Estelle Massey Riddle Osborne, a member of the board of directors of the ANA, was selected by that organization to be an official delegate to a meeting in Stockholm, Sweden. This was the first time that an Afro-American nurse had ever represented the ANA, nationally or internationally. Since then, it has not been unusual for Afro-American nurses to attend all types of nursing meetings on local, national, and international levels. Moreover, formerly all-white nursing schools began to open their doors to Afro-Americans under pressure from the civil rights movement.

On December 18 and 19, 1971, a group of Afro-American nurses, aware of the poor health status of black people, met in Cleveland, Ohio, to form the National Black Nurses' Association (NBNA). This meeting grew out of the concern of more than 150 black nurses who had formed a caucus during the 1970 ANA convention in Miami, Fla. The NBNA was not formed as part of any existing national nursing organizations. Its stated goals were: "to advance and promote the welfare of black nurses; to develop mutual strengths; and to provide leadership for the provision of optimum health care for the black community." Unlike the ANA, the NBNA accepted licensed practical nurses into its membership. Two registered nurses, Charles E. Hargett, president, and Janice E. Ruffin, vice-president, were two of its 1972 officers. *See also* DISCRIMINATION; EMPLOYMENT; HEALTH; MAHONEY, MARY E.; PHYSICIANS.

REFERENCES: Buckler, Helen, *Dr. Dan*, Little Brown, Boston, 1954; Coles, Anna B., "The Howard University School of Nursing in Historical Perspective," *Journal of the National Medical Association*, vol. 61, 1969; Elmore, Joyce, "A History of Freedmen's Hospital Training School for Nurses in Washington, D.C., 1894–1909," unpublished Master's thesis, School of Nursing, Catholic University of America, Washington, D.C., 1965; Moseley, H. Jewel, "The Status of Health Care Services by Nurses in the Black Community," *Journal of the National Pharmaceutical Association*, vol. 18, January–June 1972; Roberts, Mary M., *American Nursing History and Interpretation*, Macmillan, New York, 1963; Staupers, Mable K., *No Time for Prejudice*, Macmillan, New York, 1961.

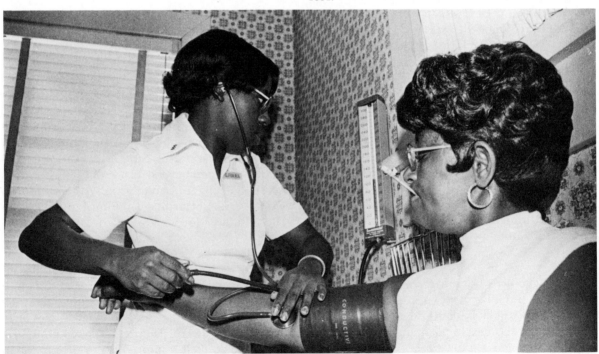

A nurse, Georgiana Fox, R.N., of Asheboro, N.C., records vital signs in 1978 before the patient sees the doctor. (*Courtesy of Daniel H. Gashler.*)

OAKWOOD COLLEGE Oakwood College, at Huntsville, Ala., was founded in 1896 by Seventh Day Adventists. A private, strongly church-related, coeducational school, Oakwood offers the bachelor's degree and provides liberal arts, teacher education, and vocational curricula. Its 1975 enrollment was 988.

O'DANIEL, THERMAN BENJAMIN (1908–), critic, educator; born in Wilson, N.C. O'Daniel received a B.A. degree from Lincoln University (Lincoln University, Pa.) and his M.A. degree from the University of Pennsylvania. He did further graduate work at Harvard University, the University of Chicago, and Pennsylvania State University. O'Daniel taught at Allen University (Columbia, S.C.), Benedict College (Columbia, S.C.) in 1939, Fort Valley State College (Fort Valley, Ga.) from 1940 to 1943, and at Morgan State University (Baltimore, Md.) after 1956. He was active in many professional organizations, including the National Council of Teachers of English and the Modern Language Association of America. His writings appeared in professional journals. O'Daniel edited *Langston Hughes, A Black Genius: A Critical Evaluation* (1971), and authored *James Baldwin: A Critical Evaluation* (1976). He was the sole editor of the *CLA Journal* (College Language Association) after its founding in 1957.

OFFICE OF MINORITY BUSINESS ENTERPRISE (OMBE) *See* BUSINESS.

OLD ORANGEBURG FEMALE COLLEGE *See* CLAFLIN UNIVERSITY.

OLIVER, EDWIN E. (1926–), pharmacist; born in Montgomery, Ala. Oliver received a B.S. degree from Xavier University (1950) and was graduated from the university's School of Pharmacy. He served as president of the National Pharmaceutical Association, and was a member of numerous professional and civic organizations.

OLIVER, JOSEPH (KING) (1885–1938), jazz cornetist, bandleader, composer; born in New Orleans, La. Oliver became the leader of the King Oliver Creole Jazz Band, considered the greatest jazz group of its era. Many leading Afro-American musicians began their careers with King Oliver's band, and Oliver became the "unofficial father" of Louis Armstrong by sharing his musical knowledge with him. In 1923 the Creole Jazz Band made the first recordings by a black jazz group. Oliver's well-known compositions include "Snake Rag," "The Chimes," "Canal Street Blues," "Working Man's Blues," "Chattanooga Stomp," and "New Orleans Stomp," most of which were written in the 1920s. *See also* ARMSTRONG, LOUIS; MUSIC: JAZZ.

O'NEAL, FREDERICK (1905–), actor, director; born in Brookville, Miss. O'Neal studied at the New Theatre School and at the American Theatre Wing in New York City. He made his professional debut after many and varied short-

Frederick O'Neal. *(Courtesy of Associated Actors and Artists of America.)*

lived jobs in St. Louis, Mo., in 1927 with the Aldridge Players, an acting group he had founded that same year. It was not until 1944 that he made his Broadway debut, as Frank in *Anna Lucasta*. Early in the 1940s O'Neal had helped to organize the American Negro Theater in New York, and toward the end of the decade he established a similar theater, the British Negro Theater, in London, England. Meanwhile, he appeared in shows in New York City and in London, including such hits as *Take a Giant Step* (1954), *The Winner* (1954), *Man with the Golden Arm* (1956), *Lost in the Stars* (1958), and others. O'Neal also played in several motion pictures and made numerous television appearances. In 1962 he served as visiting professor at Southern Illinois University and in 1963 at Clark College (Atlanta, Ga.). In the 1970s O'Neal was president of the Actors' Equity Association and international president of the Associated Actors and Artists of America. *See also* LITERATURE: DRAMA/THEATER.

O'NEILL, MILDRED   *See* NEWSPAPERS: CONTEMPORARY.

ONOMATOLOGY   The problem of giving a name to the peoples of African descent in the United States and elsewhere has been a complex and difficult one. The difficulty has much to do with the complexities of "race," culture, nationality, history, and language, wherein a valid definition in one subject may not be valid in another. Many names have been thrust upon, and some have been more or less accepted, by black people and their descendants.

Group Names

Afro-American   This term is a shortened form of "African-American," and is similar to terms used to designate such other ethnic groups as Italo-American and Franco-American. The term made its first major appearance in the nineteenth century to reflect a new dignity and a new sense of nationality. Some black writers and editors insisted upon its use. I. Garland Penn wrote a book in 1891 entitled *The Afro-American Press,* and the following year in Baltimore, Md., John Murphy began his *Afro-American* newspaper, which still bears that name. Moreover, though T. Thomas Fortune entitled his New York newspaper *The Age,* he was not averse to the use of the term "Afro-American" in his writings. An early reference book published in 1896 even took for its title *Afro-American Encyclopedia,* though the title was certainly misleading as to the quality and quantity of its contents. In the twentieth century, particularly since the 1960s, the term has gained more currency and acceptance. Richard B. Moore, president of the Afro-American Institute (based in New York City's Harlem), advocated and publicized throughout his life the need to use the term in reference to peoples of African descent in the United States.

Black American   The use of this term is relatively recent and gained much popularity during the 1960s with the rebirth and resurgence of the civil rights movement and the associated symbolism of "Black Power," "black consciousness," and "black is beautiful." The word "black," merely descriptive in slave days, took on a new meaning; either with or without the capital, it was used in a flood of writings and "rhetoric." One publisher of a respectable literary magazine (formerly *Negro Digest,* now *Black World*) substituted the word *"black"* for *"Negro"* in the title of his publication. Such new publications as *Black Enterprise, Black Essence,* and *Black Theatre* used "black" from their inception. Indeed, a virtual revolt against the use of the words "colored" and "Negro" took place throughout the 1960s and 1970s.

Negro   This term has its origins in the Latin word "niger," meaning "black." Its derivatives are numerous including the words "negritic," "negritude," and "negroid." Other derivations and corruptions are shown in the Spanish and Portuguese "negro," the French "nègre," and the German "neger." Especially when used by some white Americans, other corruptions include such offensive and hostile derivations as "nigger," "nigra," and "niggah." Equally offensive was the derivative "negress," a term referring to a black woman; the inference is clearly animal-like, as in "lioness" and "tigress." Other derivations and corruptions appear in "negrillo," a Spanish word referring to a small (diminutive) black, such as an African Pygmy or Bushman, and "negrito," referring similarly to a small black person in the Philippines, Indonesia, or Oceania.

The use of "Negro" and its many derivations carried the widespread inference that black (as opposed to white) was bad, evil, ugly, inferior, bestial, or subhuman. Even though blacks certainly did use and refer to themselves by these imposed terms, they never really accepted the meaning of the negative images and inwardly resented their use by others. Moreover, strong rejection and denial of such images occurred after the 1950s.

Colored This term was consistently employed until about the middle of the twentieth century; thereafter, its use declined sharply. The term carried connotations from physical appearances based upon skin color. It gained currency long before the findings of modern anthropology and biology became respectable and acceptable; it perpetuated the myth that skin color, like "blood", could be mixed in racial parts, like paints, revealing gradations: for example, from "jet" black to "high" yellow ("yaller"). In between were numerous words and phrases that tested the imagination: "dark brown," "light brown," "pleasing brown," "chocolate brown," "dusty black," "sooty black," "olive brown," and "tan," to mention only a few. Some groups dropped the use of the term "colored," such as the Christian Methodist Episcopal (CME) Church, which substituted the word "Christian" for "Colored". However, the National Association for the Advancement of Colored People (NAACP) still retains its use in its name. A table below documents the use of certain terms throughout the years, though it makes no claim to being definitive. The use of many of the above names often connotes abuse or derision (variable with time and place). Other names, showing stronger abuse or derision, indicating mostly a black color, included: "coon," "burrhead," "boot," "spade," "spook," "pickaninny," "shine," "darkey," "mose," and "zigaboo."

Other terms derived from skin pigmentation entered the serious lexicon of legal and literary usages: *octoroon, mulatto, creole,* and *griffe.* Indefinite and pseudoscientific, such terms have been avoided in this ENCYCLOPEDIA whenever possible.

Personal Names The names of Afro-Americans have changed since the days of the African slave trade. In the early days personal names reflected the African background. Such names as Juba, Cudjo, Mingo, Cuffee, Quashe, Sambo, and Quok (Quack) were of African origin and appear again and again in the personal names of colonial Afro-Americans. Furthermore, slave owners gave ancient or classical names, perhaps first in jest, to blacks. Popular ones included Caesar, Cato, Nero, Pliny, Primas, Neptune, Pompey, and Scipio. The names Titus, Pero, Prince, and Hannibal were also sometimes given. Such place names as Congo, Africa, Boston, and London sometimes appear. There were names that also carried a racial or color designation: Negro (as in Negro Congo, or Cato Negro) and Black.

In the course of time, names were frequently changed to indicate the slave's owner. Often the slave suggested his own name. After emancipation, Afro-Americans selected names of their own choice; and these names were often indistinguishable from other personal names that came out of the English-speaking background.

The three lists below indicate three periods of time. The first is early American, from a list of Afro-American servicemen developed from the index to the compiled military service records of the Revolutionary War, prepared by Debra Newman of the National Archives. The second list, also of servicemen, is of Afro-American second lieutenants compiled from special orders issued during World War II by the Anti-Aircraft Artillery Command. (Here the names of blacks are indistinguishable from those of whites.) The third list shows a portion of the class list of a freshman class at a predominantly black college in the 1970s. By that date some Afro-Americans, far from numerous, were adopting such Arabic or African names as Ali or Muhammad; but all on this list could be names of nonblacks.

USE OF CERTAIN TERMS FOR SELECTED YEARS

	YEARS			
	1800	1900	1950	1970
African-American	no	no	no	yes < b
Afro-American	no	yes	yes	yes < b
Black	yes > b/w	yes > b/w	no	yes < b/w
Colored	yes	yes	yes > b/w	no
Blackamoor	yes > w	no	no	no
Negro	yes (some) < b/w	yes < b/w	yes > b/w	no (some)
Nigger	yes < w/b	yes < w/b	yes > w/b	no
Sambo	yes > w	no	no	no

KEY: < w Increase in use by whites
< b Increase in use by blacks
> w Decrease in use by whites
> b Decrease in use by blacks

NAMES OF SOLDIERS FROM THE REVOLUTIONARY WAR (1770s)

Abraham (servant)	William Cuff	Pomp Lamb
Cask Africa	Cato Dedrick	Cuff Lutter
Cato Black	Caesar Dunmore	Black Minck
Juno Boding	Caeser Een	Cato Moulton
Negro Boston	Ceasar Flood	Cesar Negro
Negro Boston	Ceasar Haight	Jack Negro
Prince Cato	Cato Harris	William Negroe
Prince Cato	(Negro) Jan	Casar Osburn
Caesar Close	Negroe Jubb	Caesar Pain
David Congo	Pomp Lamb	Negro Pomp
(Negro) Cuff	Pomp Lamb	Negro Prince

NAMES OF SOLDIERS FROM WORLD WAR II (1940S)

Winthrop J. Boulware	Wilbur A. Rawlins
Ludger B. Conyers	James L. Sykes
Charles P. Jones	Elhanier W. R. Willlis, Jr.
Edward M. Martin	Virgil O. Bailey
Jesse J. Mayes	Harold R. Carney
Harry D. Rhodes, Jr.	Socrates G. Cochrane
Otto W. Williams	Franklin M. Frisby
Thomas E. Willis	John A. Johnson
Robert H. Harris, Jr.	Walter W. Leftwich
Lee A. Johnson	Frederic Mintz
Harrison E. Byrd	Robert E. Smith, Jr.
Earl W. Lewis	William H. Lathen
James H. Lyons	Clarence West
Stafford I. Pemberton	

NAMES OF ENTERING STUDENTS AT A PREDOMINANTLY BLACK COLLEGE (1970S)

Yvette A. Armstead	Jonisa Fry
Anita Bailey	Michele C. Groce
Daniel C. Beale	George E. Hill
Kimberly Ann Boone	Philip Holden
Sharon M. Byrd	Willie Holmes
Walter J. Cook	Jackie M. Holt
Gary Cox	Diane Johnson
Joyce Annette Davis	Debbie Y. Mangum
Louis J. Drone	Jesse B. Oden
Deborah Ferris	Alezia Patterson
Vanessa Fountain	Rene Y. Plummer

REFERENCES: There is no comprehensive or definitive publication on the subject. There are, however, many helpful references of varying value in McMillan, James B., *Annotated Bibliography of Southern American English* (1971), especially pp. 139–146. Another reference (with bibliography) that shows the historical evolution of personal names from "degradation to dignity" was edited by Murray Heller in 1975 (see BIBLIOGRAPHIES). There is also a chapter (6) on personal names, "Somebody Knew My Name" by Gutman, Herbert George, in his *The Black Family in Slavery and Freedom, 1750–1925* (1976).

OPERATION BREADBASKET See SOUTHERN CHRISTIAN LEADERSHIP CONFERENCE (SCLC).

OPPORTUNITIES INDUSTRIALIZATION CENTERS (OIC) OF AMERICA The OIC began as a job-training center in Philadelphia, Pa., founded by Leon H. Sullivan in 1964. With private and government aid, it expanded to seven branches in Philadelphia and into nearly 90 cities throughout the nation. The OIC Institute serves as the coordinating agency for training people in 57 different vocational areas, with centers located in the United States, Africa, and southern Central America. The program includes counseling, training, and placement.

ORGAN, CLAUDE H., JR. (1927–   ), surgeon, educator; born in Marshall, Tex. Organ received a B.S. degree from Xavier University in 1948 and his M.D. degree (1952) from Creighton University and M.S. degree in surgery (1957), School of Medicine (Omaha, Nebr.). He served as professor and as chairman of the department of surgery at Creighton University School of Medicine, and he also lectured to medical groups and surgeons in Poland and France. Organ was on the board of trustees of Fontbonne College (St. Louis, Mo.) and of Xavier University. He published many scholarly articles in medical journals.

ORY, EDWARD (KID) (1886–1973), jazz trombonist, bandleader; born in Laplace, La. Ory formed his own band in New Orleans, La., in 1911; he left New Orleans in 1919 for Los Angeles, Calif., where he founded an orchestra. In 1921 he recorded "Ory's Creole Trombone" and "Society Blues," which are the first known recordings of jazz by an Afro-American musician. See also MUSIC: JAZZ.

OVERTON, ANTHONY (1865–1946), banker, business executive, publisher; born in Monroe, La. Overton studied at Washburn College (Topeka, Kans.; now Washburn University of Topeka), and received his LL.B. degree from the University of Kansas. He served as judge of the Municipal Court in Shawnee County, Kans. In 1898 Overton established the Overton Hygienic Manufacturing Company in Kansas City, and in 1911 he moved the establishment to Chicago, Ill., where he concentrated on the production of toilet articles. In 1923 Overton organized the Douglass National Bank in Chicago, Ill., together with the Victory Life Insurance Company, and he also established the Chicago *Bee*. Overton received the Spingarn Medal in 1927 and the Harmon Business Award in 1928. During the years of the Great Depression, the bank and the life insurance company failed, but he continued to operate the manufacturing company and the Chicago *Bee*, which he administered until his death.

OWENS, JESSE (1913–80), track-and-field athlete, business executive; born in Danville, Ala. Owens made an outstanding athletic record at East Technical High School in Cleveland, Ohio, before entering Ohio State University, from which he received a B.A. degree in 1937. On a single afternoon, May 25, 1935, during his college career, he accomplished the almost incredible feat of setting world records in three track events. His autobiographical books are *Blackthink: My Life as Black Man and White Man* and *I Have Changed. See also* ATHLETES.

P

PAGE, BARBARA *See* NEWSPAPERS: CONTEMPORARY.

PAGE, INMAN EDWARD (1852–1935), educator; born a slave on a Virginia plantation. Page ran away from the plantation at the age of 10, entered a private school for Afro-Americans in Washington, D.C., and attended night school. He then enrolled in Howard University (Washington, D.C.) in 1873 and graduated from Brown University (Providence, R.I.) in 1877. Page taught at Natchez Seminary in Mississippi, was president of Lincoln Institute (Jefferson City, Mo.; now Lincoln University) for 18 years, and served as the first president of the Colored Agricultural and Normal University (Langston, Okla.; now Langston University) from 1889 to 1915. He was also president of the Colored Baptist College (Macon, Mo.), and later became president of Roger Williams University (Nashville, Tenn.).

PAIGE, LEROY ROBERT (SATCHEL) (1904–), professional baseball player; born in Mobile, Ala. Paige entered the Negro National League in the 1920s, pitching professionally for the Chattanooga Lookouts, Birmingham Black Barons, Baltimore Black Sox, Chicago American Giants, and Pittsburgh Crawfords. In 1933 he had a 31–4 record, including 21 consecutive victories and 62 consecutive scoreless innings; in 1942 he led the Kansas City Monarchs to the Negro world championship. Paige joined the Cleveland Indians of the American League in 1948, contributing six victories to their pennant drive; he was elected from the St. Louis Browns to the American League All Stars in 1952. At 65, Paige pitched for the Kansas City Athletics (American League); he retired in 1969 after serving as pitching coach for the Atlanta Braves. Paige was elected to the Baseball Hall of Fame in 1971. *See also* ATHLETES: BASEBALL.

PAINE COLLEGE Paine College, at Augusta, Ga., was founded in 1882 as Paine Institute by the Colored Methodist Episcopal Church (now the Christian Methodist Episcopal Church). Strongly church-related and coeducational, Paine offers the bachelor's degree and provides liberal arts and teacher education curricula. Its 1975 enrollment was 696.

The present campus site was acquired in 1886. For some years it looked more pastoral than collegiate, with barns, chickens, mules, and cultivated fields in addition to classrooms, a library, and residences.

In 1903 Paine Institute was rechartered as Paine College. However, since no public schools for Afro-Americans existed in that area, Paine continued to provide secondary education as well as college work for its students. It was not until 1945, in the wake of the first public high school education for blacks in Augusta, that Paine decided to discontinue its preparatory classes.

John Wesley Gilbert, Paine's first student and first graduate, became its first Afro-American faculty member in 1888. *See also* METHODISTS.

PAN-AFRICANISM

Introduction Pan-Africanism, one form of the historically significant pan-movements, has several meanings. In a general sense, the term refers to an international, social, and political movement whose goals support the concept that Africans and their identifiable kin all over the world should cooperate in all ways for the development of their own political and cultural power and for the liberation and the equality of Africans, no matter the location. More specific meanings suggest that all Africans on the African continent and their kin elsewhere must aid and support the concept of a united states of Africa modeled after the United States of America. An even more narrow definition is racially based, maintaining that black Africans and their descendants everywhere must work together in close community to end white racism, colonialism, and oppression and to seek liberation and equality of opportunity everywhere; this definition is usually considered a definition of Pan-Negroism, however.

As an international social and political movement, Pan-Africanism has two categories, unorganized and organized. The unorganized form of Pan-Africanism sometimes spelled with a small "p," denotes sympathy for the peoples, the customs, and mores of Africa and support of the general goals of Pan-Africanism. Organized Pan-Africanism includes those attempts at creating an international organization, with all the attributes of a viable social movement, including dues, officers, institutional rules, leadership, meetings, organs of communication, and ideology.

Origins and Evolution Although Pan-Africanism has been most evident since the mid-twentieth century, its roots and sources go back to the end of the eighteenth century when there were efforts to end the slave trade by humanitarians and by abolitionists.

Out of such efforts were born the beginnings of the black states of Sierra Leone in 1787, Haiti in 1804, and Liberia in 1822. Moreover, many blacks drew political meanings from the religious symbolism of the biblical story of Ethiopia, which could be defined as both a state and the continent of Africa. Thus, between 1815 and 1860 unorganized and organized Pan-Africanism focused on the African states and the continent in general as future places of black greatness. One of the first major Pan-Africanists was Paul Cuffe who in 1815 attempted to settle Afro-Americans in Africa through his own resources. Other Afro-Americans included Martin R. Delany, Henry Highland Garnet, James T. Holly, Edward Jones, and John Russwurm. All labored in the United States to dispel the myths of African inferiority associated with the enslavement of Africans and to get Afro-Americans to go back to Africa. The main organization with pan-African aims in the United States was the African Civilization Society with which both Delany and Garnet were intimately associated in the years from 1855 to 1860. Many Afro-American organizations with the word "African" in their names were founded between 1780 and 1860 but they were not pan-African oriented.

The roots of Pan-Africanism as an international social movement began to produce stems in the next 40 years. In Africa the best example of a pan-African thinker was James Africanus Beale Horton, an Ibo who became a surgeon in the British Colonial Medical Service. He published a book in 1868 calling for black unity, black self-determination, and the denial of black inferiori-

A crowd gathers on the docks in Savannah, Ga., March 1, 1896, to watch 325 Afro-American emigrants leave for Liberia. *(Library of Congress.)*

ty. However, during the next 30 years in Africa, imperialism, colonialism, oppression, and white racism brought on by the European partition of Africa stymied the development of African autonomy but not the causes of Pan-Africanism, especially abroad.

The evolution of Pan-Africanism continued in its New World beginnings. In the United States during the same 40 years, it continued to be associated with the back-to-Africa movement as it had been in the antebellum days. George Charles of Topeka, Kans., presented a memorial to the U.S. Congress in March 1886 as president of The African Emigration Association, formed in 1881. This organization may well have been the first to declare publicly that it planned to build a "United States in Africa" modeled after the United States of America. A second example is, of course, the more well-known activities of Henry M. Turner, a bishop of the African Methodist Episcopal (AME) Church, who called for a back-to-Africa movement and for the support of the black independent states. Also during these years the first African students to study in the new institutions of higher education for blacks in the United States began to arrive.

During these years the most important contributions to Pan-Africanism came from the West Indies and certain areas of Latin America. Pan-African sentiment in this region had long been certified by the repatriation of Africans, mainly from Brazil, to West Africa and by the evidence of abundant African cultural survivals. Among the personalities who originated in the West Indies and made significant and well-known contributions were Alexander Crummell and Edward Wilmot Blyden. However, their contributions were of the unorganized category. Two persons connected with the development of organized Pan-Africanism were Benito Sylvain, a Haitian diplomat, who claimed to have been one of the originators of the idea of calling the Pan-African Conference of 1900, and Henry Sylvester Williams, a Trinidadian who is generally given credit for beginning organized Pan-Africanism in calling the same conference.

The Pan-African Conference that met in London, England, in July 1900 was the first real attempt to organize the political aims of Africans in Africa and elsewhere on an international basis. Only 33 persons attended, mainly the new elite blacks, including a few from Africa. The meeting, dominated by Afro-Americans, with W. E. B. Du Bois writing the "Address to the Nations of the World," protested the declining status of blacks everywhere. Appeals were made to the European imperial rulers to administer their new African colonies justly and with an eye toward setting them free eventually. Henry Sylvester Williams hoped to establish a permanent Pan-African Association. Alexander Walters, a bishop from the United States, was elected president, a title he wore proudly thereafter. Plans were made to publish a journal and to meet biennially. But the efforts at institutionalizing the Pan-African Association failed; the interest was not there and conditions for protest did not exist in Africa. Yet, the term "Pan-African" had been created and used.

Between 1900 and 1915 very little was done to further the organization and the aims of the Pan-African Association although the sentiment remained alive. In Africa the man who came to personify black unity was a Gold Coast attorney, Joseph E. Casely-Hayford, who wrote *Ethiopia Unbound* (1911) in which he mentioned the Pan-African work of Blyden and Du Bois, as well as the programs of Booker T. Washington. In England, Duse Muhammad Ali Effendi, a writer, edited *The African Times and Orient Review*, a journal of Pan-African interests.

It was also during this period that Alain Locke, the first black Rhodes Scholar from the United States, aided in black world unity in England by serving as secretary of a Pan-African organization. Du Bois also kept interest alive by calling for a new Pan-African Association and by attending the Universal Races Congress in London in 1911, where he met others of African ancestry. In 1915 he wrote *The Negro*, a monument to the establishment of a glorious African past. He concluded this book with a renewed call for a second Pan-African movement.

In the West Indies leadership passed from Trinidad to Jamaica, where there emerged a journeyman printer, Marcus Garvey, who worked for Duse Muhammad Ali in London in 1912 and who founded in Jamaica in 1914 the Universal Negro Improvement Association (UNIA), one of whose goals was to erect a political state of Afro-Americans in Africa. The Garvey movement did not make an impact until the immediate post-World War I era.

Marcus Garvey. *(Moorland-Springarn Research Center, Howard University.)*

Between 1915 and 1920, organized Pan-Africanism was permanently implanted. The atmosphere of World War I encouraged concepts of anti-imperialism, anticolonialism, and self-determination. The world watched the excellent performances of black soldiers for France, Great Britain, Belgium, the United States, and Germany. Du Bois wanted Africa after the war to be reconstructed into two or three large states. A West Indian group, the National League of Loyal Britons, suggested the consolidation of several African areas into larger units after the war. In Africa in 1915, organized Pan-Africanism stirred in the plans of J. E. Casely-Hayford and Aki-

Memorial to Marcus Garvey, Memorial Park, Kingston, Jamaica. Garvey, who migrated from Jamaica to New York City, inspired the ill-fated back-to-Africa movement. *(Photo by Errol Harvey, Jamaica Information Service.)*

wonde Savage of Nigeria to unite all of the British West African colonies of Gambia, Sierra Leone, the Gold Coast, and Nigeria. The war, however, interrupted their plans.

Far right: W. E. B. DuBois working on the Encyclopedia Africana. His wife, the former Shirley Graham, is shown at left. *(Wide World Photos.)*

At the Versailles Peace Conference (1919), Du Bois revived interest in organized Pan-Africanism. The 57 delegates, some white, mostly from the Americas and a few from Africa, adopted a set of resolutions demanding equality, protesting colonial misrule, and calling for an African state and the internalization of the former German African colonies. No plans asked for a unification of Africa; but there was hope that a permanent organization had been founded. At the Pan-African congresses of 1921 in London, Brussels, and Paris, in 1923 in London and Lisbon, and in New York City in 1927, the same basic resolutions were readopted. Plans for meeting in 1929 on African soil were aborted by the French government, the Great Depression, and apathy. Du Bois' organizational activity in these conferences earned him the title of "Father of Pan-Africanism." The leadership was still Afro-American, and no meeting had been held on African soil.

During the 1920s the chief competitor to Du Boisian Pan-Africanism was Marcus Garvey, who aimed his slogans at the black masses of the

world while Du Bois looked to the "talented tenth" of the blacks. He used his organization to promote a back-to-Africa movement, to form the Black Star Steamship Line, and to create a United States of Africa with himself as head. He held spectacular annual meetings in New York City attended by some Africans. Although he was looked upon by many followers as a "Black Moses," his movement declined rapidly after 1925 because of his jailing upon conviction for mail fraud. Yet his ideas remained vibrant and gained more reaffirmation during the civil rights revolt of the 1960s.

Leadership and African Nationalism The only Pan-African organization in Africa in the post-World War I years was the National Congress of British West Africa. This group of black elites was an outgrowth of the wartime efforts of Casely-Hayford and Savage. They did not aim at an unified Africa, only at regional cooperation of the British areas. They also wanted more representation of Africans in the colonial government, a university, and recognition of African rights. The congress was mainly a protest organization, and it helped during its life (1920–35) to found West African nationalism. It did not know of the Pan-Africanism of Du Bois and Garvey.

Paris was another center of Pan-Africanism in the interim between World War I and World War

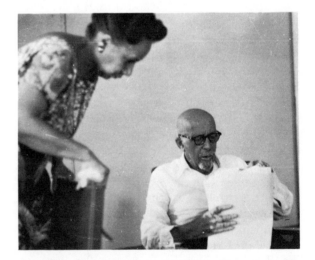

II. A group of French black colonials from Africa and the Caribbean formed Pan-African political organizations between 1924 and 1936. The main organizations were the Universal League for the Defense of the Black Race, led by Tovalou Houenou, a Dahomean who had spent most of his life in Paris; and its two successors, the Committee for the Defense of the Negro Race, headed by Lamine Senghor of Senegal, and the League for the Defense of the Negro Race, guided by Tiemoho Garan-Kouyate of the Sudan (Mali). All of these men knew of the work of Du Bois, Marcus Garvey, and George Padmore. They all dreamed of race unity and of a large state in Africa under African leadership.

After the decline of the Garvey movement in 1925 and the Du Boisian congresses in 1927, the black Communists contributed two organizations. The first was the League Against Imperialism, founded at a meeting in Brussels in 1927. Among those present as nationalists were Jawaharlal Nehru, Lamine Senghor, and delegates of the African section of the pro-Communist Profintern. The pro-Communists, now known as the International Trade Union Conference of Negro Workers, met in Hamburg, Germany, in 1930; and George Padmore became its official editor. However, Padmore, a Trinidadian, broke with the Communists in 1934 over their lack of support for African issues; he settled in London that year. From 1935 to 1945, London, with Padmore, was then the center of the movement.

Yet the difficulties of the free African states of Liberia and Ethiopia caused blacks everywhere to talk about race unity and to form organizations inspired by these countries. Among the organizations were the Ras Tafari movement in the British West Indies, founded in 1930, and the League of Colored Peoples, founded the next year in London by Harold Moody, a Jamaican physician in practice there. When Ethiopia was attacked in 1934 by Italy, Pan-African groups emerged in Africa, in the United States, and in England. The center of these groups was in London where Padmore headed a key organization called the International African Service Bureau, among whose members were C. L. R. James and Jomo Kenyatta. Moody was also connected to these groups. By the middle of World War II, a Pan-African Federation had arisen in England. Kenyatta later became head of state of the new nation of Kenya; James took up residence in the United States as a college professor; Moody remained in England.

It was the atmosphere of World War II, like that of World War I, that produced hope for better days among Africans everywhere. The Atlantic Charter, propaganda against the racial dogma of Adolf Hitler, and the four freedoms of President Franklin D. Roosevelt raised hope in the postwar period that amelioration was destined. In the same year the war ended (1945), a Pan-African Congress was held in Manchester, England. Here old standbys—Padmore, Moody, and Du Bois—were present. The new person to emerge, however, was Kwame Nkrumah of the Gold Coast, who had been educated in the United States at predominantly black Lincoln University (Lincoln University, Pa.). Nkrumah was inspired by Marcus Garvey, George Padmore, and V. I. Lenin. At this meeting in 1945 the leadership of the movement passed into African hands as the majority of the 200 delegates came as representatives of African organizations. There was little talk of a united Africa; the main focus was to protest conditions and to talk of freeing Africa from European rule.

African nationalists after 1945 worked in Africa to free their colonies from imperialists. When Ghana became free in 1957, the leadership of the Pan-African movement by Nkrumah produced two meetings in Accra, Ghana, in 1958. Padmore, in Ghana, planned both. The first meeting in April consisted of the Conference of Independent African States; it attacked imperialism, colonialism, and racism. No serious talk centered on continental unity. This subject came up at the All-African Peoples' Conference in December where 200 radical nationalists and their 60 organizations were represented. They discussed and demanded a "Commonwealth of Africa," a United States of Africa after all of Africa had been liberated. Thus two wings of the Pan-African movement, conservative and radical, appeared in 1958.

As more African colonies freed themselves between 1958 and 1963, rival concepts of continental Pan-Africanism persisted. Unions of radical (Casablanca, Morocco), conservative (Brazzaville, Congo Republic), and moderate states (Monrovia, Liberia) debated the degree of political and economic unification. These rival groups were brought together at Addis Ababa, Ethiopia, in May 1963 when the charter of the Organization of African Unity (OAU) was written. The charter was a victory for the conservatives since it based African unity on the sovereignty of African states. No political unity was achieved. Nkrumah, the leader of the radicals, who wanted immediate continental political unity, found no adherents. The OAU did succeed in setting up a Committee on Liberation; some moderates saw the committee as a device to postpone political unity until all of Africa was freed. No regional or continental units were created in Africa. However, the hopes and ideas of political and economic unity for the African continent remained very much alive in both Africa and the Americas. *See also* COLONIZATION; DELANY, MARTIN R.; DU BOIS, WILLIAM EDWARD BURGHART; GARVEY, MARCUS; NATIONAL ASSOCIATION FOR THE ADVANCEMENT OF COLORED PEOPLE (NAACP); NATIONALISM; UNIVERSAL NEGRO IMPROVEMENT ASSOCIATION (UNIA).

REFERENCES: Cervenka, Zdenek, *The Organization of African Unity and Its Charter*, Praeger, New York, 1968; Contee, Clarence G., "Du Bois, The NAACP, and the Pan-African Congress of 1919," *Journal of Negro History*, vol. 57, pp. 13–28, January 1972; Contee, Clarence G., "The Encyclopedia Project of W. E. B. Du Bois," *African Historical Studies*, vol. 4, no. 1, pp. 77–91, 1971; Cronon, E. David, *Black Moses: Marcus Garvey and the Universal Negro Improvement Association*, University of Wisconsin Press, Madison, 1955; Du Bois, W. E. B., *The World and Africa*, International Publishers, New York, 1965; Geiss, Imanuel, "Notes on the Development of Pan-Africanism," *Journal of the Historical Society of Nigeria*, June 1967, pp. 719–40; Kilson, Martin, and Adelaide Hill (eds.), *Apropos of Africa: Afro-American Leaders and the Romance of Africa*, Doubleday, Garden City, 1971; Legum, Colin, *Pan-Africanism: A Short Political Guide*, Praeger, New York, 1965; Nkrumah, Kwame, *Africa Must Unite*, Heinemann, London, 1963; Padmore, George, *Pan-Africanism or Communism?*, Dennis Dobson, London, 1956; Shepperson, George, "Pan-Africanism and 'Pan-Africanism': Some Historical Notes," *Phylon*, vol. 23, pp. 346–58, Winter 1962; and Uya, Okon Edet (ed.), *Black Brotherhood: Afro-Americans and Africa*, Heath, Boston, 1971. For an account of early Pan-Africanism, see Lynch, Hollis R., *Edward Wilmot Blyden: Pan-Negro Patriot*, Oxford Press, New York, 1970. For a brief bibliographic comment on Pan-Africanism, see Panofsky, Hans E., *A Bibliography of Africana*, Greenwood, Westport, Conn., 1975, pp. 54–56.

PARKER, BARRINGTON D. (1915–   ), lawyer, judge. Parker received a B.A. degree from Lincoln University (Lincoln University, Pa.) and his J.D. degree from the University of Chicago. He was admitted to the bar in 1947, eventually becoming judge of the U.S. District Court in Washington, D.C.

PARKER, CHARLES CHRISTOPHER (BIRD) (1920–55), jazz alto saxophonist; born in Kansas City, Mo. Parker became one of the most imitated and influential of all jazz musicians during the 1940s and 1950s. He played at Minton's Playhouse in New York City's Harlem in the 1940s during the historic developmental period of Bop, and Parker ranks as one of that jazz style's founders. Parker made many recordings with Dizzy Gillespie before his early death in New York, N.Y. *See also* MUSIC: JAZZ.

PARKS, GORDON (1912–   ), photographer, author, motion picture director; born in Fort Scott, Kans. After being forced by poverty to drop out of high school, Parks became a photog-

Gordon Parks.
(Photo by Jeannie Moutoussamy.)

rapher in the late 1930s. His photographs of Chicago's South Side ghetto won a Rosenwald Fellowship in 1941, the first ever granted in photography. He served as a staff photographer for *Life* and *Time* from 1950 to 1952, then directed such films as *Flavio* and *Shaft*, the first Afro-American to direct full-length films for a major studio. Parks was a member of the New York Newspaper Guild. His writings include two auto-biographical novels, *The Learning Tree* (1963) and *Born Black* (1971). His awards include a television "Emmy" and Photographer of the Year, 1960, and collections of his work are in the Museum of Modern Art and the Metropolitan Museum of Art, New York, N.Y. *See also* MOTION PICTURES; PHOTOGRAPHERS.

PARKS, HENRY G., JR. (1916–   ), business executive; born in Atlanta, Ga. Parks was a graduate of Ohio State University. He became director of the Resident War Production Training Center in Wilberforce, Ohio, and then president and chairman of the board of directors of H. G. Parks, Inc. (Parks sausage); national sales representative for Pabst Brewing Company; vice-president of Tuesday Publications, Inc.; and a member of the board of directors of the Magnavox Company. Parks also served as a Baltimore, Md., city coucilman.

PARKS, JAMES DALLAS *See* PREFACE: LIST OF CONTRIBUTORS; ARTISTS.

PARKS, LYMAN S. (1917–   ), clergyman, mayor; born in Princeton, Ind. Parks received a B.A. degree from Wilberforce University (Wilberforce, Ohio) in 1944 and an honorary D.D. degree from Payne Theological Seminary in 1951. He was pastor of African Methodist Episcopal (AME) churches in Indiana and Michigan from 1943 to 1966. Parks was a member of the city planning commission of Richmond, Ind., during 1951 and 1952, and was active in the civic affairs of Grand Rapids, Mich., before being elected mayor of that city in 1973. From 1971 until his election as mayor in 1973, he served as mayor of Grand Rapids, completing the term of his predecessor, who had resigned from office.

PARKS, ROSA *See* CIVIL RIGHTS: CIVIL RIGHTS MOVEMENT; WOMEN; MONTGOMERY IMPROVEMENT ASSOCIATION (MIA).

PARSONS, JAMES BENTON (1913–), educator, lawyer, judge; born in Kansas City, Mo. Parsons studied music at James Millikin University (Decatur, Ill., now Millikin University), graduating in 1934; he did graduate studies in political science at the University of Chicago, and in 1949 received a law degree from that institution. Parsons spent the years between 1934 and 1940 at Lincoln University (Jefferson City, Mo.), serving in various capacities until in 1938 he became acting head of the music department. Then he was teacher and supervisor in the public school system of Greensboro, N.C., for two years. Admitted to the Illinois bar in 1949, Parsons joined a law firm in Chicago while at the same time he taught constitutional law at John Marshall Law School. He also held the post of assistant corporation counsel for Chicago until 1951. From 1951 to 1960 he was assistant U.S. district attorney, after which he served for a year on the Superior Court in Cook County, Illinois. In 1961 Parsons was appointed by President John F. Kennedy to the U.S. District Court for the Northern District of Illinois.

PARTEE, CECIL A. (1921–), lawyer, state legislator; born in Blytheville, Ark. In 1947 Partee was admitted to the Illinois bar, a year after he received his J.D. degree from Northwestern University (Evanston, Ill.). For the next eight years he was an assistant state's attorney for Cook County, Illinois. In 1956 Partee began the first of five consecutive terms in the Illinois house of representatives, followed by election to the state senate from the 26th District (which comprises Chicago). A Democrat, he soon became majority leader and, as such, president pro tem of the senate; in 1973, the Democratic majority gone, he became minority leader.

PATERSON, BASIL ALEXANDER (1926–), lawyer, state legislator; born in New York, N.Y. Paterson received a B.S. degree from Saint John's University (Jamaica, N.Y.) in 1948, and graduated from Saint John's Law School in 1951. He joined a law firm in New York City and became involved in politics. In 1965 Paterson was elected for the first time to the New York state senate from the 27th District. He was reelected twice, serving until 1970 on committees relating to employee relations, labor and industry, housing, education, and mental retardation. In 1970 Paterson mounted an unsuccessful campaign for lieutenant governor of New York. A Democrat,

he was a delegate to the national convention in 1972, a national committeeman from New York, and vice-chairman of the Democratic National Committee. As such, he became a leader in national politics in the Democratic Party.

PATRICK, WILLIAM T., JR. (1920–), lawyer, business executive; born in Washington, D.C. A graduate of Howard University (Washington, D.C.) in 1942, Patrick received a law degree from the University of Michigan in 1946. He served as prosecuting attorney for Wayne County, Mich., from 1950 to 1953 and as special consultant to Sargent Shriver on the President's Task Force in the War Against Poverty. A lecturer at various universities in Michigan on political science, he was also director of environmental affairs for the Michigan Bell Telephone Company. Moving to New York, Patrick became director of community relations for the American Telephone and Telegraph Company.

PATTERSON, FREDERICK DOUGLASS (1901–), educator; born in Washington, D.C. Patterson received a D.V.M. degree (1923) and a M.S. degree (1927) from Iowa State University, and his Ph.D. degree from Cornell University (Ithaca, N.Y.) in 1932. He began his teaching career in the field of veterinary science at Virginia State College. In 1928 Patterson joined the faculty of Tuskegee Institute (Tuskegee Institute, Ala.) and remained there for some 30 years, rising from instructor to head of the veterinary division, then to director of the school of agriculture, and finally to president of the institute. In 1943 Patterson founded the United Negro College Fund, Inc. *See also* UNITED NEGRO COLLEGE FUND.

PATTERSON, PAT (1932–), journalist, editor, educator; born in Jamaica, N.Y. A graduate of New York University in 1957, Patterson was first employed by the New York City Department of Social Service, for which he later became a supervisor. In 1963 he moved to *Newsday*, a Long Island newspaper, as general assignment reporter, and as such was co-winner of the Silurian and Paul Tobenkin awards for excellence in journalism. Five years later he became managing editor of New York City's *Manhattan Tribune*, an interracial weekly newspaper devoted to creating and sustaining a dialogue between the races. In 1970 Patterson founded and became editor of *Black Enterprise*, a business magazine.

He left the magazine in 1974 to teach journalism at New York University and Howard University (Washington, D.C.), maintaining a post as editor-at-large for the magazine.

PATTERSON, ROLAND N. (1928–   ), educator; born in Washington, D.C. Patterson graduated from New York University, and he received his Ph.D. degree from Columbia University in 1961. He taught in the public schools of New York City; Montclair, N.J.; and Seattle, Wash. Patterson became the first Afro-American to be appointed superintendent of schools in Baltimore, Md., in 1971, a position he held until 1975.

PATTERSON, WILLIAM L. (1891– ?), lawyer, civil rights leader; born in San Francisco, Calif. Patterson was the son of a slave mother who had moved from the South to California during the Civil War. From these humble beginnings he became a lawyer, receiving his LL.B. degree from the University of California in 1919. He then pursued further studies in Moscow, U.S.S.R., returning to New York City in 1923 to take up the practice of law. In 1930 Patterson organized the International Negro Workers Conference in Hamburg, Germany; the next year he became director of the Miners and Metal Workers School in Pennsylvania; for five years after that he held the post of national executive secretary of International Labor Defense; and then he became executive secretary of the Civil Rights Congress. In 1938 Patterson served as editor of the Chicago *Record.* A member of the Communist Party, he originated and supervised the preparation of *We Charge Genocide* (1951, 1970), a petition to the United Nations charging the U.S. government with the crime of genocide against black people. He also wrote *Ben Davis: Crusader for Negro Freedom and Socialism* (1967) and his autobiography, *The Man Who Cried Genocide* (1971).

PAUL QUINN COLLEGE Paul Quinn College, at Waco, Tex. was founded in 1872 by the African Methodist Episcopal (AME) Church. Still strongly church-related, the coeducational school offers the bachelor's degree and provides liberal arts and teacher education curricula. Its 1975 enrollment was 491.

The past, present, and future of Paul Quinn are bound together in a pattern of historical development that had its beginning in a one-room

Daniel A. Payne.
*(Mother Bethel
AME Church.)*

building in Austin, Tex., in 1872, after a group of Methodist circuit riders agreed on the need for a trade school to teach newly freed slaves blacksmithing, carpentry, tanning, saddlery, and other skills to make them self-sufficient.

In 1881 Paul Quinn College—named for Bishop William Paul Quinn, African Methodist Episcopal (AME) missionary of the western states for almost 30 years—was chartered by the state of Texas and moved to its present location in Waco.

The college grew slowly, increasing its services and facilities to meet the needs of its constituency as resources became available; but it remained segregated and largely isolated from the mainstream of American education until changing cultural patterns within the last decade began to open the door to new opportunities. Then the college entered upon a program of expansion and development unparalleled in its history.

PAWLEY, THOMAS D. (1917–   ), critic, educator; born in Jackson, Miss. Pawley received a B.A. degree from Virginia State College in 1937, and a M.A. degree (1939) and his Ph.D. degree (1949) from the University of Iowa. He taught at Prairie View Agricultural and Technical College (Prairie View, Tex.) from 1939 to 1940, and was a member of the faculty of Lincoln University (Jefferson City, Mo.) after 1940, where he rose through the ranks to become professor and chairman of the division of humanities and fine arts. Pawley was the author of *Judgment Day* (1941) and *The Black Teacher and the Dramatic Arts,* with William Reardon (1970). He also contributed many articles to professional journals.

PAYNE, DANIEL ALEXANDER (1811–1893), African Methodist Episcopal bishop, educator, historian; born in Charleston, S.C. The son of free parents, Payne attended a school operated by free blacks in Charleston and the Lutheran Theological Seminary (Gettysburg, Pa.). In addition, he mastered languages and mathematics under a private tutor. Licensed to preach in 1837, he was ordained a Lutheran minister two years later. In time Payne became one of the leading figures in the African Methodist Episcopal (AME) Church, and was instrumental in raising the educational level of AME ministers and in purchasing Wilberforce University (Wilberforce, Ohio) for the denomination in 1863. Payne served as the university's president for 16 years, and its theological seminary was named for him.

He had been elected an AME bishop in 1852. His work in behalf of the church's membership also took the form of promoting literary societies and lyceums. During the Civil War, Payne visited the White House often, urging President Abraham Lincoln to free the slaves. His books include *The History of the A.M.E. Church from 1816 to 1856* (1891) and *Recollections of Seventy Years* (1883, reissued 1968). *See also* AFRICAN METHODIST EPISCOPAL CHURCH; WILBERFORCE UNIVERSITY.

PAYNE INSTITUTE See ALLEN UNIVERSITY.

PAYTON, BENJAMIN FRANKLIN (1932–   ), educator; born in Orangeburg, S.C. Payton received a B.A. degree from South Carolina State College in 1955, a B.D. degree from Harvard University in 1958, a M.A. degree from Columbia University in 1960, and his Ph.D. degree from Yale University in 1963. He taught sociology at Howard University (Washington, D.C.) from 1963 to 1965, and was a director of the Protestant Council in New York City from 1965 to 1966. Payton served as executive director of the National Council of Churches, United States, from 1966 to 1967 and as president of Benedict College (Columbia, S.C.) from 1967 to 1972. He joined the Ford Foundation in 1972.

PEEKS, EDWARD (1920–   ), journalist, author, editor; born Unadilla, Ga. Peeks received a B.S. degree from Roosevelt University (Chicago, Ill.) and a M.S. degree from Northwestern University's Medill School of Journalism (Evanston, Ill.). As a newspaperman from 1959 to 1963, he covered the civil rights movement for Afro-American newspapers. Peeks also served as the business-labor editor of the Charleston, W. Va., *Gazette,* and he wrote *The Long Struggle for Black Power* (1971).

PENN, IRVING GARLAND (1867–1940?), educator, civic leader, author; born in New Glasgow, Va. Penn received a M.A. degree from Rust College (Holly Springs, Miss.) in 1890 and his Litt.D. degree from Wiley College (Marshall, Tex.) in 1908. He was a public school principal in Lynchburg, Va., from 1886 to 1895, after which he became National Commissioner of Negro Exhibits for the Atlanta Exposition. In 1897 Penn became assistant general secretary of the Methodist Episcopal (ME) Church's Epworth League, and in 1912 corresponding secretary of the Board of Education for Negroes. Penn was the author of *The Afro-American Press and Its Editors* (1892); *The College of Life or Self-Educator* (1896); and *The United Negro* (1903).

◆◆◆

PENTECOSTALS

PENTECOSTALS Pentecostalism is uniquely the only black religious faith accepted by millions of whites in this century. Beginning in 1906, with the preaching of William J. Seymour, a black minister of a black church in Los Angeles known as the Azusa Street Mission, Pentecostalism had an estimated 40 million adherents worldwide in the mid-1970s—most strongly represented in Third World countries. In Latin America, for instance, fully 80 percent of all Protestants are Pentecostals; in Africa, nearly all of the 5,000 independent religious organizations (usually described as Natavist or Zionist) are categorized as Pentecostal. A variant form in the United States, known as the Charismatic Renewaland, includes thousands of persons in the traditional,

historic denominations (plus 3 million whites who have withdrawn, since Azusa Street days, into their own Pentecostal denominations, of which the Assemblies of God is perhaps best known). It is in the black community, however, that Pentecostalism has remained strongest and most purely African in form. It has been estimated that one out of every three black Americans is in direct contact with Pentecostalism through a family member. More specifically, the Church of God in Christ (largest of the Pentecostal bodies) has about 3 million enrolled members.

Local churches often take long and extremely novel names which do not always resemble offical denominational affiliations; but other bodies of significant size include the Pentecostal

Assemblies of the World, the United Holy Church of America, the Church of Our Lord Jesus Christ of the Apostolic Faith, Bibleway Churches Worldwide, the Fire Baptized Holiness Church, and various Churches of the Living God.

Some of these groups, including all which use

Minister leaving Pilgrim Pentecostal Church of God, ca. 1950s, in New York City. *(Museum of the City of New York.)*

the name Apostolic, reject the traditional Protestant doctrine of the Trinity and instead teach that Jesus Christ is the only person in the godhead. In other beliefs, pentecostals are distinguished by their emphasis on the perfectability of human nature, the expectation of healing from all illnesses through simple faith and the laying on of hands, the possession of the human body by the Holy Ghost with speaking in unknown tongues (technically termed *glossolalia*) as the result, and repetition of other unexplained phenomena usually described as miracles in biblical literature. (The term Pentecostal itself is derived from the scriptural festival known as the Day of Pentecost and recorded amidst similar events in Acts 2:4.) Aside from the practice of spirit possession, other African elements of Pentecostal worship include loud vocalizations, ecstatic dancing, extensive use of drums and other percussive instruments, and belief that objects touched by consecrated hands can carry benefits to others who then touch the objects.

Unlike fundamentalists, with whom they are sometimes confused, Pentecostals have been actively involved in programs of social change. Large housing projects have been completed in every major U.S. city under their auspices, as have shopping centers, supermarkets, and youth centers—all of these serving as vital additions to the often forgotten ghettos. Two Pentecostal churches served as collection centers for the "Resurrection City" protest sponsored by the Student Christian Leadership Conference. Arthur Brazier, a Pentecostal minister in Chicago, is past president of The Woodlawn Organization. Bishop Smallwood E. Williams of the Bibleway Churches in Washington, D.C., has been an active political force in that city. Martin Luther King, Jr.'s last crusade on behalf of sanitation workers in Memphis had its headquarters in a Pentecostal church—the headquarters temple of the Church of God in Christ. Other more spectacular Pentecostal ministers, such as the late Sweet Daddy Grace or Prophet Jones, have usually captured the attention of the popular media. But black Pentecostals have also fostered an accredited theological seminary, C. H. Mason Theological Seminary, which is part of the Interdenominational Theological Center in Atlanta; and they produce a scholarly journal, *Spirit: A Journal of Issues Incident to Black Pentecostalism.* See also CHURCHES; UNITED HOUSE OF PRAYER.

REFERENCES: Bartleman, Frank, *What Really Happened at Azusa Street,* Voice Publications, Northridge, Cal., 1962; Davis, Arnor S., "The Pentecostal Movement in Black Christianity," *The Black Church,* vol. II, no. I, 1972; Hollenweger, Walter J., *Pentecost Between Black and White,* Belfast, Christian Journals Ltd., 1974; Synan, Vinson, *The Holiness Pentecostal Movement,* Eerdmans, Grand Rapids, 1971; Tinney, James S., "Black Origins of the Pentecostal Movement," Christianity Today, Oct. 8, 1971, pp. 4–6; Tinney, James S., "William J. Seymour: Founder of Modern Day Pentecostalism," *Journal of the Interdenominational Theological Center,* Fall, 1971, pp. 34–44; Washington, Joseph R., *Black Sects and Cults,* Anchor, New York, 1973; Williams, Melvin D., *Community in a Black Pentecostal Church,* University of Pittsburgh Press, Pittsburgh, 1974.

PEOPLE UNITED TO SAVE HUMANITY (PUSH) See SOUTERN CHRISTIAN LEADERSHIP CONFERENCE (SCLC).

PERDUE, ROBERT EUGENE (1940–   ), historian; born in Barnesville, Ga. Perdue received the B. A. degree from Morehouse College (Atlanta, Ga.), in 1961, the M. A., from Atlanta University in 1963, and the Ph.D. degree from the University of Georgia in 1971. He taught at Fayetteville State University (N. C.) and Fort Valley State College (Ga.) before accepting a position at Spelman College, (Atlanta, Ga.) in 1972, where he became chairman of the department of history. His writings include *The Negro in Savannah, 1865–1940* (1973) and *Black Laborers and Black Professionals in Early America, 1750–1830* (1975).

PERKINS, MARION MARCHE (1908–61), sculptor; born in Marche, Ark. Beginning with the untrained whittling of bars of soap, Perkins later studied at the Community Art Center of the Illinois Art Project, and worked with Cy Gordon in learning the techniques of modeling in clay and plastic and of carving in stone. His sculpture, *Man of Sorrow,* with its emotion and sense of immensity, won the Art Institute of Chicago Purchase Award in 1951.

PERRY, LINCOLN THEODORE ANDREW *See* FETCHIT, STEPIN.

PERRY, MATTHEW JAMES, JR. (1921–   ), lawyer, judge; born in South Carolina and grew up in its capital city, Columbia. Perry was a civil rights lawyer whose legal victories helped to overturn many segregation ordinances and statutes in South Carolina during the civil rights movement of the 1960s. He won seven appeals to the U. S. Supreme Court, for example, that reversed convictions of more than 7,000 persons convicted in sit-in demonstrations. In 1976 he became a judge of the U. S. Military Court of Appeals in Washington, D. C.

PHARMACISTS *See* NATIONAL PHARMACEUTICAL ASSOCIATION.

PHARR, ERNEST *See* NEWSPAPERS: CONTEMPORARY.

PHILANDER SMITH COLLEGE Philander Smith College, at Little Rock, Ark., was founded in 1877 by the Methodist Episcopal (ME) Church. Private, strongly church-related, and coeducational, the college offers the bachelor's degree and provides liberal arts, teacher education, and vocational curricula. The 1975 enrollment was 661.

The forerunner of the college was Walden Seminary, named in honor of J. M. Walden, a white antislavery advocate and the first corresponding secretary of the Methodist Episcopal (ME) Church's Freedmen's Aid Society. The college was chartered under its present name in 1883 in honor of a donation ($10,500) made by the widow of Philander Smith of Oak Park, Ill. The institution has had several presidents,

including: James M. Cox, 1896–1924; George C. Taylor, 1924–36; Marquis L. Harris, 1936–61; Roosevelt D. Crockett, 1961–64; Ernest T. Dixon, Jr., 1965–69; and Walter R. Hazzard, 1969– *See also* METHODISTS.

PHILANTHROPY / FOUNDATIONS *See* EDUCATION: COLLEGES AND UNIVERSITIES.

PHILLIPS, CLYDE (1923–   ), surgeon; born in Chicago, Ill. Phillips received his M.D. degree from Howard University Medical College (Washington, D.C.) in 1946. He served as attending surgeon and as assistant professor in surgery at Northwestern Memorial Hospital, and became medical director of Cook County Hospital, Chicago, Ill., in 1971.

PHILLIPS, GEORGE McKENZIE (1920–   ), physician, psychiatrist; born in Tobago, British West Indies. Phillips became a licensed pharmacist in Trinidad in 1944, and received a B.S. degree (1948), a M.S. degree (1950), and his M.D. degree (1954) from Howard University (Washington, D.C.). He interned at Chester Hospital, Chester, Pa., in 1955, and completed the three-year residency requirement at Freedmen's Hospital, Washington, D.C., and at Crownsville State Hospital, Maryland, in 1958, serving as clinical director of the latter institution from 1959 to 1961. Phillips served as assistant psychiatrist at Johns Hopkins Psychosomatic Clinic, and was certified in psychiatry in 1961.

PHILLIPS, HOMER G. *See* LAWYERS.

PHILLIPS, MILDRED E. (1928–   ), pathologist, educator; born in New York, N.Y. Phillips received a B.S. degree from Hunter College of the City University of New York in 1946 and her M.D. degree from Howard University Medical College (Washington, D.C.) in 1950. She did postgraduate work at King's County Hospital, Brooklyn, N.Y., was resident at Mount Sinai and Presbyterian hospitals in New York, N.Y., and was awarded a fellowship in pathology for study in London, England. Phillips was appointed instructor in pathology and later associate professor at New York University Medical Center. She was a specialist in tumor immunology research.

PHOTOGRAPHERS The first half of the twentieth century saw the emergence and development of the professional black photographer. For

James Van Der Zee.
(Photo by Arnold Hinton.)

Ray DeCarava.
(Courtesy of the artist.)

the first time black studios and photographers received widespread patronage, especially in the large cities.

One of the best studios was maintained by Addison N. Scurlock (1883–1964) in Washington, D. C. Scurlock began his apprenticeship in 1904 and by 1911 he had opened his studio. A favorite with Washington's black elite, Scurlock was also the official photographer for Howard University and the Association for the Study of Negro Life and History. His studio was continued as a family enterprise after his death.

Other studios were maintained by James Van Der Zee in New York City, Wright in Baltimore, and Ellis and Young in St. Louis. Many of the early professional photographers, sometimes for financial reasons, affiliated with and served educational institutions or newspapers. For example, Prentiss Polk began his long career at Tuskegee Institute following World War I.

By the mid-twentieth century, individual professional photographers, though still interested in photographic portraiture, had increased their attachment and affiliation with institutions, the press, or other media. Moreover, by the 1970s the field had increased from the few hundred who were at work in the earlier generation to the nearly 3,000 (including 368 women) recorded by the U. S. Census.

Among the most outstanding were Gordon Parks, Moneta Sleet, Jr., Roy DeCarava, Leroy Henderson, Reginald McGhee, Joe Crawford, Anthony Barboza, Beuford Smith, Sa Randolph, Hugh Grannum, Arnold Hinton, and Roland Freeman. Gordon Parks was awarded the Spingarn Medal (1972). Sleet won a Pulitzer Prize (1969). DeCarava, a professor at Hunter College in New York City, was the first Afro-American to receive a Guggenheim Award in photography, and his exhibits have won recognition in the Museum of Modern Art and the Whitney Museum of American Art. Henderson, a free lance photo-journalist, has received outstanding awards, including One Show/Merit Award and Photo/Graphis International Annual Award (1974); McGhee is curator of the James Van Der Zee Institute, New York City; Crawford is in charge of *Black Photographers Annual,* which features outstanding photographers and their works; Barboza, Smith, Randolph, and Grannum have appeared in *The Black Photographers Portfolio* (1975). Roland L. Freeman, based in Washington, D.C., with Positive Images, has exhibited at the Corcoran Gallery of Art, National Gallery of Art, and the University of Maryland Baltimore County. *See also* JAMES VAN DER ZEE INSTITUTE; PARKS, GORDON; SLEET, MONETA.

REFERENCES: There is no adequate single reference. A good starting point, however, would be the scant periodical literature or this Encyclopedia.

PHYSICIANS

Early Activities Since colonial times, the black physician has been active on the American scene. In 1667 Dr. Lucas Santomée, the first Afro-American physician, was rewarded with a grant of land for his services to the colony of New Amsterdam. He was educated in Holland and practiced in New York City under both the Dutch and the British. In 1721 in Boston, Mass., an African slave of Cotton Mather named Oneissimus cited that his immunity to smallpox was due to childhood inoculation in Africa where inoculation was a custom. Mather urged Dr. Zabdiel Boylston to introduce inoculation during the Boston epidemic. In about 1740, Primus, a liberated slave of Alexander Wolcott of Windsor, Conn. was a recognized physician. In that area at about the same time an escaped slave named Simon was described in an advertisement in the *Pennsylvania Gazette* as "able to bleed and draw teeth." The first recognized American–trained-and-established physician was Dr. James Derham of New Orleans, La., who was visited by Dr. Benjamin Rush in 1783 and given high compliments on his attainments and ability. In 1792 a slave named Caesar was freed and voted a pension by the South Carolina state legislature for his "cure for rattlesnake bite." During the yellow fever epidemic in Philadelphia, Pa., of 1793, Rush enlisted the members of the African Society, who, led by Absalom Jones and Richard Allen, furnished medical aides, nurses, handlers of the dead, and other assistants, when respectability, including the national government, had fled the city. During the 1830s a few Afro-American physicians were trained in the United States under the auspices of the American Colonization Society for practice in Liberia. Most did not go. In 1833 the Georgia Infirmary was founded at Savannah, Ga. This was the first asylum and hospital established by whites solely for Afro-Americans.

The first Afro-American to obtain a medical degree was Dr. James McCune Smith of New York, who received his M.D. degree in Glasgow, Scotland, in 1837. The first to obtain a medical degree in the United States was Dr. David J. Peck, who received his M.D. degree from Rush Medical College in 1847. It is noteworthy that an American medical school graduated an Afro-American two years before any conferred the degree on a woman, white or black. In 1864 the New England Female Medical College granted the M.D. degree to Dr. Rebecca Lee. Woman's Medical College in Philadelphia, Pa., graduated Dr. Rebecca J. Cole in 1867, and Dr. Susan M. Smith-Steward received her M.D. degree from New York Medical College and Hospital for Women in 1870. Since early times the medical profession has been more open to black women than to white.

Afro-American Medical Schools It was natural that in the confusion of the Reconstruction period an attempt would be made to meet the need for Afro-American physicians through separate medical schools, but there was no organized effort to this end. Nonetheless, eight such schools came into being. The first and second to be opened are the only ones that survive today. The Medical College of Howard University (Washington, D.C.) opened in 1868 and Meharry Medical College (Nashville, Tenn.) was founded in 1876. The third school to be formed, the Leonard Medical College of Shaw University (Raleigh, N.C.) lasted 33 years from 1882 to 1915, and produced 448 graduates. Other schools were: Louisville National Medical College (Louisville, Ky.), 1888–1912; Knoxville Medical College (Knoxville, Tenn.), 1895–1909; University of West Tennessee Medical College (Memphis, Tenn.), 1900–23; Chattanooga Medical School (Chattanooga, Tenn.), 1902–1904; and Flint Medical College (New Orleans, La.), 1899–1911. A ninth medical school, that of Lincoln University (Lincoln University, Pa.), existed on paper from 1870 to 1876 but never had any students. It is worth indicating that the University of West Tennessee, which lasted 23 years and had 268 graduates, was the product of the efforts of one man, Dr. Miles Vandahurst Lynk. He also published in 1892 the first Afro-American medical journal, *The Medical and Surgical Observer*, which lasted for 18 months, and Lynk was one of the founders of the National Medical Association. At the present time Howard and Meharry

One year after its founding, Howard University (Washington, D.C.) opened its medical school, the first for Afro-Americans. By the 1970s, the University had graduated nearly half of all black physicians. *(Photo by Jacquelyn Low.)*

have produced more than half the black physicians in the United States, although the total is a painfully inadequate number.

Afro-American Hospitals Barred almost totally from hospital privileges in the early days, black physicians found ways to secure their own. Freedmen's Hospital in Washington, D.C., always federally supported, became available in 1865. Although in reality the teaching hospital of the Howard Medical College, it was not officially recognized as such until 1937. Though Meharry Medical College was opened in 1876, it did not obtain its hospital, the Hubbard Hospital, until 1910. For the decade prior to this, Meharry students had had limited access to the private 23-bed Mercy Hospital founded by Dr. Robert Fulton Boyd in 1900. Prior to this, Meharry had no hospital facilities at all.

The majority of Afro-American hospitals were operated on a semiprivate or proprietary basis.

Daniel Hale Williams in his study at Freedmen's Hospital, renamed Howard University Hospital in 1975. (*Moorland-Spingarn Research Center.*)

The first and most famous of these was Provident Hospital in Chicago, Ill., founded in 1891 by Dr. Daniel Hale Williams (known for his pioneering suture of the pericardium). This institution remains in operation.

Similar institutions that have made significant contributions include: Douglass Hospital (1895) and Mercy Hospital (1907), Philadelphia, Pa.; St. Agnes Hospital (1896), Raleigh, N.C.; Lincoln Hospital (1901), Durham, N.C.; Good Samaritan Hospital (1891), Charlotte, N.C.; Norfolk Community Hospital (1915), Norfolk, Va.; Whittaker Memorial Hospital (1908), Newport News, Va.; and Burrell Hospital (1915), Roanoke, Va.

To remove pressure for facilities and to maintain the segregated framework, public funds would sometimes be used for hospitals open to Afro-American physicians. Such hospitals were City Hospital No. 2 (now Homer G. Phillips), St. Louis, Mo., and City Hospital No. 2, Kansas City, Mo. (now absorbed into Kansas City General Hospital).

In Detroit, Mich., the fact that the city would pay for each black patient cared for gave rise to a number of proprietary hospitals, a few of which became voluntary and were modernized with public funds.

Rising standards and costs sounded the death knell of most Afro-American hospitals, but some in fortunate locations and circumstances continue to survive.

The Medical Ghetto In the early 1920s what this writer has termed "the Negro medical ghetto" seemed firmly established, and, insofar as the potentates of medicine were concerned, it seemed crystal clear that "things in general were settled forever." The medical ghetto consisted of the two medical schools, Howard and Meharry, about 10 Afro-American hospitals where the graduates of these schools could serve their internships, and up to about 100 additional Afro-American hospitals scattered throughout the country where service of variable quality was rendered. The ranks of the physicians were insignificantly swelled by an annual handful of graduates from medical schools in the North and West, which on an occasional basis would admit one or two blacks in a class.

In the 1920s, two foundations, the General Education Board and the Rosenwald Fund, made certain allocations for the improved medical education of black physicians and better hospital facilities, respectively. This was no attack on discrimination. It was an approach to *contain* the problem, not to *solve* it. In the 17 southern states and the District of Columbia at that time, medical schools, hospitals, and medical societies were to blacks like the city of Jericho, "straitly shut up: none went out and none came in."

Converging influences were presently to blast organized medicine and the general public out of their complacency toward these matters, but since shortly after the Civil War, the Afro-American physician himself, with many white supporters, had been making unremitting efforts to fight his way out.

Media Value Recognized The Afro-American physician has always seen the desirability of having some printed medium through which the general racial cause could be advocated, in addition to the example of his professional work. Dr. James McCune Smith initiated and published for a number of years a periodical that carried articles of medical and general appeal. (In one he challenged John C. Calhoun particularly.) Another early physician, Dr. Martin R. Delany, who for a time attended Harvard Medical School but began practice through the apprenticeship system, also published a newspaper. Dr. Delany served in the Union Army in the Civil War and was brevetted out a major. The publishing tradition was significantly continued in the 1970s by Dr. Carlton B. Goodlett of San Francisco, Calif., who in addition to his medical work published a newspaper and other periodicals. The National Medical Association always recognized the value of its *Journal* in communicating its point of view beyond its membership.

Separate Organizations After the opening of Howard University Medical College in 1868 with no barriers against white students or women, some liberals had hoped that there would be no barriers in medical societies either. Accordingly, in 1869 three black physicians applied for membership in the Medical Society of the District of Columbia and were rejected (they were rejected a second time in 1870). This led to a challenge to the charter of the District Medical Society through the U.S. Congress and a fight in the convention of the American Medical Association in Washington, D.C., in 1870, a fight the black physicians and their supporters lost. It was to be 80 years, in 1950, before the American Medical Association passed a resolution urging constituent societies having racially restrictive membership provisions to review them in the light of present trends with a view to their removal. Two years later in 1952 the American Medical Association reaffirmed this resolution, and in the same year the District Medical Society dropped its restrictions.

But in 1872 and in 1874, actions of the American Medical Association in convention consolidated the victory of exclusion in 1870. Hence it came about that in 1884 the Medico-Chirurgical Society of the District of Columbia was formed so as "to secure to them (black physicians) the advantages of regular meetings for medical improvement." Thus was formed the first Afro-American medical society, still hale and hearty today. It had white members at its formation and has a few at present. Similar societies began to organize throughout the South, and in 1895 a national body was formed.

The National Medical Association In Atlanta, Ga., in October 1895, during the course of the Cotton States and International Exposition, about a dozen Afro-American physicians met in the First Congregational Church and formed the National Medical Association (NMA). Its credo, stated in 1908 by Dr. C. V. Roman, was and is: "Conceived in no spirit of racial exclusiveness, fostering no ethnic antagonism, but born of the exigencies of American environment, the National Medical Association has for its object the banding together for mutual cooperation and helpfulness, the men and women of African descent who are legally and honorably engaged in the cognate professions of medicine, surgery, pharmacy, and dentistry."

In August 1970 the National Medical Association returned to the city of its birth for its 75th annual convention. The Diamond Jubilee meeting was a tremendous success. It had a record registration of 3,305, of whom 1,367 were physicians—1,167 members and 200 guests. In attendance also were 92 students, and the Women's Auxiliary had a representation of 649. In the scientific assembly 251 papers and 36 scientific exhibits were presented, in addition to panel discussions, symposia, and closed circuit television programs. At the opening session the president of the American Medical Association (AMA) presented to the president of the National Medical Association a plaque commemorating the achievements of the NMA, though this by no means symbolized an organizational wedding. Nonetheless, an AMA-NMA Liaison Committee for problems of mutual concern does exist. At the final session of the house of delegates, a group of NMA officers reported on a conference just held with President Richard M. Nixon in the White House on urgent health problems, particularly as they affected black citizens.

Annealing Forces In 1946 the nation had become so disturbed about its health situation that a national health insurance bill, the Wagner-Murray-Dingell bill, had been introduced in Congress. The National Association for the Advancement of Colored People (NAACP) decided that this legislation was in the best interests of the American people, and at its request the present writer wrote and presented the testimony of the NAACP in behalf of the bill at the committee hearings on April 16, 1946. Two days later the NMA endorsed the bill through the testimony of its president, Dr. E. I. Robinson. This proved to be a very significant stand.

The AMA was concerned that any organized segment of the profession should be dissociated from its opposition to the bill. In May 1949 the first Afro-American delegate to the house of delegates of the AMA was elected from the state of New York, but the announcement was delayed until the convention of the NMA the following August. It developed that the AMA hoped the NMA might be induced to rescind the 1946 endorsement of national health insurance, and a motion to this effect was introduced but was tabled after Dr. C. Herbert Marshall reminded the house of delegates that if it passed the motion, the NMA would get a pat on the back from the AMA and a kick in the pants from the NAACP and 11 million Afro-Americans.

In the course of events the drive for a national health bill came to be trimmed to medical aid for the elderly, commonly called Medicare, and known legislatively as the King-Anderson bill. In 1961 at its New York convention, the NMA house of delegates, with AMA prodding, decisively rejected a motion to approve this measure (North Carolina, Mississippi, and the District of Columbia being the only delegations to vote for it). But in the following year at its Chicago convention, the NMA approved Medicare by a vote of 106 to 71. The balloting on the resolution was interesting in that the delegations of some liberal states with large "inner city" populations split their votes. Illinois and Michigan split, and New York never got to cast its vote because it could not make up its mind. This state "passed" twice and before its turn came again, it had become apparent that whichever way it went its vote would make no difference.

The NMA endorsement of Medicare was a landmark action. It was the first regular national organization of physicians to endorse a measure that was in the best interests of the American people, a measure that has now become the law of the land.

This thoroughly hammered-out position was reaffirmed in 1963 and again in 1964. It brought new stature and recognition to the NMA. For the first time the White House received a NMA delegation. President John F. Kennedy met with the group on August 1, 1963. On this precedent-setting and historic occasion, he prophetically remarked in cordial and informal discussion that he could not see why the AMA was so opposed to Medicare because it would not hurt it. President Lyndon B. Johnson received NMA representatives at the White House in 1964 during the Washington, D.C., convention of that year, and in 1969 President Richard M. Nixon met briefly at San Clemente, Calif., with NMA officers at the time of the San Francisco convention.

Other Developments Following its leadership on national health insurance in 1946, the NAACP continued activity with impact in the health field. In 1947 it published a pamphlet, *Medical Care and the Plight of the Negro*, a horizontal perspective, and in 1948 another entitled *Progress and Portents for the Negro in Medicine*, a vertical or historical perspective. These publica-

tions were widely read in influential circles, and the first led Oscar Ewing, federal security administrator, to hold a series of conferences from September 1947 through January 1948 to discuss a program that would increase the number of Afro-American physicians and effectuate their distribution to places of greatest need.

Another NAACP-induced breakthrough occurred in 1948 when the University of Arkansas School of Medicine became the first southern school to admit a black student. This came as a result of the *Gaines* and *Sipuel* court decisions that separate schools had to, in fact, be equal. Arkansas decided it would be foolish to try to build a duplicate medical school for a handful of students and dropped its restrictions; other southern schools slowly followed.

Also, in 1948 the Baltimore County Medical Society, an AMA affiliate, dropped its racial bars. This was a first for a southern medical society. All societies are nominally open now.

The year 1948 might be termed a year of beginnings. At its annual fall meeting that year the Association of American Medical Colleges (AAMC) addressed the impending serious financial plight of medical schools, but refused to acknowledge that the regional school plan proposed only for Meharry Medical College was a device to relieve southern state medical schools of the necessity of admitting black students. Under the plan, a state might subsidize black residents at Meharry instead. A Senate resolution endorsing the plan was defeated, but the states found they could get along without it. Because Meharry was the first school to feel the financial pinch that later threatened most schools, it was "over a barrel" because money was sorely needed.

The AAMC continued to be coy. In 1949 and 1950 it declined to issue a statement of policy that medical schools should be open without discrimination as to ancestry or religion, stating that it had never interfered with the admission policies of member colleges. But in 1968 it sent a questionnaire to 108 medical schools in the United States to learn what programs were being mounted to assist Afro-Americans and other minority groups in order to help enlarge these programs. The AAMC was thus moved to acknowledge a problem and a responsibility to do something.

Imhotep Conferences The Hill-Burton Hospital Survey and Construction Act of 1946 and its extensions so multiplied the number of hospital beds in the country as to create a national short-age of house staff. As .a result the traditional difficulties encountered by black medical gradu-ates in obtaining internships, and especially residencies, outside the ghetto system more or less disappeared. Then came the "matching plan" for internships. Today no black graduate need go without an acceptable internship. But Afro-American physicians still face problems in securing hospital staff appointments, in spite of the antidiscrimination provisions of the Hill-Burton law.

In March 1957 the National Medical Associa-tion, the Medico-Chirurgical Society of the Dis-trict of Columbia, and the NAACP jointly spon-sored in Washington, D.C., the first Imhotep National Conference on Hospital Integration, to which all groups involved in the hospital power structure in the United States were invited to send representatives. A second conference was held in 1958 in Chicago, Ill., and the meeting was repeated for seven successive years until a final session in Atlanta, Ga., in 1963. After the second year, the NMA, the NAACP, and the National Urban League were the joint sponsors.

The name of the Egyptian demigod of medi-

cine, Imhotep, had been chosen for the meetings. It means "He who cometh in peace," and on the streets of the United States Imhotep would today be classed as a black. The peaceful attempt to solve a chronic problem through the meeting of minds was clearly symbolized.

The first Imhotep Conference had 175 regis-trants from 21 states and 49 separate localities. The delegates came from 16 constituent societies of the NMA, 26 branches of the NAACP, and 4 branches of the National Urban League. On the invitation of the sponsors, 32 organizations asso-ciated with hospital interests sent representa-tives, including the AMA, the American Hospi-tal Association, the American Nurses Association, the U.S. Public Health Service (PHS), the National Health Council, and the national AFL-CIO.

Although the hospital power groups did not send representatives with authority to act for them, the meetings had an impact. In 1964 Presi-dent Johnson had Department of Health, Educa-tion, and Welfare (HEW) Secretary Celebrezze call a conference of representatives of the NMA, the National Dental Association (NDA), and all the hospital groups. The latter this time sent

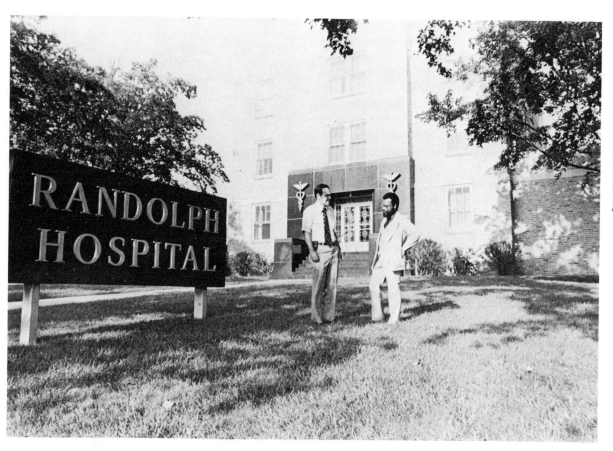

Two physicians—James B. Kinlaw, Jr., (left) and Michael A. Smith—hold an early-morning discussion as they leave the hospital in Asheboro, N.C., 1978. Though educated outside of North Carolina, Smith chose to return as a general practicioner to his native state. *(Courtesy of David H. Gashler.)*

their top officials. At the president's request, Secretary Celebrezze and ranking officers of the PHS explained in detail the significance of the Civil Rights Act of 1964 for hospital practices and expressed the hope that they would be carried out voluntarily and speedily.

Medical Manpower Shortage As in the other areas, attention had long been called to the dearth of black physicians. Federal Security Administrator Oscar Ewing's concern in 1947 has already been mentioned. In 1962 fewer Afro-American students attended medical schools other than Howard and Meharry than in 1956, and the total output of Afro-American physicians did not substantially increase in the 1960s, hovering around 180 per year. The NMA invited Dr. Ward Darley, executive director of the AAMC, to address the problem at the NMA convention in 1962. His paper, "Physicians for the Future," was promptly printed in the NMA *Journal.*

Establishment Control In 1964 the NMA launched a carefully prepared Talent Recruitment Program to enlist youngsters of promise for health careers. After two years of hard labor, the NMA council on Talent Recruitment applied for a small federal grant in support of its program and was turned down by the U.S. Office of Education on a trivial pretext. In 1968 the NMA again sought funding for a Crash Talent Recruitment Program and this time got the runaround from the Bureau of Physician Manpower.

There are today many programs throughout the country to motivate and recruit disadvantaged youth for the health professions. Most of these have been serially reported in the *Journal of the National Medical Association.* Scrutiny of these programs reveals that although Afro-Americans may be involved in these projects at different levels, all are white-controlled, whether the financing is through federal agencies or private foundations. *See also* EMPLOYMENT; HEALTH; NATIONAL MEDICAL ASSOCIATION (NMA); NURSES.

REFERENCES: The best and most comprehensive reference is the *Journal of the National Medical Association,* published from 1909 to the present. Edited by the author of this article, it is the official publication of the National Medical Association. Another reference is Morais, Herbert M., *The History of the Negro in Medicine,* Publishers Company, New York, 1968. For other references, mostly periodical, see Miller, Elizabeth W. and Mary L. Fisher (comps.), *The Negro in America: A Bibliography,* Harvard University Press, Cambridge, 1970, pp. 66–68.

PICKENS, WILLIAM (1881–1954), educator; born in Anderson County, S.C. Pickens received a B.A. degree from Talladega College (Talladega, Ala.) in 1902, a second B.A. degree from Yale University in 1904, a M.A. degree from Fisk University (Nashville, Tenn.) in 1908, and his Litt.D. from Selma University (Selma, Ala.) in 1915. He taught languages (Greek, Latin, and German) at Talladega from 1904 to 1914, sociology at Wiley College (Marshall, Tex.) from 1914 to 1915, and was dean of Morgan State College (Baltimore, Md.) from 1915 to 1920. Pickens served as field secretary for the National Association for the Advancement of Colored People (NAACP) for 22 years, from 1920 to 1942, and worked with the U.S. Treasury Department from 1942 to 1950. He wrote an autobiography, *Bursting Bonds,* in 1923. *See also* NATIONAL ASSOCIATION FOR THE ADVANCEMENT OF COLORED PEOPLE (NAACP).

PICKETT, BILL (1860s–1932), cowboy, rodeo rider. Pickett worked on ranches in South America and in the U.S. Southwest. One of the largest ranches on which he worked was the 101 Ranch, near Ponca City, Okla. Pickett claimed to have originated the rodeo technique of "bulldogging," a method of bringing a steer to submission by seizing it about the neck or horns, forcing it to the ground, and then biting into its upper lip. In 1914 Pickett performed in England before King George V and Queen Mary. He retired from active work in 1932, and died soon after from the effects of being kicked by a horse.

PICKANINNY A term used condescendingly (but not always), especially in the 1800s or early 1900s, in reference to a small black child.

PICOTT, J. RUPERT (1910–), educator; born in Suffolk, Va. Picott received a B.A. degree from Virginia Union University in 1932 and his M.Ed. degree from Temple University (Philadelphia, Pa.) in 1940. He served as executive secretary of the Virginia Teachers Association (1944–66) and as president of the American Teachers Association. Among his other activities Picott was also representative of the National Educational Association (1966–1972).

PIERCE, JOSEPH ALPHONSO (1902–), educator, mathematician; born in Waycross, Ga. Pierce received a B.A. degree from Atlanta University in 1925, and a M.S. degree (1930) and his Ph.D. degree (1938) from the University of Michigan. Before receiving his Ph.D. degree, he taught at Wiley College (Marshall, Tex.) in collaboration with a fellow Wiley professor. In 1948 Pierce joined Texas Southern University as head of the department of mathematics and chairman of the division of natural and physical sciences. He became dean of the graduate school (1952), director of the summer school (1957), and acting president (1966) and then president of the university (1967). Pierce coauthored a mathematics textbook, *Introductory College Mathematics and Applications* (1937).

PIERCE, SAMUEL RILEY, JR. (1922–   ), lawyer, judge, government official; born in Glen Cove, N.Y. Pierce received a B.A. degree (1947) and a LL.B. degree (1949) from Cornell University (Ithaca, N.Y.), and a LL.M. degree in taxation from New York University in 1952. He was admitted to the New York bar in 1949, soon becoming assistant district attorney for New York County and then assistant U.S. attorney for the Southern District of New York. Beginning in 1955, Pierce spent two years in Washington, D.C., as assistant to the undersecretary of labor and as counsel to a House antitrust subcommittee. In 1957 he returned to New York City to practice law and to teach at New York University Law School for two years. He became a judge in the New York Court of General Sessions in 1959. He returned to his law firm in New York in 1973.

PINCHBACK, PINCKNEY BENTON STEWART (1837–1921), politician; born in Holmes County, Miss., of a white planter and a freed slave. The young Pinchback was sent to Ohio with his mother to receive his education. At an early age, he began to work as a cabin boy and then as a steward on the boats that navigated the rivers and lakes of the South and the Midwest. With the beginning of the Civil War, Pinchback returned to the Union-occupied South, enlisted, and raised a company of volunteers that he led as captain. Harassment because of his race caused him to resign. He raised another company, was not permitted to lead it, and resigned a second time in disgust. He now turned his energies to the political arena. In 1867 Pinchback organized a Republican club in the Fourth Ward of Louisiana, through which he became a state committeeman. A year later he was elected to the Louisiana state senate, of which he became president pro tem in 1871. As such, Pinchback was made lieutenant governor on the death of the incumbent. Soon after, the presiding governor was unseated during impeachment proceedings, and Pinchback served as acting governor. In 1872 he was elected congressman-at-large on the Republican ticket but his seat was contested and ultimately won by a Democratic opponent. In 1873 Pinchback was elected senator by the state legislature, but this seat, too, was contested and after three years was finally denied him. About ten years later, he was appointed surveyor of customs in New Orleans, La., and in 1890 he moved to Washington, D.C., where he lived for the rest of his life.

PINKARD, MACEO (1897–1962), composer; born in Bluefield, W. Va. Pinkard studied at the Bluefield Institute, and later toured with his own orchestra. In 1914 he founded a theatrical agency in Omaha, Nebr., and later he founded one of the first Afro-American music publishing firms in New York City. Pinkard was the composer of many popular songs in the 1930s and 1940s, as well as the score of the Broadway musical *Liza*. Some of his most popular hits include "Sugar Blues," "Sweet Georgia Brown," "Them There Eyes," "Here Comes the Show Boat," "I Offer You Congratulations," "It's Right Here For You," "Is That Religion?", "Those Draftin' Blues," "Liza," "My Old Man," "Mammy o' Mine," and "Don't Cry Little Girl, Don't Cry."

PINKETT, HAROLD THOMAS (1914–   ), historian, archivist; born in Salisbury, Md. Pinkett received a B.A. degree from Morgan State University (Baltimore, Md.) in 1935, a M.A. degree from the University of Pennsylvania in 1938, and his Ph.D. degree from American University (Washington, D.C.) in 1953. In 1942, after several years of teaching, he was named archivist at the National Archives in Washington, D.C. Pinkett won the Bancroft Historical Prize in 1947 and 1948, and his writings appeared in several scholarly journals through the years. He also authored a volume on Gifford Pinchot, and was an editor of *American Archivist*. See also Contributors under PREFACE.

PITTS, LUCIUS HOLSEY educator; born in James, Ga. Pitts received a B.A. degree from Paine College (Augusta, Ga.) in 1941 and his M.A. degree from Fisk University (Nashville, Tenn.) in 1945. He served as teacher, principal, and youth worker before being named president of Miles College (Birmingham, Ala.) in 1961 and president of Paine College in 1971.

PLAYER, WILLA BEATRICE (1909–   ), educator; born in Jackson, Miss. Player received a B.A. degree (1929) and a LL.D. degree (1953) from Ohio Wesleyan, a M.A. degree from Oberlin College (Oberlin, Ohio) in 1930, a Certificat d'Etudes from Grenoble University (Grenoble, France) in 1935, and her Ed.D. degree from Columbia University in 1948. She taught French and Latin at Bennett College (Greensboro, N.C.) from 1930 to 1950, and then served as vice-president of the college from 1950 to 1955 and as president from 1955 to 1969. She also became the director, division of college support, bureau of higher education, U.S. Office of Education in 1966, and was appointed the executive administrator, Office of Education, U.S. Department of Health, Education, and Welfare (HEW) in 1973.

PLINTON, JAMES O., JR. (1914–   ), pilot, business executive; born in Westfield, N.J. Plinton received a B.S. degree from Lincoln University (Lincoln University, Pa.) in 1935, then completed a pilot training and aeronautics program at the division of aeronautics of the University of Newark (Newark, N.J.). During World War II, he served as a pilot instructor for the 99th Pursuit Squadron of the U.S. Army Air Corps, and later he helped to organize the national airline of Ecuador. Plinton became an executive with Trans World Airlines in 1950, and in 1971 he joined Eastern Airlines as a vice-president responsible for marketing affairs.

PLUMMER, JOHN O. (1880– ?), physician; born in Warrenton, N.C. Plummer received his M.D. degree from Leonard Medical School of Shaw University (Raleigh, N.C.) in 1904. He served as otologist, laryngologist, rhinologist, and ophthalmologist at St. Agnes Hospital, Raleigh, N.C., after 1905, and was a physician at the State Deaf, Dumb, and Blind Institution in Raleigh for 12 years. Plummer was also a private practitioner who specialized in diseases of the eye, ear, nose, and throat. He was president of the National Medical Association (NMA) from 1923 to 1924.

PLUMMER, NELLIE ARNOLD (1860–1924), educator; born in Ellicott's Mills, Md. Plummer was educated at the Normal Department, Wayland Seminar, Washington, D.C. (1875–78). She taught at Forestville, Md., and later served as teacher and principal in the Washington, D.C., school system for 40 years. Plummer was a member of St. Paul's Baptist Church, Bladensburg,

Md., for 56 years, where she played the organ and sang in the choir. She was especially interested in the musical development of Afro-Americans. Plummer was the author of *Out of the Depths: The Triumph of the Cross* (1927), a story of the curse of slavery. She continued to keep family records and a diary that was kept by her father for 64 years, and she was eventually able to supply documentary material over almost 100 years regarding blacks and whites living in Maryland and Washington, D.C. Plummer was one of the first to appreciate the work of the Association for the Study of Negro Life and History and annually contributed to this organization.

POGUE, ELBERT H. (1916–   ), physician; born in Bedford, Va. Pogue received a B.S. degree from Virginia State College in 1940 and his M.D. degree from Howard University Medical College (Washington, D.C.) in 1944. He interned at Harlem Hospital, New York, N.Y. and was captain in the U.S. Army Medical Corps. Pogue engaged in private practice in Elizabeth N.J., and was a staff member of St. Elizabeth, Elizabeth General, and Alexian Brothers hospitals. His brother, William Godfrey Pogue, was a highly respected physiologist. *See also* POGUE, WILLIAM GODFREY.

POGUE, WILLIAM GODFREY (1921–68), physiologist, educator; born in Bedford, Va. Pogue received a B.S. degree from Virginia State College, a M.S. degree in physiology from the University of Illinois, and his M.D. degree from Howard University Medical College (Washington, D.C.) in 1945. He was a captain in the U.S. Army Medical Corps at Frankfurt, Germany, from 1954 to 1956, and served as a faculty member of the department of psysiology at Howard University, and became a staff member of the Food and Drug Administration in 1968. His brother, Elbert H. Pogue, was an eminent New Jersey physician. *See also* POGUE, ELBERT H.

POINDEXTER, HILDRUS AUGUSTUS (1901–   ), bacteriologist, educator; born in Memphis, Tenn. Poindexter received a B.A. degree from Lincoln University (Lincoln University, Pa.) in 1924 and his M.D. degree from Harvard Medical School in 1929. He was a General Education Board Fellow at Columbia University, and received a M.S. degree (1930), his Ph.D. degree in bacteriology (1932), and a M.P.H. degree (1937) from there, and a D.Sc. degree from Dartmouth College (Hanover, N.H.) in 1956. Poindexter was assistant professor in the department of bacteriology and preventive medicine at Howard University Medical College (Washington, D.C.) from 1931 to 1934, becoming head of that department after 1934.

POINSETT, ALEX C. (1926–   ), editor, author; born in Chicago, Ill. Poinsett received a B.S. degree (1952) and his M.A. degree (1953) from the University of Illinois. He was a senior staff editor of *Ebony*, published by the Johnson Publishing Company of Chicago, Ill., and the author of *Black Power: Gary Style.*

POITIER, SIDNEY (1924–   ), actor; born in Miami, Fla. Poitier spent his childhood with his family in Nassau, British West Indies, and was educated there. He returned to Miami at the age of 15 to look for work, and eventually he traveled to New York City. There he found jobs as a dishwasher, construction worker, and longshoreman. After a four-year stint in the U.S. Army, Poitier returned to New York City in 1945, became the janitor at the American Negro Theater, and began to learn the trade that was to bring him fame. He made his stage debut at the American Negro Theater, playing small parts in several plays until, in 1946, he appeared on Broadway in a production of *Lysistrata.* The next year Poitier played in *Anna Lucasta,* after which his career shifted to motion pictures. During the 1950s he appeared in such films as *Cry, the Beloved Country* (1952), *The Blackboard Jungle* (1955), *Edge of the City* (1957), *The Defiant Ones* (1958), and *Porgy and Bess* (1959), among many others. In 1959 he returned to the Broadway stage to play Walter Lee Younger in Lorraine Hansberry's *A Raisin in the Sun.* More films followed, and in 1964 Poitier became the first Afro-American actor to win an Academy Award as best actor, scoring for his performance in *Lilies of the Field. See also* MOTION PICTURES.

POLICE   *See* CRIME.

POLITICS

Introduction Except for the brief period of Reconstruction and isolated instances thereafter, the American political system generally excluded and oppressed Afro-Americans until the middle of the twentieth century. As stated correctly by one political scientist, Samuel DuBois Cook (in Walton Hanes, Jr., *Black Political Parties: An Historical and Political Analysis,* 1972), the American political system "generated and sustained a culture of total power and participation for whites and a culture of total powerlessness and exclusivity for blacks." The system produced in whites, he continued, "a collective syndrome of insensitivity, arrogance, pride, irresponsibility, and moral conceit and pretension which corrupted their sense of justice," while it produced in blacks, the objects of the oppression, "tragic frustrations, deprivations, anger, bitterness, and alienation which corrupted their civic and political consciousness."

Though powerless objects of oppression. Afro-Americans have profoundly influenced Ameri-can politics by their everlasting presence and protest. American history abounds with examples of this truth. The politics of the enslavement of Afro-Americans, for example, was closely tied in with the politics of freedom for whites, especially in the immediate slavery controversy that preceded the Civil War. Again, the politics of civil rights for blacks in the twentieth century was related to the politics of civil rights for such other groups as women.

Whether in the politics of slavery or of civil rights, the underlying nature of the American political process (vis-à vis-blacks) has been racist. Black reaction to this harsh reality, whether as slave or "second-class citizen," was created and sustained by white and not by black power. Indeed, much of the entire political history of Afro-Americans (and by extension, much of their entire culture) was devoted to a search for ways and means to overcome the continuing heavy burden of racism.

Successes in the civil rights crusades eased

some of the burdens after the 1950s, creating in the face of massive white resistance a political and social revolution in the South, where most Afro-Americans lived or from where they or their parents had fled. One of the political keys to this revolution was the Voting Rights Act of 1965 that enabled blacks to register. Encouraged by the Voter Education Project (VEP) and by civil rights groups, black registration in the South increased dramatically in the 1960s. For example, when Dr. Martin Luther King, Jr., led the protest march from Selma to Montgomery, Ala., in 1965 to petition for the right to vote, black voter registration in the state then stood at 2.3 percent of the eligible blacks; seven years later it had reached 67 percent, a figure slightly higher than the national average. In 1965 only a few Afro-Americans had been elected to office in Alabama; in May 1975 there were 161 Afro-American officials. Nationally, black elected officials increased from 1,185 in 1969 to 3,979 in 1976, according to the Joint Center for Political Studies.

Congressional Black Caucus at the White House, 1974: (seated, left to right) Augustus Hawkins (D.-Calif.), Cardiss Collins (D.-Ill.), Charles Rangel, chairperson (D.-N.Y.), Yvonne B. Burke (D.-Calif.), William L. Clay (D.-Mo.), Parren J. Mitchell (D.-Md.); (standing, left to right) Ronald Dellums (D.-Calif.), Robert C. Nix (D.-Pa.), John Conyers (D.-Mich.), Shirley Chisholm (D.-N.Y.), Andrew Young (D.-Ga.), Stanley S. Scott, Special Assistant for Minority Affairs, Ralph H. Metcalfe (D.-Ill.), Walter Fauntroy (D.-D.C.), Barbara Jordan (D.-Tex.), Louis Stokes (D.-Ohio), and Charles Diggs (D.-Mich.). Congressmen Harold L. Ford and William H. Gray, 3d, were elected in the 1970s, after the date of this photograph. (*Courtesy of the Office of the White House.*)

Southern Politics* By the early 1950s two of the South's distinctive political institutions—disfranchisement, which had been under attack since the *Smith v. Allwright* decision of 1944, and the one-party system—showed signs of slippage, and the behavior of Southern voting groups suggested a movement toward a more participatory and class-based politics.

It was at this point that another peculiar Southern institution came under direct challenge with the *Brown v. Board of Education of Topeka* decision of May 1954. Although in its implementation decision of 1955, the U.S. Supreme Court permitted a pattern of gradual compliance, which for a decade produced the barest tokenism, the magnitude of a decision declaring the foundation of the Southern social system to be illegal was readily apparent. But in the hope that after the initial shock of social change the freeing of blacks from the caste system would also free whites from the requirement of defending it and thus would hasten the emergence of a two-party, New Deal-like politics in the South, liberally oriented political analysts had underrated the intensity of white opposition to the *Brown* decision and to the civil rights movement generally. Southern state executive officials and their malapportioned legislatures launched a program of massive resistance to school desegregation during the 1950s, and during the 1960s the white backlash against the pace and extent of civil rights progress was frequently reflected in seismic political jolts. In the face of white hostility to social change, Afro-Americans became increasingly organized and more unified in their balloting.

The racial hysteria on the part of a considerable number of Southern politicians and the racial fears on the part of many white voters drove a wedge between blacks and less affluent whites, much as in the 1890s. With prosperity increasing and memories of the Great Depression fading, many rural and lower-income whites saw themselves threatened more by social change than by economic exploitation. In state and local politics, the Folsoms and Earl Longs gave way to the Wallaces and McKeithens. Orval Faubus, George Wallace, Ross Barnett, Jimmie Davis, and John McKeithen were among those who combined racism, a white common-man campaign style, and, often, little in the way of constructive programs to rally support in rural areas and in lower-income white urban districts.

*See Preface for acknowledgments.

But massive resistance did encourage a political dialectic of its own. The two groups in Southern society most disturbed by the excesses of the movement were blacks and the affluent whites of the cities and suburbs. This coalition provided important support for some of the South's better-known moderates of the period, such men as LeRoy Collins, Carl Sanders, and DeLesseps Morrison. In the racial crisis in Little Rock, Ark., the alliance of blacks and affluent whites ultimately provided the political stability that led to the reopening of the public high schools. In Atlanta, Ga., the same coalition kept progressive Mayor Ivan Allen in office and enabled Charles Weltner to become the Democratic nominee for congressman in Atlanta's Fifth District. In Birmingham, Ala., the coalition ultimately retired Eugene "Bull" Connor from city office, although this event was delayed as the county board of registrars placed every obstacle in the path of prospective black voters and since a large proportion of the more prestigious white residential neighborhoods lay outside the city limits. The extent of the changes in voting patterns generated by the politics of massive resistance could be exaggerated, of course, but the heating up of the race question did fundamentally transform the evolution of the New Deal-like patterns that had marked the late 1940s and the early 1950s.

Similarly, the civil rights question influenced the emerging patterns of two-party politics. The first impact was temporarily to make the Republican Party the one that attracted a coalition of blacks and higher-status whites; Eisenhower carried both the affluent white precincts and the black districts in most Southern cities in 1956. But this alignment soon dissolved as Presidents John F. Kennedy and Lyndon Johnson consolidated the Democratic position among minorities by vigorously championing minority rights. The civil rights movement and federal legislation accomplished during the 1960s what federal court decisions alone had not been able to do in the 1950s—namely, the destruction of the de jure Jim Crow system, a process that sent political shock tremors throughout the region. The civil rights movement also spread northward, and what had once been quaintly regarded as a problem unique to the South now threatened to split the New Deal coalition outside the South. In this situation, the national Republicans shifted to their famed "southern strategy."

The logic and the results of the southern strategy are well known. The rural and lower-income whites, who fairly consistently supported the national Democratic ticket, also tended to vote for the Faubuses and Wallaces. Ironically, the urbane and racially liberal Adlai E. Stevenson and the equally urbane and racially liberal—and also Roman Catholic—John F. Kennedy generally ran best among the same white voter groups who evidenced the strongest concern for white supremacy and, more often than not, the greatest support for those gubernatorial candidates who most uninhibitedly vowed to thwart the liberal policies of the national Democratic party. In the presidential election of 1960 and in several senatorial contests in 1962, Republican candidates made some significant gains in areas that were normally citadels of Democratic solidarity. By abandoning civil rights in the name of states' rights, the Goldwater Republicans presumably sought to broaden these beachheads into a general polarization of southern voters along racial lines. This design was successful in the Deep South, where Goldwater won a large majority of the votes cast by whites. In the cities of the southern heartland he projected an essentially classless appeal, winning equally impressive margins in white working-class districts and affluent neighborhoods. In the peripheral South, however, Goldwater largely failed to break the Democratic voting habits of lower-income whites, while there as elsewhere driving Afro-Americans into virtually solid opposition. Nationally, of course, the Goldwater campaign was a disaster. Only in the Deep South were racial fears of sufficient salience to solidify the bulk of the white vote. Goldwater's southern strategy failed to live up to the expectations of its sponsors, but it further warped the emerging two-party system by attracting lower-income whites, especially in the Deep South, whose partisan identification had normally been Democratic and by repelling normally Republican mountain whites and highly educated suburbanites, particularly in the Rim South.

Both voter registration and voter turnout increased rapidly during the 1960s, but the long awaited and largely simultaneous enfranchisement of lower-income whites and blacks was a mixed blessing. During the decade more than 6 million new names were estimated to have been added to Southern registration rolls, of which total roughly 30 percent belonged to blacks and 70 percent to whites; clearly there appeared to be a causal relationship between the addition of some 4.5 million new white voters to the registration rolls and the election successes of Wallace, Lester Maddox, James Johnson, and other common-man, "good ole boy" segregationists.

The 1968 presidential election sharply etched the developing voting tendencies in the region. George Wallace appealed to the traditionally Democratic white voters in rural and small-town counties and in the working-class districts in the

The civil rights movement and the collapse of Jim Crow contributed to the rising political consciousness for black Americans. New coalitions emerged such as the Black Political Convention, held in Gary, Ind., 1972. Henry Marsh, then Deputy Mayor of Richmond, Va., is shown holding the Virginia placard. (Photo by Leroy Henderson.)

cities. Richard M. Nixon was the candidate of the urban bourgeoisie, and he was Wallace's chief competitor among white voters generally. Afro- American voters formed the base of Hubert Humphrey's following. In the broadest sense, both survey research data and voting patterns demonstrate that Wallace's blend of populist economics and social reaction appealed to lower-income whites; Nixon's economic conservatism and defense of social stability paralleled the attitudes of the better educated and more secure urban-suburban affluents; and Humphrey's welfare economics and racial liberalism reflected the views of blacks, liberal whites, and other minorities.

Later state elections suggested a shift away from the politics of Goldwater, Wallace, and racial turmoil. Moderate Republicans—Winthrop Rockefeller in Arkansas, A. Linwood Holton in Virginia, Howard Baker and Winfield Dunn in Tennessee, and James Holshouser in North Carolina—enjoyed at least temporary successes in the upper South, while a wave of progressive Democrats—Reuben Askew and Lawton Chiles of Florida, Dale Bumpers of Arkansas, William Waller of Mississippi, Jimmy Carter of Georgia, John West of South Carolina, and Edwin Edwards and Bennett Johnston of Louisiana, for example—were swept into office. The difficul-

ties involved in evaluating this apparent orgy of progressive moderation exemplify the problems of dealing with contemporary history. It would appear, however, that the new southern moderation was more anti-establishment than issue-oriented, a proposition that is at least indirectly supported by voting returns: New South Democrats in their primary election victories did not appeal with any consistency to specific voter groups, and liberals Ralph Yarborough and Albert Gore succumbed as readily as did more conservative contenders.

George Wallace's victories in the Democratic presidential primaries and the continuing storm over busing during 1972 evidenced the powerful strain of social conservatism that underlay the surge of New South moderation. As the vote in the Florida referenda elections suggested, white southerners had accepted desegregation but not much more than that. Attractive new faces similar to those that had fared so well in 1970 were largely unsuccessful in 1972, as Nick Galifianakis and David Pryor, among others, fell before conservative opponents. In the 1972 presidential election, Nixon combined Republican and Wallace votes to sweep the solid South with a 70.5 percent majority, leaving McGovern, like Humphrey before him, with little voter base beyond Afro-Americans and other minority groups. The New Deal coalition of have-nots that had collapsed in successive presidential elections seemed in various stages of disintegration in state politics. A notable exception was Henry Howell, who demonstrated strong appeal to urban lower-status voters (regardless of race) in his two strong but unsuccessful bids for the Virginia governorship. In Texas Frances "Sissy" Farenthold attracted a similar following in her 1972 effort for the Democratic gubernatorial nomination, although her campaign foundered when she tried again for the same office in 1974. Nevertheless, when an avowed liberal who is both female and Catholic not only wins a runoff spot in a Texas gubernatorial primary but also makes a creditable contest against a well-financed, conservative opponent, surely things are changing in southern politics.

Nonsouthern Big Cities* During the ten-year period between 1950 and 1960 nearly 2 million southern Afro-Americans moved into the nation's 12 largest nonsouthern cities. The already overcrowded black ghettos began an

*See PREFACE for acknowledgments.

almost irreversible expansion in all directions within the city. During the same ten-year period almost 2 million middle-class whites fled these cities to the suburbs. As long as they had stayed in the cities, they constituted a middle ground between the blacks and the lower-class whites. As they left, however, a situation of polarized

confrontation developed. Long-existing and patiently developed interracial contacts were broken off. Scores of cities around the country became armed camps of nervous black and white citizens.

The emergence of the so-called black central city signaled the end of the old Democratic coalition in urban America. Put together during the Great Depression by President Franklin D. Roosevelt, the coalition was a political amalgam of middle-class whites, blacks, and working-class ethnic whites. For more than 30 years the coalition constituted the backbone of the Democratic Party. In the big cities it made the party almost invincible. During the early 1950s, however, the coalition began to suffer from the defection of middle-class whites. Between 1952 and 1968, the vote in the suburbs rose 37 percent while that in the center cities dropped by 21 percent. Indeed, by 1968 the suburbs had surpassed the cities in voting power. During the national elections of that year the total vote cast in the suburbs of the nation's 12 largest nonsouthern cities was 8,591,000 as compared to 8,112,000 for the cities themselves. Moreover, reapportionment had given the suburbs electoral power commensurate with the size of their vote. They sent 20 additional representatives to the House in the Ninetieth Congress. And compounding the damage to the Democratic Party, 18 of these new congressmen were Republicans.

The working class or "ethnic" whites who remained in the center cities continued to vote Democratic in national elections but in decreased proportions. In 1968 the Democratic Party received 28 percent, or 12 million fewer votes than it did in 1964. The urban ethnics

constituted a considerable proportion of this bloc. In local and state elections the ethnic defection from the coalition frequently became wholesale. So-called liberal white candidates had little or no chance of attracting the support of this group. After 1967 this vote invariably went to the "law-and-order" candidates. If no such candidate was in the running, the ethnics voted Republican as the next best thing. In the final analysis, Afro-Americans were the only ethnic group to stick with the old coalition throughout its more than 30 years of existence. Psychologically, some of the older ones were still voting for Franklin D. Roosevelt. Even so, occasional and temporary defections occurred. In New York City, for instance, Afro-Amercians unfailingly supported the Republican John Lindsay in his successful campaigns for mayor. And while they might prefer not to be reminded of it, Afro-Americans in Baltimore, Md., in 1966 went all out for Spiro Agnew as governor of Maryland in order to defeat a law-and-order Democrat, George Mahoney.

As the black population of the center cities continued to grow, urban blacks began to look toward the election of black candidates, with less attention going to party labels or the coalition. Indeed, the coalition was increasingly coming under the attack of black dissidents and militants.

As loud and persistent as it was, however, militant rhetoric had but a secondary influence upon black political behavior during the 1960s. The results would very probably have been the same without it. Since emancipation, Afro-Americans have seldom passed up the opportunity of electing members of their own race when there was a reasonable chance to do so. Not only does the Reconstruction period provide testimony to this, but also in the first half of this century black electorates in Illinois, New York, and

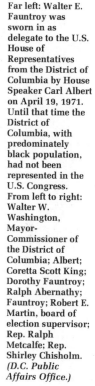

Far left: Walter E. Fauntroy was sworn in as delegate to the U.S. House of Representatives from the District of Columbia by House Speaker Carl Albert on April 19, 1971. Until that time the District of Columbia, with predominately black population, had not been represented in the U.S. Congress. From left to right: Walter W. Washington, Mayor-Commissioner of the District of Columbia; Albert; Coretta Scott King; Dorothy Fauntroy; Ralph Abernathy; Fauntroy; Robert E. Martin, board of election supervisor; Rep. Ralph Metcalfe; Rep. Shirley Chisholm. (D.C. Public Affairs Office.)

The first black cabinet members, Robert Weaver (right) was appointed Secretary of Housing and Urban Development (HUD) by Lyndon B. Johnson in 1966 and William T. Coleman was appointed Secretary of Transportation by Gerald R. Ford in 1975. (GOP National Committee.)

683

Michigan sent numerous members of the race to city councils and state legislatures. The black bloc vote antedates the black revolution by more than a half century. The mayoral elections of Carl Stokes, Richard Hatcher, and Kenneth Gibson, therefore, owed far less to militant rhetoric than to the ancient pride in race achievement. Besides, the militants as a whole seldom bothered to register and vote. However, every indication showed that the black mayors and the black center cities over which they presided were in deep trouble in the 1970s. Aside from their fiscal problems resulting principally from rapidly diminishing tax revenue, definite moves were afoot to dilute and/or to restrict the autonomy of these municipalities. The business interests and white residents remaining in these cities invariably proposed the annexation of adjacent territory ostensibly as a means of broadening the municipality's tax base but also with an eye to diluting the power of the black electorate. With few exceptions these proposals have been scuttled either by referenda, which vote them down, or by the combined pressure of the white suburbanites and black political leaders who want no diminution of their power base. The net result is that the long-range interests of the black community are invariably neglected. See also BLACK PANTHER PARTY; BLACK POWER; CIVIL RIGHTS: CIVIL RIGHTS ACTS; CIVIL RIGHTS: CIVIL RIGHTS CASES, 1865–1965; CIVIL RIGHTS MOVEMENT: CIVIL RIGHTS MOVEMENT IN SELECTED STATES; JOINT CENTER FOR POLITICAL STUDIES (JCPS); MISSISSIPPI FREEDOM DEMOCRATIC PARTY (MFDP); NATIONAL ASSOCIATION FOR THE ADVANCEMENT OF COLORED PEOPLE (NAACP); POPULISTS.

REFERENCES: Banfield, Edward C. and James Q. Wilson, *City Politics,* Harvard University Press and MIT Press, Cambridge, 1963; Bartley, Numan V. and Hugh D. Graham, *Southern Politics and the Second Reconstruction,* Johns Hopkins University Press, Baltimore, 1975; Bartley, Numan V., *The Rise of Massive Resistance: Race and Politics in the South During the 1950s,* Louisiana State University Press, Baton Rouge, 1969; Bond, Julian, *Black Candidates: Southern Campaign Experience,* Southern Regional Council, Atlanta, 1969; Brisbane, Robert H., *Black Activism: Racial Revolution in the United States, 1965–1970,* Judson Press, Valley Forge, 1974; Gosnell, Harold F. and Robert E. Martin, "The Negro as Voter and Office Holder," *Journal of Negro Education,* Fall 1963, pp. 415–25; Grossman, Lawrence, *The Democratic Party and the Negro,* University of Illinois Press, Urbana, 1976; Havard, William, *The Changing Politics of the South,* Louisiana State University Press, Baton Rouge, 1972; Holloway, Harry, *The Politics of the Southern Negro: From Exclusion to Big City Organization,* Random House, New York, 1969; Key, V. O., Jr., *Southern Politics in State and Nation* Alfred A. Knopf, New York, 1949; Ladd, Everett Carel, Jr., *Negro Political Leadership in the South,* Cornell University Press, Ithaca, 1966; Lewinson, Paul, *Race, Class, and Party: A History of Negro Suffrage and White Politics in the South,* rev. ed., Grosset & Dunlap, New York, 1965; McMillen, Neil, *The Citizens' Council: Organized Resistance to the Second Reconstruction, 1954–1964,* University of Illinois Press, Urbana, 1971; Marshall, Thurgood, "The Rise and Collapse of the 'White Democratic Primary,'" *Journal of Negro Education,* Summer 1957, pp. 249–54; Matthews, Donald R. and James W. Protho, *Negroes and the New Southern Politics,* Harcourt, Brace & World, New York, 1966; Peirce, Neal R., *The Deep South States of America: People, Politics, and Power in the Seven Deep South States,* W. W. Norton, New York, 1974; Tindall, George B., *The Disruption of the Solid South,* University of Georgia Press, Athens, 1972; U.S. Commission on Civil Rights, *Political Participation: A Study of the Participation by Negroes in the Electoral and Political Processes in 10 Southern States Since Passage of the Voting Rights Act of 1965,* U.S. Government Printing Office, Washington, D.C., 1968; U.S. Commission on Civil Rights, *Voting in Mississippi,* U.S. Government Printing Office, Washington, D.C., 1965; Walton, Hanes, Jr., *Black Political Parties: An Historical and Political Analysis,* Free Press, New York, 1972; Walton, Hanes, Jr., *Black Political Parties: A Theoretical and Structural Analysis,* J. B. Lippincott Co., Philadelphia, 1972; Watters, Pat and Reese Cleghorn, *Climbing Jacob's Ladder: The Arrival of Negroes in Southern Politics,* Harcourt, Brace & World, New York, 1967; Wilson, James Q., *Negro Politics: The Search for Leadership,* Free Press, Glencoe, 1960; Wirt, Frederick M., *Politics of Southern Equality: Law and Social Change in A Mississippi County,* Aldine Publishing Co., Chicago, 1971; and Woodward, C. Vann, *The Strange Career of Jim Crow,* 3d. ed., rev., Oxford University Press, New York, 1974.

POLK, PRENTISS See PHOTOGRAPHERS.

POLLARD, FREDERICK See ATHLETES: FOOTBALL.

POMPEY, MAURICE D. (1923–   ), lawyer, judge; born in South Bend, Ind. Pompey began his college education at Howard University (Washington, D.C.) in 1940. Upon returning from a tour of duty as a bomber pilot in the U.S. Army Air Corps, he attended Roosevelt College (Chicago, Ill.; now Roosevelt University) and received his LL.B. degree from DePaul University Law School (Chicago, Ill.) in 1951. Pompey became a judge of the Circuit Court of Cook County, Ill., in 1970.

POOR, SALEM (1747– ?), soldier; born in Andover, Mass. Poor was a freeman, and in 1775, infused with patriotic zeal, he joined a colonial militia force under Capt. Benjamin Ames. Poor first saw action on June 17, 1775, at the Battle of Bunker Hill. Fourteen officers praised him in a testimonial dated December 5, 1775.

POPULATION

Background Historians have generally agreed that the first blacks to arrive in British mainland colonies (later the continental United States), very likely about 20 in number, landed in Virginia in 1619. However, neither the exact number, date, nor the first debarkation site is conclusive. Conjecture exists that the first passengers, laborers but not slaves, may have landed before 1619; and, even if the date is accepted, the number may not have been "20 and odd." So practically nothing is known about the first and early arrivals in regard to such characteristics as age, sex, point of origin, and their destination and distribution in Virginia, which was the first and only British continental colony until the Pilgrims came to Plymouth, Mass., in 1620. It is definitely known, however, that Virginia sustained the largest Afro-American population of any colony or state for 250 years, until it was outranked by the state of Georgia during the Civil War decade of the 1860s. Either by slave importations mainly during the eighteenth century, or more important by natural increase, the modest number of "20 and odd" blacks in 1619 had grown to more than 24 million by the mid-1970s, as shown in the accompanying table.

Virginia's lead as colony and state also reflected the dominance of the South in regard to the total Afro-American population. For example, at the beginning of the Revolutionary War (1774–75), about 4 out of every 10 Afro-Americans lived in Virginia, a southern colony. If the black population of all southern colonies were included—Maryland, North Carolina, South Carolina, and Georgia—then the proportion would be more than 9 out of every 10 blacks living in the colonies. At this time, the Afro-American population of Virginia was larger than populations of four colonies—New Hampshire, Delaware, Rhode Island, and Georgia—in addition to the frontier counties of Virginia (Kentucky) and Massachusetts (Maine).

The percentage of Afro-Americans in the total population was also the highest in Virginia until 1720 when the colony was surpassed by South Carolina. In turn, after this date, whether as colony or state, South Carolina held the first rank in maintaining the highest percentages of blacks in the total American population throughout the eighteenth and nineteenth centuries (1720–1900), except for the periods of the 1810s and the 1830s when its rank was exceeded by Louisiana. Indeed, due to slave importations from 1720 to 1740, the percentages of Afro-Americans

GROWTH OF THE AFRO-AMERICAN POPULATION, 1619–1974

Year	Total number Afro-American	White	Percent Afro-American of total population
1619/20	20	2,180	1.0
1630	60	4,586	2.0
1640	597	26,037	2.2
1650	1,600	48,768	3.2
1660	2,920	72,138	3.9
1670	4,535	107,400	4.0
1680	6,971	144,536	4.6
1690	16,729	193,643	8.0

(Shown in thousands after 1690: add 000)

Year	Total number Afro-American	White	Percent Afro-American of total population
1700	27	223	11.1
1710	44	286	13.5
1720	68	397	14.8
1730	91	538	14.5
1740	160	745	17.7
1750	236	934	20.2
1760	325	1,267	20.4
1770	459	1,688	21.4
1780	575	2,204	20.7
1790	757	3,172	19.3
1800	1,002	4,306	18.9
1810	1,378	5,862	19.0
1820	1,772	7,867	18.4
1830	2,329	10,537	18.1
1840	2,874	14,196	16.8
1850	3,639	19,553	15.7
1860	4,442	26,923	14.1
1870	5,392	33,589[1]	13.5
1880	6,581	43,403	13.1
1890	7,389[1]	55,101	12.3
1900	7,760	66,809	11.6
1910	9,827	81,364	10.7
1920	10,463	94,120	9.9
1930	11,891	108,864	9.7
1940	12,865	118,214	9.7
1950	15,042	134,982	9.9
1960	18,871	158,831	10.5
1970	22,530	177,748	11.1
1974	24,038	183,823	11.4

SOURCE: See REFERENCES with asterisk (*). [1]Later revisions not shown.

within South Carolina surpassed those of whites by a ratio of 2 to 1, the highest for any colony or state in American history. However, South Carolina restricted slave importations during the last three decades of the eighteenth century, and this factor, among others, led to a decline in the high proportion of Afro-Americans. The decline was apparent in the first three federal censuses of 1790, 1800, and 1810 in which Afro-Americans were shown to comprise less than half of the state's total population. However, the decline was short-lived, and Afro-Americans continued to constitute about 60 percent of South Carolina's population until 1920.

Two additional southern states, Louisiana and Mississippi, also had percentages of Afro-Americans above the 50-percent level throughout the nineteenth century, except for a short period in Mississippi after its statehood (1817–30), and a period in Louisiana from 1890 to 1900. The black majority ended in Louisiana in 1900, in South Carolina in 1920, and in Mississippi in 1940. Despite the loss of black majorities, however, these three southern states continued to have the highest percentages of Afro-Americans in the United States. For example, the census of 1970 showed Mississippi with 37.2 percent, followed by South Carolina and Louisiana with 30.7 and 30.2 percentages, respectively.

Moreover, individual southern states not only retained the highest percentages of Afro-Americans, but also the South as a region continued to sustain the largest Afro-American population as shown in the fact that 90 percent or more of all Afro-Americans lived in the South until the beginning of the twentieth century. However, this high preponderance declined dramatically in the wake of migrations from the region following World War I (1918). With the coming of the great migrations that gained momentum after World War II, the South lost its great concentrations of blacks. For example, although the state of Georgia had the largest number of Afro-Americans after surpassing Virginia's total in 1870, New York became the first nonsouthern state to take the lead during the decade of the 1950s and to hold the first rank among states. Moreover, by 1970 New York's highest (among states) Afro-American population total of about 2.2 million was followed by two other nonsouthern states: Illinois, with slightly more than 1.4 million, and California, with 1.4 million.

Despite these population shifts, however, the South still contained a majority of the nation's Afro-Americans in the 1970s. Of the nation's 22.5 million Afro-Americans in 1970, for example, 12 million lived in the South; and five southern states—Texas, Georgia, North Carolina, Louisiana, and Florida (in this order)—each had a population numbering more than 1 million Afro-Americans. In addition, it appeared by the mid-1970s that more blacks were returning to the South than leaving it, assuring the region of a continuing large, if not increasing, black population.

Shifts in the size and distribution of the Afro-American population have reflected the main internal migrations in Afro-American history. Excluding the Atlantic slave trade, which for practical purposes ceased to be a factor affecting the size and distribution of the black population by 1810, the first great internal migration of Afro-Americans occurred in the nineteenth century. It was basically a movement associated with the expansion of slavery from the tobacco- and rice-growing areas into the developing frontier lands to the southwest—that is, into the cotton and sugar "kingdoms" of Georgia, Alabama, Mississippi, Louisiana, Arkansas, and Texas. Though not confined exclusively to these states, the movement was essentially agrarian in its nature and scope, being tied to one of the labor systems of slavery, farm tenancy, or peonage.

The second great migration, or groups of migrations that constitute a larger movement, came at times during the twentieth century, especially in the wakes of the two world wars. As a movement toward urban centers, the migrations were inspired by the hope, if not promise, of a better way of life outside of the poorer rural South. The first manifestation of this second movement was toward the industrial cities of the Northeast (Atlantic Coast), with such terminals as Baltimore, Md.; Philadelphia, Pa.; New York, N.Y.; and Boston, Mass. The second prong flowed upward from the South through the Mississippi Valley with such terminals as St. Louis, Mo.; Chicago, Ill.; and Gary, Ind. Yet a third though lesser prong of the second movement manifested itself, flowing northward out of Kentucky, Georgia, and Alabama into such inland, lake, or river cities of the Midwest as Ohio's Cincinnati, Cleveland, and Columbus and Michigan's Detroit. Before World War II, these migrations made heavy but not exclusive use of such railroad lines as the Seaboard, Atlantic Coastline, Louisville and Nashville, Rock Island, and

Illinois Central. Migrants after World War II supplemented these lines by extensive travel by bus lines or private automobiles.

The third great migration occurred almost exclusively after World War II, and in a sense it may be regarded as a phase of the second movement. The great difference in this postwar migration was one of direction. Instead of northward, the movement was westward to the Pacific, mainly to the state of California.

It is well to remember that these migrations of Afro-Americans not only corresponded in many respects to the migrations of southern whites, but also to the general American population shifts from farm to city. Therefore, whereas the most dramatic aspects of the black migrations were to northern cities, noticeable movements of Afro-Americans from southern farm to southern city occurred. The black migrations and their impact upon cities are discussed below.

Migrations and the Urban Impact The dramatic shift in the overall geographic location of the black population is documented in census data showing that during the 1960s five states—California, New York, Illinois, New Jersey, and Michigan—each added more than 100,000 Afro-Americans to their populations through migration. Conversely, seven southern states had Afro-American migration losses exceeding 100,000—Mississippi, Alabama, South Carolina, North Carolina, Louisiana, Arkansas, and Georgia. By 1970 Mississippi had lost nearly one-third of its 1960 Afro-American population; and in Alabama, South Carolina, and Arkansas as well, migration losses of Afro-Americans exceeded the natural gains in the Afro-American population. In 1970, 52 percent of the Afro-American population lived in the South, 20 percent lived in the Northeast, 20 percent in the North-central region, and 8 percent in the West.

During the period from 1960 to 1966, Afro-American migration accounted for an estimated 34 percent of metropolitan growth. Since 1966, however, an apparent slowing in the rate of movement of Afro-Americans out of the South has occurred. Indeed, for the population of the South, the shift to net in-migration occurred in the 1960s, but the region continued to send out more low-income migrants than it received until the mid-1970s, when the historic out-migration of the poor from the South was reversed.

Within central cities, Afro-Americans became increasingly concentrated in ethnically similar neighborhoods. In 20 large cities the percentage of Afro-Americans in neighborhoods in which they represented three-fourths of the population increased from 30 to 51 percent between 1950 and 1970, while the proportion of Afro-Americans in mixed neighborhoods in which they represented one-fourth or less of the population declined from 25 to 16 percent. In every one of 47 cities with Afro-American populations in excess of 50,000, the majority of Afro-Americans, and often the overwhelming majority, lived in predominantly or solidly black census tracts.

Generally speaking, cities with a smaller number of Afro-Americans have shown a lesser degree of concentration. However, exceptions do exist, as in Ft. Lauderdale, Fla., where 95 percent of 21,000 Afro-Americans have lived in concentrated black areas. Another exception is Las Vegas, Nev., where 93 percent lived in solidly black tracts.

By all measures, migrations into Chicago, Ill., effected a high degree of segregation, while those into San Francisco, Calif., Los Angeles, Calif., and New York, N.Y., effected a relatively high degree of dispersion. For some cities, the rank varied depending on the measurement used. In cities where Afro-Americans were less concentrated in solidly Afro-American areas, it cannot readily be assumed that they had had greater access to nonsegregated housing throughout the community. Instead, less concentration usually indicated that the patterns of segregation were less rigid. Thus, in cities in which there was only one ghetto area expanding at the fringes, a more rigid pattern of residential segregation existed. In those cities with two or more ghetto areas expanding at the fringes, less-segregated patterns resulted when the black housing demand was not sufficient to fill up the potentially open areas at the various ghetto fringes.

Although black segregation and concentration in central cities increased after 1950, the movement of a small but significant number of Afro-Americans to suburban areas indicated an easing of past trends. For example, a study of 15 of the largest metropolitan areas of the United States in 1971 showed that in 10 areas the suburban Afro-American population grew by more than 50 percent during the 1960s. In 9 of these 15 areas, the Afro-American population grew at a higher rate in the suburbs than it did in the central city. This new trend began relatively late in the decade of the 1960s when the annual rate of Afro-American population growth in the suburbs reached eight percent. Increases in black income in the late 1960s, changes in attitudes and behavior of blacks and whites, effects of the civil rights movement of the 1960s, and subsequent changes in public policy (in particular the federal fair housing law) all played a part in increasing black suburbanization.

In general, suburban Afro-Americans are more integrated with whites than in central cities. In most cities the majority of suburban Afro-Americans live in tracts in which the white population is predominant. However, Detroit, Mich.; Los Angeles-Long Beach, Calif.; Chicago, Ill.; St. Louis, Mo.; Gary, Ind.; Cleveland, Ohio; Jackson, Miss.; and San Francisco-Oakland, Calif., are

among metropolitan areas (SMSA's)[1] in which the majority of suburban blacks live in overwhelmingly black tracts. In some of these areas, a substantial portion of suburban blacks are concentrated in relatively older cities and towns outside central cities. These places in many respects resemble their sister central cities rather than new-growth suburban areas, and hence do not fit the common concept of suburbs. East St. Louis, Ill., with more than one-third of the St. Louis suburban blacks, Camden, N.J., and Chester, Pa., with one-third of suburban Philadelphia blacks, are outstanding examples.

The movement of Afro-Americans to the suburban areas of Washington, D.C., is fairly typical of black suburbanization elsewhere. There,

30 CITIES RANKED BY AFRO-AMERICAN POPULATION

City	Afro-American population 1970	1970 National rank		Afro-American population percentage	
		Afro-American	Total	1970	1960
New York, N.Y.	1,668,636	1	1	21.2%	14%
Chicago, Ill.	1,102,620	2	2	32.7	23
Detroit, Mich.	660,438	3	5	43.7	29
Philadelphia, Pa.	653,791	4	4	33.6	26
Washington, D.C.	537,712	5	9	71.1	54
Los Angeles, Calif.	503,606	6	3	17.9	14
Baltimore, Md.	420,210	7	7	46.4	35
Houston, Tex.	316,551	8	6	25.7	23
Cleveland, Ohio	287,841	9	10	38.3	29
New Orleans, La.	267,308	10	19	45.0	37
Atlanta, Ga.	255,051	11	27	51.3	38
St. Louis, Mo.	254,191	12	18	40.9	29
Memphis, Tenn.	242,513	13	17	38.9	37
Dallas, Tex.	210,238	14	8	24.9	19
Newark, N.J.	207,458	15	36	54.2	34
Indianapolis, Ind.	134,320	16	11	18.0	21
Birmingham, Ala.	126,388	17	48	42.0	40
Cincinnati, Ohio	125,070	18	29	27.6	22
Oakland, Calif.	124,710	19	38	34.5	23
Jacksonville, Fla.	118,158	20	23	22.3	41
Kansas City, Mo.	112,005	21	26	22.1	18
Milwaukee, Wis.	105,088	22	12	14.7	8
Pittsburgh, Pa.	104,904	23	24	20.2	17
Richmond, Va.	104,766	24	57	42.0	42
Boston, Mass.	104,707	25	16	16.3	9
Columbus, Ohio	99,627	26	21	18.5	16
San Francisco, Calif.	96,078	27	13	13.4	10
Buffalo, N.Y.	94,329	28	28	20.4	13
Gary, Ind.	92,695	29	75	52.8	39
Nashville-Davidson, Tenn.	87,851	30	30	19.6	38

SOURCE: Adapted from U.S. Department of Commerce, Bureau of the Census, *Minority Media Conference Report*, May 18, 1971, Table I: "Negro and Total Population for the 50 Cities with the Largest Negro Population: 1970 and 1960."

[1]SMSA's (Standard Metropolitan Statistical Areas) are official designations first established by the federal government (Bureau of the Budget) in 1949 in order to make use of the same boundaries in the study and analysis of statistical data relating to metropolitan problems. The general concept of the term is one of an integrated economic and social unit with a recognized large population nucleus consisting of at least one central city with 50,000 inhabitants or more, or two cities having contiguous boundaries and constituting, for general economic and social purposes, a single community with a combined population of at least 50,000, the smaller of which must have a population of at least 15,000; similarly, two or more adjacent counties with such cities within 20 miles of each other may be included in the concept. For official definitions see Bureau of the Budget, *Standard Metropolitan Statistical Areas*, U.S. Government Printing Office, Washington, D.C., 1967. For SMSA's as of July 1, 1970, numbering 233, see U.S. Bureau of the Census, *Metropolitan Area Statistics*, reprinted from *Statistical Abstract of the United States, 1970*, U.S. Government Printing Office, Washington, D.C., 1970.

increases in black population throughout the suburban areas have taken place in a very uneven pattern. Most Afro-Americans (67 percent) have moved to suburban neighborhoods of Prince George's County, Md., which are contiguous to the heavily black-populated southeast and northeast sections of Washington, D.C. Thus, the predominant pattern of suburban black settlement in Washington, D.C., has been extended ghettoization. In other Washington, D.C., metropolitan jurisdictions, Afro-Americans have located through a pattern that primarily establishes or reinforces pockets of minority population. Relatively few Afro-Americans have moved into predominantly white neighborhoods. However, this limited amount of integration is a significant change from earlier patterns in the metropolitan Washington, D.C., area. The change indicated that Afro-Americans particularly those with higher incomes, took advantage of a greater variety of housing locations than previously.

Fertility* During the early nineteenth century, death rates among Afro-Americans were very high, but fertility rates were even higher and the population annually grew at a rate of two percent or more. Beginning in the latter part of the nineteenth century, the birth rate declined; the decline continued until the late 1930s and affected all social classes in both urban and rural areas. As far as we can detect, this decrease was chiefly brought about, not by changes in marital patterns or by the increased use of contraceptives, but by alterations in health conditions that were unfavorable to fecundity. During this same period, only modest improvements in mortality occurred. Certain contagious diseases, such as yellow fever, cholera, malaria, and typhoid fever—once major causes of death—gradually disappeared as ecological changes occurred and technologies for eliminating carriers of these diseases improved. However, living conditions in southern rural areas may have deteriorated, and life expectancy among Afro-Americans was probably only a little greater in 1930 than 70 years earlier. Thus, the Afro-American population differs from many others since fertility rates declined more rapidly than mortality rates for an extended period of time. During the decade of the Great Depression, the population increased at an annual rate of well under one percent.

---

*Reynolds Farley, *Growth of the Black Population: A Study of Demographic Trends*, Chicago, Illinois. Copyright © by Markham Publishing Company, 1970, pp. 243–45.

Beginning in 1935 major efforts were made to improve health standards and during World War II income went up rapidly among Afro-Americans. In the 20-year span from 1935 to 1955, death rates were substantially reduced and life expectancy increased. Afro-Americans rapidly moved into urban areas and their socioeconomic position improved. One might have predicted that this would lead to a continuation of the low fertility rates of the Great Depression era, but this did not happen. Instead, fertility rates began to climb around 1940 and continued to increase for about 20 years. By the late 1950s the black population was growing at about 2.5 percent each year or approximately as fast as in the pre-Civil War period. This increase in fertility resulted from improved health conditions and the minimization of fertility-impairing diseases. During the 1940s and 1950s some women began using effective contraceptives, but, as the fertility studies demonstrate, many black women delayed using birth control or used ineffective methods and consequently excess childbearing frequently occurred.

Birth rates have fallen since the late 1950s, and this is an important component of the demographic transition. The further urbanization of Afro-Americans and continued improvements in educational attainment have led more couples to be aware of the possibilities and advantages of limited numbers of children. Since 1960 new contraceptive methods—the estrogen-progestin pills and the intrauterine devices—have become popular. These technological innovations have fostered a more widespread and effective use of birth control. Thus, the contemporary decline in Afro-American fertility differs from the decline that occurred prior to the Great Depression for it results from the deliberate control of childbearing.

The evidence does not permit us to predict whether racial differences in fertility will someday be nonexistent or whether the fertility of blacks may be persistently higher or lower than that of whites. We do observe that the long-run trends in white and black fertility have been quite similar, although we have not examined how the fertility of such subgroups of the white population as foreign-born whites compares to that of blacks. In addition, the patterns of rural-urban and socioeconomic differentials in fertility are the same among whites and blacks, and apparently this has been the case for a long time. The studies of fertility desires and expectations that have been conducted recently suggest there is very little racial difference in the number of children couples wish to have. However, a look at vital statistics data for any recent year finds that black fertility rates are substantially higher than those of whites. We believe there are two major reasons for this. First, among women in rural areas and among those with the characteristics of low economic status, black fertility rates exceed those of whites by a wide margin. Second, fertility rates at young ages, particularly during the teen years, are much higher among blacks than among whites. The changing characteristics of the black population and the growing use of birth control will probably lead to lower fertility rates, but it is impossible to know whether this will have the consequence of eliminating racial differences in family size. *See also* AFRICA: THE ATLANTIC SLAVE TRADE IN PERSPECTIVE; AFRO-AMERICAN HISTORY; AGRICULTURE; CIVIL DISORDERS; FAMILY; HEALTH; HOUSING; POLITICS.

REFERENCES: Craven, Wesley Frank, "Twenty Negroes to Jamestown in 1619?," *Virginia Quarterly Review*, vol. 47, pp. 416–20, 1971; Farley, Reynolds, *Growth of the Black Population: A Study of Demographic Trends*, Markham Publishing Co., Chicago, 1970; Paullin, Charles O., *Atlas of the Historical Geography of the United States*, Carnegie Institution of Washington and the American Geographical Society of New York, Washington, D.C., 1932; Price, Daniel O., *Changing Characteristics of the Negro Population*, 1960 Census Monograph, U.S. Department of Commerce, Bureau of the Census, U.S. Government Printing Office, Washington, D.C., 1969; Taeuber, Karl E. and Alma F. Taeuber, *Negroes in Cities: Residential Segregation and Neighborhood Change*, Aldine Publishing Co., Chicago, 1965; U.S. Commission on Civil Rights, *Twenty Years After Brown: Equal Opportunity in Housing*, U.S. Government Printing Office, Washington, D.C., 1975; *U.S. Department of Commerce, Bureau of the Census, 1970 Census of Population, *General Population Characteristics: United States Summary*, U.S. Government Printing Office, Washington, D.C., 1972, tables 60, 61; *U.S. Department of Commerce, Bureau of the Census, *Historical Statistics of the United States*, U.S. Government Printing Office, Washington, D.C., 1961, p.756; *U.S. Department of Commerce, Bureau of the Census, *Negro Population, 1790–1915*, U.S. Government Printing Office, Washington, D.C., 1918, chapt. IV; *U.S. Department of Commerce, Bureau of the Census, *Negroes in the United States, 1920–32*, U.S. Government Printing Office, Washington, D.C., 1935, chap. I; *U.S. Department of Commerce, Bureau of the Census, Sixteenth Census of the United States: 1940, *Population*, U.S. Government Printing Office, Washington, D.C., vol. II, 1943, pp. 52–55; and U.S. Department of Commerce, Social and Economic Statistics Administration, Bureau of the Census, *The Social and Economic Status of the Black Population in the United States, 1974*, U.S. Government Printing Office, Washington, D.C., 1974.

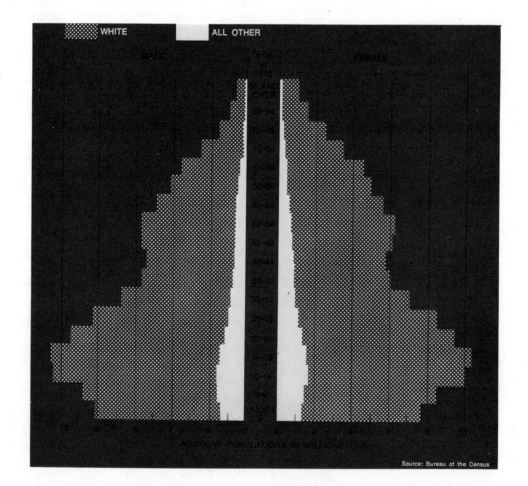

Graph showing resident populations of the United States in 1975. About 90 percent of "all other," indicated in white on the graph, would refer to the Afro-American population. Note the relative sizes in age groups: for example, about 40 percent of all blacks would be under 18 years of age compared with about 22 percent for whites.

POPULISTS

Introduction In the 1890s the majority of America's Afro-American population lived in the South. The massive disfranchisement of Afro-American voters by legal means (court decisions, new or amended state constitutions, and complex laws regulating voting) still lay ahead for most southern states. Because Afro-Americans had barely begun to migrate north and west and because they constituted such a large and well-defined minority in the South, that region's political structure was significantly influenced by the black vote. The success or failure of a political retrenchment lay, to an important degree, in the hands of the black voters.

In the antebellum South, politics had been the exclusive domain of the whites. Within that domain existed a healthy system of two-party competition between the Whigs and the Democrats. In general, the more egalitarian Democrats (the party also numbered many men of wealth in its ranks) were in the majority, while the Whigs (more aristocratic but containing numerous yeoman-farmer adherents) offered respectable opposition and frequently won elections. The polarization of the nation's attitudes toward slavery in the 1850s and the attending crisis in the election of 1860 resulted in the collapse of the southern wing of the Whig Party and domination by the Democrats. Abraham Lincoln's victory as standard bearer for the fledgling Republicans was followed by secession, the formation of the Confederate States of America, and the cataclysm of war. Whatever the Civil War accomplished or failed to accomplish, its end heralded freedom for slaves, and, in the Reconstruction period that followed, their emergence as voters and participants in government.

Southern Politics During Reconstruction In the spring of 1865 southerners, white and black, found their familiar world revolutionized, changed forever. The physical and psychological costs of the war, the abrupt changes in society, the tensions of Reconstruction, and the complex interrelationship of economics and politics were at once the difficulty of survival but no less the challenge of the future.

As the years of Reconstruction passed, action at the federal level, buttressed by state compliance (not, by any means, always voluntary), caused a political realignment in the South. The Republican Party, the party that had freed the slaves, moved into the states south of the Potomac River. Its strength in the South was based on three elements of the population. First, on native whites, many of them former Whigs, who joined the party only to be dismissed as opportunistic "scalawags" by their fellow southerners. The next category was made up of northerners who came South after Appomattox—their motivations ranging from greed for political spoils (a minority) to the idealistic desire to help improve social conditions for the southern people, especially Afro-Americans. Regardless of why they came, they were usually regarded by native southerners as grasping perpetrators of evil and stigmatized as "carpetbaggers." Neither the so-called scalawags nor the carpetbaggers represented more than a small percentage of the Republican Party's voting strength. This power resided with the third constituent group, the Afro-Americans. It was they who made up the overwhelming majority of the party, and it was upon their loyalty that the Republicans relied for success. But despite their numbers and despite certain exceptions, Afro-Americans never held positions of place and power. Instead, Republican affairs were controlled by white factions who, in fratricidal struggles of policy and personality, proceeded to destroy their organization.

Southern politicians, temporarily restored to power under President Andrew Johnson's plan of Reconstruction and then dethroned by the Radical Republican Congress that favored harsh measures for former Confederate leaders, gradually formulated a political strategy. The plan was so sound, so seemingly impregnable, that it influenced the actions of Afro-Americans and whites and the events of Populism three decades later. Simply, it called for southern whites to join together in one political party and to present as their basic goals the achievement of "redemption" or "home rule" and the establishment of white supremacy. Former Whigs and Democrats united under the Democratic Party label (in some states the organization was called the Democratic and Conservative Party, but in time the word "Conservative" was dropped). This alliance held that political power should be in the hands of native whites, and that only by maintaining white supremacy could they lift the yoke of alien rule and defeat the unholy alliance of northern whites and blacks that made up the Republican Party.

The struggle for political preeminence was on. The Republican machine—labeled the party of corruption and dishonesty, torn asunder by internecine warfare, and branded the advocate of social equality and relentless agent of the Negro—collapsed in state after state across the South. The American people, debilitated by the agony of civil war and weary of the scandals of the Grant administration and the excesses of Radical Reconstruction, were willing to turn the South back to the control of the native whites whose ideas the war had been fought to overcome. The industrial revolution, accelerated by the Civil War, was not to be denied. Mighty railroads criss-crossed the country; corporations realized staggering profits. This dazzling "gilded age" was no place for depressing stories of racial tension and political dislocations from the South.

Rural blacks in the post-Civil War South are shown discussing politics in this sketch by W.L. Sheppard for *Harper's Weekly*.

Northern consciences were salved by southerners who explained that, knowing the black man intimately, they were best equipped to look after and protect his interests. Democrats returned to the halls of Congress and to the statehouses in Jackson, Miss., Montgomery, Ala., Richmond, Va., and elsewhere. By 1877 Union soldiers had been withdrawn from their last outposts in Louisiana, Florida, and South Carolina. It was true that a Republican, Rutherford B. Hayes, was returned to the White House, but strong indications—even promises—existed that Republicans would not be averse to help fund internal improvements (mainly railroads) in the South. The Democrats had resumed the reins of control in the South in the name of strict economy and honesty in government and of white supremacy. If the Afro-American felt betrayed, he had every cause to; his future was very uncertain.

Politics of the New South The political leaders of the New South came to be called Bourbons. Scrupulously honest (with some exceptions) in governmental administration, they cut state spending to a minimum. Their program was a natural reaction to what was considered the wasteful spending of Reconstruction, and it could be justified with the argument that state treasuries were dangerously low. Yet, needed legislation in education, health, and social welfare either passed in emasculated form, failed to pass, or was not introduced at all. The Bourbons, always a minority, held a monopoly on governmental positions and passed the various offices around among themselves. That many were able people is true, but other white men, and black, who were equally capable were never given the opportunity to demonstrate their abilities. The self-righteous Bourbons contended that they alone stood between orderly, respectable government and a return to the chaos of Reconstruction. White men might differ on some issues but, the Bourbons argued, they all agreed on the necessity of maintaining white supremacy. It followed, therefore, that whites must never disagree to the point of splitting the Democratic Party. To do so invited a return to Republican misrule.

Reconstruction over, the Republican Party in the South split into two factions: the "Black and Tans," composed of Afro-Americans still loyal to the party of liberation, and the "Lily Whites," made up of white men who maintained a party structure in order to send delegates to national conventions and receive federal appointments. Republican candidates for office were rarely elected. Still constituting the bulk of the party, Afro-Americans seldom formulated policy. Bourbon nominees usually ran without opposition, and it was small wonder that they had a sense of complacency; their fallen foe had become impotent.

In the 1870s and 1880s Independent and

Greenback movements spread through the South. Committed generally to ending ring rule and bossism and to easing economic privation by a program of inflation, their success was limited. A lack of funds, program, and leadership simply could not succeed against the Democratic juggernaut. Afro-Americans did not participate significantly in the Independent and Greenback efforts.

Southern Agrarianism Throughout these years, Afro-Americans continued to vote. The Bourbons were not concerned with taking away the ballot from the blacks, but only with controlling the way they voted. As the South, desperate for capital, became gripped by its one-crop (cotton in the Deep South, tobacco in the Upper South) economy and the attendant crop-lien and tenant or sharecropping system, the landless blacks (and increasingly, the poor whites) became dependent upon their landlords and supply merchants. The Bourbons, many of whom were industry-oriented and emulative of northern business know-how, still owned large tracts of land, and were able to dictate voting patterns to their tenants. Economic sovereignty meant political sovereignty as well, and in the South, particularly in states where Afro-Americans were concentrated in regions called "Black Belts," the Bourbons were able to manipulate the black vote as they desired.

But even as the railroad bound the country to the city as never before, and even as the smoke from new factories in Chattanooga, Tenn., Birmingham, Ala., and other cities could be seen rising across the land, serious flaws in the facade of the new and prosperous America became evident. Corporate dividends went to a select few; capital itself was concentrated in the East, while the defeated South languished on an economic vine always in danger of drying up. The South's economy remained essentially rural, and the majority of its population were farmers, dependent not just on the bone-crushing labor of tilling the soil, but on unpredictable weather conditions and on market prices. The southern cotton farmer neither controlled the prices he paid for agricultural implements necessary to produce his crop—prices that tended to increase—nor the prices he received when the crop was harvested—prices that tended to decline. The farmer had to plant more in order to break even in terms of money received, yet as surpluses piled up, market prices dipped lower. Midwestern wheat farmers suffered similar difficulties but to a lesser extent, and they too would soon stir in discontent.

Farmers, both black and white, were told in patronizing terms to economize, or, more often, to move to town. Since it was hardly possible for most of them to economize any more, and since it was simply impossible for many to leave their land (although in increasing numbers they did abandon the soil) or control production, the farmers began looking for some means of redressing the wrongs inflicted upon them.

Local, county, and then state agricultural societies were formed in most southern states during Reconstruction. They hoped by collective action and mutual exchange of information to bring a return of prosperity. Most of these societies had white members only. In the depression-wracked 1870s the Patrons of Husbandry or Grange moved into the South. Unlike the Midwestern Grange, which embarked upon political as well as economic activities, the Grange in the South, where Republicans and Democrats were acting out their bitter struggle, was primarily limited to social and economic projects. It promoted nonpartisan agricultural legislation, held fairs and barbecues, conducted institutes, operated schools, and opened a number of cooperative stores. It was a precursor to the more militant organizations of the 1880s and an initial step toward the politics of Populism. Although primarily composed of farmers, both large- and small-scale, the Grange admitted businessmen and merchants to membership. A few black Granges were founded, but they were short-lived and had limited influence. However, Grange stores began to close because of mismanagement, lack of money, and underselling by more experienced rivals. The economic depression failed to lift, and the Grange's economic program languished, with a concomitant loss of enthusiasm. By the mid-1880s the Patrons had suffered a drastic decline in membership, and the tenant farmers once again had no spokesman.

As the Grange lay moribund, new organizations rose that promised salvation for the southern farmer. The Agricultural Wheel was founded at Des Arc, Ark., in 1882, spread to other southern states, and became a national order in 1885. In 1886 it absorbed another farm group, the Brothers of Freedom. The Wheel initiated cooperative ventures in buying and selling similar to those of the Grange, but it also assumed a militant tack. Wheelers, even rank-and-file members, were class conscious and recognized a common bond between themselves and industrial workers. They called for direct participation by state and national governments in the economy, and urged effective regulation of monopolies. When the order's economic program faltered, many Wheelers advocated shifting to politics to achieve their ends. There were separate Afro-American Wheels, and the economic and political interests of blacks were seen as identical to those of the whites. Although the black Wheels maintained their separate status, at conventions and various conclaves both white and black Wheelers met and voted together.

The Agricultural Wheel was gradually eclipsed by a farm organization more extensive in geographical range and better organized: the Farmers' Alliance. Founded originally in Texas about 1875, the Alliance, which was devoted to the interests of small farmers, became statewide in the late 1870s. By the mid-1880s organizers had gone into other southern states. Farmers responded with evangelical enthusiasm. Under the leadership of its president, Dr. Charles W. Macune, the Alliance became a national order with headquarters in Washington, D.C. A powerful, although smaller, Northern Farmers' Alliance also existed. At Meridian, Miss., in 1888, the Southern Farmers' Alliance absorbed the Agricultural Wheel.

The Farmers' Alliance became the most powerful agricultural organization the nation had ever seen. Besides sponsoring social and educational activities, it embarked on a bewildering number of economic schemes: operating steamboats, textile factories, fertilizer plants, banks, insurance companies, warehouses, and sprawling state exchanges for farm products. Officially eschewing politics, the Farmers' Alliance seemed to offer the long-sought relief from economic misery and to promise a place of dignity in society for the scorned agrarians.

Black Farmers' Alliance At the national meeting at Meridian in 1888, the Farmers' Alliance approved the formation of the Colored Farmers' National Alliance and Co-operative Union. The order represented the merger of several black Alliance movements and became generally known as the Colored Farmers' Alliance. The first black Alliance had been organized in Houston County, Tex., on December 11, 1886. A state organization was formed that same year, and the order followed the precedent of the white Alliance by spreading into other Southern states. General R. M. Humphrey, white, was founder and

superintendent, although Afro-Americans held office. The order was much more than a satellite of the white organization, and by 1890 more than one million Alliancemen were black.

The Colored Farmers' Alliance attempted, on a lesser scale, to duplicate the program of the white Alliance. Although many white Alliancemen looked askance at the black order's work, many approved its aims, and despite criticism from Bourbon editors and politicians, whites helped establish local orders for the blacks. The two orders were separate, but they cooperated in their economic programs. One white editor in Alabama noted that, "The white and colored Alliance are united in their war against trusts, and in promotion of the doctrine that farmers should establish cooperative stores and manufactures, and publish their own newspapers, conduct their own schools, and have a hand in everything else that concerns them as citizens or affects them personally or collectively."

As the 1880s drew to an end, it became apparent that the Farmers' Alliance was shifting its attention to politics. Since the majority of the population at that time was agrarian, a political party based on their interests would be unbeatable. In 1889 an important interracial national convention attended by Northern and Southern Alliancemen, Knights of Labor, and representatives of other working-class organizations was held at St. Louis, Mo. The convention issued the famous St. Louis "platform," calling for economic and political reform. Bourbon leaders denounced the program as false, communistic doctrine. The convention discussed the formation of a third party (a move that drew its heaviest support from Afro-Americans in the southern delegations), but nothing definite was accomplished. Afro-Americans were assured of a greater role in Alliance affairs, although their place was not one of equality. In 1890 another convention, this time at Ocala, Fla., thrust the Alliance closer to independent political action. At Ocala the Afro-American conferees were more active than before, and again voiced their desire for a separate party. Finally, after additonal meetings at Cincinnati, Ohio, in 1891, again at St. Louis, Mo., in 1892, and at Omaha, Nebr., in 1892, the People's or Populist Party was officially formed and candidates for national office nominated.

Impetus for the Populist Party came mainly from Midwestern farmers who were in a position to challenge the major parties for supremacy. But the situation for their white counterparts in the South was different and more complex. Bourbon Democrats had warned that political activity by the Alliance would split the Democratic Party and make possible the return of Republican rule. Acting on this assumption, the Southern Farmers' Alliance had attempted to take over the Democratic machinery from within. Alarmed by these developments, Democratic candidates had endorsed the Alliance program, and in the elections of 1890 Alliance candidates had won numerous offices in the South. But it soon became evident that the Bourbons could not be so easily dislodged. Campaign platforms, instead of being translated into action, had proved to be empty rhetoric, useful for winning agrarian votes but easily forgotten after the election.

Finally, in 1892, Southern white Alliancemen, facing a severe economic depression and disappointed with Democratic failures to enact a program of reform, broke the traditional barriers of race and party. They went over to the Populist Party and found many Afro-Americans ready to join them. The challenge to Democratic supremacy lasted through the election of 1896. In that year the Populist cause was doomed by the Democratic Party's nomination of William Jennings Bryan, its appropriation of reform causes (particularly that of free silver), and the subsequent election of Republican nominee William McKinley. In the South the Populist Party lingered into the twentieth century but offered no threat to the Democrats.

The Populist Revolt and the Afro-American Historians have written extensively about the movement and its place in American life. Populism has been viewed as a positive, rational program of reform whose basic concepts were later enacted into law. Other historians have assigned it a less honorable place, referring to the movement as essentially negative, unrealistic, out of touch with the emerging industrial society, and containing seeds of anti-Semitism and fascism. The important part played by Afro-Americans in the Populist upheaval has not yet been properly evaluated.

One group of historians contends that Afro-Americans received no more consideration from the Populists than from the Bourbons. The thesis is that, regardless of party, southern whites shared the same traditions of and beliefs in white supremacy, and that the only thing they sought from the black party member was his vote. In their attitudes concerning education, public transportation, jury service, lynching, and the like, it is believed that white southerners remained constant regardless of their political affiliation. Proof of this can be seen in the fact that the Populists did not reward their Afro-American supporters with public office, and even on occasion advocated total disfranchisement for blacks. The representation permitted to blacks at party conventions was token and insignificant, further evidence that the "People's Party" did not believe in either social or political equality. In fact, the very Populists who advocated rights for Afro-Americans in the 1890s became leading racists after 1900. Thus, some historians argue that although Afro-Americans were manipulated by the Republicans and controlled by the Bourbons, they had little reason to join the Populists.

Though courted politically by Populists, both black and white farmers in the post-Civil War South continued to face old problems, as shown in this sketch of black farmers unloading rice barges in South Carolina. (*Scribner's Monthly.*)

It is true that Populists courted Afro-American votes, and that Afro-American voters responded in large numbers. The black population of the 1890s was politically and economically unschooled, but it was not unintelligent. Many Afro-Americans saw an opportunity to rise from the bottom rung of southern society by political action, and they deserted the Republican and Democratic parties as a possible means to upward advancement. While it required a large measure of courage for white "dirt" farmers to forsake the Democrats, it required even more for blacks to leave the Republican fold; retribution of an unknown kind was sure to come. Yet many turned their backs on the Republicans, defied Democratic pressure, and voted Populist. They did so even though the Populists did not control the machinery of elections or count the votes. Frequently, as in North Carolina and Alabama, Afro-Americans made possible the successful fusion between Republicans and Populists. Victories by the Populists in hill counties and in piney woods counties, where there occurred a split in the white majority, can be traced directly to black votes. It can also be argued that Afro-Americans voted for the reformers because they promised political and economic improvement, dignity, and recognition. Although the Populist ranks contained racists, evidence suggests that the reformers were considerably less racist than the Bourbons. In several instances Afro-Americans held positions of leadership; John B. Rayner of Texas, for example, was extremely active in Populist councils and served on the party's executive committee. Such white men as Thomas E. Watson, who later preached race hatred in Georgia, championed the rights of blacks during the high tide of Populism; other white men, such as Joseph C. Manning of Alabama, never rejected the Populist creed of reform and political equality for blacks.

In contrast, examples abound of Democrats catering to black voters and of Populists who demanded all-white elections. Viewed superficially, such actions smack of gross hypocrisy, but a closer examination reveals the truth of these seemingly contradictory stances. Democratic appeals for Afro-American ballots frequently but not always failed. This made no difference in the black belts; the Bourbons simply resorted to fraud and intimidation by counting the votes of Afro-Americans as having been cast for Democrats. Even when Afro-Americans deliberately boycotted the polls to avoid such chicanery, the Bourbons still counted the blacks as having voted Democratic. These and other Bourbon machinations caused the desperate Populists to propose all-white elections.

With black support the Populists won numerous national and state offices in the South. The potential of uniting have-not whites and blacks together in agrarian protest was unlimited. In a few states, both black and white industrial workers also voted Populist. But control of the election machinery, strident pleas for white solidarity, appropriation of certain Populist programs, and lack of organization by the reformers assured a Democratic triumph in 1896. Conservative reaction to the Populist revolt took the form of demagogic racism and mass disfranchisement of blacks. Never again, the cry went up, should Afro-Americans be in a position to determine the outcome of elections.

However, all Democrats were not reactionaries; all Republicans were not blind to every issue

other than high tariffs and fiscal integrity; all Populists did not burn with a righteous desire to lift Afro-Americans from their lowly positions. But of the three groups, it was the Populists who offered the most to black people; it was the Populists who willingly faced political oblivion (and social and economic ostracism in some cases) to fight for election reform, economic readjustments, and political justice. Never before in American history had Afro-Americans and whites joined together in a political party based on securing for themselves a place of equity in society. *See also* AFRO-AMERICAN HISTORY: RECONSTRUCTION, 1865–77; AGRICULTURE; FRATERNAL SOCIETIES; POLITICS.

REFERENCES: Abramowitz, Jack, "The Negro in the Agrarian Revolt," *Agricultural History*, vol. 24, pp. 89–95, April 1950; Abramowitz, Jack, "The Negro in the Populist Movement," *Journal of Negro History*, vol. 38, pp. 257–89, July 1953; Bryant, Girard T., "The Populist Movement and the Negro," unpublished M.A. thesis, University of Kansas, Lawrence, 1939; Humphrey, General R. M., "History Of The Colored Farmers' National Alliance And Co-Operative Union," in N. A. Dunning (ed.), *The Farmers' Alliance History and Agricultural Digest*, Washington, 1891, pp. 288–92; Reddick, Jamie Lawson, "The Negro and the Populist Movement in Georgia," unpublished M.A. thesis, Atlanta University, Atlanta, 1937; Rogers, William Warren, "The Negro Alliance in Alabama," *Journal of Negro History*, vol. 45, pp. 38–44, January 1960; Saunders, Robert, "Southern Populists and the Negro, 1893–1895," *Journal of Negro History*, vol. 54, pp. 240–61, July 1969; Simkins, Francis B., "Ben Tillman's View of the Negro," *Journal of Southern History*, vol. 3, pp. 257–89, May 1957; and Woodward, C. Vann, "Tom Watson and the Negro," *Journal of Southern History*, vol. 3, pp. 14–33, February 1938. For a good book-length account of the Populist movement in general, see Goodwyn, Lawrence, *Democratic Promise: The Populist Moment in America*, Oxford U Pr., New York, 1976. Chapter 10, "The Populist Approach to Black America," treats mainly views by whites during the period. Racial views by whites are also stressed in a political study by Gaither, Gerald H., *Blacks & the Populist Revolt: Ballots & Bigotry in the "New South,"* U of Ala. Pr., University, 1977.

PORO A Senufo West African word relating to beliefs and uses of masks. *See also* BUSINESS; MALONE, ANNIE M. TURNBO.

PORTER, DOROTHY B. (1905–   ), librarian, author; born in Warrenton, Va. The wife of artist and author James A. Porter, she received a B.A. degree from Howard University (Washington, D.C.) in 1928 and was married the following year. Porter also received a B.S. degree (1931) and her M.S. degree (1932) from Columbia University. Until 1973 she was curator of the Moorland Foundation Library of Negro Life and History (now the Moorland-Spingarn Research Center) and of the

Founders Library at Howard University. Her many books include: *The Negro in the United States: A Working Bibliography* (1969); *The Negro in the United States: A Selected Bibliography* (1970); *North American Negro Poets: A Bibliographical Checklist of Their Writings, 1760–1944* (1945, 1963); and *Early Negro Writing 1760–1837* (1971). See also ARCHIVES; BIBLIOGRAPHIES / BIOGRAPHIES / GUIDES; PORTER, JAMES AMOS.

PORTER, EVERETTE M. (1910–), lawyer, judge; born in Franklin, La. Porter graduated from Chapman College (Orange, Calif.) and received his J.D. degree from Southwestern University (Los Angeles, Calif.) in 1940. Admitted to the California bar in 1941, he began to practice law in 1946, after having served in World War II as a captain in the infantry. In 1955 Porter left practice to serve on the board of the California Adult Authority until 1959. Two years later he was a member and vice-president of the Los Angeles Police Commission. In 1964 Porter became commissioner and judge pro tem of the Superior Court in Los Angeles. An authority on the custody of children and visitation rights, he wrote and published several works on the subject.

PORTER, HERMAN See the PREFACE: LIST OF CONTRIBUTORS.

PORTER, JAMES AMOS (1905–1971), painter, art historian, educator; born in Baltimore, Md. After receiving a B.S. degree from Howard University (Washington, D.C.) in 1927, Porter studied at Columbia University Teachers College, at the Art Students League (New York, N.Y.), at the Sorbonne, and received his M.A. degree in art history from New York University. Porter spent 40 years as professor of art at Howard University, where he influenced many modern Afro-American artists. His own work includes *Sarah*, one of the most haunting portraits ever done by a black artist; *Cuban Bus*; and a well-known portrait, *Woman Holding a Jug*, that reflects an emotional quality combined with excellent draftsmanship. Other portraits included one of his wife, Dorothy. Much exhibited, his work is in the collections of Howard University, the National Archives in Washington, D.C., and elsewhere. Among his awards were Rockefeller Foundation research grants that enabled him to study African, European, Cuban, and Haitian art in 1935 and 1945; and an award from the Sorbonne. His book, *Modern Negro Art* (1943, 1969), became a standard reference work. See also ARTISTS; PORTER, DOROTHY B.

PORTER, JOHN W. (1931–), educator; born in Fort Wayne, Ind. Porter received a B.A. degree from Albion College (Albion, Mich.) in 1953, and a M.A. degree (1957) and his Ph.D. degree (1962) from Michigan State University. He taught English and social studies in the Michigan public schools (1953–58), and was an educational consultant and research coordinator with the Michigan State Department of Public Instruction (1958–64), becoming state superintendent of public schools in 1969.

POSTON, ERSA HINES (1921–), public official; born in Paducah, Ky. Hines graduated from Kentucky State College in 1942 and received a M.A. degree in social work from Atlanta University in 1946. She began her career in the youth programs, both government-sponsored and privately endowed, of New York City, working there until 1957, when she became area director of the New York State Division for Youth. After five years Poston became youth work coordinator in that office, and in 1964 she became confidential assistant to Gov. Nelson Rockefeller. Later, Poston was appointed the director of the New York State Office of Economic Opportunity. In 1967 she was appointed president of the New York Civil Service Commission.

POUSSAINT, ALVIN FRANCES (1934–), psychiatrist, educator; born in New York, N.Y. Poussaint received a B.A. degree from Columbia University in 1956, after which he attended Cornell Medical College (Ithaca, N.Y.) from which he received a M.A. degree in psychopharmacology. He interned at the Center for Health Sciences, University of California at Los Angeles, from 1956 to 1961, and in 1966 he became assistant professor of psychiatry at Tufts University School of Medicine (Medford, Mass.). Poussaint later served as associate professor of psychiatry and associate dean for student affairs at Harvard University. He specialized in the emotional and psychological problems of Afro-Americans, and in this regard developed the "aggression-rage" theory. Poussaint contributed many articles to professional journals.

POVERTY

POVERTY The great majority of Afro-Americans lived in poverty until the decade of the 1950s. By the early 1970s this total had been reduced to approximately one-third, a poverty rate still three times that of white Americans. Black poverty is rooted in the slave system of the Old South and the caste system of the post-Civil War era that effectively excluded all but a tiny handful of Afro-Americans from occupations with sufficient income to enable them to rise above a subsistence level. Under slavery, food, clothing, and shelter were minimal, even as compared to conditions enforced in northern almshouses. These institutions were designed to receive destitute whites in northern cities and counties, and were required to provide only the absolute minimum level of food, clothing, and shelter. While precise comparison is impossible,

it appears that the quantity (but not the quality) of food was about the same as that eaten by slaves; the clothing issued was considerably better than that worn by slaves; and the shelter provided by the almshouse was dramatically superior to the average slave "cabin." Thus, the "welfare" function of the slave system did not even measure up to the harsh standards devised for the lowest class of free Americans.

Free black people living in northern cities in the antebellum period were somewhat better off than the average southern slave or southern free black, but very few were able to escape poverty. Of New York City's 11,840 Afro-American residents in 1855, the majority were domestic servants, porters, and unskilled laborers. At the other end of the occupational scale, New York City counted five black doctors and only one

Black poverty has its roots in slavery, which provided a minimal subsistence level. This early photograph shows a slave family in South Carolina in 1862. *(Library of Congress.)*

black lawyer. Frederick Douglass, visiting the city in this same decade, ruefully observed that New York's Afro-Americans were shunted into the lowest occupations "at wages so low that they could lay up little or nothing." Even in Boston, Mass., where the status of Afro-Americans was reportedly higher than that of any other city in the United States, more than two-thirds of all blacks worked in menial or common-labor occupations; and their housing conditions were among the worst in the city.

The momentous events of the Civil War, emancipation, and Reconstruction had no congruent effect on black poverty. The civil revolution of the period did not substantially alter either the concentration of the overwhelming majority of Afro-Americans in the South, or more important, the objective economic condition of Afro-Americans. The ex-slave in the New South became a landless agricultural worker whose real income was only slightly higher than the level under slavery. In the cities of the South and North, black workers, especially skilled service workers and artisans, faced increasing competition from rural whites and immigrants. Their position, never strong in these better paying occupations, further deteriorated, and access to the new occupations spawned by industrialization was retarded by the hiring practices of white employers.

After almost half a century of "freedom," black poverty had not been significantly reduced from antebellum levels, while at the same time thousands of destitute European immigrants were slowly but steadily making their way up the economic ladder. To white racists this appeared sufficient proof of black inferiority, but most white citizens simply remained ignorant of and aloof from any poverty in America.

During the Progressive Era, however, Americans discovered poverty. Muckrakers, educators, and government officials probed the plight of the lower classes. Jacob Riis' classic exposé of poverty in New York City, *How the Other Half Lives* (1890), was severely critical of Italians, Jews, and poor whites; but of New York's 60,666 Afro-Americans he had almost unqualified praise. In the face of intense discrimination in jobs and housing that forced wages down and rents up, Riis observed the city's blacks to be cleaner, more orderly, and more economically dependable "than the lower grades of foreign white people." Summing up the situation, Riis stated that in the art of "distinguishing his poverty by making a little go a long way, our negro has no

equal." The study by W. E. B. Du Bois, *The Philadelphia Negro* (1899), presented detailed figures for the turn of the century on the economic status of Afro-Americans and the rate at which they sought public and/or private charity. Noting that black recipients of charity exceeded the white rate by two to one, Du Bois indicated that this ratio was lower than might be expected: a much higher percentage of Philadelphia's blacks existed on the edge of destitution than did the white population.

In spite of these and other studies of Afro-American poverty at the turn of the century, the majority of poor southern blacks remained almost unnoticed. The central focus of poverty studies were the industrial cities of the North, which in 1910 contained less than one-tenth of the nation's black population. With the exception of Virginia and North Carolina, no southern state had even established a bureau of labor statistics to make regular reports on the living and working conditions of the laboring classes, whereas almost every northern state had done so by 1900. Within the South itself, only two out of every ten blacks lived in urban areas. The other 80 percent still lived in rural areas and were engaged primarily in cotton farming. They were thrice condemned to poverty: first, because they lived in the poorest region of the nation; second, because they were small landholders, tenants, or farm laborers; and third, because they were black.

The only major study of Afro-Americans that received national attention during the Progressive Era was Ray Stannard Baker's *Following the Color Line* (1908). Baker briefly explored the conditions of southern rural blacks, finding that a large portion were held in a relationship of economic dependency like the peasants of medieval Europe. He found evidence that rural blacks were being kept poor in order to maintain a reserve of cheap labor. As an Alabama lawyer told him, "Who will do the dirty work?. . . . In this country the white man won't, so the Negro must. There's got to be a mudsill somewhere." Herein, of course, lay the economic basis of the stereotypically lazy and petty criminal black. In an economic system designed to perpetuate black poverty so that a pool of cheap labor was continually available, laziness was logical and theft a reasonable way to secure a fair living.

Both Du Bois and Booker T. Washington agreed that black criminality and social disorganization were the results of what a later generation was to call the "culture of poverty." In

1908 Du Bois said: "Even if special legislation and organized relief intervene, freedmen always start life under an economic disadvantage which generations, perhaps centuries, cannot overcome." Certainly, neither Baker nor Du Bois realized in 1908 how rapidly the economic changes of the mid-twentieth century were to effect black poverty. No one correctly prophesied the magnitude of the black migration from farm to city and from the South to the North and to the West. This migration has been the fundamental cause of the decline of black poverty. The highest rates of poverty among local black populations and the poorest black families in the whole nation were still in the rural South in 1972.

In 1900, 22.7 percent of the Afro-American population lived in urban areas. By 1940 the figure had jumped to 48.2 percent, to 61.7 percent in 1950, and to 74 percent in 1970. For poor blacks the movement to the city provided not only economic opportunities, but also access to schools and welfare agencies that had for years been aiding European immigrants and that had remained almost unavailable in the rural South. This became particularly evident during the Great Depression of the 1930s when the entire United States was brought face to face with poverty and unemployment on a scale black people had known for generations.

The response of the New Deal during the 1930s was a massive program of welfare and unemployment relief, which aided blacks as much as whites. Some of the first detailed studies of poverty and income were made during the 1930s, and they revealed for the first time the nationwide gap between the incomes of Afro-Americans and of whites. The median income of a black family in the rural South in 1935 was approximately $330, while the median for rural whites was approximately $1,200. In Atlanta, Ga., the figures were $632 and $1,876, respectively; in Chicago, Ill., $726 and $1,687. The WPA at this time computed an "emergency budget" on the basis of prevailing prices in a cross-section of U.S. cities. The total averaged $900 per year—more than the median income of every black family in every community in the United States except that in New York City, where the median income was $980. In the rural South hardly one black family in ten reached this income standard. For those black families who could obtain welfare payments or federally sponsored relief jobs, the curse of poverty was somewhat lightened. One measure of the significance of welfare for Afro-Americans in the 1930s

was that it ranked with farming and domestic service as the three largest sources of income for blacks. Again, urban blacks had more opportunities than those in the countryside, and Afro-Americans living in the urban North had almost the same access to cash and relief jobs as did whites. Thus, the urban North held a strong economical attraction for southern blacks.

Rising prosperity after World War II convinced many whites that poverty had been finally banished. Books and articles were written on the "problems" of excess affluence and leisure. Many black leaders, however, knew this did not apply to the average black family. A. Phillip Randolph, Malcom X, and Kenneth Clark wrote and spoke eloquently about the poverty and exploitation of Afro-Americans in urban slums and rural areas, but they attracted little notice in the 1950s and early 1960s. Even many Afro-American leaders gave poverty a low priority as they bent their efforts toward the civil rights struggle in the South.

Black poverty finally attracted national attention in the 1960s—a century after emancipation. In 1963 the Kennedy administration began drawing up plans for a major federal antipoverty program that the president hoped to make the principal thrust of his 1964 campaign. Also, in 1963, Michael Harrington's book, *The Other America: Poverty in The United States,* was published; through this work, many middle-class Americans rediscovered the poor. Harrington's exposé, in contrast to those of the Progressive Era, gave prominent attention to black people, whose poverty had often been excluded from the civil rights movement and from public attention

Scene from "Resurrection City," Washington, D.C. Poverty of Afro-Americans finally attracted national attention in the 1960s. Much of the attention was focused upon a poor people's march on Washington, D.C. (1968), sponsored mainly by the Southern Christian Leadership Conference (SCLC). During this period, and extending into the 1970s, about one-third of all Afro-American families lived at poverty levels. *(Photo by Leroy Henderson.)*

as well. Indeed, the right to use hotels and restaurants, or the right to purchase a home outside the ghetto, was of no immediate benefit to black families that could not put enough food on their kitchen tables. Martin Luther King, Jr., recognized this by 1963 and turned his attention increasingly toward the elimination of poverty among blacks, calling for a "Bill of Rights for the Disadvantaged" so that Afro-Americans could afford to exercise the freedoms they had won in the civil rights movement. President Lyndon B. Johnson took up the poverty program when he assumed office after John F. Kennedy's assassination, declaring an "unconditional war on poverty in America" in his State of the Union Message in 1964. The U.S. Congress responded with the Economic Opportunity Act of 1964, which created the Job Corps, Community Action Programs, and Volunteers in Service to America (VISTA). Between 1961 and 1969 federal aid to the poor rose from $9.7 billion to $24.4 billion. Following the urban riots of 1968, the Kerner Commission published a report on ghetto poverty, unemployment, and discrimination.

The most controversial question regarding black poverty during the recent past has been the concept of a "culture of poverty." A number of social scientists, some connected with governmental poverty programs, maintain that there has arisen from the black ghettoes, a unique black culture, characterized by a low esteem for education; lack of motivation; high rates of crime, alcoholism, drug addiction, and mental illness; and a highly unstable pattern of family life. Other investigators have indicated that these patterns, described as uniquely black, are more clearly traceable to a poverty than to a racial background. Behavioral patterns among poor Afro-Americans, it is argued, more closely resemble those of poor whites than middle- or upper-income blacks. More important, those characteristics that have been labeled as cultural in origin are far from universal among the poor and may simply be the result of the immediate circumstances of material deprivation. Malnutrition, for example, may be the cause of a low level of motivation in school or at work. Moreover, low wages and unemployment, resulting in an inability to earn sufficient income to support a family, may be the cause of desertion, alcoholism, and crime. Finally, it is argued that low esteem for education may result from irrelevant and oppressive schools, or the knowledge that education still does not give many Afro-Americans equal access to jobs.

While the impact of governmental programs based on these varying theories of poverty is very difficult to assess, it is clear that black people, while lagging behind the rest of the nation, have made a dramatic ascent out of poverty since the end of World War II, particularly in the decade of the 1960s.

Using the poverty definition developed by the Social Security Administration in the 1960s, approximately two-thirds of all Afro-American families lived below the poverty level in 1947. By 1959 the figure stood at slightly more than one-half, and by 1970 poor Afro-Americans numbered 7.6 million out of 23 million, or approximately one-third. Thus, during the 1960s, poverty ceased to be the condition of the majority of Afro-Americans in the United States.

Profound as this change has been, other statistics indicate that in the 1970s blacks did not receive an equal share of the nation's wealth. The poverty rate for Afro-Americans remained stationary at a level three times that of whites. Yet, by the early 1970s white poverty was only one-tenth of the total white population. Also, poor black families remained in deeper poverty than whites. The "poverty gap" (the amount of money it would take to lift a family up to the minimum standard of living as defined by the Social Security Administration) averaged $304 more for Afro-American families than for white families in 1969.

Certain types of Afro-American families have very high poverty rates and account for most of the poor black population. Blacks living in nonmetropolitan areas in 1970 comprised 32 percent of the total black population, but accounted for almost 46 percent of all poor blacks. Most of these poor blacks still live in the South where the median income for all blacks in 1970 was only 54 percent that of whites (whereas it was 73 percent in the North and West). While only half the black families live in the South, two-thirds of all poor blacks live there. In 1970 slightly more than half of all poor black families were headed by females compared to 25 percent for whites. Similarly, 54 percent of all poor blacks were children under 18 compared to 25 percent for all poor whites. Educational level was also a major determinant of poverty. For example, in 1970, 60 percent of all male-headed poor black families were headed by a man with less than eight years of education while only 17 percent were headed by a man with four years of high school.

While it is clear that thousands of black families are working their way out of poverty each year, a significant minority appears to be trapped permanently in the inner-city poverty areas. These areas have experienced no significant improvements in employment, income, housing, or any of the other measures of material progress and social well-being. Not nearly enough is known about Afro-American poverty in these areas of intense deterioration, but some studies indicate that the areas are not producing a class of perpetually poor and hopeless individuals. Many residents achieve middle-income status and leave these slums while new families move in from rural areas and small towns. Until the "great migration" of rural blacks has run its course and the unemployment, economic discrimination, and low wages in the central cities are corrected, black poverty will remain. The most hopeful change in the 1960s was the rise of thousands of Afro-Americans to positions of power and responsibility in government and business, who have provided far more leadership in devising effective antipoverty programs. Also, poor Afro-Americans ceased to accept the economic and racial system that impoverishes them, and joined together in a variety of effective political pressure groups. See also AGRICULTURE; EMPLOYMENT; INCOME.

REFERENCES: Arnold, Joseph L., "Blacks in Cities," *Journal of Negro History*, vol. 59, April 1974, a review article of the following books: Bracey, John H., Jr., August Meier and Elliott Rudwick (eds.), *The Rise of the Ghetto*, Wadsworth Publishing Company, Belmont, 1971; Goldfield, David R., and James B. Lane (ed.), *The Enduring Ghetto: Sources and Readings*, J. B. Lippincott, Philadelphia, 1973; Forman, Robert E., *Black Ghettos, White Ghettos and Slums*, Prentice-Hall, Englewood Cliffs, 1973; Schiller, Bradley R., *The Economics of Poverty and Discrimination*, Prentice-Hall, Englewood Cliffs, 1973; Sackrey, Charles, *The Political Economy of Urban Poverty*, W. W. Norton, New York, 1973; and Groh, George, *The Black Migration: The Journey to Urban America*, Weybright and Talley, New York, 1972. See also Kain, John F. (ed.), *Race and Poverty: The Economics of Discrimination*, Prentice-Hall, Englewood Cliffs, 1969; Miller, Herman P., *Rich Man, Poor Man*, 2d. rev. ed., Thomas Y. Crowell, New York, 1971; Moynihan, Daniel P. (ed.), *On Understanding Poverty*, Basic Books, New York, 1969; Myrdal, Gunnar, *An American Dilemma*, Harper and Row, New York, 1962; Newman, Dorothy K., et al., "Perspectives on Poverty," *Monthly Labor Review*, February 1969, pp. 32–62; Thurow, Lester C., *Poverty and Discrimination*, The Brookings Institution, Washington, D.C., 1969; and U.S. Department of Commerce, Bureau of Census, *Current Population Reports: The Social and Economic Status of Negroes in the United States, 1970*, ser. P-23, no. 38, U.S. Government Printing Office, Washington, D.C., 1971.

Adam Clayton Powell, Sr. (Moorland-Springarn Research Center, Howard University.)

POWELL, ADAM CLAYTON, JR. (1908–72), U.S. Representative, clergyman, civil rights leader; born in New Haven, Conn. The young Powell was raised in New York City, leaving the city for his undergraduate studies at Colgate University (Hamilton, N.Y.) and returning after graduation in 1930 to attend Columbia University, from which he received a M.A. degree in 1932. Beginning in 1931, he assisted and later succeeded (1937) his father as minister of the Abyssinian Baptist Church in New York City's Harlem. During this period Powell received a D.D. degree from Shaw University (Raleigh, N.C.). Also during this period he revealed himself as a powerful and effective political crusader: organizing antidiscrimination demonstrations and campaigning for jobs and equal treatment for Afro-Americans. In 1941 Powell was elected to the New York City Council, and in 1942 he began to publish a weekly newspaper called the *People's Voice*. Three years later he went to Washington, D.C., as a representative from Harlem to the Seventy-ninth Congress, retaining his seat for 11 successive terms, during which time he sponsored controversial civil rights legislation. In 1960 Powell became chairman of the House Committee on Education and Labor, a post that provided him with the opportunity to exercise more power than any other Afro-American Congressman before him. Although he had a poor attendance record in Congress, his parliamentary tactics helped to pilot through the House some of the major antipoverty and aid-to-education bills of the Kennedy and Johnson administrations. Accused of irregularities in the use of public funds and involved in a defamation case in the courts, Powell was censured by his congressional colleagues and lost his House seat in 1957. However, he was seated again in 1961, but was fined and stripped of his seniority; the U.S. Supreme Court gave him the right to recover back pay, but the powerful chairmanship was not recovered. Finally, rejected by his constituency, Powell lost the congressional primary in 1970. He retired to Bimini, one of the Bahama Islands, and two years later he died in Atlanta, Ga. See also ABYSSINIAN BAPTIST CHURCH; BAPTISTS.

POWELL, ADAM CLAYTON, SR. (1865–1953), clergyman, author; born in Franklin County, Va. Powell was educated at Virginia Union University during the years 1888–92, and received his D.D. degree there in 1904; he did further study at Yale University Divinity School from 1895 to 1896, and received an honorary D.D. degree from Howard University (Washington, D.C.) in 1924.

In 1908 he became pastor of the hundred-year-old Abyssinian Baptist Church in lower Manhattan in New York City. Through his efforts, land was purchased in Harlem, on West 138th Street, in 1920, and a new church and community house were built. By the mid-1930s the church had an estimated membership of 14,000 (almost nine times the number at the outset of his tenure as its head) and had become the largest Protestant church in the United States. Powell, who retired as a minister in 1937, continued to be active as a crusader against vice and in behalf of civil rights and economic opportunity for Afro-Americans. His books include the autobiography *Against the Tide* (1938), *Picketing Hell* (1942), and *Riots and Ruins* (1945). *See also* ABYSSINIAN BAPTIST CHURCH.

POWELL, CLILAN BETHANY (1894–   ), physician, publisher, business executive; born in Suffolk, Va. Powell attended Virginia Normal College in 1913 and received his M.D. degree from Howard University Medical College (Washington, D.C.) in 1920. He interned at Bellevue Hospital, New York, N.Y., and as New York City's first black roentgenologist, he served on the staffs of Harlem and Bellevue hospitals (1922–23). Powell helped to develop and expand Victory Mutual Life Insurance Company, serving it as vice-president in 1933 and as president (1949–59), and he was the founder and president of Community Finance, the first finance company owned and operated by an Afro-American in New York City. Powell became owner, president, and editor of New York's *Amsterdam News* in 1936; and by 1962 it was one of the largest black weekly newspapers in the United States. He was named by Mayor Robert Wagner to the Citizens Advisory Committee on Cultural Affairs. Powell was also named by Gov. Nelson Rockefeller as a director of the Commission for the World's Fair.

POWELL, OZZIE   *See* SCOTTSBORO BOYS.

PRAIRIE VIEW AGRICULTURAL AND MECHANICAL (A&M) UNIVERSITY Prairie View Agricultural and Mechanical (A&M) University, at Prairie View, Tex. was founded in 1876, the first year of the Texas constitution and of the common free-school system. A state-supported, coeducational, land-grant college near Houston, Prairie View offers the bachelor's and master's degrees,

and provides liberal arts, teacher education, and vocational curricula. Its 1975 enrollment was 4,610.

The school was founded in the very beginning of public higher education in Texas. The first state institution of higher learning was the Agricultural and Mechanical College of Texas (Texas A & M), established in October 1876. Corresponding with its establishment, and under the provisions of the Second Morrill Act, the state legislature authorized a similar school in Waller County to operate under the management of the board of directors of Texas A & M College. That school was Prairie View.

Today, Prairie View is part of the Texas A & M University system. Its 1,400-acre campus is a community in itself, and has become an incorporated city. The college furnishes its own water, steam power, and sewage disposal; it also has its own telephone and telegraph system, security patrol, U.S. Post Office, college exchange store, and laboratory training school.

PRATT, CHARLES A. (1909–   ), lawyer, judge; born in Kalamazoo, Mich. Pratt received a B.A. degree (1932) and his LL.B. degree (1935) from Howard University (Washington, D.C.). In 1969 he joined the bench of the District Court of Michigan.

PREACHERS *See* cross references under CHURCHES.

PREJUDICE *See* DISCRIMINATION; RACE: RACISM; SEGREGATION.

PRENTISS NORMAL AND INDUSTRIAL INSTITUTE Prentiss Normal and Industrial Institute, at Prentiss, Miss., was founded in 1907 by Professor and Mrs. Jonas E. Johnson. An independent, coeducational school, Prentiss offers a two-year program, usually credited toward the bachelor's degree. Prentiss also retains its high school department. Its 1975 enrollment was 221.

The college remains on the site of its founding, and the little log cabin, where its first ten students met, still stands. Now the college has a sizable, contemporary physical plant.

About 40 percent of the junior college graduates enter such professions as teaching and the ministry. Others are in missionary work, law, nursing, farming, printing, and dry cleaning.

PRESBYTERIANS Presbyterian refers to some American Protestant churches of the Calvinistic or Reformed tradition whose churches are organized in a series of representative bodies governed by ordained lay and teaching elders (presbyters). The largest of these denominations are the United Presbyterian Church, U.S.A.; the Presbyterian Church, U.S. (Southern); and the Cumberland Presbyterian Church. These churches are predominantly white with a relatively small number of Afro-American members.

Like most other denominations, the Presbyterians made efforts to convert slaves in the South and free blacks in the northern cities early in the nineteenth century. The first black Presbyterian church, First African, was organized in Philadelphia, Pa., in 1807. It developed out of the missionary work of John Gloucester, who had been freed by his master in Tennessee in order to engage in religious work. Fifteen years later, Samuel Cornish organized the first Afro-American Presbyterian church in New York City with 25 members. Churches were also begun in Washington, D.C., and in Baltimore, Md., and in smaller cities in New Jersey, New York, and Pennsylvania in the era before the Civil War. There were other Afro-American leaders in the Presbyterian church besides John Gloucester. J. W. C. Pennington wrote a graphic account of his escape from slavery in Maryland and his struggles to become a minister. Elymas P. Rogers, a free Afro-American from Connecticut who had to overcome a good deal of prejudice in order to secure an education, served churches in New Jersey, took a deep interest in African colonization, and wrote protest poetry on the political problems of the day. Samuel Cornish was an associate of John Russwurm in founding the first Afro-American newspaper in the United States

in 1827, and was an officer of the American Anitslavery Society. Theodore Wright, the first Afro-American Presbyterian graduate of Princeton Theological Seminary in 1828, became active in the antislavery movement and joined Gerrit Smith in an effort to settle Afro-Americans in agriculture in New York state.

Presbyterians made efforts to convert slaves in the South, but they were not as successful as the Methodists or the Baptists. They were reluctant to adapt their patterns of church life to the needs of the masses, and were especially cool to the emotionalism of revivals, which were popular with rural people. Some churches tried to reach Afro-Americans by providing special slave galleries where they could attend services. In one case a white congregation purchased a slave to minister to blacks. A few white churches enrolled blacks as members. The earliest black Presbyterian missionary in the South was John Chavis, who was appointed in 1801. By 1831 many southern states had placed severe restrictions on black ministers out of fear of slave revolts, and Chavis was barred from his public ministry. He opened a school in North Carolina that enrolled white pupils in the morning and black pupils at night. The most active organizer of Presbyterian work for slaves in the South was Rev. C. C. Jones, a white minister in Georgia. Jones believed in working within the slave system by concentrating on the spiritual welfare of slaves rather than seeking to change their social conditions. He opposed the use of Afro-Americans as ministers and insisted that slaves be under the supervision of white pastors. Jones' *Catechism* for the oral instruction of Afro-Americans was widely used by Presbyterians.

In their attitude toward the problem of slavery, Presbyterians generally followed regional patterns. In the South they usually defended the institution of slavery. One of the most famous defenders of slavery was Rev. James H. Thornwell, who asserted that the Bible upheld slavery and that, in any event, the church could not speak out on matters of social policy but should confine its work to the regulation of personal morality. The few southern Presbyterians who opposed slavery were forced to be silent or to emigrate to the North. The great majority of Presbyterians in the North favored some compromise solution to the slavery problem. One popular idea was the African colonization movement, which proposed the resettlement of emancipated slaves in Liberia. It was supported by many prominent white Presbyterians. The first Presbyterian institution for the higher education of Afro-Americans, Ashmun Institute (later Lincoln University), was founded in 1854 by a Presbyterian minister, Rev. John Miller Dickey, of Oxford, Pa., to provide missionaries for Liberia. Most free Afro-American Presbyterians, however, were opposed to the colonization movement. The abolitionist crusade against slavery attracted only a minority of Presbyterians, but some became leaders in the movement. One of the early Presbyterian opponents of slavery was George Bourne, whose book *The Book and Slavery Irreconcilable* had a profound influence on William Lloyd Garrison. Bourne was ousted by the Lexington Presbytery in Virginia in 1818 for exposing the cruelties of the slave trade among Presbyterians. Other Presbyterians active in the antislavery movement included James G. Birney, Lewis and Arthur Tappan, Elijah Lovejoy, and Theodore Weld. The Presbyterian schism of 1837 between "Old School" and "New School" has been blamed on the slavery issue, but little evidence exists to support the contention that the two groups were so radically divided over slavery, for neither was strongly antislavery at the time. Presbyterian anitslavery sentiment was strongest in southern Ohio, which had been settled by some southern antislavery advocates. Here a small group seceded from the main Presbyterian bodies in 1846 to form the Free Presbyterian Church.

The outbreak of the Civil War resulted in the division of the Old School Presbyterians along sectional lines. The schism was not, technically, on the issue of slavery, but on the right of the church to make political pronouncements. After the war the northern Presbyterians became active in the work of Reconstruction in the South. Northern Presbyterians were most active in North Carolina, where they won some of the freedmen who had formerly been members of the southern Presbyterian churches. A few white southern Presbyterian ministers joined the northern Presbyterians to organize new churches among these freedmen. Presbyterians also became active in developing schools for Afro-Americans in the South, and many of these schools were staffed by white missionaries from the North. In addition to parochial schools for primary and secondary students, institutions of higher learning were developed. Ashmun Institute became Lincoln University and broadened its program in the liberal arts. Biddle Institute (now Johnson C. Smith University) was founded at Charlotte, N.C., in 1867 and became a center for Afro-American Presbyterians in the South. Barber-Scotia College (Concord, N.C.) and Knoxville College (Knoxville, Tenn.) were also begun in this era. The southern Presbyterian Church continued to have a small Afro-American membership that, for a time, was organized into a separate Afro-American Synod. The Cumberland Church organized its black members into a separate church, the Colored Cumberland Church, in 1869. Afro-American Presbyterian leaders in the Civil War era included Hiram H. Revels, the first Afro-American U.S. Senator from Mississippi, who served several Presbyterian churches prior to the Civil War; and Henry H. Garnet, who became one of the most famous Afro-American orators of his day and was the first Afro-American pastor invited to make a memorial address in the rotunda of the nation's Capitol, in 1865.

After the collapse of Reconstruction in the Compromise of 1877, Presbyterians tended to accept the principle of "separate but equal" in church affairs. Since Afro-American schools and churches were economically dependent upon white boards and agencies, a good deal of paternalism prevailed. In 1905 when the northern Presbyterians united with the white Cumberland Presbyterians in the South, Afro-American Presbyterians in the South were assigned to racially segregated presbyteries over the protests of black Presbyterian leaders.

A number of Afro-American Presbyterian leaders emerged in the post-Civil War period. Matthew Anderson, a graduate of Oberlin College (Oberlin, Ohio) and Princeton Seminary, advocated achieving self-respect through a study of black culture, and as a pastor in Philadelphia he was a leader establishing a number of institutions for the Afro-American community,

Francis Grimké
(Scurlock Studio.)

including a training school and a building and loan association. The outstanding Afro-American Presbyterian minister of his generation was Francis J. Grimké, who for over half a century served as pastor of the 15th Street Presbyterian Church of Washington, D.C. Although he had been born in slavery, Grimké graduated from Lincoln University (Lincoln University, Pa.) and Princeton Seminary. As a pastor in Washington, D.C., he was an ardent crusader for personal morality and for human rights, and he was active in the Niagra Movement, which led to the founding of the National Association for the Advancement of Colored People (NAACP). Grimké was a close friend of Frederick Douglass and officiated at Douglass' second marriage. He fought all forms of racial discrimination in the Presbyterian Church and led the opposition to the Cumberland union of 1905. He criticized his own college for its failure to include Afro-Americans as professors and trustees. In the South, several Afro-American Presbyterians became leaders in education. Lucy Craft Laney, who was born into slavery, opened a school for Afro-American children who had been excluded from the public schools of Augusta, Ga. This school, Haines Institute, pioneered in starting a kindergarten and in developing the first nurses' training in the area. Haines achieved a high academic standard under Laney's leadership, and she was the first Afro-American woman to be appointed head of a major Presbyterian school. Mary McLeod Bethune, another distinguished black educator, began her teaching career at Haines under Laney. Daniel J. Sanders, also an ex-slave, obtained an education at Brainerd Institute and Western Seminary. After a successful pastorate, he was appointed president of Biddle Institute, the first major Presbyterian college to be put under Afro-American leadership. Unfortunately, Sanders' appointment in 1891 led to the resignation of all but one of the white professors, so that the ideal of racial integration was not then attained.

Early in the twentieth century, an increasing migration of Afro-Americans from the rural South to the urban North began, and this caused a gradual decline in rural Afro-American Presbyterian churches in the South. In the North, Presbyterians had hopes of increasing their membership in the growing Afro-American communities. A number of new Afro-American churches were established in the northern cities, but their growth was slow. Like their white counterparts, black Presbyterians tended to appeal to middle-class groups who welcomed a more formal type of worship and an educated clergy. For this reason they made few gains among the new migrants from the South. Northern Presbyterians were conservative in their racial attitudes. In 1946 the northern Presbyterians called for the creation of a nonsegregated church in a nonsegregated society, but there was a wide gulf between what the church said and what it did.

The civil rights movement of the 1950s brought a cautious advance in the church's activity in the area of race. After the intensification of this struggle in 1963, the denomination created a special Commission on Religion and Race, headed by Gayraud Wilmore, as a sign of its commitment to the struggle for human rights. Some Presbyterians were active in sit-ins, bus boycotts, freedom rides, and the demonstrations that marked the 1960s, and at least two white Presbyterian ministers, Bruce Klunder and James Reeb, lost their lives in civil rights activities. Black Presbyterian clergy and laymen were active in all these movements. Among those who were active in the 1960s and in the 1970s were James H. Robinson, who began "Crossroads Africa," a forerunner of the Peace Corps; Edler Hawkins, who was elected the first Afro-American moderator of the Presbyterian General Assembly; and James E. Jones, of Los Angeles, Calif., who was the first Afro-American member elected to that city's school board. The movements of the 1970s toward black pride and self-determination confronted Presbyterians with new challenges to practice what they profess. See also GRIMKÉ, FRANCIS JAMES; LINCOLN UNIVERSITY (LINCOLN UNIVERSITY, PA.); SLAVERY: THE CHURCHES.

REFERENCES: Three excellent books on the subject are: Anderson, Matthew, *Presbyterianism—Its Relation to the Negro*; Barber, Jesse B., *Climbing Jacob's Ladder*; and Murray, Andrew E., *Presbyterians and the Negro—A History*.

PRESS, HARRY C., JR. (1931–   ), radiologist; born in Chesapeake, Va. Press received a B.S. degree from Virginia Union University in 1952 and his M.D. degree from the Medical College of Virginia in 1957. He interned at Homer G. Phillips Hospital, St. Louis, Mo., and was a medical officer in the U.S. Navy from 1958 to 1960. Press was a resident in radiology at Freedmen's Hospital, Washington, D.C., and at the University of Pennsylvania Hospital from 1960 to 1963, and later served as assistant professor of radiology and chief of the division of radiology at Freedmen's Hospital.

PRICE, JOSEPH C. (1854– ?), clergyman, educator; born in Elizabeth City, N.C., Price was the son of a slave father and free mother. He attended Shaw University (Raleigh, N.C.) in 1873 and graduated valedictorian from Lincoln University (Lincoln University, Pa.) in 1881. An impressive speaker, Price became a minister in the African Methodist Episcopal Zion (AMEZ) Church. He was a leading educator in North Carolina who favored liberal arts over industrial education for blacks. He served as president of Livingston College (Salisbury, N.C.) and several schools in North Carolina were named in his honor.

PRICE, (MARY) LEONTYNE (1929–), soprano; born in Laurel, Miss. Price received her B.A. degree from Central State College (Wilberforce, Ohio) in 1948. Subsequently, she studied at the Juilliard School of Music (New York, N.Y.) until 1952; at the same time she studied privately with Florence Page Kimball. Price made her New York City debut in a Broadway revival of Virgil Thomson's *Four Saints in Three Acts* in 1952, after which she appeared as Bess in *Porgy and Bess* in the touring company and then on Broadway. Following a resounding triumph in *Porgy,* during which time she met and married William Warfield, who sang the role of Porgy, she gave concerts in the United States and Europe. In 1954 her Town Hall concert in New York City evoked lyrical praises from the critics and adulation from her audience. Her first performance in grand opera came in 1955 as Floria in Puccini's *Tosca* on network television. Two years and many concerts and television appearances later, Price appeared for the first time on an opera stage in Poulenc's *Dialogues of the Carmelites* with the San Francisco Opera Company. For several years she sang with that company, with the Lyric Opera of Chicago, Ill., and in many of the large opera houses on the Continent. Meanwhile, five years after their marriage, the Warfields were divorced. In 1961 Price made her debut at the Metropolitan Opera House in New York City, singing the role of Leonora in Verdi's *Il Trovatore.* Critics commented that her magnificent soprano was one of the great operatic voices of the age. Later roles included the title role in *Aida,* Donna Anna and Donna Elvira in *Don Giovanni,* Tatiana in *Eugen Onegin,* Elvira in *Ernani,* Minnie in *The Girl of the Golden West,* and many others. In 1966 Price opened the

Metropolitan Opera season as Cleopatra in *Antony and Cleopatra,* its premiere also being the opening of the new Metropolitan Opera House in Lincoln Center. In addition to her stage roles, Price made innumerable recordings of both songs and operas, and she concertized extensively throughout the world. *See also* MUSIC: HISTORY AND DEVELOPMENT.

Joseph C. Price. *(Library of Congress.)*

PRIDE, ARMISTEAD SCOTT See NEWSPAPERS: HISTORY AND DEVELOPMENT.

PRIMM, HOWARD THOMAS (1903–), clergyman, bishop; born in Brentwood, Tenn. Primm received a B.A. degree (1924) and an honorary D.D. degree (1940), from Wilberforce University (Wilberforce, Ohio) and his B.D. degree from Payne Theological Seminary in 1927. He was pastor of African Methodist Episcopal (AME) churches in several southern states from 1926 to 1941 before becoming pastor of Union Bethel AME Church in New Orleans, La. In 1952 Primm was elected a bishop of the African Methodist Episcopal (AME) Church.

PRINCESS ANNE ACADEMY *See* MORGAN STATE UNIVERSITY.

PRITCHARD, ROBERT S. (1929–), pianist, administrator; born in Winston-Salem, N.C. Pritchard received Mus.B., Mus.M., and Ph.D. degrees from Syracuse University (Syracuse, N.Y.) and also studied piano at Juilliard, Mannes, and Manhattan schools of music, all in New York City. Pritchard acieved success as a concert pianist, making numerous tours throughout the United States, Latin America, the Middle East, and Europe. Becoming an expert in intercultural relations, Pritchard was the founder-director of the Pan American Association for the Festival of the New World in 1967, served at Syracuse University as assistant provost on minority group affairs, and planned several Afro-American arts festivals. *Isle of Springs,* a cantata (1962), and *Mass on Reconciliation* (1966) represent his work in the field of composition.

PROCTOR, HENRY H. (1868–1933), clergyman; born near Fayetteville, Tenn. The son of former slaves, Proctor received a B.A. degree from Fisk University (Nashville, Tenn.) and his B.D. degree from Yale University Divinity School. He became pastor of the First Congregational Church in Atlanta, Ga.

PROCTOR, SAMUEL DeWITT (1921–   ), clergyman, educator, government official; born in Norfolk, Va. Proctor began his higher education at Virginia Union University, from which he graduated in 1942, and received a B.D. degree from Crozer Theological Seminary in 1945 and his Th.D. degree from Boston University in 1950. He began his career as a Baptist minister in 1945 in Providence, R.I., and in 1949 Proctor joined the faculty of his alma mater, Virginia Union, as professor of religion and ethics and dean of the School of Religion. By 1960 Proctor had served that institution as vice-president and president. He then moved to North Carolina Agricultural and Technical (A & T) State University to become its president, serving until 1964; the last year of his tenure Proctor combined his academic duties with those of being the associate director of the Peace Corps. Following a year as associate general secretary of the National Council of Churches, Proctor served the Office of Economic Opportunity and the Institute for Services of Education. He joined the faculty of Rutgers University (New Brunswick, N.J.) in 1969 as professor of education, and two years later he succeeded Adam Clayton Powell, Jr., as pastor of the Abyssinian Baptist Church in New York City. His book, *The Young Negro in America, 1960–1980*, was published in 1966.

PROPHET JONES *See* Jones, James Francis Marion.

PROSSER, GABRIEL *See* Slavery: Slavery in Selected States—Virginia.

PROTESTANT EPISCOPAL CHURCH *See* Episcopalians.

PRUDHOMME, CHARLES (1908–   ), psychiatrist, educator; born in Opelousas, La. Prudhomme received a B.S. degree from Howard University in 1931 and his M.D. degree from Howard University Medical College in 1931. He interned at Freedmen's Hospital, Washington, D.C., and was a fellow in psychiatry at Billings, Cook County, and Provident hospitals, all in Chicago, Ill. Prudhomme served as psychiatrist at the Veterans Administration Hospital, Tuskegee, Ala. from 1938 to 1943, held various positions on the Howard University faculty from 1943 to 1958, and was psychiatrist for the Peace Corps in the Venezuela Training Project and for Howard University Training Projects for Niger, Togo, and Sierra Leone from 1962 to 1965.

Prudhomme was also vice-president of the American Psychiatric Association in 1970.

PRYOR, RICHARD (1940–   ), comedian, actor; born in Peoria, Ill. Pryor dropped out of school at the age of 14. Later he served in the U.S. Army, where he appeared in amateur entertainment shows. After military service he turned professional, beginning in his hometown. By 1967, he had become nationally known. Further exposure came in 1969, when his first album, *Richard Pryor*, was recorded. Another album, entitled *That Nigger's Crazy*, by Staxs Partee, came out in 1974; its sales exceeded 1 million copies. Other recordings followed, including *Is It Something I Said?* (1975). Pryor had roles in several motion pictures, including *Lady Sings The Blues* (1973) and *Hit* (1973). His artistry, enhanced by vivid facial expressions and ribaldry, often revealed great familiarity and understanding of Afro-American folk culture.

PURVIS, CHARLES BURLEIGH (1842–1929), physician, administrator; born in Philadelphia, Pa. Purvis attended Oberlin College, (Oberlin, Ohio) from 1860 to 1863 and received his M.D. degree from Western Reserve Medical School (Cleveland, Ohio; now part of Case-Western Reserve University) in 1865. Purvis served Howard University and its Medical College in various capacities for a period of 57 years, including secretary-treasurer from 1873 to 1896, president of the faculty from 1899 to 1900, and member of the board of trustees from 1908 to 1926. As secretary-treasurer, he was able to avert the closing of the Medical College during the financial panic of 1873. When President James Garfield was shot in 1881, Purvis was called by the White House to attend the president.

PUTNEY, MARTHA SETTLE (1916–   ) historian, educator; born in Norristown, Pa. Putney received a B.A. degree (1939) and a M.A. degree (1940) from Howard University (Washington, D.C.) and her Ph.D. degree from the University of Pennsylvania in 1955. She served as assistant professor at Morgan State University (Baltimore, Md.) from 1950 to 1952, as associate professor at Prairie View Agricultural and Mechanical (A & M) University (Prairie View, Tex.) from 1954 to 1955, and as professor at Bowie State College (Bowie, Md.) after 1955. Putney wrote about black merchant seamen of New England during the 1800s.

QUAKERS Known formally as the Society of Friends, Quakers can trace their origins to George Fox (1624–1691), a native of England who brought his beliefs to America. Fox and his followers believed that God is revealed directly to each individual through an "Inner Light" that can lead to truth. Their beliefs rejected orthodox, formal religious ritual and polity. Meeting informally, and maintaining silence unless motivated to speak or pray, Quakers conducted their gatherings without the assistance of priest or minister. As a group, they were severely persecuted in colonial America but found havens in New Jersey and Pennsylvania.

Quakers were known for their humanitarian views and actions. They were among the earliest supporters of abolition. In fact, the first printed protest against slavery in America has been attributed to Quakers. In face of opposition, they permitted slaves to attend their meetings, they ended slaveholding among themselves, and they made attempts to provide for the social and educational welfare of blacks. Anthony Benezet is an outstanding early example. Not only was Benezet a staunch abolitionist, but he also set up a free school for blacks in 1770. Upon his death in 1784, he bequeathed his fortune to this school, which came to be known as Benezet House and it was a landmark on Locust Street in Philadelphia.

The list of Quakers helpful to blacks includes Andrew Ellicott, who gave encouragement to Benjamin Banneker in the 1790s; Richard Humphreys, who founded Cheyney State Teachers College in 1837; Levi Coffin and J. Miller McKim, who helped finance the Underground Railroad in the 1850s; Anna T. Jeanes, who set up a fund for rural black schools in the South in 1907; and Rufus M. Jones, the Quaker philosopher, who gave inspiration to the theologian Howard Thurman in the 1920s.

Indeed, Quakers have encouraged education as

Meeting of Quakers in Philadelphia during the colonial period. *(Library of Congress.)*

well as social welfare and world peace. As a group, they have founded and supported such colleges as Bryn Mawr, Haverford, and Swathmore. Quakers have been strong friends of blacks in America. They have opposed the slave trade, slavery, caste, racism, and discrimination. *See also* CHURCHES; SLAVERY: IN SELECTED STATES / PENNSYLVANIA; SLAVERY: THE UNDERGROUND RAILROAD; SLAVERY: THE ABOLITIONISTS.

REFERENCES: There are ample studies of Quakers including classics by two older writers: Weeks, Stephen B., *Southern Quakers and Slavery: A Study in Institutional History*, Humanities, Atlantic Highlands, N.J., 1968; Jones, Rufus, *Quakers in the American Colonies*, Norton, New York, 1966. More recent selected accounts are found in Brookes, George S., *Friend Anthony Benezet*, 1937; Tolles, Frederick B., *Meeting House and Counting House*, Norton, New York, 1963, and *Quakers and the Atlantic Culture*, 1960; Drake, Thomas E., *Quakers and Slavery in America*, Peter Smith, Magnolia, Mass., 1950. For a bibliography, see Williams, Ethel L., and Clifton F. Brown, *Howard University Bibliography of African & Afro-American Religious Studies: With Locations in American Libraries*, Scholarly Res. Inc., Wilmington, Del., 1977, pp. 133–136; 273; 316.

QUARLES, BENJAMIN (1904–   ), historian, author, educator; born in Boston, Mass. Quarles received a B.A. degree from Shaw University (Raleigh, N.C.) in 1931, and a M.A. degree (1933) and his Ph.D. degree (1940) from the University of Wisconsin. He received many distinguished fellowships and grants throughout his career. Quarles taught at Shaw University and Dillard University (New Orleans, La.) before becoming professor of history and chairman of the department at Morgan State College (Baltimore, Md.) in 1953. He served with several historical organizations and on editorial boards, including that of the *Journal of Negro History.* Quarles contributed many articles to scholarly journals. His 12 books include: *Frederick Douglass* (1948, 1967); *The Negro in the Civil War* (1948, 1967); *The Negro in the American Revolution* (1961); *Lincoln and the Negro* (1962, 1969); *The Narrative Life of Frederick Douglass* (1962, 1967); *The Black American: A Documentary History,* with Leslie H. Fishel, Jr. (1970); and *Blacks on John Brown* (1972). *See also* the PREFACE: LIST OF CONTRIBUTORS; HISTORIANS.

QUARLES, NORMA R. *See* RADIO AND TELEVISION.

QUEEN, ROBERT C. *See* NEWSPAPERS: CONTEMPORARY.

QUINN, LONGWORTH M. *See* NEWSPAPERS: CONTEMPORARY.

QUINN, WILLIAM PAUL (1788–1873), clergyman. The circumstances surrounding Quinn's birth and early years are obscure. It is known, however, that he was not born in the United States and that he developed an interest in Methodism and became a local preacher early in his life. According to Daniel A. Payne, an authority on the early history of the African Methodist Episcopal (AME) Church, Quinn's name appears in the official records of an AME conference held in Baltimore in 1819. He was one of the 17 members present at the opening session; among others present were such early leaders as Richard Allen, Morris Brown, Abner Coker, and Edward Waters. Three years later, in 1822, Quinn is listed as serving with the Pittsburgh District. Ten years later, and two years after the Ohio or Western Conference was created, Quinn is listed as serving as an itinerant preacher. At this time, Quinn entered his chief service as a western circuit rider. By 1844, he is credited with having encouraged or established 47 churches west of the Mississippi River (St. Paul AME Church in St. Louis, Mo.). His services were rewarded with election to the bishopric in 1848. After his death, Paul Quinn College in Waco, Tex., was named in his honor. *See also* AFRICAN METHODIST EPISCOPAL CHURCH; PAUL QUINN COLLEGE.

Benjamin Quarles
(Courtesy of Benjamin Quarles.)

Far right:
William Paul Quinn
(Daniel A. Payne, History of the African Methodist Episcopal Church.)

R

RACE

Biology "Race" has only one scientific meaning and that is a biological one. It refers to a subdivision of a given species, members of which inherit physical characteristics that tend to distinguish that subdivision from other populations of the same species. Although this definition is as precise as one can make it, scientists realize that there are no clear-cut subdivisions in the single species called man, Homo sapiens. More people belong to categories between subdivisions than belong to the subdivisions themselves, or the same individual may have characteristics that place him in several categories simultaneously.

How Races Are Formed The discovery of the laws of heredity by Gregor Mendel in 1865 and the enunciation of the basic principles of evolution by Charles Darwin a few years earlier have thrown much light on the question of the development of races. Acquaintance with these fundamental ideas is essential to an understanding of race formation.

Biologists have ascertained that all physical characteristics—such as skin color, eye color, head shape, or stature—are determined by thousands of microscopic structures called genes. These genes are inherited from both parents through the female's egg cell and the male's sperm cell. Thus, every child will bear many resemblances to both parents. Ordinarily, genes replicate themselves exactly, but on occasion the molecular structure of a gene is spontaneously altered during the formation of sperm and eggs. This change may be reflected in the offspring as an alteration of the physical trait or traits that that particular gene determines. This spontaneous change is called mutation. Mutated genes are inheritable and can be passed on to successive generations indefinitely.

Every living thing must be able to adapt itself to its environment or perish. Certain physical traits have more adaptive value than others. The organism that acquires, through gene mutation, traits that enable it to adapt more successfully to the changing environment will live longer and reproduce more. Over a long period of time it will become the predominant type and the older less adaptive type will gradually die out.

Evolution is primarily sustained by the two processes of mutation and natural selection. Races are formed by an interaction of these forces combined with two other factors: migration and isolation. The following example will help to clarify the way in which races evolve.

Suppose a small group of light-skinned people leave an established settlement in a cool foggy climate and migrate to a hot climate where there is intense sunlight. Light skin is a liability where there is a great deal of sunlight, because some rays of the sun have a harmful effect on unpigmented skin. Now suppose that through mutation of the genes responsible for skin color a child is born with a darker skin. Since the darker skin helps him to adapt to the environment more successfully than his lighter-skinned brothers, he will live longer and reproduce more than they. Over the centuries, his descendants and those who develop even darker skins through further mutation will gradually become the dominant group, and the lighter-skinned people will eventually die out. If this migrant group becomes isolated due to the shift of a land mass or other barriers (such as a continental glacier or a great desert), it will continue to develop adaptive traits that will in time distinguish it very prominently from the group of which it was a part before their migration and isolation. In this way a new race of men is formed. Most scientists agree that all human beings are descended from the same ancestral stock that probably appeared between 600,000 and 1,000,000 years ago. They further agree that "pure" races in man never existed and cannot now exist, inasmuch as extensive migration and intermarriage have taken place continually since the beginning of the species.

Contrary to the popular view that man has descended from the ape, scientists presently hold the view that man stands at the end of a long evolutionary line from which monkeys and apes probably branched off several million years ago. Further evidence may cause this view to change; but whatever the case the assumptions concerning man's relationship to the ape have led many to conclude that some races are inferior because they are "nearer" the ape on the evolutionary scale than others. As it happens, the white man shares three primary physical traits with the ape—light skin, thin lips, and straight body hair—all of which are absent in the black man. Yet, it would be absurd to conclude that because the white man has these traits that he is "near" the ape and therefore inferior or superior.

Such expressions as "Negro blood," "half-blooded Indian," or "mixed blood" reflect a misunderstanding of the relationship between blood and race. Blood, itself, has nothing to do with the transmission of hereditary materials and should not be used to designate a racial type. Inherited physical characteristics, including blood types, are transmitted by genes and not by blood.

The blood of a mother normally does not come in contact with the growing embryo. The baby develops its own blood supply from food substances passing to it from the mother through the placenta. Because of this separation of blood systems, babies can have blood types different from their mothers.

Blood type refers to certain chemical properties of the blood. If different types are mixed, sometimes the blood cells will clump together, thereby impairing or stopping circulation. Many different blood factors are inherited. The most common types are called A, B, AB, and O. All races have the various blood types, though they appear among the races in varying frequencies. Interracial blood transfusion is therefore a perfectly sound medical practice so long as the blood types of the donor and the recipient are compatible.

For these reasons, it makes no sense to describe a person's racial ancestry in terms of blood. To say, for instance, that someone is of one-fourth "Indian blood" or has "Negro blood" coursing through his veins has no meaning based on fact.

Race-crossing or hybridization is one of the most fundamental processes of evolution. The belief that the offspring of interracial marriages might be degenerate and therefore perpetuate a deterioration of "good" racial stock has no basis in fact. The effects of race mixture depend entirely upon the inheritable physical characteristics of the individuals who have entered into the mixture. A great number of anthropological studies on race-crossing have revealed no evidence that race mixture as such produces bad results. In many cases the offspring of interracial marriages reflect qualities superior to the parental stocks. This increased "vigor" is a well-known characteristic of hybrids in general. Geneticists have utilized a scientific understanding of this effect to produce superior lines of grains, fruits, and livestock.

Not infrequently, human hybrid offspring are socially maladjusted and suffer from psychological problems. This is not due to an inherited disability, but can be traced entirely to social forces. Hybrid offspring are likely to meet with more intense forms of discrimination than do members of a given minority group because they are often rejected by members of both the racial groups from which their parents have come.

Does Race Have Anything to do with Intelligence? All races have members who are highly intelligent as well as individuals who are less intelligent. No evidence exists to show that natural selection has been operating in any way to produce a differentiation of mental capacity among various races.

Intelligence Quotient (IQ) tests, as a measure of inherited mental capacity, have so many serious limitations that comparing the average IQs computed for various racial groups as a means of proving inferiority or superiority of some races is open to serious error. Performance on IQ tests depends on so many culturally derived skills (verbal skills, mathematical ability, test-taking skills, and experience) that comparisons are meaningful *only* if all persons being compared have had similar cultural, educational, and social backgrounds. Because of prejudice and discrimination, different racial groups in some parts of the world have not had equal opportunity to acquire skills that are prerequisites to competent performance on IQ tests. As a result, IQ averages of racial groups vary widely. It should also be borne in mind that IQ tests are currently being discounted by authorities as a reliable indication of a person's ability to learn.

During World War I, the U.S. Army gave tests to all its recruits. Afro-Americans in general were found to have a lower average IQ score than whites and this led many to conclude that Afro-Americans were less intelligent than whites. However, when the recruits were roughly grouped according to educational opportunity or similar cultural experience rather than by race, a truer picture emerged. New York Afro-Americans, for instance scored as well as Alabama whites on the Alpha Test for literates, and illiterate New York Afro-Americans scored slightly higher on the average than illiterate Alabama whites.

Other factors such as preschool training, domestic security, good diet, and a home atmosphere of intellectual curiosity all have an effect on the way a child will perform on an IQ test. These factors are culturally determined and have nothing to do with inherited mental capacity. Racial groups who are the objects of discrimination are deprived of many of these opportunities, and therefore cannot be expected to perform on IQ tests as well as those who have had these opportunities. Likewise, Caucasians from underdeveloped mountain regions in our own country perform very poorly on IQ tests because of similar deprivation of opportunities and educational advantages.

All scientifically interpreted evidence indicates that all races have similar capacities for intellectual achievement. However, the similarity of these capacities will only be manifested if all have similar opportunities for health, security, and education in the broadest sense of the word.

Several investigations have shown that the average cranial capacity of the Afro-American is 1,400 cubic centimeters while the average size of the white man's is 1,450. This bit of information has been used to "prove" the superiority of one race over another, but the conclusion so reached is incorrect.

In the first place, averages are notoriously misleading because they give no indication of the range of brain size. Actually, greater differences in brain size exist among people of the same race than between races. The thousands of Afro-Americans who have larger heads than the average white man are lost in the computation of averages.

In the second place, no one has ever been able to demonstrate that brain size in man has anything to do with intelligence. The Kaffirs and Amaxosa of Africa, Eskimos, Japanese, and Polynesians all have larger average cranial capacities than the average white man. Yet, no one has ever concluded that these groups are "superior" to the white man in intelligence.

The shape of the head is likewise irrelevant to intelligence or mental capacity. That long-headed people are more intelligent than round-headed persons is another widespread belief that has no basis in fact.

Sickle-Cell Disease* Genetic diseases vary from population to population. For example, the white population in the United States is afflicted more by such conditions as phenylketonuria and cystic fibrosis of the pancreas than the black population. On the other hand, the Afro-American population is subject to sickle-cell anemia.

The anlage for the expression of the clinical effects of sickle hemoglobin was introduced into the United States when black slaves reached the shores of Virginia. Long before that time, however, the strange mutation responsible for the

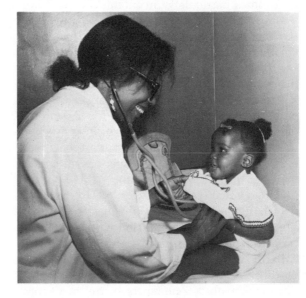

A young patient at the Sickle Cell Clinic, Jamaica Hospital, New York City, is shown with a physician, Dr. Yvette Francis. *(Arnold Hinton.)*

*See the PREFACE for acknowledgments.

disease occurred in the hemoglobin of the red blood cells of people in Africa or perhaps in response to such environmental hazards as sub-tertian malaria. There is evidence to indicate that in the malarial belts of Africa individuals bearing sickle cells appeared to be more resistant to infection by the malarial parasite than those who did not have the sickle-cell gene.

Professor J. B. Herrick of Chicago is usually given credit for the description of the first case of sickle-cell anemia in the United States in a publication that appeared in 1910.

During the next 40 years many additional cases were reported and a fairly large bibliography developed dealing essentially with descriptive clinical and pathological aspects of the disease. New interest in the syndrome occurred in 1949 when Linus Pauling and his associates, employing chemical and electrophoretic techniques, showed that an abnormal hemoglobin was responsible for the sickling phenomenon. In the same year Neel and Beet, working independently of each other, clarified the inheritance of the disease by advancement of the heterozygous–homozygous hypothesis.

In 1958 Ingraham combined the techniques of electrophoresis, chromatography, and trypsin digestion ("finger-printing") to show that the difference between hemoglobins A, C, and S was in the amino acid sequence of the polypeptide chains that made up the hemoglobin molecule.

During the next 20 years Scott and his coworkers at Howard University (Washington, D.C.), in a series of more than 50 publications, contributed to the clinical delineation of the sickle-cell syndromes particularly in infants and children.

Despite these advances, however, the disease remains incurable, and treatment is essentially episodic and symptomatic. Therefore, it is not surprising that in recent years attention has been turned to prevention through mass screening and genetic counseling. Fortunately, several laboratory techniques are available for detection of heterozygous and homozygous bearers of abnormal hemoglobins. The carrier trait occurs in eight to ten percent of Afro-Americans. Marriage between persons bearing the sickle-cell trait (heterozygous) can be expected to result in approximately 25 percent of the offspring having the homozygous condition with characteristic pathology and hazards to life and comfort.

In the United States and other parts of the world, the condition occurs predominantly, but not exclusively, in members of the black race. The condition has also been detected in other population groups including the Veddoids of Southern India, Mediterranean ethnic groups, races of African descent in the Caribbean islands and South America, as well as in people of the Middle East.

It has been estimated that among Afro-Americans the frequency of the homozygous disease affects about one in every 400 persons. This is far in excess of such other hereditary conditions as phenylketonuria (occurrence one per 10,000 live births) and cystic fibrosis of the pancreas (occurrence one per 2,000 live births), which statistically afflict predominantly the white population in the United States. Nonetheless, vast sums of money have been spent not only from research grants supported by the federal government but also from popular contributions that support national organizations interested in these and such other rare diseases as muscular dystrophy, special birth defects, hemophilia, etc. On the other hand, the more commonly occurring sickle-cell disease afflicting mainly the American black population has suffered from comparative neglect both by the federal government and the public at large.

There are compelling reasons to focus greater attention on the health needs of victims of sickle-cell disease at local and national levels. Because of the excessive mortality associated with this disease, more children and adolescents than older individuals are found as sufferers from the disease. These children, adolescents, and young adults are plagued by an array of disabilities such as crises of pain, stunted physical and sexual growth, enuresis, nocturia, leg ulcers, priapism, gallstones, strokes, increased susceptibility to infections (especially those caused by Pneumococcus and Salmonella organisms), school absenteeism, cardiac enlargement, anemia, and greater risks when surgery, anesthesia, or obstetrical delivery are contemplated.

Comprehensive care includes:

(1) Mass screening and genetic counseling for carriers of the sickling trait.

(2) Additional clinical facilities for victims of the active disease at local and state levels in clinics, hospitals, etc. Some current manuals on children with handicaps do not even mention sickle-cell anemia.

(3) Educational programs to inform the public at large (as well as victims of the disease) about the nature and needs of patients afflicted with the disease.

(4) Special schools for children handicapped neurologically and orthopedically from compli-

cations of the disease.

(5) Psychological and vocational counseling for families and patients. Victims of the disease encounter life insurance rejection and excess premiums as high-risk subjects, employer rejection for jobs, and high cost for medical care. See also DISCRIMINATION; HEALTH.

REFERENCES: For additional information, see: Bodmer, Walter F. and Luigi Luca, Cavalli-Sforza, "Intelligence and Race," Scientific American, October 1970, pp. 19–29; Dobzhansky, Theodosius, Mankind Evolving, Yale University Press, New Haven, 1962; Goldsby, Richard A., Race and Races, Macmillan, New York, 1971; Jensen, Arthur R., "How Much Can We Boost IQ and Scholastic Achievements?", Harvard Educational Review, Winter 1969, pp. 1–123; replies appear in Spring 1969 issue, pp. 273–356; Lewontin, Richard C., "Race and Intelligence," Science and Public Affairs, March 1970, pp. 2–8; and Scott, Roland B., "A Commentary on Sickle Cell Disease," Journal of the National Medical Association, January 1971. For textbook treatments, see Kirk, David, Biology Today, 2nd ed., CRM Books, 1974, pp. 204–311; and Williams, R. A., Textbook of Black Related Diseases, McGraw-Hill, New York, 1975. The latter volume has two very appropriate chapters by physicians/scientists affiliated with Howard University (Washington, D.C.): "Medical Genetics and Black-Related Diseases, "Chapter 2, by Robert F. Murray, Jr., professor of pediatrics and medicine and chief of the medical genetics unit; and "Hematology," Chapter 6, by William H. Bullock and Pongrac N. Jilly, professors of medicine and pathology, respectively. Bullock served on the National Sickle Cell Anemia Advisory Board.

Culture

Importance of Culture Culture may be said to consist of the sum total and organization of a group's behavior patterns, and it is an anthropological axiom that any cultural phenomenon must be understood and evaluated in the total cultural setting. Anthropologists assume, for example, that if an American white baby and a Chinese, or a Norwegian and a Congo black, were switched at birth and each were then fully accepted as "belonging" in its new home, each individual would grow up to accept the cultural patterns, attitudes, and beliefs of its adoptive, rather than its own family. There is equal reason to believe that if in the United States the positions of black and white people had been reversed, black people would feel the way white

people now feel and vice versa. The same thing would be true of northerners and southerners.

To be sure, not all the people of either race feel alike even when they live in the same community. In a sense, every man lives in a world of his own. Not only does each individual have his own unique genetic structure and his own inner environment (his blood pressure, his endocrine balance, and perhaps his allergy or his ulcer) but also he has his own private external world as well. In spite of a great deal of standardization, therefore, we are neither all exposed to the same stimuli, nor do we all have the same experiences even when we are members of the same family.

Recent history gave blacks more new experiences than their white counterparts (blacks were previously more restricted and had farther to go) and their position has changed more drastically. Thus the gap in the way many whites and blacks perceive themselves and their relation to one another has widened to the point of constituting a social crisis—a crisis based on "the polar attitudes of the American white, who does not yet accept the black as his equal, and the Afro-American, who is no longer satisfied with anything less."

The complexity of the race problem in sociological terms can be seen in the disparity in socioeconomic levels, in occupational distribution, in education, and in cultural levels, which is the result of generations of poor schools, job discrimination, and exclusion from cultural opportunities available to white people. There are also such psychological disparities as the long-established way of looking at the situation from the white or black point of view, of thinking in terms of "we" and "they," and of "my people" and "your people." The combined force of history, tradition, and habit serves to maintain this status quo.

Finally, myths support the situation: these myths are the socially supposed and believed-in differences that do not exist in fact but, because they are believed in, influence behavior as much as if they were actually true. Some of these myths come down as a part of history and tradition; others arise in the stress and strain of daily contact and are related to the fears that develop when established and familiar patterns are threatened. These supporting myths are allied to rumors, which are often myths in the making. Many notions about race and race mixture contrary to the article section BIOLOGY, persist as supporting myths. They are believed, not because objective evidence supports them, but because they lend credence and validity to things as they are or things as one wishes them to be.

Racial Myths Learned behavior—such as language, religion, nationality, and culture—is often confused with racial traits. Frequently, it is assumed that race is a major factor in determining behavior, and, consequently, that such behavior is inherited and not subject to change. Other myths include the belief that Afro-Americans are "naturally" lazy or immoral; that "Negro blood" is different from "white blood"; and that anyone "having Negro blood," no matter how little, is properly to be considered a Negro and may be expected to have other "Negro traits."

Race and culture are commonly confused. The images in this painting (*After Church* by Romare Bearden) are obviously "racial," but their importance is cultural. (*National Archives.*)

These and numerous other such beliefs add up to what the term "race" suggests to many people. Such conceptions, of course, bear little relation to the anthropological meaning of the term or to the biological reality for which it stands. They constitute, however, the sociological reality with which we deal when we speak of race prejudice, race attitudes, or race relations. In these areas we are dealing not so much with races in the biological sense as with what Robert Redfield has termed "socially-supposed races," that is, people who regard themselves as a race or who are so regarded by others. The extent to which the socially-supposed race corresponds to biological reality is immaterial so long as there is a believed-in difference.

Any useful analysis of race relations must take into account both biological and sociological realities and the fact that the two are commonly confused. From the practical point of view the

significant difference in the two kinds of reality lies in the fact that the biological factors are inherent in the germ plasm and hence are relatively fixed, while the sociological factors are the result of learned behavior and are, therefore, subject to modification or social manipulation. The biological and sociological factors are, of course, interrelated and they cannot always be completely separated. In general, however, we may say that the biological factors involved are important to society mainly when and because people think they are significant.

It would, of course, be naïve to assume that people can be changed by pointing out to them the fact that their beliefs and attitudes are out of harmony with objective reality. It is important, however, that the facts about race and race differences be known.

Although anthropologists do not always agree on precise definitions of race or on the specific criteria to be used in setting up racial categories, certain broad areas of general agreement exist regarding race and race differences. Some of the more important facts, in terms of practical significance, will be set forth here in the form of generalization. These statements must be oversimplified, and limitations of space will prevent their full elaboration.

(1) *There is no way by which all the individuals—or even all the populations—of the world can be classified into neat, orderly, and precise racial categories.* No "pure" races exist. Throughout human history, wherever peoples have come in contact, they have interbred, and all populations represent varying degrees of mixture of peoples of different physical types. The kind of racial categories established depends on the criteria selected, and such selection is always in some degree arbitrary. Moreover, within any racial category, however established, wide variations will occur, and the description of "a race" most certainly will not be a description of each individual belonging to that race. It is not possible to use a single criterion in establishing racial categories because the same characteristics may be found in several populations that are otherwise quite different.

This problem is well illustrated in skin color. Dark-skinned peoples are found in Africa south of the Sahara, in the area of the Pacific known as Melanesia (the islands from New Guinea to Fiji), in Australia, in parts of India, in Sri Lanka, and in scattered areas elsewhere across the world. Shall we put all these people into the racial category of Negroids? If we do, we immediately find ourselves confronted with several major difficulties.

In the first place, these populations cannot, by any reasonable procedure, be assumed to be genetically related. We have no evidence that all of these peoples had common ancestors or that they share a common gene pool. It is possible that differences in skin color may be the result of natural selection that occurred independently in different areas. In the second place, to group these populations together requires that we ignore a great many characteristics that differ: head and body hair, facial features, and other less conspicuous traits.

It is impossible to determine race by the use of any single criterion. But the fact remains that people do differ in physical features, and nobody would have much hesitation in saying a Congo Negro, a Chinese, and a blond Norwegian represent three different stocks or races. It is in this commonsense way that one should accept present day racial classifications. They are based on the fact that a fair-sized portion of the world's peoples can be grouped into categories on the basis of certain combinations of inherited physical characteristics that set them apart from other peoples having other distinguishing combinations of inherited characteristics.

Most anthropologists agree on the establishment of the broad general categories of Caucasoid, Mongoloid, Negroid, and possibly Australoid categories that are usually referred to as stocks or racial divisions and that may be thought of as subspecies of Homo sapiens. Much less agreement surrounds the subdivisions of these larger groupings into races, or varieties, and many populations do not fit into any of the conventional categories. One group of anthropologists, who listed six possible racial categories, said the names of these stocks served as useful labels so long as one realized that they were "generalized, arbitrary, tentative, and in some respects misleading." Whatever races we choose to distinguish will be almost entirely arbitrary. M. F. Ashley Montagu goes so far as to call the concept of race "an omelette which corresponds to nothing in nature." All in all, perhaps the most important thing the anthropologist can say to the nonspecialist on the subject of racial categories is that none of them should be taken too seriously.

The racial position of Afro-Americans is a case in point. Definitions of race usually involve both the idea of common ancestry and of phenotypical likeness, that is, the sharing of a certain combination of inherited physical traits. Yet observations of the effects of race mixture show clearly that common ancestry and phenotypical likeness do not necessarily go together. Neither does common ancestry guarantee likeness in genetic constitution.

Race mixture between whites and blacks has occurred since the beginning of American history. Legally, and by custom, the offspring of such unions are considered Negroes; and, in most parts of the United States today, any person known to have had a Negro ancestor is regarded as a Negro. The mechanism of biological inheritance, however, takes no account of marriage vows or of legal definitions that cannot alter biological realities. It follows that many persons in this country are legally Negroes but are genetically and phenotypically white; that is, they not only look white but they possess no genes for Negroid characteristics and cannot transmit such genes to their children.

Furthermore, it is theoretically possible for two mulattoes (mulatto here meaning an individual having one white and one black parent) to have entirely white or entirely black children. This possibility grows out of the fact that while a child receives one half of his chromosomes from each parent, he does not necessarily receive one fourth from each grandparent. In fact, as William E. Boyd points out, "a distinct though small chance" exists that a child can possess not a single chromosome of a particular grandparent.

(2) *Most of the criteria used in determining racial categories have to do with physical characteristics that are of little or no consequence in human behavior except as they are made so by the way people think and feel about them.* Color of the skin is primarily a matter of the degree to which various pigments are present, and the same thing can be said for the color of the hair and eyes. Almost all other racial differences are quantitative, being in effect a bit more or less in this or that measurement or index. In practically any measurement or index used there will be not only great variations within any designated population but also great overlapping between populations. There is no evidence that differences in skin color, hair, or features are in any way correlated with a particular kind of brain or with qualities of mind and character.

(3) *There are no known racial differences in normal human blood.* The terms "Negro blood," "mixed blood," and the saying "blood will tell," all go back to a prescientific age when it was thought that one's characteristics were deter-

mined by the blood inherited from the parents, and that the blood of the parents is combined in the child and will in turn be passed on to his offspring. According to this notion, race mixture involves the mixing of white and black blood, which suggests something like the mixing of ink and milk. Actually, of course, each organism produces its own blood, and, while blood types are inherited, blood itself is not passed from parent to child. An Rh positive infant born of an Rh positive father and an Rh negative mother may in some cases need to have its entire blood supply replaced by transfusions from unrelated donors. Such a procedure would not alter in any manner the infant's genetic constitution, its physical appearance, or the characteristics it can later transmit to its own descendents.

The ultimate absurdity in this connection was the establishment of separate blood banks during World War II for the blood of persons of different races. It is important that a person receiving a blood transfusion be of the same blood group as the donor but the race of the persons involved is of no consequence. The A, B, and O blood types are found in all races, and even in anthropoid apes. Children in the same family may have different blood types and hence a blond North European might be killed by a transfusion from his own brother but have his life saved by transfusions of matching type from a Hottentot, a Zulu, or an Australian aborigine. He would run no more risk of turning dark or having dark children as the result of receiving such blood than he would risk losing his masculine qualities by receiving a transfusion from a female donor.

(4) *No "child races" exist and no evidence is available to show that any one of the major races is more "primitive" or ape-like than another.* Many people hold to the idea that African Negroes (or for that matter American Indians or any other people whose culture is relatively simple) are a "child race," that is, they are backward or retarded and must go through a long developmental process before they can "catch up" with the more advanced peoples. Therefore, the reasoning goes, any individual of such a race must be backward, or primitive, or otherwise incapable of thinking, feeling, and acting "like a white man."

This construct is based on a number of misconceptions in which race is confused with culture and genetic equipment is confused with learned behavior. It is true that it would be diffi-

cult to teach African Negroes in an African setting to think, feel, and act like Americans. However, no evidence implies that anything other than cultural factors would be involved. Man's cultural progress is recorded not in his germ plasm but in his social institutions.

In recent years, increasing numbers of African Negroes born into simple cultures have later shown themselves quite capable of earning advanced degrees in British, European, or American universities. The causes of cultural advance or retardation are complex and obscure, but race does not play any significant role in the matter nor can one's genetic endowment be inferrred from the culture into which he was born.

The facts do not bear out the notion that any one race is more "primitive" or ape-like than another. Negroes may be more ape-like in having flat noses and dark skin, but apes have thin lips, straight hair, and a great deal of body hair—all of these being characteristics in which black people are much farther removed from the apes than are white people. Of course, no evidence exists that ties these so-called primitive traits to human behavior.

(5) *No evidence exists to indicate that any serious biological evils result from race mixture as such.* Most of the problems that arise from race mixture grow out of the way in which people think and feel about it; that is, the problems are social, not biological, in character. Common notions regarding race mixture are that the offspring of mixed unions are psychologically or emotionally unstable, that children of mixed unions inherit the worst of both parental stocks, or that the more "primitive" type determines the character of the offspring. Many people also believe that race mixture will result in "disharmonic crossings," and a common belief states that if a population becomes racially mixed cultural deterioration is sure to follow.

The notion that people of mixed racial ancestry are unstable as a consequence of such mixture confuses biological and cultural factors. Skin color, hair form, or features are in no way related to personality or temperament; and to suppose that incompatability exists in the genes of people of different races is to resort to pure speculation. When people of mixed racial ancestry are unstable—and it certainly is not true that they always are—sufficient explanation can usually be found either in the individual's particular psyche, as with persons of any race, or more commonly perhaps in the fact that the children of mixed unions frequently find themselves culturally rejected by one or both parental groups.

The notions that children of racially mixed parentage inherit the worst of both parental stocks, or that the more "primitive" type determines the character of the offspring, seem to be the result of ignorance, wishful thinking, or both.

Probably what most people who hold to these beliefs really have in mind is that the children somehow inherit the worst character defects of both racial stocks. The children do not, of course, inherit "character" at all but a specific genetic structure that is made up of particular genes and chromosomes, taken not from the races at large but from the genes and chromosomes of the two parents in question. When the parents are sound, healthy individuals, there is every reason to expect sound, healthy offspring, whether the parents belong to the same race or to different races. It is true, of course, that when interracial unions are forbidden by law or are socially unacceptable, the majority of such unions may occur between individuals who are lacking in those qualities that would make them desirable parents, whether they were to choose partners of their own or another race.

No evidence exists to support the proposition that racially mixed populations suffer cultural deterioration because of such mixture. It is true, of course, that a too rapid influx of great masses of alien people could result in disorganization in the receiving culture. This disorganization, however, would not be due to the foreign genes but to the alien habits and customs, and the prejudices and resistances involved. Present-day Afro-Americans are not of an alien culture, and the majority of them already possess varying numbers of non-Negro genes. Moreover, and more significant, they are not seeking further race mixture, but access to publicly financed community services.

(6) *No evidence exists to show that there is any such thing as an inferior or superior race.* Differences are "racial" only if genetically determined. Many characteristics that are often considered racial are the result of social and economic differences or of particular circumstances. It is assumed here that people are concerned primarily not with physical superiority but with mental traits. Physical superiority is in any case related to time and place (e.g., dark pigmentation in the tropics), to relative isolation

and exposure, and to socioeconomic standards. Unquestionably, individuals come into the world with different potentialities, but the evidence suggests that in any of the major racial groupings the whole range of individual potentialities will be found.

The absurdity of trying to "prove" racial inferiority or superiority, given the present state of our knowledge, becomes apparent when the situation is examined dispassionately. For one thing, to what "race" do we refer when we speak of "racial" inferiority or superiority? A great many Negro populations show evidence of unusual musical ability. Shall we say that the Negroid peoples are superior musically? Many people do think so, but what about the Oceanic Negroids and other Negroid peoples who show no evidence of such ability? This does not mean that musical talent is not inherited. It does mean that one cannot assume that given the genes that produce a dark skin, broad nose, and Negroid hair one will also find the genes responsible for musical ability.

Many people argue that one can measure racial differences objectively, and they point to intelligence tests as a means to prove the racial inferiority of certain groups. However, most contemporary specialists are agreed that at present we have no tests that can reveal innate racial differences in intelligence.

Other people point to cultural backwardness or inferiority as evidence of racial inferiority. But aside from the problems of definitions, one must ask when the judging is to be done, since people of different races have been in the cultural "lead" at different times.

On the practical level, it is not the average or statistical differences between races that matter but how particular individuals behave. For, however we may define them, "races" do not think, or imagine, or create. They do not work, or vote, or govern. They do not go to school, commit crimes, sing songs, or write books. They do not have a mentality, or a gift, or an IQ. Only an individual actually functions in a society, and it is the individual's gift, his ability, and his contribution to society that counts.

When people of the same race act as a unit, it can usually be demonstrated that they do so not because they are alike racially but because they have had like experiences. When people are treated alike, they act in response to that treatment. For example, other things being equal, black doctors, college professors, or businessmen are likely to think, act, and vote very much like white doctors, college professors, or businessmen. They are not likely to think, act, and vote like black porters, waiters, or day laborers unless they are so discriminated against that this fact overrides all other interests and concerns. *See also* DISCRIMINATION; SEGREGATION; SOCIAL CLASSES.

REFERENCES: Boyd, William E., *Genetics and the Races of Man*, Little, Brown, Boston, 1950; Dobzhansky, Theodosius, *Evolution, Genetics and Man*, John Wiley & Sons, New York, 1955; Dobzhansky, Theodosius, *Mankind Evolving*, Yale University Press, New Haven, 1962; Dunn, L. C. and Theodosius Dobzhansky, *Heredity, Race and Society*, Penguin Books, New York, 1946; Goldsby, Richard A., *Race and Races*, Macmillan, New York, 1971; Huxley, Julian, *Evolution in Action*, Harper Brothers, New York, 1953; Mason, Philip, *Common Sense About Race*, Macmillan, New York, 1961; Montagu, M. F. Ashley, *Man's Most Dangerous Myth: The Fallacy of Race*, Macmillan, New York, 1965; Pettigrew, Thomas F., *A Profile of the Negro American*, Van Nostrand, Princeton, 1964; Redfield, Robert, "What We Do Know About Race," *Scientific Monthly*, September 1943, pp. 193–202; and Simpson, George E. and J. Milton Yinger, *Racial and Cultural Minorities: An Analysis of Prejudice and Discrimination*, Harper and Row, New York, 1965. *See also* the references under RACE: RACISM.

Racism

Introduction Racism is difficult to define. It has many interpretations and connotations, some of them emotional, depending upon the source of the definition. However, reliable definitions are found in *Webster's Third New International Dictionary* (1965) and in a clearinghouse publication of the U.S. Commission on Civil Rights (*Racism in America and How to Combat It*, 1970). The first definition in Webster's states that racism is "the assumption that psychocultural traits and capacities are determined by biological race and that races differ decisively from one another which is usu. [usually] coupled with a belief in the inherent superiority of a particular race and its right to domination over others." The second publication defines racism in this way: "racism may be viewed as *any attitude, action, or institutional structure which subordinates a person or group because of his or their color.*" If one uses either definition, racism may be placed in numerous descriptive categories: black racism, white racism, American racism, South African racism. Two major descriptive categories that came into widespread usage during the 1960s and 1970s were institutional racism and scientific racism.

Institutional racism may not necessarily involve intent, because it may be submerged in the history, structure, and function of the institution. The fact that there are, for example, institutionalized white suburbs and black ghettoes does not necessarily mean that dwellers in either are racists, though it is conceivable and highly probable that an ample share of racists live in both. Most dwellers would have no intent or knowledge whatever of their being so, and they would resent being called racists. Yet, institutionalized racism exists and has existed in the structure and function of residential housing in the United States. To give another example, the affluent directors of an insurance company who live in the suburbs would be likely to shun the ghetto (even as they ride through it to their offices) as a poor business risk; but they may have no intent whatsoever to practice any kind of racism. The fact that the economics of racial discrimination has prevailed and does prevail in the ghetto may be viewed as an institutionalized way of life; thus, it may be defined as institutional racism.

Moreover, in scientific racism intent may also be invisible and its existence difficult to prove. Any scientific or pseudoscientific view of race that equates racial differences with racial superiority or inferiority may be defined as scientific racism. The authority of science as a discipline of study has long been called into such debatable areas as the relative importance of heredity or environment.

Whether institutional or scientific, racism has deep roots in the European and American pasts. Winthrop D. Jordan, in an important study of 1968 (*White Over Black: American Attitudes Toward the Negro, 1550–1812*), provided conclusive evidence that American racism is traceable to prejudices of Elizabethan Englishmen, whose attitudes toward blacks were shaped by their own needs for national self-consciousness and identity. With great mastery of detail, the author points out that racism preceded rather than originated with slavery, and that it persisted as a psychological as well as an economic system of exploitation. In effect, the author's central theme is that the idea of white supremacy over blacks served to provide a sense of social purpose and control for whites.

Persistence The principal reason for the persistence of antiblack racism and concomitant policies of segregation and discrimination is historical—they are too elemental and vigorous a part of the national heritage to die of their own accord. American society has always been structured along white supremacy lines, and Americans absorb the racial values of their society just as they do its economic, political, and social values.

Here are the practical consequences of anti-black racism and a major reason for its endurance. Segregation creates a vicious cycle, a self-fulfilling prophecy. Its consequences become its justification. White Americans think of their national experience as a success story. To them, America is a land of hope and opportunity, of economic abundance, social mobility, and political equality. They see their society as one that cultivates initiative, individualism, self-reliance, and self-sacrifice. They see America as a nation whose institutions are benevolent: the law protects everyone from oppression and is not itself oppressive; the fundamental rights of citizens are spelled out in the U.S. Constitution and guaranteed to all; the right of trial by an impartial jury of one's peers is so basic as to be commonplace; and every man respects his fellowman, his person and property, his womenfolk and children, and his freedom of expression and movement. This picture, of course, is over-drawn in the popular imagination, but there is an element of truth in it for whites.

For blacks the story is different; for them those ideals are honored more in the breach than in the observance. Since 1890 blacks have been relegated to a world of more-or-less rigid segregation and a deadening second-class status that saps the energies of all but the most persevering. The *racial* meaning of this must be understood. Segregation is the most important fact in the history of Afro-Americans in the twentieth century, dominating their experience as political freedom, economic opportunity, and social mobility dominated the white man's. Segregation excluded Afro-Americans from what whites call the American way of life. It tended to cultivate in them personal and social traits and moral and ethical values, which add up to a way of life notably different from that of whites. Not all Afro-Americans were so affected, but many were. Measured by the standards of the larger society, the "good" white American was one who displayed initiative, daring, independence; the "good" Afro-American was one who was imitative, humble, ingratiating, and childlike—a sycophant or a clown. The Afro-American's experience did not reward thrift and self-sacrifice as the white man's did. It offered him little hope for a better tomorrow. It encouraged irresponsibility, ignorance, servility, helplessness, and hopelessness, qualities that white Ameri-

With an estimated membership of about 5 million, members of the Ku Klux Klan, in their regalia, parade in Washington, D.C., in 1925. Founded in 1866, the Klan was not opposed to the use of terrorism in its support of white supremacy. Though national Klan membership declined after 1925, some local Klan groups could be seen in their regalia as late as the late 1970s. (*Library of Congress.*)

cans despised. His political and social status was ill-designed to inculcate respect for law and government, property rights, middle-class morality, the family, and even his fellow Afro-Americans. To him, government often seemed little more than organized tyranny; the law a device for denying him the fruits of his labor; and society a system permitting his womenfolk to be compromised, his children exploited, and his honor and self-respect undermined.

Again, the *racial* significance of this must be stressed. For whites, segregation was not even an inconvenience; for Afro-Americans it made race the supreme fact of life. At every turn it subjected the Afro-American to an invidious racial test. A ubiquitous, racial veil circumscribed his liberties, stifled his talents, and thwarted his ambition. He found it impossible, or virtually so, to exercise the responsibilities of citizenship or reap the rewards of the good life. He could not readily achieve a position of self-respect, or of independence, or of virtue.

What this means is that segregation creates ostensibly objective evidence to corroborate the segregationalist view of Afro-Americans. That at least is the conclusion white Americans have reached. Whites seem everywhere superior to Afro-Americans. They are better educated, live better, and control the instruments of power and prestige. Afro-Americans seem too often to deviate from acceptable standards of conduct. They become, in the view of whites, a race prone to violence, illegitimacy, venereal disease, and broken homes, a people who threaten property values, make low scores on intelligence tests, and lower standards in public schools.

The impact of this has been overwhelming. White Americans are preconditioned to think of Afro-Americans in racial terms, and they accordingly conclude that the Afro-American's condition is explainable only in those terms. Thus white attitudes toward Afro-Americans have always reflected the status of the race in this country, varying from time to time and section to section according to the status or condition of Afro-Americans in a given time or section. It is easy to overstate cause and effect and oversimplify a complex phenomenon, but the history of antiblack thought in America seems to follow this pattern: after Afro-Americans achieve or are relegated to a certain status, whites then develop a systematic rationale to justify that status. Only after Afro-Americans were enslaved did white Americans conclude that slavery was the natural status of the race, and only after the slave system came under systematic abolitionist attack were the most elaborate scientific, historical, and scriptural authorities cultivated to legitimate it. When Afro-Americans were segregated, the process occurred again. Racists then recognized segregation as the natural status for Afro-Americans and again cultivated authorities to support their conclusion.

The slow liberalization of racial ideas over the last generation has followed closely upon the rise of an Afro-American middle class, the emergence of independent black Africa, and new or heightened black achievement in many areas. The most excessive claims of black inferiority are no longer tenable, and have disappeared from all but the most extreme literature. The difficulty is that white attitudes are changing more slowly than black achievement and the aspiration that achievement inspires. If this analysis is correct, whites will not believe essentially in racial equality until blacks actually achieve equality. Only then will the fallacies of racist thought be apparent. But the major obstacle to equality is the white man's belief in inequality and the complex of racial policies that rest upon that belief. The way out of this impasse would seem to involve social changes fundamental enough to enable blacks to achieve actual equality. This, however, would require whites to devise social policies that run counter to deeply held racial convictions. That they will do so, with or without further violence, is problematical. The traditions of racism are strong and enduring. As a white southerner of moderate racial views once said, "the problem is not the negro, but the white man's attitude toward the negro." *See also* DISCRIMINATION; SEGREGATION; SOCIAL CLASSES.

REFERENCES: Allport, Gordon, *The Nature of Prejudice*, Addison-Wesley, Cambridge, 1954; Brink, William and Louis Harris, *Black and White: A Study of U.S. Racial Attitudes Today*, Simon and Schuster, New York, 1966; Friedman, Lawrence J. *The White Savage: Racial Fantasies in the Postbellum South*, Prentice-Hall, Englewood Cliffs, 1970; Gossett, Thomas F., *Race: The History of an Idea in America*, Southern Methodist University Press, Dallas, 1963; Jordan, Winthrop D., *White Over Black: American Attitudes Toward the Negro, 1550–1812*, University of North Carolina Press, Chapel Hill, 1968; Logan, Rayford W., *The Betrayal of the Negro, from Rutherford B. Hayes to Woodrow Wilson*, Collier Books, New York, 1965 (originally published as *The Negro in American Life and Thought, 1877–1901*); Newby, I. A., *Challenge to the Court: Social Scientists and the Defense of Segregation, 1954–1966*, Louisiana State University Press, Baton Rouge, 1967; Newby, I. A., *Jim Crow's Defense: Anti-Negro Thought in America, 1900–1930*, Louisiana State University Press, Baton Rouge, 1965; Smith, H. Shelton, *In His Image, But . . . Racism in Southern Religion, 1780–1910*, Duke University Press, Durham, 1972; Woodward, C. Vann, *The Strange Career of Jim Crow*, Oxford University Press, New York, 1966; and Zanden, James W. Vander, "The Ideology of White Supremacy," *Journal of the History of Ideas*, vol. 20, pp. 385–402, June-September 1959. For a bibliography, see Obudho, Constance E., *Black-White Racial Attitudes: An Annotated Bibliography*, Greenwood, Westport, Conn., 1976. For a comprehensive, continuing bibliography showing abstracts, see the massive *Bibliography on Racism*, 1972–1975, compiled and published (1978) by the U.S. Department of Health, Education, and Welfare (HEW), Center for Minority Group Mental Health of the National Institute of Mental Health.* See PREFACE: ACKNOWLEDGMENTS.

RACE RELATIONS INFORMATION CENTER (RRIC) Founded in 1954 in the wake of the U.S. Supreme Court's decision in *Brown v. Board of Education of Topeka* as the Southern Education Reporting Service (SERS), RRIC's objective was to collect, record, and report objectively information in regard to race relations, mainly on school desegregation. The center was based in Nashville, Tenn.; a shortage of funds forced it to close temporarily in 1972, but a grant restored its operation the same year. It permanently closed in 1974. The center published *Race Relations Reporter* bimonthly after 1969.

RACE RIOTS *See* CIVIL DISORDERS.

RACING *See* ATHLETES.

RACISM *See* RACE: CULTURE.

RADIO AND TELEVISION

RADIO AND TELEVISION Radio in its heyday reached more people daily than any other entertainment medium, and in doing so was guilty of perpetuating stereotypes of the Afro-American. In the beginning, what purported to be a black character heard over the air was in fact a white person. "Amos 'n' Andy" was a good example; its two stars were white men, Freeman Gosden and Charles Correll. In spite of its stereotyped characters, the program became one of America's favorite shows among both blacks and whites in the 1920s and 1930s. However, whether as performers before the microphone or as operators in the station, blacks were excluded from radio in its early history.

When participation came, black artists were used only as guest performers. Singing groups were the most popular, especially in the 1930s and 1940s when trios and quartets were in vogue. The Mills Brothers, the Southernaires, and the Ink Spots were popular in the 1930s. Later the King Cole Trio, featuring Nat "King" Cole, made frequent guest appearances on the "Frank Sinatra Show" and supper-club shows. The Charioteers, probably the most popular quartet in the mid-1940s, was featured on Bing Crosby's "Kraft Music Hall" for three years. Billie Holiday was one of the first and few Afro-Americans to perform regularly on a coast-to-coast network show as a band vocalist. Other vocal groups such as the Ink Spots made guest appearances on many radio programs but were never given a show of their own. The Four Vagabonds made radio history when they did commercials, the first Afro-American group to do so for a national audience.

Although the era of the big bands spanned the 1940s, such great band leaders as Count Basie and Duke Ellington made only occasional guest appearances on variety shows. The Mills Brothers, who made frequent guest appearances on the CBS network and who became a tremendous sensation, were not covered in the white press. Radio editors had a tacit agreement not to publish pictures of black radio artists, no matter how successful or popular they became.

The Mills Brothers were among the earliest black performers on radio and were very popular in the 1930s. (*National Educational Television*.)

Most radio comedy shows featured at least one Afro-American actor who figured in the action of the program. Invariably Afro-American roles were similar to those being meted out by Hollywood: maids, valets, fools, and underlings of every sort. Some prime examples were Eddie "Rochester" Anderson, a regular on the "Jack Benny Show," who played the part of the valet; Butterfly McQueen, who played maid roles; and Lillian Randolph, who played "Birdie" on "The Great Guildersleeve." While the menial acting roles were being filled by blacks, the technical and production end of the industry remained closed to Afro-Americans for many years. There were, however, a few disc jockeys and broadcasters at black stations before 1950, including Hal Jackson, Ed Pate, Mal Goode, and Roy Wood.

Toward the end of the 1940s it became increasingly apparent that radio would shortly lose much of its audience to a new medium—television. Consequently, many of the radio shows moved to television. "Amos 'n' Andy" made the transition virtually intact, except that now it had a black cast.

One of the earliest variety shows to appear on television was the "Ed Sullivan Show." Over the objections of many southern stations, Sullivan engaged talented Afro-American performers. The "Milton Berle Show" also regularly featured Afro-American performers, as did Arthur Godfrey, who presented the Mariners, an integrated quartet, as his "family of friends."

Ethel Waters was the first Afro-American performer to star in her own regular TV show, "Beulah," which was not entirely without stereotypes. She first appeared on the ABC network on October 3, 1950, and thereafter appeared on Tuesdays from 7:30 to 8 p.m. A new version of "Beulah," starring Louise Beavers, appeared on CBS in 1957. It ran Monday through Friday in the afternoon.

Nat "King" Cole also had his own show; but although the "Nat King Cole Show" maintained a popular rating on NBC, it ended in 1957 after one year because it did not attract a sponsor. A show that did obtain a national sponsor was "I Spy," starring Bill Cosby and Robert Culp as a pair of international spies. In fact, Cosby achieved a number of firsts. He was the first Afro-American to star in a network television series; he was the first Afro-American actor to win not one, but two, Emmy awards for best actor in a running series; and he was the first Afro-American actor to star on a television series that was not racially motivated. The show, "I Spy," ran on NBC from September 15, 1965, to September 2, 1968. Another Afro-American to be given an all-network show was Sammy Davis, Jr.

During the late 1960s other black stars were given their own series, including Diahann Carroll, Leslie Uggams, and Flip Wilson. Such popular black comedians as Nipsey Russell, Dick Gregory, Godfrey Cambridge, and Jackie (Moms) Mabley made frequent guest appearances on late-night talk shows, and on occasion they substituted as host for Johnny Carson or Dick Cavett. A number of series, such as "Ironsides" and "Mod Squad," also featured a black actor as a permanent member of the cast. Dramatic series—such as "The Bold Ones"—treated much more frequently themes that involved black campus radicals, militants, and poverty programs. Other individual Afro-American stars and performers made inroads. For example, Harry Belafonte produced a number of award-winning specials for television. Nipsey Russell was co-host on the "Les Crane Show" for a season, marking the first time that a regularly employed Afro-American master of ceremonies appeared on a nationally televised program. Increasingly, Afro-Americans were being used as newsmen; later Afro-American females were employed. In 1965 only three black women reported news on television: two in Philadelphia, Pa., and one in New York City. By 1976 male and female newscasters, including Toni Brown, Don Cornelius, Norma Quarles, Max Robinson, and Al Sanders, to mention a few were working for major television stations, in cities ranging from San Francisco, Calif., to Memphis, Tenn., and from Boston, Mass., to Miami, Fla.

Although individual newscasters and entertainers were important in showing the Afro-American presence on TV, the first great massive exposure of blacks came in national news broadcasts during the 1960s and 1970s, mainly in connection with the civil rights movement, civil disorders, and the war in Vietnam. To a lesser extent, coverage also came in special shows and programs that featured topics related to Afro-American history, culture, and social and economic conditions. For example, one TV station in Washington, D.C. (WTOP), beginning in 1968, established a record in having the longest continuous show ("Haranbee") that featured special topics related to blacks. Despite such coverage, however, many blacks were inclined to regard TV as a nonblack medium because white faces dominated the tube.

From the early days of TV, Afro-Americans were almost completely excluded from participation in the control and management of the industry; and blacks pointed to racial discrimination as one of the underlying causes for the

With the pronounced increase of TV shows by and about Afro-Americans in the 1970s, topical issues of the black community were discussed on programs such as "Positively Black." The program featured reporters/writers Ron Johnson (left) and Verda Williams. At right is Harry J. McNeill, producer/director. *(Courtesy of the National Broadcasting Company.)*

exclusion. Accordingly, voices of protest were raised, as shown in the two following examples.

(1) Broadcast Skills Banks, supported by such groups as the National Urban League, the National Association for the Advancement of Colored People (NAACP), the Congress of Racial Equality

State	Station and city	Year licensed*	Licensee/owner and executive/manager
Alabama	WBIL-AM (Tuskegee)	1952	George Clay
Alabama	WEUP-AM (Huntsville)	1958	Garrett Broadcasting, Inc./Leroy Garrett
Alabama	WENN-AM/FM (Birmingham)	1953	Booker T. Washington Broadcasting Co./A. G. Gaston/ K. R. Balton
California	KACE-FM (Los Angeles)	1959	Willie Davis/Bill Shearer
California	KJLH-FM (Los Angeles/ Compton)	1971	John Lamar Hill/Dalores Gardner
District of Columbia	WHUR-FM (Washington, D.C.)	1970	Howard University/Catherine Liggins
Florida	WOWD-FM (Tallahassee)	1976	Amrad Corporation/Claude Anderson/Jim Broaddus
Florida	WTMP (Tampa)	1954	Gulf South Communications, Ltd./R. A. McCleod
Georgia	WAOK (Atlanta)	1928	Broadcast Enterprise Network, Inc./Ragan Henry
Georgia	WRDW-AM (Augusta)	1930	JB Broadcasting Co./James Brown/Al Garner
Georgia	WSOK-AM (Savannah)	1947	Black Communications Corporation of Georgia, Inc./ Benjamin M. Tucker
Illinois	WJPC-AM (Chicago)	1922	Johnson Publishing Co./Marvin Dyson
Illinois	WMPP-AM (Chicago Heights)	1954	George Pinckard/Allen Wheeler
Indiana	WCMX-FM (Fort Wayne)	1971	HMH Communications Corp./Charles Hatch
Indiana	WTLC-FM (Indianapolis)	1961	Community Media Corp./Frank P. Lloyd/Al Hobbs
Kentucky	WLOU-AM (Louisville)	1949	Summers Broadcasting, Inc./Bill Summers
Kentucky	WNUU-FM (Louisville)	1967	Summers Broadcasting, Inc./William E. Summers, III/ Seretha Tinsley
Maryland	WEBB-AM (Baltimore)	1955	JB Broadcasting Co./James Brown/James Clark
Massachusetts	WILD-AM (Boston)	1947	Sheridan Broadcasting Corp./Thom McKinney/Monte Banks
Michigan	WCHB-AM (Inkster)	1957	Bell Broadcasting Corp./Wendell Cox
Michigan	WGPR-FM (Detroit)	1970	William V. Banks/Tenecia Gregory
Michigan	WGPR-TV† (Detroit)	1975	WGPR-TV, Inc./William V. Banks/Tenecia Gregory
Michigan	WJZZ-FM (Detroit)	1960	Bell Broadcasting Corp./Wendell Cox
Michigan	WWSM-FM (Saginaw)	1970	Saginaw Broadcasting Co./Robert O'Bannon
Mississippi	WORV-AM (Hattiesburg)	1969	Circuit Broadcasting Co./Vernon Floyd
Mississippi	WBAD-FM (Greenville)	1974	William D. Jackson
Mississippi	WTNK (Meridian)	1973	East-West Communication Corp./Charles Young/Len Maith
Missouri	KPRS-AM/FM (Kansas City)	1963	KPRS Broadcasting Co.
Nebraska	KOWH-AM/FM (Omaha)	1971	Reconciliation Incorporated/Keith Donald
New Jersey	WNJR (Union)	1977	Daniel Robinson/Noble Blackwell
New Jersey	WUSS-AM (Atlantic City)	1955	Edward L. Darden/John Hickman/Atlantic Business and Community Development
New York	WDKX-FM (Rochester)	1975	Monroe Broadcasting Co., Inc./Andrew Langston/Gloria M. Langston
New York	WLIB-AM/WBLS-FM (New York)	1926	Inner City Broadcasting Co./Pierre Sutton
New York	WUFO-AM (Buffalo)	1948	Sheridan Broadcasting Corp./Thom McKinney/Don Mullins
North Carolina	WBMU-FM (Asheville)	1975	Greater Ashville Education Radio Association/James Robinson
North Carolina	WGIV-AM (Charlotte)	1948	Broadcast Enterprises Network, Inc./Todd Branson/ Ken Goldbratt
North Carolina	WVOE-AM (Chadbourn)	1952	Ebony Enterprises, Inc./Lester Moore/Stacy Newkirk
Ohio	WELX-FM (Xenia)	1971	H & H Broadcasters/Harold Wright/Philip Wright
Ohio	WHBM-FM (Xenia)	1962	H & H Broadcasters, Inc./Harold Wright/Philip Wright
Pennsylvania	WAMO-FM (Pittsburgh)	1961	Sheridan Broadcasting Corp./Ronald Davenport/Thom McKinney
Pennsylvania	WYJZ-AM (Pittsburgh)		
South Carolina	WOIC-AM (Columbia)	1954	Nuance Corp./Elliott Franks, III/I. S. Leavy Johnson/J. Wade Defraffenreidt
Tennessee	WJBE-AM (Knoxville)	1968	JB Broadcasting Ltd./James Brown/Jim Clark
Tennessee	WLOK-AM (Memphis)	1946	H. A. "Art" Gilliam, Jr.
Texas	KCOH-AM (Houston)	1948	Call of Houston, Inc./Mike Petrizzo
Texas	KNOK-AM/FM (Fort Worth)	1947	EGG Dallas Broadcasting, Inc./Bill Chatman
Virginia	WOWI-FM (Norfolk)	1951	Metro Communications/L. E. Willis
Virginia	WPCE-AM (Norfolk)	1947	Metro Communications/L. E. Willis
Washington	KYAC-FM (Seattle)	1922	Dudley Communications, Ltd./Donald T. Dudley
Wisconsin	WNOV-AM (Milwaukee)	1946	Courier Communications Corp./Jerrel W. Jones
Virgin Islands	WBNB-TV† (Charlotte Amalie)	1964	Island Teleradio Service, Inc./Shirlee T. Haizlip
Virgin Islands	WVIS-FM (St. Croix)	1973	Joseph Bahr/Julio Bahr
Virgin Islands	WVIS-TV† (Christiansted)	1967	Antilles Broadcasting Corporation/Leroy Mercer

*The date refers to the year that the station was licensed; it is not necessarily the same year of acquisition by the licensee shown.
†TV stations
SOURCE: National Black Media Coalition; Federal Communications Commission; Individual stations

(CORE), and the Office of Economic Opportunity (OEO), had as their purposes to recruit minority group members, employ them in the industry on a full- or part-time basis, and give additional training where needed, including scholarships and aid for advancement in the industry. Some 24 Broadcast Skills Banks operated throughout the country in 1971 with the full cooperation of the major network channels. Later on in the 1970s, television featured an increasing number of black entertainers, black shows, and black newscasters.

(2) Specific groups were formed to challenge the renewal of broadcast licenses before the Federal Communications Commission (FCC), their challenge being based on the FCC regulation that a station must ascertain and reflect the needs of the community. The FCC, however, seemed to back away from its own regulation. In a 1971 ruling, it turned back a challenge to radio station WMAL's license renewal made by a group of Afro-Americans in Washington, D.C.

Among the specific groups interested in opening up and expanding TV to include blacks were the following: the National Black Media Coalition, an activist group founded in 1969 and later (1974) headed by Pluria Marshall; the National Black Network, based in New York City and under the leadership of Mal Goode, Eugene Jackson, and Roy Wood; the Mutual Black Network, based in Washington, D.C., and under the leadership of Paul Gates; and radio station WHUR, based at Howard University (Washington D.C.) and under the leadership of one of its principal founders, Phil Watson.

Certainly by the late 1970s, blacks were visible on TV as performers and newscasters; and many served in positions off camera. However, some Afro-Americans accused the industry of distorting black culture. Moreover, many blacks were dissatisfied with the limitations upon employment at the seat of power and control of the industry, pointing to the few blacks—the very few—who held influential positions at national levels: Stan Robertson, a director of programs at NBC; Elbert Sampson, the first Afro-American in management with the National Association of Broadcasters (NAB); and Frederick Weaver, the first Afro-American consultant for NAB.

Indeed, black control and ownership of the broadcasting industry was minimal at the end of the 1970s. With ownership being set at 51 percent or more, blacks owned and operated only one TV station out of a total of about 700 in the continental United States. (This was WGPR in Detroit, Mich., a station founded by the Masonic lodge under the leadership of William Banks, a lawyer by profession.) There were about 50 black-owned radio stations out of a total of about 7,000 in the continental United States. Black-owned radio and TV stations (1977–1978) are listed in the table on page 725. See also DISCRIMINATION; EMPLOYMENT; MOTION PICTURES; MUSIC: JAZZ.

REFERENCES: There is no single, adequate reference. This article is a good beginning point, but guides to periodical literature should be consulted. A recent, expansive bibliography can be found in Blackman, R. Dwight, The Dynamics of Black Radio, Creative Universal Products, Washington, 1977, pp. 80–93. Miller, Elizabeth and Mary L. Fisher, The Negro in America: A Bibliography, 1970, pp. 45–47. Periodical literature on the subject can be consulted in Index to Periodical Articles by and About Negroes (1950–   ) and in the printed indexes to selected periodicals compiled by the Hallie Q Brown Memorial Library and the Schomburg Collection of the New York Public Library, published after 1950 (See BIBLIOGRAPHIES/BIBLIOGRAPHIES/GUIDES).

RAGTIME See MUSIC: HISTORY AND DEVELOPMENT; MUSIC: JAZZ.

RAINEY, GERTRUDE MALISSA NIX PRIDGETT (MA) (1886–1939), blues singer; born in Columbus, Ga. "Ma" Rainey was still a teenager when she married actor William (Pa) Rainey. She then toured with Fats Chappelle's Rabbit-Foot Minstrels and Tolliver's Circus. It was while on tour with the Minstrels that she met and helped to form her successor as the greatest blues singer, Bessie Smith. During the early 1920s Rainey began recording, and by 1929 she had made more than 50 recordings. This success led to her own show in which her "Georgia" Jazz Band was featured. By this time Rainey was known as the "Mother of the Blues." See also MUSIC: HISTORY AND DEVELOPMENT; MUSIC: BLUES

RAINEY, JOSEPH HAYNE (1832–87), State legislator, U.S. Representative; born in Georgetown, S.C., Rainey began his working life as a barber, but in 1862 he was sent to Charleston, S.C., to work on Confederate fortifications. From there he escaped to the British West Indies where he remained until the end of the war. Membership on the executive committee of the newly formed Republican Party of South Carolina, and attendance at the South Carolina constitutional convention preceded his election to the state senate in 1869. In 1870, with his election to the forty-first Congress, Rainey became the first Afro-American to represent South Carolina in the House. During his five successive terms he spoke in favor of legislation to enforce the 14th

Amendment, and he demanded that the Afro-American be given all civil rights and be admitted to all public places. In 1879 Rainey was made special internal revenue agent in the U.S. Department of the Treasury. Resigning in 1881, he engaged in the banking and brokerage business for a time, and then in 1886 returned to his home in South Carolina, where he died.

RALSTON, RICHARD DAVID (1937–   ), historian, educator; born in Marietta, Ga. Ralston received a B.A. degree from Fisk University (Nashville, Tenn.) in 1958, a M.A. degree from the University of Rochester (Rochester, N.Y.) in 1961, and his Ph.D. degree from the University of California at Los Angeles in 1972. He was a Danforth Foundation Fellow (1967–69) and an assistant professor of history at Immaculate Heart College (1964–70) and at the University of Rochester after 1971. His publications include "Black Students at White Universities" (1973) and "The Future of the Black University" (1973).

RANDALL, DUDLEY (1914–   ), librarian, poet, publisher; born in Washington, D.C. Randall received a B.A. degree from Wayne State University (Detroit, Mich.) in 1949 and his M.A.L.S. degree from the University of Michigan in 1951. He began library work that year, and was a librarian in many different Michigan positions. In 1969 Randall became reference librarian for the University of Detroit, where he was also poet-in-residence. His poems appear in many anthologies, and he was the author of *Poem Counterpoint* (1966), with Margaret Danner, and *For Malcolm* (1967), with Margaret J. Burroughs. Randall also founded Broadside Press in 1965 in order to publish the work of Afro-American poets. *See also* LITERATURE: POETRY.

RANDALL, FREDERICK R. (1922–   ), surgeon, educator; born in Washington, D.C. Randall received his M.D. degree from Howard University Medical College (Washington, D.C.) in 1945, and completed his surgical training at Homer G. Phillips Hospital, St. Louis, Mo.; at the Graduate School of Medicine of the University of Pennsylvania; and at Presbyterian Hospital, New York, N.Y. He interned at and was later assistant resident in surgery and assistant in pathology at Freedmen's Hospital, Washington, D.C. Randall served as associate professor of clinical surgery at the College of Physicians and Surgeons of Columbia University, and was associate attending surgeon, Presbyterian Hospital, in 1968, and

visiting surgeon and assistant director of surgery at Harlem Hospital, New York, N.Y.

RANDOLPH, A. (ASA) PHILIP (1889–1979), labor leader, socialist; born in Crescent City, Fla. The son of a Methodist minister, Randolph made an outstanding contribution to two of the major movements of twentieth-century America: the civil rights struggle and the trade union movement. After attending high school in Jacksonville, Fla., at the Cookman Institute, Randolph came north to New York City and worked at a series of odd jobs—porter, railroad waiter, and elevator operator—while he studied at the City College of New York. Active in the socialist movement, he cofounded a socialist weekly, *The Messenger*, in 1917. Randolph taught at the New York Rand School of Social Science, and in 1921 ran unsuccessfully for the secretary of state of New York on a socialist platform. Randolph also traveled across the country delivering speeches with a socialist message. In 1925, Randolph organized the Brotherhood of Sleeping Car Porters (BSCP), and after ten years of struggle the union negotiated a collective bargaining agreement with the Pullman Palace Car Company. He was influential in getting President Franklin D. Roosevelt to form the Fair Employment Practice Committee (FEPC) in June 1941, a committee designed to curb discrimination in war production industries and government employment. Pressure was brought to bear by the threat of a march on Washington, D.C.; Randolph was able to convince Roosevelt that he could bring out 100,000 supporters. An active opponent of discrimination in the U.S. Armed Forces, he founded, in 1947, the League for Nonviolent Civil Disobedience in the Armed Forces. In 1942 New York City's Mayor Fiorella La Guardia appointed him to the New York Housing Authority. In 1955, the year the American Federation of Labor (AFL) merged with the Congress of Industrial Organizations (CIO), Randolph was appointed to the AFL-CIO executive council. In 1957 he became vice-president of the union and in 1960 he founded the Negro American Labor Council, serving as its president until 1966. Randolph often stood in opposition to George Meany and other conservatives within the AFL-CIO because of their less-than-complete support of civil rights within the unions, but Randolph remained loyal to the AFL-CIO and chose to work within its framework. Randolph joined other prominent civil rights leaders in organizing and leading the 1963 civil rights march on

Washington, D.C., which marked a turning point in the Afro-American struggle for equal rights. In later years Randolph's socialism became less militant. He began to write for *Opportunity,* the journal of the Urban League, and he affiliated with the Liberal Party, which had close ties to organized labor. Randolph was founder and president of the A. Philip Randolph Institute of New York City, which dedicated itself to educational studies and projects, as well as to the struggle for jobs within the skilled trades for minority youths. *See also* A. PHILIP RANDOLPH INSTITUTE; CIVIL RIGHTS: MOVEMENT; LABOR UNIONS.

Charles B. Rangel. *(Office of Congressman Krugel.)*

RANGEL, CHARLES BERNARD (1930–), lawyer, state legislator, U.S. Representative; born in New York, N.Y. Rangel received a B.S. degree from the New York University School of Commerce in 1957 and his LL.B degree from St. John's University School of Law (Jamaica, N.Y.) in 1960. Following his admission to the New York bar in 1960, he was named an assistant U.S. attorney for the Southern District of New York. Rangel then took the posts of associate counsel to the speaker of the New York state assembly and general counsel to the National Advisory Commission of Selective Service. In 1966 he was elected to the first two terms in the New York state assembly, representing the 72nd Assembly District, which includes most of Harlem. In 1970 Rangel was elected to the U.S. House of Representatives defeating Adam Clayton Powell, Jr. In 1974 he was named by the House Democratic and Republican leadership to the House Ways and Means Committee, becoming the first black person to sit on that committee.

RANSOM, LEON *See* LAWYERS.

RANSOM, REVERDY C. (1861–1959), African Methodist Episcopal bishop; born in Flushing, Ohio. Ransom received a B.D. degree (1886), a D.D. degree (1898), and his LL.D. degree (1912) from Wilberforce University (Wilberforce, Ohio). After having been ordained an elder in the African Methodist Episcopal (AME) Church in 1887, he served as pastor of AME churches in Ohio, Pennsylvania, Illinois, Massachusetts, and New York, and was also editor of the *AME Review* from 1912 to 1924. In 1924 Ransom began a noteworthy career as an AME bishop, following his election to that post in Louisville, Ky. Fluent and eloquent, he frequently mastered political relations in the church's highest councils.

RAY, CHARLES BENNETT (1807–86),clergyman, journalist, born in Falmouth, Mass. Ray attended local schools and studied theology at Wesleyan Academy (Wilbraham, Mass.) and at Wesleyan University (Middletown, Conn.). He served as pastor of the Bethesda Congregational Church in New York City for 20 years. In 1837 Ray became general agent for the *Colored American* under Philip A. Bell, lecturing and traveling widely to promote the interests of the newspaper and to oppose slavery. In 1838 he became coproprietor of the paper, and the following year, upon Bell's retirement. Ray took charge until the newspaper folded in 1842.

RAY, CHARLOTTE *See* LAWYERS.

RAY, SANDY FREDERICK *See* BAPTISTS.

REDDICK, LAWRENCE DUNBAR (1910–), historian, curator, author; born in Jacksonville, Fla. Reddick received a B.A. degree (1932) and a M.A. degree (1933) from Fisk University (Nashville, Tenn.), and his Ph.D. degree from the University of Chicago in 1939. Through the years he taught history at Kentucky State College; Dillard University (New Orleans, La.); Alabama State College, where he was chairman of the history department); and Coppin State College (Baltimore, Md.) where he served as chairman of the division of social studies. Beginning in 1939, Reddick served for nine years as curator of the New York Public Library's Schomburg Collection. In 1948 he began seven years as chief librarian of the Trevor Arnett Library in Atlanta, Ga. In 1970 Reddick joined the faculty of Temple University (Philadelphia, Pa.) as professor of history. His published works include *Crusader Without Violence, A Biography of Martin Luther King, Jr.* (1959) and *The Essence of Opportunities Industrialization Centers* (1971). *See also* HISTORIANS.

REDDING, JAY SAUNDERS (1906–), author, educator; born in Wilmington, Del. After attending Lincoln University, Redding received a B.A. degree (1928) and his M.A. degree (1932) from Brown University (Providence, R.I.). He taught at Morehouse College (Atlanta, Ga.) from 1928 to 1931, at the Louisville Music Conservatory (Louisville, Ky.) from 1934 to 1936, and at Southern University (New Orleans, La.) from 1936 to 1938. Redding received a Rockefeller Foundation Fellowship in 1940, taught at the Hampton Institute (Hampton, Va.) from 1943 to 1966, and received a Guggenheim Fellowship in 1944. He served as a director of the National

Endowment for the Humanities from 1966 to 1970, and then began teaching at Cornell University (Ithaca, N.Y.). His books include *To Make a Poet Black* (1939), *No Day of Triumph* (1942), *They Came in Chains* (1950), *The Lonesome Road* (1958), and *The Negro* (1967). *See also* LITERATURE: THE NOVEL.

REDDING, LOUIS *See* LAWYERS.

REDMAN, DONALD (DON) MATTHEW (1900–), bandleader, jazz saxophonist, arranger; born in Piedmont, W. Va. Redman was a child prodigy who played the trumpet at the age of three, joined a band when six years old, and later studied theory, harmony, and composition at music conservatories in Boston, Mass., and Detroit, Mich. The first important composer-arranger in jazz history, Redman achieved fame in the 1920s as a brilliant instrumentalist on several types of saxophone, and he recorded with Bessie Smith, Louis Armstrong, and other leading jazz artists. During the 1930s Redman led his own band, and in the 1940s he worked with Paul Whiteman, Jimmy Dorsey, and others, writing arrangements for both radio shows and the theater. His best-known composition was his theme song, "Chant of the Weed." *See also* MUSIC: JAZZ.

REED, THOMAS M. (1913–), lawyer, judge; born in Philadelphia, Pa. Reed received his legal education at Temple University (Philadelphia, Pa.) and from 1952 to 1965 he served as an assistant district attorney of Philadelphia. In 1956 he became chief of the Pardons and Paroles Division, and in 1964 was appointed chief of litigation. Reed later served as chief assistant district attorney. He was sworn in as judge of the Common Pleas Court in 1965.

REESE, DELLA (1932–), singer; born Deloreese Patricia Early in Detroit, Mich. Reese was singing with Mahalia Jackson's chorus by the time she was 13 years old. After attending Wayne State University (Detroit, Mich.) she sang at first in clubs in Detroit and later with Erskine Hawkins' band in New York City. Her many recordings were very successful, as were her appearances on television and in nightclubs throughout the country. In 1969 Reese became the first woman to host a television variety show, a program that was broadcast five days a week during the 1969–70 season. In the 1970s she returned to appearing in nightclubs and making records.

REESE, JAMES B. (1905–), lawyer, judge. Reese received a B.A. degree from California Western University (San Diego, Calif., now U.S. International University) and his LL.B. degree from Loyola University of Los Angeles. He was admitted to the California bar in 1934, and later he became commissioner of the Superior Court in Los Angeles County.

REID, FRANK MADISON (1900– ?), African Methodist Episcopal bishop; born in Nashville, Tenn. Reid received a B.A. degree (1921) a B.D. degree (1924), and his M.A. degree (1932) from Wilberforce University (Wilberforce, Ohio), and did additional graduate work at the University of Chicago and at Union Theological Seminary. He was a pastor for more than 20 years of African Methodist Episcopal (AME) churches in Kentucky and Missouri before being elected a bishop at the unprecedented age of 42.

REID, IRA DE AUGUSTINE (1901–68), sociologist, educator; born in Clifton Forge, Va. Reid spent his boyhood in Harrisburg, Pa. and Philadelphia, Pa., moving to Savannah, Ga., when he was about 15. He received a B.A. degree from Morehouse College (Atlanta, Ga.) in 1922, and that same year went to Texas College as an instructor. In 1925 Reid received a M.A. degree from the University of Pittsburgh and went to work for the New York Urban League. Between 1928 and 1934, he served as research director of the National Urban League. When Reid received his Ph.D. degree in 1939 from Columbia University, his dissertation, *The Negro Immigrant,* was published as a book. In 1937 he directed a federal project studying white-collar employees and skilled workers, and from 1938 to 1942 he served as consultant to the Social Security Board. From 1942 to 1943 he was a consultant to the War Manpower Commission. Reid taught at several universities here and abroad, becoming the first full-time visiting professor of Negro culture and education at New York University in 1946. He was chairman of the department of sociology and anthropology at Haverford College (Haverford, Pa.) from 1947 to 1966. Of his extensive writings, his two most important books are *In a Minor Key: Negro Youth in Story and Fact* (1940) and *Sharecroppers All* (1941) with Arthur F. Raper. Other major works include: *The Negro Population of Denver* (1929); *Social Conditions of the Negro in the Hill District of Pittsburgh, Pennsylvania* (1930); *The Negro in New Jersey* (1932); *The Problem of Child Dependency*

Among Negroes (1933); *The Negro Community in Baltimore* (1935); and *The Urban Negro Worker in the United States* (1938). *See also* SCIENTISTS: SOCIAL.

REID, WILLIAM FERGUSON (1925–), surgeon, state legislator; born in Richmond, Va. Reid received a B.S. degree from Virginia Union University and his M.D. degree from Howard University Medical College (Washington, D.C.) in 1948. He interned and was resident in surgery at Homer G. Phillips Hospital, St. Louis, Mo., and served as staff surgeon at Richmond Community and Richmond Memorial hospitals. In 1968 Reid became the first Afro-American to be seated in the Virginia house of delegates since Reconstruction.

RELIGION / RELIGIOUS BODIES See CHURCHES.

REPUBLIC OF NEW AFRICA A black separatist group founded in 1968, Republic of New Africa favors the establishment of an Afro-American republic within the boundaries of five southern states—Alabama, Georgia, Mississippi, Louisiana, and South Carolina. Annual meetings resulted in the formation in 1970 of the first "African community" in Jackson, Miss. Iman Abubakan Obadele I was named president of the republic. In 1971, a 20-acre tract of land in Hinds County, Miss. was proclaimed the capital of the nation, but the land was eventually acquired by other buyers. Also in 1971, a police raid on the group's Jackson, Miss., headquarters ended in murder charges against 11 members. Obadele I was sentenced to life imprisonment in 1972, but he was released in 1973 after 20 months in prison.

RESURRECTION CITY *See* ABERNATHY, RALPH D.

REVELS, HIRAM RHOADES (1822-1901), clergyman, U.S. Senator, civil rights advocate, educator; born in Fayetteville County, N.C. Born a free man, Revels studied at a seminary in Indiana and at Knox College (Galesburg, Ill.). He was pastor of African Methodist Episcopal (AME) churches in Illinois, Missouri, and Indiana. During the Civil War Revels recruited Afro-Americans for the Union cause and also served as chaplain of a regiment. In 1870, having settled in Mississippi, he became the first Afro-American to serve in the U.S. Senate when he was elected to the seat once occupied by Jefferson Davis, later president of the Confederate States. Revels, who served in the Senate one year, played an important part in defeating an amendment that would have ensured segregation in the public schools of the District of Columbia. In 1876 he became editor of the *Southwestern Christian Advocate*. Much of his later career was devoted to Alcorn State University (Lorman, Miss.), of which he was president. *See also* AFRO-AMERICAN HISTORY: RECONSTRUCTION; PRESBYTERIANS.

REYNOLDS, RAYMOND J. (1905–), lawyer, judge. Reynolds received B.A. and LL.B. degrees from Washburn University (Topeka, Kans.). Admitted to the bar in 1929, he later became judge of the Municipal Court in San Francisco, Calif.

RICHARD ALLEN CENTER FOR CULTURE AND ART Founded in 1976 and located in the Empire Hotel opposite Lincoln Center in New York City, the center houses the Ira Aldridge Playhouse, the Paul Robeson Concert Hall, the Henry O. Tanner Gallery, the Oscar Micheaux Media Center, the James Baldwin Library, a crafts shop, a rehearsal room, and a workshop. The center was named for Richard Allen, founder of the African Methodist Episcopal (AME) Church in Philadelphia, Pa., in 1787, the oldest Afro-American institution in continuous operation in the nation. Allen was also the first Afro-American bishop. One of the founders of the center and its first director was Hazel J. Bryant. The major sources of financial support in the establishment of the center were the AME Church, a grant from the Exxon Corporation, and a donation of 200 seats from Avery Fisher Hall of Lincoln Center. *See also* ALLEN, RICHARD; BRYANT, HAZEL J.

RICHARDSON, CLEMENT (1878– ?), educator; born in Halifax County, Va. Richardson was educated at Mt. Hermon School in Massachusetts from 1898 to 1902 and at Brown University (Providence, R.I.) from 1902 to 1905 and received a B.A. degree from Harvard University in 1907 and his M.A. degree from the University of Kansas in 1923. He taught at Morehouse College (Atlanta, Ga.) from 1907 to 1908, and at Tuskegee Institute (Tuskegee Institute, Ala.) from 1908 to 1918. Richardson served as president of Lincoln University (Jefferson City, Mo.) from 1918 to 1922 and of Western College from 1922 to 1927. In 1928 Richardson was elected treasurer of the Kansas Baptist State Convention.

RICHARDSON, GLORIA HAYS (1922–   ), civil rights activist; born in Baltimore, Md. Richardson grew up and lived in Cambridge, Md., where she founded the Cambridge Nonviolent Action Committee in 1963. She challenged the practice of segregation in places of public accommodations and helped to desegregate restaurants, bowling alleys, taverns, and other public places.

RICHARDSON, HARRY VAN BUREN (1901–   ), clergyman, educator; born in Jacksonville, Fla. Richardson received a B.A. degree from Western Reserve University Divinity School (1925), an S.T.B. from Harvard University Divinity School (1932), and his Ph.D. from Drew University (Madison, N.J.) in 1945. He was active on the boards of many influential local, regional, and national religious-related organizations. He served as chaplain at Tuskegee Institute (1934–1948) and as president of the Interdenominational Theological Center (1959–69). His books include *Dark Glory: A Picture of the Church Among Negroes in the Rural South* (1947) and *Dark Salvation: The Story of Methodism Among Blacks in America* (1976).

RIDDLE, ESTELLE MASSEY educator, nurse. Riddle received her M.S. degree with a major in nursing from Columbia University Teachers College in 1929. She became director of education at Freedman's Hospital, Washington, D.C., in 1934, and served as president of the National Association of Colored Graduate Nurses from 1934 to 1939 and as consultant to the staff of the National Nursing Council for War Service in 1943. Elected to the board of directors of the American Nurses Association (ANA), Riddle became the first Afro-American to hold office in the ANA in 1948. In 1949 she was selected by the board of the ANA as an official delegate to the International Council of Nurses, meeting in Stockholm, Sweden, the first time that an Afro-American nurse was selected as a delegate. *See also* NURSES.

RIDDLE, JOHN MORTON (ca. 1858–1943), clergyman, educator; born in Buckingham County, Va. Though he was born a slave, Riddle availed himself of the first opportunity to study in the schools of the Freedmen's Bureau following his emancipation. Soon he and his brother advanced to the rank of teachers; Riddle became the first Afro-American teacher in his home county to secure a first-class teaching certificate. In West Virginia, where he settled for a time, he had the opportunity to preach in a Baptist church, and he served as pastor of churches in several Ohio cities, including Columbus, and then of churches in California.

RIDLEY, WALTER NATHANIEL (1910–   ), educator; born in Newport News, Va. Ridley received a B.A. degree (1931) and a M.A. degree (1933) from Howard University (Washington, D.C.), and his Ed.D. degree from the University of Virginia in 1953. He served as educational adviser to the Civilian Conservation Corporation, Washington, D.C., from 1934 to 1936. Ridley then taught at Virginia State College from 1936 to 1957, was dean of St. Paul's College from 1957 to 1958, and became president of Elizabeth City State University (Elizabeth City, N.C.) in 1958.

RILES, WILSON (1917–   ), educator, public official; born in Alexandria, La. Orphaned at the age of 11, Riles was able to attend high school through the aid of friends of his parents and later worked his way through Northern Arizona State University, receiving a B.A. degree (1940) and his M.A. degree (1947) from that institution. He was affiliated with Arizona public schools for 14 years (1940–54), then joined the California department of education, where he worked on compensatory education for disadvantaged children (1958–64). Riles chaired commissions on urban education for President Lyndon B. Johnson and for President Richard M. Nixon. He held various other positions until he was elected California superintendent of public instruction in 1970), becoming the first Afro-American to be elected to a statewide office in California and the first Afro-American state superintendent of public instruction since Reconstruction. Riles was awarded the 58th Spingarn Medal in 1973.

RILLIEUX, NORBERT (1806–94), inventor; born in New Orleans, La. Rillieux received his schooling in Paris, where his great ability in engineering led to his appointment as instructor of applied mechanics at L'École Central in 1830. He invented the multiple-effect vacuum evaporation process for refining sugar. This process was first tested on the Louisiana plantation of Zenom Ramon in 1834, and it failed, as did a second attempt in 1841. However, the third attempt in 1845 was successful, and Rillieux installed his system on many plantations. He returned to Paris about 1861, and in 1881 he devised the standard refining system now used by the sugar-refining industry. His basic technique is also used in the manufacture of condensed milk, glue, and gelatin.

RIOTS *See* CIVIL DISORDERS.

RIVERS, CONRAD KENT (1933–68), poet; born in Atlantic City, N.J. Rivers graduated from Wilberforce University (Wilberforce, Ohio) and later taught at Gary, Ind. His poems were published in many magazines, including *Kenyon Review* and *Negro Digest*. His books include: *Perchance to Dream, Othello* (1959); *These Bodies and This Sunburnt Face* (1962); *Dusk at Selma* (1965); and *The Still Voices of Harlem* (1968). *Negro Digest/ Black World* offered an annual Conrad Kent Rivers Poetry Award for the best poem published each year. *See also* LITERATURE: POETRY.

RIVERS, DAVID FOOTE (1859–1941), clergyman, state legislator; born in Florence, Ala. Rivers was educated at Roger Williams University from which he received both academic and theological degrees. Settling in Tennessee, he served in the state legislature from 1883 to 1885, and was reelected in 1885 for a second term. However, he was not seated then because the election was contested. Thereafter, Rivers served as pastor of churches in Tennessee and Kansas before accepting the pastorship of Berean Baptist Church, Washington, D.C., where he was active until his death.

Paul Robeson in the Margaret Webster production of *Othello.* (Museum of the City of New York, Theatre and Music Collection.)

ROBESON, PAUL BUSTILL (1898–1976), actor, singer; born in Princeton, N.J. Robeson received a B.A. degree from Rutgers Universtiy (New Brunswick, N.J.) in 1919, where he was an honor student, a 12-letter athlete, a football All-American in 1917, and an award winner in oratory. He earned his LL.B degree from Columbia University. He was asked by Eugene O'Neill, after he had seen him in a college theater production, to appear in the playwright's *Emperor Jones.* Robeson refused, but soon after accepted a part in O'Neill's *Taboo,* which he played in the United States and London. He then joined the cast of *Emperor Jones* in 1925, and it was this play that earned him his first critical praise as a singer. At a point in the play when he was called upon to whistle, he sang instead, and thus began a new career that was to make him famous. He gave his first concert of Negro spirituals in 1925, and the next year made a tour through the United States. He acted in such plays as O'Neill's *All God's Chillun Got Wings,* Dorothy and DuBose Heyward's *Porgy, Showboat, Othello,* and O'Neill's *The Hairy Ape,* receiving consummate critical and popular praise, both in the United States and abroad. For a period of time he was absent from the stage. His political beliefs led him in the 1930s to make several trips to Russia, to speak out against the Nazis, to entertain Loyalist troops during the Spanish Civil War, to support the Committee to Aid China, and to become chairman of the Council on African Affairs. During the 1940s Robeson triumphed in *Othello* on Broadway. After World War II, he campaigned strenuously for the rights of Afro-Americans. It was at this time that Robeson was also affected by anti-Communist opinions in the United States; he was denied a passport and barred from concert halls. In 1958, however, his passport was reissued, permitting him to go abroad to concertize and appear on stage. His book, *Here I Stand,* was published in that year. Robeson returned to the United States in 1963, and he retired from an active stage career soon after. *See also* MOTION PICTURES.

ROBINSON, AUBREY EUGENE, JR. (1922–   ), lawyer, judge, civic leader; born in Madison, N.J. Robinson received a B.A. degree (1943) and his LL.B. degree (1947) from Cornell University (Ithaca, N.Y.). After admission to the District of Columbia bar in 1948, he practiced law in Washington, D.C., until 1965 when he became associate judge of the Juvenile Court in the District of Columbia. In 1966 Robinson was appointed to the U.S. District Court for the District of Columbia. Throughout his career, his efforts in behalf of civic and welfare organizations were manifold, either as counsel, board member, or trustee.

ROBINSON, BILL (BOJANGLES) (1878–1949), tap dancer; born in Richmond, Va. Orphaned as a baby and raised by a grandmother, Robinson danced for coins in the beer gardens of Richmond at the age of six. He quit school at the age of eight and hitched to Washington, D.C., to work in a stable. Wanting to be a jockey, he carried water for racehorse grooms; stable boys taught him the buck-and-wing and the other dancing steps they performed on street corners for money. Robinson began dancing professionally with minstrel Eddie Leonard for $5 a week and board, and traveled with other shows, also working as a waiter in a Richmond restaurant. By 1906 he was in nightclub and vaudeville shows. Becoming more popular with each appearance, he saw his earnings skyrocket as he played the important vaudeville houses in the country. Robinson performed in *Blackbirds of*

1928 and *Brown Buddies* (1930) on Broadway before going to Hollywood where he made 14 films, in the most popular of which he costarred with child actress Shirley Temple (*The Little Colonel*, 1935; *The Littlest Rebel*, 1935; and *Rebecca of Sunnybrook Farm*, 1937). He returned to the stage in *The Hot Mikado* in 1939, a feature at the New York World's Fair, and in 1940 he appeared on Broadway in *All in Fun*. Incomparable among tap dancers, "the Satrap of Tap," Robinson scored motion picture box-office successes with his small partner (Shirley Temple), especially when, in *The Little Colonel*, he taught her the famous "stair" dance. Although he had earned large amounts of money during his lifetime, he is reputed to have died penniless. *See also* MOTION PICTURES.

ROBINSON, CLARENCE G., JR. (1920–   ), physician, educator; born in Chicago, Ill. Robinson received his M.D. degree from Meharry Medical College (Nashville, Tenn.) in 1945, and was clinical assistant professor of medicine at the College of Medicine, State University of New York Downstate Medical Center. He served as associate attending physician at Maimonides Hospital, and as director of medicine at Coney Island Hospital, Brooklyn, N.Y., from 1967 to 1971.

ROBINSON, DAVID W. (1933–   ), scientist, administrator; born in Baltimore, Md. Robinson received a B.S. degree (1955) and his M.S. degree from Morgan State University (Baltimore, Md.). He served in the U.S. Navy from 1956 to 1960, receiving a commission, and afterward remained in the officer reserve corps while serving for two years, from 1960 to 1962, as a chemist at the American Bio-Chemical Company. Robinson was a physical science administrator for the federal government, principally at the Edgewood-Aberdeen installations in Maryland, after 1962.

ROBINSON, FRANK (1935–   ), professional baseball player, baseball manager; born in Beaumont, Tex. Robinson made his major-league debut in 1956 with the Cincinnati Reds of the National League and spent most of his playing career with that team and the Baltimore Orioles of the American League, to whom he was traded by Cincinnati in 1966. An outfielder and first baseman, Robinson led the Reds to a pennant in 1961, when he was named Most Valuable Player in the National League. In 1966 he repeated

those feats in his first season in Baltimore, and he became the first player in history to win Most Valuable Player status in both leagues. Through 1974, Robinson compiled a career batting average of .298 in the major leagues, with 574 home runs. After managing the Santurce team in the Puerto Rican winter league for five years, Robinson was named manager of the Cleveland Indians (American League), effective with the 1975 season, thus becoming the first Afro-American manager in major-league baseball; he was dismissed in June 1977. *See also* ATHLETES: BASEBALL.

ROBINSON, G. BRUCE (1907–   ), lawyer, judge; born in Washington, D.C. Robinson graduated from Williams College (Williamstown, Mass.) in 1928. He taught at Livingstone College (Salisbury, N.C.) from 1928 until 1933, when he went to Boston University Law School, graduating in 1936. Admitted to the Massachusetts bar a year later, he practiced law in Boston and served as an assistant attorney general of Massachusetts from 1942 to 1945. In 1945 Robinson became assistant corporation counsel for the City of Boston; two years later he was appointed executive secretary of the Commonwealth of Massachusetts. Robinson became judge of the Boston Juvenile Court in 1948.

ROBINSON, G. DEWEY (1910–   ), African Methodist Episcopal bishop; born in Sumter County, S.C. Robinson received a B.A. degree from Allen University (Columbia, S.C), and his B.D. degree from Howard University School of Religion (Washington, D.C.). He also attended Harvard University. Robinson was pastor of churches in North Carolina, South Carolina, Maryland, and Washington, D. C., before being elected bishop of the 15th Episcopal District of the African Methodist Episcopal (AME) Church in 1968.

ROBINSON, HENRY SHIELD, JR. (1905–   ), surgeon, educator, public official; born in Washington, D.C. Robinson received his M.D. degree from Howard University Medical College (Washington, D.C.) in 1930, and interned at Freedmen's Hospital, Washington, D.C. He first practiced in Bowie, Md., and then in Washington, D.C., and later served as associate professor of orthopedic surgery at Howard University Medical College. Robinson became a member of the city council of the District of Columbia in 1969.

ROBINSON, HUBERT NELSON (1912–), African Methodist Episcopal bishop; born in Urbana, Ohio. Robinson received a B.A. degree from Ohio State University in 1935, and later attended Hamma Divinity School and the University of Pittsburgh. He was pastor of African Methodist Episcopal (AME) churches in several Ohio cities, including Cincinnati, Columbus, and Cleveland, and in Pennsylvania and Michigan, before being elected an AME bishop in 1964.

ROBINSON, JACK ROOSEVELT (JACKIE) (1919–72), professional baseball player, business executive; born in Cairo, Ga. Robinson was educated in California at Pasadena Junior College (1937–39), and at the University of California at Los Angeles (1939–41), where he was outstanding in football, basketball, baseball, and track and field sports. After service in the U.S. Army, he played professional baseball with the Kansas City Monarchs of the Negro American League. In 1945 Branch Rickey, head of the Brooklyn Dodgers, signed Robinson for his organization. Following an apprenticeship in the minor leagues, Robinson joined the Dodgers in 1947, becoming the first Afro-American to play major-league baseball. Even without this pioneering aspect, his career would have ensured his election to the Baseball Hall of Fame (in 1962). Before he retired following the 1956 season, he had compiled a career batting average of .311, and had played for six pennant winners and one world-championship team in Brooklyn. He was named Rookie of the Year in 1947 and Most Valuable Player in the National League in 1949, the year he led the league in stolen bases. Robinson played many positions but was primarily a second baseman, and his pathbreaking efforts served to promote integration in all sports. Later, Robinson served as vice-president of Chock Full O'Nuts (1956–64); as cochairman of the Freedom National Bank of Harlem; as an aide to Gov. Nelson Rockefeller of New York; and as spokesman and fund raiser for the civil rights movement. A junior high school in East Harlem in New York City was named in his memory in March 1974. See also ATHLETES.

ROBINSON, MAGNUS L. (1852– ?), journalist, editor, publisher; born in Alexandria, Va. After some education in local schools, Robinson spent four years as an apprentice baker; he then entered Howard University School of Law (Washington, D.C.) in 1868. He worked as a reporter on a white-owned newspaper, the *Bee,* in Baltimore, Md., and wrote articles for other papers in the same city. In 1876 Robinson moved to Harrisonburg, Va., and spent three years as editor of his brother's paper, the *Virginia Post.* In 1888 he established the *National Leader* in Washington, D.C., later moving it to Alexandria, Va., and changing the paper's name to the *Weekly Leader.*

ROBINSON, PAUL TIMOTHY (1898–1966), surgeon; born in Lewisville, Ark. Robinson received a B.S. degree from Bishop College (Dallas, Tex.) in 1921 and his M.D. degree from Meharry Medical College (Nashville, Tenn.) in 1931. He interned at Flint-Goodridge Hospital, New Orleans, La., where he later held various posts in surgery from 1935 to 1952. He built the Robinson Infirmary and Clinic in New Orleans, La., in 1950. In 1953 Robinson moved to California and established a private practice.

ROBINSON, PREZELL R. (1925–), educator; born in Batesburg, S.C. Robinson received a B.A. degree from Saint Augustine's College (Raleigh, N.C.) in 1946, and a M.A. degree (1951) and his Ed.D. degree (1956) in sociology and educational administration from Cornell University (Ithaca, N.Y.). He taught at Voorhees College (Denmark, S.C.) from 1948 to 1956 and at Saint Augustine's College, becoming president of his alma mater in 1967. Robinson directed many institutes sponsored by the National Science Foundation. He received a Fulbright Fellowship to India in 1965.

ROBINSON, (SUGAR) RAY (1921–), pugilist; born Walker Smith in Detroit, Mich. Following a distinguished amateur career, Robinson boxed professionally and won the world welterweight championship in 1946. He ruled that division until 1951, and thereafter fought as a middleweight, winning the title from Jake LaMotta. Between 1951 and 1958 Robinson held the middleweight title on five separate occasions, a boxing record; from 1952 to 1955 he pursued a stage career after retiring from the ring. One of the most colorful fighters in ring history, Robinson was also recognized as one of the greatest. Robinson also had business interests in New York, N.Y.; Detroit, Mich.; Cleveland, Ohio; and Chicago, Ill. *Sugar Ray* is his autobiography. See also ATHLETES.

ROBINSON, SPOTTSWOOD WILLIAM, III (1916–   ), lawyer, educator, judge, civil rights leader; born in Richmond, Va. Robinson attended Virginia Union University, and received his LL.B. degree with honors from Howard University School of Law (Washington, D.C.) in 1939. For nearly a decade following his graduation, he taught at Howard University, while at the same time practicing law in Richmond, Va. Robinson joined Howard's law faculty in 1945, and from 1960 to 1964 he served as dean of the Howard University School of Law. (It was not until his appointment as dean that he gave up his Richmond practice.) Robinson was also counsel for the National Association for the Advancement of Colored People (NAACP) on both state and national levels. In 1964 he became judge of the U.S. District Court for the District of Columbia, and in 1966 he was elected to the U.S. Court of Appeals for the District of Columbia Circuit.

ROBINSON, WILHELMENA S. (1912–   ), educator, historian; born in Pensacola, Fla. Robinson received a B.S. degree from Tennessee State University in 1933 and her M.A. degree from Columbia University in 1934, and she did further graduate study at Boston University. She taught at Edward Waters College (Jacksonville, Fla.) from 1934 to 1935, at Florida Normal and Industrial Memorial College from 1935 to 1936, at Alabama State Teachers College from 1936 to 1940, at LeMoyne College (Memphis, Tenn.; now LeMoyne-Owen College) from 1946 to 1947, and became professor of history at Central State University (Wilberforce, Ohio) in 1947. She wrote *Historical Negro Biographies* (1967), and was coauthor of *Man In America* (1974).

ROCK AND ROLL A term that probably originated to describe the swaying rhythm and movement associated with the religious music and experience of Afro-Americans, it was later adopted as the name for a specific American popular music style with certain innovations from the Kansas City jazz style. *See also* MUSIC: JAZZ.

ROCK, JOHN SWETT *See* LAWYERS.

RODGERS, BENNIE G. *See* NEWSPAPERS: CONTEMPORARY.

RODGERS, EDELBERT *See* SCIENTISTS: SOCIAL.

RODGERS, JULIAN P., JR. (1916–   ), lawyer, judge. Rodgers received his LL.B. degree from the University of Detroit and was admitted to the Michigan bar in 1943. Later, he became a judge of the Common Pleas Court of Detroit, Mich.

ROGERS, JOEL AUGUSTUS (1883–1966), journalist, author; born in Jamaica, British West Indies. Rogers migrated to the United States in 1906 with no formal education, and was nationalized in 1917. In 1930 he reported on the coronation of Haile Selassie in Ethiopia for the Pittsburgh *Courier*, and in 1935 he covered the Italian-Ethiopian War for that paper, becoming the first Afro-American war correspondent. Rogers conducted an illustrated feature, "Your History," for the *Courier* for many years. His books include: *Superman to Man* (1917); *The Ku Klux Spirit* (1923); *World's Greatest Men of African Descent* (1931); and *World's Greatest Men of Color* (2 vols., 1946–47, 1972).

ROLARK, CALVIN *See* NEWSPAPERS: CONTEMPORARY.

ROLLINS, CHARLEMAE HILL librarian; born in Yazoo City, Miss. Rollins pursued work in library service at the Columbia University School of Library Service and at the University of Chicago. She served as a librarian with the Chicago Public Library system after 1927 and during the summers at a number of colleges, including Fisk University (Nashville, Tenn.), Morgan State University (Baltimore, Md.), and San Francisco State University. Rollins published "We Build Together," *National Council of Teachers of English*, 1941; "Children's Literature Dealing With Negro Life," *Negro College Quarterly*, 1944; and "Promoting Personal and Social Development Through Reading," 1947. *See also* LITERATURE: CHILDREN'S.

ROLLINS, SONNY (1939–   ), saxophonist; born in New York City. Rollins began his professional career after graduation from high school. He was influenced by Thelonius Monk, the pianist, and Charles (Bird) Parker, the saxophonist. Among his best-known renditions are *Saxophone Colossus* and *Sonny Rollins and the Big Brass*.

ROMAN, CHARLES VICTOR (1864–1934), physician, educator; born in Williamsport, Pa. Roman received his M.D. degree from Meharry Medical College (Nashville, Tenn.) in 1890. He practiced medicine first in Clarksville, Tenn., and then in Dallas, Tex. Roman served first as a professor in and later as head of the department of ophthalmology and otolaryngology at Meharry Medical College (Nashville, Tenn.). He was also one of the founders of the National Medical Association (NMA). *See also* NATIONAL MEDICAL ASSOCIATION (NMA); PHYSICIANS.

ROSENWALD FUND *See* EDUCATION: DEVELOPMENTS IN ELEMENTARY AND SECONDARY EDUCATION.

ROSS, DIANA (1944–　　), singer, actress, entertainer; born in Detroit, Mich. In the 1960s Ross led the singing group called the Supremes and became one of the most popular pop singers. The Supremes sold more than 12 million records before Ross left the group to continue her career as a soloist. She remained highly successful as a concert, nightclub, and television entertainer. In 1970 Ross was named Female Entertainer of the Year by the National Association for the Advancement of Colored People (NAACP), and she was cast as Billie Holiday in the movie *Lady Sings the Blues* in 1972.

ROUSSEVE, MAURICE LOUIS (1906–　　), clergyman; born in New Orleans, La. Rousseve was educated at Xavier Preparatory School (1918–20) and at Saint Augustine's Seminary (1920–34). He was ordained a priest in the Roman Catholic Church in May 1934. Rousseve engaged in pastoral work for more than 20 years. He was also a teacher, assistant provincial, master of clerical novices, and a member of the Knights of Peter Claver, 4th degree.

Carl T. Rowan.
*(WTOP-TV
Broadcast House.)*

ROWAN, CARL THOMAS (1925–　　), journalist, government official; born in Ravenscroft, Tenn. After receiving a B.A. degree from Oberlin College (Oberlin, Ohio) in 1947 and his M.A. degree in journalism from the University of Minnesota in 1948, Rowan became a writer for the Minneapolis *Tribune,* for which he worked until 1961. From 1961 to 1963 he was deputy assistant secretary of state for public affairs. In 1963 Rowan was appointed U.S. ambassador to Finland, and from 1964 to 1965 he served as head of the U.S. Information Agency, thus becoming the first Afro-American to sit in on meetings of the National Security Council. After 1965 Rowan became a syndicated columnist for the Chicago *Daily News.* His books include: *South of Free-*

dom (1953), *The Pitiful and the Proud* (1956), and *Wait Till Next Year* (1960).

ROWAN, LEVI J. (1871–1934), educator; born in Rodney, La. Rowan graduated from Alcorn College (Lorman, Miss.; now Alcorn State University) in 1893 and began teaching in a rural school in Lawrence County, Miss. He joined the faculty of Alcorn College in 1899, and served as its president from 1905 until his death.

ROYAL AFRICAN COMPANY *See* AFRICA: THE ATLANTIC SLAVE TRADE/TOBACCO COAST.

RUDOLPH, WILMA *See* ATHLETES: TRACK AND FIELD.

RUGGLES, DAVID (1810–49), hydrotherapist, abolitionist; born in Norwich, Conn. Ruggles was educated in local Connecticut schools, and then, because of his firm belief in abolitionism, he went to New York City in 1827 to work for this cause. He became the editor and publisher of *The Mirror of Liberty* in 1845. In poor health, Ruggles sought and responded well to hydrotherapeutic treatment, and desided to open his own water-cure institute in Northampton, Mass., in 1846. Though he had no medical training, his institute flourished, and he treated both Afro-American and white patients, including William Lloyd Garrison, the abolitionist leader.

RUSHING, JAMES (JIMMY) ANDREW (MISTER FIVE BY FIVE) (1903–　　), jazz singer; born in Oklahoma City, Okla. Rushing played the piano and the violin as a boy, and entered music professionally as a singer after he left high school. He sang at various spots in the Midwest until 1923 when he went to California to sing in clubs there. By 1925 Rushing had returned home, and two years later he joined Walter Page's band, which was called the "Blue Devils." His next band job began in 1929 with Bennie Moten, with whom he stayed until 1935. Subsequently, he joined Count Basie, remaining as his featured vocalist until 1948. After forming his own small band in 1950, Rushing began performing solo again in 1952, appearing in all the notable nightclubs across the country. He sang at the Brussels World's Fair in 1958 with Benny Goodman, and in 1959 he sang with Buck Clayton. Guest appearances with Count Basie, a tour with Harry James and another with Eddie Condon, jazz festivals, and recording sessions helped establish his reputation as one of the great singers in the history of jazz. *See also* Music: Jazz.

RUSSELL, CAZZIE *See* Athletes: Basketball

RUSSELL, HARVEY CLARENCE, JR. (1918–), business executive; born in Louisville, Ky. Russell received his B.S. degree from Kentucky State College in 1939, and did graduate study at Indiana University and at the University of Michigan. After World War II service in the U.S. Coast Guard, he was appointed a sales supervisor by the Pepsi-Cola Company of New York in 1950. After having been made director of the special-markets department of that firm in 1957, Russell became vice-president of the department in 1962. He was promoted to vice-president in charge of planning in 1965 and to vice-president for community affairs in 1969. He was the first Afro-American to serve at that executive level in a leading national corporation.

RUSSELL, WILLIAM FELTON (BILL) (1934–), professional basketball player, basketball coach; business executive; born in Monroe, La. Russell led the University of San Francisco basketball team to national titles in 1955 and 1956 and was a member of the 1956 Olympic Games basketball squad. As a member of the Boston Celtics of the professional National Basketball Association (NBA), he became one of the sport's great defensive players, winning the Most Valuable Player award five times in his first nine seasons. When he was made head coach of the Celtics in 1966, Russell became the first Afro-American to hold this job with a major American professional athletic team. Upon his retirement from the post in 1969, he became a television commentator on basketball and pursued business interests (rubber plantations) in Liberia. He was appointed coach and general manager of the Seattle SuperSonics of the NBA in May 1973. His autobiography is *Go Up for Glory. See also* Athletes.

RUSSWURM, JOHN BROWN (1799–1851), journalist, publisher; born in Jamaica, British West Indies. Russwurm attended school in Canada and then entered Bowdoin College (Brunswick, Maine), from which he graduated in 1826, becoming one of the first two Afro-Americans to receive an American college-level degree. With Rev. Samuel Cornish, he founded and edited *Freedom's Journal* in New York; it was one of the first Afro-American newspapers in the United States. Cornish resigned from the paper in September 1827, just six months after the first issue, but he returned in March 1829 when Russwurm's strong views in favor of resettling American blacks in Africa forced his resignation. Russwurm departed for Liberia where he became superintendent of schools, founded a newspaper (the *Liberia Herald*), and served as colonial secretary. In 1836 he became governor of the Maryland Colony at Cape Palmas (later incorporated into Liberia), a position he held until his death. *See also* Newspapers: History and Development.

RUST COLLEGE Rust College, at Holly Springs, Miss., was founded in 1866 by the Methodist Episcopal (ME) Church, North. A church-related and coeducational school, Rust offers the bachelor's degree and provides a liberal arts curricula. Its 1975 enrollment was 697.

Fewer than 50 miles from Memphis, Tenn., Rust College was named for Richard Rust, a white antislavery advocate who rendered distinguished service to the Freedmen's Aid Society of the ME Church after the Civil War. The original name of the school, Shaw University, was changed in 1890.

Over the years, Rust played a vital part in the educational system of Mississippi. First, it taught ex-slaves how to read and write. Later, it offered them, or their descendants, agricultural and domestic science courses. Then, because of the limitations of public-school training for Afro-American youth, Rust made it possible for many of these students to qualify for entrance into predominantly white colleges, either private or state, by offering them help and education. Most of these students came from culturally deprived homes and communities.

RUSTIN, BAYARD (1910–), civil rights leader; born in West Chester, Pa. After completing high school, Rustin traveled around the United States holding odd jobs and studying periodically at Wilberforce University (Wilberforce, Ohio) and Cheney State College (Cheyney, Pa.). The New York branch of the Congress of Racial Equality (CORE) was organized by Rustin in 1941, after he had joined and then left the Communist Party and had sung in New York City nightclubs. Also in this year (1941), Rustin joined the march on Washington, D.C., sponsored by A. Philip Randolph. Rustin served a prison term of almost two-and-a-half years as a conscientious objector during World War II, and in 1947 he was one of the organizers of the first freedom ride, the "journey of reconciliation," embarked upon to test Southern compliance with antidiscriminatory interstate travel laws. While participating, he was arrested and forced to serve on a chain gang. His published description of this experience triggered the final abolition of chain gangs in North Carolina. Shortly after this episode, as director of A. Philip Randolph's Committee Against Discrimination in the Armed Forces, his efforts were crucial in bringing about the 1948 presidential order to eliminate discrimination in the U.S. Armed Forces. In the 1950s, Rustin's civil rights' efforts were combined with pacifist and antiwar activi-

ties; he joined the War Resisters' League in 1953. It was during this period that Rustin began to work with Martin Luther King, Jr., first on the Montgomery bus boycott, and then in helping to conceive and draw up plans for the Southern Christian Leadership Conference (SCLC). He remained King's assistant for seven years. In the 1960s Rustin continued to organize demonstrations, the most notable of which was A. Philip Randolph's March on Washington for Jobs and Freedom in 1963, and the boycott of New York City schools in 1964. In 1964 he became executive director of the newly formed A. Philip Randolph Institute. His book, *Down the Line; The Collected Writings of Bayard Rustin*, was published in 1971. *See also* LABOR UNIONS; KING, MARTIN LUTHER, JR.

SAINT AUGUSTINE'S COLLEGE Saint Augustine's College, at Raleigh, N.C., was founded in 1867 through the joint efforts of the Freedman's Commission of the Protestant Episcopal Church and a group of clergy and laymen of the episcopal diocese of North Carolina. Church-related and coeducational, the college offers the bachelor's degree and provides liberal arts and teacher education curricula, although it also gives terminal occupation work. Its 1975 enrollment was 1,442.

The group of clergy and laymen that founded the school was headed by Bishop Thomas Atkinson, and the institution they began—with four students—was called Saint Augustine's Normal School and Collegiate Institute. In 1921 the institute became a junior college, and in 1928 the junior college became an accredited four-year school. Harold L. Trigg was named its first Afro-American president in 1947.

The student body of the college is predominantly black, and its faculty is interracial. Graduates make up a great percentage of the Afro-American professional leadership in North Carolina.

SAINT AUGUSTINE'S JUNIOR COLLEGE See SAINT AUGUSTINE'S COLLEGE.

SAINT AUGUSTINE'S NORMAL SCHOOL AND COLLEGIATE INSTITUTE See SAINT AUGUSTINE'S COLLEGE.

SAINT FRANCES ACADEMY One of the oldest Roman Catholic seminaries established for Afro-Americans, the academy has maintained a primary interest in education. Founded by four Oblate sisters in 1828 on Chase Street in Baltimore, Md., it had grown so much by the 1930s that an additional site was established in the county. The new institute became the Mount Providence Junior College in 1952.

SAINT PAUL'S COLLEGE Saint Paul's College, at Lawrenceville, Va., was founded in 1888 by the Protestant Episcopal Church and incorporated by the general assembly of Virginia two years later. Private and strongly church-related, the coeducational college offers the bachelor's degree and provides liberal arts and teacher education curricula. Its 1975 enrollment was 1,442.

In 1907 Saint Paul's became an affiliate of the American Church Institute for Negroes, an agency of the Protestant Episcopal Church. In 1922 a collegiate department of teacher training was started, and in 1926 it was accredited by the Virginia state board of education. As a result, a large percentage of the teachers in the elementary and secondary schools of Virginia and the neighboring states of North Carolina and Maryland have been graduates of St. Paul's. In 1942 a four-year degree program was started. At this time also, James A. Russell, son of the founder, was named president of the institution.

After 1950 many notable improvements were made. The college was admitted to membership in the Southern Association of Colleges and Schools, and in 1970 this accreditation was reaffirmed. In the following year, the board of trustees appointed a new preisdent, James A. Russell, Jr., the grandson of the founder. He was succeeded by Prezell R. Robinson after 1973.

SALEM, PETER (ca.1750–1816), soldier; born in Framingham, Mass. Salem, a slave belonging to the Belknap family, was given his freedom when he enlisted in the American colonial forces. He saw action on the opening day (April 19, 1775) of the Revolutionary War at Concord, Mass., but is better remembered as a participant in the Battle of Bunker Hill on June 17, 1775. Popular tradition maintains that Salem killed the first Englishman at the battle, Maj. John Pitcairn, and the "Salem" gun is preserved at Bunker Hill in memory of this deed. In his 1782 painting of the Battle of Bunker Hill, John Trumbull placed an Afro-American soldier, reputedly a likeness of Peter Salem, in the foreground of the canvas, a fact that gives support to the story of Salem's deeds. Salem served with credit in the Continental Army for the remainder of the war, but he died in Framingham in the poorhouse. *See also* WARS.

Edith Sampson. (*Moorland-Spingarn Research Center.*)

SAMPSON, EDITH SPURLOCK (1901–   ), lawyer, judge; born in Pittsburgh, Pa. After attending the New York School of Social Work and the School of Social Service Administration at the University of Chicago, Sampson received a LL.B. degree from John Marshall Law School (Chicago, Ill.) in 1925 and her LL.M. degree from Loyola University (Chicago, Ill.) in 1927, becoming the first woman to receive this degree from Loyola. She was admitted to the Illinois bar in 1927, and during the decade between 1930 and 1940 Sampson served as a referee of the Cook County Juvenile Court. At the same time she established a private law practice. In 1947 she was appointed an assistant state's attorney, and in 1950 she was appointed by President Harry S. Truman as a member of the United States delegation to the United Nations, the first Afro-American to receive this appointment. In 1955 Sampson became an assistant corporation counsel for Chicago, and she was elected associate judge of Chicago's Municipal Court in 1962. Sampson served on that bench until 1964 when she was elected associate judge of the Circuit Court of Cook County.

SAMUEL HUSTON COLLEGE *See* HUSTON-TILLOTSON COLLEGE.

SANCHEZ, SONIA *See* LITERATURE: POETRY.

SANDLER, JOAN *See also* LITERATURE: DRAMA/THEATER.

SANDS, DIANA (1934–73), actress; born in New York, N.Y. Sands studied at the Performing Arts High School and at the International Dance Studio, both in New York City. She performed in *A Raisin in the Sun* and *The Living Promise*, receiving praise and awards for both roles. Sands also received a Tony Award for her performance in *Blues for Mr. Charlie*. She had many stage triumphs during the 1960s.

SANFORD, JOHN ELROY *See* FOXX, REDD.

SAUNDERS, ELIJAH (1934–   ), cardiologist; born in Baltimore. He received a B.S. degree from Morgan State University (Baltimore, Md.) in 1956 and his M.D. degree from the University of Maryland in 1960. Having established his practice in Baltimore, he served in many professional capacities: as chief of medicinal staff and as chief of cardiology at Provident Hospital, as associate cardiologist at Maryland General Hospital, and as a faculty member of the University of Maryland. Saunders was a member of many associations and boards, including the board of directors of the American Heart Association (also president); the American College of Physicians; the American College of Cardiology, and the American College of Angiology. He wrote many articles on hypertension and a chapter on the subject in a book by Richard Allen Williams called *Textbook of Black-Related Diseases* (1975). Saunders also produced filmstrips that were accepted by the American Heart Association as a part of its national library. His awards and honors include the Bronze Service Medallion, the Presidential Award from the American Heart Association, and the Presidential Plaque from the Central Maryland chapter of the American Heart Association. He was also honored by House Resolution 15, adopted by the Maryland house of delegates in the 1976 session.

SAUNDERS, JACK *See* NEWSPAPERS: CONTEMPORARY.

SAUNDERS, MONROE RANDOLPH (1919–   ), Apostolic bishop; born in Florence, S.C. A graduate of Virginia State College in 1937, Saunders also received a B.A. degree (1953) and his B.D. degree (1957) from Howard University (Washington, D.C.). In 1957 he became the presiding bishop of the Central District of the Church of God in Christ (Apostolic). Saunders was also editor of *The Rehoboth Beacon*, the official publication of the denomination.

SAUNDERS, OTIS (1872– ?), pianist; born in Springfield, Mo. Saunders worked with Scott Joplin, with whom he toured from 1894 to 1896, and helped Joplin in the development of ragtime style. *See also* JOPLIN, SCOTT; MUSIC: HISTORY AND DEVELOPMENT.

SAUNDERS, PRINCE (ca. 1784–1839), educator. Saunders studied at Dartmouth College (Hanover, N.H.), and was recommended by the president of the college for a position as a teacher in Boston, Mass. Sent to England as a delegate of the Masonic Lodge of Africans, he met Henri Christophe, emperor of Haiti, who commissioned him to start a school system in Haiti and to help architect the change in Haiti's religion from Roman Catholicism to Protestantism. In 1816 Saunders published *Haytian Papers*, a translation of Haitian law. He briefly left the Haitian service and became a lay reader in the African Methodist Episcopal (AME) Church of St. Thomas, but upon the death of Emperor Christophe in 1820 he returned to Haiti and became attorney general. His other publications include *An Address . . . Before the Pennsylvanian Augustine Society* (1818) and *A Memoir . . . to the American Convention for Promoting the Abolition of Slavery* (1818).

SAUNDERS, WALLACE A railroad roundhouse worker in the 1890s in Jackson, Miss., Saunders, upon hearing of the wreck of No. 382 on the Illinois Central Railroad at Vaughn, Miss., composed the lines that became famous in the folk legend of the train's white engineer, John Luther (Casey) Jones:

> All the switchmen knew by the engine's moans
> That the man at the throttle was Casey Jones.

SAVAGE, AUGUSTA CHRISTINE (1900–62), sculptor, educator; born in Green Cove, Fla. Savage studied at Cooper Union (New York, N.Y.), at the Grand Chaumière (Paris, France) from 1934 to 1935, and at the Academy of Fine Arts (Rome, Italy). She was the first director of the Harlem Community Art Center, and in 1939 she was commissioned to create a sculpture that was

destined to make her famous—the harp-shaped *Lift Every Voice and Sing*, displayed at the New York World's Fair. With a forte for serious sculpture, Savage is also remembered for such works as *Gamin;* a fine head of W. E. B. Du Bois; and other pieces that show a gift for intense communication in plaster, stone, and bronze. She had work exhibited at the Harmon Foundation, New York, N.Y., 1928 and 1930–31; at the Art of the American Negro Exhibition, Chicago, Ill., 1940; and at the Société Des Artistes Français, Paris, France. Her work is part of the permanent collections of Morgan State University, Baltimore, Md.; the National Archives, Washington, D.C.; and the New York Public Library's Schomburg Collection. Savage received a Rosenwald Fellowship for 1929–31 and for 1930–32 and a Carnegie Grant to open the Savage Studio of Arts and Crafts in New York City's Harlem. *See also* ARTISTS.

Augusta Savage. *(National Archives.)*

SAVAGE, HORACE C. (1922–), clergyman, educator, publisher; born in Portsmouth, Va. Savage received a M.A. degree from New York University in 1948 and his LL.D. degree from Lane College (Jackson, Tenn.) in 1959. He was pastor of churches in Tennessee, Haiti, and Cuba, and taught at Lane College and Tennessee State University. In 1964 Savage became president of Texas College. He was also the founder and copublisher of the *Capital City Defender* of Nashville, Tenn.

SAVAGE, WILLIAM SHERMAN (1890–), historian, educator; born in Wattsville, Va. Savage received a B.A. degree from Howard University (Washington, D.C.) in 1917, a M.A. degree from the University of Oregon in 1925, and his Ph.D. degree from Ohio State University in 1934. He joined the faculty of Lincoln University (Jefferson City, Mo.) in 1921, and by 1960, when he left, he had become chairman of the history department. From 1960 to 1966 Savage taught history and chaired the social science division at Jarvis Christian College (Hawkins, Tex.). He then taught at California State College at Los Angeles, and after three years there, he returned to Lincoln as professor emeritus of history and as consultant to the school. In addition to his contributions to scholarly journals, Savage wrote *History of Lincoln University* (1941), and several pioneering studies of the role of Afro-Americans, including the role of black cowboys, in the settlement of the American West. When Savage was 86, Greenwood (Westport, Conn.) published his book, *Blacks in the West* (1976).

SAVANNAH STATE COLLEGE Savannah State College, at Savannah, Ga., was founded in 1890 by an act of the general assembly of the state of Georgia. State-supported and coeducational, the college offers the bachelor's and master's degrees, as well as terminal occupation work below the bachelor's level, and provides applied arts and sciences, business administration, teacher education, and engineering curricula. Its 1975 enrollment was 2,942.

The college was originally established as one of the departments of the state university, but one expressly for the education and training of Afro-American students. It was known as the Georgia State Industrial College for Colored Youth.

From its beginnings with 3 faculty members, a principal, 8 students, 86 acres of land, 2 buildings, and a farmhouse, Savannah State College has grown to be the largest predominantly Afro-American institution in the state, although its enrollment is now interracial. It operates as a unit of the university system of Georgia, under the supervision of the Georgia State University board of regents.

SAVORY, PHILIP MAXWELL HUGH (1889–1965), physician, publisher; born in Georgetown, British Guiana. Savory received his early education in British Guiana and worked as a compositor on newspapers there from 1906 to 1909. He then moved to Brazil, where he continued with similar work until 1911. At that time Savory emigrated to the United States, and later he went to Canada, where he received his M.D. degree from McGill University (Montreal, Que.), graduating at the head of his class. He practiced medicine in New York City and also served as copublisher and secretary-treasurer of the *Amsterdam News.*

SAWYER, BROADUS EUGENE (1921–   ), accountant, economist; born in Pinnacle, N.C. Sawyer graduated from North Carolina Agricultural and Technical (A&T) State University in 1943. He received a M.B.A. degree from the University of Pennsylvania in 1948 and his Ph.D. degree from New York University in 1955. He returned to his undergraduate alma mater to teach business administration in 1948, leaving with the rank of associate professor in 1956. That year he moved to Morgan State University (Baltimore) as an accountant, becoming a professor of economics in 1963. He later became chairman of the department.

SAWYER, GRANVILLE MONROE (1919–   ), educator, administrator; born in Mobile, Ala. Sawyer received a B.A. degree from Tennessee State University in 1947, and a M.A. degree (1952) and his Ph.D. degree (1955) from the University of Southern California. He was an assistant professor of speech and drama and a dean at Huston-Tillotson College (Austin, Tex.) from 1947 to 1956. Sawyer spent the next 12 years at Tennessee State, where he served as vice-president. In 1968 Sawyer was named president of Texas Southern University.

SAYERS, GALE *See* ATHLETES: FOOTBALL.

SCARBOROUGH, WILLIAM SANDERS (1852–1926), educator; born in Macon, Ga. Scarborough secretly attended school in Georgia out of necessity, and then studied at Atlanta University for two years before going to Oberlin College (Oberlin, Ohio), from which he received a B.A. degree (1875) and his M.A. degree (1878). He taught in Ohio and Georgia before returning to Oberlin to study theology. Scarborough was affiliated with Payne Institute in South Carolina, and taught at Wilberforce University (Wilberforce, Ohio) after 1877, and served as president of that institution from 1908 to 1920. He made a special study for the U.S. Department of Agriculture on Afro-American farms and agricultural education in the South, and was the author of *First Lesson in Greek, Our Civil Status,* and *Birds of Aristophanes: A Theory of Interpretation.*

SCHOMBURG, ARTHUR ALFONSO (1874–1938), book collector, scholar; born in San Juan, Puerto Rico. Schomburg graduated from the Institute of Instruction in San Juan, then attended St. Thomas College in the Virgin Islands, where he made a special study of Negro literature. In 1891 he moved to the United States after teaching in the Caribbean for several years. In 1911 he cofounded the Negro Society for Historical Research, and in 1922 he was head of the American Negro Academy. A lecturer and author, Schomburg wrote articles for many newspapers and magazines. He figured in the Harlem Renaissance and contributed to *The New Negro* (1925), edited by Alain Locke. Schomburg amassed more than

5,000 volumes, 3,000 manuscripts, 2,000 etchings, and several thousand pamphlets, comprising the most extensive library of Afro-American history and culture in America. In 1926 the collection was purchased by the Carnegie Corporation and given to the New York Public Library, where it was established at the 135th Street branch. In 1932 Schomburg became curator of the collection. Its official title was changed in 1973 to the Schomburg Collection of Negro Literature and History. *See also* ARCHIVES.

SCHUYLER, GEORGE SAMUEL (1895– ?), journalist, editor; born in Providence, R.I. Schuyler received a high school education and then spent eight years in the U.S. Army before becoming a civil service clerk. From 1923 to 1928 he was a staff member on *The Messenger* magazine, and in 1924 Schuyler became a columnist for the Pittsburgh *Courier,* a position he held for more than 25 years. In 1932 Schuyler

became editor of *National News,* and from 1937 to 1944 he served as business manager of the magazine of the National Association for the Advancement of Colored People (NAACP), *Crisis.* In 1931 he worked briefly as a correspondent for the New York *Post.* His books include: *Racial Intermarriage in the United States* (1930); *Slaves Today* (1931); and a novel, *Black No More* (1931).

SCHUYLER, PHILIPPA DUKE (1932–69), pianist, composer; born in New York, N.Y. Schuyler was a child prodigy who, before the age of 12, had won many awards and piano competitions, and had composed many compositions for the piano. Schuyler made her Town Hall debut in 1953 and after that pursued a career as a concert pianist. Her compositions include "Six Little Pieces" and "Eight Little Pieces" for piano; the symphonic composition "Manhattan Nocturne"; and the scherzo "Rumpelstiltskin."

Arthur Schomburg. (*New York Public Library.*)

SCIENTISTS

Biological, Physical The general assessment of the level of scientific potential among a particular group of individuals very often begins with a determination of the educational attainments of the group. Scientific accomplishments are by and large achieved through scientific research, and a determination of the scientific potential of any given group can be readily ascertained by knowing the number and percentage of research-degree holders within the group in question. While reference is made to the Ph.D. degree, it should be understood that holders of M.D., D.D.S., and D.V.M. degrees may also do research and that the possession of an earned doctorate is not necessarily a prerequisite to good output.

Precise figures on the number of Afro-Americans who have earned the doctor of philosophy (Ph.D.) and also doctorates in science (Sc.D.), public health (Dr.P.H.), and pharmacy

(Pharm.D.) do not exist. Although Edward A. Bouchet (1852–1918) earned the doctorate degree in physics at Yale University in 1876, thus becoming the first Afro-American to earn a science doctorate, a total of only 13 science doctorates were earned by Afro-Americans prior to 1930. By the end of 1943, however, close to 130 Afro-Americans had earned science doctorates. It should be noted that the greatest percentage of research output during this time was made by holders of the doctor of medicine degree (M.D.). Notable among this group were Theodore K. Lawless, Jane C. Wright, Julian H. Lewis, Charles R. Drew, W. Montague Cobb, Hildrus A. Poindexter, and others (the last four individuals held science doctorates in addition to the M.D.). Clearly, the hospital and medical school environment provided greater research opportunities than Afro-American colleges. Through 1972, it is estimated that about 850 Afro-Americans had earned science doctorates in the natural sciences (anthropology and psychology not included), with the once racially segregated universities of the South providing significant numbers. Approximately 95 percent of all Afro-American science doctorate holders were living at the beginning of 1973. Approximately 1 out of every 100 American science doctorate holders is an Afro-American.

When dealing with numbers as low as these, it is somewhat premature to expect a plethora of hard scientific accomplishments. This is brought into sharper view when one notes that approximately 75 percent of all present-day Afro-American science doctorate holders are employed by predominantly black colleges and universities, where the opportunities for serious scientific research by and large are not good. The most notable yet least appreciated contribution made by Afro-American science doctorate holders has been in the teaching of the sciences at predominantly black institutions of higher learning. Proof of the latter is to be found in the fact that 75 to 80 percent of all black science doctorate holders received their undergraduate training at these institutions.

In spite of the relatively low number of Afro-American science doctorate holders and the unproductive conditions under which they have had to endure, some noteworthy achievements have been made, and the future years should be even brighter. No Afro-American has ever won a Nobel Prize in the sciences. A singular achievement by an Afro-American scientist, however, is that of Professor David H. Blackwell, who became a member of the National Academy of Sciences in the late 1960s. The organization in question is the most prestigious body of scientists in the United States, and Blackwell was the first Afro-American member.

Numerous other achievements have been made by black scientists; some of these are noted below (with reference to biographical sketches in the *Encyclopedia*).

Notable Achievers Since space does not permit an exhaustive listing of all who have authored research papers in the professional journals, only those who fall into at least one of the following four categories are listed below: (1) recipients of awards for scientific accomplishments; (2) office holders or journal editors in scientific societies; (3) authors of books; and (4) members of scientific advisory or research grant review committees. It should be noted that these lists are not complete but are merely representative of some of the attainments of Afro-American scientists.

Alexander, Benjamin H. (chemistry): Received the Army Commendation Ribbon; received a certificate of achievement from American Chemical Society.

Amos, Harold (bacteriology): Member of National Cancer Advisory Board; professor of bacteriology and immunology at Harvard Medical School since 1970.

Barnes, Robert P. (chemistry): Member of National Science Foundation board (1950–58).

Bates, Clayton Wilson (physics): Author of many articles; professor at Stanford University, Calif. (1977).

Blackwell, David H. (mathematics, statistics): *See also* BLACKWELL, DAVID H.

Bolden, Theodore E. (pathology, dentistry): Member of National Institute of Health's advisory committee.

Branson, Herman R. (physics): *See also* BRANSON, HERMAN R.

Brown, Russell W. (bacteriology): President of southeast section, American Society for Microbiology, during late 1960s; distinguished professor of microbiology, University of Nevada at Reno.

Campbell, Hayward (virology): Section director, Eli Lilly & Company.

Carver, George W. (plant and agricultural science, 1864–1943): Most honored of all Afro-American scientists; only Afro-American scientist to have day proclaimed in his honor by U.S. Congress (January 5); only Afro-American scientist to have postage stamp issued in his memory; memorial erected in state of Missouri. *See also* CARVER, GEORGE WASHINGTON.

Cobb, W. Montague (anatomy): Vice-president, American Association of Advanced Science (1955); editor of *Journal of the National Medical Association* after 1949. *See also* COBB, W. MONTAGUE.

Coleman, John W. (biophysics): Received the David Sarnoff Award.

Cornely, Paul B. (public health): President of American Public Health Association (1969–70); received Sedgwick Memorial Medal (1972). *See also* CORNELY, PAUL BERTAU.

Drew, Charles R. (hematology, 1904–50): Developed blood bank procedures that made blood banking possible. *See also* DREW, CHARLES RICHARD.

Finley, Harold E. (parasitology): President of American Microscopical Society (1971); President of American Society of Protozoology (1966–67).

Frederick, Lafayette (mycology): Member of Committee on Undergraduate Education in Biology (1970–71).

Green, Harry James, Sr. (chemistry): *See* GREEN, HARRY JAMES, SR.

Hall, Lloyd A. (food science, 1894–1971): Received the Honor Scroll Award of the American Institute of Chemists, Chicago Chapter (1956); member of Science Advisory Board of Quartermaster (Q.M.) Corps of U.S. Army (1943–48); held many patents on food processing. *See also* HALL, LLOYD A.

Hammond, Benjamin F. (bacteriology, dentistry): Received the Hatton Award (1969); member of National Institute of Dental Research advisory council; chairman of department of microbiology, Dental School, University of Pennsylvania.

Hawthorne, Edward W. (physiology): Special consultant to National Institute of Health (1954–57); vice-president, American Heart Association (1969). *See also* HAWTHORNE, EDWARD W.

Henry, Warren E. (physics): Received the Carver Award.

Hill, Carl M. (chemistry): *See also* HILL, CARL MCCLELLAN.

Hill, Henry A. (chemistry): Civilian with Office of Scientific Research & Development (1944); first Afro-American nominee to run for national president of the American Chemical Society (1972). *See also* HILL, HENRY AARON.

Hill, Wendell T., Jr. (pharmacy): President of American Hospital Pharmaceutical Association (1972–73).

Hinton, William A. (bacteriology, immunology): Developed serologic method for detecting syphilis that bears his name. *See also* HINTON, WILLIAM AUGUSTUS.

Julian, Percy L. (chemistry): Spingarn Medal (1947); holder of at least 12 honorary doctorates; Chemical building at MacMurray College (Abilene, Tex.) named in his honor (1972). *See also* JULIAN, PERCY LAVON.

Just, Ernest E. (zoology, 1883–1941): Received the first Spingarn Medal (1914). *See also* JUST, ERNEST EVERETT.

Knox, William J. (chemistry): Section leader for the Manhattan Project at Columbia University (1943–45).

Lee, C. Bruce (malacology, microbiology): Received Meritorious Civilian Service Award

from U.S. Army for developing techniques for decontaminating missiles.

Lewis, Julian H. (physician): Received Ricketts Prize (1915); received Rush Medal (1917); author. *See also* LEWIS, JULIAN HERMAN.

Massie, S. Proctor (chemistry): *See also* MASSIE, SAMUEL PROCTOR, JR.

Milligan, Dolphus (chemistry): Received the A. Miolati Prize for free radicals research (University of Padua, Italy, 1965); received Gold Medal for Distinguished Service, U.S. Department of Commerce (1970).

Nabrit, Samuel M. (zoology): Was first and only Afro-American member of the U.S. Atomic Energy Commission (1966–67); member of National Science Foundation board (1956–60). *See also* NABRIT, SAMUEL MILTON.

Piere, Percy (physics): Dean of engineering, Howard University, Washington, D.C., (1970s).

Poindexter, Hildrus A. (public health, microbiology): Received at least three honorary doctorates; biography published; only Afro-American tropical disease specialist with U.S. Armed Forces during World War II; former chief of American Foreign Aid Health Missions to more than five countries. *See also* POINDEXTER, HILDRUS AUGUSTUS.

Proctor, Charles D. (pharmacology): Member of National Institute of Health Research Grant Advisory Group.

Sherrod, Theodore R. (pharmacology): Member of National Institute of Health Research Grant Advisory Group.

Taylor, Moddie D. (chemistry): Book Author; long tenure at Howard University (Washington, D.C.) until retirement.

Taylor, Welton I. (bacteriology): Member of editorial board, American Society for Microbiology (1968–70).

Terry, Robert J. (zoology): Member of National Institute of Health Research Grant Advisory Group.

Wallace, John H. (microbiology, immunology): Chairman, department of microbiology, University of Louisville School of Medicine.

Wilkins, J. Ernest, Jr. (mathematics, physics): Physicist on Manhattan Project at University of Chicago (1944–46). *See also* WILKINS, J. ERNEST, JR.

Woods, Geraldine (neuroembryology): Consultant to National Institute of Health.

Wright, Jane C. (medicine): Received Spence Chapin Award (1958); Mademoiselle Award (1965); Distinguished Service Award of American Medical Association (1965). *See also* WRIGHT, JANE COOKE.

Some Books Authored by Scientists, 1939–1975 The greatest output of books by black scientists came during the period following World War II, or about 150 years after the first science book was published by Benjamin Banneker. Outstanding books after the war are listed below:

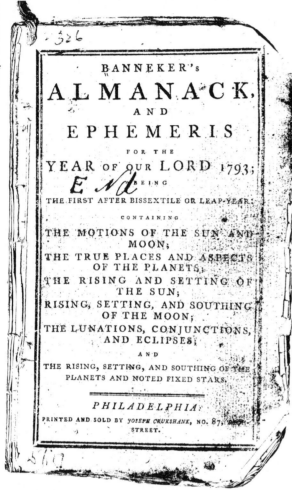

Cover of Benjamin Banneker's *Almanack*, the first science book written by an Afro-American. *(Library of Congress.)*

Blackwell, David H., and M. A. Girshick, *Theory of Games and Statistical Decisions,* John Wiley & Sons, New York, 1954; Blackwell, David H., *Basic Statistics,* McGraw-Hill, New York, 1969; Dillard, Clyde R., and D. E. Goldberg, *Chemistry: Reactions, Structure and Properties,* Macmillan, New York, 1971; Ferguson, Lloyd N., *Modern Structural Theory of Organic Chemistry,* Prentice-Hall, Englewood Cliffs, 1963; Ferguson, Lloyd N., *Textbook of Organic Chemistry,* Van Nostrand, New York, 1965; Goldsby, Richard A., *Cells and Energy,* Macmillan, New York, 1967; Goldsby, Richard A., *Race and Races,* Macmillan, New York, 1971; Graham, Horace D. (ed.), *The Safety of Foods,* Avi Pub-

lishing Co., Westport, 1968; Hinton, William A., *Syphilis and Its Treatment,* Macmillan, New York, 1936; Jay, James M., *Modern Food Microbiology,* Van Nostrand, New York, 1970; Jay, James M., *Negroes in Science: Natural Science Doctorates, 1876–1969,* Balamp Publishing Co., Detroit, 1971; Just, Ernest Everett, *Basic Methods for Experiments on Eggs of Marine Animals,* Blaikston, 1939; Just, Ernest Everett, *Biology of the Cell Surface,* Blaikston, 1939; Lewis, Julian H., *Biology of the Negro,* University of Chicago Press, Chicago, 1942; Morris, Kelso, *Principles of Chemical Equilibrium,* Van Nostrand, New York, 1967; Morris, Kelso B., *Chemical Equilibrium: Nonionic-Ionic,* Gordon Publishing, 1972; Patterson, Frederick D., and William H. Hughes, *Robert Russa Moton of Hampton and Tuskegee,* University of North Carolina Press, Durham, 1956; Poindexter, Hildrus A., *My World of Reality,* Balamp Publishing Co., Detroit, 1973; Stubblefield, Beauregard, *Intuitive Approach to Elementary Geometry,* Brooks-Cole Publishing, Belmont, 1969; Taylor, Julius H. (ed.), *The Negro in Science,* Morgan State University Press, Baltimore, 1955; and Taylor, Moddie D., *First Principles of Chemistry,* Van Nostrand, New York, 1960.

REFERENCES: With the exception of medicine, studies on Afro-American scientists are scarce; in fact, few or none exist for certain fields or scientists. However, for information on the output and for profiles of Afro-American science doctorate holders, see the following volumes: Greene, Harry W., *Holders of Doctorates Among American Negroes,* Meador Publishing Co., Boston, 1946; Jay, James M., *Negroes in Science: Natural Science Doctorates, 1876–1969,* Balamp Publishing Co., Detroit, 1971; and Taylor, Julius H., *The Negro in Science,* Morgan State College Press, Baltimore, 1955.

Social Many Afro-Americans have achieved recognition in the fields of economics, political science, psychology, anthropology, and sociology. Afro-American economists who achieved recognition in the period from the 1930s to the 1960s include such figures as Abram Harris, Booker T. McGraw. Frederick Jackson, Rodney G. Higgins, Frank G. Davis, and Winfred O. Bryson, Jr. Noteworthy political scientists of the same era include Ralph Bunche, Gwendolen Carter, G. James Fleming, Robert E. Martin, J. Erroll Miller, Robert Gill, and Alexander J. Walker. Important Afro-American psychologists of those decades were James Bayton, Mae Pullins Claytor, Kenneth B. Clark, Allison Davis, Martin D. Jenkins, John Richardson, III, Edelbert Rodgers, and Roger K. Williams. An outstanding anthropologist of that period was Laurence Foster.

Afro-American economists who have gained recognition in the 1960s and 1970s include Bernard Anderson, Andrew F. Brimmer, Samuel Myers, Ernest Murphy, Emmett J. Rice, Thomas Sowell, and Clifton R. Wharton, Jr. Political scientists include Clinton Jones, Mae King, William Nelson, Hanes Walton, and Alex Willingham. Psychologists in this category include Lillian Blake, Glenwood C. Brooks, Jr., Leslie Hicks, Clayton Stansberry, Doris Welcher, and Jerusha Wilson.

More numerous than any other group of Afro-American social scientists, the sociologists occupy a unique position in Afro-American achievement.

Sociologists Afro-Americans began systematic attempts at the study of sociology, mostly about themselves, when the science was in its infancy. W. E. B. Du Bois was the first. His study of the Philadelphia Negro was made in the 1890s and was subsequently published (1899). When Du Bois went to Atlanta University to teach at the turn of the century, he undertook a series of studies that became famous as the Atlanta University Publications. In a real sense he was the founder of the department of sociology (and social work) at Atlanta University. In later years he was followed by Ira De A. Reid, who conducted and published a number of studies on urban Afro-Americans. Reid, in turn, taught and inspired several young students or colleagues, including Tillman C. Cothran, formerly a professor of sociology at Atlanta University and editor of *Phylon* and later a dean at Western Michigan University. Reid's career came to a close at Haverford College (Haverford, Pa.) at the beginning of the end of the nation's period of legal segregation.

Another pioneer was Kelly Miller. Although he was not trained in the discipline, he introduced the study of sociology at Howard University (Washington, D.C.) and established a sociology department there. He published a study on the migration and distribution of the Afro-American population in 1905 as an occasional paper (no. 11) of the American Negro Academy. Three years later he brought out *Race Adjustment,* which was reprinted in 1924 and again in 1968.

E. Franklin Frazier came to Howard's faculty after Miller. Frazier is regarded by many observers as the preeminent Afro-American sociologist. His major studies focused on the Afro-American family and are regarded as substantial

contributions to sociological theory. His *The Free Negro Family* appeared in 1932; it was followed by *The Negro Family in Chicago* (1932) and his larger, comprehensive *The Negro Family in the United States,* which was first published in 1939 and reissued by the University of Chicago Press in 1966. Frazier also wrote a controversial volume, *Black Bourgeoisie* (1957), a critical analysis of the Afro-American middle class that influenced one of his younger colleagues, Nathan Hare, who later became editor of *The Black Scholar,* in writing *The Black Anglo-Saxons* (1965). Two younger sociologists who came to Howard through the influence and inspiration of Frazier were Harry Walker and G. Franklin Edwards. The latter served as chairman of the department from 1963 to 1970.

Meantime, another pioneer Afro-American sociologist was creating a school of sociology at Fisk University (Nashville, Tenn.). Charles S. Johnson achieved fame and recognition from the 1920s through the 1940s for his studies of rural Afro-American life (sharecropping) and of the system of segregation. Academically and theoretically oriented to the University of Chicago (as was Frazier), Johnson produced or directed numerous studies as a social scientist, remaining remarkably unbiased and aloof. His numerous writings include: *The Shadow of the Plantation* (1934), *The Negro College Graduate* (1938), *Growing up in the Black Belt* (1941), and *Patterns of Negro Segregation* (1943). Like Frazier, his contemporary, Johnson inspired younger faculty members and students at Fisk University. Those who were influenced by him include Preston Valien, G. Franklin Edwards, Clifton R. Jones, Albert N. Whiting, Lionel H. Newsom, and Hugh Smythe.

Reid at Atlanta, Frazier at Howard, and Johnson at Fisk had the resources necessary to develop strong departments of sociology and to offer graduate programs. At the same time, at institutions that did not have those kinds of resources, or whose departments offered only an undergraduate degree, many able scholars developed. Sociologists in this group include St. Clair Drake (Roosevelt College, Chicago, Ill.), Oliver C. Cox (Lincoln University, Jefferson City, Mo.), W. S. M. Banks and Earl Pierro (Fort Valley State College, Fort Valley, Ga.), George Ragland (Prairie View Agricultural and Mechanical (A&M) University, Prairie View, Tex.), Earl R. Moses (Morgan State University, Baltimore, Md.), Mozell Hill (Langston University, Langston, Okla.), Robert A. Anglin (West Virginia State College), Henry J.

McGuinn (Virginia Union University), Harry W. Roberts (Virginia State College), and C. H. Parrish (Kentucky State College).

REFERENCES The area has long remained unexplored. In the late 1960s, however, James E. Conyers, an Afro-American sociologist, began investigating other black colleagues, individually and collectively, publishing in *Phylon* (Fall 1968) an article entitled "Negro Doctorates in Sociology in America: A Social Portrait." Some of his results have also been summarized in a chapter entitled "A Profile of Black Sociologists," coauthored by Edgar G. Epps, also an Afro-American sociologist, in Blackwell, James E. and Morris Janowitz (eds.), *Black Sociologists: Historical and Contemporary Perspectives* University of Chicago Press, Chicago, 1974. Blackwell served as the first elected national chairman of the Caucus of Black Sociologists (1970–72).

SCOTIA SEMINARY See BARBER-SCOTIA COLLEGE.

SCOTIA WOMEN'S COLLEGE See BARBER-SCOTIA COLLEGE.

SCOTT, CORNELIUS ADOLPHUS See NEWSPAPERS.

SCOTT, DRED (ca. 1795–1858), bondsman; born in Southampton County, Va. Scott was a slave of Peter Blow of Virginia, who in 1827 brought his family and slaves, including Scott, to Missouri. After Blow's death, Scott became the property of Blow's daughter Elizabeth, who sold him to Dr. John Emerson in 1833. From 1833 to 1838 Scott accompanied Emerson, a surgeon in the U.S. Army, on various trips, including two that took him to Illinois and Wisconsin territories. In 1843 he was inherited by Dr. Emerson's widow, who "hired" him out to families in St. Louis, Mo. (Scott subsequently remained in St. Louis, although his owner moved to Massachusetts.) Henry Taylor Blow, the son of Scott's first master, seems to have felt a sense of responsibility to Scott, for in 1846 Blow brought a suit on Scott's behalf in the Missouri state court, alleging that Scott was free by reason of his sojourn in a free territory (*Scott, A Man of Color v. Emerson*). The Missouri judge ruled against Scott in 1852, and the case was taken to the federal courts. (Scott, for technical reasons, was nominally sold to Mrs. Emerson's brother, John Sanford.) From 1854 to 1857 the case was in federal court; meanwhile, Scott worked in St. Louis at a variety of odd jobs, and he was subject only to minimal restraints. The case went to the U.S. Supreme Court, which ruled against Scott in 1857 (*Scott v. Sanford*), finding that his status had been determined by the Missouri courts and further that Scott, as a slave, was not a citizen and therefore not entitled to sue in federal court. Henry Taylor Blow acquired Scott by means of another fictitious sale in 1857 and emancipated the bondsman and his family in May of that year. Scott continued to reside in St. Louis, working as a porter in Barnum's Hotel. He died of tuberculosis a year and a half later. *See also* AFRO-AMERICAN HISTORY: SECTIONAL CONFLICT OVER SLAVERY, 1820–60.

SCOTT, EMMETT JAY (1873–1957, administrator, author; born in Houston, Tex. Scott received a M.A. degree from Wiley College (Marshall, Tex.) in 1901. He worked for the Houston *Post* and edited the *Texas Freeman* for three years before becoming secretary to Booker T. Washington in 1897. From 1912 to 1919 Scott served as secretary of the Tuskegee Institute (Tuskegee Institute, Ala.), and from 1919 to 1934 he was secretary-treasurer and business manager of Howard University (Washington, D.C.). Scott was the author of *Tuskegee and its People* (1910) and of *The American Negro in the World War* (1919).

SCOTT, NATHAN A., JR. (1925–   ), theologian, author, educator; born in Cleveland, Ohio. Scott received a B.A. degree from the University of Michigan in 1944, a B.D. degree from Union Theological Seminary in 1946, and his Ph.D. degree from Columbia University in 1949. In 1949 he was also ordained a Protestant Episcopal priest. He was on the faculty of Howard University (Washington, D.C.) from 1948 to 1955; in the latter year he became professor of theology and literature at the University of Chicago. His books include: *Rehearsals of Discomposure: Alienation and Reconciliation in Modern Literature* (1952); *The Tragic Vision and the Christian Faith* (1957); *Reinhold Niebuhr* (1963); *The Search for Identity: Essays on the American Character* (1964); *Negative Capability: Studies in the New Literature and the Religious Situation* (1969); and *Three American Moralists: Mailer, Bellow, Trilling* (1974). He also contributed many articles to scholarly periodicals.

SCOTT, ROLAND B. (1909–   ), physician, educator; born in Houston, Tex. Scott received a B.S. degree from Howard University (Washington, D.C.) in 1931 and his M.D. degree from Howard University Medical College in 1935. He was one of the most-renowned authorities on sickle-cell anemia and contributed more scholarly articles on this subject to journals than any other physician. Scott served as chairman and as professor of pediatrics at Howard University School of Medicine, and was also chief pediatrician at Freedmen's Hospital, Washington, D.C. *See also* Contributors under Preface.

SCOTT, WENDELL See ATHELETES: AUTO RACING.

SCOTTSBORO BOYS See AFRO-AMERICAN HISTORY: RECONSTRUCTION TO REVOLT; CIVIL RIGHTS: CASES.

SCRUGGS, OTEY MATTHEW (1929–   ), historian, educator; born in Vallejo, Calif. Scruggs received a B.A. degree from the University of California at Santa Barbara in 1951, and a M.A. degree (1952; during which time he was a John Hay Whitney Fellow) and his Ph.D. degree (1958) from Harvard University. He was an instructor of history at the University of California at Santa Barbara from 1957 to 1959 and became a professor of history at Syracuse University (Syracuse, N.Y.) after 1969. Scruggs served as coeditor of *Henry Adams' History of the United States* (1963), and wrote numerous articles and reviews.

SCURLOCK, ADDISON N. See PHOTOGRAPHERS.

SEALE, ROBERT G. (BOBBY) (1937–   ), civil rights militant; born in Dallas, Tex. Seale's family moved to Oakland, Calif., when he was seven years old. After a three-year stint in the U.S. Air Force, he attended Merritt College (Oakland, Calif.), where he met Huey Newton. He founded with Newton the Black Panther Party in 1966. In 1969 Seale was indicted in Chicago, Ill., with seven others—a group that became known as the "Chicago Eight"—for conspiracy to disrupt the 1968 Democratic National Convention in Chicago. A sensational trial ensued; Seale's inflammatory behavior in the courtroom caused the judge to separate his case, declare an individual mistrial, and sentence him to four years in prison for contempt of court. Earlier in 1969 Seale had been arrested and charged with the murder of an alleged Black Panther informer in New Haven, Conn. This charge was later dismissed. His book *Seize the Time* was published in 1971. *See also* BLACK PANTHER PARTY.

SEARS, ARTHUR, JR. (1928–   ), journalist, administrator; born in Pittsburgh, Pa. Sears received his B.A. degree from the University of Pittsburgh in 1951. He served as the district managing editor of the Cleveland and Cincinnati *Call and Post* and as a reporter on the Norfolk *Journal and Guide,* and he was awarded the Columbia University Mike Berger Award for articles in the *Wall Street Journal* entitled "Kelly Street Blues." In 1972 Sears became a consultant and corporate public-relations director for General Electric.

◆◆

SEGREGATION

SEGREGATION Segregation was a way to keep Afro-Americans "in their places." It extends backward in time to the earliest periods of American history, although segregation manifested itself differently according to time and place. Slavery was essentially a system of segregation based primarily upon birth and color. Literally a racist caste system, segregation lasted in both fact and law for 100 years or more after the constitutional end of slavery. It was formalized in many Jim Crow laws following the collapse of Reconstruction. Although at times segregation was difficult to sustain, especially in the face of its own moral wrongs and of Afro-American resistance, it was a dominant feature of American society from the time of the Civil War until the beginning of its demise following World War II. This was especially true in the South where

THE FIFTEENTH AMENDMENT.

CELEBRATED MAY 19th 1870.

very large numbers of Afro-Americans lived; it was less true but no less real in other regions. Although many aspects of the system disappeared in the wake of the civil rights movement of the 1950s and 1960s, many of its features remained in fact if not in law, especially in residential housing.

Patterns The patterns of the old system of segregation and its enforcement varied from locality to locality. But generally the following manifestations prevailed.

Titles Titles of courtesy, respect, and equality were not to be used in addressing Afro-Americans. The usage of "Mr." or "Mrs." was definite-ly avoided. Afro-Americans were referred to as "uncle," "aunt," "professor," "reverend," "doctor," or "boy." The use of "nigger" and "boy" was widespread. A show of kindness or politeness, but not deference, called for the use of "nigra" or "colored." Afro-Americans were invariably addressed by their first names; conversely, they were expected to or forced to defer to whites by using "Mr." or "Mrs." or a title when addressing them.

Etiquette Shaking hands with an Afro-American was forbidden, as was sitting or dining with Afro-Americans.

Public Travel On streetcars or buses, signs

directed that: "Colored passengers will seat from the rear; white passengers will seat from the front." Afro-Americans were expected and forced by law to give up seats to whites. On trains, special Jim Crow cars were placed in the front near the baggage coach or locomotive, in locations where there was more noise, exhaust smoke, and risk of passenger injury in case of collision. No eating facilities were available to Afro-Americans on trains; if there was a dining car, blacks were not allowed at first (and when they were allowed later, a curtain was drawn around them). Passenger stations for buses and trains had separate entrances and waiting rooms, indicated by signs reading "Colored" and "White."

Public Buildings: banks, municipal buildings, theaters Use by blacks of these various public buildings was restricted to the rear areas or to balconies. In some instances, separate facilities existed; in other cases, none existed at all.

Public Schools A legally dual school system for Afro-Americans and whites was established, separate and unequal.

Hotels Afro-Americans were excluded from hotels and given no rooms and no food services. The use of a back or a servant's entrance was permitted to black servants only: maids, waiters, bellhops, porters, cooks, or other menials.

Department Stores Some stores were restricted to whites only. Others provided partial services to blacks. Garments could never be tried on and they were not returnable if purchased. Blacks were seldom provided with eating or restroom facilities.

Churches Almost all churches were completely segregated (except on special occasions) from the Civil War period to the 1960s.

Cemetaries Cemeteries were always completely segregated.

Service Businesses: barber shops, beauty shops, funeral parlors These services were completely segregated, except for occasional employment of blacks.

Employment Employment opportunities for Afro-Americans were severely restricted, largely to unskilled or menial jobs: porter, maid, cook, chauffeur, waiter, or laundress.

Intermarriage or Extramarital Relations Intermarriage or extramarital relations were the greatest taboos—they were apt causes for lynching, especially of a black male, even if only alleged. In contrast, a white male, although censure existed, could literally "get away with rape" of Afro-American women.

Police Afro-Americans were not accepted into police forces or by police forces except in special cases. Police brutality and insult to Afro-Americans were common, leaving a historic image of white policemen as being unfair, unhelpful, and oppressive.

Housing Segregated housing and separate residential areas for Afro-Americans and whites have always existed.

Afro-American Response Black response to the old system of segregation varied. The principal reactions included: avoidance; "tomming" ("playing the clown," "eating crow," or "jiving"); "passing" (escaping the color bar, where possible); flight (escape to other areas where segregation and racism were less oppressive); verbal resentment ("loudmouthing" or "putting in the dozens"); nonverbal resentment ("cussing under the breath" or "giving a mean look"); violence (hostile, overt action either on an individual or group basis); organizational dis-

Segregated facilities, 1940s. Left: A theater in Leland, Miss. Right: a railroad station in North Carolina. (*Library of Congress.*)

cussion within a church or fraternal group; and moral suasion. (Afro-Americans reiterated in speech and writing that the system was patently unfair, unjust, and un-American).

Segregation remained institutionalized in communities and churches, as shown in this photo taken in the mid-1970s. (*Ronald Duncan*.)

Conclusion A great deal of the old segregated regime remained in effect, if not in law, a quarter of a century following the legal end of segregation in the landmark case of *Brown v. Board of Education* (1954). It is true that much of the old caste system had been destroyed; for example, separate facilities and entrances, and signs indicating "white" and "colored," had disappeared. In effect, American society was far less closed—especially in public accommodations—than it had been a few decades earlier. Perhaps as important as the removal of actual and legal restrictions were the changes in the outlook and attitudes of Americans. Blacks lost many of their old inhibitions and the negative images they had of themselves; and white attitudes toward blacks grew less depreciatory.

Yet much of the old order persisted in housing and, by extension, in much of the educational and social life of Afro-Americans. Segregation remained in effect in the structure and function of society; and black Americans were inclined to relate its persistence to institutionalized racism. Although black-white attitudes toward integration changed positively after *Brown* and the civil rights movement of the 1960s, the old dilemma of what to do about an effectively segregated society with a history of racial discrimination in face of its democratic and equalitarian goals remains as a challenge and problem for the last quarter of the twentieth century. *See also* AFRO-

AMERICAN HISTORY: RECONSTRUCTION TO REVOLT, 1877–1977; CIVIL DISORDERS; CIVIL RIGHTS: MOVEMENT; CIVIL RIGHTS: CASES; DISCRIMINATION; EDUCATION: DESEGREGATION IN PERSPECTIVE; HOUSING: JIM CROW; RACE: RACISM.

REFERENCES: References are numerous for the old system of segregation, but four of the best are Johnson, Charles S., *Patterns of Negro Segregation* (1943); Myrdal, Gunnar, *An American Dilemma*, Vols. 1 & 2, Pantheon, 1975; Woodward, C. Vann, *The Strange Career of Jim Crow*, Oxford U Pr. (3rd rev. ed., 1974); and Wright, Richard, *Black Boy: A Record of Childhood and Youth*, 1969. For the later period after the 1960s, see references under HOUSING and RACE: RACISM. For an indication of the prevalence (percentages) of segregation in the largest cities, see the listing for Reynolds Farley (who cites other authors) under the references for EDUCATION: DEVELOPMENTS IN ELEMENTARY AND SECONDARY EDUCATION.

SELMA UNIVERSITY Selma University, at Selma, Ala., was founded in 1878 by Baptists to train ministers and teachers. Church-related and coeducational, Selma offers the bachelor's degree and provides liberal arts and general professional curricula. Its 1975 enrollment was 349. Its president in the mid-1970s was M. C. Cleveland, Jr., the son of an earlier leader of the college.

SENGSTACKE, JOHN HERMAN HENRY (1921–), publisher; born in Savannah, Ga. After receiving a B.S. degree from Hampton Institute (Hampton, Va.) in 1933, Sengstacke became vice-president, general manager, and president of the Robert S. Abbott Publishing Company (Chicago, Ill.). He inherited the Chicago *Defender*, one of the nation's leading Afro-American newspapers, from his uncle Robert Sengstacke Abbott. During World War II Sengstacke served as chairman of the Chicago rationing board. He also served three terms as president of the Negro Newspaper Publishers Association. *See also* ABBOTT, ROBERT SENGSTACKE; NEWSPAPERS.

SEPARATE BUT EQUAL See CIVIL RIGHTS: CASES; EDUCATION.

SEPARATISTS See AFRO-AMERICAN HISTORY: THE WEST; COLONIZATION.

SEVENTH DAY ADVENTISTS A religious group stressing the second coming of Christ. Leaders of the black conferences of the Church are Edward Dorsey (Allegheny East), D. B. Simons (Allegheny West), J. R. Wagner (Lake Region), G. R. Earle (Northeastern), R. L. Woodfork (South Atlantic), C. E. Dudley (South Central), W. J. Cleveland

(Southwest Region), and G. N. Banks (Pacific Union).

SHARECROPPERS *See* AGRICULTURE.

SHARP STREET METHODIST EPISCOPAL CHURCH *See* METHODISTS.

SHAW, HERBERT BELL (1908–   ), African Methodist Episcopal Zion bishop; born in Wilmington, N.C. Shaw studied at Fisk University (Nashville, Tenn.) and at the Howard University School of Religion (Washington, D.C.). Ordained in the African Methodist Episcopal Zion (AMEZ) Church in 1928, he held pastorships and administrative posts before being made presiding bishop of the Third Episcopal District, AMEZ Church, in 1952. Shaw was a member of the boards of trustees of Livingstone College, Clinton College, and Lomax Hannon College.

SHAW UNIVERSITY Shaw University, at Raleigh, N.C., was founded in 1865 by Baptists and supported by the American Baptist Home Mission Society. Church-related and coeducational, Shaw offers the bachelor's degree and provides liberal arts and teacher education curricula. Its 1975 enrollment was 1,227.

In its earliest days, Shaw maintained a medical school, one of the first for Afro-Americans, though now its programs emphasize the liberal arts and teacher education. Shaw has several unusual features. For example, although its student body remains mostly Afro-American, its faculty is both interracial and multicultural: more than 25 percent are natives of non-Western countries. Shaw also had one of the earliest black studies programs. King V. Cheek, Jr., and James A. Hargraves served as Shaw's presidents in the 1960s and 1970s.

SHAW UNIVERSITY (MISS.) *See* RUST COLLEGE.

SHEELER, JOHN REUBEN (ca. 1912–   ), historian, educator; born in Riceville, Tenn. Sheeler received a B.A. degree from Knoxville College (Knoxville, Tenn.) in 1934, a M.A. degree from Fisk University (Nashville, Tenn.) in 1941, and his Ph.D. degree from West Virginia University in 1952. He taught at Alabama State College (1943–45), at West Virginia State College (1948–53), and at Texas Southern University in 1953, where he served as head of the history department (1954–71) and as distinguished professor of history after 1971. His publications include:

"Unionism in East Tennessee During the Civil War," "The Struggle of the Negro in Ohio for Freedom," and "The Negro in West Virginia before 1900." *See also* PREFACE: LIST OF CONTRIBUTORS.

SHEPARD, JAMES EDWARD (1875–1947), educator; born in Raleigh, N.C. Shepard received a B.A. degree and a Ph.G. degree from Shaw University (Raleigh, N.C.) in 1894, a D.D. degree from Muskingum College (New Concord, Ohio) in 1910, a M.A. degree from Selma University (Selma, Ala.) in 1912, and his Litt.D. from Howard University (Washington, D.C.) in 1925. In 1910 he founded the National Training School for the education of Christian workers and teachers (later known as North Carolina College for Negroes, and later still as North Carolina College, and now as North Carolina Central University). He was its director and president from 1925 until his death.

SHERMAN, ODIE LEE (1897–   ), African Methodist Episcopal bishop; born in Jacksonville, Tex. Sherman attended Texas College and received his B.A. degree from Shorter College (North Little Rock, Ark.) in 1927. He was pastor of African Methodist Episcopal (AME) churches in Arkansas before being elected an AME bishop in 1956. Sherman received an award for outstanding service during the civil rights crisis in Little Rock, Ark.

SHIELDS, VAREE *See* NEWSPAPERS: CONTEMPORARY.

SHOCKLEY, ANN ALLEN (1925–   ), librarian, author; born in Louisville, Ky. Shockley received a B.A. degree from Fisk University (Nashville, Tenn.) in 1948 and her M.S.L.S. degree from Case Western Reserve University (Cleveland, Ohio) in 1960. Early in her career she served on the staff of the Louisville *Defender*, and as a columnist and as a substitute teacher. In 1966 Shockley became associate librarian at Fisk, where she was head of the special collections unit, including the Black Oral History Program that she initiated. Her books include: *Living Black American Authors*, with Sue P. Chandler (1973), and a novel, *Loving Her* (1974).

SHOCKLEY, GRANT S. (1919–   ), clergyman, educator, administrator; born in Philadelphia, Pa. Shockley received a B.A. degree from Lincoln University in 1942, a B.D. degree from Drew University (Madison, N.J.), in 1945, a M.A. degree from Union Theological Seminary in 1946 and his Ed.D. degree from Columbia University Teachers College in 1953. He was ordained an elder in 1944, and served churches in New York and Delaware. Shockley taught at Clark College, Gammon Theological Seminary, New York University, Northwestern University, Garrett Theological Seminary, and Emory University. He became president of the Interdenominational Theological Center (Atlanta, Ga.) in 1975. *See also* PREFACE: LIST OF CONTRIBUTORS.

SHORTER COLLEGE Shorter College, at North Little Rock, Ark., was founded in 1886 by the African Methodist Episcopal (AME) Church. Church-related and coeducational, the college offers a two-year program that is usually credited toward the bachelor's degree but that can also be used for terminal occupational work. The 1975 enrollment was 180.

SHUFFER, GEORGE MACON, JR. (1923–), Army officer; born in Palestine, Tex. Following high school graduation in 1940, Shuffer enlisted in the U.S. Army as a private. Completing Officer Candidate School in 1943, he was commissioned a second lieutenant and held a number of command and staff positions with the 93d Infantry Division in the Pacific theater during World War II. While on active duty, he earned an A.A. degree from Monterey Peninsular College (Monterey, Calif.) in 1953, and a B.S. degree (1956) and his M.A. degree (1959) from the University of Maryland. He was commissioned a brigadier general in 1972 and appointed assistant to the deputy chief of staff for personnel, Europe and Seventh Army. In 1973 Shuffer was assigned as assistant division commander, 3d Infantry Division. His decorations include the Silver Star with two Oak Leaf clusters, the Legion of Merit with two Oak Leaf clusters, Air Medal with five Oak Leaf clusters, the Army Commendation Medal, and the Vietnamese Cross of Gallantry with Silver Star.

SHUTTLESWORTH, FRED LEE (1922–), clergyman, civil rights leader; born in Mugler, Ala. Shuttlesworth received a B.A. degree from Selma University (Selma, Ala.) and his B.S. degree from Alabama State Teachers College. He was the pastor of several Baptist churches, including the First Baptist Church in Birmingham, Ala. (1957–1960) and the Revelation Bap-

tist Church in Cincinnati, Ohio. Shuttlesworth was very active in the civil rights movement, especially with the Alabama Christian Movement for Human Rights (ACMHR) and the Southern Christian Leadership Conference (SCLC). He was also active in the Congress of Racial Equality (CORE) and in the National Association for the Advancement of Colored People (NAACP).

SICKLE-CELL ANEMIA *See* RACE: BIOLOGY.

SIMMONS UNIVERSITY BIBLE COLLEGE Simmons University Bible College, at Louisville, Ky., was chartered in 1873 and opened in 1879 under the auspices of the Baptist Church. Church-affiliated and church-supported, the coeducational college offers the bachelor's degree and provides theology and liberal arts curricula in addition to programs leading to the Missions Certificate. Its 1975 enrollment was about 100.

The institution has been headed by one principal (E. P. Marrs) and nine presidents. The first president, after whom the college was named, was William J. Simmons, who served from 1880 to 1890. W. L. Holmes, president in the mid-1970s, began his tenure in 1955. The college is accredited by the Southern Accrediting Association of Bible Institutes, Bible Colleges, and Bible Seminaries.

SIMMONS, WILLIAM J. *See* BAPTISTS; HISTORIANS; SIMMONS UNIVERSITY BIBLE COLLEGE.

SIMPSON, ERIC O. *See* NEWSPAPERS: CONTEMPORARY.

SIMPSON, ORENTHAL JAMES (O. J.) *See* ATHLETES: FOOTBALL.

SIMS, DAVID HENRY (1886– ?). African Methodist Episcopal bishop, educator; born in Alabama. Sims received a B.A. degree from Georgia State College in 1905, a second B.A. degree from Oberlin College (Oberlin, Ohio) in 1909, a B.D. degree from Oberlin Theological Seminary in 1912, and his M.A. degree from the University of Chicago. After serving African Methodist Episcopal (AME) Churches in Ohio and Rhode Island, he was elected an AME bishop in 1932 and served in South Africa and Alabama. Sims was also a professor at Morris Brown College (Atlanta, Ga.) and dean at Allen University (Columbia, S.C.).

SIMS, WILLIAM E. (1921–   ), educator; born in Chickasha, Okla. Sims received a B.A. degree from Lincoln University (Jefferson City, Mo.) in 1949, and a M.A. degree (1952) and his Ed.D. degree (1963) from Colorado State College. He taught in Tulsa, Okla., public schools from 1948 to 1953, and then joined the faculty of Langston University (Langston, Okla.), of which institution he served as president after 1970.

SINGLETON, BENJAMIN (PAP)   See AFRO-AMERICAN HISTORY: THE WEST.

SINKFORD, JEANNE CRAIG (1933–   ), dentist, educator; born in Washington, D.C. Sinkford received a B.S. degree from Howard University (Washington, D.C.) in 1953, a D.D.S. degree from the Howard University College of Dentistry in 1958, and a M.S. degree (1962) and her Ph.D. degree in physiology (1963) from Northwestern University (Evanston, Ill.). She was associate professor of prosthodontics and served as head of the department of dentistry at the Howard University College of Dentistry after 1964, the first black woman in the United States to become head of a university department of dentistry.

SINKLER, GEORGE (1927–   ), historian, educator; born in Charleston, S.C. Sinkler received a B.A. degree from Augustana College (Rock Island, Ill.) in 1953, and a M.A. degree (1954) and his Ed.D. degree (1966) from Columbia University. After an instructorship in West Virginia, he spent 11 years as an associate professor of history at Prairie View Agricultural and Mechanical (A&M) University (Prairie View, Tex.). In 1966 Sinkler moved to Morgan State University (Baltimore, Md.), where he became a full professor in 1971. His published works include a volume entitled the *The Racial Attitudes of American Presidents from Abraham Lincoln to Theodore Roosevelt* (1971).

SIPUEL, ADA LOIS (1924–   ), lawyer, educator, civil rights activist; born in Chickasha, Okla. Sipuel was refused admission to the University of Oklahoma Law School. Her petitions, filed by the National Association for the Advancement of Colored People (NAACP) lawyers Amos T. Hall and Thurgood Marshall, for an order directing the university to admit her, were at first denied by the Oklahoma courts but later reversed. Sipuel (now Fisher) served as chairman of the department and professor of social sciences at Langston University (Langston, Okla.) after 1957. *See also* CIVIL RIGHTS: CASES, 1865–1975.

SISSLE, NOBLE (1889– ?), bandleader, lyricist; born in Indianapolis, Ind. Sissle took an early interest in music, giving performances in Baltimore, Md., and New York, N.Y. His band performed on excursion boats that sailed the Mississippi River from St. Louis, Mo. In 1915 Sissle teamed up with Eubie Blake. Two of their best-known musical shows are *Shuffle Along* (1921) and *The Chocolate Dandies* (1924). Sissle wrote the lyrics for many popular songs, including "I'm Just Wild About Harry," "Love Will Find A Way," "Dixie Moon," and "Shuffle Along." During World War II Sissle sponsored and directed a USO show. *See also* MOTION PICTURES; MUSIC: HISTORY AND DEVELOPMENT.

SIT-INS   *See* CIVIL RIGHTS: MOVEMENT IN SELECTED STATES.

SKINNER, ELLIOTT (1924–   ), anthropologist, educator, government official; born in Port-of-Spain, Trinidad. Skinner's higher education began at New York University, from which institution he received a B.A. degree in 1951. He earned a M.A. degree, several fellowships, and his Ph.D. degree in anthropology from Columbia University from 1952 to 1955, after which he won several postdoctoral fellowships and grants. In 1954 Skinner joined the faculty of Columbia University to teach anthropology, and except for a four-year association with New York University in the early 1960s he remained there. In 1969 he became Franz Boas Professor of Anthropology, and in 1972 he was named chairman of the department. His many involvements in African affairs included lecturing for the Foreign Service Institute of the U.S. Department of State. Skinner was appointed by President Lyndon B. Johnson as ambassador to Upper Volta in 1966, and he remained in that post for three years.

SLATER INDUSTRIAL ACADEMY   *See* WINSTON-SALEM STATE UNIVERSITY.

SLAVE REVOLTS   *See* AFRO-AMERICAN HISTORY: SECTIONAL CONFLICT OVER SLAVERY, 1820–60; PROSSER, GABRIEL; SLAVERY: RESTRICTIONS ON AFRO-AMERICANS; SLAVERY: THE ABOLITIONISTS; SLAVERY: SELECTED STATES: SOUTH CAROLINA; TURNER, NAT; VESEY, DENMARK.

SLAVERY

Introduction Slavery was a legacy of the Atlantic slave trade, and its origins are traceable to the colony of Virginia in the 1600s. Though the system existed throughout colonial America, it developed mainly in the South as a labor system. By the time of the Civil War, slavery was so firmly established in the southern states that it had become "the peculiar institution of the South." To a great extent, slavery meant plantation (farm) labor, and, having come into existence to meet a labor shortage, it was found mainly wherever the southerner could set up large "agricultural factories" for the raising of a staple crop—mainly cotton, but also tobacco, sugar, and hemp. It is often mistakenly thought that the whole southern population had a stake in slavery; actually, a very small percentage were slaveholders. By 1850 less than one-third of the southern white population had any direct connection with slavery, and this number was steadily decreasing.

Since the African slave trade had closed in 1808, the slaveholders had had to draw their labor supply largely from the 1 million slaves then present in the United States and their descendants. The closing of the slave trade and the gradual migration of the cotton planters westward gave rise to an interstate slave traffic. Older eastern states, especially Virginia and Maryland, no longer engaged in large-scale planting, sent their surplus supply of slaves west to be sold to the great plantation owners in the cotton and cane belts. These slaves, carried to the new markets in coastwise vessels or sent overland in coffles (caravans), fetched slave traders sums closely tied to the current selling price of cotton: when cotton sold for 13 cents per

Slaves going south after being sold in Richmond, Va., 1850s. Not to be confused with arrivals from Africa of a much earlier period (1700s), slaves in Richmond at this time came mainly from within the state which ranked first in its slave population. However, with the relative decline of tobacco culture in state and area, together with demands for slave labor in the rising "cotton kingdom" of the lower South, Richmond became the foremost slave market in the United States. This scene was painted by Eyre Crowe (1824–1910), an English artist who visited America in the 1850s. Like many foreign visitors of the period, Crowe was culturally shocked by various aspects of slavery in the United States, especially by slave auctions. He sketched scenes of sales at the markets in Richmond and Charleston, S.C. Some of his drawings were published in *The Illustrated London News*. Completed in 1853, the above painting is preserved in the Chicago Historical Society. *(Courtesy of the Chicago Historical Society.)*

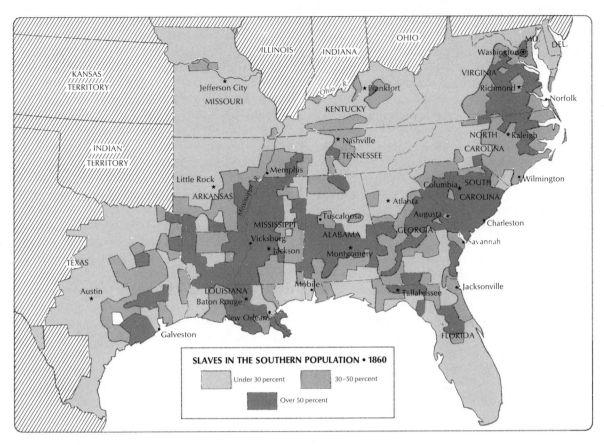

SLAVES IN THE SOUTHERN POPULATION • 1860

Under 30 percent   30–50 percent

Over 50 percent

pound in New York City in 1837, an able-bodied field hand cost his purchaser about $1,100, but when cotton reached a low of 5 cents per pound, the same slave brought only $500.

Many slaves were hired out by their owners— to small farmers too poor to buy a slave, to professional men or merchants needing helpers, or to others wanting domestic servants. Many slaves worked alongside as well as under the control of their owners. On smaller plantations and farms, where slaves were few, they worked and even ate in company with the master and his family.

Since slavery was basically a labor system, it functioned with a definite routine and discipline. Slaves were assigned tasks according to their strength and ability, serving as field hands or as blacksmiths, bricklayers, and the like. They had to observe fixed hours of labor or perform given amounts of work; a piece system was used most often on the rice coast, while time work or the gang system was best suited to sugar and cotton. The most irksome of rules involved in the system were those connected with discipline. The usual basis of discipline was a system of punishments and rewards, the rigors of which

varied with the personality of the owner or overseer. Although most slaveholders agreed that whipping was essential to order and industry, and while all discipline was based ultimately on physical force, few slaveholders indulged in cruel and unusual punishment. But behind the slaveholder stood the law, and before it the slave was a thing of little consequence. His testimony was never accepted against whites; legal statutes generally ruled to his disadvantage; and, with the passage of years, his emancipation became more and more difficult to achieve.

Food and clothing were regularly issued to the slaves, and some attention was paid to their health, amusement, and housing. Housing was seldom good; slaves usually lived in small one- or two-room cabins, windowless and unfloored. Food was adequate in quantity but unappetizing and monotonous, and probably not very nutritious. The diet almost always included pork (fatback), meal, molasses, and whatever vegetables the slaves could raise themselves. Clothing consisted of homespun cotton and shapeless brogans, the same things worn by the poorer whites. Provisions for amusement and care of health depended upon the nature of the individual slaveowner. While there were always those who neglected both, there were more who were both genuinely fond of and concerned for their slaves; in any event, the slave was at the least a financial investment to be kept in good working condition.

While the advocates of slavery emphasized the fact that slaves, once purchased, worked for nothing but their subsistence, it is not fair to ignore the economic risks involved in slavery. Not all slave children were born healthy; owners could not count on a full life of work from each slave; and the slaveholder was responsible for all slaves too old to labor. Then, many threats to his labor force existed, such as epidemics, fire, and escape. Finally, while the price of slaves rose rapidly in the years before the war, giving the planter a property wealth on the books, the price of his staple fluctuated widely, sometimes so much as to wipe out any observable profit for a given year. With the cost of slaves increasing, more and more southern planters were kept from adding to their labor supply, and thus to their yield.

Whatever the effect of slavery upon the planter and his income, the institution certainly worked hardship on the South as a whole, and particularly on its slaves.

By making manual labor disreputable, by limiting wage opportunities, by denying the average Southern farmer access to the richest lands, by withholding funds from education and general government activities, and by discouraging the diversification of industry, slavery put a blight upon the South and a stigma upon the Afro-American.

Restrictions on Afro-Americans Although slave laws, or "Black Codes," had been established and revised many times since the beginning of slavery in America, they were made more strict during the half century before the Civil War. Though each state had its own set of slave laws, they all followed a similar pattern. Some states, such as Mississippi, had special rules that forbade slaves to beat drums or to blow horns for fear that these signals might serve the purposes of slave uprisings. Slaves were chattel property and could be bought and sold at the discretion of the master. By 1800 the ways of manumission of slaves had been highly restricted by the regulations of the various states. A slave had no right to buy, to sell, or make any form of agreement without the consent and guidance of his master. Slaves were not allowed legal marriage agreements. Marriage was often no more than jumping over a broomstick,

a ceremony ludicrously conducted by the master.

The prohibition of the right to bear firearms, passed in Virginia in 1639, was the first regulation in the control of Afro-American slaves in America. The purchase or use of alcohol by slaves was also forbidden. Slaves could not assemble unless a white man was present, nor could they hold religious services unless the minister was either white or an approved black minister who officiated in the presence of a white monitoring the services to ensure that all the messages and songs related to the Bible. Slaves did not possess freedom of speech, and travel was only possible with a written pass from the master. Usually, a slave was allowed to visit another plantation for only one hour. It was also against the law to teach any slave to read or to write. During the 1850s, however, one young white woman in Wheeling, Va., was arrested 14 times for this offense. Trial in court for the slave was nonexistent. Slaves were tried in special courts of oyer set up for the purpose. In no instance were a slave's jurors his peers; instead, they were slaveholders who had to possess no less than $300 worth of slave property.

The increase in slave revolts was accompanied by an increase in the harshness of regulation of slave behavior. For example, after the Denmark Vesey revolt occurred, the South Carolina legislature required that all Afro-American sailors be locked up in jail until their vessel put out to sea. After the Nat Turner insurrection, Afro-American ministers were forbidden to preach in Virginia, education for free blacks ceased, and regulations were passed to prevent those blacks who had gone out of the state to acquire an education from returning. Organized patrols and militia were supplied by the state for the "proper" execution of these laws. Slaves called these officials "patterollers."

As the nation proceeded along its sectional division from the adoption of the Mason-Dixon Line to the Compromise of 1850, a southern justification for slavery was provided in what historians call the proslavery argument. This argument contended that God willed the black race to be an inferior one, because the people (if they *were* people) of this race were docile, happy, childlike, and incapable of caring for themselves. Consequently, slavery was a benevolent institution in which blacks were civilized and Christianized. Such prominent white southerners as Haynes, Calhoun, Dew, Fitzhugh, Priest, and Hammond held that slavery was thus a "positive good." These men and others—including writers and visitors from abroad—looked at the system of slavery from an economic or governmental viewpoint (never from the viewpoint of humanity or the aspirations of a people), and they held that the slavery system adequately clothed, housed, and fed the slaves. Slavery was usually studied from the viewpoint of econom-

---

T O   B E   S O L D

At the BALTIMORE FURNACE, near Baltimore Town, on a credit of twelve months,

Upwards of 100 NEGROES,

—CONSISTING OF—

Men, Women, Boys, Girls and Children—amongst which are, Blackfmiths, Colliers, Shoenakers, Carpenters and Laborers. Horfes, Mules, Milch Cows, about 18 yoke of Oxen, Sheep, Sows and Pigs, a quantity of Hay, Coal-Waggons, common Waggons, Carts, a Timber Carriage, two 12 ton Flats, a Batteau, Raw Hides, feveral hundred cords of wood, about 8 miles from Baltimore, and a number of other articles which would be tedious to mention. The fale will begin on Monday the 12th December, and continue until the whole is fold. Bonds on intereft, with approved fecurity will be required.

WILLIAM HAMMOND.

October 31.   eot12D

---

ics and seldom from the viewpoint of morality or from the viewpoint of the Afro-Americans actually in bondage. From 1829 onward the developing proslavery and abolitionist movements acted as counterforces, creating ever-increasing problems for the federal government.

Free blacks were never exactly free in the United States. Although they did not have masters, they also did not have the privileges, rights, and opportunities enjoyed by whites in both the South and the North. In the South their movements were often as restricted as those of slaves. Every county in the South kept a strict record of information relating to its free blacks and was ready at any time to prosecute them for any mischief (such as stealing) that might occur in the area. Most states did not permit free blacks to assemble without the presence of a white person. Even the occupations in which blacks might engage for a living were restricted. The burden of proof of his freedom rested with the free black, and he could be reenslaved for failure to pay his debts, taxes, or court fines. Neither could the free black vote nor hold office. He could neither testify in court against a white person, nor purchase

firearms or liquor without the recommendation of a "reputable" white person. Without public accommodations or the privileges of education, the free black made his living through his own ingenuity, by default, or because of the scarcity of white labor. One state (Georgia) forbade free blacks to own property. Although more restricted in the South, the free black faced great difficulties in making a living in the North. From 1830 to 1850 numerous riots and acts of violence took place in the northern states. Roaming bands of whites directed their violent wrath upon Afro-American communities in northern cities—burning homes and churches as well as beating women and children—while black men were being held in jail in order to assure the "peace" of the neighborhood. The great increase in white immigrants in the North from 1830 to 1860, as well as the beginning of efforts to organize labor, made it even more difficult for free blacks to obtain employment. These conditions led many free blacks to sympathize with and support the colonization movement, which was vigorously opposed by both abolitionists and by the majority of free blacks.

Fully aware of the racist structure of U.S. society Afro-Americans throughout this period were concerned with the separation of the church and the development of Afro-American institutions. These ranged from the founding of the African Free Society in 1787 to the National Convention of Colored Men on the eve of the Civil War. Except for the Afro-Americans themselves, for the abolitionists, and for Underground Railroad leaders, little serious concern existed in America for the freedom of Afro-Americans. From the Wilmot Proviso to the secession of the states from the Union, the South made efforts to defend and to extend slavery. While those in opposition to the South sought to prevent or to control any Afro-American settlement outside of the South, America moved westward in the spirit of manifest destiny. Afro-American history showed everywhere the ugly scars of slavery long before they appeared in the American tragedy of Civil War and Reconstruction. See also AFRO-AMERICAN HISTORY.

Slavery in Selected States

Introduction Afro-American slavery existed throughout colony and nation, and its geographic setting in selected states, or areas, illustrates the system's great diversity. Each slave state, or area, had a particular slave system with its own vari-

Far left: Advertisement for slaves in a Baltimore newspaper (1796). (Courtesy of Joseph Arnold.)

ety, character, and relative importance. Slavery differed from state to state and even from place to place within any given state. When coupled with history, demography, economics, and social conditions, the human geography of slavery varied in both time and place. This complex and dynamic system, even at state levels, has often eluded precise analysis by serious scholars whose views have differed. Yet, the vast amount of ever-growing literature on the subject of slavery is sufficient to reveal the system's scope and diversity as it existed in the individual states.

The states selected below illustrate mainly regional variations as opposed to intrastate contrasts or similarities. These selected states represent three of the nation's four census regions: South, Northeast, and North Central. Subdivisions of these three regions are represented, with the South leading in the number of states selected. The selected states according to subdivisions are: Massachusetts for New England (Northeast); Pennsylvania for the Middle Atlantic region (Northeast); Virginia, Georgia, and South Carolina for the South Atlantic region (South); Tennessee for the East South Central region (South); Arkansas for the West South Central region

(South); and Missouri and Kansas for the West North Central region (North Central).

When factors of history, demography, and economics are combined with geography in these selected states, the differences become even more dimensional. For example, by almost any criterion, Virginia would be exemplary: it was the first (oldest) province or state and had the largest Afro-American population for the longest period in American history; Virginia tobacco (the production of which depended heavily upon slave labor) was the most valuable product in colonial America. On the other hand, slavery in Massachusetts was nearly as old but of far less demographic and economic importance. The size and wealth of this maritime-oriented province and state enhanced its early importance in national political history both before and after the protracted death of slavery.

Moreover, another example can be found in the selection of Georgia. A relative latecomer to the system in contrast with Virginia and Massachusetts, slavery in Georgia nonetheless took on spectacular proportions with the shift of slave populations to the newly profitable economy of cotton during the nineteenth century.

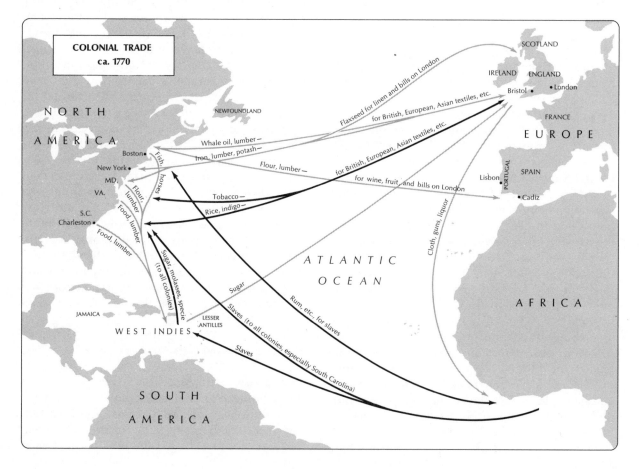

The South Atlantic system of New World slavery encompassed what is now the southern United States, waning as it approached the northern and western extremities of the South. Factors of geography, demography, economics, and politics were unfavorable for entrenchment of the system outside of the South, as will be shown in the articles treating the selected states of Missouri and of Kansas (especially), states located to the north and west of the heartland of the slave South.

Whether in the Deep South, where it was firmly entrenched, or in the North and West, where it was peripheral, the diversity of slavery was everywhere permeated with common attributes. Slavery *was* slavery, regardless of its existence in place and time. Despite individual exceptions within the vastness of the system, slavery showed unquestionably the following attributes: (1) slave societies were racist in both theory and practice: white over black (white supremacy) was axiomatic throughout the American social order; (2) slavery was dehumanizing: this "peculiar" property was constantly relegated to a subhuman status (though admittedly higher than cattle or livestock with whom slaves were classified for tax purposes); (3) slavery was coercive and oppressive, whether paternally mild or viciously violent; and (4) slaves invariably resented slavery and resisted in a variety of ways, from silent accommodation ("approval") to active rebellion.

Virginia In 1619 a "Dutch Man of War" sold "twenty and odd negars [Negroes]" to the "Cape merchant" of the Virginia Company in Jamestown. The merchant had no authority to trade with the Dutch and was, in effect, smuggling. With limited evidence, many experts have believed that these were the first blacks to arrive in the New World. They were "indentured servants" because Virginia at the time had neither a slave code nor a previous history of slavery. But Negro slavery had existed in Portugal, Spain, the Canaries, the Madeiras, and the West Indies—places all known to the English—for 100 to 200 years. The early Virginians understood black slavery, and were tough and opportunistic. The Dutch undoubtedly brought the Virginians slaves captured from the Spanish, and the Virginians were under no legal obligation to limit the service of the blacks at the time of purchase. It therefore seems likely that slavery existed informally and on a small scale from 1619 onward. This was the way in which slavery came into all of the New World colonies; laws defining slavery appeared only after the institution itself was established.

However, some of the blacks who came into Virginia were not slaves. Many free blacks, as well as slaves, worked in the major ports and served as sailors around the Atlantic. The Spanish and Portuguese often encouraged emancipation. By 1648 about 300 blacks lived in Virginia, most of them supplied illegally by the Dutch who exchanged them for Virginia tobacco. Most were slaves, but some were free; a very few even owned their own plantations.

After 1660 slavery increased rapidly. The English drove the Dutch from their colonial carrying trade, and forced their way into the African slave trade. English slavers now came directly from Africa to Virginia. Between 1660 and 1705 Virginia developed a comprehensive slave code, and in 1691 outlawed the practice of freeing Negroes unless those freed should leave the colony within six months. By 1715 Virginia had approximately 23,000 blacks among 72,500 whites. For the next 60 years the black population gained rapidly, for during this era the British dominated the Atlantic slave trade. Most of the blacks came directly from Africa in large English ships; New Englanders had only a small role in the slave trade, contrary to the popular belief. Yankees were important, however, in the carrying of food and timber from Virginia to the West Indies, and returning with tropical products, especially rum and sugar. They did bring a few thousand Negroes as well, who, having lived in the West Indies, contributed to the cosmopolitan makeup of the Virginia population. Compared to Jamaica or South Carolina, the introduction of blacks into Virginia was quite gradual, and at no time did blacks, let alone native Africans, outnumber whites.

Virginia's slave code was as harsh as any in the New World. Blacks, even if free, could not hold any civil, military, or religious office in the colony. After 1723 they were totally disfranchised. The power of masters was absolute except that murdering a slave was held a crime, and a few whites were actually hanged for it in the colonial era. But despite many suggestions from the home government and the Church of England, Virginians passed no laws to enhance the morals, education, or faith of their slaves.

Few poor whites lived in colonial Virginia. More than three-fourths of the white families in the colony owned slaves. Most of them owned farms of a few hundred acres and from one to twenty blacks. Many great estates existed in colonial Virginia that used dozens or even hundreds of slaves and that employed staffs of white artisans and overseers to train and direct them. More than half the blacks of colonial Virginia lived on family farms and worked under the direct supervision of a white farmer and his wife. Such people practiced a self-sufficient agriculture, and produced tobacco for cash or for trading purposes. The great planters did the same thing, but on a much larger scale. Though tobacco was Virginia's major export, appreciable quantities of furs, hides, grains, and lumber were shipped to England or to the West Indies. Agriculture was basic, but Negroes worked in everything. They moved goods in rafts and sailing craft, and served as carpenters, blacksmiths, coopers, masons, and grooms. Men as well as women were domestic servants. Many colonial Negroes could read, write, and keep accounts; many knew two or more languages.

No reliable records were kept on the mixing of races, but it is worth noting that Virginia continued to import white servants right up to the American Revolution. After 1691 the main reason for the growth of the free black population, besides natural increase, was a law that held that the condition of the child followed that of its mother, and many white Virginia servant girls had children by blacks. While most Virginia planters were married and appear not to have been promiscuous, thousands of single white servant men and overseers were always around. After the very early years, no one seems to have restrained them from taking black mistresses. The Virginians also enslaved Indians captured in war, or hired friendly Indians for periods of many years. Inevitably many of these mated with white servants as well as with black slaves. By the time of the American Revolution the slave population of Virginia was by no means purely African in racial descent; it may have been as much as 20 percent European and American Indian in ancestry.

Though encouraged in only a few parishes, many Afro-Americans had become practicing Christians by the 1720s, the date the bishop of London surveyed the situation. After 1750 masses of slaves became converts to the new Evangelical Christianity, and many black lay preachers appeared. In 1771 a black Baptist church formed in Williamsburg. The conversion of Afro-Americans made abolitionists out of many churchmen, and the cause of Afro-American freedom spread to intellectuals of the Enlighten-

ment. No general antislavery movement existed in white Virginia at any time, but many individuals, especially the deeply religious, wished to free their own slaves and perhaps others. Supported by the libertarian and equalitarian ideals of the American Revolution, Virginia's emancipators succeeded in 1782 in repealing the old anti-emancipation law, and the number of free blacks in the state rose from 3,000 to 13,000 in a decade. But in spite of the guarded approval of George Washington, Thomas Jefferson, George Wythe, and St. George Tucker, programs for general emancipation were never taken up (even for study) by Virginia government. In the census of 1790 Virginia (including Kentucky) had more than 300,000 Afro-Americans—almost half the total for the United States.

With the foreign slave trade ending, Virginia became the leading source of slaves for the westward movement. At first Virginia slaves stocked Kentucky and Tennessee. From these outposts and from Virginia herself slaves later poured into the lower Mississippi and the "Black Belt." Virginia lost her monopoly on the British tobacco market, and failed to keep pace with Pennsylvania in food exports after 1800. With the rise of the "Cotton Kingdom," and with agriculture lagging, surplus slaves became Virginia's most valuable export, and Richmond became a leading domestic slave market. But agriculture revived after 1830, partly because of the movement toward scientific farming led by Edmund Ruffin.

Some Afro-Americans resisted slavery throughout its history in Virginia. Records of runaways exist as far back as 1640. Rebellion first occurred in the 1680s, and a widespread revolt erupted in 1709 whose object was escape and not the overthrow of the white government. In 1800 Gabriel Prosser, a Richmond slave whose master allowed him to work on his own, organized a large conspiracy to free all the blacks of Virginia. Flooding rains and the inexperience of the leaders would have probably doomed it to failure, but on the eve of the scheduled revolt two slaves informed their masters of the conspiracy, and the leaders were captured, tried, and executed.

Frightened by Prosser's determination and by the black revolution in Haiti, Virginians again outlawed emancipation, forbade black schools, and began considering the colonization of surplus Afro-Americans, especially freedmen. Virginians never consistently obeyed the laws requiring them to supervise their slaves closely.

In 1831 Nat Turner, a black preacher, began

the most renowned slave revolt in United States history. Small compared to the many rebellions that punctuated West Indian and Brazilian history, it nevertheless terrified white southerners, especially as it coincided with the rise of William Lloyd Garrison's supercharged antislavery campaigns. The black rebels killed about 60 white Virginians and suffered more than 100 losses before they were overpowered. Nat Turner—caught, tried, and executed—had made it clear that he understood the injustice of slavery and the inherent right of revolution. He also believed himself an instrument of God's vengeance.

Though Virginia felt the growing tension of the struggle over slavery and sided with the Confederacy, the last 30 years of Virginia slavery were comparatively mild. Many blacks were freed by special acts of the state government, and the free blacks were prolific in spite of legal and economic discrimination. In 1860, 58,042 free blacks and 490,865 slaves lived in the Old Dominion—more than in any other state. Many free blacks owned their own land, and others were prosperous artisans in the towns. While most slaves remained in the country, slave labor was widely used in tobacco and iron-processing industries of the state, and in canal and railroad construction.

Many Virginia Afro-Americans fled to the Union lines during the Civil War, and part of the state never seceded at all. Still, the most heavily populated part of the state remained with the Confederacy until the fall of Richmond, and most Afro-Americans seem to have been loyal to their masters throughout the conflict, even though they welcomed emancipation by the victorious Union. *See also* AFRO-AMERICAN HISTORY: COLONIAL PERIOD, 1600s–1783; POPULATION.

REFERENCES: Ballagh, James C., *A History of Slavery in Virginia*, Johns Hopkins University Press, Baltimore, 1902; Blassingame, John W., *The Slave Community: Plantation Life in the Antebellum South*, Oxford University Press, New York, 1973; Craven, Wesley Frank, "Twenty Negroes to Jamestown in 1619?," *Virginia Quarterly Review*, vol. 47, pp. 416–20, 1971; Jackson, Luther P. *Free Negro Labor and Property Holding in Virginia, 1830–1860*, D. Appleton-Century Co., New York, 1942; Jordan, Winthrop D., *White Over Black: American Attitudes Toward the Negro, 1550–1812*, University of North Carolina Press, Chapel Hill, 1968; McColley, Robert, *Slavery and Jeffersonian Virginia*, University of Illinois Press, Urbana, 1964; Russell, John H., "Colored Freeman and Slave Owners in Virginia," *Journal of Negro History*, July 1916, pp. 233–42; Russell, John H., *The Free Negro in Virginia, 1619–1865*, Johns Hopkins University Press, Baltimore, 1913; Stealey, John Edmund, III, "Slavery and the Western Virginia Salt Industry," *Journal of Negro History*, April 1974, pp. 105–31; and Tate, Thaddeus W., *The Negro in Eighteenth Century Williamsburg*, University of Virginia Press, Charlottesville, 1965.

Deserted slave pens in Alexandria, Va., at the time of the Civil War. (*Brady Collection, National Archives.*)

South Carolina Afro-American slaves had a relatively greater impact upon the early history of South Carolina than upon any other colony or state. Peter H. Wood has shown in his book entitled *Black Majority* (1974) just how much blacks were an integral and essential part of the cattle and rice economy of the colony. Embarking from ships with the first settlers in the 1660s, the black pioneers, he suggest, bringing over an earlier African heritage (by way of Gambia), developed animal husbandry to the extent that the word "cowboy" in the American language is a "holdover reflective of the early and persistent black involvement" with cattle. Moreover, he points out that the development of South Carolina as a rice colony depended upon the skills and labor of black pioneers whose ancestors, alone of all Carolinians, had mastered its culture back in Africa. "The mastery of rice," Wood says, "paralleled closely in time the emergence of a black majority in the colony's population." Although the cultivation of rice was to spread later to other areas of the South, South Carolina produced from 60 to 80 percent of the nation's rice crop up to the Civil War (1860s).

South Carolina was the only colony in which blacks outnumbered whites (by more than two to one in the middle of the eighteenth century). The black population was and remained most dense in the lowland coastal districts (counties) of Charleston, Colleton, Beaufort, and Georgetown, destinations for spectacular importations of slaves after 1720. It has been reliably estimated that about 40 percent of all slaves coming to the American mainland entered through the port of Charleston. By the early 1800s, however, the importations had drastically declined, perhaps because of factors related to economic oversupply and fear of slave rebellion. Moreover, rice cultivation declined relatively as the cotton culture came to the state and to the entire Deep South after 1800.

Equally as important as the shifts toward cotton culture was the shift in population. The great majorities of Afro-Americans in the state declined as South Carolinians moved westward or sold their slaves to the developing areas to the south and southwest. Charleston once again, as in its colonial heyday, bustled with the sales of slaves. One writer in the Charleston *Mercury* (L. W. Spratt, who advocated the reopening of the Atlantic slave trade) stated that in the 1850s about

Slave auction in Charleston, S.C., being held at the old slave market near the wharf. A male slave (center, beneath flag) is undergoing an examination prior to being sold. Near the end of the platform (right) the auctioneer sells a mother and child. The sketch, made from an original by Theodore R. Davis, appeared in *Harper's Weekly*, July 13, 1861. (*Library of Congress*.)

1,000 slaves were drawn away from Charleston by attractive prices in the developing states west of South Carolina.

As a slave market, Charleston caught the attention of such visitors as the artist Eyre Crowe (1824–1910), who sketched a scene at the market in the 1850s, and of Theodore R. Davis, who also made a sketch in the 1860s. Slave sales also caught the attention of historian Ulrich B. Phillips, who wrote one of his early essays about Charleston, entitled "The Slave Problem in the Charleston District" (*Political Science Quarterly*, 1907). Phillips examined countless manuscript bills of sales at the archives in the state capitol in Columbia. His findings on slave prices in Charleston, still valid, show the average prices for prime (best) field hands.

Despite the emigration of and sales of slaves, the black population of South Carolina increased throughout the first half of the nineteenth century, from about 140,000 in 1800 to about 412,000 in 1860. By 1820 Afro-Americans once again outnumbered whites in the state's total population: 265,000 to 237,000; and black majorities continued throughout the remainder of the century. In 1800 the free black population of South Carolina numbered 3,185, or 2.1 percent of the total black population. In 1820 the number of

PRICES FOR BEST FIELD HANDS

Year	Price	Year	Price
1800	$500	1830	$ 450
1801	550	1831	475
1802	550	1832	500
1803	575	1833	525
1804	600	1834	650
1805	550	1835	750
1806	550	1836	1100
1807	525	1837	1200
1808	550	1838	1000
1809	500	1839	1000
1810	500	1840	800
1811	550	1841	650
1812	500	1842	600
1813	450	1843	500
1814	450	1844	500
1815	500	1845	550
1816	600	1846	650
1817	650	1847	750
1819	850	1848	700
1820	725	1849	650
1822	650	1850	700
1823	600	1851	750
1824	500	1852	800
1825	500	1853	900
1826	475	1855	900
1827	475	1858	950
1828	450	1859	1100
1829	475	1860	1200

free blacks was 6,826; in 1840 it had increased to 8,276; and in 1860 the number of free blacks in the state totaled 9,914, or 2.4 percent of the black population.

Far left: Slave tags. (The Charleston Museum.)

Charleston remained the chief city in the state throughout the slave period. Not only was it preeminent in culture and politics, it was the center of the state's largest slave and free black communities. For example, of the city's total population of 24,780 in 1820, some 12,652 were slaves and 1,475 were free blacks. In 1840, of 29,261 inhabitants, 14,673 were slaves and 1,558 free blacks. In the next 20 years the proportion of slaves declined, so that in 1860 Charleston had a population of 40,522, of whom 13,909 were slaves and 3,237 free blacks. The actual number of slaves in the city always exceeded these census figures since many were "hired out" to work in Charleston, and in addition many slaves spent a few months a year in Charleston while accompanying their master on his annual trip to the city.

To a large extent, black and white Charlestonians worked in similar occupations, often side by side. A special census of Charleston, taken in 1848, reveals the variety of occupations engaged in by artisans. Some of the selected occupations, invariably skilled or semiskilled, are shown in the table below.

In addition to these occupations, and in sharp contrast to employment of whites, many miscellaneous jobs were performed primarily by blacks: the largest single category was domestic services, employing 3,384 slave women, 1,888 slave men, and only 37 free blacks, of whom 28 were women. Surprisingly, 100 white women and 13 white males were also listed as domestic servants. Another large category listed laborers, of whom 838 were slave men, 378 were slave women, 192 were white males, and 19 were "free colored" males. The occupation employing the greatest number of "free colored" women (196) was seamstress; it was also the occupation employing the greatest number of white women (125).

Some historians suspect that slave life in South Carolina may have been relatively more harsh and rigorous than in other states, especially in the eighteenth century, due to such contributing factors as responses to population pressures, health conditions in the lowlands, and a high incidence of absentee ownership. More suspicion, however, seems to have surrounded slave revolts or conspiracies, and it is known that South Carolina had its ample share of both. Records of revolts or

OCCUPATIONAL CENSUS OF CHARLESTON FOR 1848

	Whites		Slaves		Free Blacks	
	Men	Women	Men	Women	Men	Women
Artisans						
Carpenters and joiners	120		110		27	
Masons and stonecutters	67		68		10	
Painters and plasterers	18		16		4	
Plumbers and gas fitters	9					
Wharf builders	2		10			
Boot and shoemakers	30		6		17	
Tailors and cap makers	68	6	36		42	6
Bleachers and dyers	5					
Hair braiders and wig makers	3	2				
Barbers and hairdressers		6	4	14		
Bakers	35	1	39		1	
Butchers	10		5		1	
Blacksmiths	45		40		4	
Coopers	20		61		2	
Engineers	43					
Printers	65		5			

SOURCE: J. L. Dawson and H. D. DeSaussure, *Census of Charleston for 1848*, Charleston, 1849, pp. 31–36.

unrest exist for 1711 and again for 1720. One of the best-known revolts in the eighteenth century was the Stono Rebellion in 1739, which was named after a plantation in St. Paul's Parish (about 20 miles from Charleston). Peter H. Wood, perhaps with more attention than any other historian, has examined this revolt. "It is impossible," he says, "to emphasize the small scale and ultimate failure of the uprising at Stono or to stress, on the other hand, its large potential and near success." He found that such elements as "total surprise, ruthless killing, considerable property damage, armed engagements, protracted aftermath—are singular in South Carolina's early history." The aftermath of the Stono Rebellion included another plot the following year, allegedly involving about 200 slaves; as a result, 50 slaves were publicly executed at the rate of 10 a day.

Even better known than the Stono Rebellion is the plot attributed to Denmark Vesey in 1822. Since a great deal of hysteria, rumor, hearsay, and intimidation surrounded the incident— with little or no evidence—some historians have doubted if any plot occurred at all. Certainly, Vesey and his alleged coconspirators never admitted conspiracy despite duress at their irregular trials.

More is known about the trial and its immediate aftermath than about either Vesey and his alleged plot. Fluent in several languages, Vesey, an ex-slave and seaman, was an artisan residing in Charleston in relatively comfortable circumstances. He was executed along with 34 other blacks. Many more had been arrested, including several whites and a slave belonging to the governor of the state. *See also* AFRICA: THE ATLANTIC SLAVE TRADE WITH THE CAROLINA RICE COAST; AFRO-AMERICAN HISTORY; POPULATION.

REFERENCES: For studies of the free black in Charleston, see Fritchett, E. Horace, "The Traditions of the Free Negro in Charleston, South Carolina," *Journal of Negro History*, vol. 25, pp. 139–52, 1940; Fritchett, E. Horace, "The Origin and Growth of the Free Negro Population of Charleston, South Carolina," *Journal of Negro History*, vol. 26, pp. 421–37, 1941; and Senese, Donald J., "The Free Negro and the South Carolina Courts," *South Carolina Historical Magazine*, July 1967, pp. 140–53. For additional information on slavery in South Carolina, see Aptheker, Herbert, *American Negro Slave Revolts*, 2d. ed., International Publishers, New York, 1963; Lofton, John, *Insurrection in South Carolina: The Turbulent World of Denmark Vesey*, Antioch Press, Yellow Springs, 1964; Phillips, Ulrich B., "The Slave Labor Problem in the Charleston District," *Political Science Quarterly*, September 1907, pp. 416–39; Wade, Richard C., *Slavery in the Cities: The South, 1820–1860*, Oxford University Press, New York, 1964; and Wood, Peter H., *Black Majority: Negroes in Colonial South Carolina From 1670 Through the Stono Rebellion*, Alfred A. Knopf, New York, 1974.

Massachusetts Black slaves came to Massachusetts Bay shortly after the Puritans settled in Plymouth in 1620. The date generally agreed upon for their arrival in the colony is 1638, the year in which John Winthrop recorded the return of the *Desire* from a voyage to the West Indies. The *Desire*, captained by William Pierce, had sailed for the Caribbean with captured Pequot Indians who were sold into slavery there. The vessel returned to Massachusetts with a cargo that included Negroes, in addition to cotton and tobacco. Before a year had passed, the English traveler John Josselyn learned of an unsuccessful attempt at slave breeding by Samuel Maverick on Noddles Island, one of the few such recorded instances in the province.

The number of slaves in the Bay Colony was comparatively small, in part because Massachusetts did not have the same labor needs as the plantation colonies to the south. Agriculture was on a small scale, and was only part of a diversified economy that used slave labor in a variety of occupations from the routine to the highly skilled. Slaves, for example, could be found in shipbuilding, lumbering, fishing, cooperage, farming, and domestic service.

The size of the slave population remains uncertain because the censuses, in addition to being generally unreliable, counted all Negroes in one figure, without distinguishing between slave and free. In the census of 1715, the first general census in New England by race, the Afro-American population in Massachusetts was estimated at 2,000 inhabitants. By 1776 the Afro-American population had increased to 5,249 and the white population to an estimated 343,845. Throughout this period, the largest concentration of slaves in the province was in the town of Boston. While the census of 1790 was the first federal census (and the first census analyzing the population as to free and slave), slavery had been virtually abolished in the state by that year. Accordingly, Massachusetts was reported as having 5,369 free blacks.

Beginning in the 1680s and continuing into the eighteenth century, laws were enacted that codified to a certain extent the relations of whites to blacks and masters to slaves. The General Court directed the earliest of these codes at runaway slaves by ordering in 1680 that no ship was to sail from the harbor or entertain on board "any passenger or passengers, or any servant or negro" without a permit from the governor. Conditions for emancipation were specified in Chapter I of the laws of 1703, which required every master to post a bond as security for the support of each slave freed so as to lessen the burden of indigents on the town. No doubt this proved a hindrance to emancipation because some masters failed to pay the stated sum. To prevent miscegenation, the colony passed "An Act for the Better Preventing of a Spurious and Mist Issue" (1705), which prohibited marriage between a black or "mulatto" and any member of a "Christian nation." Another section of the same law provided that any black or mulatto who struck a white man would be "severely" whipped.

The Massachusetts slave occupied the dual status of property and person before the law. In the first tax laws of the province, the slave was rated as a person on the tax lists, but this status was changed by a law of 1698 that declared "all Indian, mulatto and negro servants to be estimated as other personal estate...." (The term servant was often used to refer to a slave.) While the Afro-American slave was classified with domestic animals on tax lists and as personal possessions in wills and inventories of estates, evidence exists to show that he enjoyed such basic legal rights of a person as trial by jury and the right to legal counsel. Slaves could own property; they could receive a governor's pardon, and their testimony could be entered against whites. In trials for major as well as minor crimes, slaves generally received equitable treatment in the courts. One notable exception, however, occurred in 1681 when a slave, Maria, was burned alive after being convicted of burning her master's home and causing the death of a baby.

The slave's resistance to his bondage involved use of his legal rights. Some Afro-American slaves instituted freedom suits against their masters in which the master was sued for restraining the slave's liberty, often by questioning the validity of the master's title. Although the information about these cases is fragmentary, among the most well-known are: *Slew v. Whipple* (1766); *James v. Lechmere* (1769); and *Caesar v. Greenleaf* (1773). John Adams wrote to Rev. Jeremy Belknap, a Congregational minister, that he never knew a jury to find a Negro a slave. However, in at least one case, *Newport v. Billing* (1768), the court declared that the plaintiff was not a free man and was therefore the proper slave of the defendant.

Slaves also brought petitions to the General Court in which they related their cause to that of the American Revolution and the natural rights argument. In a petition of May 1774 a group of slaves addressed Thomas Gage, the last royal governor of Massachusetts Bay, and the Massachusetts house of representatives: "We therfor Bage . . . that you will accordingly cause an act of the legislature to be passed that we may obtain our Natural right our freedoms and our children be set at liberty at the yeare of twenty one. . . ." Another petition of January 1777 did not hesitate to note the blatant discrepancy between American demands for freedom in the struggle with Great Britain and the tolerance of domestic slavery. These efforts continually failed as Massachusetts, though having considered the issue several times, never enacted a law emancipating the slaves.

Not only did Massachusetts maintain slaves internally, but also some of her merchants engaged in the Atlantic slave trade. Laden with such commodities as dry goods, silversmiths' wares, candles, iron, and especially New England rum, a vessel would set sail for the Cape Verde Islands and the coast of West Africa where the goods would be sold and Negroes and gold dust purchased. On the return voyage slaves were sold in the West Indies, the Southern colonies, and some were brought to Massachusetts. Thus it was not uncommon to find in the local papers such an advertisement as the following from the Boston *News Letter*, June 10, 1762: "Just Imported from Africa, a Number Slaves from the Windward Coast. To be seen at a store on Mr. Griffin's Wharf." This trade in human beings was finally outlawed in 1788 when "An act to prevent the slave trade, and for granting relief to the families of such unhappy persons as may be kidnapped or decoyed away from the Commonwealth" was passed, but instances of illicit trading by shipowners and captains occurred long after.

By 1790 slavery had virtually ceased to exist within the state. Its demise came gradually, almost imperceptibly, and remains the subject of historical inquiry. While the details cannot be completely reconstructed, it is evident that the Massachusetts constitution of 1780 and the case of *Commonwealth v. Jennison* (1783) played an important part in abolition. Article I in the declaration of rights of that constitution declared "All men are born free and equal, and have certain natural, essential, and unalienable rights. . . ." Whether this article meant to free the slaves is not clear from the context, and its intent caused confusion among the people. As the status of slave property became uncertain, some instances of self-emancipation occurred. Rev. Jeremy Belknap noted shortly thereafter: "Many of the blacks, taking advantage of the publick opinion and of this general assertion in the bill of rights asked for their freedom, and obtained it. Others took it without leave." The needed exposition of Article I was provided by Chief Justice William Cushing's charge to the jury in *Commonwealth v. Jennison*. The chief justice stated that "slavery is in my judgment as effectively abolished as it can be by the granting of rights and privileges wholly incompatible and repugnant to its existence."

As we have seen, the General Court did not outlaw slavery, and no evidence exists that *Commonwealth v. Jennison* was used as a legal precedent prior to 1790. Yet in that year Massachusetts reported no slaves in the state. It should be noted that isolated instances of slaveholding may have persisted, for testimony in *Watson v. Cambridge* (1818) proved that in 1793 Venus Whittemore was sold at a public auction to William Watson of Cambridge. Nevertheless, the census of 1790 is considered, in the words of Jeremy Belknap, the "formal evidence" of slavery's abolition in Massachusetts. *See also* AFRICA: THE ATLANTIC SLAVE TRADE IN PERSPECTIVE; AFRO-AMERICAN HISTORY.

REFERENCES: Cushing, John D., "The Cushing Court and the Abolition of Slavery in Massachusetts: More Notes on 'the Quock Walker Case,'" *American Journal of Legal History*, vol. 5, April 1961; Donnan, Elizabeth, "The New England Slave Trade after the Revolution," *New England Quarterly*, vol. 3, April 1930; Greene, Lorenzo J., *The Negro in Colonial New England, 1620–1776*, Columbia University Press, New York, 1942; MacEacheren, Elaine, "Emancipation of Slavery in Massachusetts: A Reexamination, 1770–1790," *Journal of Negro History*, October 1970, pp. 289–306; Moore, George H., *Notes on the History of Slavery in Massachusetts*, D. Appleton & Company, New York, 1866; Twombley, Robert C. and Robert H. Moore, "Black Puritan: The Negro in Seventeenth Century Massachusetts," *William and Mary Quarterly*, vol. 24, April 1967; and Zilversmit, Arthur, *The First Emancipation: The Abolition of Slavery in the North*, University of Chicago Press, Chicago, 1967.

Pennsylvania Blacks were living near the Delaware River, in an area that later became a part of Pennsylvania, many years before the founding of that colony. The Swedes and Dutch, whose settlements preceded those of the English by many decades, are known to have imported blacks and to have used them as slaves. Unable to interest large numbers of Dutch settlers in their colony of New Netherland, the directors of the Dutch West India Company early decided on a policy of acquiring laborers from Africa. In 1664, the year that New Netherland fell to the English, a Dutch vessel transported a cargo of some 300 blacks to the area of the Delaware River, called by the Dutch the South River.

Thus it was not left to William Penn and other early settlers who came to Pennsylvania after 1681 to inaugurate the slave trade and the practice of employing slave labor, a practice common to all of colonial America. Building on former Dutch practices, colonists in Pennsylvania continued to rely on the services of slaves, often, it appears, preferring the labor of black slaves to the labor of white servants. Penn himself, when sending a servant from London in 1685 to serve as a gardener at his estate at Pennsbury, remarked that "It were better they were blacks, for then a man has ym [sic] while they live." Other residents were also inclined to employ slave labor, and in the last two decades of the seventeenth century small numbers of blacks filtered into Pennsylvania, most of them shipped upon request from the West Indian islands. These slaves served as agricultural laborers and house servants, and together with their white masters they began the process of carving out a new society along the shores of the Delaware River.

By 1700 somewhere between 400 and 500 blacks were living in Pennsylvania, most of them in the immediate vicinity of Philadelphia. As their numbers grew, it seemed necessary that they be controlled and circumscribed in their behavior. Already in 1693 the provincial council had expressed concern about "the tumultuous gatherings of the negroes in the towne of Philadelphia, on the first dayes of the weeke." The colonial assembly that met in 1700 enacted two statutes that can be regarded as the beginning of a slave code; one was "for regulating *Negroes* in their Morals, and Marriages," while the other dealt with "*Negroes, and their trials.*" As happened in all the English colonies, Pennsylvania had begun the process of setting blacks apart from the general community, imposing on them restrictions that were not applicable to the population at large, and providing by law for their perpetual enslavement.

The gradual circumscription of blacks, resulting finally in their enslavement by law, took place in a colony that, paradoxically, early established itself as the New World home of antislavery sentiment. Peopled at the outset by members of the Religious Society of Friends, or Quakers, Pennsylvania was noted for its early and consistent attack against buying, selling, and enslaving Africans. The first protest against the institution of slavery in the English colonies was written by a group of German settlers who had taken up homes at Germantown, on the outskirts of Philadelphia. Written in 1688, the Germantown Protest was an eloquent plea "against the traffick of mens-body." Other attacks on both the slave trade and slavery followed. In 1693, for example, a group of Quakers, followers of George Keith, published and circulated a small tract entitled *An Exhortation & Caution to Friends Concerning Buying or Keeping of Negroes.* Other Quakers, including Cadwalader Morgan, Robert Pyle, and Pentecost Teague, made public declarations against the institution of slavery before the seventeenth century ended, but their views, while they gave many Quakers pause and led to some public discussion, were not the views of the majority, not even the majority of Quakers. Pennsylvania thus entered the eighteenth century, like other English communities in America, committed to a policy of enslaving black Africans.

Yet Pennsylvania was never a flourishing slave society. Located in a temperate climatic zone, Pennsylvania did not depend on staple agricultural produce such as tobacco, rice, or indigo, and did not develop anything approximating the plantation system that emerged further south. The labor demand in Pennsylvania—where the economy was highly diversified and included agriculture, manufacturing, and commerce—was for skilled laborers capable of performing a variety of tasks.

Blacks, however, were not altogether excluded by either the climate, agricultural patterns, or labor requirements. As the eighteenth century progressed, the black population grew, due both to natural increase and to importation of slaves from other areas. Until the 1750s, most of the slaves brought into Pennsylvania were acquired in the West Indies and were shipped north in small lots, numbering at most 35 or 40 slaves.

During the middle decades of the century, however, especially during the 1760s, Philadelphia merchants sent slaving vessels directly to the west coast of Africa and brought back cargoes containing as many as 150 and 200 slaves. But the trade, compared with that conducted in the southern continental colonies and the West Indies, was small indeed; during the peak year of the slave trade (1762), no more than about 500 or 600 slaves were imported. Nevertheless, the slave population reached 2,000 by 1720, and had increased to almost 6,000 by 1770. Slavery continued to be centered in the southeastern portion of the colony, in the area of Philadelphia—including Bucks and Chester counties—and later in Lancaster, Montgomery, and York counties.

Whether employed as farm workers, in such expanding manufacturing enterprises as the iron industry, or as domestic servants in Philadelphia households, slaves were usually owned by masters who kept only small groups of slaves. Some ironmasters employed as many as 10 or 12 slaves, and such artisans as sailmakers sometimes kept as many as 6. It was much more likely, however, that the slaves were held by masters who owned no more than two or three blacks—often a man, his wife, and their children. For slaves who worked as agricultural laborers, the reality of their everyday lives meant close and extended contact with the white community. In this kind of environment it must be supposed that blacks had experiences not available to slaves who lived under the plantation regime that existed further south. In close daily contact with the white community, Pennsylvania slaves were able to acquire a facility in the English language and to assume aspects of the dominant European culture. This was no less true for slaves who served in other capacities. White artisans and craftsmen, for example, frequently owned slaves who were skilled apprentices and who worked side by side with their owners as bakers, masons, carpenters, shoemakers, tailors, and millers. In 1767 Philadelphia artisans owned slaves trained as hatters, skinners, brushmakers, sugar boilers, distillers, candlers, coopers, clockmakers, joiners, barbers, and brewers. In addition, some slaves were highly skilled goldsmiths and silversmiths. Those slaves who served as house servants commonly performed such tasks as cooking, washing, ironing, and tending children. In terms of their material well-being, slaves probably fared as well in Pennsylvania as anywhere in the English colonies; what is known about their clothing, diet,

Far left: Street scene in Philadelphia by William Birch toward the end of the 1700s. *(Library of Congress.)*

and living conditions suggests that while standards were by no means generous they were at least adequate.

The slaves posed few serious problems for the white community, although whites sometimes convinced themselves that slaves were entertaining ideas of a mass uprising or insurrection. One such occasion was in 1712, following a serious slave revolt in the neighboring colony of New York. In countless less dramatic ways, however, slaves in Pennsylvania demonstrated their opposition to the institution of slavery. The problem of runaways, for example, judging from newspaper advertisements, was persistent.

Meanwhile, opposition to slavery among whites continued to grow, with, of course, mixed motives: laborers opposed importations of additional slaves because they competed with free labor in the marketplace; others were anxious to limit slavery because of racial fears of a large black population. But the humanitarian impulse that had been sounded by Quakers also broadened during the century, in large measure the product of a group of sensitive and committed individuals who considered slavery a monstrous evil in violation of the basic laws of nature and of man. Such Quaker pamphleteers as Ralph Sandiford, Benjamin Lay, and Anthony Benezet publicized the cruelties of slavery. John Woolman, the epitome of the concerned Quaker of the eighteenth century, not only wrote extensively against slavery, but also visited Friends who owned slaves and pleaded with them to set their slaves at liberty. On the eve of the American Revolution, Benjamin Rush, another dedicated antislaveryite, could say that "Great events have been brought about by small beginnings. Anthony Benezet stood alone a few years ago in opposing Negroe slavery in Philadelphia and now three-fourths of the province as well as the City cry out against it."

The outbreak of the Revolutionary War precipitated a heated debate over the question of extending liberty to enslaved blacks. After all, it seemed inconsistent to charge the British with imposing a tyranny over Americans at the same time that Americans kept tens of thousands of Afro-Americans in chains. The discussion of the rights of man and of the institution of slavery culminated in Pennsylvania with the passage in 1780 of an "Act for the Gradual Abolition of Slavery." Although not without its defects, this act nonetheless gave to Pennsylvania the distinction of being the first state to pass a law for the abolition of slavery. The act freed no slaves immediately, for it applied only to unborn children who were to be granted their freedom after reaching the age of 28. Other weaknesses were also apparent in this statute, and eight years later, in 1788, it was amended and certain loopholes closed. In the years that followed, the slave population of Pennsylvania gradually declined, with a corresponding increase of the free black population. The federal census of 1790 reported that of 10,274 blacks, 3,737 were still held as slaves. Ten years later there were 1,706 slaves, and by 1810, 795 blacks were counted as slaves. It was not until the census of 1850 that, for the first time, Pennsylvania could correctly be labeled a free state. Slavery had never flourished there, but neither was it easily and swiftly eradicated. *See also* AFRO-AMERICAN HISTORY; QUAKERS; SLAVERY: THE ABOLITIONISTS.

REFERENCES: Drake, Thomas E., *Quakers and Slavery in America*, Yale University Press, New Haven, 1950; Turner, Edward R., *The Negro in Pennsylvania, Slavery-Servitude-Freedom, 1639–1861*, American Historical Association, Washington, D.C., 1911; Wax, Darold D., "The Demand for Slave Labor in Colonial Pennsylvania," *Pennsylvania History*, vol. 34, pp. 331–45, 1967; Wax, Darold D., "Quaker Merchants and the Slave Trade in Colonial Pennsylvania," *Pennsylvania Magazine of History and Biography*, vol. 86, pp. 143–59, 1962; and Zilversmit, Arthur, *The First Emancipation: The Abolition of Slavery in the North*, University of Chicago Press, Chicago, 1967.

Georgia Aside from being the last of the 13 English mainland colonies in America to be founded, Georgia differed from the other 12 in several significant respects. Its charter gave control of the colony to a board of 21 trustees who were to manage the affairs of the province for a stated period of time, but who were denied the right to make a personal profit from the arrangement. Projected as a bulwark against Spanish attacks from Florida upon the Carolina settlements, Georgia was designed as a place of settlement for imprisoned English debtors and persecuted Protestants. This fact helps to explain the initial ban on slavery in the colony. Slaves were excluded by the trustees in an act of 1735 "for rendering the Colony of Georgia more defensible by Prohibiting the Importation and use of Black Slaves or Negroes into the same." The expectation that the colony would serve as a defense against inroads by the Spanish precluded the introduction of Negroes who might be tempted to join the enemy. This decision of the trustees also coincided with their intention to provide an area of settlement for a class of persons presumably too indigent to buy slaves, but who would be expected to work their own small holdings of land for the benefit of themselves and the mother country.

Within five years after the arrival of the first group of settlers, discontent over the prohibition of slavery appeared. Through petitions, malcontents within the colony began to demand the privilege of importing blacks. When their requests were denied, some Georgians began the practice of hiring slaves from their South Carolina neighbors. Continued agitation against the ban brought the desired result when in 1749 the prohibition was lifted. Authorization went into effect on January 1, 1750, thus recognizing as legal a practice that to all intents and purposes already operated. It should be noted that among the early settlers of Georgia were Lutherans and Scottish Highlanders who opposed slavery for moral or economic reasons, and had no desire to see the institution introduced into the colony.

Determined to make the conditions under which slaves were brought into the colony as humane as possible, certain safeguards were written into the law that reversed the exclusion policy. The ratio of male slaves to white servants was set at four to one. Slaveholders were denied the right to exercise unlimited power over their bondsmen, while Sunday was set aside as a day of rest and attendance at church services. The sanctity of marriage was to be taught to the slaves, but intermarriage between blacks and whites was forbidden. The law also stipulated that Negroes be tried according to the laws of England.

In 1775 Georgia adopted its slave code, a body of laws based upon the slave code of South Carolina. This code, with modifications, remained in existence for the duration of the colonial period. The subsequent addition of specific laws rounded out the repressive legislation under which slaves lived and worked during the antebellum period of Georgia's history. The code was restrictive and negative in character, designed frankly to regulate and control the conduct of blacks. Despite safeguards intended to protect slaves from cruel treatment by masters, the code deprived the bondsmen of practically all civil, political, economic, judicial, and social rights. A special tribunal was established for their trial in which testimony by Negroes—slave or free—against a white person was not admissible. The provisions of the code were about the same as were those of other slave states. Slaves in Georgia were "deemed in the law to be chattels personal in the hands of their respective owners or possessors, and their administrators, executors,

and assigns, to all intents and purposes whatever." This provision vested in the master complete control of his "chattels personal" along with the unquestioned right to punish them when he deemed it necessary.

During the colonial period slave labor was utilized chiefly in the cultivation of rice in the coastal areas. The shift of emphasis to cotton culture, the invention of the cotton gin, and the nineteenth-century expansion of the upland cotton belt increased the number of slaves. This growth in the slave population is reflected in the following census figures: 1790/29,264; 1800/59,-406; 1810/105,218; 1820/149,656; 1830/217,531; 1840/289,944; 1850/381,682; and 1860/462,198.

Cotton was packed for baling by this cotton press in upland Georgia. (*Library of Congress.*)

As in other slave states, the majority of Georgians were not owners of such property. Out of a total free population of 595,088 in 1860, only 41,084 were owners of slaves. (The slave population in that year stood at 462,198.) Thus only 14.5 percent of the total free population was slaveholding. Another fact becomes clear as a result of a careful examination of census statistics for that year. The average holding of slaves was 11.2, with 78.9 percent of the owners holding fewer than 20 slaves. Despite the fact that by far the largest number of slaveholders held fewer than 20 slaves, it was the group of large owners—the planter oligarchy—that controlled the political life of the state and set its tone in the antebellum period. Defended by owners and nonowners alike, the state's "peculiar institution" persisted into the years of the Civil War.

The free blacks class in Georgia had its origin in immigration. Natural increase, manumission of slaves, self-purchase, and continued immigration were largely responsible for the growth of the group. The evidence indicates that some Afro-Americans were residing in the Georgia colony before 1750. The presence of free blacks was more definitely recognized in 1755 when the slave code took cognizance of "Negroes, Mulattoes or Mestizoes who are now free." A compilation of the births of 1,419 of the state's "free persons of color" in 1850 shows that 215 were born outside of Georgia, while in 1860 the records reveal that of the 3,500 free blacks residing in the state, 225 had been born elsewhere. During much of the antebellum period private manumission of slaves by owners was forbidden by law. Despite official disapproval of this practice, manumission continued as an important method of growth. Indeed, the census of 1860 reported that manumissions in Georgia had apparently "greatly increased," 160 slaves being set free in that year.

The rise of the abolition crusade, the growth of a proslavery sentiment, and the recurring fear of servile revolt were reflected in continuing hostility to the presence of free blacks. Although never comprising more than one percent of the total population, this class was the recipient of a disproportionate amount of official attention. Laws were enacted to confine their activities to innocuous pursuits, to keep them under constant surveillance, to nullify the possibility of their becoming too successful as competitors with white artisans, and to define for them an inferior social position and role in society. Despite these restrictions, however, the free black class showed an increase in numbers for every decade except one between 1790 and 1860, as shown in the following statistics: 1790/398; 1800/1,019; 1810/1,801; 1820/1,763; 1830/2,486; 1840/2,753; 1850/2,931; and 1860/3,500.

These figures reflect rather accurately the reaction of most white Georgians to the presence of Afro-Americans who were not slaves. This mood ranged from some commitment to the egalitarian philosophy of the American Revolution to a hardened determination to protect the institution of slavery.

As in other southern states, Georgia required free persons of color to have white guardians, while each year free blacks had to register in their respective county seats. Their certificates of freedom had to be kept on their person at all times, for the lack of such a certificate was presumption of slave status. Spasmodic enforcement of restrictive laws had the effect of mitigating the harshness of their provisions.

Achieving economic stability and independence proved extremely difficult for most free blacks, although they could own property. By custom and by law they were restricted to certain occupations. Employment, in the main, was confined to occupations involving menial and manual labor, personal services, and work as artisans. As farmers, their holdings were usually small and included more unimproved than improved acreage. Some unemployed free blacks lived on the largess of whites. Through hard work and the practice of thrift, others prospered and lived comfortably, while a handful were able to reach a position of comparative affluence. In this latter group were to be found those who had been endowed with worldly goods by their former masters at the time of their manumission.

The problem of class was complicated by the necessity of establishing what were deemed to be proper relationships between whites and free persons of color. As elsewhere, the acquisition of freedom fixed the free black's legal status but not his social status. Free blacks found most of their social contacts within their group. Family life on an institutional basis gradually evolved as property ownership increased. The majority lived a self-effacing life; a strident minority compensated for a somber existence by engaging in boisterous activities. All too often, the pattern of behavior of this latter segment has been regarded by superficial but articulate observers as characteristic of the entire class. Despite mores and legal arrangements, individual whites and individual free blacks in Georgia worked out their own patterns of social adjustment. *See also* AFRO-AMERICAN HISTORY.

REFERENCES: Blassingame, John W., *The Slave Community: Plantation Life in the Antebellum South,* Oxford University Press, New York, 1973; Bonner, James C., *A History of Georgia Agriculture, 1732–1860,* University of Georgia Press, Athens, 1964; Brown, John, *Slave Life in Georgia: A Narrative of the Life, Sufferings, and Escape of John Brown, A Fugitive Slave,* ed. by F. N. Boney, Beehive Press, Savannah, 1972; Flanders, Ralph B., *Plantation Slavery in Georgia,* University of North Carolina Press, Chapel Hill, 1933; Jones, J. Ralph, "Portraits of Georgia Slaves," *The Georgia Historical Review,* ed. by Tom Landes, Spring, 1967, Summer 1968; and Kemble, Frances Anne, *Journal of a Residence on a Georgia Plantation in 1838–1839,* Harper and Brothers, New York, 1863; rev. ed., John A. Scott (ed.), Alfred A. Knopf, New York, 1961.

Tennessee Tennessee, a geographically varied area, exhibited well the diverse nature of Afro-American slavery. In the eastern part of the state, slaveholdings were small and not numerous; in some parts of west Tennessee, a cotton economy based on relatively large holdings prevailed; and in middle Tennessee, a rather diversified economy was based on medium-sized holdings. Slaves constituted 19 percent of the population of the state in 1820; by 1860 the 276,000 slaves were 25 percent of the total population. However, the range of distribution was wide: in some parts of east Tennessee, only 1 slave existed for every 60 whites, while in the cotton counties of Haywood and Fayette slaves outnumbered whites.

The Tennessee slave code, derived originally from the relatively lenient one of North Carolina, so combined civil and common law that the slave had legal characteristics of both a chattel and a person. He was subject to transfer at the will of the owner; he had no legal marriage or property rights; his movements were circumscribed; his time and labor were not his own; and punishments for violation of the law or prescribed rules were usually whippings. On the other hand, he could contract for his freedom (during the early years of Tennessee statehood); he was recognized as the agent of his master (the courts held that the custom of allowing the slave to move about without the legally required pass had a force even above the law); he had the same personal responsibility as any other individual in the area of capital crimes; and Tennessee was one of five states that guaranteed him a trial by jury (composed of slaveholders) in such cases. The laws were made more severe and restrictive in the 1830s, but no evidence exists to show that these laws brought any actual change in the functioning of the institution. Owners, and others, did not always observe the laws, sometimes to the detriment of the slave and sometimes to his benefit. Regulations on work, punishment, and care were on occasion ignored, as were prohibitions against religious and other instruction, self-hire, living as a free person, emancipation without removal from the state after the 1830s, and the interstate slave trade between 1827 and 1855. The ameliorative or harshening effects of such actions are not easily measurable: much latitude was possible, and the government of slaves was as much—or more—by men as by laws.

Antislavery sentiment, while found in all parts of the state, was strongest in east Tennessee. The first paper in the United States devoted exclusively to antislavery, the weekly *Manumission Intelligencer,* began publication at Jonesboro in March 1819. In April 1820 Elihu Embree converted his paper to an octavo monthly, *The Emancipator,* and within eight months subscriptions had increased to 2,000 many times the number subscribing to Garrison's *Liberator* three

years after it started. After Embree's death in December 1820, citizens of the area asked Benjamin Lundy to move his *Genius of Universal Emancipation* among them; from April 1822 to August 1824 that paper was published at Greeneville. Antislavery sentiment continued to grow until 1827, when the 25 antislavery societies of the state claimed 1,000 members, two-thirds as many as claimed by the 24 societies in all the other free states. Within a decade, however, the societies had disappeared, and most of the major opponents of slavery (chiefly Quakers) had moved to the Northwest or ceased their overt opposition.

The rise of radical abolitionism and the change in southern sentiment that flowed from this agitation and the Nat Turner insurrection were primarily responsible for this decline of antislavery activity. Tennessee laws, however, did not show the effects of this change as quickly as did those of some other states. Antislavery delegates to the Tennessee constitutional convention of 1834 sought action by that body; they were unsuccessful, and the change of the constitution to deny the vote to free blacks indicates that the attitude of Tennesseans had hardened.

Most studies of slavery have relied upon plantation and legal records, private correspondence, newspapers, and a few other materials to study the above-mentioned and other facets of slavery, but for an understanding of the relation and importance of slavery to agricultural activity— the area in which the vast majority of slaves were employed—the use of the manuscript federal census schedules for 1850 and 20,558 in 1860, revealed some interesting interrelationships between landowning, slaveholding, and agricultural production and brings into question the validity of several generalizations about the social and economic structure of the antebellum South and of the relative position and role of the slaveholders and nonslaveholders. While allowance must be made for regional variations within the state, it was found that ownership of slaves depended more on landownership than the reverse. Thus, the landowners without slaves formed a larger part of the agricultural population in 1860 than in 1850. This fact, coupled with the statistical evidence that the nonslaveholder increased his improved acreage, as well as cotton and tobacco production, at a faster rate in the 1850s than did the slaveholder, raises serious doubts about the assertion that the slaveholders pushed others onto the poorer lands and were playing an ever-greater role in the economic and social life of the area. Only in the corn-producing counties did the slaveholders produce a greater percentage of the crop in 1860 than in 1850, and corn production in the state showed a decline during the decade. All evidence indicates that the small farmers—slaveholders and nonslaveholders—constituted a large yeoman-middle class, a vast majority of the total white population.

An analysis of the cotton production of 28 plantations in Haywood and Fayette counties—where cotton was dominant and slaves outnumbered whites—in 1850 and 1860 might be useful for those who ignore hard evidence in favor of speculation and models when considering the profitability of slavery. These planters held from 63 to 235 slaves, produced from 65 to 1,053 bales of cotton, operated from 430 to 4,150 improved acres, and owned farms valued from $6,840 to $339,000. In the two census years the total number of slaves owned was 3,250 and the total cotton production was 8,757 bales, or 2.7 bales per slave. Probably, the question of profitability of slavery will never be settled; the records are inadequate, and so many variables exist. As is true in evaluating other aspects of slavery, much depends upon time, place, and status of economic development.

REFERENCES: Some suggested references are: Clark, Blanche Henry, *Tennessee Yeomen, 1840–1860*, Nashville, 1942; Mooney, Chase C., *Slavery in Tennessee*, Greenwood Press, Westport, 1971; and Owsley, Frank L., *Plain Folk of the Old South*, Baton Rouge, 1949.

Arkansas Negro slavery existed in Arkansas for about 150 years, but it always bore the imprint of the frontier. It had its beginnings in 1720 in John Law's ill-fated colony in the lower Arkansas River valley; the slave population had a frontier sparseness and distribution, and Arkansas slaves lived and worked under frontier conditions. In the two decades before the Civil War, however, Arkansas began to lose its frontier character, and slavery became more like that in the older South. To the end, though, the influence of the frontier continued to be felt.

Only a few hundred of the large numbers of slaves that had been envisioned were brought to John Law's colony before it collapsed in 1721. Most of these were taken to the vicinity of New Orleans, but a few remained near Arkansas Post, where they and their descendants were used by the French and Spanish settlers in farming, trading, and military activities. Eventually, other settlements were formed, but until about 1800 the

number of slaves in Arkansas did not exceed 30. After the United States acquired Arkansas in 1803 as a part of the Louisiana Purchase, though, the slave population increased steadily—to 300 in 1810; to 1,617 in 1820, the year after Arkansas became a territory; and to 4,576 in 1830. After Arkansas became a state in 1836, growth was even more rapid—to 19,935 in 1840; to 47,100 in 1850; and to 111,115 in 1860.

Arkansas exceeded only Delaware, Maryland, and Florida in number of slaves, but the institution grew as long as it lasted. The rate of growth from 1820 to 1850 was far greater than in any other territory or state, and from 1850 to 1860 was surpassed only by that in Texas. The proportion of slaves in the total Arkansas population also increased—from 11 percent in 1820 to 25 percent in 1860. By contrast, the proportion of slaves in the total population of the South declined slightly, although in 1860 it was still more than one-third.

During territorial days a majority of the slaves lived in the more easily settled uplands north and west of the "highland line" bisecting Arkansas from northeast to southwest. But as lowland plantations were developed rapidly after 1836, slaves became increasingly concentrated in the southeast—three-quarters of the total by 1860. Slaves existed in all counties; but their distribution varied widely in density, ranging from less than 1 percent of the population in Newton County in the northwest to 81 percent in Chicot County in the extreme southeast. In 1860 half of the slaves lived in 10 of the 56 counties, all but one of which—Hempstead—were wholly in the southeastern lowlands. Slaves outnumbered whites in six counties—Phillips, Chicot, Union, Arkansas, Lafayette, and Desha. Fewer than four percent of the slaves lived in small cities and towns, the largest of which, Little Rock, had a total population of only 3,727 in 1860.

In keeping with the frontier character of the state, a smaller percentage of the white people of Arkansas owned slaves than in the South at large. Yet about 18 percent were owners or members of their immediate families, with about 43 percent of the total population—including the slaves—thus directly involved in slavery. In addition, many nonslaveholders—overseers, merchants, and artisans—were indirectly involved. Significantly, the slaveholding class controlled the state politically and economically, thus ensuring the perpetuation of slavery as long as possible.

The average Arkansas slaveholder in 1860

owned 9.6 slaves, only a fraction under the average of all slave states. But more owners held only one slave than any other number, and more than half held four or fewer. On the other hand, more than half of the slaves were in plantation-size holdings of 25 or more. One planter, Elisha Worthington of Chicot County, belonged to that elite group of 11 southerners owning more than 500 slaves. The large holdings, along with the widely distributed small ones, served to maintain a consciousness of slavery throughout the state.

Arkansas slaves worked at a wide variety of tasks, although—as the frontier was tamed—most of them worked as field hands on the plantations. Cotton was Arkansas' most important crop, but even on the large plantations some slaves cultivated food crops. Others were artisans or house servants or worked in small industries, river transportation, or road and railroad building.

Most Arkansas slaves lived in crude log cabins, ate the staple slave diet of "meat, meal, and molasses," and wore clothing of the coarsest materials. The presence of the frontier tended, however, to narrow the gulf between slaves and masters, relatively few of whom lived on the more elaborate scale of the older South.

The great demand for slaves on the new lands made Arkansas one of the heaviest slave-buying states, with prices consistently among the highest in the South. By 1860 the average value of all slaves was more than $800. "Prime field hands"—vigorous young men—were valued at $1,500 or more, and such skilled artisans as wheelwrights or blacksmiths at up to $3,000. No important slave-marketing centers developed in the state, most slaves being bought in New Orleans, La; Memphis, Tenn.; or St. Louis, Mo.

Slavery was, in general, economically profitable in Arkansas, in contrast to some of the older states, which were suffering from soil exhaustion. Large planters were especially prosperous, but almost all owners participated in the state's rapid increase in agricultural wealth—more than 500 percent in the 1850s alone—to a greater extent than nonslaveholders. Some large owners became very wealthy. For example, James Sheppard of Waterford Plantation near Pine Bluff multiplied an investment of $18,000 in 1851 to more than $160,000 in 1863. The degree to which Sheppard's prosperity was based on slave labor is indicated by the fact that almost a hundred years later Waterford Plantation was sold for only a little more than half its 1863 valuation.

Arkansas slaves were held in subjection by a legal code governing almost all aspects of their lives. Those who rebelled often were punished, but neither rigid control nor severe punishment could completely break their spirit, and most managed to maintain individualistic personal lives when free of the direct scrutiny of masters or overseers.

Slave protests against restrictions and mistreatment included passive resistance and violence against masters and overseers. Some slaves resorted to running away, made simpler by the proximity of the frontier. Most runaways never succeeded in getting out of the state, but some escaped to free states and to Indian tribes to the west. A few fled as far away as Mexico. But the majority of Arkansas slaves had neither opportunity nor resources for a break for freedom, and could only endure their lives in bondage—until the Emancipation Proclamation and the Union Army set them free. *See also* AFRO-AMERICAN HISTORY.

REFERENCES: Beatty-Brown, Florence R., "Legal Status of Arkansas Negroes Before Emancipation," *Arkansas Historical Quarterly*, Spring 1969, pp. 6–13; Taylor, Orville W., *Negro Slavery in Arkansas*, Duke University Press, Durham, 1958; and Walz, Robert B., "Arkansas Slaveholdings and Slaveholders," *Arkansas Historical Quarterly*, Spring 1953, pp. 38–74.

Missouri Slavery figured in Missouri's history from the time of its first settlement until a state-passed act of emancipation in January 1865. The "peculiar institution" began with Afro-American bondsmen digging for lead and cutting timber along the banks of the Mississippi River. An occasional large plantation existed at an early date, but the state was long characterized by few large plantations and small slaveholders.

Slavery in Missouri was largely a transplanted southern institution. Emigrants from the older states of Kentucky, North Carolina, Tennessee, and Virginia advanced to Missouri in large numbers during the late territorial period and during the first three decades of statehood. "The settlement of Missouri," one historian observed, "was marked by an effort to extend the [cotton] plantation system into the region." The cotton plantation, however, never developed during the antebellum period, though hemp and tobacco plantations did.

The majority of the southern emigrants were accustomed to slave labor and thought that it was necessary for hemp and tobacco crops—the state's staple crops. As Frederic Bancroft asserted, "a flourishing, expanding South without slavery was inconceivable" to southern settlers in Missouri. Ulrich B. Phillips remarked in his *Life and Labor in the Old South* (1929) that Missouri became a "land of promise for [slaveholding] pioneers and for stay-at-home speculators . . . who were always eager to invest anywhere ahead of boom." Many of the small farmers of the South, who realized the impossibility of competing with the large planters, found Missouri an ideal place in which to continue their agricultural pursuits and investments in slaves without the serious competition that they had previously experienced.

It should not be concluded, however, that only southerners made up the slaveholding class in Missouri. The manuscript census records for 1850 show that emigrants from the free states were also slaveholders in the state. Rev. John Mason Peck, for example, instrumental in interesting settlers in Missouri, recorded in his journal in 1819 that "many of the French inhabitants held slaves." Irish and Germans were also among the influential slaveholding class.

The territory was admitted to statehood in 1821, and its constitution sanctioned slavery and made it impossible for the state general assembly to free slaves without the consent of the owners or without compensation. Although not a member of the convention that drafted the constitution, the influential Thomas Hart Benton claimed credit for instigating the proslavery clause of the document. Senator Benton said that the clause "was adopted for the sake of peace— for the sake of internal tranquillity—and to prevent the agitation of the slavery question."

The proslavery, antiblack constitution apparently met the approval of the people of Missouri, although it was never submitted to them for ratification. It reflected the legal and social position of slavery and the attitude of the majority of white Missourians.

On the basis of the total number of slaves, Missouri ranked eleventh among the 15 slaveholding states in 1850. The largest number of slaveholders owned from one to five slaves. The census for this year showed 19,185 slaveholders with a total of 87,422 slaves. One-third of the slaveholders (5,726) held only one slave. The remaining slaveholders were divided as shown below:

SLAVEHOLDERS AND NUMBER OF SLAVES

Number of slaves	1 and under 5	5 and under 10	10 and under 20	20 and under 50	50 and under 100
Slaveholders	6,878	4,370	1,810	345	19

One slaveholding family was listed as the owner of more than 200 slaves.

Like the other slaveholding states, Missouri's small slaveholders outnumbered the large holders; and the vast majority of Missourians held no slaves at all. Yet, by natural increase and immigration, the slave population of the state increased from about 10,000 in 1820 to about 115,000 in 1860. Much available evidence suggests that the majority of Missourians had stronger social than economic interests or attachments to the slave system. Yet, the economic factor was important for slaveholders.

The largest number of slaves, no doubt, were agricultural laborers, but slaves were also used extensively as servants. The labor needs of the lead mines of Missouri and Illinois added to the economic importance of slavery in the state. Afro-American bondsmen were employed in the iron mining industry as laborers, blacksmiths, and engineers throughout the slavery era.

The early hiring practices in Missouri indicate how valuable slaves were as investments and for the labor needs of the state. Slaves could always be hired, and their labor brought comfortable sums to their owners. Many slaves were annually hired as household servants for private families, boardinghouses, and hotels. Still more numerous were the slaves hired to work in fields, forests, tobacco factories, and mines. Slaves were also among the railroad builders, and a large number of them were hired on steamboats in all capacities. Because of the demand for slave labor, domestic and outside traders in slaves found it exceedingly hard to purchase good quality slaves in Missouri. *See also* AFRO-AMERICAN HISTORY: THE WEST.

REFERENCES: Bellamy, Donnie D., "The Education of Blacks in Missouri Prior to 1861," *Journal of Negro History*, April 1974, pp. 143–57; Brown, William W., *The Narrative of William W. Brown, A Fugitive Slave*, with an introduction by Larry Gara, Reading, 1969; Bruce, Henry Clay, *The New Man: Twenty-Nine Years a Slave, Twenty-Nine Years a Free Man*, York. 1895; Dorsett, Lyle Wesley, "Slaveholding in Jackson County, Missouri," *Missouri Historical Society Bulletin*, vol. 11, pp. 25–37, October 1963; Eliot, William G., *The History of Archer Alexander, From Slavery to Freedom*, Boston, 1885; Keckley, Elizabeth, *Behind the Scenes by Elizabeth Keckley, Formerly a Slave. . . .*, New York, 1868; Nelson, Earl J., "Missouri Slavery, 1861–1865," *Missouri Historical Review*, vol. 27, pp. 260–74, July 1934; Trexler, Harrison A., *Slavery in Missouri, 1804–1865*, Baltimore, 1913; and Twelvetress, Harper (ed.), *The Story of the Life of John Anderson, the Fugitive Slave*, London, 1863.

Kansas With the passage of the Kansas-Nebraska Act of 1854, Kansas Territory became the focal point of the North-South conflict over the extension of slavery into the West. Ultimately, the antislavery forces prevailed, and Kansas entered the Union as a free state. For this reason, it is often assumed that slavery never existed in Kansas Territory. Such, however, was not the case; before 1854 slaves were found throughout the region.

Although the Missouri Compromise of 1820 barred slavery from that part of the lands received through the Louisiana Purchase (1803), its provisions did not apply to military posts and Indian reservations. Hence, as early as 1832, a Maj. R. W. Cummings resided at Shawnee Mission with a number of slaves. Later, in the 1840s and early 1850s, some of the Army officers at Fort Leavenworth, Fort Scott, and Fort Riley were accompanied by black "servants," and slaveholding existed among the Shawnees, Wyandots, Cherokees, and Osawatomies. In addition, Rev. Thomas Johnson, head of the Methodist mission at Shawnee, owned four or six slaves whom he reportedly purchased in Missouri "out of pity for their condition." Other scattered instances of slaveholding in pre-1854 Kansas could be listed as well.

The repeal of the Missouri Compromise by the Kansas-Nebraska Act of 1854 did not, then, introduce slavery into Kansas. Rather the act legalized slavery throughout Kansas for all types of residents. Only if settlers subsequently adopted a state constitution prohibiting slavery, and if the U.S. Congress approved that constitution, would slavery be banned.

Since Kansas remained a territory until early in 1861, it was officially a part of slavery's domain for nearly seven years; and, in fact, a slave code was adopted in 1855 by the first territorial legislature, which was totally dominated by Missourians determined to make Kansas a slave state free of "abolitionist contamination." To achieve their goal, the legislators not only passed "An act for the protection of slave property" (thus institutionalizing slavery), but they also proclaimed that:

If any free person, by speaking or writing, shall assert or maintain that persons have not the right to hold slaves in this territory, or shall introduce into the territory, print, publish, write, circulate . . . any denial of the right of persons to hold slaves in this territory, such persons shall be deemed guilty of felony, and punished by imprisonment at hard labor for a term of not less than two years.

At least one person, a newspaper editor, was subsequently indicted under this repressive measure, although he was never brought to trial.

An official census, taken in 1855, reported 193 slaves and 151 free Afro-Americans in the territory. Most of the slaves, and probably most of the free blacks too, were brought there by Missourians, who at the time constituted nearly one-half of the total territorial population of 8,501. However, several slaveholders from the Deep South migrated to Kansas with their human chattels.

The largest concentrations of slaves were in the northeastern border counties, although a sizable group existed in the Fort Scott area as well. The biggest single slaveholder, a man named Skaggs in Jefferson County, owned 27 slaves. The majority of Kansas slaveholders, however, possessed only a few "servants"—rarely as many as a half dozen. No known instances of slave auctions occurred in the territory, but the private sale of slaves was not uncommon, as courthouse records indicate.

For the most part, slaves and free blacks alike worked as house servants, herdsmen, and all-purpose farmhands. The soil and climate of Kansas precluded southern plantation agriculture, although partially sucessful attempts were made in the Missouri River counties to grow tobacco and hemp, the economic basis of slavery in Kentucky and western Missouri. According to one Kansas historian, most of the slaves in the territory were owned by proslavery zealots who wished to prove that the "peculiar institution" could floruish economically on the prairies of Kansas under kind masters.

Fighting actually broke out in Kansas over the question of slavery. (*Library of Congress*.)

By 1856, the number of slaves in Kansas was possibly as many as 400. That same year a bloody civil war broke out between the proslavery and antislavery parties in the territory. Not only did such abolitionist militants as John Brown terrorize proslavery inhabitants, but abolitionists encouraged slaves to run away from their masters and then aided them in their escape northward by way of the Underground Railroad. Moreover, sporadic attempts by territorial authorities to recover fugitives were frustrated by popular resistance, for a large and growing majority of the settlers were antislavery northerners. Such a state of affairs forestalled slaveholders from migrating to Kansas and compelled those already there to leave. Thus, by 1857, according to the estimate of the territorial governor, only 300 slaves were left in Kansas.

Yet Kansas nearly became a slave state. Late in 1857 a convention controlled by the proslavery faction drew up the so-called Lecompton Constitution, which declared that "The right of property is before and higher than any constitutional sanction and the right of the owner of a slave to such slave and its increase is the same and inalienable as the right of the owner of any property whatever." The antislavery settlers boycotted the ensuing referendum on the constitution, which, as a result, was ratified by a mere fraction of the territory's total population. In spite of this obvious mockery of "popular sovereignty," President James Buchanan urged the U.S. Congress to admit Kansas to statehood under the terms of the Lecompton Constitution; and some southern leaders threatened secession if Congress refused. However, Congress ordered another referendum. In this one, held on August 2, 1858, the freestaters participated, and the Lecompton Constitution was rejected by a 10 to 1 ratio.

This antislavery outcome marked the end of the slavery controversy and of slavery as such in Kansas. All but a scattered few of the remaining slaveholders either freed their slaves or else moved out of the state with them. In the latter group was the aforementioned Skaggs, who went to Texas. After the Civil War, however, Skaggs returned to Kansas with some of his former slaves, who took care of him in his destitute old age on a farm near Coffeyville.

In 1858 the territorial legislature, now firmly controlled by freestaters, repealed the 1855 slave code—only to have the repeal vetoed by the territorial governor who correctly pointed out that the code violated the terms of the Kansas-Nebraska Act of 1864. The following year the freestaters drew up the Wyandotte Constitution, which prohibited slavery in what the framers hoped would soon be the state of Kansas. However, southern opposition in Congress blocked Kansas' admission under this constitution. Then, in 1860, the territorial legislature again abolished slavery over the governor's veto. Even

so, slavery continued to be de jure (legal) in Kansas because of the Kansas-Nebraska Act of 1854. Not until January 29, 1861, when the U.S. Congress finally approved the Wyandotte Constitution, did slavery as a legal entity disappear from Kansas. At that time, according to the U.S. census of 1860, only two slaves lived in Kansas—both middle-aged women living in Anderson County. See also AFRO-AMERICAN HISTORY.

REFERENCES: Berwanger, Eugene H., The Frontier Against Slavery; Western Anti-Negro Prejudice and the Slavery Extension Controversy, University of Illinois Press, Urbana, 1967; Castel, Albert E., Frontier State at War: Kansas, 1861–1865, Cornell University Press, Ithaca, 1958; Nichols, Roy F., The Disruption of American Democracy, Macmillan, New York, 1948; Nichols, Roy F., "The Kansas-Nebraska Act: A Century of Historiography," Mississippi Valley Historical Review, September 1956; and Rawley, James A., Race and Politics: "Bleeding Kansas" and the Coming of the Civil War, J. B. Lippincott Company, Philadelphia, 1969.

On the Frontier Negro slavery existed for brief or extended periods in all of the northern frontier territories established before 1860. These areas included the states of the Old Northwest—Iowa, Minnesota, Kansas, Nebraska, Colorado, Utah, New Mexico, California, and Oregon. The duration of slavery and the numbers of slaves varied in each territory. For example, Philippe François Renault, a French mining engineer, introduced slavery into the Illinois country in 1720, and the institution was not completely abolished in the state until 1845. Slavery was legally recognized in New Mexico for about 18 months, from 1859 to 1861.

Printed U.S. census figures reveal the following numbers of slaves in frontier regions: Indiana (1820), 190; Illinois (1820), 917; Michigan Territory (1830), 32; Ohio (1830), 6; Wisconsin Territory (1840), 10; Iowa Territory (1840), 17; Kansas Territory (1860), 2; and Utah Territory (1860), 29. These figures cannot be accepted as accurate, however, for slaveholders or census takers sometimes listed slaves as free blacks if slavery was illegal in the territory. Oregon legislators, for example, attempted to pass a law protecting slave property just before Oregon became a free state in 1859, even though no slaves had been listed in the official census report. Statements by pioneers or handwritten census returns for California, Nebraska, and Colorado note the presence of slaves in these regions although printed census figures indicate there were none.

Slavery on the frontier was of three major types: domestic or personal service, mine slavery, and agricultural slave labor. Domestic and personal servants were often owned by military and civilian personnel assigned to or living near federal military installations. Dred Scott, for instance, was the slave of John Emerson, a U.S. Army surgeon, and accompanied him on his assignment to Fort Snelling in present-day Minnesota. Four slaves served as domestics to three white families at Fort Kearny, Nebr., in 1860. Like their masters, these domestic slaves were transient—their residence on frontier posts depending upon their masters' duty assignments.

In Illinois, California, and, to a lesser extent, in Colorado, slaves were used as miners. In fact, slave labor helped to establish the lead mining industry around Galena, Ill., a city in the northwestern portion of the territory. By 1820 the lead deposits were depleted and the slaves were either returned to the slave states or moved to Iowa, where they became agricultural laborers. Slave labor alone operated the salt works near Shawneetown in the southeastern part of Illinois. Because Illinoisans believed that white men could not endure the arduous labor required at the salt mines, early Illinois politicians authorized the indenture of Afro-Americans for mining until 1825, seven years after Illinois became a free state.

Nonslaveholding miners in California resented the use of slave labor in gold-mining operations. They considered it unfair competition that permitted their rivals to reap enormous, unearned profits from the goldfields. Antagonism was further intensified by the belief held by white miners that Afro-Americans had an uncanny ability to sense the locations of large gold deposits. An isolated incident involving the panning of $4,000 worth of nuggets in one week by William Manney's slaves tended to confirm the theory that Afro-Americans were more adept than whites at finding gold.

Early travelers and miners in California reported that southerners and their chattels were usually forced to leave areas occupied by nonslaveholding miners. Threats and physical force were applied if they refused to leave willingly. It was this dislike of slave labor in the mines that influenced the antislavery attitude in California. Although most miners had little interest in participating in the statehood movement of 1849, they insisted that California must be a free state.

In some instances southerners allowed their slaves to travel west and work the California gold fields on their own. The slave was then required to send back to his master the greater portion of any gold he discovered. A few purchased their freedom with nuggets they had panned in California.

A group of whites from Georgia migrated to Colorado with slaves during the Pike's Peak gold rush of 1859. Perhaps because their number was small, the presence of these blacks apparently did not cause resentment among the nonslaveholding white miners. Moreover, they did not remain long in Colorado; the majority of them were returned to the South at the outbreak of the Civil War.

While slaves were used as agricultural laborers on the frontier, nothing approximating the southern plantation system existed. The few white families who owned slaves had only one or two. Performing the same type of labor as his master, the slave in most cases worked alongside the white man. Except for his legal status, the black's living and working conditions resembled those of a hired hand.

Slavery was of limited importance in the frontier labor system because the institution was either prohibited by federal or territorial law, or was discouraged by public opinion. The sixth article of the Northwest Ordinance, passed by the U.S. Congress in 1787, forbade the further importation of slaves into the Old Northwest, but it did not free those already in the territory. Despite the existence of forced labor and the recognition that Article 6 was not rigidly enforced, slaveholders were reluctant to settle in the Old Northwest. They preferred territories where slavery was legally recognized and where continued ownership of their "property" was guaranteed. Such guaranty, however, was not given by Oregon whose territorial government in 1848 reaffirmed an earlier provisional decision of 1844.

Public opinion served as a strong force to limit slavery on the frontier. Although the Kansas-Nebraska Act of 1854 permitted slave labor, few Afro-Americans were taken into the region because of the overwhelming antislavery attitude among the settlers. In New Mexico the native population discouraged the importation of slaves even though the institution was not expressly forbidden by law. Their antislavery sentiment was motivated by the desire to exclude any labor system that might conflict with peonage. As previously stated, public opinion dictated the antislavery position of California as well. In fact, Thomas L. Clingman, a congressional representative from North Carolina, insisted that had the general public, and especially miners, not objected, slave labor could have been profitably used for both agricultural and mining purposes on the West Coast.

However, prohibition of slavery did not completely prevent attempts to use Afro-American labor. Nathaniel Ford, an Oregon farmer, held Robin Holmes and his family as slaves until the Oregon territorial court freed them in 1853. The historian Clyde A. Duniway reports that whites continued to use slaves in California despite the antislavery clause in the state constitution. Efforts were also made to nullify laws or render them ineffective. Disregarding the intent of the antislavery clause in the Northwest Ordinance of 1787, territorial legislators in Indiana and Illinois passed laws between 1803 and 1813 authorizing the lifetime indenture of Afro-Americans from the South. Some such agreements even provided for the indenture of unborn children. In 1821 Indiana state courts finally annulled all indenture contracts made during the territorial period. Illinois lawmakers prohibited slavery in the state constitution, but they permitted indenture contracts to be made until the eve of statehood and regarded them as legally binding; and, during the first decade of statehood, proslavery advocates attempted to revise the new Illinois state constitution to legalize slavery.

Attempts to skirt prohibitions against slavery were also made in New Mexico and California. The New Mexico legislature passed a slave code in 1859, but the law proved so unpopular that it was easily repealed in 1861. Throughout the 1850s southern Californians agitated for the formation of a separate state in their area; many antislavery people presumed these demands were fostered by proslavery adherents wishing to create a slave state.

In the main, proslavery groups on the frontier relied on economic arguments. They agitated for the introduction or legalization of slavery especially during times of economic depression. Proslavery advocates in both Illinois and Oregon, during the panics of 1819 and 1857, respectively, urged the legalization of slavery, and maintained that the institution would stimulate the economy by encouraging the settlement of slaveholders. In addition, these groups stressed the need for labor on the frontier, insisting that black labor was the only means of acquiring the manpower necessary to establish civilizations in the virgin forests or on the plains.

Several factors influenced antislavery sentiment on the frontier. Antislavery whites considered slavery economically unsound. When the issue of legalizing bondage arose, they countered proslavery economic arguments by declaring that the financial benefits of slavery would be only temporary. Antislavery advocates often cited figures to prove that since 1800 land values in the South had deteriorated while those in the North had increased. Some went further, stressing that slavery would bring a large black population, moral degeneration, and social burdens to whites. This racial argument carried great weight: many white people on the frontier disliked Afro-Americans more than the system of slavery. Laws prohibiting the residence of free blacks were passed in Illinois, Indiana, Oregon, and Iowa. Ohio, Michigan, and New Mexico required free blacks who wished to live in these states to post $500 bonds to ensure their good behavior and self-support. Finally, implications regarding the moral correctness of slavery were important in preventing the "peculiar institution" from becoming firmly established on the frontier. While many whites were unconcerned about the existence of slavery in the South, they opposed its spread into their area because of the moral stigma attached to human bondage.

Slavery was never an important factor on the northern frontier, neither in frontier development nor in frontier society. Indeed, the limited use of slave labor seemed to strengthen the antislavery attitudes of most white people. Whether they had emigrated from slave or free states or from Europe, the majority of settlers preferred to tame the frontier without the aid of involuntary servitude. See also AFRO-AMERICAN HISTORY: THE WEST.

REFERENCES: Beasley, Delilah L., "Slavery in California," Journal of Negro History, vol. 3, pp. 33–45, January 1918; Beller, Jack, "Negro Slaves in Utah," Utah Historical Quarterly, vol. 2, pp. 122–26, July 1929; Berwanger, Eugene H., The Frontier Against Slavery: Western Anti-Negro Prejudice and the Slavery Extension Controversy, Urbana, 1967; Dancy, John C., "The Negro People in Michigan," Michigan History Magazine, vol. 24, pp. 221–40, Spring 1940; Davidson, John N., "Negro Slavery in Wisconsin," Wisconsin State Historical Society Proceedings, vol. 40, pp. 82–86, 1892; Duniway, Clyde A., "Slavery in California After 1848," Annual Report of the American Historical Association, vol. 1, pp. 241–48, 1905; Harris, Norman D., History of Negro Slavery in Illinois, and of the Slavery Agitation in that State, 1719–1864, Chicago, 1906; Johannsen, Robert W., Frontier Politics and the Sectional Conflict: The Pacific Northwest on the Eve of the Civil War, Seattle, 1955; Pelzer, Louis, "The Negro and Slavery in Early Iowa," Iowa Journal of History and Politics, vol. 2, pp. 471–85, October 1904; Savage, Sherman W., "The Negro on the Mining Frontier," Journal of Negro History, vol. 30, pp. 30–46, January 1945 and Thornbrough, Emma Lou, The Negro in Indiana: A Study of a Minority, Indianapolis, 1957.

Slaves In Industry The early development of the southern colonies of the British in the United

States placed the black slave in an anomalous position between the poor white and the affluent slaveholding and landowning aristocracy. Slave artisans began to form a sort of rural middle class in a region where urban settlement was all but nonexistent. This social phenomenon continued to develop through the Revolutionary War and the antebellum period.

The economic decline in the late colonial period forced many planters to depend increasingly on the skilled slave laborer to produce goods. The American Revolution curtailed even more severely the importation of goods, and dependence on the mechanical skills of slaves increased. It was for these reasons that George Washington, for example, attempted the manufacture of iron with slave labor. At his Mount Vernon plantation in 1786, he had three seamstresses, four spinners, four carpenters, two blacksmiths, a knitter, and four slaves who operated his flour and grist mills. At Mount Vernon and his three adjacent plantations, nearly 20 percent of Washington's adult slaves were engaged in skilled trades or management, while several young slaves were being taught trades by white indentured servants. Likewise, Thomas Jefferson built a nail factory at his birthplace, Shadwell Plantation, employing several of his slaves. During the difficult war years, skilled slaves contributed materially to both the domestic and factory systems of manufacturing.

During the late eighteenth and early nineteenth centuries, the mechanical arts were still simple, and the slave mechanic was trained in them more readily than the illiterate and undisciplined poor white. In 1775 Thomas Heywood, a planter in the vicinity of Charleston, gathered together spinning wheels and hand looms in a large plantation shed and employed slaves in the production of cloth for the use of the Heywood plantation and for sale to neighboring planters. At about the same time a group of Williamsburg, Va., protocapitalists pooled their funds and established one of the earliest manufacturing corporations in the embryonic nation. The Williamsburg Manufacturing Society established facilities for the processing of wool and flax and produced linen cloth. The mill manager advertised in the Virginia *Gazette* for slave girls to apprentice as spinners and offered to pay "ready money" for trained slave weavers. The domestic manufacture of cloth and a variety of other items by plantation slaves expanded rapidly in the war years and during the depression of the 1780s and 1790s.

The importance and value of a slave trained in a trade gave to the slave a rank in the slave hierarchy that equaled that of the house slave. The typical plantation was "where there were ten or more prime hands," including "one man who was a jack-of-all-trades, a carpenter, blacksmith and bricklayer rolled into one": but on larger plantations "there were usually two or more slaves who had been bred to a trade." These skilled slaves were invaluable on the home plantation, and when they were not otherwise employed they were hired out to smaller planters and to yeoman farmers. Indeed, many of these slaves were so highly thought of that they were occasionally allowed to hire out on their own, in slack times, for their own profit. This process proved a constant irritation to struggling white artisans, who resented the competition; these free artisans expressed their irritation through resolutions drafted by their mechanic associations. The city fathers, not unmindful of the precarious existence of towns in an agrarian and rural society, frequently passed ordinances that prohibited slave artisans from employment within city limits. The existence of slave artisans militated against towns and hampered the emergence of a white middle class.

Meanwhile, the possibilities inherent in the new nation attracted skilled European artisans who sought opportunities to exploit the resources and markets while escaping the controls at home. The southern states, having been totally integrated into the British colonial system, faced a most difficult time after 1783. Their loss of protected markets, Parliamentary subsidies, and exclusive rights of production introduced a crisis into the entire slave-oriented system. Planters inextricably involved in a slave welfare system that held them responsible from cradle to grave were faced with the economic necessity of finding a new support for that system or abandoning it and freeing the slaves. The latter was impossible, so planter-dominated state legislatures began seeking new directions for the southern economy—most often, by encouraging European craftsmen and proto-entrepreneurs to provide a solution to their problems.

Samuel Slater was best known of the postwar immigrants. He was preceded to America by Hugh Templeton, who established a small cotton mill near Stateburg, S.C., in 1789 where slave labor was employed in the manufacture of cloth and simple textile machinery. Templeton's plan for his Stateburg factory was nullified by the constant turnover of his employees, whose owners removed them from the mill as soon as they had become proficient at spinning and weaving. Despite this, Templeton and his planter supporters kept the mill running until 1795 with the aid of the South Carolina legislature, which showed an inclination to aid entrepreneurs through state loans, tax exemptions, land grants, and direct financial assistance. James Walsh was lured by a group of Danville, Ky., capitalists to manage their cotton mill. John Hague, another Briton, went to the Indian frontier of Tennessee, where, near Nashville, he built a small cotton factory in 1791 at a new town named Manchester. Slave labor was an integral part of each of these pioneer undertakings.

At the same time, slaveholders were hectically seeking new activities in which to employ their slaves—activities that would provide themselves with an income. They experimented with the manufacture of cotton, wool, linen, iron, flour, and meal. Generally, these uncongenial activities were decelerated by Eli Whitney's invention and subsequent perfection of the cotton gin. Soon throughout the South slaves mechanics were being employed in reproducing, despite patent infringement, Whitney's gin, and giving new life to agricultural slavery.

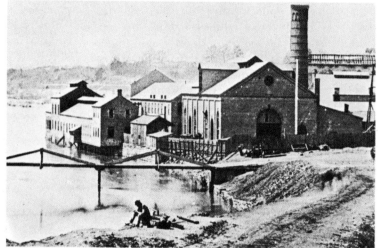

Tredegar Iron Works, a large industrial plant in Richmond, Va., employed about 700 whites and 80 slaves in 1860. Most of the slaves worked in the rolling mill and blacksmith shops; but there was an elite of skilled puddlers, heaters, and rollers. (*Library of Congress.*)

The beginnings of actual industrial activities led some southerners to continue to experiment with manufacturing as an outgrowth of the new technological age dawning in the New World. Gov. David R. Williams of South Carolina established a cotton factory at Society Hill, where he employed his own slaves and those of fellow investors. The successful efforts of such other entrepreneurs as Jacob Gregg, uncle of the more

famous William, and John J. Schley convinced a number of southerners that this was a road to rich rewards. Mill builders found that slaves were easily trained to work in this new manufacturing activity. In many cases the building of factories was financed by slaveholders who often provided slave laborers in lieu of cash investment. Mill managers found slaves easy to manage, unable to strike, and accustomed to a discipline and regularity that was difficult to inculcate in poor whites.

From 1800 to 1860 debates raged between those who wanted to employ slaves in factories and those who wished to use white labor exclusively. Paeons of praise were showered upon Afro-Americans, slave and free, for their skill, ingenuity, enterprise, imagination, and talent. The black artisan as machinist, engineer, architect, and builder was given frequent notice in the public press and more often in the private correspondence of southern entrepreneurs. The skilled slave was the most valuable member of the bonded social order and was more often held in higher esteem than the uncivilized and unchristianized piney-woods white. It was this circumstance, among others, that led Hinton R. Helper to write his antiblack diatribe in the 1850s.

By the late 1820s the idea of factory manufacturing was firmly established in the South. The foremost question, as we have seen, continued to be what race would fill the jobs created. Charles Fisher, spokesman for North Carolina Democrats and a leader in the state general assembly, produced an extensive report on the advantages of the introduction of textile manufactures into the state. This report to the legislature included a complete review of the relative merits of the employment of slaves or white labor in these factories. Fisher called Henry A. Donaldson, a native of Providence, R.I., to testify on employment of slaves in his factories at Rocky Mount and Fayetteville, N.C. Donaldson claimed that slave labor had proven cheaper and superior in his mills. The slaveholder was told that the establishment of factories offered him a better opportunity to get full value from his investment in slaves as they provided remunerative employment for women, children, and those not suited for field work.

The chief problem of using slaves in factories was the heavy investment of capital required to pay for them and the reluctance of slaveholders to rent slaves for industrial employment. James Silk Buckingham found in the late 1830s that in

Athens, Ga., both slave and white laborers were used in several of the textile mills. The mill owners there reported that slave labor was highly efficient but more expensive than white labor: the mill owner not only had to pay the slave's owner the same wages he paid the white worker, but he also had to provide the slave with room and board. The white worker had to provide for these expenses out of his monthly wage of seven dollars. In addition, factory managers complained that slaves were available in times of agricultural distress, but in periods of prosperity they were called back to the plantation regardless of the inconvenience to the mill owner.

Despite the disadvantages, mill owners evidently found slaves to be very satisfactory employees; and slaves, on their part, found the factory preferable to the unrelenting duty on the farm. Most frequently slaves were employed in grist and flour mills and in sawmills, where the need for their labor was seasonal and closely associated with the needs of agriculture and the land. They largely dominated employment in the manufacture of hempen rope and bagging in Kentucky and in the making of a variety of products in the tobacco factories of Virginia. They were also visible in Virginia's salt processing.

It is amply evident that skilled slave artisans in the South bolstered the advance of the industrial revolution. However, by the 1850s the value of slaves had become so inflated that they were generally removed from factory employment. By the end of the Civil War, Afro-American population—regardless of its skill, craftsmanship, and experience—was thrust into the position formerly occupied by the poor white, and the black man found himself persona non grata at the gates of the factories he had helped to create. *See also* AFRO-AMERICAN HISTORY; EMPLOYMENT.

REFERENCES: Dew, Charles B., *Ironmaker of the Confederacy: Joseph R. Anderson and the Tredegar Iron Works,* Yale University Press, New Haven, 1966; Dew, Charles B., "David Rose and the Oxford Iron Works: A Study of Industrial Slavery in the Early Nineteenth-Century South," *William and Mary Quarterly,* April 1974, pp. 189–224; Eaton, Clement, *A History of the Old South: The Emergence of a Reluctant Nation,* 3d ed., Macmillan, New York, 1975, chaps. 14, 15; Griffin, Richard W., "South Carolina Homespun Company, 1808–1815," *Business History Review,* Autumn 1961, pp. 402–15; Lander, Ernest M., Jr., "Charleston: Manufacturing Center of the Old South," *Journal of Southern History,* August 1960, pp. 330–51; Starobin, Robert S., *Industrial Slavery in the Old South,* Oxford University Press, New York, 1970; and Stealey, John Edmund, III, "Slavery and the Western Virginia Salt Industry," *Journal of Negro History,* April 1974, pp. 105–31.

The Churches All of the religious denominations in the British colonies claimed some slave members. However, missionary efforts by whites to convert Afro-Americans were negligible. Progress in christianization was slow, and the results of evangelistic labors up until the time of the American Revolution were meager. Some slaveholders were indifferent to the spiritual welfare of their slaves; others were outright hostile to the idea of religious instruction for blacks. Religious training and conversion, it was said, made Afro-Americans dissatisfied with their servile status and rendered them intractable and hard to control. Some masters objected for economic reasons, maintaining that evangelization of slaves would increase the cost of maintenance since much time would be consumed in language training, religious instruction, and attending worship services. The absence of efficient ecclesiastical organization in the frontier environment may partially explain why no sustained effort was made to christianize blacks during the colonial period.

However, a few churchmen were genuinely interested in Afro-Americans and sought to ameliorate their condition and to minister to their spiritual needs. The Quakers, for example, were more concerned about the blacks than were any other group in colonial America. After 1688 members of the Society of Friends expressed increasing concern for the emancipation of enslaved Afro-Americans, and by the time of the American Revolution the society had adopted a firm antislavery position. Various yearly meetings declared that slaveholders were ineligible for membership in the society of Friends.

Some Anglican missionaries, sent to America by the Society for the Propagation of the Gospel

Far left: Slaves as saltmakers numbered about 1,500 in the nation's largest plant, on the Great Kanawha River in Va., in 1850. (*Library of Congress.*)

in Foreign Parts (S.P.G.), sought to convert slaves and also to impress upon slaveholders their Christian duty to provide religious instruction for those in their care. In 1727 the bishop of London addressed a general letter to slaveholders in America urging them to baptize children of slaves and to permit their slaves to attend worship services. At the time of the Great Awakening, Samuel Davies, a Presbyterian clergyman in Virginia, tried to arouse the public conscience about the spiritual neglect of Afro-Americans. Davies preached to blacks, organized classes for their instruction, and counseled his ministerial colleagues and slaveholders to provide for the religious instruction of slaves.

During the American Revolution and the years immediately following, all of the states north of the Mason-Dixon Line enacted legislation for the emancipation of slaves, and the U.S. Congress prohibited slavery in the territory north of the Ohio River. Also in the 1780s denominational spokesmen and ecclesiastical organizations representing the major denominations—Presbyterian, Methodist, and Baptist—condemned slavery as an evil and as a denial of the natural rights of man. The initiative in these postrevolutionary antislavery statements and resolutions came from such concerned clergymen as Thomas Coke, Francis Asbury, John Leland, and David Rice, whose intent did not represent the opinions of average church members. The churches south of Pennsylvania (in the area where 90 percent of the Afro-Americans resided) generally ignored or expressed hostile reaction to the humanitarian declarations and statements of those who sought emancipation. These southern churches espoused the customs, mores, and values of the society of which they were a part. None of the emancipation resolutions proposed by various denominational spokesmen in the 1780s received a favorable response from church members. Within a short time most church leaders abandoned the hopes expressed in the Declaration of Independence and ceased to agitate for emancipation. Instead, they wrote tracts and preached sermons advising slaveholders to "give their servants that which is equal and just," to permit them to attend worship services, and to instruct them in Christian truth. Most denominations after 1793 espoused the idea that slavery was a political problem rather than a moral or religious issue, and that the discussion of emancipation should be left to politicians. This concensus prevailed for approximately a half century.

In the first half of the nineteenth century, as the nation expanded westward, church membership increased rapidly; slave members were now found in all of the major denominations, the largest number in the Baptist and Methodist churches. The informal atmosphere and preaching that prevailed in these churches, together with their emphasis on revivalism, appealed to Afro-Americans.

Although most Afro-American Christians were members of integrated congregations, some all-black churches existed. The earliest separate black congregations were formed in the South at the time of the American Revolution, and until the opening decades of the nineteenth century these black churches were independent. Their membership included both slaves and free blacks, and they were accorded membership in local and predominately white ecclesiastical organizations. However, by the 1830s state legislation, together with white fears and racial prejudices had eliminated the independent black church in the South. Autonomous black congregations, which were formed in Philadelphia, New York City, and at other places in the free states after the 1790s, have had a continuous history up to the present time. The Afro-Americans who formed separate congregations—in both the North and the South—were prompted to take this action because of racial discrimination by their white coreligionists, and by a desire to organize and conduct their own services of worship.

Although the independent Afro-American church ceased to exist in the slave South by 1830, a number of black congregations continued throughout the war and indeed long after the war had ended. These were usually Baptist or Methodist congregations, all under the control and supervision of whites; their membership was considered a part of the parent white church from which they were formed; their officials—deacons, elders, or stewards—were chosen by whites; the church property was owned by white trustees; and their pastors were all white men. The practices and procedures of these churches were patterned after white congregations. At the First African Baptist Church in Richmond, Va., men occupied the seats on the left side of the center aisle, women sat on the right side of the sanctuary, and white visitors sat in the gallery.

The vast majority of slave church members, however, attended integrated congregations. It has been estimated that there were approximately a half million slaves who were church members in 1860. These members were found in all of the denominations. However, Afro-Americans constituted a type of associate-member status since their voice in church affairs was subordinate to that of the white members. They were not permitted to vote on the policies or programs of the congregation or to participate in the business sessions of the church.

Most black members were accepted into the church on the same terms as whites: that is, upon professing their faith in Jesus Christ and after relating their religious experience. Some congregations also required a slave to present a two-part written statement from his master containing permission for the slave to join the church and a recommendation attesting to the good character of the applicant. Most slave members attended worship services and took communion with whites, but they were segregated within the sanctuary. They might occupy seats near the back of the building or on a balcony. In some congregations, where the Afro-American membership was large, separate services (conducted by white members) were held, usually on Sunday afternoon, or at the time of regular morning worship in another portion of the building or in an adjoining building. Occasionally, white supervisors would permit black congregants to hear a sermon by a preacher of their own race.

Afro-American members were subject to the same rules of church discipline as white members, and much time was consumed in the business meetings of some antebellum congregations on the subject of slave discipline. Congregational meetings for disciplinary action against Afro-Americans were usually held at the request of Afro-American members. In some instances, the Afro-American members would discipline other Afro-Americans, subject to review by the white members. Instructed that it was their duty and privilege to contribute to the financial program of the church, black members usually responded enthusiastically.

The type of gospel preached to Afro-Americans had a two-fold purpose—to save their souls and to make them better and more obedient slaves. Sermons were preached not from such a text as "the truth shall make you free," but from "slaves, be obedient to your masters." The content of sermons preached to slaves and the instruction imparted in catechisms designed for slaves emphasized the virtues of docility, obedience, honesty, and hard work. Slaves were told that in this world of sorrow, sickness, and toil it was their duty to work and to be humble, prayer-

ful, and patient. They were taught that God expected men to "work hard and wear themselves out" here in this life so that they might better appreciate rest in the life beyond the grave. Some sermons threatened the slaves with the fires of hell if they failed to stop swearing, drinking, and cheating. The humble, busy, obedient, and prayerful slave was the type of person, according to the white teachers and preachers, who would experience the joys of heaven. And heaven was described as being "better than a cool breeze, a splendid sunset or sunrise . . . where it is never dark or gloomy . . . a place where man is free." It was a place where all would be happy and pure, where there would be no storms or night. One clergyman explained to a slave congregation that if they ever had a desire to be free in this life it was because the devil was working in them. A Protestant Episcopal bishop informed the members of a slave congregation that they were responsible for their souls, even though their bodies were not their own. He assured them that their master was God's overseer and that they were to obey him as they would God. Churchmen believed that the most important item the church could teach to slaves was "obedience to masters in all things, serving them with a ready mind."

Many clergymen in the antebellum South owned slaves, and some local churches accepted gifts of slaves as part of their endowment. Churchmen, it appears, were some of the most ardent advocates of human slavery. Prominent clergymen in all of the denominations defended slavery as a part of God's design or plan. They interpreted various passages of Scripture to prove that slavery had enjoyed the favor and blessings of the deity since the beginning of history, and that the slave-master relationship was a benevolent one. Slavery was described as an institution that was ordained by the Almighty, an institution that would permit the more advanced race to christianize and civilize a helpless people.

Although most southern clergymen and denominational spokesmen defended the institution of slavery as divinely sanctioned, some did not approve of slavery and believed that the buying and selling of human beings was a sin against God and humanity. These men were convinced that the apologists for slavery who based their arguments upon Scripture were misusing the Bible.

Until the 1830s clergymen and denominational leaders in the North were almost as tolerant of slavery as their religious colleagues in the South. All major denominations had formed national organizations to coordinate and plan their programs of activities, such as missionary work and publications. Throughout the early years of the nineteenth century, those who were concerned about abolishing slavery were a minority in the churches at large. The slavery issue was dormant in all of the major denominations. It was believed that any discussion of the question might split the denomination or thwart its growth, or involve the church in a political matter.

However, as the nineteenth century moved into its second quarter, a new generation of clergy emerged in positions of influence. The slavery issue could no longer be ignored in the national gatherings of church leaders. Although abolitionists were a minority in the churches in the 1830s, they did prompt the formation of some congregations in the Midwest, in New York, and in New England—congregations that would not accept the concept of slavery. Discussions, pro and con, of the Christian merits of slavery were frequent in ecclesiastical gatherings, in denominational newspapers, and in tracts and sermons. Tensions resulting from these discussions contributed to the split in the Presbyterian Church in 1837 and precipitated division in the 1840s in the two largest denominations in the nation: the Methodist Episcopal (ME) Church and the Baptist Church.

In the years prior to the Civil War prominent churchmen were found in all denominations who were apologists for slavery and others who were leading advocates of abolition. With the majority of southern churchmen defending slavery and northern churchmen leading in the abolition movement, the consciences of many Americans were stirred, and southern churches were stimulated to devote more attention to the religious care of slaves. From the 1830s to the outbreak of the Civil War, various synods, conferences, and associations of southern churches adopted resolutions suggesting that local congregations appoint committees for the religious instruction of blacks. These resolutions frequently claimed that Afro-Americans were "missionary ground" and urged that competent teachers be appointed to instruct them in the precepts of the Bible. Similar resolutions were repeated throughout the 1840s and 1850s; however, the response to these resolutions was minimal. Although southern churchmen devoted more attention to the conversion of slaves in 1860 than they had previously, it appears that few congregations devoted much attention to their religious education. In fact, some southern churchmen believed that the Civil War was partly a manifestation of God's wrath for their failure to christianize the Negroes. They urged churches to instruct Afro-Americans in Christian teachings; ecclesiastical gatherings petitioned state governments to reform the slave code—to permit Afro-Americans to preach, to legalize slave marriages, and to allow masters to teach blacks to read and write. It was not until the war years that southern churchmen advocated minimal reforms in the slave system. But they never espoused emancipation. *See also* AFRICAN METHODIST EPISCOPAL (AME) CHURCH; AFRICAN METHODIST EPISCOPAL ZION (AMEZ) CHURCH; BAPTISTS; CHURCHES; METHODISTS/UNITED METHODIST CHURCH; PRESBYTERIANS.

REFERENCES: Daniel, W. Harrison, "Virginia Baptists and the Negro in the Antebellum Era," *Journal of Negro History*, vol. 56, January 1971; Drake, Thomas E., *Quakers and Slavery in America*, Yale University Press, New Haven, 1950; Jernegan, Marcus W., "Slavery and Conversion in the American Colonies," *American Historical Review*, vol. 21, April 1916; Mathews, Donald G., *Slavery and Methodism, A Chapter in American Morality, 1780–1845*, Princeton University Press, Princeton, 1965; Murray, Andrew E., *Presbyterians and the Negro—A History*, Presbyterian Historical Society, Philadelphia, 1966; and Rice, Madeleine H., *American Catholic Opinion in the Slavery Controversy*, Columbia University Press, New York, 1944.

The Underground Railroad The term "Underground Railroad," as popularly used, referred to assistance provided by northern abolitionists to slaves fleeing from bondage in the period before the Civil War. An American legend, composed of both fact and fancy, grew up around such efforts. According to the legend, these efforts included a highly secret and widespread network of "stations" running from the U.S. South into Canada and manned by brave and ingenious "conductors," whose devices to elude the slave catchers included secret passageways, imaginative disguises, and a variety of ruses to throw the pursuers off the track. Legendary accounts also emphasize the large numbers of slaves who rode the secret transportation system. Numerous northern communities claim a heroic record as an integral part of the underground system. In fact, the aid given to fugitive slaves was largely improvised without the benefit of an overall system: well-organized regional activity but no nationally coordinated effort existed.

Regional or local Underground Railroad activity was usually the result of some highly dedicated individual or group of individuals who made such work their special concern. Among the abolitionists who emphasized giving hospitality, financial assistance, and transportation to fugitive slaves were Levi Coffin of Cincinnati, Ohio, probably the best known; Thomas Garrett of Wilmington, Del.; and J. Miller McKim and William Still of Philadelphia, Pa. The contributions of Coffin (who also published a widely read autobiography) and Garrett tended to strengthen the popular impression that the Underground Railroad was a Quaker institution. Although both men were Quakers, they confronted some strong opposition from other members of that religious society. The contribution of Coffin and Garrett also discredits the idea that all Underground Railroad activity was done in extreme secrecy. These men were well known for their efforts in behalf of the fugitive slaves, and Coffin especially made little effort to hide his work.

J. Miller McKim and William Still belonged to the Philadelphia Vigilance Committee, one of a number of abolitionist organizations formed in various northern cities to help runaway slaves after passage of the Fugitive Slave Act of 1850. As an Afro-American, William Still readily gained the confidence of fugitives and had many contacts in Philadelphia's Afro-American community, where runaway slaves were temporarily housed in comparative safety. He kept a journal listing the names of former slaves aided by the committee, and later published it along with other documents in a large volume entitled *The Underground Rail Road*. His book indicates that about 100 fugitives a year went through Philadelphia after 1850.

The actual number of escapees is difficult to determine. Census reports for 1850 and 1860 indicate that approximately 1,000 slaves ran away per year. These figures are probably low, though both abolitionists and southern slaveholders often accepted their accuracy. Southern spokesmen frequently alleged that large numbers of slaves were enticed into fleeing the South by conniving northern abolitionists. Actually, most people who participated in Underground Railroad efforts did not work in the South. Such activity, they felt, was too dangerous and had too limited a possibility of success. Only a very few daring individuals, including the famous Harriet Tubman and Josiah Henson, who had themselves escaped from slavery, directed fugitives from the slave states.

Popular emphasis on the Underground Railroad as an abolitionist institution has caused Americans to minimize—if not overlook—the contributions made by the former slaves themselves in their flight from slavery. Those who made the break for freedom were men and women of great courage who risked terrible punishment or even death should their mission fail. Frequently, they planned and executed their escapes with little or no help from northern abolitionists. Many of them stowed away or took passage on boats running to northern ports. Some just ran away, traveling by night and hiding and resting during the daylight hours. They obtained food and shelter from other slaves, from free blacks, and occasionally even from southern whites.

Some of the escape plans were especially imaginative. Henry Brown, for example, escaped from Richmond, Va., in a box that he had shipped by express to the Vigilance Committee in Philadelphia. Ellen and William Craft left Georgia with the near-white Ellen disguised as an ailing master and William playing the part of her loyal servant. They traveled by train, eventually reaching New England. Those who were aided by the Underground Railroad had often come long distances on their own before finding abolitionists in the northern states.

Some of the former slaves became active in the abolition movement. The best known of the abolitionist fugitive slaves was Frederick Douglass, who was an unusually powerful speaker and a gifted writer. After working for a time with William Lloyd Garrison and his followers, Douglass split with Garrison and founded his own antislavery newspaper, the *North Star*. He also wrote a very popular account of his life in slavery that he eventually rewrote and published in three different editions. Other former slaves who

Far left:This well-publicized lithograph of the 1850s shows members of the Philadelphia Vigilance Committee opening the box in which Henry Brown escaped from slavery in Richmond, Va. Left to right: J. Miller McKim, William Still, Brown, Charles D. Cleveland, and Lewis Thompson. Samuel A. Smith, a white, served a jail term for boxing up Brown and two other slaves in Richmond. (*Library of Congress.*)

wrote and spoke for the abolition cause were William Wells Brown, Henry "Box" Brown, Henry Bibb, Lewis and Milton Clarke, and Samuel Ringgold Ward. These men lectured with authority about slavery. They presented the victim's picture of the South's "peculiar institution," and their emotional presentations rarely failed to move audiences. They personalized the antislavery message in a way that no white abolitionist could. They also called attention to the widespread racial discrimination practiced in northern states. Theirs was a plea for civil rights in the North as well as an end to chattel slavery in the South.

The books and pamphlets written by the former slaves supplemented their personal appearances. Although some of their narratives were taken down by abolitionists, a number of the most widely circulated were written by the fugitives themselves. They wrote of the anguish and humiliation inherent in the institution of slavery, and they told of their desire to escape and of their eventual success. Although former slaves gave due credit to abolitionists for extending aid, they placed greater emphasis on the importance of their own efforts in winning freedom. Besides Frederick Douglass, a few of the fugitive slaves gained considerable renown as writers. Henry Bibb edited a Canadian antislavery newspaper, The Voice of the Fugitive, and William Wells Brown wrote and gave public readings of an antislavery play. Brown also wrote a novel and several travel books and histories, of which the best known was The Black Man, His Antecedents, His Genius, and His Achievements.

The narratives of fugitive slaves contributed to a growing antislavery sentiment in the northern states. The sentiment, as much anti-Southern as antislavery, drew heavily upon the resentment of northerners toward the extra power southern states derived from slavery, which gave them additional representation in the House of Representatives and in the electoral college. The passage of the Fugitive Slave Law of 1850, as part of a more comprehensive sectional compromise, further embittered northerners. The law was unjust to the alleged fugitive slaves, and included an arrogant demand that northerners return to slavery those who had run away. Following its passage, many Afro-Americans left the northern states for Canada. Attempts to return fugitives often produced organized resistance by Afro-Americans and abolitionists, and Underground Railroad incidents received widespread public notice.

Such was the celebrated case of Anthony Burns, whose arrest and subsequent return in 1854 under the Fugitive Slave Law of 1850 precipitated a riot and a criminal case in Boston. A self-taught slave and preacher from Richmond, Va., Burns escaped by ship to Boston. Claimed by his master, Burns was apprehended under the Fugitive Slave Law and detained in the Boston jail. Demanding his release, an angry mob stormed the jail (located in the courthouse) and killed a guard (James Batchelder). The rescue failed, and Burns was returned to his master Later, the rioters who were charged with killing the guard were exonerated, and Burns' freedom was purchased by public subscription in Boston. Burns later attended Oberlin College (Ohio) and moved to Canada.

Moreover, the Fugitive Slave Law inspired the book that had the greatest effect of any writing in bringing the inhumanity of slavery home to thousands of Americans: Harriet Beecher Stowe's Uncle Tom's Cabin. The law and the controversy over it subverted the attempt to compromise the sectional differences and kept the antislavery issue alive until it broke out with new fury over the Kansas-Nebraska Act of 1854.

After the Civil War brought an end to slavery, the Underground Railroad became a legendary feature of the national past. Stories of heroic rescues and hairbreadth escapes were repeated verbally and were often embellished through repetition. A number of those who had been active in the Underground Railroad movement wrote memoirs of their experiences, and county histories and local newspapers related numerous tales of it. The stories told by abolitionists and their descendants tended to exaggerate the role of white abolitionists and to overlook the heroic efforts of the fugitive slaves themselves. The Underground Railroad of American legend is basically a white, paternalistic institution. The Underground Railroad of history was a combination of white aid and black self-help, of white humanitarian concern and the struggle of fugitive slaves for their own independence. See also SLAVERY: THE ABOLITIONISTS.

REFERENCES: Two old accounts are still helpful: Still, William, Underground Railroad, published in 1872 and reprinted in 1968; and Siebert, Wilbur H., Underground Railroad from Slavery to Freedom, Arno, published in 1898 and reprinted in 1967. The best recent accounts are in Campbell, Stanley W., Slave Catchers: Enforcement of the Fugitive Slave Law, 1850–1860, U of NC Pr., 1970; and Gara, Larry, Liberty Line: The Legend of the Underground Railroad, U Pr of Ky., 1967. See also references under SLAVERY: SLAVE NARRATIVES and SLAVERY: REFERENCES.

The Abolitionists Generally, people who were dedicated to the overthrow of chattel slavery were known as abolitionists. The term "abolitionist movement" is often used synonymously with "antislavery movement," although in Great Britain the term was first applied to the crusade against the Atlantic slave trade rather than against slavery itself. In America in the late 1700s, persons who campaigned actively against both slavery and slave importation called themselves abolitionists. Twentieth-century historians, however, have more commonly used the label to identify those persons who, after 1830, demanded immediate and unconditional emancipation. This latter group is thus distinguished from earlier "gradualists."

While abolitionists agreed on their major goal (emancipation), they failed to unite on subsidiary goals. For example, should they advocate equality for free blacks as well as freedom for slaves? Should their goal be the integration or separation of races? Should emancipation be followed by settlement of the freedmen in distinctly black colonies or states? Abolitionists also differed over appropriate methods or strategies: Would they be most effective by seeking gradual results, through moderate tactics of persuasion and political pressure, or by demanding immediate action in a more aggressive, militant manner? Could they accomplish the most by working through the churches to make a religious appeal based on the evil, sinful nature of slavery, or by direct political action? Should they embrace nonviolence as a philosophy, or condone the use of force as being justified and necessary? Should they join with such other reform movements as those for women's rights and peace, or should they adhere to a "single idea" and thus avoid the risks of dissipating their energies? Beset by disagreement and discord, the abolitionist movement included efforts along all of these lines at one time or another, depending on the prevailing attitudes of the period, and the different responses of succeeding generations to changing political, economic, and social pressures.

Early abolition Efforts Among the leading antislavery spokesmen of the colonial period were two black New Englanders—Prince Hall, the founder of Afro-American masonry in the United States, and Abijah Prince, one of the men who established the town of Sunderland, Vt.—and the white New England Puritan merchant and judge, Samuel Sewall. During the eighteenth century, however, it was the Quakers who assumed leadership of the cause (in fact, the Society of Friends was the first religious group to identify itself with the young antislavery movement). As early as 1715 John Hepburn wrote a pamphlet denouncing slavery as a sin. In the 1740s and 1750s his coreligionist John Woolman achieved prominence as an antislavery advocate in both North and South. By the time of the American Revolution, a Philadelphia Quaker, Anthony Benezet, had become the leading spokesman for the idea that freedom for the new nation should mean freedom for the slave as well. Before the end of the eighteenth century, two major antislavery societies were established: the New York Manumission Society (1785) and the Pennsylvania Society for Promoting the Abolition of Slavery (1775). Other state and local societies followed. After 1784 representatives from state abolition societies met annually in the American Convention to coordinate their efforts and to keep in touch with British abolitionists. They focused their attack against the foreign slave trade as well as against slavery, and in both Great Britain and the United States abolitionist pressures contributed to the passage of laws outlawing further importation of slaves after January 1, 1808.

An important aim of these early antislavery organizations was to provide education and employment for free blacks. These societies believed that as Afro-Americans were given an opportunity to demonstrate their intelligence and abilities, whites would look favorably upon some system of general emancipation. The societies tried, therefore, to avoid a militant approach that would alienate potential friends. Those who were religiously oriented had faith that God would work this out in his own good time; others put their trust in the steady progress and acceptance of the liberal idea of the natural rights of all men. They regularly sent petitions to their state legislatures as well as to the U.S. Congress on behalf of both slaves and free blacks.

In the last decade of the eighteenth century, English abolitionists established a colony in Sierra Leone in West Africa to which free blacks could be sent as settlers. One of the first Americans to advocate colonization was Paul Cuffe, a black Massachusetts shipowner who personally transported a group of settlers to the British colony. During the winter of 1816–17 the American Colonization Society was formed with the aim of sending free blacks to Africa, and within a few years the territory of Liberia was established to receive settlers. But the majority of Afro-Americans, led by Richard Allen, Absolom Jones, and James Forten in Philadelphia, Pa., rejected the American Colonization Society on the grounds that its philosophy of removal of Afro-Americans from the United States was based on racial prejudice rather than on benevolence. These leaders argued that black abolitionists should remain in the United States and not desert their "brethren in bondage." During the 1820s some abolitionists, including the black New Englander Prince Saunders and the white Benjamin Lundy, promoted the idea of colonizing Afro-Americans in the new black republic of Haiti, but with only minimal success. By the end of that decade, one of the few black leaders who still supported African colonization was John Russwurm, coeditor with Samuel Cornish of *Freedom's Journal*, an abolitionist newspaper begun in 1827 to promote the antislavery cause and to instill racial pride in Afro-Americans. As time went on, most abolitionists vehemently rejected colonization as a solution to the problem of slavery.

By the 1830s most abolitionists had become pessimistic about the slow pace of the gradualist approach: the slave trade laws were not enforced; slavery had been extended legally beyond the Mississippi River; free blacks were still denied equal rights in the North as well as in the South; efforts to boycott slave-produced goods had not gained sufficient support to be effective; and colonization had been rejected. Slavery seemed to be fastened on the nation more strongly than ever, and its defenders, such as John C. Calhoun, were claiming that it was a "positive good" rather than an evil institution.

The decision to launch a vigorous new crusade found expression in the Colored Convention Movement, which began in 1830 and culminated in the organization of the American Antislavery Society in 1833. The movement was religiously oriented, advocated nonviolence and "moral suasion," and included the goal of equal rights for free blacks as well as emancipation. It rejected the idea of financial compensation to slaveholders in return for emancipation (the British plan), arguing that if slaveholding were a sin, one should be punished rather than paid for it and that if anyone deserved compensation, it was the slave rather than the master. The American Antislavery Society was an integrated organization. Black leaders involved in its founding and elected to its offices included Robert Purvis, James McCrummell, James Barbadoes, John B. Vashon, Peter Williams, and Abraham D. Shadd, all of whom worked along with such white leaders as William Lloyd Garrison, Evan Lewis, and the Tappan brothers (Arthur and Lewis).

State and local societies and women's and juveniles' groups—many with black auxiliaries—were organized as subsidiaries to the American Antislavery Society. These societies sent out paid agents and volunteer lecturers (many of them trained by Theodore Weld), flooded the country with antislavery publications, sent petitions to the U.S. Congress, and gave what aid they could to fugitive slaves escaping to the North or to Canada. Lines of communication were established with abolitionists in Great Britain who furnished an inspiring example with the accomplishment of West Indian emancipation in the period 1833–38. August 1, which was West Indian Emancipation Day, became an annual holiday that Afro-Americans celebrated as their own "Fourth of July."

The Amistad Affair Afro-Americans could also celebrate the *Amistad* decision along with abolitionists. Under the leadership of Joseph Cinque (ca. 1811–78), a successful mutiny occurred aboard the two-masted Spanish ship *L'Amistad* in May 1839. The vessel finally appeared off the coast of Long Island, where the U.S. Navy took it into custody. The mutiners, numbering 49 with Cinque, were arrested on charges of piracy and murder.

The *Amistad* affair was the subject of impassioned controversy between antislavery and proslavery forces for nearly two years. Abolitionists, led by Lewis Tappan, conducted an extensive campaign to arouse public sympathy for the Mendians, who suddenly found themselves imprisoned by people who spoke an unfamiliar language. Tappan also recruited a team of well-known lawyers to defend the Mendians in federal court in Hartford, Conn. Afro-American religious and self-improvement societies, for their part, raised funds for the legal battle. The federal government took a clear proslavery stand in the dispute. Expecting the trial judge, A. T. Judson (who had previously handed down antiblack rulings), to decide against the blacks, President Martin Van Buren even ordered the U.S. Navy to prepare to return the Mendians to Cuba.

To the surprise of friends and foes alike, Cinque and his people were set free. The crucial testimony came from R. R. Madden, a British official stationed in Havana, who was questioned in order to make certain that Britain's treaties with Spain banning the international slave trade were not violated. Madden persuaded Judge Judson that the Mendians had been smuggled illegally into Cuba, and that they therefore were not legitimate slave property. Because of legal technicalities, the Mendians were not immediately released. But complete freedom was granted to them a year later, in January 1841, when the former U.S. president John Quincy Adams, arguing in the Africans' behalf, persuaded the U.S. Supreme Court to uphold Judson's decision.

The Mendians returned to their native land late in 1841, accompanied by two Afro-American missionaries. Back home, Cinque assumed a position of leadership among his people. Ironically, he also participated in the slave trade.

Participation by Afro-Americans Among the Afro-Americans who played prominent roles as lecturers in the antislavery cause were Frederick Douglass, David Ruggles, James McCune Smith, Henry Bibb, Charles Lennox Remond, J. W. C. Pennington, and Samuel Ringgold Ward. Two of the most militant were David Walker and Henry Highland Garnet, both of whom believed that violent revolution might be the only method of freeing the slaves. *Walker's Appeal,* a pamphlet issued in 1829, and Garnet's speech entitled "Address to the Slaves of the United States," delivered at a national convention in 1843, were both calls for slave uprisings.

Afro-American churches became antislavery centers, and black spokesmen, who were usually ministers, represented a variety of denominations: Nathaniel Paul, Baptist; Alexander Crummell, Episcopalian; Alexander W. Wayman, Methodist; J. W. C. Pennington and Samuel Ward, Congregationalist; and Henry Highland Garnet, Presbyterian, to name only a few. Afro-American women in the movement included the former slaves Harriet Tubman and Sojourner Truth, who were especially noted for their Underground Railroad activity, and such free northerners as Sarah Remond, Susan Paul, Sarah M. Douglass, and Charlotte Forten. Free black communities in northern cities furnished the main haven for fugitive slaves. Josiah Henson was a former slave who labored for years directing the refugee settlement in Canada known as Dawn. Other Canadian settlements supported by abolitionist contributions from both Great Britain and the United States were Wilberforce and Elgin. Several black abolitionists, some of them fugitives themselves, traveled to Great Britain to help raise money. One of the earliest was Rev. Nathaniel Paul, who was followed over the years by Charles and Sarah Remond, Samuel R. Ward, J. W. C. Pennington, Frederick Douglass, William and Ellen Craft, William Wells Brown, and many others who helped to awaken sympathy for the slave.

Many of those who had escaped from slavery made important contributions to antislavery literature with the publication of their autobiographies. Afro-Americans published and edited several antislavery newspapers, including: Frederick Douglass' *North Star* and *Frederick Douglass' Weekly; Freedom's Journal; The Colored American;* and *The Rights of All.* In addition, these Afro-Americans helped support many other abolitionist publications that were edited by whites, such as Benjamin Lundy's *Genius of Universal Emancipation;* William Lloyd Garrison's *Liberator; The Philanthropist; The Herald of Freedom; The Emancipator; The Anti-Slavery Standard; The Anti-Slavery Bugle;* and *The Anti-Slavery Reporter.* In the 1850s the *National Era* in Washington, D.C., became the voice of political abolitionism.

Later Abolition Efforts: 1830–60 The decade of the 1830s was one of confrontation and mob violence. Abolitionist literature was banned and burned in many southern states, and in the North mobs often prevented antislavery lecturers from speaking, egged and stoned them, burned their buildings, and destroyed their presses. Of course, abolitionists were criticized for not obeying the law of the land, which required the return of fugitives, but they stood on the philosophy of the "higher law," which held that when man-made laws violated the laws of God, one must obey his own conscience. It was dangerous to be an abolitionist, especially for Afro-Americans to actively take up the cause; it was the Afro-American who was most frequently the target of mob violence, who most suffered the consequences of economic retaliation, and who ran great risks by harboring fugitives. It was a common practice for mobs to break up antislavery meetings and then to stage general marauding expeditions against those sections of the cities where blacks lived—pillaging, looting, and setting fires.

Like most reforms, the antislavery movement had its share of internal disagreements. By 1840 several major areas of dissension had developed: whether women should be allowed to vote and hold office in the American Antislavery Society, whether abolitionists should organize politically, and whether funds for the cause should be collected centrally or locally. Many objected to what they considered William Lloyd Garrison's radicalism in espousing anticlericalism, anti-Sabbatarianism, and nonresistance, as well as his advocacy of women's rights and his call for a boycott of voting because it lent support to a proslavery government.

Unable to reach a compromise, one faction of abolitionists—led by Lewis Tappan, James G. Birney, and Joshua Leavitt—seceded from the American Antislavery Society (controlled by Garrison) in 1840 to form a new organization, the American and Foreign Antislavery Society. This new group quickly moved toward political organization, which resulted in the formation of the Liberty Party. In 1840 and again in 1844 it named James G. Birney, an ex-slaveholder from Kentucky and Alabama, as its presidential candidate. By 1848, with the addition of many northern Whigs and some northern Democrats, the Liberty Party gave way to the Free Soil Party, which stood on a platform of excluding slavery from all the western territories. This platform was later adopted by the new Republican Party.

Although many of the black abolitionists originally remained with Garrison in the old American Antislavery Society, as the years went on many of them supported the antislavery political parties. Frederick Douglass is an example of one Afro-American leader who made this shift. Unfortunately, the rivalry between the Garrisonians and the Tappanites throughout the 1840s and 1850s weakened the entire antislavery cause

and probably alienated potential support for the movement as a whole. Meanwhile, Afro-Americans continued to operate through their own Colored National conventions as well. An additional factor in strengthening this separatist movement may have been the dissatisfaction of Afro-Americans with white paternalism within the antislavery ranks.

In the 1850s prospects looked dim for either quick or peaceful emancipation and integration. The hated Fugitive Slave Act was passed in 1850; the Kansas-Nebraska Act of 1854 gave a new lease on life to the possibility of extending slavery into the western territories; the "slave power" allegedly wanted to extend it's control over the Caribbean and possibly even to reopen the African slave trade; and the *Dred Scott* decision of 1857 held that Afro-Americans were not citizens. It is not surprising, therefore, to find a resurgence of Afro-American nationalism and a reawakened interest in the possibilities of colonization. Martin R. Delany, a physician who later became prominent in the Civil War and in Reconstruction politics, emerged as a leader of a back-to-Africa movement, and Henry Highland Garnet headed the African Civilization Society. The National Emigration Convention in 1854 recommended that Haiti, Central America, and the Niger valley in Africa be investigated as possible places of refuge. But most of the black emigrants continued to go to Canada, and the majority of Afro-Americans still held to the hope of freedom and equality within American society. For most of them, the prospect of emigrating to Africa was impractical.

Some abolitionists in the last decade before the Civil War, both black and white, advocated a separation of the North from the slaveholding South; others returned to a consideration of the idea of compensated emancipation as the best method of freeing the slaves peacefully, while keeping the South in the Union. However, the abolitionist crusade did not bring about peaceful emancipation. When the Civil War came, the abolitionists exerted unrelenting pressure on President Abraham Lincoln's administration to make emancipation a war aim. Although the Emancipation Proclamation disappointed them because it was an incomplete measure motivated by military necessity, they accepted it as a step in the right direction and then bent their efforts toward the framing and adoption of the Thirteenth Amendment to the Constitution, which ended chattel slavery in the nation. *See also* AFRO-AMERICAN HISTORY: SECTIONAL CONFLICT over Slavery, 1820–60; and Afro-American History: Civil War, 1861–65; Colonization.

references: Selected references include the following: Douglass, Frederick, *The Life and Times of Frederick Douglass Written by Himself*, Grosset & Dunlap, New York, 1882; Dumond, Dwight L., *Antislavery: The Crusade for Freedom in America*, University of Michigan Press, Ann Arbor, 1961; Filler, Louis, *The Crusade Against Slavery, 1830–1860*, Harper and Row, New York, 1960; Litwack, Leon, *North of Slavery: The Free Negro in the United States, 1790–1860*, University of Chicago Press, Chicago, 1961; Mabee, Carleton, *Black Freedom: The Nonviolent Abolitionists from 1830 to the Civil War*, Maxmillan, New York, 1970; Quarles, Benjamin, *Black Abolitionists*, Oxford University Press, New York, 1969; and Woodson, Carter G. (ed.), *The Mind of the Negro as Reflected in Letters Written during the Crisis, 1800–1860*, Associated Publishers, Washington, D.C., 1926.

Slave Narratives Thousands of ex-slaves left written or dictated accounts of their experiences. As a body, these accounts constitute one of the most valuable sources for the study of the life of bondsmen. An estimated 6,000 narratives appeared in some form between 1700 and 1945. The first important account by a slave to come out of the colonial period was that of Gustavus Vassa, entitled *The Interesting Narrative of the Life of Olaudah Equiano, or Gustavus Vassa, the African; by Himself* (1790). Born in Benin (now in Nigeria, Africa) in 1745, Vassa was taken to work on a Virginia plantation at the age of 11; he purchased his freedom while working in Philadelphia, Pa., and became active in anti-slavery activities both in the colonies and in England. His two-volume autobiography was so popular that within five years it had gone through eight printings.

Slave narratives became common in the antebellum period when ex-slaves were encouraged to write their accounts for abolitionist publications. Some of these accounts were dictated and some were written down by the slaves themselves, but many were heavily edited by abolitionists. More than 300 such narratives appeared in William Lloyd Garrison's *Liberator*. Most have a repetitive theme and style and are of little value as literature, although their effectiveness as propaganda cannot be questioned.

Among the most important narratives were those written down by the slaves themselves and published as books. Such autobiographical narratives share a similar dramatic style but all are also highly individual. These narratives include those of William Wells Brown (1842); Lunsford Lane (1842); Moses Grandy (1844); Frederick Douglass (1845); Lewis Clark (1846); Julius Melbourne (1847); Henry Bibb (1849); J. W. C. Pennington (1850); Solomon Northup (1853); Austin Steward (1857); and J. W. Logan (1859).

Many of these ex-slaves were very active in the abolitionist movement; others were equally eloquent spokesmen of the Afro-American experience. Pennington was a minister of a Presbyterian Church in New York City, having escaped from slavery in the 1840s. An illiterate blacksmith while enslaved, by 1851 Pennington had achieved such renown as a preacher and lecturer that Heidelberg University (Tiffin, Ohio) awarded him an honorary D.D. degree.

William Wells Brown is remembered for his literary versatility; in his *Narrative of William W. Brown; a Fugitive Slave*, he not only gives insight into the character of the author, but also he presents a vivid account of slavery in Missouri. Wells, a prolific author, dealt with slavery in subsequent works, at least in part, by drawing on his personal experiences; notably in *Clotel: or the President's Daughter: A Narrative of Slave Life in the United States* (1853) and in his play *The Escape or A Leap For Freedom.*

The most famous and the greatest narrative from the literary and historical point of view is Frederick Douglass' *My Bondage and My Freedom* (1855). Born into slavery in 1817, Douglass became a leader in the radical reform movement. His autobiography not only relates his personal experiences, but also discusses the slave community, the meaning of slavery for the individual, and the relationship of white to black under a

Gustavus Vassa. *(Moorland-Spingarn Research Center, Howard University.)*

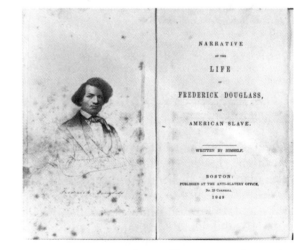

Frederick Douglass. *(Moorland-Spingarn Research Center, Howard University.)*

slave regime. Douglass offers many theoretical insights, and his style is as compelling to read now as it was a hundred years ago. His book *My Bondage and My Freedom* grew out of an abolitionist pamphlet Douglass wrote in 1845. He later incorporated the 1855 autobiography into his *Life and Times of Frederick Douglass* (1881; rev. ed. 1892).

Josiah Henson's experiences, recorded in

Truth Stranger Than Fiction, were along with Douglass' account the inspiration for much of the descriptive matter in Harriet Beecher Stowe's *Uncle Tom's Cabin.* Slave narratives were published in substantial numbers even after the Civil War.

William Still, active in the Underground Railroad, collected narratives of fugitives who came to his Underground Railroad "station." Published after the Civil War, this volume long remained an important source. In the 1930s the Library of Congress, in conjunction with the Federal Writers Project, assembled narratives from former slaves. (They were published in the 1970s under the editorship of George P. Rawick.) In the next decade Fisk University (Nashville, Tenn.) assembled a volume of slave narratives, *Social Science Source Document Number 2* (1945), which, according to Charles Johnson of Fisk, were "written down exactly as they were obtained." Ophelia Settle Egypt conducted the project. *See also* LITERATURE: THE NOVEL.

REFERENCES: For a good account of the historical background of slave narratives, see Nichols, Charles H., *Many Thousand Gone: The Ex-Slaves' Account of Their Bondage and Freedom,* Indiana University Press, Bloomington, 1969. Further commentary with a selected list of published narratives is found in Blassingame, John W., *The Slave Community: Plantation Life in the Antebellum South,* Oxford University Press, New York, 1973. Special commentary upon the Library of Congress collection is found in Botkin, B. A., *Lay My Burden Down; A Folk History of Slavery,* University of Chicago Press, Chicago, 1945; and in Rawick, George P., *The American Slave: A Composite Autobiography,* Negro Universities Press, Westport, 1970. Accounts are found in two doctoral dissertations: Jackson, Margaret Young, "An Investigation of Biographies and Autobiographies of American Slaves Published Between 1840 and 1860; Based Upon the Cornell Special Slavery Collection," Cornell University, 1954; and Starling, Marion Wilson, "The Slave Narrative: Its Place in American Literary History," New York University, 1946.

References The interpretation of slavery as an institution that grew out of the needs of white planters in the South put forth by Ulrich B. Phillips in his *American Negro Slavery* (1918) and in his *Life and Labor in the Old South* (1929) dominated scholarly studies of the subject for more than a generation. Only recently have the long-standing debates on profitability, on large v. small planters, on antebellum racial attitudes of whites, and on plantation management given way to studies of the actual life-style of slaves. Because most records and accounts of slaves were made by and for white people, much more is known about how planters tried to recover fugitive slaves than about what the slaves did when they ran away. Massive studies

exist of the effort of southern churches to convert slaves, but no one has systematically examined the religion of slaves. With the assumption that because some slave narratives were edited by abolitionists, none of them could be considered as unbiased fact, scholars have ensured the silence of these accounts by slaves.

Yet, many narrators told their stories to sympathetic ears, and countless other former slaves wrote their autobiographies after the Civil War. These primary sources, although posing the same difficulties as any bona fide primary reference, have nevertheless brought the slave forward as a witness. Charles L. Nichols, an Afro-American professor at Brown University (Providence, R.I.), wrote *Many Thousand Gone: The Ex-Slaves' Account of Their Bondage and Freedom* (1963), the first study to examine closely these illuminating works. Stanley Feldstein, in *Once a Slave; the Slaves' View of Slavery* (1971), examined more narratives than Nichols, but limited his reportage to what the slaves said about a select number of sometimes unconnected topics. Instead of making an intensive study of slave quarters, Feldstein dealt with many of the usual topics included in studies of the institutions of slavery—provisions, crops, type of slaves, and slavery as a national issue. When, however, Feldstein's narrative turns to plantation life and attitudes, it comes closer to the truth of slavery. Unfortunately, both Nichols and Feldstein treated the narratives as literature, reporting what was said without further analysis. The methodological weaknesses of both Nichols and Feldstein contrast sharply with Norman P. Yeatman's critical introduction to and careful selection of Works Project Administration (WPA) interviews for inclusion in *Life Under the "Peculiar Institution"* (1970). In spite of his diligence, Yeatman's task proved almost insurmountable. Sifting through the reminiscences of Afro-Americans who were at least 70 years removed from slavery when they were interviewed in the 1930s, he demonstrated that the selective memory of ex-slaves is such that their reminiscences generally are more valuable as folklore than as eyewitness accounts; a slave looking backward through time is a limited source of factual information. The reprinting of Afro-American autobiographies in recent years, however, presents the best opportunity to study the plantation from the slave's vantage point. Most revealing are those of Frederick Douglass, William Wells Brown, William Smalls, Henry Bibb, Josiah Henson, Olaudah Equiano (Gustavus Vassa), Austin Steward, Henry Clay Bruce, Louis Hughes, and Elizabeth Keckley.

Kenneth Stampp made a valiant effort to characterize slave life in *The Peculiar Institution* (1956), but he let the methodology of Ulrich B. Phillips set the terms of the debate, viewing slave quarters through the eyes of whites. Yet, despite methodological shortcomings, Stampp's book presents the most accurate portrait of the plantation, and stands out as one of the best books on slavery.

The most provocative study of slavery to appear in the last few decades is Stanley Elkins' *Slavery: A Problem in American Institutional and Intellectual Life* (1959). Elkins theorizes that southern slavery differed from the Latin American institution in that a distinctive personality type—the *Sambo* type—emerged on American plantations. A majority of southern slaves, Elkins argues, were *Sambos*. The childlike, docile behavior typical of the southern slave, according to Elkins, was analogous to the behavior of the survivors of the German concentration camps of World War II and explicable in terms of role psychology and interpersonal theory. Critics of Elkins have shown that more similarities than differences existed between slavery in America's South and that in Latin America, charging that he failed to support his theory with primary sources.

John W. Blassingame, in *The Slave Community: Plantation Life in the Antebellum South* (1972), examined a variety of primary sources, analogous institutions, and psychological theories in order to create a true picture of slaves and masters. According to Blassingame, interpersonal theory, analysis of the autobiographies of slaves and masters, and travel accounts lead to a complex view of the plantation and slave personality, in contrast to the deterministic view expounded by Elkins; and in contrast to other studies on the subject, Blassingame examines enslavement, the family, rebelliousness, religion, culture, and behavior from the vantage point of the slave quarters. His book tries to show what it was like to be a slave.

An earlier study by Richard Wade, *Slavery in the Cities* (1960), detailed the unique impact of urbanization on slavery. Utilizing unreliable statistics, Wade concludes that urban slavery declined in importance in the 1850s. Apparently, however, the alleged decline in the number of slaves in southern cities was due to a change in the census-taking procedure. In 1850 the slaves belonging to inhabitants of a city had been cred-ited to that city regardless of where the slaves actually resided in the state. The procedure was reversed in 1860: slaves living in a city were credited to that city regardless of where their masters lived.

Practically all studies of slavery have mentioned the issue of slave resistance. With the exception perhaps of *The Slave Community and Mullin's Flight and Rebellion* (1972), no study approaches the subject in the systematic fashion of Herbert Aptheker's *American Negro Slave Revolts* (1943). Focusing primarily on conspiracies and white fears rather than on actual revolts, Aptheker's book attempts to force Afro-American resistance into a Marxian framework, frequently leading historians to ridicule the whole idea of rebelliousness. Yet Aptheker's study has solid grounding in resource materials, and stands in sharp contrast to the undocumented volume of Nicholas Haladsz, *The Rattling Chains: Slave Unrest and Revolt in the Antebellum South* (1966). Studies of individual revolts and conspiracies include: John W. Lofton, *Insurrection in South Carolina: The Turbulent World of Denmark Vesey* (1964); Robert S. Starobin (ed.), *Denmark Vesey: The Slave Conspiracy of 1822* (1970); Herbert Aptheker, *Nat Turner's Slave Rebellion* (1966); Roy F. Turner, *The Nat Turner Slave Insurrection* (1966) and Eric Foner (ed.), *Nat Turner* (1971). Larry Gara, in *The Liberty Line: The Legend of the Underground Railroad* (1961), explores the myth and reality of organized escapes.

Fictional treatments of slavery that rise above the banal are infrequent. Although most scholars rate Harriett Beecher Stowe's *Uncle Tom's Cabin* (1852) high on the list of the most valuable, Richard Hildreth's *Archy Moore* (1836) is a more accurate portrait of the institution. Several recent treatments by Afro-American novelists are extremely perceptive: Alston Anderson's *All God's Children* (1965) and Margaret Walker's *Jubilee* (1966) are especially illuminating. The best fictionalized characterization of slave resistance is Arna Bontemps' account of Gabriel Prosser in *Black Thunder* (1936), the strength of which results from the author's broad knowledge of slave narratives.

While Bontemps depended on primary sources as the basis for his novel, William Styron used his imagination and the writings of Phillips and Elkins in composing his "Meditations on History," the Pulitzer Prize-winning *The Confessions of Nat Turner* (1966). Praised by white scholars for his historical accuracy, Styron was equally lambasted by Afro-American writers for the mental gyrations he managed in order to portray Nat Turner the rebel as Nat Turner the Sambo. Although the novel was born of ignorance, and simply repeated the errors made by Phillips and Elkins, few scholars were able to evaluate its historical accuracy. Under the theory that a novelist has the license to use his imagination to attempt to explain reality, Styron deserved his Pulitzer Prize. But when that novelist claims that he is "meditating on history," or writing a historical novel, he must be held accountable for his deviations from the facts. As a novel, the *Confessions* is superb; as a historical novel, it is absurd.

Moneta Sleet, Jr. (Photo by G. Marshall Wilson, Ebony-Jet-Black Stars.)

Having praised the novel, white historians rushed to the barricades to defend their liberal credentials when *William Styron's Nat Turner: Ten Black Writers Respond* (1968) appeared under the editorship of John Hendrik Clarke. Generally, white historians missed the essential point that the award to Styron for his emasculation of Nat Turner was acquiescence on the part of the literary community to an act (literary) that reduced the Afro-American to a position of impotence. Afro-Americans rejected Styron's effort to kill one of their folk heroes.

Unlike the slave, the antebellum free black has had few novelists or historians to chronicle his story. No general history of free blacks in the South has yet been written, and John Hope Franklin's *The Free Negro in North Carolina, 1634–1860* (1943) and Luther P. Jackson's *Free Negro Labor and Property Holding in Virginia, 1830–1860* (1942) stand alone as comprehensive state studies. Letitia Brown, in *Free Negroes in the District of Columbia* (1972), has made a pioneering study of urban free blacks. The standard monograph on northern free blacks is Leon Litwack's *North of Slavery: The Negro in the Free States, 1790–1860* (1961), but it is so concerned with race relations that it reveals little about the internal dynamics of the Afro-American community. The most essential sources for studying free blacks are the autobiographies they wrote. John Malvin, Daniel Peterson, Samuel Ringgold Ward, John Mercer Langston, Daniel A. Payne, Miflin Gibbs, John P. Green, Jeremiah Asher, and James Still present intimate pictures of their communities. Benjamin Quarles almost singlehandedly reconstructed many important activities of the free blacks in his justly acclaimed *Black Abolitionists* (1969) and in *The Negro in the American Revolution* (1961).

Robert Smalls. (Library of Congress.)

REFERENCES: For specialized references on slavery in individual states, see REFERENCES under SLAVERY IN SELECTED STATES. See also references after various entries under SLAVERY. A good, general (but not annotated) bibliography is Weinstein, Allen, Frank Otto Gatell, and Davis Sarasohn (eds.), *American Negro Slavery: A Modern Reader*, 3d ed., 1979, pp. 288–313. For bibliographical references (also not annotated) in regard to studies on quantification, especially to Robert W. Fogel and Stanley L. Engerman, *Time on the Cross: The Economics of American Negro Slavery*, 1974, see David, Paul A., et al., *Reckoning with Slavery: Critical Essays in the Quantitative History of American Negro Slavery*, Oxford U Pr., 1976, pp. 358–382.

SLEET, MONETA J., JR. (1926–), photographer; born in Owensboro, Ky. Sleet received a B.A. degree from Kentucky State College in 1947 and his M.A. degree in journalism from New York University in 1950. He also attended Columbia University and the School of Modern Photography in New York City. Sleet served as photographer for *Our World* and worked as a reporter for the New York *Amsterdam News*. He taught photography at Maryland State College (now the University of Maryland, Eastern Shore) in 1948. Sleet served as a staff photographer for the Johnson Publishing Company in Chicago, Ill., and received the Pulitzer Prize in feature photography for his photograph (1968) of Mrs. Martin Luther King, Jr., (and her daughter) at the funeral of her husband. *See also* PHOTOGRAPHERS.

SMALL, JOHN F. (1935–), business executive; born in Philadelphia, Pa. Small received a B.A. degree from Brooklyn College of the City University of New York in 1959. After service in the U.S. Air Force, he became an account executive in sales for the National Broadcasting Company in New York City. In 1969 Small formed his own New York advertising agency, among whose clients were Procter and Gamble, the Singer Company, and Joseph E. Seagram and Sons. Small was also active in civic organizations in New York City.

SMALLS, ROBERT (1839–1915), state legislator, U.S. Representative; born in Beaufort, S.C. The young Smalls moved with his master, McKee, to Charleston, S.C., in 1851. Pressed into service by the Confederates, he was assigned to the crew of the *Planter*, a transport steamer in Charleston harbor. Having learned to navigate, and having first smuggled his wife and two children aboard while the ship's officers were absent, he took command of the ship and its crew of 12 slaves and sailed it past Confederate fortifications into the hands of the Union fleet that lay outside the harbor. The exploit of Smalls and his crew made them heroes. Smalls became a pilot in the U.S. Navy, and in 1863 after more daring displays of courage, he was promoted to the rank of captain and given command of the *Planter*. He held this rank until 1866 when his ship was decommissioned, and then he returned to Charleston to enter politics. By 1868 Smalls had become a member of the state house of representatives, and in 1870 he was elected to the state senate where he served for four years. In 1875 Smalls was elected to the first of five terms in the U.S. House of Representatives. Before his first term in the U.S. Congress was completed Smalls had become a major-general in the state militia, which he had joined in 1865. He also had been convicted of accepting a bribe while a state senator, sentenced, and ultimately pardoned. During his tenure in the House, Smalls took strong positions against the election procedures in South Carolina and in favor of equal accommodations on interstate transportation. After his last term in Congress in 1887, he returned to private life, and in 1889 he was appointed collector of the port of Beaufort, S.C.

SMITH, BESSIE (1894–1937), blues singer; born in Chattanooga, Tenn. Smith began touring in 1912 with Fats Chappelle's Rabbit Foot Minstrels, which then featured Ma Rainey, the first of the great blues singers. She then toured with the Florida Cotton Pickers, and later with her own Liberty Belles act. At one time Fats Waller was her accompanist. Her first recordings were issued in 1923. They introduced a new sound in blues singing, and ultimately she was heralded as one of the innovators of modern blues jazz. Her recording of "Down Hearted Blues" sold more than 2 million copies within the year. Smith toured regularly across the country during the 1920s and 1930s in various revues and tent shows. For several years she toured with her own band and later with other name bands. Her personal appearances were interspersed with a film (*St. Louis Blues*, 1929), radio appearances, and recording sessions. Smith became known as the "Empress of the Blues." She died from injuries sustained in an automobile accident near Clarksdale, Miss. *See also* MUSIC: BLUES.

SMITH, CHARLES ZELLENDER (1927–), lawyer, judge; born in Lakeland, Fla. After military service in World War II, Smith received a

B.S. degree from Temple University (Philadelphia, Pa.) in 1952 and his LL.B. degree from the University of Washington in 1955. He then served as a law clerk in the state Supreme Court at Olympia, Wash., as deputy prosecutor for King County, and from 1961 to 1964 as attorney in the criminal division of the U.S. Department of Justice. In 1966 Smith became a judge of the Superior Court of King County, Wash.

SMITH, EMORY B. (1886–1950), lawyer, judge, educator; born in Raleigh, N.C. Smith studied at Hampton Institute (Hampton, Va.) and at the New York Evening School of Men, and he graduated from the Yale University Divinity School in 1919. A member of the District of Columbia bar, he was alumni and field secretary and later publicity director of Howard University (Washington, D.C.). From 1931 to 1941 Smith served as a faculty member of the Robert H. Terrell Law School in Washington, D.C. In 1950 he was appointed judge of the Municipal Court for the District of Columbia by President Harry S. Truman; he died a few weeks after taking office.

SMITH, EZRA EZIEKEL (1852– ?), educator, minister; born in Duplin County, N.C. Smith was educated at Shaw University (Raleigh, N.C.), and then he began teaching in North Carolina in a log schoolhouse that he built. He was ordained in the Baptist Church in 1879, and in 1888 Smith was appointed minister resident and consul general to Liberia. He also fought in the Spanish-American War. Smith is considered the founder of Fayetteville State Normal School because he donated the land for its campus and served as its principal for many years. *See also* FAYETTEVILLE STATE UNIVERSITY.

SMITH, JAMES McCUNE (1811–65), physician, abolitionist; born in New York, N.Y. Smith attended the African Free School in New York City. Unable to enroll in a medical college in the United States, he went to the University of Glasgow in Scotland, where he received a B.A. degree in 1835, a M.A. degree in 1836, and his M.D. degree in 1837, becoming the first Afro-American to obtain a medical degree. Smith then practiced medicine in New York City, and served as physician for many years to the Colored Orphan Asylum of New York. He was also the proprietor of two drugstores. An active abolitionist, Smith collaborated with Frederick Douglass in editing *North Star*, an abolitionist newspaper. Smith was a strong opponent of the colonization movement, believing that Afro-Americans should fight for their rights in America. To this end he pioneered in the scientific study of race, both lecturing and writing on the subject. *See also* SLAVERY: THE ABOLITIONISTS.

SMITH, JESSIE CARNEY (1930–   ), librarian, educator; born in Greensboro, N.C. Smith received a B.S. degree from North Carolina Agricultural and Technical (A&T) State University in 1950, a M.A. degree from Michigan State University in 1956, a M.A. degree from George Peabody College for Teachers (Nashville, Tenn.) in 1957, and her Ph.D. degree from the University of Illinois in 1964. She served on the library staff at Tennessee State University from 1957 to 1960, as a teaching assistant at the University of Illinois from 1963 to 1965, and as a professor of library science at Fisk University (Nashville, Tenn.) after 1965. Among her writings is a volume entitled *Black Academic Libraries and Research Collections: A Historical Survey* (1976).

SMITH, OTIS M. (1922–   ), lawyer; born in Memphis, Tenn. Smith studied at Fisk University (Nashville, Tenn.) and Syracuse University (N.Y.) and received his L.L.B. degree in 1950 from Catholic University (Washington, D.C.). He served in several capacities after graduation, including partner in a legal firm (1951–57), auditor general of the state of Michigan (1959–61), and justice of the Michigan State Supreme Court (1961–66). In 1967 he joined the legal staff of General Motors and, in 1977, was chosen to head General Motors' legal staff of about 125 lawyers.

SMITH, RELLIFORD STILLMAN (1889–1965), physician; born in Americus, Ga. Smith received a B.S. degree from Shaw University (Raleigh, N.C.), and two M.D. degrees, one from the University of West Tennessee in 1914 and the other from Meharry Medical College (Nashville, Tenn.) in 1916. He served as a surgeon with the U.S. Army Medical Corps in Georgia during World War I. Smith later organized and directed a venereal disease clinic at the Macon and Bibb County Hospital for eight years, and was president of the National Medical Association (NMA) from 1958 to 1959.

SMITH, RUTH CAMP (1916–   ), librarian, government official; born in Washington, D.C. Smith received a B.A. degree from Howard Uni-

versity (Washington, D.C.) in 1937, a B.L.S. degree from Hampton Institute (Hampton, Va.) in 1938, and her M.L.S. degree from Columbia University in 1948. From 1946 to 1948 she worked in the New York City Public Library system, and in 1949 she became head of the technical processing section of the Naval Ship Systems Command in Washington, D.C., a post she held until 1965. In 1971 Smith was named director of the scientific documentation division, Naval Ship Systems Command. She was a member of the Special Libraries Association, American Society for Information Science, and International Toastmistress clubs. In 1971 Smith received the Federal Woman's Award.

SMITH, SHERMAN W., JR. (1922–   ), lawyer, judge; born in Washington, D.C. Smith received a B.A. degree from West Virginia State College and his LL.B. degree from Howard University School of Law (Washington, D.C.). He was admitted to the bar in 1949, and later became a judge of the Superior Court in Los Angeles, Calif.

SMITH, WALKER *See* ROBINSON, SUGAR RAY.

SMITH, WENDELL (1914–72), sportscaster, journalist; born in Detroit, Mich. Smith graduated from West Virginia State College in 1937. After having served as sports editor and city editor of the Pittsburgh *Courier*, he became a sportswriter for the Chicago *American* from 1947 to 1963. Thereafter, he was a sports columnist for the Chicago *Sun-Times* and a commentator for the Chicago television stations WBBM-TV and WGN-TV. A specialist in boxing and baseball, Smith wrote about Afro-American stars in those sports. As a talent scout for the Brooklyn Dodgers, Smith was instrumental in Jackie Robinson's historic signing with a baseball club.

SMYTHE, HUGH H. (1914–   ), sociologist, educator, government official; born in Pittsburgh, Pa. Smythe received a B.A. degree from Virginia State College in 1936, a M.A. degree from Atlanta University in 1937, and his Ph.D. degree in anthropology from Northwestern University (Evanston, Ill.) in 1945. The recipient of several fellowships and grants, he began his career as a teacher at Fisk University (Nashville, Tenn.) in 1938. During the following decade Smythe taught and did research in sociology at several colleges for the National Association for the Advancement of Colored People (NAACP) in New York and for a private concern. In 1951 he went to Japan for two years as visiting professor of sociology and anthropology at Yamaguchi University. Upon his return to the United States, Smythe joined the faculty of Brooklyn College of the City University of New York as professor of sociology. Concurrent with his teaching, Smythe engaged in a spectrum of activities ranging from membership on several U.S. delegations to the UN to serving as U.S. ambassador to Syria from 1965 to 1969.

SOCIAL CLASSES

Background and Nature of Classes It was within the historical context of slavery that the class structure of Afro-Americans emerged. However, two things should be kept in mind. In the first place, there has historically existed a dual class system in the United States, one black and one white. In the second place, while a dual class system exists, the criteria of status are the same for both classes, with the single exception of color—an important criterion of class position among Afro-Americans through the first four decades of the twentieth century. But the major criteria of class (wealth, occupation, education, place of residence, religious affiliation, and lifestyle) function in both populations. At the same time, because of the distinctions based on race, Afro-Americans have had limited access to these criteria. Moreover, racial discrimination and segregation have resulted in their differential interpretation. For example, if a white person can lay claim to being the descendant of a person who came to America on the *Mayflower*, his family background is thereby enhanced. On the other hand, for Afro-Americans a long period of freedom before the Civil War, or being the offspring of a well-known slaveholder who had achieved a national reputation (e.g., Thomas Jefferson, the Byrds, or the Randolphs of Virginia) became sources of family pride.

For a considerable part of their history, Afro-Americans were faced with the major preoccupation of survival. Until the outbreak of World War I, for example, 90 percent of the Afro-American population lived in the southern states, more than 65 percent of whom lived a rural existence. Although a few successful farmers were numbered among this group, some of whom had large holdings, the overwhelming majority were sharecroppers, tenant farmers, and farm laborers. Their economic status was determined by the plight of southern agriculture and racial discrimination, both of which combined to keep blacks (and some whites) at a low economic level.

Afro-Americans in the cities, North and South, slowly began to raise their socioeconomic level. Perhaps the most significant achievement that occurred during this period was the rise in literacy and education. Through the efforts of religious denominations and private philanthropy, schools for Afro-Americans were established throughout the South. Afro-Americans felt that through education they could not only increase their income, but also that they could become "cultured" and learn to "behave like whites." The sacrifices that individual families made to educate at least one of their children were unbelievable. Yet, it was this pursuit of education that contributed significantly to the gradual change in the socioeconomic status of Afro-Americans.

The preoccupation of blacks with education may be noted in the following data. In 1890 the rate of literacy of Afro-Americans in the southern states was 68.8 percent; by 1930 it had risen to 90.8 percent. The college departments of Afro-American colleges graduated 137 in 1876, but the number had increased to 1,883 by 1900. In 30 Afro-American colleges in 1900 a total of 9,068 students were enrolled. Between 1868 and 1940 approximately 30,000 baccalaureate degrees were conferred on Afro-Americans.

This number of college graduates is small when compared with the number of whites during the same period. However, when one considers the fact that in 1865 more than 90 percent of the Afro-American population was illiterate, and that this educational achievement occurred

under the most discouraging circumstances, such an increase must be regarded as significant.

The real impact of this educational achievement was on social mobility within the Afro-American population. Better employment was assured with a college degree. In addition, a college degree often led to graduate education and to professional school, especially in law, medicine, and dentistry. As the numbers in these professions increased, upward mobility became more pronounced.

Another important factor in the stratification of the Afro-American population was the urbanization movement that began dramatically about the time of World War I. The exodus of Afro-Americans from the rural South to the cities of the North and the Midwest resulted in a redistribution of the black population. This mass migration was a response to at least two socioeconomic conditions. First, southern Afro-Americans were recruited by northern industry in an attempt to break the ever-increasing grip of organized labor. Second, when the United States entered World War I, the need for labor to meet the demands of war production provided Afro-Americans with employment opportunities they had never had before. When peace was made with organized labor, and when the war ended and the demand for labor declined, a considerable number of the recent migrants lost their jobs. Nevertheless, some gains were made, and the

exodus from the South continued almost unabated, even during the Great Depression of the 1930s. World War II provided employment opportunities for Afro-Americans again, and the exodus from the South once again was accelerated, with a large proportion of blacks now migrating to the cities of the West Coast, a trend that began in the early 1940s and continued through the middle 1960s. Presently, the Afro-American population is 74 percent urban, and its stratification must be considered with this characteristic in mind.

Class stratification was influenced before World War II by a strong belief in the democratic ideology that one's destiny was of one's own making and that one could rise as high as one wished if one had the will to do so. Afro-Americans embraced the "American Way" to success, by which the race could be lifted up to "respectability" and equality. "Bettering the race" was an acceptable goal, and status could be achieved through education. In the absence of the necessary family resources for education, the individual with ambition could work his way through college. One might estimate that a minimum of 40 percent of Afro-American college graduates between 1865 and 1940 paid all or part of their way through college and/or graduate and professional school by themselves. With little or no financial assistance from home, and unable to obtain employment during the summer months or part-time employment during the school year, many Afro-Americans had to drop out of college before graduation, never to return. In many other instances the pursuit of a college degree was a long, drawn-out affair, in which, out of financial necessity, students would go to school until their funds were exhausted, drop out and work for a year or two, and then return.

Throughout this period (1865–1940) Afro-Americans imitated whites in every way that, in their judgment, enhanced their status and made them more acceptable. Being like whites in dress, in manner of speech, and in life-style (to the extent that racial segregation and discrimination permitted) was a driving force for much of the Afro-American population.

By 1940 a solid middle class in the Afro-American population consisted of teachers, clergymen, doctors, dentists, lawyers, government employees, and a few businessmen. It is estimated that this group constituted 15 to 20 percent of the total black population. An Afro-American upper class (corresponding to the criteria generally accepted) constituted approximately two percent of the Afro-American population. The most conservative estimates, based on occupation and education, suggest that approximately 80 percent of the Afro-American population was in the lower socioeconomic class. This figure contrasts with the estimated 20 percent of the white population during the same period.

Changes Since World War II The change in the socioeconomic status of Afro-Americans after 1940 has been dramatic. Significant advances in civil rights, when compared with the previous 75 years, through federal civil rights acts, court decisions, and the emergence of such activist groups as the National Association for the Advancement of Colored People (NAACP), the National Urban League, the Congress of Racial Equality (CORE), and the Student Nonviolent Coordinating Committee (SNCC) have substantially changed the status of Afro-Americans in the United States. The insistent demands (rather than pleas) of these activist groups opened up opportunities for Afro-Americans that had never before existed. During a considerable portion of this period, integration was not only a wish for many, but appeared as a distinct possibility. Since integration was the goal of most Afro-Americans, whatever was regarded as approved behavior by whites was imitated by blacks. Moreover, violations of these patterns of behavior by Afro-Americans aroused the anger and contempt of those Afro-Americans who sought to rise in the class structure.

Using income as a criterion, it was estimated that in 1940 only 15 to 20 percent of the Afro-American population could be classified as middle class or above. If one uses an income of $7,000 as the lower level of the middle class, 38.7 percent of Afro-American families in 1970 qualified as members of the middle class. While this increase in income level is indeed impressive, it must be viewed with caution. For while 38.7 percent of Afro-American families had incomes of $7,000 or more, 80 percent of all white families earned such incomes in the same year. Moreover, the gap in median family incomes between Afro-Americans and whites is closing at a discouragingly slow rate. For example, in 1947 the median family income of Afro-Americans was only 51 percent of the median family income of whites. In the following 23 years (1947–70), during a period of considerable national prosperity, the median family income of Afro-Americans had risen a mere ten percentage points, to 61 percent of white median family income.

The gains in income are reflected in changes in the occupational structure in the Afro-American population. Beginning with World War II, when the demands for skilled labor were critical, blacks were employed in a wide variety of occupations from which they were excluded prior to this time. These new sources of employment broadened the income base for a fairly large number of Afro-Americans, and also resulted in the upgrading of some Afro-Americans who had been employed in certain industries for a number of years—they had seniority, but were employed at lower levels.

The broadening of employment opportunities was not voluntary either on the part of industry or of organized labor. It was only through the efforts of civil rights organizations, especially the NAACP and the National Urban League, and the threat of a march on Washington, D.C., by A. Phillip Randolph that led to the issuance of Executive Order No. 8802 in 1941, which prohibited discrimination in employment on the basis of race, creed, or color by any industry that had a government contract. Needless to say, in many cases compliance was minimal. Yet certain gains were made, most of which were retained at the conclusion of the war.

Those gains made in industry during World War II, and retained after the war, provided opportunities in business and communications at executive levels. With a history of satisfactory performance during the war and urged on by the constant pressure from civil rights organizations, Afro-Americans were employed in junior executive positions in a number of industries that previously had not employed Afro-Americans in white-collar positions. For the most part, these were token appointments (often aimed at attracting an ever-increasing number of black consumers), and, as a general rule, when this kind of appointment was made the position became a "Negro" position, a window dressing with little real authority. Nevertheless, a surprisingly large number of such appointments contributed to the increased income of the total Afro-American population.

Social gains were further reflected in the increased number of Afro-Americans in the professions, especially in medicine, dentistry, law, and college-level education. In 1940, 3,150 Negro physicians were practicing. This number had increased to 4,200 by 1950; to 5,300 by 1960; and to 6,100 by 1970. Thus, between 1940 and 1970 the number of Afro-American doctors had almost doubled. In architecture and engineering the increases were even more dramatic, as shown in the accompanying table.

AFRO-AMERICANS IN SELECTED PROFESSIONS, 1940–70

Profession	Number			
	1940	1950	1960	1970
Architects	80	180	233	1,258
Engineers	238	1,710	4,378	3,679
Lawyers	1,052	1,470	2,180	3,379
Dentists	1,586	1,680	1,998	2,098
Physicians	3,150	4,200	5,300	6,100

Life-Styles in the Afro-American Class Structure As was pointed out above, the criteria of class position operating historically in the larger society, with the exception of color, were generally accepted by Afro-Americans. Middle- and upper-middle-class behavior was emulated to the extent that the patterns of racial segregation and discrimination would permit. Middle- and upper-middle-class Afro-Americans sought to reinforce their position, or the position toward which they were striving, through conspicuous consumption in housing, dress, and entertainment, and through other displays of behavior generally associated with middle- and upper-middle-class Americans. However, the very fact of racial discrimination and segregation imposed limits on what Afro-Americans could do. Hence, their emulation of white middle- and

Far right: Typical summer scene in urban, low-income areas on the street in Harlem, New York City, 1946. The scene would also be typical for any given year in subsequent decades.

upper-middle-class behavior often resulted in innovations or distortions, and a life-style somewhat different from the generally accepted norm.

Housing discrimination forced most blacks to live in a ghetto in spite of the ability of many to purchase better housing in a better, but white, neighborhood. Only when a white neighborhood was opened for Afro-American occupancy (desegregated) could any considerable number of Afro-Americans move. In response to housing discrimination, middle- and upper-middle-class Afro-Americans sometimes spent a disproportionate amount of their income on remodeling and on home furnishings. Until very recently, most public places of entertainment were either closed to Afro-Americans or were segregated, including hotels, theaters, nightclubs, and concert halls. In such vacation spots as Atlantic City, N.J., and Miami Beach, Fla., both beaches and hotels were segregated. A small section of the public beach was occasionally reserved for Afro-Americans, but most beach-front hotels excluded blacks. When Afro-Americans frequented these spots, they either lived with friends or in the "Negro" hotel. They were, and still often are, excluded from country clubs. Hence, fraternities, sororities, and social clubs, and the social activities that these organizations promoted, became substitutes for the country club. Dress became very important to middle- and upper-middle-class Afro-Americans: it was a symbol of success. Lavish entertainment in the home, especially when it attracted prominent guests, was evidence that one had "arrived." Sending one's son or daughter to a prestigious university was as much an announcement of the

Relaxation by middle-class families is shown in this photo taken in Asheboro, N.C., in the late 1970s. Physician Michael Smith and his family (left) visit retired dentist George Jones and his wife. (*Courtesy of Daniel H. Gashler.*)

family's status as it was the desire to provide the child with a high-quality education.

The life-style of middle-class Afro-Americans, especially in regard to their expenditures on cars, on lavish entertainment, on clothes, and on liquor, has sometimes exposed them to severe criticism for establishing for themselves artificial values in a world of make-believe. E. Franklin Frazier and Nathan Hare were especially critical of these patterns of behavior on the part of the Afro-American middle class. The observations of both authors are well taken, and much of what they wrote is true, although they themselves were severely criticized for exposing the behavior of the Afro-American middle class to the public. Unfortunately, neither documented his work, and the incidence of the behavior that they criticized is unknown. Hence, perhaps the rare and the dramatic were regarded as typical rather than unique.

Critics of the life-style of the black middle- and upper-middle classes seldom suggest logical reasons for the variations from the white norm. The impression persists, therefore, that the life-style of Afro-Americans exists simply because they are Afro-Americans, and hence different. A more logical explanation would appear to be that (by virtue of the cultural definition of race) the inferior status of Afro-Americans in

American society and the formal and informal controls that preclude their full participation in that society force Afro-Americans to behave in the only ways open to them. For example, "good" housing is a symbol of middle- and upper-middle-class status. To some extent so is a Cadillac. The Afro-American can buy the latter without opposition, but he has always encountered considerable difficulty in obtaining the former. Hence, he buys the latter and continues to live in a substandard or an ordinary home. To some observers this behavior is inconsistent. More critical analysis suggests that Afro-Americans have few options. Their wishes and desires, and the patterns of behavior they employ to satisfy them, were acquired in American society. Moreover, they recognize the wide differentials between the ideals that they learn and the reality that is applied to them. Frustrations begin to run deep as Afro-Americans seek to achieve the values prescribed by the larger society but which that society simply will not permit. This may account for much of the bizarre behavior that is sometimes observed among Afro-Americans, regardless of class position.

Although gains in the quality of life may appear to be impressive when one compares the status of Afro-Americans in 1970 with their status in 1940, such gains are small when compared with the white population for the same period. G. Franklin Edwards, an Afro-American sociologist, has observed that: "While it is clear that further changes in the status of the Negro will occur in the years ahead, moving the Negro nearer to equality with other Americans, the processes by which this will be achieved are certain to be long and tortuous. . . ." Given the persistence of racial discrimination and segregation in education and employment, the attainment of parity in the social structure for Afro-Americans is not likely in the foreseeable future. See also DISCRIMINATION; EDUCATION; EMPLOYMENT; INCOME; POVERTY; SEGREGATION.

REFERENCES: Billingsley, Andrew, Black Families in White America, Prentice-Hall, Englewood Cliffs, 1968; Davis, Allison W. and John Dollard, Children of Bondage, American Council on Education, Washington, D.C., 1940; Dollard, John, Caste and Class in a Southern Town, 3d ed., Doubleday, Garden City, 1957; Edwards, G. Franklin, "Community and Class Realities: The Ordeal of Change," Daedalus, Winter 1966; Edwards, G. Franklin, The Negro Professional Class, Free Press, Glencoe, 1959; Frazier, E. Franklin, Black Bourgeoisie, Collier Books, New York, 1962; Frazier, E. Franklin, The Negro in the United States, Macmillan, New York, 1957; Hare, Nathan, The Black Anglo-Saxons, Marzani & Munsell, New York, 1965; Myrdal, Gunnar, An American Dilemma, McGraw-Hill Book Co., New York, 1964; Warner, W. Lloyd, "Social Class and Color Caste in America," in American Life: Dream and Reality, rev. ed., University of Chicago Press, Chicago, 1962; and Warner, W. Lloyd and Leo Srole, The Social Systems of American Ethnic Groups, Yale Univeristy Press, New Haven, 1946.

SOCIETY FOR THE PROPAGATION OF THE GOS-PEL IN FOREIGN PARTS (S.P.G.) Organized in 1701 by the Church of England for missionary work in the colonies and for the education and Christianization of slaves in the United States, the S.P.G. established schools toward those ends. In 1696 Thomas Bray, sent to Maryland by the Church of England, opened a school there to convert and educate slaves. In 1704 a catechizing school was established at Trinity Church in New York City. Under the tutelage of a Frenchman, Elias Neau, the school was in operation until the 1850s, interrupted only by a slave uprising in 1712 that was attributed to Neau's influence. Neau died in 1722.

SOUTHALL, HERBERT HOWARDTON, SR. (1907–), business executive; born in Richmond, Va. Southall studied at Tennessee State University and at Virginia State College. He was president of the Southern Aid Life Insurance Company, Inc., of Richmond, Va., and was on the board of directors of the Richmond Community Hospital and the Greater Richmond Chamber of Commerce.

SOUTH CAROLINA STATE COLLEGE South Carolina State College, at Orangeburg, S.C., was established in 1896 when the general assembly of South Carolina authorized the separation of the Agricultural College and Mechanic Institute from Claflin University, thus establishing the Colored, Normal, Industrial, Agricultural, and Mechanical College of South Carolina. State-supported and coeducational, the college offers the bachelor's and master's degrees and provides a liberal arts curriculum, although it also emphasizes teacher education. Its 1975 enrollment was about 2,900.

The college opened in 1896 on its present site. The school's original purpose was to train Afro-American youth in practical agriculture, mechanical arts, military tactics, and teaching. At the turn of the century, the educational needs of Afro-American youth in the state were indeed basic. The program of instruction therefore was organized into a practice school, a preparatory school, a normal school, and industrial courses.

In 1924 the institution began its first standard college course by registering 51 students in a four-year, degree-granting agricultural program. By 1932 the college offered degree programs in five major areas; by 1948 it had ten degree-granting undergraduate areas, as well as schools of law and graduate studies and an extension school. In 1954 the legal name of the college was changed to South Carolina State College. Presidents after the 1930s include Robert S. Wilkinson, Miller F. Whittaker, B. C. Turner, and M. Maceo Nance, Jr.

SOUTHERNAIRES A small vocal group with highly blended harmonies, the Southernaires were very popular on radio and in guest appearances in the 1930s and the 1940s, with a reputed repertoire of nearly 2,000 songs.

SOUTHERN BIBLE INSTITUTE See SOUTHWESTERN CHRISTIAN COLLEGE.

SOUTHERN CHRISTIAN LEADERSHIP CONFERENCE (SCLC) Founded in 1957, the SCLC is a civil rights organization that grew out of the Montgomery Improvement Association (MIA), the body formed to organize the Montgomery, Ala., bus boycott of 1956–57. In 16 border and southern states the SCLC worked to improve the economic, political, and social conditions of minority groups, "seeking full citizenship rights, equality, and the integration of the Negro in all aspects of American life, and subscribing to the Gandhian philosophy of nonviolence." Led by Martin Luther King, Jr., and Ralph D. Abernathy, the SCLC was in the vanguard of the civil rights movement in the 1960s. By 1959 it had affiliates in 22 cities. In 1960 it began a decade that was filled with activity, each year helping to achieve another milestone in the struggle for civil rights. See also ABERNATHY, RALPH D.; CIVIL RIGHTS: DISORDERS; KING, MARTIN LUTHER, JR.

SOUTHERN CONFERENCE EDUCATIONAL FUND (SEF) SEF was founded as the Southern Conference for Human Welfare in 1938 with help from Mrs. Franklin D. Roosevelt for the purpose of alleviating the economic and social plight of poor Afro-Americans and poor whites in the South. It is an interracial organization based in Louisville, Ky., and its organ, The Southern Patriot, was first published in 1942 in Nashville, Tenn. However, the organization began to decline in the 1940s, and in 1946 a new group—the Southern Conference Educational Fund, Inc.—was formed. In 1958 this group expanded its activities and made the securing of the right to vote for Afro-Americans its major goal. Publication of The Southern Patriot was continued by the new organization. See also EDUCATION: DEVELOPMENTS IN ELEMENTARY AND SECONDARY EDUCATION.

SOUTHERN, EILEEN JACKSON (1920–), musicologist, educator; born in Minneapolis, Minn. Southern received a B.A. degree (1940) and a M.A. degree (1941) from the University of Chicago, and her Ph.D. degree from New York University in 1961. Southern studied the piano professionally at Chicago Musical College, at Boston University, and at the Juilliard School of Music (New York, N.Y.). Her teaching career included appointments at Prairie View State College (Prairie View, Tex.) from 1941 to 1942; at Southern University (Baton Rouge, La.) from 1943 to 1945 and from 1949 to 1951; at Claflin College (Orangeburg, S.C.) from 1947 to 1949; at secondary schools in New York City from 1954 to 1960; at City University of New York, Brooklyn College, from 1960 to 1968; and as professor of music and chairman of the fine arts/performing arts department, York College of the City University of New York, after 1968.

Southern's books include: The Buxheim Organ Book (1963), The Music of Black Americans: A History (1971), Readings in Black American Music (1971), and Anonymous Chansons in Two Manuscripts at El Escorial. She was also the editor of The Black Perspective in Music, a scholarly journal, and the author of many scholarly articles in professional journals. See also PREFACE: LIST OF CONTRIBUTORS.

SOUTHERN ORGANIZATION OF UNIFIED LEADERSHIP (SOUL) A politically conscious civil rights group of the 1960s, SOUL was based in New Orleans, La.

SOUTHERN REGIONAL COUNCIL (SRC) The SRC was formed in 1918 largely by southern whites to improve race relations and understanding. It grew into a biracial, nonpartisan, and nonprofit information and research organization, seeking "the improvement of economic, civic, and racial conditions in the South." It seeks "to attain through research and action programs the ideals and practices of equal opportunity for all peoples in the region." To accomplish these goals the council's activities encompass voter education, community organization, urban planning, labor programs, and prison reform. A 100-member board meets annually, usually to review and establish policy.

SOUTHERN UNIVERSITY AND AGRICULTURAL AND MECHANICAL (A&M) COLLEGE Southern University and Agricultural and Mechanical (A&M) College, at Baton Rouge, La., was chartered in 1880 by the general assembly of the state of Louisiana. A state-supported, land-grant, coeducational college, the school offers the bachelor's and master's degrees, as well as terminal occupation programs. The university provides a liberal arts curriculum, although it also emphasizes teacher education and professional work. Its 1975 enrollment (at all campuses) was 12,102.

This institution was first established in New Orleans, La., for "persons of color." In 1881 the university opened with an enrollment of 12 students; in 1914 the New Orleans campus was closed and the "new" Southern University opened in Scotlandville, La.

The university's agricultural and mechanical department was organized in 1888, and the arts and sciences were departmentalized in 1940. The graduate school was established in 1958. Branch campuses were authorized by the Louisiana state legislature for New Orleans (SUNO) and Shreveport-Bossier (SUSBO) in 1956 and 1964, respectively.

Southern University, a land-grant college

since 1892, is considered the largest predominantly Afro-American institution in the United States. A few of its programs of distinction are the Afro-American executive exchange program, the congressional internship program, and the teacher corps program. A small sampling of some of its other projects includes a division of continuing education, an agricultural economics training program conducted in conjunction with the University of Cameroon, a Head Start regional training office (and related projects), a pilot program in psychology for training undergraduate majors, and a black studies program. A public affairs center on the main campus provides services to the surrounding community.

The president at the main campus in the mid-1970s was Jesse N. Stone, Jr; the vice-president at New Orleans was Emmett W. Bashful; and the vice-president at Shreveport-Bossier was Leonard C. Barnes.

SOUTHERN UNIVERSITY, NEW ORLEANS (SUNO) See SOUTHERN UNIVERSITY AND AGRICULTURAL AND MECHANICAL (A&M) COLLEGE.

SOUTHERN UNIVERSITY, SHREVEPORT-BOSSIER (SUSBO) See SOUTHERN UNIVERSITY AND AGRICULTURAL AND MECHANICAL (A&M) COLLEGE.

SOUTHWESTERN CHRISTIAN COLLEGE Southwestern Christian College, at Terrell, Tex., was founded in 1949 by George Phillip Bowser, an Afro-American pioneer minister of the Church of Christ. Church-related and coeducational, the college offers a two-year program that is usually credited toward the bachelor's degree but is also used for terminal occupational work. Its 1975 enrollment was 220.

Originally, the school was named the Southern Bible Institute. Its name was changed to Southwestern Christian College in 1950, with the goal of serving as a Christian college primarily for Afro-Americans of the Church of Christ. Its establishment was necessitated by the segregation of policies of white church-related colleges in the late 1940s and early 1950s.

The institution began by offering the last three years of high school and the first year of college. In 1951 two grades of high school were eliminated and the sophomore year of college was added. In 1952 the last grade of high school was eliminated.

SOWELL, THOMAS (1930–   ), economist, educator; born in Gastonia, N.C. Sowell received a B.A. degree from Harvard University in 1958, a M.A. degree from Columbia University in 1959, and his Ph.D. degree in economics from the University of Chicago in 1966. He served as an assistant professor of economics at Rutgers University (New Brunswick, N.J.) from 1962 to 1963, as a lecturer at Howard University (Washington, D.C.) from 1963 to 1964, as associate professor of economics at Brandeis University (Waltham, Mass.) from 1969 to 1970, and as associate professor at the University of California at Los Angeles from 1970 to 1972. Sowell was director of the Ethnic Minorities Research Project at the Urban Institute in Washington, D.C., after 1972. His publications include: *Economics: Analysis and Issues* (1971); *Say's Law: An Historical Analysis* (1972); *Black Education: Myths and Tragedies* (1972); *Classical Economics Reconsidered* (1973); and *Race and Economics* (1973).

SPAULDING, ASA T. (1902–   ), business executive; born in Columbus County, N.C. Spaulding received a B.S. degree from New York University in 1930, a M.A. degree from the University of Michigan in 1932, and his D.B.A. degree from Morgan State University (Baltimore, Md.) in 1961. He became the president of North Carolina Mutual Life Insurance Company of Durham, N.C., and served as a director of that firm as well as of the Mechanics and Farmers Bank, the Mutual Savings and Loan Association, and W. T. Grant Company. When he was appointed to the board of directors of W. T. Grant Company, Spaulding became the first Afro-American to serve on the board of a major corporation in the United States.

SPAULDING, CHARLES CLINTON (1874–1952), business executive; born in Clarkton, N.C. Spaulding rose through the ranks of the North Carolina Mutual Life Insurance Company of Durham, N.C., becoming president in 1923 and holding that position until his death. He built the company into the largest American business owned and operated by Afro-Americans. See *also* BUSINESS.

SPELLMAN, MITCHELL WRIGHT (1919–   ), surgeon, educator; born in Alexandria, La. Spellman received a B.A. degree from Dillard University (New Orleans, La.) in 1936, a M.D. degree from Howard University Medical College (Washington, D.C.) in 1944, and his Ph.D. degree in surgery from the University of Minnesota. He served on the faculty of Howard University before being appointed dean of the Charles R. Drew Postgraduate Medical School of the University of California at Los Angeles in 1969. Spellman later became a director of the Kaiser Foundation Health Plan, Inc., and of Kaiser Foundation Hospitals.

SPELMAN COLLEGE Spelman College, at Atlanta, Ga., was founded in 1881 by two New England women, Sophia B. Packard and Harriet E. Giles. Church-related and female, Spelman was founded as the first college for Afro-American women in the United States. Spelman students can also take courses at the other affiliated colleges of the Atlanta University system. On its own, the school offers the bachelor's degree and provides a liberal arts curriculum. Its 1975 enrollment was 1,135.

Spelman College grew out of a school that was started in the basement of the Friendship Baptist Church, pastored by Rev. Frank Quarles. The school was called the Atlanta Baptist Female Seminary. In 1883 it was moved to its present site, then consisting of nine acres of land and five frame buildings that had been used as drill grounds and barracks by Union troops during the Civil War and that were later secured by the American Baptist Home Mission Society. In 1884 the school's name was changed to Spelman Seminary in honor of Mr. and Mrs. Harvey Buel Spelman, the parents of Mrs. John D. Rockefeller. Her husband had paid the newly founded school's debts. In 1924 its name was changed to Spelman College by an amendment to its charter. Presidents of the institution after the 1930s have included Florence M. Read and Albert E. Manly.

SPINGARN MEDAL Begun in 1914 by Joel E. Spingarn (1875–1939), the chairman of the board of directors of the National Association for the Advancement of Colored People (NAACP), the award is a gold medal given annually for the "highest or noblest achievement by an American Negro." It is awarded by a nine-member committee, selected by the board of directors, that has free choice as to category and achievement. Traditionally, it is presented at the annual NAACP convention. Past recipients (all of whom have biographical sketches in the *Encyclopedia*) comprise the following list.

SPINGARN MEDALISTS*

Ernest E. Just (1915)
Charles Young (1916)
Harry T. Burleigh (1917)
William Stanley Braithwaite (1918)
Archibald H. Grimké (1919)
William E. B. Du Bois (1920)
Charles S. Gilpin (1921)
Mary B. Talbert (1922)
George Washington Carver (1923)
Roland Hayes (1924)
James Weldon Johnson (1925)
Carter G. Woodson (1926)
Anthony Overton (1927)
Charles W. Chesnutt (1928)
Mordecai Wyatt Johnson (1929)
Henry A. Hunt (1930)
Richard Berry Harrison (1931)
Robert Russa Moton (1932)
Max Yergan (1933)
William Taylor Burwell Williams (1934)
Mary McLeod Bethune (1935)
John Hope (1936)
Walter White (1937)
Marian Anderson (1939)
Louis T. Wright (1940)
Richard Wright (1941)
A. Philip Randolph (1942)
William H. Hastie (1943)
Charles R. Drew (1944)
Paul Robeson (1945)
Thurgood Marshall (1946)
Percy L. Julian (1947)
Channing H. Tobias (1948)
Ralph J. Bunche (1949)
Charles Hamilton Houston (1950)
Mabel Keaton Staupers (1951)
Harry T. Moore (1952)
Paul R. Williams (1953)
Theodore K. Lawless (1954)
Carl Murphy (1955)
Jack Roosevelt Robinson (1956)
Martin Luther King, Jr. (1957)
Daisy Bates and the Little Rock Nine (1958)
Edward Kennedy (Duke) Ellington (1959)
Langston Hughes (1960)
Kenneth B. Clark (1961)
Robert C. Weaver (1962)
Medgar Wiley Evers (1963)
Roy Wilkins (1964)
Leontyne Price (1965)
John H. Johnson (1966)
Edward W. Brooke, III (1967)
Sammy Davis, Jr. (1968)
Clarence M. Mitchell, Jr. (1969)

Jacob Lawrence (1970)
Leon Howard Sullivan (1971)
Gordon Parks (1972)
Wilson Riles (1973)
Damon J. Keith (1974)
Henry Louis (Hank) Aaron (1975)
Alvin Ailey (1976)
Alexander Palmer (Alex) Haley (1977)

*No award given in 1938.

SPIRITUALS See Music: Spirituals: Origins; Music: Spirituals/Performance, Collections.

SPOTTSWOOD, STEPHEN GILL (1897–1974), African Methodist Episcopal bishop; born in Boston, Mass. Spottswood was educated at Albright College (Reading, Pa.), at Gordon Divinity School, and at Yale University. After serving churches in Washington, D.C., New York, Indiana, South Carolina, Connecticut, Oregon, and Massachusetts, he was elected a bishop of the African Methodist Episcopal Zion (AMEZ) Church in 1952. Spottswood became nationally known by serving as chairman of the board of directors of the National Association for the Advancement of Colored People (NAACP), beginning in 1961.

SPURLOCK, JEANNE (1921–   ), psychiatrist, educator; born in Sandusky, Ohio. Spurlock received her M.D. degree from Howard University Medical College (Washington, D.C.) in 1947. She served as a staff psychiatrist for the Juvenile Research Institute, as a faculty member of the University of Illinois College of Medicine, as director of the Child Psychiatric Clinic of Michael Reese Hospital, and as professor of psychiatry and department chairman at Meharry Medical College (Nashville, Tenn.). Spurlock received the Strecker Award, presented to her in 1971 by the Institute of Pennsylvania, thus becoming the first Afro-American and the first woman to receive this award.

STACKOLEE A legendary bad man (ca. 1880s) whose love of gambling and blood-red Stetson hat led to his downfall and imprisonment. Entertainers enriched the legend: Ma Rainey did a special entitled "Stackolee Blues," and Sidney Bechet had a piece called "Stackolee Lament."

STAFFORD, ALPHONSO ORENZO (1871–1941), educator; born in Alexandria, Va. Stafford studied at Miner Normal School, at Howard University (Washington, D.C.), at the University of Pennsylvania, and at Columbia University. He taught in Washington, D.C., and in Baltimore, Md., served on the staff of Cheyney Training School for Teachers (Cheyney, Pa., later Cheyney State College) and then returned to Washington, D.C., where he held several positions as principal. Stafford published *Animal Fables from the Dark Continent* (1906), assisted Booker T. Washington and his staff in the study of Africa, and contributed articles to the first volume of the *Journal of Negro History* (1916).

STANLEY, FRANK L. See Newspapers: Contemporary.

STATE COLORED NORMAL AND INDUSTRIAL SCHOOL See Fayetteville State University.

STATE COLORED NORMAL SCHOOL See Fayetteville State University.

STATE NORMAL SCHOOL FOR COLORED STUDENTS See Alabama State University.

STATE NORMAL SCHOOL FOR THE NEGRO RACE See Fayetteville State University.

STATE NORMAL SCHOOL AND UNIVERSITY FOR COLORED STUDENTS AND TEACHERS See Alabama State University.

STAUPERS, MABEL KEATON (1890–   ), nurse; born in Barbados, British West Indies. The Staupers family moved to the United States in 1903, and Staupers received her R.N. degree from Freedmen's Hospital, Washington, D.C., in 1917. She was awarded a working fellowship to the Henry Phipps Institute in Philadelphia, Pa., in 1920, and she helped to organize and became superintendent of the Booker T. Washington Sanitorium, New York, N.Y., in 1920. Staupers also organized the Harlem Committee of the New York Tuberculosis and Health Association in 1922, and she served as its first executive secretary. She was consultant on nursing to Surgeon-General James C. Magee in 1941, and was president of the National Association of Colored Graduate Nurses from 1949 to 1951. She was awarded the Spingarn Medal in 1951. *See also* Nurses.

STEPHENS, ALONZO THEODORE, SR. (1919–   ), historian, educator; born in St. Petersburg, Fla. Stephens received a B.A. degree from Florida Agricultural and Mechanical (A & M) University in 1948, and a M. Litt. degree (1951) and his Ph.D. degree (1955) from the University of Pittsburgh. He taught at Florida A & M and at Savannah State College (Savannah, Ga.) before joining the faculty of Tennessee State University as professor of history in 1958. In 1963 Stephens became head of the department of history, political science, and education at Tennessee State. In addition, Stephens held positions at the United Nations, traveled and studied in the Middle East, and lectured at many American universities. His publications include *The United Nations in East Africa-Ethiopia, Kenya, Tanzania, and Zambia* (1973).

STEVENS, HAROLD A. (1907–), lawyer, judge, state legislator; born in John's Island, S.C. Stevens attended Claflin College (Orangeburg, S.C.; Now Clafin University), and received a B.A. degree from Benedict College (Columbia, S.C.) in 1930, and his LL.B. degree from Boston College Law School in 1936. After practicing law in Boston early in his career, he moved to New York City, where from 1938 to 1950 he distinguished himself at the bar with a series of partners. In 1947 Stevens began a term as assemblyman in the New York state legislature. In 1951 he became judge of the Court of General Sessions in New York City, serving on that bench until he became a justice of the New York State Supreme Court.

STEWART, MARCUS C. *See* NEWSPAPERS: CONTEMPORARY

STEWART, WILLIAM B. (1906–), educator; born in Jacksonville, Fla. Stewart received a B.A. degree from Florida Agricultural and Mechanical (A & M) College in 1930 and his M.A. degree from Hampton Institute (Hampton, Va.) in 1947. He was affiliated with several high schools in Florida before becoming president of Edward Waters College (Jacksonville, Fla.) in 1951.

STILL, JAMES (1812– ?), physician; born in Indian Mill, N.J. Still had no formal education, but about 1843 he began to make his own medicines and to sell them to neighbors, using the money to buy medical books. Prospering, Still became known as the "black doctor" and the "doctor of the pines," practicing medicine for 30 years—a respected and well-liked physician.

STILL, WILLIAM (1821–1902), abolitionist, author; born in Shainong, N.J. As a boy, Still taught himself to read and write, and at the age

of 23 he went to Philadelphia, Pa., to seek his fortune. There he joined the Pennsylvania Society for the Abolition of Slavery, becoming more and more active in helping runaway slaves during the 14 years he was there. In 1852 Still became chairman of the Vigilance Committee of Philadelphia, which provided financial help to escaped slaves. Still kept careful records of events and interviewed the slaves he helped; his records became the basis for his book *Underground Railroad*, published in 1872 and filled with the accounts of many escapes. Still helped found an orphanage for Afro-American children in Philadelphia, and in 1880 he was an organizer of one of the first Young Men's Christian Associations (YMCA) for Afro-Americans. *See also* SLAVERY: SLAVERY IN SELECTED STATES: PENNSYLVANIA; SLAVERY: THE UNDERGROUND RAILROAD.

William Still.
(Library of Congress.)

STILL, WILLIAM GRANT (1895–), composer; born in Woodville, Miss. Still studied at Wilberforce University (Wilberforce, Ohio), at Oberlin Conservatory of Music (Oberlin, Ohio), and at the New England Conservatory of Music (Boston, Mass.). As a youth, he worked for W. C. Handy's music publishing firm and played in Handy's band. Still then became a bandleader and began his long and distinguished career as a composer. His works include symphonic poems, ballets, operas, symphonies, motion-picture scores, and popular songs. Still was the first Afro-American to conduct a major symphony, the Los Angeles Philharmonic in 1936. His best-known songs include "Breath of a Rose," "Levee Land," and "Kaintuck." *Sahdji* and *La Guiablesse* (ballet scores); the symphonies *Afro-American Symphony, Africa,* and *Symphony in G Minor;* and the operas *Blue Steel* and *Troubled Island* (1949) represent the most important part of Still's output as a classical composer.

STILLMAN COLLEGE Stillman College, at Tuscaloosa, Ala., was founded in 1876 by the Presbyterian Church. Still church-related, the coeducational college offers the bachelor's degree and provides liberal arts and teacher education curricula. Its 1975 enrollment was 631.

The school was founded under the leadership of Rev. Charles A. Stillman, pastor of the First Presbyterian Church of Tuscaloosa, and was called Tuscaloosa Institute. Its purpose was to train young Afro-American men for the ministry. It opened in a rented house, with Stillman as superintendent, and in 1894 its name was changed to Stillman Institute. It subsequently occupied two other sites before it was moved to its present location—a former plantation—in 1898.

During its history the college has housed a theological seminary, a grade school, a high school, a trade school, a junior college, and a school of nursing. In 1942 the lowest level remaining was the high school, which was eventually eliminated. In 1947 the school of nursing was also discontinued, which left only the junior college. In 1948 the school's name was changed to Stillman College, and in 1949 it became a four-year college. Since the 1930s Stillman has had three presidents: A. L. Jackson, Samuel B. Hay, and Harold N. Stinson. See also PRESBYTERIANS.

STITT, HOWARD (1890–1968), physician; born in Brooklyn, N.Y. Stitt received his M.D. degree from Howard University Medical College (Washington, D.C.) in 1917, and was an officer in the U.S. Army Medical Corps during World War I. He received the Fifty Year Award from Howard University Medical College in 1967.

STOKES, CARL (1927–   ), lawyer, mayor, newscaster; born in Cleveland, Ohio. A child of the Cleveland central-city ghetto, Stokes was raised by his mother (his father died when he was three and his older brother was five). After serving in the U.S. Army, he continued his education—after an interruption of a few years as an agent of the state liquor authority. Stokes received a B.S. degree in law from the University of Minnesota in 1954, and two years later his LL.D. degree from Cleveland-Marshall College of Law of Cleveland State University. He spent the next several years as probation officer for the Cleveland Municipal Court and as assistant city prosecutor. In 1962 Stokes resigned his job as prosecutor and opened a law firm with his brother. That same year he was elected to the Ohio State legislature as a Democrat. His voting record established him as a moderate; although strongly in favor of all civil rights and aid measures, he also voted for the use of the National Guard troops in the event of serious rioting. Stokes won the mayoralty election in Cleveland in 1967 with a coalition of black and white votes, becoming the first Afro-American to be elected mayor of a major American city; he was reelected in 1969 with the same support. In 1972 Stokes joined the news staff of NBC-TV in New York City. See also STOKES, LOUIS.

STOKES, LOUIS (1925–   ), lawyer, U.S. Representative; born in Cleveland, Ohio. Educated at Western Reserve University (Cleveland, Ohio; now Case Western Reserve University) after serving in the U.S. Army, Stokes received his J.D. degree from Cleveland-Marshall College of Law of Cleveland State University in 1953. He practiced law in Cleveland until he was elected a member of the Ninety-first Congress in 1968. Louis Stokes was the older brother of Carl Stokes. See also STOKES, CARL.

STOKES, REMBERT EDWARDS (1917–   ), educator, clergyman; born in Dayton, Ohio. Stokes received a B.S. degree from Wilberforce University (Wilberforce, Ohio) in 1940, and his S.T.B. and Th.D. degrees from Boston University. He was ordained in the African Methodist Episcopal (AME) Church in 1941, and pastored churches in Rhode Island, Massachusetts, and Ohio before becoming president of Wilberforce University in 1956.

STONE, JESSE NEALAND, JR. (1924–   ), college administrator, lawyer; born in Gibsland, La. Stone attended Southern University Law School (Baton Rouge, La), where he received his J.D. degree in 1950. He became assistant state superintendent of education in Louisiana (1972), dean of Southern University Law School (1971–72), and president of the Southern University System (1974). He received several awards, including the Anne Brewster Memorial Award, NAACP (1964) and the Distinguished Service Award of the Louisiana Education Association (1969).

STONER, ELMER C. (1898–1970), painter; born in Wilkes-Barre, Pa. Stoner studied at the Pennsylvania Academy of Fine Arts in Philadelphia, Pa., and he won a Cresson Traveling Scholarship to Europe and the Prix de Rome. Stoner lived and had a studio in Greenwich Village in New York City for 46 years. His paintings are often of the anthracite coal regions in Pennsylvania including his birthplace. Stoner was commissioned to paint the portraits of three Afro-American colonels—Elmer Sawyer, Woodruff Chism, and Chauncey Harper—that now hang in the Armory at 143d Street in New York City. He created a syndicated newspaper cartoon and the railroad Train Panorama Exhibit at the 1939 World's Fair in New York City. Stoner was also the creator of the "Peanut Man" for Planters' Peanuts. Stoner was named an outstanding son of Pennsylvania in 1950. See also ARTISTS.

STOUT, JUANITA KIDD (1919–   ), lawyer, judge; born in Wewoka, Okla. Stout received a B.A. degree from the University of Iowa in 1939, and a J.D. degree (1948) and her LL.M. degree (1952) from Indiana University. After teaching elementary school, high school, and college and serving as administrative secretary to the U.S. Court of Appeals for the 3d Circuit in Philadelphia, Pa. (before completing her law degree), she was admitted to the District of Columbia bar in 1950 and to the Pennsylvania bar in 1954. By 1956 Stout had become an assistant district attorney, and in another year she became chief of the appeals, pardons, and paroles division of that office. In 1959 she was elected judge of the Municipal Court, becoming the first elected Afro-American woman to sit on a Philadelphia bench. From 1962 to 1969 Stout served as judge of the County Court, after which she became a judge of the Common Pleas Court in Philadelphia.

STOWE TEACHERS COLLEGE See HARRIS TEACHERS COLLEGE.

STRAIGHT COLLEGE See DILLARD UNIVERSITY.

STRAIGHT UNIVERSITY See DILLARD UNIVERSITY.

STRICKLAND, ARVARH E. (1930–   ), historian, educator; born in Hattiesburg, Miss. Strickland received a B.A. degree from Tougaloo College (Tougaloo, Miss.) in 1951, and a M.A. degree (1953) and his Ph.D. degree (1962) from the University of Illinois. He served as an assistant professor at Chicago State College from 1962 to 1965 and as professor there from 1968 to 1969. Strickland became professor of history at the University of Missouri in 1969. He wrote *A History of the Chicago Urban League* (1966), and he coauthored *The Black American Experience* (1974).

STUDENT NATIONAL COORDINATING COMMITTEE (SNCC; formerly STUDENT NONVIOLENT COORDINATING COMMITTEE) Formed in 1960 by black college students as a student organization dedicated to direct-action protest throughout the South, the Student National Coordinating Committee drew its membership from both black and white college campuses. In the 1960s it was particularly effective in its support of sit-in demonstrations to desegregate lunch counters and other Jim Crow facilities and in voter-registration drives; another effective tactic used by SNCC was the jail-in, in which an arrested demonstrator would refuse to pay fines and would insist upon serving the consequent jail sentence. By 1966, under the leadership of Stokely Carmichael, SNCC had changed its orientation from advocacy of nonviolent integration to militant black liberation. Carmichael's enunciation of the importance of "Black Power" in 1968 led to his departure from SNCC and his move to the Black Panther Party, an organization that reflected his belief in guerilla tactics throughout urban areas. With the increased activity of the militant urban group in the civil rights movement, SNCC lost many of its supporters, and after 1969, when it was renamed the Student National Coordinating Committee by its new leader H. Rap Brown, it became virtually defunct. *See also* BLACK POWER; CARMICHAEL, STOKELY; CIVIL RIGHTS: MOVEMENT IN SELECTED STATES: ALABAMA.

STUDENT NONVIOLENT COORDINATING COMMITTEE See STUDENT NATIONAL COORDINATING COMMITTEE.

SULLIVAN, LEON HOWARD (1922–   ), clergyman, business executive; born in Charleston, W. Va. Sullivan received a B.A. degree from West Virginia State University in 1943, his M.A. degree from Columbia University in 1947, and many honorary degrees. Ordained to the Baptist ministry in 1941, he became pastor of a church in Philadelphia, Pa. Sullivan was founder and board chairman of Opportunities Industrialization Centers and of Progress Aerospace Enterprises, Inc. He received the Freedom Foundation Award in 1960 and the Russwurm Award in 1963, and in the latter year he was named among 100 outstanding young men in the United States by *Life* magazine. Sullivan also served on the board of directors of General Motors and other corporations. He wrote *Build, Brother, Build: From Poverty to Economic Power* (1969).

SULLIVAN, MAXINE (1911–   ), jazz singer; born Marietta Williams in Homestead, Pa. Sullivan was discovered while she was doing radio work and singing with the Red Hot Peppers in Pittsburgh, Pa. Claude Thornhill arranged her first recording session, which subsequently resulted in the best-selling "Loch Lomond," a record that established Sullivan as a star. Later in the 1930s she joined John Kirby and his band.

After touring with Benny Carter's band in 1941, she retired for several years. She returned to singing in nightclubs in New York City in the mid-1940s and in Europe in 1948 and 1954. For some time after 1954, Sullivan worked as a nurse. Then, in 1958, she began a comeback that culminated in the late 1960s. *See also* MUSIC: JAZZ.

SUPREME COURT *See* CIVIL RIGHTS: CASES, 1865–1975; CIVIL RIGHTS: ENFORCEMENT; HOUSING; LAWYERS; NATIONAL ASSOCIATION FOR THE ADVANCEMENT OF COLORED PEOPLE (NAACP).

SUTHERN, ORRIN CLAYTON, II (1912–   ), organist, conductor, educator; born in Renovo, Pa. Suthern studied at Case Western Reserve University (Cleveland, Ohio), Cleveland Institute of Music, Northwestern University (Evanston, Ill.), and Columbia University. He studied organ with Edwin Arthur Kraft from 1927 to 1933, with Carl Weinrich in 1944, and with Seth Bingham in 1948. Suthern gave concerts throughout the United States. In addition, he taught at Tuskegee Institute (Tuskegee Institute, Ala.) from 1934 to 1939, at Florida Agricultural and Mechanical (A & M) College from 1940 to 1942, at Bennett College (Greensboro, N.C.) from 1942 to 1945, and at Dillard University (New Orleans, La.) after 1945. Suthern was soloist with the New Orleans Symphony Orchestra in 1945, the first time an Afro-American had performed with a white southern orchestra.

Percy Sutton.
(Courtesy of Claire Paisner.)

SUTTON, OLIVER C. (1916–   ), lawyer, judge; born in San Antonio, Tex. Sutton received a B.S. degree from Tuskegee Institute (Tuskegee Institute, Ala.) in 1937 and his LL.B. degree from New York Law School in 1951. He was admitted to the New York bar in 1954 and engaged in a general law practice until he was appointed to the Civil Court of the City of New York in 1969. *See also* SUTTON, PERCY.

SUTTON, PERCY (1920–   ), state legislator, public official; born in San Antonio, Tex. Sutton attended several colleges before he matriculated at Brooklyn Law School. He served in the Air Force during World War II, and he was an intel-

ligence officer and trial judge advocate in the Korean conflict. In 1964 Sutton was elected a member of the New York state assembly. He remained there for two years until he was chosen by the city council of New York City to fill the unexpired term of Constance Baker Motley as Manhattan borough president. The same year Sutton won the post by a large majority in a general election; he was reelected in 1969. Sutton also served as director of the National Urban League. His brother is Oliver C. Sutton. *See also* SUTTON, OLIVER C.

SWEAT, EDWARD FORREST (1912–   ), historian, educator; born in Colesburg, Ga. Sweat received a B.A. degree from Allen University (Columbia, S.C.) in 1933, a M.A. degree from Indiana University in 1948, and his Ph.D. degree from the University of Nebraska in 1957. He was an associate professor at Clark College (Atlanta, Ga.) from 1948 to 1959, and he became a professor and then Fuller E. Callaway Professor and department chairman at Clark in 1960. Sweat wrote "Frances L. Cardoza, A Profile of Integrity in Reconstruction Politics" (1961) and "Notes on the Role of Negroes in the Establishment of Public Schools in South Carolina" (1961). *See also* PREFACE: LIST OF CONTRIBUTORS.

SWEET, OSSIAN HAYES (1895– ?), physician; born in Orlando, Fla. Sweet received a B.S. degree from Wilberforce University (Wilberforce, Ohio) in 1917 and his M.D. degree from Howard University Medical College (Washington, D.C.) in 1921. He studied pediatrics and gynecology at the University of Vienna and at the Sorbonne from 1923 to 1924. Sweet practiced medicine in Detroit, Mich., where in 1925 he bought a house in a white neighborhood. Besieged and attacked by racist whites, he defended his home and family, killing an assailant. In the ensuing suit, Sweet was represented by Clarence Darrow and by Arthur Garfield Hayes, who won an acquittal. *See also* CIVIL DISORDERS: 1917–43.

SWEETS, NATHANIEL A., SR. *See* NEWSPAPERS: CONTEMPORARY.

TALLADEGA COLLEGE Talladega College, at Talladega, Ala., was founded in 1867 by the American Missionary Association (Congregational). Private, independent, and coeducational, although still strongly church-oriented, the school offers the bachelor's degree and provides a liberal arts curriculum. Its 1975 enrollment was 496.

The school began in 1867 as a primary school. The American Missionary Association purchased a colonial brick building, and with 4 teachers and 140 pupils the future college began its work. Incorporated in 1869, the college had its charter confirmed and enlarged by the legislature of Alabama 20 years later.

An outline of a course at collegiate level first appeared in the catalogue in 1890; in 1895 the first class graduated, receiving the bachelor's degree. Talladega was the first college opened to Afro-Americans in the state of Alabama. Since then, the college has shown steady growth. Its presidents since the 1930s have included Buell H. Gallagher (white) and Herman H. Long (black).

TALLEY, CORNELL E. See BAPTISTS.

TANDY, VERTNER W. (1885– ?), architect; born in New York, N.Y. Tandy studied at Tuskegee Institute (Tuskegee Institute, Ala.) and was one of the first Afro-American architects to win recognition in the United States. He also studied at Cornell University (Ithaca, N.Y.) from 1905 to 1908. Tandy was the first Afro-American to be commissioned an officer in the New York National Guard—rising to the rank of major—and was a cofounder of Alpha Phi Alpha fraternity. He designed the famous house of Madame C. J. Walker at Irvington, N.Y., on the Hudson River; St. Philip's Church in New York City; and the home of the Imperial Elks.

TANNER, HENRY OSSAWA (1859–1937), painter, educator; born in Pittsburgh, Pa. Tanner was the first Afro-American to be elected a full member of the National Academy of Design. After teaching at Clark University (Atlanta, Ga.) he went to Paris in 1891 and made his home in France. Often combining tempera and oil, Tanner did many large, dramatic paintings of religious subjects, such as *The Destruction of Sodom and Gomorrah* and *Resurrection of Lazarus*. Other works, such as *The Sabot Maker* and *The Bagpipe Lesson,* are more intimate, though they too reflect his subtle handling of light. Tanner's exhibit history includes his representation at: the Salon des Artistes Francais, Paris, 1894–1924; the Anglo-American Art Exhibition, London, 1914; the Century of Progress, Chicago, Ill., 1933–34; the Harlem Cultural Council, New York Urban League, New York, N.Y., 1967; and the Smithsonian Institution, Washington, D.C., 1969–70. His work is also included in the collections of the Louvre, Paris; the Carnegie Institute, Pittsburgh, Pa.; Howard University, Washington, D.C.; and the Metropolitan Museum of Art and the New York City Public Library (Schomburg Collection), New York, N.Y. Tanner was made a Chevalier of the Legion of Honor in 1923, after having won the 2d Medal at the Universal Exposition in Paris in 1900 and other awards. *See also* ARTISTS.

TATE, MERZE (1905–   ), historian; born in Blanchard, Mich. Tate received a B.A. degree from Western Michigan University (Kalamazoo, Mich.) in 1927; an M.A. degree from Columbia University (N.Y.C.) in 1930; a B. Litt. degree from Oxford University (London) in 1935, and her Ph.D. from Radcliffe College and Harvard University (Cambridge) in 1941. After teaching at several colleges, she came to Howard University (Washington, D.C.) in 1942. A prolific writer, her works include *The United States and the Hawaiian Kingdom,* Yale University Press, 1965, and more than a score of articles dealing mainly with the Pacific.

TATUM, REECE *See* ATHLETES: BASKETBALL.

TAYLOR, ALRUTHEUS AMBUSH (1893–1955), historian, educator; born in Washington, D.C. Taylor received a B.A. degree from the University of Michigan in 1916, and a M.A. degree (1923) and his Ph.D. degree (1935) from Harvard University. He taught at Tuskegee Institute (Tuskegee Institute, Ala.) from 1914 to 1915, and at West Virginia Collegiate Institute from 1919 to 1922. Taylor served as an associate investigator for the Study of Negro Life and History, Washington, D.C., in 1922. He became professor of history at Fisk University (Nashville, Tenn.) in 1926, and then dean of men in 1927, acting dean of the college in 1929, and dean of the college in 1930. Among his books are *The Negro in South Carolina During Reconstruction* (1924) and *The Negro in the Reconstruction of Virginia* (1926). *See also* HISTORIANS.

TAYLOR, JULIUS H. (ca. 1914–   ), physicist, educator; born in Cape May, N.J. Taylor received a B.A. degree from Lincoln University (Lincoln University, Pa.) in 1939, and a M.S. degree in physics (1942) and his Ph.D. degree in physics (1950) from the University of Pennsylvania. He became head of the department of physics at West Virginia State College in 1945, and then served as acting head of the department of physics at Morgan State University (Baltimore, Md.) from 1949 to 1951 and then as head of the department, a position he held for more than 25 years. Taylor was a member of the National Committee on Physics in Secondary Education of the American Association of Physics Teachers, and received research awards from the Office of Ordinance Research, U.S. Army, each year from 1953 to 1957. Taylor published many articles in professional journals, and he received the American Association of Physics Teachers Outstanding Service Award in 1976.

TAYLOR, MODDIE DANIEL, (1912–76), scientist, educator; born in Nymph, Ala. Taylor received a B.S. degree from Lincoln University (Jefferson City, Mo.) in 1935, and a M.S. degree (1938) and his Ph.D. degree (1941) from the University of Chicago. He was an instructor in chemistry at Lincoln University from 1935 to 1941, and served on the University of Chicago's Manhattan Project during World War II. Taylor was a Ford Foundation Fellow from 1952 to 1953, an associate chemist for Manhattan Engineers in Illinois in 1959, and a professor of chemistry from 1959 to 1969 and the chairman of the department of chemistry after 1969 at Howard University (Washington, D.C.). Taylor, who held membership in a number of scientific organizations, received many honors and awards. His career was launched with the Certificate of Merit from the U.S. secretary of war in 1945 for his work on the University of Chicago's Manhattan Project. In 1960 he received the Annual Manufacturing Chemists' Award for being one of the "Six Best Chemistry Teachers in the U.S.A." In 1972 Taylor was awarded an Honor Scroll Award from the Washington Institute of Chemists for his contributions to research and teaching. He retired as a professor emeritus of chemistry from Howard University in 1976.

TEMPLE, LEWIS (1800–54), inventor; born in Richmond, Va. Temple had no formal education. As a young man, he went to New Bedford, Mass., a major American whaling port, where he was employed as a metalsmith. As such, he invented the toggle harpoon, a type of harpoon that helped to increase the whaling catch in the nineteenth century. The new weapon, while wounding the whale also attached lines to it, thus preventing its escape. However, Temple died a poor man, never profiting from his invention.

TENNESSEE AGRICULTURAL AND INDUSTRIAL (A&I) STATE UNIVERSITY *See* TENNESSEE STATE UNIVERSITY.

TENNESSEE STATE UNIVERSITY Tennessee State University, at Nashville, Tenn., was established in 1909 by the state legislature as the Agricultural and Industrial Normal School for Negroes. State-supported and coeducational, this land-grant institution offers the bachelor's and master's degrees and provides a liberal arts curriculum, although it also emphasizes teacher education and terminal occupational programs. Its 1975 enrollment was 5,256.

Tennessee State is the only public institution of higher learning in the state that is predominantly Afro-American. Successively, the institution developed from the Agricultural and Industrial Normal School for Negroes to Tennessee Agricultural and Industrial (A & I) University and, finally, to Tennessee State University. From the 1920s to the 1940s, the affairs of the institution were dominated by its president, W. J. Hale, who was succeeded by W. S. Davis and then by Andrew P. Torrence.

TERRELL, MARY ELIZA CHURCH (1863–1954), author, civil rights activist; born in Memphis, Tenn. In 1884 Terrell entered Oberlin College (Oberlin, Ohio), and from 1888 to 1890 she studied abroad, returning to the United States to decline a post at Oberlin in 1891 as registrar and to marry Robert H. Terrell (who later became a judge in the District of Columbia). In 1895 she was appointed to a District of Columbia school board, the first Afro-American woman in the country to hold such a position. A women's rights advocate, Terrell was a charter member of the National Association of Colored Women, and from 1896 to 1901 she served as that organization's first president. In 1953 she headed a group opposing segregation in the District of Columbia that succeeded in helping to abolish it in the nation's capital. Her autobiography, *A Colored Woman in a White World,* was published in 1940. *See also* TERRELL, ROBERT HUBERTON.

TERRELL, ROBERT HUBERTON (1857–1927), educator, judge; born in Charlottesville, Va. Terrell graduated from Harvard University in 1884. He taught in Washington, D.C., served as a division chief of the U.S. Department of the Treasury, and was appointed a Municipal Court judge of the District of Columbia by President Theodore Roosevelt in 1902. Terrell was one of the founders of the Robert H. Terrell Law School in Washington, D.C. *See also* TERRELL, MARY ELIZA CHURCH.

TERRY, ROBERT *See* AVIATORS.

TEXAS COLLEGE Texas College, at Tyler, Tex., was founded in 1894 by the Christian Methodist Episcopal (CME) Church. Church-related, private, and coeducational, the college offers the bachelor's degree and provides liberal arts and teacher education curricula. Its 1975 enrollment was 558.

The school was organized as a liberal arts college by a group of ministers and laymen from the three Christian Methodist Episcopal (CME) conferences in Texas—the East Texas, the West Texas, and the Texas Mission. Instruction began in 1895 with O. T. Womack as the school's first president. In 1909 its name was changed from Texas College to Phillips University in honor of Bishop C. H. Phillips, who was chairman of the board of trustees, but in 1912 the institution reverted to the name of Texas College.

The college's first significant period of academic development was from 1915 to 1926, at which time it became fully accredited as a junior college by the Texas state department of education. The 30 years from 1931 to 1961 formed the second period of academic growth and physical expansion. In 1932 the college was accredited as a senior college. Its presidents since the 1930s include C. C. Owens, D. R. Glass, R. L. Potts, H. C. Savage, and A. C. Hancock.

TEXAS SOUTHERN UNIVERSITY Texas Southern University, at Houston, Tex. was founded in 1947 by the state legislature in response to legal pressures applied by Afro-Americans for equality in higher education. State-supported and coeducational, the school offers the bachelor's and master's degrees and provides a liberal arts curriculum, although there is heavy emphasis on teacher education, professional work, and terminal occupational programs. Its 1975 enrollment was about 6,900.

The university's growth was spectacular. In the mid-1970s it was the largest predominantly Afro-American college in the state, but like several other black schools it faced strong competition from predominantly white institutions. Its first president was Raphael O'Hara Lanier; its president in 1975 was Granville M. Sawyer.

THEATER *See* LITERATURE: DRAMA/THEATER.

THEODORE ALFRED LAWSON STATE JUNIOR COLLEGE Theodore Alfred Lawson State Junior College, at Birmingham, Ala., was founded in

Mary Eliza Church Terrell. *(Library of Congress.)*

1963 as a public institution. State-supported and coeducational, the school offers a two-year program that can be credited toward the bachelor's degree or used as terminal occupational work. Its 1975 enrollment was 2,200.

THOMAS, ANNA PERRY (1897–   ), educator; born in Wake Forest, N.C. Thomas attended Shaw University, (Raleigh, N.C.) and the Normal School at Benedict College (Columbia, S.C.), and she received her B.E. and M.E. degrees from the National College of Education (Evanston, Ill.). She was a delegate to the White House Conference on Childhood Education, and was the founder and director of the Happy Day Nursery School in Waukegan, Ill., which was recognized as one of the outstanding schools of its kind in the Midwest.

THOMAS, JESSE O. (1883–1972), civil rights leader; born in McComb, Miss. Thomas received a B.A. degree from Tuskegee Institute (Tuskegee Institute, Ala.) in 1911, and did postgraduate study at the New York School for Social Work from 1919 to 1920 and in 1923. While at Tuskegee, his intelligence, self-confidence, and ability as a speaker attracted the notice of Booker T. Washington, and immediately after graduation Thomas became a field secretary for the Institute, with his headquarters at Rochester, N.Y. In 1917 he worked as a supervisor of Afro-American economics in the offices of the New York state department of labor. Before joining the staff of the National Urban League in 1919, Thomas served as examiner in charge of the U.S. Employment Service. He was hired on the recommendation of George Haynes as field secretary for the league's southern division, and Thomas organized several league branches, including those in Tampa, Fla.; Miami, Fla.; Little Rock, Ark.; Richmond, Va.; Atlanta, Ga.; and New Orleans, La. Thomas also conducted several surveys on Afro-American living conditions in the urban South for the league. In addition, he helped organize the Atlanta University School of Social Work, a much-needed institution for the training of Afro-American social workers. He remained on the school's board of directors for many years. In 1928 Thomas served on the Mississippi Flood Relief Committee, and in the same year was a delegate to the International Conference on Social Work in Paris, France. In 1939, during the illness of Eugene Jones, he was acting executive secretary of the National Urban League, resigning in 1940 to join the staff of the American

National Red Cross. Thomas became the first Afro-American to work for that organization in a professional and policy-making capacity. *See also* NATIONAL URBAN LEAGUE.

THOMAS, RUFUS (1917–   ), entertainer, disc jockey of Memphis, Tenn. Thomas created several nationally known song-dances, including the "Funky Penguin," the "Funky Chicken," and the "Dog." His records, which made him popular in the 1960s and 1970s, include: "Cause I Love You," "The Dog," "Can Your Dog Do the Monkey," and "Walkin' the Dog."

THOMPKINS, WILLIAM JAMES (1884–1944), physician; born in Jefferson City, Mo. Thompkins received a B.A. degree from Colorado University and his M.D. degree from Howard University Medical College (Washington, D.C.). He practiced in Kansas City, Mo., where he was active in local politics and where he served as the editor of the newspaper *The American*. Thompkins was assistant commissioner of public health for Kansas City, and was appointed recorder of deeds in Washington, D.C., in 1934.

THOMPSON, CHARLES HENRY (1945–   ), educator, editor. Thompson received a B.A. degree from Virginia Union University, and a Ph.B. degree, a M.A. degree, and his Ph.D. degree (1925) from the University of Chicago. He was a Rosenwald Fellow, and served as dean of the graduate school at Howard University (Washington, D.C.). Thompson was founder and editor of the *Journal of Negro Education*, one of the oldest and most prestigious of all educational journals in the United States. *See Also* EDUCATION: COLLEGES AND UNIVERSITIES.

THOMPSON, ERA BELL author, editor; born in Des Moines, Iowa. Thompson received her B.A. degree from Morningside College (Sioux City, Iowa) in 1933 and did further study at the Medill School of Journalism of Northwestern University (Evanston, Ill.). She received honorary degrees from Morningside College in 1965 and one from the University of North Dakota in 1969. Thompson served on the editorial staff of *Ebony*, a Johnson Publication, after 1964. Her awards include the Iota Phi Lambda Outstanding Woman of the Year (1965); the Bread Loaf Writers Conference Fellowship (1949); and the Patron Saints' Award (1968) for her *American Daughter*. Her other publications include *Africa: Land of My Fathers* (1954) and *White on Black* (1963).

THORPE, EARLIE ENDRIS (1924–   ), historian; born in Durham, N.C. Thorpe received a B.A. degree from North Carolina College (Durham, N.C.) in 1948, a M.A. degree (1949) and his Ph.D. degree (1953) from Ohio State University, Columbus, O. He taught history at several black colleges (Stowe Teachers, Alabama A & M, and Southern University) before his appointment at North Carolina Central University in 1962. *See also* HISTORIANS.

THORPE, MARION DENNIS (1932–   ), educator; born in Durham, N.C. Thorpe received B.A. and M.A. degrees from North Carolina Central University and his Ph.D. degree in administration and educational services from Michigan State University in 1961. He taught educational psychology at Michigan State University from 1959 to 1961, taught at North Carolina Central University from 1961 to 1965, and then became director of the U.S. Department of Labor Neighborhood Youth Corps in 1965. Thorpe served as assistant director of the North Carolina board of higher education from 1966 to 1967, as vice-president of Central State University (Wilberforce, Ohio) from 1967 to 1968, and as president of Elizabeth City State University (Elizabeth City, N.C.) after 1968.

THURMAN, HOWARD (1900–   ), theologian, author; born in Daytona Beach, Fla. Thurman received B.A. degrees from Morehouse College (Atlanta) and Rochester Theological Seminary (1923). Ordained a Baptist minister in 1925, he served as pastor of the Mt. Zion Baptist Church, Oberlin, Ohio, from 1926 to 1928, after which he returned to Morehouse as a teacher and dean of the chapel until 1931. For the next 12 years he served as a professor and dean of the chapel at Howard University (Washington, D.C.). Thereafter, he served as pastor of the Church for Fellowship of All Peoples (San Francisco) from 1944 to 1953 and professor at Boston University from 1953 to 1967. A persuasive mystic, Thurman was in demand as a speaker, receiving honorary degrees from numerous colleges, including Morehouse College, Wesleyan University (Middletown, Conn.), Ohio Wesleyan University (Delaware), Lincoln University (Pa.), Howard University, and Oberlin College (Ohio). His sermons and writings are contained in many books and pamphlets. Among his books are *The Greatest of These* (1944), *Meditations for Apostles of Sensitiveness* (1947), *Jesus and the Disinherited* (1949), *Deep is the Hunger* (1951), *The Inward*

Journey (1961), and *The Luminous Darkness* (1965). For a bibliography, see Massey, James Earl, "Bibliographical Essay: Howard Thurman and Rufus M. Jones, Two Mystics," *Journal of Negro History*, April, 1972.

THURMOND, NATE See ATHLETES: BASKETBALL.

TILDON, JAMES TYSON (1931–   ), scientist, educator; born in Baltimore, Md. Tildon received a B.S. degree from Morgan State University (Baltimore, Md.) in 1954 and his Ph.D. degree in biochemistry from Johns Hopkins University (Baltimore, Md.) in 1965. He was a Fulbright Scholar at the University of Paris from 1959 to 1960, and held positions in research at Sinai Hospital, Baltimore, Md., from 1954 to 1959 and at Brandeis University (Waltham, Mass.) from 1967 to 1968. Tildon was a faculty member and chief of pediatric research at the University of Maryland School of Medicine after 1968, and was credited in 1972 with the discovery of a new disease in children called CoA transverse deficiency, a discovery that relates to his earlier findings that ketone bodies are an energy source for the central nervous system in infants.

TILDON, TOUSSAINT TOURGÉE (1893–1964), psychiatrist; born in Waxahachie, Tex. Tildon received his M.D. degree from Harvard Medical School in 1923, and served in the neuropsychiatric department of the Veterans Hospital, Tuskegee, Ala., beginning in 1923, thus becoming one of the first Afro-American physicians to staff that hospital. He later served as clinical director of the neuropsychiatric department and as director of the hospital.

TILLOTSON COLLEGE See HUSTON-TILLOTSON COLLEGE.

TOBIAS, CHANNING HEGGIE (1882–1961), clergyman, administrator, government official; born in Augusta, Ga. Tobias attended the public schools in his hometown and the academy connected with Paine College (Augusta, Ga.) until he entered the college itself. He received a B.A. degree in 1902, having already been ordained a minister of the Colored Methodist Episcopal (later Christian Methodist Episcopal) Church. To supplement his religious training, Tobias attended Drew Theological Seminary (Madison, N.J.), from which he received a B.D. degree in

1905. For the next six years he taught biblical literature at Paine College. In 1911 Tobias began a lifetime association with the Young Men's Christian Association (YMCA), for which he became senior secretary of the Colored Men's Department of the National Council. His position with the YMCA took him all over the world as a lecturer, an observer, and a U.S. representative to international YMCA conferences. Tobias was an active participant in community and educational activities, lecturing and serving on boards of colleges, educational projects, and citizens' committees. In 1946 he became director of the Phelps-Stokes Fund, dedicated to the betterment of educational opportunities for Afro-American students. Also concerned with race relations, Tobias served as chairman of the board of directors of the National Association for the Advancement of Colored People (NAACP). In 1950 he was named U.S. alternate delegate to the United Nations, a post he held through the following year.

TOLAN, EDDIE *See* ATHLETES: TRACK AND FIELD.

TOLES, EDWARD BERNARD (1909–), lawyer, judge; born in Columbus, Ga. Toles received a B.A. degree from the University of Illinois in 1932 and his J.D. degree from Loyola University School of Law (Chicago, Ill.) in 1936. Admitted to the Illinois bar in 1936, his 30-odd-year private law practice was interrupted only for a few years (1943–45) when Toles served as European war correspondent for the Chicago *Daily Defender.* In 1968 he became a U.S. referee in bankruptcy, appointed by the judges of the U.S. District Court in Chicago, one of only two Afro-American federal referees. Toles was the author of works on Afro-American lawyers and judges and the difficulties they face in seeking government positions.

TOLSON, MELVIN B. *See* LITERATURE: POETRY.

TOPPIN, EDGAR ALLAN (1928–), historian, educator, author; born in New York, N.Y. Toppin received a B.A. degree from Howard University (Washington, D.C.), and his M.A. and Ph.D. degrees from Northwestern University (Evanston, Ill.). He taught at Fayetteville State University (Fayetteville, N.C.), at the University of Akron (Akron, Ohio), at San Francisco State Universiy, at Alabama State University, and elsewhere. In 1964 Toppin became professor of

history at Virginia State College. He was a Northwestern University Fellow in 1951, a Hearst Foundation Fellow in 1952, and received a Whitney Fellowship in 1953. His publications include: *Pioneers and Patriots: Six Negroes in the Revolutionary Era* (1965), coauthored with Labinia Dobler; *A Mark Well Made: Negro Contributions to American Culture* (1967); and *A Biographical History of Blacks in America* (1971). *See also* HISTORIANS.

TORRENCE, ANDREW PUMPHREY (1920–), educator, administrator; born in Little Rock, Ark. Torrence received a B.S. degree from Tennessee State University in 1948, and a M.S. degree (1951) and his Ph.D. degree (1954) from the University of Wisconsin. He was an associate professor at Tennessee State University (1954–62) and also served that institution as professor and academic dean (1962–67). He was elected president of the school in 1967.

TOUGALOO COLLEGE Tougaloo College, at Tougaloo, Miss., was founded in 1869 by the Congregational Christian Church. Church-related and coeducational, the school offers the bachelor's degree and provides a liberal arts curriculum. Its 1975 enrollment was 851.

In 1869 the American Missionary Association of New York purchased a plantation of 500 acres near Jackson, Miss., and on it established a

Far right: Completed in 1881, Strieby Hall was constructed by students from bricks made on the campus. It was named for an official of the American Missionary Association. *(Courtesy of Tougaloo College.)*

school for the training of Afro-Americans. The school was to be accessible to all, irrespective of religious beliefs.

In 1871 the state legislature granted the institution a charter under the title of Tougaloo University. The normal department was recognized as a state normal school until 1892 when the institution stopped receiving financial aid from the state and ended its formal connection with the school system of Mississippi. In 1897 courses for college credit were first offered. In 1916 the name of the institution was officially changed from Tougaloo University to Tougaloo College.

TOUGALOO UNIVERSITY See TOUGALOO COLLEGE.

TRENHOLM, HARPER COUNCIL (1900–63), educator; born in Tuscumbia, Ala. Trenholm received a B.A. degree from Morehouse College (Atlanta, Ga.) in 1920, and a M.A. degree and his Ph.B. degree (1921) from the University of Chicago. He taught at the State Normal School (Montgomery, Ala.), becoming president of that institution in 1925. Trenholm was also a trustee of Selma University (Selma, Ala.).

TROTTER, WILLIAM MONROE (1872–1934), publisher, editor; born in Springfield Township, Ohio. Trotter received a B.A. degree (1895) and his M.A. degree (1896) from Harvard University. He was the first Afro-American member of Phi Beta Kappa, the national scholarship fraternity. From 1897 to 1906 Trotter was an insurance and mortgage broker in Boston, Mass. In 1901 he became publisher and editor of the *Guardian,* a crusading newspaper that he headed until his death. Trotter also edited centennial volumes on William Lloyd Garrison, Charles Sumner, and John Greenleaf Whittier. He founded the National Equal Rights League, which anticipated the civil rights movement of the 1960s by stressing voting, integration, equal rights, and the role of the federal government, and he was instrumental in having the Massachusetts motion-picture censureship laws passed as a reaction to the controversial film *Birth of a Nation.*

TRUTH, SOJOURNER (1797–1883), abolitionist; born Isabel Baumfree in Hurley, N.Y. Truth was born a slave, and at an early age she became deeply religious. She was freed by the New York State Emancipation Act of 1827. In the spring of 1843, as a result of a religious vision, Truth left her home in New York City with 25 cents, a new dress, and a new name—Sojourner Truth. Traveling to rallies on abolition in the Midwest, New England, and Middle Atlantic states, she became the first outstanding Afro-American woman to speak out publicly against slavery. Although Truth was illiterate, all who heard her speak were deeply impressed by her oratorical abilities and by her talent for reducing issues to their essentials. After the Civil War, she advocated equal treatment of Afro-Americans, particularly in matters relating to education. A champion of women's rights, Truth attended the second National Woman's Suffrage Convention held in Akron, Ohio, in 1852, where she made her famous "Ain't I A Woman" address. *See also* SLAVERY: THE ABOLITIONISTS; WOMEN.

TUBMAN, HARRIET (ca. 1821–1913), abolitionist: born in Dorchester County, Md. Tubman, sometimes called the "Moses of Her People," reputedly led more than 300 people out of bondage to freedom. The daughter of Harriet Greene and Benjamin Ross, who were not permitted to marry legally under the laws of slavery, Tubman had a brutal childhood. She was thought "stupid," and often received the standard cure, whipping. At 13 Tubman was injured by a rock thrown at her by her master, and as a result suffered from occasional blackouts for the rest of her life. She worked as a fieldhand in her late teens, developing tremendous physical strength and powers of endurance. At about the age of 25, Tubman and her two brothers planned an escape; she succeeded in getting to the North, but her brothers turned back en route. Later, in freedom, Tubman became a "conductor" for the Underground Railroad, making 19 trips back to the South to help bring slaves to freedom. After the passage of the Fugitive Slave Act in 1850, most of the escaped slaves were taken to the Canadian border because, as she told her biographer, "I wouldn't trust Uncle Sam with my people no longer, but I brought them all clear off to Canada." Though she could neither read nor write, her cleverness and shrewdness in eluding her enemies led to a bounty price of $40,000 for her capture. Northern abolitionists, such as Thomas Garrett of Wilmington, Del., gave Tubman practical assistance. Senator William Seward sold property to her in Auburn, N.Y., in 1857, and this became her permanent home where she brought her parents to live. Tubman occasionally spoke at antislavery meetings, but it was not a role in which she felt comfortable.

Harriet Tubman. *(Library of Congress.)*

During the Civil War she served as a cook for the Union troops and later as a scout; she also rendered service as a spy and, toward the end of the war, as a nurse. After the war, Tubman turned her attention to establishing an old-age home for indigent Afro-Americans, giving to this project all her funds and her energy. Although the home was never well-funded, several prominent Republicans contributed to its support, and it continued to function for some years after Tubman's death. Sarah Bradford's *Harriet Tubman: The Moses of Her People* was written to raise money for this charity (1869; reprinted in 1886). *See also* SLAVERY: THE ABOLITIONISTS; WOMEN.

TUCKER, CYNTHIA DELORES NOTTAGE (1927–), public official; born in Philadelphia, Pa. Tucker attended Temple University (Philadelphia, Pa.) and Pennsylvania State University, and she received her LL.D. degree from Villa Maria College (Erie, Pa.) in 1972. She was active in many civic organizations and served as secretary of the Commonwealth of Pennsylvania in 1974. Tucker was president of the Pennsylvania chapter of the National Association for the Advancement of Colored People (NAACP).

TUREAUD, ALEXANDER PIERRE (1899– ?), lawyer, judge; born in New Orleans, La. Tureaud received his J.D. degree from Howard University (Washington, D.C.) in 1925 and that same year he was admitted to the bar. Later, between 1960 and 1961, he initiated more than 30 public school district desegregation cases and handled suits to desegregate buses, parks, playgrounds, and public facilities. He became a judge in 1969.

TURFLEY, GEORGE GLASGO (1855– ?), physician; born in Pittsburgh, Pa. Turfley received his M.D. degree from Western Reserve Medical College (Cleveland, Ohio; now part of Case Western Reserve University) in 1897, and later set up a private practice in Pittsburgh, thus becoming the first Afro-American physician to practice in that city.

TURNER, CHARLES HENRY (1867–1923), zoologist, educator; born in Cincinnati, Ohio. Turner received B.S. and M.S. degrees from the University of Cincinnati, and his Ph.D. degree from the University of Chicago in 1907. He was a high school instructor during his entire professional career, concentrating his personal research on the study of insect behavior—especially that of ants and spiders. Turner contributed many scholarly papers to professional journals.

TURNER, HENRY McNEAL (1834–1915), African Methodist Episcopal bishop, editor; born in South Carolina. Turner was ordained a minister and bishop in the African Methodist Episcopal (AME) Church in 1853 and 1880, repectively.

Far right: Henry McNeal Turner. *(Library of Congress.)*

He served as minister in Washington, D.C., in 1862 and a year later as chaplain in the Union Army. After the Civil War, Turner worked with the Freedmen's Bureau in Georgia. Although his formal education was very limited, he began to publish and edit a newspaper in Atlanta called *Voice of Missions*, in which he advocated Afro-American colonization in Africa so that Afro-Americans could "fix" their own standards and achieve equality. Turner also preached this message from the pulpit, but his fellow bishops and communicants, though appreciative of his eloquence, were not seriously impressed with his advice to go to Africa. *See also* NATIONALISM.

TURNER, JAMES MILTON (1844–1915), educator, civic leader; born in St. Louis County, Mo. Born a slave, Turner's and his mother's freedom were purchased by his father. Though largely self-educated, Turner did attend school at Oberlin College's preparatory department for one year. He served in the Civil War and became very active in public life thereafter, including the promotion of schools for blacks in Missouri. President Grant appointed him minister to Liberia, the first significant appointment of a black to the diplomatic service.

TURNER, LORENZO DOW See AFRICA: AFRICAN LEGACY/SURVIVALS.

TURNER, NAT (1800–31), preacher, militant; born in Southampton County, Va. Turner organized and led the most successful and dramatic North American slave revolt. Born a slave to Benjamin Turner, he was sold in 1822 to Thomas Moore, also of Southampton County. A few months before the sale, Turner had run away but he had returned voluntarily 30 days later. From an early age, Turner was infused with a religious zeal; he lived an ascetic life and viewed himself as set apart by God for some great purpose. He was much respected among his fellow slaves, and there is one recorded incident of his baptizing a white overseer sometime in 1825. In January 1830 Turner became the property of Joseph Travis.

On August 13, 1831, a day-long atmospheric change occurred, during which the sun is reported to have appeared blue-green. Turner interpreted this as a sign from heaven, and on August 20, 1831, with two fellow slaves, Hark Travis and Henry Porter, he planned an insurrection. On August 21, joined by Samuel Francis and three others, Turner and the six slaves assembled at Cabin Pond. Starting at about one o'clock in the morning and continuing throughout the day of August 22, Turner and his band—which picked up followers on the way—went from house to house killing white Virginians. The group, which comprised some 60 men at its height, killed at least 57 people, many of them children. Late in the evening of August 22, the Turner group was attacked by a local militia. Though without fatalities, the revolutionary group became disorganized. A false alarm reduced the number of participants in the revolt to about 20. At daybreak on August 23, at the home of Dr. Blunt, the group was repulsed by Blunt's slaves and several men in the Turner force were killed. By midday Turner was alone; the members of his revolutionary band were either captured, dead, or in hiding. Turner himself remained in hiding in and around Southampton, Va., but he was captured on October 30, 1831. Turner's "confessions" were dictated to Thomas Gray on November 1 and 3. Found guilty on November 5, he was executed on November 11.

Turner's actions terrified southerners, and he helped to dispel the myth of the docile slave. Regulations governing slave conduct became more rigid. Slaves considered "suspicious" were examined, and some were summarily executed by increasingly nervous whites. The free black population was also adversely affected. *See also* SLAVERY: REFERENCES.

TUSCALOOSA INSTITUTE See STILLMAN COLLEGE.

TUSKEGEE INSTITUTE Tuskegee Institute, at Tuskegee Institute, Ala., was established in 1881 by an act of the general assembly of Alabama, with Booker T. Washington as its founder and first principal. Tuskegee is a private, independent, and coeducational college that offers the bachelor's and the master's degrees and that provides liberal arts, teacher education, and vocational curricula. Its 1975 enrollment was 3,171.

Founded in the one-room "log cabin" tradition, in which Washington stressed practical knowledge but at no time ignored the liberal arts, the institute grew quickly. In 1882 Washington contracted to buy a 100-acre abandoned plantation, which eventually became the nucleus of Tuskegee's present campus near Montgomery, and by 1970 the institute had grown from a single academic department to 6 schools and colleges; from 30 students to more than 3,000; and from a faculty of one to a faculty of 250. Seventy-five percent of the Afro-American veterinarians in the nation are graduates of Tuskegee. Perhaps of more importance was the historic impact that Washington and the school have made upon the nation. Presidents who followed Washington were Robert Russa Moton (1915–35), Frederick D. Patterson (1935–53), and Luther H. Foster (1953–   ). *See also* WASHINGTON, BOOKER T.

TYSON, CICELY (ca. 1942–   ), born in New York, N.Y. Tyson spent her early years in Harlem where she attended public schools, and later she attended New York University for a short time. She also went to several acting schools in New York City. Tyson was in the cast of the *Blacks*, and received the Rice Award for her performance in *Moon on a Rainbow Shawl* (1962). She appeared in *Blue Boy in Black* in 1963, and by 1973 she had won a variety of top awards for television and theater performances. Tyson's star performance in the award-winning motion picture *Sounder* (1972) was unanimously cheered as perhaps the most impressive film performance by an Afro-American in the 1970's. *See also* MOTION PICTURES.

UNCLE TOM *See* AFRO-AMERICAN HISTORY: SECTIONAL CONFLICT.

UNEMPLOYMENT *See* EMPLOYMENT.

UNITED CHURCH OF CHRIST *See* CONGREGATIONALISTS.

UNITED HOUSE OF PRAYER FOR ALL PEOPLE Developed by Daddy Grace, a very effective evangelist and revivalist during the period from the 1930s to the 1950s, the United House of Prayer for All People is the name of a religious organization referred to as a "charismatic sect" by Afro-American sociologist Albert N. Whiting. Grace is reputed to have amassed a fortune from places of worship and followers in several American cities, including Savannah, Ga.; Charlotte, N.C.; and Washington, D.C. Strong followers of the group were based in several congregations in Washington, D.C., in the 1970s. *See also* PENTECOSTALS.

UNITED METHODIST CHURCH *See* METHODISTS UNITED METHODIST CHURCH.

UNITED NEGRO COLLEGE FUND A cooperative fund-raising organization whose purpose is to provide financial aid to predominantly Afro-American colleges, the United Negro College Fund was chartered in the state of New York in 1944. With Arthur A. Fletcher as its executive director, the fund embraced a membership of 40 institutions in the early 1970s.

UNIVERSAL NEGRO IMPROVEMENT ASSOCIATION (UNIA) An organization formed in 1911 by Marcus Garvey in Jamaica, British West Indies, the Universal Negro Improvement Association was dedicated to the premise that Negroes could only achieve equality by becoming independent of white society and forming their own governments and nations. The purposes of the UNIA were stated in its official periodical, the *Negro World*, as follows: (1) to champion Negro nationhood by redemption of Africa; (2) to make the Negro race conscious; (3) to breathe the ideals of manhood and womanhood into every Negro; (4) to advocate self-determination; (5) to make all the Negro world conscious; (6) to print all the news that will be interesting and instructive to the Negro; (7) to instill racial self-help; and (8) to inspire racial love and self-respect.

In 1916, when Garvey approached the Afro-American community of New York City with his philosophy couched in a fiery oratory, he won much popular support. The "Back-to-Africa" Movement was enunciated in a 1920 convention of Garvey's followers that took place in Madison Square Garden in New York City. *See also* GARVEY, MARCUS; NATIONALISM; PAN-AFRICANISM.

Founded by Sweet Daddy Grace (C. M. Grace), the United House of Prayer in Washington, D.C. was well known both within and outside of Pentecostal congregations. *(Photo by Jacquelyn Low.)*

REFERENCES: The literature on Garvey and the UNIA has increased since 1960. A good beginning point for further reading is found under REFERENCES for NATIONALISM; especially the standard study by Cronon, E. David, *Black Moses: The*

823

Story of Marcus Garvey and *the Universal Negro Improvement Association*, U of Wis Pr, Madison, 1969. However, a more recent study of Garvey and his movement has been made by Martin, Tony, *Race First: The Ideological and Organizational Struggles of Marcus Garvey and the Universal Negro Improvement Association*, Greenwood, Westport, Conn., 1976. With educational backgrounds in England and the United States. Martin's special interest in black nationalism led him to draw upon valuable sources both in Britain and the United States for his study.

UNIVERSITIES See EDUCATION: COLLEGES AND UNIVERSITIES.

UNIVERSITY OF ARKANSAS AT PINE BLUFF The University of Arkansas at Pine Bluff was chartered in 1872 by a legislative act. State-supported and coeducational, the school offers the bachelor's degree and provides liberal arts and teacher education curricula, with emphasis also on terminal occupational programs. Its 1975 enrollment was 2,083.

Originating in a school in Pine Bluff known as Branch Normal, the college was certified to receive land-grant funds under the Second Morrill Act in 1890. Its name was also changed to Arkansas Agricultural, Mechanical, and Normal College. In 1972 the institution became a part of the state university system, and its name was changed to the University of Arkansas at Pine Bluff.

UNIVERSITY OF MARYLAND EASTERN SHORE The University of Maryland Eastern Shore (Princess Anne, Md.) was founded in 1886 by Methodists. The college offers the bachelor's degree and provides a liberal arts curriculum, in addition to offering teacher education and vocational studies. Its 1975 enrollment was 1,041. Known as Princess Anne College it was reorganized as a division of the University of Maryland. Many new faculty members were brought in to implement the reorganization, including Theodore R. Briggs, Charles O. Stout, and Furman Williams (industrial education); Claude C. Marion and John V. Strickland (agriculture); Edward N. Ferguson and George Hunter (sciences); John S. Lash (humanities); and W. Tycer Nelson (religion). In 1970 the college became the University of Maryland Eastern Shore. White students began to enroll beyond the "token" level during the 1960s, and by the early 1970s they amounted to one-fourth of the student body. Its chief executive officers since the 1930s have been Thomas H. Kiah, Robert L. Grigsby, John T. Williams, Howard E. Wright, and Archie T. Buffkins. William T. Hytche, a native of Oklahoma, was appointed chancellor in 1976. Earl Richardson, an alumnus, became an administrative associate.

UNIVERSITY OF THE DISTRICT OF COLUMBIA The university was created in 1977 from a merger of three local institutions in Washington, D.C.: District of Columbia Teachers College, Federal City College, and Washington Technical Institute. Each of the three original institutions retained its identity of location in the names of the new campuses of the university: the District of Columbia Teachers College became the campus at Georgia Avenue-Harvard Street; Federal City College became the campus at Mount Vernon Square; and Washington Technical Institute became the Van Ness campus (also the site of the central office of the university on Connecticut Avenue). The university's total enrollment in 1977–78 was about 13,900. Most of its students were black (90%), from the District of Columbia (93%), and enrolled in undergraduate programs. The university's principal executive officers were Lisle C. Carter and Wendell P. Russell. *See also* DISTRICT OF COLUMBIA TEACHERS COLLEGE; FEDERAL CITY COLLEGE.

URBAN LEAGUE See NATIONAL URBAN LEAGUE.

UTICA JUNIOR COLLEGE Utica Junior College, at Utica, Miss., was established in 1903 by William H. Holtzclaw. State-supported and coeducational, the college offers a two-year program that can be credited toward the bachelor's degree or used as terminal occupational work. Its 1975 enrollment was 705.

The school began as a normal and industrial institute called the Utica Institute, and it remained this type of institution for half a century. In 1954 the board of trustees of the institute authorized plans to proceed with the organization of a junior-college program, and, in a special session, the state legislature gave its formal approval. In 1957 the school, now Utica Junior College, was greatly expanded, and a full vocational-technical department was organized.

VALIEN, PRESTON See SCIENTISTS: SOCIAL.

VAN DER ZEE, JAMES See PHOTOGRAPHERS.

VANN, ROBERT LEE (1887–1940), lawyer, editor, publisher; born in Ahoskie, N.C. Vann studied at Virginia Union University, and received his B.A. and LL.D. degrees from the University of Pittsburgh. In 1909 he became a lawyer, but the next year he became involved in the formation of the Pittsburgh Courier Publishing Company, of which he eventually gained control. After 1912 Vann served as editor of the Pittsburgh *Courier*, a newspaper that developed rapidly into the most widely circulated Afro-American newspaper. In addition to his publishing activities, he began to participate in politics. From 1917 to 1921 he was assistant to the city solicitor of Pittsburgh; in 1924 he went to the Republican National Convention as delegate-at-large; and he served in public relations posts during the presidential campaigns of Warren G. Harding, Calvin Coolidge, and Herbert Hoover. Later, Vann changed his party affiliation and supported Franklin D. Roosevelt in 1932, and he was appointed special assistant U.S. attorney general by Roosevelt in 1933. In 1936 Vann relinquished this post to turn his full attention to his newspaper—but only after he had served again as delegate-at-large, this time at the Democratic National Convention. *See also* NEWSPAPERS: HISTORY AND DEVELOPMENT.

VAN PEEBLES, MELVIN (1932–   ), author, director, producer; born in Chicago, Ill. A graduate of Ohio Wesleyan University in 1953, Van Peebles published *The Big Heart* in 1957, a book about cable cars. Traveling to Europe after this experience, Van Peebles toured with the Dutch National Theater for a time and then went to Paris, where in 1960, on subsistence from the

Melvin Van Peebles, holding camera, about 1970. (*Courtesy of Columbia Pictures.*)

coins earned by singing and dancing in the streets, he wrote several novels, some of which eventually became films or plays. (*The Party in Harlem* became the play *Don't Play Us Cheap;*

and *La Permission* became the movie *The Story of a Three-day Pass.*) In 1970 Van Peebles became a Hollywood director, and his first film was *Watermelon Man*, a humorous satire (starring Godfrey Cambridge) of a white man who turned black. His next film was produced independently with his own money (and that of friends and supporters), an amateur cast, and a nonunion crew. The film, *Sweet Sweetback's Baadassssss Song*, revolutionized the motion picture industry and launched a new era of Afro-American films. Soon after, Van Peebles produced a musical on Broadway entitled *Ain't Supposed to Die a Natural Death* (1971), and in 1972 he produced the musical *Don't Play Us Cheap*. *See also* LITERATURE: DRAMA/THEATER; MOTION PICTURES.

VASHON, GEORGE B. (ca. 1820– ?), lawyer, educator; born in Ohio. Vashon was the first Afro-American graduate of Oberlin College (Oberlin, Ohio) in 1844. He was admitted to the bar in 1847, and he became one of the very few Afro-Americans in antebellum America to teach at a white college, New York Central College at McGrawville, N.Y. Vashon High School in St. Louis, Mo., was named in his honor. *See also* LAWYERS.

VAUGHN, GEORGE L. (1885–1950), lawyer, civic leader; born in Kentucky. Vaughn was educated at Lane College (Jackson, Tenn.) and prepared for the legal profession at Walden University (Nashville, Tenn.). After serving in the artillery as a first lieutenant in World War I, he practiced law in St. Louis, Mo. In 1936 Vaughn was appointed justice of the peace in St. Louis, and in 1941 he ran unsuccessfully for the post of alderman on the Democratic ticket. Nonetheless, he became a prominent figure in national politics by virtue of his recommendation at the Democratic National Convention in 1948 that the Mississippi delegation be unseated because of the white supremacy resolutions adopted in its state constitution. Vaughn's resolution came within 115 votes of carrying. Vaughn also helped to pilot through the St. Louis courts the case of *Shelley v. Kraemer*, in which the plaintiff opposed covenants in real estate. The U.S. Supreme Court decided in 1948 that such covenants could not be enforced in state courts because they violated the 14th Amendment by infringing upon the right of a citizen to purchase and dispose of property.

VAUGHN, OLIVIA *See* NEWSPAPERS: CONTEMPORARY.

VENABLE, ABRAHAM S. (1930–), born in Washington, D.C. Venable received his M.A. degree in economics and business administration from Howard University (Washington, D.C.), and did postgraduate study in urban problems at Princeton University's Woodrow Wilson School of Public and International Affairs. He became an authoriative spokesman on Afro-American business development, serving as director of the Office of Minority Business Enterprise from 1969 to 1972. In 1972 Venable became director of urban affairs for General Motors Corporation. He wrote *Black Business Development: Chaos in Transition* (1972).

VENABLE, H. PHILLIP (1913–), ophthalmologist; born in Windsor, Canada; Venable received his M.D. degree from Wayne State University (Detroit, Mich.) in 1940, and was the director of the department of ophthalmology after 1943 and medical director after 1965 of Homer G. Phillips Hospital, St. Louis, Mo. Venable was also director of the department of ophthalmology at St. Mary's Infirmary and at Peoples' Hospital, both in St. Louis, Mo., after 1944. In addition, he served as examiner for the American Board of Ophthalmology.

VERNON, WILLIAM TECUMSEH (1871–1944), African Methodist Episcopal bishop, educator; born in Lebanon, Mo. Vernon attended Lincoln University (Jefferson City, Mo.) and received his D.D. and LL.D. degrees from Wilberforce University (Wilberforce, Ohio). He served as president of Western University (Quindaro, Kans.) and of Campbell College (Jackson, Miss.). From 1906 to 1910 Vernon was the registrar of the U.S. Treasury. In 1920 he was elected a bishop of the African Methodist Episcopal (AME) Church, and he served the church both in the United States and in South Africa. Vernon established a church school in Basutoland (later Lesotho).

VESEY, DENMARK *See* SLAVERY IN SELECTED STATES: SOUTH CAROLINA.

VIRGINIA STATE COLLEGE Virginia State College, at Petersburg, Va., was founded in 1882 as a training institute for Afro-American citizens of Virginia. State-supported and coeducational, the college offers the bachelor's and the master's degrees (including the B.Mus. and the M.Ed.)

and provides liberal arts, teacher education, and vocational curricula. Its 1975 enrollment was 4,179. The school is the only combination of land-grant college, liberal arts college, and college of education in the state.

In 1907 the training school added a course in vocational agriculture; in 1915 it added a four-year high school and a standard normal school. The institute was selected by the state board of vocational education to train public school teachers of vocational subjects in 1918, and in 1920 it was made the state's land-grant college for Afro-American youth by legislative act. In 1930 the school was renamed the Virginia State College for Negroes, and in 1936 it received authorization to grant graduate degrees. By an act of the 1944 general assembly of Virginia, Norfolk Polytechnic College became a division of Virginia State. In 1946 the college received its present name. Preceded by James H. Johnston, John M. Gandy achieved the longest tenure as president of the college (1914–42). Following Gandy were Luther H. Foster, Robert P. Daniel, James F. Tucker, Wendell Phillips Russell, and Walter H. Quarles, Jr. See also NORFOLK STATE COLLEGE.

VIRGINIA UNION UNIVERSITY Virginia Union University, at Richmond, Va., was founded in 1865 as a result of the merger of several institutions that had been organized by the American Baptist Home Mission Societies to educate newly freed slaves: Wayland Seminary, Richmond Theological Institute, and Hartshorn Memorial College. Private and church-related, the coeducational school offers the bachelor's degree (including the B.D.) and graduate work in theology and provides a liberal arts curriculum. Its 1975 enrollment was 1,405.

In 1899 the university moved to is present site in the center of Richmond. The institution now comprises the college of liberal arts and sciences, and a graduate school of theology—from which about 10 percent of all American-educated Afro-American ministers have graduated. Its presidents have included John M. Ellison, Samuel D. Proctor, and Allix B. James.

VIRGIN ISLANDS An organized, "unincorporated" territory of the United States, the Virgin Islands is composed of three main islands—St. Thomas, St. Croix, and St. John—and more than 50 other islets in the West Indies. Extending east-west for some 60 miles between the Atlantic Ocean and the Caribbean Sea, the islands comprise the western limit of the Lesser Antilles, about 60 miles east of Puerto Rico. They are, at one and the same time, part of the Caribbean archipelago, part of the Lesser Antilles, and part of the West Indies. For 250 years, the islands were occupied by Denmark and were known as the Danish West Indies; and before that, they were held by the Netherlands, by England, and by Spain. In 1917, having been the subject of treaties sale twice before, the islands, discovered for Spain by Christopher Columbus on his second voyage to the "Indies" in 1493, were finally purchased by the United States and became known as the Virgin Islands of the United States.

Columbus found the islands peopled by peaceful Arawak and warlike Carib Indians who repulsed his landing party, but who were later overcome by Spain's forces sent to occupy the islands in 1555. By the end of the sixteenth century, most of the Indians had been killed or had disappeared, and they were superseded by African slaves. The descendants of slaves now dominate the population, as they do in most of the other islands of the West Indies.

During the days of slavery (until 1848), the population of the Danish West Indies reached a high of 43,000, but by 1917 the population had dwindled to 26,000 or less. Records show a steady increase in population since the purchase by the United States in 1917; the 1970 census numbers the population at about 63,000 but most of the key local people say it is nearer to 75,000. The population is about 80 percent black. The nonblacks include white Americans, Danes and other Europeans, Puerto Ricans, and Middle Easterners.

Slaves were first brought to St. Thomas in 1673 to work in the cane and cotton fields. The first large consignment arrived in 1681. The islands prospered as the planters and slaves increased in number, but the years were marked by several insurrections—the most noted of which was in St. John, where in 1733 slaves were in control for six months. When an international force broke the siege, many slaves committed suicide rather than return to slavery. The importation of slaves was abolished in 1803, but slavery continued until 1848 (when there was a slave revolt).

Although the islands were purchased on March 31, 1917, negotiations had been going on for months, and the first piece of American legislation concerning the islands was passed by the

U.S. Congress on March 3. This bill authorized President Woodrow Wilson to set up a temporary government and to vest military, civil, and judicial powers in such persons as he might appoint. He appointed Rear-Adm. James H. Oliver as the first governor, and the administration of the government was assigned to the U.S. Navy Department. Administration by the Navy Department continued until 1931 when President Herbert Hoover directed that the operation of the government on the Virgin Islands be made a responsibility of the Department of the Interior, and that a civilian governor be named. This historic change was brought about by the same president who had earlier called the territory America's "effective poorhouse," drawing the ire of Virgin Islanders at home and abroad. The Navy, while in control, had improved the public schools and established the first free high school; it had modernized the hospitals, had established two all-black naval bands with black bandmasters, and had sent one of the bands on a tour of the mainland. In fact, at one time, the highest-ranking black officer in the U.S. Navy was Alton A. Adams, Sr., the bandmaster of the St. Thomas Naval Band, with the rank of chief petty officer. The Navy had also started a nursing school to train native nurses, and it employed natives in many minor white-collar positions, which they had not held before.

Culturally, the islands are cosmopolitan, both European-oriented and American. In general, English is the language of the islands, though some French is spoken on St. Thomas and some Spanish on St. Croix. Although there is little indigenous music or folklore, the Virgin Islands Council of the Arts (an adjunct of the U.S. National Foundation of the Arts and Humanities) and its three community arts councils have brought in leading artists and theater companies, and they have provided courses in arts and crafts.

Religious freedom has long been respected in the islands, and all religions and denominations are represented; some congregations have existed for more than two centuries (one of the oldest synagogues under the American flag is in St. Thomas). The Lutheran (the official church of Denmark), the Roman Catholic, the Protestant Episcopal, the Moravian, and the Methodist churches have long carried on both religious and educational work. After World War II, the Christian Science and the African Methodist Episcopal (AME) churches, the Bahá'í faith, and others established congregations.

REFERENCES: Although the literature is very scant, attention is called to the following: Campbell, Albert A., *St. Thomas Negroes—A Study of Personality and Culture*, Northwestern University, Evanston, Ill., 1943; Dejnozka, Edward L., "American Educational Achievement in the Virgin Islands, 1917–1963," *Journal of Negro History* (Oct. 1972, pp. 385–394); and Harman, Jeanne Perkins, *The Virgins: Magic Islands*, Appleton-Century-Crofts, New York, 1961.

VODERY, WILL HENRY BENNETT (1885–1951), composer, bandleader; born in Philadelphia, Pa. Vodery was educated at Hugh A. Clark University and with private instructors. In 1911 he became music supervisor for Florenz Ziegfield's Follies, and held this position until 1932. During this period Vodery arranged the scores for *Show Boat* and for more than 50 other musical comedies. He also wrote many popular songs and the scores for several musical comedies. His best-known songs include "After the Ball is Over," "Oyster Man," "Two Much Isaacs," "Girls From Happy Land," and "Saucy Maid." Vodery wrote the scores for *Puerto Rico Girls, Happy Girls, Can't Get Away From It, Dark Town Poker Club,* and *Land Lady.*

VOORHEES COLLEGE Voorhees College, at Denmark, S.C., was founded in 1897 by Elizabeth Evelyn Wright, a graduate of Tuskegee Institute (Tuskegee Institute, Ala.). Church-related and coeducational, the school offers the bachelor's degree and provides a liberal arts curriculum. Its 1975 enrollment was 737.

First known as the Denmark Industrial School, after the village of Denmark, the school was renamed for a donor, Ralph Voorhees of Clinton, N.J. After the turn of the century, support was received from the Protestant Episcopal Church—mainly from the dioceses of South Carolina. Voorhees became a junior college in 1929 and a four-year college in 1942.

WADDY, JOSEPH C. (1911–   ), lawyer, judge; born in Louisa, Va. Waddy received a B.A. degree from Lincoln University (Lincoln University, Pa.) in 1935 and his LL.B. degree from Howard University (Washington, D.C.) in 1938. He was admitted to the District of Columbia bar in 1939, joined a District of Columbia law firm in 1939, and practiced there until 1962. In that year Waddy was made associate judge of the Domestic Relations Municipal Court in the District of Columbia, and in 1967 he became judge of the U.S. District Court for the District of Columbia.

WALCOTT, JERSEY JOE See ATHLETES: BOXING.

WALDEN, EMERSON COLEMAN (1923–   ), physician; born in Cambridge, Md. Walden received his M.D. degree from Howard University Medical College (Washington, D.C.) in 1947. Practicing in Baltimore, Md., he served as president of the National Medical Association, as president of the Maryland Medical Association, and as a vice-president of the Monumental City Medical Society of Baltimore. Walden was also appointed to the board of regents of the University of Maryland in the early 1970s.

WALDEN SEMINARY See PHILANDER SMITH COLLEGE.

WALDEN UNIVERSITY See MEHARRY MEDICAL COLLEGE.

WALKER, ANTONIO MACEO (1909–   ), business executive; born in Indianola, Miss. Walker received a B.A. degree from Fisk University (Nashville, Tenn.) in 1930, a M.B.A. degree from New York University in 1932, and his L.H.D. degree from Wilberforce University (Wilberforce, Ohio) in 1959. In 1946 he became president and chairman of the board of directors of Tri-State Bank of Memphis, Tenn., and he also served as president of Universal Life Insurance Company (Memphis, Tenn.), and of Memphis Mortgage Company. Walker was a member of the Tennessee Advisory Commission on Civil Rights, the Memphis Transit Authority, and the United Negro College Fund. He also served as a trustee of Fisk University.

WALKER, CORA T. (1926–   ), lawyer, civic leader; born in Charlotte, N.C. Walker received her B.S. and LL.B. degrees from Saint John's University (Jamaica, N.Y.). She practiced law in New York City's Harlem for more than 20 years, at the same time becoming involved in civic and community work. Walker served as coordinator and legal counsel for the Harlem River Consumers Cooperative, as vice-president of the National Bar Association, and as president of the Harlem Lawyers Association (the organization's only woman president). She was also organizer and president of the Harlem Involvement Project, Inc., and the director of the Morningside Heights Cooperative Housing Corporation.

WALKER, DAVID (1785–1830), author; born in Wilmington, N.C. Born of a free mother and a slave father, Walker was educated in Boston, Mass., and later owned a clothing store there. His major work was his *Appeal*, which called on Negroes to revolt against their masters. The *Appeal* was published and circulated largely through Walker's individual efforts. It was denounced by pro-slaverists, and one slaveholding state put a price on Walker's head.

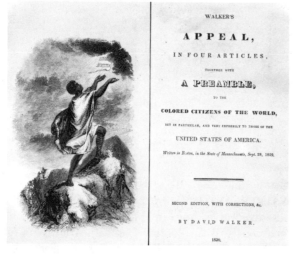

Walker's *Appeal.* (Library of Congress.)

Walker died under mysterious circumstances after refusing to flee to Canada. *See Also* SLAVERY: ABOLITIONISTS.

WALKER, ERNESTEIN (1926–), historian; born in McDonough, Ga. Walker received an A.B. degree in 1949 from Spelman College (Atlanta, Ga.), an M.A. degree in 1953 from Atlanta University (Ga.), and her Ph.D. degree in 1964 from Western Reserve University. She taught at several colleges, including Fort Valley State (Ga.), and South Carolina State (Orangeburg), before joining the faculty at Morgan State College, Baltimore, in 1965. Though her publications have treated mainly nonblack topics in English history (one of the few Afro-American professional historians to do so), she is also interested in the black woman, having published an article on the subject in the *American Negro Reference Book*, 1973.

WALKER, JOHN THOMAS (1925–), Episcopal bishop; born in Barnesville, Ga. Walker received a B.A. degree from Wayne State University (Detroit, Mich.) in 1951 and his B.D. degree from Virginia Theological Seminary in 1954. He was ordained a deacon in 1954 and became a priest in 1955. His first assignment was as locum

tenens of St. Mary's in Detroit, Mich., in 1955. Walker also taught at St. Paul's School in New Hampshire, and served at the National Cathedral in Washington, D.C. He was elected coadjutor bishop of the Episcopal Church for the District of Columbia in 1976.

WALKER, MADAME C. J. (1867–1919), business executive; born Sarah Breedlove in Delta, La. Walker attended school at night in St. Louis, Mo., and early in her career invented a metal heating comb and conditioner for straightening hair. Beginning as a door-to-door peddler of her cosmetic products, she eventually amassed a fortune. She expanded her business to Denver, Colo., and to Pittsburgh, Pa., where her daughter, A'Lelia, was placed in charge. In 1910 Walker built a factory in Indianapolis, Ind., to manufacture her hair preparations, facial creams, and other products. Arriving in New York City in 1913, she established Lelia College to train young women in the Walker beauty system and the use of Walker beauty products, and from this beginning evolved a chain of salons. Walker also promoted many other projects. She built a town house on West 136th Street in the Harlem section of New York City and a mansion on the Hudson River in Irvington, N.Y. Walker was also one of the foremost social leaders of her time. *See also* BUSINESS.

WALKER, MAGGIE (1918–), pediatrician; born in Richmond, Va. Walker received a B.S. degree from Virginia Union University in 1937 and her M.D. degree from the University of Michigan Medical School in 1941. She was an intern and resident at Provident Hospital, Chicago, Ill., and was a fellow in cardiology at Children's Memorial Hospital. Walker established a private practice in Chicago, Ill, and served as a member of the American Academy of Pediatrics.

WALKER, MAGGIE LENA (1865–1934), business executive; born in Richmond, Va. Walker attended Richmond Normal School and received her M.S. degree from Virginia Union University in 1925. She began her career as a teacher in the public schools of Richmond, serving as an insurance agent during the same period. Walker was later employed by the Consolidated Bank and Trust Company of Richmond, and eventually she became president of that institution. She was also national deputy and executive secretary of the Independent Order of St. Luke and the editor of the *St. Luke Herald*.

WALKER, MARGARET *See* ALEXANDER, MARGARET WALKER.

WALKER, WILLIAM O. (1896–), publisher, journalist; born in Selma, Ala. Walker graduated from Wilberforce University (Wilberforce, Ohio) in 1916 and from Oberlin Business College (Oberlin, Ohio) in 1918. He became secretary to the director of the Pittsburgh Urban League. Walker joined the news staff of the Pittsburgh *Courier* in 1919, the staff of the Norfolk *Journal and Guide* in 1920, helped found the Washington, D.C., *Tribune* in 1921, and took over the Cleveland *Call and Post* in 1932. He also served as director of the Ohio department of industrial relations from 1963 to 1971. *See also* NEWSPAPERS: CONTEMPORARY.

WALKER, WYATT TEE (1929–), clergyman, civil rights leader; born in Brockton, Mass. Walker received a B.S. degree (1950) and his B.D. degree (1953) from Virginia Union University. He was pastor of a Baptist church in Petersburg, Va., for eight years, and then became executive assistant to Dr. Martin Luther King, Jr., before serving as chief of staff of the Southern Christian Leadership Conference (SCLC) from 1960 to 1964. Walker was a minister at the Abyssinian Baptist Church and the Canaan Baptist Church, both in New York, N.Y. Beginning in 1966, while serving as vice-president and later as president of Educational Heritage, Inc., a publishing firm, he was also a special assistant to Gov. Nelson Rockefeller of New York on urban affairs. Walker was vice-president of the Young Men's Christian Association (YMCA) of Greater New York, and in 1972 he was appointed a visiting professor at Princeton Seminary. He received more than 100 awards and citations for his work in human relations and civil rights.

WALLACE, JOHN H. *See* SCIENTISTS: BIOLOGICAL, PHYSICAL.

WALLACE, WILLIAM JAMES LORD (1908–), educator, administrator; born in Salisbury, N.C. Wallace received a B.S. degree from the University of Pittsburgh in 1927, a M.A. degree from Columbia University in 1931, and his Ph.D. degree in chemistry from Cornell University (Ithaca, N.Y.) in 1937. He taught at Livingstone College (Salisbury, N.C.) from 1927 to 1932, at Lincoln University (Jefferson City, Mo.) from 1932 to 1933, and at West Virginia State College

beginning in 1932. He served as president of West Virginia State College from 1953 to 1973.

WALLER, THOMAS W. (FATS) (1904–43), composer, bandleader; born in Waverly, N.Y. Waller began playing the organ in his father's church when he was 10 years old, later quitting high school to become organist in a New York City theater. He learned ragtime and piano style from James P. Johnson, and wrote his first tune, "Boston Blues," in 1925. Waller formed his own band, and during the 1920s and 1930s he toured throughout the United States and Europe. In 1928 Waller wrote the score for *Keep Shufflin'* and in 1929 the score for *Hot Chocolate*. Some of his many hit tunes include "Ain't Misbehavin'," "Honeysuckle Rose," and "I've Got A Feelin' I'm Fallin'," and his best piano solos include *Minor Drag, Viper's Drag, London Suite*, and *Handful of Keys*. Waller also appeared in several films, including *Hooray for Love, King of Burlesque*, and *Stormy Weather*. *See also* MUSIC: HISTORY AND DEVELOPMENT; MUSIC: BLUES.

WALLS, JOSIAH T. *See* AFRO-AMERICAN HISTORY: RECONSTRUCTION.

WALLS, WILLIAM JACOB (1885–1975), African Methodist Episcopal Zion bishop, editor; born in Chimney Rock, N.C. Walls received B.A. and B.D. degrees from Livingstone College (Salisbury, N.C.), and his M.A. degree from the University of Chicago. He did further study at Hood Theological Seminary and at the School of Journalism of Columbia University. Walls began his clerical career as an evangelist when he was 14 years old, and later he served churches in North Carolina and Kentucky. From 1920 to 1924 he was editor of the *Star of Zion*, published in Charlotte, N.C., and in 1924 he was elected a bishop of the African Methodist Episcopal Zion (AMEZ) Church, serving in that capacity for many years until his retirement.

WALTON, HANES, JR. (1941–), political scientist, educator; born in Augusta, Ga. Walton graduated from Morehouse College (Atlanta, Ga.) in 1963, and received a M.A. degree from Atlanta University in 1964 and his Ph.D. degree from Howard University (Washington, D.C.) in 1967. He served as an associate professor at Savannah State College (Savannah, Ga.) beginning in 1967, and he became a professor there in 1971, and Galloway Professor in 1972. Walton was a Social Science Research Council Fellow

(1969–70), a Ford Foundation Fellow in 1971, and a Guggenheim Fellow in 1972. Walton's publications include: *The Negro in Third Party Politics; The Political Philosophy of Martin Luther King, Jr.; Black Poets; Black Political Parties;* and *The Poetry of Black Politics. See also* PREFACE: LIST OF CONTRIBUTORS.

WARD, CLARA *See* WARD SINGERS.

WARD, DOUGLAS TURNER (1930–   ), director, playwright, actor; born in Burnside, La. Ward studied in Paul Mann's Actors' Workshop in New York City, played the leading role in *A Raisin in the Sun* on a ten-month national tour, and starred in many plays produced by the Negro Ensemble Company, which he helped to establish, in New York City. He wrote and played in *Happy Ending* and *Day of Absence,* the latter of which ran for more than a year at the St. Marks Playhouse in New York City (1965–66). Ward also directed and played the leading role in *The First Breeze of Summer* (1975).

WARD, SAMUEL RINGGOLD (1817–64), editor, clergyman; born in Maryland. Ward escaped from slavery and went to New York City, where he taught school and became a preacher. He later served as an agent for the *Colored American* and as an editor of the *Farmer and Northern Star.* He helped to organize the Liberal and Free-Soil parties in New York, N.Y.; edited the *Impartial Citizen* in Boston, Mass., in 1850; and coedited the *Alienated American* in 1853. Ward moved to Canada in the 1850s, where he lectured for the Antislavery Society. He was the author of *The Autobiography of a Fugitive Slave* (1855). After visiting England, Ward moved to Jamaica, Britist West Indies, where he died. *See also* SLAVERY: THE ABOLITIONISTS.

WARD SINGERS Gospel singers who were popular as a group during the 1940s and 1950s. Gertrude Ward and Clara Ward were the principal leaders in organizing and developing the group. The group's extensive repertoire included *Surely God Is Able* which, recorded in the late 1940's, is reputed to be the first gospel recording to sell more than one million copies.

WARFIELD, WILLIAM (1920–   ), singer; born in West Helena, Ark. Warfield attended school in Rochester, N.Y., and received his training in voice, organ, and piano at the Eastman School of Music (Rochester, N.Y.) and at the University of Rochester. Warfield made his debut at New York City's Town Hall in 1950, and after that he performed the role of Porgy in George Gershwin's *Porgy and Bess* in many revivals both in the United States and in Europe. Between 1952 and 1959 Warfield made five international tours sponsored by the U.S. Department of State.

WARING, LAURA WHEELER (1887–1948), painter, educator; born in Hartford, Conn. After studying at the Pennsylvania Academy of Fine Arts in Philadelphia, Pa., Waring won a Cresson Memorial Scholarship and attended the Grand Chaumière in Paris, France, from 1924 to 1925. Later, she became head of the art department at Cheyney State Teachers College (Cheyney, Pa.), and she was named the director in charge of Negro Art exhibits at the Philadelphia Exposition. Her oils, watercolors, and pastels primarily depict Afro-American life. Her portraits include *Frankie* and *Anne Washington Derry.* Her work was exhibited at the Harmon Foundation, New York, N.Y., 1927–28 and 1930–31; at the Pennsylvania Academy of Fine Arts, Philadelphia, Pa., 1935; at the Art of the American Negro, Chicago, Ill., 1940; and at the Smithsonian Institution, Washington, D.C., 1933. Waring's work is in the collections of the Smithsonian Institution, the National Archives, and the National Portrait Gallery, all in Washington, D.C. Her honors include a Gold Award from the Harmon Foundation in 1927. *See also* ARTISTS.

WAR OF 1812 *See* WARS.

WARREN, SADIE (1874– ?), publisher; born in Greenfield, Ohio. Warren became manager and treasurer of New York City's *Amsterdam News* in 1921 when her husband Edward A. Warren, who had founded the paper in 1909, died.

WARS

American Revolution When Continental Congress voted to support Massachusetts farmers against the king's troops, which marked the beginning of the military aspect of the American Revolution, the expectation was that the war would be fought by white colonists. Washington had wanted no black soldiers, but the British forced Washington and the colonists to change their minds.

The British offered slaves in the South their freedom if they would rally round the king's standard, and some did. The British commanders intended to train them and use them as they saw fit to further their military action.

For the colonists, this represented an invitation to a slave insurrection, an action that would produce a bloodbath and death to soldier and civilian alike. From today's viewpoint, this is an eighteenth-century glimpse at the concept of total war. From the colonial viewpoint, this was one of the most vile ideas a man could harbor and further proof of the baseness of the enemy.

The fact that some Afro-Americans responded to the British invitation led the Americans to accept the service of free blacks in their Army. Some, by their own choice, carried a musket, and others served as substitutes for white men. Blacks, both slave and free, acted as guides, messengers, teamsters, laborers, and spies. Afro-Americans served as members of crews and as pilots in the Continental Navy.

Most of the time, Afro-Americans served in what we today would call integrated units. It has been estimated that of the total combat force of 300,000 men for the whole war, some 5,000 were Afro-Americans.

The British succeeded in recruiting a large number of slaves whom they used to help build fortifications. Although the insurrection of the slaves never materialized, the fear of one remained.

War of 1812 This same fear was revived during the War of 1812. This war was not a popular war, especially in the Northeast. Even among those who supported the war, there were unpopular assignments. One was on gunboats assigned to defend local harbors; another was service on the Great Lakes. In the gunboat service and the lakes service, the chance of supplementing one's meager pay with prize money for the capture of enemy vessels was virtually nonexistent. Money was only to be had on the high seas in the Navy or on a privateer. Afro-Americans who had the opportunity to serve on a privateer did so. The number of Afro-Americans in the Navy was not great because a regulation existed against enlisting them. When short of men, however, a captain was apt to disregard such a regulation.

In the lakes service, Afro-Americans served with Commodore Oliver H. Perry's squadron on Lake Erie, with Commodore Isaac Chauncey's on Lake Ontario, and with Commodore Thomas McDonough's on Lake Champlain.

Far left: Standing at the north end of Battle Monument Plaza on Calvert Street, an historic site in Baltimore, this statue is a memorial to Afro-Americans who served in all of the nation's wars. Sculpted by James E. Lewis, a professor of art at Morgan State University, the statue was unveiled on June 12, 1972. Its completion was a civic undertaking supported by various groups and individuals, including the mayor and other city officials, art groups, the press, and radio and television stations. *(Courtesy of James E. Lewis.)*

The general manpower situation in the Army suggests that Afro-Americans were probably used, when available, in the Northern campaigns and in various efforts to defend the East Coast from British forays in 1814. They were most conspicuous, however, in the Southwest. Free blacks responded to Andrew Jackson's call for volunteers. Two battalions of free men of color helped turn back the British in the Battle of New Orleans.

In 1820, the year of the Missouri Compromise, the Army adjutant general's office issued this order: "No Negro or Mulatto will be received as a recruit in the Army."

Mexican War Service by Afro-Americans in the Mexican War was apparently limited to those who served as crews of Navy vessels on duty off the Mexican coast and in California. By this time the old restrictions against enlisting Afro-Americans in the Navy had given way to a regulation that permitted them to constitute one-twentieth of a crew. Under no circumstances were slaves to be enlisted, although some southern officers did bring a servant to sea with them. Slaves were used, however, in laboring forces at navy yards.

Civil War The leadership of both sides in the Civil War never expected the war to last for four years. As the war dragged on and took its toll, abolitionists and others urged President Abraham Lincoln to enlist Afro-Americans. By the middle of the war, this course was being followed; but Afro-American soldiers were only gradually accepted. As members of a segregated unit, the first Afro-American volunteers were given a great deal of fatigue duty, which tended to underscore the idea that they were only laborers in uniform. It was not until the summer of 1864 that the practice of concentrating noncombatant work in Afro-American regiments was discontinued.

Other problems still remained. The Afro-American soldier received six dollars a month less in pay and uniforms than whites. He was armed with poor or obsolete weapons and received inferior medical care.

When finally given combat duty, Afro-Ameri-

Battle of Lake Erie (War of 1812). *(Library of Congress.)*

can regiments participated in 449 engagements, 39 of which may be considered as major battles.

The fact that Afro-Americans, if captured, risked being executed induced President Lincoln to try to keep them in areas where the chance of being captured was minimal. Lincoln finally had to resort to threats of retaliation before the Confederates treated Afro-Americans as official prisoners of war. Even then, the South was unwilling to exchange prisoners (involving Afro-Americans) on a man-for-man basis since this would be an admission of equality. By the

time the South did agree to a man-for-man exchange, the North had adopted a policy of no exchanges in order to deprive the South of manpower.

Service in the Union Navy was not popular during the Civil War. States did not pay bounties to men who joined the Navy; and, also, blockade duty was very boring. To meet his manpower demands, the secretary of the navy found it necessary to transfer some soldiers with maritime backgrounds to duty on board naval ships. A somewhat similar situation prevailed in relation to the gunboat service on the western waters.

Given this manpower shortage, Afro-Americans were enlisted whenever possible. In December 1862 the secretary of the navy issued an order that no "contrabands" (a black slave who had fled, had been smuggled behind the Union lines, or who had remained in territory captured by the Union Army) were to be enlisted at a rating higher than that of landsman, the lowest rating. If they were found to be qualified, they could later be advanced to the rating of coal-heaver, fireman, ordinary seaman, and seaman. If they were transferred to another vessel, they had to begin again at the lowest rating.

When all was said and done, 186,000 Afro-Americans served in the Union Army. Most

served in infantry regiments; others served engineering, light artillery, and cavalry units. In every case, it was segregated service. About 75 to 100 Afro-Americans received commissions, the highest of which was that of a lieutenant colonel.

Some 29,000 Afro-Americans served in various capacities in the Union Navy, which was an integrated service. None, however, made the rank of officer.

Despite all these restrictions, Afro-Americans won the Medal of Honor. Medal of Honor recipients in the Union Army were:

1863 Sgt. William Harvey Carney, Co. C, 54th Mass. Vols.
1864 Sgt. Maj. Christian A. Fleetwood, 4th U.S.C.T.
1864 Sgt. Alfred B. Hilton, Co. H, 4th U.S.C.T.
1864 Cpl. Charles Veal, Co. D, 4th U.S.C.T.
1864 Sgt. Milton M. Holland, Co. C, 5th U.S.C.T.
1864 1st Sgt. James E. Bronson, Co. D, 5th U.S.C.T.
1864 1st Sgt. Powhatan Beatty, Co. G, 5th U.S.C.T.
1864 1st Sgt. Robert A. Pinn, Co. I, 5th U.S.C.T.
1864 Sgt. Maj. Thomas R. Hawkins, 6th U.S.C.T.
1864 Sgt. Alexander Kelly, Co. F, 6th U.S.C.T.
1864 Cpl. Miles James, Co. B, 36th U.S.C.T.
1864 Pvt. James Gardiner, Co. I, 36th U.S.C.T.
1864 1st Sgt. Edward Ratcliffe, Co. C, 38th U.S.C.T.
1864 Sgt. James H. Harris, Co. B, 38th U.S.C.T
1864 Pvt. William H. Barnes, Co. C, 38th U.S.C.T.
1864 Sgt. Decatur Dorsey, Co. B, 39th U.S.C.T.

Medal of Honor recipients in the Union Navy were:

1863 Robert Blake, Contraband, U.S.S. *Marblehead*
1864 Joachim Pease, Seaman, U.S.S. *Kearsarge*

Far left:
A cook watches over the mess at an army rail head (Union), City Point, Virginia, during the Civil War. *(Library of Congress.)*

Sgt. William H. Carney. *(Moorland-Spingarn Research Center, Howard University.)*

Christian Fleetwood, 1860 Congressional Medal of Honor recipient. *(Lincoln University.)*

1864   John H. Lawson, Landsman, U.S.S. *Hartford*
1864   Clement Dees, Seaman, U.S.S. *Pontoosuc*
1865   Aaron Anderson, Landsman, U.S.S. *Wyandank*

Far right: *The 369th, one of the most decorated units of World War I, marches up Fifth Avenue, passing the New York Public Library, in a victory parade (1918). (The National Archives.)*

For recipients in other wars, see Robert Ewell Greene, cited in References below (pp 376–377). There were, however, some outstanding heroes who did not receive the Medal of Honor, such was Robert Lee Campbell, a captain of Infantry in World War I, who received the Distinguished Service Cross. Campbell was also a veteran of the Spanish-American War who, after World War I, served on the faculties of Tuskegee Institute and A & T College. Immediately after World War II began, Campbell volunteered his services.)

The Afro-American's service in the Civil War induced the War Department to create four Afro-American units as part of the postwar Regular Army. These were the 24th and 25th Infantry regiments and the 9th and 10th Cavalry regiments. They saw service in the Indian Wars, mainly in the Southwest.

Spanish-American War Sixteen regiments of black volunteers were raised in the Spanish-American War, but the war ended too soon for most of the volunteers to reach the front. Elements of the Regular Army Afro-American regiments did see action in Cuba, especially at San Juan Hill along with Teddy Roosevelt's dismounted Rough Riders.

The 9th cavalry, one of the oldest combat regiments, embarks for Cuba during the Spanish-American War (1898). (The National Archives.)

By this time, fewer Afro-Americans were serving in the Navy, and those in service tended to be cooks and stewards.

World War I With the beginning of World War I, 370,000 Afro-Americans (11 percent of American combat forces) enlisted or were drafted. More than half of these men were assigned to the all-black 92d and 93d Infantry divisions. Separate regiments of the 92d Division served with French troops and earned the Croix de Guerre.

The 369th Infantry Regiment ("Hell Fighters") of the 93d Infantry Division was outstanding. It was in continuous combat longer than any other American unit; and it was the first Allied regiment to reach the Rhine River in the offensive against Germany. However, the overwhelming majority of black fighting men were assigned to service units, including outfits engaged as stevedores on French docks for the American Expeditionary Force. In the Navy, Afro-American service was limited to 10,000 messmen; there were no commissioned officers. In fact, black officers numbered only about 1,400 (about one for every 2,600 black enlisted men), and the highest ranking of these officers was a colonel. By official policy, the Wilson administration and its War Department carried out rigid segregation. Black leadership protested these restrictions as discriminatory. Commissions, for example, were only reluctantly granted, and most commissions had come through the controversial all-black officers' training school in Des Moines, Iowa. See NATIONAL ASSOCIATION FOR THE ADVANCEMENT OF COLORED PEOPLE (NAACP): THE NAACP, WILSON, AND WORLD WAR I.

World War II About a million black Americans served in the armed forces in World War II, including several thousand women in the Women's Auxiliary Army Corps (WACS). By the end of the war, about 165,000 enlisted men were in the Navy. Blacks served in all theaters, largely in the service corps: quartermaster, engineer, ordinance, and transportation. About half of all enlisted men served overseas.

However, there were several black combat units. The largest in Europe was the 92d Infantry Division, known as the "Buffalo Division" because of a history of service in the post–Civil

War American West. The 93d Infantry Division was the largest combat unit in the Pacific theater. Smaller combat units, less than division strength, included the 761st Tank Batallion (highly commended for gallantry), the 614th Tank Destroyer Batallion, the 593d Field Artillery, and several anti-aircraft units (then under Coast Artillery Command). Moreover, the 99th and 332d fighter plane squadrons were outstanding.

Trained at Ft. Huachuca, Ariz., and committed to combat action with the Fifth Army, the 92d Division ended its career near the close of the war in Italy after actions in Cascina, Cinquale Canal, and La Spezia. The 93d Division, or its units, saw service in several Pacific islands, including the Solomons.

As in World War I, blacks were restricted to service in segregated units; but by the close of the war, some training schools, including some Officer Candidate Schools, were integrated. Throughout the war, segregation was enforced at all military posts: in theaters, service clubs, mess halls, living areas, transport, and other facilities. There was also discrimination in promotion and assignments. For example, black enlisted men faced difficulties in becoming commissioned officers; the Navy did not commission its first black officer (Bernard W. Robinson) until 1942 and by the end of the war had only 53 black officers. The Navy had the first national Afro-American hero of the war (Dorie Miller) in 1941 when the Japanese attacked Pearl Harbor. Also, those who were commissioned faced discrimination in promotion, especially above the rank of captain. Blacks were almost completely excluded from the command function beyond junior officer levels. Protests against segregation and discrimination were made by soldiers: sometimes by individuals "through channels"; sometimes by rioting groups in training camps or posts. Per-

Far left:
In the newly liberated city of Genoa, Italy, the 92d Division troops enter the Galleria Guiseppe Garibaldi (1945). *(U.S. Army Photograph.)*

Members of the "Suicide Six," reputedly one of the fastest gun crews in the 2d Infantry Division (Korean Conflict, 1951). *(U.S. Army Photograph.)*

haps more significant were the protests made by the black press and by the leadership of the NAACP and the Brotherhood of Sleeping Car Porters. Protests led to the beginning of integration at the end of World War II in 1945. See NATIONAL ASSOCIATION FOR THE ADVANCEMENT OF COLORED PEOPLE (NAACP): THE NAACP IN WORLD WAR II.

Military Activity after 1945 The end of World War II and the beginning of the cold war brought occupation duty in Germany, in Austria, and in Japan, and additional problems of integration. In 1948 President Harry S. Truman issued an executive order ending segregation in the Armed Forces. A new era in the history of the fighting man began. This integration was quickly completed so that by the beginning of the Korean War in June, 1950, only the 25th Infantry Regiment of the old demobilized 93d Infantry Division was still identifiable as an Afro-American unit. As members of integrated units, Afro-Americans gave a good account of themselves in Korea.

General Westmoreland is briefed by two of the advisors to the 2d Battalion, 24th Regiment of the 5th Division in Vietnam. *(U.S. Army Photograph.)*

A new problem arose out of integration. It was now possible for a black man to make a career as a soldier or sailor in an integrated unit, and many did. But this situation took on a different dimension as the American involvement in Vietnam increased. If the U.S. Army was bearing the brunt of that war, and if much of the army was Afro-American, was this the ultimate test of an integrated service? Or, was it the case of a minority group's bearing a disproportionate share of the ordeal? These questions and their implica-

tions were being discussed a long time after America's departure from Vietnam.

The following list is a breakdown by percentages of black, white, and other participation in the Armed Forces according to a Department of Defense report issued on June 30, 1972. Since that time the number of enlistees has dropped as the military has reduced its strength following the end of the Vietnam War. The category "others" includes Spanish-speaking Americans, Orientals, and American Indians.

RACIAL COMPOSITION OF THE ARMED FORCES, 1972

Races	Percent
Total in all branches of the military	2,311,194
Caucasians	87.2 percent
Afro-Americans	11.1 percent
Others	1.7 percent
Army enlisted men total	686,695
Caucasians	81.9 percent
Afro-Americans	17.0 percent
Others	1.1 percent
Army officers total	121,290
Caucasians	95.7 percent
Afro-Americans	3.9 percent
Others	.4 percent
Navy enlisted men total	510,669
Caucasians	89.0 percent
Afro-Americans	6.4 percent
Others	4.6 percent
Navy officers total	73,155
Caucasians	98.7 percent
Afro-Americans	.9 percent
Others	.4 percent
Air Force enlisted men total	599,774
Caucasians	86.6 percent
Afro-Americans	12.6 percent
Others	.8 percent
Air Force officers total	121,674
Caucasians	97.7 percent
Afro-Americans	1.7 percent
Others	.6 percent
Marine Corps enlisted men total	178,395
Caucasians	86.1 percent
Afro-Americans	12.6 percent
Others	1.3 percent
Marine Corps officers total	19,542
Caucasians	98.0 percent
Afro-Americans	1.5 percent
Others	.5 percent

Over the years, and especially during World War I and World War II, the white man's belief in the ability of Afro-American units was apt to decrease as the size of the unit increased. Thus, companies and regiments were well regarded, whereas divisions were not. Virtually everyone agrees that the quality of white officers in Afro-American divisions was very bad. As members of an integrated fighting unit, Afro-Americans performed well. Much of the problem, seemingly, stemmed directly or indirectly from leadership. In this connection, it is useful to recall a remark of Napoleon's: "There are no bad regiments, only bad colonels." *See also* AFRO-AMERICAN HISTORY: COLONIAL PERIOD, 1600s–1783; AFRO-AMERICAN HISTORY: THE WEST; AFRO-AMERICAN HISTORY: CIVIL WAR, 1861–65; AVIATORS; CIVIL RIGHTS MOVEMENT.

REFERENCES: Afro-American writers were the first to recognize the Afro-American contribution to various American war efforts. Writers of the nineteenth century—William C. Nell, George Washington Williams, and Joseph T. Wilson—wrote about Afro-American military service. More recently, good accounts are in Blassingame, John W., "Recruitment of Colored Troops in Kentucky, Maryland, and Missouri, 1863–1865," *Historian*, August, 1967; Chandler, Vera, "The Negro in World War II," *Negro Yearbook*, 1947; Lee, Ulysses, *The Employment of Negro Troops: United States Army in World War II*, 1966; McConnell, Roland C., *Negro Troops in Antebellum Louisiana: A History of the Battalion of Free Men of Color*, 1968; Quarles, Benjamin, *The Negro in the American Revolution*, 1961; and Reddick, Lawrence D., "The Negro Policy of the American Army Since World War II," *Journal of Negro History*, April, 1953. A helpful bibliographical (including periodic literature) and biographical account (with accompanying photographs) is found in Greene, Robert Ewell (ed.), *Black Defenders of America, 1775–1973: A Reference and Pictorial History*, 1974. Though the author treats all wars since and including the Revolution (except Indian campaigns), his coverage of the Vietnam war takes up more than one-third of the book.

There are other writers who have valuable accounts, including Cassell, Frank A., "Slaves of the Chesapeake Bay Area and the War of 1812," *Journal of Negro History*, April 1972; Fowler, Arlen L., *The Black Infantry in the West, 1869–1891*, 1971; Gatewood, Willard B., *"Smoked Yankees" and the Struggle for Empire*, 1971; Langley, Harold D., "The Negro in the Navy and the Merchant Service, 1789–1860," *Journal of Negro History*, October 1967; and Leckie, William H., *The Buffalo Soldiers: A Narrative of the Negro Cavalry in the West*, 1967. See also Dalfiume, Richard M., *Desegregation of the U.S. Armed Forces: Fighting on Two Fronts, 1939–1953*, 1969; Foner, Jack D., *Blacks and the Military in American History: A New Perspective*, 1974; and Motley, Mary Penick (ed.), *The Invisible Soldier: The Experience of the Black Soldier, World War II*, 1975.

WARWICK, DIONNE (1941–), singer, actress; born in East Orange, N.J. Warwick attended the University of Hartford on a music scholarship in 1959. By 1964 she was rated the top rhythm-and-blues singer in the United States. With Bert Bacharach conducting, Warwick made her singing debut at Philharmonic Hall in New York City's Lincoln Center in 1966, after which she received rave reviews. She made grand tours of the major capitals of the world, where her musical style was highly acclaimed. Warwick also appeared in *Slaves*, her first motion picture.

WASHINGTON, BOOKER T.

WASHINGTON, BOOKER TALIAFERRO (1856–1915), educator; born in Franklin County, Va.

In the mid-1890s Afro-Americans were in the throes of a national crisis that seemed to threaten their very survival. Hopes that had been inspired by emancipation and by Reconstruction lay in shambles. Abandoned by the political party of Abraham Lincoln, black citizens confronted a rising tide of racism—manifested by increasing incidents of lynching, disfranchisement, and riots—at a moment when they seemed to be without a racial spokesman. Their champion of half a century, Frederick Douglass, died in February 1895, and shortly thereafter John M. Langston, Blanche K. Bruce, and other notable Afro-American leaders died. The Afro-American press voiced grave concern about the vacuum in leadership in this critical juncture in race relations.

On September 18, 1895, seven months after the death of Douglass, ex-slave Booker T. Washington, the principal of Tuskegee Institute (Tuskegee Institute, Ala.), delivered an address at the Cotton States Exposition in Atlanta, Ga., that became famous as the "Atlanta Compromise." Notwithstanding the refusal of a few Afro-Americans to recognize Washington as Douglass' successor, the Atlanta address did in fact mark his emergence as the foremost spokesman for Afro-Americans. It was clear, however, that even if the ultimate goals of Douglass and Washington were similar, their methods and styles were substantially different. In a perceptive analysis of these differences, first published in 1903 and reflected in later interpretations, Kelly Miller of Howard University (Washington, D.C.) concluded that while the two men were in part products of their times, they were "also natural antipodes." In an "age of moral giants," Douglass was a leader of heroic proportions who was "like a lion, bold and fearless" in seeking full citizenship and integration into American society for Afro-Americans. In his pursuit of similar ends during an "era of merchant prices," according to Miller, Washington told the world what it was "disposed to listen to" rather than what it needed to hear. His were the methods of a social pacifist for whom an emphasis upon the economic uplift of Afro-Americans through industrial education offered the best way out of their predicament. Washington was more the "missionary seeking material and moral betterment of an unfortunate people" than the spontaneous leader voicing their highest aspirations in unequivocal terms.

This familiar statue of Booker T. Washington is a landmark on the campus at Tuskegee Institute (Ala.). Washington is shown "lifting the veil of ignorance from his people." *(Courtesy of Prentiss Polk, Tuskegee Institute.)*

Born a slave in 1856 on a small plantation in Virginia, the child who was to become known as Booker T. Washington was the progeny of the plantation cook and a local white man. Without a name other than Booker, he was never certain of the date of his birth and never knew the identity of his father. Only later when he became aware that other children possessed more than a single name did he add Washington to his own. His best-selling autobiography, *Up From Slavery* (1901), whatever its distortions, not only reveals much about the formative experiences in his life but also chronicles his own search for identity. Imbued with a desire to get on in a hostile world, Washington was determined to secure an education and managed to attend

school sporadically in Malden, W. Va., where his mother and stepfather, Washington Ferguson, had settled after the Civil War. Forced to work in the coal mines and salt furnaces by his exploitative stepfather, young Washington was encouraged by his mother to find a better life. He finally secured a job as a houseboy in the mansion of Gen. Lewis Ruffner, Malden's most prominent citizen. Here Washington came under the tutelage of the general's wife, a "Yankee woman from Vermont," whose lessons in cleanliness, efficiency, and order were, according to Washington, as "valuable to me as any education I have ever gotten anywhere." Mrs. Ruffner remembered Washington as the ideal servant, eager to please and "always in his place." At least one historian, in analyzing the mature Washington, claims that he "never lost the attitude of the favorite slave."

In 1871 Washington made his way across Virginia to enroll in Hampton Institute (Hampton, Va.), a school for Afro-Americans founded and directed by Gen. Samuel C. Armstrong. The son of missionaries to Hawaii and himself a former commander of Afro-American troops in the Civil War, Armstrong espoused the cause of industrial education as the means for assisting black people up the social ladder. He urged Afro-Americans to accommodate themselves to the new order in the South, a process requiring them to eschew politics and postpone the attainment of first-class citizenship. Protest and agitation were to be replaced by an emphasis upon economic progress. Although his industrial education program provided agricultural and mechanical training, Armstrong viewed it primarily as a means of endowing a backward people with the morality, discipline, and character necessary for advancement in American society. As a result, training at Hampton emphasized cleanliness, thrift, abstinence, and the dignity of manual labor as much as it did the technical aspects of various trades. As a student and later as an instructor at Hampton, Washington came under the direct influence of General Armstrong, whom he later described as "the noblest, rarest human being" he had ever known. His experiences at Hampton provided Washington with the values and rationale upon which he later acted as the spokesman of Afro-Americans. Clearly, Washington did not exaggerate when he remarked that Armstrong "made the greatest and most lasting impression" upon him.

Upon graduating in 1875, Washington returned home to West Virginia to begin a teaching career. Here he applied the lessons he had learned at Hampton. Convinced that "mere book education" did not meet the needs of his students, he taught them the proper use of the bath and the toothbrush. Indeed, he came to believe that the civilizing influence of the toothbrush was greater than that of academic subjects. Experiences during 1878 as a student at Wayland Seminary (Washington, D.C.) strengthened his belief in the superiority of practical education. In his opinion, Wayland graduated students who, though versed in Greek and Latin, knew little of the day-to-day demands of life and were little inclined to go "into the country districts of the South . . . to take up the work of our people." While in the nation's capital, he had occasion to observe Afro-American urban life in general and the behavior of Afro-American politicians in particular; and what he saw alarmed him and served to reinforce his faith in the formula prescribed by General Armstrong.

After a year at Wayland Seminary, Washington accepted an invitation to join the faculty at Hampton. During his two years there as an instructor, he served first as supervisor of a dormitory for Indian youths and later as director of a night school for black students who lacked the means of paying the cost of their education. General Armstrong, however, worked out an arrangement whereby these students were employed by day in one of the industries at Hampton so that they could earn enough money to pay their tuition. Washington described his experience in the night school as having come "providentially to help prepare me for my work at Tuskegee."

In 1881 the opportunity for Washington to direct his own institution came when General Armstrong recommended him for the position of principal of a new school for Afro-Americans at Tuskegee in Macon County, Ala. For the next 34 years Washington sought to gain his goals in the Alabama black belt. The monument to his efforts was Tuskegee Normal and Industrial Institute, which in time became the capital of black America. Consciously conceived as a replica of Hampton, his school reflected the influence of General Armstrong both in the particulars of its curriculum and in its concern for propagating the Protestant ethnic. The mission of Tuskegee was to provide Afro-Americans with the means to become economically self-supporting while inculcating the virtues necessary for leading "useful, decent" lives. Its educational program was designed to improve the economic condi-

tion of Afro-Americans but without making them dissatisfied with the existing sociopolitical order. In Washington's opinion, education that filled Afro-American citizens with nothing more than "a divine discontent" was worse than no education at all.

Beginning with neither capital nor a campus, Washington was ever aware of the pressure to demonstrate that "it was possible for Negroes to build up and control the affairs of a large educational institution." Resourcefulness and persistence enabled him to meet the challenge with such success that by 1895 Tuskegee was heralded as "the best product of Negro enterprise of the century." It was an enterprise that Washington supervised and controlled in the manner of a despot. Not the least among the factors in the development of the school was Washington's ability to sell the "Tuskegee idea" to Northern philanthropists. First introduced to men of wealth in the Northeast by General Armstrong, Washington became a remarkably effective fund raiser, who, skilled in articulating the platitudes dear to middle-class white Americans, impressed Northern industrialists and financiers as a conservative, self-made man not unlike themselves. That he was as much an entrepreneur as he was an educator served to enhance the impression that he made upon white capitalists. So complete was the faith of such men as Andrew Carnegie and William H. Baldwin in Washington and his program that they made him the arbiter of large-scale white charity.

The selection of Washington to deliver an address at the Atlanta Exposition in 1895 was a commentary on the esteem that he enjoyed among the "best" white people of the South. The formula of race relations proposed in that 20-minute speech before a biracial audience in the capital of the New South was a natural product of the lessons that Washington had learned from the Ruffners and from General Armstrong and that he had practiced for the previous 14 years at Tuskegee. It embodied what he thought was the only feasible option of Afro-American citizens in an era of deteriorating race relations and of noisy and unchecked Negrophobia. A classic example of Washington's skill in walking "the razor's edge between Negro pride and white prejudice," the address emphasized means rather than ends, the opportunities rather than the grievances of Afro-Americans, and the mutuality of interests between blacks and whites. He called upon Afro-Americans to surmount the obstacles of prejudice by focusing their energies upon economic initiative and self-help, assuring them that the acquisition of property and "high character" would bring the recognition of all other rights. To allay the fears of the whites in his audience, Washington disparaged the black man's involvement in politics, condemned the migration of Afro-Americans from "our beloved South," and repudiated any agitation for social equality. Although he urged Afro-Americans to accommodate themselves to existing circumstances in the South, he did not, according to William Dean Howells, counsel "a base submission to the Southern whites, but a manly fortitude in bearing the wrongs that cannot be righted and a patient faith in the final kindliness and ultimate justice of the Anglo-Americans." With characteristic optimism Washington closed his Atlanta address with a reference to "the higher good"— the blotting out of racial animosities—that would accompany the economic evolution of black people.

For the remainder of his life, Washington elaborated upon these views in a plethora of speeches, books, and articles. The unity, pride, and "love of race," ethnic characteristics that he observed among Jews, were, in his opinion, worthy of emulation by Afro-Americans. Washington urged black businessmen to exploit the Afro-American market and encouraged black consumers to patronize black enterprises. In spite of evidence to the contrary, he persisted in the belief that the economic success of Afro-Americans would dissipate the prejudice of whites. In the rhetoric of Social Darwinism so fashionable in his day, Washington argued that although Afro-Americans must begin "at the bottom of life," they could struggle upward to achieve the economic efficiency that underlay "every kind of success." For those overwhelmed by the dimensions of the struggle, Washington was always ready with fatherly advice. Typical was the counsel he gave in 1903 to a discouraged Tuskegee alumnus: "You must look on the bright side of life and keep up your courage; that goes a long way in the direction of bringing success." Repeatedly, Washington argued that Afro-Americans would acquire the rights and privileges of other Americans in the same degree that they made themselves economically indispensable. The means for achieving this condition lay in industrial education, which, according to Washington, "killed two birds with one stone": it secured the assistance of whites and did "the best possible thing for blacks." While he did not shut the door upon liberal education for Afro-

Americans and occasionally acknowledged the need for acquiring "culture and taste," his appeals in behalf of vocational training as more appropriate for a majority of Afro-Americans in their "present condition" displayed a disdain for Greek and Latin and other "ornamental gewgaws of life."

Washington's public utterances regarding the civil rights of Afro-American citizens were characterized by even more ambiguity and ambivalence than those on education. Accepting segregation "in all things that are purely social" as the price for racial harmony, he urged Afro-Americans to exploit every opportunity open to them within a segregated society. But within the framework of the "separate-but-equal doctrine," Washington sought equality of treatment for members of his race. Typical was his crusade for equality of accommodations on railroads. On the matter of disfranchisement, he maintained that in the South restrictions on voting were necessary but insisted that such restrictions be applied "with equal and exact justice to both races." Granting that mistakes had been made in regard to Afro-American suffrage during Reconstruction, he nonetheless expressed a belief in universal, free suffrage "as a rule" and admitted that any group permanently disfranchised under a republican form of government was "placed at a serious disadvantage." While he maintained that noisy agitation over civil rights would alienate whites and thereby hamper the progress of Afro-Americans in general, he did not abjure all protest. "When the foundation of our citizenship is attacked," he declared in 1900, "I think I have a right to speak." Washington exercised such a right, albeit unsuccessfully, in appealing to southern legislatures to apply voting restrictions equally to both races. The failure of his appeals forced Washington back upon the argument that the rights of Afro-Americans would ultimately follow their acquisition of property and character. The validity of such an argument seemed to be exemplified by Washington himself, a black who in the age of Jim Crow rode in Pullman cars, voted, dined with presidents and industrialists, and had tea with Queen Victoria. While counseling patience among Afro-Americans, Washington constantly reminded whites of the responsibilities of power. Their self-interest, he argued, required them to aid Afro-Americans, since one could not "hold another in the ditch without himself staying" there. His public statements on lynching, which were more consistently outspoken than those on any other injustice suffered by

Washington was a persuasive public speaker. *(Library of Congress.)*

Afro-Americans, not only refuted the claim that the rape of white women was the primary cause for such acts but also emphasized that a disregard for morality and legal procedures in the treatment of Afro-American citizens was more harmful to whites than to blacks.

The response to his Atlanta address cast Washington in the role of race leader. In spite of his protests to the contrary, he relished the title and skillfully consolidated his position by acquiring the power that gave it meaning. It was in this capacity as the spokesman of Afro-Americans that the nature of his personality was revealed in all its complexity and diversity. He was a man of many faces, adept at adjusting his appearance to fit the occasion and the audience. Ambitious and calculating, Washington could be as ruthless toward those whom he considered his enemies as he was magnanimous to his allies. The secrecy and deviousness that characterized his behavior as master of Tuskegee were qualities no less evident in his role as race lead-

er. If his behind-the-scenes manipulations to perpetuate his own power appeared at variance with his homilies about honesty and "high character," his clandestine activities in combating segregation, peonage, and other Jim Crow contrivances seemed to diverge no less sharply from his public image as an accomodationist. Undoubtedly, the circumspection, dissimulation, and secrecy that were so much a part of Washington's style resulted from the fact that he was a black man in a white man's world, whose earliest training had been that of a slave and house servant.

In the two decades after 1895, Washington possessed sufficient power to exercise a large measure of control over the destiny of the Afro-American community. So great was his influence with wealthy industrialists and philanthropic boards that his approval was a prerequisite for any Afro-American institution to gain their support. As the confidant of presidents Theodore Roosevelt and William Howard Taft,

Washington functioned as a political boss who distributed patronage, constructed alliances, and rooted out malcontents. Critics were always quick to point out that his performance as the "Black Warwick" was wholly inconsistent with his counsel to Afro-Americans regarding the role they should take in politics. Although he utilized this power over political appointments to consolidate what was called the "Tuskegee Machine," he also used his influence with political and governmental figures to advance the interests and welfare of Afro-Americans. Either publicly or secretly, he waged campaigns against the debt peonage system and the lily-white Republican movements in the South, attempted to secure the appointment of white officials (especially judges) who were likely to give Afro-Americans "a fair chance," and tempered party platforms and presidential utterances on racial questions. Most secret of all was his role in initiating litigation designed to protect the civil rights of Afro-Americans.

The claim that Washington was a leader of Afro-Americans selected by whites was in a sense valid, but the maintenance of his position involved a complicated interplay of forces. To be sure, his power was dependent upon the confidence that the white community placed in him and his program. Such confidence, in turn, rested in part upon his success in maintaining his image as a racial spokesman. Yet the power bestowed upon him by whites, especially in the distribution of philanthropy and political patronage, provided means for gaining and sustaining the support of blacks. With the aid of a select group of trusted allies, Washington pursued various tactics that resulted in projecting the image and in perpetuating the power he desired. A continuous flow of publicity in the form of inspired editorials, syndicated columns, articles, and books called attention to the practical achievements and popular acceptance of the Tuskegee program. The editorial allegiance of the Afro-American press to his programs, or at least to him personally, was always a matter of primary concern to Washington. With a few notable exceptions, those newspapers inclined to deviate from the Tuskegee line were brought into the fold by persuasion—if possible—and by economic coercion, subsidies, or covert ownership—if necessary. Nor did Washington fail to extend his influence among important Afro-American organizations, especially religious denominations and fraternal orders. The National Negro Business League, which he founded in 1900, proved useful not only in advertising and stimulating Afro-American capitalism but also in cementing his relations with the black entrepreneurial class in northern cities. All the while, hundreds of Tuskegee alumni, many of whom were rising young men in Afro-American communities throughout the United States, provided Washington with a constant source of reliable support. Any serious challenge to his program or personal prestige was likely to feel the full weight of the "Tuskegee Machine." Fully informed about such challenges through an elaborate and effective system of espionage, Washington used his power to undermine or isolate those engaged in anti-Tuskegee activities.

Despite the risks involved in defying Washington, opposition to his leadership steadily increased among Afro-Americans who disagreed with him ideologically, resented his power, or suffered from not having his favor. The attacks leveled against him by such articulate intellectuals as W. E. B. Du Bois and Monroe Trotter increasingly placed Washington on the defensive. Opponents who belonged to that segment of the Afro-American population that Du Bois classified as the "talented tenth" characterized his educational philosophy as a rationale for perpetuating a racial caste system and assailed his efforts to force conformity to the Tuskegee line. They also resented his use of "darkey" anecdotes and were repelled by what they considered his self-effacing, obsequious manner toward white southerners. But their basic disagreement with Washington concerned his acceptance of segregation and what they interpreted as his compromising stand on the Afro-American's civil rights. According to some critics, Washington had bargained away these rights for a skimpy mess of pottage in the form of a few "good gifts" from whites. Others claimed that the major fallacy in the Tuskegee approach was its failure to appreciate the relationship between economic and political rights. Du Bois in particular noted the paradox in Washington's attempt to transform Afro-American workers into businessmen and property owners at the same time that he called upon them to surrender the ballot—the very instrument necessary for the defense of their economic interests. Finally, those whom Washington patronizingly referred to as "a small group" of agitators were frustrated by his inconsistencies and ambiguities and by the elusive, indefinite nature of his utterances regarding the ultimate goals of his program. That Washington neither avowed nor disclaimed "in distinct terms a single plank in the platform of Douglass" was a persistent source of exasperation for his critics.

Despite Washington's frenzied efforts to neutralize or silence his critics, the opposition to his leadership gathered momentum throughout the first decade of the twentieth century. The proliferation of racial violence, dramatized by a series of bloody riots, lent credence to their charge that the status of Afro-Americans had steadily deteriorated under his tutelage. His unsuccessful attempt in 1906 to alter President Theodore Roosevelt's decision to discharge a battalion of Afro-American soldiers accused of shooting up Brownsville, Tex., played into the hands of Du Bois and other opponents who had organized the Niagara Movement in the previous year. The climactic challenge to his leadership came in 1909 with the launching of the National Association for the Advancement of Colored People (NAACP), a biracial organization that included his most effective Afro-American critic, Du Bois, as well as several prominent whites who earlier had been sympathetic to Washington. Attempts at a rapprochement between Washington and the NAACP proved to be abortive. The emergence of the NAACP, followed in 1912 by the election victory of Woodrow Wilson, which sharply curtailed Washington's role as a political boss, seriously eroded Washington's power during the last several years of his life.

Late in October 1915, while on a speaking tour of the North, Washington collapsed in New York City and had to be hospitalized. Apprised of the seriousness of his condition, he asked to go home. "I was born in the South," he declared, "I have lived and labored in the South, and I expect to die and be buried there." He returned to Tuskegee on November 13, 1915, and on the following day died at his home, "The Oaks," on the campus. His death brought forth eulogies from men of all races throughout the United States and the world. Even such men as Du Bois, who held him responsible for the deterioration of the black man's civil rights, conceded that his leadership had not been wholly barren of positive accomplishments in the educational and economic progress of his people. Although the generous assessments of Washington rendered by eulogistic biographers shortly after his death have undergone substantial alterations, the significance of his leadership has never been questioned. For nearly two decades Washington was the preeminent Afro-American, and his reputation and influence extended beyond the bounda-

ries of the United States. *See also* AFRO-AMERICAN HISTORY: RECONSTRUCTION TO REVOLT, 1877–1977; EDUCATION; DU BOIS, WILLIAM EDWARD BURGHARDT; NATIONAL ASSOCIATION FOR THE ADVANCEMENT OF COLORED PEOPLE (NAACP); TUSKEGEE INSTITUTE.

REFERENCES: Barton, Rebecca C., "Up from Slavery" in *Witnesses for Freedom: Negro Americans in Autobiography,* New York, 1948; Bontemps, Arna, *100 Years of Freedom,* New York, 1961; Cox, Oliver C., "The Leadership of Booker T. Washington," *Social Forces,* vol. 30, pp. 91–97, October 1951; Curti, Merle, *The Social Ideas of American Educators,* New York, 1935; Farrison, W. Edward, "Booker T. Washington: A Study in Educational Leadership," *South Atlantic Quarterly,* vol. 41, pp. 313–19, July 1942; Gatewood, Willard B., Jr., "Booker T. Washington and the Ulrich Affair," *Phylon,* vol. 30, pp. 286–302, Fall 1969; Harlan, Louis R., *Booker T. Washington: The Making of a Black Leader, 1856–1901,* New York, 1972; Harlan, Louis R., "Booker T. Washington and the National Negro Business League," in (eds.), *Seven on Black: Reflections on the Negro Experience in America,* Shade, William G., and Roy C. Herenkohl, Philadelphia, 1969; Harlan, Louis R., et al. (eds.), *The Booker T. Washington Papers,* vols. 1 and 2, Urbana, 1972; Harlan, Louis R., "Booker T. Washington and the White Man's Burden," *American Historical Review,* vol. 71, pp. 440–67, January 1966; Harlan, Louis R., "Booker T. Washington in Biographical Perspective," *American Historical Review,* vol. 75, pp. 1581–99, October 1970; Harlan, Louis R., *The Making of a Black Leader,* 1972; Hawkins, Hugh, *Booker T. Washington and His Critics: The Problem of Negro Leadership,* Boston, 1962; Mathews, Basil, *Booker T. Washington, Educator and Interracial Interpreter,* Cambridge, 1948; Meier, August, *Negro Thought in America, 1880–1915,* Ann Arbor, 1963; Scott, Emmett, and Lyman B. Stowe, *Booker T. Washington: Builder of a Civilization,* New York, 1916; Spencer, Samuel R., Jr., *Booker T. Washington and the Negro's Place in American Life,* Boston, 1955; Stokes, Anson Phelps, *A Brief Biography of Booker T. Washington,* Hampton, 1936; Thornbrough, Emma Lou, "More Light on Booker T. Washington and the New York Age," *Journal of Negro History,* vol. 63, pp. 34–49, January 1958; Washington, Booker T., "Is the Negro Having a Fair Chance?" *Century,* vol. 85, pp. 46–55, November 1912; Washington, Booker T., *My Larger Education,* Garden City, 1911; Washington, Booker T., "My Views of Segregation Laws," *New Republic,* vol. 5, pp. 113–15, December 4, 1915; Washington, Booker T., *The Future of the American Negro,* Boston, 1899; Washington, Booker T., *The Story of My Life and Work,* Napierville, 1900; Washington, Booker T., *Up From Slavery,* New York, 1901; Washington, Booker T., *Working with the Hands,* New York, 1904; and Washington, Booker T., *Booker T. Washington Papers,* Library of Congress, Washington, D.C.

WASHINGTON, CALVIN CARLTON (1909–   ), educator; born in Faceville, Ga. Washington received a B.S. degree from Tuskegee Institute (Tuskegee Institute, Ala.) in 1935 and his M.Ed. degree from Atlanta University in 1950. After having served as a high school principal (1944–62), he became president of Rosenwald Junior College in 1958. Wasington was also president of the Florida State Teachers Association.

WASHINGTON, CHESTER L. (1902–   ), editor, publisher; born in Pittsburgh, Pa. Washington received a B.A. degree from Virginia Union University and his M.S. degree from Duquesne University (Pittsburgh, Pa.). He served as city editor and sports editor of Pittsburgh *Courier,* and as a member of the editorial staff of the Los Angeles *Times-Mirror* from 1955 to 1960. Washington was a news commentator for radio station KWOL, editor of the Los Angeles *Sentinel,* and publisher of Central News-Wave Publications, the largest Afro-American weekly newspaper chain in the United States. He was also a ghost-writer for Joe Louis and a member of the Greater Los Angeles Press Club. Later Washington became Los Angeles County recreation and parks commissioner. *See also* NEWSPAPERS: CONTEMPORARY.

WASHINGTON, JOSEPH R., JR. (1930–), clergyman, educator; born in Iowa City, Iowa. Washington received a B.A. degree from the University of Wisconsin in 1952, a B.D. degree from Andover Newton Theological School in 1957, a Th.D. degree from Boston University in 1961, and his D.D. degree from the University of Vermont in 1969. He was minister of Congregational and Baptist churches in Maine and Massachusetts. Washington also served as a professor and dean of chapel at Dillard University (New Orleans, La.) from 1961 to 1963, as professor and chaplain at Dickinson College (Carlisle, Pa.) from 1963 to 1966, as professor and dean of chapel at Albion College (Albion, Mich.) from 1966 to 1969; and as professor and dean of chapel at Beloit College (Beloit, Wisc.), beginning in 1969. Subsequently, he served on the faculty of the University of Virginia. Washington wrote *The Politics of God: The Future of the Black Churches* (1967) and *Black and White Power Subreption* (1969).

Far right: Walter E. Washington. (Library of Congress.)

WASHINGTON, KENNY (1918–71), professional football player; Washington was an outstanding football player at the University of California at Los Angeles. In 1946, upon signing with the Los Angeles Rams of the National Football League (NFL), he broke the color barrier that had existed in professional football since the early 1930s. He remained with the Rams through the 1949 season, and thereafter he played professional baseball briefly and was a film actor. *See also* ATHLETES.

WASHINGTON, LEON H. *See* NEWSPAPERS: CONTEMPORARY.

WASHINGTON, MELVIN J. (1931–), lawyer, judge; born in Washington, D.C. Washington received his B.A. and LL.B. degrees from Howard University (Washington, D.C.). He was admitted to the District of Columbia bar in 1968, and later Washington became assistant to the corporation counsel of the District of Columbia.

WASHINGTON NORMAL SCHOOL SEE DISTRICT OF COLUMBIA TEACHERS COLLEGE.

WASHINGTON NORMAL SCHOOL NO. 2 SEE DISTRICT OF COLUMBIA TEACHERS COLLEGE.

WASHINGTON, WALTER (1923–), educator; born in Hazelhurst, Miss. Washington received a B.A. degree from Tougaloo College (Tougaloo, Miss.) in 1948, a M.S. degree from Indiana University in 1952, a Ed.S. degree from George Peabody College for Teachers (Nashville, Tenn.) in 1958, and his Ed.D. degree in school administration from the University of Southern Mississippi in 1969. He was a high school teacher and principal (1948–51; 1955–57), and then served as dean (1951–55) and as president (1957–69) of Utica Junior College (Utica, Miss.). Washington became president of Alcorn State University (Lorman, Miss.) in 1969.

WASHINGTON, WALTER E. (1915–), public official, mayor; born in Dawson, Ga. Washington received a B.A. degree from Howard University

(Washington, D.C.) in 1938 and his LL.D. degree from Howard University Law School in 1948. In 1941 he began a 25-year association with the National Capital Housing Authority in Washington, D.C.; during the last five years of this period he was executive director of the authority. In 1966 Washington was named chairman of the New York City Housing Authority by Mayor John V. Lindsay. The next year he returned to the District of Columbia as its commissioner, heading a nine-man city council with the help of an assistant commissioner. In addition, Washington was a member of innumerable boards, advisory commissions, and civic groups. In 1972 Washington began serving his first four-year term as the mayor of Washington, D.C. He was reelected to a second term beginning in 1976.

WASHINGTON, WILLIAM J. (1924–   ), physician, educator; born in Bessemer, Ala. Washington received a B.A. degree from Talladega College (Talladega, Ala.) in 1944 and his M.D. degree from Howard University Medical College (Washington, D.C.) in 1947. He interned at Freedmen's Hospital, Washington, D.C., from 1947 to 1948, and was a flight surgeon in the U.S. Air Force from 1951 to 1953. Washington served as medical officer, supervising medical officer, and chief of the treatment division of Glenn Dale Hospital, and as clinical assistant professor in medicine at Georgetown University (Washington, D.C.).

WATERS, ETHEL (1900–77), singer, actress; born in Chester, Pa. A child of poverty, Waters moved from Pennsylvania at the age of 17 and began to sing in vaudeville and nightclubs in Baltimore, Md. She then moved to New York City, where she appeared in nightclubs; Waters also starred in several traveling shows and toured with Fletcher Henderson's Black Swan Jazz Masters. She made her first big hit in New York City in 1925 as the summer replacement for Florence Mills in a revue at the Plantation Club; in 1927 she appeared in her first Broadway musical, *Africana*. Subsequently, she starred in many Broadway shows: *Blackbirds* (1930); *Rhapsody in Black* (1931, 1932); *As Thousands Cheer* (1933); *At Home Abroad* (1935); *Mamba's Daughters* (1939); *Cabin in the Sky* (1940); and *The Member of the Wedding* (1950). Waters also appeared in several films, including *Tales of Manhattan* (1941), *Cabin in the Sky* (1943), and *Pinky* (1949). Her career, having slowed some-

what between 1943 and 1949, was revived with her successes in *Pinky* and *The Member of the Wedding*. During the 1960s Waters joined the revival team of evangelist Billy Graham. Her autobiography, *His Eye Is on the Sparrow*, was published in 1951. *See also* MOTION PICTURES; RADIO AND TELEVISION.

Ethel Waters. *(Museum of the City of New York.)*

WATERS, MUDDY (1915–   ), guitarist, singer; born McKinley Morganfield in Rolling Fork, Miss. Waters was raised in Clarksdale, Miss., and he began singing and playing the harmonica at the age of ten. Discovered by folklorist Alan Lomax, Waters made several recordings for the Library of Congress. In 1943 he went to Chicago, Ill., where he performed in various nightclubs on the South Side of the city. Four years later, Waters signed with a recording company. He toured England in 1958, and the next year was featured in a folk concert at Carnegie Hall in New York City. Known as the "King of the Delta [or Country] Blues", he made between 20 and 30 appearances at colleges a year. Some of his notable albums include: *After the Rain*; *Electric Mud*; *Folk Singer*; *Muddy*; *Brass and Blues*; *Sail On*; and *Muddy Waters at Newport*. *See also* MUSIC: BLUES.

WATKINS, LEVI (1911–   ), educator; born in Montgomery, Ala. Watkins received a B.S. degree from Tennessee State University in 1933 and his M.A. degree from Northwestern University (Evanston, Ill.) in 1940. He was affiliated with high schools in Tennessee and Kentucky from 1933 to 1940 and joined Parsons Junior College from 1940 to 1948. Watkins served at Alabama State College from 1948 to 1953, and was the founding president of Owen College (Memphis, Tenn.; now LeMoyne-Owen College), serving from 1953 to 1959. He then joined Alabama State University in 1959 and became president of that school in 1963.

WATKINS, THOMAS   See NEWSPAPERS: CONTEMPORARY.

WATSON, JAMES L. (1922–   ), lawyer, state legislator, judge; born in New York, N.Y. Watson graduated from New York University in 1947, and received his LL.B. degree from Brooklyn Law School (Brooklyn, N.Y.) in 1951. In 1954 he was elected state senator from the 21st district, and he held this seat for nine years until he was elected judge of the Civil Court of New York City. In 1966 Watson's nomination to serve on the bench of the U.S. Customs Court was confirmed by the U.S. Senate.

WATSON, JAMES S. (1892–1952), lawyer, judge; born in Jamaica, British West Indies. Watson immigrated to the United States in 1905, and he graduated from New York University Law School in 1913. He was the first Afro-American lawyer to be admitted to the American Bar Association. A judge in New York City for about 20 years, Watson was appointed chairman of the Municipal Civil Service Commission by Mayor William O'Dwyer in 1950.

WATTS, ANDRE (1946–   ), concert pianist; born in Nuremberg, Germany. Watts made his debut with the New York Philharmonic in 1962, and later performed for President Richard M. Nixon's inaugural concert, for the coronation festivities of the shah of Iran, for the king and queen of Greece, and for President and Mrs. Mobutu of the Congo Republic. Born on a U.S. Army base to a Hungarian mother and American G.I. father who divorced in 1962, Watts moved with his parents from post to post in Europe until 1954 when they moved to Philadelphia, Pa. Watts studied at the Philadelphia Musical Academy, and by the age of nine he had made his first

Far right: Andre Watts. (Courtesy of Alix B. Williamson.)

public appearance with the Philadelphia Orchestra as a substitute soloist in a children's concert. He performed several times more with the Philadelphia Orchestra, studied music, and had regular schooling. In 1962 Watts won an audition to appear as soloist with the New York Philharmonic in one of Leonard Bernstein's Young People's Concerts. Devoting most of his time to study, Watts limited his engagements between 1963 and 1965. In 1966 he made his European debut in London, England, with the London Symphony Orchestra.

WATTS, ROBERT B. (1922–   ), lawyer, judge; born in Baltimore, Md. Watts was educated in his native state, receiving a B.S. degree from Morgan State University (Baltimore, Md.) in 1943 and his LL.B. degree from the University of Maryland in 1949. He was a traffic court magistrate from 1957 to 1959 and a judge on the bench of the Municipal Court of Baltimore from 1961 to 1968. In the latter year Watts was appointed to the Supreme Bench of Baltimore.

WEAVER, GEORGE LEON-PAUL (1912–   ), labor union leader, public official; born in Pittsburgh, Pa. Weaver attended Roosevelt University (Chicago, Ill.) and Howard University School of Law (Washington, D.C.). His career in the labor movement began in 1941 as a member of the War Relief Committee of the Congress of Industrial Organizations (CIO); he remained on this committee until 1955 when the CIO merged with the American Federation of Labor (AFL). Weaver then became executive secretary of the

Civil Rights Committee of the new organization (AFL-CIO). In 1958 he became assistant to the president of the International Union of Electrical, Radio, and Machine Workers, after which he served as assistant secretary of labor for international Affairs beginning in 1961. Concurrently, Weaver served as a delegate or representative of the United States at numerous international labor conferences. In 1969 he was made special assistant to the director general of the International Labor Organization (ILO).

WEAVER, ROBERT CLIFTON (1907–   ), economist, government official, educator; born in Washington, D.C. Weaver received a B.S. degree (1929), a M.S. degree (1931), and his Ph.D. degree (1934) in economics from Harvard University. His long government career began in 1933 as an aide to Secretary of the Interior Harold Ickes. Subsequently, as one of the young New Dealers brought to Washington, D.C. by President Franklin D. Roosevelt, Weaver served as an adviser (usually on minority problems) to a succession of government agencies. These assignments made Weaver a leader in what became known as the "black cabinet," a group of university-educated Afro-Americans who worked for reforms in government hiring. After World War II, Weaver lectured at Northwestern University (Evanston, Ill.) from 1947 to 1948; he directed the opportunity fellowships program of the John Hay Whitney Foundation, and served on the selection committees of several other fellowship funds. In 1955, with the election of a Democratic administration in New York state, he became New York state rent commissioner. Subsequently, in 1960, Weaver was vice-chairman of New York City's housing and redevelopment board, and in less than a year he was appointed by President Lyndon B. Johnson as secretary of housing and urban development, becoming the first Afro-American to serve in the cabinet of an American president. In 1969 he took office as president of Bernard M. Baruch College of the City University of New York, and in 1970 he joined Hunter College of the City University of New York as distinguished professor of urban affairs. Weaver was the author of several books, including *Negro Labor: A National Problem* (1946); *The Negro Ghetto* (1948); *The Urban Complex* (1964); and *Dilemmas of Urban America* (1965). *See also* POLITICS.

WELCOME, VERDA FREEMAN, educator, state legislator; born in Lake Lure, N.C. Welcome graduated from Morgan State University (Baltimore, Md.) in 1939, and received her M.A. degree from New York University in 1943. A teacher in the public schools of Baltimore from 1934 to 1945, Welcome served in Maryland's house of delegates from 1959 until 1962, when she was elected to the state senate. As a state senator, she obtained passage of a law prohibiting segregation and racial discrimination in the sale of new housing, and she introduced legislation that repealed Maryland's miscegenation laws. Welcome was the first Afro-American woman elected to the Maryland senate.

WELLS, IDA B. (IDA B. WELLS BARNETT) (1862–1931), educator, journalist, civil rights leader; born in Holly Springs, Miss. Wells began to teach in a country school at the age of 14. Moving to Memphis, Tenn., in 1884, she continued to teach while attending Fisk University (Nashville, Tenn.) during the summers. Due to a law suit involving her refusal to give up her seat in a railroad car designated for "whites only," Wells lost her teaching job and subsequently turned to journalism. For a time she wrote for a local Afro-American weekly, *Living Word*, and in 1891 she

Ida Wells. *(Moorland-Spingarn Research Center, Howard University.)*

became coowner and editor of the Memphis weekly, *Free Speech.* A year later, after she revealed in print who was responsible for the lynching of three Memphis Afro-Americans, a mob of whites demolished her printing press and office. Wells fled to New York City—where she was hired by an Afro-American weekly—and launched into an antilynching campaign. The antilynching cause took her on lecture tours across the country and twice to England. Later Wells settled in Chicago, Ill. and in 1895 she married Ferdinand L. Barnett. In Chicago she contributed to newspapers and periodicals and also founded and headed the Ida B. Wells Club. In 1898 Wells led a delegation to President William McKinley to protest lynchings, and that same year she became the secretary of the national Afro-American Council. Some ten years later Wells founded the Negro Fellowship League. In 1913 she was appointed adult probation officer in Chicago, and two years later she was elected vice-president of Chicago's Equal Rights League. Her publications, which documented facts about lynching, include *Southern Horrors* (1892) and *A Red Record* (1895). Her autobigraphy, edited in 1970 by Alfreda M. Duster, is entitled *Crusade for Justice*: The *The Autobiography of Ida B. Wells* (University of Chicago Press, 1970).

WELSING, FRANCES CRESS (1935–   ), child psychiatrist, educator; born in Chicago, Ill. Welsing received a B.A. degree from Antioch College (Yellow Springs, Ohio) and her M.D. degree from Howard University Medical College (Washington, D.C.). She was an assistant professor of pediatrics at Howard University and the author of *The Cress Theory of Color-Confrontation and Racism.* Welsing, a child psychiatrist, was a member of the National Medical Association, the American Medical Association, and the American Psychiatric Association.

WESLEY, CARTER WALKER (1892–1969), lawyer; publisher; born in Houston, Tex. Wesley received a B.A. degree from Fisk University (Nashville, Tenn.) in 1917 and his J.D. degree from Northwestern University (Evanston, Ill.) in 1922. He practiced law in Muskogee, Okla., until 1927 when he entered the construction business in Houston, Tex. While in Houston Wesley also became involved in a brokerage business, but his major interest came to be the formation of the National Negro Publishers Association. He eventually became publisher and editor of a chain of affiliated newspapers in Texas, Louisiana, Ala-

bama, and California. *See also* NEWSPAPERS: CONTEMPORARY.

WESLEY, CHARLES HARRIS (1891–   ), historian, educator, administrator; born in Louisville, Ky. Wesley received a B.A. degree from Fisk University (Nashville, Tenn.) in 1911, a M.A. degree from Yale University in 1913, and his Ph.D. degree from Harvard University in 1925. He joined the faculty of Howard University (Washington, D.C.) as an instructor in 1913 and remained there for about 30 years, during which time he became professor, department chairman, and dean of the college and the graduate school. In 1942 Wesley went to Wilberforce University (Wilberforce, Ohio) to serve as president, and in 1947 he became president of Central State University (Wilberforce, Ohio). In 1965 he was made president emeritus of Central State, and in that year became director of the Association for the Study of Negro Life and History. His published works include *Neglected History* (1965) and *The Collapse of the Confederacy* (reprint, 1968). In addition, Wesley served as an editor on both the multivolume *International Library on Negro Life and History* and the *Negro History Bulletin. See also* HISTORIANS.

WESTERFIELD, SAMUEL ZAZA, JR. (1919–1972), economist, educator, government official; born in Chicago, Ill. Westerfield received a B.A. degree from Howard University (Washington, D.C.) in 1939, and his M.A. and Ph.D. degrees in economics from Harvard University. He began 20 years of research and teaching in the field of economics in 1940 as an instructor at Howard University. Westerfield then served as assistant professor at West Virginia State College in 1945, as assistant professor of economics at Lincoln University from 1947 to 1950, as dean of the school of business administration and professor of economics at Atlanta University from 1950 to 1961, and as visiting professor in the graduate school of business administration at Harvard University from 1959 to 1960. In 1969 he became U.S. ambassador to the Republic of Liberia, a position he retained until his death.

WESTON, RUBIN FRANCIS (1921–   ), historian; born in Columbia, S.C. Weston received a B.A. degree in 1951 and an M.A. degree in 1955 from North Carolina Central University (Durham) and his Ph.D. degree from Syracuse University (New York) in 1964. After teaching at South Carolina State College (Orangeburg) from 1964 to 1968, he came to Central State University (Wilberforce, Ohio), where he became chairman of the history department in 1969. His publications include *Racism in U.S. Imperialism* (1972).

WEST VIRGINIA COLLEGIATE INSTITUTE *See* WEST VIRGINIA STATE COLLEGE.

WEST VIRGINIA COLORED INSTITUTE *See* WEST VIRGINIA STATE COLLEGE.

WEST VIRGINIA STATE COLLEGE West Virginia State College, at Institute, W. Va., was founded in 1891 by a vote of the state legislature. A state-supported, coeducational school, West Virginia State offers the bachelor's degree (including the B.S.M.A. and the B.S.T.S.) and provides liberal arts, teacher education, and vocational curricula. Its 1975 enrollment was 3,632.

The college, later acclaimed for its outstanding success with integration in reverse, originated as the West Virginia Colored Institute and began with 40 students on a small homestead in the Kanawha Valley. Today, its students, a majority of whom are white, study in classrooms and laboratories.

Until the U.S. Congress passed the Land-Grant Act (Second Morrill Act), in 1890, West Virginia had no state-supported college for its Afro-American citizens. However, since this law provided that no state could receive federal aid for its agricultural and mechanical colleges unless it provided for the education of Afro-American youth as well as white, in 1891 the state legislature voted to buy a farm and build a school. Thus, the West Virginia Colored Institute was born. A barn and a blacksmith shop were soon added, and the first school catalogue boasted that a "well-chosen library of 500 volumes is now open to the student each Saturday afternoon." By 1915 the institute had become a four-year college, and its name was changed to West Virginia Collegiate Institute; in 1929 it became West Virginia State College. For the following two decades, the leadership of President John W. Davis greatly enhanced the development of the academic program and the physical plant.

In 1953 William J. L. Wallace was elected the sixth president of the college. Under his leadership the institution was transformed from a college for Afro-Americans to a racially integrated school. Following the U.S. Supreme Court school desegregation decision of 1954, the college opened its doors to white students. West Virginia State College was the first of America's Afro-American land-grant colleges to earn full accreditation. By the mid-1970s, its student population was no longer predominantly black.

WHALEY, RUTH WHITEHEAD (1901–   ), lawyer, public official; born in Goldsboro, N.C. Whaley graduated from Livingstone College (Salisbury, N.C.) in 1919, and received her LL.B. degree with honors from Fordham University (New York, N.Y.) in 1924. After more than 30 years of practicing law in New York City, she was appointed deputy commissioner of the New York City department of housing and buildings in 1948. Her political activities led to membership from 1948 to 1968 on the New York state Democratic committee. Whaley's ideological commitments led to membership on the board of directors of the National Urban League from 1950 to 1967 and to her appointment as vice-president of the National Council of Negro Women in 1963.

WHARTON, CLIFTON REGINALD (1899–   ), lawyer, government official; born in Baltimore, Md. Wharton received his LL.B. degree from Boston University in 1920. He practiced law in Boston, Mass., for three years while concurrently working for a LL.M. degree, which he received in 1923. For the next two years, Wharton served with federal agencies in Washington, D.C., and in 1925 he entered the Foreign Service. For the first two decades of his service in the U.S. Department of State, he was the only Afro-American career diplomat in the Foreign Service. Wharton began his diplomatic career as third secretary and vice-consul in Monrovia, Liberia; rose to higher posts in West Africa and the Canary Islands; and became consul and then consul general in Portugal in 1950 and consul general in Marseilles, France, in 1953. In 1958 he was appointed by President Dwight D. Eisenhower as U.S. minister to Romania, and in 1961 President John F. Kennedy appointed him American ambassador to Norway. Wharton retired from that post in 1964. His son, Clifton Reginald Wharton, Jr., was named president of Michigan State University in 1970. *See also* WHARTON, CLIFTON REGINALD, JR.

WHARTON, CLIFTON REGINALD, JR. (1926–   ), economist, educator, administrator; born in Boston, Mass. Wharton graduated in 1947 from Harvard University, and he received a M.A. degree from the School for Advanced International Studies at Johns Hopkins University (Baltimore, Md.) in 1948 and a second M.A. degree (1956) and his Ph.D. degree (1958) in economics from the University of Chicago. His professional career began in 1948 as an executive trainee with the American International Association of Economic and Social Development. Wharton remained with that organization for five years, and then moved to the University of Chicago to become a research assistant and later a research associate in economics. In 1957 he joined the staff of the Agricultural Development Council and soon was appointed director of American University research programs and eventually vice-president of the council in 1967. In 1970 Wharton became professor of economics and president of Michigan State University, the school's first Afro-American president and the first Afro-American president of a major American university. Concurrently with these positions, Wharton served as visiting professor at the University of Malaya (1958–64) and at Stanford University (1964–65); as an advisor to the U.S. Department of State and to AID on East Asia and the Pacific (1966–69); as an advisor to the School of Advanced International Studies (1966–73); and as a member of many other educational and international councils. Wharton served on the board of directors of more than a dozen major American corporations. In 1977 he became chancellor of the State University of New York. See also WHARTON, CLIFTON REGINALD.

WHARTON, JIM See ATHLETES: BOXING.

WHARTON, ULYSSES SAMUEL (1885–1934), physician; born in Mecklenburg County, Va. Wharton attended Hampton Institute (Hampton, Va.) and Oberlin College (Oberlin, Ohio), and received his M.D. degree from Howard University Medical College (Washington, D.C.). He interned at Freedmen's Hospital, Washington, D.C., and then moved to Altoona, Pa.—becoming the first Afro-American physician to practice in that city. Arriving there just before the influenza epidemic of 1917, Wharton subsequently earned the respect of both the townspeople and the other local physicians because of his successful treatment of influenza during the epidemic. He later joined the staff of Altoona Hospital.

WHEATLEY, PHYLLIS (ca. 1753–84), born in Senegal, Africa. Wheatley was brought to America as a slave at the age of eight and sold to John Wheatley of Boston, Mass., in 1761, in whose service she learned to read and write. Her earliest surviving poem, dating from 1767, is "To the University of Cambridge in New England" (about Harvard University), but her earliest published poem was "On the Death of the Rev. Mr. George Whitefield" (1770). In 1773 Wheatley fell ill, was manumitted from slavery, and was sent to London, England, to recuperate. A London firm subsequently printed her first volume of verse, *Poems on Various Subjects, Religious and Moral.* In 1774 she returned to America to nurse John Wheatley's wife, and to attend at the deathbeds of the rest of the Wheatley family, who all died within a few years. She married John Peters, a freed slave, who later went to debtor's prison and stole the manuscript of her proposed second book. Forced afterward to work in a cheap lodging house, Wheatley found the work too much for her health and fell fatally ill. *See also* LITERATURE: POETRY.

WHEELER, JOHN H. (1908–   ), lawyer, business executive; born in Kittrell, N.C. Wheeler received a L.H.D. degree from Morehouse College (Atlanta, Ga.) and his LL.D degree from Johnson C. Smith University (Charlotte, N.C.), after studies at Shaw University (Raleigh, N.C.) and Tuskegee Institute (Tuskegee Institute, Ala.). He became president of the Mechanics and Farmers Bank of Durham, N.C., and served on the board of directors of many business, educational, and civic organizations. *See also* BANKS.

WHIPPER, WILLIAM J. lawyer, state legislator, judge; born in Michigan. Whipper joined a volunteer regiment in 1865 during the Civil War. Moving to the South following the war, he became a lawyer in Charleston, S.C., and was elected to the state legislature in 1868 and 1870. In 1875 Whipper was elected a circuit judge by the legislature, and from 1882 to 1888 he served as probate judge of Beaufort County. He was subsequently jailed for refusing to leave his post after being defeated in the election of 1888. Whipper owned the *Tribune,* a newspaper published in Beaufort, S.C., and was one of three administrators involved in the managment of the *New South,* another newspaper published in Beaufort.

WHITE, CHARLES W. (1897–   ), lawyer, judge; born in Nashville, Tenn. White graduated from Fisk University (Nashville, Tenn.) in 1921 and from Harvard University Law School in

1924. For more than 20 years he served as assistant director of law in Cleveland, Ohio. In 1955 White was appointed judge of the Court of Common Pleas, and the next year he ran for election to the same post and won. In 1966 he was appointed judge of the Ohio Court of Appeals for the Eighth District.

WHITE, CHARLES WILBERT (1918–   ), painter, graphic artist, educator; born in Chicago, Ill. In 1937 White won a tuition scholarship to the Art Institute of Chicago. Later, he studied at the Art Students League in New York City and at the Taller de Grafica in Mexico. He taught at the Chicago Community Art Center in 1941 and was artist-in-residence at Howard University (Washington, D.C.) in 1945. Among his works are an 18 × 60' mural at Hampton Institute (Hampton, Va.) entitled *The Contribution of the Negro to American Democracy.* Other notable paintings include *Wanted Poster No. 6, Birmingham Totem,* and

Preacher, each done in a realistic yet imaginative style. White's work was exhibited at the Palace of Culture, Warsaw, Poland, 1967; at Fisk University, Nashville, Tenn., 1968; at the Boston Museum of Fine Arts, Boston, Mass., 1969; at the World Festival of Negro Arts, Dakar, Senegal, 1966; and at the Metropolitan Museum of Art, New York, N.Y., 1971. Many of his works are reproduced in *Images of Dignity: The Drawings of Charles White* (1967). His works are in the collections of the Metropolitan Museum of Art; Howard University; the Library of Congress,

Washington, D.C.; and Syracuse University, Syracuse, N.Y. *See also* ARTISTS.

WHITE, CLARENCE CAMERON (1880–1960), composer, violinist, educator; born in Clarksville, Tenn. White studied at Howard University (Washington, D.C.) and at the Oberlin Conservatory of Music (Oberlin, Ohio). Afterward he studied in London, England, for three years from 1908 to 1911 with Samuel Coleridge-Taylor and then in Paris, France. White began his teaching career in the public schools of Washington, D.C., and then served as director of music at West Virginia State College from 1924 to 1931. Later he taught at Hampton Institute (Hampton, Va.) from 1931 to 1935. His compositions include operas (*Ouanga,* 1932); pieces for violin; and works for orchestra, band, organ, and voice. In addition, White arranged many Afro-American spirituals. His *Symphony in D minor* and his ballet score, *A Night in Sans Souci,* are notable.

WHITE, JOSEPH DOUGLAS (1904–   ), bishop Bible Way Church of Our Lord Jesus Christ World-Wide, Inc.; born in Macon, Ga. White attended the Church of Christ Bible Institute and the Bible Way Training School. Licensed for the ministry in 1935 and ordained in 1938, he served as pastor of churches in Georgia, Maryland, and North Carolina. White also served as director of religious education and as junior bishop in Western North Carolina, Georgia, and Florida, and as a teacher in the Bible Way Training School in Washington, D.C. He was one of the organizers of the political-action arm of the United Cafeteria Workers union in Washington, D.C.

WHITE, WALTER FRANCIS (1893–1955), civil rights leader; born in Atlanta, Ga. White graduated from Atlanta University in 1916. While working for Standard Life Insurance Company, he led efforts to form an Atlanta branch of the National Association for the Advancement of Colored People (NAACP). He was so successful that in 1918 he became assistant to the chief administrative officer of the national NAACP. Meanwhile, as a reporter, White investigated many race riots and dozens of lynchings. In 1929 he became acting secretary of the NAACP and soon thereafter directed the NAACP's fight to block confirmation of the appointment of segregationist Judge John J. Parker of North Carolina to the U.S. Supreme Court. A year later White became secretary of the national NAACP and

Far left: "Wanted Poster Number 4" by Charles White. *(Collection of the Whitney Museum of American Art.)*

began to direct campaigns for federal civil rights legislation in the form of antilynching laws, laws guaranteeing voting rights, laws banning poll taxes and discrimination in the U.S. Armed Forces, and laws in favor of equalization of schools and integration. He served as advisor to two presidents, Franklin D. Roosevelt and Harry S. Truman, helping to make both administrations more liberal in the area of civil rights. White was also instrumental in the formation of the Committee on Fair Employment Practices during World War II. In 1945 and again in 1948 he served as consultant to the U.S. delegations to the UN, one of the countless organizations he served in this capacity. His published works include the novels *Fire in the Flint* (1924) and *Flight* (1926); *Rope and Faggot: A Biography of Judge Lynch* (1929); *A Rising Wind: A Report of the Negro Soldier in the European Theater of War* (1945); his autobiography, *A Man Called White* (1948); and *How Far The Promised Land?* (1955). See also LITERATURE: THE NOVEL; NATIONAL ASSOCIATION FOR THE ADVANCEMENT OF COLORED PEOPLE (NAACP).

WHITE, WILLIAM SYLVESTER (1914–   ), lawyer, judge; born in Chicago, Ill. White received a B.A. degree (1935) and his LL.B. degree (1937) from the University of Chicago. After two years in the general practice of law, he was appointed an assistant U.S. attorney for the Northern District of Illinois. White remained in that position for 16 years until, in 1955, he was named assistant state's attorney. In 1957 he became attorney for the Chicago department of investigation, later becoming deputy commissioner of that department. As director of the Illinois department of registration and education from 1961 to 1964, White was a member of the governor's cabinet. In 1964 he was elected judge of the Circuit Court of Cook County, Ill.

WHITEHEAD, MATTHEW J. (1940–   ), lawyer; born in Wilson, N.C. Whitehead received a B.A. degree from Tufts University (Medford, Mass.) in 1962 and his LL.B. degree from the Howard University School of Law (Washington, D.C.) in 1965. He was appointed the regional counsel of International Business Machines Corporation (IBM) based in Chicago, Ill., in 1970.

WHITING, ALBERT NATHANIEL (1917–   ), sociologist, educator, administrator; born in Jersey City, N.J. Whiting received a B.A. degree from Amherst College (Amherst, Mass.) in 1938 and his M.A. degree from Fisk University (Nashville, Tenn.) in 1941. He was an instructor of sociology at Bennett College (Greensboro, N.C.) from 1941 to 1943 and again immediately after World War II from 1946 to 1947. Whiting taught sociology at Atlanta University from 1948 to 1953 while also working on his Ph.D. degree at American University (Washington, D.C.), which he received in 1952. From 1953 to 1957 Whiting served as dean of Morris Brown College of Atlanta University, and in 1957 he became assistant dean and in 1959 dean at Morgan State University (Baltimore, Md.). In 1966 Whiting became president of North Carolina Central University.

WHITING, WILLIE M. (1926–   ), lawyer, judge; born in Chicago, Ill. Whiting attended Roosevelt University (Chicago, Ill.) before she graduated from Fisk University (Nashville, Tenn.). She received her LL.B. degree from John Marshall Law School (Chicago, Ill.), and was admitted to the Illinois bar in 1951. For eight years after her admission to the bar, Whiting held a series of jobs. She worked for five years in a law firm in Chicago, for one year with the Cook County department of public welfare, and for two years as executive secretary of the National Association for the Advancement of Colored People (NAACP), Chicago branch. In 1959 Whiting was named assistant corporation counsel for the city of Chicago. Two years later she served as an assistant state's attorney for Cook County, and in 1965 she became an assistant U.S. attorney engaged in criminal litigation. In 1966 Whiting was appointed magistrate in the Circuit Court of Cook County, and in 1970 she became associate judge on that bench.

WHITMAN, ALBERY ALLSON (1851–1902), poet, clergyman; born in Munfordville, Ky. Born into slavery and freed by the Emancipation Proclamation, Whitman became a minister in the African Methodist Episcopal (AME) Church. Although he had less than three months of formal education, he wrote a major epic poem, *Not a Man, and Yet a Man,* (1877), the longest poem by an Afro-American writer published up until that time. His other books include a great many works in a wide range of metrical forms, the best known of which—*The Rape of Florida* (1884)—is about the treatment of the American Indians in that state. Whitman's last major work was *An Idyll of the South,* issued in two volumes (1901, 1902).

WHITTICO, JAMES MALACHI, JR. (1916–   ), surgeon; born in Williamson, W. Va. Whittico received a B.A. degree from Lincoln University (Lincoln University, Pa.) in 1936 and his M.D. degree from Meharry Medical College (Nashville, Tenn.) in 1940. He was an intern and resident at Homer G. Phillips Hospital, St. Louis, Mo., before becoming director of its surgical tumor clinic after 1960. Whittico served as instructor in clinical surgery at the medical schools of Washington University and St. Louis University (both in St. Louis, Mo.). He was appointed surgeon to the St. Louis police department in 1966 and commissioner of the board of health of the city of St. Louis in 1967. Whittico was also president of the National Medical Association in 1967, and he served as a consultant to the Missouri department of health, education, and welfare and to the Missouri department of vocational rehabilitation.

WIGGINS, ULYSSES SIMPSON (1896–1966), physician; born in Americus, Ga. Wiggins received a B.A. degree from Lincoln University (Lincoln University, Pa.) and his M.D. degree from the University of Michigan Medical School in 1924. He interned at Mercy Hospital, Philadelphia, Pa., and did postgraduate work at Mt. Sinai Hospital, New York, N.Y.; at the University of Michigan Medical School; and at Hahnemann Medical College and Hospital, Philadelphia, Pa. Wiggins practiced in Camden, N.J., from 1928 to 1966, and he was president of the South Jersey and New Jersey medical associations. He also served as a city highway physician for the state of New Jersey and as a medical examiner for the state athletic commission.

WILBERFORCE A black settlement in Canada founded in the nineteenth century, Wilberforce was named in honor of the English opponent of the slave trade,William Wilberforce. It is also the name given to the college (Wilberforce University) founded by the African Methodist Episcopal (AME) Church at Wilberforce, Ohio, in 1856, reputed to be the oldest Afro-American college in the United States. *See also* SLAVERY: THE UNDERGROUND RAILROAD; WILBERFORCE UNIVERSITY.

WILBERFORCE UNIVERSITY Wilberforce University, at Wilberforce, Ohio, was founded in 1856 by the African Methodist Episcopal (AME) Church. Strongly church-related, the coeducational school offers the bachelor's

degree (including the B.D.) and provides liberal arts and teacher education curricula. Its 1975 enrollment was 1,143.

The college was established and the first instruction was begun by members of the AME Church. Named for an English abolitionist, William Wilberforce, the school awarded its first baccalaureate in 1857. Thereafter, Wilberforce continued as the most important of those schools under the control and support of the African Methodist Episcopal (AME) Church. In the 1970s the university instituted a cooperative education work-study program for all degrees. The institution is accredited by the North Central Association of Colleges and Secondary Schools.

WILEY COLLEGE Wiley College, at Marshall, Tex., was founded in 1873 by the Freedman's Aid Society of the Methodist Episcopal (ME) Church. Church-related and coeducational, Wiley offers the bachelor's degree and provides liberal arts and teacher education curricula. Its 1975 enrollment was 535.

The school, founded in 1873, was chartered in 1882 by the Freedman's Aid Society, which later became the Board of Education for Negroes (it later merged with the Board of Education of the United Methodist Church). The college was named for an outstanding white bishop and medical missionary-educator.

The first nonminister to serve as president, T. W. Cole, Sr., became the college's tenth executive in 1958. During his tenure the college enjoyed continuing growth and development as evidenced by the construction of the Aaron Baker Science Building, the Thomas Winston Cole Library, and the Fred T. Long Student Union Building. Cole was succeeded as president by Robert E. Hayes, Sr.

WILKERSON, VERNON ALEXANDER (1901–68), physician, educator; born in Fort Scott, Kans. Wilkerson received a B.A. degree from the University of Kansas in 1921 and his M.D. degree from the University of Iowa Medical School in 1925. He interned at Kansas City Hospital No. 2, and served as house surgeon at Wheatley-Provident Hospital, Kansas City, and as assistant surgeon at Kansas City Hospital No. 2. Wilkerson received a General Education Board Fellowship for graduate study in biochemistry at the University of Minnesota, from which institution he received his Ph.D. degree in biochemistry in 1932. Wilkerson served on the faculty of Howard

University Medical College (Washington, D.C.) for 34 years, from 1932 to 1966.

WILKES, WILLIAM REID (1902–), bishop; born in Putnam County, Ga. Wilkes received a B.A. degree (1928) and his B.D, degree (1933) from Morris Brown College (Atlanta, Ga.). He served as college pastor of Morris Brown and as pastor of an African Methodist Episcopal (AME) church in Atlanta, and was elected an AME bishop in 1948

WILKINS J. ERNEST (1894–1959), lawyer, government official; born in Farmington, Mo. Wilkins graduated from the University of Illinois in 1918, and after infantry service in France during World War I, he received his J.D. degree from the Chicago School of Law in 1921. His lengthy private law practice in Chicago distinguished him in legal and civic circles, and he was elected president of the Cook County Bar Association in 1941. Wilkins became known nationally in 1953 when President Dwight D. Eisenhower named him vice-chairman of the Committee on Government Contracts. In this role he participated in enforcing government nondiscrimination policies in hiring and in promotions in organizations engaged in government contracts. The next year, Wilkins was named assistant secretary of labor by President Eisenhower. The first Afro-American to be appointed to a subcabinet post, he was chiefly concerned with international affairs. Wilkins left this position in 1958 and died the following year. *See also* WILKENS, J. ERNEST, JR.

WILKINS, J. ERNEST, JR. (1923–), physicist, mathematician, educator; born in Chicago, Ill. Wilkins received a B.S. degree (1940), a M.S. degree (1941), and his Ph.D. degree (1942) in mathematics from the University of Chicago. He was a Rosenwald Fellow at the Institute for Advanced Study in 1942, and received a B.M.E. degree (1957) and a M.M.E. degree (1960) from New York University. Wilkins served as a physicist on the Manhattan Project at the University of Chicago from 1944 to 1946, and worked as a mathematician for the American Optical Company from 1946 to 1950. He was a mathematician with and later a member of the Nuclear Development Corporation of America from 1950 to 1960, and an assistant chairman in the department of theoretical physics for General Dynamic Corporation from 1960 to 1965, becoming assistant director of the department in 1965. Wilkins

was also a distinguished professor of applied mathematics and physics at Howard University (Washington, D.C.) after 1970.

WILKINS, ROY (1901–), civil rights leader; born in St. Louis, Mo. Wilkins was reared in the home of an aunt and uncle in St. Paul, Minn., where he lived in a low-income, integrated community. He worked his way through the University of Minnesota with jobs as a redcap; waiter; stockyard laborer; night editor of the university newspaper; and editor of an Afro-American weekly, the St. Paul *Appeal*. In 1923 Wilkins received his B.A. degree and afterward he joined the staff of a leading Afro-American newspaper, the weekly Kansas City *Call*. Upon witnessing widespread segregation for the first time, he became active in the National Association for the Advancement of Colored People (NAACP) and was elected secretary of the Kansas City chapter. In 1931 Wilkins was hired as assistant executive secretary of the national NAACP under Walter White, and three years later he replaced W. E. B. Du Bois as editor of the *Crisis*, the NAACP's official organ. In addition to his official duties, Wilkins gave many lectures and wrote many articles on racial issues for magazines and books. He served as a consultant to the War Department in 1941 on the problems of Afro-Americans in the U.S. Armed Forces and, with White and Du Bois, he was a consultant to the American delegation at the founding conference of the United Nations in San Francisco, Calif., in 1945. During 1949, with White on a leave of absence, Wilkins served as acting executive secretary of the NAACP. At the same time, he chaired the National Emergency Civil Rights Mobilization, an organization composed of more than a hundred smaller groups. On White's return in 1950, Wilkins was appointed internal administrator of the NAACP, a post he held until White's death in 1955, when Wilkins was unanimously appointed White's successor as executive secretary. *See also* NATIONAL ASSOCIATION FOR THE ADVANCEMENT OF COLORED PEOPLE (NAACP).

WILKINSON, FREDERICK D., JR. (1921–), business executive; born in Washington, D.C. Wilkinson received his M.B.A. degree from Harvard University in 1948. Beginning as a junior assistant buyer for Macy's department store in New York City in 1949, he had risen to the post of vice-president by 1968. Wilkinson was a trustee of Jamaica Hospital, Jamaica, N.Y., and of the National Urban League, and a director of the

Jamaica Chamber of Commerce, the Freedom National Bank, and the United Cerebral Palsy Association.

WILKINSON, ROBERT SHAW (1865–1932), educator; born in Charleston, S.C. Wilkinson received his B.A. degree from Oberlin College (Oberlin, Ohio) in 1891. He taught Latin and Greek at Kentucky State College and physics and chemistry at South Carolina State College from 1891 to 1896. He became president of South Carolina State College in 1911.

WILLIAMS, A. WILBERFORCE (1865– ?), physician; born in Monroe, La. Williams received his M.D. degree from Northwestern University (Evanston, Ill.), and afterward began a private practice in Chicago, Ill. He graduated from Sheldon Business College in 1907. Williams was a frequent lecturer on diseases—particularly syphilis and tuberculosis—and wrote a health column for a newspaper, one of the first Afro-American physicians to do so. He also served on the staff of Provident Hospital, Chicago, Ill.

WILLIAMS, BERT (ca. 1874–1922), entertainer, comedian; born in Antigua, British West Indies. Williams moved with his family first to New York and then to California. A gifted mimic and singer, he sang and danced in the streets as a young boy. He began to entertain in cafes and honky-tonks in San Francisco, and in 1895 he met George Nash Walker. Together they formed a vaudeville team, were a hit in San Francisco, and moved to New York City in 1896—playing for 28 weeks at Koster and Bial's Theatre. Their subsequent reception in the music halls of London, England, was less than enthusiastic, but *The Sons of Ham*, a blackface comedy that had a New York City premiere in 1900, established for all time the two personalities they played—Walker, a dandy, and Williams, a blackface character. This revue was followed by many other hits—*In Dahomey* (1902), *The Policy Players, Bandanna Land,* and *Abyssinia*—and a command performance at Buckingham Palace, London, England, in 1903. After Walker died, Williams appeared in the *Follies* for ten years. The song "Nobody," which Williams wrote, became his trademark. His other songs include "Woodman, Spare That Tree" and "O, Death, Where is Thy Sting?" *See also* LITERATURE: DRAMA/THEATER.

WILLIAMS, CAMILLA (1925–), soprano; born in Danville, Va. Williams graduated from Virginia State College and taught in the Danville public schools. She studied voice in Philadelphia, Pa., and in 1943 and 1944 she won the Marian Anderson Prize. In 1945 Williams gave her first concert in Philadelphia; a year later she made her stage debut in *Madama Butterfly* with the New York City Opera. Following that she appeared in recitals throughout the United States, in the Caribbean islands, and, in 1950, in Central America. Williams sang in several European capitals in 1954, and became the first Afro-American singer to appear on the stage of the Vienna State Opera. A magnificent interpreter of lieder, Williams performed in many of the major musical centers of the world.

WILLIAMS, DANIEL HALE (1856–1931), surgeon; born in Hollidaysburg, Pa. Williams operated a barber shop in Wisconsin in 1873 before apprenticing himself to Dr. Henry Palmer, the surgeon-general of Wisconsin, in 1878. Williams received his M.D. degree from Chicago Medical College in 1883 and interned at Mercy Hospital, Chicago, Ill. He subsequently opened an office in Chicago, where he was also staff physician of the Protestant Orphan Asylum; surgeon at the South Side Dispensary; instructor at Chicago Medical College; surgeon of the City Railway Company; and staff member of the Illinois state board of health. In 1890 Williams launched a drive to found a biracial hospital, where Afro-American professionals could train and Afro-American patients receive treatment. As a result of his efforts, Provident Hospital was incorporated in 1891, the first hospital in the United States founded and controlled by Afro-Americans. It was at Provident Hospital in 1893 that Williams performed his famous open-heart operation, the first of its kind done successfully. Williams was appointed by President Grover Cleveland as surgeon-in-chief of Freedmen's Hospital, Washington, D.C., in 1893. He returned to Provident Hospital in 1898, and served as visiting professor at Meharry Medical College (Nashville, Tenn.) in 1899, on the surgical staff of Cook County Hospital from 1900 to 1906, and as associate attending surgeon at St. Luke's Hospital from 1907 to 1931. Williams was a founder and the first vice-president of the National Medical Association, and he was the first Afro-American to become a fellow of the American College of Surgeons in 1913. *See also* NATIONAL MEDICAL ASSOCIATION; PHYSICIANS.

REFERENCES: For an excellent feature and cover story, see W. Montague Cobb article in the September issue, 1953, of the *Journal of the Medical Association*, pp. 379–385.

WILLIAMS, DAVID W. (1910–   ), lawyer, judge; born in Atlanta, Ga. Williams graduated from the University of California at Los Angeles in 1934, and received his LL.B. degree from the University of Southern California Law School in 1937. He practiced law in Los Angeles until 1956 when he became judge of the Los Angeles Municipal Court. In 1962 Williams joined the Superior Court, a county court sitting in Los Angeles. Seven years later he was named judge of the U.S. District Court for the Central District of California.

WILLIAMS, ETHEL (1909–   ), librarian; born in Baltimore, Md. After receiving a B.A. degree from Howard University (Washington, D.C.) in 1930, Williams became librarian at Howard University School of Religion. Her works include *Biographical Directory of Negro Ministers* (1965, 1970) and *Afro-American Religious Studies: A Comprehensive Bibliography with Location in American Libraries* coauthored with Clifford L. Brown (1972). *See also* BIBLIOGRAPHIES/BIOGRA-PHIES/GUIDES.

WILLIAMS, FRANKLIN H. (1917–   ), lawyer, government official, administrator; born in Flushing, N.Y. Williams received a B.A. degree from Lincoln University (Lincoln University, Pa.) in 1941 and his LL.B. degree from Fordham University (New York, N.Y.) in 1945. He began his legal career in 1945 as assistant special counsel to the National Association for the Advancement of Colored People (NAACP). Five years later Williams went to the West Coast to serve as western director of the NAACP in San Francisco, Calif. In 1959 he became assistant attorney general of the state of California, and in 1961 he joined the Peace Corps, becoming director of the African Regional Office in 1963. Later he became president of the Phelps-Stokes Fund in New York City.

WILLIAMS, GEORGE WASHINGTON (1849–91), clergyman, journalist, historian, lawyer, state legislator, government official; born in Bedford Springs, Pa. Williams enlisted in the Union Army when he was 14 and attained the rank of sergeant major. In 1874 he graduated from New-ton Theological Institution and served the Twelfth Street Baptist Church in Boston, Mass., until the following year when he settled in Washington, D.C. In that city Williams was instrumental in founding a journal, the Com-moner. He also served briefly in the U.S. Post

George Washington Williams. (Moorland-Spingarn Research center, Howard University.)

Office Department. In 1876 Williams became pastor of the Union Baptist Church of Cincin-nati, Ohio, and while in Cincinnati he studied law and was admitted to legal practice. In 1878 he was employed in the U.S. Department of the Treasury. He also served in the Ohio state legis-lature, and in 1885 was named U.S. minister to Haiti. Williams was the author of the definitive work in Afro-American history produced in the nineteenth century: *History of the Negro Race in America from 1619 to 1880* (2 vols., 1883). Another important work is *A History of the Negro Troops in the War of the Rebellion, 1861–65* (1888). Later Williams was in the service of the Belgian government. He died in Blackpool, England. *See also* HISTORIANS.

WILLIAMS, JOHN A. (1925–   ), author; born in Jackson, Miss. Williams received a B.A. degree from Syracuse University (Syracuse, N.Y.) in 1950. In 1961 the American Academy in Rome rejected his attendance there on an Ameri-can Academy of Arts and Letters Fellowship, but Williams spent several years abroad, returning to the United States in 1967. He lectured at Sarah Lawrence College (Bronxville, N.Y.) and at the University of California, and in 1970 he became director of the Black Academy of Arts and Let-ters. He wrote for television and for many maga-zines and newspapers, serving as African corre-spondent for *Newsweek* and European correspondent for *Ebony* and *Jet*. Williams' books include *Angry Ones* (1960), *The Man Who Cried I Am* (1967), and *Captain Blackman* (1972).

WILLIAMS, JOHN TAYLOR (1904–72), educator, administrator; born in Minden, La. Williams received a B.S. degree from Langston University (Langston, Okla.) in 1928, a M.A. degree from the University of Cincinnati in 1932, and his Ed.D. degree from Indiana University in 1936. He was affiliated with Kentucky State College from 1928 to 1947, and served as president of Maryland State College (now University of Mary-land Eastern Shore) from 1947 to 1970.

WILLIAMS, KENNETH RAYNOR (1912–   ), educator; born in Norfolk, Va. Williams received a B.A. degree from Morehouse College (Atlanta, Ga.) in 1933, and a M.A. degree (1936), a S.T.B. degree (1952), and his Ph.D. degree (1962) from Boston University. He also received honorary LL.D. degrees from Wake Forest University (Winston-Salem, N.C.) and from Southern Illinois University in 1963. Williams served as an instructor of history (1936–46) and of religion (1946–61) at Winston-Salem State University (Winston-Salem, N.C.), and became president (1961) and chancellor (1974) of the university.

WILLIAMS, LEONARD L. (1934–   ), lawyer; born in Wilmington, Del. Williams received a B.A. degree from the University of Delaware in 1956 and his J.D. degree from Georgetown University (Washington, D.C.) in 1959. He established his own law office and practiced without a partner in Wilmington, and later became an associate judge of the Municipal Court in Wilmington.

WILLIAMS, LORRAINE A.   See HISTORIANS.

WILLIAMS, NOAH W. (1876– ?), African Methodist Episcopal bishop; born in Springfield, Ill. Williams attended Wilberforce University (Wilberforce, Ohio) from 1901 to 1902, Earlham College (Richmond, Ind.) from 1902 to 1903, and DePauw University (Greencastle, Ind.) in 1904. He received a D.D. degree from Payne Seminary in 1932 and his LL.D. degree from Wilberforce University in 1934. He began his career as a clergyman in the African Methodist Episcopal (AME) Church in Springfield, Ill., in 1895. Williams served as pastor of churches in Tennessee, Kentucky, and Missouri. He was ordained a presiding elder in 1895 and named a bishop in 1932.

WILLIAMS, PAUL REVERE (1894–   ), architect; born in Los Angeles, Calif. After working his way through the University of California at Los Angeles, Williams became an art instructor in Los Angeles and later attended the Beaux-Arts Institute of Design. Williams became a certified architect in 1915, and in 1923 he opened his own office and established a thriving practice. He designed more than 400 homes in California (many for movie stars) and a total of about 3,000 buildings. Williams received honorary degrees from Howard, Lincoln, and Atlanta universities, and from Hampton Institute. He received the Spingarn Medal of the National Association for the Advancement of Colored People (NAACP) in 1953.

WILLIAMS, RICHARD E. (1934–   ), naval officer, educator; born in Jacksonville, Fla. After receiving a B.S. degree in engineering from Kentucky State College in 1965, Williams entered

the U.S. Navy. Continuing his education, he received an M.A. in mathematics from Texas Agricultural and Mechanical (A&M) University in 1971. Williams rose to the rank of commander in the Navy, and in 1972, as officer in charge of Training Air Wing Three in Florida, he became the first Afro-American officer to command a naval unit in the Deep South. Williams was made a captain in 1973 and assumed the duties of professor of naval science in the NROTC unit at Florida Agricultural and Mechanical (A&M) University.

WILLIAMS, ROGER K.   See SCIENTISTS: SOCIAL.

WILLIAMS, SMALLWOOD EDMUND (1907–   ), born in Lynchburg, Va. Williams attended Howard University School of Religion (Washington, D.C.), and received his B.Th. degree from American Bible College in 1948. He organized the Bible Way Church of Our Lord Jesus Christ in Washington, D.C., and became pastor and senior bishop there. (This denomination eventually became national in scope.) Williams also served as president of the Southern Christian Leadership Conference (SCLC), and in 1958 founded a school and mission in Liberia. See also PENTECOSTALS.

WILLIAMS, THEODORE (1905–   ), lawyer, judge; born in Cleveland, Ohio. Williams attended the University of Michigan and received his J.D. and LL.B. degrees from John Marshall Law School (Chicago, Ill.). Admitted to the Ohio bar in 1932, he became judge of the Municipal Court of Cleveland, Ohio, in 1971.

WILLIAMS, WILLIAM TAYLOR BURWELL (W. T. B.) (1866–1941), educator; born in Stone Bridge, Clarke County, Va. Williams attended Hampton Institute (Hampton, Va.) from 1886 to 1888, Phillips Academy (Andover, Mass.) from 1889 to 1893, and received his B.A. degree from Harvard University in 1897. He was principal of a school in Indianapolis, Ind. (1897–1902), and served as field agent for Hampton Institute (1902–1903), for the General Education Board (1903–1906), and for the John F. Slater Fund, beginning in 1910. Williams became dean of the college department of Tuskegee Institute (Tuskegee Institute, Ala.), and then served as vice-president of the institute until his death. He was awarded the Spingarn Medal in 1934.

WILLIE, CHARLES V. (1927–   ), sociologist, educator; born in Dallas, Tex. Willie received a B.A. degree from Morehouse College (Atlanta, Ga.) in 1948, a M.A. degree from Atlanta University in 1949, and his Ph.D. degree from Syracuse University (Syracuse, N.Y.) in 1957. He joined the department of sociology of Syracuse University as an instructor in 1952, served as the chairman of the department from 1967 to 1971, and became vice-president for student affairs at Syracuse in 1972. Willie became a professor in the Graduate School of Education at Harvard University in 1974. He was the author of *Church Action in the World* (1969); *The Family Life of Black People* (1970); *Black Students at White Colleges* (1972); and *Racism and Mental Health* (1973). Willie also contributed many articles to professional journals.

WILLIS, FLOYD WILLIAMS (1885–1951), physician; born in Louisville, Ky. Willis received his M.D. degree from Meharry Medical College (Nashville, Tenn.) in 1913, and later established a general practice in Chicago, Ill. He did graduate work in roentgenology at Freedman's Hospital, Washington, D.C., in 1919, was a visiting lecturer at Meharry Medical College in 1923, and was roentgenologist at Fort Dearborn Hospital in 1924. Willis specialized in roentgenology in his practice in Chicago, Ill.

WILLIS, GERTRUDE GEDDES (? –1970), business executive. Willis was the founder and president of Gertrude Geddes Willis Life Insurance Company and Gertrude Geddes Willis Funeral Home of New Orleans, La. She was also president of Geddes and Moss Funeral Home of that city. Willis was a member of the National Association for the Advancement of Colored People (NAACP), the Young Women's Christian Association (YWCA), and the National Insurance Association.

WILLS, MAURY See ATHLETES: BASEBALL.

WILSON, CLARENCE LEON (1895–1944), physician, educator; born in Cairo, Ill. Wilson received a B.A. degree from the University of Illinois and his M.D. degree from the University of Illinois College of Medicine. He interned at Kansas City General Hospital No. 2, and did advanced medical training in obstetrics at Provident Hospital, Chicago, Ill. Wilson was on the faculty of Chicago Lying-In Hospital and Michael Reese Hospital, and served as an instructor at Provident Hospital School of Nursing. He was also senior attendant, faculty member, and staff president at Provident Hospital, and in 1938 he was recognized as a senior specialist in obstetrics by the U.S. Civil Service Commission. Wilson was a member of the American Medical Association and the American Congress of Obstetrics and Gynecology.

WILSON, FLIP (1933–   ), comedian; born Clerow Wilson in Jersey City, N.J. The tenth of 18 children growing up in destitution, Wilson lived with his family for his first eight years and in a reformatory for the next eight. At 16 he joined the U.S. Air Force, where he picked up the name "Flip" (for "flipped-out") for his barracks antics. In 1954, as a civilian, he took a job as a bellhop in a San Francisco hotel, and began to entertain during the intermissions of the professional entertainers. From there Wilson hitchhiked around the country, taking jobs in whatever nightspots hired him, until he reached New York City. In New York City he became a regular performer at the Apollo Theater in Harlem. It was not until 1965 that Wilson first appeared on television, as a guest on a late evening interview and variety show. He reappeared several times on the same show and then as a guest on many of the network shows. In 1970 the "Flip Wilson Show" had its first airing on network television. *See also* RADIO AND TELEVISION.

WILSON, FREDDY *See* NEWSPAPERS: CONTEMPORARY.

WILSON, JAMES FINLEY (1881–1952), fraternal leader; born in Nashville, Tenn. Wilson attended Fisk University (Nashville, Tenn.), and after leaving school he worked as an office boy, a railroad employee, a miner in Arizona, a gold prospector in the Klondike River valley, and a newspaper reporter. Afterward, he worked on several newspapers, including the *Plaindealer*, the *New York Age*, the *Baltimore Times*, and the Harrisburg *Advocate-Verdict*. However, Wilson is best remembered as the Grand Exalted Ruler of the Independent, Benevolent, Protective Order of Elks. He was elected to that leadership position in 1922, and was reelected annually for the next 30 years. Wilson built the small organization into a major fraternal society with more than 900 lodges. Under his leadership the Elks contributed to many worthy causes and set up a university scholarship program. Wilson also published and edited the Elks' newspaper, *The Eagle* (formerly called *The Sun*). *See also* FRATERNAL SOCIETIES.

WILSON, KENNETH E. (1919–   ), lawyer, judge; born in Tacoma, Wash. Wilson received a B.S. degree from Hampton Institute (Hampton, Va.) in 1942 and his J.D. degree from the University of Chicago Law School in 1948. He served as an assistant state's attorney for Cook County, Ill., as an assistant attorney general of Illinois, as a representative in the Illinois legislature, and as Cook County commissioner before becoming a judge of the Circuit Court of Cook County.

WILSON, MARGARET BUSH (1919–), lawyer, civic leader; born in St. Louis, Mo. Wilson received a B.A. degree from Talladega College (Ala.) in 1940 and her LL.B degree from Lincoln University School of Law (St. Louis) in 1943. She served on many commissions and boards locally and nationally before becoming president, in 1975, of the national board of the National Association for the Advancement of Colored People (NAACP).

WILSON, PRINCE EDWARD (1918–   ), historian, educator; born in Asheville, N.C. Wilson received a B.A. degree from Talladega College (Talladega, Ala.) in 1939, and a M.A. degree (1942) and his Ph.D. degree (1954) from the University of Chicago. He served as assistant professor of history at Morris Brown College (Atlanta, Ga.) where he was also professor and department chairman from 1942 to 1962; as associate professor of history and dean at Central State University (Wilberforce, Ohio) from 1962 to 1966; and as professor of history at Atlanta University after 1966. Wilson became vice-president of academic affairs at Atlanta University in 1974.

WILSON TEACHERS COLLEGE *See* DISTRICT OF COLUMBIA TEACHERS COLLEGE.

WILSON, WADE (1914–   ), educator; born in Birmingham, Ala. Wilson received a B.S. degree from Cheyney State College (Cheyney, Pa.) in 1936, a M.Ed. degree from Pennsylvania State University in 1937, a Ed.D. degree from New York University in 1954, and his LL.D. degree from Hahnemann Medical College in 1969. He taught industrial education at Maryland State College (now University of Maryland Eastern Shore) from 1939 to 1940, at Tennessee State University from 1940 to 1942, and then at Chey-

ney State College, where he first became director of development and then president in 1968. Wilson was active in many educational groups, and served as president of the Association of Pennsylvania State College Faculties from 1962 to 1965 and of the Pennsylvania State Education Association in 1967.

WINGATE, LIVINGSTON (1915–   ), lawyer, civic leader; born in Timmonsville, S.C. A leader in New York City's Harlem for more than 30 years, Wingate received a law degree from Saint John's University (Jamaica, N.Y.) by working during the day and attending classes at night. Eventually, this degree made it possible for him to become counsel to the House Committee on Education and Labor, the committee chaired by U.S. Representative Adam Clayton Powell. Subsequently, Powell engaged Wingate as his special assistant. In 1962, after having worked as assistant director of Associated Community Teams (ACT, a Harlem-based antipoverty agency), Wingate became that agency's director. When two years later it merged with HARYOU to become HARYOU-ACT, Wingate became the director of the new body. In 1968, as director of the New York chapter of the National Urban League, he continued to be a major force in the Harlem community. In fact, he emerged as the leader of an amalgam of 60 splinter groups that came to be known as the Federation of Black Community Organizations, with aspirations to be the "most authoritative, the most persuasive" voice in Harlem. Having inherited the political base and the nucleus of the powerful political machine of his former boss, Adam Clayton Powell, in 1972, Wingate resigned his post with the Urban League to run an unsuccessful campaign for the House seat occupied by U.S. Representative Charles B. Rangel.

WINGS OVER JORDAN A popular choral group of the 1930s and 1940s, Wings over Jordan sang a variety of church songs, especially spirituals and gospels, on radio shows and in concert.

WINSTON-SALEM STATE COLLEGE *See* WINSTON-SALEM STATE UNIVERSITY.

WINSTON-SALEM STATE UNIVERSITY Winston-Salem State University, at Winston-Salem, N.C., was founded in 1892 by an act of the state legislature. State-supported and coeducational, the school offers the bachelor's degree (including the B.S.Ed. and the B.S.N.) and provides liberal arts and teacher education curricula, and a school of nursing. Its 1975 enrollment was 1,653.

The university was founded as Slater Industrial Academy, one of the many schools in the South created through the John F. Slater Fund. It later became known as Winston-Salem Teachers College and then as Winston-Salem State College. Finally, in 1969, it gained university status.

Aside from the usual subject areas, the school offers a minor in black studies and also provides educational opportunities for citizens of the state through its extended services programs. These programs include evening classes and educational assistance for community organizations and schools.

WINSTON-SALEM TEACHERS COLLEGE See WINSTON-SALEM STATE UNIVERSITY.

WOMEN

WOMEN The ordeal of slavery (which lasted two and a half centuries) and of segregation (which continued for another century) have had far-reaching negative influences on Afro-American women. Practically every aspect of their lives has been influenced by these ordeals: the life-styles for survival, the relationships with mates and children, the daily coping mechanisms, and the aspirations and motivations for the future. The role of black women cannot be understood and explained adequately apart from this historical background. Afro-American women have had to endure in a society of white over black, in which, in theory if not in practice, white women were placed upon a pedestal, and white males expressed their supremacy over and chauvinism concerning females and nonwhite males. Under the systems of slavery and racial caste the Afro-American woman was subject to abuse. The sexual impulses of the white male master could be most easily satisfied at the expense of the Afro-American woman's honor, privacy, and person. Yet, the systems of slavery and caste encouraged white and black males sexually and socially to exploit black women. Thinking of profits or believing in the innate inferiority of Afro-Americans, some slave masters encouraged or ignored black male advances to black females, regarding the mating of slaves much in the same way they did that of their livestock. The Afro-American woman under slavery was further abused and dehumanized when her children were stripped from her and sold under conditions that included the likelihood that she would never see them again.

Although chattel slavery ended with emancipation, abuses under segregation continued. Especially in the former slaveholding states, where the vast majority of Afro-Americans lived, black women were at a great disadvantage in protecting themselves or their property from the abuses, excesses, and humiliations of whites. In addition, the Afro-American family still had to live for the most part in the shadows of slavery: peonage, poverty, discrimination, and unemployment. As a result, education and housing for Afro-Americans were always and still are limited, inferior, and inadequate.

A lack of understanding of these historical forces operating upon the black woman (and her children) have led some scholars to define the black family as "disorganized" or "unstable." Perhaps more important, this lack of understanding has perpetuated popular myths about the black woman's innate or "natural" promiscuity and fertility. A more accurate assessment would lead to the conclusion that an often inhospitable (and sometimes hostile) social environment created by a racist society has itself produced negative images of the Afro-American family in general and of the Afro-American woman in particular.

Another popular myth is that of the black "matriarch." The many studies that have examined this contention in detail have generally found it to be untrue as a generalization and unproven as a statement of fact. Passing beyond the simplistic definition of the matriarchal family as being one headed by a female, the black sociologist E. Franklin Frazier, in *The Negro Family in the United States* (1948), emphasized the pressures of socioeconomic influences that "developed in her [the black woman] those qualities which are associated with a 'matriarchal'

862

organization." Frazier held that the conditions of slavery were probably such that no primitive culture could survive the impact of such servitude and bondage. Melville J. Herskovits, an anthropologist, stated in his *The Myth of the Negro Past* (1941) that in those families where the mother and grandmother play important roles, one can find vestiges, albeit in diluted form, of African traditions. Hilda O. Fortune, in her "Study of the Power Position of Mothers in Contemporary Negro Family Life in New York City" (1963), pointed out that the label "matriarchal family" is a misnomer, wrongly applied to dominant women who exist in every subgroup in modern society.

In the wake of a well-publicized report by Daniel P. Moynihan, *The Negro Family: The Case for National Action* (1965), black sociologists, in conjunction with the National Urban League, responded by refuting studies that labeled Afro-American families as matriarchal, disorganized, and disintegrating. Their report, entitled "The Strengths of Black Families" (1971), stated that: "Contrary to widespread belief in 'matriarchy' among blacks, our findings reveal that most black families, whether low income or not, are characterized by an 'equalitarian' pattern in which neither spouse dominates but shares decision-making and the performance of expected tasks."

Achievements and Distinctions In spite of the ordeals that the Afro-American woman has faced, she has endured and emerged as a stable force in the family and in society. Often, she has been the sole head of the household, contributing to its economic welfare and serving as the vital force behind and the source of inspiration and motivation of her children.

Moreover, Afro-American women have been achievers throughout Afro-American history. Sadie Iola Daniel pointed out this fact in an early volume of biographies entitled *Women Builders* (1931). She identified and praised many important Afro-American women. Her subjects include: Harriet Tubman, abolitionist; Sojourner Truth, abolitionist and women's rights advocate; Phyllis Wheatley, poet; Hallie Q. Brown, librarian; Ida B. Wells, civil rights advocate; Charlotte Hawkins Brown, educator; and Mary McLeod Bethune, educator.

More recently, many Afro-American women have identified with the civil rights movement and protested against segregation and discrimination. Rosa Parks, for example, is a symbol of the many women (who never acheived her fame or publicity) who before her time spoke out and acted against the insults and humiliations of the system of segregation, or who ignored or resisted the signs on buses (or custom) that commanded blacks to defer to whites in seating.

Rosa Parks, born in Tuskegee, Ala., in 1913, was the catalyst in the historic Montgomery bus boycott. On December 1, 1955, she refused to give up her seat to a white person on a crowded bus. After her subsequent arrest and trial, a boycott was planned and successfully carried out under the leadership of Martin Luther King, Jr., who was ably assisted and supported by his wife, Coretta. Many other Afro-American women carried out both supportive and independent roles in the civil rights movement. For example, Daisy Bates was a state legislator in Arkansas during the 1950s and Gloria Richardson was a state legislator in Maryland during the 1960s.

Organizations Many women's organizations at local levels existed among free blacks as early as the eighteenth century. However, the great period of organization occurred during the nineteenth century. While local groups continued to exist at church, school, and community levels, a new national organizational activity began, largely in the 1890s. There were many leaders in this organizing effort, but some of the outstanding leaders and promoters were Ida Barnett Wells, an author; Josephine St. Pierre Ruffin, who organized the First National Conference of Colored Women in Boston, Mass., in 1895; Mary Margaret Washington of Tuskegee Institute, who helped found the National Federation of Afro-American Women; and Mary Church Terrell, leader of the National League of Colored Women. Not without rivalry for national leadership, large numbers of groups became affiliated with and then formed together the National Association of Colored Women (NACW) in 1896. Problems of health and education and the prevalence of lynching were some of the basic concerns of the NACW and its affiliates.

More members joined the NACW following the turn of the century. By the time of World War I Mary B. Talbert had become president of the NACW, and Mary McLeod Bethune was emerging as a national figure. With much prior activity in club work, and drawing some support from older organizations, Bethune founded the National Council of Negro Women (NCNW) in 1935. By the mid-1970s the NCNW had become one of the largest organized bodies of Afro-

Americans. Claiming a membership of more than 3 million, the NCNW had more than 100 affiliates in 40 states. One of its major goals was to eliminate discrimination based on race, creed, color, sex, and national origin.

Individual Women in the 1970s By 1977 a growing number of Afro-American women were making their mark in politics, business, and the professions. Only a few of the most notable examples and their accomplishments are cited here.

The top Afro-American women in law and government were: Juanita Kidd Stout, judge, and Ethel Allen, city councilwoman, both from Philadelphia; Yvonne B. Burke, U.S. congresswoman from California; Shirley Anita Chisholm, U.S. congresswoman from New York; Barbara O. Jordan, U.S. congresswoman from Texas; Patricia Roberts Harris, secretary, Department of Housing and Urban Development (HUD), Washington, D.C.; Constance B. Newman, Consumer Product Safety Commission, Washington, D.C.; Mary F. Berry, lawyer and administrator; and C. Delores Tucker, Pennsylvania secretary of state.

Others making their mark in economic and public life were: Ernesta G. Procope, who was elected to the board of directors of Avon products. In addition to becoming the second woman on the board at Avon, she was president of E. G. Bowman Company (real estate) in New York, N.Y.; Helen Jewel Moseley was elected to the board of directors of the National League for Nursing.

Other Afro-American women in prominent positions were: Juliet D. Blackburn, merchandise manager, Sears Roebuck & Co., Atlanta, Ga.; Ruth Bowen, president, Queen Booking Corp., New York, N.Y.; Julia M. Carson, Indiana state legislator; June Christmas, M.D., commissioner, New York City department of mental health and mental retardation; Louise M. Dargans, director of research, Committee on Education and Labor, U.S. House of Representatives, Washington, D.C.; Doris A. Davis, mayor, Compton, Calif.; Jean Fairfax, director of legal and community services, the Legal Defense and Educational Fund of the National Association for the Advancement of Colored People (NAACP), New York, N.Y.; Margaret Bush Wilson, president of the NAACP; Frankie Muse Freeman, commissioner, U.S. Commission on Civil Rights, Washington, D.C.; Florence S. Gaynor, executive director, Martland Hospital, Newark, N.J.; Mar-

Mary McLeod Bethune, an organizer of women's groups, is surrounded in her office by photographs of President Franklin D. Roosevelt and outstanding Afro-Americans of her generation. *(Library of Congress.)*

cia A. Gillespie, editor in chief, *Essence* magazine, one of the fastest growing women's magazines in the nation; Mercedier Goodwin, member of the Illinois state board of education; Mattelia A. Grays, past president of Alpha Kappa Alpha Sorority, Houston, Tex.; Grace Hamilton, Georgia state legislator; Dorothy I. Height, president, National Council of Negro Women, New York, N.Y.; Helen Thornton Jones, president, Joe Louis Milk Co., Chicago, Ill.; Coretta Scott King, president, Martin Luther King, Jr., Research Center, Atlanta, Ga.; Ida Lewis, publisher, *Encore* magazine, New York, N.Y.; Carmel C. Marr, commissioner, New York state public service commission; Dorothy M. McConner, administrative vice-president, Johnson Products Co., Chicago, Ill.; Ophelia D. Mitchell, publisher and editor, Columbus *Times*, Columbus, Ga.; Constance Baker Motley, judge, U.S. District Court, New York, N.Y.; Frances L. Murphy, director, Afro-American Newspapers, Baltimore-Washington, D.C.; Eleanor Holmes Norton, chairwoman, Commission on Human Rights, New York, N.Y.; Dorothy J. Orr, vice-president, Equitable Life Assurance Society, former assistant state commissioner of human rights in New York; Esra H. Poston, president, New York state civil rights commission; Joan Sandler, director, Black Theater Alliance, New York, N.Y.; Lucille Rose, commissioner, New York city department of employment; Judith Taylor, assistant vice-president, Chemical Bank, New York, N.Y.; Lynette D. Taylor, executive director, Delta Sigma Theta Sorority, Inc., Washington, D.C.; Verda Welcome, Maryland state legislator; Jane C. Wright, associate dean, New York Medical College, New York, N.Y.; and Bernice Sumlin, president, Alpha Kappa Alpha Sorority, Dayton, Ohio.

A Profile of Afro-American Women in the 1970s Afro-American women have made important strides in many aspects of life since the 1950s. Their health and education have improved, and gains have been made in entering white-collar occupations and in achieving incomes more nearly equal to those of white women. Yet much remains to be achieved, for, in most instances, Afro-American women still lag behind white women. Black women are more likely to be unemployed, to be overrepresented in low-paying jobs, to be increasingly assuming the role of family head with children to support, and to account for a larger proportion of the poor.

In March 1974, 12.5 million Afro-American women lived in the United States, an increase of 4.7 million since 1950. The black female population is characteristically younger than the white female population, and despite improvements in health status, Afro-American women continue to have a lower life expectancy than white women. The Afro-American woman is nearly six times as likely to die as a result of homicide as is the white woman, is about four and a half times as likely to die from tuberculosis, and is more than twice as likely to die from diabetes mellitus or cirrhosis of the liver, but less likely to die from suicide.

Although the proportion of Afro-American women living in the South declined from about 68 percent in 1950 to about 53 percent in both 1970 and 1974, Afro-American women are still more concentrated in the South than are white women. Also, black women continue to be overrepresented among the female residents in central cities of metropolitan areas and underrepresented in the suburbs.

Most women, both black and white, have been married at some time, but the proportion remaining single has been increasing especially rapidly for black women. Among ever-married women, only about 54 percent of Afro-Americans were living with their husbands in 1975, a substantial decline from the 1950 level of 64 percent. Corresponding to this decline has been an increase in the percentages of Afro-American women separated and divorced and in the percent of black families headed by women.

In 1974 Afro-American women had a higher rate of childbirth than white women. However, in recent years black women, on the average, have given birth to fewer children than in the past and expect to have fewer children in the future. Among the younger women (18 to 24 years old in 1974) the lifetime birth expectations of black women are the same as those for white women (2.2 children per woman).

Education is one area where Afro-American women have made major advancements. Since the mid-1960s, the number of Afro-American women enrolled at the college level has sharply increased. In 1964 slightly more than 100,000 black women under 35 years of age were attending college, compared with 392,000 in 1974. Enrollment in college among white women has also expanded over the same period; however, the growth has not been as pronounced as that for black women. Increased school enrollment and higher retention rates among black teenagers have resulted in rising educational attainment. By 1975 the proportion of black women 25 to 29 years old who were high school graduates (including those going on to college) reached 70 percent, a substantial increase over the 39 percent who were high school graduates in 1960. Yet, in 1975 an educational gap still remained between Afro-American women and white women, as 83 percent of the white women of this age group had completed high school.

For more than two decades the labor force participation rate for Afro-American women has been higher than that for white women. This pattern continued to hold true in 1974 although the labor force rate of white women has been rapidly approaching that of black women. In 1974, 49 percent of black women were in the civilian labor force, compared with 45 percent of white women. In every age group, except 16 to 19 and 20 to 24, black women were more likely than their white counterparts to be in the labor force. Also, a somewhat larger proportion of Afro-American women than white women who worked during 1974 worked year round and full time.

The presence of young children in the family affects the work status of Afro-American women to a lesser extent than white women. In 1975, 51 percent of married black women with children under six years old were in the labor force, compared with 35 percent of white women.

Unemployment has been traditionally more prevalent among Afro-American women than among white women. In 1974 the unemployment rate for black women averaged about 11 percent as compared with 6 percent for white women. The unemployment situation among Afro-American teenage girls is particularly significant.

Substantial changes have occurred since 1965 in the occupations of employed Afro-American women. The proportion of black women working in white-collar jobs increased from 24 percent in 1965 to 42 percent in 1974, whereas the percent employed in the normally low-paying private household worker positions declined from 30 percent to 11 percent.

By 1974 the median earnings of black women who worked year round and full time were approaching income parity with their white counterparts. The median earnings ratio of black to white women rose from 75 percent in 1967 to 92 percent in 1974.

In 1974, 1 million female-headed black families and 1.3 million female-headed white families were below the poverty level. Families with female heads have so accounted for an increasing proportion of all Afro-American families in poverty that by 1974 the proportion was about 67 percent. For white families the proportion was 37 percent.

A smaller proportion of Afro-American women than white women register and vote in congressional and presidential elections. Registration rates for Afro-American women in 1974 were at the lowest level reported for any of the last five general elections. In 1974 about 57 percent of black women registered to vote; for the previous four elections (1966 to 1972), the levels ranged from 61 to 66 percent. See also CIVIL RIGHTS MOVEMENT; DISCRIMINATION; EMPLOYMENT; FAMILY; HOUSING; INCOME; NURSES; POPULATION.

REFERENCES: For a good historic summary with bibliographical notes, see Lerner, Gerda, "Early Community Work of Black Club Women," *Journal of Negro History*, April 1974, pp. 158–67. More detailed references for later periods include: Cade, Toni (ed.), *The Black Woman*, New American Library, New York, 1970; Clark, John Henrik, "The Black Woman: A Figure in World History," *Essence*, June 1971; Daniel, Sadie Iola, *Women Builders*, rev. ed., Associated Publishers, Washington, D.C., 1970; Frazier, E. Franklin, *The Negro Family in the United States*, rev. ed., University of Chicago Press, Chicago, 1966; Mack, Delores E., "Where the Black-Matriarchy Theorists Went Wrong," *Psychology Today*, January 1971; McKenney, Nampeo D. R., "The Woman," *Black Enterprise*, August 1971; Strong, Augusta, "Negro Women in Freedom's Battles," *Freedomways*, Fall 1967, pp. 302–15; U.S. Bureau of the Census, *The Social and Economic Status of the Black Population in the United States, 1974*, ser. P-23, no. 54, U.S. Government Printing Office, Washington, D.C., 1975; and U.S. Bureau of the Census, *A Statistical Portrait of Women in the United States*, ser. P-23, no. 58, U.S. Government Printing Office, Washington, D.C., 1976. For a book-length bibliography, see Davis, Lenwood G. under BIBLIOGRAPHIES/BIOGRAPHIES/GUIDES.

WONDER, STEVIE (1950–   ), singer, composer; born in Saginaw, Mich. By mid-1970s Wonder had recorded more than 12 gold records. He received more awards for singing during the years 1975 and 1976 than any other popular singer. His hits include "I Call It Pretty Music," "Fingertips," and "Uptight," Wonder also played in the motion pictures *Bikini Beach* and *Muscle Beach Party*.

WOOD, HAROLD LEROY (1919–   ) lawyer, judge; born in Bridgeport, Conn. Wood received a B.A. degree from Lincoln University (Lincoln University, Pa.) in 1942, a LL.B. degree from Cornell University (Ithaca, N.Y.) in 1948, and his LL.M. degree from New York University Law School in 1952. Wood practiced law from 1950 to 1959, and in 1958 he was elected to the Westchester County board of supervisors, a post he held until 1967. During the next year he was alderman of the city of Mount Vernon, N.Y., and in 1969 he was appointed judge of the Family Court in Westchester County. Two years later Wood was named judge of the County Court of Westchester County.

WOOD, THOMAS A. (1926–   ) business executive; born in New York, N.Y. Wood received a B.A. degree from Columbia University in 1949 and his B.S. degree in electrical engineering from the University of Michigan. He also attended Massachusetts Institute of Technology and Wayne State University (Detroit, Mich.). Wood was engaged in electronics and computer development, and in 1968 he founded TAW International Leasing, Inc., a multinational leasing company of capital equipment, managed and principally owned by Afro-Americans, based in New York City but operating primarily in Africa. Wood served as president of that firm, and in 1970 was elected to the boards of the Chase Manhattan Bank of New York and its parent, Chase Manhattan Corporation. He was thus the first Afro-American to be named a director of a major U.S. bank not operated by blacks. Wood was also a trustee of the National Urban League.

WOODLAWN ORGANIZATION Formed in 1960 or 1961 in Chicago, Ill., as a Black Power group, the Woodlawn Organization is a society whose chief concern is to bring self-determination to the people of Chicago's Afro-American ghetto. The story of the organization was told by its president, Rev. Arthur M. Brazier, in *Black Self-Determination: The Story of the Woodlawn Organization* (1969).

WOODRUFF, HALE ASPACIO (1900–   ), painter, printmaker, educator; born in Cairo, Ill. Woodruff was educated at the John Herron Art Institute (Indianapolis, Ind.); at Harvard University; at the Academie Moderne, Paris; and at the Academie Scandinave in Paris, France, where he studied under Henry O. Tanner. In 1936 he studied fresco painting in Mexico with Diego Rivera, and Woodruff's work was also influenced by another Mexican painter, José Orozcó. Later, as an art instructor at Atlanta University, he drew on his observations of southern life for his paintings, etchings, and woodcuts. Two panels for a Works Project Administration (WPA) project, *Shanty-town* and *Mudhill Row*, showed such bleak poverty that the paintings produced official reaction and attention. In 1941 Woodruff initiated the important series of Atlanta University art shows. From 1946 until he retired in 1968 he was professor of art education at New York University. Woodruff's later style became remarkably flexible, as illustrated in an oil portrait of Countee Cullen, in block prints of a lynching, in the surrealistic *Man With a Balloon*, and in his famous Amistad murals in oil tempera on canvas at Talladega College (Talladega, Ala.). Woodruff's exhibit history includes shows at the Harmon Foundation, New York, N.Y., 1928, 1931, 1933, and 1935; at the Whitney Museum of American Art, New York, N.Y.; at the National Center of Afro-American Artists; and at the Boston Museum of Fine Arts, 1930. His work is in the collections of New York University; the Library of Congress, Washington, D.C.; and the Golden State Insurance Company, Los Angeles, Calif. He was awarded a bronze medal by the Harmon Foundation in 1926, a Rosenwald Fellowship in 1943, and a Great Teacher Award by New York University in 1966. *See also* ARTISTS; LITERATURE: CHILDREN'S.

WOODS, GRANVILLE T. (1856–1910), inventor; born in Columbus, Ohio. After mastering the trades of machinist and blacksmith, and after working as a railroad fireman and engineer, Woods took college courses in electrical and mechanical engineering from 1876 to 1878. He served as engineer on the British steamer *Ironsides* in 1878, and later settled in Cincinnati, Ohio. His first patent was for a steam boiler furnace in 1884. He patented a telephone transmitter in 1885, which was bought by Bell Telephone, and Woods then founded the Woods Electric Company, which manufactured and sold telephone, telegraph, and electrical instruments. His most important invention was the induction telegraph system in 1887, a method of informing an engineer of trains immediately in front of and behind him, thus ensuring safer rail travel. Woods was challenged in court by the Edison and Phelp companies—who claimed priority for Thomas Edison—but Woods eventually won the patent rights. Of the more than 50 patents that he registered, the majority were concerned with railroad telegraphs, electrical brakes, and electrical railway systems.

Granville T. Woods. *(Library of Congress.)*

WOODSON, CARTER GODWIN (1875–1950), historian, educator, author; born in New Canton, Va. The son of former slaves, James and Anne Eliza (Riddle), who needed the extra income he was able to earn by working, Woodson was unable to attend school until the age of 20. Having educated himself until that time, he received his high school diploma in less than two years. Woodson then attended Berea College (Berea, Ky.), from which he received his Litt.B. degree in 1903, after taking off three years to teach and to serve as principal of his former high school. He subsequently went to the Philippines as supervisor of schools for four years. Returning to the United States, Woodson pursued further studies at the University of Chicago, receiving a B.A. degree in 1907 and his M.A. degree a year later. A year of study in Europe and Asia, including a semester at the Sorbonne in Paris, France, was followed by further study in the fields of history and political science at Harvard University. Accepting a teaching assignment in Washington, D.C., in 1908, Woodson remained there for ten years, during which time he completed his dissertation entitled "The Disruption of Virginia" and received his Ph.D. degree from Harvard University in 1912. During this period he was the guiding force in the formation of the Association for the Study of Negro Life and History in 1915. One year later the first issue of the association's *Journal of Negro History,* with Woodson as director-editor, was published. From 1918 to 1922 Woodson served as principal of a high school in Washington, D.C., as dean of the School of Liberal Arts of Howard University (Washington, D.C.), and as dean of West Virginia Collegiate Institute. During his tenure at West Virginia he organized and became president of Associated Publishers, Inc., a company that was established to publish and circulate books about Afro-Americans that other publishers would not issue. In 1922 Woodson left West Virginia to devote his time to research; to the Association for the Study of Negro Life and History; and to the quarterly *Journal,* which he published virtually single-handedly. Called the "Father of Negro History," Woodson published many volumes. The most important include *The Education of the Negro Prior to 1861* (1915); *A Century of Negro Migration* (1918); and *The Negro in Our History* (1922), which became the standard text on Afro-American history for many years. Other works include high school texts, historical studies, studies of black Africa, and a book on the heroes and heroines of Africa. *See also* HISTORIANS.

WOOLFOLK, GEORGE RUBLE See ACKNOWLEDGMENTS.

WORK, JOHN WESLEY, JR. (1901–68), composer, educator; born in Tullahoma, Tenn. Work

was educated at Fisk University (Nashville, Tenn.), at Columbia University, at Yale University, and at the Institute of Musical Art (New York, N.Y.). After 1933 Work taught at Fisk University, and from 1948 to 1957 he directed the Fisk Jubilee Singers. Throughout his career he published articles in scholarly journals and quarterlies, and in 1940 he issued *American Folk Songs.* As a composer, Work published piano pieces, arrangements of Negro folk songs, and compositions for the voice. He remains best known for "Sassafras," "Appalachia," and "Scuppernong," all for piano; *The Singers,* a cantata for chorus and orchestra; the choral cycle *Isaac Watts Contemplates the Cross;* and *Yenvalou,* for strings. *See also* FISK JUBILEE SINGERS; MUSIC: HISTORY AND DEVELOPMENT.

WORK, MONROE NATHAN (1866–1945), historian, librarian; born in Iredell County, N.C. Work studied at Chicago Theological Seminary in 1898, and received a Ph.B. degree (1902) and his M.A. degree (1903) from the University of Chicago. He was professor of pedagogy and history at Georgia State College from 1903 to 1908, and director of the department of records and research at Tuskegee Institute (Tuskegee Institute, Ala.) from 1908 to 1939. Work participated in sociological studies of the Negro and served on numerous boards and committees. In 1912 he founded the *Negro Yearbook,* which he edited through nine editions until his death. The *Yearbook* supplied factual data on Afro-Americans and was used in schools and libraries throughout the country. Work also edited the *Bibliography of the Negro in Africa and America* (1928), the first work of its kind. *See also* BIBLIOGRAPHIES/BIOGRAPHIES/GUIDES.

WORMLEY, STANTON LAWRENCE (1909–   ), educator; born in Washington, D.C. Wormley received a B.A. degree (1930) and a M.A. degree (1931) from Howard University (Washington, D.C.), a diploma from the University of Heidelberg, (Heidelberg, Germany), and his Ph.D. degree in literature from Cornell University (Ithaca, N.Y.) in 1939. He taught at Howard, where he also served as head of the German department (1944–64), as acting dean of the graduate school (1960–64), as academic vice-president (1964–   ), and as acting president (1965–66).

WRIGHT, CHARLES (1918–   ), lawyer, judge; born in Louisiana. Wright received a B.S. degree (1944) and his LL.B. degree (1949) from Temple

University (Philadelphia, Pa.). He served as deputy attorney general in Philadelphia from 1951 to 1953. In 1965 Wright was appointed judge of the County Court of Philadelphia County, and in 1974 he became judge of the Common Pleas Court.

WRIGHT, HAROLD LOUIS (1930–), Episcopal bishop; born in Boston, Mass. Wright attended public schools in Boston and then the New England Conservatory of Music (Boston, Mass.) before matriculating at Boston University. He later received his theological degree from the Episcopal Seminary (New York, N.Y.). Wright became the sixth Afro-American bishop in the Episcopal Church when he was named a bishop in 1974. He served in the diocese of New York, the second largest in the United States. Wright's career was a testimony to a man not persuaded by a college guidance counselor (while Wright was a student at Boston University), who told him "there is no place for blacks in the Episcopal Church."

WRIGHT, JANE COOKE (1919–), surgeon, educator; born in New York, N.Y. The daughter of Dr. Louis Wright, Wright received a B.A. degree from Smith College (Northampton, Mass.) in 1942 and her M.D. degree from New York Medical College in 1945. She interned at Bellevue Hospital, New York, N.Y., and served as assistant resident in internal medicine and later as chief medical resident at Harlem Hospital, New York, N.Y. She succeeded her father as director of the Harlem Hospital Cancer Research Foundation, where she pioneered tests in the use of chemotherapy on tumors and other abnormal growths. Wright was also director of cancer chemotherapy research and instructor in research surgery at the State University of New York Downstate Medical Center in 1955, becoming associate dean and professor of surgery there in 1967. *See also* WRIGHT, LOUIS TOMPKINS; PHYSICIANS.

WRIGHT, LOUIS TOMPKINS (1891–1952), surgeon; born in La Grange, Ga. Wright received a B.A. degree from Clark College (Atlanta, Ga.) in 1911 and his M.D. degree from Harvard University Medical School in 1915. He interned at Freedmen's Hospital, Washington, D.C.; served in the U.S. Army Medical Corps from 1917 to 1918; and was in active service in France (he was later promoted to the rank of captain). Wright established a practice in New York City in 1919,

and was appointed clinical assistant in the outpatient department of Harlem Hospital in 1919, the first Afro-American physician appointed to a municipal hospital position in New York City. He served in various capacities on the staff of Harlem Hospital from 1919 to 1949, including director of the department of surgery and president of the medical board. Wright headed the team that was the first to use the "wonder drug," Aureomycin. He was regarded as an authority on head injuries, and introduced the intradermal method of vaccination. Wright was an active and outspoken opponent of racial discrimination in the entertainment media, in hospital practices vis-à-vis patient treatment and professional appointments, and in professional organizations. Wright founded the cancer research center at Harlem Hospital known as the Harlem Hospital Cancer Research Foundation. *See also* WRIGHT, JANE COOKE.

WRIGHT, RICHARD (1908–60), author; born near Natchez, Miss. Wright received nine years of public schooling in the South and in Chicago, Ill., where he moved in 1927 and where he worked as a postal clerk. He moved to New York City in 1937 and became Harlem editor for the *Daily Worker*, a Communist newspaper. In 1938 Wright worked for the Federal Writers Project and published four novellas, grouped together under the title of *Uncle Tom's Children*. A Guggenheim Fellowship in 1940 enabled him to complete *Native Son*, a landmark novel in American letters. *Native Son* was the first novel by an Afro-American writer to become a Book-of-the-Month-Club selection. The story of the economic and social conditions of "Bigger Thomas," it was also published in a Modern Library edition. In 1942 Wright broke with the Communist Party, which he had never officially joined, and in 1945 his autobiography, *Black Boy*, appeared. Gertrude Stein invited him to Paris, France, in 1946, and he left for France the next year, remaining an expatriate until his death. Wright wrote four more novels, a book of short stories, and four nonfiction works. These other works include *Black Power* (1954); *The Color Curtain; White Man, Listen!* (1957); and *Pagan Spain. See also* LITERATURE: THE NOVEL

WRIGHT, RICHARD ROBERT (1855–1947), historian, educator, banker; born in Dalton, Ga. Wright received a B.A. degree (1876) and a M.A. degree (1879) from Atlanta University, and his LL.D. degree from Wilberforce University (Wilberforce, Ohio) in 1899. He served as president of Georgia State Industrial College (1891–1921), which he developed into a progressive education center. During that time Wright participated in the Spanish-American war as a major (1898). Wright moved to Philadelphia, Pa., where he organized the Citizens' and Southern Bank and Trust Company, and served as president of the National Association of Negro Bankers (1925–47). Wright was appointed by the governor of Georgia as the historian of enlisted Afro-Americans who served in France during World War I, and he visited England, France, and Belgium (1919) to collect data for the Georgia state archives and for a book on Afro-Americans in World War I. Wright was a writer of merit, and his most important work is "Negro Companions of the Spanish Explorers" (1902). *See also* WRIGHT, RICHARD ROBERT, JR.

WRIGHT, RICHARD ROBERT, JR. (1878– ?), clergyman, sociologist, educator, editor; born in Cuthbert, Ga. Wright received a B.A. degree from Georgia State Industrial College in 1898, a B.D. degree (1901), and a M.A. degree (1904) from the University of Chicago Theological Seminary, a Ph.D. degree from the University of Pennsylvania in 1911, and his LL.D. degree from Wilberforce University (Wilberforce, Ohio) in 1920. He also attended the universities of Berlin and Leipzig. Ordained in the ministry of the African Methodist Episcopal (AME) Church in 1901, Wright served as pastor of several churches and was a bishop. He was an instructor in Hebrew at Payne Theological Seminary from 1901 to 1903, and from 1908 to 1909 served as field secretary of the Armstrong Association. From 1909 to 1936 Wright was editor of the *Christian Recorder*. He

was active in civic affairs in Philadelphia, Pa., and also supervised social services for AME churches in that city and its vicinity. From 1932 to 1936 Wright was president of Wilberforce University. Significantly, he compiled and edited a notable biographical work for the centennial of the AME church, *The Encyclopedia of the African Methodist Episcopal Church* (1916). *See also* WRIGHT, RICHARD ROBERT.

WRIGHT, STEPHEN JUNIUS (1910–), educator, administrator; born in Dillon, S.C. Wright received a B.S. degree from Hampton Institute (Hampton, Va.) in 1934, a M.A. degree from Howard University (Washington, D.C.) in 1936, and his Ph.D. degree in education from New York University in 1943. He received an honorary LL.D. degree from Colby College (Waterville, Maine) in 1962. Wright taught in high schools from 1934 to 1938, as professor of education and as director of student teaching at North Carolina Central University from 1939 to 1941, and then joined the administration at Hampton Institute (Hampton, Va.) 1943 to 1953. He was president of Bluefield State College (Bluefield, W. Va.) from 1953 to 1957, and president of Fisk University (Nashville, Tenn.) from 1957 to 1966. Wright joined the United Negro College Fund in 1966, and then became consultant to the president of the College Entrance Examination Board in 1969 and vice-president of the organization in 1970. He was a member of the board of trustees of Meharry Medical College (Nashville, Tenn.) and of the resolutions committee of the National Conference of Higher Education in 1957. Wright served with the Educational Testing Service in 1973, and was visiting professor at New York University that same year.

X,Y,Z

XAVIER UNIVERSITY OF LOUISIANA Xavier University of Louisiana, at New Orleans, La., was founded in 1915 by Katharine Drexel and the Sisters of the Blessed Sacrament, a Catholic religious order that Drexel established for the education of American minorities, especially Afro-Americans. Church-related and coeducational, the school offers the bachelor's and master's degrees and provides liberal arts and teacher education curricula. Its 1975 enrollment was 1,548.

Xavier's College of Arts and Sciences was formed in 1925, its College of Pharmacy in 1927, and its Graduate School in 1933. It moved to its current 23-acre campus in 1932.

Xavier is the only predominantly black university in the United States that is operated under Catholic auspices. Yet one-third of its students are non-Catholic. In addition, ten percent are white. The multiracial teaching faculty consists of 104 laymen, 24 nuns, and 5 priests. Traditionally, a high percentage of Xavier graduates have become teachers. In 1965, 40 percent of the teachers, 75 percent of the principals, and 90 percent of the guidance counselors in the Afro-American public schools in New Orleans were Xavier alumni.

YANCEY, ROGER M. (1904–72), lawyer, judge; born in Howardsville, Va. Yancey graduated from Hampton Institute (Hampton, Va.) and Rutgers University School of Law (New Brunswick, N.J.), and was admitted to the New Jersey bar in 1930. He served as special assistant U.S. attorney, as assistant U.S. attorney, and as assistant corporation counsel for the city of Newark, N.J. He was deputy attorney general of New Jersey; judge of the Essex County District Court; presiding judge of the Essex County District Court; and finally senior judge of that court. In 1960 Yancey became the first Afro-American judge to preside in a county court in the state of New Jersey.

YERBY, FRANK (1916–   ), author; born in Augusta, Ga. Yerby received a B.A. degree from Paine College (Augusta, Ga.) in 1937, his M.A. degree from Fisk University (Nashville, Tenn.) in 1938, and did further graduate study at the University of Chicago. He taught at Florida Agricultural and Mechanical (A & M) University in 1939 and at Southern University (Baton Rouge, La.) from 1940 to 1941. Yerby received the O'Henry Memorial Award for the best short story in 1944. His many books include: *The Foxes of Harrow* (1946), *An Odor of Sanctity* (1965), *Goat Song* (1967), *Judas, My Brother* (1968), and *Dahomean* (1971). *See also* LITERATURE: THE NOVEL.

YERGAN, LAURA H. nurse, educator. Yergan graduated from the Harlem Hospital School of Nursing (New York, N.Y.) in 1941, and completed a year in public health at New York University before receiving a B.S. degree in nursing education from Hunter College of the City University of New York in 1950. She received her M.A. degree in consultation in the administration of nursing services from Columbia University Teachers College in 1960. Yergan served on the staff of Harlem Hospital (1941–43), in the New York City department of health (1944–46), and with the U.S. Public Health Service as a Lieutenant commander assigned to Vietnàm (1953–56), to Beirut, Lebanon (1956–58), and to Karachi, Pakistan (1958–59). She became director of the study of nursing needs and resources in the Virgin Islands of the United States in 1973.

YERGAN, MAX (1893–1976), educator, civil rights leader; born in Raleigh, N.C. Yergan graduated from Shaw University (Raleigh, N.C.) in 1914 and was subsequently associated with the Young Men's Christian Association (YMCA) for 25 years. During World War I he went to Kenya to organize the YMCA among regiments recruited by the British Army. In 1936 Yergan taught black history at City College (New York, N.Y.), becoming the first Afro-American professor of such a course in a major white educational institution. He was president of the National Negro Congress, and in 1962 he served as chairman of the American Committee for Aid to Katanga Freedom Fighters. As a civil rights leader, Yergan campaigned to gain civil rights for Africans. He was awarded the Spingarn Medal in 1933.

Andrew Young, president of the Security Council, United Nations, 1977. *(United Nations/Y. Nagata.)*

YOUNG, ANDREW J., JR. (1932–   ), clergyman, U.S. Representative; born in New Orleans, La. Young was educated at Dillard University (New Orleans, La.), at Howard University (Wash-

ington, D.C.), and at Hartford Theological Seminary (Hartford, Conn.). From 1952 to 1953 he was a member of the team ministry that organized Charter Oak Community Church in Hartford, Conn., an interracial project, and from 1955 to 1957 he was pastor of Congregational churches in Georgia. From 1957 to 1961 Young served as associate director of the department of youth work of the National Council of Churches. Active in the civil rights movement in Birmingham, Ala., and in St. Augustine, Fla., he became increasingly prominent in the Southern Christian Leadership Conference (SCLC), becoming executive vice-president of that organization. In 1972 Young became the first Afro-American member of the Georgia delegation to the U.S House of Representatives since Reconstruction (1870). He was United States ambassador to the United Nations from 1977 to 1979.

YOUNG, A. S. (1924–   ), journalist, editor; born in Virginia. Young received a B.S. degree from Hampton Institute (Hampton, Va.) and attended California State University and Pepperdine College (Los Angeles, Calif.), where he studied journalism. He wrote for radio and television and was the author of several books. Young was also executive editor of the Los Angeles *Sentinel* and information director of Pepperdine College.

YOUNG, CHARLES (1864–1922), Army officer; born in Mays Lick, Ky. The son of former slaves, Young was appointed to the United States Military Academy (West Point, N.Y.), in 1884, the ninth Afro-American admitted, but only the third to graduate (1889). Brief service as a second lieutenant preceded a post as instructor in military science at Wilberforce University (Wilberforce, Ohio) from 1894–1898. In the Spanish-American War, Young commanded (with the temporary rank of major) the Ninth Ohio Regiment in Cuba. Promoted to captain, he served in the Philippines from 1901 to 1903, before becoming military attaché to Haiti in 1904. After service as staff officer in Washington, D.C., and as military attaché to Liberia, with the rank of major, Young commanded a squadron of the Tenth Cavalry under General John J. Pershing in Mexico against Pancho Villa. Heroic exploits there led to Young's promotion to lieutenant colonel in 1916. At the outbreak of World War I, U.S. Army doctors, claiming Young had high blood pressure, declared him physically unfit for active duty. To prove his fitness, he rode 500 miles on horseback from Wilberforce, Ohio, to Washington, D.C., in 16 days, but the decision was not reversed. Retired as a colonel, Young was recalled in 1918, just five days before the Armistice, and was thus the highest-ranking Afro-American officer in World War I. Sent to Monrovia to reorganize Liberia's army in 1919, he died while on a research expedition to Nigeria and was buried with full military honors in Arlington National Cemetery. A musician and composer as well as a soldier, Young wrote "The Military Morale of Races." He also wrote a pageant, poems, and a book about Haiti's liberator, Toussaint L'Ouverture.

YOUNG, CLAUDE (BUDDY) See ATHLETES: FOOTBALL.

YOUNG, COLEMAN A. (1918–), civic leader, state legislator, mayor; born in Tuscaloosa, Ala. After serving as Democratic floor leader of the Michigan state senate (he was elected in 1964), Young was elected the first Afro-American mayor of Detroit, Mich. in 1973.

YOUNG, HARDING BERNETT (1922–), educator; born in Rosston, Ark. Young received a B.S. degree from Arkansas Agricultural, Mechanical, and Normal (AM & N) College (now the University of Arkansas at Pine Bluff) in 1944 and his D.C.S. degree from the Graduate School of Business Administration at Harvard University in 1955. He served as dean and professor of business administration at Atlanta University (1961–69) and as a professor of businesss management at Georgia State University.

YOUNG, ISAAC WILLIAM (1894– ?), physician; born in Glencoa, La. Young attended Gilbert College from 1887 to 1891, was a teacher from 1892 to 1900, and received his M.D. degree from New Orleans University in 1900. He was mayor of Langston, Okla., from 1915 to 1916, and became president of Langston University (Langston, Okla.) in 1923. Young also received an honorary M.A. degree from New Orleans` University in 1924.

YOUNG, LESTER (PREZ) (1909–59), jazz tenor saxophonist. Young spent his youth on the Midwest carnival circuit with his musical family. Although he played several instruments, he chose to specialize on the tenor saxophone, and during his career he played with the orchestras of Fletcher Henderson, Andy Kirk, and Count Basie (1936–40). Young, recognized as one of the most vital influences in jazz, made the transition between a big, rich tenor style and a quiet, moody, cool style ("cool" jazz). He suffered a nervous breakdown in 1956, but made a brief European comeback before his death three years later. See also MUSIC: JAZZ.

YOUNG, LOIS A. (1934–), ophthalmologist, educator; born in Baltimore, Md. Young received a B.A. degree from Howard University (Washington, D.C.) and her M.D. degree from the University of Maryland College of Medicine in 1960, the first Afro-American woman to be admitted to that institution. She interned at the University of Maryland Hospital, and was a resident in ophthalmology at Freedmen's Hospital and at General Hospital, both in Washington, D.C. Young served as assistant professor of ophthalmology at Howard University Medical College in 1964, and also as associate professor at the University of Maryland College of Medicine.

YOUNG MEN'S/WOMEN'S CHRISTIAN ASSOCIATION (YMCA / YWCA) See CRAWFORD, HENRY ROBERT; HAYNES, GEORGE EDMUND; HEDGEMAN, ANNA ARNOLD; HOPE, JOHN; HUTCHERSON, WALTER LEONARD; JACKSON, JUANITA E.; KILGORE, THOMAS; TOBIAS, CHANNING HEGGIE; YERGEN, MAX. See also BIBLIOGRAPHIES / BIOGRAPHIES / GUIDES.

YOUNG, N. LOUISE, physician. Young attended Howard University (Washington, D.C.) and received her M.D. degree from Howard University Medical College in 1930. She interned and was resident at Freedmen's Hospital, Washington, D.C., in 1933, becoming the first Afro-American woman physician in the state of Maryland. Young served as staff physician at Maryland Training School for Girls (1933–40); as visiting physician assistant chief, and later acting chief, of obstetrics at Provident Hospital, Baltimore, Md.; and as physician for women at Morgan State University (Baltimore, Md.). She also practiced medicine, specializing in obstetrics and gynecology, in Baltimore.

YOUNG, NATHAN B. (1862–1933), educator; born in Newbern, Ala. Young received a B.A. degree (1888) and a Litt.D. degree from Talladega College (Talladega, Ala.), a M.A. degree from Oberlin College (Oberlin, Ohio) in 1891, and a Litt.D. degree and his LL.D. degree from Selma University (Selma, Ala.). He taught at Tuskegee

Coleman Young.
(Photo by Leroy Henderson.)

Institute (Tuskegee Institute, Ala.) and was head of the academic department there. Young was also a professor of English and education at Georgia State College, and served as president of Florida Agricultural and Mechanical (A & M) University for 22 years. He made a radical proposal for the establishment of a graduate school for Afro-Americans in 1915, and was the first president of Lincoln Institute upon its conversion to a university (1921–27, 1929–31). Young was frequently a controversial figure who fought for the ideal of a liberal arts college as opposed to an entirely vocational school.

YOUNG, PLUMMER B. See NORFOLK JOURNAL AND GUIDE.

YOUNG, ROSCOE CONKLING (1928–   ), surgeon, educator; born in New York, N.Y. Young received a B.S. degree from the City College of the City University of New York in 1951 and his M.D. degree from Howard University Medical College (Washington, D.C.) in 1957. He was a resident in internal medicine at Freedmen's Hospital, Washington, D.C. (1958–60) and served as instructor (1962), as assistant professor (1967), and as associate dean (1970) of Howard University Medical College. Young was also the director of the Pulmonary Function Laboratory at Freedmen's Hospital. A lieutenant colonel in the District of Columbia National Guard, he became chief of the medical service in that unit after 1966.

YOUNG, WHITNEY MOORE, JR. (1921–71), civil rights leader; born in Lincoln Ridge, Ky. Young served from 1961 until his death as the executive director of the National Urban League. He received a B.S. degree from Kentucky State College (Frankfort, Ky.) in 1941 and his M.A. degree in 1947 from the University of Minnesota. That same year Young became director of the industrial relations and vocational guidance divisions of the St. Paul, Minn., Urban League. Assuming the post of executive director of the Omaha,

Whitney M. Young, Jr. (News Voice International.)

Nebr., Urban League in 1950, he also taught social work and supervised field work in university programs. From 1950 to 1954 Young was on the faculty at the University of Nebraska School of Social Work. He lectured at Creighton University (Omaha, Nebr.) from 1950 to 1951 and from 1954 to 1960 he was at the Atlanta University School for Social Work. A grant from the Rockefeller Foundation made possible a year of postgraduate study at Harvard University from 1960 to 1961. Named executive director of the National Urban League in 1961, he greatly expanded the organization and called for a "domestic Marshall Plan," which he envisioned as a crash program that would attack directly the economic and educational problems of Afro-Americans. Young was among the organizers of the 1963 march on Washington, D.C. A moderate civil rights leader, he urged Afro-Americans to work within the system and encouraged active participation by businesses, corporations, and individual whites in the civil rights struggle during the 1960s. His book, *To be Equal*, a series of essays, was published in 1964. Among his many awards, Young received honorary LL.B. degrees from North Carolina Agricultural and Technical (A & T) State University and Tuskegee Institute. Young died in Lagos, Nigeria, while attending a meeting with African leaders sponsored by the African-American Association. The Whitney Young Magnet High School (Chicago) was later named in his honor. See also NATIONAL URBAN LEAGUE.

ZANDERS, RONALD E. (1943–   ) engineer, born in Okmulgee, Okla. Zanders received a B.S.E.E. and his M.S.E.E. from Oklahoma State University of Agriculture and Applied Science (Stillwater) in 1966. He served as an engineer with the American Telephone & Telegraph Co. and, since 1970, has been Departmental Chief of Planning and Development Engineering for Western Electric Co., with offices in New York City.

ZIGABOO See ONOMATOLOGY.

INDEX

Article titles are indicated by **boldface** page numbers; illustrations are indicated by *italicized* page numbers.

Young, Lois A., **873**
Young, N. Louise, **873**
Young, Nathan B., **873–874**
Young, Plummer B., 650
Young, Roscoe Conkling, **874**
Young, Stark, 577
Young, Trummy, 606
Young, Whitney Moore, Jr., 443, 480, **874**

Youngblood, Allen G., 541

Zanders, Ronald E., **874**
Zanuck, Darryl, 580
ZIA (Zion Investment Associates), 285
Ziegfeld, Florenz, 826
Zion Baptist Church, Cincinnati, Ohio, 165

Zion Hill Baptist Church, Los Angeles, Calif., 165
Zion Investment Associates (ZIA), 285
Zivic, Fritzie, 134
Zoar Church, Philadalphia, Pa., 32
Zoologists:
  Just, Ernest Everett, 455, **481**, 481, 615
  Turner, Charles Henry, **820**